2017 Standard Catalog of®

FIREARMS

THE COLLECTOR'S PRICE & REFERENCE GUIDE

EDITED BY
JERRY LEE

Published by

Gun Digest® Books, an imprint of F+W Media, Inc.
Krause Publications • 700 East State Street • Iola, WI 54990-0001
715-445-2214 • 888-457-2873
www.krausebooks.com

To order books or other products call toll-free 1-800-258-0929
or visit us online at www.gundigeststore.com

ISSN: 1520-4928

ISBN-13: 978-1-4402-4688-3
ISBN-10: 1-4402-4688-2

Edited by Jerry Lee and Chris Berens
Cover by Kevin Ulrich
Design by Tom Nelsen and Kevin Ulrich

Printed in the United States of America

10 9 8 7 6 5 4 3 2 1

CONTENTS

Introduction 12
About the Editor 12
Acknowledgments 13
Auction Houses 13
Contributing Editors 14
Grading System 15
Alphabetical Listings by Manufacturer 17
Classic Colt Handguns 785
Firearms Trade Names 1403
Model Index 1411

— Manufacturers Directory —

A. J. ORDNANCE 17
A.A. 17
A.A.A. 17
A-SQUARE 17
A & R SALES SOUTH 18
ABADIE 18
ABBEY, F.J. & CO. 18
ABBEY, GEORGE T. 18
ABESSER & MERKEL 18
ACCU-MATCH 19
ACCU-TEK 19
ACCURACY INTERNATIONAL 21
ACHA 21
ACME 22
ACME ARMS 22
ACME HAMMERLESS 22
ACTION ARMS LTD. 22
ADAMS / DEANE, ADAMS & DEANE .. 23
ADAMY GEBRUDER 23
ADCO ARMS 23
ADIRONDACK ARMS CO. /
  A.S. BABBITT CO. 23
ADLER 24

ADVANCED SMALL ARMS
  INDUSTRIES 24
ADVANTAGE ARMS U.S.A., INC. 24
AERO 24
AETNA ARMS CO. 24
AFC 25
AFFERBACH, W. A. 25
AGNER (SAXHOJ PRODUCTS, INC.) ... 25
AGUIRRE 26
AGUIRRE Y ARANZABAL (AYA) 26
AIR MATCH 30
AJAX ARMY 30
AKDAL 30
ALAMO RANGER 30
ALASKA 30
ALASKA MAGNUM 30
ALDAZABAL 31
ALERT 31
ALEXANDER ARMS 31
ALEXIA 31
ALFA 31
ALKARTASUNA FABRICA DE ARMAS .. 31
ALL RIGHT FIREARMS CO. 32

ALLEN, ETHAN 32
ALLEN & THURBER 36
ALLEN & WHEELOCK 36
ALLEN FIREARMS 36
ALPHA ARMS CO. 36
ALSOP, C.R. 37
AMAC 37
AMERICAN ARMS, INC. 38
AMERICAN ARMS 42
AMERICAN ARMS CO. 42
AMERICAN BARLOCK WONDER 43
AMERICAN CLASSIC 43
AMERICAN DERRINGER CORP. 44
AMERICAN FIRE ARMS
  MFG. CO., INC. 47
AMERICAN FRONTIER FIREARMS 48
AMERICAN GUN CO., NEW YORK 48
AMERICAN HISTORICAL
  FOUNDATION 48
AMERICAN INDUSTRIES 48
AMERICAN INTERNATIONAL 49
AMERICAN TACTICAL IMPORTS 49
AMERICAN WESTERN ARMS INC.
  (AWA) 50

AMES, N.P. PISTOLS 50
AMES SWORD CO. 50
AMT 51
ANCION MARX................................ 54
ANDERSON.................................... 55
ANDRUS & OSBORN......................... 55
ANSCHÜTZ, J.G. GMBH 55
ANTI GARROTTER 61
ANZIO IRON WORKS......................... 62
APACHE 62
APALOZO HERMANOS 62
AR-7 INDUSTRIES 62
ARCUS 62
ARIZAGA, G. 62
ARIZMENDI, FRANCISCO.................. 63
ARIZMENDI, ZULAICA 65
ARLINGTON ORDNANCE................... 65
ARMALITE, INC. 65
ARMAS DE FUEGO 68
ARMERO ESPECIALISTAS................. 68
ARMES DE CHASSE 69
ARMINEX LTD................................ 69
ARMINUS 69
ARMITAGE INTERNATIONAL, LTD...... 69
ARMSCO FIREARMS CORP. 70
ARMSCOR PRECISION
    INTERNATIONAL 71
ARNOLD ARMS...............................74
AROSTEGUI, EULOGIO......................75
ARRIETA S.L. 76
ARRIZABALAGA, HIJOS DE C. 78
ARSENAL, INC............................... 79
ASCASO 79
ASHEVILLE ARMORY....................... 80
ASHTON, PETER & WILLIAM............. 80
ASTON, H./H. ASTON & CO. PISTOLS.. 80
ASTRA-UNCETA SA......................... 80
ATCSA.. 84
AUBREY, A.J.................................. 84
AUER, B. 84
AUGUSTA MACHINE WORKS 84
AUSTIN & HALLECK, INC. 84
AUSTRALIAN AUTOMATIC
    ARMS LTD. 85
AUTAUGA ARMS INC. 85
AUTO MAG 85
AUTO ORDNANCE CORP. 86
AUTO POINTER............................... 89
AXTELL RIFLE CO. 89

AYA 89
AZPIRI 89
BABBIT, A. S. 90
BABCOCK, MOSES.......................... 90
BACON ARMS CO............................ 90
BAER CUSTOM, LES......................... 90
B.R.F. 90
BAFORD ARMS, INC. 98
BAIKAL 98
BAILONS GUNMAKERS, LTD. 99
BAKER GAS SEAL 100
BAKER GUN & FORGING CO.............100
BAKER, M.A. 100
BAKER, THOMAS 100
BAKER, WILLIAM 100
BALLARD, C. H. 102
BALLARD PATENT ARMS 102
BALLARD RIFLE AND
    CARTRIDGE CO. 104
BALLESTER—MOLINA....................105
BALL REPEATING CARBINE 102
BARRETT, F.A. MFG. CO..................105
BARRETT, J. B. AND A.B. & CO........106
BAR-STO PRECISION MACHINE 105
BASCARAN, MARTIN A. 107
BAUER, F. A. CORP.........................107
BAYARD 107
BAYONNE,
    MANUFACTURE D'ARMES............107
CURRENTLY IMPORTED BAIKAL
    SHOTGUNS 99
BEATTIE, J. 109
BEAUMONT 110
BEAUMONT, ADAMS 110
BECKER AND HOLLANDER 110
BEEMAN PRECISION ARMS, INC. 110
BEERSTECHER, FREDERICK 110
BEHOLLA 110
BEISTEGUI, HERMANOS 110
BENELLI 111
BENTLEY, DAVID...........................119
BENTLEY, JOSEPH 119
BERETTA, DR. FRANCO...................119
BERETTA, PIETRO 119
BERGARA 156
BERGER, JEAN MARIUS 157
BERGMANN, EINHAND 157
BERGMANN, THEODOR 157
BERNARDELLI, VINCENZO...............160

BERNARDON MARTIN 166
BERNEDO, VINCENZO.....................166
BERSA 166
BERTRAND, JULES 169
BERTUZZI....................................169
BIG HORN ARMORY........................169
BIGHORN ARMS CO. 169
BIGHORN RIFLE CO........................169
BILHARZ, HALL & CO......................170
BILLINGHURST, WILLIAM 170
BILLINGS.....................................170
BINGHAM LTD. 170
BISMARCK 170
BITTERLICH, FRANK J. 171
BITTNER, GUSTAV 171
BLAKE, J. H..................................171
BLANCH, JOHN..............................171
BLAND, THOMAS & SONS 171
BLASER JAGDWAFFEN....................171
BLISS, F. D. 173
BLISS & GOODYEAR.......................173
BLUNT & SYMS 174
BOBERG ARMS CORP. 174
BODEO 175
BOLUMBURO, G. 175
BOND ARMS INC...........................175
BOOM 176
BORCHARDT..................................176
BORSIG 177
BOSIS, LUCIANO............................177
BOSS & CO...................................177
BOSWELL, CHARLES 177
BOSWORTH, B. M. 177
BRAENDLIN ARMOURY....................177
BRAND...177
BREDA, ERNESTO..........................177
BREN 10......................................178
BRETTON.....................................179
BRIGGS, H. A. 179
BRILEY MANUFACTURING INC. 179
BRIXIA 180
BRNO ARMS 180
BROLIN ARMS 182
BRONCO.......................................186
BROOKLYN F. A. CO. 186
BROWN, E.A. MANUFACTURING CO...186
BROWN, ED PRODUCTS 187
BROWN MANUFACTURING CO. 189

BROWNING ARMS CO. 189
BROWN PRECISION, INC. 189
BRUCE & DAVIS 239
BRUCHET 239
BRUFF, R.P. 240
BRYCO ARMS 240
BSA GUNS LTD. 240
BUCO 241
BUDISCHOWSKY............................241
BULLARD REPEATING ARMS CO......242
BULLDOG SINGLE-SHOT PISTOL......242
BUL TRANSMARK LTD. 242
BURGESS GUN CO. 242
BURGSMULLER, K. 243
BURNSIDE RIFLE CO. 243
BUSHMASTER FIREARMS
    INTERNATIONAL 243
BUTLER, WM. S. 246
BUTTERFIELD, JESSE 246
CABANAS, INDUSTRIAS S.A. 247
CALICO 247
CAMEX-BLASER USA, INC................247
CAMPO GIRO 247
CARACAL 248
CARD, S. W. 248
CARLTON, M.................................248
CASARTELLI, CARLO 248
CASE WILLARD & CO. 248
CASPIAN ARMS, LTD. 248
CASULL ARMS, INC. 249
CENTURY GUN COMPANY...............249
CENTURY INTERNATIONAL
    ARMS CO...............................249
CETME...251
CHAMPLIN FIREARMS 251
CHAPMAN, CHARLES.....................251
CHAPMAN, G. & J. 251
CHAPUIS ARMES 251
CHARTER ARMS 252
CHARTER ARMS CORP. 252
CHEYTAC 256
CHIAPPA ARMS 256
CHICAGO, F. A. CO. 257
CHIPMUNK RIFLES/ROGUE
    RIFLE CO. 257
CHRISTENSEN ARMS 257
CHURCHILL 259
CHURCHILL, E. J. LTD. 259
CHYLEWSKI, WITOLD.....................260

CIMARRON, F. A. CO. 261
CLAPP, HOFFMAN & CO. CLAPP,
    GATES & CO. RIFLES.................267
CLARK, F. H. 267
CLASSIC DOUBLES 267
CLEMENT, CHAS............................268
CLERKE PRODUCTS 269
COBRA ENTERPRISES, INC............269
COBRAY INDUSTRIES.....................270
COCHRAN TURRET 270
CODY, MICHAEL & SONS...............270
COFER, T. W. 271
COGSWELL....................................271
COLTON MANUFACTURING CO. 271
COLT'S PATENT FIRE ARMS
    MANUFACTURING COMPANY 271
COLT BLACKPOWDER ARMS 336
COLUMBIA ARMORY 339
COLUMBUS F. A. MFG. CO.............339
COMANCHE.................................339
COMMANDO ARMS 339
COMPETITOR CORP. 339
CONNECTICUT ARMS CO..............340
CONNECTICUT SHOTGUN
    MANUFACTURING COMPANY 340
CONNECTICUT VALLEY ARMS CO...340
CONSTABLE, R. 344
CONTENTO/VENTUR 344
CONTINENTAL 345
CONTINENTAL ARMS CO...............345
CONTINENTAL ARMS CO...............345
COOK & BROTHER RIFLES AND
    CARBINES 345
COONAN ARMS/COONAN INC.........346
COOPER ARMS 347
COOPER, J. M. & CO. 347
COOPERATIVA OBRERA................348
COPELAND, FRANK........................348
COSMI, A. & F. 348
COSMOPOLITAN ARMS CO............349
COWLES & SON 349
CPA RIFLES 349
CRAUSE, CARL PHILLIP MUSKETS
    AND RIFLES............................349
CRESCENT F. A. CO. 350
CRISPIN, SILAS 353
CROSSFIRE 353
CRUCELEGUI, HERMANOS.............354
CUMMINGS, O. S. 354

CUMMINGS & WHEELER...............354
CUSTOM GUN GUILD.....................354
CZ 354
CZ - STRAKONICE.........................354
DAEWOO 369
DAISY 370
DAKIN GUN CO. 370
DAKOTA ARMS, INC.......................370
D. W. M. 369
DALY, CHARLES............................374
DAN ARMS OF AMERICA................382
DANCE & BROTHERS CONFEDERATE
    REVOLVERS 383
DANIEL DEFENSE 383
DANSK REKYLRIFFEL SYNDIKAT 383
DARDICK CORP.............................384
DARLING, B. & B. M. 385
DARNE, S. A. 385
DAVENPORT FIREARMS CO. 385
DAVIDSON, F.A. 385
DAVIS, A. JR................................386
DAVIS & BOZEMAN 388
DAVIS INDUSTRIES 388
DAVIS, N.R. & CO./
    DAVIS, N.R. & SONS 386
DAVIS-WARNER ARMS
    CORPORATION.........................387
DAW, G. H. 389
DEANE-HARDING...........................389
DECKER, WILHELM.........................390
DEMIRETT, J. 390
DEMRO 390
DERINGER REVOLVER
    AND PISTOL CO. 390
DERINGER RIFLES AND PISTOLS,
    HENRY...................................390
DESENZANI, LABORATORIES ARMI ..392
DESERT EAGLE.............................392
DESERT INDUSTRIES 396
DESTROYER CARBINE 396
DETONICS DEFENSE
    TECHNOLOGIES 396
DETONICS FIREARMS INDUSTRIES /
    NEW DETONICS / DECTONICS USA
    LLC 396
DEUTSCHE WERKE 397
DEVISME, F. P. 398
DIAMOND 398
DIAMONDBACK FIREARMS............398

DICKINSON, E. L. & J. 399
DICKSON, NELSON & CO. 399
DIMICK, H.E. 399
DOMINGO ACHA 399
DOMINO 399
DORNAUS & DIXON
    ENTERPRISES, INC. 399
DORNHEIM, G.C. 399
DOUBLESTAR CORP. 400
DOUBLETAP DEFENSE 401
DOUG TURNBULL
    MANUFACTURING CO. 401
DOWNSIZER CORPORATION 402
DPMS.. 402
DREYSE 406
DRISCOLL, J.B. 406
DRULOV 406
DSA, INC. 407
DUBIEL ARMS CO. 409
DUMOULIN 409
DUSEK, F. 410
84 GUN CO. 411
E.M.F. CO., INC. 411
EAGLE ARMS,
    DIVISION OF ARMALITE............ 412
ECHAVE & ARIZMENDI 412
ECHEVERRIA, STAR-BONIFACIO SA
    (STAR) 414
ECLIPSE.. 418
EL DORADO ARMS......................... 418
ELGIN CUTLASS 418
ELLS, JOSIAH................................ 419
ENDERS, CARL 419
ENFIELD AMERICAN, INC. 419
ENTREPRISE ARMS, INC. 419
ERA...421
ERICHSON, G.................................421
ERMA WERKE WAFFENFABRIK 421
ERQUIAGA 423
ERRASTI, A. 424
ESCODIN, M. 424
ESCORT 424
ESPIRIN, HERMANOS......................425
EUROARMS OF AMERICA 425
EUROPEAN AMERICAN ARMORY
    CORP./ U.S. SPORTING GOODS,
    INC..426
EVANS, J. E. 432
EVANS REPEATING RIFLE CO......... 432

EXCAM 433
EXCEL INDUSTRIES....................... 434
FABARM 438
F.A.S. 435
F.I.E. 435
FABBRI, ARMI............................... 442
FABRIQUE NATIONALE 443
FAIRBANKS, A. B. 446
FALCON FIREARMS 446
FAMARS, A. & S. 446
FARROW ARMS CO. 448
FAUSTI, STEFANO........................ 448
FAYETTEVILLE ARMORY PISTOLS
    AND RIFLES 449
FEATHER INDUSTRIES, INC. 450
FEDERAL ENGINEERING CORP........ 450
FEDERAL ORDNANCE, INC. 450
FEG
    (FEGYVER ES GAZKESZULEKGYAR)..451
FEINWERKBAU 454
FEMARU....................................... 454
FERLIB 454
FERRY, ANDREWS & CO. 455
FIALA ARMS COMPANY 455
FINNISH LION 456
FIOCCHI OF AMERICA, INC. 456
FIREARMS INTERNATIONAL 456
FIRESTORM................................... 456
FLETCHER BIDWELL, LLC 457
FLORENCE ARMORY 457
FNH USA, INC. 457
FOEHL, C...................................... 462
FOEHL & WEEKS........................... 462
FOGARTY 462
FOLSOM, H. 462
FOLSOM, H&D ARMS CO................ 462
FORBES RIFLES, LLC 462
FOREHAND & WADSWORTH 462
FOWLER, B. JR. 463
FOX, A. H. 463
FRANCHI, L. 465
FRANCOTTE, A. 472
FRANKLIN, C. W. 474
FRANKONIA JAGD......................... 474
FRASER F. A. CORP....................... 474
FREEDOM ARMS............................ 474
FREEMAN, AUSTIN T. 476
FRIGON 476
FROMMER......................................476

FRUHWIRTH 476
FUNK, CHRISTOPH......................476
FURR ARMS 476
FYRBERG, ANDREW 476
GABBET-FAIRFAX, H. 477
GABILONDO Y CIA.......................477
GABILONDO Y URRESTI..................477
GALAND, C.F. 479
GALAND & SOMMERVILLE 479
GALEF (ZABALA) 479
GALENA INDUSTRIES INC..............479
GALESI, INDUSTRIA ARMI 481
GALIL...481
GALLAGER 482
GAMBA, RENATO 482
GARAND 485
GARATE, ANITUA/G.A.C. 486
GARATE, HERMANOS.................... 487
GARBI 487
GARCIA 488
GARRET, J. & F. CO. 489
GASSER, LEOPOLD 489
GATLING ARMS CO. 489
GAUCHER 489
GAULOIS 489
GAVAGE, A. 489
GAZANAGA, ISIDRO 490
GECO 490
GEHA 490
GEM 490
GENEZ, A. G. 490
GENSCHOW, G.............................. 491
GEORGIA ARMORY 491
GERING, H. M. & CO.................... 491
GERSTENBERGER & EBERWEIN.......491
GEVARM....................................... 491
GIB 491
GIBBS 491
GIBBS GUNS, INC. 492
GIBBS, J. & G. / GIBBS, GEORGE 491
GIBBS RIFLE COMPANY 492
GIBBS TIFFANY & CO. 492
GILLESPIE 492
GLAZE, W. & CO. 493
GLOCK 493
GODDARD 497
GOLDEN EAGLE 497
GONCZ CO. 498

GOUDRY, J.F. 498

GOVERNOR 499

GRABNER G. 499

GRAND POWER 499

GRAND PRECISION, FABRIQUE D'ARMES DE 499

GRANGER, G. 500

GRAS 500

GREAT WESTERN ARMS COMPANY .. 500

GREAT WESTERN II 501

GREEN, E. 501

GREENE 501

GREENER, W. W. LTD. 501

GREIFELT & CO. 502

GRENDEL, INC. 502

GRIFFIN & HOWE 503

GRIFFON 503

GRISWOLD & GRIER 503

GRISWOLD & GUNNISON 503

GROSS ARMS CO. 504

GRUBB, J. C. & CO. 504

GRULLA 504

GUERINI, CAESAR 504

GUION, T. F. 505

GUNCRAFTER INDUSTRIES 505

GUNWORKS LTD. 506

GUSTAF, CARL 506

GWYN & CAMPBELL 506

HAENEL, C. G. 508

HAFDASA 508

HAHN, WILLIAM 509

HALE, H. J. 509

HALE & TULLER 509

HALL, ALEXANDER 509

HALL-NORTH 509

HAMBUSH, JOSEPH 509

HAMILTON RIFLE COMPANY 510

HAMMERLI, SA 511

HAMMERLI-WALTHER 514

HAMMOND BULLDOG 514

HAMMOND MFG. CO., GRANT .. 514

HANKINS, WILLIAM 514

HANUS, BILL 515

HARRINGTON & RICHARDSON, INC. .. 515

H.J.S. INDUSTRIES, INC. 507

H&R 1871, LLC 507

H-S PRECISION, INC. 507

HARRIS GUNWORKS 528

HARTFORD ARMS & EQUIPMENT CO. 531

HATFIELD RIFLE COMPANY 531

HAVILAND & GUNN 532

HAWES 532

HAWES & WAGGONER 532

HAWKEN 533

HDH, SA. 533

HEAVY EXPRESS INC. 533

HECKLER & KOCH 534

HEINZELMANN, C.E. 543

HEIZER DEFENSE 543

HELFRICHT 543

HENRION & DASSY 543

HENRY 543

HENRY, ALEXANDER 543

HENRY REPEATING ARMS COMPANY 543

HERITAGE MANUFACTURING, INC. .. 545

HEROLD 547

HERTER'S 547

HESSE ARMS 547

HEYM, F. W. 547

HIGGINS, J. C. 550

HIGH STANDARD 550

HIGH STANDARD MANUFACTURING CO. 566

HILLIARD, D. H. 567

HILL, W.J. 567

HINO-KOMURA 567

HI-POINT FIREARMS 549

HODGKINS, D. C. & SONS 567

HOFER, P. 567

HOFFMAN, LOUIS 567

HOLDEN, C. B. 567

HOLECK, EMANUEL 567

HOLLAND & HOLLAND, LTD. ... 568

HOLLOWAY ARMS CO. 568

HOLMES FIREARMS 568

HOOD F. A. CO. 568

HOPKINS & ALLEN 568

HOWA MACHINE COMPANY 569

HOWARD-WHITNEY 570

HUGLU 570

HUNGARY 572

HUNT 572

HUNTER ARMS CO. 572

HUSQVARNA 572

HYDE & SHATTUCK 574

HY-HUNTER, INC. 573

HYPER 574

IIAB 575

IAI-AMERICAN LEGENDS 575

IGA 575

I.G.I. 575

INDIAN ARMS CORP. 576

INDUSTRIA ARMI GALESI 576

INGRAM 576

INTERARMS 576

INTERARMS/HIGH STANDARD .. 578

INTERDYNAMICS OF AMERICA .. 578

INTRATEC USA, INC. 578

IRVING, W. 579

IRWINDALE ARMS, INC. 579

ISRAELI MILITARY INDUSTRIES .. 579

ITHACA GUN CO. 579

IVER JOHNSON ARMS & CYCLE WORKS 592

IVER JOHNSON ARMS, INC. 592

IXL 596

JACQUESMART, JULES 597

JACQUITH, ELIJAH 597

JAGER WAFFENFABIK 597

JEFFERY, W. J. & CO. LTD. 597

JENISON, J. & CO. 597

JENKS CARBINE 598

JENKS-HERKIMER 597

JENKS-MERRILL 598

JENNINGS 598

JENNINGS F. A., INC. 598

JERICHO 599

JIEFFCO 599

JOHNSON, STAN, BYE & CO. ... 599

JOSLYN 599

JOSLYN 599

JOSLYN FIREARMS COMPANY .. 599

JURRAS, LEE 600

JUSTICE, P. S. 600

KAHR ARMS 601

KASSNAR IMPORTS, INC. 605

KBI, INC. 605

KEBERST INTERNATIONAL 605

KEL-TEC CNC INDUSTRIES 605

KEMPER, SHRIVER & COMPANY .. 607

KENDALL, INTERNATIONAL 607

KENDALL, NICANOR 607

KENO 607

KERR 607
KESSLER ARMS CORPORATION.......607
KETTNER, EDWARD 607
K.F.C.
  (KAWAGUCHIYA FIREARMS CO.)...601
KIMBALL ARMS COMPANY..............607
KIMBER MFG., INC..........................607
KING PIN 629
KIRRIKALE, ENDUSTRISI............... 629
KLEINGUENTHER/KDF, INC............ 629
KLIPZIG & COMPANY 630
KNICKERBOCKER........................... 630
KNIGHT RIFLES 630
KNIGHT'S ARMAMENT COMPANY....631
KOHOUT & SPOLECNOST 632
KOLB, HENRY M. 633
KOLIBRI/FREDERICK PFANNL........ 633
KOMMER,
  THEODOR WAFFENFABRIK.......... 633
KONGSBERG 634
KORRIPHILA 634
KORTH 634
KRAG-JORGENSEN 635
KRAUSER, ALFRED 635
KRICO 635
KRIDER, J. H. 637
KRIEGHOFF, HEINRICH, GUN CO. 637
KRNKA, KAREL 640
KSN INDUSTRIES........................... 640
KUFAHL, G. L...............................641
KYNOCH GUN FACTORY 641
LAGRESE 642
LAHTI 642
LAKELANDER............................... 642
LAMB, H. C. & CO. 642
LAMES...................................... 642
LANBER ARMAS S.A. 643
LANCASTER, CHARLES................. 644
LANGENHAN, FRIEDRICH 644
LANG, J. 644
LAR MFG. CO. 645
LARUE TACTICAL........................... 646
LASALLE.................................... 646
LASERAIM ARMS........................... 646
LAURONA....................................647
LAW ENFORCEMENT ORDNANCE
  CORP. 649
LAZZERONI ARMS COMPANY 650
LEBEAU COURALLY 653

LEECH & RIGDON.......................... 653
LEE FIREARMS CO. 653
LEFAUCHAUX, CASIMER & EUGENE.. 653
LEFEVER, D. M., SONS & COMPANY .. 653
LE FORGERON 650
LE FRANCAIS 651
LE MAT 652
LE PAGE SA. 652
LEFEVER ARMS CO. 654
LEFEVER ARMS COMPANY, INC.
  (ITHACA)................................. 655
LEMAN, H. E. 655
LEONARD, G. 655
LES, INC. 656
LEW HORTON 656
LEWIS MACHINE & TOOL COMPANY
  (LMT) 656
LIDDLE & KAEDING...................... 656
LIEGEOISE D ARMES 656
LIGNOSE 656
LILLIPUT 657
LINDE A. 657
LINDSAY, JOHN P..........................657
LINS, A. F. 658
LITTLE SHARPS RIFLE MFG. CO. 658
LJUTIC INDUSTRIES 658
LLAMA 659
LOEWE, LUDWIG & CO. 663
LOHNER, C. 663
LOMBARD, H. C. & CO.................. 663
LONE STAR RIFLE COMPANY 663
LORCIN ENGINEERING CO., INC. 664
LOWELL ARMS CO........................ 664
LOWER, J. P. 664
LUGERS 664
LUNA 676
LWRC INTERNATIONAL.................. 676
LYMAN 677
M. B. ASSOCIATES-GYROJET 678
MAC...678
MADSEN.....................................678
MAGNUM RESEARCH, INC..............678
M.O.A. CORP. 678
MAKAROV PISTOL 679
MALIN, F. E. 679
MALTBY, HENLEY AND CO............. 680
MANHATTAN FIREARMS COMPANY.. 680
MANN, FRITZ 681
MANNLICHER PISTOL 681

MANNLICHER SCHOENAUER 681
MANUFRANCE............................. 682
MANURHIN 683
MARATHON PRODUCTS, INC. 684
MARBLE'S ARMS & MFG. CO. 684
MARGOLIN 685
MARIETTE BREVETTE.................... 686
MARLIN FIREARMS CO. 686
MAROCCHI ARMI 720
MARS..721
MARSTON, S.W............................721
MARSTON, W. W. & CO..................721
MASQUELIER, S. A. 722
MASSACHUSETTS ARMS CO. 722
MATEBA ARMS..............................724
MATRA MANURHIN DEFENSE..........724
MAUNZ MFG., INC. 724
MAUSER WERKE............................724
MAVERICK ARMS, INC.....................735
MAYNARD/PERRY...........................735
MCMILLAN & CO. INC., G. 736
MCMILLAN FIREARMS 737
MEAD & ADRIANCE........................737
MENDENHALL, JONES & GARDNER...737
MENZ, AUGUST 737
MERCURY....................................738
MERCURY(2).................................738
MERIDEN FIREARMS CO. 738
MERKEL, GEBRUDER 738
MERRILL, JAMES H. 748
MERRILL 749
MERRILL, LATROBE & THOMAS.......748
MERRIMACK ARMS.........................749
MERWIN & BRAY 749
MERWIN HULBERT & CO. 749
METROPOLITAN ARMS CO. 751
MIIDA..751
MILLER ARMS 751
MILTECH 752
MINNEAPOLIS F. A. CO. 752
MIROKU B. C. 752
MITCHELL ARMS, INC.....................752
MITCHELL'S MAUSERS....................754
MK ARMS, INC..............................754
MKE...755
MODESTO SANTOS CIA...................755
MONTENEGRAN-GASSER.................755
MOORE'S PATENT FIREARMS CO.....755

MORGAN & CLAPP........................756
MORINI 756
MORRONE 756
MORSE..756
MOSSBERG, O. F. & SONS, INC........756
MOUNTAIN ARMS 770
MOUNTAIN RIFLES, INC. 770
MUGICA, JOSE 771
MURFEESBORO ARMORY 771
MURPHY & O'CONNEL....................771
MURRAY, J. P. 771
MUSGRAVE 771
MUSKETEER RIFLES 771
NATIONAL ARMS CO. 772
NAVY ARMS COMPANY 772
NEAL, W. 801
NEPPERHAN FIREARMS CO. 801
NESIKA BAY PRECISION, INC. 801
NEW ENGLAND FIREARMS CO. 802
NEWBURY ARMS CO. 805
NEWCOMB, H. G. 805
NEWTON ARMS CO. 805
NEW ULTRA LIGHT ARMS...............804
NICHOLS & CHILDS........................805
NIGHTHAWK CUSTOM.....................805
NOBLE 807
NORINCO 809
NORTH & COUCH 810
NORTH AMERICAN ARMS...............810
NORTH AMERICAN ARMS CORP.......812
NORTH AMERICAN SAFARI
    EXPRESS................................812
NORTON ARMAMENT
    CORPORATION.........................812
NORWICH PISTOL CO. 812
NOSLER CUSTOM 812
NOWLIN MANUFACTURING
    COMPANY................................812
OBREGON....................................813
O'CONNELL, DAVID.......................813
O'DELL, STEPHEN 813
O.D.I. 813
OHIO ORDNANCE INC.....................813
OJANGUREN Y VIDOSA...................813
O.K. 813
OLD WEST GUN CO. 814
OLYMPIC ARMS, INC......................814
OMEGA 817
OMEGA FIREARMS CO. 817

OPUS SPORTING ARMS, INC. 818
ORBEA & CIA 818
ORTGIES, HEINRICH & CO. 818
ORVIS 818
OSBORN, S...................................818
OSGOOD GUN WORKS....................818
OVERTON, JOHN 818
OWA..818
P.38 819
P.A.F. 820
PAGE-LEWIS ARMS CO. 820
PALMER 821
PARA USA (PARA-ORDNANCE) 821
PARDINI......................................832
PARKER 833
PARKER BROS. 833
PARKER-HALE LTD. 832
PARKER FIELD & SONS 836
PARKER GUN 836
PARKER REPRODUCTIONS 836
PEABODY 837
PEAVY, A. J. 838
PECARE & SMITH..........................838
PEDERSEN CUSTOM GUNS.............838
PEDERSEN, JOHN D. 838
PEDERSOLI, DAVIDE 839
PERAZZI......................................845
PERRY & GODDARD 849
PERRY PATENT FIREARMS CO. 849
PERUGINI & VISINI 849
PETTINGILL C. S............................850
PFANNL, FRANCOIS........................850
PGM PRECISION 850
PHILLIPS & RODGERS INC..............851
PHOENIX 851
PHOENIX ARMS 851
PHOENIX ARMS CO. 851
PICKERT, FRIEDRICH......................851
PIEPER, HENRI & NICOLAS..............852
PIETTA, F.LLI 853
PILSEN, ZBROVKA 853
PIOTTI..853
PLAINFIELD MACHINE CO. 854
PLAINFIELD ORDNANCE CO. 854
PLANT'S MANUFACTURING CO. 854
POINTER 855
POLY-TECHNOLOGIES, INC./
    POLY-TECH 855

POND, LUCIUS, W. 855
PORTER, P. W. 856
PRAHA ZBROJOVKA........................856
PRAIRIE GUN WORKS 856
PRANDELLI & GASPARINI 856
PRATT, GEORGE 857
PRATT, H.....................................857
PRECISION SMALL ARMS...............857
PREMIER 857
PRESCOTT, E. A. 858
PRETORIA 858
PRINZ 858
PROFESSIONAL ORDNANCE, INC.....858
PROTECTION 859
PTK INTERNATIONAL, INC..............859
PULASKI ARMORY 859
PUMA...859
PURDEY, J. & SONS LTD. 860
PYRENEES....................................860
QUACKENBUSH 862
QUINABAUG MFG. CO. 862
RADOM.......................................864
RANDALL FIREARMS CO. 864
R.E. 863
R. G. INDUSTRIES 863
RANGER ARMS, INC.......................867
RAPTOR ARMS CO. 867
RAST & GASSER............................867
RAU ARMS CORP. 867
RAVELL 868
RAVEN ARMS 868
READ & WATSON...........................868
RECORD-MATCH ANSCHUTZ...........868
REEDER, GARY CUSTOM GUNS 868
REFORM......................................872
REID, JAMES 872
REISING ARMS CO. 873
REMINGTON ARMS COMPANY, INC..874
RENETTE, GASTINNE 932
RENWICK ARMS CO. 932
REPUBLIC ARMS, INC. 932
RETOLAZA HERMANOS...................933
REUNIES 933
REUTH, F.....................................933
REXIO DE ARMAS (COMANCHE) 933
RHEINMETALL...............................934
RHODE ISLAND ARMS CO. 935
RICHLAND ARMS CO. 935

RICHMOND ARMORY...................... 935
RIEDL RIFLE CO. 936
RIFLESMITH INC. 936
RIGBY, JOHN & CO., LTD. 936
RIGDON, ANSLEY & CO. 937
RIPOMANTI, GUY 937
RIVERSIDE ARMS CO. 937
RIZZINI, BATTISTA.........................937
RIZZINI, FRATELLI 939
ROBAR AND DE KIRKHAVE 940
ROBAR COMPANIES 942
ROBBINS & LAWRENCE...................942
ROBERTS DEFENSE 942
ROBINSON ARMAMENT CO. 943
ROBERTSON................................ 943
ROBINSON, ORVIL......................... 943
ROBINSON, S.C. 943
ROCK ISLAND ARMORY
   (TRADE NAME OF ARMSCOR)..... 943
ROCK RIVER ARMS, INC. 944
ROGERS & SPENCER...................... 948
ROGUE RIFLE COMPANY 948
ROGUE RIVER RIFLEWORKS 948
ROHM GMBH 948
ROHRBAUGH 949
ROMERWERKE............................. 949
RONGE, J. B. 949
ROSS RIFLE CO. 949
ROSSI, AMADEO 950
ROTH-SAUER............................... 955
ROTTWEIL.................................. 955
ROYAL AMERICAN SHOTGUNS........ 955
RUBY ARMS COMPANY 956
RUGER 956
RUPERTUS, JACOB 956
RWS... 956
SABATTI....................................957
SACKET, D. D. 957
S.A.E. 957
SAFARI ARMS...............................957
SAIGA 958
S.E.A.M.....................................957
S.W.D., INC................................957
SAKO 958
SAMCO GLOBAL ARMS, INC. 965
SAM, INC. 965
SARASQUETA, FELIX 965
SARASQUETA, J. J......................... 965

SARASQUETA, VICTOR.................. 965
SARDIUS 966
SARSILMAZ 966
SAUER & SON, J. P....................... 966
SAVAGE & NORTH........................975
SAVAGE ARMS CORPORATION........976
SAVAGE
   REVOLVING FIREARMS CO.........1004
SCATTERGUN TECHNOLOGIES.......1004
SCCY INDUSTRIES 1005
SCHALK, G. S............................1005
SCHALL & CO.............................1005
SCHMIDT & COMPANY, E. 1005
SCHMIDT, HERBERT.....................1005
SCHNEIDER & CO.........................1006
SCHNEIDER & GLASSICK 1006
SCHOUBOE................................1006
SCHUERMAN ARMS, LTD. 1006
SCHULER, AUGUST 1006
SCHULTZ & LARSEN 1006
SCHWARZLOSE, ANDREAS.............1006
SEARS, ROEBUCK & CO. BRAND....1006
SEAVER, E.R...............................1007
SECURITY INDUSTRIES 1007
SEDCO INDUSTRIES, INC. 1007
SEDGELY, R. F., INC......................1007
SEECAMP, L. W. CO., INC. 1007
SEMMERLING..............................1007
SERBU FIREARMS 1007
SHARPS ARMS CO., C..................1008
SHARPS RIFLE COMPANY 1008
SHARPS RIFLE MANUFACTURING
   COMPANY..............................1008
SHAWK & MCLANAHAN 1013
SHATTUCK, C. S. 1013
SHAW & LEDOYT 1013
SHERIDAN PRODUCTS, INC. 1014
SHILEN RIFLES, INC.....................1014
SHILOH RIFLE MFG. CO., INC.........1014
SIG 1016
SIG-HAMMERLI 1015
SIGARMS/SIG-SAUER 1017
SILMA......................................1032
SIMPLEX 1032
SIMPSON, R. J............................1032
SIMSON & COMPANY 1032
SIRKIS INDUSTRIES, LTD. 1034
SKB ARMS COMPANY 1034
SLOTTER & CO. 1039

SMITH, L. C..............................1039
SMITH, OTIS..............................1041
SMITH & WESSON 1041
SMITH AMERICAN ARMS
   COMPANY..............................1112
SNAKE CHARMER........................1112
SNEIDER, CHARLES E. 1112
SODIA, FRANZ...........................1113
SOKOLOVSKY CORP.
   SPORT ARMS 1113
SPALDING & FISHER 1113
SPANG & WALLACE 1113
SPENCER 1113
SPENCER ARMS CO. 1114
SPENCER REVOLVER....................1114
SPHINX 1114
SPIES, A. W. 1115
SPILLER & BURR 1116
SPITFIRE 1116
SPRINGFIELD ARMORY 1116
SPRINGFIELD ARMORY INC. 1116
SPRINGFIELD ARMS COMPANY 1129
SQUIBBMAN 1130
SQUIRES BINGHAM MFG. CO., INC. .1130
SSK INDUSTRIES 1130
STAFFORD, T. J. 1131
STAG ARMS...............................1131
STALCAP, ALEXANDER T.F.M.........1132
STANDARD ARMS CO....................1132
STAR, BONIFACIO ECHEVERRIA.....1132
STARR ARMS COMPANY 1132
STARR, EBAN T...........................1132
STEEL CITY ARMS, INC. 1133
STENDA WAFFENFABRIK...............1133
STERLING ARMAMENT LTD...........1134
STERLING ARMS CORPORATION ...1134
STEVENS ARMS CO., J..................1135
STEYR......................................1148
STEYR HAHN 1156
STEYR MANNLICHER 1156
STI INTERNATIONAL 1156
STOCK, FRANZ...........................1162
STOCKING & CO..........................1162
STOEGER,
   A. F./STOEGER INDUSTRIES.......1162
STREET SWEEPER 1165
STURDIVANT, LEWIS G..................1165
STURM, RUGER & CO....................1165
SUNDANCE INDUSTRIES, INC. 1198

SUPER SIX LTD. 1199
SUTHERLAND, S. 1199
SYMS, J. G. 1199
SYREN SHOTGUNS....................1199
TACONIC FIREARMS LTD...............1200
TALLASSEE 1200
TANFOGLIO 1200
TANNER, ANDRE....................1200
TARPLEY J. & F. AND
   E. T. GARRETT & CO.................1201
TAURUS INTERNATIONAL
   MFG. CO. 1201
TAYLOR, L.B. 1224
TAYLOR'S & CO., INC. 1224
TERRIER ONE 1228
TERRY, J. C. 1228
TEXAS CONTRACT RIFLES............1228
TEXAS GUNFIGHTERS..................1228
TEXAS LONGHORN ARMS, INC. 1228
THAMES ARMS CO. 1229
THIEME & EDELER 1229
THOMPSON....................1229
THOMPSON/CENTER ARMS............1229
THUNDER FIVE 1237
TIKKA 1237
TIMBER WOLF 1239
TIPPING & LAWDEN 1239
TIPPMAN ARMS....................1239
TISAS (TRABZON GUN INDUSTRY
   CORP.) 1239
TOBIN ARMS
   MANUFACTURING CO. 1240
TODD, GEORGE H....................1240
TOKAREV 1241
TOMISKA, ALOIS 1242
TORKELSON ARMS CO. 1242
TRADEWINDS....................1242
TRADITIONS....................1242
TRANTER, WILLIAM....................1245
TRIPLETT & SCOTT/MERIDEN
   MANUFACTURING COMPANY 1245
TRISTAR SPORTING ARMS............1245
TROCAOLA (TAC) 1250
TRYON, EDWARD K. & COMPANY...1250
TUCKER SHERARD & COMPANY 1250
TUFTS & COLLEY....................1250
TURBIAUX, JACQUES 1250
TURNER, THOMAS 1250
TYLER ORDNANCE WORKS 1250

U.S. ARMS CO. 1251
U.S. M1 CARBINE 1251
UBERTI, ALDO/UBERTI USA...........1252
U.S. ORDNANCE 1251
U.S. REPEATING ARMS CO. 1252
UGARTECHEA, ARMAS.................1259
UHLINGER, WILLIAM P. 1259
ULTIMATE 1259
ULTRA LIGHT ARMS....................1259
UMAREX USA 1259
UNCETA 1260
UNION....................1260
UNION FIRE ARMS COMPANY........1260
UNIQUE 1261
UNITED SPORTING ARMS, INC. 1261
UNITED STATES ARMS................1261
UNITED STATES FIRE ARMS MFG....1261
UNITED STATES REVOLVER
   ASSOCIATION 1264
UNITED STATES SMALL ARMS CO. 1264
UNIVERSAL FIREARMS 1265
URIZAR, TOMAS 1266
USAS 12 DAEWOO
   PRECISION IND., LTD................1266
USELTON ARMS INC. 1266
UZI ISRAELI MILITARY INDUSTRIES ......
   1267
VALKYRIE ARMS, LTD. 1268
VALMET, INC. 1268
VALTRO 1268
VARNER SPORTING ARMS, INC......1269
VECTOR ARMS, INC. 1269
VEKTOR 1269
VENUS WAFFENWERKE.................1271
VERNEY-CARRON 1271
VERONA 1272
VICKERS, LTD. 1273
VICTOR EJECTOR....................1273
VICTORY ARMS CO., LTD.............1273
VIRGINIAN 1274
VOERE....................1274
VOLCANIC ARMS COMPANY 1275
VOLQUARTSEN CUSTOM..............1275
VOLUNTEER ENTERPRISES 1277
VOUZELAUD 1277
WALCH, JOHN 1278
WALDMAN 1278
WALLIS & BIRCH....................1278
WALTHER, CARL....................1278

WALTHER MANURHIN 1291
WARNANT, L. AND J. 1291
WARNER, CHAS. 1291
WARNER, JAMES....................1292
WARNER ARMS CORPORATION 1292
WEATHERBY....................1293
WEAVER ARMS....................1305
WEBLEY & SCOTT, LTD. 1305
WEIHRAUCH, HANS HERMANN......1309
WEISBURGER, A. 1310
WESSON, EDWIN 1310
WESSON, FRANK....................1310
WESSON FIREARMS, DAN 1311
WESSON & LEAVITT 1311
WESSON FIREARMS CO., INC. 1318
WESTERN ARMS....................1323
WESTERN ARMS CORPORATION ...1323
WESTERN FIELD....................1323
WESTLEY RICHARDS & CO., LTD. ..1323
WHITE, ROLLIN....................1324
WHITNEY ARMS COMPANY 1324
WHITNEY FIREARMS COMPANY 1334
WHITWORTH 1334
WICHITA ARMS, INC....................1334
WICKLIFFE RIFLES....................1335
WIENER WAFFENFABRIK 1336
WILDEY FIREARMS CO., INC.........1336
WILKINSON ARMS CO. 1337
WILSON COMBAT 1337
WILLIAMSON....................1337
WILSON, J. P. 1337
WINCHESTER REPEATING ARMS ...1341
WINDSOR....................1397
WINSLOW ARMS CO. 1397
WISEMAN, BILL & CO....................1397
WITNESS....................1397
WOLF SPORTING PISTOLS 1397
WOODWARD, JAMES & SONS........1398
WURFFLEIN, ANDREW & WILLIAM ..1398
XL 1398
XPERT....................1398
ZANOTTI, FABIO 1399
Z-B RIFLE CO....................1399
ZEHNER, E. WAFFENFABRIK..........1399
ZEPHYR....................1399
ZM WEAPONS 1399
ZOLI, ANTONIO 1400
ZOLI USA, ANGELO 1401
ZULAICA, M....................1402

INTRODUCTION

Welcome to the *2017 Standard Catalog of Firearms*, the 27th annual edition of the most complete reference guide for the gun enthusiast. In these more than 1,450 pages are estimated values and detailed descriptions for virtually every rifle, shotgun and handgun manufactured in the United States or imported since the early 1800s. Values are shown for up to six condition grades with premiums added for special features. Photographs are included for most models and variants. The complete range of firearms is covered by this book, from the highly sought-after collectibles to those commonly seen on the used-gun rack at your local gun store. Current production models are updated every year, with more than 200 new models and variations added for this edition of the ever-growing *Standard Catalog*.

Keeping up with the changes in values is, of course, an ongoing process. Our contributing editors, collectors and experts in the various categories monitor the sales of used and collectible guns from numerous sources to provide us with up-to-date prices.

If this is your first edition of the book, take the time to become familiar with our Grading System section, which explains how to assess the condition of any firearm you might want to buy or sell. And remember, prices shown are *estimated retail* values. A dealer will most likely offer less to give some room for a profit margin. The retail estimates should be considered as a guide to what an individual would expect to pay.

We hope you enjoy this 27th edition of *Standard Catalog of Firearms* and that you learn something new about firearms within these pages. And thanks for your interest and support of the shooting sports.

—Jerry Lee, Editor

ABOUT THE EDITOR

Jerry Lee has been the editor of numerous gun related books and magazines. These include *Gun Digest*, which is the annual flagship of Gun Digest Books, the firearms division of Krause Publications and publisher of *Standard Catalog of Firearms*. He is also the author and editor of the recently published *Standard Catalog of Ruger Firearms*, a hard-cover book dedicated to the guns of Bill Ruger. Previously Jerry was the editor of several popular firearms magazines including *Guns*, *Rifle Shooter*, *Handguns*, and dozens of Special Interest editions of *Guns & Ammo* and *Shooting Times*. He also was editor of a group of custom newsstand magazines published for *Smith & Wesson, Remington, Ruger, Mossberg* and several other manufacturers in the industry. Jerry is an NRA Life Member and a frequent contributor to the NRA's online editions. Born and raised on a farm in West Texas, he now resides in the hills of West Virginia with his wife, Susan.

ACKNOWLEDGMENTS

The editor wishes to thank the following individuals for their input, advice and support over the years and for sharing their expertise to make contributions to this and previous editions of Standard Catalog of Firearms:

Jim Supica, Director and Phil Schreier, Senior Curator of the National Firearms Museum at NRA Headquarters in Fairfax, Virginia; auction executives/retailers/collectors Wes Dillon, Patrick Hogan, Kevin Hogan, David Moore, Dave LaRue, Jim Ciolli, Jr., Marc Murphy, Jay Hansen, Rick Verzal, Roy Marcot, Mike Clark, Alan Heldreth, John Powell, Steve Poulin, Dave Sanders and John Puglisi; and many authors who really know their guns including Tom Turpin, Terry Wieland, Garry James, Bart Skelton, Massad Ayoob, Jon Sundra, Wayne van Zwoll, Don Findley, Steve Gash, John Taffin, Jim Wilson, James House, Dick Williams, Tom Tabor, Jim Dickson, Rich Grassi, Gary Paul Johnston, Paul Scarlata, John Malloy, Layne Simpson, Larry Sterett, J.B. Wood, Kevin Muramatsu, Patrick Sweeney, Charlie Petty, Rick Hacker, Max Prasac, Holt Bodinson, Jim Foral, Wiley Clapp, Bill Hamm, Stan Trzoniec, C. Rodney James and so many others.

There are many individuals in the firearms industry who have been very helpful in providing information on their products and organizations including photographs, specifications and company history. These include industry professionals like Ken Jorgensen (Ruger), Paul Thompson (Browning), Scott Grange (Winchester), Paul Pluff, Gary Giudice and Matt Rice (Smith & Wesson), Jason Morton (CZ), Jessica Kallam (Remington/Marlin/Bushmaster), Linda Powell (Mossberg), Bud Fini (SIG-Sauer), Mike Nischalke and Karen Lutto (Steyr), Barbara Fausti (Fausti), Keith Bernkrant (European American Armory), Jamie Harvey (Cimarron), Wes Lang (Caesar Guerini), and Val Forgett (Navy Arms/Gibbs Rifle Co.).

I also would like to express my appreciation to the production staff who so ably assisted me in gathering and submitting all of the information necessary to produce this 1,472-page publication: Chris Berens, Managing Editor; Delores May, proofreader and data input specialist; and Tom Nelsen, art designer. Their long hours, professionalism and support are greatly appreciated.

AUCTION HOUSES

Among the many resources used by the editors to determine trends in firearms values are the prices realized at recent auctions. These resources include the following auction houses, which are the largest and best in the field of modern and antique firearms.

Amoskeag Auctions, 250 Commercial Street, Suite 3011, Manchester, NH 03101; **www.amoskeag-auction.com**
Bonhams & Butterfields, 220 San Bruno Ave., San Francisco, CA 94103; **www.bonhams.com**
Heritage Auctions, 3500 Maple Ave., 17th Floor, Dallas, TX 75219; **www.ha.com**
James D. Julia, Inc., 203 Skowhegan Rd., Fairfield, ME 04937; **www.juliaauctions.com**
Little John's Auctions, 1740 W. La Veta Ave., Orange, CA 92868; **www.littlejohnsauctions.com**
Poulin Antiques and Auctions, 199 Skowhegan Road, Fairfield, ME 04937, **www.poulinantiques.com**
Rock Island Auction Co., 7819 42nd Street West, Rock Island, IL 61201; **www.rockislanduaction.com**

OUR COVER GUN

The striking Colt Python revolver on the cover of this edition was manufactured in 1978 and was beautifully engraved by the late master engraver Howard Dove. The 6-inch barreled .357 Magnum features a fine scroll pattern over most of the surfaces with several gold inlayed images including the Statue of Liberty, the Iwo Jima flag raising, and an eagle holding a banner that reads "Created By God" on the left side of the barrel and "Protected by Colt" on the right. Howard Dove was one of only two engravers to do work on both Colt and Winchester firearms in the modern era. The wraparound bone grips were engraved by Leonard Francolini and feature a Rampant Colt, a gold shield and gold fleur de lis. Photo courtesy Lock, Stock & Barrel Investments (www.lsbauctions.com).

CONTRIBUTING EDITORS

J.B. Barnes
Stevens single-shot rifles and pistols
29 Ridgeview Dr.
Dry Ridge, KY 41035
859-824-5086

Holt Bodinson
Modern rifles and blackpowder rifles
Tucson, AZ

Bailey Brower, Jr.
Remington and Savage pistols
P.O. Box 111
Madison, NJ 07940
baileybrower@yahoo.com

Bud Bugni
Winchester Model 42s
P.O. Box 762
Sutter Creek, CA 95685
209-267-5402

Tom Caceci
Blackpowder revolvers
1405 Westover Drive
Blacksburg, VA 24060

Robert K. Campbell
Classic police handguns
Swt45B@aol.com

Jim Cate
J.P. Sauer pistols
406 Pine Bluff Dr.
Chattanooga, TN 37412
423-892-6320

Kevin Cherry
Winchester and Colt Commemoratives
3402 West Wendover Ave.
Greensboro, NC 27407
336-854-4182

Joseph Cornell
Browning, Colt, pre-64 Winchesters
2655 West 39th Ave.
Denver, CO 80211
303-455-1717

Jason Devine
Winchester lever-action rifles
250 Commercial Street
Unit 3011
Manchester, NH 03101
Jason@amoskeag.com

John Dougan
Ruger and Great Western single actions
102½ E. Rogers Blvd.
Skiatook, OK 74070

Don Findley
Ruger Standard Auto Pistols
5312 84th St.
Lubbock, TX 79424
donfindley@door.net

Richard Freer
Belgian Brownings and pre-64 Winchester shotguns
8928 Spring Branch Drive
Houston, TX 77080
713-467-3016

Rick Hacker
Colt SAA and 1911s
12400 Ventura Blvd., Ste. 705
Studio City, CA 91604

John Haviland
Shotguns
Missoula, MT

Karl Karash
Colt 1911/1911A1
kxkl@juno.com

George Layman
Remington Rolling Blocks
Com-bloc pistols, Auto Ord. Thompsons
bendestet@yahoo.com

Dr. Daniel Menser
Winchester Model 21 shotguns
320-522-0859
papa_menser@yahoo.com

Jon W. Miller MD, FAAEM
High Standard

Earl Minot
Lew Horton Commemoratives
erminot@lewhorton.com

Gale Morgan
Luger and Mauser pistols, and pre-WWI pistols
P.O. Box 72
Lincoln, CA 95648

Lee Newton
Ruger No. 1s
www.classicsportingarms.com

Jim Rankin
Walther pistols
Coral Gables, FL 33134
305-446-1792

Bob Rayburn
Colt Woodsman
P.O. Box 97104
Lakewood, WA 98497
rayburn@colt22.com

Phil Schreier
All categories
Senior Curator, National Firearms Museum
11250 Waples Mill Rd.
Fairfax, VA 22030

Nick Sisley
Over/under shotguns
nicksisley@hotmail.com

Jim Supica
All categories
Director, National Firearms Museum
11250 Waples Mill Rd.
Fairfax, VA 22030

John Taffin
Single-action revolvers
Boise, ID

Rick Verzal
Ruger firearms and memorabilia
www.rugercollectorsassocation.com

Terry Wieland
English and European shotguns
terrywieland@mac.com

other hand, antique firearms in this condition can be used as "wall hangers," or might be an example of an extremely rare variation or have some kind of historical significance.

Example prices are shown for the conditions described above in this format:

NIB	Exc.	V.G.	Good	Fair	Poor
2250	1800	1500	1250	1000	700

PRICING

Prices given in this book are designed as a guide, not as a quote, and the prices given reflect retail values. This is very important to remember. You will seldom realize full retail value if you trade in a gun or sell it to a dealer. In this situation, your gun will be valued at its wholesale price, which is generally substantially below retail value to allow for the seller's profit margin.

It should also be remembered that prices for firearms can vary with the time of the year, geographical location, and the general economy. As might be expected, guns used for hunting are more likely to sell in late summer or early fall as hunting season approaches. Likewise, big-game rifles chambered for powerful magnum cartridges will likely have more appeal in western states than in the Deep South, while semi-automatic rifles or shotguns will not sell well in states where their use for hunting is prohibited, such as is the case in Pennsylvania.

It is not practical to list prices in this book with regard to time of year or location. What is given here is a reasonable price based on sales at gun shows, auction houses, and information obtained from knowledgeable collectors and dealers. In certain cases there will be no price indicated under a particular condition, but rather the notation "N/A" or the symbol "—." This indicates that there is no known price available for that gun in that condition or the sales for that particular model are so few that a reliable price cannot be ascertained. This will usually be encountered only with very rare guns, with newly introduced firearms, or more likely with antique firearms in those conditions most likely to be encountered. Most antique firearms will be seen in the Good, Fair and Poor categories.

Standard Catalog of Firearms can be used as an identification guide and as a source of starting prices for a planned firearms transaction. If you begin by valuing a given firearm according to the values shown in this book, you will not be too far off the mark.

In the final analysis, a firearm is worth only what someone is willing to pay for it. New trends arise quickly, and there are many excellent bargains to be found in today's market. With patience and good judgment—and with this book under your arm—you, too, can find them.

A

A. J. ORDNANCE

This company developed one of the first double-action only semi-automatic pistols, the Thomas .45. Limited production of less than 1,000 guns in 1977. Delayed blowback action that is unique, in every shot was double-action. Pistol was chambered for .45 ACP cartridge and had a 3.5" stainless steel barrel, with fixed sights and plastic grips. Detachable magazine held 6 shots. Standard finish was matte blue. Chrome plating was available and would add approximately 15 percent to values listed.

NIB	Exc.	V.G.	Good	Fair	Poor
1250	800	600	400	250	175

A.A.
Azanza & Arrizabalaga
Eibar, Spain

A.A.

Courtesy James Rankin

NIB	Exc.	V.G.	Good	Fair	Poor
—	300	175	150	100	50

Reims

6.35mm or 7.65mm caliber semi-automatic pistol, with 6- or 8-round magazine capacity. Most pistols have their slides marked: 1914 Model Automatic Pistol "Reims" Patent.

Courtesy James Rankin

NIB	Exc.	V.G.	Good	Fair	Poor
—	200	175	150	100	50

A.A.A.
Aldazabal
Eibar, Spain

Modelo 1919

7.65mm semi-automatic pistol, with 9-round magazine capacity. Trademark of knight's head over three As is on side of slide and grips.

Courtesy James Rankin

NIB	Exc.	V.G.	Good	Fair	Poor
—	200	175	150	100	50

A-SQUARE
Bedford, Kentucky/Chamberlain, South Dakota

Hannibal Grade

Using P-17 Enfield action, with 22" to 26" barrel. Rifle chambered for 32 calibers from 7mm Rem. Magnum up to and including .500 A-Square Magnum and .577 Tyrannosaur. Blued, with checkered walnut pistol-grip stock. Introduced in 1986. Weights range from 9 to 13.25 lbs., depending on caliber. **NOTE:** Add 5 percent for Kentucky-built rifles.

NIB	Exc.	V.G.	Good	Fair	Poor
3200	2700	1800	1000	600	350

Caesar Grade

Utilizing Remington Model 700 action. Chambered for same cartridges as above, with exception that A-Square proprietary cartridges are not available. Also made in left-hand version. Introduced in 1986. Weight 8.5 to 11 lb. range.

NIB	Exc.	V.G.	Good	Fair	Poor
3200	2700	1800	1000	600	350

Hamilcar Grade

Smaller and lighter version of Hannibal Grade. Designed to be chambered for .30-06 cartridges. Weighs 8 to 8.5 lbs. Introduced in 1994.

NIB	Exc.	V.G.	Good	Fair	Poor
3200	2700	1800	1000	600	350

Genghis Khan Model

Designed for varmint shooting. Fitted with heavyweight barrel. Offered in .22-250, .243 Win., 6mm Rem., .25-06, .257 Wby. and .264 Win. Barrel length and pull are to customer's specifications. No iron sights fitted to this model. Weight about 11 lbs.

NIB	Exc.	V.G.	Good	Fair	Poor
3200	2700	1800	1000	600	350

A & R SALES SOUTH
El Monte, California

A&R Sales South also made frames for custom 1911 builds.

45 Auto

Alloy-frame version of Colt Model 1911 semi-automatic pistol.

NIB	Exc.	V.G.	Good	Fair	Poor
475	325	200	150	125	100

Mark IV Sporter

Semi-automatic copy of M-14 military rifle. Manufactured in .308-caliber (7.65mm NATO) only.

NIB	Exc.	V.G.	Good	Fair	Poor
950	650	500	375	195	100

ABADIE
Liege, Belgium

Abadie Model 1878

9mm double-action revolver, with 6-shot cylinder, octagonal barrel and integral ejector rod.

NIB	Exc.	V.G.	Good	Fair	Poor
—	550	350	175	125	90

Abadie Model 1886

Heavier version of above.

NIB	Exc.	V.G.	Good	Fair	Poor
—	575	400	200	125	90

ABBEY, F.J. & CO.
Chicago, Illinois

Abbey Brothers produced a variety of percussion rifles and shotguns, which are all individual design. Prices listed represent what a plain F.J. Abbey & Company firearm might realize.

Rifle

NIB	Exc.	V.G.	Good	Fair	Poor
—	—	1750	800	450	200

Shotgun

NIB	Exc.	V.G.	Good	Fair	Poor
—	—	2500	1750	575	150

ABBEY, GEORGE T.
Utica, New York, and Chicago, Illinois

George T. Abbey originally worked in Utica, New York from 1845 to 1852. He moved to Chicago in 1852 and was in business until 1874. He manufactured a wide variety of percussion and cartridge firearms. Values listed represent those of his most common products.

Single-Barrel Shotgun

NIB	Exc.	V.G.	Good	Fair	Poor
—	—	1750	850	550	200

Side-by-Side Shotgun

NIB	Exc.	V.G.	Good	Fair	Poor
—	—	2550	1200	675	250

Over/Under Shotgun

NIB	Exc.	V.G.	Good	Fair	Poor
—	—	2750	1300	975	250

ABESSER & MERKEL
Suhl, Germany

Crown Grade

Single-barrel trap gun, with Greener cross bolt-action and two underbolt locks. Offered in 12-gauge, with barrel lengths from 28" to 34". Ventilated rib standard. Skip line checkering. Pistol- or straight-grip stock. Weight between 7 and 7.5 lbs. Engraved receiver with game scenes.

Courtesy Dan Sheil

NIB	Exc.	V.G.	Good	Fair	Poor
—	6000	4925	3825	1000	—

Diamond Grade

Side-by-side shotgun offered in 12-, 16-, 20-, 28-gauge and .410 bore. Auto ejectors, double triggers and full coverage engraving. Artistic stock carving behind frame. Skip line checkering. Many extras offered on this grade will affect price. Barrel lengths from 25" to 32". Weight from 6.5 to 7 lbs. Prices are for standard gun with no extras. **NOTE:** Add 50 percent for 20-gauge; 100 percent for 28-gauge or .410 bore.

Courtesy Dan Sheil

NIB	Exc.	V.G.	Good	Fair	Poor
—	12000	9200	8050	3000	700

Empire Grade

Side-by-side shotgun, with Anson-Deeley action. Receiver is fully engraved, with game birds and fine scroll. Stock is carved behind action. Checkering is fine skip line-style. Auto ejectors. Pistol- or straight-grip stock, with or without Monte Carlo and cheekpiece. Prices listed are for pre-war guns, with fluid steel barrels. **NOTE:** Add 50 percent for 20-gauge; 100 percent for 28-gauge or .410 bore.

Courtesy Dan Sheil

NIB	Exc.	V.G.	Good	Fair	Poor
—	13500	11150	9200	2500	700

Excelsior Grade

Side-by-side shotgun fitted with engraved side plates. Anson-Deeley action with double triggers. Fine line checkering. Figured walnut stock. All gauges offered from 12- to 28-gauge and .410 bore. Barrel lengths from 25" to 32". Many extra cost options available. **NOTE:** Add 50 percent for 20-gauge; 100 percent for 28-gauge or .410 bore.

Courtesy Dan Sheil

NIB	Exc.	V.G.	Good	Fair	Poor
—	9000	7500	6500	3100	700

Diana Grade

Over/under combination gun, with Greener cross bolt-action. Safety located on side of pistol-grip. Iron sights. Set trigger for rifle barrel. Wide variety of centerfire calibers offered, with barrel lengths from 26" to 30".

Courtesy Dan Sheil

NIB	Exc.	V.G.	Good	Fair	Poor
—	9500	8250	6250	3200	700

Vandalia Grade

Over/under gun chambered for 2.75" 12-gauge shells. Barrel lengths from 28" to 32". Walnut stock, with pistol- or straight-grip. Skip line checkering. Double triggers with extractors. Premium for factory multi-barrel combinations.

Courtesy Dan Sheil

NIB	Exc.	V.G.	Good	Fair	Poor
—	7250	6000	4500	3300	700

Nimrod

This is a drilling, with Greener cross bolt-action and double under bolt. Safety located on side of grip. Top two barrels may be 12-, 16- or 20-gauge. Bottom barrel offered in a variety of centerfire calibers. Iron sights. Pistol- or straight-grip stock. Receiver engraved with game scenes. **NOTE:** Add 50 percent for 20-gauge.

Courtesy Dan Sheil

NIB	Exc.	V.G.	Good	Fair	Poor
—	13000	9950	6000	4995	700

Magazine Rifle

Bolt-action rifle offered in a wide variety of calibers. Barrel lengths from 24" to 30". Calibers from 6.5mm to .404 Rimless. This model may have Zeiss scope or other special order features that will affect price. **NOTE:** Add $2000 for Magnum actions.

Courtesy Dan Sheil

NIB	Exc.	V.G.	Good	Fair	Poor
—	4900	3950	3350	1100	700

ACCU-MATCH
Mesa, Arizona

Accu-Match Custom Pistol

Competition pistol built on Colt 1911 design. Chambered for .45 ACP. Fitted with 5.5" match grade stainless steel barrel, slide and frame, with extended slide release and safety. Fitted with beavertail grip safety and wraparound finger groove rubber grips. Pistol has threaded three port compensator and dual action recoil spring system, with three-dot sight system.

NIB	Exc.	V.G.	Good	Fair	Poor
1050	750	550	400	300	175

ACCU-TEK
Chino, California

AT-380SS

Introduced in 1991. Semi-automatic pistol chambered for .380 ACP cartridge. Fitted with 2.75" barrel, with adjustable rear sight for windage. Black composition grips. Stainless steel construction. Furnished with 5-round magazine. Weight about 20 oz.

NIB	Exc.	V.G.	Good	Fair	Poor
245	165	100	75	50	25

AT-380 II

Introduced in 2004. Pistol chambered for .380 ACP cartridge. Fitted with 2.8" barrel. Magazine capacity 6 rounds. Stainless steel. Magazine release on bottom of grip. Weight about 23 oz.

NIB	Exc.	V.G.	Good	Fair	Poor
255	175	125	100	75	35

CP-9SS

Semi-automatic double-action-only stainless steel pistol. Chambered for 9mm cartridge. Fitted with 3.2" barrel, with adjustable rear sight for windage. Magazine capacity 8 rounds. Grips black checkered nylon. Weight about 28 oz. Introduced in 1992.

NIB	Exc.	V.G.	Good	Fair	Poor
295	225	150	100	75	50

CP-45SS

Similar to Model CP-9SS. Chambered for .45 ACP cartridge. Furnished with 6-round magazine. Introduced in 1996.

NIB	Exc.	V.G.	Good	Fair	Poor
300	245	195	150	125	75

CP-40SS

Introduced in 1992. Similar to CP-9SS. Chambered for .40 S&W cartridge. Furnished with 7-round magazine.

NIB	Exc.	V.G.	Good	Fair	Poor
300	245	195	150	125	75

BL-9

Semi-automatic double-action-only pistol. Chambered for 9mm cartridge. Furnished with 5-round magazine. Barrel length 3". Grips black composition. Finish black. Weight about 22 oz. Introduced in 1997.

NIB	Exc.	V.G.	Good	Fair	Poor
295	225	150	100	75	50

BL-380

Similar to Model BL-9. Chambered for .380 ACP cartridge. Introduced in 1997.

NIB	Exc.	V.G.	Good	Fair	Poor
255	175	125	100	75	35

HC-380SS

Semi-automatic pistol chambered for .380 ACP cartridge, with 2.75" barrel. Stainless steel finish. Furnished with 10-round magazine. Weight about 28 oz. Introduced in 1993.

NIB	Exc.	V.G.	Good	Fair	Poor
255	175	125	100	75	35

AT-32SS

Similar to Model AT-380SS. Chambered for .32 ACP cartridge. Introduced in 1991.

NIB	Exc.	V.G.	Good	Fair	Poor
225	175	110	75	50	40

LT-380

Single-action semi-automatic pistol in .380 ACP, with 6-shot magazine and 2.8" barrel. Blued or two-tone stainless slide, with aluminum frame. Black, pink, purple or OD green grips. Introduced in 2012.

NIB	Exc.	V.G.	Good	Fair	Poor
250	225	190	150	125	90

ACCURACY INTERNATIONAL
Portsmouth, England

Manufacturer of a series of competition rifles as well as tactical rifles for law enforcement and the military. Many options and variations have been made from 1985 to the present.

Palmamaster

This bolt-action rifle was designed for competition shooting with a laminated stock in either NRA Prone or UIT style. Chambered in .308 Winchester. Discontinued in 2002.

NIB	Exc.	V.G.	Good	Fair	Poor
2750	2400	2000	1500	1000	800

Cismmaster

Target rifle chambered in .22 BR, 6mm BR, .243 Winchester, 6.5x55, 7.5x55, .308 Winchester. Made from late 1990s until 2002.

NIB	Exc.	V.G.	Good	Fair	Poor
3200	2800	2200	1550	1300	900

AE

Competition rifle chambered in .243 Winchester, .260 Remington, 6.5 Creedmoor or .308 Winchester.

NIB	Exc.	V.G.	Good	Fair	Poor
3300	2850	2400	1700	1400	1000

AT

Tactical rifle chambered in .308 Winchester. Fixed stock with adjustable cheekpiece, buttpad spacers, pistol-grip, 24" quick-change barrel. Introduced in 2014.

NIB	Exc.	V.G.	Good	Fair	Poor
3300	2850	2400	1700	1400	1000

AW

Tactical rifle chambered in .243 Winchester, .260 Remington, 6.5 Creedmoor, .308 Winchester, .300 Winchester Magnum, .338 Lapua. Features a green synthetic stock with thumbhole grip.

NIB	Exc.	V.G.	Good	Fair	Poor
5000	4400	3700	3000	2000	1200

AX

Designed primarily as a sniper rifle for law enforcement and the military. Chambered in .243, .260, 6.5 Creedmoor, .308, .300 Win. Magnum, .338 Lapua. **NOTE:** Add $1,000 for .300 Win. or .338 Lapua.

NIB	Exc.	V.G.	Good	Fair	Poor
6500	5700	4700	3500	2200	1400

AXMC

Multi-caliber variation of AX in .308, .300 Win. Magnum or .338 Lapua Magnum. Caliber can be changed in the field by switching barrel, bolt and magazine insert. **NOTE:** Add $1,000 for each additional caliber.

NIB	Exc.	V.G.	Good	Fair	Poor
7500	6750	6000	5000	—	—

AX50

The AX50 model is similar to the AX, but chambered in .50 BMG.

NIB	Exc.	V.G.	Good	Fair	Poor
9800	8500	7000	5000	3000	2000

ACHA
Domingo Acha
Vizcaya, Spain

Atlas

6.35mm semi-automatic pistol, manufactured during 1920s, in Model 1906 Browning style. Grips are plain checkered hard rubber. Some grips had ACHA trademark of Count's head. Name "Atlas" appears on slide. Later models incorporated a grip safety.

Courtesy James Rankin

NIB	Exc.	V.G.	Good	Fair	Poor
—	250	175	100	75	50

Looking Glass (Ruby-Style)

7.65mm semi-automatic pistol in Ruby-style. Pistols furnished with 7-, 9- or 12-round magazine.

Courtesy James Rankin

NIB	Exc.	V.G.	Good	Fair	Poor
—	265	195	100	75	50

Looking Glass

6.35mm or 7.65mm caliber semi-automatic pistol. Various markings seen on these pistols and their grips. They were sold in both France and Spain by different distributors. Pistol pictured has two trademarks: "Domingo Acha" on grips and "Fabrique D'Arms de Guerre De Grande Presision" on slide.

Courtesy James Rankin

NIB	Exc.	V.G.	Good	Fair	Poor
—	295	175	110	75	50

ACME

See—Davenport Arms Co., Maltby Henley & Co., and Merwin & Hulbert & Co.

ACME ARMS
New York, New York

A trade name found on .22-, .32-caliber revolvers and 12-gauge shotguns. Marketed by Cornwall Hardware Company.

.22 Revolver

7-shot single-action revolver.

NIB	Exc.	V.G.	Good	Fair	Poor
—	375	275	175	125	75

.32 Revolver

5-shot single-action revolver.

NIB	Exc.	V.G.	Good	Fair	Poor
—	400	300	200	150	100

Shotgun

12-gauge double-barrel shotgun, with external hammers.

NIB	Exc.	V.G.	Good	Fair	Poor
—	400	275	175	125	75

ACME HAMMERLESS
Made by Hopkins & Allen
Norwich, Connecticut

Acme Hammerless

.32- or .38-caliber, 5-shot revolver. Either exposed or enclosed hammer. Sometimes known as "Forehand 1891".

NIB	Exc.	V.G.	Good	Fair	Poor
—	295	225	175	50	25

ACTION ARMS LTD.
Philadelphia, Pennsylvania

AT-84, AT-88

Pistol is Swiss version of CZ-75. Built at ITM, Solothurn, Switzerland. AT-84 chambered for 9mm cartridge; AT-88 for .41 Action Express. Both have 4.75" barrel. 9mm has magazine capacity of 15 rounds; .41 AE has 10 rounds. Finish either blue or chrome. Walnut grips.

Courtesy James Rankin

NIB	Exc.	V.G.	Good	Fair	Poor
750	550	450	375	300	150

AT-84P, AT-88P

As above, with 3.7" barrel and smaller frame.

NIB	Exc.	V.G.	Good	Fair	Poor
750	550	450	375	300	150

AT-84H, AT-88H

As above, with 3.4" barrel and smaller frame.

NIB	Exc.	V.G.	Good	Fair	Poor
750	550	450	375	300	150

Timber Wolf Carbine

Introduced in 1989. Slide-action carbine features 18.5" barrel. Adjustable rear sight and blade front sight. Chambered for .357 Magnum or .44 Magnum cartridges. Offered in blue or hard chrome finish. Weight about

5.5 lbs. Built in Israel by Israel Military Industries. **NOTE:** Add 20 percent for .44 Magnum.

NIB	Exc.	V.G.	Good	Fair	Poor
850	595	395	300	200	125

Action Arms/IMI Uzi Carbine Models A and B

16" barreled semi-automatic version of Uzi sub-machine gun. Chambered in 9mm Parabellum, .41 AE, .45 ACP. Built by IMI (Israeli Military Industries). **NOTE:** Add 10 percent for nylon Uzi case and accessories.

NIB	Exc.	V.G.	Good	Fair	Poor
1700	1450	1150	850	600	250

ADAMS / DEANE, ADAMS & DEANE
London, England
London Armoury Co. (After 1856)

Revolvers based upon Robert Adams' patents, were manufactured by firm of Deane, Adams & Deane. Although more technically advanced than pistols produced by Samuel Colt, Adams' revolvers were popular primarily in England and British Empire.

Adams Model 1851 Self-Cocking Revolver

.44-caliber double-action percussion revolver, with 7.5" octagonal barrel and 5-shot cylinder. Barrel and frame blued. Cylinder case hardened. Grips walnut. Top strap marked "Deane, Adams and Deane 30 King William St. London Bridge". Revolver does not have hammer spur and functions only as double-action.

NIB	Exc.	V.G.	Good	Fair	Poor
—	4000	2975	1475	775	400

Adams Pocket Revolver

As above in .31-caliber, with 4.5" barrel.

NIB	Exc.	V.G.	Good	Fair	Poor
—	3750	2875	1375	750	400

Beaumont-Adams Revolver

As above, with Tranter Patent loading lever. Hammer made with a spur.

NIB	Exc.	V.G.	Good	Fair	Poor
—	2500	1950	950	695	300

ADAMY GEBRUDER
Suhl, Germany

Over/Under Shotgun

12- or 16-gauge double-barrel over/under shotgun, with 26" to 30" barrels. Double triggers. Walnut stock.

NIB	Exc.	V.G.	Good	Fair	Poor
—	2100	1700	1250	750	400

ADCO ARMS

This company imported several shotguns from Turkey about 2001 to 2012 under the Diamond brand. It currently imports parts for AR-style and other tactical firearms.

Diamond Double Over/Under

Available in 12- or 20-gauge, with 26" or 28" barrels, choke tubes, checkered walnut stock, selective trigger and automatic ejectors. Imperial grade has a higher-grade wood.

Field Grade

NIB	Exc.	V.G.	Good	Fair	Poor
400	350	300	250	200	150

Imperial Grade

NIB	Exc.	V.G.	Good	Fair	Poor
600	500	375	300	250	200

Double Side-by-Side

NIB	Exc.	V.G.	Good	Fair	Poor
700	600	475	400	350	250

Imperial Semi-Automatic

NIB	Exc.	V.G.	Good	Fair	Poor
400	350	300	225	175	125

Imperial Pump

NIB	Exc.	V.G.	Good	Fair	Poor
375	325	275	200	150	100

ADIRONDACK ARMS CO. / A.S. BABBITT CO.
Plattsburgh, New York

Orvil M. Robinson Patent Rifle

Robinson tube-fed repeating rifle was made in New York, between 1870 and 1874. Early models 1870-1872 marked "A.S. Babbitt"; later models 1872-1874 "Adirondack Arms Co.". Company was sold to Winchester in 1874, but they never produced Robinson after that date. Rifle has been found in two styles: first with small fingers on hammer to cock and operate mechanism; second with buttons on receiver to retract bolt and cock hammer. Rifle made in .44-caliber, with octagonal barrel usually found in 26" or 28" length. Frames predominantly brass. Some iron frames have been noted and will bring a premium of approximately 25 percent. Barrel and magazine tube have blued finish.

Courtesy Buffalo Bill Historical Center, Cody, Wyoming

First Model

NIB	Exc.	V.G.	Good	Fair	Poor
—	6500	5200	2700	1300	500

Second Model

NIB	Exc.	V.G.	Good	Fair	Poor
—	6500	5200	2700	1300	500

ADLER
Engelbrecht & Wolff
Blasii, Germany

Extremely rare and unusually designed semi-automatic pistol. Adapted for 7.25mm Adler cartridge. Striker-fired blowback pistol, with 3.4" barrel. Single-column magazine has 8-round capacity. Weight about 24 oz. Produced in a very limited number. Probably only a few hundred between 1906 and 1907.

Courtesy James Rankin

NIB	Exc.	V.G.	Good	Fair	Poor
—	—	10000	8750	2750	1250

ADVANCED SMALL ARMS INDUSTRIES
Solothurn, Switzerland

one Pro .45

Introduced in 1997. Built in Switzerland by ASAI. Pistol features 3" barrel chambered for .45 ACP cartridge. Based on short-recoil operation. Available in double-action or double-action-only. Also available is a kit (purchased separately) to convert pistol to .400 CorBon caliber. Pistol weighs about 24 oz. empty.

NIB	Exc.	V.G.	Good	Fair	Poor
1000	725	595	425	195	100

ADVANTAGE ARMS U.S.A., INC.
Distributed by Wildfire Sports
St. Paul, Minnesota

Model 422

.22- or .22-caliber Magnum four-barrel derringer, with 2.5" barrels. Entirely made of aluminum alloy. Finished in blue or nickel-plate. Manufactured in 1986 and 1987.

NIB	Exc.	V.G.	Good	Fair	Poor
225	125	100	85	65	45

AERO
Manufactura De Armas De Fuego
Guernica, Spain

Model 1914 (Aero)

7.65mm caliber semi-automatic pistol, with 3.25" barrel in Ruby design. "Aero" name on slide along with an airplane. Magazine capacity 7 rounds. Weight about 23 oz.

Courtesy James Rankin

NIB	Exc.	V.G.	Good	Fair	Poor
—	350	250	200	125	95

AETNA ARMS CO.
New York

.22-caliber spur trigger revolver, with octagonal barrel and 7-shot cylinder. Barrel marked "Aetna Arms Co. New York". Manufactured approximately 1870 to 1880. Copy of S&W No. 1.

NIB	Exc.	V.G.	Good	Fair	Poor
—	—	550	375	150	100

AFC
Auguste Francotte
Liege, Belgium

One of the most prolific makers of revolvers, in Liege, during the last half of the 19th century. Estimated over 150 different revolvers made and marketed by them, before they were forced out of business by German occupation of 1914. Francotte produced many variations from Tranter copies to pinfires, early Smith & Wesson designs to 11mm M1871 Swedish troopers revolver. They made break-open revolvers and produced only one semi-automatic, a 6.35mm blowback design. A good portion of their pistols were produced for the wholesale market and sold under other names. These particular revolvers will bear letters "AF" stamped somewhere on the frame. Because of the vast number and variety of pistols produced by this company, cataloging and pricing is beyond the scope of this or any general reference book. Suggested that any examples encountered, be researched on an individual basis. More information on Francotte, see information under that listing.

Model 1895

One of earliest Francotte pistols. Chambered for 8mm cartridge. Lever-operated repeater. Marked "A. Francotte & Co. Makers" on top of slide.

Courtesy James Rankin

NIB	Exc.	V.G.	Good	Fair	Poor
—	7000	5500	4150	2300	1500

Trainer

Single-shot target pistol. Made for competition in .22-caliber short. "AFC" trademark on left side of frame. Model probably not made by Francotte, but sold by that firm and others.

Courtesy James Rankin

NIB	Exc.	V.G.	Good	Fair	Poor
—	3800	3150	2700	2175	1500

Semi-Auto

6.35mm, 6-shot detachable magazine pocket pistol, with blue finish. Model marked "A. Francotte A Liege" on frame.

Courtesy James Rankin

NIB	Exc.	V.G.	Good	Fair	Poor
—	425	300	195	125	90

AFFERBACH, W. A.
Philadelphia, Pennsylvania

Maker known to have produced copies of Henry Derringer's percussion pocket pistols. Though uncommon, their values would be approximately as listed.

NIB	Exc.	V.G.	Good	Fair	Poor
—	—	2750	2200	995	300

AGNER (SAXHOJ PRODUCTS, INC.)
Copenhagen, Denmark

Model M 80

.22-caliber single-shot stainless steel target pistol, with 5.9" barrel, adjustable sights and walnut grips. Pistol fitted with dry fire mechanism. Also available in left-hand version. Imported from 1981 to 1986.

Courtesy James Rankin

NIB	Exc.	V.G.	Good	Fair	Poor
—	1250	875	600	450	200

AGUIRRE
Eibar, Spain

Spanish manufacturer of pistols prior to World War II.

Basculant

6.35mm semi-automatic pistol. Marked on slide "Cal. 6.35 Automatic Pistol Basculant".

NIB	Exc.	V.G.	Good	Fair	Poor
—	275	150	125	75	50

LeDragon

As above, with slide marked "Cal. 6.35 Automatic Pistol LeDragon". Patterned after Browning Model 1906. Stylized dragon molded into grips.

Courtesy James Rankin

NIB	Exc.	V.G.	Good	Fair	Poor
—	275	150	125	75	50

AGUIRRE Y ARANZABAL (AyA)
Eibar, Spain

SIDE-BY-SIDES

Matador

12-, 16-, 20-, 28-gauge or .410 bore boxlock double-barrel shotgun, with 26", 28" or 30" barrels. Single-selective trigger and automatic ejectors. Blued, with walnut stock. Manufactured from 1955 to 1963. **NOTE:** Add 100 percent for 28-gauge and .410 bore.

NIB	Exc.	V.G.	Good	Fair	Poor
—	550	415	350	300	200

Matador II

As above in 12- or 20-gauge, with ventilated rib.

NIB	Exc.	V.G.	Good	Fair	Poor
—	575	425	375	300	200

Matador III

As above, with 3" chambers. **NOTE:** Add 20 percent for 20-gauge.

NIB	Exc.	V.G.	Good	Fair	Poor
800	700	600	395	325	200

Bolero

As above, with non-selective single trigger and extractors. Manufactured until 1984.

NIB	Exc.	V.G.	Good	Fair	Poor
—	500	375	325	295	200

Iberia

12- or 20-gauge Magnum boxlock double-barrel shotgun, with 26", 28" or 30" barrels. Double triggers and extractors. Blued, with walnut stock.

NIB	Exc.	V.G.	Good	Fair	Poor
—	600	450	395	325	200

Iberia II

Similar to above in 12- or 16-gauge, with 28" barrels and 2.75" chambers.

NIB	Exc.	V.G.	Good	Fair	Poor
—	625	500	425	325	250

Model 106

12-, 16- or 20-gauge boxlock double-barrel shotgun, with 28" barrels. Double triggers and extractors. Blued, with walnut stock. Manufactured until 1985.

NIB	Exc.	V.G.	Good	Fair	Poor
—	600	500	400	300	250

Model 107-LI

As above, with receiver lightly engraved and English-style stock. In 12- or 16-gauge only.

NIB	Exc.	V.G.	Good	Fair	Poor
—	675	575	495	325	275

Model 116

12-, 16- or 20-gauge sidelock double-barrel shotgun, with 27" to 30" barrels. Double triggers and ejectors. Engraved, blued, with walnut stock. Manufactured until 1985.

NIB	Exc.	V.G.	Good	Fair	Poor
—	1095	975	800	500	350

Model 117

As above, with 3" chambers.

NIB	Exc.	V.G.	Good	Fair	Poor
—	1150	1000	850	600	400

Model 117 "Quail Unlimited"

As above in 12-gauge only, with 26" barrels. Receiver engraved "Quail Unlimited of North America". Forty-two were manufactured.

NIB	Exc.	V.G.	Good	Fair	Poor
—	1500	1200	875	650	425

Model 210

Exposed hammer 12- or 16-gauge boxlock shotgun, with 26" to 28" barrels. Double triggers. Blued, with walnut stock. Manufactured until 1985.

NIB	Exc.	V.G.	Good	Fair	Poor
—	800	675	550	400	325

Model 711 Boxlock

12-gauge boxlock double-barrel shotgun, with 28" or 30" barrels. Ventilated ribs. Single-selective trigger and automatic ejectors. Manufactured until 1984.

NIB	Exc.	V.G.	Good	Fair	Poor
—	900	800	700	500	350

Model 711 Sidelock

As above, with sidelocks. Manufactured in 1985 only.

NIB	Exc.	V.G.	Good	Fair	Poor
—	1200	1000	750	500	400

Senior

Custom order 12-gauge double-barrel sidelock shotgun. Gold inlaid and engraved. Made strictly to individual customer's specifications.

NIB	Exc.	V.G.	Good	Fair	Poor
17000	13750	9750	7000	4500	2250

OVER/UNDERS

Model 79 "A"

12-gauge boxlock over/under double-barrel shotgun, with 26", 28" or 30" barrels. Single-selective trigger and automatic ejectors. Blued, with walnut stock. Manufactured until 1985.

NIB	Exc.	V.G.	Good	Fair	Poor
—	1250	1050	925	750	500

Model 79 "B"

As above, with moderate amount of engraving.

NIB	Exc.	V.G.	Good	Fair	Poor
—	1350	1150	950	800	575

Model 79 "C"

As above, with extensive engraving.

NIB	Exc.	V.G.	Good	Fair	Poor
—	2000	1800	1500	1150	675

Model 77

As above, patterned after Merkel shotgun.

NIB	Exc.	V.G.	Good	Fair	Poor
—	3000	2700	2000	1500	1000

Coral "A"

12- or 16-gauge over/under boxlock double-barrel shotgun, with 26" or 28" barrels. Ventilated ribs, double triggers and automatic ejectors. Fitted with Kersten cross bolt. Manufactured until 1985.

NIB	Exc.	V.G.	Good	Fair	Poor
—	1250	900	700	500	300

Coral "B"

As above, with engraved French case hardened receiver.

NIB	Exc.	V.G.	Good	Fair	Poor
—	1400	1100	750	600	350

RECENTLY IMPORTED SHOTGUNS

SIDELOCK SIDE-BY-SIDES

AyA sidelock shotguns use Holland & Holland system. Feature double triggers, articulated front trigger, cocking indicators, bushed firing pins, replaceable firing pins, replaceable hinge pins and chopper lump barrels. Frame and sidelocks case-colored. Weight between 5 and 7 lbs., depending on gauge and barrel length. Barrel lengths offered in 26", 27", 28" and 29" depending on gauge. All stocks are figured walnut, with hand checkering and oil finish. Available with several extra cost options that may affect price. Also influencing price of new guns is fluctuating dollar in relation to Spanish currency.

Model No. 1

Offered in 12-, 16-, 20-, 28-gauge or .410 bore, with special English scroll engraving. Fitted with automatic ejectors and straight-grip stock. Exhibition quality wood.

NIB	Exc.	V.G.	Good	Fair	Poor
11000	10000	8000	4750	2300	700

Model No. 1 Round Body

As above, with round body action.

NIB	Exc.	V.G.	Good	Fair	Poor
12000	11000	9000	5250	—	—

Model No. 1 Deluxe

Deluxe version of No. 1, with finer wood and engraving. **NOTE:** Add $350 for round body.

NIB	Exc.	V.G.	Good	Fair	Poor
15000	12500	9000	5250	2400	700

Model No. 2

Offered in 12-, 16-, 20-, 28-gauge and .410 bore. Has automatic ejectors, straight-grip and select walnut stock.

NIB	Exc.	V.G.	Good	Fair	Poor
—	5000	4000	2500	1850	700

Model No. 2 Round Body

As above, with round body action.

NIB	Exc.	V.G.	Good	Fair	Poor
—	5200	4250	2750	1950	700

Model No. 53

Chambered for 12-, 16- and 20-gauge. Features three locking lugs, side clips, automatic ejectors and straight-grip stock.

NIB	Exc.	V.G.	Good	Fair	Poor
6900	5500	4000	2750	1000	700

Model No. 56

Available in 12-gauge only. Features three locking lugs, side clips, special wide action body and raised matted rib. Select walnut straight-grip stock.

NIB	Exc.	V.G.	Good	Fair	Poor
10500	8700	6750	5400	2000	1000

Model XXV Sidelock

Offered in all gauges. Fitted with Churchill-type rib. Automatic ejectors, select straight-grip and walnut stock standard.

NIB	Exc.	V.G.	Good	Fair	Poor
5900	5250	4250	3200	1750	1000

BOXLOCK SIDE-BY-SIDES

These AyA guns utilize Anson & Deeley system. Double locking lugs, detachable cross pin and separate trigger plate that gives access to firing mechanism. Frame case-colored. Barrels are chopper lump. Firing pins bushed. Automatic safety and ejectors standard. Barrels offered in 26", 27" and 28", depending on gauge. Weight between 5 and 7 lbs., depending on gauge.

Adarra

This model is offered in all major gauges, with the option of double non-selective or selective single triggers. Grade 2 walnut stock has a hand rubbed oil finish, cut checkering, straight-grip and a splinter fore-end. Receiver has a bold foliate engraving pattern, with choice of color case-hardened, old silver or white finish. Introduced in 2013.

NIB	Exc.	V.G.	Good	Fair	Poor
4250	3800	3000	2450	1500	500

Model XXV Boxlock

Available in 12- and 20-gauge only. Hand checkered select walnut stock, with straight-grip stock.

NIB	Exc.	V.G.	Good	Fair	Poor
—	3500	2250	800	600	350

Model No. 4

Available in 12-, 16-, 20-, 28-gauge and .410 bore. Hand checkered select walnut stock, with straight-grip. Light scroll engraving. **NOTE:** Add 75 percent for 28-gauge and .410 bore.

NIB	Exc.	V.G.	Good	Fair	Poor
—	3000	2650	1250	—	—

Model No. 4 Deluxe

Same as above, with select walnut stock and slightly more engraving coverage. **NOTE:** Add 75 percent for 28-gauge and .410 bore.

NIB	Exc.	V.G.	Good	Fair	Poor
—	5000	3995	1500	1000	550

OVER/UNDERS

These AyA shotguns are similar in design and appearance to Gebruder Merkel over/under sidelocks, with three-part fore-end, Kersten cross bolt and double under locking lugs.

Model No. 37 Super

Available in 12-, 16- or 20-gauge. Ventilated rib, automatic ejectors, internally gold-plated sidelocks. Offered with three different types of engraving patterns; ducks, scroll or deep cut engraving. Very few of this model imported into U.S.

NIB	Exc.	V.G.	Good	Fair	Poor
—	12000	9500	5000	3500	2000

Model Augusta

Top-of-the-line AyA model offered in 12-gauge only. Features presentation wood and deep cut scroll engraving. Very few imported into U.S.

NIB	Exc.	V.G.	Good	Fair	Poor
—	18000	8000	4500	3500	1500

AIR MATCH
Paris, Kentucky

Air Match 500

.22-caliber single-shot target pistol, with 10.5" barrel, adjustable sights and adjustable front-mounted counterweights. Blued, with walnut grips. Imported from 1984 to 1986.

NIB	Exc.	V.G.	Good	Fair	Poor
775	595	425	300	250	125

AJAX ARMY

Single-Action

Spur-trigger single-action solid-frame revolver. Chambered for .44 rimfire cartridge. Had 7" barrel. Blued, with walnut grips. Manufactured in 1880s.

NIB	Exc.	V.G.	Good	Fair	Poor
—	750	450	365	275	200

AKDAL
Istanbul, Turkey

This company manufactures several firearms that have recently been imported into the United States, including the Ghost pistol series and several AR-style semi-automatic shotguns.

Ghost

A 9mm striker-fired polymer-frame pistol, with features similar to the Glock. It has a 15-round magazine and interchangeable grip backstraps of different sizes.

NIB	Exc.	V.G.	Good	Fair	Poor
400	325	275	200	150	100

MKA 1919

A 12-gauge shotgun built on an AR-15 type frame. Features include a detachable 5-round magazine and three interchangeable choke tubes.

NIB	Exc.	V.G.	Good	Fair	Poor
550	450	350	285	225	150

ALAMO RANGER
Spain

Double-action Spanish copy of Colt SAA. Chambered for .38 Long Colt or .38 Special. Cylinder held 6 shots. Finish blued and grips checkered hard rubber. Maker of this pistol unknown.

NIB	Exc.	V.G.	Good	Fair	Poor
—	350	225	115	75	45

ALASKA
Norwich, Connecticut

See—Hood Firearms Co.

ALASKA MAGNUM
Fairbanks, Alaska

Manufacturer of high-grade AR-style rifles designed for hunting large game. Features include stainless steel barrels, nickel plated bolt carrier groups, free float hand guards, synthetic or laminate stocks. Chamberings include .300 Ruger, .338 Ruger, .450 Bushmaster and proprietary calibers 6.9AR Short, .375 GrizzinatAR and .460 GrizzinatAR.

Kodiak or Grizzly Model

NIB	Exc.	V.G.	Good	Fair	Poor
3400	2850	2000	1700	—	—

Wolverine Model

NIB	Exc.	V.G.	Good	Fair	Poor
2500	2000	1600	1200	—	—

ALDAZABAL
Eibar, Spain
Aldazabal, Leturiondo & CIA

Model 1919

Vest pocket semi-automatic pistol. Copied from FN Browning Model 1906. Caliber 6.35mm.

Courtesy James Rankin

NIB	Exc.	V.G.	Good	Fair	Poor
—	295	175	125	75	50

Military Model

Semi-automatic pistol in Ruby-style. Caliber 7.65mm, with 9-round magazine.

Courtesy James Rankin

NIB	Exc.	V.G.	Good	Fair	Poor
—	375	275	195	125	75

Aldazabal

Another typical low-quality "Eibar" type semi-automatic. Browning blow-back copy. Chambered for 7.65mm cartridge. Had 7-shot detachable magazine, blued finish, with checkered wood grips. Company ceased production before Spanish Civil War.

NIB	Exc.	V.G.	Good	Fair	Poor
—	295	165	115	65	40

ALERT
Norwich, Connecticut

See—Hood Firearms Co.

ALEXANDER ARMS
Radford, Virginia

This manufacturer of AR-style rifles and carbines is probably best known for developing the .50 Beowulf and 6.5 Grendel cartridges. In addition to those chamberings, rifles have been made in 5.56 NATO, .300 AAC, .338 Lapua Magnum and .17 HMR in most standard AR models and variations. Barrels are 16", 18", 20" or 24". Models are available for consumer, law enforcement and military markets. Depending on the specific model, features include forged flattop receiver with Picatinny rail, button-rifled stainless steel barrels, composite free-floating handguard, A2 flash hider, M4 collapsible stock, gas piston operating system. Listed below is a sampling of the company's many recent and current models.

R-BEOPREC .50 Beowulf Precision Rifle

NIB	Exc.	V.G.	Good	Fair	Poor
1250	1000	800	—	—	—

R-BEOENTRY .50 Beowulf Entry

NIB	Exc.	V.G.	Good	Fair	Poor
1100	950	750	—	—	—

R-50 .50 Beowulf Hunter

NIB	Exc.	V.G.	Good	Fair	Poor
1400	1100	900	—	—	—

R-65 HUNT 6.5 Grendel

NIB	Exc.	V.G.	Good	Fair	Poor
1400	1100	900	—	—	—

R-GSR 6.5 Grendel Sniper Rifle

NIB	Exc.	V.G.	Good	Fair	Poor
3000	2400	2000	—	—	—

R-338 Ulfbehrt .338 Lapua

NIB	Exc.	V.G.	Good	Fair	Poor
5500	4200	3200	—	—	—

R-556 5.56 NATO Incursion

NIB	Exc.	V.G.	Good	Fair	Poor
1000	875	650	—	—	—

R-300 16ST .300 AAC

NIB	Exc.	V.G.	Good	Fair	Poor
1000	875	650	—	—	—

R-17 .17 HMR

NIB	Exc.	V.G.	Good	Fair	Poor
900	750	550	—	—	—

ALEXIA
Norwich, Connecticut

See—Hopkins & Allen

ALFA
Eibar, Spain

See—Armero Especialistas Reunides

ALKARTASUNA FABRICA DE ARMAS
Guernica, Spain

Company began production during World War I, to help

Gabilondo y Urresti supply sidearms to the French. After hostilities ceased, they continued to produce firearms under their own name. They produced a number of variations in both 6.35mm and 7.65mm marked "Alkar". Collector interest is very thin. Factory burned down in 1920 and by 1922 business had totally ceased.

Alkar

6.35mm semi-automatic pistol, with cartridge counter in grip plates. One variation of many. Built in 6.35mm or 7.65mm.

Courtesy James Rankin

NIB	Exc.	V.G.	Good	Fair	Poor
—	295	250	195	125	100

Alkar (Ruby-Style)

7.65mm semi-automatic pistol built in Ruby-style. Pistol supplied to French government during World War I.

Courtesy James Rankin

NIB	Exc.	V.G.	Good	Fair	Poor
—	295	225	165	100	90

ALL RIGHT FIREARMS CO.
Lawrence, Massachusetts

Little All Right Palm Pistol

Squeezer-type pocket pistol, invented by E. Boardman and A. Peavy in 1876. Made in .22-caliber. Had 5-shot cylinder, with 1.625" or 2.375" barrel. Barrel octagonal, with tube on top which houses sliding trigger. Finish nickel. Black hard rubber grips have "Little All Right" & "All Right Firearms Co., Manufacturers Lawrence, Mass. U.S.A." molded into them. Several hundred produced in late 1870s.

Courtesy Milwaukee Public Museum, Milwaukee, Wisconsin

NIB	Exc.	V.G.	Good	Fair	Poor
—	4000	3250	2950	1050	300

ALLEN, ETHAN
Grafton, Massachusetts

Founded by Ethan Allen in early 1800s. It became a prolific gun-making firm, that evolved from Ethan Allen to Allen & Thurber, as well as Allen & Wheelock Company. It was located in Norwich, Connecticut and Worchester, Massachusetts, as well as Grafton. Eventually it became Forehand & Wadsworth Company in 1871, after the death of Ethan Allen. There were many and varied firearms produced under all headings described above. If one desires to collect Ethan Allen firearms, it would be advisable to educate oneself, as there are a number of fine publications available on the subject. Basic models and their values are listed.

First Model Pocket Rifle

Manufactured by Ethan Allen in Grafton, Massachusetts. Bootleg-type under-hammer single-shot pistol, chambered for .31 percussion. Larger-caliber versions have also been noted. Barrel lengths from 5" to 9" that were part-octagon in configuration. Iron mountings. Blued, with walnut grips. Barrel marked, "E. Allen/ Grafton/Mass." as well as "Pocket Rifle/ Cast Steel/Warranted". Approximately 2,000 manufactured from 1831 to 1842.

NIB	Exc.	V.G.	Good	Fair	Poor
—	—	—	1650	750	200

Second Model Pocket Rifle

Rounded-frame round-grip version of First Model.

NIB	Exc.	V.G.	Good	Fair	Poor
—	—	—	1550	650	200

Bar Hammer Pistol

Double-action pistol, with top-mounted bar hammer. Chambered for .28- to .36-caliber percussion. Half-octagon barrels were from 2" to 10" in length. They screwed out of the frame so it was possible to breech load them. Finish blued. Rounded walnut grips. They were marked, "Allen & Thurber/Grafton Mass.". Approximately 2,000 manufactured between early 1830s and 1860.

NIB	Exc.	V.G.	Good	Fair	Poor
—	—	—	1650	725	200

Tube Hammer Pistol

Version similar to Bar Hammer. Curved hammer without spur. Few hundred manufactured between early 1830s and 1840s.

NIB	Exc.	V.G.	Good	Fair	Poor
—	—	—	2900	1300	400

Side Hammer Pistol

Single-shot target-type pistol. Chambered for .34-, .41- and .45-caliber percussion. Part-octagon barrel from 6" to 10" in length. Wooden ramrod mounted under barrel. Hood quality rear sight that was adjustable. Ornate trigger guard had a graceful spur at its rear. Finish blued. Rounded walnut grip. Barrel marked, "Allen & Thurber, Worchester". Approximately 300 manufactured in late 1840s and early 1850s.

NIB	Exc.	V.G.	Good	Fair	Poor
—	—	—	1400	650	200

Center Hammer Pistol

Single-action chambered for .34-, .36- or .44-caliber percussion. Half-octagon barrel from 4" to 12" in length. Centrally mounted hammer that was offset to right side to allow for sighting the pistol. Finish blued, with walnut grips. Marked, "Allen & Thurber, Allen Thurber & Company". Some specimens marked, "Allen & Wheelock". Several thousand manufactured between late 1840s and 1860.

NIB	Exc.	V.G.	Good	Fair	Poor
—	—	—	1400	650	200

Double-Barrel Pistol

Side-by-side double-barrel pistol, with single trigger. Chambered for .36-caliber percussion, with 3" to 6" round barrels. Finish blued, with walnut grips. Examples with ramrod mounted under barrel have been noted. Flute between barrels was marked, "Allen & Thurber", "Allen Thurber & Company" or "Allen & Wheelock". Approximately 1,000 manufactured in 1850s.

NIB	Exc.	V.G.	Good	Fair	Poor
—	—	—	1250	600	150

Allen & Wheelock Center Hammer Pistol

Single-action pocket pistol, chambered for .31- to .38-caliber percussion. Octagon barrels from 3" to 6" in length. Finish blued. Square butt walnut grips. Barrel marked, "Allen & Wheelock". Approximately 500 manufactured between 1858 and 1865.

NIB	Exc.	V.G.	Good	Fair	Poor
—	—	—	1100	550	100

Allen Thurber & Company Target Pistol

Deluxe single-action target pistol. Chambered for .31- or .36-caliber percussion. Had heavy octagon barrel from 11" to 16" in length. Wooden ramrod mounted underneath barrel. Mountings were German silver. Detachable walnut stock. Deluxe engraved patchbox. Weapon was engraved and barrel marked, "Allen Thurber & Co./Worchester/Cast Steel". Firearm furnished in fitted case, with stock, false muzzle and various accessories. Considered to be a very high grade target pistol in its era. Values listed are for complete-cased outfit. Very few manufactured in 1850s. **NOTE:** Pistols without attachable stock deduct 75 percent.

NIB	Exc.	V.G.	Good	Fair	Poor
—	—	—	9000	4000	1000

Ethan Allen Pepperboxes

During the period from early 1830s to 1860s, company manufactured over 50 different variations of revolving pepperbox-type pistol. They were commercially quite successful and actually competed successfully with Colt revolving handguns for more than a decade. Widely used throughout United States, as well as Mexico and during our Civil War. They are widely collectible, because of the number of variations that exist. Potential collector should avail himself of information available on the subject. These pepperboxes can be divided into three categories.

No. 1: Manufactured from 1830s until 1842, at Grafton, Massachusetts.

No. 2: Manufactured from 1842 to 1847, at Norwich, Connecticut.

No. 3: Manufactured from 1847 to 1865, at Worchester, Massachusetts.

There are a number of subdivisions among these three basic groups, that would pertain to trigger type, size, barrel length, etc. It would be impossible to cover all 50 of these variations in a text of this type. We strongly suggest a qualified individual appraisal be secured, if contemplating a transaction. Values of these pepperbox pistols in excellent condition would be between $1,500 and $5,000. Most examples will be seen in fair to good condition and will bring $1,000 to $2,000 depending on variation.

Large Frame Pocket Revolver

Double-action pocket revolver chambered for .34-caliber percussion. Octagon barrel from 3" to 5" in length. No sights. The 5-shot unfluted cylinder was game scene engraved. Finish blued. Rounded walnut grips. Bar-type hammer. First conventional revolver manufactured by this company. Directly influenced by pepperbox pistol, for which Ethan Allen had become famous. Marked, "Allen & Wheelock" as well as "Patented April 16, 1845". Approximately 1,500 manufactured between 1857 and 1860.

Courtesy Milwaukee Public Museum, Milwaukee, Wisconsin

NIB	Exc.	V.G.	Good	Fair	Poor
—	—	—	1400	700	350

Small Frame Pocket Revolver

Version similar to Large Frame Pocket Revolver, except chambered for .31-caliber percussion. Octagon barrel length 2" to 3.5". Slightly smaller in size, but finished and marked the same. Approximately 1,000 made between 1858 and 1860.

NIB	Exc.	V.G.	Good	Fair	Poor
—	—	—	1400	700	350

Side Hammer Belt Revolver

Single-action revolver chambered for .34-caliber percussion. Octagon barrel from 3" to 7.5" in length. Featured a hammer mounted on right side of frame and 5-shot engraved unfluted cylinder. Cylinder access pin is inserted from rear of weapon. Finish blued. Case colored hammer and trigger guard. Flared butt walnut grips. Marked, "Allen & Wheelock". Two basic types. Values for early model, of which 100 manufactured between 1858 and 1861.

NIB	Exc.	V.G.	Good	Fair	Poor
—	—	—	1500	750	300

Standard Model

Second type was Standard Model. Spring-loaded catch on trigger guard, as opposed to friction catch on early model. Approximately 1,000 manufactured between 1858 and 1861.

Courtesy Milwaukee Public Museum, Milwaukee, Wisconsin

NIB	Exc.	V.G.	Good	Fair	Poor
—	—	—	1200	595	200

Side Hammer Pocket Revolver

Version chambered for .28-caliber percussion. Had 2" to 5" octagon barrel. Frame slightly smaller than belt model.

Courtesy Milwaukee Public Museum, Milwaukee, Wisconsin

Early Production

100 manufactured.

NIB	Exc.	V.G.	Good	Fair	Poor
—	—	—	1300	725	250

Standard Production

1,000 manufactured.

NIB	Exc.	V.G.	Good	Fair	Poor
—	—	2100	975	400	225

Side Hammer Navy Revolver

Large-frame military-type revolver. Similar to Side Hammer Belt Model. Chambered for .36-caliber percussion. Features octagon 5.5" to 8" barrel, with 6-shot engraved cylinder. Early production guns have friction style catch to secure trigger guard/loading lever on the left sideplate. Approximately 100 manufactured between 1858 and 1861.

Early Production

NIB	Exc.	V.G.	Good	Fair	Poor
—	—	—	4300	1975	575

Standard Model

Has a spring-loaded catch on rear of the trigger guard. 1,000 manufactured.

NIB	Exc.	V.G.	Good	Fair	Poor
—	—	—	3700	1700	475

Center Hammer Army Revolver

Large military-type single-action revolver chambered for .44-caliber percussion. Had 7.5" half-octagon barrel and 6-shot unfluted cylinder. Hammer mounted in center of frame. Finish blued. Case colored hammer and trigger guard. Walnut grips. Barrel marked, "Allen & Wheelock. Worchester, Mass. U.S./Allen's Pt's. Jan. 13, 1857. Dec. 15, 1857, Sept. 7, 1858". Approximately 700 manufactured between 1861 and 1862.

NIB	Exc.	V.G.	Good	Fair	Poor
—	—	7500	4500	1875	500

Center Hammer Navy Revolver

Similar to Army Revolver. Chambered for .36-caliber percussion, with 7.5" full-octagon barrel. Examples have been noted with 5", 6" or 8" barrels.

NIB	Exc.	V.G.	Good	Fair	Poor
—	—	—	4300	1975	475

Center Hammer Percussion Revolver

Single-action revolver chambered for .36-caliber percussion. Octagonal 3" or 4" barrel, with 6-shot unfluted cylinder. Finish blued, with walnut grips. Model supposedly was made for Providence, Rhode Island, Police Department and has become commonly referred to as "Providence Police Model". Approximately 700 manufactured between 1858 and 1862.

NIB	Exc.	V.G.	Good	Fair	Poor
—	—	2500	1750	750	200

Lipfire Army Revolver

Large military-type single-action revolver. Chambered for .44 lipfire cartridge. Had 7.5" half-octagon barrel, with 6-shot unfluted cylinder that had notches at its rear for cartridge lips. Finish blued. Case colored hammer and trigger guard. Square butt walnut grips. Barrel marked, "Allen & Wheelock, Worchester, Mass." Resembled Center Hammer Percussion Army Revolver. Two basic variations. Total of 250 Lipfire Army Revolvers manufactured in early 1860s.

Early Model

Top hinged loading gate.

NIB	Exc.	V.G.	Good	Fair	Poor
—	—	—	4500	2200	600

Late Model

Bottom hinged loading gate.

NIB	Exc.	V.G.	Good	Fair	Poor
—	—	—	4000	1700	400

Lipfire Navy Revolver

Similar to Army model. Chambered for .36 lipfire cartridge, with octagonal 4", 5", 6", 7.5" or 8" barrel. Approximately 500 manufactured in 1860s.

NIB	Exc.	V.G.	Good	Fair	Poor
—	—	—	3300	1300	400

Lipfire Pocket Revolver

Smaller version chambered for .32 lipfire cartridge, with octagonal 4", 5" or 6" barrel. Approximately 200 manufactured in early 1860s.

NIB	Exc.	V.G.	Good	Fair	Poor
—	—	—	2200	950	250

.32 Side Hammer Rimfire Revolver

Single-action spur-trigger pocket revolver chambered for .32-caliber rimfire cartridge. Octagonal barrels from 3" to 5" in length. Finish blued. Flared-butt and walnut grips. Marked, "Allen & Wheelock Worchester, Mass.". Three variations, with a total of approximately 1,000 manufactured between 1859 and 1862.

First Model
Rounded top strap.

NIB	Exc.	V.G.	Good	Fair	Poor
—	—	1125	800	450	150

Second Model
Marked on frame July 3, 1860

NIB	Exc.	V.G.	Good	Fair	Poor
—	—	1100	795	425	150

Third Model
Patent dates 1858 and 1861.

NIB	Exc.	V.G.	Good	Fair	Poor
—	—	1050	775	400	125

.22 Side Hammer Rimfire Revolver

Smaller version of .32 revolver chambered for .22 rimfire cartridge. Octagonal barrels from 2.25" to 4" in length. Has 7-shot unfluted cylinder. Many variations. Approximately 1,500 manufactured between 1858 and 1862.

Early Model First Issue
Access pin enters from rear.

NIB	Exc.	V.G.	Good	Fair	Poor
—	—	1300	850	475	100

Second Issue
Access pin enters from front.

NIB	Exc.	V.G.	Good	Fair	Poor
—	—	1300	850	475	100

Third Issue
Separate rear sight.

NIB	Exc.	V.G.	Good	Fair	Poor
—	—	1425	1250	600	150

Fourth to Eighth Issue
Very similar, values the same.

NIB	Exc.	V.G.	Good	Fair	Poor
—	—	900	750	300	100

Single-Shot Center Hammer

Single-shot derringer-type pistol. Chambered for .22-caliber rimfire cartridge. Had part-octagon barrels from 2" to 5.5" in length that swung to right side for loading. Some had automatic ejectors, others did not. Frame either brass or iron, with bird's-head or squared butt walnut grips. Marked, "Allen & Wheelock" or "E. Allen & Co.". Very few manufactured in early 1860s.

Early Issue
Full-length octagon barrel. Round iron frame. Rarely encountered.

NIB	Exc.	V.G.	Good	Fair	Poor
—	—	1275	1150	400	100

Standard Issue
Squared butt or bird's-head.

NIB	Exc.	V.G.	Good	Fair	Poor
—	—	1175	1050	300	100

.32 Single-Shot Center Hammer

Larger-frame pocket pistol chambered for .32 rimfire cartridge. Has part- or full-octagon barrel 4" or 5" in length. Swung to right side for loading. Otherwise similar to .22-caliber version.

NIB	Exc.	V.G.	Good	Fair	Poor
—	—	1175	1050	300	100

Vest Pocket Derringer

Small pocket pistol chambered for .22 rimfire cartridge. Had 2" part-octagon barrel that swung to right for loading. Cartridges were manually extracted. Featured brass frame. Blued or plated barrel and walnut bird's-head grips. Barrel marked, "Allen & Co. Makers". Extremely small firearm. Approximately 200 manufactured between 1869 and 1871.

NIB	Exc.	V.G.	Good	Fair	Poor
—	—	1595	975	425	100

.32 Derringer

Similar to Vest Pocket version. Larger in size and chambered for .32 rimfire cartridge. Had part-octagon barrel from 2" to 4" in length that swung to right for loading. Version featured automatic extractor. Barrel marked, "E. Allen & Co. Worchester, Mass.". Very rare firearm. Made between 1865 and 1871.

NIB	Exc.	V.G.	Good	Fair	Poor
—	—	1495	875	395	100

.41 Derringer

Same size and configuration as .32-caliber model, except chambered for .41 rimfire cartridge. Barrel lengths of 2.5" to 2.75". Markings the same. Approximately 100 manufactured, between 1865 and 1871.

NIB	Exc.	V.G.	Good	Fair	Poor
—	—	2200	950	350	100

Center Hammer Muzzleloading Rifle

Single-shot rifle chambered for .44-caliber percussion. Had 36" round barrel, with octagonal breech. Center-mounted hammer offset to right for sighting. Iron mountings. Finish browned. Case colored lock. Ramrod mounted under barrel. Walnut buttstock, with crescent buttplate and no forearm. Approximately 100 manufactured in 1850s.

NIB	Exc.	V.G.	Good	Fair	Poor
—	—	1850	600	250	125

Side Hammer Muzzleloading Rifle

Similar to Center Hammer model, with hammer mounted on right side of lock. Chambered for .38-caliber percussion, with octagon barrel from 28" to 32" in length. Occasionally found with a patchbox. Barrel browned. Case colored lock, walnut stock with crescent butt-plate. Several hundred manufactured from early 1840s to 1860s.

NIB	Exc.	V.G.	Good	Fair	Poor
—	—	2750	900	350	150

Combination Gun

Either over/under or side-by-side rifle. Chambered for 12-gauge and .38-caliber percussion. Barrels from 28" to 34" in length. Two hammers and double triggers. Ramrod mounted either beneath or on right side of barrels. Finish browned, with walnut stock. Examples with patchbox have been noted. Production was very limited. Over/under versions worth approximately 20 percent more than side-by-side values given. Manufactured between 1840s and 1860s.

NIB	Exc.	V.G.	Good	Fair	Poor
—	—	6000	4350	1750	600

Side Hammer Breechloading Rifle

Unique rifle chambered for .36- to .50-caliber percussion. Offered with various lengths and part-octagon barrels. Unusual breech mechanism that was activated by a rotating lever, which resembled a water faucet. Barrel browned. Case colored lock and walnut stock. Marked, "Allen & Wheelock/ Allen's Patent July 3, 1855". Approximately 500 manufactured between 1855 and 1860.

Courtesy Buffalo Bill Historical Center, Cody, Wyoming

NIB	Exc.	V.G.	Good	Fair	Poor
—	—	3550	1600	500	350

Drop Breech Rifle

Single-shot rifle chambered for .22- through .44 rimfire cartridges. Part-octagon barrel from 23" to 28" in length. Breech activated by combination trigger guard action lever. Opening breech automatically ejected empty cartridge. External hammer manually cocked. Featured an adjustable sight. Barrel blued. Case colored frame and walnut stock. Marked, "Allen & Wheelock/ Allen's Pat. Sept. 18, 1860". Approximately 2,000 manufactured between 1860 and 1871.

Courtesy Milwaukee Public Museum, Milwaukee, Wisconsin

NIB	Exc.	V.G.	Good	Fair	Poor
—	—	1550	600	200	100

Lipfire Revolving Rifle

A 6-shot cylinder-type rifle chambered for .44-caliber lipfire cartridge. Unfluted cylinder, with slots at its rear to allow for cartridge lips. Round barrels were 26" to 28" in length, with octagon breech. Finish blued. Case colored frame and walnut buttstock. Not marked with maker's name. Approximately 100 manufactured between 1861 and 1863.

Courtesy Buffalo Bill Historical Center, Cody, Wyoming

NIB	Exc.	V.G.	Good	Fair	Poor
—	—	18500	7000	2000	775

Double-Barrel Shotgun

Side-by-side shotgun chambered for 10- or 12-gauge. Barrel length 28". Loaded by means of trapdoor-type breech that had a lever handle. Finish blued, with checkered walnut stock. Few hundred manufactured between 1865 and 1871.

NIB	Exc.	V.G.	Good	Fair	Poor
—	—	1800	800	250	125

ALLEN & THURBER
See—Ethan Allen

ALLEN & WHEELOCK
See—Ethan Allen

ALLEN FIREARMS
Santa Fe, New Mexico
See—Aldo Uberti

ALPHA ARMS CO.
Flower Mound, Texas

Alpha Arms Co. produced high-grade bolt-action rifles, on a semi-custom basis. Manufactured a number of standard models, but offered many options at additional cost. Some of these options were custom sights, finishes and octagonal barrels. These extra features would add value to models listed. Company operated from 1983 until 1987.

Jaguar Grade I

Built on Mauser-type action, with barrel lengths from 20" to 24". Chambered for most calibers between .222 Rem. and .338 Win. Magnum. Stock made from a synthetic laminated material the company called "Alphawood". Introduced in 1987 and only produced that year.

NIB	Exc.	V.G.	Good	Fair	Poor
1700	1100	750	500	300	200

Jaguar Grade II

Similar to Grade I, with Douglas Premium barrel.

NIB	Exc.	V.G.	Good	Fair	Poor
1825	1275	800	500	400	250

Jaguar Grade III

Has Douglas barrel plus hand-honed trigger and action. Three-position safety like Winchester Model 70.

NIB	Exc.	V.G.	Good	Fair	Poor
1950	1500	1050	700	400	200

Jaguar Grade IV

Has all features of Grade III, with specially lightened action and sling-swivel studs.

NIB	Exc.	V.G.	Good	Fair	Poor
2000	1750	1200	900	500	250

Alpha Big-Five

Similar to Jaguar Grade IV. Chambered for .300 Win. Magnum, .375 H&H Magnum and .458 Win. Magnum. Reinforced through-bolt stock to accommodate recoil of larger caliber cartridges for which it was chambered. Had decelerator recoil pad. Manufactured in 1987 only. **NOTE:** Add 20 percent for .458.

NIB	Exc.	V.G.	Good	Fair	Poor
2200	1850	1500	950	600	300

Alpha Grand Slam

Features same high quality as Jaguar models. Available in left-hand model. Has fluted bolt, laminated stock and matte blue finish. **NOTE:** Deduct 10 percent for left-hand version.

NIB	Exc.	V.G.	Good	Fair	Poor
1700	1500	1250	700	450	250

Alpha Custom

Similar to Grand Slam, with select grade stock.

NIB	Exc.	V.G.	Good	Fair	Poor
1700	1500	1250	750	500	250

Alpha Alaskan

Similar to Grand Slam. Chambered for .308 Win., .350 Rem. Magnum, .358 Win. and .458 Win. Magnum. Features all stainless steel construction. **NOTE:** Add 20 percent for .458.

NIB	Exc.	V.G.	Good	Fair	Poor
2000	1750	1450	850	500	250

ALSOP, C.R.
Middletown, Connecticut

This firearms manufacturer made revolvers during 1862 and 1863. They made two basic models: Navy and Pocket. Some collectors consider Alsop to be a secondary U.S. martial handgun, but no verifying government contracts are known to exist.

First Model Navy Revolver

.36-caliber revolver, with 3.5", 4.5", 5.5" or 6.5" barrel length and 5-shot cylinder. Has blued finish, wood grips and peculiar hump in its backstrap. First model has a safety device, which blocks the spur trigger. This device is found on serial numbers 1-100. Markings are: "C.R. Alsop Middletown, Conn. 1860 & 1861" on barrel; cylinder, "C.R. Alsop" & "Nov. 26th, 1861"; side plate, "Patented Jan. 21st, 1862".

NIB	Exc.	V.G.	Good	Fair	Poor
—	—	3850	1300	500	350

Standard Model Navy Revolver

Exactly the same as First Model, without safety device. Serial numbered 101 to 300.

NIB	Exc.	V.G.	Good	Fair	Poor
—	—	3350	900	300	225

Pocket Model Revolver

.31-caliber 5-shot revolver, with spur trigger, 4" round barrel, blued finish and wood grips. Very similar in appearance to Navy model, but smaller in size. Marked: "C.R. Alsop Middletown, Conn. 1860 & 1861" on barrel; cylinder, "C.R. Alsop Nov. 26th, 1861". Serial numbered 1-300.

Courtesy Milwaukee Public Museum, Milwaukee, Wisconsin

NIB	Exc.	V.G.	Good	Fair	Poor
—	—	1700	700	200	125

AMAC
American Military Arms Corporation
(formerly Iver Johnson)
Jacksonville, Arkansas

Iver Johnson Arms Co. was founded in 1871 in Fitchsburg, Massachusetts. One of the oldest and most successful of old-line arms companies, on which our modern era has taken its toll. In 1984 company moved to Jacksonville, Arkansas; in 1987 it was purchased by American Military Arms Corporation. This company has released some of the older designs as well as some new models. In 1993, company went out of business. Original Iver Johnson line is listed under its own heading.

U.S. Carbine .22

Semi-automatic military-style carbine patterned after M1 of WWII fame. Chambered for .22 LR cartridge. Has 18.5" barrel. Features military-style peep sights and 15-shot detachable magazine.

NIB	Exc.	V.G.	Good	Fair	Poor
325	250	175	100	75	50

Wagonmaster Lever-Action Rifle

Chambered for .22 rimfire cartridge. Styled after Win. 94. Has an 18.5" barrel, straight-grip stock and a fore-end barrel band. Adjustable sights. Tubular magazine holds 15 LR cartridges.

NIB	Exc.	V.G.	Good	Fair	Poor
295	225	150	100	75	50

Wagonmaster .22 Magnum

Same as Wagonmaster. Chambered for .22 rimfire Magnum.

NIB	Exc.	V.G.	Good	Fair	Poor
325	250	175	125	95	50

Targetmaster Pump-Action Rifle

Model is a slide- or pump-action chambered for .22 rimfire cartridge. Has 18.5" barrel, with adjustable sights and straight-grip stock. Holds 12 LR cartridges.

NIB	Exc.	V.G.	Good	Fair	Poor
325	175	145	115	75	50

Li'L Champ Bolt-Action Rifle

Model is a scaled-down single-shot chambered for .22 rimfire cartridge. Has 16.25" barrel, adjustable sights, molded stock and nickel-plated bolt. Overall length 33". Designed to be an ideal first rifle for a young shooter.

NIB	Exc.	V.G.	Good	Fair	Poor
175	125	75	45	35	20

M .30 Cal. Carbine

Military-style carbine styled after M1 of WWII fame. Chambered for .30 Carbine cartridge. Has 18" barrel, with military-style sights and hardwood stock. Detachable 5-, 15- and 30-round magazines available.

NIB	Exc.	V.G.	Good	Fair	Poor
425	300	225	175	125	90

Paratrooper .30 Carbine

Similar to M1 model, with folding stock.

NIB	Exc.	V.G.	Good	Fair	Poor
495	395	325	250	160	100

Enforcer .30 Carbine

A 9.5" pistol version of M1 Carbine. No buttstock.

NIB	Exc.	V.G.	Good	Fair	Poor
625	500	395	300	150	100

Long Range Rifle System/AMAC Model 5100

Specialized long-range bolt-action rifle. Chambered for .50-caliber

Browning Machine gun cartridge. Has 33" barrel and special muzzle-brake system. Custom order version in .338- or .416-caliber also available.

NIB	Exc.	V.G.	Good	Fair	Poor
4100	3550	2900	2000	900	450

TP-22 and TP-25

Compact double-action pocket automatic styled after Walther TP series. Chambered for .22 rimfire or .25 centerfire cartridges. Has 2.75" barrel, fixed sights and black plastic grips. Detachable magazine holds 7 shots. Finish blue or nickel-plated. **NOTE:** Nickel-plated version worth 10 percent more than blue.

NIB	Exc.	V.G.	Good	Fair	Poor
265	195	150	100	75	50

AMAC 22 Compact or 25 Compact

Compact single-action semi-automatic pocket pistol. Chambered for .22 rimfire or .25 ACP cartridge. Has 2" barrel, 5-shot magazine, plastic grips and blue or nickel finish. **NOTE:** Add 10 percent for nickel.

NIB	Exc.	V.G.	Good	Fair	Poor
265	195	150	100	75	50

AMERICAN ARMS, INC.
North Kansas City, Missouri

SIDE-BY-SIDE SHOTGUNS

York/Gentry

These two designations cover the same model. Prior to 1988, this model was called York. In 1988, receiver was case colored and designation changed to Gentry. Model chambered for 12-, 20-, 28-gauge and .410 bore.. Had chrome-lined barrels from 26" to 30" in length, double triggers, 3" chambers and automatic ejectors. Boxlock action featured scroll engraving. Walnut stock was hand checkered. Introduced in 1986.

NIB	Exc.	V.G.	Good	Fair	Poor
750	625	450	300	200	150

10 Gauge Magnum Shotgun

10-gauge, with 3.5" chambers and 32" barrels. Featured scroll-engraved chromed boxlock action and double triggers. Imported from Spain in 1986 only.

NIB	Exc.	V.G.	Good	Fair	Poor
850	750	550	350	250	150

12 Gauge Magnum Shotgun

As above, chambered for 12-gauge 3.5" Magnum shell.

NIB	Exc.	V.G.	Good	Fair	Poor
800	700	500	300	200	150

Brittany

Chambered for 12- and 20-gauge, with 25" or 27" barrels and screw-in choke tubes. Had solid matted rib and case colored engraved boxlock action. Automatic ejectors, single-selective trigger, hand checkered walnut straight-grip stock, with semi-beavertail fore-end, were standard on this model. Introduced in 1989.

NIB	Exc.	V.G.	Good	Fair	Poor
850	750	600	450	375	200

Turkey Special

Utilitarian model designed to be an effective turkey hunting tool. Chambered for Magnum 10- and 12-gauges. Has 26" barrels. Finish Parkerized. Stock finished in non-glare matte. Sling-swivel studs and recoil pad are standard. Introduced in 1987.

NIB	Exc.	V.G.	Good	Fair	Poor
800	700	450	350	250	150

Waterfowl Special

Similar to Turkey Special. Chambered for 10-gauge only. Furnished with camouflaged sling. Introduced in 1987.

NIB	Exc.	V.G.	Good	Fair	Poor
950	850	550	350	250	150

Specialty Model

Similar to Turkey Special. Offered in 12-gauge 3.5" Magnum.

NIB	Exc.	V.G.	Good	Fair	Poor
875	750	500	300	200	150

Derby

Chambered for 12-, 20-, 28-gauge and .410 bore. Has 26" or 28" barrels, with 3" chambers and automatic ejectors. Either double- or single-selective triggers offered. Sidelock action is scroll engraved and chromed. Checkered straight-grip stock and forearm are oil-finished. Introduced in 1986. No longer imported. **NOTE:** Add 10 percent for 28 gauge or .410 bore; 50 percent for two-gauge sets.

NIB	Exc.	V.G.	Good	Fair	Poor
1150	975	850	650	450	300

Grulla #2

Top-of-the-line model. Chambered for 12-, 20-, 28-gauge and .410 bore.

Barrels are 26" or 28", with concave rib. Hand-fitted full sidelock action is extensively engraved and case-colored. Various chokes, double triggers and automatic ejectors. Select walnut straight-grip stock. Splinter fore-end is hand checkered and has a hand-rubbed oil finish. Introduced in 1989. No longer imported.

NIB	Exc.	V.G.	Good	Fair	Poor
2500	1750	1250	900	500	250

OVER/UNDER SHOTGUNS

F.S. 200

Trap or skeet model chambered for 12-gauge only. Had 26" Skeet & Skeet barrels or 32" Full choke barrels on trap model. Barrels were separated and had a ventilated rib. Boxlock action had Greener crossbolt and was black or matte chrome-plated. Featured single-selective trigger, automatic ejectors and checkered walnut pistol-grip stock. Imported in 1986 and 1987 only.

NIB	Exc.	V.G.	Good	Fair	Poor
—	675	575	465	350	150

F.S. 300

Similar to F.S. 200, with lightly engraved side plates and 30" barrel. Offered in trap grade. Imported in 1986 only.

NIB	Exc.	V.G.	Good	Fair	Poor
—	800	675	565	450	250

F.S. 400

Similar to F.S. 300, with engraved matte chrome-plated receiver. Imported in 1986 only.

NIB	Exc.	V.G.	Good	Fair	Poor
—	1100	950	800	650	350

F.S. 500

Similar to F.S. 400, with same general specifications. Not imported after 1985.

NIB	Exc.	V.G.	Good	Fair	Poor
—	1150	1000	850	700	350

Waterfowl Special

Chambered for 12-gauge Magnum, with 3.5" chambers. Has 28" barrels, with screw-in choke tubes. Automatic ejectors and single-selective trigger. Finish Parkerized, with matte finished stock, sling swivels and camouflaged sling and recoil pad. Introduced in 1987.

NIB	Exc.	V.G.	Good	Fair	Poor
875	700	500	350	300	150

Waterfowl 10 Gauge

Same as Waterfowl Special. Chambered for 10-gauge Magnum, with double triggers.

NIB	Exc.	V.G.	Good	Fair	Poor
975	850	600	400	300	200

Turkey Special

Similar to Waterfowl Special in 10-gauge, with 26" barrel and screw-in choke tubes.

NIB	Exc.	V.G.	Good	Fair	Poor
975	850	600	350	300	200

Lince

Chambered for 12- and 20-gauge. Has 26" or 28" barrels, with 3" chambers and various chokes. Boxlock action has Greener crossbolt, either blued or polished and chrome-plated. Barrels blued, with ventilated rib. Single-selective trigger and automatic ejectors. Imported in 1986 only.

NIB	Exc.	V.G.	Good	Fair	Poor
—	500	425	350	300	200

Silver Model

Similar to Lince. Plain un-engraved brushed-chrome-finished receiver. Imported in 1986 and 1987.

NIB	Exc.	V.G.	Good	Fair	Poor
—	500	425	350	300	200

Silver I

Similar to Silver. Available in 12-, 20-, 28-gauge and .410 bore. Has single-selective trigger, fixed chokes, extractors and recoil pad. Introduced in 1987. **NOTE:** Add $25 for 28-gauge and .410 bore guns.

NIB	Exc.	V.G.	Good	Fair	Poor
650	550	325	275	200	175

Silver II

Similar to Silver I, with screw-in choke tubes, automatic ejectors and select walnut. Introduced in 1987. **NOTE:** Add $25 for 28-gauge and .410 bore guns.

NIB	Exc.	V.G.	Good	Fair	Poor
750	650	450	350	300	150

Silver II Lite

Introduced in 1994. Designed as an upland game gun. Offered in 12-, 20- and 28-gauge, with 26" barrels. Chambered for both 2.75" and 3" shells. Frame made from a lightweight steel alloy. No longer imported.

NIB	Exc.	V.G.	Good	Fair	Poor
875	775	550	400	300	150

Silver Competition/Sporting

Offered in 12-gauge, with choice of 28" or 30" barrels which are made from chrome moly. Barrels have elongated forcing cones, chromed bores and are ported to help reduce recoil. Comes with interchangeable choke tubes. Single-selective trigger is mechanical. Weighs about 7.5 lbs. In

1996 a 20-gauge model was added, with 28" barrel and 3" chambers.

NIB	Exc.	V.G.	Good	Fair	Poor
950	800	600	400	300	150

Silver Hunter

Introduced in 1999. Offered in 12- and 20-gauge, with 26" and 28" barrels. Single-selective trigger with extractors. Choke tubes standard. Weight about 7 lbs.

NIB	Exc.	V.G.	Good	Fair	Poor
625	500	400	300	200	100

Bristol/Sterling

Chambered for 12- and 20-gauge. Various barrel lengths, with ventilated rib and screw-in choke tubes. Chambers are 3". Chrome-finished action is boxlock, with Greener crossbolt and game scene engraved on side plates. Automatic ejectors and single-selective trigger. Introduced in 1986. In 1989, designation was changed to Sterling. No longer imported.

NIB	Exc.	V.G.	Good	Fair	Poor
825	750	675	500	400	200

Sir

Chambered for 12- and 20-gauge, with 3" chambers, various barrel lengths, chokes and ventilated rib. Chrome-finished sidelock action has Greener crossbolt and engraved with a game scene. Automatic ejectors and single-selective trigger. Imported in 1986. No longer imported.

NIB	Exc.	V.G.	Good	Fair	Poor
—	875	750	625	500	250

Royal

Chambered for 12- and 20-gauge. Manufactured in various barrel lengths and chokes, with ventilated rib and 3" chambers. Chrome-finished sidelock action has Greener crossbolt and profusely scroll-engraved. Automatic ejectors and single-selective trigger. Select pistol-grip walnut stock is hand checkered and oil-finished. Imported in 1986 and 1987. No longer imported.

NIB	Exc.	V.G.	Good	Fair	Poor
—	1500	1275	1000	800	400

Excelsior

Similar to Royal, with extensive deep relief engraving and gold inlays. Imported in 1986 and 1987. No longer imported.

NIB	Exc.	V.G.	Good	Fair	Poor
—	1750	1500	1200	875	450

SINGLE-BARREL SHOTGUNS

AASB

Standard single-barrel break-open hammerless shotgun. Chambered for 12-, 20-gauge and .410 bore. Has 26" barrel, with various chokes and 3" chambers. Pistol-grip stock and matte finish. Introduced in 1988. No longer imported.

NIB	Exc.	V.G.	Good	Fair	Poor
100	85	75	60	45	25

Campers Special

Similar to standard model, with 21" barrel and folding stock. Introduced in 1988. No longer imported.

NIB	Exc.	V.G.	Good	Fair	Poor
110	95	85	70	50	35

Youth Model

Chambered for 20-gauge and .410 bore. Has 12.5" stock, with recoil pad. Introduced in 1989. No longer imported.

NIB	Exc.	V.G.	Good	Fair	Poor
115	100	80	65	50	35

Slugger

Version has 24" barrel, with rifle sights. Chambered for 12- and 20-gauge, with recoil pad. No longer imported.

NIB	Exc.	V.G.	Good	Fair	Poor
115	100	80	65	50	35

10 Gauge Model

Chambered for 10-gauge 3.5" Magnum. Has 32" full choke barrel and recoil pad. Introduced in 1988. No longer imported.

NIB	Exc.	V.G.	Good	Fair	Poor
175	145	100	85	60	45

Combo Model

Similar in appearance to other single-barrel models. Offered in interchangeable-barreled rifle/shotgun combination—28" barreled .22 Hornet and 12-gauge; or 26" barreled .22 LR and 20-gauge. Furnished with fitted hard case to hold interchangeable barrels. Introduced in 1989. No longer imported.

NIB	Exc.	V.G.	Good	Fair	Poor
250	200	175	145	110	75

SEMI-AUTO SHOTGUNS

Phantom Field

Chambered for 12-gauge and fitted with choice of 24", 26" or 28" barrels. Fitted with 3" chamber. Gas operated action. Choke tubes standard. Five-round magazine. Checkered walnut stock. Weight about 7 lbs. Introduced in 1999.

NIB	Exc.	V.G.	Good	Fair	Poor
400	350	300	225	125	75

Phantom Synthetic

Same as above. Furnished with checkered synthetic stock. Weight about 6.75 lbs. Introduced in 1999.

NIB	Exc.	V.G.	Good	Fair	Poor
400	350	300	225	125	75

Phantom HP

Features 19" threaded barrel for external choke tubes. Five-round magazine. Weight about 6.75 lbs. Introduced in 1999.

NIB	Exc.	V.G.	Good	Fair	Poor
400	375	325	300	150	95

RIFLES

ZCY.308

An AK-47 type design and chambered in .308 Winchester. Imported in 1988 only.

NIB	Exc.	V.G.	Good	Fair	Poor
700	600	475	375	300	200

AKY39

Semi-automatic version of Soviet AK-47. Manufactured by Yugoslavia. Offered with folding tritium night sights and wooden fixed stock. Imported in 1988.

NIB	Exc.	V.G.	Good	Fair	Poor
—	600	475	390	300	200

AKF39

Same rifle as AKY39, with metal folding stock.

NIB	Exc.	V.G.	Good	Fair	Poor
—	625	550	475	300	200

AKC47

Basically same rifle as AKY39, without tritium night sights.

NIB	Exc.	V.G.	Good	Fair	Poor
—	575	450	375	300	200

AKF47

Same rifle as AKC47, with metal folding stock.

NIB	Exc.	V.G.	Good	Fair	Poor
—	625	550	475	300	200

EXP-64 Survival Rifle

.22-caliber semi-automatic take-down rifle. Self-storing in a floating over-sized plastic stock. Rifle has 21" barrel, with open sights and crossbolt safety. A 10-shot detachable magazine. Importation by American Arms began in 1989.

NIB	Exc.	V.G.	Good	Fair	Poor
165	150	125	95	75	50

SM-64 TD Sporter

.22 LR semi-automatic, with take-down 21" barrel. Adjustable sights, checkered hardwood stock and fore-end. Importation began in 1989.

NIB	Exc.	V.G.	Good	Fair	Poor
195	155	110	85	65	45

1860 Henry

Replica of lever action Henry rifle. Brass frame. Steel half-octagon barrel, with tube magazine. Chambered for .44-40 or .45 Long Colt. Offered in 18.5" or 24" barrels. Weight with 24" barrel about 9.25 lbs. Built by Uberti.

NIB	Exc.	V.G.	Good	Fair	Poor
950	800	650	400	300	200

1866 Winchester

Replica of Winchester 1866. Offered in .44-40 or .45 Long Colt. Barrel lengths 19" or 24". Brass frame. Weight about 8.25 lbs. for 24" barrel model. Built by Uberti.

NIB	Exc.	V.G.	Good	Fair	Poor
825	700	495	300	200	100

1873 Winchester

Replica of Winchester Model 1873. Offered with choice of 24" or 30" barrels. Chambered for .44-40 or .45 Long Colt. Case hardened steel frame. Weight about 8.25 lbs. for 24" model. Built by Uberti. **NOTE:** Add $80 for 30" barrel.

NIB	Exc.	V.G.	Good	Fair	Poor
850	725	550	325	225	125

1885 Single-Shot High Wall

Chambered for .45-70 cartridge. Winchester replica fitted with 28" round barrel. Weight about 8.75 lbs. Built by Uberti.

NIB	Exc.	V.G.	Good	Fair	Poor
850	695	550	350	200	100

Sharps Cavalry Carbine

Sharps replica fitted with 22" round barrel. Chambered for .45-70 cartridge. Adjustable rear sight. Weight about 8 lbs.

NIB	Exc.	V.G.	Good	Fair	Poor
700	600	425	350	200	100

Sharps Frontier Carbine

Similar to Cavalry carbine, with 22" octagonal barrel and double-set triggers. Weight about 7.75 lbs.

NIB	Exc.	V.G.	Good	Fair	Poor
775	625	475	375	225	125

Sharps Sporting Rifle

Features 28" octagonal barrel. Chambered for .45-70 or .45-120 cartridge. Double-set triggers. Adjustable rear sight. Checkered walnut stock. Weight about 9 lbs.

NIB	Exc.	V.G.	Good	Fair	Poor
775	625	475	375	225	125

Sharps 1874 Deluxe Sporting Rifle

Similar to above, with browned barrels.

NIB	Exc.	V.G.	Good	Fair	Poor
800	650	500	395	250	150

HANDGUNS

Model EP-.380

High-quality stainless steel pocket pistol. Chambered for .380 ACP cartridge. Double-action semi-automatic that holds 7 shots and has a 3.5" barrel. Grips are checkered walnut. Imported from West Germany beginning in 1988.

NIB	Exc.	V.G.	Good	Fair	Poor
425	365	325	275	225	100

Model PK-22

Domestic semi-automatic chambered for .22 LR. Double-action with 3.5" barrel and 8-shot finger extension magazine. Made of stainless steel and has black plastic grips. Manufactured in U.S.A. by American Arms.

NIB	Exc.	V.G.	Good	Fair	Poor
245	200	150	125	100	75

Model CX-22

Compact version of PK-22, with 2.75" barrel and 7-shot magazine. Manufacture began in 1989.

NIB	Exc.	V.G.	Good	Fair	Poor
225	200	165	125	100	75

Model TT Tokarev

Yugoslavian version of Soviet Tokarev. Chambered for 9mm Parabellum, with safety added to make importation legal. Has 4.5" barrel, 9-shot magazine and blued finish. Checkered plastic grips. Importation began in 1988.

NIB	Exc.	V.G.	Good	Fair	Poor
350	225	175	150	125	100

Model ZC-.380

Scaled-down version of Tokarev. Chambered for .380 ACP. Has 3.5" barrel and holds 8 shots. Finish and grips are same as on full-sized version. Importation from Yugoslavia began in 1988.

NIB	Exc.	V.G.	Good	Fair	Poor
295	225	175	150	125	100

Aussie Model

Introduced in 1996. Australian-designed semi-automatic pistol made in Spain. Chambered for 9mm or .40 S&W cartridge. Polymer frame, with nickeled steel slide. Sold with 10-shot magazine. Barrel length 4.75"; weight 23 oz.

NIB	Exc.	V.G.	Good	Fair	Poor
400	350	300	250	200	100

Regulator

Built by Uberti. Single-action revolver has case hardened frame, polished brass trigger guard and backstrap. Barrel and cylinder are blued. One piece walnut grips. Choice of chambers in .44-40, .45 LC or .357 Magnum. Barrel lengths 4.75", 5.5" to 7.5". Weight about 34 oz., with 5.75" barrel.

NIB	Exc.	V.G.	Good	Fair	Poor
395	325	275	175	—	—

Regulator Deluxe

Same as above, with steel trigger guard and backstrap. Chambered in .45 Long Colt only.

NIB	Exc.	V.G.	Good	Fair	Poor
375	300	250	150	—	—

AMERICAN ARMS
Garden Grove, California

Eagle .380

Pistol was a stainless steel copy of Walther PPKS. Semi-automatic blowback chambered for .380 ACP. Double-action, 3.25" barrel and 6-shot detachable magazine. Optional feature a black Teflon finish, that would increase value by 10 percent. Company ceased production in 1985.

NIB	Exc.	V.G.	Good	Fair	Poor
—	325	250	195	150	100

AMERICAN ARMS CO.
Boston, Massachusetts

History of American Arms is rather sketchy. It appears the company was formed in 1853 as G. H. Fox Co., then became American Tool & Machine Co. in 1865. In 1870, they formed a new corporation called American Arms Company, with George Fox as principle stockholder. This corporation was dissolved in 1873; a second American Arms Co. was incorporated in 1877 and a third in 1890. It is unclear if these corporations had essentially the same owners, but George H. Fox appears as a principle owner in two of the three. One could assume that financial problems forced them to bankrupt one corporation and reorganize under another. American Arms manufactured firearms in Boston, Massachusetts, from 1866 until 1893. In 1893 they moved to Bluffton, Alabama and manufactured guns until 1901.

Fox Model "Swing Out" Hammer Double

Manufactured from 1870 to 1884. Designed by George H. Fox, not to be confused with A.H. Fox. Model unusual, in that barrel swings to right for loading and barrel release is located on tang. Comes in 10- and 12-gauge, 26", 28", 30" and 32" with twist Damascus or laminated barrels. Early production models have conventional soldered together barrels. Later variations after 1878, feature a unique design in that barrels are dovetailed together. Guns could be ordered with several options and choices of finish. These would add premium value to a particular gun.

NIB	Exc.	V.G.	Good	Fair	Poor
—	—	2000	950	400	150

Semi-Hammerless Double

Manufactured from 1892 to 1901. Features cocking lever that cocks an internal firing pin. Comes in 12-gauge, with 30" twist barrels.

NIB	Exc.	V.G.	Good	Fair	Poor
—	—	1500	750	350	150

Whitmore Model Hammerless Double

Manufactured from 1890 to 1901. Comes in 10-, 12- and 16-gauge, with 28", 30" or 32" twist laminated or Damascus barrels. Marked "Whitmore's Patent".

Courtesy Nick Niles, Paul Goodwin photo

NIB	Exc.	V.G.	Good	Fair	Poor
—	—	1500	775	375	150

Semi-Hammerless Single-Barrel

Manufactured from 1882 to 1901. Comes in 10-, 12- and 16-gauge, with 28", 30" or 32" twist or Damascus barrel.

NIB	Exc.	V.G.	Good	Fair	Poor
—	—	1500	750	300	100

TOP-BREAK REVOLVERS

Courtesy Milwaukee Public Museum, Milwaukee, Wisconsin

Spur Trigger Single-Action Five-Shot Revolver

Revolvers made between 1883 and 1887 in .38 S&W only. Feature an unusual manual ring extractor and double-fluted cylinder. Nickel plated, with hard rubber grips. Marked "American Arms Company Boston Mass.".

NIB	Exc.	V.G.	Good	Fair	Poor
—	550	300	100	75	25

Standard Trigger Double-Action Model 1886 Revolver

Standard trigger and trigger guard. Comes in .32 short and .38 S&W, with 3.5" barrel. Blue or nickel finish. Early models equipped with ring extractor and double-fluted cylinder. Later variations have standard star extractor and single-fluted cylinder.

NIB	Exc.	V.G.	Good	Fair	Poor
—	750	300	100	75	25

Hammerless Model 1890 Double-Action

Manufactured from 1890 to 1901. Has adjustable single- or double-stage trigger pull and several unusual safety devices. Comes in .32 and .38 S&W, with 3.25" ribbed barrel, fluted cylinder, nickel finish, hard rubber grips with logo and ivory or mother of pearl grips. Marked "American Arms Co. Boston/Pat. May 25, 1886". Top strap marked "Pat. Pending" on early models and "Pat's May 25'86/Mar 11'89/June 17'90" on later models.

NIB	Exc.	V.G.	Good	Fair	Poor
—	750	300	100	75	25

DOUBLE-BARREL DERRINGERS

American Arms Co. manufactured a two-barrel derringer-style pocket pistol. Barrels were manually rotated to load and fire the weapon. Pistol had nickel-plated brass frame, blued barrels and walnut grips. Markings were: "American Arms Co. Boston, Mass." on one barrel and "Pat. Oct. 31, 1865" on other barrel. Approximately 2,000-3,000 produced between 1866 and 1878. Beware of fakes!

Combination .22 caliber R.F. and .32 caliber R.F.

Two-caliber combination, with 3" barrel and square butt only. Most common variation.

NIB	Exc.	V.G.	Good	Fair	Poor
—	—	850	350	150	100

.32 caliber R.F., Both Barrels

3" barrel, with square butt.

Courtesy Milwaukee Public Museum, Milwaukee, Wisconsin

NIB	Exc.	V.G.	Good	Fair	Poor
—	—	1050	500	195	125

.32 caliber R.F., Both Barrels (2.625" barrel)

2.625" barrel, with bird's-head grips.

NIB	Exc.	V.G.	Good	Fair	Poor
—	—	1100	550	225	150

.38 caliber R.F., Both Barrels

2.625" barrel, with bird's-head grip. Rare variation.

NIB	Exc.	V.G.	Good	Fair	Poor
—	—	2500	1075	350	200

.41 caliber R.F., Both Barrels

2.625" barrel, with square butt only.

NIB	Exc.	V.G.	Good	Fair	Poor
—	—	1850	900	200	100

AMERICAN BARLOCK WONDER

See—Crescent Arms Co.

AMERICAN CLASSIC
(Eagle Imports)
Wanamassa, NJ

American Classic 1911-A1

Full-size 1911-A1 style semi-automatic chambered in .45 ACP. Series 70 lockwork, 8-round magazine with bumper pad, lowered ejection port, throated barrel, checkered wood grips, military-style sights, matte blue or hard chrome finish and 5" barrel. Weight 39 oz. American Classic

II has additional features including Novak-style sights, combat trigger and hammer, extended safety and slide stop front slide serrations, deep blue or hard chrome finish. **NOTE:** Add $35 for Classic II; $50 for hard chrome finish.

NIB	Exc.	V.G.	Good	Fair	Poor
435	400	350	325	250	200

American Classic Commander/Amigo

Same features as American Classic II, except 4.25" barrel, weight 35 oz. Amigo model is Officer's Model style, with 3.5" barrel, 7-round magazine. **NOTE:** Add $50 for hard chrome finish; $35 for Amigo model.

NIB	Exc.	V.G.	Good	Fair	Poor
460	425	360	335	260	200

American Classic Trophy Model

Same features as American Classic II, except 5.5" barrel, dovetail front fiber optic sight, Novak-style rear, ambidextrous safety, reverse plug recoil system with full-length guide rod, beveled mag well, checkered mainspring housing and hard chrome finish.

NIB	Exc.	V.G.	Good	Fair	Poor
650	600	550	500	400	300

American Classic .22 Model

Full-size alloy-frame 1911-style pistol. Chambered for .22 LR. Same dimensions as American Classic, with military-type sights, checkered wood grips, matte blue finish and two 10-round magazines.

NIB	Exc.	V.G.	Good	Fair	Poor
300	275	230	200	160	100

AMERICAN DERRINGER CORP.
Waco, Texas

Model 1 Derringer

Fashioned after Remington over/under derringer. High quality rugged pistol. Built from high tensile strength stainless steel. Over 60 different rifle and pistol calibers to choose from, on special order. Upper barrel can be chambered different from lower barrel, on request. Available in high polish finish or satin finish. Offered with rosewood, bacote, walnut or blackwood grips. Ivory, bonded ivory, stag or pearl are available at extra cost. Overall length 4.8"; barrel length 3"; width across frame .9"; width across grip 1.2". Typical weight 15 oz. in .45-caliber. All guns furnished with French fitted leatherette case. Prices determined by caliber. **NOTE:** Premium for rifle cartridges.

Caliber: .22 Long Rifle through .357 Magnum and .45 ACP

NIB	Exc.	V.G.	Good	Fair	Poor
550	450	350	285	225	150

Calibers: .41 Mag., .44-40, .44 Special, .44 Mag., .45 Long Colt, .410 Bore, .22 Hornet, .223 Rem., 30-30, and .45-70 Gov't.

NIB	Exc.	V.G.	Good	Fair	Poor
600	525	450	350	250	150

Model 1 Lady Derringer

Similar to Model 1. Chambered for .38 Special, .32 Magnum, .45 Colt or .357 Magnum. Offered in two grades. **NOTE:** Add $75 for .45 Colt and .45/.410; $50 for .357 Magnum.

Deluxe

High polished stainless steel. Scrimshawed ivory grips, with cameo or rose design.

NIB	Exc.	V.G.	Good	Fair	Poor
700	600	500	300	225	150

Deluxe Engraved

Same as above. Hand engraved in 1880s style.

NIB	Exc.	V.G.	Good	Fair	Poor
750	600	500	400	250	150

Model 1 NRA 500 Series

Limited edition of 500. Available in gold and blue finishes over stainless steel.

NIB	Exc.	V.G.	Good	Fair	Poor
600	450	300	150	125	100

Model 1 Texas Commemorative

Built with solid brass frame and stainless steel barrel. Dimensions same as Model 1. Grips are stag or rosewood and offered in .45 Colt, .44-40 or

.38 Special. Barrels marked "Made in the 150th Year of Texas Freedom". Limited to 500 pistols in each caliber.

Caliber: .38 Special

NIB	Exc.	V.G.	Good	Fair	Poor
425	350	250	150	100	75

Calibers: .45 Colt and .44-40

NIB	Exc.	V.G.	Good	Fair	Poor
600	450	300	200	125	100

Deluxe Engraved

Special serial number engraved on backstrap.

NIB	Exc.	V.G.	Good	Fair	Poor
700	550	395	350	175	125

Model 1 125th Anniversary Commemorative

Built to commemorate 125th anniversary of derringer, 1866 to 1991. Similar to Model 1. Marked with patent date "December 12, 1865". Brass frame and stainless steel barrel. Chambered for .44-40, .45 Colt or .38 Special.

NIB	Exc.	V.G.	Good	Fair	Poor
425	350	250	150	100	65

Deluxe Engraved

NIB	Exc.	V.G.	Good	Fair	Poor
650	475	375	250	175	100

Model 2 Pen Pistol

Introduced in 1993. Legal pistol that cannot be fired from its pen position. Requires it be pulled apart and bent 80 degrees to fire. Made from stainless steel. Offered in .22 LR, .25 ACP and .32 ACP. Length in pen form 5.6"; pistol form 4.2". Barrel length 2". Diameter varies from .500" to .625". Weight 5 oz. No longer in production.

NIB	Exc.	V.G.	Good	Fair	Poor
600	395	300	225	100	85

Model 3

Single-barrel derringer. Barrel length 2.5" and swings down to load. Frame and barrel stainless steel. Offered in .38 Special or .32 Magnum. Weighs about 8 oz. Discontinued.

NIB	Exc.	V.G.	Good	Fair	Poor
200	175	115	75	65	50

Model 4

Similar in appearance to Model 3. Fitted with 4.1" barrel. Overall length 6"; weight about 16.5 oz. Chambered for 3" .410 bore, .45 Long Colt, .44 Magnum or .357 Magnum. **NOTE:** Add $150 for .45-70; $100 for .44 Magnum.

NIB	Exc.	V.G.	Good	Fair	Poor
500	425	350	250	100	75

Engraved

NIB	Exc.	V.G.	Good	Fair	Poor
1000	900	600	400	275	150

Alaskan Survival Model

Similar to Model 4, with upper barrel chambered for .45-70 and lower barrel for .45 LC or .410. Both barrels can also be chambered for .44 Magnum or .45-70. Comes with over-sized rosewood grips.

NIB	Exc.	V.G.	Good	Fair	Poor
700	625	395	250	175	100

Model 6

Double-barrel derringer fitted with 6" barrel chambered for .45 LC or .410 bore. Weighs about 21 oz. Rosewood grips are standard. Optional calibers .357 Magnum or .45 ACP. **NOTE:** Oversize grips optional and add about $35 to value.

NIB	Exc.	V.G.	Good	Fair	Poor
750	600	450	300	150	100

Engraved

NIB	Exc.	V.G.	Good	Fair	Poor
1000	900	700	450	275	150

Double-Action Derringer

High Standard-type double-barrel double-action derringer. Chambered for .22 LR or .22 Magnum. Barrel length 3.5"; overall length 5.125". Weighs about 11 oz. Finish blue with black grips.

NIB	Exc.	V.G.	Good	Fair	Poor
295	245	175	100	85	75

DA 38 Double-Action Derringer

Similar to above. Chambered for .38 Special, .357 Magnum, 9mm Luger and .40 S&W. Finish satin stainless. Grip made from aluminum. Grips are rosewood or walnut. **NOTE:** Add $40 for .40 S&W.

NIB	Exc.	V.G.	Good	Fair	Poor
500	400	300	200	150	100

Mini Cop 4-Shot

Four-barrel derringer chambered for .22 Magnum Rimfire cartridge.

NIB	Exc.	V.G.	Good	Fair	Poor
600	395	300	225	100	85

Cop 4-Shot

Same as above. Chambered for .357 Magnum cartridge.

NIB	Exc.	V.G.	Good	Fair	Poor
1000	900	500	325	175	100

Model 7 Derringer—Lightweight

Manufactured as a backup gun for police officers. Frame and barrels made of aircraft aluminum alloy; other parts are stainless steel. Weighs 7.5 oz. Appearance and function are similar to Model 1. Finish is a gray matte, with thin matte-finished grips of rosewood or bacote. Chambered for and priced as listed.

.32 S&W Long / .32 Magnum

NIB	Exc.	V.G.	Good	Fair	Poor
500	400	250	125	100	75

.38 S&W and .380 ACP

NIB	Exc.	V.G.	Good	Fair	Poor
500	400	250	125	100	75

.22 LR and .38 Special

NIB	Exc.	V.G.	Good	Fair	Poor
500	400	250	125	100	75

.44 Special

NIB	Exc.	V.G.	Good	Fair	Poor
650	525	400	300	250	150

Model 8

Single-action two-shot target pistol, with manually operated hammer block safety. Safety automatically disengages when hammer is cocked. Barrel length 8". Chambered for .45 Colt and .410 shotshell. Weight 24 oz.

NIB	Exc.	V.G.	Good	Fair	Poor
700	600	475	350	175	100

Engraved

NIB	Exc.	V.G.	Good	Fair	Poor
1500	1000	675	450	300	125

Model 10 Derringer

Similar to Model 1, with frame of aluminum alloy. All other parts including barrels, stainless steel. Has a gray matte finish and thin grips of rosewood or bacote. Weighs 10 oz. Chambered for .38 Special, .45 ACP or .45 Colt. **NOTE:** Add $75 for .45 Colt.

NIB	Exc.	V.G.	Good	Fair	Poor
500	375	250	125	100	75

Model 11 Derringer

Stainless steel barrel and all other parts aluminum. Weighs 11 oz. Chambered for .38 Special, .380 Auto, .32 Magnum, .22 LR and .22 Magnum. Grips and finish are the same as on Model 10.

NIB	Exc.	V.G.	Good	Fair	Poor
500	375	250	125	100	75

Semmerling LM-4

LM-4 was designed as ultimate police backup/defense weapon. Manually operated 5-shot repeater only 5.2" long, 3.7" high and 1" wide. Chambered for .45 ACP. Undoubtedly smallest 5-shot .45 ever produced. LM-4 made of a special tool steel. Either blued or at extra cost hard chrome-plated. Stainless steel version also available. LM-4 is not a semi-automatic, although it physically resembles one. Slide is flicked forward and back after each double-action squeeze of the trigger. This weapon is virtually hand-built. Features high visibility sights and smooth trigger. **NOTE:** Add $200 for hard chrome; 35 percent for stainless steel.

NIB	Exc.	V.G.	Good	Fair	Poor
3500	3000	2000	1500	600	200

LM-5

Built of stainless steel. Semi-automatic chambered for .32 or .25 Auto. Barrel length 2.25"; overall length 4"; height 3". Wooden grips standard. Offered in limited quantities. Weight about 15 oz. Discontinued.

NIB	Exc.	V.G.	Good	Fair	Poor
550	450	295	150	100	50

Millennium Series 2000

Chambered for .38 Special, .45 Colt or .44-40. Single-action. Fitted with scrimshaw grips, with yellow rose of Texas on left side and Lone Star flag on right side. Weight about 15 oz. Supplied with red velvet box with silver inlay. Introduced in 1999.

NIB	Exc.	V.G.	Good	Fair	Poor
500	325	200	150	100	75

Gambler Millennium 2000

Similar to Millennium Series. Fitted with rosewood grips, with etched Lone Star of Texas. Supplied with brown leatherette box, with copper logo inlay.

NIB	Exc.	V.G.	Good	Fair	Poor
700	600	500	350	200	100

Women of Texas Series

Same features as Millennium Series 2000. Stamped "Women of Texas Series 2000".

NIB	Exc.	V.G.	Good	Fair	Poor
700	600	500	350	200	100

Cowboy Series 2000

Same features as Gambler Millennium 2000. Stamped on barrel "Cowboy Series 2000".

NIB	Exc.	V.G.	Good	Fair	Poor
700	600	500	350	200	100

AMERICAN FIRE ARMS MFG. CO., INC.
San Antonio, Texas

Company operated between 1972 and 1974, producing .25 ACP pocket pistol and stainless steel .38 Special derringer. A .380 Auto was produced on an extremely limited basis.

American .38 Special Derringer

Well-made stainless steel over/under derringer. Similar in appearance and function to old Remington over/under. Had 3" barrels that pivoted upward for loading. Single-action that had an automatic selector and spur trigger. Smooth grips were of walnut. Approximately 3,500 manufactured between 1972 and 1974.

NIB	Exc.	V.G.	Good	Fair	Poor
—	300	225	150	125	90

American .25 Automatic

Small blowback semi-automatic pocket pistol. Chambered for .25 ACP cartridge. Had 2" barrel. Made of stainless steel or blued carbon steel. Grips were plain uncheckered walnut. Detachable magazine held 7 shots. Manufactured until 1974. **NOTE:** Add 20 percent for stainless steel.

Courtesy J.B. Wood

NIB	Exc.	V.G.	Good	Fair	Poor
—	275	200	125	100	75

American .380 Automatic

Similar to .25 except larger. Barrel was 3.5". Made in stainless steel only. Grips were smooth walnut and held 8 shots. Only 10 of these .380s manufactured between 1972 and 1974. Extremely rare, but there is little collector base for this company's products. Value is difficult to estimate.

NIB	Exc.	V.G.	Good	Fair	Poor
—	600	550	475	375	200

AMERICAN FRONTIER FIREARMS
Aguanga, California

1871, 72 Open Top Standard Model

Offered in .38- or .44-caliber, with non-rebated cylinder. Barrel lengths 7.5" or 8" in round. Blued finish except silver backstrap and trigger guard. Walnut grips.

NIB	Exc.	V.G.	Good	Fair	Poor
795	625	500	400	225	100

Richards & Mason Conversion 1851 Navy Standard Model

Offered in .38- and .44-calibers, with Mason ejector assembly and non-rebated cylinder. Choice of octagon barrels in 4.75", 5.5" or 7.5". Blued finish, with blued backstrap and trigger guard. Walnut grips.

NIB	Exc.	V.G.	Good	Fair	Poor
795	625	500	400	225	100

1860 Richards Army Model

Chambered for .44 Colt and .38-caliber. Rebated cylinder with-/without ejector assembly. Barrel length 7.5". High polish blue finish, with silver trigger guard and case hardened frame. **NOTE:** Guns shipped without ejector assembly will be supplied with a ramrod and plunger, typical of the period.

NIB	Exc.	V.G.	Good	Fair	Poor
795	625	500	400	225	100

AMERICAN GUN CO., NEW YORK
Norwich, Connecticut
Maker—Crescent Firearms Co.

Side-by-Side Shotgun

Typical trade gun made around turn of the century, by Crescent Firearms Co., to be distributed by H. & D. Folsom. These are sometimes known as "Hardware Store Guns", as that is where many were sold. This particular gun chambered for 12-, 16- or 20-gauge and produced with-/without external hammers. Length of barrels varied as did chokes. Some produced with Damascus barrels; some with fluid steel. Latter are worth approximately 25 percent more. **NOTE:** Full listing of most variations of Crescent Arms Co. and shotguns marked with American Gun Co., see "Crescent F.A. Co."

Knickerbocker Pistol—See Knickerbocker

AMERICAN HISTORICAL FOUNDATION
Ashland, Virginia

American Historical Foundation, is a private organization that commissions historical commemorative's. Secondary market sales are infrequent and difficult to confirm. American Historical Foundation sells only direct and not through dealers or distributors. For information on past and current issues, contact American Historical Foundation at 10195 Maple Leaf Court, Ashland, VA 23005.

AMERICAN INDUSTRIES
Cleveland, Ohio
aka CALICO LIGHT WEAPONS SYSTEMS
Sparks, Nevada

Calico M-100

Semi-automatic carbine. Has 16.1" barrel, with flash suppressor. Chambered for .22 LR. Features folding stock, full shrouding hand guards, 100-round capacity, helical feed, detachable magazine, ambidextrous safety, pistol-grip storage compartment, black finished alloy frame and adjustable sights. Introduced in 1986.

NIB	Exc.	V.G.	Good	Fair	Poor
500	400	350	250	200	100

Calico M-100P/M-110

Similar to M-100. .22 rimfire, with 6" barrel, muzzle-brake and no shoulder stock.

NIB	Exc.	V.G.	Good	Fair	Poor
500	400	350	250	200	75

Calico M-100S Sporter/M-105

Similar to Model 100, with futuristically styled walnut buttstock and forearm.

NIB	Exc.	V.G.	Good	Fair	Poor
500	400	350	250	200	75

Calico M-101 Solid Stock Carbine

Introduced in 1994. Features 100-round magazine and composite buttstock that is removable.

NIB	Exc.	V.G.	Good	Fair	Poor
550	450	400	300	200	75

Calico M-900

Black polymer-stocked rifle similar to M-100S. Chambered for 9mm Parabellum. Has delayed blowback action. Features stainless steel bolt and alloy receiver. Cocking handle is non-reciprocating. Rear sight is fixed, with adjustable front. A 50-round magazine standard; 100-round model optional. Introduced in 1989.

NIB	Exc.	V.G.	Good	Fair	Poor
750	575	425	350	275	100

Calico M-950 Pistol

Similar to Model 900 rifle, with 6" barrel. No shoulder stock.

NIB	Exc.	V.G.	Good	Fair	Poor
750	575	425	350	275	100

Calico M-951

M-951 is a tactical carbine, with sliding buttstock. Barrel 6" in length; weighs about 7 lbs.

NIB	Exc.	V.G.	Good	Fair	Poor
750	575	425	350	275	100

Calico M-951S

Same as above. Furnished with more conventional buttstock. Referred to as light tactical carbine. Weighs about 7.25 lbs.

NIB	Exc.	V.G.	Good	Fair	Poor
750	575	425	350	275	100

AMERICAN INTERNATIONAL
Salt Lake City, Utah
aka American Research & Development

180 Carbine (SAM-180)

Firearm imported from Austria. Semi-automatic 16.5" barreled carbine. Chambered for .22 LR. Sights are adjustable and stock made of high-impact plastic. Unique drum magazine holds 177 rounds and affixed to top of receiver. A select-fire version available for law enforcement agencies, only, and optional laser lock sight system. Later manufactured by Feather Industries in Boulder, Colorado. Now known as SAM-180.

NIB	Exc.	V.G.	Good	Fair	Poor
1400	1200	650	400	200	100

AMERICAN TACTICAL IMPORTS
Summerville, So. Carolina

AT CS/FS Series

These SA/DA pistols in 9mm, .40 S&W and .45 ACP were made in Turkey. Imported into U.S. in 2010 and 2011. Model designations were CS9, CS40, C45; and FS9, FS40. Features include a high-capacity magazine, ported slide and polymer frame.

NIB	Exc.	V.G.	Good	Fair	Poor
350	300	250	200	150	100

AT MS380

Similar to Beretta Cheetah design. This .380 model was imported from Turkey in 2010.

NIB	Exc.	V.G.	Good	Fair	Poor
325	285	225	185	135	100

GSG-522

Semi-automatic tactical rifle chambered in .22 LR. Features include 16.25" barrel, black finish overall, polymer fore-end and buttstock, back-up iron sights, receiver-mounted Picatinny rail, 10-round magazine. Several other rifle and carbine versions available. This model is part of ATI's German Sporting Gun Series.

NIB	Exc.	V.G.	Good	Fair	Poor
425	365	325	250	200	100

GSG-AK

Part of the German Sporting Gun Series, this model is patterned after the AK-47. Offered in several variations and stock designs. **NOTE:** Add 25 percent for hardwood stock and gold receiver; 20 percent for adjustable polymer stock.

NIB	Exc.	V.G.	Good	Fair	Poor
325	285	225	185	135	100

FX Series

Series of 1911-style .45 ACP pistols imported from Philippines. Available in single-/double-stack magazines. Offered in various barrel lengths, with diamond-checkered wood grips, low-profile sights, blue or stainless finishes. FX Thunderbolt model has adjustable sights, Picatinny rail, competition or bull barrel. Other variations include FX Fat Boy, a high-capacity, double-stack model with 3.2" barrel; FX 45K with threaded barrel and bobbed hammer; mid-size Commander style FX GI; and Officer-size Titan model. **NOTE:** Add $200 for Thunderbolt model (shown); $100 for 45K or Fat Boy.

NIB	Exc.	V.G.	Good	Fair	Poor
500	465	425	375	250	150

ATI GSG 1911

Caliber .22 Long Rifle. Full sized 1911-style pistol chambered for .22 LR. Features include zinc alloy frame, walnut grips, 10-round magazine, ambidextrous thumb safety and extended grip safety. Target model has adjustable sights, target grips and accessory rail. **NOTE:** Add $30 for Target model.

NIB	Exc.	V.G.	Good	Fair	Poor
275	250	220	200	175	150

SX Cavalry Shotgun

This over/under series of shotguns is made in Turkey. Offered in 12-, 20-, 28-gauge and .410 bore. Features include Turkish walnut stock, five choke tubes, single-selective trigger, extractors and alloy receiver with light engraving.

NIB	Exc.	V.G.	Good	Fair	Poor
425	375	325	275	225	200

TAC-P, TAC-S Shotgun Series

This duo of tactical shotguns consists of a slide-action (TAC-P) and semi-automatic model (TAC-S) with similar features. In 12-gauge only. Barrel length 18.5", with a cylinder bore. Synthetic stock has a pistol-grip. Both models also available with an interchangeable 28" barrel, with three choke tubes. **NOTE:** Add $100 for this option.

TAC-P

NIB	Exc.	V.G.	Good	Fair	Poor
225	200	165	125	100	75

TAC-S

NIB	Exc.	V.G.	Good	Fair	Poor
325	285	225	185	135	100

AMERICAN WESTERN ARMS INC. (AWA)
Delray Beach, Florida

Lightning Rifle LE

Copy of Colt Lightning slide-action rifle. Chambered for .32-20, .38 Special, .38-40, .44-40 or .45 Colt cartridge. Choice of round barrel lengths in 20" or 24". Engraved AWA logo and stag scene on receiver. Limited edition to 500 guns.

NIB	Exc.	V.G.	Good	Fair	Poor
1200	950	775	500	300	175

Lightning Rifle

Slide-action rifle chambered for those cartridges above. Choice of 24" round or octagon barrel. Blued finish. **NOTE:** Add $40 for octagon barrel.

NIB	Exc.	V.G.	Good	Fair	Poor
800	675	500	400	300	175

Lightning Carbine

As above, with 20" round or octagon barrel. **NOTE:** Add $40 for octagon barrel.

NIB	Exc.	V.G.	Good	Fair	Poor
800	675	500	400	300	175

Lightningbolt

Handgun version of Lightning rifle, with 12" barrel and variety of finishes. Chambered in .45 Colt. Values shown are for blued version.

NIB	Exc.	V.G.	Good	Fair	Poor
1000	800	675	500	400	200

Model 1892 Lever Action

Reproduction of Winchester 1892 carbine/rifle in .357 Magnum, .44-40, .45 Colt. Carbine model has 20" octagon barrel; rifle 24" round barrel.

NIB	Exc.	V.G.	Good	Fair	Poor
750	650	500	400	300	200

Peacekeeper

Single-action revolver assembled in U.S.A. from parts made in Italy (circa 2000 - 2003). Based on Colt Single Action Army and offered in standard barrel lengths associated with that design. Calibers are .32-20, .38-40, .357 Magnum, .44-40, .44 Special and .45 Colt. Blue, case hardened or nickel finish and hard rubber grips. Engraved versions were available in various grades based on amount of coverage — add $1500 to $2000. Nickel finish would command a $150 to $200 premium.

NIB	Exc.	V.G.	Good	Fair	Poor
750	600	500	400	300	200

Longhorn

An economy variation of Peacekeeper.

NIB	Exc.	V.G.	Good	Fair	Poor
450	400	325	300	225	200

AMES, N.P. PISTOLS
Springfield, Massachusetts

Overall length 11.625"; barrel length 6"; caliber .54. Markings: on lockplate forward of hammer "N.P. AMES/SPRINGFIELD/ MASS"; on tail either "USN" or "USR" over date; on barrel standard U.S. Navy inspection marks. N. P. Ames of Springfield, Mass. received a contract from the U.S. Navy in September 1842, for delivery of 2,000 single-shot muzzle-loading percussion pistols. All are distinguished by having a lock mechanism that lies flush with right side of stock. On first 300 Ames pistols, this lock terminates in a point; balance produced made with locks with a rounded tail. This "boxlock" had been devised by Henry Nock in England and was adapted to U.S. Navy for percussion pistols they ordered from Ames and Derringer. In addition to the 2,000 pistols for Navy, U.S. Revenue Cutter Service purchased 144 (distinguished by "U S R" marks) for the forerunner of U.S. Coast Guard. Latter commands triple price over "U S N" marked pistols, while Navy pistols with pointed tails quadruple value.

NIB	Exc.	V.G.	Good	Fair	Poor
—	—	2700	1100	650	400

AMES SWORD CO.
Chicopee Falls, Massachusetts

Turbiaux Le Protector

Ames Sword Co., became one of three U.S. companies that produced this unique French palm-squeezer pistol. Design consists of a round disk, with protruding barrel on one side and lever on the other. Disk contains a cylinder that holds either seven 8mm rimfire or ten 6mm rimfire cartridges. Barrel protrudes between fingers and lever trigger is squeezed to fire the weapon. Design was patented in 1883 and sold successfully in France into 1890s. In 1892, Peter Finnegan bought the patents and brought them to Ames Sword. He contracted with them to produce 25,000 pistols for Minneapolis Firearms Company. After approximately 1,500 were delivered, Finnegan declared insolvency and after litigation, Ames secured full patent rights. Ames Company produced Protector Revolvers until at least 1917. (See Chicago Firearms Co. and Minneapolis Firearms Co.)

NIB	Exc.	V.G.	Good	Fair	Poor
—	—	3500	1800	900	550

AMT
formerly Arcadia Machine and Tool
Irwindale, California
See also—Galena Industries Inc.

AMT is one of several companies that succeeded Auto Mag Corp. Original manufacturer of Auto Mag pistols operated from approximately 1984 to 1998. Prices in this section are for these earlier AMT-built guns only. In 1998, Galena Ind., of Sturgis, South Dakota, purchased the rights to produce most of the AMT-developed firearms and manufactured several models from 1999 to 2001. In 2005, the rights to several AMT models were acquired by Crusader Gun Co. of Houston, parent company of High Standard Mfg. Co. Also see listing for Auto Mag.

HANDGUNS

Lightning

Single-action semi-automatic .22-caliber pistol. Available with barrel lengths of 5" (Bull only), 6.5", 8.5", 10.5" and 12.5" (either Bull or tapered). Adjustable sights as well as trigger. Grips are checkered black rubber. Manufactured between 1984 and 1987.

Courtesy John J. Stimson, Jr.

NIB	Exc.	V.G.	Good	Fair	Poor
—	450	350	215	125	85

Bull's Eye Regulation Target

As above, with 6.5" ventilated rib bull barrel, wooden target grips and extended rear sight. Manufactured in 1986 only.

NIB	Exc.	V.G.	Good	Fair	Poor
—	475	375	250	200	100

Baby Automag

Similar to above, with 8.5" ventilated rib barrel and Millett adjustable sights. Approximately 1,000 manufactured.

Courtesy J.B. Wood

NIB	Exc.	V.G.	Good	Fair	Poor
—	600	450	375	225	150

Automag II

Stainless steel semi-automatic .22 Magnum pistol. Available with 3.375", 4.5" and 6" barrel lengths. Millett adjustable sights and grips of black grooved plastic. First manufactured in 1987.

Courtesy J.B. Wood

NIB	Exc.	V.G.	Good	Fair	Poor
700	600	500	400	200	100

Automag III

Semi-automatic pistol chambered for .30 Carbine and 9mm Win. Magnum cartridge. Barrel length 6.37"; overall length 10.5". Magazine capacity 8 rounds. Fitted with Millett adjustable rear sight and carbon fiber grips. Stainless steel finish. Weight 43 oz.

NIB	Exc.	V.G.	Good	Fair	Poor
600	500	400	250	100	80

Automag IV

Similar in appearance to Automag III. Chambered for .45 Win. Magnum. Magazine capacity 7 rounds. Weight 46 oz.

NIB	Exc.	V.G.	Good	Fair	Poor
700	600	500	400	225	100

Automag V

Introduced in 1993. Similar in appearance to Automag models. Chambered for .50-caliber cartridge. Limited production run of 3,000 pistols, with special serial number from "1 of 3000" to "3000 of 3000". Barrel length 6.5". Magazine capacity 5 rounds. Weight 46 oz. Production stopped in 1995. **NOTE:** Add $300 each for extra conversion barrels in .45 WM or 10mm.

Courtesy J.B. Wood

NIB	Exc.	V.G.	Good	Fair	Poor
800	700	600	500	400	150

Javelina

Produced in 1992. Chambered for 10mm cartridge. Fitted with 7" barrel, with adjustable sights. Rubber wrap-around grips. Adjustable trigger. Magazine is 8 rounds. Weight about 47 oz.

Courtesy J.B. Wood

NIB	Exc.	V.G.	Good	Fair	Poor
1000	900	750	600	400	200

Back Up Pistol

Small semi-automatic pocket pistol. Chambered for .22 LR or .380 ACP cartridges. Fitted with 2.5" barrel. Offered with black plastic or walnut grips. Weighs 18 oz. Magazine capacity 5 rounds. Originally manufactured by TDE, then Irwindale Arms Inc. and then by AMT.

NIB	Exc.	V.G.	Good	Fair	Poor
450	325	175	125	100	85

.45 ACP, .40 S&W, 9mm

Courtesy J.B. Wood

NIB	Exc.	V.G.	Good	Fair	Poor
465	350	200	150	100	85

.38 Super, .357 SIG, .400 CorBon

NOTE: Prices for current production by High Standard Mfg. Co.

NIB	Exc.	V.G.	Good	Fair	Poor
475	360	250	200	150	100

9mm, .38 Super, .40 S&W, .45 ACP

NIB	Exc.	V.G.	Good	Fair	Poor
475	425	375	325	200	100

.380 Back Up II

Introduced in 1993. Similar to Back Up model. Addition of double safety extended finger grip on magazine and single-action-only. Special order pistol only.

NIB	Exc.	V.G.	Good	Fair	Poor
425	300	250	200	150	100

Hardballer/Government Model

Similar to Colt Gold Cup .45 ACP. Offered in two versions: first has fixed sights and rounded slide top; second has adjustable Millett sights and matte rib. Magazine capacity 7 rounds. Wraparound rubber grips are standard. Long grip safety, beveled magazine well and adjustable trigger common to both variations. Weight 38 oz.

Hardballer
Adjustable sights.

Courtesy J.B. Wood

NIB	Exc.	V.G.	Good	Fair	Poor
600	500	350	275	200	125

Government Model
Fixed sights.

NIB	Exc.	V.G.	Good	Fair	Poor
575	475	300	250	150	100

Longslide
Similar to Hardballer Model. Fitted with 7" barrel. Magazine capacity 7 rounds. Weight 46 oz.

NIB	Exc.	V.G.	Good	Fair	Poor
750	550	395	275	200	125

.400 Accelerator

Similar to models above. Chambered for .400 CorBon cartridge. Fitted with 7" barrel. Fully adjustable sights. Introduced in 1997.

NIB	Exc.	V.G.	Good	Fair	Poor
600	500	350	275	200	125

Commando

Built on Government model-type action. Chambered for .40 S&W cartridge. Fitted with 5" barrel and fully adjustable sights. Introduced in 1997.

NIB	Exc.	V.G.	Good	Fair	Poor
550	425	300	200	125	75

On Duty

Semi-automatic pistol. Features double-action-only trigger action or double-action with decocker. Chambered for 9mm, .40 S&W or .45 ACP calibers. Barrel length 4.5"; overall length 7.75". Finish is a black anodized matte. Carbon fiber grips are standard. Furnished with 3-dot sights. Weight 32 oz.

NIB	Exc.	V.G.	Good	Fair	Poor
675	600	500	350	150	100

Skipper

Identical to Hardballer, with 1" shorter barrel and slide. Discontinued in 1984.

NIB	Exc.	V.G.	Good	Fair	Poor
—	450	325	275	200	125

Combat Skipper

Similar to Colt Commander. Discontinued in 1984.

NIB	Exc.	V.G.	Good	Fair	Poor
—	425	300	250	200	125

RIFLES

Lightning

Patterned after Ruger 10/22. Said to have been discontinued for that reason. Rifle has 22" barrel and 25-round detachable magazine, with folding stock. Introduced in 1986.

Courtesy J.B. Wood

NIB	Exc.	V.G.	Good	Fair	Poor
375	250	175	125	75	50

Small Game Hunter

As above, with full stock and 10-round magazine. Introduced in 1986.

NIB	Exc.	V.G.	Good	Fair	Poor
350	225	175	150	125	100

Small Game Hunter II

Semi-automatic rifle chambered for .22 LR cartridge. Stock is checkered black matte nylon. Fitted with removable recoil pad for ammo, cleaning rod and knife. Rotary magazine holds 10 rounds. Stainless steel barrel and action. Barrel is a heavy weight target type, 22" long. Weight 6 lbs.

NIB	Exc.	V.G.	Good	Fair	Poor
350	225	175	150	125	100

Hunter

Semi-automatic rifle chambered for .22 Rimfire Magnum cartridge. Stock is checkered black matte nylon. Other features similar to Small Game Hunter II, including weight.

NIB	Exc.	V.G.	Good	Fair	Poor
375	250	200	150	125	100

Magnum Hunter

Similar to above. Chambered for .22 Rimfire Magnum cartridge. Fitted with 22" accurized barrel. Barrel and action are stainless steel. Comes standard with 5-round magazine and composite stock. Laminated stock was available at an extra cost, as is a 10-round magazine.

NIB	Exc.	V.G.	Good	Fair	Poor
525	400	350	250	200	150

Target Model

Semi-automatic rifle chambered for .22 LR cartridge. Fitted with 20" target barrel. Weight about 7.5 lbs. Choice of Fajen or Hogue stock. **NOTE:** Hogue stock deduct $50.

NIB	Exc.	V.G.	Good	Fair	Poor
600	500	450	300	200	—

Challenge Edition

Custom ordered .22-caliber semi-automatic rifle. Built on Ruger 10/22-like receiver. Offered in 18" or 22" barrel lengths, with all stainless steel construction. McMillan fiberglass stock. Weaver-style scope mounts.

NIB	Exc.	V.G.	Good	Fair	Poor
1050	800	550	400	300	175

Single-Shot Standard

Custom-built rifle, with choice of barrel length, composite stock, adjustable trigger, post '64 Winchester action, all in stainless and chrome moly steel. Chambered for all standard calibers. First offered in 1996.

NIB	Exc.	V.G.	Good	Fair	Poor
875	675	500	350	200	175

Single-Shot Deluxe

Custom-built rifle on Mauser-type action, with choice of match grade barrel lengths and custom Kevlar stock. Built from stainless and chrome moly steel. Chambered for all standard calibers. First offered in 1996.

NIB	Exc.	V.G.	Good	Fair	Poor
1800	1400	950	650	400	225

Bolt-Action Repeating—Standard

Similar in construction and features to Standard Single-Shot rifle.

NIB	Exc.	V.G.	Good	Fair	Poor
840	675	500	350	200	175

Bolt-Action Repeating—Deluxe

Similar in construction and features to Deluxe Single-Shot rifle.

NIB	Exc.	V.G.	Good	Fair	Poor
1800	1400	950	650	400	225

ANCION MARX
Liege, Belgium

Company began production in 1860s, with a variety of cheaply made pinfire revolvers. They later switched to solid-frame centerfire "Velo-Dog"-type revolvers, chambered for 5.5mm or 6.35mm. They were marketed in various countries under many different trade names. Some of the names they will be found under are Cobalt, Extracteur, LeNovo, Lincoln and Milady. Quality of these revolvers is quite poor and collector interest, almost non-existent. Values do not usually vary because of trade names.

NIB	Exc.	V.G.	Good	Fair	Poor
—	—	200	135	75	45

ANDERSON
Anderson, Texas

Under Hammer Pistol

Unmarked under hammer percussion pistol. Chambered for .45-caliber. Had 5" half-round/half-octagonal barrel, with all steel saw handle-shaped frame, flared butt with walnut grips. Finish blued. Little information on this pistol.

NIB	Exc.	V.G.	Good	Fair	Poor
—	—	900	400	150	100

ANDRUS & OSBORN
Canton, Connecticut

Under Hammer Pistol

Pistol of percussion type. Chambered for .25-caliber. Part-round/part-octagonal barrel is 6" long. Features small silver star inlays along its length. Barrel marked "Andrus & Osborn/Canton Conn.", with an eagle stamped beside it. Marked "Cast Steel" near breech. Grips walnut. Finish browned. Active 1863 to 1867.

NIB	Exc.	V.G.	Good	Fair	Poor
—	—	1550	625	200	100

ANSCHÜTZ, J.G. GmbH
Ulm, Germany

Originally founded in 1856, by Julius and Lusie Anschutz. Company was originally called J.G. Anschutz and manufactured a wide variety of firearms. In 1950 in Ulm, the new company was founded: J.G. Anschutz GmbH. Values for new guns fluctuate according to currency variations.

Mark 10 Target

Single-shot bolt-action rifle. Chambered for .22 LR cartridge. Has 26" heavy barrel, with adjustable target-type sights. Finish blued. Walnut target stock had an adjustable palm rest. Manufactured between 1963 and 1981.

NIB	Exc.	V.G.	Good	Fair	Poor
500	425	350	210	150	100

Model 1403D

Single-shot target rifle chambered for .22 LR cartridge. Has 26" barrel. Furnished without sights. Has fully adjustable trigger. Blued finish, with walnut target-type stock.

NIB	Exc.	V.G.	Good	Fair	Poor
850	775	675	500	375	250

Model 1407

Similar to Mark 10. Furnished without sights. Known as "I.S.U." model. Discontinued in 1981.

NIB	Exc.	V.G.	Good	Fair	Poor
525	450	375	235	175	100

Model 1408

Heavier-barreled version of Model 1407.

NIB	Exc.	V.G.	Good	Fair	Poor
525	450	375	240	180	105

Model 1411

Designed specifically to be fired from prone position.

NIB	Exc.	V.G.	Good	Fair	Poor
750	650	450	210	150	100

Model 1413 Match

High-grade competition version, with heavy target barrel. Furnished without sights; optional sights extra. Walnut stock has adjustable cheekpiece.

NIB	Exc.	V.G.	Good	Fair	Poor
775	675	550	400	275	150

Model 1416D HB Classic

Chambered for .22 LR cartridge. Magazine capacity 5 rounds. Fitted with match grade trigger and target grade barrel. Checkered walnut stock. Built on the 64 action.

NIB	Exc.	V.G.	Good	Fair	Poor
900	725	595	400	225	125

Model 1416D KL Classic

Sporting rifle chambered for .22 LR cartridge. Fitted with American-style stock of European walnut or hardwood. Built on Anschutz Match 64 action. Left-handed model also offered.

NIB	Exc.	V.G.	Good	Fair	Poor
900	725	595	300	200	100

Model 1416D Custom

Chambered for .22 LR cartridge. Features European-style stock, with Monte Carlo cheekpiece and schnabel fore-end.

NIB	Exc.	V.G.	Good	Fair	Poor
875	650	550	300	200	100

Model 1418D KL Mannlicher

Hunting rifle, with full-length Mannlicher-type stock. Made with hand-checkered walnut. Chambered for .22 LR, with 5-round magazine. Open iron sights. Weight about 5.5 lbs.

NIB	Exc.	V.G.	Good	Fair	Poor
1200	950	700	450	200	150

Model 1418/19

Lower-priced sporter model. Formerly imported by Savage Arms.

NIB	Exc.	V.G.	Good	Fair	Poor
700	650	425	200	125	85

Model 1433D

Centerfire version of Model 54 target rifle. Chambered for .22 Hornet. Special-order item. Features set trigger and 4-round detachable magazine. Finish blued, with full length Mannlicher stock. Discontinued in 1986.

NIB	Exc.	V.G.	Good	Fair	Poor
1500	950	700	400	200	100

Model 1533

Similar to Model 1433D, except chambered for .222 Remington cartridge. This model has a Mannlicher-style stock. Discontinued in mid 1990s.

NIB	Exc.	V.G.	Good	Fair	Poor
1200	1050	900	750	600	300

Model 1449D Youth

Bolt-action rifle chambered for .22 LR cartridge. Fitted with 16" barrel and adjustable rear sight. Stock is European hardwood, with 12.25" length of pull. Magazine capacity 5 rounds. No longer imported.

NIB	Exc.	V.G.	Good	Fair	Poor
450	300	250	100	75	60

Model Woodchucker

Sold by distributor RSR. Bolt-action .22-caliber. Similar to Model 1449D Youth.

NIB	Exc.	V.G.	Good	Fair	Poor
450	300	250	100	75	60

Model 1451E Target

Single-shot .22-caliber target rifle. Fitted with 22" barrel. Can be fitted with micrometer iron sights or telescope sights. Checkered pistol-grip and adjustable buttplate. Weight about 6.25 lbs.

NIB	Exc.	V.G.	Good	Fair	Poor
625	500	400	200	125	75

Model 1451R Sporter Target

Bolt-action target rifle chambered for .22 LR cartridge. Fitted with target-style stock and 22" heavy barrel. Furnished with no open sights. Two-stage target trigger is standard. Weight about 6.5 lbs.

NIB	Exc.	V.G.	Good	Fair	Poor
650	525	425	225	175	100

Model 1451D Custom

Similar to above. Fitted with checkered walnut sporting stock, with Monte Carlo comb and cheekpiece. Barrel length 22.75", with open sights. Weight about 5 lbs.

NIB	Exc.	V.G.	Good	Fair	Poor
675	550	450	250	150	100

Model 1451D Classic

Similar to Model 1451 Custom, with straight walnut stock. Weight about 5 lbs.

NIB	Exc.	V.G.	Good	Fair	Poor
700	600	500	300	150	100

Model 1516D KL Classic

Same as above. Chambered for .22 Magnum cartridge.

NIB	Exc.	V.G.	Good	Fair	Poor
775	600	500	300	200	100

Model 1516D KL Custom

Same as above. Chambered for .22 Magnum cartridge.

NIB	Exc.	V.G.	Good	Fair	Poor
850	650	550	450	250	100

Model 1517D Classic

Based on the 64 action. Bolt-action rifle chambered for .17 HMR cartridge. Fitted with 23" barrel. Checkered walnut stock. Magazine capacity 4 rounds. Weight about 5.5 lbs. Introduced in 2003.

NIB	Exc.	V.G.	Good	Fair	Poor
975	800	700	550	400	300

Model 1517D HB Classic

Similar to Model 1516D. Fitted with a heavy barrel without sights. Weight about 6.2 lbs. Introduced in 2003.

NIB	Exc.	V.G.	Good	Fair	Poor
1050	850	750	550	400	300

Model 1517D Monte Carlo

Chambered for .17 HMR cartridge. Fitted with 23" barrel. Checkered walnut stock, with schnabel fore-end and Monte Carlo comb. Weight about 5.5 lbs. Introduced in 2003.

NIB	Exc.	V.G.	Good	Fair	Poor
1000	825	725	550	400	300

Model 1517MPR Multi-Purpose Rifle

Introduced in 2003. Features 25.5" heavy barrel without sights, two-stage trigger, hardwood stock with beavertail fore-end. Chambered for .17 HMR cartridge. Weight about 9 lbs. **NOTE:** Available with a number of extra cost options.

NIB	Exc.	V.G.	Good	Fair	Poor
1100	925	800	600	450	350

Model 1518D Mannlicher

Same as above. Chambered for .22 Magnum.

NIB	Exc.	V.G.	Good	Fair	Poor
1200	950	700	350	225	125

Model 184

High-grade bolt-action sporting rifle chambered for .22 LR cartridge. Has 21.5" barrel, with folding-leaf sight. Finish blued, with checkered walnut Monte Carlo stock and schnabel fore-end. Manufactured between 1963 and 1981.

NIB	Exc.	V.G.	Good	Fair	Poor
575	425	315	225	150	100

Model 54 Sporter

High-grade bolt-action sporting rifle chambered for .22 LR cartridge. Has 24" tapered round barrel and 5-shot detachable magazine. Features folding leaf-type rear sight. Finish blued, with checkered walnut Monte Carlo stock. Manufactured between 1963 and 1981.

NIB	Exc.	V.G.	Good	Fair	Poor
750	675	600	350	250	125

Model 54M

Version chambered for .22 Rimfire Magnum cartridge.

NIB	Exc.	V.G.	Good	Fair	Poor
800	700	625	375	275	125

Model 141

Bolt-action sporter chambered for .22 LR cartridge. Has 23" round barrel, with blued finish and walnut Monte Carlo stock. Manufactured between 1963 and 1981.

NIB	Exc.	V.G.	Good	Fair	Poor
800	650	450	200	150	100

Model 141M

Chambered for .22 Rimfire Magnum cartridge.

NIB	Exc.	V.G.	Good	Fair	Poor
825	675	475	225	175	100

Model 164

Bolt-action rifle. Fitted with 23" round barrel. Chambered for .22 LR cartridge. Has Monte Carlo stock with open sights. Magazine holds 5 rounds.

NIB	Exc.	V.G.	Good	Fair	Poor
700	625	475	325	175	100

Model 164M

Same as above. Chambered for .22 Win. Magnum cartridge.

NIB	Exc.	V.G.	Good	Fair	Poor
725	650	500	225	175	100

Model 153

Bolt-action sporting rifle chambered for .222 Remington cartridge. Has 24" barrel, with folding-leaf rear sight. Finish blued, with checkered French walnut stock. Featuring rosewood fore-end tip and pistol-grip cap. Manufactured between 1963 and 1981.

NIB	Exc.	V.G.	Good	Fair	Poor
900	750	575	300	225	150

Model 153-S

Version offered with double-set triggers.

NIB	Exc.	V.G.	Good	Fair	Poor
950	775	615	350	275	150

Model 64

Single-shot bolt-action rifle. Chambered for .22 LR cartridge. Has 26" round barrel. Furnished without sights. Finish blued. Walnut target-type stock featured beavertail forearm and adjustable buttplate. Manufactured between 1963 and 1981.

NIB	Exc.	V.G.	Good	Fair	Poor
600	450	350	200	150	100

Model 64MS

Version designed for silhouette shooting. Has 21.25" barrel, blued finish and target-type walnut stock with stippled pistol-grip.

NIB	Exc.	V.G.	Good	Fair	Poor
950	850	625	400	300	200

Model 64 MPR

Multi-purpose target repeater. Chambered for .22 LR cartridge. Fitted with 25.5" heavy barrel. Offered with optional sights. Choice of stainless steel barrel, with beavertail or beavertail with swivel rail. Weight about 9 lbs.

NIB	Exc.	V.G.	Good	Fair	Poor
1100	850	700	400	300	200

Model 64P

Bolt-action pistol, with adjustable trigger. Action is grooved for scope mounts and stock is synthetic. Barrel length 10". Chambered for .22 LR cartridge. Weight about 3 lb. 8 oz. Introduced in 1998.

NIB	Exc.	V.G.	Good	Fair	Poor
595	500	450	250	175	75

Model 64P Mag

Same as above. Chambered for .22 WMR cartridge.

NIB	Exc.	V.G.	Good	Fair	Poor
650	525	475	275	175	75

Model 54.18MS

High-grade silhouette rifle chambered for .22 LR cartridge. Has 22" barrel. Match-grade action, with fully adjustable trigger. Furnished without sights. Finish blued, with target-type walnut stock.

NIB	Exc.	V.G.	Good	Fair	Poor
2150	1500	995	500	300	200

Model 54.MS REP

Repeating rifle, with 5-shot detachable magazine. Thumbhole stock, with vented forearm.

NIB	Exc.	V.G.	Good	Fair	Poor
2100	1600	1050	500	300	200

Model 2000 MK

Single-shot rifle chambered for .22 LR cartridge. Has 26" round barrel, with target-type sights. Finish blued, with walnut stock. Not imported after 1988.

NIB	Exc.	V.G.	Good	Fair	Poor
650	600	450	200	150	100

Model 2007 Supermatch

Introduced in 1993. Target rifle chambered for .22 LR cartridge. Has 19.75" barrel fitted to Match 54 action. Trigger is a two-stage. Stock is standard ISU configuration, with adjustable cheekpiece. Weight about 10.8 lbs. Offered in left-hand model.

NIB	Exc.	V.G.	Good	Fair	Poor
2350	1850	1350	750	350	200

Model 2013 Supermatch

Similar to above. Fitted with International stock, with palm rest and buttstock hook. Weight about 12.5 lbs.

NIB	Exc.	V.G.	Good	Fair	Poor
3200	2600	1850	1250	600	300

Model 1903D

Designed for advanced junior shooter. Target rifle has 25.5" barrel on Match 64 action, with single stage trigger. Walnut stock is fully adjustable. Weight about 9.5 lbs. Offered in left-hand model.

NIB	Exc.	V.G.	Good	Fair	Poor
950	800	700	400	300	200

Model 1803D

High-grade target rifle chambered for .22 LR cartridge. Has 25.5" heavy barrel, with adjustable target sights. Features adjustable trigger. Finish blued, with light-colored wood stock. Dark stippling on pistol-grip and forearm. Stock features adjustable cheekpiece and buttplate. Introduced in 1987.

NIB	Exc.	V.G.	Good	Fair	Poor
1200	1000	775	600	450	200

Model 1808D RT Super

Single-shot running-boar type rifle. Chambered for .22 LR cartridge. Has 32.5" barrel furnished without sights. Finish blued, with heavy target-type walnut stock with thumbhole. Furnished with barrel weights. Weight about 9.4 lbs. Available in left-hand version.

NIB	Exc.	V.G.	Good	Fair	Poor
1500	1300	1150	750	450	250

Model 1907ISU Standard Match

Chambered for .22 LR cartridge. Designed for both prone and position shooting. Weight 11.2 lbs. Built on Match 54 action. Fitted with 26" barrel. Two-stage trigger. Removable cheekpiece and adjustable buttstock.

NIB	Exc.	V.G.	Good	Fair	Poor
1600	1350	1000	450	300	200

Model 1910 Super Match II

High-grade single-shot target rifle chambered for .22 LR cartridge. Has 27.25" barrel. Furnished with diopter-type target sights. Finish blued, with adjustable cheekpiece and buttplate. Walnut thumbhole stock. Hand and palm rest are not included.

NIB	Exc.	V.G.	Good	Fair	Poor
2300	1850	1400	900	500	250

Model 1911 Prone Match

Version has stock designed specifically for firing from prone position.

NIB	Exc.	V.G.	Good	Fair	Poor
1850	1550	1050	650	400	250

Model 1913 Super Match

Virtually hand-built match target rifle. Chambered for .22 LR cartridge. Features single-shot action. Has adjustable diopter-type sights on 27.25" heavy barrel. Custom-made gun. Features every target option conceivable. Finish blued, with fully adjustable walnut stock.

NIB	Exc.	V.G.	Good	Fair	Poor
2700	2100	1600	1000	500	250

Model 1827B Biathlon

Repeating bolt-action target rifle chambered for .22 LR cartridge. Specially designed for biathlon competition. Production is quite limited and on a custom basis.

NIB	Exc.	V.G.	Good	Fair	Poor
1850	1500	1150	800	400	250

Model 1827BT Biathlon

Similar to above. Features straight-pull Fortner bolt system. Available in left-hand model.

NIB	Exc.	V.G.	Good	Fair	Poor
2900	2350	1750	1000	500	250

Achiever

Introduced in 1993. Target rifle chambered for .22 LR cartridge. Designed for beginner shooter. Furnished with 5-shot clip, but can be converted to single-shot with an adapter. Barrel length 19.5". Action is Mark 2000, with two-stage trigger. Stock pull is adjustable from 12" to 13". Weight about 5 lbs.

NIB	Exc.	V.G.	Good	Fair	Poor
525	400	295	150	125	100

Achiever Super Target

Designed for advanced junior shooter. Has 22" barrel. Weight about 6.5 lbs.

NIB	Exc.	V.G.	Good	Fair	Poor
575	450	325	175	125	100

Bavarian 1700

Classic-style sporting rifle chambered for .22 LR, .22 Rimfire Magnum, .22 Hornet and .222 Remington cartridges. Features 24" barrel, with adjustable sights. Has detachable magazine. Blued finish. Checkered walnut European-style Monte Carlo stock, with cheekpiece. Introduced in 1988. Values shown are for centerfire.

NIB	Exc.	V.G.	Good	Fair	Poor
1300	950	600	400	300	200

Classic 1700

Similar in appearance to Bavarian. Furnished with American-style stock, with fluted comb. Same calibers as Bavarian. Weight 6.75 lbs. **NOTE:** Add $175 for "Meister Grade" fancy wood stocks.

NIB	Exc.	V.G.	Good	Fair	Poor
1300	950	600	400	300	200

Custom 1700

Similar to Bavarian and Classic in caliber offerings, but offered with fancy European walnut stock, with roll-over cheekpiece with Monte Carlo. Pistol-grip has palm swell. Fitted with a white lined rosewood grip cap, with white diamond insert. Fore-end is schnabel type and stock checkered in ship line pattern. **NOTE:** Add $175 for "Meister Grade" fancy wood stocks.

NIB	Exc.	V.G.	Good	Fair	Poor
1650	1275	750	400	300	200

Model 1700 Mannlicher

Similar to 1700 Classic. Fitted with full-length stock. **NOTE:** Add $175 for "Meister Grade" fancy wood stocks.

NIB	Exc.	V.G.	Good	Fair	Poor
1550	1200	850	550	350	200

Model 1700 FWT

Model has same specifications as 1700 Custom. Fitted with McMillan laminated fiberglass stock. Weight about 6.25 lbs.

NIB	Exc.	V.G.	Good	Fair	Poor
1225	900	700	500	300	200

Model 1700 FWT Deluxe

Same as above. Fitted with laminated wood grain stock.

NIB	Exc.	V.G.	Good	Fair	Poor
1125	900	800	550	300	200

Model 1710 D Classic

Bolt-action .22-caliber rifle, with 23.6" barrel and no sights. Walnut stock checkered. Magazine capacity 5 rounds. Weight about 7.3 lbs.

NIB	Exc.	V.G.	Good	Fair	Poor
1300	1050	800	—	—	—

Model 1710 D HB Classic

Same as above, with heavy barrel. Weight about 8 lbs.

NIB	Exc.	V.G.	Good	Fair	Poor
1350	1050	750	475	300	150

Model 1710 D KL Monte Carlo

Same as Classic, with Monte Carlo stock. Folding leaf rear sight, with hooded front sight. Weight about 7.5 lbs.

NIB	Exc.	V.G.	Good	Fair	Poor
1300	1000	775	425	325	175

Model 1710 D HB Classic 150 Years Anniversary Version

Similar to Model 1710 D HB Classic, with heavy stainless barrel. Stock laser-engraved, with 150th Anniversary and 1901 "Germania" logos. Introduced in 2007. Only 150 units were produced.

NIB	Exc.	V.G.	Good	Fair	Poor
2100	1700	1200	700	400	200

Model 1712 Silhouette Sporter

Chambered in .22 LR. Features include two-stage trigger, deluxe walnut stock, 21.6" blued sightless barrel and 5-shot magazine.

NIB	Exc.	V.G.	Good	Fair	Poor
1150	925	675	425	200	100

Model 1702 D HB Classic

Chambered in .17 Mach 2. Features include finely-tuned double-stage trigger, walnut stock, 23" blued heavy sightless barrel and 5-shot magazine.

NIB	Exc.	V.G.	Good	Fair	Poor
1300	1150	700	450	250	125

Model 1502 D HB Classic

Similar to Model 1702 D HB, with single-stage trigger and fewer refinements. **NOTE:** Add 10 percent for beavertail fore-end.

NIB	Exc.	V.G.	Good	Fair	Poor
600	400	300	200	100	50

Model 1907 Club

Single-shot economy target rifle chambered in .22 LR. Features include target trigger, short lock time, 26" blued barrel, micrometer rear peep and hood front sights. Ambidextrous removable cheekpiece and walnut buttstock, with rubber buttplate and stock spacers. Weight 9.7 lbs.

NIB	Exc.	V.G.	Good	Fair	Poor
1800	1500	1200	900	—	—

Model 1717 D Classic

Bolt-action model chambered for .17 HMR cartridge. Fitted with 23.6" barrel, with no sights. Checkered walnut stock. Weight about 7.3 lbs.

NIB	Exc.	V.G.	Good	Fair	Poor
1375	1000	675	475	300	150

Model 1717 D HB Classic

Same as above, with heavy barrel. Weight about 8 lbs.

NIB	Exc.	V.G.	Good	Fair	Poor
1475	1200	700	495	325	175

Model 1727

Straight-pull action repeater based on Biathlon type action, with very fast lock time. Chambered for .22 Hornady Magnum Rimfire cartridge. German walnut stock, with cheekpiece and schnabel fore-end. Match-grade 22" barrel. Introduced in 2014.

NIB	Exc.	V.G.	Good	Fair	Poor
3000	2650	2100	1450	800	350

Model 1730 D Classic

Bolt-action rifle chambered for .22 Hornet cartridge. Fitted with 23.6" barrel. Magazine capacity 5 rounds. Checkered walnut stock. No sights. Weight about 7.3 lbs.

NIB	Exc.	V.G.	Good	Fair	Poor
1625	1325	750	525	350	225

Model 1730 D HB Classic

Same as above, with heavy barrel. Weight about 8 lbs.

NIB	Exc.	V.G.	Good	Fair	Poor
1550	1250	700	495	325	175

Model 1730 D KL Monte Carlo

Model has Monte Carlo stock and folding leaf rear sight, with hooded front sight. Weight about 7.5 lbs.

NIB	Exc.	V.G.	Good	Fair	Poor
1625	1325	750	525	350	225

Model 1733D KL Mannlicher

Introduced in 1993. Features Mannlicher stock built on a Match 54 action. Stock has rosewood schnabel tip. Checkering is done in a skip-line pattern. Chambered for .22 Hornet. Weight about 6.25 lbs.

NIB	Exc.	V.G.	Good	Fair	Poor
1450	1150	675	475	300	175

Model 1740 D Classic

Bolt-action model chambered for .222 Remington cartridge. Checkered walnut stock, with no sights. Magazine capacity 3 rounds. Weight about 7.3 lbs.

NIB	Exc.	V.G.	Good	Fair	Poor
1625	1325	750	525	350	225

Model 1743D

Chambered for classic .222 Remington cartridge. Model features a full-length Mannliche stock. Other features similar to 1740D series.

NIB	Exc.	V.G.	Good	Fair	Poor
1350	1150	900	700	500	250

Model 1740 D HB Classic

Same as above, with heavy barrel. Weight about 7.3 lbs.

NIB	Exc.	V.G.	Good	Fair	Poor
1550	1250	700	495	325	175

Model 1740 D KL Monte Carlo

Model fitted with Monte Carlo stock. Folding leaf rear sight and hooded front sight. Weight about 7.3 lbs.

NIB	Exc.	V.G.	Good	Fair	Poor
1625	1325	750	525	350	225

Model 1770D

Built on an action designed specifically for centerfire cartridges. Chambered for .223 Remington round. Model has a medium weight 22" barrel, detachable 3-round magazine and large bolt handle. Choice of classic Monte Carlo or German-style walnut stock. Introduced in 2009.

NIB	Exc.	V.G.	Good	Fair	Poor
2100	1700	1200	900	650	300

Model 1780D

A centerfire rifle chambered for .30-06 or .308 Winchester. Features include a 21" barrel, 5-round detachable magazine and choice of a classic sporter walnut, thumbhole or camo finished stock.

NIB	Exc.	V.G.	Good	Fair	Poor
1200	1050	900	750	600	300

Model 520/61

Blowback-operated semi-automatic rifle. Chambered for .22 LR cartridge. Has 24" barrel and 10-round detachable magazine. Finish blued, with checkered walnut stock. Discontinued in 1983.

NIB	Exc.	V.G.	Good	Fair	Poor
675	550	300	200	100	85

Model 525 Sporter

Semi-automatic rifle chambered for .22 LR cartridge. Has 24" barrel, with adjustable sights and 10-round detachable magazine. Finish blued, with checkered Monte Carlo-type stock. Introduced in 1984. Carbine version with 20" barrel was originally offered, but discontinued in 1986.

NIB	Exc.	V.G.	Good	Fair	Poor
725	600	450	250	175	100

Model RX22

An AR-style semi-automatic rifle chambered for .22LR cartridge. Features are similar to most AR-type rimfire rifles, including 16.5" barrel, Picatinny accessory rail, 10-shot magazine, folding iron backup sights, fixed or folding adjustable stock with pistol-grip and choice of black or desert tan finish. Also available with skeletonized wood stock. Made in Germany and imported by Steyr.

NIB	Exc.	V.G.	Good	Fair	Poor
850	720	600	450	300	150

Exemplar

Bolt-action pistol built on Model 64 Match Action. Chambered for .22 LR cartridge. Has 10" barrel, with adjustable sights and 5-shot detachable magazine. Features adjustable two-stage trigger, with receiver grooved for attaching a scope. Walnut stock and fore-end are stippled. Introduced in 1987, discontinued in 1997.

NIB	Exc.	V.G.	Good	Fair	Poor
500	400	300	225	175	100

Exemplar XIV

Similar to standard Exemplar, with 14" barrel. Introduced in 1988.

NIB	Exc.	V.G.	Good	Fair	Poor
600	500	400	250	200	100

Exemplar Hornet

Chambered for .22 Hornet cartridge. Introduced in 1988.

NIB	Exc.	V.G.	Good	Fair	Poor
800	650	575	300	200	100

ANTI GARROTTER
England

Percussion belt pistol marked "Balls Pat. Steel". Oval is 7" long and barrel protrudes 1.5"; approximately .45-caliber. A cord runs from lock up and through sleeve and is fired by pulling the cord. Beware of modern fakes.

NIB	Exc.	V.G.	Good	Fair	Poor
—	—	7500	3000	800	400

ANZIO IRON WORKS
St. Petersburg, Florida

This manufacturer specializes in large caliber rifles for ultra long range shooting.

Takedown Competition

Caliber .338 Lapua or .50 BMG. Five-shot detachable magazine. Many options.

.338 Lapua
Barrel lengths 26" or 29".

NIB	Exc.	V.G.	Good	Fair	Poor
4200	3800	3000	2200	1400	900

.50 BMG
Barrel length 30".

NIB	Exc.	V.G.	Good	Fair	Poor
3600	3100	2400	1750	1100	800

20/50 Rifle

Caliber 20mm or .50 BMG. Single-shot or magazine fed repeater. Barrel length 40" or 45". **NOTE:** Add $1000 for repeating model.

NIB	Exc.	V.G.	Good	Fair	Poor
7000	6000	5000	3800	2500	1000

APACHE
Eibar, Spain

See—Ojanguren Y Vidosa

APALOZO HERMANOS
Zumorraga, Spain

Spanish manufacturer from approximately 1920 to 1936. Trademark, dove-like bird normally found impressed into grips.

Apaloza

Copy of Colt Police Positive revolver.

NIB	Exc.	V.G.	Good	Fair	Poor
—	275	150	100	65	45

Paramount

Copy of Model 1906 Browning. Chambered for 6.35mm. "Paramount" stamped on slide and top of each grip plate.

Courtesy James Rankin

NIB	Exc.	V.G.	Good	Fair	Poor
—	275	175	100	50	30

Triomphe

Copy of Browning Model 1906 in caliber 6.35mm. Slide inscribed "Pistolet Automatique Triomphe Acier Comprime". "Cal. 6.35mm" stamped on each grip plate along with dove logo.

Courtesy James Rankin

NIB	Exc.	V.G.	Good	Fair	Poor
—	275	175	100	50	30

AR-7 INDUSTRIES
Meriden, Connecticut

AR-7 Explorer

Semi-automatic .22-caliber takedown rifle. Fitted with 16" barrel and 8-round magazine. Adjustable rear peep sight. Weight 2.5 lbs.

NIB	Exc.	V.G.	Good	Fair	Poor
200	150	90	65	50	25

AR-7C Explorer

Same as above, with camo stock.

NIB	Exc.	V.G.	Good	Fair	Poor
225	175	100	65	50	25

AR-7 Sporter

Similar to standard AR-7, with metal skeleton stock. Aluminum ventilated shrouded barrel. Weight about 3.8 lbs.

NIB	Exc.	V.G.	Good	Fair	Poor
250	150	120	75	65	35

AR-7 Target

Features tubular stock, with cantilever 3-9x40mm scope. Fitted with 16" bull barrel. Weight about 5.7 lbs.

NIB	Exc.	V.G.	Good	Fair	Poor
300	200	150	75	65	35

AR-7 Bolt-Action

Model similar in all respects to standard semi-automatic AR-7, with bolt-action.

NIB	Exc.	V.G.	Good	Fair	Poor
225	120	90	65	50	25

ARCUS
Bulgaria

Arcus-94

Introduced in 1998. Semi-automatic pistol chambered for 9mm cartridge. Fitted with ambidextrous safety and 10-round magazine. Imported from Bulgaria.

NIB	Exc.	V.G.	Good	Fair	Poor
425	325	275	200	150	100

ARIZAGA, G.
Eibar, Spain

Spanish manufacturer prior to World War II.

Arizaga (Model 1915)

7.65mm semi-automatic pistol. Patterned after Ruby-style military pistols. Magazine capacity 9 or 12 rounds. Wood grips.

NIB	Exc.	V.G.	Good	Fair	Poor
—	275	195	100	75	45

Mondial

Similar design to Astra pistol in 100 series. Chambered for 6.35mm cartridge. Has Owl and Mondial on each grip plate.

NIB	Exc.	V.G.	Good	Fair	Poor
—	300	190	145	75	45

Pinkerton

Arizaga's standard model known to exist, with cartridge counter. Slide marked "Pinkerton Automatic 6.35".

NIB	Exc.	V.G.	Good	Fair	Poor
—	295	175	100	75	45

Warwick

Same design as Mondial in caliber 7.65mm. "Warwick" appears on each grip plate.

NIB	Exc.	V.G.	Good	Fair	Poor
—	300	190	145	75	45

ARIZMENDI, FRANCISCO
Eibar, Spain

Originally founded in 1890s. Reformed in 1914. Manufactured semi-automatic pistols.

Singer

Singer was manufactured in a number of different variations and in calibers 6.35mm and 7.65mm. Earlier called Victor. 6.35mm model resembled Browning 1906; 7.65mm model Browning Model 1910.

6.35mm

Courtesy James Rankin

NIB	Exc.	V.G.	Good	Fair	Poor
—	225	195	100	50	35

7.65mm

Courtesy James Rankin

NIB	Exc.	V.G.	Good	Fair	Poor
—	175	125	75	50	35

Teuf Teuf

Teuf Teuf was chambered in calibers 6.35mm and 7.65mm. The 7.65mm was only slightly larger than 6.35mm model. Pistol copied its name from Browning Model 1906 and from Belgium Teuf Teuf. Pistol shown is a cartridge indicator model.

Courtesy James Rankin

6.35mm

NIB	Exc.	V.G.	Good	Fair	Poor
—	225	195	100	50	35

7.65mm

NIB	Exc.	V.G.	Good	Fair	Poor
—	225	195	100	50	35

Walman

Walman was manufactured in a number of variations and in calibers 6.35mm, 7.65mm and .380. Earliest semi-automatic production was in 1908 through 1926. Certain variations were called American Model. Model in .380-caliber had a squeeze grip safety.

6.35mm

Courtesy James Rankin

NIB	Exc.	V.G.	Good	Fair	Poor
—	225	195	100	50	35

7.65mm

Courtesy James Rankin

NIB	Exc.	V.G.	Good	Fair	Poor
—	250	200	125	60	35

.380

Courtesy James Rankin

NIB	Exc.	V.G.	Good	Fair	Poor
—	260	225	145	60	35

Arizmendi

Solid-frame folding-trigger revolver chambered for 7.65mm or .32-caliber. Normal markings are trademark "FA" and a circled five-pointed star.

NIB	Exc.	V.G.	Good	Fair	Poor
—	200	150	80	50	25

Boltun—1st Variation

Bolton semi-automatic pistol was made in both calibers 6.35mm and 7.65mm. Almost an exact copy of Belgian Pieper. 7.65mm model was only slightly larger than 6.35mm model.

6.35mm

NIB	Exc.	V.G.	Good	Fair	Poor
—	250	195	125	60	35

7.65mm

NIB	Exc.	V.G.	Good	Fair	Poor
—	250	195	125	60	35

Boltun—2nd Variation

Boltun 2nd variation chambered for 7.65mm cartridge. Almost an exact copy of Browning Model 1910. Made into 1930s.

NIB	Exc.	V.G.	Good	Fair	Poor
—	250	195	125	60	35

Roland

Chambered for 6.35 and 7.65mm cartridges. Manufactured during 1920s. The 7.65mm was only slightly larger than 6.35mm model.

Courtesy James Rankin

6.35mm

NIB	Exc.	V.G.	Good	Fair	Poor
—	250	150	90	60	35

7.65mm

NIB	Exc.	V.G.	Good	Fair	Poor
—	250	150	90	60	35

Puppy

Variation of "Velo-Dog" revolver. Barrel stamped "Puppy". Frame bearing "FA" trademark.

NIB	Exc.	V.G.	Good	Fair	Poor
—	250	195	125	60	35

Pistolet Automatique

Normal markings include "FA" trademark.

NIB	Exc.	V.G.	Good	Fair	Poor
—	250	195	125	60	35

Kaba Spezial

6.35mm semi-automatic pistol. Patterned after Browning Model 1906. Kaba Spezial was originally made by August Menz of Suhl, Germany and sold by Karl Bauer of Berlin, Germany. Name "Kaba" was derived from first two initials of Karl Bauer. These two pistols do not look alike.

Courtesy James Rankin

NIB	Exc.	V.G.	Good	Fair	Poor
—	275	150	100	50	35

Ydeal

Ydeal was made in four variations and in calibers 6.35mm, 7.65mm and .380. All four variations resemble Browning Model 1906, with 7.65mm and .380-caliber being slightly larger.

Courtesy James Rankin

6.35mm

NIB	Exc.	V.G.	Good	Fair	Poor
—	225	175	100	60	35

7.65mm

NIB	Exc.	V.G.	Good	Fair	Poor
—	225	175	100	60	35

.380

NIB	Exc.	V.G.	Good	Fair	Poor
—	225	175	100	60	35

ARIZMENDI, ZULAICA
Eibar, Spain

Cebra Pistol

Semi-automatic 7.65mm pistol. Patterned after Ruby-style of Spanish automatics. Slide marked "Pistolet Automatique Cebra Zulaica Eibar", together with letters "A.Z." in an oval. Generally found with checkered wood grips.

Courtesy James Rankin

NIB	Exc.	V.G.	Good	Fair	Poor
—	250	150	100	50	35

Cebra Revolver

Copy of a Colt Police Positive revolver marked "Made in Spain". Word "Cebra" cast in grips.

NIB	Exc.	V.G.	Good	Fair	Poor
—	250	150	125	75	50

ARLINGTON ORDNANCE
Westport, Connecticut

This company imported rebuilt M1 Garand and M1 Carbine rifles from Korea in the 1990s.

M1 Garand

Caliber .30-06 or .308 Winchester. New barrels, inspected components, rebuilt gas-operating systems.

NIB	Exc.	V.G.	Good	Fair	Poor
—	875	800	700	500	400

M1 Carbne

Caliber .30 carbine. Used models with import stamp and upgraded wood stock.

NIB	Exc.	V.G.	Good	Fair	Poor
—	800	700	600	450	300

ARMALITE, INC.
Costa Mesa, California
Geneseo, Illinois (current production)

In 1995, Eagle Arms purchased Armalite trademark and certain other assets. New companies are organized under Armalite name. Original company formed in mid 1950s, developed AR-10, which in turn led to development of M-16 series of service rifles, still in use today. All current models are produced at Geneseo, Illinois, facility.

AR-24 Pistol

15-shot, 9mm, double-action, semi-automatic pistol. Steel frame, fixed or adjustable sights. Compact version available. Introduced 2006. Pricing is for full-size pistol, with adjustable sights. **NOTE:** Deduct 15 percent for fixed sight versions.

NIB	Exc.	V.G.	Good	Fair	Poor
595	450	325	275	200	125

AR-24 Tactical Custom

Similar to above, with tactical refinements including stippled front and back straps, 3-dot luminous sights, etc. Also available in compact version (shown).

NIB	Exc.	V.G.	Good	Fair	Poor
630	475	350	300	225	150

AR-17 Shotgun

Gas-operated semi-automatic 12-gauge shotgun, with 24" barrel and interchangeable choke tubes. Receiver and barrel are made of an aluminum alloy, with an anodized black or gold finish. Stock and forearm are of plastic. Approximately 2,000 manufactured during 1964 and 1965. **NOTE:** Add 10 percent for gold finish.

NIB	Exc.	V.G.	Good	Fair	Poor
750	625	400	300	225	100

AR-7 Explorer Rifle

.22 LR semi-automatic carbine, with 16" barrel. Receiver and barrel partially made of an alloy. Most noteworthy feature of this model is it can be disassembled and component parts stored in the plastic stock. Manufactured between 1959 and 1973. Reintroduced in 1999.

NIB	Exc.	V.G.	Good	Fair	Poor
375	300	200	150	100	85

AR-7 Custom

As above, with walnut cheekpiece stock. Manufactured between 1964 and 1970.

NIB	Exc.	V.G.	Good	Fair	Poor
475	400	300	250	200	185

AR-180

Gas-operated semi-automatic rifle chambered for .223 or 5.56mm cartridge. AR-180 is civilian version of AR18, which is fully automatic. Simple and efficient rifle that was tested by various governments and found to have potential. Rifle was also manufactured by Howa Machinery Ltd. and Sterling Armament Co. of England. Most common version is manufactured by Sterling. Those built by Armalite and Howa bring a small premium.

Howa

NIB	Exc.	V.G.	Good	Fair	Poor
1500	1250	900	700	450	200

Sterling

NIB	Exc.	V.G.	Good	Fair	Poor
1150	900	700	500	350	175

AR-180B

Similar to original AR-180. Chambered for .223 cartridge. Fitted with 19.8" barrel and integral muzzle-brake. Lower receiver is polymer while upper receiver is sheet steel. Trigger group is standard M15. Accepts standard M15 magazines. Weight about 6 lbs.

NIB	Exc.	V.G.	Good	Fair	Poor
750	625	500	400	300	125

AR-10A4 Rifle

Introduced in 1995. Features 20" stainless steel heavy barrel. Chambered for .308 Win. or .243 Win. cartridge. Has a flattop receiver, optional two-stage trigger, detachable carry handle and scope mount. Equipped with two 10-round magazines. Weight about 9.6 lbs. **NOTE:** Add $100 for stainless steel barrel.

NIB	Exc.	V.G.	Good	Fair	Poor
1500	1250	900	700	500	200

AR-10A4 Carbine

Similar to above. Chambered for .308 Win. cartridge. Fitted with 16" barrel. Flattop receiver. Sold with two 10-round magazines. Weight about 9 lbs. **NOTE:** Add $100 for stainless steel barrel.

NIB	Exc.	V.G.	Good	Fair	Poor
1500	1250	900	700	500	200

AR-10A2 Rifle

Model has 20" heavy barrel. Chambered for .308 cartridge, without removable carry handle. Weight about 9.8 lbs. **NOTE:** Add $100 for stainless steel barrel.

NIB	Exc.	V.G.	Good	Fair	Poor
1500	1250	900	700	500	200

AR-10A2 Carbine

Similar to above, with 16" barrel. Weight about 9 lbs. **NOTE:** Add $100 for stainless steel barrel.

NIB	Exc.	V.G.	Good	Fair	Poor
1500	1250	900	700	500	200

AR-10B

Chambered for .308 cartridge. Fitted with 20" barrel. Trigger is single-stage or optional two-stage match type. Model has several early M16 features such as tapered handguard, pistol-grips and short buttstock in original brown color. Fitted with early charging handle. Limited production. Weight about 9.5 lbs. Introduced in 1999.

NIB	Exc.	V.G.	Good	Fair	Poor
1600	1250	900	700	500	200

AR-10(T) Rifle

Model features 24" heavy barrel, with two-stage trigger. Front sight and carry handle are removable. Handguard is fiberglass. Weight about 10.4 lbs.

NIB	Exc.	V.G.	Good	Fair	Poor
1850	1400	875	600	450	225

AR-10(T) Carbine

Similar to AR-10T, with 16.25" target weight barrel. Weight about 8.5 lbs.

NIB	Exc.	V.G.	Good	Fair	Poor
1850	1400	875	600	450	225

AR-10(T) Ultra

Chambered for .300 Remington Ultra Short Action Magnum cartridge. Barrel length 24". Two-stage National Match trigger. Offered in choice of green or black stock. Sold with 5-round magazine.

NIB	Exc.	V.G.	Good	Fair	Poor
1850	1400	875	600	450	225

AR-10 SOF

Introduced in 2003. Features M4-style fixed stock. Flattop receiver. Chambered for .308 cartridge. Offered in both A2 and A4 configurations.

NIB	Exc.	V.G.	Good	Fair	Poor
1850	1400	875	600	450	225

AR-10 .338 Federal

Similar to AR-10. Chambered in .338 Federal.

NIB	Exc.	V.G.	Good	Fair	Poor
1650	1400	1250	900	500	250

M15 SOF

Model chambered for .223 cartridge. Fitted with flattop receiver and M4-style fixed stock. Introduced in 2003. Offered in both A2 and A4 configurations.

NIB	Exc.	V.G.	Good	Fair	Poor
1150	925	675	475	300	150

M15A2 HBAR

Model introduced in 1995. Features 20" heavy barrel chambered for .223 cartridge. A2-style forward assist, recoil check brake. Formerly sold with 10-round magazine. Weight about 8.2 lbs.

NIB	Exc.	V.G.	Good	Fair	Poor
1100	850	600	500	375	125

M15A2 National Match

Chambered for .223 cartridge. Variation features 20" stainless steel match barrel, with two-stage trigger, A2-style forward assist and hard coated anodized receiver. Equipped with 10-round magazine. Weight about 9 lbs.

NIB	Exc.	V.G.	Good	Fair	Poor
1475	1200	850	600	375	200

M15A2-M4A1C Carbine

Similar to M15A2 heavy barrel, with 16" heavy barrel. Flattop receiver, with detachable carry handle. Introduced in 1995. **NOTE:** Add $100 for Match trigger.

NIB	Exc.	V.G.	Good	Fair	Poor
1100	900	700	500	300	125

M15A2-M4C Carbine

Similar to M4A1C Carbine, with flattop receiver and detachable carry handle.

NIB	Exc.	V.G.	Good	Fair	Poor
1000	850	600	500	300	125

M15A4(T) Eagle Eye

Chambered for .223 cartridge. Fitted with 24" stainless steel heavy weight barrel. Has National Match two-stage trigger, Picatinny rail and NM fiberglass handguard tube. Sold with 7-round magazine and 4-section cleaning rod with brass tip, sling, owner's manual and lifetime warranty.

NIB	Exc.	V.G.	Good	Fair	Poor
1500	1100	800	600	350	150

M15A4 Special Purpose Rifle (SPR)

Model fitted with 20" heavy barrel, detachable front sight and carry handle, NM sights and Picatinny rail. Weight about 7.8 lbs.

NIB	Exc.	V.G.	Good	Fair	Poor
1200	900	750	600	375	175

M15A4 Action Master

Variation features 20" stainless steel heavy barrel, with two-stage trigger, Picatinny rail and fiberglass handguard tube. Weight about 9 lbs.

NIB	Exc.	V.G.	Good	Fair	Poor
1450	1000	850	600	375	175

M15A4 Eagle Spirit

Similar to Action Master above, with 16" stainless steel barrel. Weight about 7.6 lbs.

NIB	Exc.	V.G.	Good	Fair	Poor
1450	1000	850	600	375	175

M15A4 Carbine 6.8 & 7.62x39

Shorty carbine version of AR-15. Chambered in 6.8 Remington and 7.62x39. 16" chrome-lined barrel with flash suppressor, front and rear Picatinny rails for mounting optics and two-stage tactical trigger. Ten-round magazine. Anodized aluminum/phosphate finish. Overall length 36.6"; weight: 7 lbs.

NIB	Exc.	V.G.	Good	Fair	Poor
950	800	650	500	350	200

M15-22

This model was made in 2011 in .22 Long Rifle caliber on a .223 lower receiver, with most standard AR-style features.

NIB	Exc.	V.G.	Good	Fair	Poor
600	500	400	350	250	150

AR-30M

Chambered for .338 Lapua, .300 Win. Magnum or .308 Winchester cartridges. Barrel length 26" with muzzle-brake. Adjustable buttstock. Weight about 12 lbs. Reduced version of AR-50. **NOTE:** Add $150 for .338 Lapua.

NIB	Exc.	V.G.	Good	Fair	Poor
2000	1700	1300	1000	500	195

AR-30A1 Standard

Introduced in 2013. This is an upgraded version of bolt-action AR-30M. Improvements include better ergonomics and versatility. Chambered in .300 Win. Magnum or .338 Lapua. **NOTE:** Add $125 for .338 Lapua caliber; $200 for target version with an adjustable fixed stock.

NIB	Exc.	V.G.	Good	Fair	Poor
3000	2400	1800	1250	700	350

AR-31

This target model in .308 Winchester has an 18" or 24" barrel, stock that's adjustable for length-of-pull and comb height, bipod, muzzle-brake and single-stage trigger. It accepts Armalite AR-10B double-stack magazines up to 25-round capacity.

NIB	Exc.	V.G.	Good	Fair	Poor
3200	2600	2000	1500	800	400

AR-50

Introduced in 2000. Chambered for .50 BMG or .416 Barrett. Fitted with 31" tapered barrel threaded for recoil check (muzzle-brake). Trigger is single-stage. Stock is 3-section type with extruded fore-end. Adjustable Pachmayr buttplate. Picatinny rail. Finish is magnesium phosphated steel and hard anodized aluminum. Bipod. Single shot. Weight about 33 lbs. **NOTE:** Add $400 for National Match Model.

NIB	Exc.	V.G.	Good	Fair	Poor
3400	2650	2000	1500	750	300

PRE-BAN MODELS

Golden Eagle

Fitted with 20" stainless extra-heavy barrel, with NM two-stage trigger and NM sights. Sold with 30-round magazine. Weight about 9.4 lbs.

NIB	Exc.	V.G.	Good	Fair	Poor
1500	1200	950	800	400	200

HBAR

Pre-ban rifle has 20" heavy barrel, 30-round magazine and sling. Weight about 8 lbs.

NIB	Exc.	V.G.	Good	Fair	Poor
1300	1000	850	700	350	175

M4C Carbine

Pre-ban variation fitted with 16" heavy barrel, collapsible stock and fixed flash suppressor. Weight about 6.2 lbs.

NIB	Exc.	V.G.	Good	Fair	Poor
1300	1000	850	700	350	175

ARMAS DE FUEGO
Guernica, Spain

See—Alkartasuna Fabrica de Armas

ARMERO ESPECIALISTAS
Eibar, Spain

Alfa

"Alfa" was a trademark given a number of revolvers based upon both Colt and Smith & Wesson designs. In calibers ranging from .22- to .44-calibers. **NOTE:** Add 50 percent for S&W N-frame copies.

NIB	Exc.	V.G.	Good	Fair	Poor
—	250	200	100	75	50

Omega

Semi-automatic 6.35 or 7.65mm pistol marked "Omega" on slide and grips.

NIB	Exc.	V.G.	Good	Fair	Poor
—	225	175	100	75	50

ARMES DE CHASSE
Chadds Ford, Pennsylvania

Importer of firearms manufactured by Franchi, P. Beretta and other arms manufactured in Germany.

Model EJ

Over/under Anson & Deeley action 12-gauge shotgun, with double triggers as well as automatic ejectors. Blued barrels, silver finished receiver and checkered walnut stock. Manufactured in Germany. Introduced in 1989.

NIB	Exc.	V.G.	Good	Fair	Poor
1500	1250	900	650	500	250

Model EU

As above, with ventilated rib barrel. Nonselective single trigger. Introduced in 1989.

NIB	Exc.	V.G.	Good	Fair	Poor
1600	1300	850	650	500	250

Highlander

Side-by-side double-barrel 20-gauge shotgun, with boxlock action. Available in various barrel lengths and choke combinations, with double triggers and manual extractors. Blued, with checkered walnut stock. Manufactured in Italy. Introduced in 1989.

NIB	Exc.	V.G.	Good	Fair	Poor
1350	800	650	350	250	125

Chesapeake

As above chambered for 3.5" 12-gauge shell. Bores are chrome-lined and suitable for steel shot. Fitted with automatic ejectors and double triggers. Manufactured in Italy. Introduced in 1989.

NIB	Exc.	V.G.	Good	Fair	Poor
1450	995	700	475	400	200

Balmoral

English-style straight-grip 12-, 16- or 20-gauge boxlock shotgun. Fitted with false side plates. Receiver and side plates case hardened. Barrels blued. Fitted with single trigger and automatic ejectors. Manufactured in Italy. Introduced in 1989.

NIB	Exc.	V.G.	Good	Fair	Poor
1200	925	725	500	400	200

Model 70E

A 12-, 16- or 20-gauge side-by-side shotgun. Fitted with 27" or 28" barrels. Action based upon Anson & Deeley design, with Greener crossbolt. Receiver case hardened. Barrels blued. Walnut stock checkered. Manufactured in Germany. Introduced in 1989.

NIB	Exc.	V.G.	Good	Fair	Poor
1225	925	725	500	400	200

Model 74E

As above, with game scene engraving. More fully figured walnut stock. Introduced in 1989.

NIB	Exc.	V.G.	Good	Fair	Poor
1475	1050	900	650	500	250

Model 76E

As above, with engraved false side plates. Fully figured walnut stock. Introduced in 1989.

NIB	Exc.	V.G.	Good	Fair	Poor
2000	1500	1100	750	600	300

ARMINEX LTD.
Scottsdale, Arizona

Tri-Fire

Semi-automatic pistol chambered for 9mm, .38 Super or .45 ACP cartridges. Fitted with 5", 6" or 7" stainless steel barrels. Presentation cases were available at an extra cost of $48. Approximately 250 manufactured from 1981 to 1985. **NOTE:** Available with conversion units that add approximately $130 if in excellent condition.

Courtesy James Rankin

NIB	Exc.	V.G.	Good	Fair	Poor
950	800	600	300	175	100

Target Model

As above, with 6" or 7" barrel.

Courtesy James Rankin

NIB	Exc.	V.G.	Good	Fair	Poor
1000	850	650	350	225	100

ARMINUS
See—Freidrich Pickert

See—Hermann Weirauch

See—F. I. E.

ARMITAGE INTERNATIONAL, LTD.
Seneca, South Carolina

Scarab Skorpion

Blowback-operated semi-automatic pistol. Patterned after Czechoslovakian Scorpion sub-machine gun. Chambered for 9mm cartridge, with 4.6" barrel having military-type sights. Fitted with 32-round detachable box magazine. Standard finish is matte black. Grips are plastic.

NIB	Exc.	V.G.	Good	Fair	Poor
650	550	400	300	175	100

ARMSCO FIREARMS CORP.
Ankara, Turkey
U.S.A.—Des Plaines, Illinois

Built by Huglu Hunting Firearms Corporation in Turkey, which was established in 1927. Armsco is U.S. representative. First year of business in U.S. was 2002.

SINGLE-SHOT

Model 301A

Single-shot model offered in 12-, 16-, 20-, 28-gauge and .410 bore. Barrel lengths from 22" to 32" depending on gauge. Checkered walnut stock. Weight varies from 5- to 5.5 lbs. depending on gauge.

NIB	Exc.	V.G.	Good	Fair	Poor
200	150	75	50	35	25

SIDE-BY-SIDES

Model 202B

Boxlock shotgun offered in 12-, 16-, 20-, 28-gauge and .410 bore. Barrel lengths from 22" to 32" depending on gauge. Double triggers. Hand engraved about 50 percent coverage. Fixed chokes or choke tubes. Checkered walnut stock with cheekpiece. Weight about 6.4- to 7.3 lbs. depending on gauge.

NIB	Exc.	V.G.	Good	Fair	Poor
550	425	325	200	125	50

Model 202A

Same as above. Offered with standard buttstock.

NIB	Exc.	V.G.	Good	Fair	Poor
775	625	450	300	175	75

Model 201A

Offered in gauges from 12-gauge to .410 bore. Sideplates with 50 percent hand engraving. Choice of single or double triggers.

NIB	Exc.	V.G.	Good	Fair	Poor
695	525	450	300	175	75

Model 200A

Boxlock in gauges 12-gauge to .410 bore, with single trigger. Hand engraved 50 percent coverage.

NIB	Exc.	V.G.	Good	Fair	Poor
750	575	450	300	175	75

Model 205A

Offered in gauges 12-gauge to .410 bore, with barrel lengths 22" to 32" depending on gauge. Boxlock frame with 60 percent hand engraved coverage. Single trigger. Checkered walnut stock. Weights are 6.1- to 6.8 lbs. depending on gauge.

NIB	Exc.	V.G.	Good	Fair	Poor
990	750	600	425	200	100

Model 210AE

Offered in 12-, 16- and 20-gauge, with single trigger and automatic ejectors. Boxlock frame is 60 percent hand engraved. Optional fixed or choke tubes.

NIB	Exc.	V.G.	Good	Fair	Poor
1250	950	700	450	300	200

Model 210BE

Same as above, with double triggers.

NIB	Exc.	V.G.	Good	Fair	Poor
1150	850	675	450	300	200

OVER/UNDERS

Model 104A

Chambered for 12-gauge through .410 bore, with double triggers. Barrel lengths from 22" to 32" depending on gauge. Ventilated rib. Checkered walnut stock. Fixed or choke tubes. Weight from 6.6- to 7.3 lbs. depending on gauge. Receiver is 15 percent hand engraved.

NIB	Exc.	V.G.	Good	Fair	Poor
425	300	250	200	125	75

Model 103D

Same as above, with single trigger and schnabel forearm.

NIB	Exc.	V.G.	Good	Fair	Poor
595	475	375	325	175	75

Model 103DE

Same as above, with automatic ejectors.

NIB	Exc.	V.G.	Good	Fair	Poor
750	575	525	425	200	75

Model 103C

Similar to Model 103D, with blued receiver, gold inlaid birds and 40 percent engraving coverage.

NIB	Exc.	V.G.	Good	Fair	Poor
720	550	525	425	200	75

Model 103CE

Same as above, with automatic ejectors.

NIB	Exc.	V.G.	Good	Fair	Poor
870	650	575	475	225	100

Model 103F

Similar to Model 103D, with 80 to 100 percent hand engraved side plates.

NIB	Exc.	V.G.	Good	Fair	Poor
850	625	550	450	225	100

Model 103FE

Same as above, with automatic ejectors.

NIB	Exc.	V.G.	Good	Fair	Poor
970	750	600	475	250	125

Model 101SE

Offered in 12-gauge only. Barrel lengths 28", 30" or 32" with ventilated rib. Single trigger and automatic ejectors. Hand engraved receiver. Checkered walnut stock. Weight from 6.6- to 7.3 lbs. depending on barrel length.

NIB	Exc.	V.G.	Good	Fair	Poor
1325	975	750	450	275	125

Model 101BE

Same as above, with adjustable comb.

NIB	Exc.	V.G.	Good	Fair	Poor
1325	975	750	450	275	125

SEMI-AUTOMATICS

Model 401A

Semi-automatic shotgun. Uses short-recoil inertia-operated system. Chambered for 12-gauge shell up to 3". Barrel lengths from 22" to 32". Ventilated rib. Plastic or walnut stock. Fixed or choke tubes. Fully engraved receiver. Weight from 6.9- to 7.2 lbs. depending on barrel length. Magazine capacity 6 rounds.

NIB	Exc.	V.G.	Good	Fair	Poor
425	350	275	225	125	75

Model 401B

Same as above, with 4-round magazine capacity.

NIB	Exc.	V.G.	Good	Fair	Poor
425	350	275	225	125	75

Model 501GA

Gas-operated shotgun chambered for 3" 12-gauge shell. Barrel lengths from 22" to 32". Black receiver with 15 percent hand engraved coverage. Magazine capacity 7 rounds. Walnut or plastic stock. Weight from 6.8- to 7.3 lbs. depending on barrel length.

NIB	Exc.	V.G.	Good	Fair	Poor
425	350	275	225	125	75

Model 501GB

Same as above, with 4-round magazine.

NIB	Exc.	V.G.	Good	Fair	Poor
425	350	275	225	125	75

Model 601GB

Same as Model 501GB, with full coverage engraved silver receiver.

NIB	Exc.	V.G.	Good	Fair	Poor
450	375	300	250	125	75

Model 601GA

Same as Model 501GA, with 7-round magazine capacity.

NIB	Exc.	V.G.	Good	Fair	Poor
450	375	300	250	125	75

Model 701GA

Model chambered for 20-gauge 3" shell. Fitted with barrel lengths from 22" to 32". Ventilated rib. Walnut stock. Fixed or choke tubes. Magazine capacity 7 rounds. Weight 6- to 6.4 lbs. depending on barrel length.

NIB	Exc.	V.G.	Good	Fair	Poor
450	375	300	225	125	75

Model 701GB

Same as above, with 4-round magazine.

NIB	Exc.	V.G.	Good	Fair	Poor
450	375	300	225	125	75

PUMP-ACTIONS

Model 801A

Slide-action 12-gauge shotgun, with plastic stock. Barrel length from 22" to 32". Fixed or choke tubes. Magazine capacity 7 rounds. Weight about 7 lbs.

NIB	Exc.	V.G.	Good	Fair	Poor
300	275	250	175	100	50

Model 801B

Same as above, with 4-round magazine.

NIB	Exc.	V.G.	Good	Fair	Poor
300	275	250	175	100	50

ARMSCOR PRECISION INTERNATIONAL
Pahrump, Nevada

Armscor Precision International imports firearms made by Arms Corporation of the Philippines.

RIFLES

M14R

Civilian version of U.S. M14 rifle. Manufactured from new and surplus parts. Introduced in 1986.

NIB	Exc.	V.G.	Good	Fair	Poor
1350	900	500	300	200	100

M14 National Match

As above. Built to A.M.T.U. MIL specifications. Introduced in 1987.

NIB	Exc.	V.G.	Good	Fair	Poor
1650	1250	800	500	400	200

FAL

Civilian version of FN FAL rifle. Assembled from new and Argentine surplus parts. Introduced in 1987.

NIB	Exc.	V.G.	Good	Fair	Poor
1600	1250	800	400	300	150

M36 Israeli Sniper Rifle

Specialized weapon built upon Armscorp M14 receiver in Bullpup style. Barrel length 22" of free floating design for accuracy. Chambered for .308 cartridge. There is an integral flash suppressor and a bipod. Furnished with 20-shot detachable magazine. This civilian version first offered for sale in 1989.

NIB	Exc.	V.G.	Good	Fair	Poor
3200	2650	2000	1500	850	400

Expert Model

.22-caliber semi-automatic rifle, with 21" barrel, open sights and 10-shot magazine. Introduced in 1989.

NIB	Exc.	V.G.	Good	Fair	Poor
225	200	175	145	100	80

Model M14P

.22-caliber bolt-action rifle. Fitted with 23" barrel, open sights and 5-shot detachable magazine. Mahogany stock.

NIB	Exc.	V.G.	Good	Fair	Poor
150	90	75	50	35	25

Model M14D

As above, with adjustable rear sight and checkered stock. Manufactured in 1987 only.

NIB	Exc.	V.G.	Good	Fair	Poor
165	100	85	60	40	25

Model 14Y

Bolt-action rifle chambered for .22 LR cartridge. Fitted with 18" barrel and 10-round magazine. Weight about 5.2 lbs.

NIB	Exc.	V.G.	Good	Fair	Poor
150	125	100	75	50	25

Model 12Y

Bolt-action rifle is a single-shot. Chambered for .22 LR. Fitted with 18" barrel. Weight about 5 lbs.

NIB	Exc.	V.G.	Good	Fair	Poor
125	100	75	50	35	25

Model 1400

Bolt-action rifle chambered for .22 LR cartridge. Fitted with 22.5" barrel and 10-round magazine. Weight about 6.5 lbs.

NIB	Exc.	V.G.	Good	Fair	Poor
225	200	150	125	100	75

Model M1500

.22 Magnum bolt-action rifle. Fitted with 22.5" barrel, open sights, 5-shot magazine and checkered mahogany stock. Weight about 6.5 lbs.

NIB	Exc.	V.G.	Good	Fair	Poor
250	200	150	125	100	75

Model M1600

.22-caliber copy of U.S. M16 rifle, with 18" barrel and detachable 15-round magazine. Weight about 6.2 lbs.

NIB	Exc.	V.G.	Good	Fair	Poor
300	200	125	100	75	50

Model M1600R

As above, with stainless steel collapsible stock and shrouded barrel. No longer in production.

NIB	Exc.	V.G.	Good	Fair	Poor
325	225	150	125	100	75

Model M1600C

As above, with 20" barrel and fiberglass stock. No longer in production.

NIB	Exc.	V.G.	Good	Fair	Poor
300	200	125	100	75	50

Model M1600W

As above, with mahogany stock. No longer in production.

NIB	Exc.	V.G.	Good	Fair	Poor
300	200	125	100	75	50

Model M1800

.22 Hornet bolt-action rifle. Fitted with 22.5" barrel, 5-shot magazine and mahogany Monte Carlo-style stock. Weight about 6.6 lbs.

NIB	Exc.	V.G.	Good	Fair	Poor
250	200	150	75	50	35

Model 20C

Chambered for .22 LR, with 15-round magazine and 18.25" barrel. Weight about 6.2 lbs.

NIB	Exc.	V.G.	Good	Fair	Poor
175	150	90	70	50	40

Model M20P

.22-caliber 15-shot semi-automatic rifle. Fitted with 20.75" barrel, open sights and plain mahogany stock. Weight about 6.3 lbs.

NIB	Exc.	V.G.	Good	Fair	Poor
175	150	90	70	50	40

Model M2000

As above, with adjustable sights and checkered stock. Weight about 6.4 lbs.

NIB	Exc.	V.G.	Good	Fair	Poor
175	150	90	70	50	40

Model AK22S

.22-caliber semi-automatic rifle resembling Russian AKA47. Barrel length 18.5", 15-round magazine and mahogany stock. Weight about 7.5 lbs.

NIB	Exc.	V.G.	Good	Fair	Poor
275	225	195	125	75	50

Model AK22F

As above, with folding stock. No longer in production.

NIB	Exc.	V.G.	Good	Fair	Poor
275	225	195	125	75	50

HANDGUNS

Hi-Power

Argentine-made version of Browning semi-automatic pistol. Chambered for 9mm, with 4.75" barrel. Matte finish, with checkered synthetic grips. Introduced in 1989.

NIB	Exc.	V.G.	Good	Fair	Poor
450	350	300	250	200	100

Detective HP—Compact

As above, with 3.5" barrel.

NIB	Exc.	V.G.	Good	Fair	Poor
475	375	350	275	200	100

P22

Copy of Colt Woodsman .22-caliber semi-automatic pistol. Available with 4" or 6" barrels and 10-shot magazine. Finish blued, grips of checkered hardwood. Introduced in 1989.

NIB	Exc.	V.G.	Good	Fair	Poor
250	150	125	100	75	50

SD9

Israeli-made 9mm double-action semi-automatic pistol, with 3" barrel. Assembled extensively from sheet metal stampings. Loaded chamber indicator and 6-round magazine. This model also known as Sirkus SD9. Manufactured by Sirkus Industries in Israel. Introduced in 1989.

Courtesy Jim Rankin

NIB	Exc.	V.G.	Good	Fair	Poor
300	250	200	150	100	75

Armscor 1911A1-45 FS GI

1911-style semi-automatic pistol. Chambered in .45 ACP (8 rounds), 9mm Parabellum, .38 Super (9 rounds). Features include checkered plastic or hardwood grips, 5" barrel, Parkerized steel frame and slide, drift adjustable sights. **NOTE:** Add $50 for Commander or Officer's model.

NIB	Exc.	V.G.	Good	Fair	Poor
400	350	300	250	200	100

Model M100

Double-action swing-out cylinder revolver. Chambered for .22, .22 Magnum and .38 Special cartridges. Has 4" ventilated rib barrel. Six-shot cylinder and adjustable sights. Blued, with checkered mahogany grips. No longer in production.

NIB	Exc.	V.G.	Good	Fair	Poor
200	175	150	110	80	50

Model 200P

Introduced in 1990. This 6-shot revolver chambered for .38 Special cartridge. Fitted with 4" barrel, fixed sights and wood or rubber grips. Weight about 26 oz.

NIB	Exc.	V.G.	Good	Fair	Poor
180	150	125	100	85	60

Model 200TC

Introduced in 1990. Similar to above. Fitted with adjustable sights and checkered wood grips. Weight about 28 oz.

NIB	Exc.	V.G.	Good	Fair	Poor
200	175	150	125	100	75

Model 200DC

Similar to Model 200P, with 2.5" barrel. Weight about 22 oz.

NIB	Exc.	V.G.	Good	Fair	Poor
175	150	125	100	85	60

Model 201S

Similar to Model 200P in stainless steel.

NIB	Exc.	V.G.	Good	Fair	Poor
200	175	150	125	100	75

Model 202

Chambered for 38 Special cartridge. This 6-shot revolver fitted with 4" barrel and fixed sights. Blued finish. Weight about 27 oz.

NIB	Exc.	V.G.	Good	Fair	Poor
150	120	95	75	50	25

Model 206

Similar to Model 202, with 2.88" barrel. Weight about 25 oz.

NIB	Exc.	V.G.	Good	Fair	Poor
180	140	110	75	50	25

Model 210

Same as Model 202, with adjustable sights. Weight about 27 oz.

NIB	Exc.	V.G.	Good	Fair	Poor
200	150	125	75	50	25

MAP1 FS

Single-/double-action 9mm semi-automatic, with 16+1 capacity. Fixed sights, 4.45" barrel, weight 40.5 oz. Nickel alloy steel frame and slide. (Shorter, lighter MS model has 3.66" barrel.) Introduced 2006.

NIB	Exc.	V.G.	Good	Fair	Poor
—	350	300	200	125	75

MAPP1 FS

Single-/double-action 9mm semi-automatic, with 16+1 capacity. Fixed sights, 4.45" barrel, weight 40.5 oz. Polymer frame with integrated accessory rail and nickel alloy steel slide. (Shorter, lighter MS model has 3.66" barrel.) Introduced 2006.

NIB	Exc.	V.G.	Good	Fair	Poor
—	350	300	200	175	75

Model 1911-A1

Semi-automatic pistol similar in design to Colt Model 1911 pistol. Chambered for .45 ACP cartridge. Fitted with 5" barrel. Blued finish. Magazine capacity 8 rounds. Weight about 39 oz. Also sold under Charles Daly name.

NIB	Exc.	V.G.	Good	Fair	Poor
500	400	300	200	150	75

Model 1911-A2

Same as above, with double column magazine and 13 round capacity. Weight about 43 oz. **NOTE:** Add $100 for two-tone finish; $130 for chrome finish.

NIB	Exc.	V.G.	Good	Fair	Poor
600	500	375	250	195	110

SHOTGUNS

Model 30D

Slide-action 12-gauge shotgun. Fitted with 28" or 30" barrels and various chokes. Magazine holds 6 cartridges. Weight about 7.6 lbs.

NIB	Exc.	V.G.	Good	Fair	Poor
200	175	150	125	100	75

Model 30DG

As above, with 20" barrel, fitted rifle sights and 7-shot magazine. Weight about 7.2 lbs.

NIB	Exc.	V.G.	Good	Fair	Poor
175	150	125	100	80	70

Model 30R

As above, with shotgun bead sights, 18.5" or 20" barrel. Weight between 7- and 7.2 lbs. depending on barrel length.

NIB	Exc.	V.G.	Good	Fair	Poor
175	150	125	100	80	70

Model 30RP

As above, with auxiliary black composition pistol-grip and 18.5" barrel.

NIB	Exc.	V.G.	Good	Fair	Poor
175	150	125	100	80	70

Model 30 SAS1

Slide-action 12-gauge, with 20" barrel and heat shield. Chambered for 3" shell. Open cylinder choke. Parkerized finish. Weight about 8 lbs.

NIB	Exc.	V.G.	Good	Fair	Poor
200	150	100	75	50	25

ARNOLD ARMS
Arlington, Washington

Company offered a wide range of rifles and calibers, including its own proprietary cartridges, from 6mm Arnold to .458 Arnold. Rifles were built on choice of actions, including Apollo, Remington, Sako and Winchester. These action choices affect base price of rifle. Out of business in 2002. Values vary with geography. **NOTE:** Add $1100 for Apollo actions to all applicable models, unless otherwise noted.

Varminter I

Model features heavy match grade barrel, with straight taper. Lengths from 24" to 26". Calibers from .222 Rem. to .257 Arnold Magnum. Choice of McMillian Varmint stock in various finishes. Pacific Research Varmint stock in flat black. Weight from 9- to 11 lbs. depending on caliber and configuration.

NIB	Exc.	V.G.	Good	Fair	Poor
2600	2000	1450	1050	700	200

Varminter II

Variation features 24" to 26" medium weight match barrel, with choice of McMillan or Pacific Research sporter stocks. Choice of triggers. Weight 7.5- to 9 lbs. depending on configuration. Calibers from .223 Rem. to .257 Arnold Magnum.

NIB	Exc.	V.G.	Good	Fair	Poor
2600	2000	1450	1050	700	200

Alaskan

Bolt-action rifle chambered for calibers .223 to .338 Win. Magnum. Barrel lengths 22" to 26" depending on caliber. Stocks are synthetic in black woodland or arctic camo. Sights optional. Rifle drilled and tapped for scope mounts. Trigger fully adjustable. Choice of chrome moly steel or stainless steel. Introduced in 1996.

NIB	Exc.	V.G.	Good	Fair	Poor
2600	2000	1450	1050	700	200

Alaskan Trophy

Similar to Alaskan Rifle. Chambered for .300 Magnum to .458 Win. Magnum. Barrel lengths 24" to 26" depending on caliber. Choice of walnut, synthetic or fibergrain stock. Fitted with iron sights. Choice of stainless or chrome moly steel. Introduced in 1996.

NIB	Exc.	V.G.	Good	Fair	Poor
3100	2500	1450	1050	700	200

Alaskan Guide

Model offered in choice of calibers .257 to .338 Magnum. Barrel lengths 22" to 26" depending on caliber. Buyer has choice of "A" English walnut stock or deluxe synthetic stock. No open sights.

Synthetic Stock

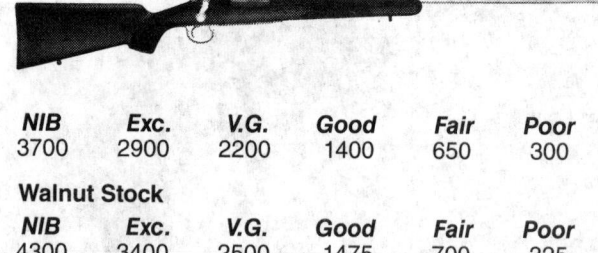

NIB	Exc.	V.G.	Good	Fair	Poor
3700	2900	2200	1400	650	300

Walnut Stock

NIB	Exc.	V.G.	Good	Fair	Poor
4300	3400	2500	1475	700	325

Grand Alaskan

Version fitted with AAA fancy select or exhibition wood. Built in calibers .300 Magnum to .458 Win. Magnum.

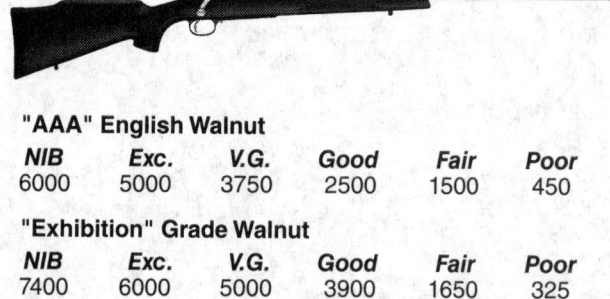

"AAA" English Walnut

NIB	Exc.	V.G.	Good	Fair	Poor
6000	5000	3750	2500	1500	450

"Exhibition" Grade Walnut

NIB	Exc.	V.G.	Good	Fair	Poor
7400	6000	5000	3900	1650	325

Safari

Introduced in 1996. Features calibers .223 to .458 Win. Magnum. Barrel lengths 22" to 26" depending on caliber. Apollo is a controlled or push feed type, with one-piece cone-head bolt. Fully adjustable trigger, with chrome moly or stainless steel construction. Sights are optional. Rifle drilled and tapped for scope mounts. Choice of A fancy English or AA fancy English walnut.

"A" Fancy English Walnut

NIB	Exc.	V.G.	Good	Fair	Poor
4300	3500	2700	1650	800	300

"AA" Fancy English Walnut

NIB	Exc.	V.G.	Good	Fair	Poor
4400	3500	2700	1650	800	300

African Trophy

Similar to Safari Rifle. Stocked in AAA fancy walnut, with wraparound checkering.

NIB	Exc.	V.G.	Good	Fair	Poor
6300	5000	3250	2500	1750	300

Grand African

Similar to Safari rifle, with addition of Exhibition Grade wood. Calibers .338 to .458 Magnum.

NIB	Exc.	V.G.	Good	Fair	Poor
7600	6100	5000	3900	1650	325

Serengeti Synthetic

Similar to Safari rifle, with fibergrain stock in classic or Monte Carlo style. Checkering or stipple finish. Calibers .243 to .300 Magnum. Introduced in 1996.

NIB	Exc.	V.G.	Good	Fair	Poor
2600	2100	1600	1150	700	225

African Synthetic

Similar to Safari rifle, with fibergrain stock, checkering or stipple finish. Calibers .338 to .458 Magnum.

NIB	Exc.	V.G.	Good	Fair	Poor
3300	2600	1800	1400	750	250

Neutralizer Mark I

Built on Remington 700 or Winchester action. Bolt-action rifle chambered in choice of calibers from .223 to .300 Win. Magnum. Barrel length 24" to 26" depending on caliber, with Magnum barrels up to 28". A fiberglass tactical stock, with adjustable cheekpiece and buttplate is standard in various finishes. **NOTE:** Deduct $400 for Winchester action.

NIB	Exc.	V.G.	Good	Fair	Poor
2900	2300	1700	1300	700	275

Neutralizer Mark II

Same as above, with Apollo action.

NIB	Exc.	V.G.	Good	Fair	Poor
4000	3200	2250	1700	900	325

Benchrest Rifles

Custom built. Unable to price individual rifles.

Prone Rifles

Custom built. Unable to price individual rifles.

X-Course Rifles

Custom built. Unable to price individual rifles.

1,000 Yard Match Rifles

Custom built. Unable to price individual rifles.

Fully Accurized Production Rifles

Rifles offered in standard blue or stainless steel, with walnut or synthetic stock. Chambered from .223 to .338 Win. Magnum. Built on Remington, Ruger or Winchester actions.

NIB	Exc.	V.G.	Good	Fair	Poor
1250	1100	750	600	400	200

AROSTEGUI, EULOGIO
Eibar, Spain

Azul Royal (Model 31)

Semi-automatic or fully automatic pistol in calibers 7.63 Mauser, 9mm Bergmann or .38 ACP. Manufactured between 1935 and 1940. Fitted with 10-round integral magazine. **NOTE:** Add 300 percent for fully automatic machine pistol version. NFA/BATFE regulations apply.

Courtesy James Rankin

NIB	Exc.	V.G.	Good	Fair	Poor
—	3000	2500	1000	500	300

Super Azul (M-34)

Semi-automatic or fully automatic pistol in 7.63mm Mauser, 9mm Bergmann and .38 ACP. Manufactured between 1935 and 1940. Has removable box magazine with capacity of 10, 20 or 30 rounds. Also known as the War Model or Standard Model. **NOTE:** Add 300 percent for fully automatic machine pistol version. NFA/BATFE regulations apply.

Courtesy James Rankin

NIB	Exc.	V.G.	Good	Fair	Poor
—	3000	2500	1000	500	300

Azul 6.35mm

6.35mm semi-automatic pistol. Copied after Model 1906 Browning. Frame marked with letters "EA" in a circle. A retriever is molded in the grips. Magazine capacity 6 or 9 rounds.

NIB	Exc.	V.G.	Good	Fair	Poor
—	250	200	150	100	75

Azul 7.65mm

7.65mm semi-automatic pistol. Copied after Model 1910 FN. Magazine capacity 7 or 9 rounds.

NIB	Exc.	V.G.	Good	Fair	Poor
—	250	200	150	100	75

Velo-Dog

Folding trigger 5.5mm or 6.35mm revolver bearing trademark "EA" on grips.

NIB	Exc.	V.G.	Good	Fair	Poor
—	175	100	75	50	30

ARRIETA S.L.
Elgoibar, Spain

Company produces a wide variety of double-barrel shotguns. Price range from $450 to more than $30,000. It is recommended that highly engraved examples, as well as small bore arms, be individually appraised. **NOTE:** For 20- or 28-gauge and .410 bore, add 10 percent to values shown.

490 Eder

Double-barrel boxlock shotgun, with double triggers and extractors. Discontinued in 1986.

NIB	Exc.	V.G.	Good	Fair	Poor
—	550	425	325	250	100

500 Titan

Holland & Holland-style sidelock double-barrel shotgun, with French case hardened and engraved locks. Double triggers on extractors. No longer imported after 1986.

NIB	Exc.	V.G.	Good	Fair	Poor
—	675	500	400	300	150

501 Palomara

As above, but more finely finished. Discontinued in 1986.

NIB	Exc.	V.G.	Good	Fair	Poor
—	800	600	500	400	200

505 Alaska

As above, but more intricately engraved. Discontinued in 1986.

NIB	Exc.	V.G.	Good	Fair	Poor
—	900	750	600	500	250

510 Montana

Holland & Holland-style sidelock double-barrel shotgun, with internal parts gold-plated.

NIB	Exc.	V.G.	Good	Fair	Poor
3800	3000	1800	950	600	350

550 Field

As above, without internal parts gold-plated.

NIB	Exc.	V.G.	Good	Fair	Poor
3200	2750	1250	850	500	250

557 Standard

As above, but more finely finished.

NIB	Exc.	V.G.	Good	Fair	Poor
5900	5000	3800	2700	1500	800

558 Patria

As above, but more finely finished.

NIB	Exc.	V.G.	Good	Fair	Poor
3650	3150	1750	1250	800	400

560 Cumbre

As above, but featuring intricate engraving.

NIB	Exc.	V.G.	Good	Fair	Poor
3800	3200	1800	1200	800	400

570 Lieja

NIB	Exc.	V.G.	Good	Fair	Poor
6200	5500	4200	3000	2000	1000

575 Sport

NIB	Exc.	V.G.	Good	Fair	Poor
6750	6000	5000	3750	2400	1100

578 Victoria

Engraved in the English manner, with floral bouquets.

NIB	Exc.	V.G.	Good	Fair	Poor
7000	6200	5200	4000	2800	1200

585 Liria

As above, but more finely finished.

NIB	Exc.	V.G.	Good	Fair	Poor
6500	5500	4250	3000	2000	1000

588 Cima

NIB	Exc.	V.G.	Good	Fair	Poor
4800	4000	2250	1500	900	400

590 Regina

NIB	Exc.	V.G.	Good	Fair	Poor
4250	3500	2700	1750	1000	500

595 Principe

As above, but engraved with relief-cut hunting scenes.

NIB	Exc.	V.G.	Good	Fair	Poor
7500	6000	4000	3000	2000	1000

600 Imperial

Double-barrel shotgun has a self-opening action.

NIB	Exc.	V.G.	Good	Fair	Poor
10000	8500	7000	4500	3200	2100

601 Imperial Tiro

As above, but nickel-plated. Fitted with self-opening action.

NIB	Exc.	V.G.	Good	Fair	Poor
11000	9500	8000	5200	3800	2200

801

Detachable sidelock self-opening action double-barrel shotgun. Engraved in manner of Churchill.

NIB	Exc.	V.G.	Good	Fair	Poor
12000	10200	7500	5000	3000	2000

802

As above, with Holland & Holland-style engraving.

NIB	Exc.	V.G.	Good	Fair	Poor
12500	11000	8000	6000	4000	2000

803

As above, with Purdey-style engraving.

NIB	Exc.	V.G.	Good	Fair	Poor
12500	1000	7000	5000	4000	2000

871

Model features hand detachable sidelocks, with Holland ejectors. Scroll engraving.

NIB	Exc.	V.G.	Good	Fair	Poor
5300	4400	2500	1500	1000	750

872

Same features as Model 871, with addition of more engraving coverage using a tighter scroll.

NIB	Exc.	V.G.	Good	Fair	Poor
14000	12500	10000	7000	5000	2000

873

Features hand detachable sidelocks and game scene engraving.

NIB	Exc.	V.G.	Good	Fair	Poor
15000	13500	11000	7000	5000	2000

874

Same features as above, with addition of blued frame and gold outlines.

NIB	Exc.	V.G.	Good	Fair	Poor
11000	9000	8000	6000	4000	2000

875

Custom manufactured sidelock double-barrel shotgun. Built solely to customer's specifications.

NIB	Exc.	V.G.	Good	Fair	Poor
17000	15000	12500	7000	5000	2000

R-1 Double Rifle

NIB	Exc.	V.G.	Good	Fair	Poor
18000	16000	12500	8000	3000	1000

R-2 Double Rifle

NIB	Exc.	V.G.	Good	Fair	Poor
40000	32000	20000	12000	5000	2000

ARRIZABALAGA, HIJOS de C.
Eibar, Spain

Arrizabalaga

7.65mm semi-automatic pistol, with 9-shot magazine. Lanyard ring fitted to butt. Checkered wood grips. "ARRIZABALAGA" on slide.

Courtesy James Rankin

NIB	Exc.	V.G.	Good	Fair	Poor
—	275	175	125	75	50

Campeon

Model 1919 6.35mm, 7.65mm or 9mm Kurtz semi-automatic pistol. Slide marked "Campeon Patent 1919"; plastic grips "Campeon". Supplied with 6- or 8-round magazines. **NOTE:** Add 25 percent for 9mm Kurtz.

Courtesy James Rankin

NIB	Exc.	V.G.	Good	Fair	Poor
—	325	275	195	75	50

Jo Lo Ar

Model 1924 semi-automatic pistol, with tip-up barrel, cocking lever and no trigger guard. Jo Lo Ar was built in five calibers: 6.35mm, 7.65mm, 9mm Kurtz, 9mm Largo and .45 ACP. "Jo-Lo-Ar" appears on slide and grips. Premium for larger calibers. **NOTE:** Add 400 percent for .45.

Courtesy James Rankin

NIB	Exc.	V.G.	Good	Fair	Poor
—	1100	925	800	450	200

Sharpshooter

6.35mm, 7.65mm or 9mm Corto (short) semi-automatic pistol. Fitted with a cocking lever. Barrel tips up for cleaning or when using as a single-shot. "SHARPSHOOTER" appears on slide.

Courtesy James Rankin

NIB	Exc.	V.G.	Good	Fair	Poor
—	400	300	225	150	100

ARSENAL, INC.
Las Vegas, Nevada

SA M-7

Semi-automatic rifles manufactured in U.S. Similar to AK-47 in appearance. Chambered for 7.62x39 cartridge. Fitted with 16" barrel. Black polymer stock.

NIB	Exc.	V.G.	Good	Fair	Poor
1000	800	550	325	200	125

SA M-7 Classic

As above, with blonde wood stock.

NIB	Exc.	V.G.	Good	Fair	Poor
1050	850	600	325	200	125

SA M-7S

Similar to SA M-7, with scope rail added.

NIB	Exc.	V.G.	Good	Fair	Poor
1025	875	575	325	200	125

SA RPK-5

Similar to SA M-7. Chambered for 5.56 NATO. Has 23.5" heavy barrel, with folding tripod and muzzle threads.

NIB	Exc.	V.G.	Good	Fair	Poor
1600	1350	1000	750	600	400

SA RPK-7

Chambered for 7.62x39 cartridge. Rifle similar to RPK. Fitted with 23" barrel with bipod. Solid blonde wood stock, with trap in stock for cleaning kit.

NIB	Exc.	V.G.	Good	Fair	Poor
975	800	595	325	200	125

SAS M-7

Based on the Bulgarian ARM1F, with under-folding stock. Chambered for 7.62x39mm. Made from 2004 to 2007.

NIB	Exc.	V.G.	Good	Fair	Poor
1000	850	650	500	300	150

SAS M-7 Classic

Based on Russian AKS-47, with heavy barrel, blonde wood and under-folding stock. Introduced in 2007.

NIB	Exc.	V.G.	Good	Fair	Poor
1650	1400	1100	825	500	200

SLR-104

Chambered for 5.45x39.5 cartridge, with Bulgarian-made receiver and barrel. Other parts made in U.S.A. Mil-spec polymer stock, with folding buttstock. Introduced in 2003.

NIB	Exc.	V.G.	Good	Fair	Poor
950	800	600	450	300	150

SLR-106

Chambered for 5.56 NATO/.223 round, with Bulgarian stamped receiver, original Bulgarian chrome lined hammer-forged barrel. U.S. made polmer stock, with left-side folding buttstock. Other features include pistol-grip, removable muzzle-brake, black or desert sand color and Picatinny rails.

NIB	Exc.	V.G.	Good	Fair	Poor
950	800	600	450	300	150

SLR-107

Chambered for 7.62x39 caliber. General features are similar to SLR-106 model.

NIB	Exc.	V.G.	Good	Fair	Poor
950	800	600	450	300	150

ASCASO
Cataluna, Spain

Spanish Rebublican Government

Copy of Astra Model 400. Chambered for 9mm Largo cartridge. Barrel marked "F. Ascaso Tarrassa" in an oval. Built by the Spanish government during Spanish Civil War. Very few were made.

Courtesy James Rankin

NIB	Exc.	V.G.	Good	Fair	Poor
—	850	750	550	300	200

ASHEVILLE ARMORY
Asheville, North Carolina

Enfield-Type Rifle

.58-caliber percussion rifle, with 32.5" barrel and full stock secured by two iron barrel bands. Finished in white brass, trigger guard and buttplate on walnut stock. Lockplate marked "Asheville, N.C." Approximately 300 made in 1862 and 1863.

Courtesy Milwaukee Public Museum, Milwaukee, Wisconsin

NIB	Exc.	V.G.	Good	Fair	Poor
—	—	42000	19200	5000	3250

ASHTON, PETER & WILLIAM
Middletown, Connecticut

Under Hammer Pistol

.28- to .38-caliber single-shot percussion revolver, with 4" or 5" half-octagonal barrels marked "P.H. Ashton" or "W. Ashton". Blued or browned, with walnut grips. Active 1850s.

NIB	Exc.	V.G.	Good	Fair	Poor
—	—	1100	500	200	100

ASTON, H./H. ASTON & CO. PISTOLS
Middleton, Connecticut

Overall length 14"; barrel length 8.5"; caliber .54. Markings: on lockplate forward of hammer "U S/H. ASTON" or "U S/H. ASTON & CO.", on tail "MIDDTN/CONN/(date)"; on barrel, standard government inspection marks. Henry Aston of Middleton, Connecticut received a contract from U.S. War Department in February 1845, for 30,000 single-shot percussion pistols. These were delivered between 1846 and 1852, after which Ira N. Johnston continued production under a separate contract. Three thousand of these pistols were purchased for Navy usage. Many of these were subsequently marked with a small anchor on barrel near breech. These Navy purchases will command a slight premium.

Courtesy Milwaukee Public Museum, Milwaukee, Wisconsin

NIB	Exc.	V.G.	Good	Fair	Poor
—	—	4700	4500	1750	500

ASTRA-UNCETA SA
Guernica, Spain

Astra is a brand name placed on guns built by Esperanza y Unceta and then Unceta y Cia. This Spanish company has now incorporated its trade name into its corporate name and is now know as Astra-Unceta SA. Firm under direction of Don Pedron Unceta and Don Juan Esperanza began business in Eibar on July 17, 1908 and moved to Guernica in 1913. Astra trademark was adopted on November 25, 1914. Esperanza began production of the Spanish Army's Campo Giro pistol in 1913. Model 1921 was marketed commercially as Astra 400. After Spanish Civil War, Unceta was one of only four handgun companies permitted to resume manufacturing operations. An interesting and informative side note is that pistols with 1000 to 5000 model numbers were made after 1945. Astra merged with Star before going out of business in 2006.

Victoria

6.35mm semi-automatic pistol, with 2.5" barrel. Blued, with black plastic grips. Manufactured prior to 1913.

NIB	Exc.	V.G.	Good	Fair	Poor
—	300	250	200	150	100

Astra 1911

6.35mm and 7.65mm semi-automatic pistol. External hammer. Checkered hard rubber grips. 7.65mm model was manufactured before 6.35mm model.

Courtesy James Rankin

NIB	Exc.	V.G.	Good	Fair	Poor
—	375	275	175	100	75

Astra 1924

6.35mm semi-automatic pistol, with 2.5" barrel. Slide marked "Esperanza y Unceta Guernica Spain Astra Cal 6.35 .25". Blued, with black plastic grips.

NIB	Exc.	V.G.	Good	Fair	Poor
—	300	200	125	100	75

Astra 100 (Old Model)

Semi-automatic pistol in caliber 7.65mm. Checkered hard rubber grips. Magazine capacity 12 rounds. Introduced after WWII.

Courtesy James Rankin

NIB	Exc.	V.G.	Good	Fair	Poor
—	550	400	300	200	100

Astra 200

6.35mm semi-automatic pistol, with 2.5" barrel and 6-shot magazine. Fitted with grip safety. Also known as "Firecat" in United States. Manufactured from 1920 to 1966. **NOTE:** Add 25 percent for factory engraving.

Courtesy James Rankin

NIB	Exc.	V.G.	Good	Fair	Poor
—	300	200	125	100	75

Astra 400 or Model 1921

9x23 Bergman (9mm Largo) caliber semi-automatic pistol, with 6" barrel. Blued, with black plastic grips. Adopted for use by the Spanish Army. Approximately 106,000 made prior to 1946. Recent importation has depressed the price of these guns. **NOTE:** Any with Nazi proofs marks are worth a 100 percent premium, but caution is advised.

NIB	Exc.	V.G.	Good	Fair	Poor
—	475	400	250	75	40

Astra 300

As above in 7.65mm or 9mm short. Those used during WWII by German forces bear Waffenamt marks. Approximately 171,000 manufactured prior to 1947. **NOTE:** Add 25 percent for Nazi-proofed.

Courtesy Orvel Reichert

NIB	Exc.	V.G.	Good	Fair	Poor
—	650	475	250	150	100

Astra 600

Similar to Model 400 in 9mm Parabellum. In 1943 and 1944 approximately 10,500 manufactured. Some of these WWII guns will have Nazi proof stamp and bring a premium. A further 49,000 were made in 1946 and commercially sold.

NIB	Exc.	V.G.	Good	Fair	Poor
—	575	375	275	175	100

Astra 700

Single-action semi-automatic pistol in caliber 7.65mm. Magazine capacity 9 rounds. Introduced in 1926.

Courtesy James Rankin

NIB	Exc.	V.G.	Good	Fair	Poor
—	500	400	300	150	100

Astra 800

Similar to Model 600, with external hammer and loaded chamber indicator. Blued, with plastic grips having trade name "Condor" cast in them. Approximately 11,400 made from 1958 to 1969.

NIB	Exc.	V.G.	Good	Fair	Poor
—	1500	1200	850	500	300

Astra 900

Modified copy of Mauser Model C96 semi-automatic pistol. Blued, with walnut grips. **NOTE:** Early examples with small Bolo grip marked "Hope" on chamber will bring a 20 percent premium. Serial numbers 32,788 through 33,774 were used by German Army in WWII and bring a 50 percent premium. Add 50 percent for matching Astra-made stock.

NIB	Exc.	V.G.	Good	Fair	Poor
—	3000	2250	1500	600	300

Astra 1000

Single-action semi-automatic pistol in caliber 7.65mm. Magazine capacity 12 rounds. Introduced after WWII.

Courtesy James Rankin

NIB	Exc.	V.G.	Good	Fair	Poor
—	750	600	450	200	100

Astra 2000

Single-action semi-automatic pistol in .22- or 6.35mm caliber. No grip safety. With external hammer. Blued, with plastic grips.

NIB	Exc.	V.G.	Good	Fair	Poor
—	225	200	175	150	90

Astra 3000

Model 300 in 7.65mm or 9mm short, with 6- or 7-shot magazine. Loaded chamber indicator. Manufactured from 1948 to 1956.

Paul Goodwin photo

NIB	Exc.	V.G.	Good	Fair	Poor
—	600	500	325	200	100

Astra 4000 Falcon

Semi-automatic pistol known later as "Falcon". Calibers were .22 LR, 7.65mm and 9mmK. Magazine capacity 7, 8 and 10 rounds. Manufactured beginning 1955.

Courtesy James Rankin

NIB	Exc.	V.G.	Good	Fair	Poor
—	575	475	325	200	100

Astra 5000 Constable

.22, 7.65mm or 9mm short semi-automatic pistol (resembling Walther PP pistol), with 3.5" barrel. Blued, chrome-plated or stainless steel, with plastic grips. Also available with 6" barrel as a sport model. Introduced in 1965. **NOTE:** Add 15 percent for Constable Sport version with 6" barrel and adjustable sight.

NIB	Exc.	V.G.	Good	Fair	Poor
—	395	300	250	200	100

Astra 7000

Enlarged version of Model 2000 in .22-caliber.

NIB	Exc.	V.G.	Good	Fair	Poor
—	575	475	325	200	100

Astra A-80

.38 Super, 9mm or .45-caliber double-action semi-automatic pistol, with 3.75" barrel. Magazine capacity 9- or 15-shot, depending on caliber. Blued or chrome-plated, with plastic grips. Introduced in 1982.

Courtesy James Rankin

NIB	Exc.	V.G.	Good	Fair	Poor
450	350	300	250	200	100

Astra A-90

As above in 9mm or .45-caliber only. Introduced in 1986.

NIB	Exc.	V.G.	Good	Fair	Poor
400	350	300	250	200	100

Constable A-60

.380-caliber double-action semi-automatic pistol, with 3.5" barrel, adjustable sights and 13-shot magazine. Blued, with plastic grips. Introduced in 1986.

NIB	Exc.	V.G.	Good	Fair	Poor
400	300	200	150	100	75

Astra Cadix

.22- or .38 Special double-action revolver, with 4" or 6" barrel. Swing-out cylinder holds 5- or 9-shots. Blued, with plastic grips. Manufactured from 1960 to 1968.

NIB	Exc.	V.G.	Good	Fair	Poor
—	225	175	125	90	70

.357 Double-Action Revolver

Similar to Cadix in .357 Magnum caliber, with 3", 4", 6" or 8.5" barrel. Adjustable sights and 6-shot cylinder. Blued or stainless steel, with walnut grips. Manufactured from 1972 to 1988. **NOTE:** Add 10 percent for stainless steel.

NIB	Exc.	V.G.	Good	Fair	Poor
295	250	175	125	100	75

.44/.45 Double-Action Revolver

As above in .41-, .44 Magnum or .45 ACP caliber, with 6" or 8.5" barrels and 6-shot cylinder. Blued or stainless steel, with walnut grips. Manufactured from 1980 to 1987. **NOTE:** Add 25 percent for stainless steel.

NIB	Exc.	V.G.	Good	Fair	Poor
—	375	325	250	200	100

Terminator

As above in .44 Special or .44 Magnum, with 2.75" barrel. Adjustable sights and 6-shot cylinder. Blued or stainless steel, with rubber grips. **NOTE:** Add 10 percent for stainless steel.

NIB	Exc.	V.G.	Good	Fair	Poor
—	380	330	255	200	100

Convertible Revolver

Similar to .357 D/A revolver. Accompanied by a cylinder chambered for 9mm Parabellum. Barrel length 3". Blued, with walnut grips. Introduced in 1986.

NIB	Exc.	V.G.	Good	Fair	Poor
—	395	325	275	150	100

RECENTLY IMPORTED PISTOLS

Model A-70

Lightweight semi-automatic pistol chambered for 9mm or .40 S&W cartridge. Fitted with 3-dot combat sights. Barrel 3.5" long. Magazine capacity 8 rounds for 9mm; 7 rounds for .40 S&W. Black plastic grips. Blue finish standard. Weight 29 oz. **NOTE:** Add $35 for nickel finish.

NIB	Exc.	V.G.	Good	Fair	Poor
350	275	225	175	150	100

Model A-75

Introduced in 1993. All standard features of Model 70 plus selective double-/single trigger action and decocking lever. Chambered for 9mm, .40 S&W or .45 ACP. Offered in blue or nickel finish, with steel or alloy frame in 9mm only. Weight: steel frame in 9mm and .40 S&W is 31 oz.; .45 ACP is 34.4 oz.; featherweight 9mm is 23.5 oz. **NOTE:** Add $35 for nickel finish.

NIB	Exc.	V.G.	Good	Fair	Poor
375	325	250	200	150	100

Model A-100

Semi-automatic service pistol. Chambered for 9mm Parabellum, .40 S&W or .45 ACP cartridges. Trigger is double-action for first shot, single-action for follow-up shots. Equipped with decocking lever. Barrel 3.8" long; overall length 7.5". Magazine capacity: 9mm is 17 rounds; .40 S&W is 13 rounds; .45 is 9 rounds. Blue or nickel finish standard. Weight about 34 oz. Also available in featherweight model 9mm at 26.5 oz. **NOTE:** Add $35 for nickel finish.

NIB	Exc.	V.G.	Good	Fair	Poor
400	350	300	250	200	100

Model A-100 Carry Comp

Similar to Model A-100, with 4.25" barrel and 1" compensator. Blue finish only. Weight about 38 oz. Magazine capacity: 9mm is 17 rounds; .40 S&W and .45 ACP is 10 rounds.

NIB	Exc.	V.G.	Good	Fair	Poor
475	375	300	250	200	100

ATCSA
Armas de Tiro y Casa
Eibar, Spain

Colt Police Positive Copy

.38-caliber 6-shot revolver resembling Colt Police Positive.

NIB	Exc.	V.G.	Good	Fair	Poor
—	250	125	100	60	40

Target Pistol

.22-caliber single-shot target pistol utilizing a revolver frame.

NIB	Exc.	V.G.	Good	Fair	Poor
—	300	175	125	100	55

AUBREY, A.J.
Meriden, Connecticut

Double-Barrel Shotguns

Good quality doubles made for Sears. Value depends on condition, grade and model. Prices range between $100 and $1,500.

AUER, B.
Louisville, Kentucky

Pocket Pistol

.60-caliber percussion pocket pistol, with 4" octagonal barrel. Long tang extending well back along grip. Browned silver furniture. Checkered walnut stock. Lock marked "B. Auer". Produced during 1850s.

NIB	Exc.	V.G.	Good	Fair	Poor
—	—	1700	700	250	100

AUGUSTA MACHINE WORKS
Augusta, Georgia

1851 Colt Navy Copy

.36-caliber percussion revolver, with 8" barrel and 6-shot cylinder. Unmarked except for serial numbers. Stop cylinder slots 6 or 12. Blued, with walnut grips. Very rare revolver.

NIB	Exc.	V.G.	Good	Fair	Poor
—	—	62500	40000	17500	5000

AUSTIN & HALLECK, INC.
Weston, Missouri; later Provo, Utah

Model 320 LR BLU

In-line percussion bolt-action rifle. Fitted with 26" half octagon/half round barrel in .50-caliber. Receiver and barrel blue. Adjustable trigger. Receiver drilled and tapped for scope mount. Stock is black synthetic, with checkering. Weight about 7.87 lbs.

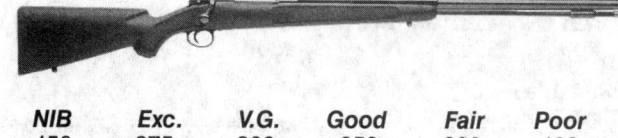

NIB	Exc.	V.G.	Good	Fair	Poor
450	375	300	250	200	100

Model 320 S/S

Similar to above, with stainless steel barrel and action.

NIB	Exc.	V.G.	Good	Fair	Poor
500	400	300	250	200	100

Model 420 LR Classic

Similar to Model 320 series. Standard lightly figured Maple stock in classic configuration. Available in blue or stainless steel. Premium for fancy wood.

NIB	Exc.	V.G.	Good	Fair	Poor
500	425	300	250	200	100

Model 420 LR Monte Carlo

Same as classic series, with Monte Carlo stock and cheekpiece. Premium for fancy wood.

NIB	Exc.	V.G.	Good	Fair	Poor
500	425	300	250	200	100

Mountain Rifle

.50-caliber percussion or flintlock rifle, with double-set triggers, 32" octagonal barrel, buckhorn sights, curly Maple stock and crescent steel buttplate. Weight about 7.5 lbs. Premium for fancy wood.

NIB	Exc.	V.G.	Good	Fair	Poor
500	400	300	250	200	100

AUSTRALIAN AUTOMATIC ARMS LTD.
Tasmania, Australia

SAR

5.56mm semi-automatic rifle, with 16.25" or 20" barrel, 5- or 20-shot magazine, black plastic stock and fore-end. Imported from 1986 to 1989.

NIB	Exc.	V.G.	Good	Fair	Poor
1200	950	650	350	250	125

SAP

10.5" barreled pistol version of above. Imported from 1986 to 1989.

NIB	Exc.	V.G.	Good	Fair	Poor
1150	900	600	325	250	125

SP

Sporting rifle version of SAR, with wood stock and 5-shot magazine. Introduced in 1989.

NIB	Exc.	V.G.	Good	Fair	Poor
975	850	575	300	250	125

AUTAUGA ARMS INC.
Prattville, Alabama

MK II

.32 ACP semi-automatic blowback pistol, with double-action trigger. Barrel length 2.25". Fixed sights. Overall length 4.25". Weight about 13.5 oz. Magazine capacity 6 rounds. Introduced in 1999.

NIB	Exc.	V.G.	Good	Fair	Poor
325	275	225	195	150	100

AUTO MAG
Various Manufacturers

Popular stainless steel semi-automatic pistol. Developed by Sanford Arms Company of Pasadena, California, in 1960s. Chambered for a special cartridge known as .44 AMP, which had a 240-grain .44-caliber bullet. Production of this arm has been carried out by a number of companies over the past 40-plus years, beginning in 1971. Believed that fewer than 10,000 have been produced by eight manufacturers involved.

.44 AMP

NIB	Exc.	V.G.	Good	Fair	Poor
2700	1850	1475	995	600	300

.44 AMP

NIB	Exc.	V.G.	Good	Fair	Poor
1950	1550	1000	800	600	300

.44 AMP

NIB	Exc.	V.G.	Good	Fair	Poor
2150	1700	1250	850	600	300

AMT "C" SERIES

There were 100 guns produced in this series. First 50 were serial numbered with a "C" prefix. Second 50 were serial numbered "LAST 1" through "LAST 50". Available with 6.5" ventilated rib or 10" tapered barrel.

.357 AMP

NIB	Exc.	V.G.	Good	Fair	Poor
1750	1300	900	700	500	300

.357 AMP

NIB	Exc.	V.G.	Good	Fair	Poor
2300	1850	1325	900	600	300

AUTO MAG, INC.
Irwindale, California

In 1998, this company was formed to produce 1,000 Harry Sanford Commemorative pistols. Chambered for .44 AMP cartridge. Each pistol comes in a walnut display case, special serial number, Harry Sanford's signature and name Auto Mag on receiver. Last retail price for Auto Mag is $2,750.

AUTO MAG CORP.
Pasadena, California

Serial number range A0000 through A3300. Made with 6.5" ventilated rib barrel. Chambered in .44 AMP only.

.44 AMP

NIB	Exc.	V.G.	Good	Fair	Poor
2700	1850	1475	995	600	300

HIGH STANDARD (2)
Hamden, Connecticut

High Standard was national distributor for Auto Mag in 1974 and 1975. These guns chambered for .44 AMP and .357 AMP. HS Cat. #9346 for .44 AMP, #9347 for .357 AMP.

High Standard sold 134 Auto Mags with "H" prefix. Serial numbers are between H1 and H198, one at H1566 and three between H17219 and H17222. Of these 108 were .44 AMP and 26 were .357 AMP.

High Standard also sold 911 Auto Mags between serial numbers A05278 and A07637. Of these, 777 were .44 AMP and 108 were .357 AMP.

NIB	Exc.	V.G.	Good	Fair	Poor
2200	1900	1350	900	600	300

KENT LOMONT

Pistols made by this maker are essentially proto-types, it is advised that potential purchasers secure a qualified appraisal.

L. E. JURRAS CUSTOM

Custom maker produced a limited number of Auto Mag pistols in 1977. These arms are worth approximately 35-50 percent more than standard production models.

TDE CORP.
El Monte, California

Serial number range A05016 through A08300. Standard 6.5" ventilated rib barrel. Also available in 8" and 10" barrel lengths. Chambered for .44 AMP and .357 AMP.

.357 AMP

NIB	Exc.	V.G.	Good	Fair	Poor
1750	1300	900	700	500	300

.44 AMP

NIB	Exc.	V.G.	Good	Fair	Poor
1950	1550	1000	800	600	300

TDE CORP.
North Hollywood, California

Serial number range A3400 through A05015. Made with 6.5" ventilated rib barrel. Chambered in .44 AMP and .357 AMP.

.357 AMP

NIB	Exc.	V.G.	Good	Fair	Poor
2300	1850	1325	900	600	300

.44 AMP

NIB	Exc.	V.G.	Good	Fair	Poor
2150	1700	1250	850	600	300

TDE-OMC

Known as solid-bolt or "B" series. Serial number range is B00001 through B00370. Either 6.5" ventilated rib or 10" tapered barrels are available.

NIB	Exc.	V.G.	Good	Fair	Poor
2550	2100	1600	1000	600	300

AUTO ORDNANCE CORP.

Auto Ordnance makes reproductions of 1911 Government Model pistol, Thompson sub-machine gun (semi-automatic only) and M-1 Carbine. Variations of 1911 are marketed under both Auto Ordnance and Thompson brand names. In 1999, the company was bought by Kahr Arms and moved from West Hurley, New York to Worcester, Massachusetts.

Auto Ordnance 1911A1

Standard model in .45 ACP with 5"barrel, Parkerized finish, fixed sights, plastic or checkered walnut grips. Also offered in 9mm, .38 Super, 10mm (all discontinued in 1996) and .40 S&W (discontinued in 1993). Blue, satin nickel and two-tone finish were optional until 2005. In 2011 a 100th Anniversary Model was introduced, with appropriate rollmarks. **NOTE:**

Add $35 for nickel, two-tone finish or 100th Anniversary Model.

NIB	Exc.	V.G.	Good	Fair	Poor
565	525	475	400	300	200

Thompson Model 1911TC

.45 ACP semi-automatic, with fixed sights and 7+1 capacity. Stainless frame and slide. 5" barrel, weight 39 oz. Laminate grips.

NIB	Exc.	V.G.	Good	Fair	Poor
650	525	395	300	200	100

Thompson Model 1911CAF

.45 ACP semi-automatic, with fixed sights and 7+1 capacity. Aluminum frame and stainless slide. 5" barrel, weight 31.5 oz. Laminate grips.

NIB	Exc.	V.G.	Good	Fair	Poor
650	525	395	300	200	100

Thompson 1911 A1—Standard

9mm, .38 Super or .45-caliber copy of Colt Model 1911 A1. Weight 39 oz. **NOTE:** Add $20 for 9mm and .38 Super (both discontinued in 1997).

NIB	Exc.	V.G.	Good	Fair	Poor
475	325	275	200	150	100

Thompson 1911 A1—Parkerized

NIB	Exc.	V.G.	Good	Fair	Poor
475	325	275	200	150	100

Thompson 1911 A1—Deluxe

Same as above in Hi-profile white 3-dot sight system. Black textured rubber wraparound grips.

NIB	Exc.	V.G.	Good	Fair	Poor
800	650	500	300	150	100

Thompson 1911 A1—Custom High Polish

Introduced in 1997. Features special high polish blued finish, with numerous special options. Stocks rosewood, with medallion. Fitted with 5" barrel. Chambered for .45 ACP. Weight about 39 oz.

NIB	Exc.	V.G.	Good	Fair	Poor
575	475	—	—	—	—

Thompson 1911 A1—10mm

Same as above. Chambered for 10mm cartridge. Magazine capacity 8 rounds. Discontinued in 1997.

NIB	Exc.	V.G.	Good	Fair	Poor
700	550	400	250	175	100

Thompson 1911 A1—Duo Tone

Chambered for .45 ACP. Slide blued. Frame satin nickel. Discontinued in 1997.

NIB	Exc.	V.G.	Good	Fair	Poor
500	425	350	225	150	100

Thompson 1911 A1—Satin Nickel

Chambered for .45 ACP or .38 Super. Finish satin nickel on both frame and slide. Blade front sight. Black checkered plastic grips. Discontinued in 1997.

NIB	Exc.	V.G.	Good	Fair	Poor
500	425	350	225	150	100

Thompson 1911 A1—Competition

Chambered for .45 ACP or .38 Super. Fitted with 5" barrel, compensator and other competition features. Such as, custom Commander hammer, flat mainspring housing, beavertail grip safety, full-length recoil guide rod, extended ejector, slide stop and thumb safety. Weight 42 oz.; 10" overall. Discontinued in 1997. **NOTE:** Add $10 for .38 Super.

NIB	Exc.	V.G.	Good	Fair	Poor
700	625	500	350	300	150

Thompson 1911 A1—Pit Bull

Chambered for .45 ACP. Fitted with 3.5" barrel. High profile sights. Black

textured rubber wraparound grips. Magazine capacity 7 rounds. Weight 36 oz.

NIB	Exc.	V.G.	Good	Fair	Poor
500	425	350	225	150	100

Thompson 1911 A1—General

Commander-size pistol, with 4.5" barrel. High profile sights. Chambered for .45 ACP or .38 Super. Weight 37 oz. Discontinued in 1997.

NIB	Exc.	V.G.	Good	Fair	Poor
500	425	350	225	150	100

ZG-51 "Pit Bull"

Same as above, with 3.5" barrel in .45-caliber. Introduced in 1988. In 1994 renamed "PIT BULL". Discontinued.

NIB	Exc.	V.G.	Good	Fair	Poor
500	425	350	225	150	100

Auto-Ordnance Thompson Semi-Automatic Model 1927 Series

First generation Auto-Ordnance Thompson Model 1927 manufactured by Colt Patent Firearms from 1927 to 1936. They were modified from original 15,000 Model 1921 Sub-Machineguns into a semi-automatic-only configuration. By removing the full-automatic rocker pivot assembly and converting the selector paddle into "single-fire" only position, allowing fire control assembly to be used as a semi-automatic only firearm. An estimated 50 such Model 1927 Semi-Automatic Carbines are believed to have been assembled and sold. Since these fire from an open bolt as the fully automatic Model 1921 and are (or can be readily converted to) full automatic, these first generation Model 1927 Thompson guns are considered to be machine guns by BATFE and must be transferred through a Class III dealer. Due to the scarcity of these firearms, a list of values would be very speculative. A base price of $35,000 is a good place to start. **NOTE:** Many thanks to George Layman for his assistance in contributing to this section. — Editor.

Second Generation Auto Ordnance Thompson Model 1927

Produced from 1975-1997 by Numrich Arms, West Hurley, N.Y. Approved for sale as a legal to own semi-automatic by BATFE on March 20, 1975. Serial numbers 1 to 29,585.

1927 A1 Deluxe Model

Features include adjustable sights, cooling fins, Cutts Compensator, 16.5" barrel, with one 20- or 30-shot box magazine. Available with choice of horizontal or vertical grip. Original price in 1980 was $489.95. Numrich Auto Ordnance guns, with all accessories including FBI reproduction hard case should add $650 to values listed.

NIB	Exc.	V.G.	Good	Fair	Poor
1850	1700	1500	1100	900	700

1927 A1 Deluxe Model (First 932 Carbines)

First 932 Thompson Model 1927 A1 Deluxe Semi-Automatic Carbines were equipped with numerous original Auto Ordnance surplus parts produced in Bridgeport, CT. in early 1940s. Genuine Lyman-manufactured adjustable rear sights and original Cutts Compensators were supplied on this first year batch of West Hurley, NY-made Thompson Deluxe Carbines.

NIB	Exc.	V.G.	Good	Fair	Poor
2800	2000	1700	1500	1350	1150

1927 A1 Standard Model

Plain barrel, banded front sight, horizontal forearm, WWII stamped steel "L" style, non-adjustable rear sight. Original 1980 price $469.95. **NOTE:** Fewer of these were manufactured than Deluxe Model and are considered scarce, thus priced accordingly.

NIB	Exc.	V.G.	Good	Fair	Poor
2200	1900	1575	1200	1000	800

1927 A3

This is a .22-caliber variation of Model 1927 A1, with 16" barrel and aluminum alloy receiver. Discontinued in 1994. **NOTE:** Add $500 for drum magazine.

NIB	Exc.	V.G.	Good	Fair	Poor
1350	900	675	550	425	250

1927 A5 .45 ACP Caliber Auto Ordnance Semi-Automatic Pistol

A 13" barrel version of M1927A1 Deluxe Carbine. Classified as a pistol and manufactured without buttstock. Original style Thompson 1927 "A" banded type front sight. Production terminated in 1995, as a result of the 1994 Assault Weapons Ban, due to certain physical characteristics, primarily the vertical fore-grip. All were grandfathered in after production had terminated. Not commonly encountered.

NIB	Exc.	V.G.	Good	Fair	Poor
2500	1900	1600	1400	1100	950

M-1 Semi-Automatic Carbine

Numrich/AO introduced this copy of WWII M-1 Thompson in 1980. Identical to simplified war-time version introduced in 1942. Features 16.5" barrel, side-mounted M-1 style bolt and frame, non-adjustable rear sight with "V" ears and horizontal front-grip. Milled from solid steel. Scarce.

NIB	Exc.	V.G.	Good	Fair	Poor
2100	1800	1500	1400	1200	1000

Third Generation Auto Ordnance Thompson Model 1927 Semi-Automatic Carbine

Successor to West Hurley, NY-made Thompson Model 1927. Kahr Arms, Worcester, MA is owner of Auto Ordnance trademark from 1999 to present.

TA5100D

Semi-Automatic Deluxe version of Thompson 1927 A1. Has aluminum receiver, 10.5" barrel, 100-round drum, cooling fins, Cutts Compensator and adjustable rear sights.

NIB	Exc.	V.G.	Good	Fair	Poor
1400	1200	1000	800	600	400

T1B

1927 A1 Deluxe Model, with finned 16.5" barrel, adjustable rear sights, detachable buttstock and Cutts Compensator.

NIB	Exc.	V.G.	Good	Fair	Poor
1800	1600	1400	1100	900	700

T150D

1927 A1 Deluxe Model, with finned barrel, adjustable rear sights, fixed buttstock, Cutts Compensator and 50-round drum.

NIB	Exc.	V.G.	Good	Fair	Poor
1550	1400	1250	1000	850	500

T5

Lightweight Deluxe Model, with 16.5" finned barrel, aluminum receiver, walnut stock, horizontal forearm, black nylon sling and 30-round magazine.

NIB	Exc.	V.G.	Good	Fair	Poor
1150	950	750	500	400	275

TA510D

1927-style pistol, which was the first of its type, reintroduced since discontinued Numrich 1927 A5 in 1995. Features 10.5" finned barrel, adjustable rear sights, 10-round drum to conform with states requiring 10-round magazine and aluminum receiver.

NIB	Exc.	V.G.	Good	Fair	Poor
1200	1000	800	550	400	300

T1SB

1927 A1 with 10.5" Short Barrel. Detachable or non-detachable buttstock. Requires Class 3 transfer. As close to original made in 1927 as possible. **NOTE:** Deduct 20 percent for non-detachable buttstock.

NIB	Exc.	V.G.	Good	Fair	Poor
2000	1700	1400	1000	700	450

M1SB

Short-barreled (10.5" finned and compensated) variant of semi-automatic M1. Does not accept drum magazines. Requires Form 3.

NIB	Exc.	V.G.	Good	Fair	Poor
1500	1150	695	400	300	150

M1 Carbine

Newly manufactured replica of military M1 carbine. Chambered in .30 Carbine. Introduced 2005. Birch stock, Parkerized finish. **NOTE:** Add 5 percent for walnut stock.

NIB	Exc.	V.G.	Good	Fair	Poor
950	800	650	500	300	125

AUTO POINTER
Yamamoto Co.
Tokyo, Japan

Auto Pointer Shotgun

12- or 20-gauge semi-automatic shotgun, with 26", 28" or 30" barrels. Aluminum alloy frame. Blued, with checkered walnut stock. Originally imported by Sloan's, no longer available. Clone of Browning A-5.

NIB	Exc.	V.G.	Good	Fair	Poor
—	475	350	250	175	100

AXTELL RIFLE CO.
Riflesmith, Inc.
Sheridan, Montana

#1 Long Range Creedmore

Single-shot rifle. Chambered for .40-50BN, .40-70SS, .40-70BN, .40-90, .45-70, .45-90 and .45-100. Weight about 10 lbs. Numerous options will affect price.

NIB	Exc.	V.G.	Good	Fair	Poor
4700	3750	3000	2200	1400	300

New Model Sharps 1877

Chambered for .45-90, .45-100 and .45-70 cartridges. Fitted with choice of 30" to 34" half round/half octagon barrel, with double-set triggers.

NIB	Exc.	V.G.	Good	Fair	Poor
5200	4000	3250	2500	1500	250

#2 Long Range

Long Range #2 rifle. Chambered for all the same calibers as #1 Long Range Creedmore. Weight about 10 lbs.

NIB	Exc.	V.G.	Good	Fair	Poor
3900	3000	1900	900	550	300

Lower Sporting Rifle

Chambered for same calibers as above. Weight between 9 and 12 lbs. depending on barrel options.

NIB	Exc.	V.G.	Good	Fair	Poor
2600	2000	1375	700	400	200

Business Rifle

Same calibers as above. Weight about 8.5 lbs.

NIB	Exc.	V.G.	Good	Fair	Poor
2400	1800	1275	700	400	200

Overbaugh Schuetzen

Chambered for .40-50BN and .40-50 straight. Weight 11 to 14 lbs. depending on barrel options.

NIB	Exc.	V.G.	Good	Fair	Poor
4400	3500	3000	2200	1400	300

AYA

For AyA shotguns, see entry under Aguirre y Aranzabal.

AZPIRI
Eibar, Spain

Spanish manufacturer of pistols prior to World War II.

Avion

6.35mm semi-automatic pistol. Copied after Model 1906 Browning. Marked "Pistolet Automatique Avion Brevete" on slide as well as on each side of grip plate along with an airplane logo. Manufactured from 1914 to 1918.

Courtesy James Rankin

NIB	Exc.	V.G.	Good	Fair	Poor
—	250	175	100	75	45

Colon

As above in 6.35mm caliber. Marked "Automatic Pistol Colon".

NIB	Exc.	V.G.	Good	Fair	Poor
—	250	175	100	75	45

B

B.R.F.
South Africa

B.R.F.

.25-caliber semi-automatic pistol. Similar to P.A.F., with 2" barrel and 6-shot magazine. "U-SA" means Union of South Africa. Little is known about manufacturer of this pistol, its origin or dates of manufacture.

NIB	Exc.	V.G.	Good	Fair	Poor
—	295	195	125	100	70

BABBIT, A. S.
Plattsburgh, New York
See—Adirondack Arms

BABCOCK, MOSES
Charlestown, Massachusetts

Babcock Under Hammer Cane Gun

.52-caliber percussion cane gun, with 27" barrel. Overall length about 33". Folding trigger under hammer, with wood handle. Hammer marked "Moses Babcock/Charlestown". Active 1850s and 1860s.

NIB	Exc.	V.G.	Good	Fair	Poor
—	—	2950	950	350	200

BACON ARMS CO.
Norwich, Connecticut

Bacon Arms operated from 1862 until 1891. They have become known primarily for production of cheaply made, solid-frame, rimfire revolvers known as "Suicide Specials". Bacon manufactured and sold under a number of different trademarks. They were: Bacon, Bonanza, Conqueror, Express, Gem, Governor, Guardian and Little Giant. Collector interest is low and values for all trademarks are quite similar.

Courtesy Milwaukee Public Museum, Milwaukee, Wisconsin

NIB	Exc.	V.G.	Good	Fair	Poor
—	295	225	100	75	50

BAER CUSTOM, LES
Hillsdale, Illinois

Long-standing 1911 pistolsmith is now producing custom quality 1911 pistols on a semi-production basis. Each pistol features a large number of custom characteristics such as forged steel frame, full slide recoil rod, double-serrated slide, beveled magazine well, checkered front strap, beavertail safety, extended magazine release button, Bo-Mar sights and many others, depending on specific model. Representative sampling of these fine Baer pistols appears below.

COMPETITION PISTOLS

Baer 1911 Ultimate Master Combat Pistol-Compensated

Chambered for .38 Super or .45 ACP. Fitted with triple-port tapered cone compensator. **NOTE:** Add $100 for .38 Super.

NIB	Exc.	V.G.	Good	Fair	Poor
2800	2000	1200	750	600	300

Baer 1911 Ultimate Master Steel Special

Designed for steel targets and Bianchi-style competition. Similar to above, but designed for light loads. Chambered for .38 Super. Hard chrome finish.

NIB	Exc.	V.G.	Good	Fair	Poor
2900	2250	1500	950	750	350

Baer 1911 Ultimate Master Combat Pistol

Similar to other Baer Master series pistols. Offered in .45 ACP, .400 Cor-Bon and .38 Super. Fitted with a large number of special features. Offered in 5" or 6" version. The 5" version also offered in 9x23 caliber.

6" Model

NIB	Exc.	V.G.	Good	Fair	Poor
2600	1950	1350	850	650	350

5" Model

NIB	Exc.	V.G.	Good	Fair	Poor
2670	1920	1425	800	600	350

Baer 1911 Ultimate Master Para

Designed for IPSC competition. Offered in Unlimited version, with compensator and scope or Limited version, with iron sights and no compensator.

Unlimited Model

.45 ACP, .38 Super, 9x23.

NIB	Exc.	V.G.	Good	Fair	Poor
3400	2700	1750	1200	850	400

Limited Model

NIB	Exc.	V.G.	Good	Fair	Poor
2900	2000	1500	900	650	300

Baer 1911 Bullseye Wadcutter Pistol

Designed for use with wadcutter loads only. Chambered for .45 ACP. **NOTE:** Add $125 for Baer Optical mount; $200 for 6" slide with LoMount BoMar sight.

NIB	Exc.	V.G.	Good	Fair	Poor
2000	1600	1000	600	500	250

Baer 1911 National Match Hardball Pistol

Designed for DCM matches. Chambered for .45 ACP.

NIB	Exc.	V.G.	Good	Fair	Poor
1900	1500	900	500	400	200

Baer 1911 Target Master

Designed for NRA centerfire matches. Chambered for .45 ACP.

NIB	Exc.	V.G.	Good	Fair	Poor
1450	1150	750	550	450	250

Baer 1911 IPSC Action Pistol

Chambered for .45 ACP, with blued slide and frame.

NIB	Exc.	V.G.	Good	Fair	Poor
1700	1350	850	600	450	300

Baer 1911 P.P.C. Distinguished Match

Introduced in 1999. Features 5" barrel, with adjustable Aristrocrat rear sight. Many, many special features such as double serrated slide, lowered and flared ejection port, extended ambi safety, checkered front strap, etc. Offered in .45 ACP and 9mm, with supported chamber. Blued finish and one magazine. **NOTE:** Add approximately $400 for 9mm model.

NIB	Exc.	V.G.	Good	Fair	Poor
2400	1850	1200	650	475	300

Baer 1911 P.P.C. Open Class

Similar to above. Fitted with 6" barrel and slide. Chambered for .45 ACP and 9mm, with supported chamber. Blued finish. Introduced in 1999. **NOTE:** Add approximately $400 for 9mm model.

NIB	Exc.	V.G.	Good	Fair	Poor
2600	1950	1300	700	500	350

DUTY & DEFENSE PISTOLS

Baer 1911 Premier II

Designed as a duty or defense pistol. Chambered for .45 ACP, .400 Cor-Bon and 9x23 cartridges. Fitted with 5" slide. **NOTE:** Add $150 for stainless steel version; $100 for .400 CorBon; $250 for 9x23.

NIB	Exc.	V.G.	Good	Fair	Poor
1790	1350	900	600	450	250

Baer 1911 Premier II—6" barrel

Same as above. Fitted with 6" match grade barrel. **NOTE:** Add $100 for .400 CorBon; $300 for .38 Super. 9x23 not offered with 6" slide.

NIB	Exc.	V.G.	Good	Fair	Poor
1990	1600	1100	900	700	350

Baer 1911 Premier II—Light Weight (LW1)

Same features as standard Premier II, with reduced weight aluminum frame. Furnished with low mount LCB adjustable rear sight. Offered in .45 ACP only.

NIB	Exc.	V.G.	Good	Fair	Poor
1900	1550	1100	900	700	350

Baer 1911 Premier II—Light Weight (LW2)

Same as above, with fixed combat-style rear sight.

NIB	Exc.	V.G.	Good	Fair	Poor
1900	1550	1100	900	700	350

Baer 1911 Premier II—Super-Tac

Similar to standard Premier II models, with low mount adjustable rear night sight and front sight. Special BEAR COAT finish. Offered in .45 ACP, .40 S&W, .400 CorBon. **NOTE:** Add $200 for dual caliber .45 ACP/.400 CorBon combo.

NIB	Exc.	V.G.	Good	Fair	Poor
2280	1700	1200	900	700	350

Baer 1911 Prowler III

Similar to Premier II, with tapered cone stub weight, full-length guide rod and reverse plug. Special order only.

NIB	Exc.	V.G.	Good	Fair	Poor
2580	1700	1200	950	700	350

Baer 1911 Prowler IV

Chambered for .45 ACP or .38 Super. Built on Para-Ordnance oversize frame. Fitted with 5" slide. Special order only. **NOTE:** Add $300 for optional 6" barrel and slide.

NIB	Exc.	V.G.	Good	Fair	Poor
2580	1900	1250	900	650	300

Baer 1911 Custom Carry—Commanche Length

Chambered for .45 ACP. Has several options including 4.5" barrel, stainless steel slide and frame, lightweight aluminum frame with blued steel slide. As of 2000, furnished with night sights. **NOTE:** Add $40 for stainless steel; $130 for lightweight frame.

NIB	Exc.	V.G.	Good	Fair	Poor
1850	1400	950	600	450	250

Baer 1911 Custom Carry—5

Same as above. Offered with 5" slide. Not offered in aluminum frame. **NOTE:** Add $40 for stainless steel.

NIB	Exc.	V.G.	Good	Fair	Poor
2120	1700	950	600	450	250

Baer 1911 Thunder Ranch Special

Features steel frame and slide, with front and rear serrations. Deluxe fixed rear sight, with tritium insert. Checkered front strap. Numerous special features. Slim line grips, with Thunder Ranch logo. Seven-round magazine standard. Special serial numbers with "TR" prefix. Offered in .45 ACP. **NOTE:** Add 10 percent for Comanche length; 5 percent for home defense model.

NIB	Exc.	V.G.	Good	Fair	Poor
1990	1500	950	600	450	250

Baer 1911 Thunder Ranch Special Engraved Model

As above, with engraved frame and slide.

NIB	Exc.	V.G.	Good	Fair	Poor
6600	4750	2500	1500	1150	650

Baer S.R.P. (Swift Response Pistol)

Chambered for .45 ACP. Built on Para-Ordnance frame. This unit similar to one supplied to FBI. Supplied with wooden presentation box. **NOTE:** Deduct $300 from NIB through Fair prices for S.R.P. models built on Baer frame or shorter 4.5" frame.

NIB	Exc.	V.G.	Good	Fair	Poor
2590	2250	1750	1200	850	400

Baer 1911 Monolith

Introduced in 1999. Features 5" barrel and slide with extra long dust cover. Chambered in .45 ACP, .400 CorBon, .40 S&W, 9x23, 9mm, or .38 Super all with supported chamber. Many special features such as BoMar sights, Commander-style hammer, speed trigger, etc. Blued finish with one magazine. Weight about 37 oz. **NOTE:** Add $250 for all other supported calibers.

NIB	Exc.	V.G.	Good	Fair	Poor
1850	1500	950	675	500	325

Baer 1911 Monolith Heavyweight

Introduced in 1999. Similar to Monolith, with addition of heavier frame that adds 3.5 oz. Same calibers as available on Monolith. Weight about 40 oz. **NOTE:** Add $200 for all other supported calibers.

NIB	Exc.	V.G.	Good	Fair	Poor
1930	1700	1100	775	425	250

Baer 1911 Monolith Tactical Illuminator

Introduced in 1999. Same features as Monolith Heavyweight, with addition of light mounted under dust cover. Offered in .45 ACP and .40 S&W with supported chamber. Weight with light about 44 oz. **NOTE:** Add $275 for all other supported calibers.

NIB	Exc.	V.G.	Good	Fair	Poor
1850	1500	1050	795	425	250

Baer 1911 Monolith Commanche

Fitted with 4.25" slide and dust cover covering length of slide. Has all features of standard Monolith. Comes with night sights and deluxe fixed rear sight. Edges rounded for tactical carry. Chambered in .45 ACP only. Introduced in 2001.

NIB	Exc.	V.G.	Good	Fair	Poor
1990	1750	1100	650	400	225

Baer 1911 Monolith Commanche Heavyweight

Exactly as above, with thicker dust cover to add an additional 2 oz. of weight. Introduced in 2001.

NIB	Exc.	V.G.	Good	Fair	Poor
2150	1800	1000	600	375	200

Baer 1911 Stinger

Features shorter Officer's grip frame and Commanche slide and barrel. Many special features. Offered in .45 ACP. Choice of aluminum frame with blued slide; aluminum frame with stainless steel slide; stainless steel frame and slide. Weight in aluminum about 28 oz.; stainless steel about 34 oz. Introduced in 1999. **NOTE:** Add $300 for aluminum frame and blued slide with supported calibers; $340 for aluminum frame with

stainless slide and supported chamber; $140 for stainless frame and slide with supported chamber.

NIB	Exc.	V.G.	Good	Fair	Poor
1890	1600	1050	750	400	225

Baer 1911 Stinger Stainless

Same as above, with stainless steel frame and slide. Introduced in 2001.

NIB	Exc.	V.G.	Good	Fair	Poor
1970	1670	1100	775	425	250

Baer 1911 .38 Super Stinger

Same as above, with blue or chrome finish.

NIB	Exc.	V.G.	Good	Fair	Poor
2650	2000	1500	1000	850	500

Black Baer 1911

Caliber 9mm. DuPont S coating on entire pistol for complete corrosion resistance. Black recon grips. Compact size with 4.25" barrel. All corners rounded for concealed carry. Many special features including slide fitted to frame, Baer speed trigger with crisp 4-lb. pull, tactical extended combat safety, beveled magazine well, polished feed ramp, throated barrel, checkered slide stop, lowered and flared ejection port, checkered front strap at 30 lpi, flat checkered mainspring housing at 20 lpi. Tuned for total reliability. Comes with two 9-round magazines. Introduced in 2016.

NIB	Exc.	V.G.	Good	Fair	Poor
2800	2300	1700	1200	900	450

NEW CONCEPT PISTOLS

Line of 1911 pistols offers custom features at slightly lower cost. Each succeeding grade offers a few more features.

Baer 1911 Concept I

Chambered for .45 ACP. Fitted with BoMar sights.

NIB	Exc.	V.G.	Good	Fair	Poor
1690	1450	975	750	550	300

Baer 1911 Concept II

Same as above. Fitted with Baer adjustable sights.

NIB	Exc.	V.G.	Good	Fair	Poor
1690	1450	975	750	550	300

Baer 1911 Concept III

Same as above, with stainless steel frame. Blued steel slide. BoMar sights.

NIB	Exc.	V.G.	Good	Fair	Poor
1840	1550	975	800	550	300

Baer 1911 Concept IV

Same as above, with Baer adjustable sights.

NIB	Exc.	V.G.	Good	Fair	Poor
1840	1550	975	800	550	300

Baer 1911 Concept V

Model has both stainless steel slide and frame. BoMar sights.

NIB	Exc.	V.G.	Good	Fair	Poor
1950	1890	975	800	550	300

Baer 1911 Concept V 6"

Identical to Concept V, with addition of 6" barrel and slide. Introduced in 1999.

NIB	Exc.	V.G.	Good	Fair	Poor
2050	1990	1075	900	650	350

Baer 1911 Concept VI

Same as above. Fitted with Baer adjustable sights.

NIB	Exc.	V.G.	Good	Fair	Poor
2050	1990	1075	900	650	350

Baer 1911 Concept VI L.W.

Same as above. Built on aluminum frame, with supported chamber. National Match barrel.

NIB	Exc.	V.G.	Good	Fair	Poor
2050	1990	1075	900	650	350

Baer 1911 Concept VII

Features all blued 4.5" steel frame and slide. Baer fixed night sights.

NIB	Exc.	V.G.	Good	Fair	Poor
2050	1990	1075	900	650	350

Baer 1911 Concept VIII

Same as above, with stainless steel slide and frame. Fixed combat night sights standard.

NIB	Exc.	V.G.	Good	Fair	Poor
2100	1850	1500	1250	700	300

Baer 1911 Concept IX

Version has lightweight aluminum frame, with 4.5" steel slide.

NIB	Exc.	V.G.	Good	Fair	Poor
2100	1850	1500	1250	700	300

Baer 1911 Concept X

Features 4.5" stainless steel slide. Lightweight aluminum frame.

NIB	Exc.	V.G.	Good	Fair	Poor
2100	1850	1500	1250	700	300

Baer Lightweight .22-caliber 1911 Models

4.5" Model with fixed sights

NIB	Exc.	V.G.	Good	Fair	Poor
1525	1400	950	800	550	300

5" Model with fixed sights

NIB	Exc.	V.G.	Good	Fair	Poor
1625	1400	950	800	550	300

5" Model with Bo-Mar sights

NIB	Exc.	V.G.	Good	Fair	Poor
1700	1475	1000	850	600	300

Baer Limited Edition Presentation Grade 1911

Fully hand engraved Baer 1911, with special bluing in presentation wooden box.

NIB	Exc.	V.G.	Good	Fair	Poor
6590	3995	2500	1750	1150	500

Model 1911 Twenty-Fifth Anniversary

Custom-engraved limited collector edition .45 ACP semi-automatic. Built on fully functional equipped Baer Premier II. Hand engraved both sides of slide and frame. Les Baer signature. Inlaid with white gold. Ivory grips. Deep blue finish. Presentation box. Introduced 2006.

NIB	Exc.	V.G.	Good	Fair	Poor
6590	3995	2500	1750	1150	500

Ultimate Recon

Semi-automatic with integral Picatinny rail, 5" barrel, .45 ACP. Blue or chrome. Comes with SureFire X-200 light. Fixed sights. 4-lb. trigger. Two 8-round magazines. Cocobolo grips. **NOTE:** Add $500 for hard chrome.

NIB	Exc.	V.G.	Good	Fair	Poor
3070	2590	1650	1100	775	450

RIFLES

AR .223 Ultimate Super Varmint

Fitted with choice of 18", 20" or 24" heavy barrels, with 1-in-12 twist. Flat top rail. Choice of single-/two-stage trigger. Aluminum free-floating handguard. Bear Coat finish. Introduced in 2000.

NIB	Exc.	V.G.	Good	Fair	Poor
1975	1600	1300	900	600	300

AR .223 Ultimate Super Match

Introduced in 2002. Wide number of custom features, with barrel lengths from 18" to 24". Special match carrier with integral rail system.

NIB	Exc.	V.G.	Good	Fair	Poor
2125	1700	1400	1000	750	500

AR .223 M4-A2 Flattop

Features flat top rail, match bolt and carrier. 16" barrel has integral compensator. Single-stage trigger. Knights Armament Systems rail adapter. Bear Coat finish. Introduced in 2000.

NIB	Exc.	V.G.	Good	Fair	Poor
2175	1725	1425	1025	675	400

AR .223 IPSC Action Model

Similar to above, with 18" Super Match heavy barrel. Integral compensator. Introduced in 2000.

NIB	Exc.	V.G.	Good	Fair	Poor
2300	1875	1550	1100	700	450

AR .223 Ultimate NRA Match

Numerous custom features. Fitted with 30" barrel. Special front and rear sights. **NOTE:** Add $750 for special sight package.

NIB	Exc.	V.G.	Good	Fair	Poor
2500	2000	1350	900	600	375

Bullpup Muzzleloader

.50-caliber muzzleloader. Fitted with 28" stainless steel barrel, Williams front sight and M16 National Match rear sight. Maple or synthetic stock. Internal ignition system. Discontinued. **NOTE:** Add $30 for maple stock and stainless steel.

NIB	Exc.	V.G.	Good	Fair	Poor
750	575	395	300	225	165

Thunder Ranch Rifle

.223 model fitted with bench-rest 16" barrel. Upper receiver has carry handle and top rail. Free-floating handguard, jewel two-stage trigger, floating front sight and many other custom features. "Thunder Ranch" logo stamped on lower receiver. Weight about 7.5 lbs. Introduced in 2004.

NIB	Exc.	V.G.	Good	Fair	Poor
2500	2000	1350	900	600	375

Monolith .308 S.W.A.T.

Military type match sniper rifle. Chambered in .308 Winchester. Solid full-length Picatinny rail for scope mounting. DuPont S coating on barrel, two-stage trigger group with choice of 18", 20" (standard) or 24" barrel. Two magazines and soft case included. Introduced in 2011.

NIB	Exc.	V.G.	Good	Fair	Poor
3500	3000	2600	2000	1000	500

BAFORD ARMS, INC.
Bristol, Tennessee

Thunder Derringer

.410 bore or .44 Special single-shot pistol, with 3" interchangeable barrels and spur trigger. Additional interchangeable barrels are chambered in calibers from .22 to 9mm. Also available with scope. Blued, with walnut grip. Introduced in 1988. **NOTE:** Add $50 for interchangeable barrel.

NIB	Exc.	V.G.	Good	Fair	Poor
175	110	85	70	55	35

Fire Power Model 35

9mm semi-automatic pistol, with 4.75" barrel, Millett adjustable sights and 14-shot magazine. Fitted with combat safety hammer and Pachmayr grips. Stainless steel. Introduced in 1988.

NIB	Exc.	V.G.	Good	Fair	Poor
550	450	365	300	250	125

BAIKAL
Izhevsk, Russia

Baikal is a Russian firearms manufacturer. A history that goes back to World War II when it made military weapons like Tokarev pistols for the old Soviet Union. After the war, company expanded into sporting firearms, mainly shotguns.

IJ-27E1C

12- or 20-gauge Magnum over/under shotgun, with 26" Skeet-Skeet or 28" Modified-Full ventilated rib barrels, single-selective trigger and extractors. Blued, with walnut stock.

NIB	Exc.	V.G.	Good	Fair	Poor
375	275	200	150	100	75

TOZ - 34

12- or 28-gauge double-barrel shotgun, with 26" or 28" barrels, double triggers, cocking indicators and extractors. Blued, with checkered walnut stock. Also available with silver-plated receiver.

NIB	Exc.	V.G.	Good	Fair	Poor
400	300	250	200	100	75

Model MC-8-0

12-gauge double-barrel shotgun, with 26" Skeet-Skeet or 28" Full-Modified barrels, hand fitted action and engraved receiver.

NIB	Exc.	V.G.	Good	Fair	Poor
2000	1250	950	700	500	250

Model MC-5-105

Model TOZ-34, with engraved receiver.

NIB	Exc.	V.G.	Good	Fair	Poor
1200	850	700	500	300	150

Model MC-7

As above, with relief engraved receiver.

NIB	Exc.	V.G.	Good	Fair	Poor
2250	1750	1200	800	550	250

IZH18/MP18

Single-barrel shotgun chambered for 12-, 20-gauge or .410 bore. Choice of 26.5" or 29.5" barrels. Hardwood stock and ejectors. Introduced in 1999.

NIB	Exc.	V.G.	Good	Fair	Poor
95	75	50	35	25	10

IZK18MAX

Similar to above, with polished nickel receiver, ventilated rib, walnut stock, screw-in chokes and ejectors. Offered in 12-, 20-gauge and .410 bore.

NIB	Exc.	V.G.	Good	Fair	Poor
170	125	100	75	50	25

IZH43

Side-by-side available in 12-, 16-, 20-, 28-gauge or .410 bore. Barrel lengths 20" to 28" depending on gauge. Internal hammers. Single-selective trigger, ejectors. Walnut stock. **NOTE:** Add $80 for 28-gauge and .410 bore.

NIB	Exc.	V.G.	Good	Fair	Poor
350	275	200	150	100	75

IZH43K

Introduced in 1999. A 12- or 20-gauge, 3" side-by-side external hammer shotgun. Barrel lengths 18.5", 20", 24", 26" and 28". Single-selective or double trigger. Engraved side plates. Walnut stock with pistol-grip. Weight about 7.3 lbs. **NOTE:** Deduct $40 for double triggers.

NIB	Exc.	V.G.	Good	Fair	Poor
375	300	250	175	125	100

MP213 Coach Gun

Similar to above, with internal hammers. Single or double triggers. Weight about 7 lbs. Barrel inserts for .45-70 were offered. **NOTE:** Add 25 percent for .45-70 inserts.

NIB	Exc.	V.G.	Good	Fair	Poor
650	500	400	350	100	75

IZH27

Over/under gun chambered for 12-, 20-, 28-gauge and .410 bore. Choice of 26.5" or 28.5" barrels. Walnut stock. Single trigger with ejectors. Fixed chokes. **NOTE:** Add $35 for screw-in chokes; $85 for 28-gauge and .410 bore.

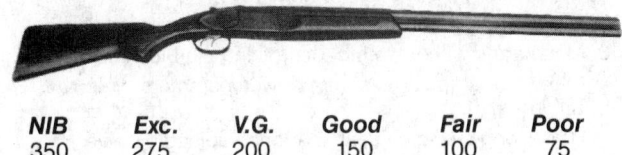

NIB	Exc.	V.G.	Good	Fair	Poor
350	275	200	150	100	75

MP233

Over/under gun chambered for 12-gauge 3" shell, with choice of 26", 28" or 30" barrels. Walnut checkered stock. Single or double triggers. Screw-in chokes. Removable trigger assembly. Weight about 7.3 lbs. Introduced in 1999.

NIB	Exc.	V.G.	Good	Fair	Poor
700	600	500	400	175	100

IZH94/MP94

Over/under combination gun, with 12-gauge upper barrel and centerfire rifle lower barrel. Barrel lengths 24" or 26". Model offered as an over/under rifle in calibers .222, .223, 6.5x55, .308, .30-06 or 7.62x39. A .410/.22LR or .410/.22 WMR model is available. Walnut stock, single or double trigger. Weight about 8 - 10 lbs. Open sights. **NOTE:** Deduct 40 percent for .410.

NIB	Exc.	V.G.	Good	Fair	Poor
525	475	425	350	300	175

IZH81

Pump-action shotgun chambered for 12-gauge 3" shells. Barrel lengths 20", 26" or 28". Five-round detachable magazine. Walnut stock. **NOTE:** Add $60 for ventilated rib.

NIB	Exc.	V.G.	Good	Fair	Poor
300	225	165	125	97	50

MP131K

Pump-action shotgun, with choice of two different feeding sources: tubular magazine or detachable 3- or 5-round box magazine.

NIB	Exc.	V.G.	Good	Fair	Poor
300	225	165	125	97	50

MP133

Slide-action shotgun chambered for 12-gauge 3.5" shell. Available barrel lengths 20", 24", 26" or 28". Ventilated rib on all barrel lengths except 20". Walnut stock. Choke tubes for all barrel lengths except 20" (Cylinder choke). Introduced in 2001.

NIB	Exc.	V.G.	Good	Fair	Poor
300	225	165	125	95	50

MP153

Semi-automatic shotgun chambered for 12-gauge 3" shell. Barrels 26" or 28". Walnut or black synthetic stock. Weight about 7.8 lbs. Screw-in chokes. Introduced in 1999.

NIB	Exc.	V.G.	Good	Fair	Poor
400	325	250	200	100	65

IZH35

Semi-automatic pistol chambered for .22 LR cartridge. Fully adjustable target-grip, adjustable trigger assembly, cocking indicator, detachable scope. Fitted with 6" barrel. Introduced in 2000.

NIB	Exc.	V.G.	Good	Fair	Poor
500	400	350	200	165	95

MP310

Originally imported as Model IZH2. Over/under now marketed as MP310. Offered in 12-, 20-gauge or .410 bore, with 26" or 28" barrels. Hammer forged barrels, machined steel receiver. Monoblock checkered walnut two-piece stock. Hard chrome-lined barrels, ventilated rib, ejectors, auto safety and single selective trigger. **NOTE:** Add $100 for Sporting Clays model.

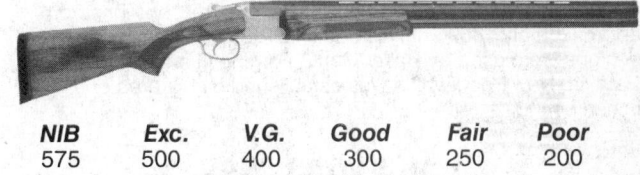

NIB	Exc.	V.G.	Good	Fair	Poor
575	500	400	300	250	200

MP220

Side-by-side field gun has single selective trigger, ejectors, machined steel boxlock receiver, checkered walnut stock with recoil pad, splinter fore-end, automatic tang safety and screw-in chokes. In 12-, 16-, 20-, 28-gauge and .410 bore. Weight 8 to 10 lbs.

NIB	Exc.	V.G.	Good	Fair	Poor
300	250	200	175	150	100

CURRENTLY IMPORTED BAIKAL SHOTGUNS
Importer—European American Armory

A custom-made over/under shotgun with detachable sidelocks. Produced in limited quantities and most often to the purchaser's specifications.

BAILONS GUNMAKERS, LTD.
Birmingham, England

Most products of this company **were** produced strictly on custom order. No longer in business.

Hunting Rifle

Bolt-action sporting rifle. Produced in a variety of calibers with 24" barrel, open sights, double-set triggers and 3- or 4-shot magazine. Blued, with well-figured walnut stock. Values listed for standard grade rifle.

NIB	Exc.	V.G.	Good	Fair	Poor
3500	2950	2450	1900	675	325

BAKER, M.A.
Fayetteville, North Carolina

In business from 1857 through 1862. Baker produced sporting arms prior to Civil War. During Civil War, Baker altered muskets and "common rifles". In addition, it is thought, Baker made rifles for State of North Carolina with lockplates stamped "M.A. Baker/Fayetteville/N.C.". These rifles resembled U.S. Model 1841 rifle and had these characteristics: overall length 51.5"; barrel length 35.125"; caliber .50.

NIB	Exc.	V.G.	Good	Fair	Poor
—	—	26000	13500	3200	1500

BAKER, THOMAS

Baker shotguns and rifles were extensively imported into United States during nineteenth and early twentieth centuries. His premises were as follows:

1 Stonecutter Street	1838-1844
Bury Street, St. James	1844-1850
34 St. James Street	1850
88 Fleet Street	1851-1881
88 Fleet Street & 21 Cockspur Street	1882-1898
88 Fleet Street & 29 Glasshouse Street	1899-1905
29 Glasshouse Street	1905-1915
64 Haymarket	1915

BAKER, WILLIAM
Marathon, Syracuse and Ithaca, New York

William Baker designed and built double barrel shotguns from approximately 1869 until his death in 1889. His hammerless designs were used by Baker Gun & Forging Company of Batavia, New York, which was established by his brother Elias in early 1890.

BAKER GAS SEAL
London, England

.577-caliber percussion revolver, with 6.5" octagonal barrel and 6-shot cylinder. When hammer is cocked, cylinder is forced forward tightly against barrel breech, thus creating a gas seal. Blued case hardened, with walnut grips.

NIB	Exc.	V.G.	Good	Fair	Poor
—	2500	1900	1500	875	350

BAKER GUN & FORGING CO.
Batavia, New York

Baker Gun & Forging Company founded in early 1890, by Elias Baker, brother of William Baker. Made from drop forged parts, Baker single-/double barrel shotguns quickly gained a reputation for strength and reliability among shooters of the period. Offered in a wide variety of grades, from plain utilitarian to heavily embellished models. Baker shotguns have in recent years become highly collectible. Company was sold on December 24, 1919, to H. & D. Folsom Arms Company of Norwich, Connecticut. Folsom Company had, for almost 20 years, been Baker Company's sole New York City agent and had marketed at least one Baker model that was only made for them. From 1919 to approximately 1923, Folsom continued to assemble and make Baker shotguns. Late model Bakers were made by Crescent Firearms Company and have serial numbers with an "F" suffix.

Baker Gun & Forging Company was the first American arms manufacturer to:

1. Make a single barrel trap shotgun.
2. Make a single barrel trap shotgun with ventilated rib.
3. Make arms with an intercepting firing pin block safety.
4. Make a double barrel shotgun, with hammers directly behind the firing pins.
5. Use a long swinging sear, that once adjusted, gave consistent trigger pull throughout the working life of an arm. Baker shotguns manufactured between 1913 and 1923, that were engraved by Rudolph J. Kornbrath, command substantial price premiums over values listed.

Baker Trap Gun

12-gauge single-barrel boxlock shotgun, with 30" or 32" barrel. Blued case hardened, with walnut stock.

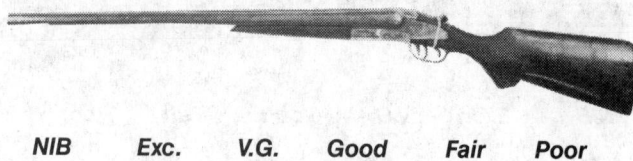

NIB	Exc.	V.G.	Good	Fair	Poor
—	1800	1450	1050	500	250

Elite Grade

Standard scrollwork. Simple game scenes engraved on receiver.

NIB	Exc.	V.G.	Good	Fair	Poor
—	3200	2750	2000	1000	600

Superba

Heavily engraved on receiver and sides of barrel breech.

NIB	Exc.	V.G.	Good	Fair	Poor
—	5500	4650	3500	2400	1200

Expert Grade Double Shotgun

Highest grade shotgun manufactured by Baker Gun & Forging Company. General specifications as above. Stock of imported English or French walnut. Engraving full coverage type and partially chiselled. Automatic ejectors and single trigger, if requested. Built on special order only.

NIB	Exc.	V.G.	Good	Fair	Poor
—	7000	5500	4000	1800	750

Deluxe Grade Double Shotgun

Designation given those Expert Grade shotguns produced by H. & D. Folsom from 1919 to 1923. Characteristics identical to those listed for Baker Expert Grade Double Shotgun. **NOTE:** Add 80 percent for this model. Very rare.

Black Beauty Double Shotgun

Made solely for H. & D. Folsom Arms Company. A 12- or 16-gauge double barrel shotgun, with sidelocks; 26", 28", 30" or 32" barrels in 12-gauge; 26", 28" or 30" barrels in 16-gauge. Barrels blued, receiver case hardened, sideplates finished with black oxide, stock is walnut. Automatic ejectors and single trigger are extra cost options.

NIB	Exc.	V.G.	Good	Fair	Poor
—	1150	1000	850	700	250

Grade S Double Shotgun

As above, with simple engraving.

NIB	Exc.	V.G.	Good	Fair	Poor
—	2400	2000	1100	500	250

Grade R Double Shotgun

As above, with case hardened sideplates. Engraved with simple scroll-work and game scenes.

NIB	Exc.	V.G.	Good	Fair	Poor
—	3200	2600	1700	1100	500

Paragon Grade Shotgun

As above, with finely cut scrollwork and detailed game scenes engraved on sideplates. Stock of finely figured walnut.

NIB	Exc.	V.G.	Good	Fair	Poor
—	5000	4000	3000	2000	800

Paragon Grade—Model NN

As above, but more finely engraved. Built on special order only. Automatic ejectors.

NIB	Exc.	V.G.	Good	Fair	Poor
—	4500	3500	2700	2000	800

Batavia Special

12- or 16-gauge double-barrel shotgun, with sidelocks; 28", 30" or 32" barrels in 12-gauge; 28" or 30" barrels in 16-gauge. Blued case hardened, with walnut stock. Double triggers.

NIB	Exc.	V.G.	Good	Fair	Poor
—	850	550	450	225	175

Batavia Brush Gun

12- or 16-gauge double-barrel shotgun, with sidelocks and 26" barrels. Blued case hardened, with walnut stock. Sling rings and swivels optional.

NIB	Exc.	V.G.	Good	Fair	Poor
—	750	600	550	225	175

Batavia Leader

12- or 16-gauge double-barrel shotgun, with sidelocks; 26", 28", 30" or 32" barrels in 12-gauge; 26", 28" or 30" barrels in 16-gauge. Blued case hardened, with walnut stock. Double triggers.

NIB	Exc.	V.G.	Good	Fair	Poor
—	1500	1000	600	400	200

Batavia Damascus

As above, with Damascus barrels.

NIB	Exc.	V.G.	Good	Fair	Poor
—	1750	1200	600	225	175

Baker Hammer Gun

10-, 12- or 16-gauge double-barrel shotgun, with sidehammers. 30" and 32" barrels in 10-gauge; 26" to 32" barrels in 12-gauge; 26" to 30" barrels in 16-gauge. Browned case hardened, with walnut stock. Double triggers.

NIB	Exc.	V.G.	Good	Fair	Poor
—	450	350	275	195	100

Batavia Automatic Rifle

.22-caliber semi-automatic rifle, with 24" round barrel. Detachable 7-shot magazine. Blued, with walnut stock.

NIB	Exc.	V.G.	Good	Fair	Poor
—	625	550	300	160	70

BALL REPEATING CARBINE
Lamson & Co.
Windsor, Vermont

Ball Repeating Carbine

.50-caliber lever-action repeating carbine, with 20.5" round barrel and 7-shot magazine. Receiver marked "E.G. Lamson & Co./Windsor, Vt./U.S./Ball's Patent/June 23, 1863/Mar. 15, 1864". Blued case hardened, with walnut stock. Late production examples of this carbine have been noted with browned or bright barrels. In excess of 1,500 made between 1864 and 1867.

Courtesy Milwaukee Public Museum, Milwaukee, Wisconsin

NIB	Exc.	V.G.	Good	Fair	Poor
—	—	5500	3000	1100	500

BALLARD, C. H.
Worcester, Massachusetts

Single-Shot Derringer

.41-caliber rimfire spur trigger single-shot pistol, with 2.75" barrel marked "Ballard's". Blued, with silver-plated frame. Walnut grips. Manufactured during 1870s. **NOTE:** Add 20 percent for iron frame model.

NIB	Exc.	V.G.	Good	Fair	Poor
—	—	1775	1450	550	225

BALLARD PATENT ARMS
(until 1873; after 1875, see MARLIN)

On Nov. 5, 1861 C.H. Ballard, of Worcester, Massachusetts, received a patent for a breechloading mechanism that would remain in production for nearly thirty years. Ballard patented a breechblock that tilted down at its front to expose breech by activating lever/triggerguard. During the twelve years that followed, Ballard rifles, carbines and shotguns were produced by five interrelated companies. Four of these were successive: Ball & Williams, R. Ball & Co. (both of Worcester, Massachusetts), Merrimack Arms & Manufacturing Co. and Brown Manufacturing Company (both of Newburyport, Massachusetts). These four companies produced Ballard arms in a successive serial range (1 through approximately 22,000), all marked on top of frame and barrel where it joins the frame. In 1863 another company, Dwight, Chapin & Company of Bridgeport, Connecticut, also produced Ballard rifles in a larger frame size, but in a different serial range (1 through about 1,900), usually marked on left side of frame below agents' mark. Large frame carbines and rifles were produced to fulfill a U.S. War Department contract initially for 10,000 of each, subsequently reduced to 1,000 of each, issued to Merwin & Bray sole agents for Ballard Patent Arms between 1862 and 1866. Most production during this period concentrated on military contracts, either for U.S. War Department or state of Kentucky, although state of New York also purchased 500 for its state militia.

Ballard (Ball & Williams) Sporting Rifles, First Type (Serial numbers 1-100)

Barrel length 24"; caliber .38 rimfire. Markings: "BALL & WILLIAMS/Worcester, Mass." and "BALLARD'S PATENT/Nov. 5, 1861" on octagonal barrel. Distinctive feature of earliest production of Ballard rifles is presence of internal extractor conforming to patent specifications. After approximately 100 rifles, this feature was dropped in favor of a manual extractor located under the barrel.

Courtesy Milwaukee Public Museum, Milwaukee, Wisconsin

NIB	Exc.	V.G.	Good	Fair	Poor
—	—	5000	3000	1250	500

Ballard (Ball & Williams) Sporting Rifles, Second Type (Serial numbers 200-1600, and 1600-14,000, interspersed with martial production)

Barrel length 24", 28" or 30" usually octagonal, but part round/part octagonal as well; calibers .32, .38 and .44 rimfire. Markings: "BALL & WILLIAMS/Worcester, Mass.", "BALLARD'S PATENT/Nov. 5, 1861" and "MERWIN & BRAY, AGT'S/ NEW YORK", on facets of barrel until about serial no. 9000. Thereafter, patent name and date on right side of frame and manufacturer and agents on left side of frame. On early production (200 to 1500), extractor knob is smaller and crescent shaped. Early production (prior to about serial no. 10,000) have solid breechblocks; after that number breechblocks are made in two halves. A few of these arms were made with bronze frames to facilitate engraving and plating. These should command a higher premium.

NIB	Exc.	V.G.	Good	Fair	Poor
—	—	2000	1650	730	280

Ballard (Ball & Williams) Sporting Rifles, Third Type (Serial numbers 14,000-15,000)

These arms essentially the same as second type in characteristics, but have Merwin & Bray's alternate percussion mechanism built into breechblock. Hammer is accordingly marked on left side "PATENTED JAN. 5, 1864".

NIB	Exc.	V.G.	Good	Fair	Poor
—	—	1400	1100	550	225

Ballard (Ball & Williams) Military Carbines (Serial numbers 1500-7500, and 8500-10500)

Overall length 37.25"; barrel (bore) length 22"; caliber .44 rimfire. Markings: same as Ballard/Ball & Williams sporting rifles second type. Additional marks on U.S. War Department purchases include inspector's initials "MM" or "GH" on left side of frame and "MM" on barrel, breechblock, buttplate and on left side of buttstock in script within an oval cartouche. Three thousand of earlier production (serial numbers 1700 through about 5000) of these carbines were sold to state of Kentucky under an August 1862 contract, extended in April 1863. In November 1863, Kentucky contracted for an additional 1,000 carbines. In the interim, state of New York purchased 500 for distribution to its militia. U.S. War Department ordered 5,000 under a contract signed in January of 1864, but Ball & Williams delivered only 1,500 (serial numbers noted in range of 9800 through 10600) while concentrating production on their more lucrative Kentucky contract. Another 600 of the federal contract were partially inspected (serial numbers about 6500 to 7100-MM in cartouche in stock only), but were rejected because barrels had been rifled prior to proofing; these were sold to Kentucky in September 1864 on an open market purchase. Carbines marked with federal inspection marks usually bring a premium.

Courtesy Milwaukee Public Museum, Milwaukee, Wisconsin

NIB	Exc.	V.G.	Good	Fair	Poor
—	—	5775	4150	1750	675

Ballard (Ball & Williams) "Kentucky" Half-Stock Rifles

Overall length 45.375"; barrel (bore) length 30"; caliber .44 rimfire. These half-stock rifles bear standard Ball & Williams markings upon their barrels. In addition they have state ownership mark "KENTUCKY" on barrel forward of rear sights. Total of 1,000 (serial numbers about 7100 through 8550) were contracted by Kentucky in November 1863 and delivered between January and April 1864.

Courtesy Milwaukee Public Museum, Milwaukee, Wisconsin

NIB	Exc.	V.G.	Good	Fair	Poor
—	—	2300	1900	800	350

Ballard (Ball & Williams) "Kentucky" Full-Stock Rifles

Overall length 45.25"; barrel (bore) length 30"; caliber .46 rimfire. Marked on frame with standard Ball & Williams manufacturer (left), agent (left) and patent (right) markings. Rifles are additionally distinguished by state ownership mark "KENTUCKY" stamped into top of frame near breech. Kentucky contracted for 3,000 of these arms in November 1863, initially in .56-caliber. However, by mutual consent of state and contractors, in February 1864 caliber of arms was changed to .46. All deliveries were made in this caliber, beginning in July 1864 and continuing until March 1865 (serial numbers 10,400 to 14,500).

Courtesy Milwaukee Public Museum, Milwaukee, Wisconsin

NIB	Exc.	V.G.	Good	Fair	Poor
—	—	2100	1750	620	295

Ballard (Dwight, Chapin & Co.) Carbines

Overall length 37.75"; barrel (bore) length 22"; caliber .56 rimfire. Markings: on left side of round-topped frame "BALLARD'S PATENT/NOV. 5 1861"; on right side of frame "DWIGHT, CHAPIN & CO./BRIDGEPORT CONN." (through serial no. about 125, deleted after that number) over "MERWIN & BRAY/AGT'S N.Y." over serial no. Inspection letters "D" frequently appear on carbines with Dwight, Chapin, & Co. markings, indicative of preliminary inspection by E. M. Dustin, of U.S. Ordnance Department. Often mistaken as early Ballard production from a fictitious Fall River, Massachusetts, factory, these carbines and their complementing rifles were in fact not placed into production until 1863, as evident by split, two-piece breechblocks. Both carbines and rifles originated from a contract entered into between U.S. War Department and Merwin & Bray in October 1862 for 10,000 of each arm, subsequently reduced to 1,000 of each by Commission on Ordnance and Ordnance Stores. Because Ball & Williams facilities were tied up with Kentucky contracts, Merwin & Bray turned to small parts maker of Dwight, Chapin & Co. in Bridgeport, Connecticut. Although they tooled for production, they fell short of scheduled delivery dates and although about 100 carbines had been inspected, no deliveries were accepted (due to caliber problems) by U.S. government, effectively bankrupting Dwight, Chapin & Co. Completed carbines and unfinished parts were sent to Worcester and assembled by Ball & Williams. Merwin & Bray sold all 1,000 carbines in Kentucky in April 1864 on an open market purchase.

Courtesy Milwaukee Public Museum, Milwaukee, Wisconsin

NIB	Exc.	V.G.	Good	Fair	Poor
—	—	2450	2000	825	350

Ballard (Dwight, Chapin & Co.) Full-Stock Rifles

Overall length 53"; barrel (bore) length 30"; caliber .56 rimfire. Markings: same as Dwight, Chapin & Co. carbines, but none found with "DWIGHT, CHAPIN & CO./BRIDGEPORT, CONN." stamping above agents marks. History of these rifles same as .56-caliber carbines, with serial numbers interspersed in production of carbines (1 through 1850). Evidently only about 650 rifles were completed of the 1,000 set up. Of these, 35 were sold to a U.S. agent in Florida in February 1864 and 600 to Kentucky in April 1864 with the 1,000 carbines.

NIB	Exc.	V.G.	Good	Fair	Poor
—	—	2450	2000	825	350

Ballard (R. Ball & Co.) Sporting Rifles

Overall length varies according to barrel length; barrel (bore) length usually 24", 28" and 30"; calibers .32, .38, .44 and .46 rimfire. Markings: frame markings of R. Ball & Co. rifles are similar to Ball & Williams production, only eliminating Ball & Williams marking on left side. Cartridge size, e.g. "No. 44", usually also stamped on top of barrel or frame. Merwin & Bray's patented alternate ignition device usually present with left side of hammer usually marked "PATENTED JAN. 5, 1864". Serial numbers (which follow in sequence with Ball & Williams production. i.e. after no. about 15,800) appear on top of barrel and frame. After William Williams withdrew from Ball & Williams partnership in mid-1865, business continued under name of R. Ball & Co., with Richard Ball's son-in-law, E.J. Halstead, in charge after the former's paralytic stroke in the fall of 1865.

Courtesy Rock Island Auction Company

NIB	Exc.	V.G.	Good	Fair	Poor
—	—	2650	2200	975	400

Ballard (R. Ball & Co.) Carbines

Overall length 37.25"; barrel (bore) length 22"; caliber .44 rimfire. Markings: same as R. Ball & Co. sporting rifles; "No. 44" on top of frame near breech. Although firm evidence is elusive, approximately 1,000 of these carbines were manufactured in anticipation of a Canadian contract, which never came to fruition. Serial numbers are interspersed with sporting rifles, in 16,400 through 17,700 range. All are equipped with Merwin & Bray dual ignition block.

NIB	Exc.	V.G.	Good	Fair	Poor
—	—	1825	1500	580	225

Ballard (Merrimack Arms & Manufacturing Co.) Sporting Rifles

Overall length varies with barrel length; usual barrel lengths 24", 28", 30"; calibers .22, .32, .44, .46, .50 rimfire. Markings: left side of frame marked with both manufacturing and patent marks, "MERRIMACK ARMS & MFG. CO./NEWBURYPORT, MASS." over "BALLARD'S PATENT/ NOV. 5, 1861". Caliber usually marked on top of barrel or frame, e.g. "No. 38" together with serial no. Left side of hammer marked "PATENTED JAN. 5, 1864" if breech fitted with Merwin & Bray's alternate ignition device. In spring of 1866 Edward Bray of Brooklyn, New York, former partner of Joseph Merwin, purchased Ballard machinery from R. Ball & Co. and set up a new plant in Newburyport, Massachusetts, primarily for production of sporting rifles. Glut of surplus arms on the market following American Civil War, however, forced him into bankruptcy in early 1869, after producing only about 2,000 Ballard rifles, carbines and a limited number of 20-gauge shotguns. Serial numbers continue in sequence of Ball & Williams/R. Ball & Co. production (serial numbers about 18,000 through 20,300). Prices of these rifles will vary considerably depending on degree of finish or engraving.

NIB	Exc.	V.G.	Good	Fair	Poor
—	—	2200	1900	775	350

Ballard (Merrimack Arms & Manufacturing Co.) Carbines

Overall length 37.25"; barrel (bore) length 22"; caliber .44 rimfire. Markings: same as Merrimack Arms & Mfg. Co. sporting rifles. In March 1866, state of New York purchased 100 Ballard carbines (serial numbers about 18,500 to 18,600) for use by its prison guards. In January 1870, an additional 70 (serial numbers 19,400 to 19,500) were purchased from New York City arms merchants Merwin, Hulbert & Co. to arm guards at Sing Sing Prison. Between these two purchases Merrimack Arms & Mfg. Co. had shortened its new "tangless" frames by .125", prime distinction between the two purchases. Despite rarity of both types of carbines, they do not command high prices.

NIB	Exc.	V.G.	Good	Fair	Poor
—	—	1750	1400	550	300

Ballard (Brown Mfg. Co.) Sporting Rifles

Dimensions: same as Merrimack Arms & Mfg. Co. sporting rifles. Markings: left side of frame marked with manufacturer, "BROWN MFG. CO. NEWBURYPORT, MASS.". Over patent, "BALLARD'S PATENT/ NOV. 5, 1861". Serial no. on top of barrel and frame. Upon the failure of Merrimack Arms & Manufacturing Company in early 1869, plant was purchased by John Hamilton Brown, who continued producing Ballard patent rifles until 1873 in a serial range consecutive with that of its three predecessors (Ball & Williams, R. Ball & Co. and Merrimack Arms & Mfg. Co.). Approximately 2,000 Ballard arms were produced during period of Brown's manufacture of Ballard (serial numbers about 20,325 through 22,100). Brown-made Ballards' tend to exhibit finer finishing than earlier produced rifles, accounting for their average higher value. Special features, such as breakdown facility and side extractors (on .22 cal. rifles) will also positively affect prices.

Courtesy Rock Island Auction Company

NIB	Exc.	V.G.	Good	Fair	Poor
—	—	2200	1825	675	350

Ballard (Brown Mfg. Co.) Full-Stock Military Rifles

Overall length 52.5"; barrel (bore) length 30"; caliber .46 rimfire. Markings: same as Brown Mfg. Co. sporting rifles, with addition of caliber marking, "No. 46", on top of barrel forward of rear sight. Cause for production of Ballard/Brown military rifle has yet to be determined, but it has been speculated that they were possibly manufactured in anticipation of a sale to France during Franco-Prussian War. In any event, sale was not culminated and many, if not most, of estimated 1,000 produced were "sporterized" by shortening fore-stock and sold by commercial dealers in United States. Serial numbers concentrate in 20,500 through 21,600 range, with sporting rifles interspersed in the sequence. Rifles that have not been sporterized command a premium.

NIB	Exc.	V.G.	Good	Fair	Poor
—	—	2350	1950	800	350

BALLARD RIFLE AND CARTRIDGE CO.
Onsted, Michigan

All models feature American black walnut stocks, case hardening and rust blued barrels. There are a number of special order features that are available with these rifles.

No. 1-1/2 Hunter's Rifle

Features 30" round barrel, single trigger, S lever, plain fore-end and rifle buttstock. Blade front sight and Rocky Mountain rear sight are standard. Calibers from .32-40 to .50-70. Weight about 10.5 lbs.

NIB	Exc.	V.G.	Good	Fair	Poor
3000	2350	1950	1200	700	300

No. 1-3/4 Far West Rifle

Offered with 30" round barrel in standard or heavy weight. Single-/double-set triggers, S lever, ring-style lever, blade front sight and Rocky Mountain rear sight. Offered in calibers from .32-40 to .50-90. Weight with standard 30" barrel about 10.5 lbs.; heavyweight barrel 11.75 lbs.

NIB	Exc.	V.G.	Good	Fair	Poor
2900	2400	1900	1200	700	300

No. 2 Sporting Model

Stock in plain walnut, with crescent butt. Offered in 24", 26", 28" or 30" octagon barrel, with blade front and Rocky Mountain rear sights. Straight-grip action with S lever, in calibers .38-40, .44-40 and .45 Colt. Discontinued.

NIB	Exc.	V.G.	Good	Fair	Poor
2050	1650	1300	1225	700	300

No. 3 Gallery Rifle

Chambered for .22-caliber rimfire cartridge. Features 24", 26" or 30" lightweight octagon barrel. Rifle-style buttstock, with steel crescent buttplate, S lever, blade and Rocky Mountain sights. Weight with standard 26" barrel about 7.5 lbs.

NIB	Exc.	V.G.	Good	Fair	Poor
3000	2650	2300	1200	700	300

No. 3F Fine Gallery Rifle

Same as above, with fancy checkered walnut stock, pistol-grip, single-/double-set triggers, full-loop lever, light Schuetzen buttstock, globe front and tang rear sight. Weight with standard 26" barrel about 7.75 lbs.

NIB	Exc.	V.G.	Good	Fair	Poor
3500	3000	2400	1500	750	300

No. 4 Perfection Model

Features plain walnut stock, with rifle or shotgun butt. Offered in 28", 30" or 32" octagon barrel, with blade front sight and Rocky Mountain rear sight. Straight-grip action, with single-/double-set triggers. S lever or ring lever. Calibers from .32-40 to .50-90.

NIB	Exc.	V.G.	Good	Fair	Poor
3400	2900	2300	1200	700	300

No. 4-1/2 Mid-Range Model

Features checkered fancy walnut stock. Standard or heavy weight half octagon barrel 30" or 32", with single-/double-set triggers. Pistol-grip hard rubber or steel shotgun butt, horn fore-end cap, full-loop lever and globe front sight. Offered in calibers from .32-40 to .40-70. Weight with standard barrel 10.75 lbs.; heavy barrel 11.5 lbs.

NIB	Exc.	V.G.	Good	Fair	Poor
3200	2650	2100	1100	600	250

No. 5 Pacific Model

Features 30" or 32" octagon barrel in standard or heavy weight. Stocks in rifle or shotgun configuration, double-set triggers, ring lever, blade front sight and Rocky Mountain rear sight. Calibers from .38-55 to .50-90. Weight with standard 30" barrel 10.75 lbs.; heavyweight barrel 12 lbs.

NIB	Exc.	V.G.	Good	Fair	Poor
3350	2600	2250	1200	700	300

No. 5-1/2 Montana Model

Model has fancy walnut stock, double-set triggers and ring lever. Shotgun steel butt. Barrels 28", 30" or 32" extra heavy octagon, in calibers .45-70, .45-110 and .50-90. Under barrel wiping rod. Weight about 14.5 lbs.

NIB	Exc.	V.G.	Good	Fair	Poor
3300	2600	2000	110	600	225

No. 6 Off-Hand Rifle Model (Schuetzen)

Features fancy walnut checkered stock, with hand rubbed finish. Heavy Schuetzen buttplate. Horn insert on fore-end. Choice of 30", 32" or 34" half-octagon barrel, with globe front sight. Straight-grip action with double-set triggers, Schuetzen ball, spur lever and deluxe rust bluing. Offered in .22 LR, .32-40, .38-55, .40-65 and .40-70 calibers.

NIB	Exc.	V.G.	Good	Fair	Poor
3300	2700	2100	1100	600	250

No. 7 Long Range Model

Features fancy walnut checkered stock, with 32" or 34" standard or heavy weight half octagon barrel. Pistol-grip stock, with rubber or steel shotgun butt, single-/double-set triggers, full-loop lever, horn fore-end cap and globe front sight. Calibers from .32-40 to .45-110. Weight with standard 32" barrel 11.75 lbs.; heavyweight barrel 12.25 lbs.

NIB	Exc.	V.G.	Good	Fair	Poor
3100	2550	2200	1100	600	250

No. 8 Union Hill Model

Features 30" or 32" half-octagon standard or heavy barrel, single-/double-set triggers, pistol-grip stock with cheekpiece, full-loop lever, hook Schuetzen buttplate and fancy walnut checkered stock. Offered in calibers from .22 LR to .40-70. Weight with standard barrel in .32-cali-

ber 10.5 lbs.; heavyweight barrel in .40-caliber 11.5 lbs. Not furnished with sights.

NIB	Exc.	V.G.	Good	Fair	Poor
3600	2000	1700	900	450	200

Model 1885 High Wall

Single-shot rifle. Chambered for a wide variety of calibers from .18 Bee to .577 Express. Barrel lengths to 34". American walnut stock. Many options to choose from that will affect price. Introduced in 2000.

NIB	Exc.	V.G.	Good	Fair	Poor
3050	2500	2000	1175	650	275

BALLESTER—MOLINA
See—Hafdasa

BAR-STO PRECISION MACHINE
Burbank, California

Bar-Sto 25

.25-caliber semi-automatic pistol, with brushed stainless steel receiver and slide. Walnut grips. Produced in 1974.

NIB	Exc.	V.G.	Good	Fair	Poor
—	325	275	175	125	100

BARRETT, F.A. MFG. CO.
Murfreesboro, Tennessee

Barrett MRAD

Chambered in .338 Lapua Magnum, with user-changeable barrel system. Match-grade trigger. Thumb-operated safety can be configured to right or left. Folding stock has adjustable cheekpiece and length of pull. Finished in Barrett's Multi-Role Brown. Introduced in 2011.

NIB	Exc.	V.G.	Good	Fair	Poor
5500	4675	3950	2500	1000	500

Model 82 Rifle

.50-caliber BMG semi-automatic rifle, with 37" barrel and 11-shot magazine. Barrel fitted with muzzle-brake. Receiver with telescope. Parkerized. Weight about 35 lbs. Manufactured from 1985 to 1987.

NIB	Exc.	V.G.	Good	Fair	Poor
6000	5500	4750	2250	1500	400

Model 82A1

As above, with 29" barrel without sights. 10-round magazine. 10X telescope and iron sights optional. Comes with hard carrying case. Weight 28.5 lbs.

NIB	Exc.	V.G.	Good	Fair	Poor
8000	7000	4000	2750	1600	400

Model 95M

Introduced in 1995. .50-caliber BMG bolt-action rifle. Features 29" barrel and 5-round magazine. Scope optional. Weight 22 lbs.

NIB	Exc.	V.G.	Good	Fair	Poor
6000	4000	3200	2000	1400	300

Model 99

Single-shot bolt-action rifle. Chambered for .50 BMG or .416 Barrett. Standard barrel length 32". Optional barrel lengths 25" or 29". Weight about 25 lbs. with 32" barrel. **NOTE:** Add $200 for fluted barrel.

NIB	Exc.	V.G.	Good	Fair	Poor
4300	3450	1700	1200	600	175

Model 107

Chambered for .50-caliber cartridge. Semi-automatic rifle fitted with 29" barrel and muzzle-brake. Bipod detachable and adjustable. M1913 accessory rail. Supplied with two 10-round magazines. Weight about 32 lbs.

NIB	Exc.	V.G.	Good	Fair	Poor
9650	8000	7000	6000	4000	1000

Model 468

Built on semi-automatic AR-15-style lower receiver. Features 16" barrel, with muzzle-brake. Chambered for 6.8 SPC cartridge. Folding front and rear sight. Integrated Rail system. Weight about 7.3 lbs.

NIB	Exc.	V.G.	Good	Fair	Poor
2800	2100	1450	975	650	225

REC7 Gen II

This piston-driven AR-style model was introduced in 2008. Chambered in 5.56 NATO or 6.8 SPC. Mag-pull MOE pistol-grip stock, 16" barrel, Barrett handguard with KeyMod rail attachment. Other features are flash suppressor, flip-up iron sights and 30-shot magazine. Offered in black, gray, Flat Dark Earth or OD green finish. **NOTE:** Deduct $400 for 2008-2013 first generation production.

NIB	Exc.	V.G.	Good	Fair	Poor
2250	1800	1200	850	500	200

Barrett Sovereign shotgun

This series of over/under and side-by-side shotguns are chambered in 12-, 20- and 28-gauge. Featuring round body steel boxlock receivers, with ornamental sideplates, scroll engraving, coin finish, AAA-grade Turkish walnut stocks with classic checkering, single selective trigger, automatic ejectors and interchangeable choke tubes. Albany is an over/under, with a slightly open Prince of Wales grip: Beltrami is a side-by-side, with a straight-grip stock (shown in photo). These classic-style shotguns are made by Fausti Stefano of Italy. Introduced in 2016. **NOTE:** Add $400 for 28-gauge.

Albany O/U

NIB	Exc.	V.G.	Good	Fair	Poor
5200	4300	3500	—	—	—

Beltrami SxS

NIB	Exc.	V.G.	Good	Fair	Poor
5700	4800	4000	—	—	—

BARRETT, J. B. and A.B. & CO.
Wytheville, Virginia

Barrett Muskets and Rifled Muskets

Overall length 57.75"; barrel length 41.5" to 42"; caliber .69. Markings: although Barretts placed no marks of their own, on their alterations most were effected on Virginia Manufactory muskets, whose lockplates are marked "VIRGINIA/Manufactory" forward of hammer and "RICHMOND/(date)" on tail. For many years collectors considered adaptations of Hall rifles and carbines from breech-loaders to muzzle-loaders to be the product of J.B. Barrett & Co. of Wytheville. Recent evidence, however, confirms that those adaptations were actually effected in Danville, Virginia, by another firm (see READ & WATSON). Nevertheless, Barretts of Wytheville did adapt arms during early years of American Civil War. Adaptation effected almost exclusively upon Virginia Manufactory flintlock muskets, consisted of percussioning by means of cone-in-barrel and rifling of barrels with seven narrow grooves. In 1861 and 1862, Barretts percussioned a total of 1250 muskets, of which 744 were rifled.

Courtesy Milwaukee Public Museum, Milwaukee, Wisconsin

NIB	Exc.	V.G.	Good	Fair	Poor
—	—	—	16500	6750	2200

BASCARAN, MARTIN A.
Eibar, Spain

Spanish manufacturer of pistols prior to World War II.

Martian 6.35mm

6.35mm semi-automatic pistol. Slide marked "Automatic Pistol Martian". Blued, with black plastic grips having monogram "MAB" cast in them.

NIB	Exc.	V.G.	Good	Fair	Poor
—	275	195	135	100	75

Martian 7.65mm

Semi-automatic pistol patterned after Ruby military pistols. "Martian" stamped on slide. Wood grips and lanyard loop.

Courtesy James Rankin

NIB	Exc.	V.G.	Good	Fair	Poor
—	275	195	135	100	75

Thunder

Semi-automatic pistol in caliber 6.35mm. Almost a duplicate of Martian. "Thunder" stamped on slide and each grip plate.

Courtesy James Rankin

NIB	Exc.	V.G.	Good	Fair	Poor
—	275	195	135	100	75

BAUER, F. A. CORP.
Fraser, Michigan

The Rabbit

.22-caliber over .410 bore combination rifle/shotgun, with tubular metal stock. Manufactured between 1982 and 1984. Similar to Garcia Bronco.

NIB	Exc.	V.G.	Good	Fair	Poor
—	325	300	225	125	75

Bauer 25 Automatic

.25-caliber semi-automatic pistol. Made of stainless steel, with 2.5" barrel and 6-shot magazine. Walnut or imitation pearl grips. Manufactured

from 1972 to 1984. After 1984, this pistol was produced under the name of Fraser for a few years. **NOTE:** Add 15 percent for NIB.

Courtesy James Rankin

NIB	Exc.	V.G.	Good	Fair	Poor
—	250	200	165	125	80

BAYARD
Herstal, Belgium
See—Pieper, H. & N. and Bergmann

BAYONNE, MANUFACTURE D'ARMES
aka MAB
Bayonne, France

Model A

Manufactured in 1921. Chambered for 6.35mm cartridge. Patterned after Browning Model 1906. Squeeze grip safety, with 6-round magazine.

Courtesy James Rankin

NIB	Exc.	V.G.	Good	Fair	Poor
—	295	175	115	75	50

Model B

Manufactured in 1932. Chambered for 6.35mm cartridge. Exposed hammer, no grip safety and 6-round magazine.

Courtesy James Rankin

NIB	Exc.	V.G.	Good	Fair	Poor
—	275	165	90	75	50

Model C

Manufactured in 1933. Chambered for 7.65mm and .380 cartridge. Patterned after Browning Model 1910. Seven-round magazine.

Courtesy James Rankin

NIB	Exc.	V.G.	Good	Fair	Poor
—	325	225	200	125	90

Model D

Manufactured in 1933. Chambered for 7.65mm and .380 cartridge. Basically a Model C, with longer barrel and 9-round magazine. **NOTE:** Add 100 percent for Nazi-marked pistols.

Courtesy James Rankin

NIB	Exc.	V.G.	Good	Fair	Poor
—	400	300	250	125	100

Model E

Manufactured in 1949. Chambered for 6.35mm cartridge. Patterned after Model D, with streamlined grips and 10-round magazine.

NIB	Exc.	V.G.	Good	Fair	Poor
—	425	325	300	150	125

Model F

Manufactured in 1950. Chambered for .22 LR cartridge. Interchangeable barrel lengths, target grips and 10-round magazine.

Courtesy James Rankin

NIB	Exc.	V.G.	Good	Fair	Poor
—	425	325	200	150	125

Model G

Manufactured in 1951. Chambered for .22 LR and 7.65mm cartridge. Some with Dural frames. Magazine capacity: 10 rounds .22 LR; 8 rounds 7.65mm.

Courtesy James Rankin

NIB	Exc.	V.G.	Good	Fair	Poor
—	450	350	225	150	125

Model GZ

Manufactured in calibers .22 LR, 6.35mm, 7.65mm and .380. Almost identical to Model G. Dural frames and two-tone finishes on some variations.

NIB	Exc.	V.G.	Good	Fair	Poor
—	450	350	275	150	125

Model P-8 & P-15

In 1966 MAB manufactured Model P-8 and Model P-15 in 9mm Parabellum, with 8- and 15-round magazines. Basically the same gun, with different magazine capacities. Model P-15 went to French military as well as some commercial sales.

Courtesy James Rankin

NIB	Exc.	V.G.	Good	Fair	Poor
—	475	350	300	250	175

Model P-15 M1 Target

MAB Model P-15 was manufactured for target shooting using 9mm Parabellum cartridge. Most M1 Target MABs were purchased by French military for their target teams.

Courtesy James Rankin

NIB	Exc.	V.G.	Good	Fair	Poor
—	875	750	500	350	175

Model R

Manufactured in caliber 7.65mm Long in 1951. Model R similar to Model D. Model R's later produced in several calibers: .22 LR furnished with 10-round magazine and two different barrel lengths; 7.65mm had 9-round magazine; .380 and 9mm Parabellum fitted with 8-round magazines. **NOTE:** Deduct 15 percent for 7.65 Long.

.22 Long Rifle

NIB	Exc.	V.G.	Good	Fair	Poor
—	350	250	225	150	125

7.65mm & 7.65mm Long & .380

NIB	Exc.	V.G.	Good	Fair	Poor
—	350	250	225	150	125

9mm Parabellum

NIB	Exc.	V.G.	Good	Fair	Poor
—	400	300	250	150	125

Model R PARA Experimental

In late 1950's, MAB began experimenting with Model R in caliber 9mm Parabellum. There were many of these experimental-type pistols. The 8-round, rotating barrel Model R shown, led directly to Model P-15 series.

Courtesy James Rankin

NIB	Exc.	V.G.	Good	Fair	Poor
—	1500	1250	1000	500	250

Model "Le Chasseur"

Manufactured in 1953. "Le Chasseur" was a target model in .22 LR. Had a 9-round magazine, external hammer, target sights and grips. **NOTE:** MAB pistols sold in U.S.A. were retailed by Winfield Arms Company of Los Angeles, California. Marked "Made in France for WAC". This does not affect value.

NIB	Exc.	V.G.	Good	Fair	Poor
—	300	200	150	125	90

BEATTIE, J.
London, England

Beattie produced a variety of revolvers during percussion period, some of which were imported into United States. During the period this firm was in business, it was located at these London addresses:

43 Upper Marylebone Street	1835-1838
52 Upper Marylebone Street	1838-1842
52 Upper Marylebone Street & 223 Regent Street	1842-1846
205 Regent Street	1851-1882
104 Queen Victoria Street	1882-1894

Beattie Gas Seal Revolver

.42-caliber single-action percussion revolver, with 6.25" octagonal barrel. When hammer is cocked, cylinder is forced forward against barrel breech, thus effecting a gas seal. Blued case hardened, with walnut grips.

NIB	Exc.	V.G.	Good	Fair	Poor
—	—	5100	3500	2200	1100

BEAUMONT, ADAMS

See—Adams

BEAUMONT

Maastrict, Netherlands

1873 Dutch Service Revolver, Old Model

9.4mm double-action 6-shot revolver. Weight 2 lbs. 12 oz.

NIB	Exc.	V.G.	Good	Fair	Poor
—	—	695	400	200	100

1873 Dutch Service Revolver, New Model

As above, with 6-shot cylinder.

NIB	Exc.	V.G.	Good	Fair	Poor
—	—	695	400	200	100

1873 KIM, Small Model

As above, with octagonal barrel. 5-shot cylinder.

NIB	Exc.	V.G.	Good	Fair	Poor
—	—	775	500	250	125

BECKER AND HOLLANDER

Suhl, Germany

Beholla

Semi-automatic pistol in caliber 7.65mm. Introduced in 1908 in Germany. Manufactured by Becker & Hollander until 1920. After that date three different companies produced Beholla under names of Stenda, Menta and Leonhardt.

Courtesy James Rankin

NIB	Exc.	V.G.	Good	Fair	Poor
—	500	350	225	175	100

BEEMAN PRECISION ARMS, INC.

Santa Rosa, California

Although primarily known as an importer and retailer of airguns, Beeman Precision Arms, Inc., has marketed several firearms.

MP-08

.380-caliber semi-automatic pistol, with 3.5" barrel and 6-shot magazine. Resembling German Luger. Blued. Introduced in 1968.

NIB	Exc.	V.G.	Good	Fair	Poor
475	375	275	225	200	125

P-08

As above in .22-caliber, with 8-shot magazine. Walnut grips. Introduced in 1969.

NIB	Exc.	V.G.	Good	Fair	Poor
475	375	275	225	200	125

SP Standard

.22-caliber single-shot target pistol, with 8" to 15" barrels. Fitted with adjustable sights and walnut grips. Imported in 1985 and 1986.

NIB	Exc.	V.G.	Good	Fair	Poor
325	225	200	175	150	100

SP Deluxe

As above, with walnut fore-end.

NIB	Exc.	V.G.	Good	Fair	Poor
350	250	225	200	150	100

BEERSTECHER, FREDERICK

Philadelphia, Pennsylvania (1846-1856)
Lewisburg, Pennsylvania (1857-1868)

Superposed Load Pocket Pistol

.41-caliber superposed load percussion pistol, with an average barrel length of 3". German silver mounts. Walnut stock. Hammer fitted with movable twin striker head so the first charge in barrel can be fired and then second fired. Lock normally marked "F. Beerstecher's/Patent 1855". Prospective purchasers are advised to secure a qualified appraisal prior to acquisition.

NIB	Exc.	V.G.	Good	Fair	Poor
—	—	6400	4800	3500	1050

BEHOLLA

See—Becker and Hollander

BEISTEGUI, HERMANOS

Eibar, Spain
See—Grand Precision

BENELLI
Italy

SHOTGUNS

SL SERIES

Model SL-121 V

Semi-automatic 12-gauge, with 3" chambers and various barrel lengths and chokes. Black anodized alloy receiver. Discontinued in 1985.

NIB	Exc.	V.G.	Good	Fair	Poor
650	500	400	350	300	150

Model SL-121 Slug

Similar to SL-121 V, with 21" cylinder-bore barrel. Rifle sights. Discontinued in 1985.

NIB	Exc.	V.G.	Good	Fair	Poor
700	550	400	350	300	150

Model SL-123 V

Model has improved fast third-generation action. Otherwise resembles earlier SL-121.

NIB	Exc.	V.G.	Good	Fair	Poor
750	600	500	400	350	200

Model SL-201

20-gauge, with 26" Improved Cylinder barrel. Similar in appearance to SL-123.

NIB	Exc.	V.G.	Good	Fair	Poor
500	475	425	350	300	150

M SERIES

M3 Super 90

Improved version of Benelli pump-action and semi-automatic inertia recoil system. Shotgun can be converted from pump to semi-automatic, by turning a spring-loaded ring located at end of forearm. Has rotating bolt system. Chambered for 12-gauge, with 3" chamber. Has 19.75" barrel, with cylinder bore, rifle sights and 7-round tubular magazine. Matte black finish, black fiberglass pistol-grip stock and forearm. Introduced in 1986. **NOTE:** Add $50 for open rifle sights.

NIB	Exc.	V.G.	Good	Fair	Poor
1300	1100	900	700	450	300

M3 Super 90 Folding Stock

Same as above. Furnished with folding tubular steel stock.

NIB	Exc.	V.G.	Good	Fair	Poor
1500	1350	1150	850	600	300

M4

Adopted by U.S. Marine Corps, this 12-gauge shotgun features a choice of three modular buttstock and two barrel configurations. Top-mounted Picatinny rail. Barrel length 18.5". Magazine capacity 6 rounds. Ghost ring sights. Weight about 8.4 lbs. Matte black finish. Introduced in 2003. Civilian version does not have collapsible buttstock.

M4 with skeleton stock with cheekpiece

M4 with standard stock

NIB	Exc.	V.G.	Good	Fair	Poor
1550	1150	875	725	500	200

M1014 Limited Edition

Introduced in 2003. Version of M4. Fitted with skeleton buttstock. Special U.S. flag engraving on receiver. Fitted with 18.5" barrel and Picatinny rail, with ghost ring sights. Limited to 2,500 shotguns.

NIB	Exc.	V.G.	Good	Fair	Poor
1600	1200	900	750	550	250

M1 Practical

Designed for IPSC events. Features over sized safety, speed loader, larger bolt handle, muzzle-brake, adjustable ghost ring sight and optics rail. Offered with extended magazine tube and 26" barrel. Weight about 7.6 lbs.

NIB	Exc.	V.G.	Good	Fair	Poor
1150	900	750	500	275	125

M1 Super 90 Tactical

Semi-automatic 12-gauge shotgun, with inertia recoil system. Features 18.5" plain barrel. Three screw-in choke tubes. Available in standard polymer or pistol-grip stock. Ghost ring sights standard. Weight 6.5 lbs. Introduced in 1993.

NIB	Exc.	V.G.	Good	Fair	Poor
900	700	600	500	450	250

M1 Super 90 Slug Gun

Equipped with standard black polymer stock and 19.75" plain barrel. Fitted with 7-shot magazine. Ghost ring sights are an option. Weight 6.7 lbs. Camo model introduced in 2000. **NOTE:** Add $100 for Camo model.

NIB	Exc.	V.G.	Good	Fair	Poor
1000	750	550	450	350	250

M1 Super 90 Entry Gun

Fitted with black polymer pistol-grip stock and 14" plain barrel. Magazine holds 5 shells. Plain or ghost ring sights available. CAUTION: NFA Weapon, Restricted sale, Class III Transfer required.

M1 Super 90 Defense Gun

Comes standard with polymer pistol-grip stock, 19.75" barrel, plain or ghost ring sights. Offered in 12-gauge only. Weight 7.1 lbs.

NIB	Exc.	V.G.	Good	Fair	Poor
900	700	600	500	450	250

M1 Super 90 Field

Similar to other Super 90 series guns, with 21", 24", 26" or 28" ventilated rib barrel and screw-in choke tubes. In 1998 this model was available

with 24" rifled bore and matte rib. Add $80 for this barrel. Left-hand model added in 2000. In 2001 this model was offered in 20-gauge as well.

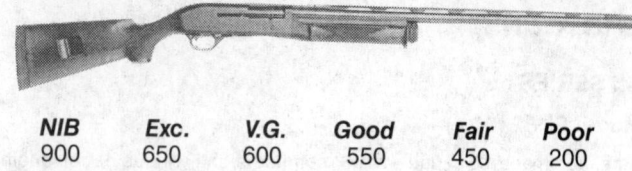

NIB	Exc.	V.G.	Good	Fair	Poor
900	650	600	550	450	200

M1 Super 90 Camo Field

Same as above, with camouflage receiver barrel, buttstock and forearm. Offered in 24", 26" and 28" ventilated rib barrels. Introduced in 1997. In 1998 this model also offered with 21" ventilated rib barrel. Left-hand model added in 2000. In 2001 this model offered in 20-gauge as well.

M1 20 gauge

M1 Field Steady Grip

Introduced in 2003. Features vertical pistol-grip, drilled and tapped receiver. Extra Full choke tube. Barrel length 24". Weight about 7.3 lbs.

NIB	Exc.	V.G.	Good	Fair	Poor
1175	900	600	325	175	100

M1 Super 90 Sporting Special

Introduced in 1993. This 12-gauge shotgun similar to Super 90, with addition of non-reflective surfaces, 18.5" plain barrel and 3 choke tubes (IC, Mod, Full). Gun fitted with ghost ring sights.

NIB	Exc.	V.G.	Good	Fair	Poor
725	600	500	400	350	200

M2 Practical with ComforTech

Introduced in 2005. Chambered for 12-gauge 3" shell. Fitted with 25" plain barrel, with compensator and ghost ring rear sight. Receiver fitted with Picatinny rail. Magazine capacity 8 rounds. Weight about 7.6 lbs.

NIB	Exc.	V.G.	Good	Fair	Poor
1200	1000	750	595	400	275

M2 Tactical

12-gauge 3" gun fitted with 18.5" barrel, with choke tubes and choice of rifle or ghost ring sights. Pistol-grip or extended pistol-grip. Black synthetic stock. Magazine capacity 5 rounds. Weight about 7 lbs. **NOTE:** Add $70 for ComforTech version; $65 for ghost ring sights.

NIB	Exc.	V.G.	Good	Fair	Poor
1250	1050	850	600	400	275

M2 Field with ComforTech

12-gauge model offered with 21", 24", 26" or 28" barrel. Black matte synthetic finish or Max-4, Timber or APG camo. 20-gauge has 24" or 26" barrel in black, Timber or APG. Average 12-gauge weight 7 lbs.; 20-gauge 5.8 lbs. **NOTE:** Add $75 for camo.

NIB	Exc.	V.G.	Good	Fair	Poor
1000	750	500	525	300	200

M2 Field without ComforTech

Same features as above, without ComforTech features. Available only in satin walnut, with 26" or 28" barrel.

NIB	Exc.	V.G.	Good	Fair	Poor
1075	825	550	525	300	200

MONTEFELTRO SERIES

Montefeltro Super 90

Introduced in 1987. Similar to Super 90 Field. Checkered walnut stock and forearm, with gloss finish. Offered with 21", 24", 26" or 28" ventilated rib barrel. Available in 12-gauge only, with 3" chambers. Offered in left-hand model also.

NIB	Exc.	V.G.	Good	Fair	Poor
900	700	600	500	450	350

Montefeltro 20 Gauge

Introduced in 1993. Features walnut checkered stock, with 26" ventilated rib barrel. In 1995 a 24" ventilated rib barrel offered. Weight 5.75 lbs. **NOTE:** Add $75 for short stock model.

NIB	Exc.	V.G.	Good	Fair	Poor
900	700	600	500	450	350

Montefeltro 20 Gauge Camo

Same as above, with Realtree Camo finish. Offered with 26" ventilated rib barrel. Introduced in 1998.

NIB	Exc.	V.G.	Good	Fair	Poor
950	750	700	600	500	400

Montefeltro 20 Gauge Limited

Introduced in 1995. Features finely etched nickel plate receiver, with scroll and game scenes highlighted in gold. Stock is select grade walnut. Fitted with 26" ventilated rib barrel.

NIB	Exc.	V.G.	Good	Fair	Poor
1750	1250	800	500	400	350

Montefeltro Silver

Same features as the standard Montefeltro model, but with bright blue nickel receiver and AA-grade walnut stock.

NIB	Exc.	V.G.	Good	Fair	Poor
1500	1250	950	700	350	200

Montefeltro (2005)

Updated version of Montefeltro series. Slight change in receiver, different trigger, upgraded wood and name "Montefeltro" in gold on receiver. Offered in 12- or 20-gauge, with 3" chambers. Checkered select walnut stock, with pistol-grip. Choice of 24", 26" or 28" ventilated rib barrel, with choke tubes. Red bar front sight. Weight for 12-gauge about 6.9 lbs.; 20-gauge about 5.6 lbs.

NIB	Exc.	V.G.	Good	Fair	Poor
1300	1000	950	700	500	350

Montefeltro Compact

In 20-gauge only. This model has a 24" or 26" barrel, shorter length-of-pull and satin finish stock. Introduced in 2012.

NIB	Exc.	V.G.	Good	Fair	Poor
1000	850	600	450	300	200

Montefeltro Synthetic

Model was introduced in 2013 in 12-gauge only, with a black synthetic stock and 26" or 28" barrel.

NIB	Exc.	V.G.	Good	Fair	Poor
1000	850	600	450	300	200

BLACK EAGLE SERIES

Black Eagle Competition Gun

Offered in 12-gauge only. Fitted with etched receiver, mid rib bead, competition stock and 5 screw-in choke tubes. Available in 26" or 28" ventilated rib barrel. Upper receiver steel while lower receiver is lightweight alloy. Weight 7.3 lbs.

NIB	Exc.	V.G.	Good	Fair	Poor
1300	800	750	700	400	275

Black Eagle

Similar to Black Eagle Competition Model, with standard grade wood. Matte black finish on receiver. Introduced in 1997.

NIB	Exc.	V.G.	Good	Fair	Poor
900	600	475	325	225	150

Black Eagle Executive Series

Offered in 12-gauge only. Special order only shotgun. Offered with 21", 24", 26", 28" ventilated rib barrels. Each grade or level of gun engraved with increasing levels of coverage. Stock is fancy walnut.

Grade I

NIB	Exc.	V.G.	Good	Fair	Poor
6200	5000	3500	2500	1500	700

Grade II

NIB	Exc.	V.G.	Good	Fair	Poor
7000	5500	4000	3000	1600	800

Grade III

NIB	Exc.	V.G.	Good	Fair	Poor
8500	6500	4750	3200	1800	900

SUPER BLACK EAGLE SERIES

Super Black Eagle

Similar to Montefeltro Super 90 Hunter, with polymer or walnut stock a⬛ forearm. Offered with 24", 26" or 28" ventilated rib barrel and 5 screw-choke tubes. Chambered for 12-gauge from 2.75" to 3.5". Introduced 1989. The 24" barrel introduced in 1993.

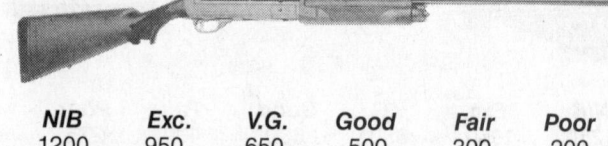

NIB	Exc.	V.G.	Good	Fair	Poor
1200	950	650	500	300	200

Super Black Eagle Left-Hand

Introduced in 1999. Same as Black Eagle in left-hand version. Cam⬛ version also available.

NIB	Exc.	V.G.	Good	Fair	Poor
1200	950	650	500	300	200

Super Black Eagle Custom Slug Gun

12-gauge model has 24" rifled barrel, with 3" chamber. Comes standa⬛ with matte metal finish. Weight 7.6 lbs.

NIB	Exc.	V.G.	Good	Fair	Poor
1100	800	750	600	500	350

Super Black Eagle Camo Gun

Introduced in 1997. Features 24", 26" or 28' ventilated rib barrels cham⬛ bered for 12-gauge shells. Has Realtree Xtra Brown Camo finish. Stoc⬛ is camo polymer as is forearm.

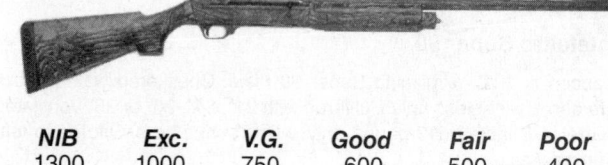

NIB	Exc.	V.G.	Good	Fair	Poor
1300	1000	750	600	500	400

Super Black Eagle Steady Grip

Similar to above. Equipped with vertical pistol-grip. Drilled and tappe⬛ receiver. Extra Full choke tube. Barrel length 24". Weight about 7.3 lb⬛ Introduced in 2003.

NIB	Exc.	V.G.	Good	Fair	Poor
1465	1100	650	575	325	225

Super Black Eagle Limited Edition

Introduced in 1997. Features 26" ventilated rib barrel, matte metal finis⬛ and satin select grade wood stock. Nickel plated receiver is finely etche⬛ with scroll and game scenes. Limited to 1,000 guns.

NIB	Exc.	V.G.	Good	Fair	Poor
2000	1500	1050	750	525	375

SUPER BLACK EAGLE II SERIES

Series of guns introduced in 2005. Major features are new butt pad, grip and cryogenically treated barrels for which specially designed longer choke tubes are required. Benelli offers this series with or without "ComforTech" features. This system reduces recoil up to 48 percent and muzzle climb by 15 percent.

Super Black Eagle II with ComforTech

Offered in 12-gauge, with 3.5" chambers. Barrel lengths 24", 26" or 28", with choke tubes and red bar front sight. Available in synthetic or various camo finishes. Magazine capacity 3 rounds. Weight about 7.2 lbs. with 26" barrel.

NIB	Exc.	V.G.	Good	Fair	Poor
1465	1100	700	600	365	250

Super Black Eagle II without ComforTech

Model without ComforTech. Same options as above, with addition of walnut stock. **NOTE:** Add $60 for walnut stock; $110 for camo models.

NIB	Exc.	V.G.	Good	Fair	Poor
1355	1000	650	575	325	225

Super Black Eagle II Rifled Slug with ComforTech

12-gauge 3" chamber gun, with 24" rifled barrel and adjustable sights. Available with synthetic stock or Timber HD camo stock. Weight about 7.4 lbs. **NOTE:** Add $120 for Camo version.

NIB	Exc.	V.G.	Good	Fair	Poor
1535	1150	650	575	325	225

Super Black Eagle II Turkey Gun

12-gauge 3" chamber shotgun (3.5" chambers on non-ComforTech guns). Fitted with 24" smooth bore barrels and choke tubes. Red bar front sight. Weight about 7.1 lbs. Available with Timber HD camo stock, with or without ComforTech. **NOTE:** Add $130 for ComforTech version.

NIB	Exc.	V.G.	Good	Fair	Poor
1455	1050	700	600	365	250

Super Black Eagle II Steady Grip

12-gauge 3.5" chamber gun. Fitted with 24" barrel and red bar front sight. Choke tubes. Stock is camo, with steady grip pistol-grip. Weight about 7.3 lbs. Model comes without ComforTech.

NIB	Exc.	V.G.	Good	Fair	Poor
1200	950	650	500	300	200

LEGACY SERIES

Legacy

Features coin finished alloy receiver. Introduced in 1998. Chambered for 12-gauge 2.75" or 3" shell. Fitted with 26" or 28" ventilated rib barrel. Mid and front sights. Weight about 7.5 lbs. Buttstock and forearm are select walnut. 20-gauge added in 1990 with 24" or 26" ventilated rib barrels. Weight 6 lbs.

NIB	Exc.	V.G.	Good	Fair	Poor
1300	800	750	700	400	275

Legacy Limited Edition

Offered in both 12- and 20-gauge. Features select walnut stock and etched game scenes with gold filled accents. 12-gauge features waterfowl scenes; 20-gauge has upland game scenes. 12-gauge fitted with 28" barrel; 20-gauge has 26" barrel. Introduced in 2000. Limited to 250 guns in each gauge.

NIB	Exc.	V.G.	Good	Fair	Poor
1600	1200	900	550	375	295

Legacy (2005)

Updated version of Legacy. Changes are in engraving pattern, upgraded wood, improved trigger and slightly different receiver style. Offered in 12- and 20-gauge, with 3" chambers. Choice of 26" or 28" ventilated rib barrel, with choke tubes. Red bar front sight. Checkered select walnut stock, with pistol-grip. Magazine capacity 4 rounds. Weight for 12-gauge about 7.4 lbs.; 20-gauge about 5.8 lbs. **NOTE:** Add $30 for 20-gauge.

NIB	Exc.	V.G.	Good	Fair	Poor
1435	1050	900	575	325	225

NOVA SERIES

Nova

"Slide-action series" introduced in 1999. Features polymer molded frame, with steel cage chambered for 3.5" shells. Choice of 24", 26" or 28" ventilated rib barrels. A 18.5" slug barrel also offered. Two- or four-shot magazine extensions offered as well. Weight with 28" barrel 8 lbs. Choice of camo or black synthetic pistol-grip stock. In 2001 offered in 20-gauge.

NIB	Exc.	V.G.	Good	Fair	Poor
350	275	225	175	150	75

Nova Slug

12-gauge shotgun has 18.5" cylinder bored barrel, with open rifle or ghost ring sights. Black synthetic stock. Chambered for 2.75" or 3" shells. Magazine capacity 4 rounds. Weight about 7.2 lbs. Introduced in 2000. **NOTE:** Add $40 for ghost ring sights.

NIB	Exc.	V.G.	Good	Fair	Poor
350	275	225	200	150	95

Nova Rifled Slug

Introduced in 2000. This 12-gauge features 24" rifled barrel, with open rifle sights. Black synthetic or Timber HD camo stock. Chambered for 2.75" or 3" shells. Magazine capacity 4 rounds. Weight about 8 lbs. **NOTE:** Add $75 for Camo version.

NIB	Exc.	V.G.	Good	Fair	Poor
525	425	350	250	175	125

Nova Field Slug Combo

12-gauge 3" gun equipped with 24" and 26" barrel. 26" barrel fitted with ventilated rib and choke tube; 24" barrel is rifled and fitted with cantilever scope mount. Black synthetic stock.

NIB	Exc.	V.G.	Good	Fair	Poor
545	425	325	250	175	125

Nova H2O Pump

Introduced in 2003. Features a largely polymer exterior, with corrosion-resistant finish. Barrel, magazine tube, magazine cap, trigger group and other internal parts are nickel plated. Chambered for 12-gauge. Fitted with 18.5" barrel. Black synthetic stock. Magazine capacity 4 rounds. Open rifle sights. Weight about 7.2 lbs.

NIB	Exc.	V.G.	Good	Fair	Poor
600	500	400	250	150	100

Supernova

Introduced in 2006. Supernova incorporates Benelli's ComforTech stock system into Nova pump shotgun. Available in 24", 26" and 28" barrel lengths in matte black synthetic; 24" and 26" barrel lengths in Advantage Timber camo; 26" and 28" barrel lengths in Max-4 camo. Weight about 8 lbs. with 28" barrel. All versions chambered for 3.5" shells. Three choke tubes. **NOTE:** Add 15 percent for camo versions.

NIB	Exc.	V.G.	Good	Fair	Poor
475	375	250	175	150	75

Supernova SteadyGrip

As above, with extended pistol-grip in 24" barrel only. Matte black synthetic or Advantage Timber stock. **NOTE:** Add 15 percent for camo model.

NIB	Exc.	V.G.	Good	Fair	Poor
455	375	250	175	150	75

Supernova Tactical

Matte black synthetic stock, with 18" barrel. Available with ComforTech or pistol-grip stock. Fixed cylinder bore. Open rifle sights. Ghost ring sights optional.

NIB	Exc.	V.G.	Good	Fair	Poor
400	325	225	150	125	75

SPORT SERIES

Sport Model

Introduced in 1997. First shotgun with removable interchangeable carbon fiber ventilated ribs. Offered in 12-gauge only with choice of 26" or 28" barrels; 20-gauge with 28" barrel. Butt pad adjustable. Weight: 7 lbs. for 26" models; 7.3 lbs. for 28" models.

NIB	Exc.	V.G.	Good	Fair	Poor
1300	1000	650	400	250	100

SuperSport with ComforTech

Introduced in 2005. Offered in 12-gauge, with 3" chamber or 20-gauge with 28" barrel. Choice of 28" or 30" carbon fiber barrel, with choke tubes and red bar front sight. Weight about 7.25 lbs.

NIB	Exc.	V.G.	Good	Fair	Poor
1670	1250	800	575	395	200

Sport II Model

Introduced in 2003. Features cryogenically treated barrels and extra-long choke tubes. Chambered for 12-gauge shell in 2.75" or 3", with 28" or 30" barrel; 20-gauge with 28" barrel. Ventilated rib and choke tubes. Magazine capacity 4 rounds. Red bar front sight. Weight about 7.9 lbs.

NIB	Exc.	V.G.	Good	Fair	Poor
1470	1100	700	475	325	150

Cordoba

Introduced in 2005. Chambered for 12-gauge 3" shell. Fitted with cryo-genically treated ported barrels in 28" or 30" lengths, with extended choke tubes. Ventilated rib is 10mm width. Synthetic stock, with adjustable length butt pads. Red bar front sight. Weight about 7.25 lbs.

NIB	Exc.	V.G.	Good	Fair	Poor
1800	1530	1200	850	375	295

Vinci

Gas-operated 12-gauge semi-automatic shotgun chambered for 2.75" and 3". Features include modular disassembly; interchangeable choke tubes; 24" to 28" ribbed barrel; black, MAX-4HD or APG HD finish; synthetic contoured stocks; optional Steady-Grip model. Weight 6.7 to 6.9 lbs.

NIB	Exc.	V.G.	Good	Fair	Poor
1200	1000	850	600	400	300

Super Vinci

Unlike Vinci, Super Vinci fires 12-gauge 2.75", 3" and 3.5" Magnum ammunition interchangeably. Barrel lengths: 26" or 28". Features Crio chokes, red bar front sight, metal bead mid sight. Receiver drilled and tapped for scope mounting. Weight about 7 lbs. Available in black synthetic, Realtree MAX-4 or Realtree APG camo finish. New in 2011. **NOTE:** Add $100 for camo finish.

NIB	Exc.	V.G.	Good	Fair	Poor
1400	1150	900	650	450	350

Ultra Light

Inertia-driven 12-gauge semi-automatic. Features alloy receiver, carbon fiber rib and small proportions to bring weight down to about 6 lbs. Walnut stock, with Weathercoat finish. Chambered for 3" shells. Offered in 24" or 26" barrel only, with 5 Crio chokes. Introduced 2006.

NIB	Exc.	V.G.	Good	Fair	Poor
1435	1050	900	575	325	225

Executive Series

Limited edition 12-gauge semi-automatic, with engraved grey lower receiver, highly polished blue barrel and upper receiver. Extra select grade walnut stock. Made in three grades, Type 1, Type 2 and Type 3, with increasing levels of engraving and wood. Limited importation.

Type 1

NIB	Exc.	V.G.	Good	Fair	Poor
6250	5000	4000	3000	—	—

Type 2

NIB	Exc.	V.G.	Good	Fair	Poor
7250	6000	5000	4000	—	—

Type 3

NIB	Exc.	V.G.	Good	Fair	Poor
8500	7200	6200	5000	—	—

Raffaello Series

Limited production 12-gauge semi-automatic, available only through Benelli World Class dealers. Offered in three grades, Standard, Deluxe and Deluxe Legacy. Deluxe grade has scroll engraving and coin finished receiver. Deluxe Legacy has gold inlaid wildlife, high-grade walnut stock and also made in 20-gauge. **NOTE:** Add 25 percent for Deluxe grade; 50 percent for Deluxe Legacy.

NIB	Exc.	V.G.	Good	Fair	Poor
1600	1450	1150	800	600	400

Ethos

Ethos features a recoil reduction system advertised as reducing felt recoil by 42 percent. The Benelli intertia-driven operating system cycles all loads. Introduced in 2014 a 12-gauge, with 20-, 28-gauge added in 2016. Barrel lengths 26" or 28", with five choke tubes and interchangeable fiber optic red, yellow and green front sights. Other features include a totally new receiver design, a two-part carrier latch for easy loading, AA-grade checkered walnut stock, and choice of engraved nickel-plated or anodized receiver. **NOTE:** Add $200 for engraved/nickel receiver.

NIB	Exc.	V.G.	Good	Fair	Poor
1800	1550	1200	850	400	200

Ethos Small Gauge

NIB	Exc.	V.G.	Good	Fair	Poor
2000	1750	1400	—	—	—

828 U

Benelli's first over/under shotgun. Features include removable trigger assembly, AA grade walnut stock with satin finish, separated barrels with carbon fiber ventilated rib, five choke tubes, fiber optic front sight and matte black or engraved and polished nickel-plated aluminum receiver. Introduced in 2015 in 12-gauge only.

NIB	Exc.	V.G.	Good	Fair	Poor
2100	1850	1500	1100	900	500

828 U w/nickel-plated receiver

NIB	Exc.	V.G.	Good	Fair	Poor
2500	2100	1800	1300	1000	500

RIFLES

Model R1 Rifle

Introduced in 2003. Chambered for .30-06 or .300 Win. Magnum cartridge. Barrels cryogenically treated. Action is gas operated. Interchangeable barrel offered in 20" and 22" in .30-06; 20" and 24" in .300 Win. Magnum. Walnut stock. Detachable magazine has 4-round capacity. Weight about 7 to 7.2 lbs. depending on caliber and barrel length. In 2005 .270 WSM and .300 WSM calibers were added.

NIB	Exc.	V.G.	Good	Fair	Poor
1080	850	675	500	350	225

R1 Limited Edition Rifle

High-grade version available from about 2010 to 2013. AAA-grade walnut stock and fore-end. Coin finished receiver, with engraving of game scenes including gold inlays and adjustable sights. In .30-06 only.

NIB	Exc.	V.G.	Good	Fair	Poor
2500	2000	1500	1100	800	500

Model R1 Carbine

As above, with 20" barrel chambered for .30-06 or .300 Win. Magnum calibers. Weight about 7 lbs.

NIB	Exc.	V.G.	Good	Fair	Poor
1080	850	675	500	350	225

Model R1 ComforTech Rifle

Similar to Model R1, with ComforTech recoil-absorbing stock. Additional chamberings .270 and .300 WSM. Introduced 2006. **NOTE:** Add 10 percent for RealTree camo and adjustable comb.

NIB	Exc.	V.G.	Good	Fair	Poor
1350	1100	700	475	325	150

Model MR1 Rifle

Gas-operated semi-automatic rifle chambered in 5.56 NATO. Features include 16" 1:9 hard chrome-lined barrel, synthetic stock with pistol-grip, rotating bolt, military-style aperture sights with Picatinny rail. Comes equipped with 5-round detachable magazine but accepts M16 magazines.

NIB	Exc.	V.G.	Good	Fair	Poor
1135	965	800	550	350	250

HANDGUNS

Model B-76

All-steel double-action semi-automatic chambered for 9mm Parabellum. Has 4.25" barrel, fixed sights and 8-round detachable magazine.

NIB	Exc.	V.G.	Good	Fair	Poor
675	500	400	300	200	100

Model B-76S

Target version of B-76. Has 5.5" barrel, adjustable sights and target grips.

NIB	Exc.	V.G.	Good	Fair	Poor
875	700	550	300	200	100

Model B-77

Similar to B-76 except chambered for .32 ACP.

NIB	Exc.	V.G.	Good	Fair	Poor
425	300	250	200	150	100

Model B-80

Similar to B-76 except chambered for .30 Luger cartridge.

NIB	Exc.	V.G.	Good	Fair	Poor
525	395	300	200	150	100

Model B-80S

Target version of B-80, with 5.5" barrel and adjustable sights. Features target-grips.

NIB	Exc.	V.G.	Good	Fair	Poor
575	475	400	300	200	100

Model MP90S Match (World Cup)

Semi-automatic single-action pistol. Chambered for .22 Short, .22 LR, .32 S&W Wadcutter. Fitted with 4.375" barrel, with walnut match style fully adjustable grips, blade front sight and fully adjustable rear sight. Barrel has adjustable weights below. Magazine capacity 5 rounds. Weighs about 39 oz. Previously imported by European American Armory, now imported by Benelli USA. **NOTE:** Add 10 percent for .32 S&W.

NIB	Exc.	V.G.	Good	Fair	Poor
1450	1250	950	700	400	200

Model MP95E Match (Atlanta)

Similar to above, with anatomically shaped grips. Choice of blue or chrome finish. Previously imported by European American Armory, now imported by Benelli U.S.A. **NOTE:** Add $60 for chrome finish.

NIB	Exc.	V.G.	Good	Fair	Poor
750	600	450	350	225	125

BENTLEY, DAVID
Birmingham, England

Bentley was a prolific maker of both percussion and cartridge arms between 1845 and 1883. Those arms in cases can be dated by addresses listed.

New Church Street	1845-1849
55 Hockley Street	1849-1854
5 Lower Loveday Street	1855-1860
61 & 62 Lower Loveday Street	1860-1863
44 Shadwell Street	1863-1871
Tower Works, Aston	1871-1883

BENTLEY, JOSEPH
Birmingham and Liverpool, England

Best known for his transitional and later patented percussion revolvers, Bentley worked at these addresses:

Birmingham11 Steelhouse Lane	1829-1837
14 St. Mary's Row	1840-1864
Liverpool143 Dale Street	1840-1842
12 South Castle Street	1842-1851
40 Lime Street & 65 Castle	1852-1857
65 Castle & 37 Russell Street	1857-1862

Bentley Revolver

.44-caliber double-action percussion revolver, with 7" barrel and 5-shot cylinder. Blued case hardened, with walnut grips.

NIB	Exc.	V.G.	Good	Fair	Poor
—	—	4500	2750	2000	750

BERETTA, DR. FRANCO
Brescia, Italy

This series of shotguns made by Beretta company in Brescia, Italy and imported under Dr. Franco Beretta name in 1980s.

Black Diamond Field Model

Over/under series offered in all standard gauges. Walnut stock, coin-finished receiver, fixed chokes, SST and auto ejectors. **NOTE:** Four embellished grades were offered, Grades One through Four, with increasing levels of scrollwork, engraving and higher grades of French walnut stocks.

NIB	Exc.	V.G.	Good	Fair	Poor
800	650	500	400	300	200

Grade One

NIB	Exc.	V.G.	Good	Fair	Poor
1400	1200	1000	850	400	200

Grade Two

NIB	Exc.	V.G.	Good	Fair	Poor
1600	1400	1200	1000	500	300

Grade Three

NIB	Exc.	V.G.	Good	Fair	Poor
2200	1900	1650	1400	600	300

Grade Four

NIB	Exc.	V.G.	Good	Fair	Poor
3500	2800	2250	1750	700	350

Gamma Standard

12-, 16- or 20-gauge boxlock over/under shotgun, with 26" or 28" barrels, single trigger and automatic ejectors. Blued French case hardened, with walnut stock. Imported from 1984 to 1988.

NIB	Exc.	V.G.	Good	Fair	Poor
900	775	600	425	250	100

Gamma Deluxe

As above, but more finely finished.

NIB	Exc.	V.G.	Good	Fair	Poor
1200	975	800	600	350	125

Gamma Target

As above in trap or skeet version. Imported from 1986 to 1988.

NIB	Exc.	V.G.	Good	Fair	Poor
1200	975	800	600	350	125

America Standard

.410 bore boxlock over/under shotgun, with 26" or 28" barrels. Blued French case hardened, with walnut stock. Imported from 1984 to 1988.

NIB	Exc.	V.G.	Good	Fair	Poor
650	475	325	275	200	100

America Deluxe

As above, but more finely finished.

NIB	Exc.	V.G.	Good	Fair	Poor
695	525	375	300	225	100

Europa

As above, with 26" barrel and engraved action. Imported from 1984 to 1988.

NIB	Exc.	V.G.	Good	Fair	Poor
800	725	575	425	275	100

Europa Deluxe

As above, but more finely finished.

NIB	Exc.	V.G.	Good	Fair	Poor
850	775	625	475	300	1005

Francia Standard

.410 bore boxlock double-barrel shotgun, with varying barrel lengths, double triggers and manual extractors. Blued, with walnut stock. Imported from 1986 to 1988.

NIB	Exc.	V.G.	Good	Fair	Poor
600	500	375	250	125	100

Alpha Three

12-, 16- or 20-gauge boxlock double-barrel shotgun, with 26" or 28" barrels, single triggers and automatic ejectors. Blued French case hardened, with walnut stock. Imported from 1984 to 1988.

NIB	Exc.	V.G.	Good	Fair	Poor
750	650	500	325	150	100

Beta Three

Single-barrel break-open field-grade gun. Chambered for all gauges and offered with ventilated rib barrel from 24" to 32" in length. Receiver is chrome-plated and stock of walnut. Imported from 1985 to 1988.

NIB	Exc.	V.G.	Good	Fair	Poor
325	225	200	175	125	40

BERETTA, PIETRO
Brescia, Italy

PISTOLS

Model 1915

7.65mm and 9mm Glisenti caliber semi-automatic pistol, with 3.5" barrel, fixed sights and 8-shot magazine. Blued, with walnut grips. The 7.65mm pistol has single-line inscription while 9mm Glisenti has double line. Various styles of wood grips on this model. Manufactured between 1915 and 1922. Replaced by Model 1915/19.

Model 1915 in 7.65mm

Courtesy James Rankin

Model 1915 in 9mm Glisenti

NIB	Exc.	V.G.	Good	Fair	Poor
—	1300	1000	800	500	250

Model 1915/1917

Improved version of above pistol. Chambered for 7.65mm cartridge. Also incorporates a new barrel-mounting method and longer cutout in top of slide. **NOTE:** Add 100 percent for Navy Model.

Courtesy Orvel Reichert

NIB	Exc.	V.G.	Good	Fair	Poor
—	500	350	275	200	100

Model 1919

Similar to Model 1915 in 6.35mm caliber. Manufactured with minor variations. Different names between 1919 and 1940s.

Courtesy James Rankin

NIB	Exc.	V.G.	Good	Fair	Poor
—	550	450	350	300	150

Model 1923

9mm Glisenti caliber semi-automatic pistol, with 4" barrel and 8-shot magazine. Blued with steel grips. Slide marked, "Brev 1915-1919 Mlo 1923". Manufactured from 1923 to 1935.

NIB	Exc.	V.G.	Good	Fair	Poor
—	1600	1200	600	265	175

Model 1931

7.65mm caliber semi-automatic pistol, with 3.5" barrel and open-top slide. Blued, with walnut grips. Marked "RM" separated by an anchor.

NIB	Exc.	V.G.	Good	Fair	Poor
—	495	425	325	250	180

Model 1934

As above with 9mm short (.380 ACP) caliber. Slide marked "P. Beretta Cal. 9 Corto-Mo 1934 Brevet Gardone VT." This inscription is followed by date of manufacture that was given numerically, followed by a Roman numeral that denoted year of manufacture on Fascist calendar, which began in 1922. Examples are marked "RM" (Navy), "RE" (Army), "RA" (Air Force) and "PS" (Police). Manufactured between 1934 and 1959. This was a main service pistol for Italian Armed Forces during WWII.

Courtesy Orvel Reichert

NIB	Exc.	V.G.	Good	Fair	Poor
—	650	550	400	175	100

Air Force "RA" marked

NIB	Exc.	V.G.	Good	Fair	Poor
—	800	650	500	250	175

Navy "RM" marked

NIB	Exc.	V.G.	Good	Fair	Poor
—	850	700	550	275	200

Model 1934 Romanian Contract

Identical to Model 1934, except slide marked "9mm Scurt" instead of 9mm Corto.

NIB	Exc.	V.G.	Good	Fair	Poor
—	700	600	450	275	175

Model 1935

As above in 7.65mm caliber. Post-war versions are known. Manufactured from 1935 to 1959.

Courtesy Orvel Reichert

NIB	Exc.	V.G.	Good	Fair	Poor
—	400	375	250	175	125

Model 318

Improved version of old Model 1919, with butt reshaped to afford a better grip. Chambered for .25 ACP cartridge. Has 2.5" barrel. Variety of finishes with plastic grips. In U.S. known as "Panthe". Manufactured between 1935 and 1946.

NIB	Exc.	V.G.	Good	Fair	Poor
—	350	275	250	175	125

Model 418

As above, with rounded grip and cocking indicator. Known as "Bantam" in U.S. Introduced in 1947.

NIB	Exc.	V.G.	Good	Fair	Poor
—	275	225	175	125	90

Model 420

Engraved and chrome-plated Model 418.

NIB	Exc.	V.G.	Good	Fair	Poor
—	350	300	275	200	150

Model 421

Engraved gold-plated Model 418, with tortoise-shell grips.

NIB	Exc.	V.G.	Good	Fair	Poor
—	475	425	325	250	150

Model 948

.22 LR version of Model 1934. Either 3.5" or 6" barrel.

NIB	Exc.	V.G.	Good	Fair	Poor
—	350	300	200	125	90

Model 949 Olympic Target

.22-caliber semi-automatic pistol, with 8.75" barrel, adjustable sights and muzzle-brake. Blued, with checkered walnut grips. Manufactured from 1959 to 1964.

NIB	Exc.	V.G.	Good	Fair	Poor
—	750	600	500	400	200

U22 Neos 4.5/6.0

Semi-automatic .22-caliber pistol. Introduced in 2002. Chambered for .22 LR cartridge. Fitted with 4.5" or 6" barrel, with integral scope rail. Magazine capacity 10 rounds. Weight about 32- to 36 oz. depending on barrel length.

NIB	Exc.	V.G.	Good	Fair	Poor
250	200	165	125	100	75

U22 Neos 4.5 Inox/6.0 Inox

Same as above, with special two-tone finish.

NIB	Exc.	V.G.	Good	Fair	Poor
300	250	195	150	100	75

U22 Neos 6.0/7.5 DLX

Introduced in 2003. Features 6" or 7.5" barrel, with target sights and polymer grips with inlays. Adjustable trigger and interchangeable sights. Laser-engraved slide. Weight about 36 oz.

NIB	Exc.	V.G.	Good	Fair	Poor
335	275	200	150	100	75

U22 Neos 6.0/7.5 Inox DLX

As above, with Inox finish.

NIB	Exc.	V.G.	Good	Fair	Poor
385	300	215	165	115	90

BERETTA 70 SERIES

These pistols began production in 1958 replacing Models 1934, 1935, 948 and 949. During late 1960s, several of these models briefly utilized a 100 series designation for U.S. market. During latter part of 1970s, a magazine safety was added to 70 series and pistols became known as Model 70S. The 70S designation replaced model designations 70 through 75 making these older model numbers obsolete. Only Model 76 designation continued.

The 70 Series design included a cross bolt safety, sear block safety, slide hold-open device and push-button magazine release. Shortly after its introduction, cross bolt safety pushbutton was replaced with lever-type sear block safety located in the same place.

NOTE: Above information was supplied by contributing editor John Stimson, Jr.

Model 70 (Model 100)

Model 948 with cross bolt safety, hold-open device and push-button magazine release. Fixed sights. There are a number of sub-variations available chambered for .22 LR, .32 ACP and .380 ACP cartridges. Available with 3.5" or 5.9" barrel. Has a detachable magazine. Also known as "Puma" when marketed in U.S. by J.L. Galef & Sons. Introduced in 1958. Discontinued in 1985.

NIB	Exc.	V.G.	Good	Fair	Poor
525	450	350	275	125	85

Model 70S

Improved Model 70. Chambered for 7.65 (.32 ACP), 9mm Corto (.380 ACP) and .22 LR cartridge. Magazine capacity 7, 8 and 9 rounds respectively.

NIB	Exc.	V.G.	Good	Fair	Poor
550	475	375	295	125	85

Model 71/Jaguar (Model 101)

Similar to above. Chambered for .22 LR cartridge. Magazine capacity 10 rounds. Frame is alloy. Fitted with 5.9" barrel. Models imported into U.S. prior to 1968 were fitted with 3.5" barrels.

NIB	Exc.	V.G.	Good	Fair	Poor
425	375	300	225	125	85

Model 72

Essentially a Model 71. Sold with two sets of barrels; 3.5" and 5.9". Fixed sights.

NIB	Exc.	V.G.	Good	Fair	Poor
450	400	325	250	150	125

Model 76 (102)

A .22 LR target pistol. Barrel shrouded with an aluminum sleeve. Rear part of sleeve extended above slide to hold an adjustable rear sight. Marketed in U.S. as "Sable". Magazine capacity 10 rounds. Briefly after 1968, imported into U.S. as Model 102 "New Sable".

Courtesy John J. Stimson, Jr.

NIB	Exc.	V.G.	Good	Fair	Poor
650	550	400	200	125	75

Model 950/Minx

.22-caliber semi-automatic pistol, with 2.25" barrel hinged at front. This could be pivoted forward for cleaning or loading, making this either a semi-automatic or single-shot pistol. Blued, with plastic grips. Introduced in 1955. A 4" barrel version also available. Known as "Minx" in U.S.

NIB	Exc.	V.G.	Good	Fair	Poor
325	250	215	145	95	50

Model 950B/Jetfire

As above in .25-caliber. Known as "Jetfire" in U.S.

NIB	Exc.	V.G.	Good	Fair	Poor
325	250	215	145	95	50

Model 950 Jetfire Inox

Same as Model 950 Jetfire, with stainless steel finish. Introduced in 2000.

NIB	Exc.	V.G.	Good	Fair	Poor
335	250	175	135	85	50

Model 3032 Tomcat

Double-action semi-automatic pistol. Similar in appearance to Model 950. Chambered for .32 ACP cartridge. Barrel length 2.45"; overall length 5". Fixed blade front sight and drift adjustable rear sight. Plastic grips. Seven-round magazine. Blued or matte black finish. Weight 14.5 oz. **NOTE:** Add $30 for blued finish.

NIB	Exc.	V.G.	Good	Fair	Poor
375	325	250	200	1350	75

Model 3032 Tomcat Inox

Same as above, with stainless steel finish. Introduced in 2000.

NIB	Exc.	V.G.	Good	Fair	Poor
400	325	250	195	125	75

Model 3032 Tomcat Titanium

Same as above, with titanium finish and plastic grips. Weight about 16 oz. Introduced in 2001.

NIB	Exc.	V.G.	Good	Fair	Poor
575	450	350	290	210	150

Alley Cat

Introduced in 2001. Special limited run promotion pistol. Chambered for .32 ACP cartridge. Model is a Tomcat, with special features such as AO Big Dot night sights. Supplied with an Alcantara inside-the-pants holster.

NIB	Exc.	V.G.	Good	Fair	Poor
575	450	350	290	210	150

Model 951

9mm caliber semi-automatic pistol, with 4.5" barrel and fixed sights. Blued, with plastic grips. Known as "Brigadier" at one time. Introduced 1952.

NIB	Exc.	V.G.	Good	Fair	Poor
—	450	375	275	150	100

Model 20

.25 ACP double-action pistol, with 2.5" barrel and 9-shot magazine. Blued, with walnut or plastic grips. Discontinued in 1985.

NIB	Exc.	V.G.	Good	Fair	Poor
300	250	195	150	90	75

Model 21 Bobcat

Small frame semi-automatic pistol. Chambered for .22 LR or .25 ACP cartridge. Features 2.4" tip-up barrel with fixed sights. Magazine capacity of 8 rounds (.25 ACP) or 7 rounds (.22 LR). Comes with plastic or walnut grips. Deluxe version with gold line engraving. Weight about 11 to 11.8 oz. depending on caliber.

Standard Model

NIB	Exc.	V.G.	Good	Fair	Poor
325	275	250	225	175	95

Model 21EL

Gold engraved model.

NIB	Exc.	V.G.	Good	Fair	Poor
395	350	325	280	195	110

Model 21 Inox

Stainless steel.

NIB	Exc.	V.G.	Good	Fair	Poor
325	250	200	140	95	75

Model 90

Double-action semi-automatic .32 auto pocket pistol, with 3.5" barrel and 8-round magazine. Manufactured from 1969 to 1983.

NIB	Exc.	V.G.	Good	Fair	Poor
—	395	350	295	200	125

Model 92

9mm caliber double-action semi-automatic pistol, with 5" barrel, fixed sights and 16-round double-stack magazine. Blued, with plastic grips. Introduced in 1976. Now discontinued.

NIB	Exc.	V.G.	Good	Fair	Poor
800	600	500	400	250	200

Model 92SB-P

As above, with polished finish. Manufactured from 1980 to 1985.

NIB	Exc.	V.G.	Good	Fair	Poor
625	475	400	325	250	200

Model 92SB Compact

As above, with 4.3" barrel and shortened grip frame that holds a 14-shot magazine. Blued or nickel-plated, with wood or plastic grips. Introduced in 1980. Discontinued in 1985. **NOTE:** Add $20 for wood grips; 15 percent for nickel version.

NIB	Exc.	V.G.	Good	Fair	Poor
500	425	375	325	250	200

Model 92FS

Current production Model 92 chambered for 9mm Parabellum cartridge. Barrel length 4.9". Rear sight is 3-dot combat drift adjustable. Magazine capacity 15 rounds. Semi-automatic pistol features double-/single-action operation. Safety is manual type. Frame is light alloy sandblasted and anodized black. Barrel slide is steel. Grips are plastic checkered, with black matte finish. Equipped with spare magazine cleaning rod and hard carrying case. Weight 34.4 oz. empty.

NIB	Exc.	V.G.	Good	Fair	Poor
550	450	350	300	200	150

Model 92FS Inox

Introduced in 2001. Chambered for 9mm cartridge. Fitted with 4.9" barrel. Slide is black stainless steel, with lightweight frame and combat-style trigger guard, reversible magazine release and ambidextrous safety. Gray wrap-around grips. Weight about 34 oz.

NIB	Exc.	V.G.	Good	Fair	Poor
695	575	425	350	225	175

Model 96

Identical to Model 92FS. Fitted with 10-round magazine. Chambered for .40 S&W. Introduced in 1992.

NIB	Exc.	V.G.	Good	Fair	Poor
550	450	350	300	200	150

Model 96 Combat

Introduced in 1997. Single-action-only, with competition tuned trigger. Developed for practical shooting competition. Barrel length 5.9". Supplied with weight as standard. Rear sight is adjustable target type. Tool kit included as standard. Weight 40 oz.

NIB	Exc.	V.G.	Good	Fair	Poor
1700	1300	950	575	350	175

Model 96 Stock

Similar to Model 96 in double-/single-action, with half-cock notch for cocked and locked carry. Fitted with 4.9" barrel with fixed sights. Three interchangeable front sights are supplied as standard. Weight 35 oz. Introduced in 1997. No longer in U.S. product line.

NIB	Exc.	V.G.	Good	Fair	Poor
1350	950	775	500	325	150

Model 96A1

An evolution of the M9 service pistol for military and law enforcement. Chambered in .40 S&W, this model comes with three 12-round magazines. Features include an integral Picatinny accessory rail, improved recoil buffer and Bruniton finish.

NIB	Exc.	V.G.	Good	Fair	Poor
700	600	475	375	250	150

Model 92/96FS Inox

Same as above except barrel, slide, trigger, extractor and other components are made of stainless steel. Frame made of lightweight anodized aluminum alloy. Model 96FS discontinued in 1993.

NIB	Exc.	V.G.	Good	Fair	Poor
650	550	450	350	300	200

Model 92/96FS Centurion

Chambered for 9mm or .40 S&W (Model 96). Features 4.3" barrel, but retains full grip to accommodate 15-round magazine (9mm); 10 rounds (.40 S&W). Weight about 33.2 oz. Introduced in 1993. Black sandblasted finish.

NIB	Exc.	V.G.	Good	Fair	Poor
550	450	400	300	200	150

Model 92FS/96 Brigadier

Same as 92FS and 96, with heavier slide to reduce felt recoil. Removable front sight. Weight about 35 oz.

NIB	Exc.	V.G.	Good	Fair	Poor
700	550	400	300	150	75

Model 92FS/96 Brigadier Inox

Same as above, with stainless steel finish. Introduced in 2000.

NIB	Exc.	V.G.	Good	Fair	Poor
750	600	475	325	175	100

Model 92G-SD/96G-SD

Introduced in 2003. Features a decock mechanism built around single-/double-action trigger system. In addition, pistol has an integral accessory rail on frame. Fitted with 9mm or .40 S&W, 4.9" barrel, with heavy slide and 3-dot tritium sights. Weight about 35 oz.

NIB	Exc.	V.G.	Good	Fair	Poor
500	400	350	300	200	150

Model 92/96 Compact "Type M"

Essentially same as Model 92FS Compact, with the exception of a single column magazine that holds 8 rounds and reduces grip thickness of pistol. Weight 30.9 oz. Discontinued in 1993, reintroduced in 1998. Model 96 version (.40 S&W) introduced in 2000. **NOTE:** Add $90 for Tritium night sights.

NIB	Exc.	V.G.	Good	Fair	Poor
700	550	350	300	200	150

Model 92/96M Compact Inox

Same as above, with stainless steel slide and frame. Introduced in 2000.

NIB	Exc.	V.G.	Good	Fair	Poor
700	550	450	350	300	200

Model 92D Compact "Type M"

Same as above, with double-action-only trigger function. **NOTE:** Add $90 for Tritium night sights.

NIB	Exc.	V.G.	Good	Fair	Poor
1000	750	500	350	195	125

Model 92F

9mm Parabellum caliber double-action semi-automatic pistol, with 4.9" barrel, fixed sights and 15-shot double-stack magazine and an extended base. Matte blued finish, with walnut or plastic grips. Introduced in 1984. No longer in production.

NIB	Exc.	V.G.	Good	Fair	Poor
500	400	350	300	200	150

Model 92F U.S. Marked Slide

A special limited edition of 100 pistols made for the Armed Forces Reserves, with BER prefix serial numbers and U.S. M9 markings on frame and slide.

NIB	Exc.	V.G.	Good	Fair	Poor
1700	1500	1250	900	—	—

Model 92F Compact

As above, with 4.3" barrel and 13-shot magazine. No longer in production.

NIB	Exc.	V.G.	Good	Fair	Poor
550	450	350	300	200	150

Model 92FS Deluxe

Identical dimensions to full size Model 92FS. Addition of gold-plated engraved frame and gold-plated extra magazine. In fitted leather presentation hard case. Grips walnut briar, with gold initial plate. Introduced in 1993.

NIB	Exc.	V.G.	Good	Fair	Poor
5500	4500	3000	2000	1500	1000

Model 92FS "470th Anniversary" Limited Edition

Limited to only 470 pistols worldwide. Features high polish finish, with stainless steel gold-filled engravings, walnut grips, Anniversary logo on top of slide and on back of chrome plated magazine. Supplied with walnut case.

NIB	Exc.	V.G.	Good	Fair	Poor
2075	1300	800	600	375	200

Model 92/96D

Same specifications as standard Model 92 and Model 96. Variation has no visible hammer. Double-action-only. No manual safety. Weight 33.8 oz.

NIB	Exc.	V.G.	Good	Fair	Poor
425	375	325	275	200	150

Model 92/96DS

Same as above, with same manual safety as found on 92FS pistol. Introduced in 1994.

NIB	Exc.	V.G.	Good	Fair	Poor
425	375	325	275	200	150

Model 92G/96G

Designed for French Gendarmerie. This model has now been adopted for French Air Force as well as other government agencies. Features hammer drop lever that does not function as safety when lever is released, but lowers hammer and returns to ready to fire position automatically. Offered to law enforcement agencies only.

NIB	Exc.	V.G.	Good	Fair	Poor
650	550	475	400	250	100

Model 92/96 Vertec

Introduced in 2002. Chambered for 9mm or .40 S&W cartridges. Fitted with 4.7" barrel. Double-/single-action trigger. Features a new vertical grip design, with shorter trigger reach and thin grip panels. Removable front sight and integral accessory rail on frame. Magazine capacity 10 rounds. Weight about 32 oz.

NIB	Exc.	V.G.	Good	Fair	Poor
700	575	425	300	225	165

Model 92 Competition Conversion Kit

Kit includes 7.3" barrel, with counterweight and elevated front sight, semi-automatic, walnut grips and fully adjustable rear sight. Comes in special carrying case, with basic pistol. **NOTE:** Kit Price Only.

NIB	Exc.	V.G.	Good	Fair	Poor
500	350	300	200	150	100

Model 92/96 Combo

Features specially designed Model 96 pistol, with extra 92FS slide and barrel assembly. Barrel lengths are 4.66". Sold with one 10-round magazine in both 9mm and .40 S&W.

NIB	Exc.	V.G.	Good	Fair	Poor
850	725	600	425	275	200

Model M9 Limited Edition

Introduced in 1995 to commemorate 10th Anniversary of U.S. military's official sidearm. This 9mm pistol limited to 10,000 units. Special engraving on slide with special serial numbers. Slide stamped "U.S. 9mm M9-BERETTA U.S.A.-65490".

Standard Model

NIB	Exc.	V.G.	Good	Fair	Poor
825	700	450	300	200	100

Deluxe Model

Walnut grips, with gold plated hammer and grip screws.

NIB	Exc.	V.G.	Good	Fair	Poor
875	750	500	350	200	100

Model 92 Billennium

Introduced in 2001. Limited production pistol of 2,000 units world wide. Chambered for 9mm cartridge. Steel frame, with checkered front and backstrap. Nickel alloy finish, with unique engraving. Carbon fiber grips. Interchangeable sights, with adjustable rear sight. Carry case standard. Single action.

NIB	Exc.	V.G.	Good	Fair	Poor
1200	1000	800	600	475	325

92 Steel-I

Steel-frame semi-automatic in 9mm or .40 S&W. Single- or single-/double-action. 15+1 capacity, 4.7" barrel, weight 42.3 oz. IDPA certified. Fixed 3-dot sights. Introduced 2006.

NIB	Exc.	V.G.	Good	Fair	Poor
1075	850	600	475	300	150

M9A1

Semi-automatic single-/double-action in 9mm developed for U.S. Marine Corps. Capacity 10+1 or 15+1. Fixed sights. Introduced 2006.

NIB	Exc.	V.G.	Good	Fair	Poor
825	650	450	300	195	125

ELITE TEAM SERIES

In 1999, Beretta introduced a new series of pistols based on company's M92/96 pistol. Each of these pistols has specific features for specific shooting requirements.

Model 92/96 Custom Carry

Fitted with 4.3" barrel, shortened grip and low profile control levers. Safety lever is left side only. Magazine capacity 10 rounds. "CUSTOM CARRY" engraved on slide. Chambered for 9mm or .40 S&W calibers.

NIB	Exc.	V.G.	Good	Fair	Poor
625	500	400	300	200	100

Model 92/96 Border Marshall

Commercial version of pistol built for Immigration and Naturalization Service. Fitted with heavy-duty steel slide and short 4.7" I.N.S. style barrel. Rubber grips and night sights are standard. "BORDER MARSHALL" engraved on slide. Offered in 9mm or .40 S&W calibers.

NIB	Exc.	V.G.	Good	Fair	Poor
750	600	475	350	225	150

Model 92G/96G Elite

Chambered for 9mm or .40 S&W calibers. Fitted with 4.7" stainless steel barrel and heavy-duty Brigadier-style slide. Action is decock only. Slide has both front and rear serrations. Hammer is skeletonized. Beveled magazine well. Special "ELITE" engraving on slide. Weight about 35 oz.

NIB	Exc.	V.G.	Good	Fair	Poor
825	650	450	375	250	165

Model 92G Elite II

Version of Elite was developed for competition shooter. Fitted with 4.7" barrel and heavy slide. Has skeletonized hammer. Beveled magazine well and extended release. Checkered front and backstrap grip. Weight about 35 oz.

NIB	Exc.	V.G.	Good	Fair	Poor
925	725	550	395	275	150

Model 92FS Inox Tactical

Model has satin matte finish on its stainless steel slide. Frame is anodized aluminum. Black rubber grips and night sights are standard. Offered in 9mm only.

NIB	Exc.	V.G.	Good	Fair	Poor
775	625	500	350	225	100

COUGAR SERIES

Model 8000/8040/8045 Cougar

Compact size pistol using a short recoil rotating barrel. Features a firing pin lock, chrome lined barrel, anodized aluminum alloy frame, with Bruniton finish. Overall length 7"; barrel length 3.6"; overall height 5.5" unloaded weight 33.5 oz. Offered in double-/single-action as well as double-action-only. Magazine holds 10 rounds. Available in 9mm or .40 S&W In 1998 Beretta added .45 ACP caliber. **NOTE:** Add $50 for .45 ACP and Inox stainless finish.

NIB	Exc.	V.G.	Good	Fair	Poor
625	525	400	350	250	150

Model 8000/8040/8045 Mini Cougar

Introduced in 1997. Similar in design to full size model. Offered in 9mm, .40 S&W or .45 ACP. Fitted with 3.6" barrel (3.7" on .45 ACP). Empty weight 27 oz. Offered in double-/single-action or double-action-only. Magazine capacity: 10 rounds for 9mm; 8 rounds for .40 S&W. Weight between 27 oz. and 30 oz. depending on caliber. **NOTE:** Add $50 for .45 ACP and Inox stainless finish.

NIB	Exc.	V.G.	Good	Fair	Poor
500	450	350	225	125	75

Model 8000F—Cougar L

Similar to above. Fitted with a shortened grip frame. Chambered for 9mm cartridge. Fitted with a 3.6" barrel. Overall height as been reduced by .4". Weight about 28 oz. Introduced in 2003.

NIB	Exc.	V.G.	Good	Fair	Poor
600	500	400	300	175	95

Model 9000F

Introduced in 2000. Chambered for 9mm or .40 S&W cartridge. Fitted with 3.4" barrel. Has polymer frame. "F" type has single-/double-action trigger. Fixed sights. Magazine capacity 10 rounds. Weight about 27 oz.; overall length 6.6"; overall height 4.8". External hammer and black finish.

NIB	Exc.	V.G.	Good	Fair	Poor
550	450	350	200	125	75

Model 9000D

Same as above, with double-action-only trigger.

NIB	Exc.	V.G.	Good	Fair	Poor
550	450	350	275	150	100

Model 9000S

Chambered for 9mm or .40 S&W cartridges. Magazine capacity 10 rounds. Optional spacer Model 92/96 magazines can also be used.

Three-dot sight system. Accessory magazine bottom that extends when griped, but retracts when holstered is standard. Steel alloy frame and slide. Weight about 27 oz. Introduced in 2001.

NIB	Exc.	V.G.	Good	Fair	Poor
550	450	350	200	125	75

CHEETAH SERIES

Model 84/Cheetah

Small semi-automatic pistol chambered for .380 cartridge. Double-column magazine that holds 13 rounds. Offered in blue or nickel finish. Grips are checkered black plastic or checkered wood.

NIB	Exc.	V.G.	Good	Fair	Poor
450	375	325	275	200	150

Model 84BB

Similar to Model 84, but incorporates different features such as a firing pin blocking device and loaded chamber indicator. Single-column magazine holds 8 rounds of .380 shells. Discontinued in 1993.

NIB	Exc.	V.G.	Good	Fair	Poor
425	375	325	275	200	150

Model 85/Cheetah

Similar in appearance to Model 84. Features single-column magazine, with capacity of 8 rounds. Available in blue or nickel finish. Grips are checkered black plastic. Weight 22 oz.

NIB	Exc.	V.G.	Good	Fair	Poor
600	475	325	275	200	150

Model 86/Cheetah

.380 ACP semi-automatic pistol has 4.4" tip-up barrel. Magazine capacity 8 rounds. Furnished with checkered wood grips. Weight 23 oz.

NIB	Exc.	V.G.	Good	Fair	Poor
675	500	300	250	200	150

Model 87/Cheetah

.22-caliber double-action semi-automatic target pistol, with 3.8" or 6" barrel, adjustable sights and 7-shot magazine. Blued, with checkered walnut grips. Introduced in 1986.

NIB	Exc.	V.G.	Good	Fair	Poor
750	625	475	350	200	150

Model 87 Target

.22-caliber single-action target pistol. Features adjustable rear sight, integral scope base and external hammer. Anodized aluminum frame. Weight about 41 oz. Introduced in 2000.

NIB	Exc.	V.G.	Good	Fair	Poor
800	700	525	400	200	150

Model 89/Gold Standard

.22-caliber semi-automatic target pistol, with adjustable sights and 10-shot detachable magazine. Matte finish, with hand-fitting walnut grips. Introduced in 1988.

NIB	Exc.	V.G.	Good	Fair	Poor
900	725	550	400	300	150

Model PX4 Storm Pistol

Introduced in 2005. Features single-/double action trigger, with decocker and chambered for 9mm, .45 ACP or .40 S&W cartridges. Fitted with 4" barrel. Interchangeable grip backstraps. Reversible magazine release button. Picatinny rail. Fixed sights. Magazine capacity; 14 rounds .40 S&W, 17 rounds 9mm. Weight about 27.5 lbs. Compact model has 3.2" barrel and smaller grip frame. Magazine capacity reduced by two rounds.

NIB	Exc.	V.G.	Good	Fair	Poor
500	450	375	250	195	125

Model PX4 Storm Inox

Same features as PX4 Storm, except for stainless steel slide. Introduced in 2015.

NIB	Exc.	V.G.	Good	Fair	Poor
575	500	400	—	—	—

Model PX4 Storm Subcompact

Similar to above, with smaller dimensions and chambered in 9mm and .40 S&W only. Round capacity: 10- (.40) or 13- (9mm). Overall length 6.2". Weight: 26.1 oz.

NIB	Exc.	V.G.	Good	Fair	Poor
500	450	375	250	195	125

Model PX4 Storm SD (Special Duty)

Similar to PX4 Storm in .45 ACP only. Matte black slide and OD polymer frame, 9- or 10-round magazine. Overall length 8.2". Weight 28.6 oz.

NIB	Exc.	V.G.	Good	Fair	Poor
900	750	575	450	300	150

90-Two

Wrap-around polymer grip standard or slim. Single-/double-action semi-automatic in 9mm (10+1, 15+1 or 17+1 capacity) or .40 S&W (10+1 or 12+1 capacity). Types D, F or G. Fixed sights. 4.9" barrel. 32.5 oz. Introduced 2006. **NOTE:** Add 10 percent for luminous sights.

NIB	Exc.	V.G.	Good	Fair	Poor
600	475	350	290	210	150

BU9 Nano

Micro-compact DA-only 9mm, with 6+1 round capacity, 3" barrel, polymer frame, adjustable sights. Weight 17 oz. Introduced 2011.

NIB	Exc.	V.G.	Good	Fair	Poor
425	375	300	225	150	100

Pico

Similar to Nano, except chambered in .380 ACP with a more compact design. Double-action-only firing system, with a 2.7" barrel. Width .725", weight 11.5 oz. Adjustable sights, ambidextrous slide release and comes with two 6+1 magazines. Introduced in 2013.

NIB	Exc.	V.G.	Good	Fair	Poor
350	320	250	200	150	100

Stampede

Introduced in 2003. Single-action revolver chambered for .45 Colt, .44-40 or .357 Magnum cartridge. Choice of 4.75", 5.5" or 7.5" barrel. Blued, with Beretta case color and black polymer grips. Weight about 2.3 lbs. depending on barrel length. Discontinued in 2013.

NIB	Exc.	V.G.	Good	Fair	Poor
525	400	275	195	125	75

Stampede Buntline

.45 Colt with 18" barrel, satin-finish grips and gold Beretta medallion. Other features similar to Stampede Blue model.

NIB	Exc.	V.G.	Good	Fair	Poor
800	700	550	475	350	250

Stampede Nickel

Similar to Stampede Blue, with brushed nickel finish and walnut grips.

NIB	Exc.	V.G.	Good	Fair	Poor
500	400	295	195	125	75

Stampede Deluxe

As above, with charcoal blue finish and Beretta case color. Select walnut grips.

NIB	Exc.	V.G.	Good	Fair	Poor
620	500	375	250	195	125

Stampede Patton Model

Similar to Deluxe model, with light engraving on case color frame, light gold inlays and faux ivory grips.

NIB	Exc.	V.G.	Good	Fair	Poor
900	800	700	600	450	350

Stampede Bisley

Single-action 6-shot Bisley. Replica revolver in .45 Colt or .357 Magnum. Blued, with 4.75", 5.5" or 7.5" barrel. Introduced 2006. **NOTE:** Add 10 percent for nickel.

NIB	Exc.	V.G.	Good	Fair	Poor
620	500	375	250	195	125

Laramie

Break-open single-action revolver. Reminiscent of S&W #3. Chambered for.45 LC or .38 Special. Six-shot cylinder. Adjustable rear sight. 5" or 6.5" barrels. Introduced 2006. Discontinued 2008. Made by Beretta subsidiary Uberti. **NOTE:** Add 10 percent for nickel finish.

NIB	Exc.	V.G.	Good	Fair	Poor
1000	875	595	375	225	145

RIFLES

1873 Renegade Short Lever-Action Rifle

Lever-action rifle chambered in .45 Colt, .357 Magnum. Patterned after 1873 Winchester. Features include 20" round barrel, blued finish, checkered walnut buttstock and fore-end, adjustable rear sight and fixed blade front. Ten-round tubular magazine.

NIB	Exc.	V.G.	Good	Fair	Poor
1400	1050	875	595	375	225

Gold Rush Slide-Action Rifle and Carbine

External replica of old Colt Lightning Magazine Rifle. Chambered in .357 Magnum and .45 Colt. Features include 20" round or 24.5" octagonal barrel, case-hardened receiver, walnut buttstock and fore-end, crescent buttplate, 13-round (rifle) or 10-round (carbine) magazine. Available as Standard Carbine, Standard Rifle or Deluxe Rifle.

NIB	Exc.	V.G.	Good	Fair	Poor
1200	1050	875	595	375	225

Cx4 Storm

Introduced in 2003. Semi-automatic carbine has 16.6" barrel. Chambered for 9mm, .40 S&W or .45 ACP cartridge. Synthetic stock, with rubber recoil pad that has adjustable stock spacers. Ghost ring rear sight, with adjustable post front sight. Forward accessory rail. Magazine capacity: 10 rounds .40 S&W or 9mm; 8 rounds .45 ACP. Weight about 5.75 lbs.

NIB	Exc.	V.G.	Good	Fair	Poor
800	650	500	350	200	100

AR-70

.223-caliber semi-automatic rifle, with 17.7" barrel, adjustable diopter sights and 8- or 30-shot magazine. Black epoxy finish, with synthetic stock. Weight about 8.3 lbs. No longer imported into U.S.

NIB	Exc.	V.G.	Good	Fair	Poor
2100	1900	1500	1000	750	400

ARX 100

Tactical semi-automatic rifle that is a civilian version of ARX-160 select-fire military rifle developed for the Italian Armed Forces. (This is not to be confused with ARX-160 .22 rimfire rifle.) Modular design allows easy maintenance. Standard configuration with four Picatinny rails. All controls are ambidextrous. Chambered for 5.56 NATO. Introduced in 2013.

NIB	Exc.	V.G.	Good	Fair	Poor
1750	1400	1050	800	550	250

ARX 160

Similar in appearance and operation to ARX 100 design, but chambered in .22 Long Rifle.

NIB	Exc.	V.G.	Good	Fair	Poor
500	425	350	250	150	100

BM-59 Garand

Gas-operated semi-automatic rifle, with detachable box magazine. Chambered for .308 cartridge. Walnut stock. Barrel length 19.3" with muzzle-brake. Magazine capacity 5, 10 or 20 rounds. Weight about 9.5 lbs.

NIB	Exc.	V.G.	Good	Fair	Poor
3000	2700	2100	1500	400	200

Model 500 Custom

Bolt-action rifle in three action lengths, 24" barrel, open sights. Chambered in .222 Rem., .223 Rem., .243 Win., .270 Win., .308 Win., .30-06. Blued finish and checkered walnut stock. Offered in several grades.

NIB	Exc.	V.G.	Good	Fair	Poor
—	600	525	400	325	275

Model 500S

NIB	Exc.	V.G.	Good	Fair	Poor
—	625	550	425	350	300

Model 500DL

NIB	Exc.	V.G.	Good	Fair	Poor
—	1400	1250	1000	775	650

Model 500DEELL

NIB	Exc.	V.G.	Good	Fair	Poor
—	1600	1450	1200	975	800

Model 500DEELLS

NIB	Exc.	V.G.	Good	Fair	Poor
—	1625	1475	1225	1000	825

Model 501

.243- or .308-caliber bolt-action rifle, with 23" barrel, furnished without sights and 6-shot magazine. Blued, with checkered walnut stock. Discontinued in 1986. Offered in same variations as Model 500 series-501S, 501DL, 501DLS, 501EELL and 501EELLS. Values for this series are same as for 500 series rifles.

Model 502

.270, 7mm Rem. Magnum and .30-06 caliber bolt-action rifle, with 24" barrel (without sights) and 5-shot magazine. Blued, with checkered walnut stock. Discontinued in 1986. Available in same variations as Model 500 and Model 501. Valued approximately 10 percent higher in each variation.

Mato Standard

Bolt-action rifles built on Mauser 98 type action, with controlled-round feed, three-position safety, adjustable trigger. Chambered in .270 Win., .280 Rem., .30-06, .300 Win. Magnum, .338 Win. Magnum. Composite stock.

NIB	Exc.	V.G.	Good	Fair	Poor
1200	1000	800	600	300	175

Mato Deluxe

Bolt-action rifle introduced into Beretta product line in 1997. Stock is XXX Claro walnut, with hand-rubbed oil finish and black fore-end tip. Chambered for .270 Win., .280, .30-06, 7mm Magnum, .300 Magnum, .338 Magnum and .375 H&H. Weight about 8 lbs.

NIB	Exc.	V.G.	Good	Fair	Poor
2000	1500	1000	750	350	200

PREMIUM RIFLES

Model S689 Sable

9.3x74R or .30-06 caliber over/under rifle, with boxlock action, 23" ribbed barrels and express-type sights. Blued case hardened or nickel-plated, with checkered walnut stock. Double triggers and automatic ejectors. Offered in three grades. **NOTE:** Add $1,200 extra 20-gauge barrel with forearm; $2,000 scope with claw mounts.

Silver Sable

NIB	Exc.	V.G.	Good	Fair	Poor
3850	3000	2500	1750	1200	300

Gold Sable

NIB	Exc.	V.G.	Good	Fair	Poor
6500	5500	4500	3000	1500	350

Diamond Sable

NIB	Exc.	V.G.	Good	Fair	Poor
12750	10000	7500	5500	2000	1000

SSO Express

.375 H&H and .458 Win. Magnum caliber over/under double barrel rifle, with 23" barrels, folding express sights, double triggers and automatic ejectors. Furnished with fitted case. Available on custom order basis. Should be individually appraised.

NIB	Exc.	V.G.	Good	Fair	Poor
18000	13000	9500	6000	3500	2500

SSO5 Express

More finely finished version of above.

NIB	Exc.	V.G.	Good	Fair	Poor
20000	15000	11000	8000	5000	3000

SSO6

Premium grade sidelock over/under express rifle. Equipped with double triggers. Offered in 9.3x74R, .375 H&H Magnum and .458 Win. Magnum. Fitted with 24" barrel, with express sights. Claw mounts for Zeiss scopes are available from factory. Receiver is case-colored, with light scroll engraving. Special select walnut used in stock and forearm, with fine line checkering. Stock comes with cheekpiece and rubber recoil pad. Furnished with leather case. Weight about 11 lbs.

NIB	Exc.	V.G.	Good	Fair	Poor
62000	52000	34000	24000	10000	3000

SSO6 EELL

Offered in same calibers as above. Furnished with hand engraved game scenes, with gold inlays. Walnut stock is special select briar, with fine diamond line checkering.

NIB	Exc.	V.G.	Good	Fair	Poor
110000	90000	70000	40000	18000	10000

Model 455

Premium grade side-by-side express rifle, with slide locks. Available in these calibers: .375 H&H Magnum, .458 Win. Magnum, .470 Nitro Express, .500 Nitro Express and .416 Rigby. Receiver is case-colored, without engraving. Walnut stock highly figured, with fine line checkering. Comes supplied with express sights. Claw mounts and Zeiss scope offered at customer's request only on .375, .458 and .416. Weight about 11 lbs.

NIB	Exc.	V.G.	Good	Fair	Poor
80000	70000	55000	40000	20000	5000

Model 455 EELL

Same as above. Furnished with case-colored game scene engraving, with gold inlays. Walnut briar stock, with fine diamond line checkering. Supplied with leather case and accessories.

NIB	Exc.	V.G.	Good	Fair	Poor
110000	85000	60000	45000	25000	10000

SHOTGUNS

Beretta shotguns are marked with a symbol or "0" stamping to indicate type of fixed choke in barrel or barrels. Usually this stamping is on side of barrel in rear, near receiver on semi-automatics and near ejectors on double-barrel shotguns. Beretta shotguns with screw-in Mobilchoke tubes will have notches cut in them to indicate amount of choke placed in tube.

BL SERIES

BL series of over/under shotguns were manufactured between 1968 and 1973. Chambered for 12-, 20- or 28-gauge. Offered with 26", 28" or 30" ventilated rib barrels, with various choke combinations. They feature boxlock actions and offered with single-/double triggers and manual extractors or automatic ejectors. Finish blued, with checkered walnut stocks. Configurations differ basically in quality of materials, workmanship and degree of ornamentation. **NOTE:** Add 50 percent for 20-gauge; 75 percent for 28-gauge.

BL-1

NIB	Exc.	V.G.	Good	Fair	Poor
—	500	450	350	225	150

BL-2

NIB	Exc.	V.G.	Good	Fair	Poor
—	425	375	300	250	200

BL-2/S (Speed Trigger)

NIB	Exc.	V.G.	Good	Fair	Poor
—	450	400	325	275	225

BL-2 Stakeout

18" barrel.

NIB	Exc.	V.G.	Good	Fair	Poor
—	400	350	275	225	175

BL-3

NIB	Exc.	V.G.	Good	Fair	Poor
—	600	550	475	425	350

BL-3 Competition

NIB	Exc.	V.G.	Good	Fair	Poor
—	650	600	525	475	400

BL-4

NIB	Exc.	V.G.	Good	Fair	Poor
—	800	750	650	525	425

BL-4 Competition

NIB	Exc.	V.G.	Good	Fair	Poor
—	850	800	700	575	450

BL-5

NIB	Exc.	V.G.	Good	Fair	Poor
—	900	850	725	575	450

BL-5 Competition

NIB	Exc.	V.G.	Good	Fair	Poor
—	950	900	775	600	475

BL-6

Sidelock.

NIB	Exc.	V.G.	Good	Fair	Poor
—	1250	1150	1000	850	675

BL-6 Competition

NIB	Exc.	V.G.	Good	Fair	Poor
—	1300	1200	1050	900	725

Model S55 B

12- or 20-gauge over/under shotgun, with 26", 28" or 30" ventilated rib barrels, various choke combinations and boxlock action with single-selective trigger and extractors. Blued, with checkered walnut stock.

NIB	Exc.	V.G.	Good	Fair	Poor
—	550	500	400	325	275

Model S56 E

As above more finely finished.

NIB	Exc.	V.G.	Good	Fair	Poor
—	600	550	450	375	325

Model S58 Competition

As above, with 26" or 30" barrels, wide ventilated ribs. Competition-type stocks.

NIB	Exc.	V.G.	Good	Fair	Poor
—	700	650	550	475	400

Silver Snipe

12-,20-, 28-gauge over/under shotgun, with 26", 28" or 30" barrels. Boxlock action, with double trigger and extractors. Blued, with checkered walnut stock. Manufactured from 1955 through 1967. Single-selective trigger version, with ventilated rib and automatic ejectors would be worth approximately an additional 50 percent. **NOTE:** Add 50 percent for 20-gauge; 80 percent for 28-gauge.

NIB	Exc.	V.G.	Good	Fair	Poor
—	700	600	500	350	200

Golden Snipe

As above, with ventilated rib and automatic ejectors. **NOTE:** Add 10 percent for single-selective trigger; 50 percent for 20-gauge; 80 percent for 28-gauge.

NIB	Exc.	V.G.	Good	Fair	Poor
—	850	700	500	350	200

Model 57 E

As above more finely finished. Manufactured between 1955 and 1967.

NIB	Exc.	V.G.	Good	Fair	Poor
—	950	800	600	475	250

ASEL Model

12- or 20-gauge over/under shotgun, with 26", 28" or 30" ventilated rib barrel and various choke combinations. Single-selective trigger and automatic ejectors. Blued, with checkered pistol-grip stock. Manufactured between 1947 and 1964. Prices listed for 20-gauge. **NOTE:** Add 30 percent for EELL grade; deduct $1000 from Exc. condition for 12-gauge.

NIB	Exc.	V.G.	Good	Fair	Poor
—	4250	2500	1200	750	400

Model 409 PB

12-, 16-, 20- and 28-gauge boxlock double-barrel shotgun, with 27", 28" or 30" barrels, double triggers and extractors. Various choke combinations. Blued, with checkered walnut stock. Manufactured between 1934 and 1964. **NOTE:** Add 50 percent for 20-gauge; 100 percent for 28-gauge.

NIB	Exc.	V.G.	Good	Fair	Poor
—	1100	850	625	500	250

Model 410

As above, with 32" Full-choke barrel. Blued, with checkered walnut stock. Introduced in 1934, 10-gauge only.

NIB	Exc.	V.G.	Good	Fair	Poor
—	1400	1200	800	600	300

Model 410 E

More finely finished version of 409PB.

NIB	Exc.	V.G.	Good	Fair	Poor
—	1600	1350	1000	750	400

Model 411 E

Model 410, with false sideplates and more heavily engraved. Manufactured between 1934 and 1964. **NOTE:** Add 25 percent for 20-gauge; 100 percent for 28-gauge.

NIB	Exc.	V.G.	Good	Fair	Poor
—	2100	1750	1250	800	425

Model 424

12- and 20-gauge boxlock shotgun, with 26" or 28" barrels, double triggers, various choke combinations and extractors. Blued, with checkered walnut stock. In 20-gauge designated Model 426 and worth an additional 50 percent.

NIB	Exc.	V.G.	Good	Fair	Poor
—	1200	950	675	500	225

Model 426 E

As above, with silver inlays and heavier engraving, single-selective trigger and automatic ejectors. Not imported after 1983.

NIB	Exc.	V.G.	Good	Fair	Poor
—	1400	1150	875	700	350

Model 625

12- or 20-gauge boxlock double-barrel shotgun, with 26", 28" or 30" barrels, various choke combinations, double triggers and extractors. Moderately engraved. Blued, with checkered walnut grip. Imported between 1984 and 1986. **NOTE:** Add 50 percent for 20-gauge.

NIB	Exc.	V.G.	Good	Fair	Poor
1200	900	750	600	500	250

Model 626 Field Grade

12- or 20-gauge boxlock double barrel shotgun, with 26" or 28" barrel, various choke combinations, single trigger and automatic ejectors. Engraved, blued with checkered walnut stock. Imported between 1984 and 1988.

NIB	Exc.	V.G.	Good	Fair	Poor
1400	1000	825	700	575	475

Model 626 Onyx

Boxlock side-by-side shotgun offered in 12- and 20-gauge. Choice of 26" or 28" solid rib barrels, with screw-in chokes. Double triggers are standard, but single trigger available on request. Receiver anti-glare black matte finish. Stock walnut, with hand checkering and pistol-grip. Weight: 12-gauge 6 lbs. 13 oz.; 20-gauge 6 lbs. 13 oz.

NIB	Exc.	V.G.	Good	Fair	Poor
1600	1250	850	750	500	400

Model 627 EL

Offered in 12-gauge only, with choice of 26" or 28" solid rib barrels. Walnut is highly figured and fine cut checkered. Receiver silver, with side plates engraved with scroll. Comes with hard case.

NIB	Exc.	V.G.	Good	Fair	Poor
2600	2000	1750	1500	1250	650

Model 627 EELL

Same as above. Fitted with scroll engraved side plates and game scenes. Walnut highly figured, with fine line checkering. Straight-grip stock also offered. Comes with hard case.

NIB	Exc.	V.G.	Good	Fair	Poor
3850	3500	3000	2500	1500	1000

GR Series

Moderately priced series of side-by-side boxlock double shotguns. Imported from 1968 to about 1976. Offered in 12- or 20-gauge, with fixed chokes. GR-2 has double triggers with folding front trigger, extractors. GR-3 has single selective trigger, better wood. GR-4 has automatic ejectors, higher grade wood. Prices shown are for 12-gauge models. **NOTE:** Add 50 percent for 20-gauge.

GR-1

NIB	Exc.	V.G.	Good	Fair	Poor
1000	850	700	600	500	350

GR-2

NIB	Exc.	V.G.	Good	Fair	Poor
1150	950	800	700	600	400

GR-3

NIB	Exc.	V.G.	Good	Fair	Poor
1250	1050	900	800	700	500

Silver Hawk

10- or 12-gauge boxlock double-barrel shotgun, with 30" barrels, double triggers and extractors. Blued, with silver-finished receiver and checkered walnut stock. 10-gauge version worth an additional 20 percent. Discontinued in 1967.

NIB	Exc.	V.G.	Good	Fair	Poor
—	700	500	375	250	150

Silver Hawk Featherweight

Similar to above. Made in 12-, 16-, 20- and 28-gauge, with 26", 28", 30" or 32" barrels. Standard choices of fixed chokes. Single-/double triggers. Automatic ejectors. **NOTE:** Add 10 percent for single trigger; 50 percent for 20-gauge; 80 percent for 28-gauge.

NIB	Exc.	V.G.	Good	Fair	Poor
1000	875	750	600	450	300

Model 470 Silver Hawk

Introduced in 1997 to commemorate Beretta's 470 years in the gunmaking business. Offered in 12- or 20-gauge configurations. Receiver silver chrome with engraving. Top lever checkered, with gold inlaid hawk's head. Fitted with straight-grip stock, splinter forearm of select walnut with oil finish. Choice of 26" or 28" barrels, with auto ejection or manual extraction. Weight: 12-gauge about 6.5 lbs.; 20-gauge about 6 lbs.

NIB	Exc.	V.G.	Good	Fair	Poor
2400	2000	1500	—	—	—

Model 470 Silver Hawk EL

Introduced in 2002. Features color case hardened frame and side plates, with gold filled game scene engraving. Offered in 12- or 20-gauge, with choice of 26" or 28" barrels. Weight: 5.9 lbs. for 20-gauge; 6.5 lbs. for 12-gauge.

NIB	Exc.	V.G.	Good	Fair	Poor
4800	4000	3000	—	—	—

Model 471 Silver Hawk

Introduced in 2003. Side-by-side shotgun has boxlock receiver. Offered in 12- and 20-gauge. Choice of 26" or 28" barrels, pistol-grip with beavertail fore-end or straight-grip stock with splinter fore-end. Straight-grip stock, with case color receiver is available at a premium. Select walnut stock with oil finish. Single-selective trigger. Weight: about 6.5 lbs. in 12-gauge; 5.9 lbs. in 20-gauge. **NOTE:** Add $350 for straight-grip stock, with case color receiver.

NIB	Exc.	V.G.	Good	Fair	Poor
3000	2500	2000	1500	900	400

Model 471 EL

High-grade variation of above. Has satin-finished Turkish walnut stock and coin-finished receiver with gold accents.

NIB	Exc.	V.G.	Good	Fair	Poor
6800	6000	4800	3500	1700	500

Model 486 Parallelo

Side-by-side model introduced in 2014. Chambered in 12-gauge only, with a round action decorated with English style scroll engraving and scalloped coin-finish. Checkered walnut stock has a straight-grip, with splinter fore-end. Other features include single selective trigger, choice of automatic ejectors or manual extractors and choke tubes or fixed chokes.

NIB	Exc.	V.G.	Good	Fair	Poor
4600	3700	2900	2200	1200	500

BERETTA "SO" SERIES & OTHER PREMIUM SHOTGUNS

Over/under shotguns fitted with side-locks, automatic ejectors, single-/double triggers. Barrel lengths from 26" to 30", with a wide variety of choke combinations. Introduced 1948 in 12-gauge only. No longer imported as production gun in 1986. Many of these SO guns were sold through firm of Garcia, a sporting goods firm and distributor. Various grades are priced according to quality of wood, finish engraving coverage and the like. Do not confuse these earlier Beretta shotguns with present line of premium grade Berettas now being imported into U.S.

SO-1

NIB	Exc.	V.G.	Good	Fair	Poor
—	3000	2400	1500	800	400

SO-2

NIB	Exc.	V.G.	Good	Fair	Poor
—	4000	2700	2000	900	500

SO-3

NIB	Exc.	V.G.	Good	Fair	Poor
—	5000	4400	3500	1500	1000

SO-4 (Garcia SO3EL)

NOTE: Add 80 percent for fully engraved Garcia Model SO3-EL.

NIB	Exc.	V.G.	Good	Fair	Poor
—	7900	6900	3500	2000	1500

SO-5 (Garcia SO-3 EELL)

NIB	Exc.	V.G.	Good	Fair	Poor
—	—	7900	5900	3500	2500

SO-6 (450 or 451 EL) Side-by-Side

Fitted with Holland & Holland-style sidelocks and third fastener.

NIB	Exc.	V.G.	Good	Fair	Poor
—	7500	6500	5500	3500	2500

SO-7 (451 EELL) Side-by-Side

NIB	Exc.	V.G.	Good	Fair	Poor
—	8900	7900	5900	4000	3000

SO-5 Trap

Premium grade Beretta over/under shotgun. Built for competition trap shooting. Available in 12-gauge, with 30" ventilated rib barrels standard. Barrels in 28" and 32" may be special ordered. Receiver silver with light scroll engraving. Stock is select highly figured walnut, with pistol-grip. Offered in International or Monte Carlo dimensions. Special trap rubber recoil pad is furnished. Weight 8 lbs. 2 oz. Furnished with leather case and tools.

NIB	Exc.	V.G.	Good	Fair	Poor
20500	16000	12000	6500	3000	600

SO-5 Trap 2 Barrel Set

NIB	Exc.	V.G.	Good	Fair	Poor
23500	18500	13000	6500	3000	600

SO-5 Sporting Clays

Offered in 12-gauge only, with 28", 30" or 32" barrels; 26" on special order. Sporting clay dimension walnut stock, with pistol-grip and rubber recoil pad. Weight 7 lbs. 8 oz.

SO-5 sidelocks

NIB	Exc.	V.G.	Good	Fair	Poor
20500	10000	7500	5000	2750	500

SO-5 Skeet

Same general specifications as SO-5 Trap. Furnished to skeet dimensions. Offered in 12-gauge only, with 26" or 28" ventilated rib barrels choked skeet. Weight 7 lbs. 8 oz.

NIB	Exc.	V.G.	Good	Fair	Poor
20500	16000	7500	5000	2750	500

SO-6 EL

Premium grade Beretta available in several different configurations. Similar to SO-5. Available in 12-gauge only. Features true side-lock action, single-selective or non-selective trigger, fixed or screw-in choke tubes. Receiver offered in silver finish or case hardened, without engraving. Highly select walnut, with fine line checkering. Choice of pistol- or straight-grip. Supplied with leather fitted hard case. Weight about 7 lbs. 4 oz. depending on barrel length.

SO-6 receiver

SO-6 Trap

NIB	Exc.	V.G.	Good	Fair	Poor
26500	13000	8500	5000	1700	500

SO-6 Skeet

NIB	Exc.	V.G.	Good	Fair	Poor
26500	13000	8500	5000	1700	500

SO-6 Sporting Clays

NIB	Exc.	V.G.	Good	Fair	Poor
26500	13000	8500	5000	1700	500

SO-6 EELL

Higher grade in SO-6 series. Features silver receiver, custom engraving with scroll or game scenes. Gold inlays are available on request. Choice of barrel lengths from 26" to 30". Choice of pistol-/straight-grip. All the same features of SO-6, with higher fit and finish. Offered in 12-gauge only.

NIB	Exc.	V.G.	Good	Fair	Poor
43750	33500	27000	20000	12000	600

SO-6 EESS

Same specifications as SO-6 EELL grade. Ruby, sapphire or emerald side plates, with diamond brilliants.

NIB	Exc.	V.G.	Good	Fair	Poor
88500	75000	55000	30000	—	—

SO-7

One of Beretta's best-grade sidelock double-barrel shotgun. Elaborately engraved. Has highest grade walnut stock. No longer in production.

NIB	Exc.	V.G.	Good	Fair	Poor
—	10500	8850	7250	5500	4500

SO-9

Model over/under is Beretta's highest grade. Offered in 12-, 20-, 28-gauge and .410 bore. True side lock (removable) receiver is highly engraved, with scroll or game scenes by Italy's finest craftsmen. Barrel lengths 26" to 30", with solid hand filed rib. Walnut stock is finest available. Either pistol-/straight-grip. Stock dimensions to customers request. A custom fitted leather case, with accessories is supplied with gun. Custom order gun. Independent appraisal is strongly suggested prior to sale.

NIB	Exc.	V.G.	Good	Fair	Poor
38000	30000	22000	15000	7500	2000

SO-10

Beretta's custom-made highest grade over/under sidelock. In 12-, 20-, 28-gauge or .410 bore. Receiver machined from a solid block of tri-alloy steel. Polishing of surfaces all done by hand. Highest grade walnut stock made to owner's specifications. Numerous engraving patterns. Introduced in 2003

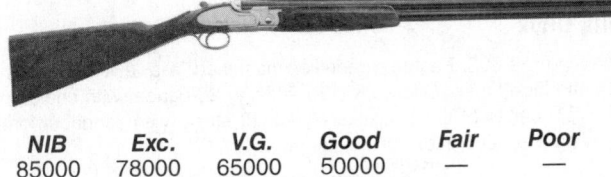

NIB	Exc.	V.G.	Good	Fair	Poor
85000	78000	65000	50000	—	—

Jubilee Field Grade (Giubileo)

Introduced in 1998. Beretta's finest boxlock over/under shotgun. Fitted with sideplates without screws. Offered in 12-, 20-, 28-gauge and .410 bore, with 26" to 30" barrel depending on gauge. Each gun richly engraved with fine scroll and signed by master engravers. Highly figured walnut, with pistol-/straight-grip. Weights range from about 7 lbs. in 12-gauge to 5.5 lbs. in .410 bore.

SO-9 with close-ups of engraving patterns

Single Gun

NIB	Exc.	V.G.	Good	Fair	Poor
14750	12000	825	4500	2200	600

Matched Pair

NIB	Exc.	V.G.	Good	Fair	Poor
32650	—	—	—	—	—

Jubilee Sporting Grade

Similar to above model in terms of finish. Offered in 12-gauge only. Choice of 30" or 32" barrels. Pistol-grip standard. **NOTE:** Add $1,500 for two barrel combination, with 20-gauge barrel and extended chokes.

NIB	Exc.	V.G.	Good	Fair	Poor
14750	12000	8250	4500	2200	600

Jubilee II (Giublio)

Side-by-side model offered in 12- or 20-gauge only, with straight-grip stocks. Choice of 26" or 28" barrels. Full coverage scroll engraving and highly figured walnut. Double triggers by special order only. Weight about: 12-gauge 6.5 lbs.; 20-gauge 6 lbs.

Single Gun

NIB	Exc.	V.G.	Good	Fair	Poor
14750	12000	8250	4500	2200	600

Matched Pair

NIB	Exc.	V.G.	Good	Fair	Poor
32650	2600	17000	9200	4000	900

ASE Deluxe Sporting

Boxlock over/under gun offered in 12-gauge only, with choice of 28" or 30" barrels. Classic European scroll engraving. Offered in both field and competition configuration. Weight about 7.5 lbs. for 12-gauge.

NIB	Exc.	V.G.	Good	Fair	Poor
25000	18500	12000	900	700	400

Model 687 EELL Gallery Special

Special version of this model. Especially engraved guns, with upgraded wood that are only made for Beretta Galleries. Offered in 12-, 20-, 28-gauge and .410 bore.

Single Gun

NIB	Exc.	V.G.	Good	Fair	Poor
8500	7300	5900	4500	3300	500

Special Combo—20/28 Gauge

NIB	Exc.	V.G.	Good	Fair	Poor
9500	8600	6700	5800	4000	600

Matched Pair

NIB	Exc.	V.G.	Good	Fair	Poor
17100	15500	11500	8000	4750	700

Imperiale Montecarlo

Side-by-side gun chambered for 12-, 20-, 28-gauge shell. True sidelock action. Choice of 26", 27" or 28" barrels, with fixed chokes. Other lengths by special request. Weight about: 7.3 lbs. for 12-gauge; 6.5 lbs. for 20-gauge; 6.2 lbs. for 28-gauge. Master engraved and signed. Beretta's top-of-the-line series built to customer's specifications. Seek qualified appraisal. MSRP from $150,000.

Diana

Side-by-side gun chambered for 12- or 20-gauge, with choice of barrel lengths. Action is true sidelock, with exposed hammers. Weight about: 12-gauge 7.2 lbs.; 20-gauge 6.4 lbs. Master engraved and signed. Hand made to customer's specifications. Seek qualified appraisal. MSRP from $170,000.

Model 451 Series

Custom order sidelock shotgun. Prospective purchasers are advised to secure a qualified appraisal prior to acquisition.

NIB	Exc.	V.G.	Good	Fair	Poor
8000	6900	5000	4000	2000	700

Model 450 Series

Model same as 451 series, with exception of being a Holland & Holland sidelock design. Prospective purchasers are advised to secure a qualified appraisal prior to acquisition.

NIB	Exc.	V.G.	Good	Fair	Poor
9000	7500	5800	4500	2500	1000

Model 452

Premium grade side-by-side shotgun fitted with sidelocks (removable). Offered in 12-gauge only. 26", 28" or 30" solid rib barrels. Receiver highly polished silver finish, without engraving. Triggers may be double-/single-selective or single non-selective. Stock and forearm special select walnut, with fine line checkering. Choice of pistol-/straight-grip. Comes with leather hard case. Weight about 6 lbs. 13 oz.

NIB	Exc.	V.G.	Good	Fair	Poor
24000	19000	14500	8500	4500	2500

Model 452 EELL

Same as above. Furnished with fine scroll or game scene engraving. Highest grade walnut furnished for stock and forearm. Leather case with accessories furnished.

NIB	Exc.	V.G.	Good	Fair	Poor
31000	27500	19500	11000	7000	600

BERETTA ONYX SERIES

Series designation first used in 2003 to simplify product line. Instead of using numeric model references, company now refers to these guns and others by series name.

Onyx

Over/under gun offered in 12-, 20- and 28-gauge. Choice of 26" or 28" barrels. Features boxlock action, with select checkered walnut stock, single-selective trigger, schnabel fore-end and auto safety. Black rubber recoil pad. Blued barrels and action. Weight about 6.8 lbs. for 12-gauge.

NIB	Exc.	V.G.	Good	Fair	Poor
1675	1350	950	650	475	200

Onyx Waterfowler 3.5

As above in 12-gauge, with 3.5" chamber. Matte black finish.

NIB	Exc.	V.G.	Good	Fair	Poor
1750	1400	1050	700	500	250

White Onyx

Introduced in 2003. Features receiver machined in a jeweled pattern, with satin nickel alloy. Offered in 12-, 20- and 28-gauge, with choice of 26" or 28" barrels. Select checkered walnut stock, with schnabel fore-end. Weight about 6.8 lbs. for 12-gauge.

NIB	Exc.	V.G.	Good	Fair	Poor
1775	1425	1250	700	500	250

Onyx Pro

Introduced in 2003. Over/under shotgun offered in 12-, 20- and 28-gauge. Choice of 26" or 28" ventilated rib barrels, with choke tubes. Single-selective trigger. Checkered X-Tra wood stock. Gel-Tek recoil pad. Supplied with plastic carry case. Weight about 6.8 lbs.

NIB	Exc.	V.G.	Good	Fair	Poor
1700	1300	1000	600	400	200

Onyx Pro 3.5

As above in 12-gauge, with 3.5" chamber. Weight about 6.9 lbs. Introduced in 2003.

NIB	Exc.	V.G.	Good	Fair	Poor
1700	1300	1000	600	400	200

BERETTA 682 SERIES

682/682 Gold

High-grade quality-built over/under shotgun. Offered in 12- and 20-gauge. Also available in some configurations in 28-gauge and .410 bore, with barrel lengths from 26" to 34" depending on type of shooting required. Fitted with single-selective trigger and automatic ejectors. Barrels fitted with ventilated rib and various fixed or screw-in choke combinations. Stock is high-grade walnut, with fine checkering in stock dimensions to fit function of gun. Frame is silver, with light scroll borders on most models. This model covers a wide variety of applications. These are listed by grade and/or function:

NOTE: Beretta Competition Series shotguns are also referred to as 682 Gold Competition Series guns, such as Model 682 Gold Trap or Model 682 Gold X Trap Combo and so forth.

682 Super Skeet

Model offered in 12-gauge only, with 28" ventilated rib barrels choked skeet and skeet. Single-selective trigger and auto ejectors standard. This Super Skeet features ported barrels and adjustable length of pull and drop. Fitted hard case standard. Weight 7 lbs. 8 oz.

NIB	Exc.	V.G.	Good	Fair	Poor
1800	1400	1100	850	650	300

682 Gold Skeet

Standard 12-gauge skeet. Features choice of 26" or 28" ventilated rib barrels, choked skeet and skeet. Walnut stock of International dimensions, with special skeet rubber recoil pad. Gun supplied with hard case. Weight 7 lbs. 8 oz.

NIB	Exc.	V.G.	Good	Fair	Poor
1700	1300	1000	800	650	300

682 4 Barrel Set

Skeet gun fitted with 4 barrels in 12-, 20-, 28-gauge and .410 bore. Each barrel is 28", choked skeet and skeet. Fitted with ventilated rib.

NIB	Exc.	V.G.	Good	Fair	Poor
4000	3500	3000	2500	2000	650

682 Super Sporting/682 Gold Sporting Ported

Built for sporting clays. This 12- or 20-gauge model features ported barrel, adjustable length of pull and drop. Fitted with 28" or 30" ventilated barrel, with screw-in chokes; fixed chokes on special order. Checkered walnut stock, with pistol-grip and recoil pad. Supplied with case. Introduced in 1993. Weight: 12-gauge 7 lbs. 8 oz.; 20-gauge 6 lbs. 3 oz.

NIB	Exc.	V.G.	Good	Fair	Poor
2400	2000	1600	1100	700	350

682 Gold Sporting

Standard version of 12- or 20-gauge Super Sporting. Choice of 28" or 30" ventilated rib barrel, with screw-in chokes. Checkered walnut stock, with recoil pad. Introduced in 1993.

NIB	Exc.	V.G.	Good	Fair	Poor
2000	1650	1400	1250	950	350

682 Sporting Combo

Similar to 682 Sporting, with addition of two 12-gauge 28" and 30" barrels, fitted with screw-in chokes. Supplied with hard case.

NIB	Exc.	V.G.	Good	Fair	Poor
3200	2700	2250	1750	1250	650

682 Super Trap

12-gauge trap model (20-gauge set of barrels is available on special order) features ported 30" or 32" ventilated rib barrels, with fixed or screw-in chokes. Automatic ejectors, single non-selective trigger, standard. Checkered walnut stock can be adjusted for length of pull and drop of comb. Offered in Monte Carlo or International dimensions. Weight about 8 lbs. 6 oz.

NIB	Exc.	V.G.	Good	Fair	Poor
2300	2000	1700	1250	950	500

682 Top Single Super Trap

Same as Super Trap. Available in single barrel configuration of 32" or 34".

NIB	Exc.	V.G.	Good	Fair	Poor
2600	2150	1700	1350	950	500

682 Top Combo Super Trap

This configuration features single barrel and over/under barrel, both interchangeable. Combinations are: 30"/32" and 30"/34".

NIB	Exc.	V.G.	Good	Fair	Poor
3300	2975	2350	1750	1250	650

682 Trap

Standard variation of Beretta trap gun. This 12-gauge comes standard with 30" ventilated rib barrels. However, 28" and 32" barrels can be special ordered. Fixed or screw-in chokes available. Three-position sliding trigger allows for adjustable length of pull. Checkered walnut stock, with recoil pad standard. Stock available in Monte Carlo or International dimensions. Customer has choice of silver or black receiver. Comes cased.

NIB	Exc.	V.G.	Good	Fair	Poor
2300	1950	1700	1250	900	450

682 Top Single Trap

12-gauge single barrel trap gun available in 32" or 34" ventilated rib barrel.

NIB	Exc.	V.G.	Good	Fair	Poor
2000	1600	1200	1000	600	450

682 Mono Combo Trap

Special configuration features single barrel, with ventilated rib set to place single barrel in bottom position of what would normally be an over/under setup. Second barrel is an over/under also provided as part of the set. Single barrel is 34" and over/under set is 32" in length.

NIB	Exc.	V.G.	Good	Fair	Poor
2500	2100	1500	1200	750	500

682 Top Combo

Trap combination features standard placement single barrel, with interchangeable over/under barrel. Barrel sets available in 30"/32", 30"/34" and 32"/34". Barrels fitted with ventilated rib.

NIB	Exc.	V.G.	Good	Fair	Poor
2500	2000	1500	1000	950	500

682 Gold Trap with Adjustable Stock

Introduced in 1998. Over/under features choice of 30" or 32" barrels, with Monte Carlo stock and adjustable drop, cast and comb. Trigger adjustable for length of pull. Selected walnut stock, with oil finish. Black rubber recoil pad standard. Weight about 8.8 lbs. **NOTE:** Add $800 for Top Combo set.

NIB	Exc.	V.G.	Good	Fair	Poor
2200	1800	1500	—	—	—

682 Gold Skeet with Adjustable Stock

Introduced in 1999. This 12-gauge features skeet stock with adjustable comb. Stock drop and cast may also be adjusted. Graystone receiver. Comes with case. Offered in choice of 28" or 30" barrels. Single-selective trigger adjustable for length of pull. Black rubber recoil pad standard. Weight about 7.5 lbs.

NIB	Exc.	V.G.	Good	Fair	Poor
2000	1700	1500	1200	900	600

682 Gold "Live Bird"

Introduced in 1995. Has gray receiver, with select walnut stock. Single-selective trigger is adjustable for length of pull. Offered in 12-gauge only, with 30" barrels. Average weight 8.8 lbs.

NIB	Exc.	V.G.	Good	Fair	Poor
2550	1950	1595	1150	850	400

S682 Gold E Trap

Chambered for 12-gauge 3", with choice of 30" or 32" barrels overbored and choke tubes. Highly select walnut stock, with black rubber pad. Single-selective trigger, with adjustable length of pull. Beavertail fore-end. Adjustable Monte Carlo stock. Front white bead with mid bead sight. Carry case standard. Weight about 8.8 lbs. Introduced in 2001.

NIB	Exc.	V.G.	Good	Fair	Poor
3900	3300	2750	1800	900	450

S682 Gold E Trap Combo

Offers same features as Trap model, with interchangeable over/under barrels. Top single barrel with under rib. Introduced in 2001.

NIB	Exc.	V.G.	Good	Fair	Poor
5600	4400	3100	1700	800	350

S682 Gold E Skeet

12-gauge skeet gun features special skeet-style stock, with beavertail fore-end. Adjustable stock. Barrel lengths 28" or 30". Single-selective trigger. Weight about 7.5 lbs. Introduced in 2001.

NIB	Exc.	V.G.	Good	Fair	Poor
4000	3600	2750	1500	625	350

S682 Gold E Sporting

12-gauge model. Choice of 28", 30" or 32" barrels, with extended choke tubes and tapered top rib. White front sight and mid bead. Sporting clay-style stock of select walnut. Weight about 7.6 lbs. Introduced in 2001.

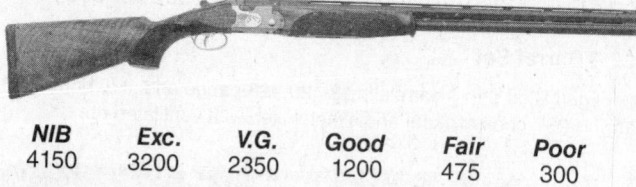

NIB	Exc.	V.G.	Good	Fair	Poor
4150	3200	2350	1200	475	300

Model 685

Lower priced over/under chambered for 12- or 20-gauge, with 3" chambers. Satin-chromed boxlock action, with single trigger and extractors. Not imported after 1986.

NIB	Exc.	V.G.	Good	Fair	Poor
—	750	675	550	375	200

BERETTA 686 SERIES

686/686 Silver Perdiz Sporting

Beretta over/under shotgun available in a number of different configurations. This basic model features ventilated rib barrels from 24" to 30"; 30" is a special order. Screw-in chokes or fixed chokes are available. All configurations offered in 12- and 20-gauge, with 28-gauge and .410 bore available in special order only. Fitted with checkered American walnut stock, with black rubber recoil pad and special grip cap. Some models have silver receiver, with scroll engraving and others have black receivers with gold-filled contours. This 686 series was renamed in 1994.

686 Essential/Silver Essential

Introduced in 1994. This 686 model designed to be an entry level 686. Offers all mechanical features of 686 series, without any frills. Offered in 12-gauge only, with 26" or 28" barrels with open-side rib. Plain walnut stock, with checkering and plain blue receiver. Weight about 6.7 lbs. Renamed Silver Essential in 1997.

Beretta 686 Silver Essential

NIB	Exc.	V.G.	Good	Fair	Poor
900	750	600	450	350	200

686 Ultra Light Onyx

Features black anodized light alloy receiver accented with an engraved gold-filled "P. Beretta" signature. Available in 12-gauge only, with 26" or 28" ventilated rib barrels. Chokes fixed or screw-in type. Weight 5 lbs. 1 oz.

NIB	Exc.	V.G.	Good	Fair	Poor
1050	850	750	600	500	400

686 Onyx

Similar in appearance to Ultra Light Onyx. Available in 12- or 20-gauge, with ventilated rib barrel lengths from 26" to 28". Chambers are 3" or 3.5". Checkered walnut stock offered in pistol-/straight-grip. Choice of choke types. Weight: 12-gauge 6 lbs.13 oz.; 20-gauge 6 lbs. 3 oz. A 12-gauge version with 3.5" chambers and 28" barrel offered (new in 1999) with matte wood finish, matte black receiver, beavertail fore-end, with fingerwells and silver finish trigger.

NIB	Exc.	V.G.	Good	Fair	Poor
1800	1350	950	650	500	400

686 Onyx 2 Barrel Set

Same as above. Supplied with 20-gauge 28" ventilated rib barrel; 28-gauge 26" ventilated rib barrel.

NIB	Exc.	V.G.	Good	Fair	Poor
2100	1650	1500	800	650	500

686 Silver Receiver

Model is basic 686. Features plain semi-matte silver receiver. Available in 12- or 20-gauge; 28-gauge available on special order. Ventilated rib barrels offered in lengths from 24" to 30", with fixed chokes or choke tubes.

NIB	Exc.	V.G.	Good	Fair	Poor
1200	895	775	650	500	400

686 L/686 Silver Perdiz

Same as above. Furnished with scroll engraved silver receiver. Offered in 28-gauge, with 26" or 28" ventilated rib barrels. Weight 5 lbs. 5 oz.

NIB	Exc.	V.G.	Good	Fair	Poor
1200	950	750	650	500	400

686 Silver Pigeon

Introduced in 1996. Replaces Silver Perdiz. Has electroless nickel finish on scroll engraved receiver. Offered in 12-, 20- and 28-gauge, with 26" or 28" barrels. Average weight 6.8 lbs. New variation introduced in 1999. Features 20-gauge gun with 28" barrels, straight-grip stock and matte nickel receiver.

NIB	Exc.	V.G.	Good	Fair	Poor
1800	1450	950	600	400	200

Sporting

NIB	Exc.	V.G.	Good	Fair	Poor
1500	1050	750	600	400	200

Trap (30")

NIB	Exc.	V.G.	Good	Fair	Poor
1400	1000	700	500	400	300

Trap Top Mono (32" or 34")

NIB	Exc.	V.G.	Good	Fair	Poor
1300	900	600	500	400	300

686 Silver Pigeon S

Essentially same as Silver Pigeon models. Packaged with carrying case that includes five choke tubes, accessory recoil pad and sling swivels. A .410-bore offering on a proportionally smaller receiver was added in 2006. **NOTE:** Add $700 for two barrel 20/28 gauge set.

NIB	Exc.	V.G.	Good	Fair	Poor
2000	1600	1275	825	575	350

686E Sporting

Offered in 12- or 20-gauge, with choice of 28" or 30" barrels. Five Beretta screw-in chokes. Modern ellipsis receiver engraving. Special carrying case. Introduced with new styling in 2001.

NIB	Exc.	V.G.	Good	Fair	Poor
2100	1700	1350	825	575	350

686 EL/Gold Perdiz

Model available in 12- or 20-gauge, with 26" or 28" ventilated rib barrels. Receiver silver, with scroll engraving fitted with side plates. Fitted hard case comes with gun.

NIB	Exc.	V.G.	Good	Fair	Poor
1900	1350	1100	800	700	350

686 Hunter Sport

Sporting clay 12- or 20-gauge shotgun. Features silver receiver, with scroll engraving. Wide 12.5mm target rib. Radius recoil pad. Offered in 26" or 28" ventilated rib barrels, with screw-in chokes. Offered first time in 1993.

NIB	Exc.	V.G.	Good	Fair	Poor
1200	950	750	600	500	250

686 Onyx Hunter Sport

Same as above. Offered in 12-gauge only, with matte black finish on receiver and barrels. Weight 6 lbs.13 oz. Introduced in 1993.

NIB	Exc.	V.G.	Good	Fair	Poor
1100	850	650	600	500	250

BERETTA WING SERIES

686 Whitewing

Introduced in fall of 1998. Over/under shotgun chambered for 12-gauge shell. Fitted with 26" or 28" barrels, with Beretta's choke system. Receiver polished nickel, with engraved game scenes and gold-plated trigger. Walnut pistol-grip stock, with gloss finish.

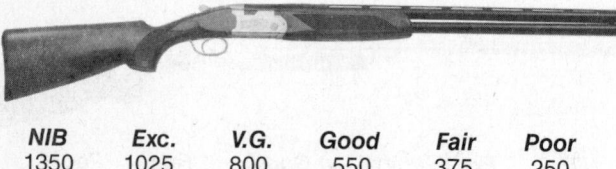

NIB	Exc.	V.G.	Good	Fair	Poor
1350	1025	800	550	375	250

686 Blackwing

Introduced in 2002. Similar to Whitewing, with exception of blued receiver and schnabel fore-end.

NIB	Exc.	V.G.	Good	Fair	Poor
1450	1100	900	600	425	300

686 Sporting Combo

Same specifications as Hunter Sport, with addition of interchangeable 30" 12-gauge barrel.

NIB	Exc.	V.G.	Good	Fair	Poor
1900	1600	1250	1000	700	325

686 Collection Trap

Introduced in 1996. Features special multi-colored stock and fore-end. Offered in 12-gauge only, with 30" barrels. Factory recoil pad standard. Average weight 7.7 lbs.

NIB	Exc.	V.G.	Good	Fair	Poor
1500	1000	750	500	400	300

686 Collection Sport

Similar to above. Offered with 28" barrels.

NIB	Exc.	V.G.	Good	Fair	Poor
1500	975	750	500	400	300

686 Quail Unlimited 2002 Covey Limited Edition

Offered in 20- or 28-gauge, with 26" or 28" ventilated rib barrels. Choke tubes. Engraved receiver with gold quail inlays. Weight about 6.8 lbs.

NIB	Exc.	V.G.	Good	Fair	Poor
1950	1550	1250	1000	700	325

686 Ringneck Pheasants Forever

Introduced in 2003. Chambered for 12- or 20-gauge. Fitted with 26 or 28" ventilated rib barrels. Checkered walnut stock, with pistol-grip Single-selective trigger. Gel-Tek recoil pad. Schnabel fore-end. Weigh about 6.8 lbs. on 12-gauge.

NIB	Exc.	V.G.	Good	Fair	Poor
2025	1550	1100	750	450	275

BERETTA ULTRALIGHT SERIES

Ultralight

Over/under chambered for 12-gauge 2.75" shells. Fitted with choice of 26" or 28" barrels. Receiver is light aluminum alloy nickel finish, with game scene engraving. Black rubber recoil pad standard. Single-selective trigger, pistol-grip and schnabel forearm. Weight about 5.75 lbs.

Ultralight receiver

NIB	Exc.	V.G.	Good	Fair	Poor
1900	1500	900	600	375	175

Ultralight Deluxe

Similar to above. Offered only with 28" barrels. Nickel receiver is gold game scene engraved. First offered in 1998.

NIB	Exc.	V.G.	Good	Fair	Poor
2400	2000	1600	1100	700	350

BERETTA 687/PIGEON SERIES

687/687 Silver Pigeon Sporting

Similar to Model 686. Slightly more ornate version. This series renamed in 1994.

687 L/Silver Pigeon

Offered in 12- or 20-gauge, with 26" or 28" ventilated rib barrels. Boxlock receiver scroll engraved with game scenes. Auto ejectors and double-/single triggers offered.

NIB	Exc.	V.G.	Good	Fair	Poor
1800	1100	950	800	650	300

687 Silver Pigeon II

Introduced in 1999. Features deep relief game scene engraving on silver receiver. Select walnut stock, with oil finish. Available in 12-gauge only. Choice of 26" or 28" ventilated rib barrels. Single-selective trigger. Weight about 6.8 lbs.

NIB	Exc.	V.G.	Good	Fair	Poor
2500	1900	1250	700	425	300

687 Silver Pigeon Sporting

Sporting clays version available in 12- or 20-gauge, with 28" or 30" barrels.

NIB	Exc.	V.G.	Good	Fair	Poor
1900	1400	1000	700	425	300

687 Silver Pigeon II Sporting

Introduced in 1999. Features deep relief engraving, with oil finished select walnut stock. Schnabel fore-end. Single-selective trigger. Offered in 12-gauge only. Choice of 28" or 30" barrels. Black rubber recoil pad. Weight about 7.7 lbs.

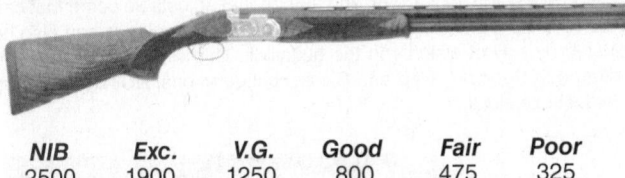

NIB	Exc.	V.G.	Good	Fair	Poor
2500	1900	1250	800	475	325

Silver Pigeon S

New in 2007. Silver Pigeon S Series features scroll and floral engraving on satin nickel-alloy finished receiver. Available in 12-, 20- and 28-gauge, with 26" or 28" barrels. .410 bore with 28" barrels. All come with five chokes. Weight about 6.8 lbs.

NIB	Exc.	V.G.	Good	Fair	Poor
1800	1475	900	600	375	275

Silver Pigeon S Combo

Combo model comes with 26" 20-gauge barrels; 28" 28-gauge barrels.

NIB	Exc.	V.G.	Good	Fair	Poor
2200	1875	100	900	600	300

687 Sporting Combo

Offered in 12-gauge only, with two sets of 12-gauge interchangeable ventilated rib barrels in 28" and 30".

NIB	Exc.	V.G.	Good	Fair	Poor
2500	2100	1850	1500	750	400

687 Silver Pigeon IV

Introduced in 2003 for U.S. market. Features black finish receiver, with full scroll engraving and gold-filled game birds. Select oil-finished walnut

stock, with Gel-Tek recoil pad. Offered in 12-, 20- or 28-gauge, with 26" or 28" barrels. Single-selective trigger, with fluted beavertail fore-end. Weight about 6.8 lbs. in 12-gauge.

NIB	Exc.	V.G.	Good	Fair	Poor
2665	1950	1850	1500	750	400

687 Silver Pigeon V

Top-of-the-line model in Silver Pigeon Series. Available in 12-, 20- and 28-gauge, with 26" and 28" barrels and .410 bore (added in 2006). Pistol-grip stock of richly figured walnut, with oil finish. Color case-hardened receiver, with gold-filled game bird inlays. English stocked versions of 20-, 28-gauge and .410 bore added in 2006.

NIB	Exc.	V.G.	Good	Fair	Poor
3595	2400	1700	1250	750	375

687 EL/687 Gold Pigeon

Model offered with scroll engraved gold inlaid game animals. Fitted with side plates. Stock highly figured walnut, with fine line checkering. Available in 12-, 20-, 28-gauge or .410 bore in 26" or 28" ventilated rib barrels, with screw-in chokes. Comes with fitted hard case. Weight: 12-gauge 6 lbs. 13 oz.; 20-gauge 6 lbs. 3 oz.; 28-gauge/.410 bore 5 lbs. 5 oz. Series renamed in 1994. In 2001, Beretta enhanced engraving on Model 687EL Gold Pigeon.

12 and 20 gauge

NIB	Exc.	V.G.	Good	Fair	Poor
3400	2450	1800	1200	750	350

28 gauge and .410 bore

NIB	Exc.	V.G.	Good	Fair	Poor
3450	2500	1850	1250	800	400

687 EL Gold Pigeon Sporting

Sporting clays model chambered for 12-gauge. Fitted with 28" or 30" ventilated rib barrels. Offered new in 1993. Comes with fitted hard case.

NIB	Exc.	V.G.	Good	Fair	Poor
3400	2450	1750	1250	900	450

687 EELL/Diamond Pigeon

Same as above including gauge and barrel offerings. Furnished with more fully figured walnut and finer checkering. Fitted with side plates that are scroll engraved with fine cut game scenes. This grade also available in straight-grip English stock version in 20-gauge as well as combo set of 20-gauge and 28-gauge interchangeable 26" barrels. All 687 EELL Models fitted with hard case. Series renamed in 1994.

12 and 20 gauge

NIB	Exc.	V.G.	Good	Fair	Poor
6500	5200	4500	3000	1500	700

28 gauge and .410 bore

NIB	Exc.	V.G.	Good	Fair	Poor
7000	5500	4500	3000	1500	700

Combo

NIB	Exc.	V.G.	Good	Fair	Poor
8000	6800	5000	3500	1300	500

687 EELL Diamond Pigeon Skeet

Same as above. Addition of skeet configuration. A 12-gauge version offered with 28" ventilated rib barrels choked skeet and skeet. Weight about 7 lbs. 8 oz. A 4 barrel set also offered with interchangeable 12-, 20-, 28-gauge and .410 bore barrels choked skeet and skeet.

12 gauge

NIB	Exc.	V.G.	Good	Fair	Poor
3500	3000	2500	1750	1450	475

4 Barrel Set

NIB	Exc.	V.G.	Good	Fair	Poor
6400	5000	4500	3750	2500	1500

With Adjustable Stock

Same as Skeet version above, with adjustable comb, drop and cast. Introduced in 1999.

NIB	Exc.	V.G.	Good	Fair	Poor
5000	4000	3200	2500	1500	500

687 EELL Diamond Pigeon Sporting

Sporting clays version of 687 EELL. In 12-gauge only, with 28" ventilated rib barrels fitted with screw-in chokes.

NIB	Exc.	V.G.	Good	Fair	Poor
6000	4750	3500	2500	1750	1200

687 EELL Trap

Fitted with International or Monte Carlo trap stock dimensions. Offered in 12-gauge, with 30" ventilated rib barrels fixed or screw-in choke tubes. Weight about 8 lbs. 6 oz.

NIB	Exc.	V.G.	Good	Fair	Poor
4000	3000	2500	2000	1500	1000

687 EELL Top Combo

Single barrel trap gun. Choice of one single barrel set and one over/under steel rod barrel. In 30"/32" or 32"/34".

NIB	Exc.	V.G.	Good	Fair	Poor
4700	3500	3000	2250	2000	1000

687 EELL King Ranch

Similar to Silver Pigeon Grade IV, with special cowboy and western engraving. In 20- or 28-gauge only. Introduced 2006. Discontinued in 2009.

NIB	Exc.	V.G.	Good	Fair	Poor
3300	2750	2200	1700	1250	800

Model 692

Introduced in 2014. Replaces 682 series with some features from that series and others from the high-grade DT10 Trident. It has a 1.6" wide receiver for improved balance and weight distribution. In 12-gauge only. Features include 30" or 32" barrels, extra long forcing cones, adjustable trigger and ejectors/extractors, and an optional adjustable comb that can be set to the shooter's drop and cast needs. Gun's balance can also be adjusted by way of weights in the buttstock. This competition-level gun is offered in Sporting, Trap and Skeet configurations. **NOTE:** Add $500 for adjustable stock.

692 Sporting

NIB	Exc.	V.G.	Good	Fair	Poor
4000	3500	3000	2500	—	—

692 Trap

NIB	Exc.	V.G.	Good	Fair	Poor
3800	3300	2800	2200	—	—

692 Skeet

NIB	Exc.	V.G.	Good	Fair	Poor
4400	3700	3200	2800	—	—

Model FS-1

Single-barrel boxlock shotgun in all gauges. A 26" or 28" full choke barrel. Blued, with checkered walnut stock. Also known as "Companion". **NOTE:** Deduct 25 percent for 12-gauge.

NIB	Exc.	V.G.	Good	Fair	Poor
—	300	225	175	125	90

TR-1 Trap

12-gauge single-barrel boxlock trap gun, with 32" ventilated rib full choke barrel. Blued, with checkered Monte Carlo stock. Manufactured between 1968 and 1971.

NIB	Exc.	V.G.	Good	Fair	Poor
—	375	250	200	150	100

TR-2 Trap

As above, with high competition-type ventilated rib. Manufactured between 1969 and 1973.

NIB	Exc.	V.G.	Good	Fair	Poor
—	400	275	225	175	125

Mark II Trap

12-gauge boxlock single-barrel trap shotgun, with 32" or 34" full-choke barrel, competition-type rib and automatic ejector. Blued, with checkered Monte Carlo type walnut stock. Manufactured between 1972 and 1976.

NIB	Exc.	V.G.	Good	Fair	Poor
—	800	625	525	450	275

MODEL ASE 90/GOLD SERIES

Competition trap model over/under shotgun. Features trigger lock assembly that is removable in the field so a spare can be used in event of failure. Single non-selective trigger has three-way adjustment. Ventilated rib is wide and side ribs are also ventilated. Walnut stock and forearms are interchangeable. Special trap recoil pad standard. Receiver silver, with gold inlays or blued on special order. ASE 90 weight about 8 lbs. 6 oz.

ASE 90 Pigeon

Equipped with 28" barrels choked Improved-Modified and Full.

NIB	Exc.	V.G.	Good	Fair	Poor
6750	5250	3750	2750	1200	500

ASE 90 Trap

Comes standard with 30" ventilated rib barrels.

NIB	Exc.	V.G.	Good	Fair	Poor
5950	5250	3750	2750	1200	500

ASE 90 Gold X Trap Combo

Introduced in 1993. Set features single barrel and interchangeable over/under barrels in 30"/32" and 30"/34" combinations.

NIB	Exc.	V.G.	Good	Fair	Poor
6950	2500	1750	1200	700	350

ASE 90 Skeet

Skeet version of ASE 90 series. Features same basic specifications as trap model. Configured for competition skeet. Offered in 12-gauge only, with 28" skeet and skeet chokes. Weight about 7 lbs. 11 oz.

NIB	Exc.	V.G.	Good	Fair	Poor
5950	2500	1750	1200	700	350

ASE 90 Sporting Clay

Configured for sporting clays competition. Offered in 12-gauge only, with 28" or 30" ventilated rib barrels.

NIB	Exc.	V.G.	Good	Fair	Poor
6950	5200	4000	3000	1500	1000

Model SL-2

12-gauge slide-action shotgun, with 26", 28" or 30" ventilated rib barrels. Various chokes. Blued, with checkered walnut stock. Manufactured between 1968 and 1971.

NIB	Exc.	V.G.	Good	Fair	Poor
—	350	300	250	200	150

Pigeon Series

As above in three grades.

Silver Pigeon

NIB	Exc.	V.G.	Good	Fair	Poor
—	300	250	200	150	110

Gold Pigeon

NIB	Exc.	V.G.	Good	Fair	Poor
—	450	400	300	250	200

Ruby Pigeon

NIB	Exc.	V.G.	Good	Fair	Poor
—	600	550	450	375	275

DT 10 TRIDENT SERIES

These shotguns feature removable trigger mechanism, overbored barrels and special choke tubes.

DT 10 Trident Trap

12-gauge over/under, with a number of options. Barrel is 30" or 32". Highly select walnut stock fitted with Monte Carlo comb. Stock also adjustable. Rib type is .375" with progressive step. Full black rubber recoil pad. Weight about 8.8 lbs. Top single model also offered with 34" barrel. Introduced in 2000.

NIB	Exc.	V.G.	Good	Fair	Poor
8000	6000	5000	2750	1600	500

DT 10 Trident Trap Combo Top

Same as above, with both over/under barrels and single barrel combo.

NIB	Exc.	V.G.	Good	Fair	Poor
10000	8000	6500	4700	3000	500

DT 10 Trident Trap Bottom Single

Introduced in 2001. Features choice of 30"/34"- or 32"/34" barrel combo. Select walnut stock. Fitted with adjustable point-of-impact rib. Weight about 8.8 lbs.

NIB	Exc.	V.G.	Good	Fair	Poor
13250	10500	7500	4700	3000	500

DT 10 Trident Skeet

12-gauge skeet model. Fitted with 28" or 30" barrel. Walnut stock is adjustable. Weight about 8 lbs. Introduced in 2000.

NIB	Exc.	V.G.	Good	Fair	Poor
8000	7000	5000	2850	1875	400

DT 10 Trident Sporting

12-gauge over/under. Fitted with 28", 30" or 32" barrels. Highly figured walnut stock, with schnabel fore-end. Weight about 8 lbs. Introduced in 2000.

NIB	Exc.	V.G.	Good	Fair	Poor
12000	10000	6000	2850	1875	400

DT 11

Top of the line Beretta competition over/under model. Upgraded from DT10 series, with an even wider frame, high-grade hand-checkered walnut stock made to customer's specifications, redesigned top lever and safety selector. In 12-gauge only. Barrel choices are 29.5", 30" or 32", with choke tubes or fixed modified and full chokes, and 2.750" chambers. Variations include Sporting, Skeet, Trap and International Trap, and several sub-categories. Values shown are for the base models in each category.

Sporting

NIB	Exc.	V.G.	Good	Fair	Poor
7900	6700	5400	4400	—	—

Skeet

NIB	Exc.	V.G.	Good	Fair	Poor
7400	6400	5300	4300	—	—

Trap

NIB	Exc.	V.G.	Good	Fair	Poor
8000	6800	5500	4500	—	—

International Trap

NIB	Exc.	V.G.	Good	Fair	Poor
7400	6400	5300	4300	—	—

SV10 Perennia

New in 2008. Perennia over/under is a 3" 12-gauge shotgun. Featuring oil-finished select walnut stock and laser-engraved nickel high-phosphorous-based finish on receiver. Barrels are 26" or 28". Features Optimachoke HP system introduced in 2008. User-selectable automatic or mechanical shell extraction. Beretta's Kick-Off recoil reduction system available on 28" Perennia. Includes five choke tubes and plastic carrying case. **NOTE:** Add $400 for Kick-Off version.

NIB	Exc.	V.G.	Good	Fair	Poor
3250	2000	1450	800	600	300

SEMI-AUTOMATIC SHOTGUNS

AL SERIES

A 12- or 20-gauge semi-automatic shotgun, with 26", 28" or 30" barrels. Various choke combinations. Blued, with checkered walnut stock. Manufactured between 1969 and 1976.

AL-1

NIB	Exc.	V.G.	Good	Fair	Poor
—	400	375	300	225	150

AL-2

NIB	Exc.	V.G.	Good	Fair	Poor
—	350	300	250	175	125

AL-2 Competition

NIB	Exc.	V.G.	Good	Fair	Poor
—	400	350	300	225	175

AL-2 Magnum

NIB	Exc.	V.G.	Good	Fair	Poor
—	425	375	325	250	200

AL-3

NIB	Exc.	V.G.	Good	Fair	Poor
—	400	350	300	225	175

AL-3 Deluxe Trap

NIB	Exc.	V.G.	Good	Fair	Poor
—	775	700	600	500	425

Model 301

Improved version of AL Series. Manufactured between 1977 and 1982. Also available as slug gun, with 22" barrel and rifle sights.

NIB	Exc.	V.G.	Good	Fair	Poor
—	400	350	300	225	175

Model 1200 Field Grade

12-gauge semi-automatic shotgun, with 28" ventilated rib barrel, screw-in choke tubes and 4-round tubular magazine. Matte blued, with checkered walnut or black synthetic stock. Introduced in 1984.

NIB	Exc.	V.G.	Good	Fair	Poor
450	400	300	250	200	150

Model 1200 Magnum

3" chamber.

NIB	Exc.	V.G.	Good	Fair	Poor
585	525	425	325	250	200

Model 1200 Riot

20" cylinder bore barrel.

NIB	Exc.	V.G.	Good	Fair	Poor
585	525	425	325	250	200

Model 1201

This 12-gauge semi-automatic shotgun, has a short recoil system. Features synthetic stock, with matte black finish and lightweight alloy receiver. Available in two basic configurations: Field Grade choice of 24", 26" and 28" ventilated rib barrel with screw-in chokes; Riot Model with 18" plain cylinder choked barrel and full or pistol-grip-only stock (introduced in 1993). Weight: Field Grade about 6 lbs. 12 oz.; Riot Model about 6 lbs.

5 oz. **NOTE:** Add $40 for Riot Model with pistol-grip; $75 for Riot Model with Tritium sights; $100 for ghost ring sights.

Field Grade

NIB	Exc.	V.G.	Good	Fair	Poor
450	400	350	300	200	150

Riot Model

NIB	Exc.	V.G.	Good	Fair	Poor
650	500	400	350	250	175

Model 1301 Comp

Designed for tactical competition. Choice of 21" or 24" barrel drilled and tapped for rail installation, Optimabore choke system, fiber optic front sight with middle bead and Blink operating system. In 12-gauge only, with 3" chamber. Tactical model is similar, but with 18.5" barrel, oversized operating controls, ghost ring sight and adjustable buttstock. Introduced in 2014.

NIB	Exc.	V.G.	Good	Fair	Poor
1000	900	750	—	—	—

Model 302

12- or 20-gauge semi-automatic shotgun. Using 2.75" or 3" shells interchangeably, various barrel lengths and screw-in choke tubes. Blued, with checkered walnut stock. Manufactured between 1982 and 1987.

NIB	Exc.	V.G.	Good	Fair	Poor
—	400	350	275	200	150

Model 302 Super Lusso

As above, with heavily engraved receiver and gold-plated contrasting parts. Presentation grade walnut used for hand checkered stock. Discontinued in 1986.

NIB	Exc.	V.G.	Good	Fair	Poor
—	2150	2000	1600	1050	850

Model Vittoria/Pintail

Semi-automatic 12-gauge shotgun. Introduced to Beretta product line in 1993. Has short recoil operation. Offered with 24" or 26" ventilated rib barrel, with screw-in chokes. A 24" rifled choke tube version for slugs is also available. Non-reflective matte finish is put on all wood and metal surfaces. Equipped with sling swivels and walnut stock. Weight about 7 lbs. Renamed in 1994.

NIB	Exc.	V.G.	Good	Fair	Poor
600	500	420	350	250	200

ES100 Pintail Synthetic

Introduced in 1999. Essentially same as Pintail above. Addition of black synthetic stock and choice of 24", 26" or 28" ventilated rib barrels, with screw-in chokes. Weight about 7 lbs.

NIB	Exc.	V.G.	Good	Fair	Poor
550	450	385	325	250	200

ES100 Pintail Rifled Slug

Introduced in 1997. Features 24" fully rifled barrel, with adjustable rear sight and removable blade front sight. Receiver is drilled and tapped for scope mount. Hardwood stock with matte finish. Anodized aluminum alloy receiver. Weight about 7 lbs. Fitted with 3" chambers.

NIB	Exc.	V.G.	Good	Fair	Poor
650	550	450	400	250	200

ES100 Rifled Slug

Variation same as Pintail Rifled Slug. Addition of black synthetic stock. Introduced in 1999.

NIB	Exc.	V.G.	Good	Fair	Poor
600	500	425	350	250	200

ES100 Rifled Slug Combo

Same as above, with addition of 28" smooth bored barrel.

NIB	Exc.	V.G.	Good	Fair	Poor
700	600	525	450	350	250

ES100 NWTF Special Camo

12-gauge fitted with 24" barrel and 3" chambers. Stock Mossy Oak camo. Metal black matte finish. Weight about 7.3 lbs. Introduced in 1999.

NIB	Exc.	V.G.	Good	Fair	Poor
975	750	550	375	210	150

A-303 SERIES

12- or 20-gauge semi-automatic shotgun, with 26", 28", 30" or 32" ventilated rib barrels and screw-in choke tubes. Blued, with checkered walnut stock. Introduced in 1987. Various models differ slightly in configuration and/or quality of materials.

Model A-303

NIB	Exc.	V.G.	Good	Fair	Poor
650	600	475	375	300	250

Model A-303 Upland

24" barrel.

NIB	Exc.	V.G.	Good	Fair	Poor
680	650	525	425	350	300

Model A-303 Sporting Clay

NIB	Exc.	V.G.	Good	Fair	Poor
735	700	575	475	400	350

Model A-303 Competition (Trap or Skeet)

NIB	Exc.	V.G.	Good	Fair	Poor
675	650	530	425	350	300

Model A-303 Slug Gun

22" barrel with sights.

NIB	Exc.	V.G.	Good	Fair	Poor
680	650	525	425	350	300

Model A-303 Youth Gun

Version of Model 303. Available in 20-gauge, with shorter length of pull 13.5", than standard. Fitted with rubber recoil pad, screw-in choke tubes and checkered walnut stock.

NIB	Exc.	V.G.	Good	Fair	Poor
500	450	400	300	250	200

Model A-303 Ducks Unlimited

Commemorative version of Model 303. Chambered for 12- or 20-gauge. Manufactured: 5,500 in 12-gauge (1986 and 1987); 3,500 in 20-gauge (1987 and 1988). Commemorative firearms are collectible when NIB, with all furnished materials.

12 Gauge

NIB	Exc.	V.G.	Good	Fair	Poor
575	500	425	325	275	225

20 Gauge

NIB	Exc.	V.G.	Good	Fair	Poor
675	600	525	425	375	325

MODEL AL390/MALLARD SERIES

Series of 12-gauge semi-automatic shotguns. Features self-compensating gas-operating recoil system. All loads from target to 3" Magnums can be used in same gun. Field Model features anodized light alloy receiver, with scroll engraving and matte black receiver top. Magazine capacity 3 rounds. Checkered walnut stock, with recoil pad. Available in ventilated rib barrel lengths from 24" to 30", with 32" on special request. A 22" or 24" slug plain barrel also available. Chokes are fixed or screw-in at customer's option. Shotgun weight about 7 lbs. Beginning in 1996 Beretta offered Silver Mallard shotguns chambered for 20-gauge shell and available with 24", 26 or 28" barrels. Average weight for these 20-gauge guns is 6.4 lbs.

Field Grade

NIB	Exc.	V.G.	Good	Fair	Poor
800	600	450	350	300	200

Slug Gun

NIB	Exc.	V.G.	Good	Fair	Poor
800	600	450	350	300	200

Synthetic Stock

NIB	Exc.	V.G.	Good	Fair	Poor
800	600	450	350	300	200

Camouflage

NIB	Exc.	V.G.	Good	Fair	Poor
800	600	450	350	300	200

Deluxe Grade/Gold Mallard

Gold-filled game animals and select walnut stock.

NIB	Exc.	V.G.	Good	Fair	Poor
700	650	500	350	300	200

AL390 Trap

NIB	Exc.	V.G.	Good	Fair	Poor
675	600	500	400	300	200

AL390 Super Trap

Features ported barrels in 30" or 32", adjustable length of pull and comb

NIB	Exc.	V.G.	Good	Fair	Poor
800	700	600	500	300	200

AL390 Skeet

NIB	Exc.	V.G.	Good	Fair	Poor
625	550	450	350	250	200

AL390 Super Skeet

Features ported barrel, adjustable cast and length of pull, with adjustable drop. 12-gauge only.

NIB	Exc.	V.G.	Good	Fair	Poor
1000	800	600	500	300	200

AL390 Sporting

NIB	Exc.	V.G.	Good	Fair	Poor
700	550	450	350	250	200

20 gauge

Same as above in 20-gauge. Introduced in 1997. Weight about 6.8 lbs.

NIB	Exc.	V.G.	Good	Fair	Poor
800	600	450	350	250	200

Ported

NIB	Exc.	V.G.	Good	Fair	Poor
725	650	550	400	300	200

AL390 Sport Gold Sporting

Introduced in 1997. Similar to above models, with silver sided receiver and gold engraving. Select walnut stock. 12-gauge only, with choice of 28" or 30" ventilated rib barrels. Weight about 7.6 lbs.

NIB	Exc.	V.G.	Good	Fair	Poor
1100	900	700	450	300	175

AL390 Sport Sporting Youth

Semi-automatic shotgun. Offered in 20-gauge only, with 26" ventilated rib barrel. Length of pull 13.5", with adjustable drop and cast on buttstock. Introduced in 1997. Weight about 6.7 lbs.

NIB	Exc.	V.G.	Good	Fair	Poor
825	675	500	350	200	175

AL390 NWTF Special Youth

Introduced in 1999. Features shortened walnut stock, with 24" 20-gauge ventilated rib barrel. Black matte finish. Weight about 6.4 lbs.

NIB	Exc.	V.G.	Good	Fair	Poor
900	700	525	375	225	175

AL390 Sport Sporting Youth Collection

Same as above, with multi-colored stock and forearm. Introduced in 1997.

NIB	Exc.	V.G.	Good	Fair	Poor
900	750	525	375	225	175

AL390 Sport Diamond Sporting

Introduced in 1998. Features silver sided receiver, with gold engraving. Select walnut stock, with oil finish and adjustable for drop and cast. Available in 12-gauge, with 28" or 30" barrels. Sold with spare trigger group and orange front sight beads. Weight about 7.6 lbs.

NIB	Exc.	V.G.	Good	Fair	Poor
3000	2600	1950	1300	600	300

AL390 Camo

12-gauge shotgun offered with 24" or 28" ventilated rib barrel. Barrel, receiver, stock and forearm have woodland camo finish. Weight about 7.5 lbs. Offered first time in 1997.

NIB	Exc.	V.G.	Good	Fair	Poor
995	775	595	450	300	150

AL390 Waterfowl/Turkey Model

Matte finish.

NIB	Exc.	V.G.	Good	Fair	Poor
550	500	450	350	300	250

AL390 NWTF Special Camo

NIB	Exc.	V.G.	Good	Fair	Poor
1100	875	625	500	325	150

AL390 NWTF Special Synthetic

NIB	Exc.	V.G.	Good	Fair	Poor
925	750	595	450	300	150

Super Trap

Ported barrels, adjustable comb and length of pull.

NIB	Exc.	V.G.	Good	Fair	Poor
975	800	650	500	325	175

Super Skeet

Ported barrels, adjustable comb and length of pull.

NIB	Exc.	V.G.	Good	Fair	Poor
950	800	650	500	325	175

3901 SERIES

Series introduced in 2005. Built around A390 shotgun. The 3901 guns feature gas operating system, choke tubes and removable trigger group.

Model 3901

Introduced in 2003. Semi-automatic shotgun offered in 12-gauge, with 26" or 28" barrel. Charcoal gray synthetic stock. Black rubber recoil pad. Non-reflective black finish. Weight about 7.5 lbs.

NIB	Exc.	V.G.	Good	Fair	Poor
730	575	450	300	225	175

Model 3901 RL

As above in 20-gauge, with reduced-length buttstock. Introduced in 2003.

NIB	Exc.	V.G.	Good	Fair	Poor
730	575	450	300	225	175

Model 3901 Camo

12-gauge offered in Mossy Oak Shadowgrass camo stock. Choice of 24" or 26" barrel. Introduced in 2003.

NIB	Exc.	V.G.	Good	Fair	Poor
840	650	475	350	250	175

Model 3901 Citizen

Offered in 12- or 20-gauge, with 26" or 28" ventilated rib barrels and choke tubes. Black synthetic stock. Rubber recoil pad. Weight about: 7.6 lbs. 12-gauge; 7 lbs. 20-gauge.

NIB	Exc.	V.G.	Good	Fair	Poor
750	600	450	300	225	175

Model 3901 Statesman

As above, with checkered walnut stock.

NIB	Exc.	V.G.	Good	Fair	Poor
850	675	475	325	250	175

Model 3901 Ambassador

Model has all features of Statesman. Fitted with select checkered X-tra wood stock, with Gel-Tek recoil pad. Weight about: 7.2 lbs. 12-gauge; 6.6 lbs. 20-gauge.

NIB	Exc.	V.G.	Good	Fair	Poor
950	750	525	450	350	200

Model 3901 Target RL

Gas-operated semi-automatic chambered in 3" 12-gauge. Specifically designed for smaller-stature shooters, with adjustable length of pull from 12" to 13". Stock adjustable for cast on or cast off. Adjustable comb and Sporting style flat rib. Available in 12-gauge only, with 26" or 28" barrel.

NIB	Exc.	V.G.	Good	Fair	Poor
895	700	550	400	295	175

AL 391 URIKA SERIES

Urika

Introduced in 2000. Semi-automatic shotgun offered in 12- and 20-gauge. Choice of barrels from 24" to 30" depending on gauge. Stock walnut, with checkered grip and fore-end. Rubber recoil pad. Gold trigger. Choke tubes. Weight about: 7.3 lbs. 12-gauge; 6 lbs. 20-gauge.

NIB	Exc.	V.G.	Good	Fair	Poor
850	750	600	450	300	175

Urika Synthetic

Same as above. Fitted with black synthetic stock and gripping inserts. Offered in 12-gauge only. Introduced in 2000.

NIB	Exc.	V.G.	Good	Fair	Poor
950	750	625	525	325	200

Urika Camo

12-gauge offered with Realtree Hardwoods camo or Advantage Wetlands camo. In 24" or 26" barrels. Weight about 7.3 lbs. First introduced in 2000.

NIB	Exc.	V.G.	Good	Fair	Poor
1050	800	650	550	300	175

Urika Gold

Features 26" or 28" barrel, with choke tubes. Black receiver model offered in both 12- and 20-gauge. Weight about 7.3 lbs. Silver receiver model (lightweight) available in 12- gauge only. Weight about 6.6 lbs. Both configurations fitted with highly figured walnut stock. Gold trigger. Introduced in 2000.

NIB	Exc.	V.G.	Good	Fair	Poor
900	825	750	675	325	200

Urika Youth

20-gauge features walnut stock, with shorter length of pull than standard and 24" barrel. Weight about 6 lbs. Introduced in 2000.

NIB	Exc.	V.G.	Good	Fair	Poor
900	800	600	450	275	195

Urika Sporting

Offered in 12- and 20-gauge. Fitted with 28" or 30" barrels. Select walnut checkered stock. Gold trigger. Chambered for 3" shells. Weight about: 7.3 lbs. 12-gauge; 6 lbs. 20-gauge. Introduced in 2000.

NIB	Exc.	V.G.	Good	Fair	Poor
1100	750	600	500	350	175

Urika Gold Sporting

Offered in 12-gauge, with black or silver receiver. The 20-gauge offered with black receiver only. Fitted with 28" or 30" barrels. Highly select checkered walnut stock. Chambered for 3" shells. Introduced in 2000. **NOTE:** Add $30 for 12-gauge silver receiver.

NIB	Exc.	V.G.	Good	Fair	Poor
1295	950	700	600	450	175

Urika Trap

12-gauge fitted with 30" or 32" barrels. Select checkered walnut stock, with Monte Carlo comb. Chambered for 3" shells. Weight about 7.2 lbs. Introduced in 2000.

NIB	Exc.	V.G.	Good	Fair	Poor
1000	750	600	500	350	175

Urika Gold Trap

Similar to standard Urika Trap, with highly selected checkered walnut stock and black receiver.

NIB	Exc.	V.G.	Good	Fair	Poor
1295	950	700	600	450	175

Urika Parallel Target RL/SL

This is a 12-gauge competition model, fitted with 28" or 30" barrels and select walnut Monte Carlo stock. The "RL" has standard stock configurations, while the "SL" has a shorter length of pull.

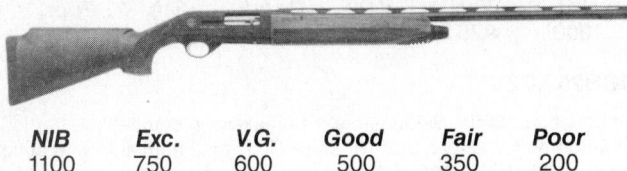

NIB	Exc.	V.G.	Good	Fair	Poor
1100	750	600	500	350	200

URIKA OPTIMA MODELS

First offered in 2003, these shotguns are similar to standard Urika model. Feature Beretta's Optima-Bore overbored barrels, with flush Optima-Choke Plus tubes.

Urika Optima

Offered in 12-gauge, with 26" or 28" ventilated rib barrel. Checkered select walnut stock. Gold trigger. Chamber is 3". Weight about 7.3 lbs.

NIB	Exc.	V.G.	Good	Fair	Poor
1500	1175	825	650	450	300

Urika Synthetic Optima

As above, with synthetic stock and rubber inserts. Weight about 7.4 lbs.

NIB	Exc.	V.G.	Good	Fair	Poor
1300	1105	750	575	400	325

Urika Optima Camo

As above, with camo stock.

NIB	Exc.	V.G.	Good	Fair	Poor
1350	1195	950	625	450	250

URIKA 2 SERIES

Introduced in 2007. Urika 2 is an enhanced version of original AL391 Urika. Improvements include addition of spinning self-cleaning action for faster cycling and longer functioning periods between cleanings.

Urika 2 X-Tra Grain

Series features Beretta's wood-enhancement treatment to highlight color contrast of wood. Offered in 3", 12- and 20-gauge, with 26" and 28" barrels. A 20-gauge youth model, with shorter stock and 24" barrel also offered.

NIB	Exc.	V.G.	Good	Fair	Poor
1000	900	725	575	400	250

Urika 2 Gold

Select oil-finished wood stock and fore-end, with gold-filled game bird inlays on receiver. 12-gauge 28" barrel; 20-gauge 26" barrel.

NIB	Exc.	V.G.	Good	Fair	Poor
1350	1075	725	500	375	250

Urika 2 Kick-Off

Waterfowl models feature Beretta's Kick-Off recoil reduction system. Matte black synthetic, Max-4 or Realtree AP finish, with 26" or 28" barrel. **NOTE:** Add 10 percent for camo finish; deduct 30 percent for models without Kick-Off.

NIB	Exc.	V.G.	Good	Fair	Poor
1200	950	700	475	350	225

Urika 2 Sporting X-Tra Grain

Sporting clay model in 12- and 20-gauge, with 28" or 30" barrel.

NIB	Exc.	V.G.	Good	Fair	Poor
1200	950	700	475	350	225

Urika 2 Gold Sporting

Enhanced wood, with gold inlays and floral motif engraving on receiver. In 12-gauge, with 28" or 30" barrel.

NIB	Exc.	V.G.	Good	Fair	Poor
1300	1025	775	525	375	275

Urika 2 Parallel Target X-Tra Grain

Target model in 12-gauge, with 28", 30" or 32" barrel.

NIB	Exc.	V.G.	Good	Fair	Poor
1250	975	750	525	375	295

Urika 2 Gold Parallel Target

Enhanced wood, with gold inlays and floral motif engraving on receiver. In 12-gauge, with 30" or 32" barrel.

NIB	Exc.	V.G.	Good	Fair	Poor
1400	1075	750	525	395	265

AL391 Covey

Introduced in 2003. Offered in 20-gauge, with 26" or 28" ventilated rib barrel. Select walnut stock. Gold-filled game scenes. Weight about 5.9 lbs. Limited to 1,000 guns.

NIB	Exc.	V.G.	Good	Fair	Poor
1350	1075	725	500	375	250

AL391 Ringneck

As above, with gold-filled pheasants. In 12-gauge only. Weight about 7.3 lbs. Limited to 1,000 guns. Introduced in 2003.

NIB	Exc.	V.G.	Good	Fair	Poor
1360	1075	800	550	400	300

AL391 Teknys

Features nickel receiver, with polished sides and anti-glare top. Offered in 12- or 20-gauge, with 26" or 28" ventilated rib barrel. Xtra-wood stock with Gel-Tek recoil. Weight about: 7.2 lbs. 12-gauge; 5.9 lbs. 20-gauge. Introduced in 2003.

NIB	Exc.	V.G.	Good	Fair	Poor
1150	900	750	500	350	250

AL391 Teknys Gold

As above, with engraved hunting scene on receiver, gold plated trigger, jeweled breech bolt and carrier. Select walnut checkered stock, with oil finish. Introduced in 2003.

NIB	Exc.	V.G.	Good	Fair	Poor
1465	1100	850	575	425	325

AL391 Teknys Gold Target

Similar to AL391 Teknys Gold, with adjustable comb, 8.5 oz. recoil reducer and additional stepped rib for trap shooting. 30" barrel.

NIB	Exc.	V.G.	Good	Fair	Poor
1665	1300	975	600	450	350

AL391 Teknys King Ranch

Introduced in 2005.

NIB	Exc.	V.G.	Good	Fair	Poor
1650	1300	1000	725	625	375

AL391 XTREMA SERIES

AL391 Xtrema 3.5

Introduced in 2002. This model is a Urika overbuilt to handle 12-gauge 3.5" super magnum loads. Offered with choice of 24", 26" or 28" ventilated rib barrels, with black synthetic stock or choice of various camo stocks. Weight about 7.8 lbs. **NOTE:** Add $100 for camo finish.

NIB	Exc.	V.G.	Good	Fair	Poor
1150	900	750	500	350	250

AL391 Xtrema2

Upgraded version of Xtrema. Additional recoil-reducing features introduced in 2005. Available with 24", 26" or 28" barrels, with black Max-4 HD or Hardwoods HD synthetic stock. Optima-Bore five choke system. Optional Kick Off recoil reduction feature available. **NOTE:** Add 10 percent for camo finish; 30 percent for Kick Off option.

NIB	Exc.	V.G.	Good	Fair	Poor
1300	950	800	650	400	300

AL391 Xtrema2 Slug Gun

24" rifled barrel version of Xtrema2. Introduced in 2006. Black synthetic only. **NOTE:** Add 10 percent for Kick Off option.

NIB	Exc.	V.G.	Good	Fair	Poor
1200	925	800	650	400	300

UGB25 XCEL

Introduced in 2005. Semi-automatic break-open competition trap gun. Chambered for 12-gauge 2.75" shell. Gun is fed from side with bottom ejection. Choice of 30" or 32" barrel, with high trap-style interchangeable rib. Choke tubes. Checkered walnut stock has adjustable comb and length of pull. Weight about 7.7 to 9 lbs. depending on barrel length and rib.

NIB	Exc.	V.G.	Good	Fair	Poor
3595	2800	2150	1675	850	450

A400 Xplor Unico

Self-regulation gas-operated shotgun. Chambered to shoot all 12-gauge loads from 2.75" to 3.5". Features include Kick-Off hydraulic damper; 26" or 28" "Steelium" barrel, with interchangeable choke tubes; anodized aluminum receiver; sculpted, checkered walnut buttstock and fore-end. **NOTE:** Add $100 for Kick-Off Recoil reduction system.

NIB	Exc.	V.G.	Good	Fair	Poor
1500	1250	1050	800	550	300

A400 Xcel Sporting

Similar to Xplor Unico, except designed for Sporting Clays competition. 12-gauge, 3" chambers, with 28" 30" and 32" barrels. Blue aluminum receiver, optional Kick-Off recoil reduction system. Gun Pod optional system available, with digital readout of temperature, ammo pressure and other information. **NOTE:** Add $100 for Kick-Off Recoil reduction system or Gun Pod.

NIB	Exc.	V.G.	Good	Fair	Poor
1600	1300	1050	800	550	300

A400 Extreme KO

Uses Beretta's Blink gas-operating system. Said to be able to handle all 12-gauge loads from 2.750" to 3.500". Includes Kick-Off recoil reduction system. Synthetic stock offered in black or camo, with non-slip rubber gripping sections.

NIB	Exc.	V.G.	Good	Fair	Poor
1500	1250	1000	800	600	350

TX4 Storm

Gas-operated semi-automatic shotgun. Chambered for 3" 12-gauge shells. Features include 18" barrel, with interchangeable choke tubes; adjustable ghost ring rear sight, with military-style front sight; adjustable length of pull; integral Picatinny rail on receiver; 5+1 capacity; soft rubber grip inlays in buttstock and fore-end.

NIB	Exc.	V.G.	Good	Fair	Poor
1200	1000	750	500	350	250

BERGARA
Bergara, Spain

This Spanish barrel maker began making sporting and tactical rifles for the U.S. market in 2013.

B-14 Hunter

This bolt-action hunting rifle is made in 6.5 Creedmoor, .270 Win., .308 Win., .30-06 and .300 Win. Magnum, with choice of synthetic or walnut stock. Values shown are for walnut stock model. **NOTE:** Deduct $100 for synthetic.

NIB	Exc.	V.G.	Good	Fair	Poor
800	700	600	—	—	—

BCR-13 Sport Hunter

Bolt-action rifle has a pillar bedded McMillan Hunter stock, with olive/black/tan finish. Shilen or Timney trigger. 22" barrel, with Weaver style two-piece scope base. Chambered in .270 Win., .308 Win., .30-06 Springfield.

NIB	Exc.	V.G.	Good	Fair	Poor
3000	2500	2000	1800	1000	500

BC-15 Long Range Hunter

Similar to BCR-13. Has McMillan A3 Sporter stock, with olive/black/tan finish. Chambered in .300 Win. Magnum or .300 Rem. Ultra Magnum, with 24" barrel

NIB	Exc.	V.G.	Good	Fair	Poor
3600	3000	2400	2000	1200	500

BX-11 Takedown Hunter

Chambered in .243 Win., .270 Win., .308 Win., .30-06 or .300 Win. Magnum, with black synthetic or walnut stock featuring rubber grip panels. Can be broken down for easy carry or storage. Introduced in 2013.

NIB	Exc.	V.G.	Good	Fair	Poor
1600	1450	1200	900	—	—

BCR-19 Tactical Rifle

Features OD Green McMillan A4 stock, with adjustable butt and comb, pillar bedding, Timney or Shilen trigger and 26" nitride finished stainless steel barrel. Chambered in .308 Win. or .300 Win. Magnum. Introduced in 2013

NIB	Exc.	V.G.	Good	Fair	Poor
3900	3400	3000	2500	—	—

BCR-17 Medium Tactical

Similar to BCR-19, with 22" barrel. McMillan A3 stock, with olive/black/tan finish. Chambered only in .308 Win.

NIB	Exc.	V.G.	Good	Fair	Poor
3600	3000	2200	1900	1000	500

Mountain Hunter

Features a Bergara custom action, lightweight fiberglass stock, 20" stainless No. 2 contour barrel, pillar-bedded action and Timney trigger. Chambered in .243 Win., .270 Win., 7mm-08 Rem., .308 Win., .30-06 or .300 Win. Magnum. Weight less than 5.9 lbs.

NIB	Exc.	V.G.	Good	Fair	Poor
3200	2700	2300	1800	—	—

Premier Series Classic

This series of rifles is advertised as being as close to custom as it can get, with many custom features. These include a choice of either high-grade hand-rubbed oil finish Grade 5 Monte Carlo walnut or hand-laid fiberglass stock, both featuring an aluminum bedding block. Premier action has a separate floating bolt head, two-positioned safety that allows bolt to operate while on safe, Timney trigger and hinged floor plate. Premier Classic chambered in 6.5 Creedmoor, .270, .280 Ackley Imp., .308, .30-06 and .300 Win. Magnum. Introduced in 2016.

NIB	Exc.	V.G.	Good	Fair	Poor
2000	1600	1250	—	—	—

BERGER, JEAN MARIUS
St. Etienne, France

Berger

Berger was a magazine-fed repeating pistol in 7.65mm. Self loader and cocker. Had all characteristics of semi-automatic except for recoil operating system.

Courtesy James Rankin

NIB	Exc.	V.G.	Good	Fair	Poor
—	5900	4750	3750	3000	2000

BERGMANN, EINHAND
See—Lignose

BERGMANN, THEODOR
Gaggenau, Germany

Theodor Bergmann was a successful industrialist, designer and sometimes inventor, with a deep interest in firearms. Based in Gaggenau, Germany, his first automatic pistol patent dates from 1892. By 1894, he had prototype pistols refined with the help of Louis Schmeisser, being evaluated by various governments. When his designs went into commercial production in 1896, however, they were actually manufactured by the firm of V. Charles Schilling in Suhl, the heart of German arms manufacture. Later he licensed manufacture of his "Mars" pistol to Anciens Establishment Pieper ("Bayard"). After WWI, affiliated with Lignose firm producing a line of .25-caliber pocket pistols first under Bergmann name, but later marketed as Lignose. Still later, several pistol designs from August Menz firm were marketed under "Bergmann Erben" trademark, though it's doubtful if Bergmann's firm actually had much part in their production or sale.

Model 1894 Bergmann Schmeisser

Made in prototype form only. Few examples surviving. Known serial numbers no higher than mid teens. Most are large framed. Chambered for

8mm Bergmann-Schmeisser cartridge. At least one was made in 7.5mm Swiss revolver for Swiss army testing. A few very compact versions, with a unique folding trigger for 5mm Bergmann. Early Bergmann pistols had no extractor, counting on gas pressure to blow the fired (rimless-groove-less) cartridge from chamber. Too rare to price.

Bergmann Schmeisser

Model 1896 Number 2

1896 Number 2 pistols were quite compact. Chambered for 5mm Bergmann cartridge. Early Number 2s also featured a folding trigger and no extractor. After serial 500 or so reverted to a more conventional in-the-frame trigger and an extractor was added. About 2000 of later model were produced. Cased sets are known. Add about 50 percent to value.

Folding Trigger

Courtesy James Rankin

NIB	Exc.	V.G.	Good	Fair	Poor
—	8000	5000	3250	1500	800

Conventional

Courtesy James Rankin

NIB	Exc.	V.G.	Good	Fair	Poor
—	5000	3500	2250	1000	600

Model 1896 Number 3

Number 3 was a larger version of Number 2. Chambered for 6.5m Bergmann cartridge. Early examples had a slim grip frame. Up to abo serial 800 were made without extractors like early Number 2s. Thes bring about 20 percent premium over later examples. Number 3 seria range to a little over 4000. Add about 20 percent for dealer marking (usually English) and 50 percent for cased sets. A few target mode with long barrel, adjustable sights and set triggers are known. Will brir about three times the price of a standard Number 3.

First Variation

Courtesy James Rankin

NIB	Exc.	V.G.	Good	Fair	Poor
—	4050	3500	2750	1650	800

Second Variation

Courtesy James Rankin

NIB	Exc.	V.G.	Good	Fair	Poor
—	3500	3200	2500	1650	800

Third Variation

Courtesy James Rankin

NIB	Exc.	V.G.	Good	Fair	Poor
—	3700	3200	2500	1650	800

Holster and Stock Model

Courtesy James Rankin

NIB	Exc.	V.G.	Good	Fair	Poor
—	6300	5700	4950	3250	2750

Model 1896 Number 4

Number 4 is identical to Number 3. Chambered for a unique 8mm Bergmann cartridge. Serialed in same series with Number 3. Both Number 4 and its cartridge are rare; probably fewer than 200 were ever made.

NIB	Exc.	V.G.	Good	Fair	Poor
—	8000	6500	5000	3700	2900

Model 1897 Number 5

Bergmann's first attempt at a more powerful arm for military market. A unique side-moving locking system and 10-shot removable box magazine. 7.8mm cartridge resembled 7.63mm Mauser, with a longer neck. **NOTE:** Add 60 percent for original metal framed leather holster-stock.

NIB	Exc.	V.G.	Good	Fair	Poor
—	8550	6900	4950	3000	2250

Model 1897 Number 5 Carbine

Limited number of approximately 1000 Bergmann Model 5s were made, with 12" barrel. Solid wood detachable buttstock and marked "Karabiner Bergmann" on action cover. Very few were made with full-length Mannlicher-type stock and sold as Bergmann Model 1897/07 Sporting Carbine; these are worth about 50 percent more than long barreled pistol, with detachable stock.

Courtesy Joe Schroeder

NIB	Exc.	V.G.	Good	Fair	Poor
—	12500	10000	6000	3000	2000

Bergmann Simplex

Simplex combined some features of 1896 pistols. Improvements developed from "Mars", resulting in a reasonable compact pocket pistol that came on the market in early 1900s. Chambered for unique Bergmann-Simplex 8mm cartridge, however, competition from better Browning and other designs doomed it to a short production life. Very early examples had checkered wood grips and bring a premium, as do very late examples (above serial 3000) that have magazine release behind magazine instead of on front of frame.

NIB	Exc.	V.G.	Good	Fair	Poor
—	3450	2950	2000	900	600

Bergmann Mars

Mars was Bergmann's first really successful pistol aimed at military market. Early examples, about 100 of total 1000 or so Mars pistols made, were chambered for 7.63mm Mauser cartridge. Later Mars pistols identified by a large "9mm" on chamber, were chambered for special 9mm cartridge that later became known as 9mm Bergmann-Bayard. Mars was adopted by Spanish government in 1905 as their first military automatic pistol, but none were ever delivered by Bergmann. At least two Mars pistols were also made in .45-caliber for U.S. Army trials in 1906, but did not perform well and were dropped from the trials; these are too rare to price. **NOTE:** Add 25 percent for low serial number guns chambered for 7.63mm Mauser; 50 percent for original Bergmann Mars holster stock.

NIB	Exc.	V.G.	Good	Fair	Poor
—	7000	5300	3850	2500	1650

Bergmann Bayard Model 1908

Shortly after receiving Spanish contract for Mars pistol, Bergmann's arrangement with Schilling to produce Bergmann pistols ended. However, he negotiated an arrangement with Anciens Establishment Pieper (Bayard) to produce Mars and after some minor modifications, AEP filled the Spanish contract. They also marketed the gun commercially and later secured a production contract from Danish Army as Model 1910. Spanish contract (proofed with a small circle divided into three segments) and very early commercial pistols have hard rubber grips that proved very fragile in service; these bring a premium as do original unmodified Danish contract guns (with a contract number and Danish letter D proof).

A few Model 1908 Bergmann Bayards were equipped with leather and wood holster stocks; a complete rig is worth at least twice the price of an unslotted pistol.

Courtesy James Rankin

NIB	Exc.	V.G.	Good	Fair	Poor
—	3500	2700	1600	775	550

Bergmann Post War Pistols

Shortly after WWI ended, Bergmann came on the market with a line of .25-caliber pocket pistols; the 2 and 3 were conventional vest pocket designs with a short and long grip frame respectively; the 2a and 3a were identical except for an "Einhand" (one-hand) feature that enabled user to cycle slide by pulling front of trigger guard with his trigger finger. Soon into production (at about serial 8000) Bergmann affiliated with Lignose firm and later Model 2 and 3 pistols were marketed under Lignose name.

Model 2 and 3

Courtesy Joe Schroeder

NIB	Exc.	V.G.	Good	Fair	Poor
—	325	275	200	150	100

Model 2a and 3a

Courtesy Joe Schroeder

NIB	Exc.	V.G.	Good	Fair	Poor
—	400	375	325	275	150

Bergmann Erben Pistols

Bergmann Erben pistols appear to be an attempt by Bergmann family to keep Bergmann name associated with firearms, without actually investing any design or production effort. Bergmann Erben pistols were all August Menz designs and were undoubtedly made by Menz as well. Most noteworthy was "Spezial" model, a very sophisticated double-action .32 pocket pistol that could be cocked for single-action fire by pulling and then releasing trigger. Also noteworthy were several compact vest pocket .25s that also bore Bergmann Erben name.

Bergmann Erben Spezial

NIB	Exc.	V.G.	Good	Fair	Poor
—	1650	1350	900	650	400

Bergmann Erben Model II Pistol

Courtesy James Rankin

NIB	Exc.	V.G.	Good	Fair	Poor
—	550	495	330	225	125

BERNARDELLI, VINCENZO
Brescia, Italy

Established in 1721, this company originally manufactured military arms. Entered commercial sporting arms market in 1928.

HANDGUNS

Vest Pocket Model

Similar to Walther Model 9. In 6.35mm caliber semi-automatic pistol, with 2.25" barrel and 5-shot magazine. An extended 8-shot version also available. Blued, with plastic grips. Manufactured between 1945 and 1948.

NIB	Exc.	V.G.	Good	Fair	Poor
—	350	250	180	125	100

Pocket Model

As above in 7.65mm caliber. Also offered with extended barrels that protruded beyond end of slide. Introduced in 1947.

NIB	Exc.	V.G.	Good	Fair	Poor
—	300	225	200	150	100

Baby Model

As above in .22 short or LR. Manufactured between 1949 and 1968.

NIB	Exc.	V.G.	Good	Fair	Poor
—	300	225	175	125	95

Sporter Model

.22-caliber semi-automatic pistol, with 6", 8" or 10" barrels and adjustable sights. Blued, with walnut grips. Manufactured between 1949 and 1968.

NIB	Exc.	V.G.	Good	Fair	Poor
—	325	250	200	150	125

Revolvers

.22 rimfire and .32-caliber double-action revolver, with 1.5", 2" or 5" barrels. A .22-caliber 7" barrel version, with adjustable sights also available. Manufactured between 1950 and 1962.

NIB	Exc.	V.G.	Good	Fair	Poor
—	250	175	150	125	100

Model 60

.22, .32 ACP or .380 ACP caliber semi-automatic pistol, with 3.5" barrel and fixed sights. Blued, with plastic grips. Manufactured since 1959.

NIB	Exc.	V.G.	Good	Fair	Poor
—	275	200	175	150	115

Model 68

.22 rimfire caliber or .25 ACP semi-automatic pistol, with 2" barrel and 5-shot magazine. Blued, with plastic grips. No longer imported into U.S.

NIB	Exc.	V.G.	Good	Fair	Poor
—	200	175	150	100	75

Model 80

.22 or .380 ACP caliber semi-automatic pistol, with 3.5" barrel and adjustable sights. Blued, with plastic grips. Imported between 1968 and 1988.

NIB	Exc.	V.G.	Good	Fair	Poor
—	250	200	150	125	95

Model AMR

As above, with 6" barrel.

NIB	Exc.	V.G.	Good	Fair	Poor
450	350	200	150	100	90

Model 69

.22-caliber semi-automatic target pistol, with 6" heavy barrel and 10-shot magazine. Blued, with checkered walnut grips.

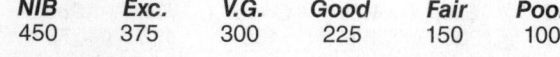

NIB	Exc.	V.G.	Good	Fair	Poor
450	375	300	225	150	100

Model PO10

.22-caliber single-action semi-automatic target pistol, with 6" barrel, adjustable target sights, barrel weights and adjustable trigger. Matte-black finish, with stippled walnut grips. Introduced in 1989. Weight 40 oz. Sold with special hard case.

NIB	Exc.	V.G.	Good	Fair	Poor
800	700	500	300	200	100

Model PO18

7.65mm or 9mm Parabellum caliber double-action semi-automatic pistol, with 4.75" barrel and 16-shot double stack detachable magazine. All-steel construction. Blued, with plastic grips. Walnut grips available for an additional $40. Introduced in 1985.

NIB	Exc.	V.G.	Good	Fair	Poor
550	450	300	275	200	100

Model PO18 Compact

As above, with 4" barrel and shorter grip frame. 14-shot double-column magazine. Introduced in 1989.

NIB	Exc.	V.G.	Good	Fair	Poor
550	450	300	275	200	100

Model P. One

Full-size semi-automatic pistol. Chambered for 9mm or .40 S&W calibers. Fitted with 4.8" barrel. Can be fired double-/single-action. Ten-shot magazine. Weight 2.14 lbs. Available in black or chrome finish. **NOTE** Add $50 for chrome finish.

NIB	Exc.	V.G.	Good	Fair	Poor
625	525	400	275	200	100

Model P. One-Compact

Same as above, with 4" barrel. Offered in .380-caliber, 9mm and .40 S&W. Weight 1.96 lbs.

NIB	Exc.	V.G.	Good	Fair	Poor
650	550	400	275	200	100

Practical VB Target

Designed for Practical shooting. This 9mm pistol has 6" barrel, with choice of 2 or 4 port compensator. Fitted with numerous extra features. Weight 2.2 lbs.

NIB	Exc.	V.G.	Good	Fair	Poor
1500	1200	850	600	400	200

Practical VB Custom

As above, but designed for IPSC rules.

NIB	Exc.	V.G.	Good	Fair	Poor
2250	1900	1400	900	600	300

Model USA

.22, .32 ACP or .380 ACP caliber semi-automatic pistol, with 3.5" barrel, adjustable sights, steel frame and loaded chamber indicator. Blued, with plastic grips.

NIB	Exc.	V.G.	Good	Fair	Poor
450	350	200	150	100	90

SHOTGUNS

MODEL 115 SERIES

12-gauge over/under boxlock double-barrel shotgun, with various barrel lengths and choke combinations. Single triggers and automatic ejectors.

Model 115

NIB	Exc.	V.G.	Good	Fair	Poor
1525	1250	900	700	550	300

Model 115S

NIB	Exc.	V.G.	Good	Fair	Poor
2000	1750	1200	800	600	300

Model 115L

NIB	Exc.	V.G.	Good	Fair	Poor
2500	2000	1500	900	650	300

Model 115E

NIB	Exc.	V.G.	Good	Fair	Poor
5200	4800	4200	3500	2500	1850

Model 115 Trap

NIB	Exc.	V.G.	Good	Fair	Poor
2200	1950	1400	950	750	600

Model 115S Trap

NIB	Exc.	V.G.	Good	Fair	Poor
2700	2450	1900	1450	1150	900

Model 115E Trap

NIB	Exc.	V.G.	Good	Fair	Poor
5250	4800	4200	3500	2500	1850

MODEL 190 SERIES

12-gauge over/under shotgun, with various barrel lengths and choke combinations. Single-selective trigger and automatic ejectors. Engraved and silver-finished, with checkered walnut stock. Introduced in 1986. Various versions differ in degree of ornamentation and quality of materials utilized in construction.

Model 190

NIB	Exc.	V.G.	Good	Fair	Poor
1050	950	750	600	475	400

Model 190MC

NIB	Exc.	V.G.	Good	Fair	Poor
1150	1050	850	700	575	500

Model 190 Special

NIB	Exc.	V.G.	Good	Fair	Poor
1350	1150	950	800	675	600

Model 190 Combo Gun

.243-, .308-, .30-06 caliber and 12-, 16-, 20-gauge combination over/under rifle shotgun, with boxlock action, double triggers and automatic ejectors. Blued, with checkered walnut stock. Introduced in 1989.

NIB	Exc.	V.G.	Good	Fair	Poor
1625	1425	925	775	650	575

ORIONE SERIES

12-gauge boxlock over/under shotgun, with various barrel lengths and choke combinations. Finishes and triggers optional, as were extractors or automatic ejectors.

Orione

NIB	Exc.	V.G.	Good	Fair	Poor
1150	900	700	500	400	200

Orione S

NIB	Exc.	V.G.	Good	Fair	Poor
1150	900	700	500	400	200

Orione L

NIB	Exc.	V.G.	Good	Fair	Poor
1250	1000	800	600	500	250

Orione E

NIB	Exc.	V.G.	Good	Fair	Poor
1350	1150	850	600	500	250

S. Uberto I Gamecock

12-, 16-, 20- or 28-gauge boxlock side-by-side shotgun, with 25.75" or 27.5" barrels, various chokes, double triggers and extractors. Automatic ejectors were available and would be worth a 20 percent premium. Blued, with checkered stock.

NIB	Exc.	V.G.	Good	Fair	Poor
—	950	700	500	350	250

Brescia

12-, 16- or 20-gauge sidelock double-barrel shotgun, with exposed hammers, various barrel lengths, choke combinations, sidelock action, double triggers and manual extractors. Blued, with English-style checkered walnut stock.

NIB	Exc.	V.G.	Good	Fair	Poor
1850	900	700	450	350	225

Italia

Higher grade version of Brescia.

NIB	Exc.	V.G.	Good	Fair	Poor
2250	1250	750	600	400	250

Italia Extra

Highest grade hammer gun Bernardelli produces.

NIB	Exc.	V.G.	Good	Fair	Poor
5900	2750	1500	1000	750	300

UBERTO SERIES

12-, 16-, 20- or 28-gauge Anson & Deeley boxlock double-barrel shotgun, with various barrel lengths and choke combinations. Increased value of various models depends on degree of engraving options and quality of materials and workmanship utilized in their construction.

S. Uberto 1

NIB	Exc.	V.G.	Good	Fair	Poor
1000	800	650	475	350	250

S. Uberto 1E

NIB	Exc.	V.G.	Good	Fair	Poor
1100	900	700	500	350	250

S. Uberto 2

NIB	Exc.	V.G.	Good	Fair	Poor
1500	1100	800	500	350	250

S. Uberto 2E

NIB	Exc.	V.G.	Good	Fair	Poor
1750	1350	950	600	400	250

S. Uberto F.S.

NIB	Exc.	V.G.	Good	Fair	Poor
2000	1500	1100	800	400	250

S. Uberto F.S.E.

NIB	Exc.	V.G.	Good	Fair	Poor
2250	1750	1200	800	400	250

ROMA SERIES

Similar to S. Uberto Series, with false sideplates. Values of respective variations result from degree of ornamentation and quality of materials and workmanship utilized in construction.

Roma 3

NIB	Exc.	V.G.	Good	Fair	Poor
1550	1200	800	600	300	200

Roma 3E

NIB	Exc.	V.G.	Good	Fair	Poor
1750	1300	900	650	300	200

Roma 4

NIB	Exc.	V.G.	Good	Fair	Poor
1950	1400	1100	750	400	250

Roma 4E

NIB	Exc.	V.G.	Good	Fair	Poor
2000	1500	1200	750	400	250

Roma 6

NIB	Exc.	V.G.	Good	Fair	Poor
2100	1750	1400	850	500	250

Roma 6E

NIB	Exc.	V.G.	Good	Fair	Poor
2200	1800	1400	850	500	250

Roma 7

NIB	Exc.	V.G.	Good	Fair	Poor
2900	2500	1800	1200	700	350

Roma 8

NIB	Exc.	V.G.	Good	Fair	Poor
3500	3000	2250	1550	850	400

Roma 9

NIB	Exc.	V.G.	Good	Fair	Poor
4000	3500	2750	1700	950	450

Elio

12-gauge boxlock double-barrel shotgun, with various barrel lengths and choke combinations, lightweight frame, double triggers and extractors. Scroll-engraved, silver-finished receiver, blued barrels and select checkered walnut stock.

NIB	Exc.	V.G.	Good	Fair	Poor
1000	800	600	500	350	250

Elio E

As above, with automatic ejectors.

NIB	Exc.	V.G.	Good	Fair	Poor
1100	900	700	550	350	250

Hemingway

As above, with coin finished receiver engraved with hunting scenes, 23.5" barrels, double-/single trigger and select checkered walnut stock. Available in 12-, 20- and 28-gauge.

NIB	Exc.	V.G.	Good	Fair	Poor
1750	1350	900	700	400	250

Hemingway Deluxe

Same as above fitted with full side plates.

NIB	Exc.	V.G.	Good	Fair	Poor
2250	1750	1200	800	400	250

Las Palomas Pigeon Model

Live pigeon gun in 12-gauge, with single trigger.

NIB	Exc.	V.G.	Good	Fair	Poor
3800	3250	2500	2000	1500	750

HOLLAND V.B. SERIES

12- or 20-gauge sidelock shotgun, with various barrel lengths, detachable Holland & Holland-type locks, single triggers and automatic ejectors. Models listed vary in amount of engraving and quality of their wood. Prospective purchasers are advised to secure a qualified appraisal prior to acquisition.

Holland V.B. Liscio

NIB	Exc.	V.G.	Good	Fair	Poor
8000	5500	4000	3000	2000	1000

Holland V.B. Inciso

NIB	Exc.	V.G.	Good	Fair	Poor
10250	7500	5250	4000	2500	1250

Holland V.B. Lusso

NIB	Exc.	V.G.	Good	Fair	Poor
11000	8000	6000	4500	2500	1250

Holland V.B. Extra

NIB	Exc.	V.G.	Good	Fair	Poor
13000	10000	7500	5500	3000	1500

Holland V.B. Gold

NIB	Exc.	V.G.	Good	Fair	Poor
45000	30000	22500	15000	7500	3000

Luck

Over/under shotgun, with single-selective trigger or double triggers and automatic ejectors. Choice of fixed chokes or choke tubes. Available in 12-gauge. Blued or coin finish receiver.

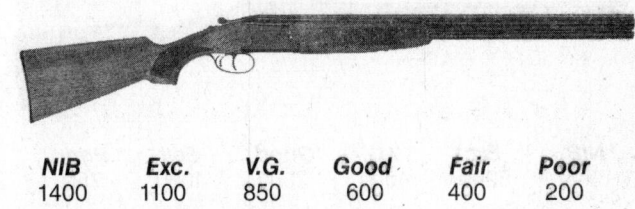

NIB	Exc.	V.G.	Good	Fair	Poor
1400	1100	850	600	400	200

Giardino/Garden Gun (9mm Rimfire)

Semi-automatic shotgun chambered for 9mm shot cartridge. Fitted with 4-round magazine. Weight 5 lbs.

NIB	Exc.	V.G.	Good	Fair	Poor
850	595	425	300	250	100

RIFLES

Carbina VB Target

Semi-automatic carbine chambered for .22 LR cartridge. Barrel is 20.8". Magazine capacity 10 rounds.

NIB	Exc.	V.G.	Good	Fair	Poor
650	550	400	300	200	100

Comb 2000

Rifle-shotgun combination in 12- or 16-gauge, with variety of centerfire calibers to choose from. Barrels are 23.5" long. Set trigger, special rib for scope mount and cheekpiece stock, with pistol-grip. Weight 6.75 lbs.

NIB	Exc.	V.G.	Good	Fair	Poor
2900	2100	1200	800	400	250

Express 2000

Over/under double rifle chambered for variety of European calibers. Fitted with automatic ejectors, double-set triggers or single trigger, muzzle adjustment device. Barrel length 23.5".

NIB	Exc.	V.G.	Good	Fair	Poor
3350	2550	1700	1200	600	300

Express VB

Side-by-side double rifle, chambered for variety of European calibers up to .375 H&H. Double-/single trigger, auto ejectors and finely engraved receiver with beavertail forearm. Cheekpiece stock with pistol-grip.

NIB	Exc.	V.G.	Good	Fair	Poor
5900	4900	3750	2000	1000	750

Express VB Deluxe

Same as above, with side plates and select walnut stock finely checkered.

NIB	Exc.	V.G.	Good	Fair	Poor
6300	5200	4000	2000	1000	750

Minerva

Side-by-side double rifle, with exposed hammers chambered for 9.3x74R cartridge. Fitted with fancy walnut stock, double triggers, hand-cut rib and other high-quality features.

NIB	Exc.	V.G.	Good	Fair	Poor
6700	5900	4550	2500	1200	750

BERNARDON MARTIN
St. Etienne, France

Small firm active between 1906 and 1912. Gun designer was Martin and money man was Bernadon.

1907/8 Model

7.65mm caliber semi-automatic pistol. Left side of slide marked "Cal. 7.65mm St. Etienne". Trademark "BM" molded into grips. Sometimes found with 32-round horseshoe magazine. Occasionally Bernardon Martin pistol will be noted with word "Hermetic" stamped on slide in letters that do not match other markings on weapon. This was but another name for Model 1907/8. Guns with this stamping were most likely assembled after company ceased operations. **NOTE:** Add 50 percent for horseshoe magazine.

Courtesy James Rankin

NIB	Exc.	V.G.	Good	Fair	Poor
—	1100	875	700	450	275

1908/9 Model

Introduced late in 1908. Similar to Model 1907/8, with addition of g safety.

NIB	Exc.	V.G.	Good	Fair	Poor
—	925	775	600	375	225

BERNEDO, VINCENZO
Eibar, Spain

B C

B C in caliber 6.35mm and most of barrel exposed. Recoil spring housed in rear of receiver. B C closely resembles Tanque pistol.

Courtesy James Rankin

NIB	Exc.	V.G.	Good	Fair	Poor
—	325	225	200	175	150

Bernado

Model 7.65mm is in Spanish style of Ruby automatic pistols.

Courtesy James Rankin

NIB	Exc.	V.G.	Good	Fair	Poor
—	225	150	125	75	50

BERSA
Ramos Mejia, Argentina

Model 644

A blowback pocket pistol chambered for .22 LR. Trigger system single action. Barrel length 3.5"; overall length 6.57"; weight empty about 2 oz. This is basic Bersa model from which its other models derive their design and function.

NIB	Exc.	V.G.	Good	Fair	Poor
275	175	150	125	100	75

Model 622

Similar to Model 644, with slightly longer barrel.

NIB	Exc.	V.G.	Good	Fair	Poor
275	175	150	125	100	75

Model 97

Slightly larger version of Model 644. Chambered for 9mm Short.

NIB	Exc.	V.G.	Good	Fair	Poor
275	175	150	125	100	75

Model 23

.22 rimfire caliber double-action semi-automatic pistol, with 3.5" barrel and 10-shot detachable magazine. Blued or satin nickel-plated, with checkered walnut grips.

NIB	Exc.	V.G.	Good	Fair	Poor
300	200	150	125	100	75

Model 223

As above, with squared trigger guard and nylon grips. Imported after 1988.

NIB	Exc.	V.G.	Good	Fair	Poor
—	275	175	125	100	75

Model 224

As above, with 4" barrel. Imported after 1988.

NIB	Exc.	V.G.	Good	Fair	Poor
—	275	175	125	100	75

Model 225

As above, with 5" barrel. Discontinued in 1986.

NIB	Exc.	V.G.	Good	Fair	Poor
—	275	175	125	100	75

Model 226

As above, with 6" barrel. Discontinued in 1988.

Courtesy John J. Stimson, Jr.

NIB	Exc.	V.G.	Good	Fair	Poor
—	275	175	125	100	75

Model 323

.32 ACP caliber single-action semi-automatic pistol, with 3.5" barrel, fixed sights and 7-shot detachable magazine. Blued, with molded plastic grips. Not imported after 1986.

NIB	Exc.	V.G.	Good	Fair	Poor
—	225	125	100	75	50

Model 383

As above in .380-caliber. Discontinued in 1988.

NIB	Exc.	V.G.	Good	Fair	Poor
—	250	150	125	90	75

Model 383A

.380 ACP caliber double-action semi-automatic pistol, with 3.5" barrel, fixed sights and 7-shot magazine. Blued, with checkered walnut grips. Overall length 6.6"; weight about 24 oz. Available in blue or nickel finish.

NIB	Exc.	V.G.	Good	Fair	Poor
300	200	150	125	100	75

Model 83

Similar to above model, with double-action operating system. Weight about 26 oz. Introduced in 1988.

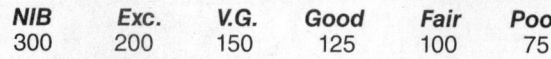

NIB	Exc.	V.G.	Good	Fair	Poor
300	200	150	125	100	75

Model 85

As above, with double-column magazine. Introduced in 1988.

NIB	Exc.	V.G.	Good	Fair	Poor
350	250	200	150	100	75

Model 86

Similar to Model 85 in .380-caliber. Features matte blue or satin nickel finish, wrap around rubber grips and three-dot sight. Magazine capacity 13 rounds

NIB	Exc.	V.G.	Good	Fair	Poor
350	250	225	200	150	100

Thunder 9

Introduced in 1993. A double-action 9mm pistol that features ambidextrous safety, reversible extended magazine release, ambidextrous slide release, adjustable trigger stop, combat-style hammer, three-dot sights and matte blue finish. Magazine capacity 15 rounds.

NIB	Exc.	V.G.	Good	Fair	Poor
350	275	250	200	150	100

Series 95/Thunder 380

Semi-automatic double-action pistol chambered for .380 cartridge. Choice of matte blue or nickel finish. Barrel length 3.5". Fixed sights. Magazine capacity 7 rounds. Weight about 23 oz. **NOTE:** Add $50 for nickel.

NIB	Exc.	V.G.	Good	Fair	Poor
260	200	150	100	75	50

Thunder 380 Matte Plus

Semi-automatic double-action blued pistol in .380, with 15-round magazine. Fixed sights and polymer grips. Introduced 2006.

NIB	Exc.	V.G.	Good	Fair	Poor
350	275	250	200	150	100

Thunder Pro Ultra Compact

Pro Ultra Compact Series features DA/SA operation, skeletonized hammer, loaded chamber indicator, checkered black polymer grips and choice of matte black, nickel, two-tone or stainless finish. Chambered in 9mm, .40 S&W or .45 ACP. Barrel lengths 3.25" for 9mm and .40; 3.50" for .45. **NOTE:** Add $40 for nickel or stainless finish.

NIB	Exc.	V.G.	Good	Fair	Poor
400	350	300	250	200	100

Thunder 9/40 High Capacity Series

Double-action semi-automatic available chambered for 9mm or .40 S&W. Matte blued or satin nickel-plate. Fixed sights and polymer grips. LOA 7.5", Barrel length 4.25". Weight 26 oz. Introduced 2006.

NIB	Exc.	V.G.	Good	Fair	Poor
395	300	250	200	150	100

Thunder Deluxe

Semi-automatic double-action pistol. Chambered for .380 cartridge. Blued finish. Fixed sights. Barrel length 3.5". Weight about 23 oz. Magazine capacity 9 rounds.

NIB	Exc.	V.G.	Good	Fair	Poor
325	225	175	100	75	50

Thunder 22

Double-action semi-automatic, with 3.5" barrel and 10-shot magazine. Matte black, satin nickel or two-tone finish.

NIB	Exc.	V.G.	Good	Fair	Poor
300	250	200	150	100	80

BERTRAND, JULES
Liege, Belgium

Le Novo

6.35mm caliber double-action revolver. Manufactured in 1890s. Only identifying markings are "JB" trademark on grips.

NIB	Exc.	V.G.	Good	Fair	Poor
—	300	225	175	100	50

Lincoln

As above in 7.65mm caliber.

NIB	Exc.	V.G.	Good	Fair	Poor
—	300	225	175	100	50

Le Rapide

6.35mm caliber semi-automatic pistol. Jules Bertrand logo on slide as well as Le Rapide. Both are on each side of grip plates.

Courtesy James Rankin

NIB	Exc.	V.G.	Good	Fair	Poor
—	350	275	200	125	50

BERTUZZI
Brescia, Italy

This maker of best quality sidelock over/under and side-by-side shotguns closed its doors in 2009, after more than 100 years in business. Values shown are approximate retail prices in recent years, depending on the wide range of optional features.

OVER/UNDER SHOTGUNS

Zeus

12-, 16-, 20- or 28-gauge sidelock shotgun, with automatic ejectors, single-selective trigger and deluxe checkered walnut stock. Custom order in various barrel lengths and chokes. Engraved. Rarely seen on used gun market. From $18,000 to $39,000

Zeus Extra Lusso

As above, with best wood and engraving. Cased. From $35,000 to $79,000.

Zeus Boss System

Chambered for 12-, 16-, 20- or 28-gauge. Fitted with Boss locking system and ejectors. One-of-a-kind gun with best quality wood and engraving. From $65,000 to $135,000.

Gull Wing

Burtuzzi's best gun, with unique sidelock design mounted on a center plate. Release located on top of safety to allow sidelock access. These shotguns usually take about three years to build. Consult distributor about options and availability. From $125,000 to $240,000.

Ariete Extra Lusso

Best quality hammer gun in all gauges from 12 to 28. Limited quantities. From $65,000 to $135,000.

SIDE-BY-SIDE SHOTGUNS

Orione

12-, 16-, 20- or 28-gauge boxlock shotgun, with Anson & Deeley through bolt. In various barrel lengths and chokes, single-selective trigger and automatic ejectors. Hand checkered walnut stock, with semi-beavertail forearm. Engraving. From $25,000 to $40,000.

Venere

Best quality sidelock gun, with traditional or round frame. Special order to customer specifications. Engraved guns bring a premium. From $30,000 to $70,000.

Ariete

Best quality hammer gun, with or without self cocking hammers and ejectors. Offered in 12-gauge through .410 bore. Many options. From $25,000 to $55,000.

Gull Wing

One-of-a-kind custom built gun, with quick release sidelocks. Delivery time about three years. Contact distributor for more information. From $85,000 to $150,000.

BIG HORN ARMORY
Cody, Wyoming

Big Horn Armory Model 89 Rifle and Carbine

Lever-action rifle or carbine chambered for .500 S&W Magnum. Features include 18" or 22" barrel; walnut or maple stocks with pistol-grip; aperture rear and blade front sights; recoil pad; sling swivels; enlarged lever loop; magazine capacity 5 (rifle) or 7 (carbine) rounds.

NIB	Exc.	V.G.	Good	Fair	Poor
1800	1500	1100	750	600	300

BIGHORN ARMS CO.
Watertown, South Dakota

Target Pistol

.22-caliber single-shot pistol resembling semi-automatic. Ventilated rib barrel 6" in length. Stock of molded plastic.

NIB	Exc.	V.G.	Good	Fair	Poor
—	275	175	100	85	65

Shotgun

Single-shot 12-gauge shotgun, with 26" barrel blued. Plastic stock.

NIB	Exc.	V.G.	Good	Fair	Poor
—	195	115	65	50	30

BIGHORN RIFLE CO.
Orem, Utah

Bighorn Rifle

A formr custom rifle manufacturer located in Orem, Utah. These made-to-order rifles were available in any caliber, with various options. Values are speculative.

NIB	Exc.	V.G.	Good	Fair	Poor
2000	1650	1200	850	650	300

BILHARZ, HALL & CO.
Location Unknown

CONFEDERATE CARBINES

Breechloading ("Rising Breech") Carbine

Overall length 40"; barrel length 21"; caliber 54. Markings: either "P" or "P/CS" on upper left side of barrel and top of rising breech. Peculiar feature of this carbine is manner in which breechblock exposes chamber. A box-like chamber at rear of barrel rises vertically to expose chamber for a paper cartridge by activating lever/trigger-guard mechanism. Only 100 of this type were delivered to Confederacy in September 1862. Two types of front sight blades are known, but neither affects value.

Courtesy Milwaukee Public Museum, Milwaukee, Wisconsin

NIB	Exc.	V.G.	Good	Fair	Poor
—	—	50000	22500	5000	2100

Muzzleloading Carbine

Overall length 37.5"; barrel length 22"; caliber .58. Markings: "P/CS" on upper left of barrel near breech; "CSA" on top near breech. Modeled after Springfield U.S. M1855 rifle carbine. Bilharz, Hall & Co. muzzleloading carbine has often been mistakenly identified as a product of D.C. Hodgkins & Sons of Macon, Georgia. Serial numbers (found internally) belie that identification. Instead these arms are part of deliveries made to Richmond from middle of 1863 until March 1864. Serial numbers, noted in excess of 700, suggest that about 1,000 were produced. Two basic types, earlier (through serial number 300) were made with brass nosecaps; later type (about serial number 310 through at least 710) have pewter nosecaps on short fore-stock; neither type affects value.

NIB	Exc.	V.G.	Good	Fair	Poor
—	—	25000	10000	3000	1650

BILLINGHURST, WILLIAM
Rochester, New York

Billinghurst originally worked for James and John Miller of Rochester. After James Miller's death in 1837, Billinghurst established his own shop where he produced revolving rifles based upon Miller's 1829 patent. While these arms were originally made with percussion ignition systems (either pill or percussion cap), later examples using self-contained metallic cartridges are sometimes encountered. Billinghurst also established a well-deserved reputation for making extremely accurate percussion target pistols and rifles.

Under Hammer Pistol

Pistol is somewhat different than most under hammers encountered. Barrels are 12" to 18" in length. Heavy octagonal construction. Chambered from .30- to .38-caliber and utilize percussion ignition system. Higher grade versions feature a part-round barrel. Important to note that no two pistols are alike. These pistols were furnished with detachable shoulder stocks and a good many were cased with telescopic sights and false muzzles. This is a high quality weapon; if encountered with optional accessories, it would definitely warrant an individual appraisal. This firearm was manufactured in 1850s and 1860s. **NOTE:** Add 50 percent for shoulder stock.

NIB	Exc.	V.G.	Good	Fair	Poor
—	—	4750	2150	800	400

Revolving Rifle

Calibers vary from .40 to .50 with barrels from 24" to 29"; walnut stocks. Barrels marked: "W. Billinghurst, Rochester, N.Y.", or "W. Billinghurst".

NIB	Exc.	V.G.	Good	Fair	Poor
—	—	7900	3700	950	400

BILLINGS
Location Unknown

Pocket Pistol

.32 rimfire caliber single-shot spur trigger pistol, with 2.5" round barrel. An unusually large grip. Barrel stamped "Billings Vest Pocket Pistol Pat. April 24, 1866". Blued, with walnut grips. Manufactured between 1865 and 1868.

NIB	Exc.	V.G.	Good	Fair	Poor
—	—	3500	1500	550	195

BINGHAM LTD.
Norcross, Georgia

PPS 50

.22 rimfire caliber semi-automatic rifle. Patterned after Soviet PPSH sub-machine gun, with 16" barrel and 50-round drum magazine. Blued, walnut or beech stock with vented hand guard. Manufactured between 1976 and 1985.

NIB	Exc.	V.G.	Good	Fair	Poor
—	575	400	275	225	100

AK-22

.22 rimfire caliber semi-automatic rifle. Patterned after Soviet AK-47, with 15- or 29-shot magazine. Walnut or beech stock. Manufactured between 1976 and 1985.

NIB	Exc.	V.G.	Good	Fair	Poor
—	365	225	150	100	75

Bantam

.22 rimfire or .22 rimfire Magnum caliber bolt-action rifle, with 18.5" barrel. Manufactured between 1976 and 1985.

NIB	Exc.	V.G.	Good	Fair	Poor
—	200	85	70	50	35

BISMARCK
Location Unknown

Pocket Revolver

.22-caliber spur trigger revolver, with 3" round ribbed barrel and 7-shot unfluted cylinder. Brass frame. Remainder plated with rosewood grips. Barrel marked "Bismarck". Manufactured in 1870s.

NIB	Exc.	V.G.	Good	Fair	Poor
—	—	550	225	90	50

BITTERLICH, FRANK J.
Nashville, Tennessee

A .41-caliber single-shot percussion pistol in a variety of octagonal barrel lengths, German silver mounts, walnut stock. Barrel and locks marked "Fr.J. Bitterlich/Nashville, Tenn." Produced between 1861 and 1867.

NIB	Exc.	V.G.	Good	Fair	Poor
—	—	5500	4900	1900	850

BITTNER, GUSTAV
Wieport, Bohemia

Bittner

7.7mm Bittner caliber repeating pistol, with 4.5" barrel. Bolt containing firing pin rotates to lock breech. Operated by finger lever that encloses trigger. Manufactured in mid-1890s. Fewer than 500 made.

NIB	Exc.	V.G.	Good	Fair	Poor
—	15000	10500	8000	4000	2000

BLAKE, J. H.
New York, New York

Blake Bolt-Action Rifle

.30-40 Krag caliber bolt-action rifle, with 30" barrel and 7-shot magazine. Stock secured by three barrel bands. Blued, with walnut stock. Manufactured between 1892 and 1910.

Courtesy Milwaukee Public Museum, Milwaukee, Wisconsin

NIB	Exc.	V.G.	Good	Fair	Poor
—	—	3500	1700	675	200

BLANCH, JOHN
London, England

Blanch Percussion Pistol

.69-caliber single-shot percussion pistol, with 5" Damascus barrel. Engraved frame and hammer, with walnut grip. Manufactured in 1830s.

NIB	Exc.	V.G.	Good	Fair	Poor
—	—	6750	2950	1450	875

BLAND, THOMAS & SONS
London, England

Established in 1840, this firm has produced or marketed a wide variety of percussion and cartridge arms. Over the years, firm has occupied a variety of premises in London, some of them concurrently.

41 Whittall Street	1840-1867
41, 42, 43 Whittall Street	1867-1886
106 Strand	1872-1900
430 Strand	1886-1900
2 William IV Street	1900-1919
4-5 William IV Street	1919-1973
New Row, St. Martin's Lane	1973-

BLASER JAGDWAFFEN
Germany

RIFLES

Model K77

Single-shot rifle chambered in a variety of calibers. A 24" barrel and silver-plated engraved receiver. Walnut stock. Introduced in 1988. Discontinued in 1990. **NOTE:** Add $750 per barrel for extra barrels.

NIB	Exc.	V.G.	Good	Fair	Poor
2400	1850	1200	850	650	300

Model R-84

Bolt-action sporting rifle. Chambered in a variety of calibers, with 23" or 24" barrel. Interchangeable barrels available for this model. Walnut stock. Imported beginning in 1988.

NIB	Exc.	V.G.	Good	Fair	Poor
2500	2000	1400	950	700	300

Model R-93 LX

A straight-pull-back bolt-action rifle, with interchangeable barrels. In calibers from .22-250 to .416 Rem. Magnum. Barrel length for standard calibers is 22" and Magnum calibers 26". Magazine capacity 3 rounds. Receiver is drilled and tapped for Blaser scope mounts. Weight about 7 lbs. Two-piece walnut stock. Introduced by SIGARMS into U.S. in 1998. **NOTE:** Add $200 for left-hand rifles; $800 for .416 Rem. Magnum.

NIB	Exc.	V.G.	Good	Fair	Poor
1700	1400	1100	800	600	300

Model R-93 Prestige

Updated and upgraded standard model, with all features of R-93 LX. Light scroll engraving on receiver.

NIB	Exc.	V.G.	Good	Fair	Poor
3275	2750	1800	1300	700	350

Model R-93 Classic

Similar to above. Choice of calibers and barrel lengths. Addition of highly figured walnut stock and game scene engraved receiver. **NOTE:** Add $200 for left-hand rifles; $800 for .416 Rem. Magnum.

NIB	Exc.	V.G.	Good	Fair	Poor
2900	2400	1750	1250	900	300

Model R-93 Luxus

Updated and upgraded model of R-93 Classic. Features high grade Turkish walnut stock, with ebony fore-end. Side plates engraved with game scenes.

NIB	Exc.	V.G.	Good	Fair	Poor
5000	4000	3000	2000	1000	500

Model R-93 Synthetic

Also available in same wide range of interchangeable barrels and calibers. Features one-piece black synthetic stock. **NOTE:** Add $200 for left-hand rifles; $800 for .416 Rem. Magnum.

NIB	Exc.	V.G.	Good	Fair	Poor
1800	1500	1000	850	600	400

Model R-93 Attache

Features custom made stock of highly figured walnut, with cheekpiece, leather covered buttplate, silver pistol-grip cap, ebony fore-end tip and custom checkering. Sold with leather carrying case. **NOTE:** Add $200 for left-hand rifles.

NIB	Exc.	V.G.	Good	Fair	Poor
5500	4650	3300	2450	1650	500

Model R-93 Safari Synthetic

Chambered for .416 Rem. Magnum cartridge. Fitted with 24" heavy barrel, with open sights. Weight 9.5 lbs. Black synthetic stock. Other Blaser barrels will interchange on this model.

NIB	Exc.	V.G.	Good	Fair	Poor
2100	1700	1250	875	500	275

Model R-93 Safari LX

Same as R-93 Safari Synthetic, with exception of two-piece walnut stock.

NIB	Exc.	V.G.	Good	Fair	Poor
2500	2000	1550	1000	750	350

Model R-93 Safari Classic

Features engraved receiver and fancy walnut stock.

NIB	Exc.	V.G.	Good	Fair	Poor
2500	2000	1550	1000	750	350

Model R-93 Safari Attache

Top-of-the-line version of R-93 series. Features engraved receiver, fancy walnut stock and other custom options found on R-93 Attache model.

NIB	Exc.	V.G.	Good	Fair	Poor
6000	5000	3950	2900	1500	400

Model R-93 Grand Luxe

Offered in same wide range of calibers as other Blaser models. Addition of high grade walnut stock, fully hand engraved receiver and matching scroll sideplates. Introduced in 1999. **NOTE:** Add $200 for left-hand rifles.

NIB	Exc.	V.G.	Good	Fair	Poor
6000	5000	4000	2000	1000	395

Model R-8 Professional

Improved variation of R-93 action, with detachable magazine. Offered in many calibers from .222 Rem. to 10.3x60R. Offered in several high grade models similar to those in R-93 series. Prices shown are for base model, with synthetic stock. **NOTE:** Add 15 to 300 percent for high grade versions.

NIB	Exc.	V.G.	Good	Fair	Poor
3000	2300	1700	1200	750	300

Model R-8 Professional Success

Similar to R-8 Professional model, except with synthetic thumbhole stock in Dark Brown or Dark Green color. Leather inlays are optional. Introduced in 2013.

NIB	Exc.	V.G.	Good	Fair	Poor
3600	3000	2300	1850	900	400

Model R-8 Professional Hunter

Chambered in most popular dangerous-game calibers. Has high-grade wood, all steel receiver, with several stock and finish options.

NIB	Exc.	V.G.	Good	Fair	Poor
6500	5400	4300	2900	1850	900

Model K-95 Standard

Single-shot model, with break-open action. Receiver is aluminum, with engraving on side plates. Barrel length 23.6" for standard calibers and 25.6" for Magnum calibers. Oil finish Turkish walnut stock. Interchangeable barrels in calibers from .243 to .300 Wby. Magnum. Weight about 5.5 lbs. Introduced in 2001.

NIB	Exc.	V.G.	Good	Fair	Poor
3500	2500	1500	1150	700	325

Model K-95 Luxus

Same as above, with fancy Turkish walnut stock. Hand engraving on receiver and side plates.

NIB	Exc.	V.G.	Good	Fair	Poor
4300	3750	2500	1900	900	400

Model K-95 Stutzen

Introduced in 2003. Break-action single-shot rifle offered in 23 calibers. Fancy walnut Mannlicher-style two-piece stock. Interchangeable barrels.

NIB	Exc.	V.G.	Good	Fair	Poor
5400	4650	3200	2250	1000	450

Ultimate Bolt-Action

Unique bolt-action design imported into U.S. in 1980s. Chambered in most popular calibers from .22-250 to .375 H&H. Features include interchangeable barrels and bolt heads, single set trigger, exposed hammer. Left-hand models at no additional cost. Available in several high-grade models. Prices shown are for standard model. **NOTE:** Add premium of 15 to 200 percent for higher grade engraving and wood.

NIB	Exc.	V.G.	Good	Fair	Poor
1500	1200	1000	800	550	300

Model R-93 Long Range Sporter

Introduced in 1998. Bolt-action rifle chambered for .308 Win. cartridge. Barrel length 24" without muzzle-brake. Removable box magazine holds 10 rounds. Stock is aluminum and fully adjustable. Weight about 10.4 lbs. No longer in production.

NIB	Exc.	V.G.	Good	Fair	Poor
2200	1775	1250	875	500	275

Model R-93 (LRS2)

Introduced in 2000. A second generation version of Long Range Sporter model above. Chambered for .300 Win. Magnum and .308, both of which are interchangeable. Also chambered for .338 Lapua cartridge which does not interchange with other calibers. Cheekpiece improved. New front rail has been added to this model. Barrel length 24" without muzzle-brake. Weight about 10.4 lbs. **NOTE:** Add $350 for .338 Lapua.

NIB	Exc.	V.G.	Good	Fair	Poor
3475	2700	1900	1275	800	375

Blaser S2 Double Rifle

Series of side-by-side double rifles offered in two different models, Standard and Safari. Standard calibers range from .22 Hornet to 9.3x74R, including several European rimmed cartridges. Safari model chamberings for .375 H&H, .470 NE, .500/416 NE and 500 NE. Both series available in standard or five higher grades offering increasing levels of wood and engraving. Higher grade models are in order: Luxus, Super Luxus, Exclusive, Super Exclusive and Imperial. Prices shown are for basic standard models. Extra sets of barrels in different calibers offered, including shotgun barrels. Barrel sets are not interchangeable between Standard and Safari models. **NOTE:** Add 15 to 200 percent or more for higher grades.

Standard

NIB	Exc.	V.G.	Good	Fair	Poor
6800	6000	5200	4200	2500	1000

Safari

NIB	Exc.	V.G.	Good	Fair	Poor
9500	8500	7000	5800	3500	1500

SHOTGUNS

F3 Series

Over/under series of shotguns. Offered in standard, sporting, skeet and trap models in 12- or 20-gauge. Available with various barrel lengths and options, including extra barrel sets. Add 40 percent for additional set of barrels. Offered in several higher grades, each with increasing levels of engraving and wood upgrades. For higher grades, add the following to prices shown below: Luxus 20 percent; Grand Lux 60 percent; Super Lux 80 percent; Baroness 100 percent; Exclusive 115 percent; Super Exclusive 200 percent; Imperial 300 percent.

NIB	Exc.	V.G.	Good	Fair	Poor
—					

Game Standard

NIB	Exc.	V.G.	Good	Fair	Poor
5500	4700	3900	3000	2000	1000

Sporting Standard and Skeet

NIB	Exc.	V.G.	Good	Fair	Poor
6500	5500	4600	3750	2500	1000

Super Trap and Super Sport

NIB	Exc.	V.G.	Good	Fair	Poor
7500	6750	5900	4500	3000	1000

HANDGUNS

Blaser HHS

Single-shot pistol has R93 receiver. Fitted with 14" barrel and pistol-grip fancy Turkish walnut stock. All R93 calibers are offered in both right-/left-hand models. Introduced in 2003. **NOTE:** Add $100 for left-hand models.

NIB	Exc.	V.G.	Good	Fair	Poor
4250	3250	2000	1300	70	400

BLISS, F. D.
New Haven, Connecticut

Bliss Pocket Revolver

.25-caliber spur trigger revolver, with 3.25" octagon barrel, 6-shot magazine and square butt. Blued, with hard rubber or walnut grips. Barrel stamped "F.D. Bliss New Haven, Ct." There was an all-brass framed version made early in production. This model would be worth approximately 50 percent more than values listed here for standard model. Approximately 3,000 manufactured circa 1860 to 1863.

NIB	Exc.	V.G.	Good	Fair	Poor
—	—	975	525	125	75

BLISS & GOODYEAR
New Haven, Connecticut

Pocket Model Revolver

.28-caliber percussion revolver, with 3" octagonal barrel, 6-shot magazine, unfluted cylinder. Solid frame, with removable side plate. Blued, with brass frame and walnut grips. Approximately 3,000 manufactured in 1860.

NIB	Exc.	V.G.	Good	Fair	Poor
—	—	1800	550	225	150

BLUNT & SYMS
New York, New York

Under Hammer Pepperbox

Pepperboxes produced by Blunt & Syms are noteworthy for the fact they incorporate a ring trigger cocking/revolving mechanism and a concealed under hammer. They were produced in a variety of calibers and standard finish was blued. Normally these pistols are found marked simply "A-C" on face of barrel group. Some examples though are marked "Blunt & Syms New York". This firm was in business from approximately 1837 to 1855.

Small Frame Round Handle .25-.28-Caliber

NIB	Exc.	V.G.	Good	Fair	Poor
—	—	1800	1300	675	175

Medium Frame Round Handle .31-Caliber

NIB	Exc.	V.G.	Good	Fair	Poor
—	—	1850	1450	725	195

Round Handle Dragoon .36-Caliber

NIB	Exc.	V.G.	Good	Fair	Poor
—	—	2900	1050	900	295

Medium Frame Saw Handle .31-Caliber

NIB	Exc.	V.G.	Good	Fair	Poor
—	—	2000	750	375	175

Saw Handle Dragoon .36-Caliber

NIB	Exc.	V.G.	Good	Fair	Poor
—	—	2800	1350	750	225

Dueling Pistol

.52-caliber percussion single-shot pistol, with octagonal barrel normally of 9" length. Steel furniture, with walnut stock. Barrel marked "B&S New York/Cast Steel".

NIB	Exc.	V.G.	Good	Fair	Poor
—	—	—	1750	725	325

Single-Shot Bar Hammer

.36-caliber single-shot percussion pistol, with 6" half-octagonal barrel and bar hammer. Blued or browned, with walnut grips. Marked as above.

NIB	Exc.	V.G.	Good	Fair	Poor
—	—	1200	700	450	200

Side Hammer Pocket Pistol

.31- or .35-caliber single-shot percussion pistol, with 2.5" to 6" octagonal barrel. Blued, with walnut grips.

NIB	Exc.	V.G.	Good	Fair	Poor
—	—	1250	650	425	195

Side Hammer Belt Pistol

As above in calibers ranging from .36 to .44, with barrel lengths of 4" or 6".

NIB	Exc.	V.G.	Good	Fair	Poor
—	—	1400	750	375	150

Ring Trigger Pistol

.36-caliber percussion single-shot pistol, with 3" to 5" half-octagonal barrel and ring trigger. Blued, with walnut grips.

NIB	Exc.	V.G.	Good	Fair	Poor
—	—	1025	650	375	150

Double Barrel Pistol

.36- to .44-caliber percussion double-barrel pistol, with 7.5" barrels and walnut grips. Ring trigger variation of this model is known.

NIB	Exc.	V.G.	Good	Fair	Poor
—	—	1350	650	275	125

Double Barrel Under Hammer Pistol

As above, with two under hammers in .34-caliber and 4" barrels.

NIB	Exc.	V.G.	Good	Fair	Poor
—	—	1750	875	425	200

Derringer Style Pistol

.50-caliber single-shot percussion pistol, with 3" barrel, German silver mounts and walnut stock. Lock marked "Blunt & Syms/New York".

NIB	Exc.	V.G.	Good	Fair	Poor
—	—	1800	675	395	200

BOBERG ARMS CORP.
White Bear Lake, Minnesota

XR9

Semi-automatic chambered in 9mm, with 3.35 (XR9-S) or 4.2" (XR9-L) barrel. Striker-fired with locked-breech action, rotating barrel, stainless steel slide, aluminum frame. Magazine capacity 7-rounds. Fixed low-profile 3-dot sights. Patented new design lifts cartridges straight into chamber, eliminating need for feed ramp and allowing for a longer barrel than other subcompact pistols. Introduced in 2013. **NOTE:** Add $350 for platinum or onyx finish.

NIB	Exc.	V.G.	Good	Fair	Poor
900	800	700	—	—	—

XR45

Similar to XR9. Chambered for .45 ACP cartridge. Magazine capacity 6 rounds. Barrel length 3.75". Aluminum frame, with stainless steel slide and polymer grip panels. Two-tone satin silver slide and black frame. Introduced in 2014. **NOTE:** Add $100 for Tritium night sights.

NIB	Exc.	V.G.	Good	Fair	Poor
1000	900	750	500	—	—

BODEO
Location Unknown

Italian Service Revolver

System Bodeo Modello 1889 (Enlisted Model)

NIB	Exc.	V.G.	Good	Fair	Poor
—	750	550	400	250	100

Modello 1889 (Officer's Model)

NIB	Exc.	V.G.	Good	Fair	Poor
—	750	550	400	250	100

BOLUMBURO, G.
Eibar, Spain

Bristol

Semi-automatic pistol in caliber 7.65mm. Made in style of Ruby military pistols. "Bristol" stamped on slide. Wood grips.

Courtesy James Rankin

NIB	Exc.	V.G.	Good	Fair	Poor
—	295	185	150	90	40

Marina 6.35mm

Semi-automatic pistol in caliber 6.35mm. "Marina" stamped on each grip's plate.

Courtesy James Rankin

NIB	Exc.	V.G.	Good	Fair	Poor
—	295	195	150	90	40

Marina 7.65mm

As above in 7.65mm, with "Marina" stamped on slide. Wood grips and lanyard loop.

Courtesy James Rankin

NIB	Exc.	V.G.	Good	Fair	Poor
—	275	195	150	90	40

Rex

Semi-automatic pistol in caliber 7.65mm. "Rex" stamped on slide. Wood grips and lanyard loop.

Courtesy James Rankin

NIB	Exc.	V.G.	Good	Fair	Poor
—	275	195	150	90	40

BOND ARMS INC.
Grandbury, Texas

Texas Defender

Stainless steel over/under derringer. Chambered for a variety of calibers such as .45 Colt/.410, .357 Magnum, 9mm, .45 ACP and .44 Magnum. Removable trigger guard. Barrels are interchangeable. Grips are laminated black ash or rosewood. Barrel length 3", with blade front sight and fixed rear sight. Weight about 21 oz. Introduced in 1997. **NOTE:** Add 300 percent for full factory engraved model.

NIB	Exc.	V.G.	Good	Fair	Poor
—	400	300	200	150	100

Bond Patriot

Features an American flag and bald eagle laser engraved on grips. Chambered for .45 Colt/.410 shotshell or .357 Magnum/.38 Special. Standard Bond features include rebounding hammer, retracting firing pins, crossbolt safety and spring-loaded cammed locking lever. Weight 22 oz.; barrel length 3". Introduced in 2015.

NIB	Exc.	V.G.	Good	Fair	Poor
500	425	375	325	250	200

Snake Slayer IV

Modern variation of Remington over/under derringer. Interchangeable 4.5" barrel assemblies, rosewood grip panels, stainless finish, fixed sights. Chambered for .410-bore shotshell/.45 LC, 9mm, 10mm, .40 S&W, .45 ACP. Weight 23 oz.

NIB	Exc.	V.G.	Good	Fair	Poor
—	400	300	200	150	100

Snake Slayer

3.5" barrels; weight 22 oz. Interchangeable barrel assemblies, rosewood grip panels, stainless fixed sights. Chambered for .410-bore shotshell/.45 LC, 9mm, 10mm, .40 S&W, .45 ACP.

NIB	Exc.	V.G.	Good	Fair	Poor
—	400	300	200	150	100

Cowboy Defender

Derringer with 3" barrels. Weight 19 oz. Interchangeable barrels, rosewood grip panels, stainless fixed sights. Variety of chambering options such as .410-bore, .45 LC, .357 Magnum, .38 Special, .45 ACP, .44 Special, .44-40 Win, .40 S&W, 10mm, etc. No trigger guard. Automatic extractor (except for 9mm, 10mm, .40 S&W, .45 ACP).

NIB	Exc.	V.G.	Good	Fair	Poor
395	350	300	225	150	75

Century 2000

Similar to Cowboy Defender, with 3.5" barrels to allow use of .410 Magnum shotshells, .357/.38 Special, .45 ACP, .44 Special, .44-40 Win, .40 S&W, 10mm, etc. Automatic extractor (except for 9mm, 10mm, .40 S&W, .45 ACP).

NIB	Exc.	V.G.	Good	Fair	Poor
425	375	300	225	150	75

BOOM
Hatfield, Massachusetts
See—Shattuck, C.S.

BORCHARDT
Berlin, Germany
Waffenfabrik Lowe

Borchardt

Forerunner of German Luger. Borchardt was a semi-automatic pistol. Chambered for 7.65mm Borchardt cartridge. Fitted with 6.5" barrel. Magazine held 8 rounds. Pistol was designed by Hugo Borchardt and manufactured by Ludwig Lowe of Berlin. Later models manufactured by DWM, Deutsch Waffen Und Munitionsfabriken, Berlin. Many Borchardts come with a case which holds shoulder stock, holster, extra magazines and numerous other accessories.

Courtesy James Rankin

Pistol Only

NIB	Exc.	V.G.	Good	Fair	Poor
—	23000	15000	8000	4000	2000

(Row at top right corner, above Cowboy Defender:)

NIB	Exc.	V.G.	Good	Fair	Poor
—	400	300	200	150	100

Pistol with Case and Accessories

NIB	Exc.	V.G.	Good	Fair	Poor
—	35000	20000	12000	7500	4000

BORSIG
East Germany

Borsig is East German version of Soviet Makarov pistol. A double-action chambered for Soviet 9x18mm cartridge. Its appearance is nearly identical to Makarov.

NIB	Exc.	V.G.	Good	Fair	Poor
—	300	225	150	100	75

BOSIS, LUCIANO
Brescia, Italy

Bosis is a maker of high-grade sidelock over/under and side-by-side guns in gauges 12, 20, 28 and .410. These guns are made on custom-order basis.

Over/Under

Values for used guns in excellent condition begin at $30,000. Secure an expert appraisal prior to sale.

Side-by-Side

Values for used guns in excellent condition begin at $20,000. Secure an expert appraisal prior to sale. **NOTE:** Small gauge guns will bring a premium of 20 percent.

BOSS & CO.
London, England

Thomas Boss worked for great British gunmaker Joseph Manton, before becoming a pieceworker to the London trade. In 1891, John Robertson was taken in as a partner and under his control the firm was established as one of London's best gunmakers, rivaled only by James Purdey. Current Boss shotgun prices begin at around £60,000 ($96,000 U.S.) and double rifles about £85,000 ($136,000 U.S.). Many of the older models are encountered on used gun market. A professional appraisal is strongly advised before establishing a buying or selling price.

A cased pair of Boss & Co. sidelock shotguns

BOSWELL, CHARLES
London, England

One of England's more established makers of best-quality rifles and shotguns. In 1988, company was purchased by an American consortium and Cape Horn Outfitters of Charlotte, North Carolina was appointed their sole agent.

Double Rifle, Boxlock

.300 H&H, .375 H&H or .458 Win. Magnum double-barrel boxlock rifle, with double triggers and walnut stock. Other features were made to customer's specifications. A .600 Nitro Express version was also available. **NOTE:** Add 25 percent for .600 Nitro Express.

NIB	Exc.	V.G.	Good	Fair	Poor
—	47000	39500	29500	19950	600

Double Rifle, Sidelock

As above, with Holland & Holland-style sidelocks. **NOTE:** Add 25 percent for .600 Nitro Express.

NIB	Exc.	V.G.	Good	Fair	Poor
—	63000	47500	35000	22000	600

BOSWORTH, B. M.
Warren, Pennsylvania

Under Hammer Pistol

.38-caliber single-shot percussion pistol, with under hammer and 6" half-octagonal barrel. Frame marked "BM Bosworth". Browned, with brass grips forming part of frame. Made circa 1850 to 1860.

NIB	Exc.	V.G.	Good	Fair	Poor
—	—	1850	800	295	125

BRAENDLIN ARMOURY
London, England

.450-caliber 8-barrel pistol, with hinged barrels, rotating firing pin and double-action lock. Manufactured during 1880s.

NIB	Exc.	V.G.	Good	Fair	Poor
—	—	8550	5500	3500	1850

BRAND
New York
Maker—E. Robinson

Brand Breech Loading Carbine

.50 rimfire caliber carbine, with 22" barrel secured by one barrel band. Frame marked "Brand's Patent July 29,1862/E. Robinson Manfr/New York". Carbine was produced in limited numbers, primarily for trial purposes.

NIB	Exc.	V.G.	Good	Fair	Poor
—	—	6800	2950	1250	550

BREDA, ERNESTO
Milan, Italy

Andromeda Special

12-gauge boxlock shotgun, with various barrel lengths and chokes, single-selective triggers and automatic ejectors. Engraved satin-finished, with checkered walnut stock.

NIB	Exc.	V.G.	Good	Fair	Poor
—	1150	775	595	425	300

Vega Special

12-gauge boxlock over/under shotgun, with 26" or 28" barrels, various choke combinations, single-selective trigger and automatic ejectors. Engraved and blued, with checkered walnut stock.

NIB	Exc.	V.G.	Good	Fair	Poor
—	850	700	600	375	275

Vega Special Trap

As above, with competition-styled stock, 30" or 32" barrels and full chokes.

NIB	Exc.	V.G.	Good	Fair	Poor
—	1350	1050	850	500	350

Sirio Standard

Similar to Vega, with extensive engraving and higher degree of finishing. There is a 28" barreled skeet version available in this model.

NIB	Exc.	V.G.	Good	Fair	Poor
—	2750	2000	1950	1350	650

Standard Semi-Automatic

12-gauge semi-automatic shotgun, with 25" or 27" ventilated rib barrels, screw-in choke tubes, engraved receiver and checkered walnut stock.

NIB	Exc.	V.G.	Good	Fair	Poor
—	375	275	225	175	125

Grade I

As above, with more engraving and finer wood.

NIB	Exc.	V.G.	Good	Fair	Poor
—	650	475	325	225	175

Grade II

A more elaborately engraved version of the Grade I.

NIB	Exc.	V.G.	Good	Fair	Poor
—	850	600	450	375	250

Grade III

The most deluxe version in this line, with select walnut and extensive engraving.

NIB	Exc.	V.G.	Good	Fair	Poor
—	1050	800	650	575	250

Magnum Model

Same as standard in 12-gauge Magnum.

NIB	Exc.	V.G.	Good	Fair	Poor
—	435	325	250	175	75

Gold Series Antares Standard

12-gauge semi-automatic shotgun, with 25" or 27" ventilated rib barrel and screw-in choke tubes. Blued, with checkered walnut stock.

NIB	Exc.	V.G.	Good	Fair	Poor
—	650	425	350	275	225

Gold Series Argus

As above, with alloy frame.

NIB	Exc.	V.G.	Good	Fair	Poor
—	650	475	375	300	250

Gold Series Aries

As above in 12-gauge Magnum.

NIB	Exc.	V.G.	Good	Fair	Poor
—	700	495	400	325	275

M1 Garand

Virtual duplicate of US M1 Garand. Chambered in .30-06. Made in mid-1950s by Breda under contract for Denmark. Values shown are for correct, non-import marked specimens. Deduct up to 50 percent for built-up parts guns or non-matching guns.

NIB	Exc.	V.G.	Good	Fair	Poor
—	2200	1595	800	400	250

BREN 10
Huntington Beach, California
See—Dornaus & Dixon Inc.

Manufactured from 1983 until 1986. Deduct 15 percent for aftermarket magazines.

Standard Bren 10

10mm caliber double-action semi-automatic pistol, with 5" barrel and 10-shot magazine. Stainless frame and satin-blued slide. Manufactured between 1983 and 1986. Value includes original factory magazine.

NIB	Exc.	V.G.	Good	Fair	Poor
2625	1925	1400	850	550	325

M & P Model

As above, with matte black finish.

NIB	Exc.	V.G.	Good	Fair	Poor
2700	2100	1550	925	595	385

Special Forces Model

Chambered for 10mm cartridge. Similar to M&P model. Offered in two models: Model D has a dark finish; Model L has a light finish. Prices listed are for Model D. **NOTE:** Add 25 percent for Model L.

NIB	Exc.	V.G.	Good	Fair	Poor
2800	2200	1750	1000	800	500

Dual-Master Presentation Model

As above, with .45-caliber extra barrel slide. Fitted walnut case.

NIB	Exc.	V.G.	Good	Fair	Poor
6125	4375	2190	1225	875	500

Marksman Model

Similar to Standard Model in .45-caliber. There were 250 manufactured for "Marksman Shop" in Chicago, Illinois.

NIB	Exc.	V.G.	Good	Fair	Poor
2450	1750	1325	700	300	275

Jeff Cooper Commemorative

Suppose to be 2,000 manufactured in 1986, but no one knows how many were actually produced. Some estimates are less than 10. Chambered for 10mm. High-gloss blue finish, with 22 kt. gold-plated details. Grips are laser engraved. Whole affair furnished in a walnut display case.

NIB	Exc.	V.G.	Good	Fair	Poor
6125	4375	—	—	—	—

Bren 10 (2010 Series)

Several Bren 10 models were manufactured by Vltor in Tucson, Arizona from 2010 to 2011. Limited production of approximately 2000 guns. Specifications similar to original Standard and Marksman models with choice of 4" or 5" barrels, 10mm or .45 ACP chambering, stainless or two-tone finish.

NIB	Exc.	V.G.	Good	Fair	Poor
1100	1000	850	700	500	300

BRETTON
Ste. Etienne, France

Baby Standard

12- or 20-gauge over/under shotgun, with various barrel lengths, choke combinations and double triggers. Blued, checkered walnut stock.

NIB	Exc.	V.G.	Good	Fair	Poor
1350	975	725	550	400	325

Deluxe Grade

12-, 16- and 20-gauge over/under shotgun. Engraved coin-finished receiver, with walnut stock.

NIB	Exc.	V.G.	Good	Fair	Poor
2150	1875	1400	800	500	325

BRIGGS, H. A.
Norwich, Connecticut

Briggs Single-Shot Pistol

.22-caliber single-shot spur trigger pistol, with 4" part-round/part-octagonal barrel and downward rotating breechblock. Blued, with walnut grips. Frame marked "H.A. Briggs/Norwich, Ct." Manufactured in 1850s and 1860s.

NIB	Exc.	V.G.	Good	Fair	Poor
—	—	2950	1250	450	200

BRILEY MANUFACTURING INC.
Houston, Texas

El Presidente Model—Unlimited

1911-style pistol can be built on a Caspian Arms STI or SVI frame. Includes scope mount, compensator, match barrel, cocking sight, lowered and flared ejection port, front and rear serrations, aluminum guide rod and numerous other custom features. Offered in most calibers. Blued finish.

NIB	Exc.	V.G.	Good	Fair	Poor
2400	2000	1450	1000	700	350

Versatility Plus Model—Limited

Built on a 1911 frame, with BoMar sight, checkered mainspring housing and checkered front strap. Many other custom features. Available in .45 ACP, .40 S&W and 9mm.

NIB	Exc.	V.G.	Good	Fair	Poor
1950	1650	1200	800	400	225

Versatility Model—Limited

Similar to above model, without several features such as checkered front strap. Available in .45 ACP, .40 S&W, 9mm.

NIB	Exc.	V.G.	Good	Fair	Poor
1475	1150	800	575	265	195

Lightning Model—Action Pistol

Built on a 1911 frame. Features many custom components including titanium compensator. Weight no more than 40 oz. Available in 9mm and .38 Super only.

NIB	Exc.	V.G.	Good	Fair	Poor
2450	1950	1300	850	425	200

Carry Comp Model—Defense

Built on a 1911 frame. Features dual port cone compensator, with many custom features. Barrel length about 5". Offered in .45 ACP only.

NIB	Exc.	V.G.	Good	Fair	Poor
2450	2000	1550	1000	500	250

BRIXIA
Brescia, Italy

Model 12

Commercial version of Model 1910 Glisenti in 9mm Glisenti caliber. Brixia was a simplified Glisenti and was made to replace Glisenti for military market. Italian military did not accept them and only a few were made for commercial market. Only markings are monogram eagle holding a shield cast in grips.

Courtesy James Rankin

NIB	Exc.	V.G.	Good	Fair	Poor
—	1300	950	7850	450	325

BRNO ARMS
Uhersky Brod, Czech Republic

Brno firearms have been manufactured since 1918 in what was once known as Czechosolvakia, now the Czech Republic. Various Brno rifles, pistols, shotguns and combination guns have been brought into U.S. since late 1940s by several importers including Continental Arms, Magnum Research, Bohemia Arms, EAA and others. There has been a close association between Brno and CZ (Ceska Zbrojovka) for many years. CZ-USA of Kansas City, Kansas, is current importer of both brands. Only Brno models currently being imported are single-shot and over/under rifles and over/under combination rifle/shotguns.

ZG-47

Bolt-action rifle based on Mauser system. Chambered for .270, 7x57, 7x64, .30-06, 8x57, 8x60, 8x64S, 9.3x62 and on special order 10.75x68.

Barrel length 23.6". Adjustable trigger. Hinged floorplate. Weight about 7.7 lbs.

Standard

NIB	Exc.	V.G.	Good	Fair	Poor
—	1000	900	800	650	400

Deluxe

NIB	Exc.	V.G.	Good	Fair	Poor
—	1100	950	850	600	450

ZH-SERIES

Double-barrel over/under boxlock series of shotguns. Interchangeable barrels in shotgun and rifle configurations, of various lengths, double triggers and automatic ejectors. Models listed represent different gauges and/or calibers offered. **NOTE:** Add $75 for ZH models with set triggers and cheekpiece; $300 to $400 for interchangeable barrels depending on gauge and caliber.

ZH-300

NIB	Exc.	V.G.	Good	Fair	Poor
—	675	575	400	325	250

ZH-301

12-gauge/12-gauge.

NIB	Exc.	V.G.	Good	Fair	Poor
—	600	500	400	350	200

ZH-302

12-gauge/12-gauge Skeet.

NIB	Exc.	V.G.	Good	Fair	Poor
—	600	550	450	400	250

ZH-303 12

12-gauge/12-gauge Trap.

NIB	Exc.	V.G.	Good	Fair	Poor
—	600	550	450	400	250

ZH-304

12-gauge/7x57R.

NIB	Exc.	V.G.	Good	Fair	Poor
—	1000	800	500	400	250

ZH-305

12-gauge/6x52R.

NIB	Exc.	V.G.	Good	Fair	Poor
—	900	700	500	400	225

ZH-306

12-gauge/6x50R Magnum.

NIB	Exc.	V.G.	Good	Fair	Poor
—	850	650	450	350	200

ZH-308

12-gauge/7x65R.

NIB	Exc.	V.G.	Good	Fair	Poor
—	850	700	500	400	225

ZH-309

12-gauge/8x57 JRS.

NIB	Exc.	V.G.	Good	Fair	Poor
—	850	700	500	400	225

ZH-321

16-gauge/16-gauge.

NIB	Exc.	V.G.	Good	Fair	Poor
—	750	625	450	400	225

ZH-324

16-gauge/7x57R.

NIB	Exc.	V.G.	Good	Fair	Poor
—	875	700	500	400	225

ZH-328

16-gauge/7x65R.

NIB	Exc.	V.G.	Good	Fair	Poor
—	850	700	500	400	225

Model 300 Combo

Model ZH-300, with 8 interchangeable barrels in a fitted case. Introduced in 1986.

NIB	Exc.	V.G.	Good	Fair	Poor
5000	4000	3000	2750	2000	1500

Model 500

Model ZH-300, with acid-etched decoration, automatic ejectors and 12-gauge.

NIB	Exc.	V.G.	Good	Fair	Poor
—	800	600	425	350	275

ZP-49

12-gauge sidelock double-barrel shotgun, with double triggers and automatic ejectors. Blued, with walnut stock. Imported in 1986 only.

NIB	Exc.	V.G.	Good	Fair	Poor
—	1050	800	650	450	325

ZP-149

As above, without engraving.

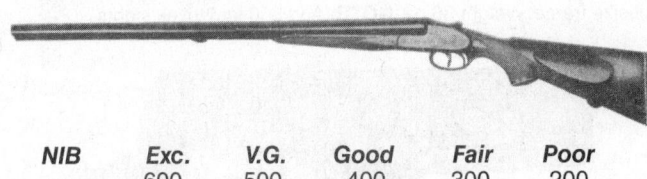

NIB	Exc.	V.G.	Good	Fair	Poor
—	600	500	400	300	200

ZP-349

As above, with buttstock having cheekpiece and beavertail forearm.

NIB	Exc.	V.G.	Good	Fair	Poor
—	800	650	500	350	250

ZBK-100

Single barrel shotgun in 12- or 20-gauge, with 27" barrel and walnut stock. Weight about 5.5 lbs.

NIB	Exc.	V.G.	Good	Fair	Poor
250	200	150	125	100	75

RIFLES

ZKW-465 (Hornet Sporter)

.22 Hornet caliber bolt-action rifle, with 23" barrel, express sights and double-set triggers. Blued, with walnut stock.

NIB	Exc.	V.G.	Good	Fair	Poor
—	1500	1100	950	800	550

Model 21H

6.5x57mm, 7x57mm or 8x57mm caliber bolt-action sporting rifle, with 23.625" barrel, express sights and double-set triggers. Blued, with walnut stock.

NIB	Exc.	V.G.	Good	Fair	Poor
—	1250	1050	900	750	600

Model 22F

As above, with Mannlicher-style stock. Barrel length 20.5".

NIB	Exc.	V.G.	Good	Fair	Poor
—	1295	1100	900	650	500

Model I

.22-caliber bolt-action rifle, with 22.75" barrel having folding leaf rear sights. Blued, with walnut stock.

NIB	Exc.	V.G.	Good	Fair	Poor
—	550	400	300	250	200

Model II

As above, with a more finely figured walnut stock.

NIB	Exc.	V.G.	Good	Fair	Poor
—	595	450	350	300	225

ZKM 611

Semi-automatic rifle chambered for .17 HMR or .22 WRM cartridge. Fitted with 20" barrel. Magazine capacity 6 rounds. Weight about 6.2 lbs.

NIB	Exc.	V.G.	Good	Fair	Poor
700	625	525	300	175	125

ZKM 451

Semi-automatic rifle chambered for .22 LR cartridge. Fitted with 22" barrel. Magazine capacity 7 rounds. Weight about 5.25 lbs.

NIB	Exc.	V.G.	Good	Fair	Poor
450	300	250	125	100	75

ZKM 451 LUX

Same as above, with select walnut stock.

NIB	Exc.	V.G.	Good	Fair	Poor
500	350	250	150	125	100

ZBK 680

.22 Hornet or .222-caliber bolt-action rifle, with 23.5" barrel, double-set triggers and 5-shot magazine. Blued, with walnut stock.

NIB	Exc.	V.G.	Good	Fair	Poor
925	750	550	400	325	225

Super Express Rifle

Over/under sidelock double-barrel rifle, with 23.5" barrels, double triggers and automatic ejectors. Engraved, blued with walnut stock. Available in 6 grades:

Standard Model

NIB	Exc.	V.G.	Good	Fair	Poor
5500	4150	3000	2500	1750	1250

Grade I

NIB	Exc.	V.G.	Good	Fair	Poor
7500	5900	4750	4500	3600	3250

Grade II

NIB	Exc.	V.G.	Good	Fair	Poor
6500	5150	4000	3500	2750	2250

Grade III

NIB	Exc.	V.G.	Good	Fair	Poor
6250	4900	3950	3250	2750	2250

Grade IV

NIB	Exc.	V.G.	Good	Fair	Poor
6000	4700	3500	3000	2500	2250

Grade V

NIB	Exc.	V.G.	Good	Fair	Poor
5750	3950	3250	2750	2250	1750

Grade VI

NIB	Exc.	V.G.	Good	Fair	Poor
4900	4250	3100	2600	1950	1500

ZH-344/348/349

Over/under rifle chambered for 7x57R, 7x65R, or 8x57JRS.

NIB	Exc.	V.G.	Good	Fair	Poor
1500	975	700	550	400	275

Model 98 Standard

Bolt-action rifle chambered for a variety of calibers from 7x64 to 9.3x62. Fitted with 23" barrel, figured walnut stock, buttplate and open sights. Weight about 7.25 lbs. **NOTE:** Add $100 for set trigger.

NIB	Exc.	V.G.	Good	Fair	Poor
800	650	400	300	200	150

Model 98 Full Stock

Same as above, with full one-piece stock and set trigger.

NIB	Exc.	V.G.	Good	Fair	Poor
1000	700	500	400	350	200

ZK 99

Tip-up centerfire rifle chambered for a wide variety of calibers from 6.5x57R to .30-06. Barrel length 23". Weight about 5.75 lbs.

NIB	Exc.	V.G.	Good	Fair	Poor
995	750	550	395	200	150

ZBK 110

Single-shot tip-open rifle chambered for .22 Hornet, .222 Rem., 5.6x50R Magnum and 5.6x52R. Barrel length 23.5". Open sights. Walnut stock without checkering. Weight about 6 lbs.

NIB	Exc.	V.G.	Good	Fair	Poor
450	350	250	200	150	75

ZBK 110 LUX

Same as above, with select walnut stock and checkering. Open sights.

NIB	Exc.	V.G.	Good	Fair	Poor
440	350	250	200	150	75

ZBK 110 Super Lux

Same as above, with fancy walnut stock and checkering. Open sights.

NIB	Exc.	V.G.	Good	Fair	Poor
650	525	400	300	150	75

HANDGUNS

ZKR 551

Double-/single-action revolver, with 6-round cylinder. Adjustable rear sight. Walnut grips. Fitted with 6" barrel. Chambered for .38, .32 S&W Long and .22 LR. Weight about 35 oz.

NIB	Exc.	V.G.	Good	Fair	Poor
1800	1350	900	700	500	275

BROLIN ARMS
La Verne, California

Brolin Arms was in business from approximately 1995 to 2000. Imported handguns from Hungary, Mauser military rifles from Europe and shotguns from China. Company also manufactured a series of 1911-pattern pistols

LEGEND SERIES—1911 AUTO PISTOL

L45—Standard Auto Pistol

Standard model, with 5" barrel chambered for .45 ACP. Fitted with throated match barrel, polished feed ramp, lowered ejection port, beveled magazine well and fixed sights. Other custom features as well. Finish matte blue, with 7-round magazine. Weight about 36 oz.

NIB	Exc.	V.G.	Good	Fair	Poor
550	400	295	200	125	75

L45C—Compact Auto Pistol

Similar to standard model, with 4.5" barrel. Weight about 32 oz.

NIB	Exc.	V.G.	Good	Fair	Poor
595	550	325	225	150	100

L45T

Version of L45 series. Introduced in 1997. Fitted with compact slide on full-size frame. Weight 36 oz. **NOTE:** Add $50 for Novak sights.

NIB	Exc.	V.G.	Good	Fair	Poor
595	550	325	200	125	75

PATRIOT SERIES—DPC CARRY-COMP PISTOLS

P45 Comp—Standard Carry Comp

Features 4" barrel, with integral compensator cut into slide. Other features are custom beavertail grip safety, adjustable aluminum trigger, flattop slide and checkered wood grips. Weight about 37 oz.

NIB	Exc.	V.G.	Good	Fair	Poor
600	550	375	225	110	95

P45C Comp—Compact Carry Comp

Similar to above. Fitted with 3.25" barrel. Weight about 33 oz. **NOTE:** Add $20 for two-tone finish.

NIB	Exc.	V.G.	Good	Fair	Poor
600	550	375	225	110	95

P45T

Addition to Patriot Series introduced in 1997. Has all features of Patriot pistols. Fitted with compact slide and full size frame. Weight about 35 oz. Available in two-tone finish for additional $20. **NOTE:** Add $50 for Novak sights.

NIB	Exc.	V.G.	Good	Fair	Poor
600	550	375	225	110	95

TAC SERIES—TACTICAL 1911 PISTOLS

TAC-11

Series and model introduced in 1997. Has all features of L45 series. Additions of special 5" conical match barrel, Novak Low Profile sights, black rubber contour grips, "iron claw" extractor and optional night sights. Chambered for .45 ACP. Supplied with 8-round magazine. Weight about 37 oz. **NOTE:** Add $90 for Tritium night sights.

NIB	Exc.	V.G.	Good	Fair	Poor
650	575	395	250	150	100

TAC SERIES—DOUBLE-ACTION PISTOLS

MS45

Full-size double-action pistol chambered for .45 ACP cartridge. Fitted with 8-round magazine and low- profile 3-dot sights. Standard finish matte blue. **NOTE:** Add $20 for royal blue finish.

NIB	Exc.	V.G.	Good	Fair	Poor
650	575	395	250	150	100

M45

Similar to above, with longer barrel. Chambered for .45 ACP and 8-round magazine. **NOTE:** Add $20 for royal blue finish.

NIB	Exc.	V.G.	Good	Fair	Poor
550	475	300	250	150	100

M40

Same as M45. Chambered for .40 S&W cartridge. Magazine capacity 10 rounds. **NOTE:** Add $50 for Novak sights.

NIB	Exc.	V.G.	Good	Fair	Poor
500	400	275	250	150	100

M90

Same as M45. Chambered for 9mm cartridge. Magazine capacity 10 rounds. **NOTE:** Add $20 for royal blue finish.

NIB	Exc.	V.G.	Good	Fair	Poor
500	400	300	250	150	100

MC40

Compact version of full-size double-action models. Fitted with full-size frame, but shorter slide. Chambered for .40 S&W cartridge. Magazine capacity 10 rounds. **NOTE:** Add $20 for royal blue finish.

NIB	Exc.	V.G.	Good	Fair	Poor
600	500	300	250	150	100

MC90

Same as above chambered for 9mm cartridge.

NIB	Exc.	V.G.	Good	Fair	Poor
500	400	275	250	150	100

MB40

Super-compact double-action pistol. Features concealed hammer. Chambered for .40 S&W cartridge. Magazine capacity 6 rounds. **NOTE:** Add $20 for royal blue finish.

NIB	Exc.	V.G.	Good	Fair	Poor
550	450	300	250	150	100

MB90

Same as above chambered for 9mm cartridge.

NIB	Exc.	V.G.	Good	Fair	Poor
550	450	300	250	150	100

PRO SERIES—COMPETITION PISTOL

Pro-Stock—Competition Pistol

Chambered for .45 ACP. Designed for competition shooter. Many special features standard such as full-length recoil guide, front strap high relief cut, serrated flat mainspring housing, ambidextrous thumb safety and fully adjustable rear sight. Barrel length 5". Weight about 37 oz. **NOTE:** Add $20 for two-tone finish.

NIB	Exc.	V.G.	Good	Fair	Poor
700	600	500	350	175	100

Pro-Comp—Competition Pistol

Similar to competition model above. Fitted with integral compensator and 4" barrel. Weight about 37 oz. **NOTE:** Add $20 for two-tone finish.

NIB	Exc.	V.G.	Good	Fair	Poor
750	650	500	375	200	100

SHOTGUNS

LAWMAN SERIES—PERSONAL SECURITY SHOTGUN

HL18SB

Pump-action 12-gauge shotgun, with 18.5" barrel, black synthetic stock and bead sights. Weight about 7 lbs. Introduced in 1997. Copy of Remington Model 870.

NIB	Exc.	V.G.	Good	Fair	Poor
295	250	195	150	95	50

HL18SR

Same as above. Fitted with rifle sights.

NIB	Exc.	V.G.	Good	Fair	Poor
325	275	225	175	125	65

HL18SBN

Same as above, with nickel finish.

NIB	Exc.	V.G.	Good	Fair	Poor
270	200	150	100	75	50

HL18WB

This version has wood stock and bead sights.

NIB	Exc.	V.G.	Good	Fair	Poor
295	250	195	150	95	50

HL18WR

Same as above. Fitted with rifle sights.

NIB	Exc.	V.G.	Good	Fair	Poor
270	200	150	100	75	50

FIELD SERIES—PUMP ACTION FIELD GUN

HF24SB

12-gauge pump action shotgun, with 24" barrel, matte finish, black synthetic stock and bead sights. Weight about 7.3 lbs. Introduced in 1997.

NIB	Exc.	V.G.	Good	Fair	Poor
270	200	150	100	75	50

HF28SB

Same as above. Fitted with 28" barrel. Weight 7.4 lbs.

NIB	Exc.	V.G.	Good	Fair	Poor
270	200	150	100	75	50

HF24WB

Features 24" barrel, with wood stock.

NIB	Exc.	V.G.	Good	Fair	Poor
270	200	150	100	75	50

HF28WB

Same as above, with 24" barrel.

NIB	Exc.	V.G.	Good	Fair	Poor
270	200	150	100	75	50

Slug Special

Slide-action shotgun chambered for 3" 12-gauge shell. Choice of 18.5" or 22" barrel, with rifle or ghost ring sights, fixed improved cylinder choke, 4" extended rifled choke or fully rifled barrel. Wood or synthetic stock.

NIB	Exc.	V.G.	Good	Fair	Poor
270	200	150	100	75	50

Turkey Special

12-gauge 3" model. Fitted with 22" extra full choke ventilated rib barrel. Wood or synthetic stock.

NIB	Exc.	V.G.	Good	Fair	Poor
270	200	150	100	75	50

FIELD COMBO—TWO BARREL COMBO SET

HC28SB

Set consists of 18.5" and 28" barrel, synthetic stock, pistol-grip, bead sight.

NIB	Exc.	V.G.	Good	Fair	Poor
300	250	200	125	75	50

HC28SR

Same as above, with rifle and bead sight.

NIB	Exc.	V.G.	Good	Fair	Poor
320	250	200	125	75	50

HC28WB

Features wood stock, pistol-grip and bead sight.

NIB	Exc.	V.G.	Good	Fair	Poor
300	250	200	125	75	50

HC28WR

Same as above, with wood stock. Rifle and bead sight.

NIB	Exc.	V.G.	Good	Fair	Poor
320	250	200	125	75	50

SEMI-AUTOMATIC SHOTGUNS

BL-12 Security

12-gauge shotgun has 3" chamber and 5-round magazine. Fitted with 18.5" ventilated rib barrel. Synthetic stock standard.

NIB	Exc.	V.G.	Good	Fair	Poor
350	325	295	200	150	75

BL-12 Field

Similar to above, with 28" ventilated rib barrel. Wood or synthetic stock.

NIB	Exc.	V.G.	Good	Fair	Poor
350	325	295	200	150	75

SAS-12 Security

12-gauge shotgun chambered for 2.75" 12-gauge shells. Fitted with 24" ventilated rib or rifle sight barrel. Detachable box magazine; 3 round standard, 5 round optional. Synthetic stock.

NIB	Exc.	V.G.	Good	Fair	Poor
350	325	295	200	150	75

RIFLES

Legacy

.50-caliber muzzleloader, with in-line ignition system. Walnut stain hardwood stock and recoil pad. Finish blue or chrome. **NOTE:** Add $20 for chrome finish.

NIB	Exc.	V.G.	Good	Fair	Poor
180	150	100	75	50	15

Mitchell PPS-50

Semi-automatic rifle chambered for .22 LR cartridge. Detachable 10-round magazine. Copy of Russian PPSh machine gun used in WWII.

NIB	Exc.	V.G.	Good	Fair	Poor
400	325	275	225	175	100

MAUSER RIFLES

All of these Mauser rifles introduced in 1998, to Brolin product line.

Lightning Model

Features sliding bolt that locks directly into barrel. Chambered for 7.62x39mm cartridge and .308 Win. Blue finish. Choice of colored synthetic stocks. Open sights standard.

NIB	Exc.	V.G.	Good	Fair	Poor
550	450	350	325	200	100

Lightning Hunter Model

Features detachable magazine, recoil pad, blued finish, checkered wood stock and choice of open or no sights, with scope mounts included. Calibers from .243 to .300 Win. Magnum. **NOTE:** Add $50 for open sights; $50 for stainless steel.

NIB	Exc.	V.G.	Good	Fair	Poor
650	500	350	325	200	100

Lightning Hunter All Weather Model

Same as above, with black synthetic stock.

NIB	Exc.	V.G.	Good	Fair	Poor
700	550	350	325	200	100

Lightning Varmint Model

Features of this model same as Lightning Hunter Model. Addition of heavy fluted barrel, with special varmint wood or synthetic stock. Chambered for .22-250 and .243 cartridges.

NIB	Exc.	V.G.	Good	Fair	Poor
900	700	550	450	300	125

Lightning Sniper

Features heavy fluted barrel, with detachable magazine. Choice of special wood or synthetic stock. Built-in bi-pod rail. Offered in .308 or 300 Win. Magnum calibers.

NIB	Exc.	V.G.	Good	Fair	Poor
1000	800	600	450	300	125

Lightning Professional

Model has heavy fluted barrel, no sights and recoil compensator. Tuned trigger system standard. All-weather adjustable stock, with pistol-grip. Available in .308 or .300 Win. Magnum calibers.

NIB	Exc.	V.G.	Good	Fair	Poor
900	700	550	395	300	125

2000 Classic

2000 Classic features interchangeable caliber system for cartridges in same action length. Detachable magazine. High-grade walnut stock, with cut checkering and rosewood fore-end. Single set trigger standard. Offered in .270, .308, .30-06, 7mm Rem. Magnum and .300 Win. Magnum.

NIB	Exc.	V.G.	Good	Fair	Poor
1500	1250	800	495	300	125

2000 Varmint

Features heavy fluted barrel, with special varmint wood stock and accessory rail. Offered in .22-250 and .243-calibers. Standard without sights.

NIB	Exc.	V.G.	Good	Fair	Poor
2200	1700	1200	800	400	200

2000 Sniper

Features interchangeable caliber system, heavy fluted barrel, no sights, single set trigger, all-weather stock, with built-in bi-pod rail. Offered in .308 and .300 Win. Magnum calibers.

NIB	Exc.	V.G.	Good	Fair	Poor
2200	1750	1250	800	400	200

2000 Professional

Has all features of Sniper rifle. Addition of recoil compensator and special all-weather pistol-grip stock. Each rifle custom built.

NIB	Exc.	V.G.	Good	Fair	Poor
3500	2750	1700	90	550	250

20/22

High-quality .22 bolt-action rifle. Chambered for .22 LR or .22 Magnum cartridge. Available in both standard and deluxe configuration. **NOTE:** Add $100 for deluxe version.

NIB	Exc.	V.G.	Good	Fair	Poor
750	575	475	395	300	125

1898 Commemorative

Celebrates 100 year anniversary of '98 Mauser. Chambered for 8mm Mauser cartridge. Limited edition rifle.

NIB	Exc.	V.G.	Good	Fair	Poor
2300	1750	1400	1000	675	300

98

Original Mauser action built to Safari calibers. Chambered for .375 H&H or .416 Rigby.

NIB	Exc.	V.G.	Good	Fair	Poor
10000	8000	6250	5000	1500	400

CUSTOM SHOP

Formula One RZ

High-performance competition race gun. Many special features such as supported barrel chamber, 6-port compensator, tuned trigger, extended magazine release and many other options as standard. Chambered for .38 Super, .40 S&W cartridges. Blue finish. **NOTE:** Add $400 for double-action.

NIB	Exc.	V.G.	Good	Fair	Poor
2500	2000	1400	1050	700	350

Formula One RS

Designed as Limited Class competition gun, with 5" barrel. Chambered for .38 Super, .40 S&W or .45 ACP calibers. Features adjustable rear sight, tuned trigger, checkered front strap, mainspring housing and other special features. **NOTE:** Add $300 for double-action.

NIB	Exc.	V.G.	Good	Fair	Poor
2000	1600	1250	875	500	350

Formula Z

Custom-built combat pistol. Chambered for .40 S&W, .400 CorBon or .45 ACP calibers. Fitted with 4" or 5" barrel. Features many extra-cost features as standard.

NIB	Exc.	V.G.	Good	Fair	Poor
1300	1000	650	425	300	150

MITCHELL SINGLE-ACTION REVOLVERS

Single-Action Army Model

Offered in 4.75", 5.5" or 7.5" barrel lengths. Chambered for .45 Long Colt,

.357 Magnum or .44-40 calibers. Offered in blue finish, with case hardened frame or nickel finish. Available with dual cylinders, i.e. .45 LC/.45 ACP. **NOTE:** Add $50 for nickel finish; $150 for dual cylinder models.

NIB	Exc.	V.G.	Good	Fair	Poor
395	350	275	175	125	75

BRONCO
Eibar, Spain

See— Echave & Arizmendi

BROOKLYN F. A. CO.
Brooklyn, New York

Slocum Pocket Revolver

.32-caliber spur-trigger revolver, with 3" round barrel. Frame silver-plated brass and scroll engraved; remainder blued or plated, with walnut grips. Barrel marked "B.A. Co. Patented April 14, 1863". Approximately 10,000 manufactured in 1863 and 1864. Cylinder has five individual tubes that slide forward to open for loading and then ejecting spent cartridges.

NIB	Exc.	V.G.	Good	Fair	Poor
—	—	975	325	120	75

Slocum Unfluted Cylinder Pocket Revolver

As above in .22- or .32-caliber, with 5- or 7-shot cylinder. Approximately 250 manufactured in .32 rimfire; 100 in .22 rimfire. **NOTE:** Add 25 percent for .22-caliber.

NIB	Exc.	V.G.	Good	Fair	Poor
—	—	1300	450	225	125

BROWN, E.A. MANUFACTURING CO.
Alexandria, Minnesota

Brown Classic Single-Shot Pistol

Falling block single-shot pistol, with 15" match grade barrel. Chambered for calibers from .17 Ackley to .45-70 Government. Walnut thumbrest grips. Handfitted. Introduced in 1998.

NIB	Exc.	V.G.	Good	Fair	Poor
1200	1000	750	600	400	200

Brown Model 97D Single-Shot Rifle

Single-shot falling block rifle. Chambered for calibers from .17 Ackley to .45-70 Government. Barrel lengths up to 26". Sporter-style stock with pistol-grip, cheekpiece and schnabel fore-end. Blue/black finish. Weight about 6 lbs. No sights.

NIB	Exc.	V.G.	Good	Fair	Poor
1200	1000	750	600	400	200

BROWN, ED PRODUCTS
Perry, Missouri

There are a number of extra options available on Ed Brown handguns and rifles that may affect values. In August of 2010, Ed Brown announced he would no longer be accepting orders for new rifles, and for an indefinite period of time, would be focusing on his core business of handguns. Rifle parts and limited services remain available.

Commander Bobtail

Features 4.25" barrel. Chambered for .45 ACP, .400 CorBon, .40 S&W, .38 Super, 9x23 or 9mm Luger cartridge. Modified Hogue grips from exotic wood standard. Completely handmade and built to customer's specifications. Many available options.

NIB	Exc.	V.G.	Good	Fair	Poor
2200	1700	1200	700	500	300

Classic Custom

Chambered for .45 ACP cartridge. Custom built pistol, with many extra features such as Videki trigger, Ed Brown wide thumb safety, stainless steel thumb safety, extended safety, adjustable rear sight, etc. All hand-fitted parts.

NIB	Exc.	V.G.	Good	Fair	Poor
3100	2400	1700	950	450	300

Class A Limited

Custom-built pistol offered in a number of different calibers from .45 ACP to 9mm Luger. Fitted with 4.25" Commander length slide. Many special features. Price listed for basic pistol.

NIB	Exc.	V.G.	Good	Fair	Poor
2450	1750	1300	800	500	325

Kobra Custom .45

Introduced in 2002. Features a snakeskin treatment on fore-strap, main-spring housing and slide. Novak night sights and Hogue checkered wood grips standard. Many other custom features.

NIB	Exc.	V.G.	Good	Fair	Poor
1995	1400	1150	675	400	250

Kobra Carry .45

Same as above, with shorter grip frame and barrel.

NIB	Exc.	V.G.	Good	Fair	Poor
2500	2000	1400	1100	500	300

Executive Target

1911 Executive Elite modified for target/range, with adjustable BoMar rear sight, ambidextrous safety. Weight 38 oz. Barrel 5". Chambered for .45 ACP. Magazine 7-rounds.

NIB	Exc.	V.G.	Good	Fair	Poor
2700	2200	1550	1200	600	300

Executive Elite

Government model 5" barrel, weight 38 oz., chambered for .45 ACP, 7-round magazine. Fixed sights. Blue/blue, stainless/blue or all-stainless.

NIB	Exc.	V.G.	Good	Fair	Poor
2450	1950	1400	1000	500	300

Executive Carry

4.25" commander model .45 ACP, with Ed Brown Bobtail. Weight 38 oz., 7-round magazine, fixed sights. Blue/blue, stainless/blue or all-stainless.

NIB	Exc.	V.G.	Good	Fair	Poor
2800	2350	1600	1100	500	300

Special Forces

Blue/blue 1911 semi-automatic, with 5" barrel and fixed 3-dot night sights. Chambered for .45 ACP. Weight 38 oz., 7-round magazine. Co-cobolo grips.

NIB	Exc.	V.G.	Good	Fair	Poor
2500	2000	1400	1100	500	300

Jim Wilson Limited Edition

Ed Brown's first special edition 1911, designed in 2006 in collaboration with Jim Wilson, popular gun writer, retired Texas Sheriff and noted singer of cowboy and American West songs. Based on Executive Elite model. Added enhancements include Tru-Ivory grips, 25 lpi checkered frame, plain black Novak sights, hand polished frame and slide. Limited production in 2007.

NIB	Exc.	V.G.	Good	Fair	Poor
2700	2200	1800	—	—	—

Jeff Cooper Commemorative Limited Edition

Limited manufacture in 2008 in memory of Jeff Cooper. Dean of 1911 school of magazine writers, WWII and Korean War veteran, professor, originator of the sport of practical pistol competition, founder of IPSC (International Practical Shooting Confederation) and Gunsite Academy. Created with input from Col. Cooper's friends and family. Virtually all Ed Brown enhancements are included, plus Cooper's pen and sword logo on the exhibition grade cocobolo grips. "DVC" on slide standing for latin phrase "Diligentia, Vis, Celeritas", meaning "Accuracy, Power, Speed", which later became the motto of IPSC.

NIB	Exc.	V.G.	Good	Fair	Poor
2700	2200	1800	—	—	—

Massad Ayoob Limited Edition

Based on Executive Carry model. Added enhancements and features suggested by renowned author, shooting champion and expert witness, Massad Ayoob. These include Ed Brown Bobtail frame, 4.25" barrel, 4.5 lb. trigger pull, 25 lpi checkering on front strap and Ayoob's signature on slide. Limited production in 2009 and 2010.

NIB	Exc.	V.G.	Good	Fair	Poor
2700	2200	1800	—	—	—

RIFLES

Savanna

Fitted with long action. Chambered for calibers from .257 Ackley to .338 Win. Magnum. Barrel lightweight 24" for standard calibers; 24" medium weight for Magnum calibers. Talley scope mounts included. Fiberglass stock, recoil pad, steel trigger guard and floorplate standard.

NIB	Exc.	V.G.	Good	Fair	Poor
3800	3000	1995	1500	900	400

Damara

Similar to Savanna in lightweight configuration, with natural-finish stainless barrel.

NIB	Exc.	V.G.	Good	Fair	Poor
3200	2650	2000	1300	650	400

Varmint

Custom-made rifle, with short single-shot action, 26" medium weight barrel or 24" heavyweight barrel. H-S Precision stock. Available in calibers from .222 to 6.5/.284.

NIB	Exc.	V.G.	Good	Fair	Poor
3500	2800	2000	1300	750	400

Bushveld

Model based on a Dakota controlled feed action. Fitted with 24" medium or heavyweight barrel. Calibers from .330 Dakota to .458 Win. Magnum. Detachable box magazine. Monte Carlo fiberglass stock, recoil pad, steel trigger and floorplate standard, as is Talley scope mounts. Weight about 8.5 lbs.

NIB	Exc.	V.G.	Good	Fair	Poor
4400	3250	2000	1500	900	400

Express

Centerfire bolt-action rifle. Chambered for a wide variety of large Africa-class calibers. Dropped box magazine, fully controlled feed, fluted bolt, McMillan stock, iron sights.

NIB	Exc.	V.G.	Good	Fair	Poor
3600	2900	2350	1600	800	400

Marine Sniper

Duplicate of Vietnam-era McMillan sniper rifle. Controlled feed, fluted bolt, hinged floorplate, woodland camo stock, blackened stainless steel barrel and receiver. Offered in .308 and .300 Win. Magnum calibers. Weight about 9.25 lbs.

NIB	Exc.	V.G.	Good	Fair	Poor
3700	2950	2350	1600	900	400

Light Tactical

Short-action rifle, with lightweight floorplate and trigger guard. Fitted with 21" medium-weight barrel. Black fiberglass stock, with aluminum bedding block. Available in calibers from .22-250 to .308.

NIB	Exc.	V.G.	Good	Fair	Poor
4100	2950	2000	1500	900	400

Tactical

Similar to above. Built on long action, with heavy weight 26" blued barrel. McMillan A-3 black tactical stock. Available in .308 and .300 Win. Magnum.

NIB	Exc.	V.G.	Good	Fair	Poor
3900	3350	2500	1600	950	400

Ozark

Rifle built on short action, with blind magazine. A 21" lightweight barrel fitted for standard calibers; medium weight 21" barrel for Magnum calibers. Chambered for calibers from .22-250 to .308. Talley scope mounts included as is fiberglass stock, recoil pad, steel trigger guard and floorplate.

NIB	Exc.	V.G.	Good	Fair	Poor
3800	3000	1995	1500	900	400

Denali

Lighter-weight version of Ozark, with 22" super light weight barrel. Chambered for calibers .25-06 to .300 WSM. Weight about 6.75 lbs.

NIB	Exc.	V.G.	Good	Fair	Poor
3800	3000	1995	1500	900	400

Peacekeeper

Single-shot long-action rifle. Chambered for .30-378 Wby., .338-378 Wby. or .338 Lapua caliber. Fitted with heavy 26" barrel with muzzlebrake. Fiberglass tactical stock with recoil pad. Leupold Mark 4 scope mounts standard. Weight about 13 lbs.

NIB	Exc.	V.G.	Good	Fair	Poor
4500	3250	2100	1300	800	400

BROWN MANUFACTURING CO.
Newburyport, Massachusetts
Also See—Ballard Patent Arms

Southerner Derringer

.41-caliber spur-trigger single-shot pocket pistol, with pivoted 2.5" or 4" octagonal barrel marked "Southerner". Silver-plated or blued, with walnut grips. Manufactured by Merrimack Arms Co. from 1867 to 1869; Brown Manufacturing Co. from 1869 to 1873.

Courtesy W. P. Hallstein III and son Chip

Brass Framed
2.5" barrel.

NIB	Exc.	V.G.	Good	Fair	Poor
—	—	875	600	325	125

Iron Frame
2.5" barrel (Brown Mfg. only).

NIB	Exc.	V.G.	Good	Fair	Poor
—	—	1025	800	500	200

Brass Frame 4" Barrel

NIB	Exc.	V.G.	Good	Fair	Poor
—	—	3700	2000	1500	500

Brown Mfg. Co./Merrill Patent Breechloading Rifles

Overall length 54.75"; barrel (bore) length 35"; caliber .577. Markings: On breechblock-bolt mechanism, "BROWN MFG. CO. NEWBURYPORT, MASS./PATANTED OCT. 17, 1871". Patent issued to George Merrill in 1871, permitted Brown Manufacturing Co. to alter probably up to 1,000 English P1853 rifle-muskets to single-shot breechloading system. Large bolt handle projecting upward at end of breech readily distinguishes these arms.

Courtesy Milwaukee Public Museum, Milwaukee, Wisconsin

NIB	Exc.	V.G.	Good	Fair	Poor
—	—	2500	1250	800	300

BROWN PRECISION, INC.
Los Molinos, California

This company pioneered manufacture of fiberglass gunstocks in 1960s. Since 1975 has been making custom rifles on various Winchester, Remington and Ruger actions. Calibers available include virtually any popular chambering available in original action. Company offers many optional features, which will affect values. Values shown are for base models of current and recent production. Deduct $1,000 for rifles made on customer-supplied action.

Custom High Country
NOTE: Add $900 for take down model.

NIB	Exc.	V.G.	Good	Fair	Poor
4250	3500	2750	1800	1000	600

Pro Hunter

NIB	Exc.	V.G.	Good	Fair	Poor
4800	4000	3000	2000	1400	1000

Pro Hunter Elite
NOTE: Add $900 for takedown model.

NIB	Exc.	V.G.	Good	Fair	Poor
6000	5200	4200	3000	2000	1200

Pro Varminter/Light Varminter

NIB	Exc.	V.G.	Good	Fair	Poor
3500	2750	2000	1200	800	500

Tactical Elite

NIB	Exc.	V.G.	Good	Fair	Poor
4250	3500	2750	1800	1000	600

EARLY PRODUCTION

Open Country Varmint Rifle (disc. 1992)

NIB	Exc.	V.G.	Good	Fair	Poor
1200	900	700	600	400	250

Law Enforcement Model (disc. 1992)

NIB	Exc.	V.G.	Good	Fair	Poor
1200	900	700	600	400	250

Blaser Action Model (disc. 1989)

NIB	Exc.	V.G.	Good	Fair	Poor
1600	1200	800	650	500	350

BROWNING ARMS CO.
Morgan, Utah

Early Semi-Automatic Pistols

In the period between 1900 and the development of Model 1935 Hi-Power Pistol, Browning had a number of semi-automatic pistols manufactured by Fabrique Nationale of Herstal, Belgium. They were Models 1900, 1903, 1905, 1910, 1922, Baby and 1935 Model Hi-Power. These firearms will be listed in more detail, with their respective values in Fabrique Nationale section of this text.

Hi-Power Modern Production

This version of FN Model 1935 is quite similar in appearance to original described in FN section. Chambered for 9mm Parabellum cartridge. Has 4.75" barrel. Models built before passage of crime bill have double column, 13-round detachable box magazine, blued, with checkered walnut grips. Has fixed sights and been produced in its present configuration since 1954. Add 10 percent premium for adjustable sights. Matte-nickel version offered between 1980 and 1984 was also available and would be worth approximately 15 percent additional. From 1994 to 2010 available in .40 S&W.
NOTE: Add $60 for adjustable sights; $350 for internal extractor (pre 1962).

Spur Hammer Version

NIB	Exc.	V.G.	Good	Fair	Poor
950	800	600	500	300	150

Round Hammer Version

NIB	Exc.	V.G.	Good	Fair	Poor
1050	900	725	600	450	200

Hi-Power—.30 Luger

Version similar to standard Hi-Power, except chambered for .30 Luger cartridge. Approximately 1,500 imported between 1986 and 1989. Slide marked "FN". Browning-marked versions are quite rare and worth approximately 30 percent additional.

NIB	Exc.	V.G.	Good	Fair	Poor
1000	900	725	450	300	200

Tangent Sight Model

Version similar to standard Hi-Power, with addition of adjustable rear sight calibrated to 500 meters. Approximately 7,000 imported between 1965 and 1978. **NOTE:** If grip frame is slotted to accept a detachable shoulder stock add approximately 20 percent to value; but be wary of fakes. Add an additional 10 percent for "T" series serial numbers.

NIB	Exc.	V.G.	Good	Fair	Poor
1200	1050	900	650	450	200

Renaissance Hi-Power

Heavily engraved version, with matte-silver finish. Features synthetic-pearl grips and gold-plated trigger. Import ended in 1979.

Spur Hammer Model

NIB	Exc.	V.G.	Good	Fair	Poor
3200	2900	2100	1750	1000	600

Ring Hammer Model

NIB	Exc.	V.G.	Good	Fair	Poor
3600	3300	2600	2000	1500	900

Adjustable Sight Spur Hammer Model

NIB	Exc.	V.G.	Good	Fair	Poor
3300	3000	2100	1750	1000	600

Renaissance .25-Caliber

NIB	Exc.	V.G.	Good	Fair	Poor
2400	2100	1700	1500	1000	600

Renaissance .380-Caliber

With pearl grips.

NIB	Exc.	V.G.	Good	Fair	Poor
2700	2400	2000	1600	1000	600

Renaissance .380-Caliber (Model 1971)

With wood grips and adjustable sights.

NIB	Exc.	V.G.	Good	Fair	Poor
2300	2000	1700	1500	900	500

Cased Renaissance Set

Features one example of fully engraved and silver-finished .25 ACP "Baby", .380 ACP pistol and Hi-Power. Set furnished in a fitted walnut case or black leatherette. Imported between 1955 and 1969. **NOTE:** Add 30 percent for early coin finish.

Courtesy Rock Island Auction Company

NIB	Exc.	V.G.	Good	Fair	Poor
9500	8000	6000	3000	—	—

Louis XVI Model

Heavily engraved Hi-Power pistol. Features leaf-and-scroll pattern, satin-finished, checkered walnut grips. Furnished in fitted walnut case. To realize its true potential, this pistol must be NIB. Imported between 1980 and 1984.

Diamond Grip Model

NIB	Exc.	V.G.	Good	Fair	Poor
3150	2500	2000	800	400	300

Medallion Grip Model

NIB	Exc.	V.G.	Good	Fair	Poor
1950	1750	1600	800	400	300

Hi-Power Centennial Model

Version similar to standard fixed-sight Hi-Power. Chrome-plated, with inscription "Browning Centennial/1878-1978" engraved on slide. Furnished with fitted case. There were 3,500 manufactured in 1978. As with all commemorative pistols, in order to realize its collector potential, this model should be NIB with all supplied material. Prices for pistols built in Belgium

NIB	Exc.	V.G.	Good	Fair	Poor
1075	875	700	450	300	200

Hi-Power Capitan

New version of Hi-Power model. Fitted with tangent sights. Introduced in 1993. Furnished with walnut grips. Weight about 32 oz. Assembled in Portugal.

NIB	Exc.	V.G.	Good	Fair	Poor
900	750	600	400	250	200

Hi-Power Practical

First introduced in 1993. Furnished with blued slide and chrome frame. Has Pachmayr wrap-around rubber grips, round-style serrated hammer and removable front sight. Available with adjustable sights. Weight 36 oz. Assembled in Portugal.

NIB	Exc.	V.G.	Good	Fair	Poor
845	625	500	300	200	175

Hi-Power Silver Chrome Model

Furnished in hard chrome. Fitted with wrap-around Pachmayr rubber grips. Assembled in Portugal. Weight 36 oz. Introduced in 1981. Dropped from Browning product line in 1984. Reintroduced in 1991. **NOTE:** Add 10 percent for models with all Belgian markings.

NIB	Exc.	V.G.	Good	Fair	Poor
750	575	500	425	225	200

Hi-Power .40 S&W

Introduced in 1994. New version of Hi-Power furnished with adjustable sights, molded grips, 5" barrel and 10-round magazine. Weight about 35 oz. Discontinued 2010.

NIB	Exc.	V.G.	Good	Fair	Poor
800	600	450	300	200	150

Hi-Power Mark III

Introduced in 1991. Matte blued or green finish, low-profile fixed sights and two-piece molded grips, with thumb rest. Weight 32 oz.

NIB	Exc.	V.G.	Good	Fair	Poor
900	700	500	300	200	175

Hi-Power Gold Classic

Limited edition model introduced in 1984. Planned production of 500, but less than 350 were made. Elaborate engraving with five gold inlays, silver/gray finish, carved and checkered wood grips.

NIB	Exc.	V.G.	Good	Fair	Poor
4500	3850	3000	2000	—	—

Hi-Power Classic

As above, except with less engraving and no gold inlays.

NIB	Exc.	V.G.	Good	Fair	Poor
2200	1650	1100	800	600	400

Baby Browning

.25-caliber semi-automatic is same as FN Baby Model. Made by Fabrique Nationale in Belgium from 1931 until 1983. Many were imported into U.S., with Browning rollmark from 1954 to 1968. See "Baby" Model under Fabrique Nationale section for more details. Prices shown for Browning-marked model.

NIB	Exc.	V.G.	Good	Fair	Poor
750	600	500	450	350	200

Browning Model 1955

Semi-automatic pistol same as FN Model 1910. From 1912 to 1983 in .32 ACP and .380 ACP. See Fabrique Nationale section for more information. Imported into U.S. by Browning from 1954 to 1968. Prices shown for Browning-marked pistols. **NOTE:** Add $200 for .32 ACP

NIB	Exc.	V.G.	Good	Fair	Poor
800	700	550	450	350	200

Pro-9/Pro-40

9mm or .40 S&W double-action pistol fitted with 4" barrel. Stainless steel slide. Grips are composite, with interchangeable backstrap inserts. Magazine capacity 16 rounds 9mm; 14 rounds .40 S&W. Weight about 30 oz.

NIB	Exc.	V.G.	Good	Fair	Poor
600	500	375	—	—	—

BDA-380

Double-action semi-automatic pistol. Chambered for .380 ACP cartridge. Features 3.75" barrel, with 14-round double-stack detachable magazine. Finish blued or nickel-plated, with smooth walnut grips. Manufactured in Italy by Beretta. Introduced in 1977. **NOTE:** Add 10 percent for nickel finish.

NIB	Exc.	V.G.	Good	Fair	Poor
625	400	325	275	200	150

BDA

Double-action semi-automatic pistol. Manufactured between 1977 and 1980 for Browning by SIG-Sauer of Germany. Identical to SIG-Sauer Model 220. Chambered for 9mm Parabellum, .38 Super and .45 ACP cartridges. **NOTE:** Add 30 percent for .38 Super.

NIB	Exc.	V.G.	Good	Fair	Poor
—	525	425	375	300	235

BDM Pistol

Double-action semi-automatic pistol. Chambered for 9mm cartridge. Fitted with selector switch that allows shooter to choose between single-/double-action model. Features 4.75" barrel, with adjustable rear sight. Magazine capacity 15 rounds. Weight 31 oz. First introduced in 1991.

NIB	Exc.	V.G.	Good	Fair	Poor
560	450	350	250	200	150

BDM Silver Chrome

Variation of BDM introduced in 1997. Features silver chrome finish on slide and frame, balance in contrasting matte blue finish.

NIB	Exc.	V.G.	Good	Fair	Poor
560	450	350	250	200	150

BDM Practical

Introduced in 1997. Same as above, with silver chrome on frame only.

NIB	Exc.	V.G.	Good	Fair	Poor
560	450	350	250	200	150

BPM-D

Introduced in 1997. New version of BDM (Browning Pistol Model Decocker) features double-action pistol, with first shot fired double-action and subsequent shots fired single-action. No manual safety. Decock lever also releases slide.

NIB	Exc.	V.G.	Good	Fair	Poor
525	400	300	250	200	150

BRM-DAO

9mm pistol is a redesigned version of Model BDM. Initials stand for "Browning Revolver Model Double-Action-Only". Has finger support trigger guard for two-handed control. All other features same as BPM-D pistol. Weight about 31 oz.

NIB	Exc.	V.G.	Good	Fair	Poor
525	400	300	250	200	150

Nomad

Blowback-operated semi-automatic pistol. Chambered for .22 LR cartridge. Offered with 4.5" or 6.75" barrel. Has 10-round detachable magazine, with adjustable sights and all-steel construction. Finish blued, with black plastic grips. Manufactured between 1962 and 1974 by FN.

NIB	Exc.	V.G.	Good	Fair	Poor
500	360	275	150	75	50

Challenger

More deluxe target pistol. Chambered for .22 LR cartridge. Offered with 4.5" or 6.75" barrel. Has 10-round magazine. Constructed entirely of steel. Adjustable sights. Finish blued, with gold-plated trigger. Checkered wraparound walnut grips. Manufactured between 1962 and 1974 by FN.

Courtesy John J. Stimson, Jr.

NIB	Exc.	V.G.	Good	Fair	Poor
600	475	300	250	200	140

Renaissance Challenger

Version fully engraved, satin-nickel finish. Furnished with fleece-lined pouch.

NIB	Exc.	V.G.	Good	Fair	Poor
2600	2300	1600	750	500	350

Gold Line Challenger

Version blued and has gold-inlaid line around outer edges of pistol. It was cased in fleece-lined pouch. Built in Belgium.

NIB	Exc.	V.G.	Good	Fair	Poor
2600	2300	1600	750	500	350

Challenger II

Blowback-operated semi-automatic pistol. Chambered for .22 LR cartridge. Has 6.75" barrel, with alloy frame. Finish blued, with phenolic impregnated hardwood grips. Manufactured between 1976 and 1982 in Salt Lake City, Utah.

NIB	Exc.	V.G.	Good	Fair	Poor
—	450	325	175	140	100

Challenger III

Version features 5.5" bull barrel, with adjustable sights. Manufactured between 1982 and 1984 in Salt Lake City, Utah. A 6.75" tapered-barrel version was available and known as Sporter.

NIB	Exc.	V.G.	Good	Fair	Poor
—	400	300	150	125	90

Browning Collector's Association Edition

Fully engraved. 100 manufactured. Fitted with two-piece grip.

NIB	Exc.	V.G.	Good	Fair	Poor
2950	2250	1650	1200	800	400

Medalist

High-grade semi-automatic target pistol. Chambered for .22 LR cartridge. Has 6.75" ventilated rib barrel, with adjustable target sights. Supplied with three barrel weights and dry-fire-practice mechanism. Finish blued, with target type thumbrest walnut grips. Manufactured between 1962 and 1974 by FN. Four additional high-grade versions of this pistol that differed in degree of ornamentation.

NIB	Exc.	V.G.	Good	Fair	Poor
1350	1000	800	675	375	250

International Medalist

About 700 sold in U.S. from 1977 to 1980. Barrels were 5.875" long. Built in Belgium.

Courtesy John J. Stimson, Jr.

NIB	Exc.	V.G.	Good	Fair	Poor
1200	900	600	450	300	150

Second Model International Medalist

Same as above, with flat-sided barrel, dull finish and adjustable palm rest. Built in Belgium.

Courtesy John J. Stimson, Jr.

NIB	Exc.	V.G.	Good	Fair	Poor
875	725	450	300	200	150

Gold Line Medalist

Introduced in 1962. Discontinued in 1974. Estimated 400 guns produced.

NIB	Exc.	V.G.	Good	Fair	Poor
3800	3000	2250	1000	750	500

Renaissance Medalist

Model built entirely in Belgium from 1970 to 1974, with one-piece grip.

NIB	Exc.	V.G.	Good	Fair	Poor
4200	3400	2600	1200	900	700

BUCK MARK SERIES

Buck Mark

Blowback-operated semi-automatic pistol. Chambered for .22 LR cartridge. Has 5.5" bull barrel, with adjustable sights; 11-round detachable magazine; matte blued, with skip-line checkered synthetic grips. Introduced in 1985. Produced in U.S. **NOTE:** Add $25 for stainless steel version, introduced in 2005.

NIB	Exc.	V.G.	Good	Fair	Poor
350	250	175	135	110	85

Buck Mark Plus

Version similar to standard, with plain wood grips. Introduced in 1987. Produced in U.S.

NIB	Exc.	V.G.	Good	Fair	Poor
395	300	200	150	100	75

Nickel

Introduced in 1991. **NOTE:** Add $35 to above prices.

Buck Mark Varmint

Version has 9.75" bull barrel, with full-length ramp to allow scope mounting. No sights. Introduced in 1987. Produced in U.S.

NIB	Exc.	V.G.	Good	Fair	Poor
395	300	250	200	175	125

Buck Mark Silhouette

Version features 9.75" bull barrel, with adjustable sights. Introduced in 1987.

NIB	Exc.	V.G.	Good	Fair	Poor
450	350	285	220	185	140

Buck Mark 22 Micro

Version of Buck Mark 22. Fitted with 4" bull barrel. Available in blue, matte blue or nickel finish. Also in Micro Plus variation, with walnut grips. Weight 32 oz. Introduced in 1992. **NOTE:** Add $25 for stainless steel version. Introduced in 2005.

NIB	Exc.	V.G.	Good	Fair	Poor
350	275	175	135	110	85

Plus

NIB	Exc.	V.G.	Good	Fair	Poor
350	275	175	150	125	90

Plus Nickel

Introduced in 1996. **NOTE:** Add $75 to above price.

Buck Mark 5.5

.22-caliber pistol has 5.5" heavy bull barrel fitted with target sights. Offered in three separate models:

Blued Target

Version has blued finish, contoured walnut grips, target sights. Weight 35.5 oz. Introduced in 1990.

NIB	Exc.	V.G.	Good	Fair	Poor
475	395	250	150	100	100

Blued Target (2005)

Introduced in 2005. Features new target-style Cocabolo grips, full length scope mount. Hooded target sights. Weight 35 oz.

NIB	Exc.	V.G.	Good	Fair	Poor
525	425	300	200	150	100

Gold Target

Same as above. Has gold anodized frame and top rib. Slide blue. Walnut grips. Introduced in 1991.

NIB	Exc.	V.G.	Good	Fair	Poor
550	425	300	200	150	125

Field

Same action and barrel as Target Model, with hoodless adjustable field sights. Slide and barrel blued; rib and frame anodized blue. Grips are walnut. Introduced in 1991.

NIB	Exc.	V.G.	Good	Fair	Poor
450	345	225	150	100	100

Field (2005)

Features new target style grips and full-length scope rail. Weight about 35 oz.

NIB	Exc.	V.G.	Good	Fair	Poor
525	425	295	225	165	100

Buck Field Plus

.22-caliber pistol has 5.5" barrel, with Truglo/Marbles' front sight. Grips laminated rosewood. Barrel polished blue. Weight about 24 oz.

NIB	Exc.	V.G.	Good	Fair	Poor
425	325	225	200	150	75

Buck Mark Bullseye

Introduced in 1996. Designed for metallic silhouette competition. Fluted barrel 7.25" long. Adjustable trigger pull and rear sight, removable barrel are some of the features. Weight about 36 oz. Choice of laminated wood or rubber grips. **NOTE:** Add $90 for rosewood target grips; $150 for stainless.

NIB	Exc.	V.G.	Good	Fair	Poor
550	425	275	175	125	75

Buck Mark Unlimited Match

Fitted with 14" barrel and top rib. Front sight hood slightly rearward of muzzle for maximum sight radius of 15". All other features same as Silhouette model. Weight 64 oz.

NIB	Exc.	V.G.	Good	Fair	Poor
700	525	375	225	175	125

Buck Mark Challenge

Introduced in 1999. Features lightweight 5.5" barrel, with adjustable rear sight. Smaller grip diameter. Matte blue finish. Magazine capacity 10-rounds. Weight about 25 oz. Buck Mark Challenge Rosewood model has laminated rosewood grips, TruGlo fiber optic front sight, gold-plated trigger. Add $85 for this model.

NIB	Exc.	V.G.	Good	Fair	Poor
350	250	200	175	125	100

Buck Mark Camper

Fitted with heavy 5.5" barrel. Matte blue finish. Magazine capacity 10-rounds. Weight about 34 oz. Introduced in 1999. **NOTE:** Add $60 for stainless steel version.

NIB	Exc.	V.G.	Good	Fair	Poor
300	225	150	125	100	75

Buck Mark Camper Cocobola UDX

Similar to above, with cocobolo Ultra DX grips and TruGlo front sight. Introduced 2008.

NIB	Exc.	V.G.	Good	Fair	Poor
375	295	245	150	100	75

Buck Mark Camper Stainless UFX

Features tapered bull 5.5" barrel, overmolded FX ambidextrous grips, with checkered panels, Pro-Target adjustable sights and gold-plated trigger.

NIB	Exc.	V.G.	Good	Fair	Poor
330	285	215	175	125	100

Buck Mark Practical URX Fiber Optic

Matte grey finish, 5.5" tapered bull barrel, Ultragrip RX ambi-grips, adjustable ProTarget rear sight, with TruGlo fiber optic front sight. Introduced 2008.

NIB	Exc.	V.G.	Good	Fair	Poor
350	300	20	150	100	75

Buck Mark Hunter

.22 LR pistol features 7.25" heavy round barrel, with TruGlo/Marbles front sights, adjustable rear sight and integrated scope base. Grips Cocabolo target-style. Weight about 38 oz. Introduced in 2005.

NIB	Exc.	V.G.	Good	Fair	Poor
375	275	225	175	125	100

Buck Mark Limited Edition 25th Anniversary

Limited to 1,000 pistols. Features 6.75" barrel, with matte blued finish and scrimshaw etched ivory grips. Pistol rug furnished as standard equipment.

NIB	Exc.	V.G.	Good	Fair	Poor
495	350	300	225	150	125

Buck Mark Bullseye Target

Blowback single action .22 LR semi-automatic. Matte blued, heavy 7.25" round and fluted stainless bull barrel. Laminated rosewood grip, adjustable sights. Introduced 2006.

NIB	Exc.	V.G.	Good	Fair	Poor
695	450	300	225	150	175

Buck Mark Bullseye Target URX

Blowback single-action semi-automatic in .22 LR. Matte blued, heavy 7.25" round and fluted bull barrel. Grooved, rubberized grip. Weight 39 oz. Adjustable sights. Introduced 2006.

NIB	Exc.	V.G.	Good	Fair	Poor
475	400	325	225	150	175

Buck Mark Contour 5.5 URX

Blowback single-action .222 semi-automatic. Matte blued, contoured 5.5" barrel. Full-length scope base. Weight 36 oz. Adjustable sights. Multiple barrel lengths and options. Introduced 2006.

NIB	Exc.	V.G.	Good	Fair	Poor
425	365	300	250	200	100

Buck Mark Contour Lite 5.5 URX

.22 LR blowback single-action semi-automatic. Matte blued, contoured 5.5" barrel. Full-length scope base. Weight 28 oz. Adjustable sights. Multiple barrel lengths and options. Introduced 2006.

NIB	Exc.	V.G.	Good	Fair	Poor
475	395	325	275	225	150

Buck Mark FLD Plus Rosewood UDX

.22 LR blowback single-action semi-automatic. "FLD" sculpted grip, with rosewood panels. Blued, contoured 5.5" barrel. Weight 34 oz. Adjustable rear sight, fiber optic front sight. Multiple barrel lengths and options. Introduced 2006.

NIB	Exc.	V.G.	Good	Fair	Poor
475	395	325	275	225	150

Buck Mark Lite Splash 5.5 URX

Blowback single-action semi-automatic. Matte blued finish, gold splash anodizing. Chambered for .22 LR, 5.5" barrel. Rubberized ambidextrous grip. Adjustable sights; fiber optic front sight. Weight 28 oz. Available with 7.5" barrel. Introduced 2006.

NIB	Exc.	V.G.	Good	Fair	Poor
450	375	325	275	225	150

Buck Mark Micro Standard Stainless URX

With 4" stainless barrel in .22 LR. Weight 32 oz. Ambidextrous rubberized grip. Adjustable sights. Available in alloy steel. Introduced 2006.

NIB	Exc.	V.G.	Good	Fair	Poor
395	350	325	275	225	150

Buck Mark Micro Bull

4" stainless bull barrel; .22 LR; weight 33 oz. Plastic grip panels. Adjustable sights. Introduced 2006.

NIB	Exc.	V.G.	Good	Fair	Poor
350	275	225	175	125	100

Buck Mark Plus Stainless Black Laminated UDX

Similar to Buck Mark Standard. Stainless UDX, with ambidextrous grips. Introduced 2007.

NIB	Exc.	V.G.	Good	Fair	Poor
495	375	300	225	150	125

Buck Mark Plus UDX

Similar to Buck Mark FLD Plus, with ambidextrous walnut grips. Introduced 2007.

NIB	Exc.	V.G.	Good	Fair	Poor
425	350	300	225	150	125

Full Line Dealer Buck Mark Plus Rosewood UDX

Similar to Buck Mark Plus UDX, with ambidextrous rosewood grips. Available only to full-line and Medallion-level Browning dealers. Introduced 2007.

NIB	Exc.	V.G.	Good	Fair	Poor
425	350	300	225	150	125

Buck Mark Plus Stainless UDX

.22 LR semi-automatic, with finger-grooved wood grips. Barrel 5.5". Weight 34 oz. Adjustable sights, fiber optic front sight. Available blued alloy steel. Introduced 2006.

NIB	Exc.	V.G.	Good	Fair	Poor
450	350	300	225	150	125

Buck Mark Standard Stainless URX

.22 LR semi-automatic. Stainless bull barrel 5.5". Weight 34 oz. Ambidextrous rubberized grip. Adjustable sights. Available in alloy steel. Introduced 2006.

NIB	Exc.	V.G.	Good	Fair	Poor
400	325	275	200	125	100

Browning 1911-22

Scaled-down version of 1911A1. Chambered in .22 LR. Aluminum slide, alloy frame, blowback operated, with single-action trigger. Controls are standard 1911 including thumb and grip safeties. Other features include 10-round magazine, brown composite grips, matte blue finish. Weight 16 oz. Barrel length 4.25". Introduced in 2011. Compact model has 3.625" barrel. **NOTE:** Add $400 for Anniversary Edition.

NIB	Exc.	V.G.	Good	Fair	Poor
500	450	400	350	300	200

Browning 1911-22 A1 Polymer Frame w/Rail

Polymer frame variation with 4.25" or 3.625" barrel. Extended grip safety, stipled black laminate grip, accessory rail, skelton trigger and hammer. Weight from 13 to 14 oz. Other features are similar to standard 1911-22. Compact model has 3.625" barrel.

NIB	Exc.	V.G.	Good	Fair	Poor
575	500	450	400	300	200

Browning 1911-22 Polymer Desert Tan

This polymer variation has a two-tone Desert Tan/Black finish. Also offered with bright pink composite grips. Other features are similar to standard 1911-22. Compact model has 3.625" barrel.

NIB	Exc.	V.G.	Good	Fair	Poor
500	425	385	350	325	180

Browning 1911-22 Black Label

Polymer frame with black laminated and stippled grips, checkered front strap, matte black finish, commander-style hammer, combat sights, optional Picatinny rail, suppressor ready. Also offered in with suppressor-ready is extended barrel and G-10 black/gray grips. Compact model has 3.625" barrel and available with Picatinny rail and suppressor-ready feature. **NOTE:** Add $100 for suppressor-ready and rail models.

NIB	Exc.	V.G.	Good	Fair	Poor
600	500	400	300	250	200

Browning 1911-380

Similar to 1911-22 models, except chambered for .380 ACP and slide is made of steel instead of an alloy as in the .22 version. Extended and ambidextrous thumb safety, extended slide release and grip safety. Introduced in 2015.

NIB	Exc.	V.G.	Good	Fair	Poor
575	485	400	—	—	—

Browning 1911-380 Black Label

Has a polymer frame, with features similar to 1911-22 Black Label. Pro model (shown) has rail, night sights and G-10 black/gray grips. Compact model offered, with limited production.

NIB	Exc.	V.G.	Good	Fair	Poor
700	600	500	380	250	200

SHOTGUNS

SUPERPOSED SHOTGUNS

Series of over/under double-barrel shotguns. Chambered for 12-, 20-, 28-gauge and .410 bore. Offered with ventilated rib barrels from 26.5" to 32" in length. Features various choke combinations. Shotgun built on boxlock action. Features double-/single-selective triggers. Automatic ejectors. A number of versions offered that differ in amount of ornamentation and quality of materials and workmanship utilized in manufacture. Values for small-bore models are generally higher. Series introduced in 1930. Manufactured by Fabrique Nationale in Belgium. Factory restored guns or very fine non-factory restorations Superposed guns will bring close to factory original prices. **NOTE:** Extra factory installed barrels add $1000 to $2500 depending on grade of gun.

PRE-WAR SUPERPOSED, 1930-1940

Browning Superposed shotgun prices are divided into three different categories. First category for pre-war guns built from 1930 to 1940. These pre-war Superposed guns manufactured in 12-gauge only from serial number 1 to around 17,000. These shotguns were offered in four different grades: Grade I, Pigeon, Diana and Midas. **NOTE:** Add 15 percent for twin-single triggers; 10 percent for ventilated rib. Deduct 25 percent for recoil pads or shorter than standard stocks.

Grade I

Rock Island Auction Company, August, 2004

NIB	Exc.	V.G.	Good	Fair	Poor
—	2800	2500	1500	700	400

Pigeon

NIB	Exc.	V.G.	Good	Fair	Poor
—	6000	4800	3000	1500	800

Diana

NIB	Exc.	V.G.	Good	Fair	Poor
—	8500	7200	4750	2000	900

Midas

NIB	Exc.	V.G.	Good	Fair	Poor
—	12500	9500	5000	2500	1000

SUPERPOSED FROM 1947-1959

Second category of Superposed produced and sold from 1947 to 1959. Built in 12- and 20-gauge; as well as 28-gauge and .410 bore which were introduced in 1959. These shotguns were graded using a Roman numeral system instead of names. They are: Grade I, Grade II, Grade III, Grade IV, Grade V and Grade VI. Values listed are for 12-gauge. Add premium or deductions as listed. Number of 28-gauge and .410 bore guns sold in late 1959 number less than 100; Grade VI sold in North America unknown, but most likely very small. This is a very rare grade. Proceed with caution. **NOTE:** Add 60 percent for 20-gauge; 100 percent for 28-gauge and .410 (1959 only). Deduct 40 percent for trap; 10 percent for standard weight 12-gauge Grade I.

Grade I

NIB	Exc.	V.G.	Good	Fair	Poor
3700	2500	1400	900	300	250

Grade II

NIB	Exc.	V.G.	Good	Fair	Poor
6500	4500	2500	1200	600	375

Grade III

NIB	Exc.	V.G.	Good	Fair	Poor
7000	6000	3900	2200	750	450

Grade IV

NIB	Exc.	V.G.	Good	Fair	Poor
10000	8500	4500	2400	1200	550

Grade V

NIB	Exc.	V.G.	Good	Fair	Poor
10000	7500	4000	2400	1200	650

Grade VI

NIB	Exc.	V.G.	Good	Fair	Poor
17000	15000	8500	4000	2200	850

SUPERPOSED FROM 1960-1976

Browning Superposed shotguns built from 1960 to 1976 revert back to older grade names. They are Grade I, Pigeon, Pointer, Diana and Midas. These shotguns were available in 12-, 20-, 28-gauge and .410 bore. This last production period is a little more complicated due to manufacturing changes that some collectors consider important, such as round knobs and long tangs.

Prices listed reflect Superposed field guns produced from 1960 to 1965 in round pistol-grip knob, with long trigger guard tang in 12-gauge. All other variations during this period one should consider:

Salt wood damage deduct a minimum of 60 percent; round knob short tang (circa 1966-1969) deduct 50 percent; flat knob short tang (circa 1969-1971) deduct 50 percent; flat knob long tang (circa 1971-1976) deduct 25 percent; New Style Skeet and Lightning Trap (recoil pad, flat knob, full beavertail forearm) with long trigger guard tang (1971-1976) deduct 35 percent; with short trigger guard tang deduct 40 percent; Broadway rib deduct an additional 10 percent; skeet chokes on field guns deduct 5 percent; recoil pads on 2.75" chambered field guns deduct 20 percent; Master engraver signed guns (Funken, Watrin, Vrancken) add 10 percent; shorter than standard stock length deduct 25 percent; barrel lengths of 32" add 10 percent; 20-gauge add 50 percent; 28-gauge add 100 percent; .410 bore add 60 percent. **NOTE:** These premiums could double for higher grade models in NIB or Excellent condition.

Grade I Standard Weight

NIB	Exc.	V.G.	Good	Fair	Poor
3000	2000	1500	700	500	250

Grade I Lightweight

NIB	Exc.	V.G.	Good	Fair	Poor
3200	2200	1600	800	600	300

Pigeon Grade

NIB	Exc.	V.G.	Good	Fair	Poor
6500	5500	3800	2000	1000	600

Pointer Grade—(Rare)

NIB	Exc.	V.G.	Good	Fair	Poor
10500	8050	5600	3000	2000	1000

Diana Grade

NIB	Exc.	V.G.	Good	Fair	Poor
11000	8250	5700	3000	2000	1000

Midas Grade

FN also built Exhibition Grades that were sold in this country under Browning name. Collectors consider a true Exhibition Grade as one not having a "C" prefix in serial number. These particular guns are considered quite desirable and should be appraised on an individual basis. Superposed in this category can range in price from $10,000 to $20,000 depending on gauge, engraving coverage and options.

Second type of Exhibition Grade known as "C" type that was first sold in U.S. from about 1973 to 1977 and is so called because of "C" prefix in serial number. There were about 225 of these guns sold in U.S. They came in quite a few grades and some were specially ordered. Although lower grades are not considered by some to be true exhibitions (pre-C series) highest "C" series grades are a match to the best of older exhibitions. In 2000, an all option Superlight 2 barrel set with sideplates engraved by Vranken sold for $22,000. Generally depending on gun, prices will range between $6,000 and $25,000. These "C" grade guns should also be appraised individually.

NIB	Exc.	V.G.	Good	Fair	Poor
15000	12000	9000	7000	5000	4000

Superposed Superlight

First introduced in 1967 in 12-gauge; 1969 in 20-gauge. Special order 28-gauge and .410 bore are also seen. Offered in 26.5" barrel lengths with 27.5" barrels in 12-gauge and 28" barrels in smaller bores available on special order. Features rounded frame and straight-grip stock with tapered, solid or ventilated rib barrels. Regular production on Superlight ended in 1976 for grades listed. Production did continue for Superlight in P-series beginning in 1977. **NOTE:** Add 50 percent premium for 20-gauge; 100 percent premium for 28-gauge; 30 percent premium for .410 bore.

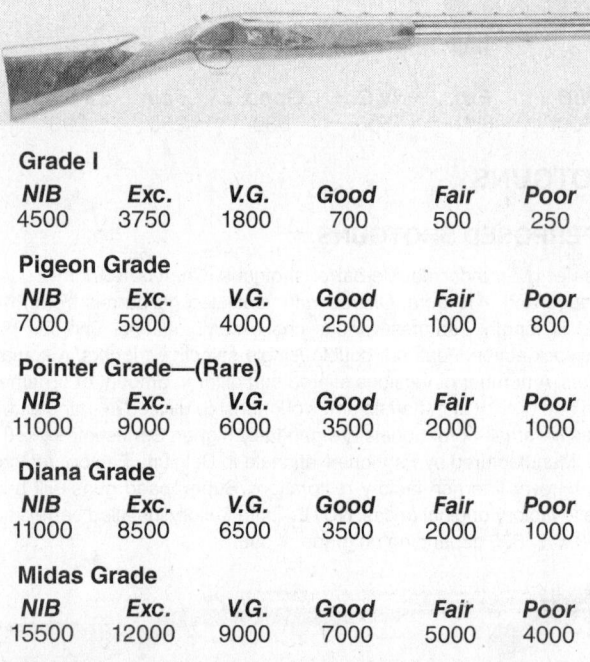

Grade I

NIB	Exc.	V.G.	Good	Fair	Poor
4500	3750	1800	700	500	250

Pigeon Grade

NIB	Exc.	V.G.	Good	Fair	Poor
7000	5900	4000	2500	1000	800

Pointer Grade—(Rare)

NIB	Exc.	V.G.	Good	Fair	Poor
11000	9000	6000	3500	2000	1000

Diana Grade

NIB	Exc.	V.G.	Good	Fair	Poor
11000	8500	6500	3500	2000	1000

Midas Grade

NIB	Exc.	V.G.	Good	Fair	Poor
15500	12000	9000	7000	5000	4000

SUPERPOSED PRESENTATION GRADE SERIES

Superposed shotguns listed were manufactured between 1977 and 1984 by FN in Belgium. Models listed differ in amount of ornamentation and quality of materials and workmanship utilized in construction. This series was also available in a Superlight configuration.

NOTE: Due to the tremendous variation of P-Series guns, prices here reflect Superlight configuration. An all option Superlight with checkered butt, oil finish and three-piece fore-end will bring 25-30 percent more. For all other variations one should consider:

Trap guns deduct 35 percent; new style skeet deduct 30 percent; skeet choked field guns deduct 5 percent; recoil pads on field guns deduct 30 percent; flat knob long tang hunting guns with no options deduct 35 percent; flat knob long tang hunting guns with all options add 25 percent; guns signed by J. Baerten add 5 percent; P-4V guns with no gold deduct 20 percent; hand filed ventilated rib add 5 percent; Presentation Grade guns with extra sets of barrels add approximately $1,500 to $2,500 depending on gauge and combination.

P1, P2, and P3 grades add premium listed:

20-gauge guns—55 percent.

28-gauge guns—100 percent.

.410 bore—30 percent.

P4 grade add premium listed:

20-gauge guns—55 percent.

28-gauge guns—100 percent.

.410 bore—40 percent.

Presentation 1 (without gold inlays)

NIB	Exc.	V.G.	Good	Fair	Poor
4500	3700	1900	1000	600	500

Presentation 1 Gold-inlaid

NIB	Exc.	V.G.	Good	Fair	Poor
7500	6000	3250	1400	700	500

Presentation 2 (without gold inlays)

NIB	Exc.	V.G.	Good	Fair	Poor
6250	5250	3700	1800	1000	600

Presentation 2 Gold-inlaid

NIB	Exc.	V.G.	Good	Fair	Poor
10000	8500	4950	2500	1500	1000

Presentation 3 Gold-inlaid

NOTE: Early hand-engraved P3 models (approximately 25 produced) add 40 percent. These early guns are rare, proceed with caution.

NIB	Exc.	V.G.	Good	Fair	Poor
12000	9500	5500	4000	2000	1300

Presentation 4 Gold-inlaid

NOTE: P4 Grade guns with no gold, deduct approximately 20 percent.

NIB	Exc.	V.G.	Good	Fair	Poor
17500	15000	9800	6750	5000	3500

SUPERPOSED WATERFOWL LIMITED EDITION SERIES

Model issued in three different versions: Mallard, Pintail and Black Duck. Each edition was limited to 500 guns, all in 12-gauge.

1981 Mallard Issue

NIB	Exc.	V.G.	Good	Fair	Poor
9500	7000	4900	3300	1900	1100

1982 Pintail Issue

NIB	Exc.	V.G.	Good	Fair	Poor
9500	7000	4900	3300	1900	1100

1983 Black Duck Issue

NIB	Exc.	V.G.	Good	Fair	Poor
10000	7000	4900	3300	1900	1100

Bicentennial Model

Produced in 1976 to commemorate 200 year Anniversary of America. Total of 53 guns built in this special edition. All of these Superposed were 12-gauge, with 28" barrels. Each was numbered for one of fifty states plus District of Columbia. Two additional guns were built for Smithsonian Institution and Liege Firearms Museum. All were fitted with side plates, with gold inlays. To reflect their true value, guns must be in unfired condition, in their original case and with all papers.

NIB	Exc.	V.G.	Good	Fair	Poor
15000	9000	5950	2750	1500	1000

FN/BROWNING SUPERPOSED

Number of FN Browning Superposed B-25 shotguns were imported into this country by Browning in various grades. These Superposed were intended originally for FN's European market. There are a large number of variations and grades. It is strongly suggested that an expert appraisal be sought prior to sale. These guns are marked with both Browning and FN barrel address.

Classic

Produced about 2,500 guns in 1986. Offered in 20-gauge, with 26" barrels. Silver gray receiver, with engraving.

NIB	Exc.	V.G.	Good	Fair	Poor
4000	3200	2650	2000	800	300

Gold Classic

Similar to above. More finely finished. Engraved with gold inlays. About 350 built in 1986.

NIB	Exc.	V.G.	Good	Fair	Poor
9000	7500	5000	2450	1750	400

Custom Shop B25 & B125 Superposed

These special order Superposed models were available from the Browning Custom Shop from mid 1980s through 1990s for Model B25 and until 2004 for B125. Several grades were offered with different levels of engraving and wood quality, all in 12- or 20-gauge. B125 models were assembled in Belgium, with components manufactured in other countries to hold down costs. B25s were made entirely in Belgium. Values shown here are for these discontinued models. For information on current Superposed high-grade models, contact the Browning Custom Shop at 801-876-2711 or on line at www.browning.com.

B-125 Hunting or Sporting Clays Model

A-Style Engraving

NIB	Exc.	V.G.	Good	Fair	Poor
3800	3200	2700	2000	1500	700

B-Style Engraving

NIB	Exc.	V.G.	Good	Fair	Poor
4100	3500	3000	2450	1800	800

C-Style Engraving

NIB	Exc.	V.G.	Good	Fair	Poor
4500	3800	3300	2750	2000	900

B-125 Trap Model

C-Style Engraving

NIB	Exc.	V.G.	Good	Fair	Poor
4800	4000	3500	2950	2000	900

B-25

Grade 1

NIB	Exc.	V.G.	Good	Fair	Poor
10000	8000	6200	4500	2500	—

Pigeon Grade

NIB	Exc.	V.G.	Good	Fair	Poor
14000	11800	8500	6700	2500	—

Pointer Grade

NIB	Exc.	V.G.	Good	Fair	Poor
15500	12000	9800	7500	3000	—

Diana Grade

NIB	Exc.	V.G.	Good	Fair	Poor
16500	13000	10800	8400	3500	—

Midas Grade

NIB	Exc.	V.G.	Good	Fair	Poor
17500	13800	11300	9000	3500	—

Custom Shop BSL

Side-by-side equipped with Browning sidelock barrel, Holland & Holland-type locks, with double trigger and automatic ejectors. Assembled and finished by Labeau-Courally. Offered in 12- and 20-gauge. Engraved grayed or case colored receiver. Introduced into Browning product line in 2001.

Case Colored Receiver (BSL Grade LC1)

NIB	Exc.	V.G.	Good	Fair	Poor
15000	12500	9000	—	—	—

Engraved Gray Receiver (BSL Grade LC2)

NIB	Exc.	V.G.	Good	Fair	Poor
18000	16000	12500	—	—	—

Liege

Over/under shotgun chambered for 12-gauge. Offered with 26.5", 28" or 30" ventilated rib barrels and various choke combinations. Features boxlock action, with non-selective single trigger and automatic ejectors. Finish blued, with checkered walnut stock. Approximately 10,000 manufactured between 1973 and 1975. U.S. versions marked Browning Arms Company on barrel.

NIB	Exc.	V.G.	Good	Fair	Poor
1500	850	650	450	300	200

B27

Improved version of Liege. Was imported into U.S., some without Browning Arms Company markings and only FN barrel address. Others may have both barrel addresses. Offered in a number of variations that differed in amount of ornamentation and quality of materials and workmanship utilized. Features same action as Liege over/under gun.

Standard

NIB	Exc.	V.G.	Good	Fair	Poor
1200	950	650	350	250	200

Deluxe

NIB	Exc.	V.G.	Good	Fair	Poor
1600	1200	850	500	350	250

Deluxe Trap

NIB	Exc.	V.G.	Good	Fair	Poor
1600	1200	850	450	300	250

Deluxe Skeet

NIB	Exc.	V.G.	Good	Fair	Poor
1600	1200	850	450	300	250

Grand Deluxe

NIB	Exc.	V.G.	Good	Fair	Poor
2000	1500	1000	650	500	400

City of Liege Commemorative

250 manufactured.

NIB	Exc.	V.G.	Good	Fair	Poor
2500	1650	1000	600	450	300

ST-100

Over/under trap gun. Features separated barrels, with adjustable point of impact. Chambered for 12-gauge. Has 30" or 32" barrel, with full choke and floating ventilated rib. Features single trigger and automatic ejectors. Finish blued, with checkered walnut stock. Manufactured by FN between 1979 and 1981.

NIB	Exc.	V.G.	Good	Fair	Poor
3750	2700	1800	1000	700	400

CITORI SERIES

Over/under double-barrel shotgun chambered for all gauges. Offered with ventilated rib barrels of 26" through 30" in length. Has boxlock action, with single-selective trigger and automatic ejectors. Various grades differ in amount of ornamentation and quality of materials and workmanship utilized in construction. Series is manufactured in Japan by B.C. Miroku. Introduced in 1973. **NOTE:** All Citori models, add 15-20 percent premium for 28-gauge and .410; 30 percent for 16-gauge.

Grade I

NIB	Exc.	V.G.	Good	Fair	Poor
1200	900	725	550	425	300

Upland Special—Grade I

Offered with straight-grip stock and 24" rib barrels. Available in 12- or 20-gauge. Weight 6 lbs. 11 oz. in 12-gauge; 6 lbs. in 20-gauge. Introduced in 1984.

NIB	Exc.	V.G.	Good	Fair	Poor
1350	950	700	600	400	300

Grade II—1978 to 1983

NIB	Exc.	V.G.	Good	Fair	Poor
—	1500	1300	1000	650	400

Grade II—Choke Tubes

NIB	Exc.	V.G.	Good	Fair	Poor
1600	1400	1000	775	650	400

Grade V—1978 to 1984

NIB	Exc.	V.G.	Good	Fair	Poor
2900	2300	1600	950	750	400

Grade V with sideplates—1981 to 1984

NIB	Exc.	V.G.	Good	Fair	Poor
2950	2500	2100	1500	800	400

Grade VI—Choke Tubes

NIB	Exc.	V.G.	Good	Fair	Poor
1950	1650	1200	1000	750	500

Citori Hunter

Features full pistol-grip stock, with beavertail forearm and high-gloss walnut. Chambered for 12-gauge with 2.75", 3" or 3.5" chambers. Choice of 26", 28" or 30" barrels. The 20-gauge choice of 26" or 28" barrels. Weight: 12-gauge from 7 lbs. 13 oz. to 8 lbs. 9 oz. depending on barrel length; 20-gauge about 6.75 lbs. **NOTE:** Add $75 for 3.5" models.

NIB	Exc.	V.G.	Good	Fair	Poor
1500	1100	850	650	550	450

Citori Sporting Hunter

Same features as Hunter, with exception of stock configuration. Sporting Hunter has Sporting model buttstock and Superposed-style forearm. Fitted with contoured sporting recoil pad. Introduced in 1998. **NOTE:** Add $75 for 3.5" models.

NIB	Exc.	V.G.	Good	Fair	Poor
1550	1400	1050	750	550	450

Citori Satin Hunter

Chambered for 12-gauge shells. Hunting-style stock. Choice of 26" or 28" barrels. Special satin wood finish, with matte black receiver and barrels. Offered in Grade I only. Weight about 8 lbs. Introduced in 1999. **NOTE:** Add $100 for 3.5" chamber.

NIB	Exc.	V.G.	Good	Fair	Poor
1250	1000	825	700	500	375

Citori Satin Hunter Micro Midas

Budget-priced Citori, with same features and handling qualities that have made other Citoris so popular. Available in 12- or 20-gauge, with 24" or 26" barrels. Satin-finished walnut stock, with 13" length of pull. Vector-Pro lengthened forcing cones. Weight: 6 lbs. 3 oz. to 6 lbs. 10 oz. New in 2011.

NIB	Exc.	V.G.	Good	Fair	Poor
1300	1050	900	800	500	300

Citori Lightning

Lightweight version that features a slimmer profile. Has checkered round-knob pistol-grip stock. Offered in all gauges. Same barrel lengths as standard Citori. Features screw-in choke tubes known as Invectors. Introduced in 1988. Offered in 12-, 16-, 20-, 28-gauge and .410 bore. Weights are 6.5 lbs. to 8 lbs. depending on gauge and barrel length. Models differ in amount of ornamentation and quality of materials and workmanship utilized. **NOTE:** Add $300 for 28-gauge and .410 bore; $150 for 16-gauge.

Grade I

NIB	Exc.	V.G.	Good	Fair	Poor
1650	1200	900	600	450	375

Grade III

NIB	Exc.	V.G.	Good	Fair	Poor
2450	1900	1400	975	600	450

Grade IV

12 Gauge

20 & 28 Ga., .410

NIB	Exc.	V.G.	Good	Fair	Poor
2610	1950	1450	1025	650	500

Grade VI

NIB	Exc.	V.G.	Good	Fair	Poor
3800	3000	2250	1500	700	550

Grade VII

12 Gauge

20 & 28 Ga., .410

NIB	Exc.	V.G.	Good	Fair	Poor
4800	4000	3000	2300	1900	1500

Citori Lightning Feather

Introduced in 1999. Features a lightweight alloy receiver. Offered in 12-gauge Grade I only, with choice of 26" or 28" barrels. Weight with 28" barrels about 7 lbs. 11 oz. In 2000, this model offered in 20-gauge, with 26" or 28" barrels and 3" chambers. Weight of 20-gauge about 6.5 lbs.

NIB	Exc.	V.G.	Good	Fair	Poor
1870	1400	975	595	400	300

Citori Lightning Feather Combo

Features 20- and 28-gauge, with 27" barrel. The 20-gauge with 3" chambers; 28-gauge with 2.75" chambers. Pistol-grip stock. Weight about 6.25 lbs. Supplied with Browning luggage case. Introduced in 2000.

NIB	Exc.	V.G.	Good	Fair	Poor
3200	2400	2000	1500	1000	500

Citori Feather XS

Offered in 12-, 20-, 28-gauge and .410 bore. Has lightweight alloy receiver. Fitted with walnut stock, pistol-grip, black recoil pad and schnabel forearm. Triple trigger system. Hi-Viz Comp sight system standard. Weight about 7 lbs. 12-gauge; 6.5 lbs. 20-gauge; 6 lbs. 28-gauge; 6 lbs. .410 bore. Introduced in 2000.

NIB	Exc.	V.G.	Good	Fair	Poor
2000	1500	1200	900	600	400

Citori Superlight Feather

Chambered for 12- or 20-gauge, with straight-grip stock and schnabel forearm. Has alloy receiver. Checkered walnut stock. Offered with 26" barrels. Weight about 6 lbs. Introduced in 2002.

NIB	Exc.	V.G.	Good	Fair	Poor
1940	1450	1100	800	550	350

Citori Super Lightning Grade I

Introduced in 2005. This 12- or 20-gauge features blued receiver, with gold line border. Checkered satin finished select walnut stock, with pistol-grip and schnabel forearm. Barrels are 26" or 28", with choke tubes. Recoil pad on 12-gauge. Weight about 8 lbs. 12-gauge; 6.75 lbs. 20-gauge.

NIB	Exc.	V.G.	Good	Fair	Poor
1865	1400	1050	750	500	300

Citori Classic Lightning Grade I

Offered in 12- or 20-gauge, with choice of 26" or 28" ventilated rib barrels and choke tubes. Receiver scroll engraved on silver nitride finish. Checkered select walnut stock, with oil finish. Forearm is Lightning style. Recoil pad on 12-gauge. Weight about 8 lbs. 12-gauge; 6.75 lbs. 20-gauge. Introduced in 2005.

NIB	Exc.	V.G.	Good	Fair	Poor
1890	1425	1075	775	525	325

Citori Classic Lightning Feather Grade I

Introduced in 2005. Features high relief engraved alloy receiver. Chambered for 12- or 20-gauge. Fitted with 26" or 28" ventilated rib barrels and choke tubes. Checkered select stock, with schnabel forearm. Recoil pad on 12-gauge. Weight about 7 lbs. 12-gauge; 6.25 lbs. 20-gauge.

NIB	Exc.	V.G.	Good	Fair	Poor
1950	1450	1100	775	525	325

Citori 525 Sporting

Introduced in 2002. Chambered for 12- or 20-gauge. Fitted with choice of 28" or 30" ventilated rib ported barrels. Stock redesigned with Euro checkering pattern and more pronounced palm swell. Weight about 8 lbs. 12-gauge; 7 lbs. 20-gauge. In 2003 offered in both 28-gauge and .410 bore. **NOTE:** Add $275 for adjustable comb.

NIB	Exc.	V.G.	Good	Fair	Poor
2320	1750	1250	800	550	350

Citori 525 Field

As above, with choice of 26" or 28" barrels. Barrels are unported. Ventilated recoil pad. Introduced in 2002. In 2003 offered in both 28-gauge and .410 bore.

NIB	Exc.	V.G.	Good	Fair	Poor
1980	1475	950	700	500	325

Citori 525 Golden Clays Sporting

Same features as 525 Sporting, with oil-finished high stock, engraved receiver and gold inlays. In 2003 offered in both 28-gauge and .410 bore.

NIB	Exc.	V.G.	Good	Fair	Poor
4450	3250	2600	1950	1200	550

Citori 525 Feather

Lightweight Citori features alloy receiver, with steel breech face and high-relief engraving. Stock and schnabel fore-end Grade II/III oil finished walnut. Available in 12-, 20-, 28-gauge and .410 bore, with 26" or 28" barrels. All but 28-gauge have 3" chambers. Weight about 6.9 lbs. 12-gauge; 5.5 to 5.7 lbs. in others. Three choke tubes.

NIB	Exc.	V.G.	Good	Fair	Poor
2300	1750	1250	800	550	350

Citori 625 Sporting

Introduced in 2008. This 2.75" 12-gauge has 28", 30" or 32" ported barrels. Browning's Vector Pro lengthened forcing cones system. Stock and schnabel fore-end Grade III/IV walnut. Steel receiver has silver nitride finish, with high-relief engraving and gold embellishment. Five choke tubes included. Weight 7.9 to 8.2 lbs. **NOTE:** Add 5 percent for adjustable comb stock.

NIB	Exc.	V.G.	Good	Fair	Poor
3500	2700	1975	1200	850	550

Citori 625 Sporting Left-Hand

As above, but configured for left-hand shooters.

NIB	Exc.	V.G.	Good	Fair	Poor
3500	2700	1975	1200	850	550

Citori 625 Field

26" or 28" barrels, gloss oil finish Grade II/III walnut stock and schnabel fore-end. Steel receiver, with silver nitride finish and high-relief engraving. Three choke tubes. Chambered for 12-, 20-, 28-gauge and .41 Weight: 7 lbs. 14 oz. to 6 lbs. 12 oz.

NIB	Exc.	V.G.	Good	Fair	Poor
2400	1900	1400	975	600	450

Citori Model 725 Field

Over/under in 12- or 20-gauge, with 28-gauge and .410 bore added in 201 with 26" or 28" barrels and Invector DS choke tubes. New action design ha lower profile than other Citori models. Single selective mechanical trigge automatic ejectors, checkered Grade II/III walnut stock, with gloss finish ar recoil pad. Silver nitride finish, with high relief engraving. Introduced in 201. Higher grade models available with more engraving and higher grade woo

NIB	Exc.	V.G.	Good	Fair	Poor
2100	1700	1250	1000	—	—

Grade III
NIB	Exc.	V.G.	Good	Fair	Poor
3300	2750	—	—	—	—

Grade V
NIB	Exc.	V.G.	Good	Fair	Poor
5200	4400	—	—	—	—

Grade VII Small Gauge
NIB	Exc.	V.G.	Good	Fair	Poor
5600	4900	—	—	—	—

725 Feather
NIB	Exc.	V.G.	Good	Fair	Poor
2200	1800	1250	1000	—	—

725 Skeet
NIB	Exc.	V.G.	Good	Fair	Poor
2800	2500	2000	1500	1000	700

725 Skeet w/adjustable comb
NIB	Exc.	V.G.	Good	Fair	Poor
3100	2800	2200	1600	1100	800

725 Sporting
NIB	Exc.	V.G.	Good	Fair	Poor
2800	2500	2000	1500	1000	700

725 Sporting w/adjustable comb
NIB	Exc.	V.G.	Good	Fair	Poor
3100	2800	2200	1600	1100	800

725 Trap
NIB	Exc.	V.G.	Good	Fair	Poor
3000	2700	2200	1750	1200	900

Citori Esprit

Introduced in 2002. Features removable decorative sideplates, schnabe forearm and high-grade walnut stock. Offered in 12-gauge only, with 28 ventilated rib barrels. Weight about 8.25 lbs.

NIB	Exc.	V.G.	Good	Fair	Poor
2450	1975	1400	975	600	450

Citori Sporting Clays

Specifically designed for sporting clay shooting. Offered in 12-gauge only. Each model is back-bored, ported and fitted with Invector-Plus choke tubes. Barrels are chrome-plated. Receiver blued, with gold inscription. Pigeon Grade has gold detailing and high grade gloss walnut stock. Signature Grade features red and black print on stock, with gold decals. Trigger is adjustable to three length of pull positions. Comes with three interchangeable trigger shoes. Each model fitted with rubber recoil pad.

NIB	Exc.	V.G.	Good	Fair	Poor
2450	1975	1400	975	600	450

Citori Lightning Sporting

Features rounded pistol-grip and Lightning forearm, with choice of high or low ventilated rib. Chambered for 3" shells. Offered in 28" or 30" barrels. Weight about 8.5 lbs. Introduced in 1989.

NIB	Exc.	V.G.	Good	Fair	Poor
1400	1000	800	600	450	300

Pigeon Grade

NIB	Exc.	V.G.	Good	Fair	Poor
1450	1100	900	650	450	300

Golden Clays

First introduced in 1994.

NIB	Exc.	V.G.	Good	Fair	Poor
2800	2250	1650	900	450	300

Citori Privilege

High-grade model features game scene engraved sideplates, unique checkering pattern oil finish high-grade walnut stock, with pistol-grip. Offered in 12-gauge only. Choice of 26" or 28" barrels. Weight about 8 lbs. Introduced in 2000. In 2001 a 20-gauge version, with 26" or 28" barrels was introduced. Discontinued in 2003.

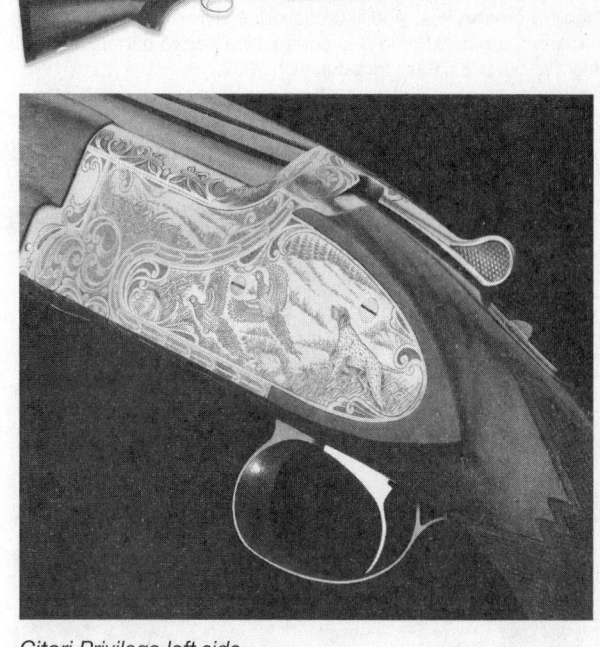

Citori Privilege left side.

NIB	Exc.	V.G.	Good	Fair	Poor
4600	4000	3000	2500	1500	1000

Citori XS Sporting Clays

Introduced in 1999. Features silver nitride receiver, gold accents and European-style stock, with schnabel fore-end. Available in 12- or 20-gauge. Choice of 28", 30" or 32" barrels. Weight varies: 8 lbs. 12-gauge to 7 lbs. 20-gauge.

NIB	Exc.	V.G.	Good	Fair	Poor
2600	2050	1450	1000	625	475

Citori Ultra XS Skeet

Model offered in 12-gauge only. Choice of 28" or 30" ported barrels. Chambered for 2.75" shells. Semi-beavertail forearm. Triple trigger system standard. Adjustable comb optional. Walnut stock, with pistol-grip. Black recoil pad. Weight about 7.75 lbs. Introduced in 2000. In 2001 a 20-gauge version with 28" or 30" barrels was introduced. **NOTE:** Add $275 for adjustable comb.

NIB	Exc.	V.G.	Good	Fair	Poor
2535	1900	1375	950	600	450

Citori XS Special

12-gauge 2.75" chamber gun. Choice of 30" or 32" ventilated rib barrels, porting and extended choke tubes. Checkered walnut stock, with adjustable comb and pistol-grip. Semi-beavertail forearm. Silver engraved receiver. Weight about 8.7 lbs.

NIB	Exc.	V.G.	Good	Fair	Poor
2825	2100	1550	1100	675	475

Citori Plus

Features adjustable point of impact from 3" to 12" above point of aim. Receiver on Grade I blued, with scroll engraving. Walnut stock is adjustable. Forearm is a modified beavertail style. Available in 30" or 32" barrels that are backbored and ported. Non-ported barrels are optional. Weight about 9 lbs. 6 oz. Introduced in 1989.

Grade I

NIB	Exc.	V.G.	Good	Fair	Poor
1300	1075	750	500	400	300

Pigeon Grade

NIB	Exc.	V.G.	Good	Fair	Poor
1850	1500	950	700	500	300

Signature Grade

NIB	Exc.	V.G.	Good	Fair	Poor
1750	1450	950	700	500	300

Golden Clays

NIB	Exc.	V.G.	Good	Fair	Poor
2850	2295	1500	900	450	300

Citori Trap Combination Set

Version offered in Grade I only. Features 34" single barrel and 32" set of over/under barrels. Furnished in fitted case. Discontinued.

NIB	Exc.	V.G.	Good	Fair	Poor
—	1950	1350	950	800	700

GTI Model

Features 13mm wide rib ventilated side ribs, pistol-grip stock, semi-beavertail forearm. Offered in 28" or 30" barrel. Weight about 8 lbs. Not offered in Pigeon Grade. Introduced in 1989.

Grade I

NIB	Exc.	V.G.	Good	Fair	Poor
1200	975	750	600	450	300

Signature Grade

NIB	Exc.	V.G.	Good	Fair	Poor
1200	975	750	600	450	300

Golden Clays

NIB	Exc.	V.G.	Good	Fair	Poor
2575	1975	1250	900	450	300

Ultra Sporter - (Sporting Clays)

Introduced in 1995. Replaces GTI model. Features 10mm to 13mm tapered rib. Offered with blued or gray receiver. Walnut stock, with pistol-grip and semi-beavertail forearm. Fitted with adjustable comb and length of pull. Offered in 12-gauge only, with 28" or 30" barrels. Average weight 8 lbs. **NOTE:** Add $200 to NIB price for Ultra Sporters with adjustable comb.

NIB	Exc.	V.G.	Good	Fair	Poor
1550	1200	800	550	400	300

Golden Clays

NIB	Exc.	V.G.	Good	Fair	Poor
2900	2300	1600	1100	750	400

Citori Superlight

Lighter-weight version of Citori. Chambered for all gauges. Offered with same features as Lightning Series. Grades differ in amount of ornamentation, quality of materials and workmanship utilized. Series introduced in 1983.

NIB	Exc.	V.G.	Good	Fair	Poor
5600	4900	—	—	—	—

Citori Superlight Feather

Introduced in 1999. Features straight-grip stock, with schnabel fore-end. Lightweight alloy receiver. Offered in 12-gauge Grade I only. Choice of 26" or 28" barrels. Weight with 28" barrels about 6 lbs. 6 oz.

NIB	Exc.	V.G.	Good	Fair	Poor
1700	1250	895	600	475	350

Micro Lightning

Offered in 20-gauge only. Has reduced dimensions for smaller shooters. Available with 24" ventilated rib barrels. Weight 6 lbs. 3 oz. Introduced in 1991.

NIB	Exc.	V.G.	Good	Fair	Poor
1100	895	700	600	400	300

Gran Lightning

Essentially a Grade I Lightning, with high grade select walnut stock and satin finish. Receiver and barrels blued. Offered in 12- and 20-gauge. Choice of 26" or 28" ventilated rib barrels. Choke tubes standard. Weight about 8 lbs. 12-gauge; 6 lbs. 11 oz. 20-gauge. Introduced in 1990. In 2004, 28-gauge and .410 bore were added. Discontinued in 2005.

NIB	Exc.	V.G.	Good	Fair	Poor
2000	1600	1200	1000	750	600

Gran Lightning 16 Gauge

This model was reintroduced in 2015, only in 16-gauge. Has Grade V/VI wood and high relief engraved receiver

NIB	Exc.	V.G.	Good	Fair	Poor
2400	2100	—	—	—	—

Citori White Lightning

Introduced in 1998. Features silver nitride scroll engraved receiver. Offered in 3" 12- and 20-gauge. Choice of 26" or 28" barrels. In 2004 available in 28-gauge and .410 bore. Weight about 8 lbs. 12-gauge; 6.8 lbs. 20-gauge. Invector-Plus chokes standard. Lightning-style stock. **NOTE:** Add $75 for 28-gauge and .410 models.

NIB	Exc.	V.G.	Good	Fair	Poor
1500	1200	950	700	600	375

Citori White Upland Special

Introduced in 2000. Features shortened straight-grip stock, schnabel forearm and 24" barrel. Fitted with 2.75" barrel. Chambered for 12- and 20-gauge only. Weight about 6.75 lbs.

NIB	Exc.	V.G.	Good	Fair	Poor
1650	1200	975	725	625	395

Citori Skeet

Series of guns chambered for all gauges. Designed for competition skeet shooting. Similar to standard Citori, with high-post target rib and 26" or 28" barrels. Versions differ in amount of engraving, quality of materials and workmanship utilized.

Grade I

NIB	Exc.	V.G.	Good	Fair	Poor
1000	925	750	550	425	350

Grade II

Discontinued 1983.

NIB	Exc.	V.G.	Good	Fair	Poor
—	1000	900	750	450	300

Grade III

NIB	Exc.	V.G.	Good	Fair	Poor
1500	1200	900	750	450	300

Grade V

Discontinued 1984.

NIB	Exc.	V.G.	Good	Fair	Poor
1600	1200	900	750	450	300

Grade VI

NIB	Exc.	V.G.	Good	Fair	Poor
2000	1750	1200	900	450	300

Golden Clays

First introduced in 1994.

NIB	Exc.	V.G.	Good	Fair	Poor
2400	2000	1500	900	450	300

3 Gauge Sets

Consists of 20-, 28-gauge and .410 bore. Interchangeable 28" ventilated rib barrels. Introduced in 1987.

Grade I

NIB	Exc.	V.G.	Good	Fair	Poor
2600	2100	1500	1250	1000	800

Grade III

NIB	Exc.	V.G.	Good	Fair	Poor
3400	2900	2300	1750	1300	1000

Grade VI

NIB	Exc.	V.G.	Good	Fair	Poor
3500	3000	2500	2000	1500	1100

4 Gauge Sets

Set has 12-, 20-, 28-gauge and .410 bore. Interchangeable ventilated rib barrels in 26" or 28" lengths. Introduced in 1981.

Grade I

NIB	Exc.	V.G.	Good	Fair	Poor
3400	2750	2250	1700	1250	900

Grade III

NIB	Exc.	V.G.	Good	Fair	Poor
3500	2900	2500	1900	1350	900

Grade VI

NIB	Exc.	V.G.	Good	Fair	Poor
3900	3300	2900	2250	1400	950

Citori Trap

Version similar to standard Citori. Offered in 12-gauge only, with 30" or 32" barrels. Features high rib, Monte Carlo-type stock, with recoil pad. Versions differ in amount of ornamentation, quality of materials and workmanship utilized.

Grade I

NIB	Exc.	V.G.	Good	Fair	Poor
1200	975	750	550	425	350

Plus Trap

Adjustable rib and stock. Introduced in 1989.

NIB	Exc.	V.G.	Good	Fair	Poor
1700	1450	1000	750	600	500

Grade II

Discontinued 1983.

NIB	Exc.	V.G.	Good	Fair	Poor
—	1200	1000	675	450	350

Grade III

NIB	Exc.	V.G.	Good	Fair	Poor
1600	1450	1000	750	600	500

Grade V

Discontinued 1984.

NIB	Exc.	V.G.	Good	Fair	Poor
—	1500	1350	900	650	450

Grade VI

NIB	Exc.	V.G.	Good	Fair	Poor
2200	1900	1550	1250	1000	800

Citori XT Trap

Introduced in 1999. Fitted with contoured beavertail Monte Carlo stock, with or without adjustable comb. Grayed receiver highlighted in gold, with light scroll work. Choice of 30" or 32" barrels. Weight about 8 lbs. 11 oz. **NOTE:** Add $275 for adjustable comb.

NIB	Exc.	V.G.	Good	Fair	Poor
2500	1700	1200	900	650	395

Golden Clays

First introduced in 1994.

NIB	Exc.	V.G.	Good	Fair	Poor
2950	2250	1500	900	450	300

Signature Grade

NIB	Exc.	V.G.	Good	Fair	Poor
2150	1750	900	600	450	300

Citori XT Trap Gold

Introduced in 2005. Features gold game scene engraving pattern on silver receiver. Choice of 30" or 32" ventilated rib ported barrels, with choke tubes. Checkered select walnut stock, with adjustable comb and semi-beavertail forearm. Stock also has adjustable length of pull and recoil reduction system. Weight about 9 lbs.

NIB	Exc.	V.G.	Good	Fair	Poor
4520	3300	2900	2250	1400	650

Model 325 Sporting Clays

Introduced in 1993. Has European design featuring scroll-engraved grayed receiver, schnabel forearm, 10mm wide ventilated rib, three interchangeable and adjustable trigger shoes. Back-bore barrels are ported. Fitted with choke tubes. Available in 12- and 20-gauge. 12-gauge offered with 28", 30" or 32" barrels; 20-gauge 28" or 30" barrels fitted with conventional chokes. Weight about: 12-gauge 7 lbs. 14 oz.; 20-gauge 6 lbs. 12 oz.

NIB	Exc.	V.G.	Good	Fair	Poor
1550	1200	900	700	450	300

Special Sporting

Similar to Sporting model. Fitted with 2.75" chamber. Choice of 28", 30" or 32" ported barrels. Fitted with high post rib. Stock has full pistol-grip. Optional adjustable comb. Weight about 8.3 lbs. depending on barrel length.

Grade I

NIB	Exc.	V.G.	Good	Fair	Poor
1350	975	750	600	450	300

Signature Grade

NIB	Exc.	V.G.	Good	Fair	Poor
1350	1000	750	600	450	300

Pigeon Grade

NIB	Exc.	V.G.	Good	Fair	Poor
1500	1300	850	600	450	300

Golden Clays

NIB	Exc.	V.G.	Good	Fair	Poor
2600	1975	1250	900	450	300

Model 425 Sporting Clays

Citori over/under gun offered in 12- and 20-gauge. Choice of 28" and 30" barrels. On 12-gauge 32" barrels available. Barrels fitted with 10mm wide rib. Invector chokes are standard. Average weight 7 lbs. 14 oz. Introduced in 1995.

NIB	Exc.	V.G.	Good	Fair	Poor
1650	1200	850	600	450	300

Model 425 Golden Clays

Same as above, with high-grade wood. Engraved receiver. **NOTE:** Add $200 to NIB price for Model 425 with adjustable comb.

NIB	Exc.	V.G.	Good	Fair	Poor
3000	2450	1650	1100	600	300

Light Sporting 802ES (Extended Swing)

Introduced in 1996. Features 28" ventilated rib barrel, with 2" stainless steel extension tubes for extended swing of 30". Additional 4" extension also included. Thus barrel can be 28", 30" or 32" according to needs. Chambered for 12-gauge, with adjustable length of pull. Walnut stock, pistol-grip and schnabel forearm. Weight about 7.5 lbs.

NIB	Exc.	V.G.	Good	Fair	Poor
—	1500	900	700	500	250

Citori Plus Combo

Features single-barrel trap and interchangeable over/under set of barrels. Other features similar to Citori Plus Grade 1. Barrel combinations: 32" over/under with 34" single barrel; 30" over/under with 32" or 34" single barrel. Introduced in 1989.

NIB	Exc.	V.G.	Good	Fair	Poor
2500	2100	1750	1100	700	450

Citori Ultra XS Prestige

New in 2008. This 12-gauge sporting clays model features adjustable comb. Grade III/IV walnut stock, with right hand palm swell. Ported barrels are 28", 30" or 32". Gold accented high relief Ultra XS Special engraving on steel/silver nitride finish receiver. Weight about 8 lbs.

NIB	Exc.	V.G.	Good	Fair	Poor
4500	3300	2900	2250	1400	600

BT-99 SERIES

BT-99

Break-open single-barrel trap gun. Chambered for 12-gauge only. Offered with 32" or 34" ventilated rib barrel, with screw-in choke tubes. Features boxlock action, with automatic ejectors. Finish blued, with checkered walnut stock and beavertail forearm. Introduced in 1968 by B.C. Miroku.

NIB	Exc.	V.G.	Good	Fair	Poor
1000	850	750	500	400	350

BT-99 Stainless

First introduced in 1993.

NIB	Exc.	V.G.	Good	Fair	Poor
1675	1250	900	700	550	350

BT-99 Signature Grade I

First introduced in 1993.

NIB	Exc.	V.G.	Good	Fair	Poor
1300	1050	700	600	500	300

BT-99 Pigeon Grade

First introduced in 1993.

NIB	Exc.	V.G.	Good	Fair	Poor
1600	1250	800	650	500	300

BT-99 Golden Clays

First introduced in 1994. In 2003 offered with adjustable comb. Weight about 9 lbs. Available with 32" or 34" barrel.

NIB	Exc.	V.G.	Good	Fair	Poor
3700	2500	1750	1100	500	300

BT-99 Plus

Version features adjustable ventilated rib and recoil reduction system. Has adjustable stock, recoil pad and back-bored barrel. Introduced in 1989.

NIB	Exc.	V.G.	Good	Fair	Poor
1350	1200	900	700	500	300

BT-99 Plus—Pigeon Grade

NIB	Exc.	V.G.	Good	Fair	Poor
1700	1300	900	800	550	350

BT-99 Plus—Signature Grade

NIB	Exc.	V.G.	Good	Fair	Poor
1600	1200	850	700	500	300

BT-99 Plus Stainless—Grade I

Same as standard version. Offered in stainless steel. First introduced in 1993. Available in 32" and 34" barrels. Weight about 8 lbs. 11 oz.

NIB	Exc.	V.G.	Good	Fair	Poor
1700	1350	900	700	500	350

BT-99 Plus—Golden Clays

First introduced in 1994.

NIB	Exc.	V.G.	Good	Fair	Poor
2700	2250	1750	900	450	300

BT-99 Plus Micro

Slightly reduced dimensions. Offered in barrel lengths from 28" to 34". Weight about 8 lbs. 6 oz. Introduced in 1991.

NIB	Exc.	V.G.	Good	Fair	Poor
1350	1100	900	700	500	300

BT-99 Grade III

New in 2008. BT-99 features gloss finish Monte Carlo Grade III/IV walnut stock. Gold accented high relief engraving on receiver. **NOTE:** Add 10 percent for adjustable comb stock.

NIB	Exc.	V.G.	Good	Fair	Poor
2400	1950	1250	750	550	350

BT-100 SERIES

BT-100

First introduced in 1995. Single-barrel trap features adjustable trigger and length of pull. Stock Monte Carlo or adjustable comb. Barrel 32" or 34". Choice blue or stainless finish. Weight about 8.9 lbs.

NIB	Exc.	V.G.	Good	Fair	Poor
2500	1900	1200	700	500	300

BT-100 Satin

Introduced in 1999. Features matte black receiver. Available in 32" or 34" barrels, without ejector selector. Grade I only.

NIB	Exc.	V.G.	Good	Fair	Poor
1950	1300	1050	600	400	200

BT-100 Thumbhole

Same as standard BT-100, with additional feature of thumbhole stock. Offered in blue and stainless.

NIB	Exc.	V.G.	Good	Fair	Poor
2575	2000	1350	1000	600	400

Recoilless Trap

First introduced in 1993. Features advanced design that eliminates recoil up to 72 percent. Receiver a special bolt-action single-shot and black anodized. Fitted with adjustable ventilated rib so point of impact can be moved. Adjustable length of pull. Standard Model a 12-gauge with 30" barrel. Micro Model fitted with 27" barrels. Choke tubes supplied. Weight: Standard Model 9 lbs. 1 oz.; Micro Model 8 lbs. 10 oz.

NIB	Exc.	V.G.	Good	Fair	Poor
1250	1100	900	700	500	350

BSS SERIES

BSS

Side-by-side double-barrel shotgun. Chambered for 12- or 20-gauge. Offered with 26", 28" or 30" barrel. Various choke combinations. Features boxlock action. Automatic ejectors. Early guns had nonselective single trigger; late production selective trigger. Finish blued, with checkered walnut stock and beavertail forearm. Manufactured between 1978 and 1987 by B.C. Miroku. **NOTE:** Add 20 percent single-selective trigger; 50 percent 20-gauge.

NIB	Exc.	V.G.	Good	Fair	Poor
1200	1000	850	750	550	400

BSS Grade II

Version features game scene engraving and satin coin finished receiver. Discontinued in 1984. **NOTE:** Add 50 percent for 20-gauge.

NIB	Exc.	V.G.	Good	Fair	Poor
3000	2500	1850	1400	1100	800

BSS Sporter

Version features English-style straight-grip stock and splinter forearm. Stock was oil-finished. Offered with 26" or 28" barrel. **NOTE:** Add 25 percent for 20-gauge.

NIB	Exc.	V.G.	Good	Fair	Poor
2400	2000	1550	975	650	400

BSS Sidelock

Version features engraved sidelock action. Offered in 12- or 20-gauge, with 26" or 28" barrel. Has straight-grip stock and splintered forearm. Manufactured in Korea between 1983 and 1987. Last few dozen 12-gauge sidelocks produced were an uncatalogued version of earlier guns. These guns had very finely engraved game scenes, with English scroll. Add 30 percent premium for this variation. **NOTE:** Add 30 percent to these prices for 20-gauge guns.

NIB	Exc.	V.G.	Good	Fair	Poor
4000	3500	2200	1750	800	500

CYNERGY SERIES

Series introduced in 2004. Browning calls it third generation over/under gun. Cynergy has a number of new design features such as monolock hinge system for lower profile, inflex recoil pad, new mechanical trigger system, adjustable comb, back-bored barrels and impact ejectors.

Cynergy Field

12-gauge 3" model features checkered walnut stock and forearm. Silver nitrate receiver with engraving. Choice of 26" or 28" ventilated rib barrels, with choke tubes. Weight about 7.75 lbs. Synthetic stock with adjustable comb offered. **NOTE:** Add $400 for Grade II/III oil-finished stock and engraved game birds on guns produced 2010 - 2014. Deduct $40 for synthetic stock.

NIB	Exc.	V.G.	Good	Fair	Poor
1600	1250	1000	800	700	600

Cynergy Classic Field

More traditionally styled 12-gauge was added to Cynergy line in 2006. Features steel receiver, with silver nitride finish and game bird scenes on each side. Satin finish walnut stock and schnabel style fore-end. Three choke tubes. Available in barrel lengths of 26" and 28". Average weight 7.75 lbs.

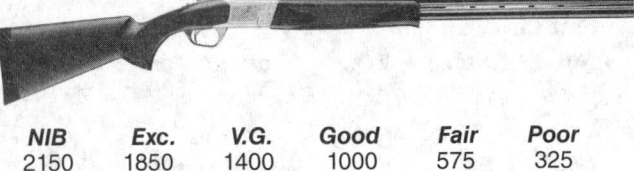

NIB	Exc.	V.G.	Good	Fair	Poor
2150	1850	1400	1000	575	325

Cynergy Field Small Gauge

Introduced in 2005. Chambered for 20-, 28-gauge and .410 bore. Choice of 26" or 28" ventilated rib barrels. Weight about 6.25 lbs.

NIB	Exc.	V.G.	Good	Fair	Poor
2100	1850	1450	1050	575	325

Cynergy Sporting

As above, with higher grade walnut stock. Choice of 28", 30" or 32" ventilated rib barrels, with choke tubes. Ported barrels. Hi-Viz front sight. Weight about 8 lbs. Synthetic stock with adjustable comb offered. **NOTE:** Deduct $40 for synthetic stock.

NIB	Exc.	V.G.	Good	Fair	Poor
2000	1600	1200	900	500	300

Cynergy Classic Sporting

New for 2006. Traditionally styled version of Cynergy Sporting. Available in 12-gauge, with 28", 30" or 32" ported barrels. Oil finish walnut stock, with schnabel fore-end. Browning logo on steel receiver, with silver nitride finish. Three Invector-Plus Midas Grade choke tubes. Average weight 7.75 lbs.

NIB	Exc.	V.G.	Good	Fair	Poor
2750	2200	1800	900	500	300

Cynergy Classic Field Grade III

Similar to Classic Cynergy Field, with full coverage high-relief engraving on receiver and top lever. Gloss finish Grade III/IV walnut.

NIB	Exc.	V.G.	Good	Fair	Poor
3400	2600	2000	1650	950	550

Cynergy Classic Field Grade VI

Similar to Cynergy Classic Field Grade III, with more extensive gold-highlighted engraving.

NIB	Exc.	V.G.	Good	Fair	Poor
5100	4200	3450	2300	1400	600

Cynergy Sporting Adjustable Comb

Similar to Cynergy Sporting, with comb adjustable for cast and drop. Average weight 8.2 lbs. Introduced 2006.

NIB	Exc.	V.G.	Good	Fair	Poor
2900	2000	1475	1050	750	450

Cynergy Sporting Small Gauge

As above in 20- or 28-gauge. Choice of 28", 30" or 32" ported barrels in 20-gauge; 28" or 30" ported barrels in 28-gauge. Weight about 6.25 to 6.5 lbs. depending on barrel length. Introduced in 2005.

NIB	Exc.	V.G.	Good	Fair	Poor
2300	1750	1200	850	625	400

Cynergy Feather

Lightweight Cynergy 12-gauge introduced in 2006; followed by 20-, 28-gauge and .410 bore versions in 2008. Satin finish walnut stock. Weight about 6.5 lbs. 12-gauge; 5 lbs. in others.

NIB	Exc.	V.G.	Good	Fair	Poor
2400	1800	1300	950	675	450

Cynergy Feather Composite

As above, with synthetic stock and fore-end. 12-gauge only.

NIB	Exc.	V.G.	Good	Fair	Poor
2300	1700	1200	950	675	450

Cynergy Euro Sporting

Sporting clays and skeet versions come in 2.75" 12- and 20-gauge, with 28", 30" or 32" barrels. Stock oil finish Grade III/IV walnut. Three choke tubes. Weight about 8 lbs. 12-gauge; 6.5 lbs. 20-gauge.

NIB	Exc.	V.G.	Good	Fair	Poor
3500	2800	2200	1650	950	550

Cynergy Euro Field

Similar to Cynergy Euro Sporting. Has Invenctor Plus tubes in 12- and 20-gauge. Standard Invector tubes on 28-gauge and .410 bore.

NIB	Exc.	V.G.	Good	Fair	Poor
2500	1900	1200	700	500	300

Cynergy Euro Sporting Composite with Adjustable Comb

Similar to Euro Sporting Composite, with adjustable comb.

NIB	Exc.	V.G.	Good	Fair	Poor
3800	3000	2000	1650	950	550

Cynergy Classic Trap Unsingle Combo

Trap shotgun in 12-gauge. Comes with double barrel set in 32/34", 32/32", 30/34" or 30/32". Gloss finish Monte Carlo Grade III/IV walnut stock, with right hand palm swell. Adjustable comb. Weight about 8.9 lbs. Four choke tubes. Aluminum fitted carrying case.

NIB	Exc.	V.G.	Good	Fair	Poor
4800	3800	2900	2250	1400	600

EARLY PRODUCTION AUTO-5

Series of recoil-operated semi-automatic shotguns. Designed by John M. Browning. Offered in 12- or 16-gauge. Barrel lengths 26", 28", 30" or 32", with various chokes and ribs. Has unique square-back action that has become instantly recognizable. Finish blued, with checkered walnut round-knob stock. Various versions differ in amount of ornamentation, type of rib, quality of materials and workmanship utilized in construction. Series manufactured in Belgium by FN between 1903 and 1939. First example appeared in U.S. in 1923. Pre-WWI 16-gauge guns introduced in 1936, had 2.5625" chambers; early models should be inspected by qualified gunsmith before firing.

NOTE: 16-gauge not converted to 2.75" chamber deduct 30 percent. Grade III or Grade IV prices are not nearly as affected by chamber length because of their rarity. Original pre-war barrels were serial numbered to gun. Extra barrels serial numbered to gun add $100 for plain barrels, $200 for matte rib barrels, $275 for ventilated rib barrels. Extra barrels on Grade IV guns add an additional 30 percent to these barrel prices. Prices given are for guns with original barrels serial numbered to gun. Remember safety is located in front of trigger guard. Deduct 10 to 25 percent for "suicide safety" in trigger guard.

Grade I—Plain Barrel

NIB	Exc.	V.G.	Good	Fair	Poor
—	850	750	600	400	275

Grade I—Matte Rib

NIB	Exc.	V.G.	Good	Fair	Poor
—	1100	975	800	550	350

Grade I—Vent Rib

NIB	Exc.	V.G.	Good	Fair	Poor
—	1000	900	725	525	325

Grade II—Plain Barrel

NIB	Exc.	V.G.	Good	Fair	Poor
—	1500	1200	1000	600	350

Grade II—Matte Rib

NIB	Exc.	V.G.	Good	Fair	Poor
—	2000	1500	1150	700	350

Grade II—Vent Rib

NIB	Exc.	V.G.	Good	Fair	Poor
—	1900	1400	1050	500	350

Grade III—Plain Barrel

NIB	Exc.	V.G.	Good	Fair	Poor
—	2800	1900	1350	775	385

Grade III—Matte Rib

NIB	Exc.	V.G.	Good	Fair	Poor
—	3600	3000	2000	900	450

Grade III—Vent Rib

NIB	Exc.	V.G.	Good	Fair	Poor
—	3500	2900	1850	800	400

Grade IV—Plain Barrel

NIB	Exc.	V.G.	Good	Fair	Poor
—	4000	3500	2500	1000	500

Grade IV—Matte Rib

NIB	Exc.	V.G.	Good	Fair	Poor
—	4500	3800	2850	1200	700

Grade IV—Vent Rib

NIB	Exc.	V.G.	Good	Fair	Poor
—	4400	3700	2750	1100	600

American Browning Auto-5

Recoil-operated semi-automatic shotgun was another variation of early-production Auto-5. Chambered for 12-, 16- or 20-gauge. Manufactured by Remington Company for Browning. Quite similar to Remington's Model 11 shotgun. Features Browning logo and different type of engraving. Approximately 45,000 manufactured between 1940 and 1942. **NOTE:** Add 20 percent for ventilated rib; 10 percent for 20-gauge.

NIB	Exc.	V.G.	Good	Fair	Poor
—	675	575	450	375	200

MID-PRODUCTION AUTO-5—FN MANUFACTURE STANDARD WEIGHT

Version of recoil-operated semi-automatic Auto-5 shotguns. Manufactured by FN in Belgium between 1952 and 1976. Offered in 12- or 16-gauge, with 26" through 32" barrels. Various chokes. Finish blued, with checkered walnut stock. Black buttplate marked "Browning Automatic" with "FN" in center oval. Guns made prior to 1967 will be found with round knob pistol-grips. Flatbottom variation introduced in 1967. **NOTE:** Add 25 percent for guns with round-knob pistol-grip; 35 percent for straight-grip stock; 20 percent for 16-gauge guns NIB or excellent condition.

Plain Barrel

NIB	Exc.	V.G.	Good	Fair	Poor
1100	900	800	650	400	300

Matte Rib

NIB	Exc.	V.G.	Good	Fair	Poor
1400	1100	900	700	500	350

Vent Rib

NIB	Exc.	V.G.	Good	Fair	Poor
1300	1000	850	650	450	325

Auto-5 Lightweight

Version chambered for 12- or 20-gauge. Featured lighter-weight scroll-engraved receiver. Manufactured between 1952 and 1976 by FN. 20-gauge introduced in 1958. **NOTE:** Add 15 percent for ventilated rib; 50 percent for 20-gauge.

NIB	Exc.	V.G.	Good	Fair	Poor
1200	900	650	550	450	350

Auto-5 Magnum

Version featured 3" chambers. Offered with 26" through 32" full-choke barrels. Manufactured between 1958 and 1976 by FN. 12-gauge introduced in 1958; 20-gauge in 1967. **NOTE:** Add 20 percent for ventilated rib; 50 percent for 20-gauge.

NIB	Exc.	V.G.	Good	Fair	Poor
1100	850	600	500	400	300

Auto-5 Skeet

Version similar to Lightweight Model. Chambered for 12- or 20-gauge, with 26" or 28" ventilated rib skeet-choked barrel. **NOTE:** Add 50 percent for 20-gauge.

NIB	Exc.	V.G.	Good	Fair	Poor
1250	1000	700	600	450	350

Auto-5 Trap Model

Version similar to standard-weight model, except chambered for 12-gauge only, with 30" ventilated rib full-choke barrel. Manufactured by FN until 1971.

NIB	Exc.	V.G.	Good	Fair	Poor
1200	900	650	550	450	350

Sweet Sixteen

Version similar to standard-weight. Chambered for 16-gauge only. Has gold-plated trigger. Manufactured by FN between 1936 and 1976. Not all A-5 16-gauges are Sweet Sixteens. Look for gold-plated trigger "Sweet Sixteen" script and lack of a suicide safety. **NOTE:** Add 50 percent for matte or ventilated rib in NIB or excellent condition; 25 percent for others.

NIB	Exc.	V.G.	Good	Fair	Poor
1650	1500	1100	900	550	400

Buck Special

Version features 24" cylinder-bore barrel, with adjustable rifle sights. Produced in 12- and 20-gauge 2.75" and 3" Magnum chambers; 16-gauge with 2.75" chambers. Manufactured by FN between 1963 and 1976. Prices for 12-gauge guns. **NOTE:** Add 50 percent for 16- or 20-gauge.

NIB	Exc.	V.G.	Good	Fair	Poor
1250	1000	800	650	450	350

Two Millionth Commemorative

Version commemorated two millionth Auto-5 shotgun produced by FN. Engraved with special high-polish blue finish. High-grade checkered wal-nut stock. Furnished in a black fitted case along with a book on Browning Company. There were 2,500 manufactured between 1971 and 1974. As with all commemoratives, it must be NIB to realize its top potential.

NIB	Exc.	V.G.	Good	Fair	Poor
3200	1850	950	625	475	300

LATE PRODUCTION AUTO-5 — B.C. MIROKU MANUFACTURE

In 1976 production of Auto-5 shotgun was begun by B.C. Miroku in Japan. This move was accomplished after approximately 2,750,000 Auto-5 shotguns were manufactured by FN in Belgium between 1903 and 1976. Japanese-manufactured guns, in the opinion of many knowledgeable people, show no less quality or functionality but are simply not as desirable from a collector's standpoint. In 1999 Browning discontinued production of Auto-5 shotgun.

NOTE: Since discontinuance of Auto-5, values for Japanese examples have risen, approaching those of Belgian guns.

Auto-5 Light 12

Version chambered for 12-gauge 2.75" chamber only. Offered with lightweight receiver. Barrel has ventilated rib and choke tubes. Introduced in 1975.

NIB	Exc.	V.G.	Good	Fair	Poor
950	800	675	500	400	350

Auto-5 Light 20

Version similar to Light 12. Chambered for 20-gauge only.

NIB	Exc.	V.G.	Good	Fair	Poor
1200	1000	850	700	500	400

Auto-5 Magnum

Version features 3" chambers. Offered with 26", 28", 30" or 32" barrels. Introduced in 1976 by Miroku. Discontinued in 1996.

NIB	Exc.	V.G.	Good	Fair	Poor
1000	800	600	450	350	300

Auto-5 Buck Special

Version has 24" barrel cylinder-bored with adjustable sights. Introduced by Miroku in 1976.

NIB	Exc.	V.G.	Good	Fair	Poor
1000	800	600	450	350	300

Auto-5 Skeet

Competition model features 26" or 28" skeet-bored barrels, with ventilated rib. Manufactured between 1976 and 1983 by Miroku.

NIB	Exc.	V.G.	Good	Fair	Poor
825	550	450	350	—	200

Sweet Sixteen

Version similar to Belgian-produced Sweet Sixteen. Offered standard with ventilated rib and screw-in Invector choke tubes. Introduced in 1988 by Miroku. Discontinued in 1992.

NIB	Exc.	V.G.	Good	Fair	Poor
1350	1100	750	550	375	225

A-5 DU 50th Anniversary

High-grade version of Auto-5. Produced to commemorate 50th Anniversary of Ducks Unlimited. Highly engraved. Features high-gloss bluing and fancy checkered walnut stock. Approximately 5,500 manufactured by Miroku in 1987. Auctioned by Ducks Unlimited chapters to raise money for their organization. Because of this fact, it is difficult to furnish an accurate value. Commemorative firearms must be NIB with all furnished materials to command premium collector value. We furnish what we feel is a general value.

NIB	Exc.	V.G.	Good	Fair	Poor
3000	2000	800	600	450	300

A-5 DU Sweet Sixteen

Special version of Miroku-manufactured Sweet Sixteen. Auctioned by Ducks Unlimited chapters in 1988. There were 5,500 produced. All specifications and cautions that were furnished for 50th Anniversary gun also apply here.

NIB	Exc.	V.G.	Good	Fair	Poor
2500	1500	850	600	400	300

Auto-5 Classic

Special limited edition series of A-5 shotguns built in 12-gauge only. Classic is photo-etched with game scenes on silver gray receiver. 5,000 of these guns were manufactured in 1984. Gold Classic similar in appearance, but features gold inlays and limited to 500 guns.

Classic

NIB	Exc.	V.G.	Good	Fair	Poor
2000	1675	1200	750	525	300

Gold Classic

Produced by FN.

NIB	Exc.	V.G.	Good	Fair	Poor
8500	7000	5000	3000	—	—

Auto-5 Light Buck Special

Lightweight version of Buck Special. Chambered for 2.75" shell. Fitted with 24" ventilated rib barrel. Conventional choked for slug or buckshot. Barrel has adjustable rear sight and ramp front sight. Weight 8 lbs.

NIB	Exc.	V.G.	Good	Fair	Poor
850	650	550	450	375	225

Auto-5 Stalker

New for 1992. Available in lightweight or Magnum version. Light Stalker available in 12-gauge, with 26" or 28" barrel and choke tubes. Magnum Stalker offered in 12-gauge (3" chamber), with 28" or 30" barrel and choke tubes. Weight: Light Stalker 8 lbs. 4 oz.; Magnum Stalker 8 lbs. 11 oz.

Light Stalker

NIB	Exc.	V.G.	Good	Fair	Poor
775	600	550	400	300	225

Magnum Stalker

NIB	Exc.	V.G.	Good	Fair	Poor
800	650	600	375	275	250

Auto-5 Final Tribute Limited Edition

Introduced in 1999. Commemorative A-5 limited to 1,000 shotguns. Represents final production of this model. Chambered for 12-gauge shell. Fitted with 28" ventilated rib barrel. Has special engraved receiver.

NIB	Exc.	V.G.	Good	Fair	Poor
5000	3750	2500	2000	1300	500

Browning A5

With squared "hump-back" receiver, A5 similar in appearance to Classic Auto-5. Totally different semi-automatic shotgun. Operates with Browning's new short-recoil Kinematic action. In 12-gauge only, with 3" chamber. A5 designed to function with a wide range of 2.75" and 3" loads. Barrel length 26", 28" or 30", with ventilated rib. Brass bead front, ivory bead middle sights and three Invector DS choke tubes. A5 Hunter model has checkered walnut stock. Also offered with black composite stock (A5 Stalker) or Mossy Oak Duck Blind or Break-Up Infinity camo finish or with black composite stock. All are shim adjustable for cast and drop. Introduced in 2012. **NOTE:** Deduct $100 for Stalker model.

NIB	Exc.	V.G.	Good	Fair	Poor
1400	1200	950	700	350	250

Browning A5 Ultimate

Higher-trade variation with brushed satin finish. Engraved receiver, with intricate scroll pheasants and mallards. Other features include: oil-finished Grade III walnut stock, ivory middle bead, fiber optic front sight and Vector Pro lengthened forcing cone.

NIB	Exc.	V.G.	Good	Fair	Poor
1600	1350	1000	750	400	250

Browning A5 Sweet Sixteen

Same features as standard A5, except chambered for 16-gauge. Offered with 26" or 28" barrel, with 2.75" chamber, and bi-tone receiver.

NIB	Exc.	V.G.	Good	Fair	Poor
1550	1300	1000	700	400	250

Double Automatic Shotgun

Short recoil-operated semi-automatic shotgun. Chambered for 12-gauge only. Offered with 26", 28" or 30" barrels plain or ventilated rib. Has various chokes. Receiver steel. Finish blued or silver, with checkered walnut stock. Tubular magazine holds only two shots—hence its name. Manufactured between 1954 and 1972. **NOTE:** Add 25 percent for ventilated rib.

NIB	Exc.	V.G.	Good	Fair	Poor
1000	800	650	550	400	250

Twelvette Double Auto

Version similar to Double Automatic, except has aircraft aluminum alloy frame color-anodized in blue, silver, green, brown or black. Red-, gold- or royal blue-colored receivers were rarest colors and would command approximately 50 to 75 percent premium. Offered with plain or ventilated rib barrel. Approximately 65,000 produced between 1954 and 1972. **NOTE:** Add 25 percent for ventilated rib.

NIB	Exc.	V.G.	Good	Fair	Poor
1050	850	725	600	450	300

Twentyweight Double Auto

Version similar in all respects to Twelvette, except .75 lb. lighter. Offered with 26.5" barrel. Manufactured between 1952 and 1971. **NOTE:** Add 25 percent for ventilated rib.

NIB	Exc.	V.G.	Good	Fair	Poor
1100	900	800	700	500	350

2000 SERIES

B-2000

Gas-operated semi-automatic shotgun. Chambered for 12- or 20-gauge. Offered with 26", 28" or 30" ventilated rib barrel and various chokes. Finish blued, with checkered walnut stock. Assembled in Portugal from parts manufactured by FN in Belgium. Approximately 115,000 imported between 1974 and 1981.

NIB	Exc.	V.G.	Good	Fair	Poor
625	550	475	300	225	175

B-2000 Magnum

Version features barrel with 3" chambers. Offered standard with recoil pad.

NIB	Exc.	V.G.	Good	Fair	Poor
775	575	500	300	225	175

B-2000 Buck Special

Version has 24" cylinder-bored barrel, with rifle sights.

NIB	Exc.	V.G.	Good	Fair	Poor
625	475	425	275	225	175

B-2000 Trap

Version has 30" full-choke barrel, with floating rib. Monte Carlo-type trap stock.

NIB	Exc.	V.G.	Good	Fair	Poor
600	475	425	275	225	175

B-2000 Skeet

Version features 26" skeet-bored barrel, with floating ventilated rib. Skeet-type stock. **NOTE:** Add 20 percent for 20-gauge gun.

NIB	Exc.	V.G.	Good	Fair	Poor
—	595	450	375	275	200

80 SERIES

B-80

Gas-operated semi-automatic shotgun. Chambered for 12- or 20-gauge. Features 3" Magnum potential by simply exchanging barrel. Features various-length barrels. Offered with screw-in Invector chokes as of 1985. Receiver steel or lightweight aluminum alloy. Finish blued, with checkered walnut stock. Assembled in Portugal from parts manufactured by Beretta in Italy. Manufactured between 1981 and 1988. **NOTE:** Add 20 percent for 20-gauge gun.

NIB	Exc.	V.G.	Good	Fair	Poor
—	550	450	375	325	225

B-80 Buck Special

Version features 24" cylinder-bored barrel, with rifle sights. Discontinued in 1984.

NIB	Exc.	V.G.	Good	Fair	Poor
—	495	400	350	300	200

B-80 DU Commemorative

Version was produced to be auctioned by American Ducks Unlimited chapters. In order to realize collector potential, it must be NIB with all supplied materials. Values supplied are general.

NIB	Exc.	V.G.	Good	Fair	Poor
950	650	550	425	325	275

GOLD SERIES

Gold 10

First introduced in 1993. Gas-operated 5-shot semi-automatic shotgun. Chambered for 10-gauge shell. Offered with 26", 28" or 30" ventilated rib barrel. Standard model has walnut stock, blued receiver and barrel.

Stalker Model fitted with graphite composite stock, non-glare finish on receiver and barrel. Both models fitted with choke tubes. Weight about 10 lbs. 10 oz.

NIB	Exc.	V.G.	Good	Fair	Poor
950	700	550	450	300	150

Gold Evolve

Introduced in 2004. Updated version of original Gold gun. Features newly designed receiver, magazine cap, ventilated rib design, checkering pattern and Hi-Viz sights. Offered in 12-gauge 3" chamber. Choice of 26", 28" or 30" barrel, with choke tubes. Weight about 7 lbs. for 28" model.

NIB	Exc.	V.G.	Good	Fair	Poor
1195	875	700	525	400	225

Gold Light 10 Gauge Camo

10-gauge offered with 26" or 28" barrels and Mossy Oak or Shadow Grass camo. Lightweight alloy receiver reduces weight to 9 lb. 10 oz. Introduced in 2001.

NIB	Exc.	V.G.	Good	Fair	Poor
1275	975	775	595	450	250

Gold 10 Gauge Combo

10-gauge has choice of two ventilated rib barrels in lengths of 24"/26" or 24"/28". Walnut stock, with black ventilated recoil pad. Weight with 28" barrels about 10 lbs. 10 oz.

NIB	Exc.	V.G.	Good	Fair	Poor
1150	800	675	500	375	250

Gold Stalker

NIB	Exc.	V.G.	Good	Fair	Poor
1025	725	550	450	300	150

Gold Classic Stalker

Introduced in 1999. Features classic Browning squared receiver and shim-adjustable stock. Chambered for 12-gauge shells. Choice of 26" or 28" ventilated rib barrels. Has 3" chambers. Black synthetic stock. Weight about 7 lbs. 3 oz.

NIB	Exc.	V.G.	Good	Fair	Poor
850	675	550	400	275	125

Gold 3-1/2" 12 Gauge

Introduced in 1997. Features 3.5" chamber. Can operate 2.75" or 3" shells as well. Choice of barrel lengths from 26" to 30". Invector-Plus chokes. Magazine capacity: 4/2.75" shells; 3/3" shells; or 3/3.5" shells. Weight about 7 lbs. 10 oz.

NIB	Exc.	V.G.	Good	Fair	Poor
1000	795	595	450	200	150

Gold 12 Gauge Hunter

Introduced in 1994. Semi-automatic shotgun built on same gas operating system as Gold 10. Offered with 26", 28" or 30" barrel. Magazine capacity: 4/3" shells. Walnut stock has full checkered pistol-grip, with black rubber recoil pad. Invector-Plus choke tubes supplied. Weight about 7.5 lbs. Available (1998) in Stalker version, with non-glare matte metal parts and stocks.

NIB	Exc.	V.G.	Good	Fair	Poor
750	525	400	300	200	150

Gold Classic Hunter

Introduced in 1999. Features squared receiver, fully adjustable selected walnut stock and deep blued barrels. Choice of 26", 28" or 30" ventilated rib barrel. Offered with 3" chamber 12-gauge only.

NIB	Exc.	V.G.	Good	Fair	Poor
850	600	500	400	275	225

Gold Classic 20 Gauge

Offered with 26" or 28" ventilated rib barrels and select walnut stock. Shim-adjustable. Squared receiver. Weight about 6 lbs. 12 oz. Introduced in 1999.

NIB	Exc.	V.G.	Good	Fair	Poor
795	600	500	400	275	225

Gold Classic High Grade

Introduced in 1999. Features traditional square receiver, with engraved silver gray finish. Offered in 12-gauge only, with 3" chambers and 28" ventilated rib barrel. Select walnut stock. Weight about 7 lbs. 6 oz.

NIB	Exc.	V.G.	Good	Fair	Poor
1500	1200	775	500	225	165

Gold Deer Hunter

Introduced in 1997. Features choice of fully rifled or smooth bore barrel and Invector choke system. Both versions come with cantilever scope mount. Stock and forearm select walnut. Receiver has non-glare black finish. Barrel satin finish. Barrel length 22" on both barrels. Weight about 7 lbs. 12 oz. Price listed for smoothbore barrel. **NOTE:** Add $40 for fully rifled version.

NIB	Exc.	V.G.	Good	Fair	Poor
875	650	500	400	200	150

Gold Deer Hunter 20 Gauge

Same as above. Chambered for 20-gauge 3" shell. Furnished with fully rifled 22" barrel. Cantilever scope mount. Introduced in 2001.

NIB	Exc.	V.G.	Good	Fair	Poor
1025	900	625	495	300	200

Gold Deer Stalker

Introduced in 1999. Same as above. Fitted with black synthetic stock.

NIB	Exc.	V.G.	Good	Fair	Poor
950	700	600	500	300	150

Gold Deer Mossy Oak

Introduced in 1999. Camo finish.

NIB	Exc.	V.G.	Good	Fair	Poor
825	675	575	450	200	125

Gold Waterfowl Mossy Oak Shadow Grass

Introduced in 1999. Camo finish.

NIB	Exc.	V.G.	Good	Fair	Poor
950	700	600	500	200	125

Gold Waterfowl Mossy Oak Breakup

Introduced in 2000. Camo finish.

NIB	Exc.	V.G.	Good	Fair	Poor
950	700	575	450	200	125

Gold Turkey/Waterfowl Mossy Oak

Introduced in 1999. Camo finish.

NIB	Exc.	V.G.	Good	Fair	Poor
950	700	575	450	200	125

Gold Turkey/Waterfowl Stalker

Introduced in 1999. Features black synthetic stock, 24" barrel, Hi-Viz sight and 3" or 3.5" chambers. Weight about 7 lbs. 4 oz.

NIB	Exc.	V.G.	Good	Fair	Poor
900	650	575	450	200	125

Gold Turkey/Waterfowl Hunter

12-gauge 3" or 3.5" chambered gun. Offered with 24" ventilated rib barrel. Select walnut stock, with black ventilated recoil pad. Weight about 7 lbs. Introduced in 1999.

NIB	Exc.	V.G.	Good	Fair	Poor
875	625	550	450	200	125

Gold NWTF Series

Model finished in Mossy Oak Breakup pattern. Bears "NWTF" logo on buttstock. Fitted with 24" barrel, Hi-Viz front sight, X-full extended Turkey choke. Offered in configurations listed.

Gold Light 10 Gauge

NIB	Exc.	V.G.	Good	Fair	Poor
1350	950	775	600	425	175

Gold 12 Gauge

3.5" Chamber, Shadow Grass

NIB	Exc.	V.G.	Good	Fair	Poor
1275	900	725	550	375	150

3" Chamber

NIB	Exc.	V.G.	Good	Fair	Poor
1100	775	650	575	375	150

3.5" Chamber Ultimate Turkey Gun

NIB	Exc.	V.G.	Good	Fair	Poor
1280	1000	900	725	375	200

Gold Hunter

Chambered for 12- and 20-gauge. Offered in 26" or 28" barrel lengths. Weight about 6.8 lbs.

NIB	Exc.	V.G.	Good	Fair	Poor
750	625	400	300	200	150

Gold Sporting Clays

Introduced in 1996. Features ported barrel in 28" or 30" lengths. Recoil pad standard. Weight about 7.5 lbs.

NIB	Exc.	V.G.	Good	Fair	Poor
800	675	475	375	200	150

Gold Ladies/Youth Sporting Clays

Offered in 12-gauge only, with 2.75" chambers. Features 28" ventilated rib barrel. Overall dimensions have been adjusted to fit women. Black solid recoil pad. Weight about 7 lbs. 6 oz. Introduced in 1999.

NIB	Exc.	V.G.	Good	Fair	Poor
1200	895	625	450	300	125

Gold "Golden Clays" Ladies Sporting Clays

Introduced in 2005. 12-gauge 2.75" chambered gun. Fitted with 28" ventilated rib ported barrel, with 4 choke tubes. Silver receiver engraved with gold enhancements. Weight about 7.75 lbs.

NIB	Exc.	V.G.	Good	Fair	Poor
1500	1375	1050	800	575	300

Gold "Golden Clays" Sporting Clays

As above, with standard stock dimensions. Choice of 28" or 30" barrels. Introduced in 2005.

NIB	Exc.	V.G.	Good	Fair	Poor
1800	1300	1050	800	575	300

Gold Micro

Introduced in 2001. Features 20-gauge gun, with 26" barrel, smaller pistol-grip, shorter length of pull. Back-bored barrel, with choke tubes. Weight about 6 lb. 10 oz.

NIB	Exc.	V.G.	Good	Fair	Poor
925	650	575	475	300	125

Gold Upland

Offered in 12- or 20-gauge. Barrel lengths: 12-gauge 24"; 20-gauge 26". Straight-grip stock with 3" chamber. Weight: 12-gauge 7 lbs.; 20-gauge 6.75 lbs. Introduced in 2001.

NIB	Exc.	V.G.	Good	Fair	Poor
950	700	600	475	300	125

Gold Fusion

Features a new style ventilated rib, adjustable comb pro-comp sight and five choke tubes. Offered in 12-gauge, 3" chambers with 26" or 28" barrels. Introduced in 2001. In 2002 offered in 20-gauge as well as 12-gauge, with choice of 26" or 28" ventilated rib barrel. Weight about: 12-gauge 7 lbs.; 20-gauge 6.5 lbs.

NIB	Exc.	V.G.	Good	Fair	Poor
900	725	650	495	300	125

Gold Fusion High Grade

Similar to Gold Fusion. Addition of high grade Turkish walnut stock, silver nitride receiver with game scene in gold. Five choke tubes and hard case standard. Introduced in 2005.

NIB	Exc.	V.G.	Good	Fair	Poor
1600	1250	900	625	450	300

Golden Clays

Introduced in 1999. Chambered for 12-gauge shell with 2.74" chamber. Choice of 28" or 30" ventilated rib ported barrels. Engraved silver gray receiver. Select walnut stock. Weight about 7 lbs. 3 oz.

NIB	Exc.	V.G.	Good	Fair	Poor
1250	1000	825	675	425	300

Gold Superlite Hunter

Introduced in 2006. Uses an aluminum alloy receiver and alloy magazine tube to reduce weight to about 7 lbs. in 12-gauge. Gloss finish walnut stock. Available with 3" or 3.5" chamber and 26" or 28" barrel. Magazine cut-off feature on 3.5" model. A 6.5 lb. 20-gauge with 3" chamber and 26" or 28" barrel also offered. Three choke tubes. **NOTE:** Add 15 percent for 3.5" chamber.

NIB	Exc.	V.G.	Good	Fair	Poor
900	650	575	475	300	125

Gold Superlite FLD Hunter

Similar to Gold Superlite Hunter, with semi-humpback style receiver, satin finish walnut stock and 3" chamber only. Magazine cut-off on 12-gauge models. Adjustable shim system and three choke tubes.

NIB	Exc.	V.G.	Good	Fair	Poor
925	650	575	475	300	125

Gold Superlite Micro

Similar to Gold Superlite Hunter, with compact dimensions for smaller shooters. Only in 20-gauge, with 26" barrel. Weight about 6.25 lbs. Three choke tubes.

NIB	Exc.	V.G.	Good	Fair	Poor
925	650	575	475	300	125

500 SERIES

A-500G/A-500R

Self-adjusting gas-operated semi-automatic shotgun. Chambered for 12-gauge only. Offered with 26", 28" or 30" barrels, with ventilated rib and screw-in Invector choke tubes. Has 3" chambers. Can fire any load interchangeably. Finish blued, with checkered walnut stock and recoil pad. Features light engraving. Introduced in 1987. The 2008 recoil version (A-500R) has a slightly better reputation for functioning than gas-operated A-500G. Values are roughly similar.

NIB	Exc.	V.G.	Good	Fair	Poor
575	490	425	350	275	225

A-500G Sporting Clays

Gas-operated version designed for sporting clays. Features choice of 28" or 30" ventilated rib barrel, with semi-gloss finish and gold lettering "Sporting Clays". Ventilated recoil pad standard. Weight about 8 lbs.

NIB	Exc.	V.G.	Good	Fair	Poor
550	425	350	300	200	150

A-500R Hunting Model

Similar in appearance to A-500G, except this model operates on a short recoil design. Buttstock features full pistol-grip. Available with 26", 28" or 30" ventilated rib barrels. Choke tubes standard. Weight about 7 lbs. 13 oz.

NIB	Exc.	V.G.	Good	Fair	Poor
475	385	300	250	200	150

A-500R Buck Special

Same as Hunting Model, with addition of adjustable rear sight, contoured front ramp sight and gold bead. Choke tubes standard, as is 24" barrel. Weight 7 lbs. 11 oz.

NIB	Exc.	V.G.	Good	Fair	Poor
500	425	350	300	225	150

SILVER SERIES

Value-priced series of gas-operated autoloaders. Introduced in 2006. All models feature semi-humpback design and aluminum alloy receiver. Weights vary from 7.25 to 7.5 lbs. depending on barrel length and stock material. Three choke tubes provided with all models.

Silver Hunter

Features satin finish walnut stock and fore-end. Available with 3" chambers in 26", 28" and 30" barrel lengths; 3.5" chamber in 26" or 28" barrel lengths. A 20-gauge version with 26" or 28" barrels became available in 2008. **NOTE:** Add 15 percent for 3.5" chamber.

NIB	Exc.	V.G.	Good	Fair	Poor
1000	850	700	500	400	250

Silver Stalker

Similar to Silver Hunter, with matte black composite stock and fore-end. Sling swivel studs. 3.5" chamber only.

NIB	Exc.	V.G.	Good	Fair	Poor
825	675	550	375	275	175

Silver Micro

20-gauge, with 26" barrel. Shorter stock dimensions for smaller shooters.

NIB	Exc.	V.G.	Good	Fair	Poor
825	695	550	375	275	175

Silver Sporting Micro

This 2.75" 12-gauge includes adjustment spacers for changing stock length. Barrel is 28". Three choke tubes included. Weight about 7 lbs.

NIB	Exc.	V.G.	Good	Fair	Poor
1150	900	725	600	375	250

Silver NWTF

New in 2008. This 3" 12-gauge turkey gun is fully camouflaged with Mossy Oak's New Break-Up pattern. Barrel 24" outfitted with fiber-optic rifle sights. Weight about 7 lbs. **NOTE:** Add 10 percent for 3.5" chamber.

NIB	Exc.	V.G.	Good	Fair	Poor
1100	900	725	600	375	250

Silver Rifled Deer

New in 2008. This 3" 12-gauge slug gun features rifled barrel, with cantilever scope mount. Finishes include satin walnut, black composite and Mossy Oak New Break-Up camo. **NOTE:** Add 10 percent for camo finish.

NIB	Exc.	V.G.	Good	Fair	Poor
1100	900	725	600	375	250

Silver–Mossy Oak

Similar to Silver Stalker. Choice of Mossy Oak New Break-Up with 26" barrel or Mossy Oak New Shadow Grass with 26" or 28" barrel.

NIB	Exc.	V.G.	Good	Fair	Poor
925	650	575	475	300	125

MAXUS SERIES

Introduced in 2009. Replacement for Gold line.

Maxus

Autoloading shotgun chambered for 3" or 3.5" shells. Aluminum receiver, lightweight profile 26" or 28" barrel with ventilated rib, composite stock, Vector Pro lengthened forcing cone, DuraTouch Armor Coating overall. Weight 6.875 lbs.

Maxus Stalker

Matte black finish overall. **NOTE:** Add $150 for 3.5" chamber.

NIB	Exc.	V.G.	Good	Fair	Poor
1200	975	800	625	475	300

Maxus Mossy Oak Duck Blind

Mossy Oak Duck Blind finish overall. **NOTE:** Add $150 for 3.5" chamber.

NIB	Exc.	V.G.	Good	Fair	Poor
1300	975	800	625	475	300

Maxus Hunter

Gas-operated auto-loader available with 3" or 3.5" Magnum chambers. Barrel lengths: 26", 28", 30" (22" for rifled version). Lengthened forcing cone. Stock is shim-adjustable for length of pull, cast and drop. Glossy-finished walnut stock, with 22 lpi checkering. Maxus Hunter and Rifled

Deer version offered in Mossy Oak Break-Up Infinity camo finish. Weight about 7 lbs. Introduced in 2011.

NIB	Exc.	V.G.	Good	Fair	Poor
1200	1000	850	650	400	300

Maxus Sporting Carbon

Gas-operated 12-gauge auto-loader, with 3" chamber. Aluminum alloy receiver has satin nickel finish, laser engraving. Barrel lengths 28" and 30". Gloss-finished high-grade walnut stock. Available with carbon fiber stock and Rifled Deer Stalker version with cantilevered scope base and 22" barrel. New 2011. **NOTE:** Deduct 15 percent for Deer Stalker/Carbon

NIB	Exc.	V.G.	Good	Fair	Poor
1390	1200	950	700	450	350

Maxus Sporting Golden Clays

Top of the Maxus line, with satin nickel finished receiver, gold enhanced engraving, grade III walnut stock and fore-end. Features include a High Viz fiber optic front sight, extra fast trigger lock time, stock adjustable for length of pull, cast and comb height.

NIB	Exc.	V.G.	Good	Fair	Poor
1700	1500	1150	850	400	250

BPS SERIES

Slide-action shotgun chambered for 10-, 12- or 20-gauge. Offered with various length ventilated rib barrels, with screw-in Invector chokes. Features 3" Magnum chambers, bottom-ejection system that effectively makes it ambidextrous. Has double slide bars and 5-shot tubular magazine. Constructed of all steel. Introduced by B.C. Miroku in 1977.

BPS Field Grade

NIB	Exc.	V.G.	Good	Fair	Poor
350	300	275	200	200	150

28 Gauge

Introduced in 1994. Weight approximately 7 lbs.

NIB	Exc.	V.G.	Good	Fair	Poor
425	325	295	225	210	150

BPS Magnum

10- or 12-gauge, 3.5" chambers.

NIB	Exc.	V.G.	Good	Fair	Poor
510	400	350	300	250	150

BPS Waterfowl 12 Gauge Camo

Introduced in 1999.

NIB	Exc.	V.G.	Good	Fair	Poor
525	425	350	300	250	150

BPS Waterfowl 12 Gauge Mossy Oak Break-Up

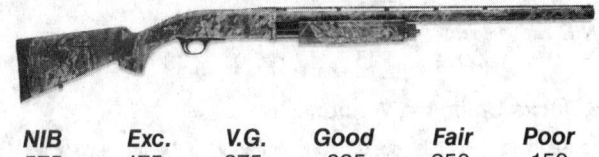

NIB	Exc.	V.G.	Good	Fair	Poor
575	475	375	325	250	150

BPS Mossy Oak New Break-up

Similar to BPS Hunter, with Mossy Oak New Break-up camo finish overall; chambers 3" and 3.5"; 12-gauge only.

NIB	Exc.	V.G.	Good	Fair	Poor
750	625	400	300	200	150

BPS Mossy Oak Duck Blind

Similar to above, with Mossy Oak Duck Blind finish overall.

NIB	Exc.	V.G.	Good	Fair	Poor
750	625	400	300	200	150

BPS Rifled Deer Mossy Oak New Break-up

Similar to BPS Rifled Deer Hunter, with Mossy Oak New Break-up camo finish overall.

NIB	Exc.	V.G.	Good	Fair	Poor
750	625	400	300	200	150

BPS NWTF Series

Model finished in Mossy Oak Breakup pattern. Bears NWTF logo on buttstock. Fitted with 24" barrel, Hi-Viz front sight, Extra Full extended turkey choke. Introduced in 2001. Offered in configurations listed.

10 Gauge

NIB	Exc.	V.G.	Good	Fair	Poor
625	475	400	325	200	125

12 Gauge 3.5" Chamber

NIB	Exc.	V.G.	Good	Fair	Poor
625	475	400	325	200	125

12 Gauge 3" Chamber

NIB	Exc.	V.G.	Good	Fair	Poor
550	450	375	325	200	125

BPS Stalker

Matte finish black stock.

NIB	Exc.	V.G.	Good	Fair	Poor
435	390	325	275	200	150

BPS Stalker—Combo

Combination of 28" ventilated rib barrel and choice of 22" fully rifle barrel or 20.5" Invector barrel, with Extra Full turkey choke. Introduced in 2000.

NIB	Exc.	V.G.	Good	Fair	Poor
650	525	475	325	200	125

BPS Game Gun

These models are designed for turkey and deer hunting. Introduced in 1992 in 12-gauge only, with 20.5" barrel. Turkey Special has fixed extra-full-choke barrel, while Deer Special originally came with 5" rifled tube. In 1998, a fully rifled barrel became an option for Deer Special. In 2007, a 20-gauge version was introduced. Turkey Special is drilled and tapped for scope mounts. Deer Special has cantilever mounting system plus iron sights. **NOTE:** Deduct 15 percent for Deer Special without a fully rifled barrel.

Game Gun Deer Special (shown above)

NIB	Exc.	V.G.	Good	Fair	Poor
600	500	425	375	325	250

Game Gun Turkey Special

NIB	Exc.	V.G.	Good	Fair	Poor
400	375	350	325	300	250

BPS 10 Gauge Mossy Oak Shadow Grass Camo

Introduced in 1999.

NIB	Exc.	V.G.	Good	Fair	Poor
575	475	375	325	175	125

BPS 10 Gauge Turkey

Fitted with 24" ventilated rib barrel, black synthetic stock and black solid recoil pad. Introduced in 1999. Weight about 9 lbs. 2 oz.

NIB	Exc.	V.G.	Good	Fair	Poor
525	425	375	325	200	125

BPS Micro 20 Gauge

Features 22" ventilated rib barrel, shorter pistol-grip stock and lighter-weight. Weight about 6.75 lbs. Introduced in 2001.

NIB	Exc.	V.G.	Good	Fair	Poor
450	350	300	250	200	125

BPS Upland Special

Chambered for 20-gauge shell. Fitted with 22" ventilated rib barrel. Walnut stock is straight-grip. Weight about 6.5 lbs. Available in 12- or

20-gauge, with 22" barrel. A 16-gauge version, with 24" or 26" barrel introduced in 2008. A very beautiful little pump.

NIB	Exc.	V.G.	Good	Fair	Poor
550	375	300	275	200	125

BPS Small Gauge

Introduced in 2000. Chambered for 28-gauge and .410 bore. The 28-gauge offered with choice of 26" or 28" ventilated rib barrel and Invector chokes. The .410 available with 26" ventilated rib barrel and Invector chokes. Weight about 6.75 lbs. each.

NIB	Exc.	V.G.	Good	Fair	Poor
525	450	325	275	200	125

BPS Pigeon Grade

Furnished in 12-gauge only, with high grade walnut stock and gold trimmed receiver.

NIB	Exc.	V.G.	Good	Fair	Poor
500	400	300	225	175	125

BPS Buck Special

24" barrel with sights.

NIB	Exc.	V.G.	Good	Fair	Poor
450	400	350	300	225	175

BPS Trap Model

NIB	Exc.	V.G.	Good	Fair	Poor
—	375	325	275	200	150

BPS Micro Trap

Similar to BPS Trap Model, with compact dimensions (13.75" length of pull, 48.25" overall length). 12-gauge only. CAUTION: Do not interchange Invector choke tubes with Invector-Plus choke tubes. May cause personal injury.

NIB	Exc.	V.G.	Good	Fair	Poor
700	—	—	—	—	—

BPS Youth Model

Short stock, 22" barrel.

NIB	Exc.	V.G.	Good	Fair	Poor
435	390	325	275	200	150

BPS Waterfowl Deluxe

Version chambered for 12-gauge 3" chamber. Features etched receiver, with gold-plated trigger. Otherwise, similar to standard BPS.

NIB	Exc.	V.G.	Good	Fair	Poor
—	600	525	425	325	250

BPS Ducks Unlimited Versions

Limited-edition guns produced to be auctioned by Ducks Unlimited. Furnished with a case. Must be NIB with furnished materials to realize their collector potential.

NIB	Exc.	V.G.	Good	Fair	Poor
650	525	425	325	250	175

MODEL 12

Grade I

Slide-action shotgun chambered for 20- and 28-gauge, with 26" modified choke and ventilated rib barrel. Reproduction of Winchester Model 12 shotgun. Has 5-round tubular magazine, with floating high-post rib and takedown feature. Blued, with walnut stock. Introduced in 1991. Total production limited to 7,000 guns.

NIB	Exc.	V.G.	Good	Fair	Poor
825	625	425	300	250	200

Grade V

Extensively engraved version of Grade I Model 12. Features select walnut stock, with deluxe checkering and high-gloss finish. Gold inlays. Introduced in 1991. Production limited to 5,000 guns. Discontinued 1992. **NOTE:** Add 30 percent for 28-gauge.

NIB	Exc.	V.G.	Good	Fair	Poor
1300	950	700	450	—	—

LIMITED EDITION MODEL 42

New version of .410 bore pump shotgun. Last produced by Winchester in 1963. Available in two grades, both fitted with 26" ventilated rib barrels. Grade I features plain blued receiver, with walnut stock. Grade V features blued receiver, with scroll engraving and gold inlays. Both models choked Full. Weight 6 lbs. 4 oz.

Grade I

NIB	Exc.	V.G.	Good	Fair	Poor
900	600	500	400	—	—

Grade V

NIB	Exc.	V.G.	Good	Fair	Poor
1450	1000	700	500	—	—

A-BOLT SHOTGUN

Introduced in 1995. Bolt-action shotgun offered in 12-gauge, with 3" chamber. Rifled barrel version 22" long, while Invector barrel version 23" long, with 5" rifle tube installed. Has 2-shot detachable magazine. Average weight about 7 lbs. Considered "Rolls Royce" of bolt shotguns and becoming quite desirable. Manufacture ceased in 1998. **NOTE:** Deduct $50 for Invector rifled choke tube model.

Hunter Version

NIB	Exc.	V.G.	Good	Fair	Poor
1000	850	750	500	300	100

Stalker Version

NIB	Exc.	V.G.	Good	Fair	Poor
900	750	650	400	200	100

RIFLES

High-Power Bolt-Action Rifle

High-grade bolt-action sporting rifle manufactured by FN in Belgium (from 1959 to 1975) or Sako of Finland (from 1961 to 1975). Built on either Mauser or Sako action. Chambered for a number of popular calibers from .222 Remington up to .458 Winchester Magnum. Three basic grades that differed in amount of ornamentation, quality of materials and workmanship utilized. Certain calibers are considered to be rare and will bring a premium from collectors of this firearm. We recommend securing a qualified appraisal on these rifles if a transaction is contemplated. We furnish general values only.

NOTE: From 1959 through 1966, FN Mauser actions with long extractors were featured. These Mauser actions will bring a premium depending on caliber. From 1967 on, FN Supreme actions with short extractors were used. Only .30-06 and .270-calibers continued with long extractor Mauser actions.

CAUTION: Buyer and seller alike, some rare calibers may be worth as much as 100 percent or more over prices listed for rare calibers such as .284 Win., .257 Roberts, 300 H&H and .308 Norma Magnum. High-Power bolt-action rifles seemed to be particularly hard hit by salt wood. That is why short extractor rifles bring less than long extractor guns. No factory replacement stocks are known to still be available. Deduct 20-25 percent for short extractor rifles. Proceed with caution.

Safari Grade
Standard model and calibers.

NIB	Exc.	V.G.	Good	Fair	Poor
1600	1350	1100	850	400	300

Medallion Grade
Scroll engraved, standard calibers.

NIB	Exc.	V.G.	Good	Fair	Poor
3200	2500	1900	1400	750	400

Olympian Grade
Extensive game scene engraving, standard calibers.

NIB	Exc.	V.G.	Good	Fair	Poor
8500	6300	5250	4250	2500	1500

Model BBR

Bolt-action sporting rifle chambered for various popular calibers. Has 24" barrel, with adjustable trigger and fluted bolt. Features detachable magazine under floorplate, furnished without sights. Finish blued, with checkered walnut Monte Carlo stock. Manufactured between 1978 and 1984 by Miroku.

NIB	Exc.	V.G.	Good	Fair	Poor
675	575	400	350	275	200

BOSS™ SYSTEM

Introduced by Browning in 1994. New accuracy system allows shooter to fine-tune his Browning rifle to particular load he is using. Consists of a tube on end of rifle muzzle that allows shooter to select best setting for ammunition type. System also reduces recoil. BOSS stands for "Ballistic Optimizing Shooting System". This option will add approximately $80 to value of particular Browning rifle on which it is fitted.

X-BOLT SERIES

Introduced in 2008. X-Bolt series of rifle features adjustable three-position Feather Trigger system, newly-designed bolt release, improved scope mounting system, tang safety. Generally slimmer sleeker profile.

X-Bolt Composite Stalker

Features include steel receiver, matte blue finish, free-floating crowned barrel, matte black composite stock with palm swell, Inflex recoil pad. Various barrel lengths depending on chambering, which include both medium and long cartridges ranging from .243 Winchester to .338 Winchester Magnum. Introduced in 2008.

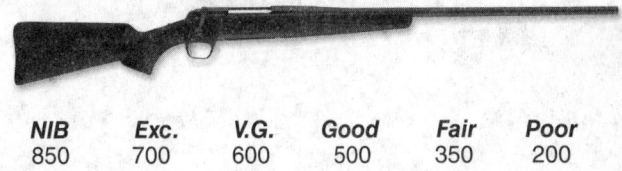

NIB	Exc.	V.G.	Good	Fair	Poor
850	700	600	500	350	200

X-Bolt Stainless Stalker

Similar to above, with stainless steel receiver and barrel. Various barrel lengths depending on chambering, which include both medium and long cartridges ranging from .243 Winchester to .375 H&H Magnum. Introduced in 2008.

NIB	Exc.	V.G.	Good	Fair	Poor
850	700	600	500	350	200

X-Bolt Hunter

Similar to above, with sculpted satin-finished walnut stock and cut checkering. Low-luster blued barrel and receiver. Various barrel lengths depending on chambering, which include both medium and long cartridges ranging from .243 Winchester to .338 Winchester Magnum. Left-hand model available.

NIB	Exc.	V.G.	Good	Fair	Poor
850	700	600	500	350	200

X-Bolt Medallion

Similar to above, with high-gloss finish. Engraved blued barrel and receiver. Various barrel lengths depending on chambering, which include both medium and long cartridges ranging from .243 Winchester to .375 H&H Magnum. Introduced in 2008. Available in left-hand version.

NIB	Exc.	V.G.	Good	Fair	Poor
1000	850	700	600	500	350

X-Bolt Micro Hunter

Similar to Browning X-Bolt Hunter, with compact dimensions (13.3125" length of pull, 41.25" overall length). Left-hand available.

NIB	Exc.	V.G.	Good	Fair	Poor
800	700	600	500	350	200

X-Bolt Eclipse Hunter

Features laminated gray satin finished thumbhole stock, with Monte Carlo cheekpiece and grooved fore-end. Same calibers and other features of standard X-Bolt Hunter models.

NIB	Exc.	V.G.	Good	Fair	Poor
900	800	675	500	350	250

X-Bolt Varmint Stalker

Similar to X-Bolt Stalker, with medium-heavy free-floated barrel, target crown, composite stock. Cartridges .223, .22-250, .243 Winchester and .308 Winchester only.

NIB	Exc.	V.G.	Good	Fair	Poor
1000	850	700	600	500	350

X-Bolt RMEF White Gold

Similar to X-Bolt Medallion, with gold-engraved matte stainless finish. Rocky Mountain Elk Foundation grip cap. Chambered in .325 WSM only.

NIB	Exc.	V.G.	Good	Fair	Poor
1300	1000	850	650	550	375

X-Bolt RMEF Special Hunter

Similar to above. Matte blued finish, without gold highlights.

NIB	Exc.	V.G.	Good	Fair	Poor
900	700	600	500	350	200

X-Bolt Hell's Canyon

Chambered in popular calibers from .243 to .300 Win. Magnum, including .26 Nosler. Free floating and fluted barrel has muzzle-brake. Stock has A-TACS AU camo, with palm swell and textured grip Finish is Cerakote Burnt Bronze.

NIB	Exc.	V.G.	Good	Fair	Poor
1050	875	650	500	350	250

A-BOLT SERIES

NOTE: In 2004, new calibers were offered for A-Bolt series depending on model. They are .25 WSSM and .223 Rem. All A-Bolt II Descriptions: "II" designation dropped from A-Bolt name in 2006.

A-Bolt Hunter

Current bolt-action rifle manufactured by B.C. Miroku. Chambered for various popular calibers. Offered with 22", 24" or 26" barrel. Has short or long action. Adjustable trigger. Detachable box magazine mounted under floorplate. Furnished without sights. Blued, with checkered walnut stock. Introduced in 1985.

NIB	Exc.	V.G.	Good	Fair	Poor
575	400	350	300	250	200

A-Bolt II Hunter

Introduced in 1994. New model features newly designed anti-bind bolt and improved trigger system. In 2001, .300 Winchester Short Magnum cartridge offered for this model. In 2003, a left-hand model introduced.

NIB	Exc.	V.G.	Good	Fair	Poor
795	575	400	300	250	200

A-Bolt II Hunter WSSM

Similar to A-Bolt Hunter. Chambered for .223 WSSM and .243 WSSM cartridges. Stock design different, with addition of longer pistol-grip and thicker forearm. Weight about 6.25 lbs. Introduced in 2003.

NIB	Exc.	V.G.	Good	Fair	Poor
795	575	400	300	250	200

A-Bolt II Micro Hunter

Introduced in 1999. Features shorter length of pull and shorter barrel length than Hunter model. Offered in .22 Hornet, .22-250, 7mm-08, .308, .243 and .260 calibers. Weight about 6 lbs. In 2003, .270 WSM, 7mm WSM and .300 WSM calibers were added for this model as well as left-hand version. **NOTE:** Add $30 for left-hand; $30 for WSM calibers.

NIB	Exc.	V.G.	Good	Fair	Poor
650	525	350	250	200	150

A-Bolt II Classic Hunter

Features Monte Carlo stock, low luster bluing, select walnut and double bordered checkering. Offered in .30-06, .270, 7mm Rem. Magnum and .300 Win. Magnum. No sights. Weight about 7 lbs. Introduced in 1999.

NIB	Exc.	V.G.	Good	Fair	Poor
675	500	395	250	200	150

A-Bolt Stainless Hunter

Features black composite stock, stainless steel receiver and barrel, no sights. Chamberings range from .243 Winchester to .300 WSM. Weight about 6.5 lbs. Introduced in 2008.

NIB	Exc.	V.G.	Good	Fair	Poor
800	650	450	300	250	200

A-Bolt Classic Hunter WSSM

As above, but chambered for .223 WSSM and .243 WSSM cartridges. Weight about 6.25 lbs. Introduced in 2003.

NIB	Exc.	V.G.	Good	Fair	Poor
800	650	450	300	250	200

A-Bolt Mountain Ti

Features lightweight stainless steel 23" barrel, titanium receiver and lightweight fiberglass stock. Chambered for .270 WSM, 7mm WSM and .300 WSM cartridges. Weight about 5.5 lbs. Calibers: .243, 7mm-08, .308, .325 WSM. Introduced in 2004.

NIB	Exc.	V.G.	Good	Fair	Poor
1695	1300	1050	800	575	350

A-Bolt Composite Stalker

Supplied with composite stock and matte finish bluing. Offered in .338 Win. Magnum, .300 Win. Magnum, 7mm Rem. Magnum, .25-06, .270, .280, .30-06. Introduced in 1988. In 2001, .300 Winchester Short Magnum cartridge was offered for this model. Calibers: .223 WSSM, .243 WSSM, .25 WSSM, .223, .243, .7mm-08, .270 WSM, 7mm WSM, .300 WSM, .325 WSM, .25-06, .270, .280, .30-06, 7mm RM, .300 WM, .338 WM. **NOTE:** Add 10 percent for BOSS or left-hand version.

NIB	Exc.	V.G.	Good	Fair	Poor
550	350	300	250	200	150

A-Bolt II Composite Stalker

Same as above, with 1994 improvements. **NOTE:** Add $80 for BOSS system.

NIB	Exc.	V.G.	Good	Fair	Poor
670	525	400	300	250	200

A-Bolt Composite Stalker WSSM

As above, but chambered for .223 WSSM or .243 WSSM cartridge. Weight about 6 lbs. Introduced in 2003.

NIB	Exc.	V.G.	Good	Fair	Poor
700	550	400	300	250	200

A-Bolt Stainless Stalker

Bolt-action rifle. Calibers: .223 WSSM, .243 WSSM, .25 WSSM, .223, .243, .7mm-08, .270 WSM, 7mm WSM, .300 WSM, .325 WSM, .25-06, .270, .280, .30-06, 7mm RM, .300 WM, .338 WM, .375 H&H. Barrel: 22", 23", 24", 26" stainless steel, sightless (except for .375 H&H). Magazine: Detachable box. Stock: Black composite. **NOTE:** Add $30 for .300 and .338 calibers; 10 percent for BOSS system and left-hand version.

NIB	Exc.	V.G.	Good	Fair	Poor
600	450	400	350	300	250

A-Bolt II Composite Stainless Stalker

Same as above, with 1994 improvements. **NOTE:** Add $30 for Magnum calibers; $110 for BOSS system.

NIB	Exc.	V.G.	Good	Fair	Poor
850	650	550	400	300	250

A-Bolt Stainless Stalker WSSM

As above, but chambered for .223 WSSM and .243 WSSM calibers. Stock design slightly different from standard A-Bolt Stalker. Weight about 6 lbs. Introduced in 2003.

NIB	Exc.	V.G.	Good	Fair	Poor
880	675	550	400	300	250

A-Bolt Carbon Fiber Stainless Stalker

Features a Christensen Arms patent carbon barrel. Chambered for .22-250 or .300 Win. Magnum. Weight about: 6.25 lbs. short action; 7 lbs. long action. Introduced in 2000. In 2001, .300 Winchester Short Magnum cartridge offered for this model.

NIB	Exc.	V.G.	Good	Fair	Poor
1400	1200	1000	900	700	350

A-Bolt II Heavy Barrel Varmint

Introduced in 1994. Features all A-Bolt II improvements in a heavy barrel varmint rifle. Offered in .22-250 and .223 Rem. calibers, with 22" barrel. Equipped with black laminated wood stock.

NIB	Exc.	V.G.	Good	Fair	Poor
685	600	525	425	325	250

A-Bolt Varmint Stalker

Introduced in 2002. Features new armor coated synthetic stock. Matte blue metal finish. Chambered for .223 Rem. and .22-250 Rem. cartridges. Fitted with 24" barrel on .223 and 26" barrel on .22-250. Weight about 8 lbs.

NIB	Exc.	V.G.	Good	Fair	Poor
790	650	525	425	325	250

A-Bolt Varmint Stalker WSSM

As above, but chambered for .223 WSSM and .243 WSSM cartridges. Weight about 7.75 lbs. Introduced in 2003.

NIB	Exc.	V.G.	Good	Fair	Poor
815	650	525	425	325	250

A-Bolt Eclipse M-1000

Thumbhole stock. Calibers: .270, .30-06, 7mm RM, .22-250, .308, .270 WSM, .7mm WSM, .300 WSM. Fitted with 26" barrel with BOSS system. Stock laminated hardwood, with gray/black finish. Forearm benchrest style. Weight about 9 lbs. 13 oz. **NOTE:** Add 10 percent for BOSS.

NIB	Exc.	V.G.	Good	Fair	Poor
1135	700	625	450	350	250

A-Bolt Eclipse M-1000 WSM & Stainless

Introduced in 2004. Offered in all WSM calibers. M-1000 blued with heavy barrel; stainless fitted with heavy bull barrel. Barrel length 26". Weight 9.85 lbs. No sights. **NOTE:** Add $200 for stainless model.

NIB	Exc.	V.G.	Good	Fair	Poor
1050	825	675	500	350	200

A-Bolt Eclipse Varmint

Introduced in 1996. Features thumbhole stock made from gray/black laminated hardwood. Offered in two versions: short-action, heavy-barrel; long and short action, with standard-weight barrel. Weight about: 9 lbs.; standard-barrel 7.5 lbs. depending on caliber.

NIB	Exc.	V.G.	Good	Fair	Poor
950	800	600	500	400	250

Euro-Bolt

First introduced in 1993. A-Bolt variation features rounded bolt shroud, Mannlicher-style bolt handle, continental-style stock. Cheekpiece and schnabel-style forearm. Finish is low-luster blue. Offered in .270, .30-06 and 7mm Rem. Magnum calibers. Weight about 7 lbs.

NIB	Exc.	V.G.	Good	Fair	Poor
650	500	450	350	250	150

A-Bolt II Euro Bolt

Same as above, with 1994 improvements.

NIB	Exc.	V.G.	Good	Fair	Poor
850	500	450	350	250	150

NRA A-Bolt Wildlife Conservation Collection

Commemorates NRA's Environment Conservation and Hunting Outreach Program. Caliber: .243 Win. Barrel: 22" blued sightless. Stock satin-finish walnut. NRA Heritage logo lasered on buttstock. MSRP: $797.

A-Bolt Medallion Model

Calibers: .223 WSSM, .243 WSSM, .25 WSSM, .223, .243, .7mm-08, .270 WSM, 7mm WSM, .300 WSM, .325 WSM, .25-06, .270, .280, .30-06, 7mm RM, .300 WM, .338 WM. **NOTE:** Add $35 for .300 and .338 calibers; 10 percent for BOSS or left-hand version.

NIB	Exc.	V.G.	Good	Fair	Poor
800	600	500	400	300	250

A-Bolt II Medallion

Same as above, with 1994 improvements. In 2003, offered in left-hand version.

NIB	Exc.	V.G.	Good	Fair	Poor
765	600	450	350	300	250

A-Bolt II Medallion WSSM

As above chambered for .223 WSSM or .243 WSSM cartridge. Weight about 6.25 lbs. Introduced in 2003.

NIB	Exc.	V.G.	Good	Fair	Poor
795	650	525	450	400	325

A-Bolt Gold Medallion

Version has fancy grade walnut stock with cheekpiece. Lightly engraved. Gold-inlaid letters. Introduced in 1988.

NIB	Exc.	V.G.	Good	Fair	Poor
690	625	550	450	400	325

A-Bolt II Gold Medallion

Same as above, with 1994 improvements.

NIB	Exc.	V.G.	Good	Fair	Poor
690	625	550	450	400	325

A-Bolt II White Gold Medallion

Features gold engraved stainless receiver and barrel, select walnut stock, with brass spacers and rosewood caps. European-style cheekpiece. No sights. Introduced in 1999. Offered in .30-06, .270, 7mm Rem. Magnum and .300 Win. Magnum. Weight about 7 lbs. 8 oz.

NIB	Exc.	V.G.	Good	Fair	Poor
1100	800	650	500	425	350

A-Bolt White Gold Medallion RMEF

Introduced in 2003. Special edition for Rocky Mountain Elk Foundation. Chambered for 7mm Rem. Magnum. Fitted with 26" barrel. Both action and barrel stainless steel. Special RMEF logo on grip cap. Weight about 7.75 lbs. **NOTE:** Add 5 percent for WSM calibers.

NIB	Exc.	V.G.	Good	Fair	Poor
1200	950	750	600	450	325

A-Bolt Custom Trophy

Introduced in 1998. Features gold highlights on barrel and receiver, select walnut stock with shadowline cheekpiece and skeleton pistol-grip. Barrel octagonal. Chambered for .270 and .30-06 with 24" barrel and 7mm Rem. Magnum and .300 Win. Magnum with 26" barrel. Weight varies from 7 lbs. 11 oz. to 7 lbs. 3 oz. depending on caliber.

NIB	Exc.	V.G.	Good	Fair	Poor
1300	1000	800	650	425	300

A-Bolt Big Horn Sheep Issue

High-grade version of A-Bolt. Chambered for .270 cartridge. Features deluxe skipline checkered walnut stock, with heavily engraved receiver and floorplate. Two gold sheep inlays. There were 600 manufactured in 1986 and 1987.

NIB	Exc.	V.G.	Good	Fair	Poor
1050	800	600	450	400	325

A-Bolt Micro-Medallion

Smaller version of A-Bolt Hunter. Chambered for popular cartridges that fit short action. Has 20" barrel without sights and 3-round magazine. Introduced in 1988.

NIB	Exc.	V.G.	Good	Fair	Poor
525	475	400	350	300	250

A-Bolt II Micro-Medallion

Same as above, with 1994 improvements.

NIB	Exc.	V.G.	Good	Fair	Poor
525	475	400	350	300	250

A-Bolt Pronghorn Issue

Deluxe version of A-Bolt. Chambered for .243 cartridge. Heavily engraved and gold inlaid. Features presentation-grade walnut stock, with skipline checkering and pearl-inlaid borders. There were 500 manufactured in 1987.

NIB	Exc.	V.G.	Good	Fair	Poor
1300	1000	750	500	400	325

A-Bolt Special Hunter RMEF

Similar to A-Bolt Hunter. Honors Rocky Mountain Elk Foundation. Chambered in .325 WSM. Satin finish. Introduced 2007.

NIB	Exc.	V.G.	Good	Fair	Poor
800	600	500	400	300	250

A-Bolt White Gold RMEF

Similar to A-Bolt Special Hunter RMEF, with stainless barrel, receiver and glossy finish. Introduced 2007.

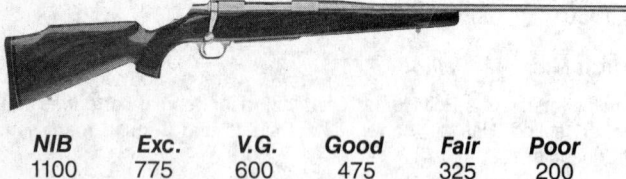

NIB	Exc.	V.G.	Good	Fair	Poor
1100	775	600	475	325	200

A-Bolt Target

Similar to A-Bolt, with 28" heavy bull blued barrel and receiver. Satin finish gray laminated stock, with adjustable comb and semi-beavertail fore-end. Chambered in .223, .308 Winchester and .300 WSM.

NIB	Exc.	V.G.	Good	Fair	Poor
1275	1000	800	650	425	300

A-Bolt Target Stainless

Similar to above, with stainless receiver and barrel.

NIB	Exc.	V.G.	Good	Fair	Poor
1500	1275	1000	800	650	425

A-Bolt .22 Grade I

Bolt-action sporting rifle. Chambered for .22 LR or .22 Magnum cartridges. Features 60-degree bolt and 22" barrel. Available with or without open sights. Has 5-round detachable magazine. Adjustable trigger. Finish blued, with checkered walnut stock. Introduced in 1986. **NOTE:** Add 15 percent for .22 Magnum.

NIB	Exc.	V.G.	Good	Fair	Poor
340	275	210	150	125	100

A-Bolt .22 Gold Medallion

Deluxe high-grade version features select stock, with rosewood pistol-grip cap and fore-end tip. Lightly engraved. Gold-filled letters. Introduced in 1988.

NIB	Exc.	V.G.	Good	Fair	Poor
450	400	350	300	225	175

AB3 Composite Stalker

Made on an A-Bolt action, with synthetic stock, matte blue finish and free-floating barrel. Stock has textured grip panels and polymer recoil pad. Picatinny rail scope mount included. The 3-round magazine is detachable. Offered in: .270 Win., 7mm Rem. Magnum, .30-06, .300 Win. Magnum, .300 WSM.

NIB	Exc.	V.G.	Good	Fair	Poor
525	450	400	350	300	200

T-BOLT SERIES

T-Bolt Model T-1

Unique straight-pull bolt-action sporting rifle. Chambered for .22-caliber cartridges. Has 22" barrel, with open sights and 5-round magazine. Finish blued, with plain walnut stock. Manufactured between 1965 and 1974 by FN. Many T-Bolt rifles affected by salt wood. Proceed with caution. Reintroduced in 2006 with rotary magazine.

NIB	Exc.	V.G.	Good	Fair	Poor
—	550	395	350	150	100

T-Bolt Model T-2

Version similar to T-1, with select checkered walnut stock and 24" barrel.

NIB	Exc.	V.G.	Good	Fair	Poor
800	600	450	375	250	200

T-Bolt (2006)

Reintroduction of classic and collectible T-bolt straight-pull .22 rifle. Introduced in 2006. Chambered for .17 HMR, .22 WMR or .22 LR.

NIB	Exc.	V.G.	Good	Fair	Poor
600	475	450	375	250	200

T-Bolt Target/Varmint

Similar to reintroduced T-Bolt, with floating heavy target barrel and other accurizing refinements. Introduced 2007.

NIB	Exc.	V.G.	Good	Fair	Poor
650	525	500	425	300	250

T-Bolt Target/Varmint Stainless

Similar to above, with stainless steel receiver and barrel. Introduced 2008.

NIB	Exc.	V.G.	Good	Fair	Poor
850	725	650	525	350	325

T-Bolt Composite Hunter

Sporter version of new T-Bolt, with black composite Monte Carlo stock and glossy blue barrel and receiver. Chambered in .17 HMR, .22 WMR or .22 LR. Scope not included. Introduced 2008.

NIB	Exc.	V.G.	Good	Fair	Poor
675	525	500	425	300	250

T-Bolt Composite Target/Varmint

Sporter version of new T-Bolt Target/Varmint, with black composite Monte Carlo stock and glossy blue barrel and receiver. Chambered in .17 HMR, .22 WMR or .22 LR. Scope not included. Introduced 2008.

NIB	Exc.	V.G.	Good	Fair	Poor
700	550	525	450	325	275

T-Bolt Composite Target/Varmint Left-Hand

Similar to T-Bolt Composite Target/Varmint in left-hand version.

NIB	Exc.	V.G.	Good	Fair	Poor
725	550	525	450	325	275

T-Bolt Sporter

Sporter version of new T-Bolt, with satin walnut stock and bright blue barrel and receiver. Scope not included. Introduced 2008.

NIB	Exc.	V.G.	Good	Fair	Poor
700	550	525	450	325	275

T-Bolt Sporter Left-Hand

Similar to Browning T-Bolt Sporter in left-hand version.

NIB	Exc.	V.G.	Good	Fair	Poor
700	550	525	450	325	275

T-Bolt Composite Sporter Left-Hand

Similar to Browning T-Bolt Sporter Left-Hand, with composite stock.

NIB	Exc.	V.G.	Good	Fair	Poor
700	550	525	450	325	275

Acera Straight Pull Rifle

Introduced in 1999. Features straight-action bolt system. Chambered for .30-06 with 22" barrel; .300 Win. Magnum with 24" barrel. Open sights optional as is BOSS system. Detachable box magazine. Checkered walnut stock. Prices listed for .30-06, with no sights and no BOSS. **NOTE:** Add $100 for .300 Win. Magnum with no sights and no BOSS.

NIB	Exc.	V.G.	Good	Fair	Poor
1100	775	600	475	325	200

Model 52 Limited Edition

Based on design of original Winchester Model 52 .22-caliber bolt-action rifle. Fitted with 24" barrel and oil finished walnut stock. Metal pistol-grip cap and rosewood fore-end tip. Drilled and tapped for scope. Five-round detachable magazine. Blued finish. Weight about 7 lbs. From 1991 to 1992, 5,000 Model 52s were built.

NIB	Exc.	V.G.	Good	Fair	Poor
1000	875	700	600	—	—

BPR-22

Short-stroke slide action rifle. Chambered for .22 LR and Magnum cartridges. Has 20.25" barrel, with open sights and 11-round tubular magazine. Finish blued, with checkered walnut stock. Manufactured between 1977 and 1982. **NOTE:** Add $100 for .22 Magnum models.

NIB	Exc.	V.G.	Good	Fair	Poor
—	500	350	215	125	95

BPR-22 Grade II

Version engraved. Select walnut stock. **NOTE:** Add 20 percent for .22 Magnum models.

NIB	Exc.	V.G.	Good	Fair	Poor
—	600	400	275	225	150

Trombone Model

Slide-action rifle chambered for .22 LR cartridge. Has 24" barrel, with open sights and takedown design. Tubular magazine and hammerless action. Approximately 150,000 manufactured by FN between 1922 and 1974. Approximately 3,200 were imported by Browning in 1960s. Marked with FN barrel address or Browning Arms address. Browning-marked guns worth approximately 40 percent additional. Values given for FN-marked guns.

NIB	Exc.	V.G.	Good	Fair	Poor
1300	1000	800	700	450	325

Semi-Automatic .22 (SA-22)

Blowback-operated semi-automatic rifle. Chambered for .22 Long Rifle or Short cartridge. Features take-down barrel design, with 19.25" barrel and 11-round tubular magazine inside buttstock. Loaded through a hole in middle of buttstock. Finish blued, with checkered walnut stock and beavertail forearm. Lightweight compact firearm manufactured by FN between 1956 and 1974 for U.S. marked guns. A number of versions that differ in amount of ornamentation, quality of materials and workmanship.

Grade I

NOTE: Add 50 percent for Grade I .22 Short; 20 percent for Early Wheel Sight manufactured 1959-1960.

NIB	Exc.	V.G.	Good	Fair	Poor
850	700	600	500	400	350

Grade II

French grayed receiver. **NOTE:** Add 300 percent for Grade II short.

NIB	Exc.	V.G.	Good	Fair	Poor
1600	1200	900	700	300	200

Grade III

French grayed receiver. **NOTE:** Premium engravers: add 40 percent to Grade III; 800 percent to Grade III short. Deduct 20 percent for unsigned Grade III, 1956-1960.

NIB	Exc.	V.G.	Good	Fair	Poor
3250	2700	1900	1200	700	400

Semi-Auto .22 (SA-22, Miroku Mfg.)

Similar to Belgian FN, except produced as of 1976 by B.C. Miroku in Japan. Collector interest not as high as in FN version.

Grade I

NIB	Exc.	V.G.	Good	Fair	Poor
600	500	400	275	125	100

Grade II

Discontinued 1984.

NIB	Exc.	V.G.	Good	Fair	Poor
900	700	525	375	225	150

Grade III

Discontinued 1983.

NIB	Exc.	V.G.	Good	Fair	Poor
1300	1000	750	500	300	200

Grade VI

Gold plated animals.

NIB	Exc.	V.G.	Good	Fair	Poor
1200	950	750	525	325	275

Semi-Auto .22 High Grade 100th Anniversary

A limited production model, with octagon barrel, high relief engraving, highly polished blueing, gold bead front sight and grade III/IV walnut stock. Engraving features John M. Browning's likeness on top of receiver, 100th Anniversary logo and small game animals. Made in Japan by Miroku during 2014, with production limited to 100 rifles. MSRP $2000.

NIB	Exc.	V.G.	Good	Fair	Poor
1800	1650	—	—	—	—

BAR-22

Blowback-operated semi-automatic rifle. Chambered for .22 LR cartridge. Has 20.25" barrel, with open sights and 15-round tubular magazine. Features polished lightweight alloy receiver. Finished blue, with checkered walnut stock. Manufactured between 1977 and 1985 by Miroku.

NIB	Exc.	V.G.	Good	Fair	Poor
—	600	525	290	160	125

BAR-22 Grade II

Deluxe version, with engraved silver-finished receiver. Select walnut stock. Discontinued in 1985.

NIB	Exc.	V.G.	Good	Fair	Poor
—	695	575	375	175	150

Buck Mark Rifle

Model uses same design as Buck Mark pistol. Fitted with 18" barrel (heavy on target model) and thumbhole pistol-grip. Magazine capacity 10 rounds. Integral rail scope mount. Introduced in 2001. Weight about: 4.25 lbs. Sporter; 5.5 lbs. Target model.

Target Model

NIB	Exc.	V.G.	Good	Fair	Poor
595	460	325	250	195	125

Sporter Model

NIB	Exc.	V.G.	Good	Fair	Poor
590	450	325	250	195	125

Buck Mark Field Target Gray Laminate

Introduced in 2003. Features lightweight carbon composite barrel, gray laminate stock and integral scope rail. Chambered for .22 cartridge. Fitted with 18" barrel. Weight: 5.5 lbs. standard; 3.75 lbs. Lite model.

NIB	Exc.	V.G.	Good	Fair	Poor
650	525	400	325	250	175

Patent 1900 High Power

Semi-automatic sporting rifle. Chambered for .35 Remington cartridge. Similar in configuration to Remington Model 8 rifle. Has 22" barrel, with open sights and 5-round integral magazine. Finish blued, with plain walnut stock. Approximately 5,000 manufactured between 1910 and 1931. Deluxe model, with ribbed barrel and checkered walnut stock available. Worth approximately 15 percent additional. Very rare in USA.

NIB	Exc.	V.G.	Good	Fair	Poor
—	1500	1000	700	475	300

BAR SERIES

Bar High Power Rifle

Gas-operated semi-automatic sporting rifle. Chambered for various popular calibers from .243 up to .338 Magnum cartridges. Offered with 22" or 24" barrel, with folding leaf sight until 1980. Finish blued, with checkered walnut stock. Various grades offered, differed in amount of ornamentation, quality of materials and workmanship utilized. Earlier models manufactured in Belgium by FN; these guns would be worth approximately 15 percent additional over guns assembled in Portugal from parts manufactured by FN. Early .338 Magnum model rarely encountered and would be worth approximately 25 percent additional. Grade I values furnished are for Portuguese-assembled guns from 1977 until introduction of BAR Mark II in 1993. This model introduced in 1967; discontinued in 1977.

Grade I

NIB	Exc.	V.G.	Good	Fair	Poor
1000	725	650	475	225	100

Grade I Magnum

NIB	Exc.	V.G.	Good	Fair	Poor
1150	750	675	400	250	125

Grade II Deluxe

1967-1974.

NIB	Exc.	V.G.	Good	Fair	Poor
1200	900	825	475	300	175

Grade II Deluxe Magnum

1968-1974.

NIB	Exc.	V.G.	Good	Fair	Poor
1275	950	850	500	325	200

Grade III

Discontinued 1984. **NOTE:** Grade III offered in two variations. First was hand-engraved and produced in Belgium. Second was photo-etched and built in Belgium and assembled in Portugal. Second variation will not be as valuable as first.

NIB	Exc.	V.G.	Good	Fair	Poor
1700	1450	1100	800	400	250

Grade III Magnum

Discontinued 1984. **NOTE:** Prices indicated are for 1970 through 1974 production. Guns assembled in Portugal deduct 30 percent. .338 Win. Magnum caliber rare in Grade III add 75 percent premium.

NIB	Exc.	V.G.	Good	Fair	Poor
1800	1550	1150	850	400	250

Grade IV

Game scene engraved. Hand-engraved from 1970 through 1976, then etched thereafter. Grade IV rifles discontinued in 1984. **NOTE:** Add 40 percent for pre-1977 rifles; 10 percent for premium engraving.

NIB	Exc.	V.G.	Good	Fair	Poor
2600	2200	1500	1000	500	400

Grade IV Magnum

NIB	Exc.	V.G.	Good	Fair	Poor
2800	2400	1600	1100	500	450

Grade V

Gold Inlaid: 1971-1974.

NIB	Exc.	V.G.	Good	Fair	Poor
6500	5800	4500	3200	1400	700

Grade V Magnum

1971-1974. **NOTE:** Add up to 100 percent for special order variations on Grade V rifles.

NIB	Exc.	V.G.	Good	Fair	Poor
6750	6000	4600	3300	1500	750

North American Deer Rifle Issue

Deluxe version of BAR. Chambered for .30-06 only. Features photo etched silver-finished receiver and deluxe checkered walnut stock. Produced and furnished 600 with walnut case and accessories. Discontinued in 1983. As with all commemorative's, it must be NIB to command premium values.

NIB	Exc.	V.G.	Good	Fair	Poor
4000	3600	2400	1800	450	250

BAR Mark II Safari Rifle

Improved version of BAR. First introduced by Browning in 1967. Announced in 1993, this Mark II design uses a new gas system, with newly designed buffering system to improve reliability. Has new bolt release lever, new easily removable trigger assembly. Available with- or with-out sights. Walnut stock, with full pistol-grip and recoil pad on Magnum gun are standard. Receiver blued, with scroll engraving. Rifles with Magnum calibers have 24" barrel; standard calibers fitted with 22" barrel. Available in .243, .308, .270, .30-06, 7mm Rem. Magnum, .300 Win. Magnum, .338 Win. Magnum. Weight: Standard calibers 7 lbs. 9 oz.; Magnum calibers 8 lbs. 6 oz. **NOTE:** Add 30 percent for .270 Wby. Magnum, which was made for one year only.

NIB	Exc.	V.G.	Good	Fair	Poor
825	750	600	450	250	150

BAR Mark II Lightweight

Version of Mark II. Introduced in 1997. Features lightweight alloy receiver and shortened 20" barrel. Offered in .30-06, .270 Win., .308 Win. and .243 Win. calibers. Not offered with BOSS system. Weight about 7 lbs. 2 oz.

NIB	Exc.	V.G.	Good	Fair	Poor
750	600	500	425	175	125

BAR Composite Stalker

Introduced in 2001. Features composite buttstock and fore-end, with removable magazine. Offered in short action (.243 and .308) with sights; standard action (.270 and .30-06) with no sights; Magnum calibers (7mm, .330 Win., and .338) with no sights and with BOSS system. **NOTE:** Add $75 for Magnum calibers; $140 for BOSS.

NIB	Exc.	V.G.	Good	Fair	Poor
900	725	550	425	175	125

BAR High Grade Models

Models will feature high grade walnut stock, with highly polished blued barrel. Receivers will be grayed with game animals: mule deer and whitetail on standard calibers (.270 and .30-06); elk and moose on Magnum calibers (7mm Magnum and .300 Win. Magnum).

NIB	Exc.	V.G.	Good	Fair	Poor
1825	1450	1100	800	550	400

BAR ShortTrac

Introduced in 2004. Features ability to chamber Magnum cartridges. Offered in .270 WSM, 7mm WSM, .325 WSM, .300 WSM, .243 and .308. Fitted with 23" barrel in Magnum calibers; 22" barrel in non-Magnum. Receiver alloy steel. Redesigned stock adjustable for length of pull. Weight about: 7.25 lbs. Magnum calibers; 6.75 lbs. others. **NOTE:** Add 10 percent for camo finish.

NIB	Exc.	V.G.	Good	Fair	Poor
950	650	450	350	250	200

BAR ShortTrac Stalker

Similar to BAR ShortTrac, with matte blue barrel. Composite stock. Introduced 2006.

NIB	Exc.	V.G.	Good	Fair	Poor
850	670	550	450	350	250

BAR ShortTrac Left-Hand

Similar to BAR ShortTrac in left-hand. Introduced 2007.

NIB	Exc.	V.G.	Good	Fair	Poor
950	650	450	350	250	200

BAR ShortTrac Mossy Oak New Break-up

Similar to BAR ShortTrac, with Mossy Oak Break-up finish overall.

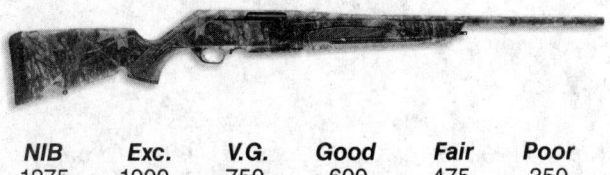

NIB	Exc.	V.G.	Good	Fair	Poor
1275	1000	750	600	475	350

BAR ShortTrac Digital Green

Similar to above, with Digital Green camo finish overall.

NIB	Exc.	V.G.	Good	Fair	Poor
1275	1000	750	600	475	350

BAR LongTrac

Similar to above. Made for long action calibers such as .270, .30-06, 7mm Rem. Magnum and .300 Win. Magnum. Barrel length 22" for .270 and .30-06; 24" for other two calibers. Weight about: 7 lbs. .270 and .30-06; 7.5 lbs. 7mm and .300. Introduced in 2004. **NOTE:** Add $75 for Magnum calibers; 10 percent for camo finish.

NIB	Exc.	V.G.	Good	Fair	Poor
950	650	450	350	250	200

BAR LongTrac Stalker

Long-action version of BAR ShortTrac Stalker.

NIB	Exc.	V.G.	Good	Fair	Poor
850	670	550	450	350	250

BAR LongTrac Left-Hand

Similar to BAR LongTrac in left-hand. Introduced 2007.

NIB	Exc.	V.G.	Good	Fair	Poor
950	1000	750	600	475	350

BAR LongTrac Mossy Oak New Break-up

Similar to BAR LongTrac, with Mossy Oak Break-up finish overall.

NIB	Exc.	V.G.	Good	Fair	Poor
1275	1000	750	600	475	350

Model BPR

Initials "BPR" stands for Browning Pump Rifle. Introduced in 1997. Similar in appearance to BAR. Offered in both long-/short-action calibers, with barrel lengths from 22" to 24". Short action calibers: .243 Win. and .308 Win. Long action calibers: .270 Win., .30-06, 7mm Rem. Magnum and .300 Win. Magnum. Weight about 7 lbs. 3 oz. Discontinued 2003.

NIB	Exc.	V.G.	Good	Fair	Poor
800	675	525	400	300	200

BL SERIES

BL-22 Grade I

Lever-action rifle chambered for .22 rimfire cartridge. Has 18" barrel, with tubular magazine and folding leaf rear sight. Western-style firearm that features an exposed hammer. Finish blued, with walnut stock. Introduced in 1970 by Miroku.

NIB	Exc.	V.G.	Good	Fair	Poor
450	350	200	150	125	100

BL-22 Grade II

Similar to above, with scroll-engraved receiver. Checkered select walnut stock.

NIB	Exc.	V.G.	Good	Fair	Poor
475	350	225	175	150	125

BL-22 Field Series Grade I

Introduced in 2005. Features satin nickel receiver, walnut stock with no checkering. Blued trigger. Magazine capacity 16 rounds. Weight about 5 lbs.

NIB	Exc.	V.G.	Good	Fair	Poor
495	375	350	200	150	100

BL-17 Field Series Grade I

As above chambered for .17 Mach 2 cartridge. Weight about 5.2 lbs.

NIB	Exc.	V.G.	Good	Fair	Poor
650	575	400	200	150	100

BL-22 Field Series Grade II

As above, with checkered stock, gold trigger. Scroll engraving on receiver.

NIB	Exc.	V.G.	Good	Fair	Poor
555	425	350	200	150	125

BL-17 Field Series Grade II

As above chambered for .17 Mach 2 cartridge.

NIB	Exc.	V.G.	Good	Fair	Poor
700	600	450	250	150	125

BL-22 Grade II Octagon

Introduced in 2005. Has 24" octagon barrel chambered for .22 Long and Long Rifle cartridges. Receiver silver nitride, with scroll engraving and gold trigger. Magazine capacity 16 rounds. Gold bead front sight. Weight about 5.25 lbs.

NIB	Exc.	V.G.	Good	Fair	Poor
725	550	375	275	200	150

BL-17 Grade II Octagon

As above, but chambered for .17 Mach 2 cartridge. Magazine capacity 16 rounds. Weight about 5.35 lbs. Introduced in 2005.

NIB	Exc.	V.G.	Good	Fair	Poor
750	575	375	275	200	150

BL-22 Classic

Introduced in 1999. Same features as BL-22 Grade I.

NIB	Exc.	V.G.	Good	Fair	Poor
425	375	275	200	175	125

BL-22 NRA Grade 1

Similar to BL-22 Grade 1, with "NRA" logo lasered on buttstock.

NIB	Exc.	V.G.	Good	Fair	Poor
500	450	350	300	—	—

BL-22 Gray Laminate Stainless

Similar to BL-22, with gray laminated stock, nickeled receiver and stainless steel barrel. Introduced 2006.

NIB	Exc.	V.G.	Good	Fair	Poor
725	550	375	275	200	150

BL-22 Micro Midas

Chambered for .22 LR. Designed for younger shooter, with 12" length of pull. Lever action, with short 33-degree throw. Full-length tubular magazine, American walnut stock, gloss finish, straight-grip. Receiver steel, with blued finish. Grooved for scope mounts. New 2011.

NIB	Exc.	V.G.	Good	Fair	Poor
400	350	300	250	200	150

Model 81 BLR

Contemporarily designed lever-action sporting rifle. Chambered for various popular calibers from .22-250 up to .358 Winchester. Has 20" barrel, with adjustable sights. Features 4-round detachable magazine and rotary locking bolt. Finish blued, with checkered walnut stock and recoil pad. Introduced in 1971. Manufactured that year in Belgium. In 1972, manufacture moved to Miroku in Japan. In 2003, straight-grip stock introduced and WSM calibers added from .270 to .300. Weight about 6.5 lbs.
NOTE: Add 20 percent for Belgian-manufactured version.

NIB	Exc.	V.G.	Good	Fair	Poor
895	675	500	300	200	150

BLR Lightning (Lightweight)

Introduced in 1996. Features lightweight aluminum receiver, with walnut stock and checkered pistol-grip. Offered in both long and short action calibers from .223 Rem. to 7mm Rem. Magnum. Barrel length 20" for short action calibers; 22" to 24" for long action calibers. Open sights standard. Weight about 7 lbs. depending on caliber. In 2003 a straight-grip stock introduced.

NIB	Exc.	V.G.	Good	Fair	Poor
740	600	450	300	200	150

BLR Lightweight '81

Features straight-grip checkered walnut stock. Fitted with 20" or 22" barrel; magazine capacity 4 or 5 rounds, both depending on caliber. Chambered for calibers .22-25-, .243, 7mm-08, .308, .358, .450 Marlin, .270 WSM, .300 WSM and .325 WSM. Offered in long action chambered for .270, .30-06, 7mm Rem. Magnum and .300 Win. Magnum. Weight from 6.5 lbs. to 7.75 lbs. depending on caliber. **NOTE:** Add 20 percent for long action; $70 for WSM calibers.

NIB	Exc.	V.G.	Good	Fair	Poor
730	550	425	325	225	125

BLR Lightweight Takedown

Similar to BLR Lightweight, with takedown feature. Introduced 2007.

NIB	Exc.	V.G.	Good	Fair	Poor
775	650	575	375	200	150

BLR Lightweight '81 Stainless Takedown

Similar to above, with stainless steel barrel and receiver. Introduced 2008.

NIB	Exc.	V.G.	Good	Fair	Poor
975	850	695	475	350	225

Model B-78

Introduced in 1973. Single-shot lever-action falling block. Offered in several calibers from .22-250 to .45-70. Barrel lengths from 24" to 26" in round or octagonal shape. No sights except .45-70. Checkered walnut stock. First built in 1973. Discontinued in 1983. **NOTE:** Add 15 percent for .45-70 caliber.

NIB	Exc.	V.G.	Good	Fair	Poor
1400	1100	850	600	350	250

Model 53

Offered in 1990. Reproduction of Winchester Model 53. Like original, chambered for .32-20 cartridge. Limited edition offering confined to 5,000 rifles. Features hand-cut checkering, high-grade walnut stock, full pistol-grip and semi-beavertail fore-end. Pistol-grip fitted with metal grip cap. Barrel length 22". Finish blue.

NIB	Exc.	V.G.	Good	Fair	Poor
900	800	650	500	325	200

Model 65 Grade I

Limited-edition lever-action rifle. Chambered for .218 Bee cartridge. Has tapered round 24" barrel, with open sights. Patterned after Winchester Model 65. Has 7-round tubular magazine. Finish blued, with plain walnut stock. Metal buttplate. Manufactured 3,500 in 1989.

NIB	Exc.	V.G.	Good	Fair	Poor
850	675	500	300	—	150

Model 65 High Grade

Deluxe version features silver-finished scroll engraved receiver, with gold animal inlays and gold-plated trigger, select checkered walnut stock. Manufactured 1,500 in 1989.

NIB	Exc.	V.G.	Good	Fair	Poor
1650	1200	825	500	—	—

Model 71 Grade I

Reproduction of Winchester Model 71. Chambered for .348 cartridge. Has 20" or 24" barrel, with open sights and 4-round tubular magazine. Finish blued, with plain walnut stock. Manufactured 4,000 20" carbines; 3,000 24" rifles, in 1986 and 1987.

NIB	Exc.	V.G.	Good	Fair	Poor
—	950	750	595	400	250

Model 71 High Grade

Version similar to Grade I. Scroll engraved grayed receiver, with gold-plated trigger and gold inlays. Manufactured 3,000 each of carbines and rifles in 1986 and 1987.

NIB	Exc.	V.G.	Good	Fair	Poor
—	1400	950	750	500	325

Jonathan Browning Centennial Mountain Rifle

Limited edition blackpowder rifle. Chambered for .50 ball. Fitted with 30" octagon barrel and single set trigger. Figured walnut stock and engraved lock plate. Cased, with powder horn. Limited to 1,000 rifles in 1978.

NIB	Exc.	V.G.	Good	Fair	Poor
1250	750	600	450	—	250

Jonathan Browning Mountain Rifle

Same as above, without fancy wood case or engraving. Chambered for .45- or .54-caliber.

NIB	Exc.	V.G.	Good	Fair	Poor
800	500	400	300	—	175

Model 1878 (Original)

Based on John M. Browning's first patent. Single-shot rifle. Only firearm manufactured by Browning brothers. Offered in several calibers. Only a few hundred probably exist with Ogden, Utah barrel address. Design later sold to Winchester. Sold under Winchester name as Model 1885 High Wall.

NIB	Exc.	V.G.	Good	Fair	Poor
—	50000	40000	30000	15000	5000

Model 1885 High Wall

Single-shot rifle, with falling block action and octagonal free-floating barrel. Similar to Model 78. Introduced in 1985. Stock is high grade walnut, with straight-grip and recoil pad. Furnished with 28" barrel. Offered in these calibers: .223, .22-250, .270, .30-06, 7mm Rem. Magnum, .45-70 Gov't. Weight about 8 lbs. 12 oz.

NIB	Exc.	V.G.	Good	Fair	Poor
1275	950	650	500	200	100

Model 1885 Low Wall

Introduced in 1995. Similar to above in a more accurate version of original Low Wall. Thin octagon barrel 24" in length. Trigger pull adjustable. Walnut stock fitted with pistol-grip and schnabel forearm. Offered in .22 Hornet, .223 Rem. and .243 Win. calibers. Weight about 6.4 lbs.

NIB	Exc.	V.G.	Good	Fair	Poor
1150	850	550	400	300	150

Model 1885 Low Wall Traditional Hunter

Introduced in 1998. Similar to Low Wall, with half-octagon half-round 24" barrel. Chambered for .357 Magnum, .44 Magnum and .45 Colt cartridges. Case colored receiver and crescent butt, with tang sight also featured. Weight about 6.5 lbs.

NIB	Exc.	V.G.	Good	Fair	Poor
1150	850	550	400	300	150

Model 1885 BPCR (Black Powder Cartridge Rifle)

Introduced in 1996 for BPCR metallic silhouette shoots. Chambered for .45-70 or .40-60 caliber. Receiver case colored, 28" round barrel fitted with vernier sight with level. Walnut stock has checkered pistol-grip. Fitted with tang sight. Weight about 11 lbs.

NIB	Exc.	V.G.	Good	Fair	Poor
1600	1300	800	400	300	150

Model 1885 BPCR Creedmoor Type

Introduced in 1998. Chambered for .45-90 cartridge. Features 34" heavy half-round barrel, with long range tang sight and wind gauge front sight. Weight about 11 lbs. 13 oz.

NIB	Exc.	V.G.	Good	Fair	Poor
1800	1500	1150	900	500	300

Model 1885 High Wall Traditional Hunter

Variation of Model 1885 series. Introduced in 1997. Fitted with an oil finish walnut stock and crescent buttplate. Barrel octagonal and 28" in length. Rear sight buckhorn. Fitted with tang-mounted peep sight. Front sight gold bead classic style. Chambered for .30-30, .38-55 and .45-70 cartridges. Weight about 9 lbs. In 1998, .454 Casull caliber added.

NIB	Exc.	V.G.	Good	Fair	Poor
1200	950	700	575	400	275

Model 1886 Grade I

Lever action sporting rifle. Patterned after Model 1886 Winchester. Chambered for .45-70 cartridge. Has 26" octagonal barrel, with full-length tubular magazine. Finish blued, with walnut stock. Crescent buttplate. Manufactured 7,000 in 1986.

NIB	Exc.	V.G.	Good	Fair	Poor
1350	950	725	600	450	300

Carbine

NIB	Exc.	V.G.	Good	Fair	Poor
950	650	550	400	325	250

Model 1886 High Grade

Deluxe version of Model 1886. Features game scene engraving, with gold accents and checkered select walnut stock. "1 of 3,000" engraved on top of barrel. Manufactured 3,000 in 1986.

NIB	Exc.	V.G.	Good	Fair	Poor
1900	1600	1000	700	—	—

Carbine

NIB	Exc.	V.G.	Good	Fair	Poor
1600	1100	900	600	—	—

Model 1886 Montana Centennial

Similar to High Grade, with different engraving pattern. Designed to commemorate Centennial of State of Montana. There were 2,000 manufactured in 1986. All commemorative's must be NIB with all supplied materials to command collector interest.

NIB	Exc.	V.G.	Good	Fair	Poor
2000	1600	1200	—	—	—

B-92 Carbine

Lever-action sporting rifle. Patterned after Winchester Model 92. Chambered for .357 Magnum and .44 Magnum cartridges. Has 20" barrel, with 11-round tubular magazine. Finish blued, with walnut stock. Discontinued in 1986. **NOTE:** Add 10 percent for Centennial Model; 30 percent for .357 Magnum.

NIB	Exc.	V.G.	Good	Fair	Poor
—	700	625	400	250	120

Model 1895 Grade I

Lever-action sporting rifle. Chambered in .30-40 Krag and .30-06 cartridge. Patterned after Model 1895 Winchester. Has 24" barrel and 4-round integral box magazine. Buckhorn rear sight and blade front. Finish blued, with walnut stock. Manufactured 6,000 in .30-06 and 2,000 chambered for .30-40 Krag, in 1984.

NIB	Exc.	V.G.	Good	Fair	Poor
—	950	675	475	375	275

Model 1895 High Grade

Deluxe engraved version of Model 1895. Has gold-inlaid game scenes and gold-plated trigger. Features checkered select walnut stock. Produced 2,000 in 1984—1,000 in each caliber.

NIB	Exc.	V.G.	Good	Fair	Poor
—	1500	1250	900	700	400

Express Rifle

Over/under superposed rifle. Chambered for .270 Winchester or .30-06 cartridges. Has 24" barrels, with folding express sights and automatic ejectors. Features a single trigger. Receiver engraved. Finish blue, with deluxe checkered walnut stock. Introduced in 1980. Discontinued in 1986.

NIB	Exc.	V.G.	Good	Fair	Poor
—	6500	3950	2000	1100	800

Custom Shop Express Rifles

Produced in two different models, Herstall and CCS 375. Both are custom-built, with choice of engraving patterns.

Herstal Express Rifle

NIB	Exc.	V.G.	Good	Fair	Poor
N/A	23000	17500	12000	5500	700

Continental Set

Consists of Express Rifle chambered for .30-06 cartridge. Furnished with an extra set of 20-gauge over/under barrels. Shotgun barrels are 26.5" in length. Single trigger, automatic ejectors and heavily engraved receiver. Select walnut stock hand checkered and oil-finished. Furnished with a fitted case. Manufactured 500 between 1978 and 1986.

NIB	Exc.	V.G.	Good	Fair	Poor
10000	9250	8000	4500	2000	1000

BRUCE & DAVIS
Webster, Massachusetts

Double-Barreled Pistol

.36-caliber double-barrel percussion pistol, with 3" to 6" round barrels. Barrel rib marked "Bruce & Davis". Blued, with walnut grips. Manufactured during 1840s.

NIB	Exc.	V.G.	Good	Fair	Poor
—	—	925	400	175	100

BRUCHET
Ste. Etienne, France

Model A Shotgun

12-gauge or .410 bore side-by-side shotgun, with double triggers and automatic ejectors. Barrel lengths and chokes to customer specifications. Produced on limited basis (50 per year) since 1982. Base price listed.

NIB	Exc.	V.G.	Good	Fair	Poor
3600	2750	1900	1450	1000	500

Model B

As above, with finer finish and spring-assisted action opener. Imported since 1982.

NIB	Exc.	V.G.	Good	Fair	Poor
6950	5250	4000	3000	2250	1250

BRUFF, R.P.
New York, New York

Pocket Pistol

.41-caliber single-shot percussion pistol, with 2.5" to 3" barrels. Marked "R.P. Bruff NY" in an arch and "Cast Steel". German silver, with checkered walnut stock. Manufactured between 1861 and 1870.

NIB	Exc.	V.G.	Good	Fair	Poor
—	—	1900	825	225	100

BRYCO ARMS
Carson City, Nevada
See—Jennings

BSA GUNS LTD.
Birmingham, England

Established in 1861, this firm has produced a wide variety of firearms over the years. Most common of these arms that are currently available in United States are listed.

SINGLE-SHOT

No. 12 Cadet Martini

.310-caliber single-shot Martini action rifle, with 29" barrel, adjustable sights and straight-grip walnut stock. Manufactured approximately 80,000 from 1911 to 1913. Many of those imported into U.S. were altered to .22-caliber.

NIB	Exc.	V.G.	Good	Fair	Poor
—	750	500	300	150	100

Centurian Match Rifle

As above in .22-caliber, with 24" barrel, adjustable sights. Pistol-grip walnut stock.

NIB	Exc.	V.G.	Good	Fair	Poor
—	600	450	300	200	100

Model 13 Sporter

As above in .22 Hornet, with hunting sights.

NIB	Exc.	V.G.	Good	Fair	Poor
—	650	425	300	225	100

Martini International Match

As above, with heavy match barrel, ISU-style sights and match stock. Manufactured from 1950 to 1953.

NIB	Exc.	V.G.	Good	Fair	Poor
—	750	575	325	250	125

Martini International Light

As above, with 26" lighter weight barrel.

NIB	Exc.	V.G.	Good	Fair	Poor
—	750	575	325	250	125

Martini International ISU

As above meeting ISU specifications, with 28" barrel. Manufactured from 1968 to 1976.

NIB	Exc.	V.G.	Good	Fair	Poor
—	850	675	400	325	200

BOLT-ACTIONS

Royal

Bolt-action sporting rifle. Manufactured in a variety of calibers. 24" barrel, with checkered French walnut stock.

NIB	Exc.	V.G.	Good	Fair	Poor
—	550	500	250	200	100

Majestic Deluxe

.22 Hornet, .222, .243, 7x57mm, .308 or .30-06 bolt-action sporting rifle, with 22" barrel. Folding rear sight, checkered walnut stock, with schnabel fore-end tip. Imported from 1959 to 1965. **NOTE:** Add 60 percent for .22 Hornet.

NIB	Exc.	V.G.	Good	Fair	Poor
—	550	350	250	200	100

Majestic Deluxe Featherweight

As above in .270 or .458 Magnum, with thinner barrel. **NOTE:** Add 25 percent for .458; 75 percent for .458.

NIB	Exc.	V.G.	Good	Fair	Poor
—	550	350	250	200	100

Monarch Deluxe

As above drilled and tapped for telescopic sight. Available in heavy barreled varmint version in .222- or .243-caliber. Imported from 1966 to 1974.

NIB	Exc.	V.G.	Good	Fair	Poor
—	550	375	275	225	100

HERTERS U9

Firm of Herters, Inc. of Waseca, Minnesota, imported BSA rifle actions beginning in 1965 that were used for custom-made rifles. Commencing in 1986, BSA began production of a new line of bolt-action sporting rifles on Model CF-2 action. Standard production models listed.

Sporter/Classic

Hunting rifle available in a variety of calibers, with checkered walnut stock. Introduced in 1986.

NIB	Exc.	V.G.	Good	Fair	Poor
—	450	325	275	200	100

Varminter

As above, with matte-finished heavy barrel in .222-, .22-250- or .243-caliber. Introduced in 1986.

NIB	Exc.	V.G.	Good	Fair	Poor
—	350	275	225	175	100

Stutzen Rifle

As above, with 20.5" barrel. Mannlicher-style stock.

NIB	Exc.	V.G.	Good	Fair	Poor
—	475	350	275	225	100

Regal Custom

As above, with engraved receiver, checkered walnut stock and ebony fore-end. Imported only in 1986.

NIB	Exc.	V.G.	Good	Fair	Poor
—	925	750	600	500	250

CFT Target Rifle

.308-caliber single-shot version of above, with 26.5" barrel and adjustable sights. Imported only in 1987.

NIB	Exc.	V.G.	Good	Fair	Poor
—	750	600	550	400	200

SHOTGUNS

Royal

Side-by-side chambered for 12- or 20-gauge 3" shells. Choice of 26" or 28" barrels, with multi-chokes. Checkered select walnut stock, with straight-grip. Splinter forearm. Case colored receiver, with side plates. Single selective trigger. Recoil pad standard. Weight about: 7.25 lbs. 12-gauge; 6.75 lbs. 20-gauge.

NIB	Exc.	V.G.	Good	Fair	Poor
1500	1150	900	675	—	—

Classic

Side-by-side offered in 12-, 16-, 20-, 28-gauge and .410 bore. Choice of 26" or 28" barrels, except for 28-gauge and .410 bore where 26" barrels are only length offered. Checkered walnut stock, with pistol-grip. Case colored box lock receiver, with scroll engraving. Semi-beavertail forearm. Recoil pad and choke tubes standard. Weight about: 7.25 lbs. 12-gauge; 6.75 lbs. 16-gauge; 6.6 lbs. 20-gauge; 6.25 lbs. 28-gauge; 6.5 lbs. .410 bore.

NIB	Exc.	V.G.	Good	Fair	Poor
1300	975	800	600	400	200

Falcon

Over/under in 12- or 20-gauge with 3" chambers. Choice of 26" or 28" barrels, with ventilated rib and choke tubes. Checkered walnut stock, with pistol-grip. Case colored scroll engraved receiver. Single selective trigger. Automatic ejectors. Recoil pad standard. Weight about: 7.25 lbs. 12-gauge; 7 lbs. 20-gauge.

NIB	Exc.	V.G.	Good	Fair	Poor
1200	900	875	500	300	150

Falcon Sporting

Similar to Falcon. Offered only in 12-gauge, with 2.75" chambers. Choice of 28" or 30" ventilated rib barrels, with 5 chokes tubes. Barrels ported. Checkered walnut stock, with schnabel forearm. Weight about 7.7 lbs.

NIB	Exc.	V.G.	Good	Fair	Poor
1250	950	775	475	275	125

Silver Eagle

Over/under chambered for 12- or 20-gauge 3" shell. Fitted with 26" or 28" ventilated rib barrels, with choke tubes. Checkered walnut stock, with pistol-grip. Single selective trigger. Blued box lock receiver. Recoil pad standard. Weight about: 7.2 lbs. 12-gauge; 6.75 lbs. 20-gauge.

NIB	Exc.	V.G.	Good	Fair	Poor
490	375	300	250	200	125

Silver Eagle II

Similar to Silver Eagle above. Addition of automatic ejectors.

NIB	Exc.	V.G.	Good	Fair	Poor
590	425	275	225	175	100

200 Series

Series of semi-automatic shotguns. Chambered for 12-, 16-, 20-, 28-gauge and .410 bore. Offered with 26" or 28" ventilated rib barrels, with choke tubes in 12-, 16- and 20-gauge; 28-gauge and .410 bore in 26" barrels only.. All gauges offered with walnut or synthetic stocks. 20-gauge offered in a youth model, with shortened stock. All gauges have 3" chambers except for 28-gauge, with 2.75" chambers. Weights range from 7.4 lbs. to 6.5 lbs. **NOTE:** Add $70 for walnut stock.

NIB	Exc.	V.G.	Good	Fair	Poor
390	290	225	200	100	75

300 SM Series

Semi-automatic series offered in 12-gauge only, with 3.5" chambers. Choice of 24", 26" or 28" ventilated rib barrels, with choke tubes. Synthetic stock. Weight about 7.3 lbs.

NIB	Exc.	V.G.	Good	Fair	Poor
420	315	250	225	175	100

BUCO
Germany

Buco Gas Pistol

Odd firearm looks more like a telescope than pistol. Chambered for 10.55mm gas cartridge. Single-shot. Overall approximately 5.5" long in its open or cocked position. Barrel is smooth bore and 3.75" in length. No sights or safety—one simply pulls inner tube back much like extending a telescope, unscrews end cap, inserts round and screws cap back into place. When needed, a thumbnail is used to depress sear and fire pistol. Marked on end cap "Buco DRGM". No more information available as to quantity or year of manufacture.

NIB	Exc.	V.G.	Good	Fair	Poor
—	—	650	500	350	150

BUDISCHOWSKY
Norton Armament Corp.
Mt. Clemens, Michigan

TP-70

.22 or .25 ACP caliber semi-automatic pistol, with 2.5" barrel, fixed sights and 6-shot magazine. Stainless steel, with plastic grips. Manufactured between 1973 and 1977.

NOTE: German-designed Budischowsky was originally made in Michigan by Norton Armament Corp. Michigan-made Budischowsky's are considered better quality than later examples made in Florida and Utah. Deduct 15% for non-Michigan manufacture.

.22 Rimfire Caliber

NIB	Exc.	V.G.	Good	Fair	Poor
550	425	350	300	225	150

.25 ACP Caliber

NIB	Exc.	V.G.	Good	Fair	Poor
525	400	325	275	175	125

BUL TRANSMARK LTD.
Tel-Aviv, Israel

Model M5

This model was brought into the USA from 1996 to 2010 by several importers, including ISA, KBI, EAA and others. Semi-automatic bears a resemblance to Model 1911. Frame polymer, slide stainless steel. Available in 9mm, .38 Super, .40 S&W and .45 ACP. Magazine limited to 10 rounds. **NOTE:** Add 40 to 60 percent for IPSC competition models.

NIB	Exc.	V.G.	Good	Fair	Poor
750	600	450	350	200	100

BULLARD REPEATING ARMS CO.
Springfield, Massachusetts

Designed by James H. Bullard. Rifles listed were manufactured in competition with those produced by Whitney Arms Company and Winchester Repeating Arms Company. Approximately 12,000 made between 1886 and 1890.

Small Frame

.32-40 and .38-45 caliber lever action rifle, with 26" octagonal barrel. Half or full length magazine tube. Blued or case hardened, with walnut stock. Receiver stamped "Bullard Repeating Arms Company/Springfield, Mass., U.S.A. Pat. Aug. 16, 1881". Caliber marked on top of frame.

Courtesy Milwaukee Public Museum, Milwaukee, Wisconsin

NIB	Exc.	V.G.	Good	Fair	Poor
—	—	4000	2050	675	300

Large Frame

.40-75 through .45-85 caliber lever action rifle, with 28" octagonal barrel. Other features and markings as above. Can be custom ordered in .50-95 and .50-115.

NIB	Exc.	V.G.	Good	Fair	Poor
—	—	5150	2500	875	400

Carbine

.45-70 caliber lever action rifle, with 22" round barrel. Sliding dust cover on receiver. Marking and finish as above.

NIB	Exc.	V.G.	Good	Fair	Poor
—	—	7950	3800	1500	500

Musket

.45-70 caliber lever action rifle, with 30" round barrel. Full-length stock secured by two barrel bands. Rod under barrel, military sights and same sliding cover on receiver as found on Carbine. Examples noted without manufacturer's markings.

NIB	Exc.	V.G.	Good	Fair	Poor
—	—	7500	3500	1500	500

BULLDOG SINGLE-SHOT PISTOL
Connecticut Arms & Manufacturing Co.
Naubuc, Connecticut

Bulldog

.44- or .50-caliber single-shot spur trigger pistol, with 4" or 6" barrels. Pivoting breechblock that moves to left for loading. Blued, case hardened and stamped "Connecticut Arms & Manf. Co. Naubuc Conn. Patented Oct. 25, 1864". Only a few hundred manufactured. Produced between 1866 and 1868. **NOTE:** Add 40 percent for .50-caliber 6" barreled versions.

NIB	Exc.	V.G.	Good	Fair	Poor
—	—	1650	675	275	150

BURGESS GUN CO.
Buffalo, New York
Also See—Colt and Whitney

One of the most prolific 19th century designers was Andrew Burgess, who established his own company in 1892. Burgess Gun Company manufactured slide action shotguns and rifles, operated by a unique pistol-grip prior to their being purchased by Winchester Repeating Arms Company in 1899. Arms based on Burgess' patents were manufactured by a variety of American gun makers. Serial numbers for all Burgess shotguns begin at 1000.

12 Gauge Slide Action Shotgun

12-gauge slide-action shotgun, with 28" or 30" barrel. Blued, with walnut stock. Available with 6 grades of engraving. Values listed are for standard plain model.

Burgess engraving grades (1-4)

NIB	Exc.	V.G.	Good	Fair	Poor
—	—	1700	700	250	125

Folding Shotgun

As above, with 19.5" barrel. Hinged so it may be folded back against buttstock.

NIB	Exc.	V.G.	Good	Fair	Poor
—	—	4550	1750	650	300

Slide Action Rifle

Extremely rare rifle based upon shotgun design described above. Manufactured in at least three calibers, with varying barrel lengths. Blued, with walnut stock.

NIB	Exc.	V.G.	Good	Fair	Poor
—	—	3950	1500	500	250

BURGSMULLER, K.
Krelensen, Germany

Burgo

Rohm RG10 under another name. It is a poor quality inexpensive .38-caliber revolver. Examples marketed by Burgsmuller are so marked. Virtually worthless.

Regent

Regent is a .22-caliber revolver that resembles Colt Police Positive in appearance. Higher quality than Burgo. Manufacturer not known.

NIB	Exc.	V.G.	Good	Fair	Poor
—	165	125	75	50	5

BURNSIDE RIFLE CO.
Bristol Firearms Co.
Bristol & Providence, Rhode Island

Bristol, Rhode Island

Historically desirable firearm for Civil War collectors. Designer, Ambrose E. Burnside, was to become a well- known Union general. Rifle, of which there were four distinct models, was used quite extensively in Civil War. This carbine was manufactured first by Bristol Firearms Co., which made entire production of first model and also some of second model. In 1862 Burnside Firearms Co. was formed. They produced remainder of second models and all third and fourth models. Production ceased entirely in 1865.

Burnside Carbine 1st Model

Produced by Bristol. Chambered for .54-caliber. Breechloader that uses percussion ignition system, but features a cartridge of sorts made of copper and a tape priming device that was located inside frame. Has 22" round barrel, with no fore-end, walnut stock and inspector's cartouche. Finish blued and case-colored. Frame stamped "Burnside's /Patent/ March 25th/1856". Approximately 250 1st Models manufactured.

NIB	Exc.	V.G.	Good	Fair	Poor
—	—	15000	6000	1500	500

2nd Model

2nd Model features an improved breechblock opening mechanism located inside trigger guard. Barrel is 21" long. Other features similar to 1st Model. Marked either "Bristol Firearm Co." or "Burnside Rifle Co./ Providence-R.I.". Barrel marked "Cast Steel 1861" and some breechblock devices marked "G.P. Foster Pat./April 10th 1860". Approximately 1,500 2nd Models manufactured in 1861 and 1862.

Courtesy Milwaukee Public Museum, Milwaukee, Wisconsin

NIB	Exc.	V.G.	Good	Fair	Poor
—	—	5500	2500	750	300

3rd Model

Differs from 2nd Model in it has a fore-end, with a barrel band and slightly modified hammer. Markings same as Burnside-manufactured 2nd Models. Approximately 2,000 produced in 1862.

NIB	Exc.	V.G.	Good	Fair	Poor
—	—	3500	1250	500	250

4th Model

Differs from others in it features a hinged breech that permits simpler loading of odd-shaped Burnside percussion cartridge. Frame marked "Burnside's Patent/Model of 1864". Other features similar to 3rd Model. Approximately 50,000 manufactured between 1862 and 1865.

Courtesy Milwaukee Public Museum, Milwaukee, Wisconsin

NIB	Exc.	V.G.	Good	Fair	Poor
—	—	4000	2000	800	400

BUSHMASTER FIREARMS INTERNATIONAL
Ilion, New York

In 2006, Bushmaster was purchased by Freedom Group, parent company of Remington, Marlin/H&R, DPMS, Para USA and Dakota Arms. In 2011, Bushmaster plant in Maine was closed and production moved to Remington facility in Ilion, New York.

ACR (Adaptive Combat Rifle)

Series of fully modular AR-15 pattern rifles in 5.56 NATO/.223 Rem., with all major components configurable to user preference, including barrel, stock and hand guard. Features include adjustable gas piston-driven system, ambidextrous controls, 16.5" barrel, A2 birdcage flash hider and 30-round magazine. Made in several variations beginning in 2010. Prices shown are for Basic Folder configuration.

NIB	Exc.	V.G.	Good	Fair	Poor
1850	1600	1200	800	400	200

ACR Enhanced

Semi-automatic Adaptive Combat Rifle chambered in 5.56 NATO. Barrel is quickly interchangeable and available in 10.5", 14.5", 16.5" and 18.5". AAC Blackout 51T flash hider, 3-rail enhanced hand guard, with 7-position folding/telescoping stock. A-TACs model has fixed A-frame composite camo stock, with rubber butt pad and sling mounts. Introduced in 2013.

NIB	Exc.	V.G.	Good	Fair	Poor
1950	1700	1300	900	500	300

XM15-E2S Target Model

Furnished with 20" heavy barrel and A-2 stock. Weight 8.35 lbs. **NOTE:** Add $10 for 24" barrel; $20 for 26" barrel; $75 for A3 carry handle.

NIB	Exc.	V.G.	Good	Fair	Poor
800	675	550	400	300	200

XM15-E2S V-Match Competition Rifle

Specially designed competition rifle, with 20", 24" or 26" barrel lengths. Fitted with black anodized aluminum handguard. Weight about 8.1 lbs. **NOTE:** Add $75 for A3 carry handle.

NIB	Exc.	V.G.	Good	Fair	Poor
950	800	700	450	350	250

XM15-E2S V-Match Carbine

As above, with 16" barrel. Weight about 6.9 lbs. **NOTE:** Add $75 for A3 carry handle.

NIB	Exc.	V.G.	Good	Fair	Poor
900	700	575	450	350	250

XM15 3-Gun Enhanced Carbine

Designed for 3-Gun competition, with crimson anodized upper and lower receiver, 16" mid-length stainless barrel, 15" carbon fiber free-float tube, Rolling Thunder compensator and Timney trigger. Other features include Boron nitride bolt carrier group, Bravo Company charging handle, ambidextrous selector switch, Magpul MIAD grip and MOE stock. Introduced in 2014.

NIB	Exc.	V.G.	Good	Fair	Poor
1485	1225	1000	750	500	250

XM15-E2S Shorty Carbine

This "post-ban" model M16 is a gas-operated semi-automatic rifle. Chambered for .223 Remington cartridge. Fitted with heavy 16" barrel and 30-round magazine. Overall length 35"; empty weight 6.72 lbs. **NOTE:** Add $50 for fluted barrel; $75 for A3-type carry handle.

NIB	Exc.	V.G.	Good	Fair	Poor
—	675	550	450	300	200

XM15-E2S Dissipator

Similar to above model, with 16" barrel. Fitted with longer plastic hand guard to give a longer sight radius. Weight 7.2 lbs. **NOTE:** Add $75 for A3 carry handle.

NIB	Exc.	V.G.	Good	Fair	Poor
950	775	600	450	300	200

XM15 Patrolman's Pistol

This law-enforcement-only model has a 7" or 10.5" barrel, with flash hider, A2 pistol-grip and knurled free-float handguard. Enhanced model has Barnes Precision free-float lightweight quad rail, Magpul MOE pistol-grip and trigger guard. **NOTE:** Add $200 for enhanced model.

NIB	Exc.	V.G.	Good	Fair	Poor
825	750	600	500	400	250

M4 Post-Ban Carbine

Introduced in 2001. Features 14.5" barrel, with permanently attached Mini Y Comp muzzle-brake (total length 16") and pinned fixed-length Tele-style stock. Chambered for .223-caliber. M16A2 rear sight. Supplied with 10-round magazine. Weight about 6.6 lbs.

NIB	Exc.	V.G.	Good	Fair	Poor
1050	900	750	450	300	200

M4A3 Post-Ban Carbine

Same as above, with removable carry handle. Introduced in 2001.

NIB	Exc.	V.G.	Good	Fair	Poor
1125	975	825	500	400	300

MOE Series

Features Magpul Original Equipment (MOE) accessories, including rifle-length hand guard, adjustable stock, grip and 30-shot magazine. Chambered for .223 (5.56) or .308. **NOTE:** Add $400 for .308.

NIB	Exc.	V.G.	Good	Fair	Poor
900	800	675	500	300	200

DCM Competition Rifle

Features 20" extra heavy barrel, with free floating fore-end. Competition sights and trigger. Supplied with buttstock weight, 10-round magazine and hard carrying case.

NIB	Exc.	V.G.	Good	Fair	Poor
1350	1075	800	600	500	350

11.5" Barrel Carbine

AR-style carbine chambered in 5.56/.223. Features include 11.5" chrome-lined barrel, with permanently attached BATF-approved 5.5" flash suppressor, fixed or removable carry handle, optional optics rail, 30-round magazine. Overall length 31.625". Weight 6.46 or 6.81 lbs.

NIB	Exc.	V.G.	Good	Fair	Poor
900	775	600	450	300	200

Heavy-Barreled Carbine

AR-style semi-automatic carbine chambered in 5.56/.223. Features include chrome-lined heavy profile 16" vanadium steel barrel, fixed or removable carry handle, six-position telestock. Overall length 32.5". Weight

6.93 lbs. to 7.28 lbs.

NIB	Exc.	V.G.	Good	Fair	Poor
1000	850	700	550	300	200

Modular Carbine

AR-style carbine chambered in 5.56/.223. Features include 16" chrome-lined chrome-moly vanadium steel barrel, skeleton stock or six-position telestock, clamp-on front sight and detachable flip-up dual aperture rear and 30-round magazine. Overall length 36.25". Weight 7.3 lbs.

NIB	Exc.	V.G.	Good	Fair	Poor
1450	1200	1000	750	400	250

M17S Bullpup

Gas-operated semi-automatic rifle in bull-pup design. Chambered for .223 cartridge. Fitted with 21.5" barrel. Weight 8.2 lbs.

NIB	Exc.	V.G.	Good	Fair	Poor
800	675	500	400	300	200

Gas Piston Rifle

Semi-automatic AR-style rifle chambered in .223. Features include 16" barrel, telescoping stock, carry handle, 30-round magazine and piston assembly rather than direct gas impingement. Overall length 32.5". Weight 7.46 lbs.

NIB	Exc.	V.G.	Good	Fair	Poor
1750	1375	1050	800	650	300

6.8 SPC Carbine

AR-style semi-automatic rifle chambered in 6.8 SPC. Features include 16" M4 profile barrel, with Izzy muzzle-brake, 26-round magazine, six-position telestock. Available in A2 (fixed carry handle) or A3 (removable carry handle) configuration. Overall length 32.75". Weight 6.57 lbs. Also chambered in 7.62x39mm.

NIB	Exc.	V.G.	Good	Fair	Poor
1200	1150	950	800	650	300

Carbon 15 9mm Carbine

Semi-automatic carbine chambered in 9mm Parabellum. Carbon fiber frame, 16" steel barrel, six-position telescoping stock, 30- round detachable magazine. Introduced 2006.

NIB	Exc.	V.G.	Good	Fair	Poor
1000	850	700	550	475	300

Carbon 15 Top Loading Rifle

Semi-automatic rifle chambered in .223. Carbon fiber frame, 16" steel barrel, retractable stock, Picatinny rail, 10-round fixed magazine. Based on AR-15. Introduced 2006.

NIB	Exc.	V.G.	Good	Fair	Poor
1000	850	700	550	475	300

Carbon 15 Quad Rail Flattop

Semi-automatic AR-style in 5.56 NATO. M4 contour 16.5" barrel, with A2 flash hider, fixed front sight bases and bayonet lug. Flat top upper receiver, with Mission First tactical pomer quad rail and four rail covers. Six-position adjustable stock. New in 2013.

NIB	Exc.	V.G.	Good	Fair	Poor
800	700	600	—	—	—

Predator

Semi-automatic rifle chambered in .223. 20" DCM-type barrel, fixed composite buttstock, 2-stage competition trigger, Picatinny rail, .500" scope risers. Based on AR-15. Introduced 2006.

NIB	Exc.	V.G.	Good	Fair	Poor
1100	900	750	600	525	325

Carbon 15 .22 Rimfire Rifle

Similar to Shorty carbine. Chambered in .22 LR. Blowback, with 10-round magazine.

NIB	Exc.	V.G.	Good	Fair	Poor
625	495	350	275	200	150

.308 Hunter

Designed for the hunter. Chambered in .308 Winchester, with 20" heavy-fluted barrel. Chrome lined bore and chamber. Features include 5-round magazine, mid-length gas system, two .75" mini risers for optics mounting, Hogue rubberized pistol-grip, standard A2 stock. Vista Hunter has A2 grip. Weight about 8.5 lbs. **NOTE:** Add $100 for Vista Hunter if NIB.

NIB	Exc.	V.G.	Good	Fair	Poor
1400	1100	925	775	500	300

ORC Series

Optics Ready Carbine series for shooters who wish to add various optical holograph, red dot or scope sights. Chambered in .223/5.56, with magazine capacity of 30 rounds or .308 with 20-round magazine. Gas piston system taps gas from barrel much like AK and FAL designs. Provides a cleaner operation with less recoil. Detented plug in gas block allows for easy cleaning. Barrel length 16"; weight 6.6 lbs. (.223) to 7.75 lbs. (.308). **NOTE:** Add $200 for .308 chambering.

NIB	Exc.	V.G.	Good	Fair	Poor
1125	965	825	700	500	300

Quick Response Carbine

This model equipped with detachable red dot sight, 16" barrel, 10-shot magazine and six-position collapsible stock.

NIB	Exc.	V.G.	Good	Fair	Poor
600	500	425	350	250	200

.450 Carbine

Chambered for .450 Bushmaster cartridge providing big-bore power in AR platform. Developed with Hornady Mfg., cartridge propels a 250-grain bullet at 2200 fps, ideal for most North American big game. Barrel length 16" or 20", A3 flattop receiver with Picatinny rail. Weight about 8.5 lbs.

NIB	Exc.	V.G.	Good	Fair	Poor
1200	1025	900	750	550	350

Bushmaster AK Carbine

AR-type rifle, with AK-type muzzle-brake and permanently pinned suppressor. 5.56 NATO caliber.

NIB	Exc.	V.G.	Good	Fair	Poor
1100	950	800	650	300	200

Bushmaster .300 AAC Blackout

AR-type rifle chambered for .300 AAC cartridge. Developed by Advanced Armament Corporation, which is now part of Freedom Group that owns Bushmaster. Round's ballistics are similar to 7.62x39 and .300 Whisper wildcat. .300 AAC is factory loaded by Remington, including a sub-sonic load. Compatible with AR-15 magazines.

NIB	Exc.	V.G.	Good	Fair	Poor
1300	1050	875	700	300	200

BA50 .50 BMG Rifle and Carbine

Bolt-action 10-round repeater intended for long-range target shooting. 30" barrel, muzzle-brake. Carbine has 20" barrel.

NIB	Exc.	V.G.	Good	Fair	Poor
5000	4200	3700	3000	—	—

Carbon 15 .223 Pistol

AR-style semi-automatic pistol chambered in 5.56/.223. Features include 7.5" stainless steel barrel, carbon composite receiver, shortened handguard, full-length optics rail, A2-type front sight with dual-aperture flip-up rear. 30-round magazine. Overall length 20". Weight 2.88 lbs.

NIB	Exc.	V.G.	Good	Fair	Poor
800	700	550	400	300	200

Carbon 15 9mm Pistol

Operating controls similar to AR-type rifles, 30 round capacity. Weight with loaded magazine 5.5 lbs. Carbon fiber receiver, fore-end and grip, with Chrome Moly steel barrel. Full length Picatinny rail.

NIB	Exc.	V.G.	Good	Fair	Poor
800	700	550	400	300	200

Type 97 Pistol

Similar to above, without hand guard.

NIB	Exc.	V.G.	Good	Fair	Poor
750	650	500	400	300	200

BUTLER, WM. S.
Rocky Hill, Connecticut

Butler Single-Shot Pistol

.36-caliber single-shot percussion pocket pistol, with 2.5" barrel. Frame and grip made in one piece. Frame marked "Wm. S. Butler's Patent/ Patented Feb.3, 1857".

NIB	Exc.	V.G.	Good	Fair	Poor
—	—	975	385	150	50

BUTTERFIELD, JESSE
Philadelphia, Pennsylvania

Butterfield Army Revolver

.41-caliber revolver, with 7" octagonal barrel and unfluted 5-shot cylinder. Features a special priming device disk that was loaded in front of trigger guard. Brass frame, blued with walnut grips. Frame stamped "Butterfield's Patent Dec. 11, 1855/Phila.". Approximately 650 manufactured in 1861 and 1862.

Courtesy Milwaukee Public Museum, Milwaukee, Wisconsin

NIB	Exc.	V.G.	Good	Fair	Poor
—	—	6000	2250	875	450

Butterfield Pocket Pistol

.41-caliber single-shot percussion pistol, with 2" to 3.5" barrel. German silver, with walnut stocks. Lock marked "Butterfield's/Patent Dec 11, 1855". Extremely rare. Manufactured in 1850s.

NIB	Exc.	V.G.	Good	Fair	Poor
—	—	9000	4250	1650	1000

CABANAS, INDUSTRIAS S.A.
Aguilas, Mexico

This company manufactures a variety of bolt-action single-shot rifles that utilize .22-caliber blanks to propel a .177-caliber pellet. Scarce, but not especially valuable.

Mini-82 Youth

NIB	Exc.	V.G.	Good	Fair	Poor
75	65	50	40	30	20

R-83 Larger Youth

NIB	Exc.	V.G.	Good	Fair	Poor
85	75	60	50	40	30

Safari A

NIB	Exc.	V.G.	Good	Fair	Poor
100	90	75	50	40	30

Varmint

NIB	Exc.	V.G.	Good	Fair	Poor
125	110	90	75	—	35

Espronceda IV

NIB	Exc.	V.G.	Good	Fair	Poor
125	110	90	75	50	35

Leyre

NIB	Exc.	V.G.	Good	Fair	Poor
140	125	100	85	65	50

Master

NIB	Exc.	V.G.	Good	Fair	Poor
150	130	110	100	75	60

CALICO
Cleveland, Ohio
See—American Industries, Inc.

CAMEX-BLASER USA, INC.
Ft. Worth, Texas
See—Blaser Jagdwaffen

CAMPO GIRO
Eibar, Spain

Esperanza y Unceta Model 1904

Designed by Lt. Col. Venancio Aguirre. This pistol was produced in limited numbers.

NIB	Exc.	V.G.	Good	Fair	Poor
—	3000	2000	1500	1000	800

Model 1910

Similar to above in 9mm Largo. Tested, but not adopted by Spanish army.

NIB	Exc.	V.G.	Good	Fair	Poor
—	2000	1500	1000	800	600

Model 1913

An improved version of above. About 1,300 made.

Courtesy James Rankin

NIB	Exc.	V.G.	Good	Fair	Poor
—	1500	1250	850	600	500

Model 1913/16

An improved version of above. About 13,000 built.

Courtesy James Rankin

NIB	Exc.	V.G.	Good	Fair	Poor
—	2000	1550	1000	600	350

CARACAL

Caracal-F

Chambered for 9mm Parabellum. Caracal has a DAO trigger and is striker-fired. Features include a polymer frame, steel slide, ambidextrous magazine release and 18-round magazine. Weight 26.5 oz. Barrel length 4.1". Finish matte blue. Caracal-C is compact variation, with 3.5" barrel. Weight 24.7 oz. Made in United Arab Emirates. Introduced in 2011.

CARACAL "F"

NIB	Exc.	V.G.	Good	Fair	Poor
535	465	400	300	200	100

CARD, S. W.
Location Unknown

Under Hammer Pistol

A .34-caliber single-shot percussion pocket pistol, with 7.75" half octagonal barrel marked "S.W. Card" and "Cast Steel". Blued, with walnut grips.

NIB	Exc.	V.G.	Good	Fair	Poor
—	—	1500	450	150	50

CARLTON, M.
Haverhill, New Hampshire

Under Hammer Pistol

A .34-caliber percussion under hammer single-shot pistol, with 3.5" to 7.75" half-octagonal barrel marked "M. Carleton & Co.". Browned, with walnut grips. Active 1830s and 1840s.

NIB	Exc.	V.G.	Good	Fair	Poor
—	—	1800	600	200	100

CASARTELLI, CARLO
Brescia, Italy

Sidelock Shotgun

Custom order sidelock shotgun. Available in any gauge, barrel length, choke, automatic ejectors, single-selective trigger and choice of engraving style.

NIB	Exc.	V.G.	Good	Fair	Poor
16000	14500	10500	8250	6000	4000

Kenya Double Rifle

Custom order full sidelock rifle that is available in all standard and Magnum calibers.

NIB	Exc.	V.G.	Good	Fair	Poor
33000	29000	24000	18900	13000	9000

Africa Model

Bolt-action rifle built on a square-bridge Magnum Mauser action. Chambered for heavy Magnum calibers and can be taken down for transport. Other features on a custom order basis.

NIB	Exc.	V.G.	Good	Fair	Poor
9750	8800	7500	5750	4750	3750

Safari Model

Built on a standard Mauser bolt-action. Chambered for non-Magnum calibers.

NIB	Exc.	V.G.	Good	Fair	Poor
8000	7200	5800	4500	3250	2500

CASE WILLARD & CO.
New Hartford, Connecticut

Under Hammer Pistol

A .31-caliber single-shot percussion pistol, with 3" half-octagonal barrel marked "Case Willard & Co./New Hartford Conn.". Blued brass frame, with walnut grips.

NIB	Exc.	V.G.	Good	Fair	Poor
—	—	1400	550	200	100

CASPIAN ARMS, LTD.
Hardwick, Vermont

This company is primarily a 1911 component manufacturer.

Vietnam Commemorative

Government Model engraved by J.J. Adams and nickel-plated. Walnut grips have a branch service medallion inlaid. Gold plating was available for an additional $350. There were 1,000 manufactured in 1986.

Courtesy James Rankin

NIB	Exc.	V.G.	Good	Fair	Poor
1800	1350	950	650	475	300

CASULL ARMS, INC.
Afton, Wyoming

CA 2000

Chambered for .22 LR cartridge. This stainless steel palm sized revolver has a 5-round cylinder, with fold-up trigger. Double-action-only. Most recently produced "Velo-Dog". Discontinued.

NIB	Exc.	V.G.	Good	Fair	Poor
550	425	350	250	200	175

CA 3800

Chambered for .38 Casull cartridge (124 gr. 1800+fps). Fitted with 6" match barrel, magazine capacity of 8 rounds and full-length two-piece guide rod. Checkering on front strap and mainspring housing is 20 lpi. Match trigger and numerous other special features. Weight about 40 oz. Introduced in 2000. Discontinued. **NOTE:** Add $300 for extra .45 ACP barrel.

NIB	Exc.	V.G.	Good	Fair	Poor
2600	2050	1700	1200	650	300

CENTURY GUN COMPANY
Evansville, Knightstown & Greenfield, Indiana

Former manufacturer of large-caliber revolvers made in Evansville or Knightstown, Indiana between 1973 and 2001 or Greenfield, Indiana between 2002 and 2004.

Model 100

Single-action revolver, with 6-round capacity. Chambered originally for .45-70 Government, later for .30-30 Win., .375 Win., .444 Marlin, .50-70 and .50-110. Barrel lengths from 6.5" to 12", weight from 5.5- to 6 lbs. Adjustable sights, crossbolt safety. Prices shown are for .45-70 caliber. **NOTE:** Add 100 percent for .50-110 caliber; 20 percent for other calibers; 100 to 200 percent if in excellent condition for early production .45-70 guns marked Evansville, Indiana.

NIB	Exc.	V.G.	Good	Fair	Poor
1200	1100	900	750	400	200

CENTURY INTERNATIONAL ARMS CO.
Delray Beach, Florida

Century International Arms is a leading importer of military firearms. It was founded in 1961 in Albans, Vermont, moved to Boca Raton, Florida in 1997 and to Delray Beach in 2004. Many models are original military surplus, others have been re-stocked or re-barreled to make satisfactory hunting rifles. Inventory changes frequently and some models are imported in limited quantities. Company also imports new handguns, rifles and shotguns from various manufacturers and countries. The listed firearms represent only a few of the many models imported recently or in the past.

Centurion 39 AK Pistol

This current production AK-47 style pistol has a 11.4" barrel, black polymer stock and pistol-grip. Other features include four Picatinny rails and M-16 type birdcage muzzle-brake.

NIB	Exc.	V.G.	Good	Fair	Poor
825	700	550	400	300	200

Centurion UC-9 Carbine

Based on UZI submachine gun in semi-automatic. Chambered in 9mm, with folding stock, 16" barrel and two 32-round magazines.

NIB	Exc.	V.G.	Good	Fair	Poor
900	750	600	500	400	250

Centurion Over/Under Shotgun

New shotgun in 12-, 20-, 28-gauge and .410 bore, with 2.75" chambers. Checkered walnut stock. Receiver is blue. Offered in 28" ventilated rib barrels in full and modified chokes. Weight about 7.35 lbs. for 12-gauge; 5.3 lbs. for .410 bore.

NIB	Exc.	V.G.	Good	Fair	Poor
—	375	325	225	175	125

Centurion 98 Sporter

Refinished and rebuilt on a surplus German Mauser 98 action, with new commercial 22" barrel. No sights. Synthetic stock, with recoil pad is standard. Chambered for .270 or .30-06. Weight about 7 lbs. 13 oz.

NIB	Exc.	V.G.	Good	Fair	Poor
—	300	250	175	150	100

Century Centurion 14

Bolt-action rifle uses an Enfield Pattern 14 action. Drilled and tapped for scope mount. Barrel is 24". Chambered for 7mm Rem. Magnum. Walnut stock checkered, with pistol-grip and Monte Carlo comb. No sights.

NIB	Exc.	V.G.	Good	Fair	Poor
350	300	250	175	150	100

C93 Pistol

Based on Hecker & Koch MP-5 in semi-automatic. Chambered in 5.56 NATO or 7.63x39mm. Barrel 8.5", with flash suppressor and two 40-round magazines.

NIB	Exc.	V.G.	Good	Fair	Poor
900	750	600	500	400	250

CZ 999 / CZ 40

Based on CZ 9 and CZ 40 pistols in 9mm or .40 S&W. Barrels 3.5" or 4.24", with 15-round double-stack magazines. Current model made by Zastava in Serbia.

NIB	Exc.	V.G.	Good	Fair	Poor
450	400	350	300	200	150

Enfield Sporter No. I Mark III

Refinished rifle has a cut down Sporter-style stock. Action and sights are original. Caliber is .303.

NIB	Exc.	V.G.	Good	Fair	Poor
—	250	200	150	100	50

Enfield Sporter No. 4 Mark I

With new walnut stock.

LEE ENFIELD
No 4 Mark I Sporter
RI682 / 10LE41S
Nov 11, 1992

NIB	Exc.	V.G.	Good	Fair	Poor
—	260	210	150	100	50

TOZ-17

An original Russian rifle chambered for .22 LR. Has 21" barrel, 5-round magazine, checkered stock and iron sights. Weight about 5.4 lbs.

NIB	Exc.	V.G.	Good	Fair	Poor
—	175	135	110	50	40

TOZ-17-1

Same as above, with hooded front sight and tangent rear sight. Receiver grooved for scope mount.

NIB	Exc.	V.G.	Good	Fair	Poor
—	185	145	120	60	50

Mexican Mauser Model 1910 Sporter

Converted from military rifle to sporter by cutting down the stock. Metal refinished, barrel re-bored and re-chambered for .30-06 cartridge. Box magazine holds 5 rounds. Barrel 23"; weight about 8 lbs.

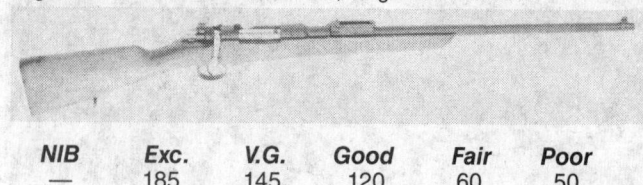

NIB	Exc.	V.G.	Good	Fair	Poor
—	185	145	120	60	50

FAL Sporter

Refinished FAL receiver and barrel installed on a synthetic thumbhole stock. Flash suppressor and bayonet lug have been removed. Barrel 20.75"; weight about 10 lbs.

NIB	Exc.	V.G.	Good	Fair	Poor
1000	850	650	450	350	150

M-14 Rifle

Imported from China by Century International. Features 22" barrel chambered for .308 Win. cartridge. Stock walnut, with rubber pad. Parkerized finish. Weight about 8.25 lbs.

NIB	Exc.	V.G.	Good	Fair	Poor
750	650	550	300	150	100

M85 Mini Mauser

Bolt action rifle in .22 Hornet, .223 Rem., or 7.62x39mm. Offered with standard Monte Carlo or full-length Mannlicher-style stock. Barrel lengths 18", 20" or 22". Current production model made in Serbia by Zastava.

NIB	Exc.	V.G.	Good	Fair	Poor
500	400	325	250	200	150

Tiger Dragunov Rifle

Shortened version of Russian SVD sniper rifle. Fitted with 20.8" barrel. Chambered for 7.62x54R cartridge. Sells with 5-round magazine and 4x range finding scope. Imported from Russia. Weight about 8.5 lbs.

NIB	Exc.	V.G.	Good	Fair	Poor
1000	850	700	500	350	150

GP WASR 10 Rifle

AK-47 design in 7.62x39mm caliber. Comes with two double-stack 30-round magazines. Available with 5- or 10-round fixed magazine. New, made by Romarm in Romania.

NIB	Exc.	V.G.	Good	Fair	Poor
500	400	325	275	200	100

Pietta SAA Millenium

Patterned after Colt Single Action Army Model of 1873. Chambered in .22 LR, .357 Magnum, .44-40 Win. or .45 Colt, with 4.75", 5.5" or 7.5" barrel, hardwood walnut-stained grips and case-colored frame. Made in Italy by Pietta

NIB	Exc.	V.G.	Good	Fair	Poor
400	350	300	250	200	150

Pietta Semi-Auto Shotgun

Made in 20-gauge only, with 28" ventilated rib barrel and four choke tubes. Stock is black polymer. Metal finish is matte black, dark nickel or bright nickel. Inertia operating system is similar to that of Benelli line.

NIB	Exc.	V.G.	Good	Fair	Poor
750	675	600	500	350	200

PW 87

Lever-action shotgun patterned after Winchester Model 1887. Made in 12-gauge only, with 19" barrel, modified choke and hardwood stock. New production model imported from China.

NIB	Exc.	V.G.	Good	Fair	Poor
350	300	250	200	150	100

Shooter's Arms 1911 Pistol

Standard 1911-A .45 ACP design in full-size version with 5" barrel or Commodore model with 4.25" barrel. Magazine capacity 8 shots. New, manufactured in Philippines.

NIB	Exc.	V.G.	Good	Fair	Poor
450	375	325	275	200	100

Saiga Semi-auto Shotgun

A 12-gauge shotgun based on AK-47 design. Five-round capacity. Weight 7.9 lbs. Has a 19" barrel, black synthetic stock, sight rail. Made in Russia.

NIB	Exc.	V.G.	Good	Fair	Poor
600	500	425	375	200	100

S.A.R. Series

AK-47 style semi-automatic rifle, with wood stock and forearm. Capacity 10 or 30 rounds. Chambered for 7.62x39mm, 5.45x39mm or .223. Made in Romania by Romarm.

NIB	Exc.	V.G.	Good	Fair	Poor
800	650	500	350	200	100

CETME
Madrid, Spain

Cetme Autoloading Rifle

A .308-caliber semi-automatic rifle, with fluted chamber, 17.74" barrel, aperture rear sight and 20-round detachable magazine. Black with military-style wood stock. Identical in appearance to H&K 91 assault rifle.

NIB	Exc.	V.G.	Good	Fair	Poor
1500	1100	800	600	350	200

CHAMPLIN FIREARMS
Enid, Oklahoma

Champlin Firearms Company manufactures custom order rifles built to customer's specifications. Prospective purchasers are advised to secure a qualified appraisal prior to purchase.

Bolt-Action Rifle

These arms featured round or octagonal barrels, set triggers, a variety of sights and well figured walnut stocks.

NIB	Exc.	V.G.	Good	Fair	Poor
5500	4500	3500	2900	2200	1500

CHAPMAN, CHARLES
Chattanooga, Tennessee

Chapman produced a limited number of percussion carbines and rifles during the Civil War. Carbines had an overall length of 39.5" and .54-caliber barrels 24" in length. Their furniture was of brass. Chapman rifles resembled the U.S. Model 1841 rifle, but did not

have patch boxes. Overall length 48.5", barrel length 33", caliber .58. Chapman rifles and carbines are marked "C. CHAPMAN" on the lockplates. Prospective purchasers are strongly advised to secure an expert appraisal prior to acquisition.

Courtesy Milwaukee Public Museum, Milwaukee, Wisconsin

NIB	Exc.	V.G.	Good	Fair	Poor
—	—	38000	17500	3000	1000

CHAPMAN, G. & J.
Philadelphia, Pennsylvania

Chapman Pocket Revolver

A .32-caliber revolver, with 4" round barrel and 7-shot cylinder. Frame made of brass, while barrel and cylinder are steel. Barrel marked "G.& J. Chapman/Philada/Patent Applied For/1861". Manufactured during 1860s.

NIB	Exc.	V.G.	Good	Fair	Poor
—	—	2550	1050	550	275

CHAPUIS ARMES
France

RGP Shotgun

A 16- or 20-gauge boxlock shotgun. Most options available on order.

NIB	Exc.	V.G.	Good	Fair	Poor
3000	2500	2000	1800	1250	900

RG Express Model 89 Rifle

A 7x65R, 8x57 JRS, 9.3x74R and .375 H&H caliber sidelock double-barreled rifle. Other features on customer's order.

NIB	Exc.	V.G.	Good	Fair	Poor
6500	5750	4800	4000	3000	1500

Utility Grade Express Model Rifle

Side-by-side boxlock-action double rifle, with case colored or coin finish receiver. Offered in a variety of calibers: 9.3x74R, 8x57JRS, 7x65R, 8x75RS and .30-06. Checkered walnut stock with pistol-grip.

NIB	Exc.	V.G.	Good	Fair	Poor
6000	4800	4000	3000	1500	750

St. Bonnet Model Shotgun

Side-by-side shotgun, with sideplates on a boxlock-action. Scroll engraved case colored receiver. Straight-grip stock and double triggers. Offered in 12-, 16- or 20- gauge.

NIB	Exc.	V.G.	Good	Fair	Poor
4000	3250	2000	1250	800	500

Super Orion Rifle Series

This series of over/under rifles was offered in a wide range of European calibers plus .30-06 and .300 Win. Magnum. Several grades were available. Prices shown are for C-15 model, which was imported in the 1990s.

These rifles also were offered with a set of shotgun barrels. Currently imported by William Larkin Moore in Scottsdale, Arizona.

NIB	Exc.	V.G.	Good	Fair	Poor
8000	7000	5200	4000	2000	1000

African PH Model Grade I Rifle

Boxlock-action double rifle offered in a wide variety of calibers which determines retail price. Hand engraved case colored receiver. Pistol-grip stock, with European-style cheekpiece.

.470 Nitro & .416 Rigby

NIB	Exc.	V.G.	Good	Fair	Poor
12500	9500	8500	6000	3750	700

.375 H&H

NIB	Exc.	V.G.	Good	Fair	Poor
9500	7500	6250	4000	2500	600

.300 Win. Magnum

NIB	Exc.	V.G.	Good	Fair	Poor
8500	6500	5250	3000	1750	500

.30-06, 9.3x74R

NIB	Exc.	V.G.	Good	Fair	Poor
8000	6000	5000	3000	1750	500

African PH Model Grade II

Same as above, with master engraving and game scenes. **NOTE:** Add 20 to 25 percent to above NIB prices.

CHARTER ARMS
Shelton, Connecticut

Founded in 1962, Charter Arms has had several name and location changes. Original production was in Stratford, Connecticut until 1991 and in Ansonia, Connecticut from 1992 to 1996. From 1998 to 2005 the company name was Charter 2000. It was located in Shelton, Connecticut, where the current company, again known as Charter Arms is headquartered.

Bulldog

Chambered for .44 Special cartridge. Fitted with 2.5" barrel. Stainless steel or blued frame, with 5-round cylinder. Round butt and fixed sights. Weight 21 oz. **NOTE:** Add $20 for stainless steel.

NIB	Exc.	V.G.	Good	Fair	Poor
320	250	175	125	75	50

Police Bulldog

Chambered for .38 Special cartridge. Fitted with 4" bull or tapered barrel. Full rubber grips. Blued finish. Weight about 24 oz. Introduced in 2002.

NIB	Exc.	V.G.	Good	Fair	Poor
320	250	175	125	75	50

Undercover

Chambered for .38 Special cartridge. Fitted with 2" barrel. Stainless steel or blued frame, with 5-round cylinder. Round butt. Weight about 20 oz. **NOTE:** Add $20 for stainless steel.

NIB	Exc.	V.G.	Good	Fair	Poor
280	225	175	150	100	75

Off Duty

This .38 Special revolver has an aluminum frame and 2" barrel. Combat grips. Double-action-only. Weight about 12 oz. Introduced in 2002.

NIB	Exc.	V.G.	Good	Fair	Poor
350	250	200	150	100	75

Pathfinder

Stainless steel revolver chambered for .22-caliber cartridge. Fitted with 2" barrel and wood grips. Weight about 17 oz. Introduced in 2002.

NIB	Exc.	V.G.	Good	Fair	Poor
265	200	165	125	75	50

Mag Pug

Chambered for .357 Magnum cartridge. Fitted with 2.2" ported barrel. Stainless steel or blued frame. Weight about 24 oz.

NIB	Exc.	V.G.	Good	Fair	Poor
320	250	175	125	75	50

Dixie Derringer

Stainless steel with 1.125" barrels. Chambered for .22 LR or .22 Magnum cartridges. Weight about 8 oz. Introduced in 2002. **NOTE:** Add $10 for .22 Magnum model.

NIB	Exc.	V.G.	Good	Fair	Poor
190	150	125	100	50	25

Field King Rifle

Available with blue or stainless steel finish. Chambered for .25-06, .270, .30-06 or .308, with 22" barrel. Magazine capacity 4 rounds. Checkered fiberglass stock with cheekpiece. Weight about 8 lbs.

NIB	Exc.	V.G.	Good	Fair	Poor
300	225	175	125	75	50

Field King Carbine

Same as above, with 18" barrel compensator (20" total). Chambered for .308.

NIB	Exc.	V.G.	Good	Fair	Poor
350	250	200	150	75	50

CHARTER ARMS CORP.
Ansonia, Connecticut/Shelton, Connecticut

Police Undercover

Chambered for .38 Special or .32 Magnum. Fitted with 2" barrel in blue or stainless steel finish. Offered with walnut or rubber grips. Overall length 6.25". Weight between 16- and 19 oz. depending on grips and finish.

NIB	Exc.	V.G.	Good	Fair	Poor
350	300	175	150	100	75

Undercover Stainless Steel

As above in stainless steel.

NIB	Exc.	V.G.	Good	Fair	Poor
390	325	225	175	125	100

Undercover Lite

Similar to Undercover, with lightweight aluminum alloy frame. Frame finishes: black/stainless, red/stainless and red/black.

NIB	Exc.	V.G.	Good	Fair	Poor
390	325	225	175	125	100

Undercoverette

As above, with a thinner grip in .32 S&W.

NIB	Exc.	V.G.	Good	Fair	Poor
350	300	250	125	100	75

Bulldog

Similar to Undercover model in .44 Special caliber, with 2.5" or 3" barrel and 5-shot cylinder. Discontinued; replaced by Target and Pug models.

NIB	Exc.	V.G.	Good	Fair	Poor
325	275	225	175	125	100

Stainless Steel Bulldog

As above in stainless steel.

NIB	Exc.	V.G.	Good	Fair	Poor
350	300	250	200	150	125

Heller Commemorative Bulldog

Fully engraved model in .44 Special, with wood presentation case and engraved knife. Commemorating U.S. Supreme Court Heller case of 2011, affirming Second Amendment rights. Only 250 made.

NIB	Exc.	V.G.	Good	Fair	Poor
1400	1200	1000	—	—	—

Target Bulldog

As above in .357 Magnum or .44 Special, with 4" barrel. Fitted with adjustable rear sights. Blued, with walnut grips. Manufactured from 1986 to 1988. Later reintroduced.

NIB	Exc.	V.G.	Good	Fair	Poor
350	300	250	200	150	125

Pathfinder

Similar to above in .22 LR or .22 Magnum caliber, with 2", 3" or 6" barrel. Adjustable sights.

NIB	Exc.	V.G.	Good	Fair	Poor
350	300	250	200	150	125

Pathfinder Stainless Steel

As above in stainless steel.

NIB	Exc.	V.G.	Good	Fair	Poor
360	310	260	210	160	135

Bulldog Pug

Chambered for .44 Special cartridge. Fitted with 2.5" barrel. Available with walnut or neoprene grips in blue or stainless steel finish. Choice of spur or pocket hammer. Cylinder holds 5 rounds. Overall length 7"; weight between 20- and 25 oz. depending on grip and finish.

NIB	Exc.	V.G.	Good	Fair	Poor
350	300	250	200	150	125

Stainless Steel Bulldog

As above in stainless steel.

NIB	Exc.	V.G.	Good	Fair	Poor
375	325	275	225	175	125

Bulldog Tracker

As above, with 2.5", 4" or 6" barrel. In .357 Magnum only.

NIB	Exc.	V.G.	Good	Fair	Poor
375	325	275	225	175	125

Police Bulldog

As above, with 3.5" or 4" barrel. In .32 H&R Magnum, .38 Special or .44 Special.

NIB	Exc.	V.G.	Good	Fair	Poor
350	300	250	200	150	125

Stainless Steel Police Bulldog

As above in stainless steel. Available in .357 Magnum.

NIB	Exc.	V.G.	Good	Fair	Poor
350	300	250	200	150	125

Off Duty

Chambered for .38 Special or .22 LR and fitted with 2" barrel. Offered with either walnut or rubber grips, blue or stainless steel finish and choice of spur or pocket hammer. Weight:.38 Special between 17- and 23 oz. depending on grip and finish; .22 LR between 19- and 22 oz. Overall length 4.75". Nickel finish with rubber grips also offered.

NIB	Exc.	V.G.	Good	Fair	Poor
325	275	225	175	125	100

Pit Bull

9mm Federal, .38 Special or .357 Magnum caliber double-action revolver, with 2.5", 3.5" or 4" barrel. Blued, with rubber grips.

NIB	Exc.	V.G.	Good	Fair	Poor
400	350	250	175	125	90

Pitbull Rimless

Improved version of above, with dual coil-spring extractor system. Design does not require use of moon clips. Chambered in 9mm (6-round capacity) or .40 S&W (5 rounds). Barrel is 2.2", stainless glass beaded finish. Black rubber grips and fixed sights.

NIB	Exc.	V.G.	Good	Fair	Poor
400	350	300	275	225	175

Pitbull .45

Similar to 9mm Pitbull Rimless, except chambered for .45 ACP. Barrel length 2.5"; weight 22 oz. Introduced in 2016.

NIB	Exc.	V.G.	Good	Fair	Poor
425	350	300	250	225	200

The Mag Pug

A 5-shot revolver chambered for .357 Magnum. Stainless or blue. Ported 2.2" barrel. Weight 23 oz. Fixed sights, rubber grips.

NIB	Exc.	V.G.	Good	Fair	Poor
350	300	250	200	150	125

Charter Arms Southpaw

Snubnose revolver chambered in .38 Special or +P. Five-shot cylinder, 2" barrel, matte black aluminum alloy frame, with stainless steel cylinder. Cylinder latch and crane assembly are on right side of frame for convenience of left-hand shooters. Rubber Pachmayr-style grips. Weight 12 oz.

NIB	Exc.	V.G.	Good	Fair	Poor
400	350	250	175	125	90

Pink Lady

Similar to Undercover Lite, with pink anodized frame. .38 Special only. Available as Chic Lady, with high polish pink finish and pink faux alligator case. DAO version also available. **NOTE:** Add $50 for Chic Lady.

NIB	Exc.	V.G.	Good	Fair	Poor
375	325	275	225	175	125

Goldfinger

Similar to Undercover Lite, with gold anodized frame. .38 Special only.

NIB	Exc.	V.G.	Good	Fair	Poor
375	325	275	225	175	125

Patriot

Built on Bulldog frame. Chambered in .327 Federal Magnum (six-shot). Rubber grips, 2.2" or 4" barrel. Comes with Kershaw "327" knife.

NIB	Exc.	V.G.	Good	Fair	Poor
425	300	225	175	150	100

Dixie Derringer, Current Production

Stainless mini-revolver chambered for .22 LR (5 oz.) or .22 Magnum (6 oz.). 5-shot, 1.175" barrel.

NIB	Exc.	V.G.	Good	Fair	Poor
175	140	100	75	50	25

Explorer II Pistol

A .22-caliber semi-automatic pistol, with 6", 8" or 10" barrels. Available with camo, black, silver or gold finish and plastic grips. Discontinued in 1986.

NIB	Exc.	V.G.	Good	Fair	Poor
225	175	125	65	45	25

Model 40

A .22-caliber double-action semi-automatic pistol, with 3.5" barrel and 8-shot magazine. Stainless steel with plastic grips. Manufactured from 1984 to 1986.

NIB	Exc.	V.G.	Good	Fair	Poor
—	275	225	200	150	100

Model 79K

A .32- or .380-caliber double-action semi-automatic pistol, with 3.5" barrel and 7-shot magazine. Stainless steel with plastic grips. Manufactured from 1986 to 1988.

NIB	Exc.	V.G.	Good	Fair	Poor
—	350	300	250	180	125

Model 42T

A .22-caliber semi-automatic pistol, with 6" barrel and adjustable sights. Blued, with walnut grips. Manufactured in 1984 and 1985.

NIB	Exc.	V.G.	Good	Fair	Poor
500	450	400	325	265	200

AR-7 Explorer Rifle

A .22-caliber semi-automatic rifle, with 16" barrel, 8-shot magazine and hollow plastic stock which can house the barrel when detached.

NIB	Exc.	V.G.	Good	Fair	Poor
175	125	80	60	40	25

CHEYTAC
Arco, Idaho

M-200

Bolt-action rifle chambered for .408 CheyTac cartridge. Detachable barrel length 30" with muzzle-brake. Magazine capacity 7 rounds. Integral bipod. No sights, but receiver has attachable Picatinny rail. Weight about 27 lbs.

NIB	Exc.	V.G.	Good	Fair	Poor
10995	8250	6900	5400	3000	700

M-310

Single-shot bolt-action rifle chambered for .408 CheyTac cartridge. Fitted with 25" barrel with muzzle-brake. McMillian A-5 stock with adjustable cheekpiece. Match grade trigger. Picatinny rail. Weight about 16.5 lbs.

NIB	Exc.	V.G.	Good	Fair	Poor
4395	3250	2750	1875	1300	500

CHIAPPA ARMS
Dayton, Ohio

1911-22

1911-style semi-automatic pistol chambered in .22 LR. Features include: alloy frame; steel barrel; matte blue-black or bright nickel finish; walnut-like grips; two 10-round magazines; fixed sights; straight blowback action. **NOTE:** Add $25 for target model with adjustable sights, $25 for OD or tan finish.

NIB	Exc.	V.G.	Good	Fair	Poor
260	225	200	150	100	75

M9

Replica of Beretta M9 pistol in 9mm or .40 S&W. Barrel length 4.9" or 4.3" (Compact model).

NIB	Exc.	V.G.	Good	Fair	Poor
500	425	375	300	225	185

M9-22

Replica of Beretta M9 9mm military pistol. Chambered for .22 Long Rifle, with checkered black plastic or checkered wooden grips. Operating features are identical to 9mm version. Tactical model has threaded barrel. **NOTE:** Add $25 for this variation.

NIB	Exc.	V.G.	Good	Fair	Poor
325	275	225	200	150	100

Rhino

Unique revolver chambered in 9x19, 9x21, .357 Magnum and .40 S&W. Features include 2", 4", 5" or 6" barrel; fixed or adjustable sights; visible hammer or hammerless design. Weight 24 to 33 oz. Walnut or synthetic grips with black frame; hexagonal-shaped cylinder. Unique design fires from bottom chamber of cylinder. **NOTE:** Add $75 for wood grips; $100 for brushed nickel finish (White Rhino model); $300 for gold finish (Rhino 60DS). Deduct $200 for polymer frame model.

NIB	Exc.	V.G.	Good	Fair	Poor
950	800	600	500	400	300

1873-22

Replica of Colt Single Action Army revolver. Chambered in .22 Long Rifle, with 6-round cylinder. Introduced in 2011 and discontinued in 2012. Available with extra cylinder in .22 WMR. **NOTE:** Add $50 for extra cylinder; $40 for target model.

NIB	Exc.	V.G.	Good	Fair	Poor
175	150	125	100	85	60

1873-22-10

Same features as above, with 10-round cylinder. Available with extra cylinder in .22 WMR. Also offered in .17 HMR caliber, with adjustable sights. **NOTE:** Add $50 for .22 WMR extra cylinder; $30 for .17 HMR model.

NIB	Exc.	V.G.	Good	Fair	Poor
200	175	150	115	90	75

Model 1886 Kodiak Rifle

Lever-action rifle chambered for .45-70 Government cartridge. Replica of Winchester 1886, with 18.5" half-octagon barrel, express sights, black synthetic stock and hard-chrome matte gray finish. Standard model has 4-round half-length tubular magazine. Trapper model 6-shot magazine, blue finish and walnut stock. **NOTE:** Deduct $150 for Trapper model.

NIB	Exc.	V.G.	Good	Fair	Poor
1500	1200	900	700	500	400

Model 1886 Rifle

Similar features as Kodiak Rifle, except has 26" octagon barrel with full-length tubular magazine, walnut stock and fore-end with crescent buttplate.

NIB	Exc.	V.G.	Good	Fair	Poor
1350	1150	900	650	400	300

Model 1892 Rifle

Replica of Winchester model 1892 lever-action rifle. Chambered for .38 Special, .357 Magnum, .38-40 WCF, .44-40 WCF, .44 Magnum, .45 Colt. Offered in several variations, with barrel lengths from 16" to 24" with different sighting options. Take-down model with octagonal barrel available. **NOTE:** Add $200 for take-down model; $100 for buckhorn rear/interchangeable blade front sights.

NIB	Exc.	V.G.	Good	Fair	Poor
900	750	600	500	400	250

Model 39 Rifle

Replica of Marlin Model 39 rifle. Chambered for .22 Short, Long and Long Rifle. Has 18.5" barrel, hardwood or synthetic stock and fore-end. Take-down model.

NIB	Exc.	V.G.	Good	Fair	Poor
350	285	225	200	175	150

Model LA322 Rifle

Similar to Model 39 Rifle, with internal changes and improvements. Lever action, with 15-shot tubular magazine. Blue or case-colored finish. Deluxe model available with oil-finished walnut stock, color-case hardened or black chrome finish. Kodiak Cub has matte chrome finish, straight-grip stock. **NOTE:** Add $150 for Deluxe model; $200 for Kodiak Cub.

NIB	Exc.	V.G.	Good	Fair	Poor
400	350	300	250	200	175

Little Sharps Rifle

Replica of Sharps single-shot rifle has been made in several rimfire and centerfire chamberings. Including .17 HMR, .17 Hornet, .22 LR, .22 WMR, .22 Hornet, .30-30, .38-55 and .45 Colt. Features include 24" or 26" octagon barrel with tang sight, walnut stock and fore-end. Target model in .17 Hornet only has heavy barrel, with spirit level front sight. Hunter model has no sights, half round and half octagon barrel and also made only in .17 Hornet. **NOTE:** Deduct $150 for Target .17 Hornet; $250 for Hunter .17 Hornet.

NIB	Exc.	V.G.	Good	Fair	Poor
1200	1000	850	600	400	200

Sharps Down Under

Replica of Sharps Model 1874 single-shot rifle. Chambered in .38-55 WCF, .45-70, .45-90, .45-110, .45-120 or .50-90. Full octagon 34" barrel, double-set triggers, walnut stock and color case-hardened finish.

NIB	Exc.	V.G.	Good	Fair	Poor
1800	1550	1200	850	600	400

Model 1887 Shotgun

Lever-action limited edition replica of Model 1887 Winchester 12-gauge, with 5-shot magazine, 22" or 28" barrel and choke tubes.

NIB	Exc.	V.G.	Good	Fair	Poor
1000	900	750	600	400	250

CHICAGO, F. A. CO.
Chicago, Illinois

Protector Palm Pistol—Standard Model

Nickel-Plated/Black Grips

A .32-caliber radial cylinder revolver. Designed to fit in the palm of your hand. Operated by a hinged lever mounted to rear of the circular frame. Sideplates are marked "Chicago Firearms Co., Chicago, Ill." and "The Protector". Blued, with hard rubber grip panels or nickel-plated, with pearl grip panels. Manufactured by Ames Manufacturing Company.

NOTE: Add 25 percent for pearl grip panels without cracks or chips; 50 percent for blued finish.

NIB	Exc.	V.G.	Good	Fair	Poor
—	—	3000	2000	1000	750

CHIPMUNK RIFLES/ROGUE RIFLE CO.
Lewiston, Idaho

Chipmunk Single-Shot Standard Rifle

A .22 or .22 rimfire Magnum caliber bolt-action rifle, with 16.25" barrel and open sights. Weight about 3.5 lbs.

NIB	Exc.	V.G.	Good	Fair	Poor
185	150	125	100	80	60

Deluxe Chipmunk

As above, with hand-checkered walnut stock.

NIB	Exc.	V.G.	Good	Fair	Poor
230	180	135	100	80	60

Chipmunk .17 HMR

Similar to Standard Model. Chambered for .17 HMR cartridge. Introduced in 2002.

NIB	Exc.	V.G.	Good	Fair	Poor
200	160	125	100	75	45

Chipmunk TM

Introduced in 2002. Features a micrometer rear sight. Stock has accessory rail installed and is adjustable for length of pull. Heavy type 18" barrel. Weight about 5 lbs.

NIB	Exc.	V.G.	Good	Fair	Poor
325	250	150	125	100	75

Silhouette Pistol

A .22-caliber bolt-action pistol, with 14.5" barrel, open sights and pistol-grip walnut stock.

NIB	Exc.	V.G.	Good	Fair	Poor
150	125	100	80	60	40

CHRISTENSEN ARMS
Gunnison, Utah

There are a number of custom options offered by this company for its rifles. Many of these options may affect price. Prices listed are for standard models with standard features.

Carbon One

Bolt-action rifle, with Remington 700 action. Chambered for .17- through .243-caliber. Fitted with a custom trigger, match-grade stainless steel barrel and black synthetic stock. Weight about 6 lbs.

NIB	Exc.	V.G.	Good	Fair	Poor
3900	2750	1900	1200	700	500

Carbon Lite

Similar to above. Weight about 5 lbs.

NIB	Exc.	V.G.	Good	Fair	Poor
3900	2750	1900	1200	700	500

Carbon King

This model utilizes a Remington 700 BDL long action. Chambered for .25-caliber through .30-06. Stainless steel barrel, custom trigger and black synthetic stock are standard. Weight about 6.5 lbs.

NIB	Exc.	V.G.	Good	Fair	Poor
3900	2750	1900	1200	700	500

Carbon Cannon

Similar to above. Chambered for belted Magnum calibers. Weight about 7 lbs.

NIB	Exc.	V.G.	Good	Fair	Poor
3900	2750	1900	1200	700	500

Carbon Challenge I

Built on a Ruger 10/22 action. Fitted with a Volquartsen trigger, stainless steel bull barrel and black synthetic stock. Weight about 3.5 lbs. **NOTE:** Add 20 percent for .17-caliber.

NIB	Exc.	V.G.	Good	Fair	Poor
1800	1300	875	600	400	175

Carbon Challenge II

Similar to above. Fitted with an AMT action and trigger. Weight about 4.5 lbs. Discontinued.

NIB	Exc.	V.G.	Good	Fair	Poor
1295	995	700	550	325	125

Carbon Tactical

Bolt-action model uses Remington 700 BDL action. Available in most any caliber. Fitted with custom trigger, match-grade stainless steel barrel and black synthetic stock. Weight about 7 lbs.

NIB	Exc.	V.G.	Good	Fair	Poor
3900	2750	1900	1200	700	500

Carbon Conquest

Chambered for .50-caliber BMG cartridge. Built on McMillan stainless steel bolt action. Magazine capacity 5 rounds. Barrel length 32" with muzzle-brake. Composite stock. Weight about 20 lbs. **NOTE:** Deduct $1,000 for single-shot model.

NIB	Exc.	V.G.	Good	Fair	Poor
6250	4000	3250	1700	875	400

Carbon One Hunter

Semi-custom bolt-action rifle built around choice of receivers; steel barrel encased in carbon alloy shroud; synthetic stock. All popular calibers. Weight 6.5- to 7 lbs.

NIB	Exc.	V.G.	Good	Fair	Poor
1500	1300	875	550	375	125

Carbon Ranger Repeater

Semi-custom bolt-action rifle chambered in .50 BMG. Five-shot magazine; steel Pac-Nor barrel encased in carbon alloy. Muzzle-brake. Weight 20 lbs.

NIB	Exc.	V.G.	Good	Fair	Poor
8000	7000	5500	4000	2000	1000

Carbon Ranger Single Shot

Similar to Repeater but single shot.

NIB	Exc.	V.G.	Good	Fair	Poor
6500	5000	3000	2000	1100	500

Summit Carbon

Bolt-action model with carbon fiber barrel, adjustable trigger, carbon stock in standard or thumbhole style. Offered in most popular calibers from .223 Rem. to .338 Lapua. Also made with steel barrel. Introduced in 2014.

NIB	Exc.	V.G.	Good	Fair	Poor
5000	4200	3700	2700	—	—

Summit Steel

NIB	Exc.	V.G.	Good	Fair	Poor
4000	3200	2700	2000	—	—

CA-15

AR-15 type semi-automatic rifle in .223 Rem., with forged aluminum upper and lower receivers. Most standard features of AR-15 style models including full Picatinny rail, Timney trigger, ambidextrous charging handle, 30-round magazine. Made in several variations. Add $500 for Recon model, with 16" or 20" carbon fiber match grade barrel, titanium "birdcage" suppressor, several camo finishes. Chambered in .204 Ruger, 6.5 Grendel, 6.8 SPC, .300 Blackout.

NIB	Exc.	V.G.	Good	Fair	Poor
2400	2000	1500	1000	750	400

CA-10 DMR

Designated Marksman Rifle originally chambered for .308 Win. Later calibers include .243 Win., .260 Rem., 6.5 Creedmoor. This is the flagship of Christensen Modern Sporting Rifle product line. Features include a Direct Impingement operating system, MagPul ACS buttstock, Hogue Overmolded pistol-grip, carbon fiber-wrapped match grade barrel with target contour M-4 style feed ramp and MagPul 20-round magazine.

NIB	Exc.	V.G.	Good	Fair	Poor
3500	2800	2000	1600	1000	500

1911 Officer

Christensen makes a series of 1911-type pistols in .45 ACP caliber. These are offered in full-size, Commander and Officers sizes (shown) in both standard and lightweight variants. Features include stainless steel slide, aerospace aluminum mainspring housing, adjustable trigger, tritium night sights, Cerakote finish, carbon-fiber grips and ambidextrous safety. **NOTE:** Add $800 for titanium frame.

NIB	Exc.	V.G.	Good	Fair	Poor
2100	1800	1400	1000	750	600

1911 Damascus

Full-size model with damascus-pattern finish, 5" barrel, titanium frame, Novak trijicon sights, skeletonized hammer and trigger, full-length guide rod with no bushing. Introduced in 2013.

NIB	Exc.	V.G.	Good	Fair	Poor
4200	3600	3000	2000	—	—

CHURCHILL, E. J. LTD.
London, England

One of One Thousand Rifle

A .270 to .458 Magnum caliber bolt-action rifle, with 24" barrel and select French walnut stock, trap pistol-grip cap and recoil pad. Only 100 actually produced for 20th Anniversary of Interarms in 1973.

NIB	Exc.	V.G.	Good	Fair	Poor
—	1750	1050	850	700	550

Premier Over/Under

Sidelock ejector gun available in 12-, 20- or 28-gauge. Single or double trigger with choice of finish. Barrel lengths built to order. Deluxe Turkish walnut with choice of grip. Fine scroll engraving. Weight about: 12-gauge 7 lbs.; 20-gauge 6.75 lbs. Many extra cost options available. **NOTE:** Add $3,000 for 28-gauge guns.

NIB	Exc.	V.G.	Good	Fair	Poor
47000	36500	26000	20000	10000	800

Premier Side-by-Side

Similar to over/under gun, with side-by-side barrels. Offered in 16-gauge as well as 12-, 20- and 28-gauge. Weight about: 6.5 lbs. 12-gauge; 6 lbs. 16-gauge; 5.8 lbs. 20-gauge. Many extra options are available. **NOTE:** Add $3,000 for 28-gauge guns.

NIB	Exc.	V.G.	Good	Fair	Poor
38000	30000	20000	16500	7000	600

Premier Double Rifle

Similar in construction to side-by-side shotgun. Rifle chambered for .300 H&H, .375 H&H or .500 Nitro Express. Weight: 9.5 lbs. .300; 9.75 lbs. .375; 12.5 lbs. .500. Many extra-cost options. **NOTE:** Add $3,000 for .500 N.E. guns.

NIB	Exc.	V.G.	Good	Fair	Poor
55000	45000	35000	20000	13000	800

Baronet Magazine Rifle

This rifle uses standard Mauser 98 action, with fully adjustable trigger, 3 position safety and box release floor plate. Barrel length is custom to order. Border engraving. Chambered for .30-06 or .375 H&H. Weight about: 8.5 lbs. .30-06; 9 lbs. .375. Many extra-cost options offered. Seek an expert opinion prior to a sale.

NIB	Exc.	V.G.	Good	Fair	Poor
13000	9750	7000	45000	2750	575

CHURCHILL
Various European Manufacturers and Importers

SIDE-BY-SIDE SHOTGUNS

Windsor I

A 10-, 12-, 16-, 20-, 28-gauge and .410 bore Anson & Deeley double-barrel boxlock shotgun. Barrel lengths from 23" through 32", various choke combinations, double triggers and extractors. Scroll-engraved silver-finished, with checkered walnut pistol-grip and fore-end.

NIB	Exc.	V.G.	Good	Fair	Poor
800	600	500	400	300	200

Windsor II

As above in 10-, 12- and 20-gauge only, with automatic ejectors. Not imported after 1987.

NIB	Exc.	V.G.	Good	Fair	Poor
800	600	550	450	350	250

Windsor VI

As above with sidelocks. Chambered for 12- and 20-gauge only, with automatic ejectors. Not imported after 1987.

NIB	Exc.	V.G.	Good	Fair	Poor
1100	800	750	650	500	350

Royal

A 12-, 20-, 28-gauge and .410 bore boxlock double-barrel shotgun, with various barrel lengths and chokes, double triggers and extractors. Case hardened, with checkered walnut stock. Introduced in 1988.

NIB	Exc.	V.G.	Good	Fair	Poor
650	500	425	350	275	125

OVER/UNDER SHOTGUNS

Monarch

A 12-, 20-, 28-gauge or .410 bore over/under shotgun, with a boxlock-action, 25", 26" or 28" ventilated rib barrels. Either double- or single-selective trigger extractors. Checkered walnut stock.

NIB	Exc.	V.G.	Good	Fair	Poor
600	475	425	375	300	150

Windsor III

A 12-, 20-gauge and .410 bore boxlock double-barrel shotgun, with 27" or 30" ventilated rib barrels, extractors, single-selective trigger, scroll-engraved, silver finished and checkered walnut stock.

NIB	Exc.	V.G.	Good	Fair	Poor
700	575	525	475	400	200

Windsor IV

As above, with screw-in choke tubes standard. Introduced in 1989.

NIB	Exc.	V.G.	Good	Fair	Poor
975	775	650	500	425	200

Regent

As above in 12- and 20-gauge, with 27" ventilated rib barrels, screw-in choke tubes, scroll-engraved false sideplates, automatic ejectors, single-selective trigger and checkered walnut stock. Not imported after 1986.

NIB	Exc.	V.G.	Good	Fair	Poor
950	750	650	550	450	250

Regent II

As above, with finer overall finishing.

NIB	Exc.	V.G.	Good	Fair	Poor
1250	1000	850	750	500	250

Regent Shotgun/Rifle Combination

A .222, .223, .243, .270, .308 or .30-06 caliber/12-gauge over/under rifle/shotgun, with 25" ventilated rib, automatic ejectors and single-selective trigger. Silver finished, scroll engraved and checkered walnut stock.

NIB	Exc.	V.G.	Good	Fair	Poor
1050	825	725	600	450	250

Windsor Grade Semi-Automatic

A 12-gauge semi-automatic shotgun, with 26", 28" or 30" ventilated rib barrels and screw-in choke tubes. An etched and anodized alloy receiver, with checkered walnut stock.

NIB	Exc.	V.G.	Good	Fair	Poor
500	375	325	275	225	175

Regent Grade Semi-Automatic

Chambered for 12-gauge, with choice of 26", 28" or 30" barrels. Standard chokes or choke tubes. Walnut stock with pistol-grip. Introduced in 1984 and discontinued in 1986. Weight about 7.5 lbs.

NIB	Exc.	V.G.	Good	Fair	Poor
500	375	325	275	225	175

Windsor Grade Slide-Action

A 12-gauge slide-action shotgun, with 26" through 30" ventilated rib barrel, various chokes, double slide rails and an anodized alloy receiver. Checkered walnut stock. Discontinued in 1986.

NIB	Exc.	V.G.	Good	Fair	Poor
—	500	375	300	250	175

RIFLES

Highlander

A .25-06 through .300-caliber Win. Magnum bolt-action rifle, with 22" barrel with or without sights, 3-shot magazine and checkered walnut stock.

NIB	Exc.	V.G.	Good	Fair	Poor
575	425	375	300	250	200

Regent

As above, with Monte Carlo-style comb and cheekpiece. Discontinued in 1988.

NIB	Exc.	V.G.	Good	Fair	Poor
—	650	500	425	350	275

CHYLEWSKI, WITOLD
Switzerland

A 6.35mm caliber semi-automatic pistol, with 6-round magazine marked "Brevete Chylewski" and bears the name "Neuhausen" on left side of pistol. Approximately 1,000 made between 1910 and 1918. Pistol was designed to be cocked with one hand.

NIB	Exc.	V.G.	Good	Fair	Poor
—	—	1250	850	550	275

CIMARRON, F. A. CO.
Fredericksburg, Texas

In business since 1984, this company imports quality firearms from Uberti, Armi San Marco, Pedersoli and others. Cimarron also sells Uberti-manufactured blackpowder Colt reproductions, from Patterson to Model 1862 Pocket. For prices and specifications on these models see Uberti section.

Model No. 3 Schofield

This version of the Schofield is manufactured for Cimarron by Armi San Marco in Italy. Its parts are interchangeable with the original. It is offered in several variations and calibers. Discontinued. Beware of latch locking problems. **NOTE:** Add $100 for standard nickel finish; $150 for custom nickel finish.

Civilian Model

Fitted with 7" barrel and offered in .38 Special, .44 Russian/.44 Special, .44 WCF, .45 Schofield, .45 Long Colt.

NIB	Exc.	V.G.	Good	Fair	Poor
875	600	525	425	300	125

Military Model

Essentially same as Civilian Model except for its markings.

NIB	Exc.	V.G.	Good	Fair	Poor
875	600	525	425	300	125

Wells Fargo

Similar to Military and Civilian Model. Fitted with 5" barrel. Calibers are the same.

NIB	Exc.	V.G.	Good	Fair	Poor
875	600	525	425	300	125

Model 1872 Open Top

This revolver offered in a number of different calibers and configurations. Chambered for .44 SP, .44 Colt, .44 Russian, .45 Schofield, .38 Colt, .38 Special. Can be fitted with Army or Navy grips. Barrel lengths are 4.75", 5.5" or 7.5". Offered in regular blued finish, charcoal blue finish or original finish. **NOTE:** Add $40 for charcoal finish; $50 for original finish; $25 for silver-plated back strap and trigger guard.

NIB	Exc.	V.G.	Good	Fair	Poor
450	400	350	300	200	100

COLT SINGLE-ACTION ARMY CONFIGURATIONS

Cimarron Arms reproduction of 1873 Colt Single-Action Army revolver comes in two basic configurations. First is "Old Model", with black powder frame, screw-in cylinder pin retainer and circular bull's eye ejector head. Second is "pre-war Model" style frame, with spring loaded cross-pin cylinder retainer and half moon ejector head. Old Model revolvers are available in authentic old style charcoal blue finish at an extra charge. Unless otherwise stated, all of these Colt reproductions are produced by Uberti of Italy. Plain walnut grips are standard unless noted. **NOTE:** Relic finish offered by Cimarron as an extra cost item on its revolvers. This finish duplicates the old worn antique finish seen on many used historical Colts. Add $40 to NIB price for any Cimarron revolver with this finish.

General Custer 7th Cavalry Model

Has U.S. military markings and fitted with 7.5" barrel on an Old Model frame. Offered in .45 LC only.

NIB	Exc.	V.G.	Good	Fair	Poor
525	450	350	300	200	100

Rough Rider U.S. Artillery Model

This version of Old Model fitted with 5.5" barrel and chambered for .45 LC.

NIB	Exc.	V.G.	Good	Fair	Poor
550	450	350	300	200	100

Frontier Six Shooter

This revolver offered with choice of 4.75", 5.5" or 7.5" barrel. Chambered for .38 WCF, .357 Magnum, .44 WCF, .45 LC or .45 LC with extra .45 ACP cylinder. **NOTE:** Add $40 to NIB price for charcoal blue finish; $30 for extra .45 ACP cylinder; $50 for stainless steel.

NIB	Exc.	V.G.	Good	Fair	Poor
450	350	300	275	175	75

Sheriff's Model no ejector

Fitted with 3" barrel. Chambered in .44 WCF or .45 LC. Built on an Old Model frame.

NIB	Exc.	V.G.	Good	Fair	Poor
450	350	300	275	175	75

New Sheriff's Model w/ejector

This variation fitted with 3.5" barrel with ejector. Available in .357 Magnum, .44 WCF, .44 Special and .45 LC. **NOTE:** Add $35 for checkered walnut grips.

NIB	Exc.	V.G.	Good	Fair	Poor
500	400	325	275	175	75

Wyatt Earp Buntline

Limited edition model fitted with 10" barrel. Chambered for .45 LC cartridge. Model P frame. Silver shield inlaid in grip.

NIB	Exc.	V.G.	Good	Fair	Poor
775	600	500	425	300	125

New Thunderer

Frame based on Old Model fitted with bird's-head grip. Choice of plain or checkered walnut grips. Originally offered in 3.5" or 4.75" barrel lengths; in 1997 5.5" barrels were offered. Chambered for .357 Magnum, .44 WCF, .44 Special or .45 LC/.45 ACP. **NOTE:** Add $35 for checkered grips.

NIB	Exc.	V.G.	Good	Fair	Poor
575	450	325	275	175	75

Thunderer Long Tom

Same as New Thunderer, except for barrel length of 7.5".

NIB	Exc.	V.G.	Good	Fair	Poor
550	425	350	275	175	75

Thunderstorm

Single-action revolver in blue or stainless finish, with checkered wood grips. Chambered in .357 Magnum or .45 Colt, with 3.5" or 4.75" barrel. Wide target sights with action smoothed for competition. **NOTE:** Add $100 for stainless finish.

NIB	Exc.	V.G.	Good	Fair	Poor
875	775	700	500	400	300

Lightning

Similar to Thunderer, with a smaller grip frame. Chambered for .38 Special cartridge or .22 LR. Fitted with 3.5", 4.75" or 5.5" barrel. Finish is blue, with case hardened frame.

NIB	Exc.	V.G.	Good	Fair	Poor
475	375	315	250	150	65

Lightning .32s

Features two cylinders chambered for .32-20 and .32 H&R cartridges. Choice of 3.5", 4.75" or 5.5" barrel. Introduced in 2004.

NIB	Exc.	V.G.	Good	Fair	Poor
550	400	350	275	175	75

New Model P

Offered in either Old Model or Pre-War styles. Choice of 4.75", 5.5" or 7.5" barrel. Chambered for .32 WCF, .38 WCF, .44 WCF, .44 Special or .45 LC.

NIB	Exc.	V.G.	Good	Fair	Poor
475	400	325	275	175	75

Stainless Frontier Model P

Model P in stainless steel. Chambered for .357 Magnum or .45 LC cartridge. Barrels are 4.75", 5.5" or 7.5". Introduced in 2004.

NIB	Exc.	V.G.	Good	Fair	Poor
550	450	400	300	200	100

A.P. Casey Model P U.S. Cavalry

Fitted with a 7.5" barrel. Chambered for .45 LC. Revolver has U.S. markings (APC) on an Old Model frame.

NIB	Exc.	V.G.	Good	Fair	Poor
550	375	325	250	150	75

Rinaldo A. Carr Model P U.S. Artillery

Model P built on an Old Model frame. Chambered for .45 LC. Fitted with 5.5" barrel. U.S. markings (RAC).

NIB	Exc.	V.G.	Good	Fair	Poor
550	425	375	275	175	100

Evil Roy Model

Features a Model P frame, with wide square-notch rear sight and wide-width front sight. Slim grips checkered or smooth. Tuned action with lightened trigger. Chambered for .357 Magnum, .45 LC or .44-40 cartridge. Barrel lengths 4.75" or 5.5". Introduced in 2004.

NIB	Exc.	V.G.	Good	Fair	Poor
625	550	475	375	250	125

Model P Jr.

Similar to Model P, but sized 20 percent smaller. Chambered for .38 Special cartridge. Fitted with 3.5" or 4.75" barrel. Blue, with case hardened frame.

NIB	Exc.	V.G.	Good	Fair	Poor
475	400	325	250	150	75

Model P Jr. .32s

Introduced in 2004. Features two cylinders chambered for .32-20 and .32 H&R cartridges. Choice of 3.5", 4.75" or 5.5" barrel.

NIB	Exc.	V.G.	Good	Fair	Poor
550	400	350	250	150	75

Cimarron 1880 Frontier Flat Top

Introduced in 1998. Target version of Colt Single-Action Army. Rear sight adjustable for windage and front adjustable for elevation. Offered with choice of 4.75", 5.5" or 7.5" barrel. Chambered for .45 LC, .45 Schofield, .44 WCF and .357 Magnum. Choice of Model P frame or Pre-War frame.

NIB	Exc.	V.G.	Good	Fair	Poor
550	450	325	225	150	100

Cimarron Bisley

Exact copy of Colt Bisley, with case-hardened frame. Choice of 4.75", 5.5" or 7.5" barrels. Calibers from .45 LC, .45 Schofield, .44 WCF to .357 Magnum. Introduced in 1998.

NIB	Exc.	V.G.	Good	Fair	Poor
550	450	325	225	150	100

Cimarron Bisley Flat Top

Offered in same barrel lengths and calibers as standard Bisley, with the addition of a windage adjustable rear sight and elevation adjustable front sight. Introduced in 1998.

NIB	Exc.	V.G.	Good	Fair	Poor
550	450	325	225	150	100

El Pistolero

Budget-priced revolver introduced in 1997. Features a brass backstrap and trigger guard, with plain walnut grips. Offered in 4.75", 5.5" and 7.5" barrel lengths. Chambered for .45 LC or .357 Magnum.

NIB	Exc.	V.G.	Good	Fair	Poor
350	250	200	125	75	50

Doc Holliday Thunderer

Nickel-plated SAA in .45 LC. Has a 3.5" barrel and Cimarron Tru Ivory grips. Comes with a matching numbered dagger and a shoulder holster designed to carry both items.

NIB	Exc.	V.G.	Good	Fair	Poor
1300	1000	800	650	450	300

Rooster Shooter SAA

Replica of SAA used by John Wayne in many movies. Chambered in .357 Magnum, .44-40 or .45 LC. Antique gray finish and artificial ivory grips. Introduced in 2010.

NIB	Exc.	V.G.	Good	Fair	Poor
800	700	525	400	300	250

Man With No Name SAA

Replica of gun used by Clint Eastwood in several "spaghetti westerns". In .45 LC, with 4.75" or 5.5" barrel, cased-colored finish, wood grips and rattlesnake inlay. Introduced in 2010.

NIB	Exc.	V.G.	Good	Fair	Poor
750	650	550	425	300	250

RICHARDS CONVERSIONS

NOTE: Relic finish offered by Cimarron as an extra cost item on its revolvers. This finish duplicates the old worn antique finish seen on many used historical Colts. **NOTE:** Add $40 to the NIB price for any Cimarron revolver with this finish.

Model 1851

Chambered for .38 Special, .38 Colt and .44 Colt. Fitted with 5" or 7" barrels.

NIB	Exc.	V.G.	Good	Fair	Poor
550	450	325	225	150	100

Model 1861

Chambered for .38 Special, .38 Colt and .44 Colt. Fitted with 5" or 7" barrels.

NIB	Exc.	V.G.	Good	Fair	Poor
550	450	325	225	150	100

Model 1860

Chambered for .38 Special, .38 Colt and .44 Colt. Fitted with 5" or 7.5" barrels.

NIB	Exc.	V.G.	Good	Fair	Poor
550	450	325	225	150	100

Model 1911A1

Manufactured by Chiappa. Standard full-size replica of Colt .45 ACP Government Model in blue, polished blue or nickel finish. **NOTE:** Add 40 percent for nickel finish; 30 percent for polished blue finish.

NIB	Exc.	V.G.	Good	Fair	Poor
525	450	400	325	250	200

Wild Bunch 1911

Replica of WWI era 1911 .45 ACP pistol with flat mainspring housing, polished blue finish, diamond-checkered walnut grips. **NOTE:** Add $100 for tanker shoulder holster which is included with new model.

NIB	Exc.	V.G.	Good	Fair	Poor
650	600	500	400	350	300

Titan Derringer

An over/under, two-shot derringer. Chambered in 9mm or .45 Colt/.410 shotshell. Made by Cobra Enterprises.

NIB	Exc.	V.G.	Good	Fair	Poor
350	300	250	200	150	100

Diablo Derringer

Chambered in .22 LR, .22 WMR, .32 H&R Magnum or .38 Special.

NIB	Exc.	V.G.	Good	Fair	Poor
200	175	150	125	100	75

RIFLES

Model 1865 Spencer

Chambered for .56-50 centerfire cartridge.

NIB	Exc.	V.G.	Good	Fair	Poor
1350	975	775	650	375	250

Henry Civil War Model

Offered in .44 WCF or .45 LC, with 24.25" barrel. **NOTE:** Add $80 for charcoal blue or white finish.

NIB	Exc.	V.G.	Good	Fair	Poor
1400	1200	1000	625	350	200

Henry Civilian Model

Same as above, without military markings.

NIB	Exc.	V.G.	Good	Fair	Poor
1200	925	750	625	350	200

Model 1866 Yellowboy Carbine

Reproduction of Winchester Model 1866. Fitted with 19" barrel. Chambered for .38 Special, .44 WCF or .45 LC. **NOTE:** Add $20 for charcoal blue.

NIB	Exc.	V.G.	Good	Fair	Poor
1000	850	600	525	300	150

Model 1866 Yellowboy Rifle

Same as above, fitted with a 24.25" barrel. **NOTE:** Add $40 for charcoal blue.

NIB	Exc.	V.G.	Good	Fair	Poor
1100	900	600	525	300	150

Model 1866 Yellowboy Trapper

As above, with 16" barrel.

NIB	Exc.	V.G.	Good	Fair	Poor
950	725	600	525	300	150

Model 1873 Winchester Rifle

Lever-action rifle offered in .357 Magnum, .44 WCF or .45 LC. Fitted with a 24.25" barrel. **NOTE:** Add $40 for charcoal blue; $140 for pistol-grip option.

NIB	Exc.	V.G.	Good	Fair	Poor
1150	925	750	675	400	200

Model 1873 Long Range Rifle

Similar to Model 1873, but fitted with a 30" barrel. **NOTE:** Add $140 for pistol-grip option; $1,250 for 1 of 1000 engraving option.

NIB	Exc.	V.G.	Good	Fair	Poor
1175	950	775	675	400	200

Model 1873 Carbine

Same as standard Model 1873, but fitted with a 19" barrel. **NOTE:** Add $40 for charcoal blue.

NIB	Exc.	V.G.	Good	Fair	Poor
1150	925	750	675	400	200

Model 1873 Short Rifle

Fitted with a 20" barrel. Production ceased in 1998. **NOTE:** Add $40 for charcoal blue.

NIB	Exc.	V.G.	Good	Fair	Poor
1150	925	750	675	400	200

Model 1873 Trapper

As above, with 16" barrel.

NIB	Exc.	V.G.	Good	Fair	Poor
1150	925	750	675	400	200

Model 1873 Deluxe Sporting Rifle

Fitted with 24" barrel, checkered walnut stock and pistol-grip.

NIB	Exc.	V.G.	Good	Fair	Poor
1220	925	850	725	400	200

Model 1873 Evil Roy Rifle

Chambered for .357 or .45 Colt cartridge. Fitted with 20" barrel.

NIB	Exc.	V.G.	Good	Fair	Poor
1450	1200	950	700	400	200

Model 1873 Larry Crow Signature Series Rifle

Chambered for .357 Magnum or .45 Colt cartridge. Fitted with 20" barrel.

NIB	Exc.	V.G.	Good	Fair	Poor
1550	1300	1050	800	400	200

Model 1892 Solid Frame Rifle

Offered with either 20" or 24" octagon barrels. Chambered for .357 Magnum, .44WCF or .45 Colt cartridges.

NIB	Exc.	V.G.	Good	Fair	Poor
850	675	575	450	300	150

Model 1892 Takedown Rifle

As above, with takedown feature.

NIB	Exc.	V.G.	Good	Fair	Poor
975	775	675	525	375	200

Model 1886

Replica of Winchester 1886. Caliber .45-70 Government.

NIB	Exc.	V.G.	Good	Fair	Poor
1400	1250	900	750	400	250

Billy Dixon Model 1874 Sharps

Reproduction of Model 1874 Sharps rifle. Chambered for .45-70 cartridge. Fitted with 32" tapered octagon barrel. Stock is hand checkered, with oil finish walnut. Double-set triggers standard.

NIB	Exc.	V.G.	Good	Fair	Poor
1650	1225	1100	700	500	250

Remington Rolling Block

Remington reproduction was introduced to Cimarron in 1997. Represents Rolling Block Sporting rifle, with 30" tapered octagon barrel. Chambered for .45-70 cartridge. Hand-checkered satin-finished walnut stock.

NIB	Exc.	V.G.	Good	Fair	Poor
1300	1000	900	550	300	175

Adobe Walls Rolling Block

Chambered for .45-70 cartridge. Fitted with 30" octagon barrel. Hand-checkered walnut stock, with hand finishing. Case colored receiver and German silver nose cap. Weight about 10- to 13 lbs. Introduced in 2004.

NIB	Exc.	V.G.	Good	Fair	Poor
1425	1050	950	600	350	225

Model 1885 High Wall

Reproduction of Winchester Model 1885. Chambered for .45-70, .45-90, .45-120, .40-65, .348 Win., .30-40 Krag or .38-55 cartridges. Fitted with 30" barrel. Walnut stock and case colored receiver.

NIB	Exc.	V.G.	Good	Fair	Poor
995	800	650	500	300	125

Model 1885 Deluxe High Wall

As above, with checkered walnut stock and pistol-grip.

NIB	Exc.	V.G.	Good	Fair	Poor
1175	875	700	550	300	125

Model 1885 Low Wall

Introduced in 2004. chambered for .22 LR, .22 Hornet, .30-30, .32-20, .38-40, .357 Magnum, .44-40 and .44 Magnum cartridges. Hand checkered walnut stock, with pistol-grip. Octagon barrel 30" long. Single-/double-set trigger.

NIB	Exc.	V.G.	Good	Fair	Poor
1175	850	700	550	300	125

Texas Ranger Carbine

Copy of Sharps Model 1859 Military Carbine. Round barrel 22" long. Receiver case colored. Stock American black walnut. Chambered for .45-70 cartridge. Marked "T*S" on barrel. Introduced in 2004.

NIB	Exc.	V.G.	Good	Fair	Poor
1200	900	725	600	350	150

Sharps Silhouette

Offered in .45-70 or .40-65 calibers, with 32" octagon barrel. Introduced in 1998.

NIB	Exc.	V.G.	Good	Fair	Poor
1095	850	700	600	350	150

Quigley Sharps Sporting Rifle

Chambered for .45-70 or .45-120 caliber. Fitted with heavy 34" octagon barrel. Introduced in 1998.

NIB	Exc.	V.G.	Good	Fair	Poor
1725	1350	1175	700	450	275

Sharp's No. 1 Sporting Rifle

Plain walnut stock with pistol-grip. Fitted with a 32" barrel. Chambered for .45-70 cartridge.

NIB	Exc.	V.G.	Good	Fair	Poor
1350	1050	900	500	300	150

Pride of the Plains Model

Based on Sharps Model 1874 Sporting Rifle. Chambered for .45-70 cartridge. Features a 32" octagon barrel, hand-checkered walnut stock with pistol-grip, coin nickel receiver, Creedmore tang sight and target front sight with inserts. Introduced in 2004.

NIB	Exc.	V.G.	Good	Fair	Poor
1620	1200	925	500	300	150

Professional Hunter Model

Basic Sharps Model 1874. Chambered for .45-70 cartridge. Fitted with a 32" barrel, case colored receiver, walnut stock with shotgun butt and double-set triggers. Introduced in 2004.

NIB	Exc.	V.G.	Good	Fair	Poor
1160	850	725	500	300	150

Big Fifty Model

Chambered for .50-90 cartridge. Fitted with a 34" half-octagon barrel. Fancy walnut stock with hand checkering and pistol-grip. Case colored receiver, German silver nose cap and Hartford-style Soule Creedmore sights, with spirit level and globe front sight. Weight about 11 lbs. Introduced in 2004.

NIB	Exc.	V.G.	Good	Fair	Poor
1890	1400	1150	700	450	275

Springfield Trapdoor Carbine

Based on the famous Springfield design. Chambered for .45-70.

NIB	Exc.	V.G.	Good	Fair	Poor
1250	1000	800	500	300	150

Springfield Trapdoor Officer's Model

Officer's version of Springfield Trapdoor model. Chambered for .45-70.

NIB	Exc.	V.G.	Good	Fair	Poor
1150	900	775	500	275	150

U.S. Shooting Team Creedmoor Sharps

Chambered in .45-70, with 34" round barrel, hand-checkered European walnut stock with hand-rubbed oil finish and color case-hardened frame. Sales of this model (a percentage) was used to win the first organized shooting event in the United States, will be donated by Cimarron to the USA Shooting Team in support of their efforts in international shooting sports. Made in Italy by Chiappa and imported by Cimarron.

NIB	Exc.	V.G.	Good	Fair	Poor
1400	1150	900	700	400	200

SHOTGUNS

1878 Coach Gun

Side-by-side double-barrel 12-gauge, with hammers, double triggers, 22" or 26" barrels. Standard or polished blue "U.S.A." finish. **NOTE:** Add $100 for U.S.A. finish.

NIB	Exc.	V.G.	Good	Fair	Poor
500	425	375	300	250	200

1881 Coach Gun

Side-by-side double-barrel in 12- or 20-gauge, with 22", 26", 28" or 30" barrels. Hammerless design. Interchangeable choke tubes. Walnut stock with straight-/pistol-grip.

NIB	Exc.	V.G.	Good	Fair	Poor
600	500	400	325	275	225

Model 1887 Shotgun

Lever-action limited edition replica of Model 1887 Winchester 12-gauge, with 5-shot magazine, 20", 22", 24" or 28" barrel. Color case-hardened frame.

NIB	Exc.	V.G.	Good	Fair	Poor
1150	975	750	600	400	250

Model 1897 Shotgun

Replica of Winchester 12-gauge pump-action model. Exposed hammer, semi-pistol-grip walnut stock, choke tubes.

NIB	Exc.	V.G.	Good	Fair	Poor
500	400	350	300	200	150

CLAPP, HOFFMAN & CO. CLAPP, GATES & CO. RIFLES
Alamance, North Carolina

Maker of Confederate Civil War rifles, 1862 - 1864. Overall length: Types I, II, & III 51.25" to 52", Type IV varies between 46.5" and 51"; barrel length: Types I, II, & III 35.25" to 36", Type IV varies between 31.25" and 35.875"; caliber: Types I, II, & III .50, Type IV .577; markings: none. Despite the absence of makers marks, the Clapp, Gates & Co. products are readily distinguished by their part-round, part-octagonal (octagonal section on Types I to III, about 4" long, 4.75" to 5.5" on Type IV rifles) barrels having only a slightly raised bolster projecting from the upper right quarter. This small bolster accommodates the boxlock that distinguished the first 100 rifles produced. This gave way to a standard percussion lock on subsequent production, which required that the hammer bend sharply to the left to strike the cone. Type I and Type II rifles were adapted to a "footprint" saber bayonet lug on the right side of the barrel; Types III and IV also had a saber bayonet lug on the right side of the barrel but of the standard pattern. Types III and IV are distinguished by their caliber, the former being .50, the latter .577. Prices reflect Type II through IV production; Type I (while extant) has never been offered for sale and would presumably bring a significantly higher premium.

NIB	Exc.	V.G.	Good	Fair	Poor
—	—	39500	19500	3900	1200

CLARK, F. H.
Memphis, Tennessee

Pocket Pistol

A .41-caliber single-shot percussion pistol, with 3.5" to 5" barrel, German silver mounts and end cap. Barrel stamped "F.H. Clark & Co./Memphis". Manufactured in 1850s and 1860s.

NIB	Exc.	V.G.	Good	Fair	Poor
—	—	5350	1900	550	200

CLASSIC DOUBLES
Tochigi City, Japan

Importer of Japanese shotguns, formerly imported by Winchester as the Model 101 and Model 23. These models were discontinued by Winchester in 1987 and imported by Classic Doubles until 1990.

Model 201 Classic

A 12- or 20-gauge boxlock side-by-side double-barrel shotgun, with 26" ventilated rib barrels, screw-in choke tubes single-selective trigger and automatic ejectors. Blued, with checkered walnut stock and beavertail forearm.

NIB	Exc.	V.G.	Good	Fair	Poor
2400	1950	1700	1500	1250	900

Model 201 Small Bore Set

As above, with a smaller receiver and two sets of barrels. Chambered for 28-gauge and .410 bore. Barrels are 28" in length.

NIB	Exc.	V.G.	Good	Fair	Poor
4100	3500	2950	2250	1750	1250

Model 101 Classic Field Grade I

A 12- or 20-gauge over/under shotgun, with 25.5" or 28" ventilated rib barrels, screw-in choke tubes, automatic ejectors and a single-selective trigger. Engraved, blued with checkered walnut stock.

NIB	Exc.	V.G.	Good	Fair	Poor
2000	1750	1500	1250	1000	700

Classic Field Grade II

As above, in 28-gauge and .410 bore. Highly engraved, with a coin-finished receiver and deluxe walnut stock. A round knob pistol-grip and fleur-de-lis checkering.

NIB	Exc.	V.G.	Good	Fair	Poor
2500	2000	1750	1500	1250	900

Classic Sporter

As above in 12-gauge only, with 28" or 30" barrels, ventilated rib and screw-in choke tubes. Frame is coin-finished, with light engraving and a matted upper surface to reduce glare. Stock is select walnut. Designed for sporting clays.

NIB	Exc.	V.G.	Good	Fair	Poor
2250	1800	1500	1250	1000	700

Waterfowl Model

As above with 30" barrels, 3" chambers, ventilated rib and screw-in choke tubes. Overall finish is a subdued matte with light engraving.

NIB	Exc.	V.G.	Good	Fair	Poor
1650	1350	1000	850	650	500

Classic Trap Over/Under

Designed for competition trap shooting, with 30" or 32" barrels, a ventilated center and top rib, automatic ejectors, screw-in choke tubes and a single trigger. Blued, with light engraving and a walnut stock in straight or Monte Carlo style.

NIB	Exc.	V.G.	Good	Fair	Poor
2250	1750	1500	1250	1000	700

Classic Trap Single

As above, with a single 32" or 34" barrel.

NIB	Exc.	V.G.	Good	Fair	Poor
2250	1800	1500	1250	1000	700

Classic Trap Combo

As above, with a single barrel and a set of over/under barrels.

NIB	Exc.	V.G.	Good	Fair	Poor
3000	2500	2000	1750	1250	1000

Classic Skeet

As above, with 27.5" barrels.

NIB	Exc.	V.G.	Good	Fair	Poor
2250	1750	1500	1250	1000	700

Classic Skeet 4 Gauge Set

As above, furnished with four sets of barrels chambered for 12-, 20-, 28-gauge, and .410 bore.

NIB	Exc.	V.G.	Good	Fair	Poor
4150	3750	3000	2500	1850	1500

CLEMENT, CHAS.
Liege, Belgium

Model 1903

A 5.5mm Glisenti caliber semi-automatic pistol. Barrel raises at muzzle to begin the loading procedure.

Courtesy James Rankin

NIB	Exc.	V.G.	Good	Fair	Poor
—	575	475	350	220	110

Model 1907

As above, in 6.35mm and 7.65mm caliber.

Courtesy Orvel Reichert

NIB	Exc.	V.G.	Good	Fair	Poor
—	475	395	325	200	100

Model 1908

Similar to Model 1907, with magazine release at the bottom of frame. Fitted with a larger grip.

Courtesy J.B. Wood

NIB	Exc.	V.G.	Good	Fair	Poor
—	575	450	295	200	125

Model 1909

Semi-automatic pistol in 6.35mm and 7.65mm calibers. Similar to Model 1908, with barrel and chamber housing in one piece.

Courtesy James Rankin

NIB	Exc.	V.G.	Good	Fair	Poor
—	575	450	300	225	100

Model 1910

Redesigned version of above, with barrel and housing all one piece. This unit is held in position by the trigger guard.

Courtesy Orvel Reichert

NIB	Exc.	V.G.	Good	Fair	Poor
—	575	475	395	350	275

Model 1912

A 6.35mm caliber semi-automatic pistol marked "Clement's Patent"; others, "Model 1912 Brevet 243839". This model is quite different from earlier Clement models.

Courtesy James Rankin

NIB	Exc.	V.G.	Good	Fair	Poor
—	425	295	250	195	100

American Model

Revolver copy of Colt Police Positive. Chambered for .38-caliber.

NIB	Exc.	V.G.	Good	Fair	Poor
—	425	295	250	150	90

CLERKE PRODUCTS
Santa Monica, California

Hi-Wall

Copy of Winchester Model 1885 High Wall rifle, with the action activated by a lever. Receiver is case colored. Chambered for almost all modern calibers. Features 26" barrel, walnut stock with a pistol-grip and schnabel fore-end. Manufactured between 1972 and 1974.

NIB	Exc.	V.G.	Good	Fair	Poor
975	850	650	425	300	200

Deluxe Hi-Wall

As above, with half-round/half-octagonal barrel, select walnut stock and recoil pad. Manufactured between 1972 and 1974.

NIB	Exc.	V.G.	Good	Fair	Poor
1100	975	750	525	400	250

COBRA ENTERPRISES, INC.
Salt Lake City, Utah

DERRINGERS

Standard Series

Offered chambered in .22 LR, .22 WMR, .25 ACP and .32 ACP. Over/under barrels are 2.4". Pearl or laminate wood grips. Weight about 9.5 oz. Introduced in 2002.

NIB	Exc.	V.G.	Good	Fair	Poor
250	200	160	125	100	75

Long Bore Series

Chambered for .22 WMR, .38 Special or 9mm cartridge. Fitted with a 3.5" barrel. Black synthetic, laminate oak or laminate rosewood grips. Chrome or black finish. Weight about 16 oz.

NIB	Exc.	V.G.	Good	Fair	Poor
250	200	160	125	100	75

Big Bore Series

Chambered for .22 WMR, .32 H&R Magnum and .38 Special. Barrel length 2.75". Choice of black synthetic, laminate oak or laminate rosewood grips. Chrome or black finish. Weight about 14 oz.

NIB	Exc.	V.G.	Good	Fair	Poor
250	200	160	125	100	75

SEMI-AUTOMATIC PISTOLS

C-32/C-380

Chambered for .32 ACP or .380 cartridges. Fitted with 2.8" barrel. Chrome or black finish. Magazine capacity 5 rounds for .380; 6 rounds for .32 ACP. Weight about 22 oz.

NIB	Exc.	V.G.	Good	Fair	Poor
175	125	80	60	40	25

C-9mm

Double-action-only pistol chambered for 9mm cartridge. Fitted with 3.3" barrel. Magazine capacity 10 rounds. Load indicator. Polymer grips. Weight about 21 oz.

NIB	Exc.	V.G.	Good	Fair	Poor
275	215	150	115	75	45

Patriot .45

Double-action-only pistol chambered for .45 ACP cartridge. Barrel length 3". Frame is black polymer. Slide is stainless steel. Magazine capacity 6 rounds. Weight about 20 oz.

NIB	Exc.	V.G.	Good	Fair	Poor
350	225	150	115	75	45

COBRAY INDUSTRIES
S.W.D., Inc.
Atlanta, Georgia

M-11 Pistol

A 9mm caliber semi-automatic pistol. Fires from the closed bolt. Made of steel stampings, with a parkerized finish. Patterned after, though a good deal smaller than, Ingram Mac 10. **NOTE:** Add $70 for stainless steel; $150 for pre-ban models.

NIB	Exc.	V.G.	Good	Fair	Poor
—	375	295	150	100	75

M-12

Same as above, but chambered for .380 ACP cartridge. **NOTE:** Add $150 for pre-ban models.

NIB	Exc.	V.G.	Good	Fair	Poor
—	375	295	150	100	75

TM-11 Carbine

As above in 9mm caliber, with 16.25" shrouded barrel and telescoping metal shoulder stock.

NIB	Exc.	V.G.	Good	Fair	Poor
—	450	350	225	150	100

TM-12 Carbine

As above, but chambered for .380 ACP cartridge.

NIB	Exc.	V.G.	Good	Fair	Poor
—	450	350	225	150	100

Terminator Shotgun

Single-shot 12- or 20-gauge shotgun that fires from an open bolt position. The cocked bolt is released to slam home on the shell when trigger is pulled. The 18" barrel is cylinder bored. There is a telescoping wire stock and finish is Parkerized. We have seen many of these advertised at sky-high prices, but junk is junk.

NIB	Exc.	V.G.	Good	Fair	Poor
—	175	125	80	60	40

COCHRAN TURRET
C. B. Allen
Springfield, Massachusetts

Under Hammer Turret Rifle

A .36- or .40-caliber percussion radial cylinder rifle, with 31" or 32" octagonal barrels and walnut stocks. Barrel marked "Cochrans/Many/Chambered/&/Non Recoil/Rifle" and top strap "C.B. Allen / Springfield". These rifles were produced in variations listed. Manufactured during late 1830s and 1840s.

1st Type

Fitted with a circular top strap secured by two screws. Serial numbered from 1 to approximately 30.

NIB	Exc.	V.G.	Good	Fair	Poor
—	—		18000	6500	2150

2nd Type

Fitted with a rectangular hinged top strap, the locking catch of which serves as the rear sight. Serial numbered from approximately 31 to 155.

NIB	Exc.	V.G.	Good	Fair	Poor
—	—	29500	15000	5100	1800

3rd Type

As above, with a smaller hammer and plain trigger guard.

NIB	Exc.	V.G.	Good	Fair	Poor
—	—	18000	15000	5100	1800

Pistol

Action similar to above with 4" to 7" barrels.

NIB	Exc.	V.G.	Good	Fair	Poor
—	—	26500	21000	9700	3000

CODY, MICHAEL & SONS
Nashville, Tennessee

Received a contract with the State of Tennessee for "Mississippi" rifles with brass patchboxes in late 1861. Barrel length 36"; caliber .54. Cody often used reworked Model 1817 rifle barrels and sporting pattern single screw lockplates. Rifles are unmarked except for large engraved serial number on top of breech plug tang.

NIB	Exc.	V.G.	Good	Fair	Poor
—	—	29500	13000	2150	775

COFER, T. W.
Portsmouth, Virginia

Cofer Navy Revolver

A .36-caliber spur trigger percussion revolver, with 7.5" octagonal barrel and 6-shot cylinder. Top strap marked "T.W. Cofer's/Patent" and barrel "Portsmouth, Va." Manufactured in limited quantities during the Civil War.

NIB	Exc.	V.G.	Good	Fair	Poor
—	—	120000	43500	6500	1500

COGSWELL
London, England

Cogswell Pepperbox Pistol

A .47-caliber 6-shot percussion pepperbox, with case hardened barrels, German silver frame and walnut grips. Normally marked "B. Cogswell, 224 Strand, London" and "Improved Revolving Pistol".

NIB	Exc.	V.G.	Good	Fair	Poor
—	—	4400	1950	975	550

COLTON MANUFACTURING CO.
Toledo, Ohio

Colton Manufacturing Co. provided Sears with its first American-made hammerless house brand double. Sears advertised their sidelock hammerless gun as "the equal of any gun made, regardless of price" in their 1900 Fall catalog No. 110. There were four models: three sideplated boxlock-types and a unique unitized coil spring driven striker assembly version. All these, especially the latter, were designed to be mass produced. Many of the distinctive sidelock-within-a-sideplated model were produced but they are seldom seen today either because they were used-up or did not hold up well and were scrapped. Sears replaced Colton with the more traditional design Fryberg gun in 1902. Values depend on grade. There appears to be at least two levels of quality and condition ranging from $300 to $1,500. Colton-marked guns are scarce.

Courtesy Nick Niles, Paul Goodwin photo

COLT'S PATENT FIRE ARMS MANUFACTURING COMPANY
Hartford, Connecticut

COLT PATERSON MODELS

Pocket or Baby Paterson Model No. 1

Paterson was the first production revolver manufactured by Colt. First made in 1837. Model 1 or Pocket Model is most diminutive of Paterson line. Revolver is serial numbered in its own range, #1 through #500. Numbers are not visible without dismantling revolver. Barrel lengths run from 1.75" to 4.75". Standard model has no attached loading lever. Chambering is .28-caliber percussion and holds 5-shots. Finish is all blued.

Grips are varnished walnut. It has a roll-engraved cylinder scene and barrel stamped "Patent Arms Mfg. Co. Paterson N.J. Colt's Pt." Cased examples in Very Good or better condition can bring upwards of $200,000.

NIB	Exc.	V.G.	Good	Fair	Poor
—	—	125000	50000	19500	5000

Belt Model Paterson No. 2

Belt Model Paterson is a larger revolver, with a straight-grip and octagonal barrel that is 2.5" to 5.5" in length. Chambered for .31-caliber percussion and holds 5-shots. Finish all blued, with varnished walnut grips and no attached loading lever. It has a roll-engraved cylinder scene and barrel stamped "Patent Arms Mfg. Co. Paterson N.J. Colt's Pt." Serial number range is #1-#850 and shared with #3 Belt Model. Made from 1837-1840. An excellent cased example was auctioned by Rock Island Auction in 2007 for $414,000.

Courtesy Buffalo Bill Historical Center, Cody, Wyoming

NIB	Exc.	V.G.	Good	Fair	Poor
—	—	225000	75000	28500	7500

Belt Model Paterson No. 3

This revolver is quite similar to Model #2, except grips are curved outward at the bottom to form a more hand-filling configuration. They are serial numbered in the same #1-#850 range. Some attached loading levers have been noted on this model, but they are extremely rare and would add approximately 35 percent to value.

NIB	Exc.	V.G.	Good	Fair	Poor
—	—	250000	95000	40000	10000

Ehlers Model Pocket Paterson

John Ehlers was a major stockholder and treasurer of Patent Arms Mfg. Co. when it went bankrupt. He seized the assets and inventory. These revolvers were Pocket Model Patersons that were not finished at the time. Ehlers had them finished and marketed them. They had an attached loading lever and abbreviation "Mfg Co." was deleted from barrel stamping. There were 500 revolvers involved in Ehlers variation totally. They were produced from 1840-1843.

NIB	Exc.	V.G.	Good	Fair	Poor
—	—	—	75000	30000	8300

Ehlers Belt Model Paterson

Same specifications apply to this larger revolver as they do to Ehlers Pocket Model. It falls within the same 500 revolver involvement and is rare.

NIB	Exc.	V.G.	Good	Fair	Poor
—	—	—	75000	30000	8000

Texas Paterson Model No. 5

This is the largest and most sought after of Paterson models, also known as Holster Model. It has been verified as actually seeing use by both military and civilians on the American frontier. It is chambered for .36-caliber percussion, holds 5-shots and has an octagonal barrel that ranges from 4" to 12" in length. It has been observed with and without the attached loading lever, but those with it are rare. Finish is blued, with a case colored hammer. Grips are varnished walnut. Cylinder is roll-engraved; barrel stamped "Patent Arms Mfg. Co. Paterson, N.J. Colts Pt." Most Texas Patersons are well used and have a worn appearance. One in excellent or V.G. condition would be highly prized. A verified military model would be worth a great deal more than standard, so a qualified appraisal would be essential. Serial number range is #1-#1000. Manufactured from 1838-1840. Attached loading lever brings approximately a 25 percent premium.

An 1836 Colt Paterson Revolver sold in September, 2011, for $977,500 at a Heritage Auction in Dallas, Texas. (Price includes a 15% buyer's premium.) This is believed to be a world record for the sale of a single American firearm. The very rare No. 5 Holster Model with a 9" barrel, ivory grips, attached loading lever and accessories in a box, is the finest known surviving example of Samuel Colt's first revolver. Two other Colt percussion revolvers were sold at the same auction for more than $800,000. (See Third Model Dragoon and Model 1861 Navy listings.) Such prices are extreme exceptions to the values of typical models.

NIB	Exc.	V.G.	Good	Fair	Poor
—	—	300000	150000	60000	17500

Colt Model 1860 Army
Fluted Cylinder

NIB	Exc.	V.G.	Good	Fair	Poor
675	575	400	300	200	125

COLT REVOLVING LONG GUNS 1837-1847

First Model Ring Lever Rifle

This was actually the first firearm manufactured by Colt; first revolver appeared a short time later. There were 200 of First Models made in 1837 and 1838. Octagonal barrel of First Model is 32" long and browned, while rest of the finish is blued. Stock is varnished walnut with a cheekpiece inlaid with Colt's trademark. Ring lever located in front of frame is pulled to rotate the 8-shot cylinder and cock the hammer. Rifle is chambered for .34-, .36-, .38-, .40- and .44-caliber percussion. Cylinder is roll-engraved and barrel is stamped "Colt's Patent/Patent Arms Mfg. Co., Paterson, N. Jersey." This model has a top strap over the cylinder. They were made both with and without an attached loading lever. Latter is worth approximately 10 percent more.

Courtesy Bonhams & Butterfields, San Francisco, California

NIB	Exc.	V.G.	Good	Fair	Poor
—	—	—	90000	40000	9750

Second Model Ring Lever Rifle

Model is quite similar in appearance to First Model. Its function is identical. Major difference is absence of top strap over the cylinder. It had no trademark stamped on the cheekpiece. Second Model offered with 28" and 32" octagonal barrel. Chambered for .44-caliber percussion, holding 8-shots. There were approximately 500 produced from 1838-1841. Presence of an attached cheekpiece would add approximately 10 percent to value.

Courtesy Bonhams & Butterfields, San Francisco, California

NIB	Exc.	V.G.	Good	Fair	Poor
—	—	—	80000	19500	8000

Model 1839 Shotgun

Model is quite similar in appearance to 1839 Carbine. Chambered for 16-gauge and holds 6-shots. It has a Damascus pattern barrel. Most notable difference is a 3.5" (instead of a 2.5") long cylinder. There were only 225 of these made from 1839-1841. Markings are same as on the Carbine.

Courtesy Bonhams & Butterfields, San Francisco, California

NIB	Exc.	V.G.	Good	Fair	Poor
—	—	37500	29500	11000	6000

Model 1839 Carbine

This model has no ring, but features an exposed hammer for cocking and rotating the 6-shot cylinder. Chambered for .525 smoothbore and comes standard with a 24" round barrel. Other barrel lengths have been noted. Finish is blued, with a browned barrel and varnished walnut stock. Cylinder is roll-engraved and barrel stamped "Patent Arms Mfg. Co. Paterson, N.J.-Colt's Pt." There were 950 manufactured from 1838-1841. Later variations of this model are found with the attached loading lever standard. Earlier models without one would bring approximately 25 percent additional. There were 360 purchased by the military and stamped "WAT" on the stock. These would be worth twice what a standard model would bring.

Courtesy Bonhams & Butterfields, San Francisco, California

NIB	Exc.	V.G.	Good	Fair	Poor
—	—	36000	25000	13500	7900

Model 1839/1848 Carbine

In 1848, Colt acquired a number of Model 1839 Carbines (approximately 40) from the state of Rhode Island. In an effort to make them marketable they were refinished and the majority fitted with plain cylinders (brightly polished) having integral ratchets around the arbor hole. Barrel length 24"; caliber .525; barrel browned; cylinder polished; frame blued; furniture case hardened; walnut stock varnished.

NIB	Exc.	V.G.	Good	Fair	Poor
—	—	70000	55000	18500	6500

Model 1854 Russian Contract Musket

In 1854, Colt purchased a large number of U.S. Model 1822 flintlock muskets that the company altered to percussion cap ignition and rifled. The reworked muskets are dated 1854 on barrel tang and at rear of the lockplate. In most instances the original manufactory marks, such as Springfield or Harpers Ferry at rear of the lockplate, have been removed, while U.S. and eagle between hammer and bolster remain. Percussion nipple bolster is marked COLT'S PATENT. Some examples have been noted with date 1858. Barrel length 42"; caliber .69; lock and furniture burnished bright; walnut stock oil finished.

NIB	Exc.	V.G.	Good	Fair	Poor
—	15000	10000	5000	1500	750

COLT WALKER-DRAGOON MODELS

Walker Model Revolver

Walker is a massive revolver. Weight 4 lbs., 9 oz. and has a 9" part-round/part-octagonal barrel. Cylinder holds 6-shots and chambered for .44-caliber percussion. There were 1,000 Walker Colts manufactured in 1847 and nearly all of them saw extremely hard use. Originally this model had a roll-engraved cylinder, military inspection marks and barrel stamping that read "Address Saml. Colt-New York City". Practically all examples noted have had these markings worn or rusted beyond recognition. Because the Walker is perhaps the most desirable and sought-after Colt from a collector's standpoint and because of the extremely high value of a Walker in any condition, qualified appraisal is definitely recommended. These revolvers were serial numbered A, B, C, D Company 1-220 and E Company 1-120. An Excellent example was auctioned by James D. Julia in 2008 for $920,000.

Courtesy Buffalo Bill Historical Center, Cody, Wyoming

NIB	Exc.	V.G.	Good	Fair	Poor
—	900000	675000	400000	200000	59500

Civilian Walker Revolver

Identical to military model, but has no martial markings. They are found serial numbered 1001 through 1100.

NIB	Exc.	V.G.	Good	Fair	Poor
—	—	500000	395000	195000	58000

Whitneyville Hartford Dragoon

A large 6-shot, .44-caliber percussion revolver. Has a 7.5" part-round/part-octagonal barrel. Frame, hammer and loading lever are case colored. Remainder is blued, with brass trigger guard and varnished walnut grips. There were only 240 made in late 1847. Serial numbers run from 1100-1340. Model is often referred to as a Transitional Walker. Some of the parts used in its manufacture were left over from Walker production run. This model has a roll-engraved cylinder scene and barrel stamped "Address Saml. Colt New York-City". An extremely rare model.

NIB	Exc.	V.G.	Good	Fair	Poor
—	—	140000	100000	55000	28500

Walker Replacement Dragoon

Extremely rare Colt (300 produced) is sometimes referred to as "Fluck", in memory of the gentleman who first identified it as a distinct and separate model. Produced by Colt as replacements to the military for Walkers that were no longer fit for service due to mechanical failures. They were large 6-shot .44-caliber percussion revolvers, with 7.5" part-round/part-octagonal barrels. Serial numbers ran from 2216 to 2515. The frame, hammer and loading lever are case-colored; remainder blued. Grips, which are longer than other Dragoons and similar to Walkers, are of varnished walnut and bear inspectors mark "WAT" inside an oval cartouche on one side and letters "JH" on the other. Frame is stamped "Colt's/ Patent/U.S." Letter "P" appears on various parts of the gun.

NIB	Exc.	V.G.	Good	Fair	Poor
—	—	75000	55000	25000	6000

First Model Dragoon

Another large 6-shot .44-caliber percussion revolver. Has a 7.5" part-round/part-octagonal barrel. Frame, hammer and loading lever are case colored; remainder blued, with a brass grip frame and square backed trigger guard. Trigger guard is silver-plated on the Civilian Model only. Another distinguishing feature on First Model is the oval cylinder stop notches. Serial number range is 1341-8000. There were approximately 7,000 made. Cylinder is roll-engraved; barrel stampings read "Address Saml. Colt, New York City." "Colt's Patent" appears on the frame. Military Models, letters "U.S." also appear on the frame.

Military Model

NIB	Exc.	V.G.	Good	Fair	Poor
—	110000	75000	40000	20000	3500

Civilian Model

NIB	Exc.	V.G.	Good	Fair	Poor
—	90000	55000	35000	18000	3000

Second Model Dragoon

Most of the improvements that distinguish this model from First Model are internal and not readily apparent. Most obvious external change is the rectangular cylinder-stop notches. This model is serial numbered from 8000-10700. Total production of approximately 2,700 revolvers manufactured in 1850 and 1851. There is a Civilian Model, Military Model and an extremely rare variation that was issued to the militias of New Hampshire and Massachusetts (marked "MS.").

Civilian Model

NIB	Exc.	V.G.	Good	Fair	Poor
—	75000	55000	35000	25000	3500

Military Model

NIB	Exc.	V.G.	Good	Fair	Poor
—	85000	62500	40000	30000	3000

Militia Model

NIB	Exc.	V.G.	Good	Fair	Poor
—	90000	75000	45000	30000	3000

Third Model Dragoon

Most common of all large Colt percussion revolvers. Approximately 10,500 were manufactured from 1851 through 1861. Quite similar in appearance to Second Model. Obvious external difference is the round trigger guard. Third Model Dragoon was first Colt revolver available with a detachable shoulder stock. There are three basic types of stocks and all are quite rare as only 1,250 were produced. There are two other major variations we will note—"C.L." Dragoon, which was a militia-issued model and is rare; late-issue model with an 8" barrel. These are found over serial number 18000 and only 50 were produced.

A historic cased Gustave Young-engraved ivory-gripped Colt Third Model Dragoon was sold for $805,000 at a Texas auction in 2011. Revolver was inscribed "Colonel P.M. Milliken". Milliken was an officer of the 1st Ohio volunteer calvary and killed leading a charge against the Confederate Army at Stone River, Tennessee in 1862. Two other Colt percussion revolvers were sold at the same auction for more than $800,000. (See Texas Paterson No. 5 and Model 1861 Navy listings.) Such prices are extreme exceptions to values of typical models.

Courtesy Buffalo Bill Historical Center, Cody, Wyoming

Courtesy Buffalo Bill Historical Center, Cody, Wyoming

Civilian Model

NIB	Exc.	V.G.	Good	Fair	Poor
—	50000	35000	15000	2500	1000

Military Model

NIB	Exc.	V.G.	Good	Fair	Poor
—	65000	47000	30000	17500	3000

Shoulder Stock Cut Revolvers

NIB	Exc.	V.G.	Good	Fair	Poor
—	70000	51000	35000	20000	3000

Shoulder Stocks

NIB	Exc.	V.G.	Good	Fair	Poor
—	15000	8000	4000	2000	

C.L. Dragoon

Hand engraved, not stamped.

NIB	Exc.	V.G.	Good	Fair	Poor
—	80000	60000	57500	17500	3000

8" Barrel Late Issue

NIB	Exc.	V.G.	Good	Fair	Poor
—	67000	55000	42500	25000	3000

Hartford English Dragoon

A variation of Third Model Dragoon. Only notable differences are British proof-marks and distinct #1-#700 serial number range. Other than these two features, description given for Third Model would apply. These revolvers were manufactured in Hartford, but were finished at Colt's London factory from 1853-1857. Some bear the hand-engraved barrel marking "Col. Colt London". Many English Dragoons were elaborately engraved and individual appraisal would be a must. Two hundred revolvers came back to America in 1861 to be used in the Civil War.

NIB	Exc.	V.G.	Good	Fair	Poor
—	50000	35000	25000	12000	3000

Model 1848 Baby Dragoon

A small 5-shot .31-caliber percussion revolver. An octagonal barrel in lengths of 3", 4", 5" and 6". Most were made without an attached loading lever, although some with loading levers have been noted. Frame, hammer and loading lever (when present) are case colored; barrel and cylinder blued. Grip frame and trigger guard are silver-plated brass. Approximately 15,500 manufactured between 1847 and 1850. Serial range is between 1-5500. Barrels are stamped "Address Saml. Colt/New York City". Some have been noted with the barrel address inside brackets. Frame is marked "Colt's/Patent". First 10,000 revolvers have Texas Ranger/Indian roll-engraved cylinder scene; later guns stagecoach holdup scene. This is a popular model and many fakes have been noted. **NOTE:** Add 15 percent for attached loading lever.

Texas Ranger/Indian Scene

Courtesy Bonhams & Butterfields, San Francisco, California

Courtesy Bonhams & Butterfields, San Francisco, California

NIB	Exc.	V.G.	Good	Fair	Poor
—	—	19500	12000	6500	2000

Stagecoach Holdup Scene

NIB	Exc.	V.G.	Good	Fair	Poor
—	—	20500	13000	7000	2000

Model 1849 Pocket Revolver

A small either 5- or 6-shot .31-caliber percussion revolver. An octagonal barrel of 3", 4", 5" or 6" in length. Most had loading gates, but some did not. Frame, hammer and loading lever are case colored; cylinder and barrel are blued. Grip frame and round trigger guard are made of brass and are silver plated. Both large and small trigger guard variations noted. Most plentiful of all Colt percussion revolvers, with approximately 325,000 manufactured over a 23-year period, 1850-1873. There are over 200 variations of this model and one should consult an expert for individual appraisals. There are many fine publications specializing in the field of Colt percussion revolvers that would be helpful in identification of the variations. Values represented here are for standard model.

Courtesy Rock Island Auction Company

NIB	Exc.	V.G.	Good	Fair	Poor
—	4000	3400	2950	1200	300

London Model 1849 Pocket Revolver

Identical in configuration to standard 1849 Pocket Revolver. London-made models have a higher quality finish and their own serial number range, 1-11000. Manufactured from 1853 through 1857. Feature a roll-engraved cylinder scene. Barrels are stamped "Address Col. Colt/London". First 265 revolvers, known as early models, have brass grip frames and small round trigger guards. They are quite rare and worth approximately 50 percent more than standard model that has a steel grip frame and large oval trigger guard.

NIB	Exc.	V.G.	Good	Fair	Poor
—	6000	5000	3500	1200	300

Model 1851 Navy Revolver

Undoubtedly, the most popular revolver Colt produced in the medium size and power range. It is a 6-shot .36-caliber percussion revolver, with 7.5" octagonal barrel. Has an attached loading lever. Basic model has a case colored frame hammer and loading lever, with silver-plated brass grip frame and trigger guard. Grips are varnished walnut. Colt manufactured approximately 215,000 of these fine revolvers between 1850 and 1873. Basic Navy features a roll-engraved cylinder scene of a battle between the navies of Texas and Mexico. There are three distinct barrel stampings—serial number 1-74000, "Address Saml. Colt New York City"; serial number 74001-101000 "Address Saml. Colt. Hartford, Ct."; and serial number 101001-215000 "Address Saml. Colt New York U.S. America". Left side of frame is stamped "Colt's/Patent" on all variations. This model also available with a detached shoulder stock. Values for shoulder stocks today are nearly as high as for the revolver itself. Careful appraisal should be secured before purchase. The number of variations within 1851 Navy model designation makes it necessary to read specialized text available on the subject.

Square Back Trigger Guard, 1st Model, Serial #1-1000

Courtesy Rock Island Auction Company

NIB	Exc.	V.G.	Good	Fair	Poor
—	—	50000	42500	27000	5500

Square Back Trigger Guard, 2nd Model, Serial #1001-4200

NIB	Exc.	V.G.	Good	Fair	Poor
—	—	37500	30000	10000	2500

Small Round Trigger Guard, 3rd Model, Serial #4201-85000

Courtesy Milwaukee Public Museum, Milwaukee, Wisconsin

NIB	Exc.	V.G.	Good	Fair	Poor
—	—	9500	8000	2500	500

Large Round Trigger Guard, 4th Model, Serial #85001-215000

NIB	Exc.	V.G.	Good	Fair	Poor
—	—	9500	8000	2500	500

Martial Model

"U.S." stamped on left side of frame; inspector's marks and cartouche on grips.

NIB	Exc.	V.G.	Good	Fair	Poor
—	—	42000	20000	7000	1000

Shoulder Stock Variations

1st and 2nd Model Revolver cut for stock only. Expert appraisal recommended prior to purchase of these very rare variations.

Stock Only

NIB	Exc.	V.G.	Good	Fair	Poor
—	—	22000	17000	7000	1250

3rd Model Cut For Stock

Revolver only.

NIB	Exc.	V.G.	Good	Fair	Poor
—	—	17500	11500	4000	1250

Stock

NIB	Exc.	V.G.	Good	Fair	Poor
—	—	12500	9000	3750	1000

London Model 1851 Navy Revolver

These revolvers are physically similar to U.S.-made model. Exception, barrel address reads "Address Col. Colt. London" and British proof-marks stamped on barrel and cylinder. There were 42,000 made between 1853 and 1857. They have their own serial number range #1-#42,000. There are two major variations of London Navy. Again, a serious purchaser would be well advised to seek qualified appraisal as fakes have been noted.

1st Model

Serial #1-#2,000, with a small round brass trigger guard and grip frame. Squareback guard worth a 40 percent premium.

NIB	Exc.	V.G.	Good	Fair	Poor
—	—	16500	8000	2150	700

2nd Model

Serial #2,001-#42,000, steel grip frame and large round trigger guard.

NIB	Exc.	V.G.	Good	Fair	Poor
—	—	15000	7500	1800	600

Hartford Manufactured Variation

Serial numbers in 42,000 range.

NIB	Exc.	V.G.	Good	Fair	Poor
—	—	15000	7500	1800	600

COLT SIDE HAMMER MODELS

Model 1855 Side Hammer "Root" Pocket Revolver

"Root", as it's popularly known, was the only solid-frame revolver Colt ever made. It has a spur trigger, walnut grips and hammer mounted on right side of frame. Standard finish is a case colored frame, hammer and loading lever, with barrel and cylinder blued. Chambered for both .28-caliber and .31-caliber percussion. Each caliber has its own serial number range—1-30000 for .28-caliber; 1-14000 for .31-caliber. Model consists of seven basic variations. Serious student should avail himself of the fine publications dealing with this model in depth. Colt produced Side Hammer Root from 1855-1870.

Model 1 and 1A Serial #1-384

3.5" octagonal barrel, .28-caliber roll-engraved cylinder. Hartford barrel address without pointing hand.

Courtesy Milwaukee Public Museum, Milwaukee, Wisconsin

NIB	Exc.	V.G.	Good	Fair	Poor
—	—	12000	6000	3500	1200

Model 2 Serial #476-25000

Same as Model 1, with pointing hand barrel address.

NIB	Exc.	V.G.	Good	Fair	Poor
—	—	7500	3500	1900	500

Model 3 Serial #25001-30000

Same as Model 2, with a full fluted cylinder.

NIB	Exc.	V.G.	Good	Fair	Poor
—	—	7500	3500	1900	500

Model 3A and 4 Serial #1-2400

.31-caliber, 3.5" barrel, Hartford address, full fluted cylinder.

NIB	Exc.	V.G.	Good	Fair	Poor
—	—	7250	3250	1800	500

Model 5 Serial #2401-8000

.31-caliber, 3.5" round barrel, address "Col. Colt New York".

NIB	Exc.	V.G.	Good	Fair	Poor
—	—	6500	2900	1300	300

Model 5A Serial #2401-8000

Same as Model 5, with a 4.5" barrel.

Courtesy Milwaukee Public Museum, Milwaukee, Wisconsin

NIB	Exc.	V.G.	Good	Fair	Poor
—	—	6500	2900	1300	300

Models 6 and 6A Serial #8001-11074

Same as Model 5 and 5A, with roll-engraved cylinder scene.

NIB	Exc.	V.G.	Good	Fair	Poor
—	—	6750	2995	1350	300

Models 7 and 7A Serial #11075-14000

Same as Models 6 and 6A, with a screw holding in cylinder pin.

NIB	Exc.	V.G.	Good	Fair	Poor
—	—	6750	2995	1350	300

COLT SIDE HAMMER LONG GUNS

Model 1855 Sporting Rifle, 1st Model

A 6-shot revolving rifle, chambered for .36-caliber percussion. Comes with 21", 24", 27" or 30" round barrel that is part octagonal where it joins the frame. Stock is walnut, with either an oil or varnish finish. Frame, hammer and loading lever are case colored; rest of the metal blued. Hammer is on right side of frame. 1st Model has no fore-end and an oiling device is attached to the barrel underlug. Trigger guard has two spur-like projections in front and back of bow. Roll-engraved cylinder scene depicts a hunter shooting at five deer and is found only on this model. Standard stampings are "Colt's Pt./1856" and "Address S. Colt Hartford, Ct. U.S.A.

Early Model

Low serial numbers, with hand-engraved barrel marking "Address S. Colt Hartford, U.S.A."

NIB	Exc.	V.G.	Good	Fair	Poor
—	—	16500	15000	5500	1500

Production Model

NIB	Exc.	V.G.	Good	Fair	Poor
—	—	15000	12000	3000	1000

Model 1855 1st Model Carbine

Identical to 1st Model Rifle. Offered with 15" and 18" barrel.

Courtesy Milwaukee Public Museum, Milwaukee, Wisconsin

NIB	Exc.	V.G.	Good	Fair	Poor
—	—	12500	9500	3000	1000

Model 1855 Half Stock Sporting Rifle

Although this rifle is quite similar in appearance and finish to 1st Model, there are some notable differences. Features a walnut fore-end that protrudes halfway down the barrel. Two types of trigger guards—a short projectionless one or a long model, with a graceful scroll. There is a 6-shot model chambered for .36- or .44-caliber or 5-shot model chambered for .56-caliber. Cylinder is fully fluted. Markings are "Colt's Pt/1856" and "Address Col. Colt/Hartford Ct. U.S.A." Approximately 1,500 manufactured between 1857 and 1864.

Courtesy Milwaukee Public Museum, Milwaukee, Wisconsin

NIB	Exc.	V.G.	Good	Fair	Poor
—	—	12500	9500	3500	1000

Model 1855 Full Stock Military Rifle

Holds 6-shots in its .44-caliber chambering and 5-shots when chambered for .56-caliber. Another side hammer revolving rifle that resembles Half Stock model. Barrels are round and part-octagonal where they join the frame. Come in lengths of 21", 24", 27", 31" and 37". Hammer and loading lever are case colored; rest of metal parts blued. Walnut buttstock and full length fore-end are oil finished with sling swivels. Cylinder is fully fluted. Military models have provisions for affixing a bayonet, military-style sights and bear "U.S." martial mark on examples that were actually issued to the military. Standard stampings found on this model are "Colt's Pt/1856" and "Address Col. Colt Hartford, Ct. U.S.A." An estimated 9,300 manufactured between 1856 and 1864.

Courtesy Milwaukee Public Museum, Milwaukee, Wisconsin

Martially Marked Models

NIB	Exc.	V.G.	Good	Fair	Poor
—	—	42500	25000	9500	2000

Without Martial Markings

NIB	Exc.	V.G.	Good	Fair	Poor
—	—	13500	9750	3500	1000

Model 1855 Full Stock Sporting Rifle

Similar in appearance to Military model, with these notable exceptions. No provision for attaching a bayonet, sling swivels and it has sporting-style sights. Buttplate is crescent shaped. This model has been noted chambered for .56-caliber in 5-shot version and chambered for .36-, .40-, .44- and .50-caliber in 6-shot variation. Quite scarce in .40- and .50-caliber and will bring a 10 percent premium. Standard markings are "Colt's Pt/1856" and "Address Col. Colt/Hartford Ct. U.S.A." Production on this model was quite limited (several hundred at most) between 1856 and 1864.

NIB	Exc.	V.G.	Good	Fair	Poor
—	—	20000	13500	4000	1000

Model 1855 Revolving Carbine

Similar in appearance to 1855 Military Rifle. Barrel lengths of 15", 18" and 21", plus absence of a fore-end make the standard Carbine Model readily identifiable. Markings are the same. Approximately 4,400 manufactured between 1856 and 1864.

NIB	Exc.	V.G.	Good	Fair	Poor
—	—	13500	9500	4000	1000

Model 1855 Artillery Carbine

Identical to standard carbine. Chambered for .56-caliber only. Has a 24" barrel, full-length walnut fore-end and bayonet lug.

NIB	Exc.	V.G.	Good	Fair	Poor
—	—	23500	17000	5500	1500

Model 1855 British Carbine

British-proofed version, with barrel lengths up to 30". Brass trigger guard, buttplate and chambered for .56-caliber only. This variation usually found in 10000-12000 serial number range.

NIB	Exc.	V.G.	Good	Fair	Poor
—	—	18500	13000	3750	1000

Model 1855 Revolving Shotgun

Very much resembles Half Stock Sporting Rifle. Made with 27", 30", 33" and 36" smoothbore barrel. Has a 5-shot cylinder chambered for .60- or .75-caliber (20- or 10-gauge). Case-colored hammer and loading lever; rest of metal blued, with an occasional browned barrel noted. Buttstock and fore-end are of walnut, either oil or varnish-finished. No rear sight and small trigger guard, with the caliber stamped on it. Some have been noted with the large scroll trigger guard; these would add 10 percent to value. Rarest shotgun variation would be a full stocked version in either gauge. Qualified appraisal would be highly recommended. Serial numbered in its own range #1-#1100. Manufactured from 1860-1863.

Courtesy Amoskeag Auction Company

.60 Caliber (20 gauge)

NIB	Exc.	V.G.	Good	Fair	Poor
—	—	22500	10000	3500	1000

.75 Caliber (10 gauge)

NIB	Exc.	V.G.	Good	Fair	Poor
—	—	22500	10000	3500	1000

Model 1861 Single-Shot Rifled Musket

With the advent of Civil War, Union army seriously needed military arms. Colt was given a contract to supply 112,500 1861-pattern percussion single-shot muskets. Between 1861 and 1865, 75,000 were delivered. They have 40" rifled barrels chambered for .58-caliber. Musket is equipped with military sights, sling swivels and bayonet lug. Metal finish is bright steel. Stock is oil-finished walnut. Military inspector marks are found on all major parts. "VP" over an eagle is stamped on breech along with a date. Colt address and a date are stamped on lockplate. A large number of these rifles were altered to Snyder breech loading system for Bey of Egypt.

Courtesy Milwaukee Public Museum, Milwaukee, Wisconsin

Production Model

NIB	Exc.	V.G.	Good	Fair	Poor
—	—	5500	2000	750	450

COLT PERCUSSION REVOLVERS

Model 1860 Army Revolver

Third most produced of Colt percussion handguns. Primary revolver used by Union Army during Civil War. Colt delivered 127,156 of these revolvers to be used during those hostilities. It is a 6-shot .44-caliber percussion revolver. Either 7.5" or 8" round barrel, with an attached loading lever. Frame, hammer and loading lever are case colored; barrel and cylinder blued. Trigger guard, front strap are brass; back-strap blued steel. Grips are one-piece walnut. Early models have barrels stamped "Address Saml. Colt Hartford Ct." Later models stamped "Address Col. Saml. Colt New-York U.S. America." "Colt's/Patent" stamped on left side of frame; ".44 Cal." on trigger guard. Cylinder is roll engraved with naval battle scene. Between 1860 and 1873, Colt manufactured 200,500 of these 1860 Army Revolvers.

Martial Marked Model

NIB	Exc.	V.G.	Good	Fair	Poor
—	14000	8500	7500	3500	900

Civilian Model

Found in either 3- or 4-screw variations. May or may not be cut for a shoulder stock. Civilian models are usually better finished.

Courtesy Milwaukee Public Museum, Milwaukee, Wisconsin

NIB	Exc.	V.G.	Good	Fair	Poor
—	10000	7500	6000	3000	800

Full Fluted Cylinder Model

Approximately 4,000 Army's were made, with full fluted cylinders. They appear in first 8,000 serial numbers.

Courtesy Milwaukee Public Museum, Milwaukee, Wisconsin

NIB	Exc.	V.G.	Good	Fair	Poor
—	20000	16500	15000	7000	2000

Model 1861 Navy Revolver

A 6-shot 7.5" round-barreled .36-caliber percussion revolver. Frame, hammer and attached loading lever are case colored. Barrel and cylinder are blued. Grip frame and trigger guard are silver-plated brass. Grips are one-piece walnut. Cylinder has roll-engraved naval battle scene and barrel stamping "Address Col. Saml. Colt New-York U.S. America." Frame is stamped "Colts/Patent" with "36 Cal." on trigger guard. Not many variations within 1861 Navy model designation. Less than 39,000 were made between 1861 and 1873.

A very exceptional cased and engraved presentation-grade Model 1861 Navy was sold at auction in 2011 for $805,000. Three Colt percussion revolvers sold for over $800,000 at auction. (See Texas Paterson No. 5 and Third Model Dragoon listings.) Such prices are extreme exceptions to values of typical models.

Courtesy Rock Island Auction Company

Fluted Cylinder Model

Approximately first 100 made with full fluted cylinders.

NIB	Exc.	V.G.	Good	Fair	Poor
—	40000	35000	30000	18000	8500

Military Model

Marked "U.S." on frame, inspector's cartouche on grip. 650 marked "U.S.N." on butt.

NIB	Exc.	V.G.	Good	Fair	Poor
—	35000	25000	15000	6000	3000

Shoulder Stock Model

Only 100 3rd-type stocks made. Appear between serial #11000-#14000. These are very rare revolvers.

Revolver

NIB	Exc.	V.G.	Good	Fair	Poor
—	—	—	—	5000	1500

Stock

NIB	Exc.	V.G.	Good	Fair	Poor
—	—	—	10000	4250	1000

Civilian Model

NIB	Exc.	V.G.	Good	Fair	Poor
—	18000	9000	6000	4000	2000

Model 1862 Pocket Navy Revolver

A smaller 5-shot .36-caliber percussion revolver. Resembles configuration of 1851 Navy. Has 4.5", 5.5" or 6.5" octagonal barrel, with attached loading lever. Frame, hammer and loading lever case colored; barrel and cylinder blued. Grip frame and trigger guard silver-plated brass; one-piece grips of varnished walnut. Stagecoach holdup scene is roll-engraved on cylinder. Frame stamped "Colt's/Patent"; barrel "Address Col. Saml. Colt New-York U.S. America". Approximately 19,000 manufactured between 1861 and 1873. Serial numbered in same range as Model 1862 Police. Because a great many were used for metallic cartridge conversions, they are quite scarce today.

NOTE: London Address Model, with blued steel grip frame would be worth more than standard model. Add 50 percent. Longer barrels will bring a premium over 4.5" length.

Standard Production Model

NIB	Exc.	V.G.	Good	Fair	Poor
—	—	6000	3750	1200	500

Model 1862 Police Revolver

A slim attractively designed revolver. Some consider it the most aesthetically pleasing of all Colt percussion designs. Has a 5-shot half-fluted cylinder chambered for .36-caliber. Offered with 3.5", 4.5", 5.5" or 6.5" round barrel. Frame, hammer and loading lever case colored; barrel and cylinder blued. Grip frame silver-plated brass; one-piece grips varnished walnut. Barrel stamped "Address Col. Saml Colt New-York U.S. America"; frame "Colt's/Patent" on left side. One of the cylinder flutes marked "Pat Sept. 10th 1850". Approximately 28,000 manufactured between 1861 and 1873. Many were converted to metallic cartridge use, so they are quite

scarce on today's market.

NOTE: London Address Model would be worth approximately twice the value of standard model. Longer barrels will bring a premium over 3.5" or 4.5" length.

Courtesy Milwaukee Public Museum, Milwaukee, Wisconsin

Standard Production Model

NIB	Exc.	V.G.	Good	Fair	Poor
—	—	6000	2950	1000	400

COLT METALLIC CARTRIDGE CONVERSIONS

Thuer Conversion Revolver

Although quite simplistic and not commercially successful, Thuer Conversion was the first attempt by Colt to convert percussion revolvers to the new metallic cartridge system. This conversion was designed around the tapered Thuer cartridge. Consists of a ring that replaced the back part of cylinder, which had been milled off. This ring stamped "Pat. Sep./15, 1868". Ejection position is marked with letter "E". These conversions have rebounding firing pins and are milled to allow loading from the front of revolver. This conversion was undertaken on six different models listed; all other specifications, finishes, markings, etc., not directly affected by the conversion would be the same as previously described. From a collectible and investment standpoint, Thuer Conversion is very desirable. Competent appraisal should be secured if acquisition is contemplated. **NOTE:** Blued models will bring higher prices than nickel models in the same condition.

Model 1849 Pocket

NIB	Exc.	V.G.	Good	Fair	Poor
—	60000	35000	15500	4000	2000

Model 1851 Navy

Courtesy Milwaukee Public Museum, Milwaukee, Wisconsin

NIB	Exc.	V.G.	Good	Fair	Poor
—	—	28000	18000	5000	2000

Model 1860 Army

NIB	Exc.	V.G.	Good	Fair	Poor
—	—	30000	19500	6000	2000

Model 1861 Navy

NIB	Exc.	V.G.	Good	Fair	Poor
—	—	30000	19500	6000	2000

Model 1862 Police

NIB	Exc.	V.G.	Good	Fair	Poor
—	—	20000	13500	3500	1500

Model 1862 Pocket Navy

NIB	Exc.	V.G.	Good	Fair	Poor
—	—	25000	16000	3500	1500

Richards Conversion, 1860 Army Revolver

Colt's second attempt at metallic cartridge conversion. It met with quite a bit more success than the first. Richards Conversion was designed for .44 Colt cartridge. Has a 6-shot cylinder and an integral ejector rod to replace the loading lever that had been removed. Other specifications pertaining to 1860 Army Revolver remain as previously described, if they are not directly altered by the conversion. Richards Conversion adds a breechplate, with a firing pin and its own rear sight. Approximately 9,000 of these Conversions manufactured between 1873 and 1878. **NOTE:** Blued models will bring higher prices than nickel models in the same condition.

Civilian Model

NIB	Exc.	V.G.	Good	Fair	Poor
—	20000	10000	3950	2000	600

Martially Marked

This variation found with mixed serial numbers and a second set of conversion serial numbers. "U.S." stamped on left side of barrel lug. Inspector's cartouche appears on grip. Very rare Colt revolver.

Courtesy Little John's Auction Service, Inc., Paul Goodwin photo

NIB	Exc.	V.G.	Good	Fair	Poor
—	30000	18000	15000	8000	2000

Transition Richards Model

Variation marked by presence of a firing pin hammer.

Courtesy Bonhams & Butterfields, San Francisco, California

NIB	Exc.	V.G.	Good	Fair	Poor
—	15000	9500	7000	3000	1200

Richards-Mason Conversion, 1860 Army Revolver

This conversion is different from Richards Conversion, in a number of readily apparent aspects. Barrel was manufactured with a small lug, much different in appearance than seen on standard 1860 Army. Breechplate does not have its own rear sight. There is a milled area to allow hammer to contact base of the cartridge. These Conversions were also chambered for .44 Colt cartridge. Cylinder holds 6-shots. There is an integral ejector rod in place of the loading lever. Barrels on some are stamped either "Address Col. Saml. Colt New-York U.S. America" or "Colt's Pt. F.A. Mfg. Co. Hartford, Ct." Patent dates 1871 and 1872 stamped on left side of frame. Finish of these revolvers and grips, were for the most part, same as on unconverted Armies; for the first time, nickel-plated guns are found. Approximately 2,100 of these Conversions produced in 1877 and 1878. **NOTE:** Blued models will bring higher prices than nickel models in same condition.

NIB	Exc.	V.G.	Good	Fair	Poor
—	22000	13500	7000	2500	800

Richards-Mason Conversions 1851 Navy Revolver

These revolvers were converted in the same way as 1860 Army previously described. Major difference being caliber .38 either rimfire or centerfire. Finishes are mostly the same as on unconverted revolvers, but nickel-plated guns are not rare. **NOTE:** Blued models will bring higher prices than nickel models in same condition.

Production Model Serial #1-3800

Courtesy Bonhams & Butterfields, San Francisco, California

NIB	Exc.	V.G.	Good	Fair	Poor
—	15000	11000	5500	2000	800

U.S. Navy Model Serial #41000-91000

"USN" stamped on butt; steel grip frame.

NIB	Exc.	V.G.	Good	Fair	Poor
—	20000	16000	9500	3000	1000

Richards-Mason Conversion 1861 Navy Revolver

Specifications for this model same as 1851 Navy Conversion described above, with base revolver being different. There were 2,200 manufactured in 1870s. **NOTE:** Blued models will bring higher prices than nickel models in same condition.

Courtesy Wallis & Wallis, Lewes, Sussex, England

Standard Production Model Serial #100-3300

NIB	Exc.	V.G.	Good	Fair	Poor
—	20000	11500	6250	1500	500

U.S. Navy Model Serial #1000-9999

NIB	Exc.	V.G.	Good	Fair	Poor
—	24000	15000	7500	3500	1000

Model 1862 Police and Pocket Navy Conversions

Conversion of these two revolver models is the most difficult to catalog of all Colt variations. Approximately 24,000 of these produced between 1873 and 1880. There are five basic variations, with a number of sub-variations. Confusion is usually caused by different ways in which these were marked. Depending upon what parts were utilized, caliber markings could be particularly confusing. One must also consider the fact that many of these conversion revolvers found their way into secondary markets, such as Mexico, Central and South America. They were either destroyed or received sufficient abuse to obliterate most identifying markings. Five basic variations are all chambered for either .38 rimfire or .38 centerfire cartridge. All held 5-shots. Most were found with round roll-engraved stagecoach holdup scene. Half-fluted cylinder from 1862 Police is quite rare on the conversion revolver and not found at all on some of the variations. Finishes on these guns were pretty much the same as they were before conversion, but not unusual to find nickel-plated specimens. Basic variations are listed. **NOTE:** Blued models will bring higher prices than nickel models in same condition. Half-fluted cylinder add 20 percent.

Round Barrel Pocket Navy with Ejector

NIB	Exc.	V.G.	Good	Fair	Poor
—	—	7500	3500	1600	800

3.5" Round Barrel Without Ejector

NIB	Exc.	V.G.	Good	Fair	Poor
—	—	5500	2500	1000	300

4.5" Octagonal Barrel Without Ejector

NIB	Exc.	V.G.	Good	Fair	Poor
—	—	6500	3500	1200	400

Model 1862 Pocket Navy Octagon Barrel with Ejector

NIB	Exc.	V.G.	Good	Fair	Poor
—	—	7500	3850	1500	600

Model 1862 Police Round Barrel with Ejector

NIB	Exc.	V.G.	Good	Fair	Poor
—	—	7500	3850	1500	600

Model 1871-1872 Open Top Revolver

First revolver Colt manufactured especially for a metallic cartridge. It was not a conversion. Frame, 7.5" or 8" round barrel and 6-shot cylinder were produced for .44 rimfire metallic cartridge. Grip frame and some internal parts were taken from 1860 Army and 1851 Navy. Although this model was not commercially successful and not accepted by U.S. Ordinance Department, it did pave the way for Single-Action Army that came out shortly thereafter, and was an immediate success. Model is all blued, with case colored hammer. There are some with silver-plated brass grip frames, but most are blued steel. One-piece grips are of varnished walnut. Cylinder is roll-engraved with naval battle scene. Barrel stamped "Address Col. Saml. Colt New-York U.S. America." Later production revolvers are barrel stamped "Colt's Pt. F.A. Mfg. Co. Hartford, Ct. U.S.A." First 1,000 revolvers were stamped "Colt's/Patent." After that, 1871 and 1872 patent dates appeared on the frame. There were 7,000 revolvers manufactured in 1872 and 1873.

1860 Army Grip Frame

NIB	Exc.	V.G.	Good	Fair	Poor
—	—	27500	15000	4500	800

1851 Navy Grip Frame

NIB	Exc.	V.G.	Good	Fair	Poor
—	—	29000	17500	4000	1200

COLT DERRINGERS AND POCKET REVOLVER

First Model Derringer

Small all-metal single-shot. Chambered for .41 rimfire cartridge. The 2.5" barrel pivots to left and downward for loading. Model engraved with a scroll pattern and been noted blued, silver or nickel-plated. Barrel stamped "Colt's Pt. F.A. Mfg. Co./Hartford Ct. U.S.A/ No.1". ".41 Cal." stamped on frame under release catch. Approximately 6,500 manufactured from 1870-1890. First single-shot pistol Colt produced.

Courtesy Rock Island Auction Company

NIB	Exc.	V.G.	Good	Fair	Poor
—	3500	2500	1200	800	400

Second Model Derringer

Although this model has the same odd shape as First Model, it is readily identifiable by checkered varnished walnut grips and "No 2" on barrel after address. A .41 rimfire with 2.5" barrel that pivots in the same manner as First Model. Approximately 9,000 manufactured between 1870 and 1890. **NOTE:** Add 100 percent for .41 Centerfire model.

Courtesy Wallis & Wallis, Lewes, Sussex, England

NIB	Exc.	V.G.	Good	Fair	Poor
—	1800	1300	800	400	250

Third Model Derringer

Designed by Alexander Thuer, who was also responsible for Colt's first metallic cartridge conversion. Often referred to as "Thuer Model" for this reason. Chambered for .41 rimfire cartridge, has a 2.5" barrel that pivots to the right (but not down) for loading. Third Model has a more balanced appearance than its predecessors and its commercial success (45,000 produced between 1875 and 1910) reflects this. Barrel on this model stamped "Colt" in small block letters on first 2,000 guns. Remainder of production features "COLT"in large italicized print. ".41 Cal." stamped on left side of frame. Model will be found with barrel blued or plated in either silver or nickel and the bronze frame plated. Grips are varnished walnut. **NOTE:** Blued models will bring a premium over nickel in same condition. Add 25 percent for .41 Centerfire model.

First Variation, Early Production

Has a raised area ("pregnant frame") on underside of frame through which barrel screw passes. Spur is not angled. Small block "Colt" lettering on barrel.

NIB	Exc.	V.G.	Good	Fair	Poor
—	3500	2500	2000	1200	600

First Variation, Late Production

Similar to early production. Has large italicized "COLT" on barrel.

NIB	Exc.	V.G.	Good	Fair	Poor
—	3000	2000	1200	800	400

Production Model

NIB	Exc.	V.G.	Good	Fair	Poor
—	1800	1300	800	400	250

House Model Revolver

There are two basic versions of this model. Both chambered for .41 rimfire cartridge. 4-shot version is known as "Cloverleaf" due to shape of the cylinder when viewed from front. Approximately 7,500 of nearly 10,000 House revolvers were 4-shot configuration. Offered with 1.5" or 3" barrel. The 1.5" length is quite rare. Some octagonal barrels in this length have been noted. 5-shot round-cylinder version accounts for the rest of production. Found with serial numbers over 6100 and offered with 2.875" length barrel only. Model stamped on top strap "Pat. Sept. 19, 1871". Has brass frames that were sometimes nickel-plated. Barrels are found either blued or plated. Grips are varnished walnut or rosewood. Slightly fewer than 10,000 of both variations manufactured from 1871-1876. **NOTE:** Blued models will bring a premium over nickel in same condition.

Cloverleaf with 1.5" Round Barrel

NIB	Exc.	V.G.	Good	Fair	Poor
—	3750	3000	2000	1250	400

Cloverleaf with 3" Barrel

Courtesy Buffalo Bill Historical Center, Cody, Wyoming

NIB	Exc.	V.G.	Good	Fair	Poor
—	—	1750	1500	500	200

House Pistol with 5-Shot Round Cylinder

NIB	Exc.	V.G.	Good	Fair	Poor
—	—	1550	1300	500	200

Open Top Pocket Revolver

A .22-caliber rimfire 7-shot revolver, that was offered with either 2.375" or 2.875" barrel. Model was a commercial success, with over 114,000 manufactured between 1871 and 1877. Would undoubtedly been a great deal more sold had not the cheap copies begun to flood the market at that time, forcing Colt to drop this model from the line. Revolver has a silver or nickel-plated brass frame and nickel-plated or blued barrel and cylinder. Grips are varnished walnut. Cylinder bolt slots are found toward the front on this model. "Colt's Pt. F.A. Mfg. Co./Hartford, Ct. U.S.A." stamped on barrel; "22 Cal." on left side of frame. **NOTE:** Blued models will bring a premium over nickel in same condition.

Early Model with Ejector Rod

Courtesy Bonhams & Butterfields

NIB	Exc.	V.G.	Good	Fair	Poor
—	—	2000	1750	800	400

Production Model without Ejector Rod

NIB	Exc.	V.G.	Good	Fair	Poor
—	—	1250	600	300	150

New Line Revolver .22

This was smallest framed version of five distinct New Line Revolvers.

A 7-shot cylinder and 2.25" octagonal barrel. Frame is nickel-plated and balance of revolver either nickel-plated or blued. Grips are of rosewood. Approximately 55,000 of these made from 1873-1877. Colt also stopped production of New Lines rather than try to compete with "Suicide Specials". "Colt New .22" is found on barrel; ".22 Cal." on frame. Barrel also stamped "Colt's Pt. F.A. Mfg.Co./Hartford, Ct. U.S.A." **NOTE:** Blued models will bring higher prices than nickel models in same condition.

1st Model

Short cylinder flutes.

NIB	Exc.	V.G.	Good	Fair	Poor
—	—	1300	600	300	150

2nd Model

Long cylinder flutes.

Courtesy Bonhams & Butterfields, San Francisco, California

NIB	Exc.	V.G.	Good	Fair	Poor
—	—	750	500	250	125

New Line Revolver .30

Larger version of .22 New Line. Basic difference is size, caliber, caliber markings and offering of a blued version with case colored frame. Approximately 11,000 manufactured from 1874-1876. **NOTE:** Prices are for nickel finish. Blued models will bring a premium of 100 percent.

Courtesy Wallis & Wallis, Lewes, Sussex, England

NIB	Exc.	V.G.	Good	Fair	Poor
—	—	1000	750	300	150

New Line Revolver .32

Same basic revolver as .30-caliber, except chambered for .32-caliber rimfire and .32-caliber centerfire and is so marked. There were 22,000 manufactured from 1873-1884. Model was offered with rare 4" barrel. This variation would be worth nearly twice the value of a standard model. **NOTE:** Prices are for nickel finish. Blued models will bring a premium of

100 percent.

Courtesy Bonhams & Butterfields, San Francisco, California

NIB	Exc.	V.G.	Good	Fair	Poor
—	—	1550	850	300	150

New Line Revolver .38

Approximately 5,500 manufactured between 1874 and 1880. Chambered for either .38 rimfire or .38 centerfire caliber and is so marked. This model in a 4" barrel would also bring twice the value. **NOTE:** Prices are for nickel finish. Blued models will bring a premium of 100 percent.

Courtesy Rock Island Auction Company

NIB	Exc.	V.G.	Good	Fair	Poor
—	—	1500	800	400	200

New Line Revolver .41

The "Big Colt", as it was sometimes known in advertising of its era. Chambered for .41 rimfire and .41 centerfire and is so marked. Large caliber of this variation makes this the most desirable of New Lines to collectors. Approximately 7,000 manufactured from 1874-1879. A 4"-barreled version would again be worth a 100 percent premium. **NOTE:** Prices are for nickel finish. Blued models will bring a premium of 100 percent.

NIB	Exc.	V.G.	Good	Fair	Poor
—	—	2000	1375	650	300

New House Model Revolver

Revolver similar to other New Lines. Features a square-butt instead of bird's-head configuration, 2.25" round barrel without ejector rod and a thin loading gate. Chambered for .32 (rare), .38 and .41 centerfire cartridges. Finish was either full nickel-plated or blued, with case colored frame. Grips are walnut, rosewood or (for the first time on a Colt revolver) checkered hard rubber, with an oval around the word "Colt". Barrel address is same as on other New Lines. Frame marked "New House" with caliber. Approximately 4,000 manufactured between 1880-1886. .32-caliber model would bring a 10 percent premium. **NOTE:** Prices are for nickel finish. Blued models will bring a premium of 100 percent.

Courtesy Milwaukee Public Museum, Milwaukee, Wisconsin

NIB	Exc.	V.G.	Good	Fair	Poor
—	—	1495	1000	450	250

New Police Revolver

Final revolver in New Line series. Chambered for .32, .38 and .41 centerfire caliber. The .32 and .41 are quite rare. Offered in barrel lengths of 2.25", 4.5", 5.5" and 6.5". An ejector rod is found on all but the 2.5" barrel. Finish is either nickel or blued and case colored. Grips are hard rubber, with scene of a policeman arresting a criminal embossed on them; thusly the model became known to collectors as "Cop and Thug" model. Barrel stamping as other New Lines; frame stamped "New Police .38". Approximately 4,000 manufactured between 1882-1886. **NOTE:** The .32- and .41-caliber versions will bring a 40- to 50 percent premium. Blued and models with 5.5" or 6.5" barrels will bring a premium. Short barrel model will bring about 50 percent of listed prices.

Courtesy Milwaukee Public Museum, Milwaukee, Wisconsin

Long Barrel Model with Ejector

NIB	Exc.	V.G.	Good	Fair	Poor
—	—	—	3250	1400	700

COLT SINGLE ACTION ARMY REVOLVER

Colt Single Action Army or Peacemaker, as it is sometimes referred to, is one of the most widely collected and recognized firearms in the world. Few interruptions or changes in design, it has been manufac-

tured from 1873 until the present. Variations in this model are myriad. Produced in 30 different calibers; barrel lengths from 2.5" to 16", with 4.75", 5.5" and 7.5" standard. The standard finish is blued, with case colored frame. Many are nickel-plated. Examples have been found silver-/gold-plated, with combinations thereof. Finest engravers in the world have used SAA as a canvas to display their artistry. Standard grips from 1873-1883 were walnut, either oil-stained or varnished. From 1883 to approximately 1897 standard grips were hard rubber, with eagle and shield. After this date, at serial number 165000, hard rubber grips featured Rampant Colt. Many special-order grips were available, notably pearl and ivory, which were often checkered or carved in ornate fashion. Variables involved in establishing values on this model are extreme. Added to this, one must also consider historical significance, since SAA played a big part in formative years of the American West. Fortunately for those among us interested in SAA, there are a number of fine publications available dealing exclusively with this model. It is my strongest recommendation that they be acquired and studied thoroughly to prevent extremely expensive mistakes. Colt factory records are nearly complete for this model and research should be done before acquisition of rare or valuable specimens. Colt factory will provide a letter documenting the history of a particular model for a fee of $100, as of 2014. For historically significant, factory engraved or celebrity owned guns, fees may be higher. Archive department's address is: Colt Archive Properties, P. O. Box 1868, Hartford, CT 06144. Some research data can be obtained by telephone: 800-962-2658 ext. 1343.

For our purposes we will break down Single-Action Army production as follows:

Antique or Black Powder, 1873-1898, serial number 1-175000

Cylinder axis pin is retained by a screw in front of frame.

Pre-war, 1899-1940, serial number 175001-357859

Cylinder axis pin is retained by a spring-loaded button through side of frame. This method is utilized on the following models, as well.

Post-war 2nd Generation, 1956-1978, serial number 0001SA-99999SA

3rd Generation, 1978-Present, serial #SA1001.

Breakdown of production by caliber will follow the chapter. It is important to note that the rarer calibers and larger calibers bring higher values in this variation.

NOTE: As a rule of thumb, nickel guns will bring a deduction of 20- to 30 percent. Revolvers with 4.75" barrels add 10- to 15 percent. Checkered grips add 20 percent.

COLT ANTIQUE SINGLE-ACTION ARMY REVOLVER

1st Year Production "Pinched Frame" 1873 Only

It is necessary to categorize this variation on its own. This is one of the rarest and most interesting of all SAAs—not to mention that it is the first. On this model, top strap is pinched or constricted approximately .5" up from hammer to form the rear sight. Highest surviving serial number having this feature is #156, lowest #1. From these numbers it is safe to assume that the first run of SAAs were all pinched-frame models; but there is no way to tell how many there were, since Colt did not serial number the frames in the order that they were manufactured. An educated guess would be there were between 50 and 150 pinched frame guns in all and that they were all made before mid-July 1873. Reason for change came about on the recommendation of Capt. J.R. Edie, a government inspector who thought that the full fluted top strap would be a big improvement in sighting capabilities of the weapon. Barrel length of first model is 7.5"; standard caliber .45 Colt; proper grips were of walnut. Front sight blade is German silver. Needless to say, this model will rarely be encountered, and if it is, it should never be purchased without competent appraisal.

NIB	Exc.	V.G.	Good	Fair	Poor
—	—	275000	250000	125000	90000

Early Military Model 1873-1877

Serial number range on this first run of military contract revolvers extends to #24000. Barrel address is in early script style, with # symbol preceding and following. Frame bears martial marking "US" and walnut grips have inspector's cartouche stamped on them. Front sight is steel as on all military models; barrel length 7.5"; caliber .45 Colt; ejector rod head is bull's-eye or donut style, with a hole in the center of it. Finish features military polish and case colored frame, with remainder blued. Authenticate any potential purchase; many spurious examples have been noted.

NIB	Exc.	V.G.	Good	Fair	Poor
—	115000	75000	40000	30000	15000

Early Civilian Model 1873-1877

Identical to Early Military Model, but has no military acceptance markings or cartouches. Some could have German silver front sight blade. Early bull's-eye ejector rod head is used on this model. Civilian Model has a higher degree of polish than is found on military models. Finish on these early models could be plated or blued, with case colored frame. Has a script barrel address. Grips are standard one-piece walnut. Ivory-grip models are worth a premium.

NIB	Exc.	V.G.	Good	Fair	Poor
—	75000	60000	45000	25000	12500

.44 Rimfire Model 1875-1880

Model made to fire .44 Henry Rimfire cartridge. It was to be used as a compatible companion sidearm to Henry and Winchester 1866 rifles, that were used extensively during this era. However, this was not the case; and .44 Rimfire was doomed to economic failure as soon as it appeared on the market. By that time, it had already been established that large-caliber centerfire cartridges were a good deal more efficient than their rimfire counterparts. Large-caliber rimfires were deemed obsolete before this Colt ever hit the market. The result of this was that Colt's sales representatives sold most of the production to obscure banana republics in South and Central America, where this model received much abuse. Most had original 7.5" barrels cut down; nearly all were denied even the most basic maintenance, making the survival rate of this model quite low. All this adds to its desirability as a collector's item and makes the risk of acquiring a fake that much greater. This model is unique in that it was the only SAA variation to have its own serial number range, starting with #1 and continuing to #1892, the latest known surviving specimen. Block style barrel markings were introduced during this production run. At least 90 of these revolvers were converted by the factory to .22 rimfire and one was shipped chambered for .32 rimfire.

NIB	Exc.	V.G.	Good	Fair	Poor
—	—	75000	50000	30000	15000

Late Military Model 1878-1891

Later Military Models are serial numbered to approximately #136000. They bear block-style barrel address without the # prefix and suffix. Frames are marked "US"; grips have inspector's cartouche. Finish is military-style polish, case colored frame and remainder blued. Grips are oil-stained walnut. On military marked Colts, it is imperative that potential purchases be authenticated as many fakes have been noted. **NOTE:**

Revolvers produced from 1878 to 1885 will command a premium. Seek an expert appraisal prior to sale.

NIB	Exc.	V.G.	Good	Fair	Poor
—	68000	39500	14000	10000	6000

Artillery Model 1895-1903

A number of "US" marked SAAs were returned either to the Colt factory or to the Springfield Armory, where they were altered and refinished. These revolvers have 5.5" barrels and any combination of mixed serial numbers. They were remarked by inspectors of the era. They have case colored frame, blued cylinder and barrel. Some have been noted all blued within this variation. This model, as with other military marked Colts, should definitely be authenticated before purchase. Some of these revolvers fall outside the 1898 antique cutoff date that has been established by the government. In our experience are not quite as desirable to investors. They are generally worth approximately 20 percent less. Add a 50 percent premium for specimens marked "New York State Militia". These have 7.5" barrels and only 800 are documented in Colt records. Be sure to obtain documentation from the factory for these models.

NIB	Exc.	V.G.	Good	Fair	Poor
—	18000	12500	8000	4000	3000

London Model

These SAAs were manufactured to be sold through Colt's London Agency. Barrel stamped "Colt's Pt. F.A. Mfg. Co. Hartford, Ct. U.S.A. Depot 14 Pall Mall London". This model is available in various barrel lengths. They are generally chambered for .45 Colt, .450 Boxer, .450 Eley, .455 Eley and rarely .476 Eley, largest of the SAA chamberings. A good many of these London Models were cased and embellished and should be individually appraised. This model should be authenticated as many spurious examples have been noted.

NIB	Exc.	V.G.	Good	Fair	Poor
—	22000	15000	10000	4500	2000

Frontier Six-Shooter 1878-1882

Several thousand SAAs were made with the legend "Colt's Frontier Six Shooter" acid-etched into left side of barrel instead of being stamped. This etching is not deep and today collectors will become ecstatic if they discover a specimen with mere vestiges of the etched panel remaining. These acid-etched SAAs are serial numbered #45000-#65000. They have various barrel lengths and finishes, but all are chambered for .44-40 caliber.

Courtesy Little John's Auction Service, Inc., Paul Goodwin photo

NIB	Exc.	V.G.	Good	Fair	Poor
—	40000	20000	14000	7000	5000

Sheriff's or Storekeeper's Model 1882-1898

Made in several barrel lengths: 2.5", 3", 3.5", 4", 4.75" and 7.5". The 2.5" and 7.5" guns are very rare and can bring premiums of 25 to 50 percent, depending on condition. Most have 4" barrels. Features no ejector rod or housing and frame is made without the hole in right forward section to accommodate ejector assembly. Sheriff's or Storekeeper's Model is numbered above serial #73000. Manufactured with various finishes and chambered for numerous calibers. This model continued after 1898 into smokeless or modern era. Examples with smokeless-powder frame made after 1898 are worth approximately 20 percent less. Although faking this model is quite difficult, it has been successfully attempted. **NOTE:** Nickel models will command a premium.

Courtesy Little John's Auction Service, Inc., Paul Goodwin photo

NIB	Exc.	V.G.	Good	Fair	Poor
75000	65000	50000	38000	22000	8000

Flattop Target Model 1888-1896

Model highly regarded and sought after by collectors. It is not only rare (only 925 manufactured), but an extremely attractive and well-finished variation. Chambered for 22 different calibers from .22 rimfire to .476 Eley. The .22 rimfire, .38 Colt, .41 and .45 Colt are the most predominant chamberings. The 7.5" barrel length is most commonly encountered. Serial number range between #127000-#162000. Some have been noted in higher ranges. Finish is all blued, with case colored hammer. Checkered grips are either hard rubber or walnut. Most identifying feature of flattop is lack of a groove in the top strap and sight blade dovetailed into the flattop. Front sight has a removable blade insert. Values given are for a standard production model chambered for calibers previously mentioned as being the most common. It is important to have other calibers individually appraised, as variance in values can be quite extreme.

NIB	Exc.	V.G.	Good	Fair	Poor
—	35000	25000	15000	8000	4000

Bisley Model 1894-1915

Named for target range in Great Britain where their National Target Matches were held, since the nineteenth century. Designed as a target revolver, with an odd humped-back grip that was supposed to better fill the hand while target shooting. Easily identified by wide low profile hammer spur, wide trigger and name "Bisley" stamped on barrel. Bisley production fell within serial number range #165000-#331916. There were 44,350 made. Offered in 16 different chamberings from .32 Colt to .455 Eley. Most common calibers were .32-20, .38-40, .41, .44-40 and .45 Colt. Barrel lengths 4.75", 5.5" and 7.5". Frame and hammer are case-colored; remainder blued. Smokeless-powder models produced after 1899 utilized push-button cylinder pin retainer. Grips are checkered hard rubber. This model was actually designed with English sales in mind; though it did sell well over there, American sales accounted for most of Bisley production. Values we provide here cover the standard calibers and barrel lengths. Rare calibers and/or other notable variations can bring greatly fluctuating values.

NIB	Exc.	V.G.	Good	Fair	Poor
—	9000	6500	4500	2500	1200

Bisley Model Flattop Target 1894-1913

Model quite similar to Standard Bisley, with flattop frame and dovetailed rear sight feature. Has removable front sight insert, all-blued finish with case-colored hammer only. Available with 7.5" barrel. Smokeless-powder models produced after 1899 utilized push-button cylinder pin retainer. Calibers same as standard Bisley. Colt manufactured 976 of these revolvers. Advice regarding appraisal would also apply.

NIB	Exc.	V.G.	Good	Fair	Poor
—	25000	16000	9500	3500	1800

Standard Civilian Production Models 1876-1898

Final designated category for black powder or antique SAAs includes all revolvers not previously categorized. Barrel lengths 4.75", 5.5" and 7.5" are chambered for any one of 30 different calibers. Finishes could be blued, blued and case colored or plated in nickel, silver, gold or combinations thereof. Grips could be walnut, hard rubber, ivory, pearl, stag or bone. Possibilities are endless. Values given here are for basic model and we again strongly advise securing qualified appraisal when not completely sure of any model variation.

NOTE: Add 20 percent premium for serial numbers between 54000 and 130000; 40 percent for serial numbers between 22000 and 54000; 20 to 30 percent for original box, depending on condition; 10 percent for 4.75" barrel.

NIB	Exc.	V.G.	Good	Fair	Poor
—	35000	24000	12000	8000	3000

COLT PRE-WAR SINGLE ACTION ARMY REVOLVER 1899-1940

Standard Production Pre-war Models (1899-1940)

The 1899 cutoff has been thoroughly discussed, but it is interesting to note that the actual beginning production date for smokeless models was 1900. Pre-war Colts, all in all, are quite similar to the antiques—finishes, barrel lengths, grips, etc. Calibers are also similar, with the exception of obsolete ones being dropped and new discoveries added. Most apparent physical difference between smokeless-powder and black-powder models is previously discussed method of retaining the cylinder axis pin. Pre-war Colts utilized the spring-loaded button through side of the frame. Black-powder models utilized a screw in front of the frame. Values we furnish for this model designation are for these standard models only. Serial number range on pre-war SAAs is 175001-357859. Any variation can have marked effects on value fluctuations. Qualified appraisal should be secured. **NOTE:** Scarce chamberings command 30 percent to 100 percent premium. Early production guns can also bring a premium. Add 10- to 25 percent for original box, depending on condition; 25 percent for original ivory, pearl or checkered wood grips; 35 percent for stag grips.

1896-1899, Serial numbers 165000-182000

NIB	Exc.	V.G.	Good	Fair	Poor
—	28000	17500	12000	5000	2500

1899-1908, Serial numbers 182000-300000

NIB	Exc.	V.G.	Good	Fair	Poor
—	25000	15000	10000	3500	2000

1908-1914, Serial numbers 300000-328000

NIB	Exc.	V.G.	Good	Fair	Poor
—	20000	10000	8000	3000	2000

1914-1920, Serial numbers 328000-339000

NIB	Exc.	V.G.	Good	Fair	Poor
—	18000	9000	7000	3500	2000

1920-1940, Serial numbers 339000-357000

NIB	Exc.	V.G.	Good	Fair	Poor
—	12000	7500	6000	3000	2000

Long Fluted Cylinder Model (1913-1915)

Strange as it may seem, Colt Company has an apparent credo they followed to never throw anything away. That credo was never more evident than with this model. These Long Flute Cylinders were actually left over from model 1878 Double-Action Army Revolvers. Someone in the hierarchy at Colt had an inspiration that drove gunsmiths on the payroll slightly mad: to make these cylinders fit SAA frames. There were 1,478 of these Long Flutes manufactured. Chambered for .45 Colt, .38-40, .32-20, .41 Colt and .44 Smith & Wesson Special. Offered in three standard barrel lengths and were especially well-polished, having what has been described as Colt's "Fire Blue" on the barrel and cylinder. Frame and hammer are case colored. Fitted with checkered hard rubber grips. Particularly fine examples of Colt's craft. Rare.

NIB	Exc.	V.G.	Good	Fair	Poor
—	17500	10000	6000	3250	2000

COLT POST-WAR SINGLE ACTION ARMY REVOLVER (AKA SECOND GENERATION)

Standard Post-war Model (1956-1975)

In 1956, shooting and gun-collecting fraternity succeeded in convincing Colt there was a market for a re-introduced SAA. Revolver was brought back in the same external configuration. Only changes were internal. Basic specifications as to barrel length and finish availability were the same. Calibers available were .38 Special, .357 Magnum, .44 Special and .45 Colt. Serial number range of re-introduced 2nd Generation Colt is #000ISA-73000SA. Values are established by four basic factors: caliber (popularity and scarcity), barrel length, finish and condition. The .38 Special is rarest caliber; .45 Colt and .44 Special are more sought after than .357 Magnum. Special feature revolvers such as 350 factory-engraved guns produced during this period, must be individually appraised. Ivory situation in the world today has become quite a factor, as ivory grips are found on many SAAs. Remember as always, when in doubt secure a qualified appraisal. **NOTE:** Values shown are for 5.5" barrel models. Add 15 percent for 4.75"; 10 percent for 7.5"; 20 percent for nickel finish; $250 for ivory grips.

.38 Special

NIB	Exc.	V.G.	Good	Fair	Poor
3000	2500	1700	1100	800	600

.357 Magnum

NIB	Exc.	V.G.	Good	Fair	Poor
2500	2000	1200	900	700	600

.44 Special

NIB	Exc.	V.G.	Good	Fair	Poor
3250	2600	1800	1100	1000	750

.45 Colt

NIB	Exc.	V.G.	Good	Fair	Poor
3400	2900	2000	1500	1000	750

Sheriff's Model (1960-1975)

Between 1960 and 1975, approximately 500 Sheriff's Models manufactured. First of these were marketed by Centennial Arms. They have 3" barrels and no ejector rod assemblies. Frames were made without the hole for ejector rod to pass through. Blued, with case colored frames; 25 revolvers were nickel-plated and would bring a sizable premium if authenticated. Barrels marked "Colt Sheriff's Model". Serial number has an "SM" suffix. Chambered for .45 Colt cartridge. **NOTE:** Add 100 percent for nickel finish.

NIB	Exc.	V.G.	Good	Fair	Poor
2500	2000	1500	1000	750	500

Buntline Special (1957-1975)

"Buntline Special" was named after a dime novelist named Ned Buntline, who supposedly gave this special long barrel revolver to Wyatt Earp.

Story is suspected to be purely legend as no Colt records exist to lend it credence. Be that as it may, Colt factory decided to take advantage of the market and produced 12" barreled SAA from 1957-1974. Approximately 3,900 were manufactured. Chambered for .45 Colt cartridge. Offered in blued and case colored finish. Only 65 Buntlines are nickel-plated, making this an extremely rare variation that definitely should be authenticated before purchase. Walnut grips are most commonly noted. Also offered with checkered hard rubber grips. Barrels marked on left side "Colt Buntline Special .45". **NOTE:** Add 100 percent for nickel finish.

NIB	Exc.	V.G.	Good	Fair	Poor
2400	1600	1250	850	600	500

New Frontier (1961-1975)

New Frontier is readily identified by its flattop frame and adjustable sight. Has a high front sight. Colt manufactured approximately 4,200 of them. Chambered for .357 Magnum, .45 Colt, .44 Special (255 produced) and rarely (only 49 produced) in .38 Special. A few were chambered for .44-40 cartridge. The 7.5" barrel length is by far the most common, but 4.75" and 5.5" barrels are also offered. Standard finish is case colored and blued. Nickel-plating and full blue are offered, but are rarely encountered. Standard grips are walnut. Barrel stamped on left side "Colt New Frontier S.A.A." Serial number has "NF" suffix. **NOTE:** Add 25 percent for 4.75" barrel; 20 percent for 5.5" barrel; 50 percent for full blue and .38 Special; 30 percent for .44 Special and .44-40.

NIB	Exc.	V.G.	Good	Fair	Poor
1750	1250	900	800	600	500

New Frontier Buntline Special (1962-1967)

Rare model, as Colt only manufactured 70 during this five-year period. Similar to standard Buntline, with 12" barrel. Chambered for .45 Colt only.

NIB	Exc.	V.G.	Good	Fair	Poor
3500	2750	2000	1500	1000	700

COLT THIRD GENERATION SINGLE ACTION ARMY 1976-1981

Colt made some internal changes in 1976 to the SAA. External configuration was not altered. Serial number range began in 1976 with #80000SA and in 1978 #99999SA was reached. At this time the suffix became a prefix. New serial range began with #SA01001. Value is determined, in much the same manner, as described in section on 2nd Generation SAAs. Caliber, barrel length, finish and condition are once again the four main determining factors. Prevalence of special-order guns was greater during this period and many more factory-engraved SAAs were produced. Colt's Custom Shop was quite active during this period. Custom guns are valued according to the prevailing market. **NOTE:** Add 10 percent for 4.75" barrel and nickel plated; $250 for ivory grips.

Colt Single-Action Army Production Breakdown by Caliber Antique and Pre-war

NOTE: Rare calibers can increase values 300-500 percent in extreme cases.

CALIBER	SAA	FLATTOP SAA	BISLEY	FLATTOP BISLEY
.22 R.F.	107	93	0	0
.32 R.F.	1	0	0	0
.32 Colt	192	24	160	44
.32 S&W	32	30	18	17
.32-44	2	9	14	17
.32-20	29,812	30	13,291	131
.38 Colt (1914)	1,011	122	412	96
.38 Colt (1922)	1,365	0	0	0
.38 S&W	9	39	10	5
.38 Colt Sp.	82	7	0	0
.38 S&W Sp.	25	0	2	0
.38-44	2	11	6	47
.357 Mag.	525	0	0	0
.380 Eley	1	3	0	0
.38-40	38,240	19	12,163	98
.41	16,402	91	3,159	24
.44 SmBr.	15	0	1	0
.44 R. F.	1,863	0	0	0
.44 Germ.	59	0	0	0
.44 Russ.	154	51	90	62
.44 S&W	24	51	29	64
.44 S&W Sp.	506	1	0	0
.44-40	64,489	21	6,803	78
.45 Colt	150,683	100	8,005	97
.45 SmBr.	4	0	2	0
.45 ACP	44	0	0	0
.450 Boxer	729	89	0	0
.450 Eley	2,697	84	5	0
.455 Eley	1,150	37	180	196
.476 Eley	161	2	0	0
Total	**310,386**	**914**	**44,350**	**976**

The above chart covers the production by caliber of the Single-Action Army Revolvers manufactured between 1873 and 1940. These are the antique and the pre-war firearms. This chart readily informs us as to which are the rare calibers.

.357 Magnum

NIB	Exc.	V.G.	Good	Fair	Poor
1200	950	800	700	600	500

.44-40

NIB	Exc.	V.G.	Good	Fair	Poor
1300	1100	900	750	600	500

.44-40 Black Powder Frame (Screw Retaining Cylinder Pin)

NIB	Exc.	V.G.	Good	Fair	Poor
1425	1200	1000	800	650	550

.44 Special

NIB	Exc.	V.G.	Good	Fair	Poor
1500	1300	1100	900	700	600

.45 Colt

NIB	Exc.	V.G.	Good	Fair	Poor
1450	1250	1050	850	650	550

Sheriff's Model 3rd Generation

Similar to 2nd Generation Sheriff's Model. Serial number and the fact this model is also chambered for .44-40, are the only external differences. Colt offered this model with interchangeable cylinders—.45 Colt/.45 ACP or .44-40/.44 Special—available in 3" barrel, blued and case colored finish standard. NOTE: Add 30 percent for interchangeable cylinders; 10 percent for nickel finish; $250 for ivory grips.

NIB	Exc.	V.G.	Good	Fair	Poor
1300	1075	900	750	600	500

Buntline Special 3rd Generation

Same basic configuration as 2nd Generation, with 12" barrel. Standard finish blued and case-colored. Chambered for .45 Colt, with checkered hard rubber grips. NOTE: Add 20 percent for nickel finish.

NIB	Exc.	V.G.	Good	Fair	Poor
1500	1275	1000	900	700	600

New Frontier 3rd Generation

Similar in appearance to 2nd Generation guns. 3rd Generation New Frontiers have five-digit serial numbers; 2nd Generation guns four-digit numbers. That and calibers offered are basically the only differences. 3rd Generations are chambered for .44 Special and .45 Colt and rarely found in .44-40. Barrel lengths 7.5" standard, with 4.75" and 5.5" rarely encountered. NOTE: Add 20 percent for .44-40; 35 percent for 4.75" barrel; 25 percent for 5.5" barrel.

NIB	Exc.	V.G.	Good	Fair	Poor
1650	1225	750	550	500	400

COLT RECENT PRODUCTION
SINGLE ACTION ARMY 1982-PRESENT

Standard Single Action Army Optional Features:

Add $125 for nickel finish; $200 for Royal Blue finish; $225 for mirror brite finish; $365 for gold plate and silver plate; $875 for class A engraving; $1,200 for class B engraving; $1,500 for class C engraving; $1,750 for class D engraving; 15 percent for buntline engraving.

NIB	Exc.	V.G.	Good	Fair	Poor
1250	950	850	650	500	300

Colt Cowboy (CB1850)

Introduced in 1998, this model is a replica of Single Action Army. Features a modern transfer bar safety system. Made in USA using some Canadian-built parts. Offered with 5.5" barrel. Chambered for .45 Colt. Sights are fixed, with walnut grips. Blued barrel with case colored frame. Discontinued in 2003.

NIB	Exc.	V.G.	Good	Fair	Poor
850	650	500	400	300	200

Colt Single Action Army "Legend Rodeo"

A limited-edition revolver built to commemorate Colt's official PRCA sponsorship. Limited to 1,000. Chambered for .45 LC. Fitted with a 5.5" barrel. Nickel finish Buffalo horn grips, with gold medallions. Machine engraved and washed in gold. Discontinued 1998.

NIB	Exc.	V.G.	Good	Fair	Poor
2750	2250	—	—	—	—

Frontier Six Shooter (2008)

New re-introduction of classic .44-40 Peacemaker. Black powder-style frame and 4.75", 5.5" and 7.5" barrel lengths. Blued finish, with color case-hardened frame or nickel. Discontinued 2010.

NIB	Exc.	V.G.	Good	Fair	Poor
1550	1100	750	600	400	200

Sheriff's and Storekeeper's Model (2008)

New re-introduction of classic Sheriff's (4" barrel) and Storekeeper's Model (3" barrel), without ejector assembly. Black powder-style frame. Blued finish, with color case-hardened frame or nickel. .45 Colt or .44-40. Discontinued 2010.

NIB	Exc.	V.G.	Good	Fair	Poor
1550	1100	750	600	400	200

175th Anniversary SAA Limited Edition

From Colt Custom Shop to celebrate 175th Anniversary of the Colt Company. Introduced in 2011, with production limited to 175 units in each of three standard barrel lengths; 4.75", 5.5" and 7.5". In .45 Colt only features include a black powder frame, Royal Blue finish, 24 karat Gold plated scroll on the frame, cylinder and barrel depicting Rampant Colt icon, Colt Dome, Serpentine Colt, Sam Colt signature and a banner with the text "1836 — 175th Anniversary — 2011".

NIB	Exc.	V.G.	Good	Fair	Poor
2500	1500	1200	1000	700	400

New Frontier Third Generation, Current Production

Re-introduction of adjustable-sighted, flattop-frame version of Single Action Army, last made in 1983. Chambered in .357 Magnum, .44 Special or .45 Colt in all three standard barrel lengths. Rear sight is adjustable for windage and elevation. There is a ramp style front sight. Finish is Colt's Royal Blue on both barrel and cylinder, with color case-hardened frame. Two-piece walnut grips are decorated with a gold medallion. Introduced in 2011.

NIB	Exc.	V.G.	Good	Fair	Poor
1300	1225	900	700	600	500

COLT SCOUT MODEL

A surprising number of Colt pistols are still found in their original boxes, even older models. This can add 100 percent value to the pistol. My thanks to Bruce Buckner, Jr., for his suggestions for and corrections to this section. Anyone wishing to procure a factory letter authenticating a Single Action Army should do so by writing to: COLT HISTORIAN, P.O. BOX 1868, HARTFORD, CT 06144. There is a charge of $75 per serial number for this service. If Colt cannot provide the desired information, $10 will be refunded. Enclose the Colt model name, serial number and your name and address, along with the check.

Frontier Scout (1957-1971)

Scaled-down version of SAA. Chambered for .22 LR with an interchangeable .22 Magnum cylinder. Offered with 4.75" or 9.5" barrel. Frame is alloy. First year production frames were duotone, with frame left in white and balance of revolver blued. All blue models and wood grips became available in 1958. In 1961 duotone model was dropped from production. All Q series guns were offered in duotone finish; F series guns were made in duotone and full blue. A .22 Magnum model was first offered in 1959. In 1964 dual cylinders were introduced. These revolvers have "Q" or "F" serial number suffixes. In 1960 the "K" series Scout was introduced and featured a heavier frame, nickel plating and wood grips. Majority of commemorative revolvers are of this type. This series was discontinued in 1970. Prices are about 15 percent higher than for "Q" and "F" series guns. **NOTE:** Add 50 percent for 9.5" Buntline; 10 percent for extra cylinder.

NIB	Exc.	V.G.	Good	Fair	Poor
450	325	200	175	125	90

Peacemaker & New Frontier .22

Similar to Frontier Scout, with a steel case colored or blued frame. Fitted with old style black plastic eagle grips. Peacemaker .22 and New Frontier .22 revolvers were initially offered with 4.75", 6" and 7.5" barrels (Buntline). After about one year of production 4.75" barrel was discontinued and a 4.4" barrel was offered in each model. Also has an interchangeable .22 Magnum cylinder.

Peacemaker .22 was only available with a steel receiver and color case-hardened finish. Grip frames were alloy. Same is true of New Frontier .22 revolvers except that (as noted in the book), New Frontier .22 GS series was available with color case-hardened or blue receivers. Both Peacemaker .22 and New Frontier .22 revolvers were available in single caliber (.22 LR only) and dual caliber (.22 LR and .22 Magnum) models. The factory had separate model numbers for these variations. Also, the factory offered "P" series or "62" model Frontier Scouts and Buntline Scouts. This was a significant model variation. Most of these revolvers had a "G" suffix although some built in 1974 had a "L" suffix. In 1982 through 1986 a New Frontier model with cross-bolt safety was offered. This model is often referred to as "GS" series. This revolver was offered with adjustable sights only. No Peacemakers were offered in this series.

NIB	Exc.	V.G.	Good	Fair	Poor
550	475	300	200	150	100

Scout Model SAA (1962-1971)

Basically a scaled-down version of SAA. Chambered for .22 LR cartridge. Offered with 4.75", 6" or 7" barrel. Earlier production has case colored frames with remainder blued; later production is all blued. Grips are checkered hard rubber. Discontinued in 1986.

NIB	Exc.	V.G.	Good	Fair	Poor
400	275	200	150	100	75

COLT ANTIQUE LONG ARMS

Berdan Single-Shot Rifle

A scarce rifle on today's market. Approximately 30,200 manufactured, but nearly 30,000 were sent to Russia. Produced from 1866-1870. A trapdoor-type action chambered for .42 centerfire. Standard model has 32.5" barrel; carbine 18.25". Finish blued, with walnut stock. Rifle was designed and patent held by Hiram Berdan, Commander of Civil War "Sharpshooters" Regiment. This was actually Colt's first cartridge arm. The 30,000 rifles and 25 half-stocked carbines that were sent to Russia were in Russian Cyrillic letters. Few examples made for American sales have Colt's name and Hartford address on the barrel.

Courtesy Milwaukee Public Museum, Milwaukee, Wisconsin

Russian Order

30,000 manufactured.

NIB	Exc.	V.G.	Good	Fair	Poor
—	15000	10000	5000	1500	750

Carbine Russian Order

25 manufactured.

NIB	Exc.	V.G.	Good	Fair	Poor
—	18000	12500	6500	1800	750

U.S. Sales

100 manufactured.

NIB	Exc.	V.G.	Good	Fair	Poor
—	15000	10000	5000	1500	750

Carbine U.S. Sales

25 manufactured.

NIB	Exc.	V.G.	Good	Fair	Poor
—	18000	12500	6500	1800	750

Colt-Franklin Military Rifle

Rifle was not a successful venture for Colt. Patents were held by William B. Franklin, a vice-president of the company. Bolt-action rifle, with a primitive gravity-fed box magazine. Chambered for .45-70 government cartridge. Has a 32.5" barrel. Blued, with walnut stock. Rifle has Colt Hartford barrel address and stamped with an eagle's head and U.S. inspectors marks. There were only 50 of these rifles produced and it is believed they were prototypes intended for government sales. This was not to be and production ceased after approximately 50 were manufactured in 1887 and 1888.

NIB	Exc.	V.G.	Good	Fair	Poor
—	—	9500	5000	2000	1100

Colt-Burgess Lever-Action Rifle

Represented Colt's only attempt to compete, with Winchester, for lever-action rifle market. It is said when Winchester started to produce revolving handguns for prospective marketing, Colt dropped the Burgess from its line. Chambered for .44-40. Has 25.5" barrel and 15-shot tubular magazine. Carbine version has 20.5" barrel and 12-shot magazine. Finish blued, with case-colored hammer and lever. Stock is walnut, with an oil finish. Colt Hartford address is on barrel and "Burgess Patents" stamped on bottom of lever. There were 3,775 rifles manufactured—1,219 with round barrels and 2,556 with octagonal barrels. Also, 2,593 Carbines. Burgess was produced from 1883-1885.

Courtesy Buffalo Bill Historical Center, Cody, Wyoming

Rifle - Octagonal Barrel

NIB	Exc.	V.G.	Good	Fair	Poor
—	—	12500	10000	5000	2000

Rifle - Round Barrel

NIB	Exc.	V.G.	Good	Fair	Poor
—	—	12000	9500	4700	1800

Carbine

NIB	Exc.	V.G.	Good	Fair	Poor
—	—	17500	13000	6500	2500

Baby Carbine

Lighter frame and barrel (RARE).

NIB	Exc.	V.G.	Good	Fair	Poor
—	—	20000	15000	7500	3000

Lightning Slide-Action, Medium-Frame

First slide-action rifle Colt produced. Chambered for .32-20, .38-40 and .44-40. Intended to be a companion piece to SAAs in same calibers. Has a 26" barrel with 15-shot tube magazine; carbine 20" barrel with 12-shot magazine. Finish blued, with case colored hammer; walnut stock is oil-finished; fore-end usually checkered. Colt name and Hartford address stamped on barrel along with patent dates. Approximately 89,777 manufactured between 1884 and 1902.

Courtesy Bonhams & Butterfields, San Francisco, California

Rifle

NIB	Exc.	V.G.	Good	Fair	Poor
—	—	5500	3500	2000	1000

Carbine

NIB	Exc.	V.G.	Good	Fair	Poor
—	—	7500	4000	2500	1500

Military Rifle or Carbine

.44-40 caliber, short magazine tube, bayonet lug and sling swivels.

NIB	Exc.	V.G.	Good	Fair	Poor
—	—	7000	4000	2000	1500

Baby Carbine

1 lb., lighter version of standard carbine.

Courtesy Richard M. Kumor Sr.

NIB	Exc.	V.G.	Good	Fair	Poor
—	—	8750	5500	3000	2000

San Francisco Police Rifle

.44-40 caliber, #SFP 1-SFP401 on bottom tang.

NIB	Exc.	V.G.	Good	Fair	Poor
—	—	9000	6000	3000	2000

Lightning Slide-Action Small-Frame

Well-made rifle and first of its type Colt manufactured. Chambered for .22 Short and Long. Standard barrel length 24"; finish blued with case-colored hammer. Stock walnut; some checkered, some not. Barrel stamped with Colt name, Hartford address and patent dates. There were 89,912 manufactured between 1887 and 1904.

Courtesy Bonhams & Butterfields, San Francisco, California

NIB	Exc.	V.G.	Good	Fair	Poor
—	6000	4800	2500	1500	1000

Lightning Slide-Action, Large-Frame (Express)

Similar in appearance to medium-frame Lightning, though larger in size. Chambered in larger rifle calibers of the era, from .38-56 up to .50-95 Express. Larger calibers are more desirable from a collector's standpoint. Has a 28" barrel; carbine a 22" barrel. Finish blued, with case colored hammer. Stock is oiled walnut; fore-end checkered. Colt name and Hartford address stamped on barrel along with patent dates. Rifle is quite large and has come to be known as "Express Model." Colt manufactured 6,496 between 1887 and 1894.

Rifle - Octagonal Barrel

NIB	Exc.	V.G.	Good	Fair	Poor
—	—	10500	5500	2000	1000

Rifle - Round Barrel

NIB	Exc.	V.G.	Good	Fair	Poor
—	—	10500	5500	2000	1000

Carbine

22" barrel.

NIB	Exc.	V.G.	Good	Fair	Poor
—	—	12500	6500	2500	1000

Baby Carbine

22" barrel 1 lb. lighter.

NIB	Exc.	V.G.	Good	Fair	Poor
—	—	12500	6500	2500	950

Model 1878 Double-Barrel Shotgun

Chambered in 10- or 12-gauge. Has 28", 30" or 32" barrel. It is a sidelock double trigger hammer gun, with case colored locks and breech. Barrels are browned Damacus-patterned. Checkered walnut stock is varnished or oil-finished. Colt's Hartford address stamped on barrel rib; Colt's name on lock. This has been regarded as one of the finest shotguns made in America, although Colt had difficulty competing with the less expensive European imports of the day. Production ceased after only 22,690 were manufactured between 1878 and 1889. **NOTE:** Add 300 percent for fully engraved model.

NIB	Exc.	V.G.	Good	Fair	Poor
—	—	4500	2250	750	300

Model 1883 Double-Barrel Shotgun

A hammerless boxlock, chambered for 8-, 10- or 12-gauge. Barrels are 28", 30" or 32"; features double triggers. Frame and furniture are case colored; barrels browned with Damascus pattern. Checkered walnut stock is varnished or oil-finished. Colt's Hartford address stamped on barrel rib. "Colt" stamped on each side of frame. Again, as in Model 1878, this is rated as one of the finest of all American-made shotguns. There were many special orders and they require individual appraisal. Colt manufactured 7,366 of these guns between 1883 and 1895. **NOTE:** Add 300 percent for fully engraved model; 200 percent for 8-gauge.

NIB	Exc.	V.G.	Good	Fair	Poor
—	3000	2000	1400	775	400

Double-Barrel Rifle

One of the rarest of all Colt firearms. A prize for the Colt collector. Only 35 of these guns manufactured. They were said to be the special interest of Caldwell Hart Colt, Samuel Colt's son, who was an avid arms collector. It is said that most of the 35 guns produced wound up in his collection or those of his friends. Chambered for .45-70 or one of the larger variations thereof. It is an exposed hammer sidelock with double triggers. Locks, breech and furniture are case colored; barrels browned or blued. Barrels are 28" in length and checkered stock was oil-finished or varnished walnut. Barrel rib stamped with Colt name and Hartford address. Locks are also stamped "Colt." One must exercise extreme caution in dealing with this model as there have been Model 1878 shotguns converted into double rifles. Colt manufactured 35 guns from 1879-1885.

Courtesy Bonhams & Butterfields, San Francisco, California

NIB	Exc.	V.G.	Good	Fair	Poor
—	95000	75000	35500	—	—

COLT DOUBLE-ACTION REVOLVERS

Model 1877 "Lightning" and "Thunderer"

Model 1877 was Colt's first attempt at manufacturing a double-action revolver. Shows a striking resemblance to Single Action Army. Sales on this model were brisk, with over 166,000 produced between 1877 and 1909. Chambered for two different cartridges; .38 Colt known as "Lightning" and .41 Colt as "Thunderer." Standard finishes are blued, with case colored frame and nickel plate. Bird's-head grips are of checkered rosewood on early guns and hard rubber on majority of the production run. Barrel lengths most often encountered are 2.5" and 3.5" without an ejector rod and 4.5" and 6" with rod. Other barrel lengths from 1.5" through 10" were offered. Model 1877 holds 6-shots in either caliber. There are quite a few different variations found within this model designation. Values furnished are for standard variations. Antiques made before 1898 would be more desirable from an investment standpoint. These revolvers have a reputation as "watchmaker's nightmares" and non-functioning examples command substantially reduced prices. **NOTE:** Add 25 percent premium for blued guns; 50 percent premium for shorter than 2.5"; 10 percent for .41-caliber "Thunderer"; 50 percent for over 6" barrel; 20 percent for London barrel address; 50 percent for .32-caliber; 10 percent for rosewood grips.

Without Ejector, 2.5" and 3.5" Barrel

NIB	Exc.	V.G.	Good	Fair	Poor
—	3000	2000	800	500	350

With Ejector, 4.5" and 6" Barrel

NIB	Exc.	V.G.	Good	Fair	Poor
—	3000	1800	800	750	450

Model 1878 "Frontier"

A large and somewhat ungainly looking revolver. Solid frame with removable trigger guard. Cylinder does not swing out and there is a thin loading gate. Bird's-head grips made of checkered hard rubber; walnut would be found on early models. Finish either blued and case colored or nickel-plated. Model 1878 holds 6-shots and standard barrel lengths are 4.75", 5.5" and 7.5" with an ejector assembly and 3", 3.5" and 4" without. Standard chamberings for Model 1878 are .32-20, .38-40, .41 Colt, .44-40 and .45 Colt. This model was fairly well received because it is chambered for large calibers that were popular in that era. Colt manufactured 51,210 between 1878 and 1905. Antique models made before 1898 would be more desirable from an investment standpoint. **NOTE:** Add 15 percent premium for blued revolvers; 10- to 50 percent premium for calibers other than .44-40 or .45.

Standard

Courtesy Bonhams & Butterfields, San Francisco, California

NIB	Exc.	V.G.	Good	Fair	Poor
—	5000	3200	1600	800	400

Omnipotent

Special order version of above, with name "Omnipotent" stamped on barrel.

NIB	Exc.	V.G.	Good	Fair	Poor
—	8000	7000	6000	3000	1000

Sheriff's Model

Chambered for .44-40 or .45 Colt. Barrel lengths 3.5" or 4".

NIB	Exc.	V.G.	Good	Fair	Poor
—	6000	4000	2000	1000	800

Model 1902 (Philippine or Alaskan Model)

U.S. Ordnance contract Model 1878. Has a 6" barrel and chambered for .45 Colt. Finish blued and there is a lanyard swivel on the butt. Model bears U.S. inspector's marks. Sometimes referred to as Philippine or Alaskan model. Trigger guard is quite a bit larger than standard.

Courtesy Bonhams & Butterfields

NIB	Exc.	V.G.	Good	Fair	Poor
—	5500	3500	1800	1000	600

Model 1889 Navy—Civilian Model

1889 Navy is an important model from a historical standpoint. It was the first double-action revolver Colt manufactured, with a swing-out cylinder. They produced 31,000 of them between 1889 and 1894. Chambered for .38 Colt and .41 Colt cartridges. Cylinder holds 6-shots. Offered with 3", 4.5" or 6" barrel; finish was either blued or nickel-plated. Grips are checkered hard rubber, with "Rampant Colt" in an oval molded into them. Patent dates 1884 and 1888 appear in the barrel marking and serial numbers stamped on the butt. **NOTE:** Add premium for blued models; 20 percent for 3" barrel

NIB	Exc.	V.G.	Good	Fair	Poor
—	2250	1500	1000	600	300

Model 1889 U.S. Navy—Martial Model

This variation has a 6" barrel, chambered for .38 Colt and offered in blued finish only. "U.S.N." stamped on the butt. Most Navy models were altered at the Colt factory to add Model 1895 improvements. Original unaltered specimen would be worth as much as 50 percent premium over altered values listed.

Courtesy Bonhams & Butterfields, San Francisco, California

NIB	Exc.	V.G.	Good	Fair	Poor
—	6000	5000	2500	1000	500

Model 1892 "New Army and Navy" —Civilian Model

Similar in appearance to 1889 Navy. Main differences are improvements to lock-work function. Has double bolt stop notches, double cylinder locking bolt and shorter flutes on the cylinder. The .38 Smith & Wesson and .32-20 were added to .38 Colt and .41 Colt chamberings. Checkered hard rubber grips are standard, with plain walnut grips found on some contract series guns. Barrel lengths and finishes are the same as described for Model 1889. Patent dates 1895 and 1901 appear stamped on later models. Colt manufactured 291,000 of these revolvers between 1892 and 1907. Antiques before 1898 are more desirable from an investment standpoint. **NOTE:** Add 20 percent for 3" barrel.

NIB	Exc.	V.G.	Good	Fair	Poor
—	1500	800	500	200	100

Model 1892 U.S. Navy—Martial Model

NIB	Exc.	V.G.	Good	Fair	Poor
—	2500	2000	800	600	400

Model 1892 U.S. Army—Martial Model

NIB	Exc.	V.G.	Good	Fair	Poor
—	2500	2000	800	600	400

Model 1894/1896 Army

NIB	Exc.	V.G.	Good	Fair	Poor
—	2200	2000	800	600	400

Model 1905 Marine Corps

Variation of New Army and Navy Model. Derived from late production, with its own serial range #10001-10926. Only 926 produced between 1905 and 1909. Quite rare on today's market and is eagerly sought after by Colt Double-Action collectors. Chambered for .38 Colt and .38 Smith & Wesson Special cartridges. Holds 6-shots, has a 6" barrel and offered in blued finish only. Grips are checkered walnut and quite different than those found on previous models. "U.S.M.C." stamped on the butt; patent dates of 1884, 1888 and 1895 stamped on barrel. Of these revolvers 125 were earmarked for civilian sales and do not have Marine Corps markings; these will generally be found in better condition. Values are similar.

Courtesy Faintich Auction Services, Inc., Paul Goodwin photo

NIB	Exc.	V.G.	Good	Fair	Poor
—	3000	2500	2000	1500	750

New Service Model

This model was in continual production from 1898 through 1944. Chambered for 11 different calibers: .38 Special, .357 Magnum, .38-40, .44 Russian, .44 Special, .44-40, .45 ACP, .45 Colt, .450 Eley, .455 Eley and .476 Eley. Offered in barrel lengths from 2" to 7.5", either blued or nickel-plated. Checkered hard rubber grips were standard until 1928. Then checkered walnut grips were used, with an inset Colt medallion. This was the largest swing-out cylinder double-action revolver that Colt ever produced. Approximately 356,000 were manufactured over the 46 years they were made. There are many different variations of this revolver and one should consult a book dealing strictly with Colt for a thorough breakdown and description. **NOTE:** Add 30 percent for nickel finish; 40 percent for factory ivory or pearl grips.

Courtesy Cherry's Collector Firearms Auction, Paul Goodwin photo

Early Model, #1-21000

NIB	Exc.	V.G.	Good	Fair	Poor
—	2250	1800	1200	600	300

Early Model Target, #6000-15000

Checkered walnut grips, flattop-frame, 7.5" barrel.

Courtesy Faintich Auction Services, Inc., Paul Goodwin photo

NIB	Exc.	V.G.	Good	Fair	Poor
—	3000	1500	550	300	200

Improved Model, #21000-325000

Has internal locking improvements.

Courtesy Faintich Auction Services, Inc., Paul Goodwin photo

NIB	Exc.	V.G.	Good	Fair	Poor
—	1850	1500	800	400	200

Improved Target Model, #21000-325000

Courtesy Faintich Auction Services, Inc., Paul Goodwin photo

NIB	Exc.	V.G.	Good	Fair	Poor
—	2250	1500	550	300	200

U.S. Army Model 1909, #30000-50000

5.5" barrel, .45 Colt, walnut grips, "U.S. Army Model 1909" on butt.

NIB	Exc.	V.G.	Good	Fair	Poor
—	2350	1900	1400	700	350

U.S. Navy Model 1909, #50000-52000

Same as above with "U.S.N." on butt.

NIB	Exc.	V.G.	Good	Fair	Poor
—	3000	2400	1700	1000	500

U.S. Marine Corps Model 1909, #21000-23000

Checkered walnut grips, "U.S.M.C." on butt.

NIB	Exc.	V.G.	Good	Fair	Poor
—	3500	2900	2200	1500	700

U.S. Army Model 1917, #150000-301000

Smooth walnut grips, 5.5" barrel, .45 ACP. Model designation stamped on butt.

Courtesy Faintich Auction Services, Inc., Paul Goodwin photo

NIB	Exc.	V.G.	Good	Fair	Poor
—	1300	900	600	300	225

Model 1917 Civilian, #335000-336000

Approximately 1,000 made in .45 ACP only, from Army parts overrun. No military markings.

NIB	Exc.	V.G.	Good	Fair	Poor
—	1500	950	600	250	200

Late Model New Service, #325000-356000

Checkered walnut grips and internal improvements.

NIB	Exc.	V.G.	Good	Fair	Poor
—	1550	975	650	300	225

Shooting Master, #333000-350000

Round-butt, checkered walnut grips with Colt medallion, 6" barrel, "Colt Shooting Master" on barrel, flattop-frame with target sights. Chambered for .38 Special cartridge. **NOTE:** Add 100 percent premium for .44 Special, .45 ACP and .45 Colt.

Courtesy Faintich Auction Services, Inc., Paul Goodwin photo

NIB	Exc.	V.G.	Good	Fair	Poor
—	1950	1200	850	400	300

Magnum Model New Service, Over #340000
Chambered for .357 Magnum, .38 Special.

NIB	Exc.	V.G.	Good	Fair	Poor
—	2400	2000	1000	500	200

New Pocket Model

First swing-out cylinder, double-action pocket revolver made by Colt. Chambered for .32 Colt and .32 Smith & Wesson. Holds 6-shots and offered with barrel lengths of 2.5", 3.5", 5" and 6". Finish blued or nickel-plated. Grips are checkered hard rubber, with oval Colt molded into them. "Colt's New Pocket" stamped on frame. Patent dates 1884 and 1888 stamped on barrel of later-production guns. Approximately 30,000 of these manufactured between 1893 and 1905. Antiques made before 1898 are more desirable. **NOTE:** Add 25 percent for early production without patent dates; 10 percent for 5" barrel.

NIB	Exc.	V.G.	Good	Fair	Poor
1200	1000	750	600	400	200

Pocket Positive

Externally, same revolver as New Pocket, but has positive lock feature. Manufactured between 1905 and 1940.

NIB	Exc.	V.G.	Good	Fair	Poor
1100	900	700	550	350	200

Army Special Model

Heavier-framed improved version of New Army and Navy revolver. Chambered for .32-20, .38 Colt, .38 Smith & Wesson and .41 Colt. Offered with 4", 4.5", 5" and 6" barrel. Finish blued or nickel-plated. Grips checkered hard rubber. Serial number range #291000-#540000. Manufactured between 1908-1927.

NIB	Exc.	V.G.	Good	Fair	Poor
1000	850	650	500	350	200

New Police Model

Appears similar to New Pocket Model. Frame stamped "New Police". Chambered for .32 Colt, .32 Colt New Police and .32 Smith & Wesson cartridges. Barrel lengths 2.5", 4" and 6". Finishes blued or nickel-plated. Colt manufactured 49,500 of this model from 1896-1907. New York City Police Department purchased 4,500 of these revolvers and backstraps are so marked. Also, a target model of 5,000 were produced. Features 6" barrel, with flattop-frame and target sights. **NOTE:** Add 30 percent for New York Police marked; 20 percent for target model.

NIB	Exc.	V.G.	Good	Fair	Poor
1050	900	700	550	350	200

Police Positive

Externally same as New Police. Additions of positive lock feature and two new chamberings—.38 New Police and .38 Smith & Wesson. Manufactured from 1905-1947.

NIB	Exc.	V.G.	Good	Fair	Poor
—	700	475	250	200	150

Police Positive Target

Basically same as New Police Target, with positive lock feature. Chambered in .22 LR, .22 WRF as well as other cartridges offered in earlier model. **NOTE:** Deduct 20 percent for WRF. A .22-caliber Police Positive chambered for .22 Short and Long cartridge may be seen with British proofs. Several such revolvers were sold to London Armory in this configuration during the late 1920s. A NIB example recently sold for $1,200.

NIB	Exc.	V.G.	Good	Fair	Poor
—	800	600	300	175	100

Police Positive Special

Similar to Police Positive. Has a slightly larger frame to accept longer cylinder needed to chamber more powerful cartridges such as .38 Special, in addition to original chamberings. Manufactured from 1907-1973.

NIB	Exc.	V.G.	Good	Fair	Poor
—	600	450	250	150	100

Police Positive Special Mark V

Introduced in 1994, this is an updated version of Police Positive Special. Features an underlug 4" barrel, with rubber grips and fixed sights. Butt is rounded. Revolver is rated to fire .38-caliber +P rounds. Overall length 9". Weight about 30 oz.

NIB	Exc.	V.G.	Good	Fair	Poor
550	400	300	150	100	85

Officer's Model Target 1st Issue

Chambered for .38 Special cartridge. Has a blued 6" barrel. Flattop-frame with adjustable target sights. Colt manufactured this model from 1904-1908.

NIB	Exc.	V.G.	Good	Fair	Poor
1800	1450	1000	800	500	250

Officer's Model Target 2nd Issue

Similar to 1st Issue, but offered in .22 LR, .32 Police Positive caliber and .38 Special. Furnished with 4", 4.5", 5", 6" and 7.5" barrel in .38 Special only. Checkered walnut grips. Colt manufactured this model between 1908 and 1940.

Courtesy Faintich Auction Services, Inc., Paul Goodwin photo

NIB	Exc.	V.G.	Good	Fair	Poor
1700	1350	950	700	400	225

Camp Perry Single-Shot

Created by modifying an Officer's Model frame to accept a special flat single-shot "cylinder". This flat chamber pivots to the left side and downward for loading. Chambered for .22 LR and offered with an 8" (early production) or 10" (late production) barrel. Finish blued, with checkered walnut grips. Name "Camp Perry Model" stamped on left side of chamber; caliber on the barrel. Colt named this model after the site of U.S. Target Competition held annually at Camp Perry, Ohio. Colt manufactured 2,525 of these between 1920 and 1941. **NOTE:** This gun serial numbered 101-2525 with 2488 produced from 1926-1941. In 1934 standard barrel length was reduced from 10" to 8" at approximately serial number 2150. Add 100 percent premium for 10" barrel; 50 percent premium for original box.

NIB	Exc.	V.G.	Good	Fair	Poor
—	2500	1750	950	600	400

Officer's Model Match

Introduced in 1953, this model similar to Officer's Model Target. Chambered for either .22-caliber cartridge or .38 Special, with 6" barrel. Revolver fitted with a heavy tapered barrel, wide hammer spur, with adjustable rear sight and ramp front sight. Sold with checkered walnut target grips.

Blued finish is standard. Discontinued in 1970. Standard of long action could be fired both double- or single-action. The .22-caliber version prices are listed. Officer's Model Match in .38-caliber will bring approximately 20 percent less. **NOTE:** This model also produced in .22 Magnum. Rather a rare gun in this caliber, with approximately 800 produced.

NIB	Exc.	V.G.	Good	Fair	Poor
—	750	600	450	350	250

.22 Caliber in Short Action—Single-Action-Only

NIB	Exc.	V.G.	Good	Fair	Poor
—	1000	750	600	500	350

Official Police

Popular revolver in Colt line for many years. Manufactured from 1927 to 1969. Chambered for .32-20 and .41 Colt. These calibers were discontinued in 1942 and 1930, respectively. The .38 Special was chambered throughout the entire production run and .22 LR was added in 1930. Holds 6-shots, has a square-butt and offered with 2", 4", 5" and 6" barrel lengths. Grips are checkered walnut. Finish either blued or nickel-plated. **NOTE:** Add 10 percent for nickel-plated; 20 percent for .22 LR; 80- to 100 percent for rare round-butt model. Deduct 10 percent for 1947-1969 production. These barrels have no patent dates.

NIB	Exc.	V.G.	Good	Fair	Poor
1000	850	600	400	300	200

Commando Model

This model, for all intents and purposes, is an Official Police. Chambered for .38 Special, with 2", 4" or 6" barrel. Parkerized and stamped "Colt Commando" on the barrel. Approximately 50,000 manufactured between 1942-1945 for use in World War II. **NOTE:** Add 30 percent for 2" barrel.

Courtesy Richard M. Kumor, Sr.

NIB	Exc.	V.G.	Good	Fair	Poor
2000	1600	1000	750	500	300

Marshal Model

Official Police marked "Colt Marshal" on barrel and an "M" suffix in the serial number. Has 2" or 4" barrel and round butt. Finish is blued. Approximately 2,500 manufactured between 1954 and 1956.

NIB	Exc.	V.G.	Good	Fair	Poor
1950	1500	1000	800	500	250

Colt .38 SF-VI

Introduced in 1995, this model is essentially a Detective Special in stainless steel, with a new internal mechanism. Has a transfer bar safety mechanism. Fitted with 2" barrel and cylinder holds 6 rounds of .38 Special. A 4" barrel in bright stainless steel also available. Weight 21 oz.; overall length 7".

NIB	Exc.	V.G.	Good	Fair	Poor
650	475	350	225	150	100

Colt .38 SF-VI Special Lady

Introduced in 1996, this 2" barrel version similar to above model. Addition of a bright finish and bobbed hammer. Weight 21 oz.

NIB	Exc.	V.G.	Good	Fair	Poor
650	450	300	200	150	100

Detective Special 1st Issue / 2nd Issue

Actually a Police Positive Special, with 2" barrel. Originally chambered for .32 New Police, .38 New Police (which were discontinued) and .38 Special, which continued until end of production run. Finish blued or nickel and offered with wood or plastic grips. Over 400,000 manufactured between 1926 and 1972. A few 2nd issue (post WWII) units came with 3" barrels. **NOTE:** Add 50 percent for pre-war 1st issue (serial number 331000 - 490000); 25 percent for nickel finish; 30 percent for 3" barrel.

NIB	Exc.	V.G.	Good	Fair	Poor
1600	1100	800	700	450	225

Detective Special 3rd Issue

Basically a modernized, streamlined version. Features 2" or 3" barrel, shrouded ejector rod, wrap-around checkered walnut grips and chambered for .38 Special. Finished in blue or nickel plate. Made from 1973 to 1986 and 1993 to 1995. **NOTE:** Add $50 for nickel finish.

NIB	Exc.	V.G.	Good	Fair	Poor
950	800	700	600	500	250

Detective Special II (DS-II)

Introduced in 1997, this version of Detective special, features new internal lock work and a transfer bar safety mechanism. Fitted with 2" barrel, capacity of 6 rounds and chambered for .38 Special. In 1998 this model was offered chambered for .357 Magnum cartridge as well. Rubber combat style grips are standard. Stainless steel finish. Weight about 21 oz.

NIB	Exc.	V.G.	Good	Fair	Poor
650	475	300	225	—	—

Colt Magnum Carry

Introduced in 1999, this model is essentially a renamed Detective Special II. Stainless steel finish. Weight 21 oz.

NIB	Exc.	V.G.	Good	Fair	Poor
650	475	300	250	—	—

Banker's Special

Bankers Special is a 2" barreled, easily concealed revolver. Designed with bank employees in mind. Chambered for .38 Special. Offered in blued finish and .22-caliber. Grips are rounded but full-sized. Colt utilized this feature in advertising this model. U.S. Postal Service equipped its railway mail clerks with this model. Approximately 35,000 manufactured between 1926 and 1943. **NOTE:** Nickel models will command a premium. .22-caliber will command a premium of up to 50 percent.

NIB	Exc.	V.G.	Good	Fair	Poor
2100	1500	975	500	250	150

Cobra 1st Issue

Cobra 1st Issue is simply an alloy-framed lightweight version of Detective Special. Weight only 15 oz. Chambered for .32, .38 Special and .22 LR. Available in either round- or square-butt version, with 4" barrel only. Manufactured between 1950 and 1973.

NIB	Exc.	V.G.	Good	Fair	Poor
1000	850	650	525	200	100

Cobra 2nd Issue

Same as Cobra 1st Issue in .38 Special only. Streamlined with wraparound walnut grips and shrouded ejector rod. **NOTE:** Add 30 percent for nickel.

NIB	Exc.	V.G.	Good	Fair	Poor
900	800	600	450	350	250

Agent 1st Issue

Basically same as Cobra 1st Issue, with shortened grip frame. This was done to make Agent more concealable. Colt manufactured Agent 1st Issue from 1955-1973.

NIB	Exc.	V.G.	Good	Fair	Poor
900	800	600	450	350	250

Border Patrol

Model is quite rare, as Colt manufactured only 400 of them in 1952. Basically a Police Special, with heavy 4" barrel. Chambered for .38 Special and built to be strong. Finish is blued. Serial numbered in 610000 range.

NIB	Exc.	V.G.	Good	Fair	Poor
3750	3500	2800	2000	1000	500

Agent L.W. 2nd Issue

Streamlined version, with shrouded ejector rod. Last four years of its production was matte finished. Manufactured between 1973 and 1986.

NIB	Exc.	V.G.	Good	Fair	Poor
—	550	400	275	175	150

Aircrewman Special

Especially fabricated for the Air Force, to be carried by their pilots for protection. Extremely lightweight at 11 oz. Frame and cylinder are made of aluminum alloy. Has 2" barrel and chambered for .38 Special. Finish was blued, with checkered walnut grips. Approximately 1,200 manufactured in 1951 and marked "U.S." or "A.F."

NIB	Exc.	V.G.	Good	Fair	Poor
4500	3500	3000	1500	800	400

Courier

Another version of the Cobra. Features shorter grip frame and 3" barrel. Chambered for .32 and .22 rimfire. Approximately 3,000 manufactured in 1955 and 1956. **NOTE:** Add 20 percent for .22 Rimfire.

NIB	Exc.	V.G.	Good	Fair	Poor
1300	750	600	500	350	150

Trooper

Designed specifically by Colt to fill the need for a large heavy-duty powerful revolver, that was accurate. Trooper filled that need. Offered with 4" or 6" barrel, blued or nickel finishes and checkered walnut grips. Trooper chambered for .38 Special, .357 Magnum and there is a .22 rimfire version for target shooters. Manufactured between 1953 and 1969. **NOTE:** Add 10 percent for .357 or .22.

NIB	Exc.	V.G.	Good	Fair	Poor
—	600	475	300	150	100

Colt .357 Magnum

Deluxe version of Trooper. Offered with a special target, wide hammer and large target-type grips. Sights are same as Accro target model. Features 4" or 6" barrel and blued finish. Manufactured between 1953 and 1961. Fewer than 15,000 produced.

NIB	Exc.	V.G.	Good	Fair	Poor
—	675	495	300	200	150

Diamondback

Medium-frame, duty-type weapon suitable for target work. Has a short frame of Detective Special, with ventilated rib 2.5", 4" or 6" barrel. Chambered for .38 Special and .22 rimfire for target shooters. Finish blued or nickel-plated, with checkered walnut grips. Diamondback features adjustable target sights, wide target hammer and steel frame. Manufactured between 1966 and 1986. Very few Diamondbacks were chambered for .22 WMR. Another premium should be added for these models. Since fakes exist, a factory letter documenting this chambering is strongly advised. **NOTE:** Premium of 100 percent for 2.5" barrel or nickel finish in .22 LR caliber; 20 percent in .38 Special.

.38 Special

NIB	Exc.	V.G.	Good	Fair	Poor
1200	1000	650	550	400	250

.22 Long Rifle

NIB	Exc.	V.G.	Good	Fair	Poor
1800	1500	1000	750	500	300

Viper

Alloy-framed revolver chambered for .38 Special. Has a 4" barrel. Manufactured between 1977 and 1984. Viper is essentially a lightweight version of Police Positive.

NIB	Exc.	V.G.	Good	Fair	Poor
1000	750	500	200	125	100

Python

Python was often described as the Cadillac of Colt double-action revolver line. Originally designed to be a large-frame .38 Special target revolver, but shortly before Python was introduced in 1955, Colt management decided to chamber it for .357 Magnum. (A .38 Special 8" barrel variation was made in early 1980s. See separate listing.) Python was offered in barrel lengths of 2.5", 3" (very rare), 4", 6" and 8". Features included a ventilated rib, full lug barrel and adjustable rear sight. Finish choices were Royal Blue, nickel plated, matte stainless and high polished "Ultimate" stainless. Python remained in the catalog as a regular production item until 1996. The following year Colt Custom Shop started making Python on a special-order-only basis. Known as Python Elite, it was produced by the Custom Shop until 2006.

Blue or Royal Blue Finish

NOTE: Add 10- to 15 percent for early production from 1955 to 1969 with checkered wood grips (serial number 1 — 99999); 50 percent for rare 3" barrel.

NIB	Exc.	V.G.	Good	Fair	Poor
3500	3200	2500	1600	900	600

Polished Nickel Finish

NOTE: Add 30 percent for satin nickel instead of polished nickel; 25 percent for 2.5" or 8" barrel; 200- to 250 percent for 3" barrel. A Colt Archive Letter is recommended for 3" model.

NIB	Exc.	V.G.	Good	Fair	Poor
3400	3100	2400	1500	800	500

Matte Stainless Steel

NOTE: Add 30 percent for 2.5" barrel; 10 percent for 8".

NIB	Exc.	V.G.	Good	Fair	Poor
3500	3200	2500	1600	900	600

Ultimate Bright Stainless

NOTE: Add 30 percent for 2.5" barrel; 10 percent for 8".

NIB	Exc.	V.G.	Good	Fair	Poor
3500	3000	2200	1600	900	600

Python Elite

Custom Shop model features stainless steel satin finish or blued. Adjustable red ramp front sight. Custom wood grips. Choice of 4" or 6" barrel. **NOTE:** Value estimates shown are for Royal Blue finish. Deduct 20 percent for more common stainless Elite model.

NIB	Exc.	V.G.	Good	Fair	Poor
3900	3500	2800	2200	1200	800

Python .38 Special

An 8" barreled Python chambered for .38 Special only. Limited-production venture was not a success. Offered in blue only. **NOTE:** Add 40- to 50 percent for nickel finish.

NIB	Exc.	V.G.	Good	Fair	Poor
2900	2400	2000	1600	900	600

Python Hunter

Hunter was a special 8" .357 Magnum Python, with an extended eye relief Leupold 2X scope. Grips are neoprene, with gold Colt medallions. Revolver with mounted scope and accessories. Fitted into a Halliburton extruded aluminum case. Hunter was manufactured in 1981 only.

NIB	Exc.	V.G.	Good	Fair	Poor
4200	3750	2800	2000	1350	700

Python Silhouette

In .357-caliber, with 8" barrel. Similar to Python Hunter, except for Silhouette barrel markings. As with Hunter, Leupold 2x scope is included.

NIB	Exc.	V.G.	Good	Fair	Poor
4300	3850	2900	2050	1400	750

Python Ten Pointer

Similar to Hunter model, except it came from the factory with a 3x Burris scope and two sets of grips, wood and composite.

NIB	Exc.	V.G.	Good	Fair	Poor
4200	3750	2800	2200	1200	800

Python Grizzly

Hybrid limited edition from Colt Custom Shop in mid '90s. Only 999 were made. Featured a Python Magna-Ported barrel and Colt King Cobra frame.

NIB	Exc.	V.G.	Good	Fair	Poor
4300	3850	2900	2400	1500	800

Metropolitan MK III

Basically a heavier-duty version of Official Police. Chambered for .38 Special. Fitted with 4" heavy barrel. Finished in blue only. Manufactured from 1969-1972.

NIB	Exc.	V.G.	Good	Fair	Poor
750	525	350	250	100	75

Lawman MK III

Offered chambered for .357 Magnum, with 2" or 4" barrel. Checkered walnut grips. Either blued or nickel-plated. Manufactured Lawman between 1969 and 1983.

NIB	Exc.	V.G.	Good	Fair	Poor
750	550	400	300	200	100

Lawman MK V

Improved version of MK III. Entailed a redesigned grip, shorter lock time and improved double-action. Manufactured 1982-1985.

NIB	Exc.	V.G.	Good	Fair	Poor
850	700	600	400	250	150

Trooper MK III

Revolver intended to be target-grade version of MK III series. Offered with 4", 6" or 8" ventilated rib barrel, with a shrouded ejector rod similar in appearance to Python. Chambered for .22 LR, .22 Magnum and .357 Magnum. Features adjustable target sights, checkered walnut target grips and either blued or nickel-plated. Manufactured between 1969 and 1983. **NOTE:** Add $100 for .22 LR; $200 for .22 WMR.

NIB	Exc.	V.G.	Good	Fair	Poor
750	400	325	200	150	100

Trooper MK V

Improved version of MK III. Manufactured between 1982 - 1985.

NIB	Exc.	V.G.	Good	Fair	Poor
825	550	375	200	150	100

Boa

Basically a deluxe version of Trooper MK V. Has all the same features plus high polished blue found on Python. Manufactured 1,200 of these revolvers in 1985. Entire production was purchased and marketed by Lew Horton Distributing Company in Southboro, Massachusetts.

NIB	Exc.	V.G.	Good	Fair	Poor
9500	8500	6500	5000	4000	2000

Peacekeeper

Designed as a duty-type weapon, with target capabilities. Offered with 4" or 6" barrel chambered for .357 Magnum. Features adjustable sights and neoprene combat-style grips. Matte blued finish. Manufactured between 1985 - 1987.

NIB	Exc.	V.G.	Good	Fair	Poor
1000	850	650	500	350	250

King Cobra

King Cobra has a forged steel frame, barrel and full length ejector rod housing. Barrel fitted with a solid rib. Model equipped with an adjustable white outline rear sight and red insert front sight. Colt black neoprene combat style grips are standard. Discontinued. **NOTE:** In 1998 all King Cobras were drilled and tapped for scope mounts. Add 20 percent for 2.5" barrel.

Blued

NIB	Exc.	V.G.	Good	Fair	Poor
1800	1500	1100	900	700	500

Stainless Steel

Offered in 4" or 6" barrel lengths. In 1997, introduced with optional barrel porting. No longer in production.

NIB	Exc.	V.G.	Good	Fair	Poor
2000	1700	1250	1000	800	600

High Polish Stainless Steel

NIB	Exc.	V.G.	Good	Fair	Poor
2900	2300	1700	1200	900	700

Anaconda

Double-action .44 Magnum revolver introduced in 1990. Offered with 4", 6" or 8" barrel lengths. Weight: 4" model 47 oz.; 6" model 63 oz.; 8" model 59 oz. Anaconda holds 6 rounds and available with matte stainless steel finish. For 1993, a new chambering in .45 Colt was offered with 6" or 8" barrel in matte stainless steel finish. Revolver chambered for .44 Remington Magnum cartridge. Constructed of matte-finished stainless steel and black neoprene finger groove grips, with gold Colt medallions. In 1996, Realtree model was offered with 8" barrel. Chambered for .44 Magnum cartridge. Furnished with either adjustable rear and ramp front sights or with Redfield 2.5-7x scope. No longer in production. Re-introduced in 2001, in .44 Magnum with 4", 6" or 8" barrel. Once again, discontinued. **NOTE:** In 1998, Anaconda was drilled and tapped for scope mounts and buyers had the option of barrel porting.

.44 Magnum

NIB	Exc.	V.G.	Good	Fair	Poor
2200	1600	1200	1000	700	400

.45 Colt

NIB	Exc.	V.G.	Good	Fair	Poor
2500	1900	1450	1200	800	500

Realtree Camo Model—Adjustable Sights

NIB	Exc.	V.G.	Good	Fair	Poor
2400	1800	1300	1100	750	450

Realtree Camo Model—Scope Mounts

NIB	Exc.	V.G.	Good	Fair	Poor
2450	1850	1400	1200	800	500

COLT SEMI-AUTOMATIC PISTOLS

Colt Firearms Co. was the first of American gun manufacturers to take advent of the semi-automatic pistol seriously. This pistol design was becoming popular among European gun makers in late 1880s and early 1900s. In the United States, however, the revolver was firmly ensconced as the accepted design. Colt realized that if the semi-automatic could be made to function reliably, it would soon catch on. Powers that be at Colt were able to negotiate with some of the noted inventors of the day, including Browning, to secure or lease the rights to manufacture their designs. Colt also encouraged creativity of their employees, with bonuses and incentives. Through this innovative thinking, Colt soon became the leader in semi-automatic pistol sales—a position that they have never really relinquished to any other American gun maker. Colt semi-automatic pistols represent an interesting field for the collector of Colt handguns. There are many variations with high enough production to make it worthwhile to seek them out. There are a number of fine books on Colt semi-automatics and anyone wishing to do so will be able to learn a great deal about them. Collector interest is high in this field and values are definitely on the rise.

Model 1900

First of Colt automatic pistols. Actually a developmental model, with only 3,500 being produced. Model 1900 was not really a successful design. Quite clumsy and out of balance in the hand, however, it was reliable in function during Army trials. Chambered for .38 Rimless smokeless cartridge. A detachable magazine that holds seven cartridges. Barrel length 6". Finish blued, with case-colored hammer and safety/sight combination. Grips are either plain walnut, checkered walnut or hard rubber. Pistol is a Browning design and left side of slide stamped "Browning's Patent" with 1897 patent date. Colt sold 200 pistols to the Navy and 200 to the Army for field trials and evaluation. Remaining 3,300 were sold on the civilian market. Manufactured from 1900-1903. **NOTE:** Many of the original 1900 pistols had the original sight/safety converted to Model 1902 configuration. These are worth about 50 percent less than unconverted pistols.

Standard Civilian Production

NIB	Exc.	V.G.	Good	Fair	Poor
—	15000	12000	5000	2500	1000

U.S. Navy Military Model

NIB	Exc.	V.G.	Good	Fair	Poor
—	25000	20000	8500	4200	1650

U.S. Army Military Model—1st Contract

NIB	Exc.	V.G.	Good	Fair	Poor
—	30000	24000	10000	4500	1800

U.S. Army Military Model—2nd Contract

NIB	Exc.	V.G.	Good	Fair	Poor
—	24000	18500	7500	4000	1500

Model 1902 Sporting Pistol

Chambered for .38 ACP cartridge. Has a 7-round detachable magazine, 6" barrel and blued. Checkered hard rubber grips featuring "Rampant Colt" molded into them. Most notable features of 1902 Sporting Model are rounded butt, rounded hammer spur, dovetailed rear sight and 1897-1902 patent dates. Manufactured approximately 7,500 of these pistols between 1903 and 1908.

Paul Goodwin photo

NIB	Exc.	V.G.	Good	Fair	Poor
—	5000	3500	2500	1200	800

Model 1902 Military Pistol

Early Model with Front of Slide Serrated

NIB	Exc.	V.G.	Good	Fair	Poor
—	6000	5000	4000	1500	750

Standard Model with Rear of Slide Serrated

NIB	Exc.	V.G.	Good	Fair	Poor
—	5000	4000	3000	1000	400

U.S. Army Marked, #15001-15200 with Front Serrations

NIB	Exc.	V.G.	Good	Fair	Poor
—	18000	15000	10000	5000	2000

Model 1903 Pocket Hammer Pistol

First automatic pocket pistol Colt produced. Essentially identical to 1902 Sporting Model, with a shorter slide. Barrel length 4.5". Chambered for .38 ACP cartridge. Blued, with case-colored hammer. Checkered hard rubber grips have "Rampant Colt" molded into them. Detachable magazine holds 7 rounds. Approximately 26,000 manufactured between 1903 - 1929.

Paul Goodwin photo

NIB	Exc.	V.G.	Good	Fair	Poor
—	4000	3000	1200	800	400

NIB	Exc.	V.G.	Good	Fair	Poor
2400	2000	1500	1000	750	400

Model 1903 Hammerless, .32 Pocket Pistol (Model M)

Second pocket automatic Colt manufactured. Another of John Browning's designs, it developed into one of Colt's most successful pistols. Chambered for .32 ACP cartridge. Initially barrel length was 4", then shortened to 3.75". Detachable magazine holds 8 rounds. Standard finish blue, with quite a few nickel plated. Early model grips are checkered hard rubber, with "Rampant Colt" molded into them. Many of the nickel plated pistols had pearl grips. In 1924 grips were changed to checkered walnut, with Colt medallions. Name of this model can be misleading as it is not a true hammerless, but a concealed hammer design. Features a slide stop and grip safety. Manufactured 572,215 civilian versions of this pistol and approximately 200,000 more for military contracts. Manufactured between 1903 and 1945. **NOTE:** Add 40 percent for Early Model 1897 patent date; $100 for nickel-plated with pearl grips; 20 percent for 4" barrel to #72,000.

Courtesy Richard M. Kumor, Sr.

Courtesy Orvel Reichert

NIB	Exc.	V.G.	Good	Fair	Poor
1200	1000	500	450	300	200

U.S. Military Model

Serial prefix M, marked "U.S. Property" on frame, Parkerized finish. **NOTE:** Premium of 50 percent for pistols issued to General Officers.

Model 1908 Hammerless .380 Pocket Pistol

Essentially same as .32 Pocket Pistol. Chambered for more potent .380 ACP, also known as 9mm Browning short. Other specifications are the same. Manufactured approximately 138,000 in this caliber for civilian sales. An unknown number were sold to the military. **NOTE:** Add $100 for nickel with pearl grips.

Standard Civilian Model

NIB	Exc.	V.G.	Good	Fair	Poor
1600	1300	1000	700	500	350

Military Model

Serial prefix M, marked "U.S. Property" on frame, blue finish. **NOTE:** Add 50 percent for General Officer's pistol.

NIB	Exc.	V.G.	Good	Fair	Poor
—	4000	3000	2000	800	400

Model 1908 Hammerless .25 Vest Pocket Model

Smallest automatic Colt made. Chambered for .25 ACP cartridge. Has 2" barrel and is 4.5" long overall. Weight a mere 13 oz. A true pocket pistol. Detachable magazine holds 6-shots. Offered in blue or nickel-plate, with grips of checkered hard rubber and checkered walnut on later versions. Has a grip safety, slide lock and magazine disconnect safety. Another Browning design. Fabrique Nationale manufactured this pistol in Belgium before Colt picked up the rights to make it in the U.S. A commercial success by Colt's standards, with approximately 409,000 manufactured between 1908 and 1941. **NOTE:** Add 30 percent for nickel finish; 50 percent for factory pearl grips.

Courtesy Orvel Reichert

Civilian Model

NIB	Exc.	V.G.	Good	Fair	Poor
—	750	500	300	200	100

Military Model

"U.S. Property" marked on right frame. Very rare.

NIB	Exc.	V.G.	Good	Fair	Poor
—	3500	2500	1350	450	300

Model 1905 .45 Automatic Pistol

Spanish American War and experiences with the Moros in Philippine campaign, taught a lesson about stopping power or lack of it. United States Army was convinced they needed a more powerful handgun cartridge. This led Colt to the development of a .45-caliber cartridge suitable for the semi-automatic pistol. Model 1905 and .45 rimless round were the result. In actuality, this cartridge was not nearly powerful enough to satisfy the need, but it led to the development of .45 ACP. Colt believed this pistol/cartridge combination would be a success and was geared up for mass production. Army actually bought only 200 of them and total production was approximately 6,300 from 1905 to 1911. Has a 5" barrel and detachable 7-shot magazine. Blued, with case-colored hammer. Grips are checkered walnut. Hammer was rounded on first 3,600 pistols and changed to a spur hammer on later models. Right side of slide stamped "Automatic Colt / Caliber 45 Rimless Smokeless". Not a commercial success for Colt—possibly because it has no safety, whatsoever, except for the floating inertia firing pin. The 200 military models have grip safeties only. A small number (believed to be less than 500) were grooved to accept a shoulder stock. Stocks were made of leather and steel, and double as a holster. These pistols have been classified "Curios and Relics" under the provisions of the Gun Control Act of 1968.

Civilian Model

NIB	Exc.	V.G.	Good	Fair	Poor
—	7000	5000	3000	1500	800

Military Model, Serial #1-201

NIB	Exc.	V.G.	Good	Fair	Poor
—	15000	12000	8000	4000	1000

COLT 1911/1911A1

Soon after the first Military 1911 pistol was shipped, in Jan. 1912, first Commercial equivalent pistol called "GOVERNMENT MODEL" was also shipped. Strictly speaking, "GOVERNMENT MODEL" is not a "MODEL OF 1911" and "MODEL OF 1911" is not a "GOVERNMENT MODEL". Yet between these two models, most parts will interchange. Main differences are finish and markings.

Colt Government (Commercial) models all had VP (Verified Proof) mark on trigger guard bow. Colt-made 1911 Military pistols did not have verified proof mark, unless pistol was returned to Colt for repair where they replaced barrel and re-proofed (fired) the pistol. Colt-made 1911A1 pistols (with exception of 1924 Transition contract) all had the verified proof mark.

Collectors of Commercial Government Model pistols, usually have a different perspective regarding pistols that they wish to collect than do collectors of Military "MODEL OF 1911". Since military pistols have been presumed to have gone through a war, most examples that one sees are usually in considerably worse condition than contemporary commercial pistols. Indeed, the commercial collector usually expects to see typical examples that are in far better condition than typical military examples. Many commercial collectors purchase only "Near New" or "New in Box" examples.

Prices listed for commercial Government Models have the same condition categories as do military pistols, but NIB, Exc. and V.G. are the only ones that have much collector interest, as Good, Fair and Poor categories are often relegated as "Shooters without any significant collector interest". Reality is, pistols in these three later categories are often very difficult to sell, except at a shooter price, despite the numbers quoted in this guide. Commercial collectors are often as fixated about originality as with condition, to the point that a whole cottage industry has grown up that specializes in creating reproduction boxes that are represented as ORIGINAL boxes.

Yet, the beginning collector has few tools to determine if pistol is original or has original finish. Black and white photos in books are of little use in showing what original finish looks like. Only by looking at original pistols can one's eyes become calibrated as to what original finish looks like.

Until then, the beginner collector will be at the mercy of fakers and counterfeiters. Buy the best books and read them. Look at as many pistols as you can manage. — Karl Karash

Early Colt 1911 "Commercial Government Model"

Serial numbers through about C4500. High polish on all parts and fire-blue finish on trigger, slide stop, thumb safety, hammer pins, ejector and stock screws. Pistols in latter part of serial range did not have fire-blued stock screws. Pistols through about serial C350 had the dimpled magazine catch. Main spring housing pin was rounded on both ends in pistols through about serial C2000. Keyhole (punch and sawcut) magazines were shipped on pistols through serial C3500. **NOTE:** Add 30 percent for three-digit serial number; 60 percent for two-digit serial number; 50- to 100 percent for finish 99-100 percent.

Courtesy Karl Karash

NIB	Exc.	V.G.	Good	Fair	Poor
—	15000	10000	7500	3500	2000

Standard Colt "1911 Commercial Model" with Un-numbered Slide

From about serial #C4500 to about serial #C127300 with un-numbered slide. No fire-blue. Polished finished but not mirror finish. Loop magazine until about C90000. **NOTE:** Add 20- to 50 percent for finish 99-100 percent.

NIB	Exc.	V.G.	Good	Fair	Poor
8000	5000	2500	1500	1100	850

Standard Colt 1911 Commercial "Government Model" with Numbered Slide

Colt started to number the slide, with receiver's serial number at about #C127300. This practice continued for commercial production through WWII. All 1911 commercial pistols after about serial C127300 to about C136000 (when 1911A1 production changes were phased in). First numbered slide pistols (in the C127xxx range) had the slide numbered on the bottom of slide rail. This only lasted a short time and numbering was moved to behind firing pin stop plate by serial C128000. Deduct 20 percent for a mismatched slide number. Changes between 1911 Commercial Government Model and 1911A1 Commercial Government were phased in during this period. A number of variations within these serial number ranges are of specific interest and are listed separately below. **NOTE:** Add 20- to 50 percent for finish 99-100 percent.

NIB	Exc.	V.G.	Good	Fair	Poor
8500	5300	2700	1600	1200	950

FOREIGN CONTRACTS

Colt 1911 Commercial "Government Model" Argentine Contracts

Multiple contracts were awarded by Argentina between 1914 and 1948 to supply .45-caliber pistols to their armed forces, police and government agencies. These contracts totaled 21,616 pistols, of which 2,151 were 1911 model. Pistols differ from Standard Government Model in that they are usually marked with an Argentine crest as well as normal Colt commercial markings including C prefix serial number. Colt also supplied Argentina 1911A1 model "modelo 1927" that had its own serial number range of #1 to #10000 with no C prefix. Most of these pistols are well used, reblued, had mixed parts and have import markings. Prices listed are for completely original pistols. Reblue=Fair/Poor. **NOTE:** Add 20- to 100 percent for finish 99-100 percent.

NIB	Exc.	V.G.	Good	Fair	Poor
2400	1500	1100	750	500	400

Colt 1911 Commercial "Government Model" Russian Order

This variation chambered for .45 ACP and has Russian version of "Anglo Zakazivat" stamped on frame. About 51,000 of these blued pistols manufactured in 1915-1916. Found between serial numbers C21000 and C89000. Rarely encountered today, but a few have recently been imported and advertised. One should be extremely cautious and verify authenticity if contemplating a purchase, as fakes have been noted. Despite market uncertainties, demand for original pistols is high. (Reblue=Fair/Poor)

NIB	Exc.	V.G.	Good	Fair	Poor
—	15000	11000	7500	5000	2000

Colt 1911 Commercial "Government Model" Canadian Contract

This group of 5,099 pistols, serial numbered between about C3077 and C13500, were purchased by the Canadian Government in 1914. Most observed pistols appear to be unmarked and can be identified only by a Colt factory letter. Others have been observed with Canadian Broad Arrow property mark, as well as unit markings. Often these unit markings are applied in a very rudimentary manner that detracts considerably from the appearance. (Any applied markings done crudely, deduct 10-50 percent.) Due to the nature of these markings, a Colt factory letter is probably a requirement to authenticate these pistols. Refinish=Fair/Poor. **NOTE:** Add 20- to 50 percent for finish. 99-100 percent.

NIB	Exc.	V.G.	Good	Fair	Poor
—	5100	3500	2200	1750	1200

Colt 1911 Commercial "Government Model" British Contract

Chambered for British .455 cartridge. Marked on right side of slide British "Broad Arrow" proofmark will often be found. Pistols were made in 1915-1919 and follow same numeric serial number sequence as normal Government models, except "C" prefix was replaced with a "W." They are commercial series pistols. Magazine well of these .455 pistols is slightly larger than a standard Cal. .45 Auto pistol and will accept a Cal. .45 magazine, but a standard Cal. .45 will not accept a Cal. .455 magazine. All pistols in W19001 to W19200 range, as well as some in W29000 range, are believed to be JJ marked above left trigger guard bow. Add 25 percent for JJ marked. Some pistols in C101000 to about C109000 range have RAF marks as well as a welded ring in the lanyard loop. Most RAF pistols have been refinished and many have been converted to .45-cal. by changing barrels. Refinish=Fair/Poor. **NOTE:** Add 20- to 50 percent for finish 99-100 percent; 25 percent for RAF. Deduct 35 percent for wrong barrel.

Colt 1911 Versus 1911A1 Distinguishing Features
Photos courtesy of Karl Karash

Arched mainspring 1911A1   Flat mainspring 1911

Long grip safety 1911A1   Short grip safety 1911

Finger cutout 1911A1   No finger cutout 1911

NIB	Exc.	V.G.	Good	Fair	Poor
—	7000	5000	3500	2300	1750

Norwegian Kongsberg Vapenfabrikk Pistol Model 1912 (Extremely Rare)

Serial number 1-96. **NOTE:** Pistols are so rare that almost any price would not be out of order for an original pistol. Add 20- to 30 percent for finish 99-100 percent.

NIB	Exc.	V.G.	Good	Fair	Poor
—	10000	6500	4400	3200	2500

Norwegian Kongsberg Vapenfabrikk Pistol Model 1914

Serial number 97-32854. **NOTE:** Add 20- to 50 percent for finish 99-100 percent.

NIB	Exc.	V.G.	Good	Fair	Poor
—	2000	1500	1200	1000	800

Norwegian Kongsberg Vapenfabrikk Model 1914 (Copy)

Serial number 29615 to 30535. Waffenamt marked on slide and barrel. CAUTION: Fakes have been reported. Any Waffenamt-marked pistol outside this serial range is probably counterfeit. **NOTE:** Add 20- 30 percent for finish 99-100 percent.

NIB	Exc.	V.G.	Good	Fair	Poor
—	9000	6000	4000	2800	1900

MODEL 1911 U.S. MILITARY SERIES

For a complete look at the many variations of Colt Model 1911 that were made for U.S. Military forces, *see Standard Catalog of Military Firearms, 8th Edition*. This publication covers history, technical data, photos and values of the world's military arms and accessories. Following is a brief summary of estimated values for Model 1911 pistols manufactured for U.S. forces between 1912 and 1919.

Colt 1912

Serial number range 1-17250.

NIB	Exc.	V.G.	Good	Fair	Poor
—	12500	8500	5500	3000	1500

Colt 1913-1915

Serial number ranges 17251-72570, 83856-102596, 107597-113496, 120567-125566, 133187-137400.

NIB	Exc.	V.G.	Good	Fair	Poor
—	7500	6000	4000	2000	1400

Colt 1917-1918

Serial number range 137401-594000.

NIB	Exc.	V.G.	Good	Fair	Poor
—	4500	3000	2000	1000	500

Springfield Armory 1914-1916

Serial number ranges 72751-83855, 102597-107596, 113497-120566, 125567-133186.

NIB	Exc.	V.G.	Good	Fair	Poor
—	9000	6000	4500	2750	1600

Remington-UMC 1918-1919

Serial number range 1-21676.

NIB	Exc.	V.G.	Good	Fair	Poor
—	7500	4750	3500	2000	1300

North American Arms 1918

Less than 100 manufactured in Canada, but none delivered to U.S. government. One of the most rare 1911 models, so beware of fakes. Get an expert appraisal before buying or selling.

NIB	Exc.	V.G.	Good	Fair	Poor
—	110000	55000	40000	25000	10000

PRE AND POST WWII COLT "1911A1 COMMERCIAL GOVERNMENT MODEL"

"Commercial Government Models" made by Colt between the wars may be the best pistols Colt ever produced. Civilian configurations of 1911 and 1911A1 were known as "Government Models". Identical to military models, with exception of fit, finish and markings. However, commercial production of 1911A1 pistols stopped when WWII started. Therefore, production changes of 1911A1 pistols were not carried over to contemporary commercial pistols, because there was no contemporary commercial production. "C" serial number prefix designated commercial series until 1950, when it was changed to a "C" suffix. "Government Model" pistols were polished and blued until about serial number C230,000, when top, bottom and rear were matte finished. Words "Government Model" as well as "Verified Proof" mark were stamped on all but about the first 500 pistols, when post-war production commenced at C220,000. Some of these first 500 also lacked verified proof mark. First post-war pistols used some left-over military parts such as triggers and stocks. Pre-war pistols all had checkered walnut grips. Post-war pistols generally had plastic grips until "midrange" serial when wood grips returned. There were a number of different commercial models manufactured. They are individually listed.

Manufactured by Colt from 1925-1942 from about serial number C136000 to about serial number C215000. Only a few pistols from serial #C202000 to C215000 were shipped domestically, as most were shipped to Brazil or renumbered into military models. See Model 1911A1 commercial to military conversions.

Standard Colt "1911A1 Commercial Government Model" Domestic Sales

These pistols have numbered slides. NO foreign markings, NO Swartz safeties or additions. **NOTE:** Add 30- to 60 percent for finish 99-100 percent.

NIB	Exc.	V.G.	Good	Fair	Poor
—	4500	3500	2500	1000	500

Standard Colt "1911A1 Commercial Government Model" Export Sales

Usually with foreign crest or foreign inscription of a county such as Argentina or Brazil. Pistol has a numbered slide. Some variations with foreign markings are more rare than standard domestic pistols. Argentine pistols do not have collector interest that others or "Standard" domestic pistols have, because the market has been flooded with Argentine imports in recent years.

Argentine Colt-made 1911A1 model pistols without Swartz safeties

NOTE: Add 20- to 30 percent for finish 99-100 percent.

NIB	Exc.	V.G.	Good	Fair	Poor
—	2000	1450	850	650	550

Brazilian, Mexican, and other South American (except Argentina)

Colt-made "1911A1 Commercial Government Model" pistols. **NOTE:** Add 20- to 100 percent for finish 99-100 percent.

NIB	Exc.	V.G.	Good	Fair	Poor
—	6500	4500	2800	1700	1000

Colt National Match Caliber .45, Pre-WWII, .45 (without Swartz safeties)

A National Match Commercial pistol, was introduced by Colt at the 1930 National Matches at Camp Perry. Production began in 1932. Right side of slide marked "NATIONAL MATCH" and mainspring housing had no lanyard loop. National Match modifications to standard pistol, as described in Colt literature included: Tighter barrel, better sights and a hand polished action. Tighter barrel probably amounted to a tighter fit between barrel bushing and barrel. Hand polishing of action probably produced a greatly improved trigger pull, but overall, barrel slide lockup was probably only superficially improved. Colt also advertised a "Selected Match Grade" barrel. Colt advertising indicated that scores using National Match pistols improved greatly and probably did to a degree, but most of the improvement was probably due to the improved (wider) sights and improved trigger pull. The very first

pistols had fixed sights, but by about SN C177,000 the "Stevens Adjustable Rear Target Sight" was available. Both fixed and adjustable sights were available thereafter throughout production. Total number of National Match pistols, with each type of sight is not known, but one author (Kevin Williams, Collecting Colt's National Match Pistols) estimates that the percentage of adjustable sight equipped National Match pistols may have been only 20 percent. Note that the Colt National Match pistol is not referred to here as a "1911A1", because this pistol lacks the military lanyard loop that is present in all Standard Government Models. Also note that "Colt National Match" Pre-war pistols are also "Government Models" as the receiver was marked as such throughout production. **NOTE:** Add 30- to 60 cercent for finish 99-100 percent.

With Adjustable Sights

NIB	Exc.	V.G.	Good	Fair	Poor
—	12000	7500	4500	2500	900

Fixed Sights

NIB	Exc.	V.G.	Good	Fair	Poor
—	9000	6000	3000	1750	750

Swartz Safeties, Pre-WWII, Firing Pin and Hammer/Sear

The "Swartz Safeties" are a pair of devices that Colt installed in 1911A1 commercial "Government Models" and 1911A1 Commercial National Match pistols in the late 1930s and early 1940s. First device, a firing pin block that was actuated by the grip safety, prevented the firing pin from moving forward unless the grip safety was squeezed. Second, Swartz Safety Device the Hammer/Sear safety prevented a possible unsafe half cock position. Swartz firing pin block safety can be observed by pulling the slide back all the way and looking at the top of the frame. A Swartz-safety-equipped 1911A1 pistol will have a second pin protruding up next to the conventional disconnect pin. A second Swartz safety (the Swartz Sear Safety), is usually built into pistols equipped with the Swartz firing pin block safety. The sear safety can sometimes be detected by the drag marks of the notched sear on the round portion of the hammer that the sear rides on. Pulling the hammer all the way back will expose these drag marks if they are visible. Presence of the drag marks, however, does not ensure that the Swartz-modified sear safety parts are all present. Disassembly may be required to verify the correct parts are all present.

The Swartz Safeties are referred to in Colt Factory letters as the "NSD" (New Safety Device). (From SN C162,000 to C215,000 about 3,000 total National Match pistols were made with and without Swartz safeties.) The number of National Match pistols having the Swartz safeties is unknown. However, only a few pistols below serial C190000 had the safeties installed and of the pistols made after C190000, most were Standard Models shipped to Brazil and Argentina. Brazilian pistols were without the safeties or the cutouts. Argentine pistols were shipped in two batches of 250 pistols each. Both of these Argentine batches appear to have had the safeties installed as a number of them have recently been imported into the U.S.A. Probably much less than half of the total Colt made National Match pistols had the Swartz safeties. Total number of pistols (both Standard Government Model and National Match) shipped with Swartz safeties may be less than 3,000. And, probably much less than half of the total Colt made National Match pistols had the Swartz safeties. Swartz safeties were also installed in late Super .38 and Super Match .38 pistols.

Standard Colt 1911A1 Commercial "GOVERNMENT MODEL" Marked Pistol with Numbered Slide and Swartz Safeties

No foreign markings. Fixed sights only, no additions whatsoever. Rare, seldom seen. **NOTE:** Add 20- 50 percent for finish 99-100 percent.

NIB	Exc.	V.G.	Good	Fair	Poor
—	7500	4500	3000	1500	1000

Colt National Match Caliber Pre-WWII, .45. Pre-WWII (with "Swartz Safeties")

Serial number C186,000-C215,000 probably less than 1,500 pistols. Colt would rework fixed sights equipped pistols on a repair order, with Stevens adjustable sight. Therefore, a Colt letter showing that the pistol was originally shipped with adjustable sights is in order for any adjustable sight-equipped pistol. **NOTE:** Add 30- to 60 percent for finish 99-100 percent.

Stevens Adjustable Sights

NIB	Exc.	V.G.	Good	Fair	Poor
—	15000	11000	7000	4000	2200

Fixed Sights

NIB	Exc.	V.G.	Good	Fair	Poor
—	12000	9000	6000	3750	1500

Standard 1911A1 Pre-WWII, "GOVERNMENT MODEL" Export Sales

With "Swartz Safeties" and usually a foreign crest or foreign inscription mainly from Argentina. Vast majority of Swartz equipped foreign contract pistols were shipped to Argentina, but Argentine pistols do not have the collector interest that others or the plain domestic pistols have, because the market has been flooded with Argentine imports in recent years.

The few Argentine Swartz equipped pistols that remain in original and excellent or better condition, usually sell for less than their "plain Jane" domestic counterparts and for much less than the much rarer Brazilian and Mexican pistols. Perhaps these depressed prices represent a bargain for collectors, with an eye to the future when the supply of these extremely rare pistols dries up. Reblue = Fair/Poor. **NOTE:** Add 20- to 30 percent for finish 99-100 percent.

NIB	Exc.	V.G.	Good	Fair	Poor
—	2000	1500	1200	900	750

Normal Brazilian and Mexican Pistols

These pistols do not have Swartz safeties. Most examples seen are refinished = Fair/Poor. **NOTE:** Add 20- 30 percent for finish 99-100 percent.

NIB	Exc.	V.G.	Good	Fair	Poor
—	7500	5000	3500	2750	1750

Argentine Contract Pistols "Modelo Argentino 1927, Calibre .45"

These pistols delivered to Argentina in 1927. Right side of slide marked with the two-line inscription "Ejercito Argentino Colt Cal .45 Mod. 1927". Also the Argentine National Seal and "Rampant Colt". SN 1-10,000. Verified proof, Assembler's mark and Final inspectors mark under left stock by upper bushing. None had Swartz Safeties. Most of these pistols were reblued. Reblued = Fair/Poor. **NOTE:** Abundance of these and other refinished Argentine pistols has depressed the prices of all original finish Argentine pistols. Add 20- to 50 percent for finish 99-100 percent.

NIB	Exc.	V.G.	Good	Fair	Poor
—	1800	1350	950	700	600

Military to Commercial Conversions

Some 1911 Military pistols that were brought home by GIs, were subsequently returned to the Colt factory by their owners for repair or refinishing. If the repair included a new barrel, the pistol would have been proof fired and a normal Verified proof mark affixed to the trigger guard bow in the normal commercial practice. If the pistol was refinished between about 1920 and 1942, the slide would probably be numbered to the frame again in the normal commercial practice. These pistols are really remanufactured Colt pistols of limited production and should be valued at least that of a contemporary 1911A1 commercial pistol, but usually sell for less. Only pistols marked with identifiable Colt markings should be included in this category. Very seldom seen. Since Colt rework records are lost, reworked and refinished pistols without identifiable Colt applied markings are probably not verifiable as Colt reworks and should be considered refinished pistols of unknown pedigree. **NOTE:** Finish 99-100 percent add 30 percent.

NIB	Exc.	V.G.	Good	Fair	Poor
—	2800	1900	1500	1000	875

Super .38 1929 Model, Pre-WWII

Pistol is identical in outward physical configuration to .45 ACP Colt Commercial. Chambered for .38 Super cartridge. Magazine holds 9 rounds. Right side of slide marked "Colt Super .38 Automatic" in two lines, followed by "Rampant Colt". Last few thousand pre-war Super .38 pistols made, had Swartz Safety parts installed. Some pistols were assembled post-war, with leftover parts. Post-war-assembled pistols did not have Swartz safeties installed but most (possibly all) had the cutouts. In 1945, 400 pistols were purchased by the U.S. Government. These 400 pistols bear the G.H.D. acceptance mark as well as Ordnance crossed cannons. (G.H.D. and Ordnance marked add 30-50 percent. A factory letter is probably necessary here.) Some collectors feel that post-war assembly and post-war chemical tank bluing adds a premium, others feel that it requires a deduction. **NOTE:** Add 33 percent for finish 99-100 percent; 20 percent for Swartz Safeties; 50 percent for nickel finish.

NIB	Exc.	V.G.	Good	Fair	Poor
10000	7000	5000	3000	2000	1000

Super Match .38 1935 Model, Pre-WWII

Only 5,000 of these specially fit and finished target-grade pistols were manufactured. Have fixed sights or Stevens adjustable sights. Top surfaces are matte-finished to reduce glare. Twelve hundred pistols were purchased and sent to Britain in 1939, at the then-costly rate of $50 per unit. Last few thousand pre-war Super .38 pistols made had Swartz safety parts installed, but some pistols were assembled post-war with leftover parts. Post-war-assembled pistols did not have Swartz safeties installed, but most (possibly all) had the cutouts. In 1945, 400 pistols were purchased by the U.S. Government. These 400 pistols bear the G.H.D. acceptance mark as well as Ordnance crossed cannons. G.H.D. and Ordnance marked add 30-50 percent. A factory letter is probably necessary here. Swartz Safeties add 20 percent. Some collectors feel that post-war assembly and post-war chemical tank bluing adds a premium, others feel that it requires a deduction. **NOTE:** Add 20- 75 percent for both models for finish 99-100 percent.

Adjustable Sights

NIB	Exc.	V.G.	Good	Fair	Poor
—	11500	8000	5000	3000	2000

Fixed Sights

NIB	Exc.	V.G.	Good	Fair	Poor
—	10000	6500	4000	2000	1250

MODEL 1911A1 U.S. MILITARY SERIES

A complete look at the many variations of Colt Model 1911A1 that were made for U.S. Military forces, *see Standard Catalog of Military Firearms, 8th Edition*. This publication covers history, technical data, photos and values of the world's military arms and accessories. Following is a summary of estimated values for Model 1911A1 pistols manufactured for U.S. forces between 1924 and end of WWII in 1945.

Colt

NOTE: Add 100- to 400 percent for Army or Navy variations, with blue finish made between 1937 and 1941. Serial number range 710000-734xxx.

NIB	Exc.	V.G.	Good	Fair	Poor
—	3500	3200	2500	1000	500

Ithaca

NIB	Exc.	V.G.	Good	Fair	Poor
—	2500	1800	1200	900	600

Remington Rand

NIB	Exc.	V.G.	Good	Fair	Poor
—	2250	1700	1200	900	600

Union Switch & Signal

NIB	Exc.	V.G.	Good	Fair	Poor
—	7000	4800	3800	3000	2000

Singer Mfg. Co.

NOTE: Highly collectible model and fakes are known to exist. 500 of these guns were made, with serial numbers from S800001 to S800500. An appraisal from a recognized Colt expert is strongly suggested, whether buying or selling. Deduct 50 percent for unserialed or presentation pistols.

NIB	Exc.	V.G.	Good	Fair	Poor
—	100000	70000	50000	29000	15000

COLT 1911A1 POST WWII COMMERCIAL PRODUCED, DOMESTIC SALES, 1946-1969

SN C220,000 to about C220,500

No "GOVERNMENT MODEL" marking. Few have no verified proof. Many parts are leftover military. **NOTE:** Add 20- to 50 percent for finish 99-100 percent.

NIB	Exc.	V.G.	Good	Fair	Poor
8500	6000	4000	2500	1500	1000

SN C220,500 to about C249,000 verified proof and "GOVERNMENT MODEL" marking

Many parts are leftover military in first few thousand pistols. No foreign markings. **NOTE:** Add 20- to 30 percent for finish 99-100 percent. Deduct 30 percent for foreign markings.

NIB	Exc.	V.G.	Good	Fair	Poor
4500	3500	2500	1500	1000	750

SN 255,000-C to about 258,000-C Slide Factory Roll Marked "PROPERTY OF THE STATE OF NEW YORK", verified proof, and "GOVERNMENT MODEL" marking (250 pistols total)

Few leftover military parts are still used. Few pairs of pistols remain as consecutive pairs. **NOTE:** Add 20- to 50 percent for finish 99-100 percent; 10 percent for consecutive pairs.

Courtesy Karl Karash

NIB	Exc.	V.G.	Good	Fair	Poor
—	4000	2500	1600	1100	800

SN 249,500-C to about 335,000-C, verified proof and "GOVERNMENT MODEL" marking

No foreign markings. **NOTE:** Add 20- to 30 percent for finish 99-100 percent. Deduct 30 percent for foreign markings.

NIB	Exc.	V.G.	Good	Fair	Poor
—	1600	1100	750	500	400

SN 334,500-C to about 336,169-C, BB (Barrel Bushing) marked

About 1000 pistols. Verified proof and "GOVERNMENT MODEL" marking. **NOTE:** Add 20- to 50 percent for finish 99-100 percent.

NIB	Exc.	V.G.	Good	Fair	Poor
3300	2200	1750	1350	1000	750

ACE and SERVICE MODEL ACE

Ace Model .22 Pistol

Starting on June 21, 1913, U.S. Military along with "Springfield Armory" and "Colt Patented Firearms Manufacturing Co." attempted to develop a .22-cal. rimfire pistol that could be used for training purposes. By 1927, the military became convinced that a pistol identical to standard "Service Pistol", but in .22-cal. rimfire was impractical and dropped the idea. In 1930 Colt purchased advertising that, in effect, requested the shooting public to let the company know if they would be interested in a .22 rimfire pistol built similar to "Government Model". The response must have been positive, because in 1931 Colt Ace appeared on the market. Ace uses a frame similar to the frame of "Government Model", with a highly modified slide and heavy barrel. Chambered for .22 LR cartridge only. Size is the same as larger-caliber version and weight is 36 oz. Operation is straight blowback. Ace has a 10-round detachable magazine and features "Improved Ace Adjustable Target Sight". Markings on left side of slide are the same as on "Government Model"; right side reads "Colt Ace 22 Long Rifle". The Army purchased a few pistols (totaling 206) through 1936. The Army concluded that the function of Ace was less than perfect, as they concluded the .22 rimfire lacked the power to consistently and reliably operate the slide. Approximately 11,000 Ace pistols were manufactured and in 1941 they were discontinued. Many owners today find that although ACE is somewhat selective to ammunition, with full power loads it is a highly reliable pistol that does not require the constant cleaning needed by the "Service Model Ace". **NOTE:** Add 33 percent for finish 99-100 percent.

NIB	Exc.	V.G.	Good	Fair	Poor
7000	4500	3000	1800	950	700

Pre-1945 Service Model Ace .22 R. F. Pistol

In 1937, Colt introduced this improved version of the Ace Pistol. It utilizes a floating chamber, invented by David "Carbine" Williams the firearm's designer who invented the "Short Stroke Gas Piston", that is the basis of the MI carbine, while serving time on a Southern chain gang. Colt advertised that this pistol, with its floating chamber would give the Service Model Ace the reliability and "feel" of a .45 Auto. Today, owners of Service Model ACE pistols find they require regular maintenance and cleaning in order to keep the close-fitting floating chamber from binding. Furthermore, fouling appears to be much worse with some brands and types of ammunition. Most owners feel that although the perceived recoil of Service Model ACE is noticeably greater than that of ACE, it falls far short of a .45 Auto's recoil. Serial number is prefixed by letters "SM". External configuration is the same as Ace. Slide is marked "Colt Service Model Ace .22 Long Rifle". Most were sold to the Army and some on a commercial basis. There were a total of 13,803 manufactured before production ceased in 1945. **NOTE:** Add 20- to 30 percent for both models for finish 99-100 percent; 35 percent for "US Property" marking on blued pistols.

Blued pistols (before about SN SM 3840)

NIB	Exc.	V.G.	Good	Fair	Poor
—	11000	7500	4000	1500	1000

Parkerized pistols (after about SN SM 3840)

NIB	Exc.	V.G.	Good	Fair	Poor
—	5000	3000	1800	950	700

Service Model Ace-Post-War

Introduced in 1978. Similar to pre-war model. Production ceased in 1982. **NOTE:** Add 20- to 30 percent for finish 99-100 percent.

NIB	Exc.	V.G.	Good	Fair	Poor
—	1400	1050	950	700	600

Conversion Units .22-.45, .45-.22

In 1938, Colt released a .22-caliber conversion unit. With this kit, one who already owned a "Government Model" could simply switch the top half and fire inexpensive .22 rimfire ammunition. Unit consists of a slide marked "Service Model Ace" barrel, with floating chamber, ejector, slide lock, bushing, recoil spring, 10-shot magazine and box. Conversion Units feature the Stevens adjustable rear sight. Later that same year a kit to convert Service Model Ace to .45 ACP was offered. In 1942 production of these units ceased. The .22 kit was reintroduced in 1947; .45 kit was not brought back. Be alert, as sometimes a conversion unit is found on a Service Model ACE receiver and a Service model Ace upper is sold as a "Conversion Unit". Conversion Units are ALWAYS marked "Conversion Unit". "Service Model ACE" pistols lack the "Conversion Unit" marking. **NOTE:**

Finish 99-100 percent add 20-30 percent. Deduct 20 percent if box is missing.

Pre-war and Post-war "U" numbered Service Model Ace Conversion Unit, .22-.45 (to convert .45 cal. to .22 cal.)

Pre-war conversion units were serial numbered U1-U2000.

Courtesy Karl Karash

NIB	Exc.	V.G.	Good	Fair	Poor
2000	1500	1000	550	500	450

Post-war Conversion Units

These were serial numbered U2001-U2670.

NIB	Exc.	V.G.	Good	Fair	Poor
1200	800	550	500	450	425

Pre-war Service Model Ace (Re-) Conversion Unit, .45-22

To convert SMA .22 Cal. to .45 Cal. SN 1-SN 112. Watch out for fakes.

NIB	Exc.	V.G.	Good	Fair	Poor
5000	3500	2500	1500	750	550

Post-war .22 Conversion Unit Unnumbered

30 percent premium for Stevens adjustable sights, 1946 only.

NIB	Exc.	V.G.	Good	Fair	Poor
600	400	350	250	225	175

Military National Match .45 Pistols

Rebuilt from service pistols at Springfield Armory, between 1955 and about 1967 and Rock Island in 1968. Pistols were built and rebuilt each year, with a portion being sold to competitors by the NRA. Each year improvements were added to the rebuild program. Four articles in "National Rifleman" document these pistols well: August 1959, April 1963, June 1966 and July 1966. Many parts for these pistols have been available and many "Look Alike" pistols have been built by basement armorers. Pistols generally came with a numbered box and shipping papers. Prices listed are for pistols with numbered box or papers. Less box and papers deduct 30 percent. When well-worn, these pistols will offer little over a standard pistol. Early pistols are much less commonly seen, but seem to be less sought after since they look largely like normal issue pistols. **NOTE:** Add 20- to 30 percent for finish 99-100 percent.

Paul Goodwin photo

NIB	Exc.	V.G.	Good	Fair	Poor
2500	2000	1300	1100	700	475

Military National Match Pistols (Drake Slide)

In 1964, Springfield Armory used some of these specially machined and hardened slides to build the Military National Match pistols that year. This year's pistol are perhaps the most identifiable NM pistol due to the unique slide marking. However, Drake was the only supplier of slides that year. Colt supplied slides in the following year (1965). **NOTE:** Add 20- to 30 percent for finish 99-100 percent.

Courtesy Karl Karash

NIB	Exc.	V.G.	Good	Fair	Poor
2700	2100	1300	1100	700	485

Gold Cup National Match (pre-Series 70)

Chambered for .45 ACP. Features flat mainspring housing of 1911. Has a match-grade barrel and bushing. Parts were hand fitted and slide has

an enlarged ejection port. Trigger is the long version, with an adjustable trigger stop and sights are adjustable target type. Finish blued, with checkered walnut grips and gold medallions. Slide marked "Gold Cup National Match". Serial number is prefixed by letters "NM". Pistol manufactured from 1957 to 1970. **NOTE:** Add 20- to 30 percent for finish 99-100 percent.

NIB	Exc.	V.G.	Good	Fair	Poor
1750	1400	1000	700	500	400

Gold Cup MKIII National Match

Pistol is identical to Gold Cup .45, except chambered for .38 Mid-Range Wad Cutter round. Manufactured from 1961 until 1974. **NOTE:** Add 20- to 30 percent for finish 99-100 percent.

Courtesy John J. Stimpson

NIB	Exc.	V.G.	Good	Fair	Poor
1800	1500	1000	600	450	350

Colt 1911A1 AMU (Army Marksmanship Unit)

NOTE: Deduct 70 percent for Army modified pistols.

NIB	Exc.	V.G.	Good	Fair	Poor
—	2700	2250	1450	900	400

COLT LICENSED AND UNLICENSED FOREIGN-MADE 1911A1 AND VARIATIONS

Argentine D.G.F.M.

Direccion General de Fabricaciones Militares made at the F.M.A.P. (Fabrica Militar de Arms Portatiles [Military Factory of Small Arms]). Licensed copies SN 24,000 to 112,494. Parts are generally interchangeable with Colt-made 1911A1 type pistols. Most pistols were marked "D.G.F.M. - (F.M.A.P.)". Late pistols marked FM within a cartouche on right side of slide. Pistols are found both with and without import markings, often in excellent condition, currently more often in refinished condition and with a seemingly endless variety of slide markings. None of these variations have yet achieved any particular collector status or distinction, unless new in box. In fact, many of these fine pistols have and continue to be used as platforms for the highly customized competition and target pistols that are currently popular. Refinished=Fair/Poor. **NOTE:** Add 10- to 30 percent for finish 99-100 percent-NIB.

Courtesy Karl Karash

NIB	Exc.	V.G.	Good	Fair	Poor
2000	1400	900	675	525	475

Argentine-Made Ballester Molina

Un-licensed Argentine redesigned versions. (Parts are NOT interchangeable with Colt except for barrel and magazine.) These pistols are found both with and without import markings. Pistols without import markings usually have a B prefix number stamped on left rear part of the mainspring housing and are often in excellent to new original condition. Vast majority of currently available pistols are found in excellent but refinished condition. Only pistols with no import markings that are in excellent-to-new original condition have achieved any particular collector status. Most of these pistols that are being sold today are being carried and shot rather than being collected. Refinished = Fair/Poor. **NOTE:** Add 10- to 30 percent for finish 99-100 percent-NIB.

Courtesy Karl Karash

NIB	Exc.	V.G.	Good	Fair	Poor
800	600	375	300	215	190

Brazilian Models 1911A1

Made by "Fabrica de Itajuba" in Itajuba, Brazil. The Imbel Model 973, made by "Industriade Material Belico do Brazil" in Sao Paulo, Brazil. The Itajuba is a true copy of Colt 1911A1 and the Imbel is also believed to be a true copy. However, an Imbel has yet to be examined by the author. Too rarely seen in U.S.A. to establish a meaningful price.

COLT MODEL 1911A1
1970 - CURRENT

Model 1911A1 was manufactured by Colt until 1971, when the Series 70 Government Model superseded it. Modifications in the new model were slightly heavier slide and slotted collet barrel bushing. In 1983, Colt introduced Series 80 models, which had an additional passive firing pin safety lock. Half-cock notch was also redesigned. Beginning of 1992 another change was made to Model 1911A1 in the form of an enhanced pistol. Included were Government models, Commander, Officer's, Gold Cup and Combat Elite. These modifications are the result of Colt's desire to meet the shooters demand for a more "customized" pistol. Colt chose some of the most popular modifications to perform on their new enhanced models. They include beavertail safety grip, slotted Commander-style hammer, relief cut under the trigger guard, beveled magazine well, slightly longer trigger, flat top rib and angled slide serrations. Model 1911A1 may be the most modified handgun in the world.

MKIV Series 70 Government Model

Model is essentially a newer version of 1911A1. Has prefix "70G" from 1970-1976, "G70" from 1976-1980 and "70B" from 1980-1983, when production ceased. Offered in blue or nickel plate. Checkered walnut grips, with Colt medallion. Chambered for .45 ACP, .38 Super, 9mm and 9mm Steyr (foreign export only). **NOTE:** Add 35 percent for bright nickel finish; 10 percent for satin nickel; 10 percent for .38 Super, 9mm Parabellum or 9mm Steyr.

NIB	Exc.	V.G.	Good	Fair	Poor
1500	1000	800	600	500	400

MKIV Series 70 Gold Cup National Match

Newer version of 1957 National Match. Features a slightly heavier slide and Colt Elliason sights. Chambering is .45 ACP only. Accurizer barrel and bushing was introduced on this model. Manufactured from 1970-1983.

NIB	Exc.	V.G.	Good	Fair	Poor
2200	1750	1500	1100	750	500

Series 70 Gunsite Pistol

Features 5" barrel, thin rosewood grips, Gold Cup serrations, Heinie front sight and Novak rear sight, plus several other special features. Available in blue or stainless steel. Introduced in 2004.

NIB	Exc.	V.G.	Good	Fair	Poor
1200	1050	825	600	400	200

Series 70 Gunsite Pistol Commander

As above, with 4.25" barrel.

NIB	Exc.	V.G.	Good	Fair	Poor
1200	1050	825	600	400	200

COLT ENHANCED GOVERNMENT MODELS

In 1992, Colt introduced a new set of features for its Model 1911A1 series pistols. New features include: a flattop slide, angled rear slide serrations, scalloped ejection port, combat style hammer, beavertail grip safety, relief cut-under trigger guard and long trigger. Models that are affected by this new upgrade are: Delta Elite, Combat Elite, Government Model, Combat Commander, Lightweight Commander, Officer's ACP, Officer's ACP Lightweight.

COMMANDER SERIES

A shortened version of Government model. Has a 4.25" barrel, lightweight alloy frame and rounded spur hammer. Total weight of the Commander is 27.5 oz. Serial number has suffix "LW". Chambered for .45 ACP, 9mm, .38 Super and some for 7.65 Parabellum for export only. Introduced in 1949.

Pre-70 Series (1949-1969)

NOTE: Deduct 20 percent for 9mm.

NIB	Exc.	V.G.	Good	Fair	Poor
1500	1250	1000	800	600	400

Series 70 (1970-1983)

NIB	Exc.	V.G.	Good	Fair	Poor
1200	1000	850	700	600	300

Series 80 (1983-1996)

NIB	Exc.	V.G.	Good	Fair	Poor
900	750	600	500	400	300

Combat Commander

Combat Commander was produced in response to complaints from some quarters about the excessive recoil and rapid wear of the alloy-framed Commander. This model is simply a Commander, with a steel frame. Combat Commander weight 32 oz. and offered in blue or satin nickel, with walnut grips. No longer in production. **NOTE:** Add 40 percent for Series 70 model

NIB	Exc.	V.G.	Good	Fair	Poor
850	550	475	375	300	200

MK IV Series 80 Government Model

Introduced in 1983. It is, for all purposes, externally the same as Series 70. Basic difference is the addition of the new firing pin safety on this model. No longer in production.

Blued

NIB	Exc.	V.G.	Good	Fair	Poor
850	725	600	500	400	250

Nickel Plated

NIB	Exc.	V.G.	Good	Fair	Poor
1000	800	650	500	400	250

Stainless Steel

NIB	Exc.	V.G.	Good	Fair	Poor
950	800	650	500	400	250

Polished Stainless Steel

NIB	Exc.	V.G.	Good	Fair	Poor
1000	800	700	500	400	250

Colt 1991A1

The 1991 Series is a direct descendant of original Model 1911. The long trigger, flat mainspring housing and recoil spring system are like the original design. Upgrades include high profile white dot sights and lowered ejection port. Based on Series 80 MKIV Colt design, it was introduced in 1992. Early models were offered in 9mm. Standard model in .45 ACP, with a 7+1 capacity. A .38 Super version is available. See separate listing.

NIB	Exc.	V.G.	Good	Fair	Poor
750	675	550	350	150	125

M1991A1 Commander

Chambered for .45 ACP, this model has all the same features as standard M1991A1, with a slightly shorter 4.25" barrel. Reintroduced in 2004. **NOTE:** In 1997, Colt offered this model in stainless steel, with fixed white dot sights. Add $100 to NIB price.

NIB	Exc.	V.G.	Good	Fair	Poor
800	550	400	300	225	125

M1991A1 Compact

Chambered for .45 ACP, this model has a 3.25" barrel. It is 1.5" shorter than standard M1991A1 model and .375" shorter in height. Magazine holds 6 rounds. No longer in production. **NOTE:** In 1997, Colt offered this model in stainless steel, with fixed white dot sights. Add $50 to NIB price.

NIB	Exc.	V.G.	Good	Fair	Poor
850	600	425	300	150	125

M1991A1 .38 Super

Has the same features as .45 ACP M1991A1 Government Model, except chambered for .38 Super cartridge. Magazine capacity is 9 + 1. Available only with bright stainless steel finish.

NIB	Exc.	V.G.	Good	Fair	Poor
900	800	650	500	375	300

MK IV Series 80 Gold Cup National Match

Externally same as Series 70 Gold Cup, with new firing pin safety.

Blued

NIB	Exc.	V.G.	Good	Fair	Poor
1200	900	675	500	350	250

Stainless Steel

NIB	Exc.	V.G.	Good	Fair	Poor
1200	900	675	500	350	250

Polished Stainless Steel

NIB	Exc.	V.G.	Good	Fair	Poor
1200	900	675	500	350	250

Officer's ACP

Shortened version of Government Model. Barrel 3.5"; weight 37 oz. Chambered for .45 ACP only, with checkered walnut grips. Officer's ACP introduced in 1985. No longer in production.

Blued

NIB	Exc.	V.G.	Good	Fair	Poor
1000	700	525	325	250	200

Matte Blued

NIB	Exc.	V.G.	Good	Fair	Poor
1000	700	525	325	250	200

Satin Nickel

Discontinued 1985.

NIB	Exc.	V.G.	Good	Fair	Poor
1050	750	575	375	295	200

Stainless Steel

NIB	Exc.	V.G.	Good	Fair	Poor
1100	800	625	425	345	200

Lightweight Officer's ACP

An alloy-framed version. Weight 24 oz. Introduced in 1986. No longer in production.

NIB	Exc.	V.G.	Good	Fair	Poor
1000	700	525	325	250	200

Concealed Carry Officer's Model

Features a lightweight aluminum frame, with stainless steel Commander slide. Barrel length 4.25". Chambered for .45 ACP cartridge. Fitted with lightweight trigger, combat style hammer and Hogue grips. Weight about 34 oz. Introduced in 1998. No longer in production.

NIB	Exc.	V.G.	Good	Fair	Poor
1000	700	525	325	250	200

Delta Gold Cup

Introduced in 1992. Chambered for 10mm. Features 5" barrel, stainless steel finish, adjustable Accro sights, special trigger and black rubber wrap-around grips. Features all of the new "Enhanced" model features. No longer in production.

NIB	Exc.	V.G.	Good	Fair	Poor
1050	875	700	600	400	200

Delta Elite

Chambered for 10mm Norma cartridge. Offered in blue or stainless steel. Grips are black neoprene, with the Delta medallion. Features a high-profile three-dot combat sight system. Delta Elite introduced in 1987. Discontinued in 1996 and reintroduced in 2008. **NOTE:** Deduct 20 percent for current production model.

Blued

NIB	Exc.	V.G.	Good	Fair	Poor
1200	925	650	425	300	250

Stainless Steel

NIB	Exc.	V.G.	Good	Fair	Poor
1250	950	675	400	300	250

Polished Stainless Steel

NIB	Exc.	V.G.	Good	Fair	Poor
1250	950	675	400	300	250

Combat Elite

Specialized Government model. Has a 5" barrel and adjustable Accro sights. Chambered either in .45 ACP or .38 Super. Weight 38 oz. Has an 8-round magazine for .45 ACP; 9-round magazine for .38 Super. Finish either blue or matte stainless steel. No longer in production. (Colt issued a recall notice for the safety on this model in June 2009. Pistols with serial numbers from CG10000E to CG11293E should be sent to the factory for parts replacement.)

NIB	Exc.	V.G.	Good	Fair	Poor
1050	875	700	600	400	200

Combat Target Model

Introduced in 1996, this 5" barrel 1911 model features a fitted barrel, Gold Cup-style trigger, tuned action, flat top slide, relieved ejection port, skeletonized hammer, wide grip safety, high cut trigger guard, beveled magazine well, and adjustable sights. Weight 39 oz. Offered in both blue and stainless steel. Chambered for the new 9x23 cartridge as well as .45 ACP and .38 Super. No longer in production. In 1997, Colt expanded Target Model to include a number of different variations. They are listed. **NOTE:** Add $50 for stainless steel version.

NIB	Exc.	V.G.	Good	Fair	Poor
1050	875	700	600	400	200

Combat Target Commander

Barrel length 4.25". Chambered for .45 ACP. Stainless steel finish. Weight 36 oz. Has all other Combat Target features. No longer in production.

NIB	Exc.	V.G.	Good	Fair	Poor
1050	875	700	600	400	200

Combat Target Officer's ACP

Fitted with a 3.5" barrel and chambered for .45 ACP. Stainless steel finish. Weight about 34 oz. Has all other Combat Target features. No longer in production.

NIB	Exc.	V.G.	Good	Fair	Poor
1050	875	700	600	400	200

Special Combat Government

Pistol features a 5" barrel, double diamond rosewood grips, extended ambidextrous thumb safety. Steel checkered mainspring housing, with extended magazine well. Chambered for .45 ACP or .38 Super cartridges. Adjustable Bomar rear sight. Magazine capacity 8 rounds. Choice of hard chrome or blue/satin nickel finish.

NIB	Exc.	V.G.	Good	Fair	Poor
2000	1700	1500	1200	800	400

Special Combat Government Carry Model

1911-style semi-automatic pistol, chambered in .45 ACP (8+1) or .38 Super (9+1). Semi-custom features include Novak front and rear night sights, skeletonized three-hole trigger, slotted hammer, black/silver synthetic grips, Smith & Alexander upswept beavertail grip, palm swell safety and extended magazine well. Wilson tactical ambidextrous safety. 5" barrel. Available blued, hard chrome, or blue/satin nickel finish depending on chambering.

NIB	Exc.	V.G.	Good	Fair	Poor
1450	1100	900	650	400	300

Close Quarters Battle (CQB) Pistol

From Colt Custom Shop, this .45 ACP model was designed for and is primarily manufactured for U.S. Marine Corps. Features a Desert Tan Cerakoted receiver and slide, 5" National Match barrel with accessory rail and a flat, serrated mainspring housing with extended grip safety and lanyard loop. Grips are G-10 composite and sights are Novak 3-Dot Night Sights.

NIB	Exc.	V.G.	Good	Fair	Poor
1850	1700	1500	1200	800	400

XSE SERIES MODEL O PISTOLS

Introduced in 1999, these models are an enhanced version of Colt 1911. Features front slide serrations, checkered double diamond rosewood grips, adjustable McCormick trigger, three-dot dovetail rear sights, ambidextrous safety, enhanced tolerances, aluminum frame and stainless steel slide. Chambered for .45 ACP cartridge.

XSE Model O Government (01070XS)

Fitted with 5" barrel and 8-round magazine.

NIB	Exc.	V.G.	Good	Fair	Poor
950	800	595	475	350	200

XSE Model O Concealed Carry Officer's (09850XS)

Fitted with 4.25" barrel and 7-round magazine.

NIB	Exc.	V.G.	Good	Fair	Poor
1000	850	625	475	350	200

XSE Model O Commander (04012XS)

Fitted with 4.25" barrel and 8-round magazine.

NIB	Exc.	V.G.	Good	Fair	Poor
950	800	595	475	350	200

XSE Model O Lightweight Commander (04860XS)

Fitted with 4.25" barrel and 8-round magazine. Weight about 26 oz.

NIB	Exc.	V.G.	Good	Fair	Poor
950	800	595	475	350	200

Colt Defender

Single-action pistol introduced in 1998. Features a lightweight aluminum alloy frame and stainless steel slide. Chambered for .45 ACP or .40 S&W cartridge. Fitted with a 3" barrel. Magazine capacity 7 rounds. Rubber wrap-around grips. Weight about 23 oz.; overall length 6.75".

NIB	Exc.	V.G.	Good	Fair	Poor
850	650	475	300	250	200

Colt Defender Model O (07000D)

Takes the place of Defender. Introduced in 2000. Brushed stainless finish, with 3" barrel. Skeletonized composite trigger, beveled magazine well, extended thumb safety and upswept beavertail, with palm swell. Chambered for .45 ACP only. (Colt issued a recall notice for the guide pad on this model in June 2009. Pistols with serial numbers from DR33036 to DR35948 should be sent to the factory for parts replacement.)

NIB	Exc.	V.G.	Good	Fair	Poor
950	700	525	350	200	145

1911 – WWI Replica

Single-action semi-automatic, chambered in .45 ACP. Faithful external reproduction of WWI-era service pistol, with original-style rollmarks grips, sights, carbonia blue finish, etc. Series 70 lockwork. Made from 2003 - 2009.

NIB	Exc.	V.G.	Good	Fair	Poor
1025	850	625	575	400	200

1911 - WWI 1918 Replica

Based on military model made in 1918. Black finish and WWI rollmarks. Offered in a Presentation Grade, with blue or nickel finish and Colt Custom Shop "A" engraving. Excellent or new condition could add a premium of 100 percent. Made in 2008 and 2009. (Colt issued a recall notice for the safety on this model in June of 2009. Pistols with serial numbers from 1001WWI to 3431WWI should be sent to the factory for parts replacement.)

NIB	Exc.	V.G.	Good	Fair	Poor
1400	1075	850	700	500	400

1911A1 - WWII Replica

Replica of U.S. Military sidearm of WWII. Parkerized finish, WWII-ear rollmarks, lanyard loop, original style composite grips and packaging. Made in .45 ACP only, by Colt Custom Shop from 2001 to 2004. Series 70 lockwork. (Colt issued a recall notice for the safety on this model in June 2009. Pistols with serial numbers from 4597WMK to 5414WMK should be sent to the factory for parts replacement.)

NIB	Exc.	V.G.	Good	Fair	Poor
1075	950	700	575	400	200

Colt New Agent Double Action Only

Similar to New Agent single action, except has double-action-only operating system. Spur-less hammer design, with second-strike capability and no manual safety. Double-diamond slim fit grips, snag free trench sighting system, 7-shot magazine. In .45 ACP only. (Colt issued a recall notice for the safety and guide pad on this model in June of 2009. Pistols with serial numbers from GT01001 to GT04505 should be sent to the factory for parts replacement.)

NIB	Exc.	V.G.	Good	Fair	Poor
850	750	600	500	400	200

Colt Model 1991 DAO

Double-action-only version of Lightweight Government Model. Spur-less hammer design, with second-strike capability and no manual safety. Double-diamond slim fit grips, 7-shot magazine. In .45 ACP only. Introduced in 2011.

NIB	Exc.	V.G.	Good	Fair	Poor
950	800	700	550	400	250

Colt Model 1911 100th Anniversary Series

These two limited edition Model 1911s, were introduced in 2011 to commemorate 100th Anniversary of the legendary pistol. Model 1911ANVIII is based on 1918 configuration, with custom rollmarks on receiver relating to 100th Anniversary. Higher grade version, Model 1911ANVII, features scroll engraving and historic Colt symbols highlighted in 24 karat gold. Comes in a glass-topped walnut display case. Production was limited to 750 units. Higher grade variants limited to 100 units, with A, B, C or D levels of engraving scheduled at prices ranging from $2640 to $6528.

1911ANVII

NIB	Exc.	V.G.	Good	Fair	Poor
2150	1800	1500	—	—	—

1911ANVIII

NIB	Exc.	V.G.	Good	Fair	Poor
1075	900	750	—	—	—

Gunsite Model 1911

Made from 2003 to 2005 to commemorate Gunsite Shooting Academy. Special features include: Heinie front and Novak rear sights, Chip McCormick hammer and sear, checkered rosewood grips and flat serrated mainspring housing. Chambered in .45 ACP, with two 8-shot magazines.

NIB	Exc.	V.G.	Good	Fair	Poor
1350	1050	900	800	650	350

Colt Government Model 1911 .22 LR Series

Licensed reproduction of 1911A1 in .22 LR, manufactured by Umarex USA. Blow-back action, with 12-shot magazine. Other standard 1911 specifications including 5" barrel, thumb and grip safeties, diamond checkered wood grips, blue finish and drift-adjustable rear sight. (Gold Cup has fully adjustable sight.) Weight about 33 oz. Offered in three variants: standard model, Rail Gun and Gold Cup. Introduced in 2011. Prices below are for standard model.

NIB	Exc.	V.G.	Good	Fair	Poor
350	300	275	225	175	100

Colt Concealed Carry

Chopped lightweight 1911-style semi-automatic, chambered in .45 ACP. Weight 25 oz. unloaded; overall length 6.75"; 7+1 capacity; Series 80 lockwork; black anodized aluminum frame, with double-diamond wood grips. Introduced 2007.

NIB	Exc.	V.G.	Good	Fair	Poor
950	700	525	350	200	150

New Agent

7+1 .45 ACP semi-automatic, with aluminum frame, fixed sights, Series 80 action, slim-fit grips and 6.75" overall length. Introduced 2007.

NIB	Exc.	V.G.	Good	Fair	Poor
950	700	525	350	200	150

Colt Rail Gun

1911-style semi-automatic pistol, chambered in .45 ACP. Stainless steel frame and slide, front and rear slide serrations, skeletonized trigger, integral accessory rail, Smith & Alexander upswept beavertail grip, palm swell safety, white dot front sight and Novak rear. Rosewood double diamond grips, tactical thumb safety, National Match barrel. Capacity 8+1. **NOTE:** Add $300 for Cerakote Desert Tan finish.

NIB	Exc.	V.G.	Good	Fair	Poor
950	700	525	350	200	150

Competition Pistol

Full-size 1911A1 Government Model in 9mm or .45 ACP, with competition enhanced features including National Match barrel, Novak adjustable rear and fiber optic front sights, extended grip safety. Introduced in 2016.

NIB	Exc.	V.G.	Good	Fair	Poor
800	700	600	400	—	—

Double Eagle

Chambered for 9mm, .38 Super, 10mm Auto and .45 ACP cartridges. Has 5" barrel and 8-round detachable box magazine. Constructed of stainless steel and checkered black synthetic grips. Sights are fixed and utilize the three-dot system. Manufactured from 1990 to 1996. **NOTE:** Add 20 percent for 9mm, .38 Super or 10mm.

NIB	Exc.	V.G.	Good	Fair	Poor
1000	800	650	500	400	300

Double Eagle Officer's Model

Compact version of double-action Double Eagle pistol. Chambered for .45 ACP only. No longer in production.

NIB	Exc.	V.G.	Good	Fair	Poor
1025	850	625	575	400	200

Double Eagle Combat Commander

Based on standard Double Eagle design, with a slightly shorter 4.25" barrel. Double Eagle Combat Commander fits between standard model and smaller Officer's Model. Available in .45 ACP and .40 S&W (1993). Weight 36 oz., holds 8 rounds, has white dot sights and checkered Xenoy grips. Finish is matte stainless steel. No longer in production.

NIB	Exc.	V.G.	Good	Fair	Poor
1025	850	625	575	350	200

Double Eagle First Edition

This version of double-action Double Eagle pistol is chambered for 10mm Auto. Furnished with Cordura holster, double-magazine pouch,

three magazines and zippered black Cordura case.

NIB	Exc.	V.G.	Good	Fair	Poor
1100	875	650	500	375	300

Pocket Nine

Double-action semi-automatic pistol, chambered for 9mm cartridge. Frame is aluminum alloy and slide stainless steel. Barrel length 2.75". Magazine capacity 6 rounds. Wrap-around rubber grips standard. Overall length 5.5". Weight about 17 oz. No longer in production.

NIB	Exc.	V.G.	Good	Fair	Poor
950	700	525	350	250	175

Tac Nine

Introduced in 1999. This double-action-only semi-automatic pistol is chambered for 9mm cartridge. Has 2.75" barrel, with an aluminum alloy frame and stainless steel slide. Tritium night sights. Wrap-around rubber grips are standard. Finish is black oxide. Enhanced tolerances. Weight about 17 oz. No longer in production.

NIB	Exc.	V.G.	Good	Fair	Poor
975	725	550	375	250	175

Mustang

More compact version of .380 Government Model. Has 2.75" barrel and 5-round detachable magazine. No longer in production. **NOTE:** Add 10 percent for nickel finish and stainless steel.

NIB	Exc.	V.G.	Good	Fair	Poor
850	650	475	300	250	200

Mustang PocketLite

Lightweight version of Mustang. Features an aluminum alloy receiver. Finish is blued only and has synthetic grips. Introduced in 1987. Discontinued 1999. Reintroduced 2012. **NOTE:** Deduct 20 percent for 2012 model.

NIB	Exc.	V.G.	Good	Fair	Poor
800	600	475	300	250	200

Mustang Lite

Similar to Pocket Lite, except has black polymer frame with ribbed grips, matte black stainless slide.

NIB	Exc.	V.G.	Good	Fair	Poor
450	400	365	325	275	250

Government Pocketlite LW

Similar to Mustang, but fitted with a 3.25" barrel and 7-round magazine. Has an aluminum frame and stainless steel slide. Fixed sights. Black composition grips. Weight about 15 oz. No longer in production.

NIB	Exc.	V.G.	Good	Fair	Poor
850	650	475	300	250	200

Mustang Pocketlite XSP

Similar in design and operation to standard Mustang Pocketlite model, except it has a polymer receiver, black finish and squared trigger guard. Introduced in 2013.

NIB	Exc.	V.G.	Good	Fair	Poor
550	500	400	300	250	200

Mustang Plus II

This version of Mustang pistol features 2.75" barrel, with longer grip frame that accommodates a 7-round magazine. Introduced in 1988. Offered in blue and stainless steel. No longer in production. **NOTE:** Add 10 percent for stainless steel.

NIB	Exc.	V.G.	Good	Fair	Poor
850	650	475	300	250	200

Colt Pony

Introduced in 1997. Semi-automatic pistol chambered for .380 ACP. Fitted with a 2.75" barrel and bobbed hammer. Double-action-only. Grips are black composition. Sights are ramp front with fixed rear. Finish is Teflon and stainless steel. Magazine capacity 6 rounds. Overall length 5.5". Weight 19 oz. No longer in production.

NIB	Exc.	V.G.	Good	Fair	Poor
850	650	475	300	250	200

Colt Pony PocketLite

Same as above, with aluminum and stainless steel frame. Weight about 13 oz. No longer in production.

NIB	Exc.	V.G.	Good	Fair	Poor
850	650	475	300	250	200

.380 Series 80 Government Model

Single-action blowback-operated semi-automatic pistol, chambered for .380 ACP cartridge. Has a 3.25" barrel and 7-round magazine. Sights are fixed. Available either blued, nickel plated or stainless steel. Synthetic grips. Introduced in 1985. No longer in production. **NOTE:** Add 10 percent for nickel finish and stainless steel.

NIB	Exc.	V.G.	Good	Fair	Poor
875	675	500	325	275	200

Colt CZ40

Introduced in 1998, this double-action .40 S&W pistol was built for Colt by CZ in Czech Republic. Fitted with a 4" barrel and black polymer grips. Frame is alloy, with carbon steel slide and blue finish. Magazine capacity 10 rounds. Weight about 34 oz. No longer in production.

NIB	Exc.	V.G.	Good	Fair	Poor
900	750	600	500	400	225

Colt Model 2000

Introduced in 1992, Model 2000 was a new departure for Colt from its traditional service style semi-automatic pistols. Chambered for 9mm, Model 2000 is a double-action-only pistol, with 4.5" barrel and choice between polymer or aluminum alloy frame. Polymer frame model weighs 29 oz.; aluminum alloy frame 33 oz. Grips are black composition and sights are white dot. Pistol dropped from Colt line in 1994.

NIB	Exc.	V.G.	Good	Fair	Poor
700	595	400	300	250	200

COLT .22 RIMFIRE SEMI-AUTOMATIC PISTOLS

For Colt Ace, see Model 1911 section.

COLT WOODSMAN

Text and photos by Bob Rayburn

The original Colt .22 Target Model was designed by John Moses Browning and improved by engineers at Colt Firearms prior to the start of production in 1915, and major design updates were made in 1947 and again in 1955. Those three designs constitute what collectors call the three series of Woodsman pistols. First Series refers to all those built on the frame used prior to and during WWII. Second Series includes all versions built on the second frame design from 1947 until 1955 and Third Series means the third frame design as used from 1955 to the end of production in 1977.

Each series had a Target Model, Sport Model and Match Target Model. All models are very similar: Sport Model for example, is merely Target Model with a short barrel, and in some cases different sights or grips. Match Target is nearly the same as Sport or Target Model, but with a heavier slab-sided barrel, squared-off frame at the front of receiver to mate with the heavy barrel and improved sights. In the post-war years there were also three very similar economy models: First the Challenger, then Huntsman and finally Targetsman. The actions of these economy models are identical to higher-end models of the same period internally; they lack only some of the refinements.

These guns were not assembled in strict numerical sequence. Furthermore, even when changes were made, old parts were used up at the same time new parts were being introduced. As a result, there is no hard and fast serial number dividing line for any particular feature and serial number overlaps of several thousand are common.

All models of the Woodsman line, in all three series, are discussed here, but there are numerous variations in details that are primarily of interest to specialized collectors. For more details see Bob Rayburn's Colt Woodsman Pocket Guide, a 96-page pocket-sized guide to the Colt Woodsman line, available for $11 (including shipping) from:

Bob Rayburn
PO Box 97104
Lakewood, WA 98497 or online at www.colt22.com or www.coltwoodsman.com

Except for NIB, values listed here are for the pistol only, without extras, for guns in the middle of each condition range. These are guidelines to the prevailing retail values for collector or shooter who is buying it as the end user, not what one might expect to receive from a gun dealer who is buying it to resell. Furthermore, within the Excellent and Very Good condition categories, there is a considerable spread in value, especially for the older and more collectible versions. Excellent, for example, means 98 percent or more original blue, but a very nice pre-Woodsman with 100 percent of the original blue would likely be worth twice as much to a serious collector as one with only 98 percent. At the other end of the condition scale, in the Fair and Poor categories, the individual values of component parts become significant, and effectively set a floor value. A poor condition, rusty, pitted pre-Woodsman or First Series Match Target would still have good value if it included the original magazine and grips in nice condition, for example. In addition, there are sometimes rare variations within the broad categories that can significantly enhance the value. Include the original crisp condition box, instructions, and tools, and the value goes up more, especially for high condition early guns. On the other hand, rust, pitting (even very minor), rebluing, or other non-factory modifications will significantly reduce the values from those listed in the Very Good category or better.

FIRST SERIES

In 1915, intended market was the target shooter and there was only one model: Colt .22 LR Automatic Target Pistol. That model, however, proved to be very popular not only with target shooters, but also with hunters, trappers, campers and other outdoorsmen. Management at Colt noticed this, of course, and decided to give the pistol a new name that more closely reflected its widespread use. THE WOODSMAN, was name chosen and that roll mark was added to side of receiver in 1927, at approximately serial number 54000. To further satisfy the broader market, Colt introduced the Sport Model in 1933 and Match Target Model in 1938. Compact and beautifully balanced Sport Model was a near perfect "kit gun" for the outdoorsman. Match Target was designed for special needs of the serious target shooters. Approximately 54,000 pre-Woodsmans (all with 6.625" barrels) and a combined total of approximately 110,000 Woodsman marked Sport and Target Models were produced in the first series. Sport Model and Target Model were serial numbered together after Sport Model was added to the line in 1933. It was not possible to easily determine how many of each were manufactured. Safe to say Target Model far outnumbered Sport Model. During the war years of 1942-45, Match Target was the only Woodsman model built. Virtually the entire production was for the US military.

Pre-Woodsman

Model made from 1915-1927. Has a 10-round magazine, blue finish, checkered walnut grips and 6.625" barrel. Designed for .22 LR standard velocity ammunition. Rear sight adjustable for windage, front sight for elevation. Up until approximately serial number 31000 the barrel was a very thin, so-called "pencil barrel." Barrel weight and diameter were increased slightly in 1922, to what collectors now call the "medium weight barrel." Also numerous small changes in grips, magazines and markings over the years. Approximately 54,000 were made in all variations.

An early pre-Woodsman

A checkered pattern in an oval on the mainspring housing (left) indicates a pre-Woodsman or First Series Woodsman Target model that was designed for standard velocity .22 Long Rifle ammunition only. A series of horizontal parallel lines in a rectangular pattern (right) indicates one that was designed for high-velocity .22 Long Rifle ammunition. All guns in the series made after 1932 were designed for high-velocity ammunition, and that includes all Sport, Match Target, Challenger, Huntsman, and Targetsman models. The post-WWII guns have no pattern on the mainspring housing but they were all made for high-velocity ammunition.

The three barrel profiles used with the Colt pre-Woodsman and First Series Target Model: from left to right, in order used, the pencil barrel, medium weight barrel and straight taper barrel.

NIB	Exc.	V.G.	Good	Fair	Poor
2800	2200	1400	850	350	200

Woodsman Target

Initially, this was exactly the same as late pre-Woodsman, with the exception of THE WOODSMAN marking on side of receiver. Later there were small changes in sights, trigger and markings. In 1934, barrel profile was again modified to a larger diameter, heavier barrel. This third and final pre-WWII barrel profile lacked the fillet or step-down, as was present on earlier pencil barrel and medium barrel, therefore commonly called the "straight taper" barrel. A significant modification occurred in 1932, when a new heat-treated mainspring housing and stiffer recoil spring were phased in to allow use of increasingly popular high velocity .22 LR ammunition. While this change had widely reported to have taken place at serial number 83790, it was actually phased in over a period of time and a range of serial numbers, spanning at least 81000-86000, within which range both standard and high speed versions can be found. Fortunately, Colt changed the marking on back of mainspring housing (see photo) to allow visual differentiation. Colt also sold a conversion kit to modify older guns for use with high velocity ammunition. Kit consisted of a new style mainspring housing, stiffer recoil spring and coil type magazine spring for use in the very early guns that had a Z type magazine spring.

NIB	Exc.	V.G.	Good	Fair	Poor
2500	1700	1100	500	250	200

Woodsman Sport

THE WOODSMAN, proving to be increasingly popular with outdoorsmen of all types, Colt decided to market a Woodsman better suited for "take along" gun for hiking, camping, etc. This was accomplished in 1933, by merely shortening the barrel from 6.625" to 4.5" and announcing the new Sport Model. Other than barrel length, the only difference between Target Model and Sport Model was an adjustable front sight on Target Model and fixed front sight on Sport Model. Later, a front sight adjustable for elevation would be an available option for Sport Model. Colt called this arrangement "Target Sights." Indeed, it was the same front sight used on Target Model. First Series Sport Model, with adjustable front sight will command a premium of approximately 25 percent over values listed.

NIB	Exc.	V.G.	Good	Fair	Poor
2600	1800	1300	600	250	200

Woodsman Match Target

Colt introduced Match Target Woodsman in 1938, with its own serial number series beginning at MT1 and continuing until 1944 with serial number MT16611. New features included larger grips, heavier barrel (6.625") and rear sight fully adjustable for both windage and elevation. To signify its intended market, a Bullseye Target pattern was placed on side of barrel. That led to its nickname "Bullseye Match Target". Elongated one-piece wraparound walnut grips also picked up a nickname due to their unusual shape. Unfortunately, the so-called "Elephant Ear" grips are somewhat fragile and often broken. In addition, many serious target shooters of the day replaced them with custom grips with thumb rest and palm swell. Original grips were set aside and eventually lost or discarded. For those reasons, original grips are often missing and that severely affects value. Values listed assume original one-piece walnut wraparound Elephant Ear grips, no cracks, repairs or modifications and a correct Match Target marked magazine. Values listed for Fair and Poor condition are primarily salvage value and reflect the high value of original "Elephant Ear" grips and Match Target marked magazines for spare parts. Approximately 11,000 produced for civilian market from 1938-1942.

NIB	Exc.	V.G.	Good	Fair	Poor
4000	3500	2200	1500	700	600

Military Woodsman Match Target

After U.S. entered WWII at the end of 1941, civilian production at Colt stopped and total effort was devoted to U.S. military. Slightly more than 4000 First Series Match Target Woodsman's were delivered on U.S. Government contract from 1942-1944. Most of them, but not all, had serial numbers above MT12000. With possible rare exceptions, they all had U.S. Property or U.S. military markings, standard blue finish, 6.625" barrel and extended length plastic stocks. Plastic stocks are sometimes erroneously called elephant ear stocks. Military plastic stocks are still relatively easy to find and inexpensive. Since they will fit any First Series Colt Woodsman, they are often used as replacement grips on non-military guns. Since military guns had plastic grips, rather than costly and desirable "Elephant Ear" grips, salvage value in Fair and Poor condition range is less than that for civilian model.

NIB	Exc.	V.G.	Good	Fair	Poor
4400	3500	2000	1100	500	400

SECOND SERIES

After WWII, Colt entered a lengthy period of clearing up government contracts and retooling for the civilian market. Woodsman line was extensively revised and modernized. Second Series guns began appearing near the end of 1947, although no appreciable numbers were shipped until 1948. Second Series Woodsman had essentially same action and many of the same internals as First Series guns, but larger, heavier and a longer grip frame. New features included a magazine safety, automatic slide stop when magazine was emptied, fully adjustable rear sight, heavier barrels and 6" barrel length on Target and Match Target Models, rather than 6.625" as on First Series. Other new features included a push button magazine release just aft of trigger guard like that on large frame Government Model semi-automatics, lanyard ring concealed in butt and provision for attaching a plastic grip adapter to the backstrap, thereby accommodating different sized hands. Elevation adjustment was incorporated into rear sight of all Woodsman models and adjustable front sight replaced with a fixed blade. Serial numbers restarted at 1-S and are intermixed for all three models. Approximately 146,000 of the three models were produced.

In 1950, Colt added Challenger to Second Series pistols, first of the economy models. Internally, Challenger is nearly identical to Woodsman pistols of same era, but externally lacks most of the refinements introduced with Second Series Woodsman. Has no magazine safety, automatic slide stop, adjustable sights, push button magazine release, lanyard ring or grip adapters. Available with either 4.5" or 6" barrel and had its own serial number series beginning with 1-C. Approximately 77,000 were produced.

Woodsman Target 6" barrel

NIB	Exc.	V.G.	Good	Fair	Poor
1800	1400	1000	750	350	200

Woodsman Sport 4.5" barrel

NIB	Exc.	V.G.	Good	Fair	Poor
2000	1500	1050	800	350	200

Woodsman Match Target 6" barrel

NIB	Exc.	V.G.	Good	Fair	Poor
2200	1700	1400	950	600	350

Woodsman Match Target 4.5" barrel

Introduced in 1950.

Second Series Match Target Model with 4.5" barrel.

NIB	Exc.	V.G.	Good	Fair	Poor
2500	1800	1500	1100	650	400

Challenger 4.5" barrel

NIB	Exc.	V.G.	Good	Fair	Poor
1050	900	600	450	300	200

Challenger 6" barrel

NIB	Exc.	V.G.	Good	Fair	Poor
950	800	500	400	250	200

THIRD SERIES

In 1955, Colt again redesigned the Woodsman line. Most obvious change was location of magazine release, which was again placed at heel of butt, just like First Series guns. Other changes made over time in markings, grips, sights and trigger. Sport, Target and Match Target models continued. Challenger was replaced by very similar Huntsman, with either 4.5" or 6" barrel. In 1959, Targetsman was added to line. Targetsman differs from Huntsman only in having an adjustable rear sight and thumbrest on left grip panel. Available with 6" barrel only. All Third Series models had black plastic grips until 1960 and checkered walnut grips thereafter. Huntsman has no thumbrest on grips. All other Third Series models have a thumbrest on left grip panel.

It is difficult to impossible to determine how many of each model was produced in Third Series, due to a very complex serial numbering scheme. Approximately 1000 Third Series Sport, Target and Match Target Models were numbered at the end of Second Series serial number range, from 146138-S to 147138-S. Numbers were then restarted at 160001-S, so there are no post-WWII Woodsmans with numbers in 148xxx-S to 159xxx-S range. Challenger serial numbers, meantime, had reached approximately 77143-C prior to Challenger being replaced by Huntsman (note C suffix, for Challenger). Huntsman initially continued in Challenger serial number series, although numbers skipped forward to 90000-C before restarting. Targetsman, when added to the line early in 1959, joined Huntsman in using -C suffix serial numbers, which were by then up to 129300-C. Then in 1969, when Woodsman serial numbers had reached 241811-S and -C numbers had reached 194040-C, Colt decided to integrate the serial numbers for all versions of Woodsman, Huntsman and Targetsman and restart numbering again. This time they started with 001001S. That worked fine until numbers reached 099999S and rolled over to 100000S. Numbers used in 1951-52 were then being inadvertently duplicated, with one small exception: earlier guns had -S suffix while later ones had only an S (no hyphen before the S). Apparently that was not enough of a distinction to satisfy federal regulations, so when Colt discovered the error after approximately 1,330 had already been numbered, the existing "double headers" were hand stamped with an S prefix, in addition to S suffix, in order to salvage them. Serial numbers were then restarted yet again, this time at 300000S, and continued to 317736S, when production ended.

Woodsman Target 6" barrel

NIB	Exc.	V.G.	Good	Fair	Poor
1200	1000	700	450	275	175

Woodsman Sport 4.5" barrel

NIB	Exc.	V.G.	Good	Fair	Poor
1400	1100	750	500	300	200

Woodsman Match Target 6" barrel

NIB	Exc.	V.G.	Good	Fair	Poor
1900	1600	950	725	500	300

Woodsman Match Target 4.5" barrel

Added to line in 1950.

With the introduction of Third Series guns, Colt moved the magazine catch back to the heel of the butt, where it had been on the First Series.

NIB	Exc.	V.G.	Good	Fair	Poor
2100	1800	1050	800	550	350

Huntsman 6" or 4.5" barrel

NIB	Exc.	V.G.	Good	Fair	Poor
850	750	500	365	225	175

Targetsman 6" barrel

NIB	Exc.	V.G.	Good	Fair	Poor
950	800	550	400	250	200

Colt Junior Pocket Model

This diminutive unit is only 4.5" long overall and weighs 12 oz. Colt did not manufacture this pistol, but rather had it made for them by Astra in Spain. Introduced in 1958 and chambered for .25 ACP. One year later .22 Short version appeared. Both had external hammers and detachable 6-round magazines. Passage of 1968 Gun Control Act, made import of a weapon this size illegal, so Colt discontinued its relationship with Astra. Pistol was re-introduced in 1970 as an American-made product and produced for two more years. Production ceased in 1972. Astra also made this pistol and called it the Cub. **NOTE:** Add 25 percent for .22 Short.

NIB	Exc.	V.G.	Good	Fair	Poor
525	375	250	175	125	75

Cadet / Colt .22

Introduced in 1994, this .22-caliber semi-automatic pistol offered with 4.5" barrel and stainless steel finish. Model was renamed Colt .22 in 1995. Sights are fixed and magazine capacity 11 rounds. Overall length 8.625". Weight about 33 oz.

NIB	Exc.	V.G.	Good	Fair	Poor
350	300	265	225	125	50

Colt .22 Target

Introduced in 1995. Features 6" bull barrel, removable front sight and adjustable rear sight. Black composite monogrip stock. Stainless steel finish. Weight 40.5 oz.

NIB	Exc.	V.G.	Good	Fair	Poor
475	325	300	250	150	75

COLT MODERN LONG ARMS

Colteer I-22

Single-shot bolt-action rifle, chambered for .22 LR or .22 Magnum. Plain unchecked walnut stock, 20" barrel and adjustable sights. Approximately 50,000 manufactured between 1957 and 1966.

NIB	Exc.	V.G.	Good	Fair	Poor
350	300	175	125	90	25

Stagecoach

Semi-automatic saddle ring carbine. Chambered for .22 LR, 16.5" barrel and 13-shot tubular magazine. Stock is fancy walnut and receiver has stagecoach holdup scene roll-engraved on it. Approximately 25,000 manufactured between 1965 and 1975.

NIB	Exc.	V.G.	Good	Fair	Poor
450	400	350	200	150	100

Courier

Similar to Stagecoach, with pistol-grip stock and beavertail forearm. Manufactured between 1970 and 1975.

NIB	Exc.	V.G.	Good	Fair	Poor
425	400	300	200	125	90

Colteer

Less-expensive version of Stagecoach. Features 19.5" barrel, 15-shot tubular magazine. Stock in a plainer grade walnut. No roll engraving. Approximately 25,000 manufactured between 1965 and 1975. **NOTE:** Add 50 percent for .22 rimfire Magnum.

NIB	Exc.	V.G.	Good	Fair	Poor
425	400	300	175	100	90

Colt "57" Bolt-Action Rifle

Rifle manufactured for Colt by Jefferson Mfg. Co of New Haven, Connecticut. Utilizes a Fabrique Nationale Mauser action. Checkered American walnut stock, with Monte Carlo comb. Offered with adjustable sights. Chambered for .243 or .30-06. Also, a deluxe version features higher-grade wood. Approximately 5,000 manufactured in 1957. **NOTE:** Add 20 percent for deluxe version.

NIB	Exc.	V.G.	Good	Fair	Poor
675	550	450	350	300	225

Coltsman Bolt-Action Rifle

Coltsman was manufactured for Colt by Kodiak Arms. Utilizes either Mauser or Sako action. Offered in .243, .308, .30-06 and .300 Winchester Magnum. Barrel length of 22" or 24" in the Magnum chambering. Stock is checkered American walnut. Approximately 10,000 manufactured between 1958 and 1966. Deluxe version features a higher-grade skipline-checkered walnut stock and rosewood fore-end tip; called "The Coltsman Custom". **NOTE:** Add 50 percent for Coltsman Custom.

NIB	Exc.	V.G.	Good	Fair	Poor
700	650	550	450	350	250

Coltsman Pump Shotgun

Manufactured by Jefferson Arms, utilizing an aluminum alloy frame made by Franchi. Chambered for 12-, 16- and 20-gauge. Has 26" or 28" plain barrel. Approximately 2,000 manufactured between 1961 and 1965.

NIB	Exc.	V.G.	Good	Fair	Poor
375	350	300	275	200	150

Semi-Automatic Shotgun

Manufactured for Colt by the firm of Luigi Franchi in Italy. Features an aluminum alloy receiver and chambered for 12- or 20-gauge. Barrel length 26", 28", 30" or 32"—either ventilated rib or plain. Deluxe version "The Custom Auto" features a fancy walnut stock and hand engraved receiver. Approximately 5,300 manufactured between 1962 and 1966. **NOTE:** Add 25 percent for Custom Auto.

NIB	Exc.	V.G.	Good	Fair	Poor
400	375	325	300	225	175

Double-Barrel Shotgun

During 1961 and 1962, Colt had approximately 50 side-by-side shotguns made for them by a French gun manufacturer. They have the Colt name on breech area of barrels and are in 467000-469000 serial range. There is little information available on this gun. Colt never went past the test-market stage.

NIB	Exc.	V.G.	Good	Fair	Poor
—	1200	950	650	500	400

Colt Light Rifle

Introduced in 1999, this bolt-action rifle offered in both long and short action calibers from .243 to .300 Win. Magnum. Fitted with 24" barrel and adjustable trigger. Stock is black synthetic. Action and barrel are matte black. Long action calibers. Weight about 6 lbs., with short action rifle about 5.4 lbs. Adjustable trigger. No sights.

NIB	Exc.	V.G.	Good	Fair	Poor
—	700	600	500	400	200

Colt Sauer Bolt-Action Rifle

High quality and unique rifle, manufactured for Colt by J.P. Sauer & Son of Germany. Rifle features a non-rotating bolt, that makes Colt Sauer action smoother functioning than most. Has 24" barrel, skipline-checkered walnut stock, rosewood fore-end tip, pistol-grip cap and recoil pad. There are five basic configurations: Standard Action chambered for .25-06, .270 Winchester and .30-06; Short Action chambered for .22-250, .243 Winchester and .308 Winchester; Magnum Action chambered for .7mm Remington Magnum, .300 Winchester Magnum and .300 Weatherby Magnum; "Grand Alaskan" and "Grand African" heavier versions chambered for .375 H&H Magnum and .458 Winchester Magnum, respectively. All discontinued by Colt in 1985.

Colt Sauer Short Action

NOTE: Add $50 for Standard Action; 20 percent for Magnum Action; 50 percent for "Grand Alaskan"; 75 percent for "Grand African".

NIB	Exc.	V.G.	Good	Fair	Poor
2000	1950	1850	1500	800	500

Colt Model 2012 SA308

This precision rifle series is offered in several configurations. The 2012 SA308 is a tactical model in .308 Winchester, with 22" spiral fluted heavy stainless steel match-grade barrel with muzzle-brake. Other fetures are an aluminum stock with pistol-grip, aluminum handguard with 2/3-length Picatinny rail and an ajustable Timney single stage trigger. Weight about 13 lbs. The 2012 MT308T model has similar features, with a custom Manners composite stock in Coyote Tan finish. Weight 10.25 lbs. The 2012 LT available in .308 or 260 Remington, with gray laminate stock, medium heavy 22" barrel. Weight 8.5 lbs. These rifles are a joint effort, with Colt Custom Shop and Cooper Firearms of Montana.

SA308

NIB	Exc.	V.G.	Good	Fair	Poor
3250	2750	2200	1750	900	400

MT308T

NIB	Exc.	V.G.	Good	Fair	Poor
2800	2350	1850	1400	600	300

LT

NIB	Exc.	V.G.	Good	Fair	Poor
2400	1950	1450	1000	500	250

Colt Sauer Drilling

Rather unique firearm. One which many American enthusiasts are not familiar—a 3-barreled gun. Features side-by-side shotgun in 12-gauge, over a .30-06 or .243 rifle barrel. Name based on German word for three, as this is where the concept was developed. Quite popular in Europe where game preserve style of hunting is prevalent, but has little use in America where our hunting seasons don't often overlap. Drilling has 25" barrels and pop-up sights for rifle barrel and nicely engraved. Discontinued by Colt in 1985.

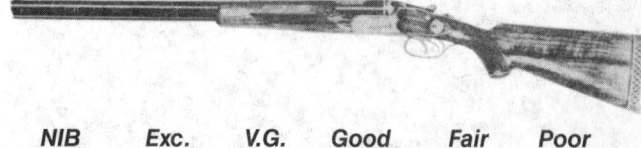

NIB	Exc.	V.G.	Good	Fair	Poor
4500	4000	3000	2000	1500	1100

Colt-Sharps Rifle

Introduced in 1970 as the last word in sporting rifles. Colt-Sharps is a falling-block action that was advertised as a modern Sharps-Borchardt. Undertaking was first-class all the way. Finish is high polish blue, with deluxe-grade hand-checkered walnut stock and fore-end. Chambered for .17 Remington, .22-250, .243, .25-06, 7mm Remington Magnum, .30-06 and .375 H&H Magnum. Offered cased with accessories. Manufactured between 1970 and 1977. **NOTE:** Add 25 percent for .375.

NIB	Exc.	V.G.	Good	Fair	Poor
6000	4900	3200	1550	800	500

COLT AR-15 AND COLT SPORTER TERMINOLOGY

There are three different and distinct manufacturing cycles that not only affect the value of these rifles but also the legal consequences of their modifications.

Pre-Ban Colt AR-15 rifles (Pre-1989): Fitted with bayonet lug, flash hider, and stamped AR-15 on lower receiver. Rifles that are NIB have a green label. It is legal to modify this rifle with any AR-15 upper receiver. These are the most desirable models because of their pre-ban features.

Colt Sporters (Post-1989-pre-September 1994): This transition model has no bayonet lug, but it does have a flash hider. There is no AR-15 designation stamped on the lower receiver. Rifles that are NIB have a blue label. It is legal to modify this rifle with upper receivers made after 1989, i.e. no bayonet lug. These rifles are less desirable than pre-ban AR-15s.

Colt Sporters (Post-September 1994): This rifle has no bayonet lug, no flash hider, and does not have the AR-15 designation stamped on the lower receiver. Rifles that are NIB have a blue label. It is legal to modify this rifle only with upper receivers manufactured after September 1994. These rifles are the least desirable of the three manufacturing periods because of their lack of pre-ban military features and current manufacture status.

COLT AR-15 & SPORTER RIFLES

PRICING NOTICE: It is estimated the value of pre-ban AR-15s declined 10-15 percent, since 1994-2004 Assault Weapons ban has lapsed, but market has once again spiked due to demand. Pricing status of AR-15 is still volatile.

COLT AR-15 PRE-BAN PRODUCTION 1964 TO 1989

AR-15 Sporter (Model #6000)

Semi-automatic rifle firing from a closed bolt. Introduced into Colt product line in 1964. Similar in appearance and function to military version M-16. Chambered for .223 cartridge. Fitted with standard 20" barrel, no forward assist, no case deflector, but with a bayonet lug. Weight about 7.5 lbs. Dropped from production in 1985.

NIB	Exc.	V.G.	Good	Fair	Poor
2150	1800	1600	1500	600	400

AR-15 Sporter w/Collapsible Stock (Model #6001)

Same as above, fitted with 16" barrel and folding stock. Weight about 5.8 lbs. Introduced in 1978, discontinued in 1985.

NIB	Exc.	V.G.	Good	Fair	Poor
2750	2450	2100	1800	600	400

AR-15 Carbine (Model #6420)

Introduced in 1985. Has 16" standard weight barrel. All other features same as previous discontinued AR-15 models. Version dropped from Colt product line in 1987.

NIB	Exc.	V.G.	Good	Fair	Poor
2200	1900	1700	1600	600	400

AR-15 9mm Carbine (Model #6450)

Same as above. Chambered for 9mm cartridge. Weight 6.3 lbs.

NIB	Exc.	V.G.	Good	Fair	Poor
2250	1950	1750	1650	700	400

AR-15A2 Sporter II (Model #6500)

Introduced in 1984. An updated version, with heavier barrel and forward assist. AR sight still utilized. Weight about 7.8 lbs.

NIB	Exc.	V.G.	Good	Fair	Poor
1850	1500	1300	1050	550	400

AR-15A2 Government Model Carbine (Model #6520)

Added to Colt line in 1988, this 16" standard barrel carbine featured for the first time a case deflector and improved A2 rear sight. Fitted with 4-position telescoping buttstock. Weight about 5.8 lbs.

NIB	Exc.	V.G.	Good	Fair	Poor
2300	2000	1750	1650	700	400

AR-15A2 Government Model (Model #6550)

Introduced in 1988. Rifle equivalent to the Carbine. Features 20" A2 barrel, forward assist, case deflector, but still retains the bayonet lug. Weight about 7.5 lbs. Discontinued in 1990. USMC model.

NIB	Exc.	V.G.	Good	Fair	Poor
2300	2000	1750	1650	700	400

AR-15A2 H-BAR (Model #6600)

Introduced in 1986. This version features special 20" heavy barrel. All other features the same as A2 series of AR15s. Discontinued in 1991. Weight about 8 lbs.

NIB	Exc.	V.G.	Good	Fair	Poor
1950	1750	1500	950	700	500

AR-15A2 Delta H-BAR (Model #6600DH)

Same as above. Fitted with 3x9 scope and detachable cheekpiece. Dropped from Colt line in 1990. Weight about 10 lbs.

NIB	Exc.	V.G.	Good	Fair	Poor
2350	2100	1800	1650	850	600

COLT AR-15 PRE-BAN PRODUCTION 1989 TO 1994

Sporter Lightweight Rifle

Lightweight model has 16" barrel and finished in matte black. Available in: .223 Rem. caliber (Model #6530) weighs 6.7 lbs.; 9mm caliber (Model #6430) weighs 7.1 lbs.; 7.65x39mm (Model #6830) weighs 7.3 lbs. All furnished with two 5-round box magazines. Cleaning kit and sling are also supplied with each new rifle. Buttstock and pistol-grip are made of durable nylon. Handguard is reinforced fiberglass and aluminum lined. Rear sight is adjustable for windage and elevation. Newer models are referred to simply as Sporters. Not fitted with a bayonet lug and receiver block. Has different size pins. **NOTE:** Model 6830 will bring about $25 less than these prices.

NIB	Exc.	V.G.	Good	Fair	Poor
1650	1500	1100	850	750	600

Sporter Target Model Rifle (Model #6551)

This 1991 model is a full size version of Lightweight Rifle. Weight 7.5 lbs. Has a 20" barrel. Offered in .223 Rem. caliber only, with target sights adjustable to 800 meters. New rifles furnished with two 5-round box magazines, sling and cleaning kit. **NOTE:** Deduct 30 percent for post-9/94 guns.

NIB	Exc.	V.G.	Good	Fair	Poor
1700	1400	1100	650	400	300

Sporter Match H-BAR (Model #6601)

This 1991 variation of AR-15 is similar to Target Model. Has 20" heavy barrel, target type sights adjustable out to 800 meters and chambered for .223-caliber. Supplied with two 5-round box magazines, sling and cleaning kit. Weight 8 lbs.

NIB	Exc.	V.G.	Good	Fair	Poor
1700	1400	1100	650	400	300

AR-15 (XM16E1)

Rifle made upon request for foreign contracts. Very rare. Proceed with caution. Variation will command a premium price over standard AR-15 rifle. Secure an appraisal before purchase.

Courtesy Richard M. Kumor, Sr.

Sporter Match Delta H-BAR (Model #6601 DH)

Same as above, but supplied with a 3x9 scope. Weight about 10 lbs. Discontinued in 1992.

NIB	Exc.	V.G.	Good	Fair	Poor
2300	1900	1600	1300	600	400

Match Target H-BAR Compensated (Model #6601C)

Same as regular Sporter H-BAR, with addition of a compensator.

NIB	Exc.	V.G.	Good	Fair	Poor
2200	1900	1600	1300	600	400

Colt Match Target M4

Similar to above, with carbine-length barrel.

NIB	Exc.	V.G.	Good	Fair	Poor
2200	1900	1600	1300	600	400

Sporter Competition H-BAR (Model #6700)

Introduced in 1992. Competition H-BAR available in .223-caliber, with 20" heavy barrel counterbored for accuracy. Carry handle is detachable, with target sights. With carry handle removed the upper receiver is dovetailed and grooved for Weaver-style scope rings. New rifles furnished with two 5-round box magazines, sling and cleaning kit. Weight abut 8.5 lbs. **NOTE:** Deduct 35 percent for post-9/94 guns.

NIB	Exc.	V.G.	Good	Fair	Poor
1800	1500	1300	1000	500	350

Sporter Competition H-BAR Select w/scope (Model #6700CH)

This variation identical to Sporter Competition, with addition of factory mounted scope. Rifle has also been selected for accuracy. Comes complete with 3-9X rubber armored variable scope, scope mount, carry handle with iron sights and nylon carrying case.

NIB	Exc.	V.G.	Good	Fair	Poor
2000	1800	1400	1000	600	400

Match Target Competition H-BAR Compensated (Model #6700C)

Same as Match Target, with compensator.

NIB	Exc.	V.G.	Good	Fair	Poor
2000	1800	1400	1000	600	400

AR-15 Carbine Flat-top Heavyweight/Match Target Competition (Model #6731)

This variation in Sporter series features heavyweight 16" barrel, with flat-top receiver. Chambered for .223 cartridge. Equipped with a fixed buttstock. Weight about 7.1 lbs.

NIB	Exc.	V.G.	Good	Fair	Poor
1200	1000	800	600	400	300

AR-15 Tactical Carbine (Model #6721)

Similar to above model, with exception of buttstock which is telescoping and adjusts to 4 positions. Chambered for .223 cartridge. Weight about 7 lbs. Majority of these guns were for law enforcement only. Only 134 rifles are pre-ban. **NOTE:** Add 100 percent premium if serial number is below BD000135.

NIB	Exc.	V.G.	Good	Fair	Poor
1400	1200	1000	800	600	400

Sporter H-BAR Elite/Accurized Rifle (Model #6724)

Introduced in 1996. Features a free floating 24" stainless steel match barrel, with an 11 degree target crown and special Teflon coated trigger group. Hand guard is all-aluminum, with twin swivel studs. Weight about 9.26 lbs.

NIB	Exc.	V.G.	Good	Fair	Poor
1500	1250	900	550	400	300

COLT AR-15 POST-BAN PRODUCTION 1994 TO PRESENT

Colt SP6920

Sporter version of classic Colt M4 carbine. Chambered for .223 Remington. Chrome-lined bore with 6 grooves, 1" to 7" right hand twist. Four-position collapsible stock. Flattop receiver with removable carry handle. Matte black finish. Introduced in 2011. Discontinued.

NIB	Exc.	V.G.	Good	Fair	Poor
975	850	725	600	400	200

Colt SP6940

Same gun as SP6920, with one-piece upper receiver. Fully floated barrel, which allows easier mounting of optical, laser or light accessories. No carry handle. Matte black finish. Introduced in 2011. Discontinued.

NIB	Exc.	V.G.	Good	Fair	Poor
1275	1075	900	700	500	300

Match Target Competition H-BAR (Model 6700)

This 5.56 NATO model has a flat-top upper receiver grooved for Weaver scope mounts, 20" heavy barrel, detachable carry handle with 600 meter rear sight system. Weight 8.5 lbs. Introduced in 1992, discontinued 2013.

NIB	Exc.	V.G.	Good	Fair	Poor
1000	850	700	500	400	325

Match Target Lightweight

Chambered in 5.56 NATO, 7.62x39 or 9mm. Has 16" barrel and hand guard, with adjustable rear sight. Weight 7 lbs.

NIB	Exc.	V.G.	Good	Fair	Poor
900	800	650	475	400	325

Match Target M4 Carbine

Chambered in 5.56 NATO/.223 Rem., with 16.1" barrel, fixed tube buttstock and detachable carring handle. This model is a semi-automatic version of the one currently issued to U.S. armed forces. Introduced in 2002, discontinued 2013.

NIB	Exc.	V.G.	Good	Fair	Poor
1000	850	700	500	400	325

Match Target H-BAR Rifle

Similar to Match Target M4 Carbine, but with 20" heavy barrel. Introduced in 1986, discontinued 2010.

NIB	Exc.	V.G.	Good	Fair	Poor
1100	950	800	550	450	350

Colt Carbine

Chambered in 9mm with 32-shot magazine, 16.1" barrel with flash suppressor. Muddy Girl or matte black finish. **NOTE:** Deduct $300 for matte black finish.

NIB	Exc.	V.G.	Good	Fair	Poor
1400	1200	900	750	600	450

M.A.R.C. 901

This family of modular AR carbines are chambered in .308 Winchester caliber, with 16.1" heavy barrels. Adapter kit available to allow mounting of .223/5.56 NATO upper receiver. Picatinny rail-mounted accessories for .223 models can be used. LE901 has one-piece upper receiver with BUIS, bayonet lug and flash hider, ambidextrous controls, VLTOR buttstock. AR901 has tubular handguard, B5 Bravo buttstock. Introduced in 2015.

LE901

NIB	Exc.	V.G.	Good	Fair	Poor
1850	1700	1600	—	—	—

AR901

NIB	Exc.	V.G.	Good	Fair	Poor
1300	1200	1100	—	—	—

LE6920

Colt's basic version of Modern Sporting Rifle. Features Magpul MOE SL handguards, MOE SL carbine stock and pistol-grip, and MOE back up sight. Offered in several variations, all with 16.1" barrel, 5.56 NATO chambering, chromed 6-groove barrel and direct gas operating system. Introduced in 2015.

NIB	Exc.	V.G.	Good	Fair	Poor
900	800	700	—	—	—

LE6940

Similar to LE6920 with free floating barrel, fixed four-position rail system, 30-round magazine, MBUS Gen 2 rear sight. Introduced in 2015.

NIB	Exc.	V.G.	Good	Fair	Poor
1300	1200	1100	—	—	—

Expanse M4

Entry-level AR-15 style rifle, with standard features including a 16" barrel chambered for .223/5.56 NATO. Mil Spec grip, trigger and collapsible stock, direct impingement gas operation and 30-round magazine. Introduced in 2016.

NIB	Exc.	V.G.	Good	Fair	Poor
625	550	485	400	325	250

COLT CUSTOM SHOP

Colt Custom Shop offers various customizing, upgrading and engraving services on current catalog models For information, contact Colt at www.colt.com or 800-962-2658. Shown here is a sampling of previously customized models.

Special Combat Government Model (Competition)

Competition ready model. Chambered for .45 ACP. Fitted with skeletonized trigger, upswept grip safety, custom tuned action, polished feed ramp, throated barrel, flared ejection port, cutout commander hammer, two 8-round magazines, hard chromed slide and receiver, extended thumb safety, Bomar rear sight, Clark dovetail front sight and flared magazine funnel. Pistol has been accurized and shipped with a certified target.

NIB	Exc.	V.G.	Good	Fair	Poor
1750	1200	800	500	300	200

Special Combat Government Model (Carry)

Has all the same features as competition model, except it has a royal blue finish, special bar-dot night sights, ambidextrous safety. Also been accurized and shipped with a certified target.

NIB	Exc.	V.G.	Good	Fair	Poor
1550	1000	700	400	300	200

Gold Cup Commander

Chambered for .45 ACP. Features heavy-duty adjustable target sights, beveled magazine well, serrated front strap, checkered mainspring housing, wide grip safety, Palo Alto wood grips and stainless steel or royal blue finish.

NIB	Exc.	V.G.	Good	Fair	Poor
1400	875	650	600	500	375

U.S. Shooting Team Gold Cup

Limited edition Gold Cup .45 ACP, with special blue, sights, grips. U.S. Shooting Team logo rolled on the slide. Limited to 500 pistols and built for

Lew Horton..

NIB	Exc.	V.G.	Good	Fair	Poor
1400	875	650	600	500	375

Gold Cup Trophy

Introduced in 1997. Features 1911 .45 ACP 5" barrel, with choice of stainless steel or blue finish. Several custom features such as skeletonized hammer and trigger. Adjustable rear sight and wrap around rubber grips are standard. Pistol has been accurized and shipped with a target. Magazine capacity 7 or 8 rounds. Weight about 39 oz.

NIB	Exc.	V.G.	Good	Fair	Poor
1000	900	675	625	525	400

McCormick Commander

Limited edition pistol made for Lew Horton in 1995. Limited to 100 pistols. Has many special features. Slide is engraved and there is a gold rampant colt on the slide.

NIB	Exc.	V.G.	Good	Fair	Poor
1600	1000	750	600	500	375

McCormick Officer

Lew Horton exclusive pistol, has factory installed McCormick parts and hard chrome finish. Total of 500 guns built in 1995.

NIB	Exc.	V.G.	Good	Fair	Poor
1500	875	650	600	500	375

McCormick Factory Racer

Limited edition pistol from Lew Horton. Full size government model, with hard chrome finish, special barrel, trigger safety and other custom features. Each gun rollmarked "McCormick Factory Racer" on the slide. Special serial numbers from MFR001 to MFR500.

NIB	Exc.	V.G.	Good	Fair	Poor
1300	775	650	600	500	375

Colt Classic .45 Special Edition

Lew Horton model limited to 400 pistols. Features a royal blue polish with special "Classic .45" gold etched on the slide. Pearlite grips.

NIB	Exc.	V.G.	Good	Fair	Poor
1300	775	650	600	500	375

125th Anniversary Edition Peacemaker

Introduced in 1998. Features a V-shaped rear sight, with two-line patent date. Barrel is 4.75" and chambered for .45 Colt cartridge. Cylinder is second generation type and hammer is knurled. Frame and hammer are case colored, with blue barrel. Grips are two piece walnut, with oil finish. Special serial number range SA74000 to SA75999.

NIB	Exc.	V.G.	Good	Fair	Poor
1950	1350	950	600	500	375

Custom Anaconda

Custom-tuned action, Magnaported barrel, with Elliason rear sight. Contoured trigger is polished smooth. Comes with Pachmayr grips and brushed stainless steel finish.

NIB	Exc.	V.G.	Good	Fair	Poor
1950	1275	800	600	300	200

Ultimate Python

Custom tuned action, with both Elliason and Accro sighting systems. Both rubber and walnut grips are included. Bright stainless steel or royal blue finish. Available only with 6" barrel.

NIB	Exc.	V.G.	Good	Fair	Poor
1800	1275	800	600	300	200

Anaconda Hunter

Comes with a Leupold 2X scope, heavy-duty mounts, cleaning accessories, both walnut and rubber grips, in a hard case. Furnished only with an 8" barrel.

NIB	Exc.	V.G.	Good	Fair	Poor
1800	1275	800	600	300	200

Bobbed Detective Special

First offered in 1994. Features bobbed hammer, front sight with night sight and honed action. Available in either chrome or blue finish.

NIB	Exc.	V.G.	Good	Fair	Poor
775	600	450	300	150	100

Limited Class .45 ACP

1911 auto. Designed for tactical competition. Supplied with a parkerized matte finish, lightweight composite trigger, extended ambidextrous safety, upswept grip safety, beveled magazine well. Accurized and shipped with a signed target. Introduced in 1993.

NIB	Exc.	V.G.	Good	Fair	Poor
1450	1050	650	450	300	200

Compensated Model .45 ACP

Competition pistol has a hard chrome receiver, bumper on magazine, extended ambidextrous safety, blue slide with full profile BAT compensator, Bomar rear sight and flared funnel magazine well. Introduced in 1993.

NIB	Exc.	V.G.	Good	Fair	Poor
1450	1050	650	450	300	200

Compensated .45 ACP Commander

Introduced in 1998 and limited to 500 pistols. Fitted with a full-length guide rod, extended beavertail safety, skeletonized hammer, Novak-style sights and checkered walnut double-diamond grips.

NIB	Exc.	V.G.	Good	Fair	Poor
1350	975	575	400	300	200

Nite Lite .380

Supplied with a bar-dot night sight, special foil mark on barrel slide, Teflon-coated alloy receiver, stainless slide, high-capacity grip-extension magazine and standard magazine. Shipped with a soft carrying case. Introduced in 1993.

NIB	Exc.	V.G.	Good	Fair	Poor
1350	975	575	400	300	200

Standard Tactical Model

Built for 20th Anniversary of IPSC competition shooting in 1996. Built on Colt Government model, with round top slide and chambered for .45 ACP. Many special features and serial numbers. Limited to 1,500 pistols.

NIB	Exc.	V.G.	Good	Fair	Poor
1450	875	600	450	300	200

Superior Tactical Model

Same as above. Built on an enhanced frame, with many custom features. Special serial numbers limited to 500 pistols.

NIB	Exc.	V.G.	Good	Fair	Poor
1550	975	700	550	400	200

Deluxe Tactical Model

Same as above, with added features. Limited to 250 pistols.

NIB	Exc.	V.G.	Good	Fair	Poor
1650	1075	800	650	500	300

COLT COMMEMORATIVES

The field of commemorative's can be fascinating and frustrating, depending on one's point of view. For someone who collects things from purely an aesthetic sense, commemorative's are quite desirable. Most are embellished and have had great care put into their fit and finish. They are attractively cased, and the proliferation of them makes acquisition relatively simple except from a financial standpoint. On the other hand, the collector who has an eye for the investment potential of his collections has found that the commemorative market has been soft and as investments they historically have not done well. The reason for this is twofold. The limited production appeal is not always what it seems. Many times the amounts produced are greater than one would consider limited. It is also a fact that if one fires a commemorative, its collectability is gone. Even excessive handling can cause this problem. This means that since the majority of these firearms are kept new in the original boxes, the supply will usually outstrip the demand.

Because of the limited numbers built, it is difficult to furnish accurate prices for the secondary market. Today's collectors are attracted to those Commemorative's with low production numbers and are willing to pay modest premiums for those where production was 2,500 or less. Few commemorative's are ever lost or worn out. Collectors who seek firearms for their historic significance are usually not interested in the commemorative's, as even though they may have been issued to commemorate a specific historic person or event, they are not a part of the era and are regarded as "instant"

collectibles. In some areas one will find that the Colt Commemorative's are not as desirable, salable, or expensive as the plain out-of-the-box versions. This is especially true in the Single-Action Army Models. We list the commemorative's made by Colt in chronological order. Remember that the prices reflect new-in-the-box as it came from the factory—all papers, books, etc., intact and included. We also include the issue price for comparison. If the model with which you are concerned has been fired or is not in its original casing or box, deduct as much as 50 percent from these prices. It is interesting to note that in some areas shooters are taking advantage of the soft commemorative market and are buying SAAs at lower prices than the plain 3rd Generation guns—then shooting them. This can perhaps have a positive effect on appreciation.

One final note. There are a number of Colt Commemorative's that were produced by Colt but offered for sale by private companies to commemorate an event of their choosing. This publication does not cover most of these private commemorative's because it is difficult, if not impossible, to determine a secondary market value. It is also difficult to construct any meaningful comprehensive list of these private offerings. While the market for Colt factory remains soft the market for private commemorative's is usually very soft. the few that come on the market sometimes sell for less than half of their initial offering price. For those who enjoy collecting these firearms without investment goals these private commemorative's offer an additional outlet.

1961	Issue Price	NIB	Amount Mfg.
Guneseo, IL. 125th Anniv. Derringer	$28	$650	104
Sheriff's Model (Blue & Case)	130	3000	478
Sheriff's Model (Nickel)	140	6000	25
Kansas Statehood Scout	75	500	6,197
125th Anniv. Model SAA .45	150	1600	7,390
Pony Express Cent. Scout	80	500	1,007
CIvil War Cent. Pistol	75	300	24,114

1962	Issue	NIB	Amount Mfg.
Rock Island Arsenal Cent. Scout	$250	$250	550
Columbus, OH. Sesquicent. Scout	100	700	200
Ft. Findlay, OH. Sesquicent. Scout	90	650	110
Ft. Findlay, OH. Cased Pair	185	2500	20
New Mex. Golden Anniv. Scout	80	550	1,000
Ft. McPherson, Nebraska Cent. Derringer	29	500	300
West Virginia Statehood Cent. Scout	75	550	3,452

1963	Issue	NIB	Amount Mfg.
West Virginia Statehood Cent. SAA .45	$150	$1495	600
Ariz. Terr. Cent. Scout	75	550	5,355
Ariz. Terr. Cent. SAA .45	150	1495	1,280
Carolina Charter Tercent Scout	75	550	300
Carolina Charter Tercent .22/.45 Comb.	240	2200	251
H. Cook 1 to 100 .22/.45 Comb.	275	2500	100
Ft. Stephenson OH. Sesquincent. Scout	75	550	200
Battle of Gettysburg Cent. Scout	90	650	1,019
Idaho Terr. Cent. Scout	75	550	902
Gen. J.H. Morgan Indiana Raid Scout	75	650	100

1964	Issue	NIB	Amount Mfg.
Cherry's 35th Anniv. .22/.45 Comb.	$275	$2500	100
Nevada Statehood Cent. Scout	75	450	3,984
Nevada Statehood Cent. SAA .45	150	1600	1,688
Nevada Statehood Cent. .22/.45 Comb.	240	2100	189
Nevada Statehood Cent. .22/.45 w/extra cyls.	350	2200	577
Nevada Battle Born Scout	85	550	981
Nevada Battle Born SAA .45	175	1900	80
Nevada Battle Born .22/.45 Comb.	265	2595	20
Montana Terr. Cent. Scout	75	550	2,300
Montana Terr. Cent. SAA .45	150	1600	851
Wyoming Diamond Jubilee Scout	75	550	2,357
General Hood Cent. Scout	75	550	1,503
New Jersey Tercent Scout	75	450	1,001
New Jersey Tercent SAA .45	150	1600	250
St. Louis Bicent. Scout	75	450	802
St. Louis Bicent. SAA .45	150	1600	200
St. Louis Bicent. .22/.45 Comb.	240	2100	250
California Gold Rush Scout	80	575	500
Pony Express Pres. SAA .45	250	1750	1,004
Chamizal Treaty Scout	85	550	450
Chamizal Treaty SAA .45	170	1700	50
Chamizal Treaty .22/.45 Comb.	280	2400	50
Col. Sam Colt Sesquicent. SAA .45	225	1600	4,750
Col. Sam Colt Deluxe SAA .45	500	3500	200
Col. Sam Colt Soecial Deluxe SAA .45	1000	5000	50
Wyatt Earp Buntline SAA .45	250	2750	150

1965	Issue	NIB	Amount Mfg.
Oregon Trail Scout	$75	$550	1,995
Joaquin Murietta .22/.45 Comb.	350	2100	100
Forty-Niner Miner Scout	85	550	500
Old Ft. Des Moines Reconst. Scout	90	600	700
Old Ft. Des Moines Reconst. SAA .45	170	1600	100
Old Ft. Des Moines Reconst. .22/.45 Comb.	290	2100	100
Appomattox Cent. Scout	75	600	1,001
Appomattox Cent. SAA .45	150	1600	250
Appomattox Cent. .22/.45 Comb.	240	2200	250
General Meade Campaign Scout	75	550	1,197
St. Augustine Quadracent. Scout	85	550	500
Kansas Cowtown Series Wichita Scout	85	500	500

1966	Issue	NIB	Amount Mfg.
Kansas Cowtown Series Dodge City Scout	$85	$550	500
Colorado Gold Rush Scout	85	600	1,350
Oklahoma Territory Scout	85	550	1,343
Dakota Territory Scout	85	600	1,000
General Meade SAA .45	165	1600	200
Abercrombie & Fitch Trailblazer N.Y.	275	1400	200
Abercrombie & Fitch Trailblazer Chic.	275	1400	100
Abercrombie & Fitch Trailblazer S.F.	275	1400	100
Kansas Cowtown Series Abilene Scout	95	550	500
Indiana Sesquicent. Scout	85	600	1,500
Pony Express 4-Square Set .45 4 Guns	1,400	7000	N/A
California Gold Rush SAA .45	175	1700	130

1967	Issue	NIB	Amount Mfg.
Colorado Gold Rush Scout	$90	$600	3,000
Oklahoma Territory Scout	180	1700	500
Dakota Territory Scout	85	500	4,250
Alamo SAA .45	165	1650	750
Alamo .22/.45 Comb.	265	2100	250
Kansas Cowtown Series Coffeyville Scout	95	450	500
Kansas Trail Series Chisolm Trail Scout	100	450	500
WWI Series Chateau Thierry .45 Auto	200	1000	7,400
WWI Series Chateau Thierry Deluxe	500	1350	75
WWI Series Chateau Thierry Sp. Deluxe	1000	2950	25

1968	Issue	NIB	Amount Mfg.
Nebraska Cent. Scout	$100	$450	7,001
Kansas Trail Series Chisolm Trail Scout	100	450	500
WWI Series Belleau Wood .45 Auto	200	1000	7,400
WWI Series Belleau Wood Deluxe	500	1350	75
WWI Series Belleau Wood Sp. Deluxe	1000	2950	25
Lawman Series Pat Garrett Scout	110	600	3,000
Lawman Series Pat Garrett SAA .45	220	1700	500

1969	Issue	NIB	Amount Mfg.
Nathan B. Forrest Scout	$110	$450	3,000
Kansas Trail Series Santa Fe Trail Sct.	120	450	501
WWI Ser. 2nd Battle of Marine .45 Auto	220	1000	7,400
WWI Ser. 2nd Battle of Marine Deluxe	500	1350	75
WWI Ser. 2nd Battle of Marine Sp. Deluxe	1000	2950	25
Alabama Sesquicent. Scout	110	450	3,001
Alabama Sesquicent. SAA .45	N/A	15000	1
Golden Spike Scout	135	550	11000
Kansas Trail Ser. Shawnee Tr. Scout	120	450	501
WWI Ser. Meuse-Argonne .45 Auto	220	1000	7,400
WWI Ser. Meuse-Argonne Deluxe	500	1350	75
WWI Ser. Meuse-Argonne Sp. Deluxe	1000	2950	25
Arkansas Terr. Sesquicent Scout	110	450	3,500
Lawman Ser. Wild Bill Hickok Scout	117	600	3,000
Lawman Ser. Wild Bill Hickok SAA .45	220	1650	500
California Bicent. Scout	135	550	5,000

1970	Issue	NIB	Amount Mfg.
Kansas Ft. Ser. Ft. Larned Scout	$120	$450	500
WWII Ser. European Theatre	250	1000	11,500
WWII Ser. Pacific Theatre	250	1000	11,500
Texas Ranger SAA .45	650	2250	1,000
Kansas Ft. Ser. Ft. Hays Scout	130	450	500
Marine Sesquicent. Scout	120	450	3,000
Missouri Sesquicent. Scout	125	450	3,000
Missouri Sesquicent. SAA .45	220	1600	900
Kansas Ft. Ser. Ft. Riley Scout	130	450	500
Lawman Ser. Wyatt Earp Scout	125	600	3,000
Lawman Ser. Wyatt Earp SAA .45	395	3000	500

1971	Issue	NIB	Amount Mfg.
NRA Centennial SAA .45	$250	$1600	5,000
NRA Centennial SAA .357 Mag.	250	1600	5,000
NRA Centennial Gold Cup .45 Auto	250	1295	2,500

1971	Issue	NIB	Amount Mfg.
U.S. Grant 1851 Navy	250	750	4,750
Robt. E. Lee 1851 Navy	250	750	4,750
Lee - Grant Set 1851 Navies	500	1500	250
Kansas Ft. Ser. Ft. Scott Scout	130	450	500

1972	Issue	NIB	Amount Mfg.
Centennial Cased Set Florida Terr. Sesquicent. Scout	$125	$550	2,001
Arizona Ranger Scout	135	550	3,001

1975	Issue	NIB	Amount Mfg.
Peacemaker Centennial SAA .45	$300	$1700	1,500
Peacemaker Centennial SAA .44-40	300	1700	1,500
Peacemaker	625	3600	500

1976	Issue	NIB	Amount Mfg.
U.S. Bicentennial Set (SAA .45 Python .357 Mag., Dragoon black powder)	$1695	$6000	1,776

1977	Issue	NIB	Amount Mfg.
2nd Amendment .22	$195	$450	3,020
U.S. Cavalry 200th Anniversary Set	995	1450	3,000

1978	Issue	NIB	Amount Mfg.
Statehood 3rd Model Dragoon	$12500	$7500	52

1979	Issue	NIB	Amount Mfg.
Ned Buntline SAA N.F. .45	$895	$1295	3,000
Ohio President's Spec. Edit. .45 Auto	N/A	995	250
Tombstone Cent. .45 SAA	550	1500	300

1980	Issue	NIB	Amount Mfg.
Drug Enforcement Agency .45 Auto	$550	$1100	910
Olympics Ace Spec. Edition .22	1000	1295	200
Heritage Walker .44 Percussion	1495	950	1,847

1981	Issue	NIB	Amount Mfg.
John M. Browning .45 Auto	$1100	$995	3,000
Ace Signature Series .22	1000	1350	1,000

1982	Issue	NIB	Amount Mfg.
John Wayne SAA	$2995	$2250	3,100
John Wayne SAA Deluxe	10000	7500	500
John Wayne SAA Presentation	20000	13500	100

1983	Issue	NIB	Amount Mfg.
Buffalo Bill Wild West Show Cent. SAA	$2995	$1595	500

1984	Issue	NIB	Amount Mfg.
1st Edition Govt. Model .380 ACP	$425	$750	1,000
Duke Frontier .22	475	850	1,000
Winchester/Colt SAA .44-40	N/A	2500	4,000
USA Edition SAA .44-40	4995	3500	100
Kit Carson New Frontier .22	550	550	1,000
2nd Edition Govt. Model .380 ACP	525	750	1,000
Officer's ACP Commencement Issue	700	1000	1,000
Theodore Roosevelt SAA .44-40	1695	1995	500

1984	Issue	NIB	Amount Mfg.
No Amer. Oilmen Buntline SAA .45	3900	3500	200

1985	Issue	NIB	Amount Mfg.
Mustang 1st Edition .380 ACP	$475	$750	1,000
Officer's ACP Heirloom Edition	1575	1550	N/A
Klay-Colt 1851 Navy	1850	1850	150
Klay-Colt 1851 Navy Engraved Edit.	3150	3150	50
Double Diamond Set .357 Python and .45 ACP Officer's Model	1575	6000	1,000
Texas 150th Sesquicent. SAA	1836	1600	1,000
Texas 150th Sesquicent. SAA Premier	7,995	5000	75

1986	Issue	NIB	Amount Mfg.
150th Anniversary SAA .45	$1595	$1995	1,000
150th Anniversary Engraving Sampler	1613	3500	N/A
150th Anniversary Engraving Sampler .45 Auto	1155	2000	N/A
Texas 150th Sesquicent. Sheriff's .45	836	1695	N/A

1987	Issue	NIB	Amount Mfg.
Combat Elite Custom Edition .45 Auto	$900	$1100	500
12th Man Spirit of Aggieland .45 Auto	950	995	999

1989	Issue	NIB	Amount Mfg.
Snake Eyes Ltd. Edit. 2-2.5" Pythons	$1000	$3500	500

1990	Issue	NIB	Amount Mfg.
Joe Foss Limited Edition .45 Gov't Model	$1375	$1900	300

COLT REPRODUCTION PERCUSSION REVOLVERS

Revolvers listed were manufactured in a variety of styles (cylinder form, stainless steel, etc.) that affect prices. Factory engraved examples command a considerable premium over prices listed. Imported from Italy.

Walker

Made from 1979 to 1981; serial numbers 1200-4120 and 32256 to 32500.

NIB	Exc.	V.G.	Good	Fair	Poor
950	750	500	—	—	—

Walker Heritage Model

NIB	Exc.	V.G.	Good	Fair	Poor
1000	—	—	—	—	—

First Model Dragoon

Made from 1980 to 1982; serial numbers 24100-34500.

NIB	Exc.	V.G.	Good	Fair	Poor
595	400	300	—	—	—

Second Model Dragoon

Made from 1980 to 1982; serial numbers as above.

NIB	Exc.	V.G.	Good	Fair	Poor
595	400	300	—	—	—

Third Model Dragoon

Made from 1980 to 1982; serial numbers as above.

NIB	Exc.	V.G.	Good	Fair	Poor
595	400	300	—	—	—

Model 1848 Pocket Pistol

Made in 1981; serial numbers 16000-17851.

NIB	Exc.	V.G.	Good	Fair	Poor
600	425	325	—	—	—

Model 1851 Navy Revolver

Made from 1971 to 1978; serial numbers 4201-25100 and 24900-29150.

NIB	Exc.	V.G.	Good	Fair	Poor
595	400	300	—	—	—

Model 1860 Army Revolver

Made from 1978 to 1982; serial numbers 201000-212835.

NIB	Exc.	V.G.	Good	Fair	Poor
595	400	300	—	—	—

Model 1861 Navy Revolver

Made during 1980 and 1981; serial numbers 40000-43165.

NIB	Exc.	V.G.	Good	Fair	Poor
595	400	300	—	—	—

Model 1862 Pocket Pistol

Made from 1979 to 1984; serial numbers 8000-58850.

NIB	Exc.	V.G.	Good	Fair	Poor
595	400	300	—	—	—

Model 1862 Police Revolver

Made from 1979 to 1984; serial numbers in above range.

NIB	Exc.	V.G.	Good	Fair	Poor
595	400	300	—	—	—

COLT BLACKPOWDER ARMS
Brooklyn, New York

These blackpowder revolvers and rifles were made under license from Colt. Imported from Italy. No longer in business.

1842 Paterson Colt No. 5 Holster Model

A copy of No. 5 Holster model. Chambered for .36-caliber ball. Fitted with 7.5" octagon barrel. Hand engraved. Special order revolver.

NIB	Exc.	V.G.	Good	Fair	Poor
1900	1200	900	600	450	200

Walker

This .44-caliber large-frame revolver fitted with 9" barrel.

NIB	Exc.	V.G.	Good	Fair	Poor
975	600	350	300	200	150

Walker 150th Anniversary Model

Marked "A Company No. 1" in gold. Introduced 1997.

NIB	Exc.	V.G.	Good	Fair	Poor
975	600	350	300	200	150

Whitneyville Hartford Dragoon

Similar in appearance to Walker colt. Revolver fitted with 7.5" barrel and silver plated iron backstrap and trigger guard. Limited edition, with a total of 2,400 guns built. Serial numbers between 1100 through 1340.

NIB	Exc.	V.G.	Good	Fair	Poor
1075	700	450	32	225	200

Marine Dragoon

Special limited edition presentation grade in honor of U.S. Marine Corps.

NIB	Exc.	V.G.	Good	Fair	Poor
1100	725	450	32	225	200

3rd Model Dragoon

Another large-frame revolver, with 7.5" barrel, brass backstrap, 3-screw frame and unfluted cylinder.

NIB	Exc.	V.G.	Good	Fair	Poor
675	500	350	300	200	150

Steel Backstrap

NIB	Exc.	V.G.	Good	Fair	Poor
600	425	375	325	200	150

Fluted Cylinder

NIB	Exc.	V.G.	Good	Fair	Poor
610	435	375	325	200	150

Cochise Dragoon

Commemorative issue Third Model, with gold inlay frame and barrel with special grips.

NIB	Exc.	V.G.	Good	Fair	Poor
975	600	350	300	200	150

Colt 1849 Model Pocket

Small-frame revolver chambered in .31-caliber, with 4" barrel. Fitted with one-piece walnut grips.

NIB	Exc.	V.G.	Good	Fair	Poor
575	475	325	275	200	150

Colt 1851 Model Navy

Medium-frame revolver chambered in .36-caliber, with 7.5" barrel. Walnut grips and case color frame.

NIB	Exc.	V.G.	Good	Fair	Poor
635	575	400	300	200	125

Dual Cylinder

NIB	Exc.	V.G.	Good	Fair	Poor
675	595	400	300	200	125

Colt Model 1860 Army

Model chambered in .44-caliber, with roll engraved cylinder and one piece walnut grips. Barrel length 8".

NIB	Exc.	V.G.	Good	Fair	Poor
675	575	400	300	200	125

Dual Cylinder

NIB	Exc.	V.G.	Good	Fair	Poor
700	600	450	350	225	150

Colt 1860 Officer's Model

Deluxe version of standard 1860. Special blued finish and gold crossed sabres. This is a 4-screw frame, with 8" barrel and 6-shot rebated cylinder.

NIB	Exc.	V.G.	Good	Fair	Poor
675	575	450	375	250	150

Colt Model 1860 Army Gold U.S. Cavalry

Features a gold engraved cylinder and gold barrel bands.

NIB	Exc.	V.G.	Good	Fair	Poor
650	575	450	375	250	150

Stainless Steel

NIB	Exc.	V.G.	Good	Fair	Poor
575	400	350	300	200	150

Colt 1860 Heirloom Edition

Elaborately engraved revolver done in Tiffany-style. Fitted with Tiffany-style grips.

NIB	Exc.	V.G.	Good	Fair	Poor
4100	3000	2175	1400	850	450

Colt Model 1861 Navy

This .36-caliber revolver features 7.5" barrel, with engraved cylinder, case colored frame and one piece walnut grips.

NIB	Exc.	V.G.	Good	Fair	Poor
700	550	350	300	200	150

General Custer

Same as above, with engraved frame and cylinder.

NIB	Exc.	V.G.	Good	Fair	Poor
975	850	700	500	300	200

Colt Model 1862 Pocket Navy

Small-frame revolver. Fitted with round engraved cylinder, 5" octagon barrel and hinged loading lever. Chambered for .36-caliber.

NIB	Exc.	V.G.	Good	Fair	Poor
550	475	325	275	200	150

Colt Model 1862 Trapper-Pocket Police

Small-frame revolver. Fitted with 3.5" barrel, silver backstrap and trigger guard. Cylinder is semi-fluted. Chambered in .36-caliber.

NIB	Exc.	V.G.	Good	Fair	Poor
600	475	325	275	200	150

Colt 1861 Musket

Civil War musket chambered in .58-caliber. Lockplate, hammer, buttplate, three barrel bands and 40" barrel are finished bright. Stock is a one-piece oil-finish affair. Bayonet and accessories are extra.

NIB	Exc.	V.G.	Good	Fair	Poor
800	650	500	325	275	150

Artillery Model

Same as above, fitted with 31.5" barrel.

NIB	Exc.	V.G.	Good	Fair	Poor
800	650	500	325	275	150

Presentation 1 of 1000

Limited to 1,000 guns. Special finished with a high polish and Colt's signature in gold on trigger guard. Sold with special custom wooden case.

NIB	Exc.	V.G.	Good	Fair	Poor
1650	1300	750	600	450	300

Presentation 1 of 1000 - Artillery Model

Same as above, with 31.5" barrel.

NIB	Exc.	V.G.	Good	Fair	Poor
1650	1300	750	600	450	300

Colt Gamemaster .50

Introduced in 1997. Rifle similar to above in general outline and in .50-caliber. Fitted with 31.5" barrel. Weight about 13 lbs.

NIB	Exc.	V.G.	Good	Fair	Poor
800	650	475	300	225	125

COLUMBIA ARMORY
Columbia, Tennessee

Trade name applied to a variety of solid frame cartridge revolvers made by John T. Smith Company of Rock Falls, Connecticut. They were marked "SAFETY HAMMERLESS REVOLVER". Model made under several trade names.

NIB	Exc.	V.G.	Good	Fair	Poor
—	—	225	110	75	50

COLUMBUS F. A. MFG. CO.
Columbus, Georgia

Columbus Revolver

A .36-caliber double-action percussion revolver, with 6-shot unfluted cylinder and 7.5" octagonal barrel. Similar in appearance to 1851 Colt Navy. Pistol is browned steel, with brass gripstraps and walnut grips. Barrel marked "Columbus Fire Arms Manuf. Co/Columbus Ga.". Manufactured 100 in 1863 and 1864.

NIB	Exc.	V.G.	Good	Fair	Poor
—	—	115000	55000	35000	12500

COMANCHE
Buenos Aires, Argentina
See—Firestorm

Comanche I

Single-/double-action revolver chambered in .22 LR. Nine-shot cylinder, 6" barrel, adjustable sights, blued or stainless steel construction with rubber grips.

NIB	Exc.	V.G.	Good	Fair	Poor
225	150	100	65	35	15

Comanche II

Similar to above in .38 Special, with 2", 3" or 4" barrel.

NIB	Exc.	V.G.	Good	Fair	Poor
225	150	100	65	35	15

Comanche III

Similar to above in .357 Magnum. Additional 6" barrel option.

NIB	Exc.	V.G.	Good	Fair	Poor
250	150	100	65	35	15

Super Comanche

Single-shot break-action pistol chambered in .410/.45 Colt. Matte black finish, rubber grips.

NIB	Exc.	V.G.	Good	Fair	Poor
195	150	125	85	50	25

COMMANDO ARMS
Knoxville, Tennessee

Formerly known as Volunteer Enterprises. Name change took place in 1978.

Mark III Carbine

A .45 ACP caliber semi-automatic rifle, with 16.5" barrel, peep rear sight and vertical fore-grip. Manufactured between 1969 and 1976.

NIB	Exc.	V.G.	Good	Fair	Poor
675	550	375	300	225	150

Mark 9 Carbine

As above in 9mm caliber.

NIB	Exc.	V.G.	Good	Fair	Poor
675	550	375	300	225	150

Mark .45

New designation for Mark III after the company changed its name.

NIB	Exc.	V.G.	Good	Fair	Poor
675	550	375	300	225	150

COMPETITOR CORP.
New Ipswich, New Hampshire

Competitor Single-Shot

Single-shot pistol chambered for calibers from .22 LR to .50 Action Express. Choice of barrel lengths from 10.5", 14" and 16". Ramp front sight. Adjustable single stage trigger. Interchangeable barrels. Matte blue finish. Weight about 59 oz. depending on barrel length. Introduced in 1988.

NIB	Exc.	V.G.	Good	Fair	Poor
465	325	275	225	175	125

CONNECTICUT ARMS CO.
Norfolk, Connecticut

Pocket Revolver

A .28-caliber spur trigger revolver, with 3" octagonal barrel, 6-shot un-fluted cylinder, using a cup-primed cartridge and loads from front of the cylinder. There is a hinged hook on side of the frame under the cylinder that acts as the extractor. Silver-plated brass blued, with walnut grips. Barrel marked "Conn. Arms Co. Norfolk, Conn." Approximately 2,700 manufactured in 1860s.

NIB	Exc.	V.G.	Good	Fair	Poor
—	—	950	750	300	100

CONNECTICUT SHOTGUN MANUFACTURING COMPANY
New Britain, Connecticut

RBL Side-By-Side Shotgun

Round-action SXS shotguns made in the USA. Chambered in 12-, 16-, 20-, 28-gauge and .410 bore with scaled frames. Barrel lengths 26", 28", 30" and 32", with five TruLock choke tubes. Deluxe fancy-grade walnut buttstock and fore-end, Quick Change recoil pad in two lengths. Various dimensions and options available depending on gauge. Values shown are for 12-gauge. **NOTE:** Add 20 percent for 20-gauge; 30 percent for 28-gauge; 75 percent for .410 bore.

NIB	Exc.	V.G.	Good	Fair	Poor
4000	2950	2000	1275	800	400

A-10 American

Sidelock design in 12-, 20- or 28-gauge with XX grade walnut stock and light scroll engraving. Offered in standard barrel lengths from 26" to 32". Options include higher-grade wood and engraving. Prices shown are for standard model. Introduced in 2010

NIB	Exc.	V.G.	Good	Fair	Poor
7500	6000	4500	3500	—	—

Model 21

A faithful rendition of famous Winchester side-by-side shotgun that was in production from 1931 to 1959. On custom-order from 1960 to 1993. Made in all gauges and standard barrel lengths, with many options. Each gun is custom made to order. Introduced in 2002. Prices are for standard 12-, 16- and 20-gauge models. **NOTE:** Add $3000 for 28-gauge or .410 bore, plus $10,000 if made on optional small frame.

NIB	Exc.	V.G.	Good	Fair	Poor
15000	12000	9500	7000	3500	—

Model 21 Grand American

As above with high-grade gold-inlayed engraving, AAA-grade walnut stock, with elaborate checkering and carving patterns. Comes with two sets of barrels. **NOTE:** Add $3000 for 28-gauge or .410 bore, plus $10,000 if made on optional small frame.

NIB	Exc.	V.G.	Good	Fair	Poor
25000	20000	17500	15000	8000	—

Model 21 Over/Under

An over/under model patterned after classic Winchester side-by-side. Made on the same machining and tooling, with the same manufacturing techniques as SxS model, resulting in virtually the same balance, feel and appearance. Features include automatic ejectors, single-selective trigger, American walnut stock with straight- or pistol-grip. Made only in 20-gauge, with 26", 28", 30" or 32" barrels that are steel-shot compatible. Comes with five choke tubes. Wood upgrades are available at prices up to $900.

NIB	Exc.	V.G.	Good	Fair	Poor
3400	2900	2450	1900	1350	750

Model 21 Side-By-Side Rifle

In .22 Long Rifle caliber, this very unique double rifle is built on a frame even smaller than the .410 frame. Each gun is custom made, with many upgrades and engraving options available. Higher grades have a MRSP from $30,000 to $34,000. **NOTE:** A few custom made-to-order models in various centerfire calibers have been built in the past, with very limited production. Values are estimated to be approximately 50 percent higher than the rimfire model.

NIB	Exc.	V.G.	Good	Fair	Poor
22500	18000	14000	—	—	—

A.H. Fox

Conn. Shotgun Co. also makes high-grade side-by-side shotguns, based on classic A.H. Fox models of early 20th century. These are CE and DE grades, with many available options and upgrades. Prices shown are for base CE model.

NIB	Exc.	V.G.	Good	Fair	Poor
16500	12000	9500	—	—	—

CONNECTICUT VALLEY ARMS CO.
Norcross, Georgia

RIFLES

Express Rifle

A .50-caliber double-barrel percussion rifle, with 28" barrels. Blued, with walnut stock. **NOTE:** Add 25 percent for deluxe version.

NIB	Exc.	V.G.	Good	Fair	Poor
625	475	425	375	325	200

Over/Under Rifle

A .50-caliber double-barrel over/under rifle, with 26" barrels. Blued, with walnut stock.

NIB	Exc.	V.G.	Good	Fair	Poor
600	475	425	375	325	200

Hawken Rifle

A .50-caliber with 28" octagonal barrel, double-set triggers and walnut stock.

NIB	Exc.	V.G.	Good	Fair	Poor
450	325	275	225	150	100

Presentation Grade Hawken

As above, with engraved lock, patchbox and finely figured stock.

NIB	Exc.	V.G.	Good	Fair	Poor
550	425	375	325	275	200

Pennsylvania Long Rifle

A .50-caliber flintlock rifle, with 40" octagonal barrel, double-set triggers and walnut stock.

NIB	Exc.	V.G.	Good	Fair	Poor
475	400	350	300	250	175

Kentucky Rifle

A .45-caliber percussion rifle, with 33.5" octagonal barrel and walnut stock.

NIB	Exc.	V.G.	Good	Fair	Poor
275	225	175	150	100	75

Mountain Rifle

A .50- or .54-caliber percussion half-stock rifle.

NIB	Exc.	V.G.	Good	Fair	Poor
300	225	175	125	100	75

Blazer Rifle

A .50-caliber percussion rifle, with 28" octagonal barrel and walnut stock.

NIB	Exc.	V.G.	Good	Fair	Poor
150	125	100	85	65	45

Apollo Shadow SS

Introduced in 1993. Rifle features an in-line stainless steel bolt spring-action. A 24" blued round barrel with octagonal one piece receiver drilled and tapped. Stock is black hardwood-textured with Dura Grip. Pistol-grip and recoil pad. Offered in either .50- or .54-caliber. Weight about 9 lbs.

NIB	Exc.	V.G.	Good	Fair	Poor
175	150	125	100	75	50

Apollo Classic

Similar to above Apollo, with dark brown stained laminated hardwood stock. Pistol-grip, raised comb and recoil pad. Weight about 8.5 lbs.

NIB	Exc.	V.G.	Good	Fair	Poor
215	175	150	125	100	75

Apollo Carbelite

Offered in .50-caliber, with percussion bolt and 27" blued round taper barrel. Octagonal receiver drilled and tapped. Fitted with Carbelite composite stock with Monte Carlo and cheekpiece with pistol-grip. Weight about 7.5 lbs.

NIB	Exc.	V.G.	Good	Fair	Poor
280	225	175	150	100	75

Apollo Starfire

Chambered for .50-caliber bullet. Rifle is an in-line type, with 24" stainless steel barrel. Synthetic stock, checkered pistol-grip, raised comb and cheekpiece. Weight about 6.5 lbs.

NIB	Exc.	V.G.	Good	Fair	Poor
225	175	150	125	100	75

Apollo Eclipse Rifle

Offered in either .50- or .54-caliber, with 24" round barrel and blued steel receiver. Synthetic stock, with checkered pistol, raised comb and cheekpiece. Weight about 6.5 lbs.

NIB	Exc.	V.G.	Good	Fair	Poor
175	150	125	100	85	65

Apollo Dominator

Fitted with a synthetic thumbhole stock and 24" round barrel. Chambered for .50-caliber bullet. Introduced in 1996. Weight about 8.5 lbs.

NIB	Exc.	V.G.	Good	Fair	Poor
300	225	175	150	100	75

Apollo Brown Bear

This .50-caliber rifle fitted with a hardwood stock, pistol-grip, raised comb and cheekpiece. Round 24" barrel. Introduced in 1996. Weight about 6.5 lbs.

NIB	Exc.	V.G.	Good	Fair	Poor
200	175	150	125	100	75

Frontier Carbine

Fitted with 24" blued barrel, Offered in .50-caliber percussion or flintlock. Case-hardened lock, with hardwood stock. Weight about 6.75 lbs.

NIB	Exc.	V.G.	Good	Fair	Poor
150	125	100	85	75	50

Plainsman Rifle

This .50-caliber percussion rifle has 26" octagonal barrel, with case-hardened lock and hardwood stock. Weight about 6.5 lbs.

NIB	Exc.	V.G.	Good	Fair	Poor
130	115	100	85	75	50

Panther Carbine

Percussion rifle available in either .50- or .54-caliber. Fitted with 24" blued octagonal barrel and Hawken-style case-hardened lock. Stock is textured black Dura Grip over hardwood, with Monte Carlo comb, cheekpiece and pistol-grip. Weight about 7.5 lbs.

NIB	Exc.	V.G.	Good	Fair	Poor
150	125	100	85	75	50

Bushwacker Rifle

This .50-caliber percussion rifle fitted with 26" octagonal barrel. Case-hardened engraved lock, brown stained hardwood stock and rounded nose. Weight about 7.5 lbs.

NIB	Exc.	V.G.	Good	Fair	Poor
135	115	100	85	75	50

Trophy Carbine

Fitted with 24" half-round/half-octagon barrel and Hawken-style lock. Stock is walnut with Monte Carlo comb, cheekpiece and pistol-grip. Offered in .50- or .54-caliber percussion. Weight about 6.75 lbs.

NIB	Exc.	V.G.	Good	Fair	Poor
215	175	150	125	100	75

Varmint Rifle

Lightweight percussion rifle in .32-caliber, with 24" octagon barrel and case colored lock. Stock is hardwood. Weight about 6.75 lbs.

NIB	Exc.	V.G.	Good	Fair	Poor
175	150	125	100	85	75

Woodsman Rifle LS

Introduced in 1994. Features 26" blued octagon barrel, with dark brown stained laminated hardwood stock. Offered in .50- or .54-caliber percussion. Weight about 6.5 lbs.

NIB	Exc.	V.G.	Good	Fair	Poor
135	115	100	85	75	50

Frontier Hunter Carbine

Offered in either .50- or .54-caliber, this percussion rifle fitted with 24" blued octagon barrel. Case-hardened 45° offset hammer. Stock is dark stained laminated hardwood. Weight about 7.5 lbs.

NIB	Exc.	V.G.	Good	Fair	Poor
170	150	125	100	75	50

Grey Wolf Rifle

Offered in either .50- or .54-caliber, this percussion rifle fitted with 26" matte blue octagon barrel. Case-hardened engraved lock. Stock is matte gray composite, with raised comb, checkered pistol-grip and buttplate. Weight about 6.5 lbs.

NIB	Exc.	V.G.	Good	Fair	Poor
160	125	100	85	75	50

Lone Grey Wolf Rifle

Introduced in 1994. This .50-caliber percussion rifle features 26" matte blued octagon barrel. Trigger guard is oversized. Composite stock is black and has a raised comb, checkered pistol-grip and recoil pad. Weight about 6.5 lbs.

NIB	Exc.	V.G.	Good	Fair	Poor
185	150	125	100	75	50

Timber Wolf Rifle

Introduced in 1994. Similar to above model, but furnished with Realtree composite stock. Raised comb, checkered pistol-grip and buttplate. Weight about 6.5 lbs.

NIB	Exc.	V.G.	Good	Fair	Poor
185	165	140	100	75	50

Tracker Carbine LS

Introduced in 1994. Fitted with 21" blued half-round/half-octagon barrel. Hawken-style lock. Stock is laminated dark brown with matte finish and straight-grip. Chambered for .50-caliber percussion. Weight about 6.5 lbs.

NIB	Exc.	V.G.	Good	Fair	Poor
185	165	140	100	75	50

Stag Horn

Introduced in 1996. This in-line rifle chambered for .50- or .54-caliber bullet. Round barrel is 24", with blued finish. Stock is synthetic, with checkered pistol-grip, raised comb and cheekpiece. Weight about 6.5 lbs.

NIB	Exc.	V.G.	Good	Fair	Poor
175	150	125	100	85	65

Electra

A .50-caliber inline muzzle-loader that uses electronic-arc ignition rather than caps or primers. Powered by common 9v battery. Finishes include stainless/camo, stainless/black composite and blued/black composite. Introduced in 2007. Price given for stainless/camo version.

NIB	Exc.	V.G.	Good	Fair	Poor
600	500	400	300	200	100

Accura MR

Break-action .50-caliber in-line ignition muzzle-loading rifle, with weather guard finish, adjustable trigger, quick release breech plug, 416 stainless steel barrel and camo polymer stock. Barrel length 25", weight 6.2 lbs. Introduced 2012.

NIB	Exc.	V.G.	Good	Fair	Poor
525	450	400	350	300	250

Optima V2

Break-action .50-caliber in-line ignition muzzle-loading rifle, with black or Realtree camo finish, quick release breech plug, 416 stainless steel barrel and polymer standard or thumb-hole stock. Barrel length 26", weight 6.7 lbs. **NOTE:** Add $25.00 for thumbhole stock.

NIB	Exc.	V.G.	Good	Fair	Poor
360	300	275	235	200	185

SHOTGUNS

Brittany 11 Shotgun

A .410 bore double-barrel percussion shotgun, with 24" barrels, double triggers and walnut stock.

NIB	Exc.	V.G.	Good	Fair	Poor
425	350	250	150	125	75

Trapper Shotgun - #1

A 12-gauge percussion single-barrel shotgun, with 28" barrel threaded for choke tubes and walnut stock.

NIB	Exc.	V.G.	Good	Fair	Poor
275	250	225	175	150	100

Classic Turkey Double-Barrel Shotgun

A 12-gauge percussion breech-loading shotgun, with 28" barrel. Checkered stock is European walnut with straight-grip. Weight about 9 lbs.

NIB	Exc.	V.G.	Good	Fair	Poor
495	375	275	200	175	100

Trapper Shotgun #2

A single-barrel 12-gauge shotgun, with 28" barrel. Stock is straight-grip hardwood with checkering. Supplied with three interchangeable chokes. Weight about 6 lbs.

NIB	Exc.	V.G.	Good	Fair	Poor
295	250	200	150	100	75

PISTOLS

Made by Pedersoli, Uberti and other Italian makers.

Siber

A .45-caliber percussion pistol patterned after Swiss Siber.

NIB	Exc.	V.G.	Good	Fair	Poor
450	325	275	225	150	100

Kentucky

A .45-caliber single-shot percussion pistol, with 10" barrel and walnut stock.

NIB	Exc.	V.G.	Good	Fair	Poor
140	125	100	80	60	40

Philadelphia Derringer

A .45-caliber single-shot percussion pistol, with 3.25" barrel and walnut stock.

NIB	Exc.	V.G.	Good	Fair	Poor
125	95	50	40	30	20

Sheriff's Model

A .36-caliber percussion revolver, nickel-plated with walnut grips.

NIB	Exc.	V.G.	Good	Fair	Poor
225	200	175	150	125	100

3rd Model Dragoon

NIB	Exc.	V.G.	Good	Fair	Poor
225	200	175	150	125	100

Colt Walker Replica

NIB	Exc.	V.G.	Good	Fair	Poor
425	295	225	200	175	150

Remington Bison

NIB	Exc.	V.G.	Good	Fair	Poor
250	225	200	175	150	125

Pocket Police

NIB	Exc.	V.G.	Good	Fair	Poor
135	110	100	85	65	45

Pocket Revolver

Chambered for .31-caliber. Fitted with 4" octagon barrel. Cylinder holds five bullets. Solid brass frame. Weight about 15 oz.

NIB	Exc.	V.G.	Good	Fair	Poor
225	150	85	75	60	50

Wells Fargo

NIB	Exc.	V.G.	Good	Fair	Poor
225	150	85	75	60	50

1851 Navy

NIB	Exc.	V.G.	Good	Fair	Poor
250	225	200	175	150	125

1861 Navy

NIB	Exc.	V.G.	Good	Fair	Poor
250	225	200	175	150	125

1860 Army

NIB	Exc.	V.G.	Good	Fair	Poor
250	225	200	175	150	125

1858 Remington

NIB	Exc.	V.G.	Good	Fair	Poor
275	225	125	100	75	50

1858 Remington Target

As above, but fitted with adjustable sights.

NIB	Exc.	V.G.	Good	Fair	Poor
275	225	125	100	75	50

Bison

A 6-shot .44-caliber revolver, with 10.25" octagonal barrel. Solid brass frame. Weight about 48 oz.

NIB	Exc.	V.G.	Good	Fair	Poor
275	225	125	100	75	50

Hawken Pistol

A .50-caliber percussion pistol, with 9.75" octagon barrel. Stock is hardwood. Weight about 50 oz.

NIB	Exc.	V.G.	Good	Fair	Poor
250	180	115	75	65	50

CONSTABLE, R.
Philadelphia, Pennsylvania

Pocket Pistol

Single-shot percussion pistol, with 3" round or octagonal barrel. German-silver mounts and walnut stock. Pistols are marked "R. Constable Philadelphia". Manufactured during late 1840s and 1850s.

NIB	Exc.	V.G.	Good	Fair	Poor
—	—	2200	1100	550	200

CONTENTO/VENTUR
SIDE-BY-SIDES

Model 51

A 12-, 16-, 20-, 28-gauge and .410 bore boxlock double-barrel shotgun, with 26", 28", 30" and 32" barrels. Various chokes, extractors and double triggers. Checkered walnut stock. Introduced in 1980, discontinued 1985.

NIB	Exc.	V.G.	Good	Fair	Poor
—	500	350	300	225	150

Model 52

As above in 10-gauge.

NIB	Exc.	V.G.	Good	Fair	Poor
—	500	350	300	225	150

Model 53

As above, with scalloped receiver, automatic ejectors and available with single-selective trigger. Discontinued in 1985. **NOTE:** Add 25 percent for single-selective trigger.

NIB	Exc.	V.G.	Good	Fair	Poor
—	550	400	350	250	200

Model 62

A 12-, 20- or 28-gauge H&H sidelock shotgun, with various barrel lengths and chokes. Automatic ejectors, cocking indicators, floral engraved receiver and checkered walnut stock. Discontinued in 1982.

NIB	Exc.	V.G.	Good	Fair	Poor
—	1150	800	750	600	450

Model 64

As above, but more finely finished. No longer in production.

NIB	Exc.	V.G.	Good	Fair	Poor
—	1250	900	850	700	550

OVER/UNDERS

A 12-gauge over/under shotgun, with 32" barrels, screw-in choke tubes, high ventilated rib, automatic ejectors and standard single-selective trigger. Checkered with Monte Carlo walnut stock.

NIB	Exc.	V.G.	Good	Fair	Poor
—	1250	900	750	600	500

Mark 2

As above, with an extra single-barrel. Fitted in a leather case.

NIB	Exc.	V.G.	Good	Fair	Poor
—	1500	1200	1050	900	800

Mark 3

As above, but engraved with a finely figured walnut stock.

NIB	Exc.	V.G.	Good	Fair	Poor
—	1850	1500	1250	1100	950

Mark 3 Combo

As above, with an extra single-barrel. Fitted in a leather case.

NIB	Exc.	V.G.	Good	Fair	Poor
—	3200	2600	2250	1750	1300

CONTINENTAL
RWM
Cologne, Germany

Continental Pocket Pistol (6.35mm)

A 6.35mm caliber semi-automatic pistol, with 2" barrel, internal hammer and 7-shot detachable magazine. Blued, with plastic grips and slide marked "Continental Kal. 6.35". Produced during 1920s.

NOTE: Pistol may have been manufactured in Spain and carried German proof marks, because it was sold by RWM in Germany.

NIB	Exc.	V.G.	Good	Fair	Poor
—	300	150	125	100	75

Continental Pocket Pistol (7.65mm)

German-made pistol chambered for 7.65mm cartridge. Fitted with 3.9" barrel. Rear sight is a U-notch in slide. Magazine capacity 8 rounds. Weight about 20 oz. Made prior to 1914.

NIB	Exc.	V.G.	Good	Fair	Poor
—	500	300	225	150	100

CONTINENTAL ARMS CO.
Norwich, Connecticut

Pepperbox

.22-caliber 5-barrel pepperbox, with spur trigger and 2.5" barrels marked "Continental Arms Co. Norwich Ct. Patented Aug. 28, 1866". Some examples found marked "Ladies Companion".

Courtesy Milwaukee Public Museum, Milwaukee, Wisconsin

NIB	Exc.	V.G.	Good	Fair	Poor
—	—	2250	1000	350	250

CONTINENTAL ARMS CO.
Leige, Belgium

Double Rifle

A .270, .303, .30-40, .30-06, .348, 375 H&H, .400 Jeffreys, .465, .475, .500 and .600 Nitro Express caliber Anson & Deeley boxlock double-barreled rifle, with 24" or 26" barrels. Double triggers and checkered walnut stock.

NIB	Exc.	V.G.	Good	Fair	Poor
—	6500	4500	3750	3000	2250

COOK & BROTHER RIFLES AND CARBINES
New Orleans, Louisiana

In early 1861, Ferdinand W.C. Cook and his brother Francis L. Cook, both English emigres, joined to form Cook & Brother in New Orleans to manufacture rifles and carbines following the English P1853 series for the newly seceded state of Louisiana and its neighbors. Between June 1861 and the federal occupation of New Orleans in April 1862, this firm produced about 200 cavalry and artillery carbines and about 1000 rifles. Having successfully moved the armory's machinery before federal occupation, the firm continued manufacture of rifles in Selma, Alabama during 1862, probably completing another 1,000 rifles with the New Orleans lock markings from the parts brought with them. Re-established in Athens, Georgia in early 1863, the firm continued to build both carbines and rifles, manufacturing more than 5,500 above the New Orleans production through 1864. The firm's products were clearly among the best small arms made within the Confederacy.

Cook & Brother Rifles (New Orleans & Selma production)

Overall length 48.75"; barrel length 33"; caliber .58. Markings: representation of a Confederate flag ("Stars & Bars") and "COOK & BROTHER/N.O./1861 (or) 1862" on lock; same usually on barrel together with serial number and "PROVED" near breech. Rifles in the early production have long range rear sights and unusual two piece block and blade front sights as well as an integral bayonet lug with guide on right side of barrel. Later production utilizes a brass clamping ring for the bayonet, a block open rear sight and a simple block and blade front sight. Earlier production will claim a premium if in good condition.

Courtesy Milwaukee Public Museum, Milwaukee, Wisconsin

NIB	Exc.	V.G.	Good	Fair	Poor
—	—	35000	15500	3000	1650

Cook & Brother Carbines (New Orleans production)

Overall length 40" (artillery), 37" (cavalry); barrel length 24" (artillery), 21" to 21.5" (cavalry); caliber .58. Markings: As on Cook & Brother rifles (New Orleans production) artillery and cavalry carbines were produced in New Orleans in a separate serial range from the rifles. Total production is thought not to have exceeded 225, divided evenly between 1861 and 1862 dates. In addition to the overall and barrel lengths, the main difference between the artillery and cavalry carbines is the manner in which they were carried. The former bears standard sling rings on the upper band and the trigger guard strap, the latter has a bar with a ring on the left side of the stock. Both are exceedingly rare.

NIB	Exc.	V.G.	Good	Fair	Poor
—	—	20000	8500	5000	1500

Cook & Brother Rifles (Athens production)

Overall length 49"; barrel length 33"; caliber .58. Markings: representation of a Confederate flag ("Stars & Bars") and "COOK & BROTHER/ATHENS GA./date (1863 or 1864) and serial number on lock; "PROVED" on barrel near breech; serial number on various metal parts. After re-establishing their plant at Athens, Georgia, in the spring of 1863, Cook & Brother continued to manufacture rifles in a consecutive serial range after their New Orleans/Selma production (beginning about serial number 2000) and continued to make arms well into 1864 (through at least serial number 7650) until Sherman's army threatened the plant and necessitated the employment of its workforce in a military capacity as the 23rd Battalion Georgia State Guard.

Courtesy Milwaukee Public Museum, Milwaukee, Wisconsin

NIB	Exc.	V.G.	Good	Fair	Poor
—	—	21000	9300	3000	900

Cook & Brother Carbines (Athens production)

Overall length 40" (artillery) or 37" (cavalry); barrel lengths 24" (artillery) or 21" to 21.5" (cavalry); caliber .58. Markings: same as on Athens production rifles. Artillery and cavalry carbines were manufactured in the same serial range as the Athens production rifles (about 2000 through 7650). As in New Orleans production, the artillery and cavalry carbines are distinguished from one another by their respective lengths. Unlike New Orleans/Selma production, however, some of the cavalry carbines are mounted with sling swivels of the artillery style, while others bear the sling ring on the left side and additionally have a swivel ring to secure the ramrod.

NIB	Exc.	V.G.	Good	Fair	Poor
—	—	27500	9800	3900	1250

COONAN ARMS/COONAN INC.
Blaine, Minnesota

Original Coonan Arms was based in St. Paul, Minnesota from 1983 to 1994 and in Maplewood, Minnesota from 1994 to 1998. That company ceased operations in 1998. Current manufacturer was established as Coonan Inc. in 2009 and is located in Blaine, Minnesota. **NOTE:** Add $40 for 6" barrel; $130 for Bomar adjustable sights; $40 for .38 Special conversion; $40 for checkered walnut grips; $100 with Teflon slide; $100 with Teflon frame.

Model A

A .357 Magnum semi-automatic pistol, with 5" barrel, 7-shot detachable magazine and fixed sights. Stainless steel with walnut grips. Introduced in 1981, discontinued 1984.

NIB	Exc.	V.G.	Good	Fair	Poor
1200	1000	875	500	350	275

Model B

An improved version of Model A, with a linkless barrel system, extended grip safety, enclosed trigger bar and more contoured grip. A 6" barrel is available, as are adjustable sights, as extra cost options. A .38

Special conversion is also available. Introduced in 1985. A number of other options are also available that will affect value.

NIB	Exc.	V.G.	Good	Fair	Poor
1300	1175	925	675	500	300

Comp I

As above, with 6" barrel, attached compensator and stippled front grip strap. Introduced in 1989.

NIB	Exc.	V.G.	Good	Fair	Poor
1600	1250	1000	700	550	350

Comp I Deluxe

As above, with blued stainless steel slide, checkered grip straps and finer finishing.

NIB	Exc.	V.G.	Good	Fair	Poor
1650	1300	1050	750	600	400

Classic (Current Production)

Features an integrated compensator, with 5" barrel. Supplied with checkered walnut grips, Millett adjustable rear sight and two-tone Teflon finish. Magazine capacity 7 rounds; weight 42 oz.; overall length 8.3".

NIB	Exc.	V.G.	Good	Fair	Poor
1000	900	700	600	—	—

Cadet

Chambered for .357 Magnum cartridge, Has 3.9" barrel, with smooth walnut grips and fixed rear sight. Magazine capacity 6 rounds; weight about 39 oz.; overall length 7.8"; height 5.3". Coonan Arms refers to this model as "Short Grip".

NIB	Exc.	V.G.	Good	Fair	Poor
1150	875	675	500	400	400

Cadet II

Same as above, with standard grip. Magazine capacity 7 rounds.

NIB	Exc.	V.G.	Good	Fair	Poor
1150	875	675	500	400	200

Coonan .45 ACP

A 1911-style pistol similar to Coonan .357 models, except chambered in .45 ACP. Features 5" linkless barrel, pivoting trigger, external extractor, Novak style sights, smooth walnut grips and stainless finish. Introduced in 2016.

NIB	Exc.	V.G.	Good	Fair	Poor
1300	1050	900	—	—	—

COOPER, J. M. & CO.
Philadelphia, Pennsylvania

Pocket Revolver

A .31-caliber percussion double-action revolver, with 4", 5" or 6" octagonal barrel and 6-shot unfluted cylinder. Blued, with walnut grips. During first two years of production they were made in Pittsburgh, Pennsylvania and were so marked. Approximately 15,000 manufactured between 1864 and 1869. **NOTE:** Add 20 percent for Pittsburgh-marked models.

Courtesy Milwaukee Public Museum, Milwaukee, Wisconsin

NIB	Exc.	V.G.	Good	Fair	Poor
—	—	1850	775	200	100

COOPER ARMS
Stevensville, Montana

Model 36 Marksman

Premium bolt-action repeating rifle chambered for .22 LR cartridge. In centerfire calibers .17 CCM and .22 Hornet. The 23" Shilen barrel is mated to a solid bar stock receiver. High grade walnut used in stocks that are fine-lined checkered. Manufactured from 1992 to 1999.

Standard

NIB	Exc.	V.G.	Good	Fair	Poor
1100	900	700	500	300	200

Classic

NIB	Exc.	V.G.	Good	Fair	Poor
1800	1200	800	600	400	200

Custom Classic

NIB	Exc.	V.G.	Good	Fair	Poor
2000	1650	1150	850	600	300

Western Classic

Octagon barrel and case color metal.

NIB	Exc.	V.G.	Good	Fair	Poor
2800	2200	1500	850	600	300

BR-50 w/Jewell Trigger

NIB	Exc.	V.G.	Good	Fair	Poor
1800	1450	1100	800	600	300

IR-50-50 w/Jewell Trigger

NIB	Exc.	V.G.	Good	Fair	Poor
1800	1450	1100	800	600	300

Featherweight w/Jewell Trigger

NIB	Exc.	V.G.	Good	Fair	Poor
1800	1450	1100	800	600	300

Model 38/40

Bolt-action rifle chambered for .17 AK Hornet, .22 K Hornet or .22 Hornet. Made as a repeater in early '90s, single-shot from 1997 to present. Model 40 has a 3-lug bolt and some Anschutz parts.

Classic

NIB	Exc.	V.G.	Good	Fair	Poor
1800	1500	1100	800	600	300

Custom Classic

NIB	Exc.	V.G.	Good	Fair	Poor
2000	1750	1250	850	600	300

Western Classic (octagon barrel)

NIB	Exc.	V.G.	Good	Fair	Poor
2900	2300	1750	1300	700	350

Mannlicher Model

NIB	Exc.	V.G.	Good	Fair	Poor
3650	3000	2450	1850	800	450

Model 21

Bolt-action single-shot rifle chambered for these cartridges: .221 Fireball, .222, .223, 6x45, 6x47, .17 Mach IV and .17 Rem. A 24" stainless steel Shilen match grade barrel is fitted. AAA claro walnut is used. Oval forearm, ambidextrous palm swell, 22 lpi checkering, oil finish and Pachmayr buttpad are all standard features. Weight about 8 lbs.

Varmint Extreme

NIB	Exc.	V.G.	Good	Fair	Poor
2000	1600	1200	900	500	250

Classic

NIB	Exc.	V.G.	Good	Fair	Poor
1800	1400	1000	800	500	250

Custom Classic

NIB	Exc.	V.G.	Good	Fair	Poor
2100	1700	1300	900	600	300

Western Classic

NIB	Exc.	V.G.	Good	Fair	Poor
2800	2200	1500	850	600	300

Benchrest w/Jewell Trigger

NIB	Exc.	V.G.	Good	Fair	Poor
2100	1800	1250	850	600	300

Model 22

Bolt-action single-shot rifle chambered for a variety of calibers: 6mm PPC, .22-250, .220 Swift, .243, .25-06, .308, .22 BR, 7.62x39, 6.5x55. Pachmayr decelerator pad standard. Weight about 8.5 lbs.

Pro Varmint Extreme

NIB	Exc.	V.G.	Good	Fair	Poor
1750	1500	1200	800	600	300

Benchrest w/Jewell Trigger

NIB	Exc.	V.G.	Good	Fair	Poor
2100	1800	1300	900	650	300

Model 22 Repeater

Same as above, with magazine. Chambered for .22-25, .308, 7mm-08 and .243.

Classic

NIB	Exc.	V.G.	Good	Fair	Poor
2400	2000	1750	1250	800	325

Custom Classic

NIB	Exc.	V.G.	Good	Fair	Poor
2650	2200	1850	1400	900	400

Western Classic

NIB	Exc.	V.G.	Good	Fair	Poor
3000	2350	1950	1500	900	400

Model 52 Classic

Long-action repeater offered virtually in any centerfire caliber from .22-250 to .340 Weatherby. Has oil-finished AA Claro walnut stock, hand checkering, matte finish. Also offered with synthetic stock as Excalibur. Custom Classic has more extensive checkering, ebony fore-end cap. Western Classic available in any caliber has octagon barrel, case-hardened action, engraving. Introduced in 2007. **NOTE:** Add $150 for Excalibur, $1200 for Custom Classic, $2000 for Western Classic.

NIB	Exc.	V.G.	Good	Fair	Poor
1500	1300	1000	800	500	300

Model 54

Similar to above except with short action and in these calibers: .22-250, .243 Win., .250 Savage, .260 Rem., 7mm-08 Rem., .308 Win. Optional models same as Model 52 plus three varmint variants. **NOTE:** Add $150 for Excalibur, $400 for Varmint Extreme, $1200 for Custom Classic, $2000 for Western Classic.

NIB	Exc.	V.G.	Good	Fair	Poor
1500	1300	1000	800	500	300

Model 57

Bolt-action repeater chambered for the following rimfire calibers: .17 Mach II, .17 HMR, .22 LR or .22 Win. Magnum. Offered in several versions including standard model, with checkered walnut stock, matte finish, steel grip cap. **NOTE:** Add $500 for Custom Classic, $1200 for Western Classic

NIB	Exc.	V.G.	Good	Fair	Poor
1800	1400	1000	800	500	300

Model 58 Classic

Similar to Model 52 Classic, with most of the same options available. Chambered for .375 H&H, .404 Jeffery, .416 Rigby, .416 Rem., .458 Win., .458 Lott, .505 Gibbs. **NOTE:** Add $1,000 for Custom Classic; $1,200 for Western Classic.

NIB	Exc.	V.G.	Good	Fair	Poor
2500	2100	1750	1200	800	400

COOPERATIVA OBRERA
Eibar, Spain

Longines

A 7.65mm caliber semi-automatic pistol. Slide marked "Cal. 7.65 Automatic Pistol Longines".

NIB	Exc.	V.G.	Good	Fair	Poor
—	275	175	150	110	85

COPELAND, FRANK
Worcester, Massachusetts

Copeland Pocket Revolver .22

A .22 cartridge spur trigger revolver, with 2.5" barrel, 7-shot magazine, unfluted cylinder and lock notches on front. Frame is brass blued, walnut or rosewood grips. Barrel marked "F. Copeland, Worcester, Mass." Manufactured in 1860s.

NIB	Exc.	V.G.	Good	Fair	Poor
—	—	700	300	125	100

Copeland .32 Revolver

A .32-caliber spur trigger revolver, with 5-shot fluted cylinder and iron frame. Nickel-plated. Barrel marked "F. Copeland, Sterling, Mass." Manufactured in 1860s.

NIB	Exc.	V.G.	Good	Fair	Poor
—	—	700	300	150	75

COSMI, A. & F.
Torrette, Italy

Semi-Automatic

A 12- and 20-gauge top-break semi-automatic shotgun, with various barrel lengths and chokes. An 8-shot magazine and ventilated rib. Basically a custom-built made-to-order gun. There is a standard and deluxe model, with differences in degree of embellishment.

Standard Model

NIB	Exc.	V.G.	Good	Fair	Poor
14000	8500	4750	3250	2200	1500

Deluxe Model

NIB	Exc.	V.G.	Good	Fair	Poor
15500	9500	6000	4250	3250	1750

COSMOPOLITAN ARMS CO.
Hamilton, Ohio

Breech Loading Rifle

A .52-caliber single-shot percussion rifle, with 31" round barrel. Frame marked "Cosmopolitan Arms Co. Hamilton 0. U.S./Gross Patent". Blued, with walnut buttstock. Approximately 100 made between 1859 and 1862.

NIB	Exc.	V.G.	Good	Fair	Poor
—	—	7000	2750	775	450

COWLES & SON
Chicopee, Massachusetts

Single-Shot

A .22- or .30-caliber single-shot spur trigger pistol, with 3.25" round barrel. Silver-plated brass frame blued, with walnut grip. Approximately 200 manufactured in 1865.

Courtesy Richard M. Kumor Sr.

NIB	Exc.	V.G.	Good	Fair	Poor
—	—	1500	775	250	100

CPA RIFLES
Dingman's Ferry, Pennsylvania

This company builds rifles based on Stevens Model 44-1/2. Several different configurations are offered, which are listed. **NOTE:** There are a number of special order options and custom features available at extra charge that will affect value.

Schuetzen Rifle

This model is usually built to order as to stock style, caliber, barrel size, shape and length. Many calibers are available from .22 Short to .40-65 Winchester. Sights are extra.

NIB	Exc.	V.G.	Good	Fair	Poor
2900	2250	1600	975	600	300

Silhouette Rifle

This model as produced is approved for BPCR competition by NRA. Has either sporting-style stock with low comb or Model 52 style with more drop. Calibers are from .38-55 to .45-110, with other calibers available. Standard barrel #4 part octagon 30" in length. Sights are extra.

NIB	Exc.	V.G.	Good	Fair	Poor
2550	1900	1350	700	550	250

Sporting Rifle

This model uses a sporting-style stock, with standard forearm and schnabel tip. Offered in rimmed calibers including .222, .225, .22 Hornet and others. Standard barrels are round or part octagon, with weights from #1 to #5 and up to 28" in length. Sights are extra.

NIB	Exc.	V.G.	Good	Fair	Poor
2475	1900	1350	700	550	250

Varmint Rifle

As above, with a semi-beavertail forearm.

NIB	Exc.	V.G.	Good	Fair	Poor
2475	1900	1350	700	550	250

CRAUSE, CARL PHILLIP MUSKETS AND RIFLES
Herzberg, Germany

Carl Phillip Crause (who signed his products only with his last name) operated a gun manufactory in Herzberg on the Harz in northwestern German kingdom of Hannover from the close of Napoleonic Wars until 1857. Main production of his factory was devoted to military arms for Hannover and surrounding principalities. Weapons of his manufacture included Brunswick M1835 and M1848 rifles, Hannovarian M1850 and M1854 rifle-muskets and yager rifles, and M1840 and M1849 rifle-muskets of Hanseatic League (a coalition of north German states of Oldenberg, Hamburg, Bremen, and Lubeck). Latter two arms were subsequently altered to accept the elongated projectiles popular during 1850s. A few thousand evidently were imported into the United States and saw service during American Civil War.

Hanseatic League M1840 Rifled Musket

Overall length 55.5"; barrel length 40.25"; caliber .70. Markings: on lock-plate forward of hammer, "Crause in Herzberg" in script, the "s" in the archaic form, appearing as an "f". Of the 6,000 muskets of this type made, approximately half were sent to the United States in 1861 during the arms crisis that accompanied the outbreak of the American Civil War. A total of 2,680 of these were issued to Ohio and at least one regiment (the 56th Ohio) was armed with these rifled muskets. These arms were mistakenly identified during the period as being Saxon due to the similarity of the large squared off foresection of the lockplate.

Courtesy Milwaukee Public Museum, Milwaukee, Wisconsin

NIB	Exc.	V.G.	Good	Fair	Poor
—	—	1700	800	375	200

Oldenberg M1849 Rifled Musket

Overall lengths 55.5" to 56.625" (long version), 49.5" (short version); barrel lengths 39" to 39.125" (long version), 33" (short version); caliber .69-.72 (rifled). Markings: "Crause in Herzberg" inscribed in script on the backstrap of the hammer housing, the "s" in archaic form, appearing as an "f". Nicknamed the "Cyclops" because its large center-hung hammer is pierced with a large window that served as its rear sight. A few hundred of these clumsy rifled muskets may have been intermixed with the shipments of "Saxon" muskets imported in 1861 or 1862 into the United States during the American Civil War.

Courtesy Milwaukee Public Museum, Milwaukee, Wisconsin

NIB	Exc.	V.G.	Good	Fair	Poor
—	—	1975	850	400	250

CRESCENT F. A. CO.
Norwich, Connecticut

Company made good quality inexpensive single- and double-barrel shotguns at its Norwich works, beginning about 1892. It was bought by H&D Folsom of New York City, large importers and distributors of firearms and sporting goods, so they could add an American-made sidelock hammer side-by-side to their extensive range of imported guns. Crescent guns were offered in 12-, 16-, 20- and 28-gauges and later, 44XL shot caliber with Damascus twist laminated or Armory steel barrels depending on the shooter's wants. In 1898 VL&D said these were the best American hammer guns in the market for the money.

Huge quantities of these "Hardware Guns" were produced in a profusion of private brands as well as in Folsom's house brand "American Gun Co. of NY". In 1922 Crescent brand replaced "American Gun Co. of NY" and can be found on many thousands of doubles. In 1905 Crescent's first hammerless sidelock was introduced as the American Gun Co. "Knickerbocker" Model No. 6. This very popular model became the Crescent "Peerless" No. 6 in 1922. In 1928 it became the Crescent "Empire" No. 60 and in 1931 the Crescent-Davis "New Empire" No. 88, "New Empire" No. 9 and "Empire" No. 9.

Crescent was bought by J. Stevens Arms Co., Division of Savage Arms Corp. about 1930. It was merged with Davis-Warner Arms Corp. successors to N.R. Davis & Sons Co. and became Crescent-Davis Arms Corp. In 1932 the operation was moved to the Stevens plant at Springfield, Mass. where some sidelock doubles were assembled. Crescent-Davis brand guns remained in Steven's full line catalog until 1941, but from 1937 to 1941 the doubles sold in the C-D brand were on either Stevens or Davis boxlock frames.

DOUBLES

Triumph—Hammerless Boxlock

NIB	Exc.	V.G.	Good	Fair	Poor
—	800	650	425	300	200

Model 2655—Laminated Barrels Hammer Sidelock

NIB	Exc.	V.G.	Good	Fair	Poor
—	575	450	325	200	150

Model 2665—Damascus Barrels Hammer Sidelock

NIB	Exc.	V.G.	Good	Fair	Poor
—	575	450	325	200	150

Crescent American Hammer Gun No. 0—Hammer Sidelock

NIB	Exc.	V.G.	Good	Fair	Poor
—	400	325	250	200	100

American Machine Made 2641—Hammer Sidelock

NIB	Exc.	V.G.	Good	Fair	Poor
—	450	350	300	250	200

American Machine Made 2650—Hammer Sidelock

NIB	Exc.	V.G.	Good	Fair	Poor
—	575	450	325	200	150

American Machine Made 2660—Damascus Barrels Hammer Sidelock

NIB	Exc.	V.G.	Good	Fair	Poor
—	700	550	400	275	175

American Gun Co. NY No. 1 Armory—Hammerless Sidelock

NIB	Exc.	V.G.	Good	Fair	Poor
—	450	325	250	200	100

American Gun Co. NY No. 2—Hammerless Sidelock

NIB	Exc.	V.G.	Good	Fair	Poor
—	575	450	300	250	200

American Gun Co. No. 3—Damascus Barrels Hammer Sidelock

NIB	Exc.	V.G.	Good	Fair	Poor
—	700	550	425	300	250

American Gun Co. No. 4—Hammer Sidelock

NIB	Exc.	V.G.	Good	Fair	Poor
—	800	650	525	400	300

American Gun Co. No. 5—Damascus Barrels Hammer Sidelock

NIB	Exc.	V.G.	Good	Fair	Poor
—	925	800	650	450	350

Folsom Arms Co. No. 0 Armory—Hammer Sidelock

NIB	Exc.	V.G.	Good	Fair	Poor
—	450	325	250	200	100

Folsom Arms Co. No. 2—Hammer Sidelock

NIB	Exc.	V.G.	Good	Fair	Poor
—	575	450	300	200	150

Folsom Arms Co. No. 3—Damascus Barrel

NIB	Exc.	V.G.	Good	Fair	Poor
—	700	550	425	300	200

Knickerbocker No. 6 Armory—Hammerless Sidelock

Courtesy Nick Niles, Paul Goodwin photo

NIB	Exc.	V.G.	Good	Fair	Poor
—	450	325	250	200	100

Knickerbocker No. 7—Hammerless Sidelock

NIB	Exc.	V.G.	Good	Fair	Poor
—	450	325	250	200	100

Knickerbocker No. 8—Damascus Barrels Hammerless Sidelock

NIB	Exc.	V.G.	Good	Fair	Poor
—	575	450	300	250	200

New Knickerbocker Armory—Hammerless Sidelock

NIB	Exc.	V.G.	Good	Fair	Poor
—	450	325	250	200	100

New Knickerbocker WT—Hammerless Sidelock

Courtesy Nick Niles, Paul Goodwin photo

NIB	Exc.	V.G.	Good	Fair	Poor
—	500	375	250	200	150

New Knickerbocker Damascus Barrels—Hammerless Sidelock

NIB	Exc.	V.G.	Good	Fair	Poor
—	575	450	300	250	200

American Gun Co. Small Bore No. 28—Straight Stock Hammer Sidelock

NIB	Exc.	V.G.	Good	Fair	Poor
—	925	775	650	400	300

American Gun Co. Small Bore No. 44—Straight Stock Hammer Sidelock

NIB	Exc.	V.G.	Good	Fair	Poor
—	1025	825	700	475	350

American Gun Co. No. 0—Armory Straight Stock—Hammer Sidelock

Courtesy Nick Niles, Paul Goodwin photo

NIB	Exc.	V.G.	Good	Fair	Poor
—	400	300	250	200	100

American Gun Co. No. 28—Nitro Straight Stock—Hammer Sidelock

NIB	Exc.	V.G.	Good	Fair	Poor
—	925	775	650	400	300

American Gun Co. No. 44—Nitro Straight Stock—Hammer Sidelock

NIB	Exc.	V.G.	Good	Fair	Poor
—	1025	825	700	475	350

American Gun Co. Midget Field No. 28—Hammer Sidelock

NIB	Exc.	V.G.	Good	Fair	Poor
—	925	775	650	400	300

American Gun Co. Midget Field No. 44—Hammer Sidelock

Courtesy Nick Niles, Paul Goodwin photo

NIB	Exc.	V.G.	Good	Fair	Poor
—	1025	825	700	500	350

Crescent 1922 Model No. 66—Quail—Hammerless Sidelock

NIB	Exc.	V.G.	Good	Fair	Poor
—	700	550	400	275	175

Crescent Firearms Co. No. 0—Hammer Sidelock

NIB	Exc.	V.G.	Good	Fair	Poor
—	450	350	250	200	150

Crescent Firearms Co. No. 0—Nickel—Hammer Sidelock

NIB	Exc.	V.G.	Good	Fair	Poor
—	600	450	350	250	200

Crescent Firearms Co. No. 6—Peerless—Hammerless Sidelock

NIB	Exc.	V.G.	Good	Fair	Poor
—	450	350	250	200	150

Crescent Firearms Co. No. 6E—Peerless Engraved—Hammerless Sidelock

NIB	Exc.	V.G.	Good	Fair	Poor
—	700	550	400	275	175

Crescent Firearms Co. No. 66—Quail—Hammerless Sidelock

NIB	Exc.	V.G.	Good	Fair	Poor
—	750	550	425	300	200

Crescent Firearms Co. No. 60—Empire—Hammerless Sidelock

Courtesy Nick Niles, Paul Goodwin photo

NIB	Exc.	V.G.	Good	Fair	Poor
—	500	400	350	300	200

Crescent Firearms Co. No. 6—Peerless—Hammerless Sidelock

Courtesy Nick Niles, Paul Goodwin photo

NIB	Exc.	V.G.	Good	Fair	Poor
—	450	350	300	200	150

Crescent Firearms Co. No. 44—Improved—Hammer Sidelock

NIB	Exc.	V.G.	Good	Fair	Poor
—	800	600	500	400	300

Crescent Empire No. 60—Hammerless Sidelock

NIB	Exc.	V.G.	Good	Fair	Poor
—	400	300	250	200	100

New Crescent Empire Red Butt—Hammerless Sidelock

NIB	Exc.	V.G.	Good	Fair	Poor
—	450	350	250	200	150

Crescent New Empire No. 88—Hammerless Sidelock

NIB	Exc.	V.G.	Good	Fair	Poor
—	450	350	250	200	150

Crescent New Empire No. 9—Hammerless Sidelock

Courtesy Nick Niles, Paul Goodwin photo

NIB	Exc.	V.G.	Good	Fair	Poor
—	400	300	250	200	100

Crescent Certified Empire No. 60—Hammerless Sidelock

NIB	Exc.	V.G.	Good	Fair	Poor
—	450	300	250	200	150

Crescent Certified Empire No. 9—Hammerless Sidelock

NIB	Exc.	V.G.	Good	Fair	Poor
—	500	375	300	250	200

Crescent Certified Empire No. 88—Hammerless Sidelock

Courtesy Nick Niles, Paul Goodwin photo

NIB	Exc.	V.G.	Good	Fair	Poor
—	575	450	400	350	300

Crescent Davis No. 600—Hammerless Boxlock

Courtesy Nick Niles, Paul Goodwin photo

NIB	Exc.	V.G.	Good	Fair	Poor
—	450	350	300	250	200

Crescent Davis No. 900—Hammerless Boxlock

NIB	Exc.	V.G.	Good	Fair	Poor
—	575	450	400	350	300

Single-Shot

Made in 12-, 16-, 20-, 28-gauge and .410. Barrel lengths were 26", 28", 30" and 32", with various chokes. Had an exposed hammer, fluid steel barrel and walnut pistol-grip stock.

NIB	Exc.	V.G.	Good	Fair	Poor
—	200	125	100	75	50

Revolver

Typical S&W copy made by Crescent in Norwich, Connecticut. A top-break double-action, that was found either blued or nickel-plated, with checkered black hard rubber grips. Cylinder held 5 shots. Chambered for .32 S&W cartridge.

NIB	Exc.	V.G.	Good	Fair	Poor
—	250	150	125	85	40

Crescent Certified Shotgun NFA, Curio or Relic

Crescent Certified Shotgun is a .410 smooth bore pistol with 12.25" barrel. Manufactured from approximately 1930 to 1932 by Crescent-Davis Arms Corp., Norwich, Connecticut, and possibly thereafter until 1934 by J. Stevens Arms Co., which purchased the company. In various distributor catalogs, it is termed "Ever-Ready" Model 200 and advertised with a blued frame. Specimens have been observed with "tiger-stripe" (like an H&R Handy-Gun) or Colt SAA or Winchester-type case hardening. Total production is unknown but serial numbers ranging from 1305 to 3262 have been observed, suggesting it may have been fewer than 4,000. Treasury Department ruled .410 Crescent to be a "firearm" in the "any other weapon" category under NFA in 1934, when its retail price was about $11.

Barrel is marked proof tested .410 gauge on top and 2-1/2 IN SHELLS on the middle left side. Receiver's left side is stamped crescent certified shotgun/ crescent-davis arms corporation/norwich, conn., u.s.a. Earliest guns also have .410 stamped at the top of the left side of the receiver near the breech,

but this marking does not appear on later guns. It is a rather heavy (57 oz. unloaded) handgun. **NOTE:** Add $100 to $300 for original cardboard box.

NIB	Exc.	V.G.	Good	Fair	Poor
—	975	725	550	350	250

Brand Names Used by Crescent Arms

American Bar Lock Wonder made for Sears, Roebuck & Co.
American Boy made for Townley Metal & Hardware Co.
American Gun Co. (H & D Folsom house brand)
American Gun Company of New York
American Nitro
Armory Gun Co.Baker Gun Co. (if no foreign proof marks)
T. Barker New York-if a sidelock hammerless double without proofs.
Bellmore Gun Co.Berkshire No. 3000 made for Shapleigh Hardware Co. of St. Louis, MO
Black Beauty-hammerless doubles
Bluefield Clipper
Bluegrass Arms Co. made for Belknap Hardware Co. of Louisville, KY
Blue Whistler
Bridge Black PrinceBridge Gun Co.
Bridge Gun Works
Bridgeport Arms Co. (if no foreign proof marks)
Bright Arms Co.
Canadian Belle
Carolina Arms Co. made for Smith Wadsworth Hardware Co. of Charlotte, NC
Caroline Arms
Central Arm Co. made for Shapleigh Hardware Co. of St. Louis, MO
Chatham Arms Co.
Cherokee Arms Co. made for C. M. McClung Co. of Knoxville, TN
Chesapeake Gun Co.
Chicago Long Range Wonder 1908-1918 made for Sears, Roebuck & Co. of Chicago, IL
Colonial
Columbian New York Arms Co.
Compeer made for Van Camp Hardware & Iron Co. of Indianapolis, IN
Connecticut Arms Co.
Cumberland Arms Co.
Crescent Fire Arms Co.
Creve Cour (if no foreign proof marks) made for Isaac Walker Hardware Co. of Peoria, IL
CrusoDaniel Boone Gun Co. made for Belknap Hardware Co. of Louisville, KY
Delphian Arms Co. (some models without foreign proof marks) made for Supplee-Biddle Hardware Co. of Philadelphia, PA
Delphian Manufacturing Co. (some models)
Diamond Arms Co. (some models) made for Shapleigh Hardware Co. of St. Louis, MO
Dunlap Special made for Dunlap Hardware Co. of Macon, GAE.C. Mac made for E.C. Meacham Arms Co. of St. Louis, MO
Elgin Arms Co. made for Strauss & Schram and Fred Biffar & Co. both of Chicago, IL
Elmira Arms Co.
Empire Arms Co. made for Sears, Roebuck & Co. of Chicago, IL
Empire State Arms Co.
Enders Oakleaf made for Shapleigh Hardware Co. of St. Louis, MO
Enders Special Service made for Shapleigh Hardware Co.
Enders Royal Service made for Shapleigh Hardware Co.
Essex made for Belknap Hardware Co. of Louisville, KY
Excel made for Montgomery Ward & Co. of Chicago, IL
Farwell Arms Co. made for Farwell, Ozmun & Kirk of St. Paul, MN
Faultless made for John M. Smythe Co. of Chicago, IL
Faultless Goose Gun made for John M. Smyth Co. of Chicago, IL
The Field after 1894
Folsom Arms Co. (also used by H & D Folsom on Belgian imports)
F.F. Forbes (H & D Folsom house brand)
Fort Pitt Arms Co.
Fremont Arms Co. (also used on Belgian imports)
Gold Medal Wonder
Greenfield (some models) made for Hibbard, Spencer, Bartlett & Co. of Chicago, ILH.B.C. (some models) made for Hudson's Bay Co. of Canada
H.S.B. & Co. (some models) made for Hibbard, Spencer,Bartlett & Co. of Chicago, IL

Hanover Arms Co. (if no foreign proof marks)

S.H. Harrington (if no foreign proof marks)

Hartford Arms Co. made for both Simmons Hardware and Shapleigh Hardware Co. of St. Louis, MO

Harvard (H & D Folsom house brand)

Hermitage (some models) made for Grey-Dusley Hardware Co. of Nashville, TN

Hip Spe Bar (some models) made for Hibbard, Spencer, Bartlett & Co. of Chicago, IL

Hibbard (some models) made for Hibbard, Spencer, Bartlett & Co. of Chicago, IL

Howard Arms Co. made for Fred Biffar & Co. of Chicago, IL

Hudson (some models) made for Hibbard, Spencer, Bartlett & Co. of Chicago, IL

Hunter made for Belknap Hardware Co. Louisville, KY

Interstate Arms Co. made for Townley Metal & Hardware Co. of Kansas City, MO

Jackson Arms Co. made for C.M. McClung & Co. of Knoxville, TN

Joseph Arms Co. Norwich, Conn.

K K and Keen Kufter (some models) made for Shapleigh Hardware Co. of St. Louis, MO

Kingsland Special and Kingsland 10 Star made for Geller, Ward & Hasner of St. Louis, MO

Kirk Gun Co. made for Farwell, Ozmun & Kirk of St. Paul, MN

Knickerbocker (up to 1915, H & D Folsom house brand)

Knockabout (before 1925) made for Montgomery Ward & Co. of Chicago, IL

Knoxall (only hammerless doubles)

Laclede Gun Co.

Lakeside made for Montgomery Ward & Co. of Chicago, IL

Leader Gun Co. made for Charles Williams Stores of New York, NY

Lee's Special and Lee's Munner Special made for Lee Hardware Co. of Salina, KS

Long Range Marvel, Long Range Winner, and Long Range Wonder made between 1893 to 1909 for Sears, Roebuck & Co. of Chicago, IL

F.A. LoomisMarshwoodMassachusetts Arms Co. made before 1920 for Blish, Mizet and Silliman Hardware Co. of Atchison, KS

Mears (if no foreign proof marks)

Metropolitan made for Siegal-Cooper Co. of New York, NY

Minnesota Arms Co. made for Farwell, Ozmun, Kirk & Co. of St. Paul, MN

Mississippi Arms Co. St. Louis (some models) made for Shepleigh Hardware Co. of St. Louis, MO

Mississippi Valley Arms Co. (some models) made for Shapleigh Hardware Co. of St. Louis, MO

Mohawk made for Glish, Mizet and Lilliman Hardware Co. of Atchinson, KS

Monitor

R. Murdock, National Firearms Co. (some models)

National Arms Co. hammer doubles (without foreign proof marks) and hammerless doubles made for May Hardware Co. of Washington, D.C. and Moskowitz and Herbach Co. of Philadelphia, PA

New Britain Arms Co.'s Monarch

New Elgin Arms Co.

New EmpireNew England (some models after 1914) made for Sears, Roebuck & Co.

New England Arms Co. (some models)

Newport Model CN made for Hibbard, Spencer, Bartlett and Co. of Chicago

Newport Model WN (some models) made for Hibbard, Spencer, Bartlett and Co. of Chicago

New Rival made for Van Camp Hardware and Iron Co. of Indianapolis, IN

New York Arms Co. made for Garnet Carter Co. of Chattanooga, TN

New York Machine Made (some models)

New York Match Gun (some models)

New York Nitro Hammerless

Nitro Bird made for Conover Hardware Co. of Kansas City, MO

Nitro Hunter made for Belknap Hardware Co. of Louisville, KY

Nitro King 1908 to 1917 made for Sears, Roebuck & Co. of Chicago, IL

Norwich Arms Co.

Not-Noc Manufacturing Co. made for Belknap Hardware Co. of Louisville, KY and Canton Hardware Co. of Canton, OH

Osprey made for Lou J. Eppinger, Detroit, MI

Oxford made for Belknap Hardware Co. of Louisville, KY

Peerless (H & D Folsom house brand)

Perfection made for H. G. Lipscomb & Co. of Nashville, TN

Piedmont made for Piedmont Hardware Co. of Danville, PA

Piedmont Arms Co.

Pioneer Arms (if no foreign proof marks) made for Kruse and Baklmann Hardware Co. of Cincinnati, OH

Quail (H & D Folsom house brand)

Queen City made for Elmira Arms Co. of Elmira, NY

Red Chieftan (model 60) made for Supplee Biddle Hardware Co. of Philadelphia, PARev-O-Noc (some models) made for Hibbard, Spencer, Bartlett & Co. of Chicago, IL

Rich-Con made for Richardson & Conover Hardware Co.Charles Richter

(some models) made for New York Sporting Goods Co. of New York, NY

Rickard Arms Co. made for J. A. Rickard Co. of Schenectady, NYRival (some models) made for Van Camp Hardware and Iron Co. of Indianapolis, IN

Rocket SpecialRoyal Service made for Shapleigh Hardware Co. of St. Louis, MO

Rummel Arms Co. made for A. J. Rummel Arms Co. of Toledo, OH

Ruso (if no foreign proof marks)St. Louis Arms Co. (sidelock hammerless doubles) made for Shapleigh Hardware Co. of St. Louis, MO

Seminole (hammerless) unknown

Shue's Special made for Ira M. Shue of Hanover, PA

Smithsonian (some models)

John M. Smythe & Co. made for John M. Smythe Hardware Co. of Chicago, IL

Southern Arms Co. (some models)

Special Service made for Shapleigh Hardware Co. of St. Louis, MO

Spencer Gun Co. made for Hibbard, Spencer, Bartlett & Co. of Chicago, IL

Sportsman (some models) made for W. Bingham & Co. of Cleveland, OH

Springfield Arms Co. used until 1930. (H & D Folsom house brand). This brand was also used by Stevens and James Warner guns.Square Deal made for Stratton, Warren Hardware Co. of Memphis, TN

Star Leader (some models)

State Arms Co. made for J.H. Lau & Co. of New York, NY

Sterling Arms Co.

Sullivan Arms Co. made for Sullivan Hardware Co. of Anderson, SC

Superior (some models) made for Paxton & Gallagher Co. of Omaha, NE

Syco (some models) made for Wyeth Hardware Co. of St. Joseph, MO

Ten Star & Ten Star Heavy Duty (if no foreign proof marks) made for Geller, Ward & Hasner Co. of St. Louis, MO

Tiger (if no foreign proof marks) made for J.H. Hall & Co. of Nashville, TN

Townley's Pal and Townley's American Boy made for Townley Metal & Hardware Co. of Kansas City, MO

Trap's Best made for Watkins, Cottrell Co. of Richmond, VA

Triumph (some models) made for Sears, Roebuck & Co. of Chicago, IL

Tryon Special (some models) made for Edward K. Tryon Co. of Philadelphia, PA

U.S. Arms Co. (if no foreign proof marks) made for Supplee-Biddle Hardware Co. of Philadelphia, PA

U.S. FieldUtica Firearms Co. (some models) made for Simmons Hardware Co. of St. Louis, MO

Victor & Victor Special made for Hibbard, Spencer, Bartlett & Co. of Chicago, IL

Virginia Arms Co. made for Virginia-Carolina Co. of Richmond, VA

Volunteer (some models) made for Belknap Hardware Co. of Louisville, KY

Vulcan Arms Co. made for Edward K. Tryon Co. of Philadelphia, PA

Warren Arms Co. (if no foreign proof marks)

Washington Arms Co. (some models)

Wauregan (some models)

Wautauga (some models) made for Wallace Hardware Co. Morristown, TN

Wildwood made for Sears, Roebuck & Co. of Chicago, IL

Wilkinson Arms Co. (if no foreign proof marks) made for Richmond Hardware Co. of Richmond, VA

Wilshire Arms Co. made for Stauffer, Eshleman & Co. of New Orleans, LA

Winfield Arms Co. (H & D Folsom house brand)

Winoca Arms Co. made for Jacobi Hardware Co. of Philadelphia, PA

Witte Hardware Co. (some models) made for Witte Hardware Co. of St. Louis, MO

Wolverine Arms Co. made for Fletcher Hardware Co. of Wilmington, NC

Worthington Arms Co. made for George Worthington Co. of Cleveland, OH

CRISPIN, SILAS
New York, New York

Crispin Revolver

A .32 Crispin caliber 5- or 6-shot revolver produced in limited quantities. Some are marked "Smith Arms Co., New York City. Crispin's Pat. Oct. 3, 1865". Most noteworthy feature of these revolvers is the cylinder is constructed in two pieces so that the belted Crispin cartridge can be used. It is believed that these revolvers were only made on an experimental basis, between 1865 and 1867.

NIB	Exc.	V.G.	Good	Fair	Poor
—	—	19000	7500	2500	1000

CROSSFIRE
LaGrange, Georgia

This combination rifle/shotgun is manufactured by Saco Defense, Inc. for Crossfire. It is the first production firearm to combine the shotgun and rifle into a pump action multi-shot weapon.

MK-1

Designed to fire both .223 Rem. cartridge and 12-gauge 3" shotgun shell from two different barrels. A dual action long gun operated with a pump action. Overall length 38". Shotgun has 4-round detachable magazine; rifle has AR-15 type 5-round magazine. Shotgun barrel furnished with choke tubes. Offered in black oxide finish or camo finish. Weight about 8.6 lbs. Introduced in 1999. **NOTE:** Add $100 for camo finish.

NIB	Exc.	V.G.	Good	Fair	Poor
2200	1700	1350	775	500	250

CRUCELEGUI, HERMANOS
Eibar, Spain

A 5mm, 6.35mm, 7.65mm and 8mm caliber double-action revolver. Trade names used were; Puppy, Velo-Mith, Le-Brong, Bron-Sport, C.H. and Brong-Petit.

NIB	Exc.	V.G.	Good	Fair	Poor
—	250	150	80	60	35

CUMMINGS, O. S.
Lowell, Massachusetts

Cummings Pocket Revolver

A .22-caliber spur trigger revolver, with 3.5" ribbed round barrel and 7-shot fluted cylinder. Nickel-plated with rosewood grip. Barrel stamped "O.S. Cummings Lowell, Mass." Approximately 1,000 manufactured in 1870s.

NIB	Exc.	V.G.	Good	Fair	Poor
—	—	675	300	150	100

CUMMINGS & WHEELER
Lowell, Massachusetts

Pocket Revolver

Similar to Cummings Pocket Revolver, with subtle differences: such as length of flutes on cylinder; size and shape of grip. Barrel slightly longer and marked "Cummings & Wheeler, Lowell, Mass.

NIB	Exc.	V.G.	Good	Fair	Poor
—	—	750	350	150	100

CUSTOM GUN GUILD
Doraville, Georgia

Wood Model IV

Falling block single-shot rifle produced in a number of popular calibers. Barrel lengths from 22" to 28". Stock of select checkered walnut. Lightweight, about 5.5 lbs. Manufactured in 1984 only. Not often encountered on today's market.

NIB	Exc.	V.G.	Good	Fair	Poor
—	3750	2750	2500	1750	1000

CZ - Strakonice
Strakonice, Czech Republic

This firm is a separate company from the one located in Uhershy Brod. Prior to the collapse of the Soviet Union both companies were owned and operated by the state.

Model TT 40/45/9

Semi-automatic pistol chambered for .40 S&W, .45 ACP or 9mm cartridges. Fitted with 3.8" barrel. Trigger is single-/double-action or double-action-only. Magazine capacity 10 rounds. Weight about 26 oz.

NIB	Exc.	V.G.	Good	Fair	Poor
575	425	300	200	125	100

CZ
(Ceska Zbrojovka)
Uhersky Brod, Czech Republic

Established by Karel Bubla and Alois Tomiska in 1919. This company later merged with Hubertus Engineering Company. In 1949, company was nationalized. CZ regularly exports 90 percent of its production to over 80 countries.

NOTE: As of 1998, CZ firearms have been imported exclusively by CZ-USA, a wholly-owned distribution subsidiary of Ceska Zbrojovka a.s. Uhersky Brod, (CZUB) of the Czech Republic.

Fox

A 6.35mm caliber semi-automatic pistol, with 2.125" barrel, tubular slide, folding trigger and no trigger guard. Fox and CZ are inscribed on slide. CZ logo on each grip plate. Blued, with plastic grips. Manufactured between 1919 and 1936.

Courtesy James Rankin

NIB	Exc.	V.G.	Good	Fair	Poor
—	900	750	600	400	200

CZ 1921 Praga

Semi-automatic pistol in 7.65mm caliber. First service pistol manufactured in Czechoslovakia. Production began in 1920. Praga stamped on slide and on each grip plate for commercial models. Service models fitted with wood grips.

Courtesy James Rankin

NIB	Exc.	V.G.	Good	Fair	Poor
—	650	550	475	350	200

Army Pistol 1922 (Nickl-Pistole)

Designed by Josef Nickl of Mauser. First approved by Army in 1921. Chambered for .380 ACP (9mmKurtz/9x17mm) cartridge. Plagued by design problems. Produced only in 1922 and 1923. Fewer than 22,000 built.

NIB	Exc.	V.G.	Good	Fair	Poor
—	650	500	350	200	150

CZ 1922

Semi-automatic pistol in 6.35mm caliber. Very similar to Fox above. Has no sights but fitted with a conventional trigger guard. CZ stamped on slide and CZ logo on each grip plate. Grips are plastic or wood. Manufactured between 1922 and 1936.

Courtesy James Rankin

NIB	Exc.	V.G.	Good	Fair	Poor
—	550	450	350	300	200

CZ 1924

First large-production military pistol produced by CZ. Chambered for 9mmK cartridge. First of CZ models with wrap-around grips of both wood and plastic. CZ logo seen on plastic grips. Lanyard loop attached to base of butt. Manufactured from 1925 to 1932.

Courtesy James Rankin

NIB	Exc.	V.G.	Good	Fair	Poor
—	650	500	400	300	200

CZ 1927

Semi-automatic pistol chambered for 7.65mm cartridge. Marked same as CZ 1924, but cocking grooves on slide are cut vertically instead of sloped as on earlier model. This model was blued, with checkered wrap-around plastic grips. These early guns were beautifully made and marked, "Ceska Zbrojovka AS v Praze". After the war, these pistols continued in production until 1951. More than 500,000 manufactured.

NOTE: Some of these pistols were made with an extended barrel for the use of a silencer. This variation brings a large premium. Fewer than 10 CZ27s were made in .22-caliber. An expert opinion is suggested if a sale is contemplated. **NOTE:** Add 50 percent for Nazi-proofed.

NIB	Exc.	V.G.	Good	Fair	Poor
—	650	475	300	200	165

CZ 1936

A 6.35mm caliber semi-automatic pistol, with 2.5" barrel and double-action-only lockwork. Has plastic wrap-around grips, with CZ logo on each side. Replaced Model 1922 in 1936. Discontinued in 1940, because of wartime production.

Courtesy James Rankin

NIB	Exc.	V.G.	Good	Fair	Poor
—	450	350	300	200	100

CZ 1938

Semi-automatic double-action pistol in 9mmK caliber. Manufactured for Czechoslovakian military from 1938 to 1940. Barrel length 4.7"; weight about 32 oz.; magazine capacity 8 rounds. Wrap-around plastic grips, with CZ logo on each side.

Courtesy James Rankin

NIB	Exc.	V.G.	Good	Fair	Poor
—	550	500	400	300	200

CZ 1945

A small .25-caliber (6.35mm) pocket pistol that is double-action-only. Produced and sold after World War II. Modified version of CZ 1936. Approximately 60,000 built between 1945 and 1949.

NIB	Exc.	V.G.	Good	Fair	Poor
—	350	300	250	175	125

CZ 1950

Blowback-operated semi-automatic double-action pistol chambered for 7.65mm cartridge. Patterned after Walther Model PP, with a few differences. Safety catch is located on frame instead of slide; trigger guard is not hinged as on Walther. Dismantled by means of a catch on side of the frame. Intended to be a military pistol designed by Kratochvil brothers, it proved to be underpowered and was adopted by the police. Few were released on the commercial market.

Courtesy James Rankin

NIB	Exc.	V.G.	Good	Fair	Poor
—	250	150	125	100	50

CZ 1952

Czech army sidearm, is a semi-automatic pistol chambered for 7.62mm cartridge. Fitted with 4.7" barrel. Has a very complex locking system using two rollers inside the frame. Magazine capacity 8 rounds; weight about 34 oz. Production ended in 1956.

NIB	Exc.	V.G.	Good	Fair	Poor
—	300	275	225	125	75

Model 1970

This model was an attempt to correct dependability problems with Model 50. There is little difference to see externally between the two except for markings and grip pattern. Production began during 1960s, ended in 1983.

Courtesy Rock Island Auction Company

NIB	Exc.	V.G.	Good	Fair	Poor
—	250	200	150	100	75

RIFLES

Model 52 (7.62 x 45) Carbine

NIB	Exc.	V.G.	Good	Fair	Poor
—	450	300	250	200	125

Model 52/57 (7.62 x 39)

NIB	Exc.	V.G.	Good	Fair	Poor
—	525	325	275	225	150

CZ-USA - Kansas City, Kansas

CZ first entered U.S. market in 1990 through various distributors. In January 1998, CZ-USA opened its office in Kansas City, Kansas. This office includes full sales and warranty service as well as an on-site gunsmith.

RIFLES

CZ Model 3

Bolt-action rifle introduced in 2004. Produced in U.S.A. Offered in both right- and left-hand configurations. Chambered for Winchester Short Magnums: .270, 7mm and .300. Walnut stock, with choice of stainless steel or blue finish. Fitted with 24" barrel. No sights. Magazine capacity 3 rounds; weight about 7.5 lbs. **NOTE:** Add $30 for stainless steel.

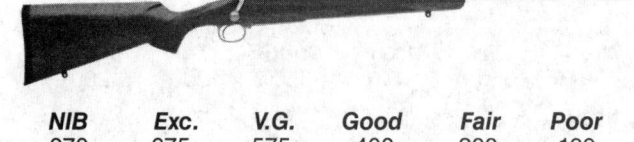

NIB	Exc.	V.G.	Good	Fair	Poor
970	675	575	400	200	100

CZ 452-2E LUX

Bolt-action rifle chambered for .22 LR or .22 Win. Magnum cartridge. Fitted with 24.8" barrel. Hooded front and adjustable rear sight. Trigger adjustable for pull. Pistol-grip stock is a European-style Turkish walnut. Supplied with a 5-round magazine. Blued finish. Weight about 6.6 lbs. **NOTE:** Add $40 for .22 WMR.

NIB	Exc.	V.G.	Good	Fair	Poor
490	350	225	150	125	100

CZ ZKM-452D

As above, with walnut Monte Carlo-style stock.

NIB	Exc.	V.G.	Good	Fair	Poor
—	425	300	225	150	100

CZ 452-2E ZKM Style

Similar to above model, but chambered for .22 LR only. Fitted with black synthetic stock, matte nickel finish and 22.5" barrel. Weight about 6 lbs.

NIB	Exc.	V.G.	Good	Fair	Poor
475	325	225	175	125	100

CZ 452 Training Rifle

Chambered for .22 LR cartridge and fitted with 24.8" barrel. Detachable magazine has 5-round capacity. Beechwood stock. Adjustable sights. Weight about 5.4 lbs.

NIB	Exc.	V.G.	Good	Fair	Poor
375	275	175	150	125	100

CZ 452 American Classic

Chambered for .22 LR and .22 Win. Magnum cartridge. Features American-style Circassian walnut stock, with 18 lpi checkering. Fitted with 21" barrel, with recessed target crown. Supplied with a 5-round magazine. Blued finish. Weight about 6.5 lbs. Introduced in 1999. In 2005 .17 Mach 2 caliber was offered. **NOTE:** Add $40 for .22 WMR. or .17 HMR.

NIB	Exc.	V.G.	Good	Fair	Poor
465	350	250	150	12	100

CZ 452 Varmint

Bolt-action rifle chambered for .22 LR cartridge and fitted with 20" barrel. American-style Turkish walnut stock. Blued finish. Weight about 7.5 lbs. In 2005 .17 Mach 2 was offered. **NOTE:** Add $20 for .17 Mach 2 caliber.

NIB	Exc.	V.G.	Good	Fair	Poor
420	300	250	200	150	125

CZ 452 Scout

Designed for the younger shooter. Features shortened buttstock, 16.2" barrel and reduced weight receiver. Chambered for .22 LR cartridge. Open adjustable sights. Weight 3.9 lbs. Introduced in 2000.

NIB	Exc.	V.G.	Good	Fair	Poor
275	200	150	125	100	75

CZ 452 Style

Chambered for .22 LR cartridge and fitted with 22.5" barrel. Features synthetic stock, with matte nickel finish. Magazine capacity 5 or 10 rounds. Weight about 5.3 lbs.

NIB	Exc.	V.G.	Good	Fair	Poor
400	300	250	225	125	75

CZ 452 Silhouette

Designed for small silhouette competition shooting. This .22-caliber rifle has synthetic stock and blued finish. Barrel length 22.5". Weight about 5.3 lbs.

NIB	Exc.	V.G.	Good	Fair	Poor
400	300	250	225	125	75

CZ 452 FS

Introduced in 2004. Chambered for .22 LR or .22 WMR cartridge. Fitted with full-length Turkish walnut stock. Barrel length 20.5". Adjustable sights. Weight about 6.5 lbs.

NIB	Exc.	V.G.	Good	Fair	Poor
475	350	265	200	150	100

CZ 455 American

Updated version of popular CZ 452. Action forged from steel billets. Walnut stock, cut checkering, oil finish. No sights furnished, 20.5" barrel. Trigger adjustable for weight and pull. Detachable magazine. Available with CZ Switch Barrel Set in .22 LR and .17 HMR. Single-barrel guns chambered for .22LR, .22 WMR or .17 HMR. Thumbhole Varmint Model available, with thumbhole camo stock, single-set trigger, fluted barrel. **NOTE:** Add $150 Thumbhole Varmint Model; $100 Switch Barrel set.

NIB	Exc.	V.G.	Good	Fair	Poor
350	300	250	220	170	100

CZ 512

Rimfire semi-automatic rifle. Dual guide rods for smooth operation. Hammer forged barrel, adjustable sights. Receiver machined for 11mm dovetail mounts. Field stripping via a coin modular design for simple takedown. Aluminum upper receiver with polymer lower. Beechwood stock. Chambered for .22LR and .22 WMR.

NIB	Exc.	V.G.	Good	Fair	Poor
400	350	295	220	185	125

CZ 513 Basic

Simplified version of CZ 452. Features plain beechwood stock, with no checkering. Iron sights. Chambered for .22 LR cartridge. Barrel length 21". Weight about 5.4 lbs. Introduced in 2004.

NIB	Exc.	V.G.	Good	Fair	Poor
275	200	170	125	100	75

CZ 511

Semi-automatic rifle chambered for .22 LR cartridge. Fitted with 22" barrel. Two-position rear sight. Supplied with an 8-round magazine. Cross bolt safety. Turkish walnut stock. Blued finish. Weight about 5.4 lbs.

NIB	Exc.	V.G.	Good	Fair	Poor
400	335	250	175	125	75

CZ 527

Bolt-action model chambered for .22 Hornet, .222 Rem. and .223 Rem. Rear sight adjustable. Checkered walnut stock. Barrel length 23.6"; magazine capacity 5 rounds; weight about 6.2 lbs.

NIB	Exc.	V.G.	Good	Fair	Poor
600	500	400	300	225	125

CZ 527 American Classic

Introduced in 1999. Features 20.5" barrel, with American-style Turkish walnut stock. Weight about 7.6 lbs. Blued finish. In 2005, this model chambered for .204 Ruger cartridge with 22" barrel. **NOTE:** Add $170 for English walnut stock; $200 for fancy American walnut; $30 for maple; $30 for laminate stock.

NIB	Exc.	V.G.	Good	Fair	Poor
600	500	400	300	200	100

CZ 527 Lux

Bolt-action center fire rifle. Chambered for .22 Hornet, .222 Rem. or .223 Rem. cartridge. Fitted with 23.6" barrel, with hooded front sight and fixed rear sight. Trigger is an adjustable single-set type. Turkish walnut stock in Bavarian-style. Blued finish. Supplied with a 5-round magazine. Weight about 6.6 lbs.

NIB	Exc.	V.G.	Good	Fair	Poor
600	475	350	250	150	100

CZ 527 Premium (Lux)

Introduced in 2000. Features hand fitted actions, fancy walnut stock, 18 lpi checkering and satin finish. Offered in .22 Hornet and .223 Rem. Barrel length 22". Magazine capacity 5 rounds. Weight about 6.2 lbs.

NIB	Exc.	V.G.	Good	Fair	Poor
650	525	400	300	175	125

CZ 527 FS

Similar to above model, but fitted with 20.5" barrel and Mannlicher-style stock. Blued finish. Weight about 6 lbs.

NIB	Exc.	V.G.	Good	Fair	Poor
690	525	400	300	175	125

CZ 527 Varmint

Chambered for .17 Hornet, .17 Remington, .204 Ruger, .222 Remington and .223 Remington cartridges. Fitted with 24" heavy barrel. Checkered Turkish walnut, gray laminate or black H-S Precision Kevlar stock. No sights. Detachable magazine. Weight about 7.2 lbs. **NOTE:** Add $50 for laminate; $150 for Kevlar stock.

NIB	Exc.	V.G.	Good	Fair	Poor
600	475	350	175	125	100

CZ 527 Carbine

Introduced in 2000. Chambered for 7.62x39 cartridge. Fitted with 18.5" barrel. Detachable magazine capacity 5 rounds. Open sights. Weight about 6 lbs.

NIB	Exc.	V.G.	Good	Fair	Poor
600	475	350	225	175	100

CZ 527 Prestige

Upgraded CZ 527 American, with jeweled bolt. Semi-fancy Turkish walnut, with hand rubbed finish. Chambered for .22 Hornet or .223 Remington cartridges. Barrel length 21.9". Weight about 6.2 lbs. Introduced in 2001.

NIB	Exc.	V.G.	Good	Fair	Poor
880	675	600	475	275	150

CZ 537

Bolt-action rifle chambered for .270, .308 and .30-06 cartridges. Rear sight is adjustable. Stock checkered walnut. Barrel length 23.6". Magazine capacity 5 rounds. Weight about 7.9 lbs. Discontinued.

NIB	Exc.	V.G.	Good	Fair	Poor
600	475	375	250	200	100

CZ 550 American Classic

Similar to Model CZ 550. Chambered for .243, .308, .270 and .30-06 cartridges. Fitted with 20.5" barrel. American-style Turkish walnut stock. No sights. Supplied with 5-round internal magazine. Blued finish. Weight about 7.6 lbs. Introduced in 1999.

NIB	Exc.	V.G.	Good	Fair	Poor
620	500	400	300	200	100

CZ 550

Chambered for .243, .270, .30 and .30-06 cartridges. Bolt-action features 24" barrel and high comb walnut stock. No open sights. Weight about 7.25 lbs.

NIB	Exc.	V.G.	Good	Fair	Poor
700	525	400	300	200	100

CZ 550 Battue Lux

Chambered for .30-06 cartridge. Ramp rear sight. Barrel length 20.25". Checkered walnut stock. Weight about 7.25 lbs.

NIB	Exc.	V.G.	Good	Fair	Poor
700	525	400	300	200	100

CZ 550 FS Battue

Same as above, with full-length stock.

NIB	Exc.	V.G.	Good	Fair	Poor
750	600	500	375	200	100

CZ 550 Minnesota

Chambered for .270 Win. and .30-06 calibers. Barrel length 23.5". No sights. Supplied with recoil pad. Weight about 7.25 lbs.

NIB	Exc.	V.G.	Good	Fair	Poor
650	550	450	325	225	125

CZ 550 Minnesota DM

Same as above, with detachable magazine. Calibers .270 Win. and .308.

NIB	Exc.	V.G.	Good	Fair	Poor
725	575	475	350	225	125

CZ 550 Prestige

Similar to CZ 550 American. Added features of jeweled bolt, semi-fancy

walnut and hand rubbed finish. Chambered for .270 or .30-06 cartridges, with 23.6" barrel. Weight about 7.3 lbs. Introduced in 2001.

NIB	Exc.	V.G.	Good	Fair	Poor
700	625	550	425	300	175

CZ 550 Lux

Chambered for 7x57, 6.5x55 SE and 9.3x62 cartridges. Barrel length 23.6". Fixed magazine capacity 5 rounds. Bavarian-style stock, with Turkish walnut. Open sights. Weight about 7.3 lbs.

NIB	Exc.	V.G.	Good	Fair	Poor
575	450	375	200	150	75

CZ 550 Varmint

Chambered for .308 Win. cartridge. Fitted with 25.6" heavy barrel. No sights. Checkered walnut varmint-style stock. Ventilated recoil pad. Single-set trigger. Detachable magazine holds 4 rounds. Weight about 9.3 lbs. In 2004 an HS Precision Kevlar stock was also offered. **NOTE:** Add $200 for Kevlar stock.

NIB	Exc.	V.G.	Good	Fair	Poor
650	500	400	300	200	100

CZ 550 Varmint Laminate

As above, with gray laminate stock. Offered in .22-250. Introduced in 2002.

NIB	Exc.	V.G.	Good	Fair	Poor
750	600	450	350	200	125

CZ 550 Safari Magnum

Chambered for .300 Win. Magnum, .375 H&H, .458 Win. Magnum and .416 Rigby cartridges. Bolt-action rifle fitted with 25" barrel and 5-round internal magazine. Sights are one standing and two folding express rear, with hooded front sight. Blued finish. Bavarian-style Turkish walnut stock. Weight about 9.2 lbs.

NIB	Exc.	V.G.	Good	Fair	Poor
925	750	500	400	300	200

CZ 550 American Safari Magnum

Introduced in 2004. Similar to Safari Magnum above, with American pattern stock. Offered with American walnut, brown laminate or camo laminate and fancy American walnut stock. **NOTE:** Add $200 for laminate stock; $600 for fancy wood stock.

NIB	Exc.	V.G.	Good	Fair	Poor
925	750	500	400	300	200

CZ 550 Ultimate Hunting Rifle

Similar to CZ550 Safari Magnum, but chambered for .300 Win. Magnum only. Custom select wood and 23.6" barrel. Accuracy guaranteed at one MOA to 1000 yards. Introduced 2006.

NIB	Exc.	V.G.	Good	Fair	Poor
3600	3000	2450	1500	675	300

CZ 550 Premium

Introduced in 2000. Features hand fitted action, fancy walnut stock and 18 lpi checkering. Chambered for .30-06 and .270 Win. cartridges. Barrel length 23.6". Weight about 7.3 lbs.

NIB	Exc.	V.G.	Good	Fair	Poor
925	750	500	400	300	200

CZ 550 Medium Magnum

Designed around a mid-sized Magnum action. Fitted with 23.6" barrel. Fixed magazine capacity of 5 rounds. Chambered for .300 Win. Magnum or 7mm Rem. Magnum. Single-set trigger and adjustable rear sight. Weight about 7.3 lbs. Introduced in 2001.

NIB	Exc.	V.G.	Good	Fair	Poor
700	575	425	300	200	100

CZ 550 Safari Classic Custom

Chambered for .404 Jeffery, .450 Rigby or .505 Gibbs. Fancy grade checkered walnut stock. Single-set trigger. Express sights. **NOTE:** Add $100 for .505 Gibbs.

NIB	Exc.	V.G.	Good	Fair	Poor
2400	2000	1400	750	400	300

CZ 557

Bolt-action carbine with 20.5" barrel, steel receiver with integral scope rails. Oil-finished walnut or synthetic stock with cheekpiece. Adjustable rear and fiber optic front sights. Chambered in .243 Win., 6.5x55, .270 Win., .308 Win., .30-06. Introduced in 2014.

NIB	Exc.	V.G.	Good	Fair	Poor
700	600	525	425	350	300

CZ 584

Combination 12-gauge/7x57Rmm, .222- or .308-caliber over/under combination rifle/shotgun. Automatic ejectors, 24.5" ventilated rib barrels and single triggers. Blued, with walnut stock.

NIB	Exc.	V.G.	Good	Fair	Poor
1000	775	600	500	400	200

CZ ZKK 600

Offered in 7x57mm, 7x64mm, .270 or .30-06. Features Mauser-type bolt-action, with controlled feed, non-rotating extractor and dovetailed receiver in three action lengths. **NOTE:** Add $100 to prices for pop-up receiver sight that was discontinued in 1977.

NIB	Exc.	V.G.	Good	Fair	Poor
750	625	500	425	325	175

CZ ZKK 601

As above, in .243- or .308-caliber.

NIB	Exc.	V.G.	Good	Fair	Poor
700	600	500	425	325	175

CZ ZKK 602

As above, in .300 H&H, .375 H&H, .458 Win. Magnum.

NIB	Exc.	V.G.	Good	Fair	Poor
800	700	600	500	400	200

CZ 700 Sniper M1

Introduced in 2001. Chambered for .308 Winchester cartridge. Fitted with 25.6" heavy barrel. Receiver has permanently attached Weaver rail. Laminated stock has adjustable cheekpiece and buttplate, with adjustable trigger. Magazine capacity 10 rounds. Weight about 12 lbs.

NIB	Exc.	V.G.	Good	Fair	Poor
2350	1800	1300	700	400	200

CZ 750 Sniper

Bolt-action rifle; .308 Win. 10-shot detachable magazine, 26" blued barrel, two scope mount systems, polymer stock, weight 12 lbs. Introduced 2006.

NIB	Exc.	V.G.	Good	Fair	Poor
2000	1750	1550	1050	600	325

CZ 550 Urban Sniper

Compact profile in a modern sniper rifle. Free floating 16" barrel, with target crown. Surefire muzzle-brake, with suppressor compatibility. Bell & Carlson fiberglass stock, aluminum bedding block, oversized bolt handle and single-stage trigger. Available with 5- or 10-round magazine. Chambered for .308 Winchester, with other calibers on request.

NIB	Exc.	V.G.	Good	Fair	Poor
2000	1725	1400	950	500	300

SHOTGUNS

CZ 581

A 12-gauge over/under double-barrel boxlock shotgun, with 28" ventilated rib barrels, single trigger and automatic ejectors. Blued, with walnut stock.

NIB	Exc.	V.G.	Good	Fair	Poor
875	700	600	450	400	200

CZ 712

Gas-operated semi-automatic 12-gauge 3" chamber shotgun, built on a lightweight alloy receiver. Offered with choice of 26" or 28" ventilated rib barrels. Magazine is 4 rounds. Checkered walnut stock, with blued finish. Weight about 7 lbs. Introduced in 2004.

NIB	Exc.	V.G.	Good	Fair	Poor
425	325	275	200	150	100

CZ 712 3-Gun

Semi-automatic 12-gauge designed for 3-gun competition. Black synthetic stock, matte black chrome finish, 22" barrel with 9-shot magazine extension and three choke tubes. Introduced in 2016.

NIB	Exc.	V.G.	Good	Fair	Poor
575	500	425	375	—	—

CZ 720

Similar to CZ 712. Chambered for 20-gauge 3" shell. Offered with choice of 26" or 28" ventilated rib barrels. Walnut stock. Weight about 6 lbs. Introduced in 2004.

NIB	Exc.	V.G.	Good	Fair	Poor
425	325	275	200	150	100

CZ 612/620

This family of slide-action shotguns comes in 12-gauge (CZ 612) and 20-gauge (620). Offered in Field, Home Defense, Turkey, Waterfowl, Trap, Big Game and Youth models. **NOTE:** Add $50 for Turkey and Waterfowl; $100 for Trap.

NIB	Exc.	V.G.	Good	Fair	Poor
325	300	275	235	200	185

Redhead

This over/under available in 12-, 20- or 28-gauge, with choke tubes and .410 bore with fixed chokes. Barrel lengths are 26" or 28". Single-selective trigger with extractors on 28-gauge and .410 bore models. Checkered walnut stock with pistol-grip. Receiver finish is silver. Weight from 6 lbs. to 8 lbs. depending on gauge.

NIB	Exc.	V.G.	Good	Fair	Poor
795	625	500	350	200	150

Canvasback

Over/under gun offered in 12- or 20-gauge. Fitted with 26" or 28" barrels, with choke tubes. Single-selective trigger with extractors. Black receiver finish. Weight about 7.5 lbs.

NIB	Exc.	V.G.	Good	Fair	Poor
695	550	450	350	200	150

Woodcock

Available in 12-, 20-, 28-gauge and .410 bore, with 26" or 28" barrel, choke tubes except for fixed chokes on .410 bore. Single-selective trigger with ejectors except 12- and 20-gauge. Receiver case colored with sideplate. Checkered walnut stock with pistol-grip. **NOTE:** Add $75 for 28-gauge and .410 bore models.

NIB	Exc.	V.G.	Good	Fair	Poor
1055	825	625	450	300	225

Woodcock Custom Grade

Similar to Woodcock model, but stocked with Grade IV walnut. Offered only in 20-gauge with 28" barrels.

NIB	Exc.	V.G.	Good	Fair	Poor
1500	1250	975	600	400	200

Mallard

This 12- or 20-gauge over/under gun is fitted with double triggers and extractors. Barrel length 28". Checkered walnut stock with pistol-grip. Coin finish receiver.

NIB	Exc.	V.G.	Good	Fair	Poor
695	550	450	350	200	150

Durango

Side-by-side gun offered in 12- or 20-gauge, with 20" barrels and choke tubes. Extractors. Case colored receiver. Single trigger. Checkered walnut with pistol-grip.

NIB	Exc.	V.G.	Good	Fair	Poor
795	625	550	400	300	200

Amarillo

As above, with double triggers.

NIB	Exc.	V.G.	Good	Fair	Poor
700	550	425	350	250	150

Ringneck

Side-by-side gun chambered for 12-, 16-, 20-, 28-gauge and .410 bore, with 26" or 28" barrels and choke tubes. Case colored receiver with side plates. Single-selective trigger with extractors. Checkered walnut stock with pistol-grip. **NOTE:** Add $100 for 16-gauge; $175 for 28-gauge and .410 bore.

NIB	Exc.	V.G.	Good	Fair	Poor
870	675	575	400	300	200

Ringneck Custom Grade

Select Grade IV walnut used in manufacture of this 20-gauge, with 28" barrels.

NIB	Exc.	V.G.	Good	Fair	Poor
1200	1000	700	450	300	200

Bobwhite

As above, with straight-grip stock and double triggers.

NIB	Exc.	V.G.	Good	Fair	Poor
795	625	550	400	300	200

Partridge

New in 2008, this side-by-side is available in 12-, 20-, 28-gauge and .410 bore, with 3" chambers (2.75" in 28-gauge), each with a frame scaled to its bore size. White chrome-plated receiver with scroll engraving. Boxlock action and double triggers. Straight-grip stock and splinter fore-end. Barrels are 28" in 12- and 20-gauge; 26" in 28-gauge and .410 bore. Includes five choke tubes (.410 bore is choked IC/MOD). **NOTE:** Add 20 percent for 28-gauge and .410 bore.

NIB	Exc.	V.G.	Good	Fair	Poor
795	625	550	400	300	200

Grouse

New in 2008, the Grouse is a single trigger side-by-side in 12-, 20-, 28-gauge and .410 bore, with 3" chambers (2.75" in 28-gauge). White chrome-plated receiver with scroll engraving. Prince of Wales grip and semi-beavertail schnabel fore-end. Barrels are 28" in 12- and 20-gauge; 26" in 28-gauge and .410 bore. Includes five choke tubes (.410 is choked IC/MOD). **NOTE:** Add 20 percent for 28-gauge and .410 bore.

NIB	Exc.	V.G.	Good	Fair	Poor
995	800	700	550	450	300

CZ Sporting

This dedicated sporting clays over/under is a 12-gauge, with adjustable comb stock and fore-end of #3 Circassian walnut. Features chrome-lined barrels back-bored to .736 and automatic ejectors. Barrels are 30" or 32". Five choke tubes included. Weight about 9 lbs.

NIB	Exc.	V.G.	Good	Fair	Poor
2400	1800	1300	700	400	200

Hammer Coach

12-gauge cowboy gun, with double triggers, color case-hardened receiver, external hammers and Turkish walnut pistol-grip stock and fore-end. Fixed IC and modified chokes. Introduced 2006.

NIB	Exc.	V.G.	Good	Fair	Poor
795	625	550	400	300	200

PISTOLS

All currently imported CZ pistols can be ordered with tritium night sights with the exception of models CZ 97B and CZ 100. Add $80 for this option. **NOTE:** Substantial premium for factory-engraved examples.

CZ 75

Designed by Koucky brothers in 1975, this model bears little resemblance to previous CZ pistols. Considered by many, including the late Jeff Cooper, to be the best pistol ever to come from Czech Republic. One of the finest semi-automatics in the world. Chambered for 9mm Parabellum cartridge, it is copied in many countries. Has a breechlock system utilizing a Browning-style cam. Slide rides on inside of the slide rails. Magazine capacity 15 rounds; barrel length 4.72"; overall length 8". Empty pistol weighs 34.5 oz. Offered in black paint, matte or polished blue finish.

NIB	Exc.	V.G.	Good	Fair	Poor
500	450	425	400	325	250

CZ 75 B

Introduced in 1994. An updated version of original CZ 75. Features pinned front sight, commander hammer, non-glare ribbed barrel and squared trigger guard. Also offered in .40 S&W chamber. **NOTE:** Add $20 for glossy blue; $25 for dual tone finish; $25 for nickel; $80 for tritium night sights; $30 for .40 S&W.

NIB	Exc.	V.G.	Good	Fair	Poor
510	400	300	250	175	125

CZ 75 30th Anniversary

Introduced in 2005. Features special 30th Anniversary engraving, gold inlays, gold plated controls, high gloss blue finish, engraved blonde finished birch grips. Magazine capacity 15 rounds. Limited to 1,000 pistols.

NIB	Exc.	V.G.	Good	Fair	Poor
850	675	500	400	300	200

CZ 75 Compact

Introduced in 1992. Compact version of CZ 75. Offered in black paint, matte or polished blue finish. Traditional single-/double-action. Barrel length 3.9"; overall length 7.3"; weight about 32 oz. In 2005, offered with accessory rail and ambidextrous manual safety. Add $50 to prices. **NOTE:** Add $20 for glossy blue; $25 for dual tone finish; $25 for nickel; $80 for tritium night sights; $30 for .40 S&W.

NIB	Exc.	V.G.	Good	Fair	Poor
475	425	300	250	175	125

CZ 75 Compact D

Essentially same as CZ 75 Compact, with decocking double-action system and lightweight alloy frame. Weight about 25 oz. **NOTE:** Only 20 of these pistols imported into U.S. No longer in production. Expert appraisal suggested prior to sale.

NIB	Exc.	V.G.	Good	Fair	Poor
555	450	300	225	150	100

CZ 75 B Tactical

Chambered for 9mm Luger cartridge. Fitted with 4.7" barrel. Has a single-/double-action trigger. Fixed sights. Rubber grips. Slide is black polycoat. Frame a military green finish. Weight about 35 oz. **NOTE:** Add 10 percent for night sights.

NIB	Exc.	V.G.	Good	Fair	Poor
475	400	325	250	175	125

CZ 75 Tactical Sport

Large steel frame CZ 75 variant in 9mm or .40 S&W, with 5.3" barrel, checkered wood grips and fixed sights. Weight 45 oz. Introduced in 2016.

NIB	Exc.	V.G.	Good	Fair	Poor
1200	1000	800	—	—	—

CZ 75 BD

Has all the same features as Model 75 B, with addition of a decocking double-action. Black polycoat finish.

NIB	Exc.	V.G.	Good	Fair	Poor
450	400	300	225	150	100

CZ BD Compact

Introduced in 2001. Features 3.9" barrel, with decocking lever. Chambered for .40 S&W cartridge. Blued finish. Magazine capacity 10 rounds. Weight about 32 oz. All other features same as CZ 75 B Compact.

NIB	Exc.	V.G.	Good	Fair	Poor
400	350	300	225	150	100

CZ BD Compact Carry

Same as above model, with rounded edges including trigger guard.

NIB	Exc.	V.G.	Good	Fair	Poor
425	375	300	225	150	100

CZ 75 B SA

Introduced in 2000. Features single-action trigger designed for competitive shooting that can be carried in condition one. Fitted with straight trigger and manual safety. Chambered for 9mm cartridge. Weight about 35 oz.

NIB	Exc.	V.G.	Good	Fair	Poor
520	400	325	225	150	100

CZ 75 Semi-Compact

Introduced in 1994. Same barrel length as Compact (3.9"), but same full-size grip as CZ 75. Magazine capacity 15 rounds of 9mm. Overall length 7.3".

NIB	Exc.	V.G.	Good	Fair	Poor
495	350	300	250	175	100

CZ 75 D PCR Compact

Introduced in 2000. Chambered for 9mm cartridge. Features light alloy frame and 3.9" barrel. Trigger both single-/double-action with decocking lever. Low profile sights. Serrated front and rear backstrap. Designed for Czech national police force. Magazine capacity 10 rounds. Weight about 27 oz.

NIB	Exc.	V.G.	Good	Fair	Poor
525	425	350	225	150	100

CZ 75 Champion

Chambered for .40 S&W, 9mm and 9x21 cartridges. Single-action-only trigger with straight trigger. Fitted with 4.5" barrel, low profile adjustable sights and three port compensator. Furnished with blue slide and nickel frame. Hand fitted. Weight about 36 oz.

NIB	Exc.	V.G.	Good	Fair	Poor
1475	1150	975	675	500	300

CZ 75 DAO

Similar to CZ 75, with double-action-only trigger, no safety lever and spurless hammer. Offered in 9mm and .40 S&W. Barrel length 4.7". Weight about 35 oz. Introduced in 2000.

NIB	Exc.	V.G.	Good	Fair	Poor
695	525	450	350	250	175

CZ P-01

Introduced in 2002, this pistol replaced CZ 75 with Czech National Police. Features forged aluminum alloy frame and 3.8" barrel. Decocker single-/double-action. Fixed sights. Fitted with M3 accessory rail. Rubber grips and 14-round magazine. Black polycoat finish. Weight about 29 oz.

NIB	Exc.	V.G.	Good	Fair	Poor
525	475	400	335	300	275

CZ P-06

The .40 S&W version of P-01. Magazine capacity 10 rounds.

NIB	Exc.	V.G.	Good	Fair	Poor
585	525	450	400	350	300

CZ P-09 Duty

Full-size high-capacity variation of P-01/P-06 series. Chambered in 9mm (19-round magazine) or .40 S&W (15-rounds). Low-profile sights, Picatinny rail, black polymer frame and black steel slide. P-07 model is single-stack variation

NIB	Exc.	V.G.	Good	Fair	Poor
475	425	385	325	300	260

CZ 75 Standard IPSC (ST)

Designed and built for IPSC competition. Chambered for .40 S&W and fitted with 5.4" barrel. Single-action-only trigger. Special high-profile sights. Weight about 45 oz.

NIB	Exc.	V.G.	Good	Fair	Poor
1000	850	775	625	500	300

CZ 75 M IPSC

Similar to CZ 75 Standard IPSC, with addition of two-port compensator and blast shield to protect frame-mounted optics. Slide racker standard. Red Dot optics. Barrel length 3.9". Weight about 45 oz. Introduced in 2001.

NIB	Exc.	V.G.	Good	Fair	Poor
1350	1200	1050	675	550	325

CZ 75 Silver Anniversary

Commemorates 25th Anniversary of CZ Model 75 pistol. Features high polish nickel finish, with walnut grips. Number "25" inlaid in grips. Total of 1000 pistols will be produced, with about 500 allocated for U.S. market.

NIB	Exc.	V.G.	Good	Fair	Poor
850	700	600	500	400	225

CZ 75 Stainless

All steel construction, double-stack magazines, 3-dot fixed sights. Chambered for 9mm., 16+1 or 10+1 capacity and 4.72" barrel. First stainless from CZ. Introduced 2006.

NIB	Exc.	V.G.	Good	Fair	Poor
675	550	425	350	275	150

CZ 75 SP-01 Shadow

Chambered 9mm for IPSC "Production" Division competition. 19+1 capacity, 4.72" barrel., 41 oz., wood grip. Introduced 2006.

NIB	Exc.	V.G.	Good	Fair	Poor
650	600	500	400	300	175

CZ 75 SP-01 Shadow Custom

Chambered in 9mm Parabellum. Steel slide and frame, CZ Custom Shop trigger job. Cold hammer-forged barrel, fiber-optic front sight, aluminum grips and 19-round magazine. Weight 36 oz., 4.7" barrel and dual-tone finish. Customized for IPSC Production division. Introduced in 2011.

NIB	Exc.	V.G.	Good	Fair	Poor
585	525	450	400	350	300

CZ 75 TS Czechmate

Comes with all parts necessary to compete in IPSC Open or Limited divisions. Chambered in 9mm Parabellum. Steel slide and frame, single-action grips. Comes with compensator and C-More red dot sight installed and ambidextrous slide racker. Includes front-sight adapter that replaces compensator, rear sight, ambidextrous safeties, aluminum grips, magazine well, one 26- and three 20-round magazines. Weight 48 oz., 5.4" barrel, matte blue finish. Introduced in 2011.

NIB	Exc.	V.G.	Good	Fair	Poor
2900	2500	2000	1500	800	350

CZ 75 Tactical Sport

Single-action for IPSC competition. Chambered in 9mm and .40 S&W. Dual tone (nickel/blued). Capacity 20+1 (9mm) or 16+1 (.40 S&W). 5.4" barrel; 45 oz. Introduced 2006.

NIB	Exc.	V.G.	Good	Fair	Poor
1100	900	675	500	400	200

CZ 85 B

Similar in appearance to CZ 75. Offers some new features such as ambidextrous safety and slide stop levers, squared trigger guard, adjustable sight and ribbed slide. Caliber, magazine capacity and weight same as CZ 75. **NOTE:** Add $20 for glossy blue; $25 for dual tone and nickel finish; $30 for .40 S&W.

NIB	Exc.	V.G.	Good	Fair	Poor
525	475	425	300	250	175

CZ 85 Combat

Similar to CZ 85, with addition of adjustable sights, walnut grips, round hammer and free dropping magazine. **NOTE:** Add $20 for glossy blue; $25 for dual tone and nickel finish; $30 for .40 S&W.

NIB	Exc.	V.G.	Good	Fair	Poor
500	450	325	250	175	125

CZ 40B

Introduced in 2002 and similar to CZ 75. Features an alloy frame similar in shape to Colt Model 1911. A single-/double-action design. Barrel length 4.7". Magazine capacity 10 rounds. Chambered for .40 S&W cartridge. Weight about 35 oz.

NIB	Exc.	V.G.	Good	Fair	Poor
625	500	400	300	200	125

CZ Kadet

Chambered for .22 LR cartridge. Fitted with 4.7" barrel. A fixed barrel blowback semi-automatic pistol. Adjustable sights and blue finish. Weight about 36 oz.

NIB	Exc.	V.G.	Good	Fair	Poor
510	400	300	225	175	100

CZ 75 Kadet Conversion

A separate conversion kit for CZ 75/85 series. Converts these pistols to .22 LR. Adjustable rear sight. Supplied with 10-round magazine.

NIB	Exc.	V.G.	Good	Fair	Poor
300	225	200	150	100	50

CZ 2075 RAMI

Introduced in 2004, this 9mm or .40 S&W pistol fitted with 3" barrel. Has single-/double-action trigger. Design based on CZ 75. Magazine capacity: 10 rounds 9mm; 8 rounds .40 S&W. Weight about 25 oz.

NIB	Exc.	V.G.	Good	Fair	Poor
450	400	350	300	250	175

CZ 83

Fixed-barrel .380-caliber pistol. Features ambidextrous safety and magazine catch behind trigger guard. Stripped by means of a hinged trigger guard. Barrel length 3.8"; overall length 6.8"; weight about 23 oz. **NOTE:** Add $5 for nickel finish. In 1993, Special Editions of this pistol were introduced. These Special Editions consist of special finishes for then-currently imported CZ pistols. These are high polish blue, nickel, chrome, gold and combination of these finishes. These Special Edition finishes may affect price; they add between $100 and $250 to cost of the pistol when new.

NIB	Exc.	V.G.	Good	Fair	Poor
475	325	200	175	150	125

CZ 97 B

Planned for production in summer of 1997. Chambered for .45 ACP cartridge. Fitted with 4.8" barrel. Has single-/double-action mode. Magazine capacity 10 rounds. Wood grips with blue finish. Weight about 40 oz.

NIB	Exc.	V.G.	Good	Fair	Poor
665	525	400	300	175	100

CZ 100

Semi-automatic pistol introduced in 1996. Chambered for 9mm or .40 S&W cartridge. Has plastic frame and steel slide. Barrel length 3.75". Weight about 24 oz. U.S. magazine capacity 10 rounds.

NIB	Exc.	V.G.	Good	Fair	Poor
525	450	325	2000	150	100

CZ 1911 A1

Classic full-size 1911 A1 in .45 ACP, with 5" barrel, steel slide and frame with black oxide finish. Checkered walnut grips and fixed sights. Made in U.S.A. Introduced in 2015

NIB	Exc.	V.G.	Good	Fair	Poor
750	700	650	—	—	—

CZ Scorpion Evo

Blowback-operated 9mm semi-automatic, with 7.75" barrel. Imported as a pistol, it's a civilian version of CZ Scorpion EVO 3-A1 sub-gun. Low-profile sights, with four aperture sizes on an 11" Picatinny rail. Features include ambidextrous controls, and an arm brace adapter which adds an AR-style pistol buffer tube to rear of the action. Introduced in 2015.

NIB	Exc.	V.G.	Good	Fair	Poor
750	700	650	—	—	—

D

D. W. M.
Berlin, Germany
See—Luger & Borchardt

Model 22

A 7.65mm caliber semi-automatic pistol, with 3.5" barrel. Blued with walnut grips; later changed to plastic grips. Approximately 40,000 manufactured between 1921 and 1931.

NIB	Exc.	V.G.	Good	Fair	Poor
—	950	775	500	400	250

DAEWOO
Pusan, Korea

DH-40

Semi-automatic pistol chambered for .40 S&W cartridge. Has 4.13" barrel and magazine capacity of 11 rounds. Weight about 32 oz.

NIB	Exc.	V.G.	Good	Fair	Poor
495	375	300	250	175	100

DP-51B

Semi-automatic pistol chambered for 9mm cartridge. Fitted with 4.13" barrel. Magazine capacity 13 rounds; overall length 7.5"; weight about 28 oz.

NIB	Exc.	V.G.	Good	Fair	Poor
400	325	275	225	175	100

DP-51SB

More compact design, with 3.6" barrel and 10-round magazine. Weight 27 oz. Stainless steel finish.

NIB	Exc.	V.G.	Good	Fair	Poor
450	395	275	225	175	100

DP-51CB

Same as above, fitted with a 3.6" barrel. Magazine capacity 10 rounds. Weight about 26 oz.

NIB	Exc.	V.G.	Good	Fair	Poor
450	375	300	250	175	100

DP-52

Semi-automatic pistol chambered for .22 LR cartridge. Has 3.82" barrel length; magazine capacity 10 rounds. Operates in double/single-action modes. Overall length 6.7"; weight about 23 oz.

NIB	Exc.	V.G.	Good	Fair	Poor
395	325	250	200	150	100

DH380

Introduced in 1996. Semi-automatic pistol chambered for .380 ACP cartridge. Fitted with 3.8" barrel; magazine capacity 8 rounds. Firing is double/single-action. Weight about 24 oz.

NIB	Exc.	V.G.	Good	Fair	Poor
425	375	275	225	150	100

DR200

Introduced in 1996. Post-ban semi-automatic rifle chambered for .223 Rem. cartridge. Features black matte finish, with synthetic thumbhole stock. Barrel length 18.3". Uses AR-15 magazines, not included with rifle. Weight about 9 lbs.

NIB	Exc.	V.G.	Good	Fair	Poor
975	875	500	400	300	150

K-2/AR-100 (Max I)

A 5.56mm caliber pre-ban semi-automatic rifle, with 18" barrel. Gas-operated rotary bolt-action, magazines interchangeable with those from M-16. Black. Introduced in 1985. No longer imported.

NIB	Exc.	V.G.	Good	Fair	Poor
1450	1200	950	700	500	400

K1A1 (Max II)

Rifle is quite similar to K-2/AR-100, with a folding composite stock.

NIB	Exc.	V.G.	Good	Fair	Poor
1450	1200	950	700	500	400

DAISY
Rogers, Arkansas

VL Rifle

A .22 combustible cartridge single-shot rifle, with 18" barrel and plastic stock. Cartridge ignited by compressed air. Manufactured during 1968 and 1969. Believed fewer than 20,000 made. Add considerable premium if large quantity of VL ammunition is present.

NIB	Exc.	V.G.	Good	Fair	Poor
275	100	85	75	50	25

VL Presentation Model

As above, with walnut stock. Approximately 4,000 made in 1968 and 1969.

NIB	Exc.	V.G.	Good	Fair	Poor
275	150	125	100	75	50

VL Cased Presentation Model

As above, with gold plaque inlaid in the stock. Fitted case containing 300 VL cartridges.

NIB	Exc.	V.G.	Good	Fair	Poor
325	200	175	125	100	75

Model 2201/2211

Bolt-action single-shot rifle chambered for .22 LR cartridge. Fitted with a 19" barrel and octagon shroud. Ramp blade front sight, with adjustable notch rear sight. Synthetic stock Model 2211 and walnut stock Model 2201. Trigger is adjustable. Weight about 6.5 lbs.

NIB	Exc.	V.G.	Good	Fair	Poor
200	150	100	60	50	25

Model 2202/2212

Similar to above model in appearance, but fitted with 10-round rotary magazine. Synthetic stock Model 2212 and walnut stock Model 2202. Weight about 6.5 lbs.

NIB	Exc.	V.G.	Good	Fair	Poor
200	150	100	60	50	25

Model 2203/2213

Semi-automatic rifle chambered for .22 LR cartridge. Has 7-round magazine and 19" barrel. Synthetic stock Model 2213 and walnut stock Model 2203. Weight about 6.5 lbs.

NIB	Exc.	V.G.	Good	Fair	Poor
225	175	125	75	75	50

DAKIN GUN CO.
San Francisco, California

Model 100

A 12- and 20-gauge boxlock double-barrel shotgun, with 26" or 28" barrels, various chokes, extractors and double triggers. Engraved, blued, with a checkered walnut stock. Manufactured in the 1960s.

NIB	Exc.	V.G.	Good	Fair	Poor
—	475	325	275	200	100

Model 147

As above, with ventilated rib barrels.

NIB	Exc.	V.G.	Good	Fair	Poor
—	450	375	250	200	100

Model 160

As above, with single-selective trigger.

NIB	Exc.	V.G.	Good	Fair	Poor
—	700	600	450	250	150

Model 215

As above, but more finely finished.

NIB	Exc.	V.G.	Good	Fair	Poor
—	1800	1600	1100	500	250

Model 170

A 12-, 16- and 20-gauge over/under shotgun, with 26" or 28" ventilated rib barrels, various chokes and double triggers. Blued and lightly engraved. Discontinued in the 1960s.

NIB	Exc.	V.G.	Good	Fair	Poor
—	500	425	350	275	150

DAKOTA ARMS, INC.
Sturgis, South Dakota

This company was formed by Don Allen. He was a fine craftsman in the field of custom rifles. The company offers four basic models, with a number of options to fit the customers' needs or wants. Workmanship and materials are of the highest quality. In business since 1987, the company was purchased by Remington Arms Co. in 2009. **NOTE:** All prices are base prices. Dakota offers a number of extra cost options that can greatly affect the value of its rifles and shotguns.

RIFLES

Dakota 76 Classic

A .257 Roberts, .270 Winchester, .280 Remington, .30-06, 7mm Remington Magnum, .338, .300 Winchester Magnum and .458 Winchester Magnum bolt-action rifle, with 23" barrel and Mauser-type extractor. Checkered walnut stock. Manufactured in 1987.

NIB	Exc.	V.G.	Good	Fair	Poor
5500	4500	3250	2400	1200	500

Dakota 76 Professional Hunter

Features 23" Douglas premium stainless barrel, quarter rib with fixed blade rear and handed/hooded front sight, pillar-bedded fiberglass stock. Calibers are .375 H&H, .404 Jeffery, .416 Remington, .416 Rigby, .450 Dakota, .450 Rigby or .458 Lott. Introduced in 2013

NIB	Exc.	V.G.	Good	Fair	Poor
7500	6500	5000	4000	—	—

Dakota 76 Varmint Grade

Introduced in 1996. Chambered for a variety of cartridges from .17 Rem. to 6mm PPC. Single-shot bolt-action design available in right-/left-hand versions. Barrel length 24". Varmint-style stock is semi-fancy walnut, with oil finish and no checkering. Many extra cost options offered for this model.

NIB	Exc.	V.G.	Good	Fair	Poor
2500	2000	1500	1100	800	400

Model 97 Varmint Hunter

Built on Model 97 action. Standard features are fiberglass stock, round-action single-shot, adjustable trigger and black recoil pad. Barrel length 24". Offered in calibers from .220 Swift to .308 Winchester. Weight about 8 lbs. Introduced in 1999.

NIB	Exc.	V.G.	Good	Fair	Poor
2195	1750	1000	750	600	300

Model 76 Safari Grade

Chambered in .375 H&H, .458 Winchester Magnum and other short Magnum calibers. Features ebony fore-end tip, one-piece magazine assembly and open sights. Weight about 8.5 lbs.

NIB	Exc.	V.G.	Good	Fair	Poor
7800	6500	5000	3800	1500	750

Model 76 Alpine Grade

As above, but lighter in weight. Chambered for .22-250, .243, 6mm, .250-3000, 7mm/08, .308 and .358. Introduced in 1989.

NIB	Exc.	V.G.	Good	Fair	Poor
5600	4500	3600	2800	1000	500

Model 76 African Grade

As above in .416 Rigby, .416 Dakota, .404 Jeffery and .450 Dakota. Walnut especially selected for strength, with crossbolts through the stock. Weighs between 9 and 10 lbs.

NIB	Exc.	V.G.	Good	Fair	Poor
8000	7000	5800	4000	1600	800

Model 10 Single Shot

Built on a single-shot falling action. Features 23" barrel and choice of XX grade wood with oil finish. Fine line checkering, steel grip cap and .5" recoil pad are also standard. Weight about 5.5 lbs.

NIB	Exc.	V.G.	Good	Fair	Poor
4500	4000	2750	1550	900	400

Model 10 Single Shot Magnum

Same as above, in calibers .338 Win. Magnum to .416 Dakota. Weight about 6.5 lbs.

NIB	Exc.	V.G.	Good	Fair	Poor
5895	4600	3200	1900	1000	450

Dakota .22 Long Rifle Sporter

Fitted with 22" barrel, X grade oil finish walnut, with fine line checkering and steel grip cap. A .5" black recoil pad standard. Weight about 6.5 lbs. Ceased production in 1998.

NIB	Exc.	V.G.	Good	Fair	Poor
1750	1300	800	650	500	275

Dakota .22 Long Rifle Sporter (New Model)

Reintroduction (2003) of Dakota .22 rifle.

NIB	Exc.	V.G.	Good	Fair	Poor
2800	2500	2000	1350	700	350

Model 97 Long Range Hunter

Introduced in 1997. Bolt-action rifle offered in 13 calibers: .250-6, .257 Roberts, .270 Win., .280 Rem., 7mm Rem. Magnum, 7mm Dakota

Magnum, .30-06, .300 Win. Magnum, .300 Dakota Magnum, .338 Win. Magnum, .330 Dakota Magnum, .375 H&H and .375 Dakota Magnum. Barrel length depends on caliber, but are either 24" or 26". Trigger is fully adjustable. Many other special features. Stock is black synthetic, with one-piece bedding. Black recoil pad standard. Weight about 7.7 lbs.

NIB	Exc.	V.G.	Good	Fair	Poor
2800	2400	2200	1500	800	375

Model 97 Lightweight Hunter

Introduced in 1998. Features barrel lengths from 22" to 24" in both short-/long-actions. Special lightweight composite stock is used. Calibers offered range from .22-250 to .330 Dakota Magnum. Weights are between 6.15 to 6.5 lbs., depending on caliber and barrel length. **NOTE:** Add 50 to 70 percent for Deluxe with AAA grade wood.

NIB	Exc.	V.G.	Good	Fair	Poor
2000	1500	1100	800	500	375

Model T-76 Longbow Tactical Rifle

Long range tactical bolt-action rifle available in 3 calibers: .338 Lapua, .300 Dakota Magnum and .330 Dakota Magnum. Fiberglass stock is an A-2 McMillan in black or olive green. Adjustable length of pull, with bi-pod spike in forearm. The 28" stainless steel barrel is .950 diameter at the muzzle, with muzzle-brake. Rifle sold with a number of accessories; case with bipod, tool kit and tool box. Weight about 13.7 lbs.

NIB	Exc.	V.G.	Good	Fair	Poor
4600	4250	3000	1650	800	400

Model 76 Traveler

Introduced in 1999. Built on a modified Model 76 design. Stock is wood. Disassembly is threadless. Offered in standard length action, short Magnum-action and long-action in both left-/right hand. Offered in three grades.

Classic

NIB	Exc.	V.G.	Good	Fair	Poor
6200	5500	4000	2700	1800	900

Safari

NIB	Exc.	V.G.	Good	Fair	Poor
7800	6500	4200	3000	2000	1200

African

NIB	Exc.	V.G.	Good	Fair	Poor
9000	7500	5000	3200	2000	1200

Classic Predator

Bolt-action rifle chambered for .17 VarTarg, .17 Rem., .17 Tactical, .20 VarTarg, .20 Tactical, .20 PPC, .204 Ruger, .221 Rem. Fireball, .222 Rem., .222 Rem. Magnum, .223 Rem., .22 BR, 6 PPC and 6 BR. Fitted with a 22" stainless steel barrel, checkered special select Claro walnut stock, with cheekpiece.

NIB	Exc.	V.G.	Good	Fair	Poor
3800	3000	2200	1700	800	375

Serious Predator

As above, with AAA Claro walnut stock.

NIB	Exc.	V.G.	Good	Fair	Poor
3000	2250	2000	1650	800	400

All-Weather Predator

As above, with varmint style composite stock.

NIB	Exc.	V.G.	Good	Fair	Poor
2500	2000	1600	1000	500	300

Double Rifle

Available in most common calibers. Fitted with exhibition walnut, with pistol-grip. Barrel is 25". Round-action with selective ejectors, recoil pad and hard case. Prices listed for guns without engraving.

NIB	Exc.	V.G.	Good	Fair	Poor
30000	24000	18000	10000	3500	800

Little Sharps Rifle

Introduced in 2003. Smaller version (20 percent) of full size Sharps rifle. Standard rifle has 26" octagon barrel, straight-grip stock with XX walnut, steel buttplate and blade front sight. Offered in calibers from .17 HMR to .30-40 Krag. Weight around 8 lbs.

NIB	Exc.	V.G.	Good	Fair	Poor
5500	3950	2750	2000	1500	400

Limited Edition .30-06 Model 76

Ultra-decked-out version of Model 76; commemorates 100th anniversary of .30-06 cartridge; production limited to 101 units. Introduced 2006.

NIB	Exc.	V.G.	Good	Fair	Poor
8000	5500	4000	2650	1700	500

Limited Edition .30-06 Model 10

Ultra-decked-out version of Model 10; commemorates 100th anniversary of .30-06 cartridge; production limited to 101 units. Introduced 2006.

NIB	Exc.	V.G.	Good	Fair	Poor
8000	5500	4000	2650	1700	500

SHOTGUNS

Classic Grade

Grade features case colored round-action, with straight-grip and fancy walnut oil finish stock. Forearm is splinter type. Double trigger standard, with choice of chokes. No longer in production.

NIB	Exc.	V.G.	Good	Fair	Poor
7950	5200	4400	3000	2000	600

Premier Grade

Grade features case colored round-action, with 50 percent engraving coverage. Exhibition grade English walnut stock, with straight-grip and splinter forearm. Oil rubbed finish. Double triggers are standard, with choice of chokes. **NOTE:** Add 10 percent for 28-gauge and .410 bore.

NIB	Exc.	V.G.	Good	Fair	Poor
13950	9500	7000	4750	2900	500

Dakota American Legend

Introduced in 1996. Side-by-side shotgun offered in 12-, 20-, 28-gauge and .410 bore. Concave rib, splinter forearm, double triggers, straight-grip stock, 27" barrels and full scroll engraving on frame. Many additional extra cost options are offered that can greatly affect price. Base price listed.

NIB	Exc.	V.G.	Good	Fair	Poor
18000	14000	11500	7900	5000	600

Dakota Shotgun

Similar to American Legend. Offered in two grades of finish. New grades first offered in 1997.

DAKOTA ARMS INC.—FERLIB SHOTGUNS

In 2000, Dakota Arms Inc. became the exclusive importer of Ferlib shotguns in the U.S. Models listed are imported and sold by Dakota Arms Inc.

Model 7

NIB	Exc.	V.G.	Good	Fair	Poor
10950	8000	6500	5000	4000	700

Prince Model

NIB	Exc.	V.G.	Good	Fair	Poor
11950	9000	7500	6000	4500	700

Prince Model Side-Lever

NIB	Exc.	V.G.	Good	Fair	Poor
14500	10500	8500	7000	5500	700

Rex

NIB	Exc.	V.G.	Good	Fair	Poor
14950	11000	8500	7000	5500	700

Premier

NIB	Exc.	V.G.	Good	Fair	Poor
16950	12500	10000	7200	5500	600

Sideplate Model

NIB	Exc.	V.G.	Good	Fair	Poor
14400	10500	8500	7000	5500	700

Sideplate Model with Gold

NIB	Exc.	V.G.	Good	Fair	Poor
15100	11250	10000	7200	5500	600

Sideplate with Scroll

NIB	Exc.	V.G.	Good	Fair	Poor
14000	10500	8500	7000	5500	700

Hammer Gun

NIB	Exc.	V.G.	Good	Fair	Poor
19000	14000	12000	10000	5000	700

H.H. Model—no engraving

NIB	Exc.	V.G.	Good	Fair	Poor
20000	15000	13000	11000	570	675

Esposizione

NIB	Exc.	V.G.	Good	Fair	Poor
25500	18000	13000	10000	7000	700

L'Inglesina

NIB	Exc.	V.G.	Good	Fair	Poor
25500	18000	13000	10000	7000	700

Model E "Fantasy

NIB	Exc.	V.G.	Good	Fair	Poor
39500	27500	22000	15500	11000	700

Boss—no engraving

NIB	Exc.	V.G.	Good	Fair	Poor
29500	20000	15000	10000	7000	750

DAKOTA ARMS INC.—SIACE SHOTGUNS

Imported from Italy in 2004 and called Dakota SuperLight. Shotguns are side-by-sides, with boxlock actions.

Field

Available in 12-, 16-, 20-, 24-, 28- and 32-gauge as well as .410 bore. Case colored receiver with select Turkish walnut. Checkering is 24 lpi. Double triggers. Border engraving. Weight about 5.5 lbs. for 20-gauge. **NOTE:** Add $600 for 16-, 32-gauge and .410 bore.

NIB	Exc.	V.G.	Good	Fair	Poor
4500	3500	2400	1775	1100	500

Grade II

As above, with 65 percent coverage of English scroll. **NOTE:** Add $700 for 16-, 32-gauge and .410 bore.

NIB	Exc.	V.G.	Good	Fair	Poor
5500	4250	3200	1600	800	400

Grade III

As above, with deeply cut vine and leaf scroll. Deluxe Turkish walnut and 65 percent coverage of English scroll. **NOTE:** Add $800 for 16-, 32-gauge and .410 bore.

NIB	Exc.	V.G.	Good	Fair	Poor
6500	5000	4000	3000	1650	400

DALY, CHARLES

Charles Daly was co-founder of Schoverling & Daly sporting goods company in New York City in 1865. The company imported some of the better-made shotguns from Europe and Charles Daly was used as the brand name. Daly trademark was sold several times over the years, with various owners importing guns from Belgium, Germany, Japan, Italy and other countries.

EARLY PRUSSIAN GUNS

Commander Over/Under Model 100

Boxlock over/under Anson & Deeley action shotgun chambered for all gauges. Choice of barrel length and chokes, double triggers (standard) or single-selective trigger. Blued, with a checkered walnut stock. Manufactured in Belgium in late 1930s.

NIB	Exc.	V.G.	Good	Fair	Poor
—	1000	750	475	275	200

Commander Over/Under Model 200

As above, with a better-grade walnut stock.

NIB	Exc.	V.G.	Good	Fair	Poor
—	1100	850	550	300	200

Superior Side-by-Side

As above, with an Anson & Deeley boxlock action and double triggers. Blued, with a walnut stock. Not manufactured after 1933. **NOTE:** Add $600 for 20-gauge; $1000 for 10-gauge.

NIB	Exc.	V.G.	Good	Fair	Poor
—	1400	950	650	450	250

Empire Side-by-Side

As above, but engraved with a better grade of walnut.

NIB	Exc.	V.G.	Good	Fair	Poor
—	3750	3000	2250	1250	600

NOTE: Prices shown for Empire and Diamond grade models are for those manufactured by Sauer. Add 20 to 30 percent for Linder manufacture.

Diamond Grade Side-by-Side

A deluxe version of above.

NIB	Exc.	V.G.	Good	Fair	Poor
—	5750	4500	3750	3000	1200

Regent Diamond Grade Side-by-Side

Custom order version of above.

NIB	Exc.	V.G.	Good	Fair	Poor
—	11500	8500	7000	5500	2500

Empire Over/Under

A 12-, 16- and 20-gauge Anson & Deeley boxlock shotgun. Choice of barrel length and choke, double triggers and automatic ejectors. Engraved with fine quality scrollwork and walnut stock. Discontinued in 1933.

NIB	Exc.	V.G.	Good	Fair	Poor
—	3500	2750	2000	1150	500

Diamond Grade Over/Under

As above, but more finely finished.

NIB	Exc.	V.G.	Good	Fair	Poor
—	5500	3750	3250	2500	1250

SEXTUPLE SINGLE-BARREL TRAP

Empire Grade

A 12-gauge boxlock single-barrel shotgun, with 30"-34" Full choke barrels, ventilated rib and automatic ejectors. Strong action features six locking lugs. Engraved with a walnut stock. Manufactured after 1933.

NIB	Exc.	V.G.	Good	Fair	Poor
—	2950	2450	1850	1500	750

Regent Diamond Grade

As above, with more engraving and better grade walnut stock.

NIB	Exc.	V.G.	Good	Fair	Poor
—	7500	6300	5500	4500	2000

DRILLINGS

Superior Grade

A 12-, 16- and 20-gauge over/under rifle/shotgun, with a rifle barrel in .25-20, .25-35 or .30-30. Engraved with a walnut stock. Not manufactured after 1933.

NIB	Exc.	V.G.	Good	Fair	Poor
—	3700	2450	1800	1450	800

Diamond Grade

As above, with more engraving and better grade of walnut in the stock.

NIB	Exc.	V.G.	Good	Fair	Poor
—	5250	4500	3750	3000	1500

Regent Diamond Grade

As above, with elaborate engraving and highest quality walnut stock.

NIB	Exc.	V.G.	Good	Fair	Poor
—	12500	9500	7200	5800	3000

B.C. MIROKU GUNS

Empire Grade Side-by-Side

A 12-, 16- and 20-gauge Anson and Deeley boxlock shotgun, with 26", 28" and 30" barrels, various chokes, extractors and a single trigger. Blued, with a checkered walnut stock. Manufactured between 1968 and 1971. **NOTE:** Add 10 percent for ventilated rib barrels and/or 20-gauge.

NIB	Exc.	V.G.	Good	Fair	Poor
—	750	550	375	200	100

Superior Grade Single Barrel Trap

A 12-gauge boxlock shotgun, with 32" or 34" ventilated rib barrels, Full choke and automatic ejector. Blued, with Monte Carlo walnut stock. Manufactured between 1968 and 1976.

NIB	Exc.	V.G.	Good	Fair	Poor
—	675	525	450	350	200

Over/Unders

A 12-, 20-, 28-gauge and .410 bore boxlock shotgun, with 26", 28" and 30" barrels and ventilated ribs. Various choke combinations were offered, with single-selective triggers and automatic ejectors. Blued, with checkered walnut stocks. Differences between grades are degree and quality of engraving and grade of walnut used for stock. Smaller-bore guns bring a premium as listed. Manufactured between 1963 and 1976 by B.C. Miroku. **NOTE:** Add 10 percent 20-gauge; 20 percent 28-gauge; 30 percent .410.

Venture Grade

NIB	Exc.	V.G.	Good	Fair	Poor
—	900	675	500	375	200

Venture Grade Skeet or Trap

Offered with either 26" Skeet & Skeet or 30" Full choke.

NIB	Exc.	V.G.	Good	Fair	Poor
—	800	550	475	375	200

Field Grade

Chambered for 12- and 20-gauge only.

NIB	Exc.	V.G.	Good	Fair	Poor
—	900	700	500	425	200

Superior Grade

NIB	Exc.	V.G.	Good	Fair	Poor
—	1200	900	600	525	200

Superior Grade Trap

NIB	Exc.	V.G.	Good	Fair	Poor
—	800	600	525	425	200

Diamond Grade

NIB	Exc.	V.G.	Good	Fair	Poor
—	1800	1400	975	650	300

Diamond Grade Trap or Skeet

With either 26" Skeet & Skeet or 30" Full choke barrels and Monte Carlo stocks. **NOTE:** Add 5 percent for wide rib.

NIB	Exc.	V.G.	Good	Fair	Poor
—	1500	1100	800	650	350

ITALIAN MANUFACTURE
SEMI-AUTOMATIC SHOTGUNS

Manufactured by the firm Breda in Milan, Italy. Semi-automatic "Novamatic" produced in 1968. All other models began Italian production in 1976. Imported by KBI, Inc. until 2010.

Novamatic Lightweight

A 12-gauge semi-automatic shotgun, with 26" or 28" ventilated rib barrel and screw-in choke tubes. Receiver is alloy, with checkered walnut stock. Imported under the Daly name in 1968 only.

NIB	Exc.	V.G.	Good	Fair	Poor
—	400	325	275	175	125

Novamatic Trap

As above, with Monte Carlo stock and 30" full choke barrel.

NIB	Exc.	V.G.	Good	Fair	Poor
—	415	340	290	200	150

Charles Daly Automatic

A 12-gauge Magnum semi-automatic shotgun, with 26" or 28" ventilated rib barrels, screw-in choke tubes and 5-shot magazine. A slug gun is available, with rifle sights. Checkered walnut grip in two versions—pistol-grip and English-style straight-grip. **NOTE:** Choke-tube model would be worth a 10 percent premium.

NIB	Exc.	V.G.	Good	Fair	Poor
—	475	395	300	225	150

Field Grade

Introduced in 1999, this model has several variations all in 12-gauge. Standard gun choice of 24", 26", 28" or 30" barrels, with screw-in chokes and synthetic stocks. Slug gun offered with 22" barrel in blue or nickel finish. A full coverage camo model offered in same configurations as field grade. **NOTE:** Add $30 for nickel slug gun; $100 for camo gun.

NIB	Exc.	V.G.	Good	Fair	Poor
425	365	255	200	150	100

Superior Grade Hunter

Offered in 12-gauge, with choice of 26", 28" or 30" ventilated rib barrels. Walnut stock, with hand checkering. Gold trigger and highlights. Introduced in 1999.

NIB	Exc.	V.G.	Good	Fair	Poor
550	425	365	245	160	100

Superior Grade Sporting

Same as above, with 28" or 30" ported barrel and select walnut stock.

NIB	Exc.	V.G.	Good	Fair	Poor
570	450	365	245	160	100

Superior Grade Trap

This 12-gauge model offered with a choice of 30" or 32" ventilated rib barrel. Walnut stock with hand checkering. Introduced in 1999.

NIB	Exc.	V.G.	Good	Fair	Poor
625	475	390	270	185	100

Field Hunter VR-MC

This series of 3" semi-automatic 12-gauges is finished in one of four Realtree/Advantage camo patterns or matte black. Barrels are 24", 26" or 28". Advantage Timber model available in 20-gauge and black matte available in 20- and 28-gauge. **NOTE:** Add 15 percent for camo.

NIB	Exc.	V.G.	Good	Fair	Poor
425	365	255	200	150	100

Field Hunter VR-MC Youth

As above, with 1.6" shorter stock and 22" barrel. 20-gauge only.

NIB	Exc.	V.G.	Good	Fair	Poor
400	345	230	165	125	100

Superior II

New in 2007, Superior II line of semi-automatics features oil-finished Turkish walnut stocks and three chokes.

NIB	Exc.	V.G.	Good	Fair	Poor
600	525	395	275	200	100

Hunter

Available in 12- and 20-gauge, with 26" or 28" barrel. 28-gauge with 26" barrel.

NIB	Exc.	V.G.	Good	Fair	Poor
600	525	395	275	200	100

Sport

In 12-gauge only, with 28" or 30" ported barrel and wide rib.

NIB	Exc.	V.G.	Good	Fair	Poor
600	525	395	275	200	100

Trap

In 12-gauge 30" ported barrel only, with Monte Carlo comb and wide rib.

NIB	Exc.	V.G.	Good	Fair	Poor
650	550	425	275	200	100

Field Hunter Maxi-Mag VR-MC Semi-Auto

This 3.5" 12-gauge comes in one of three Realtree/Advantage camos and matte black, with 24", 26" or 28" ported barrel. **NOTE:** Add 15 percent for camo.

NIB	Exc.	V.G.	Good	Fair	Poor
425	365	255	200	150	100

TURKISH SHOTGUNS

Model 105

This 3" 12-gauge over/under features an engraved nickel-plated steel receiver, double triggers and extractors. Chokes are fixed Modified and Full with 28" barrels; or Modified and Improved Cylinder with 26" barrels.

NIB	Exc.	V.G.	Good	Fair	Poor
600	450	395	300	175	100

Model 106/206

Similar to Model 105, but in 12-, 20- and 28-gauge and .410 bore. Model 106 has a blued receiver, with raised gold ducks and rounded pistol-grip. All but the .410 include three screw-in chokes. Barrels are 26" or 28" in 12- and 20-gauge and 26" in 28-gauge and .410. Frames are scaled to gauge. **NOTE:** Add $50 for 28-gauge and .410 bore; $50 for model 206 with SST, ejectors.

NIB	Exc.	V.G.	Good	Fair	Poor
650	495	395	300	175	100

Model 306

This 3" side-by-side is offered in 12- and 20-gauge, with 26" or 28" barrels. Turkish walnut stock, gold-plated single selective trigger and extractors. Three choke tubes.

NIB	Exc.	V.G.	Good	Fair	Poor
400	350	295	175	115	75

PUMP SHOTGUNS

Field Grade

This 12-gauge pump gun offered with 24", 26", 28" or 30" barrels. Fixed chokes. A slug gun offered with 18.5" barrels, with blue or nickel finish. Camo version also offered. First introduced in 1999. Model also offered in 20-gauge in both full size and youth. **NOTE:** Add $10 for nickel gun; $80 for full camo gun.

NIB	Exc.	V.G.	Good	Fair	Poor
300	225	165	125	100	65

Field Tactical

This pump gun chambered for the 12-gauge shell. Fitted with an 18.5" barrel and fixed blade front sight. An 18.5" slug barrel with adjustable sights is also offered. Black synthetic stock. Blued or nickel finish. **NOTE:** Add $30 for nickel finish.

NIB	Exc.	V.G.	Good	Fair	Poor
350	275	190	150	125	75

Field Hunter MM (Maxi-Mag)

This 12-gauge pump gun chambered for 3.5" Magnum shell. Offered with choice of 24", 26" or 28" ventilated rib ported barrels. Black synthetic stock, with camo stock also available. Weight about 6.75 lbs. **NOTE:** Add $50 for camo finish.

NIB	Exc.	V.G.	Good	Fair	Poor
275	225	150	125	100	65

Field Hunter Maxi-Mag VR-MC Pump

Newer versions of Maxi-Mag are recognized by an updated fore-end and availability in Timber or Hardwoods camo or matte black. All are 3.5" 12-gauge, with a 24", 26" or 28" ported barrel. **NOTE:** Add 15 percent for camo.

NIB	Exc.	V.G.	Good	Fair	Poor
350	300	255	200	150	100

OVER/UNDER GUNS

Country Squire Over/Under Folding

Features a folding stock ,with over/under ventilated rib barrels 25.5" in length. Gold double triggers and walnut stock. Chokes are Full and Full.

NIB	Exc.	V.G.	Good	Fair	Poor
550	450	325	250	175	125

Field II Hunter

A 12-, 20-, 28-gauge and .410 bore over/under shotgun, with 26" or 28" chrome-lined ventilated rib barrels. Crossbolt boxlock-action, single-selective trigger and extractors. Blued, with a stamped checkered walnut stock. Introduced in 1989. Weight: 12-gauge about 7 lbs.; 28-gauge and .410 bore about 6.75 lbs. **NOTE:** Add $150 for ejectors.

NIB	Exc.	V.G.	Good	Fair	Poor
900	775	575	400	250	200

Field Ultra Light

Introduced in 1999. Offered in either 12- or 20-gauge, with 26" barrel choked Improved Cylinder/Modified. Receiver is aluminum alloy. Walnut stock, with pistol-grip and slim fore-end. Weight about 5.5 lbs.

NIB	Exc.	V.G.	Good	Fair	Poor
950	850	650	450	—	—

Field III

An economy level model in 12- or 20-gauge, imported from Turkey in the 1980s.

NIB	Exc.	V.G.	Good	Fair	Poor
400	350	300	250	200	150

Empire

Similar to Field II Hunter, with automatic ejectors, screw-in choke tubes and a silver-finished receiver. Walnut stock is hand-checkered. Introduced in 1989.

NIB	Exc.	V.G.	Good	Fair	Poor
1150	1000	750	500	400	200

Empire II EDL Hunter

Offered in 12-, 20-, 28-gauge and .410 bore. Features 26" or 28" ventilated rib barrels (26" only on 28-gauge or .410). Choke tubes on 12- and 20-gauge and fixed chokes on 28-gauge and .410 guns. Receiver has game scene engraving, with nine gold inlays. Weight 6.25 to 7.25 lbs. depending on gauge.

NIB	Exc.	V.G.	Good	Fair	Poor
2000	1500	1100	700	375	200

Empire Sporting

Offered in 12-gauge, with choice of 28" or 30" barrels. Fitted with a Monte Carlo stock and automatic ejectors.

NIB	Exc.	V.G.	Good	Fair	Poor
1850	1425	1000	600	375	200

Empire Grade Combination

An over/under, with 12-gauge top barrel and rifle lower barrel. Rifle calibers are .22 Hornet, .223 Rem., .22-250, .243, .270, .308 and .30-06. Barrel length 23.5". Weight about 7.25 lbs.

NIB	Exc.	V.G.	Good	Fair	Poor
2190	1600	1150	800	375	200

Empire Trap

This 12-gauge features Monte Carlo stock with 30" barrels.

NIB	Exc.	V.G.	Good	Fair	Poor
2250	1650	1200	750	325	150

Empire Grade Trap Combo

Features 30" over/under barrel, with an additional 32" single barrel. Buttstock has fully adjustable comb. Introduced in 1999. **NOTE:** Deduct $600 for non-adjustable stock.

NIB	Exc.	V.G.	Good	Fair	Poor
4000	3000	2000	1450	675	375

Diamond GTX DL Hunter

As above in 12- and 20-gauge Magnum. Various barrel lengths and screw-in choke tubes, single trigger, automatic ejectors and select walnut stock. Extra fancy walnut stock and hand engraved frame.

NIB	Exc.	V.G.	Good	Fair	Poor
9000	8000	6000	5000	2000	1000

Diamond GTX Sporting

This 12-gauge features a choice of 28" or 30" barrels, with automatic ejectors and Monte Carlo stock.

NIB	Exc.	V.G.	Good	Fair	Poor
5900	4500	2750	1250	900	450

Diamond GTX Trap or Skeet

As above, with 26" or 30" barrels. Available in 1989. **NOTE:** Add 5 percent for wide rib.

NIB	Exc.	V.G.	Good	Fair	Poor
5900	4500	2750	1250	900	400

Diamond GTX Trap Combo

This model has a fully adjustable stock. Choice of 30" over/under barrels and 32" single barrel.

NIB	Exc.	V.G.	Good	Fair	Poor
7500	5700	4250	2650	1000	450

Presentation Grade

As above, with a Purdey-type boxlock action and engraved false sideplates. Stock of deluxe French walnut. Discontinued in 1986.

NIB	Exc.	V.G.	Good	Fair	Poor
—	5500	3750	1650	900	450

Superior II

A 12-, 20-, 28-gauge and .410 bore over/under shotgun, with 26" or 28" ventilated rib barrels. Various chokes, single trigger and automatic ejec-tors. Engraved blued, with walnut stock. Weight: 12- and 20-gauge about 7 lbs.; 28-gauge and .410 about 6.75 lbs.

NIB	Exc.	V.G.	Good	Fair	Poor
625	550	350	300	200	150

Superior II Sporting

This 12-gauge fitted with choice of 28" or 30" barrels, Monte Carlo stock and automatic ejectors.

NIB	Exc.	V.G.	Good	Fair	Poor
650	575	375	325	225	165

Superior Grade Trap

This 12-gauge fitted with 30" barrels, Monte Carlo stock and automatic ejectors.

NIB	Exc.	V.G.	Good	Fair	Poor
1700	1250	900	625	425	200

Superior Grade Combination

This is an over/under, with 12-gauge top barrel and rifle lower barrel. Rifle calibers are .22 Hornet, .223 Rem. and .30-06. Barrel length 23.5". Weight about 7.25 lbs.

NIB	Exc.	V.G.	Good	Fair	Poor
1480	1100	800	550	350	175

SINGLE-BARREL SHOTGUNS

Empire Trap Mono

Single barrel trap gun, with choice of 30" or 32" barrels. Automatic ejectors and Monte Carlo fully adjustable stock. **NOTE:** Deduct $600 for non-adjustable stock.

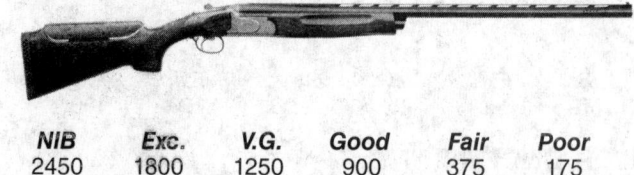

NIB	Exc.	V.G.	Good	Fair	Poor
2450	1800	1250	900	375	175

Diamond GTX Mono

Model has fully adjustable stock. Barrel choice 30". Automatic ejectors are standard.

NIB	Exc.	V.G.	Good	Fair	Poor
6500	5250	3750	1750	900	400

SIDE-BY-SIDE GUNS

Field Hunter

A side-by-side boxlock gun chambered for 10-, 12-, 20-, 28-gauge and .410 bore. Barrel length from 26" to 32" depending on gauge. Extractors are standard. Weight from 6.75 lbs. to 8.75 lbs. depending on gauge. Nickel receiver, with game scene engraving. **NOTE:** Add $40 for 28-gauge and .410 guns; $100 for automatic ejectors.

NIB	Exc.	V.G.	Good	Fair	Poor
1190	850	600	400	250	100

Superior Hunter

A 12-, 20-, 28-gauge and .410 bore boxlock double-barrel shotgun, with 26" or 28" barrels, various chokes, boxlock action and single trigger. Blued, with walnut stock. In 2002, offered in 10-gauge with 28" barrels. **NOTE:** Add $50 for 28-gauge and .410 guns.

NIB	Exc.	V.G.	Good	Fair	Poor
1660	1200	850	600	350	150

Empire Hunter

Offered in 12- and 20-gauge, with 26" or 28" barrels. Chokes are fixed. Weight about 7 lbs. Silver receiver with game scene engraving, straight stock, splinter forearm, automatic ejectors.

NIB	Exc.	V.G.	Good	Fair	Poor
2120	1500	1100	700	400	200

Diamond DL

Offered in 12-, 20-, 28-gauge and .410 bore, with 26" or 28" barrels and fixed chokes. Fancy walnut straight-grip stock, hand detachable sidelocks, 100 percent hand engraving coverage. Hand fit and finished. Weight: 12- and 20-gauge about 6.75 lbs.; 28-gauge and .410 about 5.75 lbs. Model generally made on special order only. **NOTE:** Add $450 for 28-gauge and .410 bore.

NIB	Exc.	V.G.	Good	Fair	Poor
6700	5000	3500	1500	750	350

Diamond Regent DL

High grade model of above, with best quality engraving, hand-checkered AAA-grade walnut stock, fixed chokes. Limited importation in 1997.

NIB	Exc.	V.G.	Good	Fair	Poor
18000	16000	12500	—	—	—

Country Squire Side-by-Side Folding

Features a folding stock, with 25.5" barrels, gold double triggers and walnut stock. Chokes are Full and Full.

NIB	Exc.	V.G.	Good	Fair	Poor
475	375	275	200	145	100

Model 306

In 12- or 20-gauge, with 26" or 28" barrels, choke tubes, single trigger and extractors. Imported from Turkey from 2006 to 2008.

NIB	Exc.	V.G.	Good	Fair	Poor
600	525	450	300	200	150

Classic Coach

Same features as Model 306 above, except with 20" barrels and 12-gauge only.

NIB	Exc.	V.G.	Good	Fair	Poor
650	575	500	350	200	150

RIFLES

Field Grade Mauser 98

Bolt-action rifle offered in a wide variety of calibers from .243 Win. to .458 Win. Magnum. Barrel length 23" for all calibers. Stock is black synthetic. Open sights. **NOTE:** Add $175 for .375 H&H and .458 Win. Magnum; $50 for stainless steel.

NIB	Exc.	V.G.	Good	Fair	Poor
460	350	300	225	150	100

Field Grade Mini-Mauser 98

Version chambered for short cartridges such as .22 Hornet, .223, .22-250 and 7.62x39mm. Barrel length 19.25". Magazine capacity 5 rounds.

NIB	Exc.	V.G.	Good	Fair	Poor
600	475	350	250	175	125

Superior Grade Mauser 98

Similar to Field Grade Mauser, with addition of hand-checkered walnut stock.

NIB	Exc.	V.G.	Good	Fair	Poor
600	425	325	225	165	100

Superior Grade Mini-Mauser 98

Same as Field Grade Mini-Mauser, with addition of hand-checkered walnut stock.

NIB	Exc.	V.G.	Good	Fair	Poor
600	450	325	250	150	100

Field Grade Rimfires

Chambered for .22 LR cartridge. Fitted with a 22" barrel bolt-action version; 20" barrel in semi-automatic or 17.5" barrel in bolt-action. True Youth model 16.25" barrel in bolt-action single-shot. **NOTE:** Add $25 for True Youth model.

NIB	Exc.	V.G.	Good	Fair	Poor
120	100	75	50	25	10

Superior Grade Rimfires

Chambered for .22, .22 Magnum or .22 Hornet in bolt-action or .22 LR semi-automatic. Walnut stock with checkering. Open sights. **NOTE:** Add $20 for .22 Magnum; $170 for .22 Hornet.

NIB	Exc.	V.G.	Good	Fair	Poor
175	125	100	75	50	25

Superior II Grade Rimfire

Introduced in 2005. Chambered for .22 LR, .22 WMR or .17 HMR cartridges. Fitted with a 22" barrel. Open sights on .22 LR. Drilled and tapped for scope mounts on .22 WMR and .17 HMR. Oiled walnut stocks with checkering. **NOTE:** Add $40 for .22 Magnum; $75 for .17 HMR.

NIB	Exc.	V.G.	Good	Fair	Poor
260	200	175	150	125	100

Empire Grade Rimfires

Empire Grade has select walnut stock, with 24 lpi hand-cut checkering. Grip and forearm caps highly polished and blued metal finish. Same configurations as Superior Grade rifles. **NOTE:** Add $20 for .22 Magnum; $100 for .22 Hornet.

NIB	Exc.	V.G.	Good	Fair	Poor
335	275	225	175	125	100

Superior Grade Express

Chambered for .30-06 cartridge and fitted with 23.5" barrel. Open sights, with dovetail receiver for scope mounting. Silver receiver with game scene engraving. Checkered walnut stock with sling swivels. Weight about 7.75 lbs.

NIB	Exc.	V.G.	Good	Fair	Poor
3250	2700	1800	1475	1000	500

Empire Express

Chambered for .30-06, .375 H&H or .416 Rigby cartridge, with open sights and dovetail receiver for scope mounting. Barrel length 23.5". Checkered walnut stock, with Bavarian-style cheekpiece. Silver game scene engraved receiver. Weight about 8 lbs. **NOTE:** Add $700 for .375 H&H and .416 Rigby.

NIB	Exc.	V.G.	Good	Fair	Poor
3600	3000	2300	1775	1250	600

DM-4 Series

This series of rifles and carbines were manufactured in 2008 and 2009, with forged aluminum alloy receivers, manganese phosphate or stainless barrels, forward assist and other features typically found on quality made AR-type models. All were chambered in 5.56 NATO. Many of the popular AR configurations were offered with 16" or 20" barrels, sighting and grip options, mounting rails, finishes and other regular features found in the AR family. Prices shown are for standard DM-4 Carbine. Many available options can double these values.

NIB	Exc.	V.G.	Good	Fair	Poor
950	825	700	500	—	—

HANDGUNS

Daly ZDA

Introduced in 2005. Chambered for 9mm or .40 S&W cartridge. Fitted with 4.5" ramped barrel. Ambidextrous slide release/decocker/lock as well as magazine release. Loaded chamber indicator. Magazine capacity: 15 rounds 9mm; 12 rounds .40 S&W.

NIB	Exc.	V.G.	Good	Fair	Poor
590	450	375	300	175	100

Field 1911-A1 FS/MS/CS

Chambered for .45 ACP, with choice of 5" (FS), 4" (MS) or 3.5" (CS) barrel. Various special features such as front and rear slide serrations, extended beavertail safety and lightweight trigger. Magazine capacity 8 rounds. Overall length 8.75".

NIB	Exc.	V.G.	Good	Fair	Poor
575	400	300	200	175	115

Superior 1911-A1 EFS/EMS/ECS

Same as Field Grade described above, with blued frame and stainless steel slide. Introduced in 1999.

NIB	Exc.	V.G.	Good	Fair	Poor
550	450	350	200	175	115

Empire 1911-A1 EFS

Same as Field Grade. Full stainless, with both stainless steel slide and frame. Introduced in 1999.

NIB	Exc.	V.G.	Good	Fair	Poor
630	475	350	225	195	125

Field 1911-A2P

Same as above, with 10-round magazine.

NIB	Exc.	V.G.	Good	Fair	Poor
570	450	350	225	195	125

.22 Caliber Conversion Kit

Offered with adjustable sights for models with 5" barrel only. First offered in 1999.

NIB	Exc.	V.G.	Good	Fair	Poor
200	150	100	65	45	25

Field 1911-A1 PC

Fitted with 4" barrel and slide. Polymer frame. Produced under license from STI. Introduced in 1999.

NIB	Exc.	V.G.	Good	Fair	Poor
575	400	300	200	175	115

Superior 1911-A1 PC

Same as model above, with stainless steel slide and black polymer frame. Introduced in 1999.

NIB	Exc.	V.G.	Good	Fair	Poor
595	425	325	225	195	125

Field 1911 Target EFST

Fitted with 5" barrel. Chambered for .45 ACP cartridge. Eight-round magazine. Blued finish. Fully adjustable rear sight, with dovetail front sight. Weight about 40 oz.

NIB	Exc.	V.G.	Good	Fair	Poor
620	475	350	240	195	125

Empire 1911 Target EFST

As above, with stainless steel finish.

NIB	Exc.	V.G.	Good	Fair	Poor
790	600	475	350	240	125

Empire Custom Match Target

Same as Empire Target, with hand polished stainless steel finish and 20 lpi checkered front strap.

NIB	Exc.	V.G.	Good	Fair	Poor
800	600	500	375	255	135

Daly HP

Introduced in 2003. This U.S.-made 9mm pistol is similar to the famous Browning Hi-Power. Fitted with 5" barrel. XS sighting system. Weight about 35 oz.

NIB	Exc.	V.G.	Good	Fair	Poor
550	400	350	225	195	125

Daly M-5 Government

Polymer frame pistol chambered for 9mm, .40 S&W or .45 ACP cartridge. Fitted with 5" barrel, high rise beavertail and ambidextrous safety.

Low profile sights. Weight about 34 oz. Made in Israel by BUL. Introduced in 2003.

NIB	Exc.	V.G.	Good	Fair	Poor
720	575	400	275	225	100

Daly M-5 Commander

Same as above. Fitted with 4.375" barrel. Weight about 30 oz.

NIB	Exc.	V.G.	Good	Fair	Poor
720	575	400	275	225	100

Daly M-5 Ultra-X

An ultra compact model.

NIB	Exc.	V.G.	Good	Fair	Poor
720	575	400	275	225	100

Daly M-5 IPSC

Has a 5" barrel. Fitted with a stainless steel slide and adjustable sights. Flared and lowered ejection port. Extended magazine release. Weight about 34 oz.

NIB	Exc.	V.G.	Good	Fair	Poor
1500	1150	725	600	325	125

Daly Classic 1873 Single-Action Revolver

Chambered for .45 Colt or .357 Magnum. Revolver offered with 4.75", 5.5" or 7.5" barrel. Choice of walnut or simulated ivory grips. Stainless steel, blue or case colored finish. Introduced in 2005. Imported from Italy. **NOTE:** Add $30 for steel backstrap and trigger guard; $200 for stainless steel.

NIB	Exc.	V.G.	Good	Fair	Poor
450	350	285	250	195	150

SHOTGUNS - 2013 AND CURRENT

Model 600

In 2013, Samco Global Arms of Miami, FL. purchased the Charles Daly trademark from the previous importer K.B.I. of Harrisburg, PA. and began importing a series of shotguns. Among these are the Model 600 semi-automatic, offered in several variations including field and sporting clays, with synthetic, camo or wood stocks, in 12-, 20- and 28-gauges. These are gas-operated guns, with standard barrel lengths with choke tubes that are cmpatible with Remington's REM-choke series. Values shown are for field model. **NOTE:** Add $50 for camo; $100 for sporting.

NIB	Exc.	V.G.	Good	Fair	Poor
525	450	400	350	300	250

Model 300

Pump-action series, with features similar to Model 600.

NIB	Exc.	V.G.	Good	Fair	Poor
400	375	300	250	200	150

Model 206

An over/under series including field, sporting and trap models, all in 12-gauge only. Features include 28", 30" and 32" barrels, automatic ejectors, single selective trigger, choke tubes, ventilated rib, checkered oil-finished walnut stock and fore-end. Made in Turkey by Akkar Silah Sanayi.

206 Field Grade

NIB	Exc.	V.G.	Good	Fair	Poor
900	800	650	550	475	400

206S Sporting Model

NIB	Exc.	V.G.	Good	Fair	Poor
1100	1000	800	650	550	450

206T Trap Model

NIB	Exc.	V.G.	Good	Fair	Poor
1200	1050	900	750	650	500

DAN ARMS OF AMERICA
Allentown, Pennsylvania

These are Italian-made shotguns. Manufactured by Silmer and imported by Dan Arms of America. Production ceased in 1988.

SIDE-BY-SIDES

Field Grade

Boxlock shotgun chambered for all gauges, with 26" or 28" barrels. Various choke combinations, double triggers and extractors. Blued, with walnut stock.

NIB	Exc.	V.G.	Good	Fair	Poor
—	325	265	225	150	125

Deluxe Field Grade

As above, with single trigger and automatic ejectors.

NIB	Exc.	V.G.	Good	Fair	Poor
—	465	400	325	250	200

OVER/UNDERS

Lux Grade I

12- and 20-gauge over/under shotgun, with 26", 28" or 30" ventilated rib barrels, double triggers and extractors. Blued finish, with walnut stock.

NIB	Exc.	V.G.	Good	Fair	Poor
—	325	265	200	150	100

Lux Grade II

As above in 12-gauge only, with single trigger.

NIB	Exc.	V.G.	Good	Fair	Poor
—	350	300	250	200	150

Lux Grade III

As above in 20-gauge only, with automatic ejectors.

NIB	Exc.	V.G.	Good	Fair	Poor
—	400	325	275	225	175

Lux Grade IV

As above in 12-gauge only, with screw-in choke tubes.

NIB	Exc.	V.G.	Good	Fair	Poor
—	450	375	325	275	200

Silver Snipe

Shotgun in 12- or 20-gauge. Manufactured to custom order, with engraved false sideplates and select walnut stock.

NIB	Exc.	V.G.	Good	Fair	Poor
—	1250	1000	800	600	350

DANCE & BROTHERS CONFEDERATE REVOLVERS
Columbia, Texas

J.H., G.P. and D.E. Dance began production of percussion revolvers for the Confederate States of America in Columbia, Texas, in mid-1862, moving to Anderson, Texas in early 1864. Based on surviving serial numbers, combined output at both places did not exceed 350 pistols. Most of these were in the "Army" (.44-caliber) size but a limited number of "Navy" (.36-caliber) were also manufactured. Nearly all are distinguished by the absence of a "recoil shield" on the frame behind the cylinders. As Colt M1851 "Navy" revolvers closely resemble the Dance Navy revolvers, great care must be exercised in examining revolvers purported to be Dance Navies.

.36 Caliber

Courtesy Milwaukee Public Museum, Milwaukee, Wisconsin

NIB	Exc.	V.G.	Good	Fair	Poor
—	—	85000	67500	20000	7000

.44 Caliber

NIB	Exc.	V.G.	Good	Fair	Poor
—	—	90000	68000	20000	5500

DANIEL DEFENSE
Savannah, Georgia

DDM4

This series of AR-type carbines comes in six variations. Different receiver and stock configurations, and rail/sight systems. All have 16" barrels and available in 5.56 NATO, with some offered in 6.8 SPC or .300 Blackout calibers.

NIB	Exc.	V.G.	Good	Fair	Poor
1450	1250	1000	800	500	300

MK 12

New in 2014, this model is in 5.56 NATO caliber, with 20-round Magpul magazine, 18" barrel, glass-filled polymer stock, with Soft Touch over-molding and pistol-grip.

NIB	Exc.	V.G.	Good	Fair	Poor
1875	1600	1300	500	400	250

DANSK REKYLRIFFEL SYNDIKAT
Copenhagen, Denmark

This firm was founded in 1896. In 1936 it became known as Madsen, makers of the famous Madsen light machine gun. Schouboe pistols were designed by Jens Schouboe, chief engineer for Dansk. They were developed in 1900-1902. First year of manufacture was in 1902.

Schouboe Model 1902

A 7.65mm caliber semi-automatic pistol, with conventional blowback design. Production began in 1903 and ended in 1908, with fewer than 1,000 manufactured.

Courtesy James Rankin

NIB	Exc.	V.G.	Good	Fair	Poor
—	15500	12000	8200	5000	3000

Schouboe Model 1904

A semi-automatic pistol in caliber 11.35mm. Model 1904 was an enlarged Model 1902. Name Dansk Rekylriffel is stamped on the slide.

Courtesy James Rankin

NIB	Exc.	V.G.	Good	Fair	Poor
—	24500	20500	16500	11000	5000

NIB	Exc.	V.G.	Good	Fair	Poor
—	24500	21500	16500	11000	5000

Schouboe Model 1907

An 11.35mm caliber semi-automatic pistol. Designed to fire a 55-grain, copper-aluminum-and-wood projectile at a velocity of 1625 fps. Pistol has the name Dansk Rekylriffel and Schouboe stamped on slide. Some of these pistols had grip frames slotted for stocks. Five hundred were manufactured before production stopped in 1917. **NOTE:** Combination holster/shoulder stocks were made for this model, but are extremely rare. If present with a pistol, they would add approximately $5,000 to the value.

Courtesy James Rankin

NIB	Exc.	V.G.	Good	Fair	Poor
—	24000	20000	16000	10500	5000

Schouboe Model 1907 9mm

As above, but chambered for 9mm cartridge. Very few of these pistols were built.

Courtesy James Rankin

NIB	Exc.	V.G.	Good	Fair	Poor
—	14000	11000	8250	5500	3000

Schouboe Model 1910/12

Chambered for 11.35mm cartridge. Involved in U.S. military tests in 1912.

Courtesy James Rankin

Schouboe Model 1916

Also chambered for 11.35mm cartridge. Fitted with a very large slide release and safety lever on left side of pistol. Name of manufacturer stamped on slide.

Courtesy James Rankin

NIB	Exc.	V.G.	Good	Fair	Poor
—	24000	21050	16500	11000	5000

DARDICK CORP.
Hamden, Connecticut

Perhaps one of the most unusual firearms to have been designed and marketed in the United States during the 20th century. It utilizes a "tround" which is a triangular plastic case enclosing a cartridge. Action of these arms consists of a revolving carrier that brings the trounds from the magazine into line with the barrel. Discontinued in 1962. Values below are for boxed examples, with a supply of tround ammunition. Deduct 50 to 75 percent for un-boxed loose examples, without ammunition.

Series 110

3" barrel. Chambered in .38 Dardick only.

NIB	Exc.	V.G.	Good	Fair	Poor
—	2500	1650	1500	1100	500

Series 1500

6" barrel. Chambered for .22, .30 and .38 Dardick. **NOTE:** Carbine conversion kit consisting of a long barrel and shoulder stock was available and would bring a premium of $750 to $1400 depending on the condition.

NIB	Exc.	V.G.	Good	Fair	Poor
—	5000	3000	1750	1500	900

DARLING, B. & B. M.
Belingham, Massachusetts

Pepperbox Pistol

A .30-caliber percussion 6-shot pepperbox, with 3.25" length barrels. Blued, with walnut grips. One of the rarest American pepperboxes and copies are known to have been made. Consequently, prospective purchasers are advised to secure a qualified appraisal prior to acquisition. Manufactured during the late 1830s.

NIB	Exc.	V.G.	Good	Fair	Poor
—	—	4950	1950	600	600

DARNE, S. A.
St. Etienne, France

SIDE-BY-SIDE SHOTGUNS

A 12-, 16-, 20- or 28-gauge sliding breech double-barrel shotgun. Manufactured in a variety of barrel lengths and numerous optional features. Manufactured from 1881 to 1979. **NOTE:** Darnes have been undergoing a surge in popularity the last few years, because of their unique design. Depending on circumstances and amount of factory engraving and ornamentation present, individual examples may bring considerably in excess of values listed below. Deduct 25 percent for 2.5" chambers.

Model R11

NIB	Exc.	V.G.	Good	Fair	Poor
—	2500	2000	1200	800	550

Model R13

NIB	Exc.	V.G.	Good	Fair	Poor
—	3000	2600	2250	1100	750

Model R15

NIB	Exc.	V.G.	Good	Fair	Poor
—	4000	3000	2450	1500	750

Model V19

NIB	Exc.	V.G.	Good	Fair	Poor
—	4500	3600	2950	2050	1250

Model V22

NIB	Exc.	V.G.	Good	Fair	Poor
—	5000	4100	3500	2500	1700

Model V Hors Series No. I

NIB	Exc.	V.G.	Good	Fair	Poor
—	7500	5500	4050	3250	1500

DAVENPORT FIREARMS CO.
Providence, Rhode Island
Norwich, Connecticut

Double-Barrel Shotguns

Text and prices by Nick Niles. William Hastings Davenport's company, also made and marked double-barrel, visible hammer guns in Providence, R.I. on Orange St., 1880-1882 and in Norwich, Conn. ca. 1890-1909. All are monbloc designs of which there were four models. 1st model, made at Providence, ca. 1881, had hammers rising out of the boxlock frame. 2nd model, made in Norwich, Conn. about 1898, is a typical boxlock. 3rd model, made in Norwich, Conn., ca. 1909, has small sidelocks set in larger boxlock frames. Its barrels have un-notched extensions and notched underlugs. 4th model, also from Norwich, possibly made after the 1901 takeover by Hopkins & Allen, also has sidelocks set in boxlock frames, but the barrels have half moon lugs and notched barrel extensions. Few Davenport doubles are seen, although single barrel guns are often found.

1st Model

NIB	Exc.	V.G.	Good	Fair	Poor
—	1200	875	500	400	300

2nd Model

NIB	Exc.	V.G.	Good	Fair	Poor
—	700	450	300	200	150

3rd Model

NIB	Exc.	V.G.	Good	Fair	Poor
—	1200	875	500	400	300

4th Model

NIB	Exc.	V.G.	Good	Fair	Poor
—	900	450	300	250	200

Single-Barrel Shotgun

A 10-, 12-, 16- or 20-gauge side-hammer single-barrel shotgun, with 26" to 36" barrels and extractors. Blued, case-hardened, with walnut stock. Manufactured from approximately 1880 to 1915.

NIB	Exc.	V.G.	Good	Fair	Poor
—	—	450	300	150	75

8 Gauge Goose Gun

As above in 8-gauge.

NIB	Exc.	V.G.	Good	Fair	Poor
—	—	550	250	175	100

Falling Block Single-Shot Rifle

A .22, .25 or .32 rimfire single-shot rifle, with 24" round barrel and exposed hammer. Blued, with walnut stock. Barrel marked "The W.H. Davenport Fire Arms Co. Norwich, Conn. U.S.A. Patented Dec. 15, 1891". Manufactured between 1891 and 1910.

NIB	Exc.	V.G.	Good	Fair	Poor
—	—	675	425	325	200

DAVIDSON, F.A.
Eibar, Spain

Arms bearing this name were manufactured in Spain by Fabrica De Armas.

Model 63B

A 12-, 16-, 20-, 28-gauge or .410 bore double-barrel boxlock shotgun, with 25" to 30" barrels. Engraved, nickel-plated with a walnut stock. Made from 1963 to 1976.

NIB	Exc.	V.G.	Good	Fair	Poor
—	350	225	200	150	100

Model 69 SL

A 12- or 20-gauge sidelock double-barrel shotgun, with 26" or 28" barrels and finished as above.

NIB	Exc.	V.G.	Good	Fair	Poor
—	425	350	300	225	125

Stagecoach Model 73

A 12- or 20-gauge Magnum sidelock double-barrel shotgun, with 20" barrels and exposed hammers.

NIB	Exc.	V.G.	Good	Fair	Poor
—	300	250	175	150	100

DAVIS, A. JR.
Stafford, Connecticut

Under Hammer Pistol

A .31-caliber single-shot under hammer percussion pistol, with 7.5" half octagonal barrel and brass frame. Grips are maple and formed with a bottom tip. Top strap marked "A. Davis Jr./Stafford Conn.".

NIB	Exc.	V.G.	Good	Fair	Poor
—	—	1250	775	350	100

DAVIS, N.R. & CO./
DAVIS, N.R. & SONS
(See also Davis-Warner Arms Corporation)

Manufacturer of percussion and later cartridge shotguns, from 1853 to 1919. Cartridge shotguns embodied Nathan R. Davis' patented improvements of 1879, 1884 and 1886. Though only made in plain serviceable grades, Davis shotguns were extremely well made and lived up to the company's motto "As Good as the Best".

Grade A and B Hammerless Shotguns

Made in 12- or 16-gauge, with 28", 30" or 32" barrels.

NIB	Exc.	V.G.	Good	Fair	Poor
—	900	675	400	200	100

Grade C Hammerless Shotgun

Made in 10-gauge, with 30" or 32" barrels.

NIB	Exc.	V.G.	Good	Fair	Poor
—	900	675	400	200	100

Grade D and DS Hammer Shotguns

Made in 12- or 16-gauge, with 28", 30" or 32" barrels.

NIB	Exc.	V.G.	Good	Fair	Poor
—	875	675	425	200	100

Grade E and F Single-Barrel Shotguns

Made in 12- or 16-gauge, with 30" or 32" barrels.

NIB	Exc.	V.G.	Good	Fair	Poor
—	350	250	125	75	50

N.R. DAVIS BRANDS

1st Button Opener—Hammer Boxlock

NIB	Exc.	V.G.	Good	Fair	Poor
—	475	325	250	150	100

1st Sidelever—Hammer Boxlock

NIB	Exc.	V.G.	Good	Fair	Poor
—	475	325	250	150	100

2nd Sidelever—Hammer Boxlock

Courtesy Nick Niles, Paul Goodwin photo

NIB	Exc.	V.G.	Good	Fair	Poor
—	475	325	250	150	100

1st Toplever—Hammer Boxlock

Courtesy Nick Niles, Paul Goodwin photo

NIB	Exc.	V.G.	Good	Fair	Poor
—	475	325	250	150	100

2nd Toplever—Hammer Boxlock

NIB	Exc.	V.G.	Good	Fair	Poor
—	475	325	250	150	100

3rd Toplever—Hammer Boxlock

NIB	Exc.	V.G.	Good	Fair	Poor
—	475	325	250	150	100

1879 1st Model—Hammer Boxlock

NIB	Exc.	V.G.	Good	Fair	Poor
—	475	325	250	150	100

1879 2nd Model—Damascus Barrel—Hammer Boxlock

NIB	Exc.	V.G.	Good	Fair	Poor
—	475	325	250	150	100

1885—Hammerless Boxlock

NIB	Exc.	V.G.	Good	Fair	Poor
—	475	325	250	150	100

1886 Rival—Hammerless Boxlock

NIB	Exc.	V.G.	Good	Fair	Poor
—	350	275	200	150	100

1886 Rival Improved—Hammerless Boxlock

NIB	Exc.	V.G.	Good	Fair	Poor
—	350	275	200	150	100

1897 "G" —Hammer Sidelock

NIB	Exc.	V.G.	Good	Fair	Poor
—	350	275	200	150	100

N.R. DAVIS & SONS BRAND

Hammerless 1900—Boxlock

NIB	Exc.	V.G.	Good	Fair	Poor
—	350	275	200	150	100

Hammerless A—Damascus Barrel—Boxlock

NIB	Exc.	V.G.	Good	Fair	Poor
—	350	275	200	150	100

Hammerless B—Boxlock

NIB	Exc.	V.G.	Good	Fair	Poor
—	350	275	200	150	100

Hammerless C—Engraved Damascus Barrel—Boxlock

NIB	Exc.	V.G.	Good	Fair	Poor
—	400	325	250	150	100

Hammerless D—Engraved—Boxlock

NIB	Exc.	V.G.	Good	Fair	Poor
—	475	375	300	250	200

New Model—Hammerless Boxlock

NIB	Exc.	V.G.	Good	Fair	Poor
—	350	275	200	150	100

"D.S." Straight Stock—Engraved—Hammerless Boxlock

NIB	Exc.	V.G.	Good	Fair	Poor
—	350	275	200	150	100

Davis Special—Hammerless Boxlock

NIB	Exc.	V.G.	Good	Fair	Poor
—	925	650	500	400	250

Davis "B" Manga Steel—Hammerless Boxlock

NIB	Exc.	V.G.	Good	Fair	Poor
—	925	650	500	400	250

CRESCENT-DAVIS BRANDS

Model No. 600—Hammerless Boxlock

NIB	Exc.	V.G.	Good	Fair	Poor
—	700	550	300	200	100

Model No. 900—Hammerless Boxlock

NIB	Exc.	V.G.	Good	Fair	Poor
—	700	550	300	200	100

DAVIS-WARNER ARMS CORPORATION
Norwich, Connecticut

Established in 1917, when N.R. Davis & Sons purchased the Warner Arms Company. Manufactured shotguns, as well as revolvers and semi-automatic pistols. Ceased operations in 1930. Crescent Arms Company purchased the proprietary rights to the name and briefly assembled shotguns under the name (probably from parts acquired in the purchase), until Crescent was in turn purchased by J.C. Stevens. Initially, Davis-Warner shotguns were identical to those made by Davis, but they subsequently made a Davis Grade B.S. Hammerless, Davis-Warner Expert and Davis Grade D.S. Pistols made by the company included .32-caliber revolvers and two Browning Patent semi-automatics made in Belgium for the company.

Davis Grade B.S. Hammerless Shotgun

Made in 12-, 16- or 20-gauge, with 28", 30" or 32" barrels.

Courtesy William Hammond

NIB	Exc.	V.G.	Good	Fair	Poor
—	875	650	400	200	100

Davis-Warner Expert Hammerless

Made in 12-, 16- or 20-gauge, with 26", 28", 30" or 32" barrels.

Courtesy Nick Niles, Paul Goodwin photo

NIB	Exc.	V.G.	Good	Fair	Poor
—	875	650	400	200	100

"BS"—Hammerless Boxlock

NIB	Exc.	V.G.	Good	Fair	Poor
—	350	275	200	150	100

"Maximin"—Hammerless Boxlock

Courtesy Nick Niles, Paul Goodwin photo

NIB	Exc.	V.G.	Good	Fair	Poor
—	475	325	250	200	150

"DS"—Hammerless Boxlock

NIB	Exc.	V.G.	Good	Fair	Poor
—	350	275	200	150	100

Deluxe—Hammerless Boxlock

NIB	Exc.	V.G.	Good	Fair	Poor
—	350	275	200	150	100

Premier—Hammerless Boxlock

NIB	Exc.	V.G.	Good	Fair	Poor
—	350	275	200	150	100

Peerless Ejector—Hammerless Boxlock

Courtesy Nick Niles, Paul Goodwin photo

NIB	Exc.	V.G.	Good	Fair	Poor
—	475	325	250	200	150

Hypower—Hammerless Boxlock

NIB	Exc.	V.G.	Good	Fair	Poor
—	475	325	250	200	150

Ajax (Model 800)

Courtesy Nick Niles, Paul Goodwin photo

NIB	Exc.	V.G.	Good	Fair	Poor
—	475	325	250	150	100

Ajax—Hammerless Boxlock

Courtesy Nick Niles, Paul Goodwin photo

NIB	Exc.	V.G.	Good	Fair	Poor
—	350	275	200	150	100

Certified (Savage)

Courtesy Nick Niles, Paul Goodwin photo

NIB	Exc.	V.G.	Good	Fair	Poor
—	475	325	250	150	100

Deluxe Special (Model 805)

Automatic ejectors.

NIB	Exc.	V.G.	Good	Fair	Poor
—	575	450	300	200	150

Premier Special (Model 802)

NIB	Exc.	V.G.	Good	Fair	Poor
—	575	450	300	200	150

Premier (Model 801)

NIB	Exc.	V.G.	Good	Fair	Poor
—	475	325	250	150	100

Warner Infallible Semi-Automatic Pistol

Fyrberg Patent .32 ACP. Not a particularly robust design.

NIB	Exc.	V.G.	Good	Fair	Poor
—	350	275	175	125	75

Davis-Warner Swing-Out Revolver

Double-action .32-caliber revolver, with 5" or 6" barrel.

NIB	Exc.	V.G.	Good	Fair	Poor
—	200	150	120	75	50

Davis-Warner Semi-Automatic Pistols

Browning Patent .25 ACP, .32 ACP or .380-caliber pistols.

NIB	Exc.	V.G.	Good	Fair	Poor
—	350	275	175	125	75

DAVIS & BOZEMAN
Central, Alabama

Pattern 1841 Rifle

A .58-caliber single-shot percussion rifle, with 33" round barrel, full walnut stock, two barrel bands, brass furniture and an iron ramrod. Lock marked "D. & B. Ala." as well as serial number and date of manufacture.

NIB	Exc.	V.G.	Good	Fair	Poor
—	—	40000	16500	3500	1750

DAVIS INDUSTRIES
Mira Loma, California

This company was founded in 1987 by Jim Davis in Chino, California. Company ceased operations in 2001. Remaining stocks and production machinery purchased by Cobra Enterprises, 1960 S. Milestone Drive, Suite F, Salt Lake City, UT 84104.

D-Series Deringer

A .22 LR, .22 WMR, .25 ACP and .32 ACP caliber double-barrel over/under derringer, with 2.4" barrels. Black Teflon or chrome-plated finish, with laminated wood grips. Weight about 9.5 oz.

NIB	Exc.	V.G.	Good	Fair	Poor
150	75	40	30	25	20

Big Bore D-Series

Similar to above, but chambered for .38 Special and .32 H&R Magnum. Barrel length 2.75". Weight about 11.5 oz.

NIB	Exc.	V.G.	Good	Fair	Poor
150	75	40	30	25	20

Long Bore D-Series

Introduced in 1994. This two-shot pistol chambered for .22 LR , .22 WMR, .32 ACP, .32 H&R Magnum, .380 ACP, 9mm and .38 Special cartridges. Barrel length 3.75"; overall length 5.65"; weight about 13 oz.

NIB	Exc.	V.G.	Good	Fair	Poor
150	75	40	30	25	20

P-32

A .32-caliber semi-automatic pistol, with 2.8" barrel and 6-shot magazine. Black Teflon or chrome-plated finish, with laminated wood grips. Overall length 5.4". Weight about 22 oz.

NIB	Exc.	V.G.	Good	Fair	Poor
150	75	40	30	25	20

P-380

As above, in .380-caliber.

NIB	Exc.	V.G.	Good	Fair	Poor
175	85	65	50	40	30

DAW, G. H.
London, England
Daw Revolver

A .38-caliber double-action percussion revolver, with 5.5" barrel marked "George H. Daw, 57 Threadneedle St. London, Patent No. 112". Blued, with walnut grips. Manufactured in the 1860s.

NIB	Exc.	V.G.	Good	Fair	Poor
—	—	5750	3500	1975	1000

DEANE-HARDING
London, England
Revolver

A .44-caliber percussion revolver, with 5.25" barrel and 5-shot cylinder. Blued case-hardened, with walnut grips. Manufactured during late 1850s.

Courtesy Bonhams & Butterfields, San Francisco, California

NIB	Exc.	V.G.	Good	Fair	Poor
—	—	8500	2750	1475	850

DECKER, WILHELM
Zella St. Blasii, Germany

A 6.35mm double-action revolver, with 6-shot cylinder and concealed hammer. Unusual bar-type trigger design. Blued, with plastic grips. Manufactured prior to 1914. Very few of these revolvers were produced.

Revolver

NIB	Exc.	V.G.	Good	Fair	Poor
—	2100	1500	750	325	100

DEMIRETT, J.
Montpelier, Vermont
Under-Hammer Pistol

A .27-caliber single-shot percussion pistol, with 3" to 8" barrels and an under hammer. Barrel marked "J. Demerrit / Montpelier / Vermont". Blued, with maple, walnut or stag horn grips. Active from 1866 to mid-1880s.

NIB	Exc.	V.G.	Good	Fair	Poor
—	—	2700	825	350	200

DEMRO
Manchester, Connecticut
XF-7 Wasp Carbine

A 9mm or .45-caliber semi-automatic carbine, with 16.5" barrel and folding stock. Fires from open bolt.

NIB	Exc.	V.G.	Good	Fair	Poor
—	750	600	450	300	150

T.A.C. Model 1

As above, with fixed stock.

NIB	Exc.	V.G.	Good	Fair	Poor
—	750	600	450	300	150

DERINGER REVOLVER AND PISTOL CO.
Philadelphia, Pennsylvania

After Henry Deringer's death, his name was used by I.J. Clark, who manufactured rimfire revolvers on Charles Foehl's patents between 1870 and 1879.

Deringer Model I

A .22-caliber spur trigger revolver, with hinged octagonal barrel and 7-shot cylinder. Manufactured circa 1873.

NIB	Exc.	V.G.	Good	Fair	Poor
—	—	—	650	275	150

Deringer Model II

As above, with round barrel and also available in .32-caliber.

NIB	Exc.	V.G.	Good	Fair	Poor
—	—	—	425	200	100

Centennial 1876

A .22-, .32- or .38-caliber solid frame revolver.

NIB	Exc.	V.G.	Good	Fair	Poor
—	—	—	900	450	200

DERINGER RIFLES AND PISTOLS, HENRY
Philadelphia, Pennsylvania

Henry Deringer Sr. and his son, Henry Jr., were well established in Philadelphia by the close of the War of 1812, having made both sporting and military rifles at that place since the turn of the century. Henry Jr. continued in the gun trade until the outbreak of the American Civil War, primarily producing flintlock and percussion military rifles. At least 2,500 "Northwest guns" and 1,200 rifles for the Indian trade, a few percussion martial pistols, but most importantly the percussion pocket pistols that became so popular they took on his misspelled name as a generic term, the "derringers".

Deringer U.S. M1814 Military Rifle

Overall length 48.5"; barrel length 32.75"; caliber .54. Markings: on lockplate, "US/H. DERINGER/PHILADA"; on top flat of barrel, "H. DERINGER/PHILADA" and standard U.S. proofmarks. U.S. M1814 rifle is distinguished by its part octagonal barrel, whose bands were secured by wedge-shaped spring bands and distinctive finger ridges on triggerguard strap. Henry Deringer Sr. received a contract for 2,000 of these rifles in 1814, but delivered only 50 that year, devoting his resources instead to a more lucrative Pennsylvania state contract for rifles.

NIB	Exc.	V.G.	Good	Fair	Poor
—	—	9000	2950	1500	850

Deringer U.S. M1817 Military Rifle (Types I & II)

Overall length 51.25"; barrel length 36"; caliber .54. Markings: on lockplate, "US/H. DERINGER/PHILADA" forward of cock, date on tail; standard U.S. proofmarks on barrel. U.S. M1817 "common" rifle followed much the same design elements as its predecessor, U.S. M1814 rifle; however, barrel is fully round, with its bands secured by full band springs and on earlier production, finger ridges on triggerguard strap were eliminated in favor of a plain strap formed into a handgrip. On the 6,000 rifles manufactured under his 1840 contract, Deringer eliminated the "pistol-grip" in favor of a plain strap, distinguishing Type II production from Type I. As one of four major contractors for the U.S. M1817 rifle, Deringer produced a total of 111,000 rifles for the U.S. War Department. Many of the rifles from the first two contracts (2,000 in 1821, 3,000 in 1823) were distributed to Southern states under the 1808 Militia Act. Accordingly, Deringer M1817 rifles altered to percussion by traditional Southern methods may generate a premium.

In Flintlock

NIB	Exc.	V.G.	Good	Fair	Poor
—	—	8000	3500	1750	800

Altered to Percussion

NIB	Exc.	V.G.	Good	Fair	Poor
—	—	4000	1250	600	400

Deringer Original Percussion Martial Rifles (Types I & II)

Overall length 51.25"; barrel length 36"; caliber .54. Markings: Type I-on lockplate forward of hammer "DERINGER/PHILA"; also known to exist with standard U.S. M1817 lock markings and barrel marks; Type II-on lockplate forward of hammer "US/DERINGER/PHILADELA" or "DERINGER/PHILADELA" and same on top of barrel. Although Type I rifle of this series appears at first glance to be a late contract rifle altered to percussion by means of the cone-in-barrel method, in fact, it is an original percussion rifle made by Deringer from modified spare parts that remained after the completion of his 1840 contract. Type II rifle also evidences having been made from modified parts; however, its cone is set in an elongated bolster brazed to the right side of barrel. Speculation concerning these rifles is rampant; however, available evidence indicates that Deringer produced about 600 of these, most likely produced at the beginning of American Civil War.

Courtesy Milwaukee Public Museum, Milwaukee, Wisconsin

NIB	Exc.	V.G.	Good	Fair	Poor
—	—	4750	1550	800	450

Deringer Original Percussion Rifle-Muskets

Overall length 57.75"; barrel length 42"; caliber .69. Markings: on lock forward of hammer, "US/DERINGER/PHILADELA". Just as original percussion rifle appears to be an altered arm, the rare Deringer rifle muskets at first appear to have been flintlocks. However, these arms are original percussion, having been made from spare or rejected parts from the U.S. M1816 muskets. Brazed bolsters are identical in style to that of Type II original percussion rifles made by Deringer. Barrels are rifled with seven grooves and barrels accordingly bear a rear sight. Deringer probably assembled a hundred of these rifles in 1861 to arm some company of Pennsylvania's early war regiments.

Courtesy Milwaukee Public Museum, Milwaukee, Wisconsin

NIB	Exc.	V.G.	Good	Fair	Poor
—	—	4000	1300	725	450

Deringer U.S. Navy Contract "Boxlock" Pistols

Overall length 11.625"; barrel length 6"; caliber .54. Markings: on lockplate, "US/DERINGER/ PHILADELIA" or merely "DERINGER/PHILADEL\" in the center; tail either plain or marked "U.S.N./(date)"; barrels sometimes marked with U.S. Navy inspection marks. Deringer was granted a contract with the U.S. Navy in 1845 for 1,200 of the new "boxlock" percussion pistols also made by Ames. All of these appear to have been delivered. From the extra parts, Deringer is thought to have assembled several hundred extra pistols, some of which he rifled. The latter bring a premium, even though quantities remain enigmatic.

NIB	Exc.	V.G.	Good	Fair	Poor
—	—	4050	1550	1225	750

Deringer Percussion Pocket Pistols

The most famous of Henry Deringer's products, an estimated 15,000 were produced between the Mexican War through the Civil War, usually in pairs. Popularity of the pistol is attested in large number of imitations and nickname "Derringer" applied to them, even when clearly not Deringer's products. Prices can fluctuate widely based on agent marks occasionally found on barrel. Care is advised in purchasing purported "true" derringers. Beware of fakes!

Courtesy Milwaukee Public Museum, Milwaukee, Wisconsin

NIB	Exc.	V.G.	Good	Fair	Poor
—	—	7000	2250	1600	800

Principal Makers of Deringer-Style Pocket Pistols

William AFFLERBACH, Philadelphia, PA
Balthaser AUER, Louisville, KY
Frederick BEERSTECHER, Philadelphia and Lewisburg, PA
Franz J. BITTERLICH, Nashville, TN
BLUNT & SYMS, New York, NY
Richard P. BRUFF, New York, NY
Jesse S. BUTTERFIELD, Philadelphia, PA
Daniel CLARK, Philadelphia, PA
Richard CONSTABLE, Philadelphia, PA
DELONG & SON, Chattanooga, TN
MOSES DICKSON, Louisville, KY
Horace E. DIMICK, St. Louis, MO
Gustau ERICHSON, Houston, TX
B.J. EUSTACE & Company, St. Louis, MO
James E. EVANS, Philadelphia, PA
W.S. EVANS, Philadelphia, PA
FIELD, LANGSTROTH & Company, Philadelphia, PA
Daniel FISH, New York, NY
FOLSOM BROTHERS & Company, New Orleans, LA
August G. GENEZ, New York, NY
George D. H. GILLESPIE, New York, NY
Frederick G. GLASSICK, Memphis, TN
James GOLCHER, Philadelphia, PA
Joseph GRUBB & Company, Philadelphia, PA
John H. HAPPOLDT, Charlestown, SC
John M. HAPPOLDT, Columbus, GA & Charlestown, SC
HAWS & WAGGONER, Columbia, SC
HODGKINS & SONS, Macon, GA
Louis HOFFMAN, Vicksburg, MS
HYDE & GOODRICH, New Orleans, LA
Joseph JACOB, Philadelphia, PA
William W. KAYE, Philadelphia, PA
Benjamin KITTERIDGE, Cincinnati, OH
Peter W. KRAFT, Columbia, SC
John KRIDER, Philadelphia, PA
Jacob KUNTZ, Philadelphia, PA
Martille La FITTE, Natchitoches, LA
A. Frederich LINS, Philadelphia, PA
C. LOHNER, Philadelphia, PA
John P. LOWER, Denver, CO
A.R. MENDENHALL, Des Arc, AK
John MEUNIER, Milwaukee, WI
William D. MILLER, New York, NY
MURPHY & O'CONNELL, New York, NY
— — NEWCOMB, Natchez, MS
Charles A. OBERTEUFFER, Philadelphia, PA
Stephen O'DELL, Natchez, MS
Henry C. PALMER, St. Louis, MO
R. PATRICK, New York, NY
REID & TRACY, New York, NY
William ROBERTSON, Philadelphia, PA
ROBINSON & KRIDER, Philadelphia, PA
Ernst SCHMIDT & Company, Houston, TX
SCHNEIDER & GLASSICK, Memphis, TN
W.A. SEAVER, New York, NY
Paul J. SIMPSON, New York, NY

SLOTTER & Company, Philadelphia, PA
Patrick SMITH, Buffalo, NY
SPRANG & WALLACE, Philadelphia, PA
Adam W. SPIES, New York, NY
Casper SUTER, Selma, AL
Jacob F. TRUMPLER, Little Rock, AK
Edward TRYON, Jr., Philadelphia, PA
George K. TRYON, Philadelphia, PA
TUFTS & COLLEY, New York, NY
WOLF, DASH & FISHER, New York, NY
Alfred WOODHAM, New York, NY
Andrew WURFFLEIN, Philadelphia, PA
John WURFFLEIN, Philadelphia, PA

Agent Names Found On Deringer Pocket Pistols

W.C. ALLEN, San Francisco, CA
W.H. CALHOUN, Nashville, TN
CANFIELD & BROTHERS, Baltimore, MD
F. H. CLARK & CO., Memphis, TN
COLEMAN & DUKE, Cahaba, AL
M.W. GALT & BROTHER, Washington, DC
J.B. GILMORE, Shreveport, LA
A.B. GRISWOLD & CO., New Orleans, LA
HYDE & GOODRICH, New Orleans, LA
LULLMAN & VIENNA, Memphis, TN
A.J. MILLSPAUGH, Shreveport, LA
H.G. NEWCOMB, Natchez, MS
A.J. PLATE, San Francisco, CA
J.A. SCHAFER, Vicksburg, MS
S.L. SWETT, Vicksburg, MS
A.J. TAYLOR, San Francisco, CA
WOLF & DURRINGER, Louisville, KY

DESENZANI, LABORATORIES ARMI
Brescia, Italy

Over/Under

These custom made guns are all unique. Used guns in excellent condition will bring $35,000. Values increase depending on the small gauges, amount and coverage of engraving.

Side-By-Side

These custom made guns are all unique. Used guns in excellent condition will bring $25,000. Values increase depending on the small gauges, amount and coverage of engraving.

DESERT EAGLE

Desert Eagle is a semi-automatic gas-operated pistol chambered for the .357 Magnum, .41 Magnum, .44 Magnum and .50 Action Express. Produced by Israel Military Industries until 2009 and now made in U.S. Pistols furnished with a standard 6" barrel, but 10" and 14" interchangeable barrels are offered as options. Also available are these interchangeable barrels that are Mag-Na-Ported. Standard material used for frame is steel, but stainless and aluminum are also available. Standard finish for these pistols is black oxide, but custom finishes are available on special order. These special finishes are: gold, stainless steel, satin nickel, bright nickel, polished blue, camo, matte chrome, polished chrome, brushed chrome and matte chrome with gold. All of these special order finishes, as well as the optional barrels, will affect the price of these pistols. Prices listed here will reflect standard pistols only.

Desert Eagle .357 Magnum

Standard with 6" barrel and black oxide finish. Magazine capacity 9 rounds. Standard weight 58 oz.

NIB	Exc.	V.G.	Good	Fair	Poor
1250	900	700	500	400	250

Desert Eagle .41 Magnum/.44 Magnum

Standard barrel length 6", with black oxide finish. Magazine capacity 8 rounds. Weight for standard 63 oz. **NOTE:** Add 10 percent for .41.

NIB	Exc.	V.G.	Good	Fair	Poor
1350	900	700	500	400	250

Desert Eagle .50 Action Express

Standard barrel length 10", with black oxide finish. Magazine capacity 7 rounds. Standard weight 72 oz.

Interchangeable barrels make the Desert Eagle a truly versatile handgun. The .50 AE shown here will handle the biggest game in North America.

NIB	Exc.	V.G.	Good	Fair	Poor
1450	900	700	500	400	250

Desert Eagle Mark XIX

Introduced in 1996. This new design is manufactured in U.S. and allows interchangeability of barrels to switch calibers between the same receiver. Single receiver can be turned into six different pistols in three Magnum calibers. Available are .50 A.E., .44 Magnum and .357 Magnum in barrel lengths of 6" or 10". Separate magazines are also required. Eight different finishes offered as well. Separate bolt assembly is necessary to convert .44/.50 calibers to .357. There are so many different possibilities with this design that only basic pistol prices are given. Extra barrel assemblies are an additional cost. Prices range from $160 to $280 depending on caliber and length. **NOTE:** These custom shop finishes for Desert Eagle pistols are available in: satin nickel, bright nickel, polished and deep blued matte hard chrome, polished hard chrome, brushed hard chrome, 24K gold. All finishes except gold add $195 to price of pistol; $500 for gold finish; $195 for gold appointments.

.50A.E. w/6" Barrel

NIB	Exc.	V.G.	Good	Fair	Poor
1450	900	700	500	300	200

.50A.E. w/10" Barrel

NIB	Exc.	V.G.	Good	Fair	Poor
1350	1000	750	500	300	200

.44 Mag. w/6" Barrel

NIB	Exc.	V.G.	Good	Fair	Poor
1250	900	700	450	300	200

.44 Mag. w/10" Barrel

NIB	Exc.	V.G.	Good	Fair	Poor
1350	1000	750	500	300	200

.357 Mag. w/6" Barrel

NIB	Exc.	V.G.	Good	Fair	Poor
1250	900	700	450	300	200

.357 Mag. w/10" Barrel

NIB	Exc.	V.G.	Good	Fair	Poor
1350	1000	750	500	300	200

.440 CorBon w/6" Barrel (1999)

NIB	Exc.	V.G.	Good	Fair	Poor
1200	950	700	600	500	300

.440 CorBon w/10" Barrel (1999)

NIB	Exc.	V.G.	Good	Fair	Poor
1300	1000	750	650	550	325

Bolt Assembly—.44/.50 or .357

NIB	Exc.	V.G.	Good	Fair	Poor
220	175	150	100	75	50

Mark XIX Component System

Introduced in 2000. This system features Mark XIX frame with .44 Magnum 6" and 10" barrels; .50AE with 6" and 10" barrel; .357 Magnum with 6" and 10" barrel. Supplied with ICC aluminum case. Also offered with 6" only barrel components or 10" only barrel components.

6" & 10" Component System

NIB	Exc.	V.G.	Good	Fair	Poor
3990	2990	2500	1875	1150	500

6" Component System

NIB	Exc.	V.G.	Good	Fair	Poor
2575	1900	1500	1200	700	350

10" Component System

NIB	Exc.	V.G.	Good	Fair	Poor
2815	2100	1600	1325	725	400

Baby Eagle

Baby Eagle is a smaller version of Desert Eagle. All-steel construction, extra long slide rail, nylon grips, combat style trigger guard, ambidextrous thumb safety and decocking safety. Double-action design and available in 9mm, .40 S&W, .41 Action Express. Standard finish is black oxide, but matte chrome and brushed are offered as optional finishes. Fixed sights are standard. Fixed night sights and adjustable night sights are options.

.40 S&W (Standard)

Supplied with 4.5" barrel and black oxide finish. Magazine capacity 10 rounds. Empty weight 38 oz.

NIB	Exc.	V.G.	Good	Fair	Poor
500	400	350	300	250	200

9mm (Standard)

Fitted with 4.5" barrel and black oxide finish. Magazine capacity 16 rounds. Empty weight 38 oz.

NIB	Exc.	V.G.	Good	Fair	Poor
500	400	350	300	250	200

.41 Action Express

Has 4.7" barrel and black oxide finish. Magazine capacity 11 rounds. Empty weight 38 oz.

NIB	Exc.	V.G.	Good	Fair	Poor
500	400	350	300	250	200

Short Barrel (Semi-Compact)

This 9mm, .40 S&W or .45 ACP model features 3.6" barrel, with frame-mounted safety. Weight about 36 oz. Magazine holds 10 rounds.

NIB	Exc.	V.G.	Good	Fair	Poor
500	400	350	300	250	200

Short Barrel/Short Grip (Compact)

This 9mm or .40 S&W version has 3.6" barrel and shorter grip (3.25") than standard. Magazine capacity still 10 rounds. Weight about 38 oz. Frame-mounted safety.

NIB	Exc.	V.G.	Good	Fair	Poor
500	400	350	300	250	200

Semi-Compact Polymer

Pistol has a polymer frame and 3.9" barrel chambered for 9mm or .40 S&W cartridge. Weight about 29 oz.

NIB	Exc.	V.G.	Good	Fair	Poor
500	400	325	285	225	175

Compact Polymer

As above, with 3.6" barrel and short grip. Weight about 27 oz.

NIB	Exc.	V.G.	Good	Fair	Poor
500	400	325	285	225	175

Mountain Eagle

Semi-automatic pistol chambered for .22 LR cartridge. Features 6.5" barrel, with adjustable rear sight. Grip is a one-piece molded checkered plastic, with raised side panels. Magazine capacity 15 rounds; 20-round magazine available as an option. Black oxide finish standard. Weight 21 oz.

NIB	Exc.	V.G.	Good	Fair	Poor
275	175	150	125	100	75

Mountain Eagle Target Edition

Similar to standard Mountain Eagle. Fitted with 8" accurized barrel, two-stage target trigger, jeweled bolt, adjustable sights with three interchangeable blades and range case.

NIB	Exc.	V.G.	Good	Fair	Poor
295	225	195	150	125	85

Mountain Eagle Compact Edition

Similar to above, with 4.5" barrel and short grip.

NIB	Exc.	V.G.	Good	Fair	Poor
295	225	195	150	125	85

Desert Eagle L5

This is the smallest and lightest of Desert Eagle family, with alloy frame and heavily milled slide and barrel assembly. Barrel length 5", with integral muzzle-brake. Chambered in .357 Magnum, with 9-round magazine capacity. Finish black; weight 49.6 oz.; overall length 9.7". Introduced in 2006.

NIB	Exc.	V.G.	Good	Fair	Poor
1700	1500	1400	—	—	—

Lone Eagle

Single-shot rotating breech pistol designed to fire centerfire cartridges. Standard finish black oxide blue luster. Barrel drilled and tapped for scope mounts. Standard barrel length 14". Fixed, adjustable or silhouette sights are offered as options. Stock assembly made from Lexan. Handgun offered in these calibers: .22-250, .223, .22 Hornet, .243, .30-30, .30-06, .308, .357 Magnum, .358 Win., .35 Rem., .44 Magnum, .444 Marlin, 7mm-08, 7mm Bench Rest. Weight between 4 lbs. 3 oz. to 4 lbs. 7 oz. depending on caliber.

NIB	Exc.	V.G.	Good	Fair	Poor
400	300	275	250	200	125

Lone Eagle (New Model)

Introduced in 1996, this improved Lone Eagle model features 15 interchangeable barreled actions from .22 Hornet to .444 Marlin. Available in both black and chrome actions, with or without muzzle-brake. The 7.62x39 action introduced in 1996 also. Sights can be fixed, adjustable or silhouette type. Weight from 4 lbs. 3 oz. to 4 lbs. 7 oz. depending on caliber. Prices listed reflect black action and fixed sights. **NOTE:** Add $100 for muzzle-brake;

$30 for chrome action; $35 for adjustable sights; $130 for silhouette sights.

NIB	Exc.	V.G.	Good	Fair	Poor
425	325	175	150	125	100

Micro Desert Eagle Pistol

Small-frame DAO pocket pistol chambered in .380 ACP. Features include 2.22" barrel, fixed low-profile sights, steel slide, aluminum alloy frame, nickel-teflon finish, 6-round capacity. Overall length 4.52"; weight 14 oz.

NIB	Exc.	V.G.	Good	Fair	Poor
450	350	250	200	150	100

Model 1911 Desert Eagle

Based on classic 1911 design. This model comes in two sizes: 1911 G full-size (5"); 1911 C mid-size (4.33"). Custom-type features like extended beavertail grip safety, extended thumb safety and mag release, enlarged ejection port, beveled mag well and double-diamond wood grips. Comes with black finish, fixed sights and two 8-shot magazines. A 3" barrel model (Undercover) also available, with aluminum frame, 6-shot magazine and ajustable sights. **NOTE:** Add $50 for Undercover.

NIB	Exc.	V.G.	Good	Fair	Poor
750	650	500	400	300	200

MR9 / MR40

This family of pistols has a Walther polymer frame, with Magnum Research stainless slide and barrel made in U.S.A. Striker-fired operation, with internal safeties. Offered in 9mm or .40 S&W, with 4", 4.15" or 4.5" barrels. The integral polymer grips have interchangeable palm swells of different sizes.

NIB	Exc.	V.G.	Good	Fair	Poor
500	400	325	250	200	125

Mountain Eagle Rifle

Limited edition rifle (1,000), with Sako action and composite stock. Chambered for .270, .280, .30-06, .300 Win., .338 Win, 7mm Magnum. Introduced in 1994. Additional calibers are .300 Weatherby, .375 H&H, .416 Rem. and 7mm STW. Barrel length 24". Average weight about 7.74 lbs. **NOTE:** Add $150 for muzzle-brake; $300 for .375 H&H and .416 Rem.; $100 for left-hand actions.

NIB	Exc.	V.G.	Good	Fair	Poor
2295	1700	1150	800	400	175

Mountain Eagle Varmint Edition

Chambered for .222 Rem. and .223 Rem. cartridges. Fitted with 26" stainless Krieger barrel. Kevlar-graphite stock. Weight about 9 lbs. 13 oz.

NIB	Exc.	V.G.	Good	Fair	Poor
2295	1750	1150	800	400	175

Magnum Lite Rimfire Rifles

These rifles are built with Ruger 10/22 actions and graphite barrels. There are several variations depending on stock configuration. **NOTE:** For Clark Custom Upgrades add $130 to price of each Magnum Lite rifle.

Hogue and Fajen Scope-Hi Stock

NIB	Exc.	V.G.	Good	Fair	Poor
650	495	400	300	200	125

Fajen Thumbhole Sporter

NIB	Exc.	V.G.	Good	Fair	Poor
700	550	450	300	200	125

Fajen Thumbhole Silhouette

NIB	Exc.	V.G.	Good	Fair	Poor
800	650	500	300	200	125

Turner Barracuda

NIB	Exc.	V.G.	Good	Fair	Poor
800	650	500	300	200	125

Magnum Lite Centerfire Rifles

These rifles built on Sako actions. Fitted with graphite barrels. Introduced in 1999. Offered in two configurations, both with synthetic stock.

Heavy Barrel

Fitted with 26", 1.2" diameter. barrel, with 1-in-14 twist. Chambered for .223 cartridge. Weight about 7.8 lbs

NIB	Exc.	V.G.	Good	Fair	Poor
2295	1700	1150	800	400	295

Sport Taper Barrel

Fitted with 24" tapered barrel. Chambered for .280 Rem., 7mm Magnum, .30-06, .300 Win. Magnum. Weight about 6.4 lbs.

NIB	Exc.	V.G.	Good	Fair	Poor
2295	1700	1150	800	400	295

Tactical Rifle

Introduced in 2000. Features 26" match grade barrel. Chambered for .223, .22-250, .308 or .300 Win. Magnum cartridges. Barrel made from carbon fiber. Action is Remington Model 700. H-S Precision tactical stock, with adjustable comb. Adjustable trigger. Weight about 8.3 lbs.

NIB	Exc.	V.G.	Good	Fair	Poor
2400	1800	1250	850	400	295

DESERT INDUSTRIES
Las Vegas, Nevada
See—Steel City Arms

DESTROYER CARBINE
Spain

Destroyer Carbine

A 9mm Bayard/Large caliber bolt-action rifle, with 20" barrel and 7-shot magazine. Full length stock, with two barrel bands.

NIB	Exc.	V.G.	Good	Fair	Poor
—	500	395	200	100	35

DETONICS DEFENSE TECHNOLOGIES
Millstadt, Illinois

Most recent manufacturer of Detonics 1911-style pistols. As of mid 2016, all models listed below are no longer in production.

Combat Master

Latest version of very first compact 1911 developed in the 1970s by original Detonics company. In .45 ACP, with 3.5" octagonal barrel, two-tone finish, aluminum/Dymondwood grips, 6+1 capacity, stainless steel frame and slide. Weight 30 oz. Introduced in 2010.

NIB	Exc.	V.G.	Good	Fair	Poor
850	775	700	550	—	—

Nemesis HT

Full-size with 5" barrel, chambered in .40 S&W. Weight 38 oz., capacity 9+1. Other features same as above. Introduced in 2011.

NIB	Exc.	V.G.	Good	Fair	Poor
1950	1800	1500	1100	—	—

DTX

Polymer frame double-action-only pistol. Chambered in 9mm or .40 S&W. Barrel 4.25"; weight 25 oz.; capacity 16+1 (9mm), 14+1 (.40). Introduced in 2011.

NIB	Exc.	V.G.	Good	Fair	Poor
975	900	775	625	450	250

DETONICS FIREARMS INDUSTRIES / NEW DETONICS / DECTONICS USA LLC
Bellevue, Washington / Phoenix, Arizona / Pendergrass, Georgia

This series of compact 1911-type pistols, was first manufactured by Detonics Firearms Industries in Bellvue, WA from 1976 to 1988. That firm was sold to New Detonics Mfg. Corp. of Phoenix, AZ, which operated from 1989 to 1992. In 2004, the brand was resurrected and returned to production by Detonics USA in Pendergrass, GA. Then in 2007, Detonics USA and all if its predecessors was sold to a group of investors who established the current company, known only as Detonics, in Millstadt, IL. The company name was changed in 2013 to Detonics Defense Technologies.

Mark I

A .45-caliber semi-automatic pistol, with 3.25" barrel and 6-shot magazine. Matte blued with walnut grips. Discontinued in 1981.

NIB	Exc.	V.G.	Good	Fair	Poor
—	550	450	400	300	200

Mark II

As above, with satin nickel-plated finish. Discontinued in 1979.

NIB	Exc.	V.G.	Good	Fair	Poor
—	550	450	400	300	200

Mark III

As above, with hard chrome plating. Discontinued in 1979.

NIB	Exc.	V.G.	Good	Fair	Poor
—	600	500	450	350	250

Mark IV

As above, with polished blue finish. Discontinued in 1981.

NIB	Exc.	V.G.	Good	Fair	Poor
—	550	450	400	300	200

Combat Master

The Mark I in 9mm, .38 Super or .45-caliber.

NIB	Exc.	V.G.	Good	Fair	Poor
975	800	600	500	400	250

Combat Master Mark V

As above, in stainless steel with a matte finish. Discontinued in 1985.

NIB	Exc.	V.G.	Good	Fair	Poor
975	800	600	500	400	250

Combat Master Mark VI

As above, with adjustable sights and sides of slide polished. 1,000 were made in .451 Detonics Magnum caliber. **NOTE:** Add 40 percent for .451 Detonics Magnum.

NIB	Exc.	V.G.	Good	Fair	Poor
900	750	600	500	400	250

Combat Master Mark VII

As above, without sights. **NOTE:** Add 40 percent for .451 Detonics Magnum.

NIB	Exc.	V.G.	Good	Fair	Poor
900	750	600	500	400	250

Military Combat MC2

As above, in 9mm, .38 Super or .45-caliber. Fixed sights, dull finish and Pachmayr grips. Discontinued in 1984.

NIB	Exc.	V.G.	Good	Fair	Poor
675	600	500	425	300	200

Scoremaster

As above, in .45- or .451 Detonics Magnum, with 5" or 6" barrel, Millet sights and grip safety.

NIB	Exc.	V.G.	Good	Fair	Poor
1250	1000	800	600	400	250

Janus Competition Scoremaster

As above, in .45-caliber with compensated barrel. Introduced in 1988.

NIB	Exc.	V.G.	Good	Fair	Poor
1750	1450	1250	850	650	300

Servicemaster

As above, with a 4.25" barrel, interchangeable sights and matte finish. Discontinued in 1986.

NIB	Exc.	V.G.	Good	Fair	Poor
—	1000	800	600	400	200

Pocket 9

A 9mm double-action semi-automatic pistol, with 3" barrel and 6-shot magazine. Matte finish stainless steel. Discontinued in 1986.

NIB	Exc.	V.G.	Good	Fair	Poor
—	400	350	275	225	175

Combat Master

Fitted with a 3.5" barrel chambered for the .45 ACP, .40 S&W, .357 SIG, .38 Super or the 9mm Para cartridges. Checkered rosewood grips. Low profile fixed sights. Magazine capacity 6 rounds. Height of pistol 4.75". Overall length 7". Weight about 34 oz. All stainless steel including springs. Introduced in 2005, by Detonics USA.

NIB	Exc.	V.G.	Good	Fair	Poor
1300	1050	650	425	300	175

Street Master

Chambered for .45 ACP cartridge and fitted with a 5" barrel. Checkered rosewood grips. All stainless steel including springs. Height 4.75". Overall length 8.5". Weight about 39 oz. Magazine capacity 6 rounds. Fixed sights. Introduced in 2005, by Detonics USA.

NIB	Exc.	V.G.	Good	Fair	Poor
1200	950	675	450	325	195

Model 9-11-01

Introduced in 2005, by Detonics USA. Chambered for .45 ACP cartridge and fitted with a 5" barrel. All stainless steel construction. Checkered rosewood grips. Height about 5.5". Overall length 8.625". Weight about 43 oz. Magazine capacity 7 rounds. Fixed sights.

NIB	Exc.	V.G.	Good	Fair	Poor
1200	950	675	450	325	195

DEUTSCHE WERKE
Erfurt, Germany

Ortgies

Semi-automatic pistol in 6.35mm and 7.65mm. The 6.35mm pistol manufactured in 1921 and 7.65mm model in 1922 by Ortgies Company. Pistols had "HO" logo for Heinrich Ortgies on each grip. Later, Ortgies Company was bought by Deutsche Werke. Grip logo was "D". Over the period Ortgies were manufactured with four different slide legends.

Courtesy James Rankin

NIB	Exc.	V.G.	Good	Fair	Poor
—	450	325	275	200	100

Ortgies 9mm

As above, with addition of a hold-open button on left side of slide. Caliber is 9mmK, aka .380 ACP.

Courtesy James Rankin

NIB	Exc.	V.G.	Good	Fair	Poor
—	450	375	250	175	100

DEVISME, F. P.
Paris, France

One of the more popular French gunsmiths of the mid-19th century. F.P. Devisme manufactured a wide variety of firearms, including single-shot percussion pistols, double-barrel percussion rifles and shotguns, percussion revolvers and cane guns. After 1858, this maker manufactured cartridge weapons of the same style as his percussion arms. Quality of all his products is uniformly high and impossible to provide a generalized price guide.

DIAMOND
Turkey

Gold Series Semi-Automatic Shotgun

Chambered for 12-gauge shell, with 3" chamber. Barrel length 28". Turkish walnut stock or synthetic stock. Black receiver, with gold-filled engraving. Also available with 24" slug barrel with sights. **NOTE:** Add $50 for walnut stock.

NIB	Exc.	V.G.	Good	Fair	Poor
350	300	200	150	100	75

Gold Series Pump-Action Shotgun

Offered with same features as semi-automatic Gold gun, with slide-action. **NOTE:** Add $25 for walnut stock.

NIB	Exc.	V.G.	Good	Fair	Poor
300	250	175	125	100	75

Silver Series Mariner Semi-Automatic Shotgun

A 12-gauge stainless steel and anodized alloy semi-automatic gun, with 3" chambers. Fitted with 22" ventilated rib barrel and synthetic stock.

NIB	Exc.	V.G.	Good	Fair	Poor
425	350	275	200	150	100

Silver Series Mariner Pump-Action Shotgun

A 12-gauge pump gun, with 20" slug barrel and synthetic stock. Stainless steel and alloy.

NIB	Exc.	V.G.	Good	Fair	Poor
350	275	200	150	100	75

Diamond Elite Semi-Automatic Shotgun

A 12-gauge 3" chamber shotgun. Offered with 22" to 28" barrels, with 3 choke tubes. Engraved receiver.

NIB	Exc.	V.G.	Good	Fair	Poor
325	275	200	150	100	75

Diamond Panther Pump-Action Shotgun

As above, in a slide-action configuration.

NIB	Exc.	V.G.	Good	Fair	Poor
250	200	200	150	100	75

Diamond Panther Semi-Automatic Shotgun

A 12-gauge gun, with 3" chambers and 20" or 28" ventilated rib barrel. Furnished with 3 choke tubes. Synthetic stock.

NIB	Exc.	V.G.	Good	Fair	Poor
325	275	200	150	100	75

Diamond Elite Pump-Action Shotgun

As above, with slide-action. Offered with 18.5" slug barrel.

NIB	Exc.	V.G.	Good	Fair	Poor
300	250	175	125	100	75

DIAMONDBACK FIREARMS
Cocoa, Florida

DB9 Semi-Automatic Pistol

Polymer-frame striker-fired mini-compact 9mm, with 6+1 capacity. Weight 11 oz. Very compact design, with 3" barrel, overall length 5.6", height 4" and width .80". Available in several sight and finish options including black, stainless, pink, orange and teal. Introduced in 2011. **NOTE:** Add $200 for Crimson Trace laser grip.

NIB	Exc.	V.G.	Good	Fair	Poor
360	335	300	250	200	125

DB380 Semi-Automatic Pistol

Small variation of DB9. Chambered for .380. Barrel length 2.8"; weight 8.8 oz. Introduced in 2011. **NOTE:** Add $200 for Crimson Trace laser grip.

NIB	Exc.	V.G.	Good	Fair	Poor
385	325	285	250	—	—

DB9 FS

Full-size variation of DB9, with 4.75" barrel and 15-round magazine. Weight 21.5 oz.

NIB	Exc.	V.G.	Good	Fair	Poor
385	350	300	250	200	125

DB15

AR-15 style rifle in .223/5.56 NATO. Has standard features of other AR models: M4 contour free-floating 16" barrel, with A2 flash hider; M4 4-position stock, flattop upper receiver, four-rail or standard hand guard. **NOTE:** Add $200 for four-rail hand guard; $125 for Magpul sights.

NIB	Exc.	V.G.	Good	Fair	Poor
350	325	275	200	175	125

DB15 NB

Upgraded model of DB15, with nickel boron coated barrel, upper and lower receivers. Magpul six-position stock and pistol-grip. Variety of finish and sight options.

NIB	Exc.	V.G.	Good	Fair	Poor
1050	900	700	550	400	200

DB10

AR-10 style rifle in .308 Win., with 18" HBAR barrel, Magpul ACS stock and MOE Plus pistol-grip. Features include black anodized or Flat Dark Earth finish and low profile gas block.

NIB	Exc.	V.G.	Good	Fair	Poor
1600	1400	1150	750	500	250

DICKINSON, E. L. & J.
Springfield, Massachusetts

Ranger

A .32-caliber spur trigger revolver, with 6-shot cylinder.

NIB	Exc.	V.G.	Good	Fair	Poor
—	—	525	450	200	100

Single-Shot

A .32-caliber single-shot pistol, with 3.75" hinged barrel, silver plated brass frame, blued barrel and walnut grips.

NIB	Exc.	V.G.	Good	Fair	Poor
—	—	775	650	250	100

DICKSON, NELSON & CO.
Dawson, Georgia

Rifle

A .58-caliber single-shot percussion rifle, with 34" barrel, full stock secured by two barrel bands, brass furniture and iron loading rod. Lock marked "Dickson/Nelson & Co./C.S." as well as "Ala." and date of manufacture. Prospective purchasers are advised to secure a qualified appraisal prior to acquisition. Carbine version of this arm known and has a 24" barrel.

NIB	Exc.	V.G.	Good	Fair	Poor
—	—	39500	14000	3000	2000

DIMICK, H.E.
St. Louis, Missouri

Percussion Pistol

This maker primarily known for half stock Plains Rifles. He also manufactured a limited number of percussion pistols. These vary in length, caliber, stock form and type of furniture. Values listed should only be used as a rough guide. Prospective purchasers should secure a qualified appraisal prior to acquisition. Active 1849 to 1873.

NIB	Exc.	V.G.	Good	Fair	Poor
—	—	—	7500	2750	900

DOMINGO ACHA
See—Acha

DOMINO
Brescia, Italy

Model OP 601 Match Pistol

A .22-caliber short semi-automatic pistol, with 5.6" vented barrel, target sights, adjustable and removable trigger. Blued, with adjustable walnut grips.

NIB	Exc.	V.G.	Good	Fair	Poor
1700	1200	800	550	300	175

Model SP 602 Match Pistol

As above, in .22 LR caliber.

Courtesy John J. Stimsom, Jr.

NIB	Exc.	V.G.	Good	Fair	Poor
1700	1200	800	550	300	175

DORNAUS & DIXON ENTERPRISES, INC.
Huntington Beach, California
See—Bren 10

DORNHEIM, G.C.
Suhl, Germany

Gecado Model 11

A 6.35mm semi-automatic pistol, bearing the name "Gecado" on the slide. Fitted with a 2.2" barrel. Magazine capacity 6 rounds. Weight about 15 oz. Marketed by G.C. Dornheim. Copy of FN Browning Model 1906.

Courtesy James Rankin

NIB	Exc.	V.G.	Good	Fair	Poor
—	300	225	125	75	50

Gecado 7.65mm

A 7.65mm semi-automatic pistol bearing the name "Gecado" on the slide. Fitted with 2.6" barrel. Magazine capacity 7 rounds. Weight about 21 oz. Marketed by G.C. Dornheim.

NIB	Exc.	V.G.	Good	Fair	Poor
—	275	150	125	75	50

DOUBLESTAR CORP.
Winchester, Kentucky

Star EM-4

Chambered for .223 cartridge. Fitted with 16" barrel. Rifle supplied with A-2 or flat top upper and Colt M-4 hand guard.

NIB	Exc.	V.G.	Good	Fair	Poor
915	750	600	500	275	125

Star-15

Has 20" barrel, A-2 buttstock and hand guard. Supplied with A-2 or flat top upper. In .223 or 7.62x39 calibers.

NIB	Exc.	V.G.	Good	Fair	Poor
775	625	575	450	225	100

Star Lightweight Tactical Rifle

Fitted with 15" fluted barrel, permanently attached muzzle-brake and short tactical buttstock. Supplied with A-2 or flat top upper.

NIB	Exc.	V.G.	Good	Fair	Poor
880	700	575	450	225	100

Star Carbine

Has 16" match grade barrel. Supplied with either A-2 or non-collapsing CAR buttstock. Upper receiver A-2 style or flat top. In .223 or 7.62x39 calibers.

NIB	Exc.	V.G.	Good	Fair	Poor
775	625	575	450	225	100

Star DS-4 Carbine

Features 16" M-4 barrel, with 6-position buttstock, oval hand guard and A-2 flash hider. Weight about 6.75 lbs. Choice of A-2 or flattop upper receiver.

NIB	Exc.	V.G.	Good	Fair	Poor
875	700	575	450	225	100

Star Super Match Rifle

Choice of match grade barrel lengths; 16", 20", 22" or 24". Supplied with flat top upper or tactical Hi-Rise upper. **NOTE:** Add $50 for .204 Ruger or 6.8 SPC; $100 for 6.5 Grendel, all discontinued.

NIB	Exc.	V.G.	Good	Fair	Poor
950	800	675	450	225	100

Star Critterslayer

Fitted with 24" fluted super match barrel, with flat top upper and free floating hand guard. Match 2 stage trigger. Fitted with Harris LMS swivel bipod and Ergo grip, with palm swell.

NIB	Exc.	V.G.	Good	Fair	Poor
1300	1000	750	600	395	175

DSC Expedition Rifle

Offered with 16" or 20" lightweight barrel and integral muzzle-brake. Stock sights and receiver are A-2 configuration.

NIB	Exc.	V.G.	Good	Fair	Poor
825	650	575	450	225	100

DSC Star-15 CMP Service Rifle

Fitted with 20" chrome lined heavy match barrel. National Match front and rear sights. CMP free float handguard. National Match trigger. A-2 upper receiver.

NIB	Exc.	V.G.	Good	Fair	Poor
1000	750	650	575	450	225

DSC Star CMP Improved Service Rifle

Similar to above model, with 20" Wilson Arms premium grade heavy match barrel. McCormick single- or two-stage Match trigger and Tippie Competition rear sight.

NIB	Exc.	V.G.	Good	Fair	Poor
1299	975	825	650	575	300

DSC Star 15 Lightweight Tactical

Fitted with 16" fluted heavy barrel and tactical "shorty" A-2 buttstock.

NIB	Exc.	V.G.	Good	Fair	Poor
880	700	575	450	225	100

DSC Star Dissipator

Features 16" barrel, with full length hand guard. Available with A-2 or flattop upper receiver.

NIB	Exc.	V.G.	Good	Fair	Poor
875	700	575	450	225	100

DSC Star 15 9mm Carbine

Chambered for 9mm cartridge. Fitted with 16" heavy barrel. A-2 or flattop upper receiver. Available with A-2 or CAR buttstock.

NIB	Exc.	V.G.	Good	Fair	Poor
995	750	650	575	450	225

1911 Combat Pistol

Full-size Government Model .45 ACP, with 5" barrel, stainless slide, forged frame, black finish. Novak white-dot LoMount sights, Picatinny rail, 8-shot magazine, checkered wood grips. Introduced 2010.

NIB	Exc.	V.G.	Good	Fair	Poor
1600	1350	1100	800	500	300

1911 C2

Commander size .45 ACP, with 4.25" barrel, round butt or bobtail grip, black or gray Ion Bond finish, Novak 3-dot sights and 8-round magazine. **NOTE:** Add $150 for bobtail grip.

NIB	Exc.	V.G.	Good	Fair	Poor
1800	1600	1300	950	600	325

1911 C2G

Upgraded full size 1911 .45, with features of 1911 C2. Plus 5" hand fitted match barrel, with optional Picatinny rail. Also available in 10mm. **NOTE:** Add $200 for 10mm.

NIB	Exc.	V.G.	Good	Fair	Poor
1800	1600	1300	950	600	325

DSC .300 Blackout AR Pistol

AR-style pistol in .300 AAC caliber, with 7.5" or 9" barrel. A2 muzzle-brake, free-float aluminum hand guard and pistol-grip.

NIB	Exc.	V.G.	Good	Fair	Poor
1200	1000	750	600	450	300

DOUBLETAP DEFENSE
St. Louis, Missouri

Doubletap

An over/under model, with tip-up action double action trigger. Chambered in 9mm or .45 ACP. Grip has space to carry two extra rounds. Weight 12 to 14 oz. **NOTE:** Add $100 for ported barrels; $200 for titanium frame.

NIB	Exc.	V.G.	Good	Fair	Poor
425	350	300	250	200	165

DOUG TURNBULL MANUFACTURING CO.
Bloomfield, New York

Company began operation in 1983 as a one-man shop. Today the company numbers 14 people and does finish work for most major firearms manufacturers. Company also installs Miller single triggers. Models listed are a series of special run firearms produced by Turnbull.

DT COLT

This model is a current Colt SAA reworked to look like the pre-1920 SAA. Assigned serial numbers beginning with 001DT. Revolvers are offered in .45 Colt, .44-40 and .38-40 calibers. Barrel lengths 4.75", 5.5" and 7.5". Standard DT has color case-hardened frame, rest of gun charcoal blue. Cylinder flutes are enlarged and front of cylinder is beveled. Many special options offered which will affect cost. Prices listed are for standard revolvers. Values for these very special guns is strictly what the market will bear.

Year Offered—1998

NIB	Exc.	V.G.	Good	Fair	Poor
1795	—	—	—	—	—

Year Offered—1999

NIB	Exc.	V.G.	Good	Fair	Poor
2250	—	—	—	—	—

Year Offered—2000

NIB	Exc.	V.G.	Good	Fair	Poor
2500	—	—	—	—	—

EHBM Colt

A Colt SAA current production revolver, limited to 50 guns. Chambered for .45 Colt. Fitted with 5.5" barrel. Special features. Serial numbers EHBM01 to EHBM50. First offered in 2000.

NIB	Exc.	V.G.	Good	Fair	Poor
2650	2300	1600	1250	700	500

Smith & Wesson No. 3 Schofield

Introduced in 2002, a special new production S&W Schofield. Special serial numbers with "DTR" prefix starting with serial number 0001. Frame, barrel and cylinder are charcoal blued. Trigger, trigger guard and barrel latch are bone color case-hardened. Factory wood grips are standard. Engraving is optional.

NIB	Exc.	V.G.	Good	Fair	Poor
2300	2450	1900	1550	875	500

Colt/Winchester Cased Set

Cased set, with Colt Model 1873 engraved revolver and Winchester Model 1894. Colt chambered for .45 Colt cartridge, fitted with 7.5" barrel, engraving "B" coverage; Model 1894 chambered for .45 Colt cartridge, in saddle ring configuration, engraving pattern #9 with deer. Checkered walnut stock. Limited to five sets total. Serial numbers 160DT to 164DT.

NIB	Exc.	V.G.	Good	Fair	Poor
5750	4300	3750	2500	1500	600

General Patton Colt

Limited run of engraved Colt Model 1873 Single Action Army revolvers. Helfricht-style full-coverage engraving. Chambered for .45 Colt cartridge, fitted with 4.75" barrel and ivory grips. Silver-plated finish. Limited to 10 revolvers total. Serial numbers GP01 to GP10.

NIB	Exc.	V.G.	Good	Fair	Poor
5250	4000	3250	2000	1000	400

Theodore Roosevelt Colt

Colt SAA revolver features carved ivory grips, Nimschke-style full coverage engraving, with gold cylinder, hammer and ejector rod. Chambered for .44-40 cartridge, fitted with 7.5" barrel. Balance of gun silver plated. Supplied with fitted case. Limited to 25 revolvers total. Serial numbers TR01 to TR25.

NIB	Exc.	V.G.	Good	Fair	Poor
7750	6000	5000	4000	3000	600

Theodore Roosevelt Winchester Model 1876

Custom rifle limited to 25 units. Serial numbered from TR01 to TR-25. Each rifle engraved and checkered in style of original. Chambered for .45-70 cartridge. Fitted with 28" half round barrel. Gold inlaid stock oval. Portion of the proceeds of each rifle goes to benefit Doug Turnbull Conservation Laboratory at the National Firearms Museum.

NIB	Exc.	V.G.	Good	Fair	Poor
29000	—	—	—	—	—

Cowboy Classic

Custom-tuned and authentically finished USFA 1873-style single-action revolver. Chambered in virtually all historically-correct centerfire cartridges. Barrel: 4.75", 5.5" and 7.5". Black hard rubber grips standard. Bone charcoal case-hardened and charcoal blue finish. Introduced 2006.

NIB	Exc.	V.G.	Good	Fair	Poor
1650	1300	950	675	400	300

Model 1911 Heritage

Made-to-order reproduction of original design in the year 1911, is made to have the look and feel of pistols made during WWI. Chambered in .45 ACP, features include hand-checkered American black walnut double-diamond grips, color case-hardened frame and hammer, a short and wide checkered spur hammer and two two-tone magazines. Several other variants are offered including Commander size and engraved models

NIB	Exc.	V.G.	Good	Fair	Poor
2075	1750	1200	700	400	250

DOWNSIZER CORPORATION
Santee, California

Model WSP

Introduced in 1999. Billed as world's smallest pistol by manufacturer. Single-/double-action-only pistol, with tip-up barrel. Chambered for .22 Magnum, .32 Magnum, .357 Magnum, 9mm, .40 S&W and .45 ACP cartridges. Barrel length 2.1"; overall length 3.25"; height 2.25"; thickness .9"; weight about 11 oz. Built from stainless steel.

NIB	Exc.	V.G.	Good	Fair	Poor
400	325	275	225	175	125

DPMS
St. Cloud, Minnesota

Panther Bull A-15

AR-15 type rifle chambered for .223 cartridge. Fitted with 20" stainless steel bull barrel. A-2 style buttstock. No sights. Barrel has 1:9 twist. Flat top receiver. Hand guard is aluminum free float tube. Upper and lower receivers are hard coated black. Weight about 9.5 lbs. Each rifle comes standard with two 7-round magazines, sling and cleaning kit.

NIB	Exc.	V.G.	Good	Fair	Poor
900	700	550	400	275	125

Panther Bull 24

Similar to model above. Fitted with 24" bull barrel. Flat top receiver. Weight about 10 lbs.

NIB	Exc.	V.G.	Good	Fair	Poor
950	750	600	400	275	125

Panther Deluxe Bull 24 Special

Fitted with 24" stainless steel fluted bull barrel. Adjustable A-2 style butt-stock. Flat top receiver. Adjustable sniper pistol-grip. Weight about 10 lbs.

NIB	Exc.	V.G.	Good	Fair	Poor
1150	900	750	400	275	125

Panther Extreme Super Bull 24

Fitted with 24" stainless steel extra heavy bull barrel (1.150" dia.). Skeletonized stock. Flat top receiver. Weight about 11.75 lbs.

NIB	Exc.	V.G.	Good	Fair	Poor
1200	800	650	400	275	125

Panther Bulldog

Fitted with 20" stainless steel fluted bull barrel. Black synthetic A-2-style buttstock. Flat top receiver. Adjustable trigger. Weight about 10 lbs.

NIB	Exc.	V.G.	Good	Fair	Poor
1200	975	800	400	275	125

Panther Bull Sweet 16

Fitted with 16" stainless steel bull barrel. Flat top receiver. Weight about 7.75 lbs.

NIB	Exc.	V.G.	Good	Fair	Poor
1100	900	550	400	275	125

Panther Bull SST 16

Similar to model above, with stainless steel lower receiver. Weight about 9 lbs.

NIB	Exc.	V.G.	Good	Fair	Poor
1300	975	650	400	275	125

Panther Bull Classic

Fitted with 20" 4150 steel bull barrel. Square front post sight, adjustable A-2 rear sight. Weight about 9.75 lbs.

NIB	Exc.	V.G.	Good	Fair	Poor
1200	800	650	400	275	125

TAC 2/TAC 20

This model in 5.56 NATO, with 16" barrel, Magpul ACS stock with MOE pistol-grip and A2 front and rear sights. Weight about 8.5 lbs. TAC 20 model similar, but in .308 Winchester with 20" heavy barrel. Introduced in 2012.

NIB	Exc.	V.G.	Good	Fair	Poor
1100	950	800	600	400	300

GII AP4

Chambered in .308 Win., with 16" lightweight chrome-lined barrel. M4 6-position collapsible stock, A2 pistol-grip, carbine-length Glacier Guard hand guard, Magpul Gen 2 rear sight, anodized and Teflon-coated upper and lower receivers.

NIB	Exc.	V.G.	Good	Fair	Poor
1300	1100	925	700	400	250

GII Hunter

Chambered in .243 Win., .260 Rem., .308 Win. or .338 Federal. Has 20" stainless steel barrel with no sights, Magpul MOE stock with pistol-grip and a free-float tube hand guard. Compact model identical except with 18" barrel. Introduced in 2014.

NIB	Exc.	V.G.	Good	Fair	Poor
1400	1250	1000	750	450	325

Panther Arctic

Similar to Bull Classic, with 20" fluted bull barrel and flat top receiver. Black A-2 style buttstock, with white coat finish on receiver and hand guard. Black Teflon finish on barrel. Weight about 8.25 lbs.

NIB	Exc.	V.G.	Good	Fair	Poor
1075	850	700	400	275	125

Panther Classic

Fitted with 20" 4150 steel heavy barrel. Square front post sight and A-2 rear sight. A-2 round hand guard. Weight about 9.5 lbs.

NIB	Exc.	V.G.	Good	Fair	Poor
800	600	500	400	275	125

Panther DCM

Similar to model above, with 20" stainless steel heavy barrel and NM rear sight. DCM free-float hand guard. Adjustable trigger. Weight about 9.5 lbs.

NIB	Exc.	V.G.	Good	Fair	Poor
950	750	600	400	275	125

Panther Classic 16 Post Ban

Fitted with 1" 4150 steel heavy barrel. A-2 style sights. Round hand guard. Weight about 7.25 lbs.

NIB	Exc.	V.G.	Good	Fair	Poor
775	600	500	400	275	125

Panther Free Float 16 Post Ban

Similar to model above, with 16" barrel. Fitted with vented free-floated barrel and tube hand guard. Weight about 7.25 lbs.

NIB	Exc.	V.G.	Good	Fair	Poor
825	650	550	400	275	125

Panther Southpaw Post Ban

Fitted with 20" 4150 steel heavy barrel. A-2 style sights. Upper receiver modified for left-hand ejection. Weight about 9.5 lbs.

NIB	Exc.	V.G.	Good	Fair	Poor
875	700	600	400	275	125

Panther Race Gun

Similar to Panther Bull, with 24" fluted bull barrel. Sights: JP Micro adjustable rear, JP front sight adjustable for height. Includes Lyman globe and Shaver inserts.

NIB	Exc.	V.G.	Good	Fair	Poor
1875	1500	800	500	275	125

Panther Tuber

Similar to Panther Bull 24, with 16" barrel and cylindrical aluminum shroud.

NIB	Exc.	V.G.	Good	Fair	Poor
700	600	500	400	275	125

Single Shot Rifle

AR-15 style single-shot rifle, with manually-operated bolt. No magazine.

NIB	Exc.	V.G.	Good	Fair	Poor
775	500	400	275	125	100

Panther Pardus

Similar to Panther Post Ban, with 16" bull barrel, telescoping buttstock and tan Teflon finish. Introduced 2006.

NIB	Exc.	V.G.	Good	Fair	Poor
1200	850	700	400	275	200

Panther 20th Anniversary Rifle

Similar to Panther Post-ban, with 20" bull barrel and engraved chrome-plated lower receiver. Introduced 2006.

NIB	Exc.	V.G.	Good	Fair	Poor
2500	2000	1550	800	500	300

Panther 6.8 Rifle

Similar to Panther DCM, with 20" chrome-moly barrel. Chambered for 6.8x43 Remington SPC. Introduced 2006.

NIB	Exc.	V.G.	Good	Fair	Poor
1000	850	700	400	275	125

Panther Mark 12

Similar to other Panthers, with flash hider and other refinements. Introduced 2007.

NIB	Exc.	V.G.	Good	Fair	Poor
1300	850	700	400	275	125

Panther SDM-R

Similar to other Panthers, with stainless steel barrel and Harris bipod. Introduced 2007.

NIB	Exc.	V.G.	Good	Fair	Poor
1200	850	700	400	275	125

LRT-SASS

Semi-automatic rifle based on AR-15 design. Chambered in .308 Win., 18" stainless steel barrel with flash hider. Collapsible Vitor Clubfoot carbine stock and 19-round detachable magazine. Introduced 2006.

NIB	Exc.	V.G.	Good	Fair	Poor
1900	1600	1475	1000	600	350

LR-260

Similar to LRT-SASS, with 24" stainless steel barrel. Chambered in .260 Remington. Also available with 20" chrome-moly barrel as LR-260H. Introduced 2006.

NIB	Exc.	V.G.	Good	Fair	Poor
1300	1000	900	800	500	300

LR-243

Similar to LR-260, with 20" chrome-moly barrel. Chambered in .243 Win. Introduced 2006.

NIB	Exc.	V.G.	Good	Fair	Poor
1150	950	800	650	500	300

LR-204

Similar to LRT-260. Chambered in .204 Ruger. Introduced 2006.

NIB	Exc.	V.G.	Good	Fair	Poor
1000	800	650	500	400	300

Panther Arms 5.56 Oracle

Semi-automatic AR-style rifle chambered in 5.56 NATO. Features include 16" 4140 chrome-moly 1:9 barrel; phosphated steel bolt; oval Glacier Guard hand guard; flattop upper with Picatinny rail; aluminum lower; two 30-round magazines; Pardus 6-position telescoping stock. Also available on larger platform in .308 Winchester/7.62 NATO.

NIB	Exc.	V.G.	Good	Fair	Poor
700	575	500	400	300	200

Panther 3G1

Semi-automatic AR-style rifle chambered in 5.56 NATO. Features include 18" 416 stainless 1:9 barrel; phosphated steel bolt; VTAC modular hand guard; flattop upper with Picatinny rail; aluminum lower; two 30-round magazines; Magpul CTR adjustable stock.

NIB	Exc.	V.G.	Good	Fair	Poor
1000	850	700	600	400	300

Prairie Panther

Semi-automatic AR-style rifle chambered in 5.56 NATO. Features include 20" 416 stainless fluted heavy 1:8 barrel; phosphated steel bolt; free-floated carbon fiber hand guard; flattop upper with Picatinny rail; aluminum lower; two 30-round magazines; skeletonized Zytel stock; finished in King Desert Shadow camo overall.

NIB	Exc.	V.G.	Good	Fair	Poor
1150	1000	850	700	450	300

Panther RAPTR

Semi-automatic AR-style rifle chambered in 5.56 NATO. Features include 16" 4140 chrome-moly 1:9 barrel; phosphated steel bolt; ERGO Z-Rail 4-rail hand guard; front vertical grip; standard A-2 sights; aluminum lower; four 30-round magazines. Discontinued 2012.

NIB	Exc.	V.G.	Good	Fair	Poor
1350	1025	800	625	350	250

Panther REPR

Semi-automatic AR-style rifle chambered in .308 Win./7.62 NATO. Features include 18" 416 stainless steel 1:10 barrel; phosphated steel bolt; 4-rail free-floated hand guard; no sights; aluminum lower; two 19-round magazines; Coyote Brown camo finish overall.

NIB	Exc.	V.G.	Good	Fair	Poor
2100	1850	1400	1000	650	350

Panther 308 Mk12

Semi-automatic AR-style rifle chambered in .308 Win./7.62 NATO. Features include 16" 4140 chrome-moly heavy 1:10 barrel; phosphated steel bolt; 4-rail free-floated hand guard; flip-up front and rear sights; aluminum lower; two 19-round magazines; matte black finish overall; Magpul CTR adjustable stock.

NIB	Exc.	V.G.	Good	Fair	Poor
1500	1100	850	700	450	300

Panther A-15 Pump Rifle

Model has 20" 4150 steel heavy barrel, with A-2 style sights. Fitted with A-2 compensator and modified to slide-action. Weight about 8.5 lbs.

NIB	Exc.	V.G.	Good	Fair	Poor
1400	1050	700	600	500	300

Panther A-15 Pump Pistol

Same as above. Fitted with 10.5" barrel. Weight about 5 lbs.

NIB	Exc.	V.G.	Good	Fair	Poor
1450	1100	750	575	450	300

Panther DCM .22 LR

Rimfire version of Panther series, with 20" fluted stainless H-Bar barrel, A-2 upper receiver, National Match sights. Also available with 16" barrel (Panther AP4) and flat-top receiver. **NOTE:** Deduct $75 for AP4 model

NIB	Exc.	V.G.	Good	Fair	Poor
850	750	600	450	300	150

Panther Lite 308/338

Chambered for .308 Win. or .338 Federal. A-3 Flattop design, with 20" free-floated barrel and hand guard. Various options offered.

NIB	Exc.	V.G.	Good	Fair	Poor
1350	1200	900	650	400	200

Panther 6.5

Basic Panther model chambered for 6.5 Creedmoor. Stainless steel free-floated 24" barrel, A-3 Flattop upper, mil-spec stock.

NIB	Exc.	V.G.	Good	Fair	Poor
1100	975	750	550	350	200

6.8 SPCII Hunter

Chambered for Remington 6.8 SPC cartridge, with 18" barrel and Miculek compensator. A-3 Flattop design with forward assist. Skeletonized stock.

NIB	Exc.	V.G.	Good	Fair	Poor
1150	1025	800	600	400	250

300 AAC Blackout

Chambered for .300 AAC cartridge. Chrome-lined 16" heavy barrel comes with Blackout suppressor adapter. AP4 stock, free-float hand guard.

NIB	Exc.	V.G.	Good	Fair	Poor
1100	975	750	550	350	200

308 Recon

Similar to 300 AAC Blackout model, except chambered for .308 Winchester. Standard weight, 16" barrel with Blackout suppressor adapter. A-3 Flattop upper receiver, Magpul MOE stock with 4-Rail hand guard.

NIB	Exc.	V.G.	Good	Fair	Poor
1350	1200	1000	750	500	250

DREYSE

See—Rheinmetall

DRISCOLL, J.B.
Springfield, Massachusetts

Single-Shot Pocket Pistol

Small pistol chambered for .22 rimfire. Has 3.5" octagonal barrel that pivots downward for loading after trigger-like hook under breech is pulled. Spur trigger, silver-plated brass frame and blued barrel. Square butt is flared at bottom and grips are walnut. Approximately 200 manufactured in late 1860s.

NIB	Exc.	V.G.	Good	Fair	Poor
—	—	1000	375	100	50

DRULOV
Czech Republic

This Company was part of the national co-operative under communist rule when Czech Republic was part of Czechoslovakia. Formed in 1948 and specialized in low-cost but well made rimfire target pistols.

Model 70 Standard

A bolt-action single-shot pistol chambered for .22 LR. Knob at rear of frame opened the bolt. When bolt is closed firing pin is cocked. Barrel 9.75" long, with an adjustable front sight for windage. Rear sight is adjustable for elevation. Wooden wrap-around grips with thumb rest are standard. Weight about 44 oz.

NIB	Exc.	V.G.	Good	Fair	Poor
—	300	200	175	100	75

Model 70 Special

Same as above, with addition of set trigger.

NIB	Exc.	V.G.	Good	Fair	Poor
—	350	250	200	150	100

Model 75

Features set trigger, better sights and grip. Rear sight is fully adjustable.

NIB	Exc.	V.G.	Good	Fair	Poor
—	400	300	250	200	150

Pav

Target pistol introduced between WWI and WW II. Inexpensive pistol, with fixed front sight and notch for rear sight. Also a single-shot chambered for .22 LR cartridge. Barrel is 10.25"; weight about 35 oz.

Courtesy Orvel Reichert

NIB	Exc.	V.G.	Good	Fair	Poor
—	175	150	100	75	50

DSA, INC.
Barrington, Illinois

DSA, Inc. began selling its rifles to the public in 1996. Based on actual blueprints of famous FN/FAL rifle, SA58 rifles are made in the U.S. All SA58 rifles are fitted with fully adjustable gas system, Type I, II or III forged receiver, hand-lapped barrel, muzzle-brake, elevation adjustable post front sight, windage adjustable rear peep sight with 5 settings from 200 to 600 meters, detachable metric magazine, adjustable sling and hard case. DSA also manufactures a series of AR-15 type rifles and carbines. Virtually all parts are made by DSA.

SA58

SA58 24" Bull

Fitted with 24" stainless steel barrel and .308 match chamber. Overall length 44.5". Weight about 11.5 lbs.

NIB	Exc.	V.G.	Good	Fair	Poor
1750	1500	1150	800	500	300

SA58 21" Bull

Same as above. Fitted with 21" stainless steel barrel. Weight about 11.1 lbs.

NIB	Exc.	V.G.	Good	Fair	Poor
1750	1500	1150	800	500	300

SA58 Medium Contour

Offered with 21" barrel either stainless or blued steel. Weight about 10.5 lbs. **NOTE:** Add $250 for stainless steel.

NIB	Exc.	V.G.	Good	Fair	Poor
1550	1300	1150	800	500	300

SA58 Carbine

Fitted with 16.25" barrel cut for factory light bipod. Blued finish. Stainless steel version also available. Overall length 37.5". Weight about 8.35 lbs. **NOTE:** Add $250 for stainless steel.

NIB	Exc.	V.G.	Good	Fair	Poor
1600	1400	1150	800	500	300

SA58 Standard

Model has 21" barrel cut for factory light bipod. Weight about 8.75 lbs. Blued finish.

NIB	Exc.	V.G.	Good	Fair	Poor
1600	1400	1150	800	500	300

SA58 Tactical

Fitted with 16.25" fluted barrel, black synthetic stock, Type I receiver, adjustable sights and detachable magazine. Blued finish. Weight about 8.25 lbs.

NIB	Exc.	V.G.	Good	Fair	Poor
1600	1400	1150	800	500	300

SA58 Congo

This .308 model features 18" bipod-cut barrel, with short Belgian-style flash hider. Type I receiver with carry handle. Synthetic buttstock and pistol-grip. Aluminum lower. Detachable magazine. Adjustable sights. Weight about 8.6 lbs.

NIB	Exc.	V.G.	Good	Fair	Poor
1800	1550	1250	800	500	300

SA58 Para Congo

Fitted with Type II receiver, carry handle and 18" bipod-cut barrel. Short Belgian-style flash hider. Steel lower. Folding steel Para stock. Adjustable sights. Weight about 9.85 lbs.

NIB	Exc.	V.G.	Good	Fair	Poor
1800	1550	1250	800	500	300

SA58 Predator

Offered in .308, .260 Rem. or .243. Has Type I receiver, 16" or 19" medium carbine barrel with target crown. Green furniture. Aluminum lower. Picatinny rail. Weight about 9 lbs. with 16" barrel.

NIB	Exc.	V.G.	Good	Fair	Poor
1600	1450	1100	800	475	200

SA58 Graywolf

This .308 model fitted with 21" match grade barrel and target crown. Type I receiver. Aluminum lower. Extended safety. Picatinny rail. Target pistol-grip with standard or X-series buttstock. Versa-pod bipod. Weight about 13 lbs.

NIB	Exc.	V.G.	Good	Fair	Poor
2100	1600	1250	800	500	300

SA58 T48 Replica

Chambered for .308 cartridge and fitted with 21" barrel. Replica Browning flash hider. Supplied with 10- or 20-round fixed magazine and stripper clip top cover. Wooden stock. Weight about 9.7 lbs.

NIB	Exc.	V.G.	Good	Fair	Poor
1600	1400	1250	800	475	200

DS-AR
S1 Rifle

Introduced in 2004, this 5.56-caliber rifle features 20" or 24" bull barrel. Picatinny gas black sight base. Flattop receiver. Free-floating aluminum hand guard. A-2 stock. Ten-round magazine. Discontinued.

NIB	Exc.	V.G.	Good	Fair	Poor
950	750	600	425	225	150

CVI Carbine

Similar to model above, with 16" barrel, forged front sight base and integral muzzle-brake. D-4 hand guard. Fixed CAR buttstock. Ten-round magazine. Discontinued.

NIB	Exc.	V.G.	Good	Fair	Poor
900	700	600	425	225	150

LE4 Carbine

As above, with pre-ban features. For law enforcement only. Discontinued.

NIB	Exc.	V.G.	Good	Fair	Poor
1150	850	600	425	225	150

DS-AR S Series Rifle

Introduced in 2005. Chambered for .223 cartridge. Fitted with choice of 16", 20" or 24" stainless steel match grade bull barrel. A-2 stock with free-floating hand guard. Flattop receiver, National Match 2 stage trigger. Magazine capacity 10, 20 or 30 rounds.

NIB	Exc.	V.G.	Good	Fair	Poor
1350	1050	800	525	225	150

DS-AR Carbine

Chambered for .223 cartridge. Fitted with 16" D4 barrel and flash hider. Choice of: fixed or collapsible stock; forged flattop or A-2 upper receiver. Magazine capacity 10, 20 or 30 rounds. Introduced in 2005.

NIB	Exc.	V.G.	Good	Fair	Poor
1350	1050	800	525	225	150

DS-AR Rifle

As above, with 20" heavy barrel, flash hider and fixed stock. Introduced in 2005.

NIB	Exc.	V.G.	Good	Fair	Poor
1350	1050	800	525	225	150

DS-AR DCM Rifle

Chambered for .223 cartridge with Wylde chamber. Fitted with 20" match grade Badger barrel. DCM free-float hand guard system. National Match two-stage trigger. National Match rear sight. A-2 upper receiver. Introduced in 2005.

NIB	Exc.	V.G.	Good	Fair	Poor
1595	1250	950	625	425	225

DS-AR CQB MRP

Introduced in 2005. Features 16" chrome lined barrel and A-2 flash hider. Collapsible stock with MRP quad rail. Monolithic rail platform upper. Flattop or A-2 upper receiver. Supplied with 30-round magazine.

NIB	Exc.	V.G.	Good	Fair	Poor
2595	1850	1400	1025	600	300

DSA Z4 Gas Trap Carbine (GTC)

Introduced in 2005. Fitted with 16" chrome lined barrel, M4 profile fluted and Vortec flash hider. Collapsible 6-position stock, with free float tactical rail. Gas trap system. Flattop upper receiver. Magazine capacity 10, 20 or 30 rounds.

NIB	Exc.	V.G.	Good	Fair	Poor
1675	1250	950	625	425	225

ZM-4 Series

Series of AR-15 type models. Features forged upper and lower receivers, flattop upper, fixed or collapsible stocks, 16" or 20" barrels, black finish or OD Green. **NOTE:** Add $200 for Spartan model with Robar bolt, Magpul trigger guard, Phantom Flashider, 30-round magazine.

NIB	Exc.	V.G.	Good	Fair	Poor
750	650	600	500	300	150

RPD Traditional Rifle

Chambered for 7.62x39 cartridge, this belt-fed semi-automatic rifle comes with two 100-round belt and drum sets. Barrel length 20.5". Stock is wood. Weight about 17 lbs. Introduced in 2013.

NIB	Exc.	V.G.	Good	Fair	Poor
1800	1600	1250	900	750	500

RPD Carbine

Similar to Traditional Rifle, with 17.5" fluted barrel, fully adjustable AR-style stock with SAW-style pistol-grip and lighter weight alloy frame. Weight about 14 lbs. Introduced in 2013.

NIB	Exc.	V.G.	Good	Fair	Poor
2400	2100	1500	1200	850	600

BOLT-ACTION RIFLES

DS-MP1

Bolt-action rifle chambered for .308 cartridge. Built on custom Remington 700 action. Fitted with 21" Badger barrel, with target crown. Black McMillan A5 stock. Matte black finish. Introduced in 2004.

NIB	Exc.	V.G.	Good	Fair	Poor
2800	2100	1675	1050	650	425

HANDGUNS

B&T TP9 Tactical Pistol

Swiss made recoil-operated rotating-bolt semi-automatic. Chambered in 9mm Parabellum. Semi-automatic civilian-legal version of B&T TP9SF select-fire sub-machine gun. Imported from Switzerland by DSA from 2008 to 2011.

NIB	Exc.	V.G.	Good	Fair	Poor
1100	950	775	600	475	350

SA58TAC

Based on FAL design with 8" barrel. Chambered in 7.62x39. This is considered a pistol. Features include a 20-shot magazine, alloy lower receiver, SAW pistol-grip, Para extended scope mount and black nylon stock. Introduced in 2013.

NIB	Exc.	V.G.	Good	Fair	Poor
1500	1200	1000	750	450	325

DUBIEL ARMS CO.
Sherman, Texas

Dubiel Arms was a manufacturer of custom bolt-action rifles in Sherman, Texas from 1975 to about 1987. Joseph Dubiel and Dr. John Tyson were founders and co-owners of the company. Dubiel's father was John Dubiel, a well-known gunsmith in Oklahoma in the 1920s and '30s. It is believed that Texas rifles were based on his original designs. Actions featured a bolt with five locking lugs and a short 36-degree bolt rotation. Rifles were available with many options, stock designs and custom

features. Made in most popular centerfire calibers. Several Dubiel rifles are on display at the Buffalo Bill Historical Center in Cody, Wyoming. In May of 2012, co-founder Dr. John Tyson, made a presentation of nine rifles to the NRA National Firearms Museum in Fairfax, Virginia. Prices shown are estimated values of basic models. Various options would increase these values significantly.

NIB	Exc.	V.G.	Good	Fair	Poor
5000	3500	2800	2000	—	—

DUMOULIN
Herstal, Belgium

Guns produced by Ernest Dumoulin are essentially handmade to customer's order. They are of highest quality, both in materials and workmanship. There are many options available that have a tremendous impact on value fluctuations. Models and values listed here are base prices.

SHOTGUNS

Europa Model

Side-by-side double-barrel chambered for 12-, 20-, 28-gauge and .410 bore. Available in any length barrel and choke combination. Anson & Deeley boxlock action and automatic ejectors. One has the option of double- or single-selective triggers and choice of six different moderate engraving patterns. Select walnut stock is oil-finished. Introduced in 1989.

NIB	Exc.	V.G.	Good	Fair	Poor
3500	2750	1950	1250	800	400

Leige Model

Side-by-side double-barrel chambered for 12-, 16-, 20- and 28-gauge. Similar to Europa, with greater degree of finish and more engraving. Walnut is of a higher grade. Introduced in 1986.

NIB	Exc.	V.G.	Good	Fair	Poor
5750	4200	2750	1500	950	425

Continental Model

Side-by-side chambered for 12-, 20-, 28-gauge and .410 bore. Barrel lengths and chokes are on custom-order basis. A true sidelock action, with automatic ejectors and choice of triggers. Six different engraving patterns. Stock is made of high grade hand-checkered oil-finished walnut. Introduced in 1989.

NIB	Exc.	V.G.	Good	Fair	Poor
7500	6000	4500	3000	1500	400

Etendart Model

Side-by-side chambered for 12-, 20- and 28-gauge. Best grade side-by-side built on purely made-to-order basis. Profusely engraved and uses exhibition grade walnut in its stock. There are 12 different engraving patterns from which to choose. Cost is according to embellishments chosen. Values given here are for basic model.

NIB	Exc.	V.G.	Good	Fair	Poor
14500	11000	8500	4000	3000	700

Superposed Express International

An over/under chambered for 20-gauge. Furnished with a set of rifle barrels. Customer's choice of seven calibers. Walnut is a deluxe grade and engraving available at extra cost. Made-to-order gun. Value here for the most basic model. Discontinued in 1985

NIB	Exc.	V.G.	Good	Fair	Poor
—	2500	2000	1250	750	400

Boss Royal Model

Best grade over/under chambered for 12-, 20- and 28-gauge. Full side-lock gun made to customer's specifications, using finest materials and workmanship available. Introduced in 1987.

NIB	Exc.	V.G.	Good	Fair	Poor
18500	15000	12000	8000	4500	700

Eagle Model Combination Gun

This model has a rifle or shotgun barrel that is chambered for 12- or 20-gauge. Rifle calibers available are .22 Hornet, .222 Remington, .222 Remington Magnum, 6mm, .243, .25-06, .30-06, 6.5 x 57R, 7 x 57R, 8 x 57JRS and 9.3 x 74R. Action is boxlock, with automatic ejectors. Other specifications are on custom-order basis. Introduced in 1989.

NIB	Exc.	V.G.	Good	Fair	Poor
2750	2250	1500	950	750	400

DOUBLE RIFLES

Europa I

Made-to-order over/under double-barreled rifle. Available in same calibers as Eagle Combination gun. Has Anson & Deeley boxlock. All other options to customer's specifications.

NIB	Exc.	V.G.	Good	Fair	Poor
6000	4700	3500	4000	1250	500

Continental I Model

More deluxe over/under rifle, with true sidelock-action. Calibers the same as Europa. Specifications are to customer's order, with 12 engraving patterns to choose from at extra cost. Introduced in 1989.

NIB	Exc.	V.G.	Good	Fair	Poor
9000	7150	5500	4000	2000	600

Pionnier Express Rifle

Side-by-side double rifle chambered for .22 Hornet through .600 Nitro Express. Anson & Deeley boxlock-action and quite deluxe throughout. Specifications are to customer's order. There are basically 12 models available (P-1 through P-XII). Differences among these models are in degree of ornamentation and quality of walnut used for the stock. Values range from approximately $10,000 to $15,000 for basic models.

Aristocrat Model

Low-profile single-shot chambered for all calibers up to .375 H&H. Deluxe made-to-order rifle, with exhibition-grade walnut and 12 engraving patterns available.

NIB	Exc.	V.G.	Good	Fair	Poor
—	9500	7500	5800	3000	700

BOLT-ACTION RIFLES

Centurion Model

Custom-order rifle built on Mauser or Sako action. Chambered for all calibers from .270 to .458 Winchester Magnum. Barrel lengths available were 21.5", 24" and 25.5"; many engraving options from which to choose. Stock of deluxe French walnut, with rosewood fore-end tip and pistol-grip cap. Discontinued in 1986.

NIB	Exc.	V.G.	Good	Fair	Poor
7500	6000	5000	4000	—	—

Centurion Classic

Similar to Mauser-actioned Centurion. Chambered for non-Magnum calibers only. Walnut used for stock is a better grade.

NIB	Exc.	V.G.	Good	Fair	Poor
1275	950	750	600	500	400

Diane

More deluxe version of Centurion Classic.

NIB	Exc.	V.G.	Good	Fair	Poor
1800	1550	1250	900	650	500

Amazone

A 20" barreled full-length stocked upgraded version of Diane.

NIB	Exc.	V.G.	Good	Fair	Poor
2100	1750	1400	950	700	500

Bavaria Deluxe

Similar to Centurion, with same barrel lengths and calibers available. Engraving styles available are more deluxe. Discontinued in 1985.

NIB	Exc.	V.G.	Good	Fair	Poor
2350	1800	1400	950	700	500

Safari Model

Similar to Bavaria Deluxe. Chambered for heavy Magnum calibers only.

NIB	Exc.	V.G.	Good	Fair	Poor
3275	2700	1900	1450	900	500

Safari Sportsman

Built on a Magnum Mauser action. Chambered for .375 H&H, .404 Jeffreys, .416 Rigby and .505 Gibbs. A true big game rifle. Made available in 1986.

NIB	Exc.	V.G.	Good	Fair	Poor
4500	3650	2400	1550	1100	—

African Pro

More deluxe version of Safari Sportsman. Folding leaf rear sight, hooded front sight and ebony or buffalo horn fore-end tip.

NIB	Exc.	V.G.	Good	Fair	Poor
5200	3950	2700	1700	1300	750

DUSEK, F.
Opocno, Czech Republic

Dusek commenced business in mid-1920s and continued to make firearms through WWII. They manufactured pistols for Nazi Germany under the contract code "aek". After the war, the communists took over and Dusek's designs were redelegated to the CZ factory.

Perla

This 6.35mm pistol has a fixed barrel and open-topped slide. Resembles a Walther design and is striker-fired. Slide is marked "Automat Pistole Perla 6.35mm"; grips "Perla 6.35". Dusek made this model from early 1930s until WWII.

NIB	Exc.	V.G.	Good	Fair	Poor
—	335	225	165	100	80

Duo

DAK-5 replace with DAK-6-7. **NOTE:** Nazi-marked examples will bring a 25 percent premium.

Courtesy J.B. Wood

NIB	Exc.	V.G.	Good	Fair	Poor
—	375	250	195	100	80

84 GUN CO.
Eighty Four, Pennsylvania

In business for a brief time in early 1970s. Company produced three basic bolt-action rifles—each in four grades that differ in amounts of embellishment and grades of wood. There is little known about this company and its products. Basic models are listed and values are approximate.

Classic Rifle

Grade 1 - Grade 4 available. $650—$1800

Lobo Rifle

Grade 1 - Grade 4 available. $625—$2700

Pennsylvania Rifle

Grade 1 - Grade 4 available. $625—$2800

E.M.F. CO., INC.
Santa Ana, California
See—Uberti, Aldo

An importer and distributor of quality Italian-made reproduction firearms. Most of its offerings are listed in the section dealing with Aldo Uberti firearms. E.M.F. also markets a line of 1911 pistols made in the Philippines.

HANDGUNS

Hartford Bisley

Single-action revolver fitted with Colt Bisley grip. Chambered for .45 Long Colt as well as .32-20, .357 Magnum, .38-40 and .44-40 calibers. Barrel lengths 4.75", 5.5 and 7.5". Plain walnut grips.

NIB	Exc.	V.G.	Good	Fair	Poor
525	425	300	225	145	105

Hartford Express

Single-action Colt SAA frame and barrel, with Colt Lightning-style grip. Chambered for .45 Long Colt in 4.75", 5.5" or 7.5" barrel lengths.

NIB	Exc.	V.G.	Good	Fair	Poor
525	425	300	225	145	105

Hartford Pinkerton

Features 4" barrel, with ejector and bird's-head grip. Chambered for 45 Long Colt, .32-20, .357 Magnum, .38-40, .44-40 and .44 Special.

NIB	Exc.	V.G.	Good	Fair	Poor
525	425	300	225	145	105

Russian Model 1875

Top-break action in .44 Russian or .45 Colt, with various barrel lengths. Imported from 2006 to 2008.

NIB	Exc.	V.G.	Good	Fair	Poor
750	650	500	400	300	200

Remington Model 1875 Army Frontier

Offered in .357 Magnum, .44-40 or .45 Colt, with 5.5" or 7.5" barrel. Imported from 2003 to 2013. **NOTE:** Add $200 to $250 for engraved models or nickel finish.

NIB	Exc.	V.G.	Good	Fair	Poor
450	375	325	275	200	150

Schofield Model

Replica of Smith & Wesson Schofield in .45 Colt. Made by Uberti and imported from 2000 to 2003.

NIB	Exc.	V.G.	Good	Fair	Poor
600	500	450	350	275	200

DAKOTA SAA SERIES

E.M.F. has imported this brand of Colt-style single-action revolvers made by several Italian manufacturers since the 1970s. Made in standard SAA calibers and barrel lengths.

Dakota Old Model

With brass backstrap and trigger guard. **NOTE:** Add 50 to 75 percent for engraved models.

NIB	Exc.	V.G.	Good	Fair	Poor
425	350	300	250	200	175

Dakota New Model

With black nickel backstrap and trigger guard. **NOTE:** Add 35 percent for satin nickel finish; 45 percent for bright nickel finish.

NIB	Exc.	V.G.	Good	Fair	Poor
450	375	300	250	200	175

Dakota II

With brass backstrap and trigger guard. Matte black finish.

NIB	Exc.	V.G.	Good	Fair	Poor
350	300	275	225	175	150

Citadel 1911

These 1911 A1-type pistols are chambered in .45 ACP or 9mm, with 3.5" or 5" barrels. Matte black, satin nickel, bright nickel finish. Optional Hogue green, black or sand grips. **NOTE:** Add $50 for Hogue grips.

NIB	Exc.	V.G.	Good	Fair	Poor
500	425	350	300	250	200

RIFLES

Lightning Standard

This replica of Colt Lightning slide-action rifle was chambered in .357 Magnun, .44-40 Win., or .45 Colt. Choice of 20", 24" or 26" round or octagon barrel. Straight-grip walnut stock and fore-end, semi-buckhorn rear sight. Deluxe model has color case-hardened finish, checkered stock. Super Deluxe model has coin-finished frame with engraving and high grade checkered walnut. Made by Pedersoli and imported from 2008 to 2013. **NOTE:** Add $150 for Deluxe; $250 for Super Deluxe.

NIB	Exc.	V.G.	Good	Fair	Poor
1250	1050	800	625	500	400

Rolling Block

Replica of Remington Rolling Block rifle in .45-70 caliber, with 26" (carbine) or 30" octagon barrel. Target Deluxe model has checkered grip, case-hardened finish, silver fore-end cap. Made by Pedersoli and imported from 1991 to 2013. **NOTE:** Add $300 for Target Deluxe.

NIB	Exc.	V.G.	Good	Fair	Poor
850	750	600	400	325	250

1874 Sharps Sporting or Militay Rifle

In .45-70, .45 Colt or .45-120 calibers. Reproduction of Sharps Single Shot was imported from 1999 to 2008 and reintroduced in 2013. **NOTE:** Deduct 20 percent for older model.

NIB	Exc.	V.G.	Good	Fair	Poor
1350	1200	850	700	350	300

Down Under Sharps Model 1874

This reproduction of Model 1874 Sharps rifle popularized in the 1990 movie "Quigley Down Under" starring Tom Selleck. Chambered in .45-70, .45-90, .45-110 and .45-120, with 34" heavy octagon barrel, double-set triggers and deluxe checkered walnut stock. Values shown are for .45-70. **NOTE:** Add $100 for other calibers.

NIB	Exc.	V.G.	Good	Fair	Poor
2000	1700	1350	1000	400	300

Winchester Lever Actions

E.M.F. has imported reproductions of several famous Winchester lever-action rifles and carbines since 1987. Among these are: Model 1860 in .44-40 or .45 Colt; 1866 Yellow Boy in .22 LR and WMR, .32-20, .38-40, .38 Special, .44-40 and .45 Colt; 1873 in .22 WMR, .32-20, .38-40, .44 Special, .44-40 and .45 Colt; 1886/71 in .45-70; and Model 1892 in .357 Magnum, .44 Magnum and .45 Colt.

Model 1860

NIB	Exc.	V.G.	Good	Fair	Poor
900	750	550	400	300	200

Model 1866

NIB	Exc.	V.G.	Good	Fair	Poor
750	625	500	350	250	200

Model 1873

NIB	Exc.	V.G.	Good	Fair	Poor
900	750	550	400	300	200

Model 1886/71

NIB	Exc.	V.G.	Good	Fair	Poor
1700	1500	1350	1000	400	300

Model 1892

NIB	Exc.	V.G.	Good	Fair	Poor
450	400	350	300	200	150

EAGLE ARMS, DIVISION OF ARMALITE
Geneseo, Illinois

Previous manufacturer of AR-15 type rifles from 1990 to 2005. From 1995 to 2002, a division of ArmaLite, Inc.

PRE-BAN MODELS

Golden Eagle

Model identical in design to AR-15. Fitted with 20" stainless steel extra-heavy barrel. National Match sights and two-stage trigger. Weight about 9.4 lbs.

NIB	Exc.	V.G.	Good	Fair	Poor
1050	950	750	575	400	225

HBAR

Similar to above, with heavy 20" barrel. Weight about 8 lbs.

NIB	Exc.	V.G.	Good	Fair	Poor
1250	950	750	575	400	225

SPR

Similar to above, with exception of detachable carry handle. Weight about 7.6 lbs.

NIB	Exc.	V.G.	Good	Fair	Poor
1250	950	750	575	400	225

M4C Carbine

Features 16" barrel, with 4.33" flash suppressor. Retractable stock. Weight about 6.2 lbs.

NIB	Exc.	V.G.	Good	Fair	Poor
1250	950	750	575	400	225

M4A1C Carbine

Similar to above, with detachable carry handle. Weight about 6 lbs.

NIB	Exc.	V.G.	Good	Fair	Poor
1250	950	750	575	400	225

POST-BAN MODELS

Golden Eagle

Reintroduction of earlier model. Limited production in 2002.

NIB	Exc.	V.G.	Good	Fair	Poor
1050	850	750	575	400	225

AR-10 Match Rifle

Chambered for .308 Win., with 20" or 24" chrome-moly barrel. Features include flattop upper receiver, black stock and forearm, 10-round magazine.

NIB	Exc.	V.G.	Good	Fair	Poor
1000	900	750	500	400	200

Model M15 Series

Chambered for .223 or .308 in various AR-15 type configurations. Manufactured from 2002 to 2005. **NOTE:** Add $200 for .308-caliber; $150 for Eagle Spirit model with National Match accessories.

ECHAVE & ARIZMENDI
Eibar, Spain

Basque, Echasa, Dickson, or Dickson Special Agent

These four pistols are the same semi-automatic pistols. Chambered in .22 LR, 6.35mm, 7.65mm and 9mmK respectively. Magazine capacities are 10, 9, 7 and 6 rounds. Manufactured with alloy frames and various finish combinations. Specific model names are stamped on slides and grip plates.

Courtesy James Rankin

NIB	Exc.	V.G.	Good	Fair	Poor
—	295	185	125	90	50

Bronco Model 1913

Semi-automatic pistol in caliber 6.35mm. Patterned after Browning Model 1906, with squeeze grip safety. "Bronco" stamped on slide and each side of grip plate.

Courtesy James Rankin

NIB	Exc.	V.G.	Good	Fair	Poor
—	295	185	125	90	50

Bronco Model 1918

Semi-automatic pistol chambered for both 6.35mm or 7.65mm. Both are patterned after Browning Model 1906, with squeeze grip safety. The 7.65mm pistol approximately .5" longer and higher than 6.35mm. Magazine capacity: 7.65mm 7 rounds; 6.35mm 6 rounds.

Courtesy James Rankin

NIB	Exc.	V.G.	Good	Fair	Poor
—	295	185	125	90	50

Echasa

Similar to 6.35mm Bronco, without grip safety. Marked "Model 1916".

NIB	Exc.	V.G.	Good	Fair	Poor
—	295	185	125	90	50

Lightning

Renamed version of Bronco in 6.35mm.

NIB	Exc.	V.G.	Good	Fair	Poor
—	295	185	125	90	50

Lur Panzer

Copy of Luger toggle-lock-action chambered for .22 rimfire. Almost an exact copy, except for different trigger assembly and less robust mainspring. Marked "Lur Cal.22 LR Made in Spain". Plastic grips have "Panzer" molded into them.

NIB	Exc.	V.G.	Good	Fair	Poor
—	265	225	150	125	100

Pathfinder

Semi-automatic pistol similar to above Bronco. In calibers 6.35mm and 7.65mm. Sold in U.S. by Stoeger. The 7.65mm Pathfinder holds 12 rounds. Values listed are for both pistol models.

NIB	Exc.	V.G.	Good	Fair	Poor
—	295	185	125	90	50

Protector Model 1915 and 1918

Semi-automatic pistol in caliber 6.35mm. Similar to Echasa model. "Protector" stamped on slide while grip plates have various logos of firms that marketed the pistol.

Courtesy James Rankin

NIB	Exc.	V.G.	Good	Fair	Poor
—	275	185	100	70	40

Selecta Model 1918

Semi-automatic pistol chambered for 7.65mm cartridge. Patterned after Protector, but chambered for 7.65mm. "Selecta" stamped on slide and Echave Arizmendi logo on each of grip plates.

Courtesy James Rankin

NIB	Exc.	V.G.	Good	Fair	Poor
—	295	185	125	90	50

ECHEVERRIA, STAR-BONIFACIO SA (STAR)
Eibar, Spain

An old-line Spanish company that survived Spanish Civil War. Founded in 1908 by Jean Echeverria, but early records of the company were lost during the civil war. Early pistols the company produced were patterned after Mannlicher designs and trade name Star was the closest thing to Steyr that could be used. After the close of WWI, the company began production of open-topped slide Star for which they have become known. They also produced a large 1911-type pistol that was successful. During the civil war, the plant was damaged and company records destroyed; but after cessation of hostilities, they were one of only three gun companies that were allowed to remain in business. Company is now defunct.

Star Model 1908

First pistol produced under Star banner. A Mannlicher copy chambered for 6.35mm, 3" fixed barrel and open-topped slide. Detachable magazine holds 8 shots. Finish blued, grips are checkered plastic. Slide marked "Automatic Pistol Star Patent".

Courtesy James Rankin

NIB	Exc.	V.G.	Good	Fair	Poor
—	350	275	200	150	100

Star Model 1914

Similar to Model 1908, with 5" barrel and larger grips that have Star name molded into them. Model was first to have six-pointed star surrounded by rays of light (that became Star trademark) stamped on its slide.

Courtesy James Rankin

NIB	Exc.	V.G.	Good	Fair	Poor
—	350	275	200	150	100

Star Model 1919

Copy of Mannlicher design. Differs from its predecessors chiefly in the way pistol is disassembled. Has a spring catch at top of trigger guard, a small spur on hammer and magazine release was relocated to a button behind the trigger guard instead of a catch at bottom of butt. Chambered for 6.35mm, 7.65mm and 9mm short, with various barrel lengths offered. Maker's name, as well as Star trademark stamped into slide. Produced until 1929.

Courtesy James Rankin

NIB	Exc.	V.G.	Good	Fair	Poor
—	350	275	200	150	100

Star Model 1919 New Variation

Same as above, with full spur hammer.

Courtesy James Rankin

NIB	Exc.	V.G.	Good	Fair	Poor
—	350	275	200	150	100

Modelo Militar

Represents the first pistol Star produced that was not a Mannlicher design copy. Copied from Colt 1911. Chambered initially for 9mm Largo in hopes of securing a military contract. When this contract was awarded to Astra, Star chambered Model 1919 for .38 Super, .45 ACP and put it on the commercial market. Model like Colt 1911—has a Browning-type swinging link and same type of lock up. However, there is no grip safety and thumb safety functions differently. **NOTE:** Add 30 percent for guns marked .38 Super.

NIB	Exc.	V.G.	Good	Fair	Poor
—	425	325	245	175	125

Star Model A

Modification of Model 1919. Chambered for 7.65mm, 7.63mm Mauser, 9mm Largo and .45 ACP cartridge. Slide similar in appearance to 1911 Colt. Spur hammer has a small hole in it. Early models had no grip safety, but later production added this feature. Some models slotted for addition of shoulder stock.

NIB	Exc.	V.G.	Good	Fair	Poor
—	425	325	245	175	125

Star Model B

Similar to Model A, except almost an exact copy of Colt 1911. Chambered for 9mm Parabellum. Has a spur hammer with no hole. Introduced in 1928.

Courtesy Orvel Reichert

NIB	Exc.	V.G.	Good	Fair	Poor
—	425	325	245	175	125

Star Model C

Model B chambered for 9mm Browning Long cartridge. Manufactured in 1920s.

NIB	Exc.	V.G.	Good	Fair	Poor
—	350	265	175	125	90

Star Model CO

Pocket pistol similar to early open-topped Star pistols. Chambered for 6.35mm cartridge. Finish blued, with checkered plastic grips that bear Star name and logo. Manufactured between 1930 and 1957.

Courtesy James Rankin

NIB	Exc.	V.G.	Good	Fair	Poor
—	275	195	125	100	75

Star Model D

Medium-sized pistol similar in appearance to smaller Model A. Chambered for 9mm Short cartridge. Called "Police and Pocket Model" after it was adopted by the Spanish police. Manufactured between 1930 and 1941.

NIB	Exc.	V.G.	Good	Fair	Poor
—	500	400	300	200	100

Star Model DK Starfire

Single-action .380, with 3.125" barrel, fixed sights, brown plastic grips. Imported from 1957 until 1968. Alloy frame available in blue finish or various colors. **NOTE:** Add $100 for colored frame.

Courtesy James Rankin

NIB	Exc.	V.G.	Good	Fair	Poor
550	425	400	350	300	150

Star Model E

Pocket pistol chambered for 6.35mm cartridge. A 2.5" barrel and external hammer. Detachable magazine holds 5 rounds. Finish blued, with checkered plastic grips. Manufactured between 1932 and 1941.

NIB	Exc.	V.G.	Good	Fair	Poor
—	250	195	165	110	80

Star Model F

First of .22-caliber Star pistols. Has a 4" barrel, 10-shot magazine and fixed sights. Finish blued and plastic grips checkered. Manufactured between 1942 and 1967.

NIB	Exc.	V.G.	Good	Fair	Poor
—	300	265	200	110	75

Star Model F Target

Similar to Model F, with 6" barrel.

NIB	Exc.	V.G.	Good	Fair	Poor
—	325	275	210	125	100

Star Model F Sport

Has a 5" barrel. Manufactured between 1962 and 1967.

NIB	Exc.	V.G.	Good	Fair	Poor
—	325	275	210	125	100

Star Model F Olympic

Has a 6" barrel and adjustable sights. Furnished with muzzle-brake and barrel weights. Manufactured between 1942 and 1967.

Courtesy James Rankin

NIB	Exc.	V.G.	Good	Fair	Poor
—	350	265	175	125	90

Star Model F Olympic Rapid Fire

Similar to Olympic. Chambered for .22 Short only.

NIB	Exc.	V.G.	Good	Fair	Poor
—	375	295	185	150	125

Star Model FR

Has an adjustable sight and a slide stop. The 4" barrel is heavier with flattened sides. Manufactured between 1967 and 1972.

NIB	Exc.	V.G.	Good	Fair	Poor
—	325	275	210	125	100

Star Model FRS

Similar to Model FR, with 6" barrel. Also available chrome-plated, with white checkered plastic grips. Introduced in 1967.

NIB	Exc.	V.G.	Good	Fair	Poor
—	295	225	175	125	100

Star Model FM

Heavier-framed version of Model FRS. Has a 4.5" barrel. Available in blue or chrome-plated. Introduced in 1972.

NIB	Exc.	V.G.	Good	Fair	Poor
—	325	275	210	125	100

Star Model H

Similar to old Model CO—only larger in size. Chambered for 7.65mm cartridge. Manufactured between 1932 and 1941.

NIB	Exc.	V.G.	Good	Fair	Poor
—	250	195	150	125	100

Star Model HK

Pocket-sized version of Model F. Chambered for .22 Short. Has a 2.5" barrel. Quite scarce on today's market.

NIB	Exc.	V.G.	Good	Fair	Poor
—	325	275	210	125	100

Star Model HN

Simply Model H chambered for 9mm Short cartridge. Manufactured and discontinued same time as Model H was.

NIB	Exc.	V.G.	Good	Fair	Poor
—	275	202	165	125	100

Star Model I

Improved version of Model H, with 4" barrel and re-contoured grip. Chambered for 7.65mm and produced until 1941. After the war it was resumed and survived until mid-1950s. Replaced by modernized Model IR that would be valued approximately the same.

NIB	Exc.	V.G.	Good	Fair	Poor
—	250	195	150	125	100

Star Model M

Similar to Model B. Chambered for .38 Auto (NOT .38 Super) cartridge.

NIB	Exc.	V.G.	Good	Fair	Poor
—	375	295	185	150	125

Star Model P

Post-war version of Model B. Fitted with 5" barrel. Chambered for .45 ACP cartridge. Checkered walnut grips and blued finish.

NIB	Exc.	V.G.	Good	Fair	Poor
—	400	350	265	195	125

Star Model CU "Starlet"

Similar to Model CO, with an alloy frame that was anodized in black, blue, gray, green or gold. A steel slide that is blued or chrome-plated. Checkered white plastic grips. Chambered for .25 ACP cartridge. Has a 2.5" barrel, fixed sights and 5-shot magazine. Introduced in 1975 and not imported after 1986.

NIB	Exc.	V.G.	Good	Fair	Poor
—	250	175	145	100	75

Star Model 1941 S

Add 100 percent to prices listed for pistols issued to Spanish Air Force, with box cleaning rod, instruction sheet and two numbered magazines.

Courtesy Richard M. Kumor Sr.

NIB	Exc.	V.G.	Good	Fair	Poor
—	250	210	175	125	75

Star Model BKS "Starlight"

Smallest locked-breech automatic chambered for 9mm cartridge at the time. Has an alloy frame and 4.25" barrel. Similar in appearance to scaled-down Colt 1911, without grip safety. Has an 8-shot magazine. Either blued or chrome-plated, with checkered plastic grips. Manufactured between 1970 and 1981.

NIB	Exc.	V.G.	Good	Fair	Poor
—	325	275	210	125	100

Star Model PD

Chambered for .45 ACP cartridge. Has a 4" barrel, alloy frame, 6-shot magazine, adjustable sights. Blued, with checkered walnut grips. Introduced in 1975.

NIB	Exc.	V.G.	Good	Fair	Poor
400	325	275	225	175	125

Star Model BM

Steel-framed 9mm styled after Colt 1911. Has an 8-shot magazine and 4" barrel. Available either blued or chrome-plated.

NIB	Exc.	V.G.	Good	Fair	Poor
350	300	250	200	150	125

Star Model BKM

Similar to Model BM, with alloy frame.

NIB	Exc.	V.G.	Good	Fair	Poor
375	325	275	225	175	125

Star Model 28

First of Star's Super 9s. Double-action semi-automatic chambered for 9mm Parabellum cartridge. Has a 4.25" barrel and steel frame. Magazine holds 15 shots. Construction of this pistol was totally modular and has no screws in its design. Blued, with checkered synthetic grips. Manufactured in 1983 and 1984.

NIB	Exc.	V.G.	Good	Fair	Poor
425	365	295	200	150	100

Star Model 30M

Improved version of Model 28, that is quite similar in appearance. Introduced in 1985.

NIB	Exc.	V.G.	Good	Fair	Poor
450	350	300	250	200	125

Star Model 30/PK

Similar to Models 28 and 30M, with lightweight alloy frame.

NIB	Exc.	V.G.	Good	Fair	Poor
450	350	300	250	200	125

Megastar

Double-action semi-automatic pistol chambered for 10mm or .45 ACP cartridge. Features a three-position ambidextrous selective decocking lever, rubber grips, combat-style trigger guard, slotted hammer and checkered mainspring housing. Barrel length 4.6"; magazine capacity 12 rounds. Available in blue or Starvel (brushed chrome). Weight 47.6 oz.

NIB	Exc.	V.G.	Good	Fair	Poor
500	450	350	250	200	100

Firestar M43, M40, and M45

Compact large caliber semi-automatic pistol offered in: M43 9mm; M45 .45 ACP; M40 .40 S&W. Features an ambidextrous safety, steel frame and slide, checkered rubber grips. Barrel: 3.4" on M43 and M40; 3.6" on M45. Choice of blue or Starvel (brushed chrome) finish. Finger rest magazine optional. Weight: M43 and M40 30 oz.; M45 35 oz. Introduced in 1990.

NIB	Exc.	V.G.	Good	Fair	Poor
400	300	250	200	150	100

Starfire Model 31P

Evolved from Models 28 and 30. Chambered for either 9mm Parabellum or .40 S&W. Trigger action is double-/single-action. Barrel length 3.9". Fitted with two-position safety/decocking lever. Magazine capacity: 9mm 15 rounds; .40 S&W 11 rounds. Weight 39 oz.

NIB	Exc.	V.G.	Good	Fair	Poor
425	350	300	250	200	100

Starfire Model 31PK

Similar to Model 31P. Built on an alloy frame. Chambered for 9mm only, with 15-round magazine capacity. Weight 30 oz.

NIB	Exc.	V.G.	Good	Fair	Poor
400	325	275	225	200	100

Ultrastar

Introduced in 1994. Compact 9mm or .40 S&W semi-automatic pistol. Polymer frame features 3.57" barrel, 9-round magazine, blued finish and overall length of 7". Weight about 26 oz. Has a double-action operating system, windage adjustable rear sight and ambidextrous two-position safety.

NIB	Exc.	V.G.	Good	Fair	Poor
400	365	305	275	200	100

ECLIPSE
Enterprise Gun Works
Pittsburgh, Pennsylvania

Single-Shot Derringer

Pocket pistol made by the firm of James Bown & Son, doing business as Enterprise Gun Works. Chambered for .22- or .32-caliber rimfire cartridges. A few in .25 rimfire have been noted and would add approximately 25 percent to values listed. Barrel 2.5" in length and part-round/part-octagonal. Pivots sideways for loading. Spur trigger and bird's-head grip. Barrel stamped "Eclipse". Made of nickel-plated iron, with walnut grips. Approximately 10,000 manufactured between 1870 and 1890.

NIB	Exc.	V.G.	Good	Fair	Poor
—	—	650	250	100	75

EL DORADO ARMS
See—United Sporting Arms, Inc.

ELGIN CUTLASS
(C.B. Allen / Merrill, Mossman and Blair)
Springfield and Amherst, Massachusetts

Manufactured by two companies—C.B. Allen of Springfield, Massachusetts and Morill, Mosman and Blair of Amherst, Massachusetts. A unique pistol that has an integral knife attachment affixed to the gun barrel. Designed and patented by George Elgin and simultaneously produced by the two companies. Inspiration for this weapon was supposedly Jim Bowie, who at that time had made a name as a knife fighter with his large "Bowie" knife. Blades for these pistols were supplied by N.P. Ames of the famed Ames Sword Co. These pistols are much sought after and one must exercise caution as fraudulent examples have been noted.

C. B. ALLEN-MADE PISTOLS

U.S. Navy Elgin Cutlass Pistol

Chambered for .54-caliber percussion. Has a 5" octagonal smooth-bore barrel. Bowie-style blade is 11" long by 2" wide. Forged together with trigger guard and knuckle guard that protects the grip. Handle is walnut. Pistol issued to U.S. Navy's Wilkes-South Sea Exploration Expedition. Markings are "C.B. Allen / Springfield / Mass." "Elgin's Patent" and letters "CB", "CBA" along with date 1837. If the sheath that was issued with this knife pistol is included and in sound condition, it would add approximately $700 to value. There were 150 manufactured for U.S. Navy in 1838.

NIB	Exc.	V.G.	Good	Fair	Poor
—	—	35500	14000	7500	4750

Civilian Model

Chambered for .35- or .41-caliber percussion. Has a 4" octagonal barrel, with 7.5"-10" knife blade, round trigger guard, but does not have knuckle bow across the grip, as found on military model. Marked "C.B. Allen Springfield, Mass." Blades marked "N.P. Ames" have been noted. Approximately 100 manufactured in 1837.

NIB	Exc.	V.G.	Good	Fair	Poor
—	—	33500	13000	6250	3250

MORILL, MOSMAN AND BLAIR-MADE PISTOLS

Small Model

Main difference in pistols of the two makers is; this model has a round barrel and square-back trigger guard, that comes to a point at the rear. This version chambered for .32-caliber percussion and has 2.75" barrel. Knife blade is 7.5" in length and screwed to frame. Model is unmarked except for a serial number. Number produced is unknown. Manufactured in 1837.

NIB	Exc.	V.G.	Good	Fair	Poor
—	—	33500	13000	6250	3250

Large Model

Chambered for .36-caliber percussion. Has 4" round barrel and 9" knife blade. Pistol usually marked "Cast Steel" and serial numbered. Blade etched with an American eagle, stars and urn with flowers. "Elgin Patent" etched in center. Manufactured in 1837.

Courtesy Milwaukee Public Museum, Milwaukee, Wisconsin

NIB	Exc.	V.G.	Good	Fair	Poor
—	—	37000	14500	7000	3900

ELLS, JOSIAH
Pittsburgh, Pennsylvania
POCKET REVOLVER

Three distinct variations of this percussion revolver. Chambered for .28- and .31-caliber; have 6-shot unfluted cylinders; have been noted with 2.5", 3" and 3.75" octagonal barrels.

Model 1

Have an open-topped frame. Chambered for .28-caliber. Cylinder holds 5- or 6-shots. Hammer is of the bar type. Offered with 2.5" or 3" barrel. Markings are "J. Ells; Patent; 1854". Approximately 625 manufactured between 1857 and 1859.

Courtesy Milwaukee Public Museum, Milwaukee, Wisconsin

NIB	Exc.	V.G.	Good	Fair	Poor
—	—	1700	875	375	200

Model 2

Similar to first, with solid-topped frame. Have 5-shot cylinders and 3.75" long barrels. Approximately 550 manufactured.

Courtesy Milwaukee Public Museum, Milwaukee, Wisconsin

NIB	Exc.	V.G.	Good	Fair	Poor
—	—	1750	750	365	200

Model 3

Radically different from its forerunners. Closed-top frame and conventional spur-type hammer that strikes from right side. Functions either as a double-/single-action. Chambered for .28-caliber, 5-shot cylinder and 3.75" barrel. About 200 manufactured between 1857 and 1859.

NIB	Exc.	V.G.	Good	Fair	Poor
—	—	1850	995	425	200

ENDERS, CARL
Suhl, Germany

Side-by-Side Shotgun

Percussion damascus double-barrel side-by-side in 12-gauge. Ornate checkering, with cheekpiece and engraved metal work. This firm made high-quality firearms, mostly side-by-side guns. Gun pictured was made circa 1850-1860. Firm in business about 1835 to approximately 1890.

Courtesy Jim Cate

NIB	Exc.	V.G.	Good	Fair	Poor
—	—	1250	550	300	150

ENFIELD AMERICAN, INC.
Atlanta, Georgia

MP-45

Blowback-operated semi-automatic assault pistol. Chambered for .45 ACP cartridge. Offered barrel lengths 4.5" through 18.5". Long barrel features a shroud. Finish is Parkerized. Four different magazines available in 10, 20, 30 and 50 round capacities. Manufactured in 1985 only.

NIB	Exc.	V.G.	Good	Fair	Poor
—	575	475	295	175	125

ENTREPRISE ARMS, INC.
Irwindale, California

ELITE SERIES

Basic model with stainless steel barrels, fixed sights, squared trigger guard, adjustable match trigger, checkered slide release, high ride grip safety, flat mainspring housing and a number of other special features. Magazine capacity 10 rounds.

Elite P500

Chambered for .45 ACP. Fitted with 5" barrel. Weight about 40 oz.

NIB	Exc.	V.G.	Good	Fair	Poor
600	500	400	350	200	100

Elite P425

Has 4.25" barrel. Weight about 38 oz.

NIB	Exc.	V.G.	Good	Fair	Poor
600	500	400	350	200	100

Elite P325

Has 3.25" barrel. Weight 36 oz.

NIB	Exc.	V.G.	Good	Fair	Poor
600	500	400	350	200	100

TACTICAL SERIES

Models have ambidextrous thumb lock, lightweight match hammer and matching sear. National match barrel with match extractor, full length one-piece guide rod, Novak sights, dovetail front sight, matte black finish and host of other features. Magazine capacity 10 rounds.

Tactical P500

Chambered for .45 ACP cartridge. Barrel 5". Weight about 40 oz.

NIB	Exc.	V.G.	Good	Fair	Poor
900	795	600	495	350	100

Tactical P425

Fitted with 4.25" barrel. Weight about 38 oz.

NIB	Exc.	V.G.	Good	Fair	Poor
900	795	600	495	350	100

Tactical P325

Fitted with 3.25" barrel. Weight 36 oz.

NIB	Exc.	V.G.	Good	Fair	Poor
900	795	600	495	350	100

Tactical P325 Plus

Features 3.25" barrel. Fitted to full size Government model frame. Weight about 37 oz.

NIB	Exc.	V.G.	Good	Fair	Poor
950	800	615	500	365	105

TITLEIST NATIONAL MATCH SERIES

Model chambered for either .45 ACP or .40 S&W cartridge. Has all features of Elite Series. Adjustable rear sight and dovetail Patridge front sight. Many other special features.

Titleist P500

Fitted with 5" barrel. Weight about 40 oz. **NOTE:** Add $20 for .40 S&W chambering.

NIB	Exc.	V.G.	Good	Fair	Poor
900	795	600	495	350	100

Boxer Model

Chambered for .45 ACP cartridge. Fitted with 5" barrel. Features a ramped bull barrel, wide ambi safety and high-mass chiseled slide. Weight about 44 oz.

NIB	Exc.	V.G.	Good	Fair	Poor
1200	975	750	600	375	125

TOURNAMENT SERIES

These are top-of-the-line models. They have all features of Elite Series, plus over-sized magazine release button, checkered front strap and flared extended magazine well.

TSM I

Limited class competition pistol. All models are hand crafted. Fitted with 5" barrel and choice of calibers. Weight about 40 oz.

NIB	Exc.	V.G.	Good	Fair	Poor
1900	1750	1375	900	675	300

TSM II

Long slide model, with cocking serrations on front and rear of slide. Barrel 6"; weight about 44 oz.

NIB	Exc.	V.G.	Good	Fair	Poor
2300	1750	1375	900	675	300

TSM III

Open class pistol designed for scope mount. Fitted with 7-port compensator. Many other custom features. Barrel 5.5"; weight about 44 oz.

NIB	Exc.	V.G.	Good	Fair	Poor
2500	2000	1525	1050	700	310

ERA
Brazil

ERA Side-by-Side Shotgun

Inexpensive shotgun chambered for 12-, 20-gauge and .410 bore. Offered with 26", 28" or 30" barrels and various choke combinations. Double triggers and extractors, with checkered hardwood pistol-grip stock. Also available as Quail model, with 20" barrel; Riot model with 18" barrel. These two models not offered in .410 bore.

NIB	Exc.	V.G.	Good	Fair	Poor
—	200	150	125	100	75

ERA Over/Under Shotgun

Chambered for 12- or 20-gauge, with 28" ventilated rib barrels that were choked full and modified. Boxlock with double triggers, extractors and hardwood stock. Also offered in trap and skeet model, chambered for 12-gauge only and appropriately choked. **NOTE:** Latter two models would be worth 10 percent premium over values listed.

NIB	Exc.	V.G.	Good	Fair	Poor
—	325	275	250	200	150

ERICHSON, G.
Houston, Texas

Pocket Pistol

Close copy of Philadelphia-style Henry Deringer. Chambered for .45-caliber percussion. Has 3.25" barrel. Mountings are German silver and not engraved. Stock is walnut. Hammer is deeply fluted and fore-end carved. Barrel marked "G. Erichson / Houston, Texas". Number produced unknown, but examples are scarce. Manufactured in 1850s and 1860s.

NIB	Exc.	V.G.	Good	Fair	Poor
—	—	6500	3000	1000	400

ERMA WERKE WAFFENFABRIK
Erfurt, Germany
Post-war Dachau, Germany

Known primarily as a manufacturer of sub-machine guns, they are also in the handgun and rifle business. In 1933, they answered the German army's need for an inexpensive practice weapon by producing a .22 rimfire conversion unit for the Luger pistol. This was marketed commercially and available for many years. Success of this unit led the company to produce other inexpensive target and plinking pistols. After the war, they were reorganized in the western sector and resumed sub-machine gun production. In 1964, they returned to the sporting firearms business, with the introduction of their .22 rimfire Luger-lookalike pistol. Since then, they have produced many like-quality firearms. They were imported by Excam of Hialeah, Florida. This association is now terminated and they are currently imported by Beeman Precision in Santa Rosa, California and Mandell Shooting Supplies in Scottsdale, Arizona.

PISTOLS

Erma .22 Luger Conversion Unit

Produced for the German army in 1933 and then became a successful commercial item. It would turn a standard 9mm or 7.65mm Luger into an inexpensive-to-shoot .22 rimfire. Unit consists of barrel insert, breech block and toggle unit, with its own lightened recoil spring and .22 magazine. Unit

was furnished with a wooden box. There were many different sized units to fit various caliber and barrel-length Lugers, but all used the same parts and concept. These units have become desirable to Luger collectors.

NIB	Exc.	V.G.	Good	Fair	Poor
—	500	425	350	275	200

.22 Target Pistol (Old Model)

Semi-automatic target pistol in caliber .22 LR. Offered with 4", 6" or 8" barrels. Frame made from cast zinc alloy and there is an external hammer. Adjustable sights and balance weights were available. Magazine capacity 10 rounds. Weight about 35 oz. Manufactured in 1936 and 1937.

Courtesy James Rankin

NIB	Exc.	V.G.	Good	Fair	Poor
—	800	725	500	350	100

.22 Target Pistol (New Model) Master Model

Improved version of old model. Features new grip angle, magazine and takedown device like that of the Luger. There were interchangeable barrels and three basic models — "Sport", "Hunter" and "Master". Difference was length of barrels — 4", 8" and 12" respectively. Magazine capacity 10 rounds. Weight about 39 oz. Manufactured between 1937 and 1940. Discontinued due to Erma's involvement in the war effort.

Courtesy James Rankin

NIB	Exc.	V.G.	Good	Fair	Poor
—	850	700	500	400	125

KGP SERIES

Made to resemble the Luger quite closely. They utilized mechanical features of the .22 conversion unit and developed a pistol around it. Many different versions of this pistol chambered for .22 rimfire, .32 ACP and .380 ACP. Original designation was KGP-68; but the Gun Control Act of 1968 required that a magazine safety be added and model was re-designated KGP-68A. Last designations for the three calibers are KGP-22, KGP-32 and KGP-38. Manufactured between 1964 - 1986 and their values listed.

KGP-68

A 4" barrel and chambered for .32 ACP and .380 ACP cartridges. Has a 6-shot magazine and anodized alloy receiver. Weight about 23 oz. Model also known as Beeman MP-08.

NIB	Exc.	V.G.	Good	Fair	Poor
—	450	400	300	200	100

KGP-69

A .22 rimfire version of this series, with 8-shot magazine capacity. Weight about 30 oz. Also known as Beeman P-08.

NIB	Exc.	V.G.	Good	Fair	Poor
—	300	200	150	100	75

KGP-22

Later version of KGP-69 chambered for .22 rimfire.

NIB	Exc.	V.G.	Good	Fair	Poor
—	350	300	250	200	125

KGP-32 & KGP-38

Two designations are later versions of KGP-68 and 68A.

NIB	Exc.	V.G.	Good	Fair	Poor
—	350	300	250	200	125

ET-22 "Navy Luger" Long-Barreled Pistol

A rare firearm. According to some estimates only 375 were produced. Features a 11.75" barrel and chambered for .22 rimfire cartridge. Artillery Luger-type rear sight and checkered walnut grips, with a smooth walnut fore-end. Pistol furnished with a red-felt-lined black leatherette case.

NIB	Exc.	V.G.	Good	Fair	Poor
—	900	675	400	250	150

ESP 85A

High-quality target pistol imported by Mandall Shooting Supply. Features an interchangeable barrel system that converts chambering from .22 rimfire to .32 S&W long wad cutter. Barrels are both 6" in length. Adjustable and interchangeable sights and 5- or 8-shot detachable magazine. Weight about 41 oz. Finish blued and grips are stippled target types. Gun furnished in padded hard case, with two extra magazines and takedown tools. Introduced in 1989.

NIB	Exc.	V.G.	Good	Fair	Poor
1100	1000	850	700	550	450

EP-25

Semi-automatic pistol in caliber 6.35mm. Fitted with 2.75" barrel. Weight about 18 oz. Mostly marketed outside of Germany. Polished blue finish and wood grips. Erma stamped on slide and on each grip plate.

Courtesy James Rankin

NIB	Exc.	V.G.	Good	Fair	Poor
—	275	195	150	100	75

RX-22 and PX-22

Semi-automatic .22 rimfire copy of Walther PPK. Has a 7-round magazine. Assembled in U.S., with parts from Germany by various companies that marketed the pistol in U.S. Black plastic wrap-around grips, with Erma logo on each side.

Courtesy James Rankin

NIB	Exc.	V.G.	Good	Fair	Poor
—	240	175	150	100	75

REVOLVERS

ER-772 Match

Target revolver chambered for .22 rimfire. Has 6" shrouded barrel with solid rib. Swing-out cylinder holds 6-shots and sights are adjustable. Finish blued, with stippled target grips. Introduced in 1989.

NIB	Exc.	V.G.	Good	Fair	Poor
1000	800	600	350	250	200

ER-773 Match

Similar to ER-772, except chambered for .32 S&W long cartridge.

NIB	Exc.	V.G.	Good	Fair	Poor
900	750	500	375	250	200

ER-777

Basically similar revolver to ER-773, except it has 4.5" or 5" barrel and chambered for .357 Magnum cartridge. Revolver is larger and has standard sport grips. Introduced in 1989.

NIB	Exc.	V.G.	Good	Fair	Poor
800	600	450	350	250	200

RIFLES

EM1.22

Semi-automatic .22 rimfire version of M1 Carbine. Has an 18" barrel and 15-round magazine. Manufactured between 1966 and 1976.

NIB	Exc.	V.G.	Good	Fair	Poor
—	350	225	150	125	100

EG-72, EG-722

A 15-shot slide-action carbine chambered for .22 rimfire. A 18.5" barrel and open sights. Finish is blued. Manufactured between 1970 and 1985.

NIB	Exc.	V.G.	Good	Fair	Poor
—	250	165	100	75	50

EG-712, EG-73

Lever copy of Winchester 94 Carbine. Chambered for .22 rimfire or .22 rimfire Magnum (EG-73). Has an 18.5" barrel and holds 15-shots in a tubular magazine. Manufactured between 1973 and 1985.

NIB	Exc.	V.G.	Good	Fair	Poor
—	250	175	150	125	100

SR-100

Long-range precision bolt-action rifle, chambered for .308 Win., .300 Win. Magnum or .338 Lapua calibers. Barrel length on .308 Win. is 25.25", other calibers 29.25". All barrels fitted with muzzle-brake. Trigger is adjustable. Stock laminated, with thumbhole and adjustable recoil pad and cheekpiece. Weight about 15 lbs.

NIB	Exc.	V.G.	Good	Fair	Poor
8800	7000	5000	2750	1300	600

ERQUIAGA
Eibar, Spain

Another Spanish company that commenced business during WWI, as a subcontractor on the French "Ruby" contract. They manufactured the usual poor quality, 7.65mm Eibar-type pistol.

Fiel

Trade name found on Ruby subcontract pistol described above. Marked "Erquiaga y Cia Eibar Cal. 7.65 Fiel".

Courtesy James Rankin

NIB	Exc.	V.G.	Good	Fair	Poor
—	200	150	125	100	75

Fiel 6.35

After the end of WWI, a 1906 Browning copy was made. Chambered for 6.35mm cartridge. Markings are "Automatic Pistol 6.35 Fiel No. 1". Later models had "EMC" molded into grip.

NIB	Exc.	V.G.	Good	Fair	Poor
—	195	135	100	75	50

Marte

Another poor-quality "Eibar"-type pistol. Chambered for 6.35mm. Made in early 1920s.

NIB	Exc.	V.G.	Good	Fair	Poor
—	195	135	100	75	50

ERRASTI, A.
Eibar, Spain

Errasti manufactured a variety of inexpensive yet serviceable pistols, from early 1900s until the Spanish Civil War.

Velo Dog

Usual cheap solid-frame folding-trigger revolvers one associates with model designation. Chambered in 5.5mm and 6.35mm. Made in early 1900s.

NIB	Exc.	V.G.	Good	Fair	Poor
—	195	135	100	75	50

M1889

In 1915-1916 Errasti produced the 10.4mm Italian army service revolver. Quality was reasonably good. Marked "Errasti Eiber" on the right side of frame.

NIB	Exc.	V.G.	Good	Fair	Poor
—	400	295	200	125	75

Errasti

Two "Eibar"-type Browning copies were made under this trade name. One chambered for 6.35mm the other 7.65mm. Both marked "Automatic Pistol Errasti".

Courtesy James Rankin

NIB	Exc.	V.G.	Good	Fair	Poor
—	195	135	110	75	50

Errasti Oscillante

Manufactured in the 1920s, these revolvers were copied from Smith & Wesson Military & Police design. Chambered for .32-, .38- and .44-calibers, with .38 being most frequently encountered. **NOTE:** Add 30 percent for .44-caliber.

NIB	Exc.	V.G.	Good	Fair	Poor
—	250	195	125	95	50

Dreadnaught, Goliath and Smith Americano

These three trade names found on a group of poor quality nickel-plated revolvers. Made from 1905 through 1920. Obvious copies of Iver Johnson design. They had break-open actions, ribbed barrel and chambered for .32-, .38- and .44-calibers. They are scarce today, as most have long since fallen apart. **NOTE:** Add 30 percent for .44-caliber.

NIB	Exc.	V.G.	Good	Fair	Poor
—	225	175	100	75	50

ESCODIN, M.
Eibar, Spain

This company made a Smith & Wesson revolver copy from 1924 through 1931. Chambered for .32 and .38 Special. Only marking is a coat of arms stamped on left side of frame.

NIB	Exc.	V.G.	Good	Fair	Poor
—	175	125	100	75	50

ESCORT
Turkey

SEMI-AUTOMATIC SHOTGUNS

Model AS

This 12-gauge 3" model fitted with 28" ventilated rib barrel and choke tubes. Walnut stock. Black finish. Magazine capacity 4 rounds. Weight about 7 lbs.

NIB	Exc.	V.G.	Good	Fair	Poor
450	365	245	200	150	100

Model PS

This 12-gauge 3" model similar to above, with black polymer stock and finish. Also offered in Shadow Grass camo or Mossy Oak Break-Up camo. Choice of Spark or TriViz front sights. Barrel length 28" except for TriViz variation with 24" barrel. Weight about 7 lbs. **NOTE:** Add $100 for camo coverage; $45 for TriViz model.

NIB	Exc.	V.G.	Good	Fair	Poor
500	400	300	200	150	100

Model PS AimGuard

This 12-gauge 3" model is fitted with 20" fixed choke barrel in Cylinder bore. Black polymer stock and finish. Magazine capacity 5 rounds. Weight about 6.4 lbs.

NIB	Exc.	V.G.	Good	Fair	Poor
400	295	200	125	100	75

Combo Model

This 12-gauge 3" model is offered with two sets of barrels: one 28" with Full choke tube; the other 24" with Turkey choke tube. Polymer stock with Mossy Oak Break-Up. Receiver is fitted with a dovetail mount. Weight about 7 lbs.

NIB	Exc.	V.G.	Good	Fair	Poor
575	425	365	295	200	100

Escort Semi-Auto Slug Gun

Slug gun available in 12- or 20-gauge. Rifled barrel 22" long with 1:26 twist. Self-regulating gas piston. Has Hi-Viz sights and equipped with a cantilevered scope base. Black synthetic stock. Overall length, 42". Weight: 6.3 lbs. (20-gauge); 7 lbs. (12-gauge).

NIB	Exc.	V.G.	Good	Fair	Poor
530	475	375	300	250	200

Escort Extreme Series

Available for either 12-gauge 3" or 3.5" Magnum, with 28" barrel, Hi-Viz sights and choke tubes. Several camo patterns for turkey or waterfowl hunting. Extreme Waterfowl Youth model available in 20-gauge with 22" barrel.

Extreme 3.5

NIB	Exc.	V.G.	Good	Fair	Poor
800	675	500	400	300	200

Extreme 3

NIB	Exc.	V.G.	Good	Fair	Poor
700	600	450	400	300	150

Extreme Waterfowl Youth

NIB	Exc.	V.G.	Good	Fair	Poor
600	525	400	350	300	150

PUMP-ACTION SHOTGUNS

Field Hunter

This 12-gauge 3" model fitted with 28" ventilated rib barrel and choke tubes. Offered with black polymer stock of Mossy Oak Break-Up or Shadow Grass camo pattern. A 24" barrel with TriViz also offered. Magazine capacity 4 rounds. Weight about 7 lbs. **NOTE:** Add $50 for camo finish; $100 for TriViz sights.

NIB	Exc.	V.G.	Good	Fair	Poor
325	225	165	135	100	75

AimGuard

This 12-gauge 3" model fitted with 20" barrel and fixed Cylinder bore choke. Black polymer stock. Magazine capacity 5 rounds. Weight about 6.4 lbs. **NOTE:** Add 10 percent for 18" barrel and nickel finish.

NIB	Exc.	V.G.	Good	Fair	Poor
325	225	165	135	100	75

Escort Pump Slug Gun

Same specifications as semi-automatic except slide-action. Weight: 6 lbs. (20-gauge); 6.7 lbs. (12-gauge).

NIB	Exc.	V.G.	Good	Fair	Poor
430	385	290	250	200	150

ESPIRIN, HERMANOS
Eibar, Spain

Euskaro

Poor-quality often unsafe revolver. Manufactured from 1906 until WWI. They are copies of Iver Johnson design break-open actions. Chambered for .32-, .38- and .44-calibers. Product epitomizes the worst Eibar had to offer during pre-Civil War era. **NOTE:** Add 30 percent for .44-caliber.

NIB	Exc.	V.G.	Good	Fair	Poor
—	200	125	75	50	25

EUROARMS OF AMERICA
Winchester, Virginia

An importer of blackpowder muzzle-loading firearms, primarily replicas of early American weapons.

REVOLVERS

1851 Navy

Replica of Colt revolver chambered for .36- or .44-caliber percussion. Has a squareback silver-plated trigger guard and 7.5" barrel.

NIB	Exc.	V.G.	Good	Fair	Poor
275	225	170	110	75	45

1851 Navy Police Model

Chambered for .36-caliber, with 5-shot fluted cylinder and 5.5" barrel.

NIB	Exc.	V.G.	Good	Fair	Poor
275	225	170	110	75	45

1851 Navy Sheriff's Model

A 5" barreled version of Navy Model.

NIB	Exc.	V.G.	Good	Fair	Poor
275	225	170	110	75	45

1851 "Schneider & Glassick" Navy

Replica of Confederate revolver chambered for .36- or .44-caliber percussion.

NIB	Exc.	V.G.	Good	Fair	Poor
150	100	80	60	50	35

1851 "Griswold & Gunnison" Navy

Replica of Confederate revolver chambered for .36- or .44-caliber percussion.

NIB	Exc.	V.G.	Good	Fair	Poor
285	235	170	110	75	45

1862 Police

Replica of Colt Model 1862 chambered for .36-caliber percussion, with 7.5" barrel and steel frame.

NIB	Exc.	V.G.	Good	Fair	Poor
275	225	170	110	75	45

1860 Army

Replica of Colt revolver chambered for .44-caliber percussion. Offered with 5" or 8" barrel.

NIB	Exc.	V.G.	Good	Fair	Poor
275	225	170	110	75	45

1861 Navy

Replica of Colt revolver chambered for .36-caliber percussion.

NIB	Exc.	V.G.	Good	Fair	Poor
275	225	170	110	75	45

1858 Remington Army or Navy

Replicas of Remington percussion revolvers chambered for .36- or .44-caliber.

NIB	Exc.	V.G.	Good	Fair	Poor
275	225	170	110	75	45

RIFLES

Rifles listed are modern replicas of early American and British firearms. They are good quality and quite serviceable.

Cook & Brother Carbine

NIB	Exc.	V.G.	Good	Fair	Poor
595	500	375	250	195	100

1863 J.P. Murray

NIB	Exc.	V.G.	Good	Fair	Poor
595	500	375	250	195	100

1853 Enfield Rifled Musket

NIB	Exc.	V.G.	Good	Fair	Poor
610	525	375	250	195	100

1858 Enfield Rifled Musket

NIB	Exc.	V.G.	Good	Fair	Poor
610	525	375	250	195	100

1861 Enfield Musketoon

NIB	Exc.	V.G.	Good	Fair	Poor
500	375	250	195	100	65

1803 Harper's Ferry

NIB	Exc.	V.G.	Good	Fair	Poor
595	500	375	250	195	100

1841 Mississippi Rifle

NIB	Exc.	V.G.	Good	Fair	Poor
595	500	375	250	195	100

Pennsylvania Rifle

NIB	Exc.	V.G.	Good	Fair	Poor
400	350	275	225	150	100

Hawken Rifle

NIB	Exc.	V.G.	Good	Fair	Poor
400	350	275	225	150	100

Cape Gun

NIB	Exc.	V.G.	Good	Fair	Poor
450	395	325	275	200	150

Buffalo Carbine

NIB	Exc.	V.G.	Good	Fair	Poor
450	395	325	275	200	150

1862 Remington Rifle

NIB	Exc.	V.G.	Good	Fair	Poor
450	395	325	275	200	150

Zouave Rifle

NIB	Exc.	V.G.	Good	Fair	Poor
450	395	325	275	200	150

SHOTGUNS

Duck Gun

Single-barreled percussion fowling piece chambered for 8-, 10- or 12-gauge. Has a 33" smoothbore barrel and case-colored hammer and lock. Stock is walnut with brass mountings. Introduced in 1989. **NOTE:** Add 20 percent for 8-gauge.

NIB	Exc.	V.G.	Good	Fair	Poor
450	395	325	275	200	150

Standard Side-by-Side

Side-by-side chambered for 12-gauge percussion. Has 28" barrels, with engraved locks and walnut stock.

NIB	Exc.	V.G.	Good	Fair	Poor
475	400	350	295	200	125

EUROPEAN AMERICAN ARMORY CORP./ U.S. SPORTING GOODS, INC.
Rockledge, Florida

EAA WITNESS PISTOLS

EAA Witness P-Series Full Size

Introduced in 1998, P-Series is a polymer-frame variation of original steel-frame Witness DA/SA pistols. Chambered for 9mm, .40 S&W, .45 ACP, .38 Super and 10mm cartridges. Barrel length 4.55". Overall length 8.5" with an empty weight of 31 oz. Rear sight adjustable for windage. Magazine capacity: 9mm 28 rounds; .40 S&W 15 rounds; .45 ACP 10 rounds; 10mm 15 rounds. **NOTE:** Add $30 for ported barrel.

NIB	Exc.	V.G.	Good	Fair	Poor
525	425	325	225	180	100

EAA Witness P-Series Carry-Comp

Fitted with a 4.25" ported barrel. Chambered for .45 ACP.

NIB	Exc.	V.G.	Good	Fair	Poor
470	375	275	200	150	100

EAA Witness P-Series Compact

Similar to above, with barrel length of 3.55". Weight about 26 oz. **NOTE:** Add $30 for ported barrel.

NIB	Exc.	V.G.	Good	Fair	Poor
450	350	250	200	150	100

EAA Witness P-S Series

Built on a different frame size from P-Series pistols. Chambered for .22 LR, 9mm or .40 S&W cartridges. Barrel length 4.55". Weight about 31 oz.

NIB	Exc.	V.G.	Good	Fair	Poor
400	325	275	200	150	100

EAA Witness Carry Comp

Offered in 9mm, .41 AE, .40 S&W and .45 ACP. Features 1" steel compensator. Barrel 4.1" long. Overall length same as standard model as is magazine capacity. Offered in blue or blue chrome finish. Weight 34 oz. **NOTE:** Add 15 percent for .45 ACP.

New Configuration

NIB	Exc.	V.G.	Good	Fair	Poor
500	450	375	325	250	175

EAA Witness Standard

This is the original Witness model with a steel frame. Based on CZ-75 design. Made by Tanfoglio in Italy, it has been imported by EAA since 1990. Available in 9mm, .41 AE, .40 S&W and .45 ACP, with 4.5" barrel. Magazine capacity: 9mm 16 rounds; .41 AE 11 rounds; .40 S&W 12 rounds; .45 ACP 10 rounds. Offered in blue, chrome, two-tone and stainless steel. Weight about 33 oz. **NOTE:** Add 5 percent for chrome, two-tone and stainless steel.

New Configuration

NIB	Exc.	V.G.	Good	Fair	Poor
500	375	295	225	175	125

EAA Witness Subcompact

Offered in same calibers as standard model. Fitted with 3.66" barrel and shorter grip. Magazine capacity: 9mm 13 rounds; .41 AE 9 rounds; .40 S&W 9 rounds; .45 ACP 8 rounds. Weight about 30 oz. Offered in blue, chrome, two-tone and stainless steel. **NOTE:** Add 5 percent for chrome, two-tone and stainless steel.

New Configuration

NIB	Exc.	V.G.	Good	Fair	Poor
460	350	275	225	175	125

EAA Witness Sport L/S

Features longer slide for its 4.75" barrel. Offered in 9mm, .41 AE, .40 S&W and .45 ACP. Magazine capacity: 9mm 19 rounds; .41 AE 13 rounds; .40 S&W 14 rounds; .45 ACP 11 rounds. Also fitted with adjustable rear sight and extended safety. Available in two-tone finish. Weight about 34.5 oz. A ported barrel offered as an option. **NOTE:** Add 10 percent for .45 ACP.

New Configuration

NIB	Exc.	V.G.	Good	Fair	Poor
625	550	500	400	300	200

EAA Witness Combo 9/40

Offers a 9mm and .40 S&W conversion kit. Kits consist of a slide, barrel, recoil spring, guide and magazine. Available in standard or subcompact size in blue, chrome or two-tone finish. **NOTE:** Add 5 percent for chrome or two-tone finish.

NIB	Exc.	V.G.	Good	Fair	Poor
595	495	425	350	275	175

EAA Witness Silver Team Match

Designed as a competition pistol. Fitted with 5.25" barrel. Features dual chamber compensator, single-action trigger, extended safety, competition hammer, paddle magazine release, checkered walnut grips and adjustable rear sight or drilled and tapped for scope mount. Offered in: 9mm 19 rounds; .40 S&W 14 rounds; .41 AE 13 rounds; .45 ACP 11 rounds and 9 x 21. Finish is blue. Weight about 34 oz.

NIB	Exc.	V.G.	Good	Fair	Poor
900	800	700	600	450	300

EAA Witness Sport

Built on standard Witness frame. Addition of an adjustable rear sight and extended safety. Offered in 9mm, .41 AE, .40 S&W, .45 ACP in standard model magazine capacity. Weight 33 oz. Available in two-tone finish. **NOTE:** Add 10 percent for .45 ACP.

New Configuration

NIB	Exc.	V.G.	Good	Fair	Poor
550	475	400	300	200	150

EAA Witness Hunter

Features camo finish with 6" barrel. Chambered for .45 ACP or 10mm cartridge. Drilled and tapped for scope mount and adjustable sights. Magazine capacity 10 rounds. Weight about 41 oz. Also available with blued finish.

NIB	Exc.	V.G.	Good	Fair	Poor
975	800	575	395	250	150

EAA Witness Gold Team Match

This is a full race competition pistol. Features triple chamber compensator, beaver tail grip safety, beveled magazine well, adjustable rear sight or drilled and tapped for scope mount, extended safety and magazine release, competition hammer, square trigger guard, checkered front and backstrap, competition grips and hard chrome finish. Same barrel length, magazine capacity and calibers as Silver Team Match. Weight 38 oz.

NIB	Exc.	V.G.	Good	Fair	Poor
1700	1250	900	750	600	400

EAA Witness Limited Class Pistol

Built on Witness Match frame. Features competition grips, high-capacity magazine, extended safety and magazine release, single-action trigger, long slide with adjustable rear sight and match grade barrel. Offered in 9mm, .40 S&W, .38 Super and .45 ACP, with blue finish.

NIB	Exc.	V.G.	Good	Fair	Poor
1200	975	725	550	400	300

EAA Witness Stock

Introduced in 2005 Features 4.5" tapered cone barrel chambered for 9mm, .40S&W, .45ACP or .10mm cartridge. Hard chrome finish, extended safety, wood checkered grips and fully adjustable sights. Weight about 33 oz.

NIB	Exc.	V.G.	Good	Fair	Poor
825	695	595	400	200	100

EAA Witness Multi Class Pistol Package

This package consists of one Witness Limited Class pistol, with a complete unlimited class top half. Top half is made up of standard length slide with super sight, recoil guide and spring, match grade competition barrel (threaded for compensator) and a dual chamber compensator. Available in 9mm, .40 S&W, 9 x 21, .45 ACP, 9 x 23 and .38 Super. Finish is blue.

NIB	Exc.	V.G.	Good	Fair	Poor
1700	1350	850	600	300	200

EAA Witness Elite Match

Single-action semi-automatic featuring 4.5" polygonal rifled steel barrel, adjustable rear sights, rubber grips. Two-tone finish. Chambered for 9 mm (18+1), 10 mm (15+1), 38 Super (15+1), .40 S&W (15+1) and .45 ACP (10+1). Weight 33 oz. Introduced 2006.

NIB	Exc.	V.G.	Good	Fair	Poor
725	600	450	300	200	100

EAA Witness 1911

Made by Tanfoglio in Italy. This is a standard size 1911 in .45 ACP. Made in two variations, one with a steel frame (shown) and the other is polymer. Operating controls are standard 1911, with added features like an accessory rail, flat mainspring housing, skeleton hammer and trigger, extended grip safety and ambidextrous manual safety. Introduced in 2014. Values shown are for polymer model. **NOTE:** Add $250 for steel frame.

NIB	Exc.	V.G.	Good	Fair	Poor
525	435	350	275	200	150

Zastava EZ Pistol

CZ-75 clone. Single-/double-action pistol, with 4" (Full Size) or 3.5" (Compact) barrel and polymer frame. Chambered in 9mm, .40 S&W or .45 ACP. Magazine capacity varies from 7 rounds (.45 ACP) to 15 (9mm).

NIB	Exc.	V.G.	Good	Fair	Poor
450	400	325	275	165	100

Thor

Single-shot pistol chambered for .223 Rem., .270 Win., .30-06, .300 Win., .308, .375 Win., .44 Magnum, .45-70, .50 S&W, .7mm-08 or .7mm Rem. Magnum. Fitted with 14" barrel. Receiver has an integral top rail for scope mount. Weight about 5 lbs.

NIB	Exc.	V.G.	Good	Fair	Poor
1150	850	675	500	355	145

OTHER EAA IMPORTED FIREARMS

BUL 1911 SERIES

BUL Government

Chambered for .45 ACP cartridge. Fitted with 4.8" barrel, polymer frame, tactical rear sight, with dovetail front sight, fully checkered grip. Black or stainless steel slide. Weight about 24 oz. Magazine capacity 10 rounds. Introduced in 2002. **NOTE:** Add $50 for stainless steel slide.

NIB	Exc.	V.G.	Good	Fair	Poor
550	450	300	200	125	75

Commander

Same as above. Fitted with 3.8" barrel.

NIB	Exc.	V.G.	Good	Fair	Poor
550	450	300	200	125	75

Stinger

This model has a 3" barrel.

NIB	Exc.	V.G.	Good	Fair	Poor
550	450	300	200	125	75

EAA Big Bore Bounty Hunter

Single-action revolver made in Germany. Features three-position hammer, forged barrel and walnut grips. Offered in .357 Magnum, .45 Long Colt and .44 Magnum. Barrel lengths 4.5", 5.5" or 7.5". Choice of finish includes blue or case-colored frame, chrome, gold or blue and gold. **NOTE:** Add 20 percent for chrome, gold or blue and gold finish.

NIB	Exc.	V.G.	Good	Fair	Poor
400	300	225	175	150	125

EAA Small Bore Bounty Hunter

Single-action .22-caliber revolver. Wood grips and available in blue or blue and brass finish. Barrel lengths 4.75", 6" and 9". Chambered for .22 LR or .22 Winchester Rimfire Magnum.

NIB	Exc.	V.G.	Good	Fair	Poor
275	200	145	125	75	60

EAA Bounty Hunter Shotgun—External Hammers

Side-by-side shotgun with external hammers. Chambered for 10-, 12-, 16-, 20-, 28-gauge and .410 bore. Offered in barrel lengths of 20", 24" and 26".

NIB	Exc.	V.G.	Good	Fair	Poor
375	300	250	175	150	125

EAA Bounty Hunter Shotgun—Traditional

Same as above, with internal hammers. Offered in 12- or 20-gauge.

NIB	Exc.	V.G.	Good	Fair	Poor
300	250	200	150	100	75

EAA F.A.B. 92 Pistol

Semi-automatic pistol similar to Witness. Fitted with hammer drop safety and slide mounted safety, that is both double-/single-action. Available in either full size (33 oz.) or compact size (30 oz.). Full size version has 4.5" barrel while compact is fitted with 3.66" barrel. Offered in 9mm or .40 S&W in blue, two-tone or chrome finish.

NIB	Exc.	V.G.	Good	Fair	Poor
395	300	225	175	125	100

EAA European Standard Pistol

Single-action semi-automatic pistol, with external hammer, slide grip serrations, wood grips and single column magazine. Barrel length 3.2" and overall length 6.5". Chambered for .22 LR, 380 ACP and .32 ACP. Magazine capacity: 10 rounds .22 LR; 7 rounds .380 and .32. Offered in blue, blue/chrome, chrome, blue/gold. Weight 26 oz.

NIB	Exc.	V.G.	Good	Fair	Poor
195	155	110	95	75	50

EAA European Target Pistol

Features adjustable rear sight, external hammer, single-action trigger, walnut target grips and adjustable weight system. Chambered for .22 LR. Offered in blue finish. Weight 40 oz.

NIB	Exc.	V.G.	Good	Fair	Poor
355	295	225	175	150	100

EAA Windicator Standard Grade

German-built model is a double-action revolver chambered for .22 LR, .22 Winchester Rimfire Magnum, .32 H&R and .38 Special. Offered in 2", 4" and 6" barrel lengths. Cylinder capacity: .22 LR/.22 WRM 8 rounds; .32 H&R 7 rounds; .38 Special 6 rounds. Cylinder is unfluted, finish blue.

NIB	Exc.	V.G.	Good	Fair	Poor
275	165	135	110	75	60

EAA Windicator Basic Grade

Chambered for .38 Special or .357 Magnum, with 2" barrel. Fluted cylinder holds 6 rounds. Finish is blue.

NIB	Exc.	V.G.	Good	Fair	Poor
275	165	135	110	75	60

EAA Windicator Tactical Grade

Similar in appearance to standard grade. Chambered for .38 Special, with 2" or 4" barrel. The 4" barrel has an integral compensator. Finish is blue.

2" Barrel

NIB	Exc.	V.G.	Good	Fair	Poor
190	150	125	100	80	60

4" Barrel

NIB	Exc.	V.G.	Good	Fair	Poor
250	200	150	125	100	75

EAA Windicator Target Grade

Model has these special features: adjustable trigger pull, walnut grips, adjustable rear sight, drilled and tapped for scope mount, target hammer, adjustable trigger stop. Fitted with 6" target barrel. Chambered for .22 LR, .38 Special, .357 Magnum. Blue finish.

NIB	Exc.	V.G.	Good	Fair	Poor
350	275	225	200	150	100

EAA PM2 Shotgun

Pump-action 12-gauge shotgun, with 6-round box magazine. Barrel length 20". Finish either blue or chrome. Stock is black composite. Weight 6.8 lbs. Discontinued in 1993. **NOTE:** Add $100 for optional night sights.

NIB	Exc.	V.G.	Good	Fair	Poor
450	350	300	250	200	150

EAA HW 60 Rifle

German-made target rifle chambered for .22 LR. Features an adjustable trigger and other target and match grade components. Barrel length 26.8", stock stippled walnut and finish blue. Weight about 10.8 lbs.

Target Grade

NIB	Exc.	V.G.	Good	Fair	Poor
700	595	500	400	300	200

Match Grade

NIB	Exc.	V.G.	Good	Fair	Poor
795	675	550	450	350	250

EAA SABATTI

These firearms are made by Sabatti firm in Gardone, Italy. It is an old line company, having been in the firearms business since 1674. Company also produces and supplies component parts to many of Italy's premier gun makers. These shotguns and rifles are manufactured for the cost-conscious buyer.

EAA Sabatti Falcon

Field grade over/under shotgun, with checkered walnut stock and pistol-grip, boxlock action, double triggers and extractors. Offered in 12- or 20-gauge with 3" chambers. Also available in 28-gauge and .410 bore with 26" or 28" barrels. Barrel lengths are available in 26", 28" or 30". Chokes are fixed.

12/20 Gauge

NIB	Exc.	V.G.	Good	Fair	Poor
575	425	400	350	300	250

28/.410

NIB	Exc.	V.G.	Good	Fair	Poor
625	480	425	375	325	275

EAA SP 1822

Sabatti rifle chambered for .22 LR. Semi-automatic carbine, with two-piece adjustable stock.

NIB	Exc.	V.G.	Good	Fair	Poor
225	175	125	100	85	60

EAA SP 1822H

Heavy barrel version of above model without sights. Receiver fitted with scope mount base.

NIB	Exc.	V.G.	Good	Fair	Poor
225	175	125	100	85	60

EAA SP 1822TH

This variation also has a heavy barrel without sights, with base mounts. One-piece Bell and Carlson thumbhole stock is feature of this model.

NIB	Exc.	V.G.	Good	Fair	Poor
350	260	225	175	125	90

EAA Sporting Clay Basic

Features single-selective trigger, extractors, checkered walnut stock and pistol-grip, extra wide rib. Flued receiver with scroll engraving. Offered in 12-gauge only, with 28" fixed choke barrel.

NIB	Exc.	V.G.	Good	Fair	Poor
350	275	250	200	150	100

EAA Sporting Clay Pro

Similar to basic sporting clay. Addition of a select walnut stock, screw-in choke tubes, automatic ejectors, recoil pad. Comes with hard shell case.

NIB	Exc.	V.G.	Good	Fair	Poor
950	720	650	550	450	300

EAA Sporting Clay Pro Gold

Same as above, with gold inlay receiver.

NIB	Exc.	V.G.	Good	Fair	Poor
1000	750	650	550	450	300

EAA Saba

A side-by-side shotgun. Features an engraved silver boxlock receiver, double-/single triggers, selective ejectors, solid raised matted rib and select European walnut checkered stock. Offered in 12-, 20-, 28-gauge and .410 bore. Barrel length 26" or 28" with fixed chokes.

NIB	Exc.	V.G.	Good	Fair	Poor
775	600	500	400	300	250

EAA/Saiga Shotgun

Semi-automatic shotgun based on AK-47 design. Chambered for 12-, 20-gauge and .410 bore. Barrel lengths 20", 24", 26" or 28". Blued finish with optional camo finish. Detachable 5-round box magazine. Introduced in 1999. **NOTE:** Deduct $175 for .410 variation.

NIB	Exc.	V.G.	Good	Fair	Poor
600	525	450	350	200	125

EAA/Saiga Rifle

Same as above, but chambered for 7.62x39 or .308 cartridge. Fitted with 20" barrel. Choice of wood or synthetic stock. Introduced in 1999. **NOTE:** Add $100 for .308 caliber.

NIB	Exc.	V.G.	Good	Fair	Poor
550	450	300	200	125	75

EAA Rover 870

High-quality bolt-action rifle. Walnut stock is checkered, with rubber recoil pad. Adjustable rear sight and receiver is drilled and tapped for scope mount. Barrel length 22". Chambered for these cartridges: .22-250, .243, .25-06, .270, .308, .30-06, 7mm Rem. Magnum, .300 and .338 Win. Magnum.

NIB	Exc.	V.G.	Good	Fair	Poor
585	445	375	300	200	125

EAA Benelli Silhouette Pistol

Specialized competition pistol, with a semi-automatic action. Stocks are match type walnut with stippling. Palm shelf is adjustable. Barrel 4.3" long. Fully adjustable sights. Chambered for .22 LR, .22 Short and .32 WC. Supplied with loading tool and cleaning rod. The .22-caliber version weighs 38.5 oz. Overall length 11.7".

NIB	Exc.	V.G.	Good	Fair	Poor
2000	1350	995	750	600	400

MP94 Combo Gun

An over/under combination model, with a 12-gauge shotgun barrel atop a rifle barrel. Chambered for either .223 or .308. A .410/22 LR version is also available. Barrels are 20". Stock is checkered walnut. Sights are an adjustable rear and ramp front with bead. Other features include double triggers, Picatinny scope rail and four choke tubes for the shotgun barrel.

NIB	Exc.	V.G.	Good	Fair	Poor
675	525	400	300	250	125

Model .410/22 LR

NIB	Exc.	V.G.	Good	Fair	Poor
485	400	325	250	200	125

Model 221 Double Rifle

An affordable side-by-side double rifle in .30-06 or .45-70, with 23.5" barrels, checkered walnut stock, double triggers and extractors. Sights are an adjustable rear and ramp front with bead, plus a Picatinny or 11mm scope rail.

NIB	Exc.	V.G.	Good	Fair	Poor
1000	850	650	500	400	350

EVANS, J. E.
Philadelphia, Pennsylvania

Pocket Pistol

Copy of Philadelphia-made Henry Deringer pistol. Chambered for .41-caliber. Utilizes the percussion ignition system. Barrels from 2.5" to 3" in length. Stock is walnut, with checkered grip and mountings are scroll engraved German silver. Barrel marked "J.E. Evans Philada." Manufactured in 1850s.

NIB	Exc.	V.G.	Good	Fair	Poor
—	—	1250	1850	775	350

EVANS REPEATING RIFLE CO.
Mechanic Falls, Maine

Incorporated in 1873, this firm produced repeating rifles based upon patents issued to Warren R. Evans (1868-1871) and later George F. Evans (1877, 1878 and 1879). Most distinctive feature of these arms is they used a butt magazine operating on the principle of an Archimedean screw. Distributed by Merwin, Hulbert & Company, as well as Schuyler, Hartley & Graham, Evans rifles met with some success. One of their earliest advocates was William F. Cody (Buffalo Bill). Company ceased operations in 1879, after approximately 15,000 arms had been made.

LEVER-ACTION RIFLES

Rifle is totally unique for a number of reasons. Holds the most rounds of any repeating rifle that did not have a detachable magazine, with capacities up to 38 rounds on some models. Rifle was chambered for its own cartridge—the .44 Evans of which there were two versions: a 1" cartridge in the "Old Model" and "Transition Model" and a 1.5" cartridge in "New Model". Finish on these rifles is blued, with nickel-plated levers and buttplates noted on some examples. Stocks are walnut. Approximately 12,250 models manufactured between 1873 and 1879.

Old Model

This variation chambered for 1" .44 Evans cartridge. Has a butt stock that covers only the top half of revolving 34-shot magazine located in butt of rifle. Buttplate appears as if it is reversed and markings on the "Old Model" are "Evans Repeating Rifle/Pat. Dec. 8, 1868 & Sept. 16, 1871". There are three versions of Old Model listed. Manufactured between 1874 and 1876 and serial numbered 1-500.

Military Musket

This version has 30" barrel, with two barrel bands and provisions for a bayonet. Only 50 estimated manufactured.

NIB	Exc.	V.G.	Good	Fair	Poor
—	—	3750	1700	500	200

Sporting Rifle

Approximately 300 of this model produced, with 26", 28" or 30" octagonal barrel.

NIB	Exc.	V.G.	Good	Fair	Poor
—	—	1950	900	500	200

Carbine

This variation has 22" barrel, with one barrel band and sling swivel. There were 150 produced.

NIB	Exc.	V.G.	Good	Fair	Poor
—	—	3500	1450	500	200

Transitional Model

Has a buttstock that covers both top and bottom of rotary magazine, with an exposed portion in middle of the butt. Buttplate does not have backward appearance and barrel marked "Evans Repeating Rifle Mechanic Falls Me./Pat Dec. 8, 1868 & Sept. 16, 1871". This version manufactured in 1876 and 1877. Serial numbered between 500-2185, for a total of approximately 1,650 manufactured.

Military Musket

Has a 30" barrel and two barrel bands. 150 were produced.

NIB	Exc.	V.G.	Good	Fair	Poor
—	—	3000	1750	650	200

Carbine

Produced 450, with 22" barrel and one barrel band.

NIB	Exc.	V.G.	Good	Fair	Poor
—	—	2950	1700	600	200

Sporting Rifle

Has 26", 28" or 30" barrel. There were 1,050 produced.

NIB	Exc.	V.G.	Good	Fair	Poor
—	—	2250	1000	300	150

Montreal Carbine

Special issue marked "Montreal", sold by R.H. Kilby, Evans' Canadian sales agent. Between 50 and 100 produced.

NIB	Exc.	V.G.	Good	Fair	Poor
—	—	3250	1150	450	250

New Model

Approximately 10,000 New Model were produced. Chambered for 1.5" .44 Evans cartridge, with magazine capacity reduced to 28. Frame was redesigned and rounded at top and fore-end fit flush to receiver. Lever and hammer are streamlined and a dust cover over loading gate. Markings are same as on Transitional Model, with "U.S.A." added to last line. This version was not serial numbered and any numbers found are assembly numbers only

Military Musket

3,000 produced, with 30" barrel and two barrel bands.

Courtesy Bonhams & Butterfields, San Francisco, California

NIB	Exc.	V.G.	Good	Fair	Poor
—	—	3950	1750	450	275

Carbine

4,000 produced, with 22" barrel, one barrel band and sling swivel.

Courtesy Buffalo Bill Historical Center, Cody, Wyoming

NIB	Exc.	V.G.	Good	Fair	Poor
—	—	2150	950	500	250

Sporting Rifle

3,000 produced, with 26", 28" or 30" octagonal barrels.

NIB	Exc.	V.G.	Good	Fair	Poor
—	—	2500	2000	800	300

EXCAM
Hialeah, Florida

An importer of firearms, not a manufacturer. Erma and Uberti products imported by this company are under their own heading in this book. Other products that they imported are listed here. No longer in business.

TA 76

Patterned after Colt Single Action Army and chambered for .22 rimfire cartridge. Has a 4.75", 6" or 9" barrel and blue finish, with wood grips. Offered with brass trigger guard and backstrap. Also offered chrome-plated. A combo model with an extra .22 Magnum cylinder is available and would add 10 percent to listed values.

NIB	Exc.	V.G.	Good	Fair	Poor
—	100	75	65	40	25

TA 38 Over/Under Derringer

Two-shot derringer patterned after Remington derringer. Chambered for .38 Special cartridge. Has 3" barrels that pivot upward for loading. Blued, with checkered nylon grips. Discontinued in 1985.

NIB	Exc.	V.G.	Good	Fair	Poor
—	100	75	65	40	25

TA 90

Double-action semi-automatic copy of CZ-75, that some experts rate as the finest combat handgun in the world. Chambered for 9mm Parabellum and has a 4.75" barrel. Constructed of steel and finished with matte blue or chrome. Checkered wood or rubber grips. Detachable magazine holds 15 rounds.

NIB	Exc.	V.G.	Good	Fair	Poor
425	375	325	275	200	150

BTA-90B

Compact version of TA 90. Has a 3.5" barrel and 12-round detachable magazine. Similar in all other respects to standard model. Rubber grips only.

NIB	Exc.	V.G.	Good	Fair	Poor
425	375	325	275	200	150

TA 90 SS

Competition version of TA 90. Similar to standard model, except it is compensated and features adjustable sights. Offered either blued or chrome-plated. Introduced in 1989.

NIB	Exc.	V.G.	Good	Fair	Poor
650	575	500	400	325	225

TA 41, 41C, and 41 SS

Series of pistols identical to TA 90 series, except they are chambered for .41 Action Express cartridge. Values are about 10 percent higher than 9mm versions. Introduced in 1989.

Warrior Model W 722

Double-action revolver chambered for .22 rimfire and .22 rimfire Magnum, with an interchangeable cylinder. Has a 6" barrel, adjustable sights and 8-shot cylinder capacity. Blued, with checkered plastic grips. Model not imported after 1986.

NIB	Exc.	V.G.	Good	Fair	Poor
—	100	75	50	35	20

Model W384

Double-action revolver chambered for .38 Special cartridge, with 4" or 6" ventilated rib barrel. Blued finish and plastic grips. Discontinued in 1986.

NIB	Exc.	V.G.	Good	Fair	Poor
—	175	125	100	75	50

Model W357

Similar to W384, except chambered for .357 Magnum cartridge. Discontinued in 1986.

NIB	Exc.	V.G.	Good	Fair	Poor
—	200	150	125	100	75

Targa GT 26

A blowback-operated semi-automatic pistol, chambered for .25 ACP cartridge. Has a 2.5" barrel and 6-shot detachable magazine. Finished in blue or matte chrome, with choice of alloy or steel frame. Grips are wood.

Steel Frame Version

NIB	Exc.	V.G.	Good	Fair	Poor
125	90	75	50	40	30

Alloy Frame Version

NIB	Exc.	V.G.	Good	Fair	Poor
100	75	50	35	30	25

GT 22

Semi-automatic pistol, chambered for .22 LR cartridge. Has a 4" barrel, fixed sights and 10-round magazine. Available either blued or matte chrome-plated, with wooden grips.

NIB	Exc.	V.G.	Good	Fair	Poor
200	175	150	125	90	70

GT 22T

Similar to GT 22, with 6" barrel and adjustable target-type sights.

NIB	Exc.	V.G.	Good	Fair	Poor
225	200	175	150	100	75

GT 32

Blowback-operated semi-automatic pistol, chambered for .32 ACP cartridge. Has a 7-round magazine and either blued or matte chrome-plated, with wood grips.

NIB	Exc.	V.G.	Good	Fair	Poor
200	175	150	125	90	75

GT 380

Similar to GT 32, except chambered for .380 ACP cartridge.

NIB	Exc.	V.G.	Good	Fair	Poor
225	175	150	125	100	75

GT 380XE

Similar to GT 380, with 11-shot high-capacity detachable magazine.

NIB	Exc.	V.G.	Good	Fair	Poor
225	200	175	150	125	100

EXCEL INDUSTRIES
Ontario, California

Accelerator Pistol

Semi-automatic pistol currently available in .22 WMR or 5.7x28mm. Previously chambered for .22 LR, .17 HMR and .17 Mach 2. Barrel length 6.5" or 8.5" and diameter .875". Stainless steel with polymer grip. Barrel fitted with an aluminum rib, target sights and Weaver base. Magazine capacity 9 rounds. Weight about 54 oz. Introduced in 2004. **NOTE:** Add $50 to $75 for red dot optical sight or factory-mounted scope; $100 for 5.7x28mm chambering.

NIB	Exc.	V.G.	Good	Fair	Poor
425	320	250	165	125	75

Accelerator Rifle

As above, with 18" fluted stainless steel barrel and black polymer pistol-grip stock. Fully adjustable removable sights on a Weaver rail. Weight about 8 lbs. Introduced in 2004.

NIB	Exc.	V.G.	Good	Fair	Poor
465	350	275	195	150	100

X-22

Blow-back semi-automatic in .22 LR, with 10- or 25-round magazine. Barrel is 4.375", overall length 12". Sights are fully adjustable. Frame is CNC-machined aluminum, with accessory rail. Rifle variation with 18" barrel is also available, with comparable values.

NIB	Exc.	V.G.	Good	Fair	Poor
385	300	250	200	150	100

X-57 / X-30

Centerfire series of AR-type pistols, chambered in 5.7x28mm or .30 Carbine. Magazine capacity: 25-rounds 5.7; 20-rounds .30 Carbine; 10-rounds where required by law. Features are similar to X-22 model, except barrel length is 8.5", overall length 16". Rifle variation with 18" barrel is also available, with comparable values.

NIB	Exc.	V.G.	Good	Fair	Poor
600	515	425	350	250	150

F

F.A.S.
Italy

Model 601

High-grade competition target pistol, chambered for .22 Short cartridge. Semi-automatic, with 5.5" barrel and adjustable target sights. Detachable magazine holds 5 rounds. Finish is blued, with wrap-around target grips. Discontinued in 1988.

NIB	Exc.	V.G.	Good	Fair	Poor
—	1450	1150	775	550	300

Model 602

Similar to Model 601, except chambered for .22 LR. Discontinued in 1987.

NIB	Exc.	V.G.	Good	Fair	Poor
—	1250	975	725	500	250

Model 603

Chambered for .32 S&W Wadcutter cartridge. Features adjustable grips. Discontinued in 1987.

NIB	Exc.	V.G.	Good	Fair	Poor
—	1350	1075	775	500	250

F.I.E.
Hialeah, Florida

Firearms Import and Export engaged in the business of importing Franchi shotgun (which is listed under its own heading) and Arminius revolver (which is made in Germany). They were also distributors for Titan semi-automatic pistols, which are manufactured in U.S.A. They were also importing a series of 9mm pistols from Italy, that are produced by Tanfoglio and known as TZ series. F.I.E. no longer in business as of 1990.

HANDGUNS

TZ 75

Copy of CZ 75 Czechoslovakian combat pistol, produced by Tanfoglio in Italy. A 9mm double-action semi-automatic, with 4.75" barrel, all-steel construction, fixed sights and 15-shot magazine. Offered either blued or matte chrome plated, with wood or rubber grips.

NIB	Exc.	V.G.	Good	Fair	Poor
450	350	300	250	200	150

TZ 75 Series 88

Improved version that is also chambered for .41 Action Express cartridge. Has a firing pin safety and can be carried cocked and locked. Few other minor changes. Introduced in 1988.

NIB	Exc.	V.G.	Good	Fair	Poor
500	375	325	250	200	150

KG-99

Blowback-operated semi-automatic assault pistol, chambered for 9mm Parabellum cartridge. Has a 36-round magazine. Discontinued in 1984.

NIB	Exc.	V.G.	Good	Fair	Poor
550	450	350	250	200	150

Spectre Assault Pistol

Assault-type semi-automatic pistol, chambered for 9mm Parabellum. Has a 30- or 50-round magazine available. Introduced in 1989.

NIB	Exc.	V.G.	Good	Fair	Poor
800	675	575	400	300	200

Titan II .22

Semi-automatic pistol chambered for .22 LR. Has a 10-shot magazine and blued finish, with walnut grips. Made in the U.S.A.

NIB	Exc.	V.G.	Good	Fair	Poor
275	150	100	75	50	25

Titan E32

Single-action blowback-operated semi-automatic pistol, that was chambered for .32 ACP and now chambered for .380 ACP cartridge. Finish is blue or chrome-plated. Grips are walnut.

NIB	Exc.	V.G.	Good	Fair	Poor
300	175	150	125	100	75

Super Titan 11

Similar to Titan, except it has a 12-round high-capacity magazine.

NIB	Exc.	V.G.	Good	Fair	Poor
325	200	175	150	100	75

Titan 25

Smaller version of Titan Series, chambered for .25 ACP cartridge. Blued or chrome-plated.

NIB	Exc.	V.G.	Good	Fair	Poor
200	75	50	40	30	20

Titan Tigress

Similar to Titan 25, except gold-plated and cased.

NIB	Exc.	V.G.	Good	Fair	Poor
225	115	90	75	50	30

D38 Derringer

Two-shot over/under Remington-style derringer. Chambered for .38 Special cartridge and chrome-plated. Dropped from line in 1985.

NIB	Exc.	V.G.	Good	Fair	Poor
145	75	45	35	25	20

D86 Derringer

Single-shot derringer with 3" barrel. Chambered for .38 Special cartridge and chrome-plated. An ammunition storage compartment in butt and transfer bar safety makes it safer to carry. Introduced in 1986.

NIB	Exc.	V.G.	Good	Fair	Poor
150	80	65	50	35	20

SINGLE ACTION ARMY REPLICA REVOLVERS

There is a series of single-action .22-caliber revolvers, that were patterned after Colt Single Action Army. Manufactured in U.S.A. or Brescia, Italy. They are inexpensive and of fair quality. Differences between these models are basically barrel lengths, type of sights and finish. All are chambered for .22 LR and have interchangeable .22 Magnum cylinders. We list them for reference purposes.

Cowboy

NIB	Exc.	V.G.	Good	Fair	Poor
250	125	100	80	75	50

Gold Rush

NIB	Exc.	V.G.	Good	Fair	Poor
250	125	100	80	75	50

Texas Ranger

NIB	Exc.	V.G.	Good	Fair	Poor
200	85	75	50	35	20

Buffalo Scout

NOTE: Add 50 percent for faux "gold" -plated Yellow Rose of Texas variant.

NIB	Exc.	V.G.	Good	Fair	Poor
175	80	70	50	35	20

Legend S.A.A.

NIB	Exc.	V.G.	Good	Fair	Poor
250	125	100	80	75	50

ARMINIUS REVOLVERS

Hombre

Single-action made in Germany by Arminius. Patterned after Colt Single Action Army revolver. Hombre chambered for .357 Magnum, .44 Magnum and .45 Colt cartridges. Offered with 5.5", 6" or 7.5" barrel. Case colored frame, blued barrel and cylinder, with smooth walnut grips. Backstrap and trigger guard offered in brass will bring a 10 percent premium.

NIB	Exc.	V.G.	Good	Fair	Poor
325	225	175	125	100	75

Model 522TB

Swing-out cylinder double-action revolver, chambered for .22 rimfire cartridge. Has a 4" barrel and blued, with wood grips.

NIB	Exc.	V.G.	Good	Fair	Poor
250	125	100	75	50	30

722

Similar to 522, with an 8-shot cylinder and 6" barrel. Available with chrome finish.

NIB	Exc.	V.G.	Good	Fair	Poor
250	125	100	75	50	30

532TB

A 7-shot double-action revolver, chambered for .32 S&W cartridge. Has a 4" barrel, adjustable sights and finished in either blue or chrome.

NIB	Exc.	V.G.	Good	Fair	Poor
250	130	110	80	60	40

732B

Similar to 532TB, with 6" barrel and fixed sights. Discontinued in 1988.

NIB	Exc.	V.G.	Good	Fair	Poor
225	100	80	65	50	35

Standard Revolver

Double-action swing-out cylinder revolver. Chambered for .32 Magnum or .38 Special. Has a 4" or 6" barrel. Fixed sights and blued, with wood grips. Model made in U.S.A. Introduced in 1989.

NIB	Exc.	V.G.	Good	Fair	Poor
225	100	75	50	35	20

Models 384TB and 386TB

These two models are double-action. Chambered for .38 Special cartridge. The 384 has a 4" barrel; 386 a 6" barrel. Available in blue or chrome plate. Both discontinued in 1985.

NIB	Exc.	V.G.	Good	Fair	Poor
250	125	100	85	65	50

Model 357TB

Similar to 384TB, except chambered for .357 Magnum cartridge. Offered with 3", 4" or 6" barrel.

NIB	Exc.	V.G.	Good	Fair	Poor
250	125	100	85	65	50

222, 232, and 382TB

These models are double-action swing-out cylinder revolvers. Chambered for .22 rimfire, .32 S&W and .38 Special. They are 2"-barreled snub-nosed revolvers, with either blued or chrome-plated finishes. Discontinued in 1985.

NIB	Exc.	V.G.	Good	Fair	Poor
200	100	75	50	40	25

Model 3572

Similar revolver to 382TB, except chambered for .357 Magnum cartridge. Discontinued in 1984.

NIB	Exc.	V.G.	Good	Fair	Poor
250	125	100	85	65	50

SHOTGUNS AND RIFLES

Model 122

Bolt-action rifle chambered for .22 rimfire, with 21" barrel and adjustable sights. Has a 10-shot magazine and walnut Monte Carlo stock. Introduced in 1986.

NIB	Exc.	V.G.	Good	Fair	Poor
200	100	75	50	35	25

Single-Shot

Brazilian made chambered for 12- or 20-gauge and .410 bore. Single-barrel break-open, with 25" through 30" barrel lengths. Various chokes. Blued, with a wood stock. Introduced in 1985.

NIB	Exc.	V.G.	Good	Fair	Poor
150	100	60	45	35	25

S.O.B.

Similar to single-shot, with 18.5" barrel and pistol-grip instead of standard stock. Discontinued in 1984.

NIB	Exc.	V.G.	Good	Fair	Poor
165	110	60	45	35	25

Sturdy Over/Under

Chambered for 12- and 20-gauge. Has 3" chambers and 28" ventilated rib barrels, with various chokes. An over/under with double triggers and extractors. Frame is engraved and silver finished. Manufactured in Italy by Maroccini and imported between 1985 and 1988.

NIB	Exc.	V.G.	Good	Fair	Poor
400	300	225	175	150	100

Brute

Side-by-side chambered for 12- or 20-gauge and .410 bore. Has 19" barrels, double triggers and extractors, with a wood stock. Dropped from line in 1984.

NIB	Exc.	V.G.	Good	Fair	Poor
300	200	125	100	75	50

SPAS-12

A unique shotgun in that it can function as a pump or automatic, with the touch of a button. A paramilitary-type shotgun. Chambered for 12-gauge, with 21.5" barrel and 9-shot tube magazine. Has an alloy receiver and optional folding stock. Finish is all black. Manufactured by Franchi in Italy. **NOTE:** Some early models had detachable wood stocks. These are rarely encountered. Seek a qualified appraiser for evaluations.

NIB	Exc.	V.G.	Good	Fair	Poor
1500	1100	900	700	400	300

LAW-12

A paramilitary-type 12-gauge semi-automatic shotgun, that is gas-operated. Has a 9-shot tube magazine. Barrel is 21.5" in length and choked cylinder bore. Has a military special black finish and black synthetic stock.

NIB	Exc.	V.G.	Good	Fair	Poor
850	650	400	300	200	100

SAS-12

A paramilitary-type slide-action shotgun, chambered for 12-gauge. Has a 21.5" barrel and choked cylinder bore. Finish is similar to LAW-12. Manufactured by Franchi in Italy.

NIB	Exc.	V.G.	Good	Fair	Poor
850	650	500	400	300	200

FABARM
Brescia, Italy

In 1998, H&K took over importation of Fabarm shotgun line in U.S. Imported by Tristar and Sig Arms from 2005 - 2009. Currently imported by Fabarm USA.

SEMI-AUTOMATIC SHOTGUNS

Ellegi Standard

Gas-operated semi-automatic shotgun, chambered for 12-gauge. Has a 28" ventilated rib barrel, with choice of choke. Receiver is blue anodized alloy, with a photo-etched game scene. Stock and forearm are checkered walnut. Introduced in 1989. Ellegi Model available in six other configurations. Differences are in barrel length and choke, type of choke tubes and finish. Basically the guns are quite similar to standard model. These variations are listed.

NIB	Exc.	V.G.	Good	Fair	Poor
700	625	525	450	350	250

Ellegi Multichoke

NIB	Exc.	V.G.	Good	Fair	Poor
700	625	525	450	350	250

Ellegi Innerchoke

NIB	Exc.	V.G.	Good	Fair	Poor
725	650	550	475	375	275

Ellegi Magnum

NIB	Exc.	V.G.	Good	Fair	Poor
725	650	550	475	375	275

Ellegi Super Goose

NIB	Exc.	V.G.	Good	Fair	Poor
800	725	625	550	450	350

Ellegi Slug

NIB	Exc.	V.G.	Good	Fair	Poor
775	700	600	525	425	325

Ellegi Police

NIB	Exc.	V.G.	Good	Fair	Poor
575	500	450	400	300	225

XLR5 Velocity

Semi-automatic 12-gauge shotgun, designed for clay target shooting. With 2.75" chamber, Turkish walnut stock, adjustable comb and rib, 30" or 32" barrel and five choke tubes. Also available in left-hand configuration. Velocity Silver model has titanium receiver. **NOTE:** Add $150 for left-hand model; $300 for Velocity Silver.

NIB	Exc.	V.G.	Good	Fair	Poor
1750	1600	1200	900	750	400

LR (Long Rib)

NIB	Exc.	V.G.	Good	Fair	Poor
1900	1750	1300	1000	750	400

AR (Adjustable Rib)

NIB	Exc.	V.G.	Good	Fair	Poor
2350	2050	1700	1200	750	400

L4S Initial Hunter

Semi-automatic shotgun in 12-gauge, with 26" or 28" barrel, black anodized frame and Turkish walnut stock with hand-oiled finish. Innovative feature allowing removal of fore-end to clean the action without removing barrel. Grey Hunter and Deluxe Hunter models feature engraved receivers and higher-grades of wood. **NOTE:** Add $400 for Grey Hunter; $700 for Deluxe Hunter.

NIB	Exc.	V.G.	Good	Fair	Poor
1050	850	650	500	400	300

SLIDE-ACTION SHOTGUNS

Model S.D.A.S.S.

Chambered for 12-gauge with 3" chamber. Offered with 20" or 24.5" barrel, threaded for external choke tubes. Has 8-shot tube magazine, twin action bars, alloy receiver and matte black finish. Defensive-type shotgun and imported since 1989. Special Police and Martial Model are variations of basic slide-action. Differ in barrel length and choke. Police Model has a shrouded barrel.

NIB	Exc.	V.G.	Good	Fair	Poor
350	275	200	150	100	75

Special Police

NIB	Exc.	V.G.	Good	Fair	Poor
525	475	425	350	275	200

Martial Model

NIB	Exc.	V.G.	Good	Fair	Poor
475	425	375	300	225	175

SINGLE-SHOT SHOTGUNS

Omega Standard

Has an alloy receiver chambered for 12- or 20-gauge and .410 bore. Has 26" or 28" barrels, with various chokes. Finish is black, with a beech stock. Introduced in 1989.

NIB	Exc.	V.G.	Good	Fair	Poor
150	125	100	75	50	40

Omega Goose Gun

Chambered for 12-gauge only, with 35.5" full-choke barrel.

NIB	Exc.	V.G.	Good	Fair	Poor
195	140	125	100	75	50

SIDE-BY-SIDE SHOTGUNS

Beta Model

Double-barrel is chambered for 12-gauge only, with choice of barrel length and choke. Boxlock action, with false side plates, single trigger and automatic ejectors. Finish is blued, with checkered select walnut stock. Introduced in 1989.

NIB	Exc.	V.G.	Good	Fair	Poor
925	850	750	600	450	300

Beta Europe

Deluxe version features single-selective triggers. A game scene engraved coin-finished receiver. Stock is straight English style, with a splinter fore-end. Introduced in 1989.

NIB	Exc.	V.G.	Good	Fair	Poor
1750	1500	1250	1000	750	500

OVER/UNDER SHOTGUNS

Field Model

Chambered for 12-gauge. Has 29" ventilated rib barrels, with various chokes. Receiver is coin-finished and stock checkered walnut. Discontinued in 1985.

NIB	Exc.	V.G.	Good	Fair	Poor
900	700	600	500	400	300

Gamma Field

Chambered for 12- or 20-gauge. Offered with 26", 28" or 29" ventilated rib barrels and various choke combinations. Screw-in choke tubes are available and would be worth a 10 percent premium. Has a boxlock coin-finished receiver that is moderately engraved and checkered walnut stock.

NIB	Exc.	V.G.	Good	Fair	Poor
925	850	775	650	500	350

Gamma Paradox Gun

Chambered for 12-gauge only. Top barrel is rifled for accurate placement of slugs. Barrels are 25" long, with ventilated rib. Bottom barrel has three screw-in choke tubes. Has a single-selective trigger and automatic ejectors. Finish is similar to Field Model. Introduced in 1989.

NIB	Exc.	V.G.	Good	Fair	Poor
1000	900	825	750	600	450

Gamma Trap or Skeet

Competition-grade guns. Either with 27.5" barrel and five screw-in choke tubes on skeet model, or 29" barrel with screw-in trap chokes. Both models feature single-selective triggers and automatic ejectors; trap model has Monte Carlo stock. Moderately engraved and coin-finished boxlock actions. Introduced in 1989.

NIB	Exc.	V.G.	Good	Fair	Poor
1000	900	825	750	600	450

Gamma Sporting Competition Model

Designed for Sporting Clays and chambered for 12-gauge only. The 29" barrel has a wide rib and furnished with five screw-in choke tubes. It has single-selective trigger, automatic ejectors and checkered walnut stock, with a competition recoil pad. Finished like skeet and trap models. Introduced in 1989.

NIB	Exc.	V.G.	Good	Fair	Poor
1000	900	825	750	600	450

Elos

Over/under offered only in 20- or 28-gauge, with round action, 28" barrels, 5 choke tubes, steel or aluminum alloy frame, with case colored or titanium finish. Stock and fore-end are checkered Turkish walnut, with hand-rubbed oil finish. Deluxe model features game scene engraving and premium grade Turkish walnut. Values shown are for standard 20-gauge. New in 2013. **NOTE:** Add $150 for 28-gauge; $500 for Deluxe model.

NIB	Exc.	V.G.	Good	Fair	Poor
2050	1750	1425	1100	850	450

Axis Competition

Competition-grade over/under in 12-gauge only. Two variants are offered: Sporting and Trap. Both feature Turkish walnut stocks, with adjustable comb. Sporting model has 30" or 32" barrels; Trap barrels are 32" or 34", with high-profile adjustable rib and Fabarm's removable Kinetik recoil reduction system. New in 2013.

Sporting

NIB	Exc.	V.G.	Good	Fair	Poor
2600	2200	1800	1250	900	450

Trap

NIB	Exc.	V.G.	Good	Fair	Poor
3700	3000	2500	1850	1100	550

H&K 1997-2004 IMPORTED SHOTGUNS

Camo Lion

Introduced in 1999, this 12-gauge model features a ported barrel system in 24", 26" or 28" lengths. Wetlands camo finish. Five choke tubes and hard plastic case included. Weight about 7 lbs.

NIB	Exc.	V.G.	Good	Fair	Poor
800	650	450	300	175	100

Red Lion

A 12-gauge semi-automatic, with 3" chambers. Has a three-shot magazine, matte finish and walnut stock. Rubber ventilated recoil pad, with leather cover and set of five choke tubes. Available with 24", 26" or 28" ventilated rib barrel. Weight about 7 lbs.

NIB	Exc.	V.G.	Good	Fair	Poor
800	650	450	300	175	100

Red Lion Ducks Unlimited 2001

Offered only through Ducks Unlimited banquet program. This is a 12-gauge, 28" barrel, with select walnut stock. Oil-finish. Unique serial numbers from 0001DU2001 to 3600DU2001. Receiver engraved with waterfowl scene and DU logo. Comes with lockable case. Limited to 3,600 shotguns.

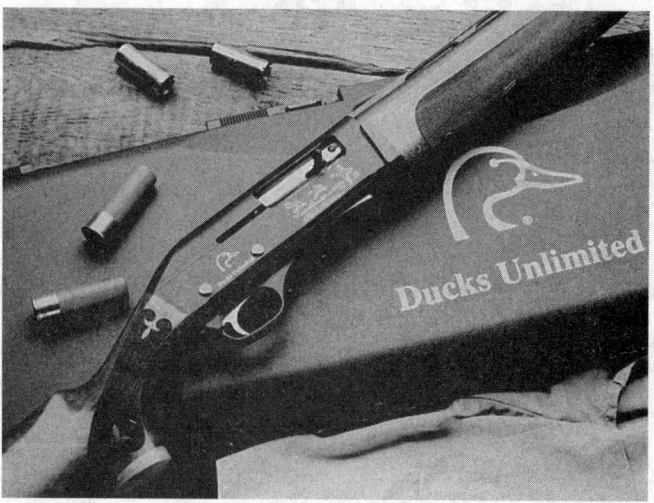

NIB	Exc.	V.G.	Good	Fair	Poor
975	775	625	500	325	200

Gold Lion

Has many features of Red Lion model, with addition of high-grade oil-finished walnut stock and olive wood pistol-grip cap. Trigger is gold plated.

NIB	Exc.	V.G.	Good	Fair	Poor
800	650	450	300	175	100

Gold Lion Mark III

Semi-automatic model is an improved version of Gold Lion. Addition of enhanced walnut stock, lightweight receiver with scroll engraving and gold inlays. Fitted with 28" TriBore barrel and chambered for 3", 12-gauge shell. Supplied with five choke tubes. Weight about 7.2 lbs.

NIB	Exc.	V.G.	Good	Fair	Poor
975	775	625	500	325	200

Sporting Clays Lion

Introduced in 1999. Features a ported barrel and special "TriBore" system. Offered in 12-gauge with 28" barrel. Walnut stock with rubber recoil pad, gold-plated trigger, matte blue finish, red front sight bar, 10mm channeled rib, two extra front sights (green and white) and set of five choke tubes. Weight about 7.2 lbs.

NIB	Exc.	V.G.	Good	Fair	Poor
975	775	625	500	325	200

Rex Lion

Introduced in 2002. Features 12-gauge, with 3" chambers and 26" or 28" ventilated rib barrel. Choke tubes. High-grade walnut stock, with olive wood grip cap. Silver and black frame, with scroll engraving and gold inlay. Weight about 7 lbs. Limited edition.

NIB	Exc.	V.G.	Good	Fair	Poor
1050	800	650	450	300	175

Sporting Clays Extra

Introduced in 2000. Features 28" or 30" ventilated rib barrel, with carbon fiber finish on both barrel and receiver. Also supplied with eight competition choke tubes and fitted luggage case. Stock is adjustable. Weight about 7.3 lbs.

NIB	Exc.	V.G.	Good	Fair	Poor
850	675	450	300	175	100

Tactical Semi-Auto

A 12-gauge semi-automatic shotgun, fitted with 20" barrel threaded for chokes. Receiver-mounted Picatinny rail. Flip-up front sight. Optional magazine extension has 7-round capacity. Optional pistol-grip. Weight about 6.6 lbs. Introduced in 2001.

NIB	Exc.	V.G.	Good	Fair	Poor
650	550	400	265	150	100

Home Security HD

Semi-automatic shotgun chambered for 12-gauge 3" shell. Fitted with 20" plain barrel, with cylinder screw-in choke. Matte black finish. Black polymer stock. Magazine capacity 5 rounds. Weight about 7.5 lbs.

NIB	Exc.	V.G.	Good	Fair	Poor
600	475	300	225	150	100

H368

This 12-gauge 3" model, features 28" TriBore ventilated rib barrel, matte black synthetic stock or Realtree camo stock. Lightweight alloy matte black receiver. Magazine capacity 2 rounds. Weight about 7.2 lbs. Introduced in 2003. Available in a left-hand model. **NOTE:** Add $60 for camo stock; $90 for left-hand model.

NIB	Exc.	V.G.	Good	Fair	Poor
650	550	400	265	150	100

FP6 Field Pump

Introduced in 2001. Features black alloy receiver with screw-in chokes. Chambered for 12-gauge with 28" barrel. Black synthetic stock. Optional 24" rifled barrel. Weight about 7 lbs. Available in Mossy Oak Break-up Camo.

NIB	Exc.	V.G.	Good	Fair	Poor
375	350	275	225	175	100

FP6

A 12-gauge slide-action shotgun, with 3" chamber, 20" barrel, heat shield black polymer stock and threaded barrel for exterior chokes. Weight about 6.6 lbs. Available with carbon fiber finish.

NIB	Exc.	V.G.	Good	Fair	Poor
500	400	300	200	125	100

FP6 with Rail

Introduced in 1999. Similar to standard FP6, with addition of Picatinny rail mounted on top of receiver. Also fitted with flip-up front sight. In 2003 this model offered with 20" TriBore barrel, with barrel threaded choke, new style front sight and ghost ring rear sight. **NOTE:** Available with 14" barrel. Requires BATF tax and all NFA rules apply to purchase and sale of this restricted shotgun. Accessory wire stock and pistol-grip available for an additional $150.

NIB	Exc.	V.G.	Good	Fair	Poor
510	410	300	200	125	100

Max Lion

This over/under gun chambered for 12- or 20-gauge, 3" shell. Fitted with single-selective trigger, auto ejectors, high grade walnut stock, leather covered recoil pad, set of five choke tubes and fitted luggage-style case. Choice of 26", 28" or 30" barrels on 12-gauge; 26" or 28" on 20-gauge. Weight about 7.5 lbs. for 12-gauge; 7 lbs. for 20-gauge. **NOTE:** In 1999 Max Lion was offered with TriBore barrel system. Models with this system add $70 to NIB price.

NIB	Exc.	V.G.	Good	Fair	Poor
1200	900	700	550	300	175

Max Lion Light

Introduced in 2000. Features 24" barrels in both 12- and 20-gauge. Receiver has gold game bird inlay. Single trigger, automatic ejectors and select walnut stock. Weight about 7 lbs.

NIB	Exc.	V.G.	Good	Fair	Poor
1200	900	700	550	300	175

Max Lion Paradox

Introduced in 2002. Features 12-gauge 3" gun, with 24" barrels. Bottom barrel is rifled. Case-hardened receiver, with checkered walnut stock. Weight about 7.6 lbs.

NIB	Exc.	V.G.	Good	Fair	Poor
1425	1175	900	700	550	300

Sporting Clays Competition Lion

Available in 12- or 20-gauge, with 28" 10mm channeled rib barrels. Single-selective trigger and automatic ejectors. Recoil reducer installed in

buttstock. Ported barrels. Set of 5 choke tubes standard. Leather covered recoil pad. High grade walnut stock. Introduced in 1999.

NIB	Exc.	V.G.	Good	Fair	Poor
925	825	600	500	300	150

Sporting Clays Max Lion

Chambered for 12-gauge 3" shell and fitted with 32" TriBore ventilated rib barrel. Select walnut stock with hand checkering, adjustable trigger and leather covered recoil pad. Engraved gold inlay receiver is case colored. Supplied with eight choke tubes. Weight about 7.9 lbs. Introduced in 2003.

NIB	Exc.	V.G.	Good	Fair	Poor
925	825	600	500	300	150

Sporting Clays Competition Extra

This 12-gauge model features a choice of 28" or 30" barrels. Walnut stock adjustable. Finish carbon fiber. Gun supplied with set of eight choke tubes. Introduced in 2000. Weight about 7.8 lbs.

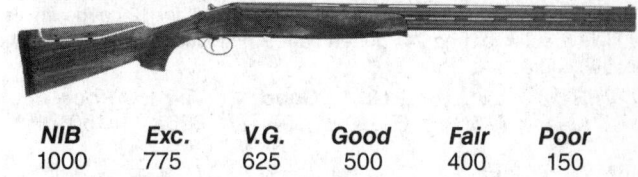

NIB	Exc.	V.G.	Good	Fair	Poor
1000	775	625	500	400	150

Black Lion Competition

Similar to Max Lion. Choice of gauges, barrel lengths and features. Less figured walnut stock and black receiver finish.

NIB	Exc.	V.G.	Good	Fair	Poor
1050	795	650	525	425	175

Monotrap

Single barrel trap gun, with 30" ventilated rib barrel. Forearm has built-in recoil reduction system. Single-selective trigger and automatic ejectors. Adjustable comb. Shotgun is 12-gauge built on 20-gauge receiver. Weight about 6 lbs. Introduced in 2000.

NIB	Exc.	V.G.	Good	Fair	Poor
1800	1350	1100	750	600	500

Silver Lion

Model available in both 12- and 20-gauge, with 26" or 28" barrel. 30" barrels in 12-gauge. Silver finish receiver etched and stock high quality walnut, with leather covered pad. Scalable forearm standard. Single-selective trigger and auto ejectors. Five chokes tubes are included. Weight about: 7.5 lbs. 12-gauge; 7 lbs. 20-gauge.

NIB	Exc.	V.G.	Good	Fair	Poor
925	825	600	500	300	150

Silver Lion Youth

This 20-gauge over/under features shortened buttstock and 24" ported barrels. Single-selective trigger and automatic ejectors standard. Walnut stock. Rubber recoil pad. Silver steel receiver. Weight about 6 lbs. Introduced in 1999.

NIB	Exc.	V.G.	Good	Fair	Poor
800	775	675	500	325	150

Super Light Lion Youth

Similar to Silver Lion Youth model, but chambered for 12-gauge shells. Aluminum receiver and 24" ported barrels. Introduced in 1999. Weight about 6.5 lbs.

NIB	Exc.	V.G.	Good	Fair	Poor
800	775	675	500	325	150

Ultra Mag Lion

This model is a 12-gauge, with 3.5" chambers, black receiver, single-selective trigger, auto ejectors, blackened walnut stock, leather covered recoil pad and set of five choke tubes. Barrel length 28". Weight 7.9 lbs.

NIB	Exc.	V.G.	Good	Fair	Poor
800	775	675	500	325	150

Super Light Lion

Features lightweight alloy receiver, with 12 gauge 24" barrels, single-selective trigger, non-auto ejectors, walnut stock, five choke tubes and leather covered recoil pad. Weight about 6.5 lbs. **NOTE:** Add $125 for TriBore system.

NIB	Exc.	V.G.	Good	Fair	Poor
800	775	675	500	325	150

Camo Turkey Mag

Introduced in 1999. Features unported TriBore 20" barrel. Receiver has Picatinny rail on top. Full extra brown camo finish. Chambered for 12-gauge with 3.5" chambers. Weight about 7.5 lbs.

NIB	Exc.	V.G.	Good	Fair	Poor
925	825	600	500	300	150

Ultra Camo Mag Lion

This 12-gauge 3.5" model fitted with 28" barrels. Wetlands camo pattern finish. Non-automatic ejectors. Weight about 8 lbs. Introduced in 1999. Standard with steel screw-in chokes and regular screw-in chokes.

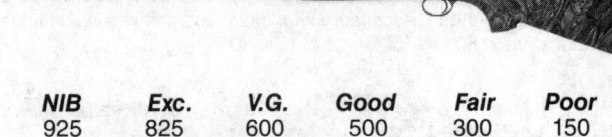

NIB	Exc.	V.G.	Good	Fair	Poor
925	825	600	500	300	150

Classic Lion Grade I

Offered in 12-gauge with 3" chambers. Single-selective trigger, auto-ejectors, walnut stock and buttplate. Fitted with 26" barrels. Weight about 7 lbs.

NIB	Exc.	V.G.	Good	Fair	Poor
1200	925	825	600	500	300

Classic Lion Grade II

Similar to Grade I, with addition of oil-finished stock and removable sideplates. Game scene engraving. Weight 7.2 lbs.

NIB	Exc.	V.G.	Good	Fair	Poor
1200	925	825	600	500	300

Classic Lion Elite

Introduced in 2002, this 12-gauge model features 26" or 28" barrels. Case colored receiver and straight-grip stock. Fixed chokes. Weight about 7 lbs.

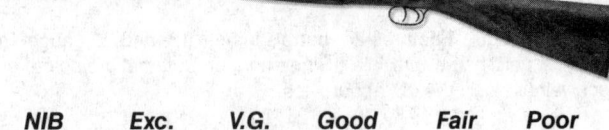

NIB	Exc.	V.G.	Good	Fair	Poor
1300	1025	850	650	525	315

FABBRI, ARMI
Gardone V.T., Italy

Fabbri Armi currently manufactures one of the best shotguns in the world. Available as a custom made-to-order item and are not often seen in the used gun market. Values for guns of this nature and quality are impossible to accurately establish in a book of this nature. There are so many options and conditions that make prices fluctuate greatly. We give an estimated figure, as a base starting point. See Karl Lippard's book *Fabbri Shotguns*, Colorado Springs, Colorado, VM Publications 1998, for more value details.

Side-by-Side Shotgun

Chambered for 12- or 20-gauge, with all other features on custom-order basis. Model no longer in production. **NOTE:** Deduct $10,000 for Type One Model.

NIB	Exc.	V.G.	Good	Fair	Poor
39500	27000	18500	15000	10000	8000

Over/Under Shotgun

Chambered for 12- or 20-gauge, with all other features on custom-order basis. Prices listed are for Boehler barrels. **NOTE:** Add 50 percent for vacuum arc remelted steel barrels. Deduct 50 percent for Phoenix barrels.

NIB	Exc.	V.G.	Good	Fair	Poor
41500	26000	18500	15000	10000	8000

FABRIQUE NATIONALE
Herstal, Belgium

In 1889, Fabrique Nationale (or FN) was founded by a group of Belgian investors for the purpose of manufacturing Mauser rifles for Belgian army. This was to be accomplished under the license from Mauser, with technical assistance of Ludwig Loewe of Berlin. A few years later, in late 1890s, John Browning arrived in Europe seeking a manufacturer for his semi-automatic shotgun. He had severed his ties with Winchester, after a disagreement. This led to a long association that worked out extremely well for both parties. Later Browning became associated with Colt and the world market was divided—with Eastern Hemisphere going to FN and Western Hemisphere to Colt. In this section, we list arms that bear the FN banner. FN-manufactured firearms produced under the Browning banner, are listed in Browning section of this book.

PISTOLS

Model 1900

Blowback-operated semi-automatic pistol, chambered for 7.65mm cartridge. Has 4" barrel and fixed sights. Blued, with molded plastic grips. Manufactured between 1899 and 1910. Model referred to as "Old Model". **NOTE:** Add premium of 30 to 50 percent for factory nickel finish.

NIB	Exc.	V.G.	Good	Fair	Poor
—	1000	850	400	300	200

Model 1903

Considerable improvement over Model 1900. Also a blowback-operated semi-automatic; recoil spring located under barrel and firing pin travels through slide after being struck by a hidden hammer. Barrel is held in place by five locking lugs that fit into five grooves in frame. Pistol chambered for 9mm Browning long cartridge and has a 5" barrel. Finish is blued, with molded plastic grips. Detachable magazine holds 7 rounds. There is a detachable shoulder stock/holster along with a 10-round magazine that was available for this model. Accessories are extremely rare and if present, would make the package worth approximately five times that of the pistol alone. Approximately 58,000 manufactured between 1903 and 1939. **NOTE:** Add premium of 30 to 50 percent for factory nickel finish.

NIB	Exc.	V.G.	Good	Fair	Poor
—	1750	1400	900	600	400

Model 1905

A smaller version of Model 1903. Designed to be a pocket pistol. Chambered for 6.35mm cartridge. Became known as "Vest Pocket" and was also basis for many Eibar copies. Has 2.5" barrel and produced in two distinct variations. First variation had no safety lever or slide lock and relied on grip safety. Second variation, that occurred at approximately serial number 100000, added this safety lever and slide lock, which helped simplify dismantling of pistol. Available either blued or nickel-plated. Plated models would bring 30 to 50 percent premium. Approximately 1,086,100 manufactured between 1906 and 1959. Known in U.S. as Model 1905 and in Europe as Model 1906.

1st Variation, Under Serial Number 100000

NIB	Exc.	V.G.	Good	Fair	Poor
750	650	500	350	200	125

2nd Variation, Over Serial Number 100000

NIB	Exc.	V.G.	Good	Fair	Poor
650	550	400	300	175	100

Model 1910

Chambered for 7.65mm and 9mm short. Has a 3.5" barrel, blued and molded plastic grips. Principal difference between this model and its predecessors, is the recoil spring on Model 1910 is wrapped around the barrel. This gives the slide a more graceful tubular appearance, instead of old slab-sided look. Has triple safety features of 1906 Model, 2nd variation. This model adopted by police forces around the world. Manufactured between 1912 and 1954. **NOTE:** Add $100 for .380 (9mm Short) chambering.

Courtesy Orvel Reichert

NIB	Exc.	V.G.	Good	Fair	Poor
675	600	500	400	300	175

Model 1922

Variation of Model 1910. Made for military and police use in several European countries, between 1922 and 1944. **NOTE:** Add 75 percent if Nazi marked with original magazine; 100 percent for "WaA613" marking.

NIB	Exc.	V.G.	Good	Fair	Poor
550	400	300	200	150	125

"Baby" Model

Smaller and lighter version of Model 1906. Chambered for 6.35mm cartridge. Has 2" barrel. No grip safety or slide lock on this model. Appears to be more square in shape than Model 1906. Offered in blue, with molded plastic grips. Early models have word "Baby" molded into grips; post-1945 versions do not. Also a nickel-plated version with pearl grips. Over 500,000 of these manufactured between 1931 and 1983. Late-production specimens command a slight premium.

NIB	Exc.	V.G.	Good	Fair	Poor
800	650	500	300	225	150

MODEL 1935/HI-POWER/GP

Last design from John Browning developed between 1925 and 1935. Pistol known as Model 1935, P-35, Hi-Power or HP and also GP (which stood for "Grand Puissance") and referred to by all those names at one time or another. HP is essentially an improved version of Colt 1911 design. Swinging link replaced with fixed cam, which was less prone to wear. Chambered for 9mm Parabellum and has a 13-round detachable magazine. Only drawback to the design, that the trigger pull is not as fine as that of the 1911, as there is a transfer bar instead of stirrup arrangement. This is necessary, due to increased magazine capacity resulting in thicker grip. Barrel is 4.75" in length. External hammer with manual and magazine safety. Available with various finishes and sight options. Furnished with shoulder stock. Model 1935 used by many countries as their service pistol, as there are many variations. We list these versions and their approximate values.

Pre-War Commercial Model

Found with sliding tangent rear sight and slotted for detachable shoulder stock. Manufactured from 1935 until 1940.

Tangent Sight Version

NOTE: Add 50 percent for Wood holster stock..

NIB	Exc.	V.G.	Good	Fair	Poor
2800	2000	1800	1500	1000	400

Pre-War Military Contract

Model 1935 adopted by many countries as a service pistol. Following, is a list:

Belgium

NIB	Exc.	V.G.	Good	Fair	Poor
—	3000	2600	2000	600	375

Canada and China

NIB	Exc.	V.G.	Good	Fair	Poor
—	2500	2000	950	650	400

Great Britain

NIB	Exc.	V.G.	Good	Fair	Poor
—	2500	1700	1000	550	325

Estonia

NIB	Exc.	V.G.	Good	Fair	Poor
—	3750	3100	2000	600	375

Holland

NIB	Exc.	V.G.	Good	Fair	Poor
—	3000	2600	2000	650	400

Latvia

NIB	Exc.	V.G.	Good	Fair	Poor
—	3000	2600	2000	775	500

Lithuania

NIB	Exc.	V.G.	Good	Fair	Poor
—	3600	2500	1200	650	400

Romania

NIB	Exc.	V.G.	Good	Fair	Poor
—	3000	2600	2000	775	500

German Military Pistole Model 640(b)

In 1940, Germany occupied Belgium and took over the FN plant. Production of Model 1935 continued, with Germany taking the output. FN plant was assigned production code "ch" and many thousands were produced. Finish on these Nazi guns runs from as fine as Pre-war Commercial series to downright crude. Possible to see how war was progressing for Germany by finish on their weapons. One must be cautious with some of these guns as there have been fakes noted, with their backstraps cut for shoulder stocks, producing what would appear to be a more expensive variation. Individual appraisal should be secured if any doubt exists.

Fixed Sight Model

NIB	Exc.	V.G.	Good	Fair	Poor
—	1000	750	400	300	250

Tangent Sight Model

50,000 manufactured.

Courtesy Orvel Reichert

NIB	Exc.	V.G.	Good	Fair	Poor
—	2200	1600	1000	550	400

Captured Pre-war Commercial Model

These pistols were taken over when plant was occupied. Slotted for stocks and have tangent sights. Few produced between serial number 48,000 and 52,000. All noted have WA613 Nazi proof mark. Beware of fakes!

NIB	Exc.	V.G.	Good	Fair	Poor
—	1700	1400	1150	750	500

Post-War Military Contract

Manufactured from 1946, they embody some design changes—such as improved heat treating and barrel locking. Pistols produced after 1950 do not have barrels that can interchange with earlier models. Earliest models have an "A" prefix on serial number and do not have the magazine safety. Pistols were produced for many countries and there were many thousands manufactured.

Fixed Sight

NIB	Exc.	V.G.	Good	Fair	Poor
—	750	425	375	300	250

Tangent Sight

NIB	Exc.	V.G.	Good	Fair	Poor
—	1000	675	575	400	300

Slotted and Tangent Sight

NIB	Exc.	V.G.	Good	Fair	Poor
—	1500	1050	750	500	400

Post-War Commercial Model

Introduced in 1950 and 1954. Those imported into U.S.A. are marked Browning Arms Co. These pistols have commercial polished finish.

Fixed Sight

NIB	Exc.	V.G.	Good	Fair	Poor
—	850	500	350	300	250

Tangent Sight

NIB	Exc.	V.G.	Good	Fair	Poor
—	1000	650	500	400	350

Slotted and Tangent Sight

NIB	Exc.	V.G.	Good	Fair	Poor
—	1500	1100	800	550	450

RIFLES

Model 1889

NIB	Exc.	V.G.	Good	Fair	Poor
—	350	250	200	125	100

Model 1949 or SAFN 49

NIB	Exc.	V.G.	Good	Fair	Poor
—	600	500	300	225	150

Model 30-11 Sniper Rifle

NIB	Exc.	V.G.	Good	Fair	Poor
—	5000	4500	3500	2750	2000

FN-FAL

50.00—21" Rifle Model

NIB	Exc.	V.G.	Good	Fair	Poor
3000	2750	2250	2000	1850	1000

50.63—18" Paratrooper Model

NIB	Exc.	V.G.	Good	Fair	Poor
3800	3350	2950	2750	2450	1100

50.64—21" Paratrooper Model

NIB	Exc.	V.G.	Good	Fair	Poor
3300	3000	2700	2200	1900	1000

50.41—Synthetic Butt H-Bar

NIB	Exc.	V.G.	Good	Fair	Poor
2800	2400	2000	1800	1200	1000

50.42—Wood Butt H-Bar

NIB	Exc.	V.G.	Good	Fair	Poor
2800	2400	2000	1800	1200	1000

FN-FAL "G" Series (Type I Receiver)

Standard

NIB	Exc.	V.G.	Good	Fair	Poor
6500	5000	4000	3000	2000	1000

Lightweight

NIB	Exc.	V.G.	Good	Fair	Poor
6500	5000	4000	3000	2000	1000

FN CAL

NIB	Exc.	V.G.	Good	Fair	Poor
7000	6500	5000	3000	1500	1000

FNC

NOTE: Prices are for Belgian-made guns only.

Standard

Fixed stock, 16" or 18" barrel.

NIB	Exc.	V.G.	Good	Fair	Poor
3000	2800	2500	2000	1500	1000

Paratrooper Model

Folding stock, 16" or 18" barrel.

NIB	Exc.	V.G.	Good	Fair	Poor
3000	2800	2500	2000	1500	1000

Musketeer Sporting Rifles

Bolt-action rifle built on Mauser-action. Chambered for various popular cartridges. Has a 24" barrel and blued, with checkered walnut stock. Manufactured between 1947 and 1963.

NIB	Exc.	V.G.	Good	Fair	Poor
—	450	350	300	250	200

Deluxe Sporter

Higher-grade version of Musketeer, with same general specifications. Manufactured between 1947 and 1963.

NIB	Exc.	V.G.	Good	Fair	Poor
—	550	450	400	275	200

FN Supreme

Chambered for popular standard calibers. Has a 24" barrel, with an aperture sight and checkered walnut stock. Manufactured between 1957 and 1975.

NIB	Exc.	V.G.	Good	Fair	Poor
—	800	650	500	450	400

Supreme Magnum Model

Similar to standard Supreme, except chambered for .264 Win. Magnum, 7mm Rem. Magnum and .300 Win. Magnum. Furnished with recoil pad. Manufactured between same years as standard model.

NIB	Exc.	V.G.	Good	Fair	Poor
—	800	650	500	400	400

FAIRBANKS, A. B.
Boston, Massachusetts

Fairbanks All Metal Pistol

Odd pistol was produced of all metal. A one-piece cast brass frame, handle, an iron barrel and lock system. Chambered for .33-caliber and utilizes percussion ignition system. Barrel lengths noted are 3" to 10". Barrels are marked "Fairbanks Boston. Cast Steel". Manufactured between 1838 and 1841.

NIB	Exc.	V.G.	Good	Fair	Poor
—	—	1050	350	150	75

FALCON FIREARMS
Northridge, California

Portsider

Copy of Colt 1911. Built for left-handed individual. Constructed of stainless steel and similar in all other respects to Colt. Introduced in 1986. A scarce 1911.

NIB	Exc.	V.G.	Good	Fair	Poor
700	575	450	375	300	225

Portsider Set

Matching serial numbered pair. Consisting of left- and right-handed version, in a case. Only 100 manufactured in 1986 and 1987.

NIB	Exc.	V.G.	Good	Fair	Poor
1400	1250	1000	750	600	475

Gold Falcon

Frame machined from solid 17-karat gold. Slide is stainless steel and sights have diamond inlays. Engraved to customer's order. Only 50 manufactured.

NIB	Exc.	V.G.	Good	Fair	Poor
50000	30000	25000	15000	7500	700

FAMARS, A. & S.
Brescia, Italy

A. Famars shotgun is one of the world's finest and was available on a custom order basis. This makes it quite difficult to accurately establish values in a book of this nature. We list them and give an estimated value in their basic form only. The company ceased production in 2012.

Engraving Pattern Descriptions
(Older Discontinued Patterns)

S2—Traditional fully engraved fine English scroll, with coverage highlighting selected areas of receiver and fore-end metal. Wood grade AA.

S3—Traditional hand-engraved scroll, with some open areas around scroll coverage on receiver and fore-end metal. Wood grade AAA.

S4—Traditional full coverage, intricate and high in detail. Patterns may be English, German or game scene. Wood grade AAAA.

S5—Grade S4 patterns with animals inlaid in 24k gold. Wood grade AAAAA.

S4E—Extremely high detail scenes and elaborate ornamental work where subject matter is selected by customer. Wood grade AAAAA.

S5E—Similar to S4E level, but with raised or flush gold inlay work. Wood grade AAAAA.

SXO—Best work by world's best engravers. Museum quality. Wood grade AAAAAA.

Zeus

Engraved side-by-side boxlock in 12-, 20-, 28-gauge and .410 bore.
NOTE: Add 10 percent for smaller gauges.

In the white

NIB	Exc.	V.G.	Good	Fair	Poor
19000	12000	9000	6500	4750	750

D2 pattern

NIB	Exc.	V.G.	Good	Fair	Poor
20000	12000	9000	6500	4750	750

S3 pattern

NIB	Exc.	V.G.	Good	Fair	Poor
22000	20000	12000	9000	6500	900

Tribute

Engraved side-by-side droplock, offered in 12- or 20-gauge.

In the white

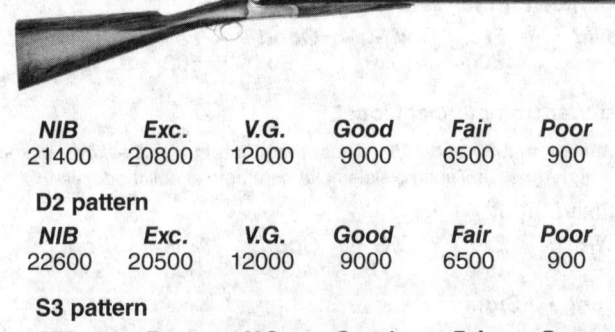

NIB	Exc.	V.G.	Good	Fair	Poor
21400	20800	12000	9000	6500	900

D2 pattern

NIB	Exc.	V.G.	Good	Fair	Poor
22600	20500	12000	9000	6500	900

S3 pattern

NIB	Exc.	V.G.	Good	Fair	Poor
24300	22000	12000	9000	6500	900

Venus

Side-by-side sidelock shotgun, with choice of engraving patterns and coverage. Offered in 12-, 20-, 28-gauge or .410 bore.

In the white

NIB	Exc.	V.G.	Good	Fair	Poor
32700	30500	20000	12000	9000	900

D2 pattern

NIB	Exc.	V.G.	Good	Fair	Poor
33900	31500	—	—	—	—

D3 pattern

NIB	Exc.	V.G.	Good	Fair	Poor
37000	10500	—	—	—	—

D4 pattern

NIB	Exc.	V.G.	Good	Fair	Poor
42800	39000	—	—	—	—

D5 pattern

NIB	Exc.	V.G.	Good	Fair	Poor
48200	42000	—	—	—	—

D4E pattern

NIB	Exc.	V.G.	Good	Fair	Poor
53500	47500	—	—	—	—

D5E pattern

NIB	Exc.	V.G.	Good	Fair	Poor
58500	51500	—	—	—	—

DXO pattern

NIB	Exc.	V.G.	Good	Fair	Poor
85000	55000	—	—	—	—

Veneri

Side-by-side sidelock shotgun.

NIB	Exc.	V.G.	Good	Fair	Poor
32000	30000	—	—	—	—

D2 pattern

NIB	Exc.	V.G.	Good	Fair	Poor
32700	30500	—	—	—	—

Jorema Royal

An over/under shotgun with sidelocks. Offered in 12-, 20-, 28-gauge and .410 bore. **NOTE:** Add 15 percent for smaller gauges.

In the white

NIB	Exc.	V.G.	Good	Fair	Poor
32700	26000	—	—	—	—

S2 pattern

NIB	Exc.	V.G.	Good	Fair	Poor
33900	20000	—	—	—	—

S3 pattern

NIB	Exc.	V.G.	Good	Fair	Poor
37300	29500	—	—	—	—

S4 pattern

NIB	Exc.	V.G.	Good	Fair	Poor
42900	33500	—	—	—	—

S5 pattern

NIB	Exc.	V.G.	Good	Fair	Poor
48200	29500	—	—	—	—

S4E pattern

NIB	Exc.	V.G.	Good	Fair	Poor
53500	42500	—	—	—	—

S5E pattern

NIB	Exc.	V.G.	Good	Fair	Poor
53500	42500	—	—	—	—

SXO pattern

NIB	Exc.	V.G.	Good	Fair	Poor
85000	66500	—	—	—	—

Excaliber BL

An over/under shotgun, with single trigger and removable trigger group. Offered in 12-, 20-, 28-gauge and .410 bore.

NIB	Exc.	V.G.	Good	Fair	Poor
11800	6500	—	—	—	—

Excalibur BL Extra

Finer engraving than standard.

NIB	Exc.	V.G.	Good	Fair	Poor
15455	8900	—	—	—	—

Excalibur BL Prestige

Finer engraving than BL Extra.

NIB	Exc.	V.G.	Good	Fair	Poor
17820	10750	—	—	—	—

Excalibur BLX

Over/under shotgun with sideplates.

NIB	Exc.	V.G.	Good	Fair	Poor
11150	9000	—	—	—	—

Excalibur BLX Extra

Same as above, with finer engraving.

NIB	Exc.	V.G.	Good	Fair	Poor
16759	14000	—	—	—	—

Excalibur BLX Prestige

Finer engraving than BLX Extra.

NIB	Exc.	V.G.	Good	Fair	Poor
16900	13750	—	—	—	—

Excalibur SL

Over/under shotgun with sidelocks.

NIB	Exc.	V.G.	Good	Fair	Poor
26125	14800	—	—	—	—

Excalibur SL Extra

Same as above, with finer engraving.

NIB	Exc.	V.G.	Good	Fair	Poor
30000	16000	—	—	—	—

Excalibur SL Prestige

Finer engraving than SL Extra.

NIB	Exc.	V.G.	Good	Fair	Poor
33000	18000	—	—	—	—

Excalibur Express

An over/under double rifle in calibers from 7x65R to .375 H&H.

NIB	Exc.	V.G.	Good	Fair	Poor
20196	11500	—	—	—	—

Excalibur Express Extra

Same as above, with finer engraving.

NIB	Exc.	V.G.	Good	Fair	Poor
27060	12000	—	—	—	—

Excalibur Express Prestige

Finer engraving than Express Extra.

NIB	Exc.	V.G.	Good	Fair	Poor
32065	15250	—	—	—	—

African Express

Side-by-side boxlock double rifle. Calibers from .22 Long Rifle to .600 NE.

NIB	Exc.	V.G.	Good	Fair	Poor
34000	17500	—	—	—	—

Venus Express Professional

Side-by-side double rifle with sidelocks.

NIB	Exc.	V.G.	Good	Fair	Poor
45000	34500	—	—	—	—

Venus Express Extra

Side-by-side double rifle with sidelocks. Calibers from .375 H&H to .500 NE.

NIB	Exc.	V.G.	Good	Fair	Poor
95750	50000	—	—	—	—

FARROW ARMS CO.
Holyoke, Massachusetts
Mason, Tennessee

Farrow Falling Block Rifle

Designed by W.M. Farrow, a target shooter, who had worked on Ballard rifles for Marlin Company. Farrow rifles are chambered for various calibers and have barrel lengths from 28"- 36" of octagonal configuration. Feature tang sights and are either all blued or have a nickel-plated receiver. Stocks are walnut. Two grades offered, that varied according to grade of wood used. Rifles are quite scarce on today's market. Number manufactured between 1885 and 1900 is unknown.

No. 1 Model

Fancy walnut with checkering and Schutzen buttplate.

NIB	Exc.	V.G.	Good	Fair	Poor
—	—	13500	4500	1950	750

No. 2 Model

Plainer wood and no checkering.

NIB	Exc.	V.G.	Good	Fair	Poor
—	—	11000	3300	1600	500

FAUSTI, STEFANO
Italy

Fausti has been manufacturing quality over/under and side-by-side shotguns in Italy, for the European market since 1948. In 2009, the company established an office in Fredericksburg, Virginia and now imports a wide range of models

OVER/UNDER SHOTGUNS

Low-profile boxlock design scaled to various gauges. All standard barrel lengths with five choke tubes (.410 has fixed M/F). Offered in 12-, 16-, 20-, 28-gauge and .410 bore in four grades: Caledon (shown), Caledon SL, Class and Class SL, each with increased level of walnut, laser engraving and inlays. Features include automatic ejectors, single selective trigger, rounded pistol-grip. SL models have false side plates. Prices shown are for 12- and 20-gauge models. **NOTE:** Add $500 for 16-, 28-gauge or .410 bore.

Caledon

NIB	Exc.	V.G.	Good	Fair	Poor
1800	1450	1200	950	600	400

Caledon SL

NIB	Exc.	V.G.	Good	Fair	Poor
2500	2000	1600	1350	900	500

Class

NIB	Exc.	V.G.	Good	Fair	Poor
2200	1750	1400	1100	750	500

Class SL

NIB	Exc.	V.G.	Good	Fair	Poor
2900	2250	1700	1450	1000	500

Round Body

Similar to other over/under models, except built on Fausti-designed rounded receiver. AAA grade oil-finished walnut stock. Not available in 12-gauge. Prices shown are for 20-gauge. **NOTE:** Add $500 for 16-, 28-gauge or .410 bore.

NIB	Exc.	V.G.	Good	Fair	Poor
3750	3200	2600	2000	1200	500

MAGNIFICENT SERIES

Higher grade series with AAA+ walnut stock and deep-sculpted engraving. Offered in a field version and sporting clays model (shown). Prices shown are for 12- or 20-gauge. **NOTE:** Add $500 for 16-, 28-gauge or .410 bore.

Magnificent Field

NIB	Exc.	V.G.	Good	Fair	Poor
4500	3600	3000	2400	1600	700

Magnificent Sporting

NIB	Exc.	V.G.	Good	Fair	Poor
5400	4500	3750	3000	2000	900

SIDE-BY-SIDE SHOTGUNS

Model DEA

Built on a low boxlock action, with modified Anson & Deeley mechanism. Straight-grip AAA-grade oil-finished walnut stock. Automatic ejectors, non-selective single trigger. Made in 12-, 16-, 20-, 28-gauge and .410 bore. Also offered as Duetto model, with interchangeable 28-gauge and .410 bore barrel sets. Prices shown are for 12- or 20-gauge. **NOTE:** Add $500 for other gauges; $1800 for Duetto model.

NIB	Exc.	V.G.	Good	Fair	Poor
3000	2500	2000	1600	1000	500

RIFLES

Classic Express Rifle

Over/under design, with oil-finished walnut stock, automatic ejectors and choice of double or single trigger. Calibers are .30-06, .444 Marlin, .45-70, 30R Blaser, 8x57 JRS and 9.3x74R. Barrels are 24" with adjustable fiber optic sight.

NIB	Exc.	V.G.	Good	Fair	Poor
4500	3600	3000	2400	1600	700

FAYETTEVILLE ARMORY PISTOLS AND RIFLES
Fayetteville, North Carolina

In 1861, U.S. Arsenal at Fayetteville, North Carolina, was seized by officials of that state and later turned over to the government of Confederate States of America. While still controlled by the state of North Carolina, a number of inferior flintlock arms were altered at the arsenal from flint to percussion, including a number of U.S. M1836 pistols and U.S. M1819 Hall rifles (latter also shortened and remodeled into cavalry carbines). In accordance with an agreement between the governors of Virginia and North Carolina, rifle machinery seized at the former U.S. Armory at Harpers Ferry, Virginia, was also sent to Fayetteville, where in 1862 the Confederacy began construction of rifles modeled after U.S. M1855 rifle. Production continued until 1865, when the advance of Sherman's armies necessitated evacuation of the armory.

Fayetteville Armory Percussion Pistols

(U.S. M1836 Pistols, Altered)

Overall length 13.25"; barrel length 8.5"; caliber .54. Markings: same as U.S. M1836 contact pistols, i.e. the locks either marked with eagle head over "A. WATERS/MILBURY MS./(date)" or "US/R. JOHNSON/MIDDN CONN./(date)" and various barrel proofmarks; also occasionally marked "N. CAROLINA".

Fayetteville Armory altered approximately 900 U.S. M1836 pistols from flintlock to percussion. These arms were altered by enlarging the flint touchhole and screwing in a cylindrical drum in place of the pan and frizzen. Distinguishing feature of Fayetteville alteration is the clean-out screw at face of cylinder and "S" shaped hammer, not unlike that used on post-1862 dated rifles.

Courtesy Milwaukee Public Museum, Milwaukee, Wisconsin

NIB	Exc.	V.G.	Good	Fair	Poor
—	—	3250	1350	950	400

Fayetteville Armory Rifles (Types I through IV)

Overall length 49.125"; barrel length 33"; caliber .58. Markings: on barrel, an eagle over "C.S.A./FAYETTEVILLE" forward of the hammer and date on rounded tail. "CSA" also found on buttplates; date on top of barrel; proofmarks (eagle head, "V" and "P") on left quarter of barrel near breech.

From 1862 to early 1865, Fayetteville Armory produced four variants of old U.S. M1855 rifle on machinery that had been lent to North Carolina by Virginia, after its capture in April 1861. Earliest 1862 production (Type I) utilized unmilled lockplates captured at Harpers Ferry and distinguished by having a "hump" (where the Maynard primer would have been milled) that extends to arc of hammer. Type II production utilized newly made locks received from Richmond during balance of 1862; they had a relatively low "hump" whose upper surface matched contour of stock. By end of 1862, Fayetteville was producing its own lock, the plate of which resembled U.S. M1861 rifle musket, but with a distinctive "S" shaped hammer. This lock distinguishes both type III and type IV production. All rifles made through 1863 continued to bear a saber bayonet lug on right side of barrel. In 1864, however, this was eliminated in favor of a triangular socket bayonet. Absence of the saber bayonet lug and remodeled front sight distinguishes type IV production. Because the barrel machinery went to Richmond, production at Fayetteville was continually hindered, seldom reaching more than 300 per month in three years that Fayetteville rifle was manufactured. (Note: Rarity of Type I production will usually generate a premium for that variant.)

NIB	Exc.	V.G.	Good	Fair	Poor
—	—	27500	10500	4000	800

FEATHER INDUSTRIES, INC.
Trinidad, Colorado

AT-22

Blowback-operated semi-automatic chambered for .22 LR cartridge. Removable shrouded 17" barrel and folding metal stock. Adjustable sights and finish is black. Detachable 20-round magazine. Introduced in 1986.

NIB	Exc.	V.G.	Good	Fair	Poor
450	200	175	150	110	75

AT-9

Similar to AT-22, except chambered for 9mm Parabellum cartridge. Has a 16" barrel and 32-round magazine. Introduced in 1988.

NIB	Exc.	V.G.	Good	Fair	Poor
800	675	300	250	175	125

KG-9

A 9mm semi-automatic assault rifle. Introduced in 1989.

NIB	Exc.	V.G.	Good	Fair	Poor
725	500	425	375	300	250

KG-22

Similar in appearance to KG-9, except chambered for .22 LR. Has a 20-round detachable magazine. Introduced in 1989.

NIB	Exc.	V.G.	Good	Fair	Poor
400	275	225	175	125	100

SAR-180

Current incarnation of old American 180, which was manufactured in Austria a number of years ago. Chambered for .22 LR and has a 17.5" barrel. Blowback-operated semi-automatic, that has a 165-round drum magazine that sits on top of the action on flat side. Rear sight is adjustable. Finish is blued, with walnut stock, pistol-grip and fore-end. Model revived by Feather Industries in 1989.

NIB	Exc.	V.G.	Good	Fair	Poor
750	675	600	475	300	200

Mini-AT

Blowback-operated semi-automatic pistol, chambered for .22 LR cartridge. A 5.5"-barreled version of AT-22 rifle and has a 20-round magazine. Manufactured between 1986 and 1989.

NIB	Exc.	V.G.	Good	Fair	Poor
375	250	175	150	125	100

Guardian Angel

Two-shot over/under derringer-style pistol. Chambered for 9mm Parabellum. Can be converted to fire .38 Super cartridge. Constructed of stainless steel and has an internal hammer and fully enclosed trigger. Introduced in 1988.

NIB	Exc.	V.G.	Good	Fair	Poor
225	125	100	75	50	40

FEDERAL ENGINEERING CORP.
Chicago, Illinois

XC-220

Blowback-operated semi-automatic rifle, chambered for .22 LR cartridge. Has a 16.5" barrel and steel receiver that is blued. Stock is black synthetic. Introduced in 1984.

NIB	Exc.	V.G.	Good	Fair	Poor
650	450	375	225	175	125

XC-450

Similar in appearance to XC-220, except chambered for .45 ACP cartridge. Has a 30-round detachable magazine.

NIB	Exc.	V.G.	Good	Fair	Poor
750	525	450	400	300	250

XC-900

A 9mm Parabellum version of same basic firearm. Has a 32-round magazine. Introduced in 1984.

NIB	Exc.	V.G.	Good	Fair	Poor
750	525	450	400	300	250

FEDERAL ORDNANCE, INC.
South El Monte, California

An importer, as well as a manufacturer, that basically fabricates new and custom firearms out of existing older military parts. Firearms they import are military surplus weapons. Firearms covered here are of Federal Ordnance manufacture.

M-14 Semi-Automatic

Semi-automatic version of M-14 service rifle. Constructed of a newly manufactured receiver, that has no selector and select surplus G.I. parts.

Refinished to original specifications. Furnished with 20-round magazine. Has either wood or fiberglass stock. Introduced in 1986. Although this model is a battle rifle and falls into the category affected by, wild price fluctuations, we have been experiencing prices for this gun staying fairly stable due to a fairly constant supply. Manufactured since 1986.

NIB	Exc.	V.G.	Good	Fair	Poor
—	750	600	550	450	375

Model 714 Broomhandle Mauser

Remanufactured C96-type pistol, chambered for 7.63mm or 9mm Parabellum. Utilizes a new manufactured frame and surplus parts. Features a 10-round detachable magazine, adjustable sights and walnut grips. Manufactured 1986 to 1991. Bolo Model, with a smaller grip, produced in 1988 only.

NIB	Exc.	V.G.	Good	Fair	Poor
650	500	400	300	250	100

Model 713 Mauser Carbine

A 16"-barreled version of Mauser, with fixed walnut stock. Standard magazine and chambered for 7.63mm or 9mm Parabellum. Refinished and introduced in 1987.

NIB	Exc.	V.G.	Good	Fair	Poor
—	1250	1000	900	700	575

Model 713 Deluxe

Chambered for 7.63mm. Has 16" barrel, with detachable shoulder stock made of deluxe walnut. Modified to accept detachable magazines. Furnished with two 20-shot units. Has 1000-meter adjustable sight. Furnished in a fitted leather case. Only 1,500 manufactured in 1986.

NIB	Exc.	V.G.	Good	Fair	Poor
2000	1750	1500	1250	1000	800

Standard Broomhandle

Refurbished surplus C-96 Mauser pistol, with new 7.63mm or 9mm barrel. All springs are replaced and entire gun refinished. Furnished with shoulder stock/holster of Chinese manufacture.

NIB	Exc.	V.G.	Good	Fair	Poor
800	650	525	450	350	275

Ranger 1911A1

Federal Ordnance's version of 1911A1 Colt service pistol. Made of all steel, chambered for .45 ACP, has checkered walnut grips and phiosphate-style finish. Introduced in 1988.

NIB	Exc.	V.G.	Good	Fair	Poor
500	375	325	275	225	150

FEG (FEGYVER ES GAZKESZULEKGYAR)
Budapest, Hungary

Rudolf Frommer, was a first-class engineer, who became associated with Fegyvergyar in 1896. In 1900, he became manager and held that position until his retirement in 1935. He died one year later in 1936. His designs were successful and prolific. They were used militarily and sold on the commercial market as well.

PISTOLS

Model 1901

An odd pistol that was not successful at all. Chambered for 8mm cartridge, that was the forerunner of 8mm Roth Steyr. Has long slender barrel, which was actually a collar with the barrel within. A rotary bolt, external hammer and is recoil-operated. There is a 10-round integral magazine and is loaded from top via a stripper clip. Manufactured from 1903 to 1905.

Courtesy James Rankin

NIB	Exc.	V.G.	Good	Fair	Poor
—	2450	1795	1000	700	350

Model 1906

Improved version of 1901, chambered for 7.65mm Roth-Sauer cartridge. For all intents and purposes, the same action; on later models a detachable 10-round magazine was adopted. Manufactured between 1906 and 1910 in small quantities.

NIB	Exc.	V.G.	Good	Fair	Poor
—	2300	1750	1000	700	350

Model 1910

Final version in this series of pistols, with the addition of grip safety. Chambered for 7.65mm Browning.

NIB	Exc.	V.G.	Good	Fair	Poor
—	2600	1950	1100	700	350

Frommer Stop Model 1912

Semi-automatic pistol in caliber 7.65mm or 9mmK. Unusual, in that it operates on a long recoil system. Frommer is stamped on the slide, as well as Frommer Stop logo on each side of wood or plastic grip plates.

Courtesy James Rankin

NIB	Exc.	V.G.	Good	Fair	Poor
—	450	300	225	150	50

Frommer Baby Model

Smaller version of Stop Model 1912. Designed as a pocket pistol, with 2" barrel and chambered for same calibers. Manufactured at the same time as Stop Model.

Courtesy James Rankin

NIB	Exc.	V.G.	Good	Fair	Poor
—	375	250	200	125	75

Frommer Lilliput

Pocket pistol chambered for 6.35mm and outwardly resembles Baby. Actually a simple blowback-operated semi-automatic pistol. A good deal less complex to produce. Introduced in 1921.

Courtesy James Rankin

NIB	Exc.	V.G.	Good	Fair	Poor
—	350	225	175	125	75

Model 1929

Semi-automatic pistol in 9mmK. Based on Browning designed blowback-action. Pistol replaced earlier models. Few made in .22 LR.

Courtesy James Rankin

NIB	Exc.	V.G.	Good	Fair	Poor
—	450	350	225	175	100

.22 Caliber

NIB	Exc.	V.G.	Good	Fair	Poor
—	975	825	725	450	250

Model 1937

Semi-automatic pistol in caliber 7.65mm or 9mmK. Pistol was designed by Frommer and manufactured by Femaru. Also known as Model 1937.

Courtesy James Rankin

Nazi Proofed 7.65mm Version

NIB	Exc.	V.G.	Good	Fair	Poor
—	450	350	225	175	100

9mm Short Hungarian Military Version

NIB	Exc.	V.G.	Good	Fair	Poor
—	425	325	200	175	100

Model R-9

Copy of Browning Hi-Power semi-automatic pistol. Chambered for 9mm Parabellum and has a 4.75" barrel. Frame is steel and finish is blued, with checkered wood grips. Detachable magazine holds 13 shots and sights are fixed. Imported in 1986 and 1987 only.

NIB	Exc.	V.G.	Good	Fair	Poor
—	375	250	225	175	100

Model AP-9

Pistol has been manufactured in Hungary, under a number of different names. Known as AP-9, Walam 48, AP-66 and Attila. Semi-automatic pistol in calibers 7.65mm and 9mmK. Similar to Walther Model PP. Has a 7-round magazine and alloy frame. Various styles of grip plates.

Courtesy James Rankin

NIB	Exc.	V.G.	Good	Fair	Poor
—	325	200	150	100	50

Model PPH

Copy of Walther PP, chambered for .380 ACP cartridge. Double-action semi-automatic, with 3" barrel. Alloy frame, blued finish, with thumb rest checkered plastic grips. Imported in 1986 and 1987 only.

NIB	Exc.	V.G.	Good	Fair	Poor
—	350	200	175	100	75

Model B9R

Semi-automatic pistol, chambered for .380 ACP cartridge. Fitted with a 4" barrel. Features double-/single-action trigger operation. Frame is alloy and weight about 25 oz. Magazine capacity 15 rounds.

NIB	Exc.	V.G.	Good	Fair	Poor
375	225	200	175	125	75

Model PA-63

Same as above, but chambered for 9mm Makarov (9x18mm) cartridge.

NIB	Exc.	V.G.	Good	Fair	Poor
—	275	175	125	100	50

Model FP-9

Copy of Browning Hi-Power pistol. Chambered for 9mm Luger cartridge. Features walnut checkered grip, with blue finish. Barrel 5" and overall length 8". Top of slide features full-length ventilated rib, with fixed sights. Weight 35 oz. Magazine capacity 14 rounds.

NIB	Exc.	V.G.	Good	Fair	Poor
300	175	150	125	90	70

Model P9R

Similar to model above and follows Browning Hi-Power lines, with exception of ventilated rib. Barrel length 4.66". Pistol offered in blue or chrome finish. Magazine capacity 15 rounds.

Blue

NIB	Exc.	V.G.	Good	Fair	Poor
450	400	325	250	200	150

Chrome

NIB	Exc.	V.G.	Good	Fair	Poor
475	425	350	285	235	160

Model P9RK

Similar to model above. Fitted with 4.12" barrel and 7.5" overall length. Finger grooves on front strap and backstrap is serrated. Weight about 34 oz.

NIB	Exc.	V.G.	Good	Fair	Poor
300	200	150	125	90	70

RIFLES

SA-2000-M

Introduced in 1999. Model is a semi-automatic rifle, chambered for 7.62x39mm or .223 cartridge. Fitted with detachable 10-round magazine, synthetic stock and muzzle-brake.

NIB	Exc.	V.G.	Good	Fair	Poor
575	450	350	250	150	95

AMD-65 AK47

Hungarian AK-47 clone, chambered in 7.62xc39. Fixed or folding-stock versions are available.

NIB	Exc.	V.G.	Good	Fair	Poor
650	495	375	275	175	125

FEINWERKBAU
Oberndorf, Germany

Known predominately for production of high quality, extremely accurate air rifles and pistols. They also produce some of the most accurate target .22-caliber firearms in the world today. These firearms are listed:

Model 2000 Universal

Single-shot bolt-action target rifle, chambered for .22 rimfire cartridge. Has a 26.5" barrel, with adjustable aperture sights and fully adjustable trigger. There were four different stock configurations offered, with stippled pistol-grips and forearms. An electronic trigger was available as a $450 option. Discontinued in 1988.

NIB	Exc.	V.G.	Good	Fair	Poor
—	1800	1250	950	650	550

Mini 2000

Has a 22" barrel. Electronic trigger available at additional cost.

NIB	Exc.	V.G.	Good	Fair	Poor
—	1550	1050	850	550	450

Running Boar Rifle

Has a thumbhole stock, with an adjustable cheekpiece. Furnished without sights. Specially designed for offhand Running Boar Competitions.

NIB	Exc.	V.G.	Good	Fair	Poor
—	1800	1250	950	650	550

Match Rifle

Has 26.75" barrel and adjustable cheekpiece stock.

NIB	Exc.	V.G.	Good	Fair	Poor
—	1650	1095	850	550	450

Model 2600 Ultra Match Free Rifle

Similar to Model 2000, with laminated thumbhole stock. Heavy 26" barrel, fully adjustable sights and trigger. Offered with electronic trigger for an additional $400. Introduced in 1986.

NIB	Exc.	V.G.	Good	Fair	Poor
1950	1400	1150	850	650	550

FEMARU
Budapest, Hungary

Hungary became a communist satellite in the mid-1950s. At this time, Femaru company was designated to replace the firm of Fegyvergyar, as the official Hungarian arms manufacturer. The products are of good quality.

Model 37

Semi-automatic pistol built in both 7.65mm and 9mm Short calibers. Well designed pistol of quality construction. Fitted with a grip safety and exposed hammer. Hungarian military adopted the pistol in 1937. Produced until late 1940s. Early guns were marked "Femaru Fegyver es Gepgyar RT Budapest". During the war, Nazi code for these guns was "jhv". The 9mm have a 7-round magazine; 7.65mm an 8-round. During World War II the Germans designed this pistol the "Pistol Mod 37 Kal 7.65 (Ung)". **NOTE:** Add 75 percent for Nazi proofed examples.

Courtesy Richard M. Kumor, Sr.

NIB	Exc.	V.G.	Good	Fair	Poor
—	350	275	225	150	100

Hege

Complete copy of Walther PP. Chambered for 7.65mm. Manufactured to be sold by Hegewaffen of Germany. Slide is so marked along with Pegasus in a circle. Designation "AP 66 Cal.7.65" also appears. Pistol intended for export sales in U.S. and other western countries.

NIB	Exc.	V.G.	Good	Fair	Poor
—	350	225	175	125	100

Tokagypt

15,000 of these pistols built in 1958, under contract for the Egyptian army. Modified version of Soviet TT-33 Tokarev, chambered for 9mm Parabellum, with a safety added. Balance were sold commercially, some under trademark "Firebird".

NIB	Exc.	V.G.	Good	Fair	Poor
—	475	350	275	200	125

Walam

Another Walther PP copy of excellent quality. Chambered for 9mm short or .380 ACP. Pistols sold on commercial market—some designated Model 48.

NIB	Exc.	V.G.	Good	Fair	Poor
—	350	225	175	125	100

FERLIB
Gardone V.T., Italy

From 2000 to 2005, Dakota Arms Inc. was the importer and distributor of Ferlib shotguns into the United States. See Dakota Arms Inc. listing in this edition for more information on models distributed by Dakota Arms.

Model F.VI

High-grade side-by-side shotgun. Chambered for all gauges and essentially custom-ordered. Available in various barrel lengths and chokes. Anson and Deeley boxlock-action, double triggers and automatic ejectors. Action is case colored and stock is hand-checkered select walnut.

Single-selective triggers are available for an additional $375. **NOTE:** Add 10 percent for 28-gauge and .410 bore.

NIB	Exc.	V.G.	Good	Fair	Poor
4750	3600	—	—	—	—

Model F.VII

Has scroll-engraved coin-finished frame, but otherwise similar to Model F.VI. Single trigger option and small gauge premium are same.

NIB	Exc.	V.G.	Good	Fair	Poor
12000	8500	—	—	—	—

Model F.VII/SC

More deluxe version, with gold inlays and game scene-engraved receiver. Options and premium are same.

NIB	Exc.	V.G.	Good	Fair	Poor
13000	9500	—	—	—	—

Model F.VII Sideplate

Features false sideplates that are completely covered with game scene engraving. Model is standard, with single-selective trigger. Small gauge premium is applicable.

NIB	Exc.	V.G.	Good	Fair	Poor
15000	10500	—	—	—	—

Model F.VII/SC Sideplate

False sideplate model, with gold inlays accenting the full coverage engraving. **NOTE:** Add 10 percent for 28-gauge and .410.

NIB	Exc.	V.G.	Good	Fair	Poor
16000	11500	—	—	—	—

Hammer Gun

Features boxlock action with external hammers. Other features are custom ordered to purchaser's specifications.

NIB	Exc.	V.G.	Good	Fair	Poor
20000	14500	—	—	—	—

FERRY, ANDREWS & CO.
Stafford, Connecticut

Under Hammer Pistol

Boot pistol chambered for .36-caliber percussion. Has 3" part-round, part-octagonal barrel. Similar to other under hammer pistols that were produced in Connecticut and Massachusetts. Top strap marked "Andrews Ferry & Co." Number manufactured unknown. Produced in 1850s.

NIB	Exc.	V.G.	Good	Fair	Poor
—	—	1550	700	395	125

FIALA ARMS COMPANY
New Haven, Connecticut

Fiala Repeating Target Pistol

Different type of pistol than what is commonly encountered. Outwardly it resembles a semi-automatic Colt Woodsman; in actuality it is a manually operated firearm that must be cycled by hand after every shot. Chambered for .22 rimfire and offered with interchangeable barrels in lengths of 3", 7.5" and 20". Also offered a detachable buttstock. Finish is blued and grips are found in both smooth and ribbed walnut. Rear sight is a square-notched blade that tips up into an elevation-adjustable peep sight. Marked "Fiala Arms and Equipment Co. Inc. / New Haven Conn. / Patents Pending" on right side of frame behind grip and Model 1920/ Made in U.S.A. on right side of frame above trigger guard. Left side of frame marked "FIALA ARMS" above image of polar bear with "TRADE MARK" below polar bear in area above trigger guard. Pistol furnished in one of three variations of cases that were optionally available: canvas case, black leatherette case velvet-lined and fitted with a lock and key, and tan leather version of leatherette case. A fixed 7.5" barrel variation was also produced. A 7.5" smoothbore barrel was cataloged as a silencer. Some 20" smoothbore barrels were produced. Some pistols bear the names "Columbia Arms Company" and "Botwinik Brothers". Government has classified this pistol with its stock as a "Curio or Relic" and in its complete state a very desirable collectible. **NOTE:** See also Schall & Co.

Courtesy Butterfield & Butterfield, San Francisco, California

Complete, Three Barrels, Stock, Tools, and Case

NIB	Exc.	V.G.	Good	Fair	Poor
—	2500	2100	1250	675	550

Gun Only

Courtesy Dr. Jon Miller

NIB	Exc.	V.G.	Good	Fair	Poor
—	800	700	450	275	175

FINNISH LION
Valmet, Sweden

ISU Target Rifle

Single-shot bolt-action rifle, chambered for .22 rimfire cartridge. Has a 27" heavy barrel and target stock with accessories. Features target adjustable sights. Manufactured between 1966 and 1977.

NIB	Exc.	V.G.	Good	Fair	Poor
—	475	325	275	200	125

Champion Free Rifle

Has a 29" heavy barrel and double-set triggers. Otherwise similar to ISU model. Manufactured between 1965 and 1972.

NIB	Exc.	V.G.	Good	Fair	Poor
—	900	750	600	375	275

Match Rifle

Similar to Champion rifle, with thumbhole stock and adjustable buttplate. Manufactured between 1937 and 1972.

NIB	Exc.	V.G.	Good	Fair	Poor
—	900	750	600	375	275

FIOCCHI OF AMERICA, INC.
Ozark, Missouri
See—Pardini and A. Zoli

Imports above firearms. They are listed in their own respective sections.

FIREARMS INTERNATIONAL
Washington, D.C.
See—Star and Garcia

Once importer of Star Model D, as it was sold in U.S.A. They also imported various other .25-caliber Colt copies, that are not considered collectible and would be valued in the $150-and-under range. For the .22/.410 Bronco, see "Garcia".

FIRESTORM
Argentina

Firestorm .22 LR

Semi-automatic pistol, chambered for .22 LR cartridge. Ten-round magazine capacity. Matte blue finish or duotone.

NIB	Exc.	V.G.	Good	Fair	Poor
250	185	135	100	75	45

Firestorm .32

Double-action semi-automatic chambered for .32 with 10+1 capacity. Blued, 3.5" barrel, weight 23 oz. Fixed sights and rubber grips. Introduced 2006.

NIB	Exc.	V.G.	Good	Fair	Poor
275	215	155	125	95	50

Firestorm .380

Semi-automatic double-action pistol. Chambered for .380 ACP cartridge and fitted with 3.5" barrel. Fixed three-dot combat sights. Matte blue or duotone finish. Magazine capacity 7 rounds. Weight about 23 oz.

NIB	Exc.	V.G.	Good	Fair	Poor
295	225	195	150	95	50

Mini Firestorm 9mm

This 9mm semi-automatic double-action pistol, fitted with 3.5" barrel. White outline drift adjustable target sights. Matte blue finish. Polymer grips. Magazine capacity 10 rounds. Weight about 25 oz.

NIB	Exc.	V.G.	Good	Fair	Poor
350	275	215	165	115	75

Mini Firestorm .40 S&W

As above, but chambered for .40 S&W cartridge.

NIB	Exc.	V.G.	Good	Fair	Poor
350	275	215	165	115	75

Firestorm .45 Government

Single-action semi-automatic pistol, chambered for .45 ACP cartridge. Fitted with 5.125" barrel and 3 dot fixed combat sights. Magazine capacity 7 rounds. Black rubber grips. Matte blue, nickel or duotone finish. Weight about 36 oz.

NIB	Exc.	V.G.	Good	Fair	Poor
350	275	215	165	115	75

Compact Firestorm .45 Government

As above, with 4.25" barrel. Weight about 34 oz.

NIB	Exc.	V.G.	Good	Fair	Poor
350	275	215	165	115	75

Mini Firestorm .45 Government

As above, with 3.14" barrel. Black polymer grips. Magazine capacity 10 rounds. Weight about 31 oz.

NIB	Exc.	V.G.	Good	Fair	Poor
350	275	215	165	115	75

1911 Mil-Spec Standard Government

1911A1-style single-action semi-automatic. Chambered in .45 ACP; 5.125" barrel, steel frame, 7- or 8-round magazine. Plastic or wood grips, matte blue or deluxe polished blue finish.

NIB	Exc.	V.G.	Good	Fair	Poor
350	275	215	165	115	75

FLETCHER BIDWELL, LLC
Viroqua, Wisconsin

Spencer 1860 Military Carbine

Introduced in 2001, this is a faithful reproduction of original Spencer Carbine. Chambered for .56-50 black powder cartridge but in centerfire. Fitted with blued, 22" round barrel. Magazine capacity 7 rounds in butt tube. Bone charcoal case hardened receiver. Walnut stock. Blade front sight with ladder rear sight, adjustable to 800 yards. Weight about 9 lbs. Built in U.S.

NIB	Exc.	V.G.	Good	Fair	Poor
2750	1950	1500	900	625	400

FLORENCE ARMORY
Florence, Guilford County, North Carolina

Founded in 1862, as a repair facility to alter sporting arms for military use. Majority of work done by H.C. Lamb & Company. In 1862, Captain Z. Coffin ordered stocks, barrels and locks to assemble newly made rifles. Furniture of these arms varied, either being supplied by Glaze & Company or being remainders from Searcy & Moore's production. Number made estimated to be in excess of 300 rifles in both .50- and .54-calibers. These arms (particularly the barrels) exhibit characteristics of North Carolina contract pieces.

NIB	Exc.	V.G.	Good	Fair	Poor
—	—	29500	12500	4000	1450

FNH USA, INC.
McLean, Virginia

Company is a subsidiary of FN Herstal in Belgium. Essentially the sales and marketing arm for FN in U.S. market.

PISTOLS

Model Forty-Nine

Pistol built by FN Manufacturing, Inc. in Columbia, S.C. Has a polymer frame and stainless steel slide. Chambered for 9mm or .40 S&W cartridge. Barrel length 4.25". Magazine capacity: 16 rounds for law enforcement; 10 rounds for commercial sales. Features a repeatable secure striker trigger system. Offered in stainless steel or black coated slide. Weight about 26 oz. Offered primarily for sale to law enforcement agencies. Introduced in 2000.

NIB	Exc.	V.G.	Good	Fair	Poor
470	375	300	250	225	135

Model FNP-9/FNP-40

Introduced in 2003, this pistol chambered for 9mm or .40 S&W cartridge. Fitted with 4" barrel and featuring a polymer frame. Action is double-/single-action design, with ambidextrous manual decocking lever. Fixed sights. Ten-round magazine capacity. Weight about 33 oz.

NIB	Exc.	V.G.	Good	Fair	Poor
550	425	375	300	250	125

FNP-45

Longer-frame version of FNP-9, chambered for .45 ACP. Barrel length 4.5" and weight 33.3 oz. Ambidextrous mag release and decocker/safety, forward slide serrations. Magazine capacity: 10 or 15 rounds. Black or Flat Dark Earth finish. Interchangeable backstrap inserts.

NIB	Exc.	V.G.	Good	Fair	Poor
700	625	500	375	250	150

FNP-45 Tactical

Developed for U.S. Joint Combat Pistol Program, this .45 ACP tactical model has 5.3" threaded barrel for a suppressor or other accessories. High-profile combat sights, two mounting bases for optional red dot sights, MIL-STD 1913 rail. Black or Flat Dark Earth finish. Weight 33.6 oz.

NIB	Exc.	V.G.	Good	Fair	Poor
1250	1050	850	625	350	250

FNP-45 Competition

Designed as a major caliber competition pistol. Same overall features as FNP-45, plus fiber optic front sight and Picatinny rail. Introduced in 2011.

NIB	Exc.	V.G.	Good	Fair	Poor
1050	850	700	500	300	250

FNX-9, FNX-40

Chambered in 9mm or .40 S&W. Magazine capacity: 17 (9mm), 14 (.40). Weight 22 to 24 oz. Stainless steel slide has front and rear cocking serrations. Other features include ambidextrous operating controls. Four interchangeable back-strap inserts.

NIB	Exc.	V.G.	Good	Fair	Poor
600	535	450	325	250	150

FNX-45

.45 ACP variation of FNX series. Magazine capacity 15-rounds. **NOTE:** Add $100 for night sights; $300 Competition model; $400 Tactical model.

NIB	Exc.	V.G.	Good	Fair	Poor
700	625	550	500	450	350

FNS-9

Striker-fired polymer-frame full-size pistol. Chambered in 9mm or .40 S&W (FNS-40). Capacity: 18 rounds (9mm), 15 (.40). Black or matte silver slide, black polymer frame, ambidextrous safety, magazine release and slide lock. Fixed 3-dot sights. Night sights optional.

NIB	Exc.	V.G.	Good	Fair	Poor
600	525	450	400	350	300

FNH Five-seveN

Single-action design chambered for 5.7x28mm round. Magazine capacity 10 or 20 rounds. Matte black, olive drab green or Flat Dark Earth finish. Ambidextrous safety and accessory mounting rail. Barrel length 4", weight 21 oz. Three-dot combat sights, adjustable rear.

NIB	Exc.	V.G.	Good	Fair	Poor
1100	975	800	575	250	150

Model HP-SA

Famous John Browning design Hi-Power pistol. Chambered for 9mm or .40 S&W cartridge. Barrel length 4.6". Magazine capacity 10 rounds. Weight about 32 oz. Blued finish.

NIB	Exc.	V.G.	Good	Fair	Poor
900	750	595	400	200	125

Model HP-SA-SFS

Introduced in 2003, this variant of Hi-Power pistol features single-/double-action mechanism, that allows cocked-and-locked carry, with hammer and slide locked. When safety is pushed off hammer is set in cocked position and fired single action.

NIB	Exc.	V.G.	Good	Fair	Poor
900	750	595	400	200	125

Model HP-DA/HP-DAO

Model offered in two different configurations. First with double-/single-action trigger; second is double-action-only. Chambered for 9mm cartridge. Fitted with fixed sights. Magazine capacity: 15 rounds for law enforcement; 10 rounds for commercial sales. Weight about 31 oz. Intended primarily for law enforcement sales. Introduced in 2000.

NIB	Exc.	V.G.	Good	Fair	Poor
900	750	595	400	200	125

Model HP-DA/HP-DAO Compact

As above in smaller and lighter package.

NIB	Exc.	V.G.	Good	Fair	Poor
900	750	595	400	200	125

Model BDA/BDAO Compact

Short recoil compact pistol, chambered for 9mm Parabellum cartridge. Fitted with double-/single-action trigger or double-action-only trigger. Each configuration has 10-round magazine capacity. Weight about 28 oz. Corrosion-resistant finish. Fixed sights.

NIB	Exc.	V.G.	Good	Fair	Poor
800	650	500	395	200	125

RIFLES

Rifles produced at FN manufacturing in U.S.

SPECIAL POLICE RIFLES (FN SPR)

FNAR

Semi-automatic chambered in .308 Winchester. Cold hammer-forged 16" standard or 20" heavy barrel. Magazine capacity 5 or 10 rounds. Weight 8.5 to 10 lbs. Receiver-mounted optical rail, with additional rails on fore-end. Matte black synthetic stock, with fully adjustable comb and length of pull via interchangeable inserts. Match-grade model available.

NIB	Exc.	V.G.	Good	Fair	Poor
1600	1350	1050	800	450	300

FN A1 SPR

Chambered for .308 and 7.62x51mm cartridge. Bolt-action. Fitted with 24" heavy barrel and no sights. Choice of hinged floorplate or detachable box magazine. Stock is McMillan A3 tactical. Weight about 10.75 lbs.

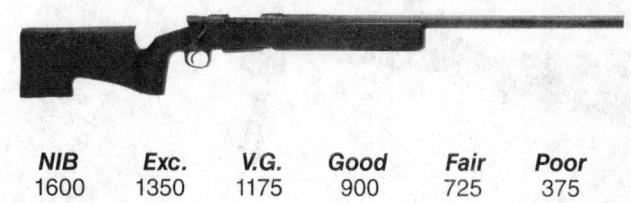

NIB	Exc.	V.G.	Good	Fair	Poor
1600	1350	1175	900	725	375

FN A1a SPR

Similar to above model. Fitted with 20" heavy fluted barrel. McMillan A3 tactical stock. Weight about 9.75 lbs.

NIB	Exc.	V.G.	Good	Fair	Poor
1600	1350	1175	900	725	375

FN A2 SPR

Fitted with 24" heavy barrel. McMillan A4 tactical stock. Badger Ordinance scope base. Weight about 10.75 lbs.

NIB	Exc.	V.G.	Good	Fair	Poor
2190	1750	1550	1275	900	400

FN A3 SPR

Model has 24" heavy barrel, with McMillan A4 adjustable stock. Badger Ordinance scope base and Badger Ordinance or FN scope rings. Supplied with FNH Parker-Hale type or Harris bipod. Weight about 10.75 lbs.

NIB	Exc.	V.G.	Good	Fair	Poor
2450	1950	1650	1375	950	450

FN A4 SPR

Fitted with 24" heavy barrel. McMillan A4 adjustable tactical stock. Scope base and rings standard. Choice of several tactical scopes. Bipod, sling, drag bag, kill flash, tool kit, cleaning kit, hard case. Weight about 10.75 lbs.

NIB	Exc.	V.G.	Good	Fair	Poor
5000	4250	3500	2800	2200	1700

FN A5 SPR

Model has 20" heavy fluted barrel threaded for a suppressor. Special McMillan tactical stock. Rest of features same as FN A4 model.

NIB	Exc.	V.G.	Good	Fair	Poor
6500	5750	4500	3700	2900	2000

FN A5M

Similar to FN A5 SPR, with McMillan fiberglass tactical stock, standard optics rail. Chambered in .300 WSM or .308 Win. Barrel length 20" to 24", standard or fluted.

NIB	Exc.	V.G.	Good	Fair	Poor
3000	2600	2200	1800	1400	1000

FN PS90

Semi-automatic bullpup model chambered for 5.7x28mm caliber, with 10- or 30-round magazine. Barrel is 16", with integrated muzzle-brake. Design features downward ejection, three M1913 accessory rails.

NIB	Exc.	V.G.	Good	Fair	Poor
2000	1500	1200	1000	800	500

FNH-USA Ballista

Modular multi-caliber bolt-action tactical rifle. Chambered for .308 Win., .300 Win. Magnum or .338 Lapua. Accessory conversion kits available for each caliber. Aluminum alloy receiver, adjustable trigger, fluted 24" or 25" barrel. Ambidextrous folding stock adjustable for length of pull, comb height, buttplate height, cast-on and cast-off. New in 2012.

NIB	Exc.	V.G.	Good	Fair	Poor
6250	5700	5000	4000	—	—

FNH-USA SCAR 16S/17S

Semi-automatic tactical rifle chambered for .223 (16S) or .308 Win. (17S), with 10- or 30-round magazines. Black or FDE finish, hard anodize aluminum receiver, telescoping side-folding polymer stock, integrated optics rail. Barrel length 16.25".

NIB	Exc.	V.G.	Good	Fair	Poor
3000	2400	2000	1500	1100	700

FN A5a SPR

Model has 20" heavy fluted barrel threaded for a suppressor. Special SPR McMillan adjustable tactical stock. Weight about 9.75 lbs.

NIB	Exc.	V.G.	Good	Fair	Poor
2460	1975	1650	1375	950	450

FN PBR (Patrol Bolt Rifle)

Introduced in 2004. Rifle chambered for .308 or .300 WSM. Offered with four different barrel lengths: 18", 20", 22" or 24". Fitted with two-piece MIL spec M1913 rail. Black Hogue stock. Magazine capacity 4 rounds. Weight about 9 lbs.

NIB	Exc.	V.G.	Good	Fair	Poor
1000	950	900	800	700	400

PGM PRECISION RIFLES

Rifles made by PGM Precision, a subsidary of FN, in Poisy Cedex, France.

Ultima Ratio Intervention

Bolt-action rifle, chambered for .308 and 7.62x51mm cartridge. Fitted with 23.6" ribbed barrel and integral muzzle-brake. Folding bipod. Stock trigger group and action are fixed to a rigid metal girder. Stock is adjustable. No sights. Magazine capacity 5 or 10 rounds. Weight about 13.25 lbs., depending on configuration.

NIB	Exc.	V.G.	Good	Fair	Poor
9000	7995	6000	3250	1795	700

Ultima Ratio Commando I

Similar to above model, with 18.5" fluted barrel and muzzle-brake. Weight about 12 lbs.

NIB	Exc.	V.G.	Good	Fair	Poor
9100	8050	6100	3250	1795	700

Ultima Ratio Commando II

Similar to Commando I, with folding stock.

NIB	Exc.	V.G.	Good	Fair	Poor
8320	—	—	—	—	—

FN-Mini-Hecate

Chambered for .308 cartridge. Bolt-action rifle features free-loading interchangeable 18.5", 19.7", 21.7" or 23.6" match-grade barrel. Collapsible buttstock. Magazine capacity 10 rounds. Weight about 14 lbs. Introduced in 2001.

NIB	Exc.	V.G.	Good	Fair	Poor
9100	8050	6100	3250	1795	700

.338 Lapua

Similar to Mini-Hecate, but chambered for .33 Lapua cartridge. Fitted with 27.2" barrel and integral muzzle-brake. Collapsible buttstock. Weight about 15 lbs. Magazine capacity 10 rounds.

NIB	Exc.	V.G.	Good	Fair	Poor
10500	9000	7750	6000	3750	1475

FS 2000

Semi-automatic bullpup-style carbine, chambered in 5.56 NATO/.223 Rem. Features include gas-operated action with rotating bolt lockup, 17.4" barrel with muzzle-brake, and fully ambidextrous polymer stock. Fired cases are ejected forward, away from shooter. A civilian version of selective fire model used by military and law enforcement. Introduced in 2006.

NIB	Exc.	V.G.	Good	Fair	Poor
2400	1850	1500	1200	600	300

SHOTGUNS

FNH-USA SC1

Over/under shotgun designed for competition. 12-gauge only, with 28" or 30" ported and back-bored barrels, Invector-Plus choke tubes, ventilated rib and mid-bead. Checkered wood, laminate wood or blue stock adjustable for comb height, cast and length of pull. Weight 8 to 8.2 lbs.

NIB	Exc.	V.G.	Good	Fair	Poor
2000	1700	1450	1100	900	500

FN Police Shotgun

Slide-action 12-gauge shotgun, chambered for 3" 12-gauge shell. Barrel length 18". Magazine capacity 7 rounds. Black synthetic stock. Corrosion-resistant finish. Weight about 6.5 lbs.

NIB	Exc.	V.G.	Good	Fair	Poor
350	275	200	150	125	100

FN Tactical Police

Similar to standard model, with ported barrel, collapsible stock and pistol-grip. Weight about 6.5 lbs.

NIB	Exc.	V.G.	Good	Fair	Poor
550	475	400	300	200	100

FN Self-Loading Police

Gas-operated semi-automatic shotgun. Fitted with Picatinny rail and short stock. Chambered for 12-gauge shell. Magazine capacity 6 rounds. Weight about 7.75 lbs.

NIB	Exc.	V.G.	Good	Fair	Poor
1000	800	600	400	300	200

FOEHL, C.
Philadelphia, Pennsylvania

Derringer

A .41-caliber percussion single-shot pistol, with 2" barrel, German silver mounts and walnut stock. Lock marked "C. Foehl".

NIB	Exc.	V.G.	Good	Fair	Poor
—	—	1950	750	300	110

FOEHL & WEEKS
Philadelphia, Pennsylvania

Columbian

A .32- or .38-caliber revolver, marked with patent date "20 January 1891".

NIB	Exc.	V.G.	Good	Fair	Poor
—	—	350	150	75	50

Columbian Automatic

A .38-caliber revolver, with hinged barrel and cylinder assembly.

NIB	Exc.	V.G.	Good	Fair	Poor
—	—	400	200	100	75

Perfect

As above, with concealed hammer. Also in .32-caliber.

NIB	Exc.	V.G.	Good	Fair	Poor
—	—	400	200	100	75

FOGARTY
American Repeating Rifle Co.
Boston, Massachusetts

Fogarty Repeating Rifle and Carbine

Limited number of repeating rifles and carbines, based upon Valentine Fogarty's patents. Produced between 1866 and 1867. Calibers of these arms varies. Normal barrel lengths are 20" and 28". Blued, case-hardened, with walnut stocks. American Repeating Rifle Company purchased by Winchester Repeating Arms Company in 1869.

Rifle

Courtesy Buffalo Bill Historical Center, Cody, Wyoming

NIB	Exc.	V.G.	Good	Fair	Poor
—	—	9500	4050	1250	450

Carbine

Courtesy Buffalo Bill Historical Center, Cody, Wyoming

NIB	Exc.	V.G.	Good	Fair	Poor
—	—	9500	4050	1250	450

FOLSOM, H&D ARMS CO.

Large distributor of double-/single barrel shotguns, produced by Crescent Firearms Co., Norwich, Connecticut. Folsom owned and later sold to Savage Arms Co. the Crescent Firearms Co., Davis Warner Co. and Baker Gun Co. around 1930. For more information see Crescent Firearms Co.

FOLSOM, H.
St. Louis, Missouri

Derringer

A .41-caliber single-shot percussion pocket pistol, with 2.5" barrel. German silver mounts and walnut stock. Barrel marked "H. Folsom".

NIB	Exc.	V.G.	Good	Fair	Poor
—	—	1150	800	350	275

FORBES RIFLES, LLC
Westbrook, Maine

Model 24B

A production version of Model 24 made by New Ultra Light Arms Co. Chambered in .25-06, .270, 7mm Rem. Magnum, .30-06 and .300 Win. Magnum. Barrel length 24", black composite stock, no sights. Introduced 2011. **NOTE:** Add $100 for stainless and/or left-hand version.

NIB	Exc.	V.G.	Good	Fair	Poor
1300	1200	1100	900	700	350

FOREHAND & WADSWORTH
Worcester, Massachusetts

Established in 1871 and operated under the above name until 1890, when it became Forehand Arms Company. Hopkins & Allen purchased the company in 1902.

Single-Shot Derringer

A .22-caliber single-shot pocket pistol, with 2" half-octagonal pivoted barrel. Spur trigger and nickel- or silver-plated frame. Walnut grips. Barrel marked "Forehand & Wadsworth Worcester".

NIB	Exc.	V.G.	Good	Fair	Poor
—	—	1450	600	250	100

Single-Shot .41 Derringer

As above in .41-caliber, with 2.5" round barrel.

Courtesy Milwaukee Public Museum, Milwaukee, Wisconsin

NIB	Exc.	V.G.	Good	Fair	Poor
—	—	1000	850	450	200

Side-Hammer .22

A .22-caliber spur trigger revolver, with 2.25" to 4" octagonal barrel. 7-shot cylinder. Blued or nickel-plated, with walnut grips.

NIB	Exc.	V.G.	Good	Fair	Poor
—	—	675	475	200	100

Center Hammer

A .32-caliber spur trigger revolver, with 3.5" octagonal barrel and 6-shot cylinder. Blued or nickel-plated, with rosewood or walnut grips. Top strap commonly found marked "Terror".

Courtesy Milwaukee Public Museum, Milwaukee, Wisconsin

NIB	Exc.	V.G.	Good	Fair	Poor
—	—	400	300	200	100

Old Model Army Single-Action Revolver

A .44 Russian caliber revolver, with 7.5" round barrel and 6-shot cylinder. Barrel marked "Forehand & Wadsworth, Worchester, Mass. U.S. Patd. Oct. 22, '61, June 27, '71 Oct. 28, '73". Blued with walnut grips. Approximately 250 manufactured between 1872 and 1878.

NIB	Exc.	V.G.	Good	Fair	Poor
—	—	4000	3250	2000	500

New Model Army Single-Action Revolver

Similar to above, with 6.5" barrel and half-cock notch on hammer. Approximately 250 made between 1878 and 1882. Interesting Note: In 2008, United States Fire Arms announced plans to remanufacture this model.

NIB	Exc.	V.G.	Good	Fair	Poor
—	—	3750	3000	2250	500

Double-Action Revolver

A .32 or .38 centerfire or rimfire caliber double-action revolver, with 3.5" barrel and 6- or 7-shot cylinder. The .32-caliber version marked "Forehand & Wadsworth Double-Action" and .38-caliber "American Bulldog". Manufactured from 1871 to 1890.

NIB	Exc.	V.G.	Good	Fair	Poor
—	400	300	200	100	35

British Bulldog

A .32 or .38 centerfire solid frame double-action revolver, resembling Webley Bulldog.

NIB	Exc.	V.G.	Good	Fair	Poor
—	—	395	300	150	75

British Bulldog .44

As above in .44 Webley caliber, with 5" barrel and 5-shot cylinder.

NIB	Exc.	V.G.	Good	Fair	Poor
—	—	450	325	175	100

Swamp Angel

A .41-caliber single-action revolver, with 3" barrel and 5-shot cylinder. Top strap marked "Swamp Angel".

NIB	Exc.	V.G.	Good	Fair	Poor
—	—	425	275	100	50

FOREHAND ARMS CO. 1898-1902

Perfection Automatic

A .32- or .38-caliber double-action revolver, with hinged barrel and cylinder assembly. Varying barrel lengths. Blued or nickel-plated, with hard rubber grips.

NIB	Exc.	V.G.	Good	Fair	Poor
—	275	250	100	75	50

Double-Barrel Shotguns

Good quality hammer and hammerless doubles, but few produced until taken over by Hopkins and Allen Firearms Co. Values from $100 to $1,000 depending on grade and condition.

FOWLER, B. JR.
Hartford, Connecticut

Percussion Pistol

A .38-caliber single-shot percussion pistol, with 4" half octagonal barrel, iron frame and maple grips. Barrel marked "B. Fowler, Jr.". Manufactured between 1835 and 1838.

NIB	Exc.	V.G.	Good	Fair	Poor
—	—	995	550	325	150

FOX, A. H.
Philadelphia, Pennsylvania

Ansley H. Fox established Fox Gun Company, in Baltimore, Maryland, in 1896. Subsequently, he made arms under the name Philadelphia Gun Company. As of 1905, he operated under the name A.H. Fox. In 1930, this company was purchased by Savage Arms Company, who continued manufacturing all grades of Fox shotguns. As of 1942, Savage Company only made plainer grades.

NOTE: Fox Model B double shotguns see Savage Arms Co.

Sterlingworth

A 12-, 16- or 20-gauge boxlock double-barrel shotgun, with 26", 28" or 30" barrels. Double triggers and extractors. Automatic ejectors were also available and would add approximately 30 percent to values listed. Blued, case-hardened, with walnut stock. Manufactured from 1911 to 1946. **NOTE**: Add 50 percent for 20-gauge; 25 percent for 16-gauge.

Courtesy Nick Niles, Paul Goodwin photo

NIB	Exc.	V.G.	Good	Fair	Poor
—	2000	1600	1000	500	275

Sterlingworth Deluxe

As above, with an ivory bead recoil pad and optional 32" barrel. **NOTE**: Add 50 percent for 20 gauge; 25 percent for 16-gauge.

NIB	Exc.	V.G.	Good	Fair	Poor
—	2500	1900	1250	700	400

SP Grade

A 12-, 16- or 20-gauge boxlock double-barrel shotgun, with varying length barrels. Double triggers and extractors. **NOTE**: Add 35 percent for 20-gauge; 15 percent for Automatic ejectors; 25 percent for 16-gauge.

NIB	Exc.	V.G.	Good	Fair	Poor
—	1600	1325	1050	450	225

HE Grade

Similar to early A Grade and offered in 12- and 20-gauge. Chambers were 2.25" standard, with 3" chambers available on request. Marked on the barrel "Not Warranted". This referred to pattern density, not barrel quality. Only sixty 20-gauge HE Grades appear in factory records. Manufactured from 1923 to 1942. **NOTE**: Add 20 percent for single-selective trigger; 100 percent premium for 20-gauge.

NIB	Exc.	V.G.	Good	Fair	Poor
—	5000	4200	3200	2000	1000

High Grade Guns A-FE

Fox Company as well as Savage Arms Company, produced a variety of shotguns decorated in varying grades. Available in 12-, 16- and 20-gauge. Value depends on particular features of these arms. Prospective purchasers are advised to secure a qualified appraisal prior to acquisition. **NOTE**: A 25 percent premium should be added to grades below, for small gauge and guns with single selective trigger.

A Grade

Built from 1905 to 1942.

NIB	Exc.	V.G.	Good	Fair	Poor
—	2100	1700	1225	600	400

AE Grade (Automatic Ejectors)
Built from 1905 to 1946.

NIB	Exc.	V.G.	Good	Fair	Poor
—	2400	2000	1600	900	700

B Grade
Built from 1905 to 1918.

NIB	Exc.	V.G.	Good	Fair	Poor
—	3100	2700	1950	1100	500

BE Grade
Built from 1905 to 1918.

NIB	Exc.	V.G.	Good	Fair	Poor
—	4500	3600	3000	2000	1000

C Grade
Built from 1905 to 1913.

NIB	Exc.	V.G.	Good	Fair	Poor
—	3300	2700	2150	1100	550

CE Grade
Built from 1905 to 1946.

NIB	Exc.	V.G.	Good	Fair	Poor
—	5500	4500	3750	2500	1200

XE Grade
Built from 1914 to 1945.

Courtesy William Hammond

NIB	Exc.	V.G.	Good	Fair	Poor
—	7500	6700	5000	3000	1500

D Grade
Built from 1906 to 1913.

NIB	Exc.	V.G.	Good	Fair	Poor
—	9300	8000	5150	2750	1000

DE Grade
Built from 1906 to 1945.

NIB	Exc.	V.G.	Good	Fair	Poor
—	12500	11000	8000	3750	1800

F Grade
Built from 1906 to 1913.

NIB	Exc.	V.G.	Good	Fair	Poor
—	25000	16800	9000	5700	3000

FE Grade
Built from 1906 to 1940.

NIB	Exc.	V.G.	Good	Fair	Poor
—	28000	21000	11500	7700	5000

Single Barrel Trap Guns

A 12-gauge single-barrel boxlock shotgun, with 30" or 32" ventilated rib barrels and automatic ejector. Approximately 571 single-barrel trap guns manufactured. Produced in four grades as listed:

J Grade
Built from 1919 to 1936.

NIB	Exc.	V.G.	Good	Fair	Poor
—	3100	2400	1750	1050	600

K Grade
Built from 1919 to 1931. Approximately 75 built.

NIB	Exc.	V.G.	Good	Fair	Poor
—	4350	3300	2450	1650	950

L Grade
Built from 1919 to 1931. Approximately 25 built.

NIB	Exc.	V.G.	Good	Fair	Poor
—	5750	3900	3150	2150	1200

M Grade
Built from 1919 to 1932. A total of 9 guns built.

NIB	Exc.	V.G.	Good	Fair	Poor
—	15000	10000	6500	4700	2500

RECENTLY MANUFACTURED A.H. FOX SHOTGUNS

In 1993, Connecticut Shotgun Manufacturing Company of New Britain, Connecticut, announced production of A.H. Fox shotgun in 20-gauge exclusively. Gun is hand-built and constructed to same dimensions and standards as original Fox. Gun offered in five grades, with many standard features and several optional ones as well. Each shotgun built to order. Because these guns are newly built and have no pricing history, only manufacturer's retail price for base gun will be given. Extra sets of barrels, single triggers and other extra costs options will greatly affect price.

CE Grade

Retail price: $19,500

XE Grade

Retail price: $22,000

DE Grade

Retail price: $25,000

FE Grade

Retail price: $30,000

Exhibition Grade

This is the company's highest grade. Features any optional detail the customer desires, including custom engraving and exhibition quality wood. Retail price: On request from CSMC.

FRANCHI, L.
Brescia, Italy

BOXLOCK SIDE-BY-SIDE-SHOTGUNS

Astore

A 12-gauge boxlock shotgun. Manufactured in a variety of barrel lengths, with double triggers and automatic ejectors. Blued, with straight walnut stock. Manufactured from 1937 to 1960.

NIB	Exc.	V.G.	Good	Fair	Poor
2900	1600	750	500	350	200

Astore II

As above, but more finely finished.

NIB	Exc.	V.G.	Good	Fair	Poor
3150	1850	900	700	450	250

Astore 5

As above, but more finely finished.

NIB	Exc.	V.G.	Good	Fair	Poor
3350	2150	1250	950	600	300

Airone

Similar to Astore. Manufactured during 1940s.

NIB	Exc.	V.G.	Good	Fair	Poor
2900	1600	750	500	350	200

SIDELOCK SIDE-BY-SIDE SHOTGUNS

A 12- 16- or 20-gauge sidelock double-barrel shotgun. Manufactured in a variety of barrel lengths, with single-selective trigger and automatic ejectors. Produced in the following grades, they differ as to engraving, coverage and quality of wood:

Condor

NIB	Exc.	V.G.	Good	Fair	Poor
7500	6500	4500	3500	2500	1250

Imperial

NIB	Exc.	V.G.	Good	Fair	Poor
10000	8500	6000	4500	3250	1500

Imperiales

NIB	Exc.	V.G.	Good	Fair	Poor
10500	9000	6500	5000	3500	1500

No. 5 Imperial Monte Carlo

NIB	Exc.	V.G.	Good	Fair	Poor
15000	12500	9000	7500	5000	2000

No. 11 Imperial Monte Carlo

NIB	Exc.	V.G.	Good	Fair	Poor
16000	13500	10000	8000	5500	2000

Imperial Monte Carlo Extra

NIB	Exc.	V.G.	Good	Fair	Poor
20000	17500	12500	9500	7500	3500

Highlander

Introduced in 2003. Features either 12-, 20- or 28-gauge, fitted with 26" barrels and fixed chokes. Select walnut straight-grip stock, with splinter fore-end. Coin finished steel receiver. Single trigger. Weight: 6.4 lbs. 12-gauge; 5.8 lbs. 20-gauge; 5.7 lbs. 28-gauge. **NOTE:** Add $150 for 28-gauge.

NIB	Exc.	V.G.	Good	Fair	Poor
1800	1600	1200	850	475	300

OVER/UNDER SHOTGUNS

Priti Deluxe Model

A 12- or 20-gauge over/under boxlock double-barrel shotgun, with 26" or 28" ventilated rib barrels. Single trigger and automatic ejectors. Introduced in 1988.

NIB	Exc.	V.G.	Good	Fair	Poor
400	350	300	250	200	150

Falconet

A 12-, 16-, 20-, 28-gauge and .410 bore boxlock double-barrel shotgun, with single-selective trigger and automatic ejectors. Receiver was anodized in tan, ebony or silver finishes. Manufactured from 1968 to 1975. **NOTE:** Add 10 percent for silver receiver; 25 percent 28-gauge and .410 bore.

NIB	Exc.	V.G.	Good	Fair	Poor
650	550	425	350	250	200

Falconet Skeet

As above, with 26" skeet barrel. Wide rib and receiver case-hardened. Manufactured from 1970 to 1974.

NIB	Exc.	V.G.	Good	Fair	Poor
950	850	700	550	450	250

Falconet International Skeet

As above, but more finely finished.

NIB	Exc.	V.G.	Good	Fair	Poor
1050	950	750	600	475	250

Falconet Trap

As above, with 30" Modified Full choke barrel and trap stock. Manufactured from 1970 to 1974.

NIB	Exc.	V.G.	Good	Fair	Poor
1000	900	700	550	450	250

Falconet International Trap

As above, but more finely finished.

NIB	Exc.	V.G.	Good	Fair	Poor
1050	950	750	600	475	250

Peregrine Model 451

A 12-gauge boxlock double-barrel shotgun, with 26" or 28" ventilated rib barrels. Alloy receiver, single-selective trigger and automatic ejectors. Manufactured in 1975.

NIB	Exc.	V.G.	Good	Fair	Poor
800	675	495	375	275	200

Peregrine Model 400

As above, with steel frame.

NIB	Exc.	V.G.	Good	Fair	Poor
850	775	600	400	300	200

Aristocrat

Similar to above, with 26", 28" or 30" ventilated rib barrels. Manufactured from 1960 to 1969.

NIB	Exc.	V.G.	Good	Fair	Poor
850	725	600	400	300	200

Aristocrat Magnum

As above, with 3" chambers and 32" Full choke barrels.

NIB	Exc.	V.G.	Good	Fair	Poor
895	775	675	450	300	200

Aristocrat Silver King

As above, with French case-hardened receiver. Available in four grades of decoration.

NIB	Exc.	V.G.	Good	Fair	Poor
950	875	775	475	350	200

Aristocrat Deluxe

NIB	Exc.	V.G.	Good	Fair	Poor
1250	1000	875	575	400	200

Aristocrat Supreme

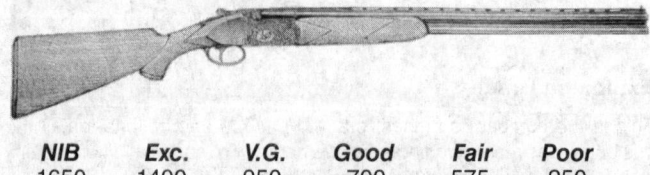

NIB	Exc.	V.G.	Good	Fair	Poor
1650	1400	950	700	575	250

Aristocrat Imperial

NIB	Exc.	V.G.	Good	Fair	Poor
2950	2450	1950	1250	950	450

Aristocrat Monte Carlo

NIB	Exc.	V.G.	Good	Fair	Poor
3750	3200	2950	2000	1500	750

Model 2003 Trap

A 12-gauge boxlock double-barrel shotgun, with 30" or 32" ventilated rib barrels. Single-selective trigger and automatic ejectors. Manufactured in 1976.

NIB	Exc.	V.G.	Good	Fair	Poor
1450	1300	900	650	500	250

Model 2004 Trap

A single-barreled version of Model 2003.

NIB	Exc.	V.G.	Good	Fair	Poor
1450	1300	900	650	500	250

Model 2005 Combination Trap

Model 2003, with both single and set of over/under barrels.

NIB	Exc.	V.G.	Good	Fair	Poor
2800	2400	1950	1200	950	450

Model 3000 "Undergun"

As above, with single-barrel fitted with high ventilated rib so it fires from lower barrel position.

NIB	Exc.	V.G.	Good	Fair	Poor
3050	2850	2200	1500	1200	600

Alcione Classic

Introduced in 2004, this 12-gauge 3" model features 26" or 28" ventilated rib barrels. Side rib ventilated. Walnut stock with schnabel fore-end. Optional 20-gauge barrels. Weight about 7.5 lbs.

NIB	Exc.	V.G.	Good	Fair	Poor
1300	975	800	600	500	250

Alcione T (Titanium)

Introduced in 2002, this model is similar to Alcione Field. Has an aluminum alloy frame, with titanium inserts. Available in 12- and 20-gauge with 3" chambers. Choice of 26" or 28" ventilated rib barrels, with choke tubes. Weight about 6.8 lbs. for 12- and 20-gauge.

NIB	Exc.	V.G.	Good	Fair	Poor
1400	1150	950	700	600	300

Alcione T Two-Barrel Set

As above, with two-barrel set: one 12-gauge 28"; other 20-gauge 26". Introduced in 2004.

NIB	Exc.	V.G.	Good	Fair	Poor
1600	1275	1100	800	650	350

Alcione Field Model

A 12-gauge boxlock double-barrel shotgun, with 26" or 28" ventilated rib barrels. Single-selective trigger and automatic ejectors. Engraved silver receiver. Weight about 7.5 lbs.

NIB	Exc.	V.G.	Good	Fair	Poor
1200	995	800	525	300	150

Alcione Sporting

This over/under gun designed for sporting clays competition. Fitted with mechanical triggers and ported barrels. Offered in 12-gauge only, with 30" barrels. Select walnut stock. Removable sideplates. Weight about 7.5 lbs.

NIB	Exc.	V.G.	Good	Fair	Poor
1550	1250	995	775	400	200

Alcione LF

This 12- or 20-gauge model, features barrels of 26" in 20-gauge; 28" in 12-gauge. Both gauges are chambered for 3" shells. Walnut stock. Receiver is aluminum alloy, with etched games scenes and gold fill. Weight about 6.8 lbs.

Alcione LF receiver—Right side view

NIB	Exc.	V.G.	Good	Fair	Poor
1300	1050	700	450	300	200

Alcione SL Sport

As above, but more finely finished. French case-hardened receiver.

NIB	Exc.	V.G.	Good	Fair	Poor
1375	1125	775	525	375	275

Alcione SP

Chambered for 12-gauge shell and fitted with 28" ventilated rib barrels and choke tubes. Full slide lock-style side plates, with engraving of gold pheasants and mallards. Weight about 7.5 lbs. Introduced in 2003.

NIB	Exc.	V.G.	Good	Fair	Poor
1700	1450	975	700	575	345

ALCIONE SIDEPLATES

Alcione Classic SX

This 12-gauge 3" model similar to Alcione Field SX above, with blued receiver. Available with choice of 26" or 28" ventilated rib barrels. An extra 12-gauge 30" ported barrel and 20-gauge barrels are also optional. Weight about 7.5 lbs. Introduced in 2004.

NIB	Exc.	V.G.	Good	Fair	Poor
1400	1150	950	700	600	300

Alcione Field SX

Model fitted with high grade walnut stock, fine checkering and engraved receivers. Gold filled etched side plates. Offered with 26" or 28" barrels. Weight about 7.3 lbs.

NIB	Exc.	V.G.	Good	Fair	Poor
1600	1250	995	775	400	200

Veloce

Introduced in 2001. Chambered for 20- or 28-gauge only. Barrels: 20-gauge 28"; 28-gauge 26". Aluminum alloy receiver. Engraved side plates, with gold filled game scenes. Mechanical trigger. Select walnut stock. Weight about: 20-gauge 5.8 lbs.; 28-gauge 5.5 lbs.

NIB	Exc.	V.G.	Good	Fair	Poor
1375	1125	775	525	375	275

Veloce English Stock

Introduced in 2002. Similar to Veloce, with straight-grip stock. Offered in 20- and 28-gauge, with 26" ventilated rib barrels. Choke tubes. Weight about: 20-gauge 5.7 lbs.; 28-gauge 5.5 lbs.

NIB	Exc.	V.G.	Good	Fair	Poor
1400	1150	950	700	600	300

Veloce Grade II

This 20- or 28-gauge model, features extra-select-grade walnut stock, with gold-filled birds and scroll engraving. The 20-gauge offered with either 26" or 28" ventilated rib barrel; 28-gauge fitted with 26" ventilated rib barrel. Weight about: 20-gauge 5.75 lbs.; 28-gauge 5.5 lbs.

NIB	Exc.	V.G.	Good	Fair	Poor
1600	1275	1100	800	650	350

Veloce Squire Set

Model features a two-barrel set in 20- and 28-gauge. Each barrel set fitted with 26" ventilated rib barrels. Select walnut stock, gold-emblished game scenes, jeweled monoblocs and filigreed top lever. Weight about 5.5 lbs. Introduced in 2003.

NIB	Exc.	V.G.	Good	Fair	Poor
2100	1775	1600	1200	800	400

Renaissance

Renaissance Series introduced in 2006. These over/unders feature ultra-light alloy receivers, oil-finished walnut stocks, Prince of Wales pistol-grips, cut checkering and Twin Shock Absorber recoil pads with gel insert. The 3" 12- and 20-gauges have 26" or 28" barrels; 28-gauge has 26" barrel. Weights average 6.2 lbs. 12-gauge, 5.8 lbs. 20-gauge and 5.5 lbs. 28-gauge. **NOTE:** Add 5 percent to values shown for 28-gauge.

Field

Walnut stock, with engraved receiver.

NIB	Exc.	V.G.	Good	Fair	Poor
1600	1250	995	775	400	200

Classic

A-Grade walnut, with gold inlaid receiver.

NIB	Exc.	V.G.	Good	Fair	Poor
1650	1300	1050	825	450	250

Elite

AA-Grade Walnut, with gold inlaid receiver.

NIB	Exc.	V.G.	Good	Fair	Poor
1900	1550	1295	1050	650	275

Sporting

This 3" 12-gauge model introduced in 2007. Features 30" barrel, A-Grade walnut stock, engraved receiver with gold inlay and adjustable comb. Weight about 7.9 lbs.

NIB	Exc.	V.G.	Good	Fair	Poor
1975	1625	1350	1300	825	325

Aspire

This diminutive over/under is made only in 28-gauge and .410 bore, for the discerning small-bore shooter. Features include round-action receiver and standard items expected for a quality over/under, such as single-selective trigger, automatic ejectors, AA-grade oil-finished walnut stock, ventilated rib and choke tubes. Barrels are 28" and weight just under 6 lbs.

NIB	Exc.	V.G.	Good	Fair	Poor
1950	1675	1425	1200	950	450

Instinct

In 12- or 20-gauge. Features 26" or 28" barrels with 3" chambers, five choke tubes, automatic ejectors, single-selective trigger, checkered A-grade walnut stock with satin finish. Available with AA-grade wood; add $200. Sporting model has 30" barrels with extended choke tubes, nickel receiver, target stock with squared pistol-grip; add $350. Introduced in 2012.

NIB	Exc.	V.G.	Good	Fair	Poor
1000	850	700	550	400	300

SEMI-AUTOMATIC SHOTGUNS

AL48

A 12- or 20-gauge semi-automatic shotgun, with 24" to 30" ventilated rib barrels (those made after 1989, threaded for choke tubes) and an alloy receiver. Walnut stock. Manufactured since 1950. Values shown are for current production. **NOTE:** Add 10 percent for Magnum Model; $75 for 28-gauge model.

NIB	Exc.	V.G.	Good	Fair	Poor
725	550	300	250	150	100

AL 48 Short Stock (Modern)

Same as above in 20-gauge, with shorter length of pull. First imported in 2000.

NIB	Exc.	V.G.	Good	Fair	Poor
700	525	275	250	150	100

AL 48 Deluxe English Stock (Modern)

Similar to standard AL 48, with straight-grip stock. Offered in 20- and 28-gauge, with 26" ventilated rib barrel and choke tubes. Weight about 5.5 lbs. Introduced in 2002.

NIB	Exc.	V.G.	Good	Fair	Poor
800	625	375	275	175	100

Hunter Model AL48 (1950-1970)

As above, with an etched receiver and more finely figured wood. **NOTE:** Add 10 percent for Magnum model.

NIB	Exc.	V.G.	Good	Fair	Poor
550	350	300	250	200	150

Eldorado AL48 (1954-1975)

As above, but more finely finished. Manufactured from 1954 to 1975.

NIB	Exc.	V.G.	Good	Fair	Poor
600	425	325	250	200	150

Crown Grade

As above, with hand-done engraving and finely figured walnut stocks.

NIB	Exc.	V.G.	Good	Fair	Poor
1800	1450	1200	800	475	250

Diamond Grade

As above, with hand-done engraving and finely figured walnut stocks.

NIB	Exc.	V.G.	Good	Fair	Poor
2300	1850	1375	900	575	300

Imperial Grade

As above, with hand-done engraving and finely figured walnut stocks.

NIB	Exc.	V.G.	Good	Fair	Poor
2800	2450	1850	1250	950	450

Model 500

A 12-gauge semi-automatic shotgun, with 28" ventilated rib barrel and walnut stock. Introduced in 1976. **NOTE:** Add 10 percent for deluxe version.

NIB	Exc.	V.G.	Good	Fair	Poor
500	425	375	295	150	100

Model 520 "Eldorado Gold"

An engraved and gold-inlaid version of above.

NIB	Exc.	V.G.	Good	Fair	Poor
1250	1050	850	550	300	150

Model 530 Trap

Model 500, with 30" or 32" ventilated rib barrel and trap stock.

NIB	Exc.	V.G.	Good	Fair	Poor
675	600	500	400	300	150

Prestige Model

A 12-gauge semi-automatic shotgun, manufactured in a variety of barrel lengths. After 1989 barrels threaded for choke tubes. Alloy receiver and walnut stock.

NIB	Exc.	V.G.	Good	Fair	Poor
675	550	475	350	250	150

Elite Model

As above, with etched receiver and more finely figured stock.

NIB	Exc.	V.G.	Good	Fair	Poor
700	600	525	350	250	150

SPAS12

A 12-gauge slide-action semi-automatic shotgun, with 21.5" barrel and 9-shot magazine. Anodized black finish, with composition folding or fixed stock.

NIB	Exc.	V.G.	Good	Fair	Poor
1450	1000	800	600	475	300

Black Magic Game Model

A 12-gauge Magnum semi-automatic shotgun, with 24" to 28" ventilated rib barrels. Threaded for choke tubes, gold anodized alloy receiver, blackened barrel and walnut stock. Also available in trap or skeet configuration. **NOTE:** Add 10 percent for Skeet Model; 15 percent for Trap Model.

NIB	Exc.	V.G.	Good	Fair	Poor
750	600	525	300	250	100

Black Magic Hunter

A 12- or 20-gauge Magnum double-barrel shotgun, with 28" ventilated rib barrels. Threaded for choke tubes, single-selective triggers and automatic ejectors. Blued, with a walnut stock. Introduced in 1989.

NIB	Exc.	V.G.	Good	Fair	Poor
700	550	475	300	250	100

Black Magic Lightweight Hunter

As above, with 26" barrels and 2.75" chambers.

NIB	Exc.	V.G.	Good	Fair	Poor
975	850	650	400	300	150

Variomax 912

Introduced in 2001, this model chambered for 12-gauge 3.5" shell. Offered with choice of 24", 26", 28" or 30" barrels with ventilated rib. Black synthetic stock. Weight about 7.6 lbs. Choke tubes. In 2002 a walnut stock added as an option. **NOTE:** Add $50 for walnut stock.

NIB	Exc.	V.G.	Good	Fair	Poor
700	550	475	300	250	100

Variomax 912 Camo

Same as above, with Advantage Timber camo finish.

NIB	Exc.	V.G.	Good	Fair	Poor
750	600	525	300	250	100

Variomax 912 SteadyGrip

Introduced in 2005. Features extended pistol-grip Advantage H-D camo stock, with 24" ventilated rib barrel and choke tubes. Weight about 8 lbs.

NIB	Exc.	V.G.	Good	Fair	Poor
775	625	550	325	265	100

Variopress 612 Sporting

A 12-gauge semi-automatic gas-operated shotgun, with 30" ported barrel. Extended choke tubes. Select walnut stock, with stock drop kit. Magazine capacity 5 rounds. Weight about 7 lbs. First imported in 2000.

NIB	Exc.	V.G.	Good	Fair	Poor
700	550	475	300	250	100

Variopress 612 Field

This 12-gauge model offered with barrel lengths from 24" to 28". Stock configurations are walnut, synthetic or camo. Magazine capacity 5 rounds. Weight about 7 lbs., depending on barrel length.

NIB	Exc.	V.G.	Good	Fair	Poor
700	550	475	300	250	100

Variopress 612 Defense

This 12-gauge gun fitted with 18.5" barrel and black synthetic stock. Matte black finish. Choke is cylinder. Weight about 6.5 lbs. Magazine capacity 5 rounds. First imported in 2000.

NIB	Exc.	V.G.	Good	Fair	Poor
600	500	425	350	250	150

Variopress 620 Field

Model offered in 20-gauge, with choice of walnut or camo stock. Barrel lengths from 24" to 28". Magazine capacity 5 rounds. Weight about 6 lbs. **NOTE:** Add $50 for camo stock.

NIB	Exc.	V.G.	Good	Fair	Poor
700	550	475	300	250	100

Variopress 620 Short Stock

Same as above, with 12.5" length of pull and walnut stock. First imported in 2000.

NIB	Exc.	V.G.	Good	Fair	Poor
700	550	475	300	250	100

Model 712

Semi-automatic shotgun, chambered for 12-gauge 3" shell. Choice of 24", 26" or 28" ventilated rib barrels with choke tubes. Offered in several different finishes: Weathercoat (synthetic wood), Max-4 camo and Timber HD. Choice of synthetic wood, black synthetic or camo stock. Weight about 6.8 lbs. to 7 lbs., depending on stock and barrel length. Introduced in 2004.

Weathercoat

NIB	Exc.	V.G.	Good	Fair	Poor
700	600	500	375	200	100

Camo

NIB	Exc.	V.G.	Good	Fair	Poor
725	625	525	400	225	125

Synthetic

NIB	Exc.	V.G.	Good	Fair	Poor
775	650	550	425	250	150

Model 720

Similar to Model 712, but chambered for 20-gauge 3" shell. Offered with 24", 26" or 28" ventilated rib barrels. Choice of Max-4, Timber HD finish or walnut stock, with 12.5" lop. Introduced in 2004.

Camo

NIB	Exc.	V.G.	Good	Fair	Poor
750	650	550	425	250	150

Walnut Short Stock

NIB	Exc.	V.G.	Good	Fair	Poor
725	625	525	400	225	125

Weathercoat

Introduced in 2005, with 28" ventilated rib barrel. Weight about 6.2 lbs.

NIB	Exc.	V.G.	Good	Fair	Poor
775	650	550	425	250	150

I-12

Introduced in 2005, this 12-gauge model offered with 3" chambers and choice of 24", 26" or 28" ventilated rib barrels. Available with synthetic, walnut, Max-4 or Timber H-D stock. Choke tubes. Weight about 7.5 lbs., depending on barrel length.

NIB	Exc.	V.G.	Good	Fair	Poor
1200	900	600	500	350	200

I-12 White Gold

Similar to Inertia I-12, with highly figured walnut stock. White gold game bird scene on a satin nickel receiver. Introduced in 2006. Available only with 28" barrel. Weight about 7.7 lbs.

NIB	Exc.	V.G.	Good	Fair	Poor
1400	1050	750	600	425	250

Fenice

Small-frame semi-automatic built on Franchi's classic recoil-operated AL-48 design. No recoil problem, however, Fenice is only in 28-gauge and .410 bore. Among the quality features are AA-grade European walnut stock, 26" or 28" barrel with ventilated rib and nickel-plated receiver with scroll engraving and inlayed game bird scene. Weight: 20-gauge 5.75 lbs.; 28-gauge 5.4 lbs.

NIB	Exc.	V.G.	Good	Fair	Poor
1150	1000	850	620	450	300

Intensity

Semi-automatic operates on Inertia Driven system, which is designed to operate with 2.75", 3" and 3.5" 12-gauge shells. Barrel lengths are 26", 28" or 30" and weight of all three length models is between 6.7 and 6.9 lbs. Synthetic stock makes it ideal for all weather conditions. Several Realtree and Mossy Oak camo designs are available. **NOTE:** Add $100 for camo models if in good or better condition.

NIB	Exc.	V.G.	Good	Fair	Poor
975	800	675	500	375	300

Affinity

Semi-automatic in 12- or 20-gauge with 3" chambers and three choke tubes. Black finish or 100 percent camo coverage. Sporting model in 12-gauge only, with 30" barrel and nickel receiver. Introduced in 2012. **NOTE:** Add $100 for camo finish; $300 for Sporting model.

NIB	Exc.	V.G.	Good	Fair	Poor
750	650	500	400	300	250

RIFLES

Centennial Semi-Automatic

A .22-caliber semi-automatic rifle, with 21" barrel, adjustable sights, Alloy receiver and walnut stock. Manufactured in 1968 only. **NOTE:** Add 20 percent for deluxe engraved model.

NIB	Exc.	V.G.	Good	Fair	Poor
550	375	325	250	175	125

FRANCOTTE, A.
Liege, Belgium

For pistols and revolvers See—AFC.

Jubilee

A 12-, 16-, 20- and 28-gauge Anson & Deeley boxlock double-barrel shotgun, with various barrel lengths and chokes. Automatic ejectors, double triggers and walnut stock.

NIB	Exc.	V.G.	Good	Fair	Poor
—	2000	1350	1100	850	450

No. 14

Courtesy William Hammond

NIB	Exc.	V.G.	Good	Fair	Poor
—	3000	2050	1700	1300	650

No. 18

NIB	Exc.	V.G.	Good	Fair	Poor
—	3500	3000	2200	1500	750

No. 20

NIB	Exc.	V.G.	Good	Fair	Poor
—	4000	3600	2250	1750	900

No. 25

NIB	Exc.	V.G.	Good	Fair	Poor
—	5000	3900	2750	2000	1000

No. 30

Courtesy William Hammond

NIB	Exc.	V.G.	Good	Fair	Poor
—	6000	4200	3500	3000	1500

Eagle Grade No. 45

NIB	Exc.	V.G.	Good	Fair	Poor
—	9000	7000	3500	2000	1000

Knockabout

Plain version of Jubilee Model, in 12-, 16-, 20-, 28-gauge and .410 bore.
NOTE: Add 20 percent for 20-gauge; 30 percent for 28-gauge; 40 percent for .410 bore.

NIB	Exc.	V.G.	Good	Fair	Poor
—	2700	2000	1000	650	500

Sidelock Side-by-Side

A 12-, 16-, 20-, 28-gauge and .410 bore sidelock shotgun, ordered per customer's specifications. Extensive scroll engraving, deluxe walnut stock and finely checkered. **NOTE:** The .410 will bring a premium from $1,200 - $1,500.

NIB	Exc.	V.G.	Good	Fair	Poor
25000	20000	12000	6500	5000	3500

Deluxe Sidelock Side-by-Side

As above, with gold-inlaid hunting scenes.

NIB	Exc.	V.G.	Good	Fair	Poor
30000	24000	16000	8000	5750	4800

CUSTOM MADE SHOTGUNS & RIFLES

These shotguns and rifles were all custom built to customer's specifications. Gauge (including 24- and 32-gauge), caliber, barrel length, engraving, wood type and style are all individually produced. No two are alike. These shotguns and rifles should be individually appraised before sale. Prices listed are subject to fluctuations in international currency.

Custom Side-by-Side Shotguns

Available in 12-, 16-, 20-, 28-gauge and .410 bore, in either boxlock or sidelock actions. Barrel length, engraving, wood type and style are at customer's discretion. Retail prices range from:

Basic Boxlock with 27.5" barrels and walnut stock with double triggers in 12-, 16- and 20-gauge without engraving—$18,000

Basic Boxlock in 28-gauge or .410 bore without engraving—$14,000

Basic Boxlock with 26.5" or 28" barrels and deluxe walnut stock, with scroll engraving and double triggers in 12-, 16- and 20-gauge—$23,000

Basic Boxlock in 28-gauge or .410 bore—$28,000

Prices for 24- and 32-gauge are extra. These prices do not include engraving.

Custom Double Rifles

These custom built double rifles were offered, in calibers from 9.3x74R to .470 Nitro Express, in boxlock or sidelock actions. Barrel length, engraving, wood type and style are at customer's discretion. Retail prices range from:

Prices for 24- and 32-gauge are extra. These prices do not include engraving.

Boxlock in 9.3x74R, 8x57JRS and other European calibers-$14,000

Boxlock in .375 H&H and .470 NE—$19,000

Sidelock in 9.3x74R, etc.—$23,700

Sidelock in large calibers—$32,000

Custom Single-Shot Mountain Rifles

These single-shot rifles were offered in rimmed cartridges, but rimless cartridge rifles can be built on special request. Barrel length, engraving, wood type and style are at customer's discretion. Retail prices range from:

Boxlock in rimmed calibers—Prices start at $13,000

Sidelock in 7x65R and 7mm Rem. Magnum—Prices start at $24,000

Custom Bolt-Action Rifles

These bolt-action rifles utilize a Mauser 98 type action, with adjustable trigger. Offered in calibers from .17 Bee to .505 Gibbs. Barrel lengths are

21" to 24.5". Engraving, wood type and style are at customers' discretion. Retail prices range from:

Standard bolt-action calibers: .270, .30-06, 7x64, 8x60S and 9.3x62—Prices start at $7,650

Short-action calibers: .222, .223—Prices start at $9,100

Magnum-action calibers: 7mm Rem. Magnum, .300 Win. Magnum, .338 Win. Magnum, .375 H&H and .458 Win. Magnum—Prices start at $8,400

African calibers: .416 Rigby, .460 Wby., .505 Gibbs—Prices start at $12,250

PLEASE NOTE: Prices listed are for basic models. They do not reflect the extensive list of options available on these custom firearms.

FRANKLIN, C. W.
Liege, Belgium

Manufacturer of utilitarian shotguns, with either exposed or enclosed hammers. Circa 1900.

Single-Barrel

NIB	Exc.	V.G.	Good	Fair	Poor
—	150	75	50	35	20

Damascus Barrel Double

NIB	Exc.	V.G.	Good	Fair	Poor
—	250	150	125	100	65

Steel Barrel Double

NIB	Exc.	V.G.	Good	Fair	Poor
—	300	175	150	125	90

FRANKONIA JAGD
Favorit, Germany

Seldom seen in U.S.A. Values extremely variable, based on local market, chambering and other factors.

Favorit Standard

Chambered for various European calibers, this bolt-action rifle has 24" barrel and set triggers. Blued, with checkered walnut stock.

NIB	Exc.	V.G.	Good	Fair	Poor
—	450	295	260	175	125

Favorit Deluxe

As above, with more finely figured stock.

NIB	Exc.	V.G.	Good	Fair	Poor
—	475	325	275	200	150

Safari Model

As above, in Magnum calibers.

NIB	Exc.	V.G.	Good	Fair	Poor
—	1400	950	675	275	200

Heeren Rifle

Best quality single-shot rifle, with 26" octagonal barrel, double-set triggers and adjustable sights. Engraved with hand checkered high-grade walnut. Blued. Produced in a variety of calibers.

NIB	Exc.	V.G.	Good	Fair	Poor
—	5000	3050	2500	1700	1250

FRASER F. A. CORP.
Fraser, Michigan

Fraser .25 cal.

A .25 ACP caliber semi-automatic pistol, with 2.25" barrel and 6-round magazine. Stainless steel with black nylon grips. There is a 24 kt. gold-plated model, that is worth approximately $100 additional. Later made under Fraser name, by a different company in 1990.

NIB	Exc.	V.G.	Good	Fair	Poor
250	175	125	100	50	35

FREEDOM ARMS
Freedom, Wyoming

Percussion Mini-Revolver

A .22-caliber spur trigger revolver, with 1", 1.75" or 3" barrel lengths, 5-shot cylinder and bird's-head grip. Stainless steel. Belt buckle available that houses pistol for additional $40.

NIB	Exc.	V.G.	Good	Fair	Poor
300	250	195	125	100	75

Bostonian (aka Boot Gun)

As above, with 3" barrel in .22 Magnum. Discontinued 1992.

NIB	Exc.	V.G.	Good	Fair	Poor
375	300	225	150	80	60

Patriot (aka Boot Gun)

As above, in .22 LR caliber. Discontinued 1992.

NIB	Exc.	V.G.	Good	Fair	Poor
375	300	225	150	80	60

Minuteman

As above, with 3" barrel. Discontinued in 1988.

NIB	Exc.	V.G.	Good	Fair	Poor
375	300	225	150	80	60

Ironsides

As above in .22 Magnum, with 1" or 1.75" barrel.

NIB	Exc.	V.G.	Good	Fair	Poor
375	300	225	150	80	60

Celebrity

As above, with belt buckle mount for either .22 or .22 Magnum revolvers. **NOTE:** Add $25 for .22 Magnum model.

NIB	Exc.	V.G.	Good	Fair	Poor
400	325	275	225	150	100

PREMIER AND FIELD GRADE REVOLVERS

Both grades use the same materials and machining tolerances. Difference is in finish, standard components and warranty.

Premier Grade has a bright brushed finish, screw adjustable rear sight, laminated hardwood grips and limited lifetime warranty.

Field Grade has matte finish, adjustable rear sight for elevation only, Pachmayr rubber grips and one year warranty.

Casull Field Grade Model 83

A .454 Casull Magnum revolver, with 4.75", 6", 7.5" and 10" barrel. Standard fixed sights. Fires a 225-grain bullet. Also offered in .50 AE, .475 Linebaugh, .44 Rem. Magnum, .41 Magnum and .357 Magnum. Adjustable sights available as a $75 option. Matte stainless steel with black rubber Pachmayr grips. Introduced in 1988. **NOTE:** Add $75 for .454 Casull, .475 Linebaugh or .50 AE calibers.

NIB	Exc.	V.G.	Good	Fair	Poor
1825	1400	800	550	—	—

Casull Premier Grade Model 83

A .454 Magnum, .44 Rem. Magnum, .45 Win. Magnum, .475 Linebaugh and .50 AE, with replaceable forcing and walnut grips. Finish is brush stainless steel. Adjustable sights are an extra cost option on this model as well. Offered in barrel lengths of 4.75", 6", 7.5" and 10" except for .475 Casull. .55 Wyoming Express added in 2006. **NOTE:** Extra cylinders are available for these models in .45 Colt, .45 Win. Magnum and .45 ACP. Add $250 to price of gun for each cylinder. Add $75 for .454 Casull, .475 Linebaugh or .50 AE calibers.

NIB	Exc.	V.G.	Good	Fair	Poor
2150	1800	1250	850	500	350

Model 97

Revolver chambered for either .357 Magnum, .45 Colt, .44 Special and .22 LR cartridges. Available in Field or Premier grades, with choice of 4.25", 5.5" or 7.5" barrel. Optional .45 ACP cylinder of .45 Colt and .38 Special cylinder for .357 Magnum model. In 2004 this model was also offered in .17 HMR and .32 H&R Magnum calibers. **NOTE:** There are a number of extra-cost options that will affect price. Some of these options are sights, grips, Mag-Na-Port barrels, slings and trigger over-travel screws. Add $265 for extra .38 Special, .45 ACP cylinder or .22 WMR cylinder. Add $475 for extra fitted .22 LR match grade cylinder. Add $215 for match grade chambered, instead of .22 LR sport chamber.

NIB	Exc.	V.G.	Good	Fair	Poor
1800	1350	1000	600	400	300

Model 353

Chambered for .357 Magnum cartridge, with choice of 4.75", 6", 7.5" or 9" barrel length. Adjustable sights. Model designation no longer used; see Model 97.

Field Grade

NIB	Exc.	V.G.	Good	Fair	Poor
1650	1300	950	550	350	250

Premier Grade

NIB	Exc.	V.G.	Good	Fair	Poor
2150	1800	1250	700	500	300

Signature Edition

As above, with highly polished finish, rosewood grips, 7.5" barrel only and fitted case. Serial numbers are DC1-DC2000. (DC represents Dick Casull, designer of firearm.) Total of 2,000 made.

NIB	Exc.	V.G.	Good	Fair	Poor
2500	1950	1300	750	550	350

Model 252

Stainless steel version of large frame revolver, chambered for .22 LR cartridge. Available in 5.12", 7.5" or 10" barrel lengths. Matte finish. Designation no longer used; see Model 97. **NOTE:** Optional .22 Magnum cylinder available for $250.

Silhouette Class

10" barrel.

NIB	Exc.	V.G.	Good	Fair	Poor
1700	1150	850	600	450	250

Varmint Class

5.12" or 7.5" barrel.

NIB	Exc.	V.G.	Good	Fair	Poor
1700	1150	850	600	450	250

Model 757

Introduced in 1999, this 5-shot revolver chambered for .475 Linebaugh cartridge. Fitted with adjustable sights. Offered in both Field and Premier grades. Choice of 4.75", 6" or 7.5" barrel lengths. Designation no longer used; see Model 83.

Field Grade

NIB	Exc.	V.G.	Good	Fair	Poor
1400	1100	750	500	400	300

Premier Grade

NIB	Exc.	V.G.	Good	Fair	Poor
1800	1450	1100	750	500	400

Model 654

This 5-shot revolver chambered for .41 Magnum cartridge. Adjustable sights. Introduced in 1999. Designation no longer used; see Model 97.

Field Grade

NIB	Exc.	V.G.	Good	Fair	Poor
1325	1050	750	500	400	300

Premier Grade

NIB	Exc.	V.G.	Good	Fair	Poor
1750	1400	1100	750	500	400

Model 83 .500 Wyoming Express

Similar to Model 83, but chambered in .500 Wyoming Express. Introduced 2007.

NIB	Exc.	V.G.	Good	Fair	Poor
2150	1800	1250	700	500	300

FREEMAN, AUSTIN T.
Hoard's Armory
Watertown, New York

Freeman Army Model Revolver

A .44-caliber percussion revolver, with 7.5" round barrel, 6-shot unfluted cylinder with recessed nipples. Blued, walnut grips, case-hardened rammer and hammer. Frame marked "Freeman's Pat. Dec. 9, 1862/Hoard's Armory, Watertown, N.Y." Several thousand manufactured in 1863 and 1864.

NIB	Exc.	V.G.	Good	Fair	Poor
—	—	5800	2200	550	200

FRIGON
Clay Center, Kansas

An importer of guns manufactured by Marocchi of Italy.

FT I

A 12-gauge boxlock single-barrel shotgun, with 32" or 34" ventilated rib barrel. Full choke, automatic ejector and interchangeable stock. Blued. Introduced in 1986.

NIB	Exc.	V.G.	Good	Fair	Poor
950	750	650	550	450	300

FTC

As above, with two sets of barrels (a single ventilated rib trap barrel and a set of over/under ventilated rib barrels). In a fitted case. Introduced in 1986.

NIB	Exc.	V.G.	Good	Fair	Poor
1750	1400	1150	800	650	500

FS-4

A four gauge set (12-, 20-, 28-gauge and .410 bore). Introduced in 1986.

NIB	Exc.	V.G.	Good	Fair	Poor
2500	2100	1750	1500	1100	750

FROMMER
See—FEG (Fegyver Es Gazkeszulekgyar)

FRUHWIRTH
Austria

M1872 Fruhwirth System Rifle

An 11mm bolt-action rifle, with 25" barrel and 6-shot magazine. Blued, with full-length walnut stock.

NIB	Exc.	V.G.	Good	Fair	Poor
—	650	425	300	195	100

FUNK, CHRISTOPH
Suhl, Germany

Christoph Funk began his gun business before 1900. The vast majority of long guns were the best quality. Some collectors believe that J.P. Sauer built receivers for Funk, but this is not known for certain. Funk produced shotguns, shotgun-rifle combinations and double rifles. Some were exported to England and U.S. Most of U.S. imports are in the more common North American calibers, such as .300 Savage, 30-30, 32-20 Winchester and 12- or 16-gauge. Most are found with only a right-hand extension arm, which locks into the receiver, but some higher grades have both extension arms. Quality of these guns is extremely high. Guns were probably not made after 1940. Quality of engraving and caliber determines value. American calibers will command a higher price. Prices listed are for American calibers.

Double Rifles

Courtesy Jim Cate

NIB	Exc.	V.G.	Good	Fair	Poor
—	2950	2250	1450	600	400

Prewar Drilling in 16 or 12 gauge

Courtesy Jim Cate

NIB	Exc.	V.G.	Good	Fair	Poor
—	4500	3750	2500	1200	—

FURR ARMS
J. & G. Sale, Inc.
Prescott, Arizona

In addition to producing reproductions of various cannon, this company also manufactured one-tenth to three-quarter scale reproductions of Gatling guns. Furr products are highly desirable in some circles, with the Gatling .22 reproductions typically commanding prices in excess of $18,000 in mint, unfired condition.

FYRBERG, ANDREW
Worcester and Hopkinton, Massachusetts

Double-Barrel Shotguns

Fyrberg did work for Iver Johnson and C.S. Shattuck Co. of Hatfield, Mass. He began producing a hammerless double about 1902, a well designed boxlock with coil mainsprings. An estimated 2,000 were produced at Hopkinton and Worcester, Mass. Some have been made at Meriden, Conn. Sears cataloged the Fyrberg guns in 1902 to about 1908.

NIB	Exc.	V.G.	Good	Fair	Poor
—	525	425	300	200	150

Revolvers

A 3" barreled .32-caliber and 3.5" .38-caliber revolver, with round ribbed barrels and round butts. Grips bear trademark "AFCo". Model most likely made by Iver Johnson for Andrew Fyrberg.

NIB	Exc.	V.G.	Good	Fair	Poor
—	250	145	100	75	50

GABBET-FAIRFAX, H.
Birmingham, England

Mars

Designed by Hugh Gabbet-Fairfax, this semi-automatic pistol first produced on an experimental basis by Webley & Scott Revolvers in the 1890s. After Webley gave up on the idea an extremely limited number were built by Mars Automatic Pistol Syndicate, Ltd., 1897 to 1905. Pistol produced in four calibers; 8.5mm Mars, 9mm Mars, .45 Mars Short Case and .45 Mars Long Case. Most powerful handgun cartridge of its time and remained so until well after World War II. It is estimated that only about 80 of these pistols were ever produced. **NOTE:** Webley examples are worth a premium.

Courtesy James Rankin

NIB	Exc.	V.G.	Good	Fair	Poor
—	45000	30500	19500	9200	6000

GABILONDO Y CIA
See—Llama

GABILONDO Y URRESTI
Guernica, Spain
Elgoibar, Spain
See—Llama

Spanish firm founded in 1904 to produce inexpensive revolvers of Velo-Dog type. Sometime around 1909 the firm began to manufacture Radium revolver. In 1914 the company produced a semi-automatic pistol distributed as Ruby. This pistol soon became the mainstay of the company, with orders of 30,000 pistols a month for the French army. End of WWI Gabilondo Y Urresti moved to Elgoeibar, Spain. Company produced a Browning 1910 replica pistol until early 1930s. It was at this point that Gabilondo began to manufacture a Colt Model 1911 copy that became known as Llama. For information of specific Llama models see Llama section. Pistols listed reflect pre-Llama period and are so marked, with the trade name of that particular model. Monogram "GC" frequently appears on grips but not on slide.

Velo-Dog Revolver

A 6.35mm double-action revolver with 1.5" barrel, folding trigger and concealed hammer. Blued, with walnut grips. Manufactured from 1904 to 1914.

NIB	Exc.	V.G.	Good	Fair	Poor
—	295	195	125	75	50

Radium

Semi-automatic pistol in caliber 7.65mm. Produced both for commercial and military market in Ruby style. "Radium" stamped on slide as well as top of each grip plate.

Courtesy James Rankin

NIB	Exc.	V.G.	Good	Fair	Poor
—	295	195	125	100	70

Ruby

A 7.65mm caliber semi-automatic pistol. Discontinued in 1930.

NIB	Exc.	V.G.	Good	Fair	Poor
—	250	175	150	100	75

Bufalo 6.35mm

Semi-automatic pistol in caliber 6.35mm. Copy of Browning Model 1906, with squeeze grip safety. Has "Bufalo" stamped on slide and Gabilondo logo along with a buffalo's head on each side of grip plates. Manufactured between 1918 and 1925. **NOTE:** Spelling of "Bufalo" as it appears on pistol.

Courtesy James Rankin

NIB	Exc.	V.G.	Good	Fair	Poor
—	275	175	150	100	75

Bufalo 7.65mm

Semi-automatic pistol in caliber 7.65mm. Patterned after Browning Model 1910, with squeeze grip safety. There were two models, with either 7- or 9-round magazine. Model with 9-round magazine usually fitted with wood grips and lanyard ring. Buffalo's head is inset in each grip plate. Manufactured between 1918 and 1925.

Courtesy James Rankin

NIB	Exc.	V.G.	Good	Fair	Poor
—	275	175	125	100	75

Bufalo 9mmK

Semi-automatic pistol in caliber 9mmK. Nearly same pistol as 7.65mm model, but fitted with grip safety. "Bufalo" stamped on slide and Gabilondo logo and buffalo's head are on each grip plate. Manufactured between 1918 and 1925.

Courtesy James Rankin

NIB	Exc.	V.G.	Good	Fair	Poor
—	295	205	145	105	70

Danton 6.35mm

Semi-automatic pistol in caliber 6.35mm. Patterned after Browning Model 1906, with grip safety. "Danton" appears on slide as well as grips. Gabilondo logo on each grip plate. Manufactured between 1925 and 1931.

Courtesy James Rankin

NIB	Exc.	V.G.	Good	Fair	Poor
—	275	175	125	100	75

Danton War Model

Semi-automatic pistol in caliber 7.65mm. Similar to Bufalo above and made with-/without grip safety. Came in two models, with 9- and 20-round magazines. Fitted with lanyard ring. "Danton" stamped on slide and grips. Gabilondo logo on each side of grip plate. Manufactured between 1925 and 1931.

Courtesy James Rankin

Nine-Round Magazine

NIB	Exc.	V.G.	Good	Fair	Poor
—	275	175	125	100	75

Twenty-Round Magazine

NIB	Exc.	V.G.	Good	Fair	Poor
—	550	325	250	200	100

Perfect

Semi-automatic pistol chambered for 6.35mm and 7.65mm cartridges. Cheap low-priced pistol marketed by Mugica. Pistols usually have the word "Perfect" on grips. Slide may be stamped with the name MUGICA, but many are not.

NIB	Exc.	V.G.	Good	Fair	Poor
—	275	175	125	100	75

Plus Ultra

Pistol chambered for 7.65mm cartridge and built from 1925 to 1933. Had a 20-round magazine that gave the pistol an unusual appearance. "Plus Ultra" appears on slide and grips. Gabilondo logo on each grip plate. Equipped with lanyard ring.

Courtesy James Rankin

NIB	Exc.	V.G.	Good	Fair	Poor
—	1200	875	650	425	250

GALAND, C.F.
Liege, Belgium

Galand, Galand & Sommerville, Galand Perrin (Galand M1872)

A 7mm, 9mm and 12mm caliber double-action revolver, with 6-shot cylinder and open frame. A unique ejection system that by means of rotating a lever downward from the trigger guard, causes barrel and cylinder to slide forward leaving ejector and spent cases behind. Circa 1872.

Courtesy Bonhams & Butterfields

NIB	Exc.	V.G.	Good	Fair	Poor
—	—	1350	875	550	150

Velo-Dog

A 5.5mm Velo-Dog caliber fixed trigger and guard double-action revolver, with open-top design. Later models (.22 and 6.35mm caliber) feature folding triggers and no trigger guards.

NIB	Exc.	V.G.	Good	Fair	Poor
—	250	165	125	75	50

Le Novo

As above, with concealed hammer and in 6.35mm caliber.

NIB	Exc.	V.G.	Good	Fair	Poor
—	250	165	125	75	50

Tue-Tue

A .22 short 5.5mm Velo-Dog and 6.35mm caliber double-action revolver. Concealed hammer, folding trigger and swing-out cylinder, with central extractor. Introduced in 1894.

NIB	Exc.	V.G.	Good	Fair	Poor
—	250	165	125	75	50

GALAND & SOMMERVILLE
Liege, Belgium

See—Galand

GALEF (ZABALA)
Zabala Hermanos & Antonio Zoli
Spain

Zabala Double

A 10-, 12-, 16- and 20-gauge boxlock shotgun, with 22" to 30" barrel and various chokes. Hardwood stock. **NOTE:** Add 50 percent for 10-gauge.

NIB	Exc.	V.G.	Good	Fair	Poor
—	450	300	175	100	75

Companion

Folding 12-gauge to .410 bore single-shot underlever shotgun, with 28" or 30" barrel.

NIB	Exc.	V.G.	Good	Fair	Poor
—	200	145	105	50	25

Monte Carlo Trap

A 12-gauge underlever single-shot shotgun, with 32" ventilated rib barrel.

NIB	Exc.	V.G.	Good	Fair	Poor
—	325	275	150	100	75

Silver Snipe, Golden Snipe, and Silver Hawk

See—Antonio Zoli

GALENA INDUSTRIES INC.
Sturgis, South Dakota

In 1998, Galena Industries purchased the rights to use AMT trademark and manufacturing rights to many, but not all, AMT designs. For AMT models made by AMT see that section. This company's designs have been acquired by Crusader/High Standard of Houston, Texas.

AMT Backup

Model features double-action-only trigger system and offered in both stainless steel and matte black finish. Small frame .380 Backup weighs 18 oz. with its 2.5" barrel. Large frame Backups are fitted with 3" barrel and offered in 9mm, .38 Super, .357 Sig., .40 S&W, .400 CorBon and .45 ACP. Weight about 23 oz.; magazine capacity 5 to 6 rounds, depending on caliber. **NOTE:** Add $50 for .38 Super, .357 Sig, and .400 CorBon.

Galena .380 DAO Backup

NIB	Exc.	V.G.	Good	Fair	Poor
525	375	275	200	125	100

Automag II

Semi-automatic pistol chambered for .22 WMR cartridge. Offered in 3.38", 4.5" or 6" barrel lengths. Magazine capacity 9 rounds, except for 3.38" model is 7 rounds. Weight about 32 oz.

Automag II with 4.5" barrel

NIB	Exc.	V.G.	Good	Fair	Poor
695	550	325	225	125	100

Automag III

Pistol chambered for .30 Carbine cartridge. Barrel length 6.38". Weight about 43 oz. Stainless steel finish.

NIB	Exc.	V.G.	Good	Fair	Poor
800	675	375	250	150	100

Automag IV

Model chambered for .45 Winchester Magnum cartridge. Fitted with 6.5" barrel. Magazine capacity 7 rounds. Weight about 46 oz.

NIB	Exc.	V.G.	Good	Fair	Poor
800	675	375	250	150	100

Automag .440 CorBon

Semi-automatic pistol chambered for .440 CorBon cartridge and fitted with 7.5" barrel. Magazine capacity 5 rounds. Finish matte black. Weight about 46 oz. Checkered walnut grips. Introduced in 2000. Special order only.

NIB	Exc.	V.G.	Good	Fair	Poor
1000	900	750	575	400	175

Galena Accelerator

Model has 7" barrel built on 1911 frame. Chambered for .400 CorBon. Magazine capacity 7 rounds. Weight about 46 oz. Finish stainless steel.

NIB	Exc.	V.G.	Good	Fair	Poor
850	725	550	400	300	100

Galena Hardballer

Pistol based on Colt Model 1911 design. Chambered for .45 ACP cartridge. Fitted with 5" barrel. Magazine capacity 7 rounds. Finish stainless steel. Adjustable trigger and beveled magazine well. Offered chambered for .40 S&W and .400 CorBon cartridges. Weight about 38 oz.

NIB	Exc.	V.G.	Good	Fair	Poor
1000	900	750	575	400	175

Galena Longslide

Model chambered for .45 ACP cartridge and fitted with 7" barrel. Magazine capacity 7 rounds. Weight about 46 oz. Finish stainless steel.

NIB	Exc.	V.G.	Good	Fair	Poor
850	725	550	400	300	10

Galena Commando

Commando chambered for .40 S&W cartridge. Fitted with 4" barrel. Magazine capacity 8 rounds. Weight about 38 oz. Finish stainless steel.

NIB	Exc.	V.G.	Good	Fair	Poor
550	400	295	225	175	100

GALESI, INDUSTRIA ARMI
Brescia, Italy

Rino Galesi Armi, Collebeato, Italy, manufactured shotguns, revolvers and automatic pistols. Firm's name changed from Rino Galesi Armi to Industria Armi Galesi to Rigarmi di Rino Galesi. Their semi-automatic pistols were designated by model year, model number and a 500 Series. Most models named in the 500 Series came after the firm changed its name to Industria Armi Galesi.

Model 1923

A 6.35mm and 7.65mm caliber semi-automatic pistol. Has a squeeze grip safety and wood grip plates with crest. Model 1923 stamped on slide.

Courtesy James Rankin

NIB	Exc.	V.G.	Good	Fair	Poor
—	275	195	145	75	50

Model 1930

A 6.35mm and 7.65mm caliber semi-automatic pistol. Very few were made in 1946 in 9mm Parabellum. Based on 1910 Browning design. Blued, with plastic grips. Slide marked "Brevetto Mod. 1930".

Courtesy James Rankin

NIB	Exc.	V.G.	Good	Fair	Poor
—	275	195	145	75	50

9mm Parabellum

NIB	Exc.	V.G.	Good	Fair	Poor
—	600	500	400	300	100

Model 6

Updated Model 1930. Manufactured approximately 1938 to 1948 in calibers; 22 Short, .22 Long, .22 LR, 6.35mm, 7.65mm and 9mm Short.

Courtesy James Rankin

NIB	Exc.	V.G.	Good	Fair	Poor
—	350	175	100	75	50

Model 9

Manufactured from approximately 1947 to 1956 in calibers .22 Short, .22 Long, .22 LR, 6.35mm, 7.65mm and 9mm Short. Also listed under 500 Series. The .22 versions were marketed as "the smallest .22 pistols ever built".

Courtesy James Rankin

NIB	Exc.	V.G.	Good	Fair	Poor
—	295	175	100	75	50

GALIL
Israel Military Industries
Israel

Model AR (.223)

NOTE: Add $600 for .308-caliber.

NIB	Exc.	V.G.	Good	Fair	Poor
3000	2400	2000	1500	900	700

Model ARM

NIB	Exc.	V.G.	Good	Fair	Poor
3400	2700	2000	1500	900	700

Sniper Rifle

NIB	Exc.	V.G.	Good	Fair	Poor
8500	7500	6000	4000	3000	2000

Hadar II

NIB	Exc.	V.G.	Good	Fair	Poor
1300	1100	800	650	500	400

GALLAGER
Richardson & Overman
Philadelphia, Pennsylvania

Gallager Carbine

A .50-caliber single-shot percussion carbine, with 22.25" barrel, saddle ring and walnut stock. Blued and case-hardened. Approximately 23,000 made during Civil War.

Percussion Model

As above, in .56-62 rimfire caliber. Approximately 5,000 made.

Courtesy Milwaukee Public Museum, Milwaukee, Wisconsin

NIB	Exc.	V.G.	Good	Fair	Poor
—	—	3900	2450	1500	500

Spencer Cartridge Model

NIB	Exc.	V.G.	Good	Fair	Poor
—	—	3425	1950	1350	400

GAMBA, RENATO
Gardone V. T., Italy

SIDE-BY-SIDE SHOTGUNS

Hunter Super

A 12-gauge Anson & Deeley boxlock double-barrel shotgun. Variety of barrel lengths and chokes, double triggers and extractors. Engraved and silver-plated.

NIB	Exc.	V.G.	Good	Fair	Poor
1250	900	700	550	450	250

Principessa

A 12-, 20- or 28-gauge boxlock shotgun. Engraved checkered stock.

NIB	Exc.	V.G.	Good	Fair	Poor
1850	1250	900	700	500	250

Oxford 90

A 12- or 20-gauge sidelock shotgun, with various barrel lengths and chokes. Purdey locking system, double triggers and automatic ejectors. Walnut stock.

NIB	Exc.	V.G.	Good	Fair	Poor
4250	3250	1700	900	600	300

Oxford Extra

Same as above, with fine engraving.

NIB	Exc.	V.G.	Good	Fair	Poor
5200	4000	2250	1500	900	450

Gamba 624 Prince

Fitted with Wesley Richards-type frame, select walnut stock and fine hand engraving. Offered in 12-gauge with 28" barrels.

NIB	Exc.	V.G.	Good	Fair	Poor
4800	3900	2500	1500	850	400

Gamba 624 Extra

Same as above, with deep floral engraving.

NIB	Exc.	V.G.	Good	Fair	Poor
8000	5000	4500	2500	1250	600

London

A 12- or 20-gauge H&H sidelock shotgun, with various barrel lengths and chokes. Double-/single-selective trigger, automatic ejectors. Walnut stock.

NIB	Exc.	V.G.	Good	Fair	Poor
7000	5500	4500	2500	1250	700

London Royal

As above, with engraved hunting scenes.

NIB	Exc.	V.G.	Good	Fair	Poor
8000	6500	5000	3750	2000	950

Ambassador Gold and Black

A 12- and 20-gauge H&H sidelock shotgun, with various barrel lengths and choke combinations. Single-selective trigger, automatic ejectors and a single gold line engraved on barrels and frame. Walnut stocks.

NIB	Exc.	V.G.	Good	Fair	Poor
25000	19000	13500	9500	5000	2500

Ambassador Executive

Gamba's best quality shotgun produced in 12- or 20-gauge to customer's specifications.

NIB	Exc.	V.G.	Good	Fair	Poor
28000	20000	15000	10000	5000	2500

OVER/UNDER SHOTGUNS

Country Model

A 12- and 20-gauge over/under shotgun, with 28" or 30" ventilated rib barrels, double triggers, extractors. Walnut stock.

NIB	Exc.	V.G.	Good	Fair	Poor
650	550	400	300	275	200

Grifone Model

A 12- and 20-gauge over/under shotgun, with 26", 28" or 30" ventilated rib barrels, single-selective trigger and automatic ejectors. Boxlock action silver-plated, with walnut stock. Available with screw-in chokes. This would add 10 percent to values.

NIB	Exc.	V.G.	Good	Fair	Poor
800	650	550	350	250	200

Europa 2000

A 12-gauge over/under shotgun in various barrel lengths and choke combinations. Single-selective trigger and automatic ejectors. Engraved silver-plated boxlock action, with false sideplates and walnut stock.

NIB	Exc.	V.G.	Good	Fair	Poor
1250	900	700	550	350	250

Grinta Trap and Skeet

A 12-gauge over/under shotgun, with 26" Skeet or 30" Full choke barrels, single-selective trigger, automatic ejectors and some engraving. Walnut stock.

NIB	Exc.	V.G.	Good	Fair	Poor
1350	900	700	550	350	250

Victory Trap and Skeet

As above, but more finely finished.

NIB	Exc.	V.G.	Good	Fair	Poor
1650	1150	850	600	400	250

Edinburg Match

As above, with slightly different engraving patterns.

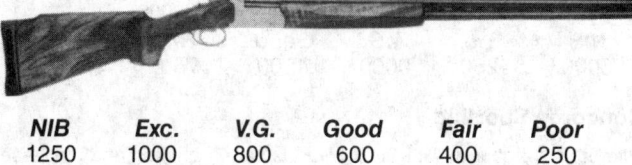

NIB	Exc.	V.G.	Good	Fair	Poor
1250	1000	800	600	400	250

Boyern 88 Combination Gun

A 12-gauge combination over/under rifle/shotgun, with double triggers and extractors. Engraved game scenes and coin-finished, with walnut stock.

NIB	Exc.	V.G.	Good	Fair	Poor
1250	900	700	500	400	250

DAYTONA SERIES

Competition shotgun first introduced into U.S. in 1986 as Type I. Type I available in different configurations, with base model selling for about $4,000 until 1991. In 1994 Gamba introduced Daytona in a wide variety of configurations and grades under a new designation called Type II. Primary difference was in location of stock bolt. Only about 80 Daytona Type II shotguns are allocated to U.S. per year. High quality shotgun with an excellent reputation. Prices listed are for 12-gauge. 20-gauge guns available on special request.

Daytona Trap

Offered in 12-gauge with 30" or 32" barrels. Select walnut stock with hand checkering. Removable trigger group, improved Boss lock-up and boxlock receiver.

NIB	Exc.	V.G.	Good	Fair	Poor
5900	4750	3000	2250	1200	600

Daytona Sporting

Available in 12-gauge, with 30" barrel, screw-in chokes and single-selective trigger.

NIB	Exc.	V.G.	Good	Fair	Poor
4000	3250	2500	1900	1200	700

Daytona Skeet

Offered in 12-gauge, with 29" barrels and single-selective trigger.

NIB	Exc.	V.G.	Good	Fair	Poor
4000	3250	2500	1900	1200	700

Daytona America Trap

Offered in 12-gauge, with 30" or 32" barrels, high adjustable rib, adjustable stock and single trigger.

NIB	Exc.	V.G.	Good	Fair	Poor
4000	3250	2500	1900	1200	700

Daytona Game

Offered in 12-gauge, with 28" barrels and single trigger. **NOTE:** Add $300 for black frame with gold inlaid names and logo.

NIB	Exc.	V.G.	Good	Fair	Poor
3900	3500	3000	2250	1200	700

Daytona Grade 6 Engraving

Fine English scroll hand engraving, edged with gold line work.

Daytona Trap and Skeet Models

NIB	Exc.	V.G.	Good	Fair	Poor
13000	5000	4000	3000	1500	700

Daytona Sporting Model

NIB	Exc.	V.G.	Good	Fair	Poor
13500	5000	4000	3000	1500	700

Daytona Grade 5 Engraving

Deep relief floral engraving, with gold inlaid griffons.

Daytona Trap and Skeet Models

NIB	Exc.	V.G.	Good	Fair	Poor
14000	9000	6500	5000	2500	1200

Daytona Sporting Model

NIB	Exc.	V.G.	Good	Fair	Poor
14500	9000	6500	5000	2500	1200

Daytona Grade 4 Engraving

Flying eagle in a landscape and very fine English scroll by master engravers.

Daytona Trap and Skeet Models

NIB	Exc.	V.G.	Good	Fair	Poor
16250	10000	7500	5500	3000	1500

Daytona Sporting Model

NIB	Exc.	V.G.	Good	Fair	Poor
16750	10000	7500	5500	3000	1500

Daytona SL Grade 3 Engraving

Fitted with engraved game scene sideplates and fine English scroll by master engravers.

Daytona Trap and Skeet Models

NIB	Exc.	V.G.	Good	Fair	Poor
18750	15000	11000	7500	3500	1750

Daytona Sporting Model

NIB	Exc.	V.G.	Good	Fair	Poor
19250	11000	9000	6500	3500	1750

Daytona Game

NIB	Exc.	V.G.	Good	Fair	Poor
18750	11000	9000	6500	3500	1750

Daytona SLHH Grade 2 Engraving

Fitted with sideplates and Boss lock-up system, automatic ejectors, figured walnut stock. Fine game scene engraving signed by a master. Offered in 12-gauge with 28" barrels.

NIB	Exc.	V.G.	Good	Fair	Poor
36250	16000	12500	9500	6000	3000

Daytona SLHH Grade 1 Gold Engraving

Same as above, with gold inlaid game scenes and floral-style engraving signed by master engraver. Offered in 12-gauge with 28" barrels.

NIB	Exc.	V.G.	Good	Fair	Poor
43500	17000	13000	9500	5500	2500

Daytona SLHH "One of Thousand"

Same as above, but game scene is executed at customers direction. A totally custom ordered gun. Available in all configurations.

NIB	Exc.	V.G.	Good	Fair	Poor
125000	70000	35000	15500	7500	600

CONCORDE GAME SHOTGUNS

This over/under model offered as a slightly less expensive alternative to Daytona Series guns. Base gun available with blued or chromed action. Extra barrel are interchangeable in both 12- and 20-gauge, with 28" barrels and single triggers.

NIB	Exc.	V.G.	Good	Fair	Poor
6000	4250	3000	1500	750	450

Concorde Trap

Available in 12-gauge, with 30" or 32" barrels, single trigger.

NIB	Exc.	V.G.	Good	Fair	Poor
—	2000	1500	1000	600	450

Concorde Skeet

Available in 12-gauge, with 29" barrels and single trigger.

NIB	Exc.	V.G.	Good	Fair	Poor
6000	4250	3000	1500	750	450

Concorde Sporting

Offered in 12-gauge, with 30" barrels, screw-in chokes and single-selective trigger.

NIB	Exc.	V.G.	Good	Fair	Poor
6100	2900	2000	1500	900	500

Concorde Game Grade 7 Engraving

Game scene engraving, with fine English scroll.

NIB	Exc.	V.G.	Good	Fair	Poor
8700	4000	3250	2250	1200	600

Concorde Game Grade 8 Engraving

English scroll engraving.

NIB	Exc.	V.G.	Good	Fair	Poor
6250	3000	2500	1750	1000	500

Concorde 2nd Generation

Similar to Concorde series, with fixed trigger group. Black or chrome frame. Automatic ejectors. Select walnut stock. Choice of 12- or 20-gauge, with 28" or 30" barrels and single trigger. Introduced in 2002.

NIB	Exc.	V.G.	Good	Fair	Poor
6100	4850	3200	1950	750	300

Le Mans

Model chambered for 12-gauge shell and fitted with choice of 28" or 30" barrels. Automatic ejectors. Single-selective trigger. Five choke tubes. Introduced in 2002.

NIB	Exc.	V.G.	Good	Fair	Poor
1750	1200	850	625	475	200

Hunter II

This 12-gauge model has an alloy frame, with reinforced barrel and automatic ejectors. Five choke tubes. Single-selective trigger. Barrel lengths of 26" to 27.5". Introduced in 2002.

NIB	Exc.	V.G.	Good	Fair	Poor
1600	1100	750	525	375	150

RIFLES

Safari Express

A 7x65R, 9.3x74R or .375 H&H caliber boxlock double-barrel rifle, with 25" barrels, open sights, double triggers, automatic ejectors and coin-finished scroll engraved receiver. Walnut stock.

NIB	Exc.	V.G.	Good	Fair	Poor
8500	6500	4500	1750	750	350

Mustang

A 5.6x50, 6.5x57R, 7x65R, .222 Rem., .270 Win. or .30-06 caliber side-lock single barrel rifle, with double-set triggers, engraved sidelock action and walnut stock.

NIB	Exc.	V.G.	Good	Fair	Poor
8500	6500	4500	1750	750	350

RGZ 1000

7x64, .270 Win., 7mm Rem. Magnum and .300 Win. Magnum caliber Mauser 98 bolt-action, with 20.5" barrel. Walnut pistol-grip stock and cheekpiece.

NIB	Exc.	V.G.	Good	Fair	Poor
1100	900	750	550	400	200

RGX 1000 Express

As above, with double-set triggers and 23.75" barrel.

NIB	Exc.	V.G.	Good	Fair	Poor
1250	950	750	550	400	200

PISTOLS

SAB G90

A 7.65 Parabellum or 9mm caliber double-action semi-automatic pistol, with 4.75" barrel and 15-shot magazine. Blued or chrome-plated, with walnut grips.

NIB	Exc.	V.G.	Good	Fair	Poor
575	450	350	300	250	175

SAB G91 Compact

As above, with 3.5" barrel and 12-shot magazine.

NIB	Exc.	V.G.	Good	Fair	Poor
550	400	325	275	225	150

Trident Fast Action

A .32 S&W or .38 Special caliber double-action revolver, with 2.5" or 3" barrel and 6-shot cylinder. Blued, with walnut grips.

NIB	Exc.	V.G.	Good	Fair	Poor
500	400	300	250	200	150

Trident Super

As above, with 4" ventilated rib barrel.

NIB	Exc.	V.G.	Good	Fair	Poor
550	400	325	275	225	150

Trident Match 900

As above, with 6" heavy barrel, adjustable sights. Target type walnut grips.

NIB	Exc.	V.G.	Good	Fair	Poor
850	700	550	400	350	200

GARAND
(U.S. M-1 Rifle)

This was the standard issue rifle for U.S. military services from 1936 to 1957. In .30-06 caliber, it is a gas-operated semi-automatic, fed by an 8-round clip that is inserted in the open action from above. Garand series was made in several variants and manufactured by many different companies over its 20 years of service. A complete history of John Garand's great rifle, see Standard Catalog of Military Firearms, published by Gun Digest Books/Krause Publications. Prices shown below are for rifles in original, unaltered condition. Many rifles seen on today's market have been restored or refinished and values should be reduced from 30 to 50 percent.

Rebuilt Rifle, any manufacture

NIB	Exc.	V.G.	Good	Fair	Poor
1200	1000	800	600	—	—

DCM Rifles

NIB	Exc.	V.G.	Good	Fair	Poor
—	850	575	450	—	—

Navy Trophy Rifles U.S.N. Crane Depot Rebuild

NIB	Exc.	V.G.	Good	Fair	Poor
—	1800	1000	900	—	—

AMF Rebuild

NIB	Exc.	V.G.	Good	Fair	Poor
—	1000	900	750	—	—

H&R Rebuild

NOTE: These rifles MUST be original and validated by experts.

NIB	Exc.	V.G.	Good	Fair	Poor
—	900	800	700	—	—

SPRINGFIELD ARMORY PRODUCTION

Gas trap sn: ca 81-52,000

NIB	Exc.	V.G.	Good	Fair	Poor
—	40000	35000	25000	—	—

Gas trap/modified to gas port

NIB	Exc.	V.G.	Good	Fair	Poor
—	5000	3500	2500	—	—

Pre-Dec. 7, 1941 gas port production sn: ca 410,000

NIB	Exc.	V.G.	Good	Fair	Poor
—	4000	2200	1300	900	400

WWII Production sn: ca 410,000-3,880,000

NIB	Exc.	V.G.	Good	Fair	Poor
—	1400	1100	900	750	500

Post-WWII Production sn: ca 4,200,000-6,099,361

NIB	Exc.	V.G.	Good	Fair	Poor
—	1100	850	650	500	450

Winchester Educational Contract sn: 100,000-100,500

NIB	Exc.	V.G.	Good	Fair	Poor
—	10000	6000	4500	2000	700

Winchester sn: 100,501-165,000

NIB	Exc.	V.G.	Good	Fair	Poor
—	6500	4500	3000	1100	550

Winchester sn: 1,200,00-1,380,000

NIB	Exc.	V.G.	Good	Fair	Poor
—	5500	4500	2500	750	400

Winchester sn: 2,305,850-2,536,493

NIB	Exc.	V.G.	Good	Fair	Poor
—	3500	2800	1500	500	300

Winchester sn: 1,601,150-1,640,000 "win-13"

NIB	Exc.	V.G.	Good	Fair	Poor
—	3500	2200	1800	1500	850

Harrington & Richardson Production

NIB	Exc.	V.G.	Good	Fair	Poor
—	1800	1200	900	600	300

International Harvester Production

NIB	Exc.	V.G.	Good	Fair	Poor
—	2200	1500	800	500	250

International Harvester/with Springfield Receiver (postage stamp)

NIB	Exc.	V.G.	Good	Fair	Poor
—	2800	1500	1000	—	—

International Harvester/with Springfield Receiver (arrow head)

NIB	Exc.	V.G.	Good	Fair	Poor
—	2800	1500	1000	—	—

International Harvester/with Springfield Receiver (Gap letter)

NIB	Exc.	V.G.	Good	Fair	Poor
—	2800	1500	1000	—	—

International Harvester/with Harrington & Richardson Receiver

NIB	Exc.	V.G.	Good	Fair	Poor
—	1900	1200	900	—	—

British Garands (Lend Lease)

NIB	Exc.	V.G.	Good	Fair	Poor
—	1300	1200	875	500	275

M1 Garand Cutaway

NOTE: Add 300 percent for examples with documentation.

NIB	Exc.	V.G.	Good	Fair	Poor
—	3000	2500	1000	600	500

SCOPED VARIANTS (SNIPER RIFLES)

NOTE: Sniper rifles must have sales or verification papers.

M1C

NIB	Exc.	V.G.	Good	Fair	Poor
—	10000	8000	5000	—	—

M1D (USMC Issue) MC 1952

NIB	Exc.	V.G.	Good	Fair	Poor
—	3800	3000	2000	—	—

National Match

Type I

NIB	Exc.	V.G.	Good	Fair	Poor
—	4500	2500	1800	—	—

Type II

NIB	Exc.	V.G.	Good	Fair	Poor
—	3200	2200	1500	—	—

GARATE, ANITUA/G.A.C.
Eibar, Spain

Charola

A 5.5mm Clement semi-automatic pistol, with magazine located in front of trigger and exposed hammer.

Courtesy James Rankin

NIB	Exc.	V.G.	Good	Fair	Poor
—	1500	1200	750	500	400

Cosmopolite

A .38-caliber copy of Colt Police Positive. Manufactured from 1920 to 1930.

NIB	Exc.	V.G.	Good	Fair	Poor
—	275	165	125	100	75

El Lunar

Resembling Colt Police Positive in 8mm Lebel caliber. Revolver made for French government in 1915 and 1916.

NIB	Exc.	V.G.	Good	Fair	Poor
—	300	175	150	125	100

G.A.C.

Copy of Smith & Wesson Military & Police revolver. Manufactured between 1930 and 1936 in .32-20 caliber. Marked "G.A.C. Firearms Mfg. Co.".

NIB	Exc.	V.G.	Good	Fair	Poor
—	250	150	125	100	75

Modelo Militar

Close copy of Smith & Wesson Triple Lock/New Century N-frame revolver. Chambered in .44 Special. Marked "G.A.C."

NIB	Exc.	V.G.	Good	Fair	Poor
—	325	250	200	175	75

Express or Danton

A 7.65mm caliber "Eibar" semi-automatic pistol, with 9-shot magazine.

NIB	Exc.	V.G.	Good	Fair	Poor
—	275	150	100	75	50

British Service Old Pattern No.2 Mk. I Trocaola Aranzabal Military Revolver

A .455-caliber double-action break-open revolver, with 5" barrel. Adopted by Royal Army in November of 1915 and known as "Pistol OP No. 1 Mark 1".

NIB	Exc.	V.G.	Good	Fair	Poor
—	450	250	200	150	100

L'Eclair

A 5.5mm Velo-Dog caliber folding-trigger double-action revolver, with 6-shot cylinder. Manufactured from 1900 to 1914. Not to be confused with the chocolate confectionary.

NIB	Exc.	V.G.	Good	Fair	Poor
—	250	145	100	75	50

Sprinter

A 6.35mm caliber semi-automatic pistol marked "The Best Automatique Pistol Sprinter Patent 6.35mm Cartridge". Manufactured before WWI.

NIB	Exc.	V.G.	Good	Fair	Poor
—	250	145	125	75	50

La Lira

Copy of Mannlicher Model 1901 in .32 ACP caliber, with removable magazine marked "System La Lira" on breech; "Para Cartoucho Browning 7.65mm" on barrel; "G.A.C." on grips. Produced prior to WWI.

Courtesy James Rankin

NIB	Exc.	V.G.	Good	Fair	Poor
—	1200	1000	700	400	300

Triumph

Identical to La Lira model marked "Triumph Automatic Pistol".

NIB	Exc.	V.G.	Good	Fair	Poor
—	1200	1000	700	400	300

GARATE, HERMANOS
Ermua, Spain

Cantabria

A 6.35mm caliber folding-trigger double-action revolver, with concealed hammer, cocking spur and short barrel resembling slide on a semi-automatic. Name "Cantabria" stamped on left side.

NIB	Exc.	V.G.	Good	Fair	Poor
—	300	175	125	100	75

Velo-Stark

Double-action folding-trigger revolver, with concealed hammer.

NIB	Exc.	V.G.	Good	Fair	Poor
—	250	150	100	75	50

GARBI
Eibar, Spain

Model 51-B

A 12-gauge boxlock shotgun. Also available in 16- and 20-gauge, with double triggers, automatic ejectors, case-hardened or coin-finished receiver and walnut stock.

NIB	Exc.	V.G.	Good	Fair	Poor
1750	1200	850	600	—	—

Model 62-B

A 12-gauge sidelock shotgun. Also chambered for 16- and 20-gauge, with double triggers, extractors and cocking indicators. Engraved case-hardened or coin-finished receiver and walnut stock.

NIB	Exc.	V.G.	Good	Fair	Poor
1500	1050	850	650	325	175

Model 71

A 12-, 16- or 20-gauge H&H sidelock shotgun, with various barrel lengths and choke combinations. Automatic ejectors and single-selective trigger. Engraved with fine English-style scrollwork and walnut stock. Discontinued in 1988.

NIB	Exc.	V.G.	Good	Fair	Poor
2500	2000	1800	1500	700	225

Model 100

A 12-, 16- or 20-gauge H&H sidelock shotgun, with chopper-lump barrels, automatic ejectors and single trigger. Engraved in Purdey style, with walnut stock.

NIB	Exc.	V.G.	Good	Fair	Poor
4500	4000	3000	2000	900	250

Model 101

As above, with floral engraving. Discontinued in 1988 in this form, then furnished with hand-engraved Continental scroll and round body action.

NIB	Exc.	V.G.	Good	Fair	Poor
9500	8000	6000	4500	2000	1000

Model 102

As above, with H&H style engraving. Also in 28-gauge. Discontinued in 1988.

NIB	Exc.	V.G.	Good	Fair	Poor
4500	3750	3200	1600	600	250

Model 103A

Model has Purdey-style engraving, with high grade wood and checkering.

NIB	Exc.	V.G.	Good	Fair	Poor
17500	13000	9000	7500	2750	1000

Model 103A Royal

Same as above, with special high quality engraving, very fancy wood, hand matted rib.

NIB	Exc.	V.G.	Good	Fair	Poor
18500	16000	13000	8750	3750	1200

Model 103B

In 12-, 16-, 20- or 28-gauge H&H sidelock shotgun. Various barrel lengths and choke combinations. Chopper-lump barrels, H&H easy-opening mechanism, automatic ejectors, single-selective trigger and Purdey-type scroll engraving.

NIB	Exc.	V.G.	Good	Fair	Poor
22500	18000	14000	9500	6000	1500

Model 103B Royal

Same as above, with high quality engraving, very fancy wood, hand matted rib.

NIB	Exc.	V.G.	Good	Fair	Poor
25000	20000	15000	10500	4000	1500

Model 120

As above, with engraved hunting scenes. Discontinued in 1988.

NIB	Exc.	V.G.	Good	Fair	Poor
22500	18000	14000	9500	4000	1300

Model 200

As above, Magnum proofed double locking screws and 100 percent floral scroll engraving.

NIB	Exc.	V.G.	Good	Fair	Poor
20000	15000	10000	7500	3000	1300

Model Special

A special order gun. Too rare to price.

Express Rifle

Best-quality sidelock side-by-side double rifle. Stock has pistol-grip and cheekpiece. Choice of English scroll or floral engraving. Calibers are 7x65R, 9.3x74R or .375 H&H.

NIB	Exc.	V.G.	Good	Fair	Poor
21000	15000	12000	7750	6000	1500

GARCIA
(formerly Firearms International of Wash., D.C.)

Garcia Bronco

Single-shot .410 bore shotgun or .22 LR or .22 Magnum rifle, with swing out action. Modeled somewhat after old Hamilton No. 7. Barrel length 18.5". Stock is one-piece metal skeletonized affair. Weight about 3.5 lbs. Introduced in 1968, discontinued 1978. Built in U.S.A.

NIB	Exc.	V.G.	Good	Fair	Poor
350	250	225	125	90	50

Garcia Bronco .22/.410

Over/under shotgun/rifle combination. Over barrel .22 LR; under barrel chambered for .410 bore. Barrel length 18.5". One-piece metal skeletonized stock. Introduced in 1976, discontinued 1978. Weight about 4 lbs.

NIB	Exc.	V.G.	Good	Fair	Poor
500	375	295	200	115	75

Garcia Musketeer

Bolt-action rifle chambered for .243, .264, .270, .30-06, .307 Win. Magnum, .308 Norma, 7mm Rem. Magnum and .300 Win. Magnum. Fitted with checkered walnut stock, open sights, pistol-grip, hinged floorplate and adjustable trigger. Introduced in 1970, discontinued 1972.

NIB	Exc.	V.G.	Good	Fair	Poor
600	500	350	250	200	150

GARRET, J. & F. CO.
Greensboro, North Carolina

Garrett Single-Shot Pistol

A .54-caliber single-shot percussion pistol, with 8.5" round barrel, swivel ramrod, walnut stock and brass mounts. Marked on barrel breech "G.W." or "S.R." Approximately 500 made in 1862 and 1863.

Courtesy Bonhams & Butterfields

NIB	Exc.	V.G.	Good	Fair	Poor
—	—	4550	165	1000	500

GASSER, LEOPOLD
Ottakring, Austria

M1870

An 11mm caliber double-action revolver, with 9.3" or 14.75" barrel and 6-shot cylinder. Marked "Gasser Patent, Guss Stahl". Bears an Austrian eagle and apple pierced by an arrow, with words "Schutz Mark".

NIB	Exc.	V.G.	Good	Fair	Poor
—	650	425	230	175	125

M1870/74

As above, with steel frame.

NIB	Exc.	V.G.	Good	Fair	Poor
—	650	425	350	175	125

Gasser-Kropatschek M1876

A 9mm caliber M1870/74. Weight 1 lb. 11 oz.

NIB	Exc.	V.G.	Good	Fair	Poor
—	600	400	300	150	100

Montenegrin Gasser

A 10.7mm caliber double-action revolver, with 5" or 6" barrel and 5-shot cylinder. Engraved silver and gold inlay. Ivory or bone grips. Values given are for plain, unadorned model. Embellished models will need individual appraisal.

NIB	Exc.	V.G.	Good	Fair	Poor
—	650	425	350	200	150

Rast & Gasser M1898

A 8mm caliber double-action revolver, with 4.75" barrel, 8-shot cylinder, solid-frame with loading gate and integral ejector rod.

NIB	Exc.	V.G.	Good	Fair	Poor
—	650	425	350	175	125

GATLING ARMS CO.
Birmingham, England

Established in 1888, this company remained in operation until approximately 1890. Although primarily involved with marketing of Gatling Guns, it did market one revolver listed.

Kynoch-Dimancea

A .38- or .45-caliber double-action hammerless revolver, with 6-shot cylinder. Loading system rather unusual—a spur that resembles a hammer is pulled down allowing barrel and cylinder to pivot and to be pulled forward. During this motion empty cases are ejected and new ones could be inserted. Marked "The Gatling Arms and Ammunition Co. Birmingham"; also marked "Dimancea Patent".

NIB	Exc.	V.G.	Good	Fair	Poor
—	—	2400	1275	750	350

GAUCHER
France

GN 1

Single-shot bolt-action pistol chambered for .22 LR. Fitted with 10" barrel, blade front sight and adjustable rear sight. Adjustable trigger. Hardwood target grips. Weight about 38 oz. Introduced in 1990.

NIB	Exc.	V.G.	Good	Fair	Poor
525	425	350	225	145	100

GAULOIS
St. Etienne, France

See—Le Francais

GAVAGE, A.
Liege, Belgium

A 7.65mm caliber semi-automatic pistol, with fixed barrel and concealed hammer. Similar in appearance to Clement. Markings with "AG" molded into grips. Some have been found bearing German Waffenamts. Manufactured from 1930s to 1940s.

Courtesy James Rankin

NIB	Exc.	V.G.	Good	Fair	Poor
—	450	325	250	150	100

GAZANAGA, ISIDRO
Eibar, Spain

Destroyer M1913

A 6.35mm or 7.65mm caliber semi-automatic pistol. The 6.35mm model copied after 1906 Browning. "Destroyer" stamped on slide and Isidro logo on each side of grip plate. Produced through WWI.

Courtesy James Rankin

NIB	Exc.	V.G.	Good	Fair	Poor
—	295	195	145	75	50

Destroyer M1916

A 7.65mm caliber semi-automatic pistol, with 7- or 9-shot magazine. Ruby style pistol manufactured by the Spanish during WWI. "Destroyer" stamped on slide. Wood grips.

Courtesy James Rankin

NIB	Exc.	V.G.	Good	Fair	Poor
—	325	225	125	75	50

Destroyer Revolver

A good quality .38-caliber copy of Colt Police Positive.

NIB	Exc.	V.G.	Good	Fair	Poor
—	295	165	155	100	75

Super Destroyer

A 7.65mm caliber copy of Walther PP. Slide stamped "Pistola Automatica 7.65 Super Destroyer".

NIB	Exc.	V.G.	Good	Fair	Poor
—	325	195	175	100	75

Surete

As above in 7.65mm caliber. Marked "Cal. 7.65 Pistolet Automatique Surete", with "IG" stamped on frame.

NIB	Exc.	V.G.	Good	Fair	Poor
—	295	165	155	100	75

GECO
See—Genschow, G.

GEHA
Germany

An altered Mauser 98 rifle re-barreled for use with 12-gauge shotgun shells. Barrel length 26.5", military stock shortened to half length and butt inlaid with a brass medallion marked "Geha". Manufactured from approximately 1919 to 1929.

NIB	Exc.	V.G.	Good	Fair	Poor
—	375	225	150	100	75

GEM
Bacon Arms Company
Norwich, Connecticut
See—Bacon Arms Company

Gem Pocket Revolver

A .22-caliber spur trigger revolver, with 1.25" octagonal barrel. Frame is iron, engraved nickel-plated, with walnut or ivory grips. Barrel marked "Gem". Manufactured between 1878 and 1883.

NIB	Exc.	V.G.	Good	Fair	Poor
—	—	1950	700	300	145

GENEZ, A. G.
New York, New York

Located at 9 Chambers Street, Genez made a wide variety of firearms during his working life (ca. 1850 to 1875). Most commonly encountered of his arms today are single-shot percussion pistols and percussion double-barrel shotguns. More rarely seen are single-shot percussion target rifles. A number of arms he made were decorated by Louis D. Nimschke. Genez products signed by Nimschke command considerable premiums over values for standard firearms listed.

Double-Barrel Shotgun

Most often encountered in 12-gauge. Varying barrel lengths, blued steel furniture and walnut stock.

NIB	Exc.	V.G.	Good	Fair	Poor
—	—	2800	1950	500	250

Pocket Pistol

A .41-caliber single-shot percussion pistol, with 3" barrel, German silver mountings and walnut stock. Manufactured in 1850s and 1860s.

NIB	Exc.	V.G.	Good	Fair	Poor
—	—	3950	1850	500	175

GENSCHOW, G.
Hamburg, Germany

Geco

A 6.35mm, 7.65mm, .32 Long and 8mm Lebel caliber folding trigger double-action revolver.

NIB	Exc.	V.G.	Good	Fair	Poor
—	275	175	100	75	50

German Bulldog

A .32-, .38- and .45-caliber folding trigger double-action revolver, with solid frames, integral ejector rods and loading gates. Proofmarks indicate Belgian manufacture.

NIB	Exc.	V.G.	Good	Fair	Poor
—	275	175	110	75	50

GEORGIA ARMORY
Milledgeville, George

Established in 1862, this concern produced a rifle based upon U.S. Model 1855 Harper's Ferry Rifle. Nearly identical in all respects to Harpers Ferry, Georgia Armory rifle had a lockplate patterned after U.S. Model 1841 Rifle. Lock marked "G.A. ARMORY" over date (1862 or 1863). Buttplate tangs marked with serial numbers. Highest known serial number is 309. Rifles were fitted with saber bayonets.

NIB	Exc.	V.G.	Good	Fair	Poor
—	—	65000	22000	10500	3000

GERING, H. M. & CO.
Arnstadt, Germany

Leonhardt

Semi-automatic pistol in caliber 7.65mm. Almost identical to Beholla pistol made by Becker. Leonhardt stamped on slide. These pistols were made for the German Army during WWI.

Courtesy James Rankin

NIB	Exc.	V.G.	Good	Fair	Poor
—	425	325	250	200	100

GERSTENBERGER & EBERWEIN
Gussenstadt, Germany

Em-Ge, G.& E., Omega & Pic

Series of poor-quality revolvers sold in U.S.A. before 1968. .22- and .32-calibers, with 2.25" barrels and 6-shot cylinder. Editor does not consider these safe to shoot, even if new in box.

NIB	Exc.	V.G.	Good	Fair	Poor
—	Worthless.	—	—	—	—

GEVARM
St. Etienne, France

Model A-6

This .22-caliber semi-automatic rifle fires from an open bolt. Fitted with a one-piece stock. Furnished with 8-round magazine. The E-1 20-magazine will not fit A-6 without hand fitting. Add 15 percent for higher-end A7 model. These rifles are increasingly popular on the secondary market because of their open-bolt design.

NIB	Exc.	V.G.	Good	Fair	Poor
—	800	695	475	275	165

E-1 Autoloading Rifle

A .22-caliber semi-automatic rifle, with 19" barrel, 8-shot magazine, blued with walnut grips. Two-piece stock. A 20-round magazine is an option.

NIB	Exc.	V.G.	Good	Fair	Poor
—	550	450	295	200	150

GIB
Eibar, Spain

10 Gauge Shotgun

A 10-gauge Magnum boxlock double-barrel shotgun, with 32" matte-ribbed barrels. Case-hardened, blued with walnut grips.

NIB	Exc.	V.G.	Good	Fair	Poor
—	700	495	275	150	100

GIBBS, J. & G. / GIBBS, GEORGE
Bristol, England

Established in 1835, this concern continues in business to this day. J. & G. Gibbs 4 Redcliffe Street 1835-1842; George Gibbs 142 Thomas Street; Clare Street; 39 Corn Street. While initially known for exceptionally accurate single-shot rifles, the firm subsequently established a reputation for first quality bolt-action magazine rifles in a variety of large bore calibers. Bolt rifles by Gibbs, Rigby and others have become extremely desirable, especially in the African chamberings.

GIBBS
New York, New York

Gibbs Carbine

A .52-caliber single-shot percussion carbine, with sliding 22" round barrel. Blued case-hardened with walnut stock. Lock marked with American eagle and "Wm. F. Brooks/Manf New York/1863". Breech marked "L.H. Gibbs/Patd/Jany 8, 1856". Only 1,050 produced.

Courtesy Milwaukee Public Museum, Milwaukee, Wisconsin

NIB	Exc.	V.G.	Good	Fair	Poor
—	—	5950	2200	900	350

Gibbs Pistol

A caliber percussion pistol made by Hull & Thomas of Ilion, New York, in 1855 or 1856.

Courtesy Milwaukee Public Museum, Milwaukee, Wisconsin

NIB	Exc.	V.G.	Good	Fair	Poor
—	—	3600	2750	1250	400

GIBBS GUNS, INC.
Greenback, Tennessee

Mark 45 Carbine

A .45 ACP caliber semi-automatic rifle, with 16.5" barrel, 5-, 15-, 30- or 90-shot magazine. Blued, with walnut buttstock and fore-end. Nickel-plated model available as an option. Would bring approximately $25 additional. Discontinued in 1988.

NIB	Exc.	V.G.	Good	Fair	Poor
650	475	275	200	125	100

GIBBS RIFLE COMPANY
Martinsburg, West Virginia

Gibbs Rifle Company was founded in 1991, by Val Forgett III, originally to refurbish and distribute various older military firearms. The company over the years has imported numerous black powder replicas from Europe and has also produced historical remakes and specialty rifles.

Enfield No. 5 Jungle Carbine

Remake of original British rifle. Chambered for .303 cartridge and fitted with 20" barrel and flash hider. Magazine capacity 10 rounds. Weight about 7.75 lbs. New stock.

NIB	Exc.	V.G.	Good	Fair	Poor
350	295	200	150	100	50

Enfield No. 7 Jungle Carbine

Model chambered for .308 Winchester cartridge. Fitted with 20" barrel and flash hider. Magazine capacity 12 rounds. Adjustable rear sight. Original wood. Weight about 8 lbs.

NIB	Exc.	V.G.	Good	Fair	Poor
650	575	475	350	250	200

Quest Extreme Carbine

An updated design of No. 5 Jungle Carbine. Chambered for .303 cartridge with 20" barrel. Nickel finish and new hardwood stock. Brass butt trap. Weight about 7.75 lbs.

NIB	Exc.	V.G.	Good	Fair	Poor
350	295	200	150	100	50

Quest II Extreme Carbine

Updated version of No. 7 Jungle Carbine, with nickel finish, see-through scope mount and hardwood stock. Chambered for .308 cartridge. Magazine capacity 12 rounds. Barrel length 20". Weight about 8 lbs.

NIB	Exc.	V.G.	Good	Fair	Poor
350	295	200	150	100	50

Quest III Extreme Carbine

Similar to Quest II, with synthetic stock.

NIB	Exc.	V.G.	Good	Fair	Poor
400	325	200	150	100	50

Summit 45-70 Carbine

Bolt-action built on Enfield No. 4 action. Re-barreled to .45-70 caliber. Fitted to 21" barrel. MIL SPEC peep sight and checkered walnut stock. Weight about 8.5 lbs.

NIB	Exc.	V.G.	Good	Fair	Poor
400	325	225	175	125	75

Mauser M71/84

Chambered for 11mm Mauser cartridge and fitted with 31.5" barrel. Model has been arsenal reconditioned, but otherwise original. Weight about 10 lbs.

NIB	Exc.	V.G.	Good	Fair	Poor
300	250	175	150	100	50

Mauser M88 Commission Rifle

Fitted with 30" barrel and chambered for 8mm cartridge. Model has been arsenal reconditioned, but otherwise original. Weight about 10 lbs.

NIB	Exc.	V.G.	Good	Fair	Poor
200	175	120	100	65	50

M98K Israeli Mauser

Re-barreled to .308 Win. by Israeli Arsenal. Made in three grades; Standard, Grade 2 and Grade 1 (best grade). **NOTE:** Add $50 for Grade 2, $100 for Grade 1.

NIB	Exc.	V.G.	Good	Fair	Poor
350	300	250	200	150	100

M1903-A4 Springfield Sniper Model

Replica of 1903-A3, with original Remington action, new barrels in .30-06, C model stock. New copy of M73B1 scope with Redfield-type rings and mounts. Parkerized finish.

NIB	Exc.	V.G.	Good	Fair	Poor
900	800	650	500	300	150

GIBBS TIFFANY & CO.
Sturbridge, Massachusetts

Under Hammer Pistol

A .28-caliber single-shot percussion pistol, with 3" to 8" barrels. Browned iron frame, walnut or maple pointed handle trimmed with brass. Top strap marked "Gibbs Tiffany & Co." Active 1820 to 1838.

NIB	Exc.	V.G.	Good	Fair	Poor
—	—	1250	650	250	100

GILLESPIE
New York, New York

Derringer Type Pocket Pistol

A .41-caliber single-shot percussion pistol, with 2.5" barrel and walnut stock. Manufactured from 1848 to 1870.

NIB	Exc.	V.G.	Good	Fair	Poor
—	—	2950	1350	500	200

GLAZE, W. & CO.
Columbia, South Carolina
See—B. & B. M. Darling

GLOCK
Deutsch-Wagram, Austria
Smyrna, Georgia

First imported into U.S.A. in 1985. Completely manufactured in Austria until 2004 when Glock opened its plant in Georgia to produce polymer frames. Offered in many models, but main differences are caliber, sighting systems, barrel, slide and grip length, and magazine capacity. Common features include a striker-fired action with a consistent DA-only trigger pull, trigger safety within main trigger, no grip or thumb safety, polymer frame with integral grips and steel slide. In 2010, Gen4 (fourth generation) of Glock pistols was introduced. Gen4 features include three interchangeable back-straps, reversible magazine release button, improved recoil spring assembly and rough-textured frame (RTF) to enhance grip traction. As of 2016, all new-production units of the following models had Gen4 features: M17, M19, M20, M21, M22, M23, M26, M27, M29, M30, M31, M32, M33, M34, M35, M37, M40, M41, M42, M43. **NOTE:** Add $70 if equipped with Meprolight night sights; $90 if equipped with Trijicon night sights; $30 if equipped with adjustable sights; 10 percent for Gen4 if NIB.

Glock 17

Chambered for 9mm Parabellum cartridge. Double-action-only semi-automatic has 4.49" barrel and 17-shot detachable magazine. Empty weight 21.91 oz. **NOTE:** Add $50 for Model 17 Gen4; $200 for Silver Anniversary Limited Edition.

NIB	Exc.	V.G.	Good	Fair	Poor
500	425	325	300	275	175

Glock 17C

Similar to Model 17, with additional feature of an integral ported barrel. Specifications are same except for weight: 17C weight 21.9 oz. Available with OD green frame.

NIB	Exc.	V.G.	Good	Fair	Poor
525	475	350	300	275	175

Glock 17CC

Introduced in 1998. Compensated competition version of C variation. Fitted with extended slide stop lever, extended magazine release, adjustable sights and target trigger pull. This is a special order item only.

NIB	Exc.	V.G.	Good	Fair	Poor
650	600	500	400	300	200

Glock 17L Competition Model

Version features 6" compensated barrel and adjustable sights. Trigger is fine-tuned to provide between 5- to 8-lbs. trigger pull. Introduced in 1988.

In 1990 this pistol won I.P.S.C. World Stock Gun Championship. Pistol has limited availability in U.S. Available with OD green frame.

NIB	Exc.	V.G.	Good	Fair	Poor
700	600	475	350	300	225

Glock 19

Similar in appearance to Model 17. Compact version, with 4" barrel and smaller grip that will accept either 15-round or standard 17-round magazine that protrudes a bit. Weight 20.99 oz. empty. Grip straps on this model are serrated as they are on other Glock models. Introduced in 1988 and currently in production. Available with OD green frame. **NOTE:** Add $50 for Gen4; $100 for Competition model.

NIB	Exc.	V.G.	Good	Fair	Poor
525	475	350	300	275	175

Glock 19C

Same as above, with integral ported barrel. Weight 20.7 oz. Available with OD green frame.

NIB	Exc.	V.G.	Good	Fair	Poor
550	475	350	300	275	175

Glock 19CC

Introduced in 1998, this is a compensated competition version of C variation. Fitted with extended slide stop lever, extended magazine release, adjustable sights and target trigger pull. This is special order item only.

NIB	Exc.	V.G.	Good	Fair	Poor
700	600	500	350	300	275

Glock 20 and Glock 21

Both of these models are identical in physical appearance except for caliber: Model 20 chambered for 10mm cartridge; Model 21 for .45 ACP. Barrel length on both is 4.60". Model 20 has 15-round clip, weight 26.35 oz.; Model 21 has 13-round clip, weight 25.22 oz. Available with OD green frame. **NOTE:** Add $25 for Gen4.

NIB	Exc.	V.G.	Good	Fair	Poor
550	425	350	300	250	200

Glock 20 SF Short Frame Pistol

DAO semi-automatic similar to Glock Model 20, with short-frame design. Chambered in 10mm Auto. Features include 4.61" barrel, with hexagonal rifling, fixed sights, extended sight radius. Overall length 8.07". Weight 27.51 oz.

NIB	Exc.	V.G.	Good	Fair	Poor
550	475	350	300	275	175

Glock 21 SF

Slenderized version of Model 21, with slimmer frame and ambidextrous magazine catch. Introduced 2007.

Courtesy Ken Lunde

NIB	Exc.	V.G.	Good	Fair	Poor
550	475	350	300	275	175

Glock 20C and 21C

Same as Models 20 and 21, with integral ported barrel. Available with OD green frame.

NIB	Exc.	V.G.	Good	Fair	Poor
600	475	400	325	250	200

Glock 20CC and 21CC

Introduced in 1998, this is a compensated competition version of C variation. Fitted with extended slide stop lever, extended magazine release, adjustable sights and target trigger pull. This is special order item only.

NIB	Exc.	V.G.	Good	Fair	Poor
700	600	500	350	300	275

Glock 22

Almost identical in appearance to Model 17. Model 22 chambered for .40 S&W cartridge. Standard with 15-round clip. Slightly larger and heavier slide. Weight 22.36 oz. Available with OD green frame. **NOTE:** Add $25 for Gen4.

NIB	Exc.	V.G.	Good	Fair	Poor
525	475	350	300	275	175

Glock 22C

Same as Glock 22 model, with addition of integral ported barrel. Weight 22.5 oz. Available with OD green frame.

NIB	Exc.	V.G.	Good	Fair	Poor
550	475	350	300	275	175

Glock 22CC

Introduced in 1998, this is a compensated competition version of C variation. Fitted with extended slide stop lever, extended magazine release, adjustable sights and target trigger pull. This is special order item only.

NIB	Exc.	V.G.	Good	Fair	Poor
700	600	500	350	300	275

Glock 23

Chambered for .40 S&W cartridge. Slide is slightly heavier and larger than Model 19. Weight 21.67 oz. Glock 23 magazine holds 13 rounds. Available with OD green frame. **NOTE:** Add $25 for Gen4.

NIB	Exc.	V.G.	Good	Fair	Poor
525	475	350	300	275	175

Glock 23C

Same as above, with integral ported barrel. Weight 20.9 oz. Available with OD green frame.

NIB	Exc.	V.G.	Good	Fair	Poor
550	475	350	300	275	175

Glock 23CC

Introduced in 1998, this is a compensated competition version of C variation. Fitted with extended slide stop lever, extended magazine release, adjustable sights and target trigger pull. This is special order item only.

NIB	Exc.	V.G.	Good	Fair	Poor
700	600	500	350	300	275

Glock 24

Chambered for .40 S&W cartridge. Fitted with 6" barrel. Weight 26.5 oz.

NIB	Exc.	V.G.	Good	Fair	Poor
675	550	400	350	300	175

Glock 24C

Same as above, with ported barrel.

NIB	Exc.	V.G.	Good	Fair	Poor
700	525	400	300	250	200

Glock 24CC

Introduced in 1998, this is a compensated competition version of C variation. Fitted with extended slide stop lever, extended magazine release, adjustable sights and target trigger pull. This is special order item only.

NIB	Exc.	V.G.	Good	Fair	Poor
700	600	500	350	300	275

Glock 26 and Glock 27

Both of these models are identical except for caliber. Introduced in 1995, these are subcompact versions of full-size Glocks. Model 26 chambered for 9mm cartridge; Model 27 for .40 S&W. Magazine capacity; 9mm 10 rounds; .40-caliber 9 rounds. Overall length 6.25"; barrel length 3.5"; height 4.1875"; width 1.25". Weight for both models about 20 oz. Standard are a dot front sight and white outline rear adjustable sight. Available with OD green frame. **NOTE:** Add $25 for Gen4.

NIB	Exc.	V.G.	Good	Fair	Poor
550	475	350	300	275	175

Glock 29 and Glock 30

These two pistols were introduced in 1997. Model 29 chambered for 10mm cartridge; Model 30 for .45 ACP. Barrel length 3.78"; weight about 24 oz.; overall length 6.77". Model 29 magazine capacity 10 rounds; Model 30 has standard capacity of 10 rounds, with optional capacity of

9 rounds. Model 30 with 10-round magazine in place protrudes slightly below grip. With 9-round magazine in place fits flush with bottom of grip. Available with OD green frame. **NOTE:** Add $25 for Gen4.

NIB	Exc.	V.G.	Good	Fair	Poor
550	475	350	300	275	175

Glock 29 SF Short Frame Pistol

DAO semi-automatic similar to Glock Model 29, with short-frame design. Chambered in 10mm Auto. Features include 3.78" barrel with hexagonal rifling, fixed sights, extended sight radius. Overall length 6.97"; weight 24.52 oz.

NIB	Exc.	V.G.	Good	Fair	Poor
575	495	350	300	275	175

Glock 31

Chambered for .357 SIG cartridge, this pistol fitted with 4.5" barrel and magazine capacity of 10 rounds (15 rounds law enforcement). Overall length 7.3", height 5.4", weight about 23.3 oz. Introduced in 1998. Available with OD green frame. **NOTE:** Add $25 for Gen4.

NIB	Exc.	V.G.	Good	Fair	Poor
550	475	350	300	275	175

Glock 31C

Same as Model 31, with integral compensator. Available with OD green frame.

NIB	Exc.	V.G.	Good	Fair	Poor
575	495	350	300	275	175

Glock 31CC

Introduced in 1998, this is a compensated competition version of C variation. Fitted with extended slide stop lever, extended magazine release, adjustable sights and target trigger pull. This is special order item only.

NIB	Exc.	V.G.	Good	Fair	Poor
700	600	500	350	300	275

Glock 32

Similar to Glock 31 except fitted with 4" barrel. Overall length 6.85"; height 5". Magazine capacity 10 rounds (13 rounds law enforcement). Weight about 21.5 oz. Introduced in 1998. Also available with OD green frame. **NOTE:** Add $25 for Gen4.

NIB	Exc.	V.G.	Good	Fair	Poor
575	495	350	300	275	175

Glock 32C

Same as above, with integral ported barrel and slide. Available with OD green frame.

NIB	Exc.	V.G.	Good	Fair	Poor
700	600	500	350	300	275

Glock 32CC

Introduced in 1998. Compensated competition version of C variation. Fitted with extended slide stop lever, extended magazine release, adjustable sights and target trigger pull. This is special order item only.

NIB	Exc.	V.G.	Good	Fair	Poor
700	600	500	350	300	275

Glock 33

This .357 SIG model has 3.5" barrel. Overall length 6.3"; height 4.2"; weight about 17.7 oz. Introduced in 1998. Available with OD green frame. **NOTE:** Add $25 for Gen4.

NIB	Exc.	V.G.	Good	Fair	Poor
575	495	350	300	275	175

Glock 34

Chambered for 9x19 cartridge. Has 5.3" barrel. Overall length 8.2". Magazine capacity 10 rounds. Empty weight about 23 oz. Available with OD green frame. **NOTE:** Add $25 for Gen4; $50 to $75 for Gen4 Competition if in excellent or better condition.

NIB	Exc.	V.G.	Good	Fair	Poor
575	495	350	300	275	175

Glock 35

Chambered for .40 S&W cartridge. Same dimensions as Glock 34 except weight is 24.5 oz. Available with OD green frame. **NOTE:** Add $25 for Gen4; $50 to $75 for Gen4 Competition if in excellent or better condition.

NIB	Exc.	V.G.	Good	Fair	Poor
700	600	500	350	300	275

Glock 36

Introduced in 1999. Similar to Model 30. Fitted with single-column magazine capacity 6 rounds. Width .14" less than Model 30; barrel length 3.78"; weight 20 oz. Available with OD green frame.

NIB	Exc.	V.G.	Good	Fair	Poor
575	495	350	300	275	175

Glock 37

Semi-automatic pistol chambered for .45 G.A.P. cartridge, which is slightly shorter than .45 ACP. Cartridge has a muzzle speed of 951 fps and muzzle energy of 405 ft. lbs. Fitted with 4.49" barrel; height 5.5"; overall length 7.3"; weight about 26 oz. Available with OD green frame. **NOTE:** Add $25 for all Gen4 variations.

NIB	Exc.	V.G.	Good	Fair	Poor
575	495	350	300	275	175

Glock 38

This .45 G.A.P. pistol fitted with 4" barrel. Height 5"; overall length 6.85". Magazine capacity 8 rounds. Weight about 24 oz. Introduced in 2005. Available with OD green frame.

NIB	Exc.	V.G.	Good	Fair	Poor
575	495	350	300	275	175

Glock 39

Introduced in 2005, this sub-compact .45 G.A.P. pistol has 3.46" barrel. Height 4.17"; overall length 6.3". Magazine capacity 8 rounds. Weight about 19.3 oz. Available with OD green frame.

NIB	Exc.	V.G.	Good	Fair	Poor
575	495	350	300	275	175

Glock 41 Sport/Service Competition

Much like Gen4 Model 21, with 5.3" barrel, RTF frame, octagonal rifling, interchangeable backstraps, dual recoil spring and new trigger system. Introduced in 2014. Chambered for .45 ACP. Model 40 is similar, except chambered in 10mm, with 6" barrel. **NOTE:** Add $50 for Model 40 in 10mm.

NIB	Exc.	V.G.	Good	Fair	Poor
650	550	425	325	—	—

Glock 42

Sub-compact model chambered in .380 ACP. Barrel 3.5" with hexagonal rifling. Has new trigger system, dual spring operating assembly and slimmest frame of any Glock, less than 1" in diameter. New in 2014.

NIB	Exc.	V.G.	Good	Fair	Poor
575	475	400	300	—	—

Glock 43

Long anticipated model from Glock is this single-stack 9mm compact. Magazine capacity 6 rounds. General features same as other Glock compacts. Barrel length 3.4"; overall length 6.26"; height 4.25"; width 1.02"; weight unloaded 17.95 oz. Introduced in 2015.

NIB	Exc.	V.G.	Good	Fair	Poor
575	475	400	300	—	—

GODDARD
See—B. & B. M. Darling

GOLDEN EAGLE
Nikko Limited
Tochigi, Japan

SHOTGUNS

Golden Eagle Model 5000 Grade I

A 12- or 20-gauge over/under shotgun, with 26", 28" and 30" barrels, ventilated ribs and various choke combinations. Single-selective trigger and automatic ejectors. Blued, with walnut stock that has an eagle's head inlaid into pistol-grip cap. Manufactured between 1976 and early 1980s.

NIB	Exc.	V.G.	Good	Fair	Poor
1000	900	750	600	475	250

NIB	Exc.	V.G.	Good	Fair	Poor
—	—	6500	2000	1000	500

GOVERNOR
Norwich, Connecticut

Governor Pocket Revolver

A .22-caliber spur trigger revolver, with 3" barrel and 7-shot cylinder. Revolvers were made from modified Bacon pepperboxes. Top strap marked "Governor". Manufactured from approximately 1868 to 1874.

NIB	Exc.	V.G.	Good	Fair	Poor
—	—	725	650	250	100

GRABNER G.
Kolibri Rehberg, Austria
See—Kolibri

GRAND POWER
Lupca, Slovakia

K100 Mk12

Made in Slovakia, this is a polymer frame 9mm pistol with a steel slide and 4.25" rotating barrel. Traditional double-/single-action design, with ambidextrous controls, 15-round magazine and fixed 3-dot sights. Front sight comes with two extra inserts of different heights. Unique rotating barrel design is said to reduce felt recoil and provide better accuracy. Introduced in 2015. Imported by Eagle Imports.

NIB	Exc.	V.G.	Good	Fair	Poor
575	500	400	300	225	200

GRAND PRECISION, FABRIQUE D'ARMES DE
Eibar, Spain

Bulwark Model 1913

Chambered for 6.35mm cartridge. Exact copy of Browning Model 1906. Complete with squeeze grip safety. Marketed by Beistegui Hermanos. Bulwark stamped on slide and B.H. stamped on grip plate.

Courtesy James Rankin

NIB	Exc.	V.G.	Good	Fair	Poor
—	295	195	150	75	40

Bulwark Model 1914

Chambered for 7.65mm cartridge. Style Ruby military pistols of WWI. Magazine capacity 9 rounds.

Courtesy James Rankin

NIB	Exc.	V.G.	Good	Fair	Poor
—	275	225	150	75	40

Bulwark 6.35mm

Semi-automatic pistol in caliber 6.35mm. Patterned after Browning Model 1906. Marketed by Beistegue Hermanos.

Courtesy James Rankin

NIB	Exc.	V.G.	Good	Fair	Poor
—	250	175	115	75	40

Libia 6.35mm

Also patterned after Browning Model 1906, with squeeze safety. Libia stamped on slide and each grip plate. Marketed by Beistegui Hermanos.

Courtesy James Rankin

NIB	Exc.	V.G.	Good	Fair	Poor
—	275	225	150	750	40

Libia 7.65mm

Similar to model above. Chambered for 7.65mm cartridge.

Courtesy James Rankin

NIB	Exc.	V.G.	Good	Fair	Poor
—	275	225	150	75	40

GRANGER, G.
St. Etienne, France

Side-by-Side Shotgun

Custom-order 12-, 16- and 20-gauge boxlock double-barrel shotgun. Manufactured since 1902. Because gun is imported, value of dollar frequently determines price movement.

NIB	Exc.	V.G.	Good	Fair	Poor
—	16500	13000	8500	4250	1500

GRAS
France

Model 1874

An 11mm caliber bolt-action rifle, with 32" barrel, walnut stock, barrel band and metal tip. Bayonet is a spike blade, with wood handle and brass butt cap.

NIB	Exc.	V.G.	Good	Fair	Poor
—	500	375	225	150	75

GREAT WESTERN ARMS COMPANY
Los Angeles, California

Popularity of western television programs in early 1950s, spawned a renewed interest in guns that were seen in almost every episode, primarily the Single Action Army revolver. At about the same time that Bill Ruger was designing his company's first single-action, Single Six, a group of investors in the Los Angeles area, were preparing to launch Great Western Arms Company. Among this group was Dan Reeves, owner of the Los Angeles Rams professional football team, and several other prominent area businessmen.

Ruger's .22 LR Single Six hit the market in 1953 and by spring of 1954, Great Western unveiled a faithful copy of the Colt Single Action Army, chambered in several centerfire calibers, including .38 Special, .357 Magnum, .357 Atomic, .44 special, .44-40, .44 Magnum, .45 Colt and .22 Long Rifle. This was the first of many Colt SAA clones. (.357 Atomic was a propriety cartridge that never got off the ground, a .357 with a slightly lengthened case. It apparently was never commercially loaded.) Standard single-action was known as Frontier Model and was made in the same barrel lengths as the original: 4.750", 5.500" and 7.500", plus a 12" Buntline Model. Grips were faux stag, with optional real stag, walnut, ivory and other materials on the handful of presentation grade engraved models. Some of the high-grade models were made for prominent political leaders and celebrities, including President Dwight D. Eisenhower, John Wayne and Elvis Presley. In addition to Frontier Model, Great Western offered several other single-action variations that are listed below, as well as a copy of Remington Double Derringer in either .38 S&W or .38 Special.

The company went through several ownership changes and had a tough time competing with Ruger and later Colt, which resurrected the original SAA in 1956. In 1959, the name and assets of the company were purchased by EMF (Early and Modern Firearms Co.) and in 1964 Great Western products were discontinued. The name was resurrected in 2003, when EMF imported a series of single-action revolvers, known as Great Western II 1873 SA, until about 2009. See separate listing below for these firearms.

Centerfire Single-Action

Courtesy John C. Dougan

NIB	Exc.	V.G.	Good	Fair	Poor
800	725	500	350	250	200

.22 Long Rifle Single-Action

NIB	Exc.	V.G.	Good	Fair	Poor
600	525	450	375	300	200

Target Model (.22 LR)

NIB	Exc.	V.G.	Good	Fair	Poor
700	625	500	350	300	200

Fast Draw Model

Brass backstrap and trigger guard.

NIB	Exc.	V.G.	Good	Fair	Poor
750	675	550	400	300	225

Deputy Model

4"barrel with full length sight rib. **NOTE:** Calibers other than standard such as .22 Hornet, .32-20, .45 ACP, .22 Magnum, .30 Carbine or .357 Atomic add 10 percent premium. Factory plated pistols add 10 percent. Factory cased pistols add 20 percent. Sheriff's Model or Buntline Special add 15 percent. Factory ivory grips add $175; stag grips add $95 and pearl grips add $150. Factory-engraved guns will add $750 to $3,500 to prices depending on coverage.

NIB	Exc.	V.G.	Good	Fair	Poor
1000	850	600	425	250	—

Derringer Models

These two-shot over/unders were based on Remington Derringer of late 19th Century. Chambered for either .38 S&W or .38 Special. Some models were factory engraved and presented to Hollywood celebrities.

Engraved Model

Courtesy John C. Dougan

NIB	Exc.	V.G.	Good	Fair	Poor
1300	1100	900	700	400	150

Standard Model

Courtesy John C. Dougan

NIB	Exc.	V.G.	Good	Fair	Poor
650	550	475	275	175	100

GREAT WESTERN II
Santa Ana, California

These single-action revolvers were made by Pietta in Italy. EMF, owner of the Great Western name, began importing these guns in 2003.

Custom 1873 SA

Chambered in .357, .44-40 and .45 Colt in standard SAA barrel lengths. Offered in blue, blue with color case-hardening, satin nickel or bright nickel finish. Ivory or stag grips. Engraved models were available. Imported from 2003 to 2010. **NOTE:** Add a premium of up to $100 for stag grips.

NIB	Exc.	V.G.	Good	Fair	Poor
750	625	500	400	300	200

Stainless 1873 SA

NIB	Exc.	V.G.	Good	Fair	Poor
800	650	550	450	300	200

Paladin Model

In .45 Colt, with 3.5", 5.5" or 7.5" barrel, ivory grips, blue finish. Introduced in 2013.

NIB	Exc.	V.G.	Good	Fair	Poor
480	400	325	275	200	175

Liberty Model

Similar to Paladin Model, except with laser engraving. Made in .357 Magnum and .45 Colt.

NIB	Exc.	V.G.	Good	Fair	Poor
550	475	400	350	300	200

GREEN, E.
Cheltenham, England

Green

A .450- and .455-caliber double-action revolver. Popular with military users in late 1800s.

NIB	Exc.	V.G.	Good	Fair	Poor
—	—	2000	875	550	300

GREENE
Milbury, Massachusetts

Greene Breechloading Rifle

A .53-caliber single-shot bolt-action percussion rifle, with 35" barrel, under hammer and full length walnut stock secured by three barrel bands. Marked "Greene's Patent/Nov. 17, 1857". Approximately 4,000 made by A.H. Waters Armory between 1859 and 1862.

Courtesy Milwaukee Public Museum, Milwaukee, Wisconsin

NIB	Exc.	V.G.	Good	Fair	Poor
—	—	3250	1050	400	200

GREENER, W. W. LTD.
Birmingham, England

Perhaps the best known manufacturer of double-barrel shotguns in England during 19th Century. Greener was also a prolific author. His name will forever be associated with "Greener Crossbolt". Greener hammer-model shotguns were quite popular in United States during last half of 19th century. Company is still in business in Birmingham and makes a limited number of custom guns. Current prices on used gun market range for basic boxlock non-ejector models in the $1,500 to $2,000 range. Top of the line models from first half of 20th century can bring $100,000 or more. Because of the wide range of models and grades, a professional appraisal would be necessary before any transaction.

GREIFELT & CO.
Suhl, Germany

OVER/UNDER SHOTGUNS

Grade No. 1

NOTE: Add 25 percent for 28-gauge and .410 bore.

NIB	Exc.	V.G.	Good	Fair	Poor
—	3750	3250	2950	1750	1000

Grade No. 3

Similar to No. 1, with less engraving. Manufactured prior to WWII. **NOTE:** Add 25 percent for 28-gauge and .410 bore.

NIB	Exc.	V.G.	Good	Fair	Poor
—	3250	2700	1850	1250	750

Model 143E

Post-war version of No. 1. Not made in 28-gauge or .410 bore.

NIB	Exc.	V.G.	Good	Fair	Poor
—	2750	2300	1650	1200	750

Combination Gun

Combination over/under rifle/shotgun. Manufactured in all bores and variety of rifle calibers, with 24" or 26" barrels. Made prior to 1939. **NOTE:** Add 25 percent for 28-gauge and .410 bore; 10 percent for automatic ejectors. Deduct 40 percent if rifle caliber is obsolete

NIB	Exc.	V.G.	Good	Fair	Poor
—	5800	4750	3950	2500	1250

SIDE-BY-SIDE SHOTGUNS

Model 22

A 12- or 20-gauge boxlock double-barrel shotgun, with 28" or 30" barrels, sideplates, double triggers and extractors. Blued, case-hardened with walnut stock. Manufactured after 1945.

NIB	Exc.	V.G.	Good	Fair	Poor
—	2500	1950	1500	500	200

Model 22E

As above, with automatic ejectors.

NIB	Exc.	V.G.	Good	Fair	Poor
—	2750	2300	1650	550	225

Model 103

A 12- and 16-gauge boxlock shotgun, with 28" or 30" barrel, double triggers and extractors. Walnut stock, with pistol-, straight- or English-style-grip. Post-war model.

NIB	Exc.	V.G.	Good	Fair	Poor
—	2250	1800	1350	400	175

Model 103E

As above, with automatic ejectors.

NIB	Exc.	V.G.	Good	Fair	Poor
—	2500	1950	1500	500	200

Drilling

A 12-, 16- or 20-gauge double-barrel shotgun. Fitted with a rifle barrel. Chambered for variety of cartridges. Barrel length 26", boxlock-action, double triggers, extractors and folding rear sight. Manufactured prior to 1939. **NOTE:** Add 10 percent for 20-gauge. Deduct 40 percent if rifle caliber is obsolete.

NIB	Exc.	V.G.	Good	Fair	Poor
—	3750	3200	2950	900	300

GRENDEL, INC.
Rockledge, Florida

P-10 Pistol

A .380-caliber semi-automatic pistol, with 3" barrel, 11-shot magazine, matte black finish and black plastic grips. Pistol has plastic frame and magazine. Offered in electroless nickel-plate, as well as a green Teflon finish for slightly higher price. **NOTE:** Add $5 for green finish; $15 for electroless nickel.

NIB	Exc.	V.G.	Good	Fair	Poor
295	250	195	150	125	75

P-12

Semi-automatic double-action pistol, chambered for .380 ACP cartridge. Fitted with 3" barrel, checkered polymer grips, and blued finish. Magazine capacity 10 rounds. Weight about 13 oz. Introduced in 1992.

NIB	Exc.	V.G.	Good	Fair	Poor
295	250	195	150	125	75

P-30

Introduced in 1990, this double-action semi-automatic pistol chambered for .22 WMR cartridge. Fitted with 5" or 8" barrel. Fixed sights. Magazine capacity 30 rounds. Weight about 21 oz. Discontinued in 1994.

NIB	Exc.	V.G.	Good	Fair	Poor
450	350	275	125	85	75

P-30L

Same as above, in 8" barrel only. Discontinued in 1994.

NIB	Exc.	V.G.	Good	Fair	Poor
450	350	275	125	85	75

P-30M

Similar to P-30. Fitted with removable muzzle-brake.

NIB	Exc.	V.G.	Good	Fair	Poor
450	350	275	125	85	75

P-31

Semi-automatic pistol chambered for .22 WMR cartridge. Fitted with 11" barrel, muzzle-brake. Black matte finish. Weight about 48 oz. Introduced in 1991. No longer in production.

NIB	Exc.	V.G.	Good	Fair	Poor
450	350	275	125	85	75

RIFLES

SRT-20F Compact Rifle

A .308-caliber bolt-action rifle, with 20" finned match grade barrel, 9-shot magazine, folding synthetic stock, integral bipod and no sights.

Courtesy Jim Supica, Old Town Station

NIB	Exc.	V.G.	Good	Fair	Poor
575	500	425	325	250	100

SRT-24

As above, with 24" barrel. Discontinued in 1988.

NIB	Exc.	V.G.	Good	Fair	Poor
600	525	450	350	275	100

R-31 Carbine

Semi-automatic carbine introduced in 1991. Chambered for .22 WMR cartridge. Fitted with 16" barrel. Muzzle-brake and telescoping tubular stock. Magazine capacity 30 rounds. Weight about 4 lbs. Discontinued in 1994.

NIB	Exc.	V.G.	Good	Fair	Poor
300	250	200	150	125	100

GRIFFIN & HOWE
Bernardsville, New Jersey

Established in 1923, this firm manufactures on custom order a variety of bolt-action sporting rifles. These rifles have an excellent reputation and are quite desirable. Starting prices for currently manufactured rifles is around $15,000. Values of older models in excellent condition range from $4,000 to $10,000 and much higher for engraved rifles. Griffin & Howe also are agents for various European shotgun makers.

GRIFFON
South Africa

Griffon 1911 A1 Combat

Semi-automatic single-action pistol, chambered for .45 ACP cartridge. Fitted with 4" ported barrel. Aluminum trigger and high-profile sights are standard. Frame is chrome and slide blued. Magazine capacity 7 rounds.

NIB	Exc.	V.G.	Good	Fair	Poor
600	500	400	295	200	125

GRISWOLD & GRIER
See—Griswold & Gunnison

GRISWOLD & GUNNISON
Griswoldville, Georgia

1851 Navy Type

A .36-caliber percussion revolver, with 7.5" barrel and 6-shot cylinder.

Frame and grip straps made of brass. Barrel and cylinder made of iron. Approximately 3,700 made between 1862 and 1864 for Confederate government. **NOTE:** This revolver sometimes referred to as Griswold and Grier.

Courtesy Milwaukee Public Museum, Milwaukee, Wisconsin

NIB	Exc.	V.G.	Good	Fair	Poor
—	—	38500	14000	2750	1350

GROSS ARMS CO.
Tiffin, Ohio

Pocket Revolver

A .25- and .30-caliber spur trigger revolver, with 6" octagonal barrel, 7-shot cylinder and marked "Gross Arms Co., Tiffin, Ohio". Blued, with walnut grips. Only a few hundred manufactured between 1864 and 1866.

NIB	Exc.	V.G.	Good	Fair	Poor
—	—	1700	600	300	150

GRUBB, J. C. & CO.
Philadelphia, Pennsylvania

Pocket Pistol

A .41-caliber single-shot percussion pistol, with various barrel lengths. German silver walnut stock and engraved lock and trigger guard. Lock marked "J.C. Grubb". Several hundred manufactured between 1860 and 1870.

NIB	Exc.	V.G.	Good	Fair	Poor
—	—	1550	800	650	170

GRULLA
Eibar, Spain

Model 216RL

Side-by-side shotgun offered in 12-, 16-, 20-, 28-gauge and .410 bore. Barrel length 28". Articulated double triggers. Action body is H&H side locks. Select walnut, with straight-grip and splinter fore-end. Fixed chokes. Choice of different styles of engraving. Weight range from 7.1 lbs. for 12-gauge to 6 lbs. for .410 bore. **NOTE:** Add $300 for 28-gauge and .410 bore.

NIB	Exc.	V.G.	Good	Fair	Poor
9000	5750	3500	2000	1350	500

Royal

High-grade side-by-side series offered in all standard gauges. Featuring H&H seven-pin style sidelock and H&H, Purdey or Churchill style engraving. Custom made to buyer's specifications, with select exhibition grade walnut stock and forearm. Choice of several metal finishes. **NOTE:** Add $1000 for Purdey-style engraving; $2000 for Churchill.

NIB	Exc.	V.G.	Good	Fair	Poor
22750	19500	16000	10000	—	—

Consort

Side-by-side model, with double triggers, H&H style assisted-opening action, drop forged demi-block chopper lump barrels with concave rib and choice of old silver or case-hardened finish. This is a true sidelock action, with five pins, double safety sears and extensive engraving. Stock and forearm are hand checkered, with hand rubbed oil-finish. Chamberings are available in all standard gauges.

NIB	Exc.	V.G.	Good	Fair	Poor
11500	9800	8000	5500	—	—

GUERINI, CAESAR
Italy

This line of Italian over/under guns was introduced into U.S.A. in 2004.

Flyway

Over/under 12-gauge 3" gun offered with either 28" or 30" ventilated rib barrels, with choke tubes. Checkered walnut stock with pistol-grip. Trap-style forearm with finger grooves. Single-selective trigger and ejectors. Weight about 8 lbs. depending on barrel length.

NIB	Exc.	V.G.	Good	Fair	Poor
2795	2300	1750	1300	900	500

Woodlander

Offered in 12-, 20- and 28-gauge, with choice of 26" or 28" ventilated rib barrels and choke tubes. Frame case-hardened, with gold ruffed grouse on bottom of receiver. Checkered Circassian walnut stock, with straight-grip and oil-finished. Single-selective trigger and ejectors. Weight about: 6.25 lbs. 20-gauge; 6.15 lbs. 28-gauge.

NIB	Exc.	V.G.	Good	Fair	Poor
3000	2400	1750	1300	900	500

Magnus Light

Offered in 12-, 20- or 28-gauge, with choice of 26" or 28" ventilated rib barrels and choke tubes. Alloy frame with Tinaloy finish and side plates. Scroll engraved with gold game birds. Checkered walnut stock with Prince of Wales-style pistol-grip. Weight about: 6 lbs. 12-gauge; 5.4 lbs. 20-gauge; 5.25 lbs. 28-gauge.

NIB	Exc.	V.G.	Good	Fair	Poor
3800	2995	2000	1500	1000	500

Magnus

Similar to Magnus Light, with case-hardened steel receiver. Weight about: 6.75 lbs. 12-gauge; 6.5 lbs. 20-gauge; 6.25 lbs. 28-gauge.

NIB	Exc.	V.G.	Good	Fair	Poor
3800	2995	2000	1500	1000	500

Magnus Sporting

Similar to Summit, with upgraded wood and sidelock-style receiver. Scroll engraving and gold game birds.

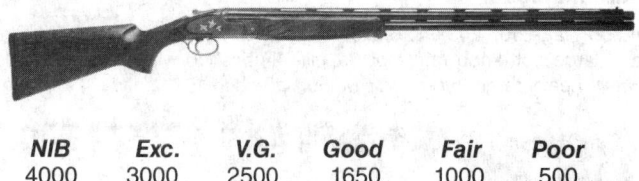

NIB	Exc.	V.G.	Good	Fair	Poor
4000	3000	2500	1650	1000	500

Maxum

Offered in 12-, 20- and 28-gauge, with hand-polished coin finish receiver, hand-rubbed oil walnut stock, deep relief floral scroll hand-finished engraving on receiver, side plates and fore-end assembly. Comes with velvet-lined lockable hard case and five choke tubes.

NIB	Exc.	V.G.	Good	Fair	Poor
5400	4500	3200	2400	1200	600

Tempio

Over/under gun offered in 12-, 20- and 28-gauge, with choice of 26" or 28" barrels and choke tubes. Checkered Circassian walnut stock, with Prince of Wales-style pistol-grip. Alloy receiver is a gray finish of Tinaloy. Engraved with scroll and gold game birds. Single-selective trigger with ejectors. Weight about: 6.8 lbs. 12-gauge; 6.4 lbs. 20-gauge; 6.25 lbs. 28-gauge.

NIB	Exc.	V.G.	Good	Fair	Poor
3200	2000	1500	1050	600	250

Forum/Forum Sporting

Offered in 12-, 20- and 28-gauge, with choice of 26" or 28" barrels on Forum. Forum Sporting has 30", 32" or 34" barrels. Gun has silver receiver, with scroll and game scene engraving and side plates. NOTE: Add $300 for Forum Sporting.

NIB	Exc.	V.G.	Good	Fair	Poor
8000	6000	4750	3250	1600	700

Summit Sporting/Summit Limited

Offered in 12-, 20- or 28-gauge, with choice of 30" or 32" ventilated rib barrels and extended choke tubes. Alloy receiver with engraving. Single-selective trigger adjustable for length of pull. Ejectors. Checkered walnut stock, with pistol-grip. Weight about: 8 lbs. 12-gauge; 7.5 lbs. 20-gauge; 7.45 lbs. 28-gauge. NOTE: Add $300 for Summit Limited.

NIB	Exc.	V.G.	Good	Fair	Poor
2950	2300	1650	1200	750	300

Essex

Over/under with oil-finished stock and coin finished receiver. Scroll engraving. Available in 12-, 20-, 28-gauge and .410 bore all with 3" chambers. New in 2006.

NIB	Exc.	V.G.	Good	Fair	Poor
4250	3500	2300	1650	1000	500

Ellipse Evo

Rounded action in 12-, 20- or 28-gauge, with coin-finished receiver, hand-rubbed oil-finished stock with rounded grip, choke tubes and 28" barrels. Choice of selective or non-selective trigger, manual or automatic safety. Also offered in 12-gauge sporting (Evolution) and Limited versions. NOTE: Add $1800 for Evolution; deduct $1500 for Limited.

NIB	Exc.	V.G.	Good	Fair	Poor
5000	4000	2800	2000	1500	700

Apex

This over/under series is offered in 12-, 20-, 28-gauge and .410 bore, with coin-finished scroll-engraved receiver and hand-rubbed oil-finished walnut stock. Barrels are currently only 28", but early models were made with 26" and 30". Five choke tubes are included. A Sporting Clays model is available, with 32" barrels in 12-gauge only, with high-grade walnut stock. NOTE: Add $500 for Sporting Clays model if excellent or better condition.

NIB	Exc.	V.G.	Good	Fair	Poor
6900	5800	4900	3500	2250	900

Invictus I Sporting

12-gauge Sporting Clays model with 30" or 32" barrels. Ventilated rib, hand rubbed oil-finished walnut stock and fore-end, coin finished receiver and some light scroll engraving. Introduced in 2014. NOTE: Add $1500 for Invictus V Sporting, with high-grade hand engraving.

NIB	Exc.	V.G.	Good	Fair	Poor
6200	4900	3700	—	—	—

GUION, T. F.
New Orleans, Louisiana

Pocket Pistol

A .41-caliber single-shot percussion pistol, with 2.5" barrel, German silver mountings and walnut stock. Manufactured in 1850s.

NIB	Exc.	V.G.	Good	Fair	Poor
—	—	2150	1850	550	275

GUNCRAFTER INDUSTRIES
Huntsville, Arkansas

This manufacturer of 1911-style pistols offers several different models, with typical 1911 features.

Model No. 1

Chambered in 9mm, .45 ACP and manufacturer's own proprietary .50 GI caliber. Barrel lengths include standard 5" plus 4.25" and 6". All guns are made-to-order. NOTE: Add 50 percent for 6" model.

NIB	Exc.	V.G.	Good	Fair	Poor
2850	2100	1500	1000	450	300

GUNWORKS LTD.
Buffalo, New York

Model 9 Derringer

Over/under derringer chambered in 9mm, .38 Special, .38 Super and .357 Magnum caliber. Barrels 2.5", with spur trigger and Millet sights. Nickel-plate with walnut grips. Manufacturing ceased in 1986.

NIB	Exc.	V.G.	Good	Fair	Poor
—	175	125	90	75	50

GUSTAF, CARL
Eskilstuna, Sweden

Bolt-Action Rifle

A 6.5x55, 7x64, .270, 7mm Magnum, .308, .30-06 and 9.3x62 caliber bolt-action rifle, with 24" barrel. Blued, with walnut stock in either classic style or with Monte Carlo cheekpiece. Manufactured between 1970 and 1977.

NIB	Exc.	V.G.	Good	Fair	Poor
—	700	600	450	325	150

Grade II

As above, with better walnut, rosewood pistol-grip cap and fore-end tip.

NIB	Exc.	V.G.	Good	Fair	Poor
—	850	650	475	375	175

Grade III

As above, with high-gloss finish and finely figured walnut stock.

NIB	Exc.	V.G.	Good	Fair	Poor
—	950	700	550	475	275

Deluxe Bolt-Action

As above, with engraved floorplate and trigger guard, Damascened bolt and high-grade French walnut stock. Manufactured between 1970 and 1977.

NIB	Exc.	V.G.	Good	Fair	Poor
—	1250	900	650	450	300

Varmint Model

A .222, .22-250, .243 and 6.5x55 caliber bolt-action rifle, with 27" barrel and large bolt knob made of Bakelite. Furnished without open sights. Has a heavy target-type stock. Manufactured in 1970 only.

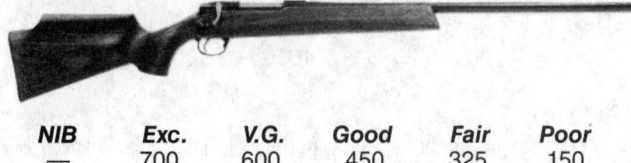

NIB	Exc.	V.G.	Good	Fair	Poor
—	700	600	450	325	150

Grand Prix Target

A .22-caliber single-shot bolt-action rifle, with 27" barrel. Adjustable weights and butt target stock. Furnished without sights. Only manufactured in 1970.

NIB	Exc.	V.G.	Good	Fair	Poor
—	700	600	450	325	150

Model 2000

A 6.5x55, .243, .270, .308 and .30-06 caliber bolt-action rifle, with 60 percent bolt lift. Cold swagged barrel and action. Furnished with open sights. Blued, walnut stock with Monte Carlo cheekpiece. Manufactured until 1985.

NIB	Exc.	V.G.	Good	Fair	Poor
—	675	575	400	300	150

GWYN & CAMPBELL
Hamilton, Ohio

Union Carbine

A .52-caliber single-shot breech loading percussion carbine, with round/octagonal 20" barrel marked "Gwyn & Campbell/ Patent/1862/ Hamilton,O". Blued, case-hardened with walnut stock. Approximately 8,500 made between 1862 and 1865.

Courtesy Milwaukee Public Museum, Milwaukee, Wisconsin

NIB	Exc.	V.G.	Good	Fair	Poor
—	—	4000	1975	500	300

H&R 1871, LLC
Gardner, Massachusetts
See—Harrington & Richardson

H.J.S. INDUSTRIES, INC.
Brownsville, Texas

Frontier Four Derringer

A .22-caliber four-barreled pocket pistol, with 2.5" sliding barrels, stainless steel frame, barrel grip and walnut grips. Recalled due to risk of unintentional discharge.

NIB	Exc.	V.G.	Good	Fair	Poor
—	450	400	275	150	50

Lone Star Derringer

A .38 Special caliber single-shot spur trigger pistol, with 2.5" barrel. Stainless steel with wood grips.

NIB	Exc.	V.G.	Good	Fair	Poor
—	300	250	175	125	50

H-S PRECISION, INC.
Rapid City, South Dakota

SPR Sporter Rifle

Bolt-action rifle offered in long and short actions, with any standard SAAMI caliber. Match grade stainless steel barrel lengths are 22", 24" or 26", with optional muzzle-brake available. Synthetic stock offered in various colors. Weight between 7.5 and 7.75 lbs. depending on barrel length. Magazine capacity: 4 rounds standard calibers; 3 rounds Magnum calibers.

NIB	Exc.	V.G.	Good	Fair	Poor
2375	1800	1400	900	500	250

SPL Lightweight Sporter

Introduced in 2005. Features 22", 24" or 26" fluted barrel, with choice of short or long action calibers. Detachable magazine. No sights. Pro-series synthetic stock. Weight under 7 lbs.

NIB	Exc.	V.G.	Good	Fair	Poor
2400	1825	1425	925	525	275

PHR Professional Hunter Rifle

Bolt-action rifle chambered for Magnum calibers only. Fitted with 24" or 26" stainless steel match grade fluted barrel (except .416 Rigby). Built in recoil reduced in synthetic stock with choice of colors. Matte black finish. Weight between 7.75 lbs. and 8.25 depending on barrel length and caliber. Offered in any standard SAAMI caliber. Magazine capacity 3 rounds.

NIB	Exc.	V.G.	Good	Fair	Poor
3000	2400	1650	1050	575	300

BHR Big Game Professional Hunter Rifle

Introduced in 2005. Same features as PHR series, with addition of adjustable iron sights and specially designed stock. Weight about 7.75 to 8.25 lbs. depending on caliber and barrel length.

NIB	Exc.	V.G.	Good	Fair	Poor
3100	2500	1850	1175	625	350

PHL Professional Hunter Lightweight Rifle

Features weight of 5.75 lbs. Fitted with Pro-Series stock and choice of 20" or 22" contoured fluted stock. Matte black teflon finish. Detachable magazine. Chambered for short action calibers. Introduced in 2005.

NIB	Exc.	V.G.	Good	Fair	Poor
3100	2500	1850	1175	625	350

VAR Varmint Rifle

Offered in long or short action, with .17 Rem., 6mm PPC and .223 Rem. in single-shot. Fitted with match grade stainless steel fluted barrel in 24" or 26" lengths. Available in a lightweight 20" barrel. Synthetic stock in choice of colors, with 20" barrel guns offered with thumbhole stocks. Black matte finish. Weight between 8 and 8.25 lbs. for standard rifles and 7.5 and 7.75 lbs. for 20" barrel guns. Available in any standard SAAMI caliber.

NIB	Exc.	V.G.	Good	Fair	Poor
2600	2050	1650	1050	575	300

Varmint Take-Down Rifle

Take-down bolt-action rifle offered in stainless steel long or short action, with 24" stainless steel match grade fluted barrel. Matte black finish. Weight between 8.5 and 9 lbs. **NOTE:** Add $1,000 for extra barrel with same head size caliber; $1,200 for extra barrel with different head size caliber.

NIB	Exc.	V.G.	Good	Fair	Poor
3700	2900	2050	1450	600	400

Professional Hunter Take-Down Rifle

Take-down rifle offered in Magnum and Super Magnum calibers, with 24" fluted stainless steel barrel. Built in recoil reducer. Matte black finish. Weight between 8.25 and 8.75 lbs.

NIB	Exc.	V.G.	Good	Fair	Poor
4500	3200	2400	1650	750	450

Varmint Pistol

Bolt-action single-shot pistol chambered for a wide variety of calibers from .17 Rem. to 7mm BR. Fitted with heavy contour fluted stainless steel match barrel. Synthetic stock with center grip. Matte black finish. Weight about 5.25 to 5.5 lbs.

NIB	Exc.	V.G.	Good	Fair	Poor
2200	1500	950	600	400	225

Silhouette Pistol

Same as above, with sporter contoured barrel. Weight about 4.5 lbs.

NIB	Exc.	V.G.	Good	Fair	Poor
2100	1400	950	600	400	225

HTR Heavy Tactical Rifle

Bolt-action model features stainless steel long or short action, with fluted stainless steel 24" heavy barrel. Stock is synthetic, with adjustable cheekpiece and length of pull. Any standard SAAMI caliber available. Weight about 10.75 to 11.25 lbs. Matte black finish.

NIB	Exc.	V.G.	Good	Fair	Poor
2750	2250	1850	1175	625	350

Short Tactical

Chambered for .308 cartridge. Fitted with 20" fluted barrel. Matte teflon finish. Pro-Series tactical stock.

NIB	Exc.	V.G.	Good	Fair	Poor
2750	2250	1850	1175	625	350

RDR Rapid Deployment Rifle

Similar to model above, with 20" stainless steel fluted barrel and smaller stock. Thumbhole stock on request. Magazine is 4 rounds. Matte black finish. Offered in any short action SAAMI calibers. Weight between 7.5 and 7.75 lbs.

NIB	Exc.	V.G.	Good	Fair	Poor
2750	2250	1850	1175	625	350

TTD Tactical Take-Down System

Take-down rifle chambered for any standard SAAMI caliber. Fitted with 24" fluted heavy stainless steel barrel. Magazine capacity: 4 rounds standard calibers; 3 rounds Magnum calibers. Synthetic stock adjustable for length of pull and cheekpiece. Matte black finish. Weight between 11.25 and 11.75 lbs.

NIB	Exc.	V.G.	Good	Fair	Poor
4600	3800	2400	1650	750	450

HAENEL, C. G.
Suhl, Germany

Established in 1840, this company began to manufacture semi-automatic pistols after Hugo Schmeisser joined the firm in 1921 as its chief engineer.

Model 1

A 6.35mm caliber semi-automatic pistol, with 2.48" barrel, striker-fired, 6-shot magazine. Weight about 13.5 oz. Left side of slide stamped "C.G. Haenel Suhl-Schmeisser Patent". Each grip panel marked "HS" in an oval.

NIB	Exc.	V.G.	Good	Fair	Poor
—	500	400	295	200	125

Model 2

As above, but shorter (2" barrel) and lighter in weight (12 oz.). "Schmeisser" molded into grips.

Courtesy Orvel Reichert

NIB	Exc.	V.G.	Good	Fair	Poor
—	550	425	350	225	150

HAFDASA
Buenos Aires, Argentina

Ballester-Molina

Copy of Colt Model 1911 semi-automatic pistol. Differing only in absence of grip safety, smaller grip and finger grooves on slide. Slide stamped "Pistola Automatica Cal. .45 Fabricado por HAFDASA Patentes Internacional Ballester Molina Industria Argentina". Introduced in 1941.

Courtesy James Rankin

NIB	Exc.	V.G.	Good	Fair	Poor
—	475	400	300	225	100

Criolla

A .22-caliber automatic pistol similar to Ballester-Molina. Some were sold commercially under trademark "La Criolla".

NIB	Exc.	V.G.	Good	Fair	Poor
—	1000	800	650	500	250

Hafdasa

A .22-caliber semi-automatic pistol with tubular receiver. A true hammerless striker-fired, with angled grip. Markings are "HA" on butt.

NIB	Exc.	V.G.	Good	Fair	Poor
—	400	325	275	200	100

Zonda

As above marked "Zonda".

NIB	Exc.	V.G.	Good	Fair	Poor
—	400	325	275	200	100

Rigaud

A semi-automatic copy of Colt Model 1911, with no grip safety. Caliber is .45 ACP and later .22 LR. Barrel length 5". Magazine capacity 7 rounds. The .22-caliber introduced in 1940.

Courtesy James Rankin

NIB	Exc.	V.G.	Good	Fair	Poor
—	475	400	300	225	100

Campeon

Same as Ballester-Molina, with floating chamber to accommodate .22 LR cartridge. Three variations of target model: sights, trigger and barrel lengths. Pistol first introduced in 1941 and produced until 1953.

Courtesy James Rankin

NIB	Exc.	V.G.	Good	Fair	Poor
—	750	550	400	300	200

HAHN, WILLIAM
New York, New York

Pocket Pistol

A .41-caliber single-shot percussion pistol, with 2.5" round barrel, German silver mountings and walnut stock. Manufactured in 1860s and 1870s.

NIB	Exc.	V.G.	Good	Fair	Poor
—	—	1950	1050	475	250

HALE, H. J.
Bristol, Connecticut

Under Hammer Pistol

A .31-caliber single-shot under hammer percussion pistol, with 5" or 6" part-round/part-octagonal barrel. Iron frame, with either pointed or round walnut butt. Markings read "H.J.Hale/Warranted/Cast Steel". Manufactured during 1850s.

NIB	Exc.	V.G.	Good	Fair	Poor
—	—	995	375	245	125

HALE & TULLER
Hartford, Connecticut

Under Hammer Pistol

A .44-caliber single-shot under hammer percussion pistol, with 6" tapered round barrel and pointed walnut grip. Manufactured at Connecticut State Prison between 1837 and 1840.

NIB	Exc.	V.G.	Good	Fair	Poor
—	—	975	450	200	125

HALL, ALEXANDER
New York, New York

Revolving Rifle

A .58-caliber percussion revolving rifle, with 15-shot open centered cylinder. Frame was made of brass. Barrel and cylinder of iron. Stock of walnut. Manufactured during 1850s in limited quantities. Very rare firearm.

NIB	Exc.	V.G.	Good	Fair	Poor
—	—	27500	12500	3750	1300

HALL-NORTH
Middletown, Connecticut

MODEL 1840 CARBINE

Carbine manufactured by Simeon North. Chambered for .52-caliber percussion. Single-shot breech-loading smoothbore, with 21" round barrel. Full-length stock held on by two barrel bands. Ramrod mounted under barrel and mountings are of iron. Lock is case-hardened and barrel brown. Stock is walnut. Markings are "US/S. North/Midltn/ Conn." Two distinct variations, both produced under military contract.

Type 1 Carbine

Has squared right-angled breech lever mounted on trigger plate. There were 500 manufactured in 1840.

NIB	Exc.	V.G.	Good	Fair	Poor
—	—	9000	4000	1750	1000

Type 2 Carbine

Variation features curved breech-operating lever known as fishtail. Approximately 6,000 manufactured from 1840 to 1843. Some have an 8" bar and ring.

NIB	Exc.	V.G.	Good	Fair	Poor
—	—	7500	2500	1100	550

HAMBUSH, JOSEPH
Ferlach, Austria

Boxlock Side-by-Side Shotgun

Custom-order boxlock double-barrel shotgun chambered for all gauges. Single-selective or double trigger and automatic ejectors. Features workmanship of high order. All specifications could vary with customer's wishes. Engraved with hunting scenes. Rare gun and not often encountered on today's market. **NOTE:** Pricing only estimated as not enough are traded to provide accurate values.

NIB	Exc.	V.G.	Good	Fair	Poor
—	1950	1100	950	575	375

Sidelock Side-by-Side Shotgun

Similar to above. Features full sidelock-action.

NIB	Exc.	V.G.	Good	Fair	Poor
—	3800	2500	1750	1600	1350

HAMILTON RIFLE COMPANY
Plymouth, Michigan

Manufacturer of inexpensive .22-caliber rifles. Established by Clarence J. Hamilton and his son Coello, in 1898 in Plymouth, Michigan. Company ceased production in 1945. Over 1 million rifles were produced between 1900 and 1911.

NOTE: Despite the fact there were many Hamilton rifles sold, most of these little guns were used hard and many did not survive. Hamilton rifles in excellent condition are hardly ever encountered. No prices are quoted for rifles in this condition as few exist. Further information about these rifles is gratefully accepted by the editor.

Model 7

First rifle produced by this company. Made entirely of castings and stampings. Nickel plated. Chambered for .22 Short cartridge, with 8" brass-lined barrel that pivots for loading. Stock was metal skeleton. Production ceased in 1901. Total of 44,000 rifles produced.

Courtesy William F. Krause

NIB	Exc.	V.G.	Good	Fair	Poor
—	750	500	450	300	195

Model 11

Similar to Model 7. Fitted with board-like walnut stock. Markings stamped into buttstock: "Hamilton Rifles Co., Plymouth, Mich., Pat. Pending No. 11". Produced from 1900 to 1902. Approximately 22,000 were sold.

NIB	Exc.	V.G.	Good	Fair	Poor
—	700	475	300	200	150

Model 15

Produced from 1901 to 1910, Chambered for .22 Short, with 8" brass lined barrel. Walnut stock. Design was an under lever single-shot, with loading port under barrel. Cocking knob located at rear of frame. Blued finish. Approximately 234,000 were sold.

NIB	Exc.	V.G.	Good	Fair	Poor
—	675	400	200	150	100

Model 19

Similar to Model 15, with modified loading port and 12" barrel. Few Model 19s have been seen with 13" barrels. These will bring a premium. Produced from 1903 to 1910. About 59,000 were sold.

NIB	Exc.	V.G.	Good	Fair	Poor
—	700	475	300	200	150

Model 23

First bolt-action rifle made by this company. Receiver is steel tube with loading port in top where barrel joins receiver. Bolt handle located at extreme rear of bolt. Cocking knob must be operated manually. Walnut stock either rounded or flat. Chamberd for .22 Short and .22 Long cartridges. 15" brass lined barrel. Blued finish. Weight about 3 lbs. Produced from 1905 to 1909. About 25,000 were sold.

NIB	Exc.	V.G.	Good	Fair	Poor
—	700	475	300	200	150

Model 27

Single-shot tip-up .22-caliber rifle, with stamped steel receiver. Barrel length 16" brass lined or 14.875"; overall length 30". First produced in 1906.

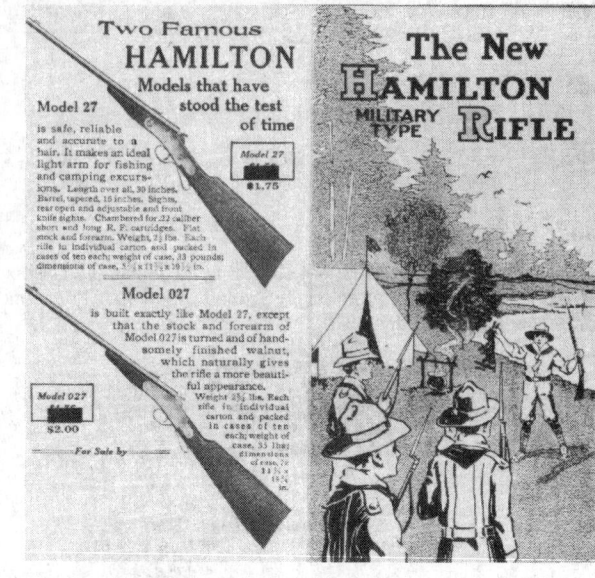

NIB	Exc.	V.G.	Good	Fair	Poor
—	475	300	200	150	100

Model 027

As above with walnut stock. First produced in 1908.

NIB	Exc.	V.G.	Good	Fair	Poor
—	495	300	200	150	100

Model 31

Introduced in 1910. Single-shot rifle chambered for .22 Short and Long cartridge. Fitted with 15.75" barrel, with brass liner. A tip-up design. Blued finish. Weight about 2.25 lbs.

NIB	Exc.	V.G.	Good	Fair	Poor
—	725	575	400	250	200

Model 35 or Boys' Military Rifle

Single-shot .22-caliber rifle, with full-length oval walnut straight-grip stock and 15.75" brass lined barrel. Produced from 1915 to 1918. Sold with stamped steel bayonet. Few bayonets survive. **NOTE:** Add $150 for bayonet to prices.

NIB	Exc.	V.G.	Good	Fair	Poor
—	950	700	450	250	125

Model 39

Only repeating rifle built by this company. Hammerless slide-action design, with tubular magazine. Magazine capacity 15 rounds of .22 Short. Barrel length 16", with brass liner. Walnut stock, with blade front sight. Produced from 1922 to 1930. Weight about 4 lbs.

NIB	Exc.	V.G.	Good	Fair	Poor
—	575	300	200	150	100

Model 43

Bolt-action design with loading port on top of barrel. No external cocking knob, but bolt is pulled to rear when in locked position. Chambered for .22 Short and .22 Long cartridges. 15.75" brass lined barrel. Fitted with an oval walnut stock, with blade front sight and open non-adjustable rear sight. Weight about 3 lbs. Built from 1924 to 1932.

NIB	Exc.	V.G.	Good	Fair	Poor
—	575	300	200	150	100

Model 47

Bolt-action single-shot rifle, with loading port located on top of barrel. Chambered for .22 Short and Long cartridges. Cocking knob located at rear of bolt handle. Early Model 47 were built with 16" brass lined barrels. Later examples were fitted with 18.25" steel lined barrels. Early guns had an oval buttstock while later guns had a pistol-grip stock. Very late guns had an all-steel barrel. Produced from 1927 to 1932.

NIB	Exc.	V.G.	Good	Fair	Poor
—	575	475	300	200	150

Model 51

Conventional type bolt-action rifle, with cocking knob located at rear of bolt. Two styles of buttstocks were used: flat style and later an oval shape. First Hamilton rifle chambered for .22 LR cartridge. Barrel was 20" steel. Finish was blue. Weight about 3.5 lbs. Produced from 1935 to 1941.

NIB	Exc.	V.G.	Good	Fair	Poor
—	550	400	250	200	150

Model 55

Bolt-action rifle chambered for .22 Short, Long and LR cartridges. Fitted with 20" steel barrel, with bead front sight and open adjustable rear sight. Walnut stock. Rarest Hamilton rifle. Only one example is known. Produced from late 1941 to early 1942.

NIB	Exc.	V.G.	Good	Fair	Poor
—	1000	—	—	—	—

HAMMERLI, SA
Lenzburg, Switzerland

RIFLES

Model 45 Smallbore Rifle

A .22-caliber bolt-action single-shot, with 27.5" heavy barrel, aperture rear and globe target front sight. Match rifle-type thumbhole stock. Manufactured between 1945 and 1957.

NIB	Exc.	V.G.	Good	Fair	Poor
—	825	700	595	450	250

Model 54 Smallbore Rifle

As above, with adjustable buttplate. Manufactured between 1954 and 1957.

NIB	Exc.	V.G.	Good	Fair	Poor
—	850	725	625	475	275

Model 503 Smallbore Free Rifle

Similar to Model 54, with free rifle-style stock.

NIB	Exc.	V.G.	Good	Fair	Poor
—	800	675	575	450	225

Model 506 Smallbore Match Rifle

Later version of Smallbore target series. Manufactured between 1963 and 1966.

NIB	Exc.	V.G.	Good	Fair	Poor
—	850	725	625	475	275

Olympic 300 Meter

A 7x57, .30-06 or .300 H&H Magnum caliber bolt-action single-shot rifle, with 20.5" heavy barrel. Aperture rear globe target front sight, double-set triggers and free rifle-type adjustable thumbhole stock. Wide beavertail forearm and schuetzen-style buttplate. Manufactured between 1945 and 1959.

NIB	Exc.	V.G.	Good	Fair	Poor
—	1050	900	725	550	325

Sporting Rifle

Bolt-action single-shot rifle chambered for many popular calibers (American and European). Double-set triggers and classic-style stock.

NIB	Exc.	V.G.	Good	Fair	Poor
—	800	675	575	450	225

PISTOLS

Model 100 Free Pistol

A .22-caliber single-shot Martini-action target pistol, with 11.5" octagonal barrel, adjustable sights, single-set trigger and walnut stocks. Manufactured from 1933 to 1949.

NIB	Exc.	V.G.	Good	Fair	Poor
—	1000	825	700	550	325

Model 101

As above, with heavy round barrel and more sophisticated target sights. Matte-blued finish. Manufactured between 1956 and 1960.

NIB	Exc.	V.G.	Good	Fair	Poor
—	1000	825	700	550	325

Model 102

As above, with highly polished blue finish. Manufactured between 1956 and 1960.

NIB	Exc.	V.G.	Good	Fair	Poor
—	1000	825	700	550	325

Model 103

Similar to Model 101, with lighter-weight octagonal barrel, high-polished blued finish. Manufactured between 1956 and 1960.

NIB	Exc.	V.G.	Good	Fair	Poor
—	1100	925	825	650	425

Model 104

As above, with lightweight round barrel. Manufactured between 1961 and 1965.

NIB	Exc.	V.G.	Good	Fair	Poor
—	950	625	550	450	300

Model 105

As above, with redesigned stock and improved action. Manufactured between 1962 and 1965.

NIB	Exc.	V.G.	Good	Fair	Poor
—	950	625	550	450	300

Model 106

As above, with improved trigger.

NIB	Exc.	V.G.	Good	Fair	Poor
—	950	625	550	450	300

Model 107

Variation fitted with five-level set trigger. Introduced in 1965, discontinued 1971.

NIB	Exc.	V.G.	Good	Fair	Poor
—	950	625	550	450	300

Model 107 Deluxe

As above, but engraved with carved stock.

NIB	Exc.	V.G.	Good	Fair	Poor
—	1500	1250	900	800	500

Model 120-1 Free Pistol

Bolt-action single-shot pistol in .22 LR caliber, with 9.9" barrel. Adjustable target sights activated for loading and cocking by an alloy lever on side of bolt. Blued, with checkered walnut grips

NIB	Exc.	V.G.	Good	Fair	Poor
—	1200	975	600	425	250

Model 120-2

As above, with contoured grips.

NIB	Exc.	V.G.	Good	Fair	Poor
—	1200	975	600	425	250

Model 120 Heavy Barrel

As above, with 5.7" heavy barrel.

NIB	Exc.	V.G.	Good	Fair	Poor
—	1200	975	600	425	250

Model 150

Single-shot Martini-action .22-caliber pistol, with 11.25" barrel, adjustable sights, contoured grips and single-set trigger. Blued, with walnut stocks.

NIB	Exc.	V.G.	Good	Fair	Poor
—	1500	1100	775	500	350

Model 152

As above, with 11.25" barrel and electronic release trigger.

NIB	Exc.	V.G.	Good	Fair	Poor
—	1800	1300	1050	600	450

International Model 206

A .22-caliber semi-automatic pistol, with 7.5" barrel, integral muzzle-brake, adjustable sights and walnut grips. Manufactured between 1962 and 1969.

NIB	Exc.	V.G.	Good	Fair	Poor
—	825	700	575	425	300

International Model 207

As above, with adjustable grips.

NIB	Exc.	V.G.	Good	Fair	Poor
—	850	725	600	450	325

International Model 208

A .22-caliber semi-automatic pistol, with 6" barrel, adjustable sights and 8-shot magazine. Adjustable trigger and target grips. Barrel drilled and tapped for addition of barrel weights. Manufactured between 1966 and 1988.

NIB	Exc.	V.G.	Good	Fair	Poor
—	1850	1550	1250	1000	750

International Model 208 Deluxe

As above, with engraved receiver and carved grips. Discontinued in 1988.

NIB	Exc.	V.G.	Good	Fair	Poor
—	3250	2750	2500	2000	1500

International Model 209

A .22 Short caliber semi-automatic pistol, with 4.75" barrel, muzzle-brake, adjustable target sights and 5-shot magazine. Blued, with walnut grips. Manufactured between 1966 and 1970.

NIB	Exc.	V.G.	Good	Fair	Poor
—	1200	975	600	425	250

International Model 210

As above, with adjustable grips.

NIB	Exc.	V.G.	Good	Fair	Poor
—	1225	1000	625	450	275

International Model 211

As above, with non-adjustable thumb rest grips.

NIB	Exc.	V.G.	Good	Fair	Poor
—	1300	1075	700	475	300

Model 212

A .22-caliber semi-automatic pistol, with 5" barrel and adjustable sights. Blued, with walnut grips.

NIB	Exc.	V.G.	Good	Fair	Poor
—	1300	1075	700	475	300

Model 230

A .22 Short caliber semi-automatic pistol, with 6.3" barrel, 5-shot magazine, adjustable sights and walnut grip. Manufactured between 1970 and 1983.

NIB	Exc.	V.G.	Good	Fair	Poor
—	1350	1125	750	525	325

Model 232

A .22 Short caliber semi-automatic pistol, with 5" barrel, adjustable sights and 6-shot magazine. Contoured walnut grips. Introduced in 1984.

NIB	Exc.	V.G.	Good	Fair	Poor
—	1300	1075	700	475	300

Model 280

New state-of-the-art target pistol from Hammerli. Features a modular design. Frame of carbon fiber material. Has 4.6" barrel, with adjustable sights, trigger and grips. Chambered for .22 LR or .32 Wadcutter. Magazine holds 5 rounds. Introduced in 1988.

NIB	Exc.	V.G.	Good	Fair	Poor
—	1800	1500	1350	1000	600

Model SP 20

Introduced in 1998, this pistol has a very low sight line. Features a wide variety of special items such as adjustable buffer system, anatomically shaped trigger in various sizes and receiver colors. Change over caliber system from .22 LR to .32 S&W.

NIB	Exc.	V.G.	Good	Fair	Poor
1750	1325	900	800	500	—

HAMMERLI-WALTHER
Lenzburg, Switzerland

These target pistols were produced by Hammerli under license from Walther after WWII. This project continued until approximately 1963, when production ceased.

Olympia Model 200 Type 1952

A .22-caliber semi-automatic pistol, with 7.5" barrel, 10-shot magazine, adjustable target sights. Blued, with walnut grips. Manufactured between 1952 and 1958.

NIB	Exc.	V.G.	Good	Fair	Poor
—	900	775	575	475	350

Model 200 Type 1958

As above, with integral muzzle-brake. Manufactured between 1958 and 1963.

NIB	Exc.	V.G.	Good	Fair	Poor
—	950	725	625	495	350

Model 201

Model 200 Type 1952, with 9.5" barrel. Manufactured between 1955 and 1957.

NIB	Exc.	V.G.	Good	Fair	Poor
—	950	725	625	495	350

Model 202

Similar to Model 201, with adjustable walnut grips. Manufactured between 1955 and 1957.

NIB	Exc.	V.G.	Good	Fair	Poor
—	950	725	625	495	350

Model 203

Similar to Model 200, with adjustable grips. Available with or without muzzle-brake.

NIB	Exc.	V.G.	Good	Fair	Poor
—	950	725	625	495	350

Model 204

A .22-caliber semi-automatic pistol, with 7.5" barrel, muzzle-brake and barrel weights. Manufactured between 1956 and 1963.

NIB	Exc.	V.G.	Good	Fair	Poor
—	975	750	650	525	375

Model 205

As above, with adjustable target grips. Manufactured between 1956 and 1963.

NIB	Exc.	V.G.	Good	Fair	Poor
—	1000	775	675	575	450

HAMMOND BULLDOG
Connecticut Arms & Mfg. Co.
Naubuc, Connecticut

Hammond Bulldog

A .44 rimfire single-shot spur trigger pistol, with 4" octagonal barrel that pivots to open. Blued, with checkered walnut grips. Manufactured from 1864 to approximately 1867.

NIB	Exc.	V.G.	Good	Fair	Poor
—	775	550	375	250	100

HAMMOND MFG. CO., GRANT
New Haven, Connecticut

Military Automatic Pistol

A .45 ACP caliber semi-automatic pistol, with 6.75" barrel and 8-shot magazine. Blued, with checkered walnut grips. Marked on right of slide "Grant Hammond Mfg. Corp. New Haven, Conn." Left side shows patent dates. Manufactured in 1917. As all known specimens of this pistol exhibit differences, it is believed they were only made as prototypes. Highest serial number known is under 20. TOO RARE TO PRICE.

Courtesy Horst Held

Grant Hammond 7.65mm Pistol

A semi-automatic pistol in 7.65mm caliber. Has a blow-forward action and spur hammer. TOO RARE TO PRICE.

Courtesy James Rankin

HANKINS, WILLIAM
Philadelphia, Pennsylvania

Pocket Revolver

A .26-caliber spur trigger percussion revolver, with 3" octagonal barrel and 5-shot unfluted cylinder. Blued, with walnut grips. Approximately 650 manufactured in 1860 and 1861.

Courtesy Milwaukee Public Museum, Milwaukee, Wisconsin

NIB	Exc.	V.G.	Good	Fair	Poor
—	—	3250	1700	600	200

HANUS, BILL
Newport, Oregon

Bill Hanus Classic

The late Bill Hanus, was a dealer and importer of various European shotguns until his passing in 2012. In the 1980s and 1990s, he imported his own private brand of side-by-side doubles from Ignacio Ugartechea and several other manufacturers in Italy. These guns in 16-, 20-, 28-gauge and .410 bore had double trigger ejectors and English-style stocks.

NIB	Exc.	V.G.	Good	Fair	Poor
2500	2000	1350	900	625	350

HARRINGTON & RICHARDSON, INC.
Madison, North Carolina

One of the oldest manufacturers of firearms in the United States. Original Harrington and Richardson started in 1871 and was in existence until 1986. For all those years, the company was located in Worcester, Massachusetts. After the original company closed, in 1991 a new company, H&R 1871 was formed in Gardner, Massachusetts. In 2000, H&R 1871 was purchased by Marlin Firearms. The assets of Marlin, including H&R 1871 and its subsidiary, New England Firearms (NEF), were bought by Remington in 2007. H&R's corporate office is now located with Remington and Marlin in Madison, North Carolina, while the production facilities are at the former Remington plant in Ilion, New York. New England Firearms brand has been used for marketing some H&R products in recent years. See separate listing under New England Firearms (NEF).

Model No. 1

A .32- or .38-caliber spur-trigger single-action revolver, with 3" octagonal barrel, solid frame, 7- or 5-shot cylinder depending on caliber. Nickel-plated, with checkered rubber bird's-head grips. Barrel marked "Harrington & Richardson Worcester, Mass." Approximately 3,000 manufactured in 1877 and 1878.

NIB	Exc.	V.G.	Good	Fair	Poor
—	300	250	200	125	75

Model No. 1-1/2

A .32-caliber spur-trigger single-action revolver, with 2.5" octagonal barrel and 5-shot cylinder. Nickel-plated, round-butt rubber grips with an "H&R" emblem molded in. Approximately 10,000 manufactured between 1878 and 1883.

NIB	Exc.	V.G.	Good	Fair	Poor
—	300	150	125	75	50

Model No. 2-1/2

As above, with 3.25" barrel and 7-shot cylinder. Approximately 5,000 manufactured between 1878 and 1883.

NIB	Exc.	V.G.	Good	Fair	Poor
—	300	150	125	75	50

Model No. 3-1/2

Similar to Model 2-1/2 except in .38 rimfire caliber, with 3.5" barrel and 5-shot cylinder. Approximately 2,500 manufactured.

NIB	Exc.	V.G.	Good	Fair	Poor
—	300	175	150	100	75

Model No. 4-1/2

A .41 rimfire caliber spur trigger revolver, with 2.5" barrel and 5-shot cylinder. Approximately 1,000 manufactured.

NIB	Exc.	V.G.	Good	Fair	Poor
—	600	400	200	125	90

Model 1880

A .32 or .38 S&W caliber centerfire double-action revolver, with 3" round barrel, solid frame and 5- or 6-shot cylinder depending on caliber. Nickel-plated, with hard rubber grips. Marked "Harrington & Richardson Worchester, Mass." Approximately 4,000 manufactured between 1880 and 1883.

NIB	Exc.	V.G.	Good	Fair	Poor
—	250	200	175	125	90

The American Double-Action

A .32-, .38- or .44-caliber centerfire double-action revolver, with 2.5", 4.5" or 6" round or octagonal barrel, 5- or 6-shot fluted cylinder depending on caliber. Solid frame nickel-plated, with some blue models noted. Grips are hard rubber. Marked "The American Double Action." Some noted are marked "H&R Bulldog". Approximately 850,000 manufactured between 1883 and 1940. **NOTE:** Add 150 percent for .44.

NIB	Exc.	V.G.	Good	Fair	Poor
—	250	125	100	85	65

The Young America Double-Action

A .22 rimfire or .32 S&W caliber centerfire double-action revolver, with 2", 4.5" or 6" round or octagonal barrels. Solid frame and 5- or 7-shot cylinder depending on caliber. Blued or nickel-plated, with hard rubber grips. Marked "Young America Double Action" or "Young America Bulldog". Approximately 1,500,000 manufactured between 1884 and 1941.

NIB	Exc.	V.G.	Good	Fair	Poor
—	200	125	100	85	65

Hunter

A .22-caliber double-action revolver, with 10" octagonal barrel and 9-shot fluted cylinder. Blued, with checkered walnut grips.

Courtesy Mike Stuckslager

NIB	Exc.	V.G.	Good	Fair	Poor
—	400	300	200	150	100

Trapper

As above, with 6" octagonal barrel and 7-shot cylinder. Otherwise similar to Hunter.

Courtesy Mike Stuckslager

NIB	Exc.	V.G.	Good	Fair	Poor
—	300	200	125	100	75

Self-Loader

A 6.35mm or 7.65mm semi-automatic pistol, with 2" or 3.5" barrel, 6- or 8-shot magazine. Similar in outline to Webley. Larger 7.65 model has a grip safety. Blued or nickel-plated, with checkered hard rubber grips that bear the H&R monogram. Slide marked "H&R Self-Loading", with 1907 or 1909 patent dates. Approximately 16,500 manufactured in 6.35mm between 1912 and 1916; 34,500 in 7.65mm between 1916 and 1924. **NOTE:** Add 10 percent for .32.

Courtesy Orvel Reichert

NIB	Exc.	V.G.	Good	Fair	Poor
—	500	400	275	200	125

First Model Hand Ejector

A .32- or .38-caliber centerfire double-action revolver, with 3.25" ribbed round barrel. Version does not feature automatic ejection found on later models. Nickel-plated, with hard rubber grips. Company name marked on barrel. Approximately 6,000 manufactured between 1886 and 1888.

NIB	Exc.	V.G.	Good	Fair	Poor
—	200	150	125	90	65

Model 1 Double-Action Revolver

A .32, .32 Long and .38 S&W caliber double-action revolver, with 3.25" ribbed round barrel and 5- or 6-shot cylinder depending on caliber.

Nickel-plated, with hard rubber grips. Approximately 5,000 manufactured between 1887 and 1889.

NIB	Exc.	V.G.	Good	Fair	Poor
—	175	145	110	80	50

Model 2

Similar to Model 1, with 2.5", 3.25", 4", 5" or 6" barrels. Grips feature H&R target logo. Approximately 1,300,000 manufactured between 1889 and 1940.

NIB	Exc.	V.G.	Good	Fair	Poor
—	125	100	80	65	40

Knife Model

Model 2, with 4" ribbed round barrel having a folding 2.25" double-edged knife mounted under barrel. Blued or nickel-plated. Approximately 2,000 manufactured between 1901 and 1917.

NIB	Exc.	V.G.	Good	Fair	Poor
2000	1500	1000	700	500	150

Model 922 First Issue

A .22-caliber double-action revolver, with 2.5", 4" or 6" barrel. Blued, with checkered walnut grips.

NIB	Exc.	V.G.	Good	Fair	Poor
—	150	125	100	75	50

Target Model

A .22 LR or .22 WRF caliber double-action revolver, with 7-shot cylinder, break-open frame and 6" barrel. Fixed sights. Blued, with checkered walnut grips.

NIB	Exc.	V.G.	Good	Fair	Poor
—	150	125	100	75	50

.22 Special

A .22 LR or .22 WRF double-action break-open revolver, with 6" barrel and 7-shot cylinder. Blued, with checkered walnut grips.

NIB	Exc.	V.G.	Good	Fair	Poor
—	300	200	125	90	65

Expert

As above, with 10" barrel.

NIB	Exc.	V.G.	Good	Fair	Poor
—	400	300	200	100	50

No. 199 Sportsman

A .22-caliber single-action break-open revolver, with 6" barrel, adjustable target sights and 9-shot cylinder. Blued, with checkered walnut grips.

NIB	Exc.	V.G.	Good	Fair	Poor
—	275	200	150	100	75

Ultra Sportsman

As above, but more finely finished. Special wide target hammer and improved action.

NIB	Exc.	V.G.	Good	Fair	Poor
—	325	215	175	125	90

Defender

A .38 S&W caliber double-action break-open revolver, with 4" or 6" barrel and fixed sights. Blued, with plastic grips.

NIB	Exc.	V.G.	Good	Fair	Poor
—	275	200	145	75	50

New Defender

A .22-caliber double-action break-open revolver, with 2" barrel and 9-shot cylinder. Blued, with checkered walnut round-butt grips.

NIB	Exc.	V.G.	Good	Fair	Poor
—	225	200	175	125	90

.22 U.S.R.A./Model 195 Single-Shot Match Target Pistol

Also called Model 195, this pistol underwent nearly constant modifications from its inception in 1928 until production ceased in 1941. Its development was greatly influenced by the United States Revolver Association (USRA), which established certain rules for target pistol shooting. Lack of any H&R-published model chronology for estimated 3,500 guns manufactured, makes model determination by examination complicated; further difficulty is that H&R supplied newly designed parts to owners of older variations, who would then retrofit their pistols with newer triggers, hammers, sights and trigger guards. Extracted from available literature, the parts represent approximately: 14 different stocks and virtually endless custom variations by Walter F. Roper; 5 different trigger guards; 3 different triggers; 2 different hammers; 2 different extractors; 3 barrel lengths (7", 8", 10"); and 3 barrel rib styles. From this array of potential characteristics, at least four distinct variations can be identified.

.22 U.S.R.A./Model 195 Pistol, Variations 1 to 3

NIB	Exc.	V.G.	Good	Fair	Poor
—	2500	1800	1000	600	200

.22 U.S.R.A./Model 195 Pistol, Variation 4

NIB	Exc.	V.G.	Good	Fair	Poor
—	2200	1500	800	325	250

VARIATION 1, PRE-U.S.R.A., 1928-30: Not marked U.S.R.A., and known as "H&R Single-Shot Pistol." There is no finger rest between trigger guard and front grip strap; it was advertised with "sawhandle" shape grip copied from Model 1 or 2 smooth bore H&R Handy-Gun, manufactured with 10" "hourglass" barrel with a deeply undercut rib. These are the first 500 pistols.

VARIATION 2, U.S.R.A. KEYHOLE BARREL, 1930-31: This is standard "early" model marked U.S.R.A., has a finger rest and non-sawhandle grips; however, several grip shapes were offered as options. Grip screw goes from rear of grip into threaded hole in back grip strap.

VARIATION 3, MODIFIED KEYHOLE BARREL, 1931: Modification of Variation 2 to improve rear sight, barrel catch changed, reduced spent cartridge force by replacing cylindrical extractor with less powerful hinged type and hammer cocking spur and finger rest were made wider. The 8" barrel was offered as an option to standard 10" length and number of different grip shapes was increased. This is a transition model between "early" Variation 2 and "final" Variation 4 designs.

VARIATION 4, TAPERED SLABSIDE BARREL, 1931-41: New "truncated teardrop" barrel cross section shape; new standard barrel length of 7", with 10" optional; adjustable trigger; new sear; grip screw location was changed to front of grip; and front sight was adjustable for elevation. Trigger design was changed from curved to straight beveled type with relocated cocking surfaces and number of grip shapes increased further to 13 types. A front sight protector was supplied as standard equipment and luggage style case offered as an option. It appears that Variation 4 was introduced around 1931; 1932 advertisements describe the fully redesigned gun, but picture Variation 2, indicating H&R probably did not re-photograph the new design. Final variation has a special, tight bore .217" in diameter, with bullet seating .03125" (1/32") into rifling and is among the most accurate of single-shot .22-caliber pistols. Model 195/U.S.R.A. was relatively expensive, costing approximately $30 in 1932 and increased to slightly more than $36 by the time production ended in 1941, yet was the least expensive of all single-shot .22 target pistols of quality.

Model 504

A .32 H&R Magnum caliber double-action swing-out cylinder revolver, with 4" or 6" heavy barrel, adjustable sights and 5-shot cylinder. Blued, with either black plastic or walnut grips. Smaller version manufactured with 3" or 4" barrel and round butt.

NIB	Exc.	V.G.	Good	Fair	Poor
—	350	275	150	90	65

Model 532

As above, with a cylinder that has to be removed for loading. Manufactured in 1984 and 1985.

NIB	Exc.	V.G.	Good	Fair	Poor
—	275	175	125	75	50

Model 586

A .32 H&R Magnum caliber double-action revolver, with 4.5", 5.5", 7.5" or 10" barrel, adjustable sights and 5-shot cylinder. Blued, with either black plastic or walnut grips.

NIB	Exc.	V.G.	Good	Fair	Poor
—	325	275	175	150	100

Model 603

A .22 rimfire Magnum caliber double-action revolver, with 6" flat-sided barrel and swing-out 6-shot cylinder. Blued, with smooth walnut grips.

NIB	Exc.	V.G.	Good	Fair	Poor
—	225	165	140	110	85

Model 604

As above, with 6" ribbed heavy barrel.

NIB	Exc.	V.G.	Good	Fair	Poor
—	295	215	175	125	100

Model 622

A .22-caliber solid-frame double-action revolver, with 2.5" or 4" barrel. Blued, with round-butt plastic grips.

NIB	Exc.	V.G.	Good	Fair	Poor
—	150	100	65	50	25

Model 623

As above, but nickel-plated.

NIB	Exc.	V.G.	Good	Fair	Poor
—	165	110	80	60	40

Model 632

As above, in .32 centerfire.

NIB	Exc.	V.G.	Good	Fair	Poor
—	150	90	75	60	30

Model 642

As above, in .22 rimfire Magnum.

NIB	Exc.	V.G.	Good	Fair	Poor
—	150	80	65	50	25

Model 649

Model 622, with 5.5" or 7.5" barrel.

NIB	Exc.	V.G.	Good	Fair	Poor
—	150	125	100	75	50

Model 650

As above, but nickel-plated.

NIB	Exc.	V.G.	Good	Fair	Poor
—	175	150	125	75	50

Model 660

A .22-caliber solid-frame Western-style revolver, with 5.5" barrel and double-action. Blued, with walnut grips. Also known as "Gunfighter".

NIB	Exc.	V.G.	Good	Fair	Poor
—	150	125	100	50	25

Model 666

A .22 or .22 rimfire Magnum caliber double-action revolver, with 6" barrel and 6-shot cylinder. Blued, with plastic grips. Manufactured between 1976 and 1982.

NIB	Exc.	V.G.	Good	Fair	Poor
—	150	125	100	50	25

Model 676

Similar to Model 660. Blued, with case colored frame and walnut grips. Manufactured between 1976 and 1982.

NIB	Exc.	V.G.	Good	Fair	Poor
—	175	150	100	75	50

Model 686

Similar to Model 660 "Gunfighter", with 4.5", 5.5", 7.5", 10" or 12" barrel.

NIB	Exc.	V.G.	Good	Fair	Poor
—	175	150	125	100	75

Model 732

A .32-caliber double-action solid-frame revolver, with swingout cylinder, 2.5" or 4" barrel and 6-shot cylinder. Blued, with black plastic grips. Also known as "Guardsman".

NIB	Exc.	V.G.	Good	Fair	Poor
—	150	125	90	65	45

Model 733

As above, but nickel-plated and 2.5" barrel.

NIB	Exc.	V.G.	Good	Fair	Poor
—	175	150	100	75	50

Model 900

A .22-caliber solid-frame revolver, with removable cylinder, 2.5", 4" or 6" barrel and 9-shot cylinder. Blued, with black plastic grips. Manufactured between 1962 and 1973.

NIB	Exc.	V.G.	Good	Fair	Poor
—	150	125	90	60	40

Model 901

As above, but chrome-plated with white plastic grips. Manufactured in 1962 and 1963 only.

NIB	Exc.	V.G.	Good	Fair	Poor
—	150	125	90	60	40

Model 903

As above, with swing-out cylinder, flat-sided 6" barrel and 9-shot cylinder. Blued, with walnut grips.

NIB	Exc.	V.G.	Good	Fair	Poor
—	150	125	90	75	50

Model 904

As above, with ribbed heavy barrel.

NIB	Exc.	V.G.	Good	Fair	Poor
—	175	150	125	100	50

Model 905

As above, but nickel-plated.

NIB	Exc.	V.G.	Good	Fair	Poor
—	200	175	150	80	65

Model 922 Second Issue

A .22-caliber rimfire solid-frame revolver, with 2.5", 4" or 6" barrel. Blued, with black plastic grips. Manufactured between 1950 and 1982.

NIB	Exc.	V.G.	Good	Fair	Poor
—	150	90	80	60	40

Model 923

As above, but nickel-plated.

NIB	Exc.	V.G.	Good	Fair	Poor
—	160	90	80	60	40

Model 925

A .38 S&W caliber double-action break-open hand ejector revolver, with 2.5" barrel, adjustable sights and 5-shot cylinder. Blued, with one-piece wrap-around grip. Manufactured between 1964 and 1984.

NIB	Exc.	V.G.	Good	Fair	Poor
—	250	175	125	75	50

Model 935

As above, but nickel-plated.

NIB	Exc.	V.G.	Good	Fair	Poor
—	260	200	150	100	50

Model 929

A .22 rimfire solid-frame swing-out revolver, with 2.5", 4" or 6" barrel and 9-shot cylinder. Blued, with plastic grips. Also known as "Sidekick". Manufactured between 1956 and 1985.

NIB	Exc.	V.G.	Good	Fair	Poor
—	225	150	125	65	45

Model 929 Sidekick—New Model

Reintroduced in 1996, this single-/double-action revolver chambered for .22 Short, Long or LR cartridges. Cylinder holds 9 rounds. Sold with lockable storage case, nylon holster, gun oil and grease samples. Weight about 30 oz. Made from 1996 - 1999. Discontinued.

NIB	Exc.	V.G.	Good	Fair	Poor
250	175	150	100	75	50

Model 929 Sidekick Trapper Edition

As above, with gray laminate grips and special "NTA" Trapper Edition roll stamp on barrel. Made in 1996.

NIB	Exc.	V.G.	Good	Fair	Poor
275	175	150	100	75	50

Model 930

As above, but nickel-plated. Not available with 6" barrel.

NIB	Exc.	V.G.	Good	Fair	Poor
—	250	150	125	65	45

Model 939 Ultra Sidekick

As above, with ventilated rib, flat sided 6" barrel, adjustable sights, thumb rest grips. Features a safety device whereby pistol could not be fired unless it was unlocked by a furnished key. Manufactured between 1958 and 1982.

NIB	Exc.	V.G.	Good	Fair	Poor
—	225	200	150	75	50

Model 939 Premier

Similar to above models, but fitted with 6" barrel, sighting rib, adjustable rear sight, hard wood grips, high polished blued finish. Weight about 36 oz. Made from 1995 - 1999.

NIB	Exc.	V.G.	Good	Fair	Poor
250	225	200	125	75	50

Model 940

Round-barreled version of above.

NIB	Exc.	V.G.	Good	Fair	Poor
—	225	200	125	75	50

Model 949

A .22-caliber double-action Western-type revolver, with 5.5" barrel, ejector rod, 9-shot gate-loaded cylinder and adjustable sights. Blued, with walnut grips. Manufactured between 1960 and 1985.

NIB	Exc.	V.G.	Good	Fair	Poor
—	200	175	150	75	50

Model 949 Western

Similar to above model. This revolver is offered with choice of 5.5" or 7.5" barrel, adjustable rear sight, walnut grips. Case colored frame and backstrap, with blued cylinder and barrel. Weight about 36 oz.

NIB	Exc.	V.G.	Good	Fair	Poor
250	200	150	100	75	50

Model 950

As above, but nickel-plated.

NIB	Exc.	V.G.	Good	Fair	Poor
—	250	175	125	75	50

Model 976

As above, with case-hardened frame.

NIB	Exc.	V.G.	Good	Fair	Poor
—	200	150	100	75	50

Model 999 Sportsman

A .22-caliber rimfire double-action break-open self ejecting revolver, with 4" or 6" barrel ventilated rib barrel and windage adjustable sights. Blued, with walnut grips. Weight about: 30 oz. 4" barrel; 34 oz. 6" barrel.

NIB	Exc.	V.G.	Good	Fair	Poor
500	425	350	295	175	100

Model 999 Engraved

As above, but engraved.

NIB	Exc.	V.G.	Good	Fair	Poor
550	450	375	300	200	125

Amtec 2000

German-designed (Erma) and American-built double-action revolver. Introduced in 1996. Offered in 2" or 3" barrel. Chambered for .38 Special cartridge. Pachmayr composition grips. Cylinder holds 5 rounds. Weight about 25 oz. Discontinued.

NIB	Exc.	V.G.	Good	Fair	Poor
250	200	200	150	75	50

SHOTGUNS

Hammerless Double

A 10- or 12-gauge Anson & Deeley hammerless boxlock double-barrel shotgun, with 28", 30" or 32" Damascus barrels in various choke combinations, double triggers and extractors. Engraved, case-hardened and walnut stock. Four grades were available. They differ in amount of engraving and quality of materials and workmanship utilized. Approximately 3,500 manufactured between 1882 and 1885.

D Grade

NIB	Exc.	V.G.	Good	Fair	Poor
—	650	550	425	300	175

C Grade

NIB	Exc.	V.G.	Good	Fair	Poor
—	750	650	500	400	275

B Grade

NIB	Exc.	V.G.	Good	Fair	Poor
—	900	750	600	500	350

A Grade

NIB	Exc.	V.G.	Good	Fair	Poor
—	2000	1750	1500	1000	550

Harrich No. 1

A 12-gauge boxlock single-barrel shotgun, with 32" or 34" ventilated rib, full-choke barrel and automatic ejector. Engraved, blued with checkered walnut stock. Imported between 1971 and 1975.

NIB	Exc.	V.G.	Good	Fair	Poor
—	1750	1500	1150	850	650

Single-Barrel Shotguns

H&R manufactured a series of single-barrel break-open shotguns, between 1908 and 1942. Chambered for various gauges, barrel lengths and chokes. Finishes were blued with walnut stocks. Little collector interest in these guns. If in sound condition are desirable as shooters only. They are Models 3, 5, 6, 7, 8, 9, as well as hinged-frame folding design.

NIB	Exc.	V.G.	Good	Fair	Poor
—	125	100	85	65	40

Turkey Mag

Single-shot break-open side release gun chambered for 12-gauge 3.5" shell, with screw-in Full choke. Hardwood stock has Mossy Oak finish. Barrel length 24", with bead front sight. Weight about 6 lbs.

NIB	Exc.	V.G.	Good	Fair	Poor
175	150	125	100	75	50

Youth Turkey Gun

Similar in appearance to Turkey Mag, but on a smaller scale. Chambered for 20-gauge 3" shell, with 22" barrel. Weight about 5.5 lbs.

NIB	Exc.	V.G.	Good	Fair	Poor
165	140	115	90	60	40

Topper (New Production)

Break-open side release single-shot, available in 12-, 20-gauge and .410 bore. The 12-gauge offered with 28" barrel while others are fitted with 26" barrel. Blued finish, with hardwood stock in black finish and semi-pistol grip. Weight about 6 lbs.

NIB	Exc.	V.G.	Good	Fair	Poor
150	100	80	60	45	30

Topper Deluxe

NIB	Exc.	V.G.	Good	Fair	Poor
170	125	90	70	50	40

Topper Jr. in 20 Gauge and .410 Bore Only

NIB	Exc.	V.G.	Good	Fair	Poor
150	100	80	60	45	30

Topper Jr. Classic

Similar to Topper Jr. Features black walnut stock, with butt checkering, white line spacer and black recoil pad. Weight about 7.5 lbs.

NIB	Exc.	V.G.	Good	Fair	Poor
150	100	80	60	45	30

Topper Deluxe Slug

This 12-gauge single-shot has 24" fully rifled barrel, with built-in compensator.

NIB	Exc.	V.G.	Good	Fair	Poor
150	115	90	70	50	40

Topper Deluxe Classic

Introduced in 2004. This 12-gauge 3" single-shot gun fitted with 28" ventilated rib barrel and screw-in modified choke. American black walnut stock, with pistol-grip and ventilated recoil pad. Barrel has black finish while receiver nickel finish. Weight about 5.5 lbs. In 2005, offered in 20-gauge.

NIB	Exc.	V.G.	Good	Fair	Poor
245	200	150	100	75	50

Topper Trap Gun

Similar to above, with select checkered walnut stock, fore-end with fluted comb and full pistol-grip; 30" barrel with two white beads and screw-in chokes (Improved Modified Extended included); deluxe Pachmayr trap recoil pad.

NIB	Exc.	V.G.	Good	Fair	Poor
350	275	200	165	145	75

Tamer

Single-shot gun chambered for .410 shell with 3" chamber. Fitted with 19.5" barrel and matte nickel finish. Stock is matte black polymer. Weight about 6 lbs.

NIB	Exc.	V.G.	Good	Fair	Poor
160	125	90	60	45	30

Ultra Slug Hunter

Introduced in 1995. Uses heavy 10-gauge action fitted with 24" 12-gauge barrel. Weight about 8 lbs.

NIB	Exc.	V.G.	Good	Fair	Poor
150	115	90	70	50	40

Ultra Slug Hunter Deluxe 20 Gauge

Introduced in 1997. Chambered for 20-gauge shells. Features hand checkered camo laminated wood stock. Fitted with fully rifled heavy slug barrel 24" long.

NIB	Exc.	V.G.	Good	Fair	Poor
315	250	200	150	100	75

Ultra Slug Hunter Deluxe 12 Gauge

As above, in 12-gauge with 3" chamber.

NIB	Exc.	V.G.	Good	Fair	Poor
315	250	200	150	100	75

Ultra Slug Youth Model

As above chambered for 20-gauge shell. Weight about 7 lbs.

NIB	Exc.	V.G.	Good	Fair	Poor
260	200	150	100	60	45

Ultra Slug Hunter Bull Barrel

As above chambered for 20-gauge.

NIB	Exc.	V.G.	Good	Fair	Poor
150	100	80	60	45	30

Ultra Slug Hunter Thumbhole Stock

Similar to above, with laminated thumbhole stock and blued or stainless steel finish. Weight 8.5 lbs. **NOTE:** Add 10 percent for stainless.

NIB	Exc.	V.G.	Good	Fair	Poor
—	150	125	100	75	50

Model 401

As above, with variable choke device. Manufactured between 1956 and 1963.

NIB	Exc.	V.G.	Good	Fair	Poor
—	175	150	125	90	65

Model 402

As above, in a .410 bore. Manufactured between 1959 and 1967.

NIB	Exc.	V.G.	Good	Fair	Poor
—	175	150	125	90	65

Model 440

A 12-, 16- or 20-gauge slide-action shotgun, with 26", 28" or 30" barrel in various chokes. Blued, with hardwood stock. Manufactured between 1968 and 1973.

NIB	Exc.	V.G.	Good	Fair	Poor
—	150	125	100	75	50

Model 442

As above, with ventilated rib barrel and checkered stock. Manufactured between 1969 and 1973.

NIB	Exc.	V.G.	Good	Fair	Poor
—	175	150	125	90	65

Model 403

A .410 bore semi-automatic shotgun, with 26" Full choke barrel. Blued, with hardwood stock. Manufactured in 1964.

NIB	Exc.	V.G.	Good	Fair	Poor
—	300	250	175	100	75

Model 404

A 12-, 20-gauge or .410 bore boxlock double-barrel shotgun, with 26" or 28" barrels, double triggers and extractors. Blued, with walnut stock. Manufactured by Rossi in Brazil and imported between 1969 and 1972.

NIB	Exc.	V.G.	Good	Fair	Poor
—	175	150	125	90	65

Pardner Pump Field Gun Full-Dip Camo

Pump-action shotgun, with steel receiver, double action bars, cross-bolt safety, easy take-down. 28" barrel with 3" chamber and ventilated rib, screw-in Modified choke tube. Synthetic stock, with ventilated recoil pad and grooved fore-end. Realtree APG-HDTM full camo dip finish. Overall length 48.125"; weight 7.5 lbs. Also available in several variations, with hardwood or black synthetic stock. Suggested retail for full camo version $278.

Topper (Old Production)

Single-shot break-open shotgun, chambered for various gauges, barrel lengths, chokes. Blued, with hardwood stock. Introduced in 1946.

NIB	Exc.	V.G.	Good	Fair	Poor
—	145	95	75	60	40

Model 088

An external hammer single-shot break-open shotgun chambered for all gauges. Various barrel lengths, chokes and an automatic ejector. Blued, with case colored frame and hardwood stock.

NIB	Exc.	V.G.	Good	Fair	Poor
—	80	65	50	40	30

Model 099

As above, but matte electroless nickel-plated.

NIB	Exc.	V.G.	Good	Fair	Poor
—	110	95	75	60	40

Model 162

A 12- or 20-gauge boxlock single-shot, with 24" barrel and rifle sights.

NIB	Exc.	V.G.	Good	Fair	Poor
—	125	100	80	65	45

Model 176

A 10-gauge 3.5" Magnum caliber boxlock single-barrel shotgun, with heavyweight 36" barrel and Full choke. Manufactured between 1977 and 1985.

NIB	Exc.	V.G.	Good	Fair	Poor
—	225	175	115	75	45

Model 400

A 12-, 16- or 20-gauge slide-action shotgun, with 28" Full choke barrel. Blued, with hardwood stock. Manufactured between 1955 and 1967.

Excell

Introduced in 2005, this semi-automatic shotgun chambered for 12-gauge 3" shell. Fitted with 28" ventilated rib barrel and choke tubes. Checkered black synthetic stock. Magazine capacity 5 rounds. Weight about 7 lbs.

NIB	Exc.	V.G.	Good	Fair	Poor
400	365	295	200	150	100

Excell Waterfowl

As above, with Realtree Advantage Wetlands camo finish. Introduced in 2005.

NIB	Exc.	V.G.	Good	Fair	Poor
425	375	325	225	175	125

Excell Turkey

Fitted with 22" barrel, choke tubes and fiber optic front sight. Realtree Advantage Hardwoods camo finish. Weight 7 lbs. Introduced in 2005.

NIB	Exc.	V.G.	Good	Fair	Poor
425	375	325	225	175	125

Excell Combo

Has black synthetic stock and two barrels: 28" ventilated rib with choke tubes and 24" rifled barrel. Weight about 7 lbs. depending on barrel length. Introduced in 2005.

NIB	Exc.	V.G.	Good	Fair	Poor
450	395	350	250	195	145

Pinnacle

Over/under gun chambered for 12- or 20-gauge with 3" chambers. Barrel length for 12-gauge 28"; 20-gauge 26"; both with ventilated ribs and choke tubes. Checkered walnut stock, with recoil pad and pistol-grip. Weight about: 6.75 lbs. 12-gauge; 6.25 lbs. 20-gauge. Introduced in 2005.

NIB	Exc.	V.G.	Good	Fair	Poor
700	600	500	325	175	125

Model 1212

A 12-gauge over/under boxlock shotgun, with 28" ventilated rib barrels. Blued, with walnut stock. Also available with 30" barrels having 3" chambers. Manufactured by Lanber Arms of Spain and imported after 1976.

NIB	Exc.	V.G.	Good	Fair	Poor
—	450	375	325	200	125

Long Tom Classic

Introduced in 1996, this limited edition single-barrel shotgun features case-hardened frame, with 32" Full choked barrel. Stock hand-checkered black walnut, with crescent buttplate. Chambered for 12-gauge. Weight about 7.5 lbs.

NIB	Exc.	V.G.	Good	Fair	Poor
425	395	325	250	175	125

H&R/NEF Handi-Rifle/Slug Gun Combo

Single-shot break-open rifle/shotgun combos (one rifle barrel, one shotgun barrel per combo) chambered in .44 Magnum/12-gauge rifled slug and .357 Magnum/20-gauge rifled slug. Rifle barrels are not interchangeable; shotgun barrels are interchangeable. Stock black matte high-density polymer, with sling swivel studs, molded checkering and recoil pad. Rifle barrel 22" for both calibers; shotgun barrels 28" (12-gauge) and 24" (20-gauge) fully rifled. No iron sights; scope rail included. Overall length 38" (both rifle chamberings); 42" (12-gauge); 40" (20-gauge). Weight 7 - 8 lbs.

NIB	Exc.	V.G.	Good	Fair	Poor
—	300	250	175	100	75

RIFLES

Model 058

A 20-gauge .22 Hornet, .30-30, .357 Magnum or .44 Magnum caliber rifle/shotgun outfit, with interchangeable barrels. Blued, with hardwood stock.

NIB	Exc.	V.G.	Good	Fair	Poor
—	200	150	100	75	50

Model 258

As above, with matte electroless nickel-plate finish.

NIB	Exc.	V.G.	Good	Fair	Poor
—	225	175	125	100	75

Reising Model 60

A .45 ACP caliber semi-automatic rifle, with 18.25" barrel and 12- or 20-round detachable magazine. Blued, with walnut stock. Operates on retarded blowback system and developed to be used as police weapon. Manufactured between 1944 and 1946.

Courtesy Richard M. Kumor, Sr.

NIB	Exc.	V.G.	Good	Fair	Poor
—	2000	1600	1000	450	250

Model 65 Military (Model 58C)

A .22 LR caliber semi-automatic rifle, with 23" barrel and Redfield peep sights. Blued, with walnut stock. Manufactured between 1944 and 1956. **NOTE:** Add 100 percent if USMC marked.

Courtesy Richard M. Kumor, Sr.

NIB	Exc.	V.G.	Good	Fair	Poor
—	500	300	200	125	90

Model 150

A .22 LR caliber semi-automatic rifle, with 20" barrel and 5-shot magazine. Blued, with walnut stock. Manufactured between 1949 and 1953.

NIB	Exc.	V.G.	Good	Fair	Poor
—	100	80	60	45	30

Model 155 (Shikari)

Single-shot break-open rifle chambered for .44 Magnum or .45-70 cartridge. Has 20" barrel with fixed sights. Finish blued, with full-length walnut stock. Introduced in 1972.

NIB	Exc.	V.G.	Good	Fair	Poor
—	375	300	225	150	100

Model 157

As above in .22 Magnum, .22 Hornet and .30-30 caliber.

NIB	Exc.	V.G.	Good	Fair	Poor
—	350	275	200	125	75

Model 158

A .357 or .44 Magnum single-shot side lever rifle, with 22" barrel. Blued case-hardened, with walnut stock. Available with interchangeable 26" 20-gauge barrel. Manufactured prior to 1986.

NIB	Exc.	V.G.	Good	Fair	Poor
—	350	275	200	125	75

Model 300 Ultra

A .22-250 up to .300 Winchester Magnum caliber bolt-action rifle, with 22" or 24" barrel without sights. High polished blue and checkered walnut stock. Manufactured between 1965 and 1978.

NIB	Exc.	V.G.	Good	Fair	Poor
—	450	400	350	275	175

Model 301 Carbine

As above, with 18" barrel and full-length Mannlicher-style stock.

NIB	Exc.	V.G.	Good	Fair	Poor
—	450	400	350	275	175

Model 317 Ultra Wildcat

A .17 Rem., .17-223, .222 Rem. and .223 Rem. caliber short Sako bolt-action rifle, with 20" barrel furnished without sights. Blued, with checkered walnut stock. Manufactured between 1968 and 1976.

NIB	Exc.	V.G.	Good	Fair	Poor
—	550	400	350	275	175

HANDI-RIFLE SERIES

Break-action single-shot rifle, that's been around in one form or another since 1960s. Side lever release, automatic ejection, hardwood stock, transfer bar passive safety. Available in nearly every conceivable rimfire and centerfire chambering (except the biggest centerfires) and now made under auspices of Marlin. Rifle is as good a bargain today as it ever was. Some newer models feature factory scopes, bull barrels, thumbhole stocks and other niceties, but are still Handi-Rifles. Value generally under $300 even in New or Excellent condition, sometimes remarkably under.

H&R Handi-Rifle (current production)

Single-shot rifle offered in a wide range of calibers from .204 Ruger to .500 S&W. Barrel lengths from 20" to 26", with walnut-finished hardwood or synthetic stock and fore-end. **NOTE:** Add $25 for thumbhole stock.

NIB	Exc.	V.G.	Good	Fair	Poor
265	225	175	150	125	75

H&R Survivor

Variation of Handi-Rifle in .223 Rem., .308 Win., or .45 Colt/.410 shotshell combo. Black polymer thumbhole stock, with pistol-grip, accessory rail, sling and swivels. Storage compartment in buttstock and fore-end.

NIB	Exc.	V.G.	Good	Fair	Poor
290	250	200	175	150	100

Synthetic

Basic Handi-Rifle design, with synthetic buttstock and fore-end (either grooved or beavertail). Available with iron sights or Picatinny rail for mounting optics.

NIB	Exc.	V.G.	Good	Fair	Poor
275	200	175	150	100	50

Stainless

Similar to above, with stainless barrel. Chambered in .223, .270 or .30-06.

NIB	Exc.	V.G.	Good	Fair	Poor
295	225	200	175	115	75

Synthetic Handi-Rifle/Slug Gun Combo

Similar to above, with extra slug barrel. Available in .44 Magnum/12-gauge and .357 Magnum/20-gauge. Introduced in 2008.

NIB	Exc.	V.G.	Good	Fair	Poor
—	325	300	225	175	100

Superlite Compact

Similar to Synthetic Handi-Rifle. Weight only 5.5 lbs. Chambered in .223 and .243. Available with optional scope.

NIB	Exc.	V.G.	Good	Fair	Poor
295	225	200	175	115	75

Ultra Varmint Rifle

Single-shot rifle chambered for .223 Rem. or .22-250 cartridge. Fitted with 22" heavy barrel. Stock hand checkered curly maple (older models) or laminated (newer models), with Monte Carlo cheekpiece. Comes with Picatinny rail for mounting optics. Weight about 7.5 lbs.

NIB	Exc.	V.G.	Good	Fair	Poor
350	295	175	125	75	50

Ultra Varmint Thumbhole

Similar to above, with laminated thumbhole stock.

NIB	Exc.	V.G.	Good	Fair	Poor
375	325	200	150	100	75

Stainless Steel Ultra Varmint Thumbhole

Similar to above, with stainless steel barrel and matte nickel receiver.

NIB	Exc.	V.G.	Good	Fair	Poor
375	325	200	150	100	75

Ultra Varmint Fluted

Introduced in 2005. Chambered for .204 Ruger, .22-250 or .223 Rem. cartridge. Fitted with 24" fluted barrel with no sights. Stock is black synthetic, with vertical adjustable knob, recoil pad and adjustable bipod mount. Weight about 7 lbs.

NIB	Exc.	V.G.	Good	Fair	Poor
350	295	175	125	75	50

Model 317P

As above, but more finely finished. Manufactured between 1968 and 1976.

NIB	Exc.	V.G.	Good	Fair	Poor
—	500	475	425	375	250

Ultra Rifle—Hunting

Single-shot chambered for .25-06, .308 Win. and .357 Rem. Max. The .25-06 has 26" barrel; other two fitted with 22" barrels. Cinnamon laminated stock standard. Weight about 7 lbs. In 2001 .450 Marlin cartridge was added.

NIB	Exc.	V.G.	Good	Fair	Poor
275	200	175	150	100	50

Harrington & Richardson/New England Firearms Stainless Ultra Hunter with Thumbhole Stock

Single-shot break-open rifle chambered in .45-70 Government. 24" stainless steel barrel and receiver with scope mount rail; hammer extension; cinnamon laminate thumbhole stock. Overall length 40"; weight 8 lbs.

NIB	Exc.	V.G.	Good	Fair	Poor
375	325	200	150	100	75

Ultra Rifle—Varmint

Same as above, chambered for .223 Rem. with 22" barrel. Laminated stock, with checkered pistol-grip.

NIB	Exc.	V.G.	Good	Fair	Poor
375	325	200	150	100	75

Ultra .22 Magnum Rifle

Same as above, chambered for .22 Win. Magnum. Introduced in 2001.

NIB	Exc.	V.G.	Good	Fair	Poor
295	225	200	175	115	75

Ultra Rifle—Comp

Introduced in 1997, this single-shot rifle features an integral muzzlebrake on barrel end. Available in .270 Win. and .30-06 calibers, with 24" barrels. Camo laminated stock.

NIB	Exc.	V.G.	Good	Fair	Poor
295	225	200	175	115	75

Ultra Rifle Rocky Mountain Elk Foundation Commemorative

Limited edition single rifle chambered for .35 Whelen cartridge. Selected laminated stock with Monte Carlo. Barrel length 26".

NIB	Exc.	V.G.	Good	Fair	Poor
—	450	400	350	275	175

Sportster .17 HMR

A .17 HMR version of Handi-Rifle, with black polymer Monte Carlo stock and Picatinny rail for moutning optics. Overall length 38.25".

NIB	Exc.	V.G.	Good	Fair	Poor
—	250	200	150	100	50

Sportster

A .22 LR or .22 WMR version of Handi-Rifle, with black polymer stock, fluted fore-end and iron sights. Overall length 36.25".

NIB	Exc.	V.G.	Good	Fair	Poor
—	175	150	100	75	50

Sportster Compact

Similar to above, in .22 LR only and 2" shorter length of pull.

NIB	Exc.	V.G.	Good	Fair	Poor
—	150	125	100	75	50

Buffalo Classic

Rifle first produced in 1995. Chambered for .45-70 and .38-55 cartridges. Barrel length 32" with no sights, but dovetail front, drilled and tapped rear. Hand checkered walnut stock, with case colored crescent steel buttplate. Weight about 8 lbs. Since its introduction in 1995, about 2,000 guns produced. Factory anticipates about 1,000 rifles being built each year.

NIB	Exc.	V.G.	Good	Fair	Poor
375	315	225	175	125	50

Wesson & Harrington Brand 125th Anniversary Rifle

Introduced in 1996. Commemorates 125th Anniversary of partnership. Special rifle chambered for .45-70 Government cartridge. Receiver hand engraved. Barrel length 32". Stock American black walnut, with crescent steel butt.

NIB	Exc.	V.G.	Good	Fair	Poor
395	325	250	200	150	75

Ultra Rifle Whitetails Unlimited 1997 Commemorative Edition

Introduced in 1997. Chambered for .45-70 Govt. cartridge. Features hand checkered black walnut stock. Special laser engraving on action and pewter finished medallion in-letted into stock. Barrel length 22".

NIB	Exc.	V.G.	Good	Fair	Poor
325	275	225	175	125	75

CR Carbine

Single-shot rifle based on Handi-Rifle design. Two-piece checkered walnut stock, with schnabel fore-end. Marble front and rear sights, Crescent steel buttplate. Chambered in .45 Colt. Introduced in 2007.

NIB	Exc.	V.G.	Good	Fair	Poor
375	315	225	150	100	50

Model 333

Model 300 in 7mm Magnum caliber. Manufactured in 1974.

NIB	Exc.	V.G.	Good	Fair	Poor
—	250	200	175	125	100

Model 340

A .243 to .308 Winchester caliber bolt-action rifle, with 22" barrel and 5-shot magazine. Blued, with checkered walnut stock.

NIB	Exc.	V.G.	Good	Fair	Poor
—	400	350	300	225	150

Model 360 Ultra Automatic

A .243 Win. and .308 Win. caliber semi-automatic rifle, with 22" barrel, adjustable sights and 3-shot detachable magazine. Blued, with checkered walnut stock. Manufactured between 1965 and 1978.

NIB	Exc.	V.G.	Good	Fair	Poor
—	425	375	275	195	100

Model 451 Medalist

A .22 LR caliber bolt-action rifle, with 26" barrel, open sights and 5-shot detachable magazine. Blued, with walnut stock. Manufactured between 1948 and 1961.

NIB	Exc.	V.G.	Good	Fair	Poor
—	175	150	125	100	75

Model 700

A .22 rimfire Magnum caliber semi-automatic rifle, with 22" barrel, adjustable sights and 5-round detachable magazine. Blued, with checkered walnut stock. Manufactured between 1977 and 1985.

NIB	Exc.	V.G.	Good	Fair	Poor
—	225	200	150	125	85

Model 700 DL

As above, with checkered walnut stock and 4X scope. Manufactured until 1985.

NIB	Exc.	V.G.	Good	Fair	Poor
—	300	250	200	150	100

Model 750

A .22 LR bolt-action single-shot rifle, with 22" barrel, sights and short stock. Blued, with hardwood stock.

NIB	Exc.	V.G.	Good	Fair	Poor
—	100	80	60	45	25

Model 865

A .22 LR caliber bolt-action rifle, with 22" barrel, open sights and 5-shot magazine. Blued, with hardwood stock.

NIB	Exc.	V.G.	Good	Fair	Poor
—	100	80	60	45	25

Model 5200

A .22 LR caliber bolt-action single-shot rifle, with 28" heavy barrel without sights and adjustable trigger. Blued, with target-type walnut stock.

NIB	Exc.	V.G.	Good	Fair	Poor
—	400	350	300	225	125

Model 5200 Sporter

A .22 LR caliber bolt-action rifle, with 24" barrel, adjustable sights and 5-shot magazine. Blued, with walnut stock. Not manufactured after 1983.

NIB	Exc.	V.G.	Good	Fair	Poor
—	400	350	300	225	125

100th Anniversary Officer's Model

Commemorative replica of Officer's Model 1873 Trapdoor Springfield Rifle, with 26" barrel. Engraved and anniversary plaque mounted on stock. Blued, with case colored receiver and pewter fore-end tip. There were 10,000 manufactured in 1971. As with all commemorative's, this model most desirable when NIB with all supplied material.

NIB	Exc.	V.G.	Good	Fair	Poor
850	695	500	375	250	175

Custer Memorial Issue

Limited production issue commemorating George Armstrong Custer's Battle of Little Bighorn. Heavily engraved and gold inlaid, with high-grade checkered walnut stock. Furnished in mahogany display case, that included two books dealing with the subject. Two versions produced: Officer's Model, of which 25 were issued commemorating 25 officers that fell with Custer; another version commemorating 243 enlisted men who lost their lives at Little Bighorn. As with all commemorative's to be collectible, they must be NIB with all furnished material.

Officer's Model

25 manufactured.

NIB	Exc.	V.G.	Good	Fair	Poor
4000	3000	2000	1200	500	200

Enlisted Men's Model

243 manufactured.

NIB	Exc.	V.G.	Good	Fair	Poor
2000	1500	1000	400	250	150

Model 171

Reproduction of Model 1873 Trapdoor Springfield Carbine, with 22" barrel. Blued, with case colored receiver and walnut stock.

NIB	Exc.	V.G.	Good	Fair	Poor
—	500	450	300	200	125

Model 171-DL

As above, but more finely finished.

NIB	Exc.	V.G.	Good	Fair	Poor
—	550	500	325	250	175

Model 174

Plain copy of Springfield Model 1873 Carbine in .45-70 caliber, with 22" barrel. Manufactured in 1972.

NIB	Exc.	V.G.	Good	Fair	Poor
—	525	400	325	250	175

Model 178

Copy of Springfield Model 1873 rifle, with 32" barrel. Manufactured from 1973 to 1984.

NIB	Exc.	V.G.	Good	Fair	Poor
—	525	400	325	250	175

HARRIS GUNWORKS
Phoenix, Arizona

There are a wide range of extra costs options for all Harris Gunworks models, that in many cases will dramatically affect price.

National Match Rifle

Introduced in 19809. Features bolt-action rifle chambered for 7mm-08 Rem. or .308 Win., with 5-round magazine. Fitted with 24" stainless steel match grade barrel, with Canjar trigger. Stock is fiberglass, with adjustable buttplate. Weight about 11 lbs.

NIB	Exc.	V.G.	Good	Fair	Poor
3500	2750	1750	950	600	300

Model 86 Sniper Rifle

Chambered for .308, .30-06, .300 Win. Magnum, with 24" heavy match grade barrel. Stock is a special design McHale fiberglass, with textured grip and forearm. Fitted with recoil pad. Supplied with bipod. Weight about 11.25 lbs. **NOTE:** Add $100 for take-down model.

NIB	Exc.	V.G.	Good	Fair	Poor
2700	2100	1600	1000	600	350

Model 87 Series

Single-shot rifles chambered for .50 BMG. Fitted with 29" barrel and muzzle-brake. Fiberglass stock. Introduced in 1987. Weight about 21.5 lbs. **NOTE:** Add $600 for Model 87R 5-shot repeater; $400 for Model 87 5-shot repeater; $300 for Model 92 Bullpup.

NIB	Exc.	V.G.	Good	Fair	Poor
6000	4750	3000	2000	1000	500

Model 88

Bolt-action .50 BMG rifles offered in two different configurations. First variation: fitted with 20" carbon graphite barrel, with add-on recoil arrestor and black teflon finish; second variation: fitted with 16.5" stainless steel barrel, with integral recoil arrestor. Both rifles weigh about 14 lbs. Titanium action available for further weight reduction.

NIB	Exc.	V.G.	Good	Fair	Poor
6000	4750	3000	2000	1000	500

Model 89 Sniper Rifle

Bolt-action rifle chambered for .308 cartridge. Fitted with 28" barrel. Supplied with bipod. Stock is fiberglass, with adjustable length of pull and fitted with recoil pad. Weight about 15.25 lbs.

NIB	Exc.	V.G.	Good	Fair	Poor
2700	2100	1600	1000	600	350

Model 93

Bolt-action .50 BMG rifle, with folding hinge stock assembly. Furnished with 10- or 20-round magazine. Barrel length 29". Weight about 21 lbs.

Model 93 folding model

NIB	Exc.	V.G.	Good	Fair	Poor
6000	4750	3000	2000	1000	500

Model 95

Lightweight variation of .50 BMG models featuring Titanium and graphite. Supplied with bipod. Barrel length 29". Weight about 18 lbs.

NIB	Exc.	V.G.	Good	Fair	Poor
6000	4750	3000	2000	1000	500

Model 96

Gas-operated semi-automatic .50 BMG sniper rifle. Barrel length 29". Detachable 5-round magazine. Weight about 25 lbs.

NIB	Exc.	V.G.	Good	Fair	Poor
7500	6500	4000	2500	1500	750

Long Range Rifle

Chambered for a variety of cartridges such as .300 Win. Magnum, 7mm Rem. Magnum, .300 Phoenix, .338 Lapua. Single-shot rifle fitted with 26" match grade stainless steel barrel. Fiberglass stock, with adjustable buttplate and cheekpiece. Weight about 14 lbs.

NIB	Exc.	V.G.	Good	Fair	Poor
3900	2850	1500	1000	700	350

Target/Benchrest Rifle

Offered in .243, .308, 6mm BR, 6mm PPC and 6mm Rem. Custom built for customer. Available in both left-/right-hand. Weight about 11 lbs.

NIB	Exc.	V.G.	Good	Fair	Poor
3500	2750	1750	950	600	300

Antietam Sharps Rifle

Replica of Sharps Model 1874 sidehammer, introduced in 1994. Chambered for .40-65 or .45-70. Choice of 30" or 32" octagon or round barrel. Stock fancy walnut. Either straight-/pistol-grip or Creedmoor, with schnabel forearm. Many optional sights offered. Weight about 11.25 lbs.

NIB	Exc.	V.G.	Good	Fair	Poor
2600	1950	1200	800	450	200

Signature Classic Sporter

Left-/right-handed bolt-action model, introduced in 1987. Choice of calibers from .22-250 to .375 H&H. Barrel lengths 22", 24" or 26" depending on caliber. Choice of fiberglass stocks in green, beige, brown or black. Wood stock optional. Weight about 7 lbs. for short action calibers.

NIB	Exc.	V.G.	Good	Fair	Poor
3150	2550	1500	1150	500	250

Signature Classic Stainless Sporter

Same as above, with barrel and action made from stainless steel. A .416 Rem. Magnum available in this variation. Available with interchangeable barrels. **NOTE:** Add $600 for interchangeable barrels.

NIB	Exc.	V.G.	Good	Fair	Poor
3200	2650	1600	1250	600	300

Signature Super Varminter

Similar to Classic Sporter, except fitted with a heavy contoured barrel, adjustable trigger and special hand-bedded fiberglass stock. Chambered for .223, .22-250, .220 Swift, .243, 6mm Rem., .25-06, 7mm-08, 7mm BR, .308, .350 Rem. Introduced in 1989.

NIB	Exc.	V.G.	Good	Fair	Poor
2900	2250	1600	1050	700	350

Signature Alaskan

Similar to Classic Sporter, except fitted with match grade barrel and single leaf rear sight. Nickel finish. Walnut Monte Carlo stock, with cheekpiece and palm swell grip. Chambered for .270 to .375 H&H. Introduced in 1989.

NIB	Exc.	V.G.	Good	Fair	Poor
3950	3200	2200	1500	700	350

Signature Titanium Mountain Rifle

Similar to Classic Sporter, except action is made of titanium alloy and barrel of chrome-moly steel. Stock is graphite reinforced fiberglass. Chambered for .270 to .300 Win. Magnum. Weight about 5.5 lbs. Introduced in 1989. **NOTE:** Add $400 for graphite steel barrel.

NIB	Exc.	V.G.	Good	Fair	Poor
3500	2750	1750	950	600	300

Sportsman 97

Bolt-action rifle chambered for a variety of calibers from .270 Win. to .338 Win. Stock is fancy grade walnut, Bastogne or English. Talon action is fitted.

NIB	Exc.	V.G.	Good	Fair	Poor
2900	2250	1600	1050	700	350

Talon Safari Rifle

Bolt-action rifle chambered for 16 different calibers from .300 Win. Magnum to .460 Weatherby Magnum. Finish is matte black, with fiberglass Safari stock. Weight between 9 and 10 lbs. depending on caliber.

NIB	Exc.	V.G.	Good	Fair	Poor
4200	3350	2200	1600	1200	600

Talon Sporter Rifle

Bolt-action rifle, introduced in 1991. Uses a pre-64 Model 70 type action, with cone breech. Barrel and action are stainless steel. Chambered for a wide variety of calibers from .22-250 to .416 Rem. Magnum. Choice of walnut or fiberglass stock. Most barrel lengths are 24". Weight about 7.5 lbs. depending on caliber.

NIB	Exc.	V.G.	Good	Fair	Poor
3150	2550	1500	1150	500	250

Double Rifle/Shotgun

Side-by-side gun offered in .470 NE or .500 NE, as well as 12- and 20-gauge guns. Engraved receiver, AAA fancy walnut stocks and 3-leaf express sights are standard. Offered in boxlock and sidelock models.

Boxlock

NIB	Exc.	V.G.	Good	Fair	Poor
15000	12500	9000	5000	2750	1500

Side Lock

NIB	Exc.	V.G.	Good	Fair	Poor
21000	16500	12000	7500	3100	1750

HARTFORD ARMS & EQUIPMENT CO.
Hartford, Connecticut

Established in 1925, this firm was purchased by High Standard Company in 1932.

Single-Shot Target

A .22-caliber single-shot pistol, with 6.75" round barrel, fixed sights and either walnut or composition grips. Frame marked "Manfd. by the/ Hartford Arms and Equip. Co./ Hartford, Conn./ Patented .22 cal./ l.r." on left side in front of their breech. Although this pistol resembles a semi-automatic, it is in fact a single-shot manually operated pistol. **NOTE:** Add $150 premium for guns in original Hartford Arms box numbered to gun; $250 premium for guns in original High Standard box numbered to gun.

Courtesy John J. Stimson, Jr.

NIB	Exc.	V.G.	Good	Fair	Poor
—	595	450	325	250	150

Model 1925

Semi-automatic pistol chambered for .22-caliber, with 6.75" round barrel, checkered hard black rubber grips or ribbed walnut grips. Magazine capacity 10 rounds. Frame marked, "manfd. by/ the hartford arms and equip. co./ hartford, conn./ patented/ .22 cal/long rifle" on left side in front of breech. Approximately 5,000 produced from 1925 to 1932. **NOTE:** Add $150 premium for guns in original Hartford Arms box numbered to gun.

Courtesy John J. Stimson, Jr.

NIB	Exc.	V.G.	Good	Fair	Poor
—	600	475	365	225	175

HATFIELD RIFLE COMPANY
St. Joseph, Missouri

Squirrel Rifle

Flintlock or percussion rifle in .32- to .50-caliber, with 39" barrel, double-set triggers, adjustable sights, brass mounts and maple stocks. Available in a wide variety of forms, which affect values. Values listed are for plain standard models.

NIB	Exc.	V.G.	Good	Fair	Poor
550	400	350	300	225	150

SHOTGUNS

Uplander Grade I

A 20-gauge boxlock double-barrel shotgun, with 26" improved cylinder and modified barrel. Matte raised rib, single-selective trigger and automatic ejectors. Case-hardened blued, with deluxe-grade hand-checkered walnut stock. Introduced in 1987.

NIB	Exc.	V.G.	Good	Fair	Poor
1250	1050	750	600	475	200

Uplander Pigeon Grade II

As above, with scroll engraving. Fitted leather case.

NIB	Exc.	V.G.	Good	Fair	Poor
2250	1750	1275	900	650	500

Uplander Super Pigeon Grade III

As above, with deep-relief cut engraving and leather case.

NIB	Exc.	V.G.	Good	Fair	Poor
2500	2200	1700	1400	1000	700

Uplander Golden Quail Grade IV

Gold-inlaid version of above.

NIB	Exc.	V.G.	Good	Fair	Poor
4000	3500	2750	2000	1700	1300

Uplander Woodcock Grade V

As above, with seven 24 kt. gold inlays and best quality engraving. Furnished with leather case.

NIB	Exc.	V.G.	Good	Fair	Poor
5600	5000	4250	3500	2750	2000

HAVILAND & GUNN
Ilion, New York

Gallery Pistol

A .17-caliber rimfire single-shot pistol, with 5" barrel. Barrel and frame made of one piece iron and nickel plated. No markings on these pistols whatsoever. Believed to have been made during 1870s.

NIB	Exc.	V.G.	Good	Fair	Poor
—	—	1150	550	175	100

HAWES & WAGGONER
Philadelphia, Pennsylvania

Pocket Pistol

A .41-caliber single-shot percussion pistol, with 3" barrel, German silver mountings and walnut stock. Manufactured in 1850s.

NIB	Exc.	V.G.	Good	Fair	Poor
—	—	2250	925	475	275

HAWES
Los Angeles, California

Importer of handguns primarily made in Europe.

Courier

A .25-caliber blowback semi-automatic pocket pistol. Manufactured by Galesi.

NIB	Exc.	V.G.	Good	Fair	Poor
—	125	100	75	50	25

Diplomat

A .380 ACP pistol, with external hammer.

NIB	Exc.	V.G.	Good	Fair	Poor
—	150	125	100	75	50

Trophy

J.P. Sauer & Sohn manufactured revolver, with swing-out cylinder and 6" barrel. Chambered for .22 LR and .38 Special. Adjustable sights.

NIB	Exc.	V.G.	Good	Fair	Poor
—	250	200	175	125	90

Medalion

As above, with 3", 4" or 6" barrel and fixed sights.

NIB	Exc.	V.G.	Good	Fair	Poor
—	200	175	125	100	75

Tip-Up Target Pistol

Replica of Stevens Model 35 .22 LR single-shot. Globe front sight, adjustable rear.

NIB	Exc.	V.G.	Good	Fair	Poor
—	275	200	135	75	35

MARSHAL SINGLE-ACTION ARMY REVOLVERS

J. P. Sauer made a Western-styled series for Hawes. Based in appearance on Colt Single-Action Army.

Silver City

A .22 LR or .22 rimfire Magnum caliber single-action revolver, with 5.5" barrel, 6-shot cylinder and fixed sights.

NIB	Exc.	V.G.	Good	Fair	Poor
—	150	125	95	50	25

Western

A .357 Magnum, .44 Magnum, .45 Colt, .45 ACP, .44-40, 9mm, .22 LR and .22 rimfire Magnum single-action revolver, with fixed sights. Blued.

NIB	Exc.	V.G.	Good	Fair	Poor
—	350	275	195	100	75

Texas

As above, but nickel-plated.

NIB	Exc.	V.G.	Good	Fair	Poor
—	350	275	195	100	75

Montana

Western Marshal, with brass backstrap and trigger guard.

NIB	Exc.	V.G.	Good	Fair	Poor
—	350	275	195	100	75

Deputy

A .22 LR and .22 rimfire Magnum single-action revolver, with 5.5" barrel and 6-shot cylinder.

NIB	Exc.	V.G.	Good	Fair	Poor
—	150	125	95	50	25

Chief

A .357 Magnum, .44 Magnum and .45 Colt caliber revolver, with 6.5" barrel, 6-shot cylinder and adjustable sights. Blued.

NIB	Exc.	V.G.	Good	Fair	Poor
—	350	275	195	100	75

Federal

A 6-shot single-action revolver in .357 Magnum, .44 Magnum and .45 Colt caliber.

NIB	Exc.	V.G.	Good	Fair	Poor
—	350	275	195	100	75

HAWKEN
St. Louis, Missouri

During early part of 19th century, Jacob and Samuel Hawken manufactured a variety of flintlock, percussion and cartridge rifles, shotguns and pistols. They are best known, however, for half stock Plains Rifles. Though of a plain nature, these arms were recognized for their accuracy and dependability. Early Hawken rifles will be worth a substantial premium over later examples. Some examples in very good condition may be worth as much as $50,000. Proceed with caution.

HDH, SA.
Henrion, Dassy & Heuschen
Liege, Belgium

Cobold

A 9.4mm Dutch, 10.6mm German, .38- and .45-caliber double-action five-shot revolver, with solid frame, octagonal barrel and an odd safety catch that locks the cylinder.

NIB	Exc.	V.G.	Good	Fair	Poor
—	500	325	275	150	100

Puppy

A 5.5mm to 7.65mm caliber folding trigger double-action revolver. Most are "Velo-Dogs".

NIB	Exc.	V.G.	Good	Fair	Poor
—	200	150	100	75	50

Lincoln

A .22-caliber folding trigger double-action revolver, with solid frame, imitation pearl or ivory grips and engraving.

NIB	Exc.	V.G.	Good	Fair	Poor
—	200	150	100	75	50

Lincoln-Bossu

A 5.5mm or 6.35mm caliber folding trigger double-action revolver ("Velo-Dog" type), with solid-frame and hammerless.

NIB	Exc.	V.G.	Good	Fair	Poor
—	200	150	100	75	50

Left Wheeler

A Colt Police Positive copy in .32- or .38-caliber. Last revolver HDH manufactured.

NIB	Exc.	V.G.	Good	Fair	Poor
—	200	150	125	100	75

HEAVY EXPRESS INC.
Colorado Springs, Colorado

This company custom-built rifles, using its proprietary nonbelted cartridges from .260 Heavy Express Magnum to .416 Heavy Express Magnum. Company's rifles were built on Ruger Model 77 Mark II and Winchester Model 70 Classic actions. Barrels are 4140 chrome-moly blue and 416R stainless steel. Stocks include factory walnut, laminated or composite designs.

Prices listed are for basic guns. Options are not included and will affect price.

Heavy Express Premier—Ruger M77 Mk II

Chambered for .260 HE Magnum, .284 HE Magnum or .300 HE Magnum. Choice of walnut, laminated or composite stocks. **NOTE:** Add $200 for stainless steel.

NIB	Exc.	V.G.	Good	Fair	Poor
1500	1150	800	600	350	175

Heavy Express Monarch—Winchester M70 Classic

Same as above. Built on Winchester M70 Classic action. Choice of stocks. **NOTE:** Add $200 for stainless steel.

Close-up of Model 70 Classic stainless steel action.

NIB	Exc.	V.G.	Good	Fair	Poor
1775	1400	1000	750	500	250

Heavy Express Monarch—Ruger 77 MK II

Built on Ruger M77 action. Chambered for .338, .350, .375, .416 and .460 HE Magnum cartridges. Choice of stocks. **NOTE:** Add $200 for stainless steel.

NIB	Exc.	V.G.	Good	Fair	Poor
1775	1400	1000	750	500	250

Heavy Express Single-Shot—Ruger #1

Chambered in .300, .338, .350 and .416 HE Magnum cartridges. Choice of stocks. **NOTE:** Add $200 for stainless steel.

NIB	Exc.	V.G.	Good	Fair	Poor
1775	1400	1000	750	500	250

HECKLER & KOCH
Oberndorf/Neckar, Germany

End of WWII, the French dismantled Mauser factory as part of their reparations; buildings remained idle until 1949, when firearms production was again allowed in Germany. Heckler & Koch was formed as a machine tool enterprise and occupied vacant Mauser plant. In early 1950s, Edmund Heckler and Theodor Koch began to produce G3 automatic rifle based on Spanish CETME design and progressed to machine guns and sub-machine guns, eventually to production of commercial civilian rifles and pistols. In 1990, company got into financial difficulties because of a failed contract bid. In December 1990, French state consortium GIAT announced the purchase of Heckler and Koch, but a little more than a year later contract was canceled. Later in 1991, company was purchased by Royal Ordnance of Britain. In 2002, company was sold to a combined group of European investors and long-time company managers.

Model 91 A2

Recoil-operated rifle, with delayed-roller lock bolt. Chambered for .308 Winchester cartridge. Has 17.7" barrel, with military style aperture sights. Furnished with 20-round detachable magazine. Finished in matte black, with black plastic stock. Some areas of the country have made its ownership illegal.

NIB	Exc.	V.G.	Good	Fair	Poor
2800	2400	2000	1500	1150	800

Model 91 A3

Simply Model 91, with retractable metal stock.

NIB	Exc.	V.G.	Good	Fair	Poor
3100	2700	2250	1700	1350	900

Model 93 A2

Similar to Model 91, except chambered for .223 cartridge with 16.4" barrel. Magazine holds 25 rounds. Specifications same as Model 91.

NIB	Exc.	V.G.	Good	Fair	Poor
3000	2500	2000	1500	1150	800

Model 93 A3

Model 93 with retractable metal stock.

NIB	Exc.	V.G.	Good	Fair	Poor
3250	2650	2250	1700	1350	900

Model 94 A2

Carbine version chambered for 9mm Parabellum cartridge, with 16.5" barrel. Smaller-scaled weapon, with 15-shot magazine.

NIB	Exc.	V.G.	Good	Fair	Poor
4000	3750	3500	3100	2500	1250

Model 94 A3

Variation of Model 94, with addition of retractable metal stock.

NIB	Exc.	V.G.	Good	Fair	Poor
4200	3950	3750	3300	2700	1000

Model 270

Chambered for .22 LR cartridge. Sporting-styled rifle, with 16.5" barrel. Furnished with either 5- or 20-round magazine. Blued, with checkered walnut stock. Discontinued in 1985.

NIB	Exc.	V.G.	Good	Fair	Poor
800	675	500	350	250	150

Model 300

Similar to Model 270, except chambered for .22 rimfire Magnum cartridge. Not imported after 1988.

NIB	Exc.	V.G.	Good	Fair	Poor
1000	800	500	350	250	150

Model 630

Chambered for .223. Features same roller-delayed semi-automatic action as found on paramilitary-type weapons. Sporting-style rifle with polished blue finish and checkered walnut stock. Barrel 17.7" long. Magazines offered hold either 4- or 10-rounds. Importation discontinued in 1986.

NIB	Exc.	V.G.	Good	Fair	Poor
1795	1350	900	650	450	300

Model 770

Similar to Model 630 except chambered for .308 Winchester cartridge and 19.7" barrel. Not imported after 1986.

NIB	Exc.	V.G.	Good	Fair	Poor
1795	1350	900	650	450	300

Model 940

Essentially same as Model 770 except chambered for .30-06 cartridge, with 21" barrel. Not imported after 1986.

NIB	Exc.	V.G.	Good	Fair	Poor
2000	1600	1000	600	400	300

Model SL6

Heckler & Koch's current sporting rifle chambered for .223 cartridge, with 17.7" barrel. Features same basic action as military versions. Matte black finish, walnut stock, with vented walnut hand guard. Magazine holds 4 rounds.

NIB	Exc.	V.G.	Good	Fair	Poor
1600	1300	950	650	350	300

Model SL7

Similar to SL6 except chambered for .308 Winchester cartridge and 3-round magazine.

NIB	Exc.	V.G.	Good	Fair	Poor
1600	1300	950	650	350	300

Model SR9

Introduced into U.S. market after the federal government prohibited importation of H&K's other semi-automatic rifles. SR9 similar to HK91, but certified by BATF as a sporting rifle. Features special thumbhole stock made of Kevlar reinforced fiberglass. Action is a delayed-roller locked bolt semi-automatic design chambered for .308 Winchester cartridge. Barrel 19.7" in length and features adjustable rear sight, with hooded front sight. Weight 10.9 lbs.

NIB	Exc.	V.G.	Good	Fair	Poor
2900	2400	2000	1400	700	500

Model SR9 (T) Target

Similar to standard model SR9, with addition of special MSG90 adjustable buttstock, PSG-1 trigger group and PSG-1 contoured hand grip. Weight 10.6 lbs.

NIB	Exc.	V.G.	Good	Fair	Poor
3000	2500	2200	1650	950	600

Model SR9 (TC) Target Competition

Similar to Model SR9 (T), with addition of PSG-1 adjustable buttstock. Weight 10.9 lbs.

NIB	Exc.	V.G.	Good	Fair	Poor
3300	3000	2300	1950	1100	700

BASR Model

Bolt-action rifle chambered for various popular calibers. Stainless steel barrel. Essentially custom built to customer's specifications. Stock is of Kevlar. Quite rare. Only 100 manufactured in 1968.

NIB	Exc.	V.G.	Good	Fair	Poor
—	4000	3600	2750	1300	800

PSG-1

High precision sniping rifle. Features delayed-roller semi-automatic action. Chambered for .308 Winchester cartridge and 5-shot magazine. Barrel length 25.6". Furnished with complete array of accessories including 6x42-power illuminated Hensoldt scope. Weight 17.8 lbs.

NIB	Exc.	V.G.	Good	Fair	Poor
14500	12500	9000	7500	6000	4000

Model SL8-1

New generation .223 rifle modeled after military Model G36. Introduced in 2000. Built of carbon fiber polymer and gas operated. Thumbhole stock with cheekpiece. Barrel length 20.8". Magazine capacity 10 rounds. Adjustable sights. Weight about 8.6 lbs.

NIB	Exc.	V.G.	Good	Fair	Poor
1800	1625	1050	700	500	325

SLB 2000

Introduced in 2001. Gas-operated semi-automatic rifle chambered for .30-06 cartridge. Receiver built of lightweight alloy. Barrel 16.7" in length and will accept interchangeable barrels, at some future date. Oil-finished walnut stock. Open sights, with both barrel and receiver drilled and tapped for scope mounts. Magazine capacity 2, 5 or 10 rounds. Weight about 7.25 lbs.

NIB	Exc.	V.G.	Good	Fair	Poor
1200	1000	800	600	400	225

Model USC

Introduced in 2000. Semi-automatic blowback carbine derived from H&K's UMP sub-machine gun. Chambered for .45 ACP cartridge. Fitted with 16" barrel. Skeletonized stock. Accessory rail on top of receiver. Adjustable sights. Magazine capacity 10 rounds. Weight about 6 lbs.

NIB	Exc.	V.G.	Good	Fair	Poor
1700	1275	1000	750	400	200

Model MR556A1

Direct descendant of HK416. Semi-automatic gas-piston operating system. Free floating rail hand-guard system, with four Picatinny rails for mounting of optical or lighting accessories. Two-stage trigger. Retractable butt-stock can be locked in any position to suit individual requirements. Chambered for 5.56x45mm NATO round. Magazine capacities: 10, 20 or 30 rounds.

NIB	Exc.	V.G.	Good	Fair	Poor
2900	2475	2100	1300	650	300

MR762A1 Carbine

Similar to MR556A1, except 7.62x51mm chambering, 10- or 20-shot magazine, upper and lower accessory rails. Also made in LRP (Long Rifle Package), with Leupold 3-9x40mm VXR Patrol scope, LaRue Tactical BRM-6 bipod, collapsible stock with adjustable cheekpiece. **NOTE:** Add $2500 for LRP model.

NIB	Exc.	V.G.	Good	Fair	Poor
3500	2900	2200	1750	1000	500

PISTOLS

HK4

Blowback-operated semi-automatic pistol based on Mauser HSc design. Chambered for .22 LR, .25 ACP, .32 ACP and .380. These calibers easily converted by switching barrels, recoil springs and magazines. Rimfire model could be changed by rotating breechface. Conversion kits available for all calibers. Barrel 3" long; finish blued, with molded plastic thumb rest grips. Pistol sold from 1968-1973 as Harrington & Richardson HK4 and so marked. Discontinued in 1984.

.22 Caliber or .380 Caliber

NIB	Exc.	V.G.	Good	Fair	Poor
—	475	350	250	200	100

.25 Caliber or .32 Caliber

NIB	Exc.	V.G.	Good	Fair	Poor
—	350	300	250	200	100

Conversion Units

NIB	Exc.	V.G.	Good	Fair	Poor
—	150	125	90	60	30

P9

Single-action delayed-blowback semi-automatic pistol chambered for 9mm or 7.65mm Parabellum. Action based on G-3 rifle mechanism. Barrel length 4". Pistol has internal hammer, thumb-operated hammer drop and de-cocking lever. Also a manual safety and loaded-chamber indicator. Finish is Parkerized. Grips are molded plastic and well contoured. Fixed sights. Manufactured between 1977 and 1984. Model rarer than P9S model.

NIB	Exc.	V.G.	Good	Fair	Poor
800	650	500	400	300	200

P9S

Similar to Model P9 except action features double-action capability. Chambered for .45 ACP and 9mm Parabellum, with 5.5" barrel. Manufactured between 1977 and 1984.

NIB	Exc.	V.G.	Good	Fair	Poor
800	650	500	400	300	200

P9S Target Model

Similar to model P9S. Chambered for 9mm or .45 ACP cartridges. Adjustable sights and trigger. Discontinued in 1984.

NIB	Exc.	V.G.	Good	Fair	Poor
1400	1100	900	600	500	300

P9S Competition

Similar to P9S target, with addition of barrel weights and special competition grips.

NIB	Exc.	V.G.	Good	Fair	Poor
3000	2000	1200	750	500	275

VP 70Z

Blowback-operated semi-automatic chambered for 9mm Parabellum cartridge. Striker-fired and double-action-only. Barrel 4.5" long. Double-column magazine holds 18 rounds. Finish blued. Receiver and grip molded from plastic. Discontinued in 1984.

NIB	Exc.	V.G.	Good	Fair	Poor
700	500	350	300	250	200

P7 PSP

First of squeeze-cocked H&K pistols. Single-action semi-automatic placed in firing position by pressure on front of grip strap. This moves striker into battery; firing is then accomplished by single-action pressure on trigger, releasing grip strap cocking device and decocking mechanism. This particular model does not have extended finger guard on trigger. Does not have ambidextrous safety. Discontinued in 1984.

NIB	Exc.	V.G.	Good	Fair	Poor
1100	900	700	600	500	400

P7 K3

This is "Squeeze Cocker" chambered for either .380 or .22 LR caliber.

Has a recoil buffer that is oil-filled and 3.8" barrel. Magazine holds 8 rounds. Introduced in 1988.

NIB	Exc.	V.G.	Good	Fair	Poor
1800	1600	1350	900	500	300

.22 Caliber Conversion Kit

This unit will convert P7 K3 to fire .22 LR cartridge.

NIB	Exc.	V.G.	Good	Fair	Poor
1500	1200	650	300	150	75

.32 ACP Caliber Conversion Kit

NIB	Exc.	V.G.	Good	Fair	Poor
1000	900	400	100	75	50

P7 M8

This is an 8-shot newer version of "Squeeze Cocker". Has heat-shield finger guard, ambidextrous safety, 4" barrel and 3-dot sight system. Finish is matte blue or nickel, with stippled black plastic grips. No longer in production. **NOTE:** Add $100 for night sights introduced in 1993.

NIB	Exc.	V.G.	Good	Fair	Poor
1500	1200	900	700	500	300

P7 M10

New addition to P7 series in 1993. Variation chambered for .40 S&W cartridge. Magazine holds 10 rounds. Finish available either blue or nickel. Weight 2.69 lbs. **NOTE:** Add $100 for night sights.

NIB	Exc.	V.G.	Good	Fair	Poor
2750	2250	1600	1100	500	300

P7 M13

Version similar to P7 M8 except it has a double column 13-shot magazine. **NOTE:** Add $100 for night sights.

NIB	Exc.	V.G.	Good	Fair	Poor
2200	1750	1200	650	500	300

SP89

Introduced in early 1990s. Large frame semi-automatic pistol chambered for 9mm cartridge. Features 15-round magazine and square notch rear sight ,with hooded front sight. Has 4.5" barrel; 13" overall; weight 4.4 lbs. In August 1993 no longer imported due to ban on assault pistols.

NIB	Exc.	V.G.	Good	Fair	Poor
4000	3600	3200	2500	1800	1000

USP SERIES

Late in 1999, H&K began shipping its USPs and Mark 23s with an internal locking system. This lock-out is installed in the grip and blocks movement of hammer, trigger and slide. Operated with two pronged key supplied with pistol. This system is in addition to traditional trigger lock that is sold with each H&K firearm. In 2001 stainless steel version of these pistols was discontinued.

In 2005 H&K offered a limited edition run of color frame variations for USP line. These colors are Desert tan, green and gray.

Gray: USP 45 and USP 40 Compact

Green: USP 45, USP 40, USP 40 Compact and USP 45

Tactical Desert Tan: USP 45, USP 40, USP 40 Compact and USP 45 Tactical and Mark 23

Retail prices are same for these color variations as standard black frame pistols

USP 40

Introduced in 1993, this new semi-automatic H&K pistol features a new design that incorporates a short recoil modified Browning action. Chambered for .40 S&W cartridge, this model has 4.13" barrel and magazine capacity of 13 rounds. Stainless steel model introduced in 1996. Weight 1.74 lbs. Available in seven different variations from traditional double-action to double-action-only and various safety locations and styles. Variants numbered by H&K are listed.

1. DA/SA with safe position and control lever on left side of frame.

2. DA/SA with safe position and control lever on right side of frame.

3. DA/SA without safe position and decocking lever on left side of frame.

4. DA/SA without safe position and decocking lever on left side of frame.

5. DA only with safe position and safety lever on left side of frame.

6. DA only with safe position and safety lever on right side of frame.

7. DA only without control lever.

9. DA/SA with safe position and safety lever on left side of frame.

10. DA/SA with safety lever on the right side of frame.

NOTE: Add $45 for stainless steel model.

NIB	Exc.	V.G.	Good	Fair	Poor
900	800	650	300	250	125

USP 9

Same as USP 40, but chambered for 9mm cartridge. Magazine holds 16 rounds. Weight 1.66 lbs. Choice of seven variations as listed above

for USP 40. New for 1993. **NOTE:** Add $45 for stainless steel.

NIB	Exc.	V.G.	Good	Fair	Poor
900	800	650	300	250	125

USP 9SD

Variation of USP 9 fitted with target sights to see over an optional sound suppressor. Barrel threaded left-hand. Does not have O-ring and does not require thread cap. Introduced in 2004.

NIB	Exc.	V.G.	Good	Fair	Poor
975	825	675	325	275	150

USP 40 Compact

Same as 9mm Compact model. Chambered for .40 S&W cartridge. Weight about 27 oz. All other dimensions the same.

NIB	Exc.	V.G.	Good	Fair	Poor
900	800	650	300	250	125

USP 45

Introduced in 1995. Slightly larger than 9mm and .40 S&W models. Barrel length 4.41"; overall 7.87"; weight 1.9 lbs. USP 45 available in same variants as other USP models. Magazine capacity 12 rounds. **NOTE:** Add $45 for stainless steel.

NIB	Exc.	V.G.	Good	Fair	Poor
1100	950	775	500	350	200

USP 9 Compact

Introduced in 1997, this 9mm model is smaller version of full size USP 9. Internal differences due to size. Barrel length .58"; overall length 6.81". Magazine capacity 10 rounds. Weight about 26 oz. Available with stainless steel slide. **NOTE:** Add $45 to NIB price.

NIB	Exc.	V.G.	Good	Fair	Poor
800	600	450	300	200	150

USP Compact LEM (Law Enforcement Modification)

Introduced in 2002. Identical to USP Compact .40 S&W Variant 7, with double-action-only trigger. Special trigger mechanism improves double-action trigger performance and reduces weight of pull between 7.5 and 8.5 lbs. Offered in blued finish.

NIB	Exc.	V.G.	Good	Fair	Poor
1150	1000	750	500	300	150

USP 45 Match

Introduced in 1997, model is match grade variation of USP. Chambered for .45 ACP cartridge. Fitted with 6.02" barrel, with barrel weight assembly. Adjustable rear sight and target front sight. Adjustable trigger stop. Blued finish. Weight about 38 oz. Available in stainless steel version. **NOTE:** Add $60 for stainless steel.

NIB	Exc.	V.G.	Good	Fair	Poor
1500	1300	1050	800	475	275

USP 45 Compact

Introduced in 1997. Chambered for .45 ACP cartridge. Has 3.8" barrel; overall length 7.1"; weight about 28 oz. Magazine capacity 8 rounds.

NIB	Exc.	V.G.	Good	Fair	Poor
1100	950	775	500	350	200

USP 45 Compact Tactical

Blued semi-automatic .45 ACP. Double-action with 4.46" barrel, 8 round capacity. Polymer grip. Weight about 27.5 oz.

NIB	Exc.	V.G.	Good	Fair	Poor
1100	950	775	500	350	200

USP .357 Compact

Introduced in mid-1998. Pistol built on same frame as .40 S&W Compact. Chambered for .357 SIG cartridge. Magazine capacity 10 rounds. Weight about 28 oz.

NIB	Exc.	V.G.	Good	Fair	Poor
1000	850	4675	375	250	150

USP 45 Expert

Introduced in fall of 1998. This .45 ACP pistol fitted with 5.2" barrel and slide, with 10-round magazine. Overall length 8.7"; height 1.87"; weight about 30 oz. Adjustable low-profile sights. Limited availability between 1,000 and 2,500 pistols. In 2003 offered chambered for 9mm and .40 S&W cartridge. **NOTE:** H&K price reduction in 2005.

NIB	Exc.	V.G.	Good	Fair	Poor
1355	1200	900	600	300	150

USP 45 Tactical

Introduced in 1998. Enhanced version of USP 45. Fitted with 4.9" threaded barrel, with adjustable high profile target sights. Overall length 8.6"; weight about 36 oz. Magazine capacity 10 rounds. Availability limited to 1,000 and 2,500 pistols.

NIB	Exc.	V.G.	Good	Fair	Poor
1100	850	625	425	300	175

USP Elite

Introduced in 2003. Features 6.2" barrel chambered for 9mm or .45 ACP cartridge. Fitted with match trigger, adjustable trigger stop, adjustable micrometer rear target sights, extended floorplate and loaded chamber indicator. Weight about 30 oz. empty. Magazine capacity 10 rounds. **NOTE:** H&K price reduction in 2005.

NIB	Exc.	V.G.	Good	Fair	Poor
1400	1150	800	575	250	135

USP 45 50th Anniversary Commemorative

Limited to 1,000 pistols. Features high polish blue with 50th Anniversary logo engraved in gold and silver. Supplied with custom-made wooden box and commemorative coin. Introduced in 2000.

NIB	Exc.	V.G.	Good	Fair	Poor
1100	850	625	425	300	175

P2000 GPM

Introduced in 2003. Similar to USP compact LEM pistol. Several modular features, such as interchangeable back straps, ambidextrous slide release and short trigger reset distance. Chambered for 9mm or .40 S&W cartridge. Fitted with 3.62" barrel. Fixed sights. Magazine capacity: 12 rounds .40 S&W and .357 SIG; 13 rounds 9mm. Weight about 22 oz. **NOTE:** Add $30 for magazine disconnect.

NIB	Exc.	V.G.	Good	Fair	Poor
875	700	500	350	250	125

P2000 SK

Semi-automatic double-action pistol is a subcompact version of P2000. Chambered for 9mm or .40 S&W cartridge as well as .357 SIG. Has 2.5" barrel; overall length 6.4". Magazine capacity: 10 rounds 9mm; 12 rounds .357 SIG; 9 rounds .40 S&W. Weight about 21 oz. Introduced in 2004.

NIB	Exc.	V.G.	Good	Fair	Poor
1100	850	625	425	300	175

Mark 23

Very similar to H&K's US government contract pistol. Developed for special Operation Units. Chambered for .45 ACP. Fitted with 5.87" barrel. Pistol has polymer frame, with steel slide. Magazine capacity 10 rounds on civilian models; 12 rounds on law enforcement models. Barrel threaded for noise suppressor. Weight about 42 oz.

NIB	Exc.	V.G.	Good	Fair	Poor
2200	1850	1200	875	500	250

HK45

Full-size autoloader chambered in .45 ACP. Features include polygonal bore, front and rear slide serrations, integrated Picatinny rail, ambi mag release levers, interchangeable backstrap panels, polymer frame, modular action design allowing for double-/single-action or double-action-only operation. Measures 7.52" overall length. 10+1 capacity.

NIB	Exc.	V.G.	Good	Fair	Poor
1100	850	625	425	300	175

HK45 Compact

Similar to above, with 8 round capacity; overall length 7.2".

NIB	Exc.	V.G.	Good	Fair	Poor
1100	850	625	425	300	175

P30

Polymer-frame 9mm autoloader. Features include loaded chamber indicator, integral Picatinny rail, oversized trigger guard, double-/single-action firing mode with decocker, "Hostile Environment" black finish, ambidextrous, oversized controls. **NOTE:** Add 10 percent for longslide variant. Deduct $200 for subcompact P30SK.

NIB	Exc.	V.G.	Good	Fair	Poor
950	750	600	450	250	150

VP9/VP40

This 9mm model is first HK striker-fired pistol since P7 series of 1980s. Similar in appearance and operation as P30, VP9 trigger has a short light take-up, with solid single-action break. It uses HK ergonomic grip design that comes with three interchangeable backstraps and six side panels to accommodate all hand sizes. Other features include an extended Picatinny accessory rail, machined steel slide and HK's hostile environment finish. Magazine has 15-round capacity. Introduced in 2014. A .40 S&W chambering was added in 2016.

NIB	Exc.	V.G.	Good	Fair	Poor
600	525	450	375	—	—

HEINZELMANN, C.E.
Plochipnam Neckar, Germany

Heim

A 6.35mm semi-automatic pistol, with 2" barrel. Detachable magazine holds 6 rounds. Weight about 11 oz. Manufactured during 1930s. Marked on frame "C.E. Heinzelmann Plochingen A.N. Patent Heim-6.35".

NIB	Exc.	V.G.	Good	Fair	Poor
—	800	675	550	400	200

HEIZER DEFENSE
Pevely, Missouri

PS1 Pocket Shotgun

Single-shot pistol chambered for .45 Colt/.410 shotshell rounds. Tip-up barrel with titanium frame. Choice of black, polished silver or several bright color finishes. Introduced in 2013.

NIB	Exc.	V.G.	Good	Fair	Poor
400	350	300	250	200	150

HELFRICHT
Zella-Mehlis, Germany

Model 3 Pocket Pistol

A 6.35mm semi-automatic pistol, with 2" barrel and 6-shot magazine. Weight about 11 oz. Blued, with checkered black plastic grips having monogram "KH" cast in them. Pistols have no external sights.

Courtesy James Rankin

NIB	Exc.	V.G.	Good	Fair	Poor
—	500	400	300	200	100

Model 4 Pocket Pistol

Semi-automatic pistol in caliber 6.35mm. Checkered black plastic grips, with "KH" logo on each grip.

Courtesy James Rankin

NIB	Exc.	V.G.	Good	Fair	Poor
—	400	300	200	150	100

HENRION & DASSY
Liege, Belgium

Semi-Automatic

A 6.35mm semi-automatic pistol, with 2.5" barrel and 5-shot magazine. Blued, with black plastic grips marked "H&D".

NIB	Exc.	V.G.	Good	Fair	Poor
—	600	500	450	375	275

HENRY, ALEXANDER
Edinburgh, Scotland

Noted for both the rifling system he developed and falling block single-shot rifles he made.

Single-Shot Rifle

High-grade single-shot features true falling-block action that is activated by a side lever on action. Available in popular European cartridges of the era. Barrel length varies from 22" to 28". Rifle exhibits fine quality materials and workmanship. Select-grade walnut stock and schnabel fore-end are hand checkered. Finish scroll-engraved and blued. Company manufactured firearms from 1869 until 1895.

NIB	Exc.	V.G.	Good	Fair	Poor
—	—	3800	1500	700	400

Double Rifle

Side-by-side double-barreled Express Rifle chambered for .500/450 Black Powder Express cartridge. Damascus barrels and double triggers. Gun is hammerless and features ornate scroll engraving as well as a high-grade hand checkered walnut stock and fore-end. Furnished with fitted leather case and accessories. Manufactured in 1890s.

NIB	Exc.	V.G.	Good	Fair	Poor
—	—	9000	5000	1750	800

HENRY
See—Winchester

HENRY REPEATING ARMS COMPANY
Bayonne, New Jersey

Lever-Action

Chambered for .22 LR, Long and Short cartridges. Fitted with 18.25" barrel. Weight 5.5 lbs. Magazine capacity 15 rounds for .22 LR cartridge. Rear sight adjustable and front sight hooded.

NIB	Exc.	V.G.	Good	Fair	Poor
280	200	155	125	75	50

Carbine

Similar to above, with overall length of 34". Features large loop lever.

NIB	Exc.	V.G.	Good	Fair	Poor
280	200	155	125	75	50

Youth Model

Similar to carbine above, with overall length of 33".

NIB	Exc.	V.G.	Good	Fair	Poor
280	200	155	125	75	50

Lever-Action .22 Magnum

Fitted with 19.5" barrel. Tubular magazine capacity 11 rounds. Checkered deluxe walnut stock. Weight about 5.5 lbs.

NIB	Exc.	V.G.	Good	Fair	Poor
350	300	250	195	125	75

Lever-Action Frontier Model

Similar to Lever Action, with 20" octagon barrel. Chambered in .22 WMR and .17HMR. Introduced 2006.

NIB	Exc.	V.G.	Good	Fair	Poor
375	300	250	175	115	85

Golden Boy

Lever-action rifle chambered for .22 LR, Short or Long cartridges as well as .22 WRM cartridge, in a separate model. Fitted with brass receiver and 20" octagon barrel. Walnut stock. Weight about 6.75 lbs. **NOTE:** Add $70 for .22 WRM or .17 HMR; $20 for large loop lever; $600 for hand-engraved model.

NIB	Exc.	V.G.	Good	Fair	Poor
550	400	295	200	125	85

Golden Boy Deluxe

Chambered for .22 LR cartridge. Fitted with 20" octagon barrel. Fancy walnut stock. Deeply engraved receiver.

NIB	Exc.	V.G.	Good	Fair	Poor
1250	995	650	400	200	125

Deluxe Engraved Golden Boy Magnum

Similar to Golden Boy Deluxe, but chambered in .22 WMR. Features deluxe deep-cut German-style engraving on receiver. Introduced 2006.

NIB	Exc.	V.G.	Good	Fair	Poor
1275	1000	675	425	225	150

Silver Boy

Lever-action rimfire rifle similar to Golden Boy, but has a nickel-plated receiver, barrel band and buttplate. The 20" blued barrel is octagon

---

shaped, with Buckhorn adjustable rear sight and bead front. Chambered in .22 LR, .22 WMR or .17 HMR. Also made in youth model with 16.5" barrel, shorter length of pull. **NOTE:** Add $50 for .22 Magnum; $75 for .17 HMR.

NIB	Exc.	V.G.	Good	Fair	Poor
525	450	400	350	300	275

Varmint Express

Lever-action rifle chambered for .17 HMR cartridge and fitted with 20" round barrel. Checkered American walnut stock. Scope mount included. Magazine capacity 11 rounds. Weight about 5.75 lbs.

NIB	Exc.	V.G.	Good	Fair	Poor
45	350	225	175	100	75

Big Boy

Lever-action model chambered for .44 Magnum or .45 Colt cartridge. Octagonal barrel is 20". Magazine capacity 10 rounds. American walnut stock, with straight-grip. Weight about 8.7 lbs. .357 Magnum added 2006.

NIB	Exc.	V.G.	Good	Fair	Poor
725	595	400	300	200	150

Big Boy Deluxe Engraved .44 Magnum

Similar to Big Boy, with deluxe deep-cut German-style engraving on receiver. Introduced 2006.

NIB	Exc.	V.G.	Good	Fair	Poor
1350	1100	850	550	275	175

Big Boy .44 Magnum "Wildlife Edition"

Similar to Big Boy .44 Magnum. Fore-end and buttstock laser-engraved with whitetail deer scenes. Introduced in 2007.

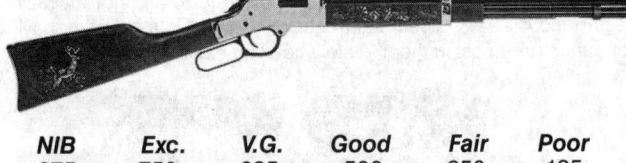

NIB	Exc.	V.G.	Good	Fair	Poor
875	750	625	500	250	125

Big Boy .45 Colt "Cowboy Edition"

Similar to Big Boy .45 Colt. Fore-end and buttstock laser-engraved with Old West scenes. Introduced in 2007.

NIB	Exc.	V.G.	Good	Fair	Poor
1350	1100	850	550	275	175

.30-30

.30-30 caliber Winchester. Features 20" barrel, straight-grip American walnut stock with rubber butt-pad, XS ghost ring sights, blue finish, weight 7 lbs. Also available with brass receiver, octagon barrel and adjustable Marble's buck-horn rear sight, bead front. **NOTE:** Add 30 percent for brass receiver/octagon barrel.

NIB	Exc.	V.G.	Good	Fair	Poor
650	575	500	400	300	200

Mare's Leg

Caliber: .45 Colt or .22 S/L/LR. Has large-loop lever based on rifle seen in classic Steve McQueen western TV series "Wanted: Dead or Alive". Barrel length 12.9"; overall length 25"; weight: 5.8 lbs. (.45 Colt), 4.5 lbs. (.22). Lanyard ring, blue finish, straight-grip walnut stock. Sights are Marble's adjustable semi-buckhorn rear and brass bead front (.45 Colt): adjustable rear and hooded front (.22).

.45 Colt

NIB	Exc.	V.G.	Good	Fair	Poor
800	675	500	400	300	200

.22

NIB	Exc.	V.G.	Good	Fair	Poor
315	275	220	175	110	85

Original Henry Rifle

This rifle is virtually identical to the original 1860 version, except for caliber. Chambered for .44-40 (.44 WCF) cartridge, it has a 13-round magazine, hardened brass receiver with blued steel 24" barrel, folding ladder rear and blade front sights. Buttstock is high grade American walnut. Serial number prefix "BTH" honors Benjamin Tyler Henry, inventor of the rifle that went on to become one of the most legendary firearms in history. Introduced in 2014, original Henry is made in America for the first time since 1864. **NOTE:** Add $1,000 for limited edition model, with deluxe scroll engraving. Limited to 1,000 rifles.

NIB	Exc.	V.G.	Good	Fair	Poor
2000	1700	1400	1000	—	—

Long Ranger

Totally new lever-action design. Featuring an alloy receiver, checkered oil-finished walnut stock, 20" free-floating barrel, detachable magazine, side ejection and gear-operated action. Calibers include .223 Rem., .243 Win. and .308 Win. Introduced in 2016.

NIB	Exc.	V.G.	Good	Fair	Poor
875	800	650	—	—	—

Pump-Action Rifle

Introduced in 1999. .22-caliber fitted with 18.25" barrel and chambered for .22 LR cartridge. Walnut stock and adjustable rear sight. Weight about 5.5 lbs.

NIB	Exc.	V.G.	Good	Fair	Poor
350	250	185	135	100	75

U.S. Survival Rifle

Improved version of AR-7 .22-caliber survival rifle issued to Air Force. Breakdown design and features waterproof stock, steel-lined barrel and adjustable sights. Furnished with two 8-round magazines. Overall length when broken down is 16.5".

NIB	Exc.	V.G.	Good	Fair	Poor
250	175	115	85	65	40

Pump-Action .22 Octagon Rifle

Similar to Pump-Action Rifle, with 20" octagon barrel. Introduced 2006. **NOTE:** Add 10 percent for .22 WMR.

NIB	Exc.	V.G.	Good	Fair	Poor
495	350	225	150	125	75

Mini Bolt

Single-shot bolt-action .22-caliber rifle designed for young shooters. Barrel length 16.25"; overall 30.25". Stainless steel barrel and receiver. Colored stocks available. Adjustable sights. Weight about 3.25 lbs.

NIB	Exc.	V.G.	Good	Fair	Poor
210	165	100	75	50	25

Acu-Bolt

Chambered for .22 LR, .22 WMR or .17 HMR cartridges. Fitted with 20" barrel. Fiberglass stock. Scope mounts. Weight about 4.25 lbs. **NOTE:** Add 10 percent for factory scope.

NIB	Exc.	V.G.	Good	Fair	Poor
315	275	200	150	100	75

HERITAGE MANUFACTURING, INC.
Opa Locka, Florida

Stealth

Semi-automatic pistol chambered in 9mm and .40 S&W. Black polymer frame, with stainless steel slide. Barrel length 3.9"; overall 6.3". Magazine capacity 10 rounds. Weight about 20 oz. Offered with black finish, two-tone black chrome, with stainless steel side panels or black chrome.

NIB	Exc.	V.G.	Good	Fair	Poor
275	225	175	150	125	100

Model H25S

Semi-automatic pistol chambered for .25 ACP cartridge. Barrel length 2.25"; overall 4.58"; weight about 13.5 oz. Frame mounted safety. Single-action-only. Available in blue or nickel.

NIB	Exc.	V.G.	Good	Fair	Poor
150	125	100	85	65	50

Sentry

Double-action revolver chambered for .38 Special. Cylinder holds 6 rounds. Barrel length 2". Weight about 23 oz. Blue or nickel finish.

NIB	Exc.	V.G.	Good	Fair	Poor
130	100	85	65	50	30

Rough Rider

Single-action revolver chambered for .22-caliber cartridges. Barrel lengths 4.75", 6.5" and 9". Cylinder holds 6 rounds. Weight about 34 oz. Available in blue or nickel finish.

NIB	Exc.	V.G.	Good	Fair	Poor
250	215	180	130	100	80

With Combination Cylinder—.22 Magnum

NIB	Exc.	V.G.	Good	Fair	Poor
275	235	200	150	125	100

With Bird's-Head Grip & Combo Cylinder

NIB	Exc.	V.G.	Good	Fair	Poor
285	250	200	150	125	100

Rough Rider .17 HMR

Introduced in 2004.

NIB	Exc.	V.G.	Good	Fair	Poor
300	260	220	185	125	100

Rough Rider .32

Six-shot revolver chambered for .32 H&R Magnum centerfire (inter-changeably .32 S&W, .32 S&W Long). Black satin finish. Offered with 3.5", 4.75" or 6.5" barrels. Weight 35 oz. (6.5" bbl.). 11.785" LOA. Fixed sights. Bird's-head grip available. Discontinued.

NIB	Exc.	V.G.	Good	Fair	Poor
240	190	140	95	75	50

Rough Rider Big-Bore Series

Six-shot steel-frame revolver chambered for .357, .44-40 or .45 Long Colt. Barrel lengths 4.75", 5.5" or 7.5". Weight 36 oz. Fixed sights. **NOTE:** Add 10 percent for chrome finish.

NIB	Exc.	V.G.	Good	Fair	Poor
400	350	300	250	200	150

HEROLD
Franz Jaeger
Suhl, Germany

Bolt-Action Rifle

A .22 Hornet bolt-action sporting rifle, with 24" ribbed barrel, adjustable sights, double-set triggers and walnut stock. Imported by Charles Daly and Stoeger Arms prior to WWII.

NIB	Exc.	V.G.	Good	Fair	Poor
—	1500	850	600	400	250

HERTER'S
Waseca, Minnesota

An importer and retailer of European-made firearms. Active until approximately 1980.

REVOLVERS

Guide

A .22-caliber double-action swing-out cylinder revolver, with 6" barrel and 6-shot cylinder. Blued, with walnut grips.

NIB	Exc.	V.G.	Good	Fair	Poor
—	125	95	70	45	30

Power-Mag Revolver

A .357 Magnum, .401 Herter Power Magnum and .44 Magnum caliber single-action revolver, with 4" or 6" barrel and 6-shot cylinder. Blued, with walnut grips. **NOTE:** Add 10 percent for .401.

NIB	Exc.	V.G.	Good	Fair	Poor
—	400	325	200	125	75

Western

As above, in .22-caliber.

NIB	Exc.	V.G.	Good	Fair	Poor
—	200	150	125	75	50

RIFLES

J-9 or U-9 Hunter

Mauser-action sporting rifles manufactured in England (J-9) and Yugoslavia (U-9), with 24" barrels and Monte Carlo-style walnut stocks.

NIB	Exc.	V.G.	Good	Fair	Poor
—	475	200	155	100	75

J-9 or U-9 Presentation or Supreme

As above, with checkering and sling swivels.

NIB	Exc.	V.G.	Good	Fair	Poor
—	550	325	200	150	100

HESSE ARMS
Inver Grove Heights, Minnesota

This previous manufacturer of military style firearms was succeeded by Vulcan Armament, which is no longer in business. Values of Hesse Arms products can vary widely.

HEYM, F. W.
Gleichamberg, Germany

Established 1865 in Suhl, Germany, this company was re-established after WWII in Munnerstadt. Company remained there until 1996 when it moved back to a suburb of Suhl. Post-war arms were originally imported by Paul Jaeger of Grand Junction, Tennessee. Double Gun Imports in Dallas, Texas, is the current importer of Heym firearms.

SINGLE-SHOT RIFLES

Model HR-30

Built on Ruger No. 1 falling-block-action. Chambered for most calibers, with 24" round barrel or 26" barrel in Magnum calibers. There is a quarter rib with express sights. Single-set trigger made by Canjar. Rifle engraved with game scene motif. Stock is deluxe hand checkered French walnut, with classic European-style cheekpiece. French case-hardened and blued.

NIB	Exc.	V.G.	Good	Fair	Poor
4000	3500	3000	2500	2000	1000

Model HR-38

As above, with octagonal barrel.

NIB	Exc.	V.G.	Good	Fair	Poor
4600	4200	3600	3000	2300	1200

DOUBLE RIFLES

Model 22 Safety

Over/under combination rifle/shotgun chambered for 16- or 20-gauge over .22 Hornet, .22 WMR, .222 Remington, .222 Remington Magnum, .223, 5.6x50Rmm, 6.5x57Rmm and 7x57Rmm, with 24" barrels. Boxlock action with single trigger, automatic ejectors and automatic decocking mechanism. French case-hardened, blued, with walnut stock.

NIB	Exc.	V.G.	Good	Fair	Poor
—	3500	3000	2750	1200	900

Model 77B/55B Over/Under Rifle

Over/under rifle manufactured in a variety of calibers, with 25" barrels. Has open sights and boxlock-action, with Kersten double cross bolts. Action is heavily engraved with game scene motif and silver plated. Has double triggers, cocking indicators, automatic ejectors and select walnut stock. Barrels machined to accept Zeiss scope, with claw mounts.

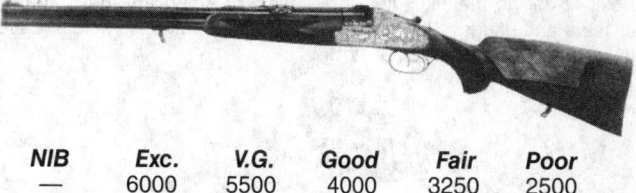

NIB	Exc.	V.G.	Good	Fair	Poor
—	6000	5500	4000	3250	2500

Model 55BSS

As above with sidelocks.

NIB	Exc.	V.G.	Good	Fair	Poor
—	10500	9500	8500	5000	3500

Model 55BF/77BF

Similar to Model 55B, except one barrel rifled and other smooth in 12-, 16- or 20-gauge.

NIB	Exc.	V.G.	Good	Fair	Poor
—	6000	5500	5000	3250	2500

Model 55BFSS

As above, with sidelocks.

NIB	Exc.	V.G.	Good	Fair	Poor
—	10500	9500	8500	5000	3500

Model 88 B

Large bore double-barrel boxlock rifle, with 24" barrels, automatic ejectors, double triggers and select walnut stock.

NIB	Exc.	V.G.	Good	Fair	Poor
—	12500	9750	8750	5500	4000

Model 88 BSS

As above with sidelocks.

NIB	Exc.	V.G.	Good	Fair	Poor
20000	18000	15000	10500	6500	5250

Model 88 Safari

As above, but chambered for .375 H&H, .458 Winchester Magnum, .470 or .500 Nitro Express calibers, with 25" barrels.

NIB	Exc.	V.G.	Good	Fair	Poor
20000	18000	15000	10000	7000	4750

DRILLINGS

Model 33

Boxlock drilling manufactured in a variety of American and European calibers and gauges. 25" barrels, double triggers and extractors. Case-hardened, blued, with walnut stock.

NIB	Exc.	V.G.	Good	Fair	Poor
—	7000	6000	5250	3750	2000

Model 33 Deluxe

Same as above, with game scene engraving.

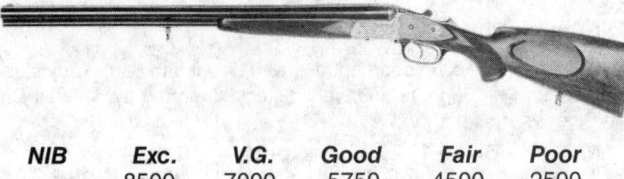

NIB	Exc.	V.G.	Good	Fair	Poor
—	8500	7000	5750	4500	2500

Model 37

Similar to Model 33 Standard, with full sidelocks.

NIB	Exc.	V.G.	Good	Fair	Poor
—	17500	13000	9500	6000	2500

Model 37 Deluxe

Similar to Model 37, with hand engraved scroll work and fancy walnut stock.

NIB	Exc.	V.G.	Good	Fair	Poor
—	20000	16500	12000	6000	3000

BOLT-ACTION RIFLES

Model SR-20

Mauser-action sporting rifle manufactured in a variety of calibers, with 21", 24" or 26" barrels, open sights, adjustable or set trigger. Blued, with walnut stock.

NIB	Exc.	V.G.	Good	Fair	Poor
2450	2250	1650	750	600	450

Model SR-20 Alpine

As above, with 20" barrel and Mannlicher stock. Introduced in 1989.

NIB	Exc.	V.G.	Good	Fair	Poor
—	2500	2000	1250	850	600

SR-20 Classic Safari

As above, but chambered for .404 Jeffries, .425 Express and .458 Win. Magnum, with 24" barrel having express sights. Introduced in 1989.

NIB	Exc.	V.G.	Good	Fair	Poor
—	3000	2500	2000	1250	750

SR-20 Classic Sportsman

Features round barrel without sights. Chambered for many calibers from .243 to .375 H&H. Introduced in 1988. **NOTE:** Add $100 for Magnum calibers.

NIB	Exc.	V.G.	Good	Fair	Poor
2650	2250	1900	900	500	300

SR-20 Trophy

Similar to above Classic Sportsman, with German bead ramp sight and open quarter rib rear sight. Select walnut stock, with oil-finish. Octagonal barrel and rosewood grip cap.

NIB	Exc.	V.G.	Good	Fair	Poor
3000	2500	2250	1800	900	300

Heym Magnum Express

Bolt-action rifle chambered for .338 Lapua, .375 H&H, .416 Rigby, .500 Nitro Express, .500 A-Square and few were built in .600 Nitro Express. Fitted with 24" barrel. Adjustable front sight, three leaf rear express sight. Select hand checkered European walnut stock and many other special features. Introduced in 1989. **NOTE:** Add $4,000 for .600 N.E.

NIB	Exc.	V.G.	Good	Fair	Poor
10000	8000	5000	2500	1750	500

HI-POINT FIREARMS
MKS Supply
Dayton, Ohio

Model C

A 9mm single-action compact semi-automatic pistol, with 3.5" barrel. Magazine capacity 8 rounds. Black or chrome finish. Weight 32 oz.

NIB	Exc.	V.G.	Good	Fair	Poor
125	100	85	75	65	50

Model C Polymer

Same as above, with polymer frame. Weight 28 oz.

NIB	Exc.	V.G.	Good	Fair	Poor
140	110	85	75	65	50

Model C Comp

Introduced in 1998, this 9mm model features 4" barrel with compensator, adjustable sights and 10-round magazine.

NIB	Exc.	V.G.	Good	Fair	Poor
170	130	100	90	75	50

Model JH

All steel construction chambered for .45 ACP, with 4.5" barrel. Magazine capacity 7 rounds. Weight 39 oz.

NIB	Exc.	V.G.	Good	Fair	Poor
180	135	100	85	75	50

Model 40SW

Same as above. Chambered for .40 S&W cartridge, 8-round magazine. Weight 39 oz.

NIB	Exc.	V.G.	Good	Fair	Poor
180	135	100	85	75	50

Model 9mm Polymer (Model 916)

Polymer-frame 9mm. Similar to .40- and .45-caliber models.

NIB	Exc.	V.G.	Good	Fair	Poor
160	140	120	100	80	60

Model .45 Polymer

Polymer frame and 4.5" barrel. Chambered for .45 ACP cartridge. Magazine capacity 9 rounds. Weight about 32 oz.

NIB	Exc.	V.G.	Good	Fair	Poor
180	135	100	85	75	50

Model .40 Polymer

As above, but chambered for .40 S&W cartridge, with magazine capacity of 10 rounds. Weight about 32 oz.

NIB	Exc.	V.G.	Good	Fair	Poor
180	135	100	85	75	50

Model CF

Chambered for .380 ACP cartridge. Fitted with polymer frame. Magazine capacity 8 rounds. Barrel length 3.5". Weight 29 oz. **NOTE:** Add $25 for compensator model.

NIB	Exc.	V.G.	Good	Fair	Poor
120	95	65	40	30	25

.380 ACP Compensated

Semi-automatic with fully-adjustable 3-dot sights, muzzle compensator, 4" barrel, 31 oz. polymer frame. Two magazines 8 and 10 rounds. **NOTE:** Add 50 percent for laser sight.

NIB	Exc.	V.G.	Good	Fair	Poor
150	125	100	85	75	50

Model 4095 Carbine

.40 S&W semi-automatic carbine. Features include all-weather black polymer stock, 10-shot magazine, 17.5" barrel, sling swivels, grip mounted clip release, quick on & off thumb safety, rear peep sight, 32.5" OAL and scope mount. **NOTE:** Add $85 for red dot sight.

NIB	Exc.	V.G.	Good	Fair	Poor
275	200	150	100	75	50

Model 995 Carbine

Similar to .40 S&W Carbine. Chambered for 9mm Parabellum.

NIB	Exc.	V.G.	Good	Fair	Poor
250	190	150	100	75	50

Model 4595 Carbine

Similar to 995 and 4095 models. Chambered in .45 ACP.

NIB	Exc.	V.G.	Good	Fair	Poor
300	265	200	150	125	100

HIGGINS, J. C.
Chicago, Illinois

Sears, Roebuck & Company of Chicago used trade name J.C. Higgins on firearms and other sporting goods it sold between 1946 and 1962. Arms bearing this trade name were manufactured by a variety of American gun makers. See High Standard, Mossberg, etc.

HIGH STANDARD
New Haven, Connecticut 1932-1945
Hamden, Connecticut 1946-1977
East Hartford, Connecticut 1977-1984

See High Standard Manufacturing Co., Houston, TX at the end of this section.

LETTER MODELS

Model B

A .22 LR caliber semi-automatic pistol, with 4.5" or 6.75" round barrel and 10-shot magazine. Blued came with checkered hard rubber grips (later production versions have checkered grips impressed with High Standard monogram). Introduced 1932, with serial numbers beginning at 5000. Early production utilized Hartford parts. Approximately 65,000 made. **NOTE:** Add $75 premium for Type-I-B takedown; $75 premium for early models with Hartford Arms front sight, safety and takedown levers; 15 percent premium for box with papers. C&R eligible. Most guns are found in serial number ranges from 5,000 to about 95,894 and 148198 to about 151021.

NIB	Exc.	V.G.	Good	Fair	Poor
—	675	550	350	250	150

Model B-US

Version of Model B, with slight contour modifications to back of frame. Approximately 14,000 made for U.S. government in 1942-1943. Most are marked "PROPERTY OF U.S." on top of barrel and on right side of frame. Monogrammed hard rubber grips. Most guns found in serial number range 92344 to about 111631. **NOTE:** Add 20 percent premium for box with papers.

NIB	Exc.	V.G.	Good	Fair	Poor
—	875	750	400	300	200

Model C

Like Model B except in .22 Short. Introduced 1936; approximately 4,700 made. Both plain and monogrammed hard rubber grips. Available with 4.5" or 6.75" round barrel. **NOTE:** Add $75 premium for I-A takedown; $175 premium for I-B takedown; 15 percent premium for box with papers.

NIB	Exc.	V.G.	Good	Fair	Poor
—	900	800	450	350	250

Model A

Similar to Model B, with checkered walnut grips over an extended grip and adjustable sight. Introduced 1938; approximately 7,300 made. Available with 4.5" or 6.75" round barrel. Same light barrel as Model B. **NOTE:** Add $175 premium for I-B takedown; 15 percent premium for box with papers.

NIB	Exc.	V.G.	Good	Fair	Poor
—	850	700	375	300	200

Model D

Similar to Model A, with heavier weight barrel (middle weight barrel). Available with 4.5" or 6.75" barrel and optional checkered walnut grips. Introduced 1938; approximately 2,500 made. **NOTE:** Add $175 premium for I-B takedown; 15 percent premium for box with papers.

NIB	Exc.	V.G.	Good	Fair	Poor
—	1000	850	500	400	300

Model E

Like Model D, with still heavier weight barrel (heavy weight barrel). Available with 4.5" or 6.75" barrel. Checkered walnut grips, with thumb rest.

Introduced 1938; approximately 2,600 made. **NOTE:** Add $175 for I-B takedown; 18 percent premium for box with papers.

NIB	Exc.	V.G.	Good	Fair	Poor
—	1400	1000	750	500	350

Model S

Not a production model. Like Model B, with a smooth bore. Nine registered as Model S. Additional five with Model C slides are registered, Model C/S. Note ivory bead front sight. Others may exist but only 14 are registered with BATF. Manufactured in 1939 and 1940. Values for both variations are equal. 6.75" barrels. **NOTE:** Serial numbers for registered samples. Model S: 48142; 48143; 48144; 48145; 48146; 59458; 59459; 59474 Model C/S: 59279; 59460; 59469; 59473; 59478. This model is too rare to accurately price. Last one sold at auction for $7,500 in 2012.

NIB	Exc.	V.G.	Good	Fair	Poor
—	5250	3950	3000	—	—

HAMMER LETTER MODELS

Second models made. Like letter models, with external hammers.

Model H-B, Type 1 Pre-War

Like Model B, with exposed hammer. Introduced 1940; approximately 2,100 made. **NOTE:** Add 15 percent premium for box with papers.

NIB	Exc.	V.G.	Good	Fair	Poor
—	1000	900	750	500	300

Model H-B, Type 2 Post-War

Post-war variation has external safety. Approximately 25,000 made. **NOTE:** Add 15 percent premium for box with papers.

NIB	Exc.	V.G.	Good	Fair	Poor
—	650	575	425	350	200

Model H-A

Like Model A, with exposed hammer. Introduced 1940; approximately 1,040 made. **NOTE:** Add 15 percent premium for box with papers.

NIB	Exc.	V.G.	Good	Fair	Poor
—	1850	1400	900	750	400

Model H-D

Like Model D, with exposed hammer. Introduced 1940; approximately 6,900 made. **NOTE:** Add 15 percent premium for box with papers.

NIB	Exc.	V.G.	Good	Fair	Poor
—	2250	1750	1100	850	400

Model H-E

Like Model E, with exposed hammer. Introduced 1940; approximately 2,100 made. **NOTE:** Add 15 percent premium for box with papers.

NIB	Exc.	V.G.	Good	Fair	Poor
—	2200	1700	1050	800	400

Model USA—Model HD

Similar to Model HD, with 4.5" barrel only. Has fixed sights, checkered black hard rubber grips and external safety. Early models blued; later model Parkerized. Introduced 1943; approximately 44,000 produced for U.S. government. **NOTE:** Add 20 percent premium for box with papers.

NIB	Exc.	V.G.	Good	Fair	Poor
—	950	850	700	500	300

Model USA—Model HD-MS

Silenced variation of USA Model HD. Approximately 2,000 produced for OSS during 1944 and 1945. 6.75" shrouded barrel. Early models blued; later model Parkerized. Only a few registered with BATFE or civilian ownership. This model is too rare to accurately price.

Model H-D Military

Similar to HD, with external safety. Early production had checkered plastic grips; later production changed to checkered walnut. Introduced 1945; approximately 150,000 produced. **NOTE:** Add 15 percent premium for box with papers.

NIB	Exc.	V.G.	Good	Fair	Poor
—	850	750	550	350	200

LEVER LETTER MODELS

Third design models incorporate interchangeable barrels, with lever takedown.

G-.380

A .380-caliber semi-automatic pistol, with 5" barrel and 6-shot magazine. Blued, with checkered plastic grips. Fixed sights. Introduced 1947, discontinued 1950; approximately 7,400 made. High Standard's only production centerfire pistol. **NOTE:** Add 10 percent premium for box with papers.

NIB	Exc.	V.G.	Good	Fair	Poor
—	750	550	450	350	200

G-B

Similar characteristics like Model B. with interchangeable 4.5" or 6.75" barrels. Sold with either barrel or as combination with both barrels. Fixed sights. Blued, with monogrammed plastic grips. Last short frame model produced. Introduced 1949, discontinued 1950; approximately 4,900 produced. **NOTE:** Add $225 premium for factory combination; 15 percent premium for box with papers.

NIB	Exc.	V.G.	Good	Fair	Poor
—	650	550	450	350	200

G-D

Similar characteristics like Model D, with interchangeable 4.5" or 6.75" barrels. Sold with either barrel or as combination with both barrels. Adjustable sights. Blued, with checkered walnut grips. Optional checkered thumb rest walnut grips. Introduced 1949, discontinued 1950; approximately 3,300 produced. **NOTE:** Add $325 premium for factory combination; $50 premium for factory target grips; 15 percent premium for box with papers.

NIB	Exc.	V.G.	Good	Fair	Poor
—	1050	950	600	400	300

G-E

Similar characteristics like Model E, with interchangeable 4.5" or 6.75" barrels. Sold with either barrel or as combination with both barrels. Adjustable sights. Blued, with checkered thumb rest walnut grips. Introduced 1949, discontinued 1950; approximately 2,900 produced. **NOTE:** Add $375 premium for factory combination; 15 percent premium for box with papers.

NIB	Exc.	V.G.	Good	Fair	Poor
—	1550	1200	800	450	300

Olympic (commonly called "G-O")

New gun design for competitive shooting in .22 Short caliber. 4.5" or 6.75" barrels. Sold with either barrel or as combination with both barrels. Grooved front and back straps on frame. Adjustable sights. Blued, with checkered thumb rest walnut grips. Introduced 1949, discontinued 1950; approximately 1,200 produced. Model uses a special curved magazine. Few guns will utilize a straight-back magazine. Majority of these Olympics use curved magazine, with a humped back. **NOTE:** Add $375 premium for factory combination; $300 for straight magazine variation; 15 percent premium for box with papers.

NIB	Exc.	V.G.	Good	Fair	Poor
—	1800	1450	900	500	300

LEVER NAME MODELS

Fourth design models evolving from lever letter series, with slight changes.

Supermatic

.22 LR caliber pistol, with 10-shot magazine. Heavy round barrel, blued finish, adjustable sights and brown plastic thumb rest grips. Grooved front and back straps on frame. Available with 4.5" or 6.75" barrels or combination with both barrels. Ribbed barrels and provisions for weights. A 2 and 3 oz. weight were provided with this model, as was a filler strip for when weights were not used. **NOTE:** Add $250 for factory combination; 15 percent premium for box with papers.

NIB	Exc.	V.G.	Good	Fair	Poor
—	875	725	625	425	200

Olympic

.22 Short caliber pistol, with 10-shot magazine. Heavy round barrel, blued finish, adjustable sights and brown plastic thumb rest grips. Grooved front and back straps on frame. Available with 4.5" or 6.75" barrels or combination with both barrels. Ribbed barrels and provisions for weights. Weights of 2 and 3 oz. were provided with this model, as was a filler strip for when weights were not used. **NOTE:** Add $250 for factory combination; 15 percent premium for box with papers.

NIB	Exc.	V.G.	Good	Fair	Poor
—	1250	925	775	650	250

Field King

.22 LR caliber pistol, with 10-shot magazine. Heavy round barrel, blued finish, adjustable sights and brown plastic thumb rest grips. Available with 4.5" or 6.75" barrels or combination with both barrels. No rib on barrels or provisions for weights. **NOTE:** Add $225 premium for factory combination; 15 percent premium for box with papers.

NIB	Exc.	V.G.	Good	Fair	Poor
—	650	550	450	350	150

Sport King

.22-caliber pistol, with 10-shot magazine. Lightweight round barrel, blued finish, fixed sights and brown plastic thumb rest grips. Available with 4.5" or 6.75" barrels or combination with both barrels. Early models did not have slide holdback when magazine was empty. Early variation without holdback was produced in about twice the quantity as later models incorporating this feature. **NOTE:** Add $200 premium for factory combination; $25 premium for guns with holdback feature; 15 percent premium for box with papers.

NIB	Exc.	V.G.	Good	Fair	Poor
—	500	425	350	250	150

100 SERIES MODELS

Fifth design models evolving from lever name series. Series introduced small pushbutton barrel release takedown and deletes shrouded breech.

Supermatic S-100

Like lever takedown Supermatic, with new takedown. Available with 4.5" or 6.75" barrels or combination with both barrel lengths. Grooved front and back straps on frame. Model produced briefly in 1954. Weights of 2 and 3 oz. were provided with this model, as was filler strip for when weights were not used. **NOTE:** Add $250 for factory combination; 15 percent premium for box with papers.

NIB	Exc.	V.G.	Good	Fair	Poor
—	850	750	550	400	200

Olympic O-100

Like lever takedown Olympic, with new takedown. Available with 4.5" or 6.75" barrels or combination with both barrel lengths. Grooved front and back straps on frame. Model produced briefly in 1954. Weights of 2 and 3 oz. were provided with this model, as was filler strip for when weights were not used. **NOTE:** Add $250 for factory combination; 15 percent premium for box with papers.

NIB	Exc.	V.G.	Good	Fair	Poor
—	1200	950	650	500	300

Field King FK-100

Like lever takedown Field King, with new takedown. Available with 4.5" or 6.75" barrels or combination with both barrel lengths. Model produced briefly in 1954. **NOTE:** Add $225 premium for factory combination; 15 percent premium for box with papers.

NIB	Exc.	V.G.	Good	Fair	Poor
—	750	650	400	300	200

Sport King SK-100

Like lever takedown Sport King, with new takedown. Available with 4.5" or 6.75" barrels or combination with both barrel lengths. Produced 1954 to 1957. In late 1958, Col. Rex Applegate imported about 300 of these pistols into Mexico. Guns are marked with his company's name "ARMAMEX". Marked "ARMAMEX, MEXICO" on right side of barrel and "SPORT KING/CAL .22 L.R." on left side of barrel. Serial numbers around 870,084-870,383. Note that Applegate guns were made after 102 series was in production. Armamex catalog number 1910. **NOTE:** Add $200 premium for factory combination; $250 premium for Armamex version; 10 percent premium for box with papers.

NIB	Exc.	V.G.	Good	Fair	Poor
—	450	400	300	200	150

Sport King Lightweight SK-100

Aluminum frame like Flite King LW-100 in .22 LR caliber. Produced 1956 to 1964. Also available nickel plated 1957 to 1960. **NOTE:** Add $150 premium for nickel finish; $200 premium for factory combination; 12 percent premium for box with papers.

NIB	Exc.	V.G.	Good	Fair	Poor
—	525	450	350	275	200

Flite King LW-100

.22 Short caliber semi-automatic pistol, with 10-shot magazine. Blued finish, with black anodized aluminum frame and slide. Brown plastic checkered thumb rest grips. Fixed sights. Available with 4.5" or 6.75" barrels or combination with both barrel lengths. Produced 1954 to 1957. **NOTE:** Add $200 for factory combination; 12 percent premium for box with papers.

NIB	Exc.	V.G.	Good	Fair	Poor
—	625	525	400	300	200

Dura-Matic M-100

.22 LR caliber semi-automatic pistol, with 10-shot magazine. Striker-fired, fixed sights, blued finish, brown checkered plastic one-piece grip. Takedown by thumb nut. Available with 4.5" or 6.5" barrls or combination with both barrel lengths. Produced briefly in 1954. **NOTE:** Add $150 premium for factory combination; 12 percent premium for box with papers.

NIB	Exc.	V.G.	Good	Fair	Poor
—	500	350	300	250	175

101 SERIES MODELS

Sixth design models evolving from 100 series. Series continued small pushbutton barrel release takedown.

Olympic O-101

.22 Short caliber semi-automatic pistol, with 10-shot magazine. Heavy round barrel, blued finish, adjustable sights and brown plastic thumb rest grips. Grooved front and back straps on frame. Available with 4.5" or 6.75" barrels or combination with both barrel lengths. The 6.75" barrel incorporates a muzzle-brake with one slot on either side of front sight. **NOTE:** Add $250 premium for factory combination; 13 percent premium for box with papers.

NIB	Exc.	V.G.	Good	Fair	Poor
—	1150	950	800	500	300

Supermatic S-101

.22 LR caliber semi-automatic pistol, with 10-shot magazine. Heavy round barrel, blued finish, adjustable sights and brown plastic thumb rest grips. Grooved front and back straps on frame. Available with 4.5" or 6.75" barrels or combination with both barrel lengths. The 6.75" barrel incorporates a muzzle-brake with one slot on either side of front sight. Produced with U.S. marking for military. **NOTE:** Add $250 premium for factory combination; 13 percent premium for box with papers.

NIB	Exc.	V.G.	Good	Fair	Poor
—	775	700	600	425	250

Field King FK-101

.22 LR caliber semi-automatic pistol, with 10-shot magazine. Heavy round barrel, blued finish, adjustable sights and brown plastic thumb rest grips. Available with 4.5" or 6.75" barrels or combination with both barrel lengths. **NOTE:** Add $225 premium for factory combination; 15 percent premium for box with papers.

NIB	Exc.	V.G.	Good	Fair	Poor
—	675	550	500	300	200

Dura-Matic M-101

Like Dura-matic M-100, with slightly different locking method for thumb nut takedown. Produced 1954 to 1970. Later appeared renamed "Plinker" M-101 in 1971 to 1973. Plinker not available with both barrel combinations. Slightly modified version was sold by Sears Roebuck & Co. as J. C. Higgins M-80. **NOTE:** Add $150 premium for factory combination; 10 percent premium for box with papers.

NIB	Exc.	V.G.	Good	Fair	Poor
—	375	325	250	175	100

Conversion Kits

Kits convert .22 LR to .22 Short and include barrel, aluminum slide and magazine for .22 Short to .22 LR, in which case slide is steel. Prices for kit in original factory boxes. **NOTE:** First advertised for 101 Series guns. Later versions were produced for lever takedown guns. Catalog numbers are unknown for conversion kits for lever takedown guns.

NIB	Exc.	V.G.	Good	Fair	Poor
—	600	475	—	—	—

102 & 103 SERIES MODELS

The 102 Series was a major design change. Incorporating a new frame with large pushbutton takedown release. Also new was a superb adjustable sight. Little difference between the two series.

Supermatic Trophy

.22 LR caliber semi-automatic pistol, with 10-shot magazine. Tapered barrel with enlarged register at muzzle end to hold a removable muzzle-brake. Super polished blue finish; adjustable sights; 2 and 3 oz. adjustable weights and checkered walnut thumb rest grips. Grooved front and back straps on frame. Available with 6.75", 8" or 10" barrels. Occasionally sold as combination including two barrels. Premiums for 10" barrels and combinations in original boxes. 5.5" bull barrel available in 103s after April 1962, 7.25" fluted barrels available in 103s after April 1963. **NOTE:** Add $125 premium for 8" barrel; $225 premium for 10" barrel; 12 percent premium for box with papers; 14 percent premium for light oak case.

NIB	Exc.	V.G.	Good	Fair	Poor
—	1350	1100	825	500	250

Supermatic Citation

Like Supermatic Trophy, with checkered plastic grips. Blued finish, without trophy's super polished finish. Grooved front and back straps on frame. 5.5" bull barrel available in 103s after April 1962. Also produced with U.S. marking for military. **NOTE:** Add $100 premium for 8" barrel; $200 premium for 10" barrel; 12 percent premiun for box with papers; 18 percent premium for light oak case.

NIB	Exc.	V.G.	Good	Fair	Poor
—	900	825	675	400	200

Supermatic Tournament

.22 LR caliber semi-automatic pistol, with 10-shot magazine. Barrels are round and tapered. Blued finish, adjustable sights and checkered plastic grips. Available with 4.5", 6.75" or combination with both barrels. Combinations available in 102 Series only. 5.5" bull barrel replaced the 4.5" barrel in early 1962. Also produced with U.S. marking for military. **NOTE:** Add $200 premium for factory combination; 12 percent premium for box with papers.

NIB	Exc.	V.G.	Good	Fair	Poor
—	725	600	450	300	200

Olympic

.22 Short caliber version of Supermatic Citation. Early models marked "Olympic Citation", changed to "Olympic" only in 1960. Grooved front and back straps on frame. 6.75", 8" and 10" barrels produced. 5.5" bull barrel available on later 103 production. **NOTE:** Add $125 premium for 8" barrel; $225 premium for 10" barrel; $150 premium for "Olympic Citation" marked guns; 12 percent premium for box with papers.

NIB	Exc.	V.G.	Good	Fair	Poor
—	1150	900	750	450	225

Olympic ISU

Like an Olympic only available with 6.75" barrel and integral muzzle-brake. Grooved front and back straps on frame. **NOTE:** Add 12 percent premium for box with papers.

NIB	Exc.	V.G.	Good	Fair	Poor
—	1250	950	800	550	250

Olympic Trophy ISU

Olympic ISU with Supermatic Trophy finish. Grooved front and back straps on frame. Produced in 103 Series only. Fewer than 500 produced. **NOTE:** Add 10 percent premium for box with papers.

NIB	Exc.	V.G.	Good	Fair	Poor
—	2250	1450	800	550	250

Sport King

.22 LR caliber semi-automatic pistol, with 10-shot magazine. Barrels are lightweight, round and tapered. Blued finish, fixed sights and checkered plastic grips. Available with 4.5", 6.75" or combination with both barrel lengths. Produced 1957 to 1970 and 1974 to 1977. Also available 1974 to 1977 with nickel finish. **NOTE:** Add $100 premium for nickel finish; $200 premium for factory combination; 20 percent premium for box with papers.

NIB	Exc.	V.G.	Good	Fair	Poor
—	425	350	300	200	150

Flite King

.22 Short caliber version of Sport King Models 102 and 103. Models have steel frames. **NOTE:** Add $200 premium for factory combination; 12 percent premium for box with papers.

NIB	Exc.	V.G.	Good	Fair	Poor
—	525	450	350	300	200

Sharpshooter

.22 LR caliber semi-automatic pistol, with 10-shot magazine. 5.5" bull barrel, blued finish, adjustable sights, checkered plastic grips. Some produced with Model 103-marked slides. Although the 103-marked guns have 1969 and later serial numbers they were shipped after introduction of Sharpshooter in 1971 and were probably converted from unsold Sport Kings. No premium for 103-marked. Variation without series marked on slide is most plentiful. Produced 1971 to 1977. **NOTE:** Add 15 percent premium for box with papers.

NIB	Exc.	V.G.	Good	Fair	Poor
—	600	475	400	300	200

Conversion Kits

Kits convert .22 LR to .22 Short and include barrel, aluminum slide and magazine. Prices for kits in original boxes.

NIB	Exc.	V.G.	Good	Fair	Poor
900	700	575	—	—	—

104 SERIES MODELS

Last of slant grip gun designs. Early production marked "Model 104". Later production unmarked.

Supermatic Trophy

.22 LR caliber semi-automatic pistol, with 10-shot magazine. Super polished blue finish; adjustable sights; 2 and 3 oz. adjustable weights; checkered walnut thumb rest grips. Grooved front and back straps on frame. Available with 5.5" bull or 7.25" fluted barrels. Both barrels accept removable muzzle-brake. **NOTE:** Add $150 premium for high polish blue finish; 12 percent premium for box with papers.

NIB	Exc.	V.G.	Good	Fair	Poor
—	1175	1050	800	450	225

Supermatic Citation

.22 LR caliber semi-automatic pistol, with 10-shot magazine. Blue finish, adjustable sights, 2 and 3 oz. adjustable weights, checkered walnut thumb rest grips. Grooved front and back straps on frame. **NOTE:** Add 12 percent premium for box with papers.

NIB	Exc.	V.G.	Good	Fair	Poor
—	850	750	625	350	175

Olympic

Like 103 Series 8" barrel models. **NOTE:** Add 12 percent premium for box with papers.

NIB	Exc.	V.G.	Good	Fair	Poor
—	1300	1150	850	550	300

Olympic ISU

Like 103 model. 6.75" barrel with integral brake. 5.5" version introduced in 1964. Catalogs and price list refer to 9295 as both Olympic and Olympic ISU. Met ISU regulations and included removable muzzle-brake and weights. **NOTE:** Add 12 percent premium for box with papers.

NIB	Exc.	V.G.	Good	Fair	Poor
—	1200	1000	850	450	250

Victor (Slant Grip)

.22 LR caliber semi-automatic pistol, with 10-shot magazine. 4.5" and 5.5" slab-sided barrels with either ventilated or solid ribs. Adjustable sights are integral with rib. Blue finish, barrel tapped for weight, checkered walnut thumb rest grips. Grooved front and back straps on frame. Probably fewer than 600 of these slant grip Victors in all configurations. Probably fewer than 40 each of 4.5" guns. Trigger adjustable for both pull and over-travel. Most guns in serial number range above 2401xxx with few in ML serial number series. **NOTE:** Early ventilated rib barrels were steel and later ones aluminum, without a change in catalog numbers. **BEWARE**—fakes exist. **NOTE:** Add $75 premium for steel rib; $200 premium for solid rib; $200 premium for 4.5" barrel; 15 percent premium for box with papers.

Victor with 4.5" solid rib barrel

Victor with 5.5" ventilated rib barrel

NIB	Exc.	V.G.	Good	Fair	Poor
—	2750	2150	1000	650	350

106 SERIES MODELS

Referred to as military models, this series was designed to provide same grip angles and feel of Colt military model 1911. Design introduced in 1965 and continued through most of 1968.

Supermatic Trophy

Like 104 Series Supermatic Trophy, with new military frame. Stippled front and back straps on frame. **NOTE:** Add $100 premium for high polish blue finish; $200 premium for guns with boxes and accessories if factory records verify model numbers; 12 percent premium for box with papers.

NIB	Exc.	V.G.	Good	Fair	Poor
—	1100	850	600	450	200

Supermatic Citation

Like 104 Series Supermatic Citation, with new military frame. Stippled front and back straps on frame. **NOTE:** Add $150 premium for guns with boxes and accessories if factory records verify model numbers; 12 percent premium for box with papers.

NIB	Exc.	V.G.	Good	Fair	Poor
—	850	750	500	300	175

Supermatic Tournament

Like 104 Series Supermatic Tournament, with new military frame. Stippled front and back straps on frame. **NOTE:** Add $125 premium for guns with boxes and accessories if factory records verify model numbers; 12 percent premium for box with papers.

NIB	Exc.	V.G.	Good	Fair	Poor
—	725	650	400	250	175

Olympic

Listed in catalog not in shipping records. Catalog number 9235 for 5.5" barrel. **WARNING:** There is no evidence this model was actually produced.

Olympic ISU

Like 104 Series Olympic ISU, with new military frame. Stippled front and back straps on frame. **NOTE:** Add $200 premium for guns with boxes and accessories if factory records verify model numbers; 12 percent premium for box with papers.

NIB	Exc.	V.G.	Good	Fair	Poor
—	1200	900	700	450	200

107 SERIES MODELS

Evolutionary successor to 106 Series. Series had frame redesigned to eliminate plugging of spring hole produced with old tooling. During time of this series production, MILITARY marking on frame was removed and then later reappeared near the end of traditional serial number series. MILITARY marking is absent from guns with ML prefixed serial numbers. No premium associated with these variations.

Olympic ISU

Like 106 Series Olympic ISU. **NOTE:** Add 12 percent premium for box with papers.

NIB	Exc.	V.G.	Good	Fair	Poor
—	1200	900	700	450	200

Olympic ISU 1980 Commemorative

Limited edition of 107 Olympic ISU, with 1,000 produced. "USA" prefix on serial numbers from 0001 to 1000. Engraved right side of slide has five gold ring Olympic logo. Offered with lined presentation case. **NOTE:** Prices are for guns with box, papers and presentation case; otherwise deduct $250 for guns in excellent condition.

NIB	Exc.	V.G.	Good	Fair	Poor
—	1750	1250	650	—	—

Supermatic Trophy

Like 106 Series Supermatic Trophy. **NOTE:** Add 12 percent premium for box with papers.

NIB	Exc.	V.G.	Good	Fair	Poor
—	975	750	500	250	175

Supermatic Trophy 1972 Commemorative

Limited edition of 107 Supermatic Trophy, with 1000 planned. "T" prefix on serial numbers from 0000 to 999. Engraved right side of slide has five gold ring Olympic logo. Offered with lined presentation case. Only 107 guns listed in shipping records, plus one frame. Couple of proto-types believed to exist in regular serial number series. Prices are for guns in original presentation cases. **NOTE:** One fully engraved gun is known.

NIB	Exc.	V.G.	Good	Fair	Poor
7500 (based on rarity and last sale price)					

Supermatic Citation

Like 106 Series Supermatic Citation. **NOTE:** Add 12 percent premium for box with papers.

NIB	Exc.	V.G.	Good	Fair	Poor
—	850	650	500	250	175

Supermatic Tournament

Like 106 Series Supermatic Tournament. Smooth front and back straps on frame. **NOTE:** Add 12 percent premium for box with papers.

NIB	Exc.	V.G.	Good	Fair	Poor
—	700	550	400	300	175

Sport King

Like 103 Series Sport King, with military frame. **NOTE:** Add 12 percent premium for box with papers.

NIB	Exc.	V.G.	Good	Fair	Poor
—	450	400	350	300	175

Sharpshooter

Like 103 Series Sharpshooter, with military frame. **NOTE:** Add 12 percent premium for box with papers.

NIB	Exc.	V.G.	Good	Fair	Poor
—	550	450	400	350	175

Survival Kit

An electroless nickel Sharpshooter, with 5.5" barrel in canvas carrying case and extra electroless nickel magazine. **NOTE:** Deduct $100 for guns without case; $65 for guns without extra magazine, for guns in excellent condition.

NIB	Exc.	V.G.	Good	Fair	Poor
—	600	475	400	300	175

Victor

.22 LR caliber semi-automatic pistol, with 10-shot magazine. 4.5" and 5.5" slab-sided barrels with ventilated or solid ribs. Adjustable sights are integral with rib. Blue finish, barrel tapped for weight, checkered walnut thumb rest grips. Stippled front and back straps on frame. Early ventilated ribs were steel; aluminum replaced steel on later ventilated ribs. Still later a clearance groove was added for spent shell ejection behind barrel. Early models marked THE VICTOR on left side of barrel; later guns marked simply VICTOR on left side of frame. Few transition guns marked in both locations. **NOTE:** Add $125 premium for steel ribs; $125 premium for solid rib guns, premium for 4.5" barreled guns; $140 premium for Hamden guns (7-digit serial numbers and ML prefix serial numbers below ML 25,000); 12 percent premium for box with papers.

NIB	Exc.	V.G.	Good	Fair	Poor
—	1025	800	700	450	200

10-X

.22 LR caliber semi-automatic pistol, with 10-shot magazine. Matte blue finish, adjustable sights, checkered walnut thumb rest grips painted black. Stippled front and back straps on frame. Available with 5.5" bull barrel. Assembled by a master gunsmith. Gunsmith's initials stamped in frame under left grip panel. Produced in 1981. **NOTE:** Prices are for guns with box and papers including test target, otherwise deduct $175.

NIB	Exc.	V.G.	Good	Fair	Poor
—	2800	2350	1700	800	300

SH SERIES MODELS

Final design produced by High Standard. Change in takedown from large pushbutton introduced with 102 Series and continuing through 107 Series, to hex socket head cap screw takedown.

Supermatic Trophy

Like 107 Supermatic Trophy, with new takedown. **NOTE:** Add 10 percent premium for box with papers.

NIB	Exc.	V.G.	Good	Fair	Poor
—	750	700	600	450	200

Supermatic Citation

Like 107 Supermatic Citation, with new takedown. **NOTE:** Add 10 percent premium for box with papers.

NIB	Exc.	V.G.	Good	Fair	Poor
—	700	625	550	400	200

Citation II

New gun like Supermatic Citation, with barrel slabbed on sides like Victor and smooth front and back straps on frame. 5.5" and 7.25" barrels available. Blued finish, adjustable sights. Electroless nickel version utilized in some survival kits. **NOTE:** Add 10 percent premium for box with papers.

NIB	Exc.	V.G.	Good	Fair	Poor
—	550	500	400	300	200

Sport King-M

Like 107 Sport King, with new takedown. Electroless nickel finish also available. **NOTE:** Add 10 percent premium for box with papers.

NIB	Exc.	V.G.	Good	Fair	Poor
—	350	275	190	150	100

Victor

Like 107 Victor, with new takedown. Only available with 5.5" barrel. **NOTE:** Add 10 percent premium for box with papers.

NIB	Exc.	V.G.	Good	Fair	Poor
—	800	700	575	400	200

Sharpshooter-M

Like 107 Sharpshooter, with new takedown. Electroless nickel version utilized in some survival kits. **NOTE:** Add 10 percent premium for box with papers.

NIB	Exc.	V.G.	Good	Fair	Poor
	425	375	300	200	100

10-X

Like 107 10-X, with new takedown. Also available with 7.25" fluted barrel and 5.5" ribbed barrel like Victor. **NOTE:** Add $500 premium for 7.25" barrel; $1,000 for ribbed barrel like Victor. Prices are for guns with box and papers including test target, otherwise deduct $150.

NIB	Exc.	V.G.	Good	Fair	Poor
—	2325	1900	1200	750	300

Survival Kit (with carrying case)

Either electroless nickel Sharpshooter or electroless nickel Citation II, with 5.5" barrel in canvas carrying case, with an extra electroless nickel magazine. Two different fabrics utilized during production. **NOTE:** Deduct $100 for guns without case; $65 for guns without extra magazine, for guns in excellent condition.

NIB	Exc.	V.G.	Good	Fair	Poor
—	625	575	475	300	200

Conversion Kits for Military Frame Guns

Kits convert .22 LR to .22 Short and include barrel, aluminum slide and 2 magazines. **NOTE:** Prices are for kits in original boxes.

NIB	Exc.	V.G.	Good	Fair	Poor
—	625	390	—	—	—

DERRINGERS

A .22-caliber or .22 Magnum caliber over/under double-action-only derringer, with 3.50" barrels. Found with three different types of markings.

Type 1 Markings

Type 1 Markings are found on early models which are marked "HI-STANDARD" / "DERRINGER" and have EAGLE logo on left side of barrel. Models marked "D-100" for .22-caliber and "DM-101" for .22 Magnum on left side of barrel. Date range 1962 to about 1967.

Type 2 Markings

Type 2 Markings are found on later models marked "HI- STANDARD" / "DERRINGER" and had TRIGGER logo. Early .22-caliber models marked "D-100" and later .22-caliber models beginning about 1969 were marked "D-101" on left side of barrel. .22 Magnum models marked "DM-101" on left side of barrel. Date range 1967 to about 1970.

Type 3 Markings

Type 3 Markings are found on latest models marked simply "DERRINGER" without HI STANDARD or either logo. These models also marked "D-101" for .22-caliber and "DM-101" for .22 Magnum on left side of barrel.

Blued finish, white or black grips, 1962-1984

NIB	Exc.	V.G.	Good	Fair	Poor
—	450	350	250	125	75

Nickel Finish black grips, introduced 1970

NIB	Exc.	V.G.	Good	Fair	Poor
—	450	350	250	125	75

Electroless Nickel Finish with checkered walnut grips

NIB	Exc.	V.G.	Good	Fair	Poor
—	475	375	250	125	75

Silver-Plated Derringer

A .22 Magnum derringer, with presentation case. Faux black mother of pearl grips. 501 made. Serial numbers SP 0 through SP 500. Produced in 1981.

NIB	Exc.	V.G.	Good	Fair	Poor
—	750	700	500	200	150

Gold-Plated Derringer

NOTE: Prices for GP serial number guns with presentation case. $100 premium for DM prefix guns in Exc. condition with presentation case; $150 premium for 1960s gold guns in Exc. condition with presentation cases.

NIB	Exc.	V.G.	Good	Fair	Poor
—	800	725	550	200	150

REVOLVERS

POLICE-STYLE REVOLVERS

Revolvers begin with R-100 design series and continue through R-109. Later steel-framed Sentinels carry no design series markings. Changes of design series designations indicate design changes to guns. Only R-105 known to date is a private label gun made for Sears. Design series designations and associated catalog numbers listed are best estimates at time of publication.

Earliest Sentinels in 1955 were in separate serial number series from 1 through approximately 45000. They were included in serial number series common to all handguns. In 1974 they were again put in separate serial number series with S prefix: S101 through S79946. Many later guns had V suffix which indicated gun was visually imperfect, but guaranteed to work properly.

Sentinel Aluminum Frames

A 9-shot single-/double-action revolver, with swing-out cylinder for .22 Short, Long or LR cartridges. Fixed sights. Sentinel snub 2.375" barrel

model had bobbed hammer from its introduction until 1960. Beginning in 1961 this changed to standard spur hammer with no change in catalog number. Beginning with R-102 series ejector had a spring return. Available in configurations listed.

High Standard private-labeled aluminum-framed Sentinels for both Sears and Western Auto. From 1957 through 1962 High Standard offered 2.375" snub-barreled Sentinel in three different color anodized frames. These guns had nickel-plated cylinders, triggers and hammers. Grips were round-butt ivory-colored plastic. **NOTE:** Add $20 premium for nickel; $20 for R-102 marked guns. Deduct $15 for early models without spring return ejector.

NIB	Exc.	V.G.	Good	Fair	Poor
—	350	275	175	125	100

Gold

NIB	Exc.	V.G.	Good	Fair	Poor
—	1000	850	500	300	200

Turquoise

NIB	Exc.	V.G.	Good	Fair	Poor
—	1200	900	650	300	200

Pink

NIB	Exc.	V.G.	Good	Fair	Poor
—	1200	900	650	300	200

Sentinel Imperial

Has two-piece walnut square-butt grips, ramp front and adjustable rear sights. **NOTE:** Add $15 premium for nickel.

NIB	Exc.	V.G.	Good	Fair	Poor
—	375	325	275	150	100

Sentinel Deluxe

Has two-piece walnut square-butt grips and fixed sights. **NOTE:** Add $20 premium for nickel.

NIB	Exc.	V.G.	Good	Fair	Poor
—	375	325	275	150	100

Sentinel Snub

Has 2.375" barrel, with round-butt grips. **NOTE:** Add $20 premium for nickel.

NIB	Exc.	V.G.	Good	Fair	Poor
—	375	325	275	150	100

Sentinel Steel Frames

Model like Mark I sentinels without Mark I markings. Offered as a combination with cylinders for .22 LR and .22 Win. Magnum. Prices for guns with both cylinders. **NOTE:** Add $25 premium for adjustable sights. Deduct $50 for guns with only one cylinder.

NIB	Exc.	V.G.	Good	Fair	Poor
—	425	375	300	150	100

Kit Gun

A 9-shot single-/double-action revolver, with swing-out cylinder for .22 Short, Long or LR cartridges. Blue finish, aluminum frame, 4.0" barrel and adjustable sights. Wood round-butt grips.

NIB	Exc.	V.G.	Good	Fair	Poor
—	350	300	200	150	100

Camp Gun

A 9-shot single-/double-action revolver, with swing-out cylinder for .22 Short, Long, LR cartridges or .22 Magnum. Available as combination with both cylinders. Blue finished steel frame, adjustable sights. **NOTE:** Add $50 premium for combination with both cylinders.

NIB	Exc.	V.G.	Good	Fair	Poor
—	350	300	200	150	100

Sentinel Mark I

A 9-shot single-/double-action revolver, with swing-out cylinder for .22 Short, Long or LR cartridges. Steel frame and fixed sights. Available with blue and nickel finishes in 2", 3" and 4" barrels. Adjustable sights available on 3" and 4" barreled guns only. Wood square-butt grips. **NOTE:** Add $25 premium for adjustable sights; $25 for nickel.

NIB	Exc.	V.G.	Good	Fair	Poor
—	350	300	200	150	100

Sentinel Mark IV

Like Mark I above except in .22 Magnum. **NOTE:** Add $25 premium for nickel; $25 premium for adjustable sights.

NIB	Exc.	V.G.	Good	Fair	Poor
—	400	350	250	175	125

Sentinel Mark II

A .357 Magnum single-/double-action 6-shot revolver, with swing-out cylinder. Blue finish, steel frame, fixed sights. Produced by Dan Wesson for High Standard. Sold 1974 through 1975.

NIB	Exc.	V.G.	Good	Fair	Poor
—	475	400	325	250	200

Sentinel Mark III

Like Mark II above except with adjustable sights. Sold 1974 through 1975.

NIB	Exc.	V.G.	Good	Fair	Poor
—	500	425	350	275	200

Power Plus

A 5-shot single-/double-action revolver, with swing-out cylinder for .38 Special cartridges. Blue finished steel frame. Only 177 guns produced. Serial numbers between PG 1010 and PG 1273.

NIB	Exc.	V.G.	Good	Fair	Poor
—	650	575	475	300	250

Crusader

A .44 Magnum or .45 Colt caliber double-action swing-out cylinder revolver, with unique geared action. Adjustable sights. 6-shot cylinder. First 51 guns had long barrels, special engraving, gold crusader figure on side plate and anniversary rollmark to commemorate High Standard's 50th Anniversary.

.45 Colt (s/n 000 to 050)

NOTE: Values are for .45 Colt with serial numbers 000 to 050. Add 10 percent for .44 Magnum; $1,000 for serial numbers 000 and 001 or proto-types C001, C002, C003.

NIB	Exc.	V.G.	Good	Fair	Poor
2500	2000	1500	750	—	—

.45 Colt (s/n over 050)

NOTE: Prices for serial numbers over 050 in .45 Colt. Add 10 percent for .44 Magnum. Expect to pay a premium for matching set.

NIB	Exc.	V.G.	Good	Fair	Poor
1750	1500	1000	650	—	—

WESTERN-STYLE REVOLVERS

Western-style revolvers begin with W-100 design series and continue through W-106. Later steel-framed Sentinels carry no design series markings. Changes of design series designations indicate design changes to guns. Design series designations and associated catalog numbers listed are best estimates at time of publication.

Double Nine with Aluminum Frame

A 9-shot single-/double-action revolver for .22 Short, Long, LR cartridges and all aluminum frame guns. One model has grip straps and trigger guard, with gold plating contrasting with blue frame. **NOTE:** Add $50 premium for nickel.

NIB	Exc.	V.G.	Good	Fair	Poor
—	400	325	200	150	100

Double Nine with Steel Frame

Available as .22 Short/Long/LR, .22 Magnum or combination with both cylinders. **NOTE:** Add $45 premium for combination models; $50 premium for nickel.

NIB	Exc.	V.G.	Good	Fair	Poor
—	400	325	200	150	100

Longhorn

A 9-shot single-/double-action revolver for .22 Short, Long, LR cartridges and all aluminum frame guns. Blue finish, fixed sights and square-butt grips. One model has grip straps and trigger guard, with gold plating contrasting with blue frame. Sears version exists.

NIB	Exc.	V.G.	Good	Fair	Poor
—	475	450	350	275	200

Longhorns with Steel Frame

Guns available as .22 Short/Long/LR, .22 Magnum or combination with both cylinders. **NOTE:** Add $45 premium for combination models; $25 premium for adjustable sights.

NIB	Exc.	V.G.	Good	Fair	Poor
—	475	450	350	275	200

Marshal

A 9-shot single-/double-action revolver for .22 Short, Long or LR cartridges. Blue finish. Aluminum frame, 5.5" barrel, fixed sights and square-butt stag style plastic grips. Offered in special promotion package, with holster, trigger lock and spray can of G-96 gun scrubber. Price for gun only. **NOTE:** Add $40 premium if box, papers and accessories are present and in excellent condition.

NIB	Exc.	V.G.	Good	Fair	Poor
—	350	250	200	150	100

Posse

A 9-shot single-/double-action revolver for .22 Short, Long or LR cartridges. Blue finish, with brass colored grip straps and trigger guard. Aluminum frame, 3.5" barrel, fixed sights and square-butt walnut grips.

NIB	Exc.	V.G.	Good	Fair	Poor
—	450	375	275	150	100

Natchez

A 9-shot single-/double-action revolver for .22 Short, Long or LR cartridges. Aluminum frame, 4.5" barrel, fixed sights and bird's-head-style ivory-colored plastic grips.

NIB	Exc.	V.G.	Good	Fair	Poor
800	750	650	500	350	200

Hombre

A 9-shot single-/double-action revolver for .22 Short/Long/LR cartridges. Blue or nickel finish. Aluminum frame, 4" barrel, fixed sights and square-butt walnut grips. **NOTE:** Add $20 premium for nickel.

NIB	Exc.	V.G.	Good	Fair	Poor
—	425	375	300	250	175

Durango

A 9-shot single-/double-action revolver for .22 Short/Long/LR cartridges. Blue or nickel finish. Aluminum or steel frame, 4.5" or 5.5" barrel, fixed or adjustable sights and square-butt walnut grips. Two models have their grip straps and trigger guard with contrasting plating to blue frame. **NOTE:** Add $50 premium for nickel; $25 premium for steel frame; $25 premium for adjustable sights.

NIB	Exc.	V.G.	Good	Fair	Poor
—	425	375	300	250	175

The Gun/High Sierra

A 9-shot single-/double-action revolver for .22 Short, Long or LR cartridges. Available as combination model, with second cylinder in .22 Magnum. Blued finish, with gold plated grip straps and trigger guard. Steel frame, 7" octagonal barrel, fixed or adjustable sights and square-butt walnut grips. Revolver introduced as "The Gun" in February 1973 price list and name changed to "High Sierra" by November 1973 price list. Note that early "The Gun" had neither "High Sierra" markings nor any other name. **NOTE:** Add $60 premium for presentation case; $55 premium for combination models; $25 for adjustable sights.

NIB	Exc.	V.G.	Good	Fair	Poor
—	475	425	350	275	200

BLACKPOWDER REVOLVERS

Guns were series of .36-caliber cap-and-ball revolvers that began production in 1974 and ran through 1976. These are reproductions of Confederate copies of Colt Model 1851 Navy. **NOTE:** Most Confederate copies of Colt had round barrels not octagonal as found on Colts. Frames were made by High Standard and balance of parts by Uberti. Guns were assembled and finished by High Standard.

Griswold & Gunnison

Blued finish with brass frame. Six-shot single-action. Commemorative gun came with pine presentation case and brass belt plate depicting Georgia state seal. **NOTE:** Price is for gun in case with accessories. Deduct $100 for gun only in Exc. condition.

NIB	Exc.	V.G.	Good	Fair	Poor
—	450	375	300	175	100

Leech & Rigdon

Blued finish with steel frame. Six-shot single-action. Commemorative gun came with presentation case and reproduction of Civil War belt buckle. **NOTE:** Price is for gun in case with accessories. Deduct $100 for gun only in Exc. condition.

NIB	Exc.	V.G.	Good	Fair	Poor
—	450	375	300	175	100

Schneider & Glassick

Blued finish, with steel frame. Six-shot single-action. Commemorative gun came with presentation case and modern version of Confederate "D" guard Bowie knife. **NOTE:** Add $450 for Confederate "D" Bowie knife.

NIB	Exc.	V.G.	Good	Fair	Poor
—	450	375	300	175	100

Bicentennial 1776-1976

Blued finish, with steel frame. Six-shot single-action. Guns came with two versions of presentation case. One case is pine marked "High Standard" and trigger logo on lid, with powder flask and silver dollar-sized medallion inside; other a brown leatherette covered case with "American Bicentennial 1776-1976" and contains a pewter Bicentennial belt buckle.

NIB	Exc.	V.G.	Good	Fair	Poor
—	450	375	300	175	100

Special Presentation Bicentennial

100 guns were available in presentation cases, with "US" serial number prefixes. Serial numbers US 11 through US 50 are in walnut presentation cases, with purple fitted lining and pewter Bicentennial belt buckle. Top of case marked "Limited Edition / American Bicentennial / 1776 – 1976". Guns are engraved on frame, cylinder barrel, loading lever, and hammer. Catalog number 9339 has a steel frame, with round barrel; catalog number 9340 has a brass frame, with octagonal barrel.

NIB	Exc.	V.G.	Good	Fair	Poor
—	700	500	350	175	125

SHOTGUNS

High Standard made a series of semi-automatic and slide-action shotguns for Sears, Roebuck & Co. under the J. C. Higgins brand name from late 1940s to late 1950s. Beginning in 1960, similar models were made under the High Standard name. Most of these remained in production until mid 1970s.

SEMI-AUTOMATIC SHOTGUNS

Supermatic Field

Gas-operated semi-automatic shotgun. Blued finish, plain pistol-grip walnut stock and forearm, 4-round magazine capacity. Supermatic Field models were superseded by models in Supermatic Deluxe group beginning in 1966. 12-gauge guns have 2.75" chambers; 20-gauge 3" chambers. **NOTE:** Slight premium for 20-gauge.

NIB	Exc.	V.G.	Good	Fair	Poor
—	325	300	250	200	100

Supermatic Special

Like Supermatic Field except with 27" barrel and 6-position click-stop adjustable choke. Supermatic Special models were superseded by models in Supermatic Deluxe group beginning in 1966. 12-gauge guns have 2.75" chambers.

NIB	Exc.	V.G.	Good	Fair	Poor
—	325	300	250	200	100

Supermatic Deluxe

Gas-operated semi-automatic shotgun. Blued finish, checkered pistol-grip walnut stock and forearm, 4-round magazine. Adjustable choke had 6-click-stop positions. Recoil pad beginning 1966. 12-gauge guns have 2.75" chambers; 20-gauge 3". **NOTE:** Add $20 premium for ventilated rib versions.

NIB	Exc.	V.G.	Good	Fair	Poor
—	350	325	275	200	100

Supermatic Citation

Same as Trophy, without ventilated rib. 6-click-stop adjustable choke. Catalog #8220 has compensator integral, with adjustable choke. 12-gauge guns have 2.75" chambers.

NIB	Exc.	V.G.	Good	Fair	Poor
—	325	300	250	200	100

Supermatic Trophy

Gas-operated semi-automatic shotgun. Blued finish, checkered walnut stock and fore-end, 4-round magazine, 6-click-stop adjustable choke. Catalog #8230 has compensator integral, with adjustable choke. 12-gauge guns have 2.75" chambers; 20-gauge 3".

NIB	Exc.	V.G.	Good	Fair	Poor
—	325	300	250	200	100

Supermatic Duck

Gas-operated semi-automatic shotgun. Chambered for 3" Magnum. Suitable for all 2.75" shells. Blued finish. Checkered pistol-grip walnut stock and forearm. Magazine capacity: five 2.75" shells; four 3" shells. Recoil pad. **NOTE:** Add $20 premium for ventilated rib versions.

NIB	Exc.	V.G.	Good	Fair	Poor
—	350	325	275	250	130

Supermatic Deer

Like Supermatic Deluxe, with rifle sight. Recoil pad. Receiver tapped for peep sight on catalog #8246. 12-gauge guns have 2.75" chambers.

NIB	Exc.	V.G.	Good	Fair	Poor
—	325	300	250	200	100

Supermatic Skeet

Same features as Supermatic Deluxe except select American walnut stock and forearm. No recoil pad. 12-gauge 2.75" chambers; 20-gauge 3".

NIB	Exc.	V.G.	Good	Fair	Poor
—	350	325	275	200	100

Supermatic Trap

Same features as Supermatic Deluxe except select American walnut stock and forearm. Recoil pad. Catalog #8266 is Executive Trap model, with Fajen Monte Carlo stock. 12-gauge guns have 2.75" chambers.

NIB	Exc.	V.G.	Good	Fair	Poor
—	350	325	275	200	100

PUMP SHOTGUNS

Model 200

Economy 12-gauge pump shotgun, sold as part of a promotional package beginning in 1971. Package included Model 200, zippered gun case, plastic trigger lock and G-96 gun lubricant. Prices are for gun alone. **NOTE:** Add $30 for gun with complete promotional package.

NIB	Exc.	V.G.	Good	Fair	Poor
—	200	150	125	100	80

Flite King Field

Slide-action shotgun. Blued finish, plain pistol-grip walnut stock and forearm. Catalog #8450, magazine capacity: five 2.5" shells; four 3" shells. 12-gauge guns have 2.75" chambers; 20 gauge 3". **NOTE:** Add 50 percent for .410 bore.

NIB	Exc.	V.G.	Good	Fair	Poor
—	250	225	175	135	100

Flite King Brush

Like Flite King Field, with adjustable rifle sights. Receiver tapped for Williams sight and provision exists for sling swivels. Deluxe models have Williams receiver sight, leather sling with swivels and recoil pad. 12-gauge guns have 2.75" chambers. **NOTE:** Add $10 premium for deluxe model.

Flite King Brush Deluxe

NIB	Exc.	V.G.	Good	Fair	Poor
—	275	240	200	175	135

Flite King Special

Like Flite King Field, with 27" barrel and 6-click-stop adjustable choke. 12-gauge guns have 2.75" chambers; 20-gauge 3".

NIB	Exc.	V.G.	Good	Fair	Poor
—	275	225	175	135	100

Flite King Deluxe

Slide-action shotgun. Blued finish, checkered pistol-grip walnut stock and forearm, 5-round magazine. Available with-/without ventilated rib. #8411 and #6411 were boys "Converta Pump" sold with two stocks: one youth size, one full. Adjustable choke had 6-click-stop positions. Recoil pad beginning 1966 except .410 models. 12-gauge guns have 2.75" chambers; 16- gauge 2.75"; 20-gauge 3"; 28-gauge 2.75"; .410 bore 3". **NOTE:** Add $20 for ventilated rib.

NIB	Exc.	V.G.	Good	Fair	Poor
—	285	250	210	175	135

Flite King Citation

Like Flite King Trophy without ventilated rib. Catalog #8130 has compensator integral, with 6-click-stop position adjustable choke. 12- and 16-gauge guns have 2.75" chambers.

NIB	Exc.	V.G.	Good	Fair	Poor
—	275	225	175	135	100

Flite King Trophy

Slide-action shotgun. Blued finish, checkered pistol-grip walnut stock and forearm, 5-round magazine, ventilated rib. Catalog #8140 has compensator integral, with adjustable choke. 12-gauge guns have 2.75" chambers; 20-gauge 3".

NIB	Exc.	V.G.	Good	Fair	Poor
—	275	225	200	175	135

Flite King Skeet

Same features as Flite King Deluxe, except select American walnut stock and forearm. No recoil pad. 12-gauge guns have 2.75" chambers; 20-gauge 3"; 28-gauge 2.75"; .410 bore 3".

NIB	Exc.	V.G.	Good	Fair	Poor
—	325	275	225	175	135

Flite King Trap

Same features as Flite King Deluxe, except select American walnut stock and forearm. Recoil pad. #8166 is Executive Trap model, with Fajen Monte Carlo stock. Catalog #6165 model has provisions for interchangeable barrels. 12-gauge guns have 2.75" chambers. **NOTE:** Add $25 for Fajen Monte Carlo stock.

NIB	Exc.	V.G.	Good	Fair	Poor
—	300	250	200	175	135

BOLT-ACTION SHOTGUNS

Model 514

Sears version of this shotgun was recalled for safety considerations in late 1990s.

NIB	Exc.	V.G.	Good	Fair	Poor
—	135	85	60	45	25

POLICE SHOTGUNS

Semi-Automatic

Gas-operated semi-automatic 12-gauge shotgun. Plain oiled pistol-grip walnut stock and forearm. Magazine capacity 4 rounds. Recoil pad.

NIB	Exc.	V.G.	Good	Fair	Poor
—	300	250	200	175	125

Model 10-A

Gas-operated semi-automatic 12-gauge shotgun. Bullpup configuration with pistol-grip. Integral carrying handle and flashlight on top of gun. Magazine capacity 4 rounds.

NIB	Exc.	V.G.	Good	Fair	Poor
—	1850	1150	800	550	250

Model 10-B

Gas-operated semi-automatic 12-gauge shotgun. Bullpup configuration with pistol-grip. Fitted with integral folding carrying handle and mounting provisions for flashlight. Magazine capacity 4 rounds. Carrying case catalog #50284 and attachable flashlight catalog #50285, sold optionally. **NOTE:** Values for gun with flashlight.

NIB	Exc.	V.G.	Good	Fair	Poor
—	1700	1000	700	450	200

Pump

Slide-action 12-gauge shotgun. Plain pistol-grip oiled walnut stock and forearm—changed from walnut to stained and lacquered birch in mid 1970s. Magazine capacity: #8111/8113 6-rounds; #8104/8129 5-rounds. A 1963 flyer mentions #8105 Flite King Brush 20" and #8107 Flite King Deluxe 20" as riot guns. Data on #8105 and #8107 listed under Flite King Brush.

NIB	Exc.	V.G.	Good	Fair	Poor
—	300	225	150	125	100

IMPORTED SHOTGUNS

Supermatic Shadow Automatic

Gas-operated semi-automatic shotgun in 12- and 20-gauge. Interchangeable barrels. Checkered walnut stock and forearm. Special "airflow" rib. Imported from Nikko in Japan.

NIB	Exc.	V.G.	Good	Fair	Poor
—	450	350	265	200	175

Supermatic Shadow Indy Over/Under

Boxlock over/under 12-gauge shotgun, with selective automatic ejectors and single trigger. Receiver fully engraved. Skipline checkered walnut stock, with pistol-grip. Ventilated forearm. Recoil pad. Special "airflow" rib. Imported from Nikko in Japan.

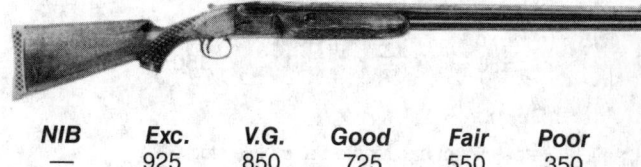

NIB	Exc.	V.G.	Good	Fair	Poor
—	925	850	725	550	350

Supermatic Shadow Seven Over/Under

Like Shadow Indy, with standard size ventilated rib, conventional forearm, no recoil pad, standard checkering and less engraving. Imported from Nikko in Japan.

NIB	Exc.	V.G.	Good	Fair	Poor
—	725	650	525	400	325

RIFLES

Sport King/Flite King

.22-caliber slide-action rifle capable of using Short/Long/LR ammunition interchangeably. 24" barrel, open sights and tubular magazine. Magazine capacity 21 Short, 17 Long or 15 LR.

NIB	Exc.	V.G.	Good	Fair	Poor
—	225	150	80	60	50

Sport King Field

.22-caliber semi-automatic rifle capable of using Short/Long/LR ammunition interchangeably. 22.25" barrel, open sights and tubular magazine. Magazine capacity 21 Short, 17 Long, 15 LR. Walnut stock.

NIB	Exc.	V.G.	Good	Fair	Poor
—	250	200	100	80	50

Sport King Special

Like Sport King Field except Monte Carlo walnut stock, with pistol-grip.

NIB	Exc.	V.G.	Good	Fair	Poor
—	225	150	125	100	80

Sport King Deluxe/Sport King Rifle

Sport King Special with a new name. Catalog #6005 is the same gun but called just Sport King. Promotional package offered that included Sport King rifle, zippered gun case, plastic trigger lock and G-96 gun lubricant. This package was catalog #8007. **NOTE:** Add a 10 percent premium for complete 8007 package in original box.

NIB	Exc.	V.G.	Good	Fair	Poor
—	275	220	140	100	80

Sport King Carbine

.22 carbine semi-automatic rifle capable of using Short/Long/LR ammunition interchangeably. 18.25" barrel, open sights and tubular magazine. Magazine capacity 17 Short, 14 Long, 12 LR. Straight-grip walnut stock, with barrel band and sling.

NIB	Exc.	V.G.	Good	Fair	Poor
—	225	175	150	100	80

Hi-Power Field Grade

A .270 or .30-06 caliber bolt-action rifle, with 22" barrel, open sights and 4-shot magazine. Blued, with walnut stock.

NIB	Exc.	V.G.	Good	Fair	Poor
—	500	425	300	150	100

Hi-Power Deluxe

Like Field Grade except has Monte Carlo-style stock.

NIB	Exc.	V.G.	Good	Fair	Poor
—	575	500	375	225	150

HIGH STANDARD MANUFACTURING CO.
Houston, Texas

Company established in 1993. Among its employees are several who worked for High Standard Company that closed its doors in Connecticut in 1984. Remaining semi-automatic pistols in this section were made in Houston. This firm expanded in 2004, by purchasing the assets of AMT-Auto Mag and Interarms.

Supermatic Citation

Chambered for .22 LR. Fitted with 5.5" barrel. Matte blue or Parkerized finish. Weight about 44 oz. Discontinued.

NIB	Exc.	V.G.	Good	Fair	Poor
425	325	275	225	175	100

Supermatic Citation MS

Designed for metallic silhouette shooting. Introduced in 1996. Fitted with 10" barrel. Weight about 49 oz. Discontinued.

NIB	Exc.	V.G.	Good	Fair	Poor
800	650	500	400	325	200

Supermatic Tournament

Chambered for .22 LR. Fitted with 5.5" barrel. Matte blue finish. Weight about 44 oz.

NIB	Exc.	V.G.	Good	Fair	Poor
900	750	600	450	325	200

Supermatic Trophy

Offered with 5.5" or 7.25" barrels. Chambered for .22 LR. Adjustable trigger, barrel weights, gold-plated trigger safety, slide stop and magazine catch. Matte blue or Parkerized finish. Weight about 45 oz. **NOTE:** Add 10 percent for 7.25 barrel.

NIB	Exc.	V.G.	Good	Fair	Poor
800	650	500	400	325	200

Olympic Model

Chambered for .22 Short. Fitted with 5.5" bull barrel. Blued finish. Weight about 44 oz.

NIB	Exc.	V.G.	Good	Fair	Poor
900	750	600	450	300	150

Olympic ISU

Similar to previous model. Fitted with 6.75" barrel with internal stabilizer. Magazine capacity 5 rounds. Checkered walnut grips. Weight about 45 oz. Discontinued in 1995.

NIB	Exc.	V.G.	Good	Fair	Poor
600	500	350	300	200	150

Olympic Rapid Fire

Introduced in 1996. Chambered for .22 Short cartridge, with 4" barrel, integral muzzle-brake and forward mounted compensator. Special grips. Weight about 46 oz. Discontinued.

NIB	Exc.	V.G.	Good	Fair	Poor
1000	850	700	500	425	300

Sport King

Chambered for .22 LR. Fitted with 4.5" or 6.75" barrel. Adjustable rear sight. Weight about 44 oz. Limited edition.

NIB	Exc.	V.G.	Good	Fair	Poor
650	400	225	150	100	80

Victor

With 4.5" barrel and blue or Parkerized finish. **NOTE:** Add $75 for adjustable sights.

NIB	Exc.	V.G.	Good	Fair	Poor
800	650	500	400	325	200

10-X

Fitted with 5.5" barrel. Weight about 44 oz. From HS Custom Shop.

NIB	Exc.	V.G.	Good	Fair	Poor
1100	950	800	600	425	300

10-X—Shea Model

Fitted with 4.5" or 5.5" barrel. Limited to 150 pistols per year. **NOTE:** Add 10 percent for 5.5 barrel.

NIB	Exc.	V.G.	Good	Fair	Poor
1400	1200	850	750	500	350

Olympic Trophy Space Gun

Semi-automatic pistol chambered in .22 LR. Re-creation of famed competition "Space Gun" from 1960s. Features include 8" or 10" barrel; 10-round magazine; adjustable sights; barrel weight; adjustable muzzlebrake; blue-black finish with gold highlights.

NIB	Exc.	V.G.	Good	Fair	Poor
1200	900	800	650	500	200

Model 1911A1

Reproduction of standard Colt design imported from the Philippines, where it is made by Armscor. Chambered in .45 ACP or .38 Super. Has 5" barrel with fixed, adjustable or Novak Night Sights. **NOTE:** Add $40 for .38 Super; $300 for adjustable or Novak sights.

NIB	Exc.	V.G.	Good	Fair	Poor
450	400	375	350	300	150

HAS-15

An A2 configuration AR-15 style rifle, with 16" or 20" barrel with muzzlebrake, 30-shot magazine, fixed or folding stock (carbine). Chambered in .223/5.56 NATO. Previously chambered in 6x45mm.

NIB	Exc.	V.G.	Good	Fair	Poor
800	700	575	425	325	225

HAS-15 Enforcer

M4-style carbine, with 16" barrel. Chambered for 5.56 NATO or .300 Blackout. Features include A2 flash hider, forged aluminum upper and lower receiver, six-position adjustable stock, Picatinny rail.

NIB	Exc.	V.G.	Good	Fair	Poor
1000	850	700	500	400	250

HAS-15 National Match

Chambered in 5.56 NATO, with 20" or 24" heavy fluted barrel. Knight two-stage trigger.

NIB	Exc.	V.G.	Good	Fair	Poor
1100	950	800	650	300	200

HILL, W.J.
Birmingham, England

Hill's Self-Extracting Revolver

.32-caliber double-action folding trigger revolver, with 3.75" barrel and 6-shot cylinder. Marked "Hill's Patent Self Extractor". Blued, with walnut grips.

NIB	Exc.	V.G.	Good	Fair	Poor
—	—	1025	495	295	150

HILLIARD, D. H.
Cornish, New Hampshire

Under Hammer Pistol

.34-caliber under hammer percussion pistol, with varying barrel lengths. Blued, with walnut grips. Active 1842 to 1877.

NIB	Exc.	V.G.	Good	Fair	Poor
—	—	950	475	200	100

HINO-KOMURA
Tokyo, Japan

7.65mm or 8mm Nambu semi-automatic pistol manufactured in limited quantities between 1905 and 1912. Operation of this pistol involves pulling muzzle forward until slide engages a catch on trigger assembly. Pulling trigger at this point allows barrel to move back and engage cartridge nose into chamber. Squeezing grip safety then allows barrel to slam back into fixed firing pin on breechblock. Prospective purchasers are advised to secure a qualified appraisal prior to acquisition.

NIB	Exc.	V.G.	Good	Fair	Poor
—	3850	3600	3000	2250	1000

HODGKINS, D. C. & SONS
Macon, Georgia
See—Bilharz, Hall & Co.

HOFER, P.
Feriach, Austria

Gunmaker specializing in double-barrel rifles made strictly to custom order. Value depends on local demand, chamberings and other factors.

HOFFMAN, LOUIS
Vicksburg, Mississippi

Pocket Pistol

.41-caliber percussion pocket pistol, with 3" barrel, German silver mounts and walnut stock. Active 1857 to 1886.

NIB	Exc.	V.G.	Good	Fair	Poor
—	—	900	525	200	100

HOLDEN, C. B.
Worcester, Massachusetts

Open Frame Rifle

.44 rimfire single-shot rifle, with 28" barrel, open sights, silver plated bronze frame and walnut stock. Barrel marked "C.B. Holden Worcester-Mass.". Produced in limited quantities during mid-1860s.

NIB	Exc.	V.G.	Good	Fair	Poor
—	—	2600	1850	675	300

HOLECK, EMANUEL
Czechoslovakia

Holeck Rifle

Chambered for .276 cartridge. Semi-automatic rifle submitted for testing for U.S. military trials in 1920s. Barrel length 21.5", with upper portion slotted for operating handle. Rotating dial at barrel band. Rarely encountered. **NOTE:** Thanks to Jim Supica for research found in his Old Town Station Dispatch, in which one of these rifles was offered for sale.

NIB	Exc.	V.G.	Good	Fair	Poor
—	4250	—	—	—	—

HOLLAND & HOLLAND, LTD.
London, England

Established in 1835, Holland & Holland has manufactured a wide variety of shotguns and rifles during its existence. Greater part of these arms are made to custom order.

DOUBLE RIFLES

No. 2 Grade Double Rifle

Sidelock double-barrel rifle produced in a variety of calibers, with 24" barrels, double triggers, automatic ejectors and express sights. Obsolete cartridges could be worth less. **NOTE:** Add 50 percent for calibers from .400 to .500; 100 percent for over .500.

NIB	Exc.	V.G.	Good	Fair	Poor
20000	17000	12500	10000	—	—

Royal Side-by-Side Rifle

Higher grade version of No. 2, with more elaborate engraving. Values shown are for .300 H&H. **NOTE:** Add 25 percent for larger calibers; 50 to 100 percent for Nitro Express calibers.

NIB	Exc.	V.G.	Good	Fair	Poor
29500	25000	18000	13500	—	—

H&H .700 Bore Side-by-Side Rifle

.700 H&H double-barrel rifle. Weight about 18 lbs. Currently manufactured. Because of its uniqueness, buyers should seek a qualified appraisal. Current base price approximately $200,000.

BOLT-ACTION RIFLES

Best Quality Rifle

Price depends on caliber and extra cost options. Retail prices for magazine rifles begin around $41,500, depending on value of the dollar. Due to uniqueness of each rifle an independent appraisal is a must prior to sale.

SHOTGUNS

Holland & Holland has been one of Britain's most prestigious makers of custom-made shotguns, all the way back to mid-19th Century. Currently the company makes several side-by-side and over/under models, with prices starting at approximately $75,000. Values of older models range from $8,000 to $10,000 for boxlock designs; $25,000 to $100,000 for sidelocks.

HOLLOWAY ARMS CO.
Ft. Worth, Texas

HAC Model 7

7.62x54mm semi-automatic rifle, with 20" barrel, adjustable sights, integral telescope mount and 20-shot magazine. Black anodized finish, with folding stock. No longer in production.

NIB	Exc.	V.G.	Good	Fair	Poor
2500	2000	1750	1200	600	500

HAC Model 7C

As above, with 16" barrel.

NIB	Exc.	V.G.	Good	Fair	Poor
2750	2500	2000	1400	700	500

HAC Model 7S

As above, with heavy barrel.

NIB	Exc.	V.G.	Good	Fair	Poor
2850	2650	2100	1500	700	500

HOLMES FIREARMS
Wheeler, Arkansas

MP-22

.22-caliber semi-automatic pistol, with 6" barrel and alloy receiver. Anodized black finish, with walnut grip. Manufactured in 1985.

NIB	Exc.	V.G.	Good	Fair	Poor
425	325	250	200	150	100

MP-83

Similar to above in 9mm or .45-caliber. Manufactured in 1985. **NOTE:** Several of Holmes pistols have been declared machine guns by BATFE, because of their easy conversion to full automatics. Make sure before purchase that a Class III license is not required.

NIB	Exc.	V.G.	Good	Fair	Poor
550	425	325	250	200	125

HOOD F. A. CO.
Norwich, Connecticut

Manufacturer of spur trigger .22- or .32-caliber revolvers, with varying length barrels and finishes. Many of these revolvers are found stamped only with trade names. This type of handgun is often referred to as a suicide special to denote its poor quality and lack of reliability.

NIB	Exc.	V.G.	Good	Fair	Poor
—	—	250	145	75	50

HOPKINS & ALLEN
Norwich, Connecticut
See—Bacon Arms Co. & Merwin Hulbert & Co.

Established in 1868, this company produced a variety of spur trigger revolvers in .22-, .32-, .38- or .41-caliber. Often marked with trade names such as: Acme, Blue Jacket, Captain Jack, Chichester, Defender, Dictator, Hopkins & Allen, Imperial Arms Co., Monarch, Mountain Eagle, Ranger, Tower's Police Safety, Universal and XL.

Some of these revolvers are hinged-frame double-action break-opens, with round-ribbed barrels of various lengths. Blued or nickel-plated, with checkered plastic grips.

Courtesy Milwaukee Public Museum, Milwaukee, Wisconsin

NIB	Exc.	V.G.	Good	Fair	Poor
—	—	550	275	125	75

Dictator

.36-caliber percussion or .38 rimfire single-action revolver, with 4" barrel and 5-shot cylinder. Blued, with walnut grips. Barrel marked "Dictator". Made approximately 6,000 percussion; 5,000 rimfire.

NIB	Exc.	V.G.	Good	Fair	Poor
—	—	1000	725	400	125

Falling Block Rifle

.22 to .38-55 caliber single-shot rifle, with 24", 26" or 28" octagonal barrel. Blued, with walnut stock. Manufactured between 1888 and 1892.

NIB	Exc.	V.G.	Good	Fair	Poor
—	—	1250	650	325	175

Schuetzen Rifle

.22 or .25-20 caliber single-shot rifle, with 26" octagonal barrel, double-set trigger and Schuetzen-type buttplate. Blued, with walnut stock.

NIB	Exc.	V.G.	Good	Fair	Poor
—	—	2750	1025	550	200

Navy Revolver

.38-caliber rimfire single-action revolver, with 6.5" barrel marked "Hopkins & Allen Mfg. Co., Pat. Mar. 28, 71, Apr. 27, 75" and 6-shot cylinder. Top strap marked "XL Navy". Blued or nickel-plated, with walnut grips. Several hundred made between 1878 and 1882.

NIB	Exc.	V.G.	Good	Fair	Poor
—	—	1950	1650	675	175

Army Revolver

As above in .44 rimfire, with 4.5", 6" or 7.5" barrel. Top strap marked "XL No. 8". Several hundred manufactured between 1878 and 1882.

NIB	Exc.	V.G.	Good	Fair	Poor
—	—	2800	2500	925	350

Derringer

.22-caliber single-shot pistol, with hinged 1.75" barrel that pivots downwards for loading. Blued or nickel-plated, with walnut, ivory or pearl grips. Frame marked "Hopkins & Allen Arms Co., Norwich, Conn. U.S.A." Several hundred manufactured in 1880s and 1890s.

NIB	Exc.	V.G.	Good	Fair	Poor
—	—	2750	950	330	150

Double-Barrel Shotguns

Hopkins & Allen also made good quality single-/double-barrel shotguns in large numbers. Many sold under private brand names such as Seminole and King Nitro. Both hammer and hammerless versions were offered. Values vary from $100 to $1,000 depending on model and condition.

HOWA MACHINE COMPANY
Japan

Company manufactured bolt-action rifles for Smith & Wesson until 1985 and then for Mossberg in 1986 and 1987. From 1988 to 2000, Howa firearms were imported by Interarms of Alexandria, Virginia. These rifles are now imported by Legacy Sports of Alexandria, Virginia.

Model 1500 Hunter

.22-250, .223, .243, .270, 7mm Rem. Magnum .308, .30-06, .300 Win. Magnum and .338 Win. Magnum caliber bolt-action sporting rifle, with 22" or 24" barrel and 3- or 5-shot magazine. Blued or stainless steel, with checkered walnut stock. In 2002, offered with black polymer stock. Weight about 7.6 lbs. **NOTE:** Add $70 for stainless steel.

NIB	Exc.	V.G.	Good	Fair	Poor
600	500	450	325	225	175

Model 1500 JRS Classic

Offered in blue or stainless steel, with laminated stock. Chambered for .223 through .338 Win. Magnum calibers. Barrel length 22" or 24" depending on caliber. Weight about 8 lbs. **NOTE:** Add $70 for stainless steel.

NIB	Exc.	V.G.	Good	Fair	Poor
650	575	500	375	250	195

Model 1500 Mountain

Introduced in 2004. Bolt-action chambered for .243, .308 or 7mm-08 cartridges. Fitted with 20" contoured barrel, no sights, blued finish, black hardwood stock. Stainless steel offered in .308 only. Magazine capacity 5 rounds. Weight about 6.4 lbs. **NOTE:** Add $115 for stainless steel.

NIB	Exc.	V.G.	Good	Fair	Poor
600	500	450	325	225	175

Model 1500 Trophy

As above, with more finely figured walnut stocks and checkering. Introduced in 1988. No longer imported.

NIB	Exc.	V.G.	Good	Fair	Poor
650	525	450	375	250	195

Model 1500 Varmint

As above in .22-250 or .223 caliber, with 24" heavy barrel. Choice of walnut or synthetic stock in blue or stainless. Weight about 9.3 lbs. Introduced in 1988. **NOTE:** Add $70 for stainless steel; $20 for walnut stock.

NIB	Exc.	V.G.	Good	Fair	Poor
650	600	500	375	250	195

Model 1500 Varmint Supreme

Features stainless steel barrel. Chambered for .223, .22-250, .308 and .243. No sights. Choice of black synthetic or laminated stock, with Monte Carlo comb. **NOTE:** Add $110 for thumbhole stock.

NIB	Exc.	V.G.	Good	Fair	Poor
650	525	450	375	250	195

Model 1500 Lightning Rifle

Introduced in 1993. Has black composite checkered stock, with schnabel fore-end. Buttstock is Monte Carlo. Choice of blue or stainless steel. Offered in .223, .22-250, .243, .270, .308, .30-06, 7mm Rem. Magnum, .300 and .338 Win. Magnum. Weight about 7.5 lbs. **NOTE:** Add $70 for stainless steel.

NIB	Exc.	V.G.	Good	Fair	Poor
600	525	450	325	225	175

Model 1500 Youth

Chambered for .243, .308 or 7mm-08 cartridge. Barrel length 20". Black hardwood stock, with 1" shorter length of pull than standard. Weight about 6.3 lbs. Introduced in 2004. **NOTE:** Add $115 for stainless steel .308 version.

NIB	Exc.	V.G.	Good	Fair	Poor
600	500	400	275	175	125

Model 1500 Thumbhole Sporter

As above, with thumbhole stock. Weight about 8.25 lbs. **NOTE:** Add $70 for stainless steel.

NIB	Exc.	V.G.	Good	Fair	Poor
750	625	500	400	275	150

Model 1500 Custom

Chambered for .300 WSM or .300 Win. Magnum cartridge. Fitted with 22" or 24" barrel, depending on caliber. Polymer or laminated stock. Weight about 8 lbs. Blued or stainless steel. **NOTE:** Add $70 for stainless steel.

NIB	Exc.	V.G.	Good	Fair	Poor
950	800	700	495	325	175

Realtree Camo Rifle

Introduced in 1993. Bolt-action features composite stock and 22" barrel. Both metal and stock finish are brown leaf pattern. Receiver is mono-block system, drilled and tapped for scope mounts. Floorplate hinged and magazine holds 5 rounds. Fitted with sling swivel and recoil pad. Offered in .30-06 and .270 calibers. Weight 8 lbs.

NIB	Exc.	V.G.	Good	Fair	Poor
650	525	400	275	175	125

Texas Safari Rifle

Chambered for .270 Win. or .300 Win. Magnum cartridge. Rifle is modified by gunsmith Bill Wiseman. Blue Teflon finish and 22" or 24" barrel depending on caliber. Laminated stock. Weight about 7.8 lbs.

NIB	Exc.	V.G.	Good	Fair	Poor
1200	800	650	525	400	150

Model 1500 PCS (Police Counter Sniper)

Bolt-action offered in .308 Winchester. Fitted with 24" heavy barrel. Magazine capacity 5 rounds. Available in blue or stainless steel. Walnut or synthetic stock. Weight about 9.3 lbs.

NIB	Exc.	V.G.	Good	Fair	Poor
1200	800	650	525	400	150

HOWARD-WHITNEY
New Haven, Connecticut
See—Whitney Arms Co.

HUGLU
Turkey

SIDE-BY-SIDES

Bobwhite

Offered in 12-, 20-, 28-gauge and .410 bore, with 26" or 28" barrels with choke tubes. The .410 bore has fixed chokes. Double triggers with no auto ejectors. Manual safety. Box lock receiver, with silver finish. Walnut stock, with round knob pistol-grip and splinter schnabel fore-end. **NOTE:** Add $200 for 28-gauge or .410 models.

NIB	Exc.	V.G.	Good	Fair	Poor
700	550	400	275	175	125

Ringneck

Similar to Bobwhite, with single trigger, case colored frame and side plates. Choice of round knob pistol-/straight-grip. Fore-end is beavertail schnabel. **NOTE:** Add $200 for 28-gauge or .410 models.

NIB	Exc.	V.G.	Good	Fair	Poor
1000	750	600	495	300	150

OVER/UNDERS

Woodcock

Available in 12-, 20-, 28-gauge and .410 bore. Choice of 26" or 28" ventilated rib barrels, with choke tubes. Fixed chokes on .410. Single trigger. No auto ejectors. Manual safety. Receiver finish is case colored. Checkered walnut stock, with round knob pistol-grip and schnabel fore-end. **NOTE:** Add $150 for 28-gauge or .410 models.

NIB	Exc.	V.G.	Good	Fair	Poor
1050	825	600	495	300	150

Woodcock Deluxe

As above in 12-gauge, with auto ejectors and side plates.

NIB	Exc.	V.G.	Good	Fair	Poor
1200	900	750	550	350	185

Redhead

Available in 12-, 20-, 28-gauge and .410 bore. Choice of 26" or 28" ventilated rib barrels, with choke tubes. Fixed chokes on .410. The 20-gauge offered with 24" barrels. Single trigger, no auto ejectors and manual safety. Boxlock receiver with silver finish. Checkered walnut stock, with round knob pistol-grip and schnabel fore-end. **NOTE:** Add $150 for 28-gauge or .410 models.

NIB	Exc.	V.G.	Good	Fair	Poor
800	625	500	400	275	150

Redhead Deluxe

As above in 12- and 20-gauge only, with 26" or 28" barrels. Auto ejectors.

NIB	Exc.	V.G.	Good	Fair	Poor
900	750	675	395	200	100

Mallard

12- or 20-gauge gun fitted with 28" ventilated rib barrels and choke tubes. Double triggers and no auto ejectors. Silver receiver. Checkered walnut stock, with round knob pistol-grip and schnabel fore-end.

NIB	Exc.	V.G.	Good	Fair	Poor
550	425	300	200	150	75

Canvasback

Available in 12-, 20-, 28-gauge and .410 bore. Choice of 26" or 28" ventilated rib barrels, with choke tubes. Fixed chokes on .410. Single trigger, no auto ejectors and manual safety. Black boxlock receiver. Checkered walnut stock, with round knob pistol-grip and schnabel fore-end. **NOTE:** Add $150 for 28-gauge or .410 models.

NIB	Exc.	V.G.	Good	Fair	Poor
800	625	500	400	275	150

Canvasback Deluxe

As above in 12- and 20-gauge only, with auto ejectors.

NIB	Exc.	V.G.	Good	Fair	Poor
900	750	675	395	200	100

COWBOY & SINGLE-SHOTS

Cottontail

Single-barrel shotgun in 12- or 20-gauge and .410 bore. Choice of 24" or 28" barrels. Modified choke. No auto ejectors. Silver receiver, with blued barrel. Checkered walnut stock, with pistol-grip.

NIB	Exc.	V.G.	Good	Fair	Poor
200	150	100	75	50	25

Durango

Side-by-side shotgun chambered for 12- or 20-gauge, with single trigger and choke tubes. Barrel lengths 20". No auto ejectors. Boxlock receiver is case colored. Checkered walnut grips, with round knob pistol-grip and schnabel fore-end.

NIB	Exc.	V.G.	Good	Fair	Poor
850	650	500	400	275	150

Amarillo

Similar to Durango, with flat-side receiver.

NIB	Exc.	V.G.	Good	Fair	Poor
700	525	400	300	195	125

SEMI-AUTOMATICS

Sharptail

12-gauge 3" gun fitted with choice of 26" or 28" ventilated rib barrels and choke tubes. Black receiver. Checkered walnut stock, with pistol-grip. Weight about 7.3 lbs.

NIB	Exc.	V.G.	Good	Fair	Poor
550	425	300	200	150	95

Canadian

As above, with alloy frame and matte black finish. Weight about 7 lbs.

NIB	Exc.	V.G.	Good	Fair	Poor
650	525	400	275	165	115

Teal

A 20-gauge, with 3" chambers. Choice of 26" or 28" ventilated rib barrels, with choke tubes. Black alloy receiver. Checkered walnut stock, with pistol-grip.

NIB	Exc.	V.G.	Good	Fair	Poor
550	425	300	200	150	95

COMPETITION GUNS

Vandalia Trap

A 12-gauge trap gun offered with single-/double-barrel combo: single-barrel only; double-barrel only. Five choke tubes. Engraved silver receiver. Checkered walnut stock, with pistol-grip and adjustable comb. **NOTE:** Add $300 for Combo model.

NIB	Exc.	V.G.	Good	Fair	Poor
1900	1400	995	650	395	200

English Sporter

Sporting clays model chambered for 12-gauge shell. Fitted with 30" barrel. Ten choke tubes. Black receiver. Adjustable comb. Checkered walnut stock, with pistol-grip.

NIB	Exc.	V.G.	Good	Fair	Poor
1900	1400	995	650	395	200

CUSTOM GRADES

Custom Grade II

Custom-built side-by-side gun in customer's choice of gauge. Engraved case colored receiver, with side plates. Choice of barrel lengths. Select walnut stock, with hand checkering and round knob pistol-grip.

NIB	Exc.	V.G.	Good	Fair	Poor
2200	1600	1200	950	500	300

Custom Grade IV

Custom-built side-by-side features silver scroll engraved receiver, with side plates. Straight-grip stock. Choice of bore and barrel lengths.

NIB	Exc.	V.G.	Good	Fair	Poor
2800	1900	1400	650	600	350

Custom Grade IV with Upgrade

An over/under gun, with extra fancy walnut stock and elaborately engraved silver receiver. Choice of gauge and barrel lengths.

NIB	Exc.	V.G.	Good	Fair	Poor
3150	2200	1600	750	650	350

Custom Grade VI

Highest grade offered, with finest walnut stock and engraving.

NIB	Exc.	V.G.	Good	Fair	Poor
3500	2650	1900	950	775	475

HUNGARY

SA-85M

Pre-ban semi-automatic copy of AKM rifle. Chambered for 7.62x39mm cartridge. Fixed or folding stock.

NIB	Exc.	V.G.	Good	Fair	Poor
1800	1600	1200	850	600	500

HUNT
New Haven, Connecticut
See—Winchester Repeating Arms Co.

HUNTER ARMS CO.
Fulton, New York
See—L. C. Smith

HUSQVARNA
Husqvarna, Sweden

PISTOLS

Model 1907

Copy of FN Browning Model 1903 made for Swedish Army. Identical in every way to FN model. Many converted to .380-caliber and imported into U.S. **NOTE:** If converted to .380-caliber reduce values by 50 percent.

Courtesy Orvel Reichert

NIB	Exc.	V.G.	Good	Fair	Poor
—	400	325	225	150	100

Lahti

9mm caliber semi-automatic pistol, with 5.5" barrel and 8-shot magazine. Designed by Aino Lahti and adopted as standard Swedish sidearm in 1940. **NOTE:** Add 75 percent for complete military rig, with holsters and magazines.

NIB	Exc.	V.G.	Good	Fair	Poor
—	800	675	475	225	150

BOLT-ACTION RIFLES

Hi-Power

Bolt-action sporting rifle. Manufactured in a variety of calibers, with 24" barrel, open sights and beechwood stock. Manufactured between 1946 and 1951.

NIB	Exc.	V.G.	Good	Fair	Poor
—	500	375	275	200	150

Model 1100 Deluxe

As above, with walnut stock. Manufactured between 1952 and 1956.

NIB	Exc.	V.G.	Good	Fair	Poor
—	550	400	325	250	200

Model 1000 Super Grade

As above, with Monte Carlo-style stock. Manufactured between 1952 and 1956.

NIB	Exc.	V.G.	Good	Fair	Poor
—	575	475	350	250	200

Model 3100 Crown Grade

Bolt-action sporting rifle manufactured in a variety of calibers, with 24" barrel. Walnut stock, with black composition fore-end tip and pistol-grip cap. Manufactured between 1954 and 1972.

NIB	Exc.	V.G.	Good	Fair	Poor
—	575	475	350	300	200

Model 4100 Lightweight

As above, with schnabel fore-end tip. Manufactured between 1954 and 1972.

NIB	Exc.	V.G.	Good	Fair	Poor
—	575	475	350	300	200

Model 456

As above, with full length Mannlicher-style stock. Manufactured between 1959 and 1970.

NIB	Exc.	V.G.	Good	Fair	Poor
—	600	500	375	325	200

Model 6000

Model 4100, with express folding sights and finely figured walnut stock. Manufactured between 1968 and 1970.

NIB	Exc.	V.G.	Good	Fair	Poor
—	600	500	400	300	200

Model 9000 Crown Grade

Bolt-action sporting rifle. Manufactured in a variety of calibers, with 23.5" barrel, open sights, adjustable trigger and walnut stock. Manufactured in 1971 and 1972.

NIB	Exc.	V.G.	Good	Fair	Poor
—	500	425	350	300	250

Model 8000 Imperial Grade

As above, with engraved magazine floor plate, machine jeweled bolt. Finely figured walnut stock. Manufactured in 1971 and 1972.

NIB	Exc.	V.G.	Good	Fair	Poor
—	675	550	475	400	300

DOUBLE SHOTGUNS

Number of pre-war Husqvarna side-by-side shotguns have been imported over the years. While sturdy excellent shotguns, their collector value is rather limited. Those following values apply only to modern fluid-steel (nitro proofed) guns.

NIB	Exc.	V.G.	Good	Fair	Poor
—	500	425	350	300	250

HY-HUNTER, INC.
Burbank, California

Chicago Cub

.22-caliber folding trigger double-action revolver, with 2" barrel and 6-shot cylinder.

NIB	Exc.	V.G.	Good	Fair	Poor
—	50	40	30	25	20

Detective

.22 or .22 WMR caliber double-action revolver, with 2.5" barrel and 6-shot cylinder. Blued, with plastic grips.

NIB	Exc.	V.G.	Good	Fair	Poor
—	65	50	40	30	25

Frontier Six Shooter (rimfire)

.22 or .22 WMR caliber single-action revolver, with 6-shot cylinder.

NIB	Exc.	V.G.	Good	Fair	Poor
—	125	95	50	40	30

Frontier Six Shooter(centerfire)

As above in .357 Magnum, .44 Magnum or .45 Colt.

NIB	Exc.	V.G.	Good	Fair	Poor
—	225	195	175	100	50

Maxim

.25-caliber semi-automatic pistol, with 2" barrel and 5-shot magazine.

NIB	Exc.	V.G.	Good	Fair	Poor
—	75	65	50	40	30

Military

.22-, .32- or .380-caliber double-action semi-automatic pistol, with 4" barrel and 6-shot magazine.

NIB	Exc.	V.G.	Good	Fair	Poor
—	100	80	60	50	40

Stingray

.25-caliber semi-automatic pistol, with 2.5" barrel and 5-shot magazine.

NIB	Exc.	V.G.	Good	Fair	Poor
—	75	65	50	40	30

Panzer

.22-caliber semi-automatic pistol, with 4" barrel and 7-shot magazine.

NIB	Exc.	V.G.	Good	Fair	Poor
—	75	65	50	40	30

Stuka

Similar to above.

NIB	Exc.	V.G.	Good	Fair	Poor
—	75	65	50	40	30

Automatic Derringer

.22-caliber over/under pocket pistol patterned after Remington Double Derringer.

NIB	Exc.	V.G.	Good	Fair	Poor
—	50	40	30	25	20

Accurate Ace

.22-caliber Flobert-action pistol.

NIB	Exc.	V.G.	Good	Fair	Poor
—	50	40	30	25	20

Favorite

.22 or .22 WMR caliber copy of Steven's single-shot pistol, with 6" barrel and nickel-plated frame.

NIB	Exc.	V.G.	Good	Fair	Poor
—	100	80	70	50	25

Gold Rush Derringer

.22-caliber spur trigger single-shot pistol, with 2.5" barrel.

NIB	Exc.	V.G.	Good	Fair	Poor
—	100	80	70	50	25

Target Model

.22 or .22 WMR bolt-action single-shot pistol, with 10" barrel, adjustable sights and walnut grip.

NIB	Exc.	V.G.	Good	Fair	Poor
—	50	40	30	25	20

HYDE & SHATTUCK
Hatfield, Massachusetts

Queen Derringer

.22-caliber spur trigger single-shot pistol, with 2.5" half octagonal barrel. Blued or nickel-plated, with walnut grips. Barrel normally marked "Queen" sometimes "Hyde & Shattuck". Manufactured between 1876 and 1879.

NIB	Exc.	V.G.	Good	Fair	Poor
—	—	650	400	300	150

HYPER
Jenks, Oklahoma

Single-Shot Rifle

Custom made falling-block action single-shot rifle. Manufactured in a variety of calibers, barrel lengths, barrel types, and stock styles. Manufactured until 1984.

NIB	Exc.	V.G.	Good	Fair	Poor
—	2750	2000	1750	1450	800

I

I.G.I.
Itaiguns International
Zingone de Tressano, Italy

Domino SP602

.22-caliber semi-automatic target pistol, with 6" barrel and 5-shot magazine (inserted into action from top), adjustable trigger and customized grips.

NIB	Exc.	V.G.	Good	Fair	Poor
—	950	725	625	450	250

Domino OP601

As above in .22 short caliber.

NIB	Exc.	V.G.	Good	Fair	Poor
—	950	725	625	450	250

IAB
Industria Armi Bresciane
Brescia, Italy

S-300

12-gauge boxlock single-barrel trap gun, with 30" or 32" barrels having wide ventilated rib. Walnut trap-style stock.

NIB	Exc.	V.G.	Good	Fair	Poor
—	1600	1325	1050	850	450

C-300 Combo

12-gauge over/under boxlock double-barrel shotgun, with 30" or 32" barrels. Single-selective trigger, automatic ejectors, trap-style walnut stock, accompanied by two extra single barrels.

NIB	Exc.	V.G.	Good	Fair	Poor
—	2850	2300	1875	1500	800

C-300 Super Combo

As above, but more finely finished.

NIB	Exc.	V.G.	Good	Fair	Poor
—	3600	2800	2275	1750	900

IAI-AMERICAN LEGENDS
Houston, Texas

RIFLES

M-888 M1 Carbine

Re-creation of U.S. M1 Carbine in .30-caliber. Barrel length 18". Weight about 5.5 lbs. Uses surplus magazines of 15 to 30 rounds. Comes with 10-round magazine. Options: wooden or metal hand guard; walnut or birchwood stock.

NIB	Exc.	V.G.	Good	Fair	Poor
675	575	400	325	200	100

M-333 M1 Garand

Re-manufactured to GI specifications. Fitted with 24" barrel and GI wood stock. Eight-round capacity. Parkerized finish. Weight about 9.5 lbs.

NIB	Exc.	V.G.	Good	Fair	Poor
900	800	625	495	350	150

PISTOLS

M-2000

Government model .45 ACP pistol, fitted with 5" barrel and 7-round magazine. Fixed sights, wood grips and Parkerized finish. Weight about 38 oz.

NIB	Exc.	V.G.	Good	Fair	Poor
475	375	325	250	175	100

M-999

Similar to above model, with rubber-style combat grips, extended slide stop safety and magazine release. Fixed sights. Offered with stainless steel slide and blued frame or all stainless steel. Supplied with 7-round magazine. Weight about 38 oz. **NOTE:** Add $25 for stainless steel frame.

NIB	Exc.	V.G.	Good	Fair	Poor
475	350	275	200	125	75

M-777

Same as M-999, fitted with 4.25" barrel. Weight about 36 oz. **NOTE:** Add $25 for stainless steel frame.

NIB	Exc.	V.G.	Good	Fair	Poor
475	350	275	200	125	75

M-6000

This .45 ACP pistol, fitted with 5" barrel, plastic grips, extended slide stop safety and magazine release. Safety is ambidextrous. Magazine capacity 8 rounds. Fixed sights. Weight about 38 oz.

NIB	Exc.	V.G.	Good	Fair	Poor
475	375	325	250	175	100

M-5000

Similar to M-6000. Fitted with 4.25" barrel. Weight about 36 oz.

NIB	Exc.	V.G.	Good	Fair	Poor
475	375	325	250	175	100

IGA
Veranopolis, Brazil

Single-Barrel Shotgun

A 12-, 20-gauge or .410 bore single-barrel shotgun, with exposed hammer, 28" barrel and hardwood stock.

NIB	Exc.	V.G.	Good	Fair	Poor
150	90	75	50	40	30

Single-Barrel Shotgun Youth Model

Offered in 20-gauge and .410 bore. Features 22" barrel and shorter than standard buttstock. Weight 5 lbs.

NIB	Exc.	V.G.	Good	Fair	Poor
150	100	80	60	50	35

Coach Gun

A 12- or 20-gauge and .410 bore boxlock double-barrel shotgun, with 20" barrels, double triggers and extractors. Blued, with hardwood stock. **NOTE:** Add $50 for nickel finish; $60 for engraved butt stock.

NIB	Exc.	V.G.	Good	Fair	Poor
425	325	250	150	100	75

Standard Side-by-Side Uplander

Offered in 12-, 20-, 28-gauge and .410 bore, with 26" and 28" barrels. Checkered hardwood stock, with pistol-/straight-grip. Weight 6.75 lbs. **NOTE:** Add $40 for choke tubes.

NIB	Exc.	V.G.	Good	Fair	Poor
425	325	250	150	100	75

Uplander Youth

Same as above. Offered in 20-gauge or .410 bore with 24" barrels. Shorter length of pull. Recoil pad standard.

NIB	Exc.	V.G.	Good	Fair	Poor
450	325	250	150	100	75

Uplander Supreme

Introduced in 2000. Features high grade walnut stock with checkering, single-selective trigger, choke tubes and automatic ejectors. Offered in 12- and 20-gauge, with 26" or 28" barrels. Chambered for 3" shells. Soft rubber recoil pad standard.

NIB	Exc.	V.G.	Good	Fair	Poor
600	450	375	300	200	100

Standard Over/Under Condor I

Offered in 12- or 20-gauge, with 26" or 28" barrels. Fitted with extractors and single trigger. Choke tubes are standard. Checkered hardwood stock, with pistol-grip and recoil pad. Weight 8 lbs.

NIB	Exc.	V.G.	Good	Fair	Poor
425	300	225	200	150	100

Condor II

Same as above, with double triggers and plastic buttplate.

NIB	Exc.	V.G.	Good	Fair	Poor
400	250	200	150	100	75

Condor Supreme Deluxe

Similar to standard Condor. Has high grade walnut stock, hand checkering, recoil pad, single-selective trigger and automatic ejectors. Offered in 12- and 20-gauge, with 26" or 28" ventilated rib barrels. Chambered for 3" shells. Choke tubes standard. First offered in 2000.

NIB	Exc.	V.G.	Good	Fair	Poor
550	400	325	200	150	100

Deluxe Over/Under ERA 2000

Offered in 12-gauge only, with 26" or 28" barrels. Fitted with single trigger and extractors. Choke tubes are standard. Barrels are chrome lined and stock is hand checkered.

NIB	Exc.	V.G.	Good	Fair	Poor
450	325	250	150	100	75

INDIAN ARMS CORP.
Detroit, Michigan

Indian Arms .380

.380-caliber semi-automatic pistol, with 3.25" barrel and 6-shot magazine. Made of stainless steel. Finished in white or blued, with walnut grips. Manufactured from 1975 to 1977.

NIB	Exc.	V.G.	Good	Fair	Poor
—	350	250	200	150	100

INDUSTRIA ARMI GALESI
Brescia, Italy
See—Galesi

INGRAM
Military Armament Corp.
Atlanta, Georgia

MAC 10

9mm or .45-caliber open-bolt semi-automatic pistol, with 5.75" barrel and 32-shot magazine. Anodized, with plastic grips. Discontinued. **NOTE:** Add 20 percent for accessory kit (barrel extension and extra magazine).

NIB	Exc.	V.G.	Good	Fair	Poor
750	500	375	250	175	100

MAC 10AI

As above, but firing from closed-bolt. **NOTE:** Add 300 percent for earlier open-bolt model; 20 percent for accessory kit.

NIB	Exc.	V.G.	Good	Fair	Poor
750	600	250	200	150	100

MAC 11

As above in smaller version. Chambered for 9mm cartridge. **NOTE:** Add 300 percent for earlier open-bolt model; 20 percent for accessory kit.

NIB	Exc.	V.G.	Good	Fair	Poor
800	650	350	150	100	50

INTERARMS
Alexandria, Virginia

Importer of arms made by Howa Machine, Star and Walther. This firm no longer in business.

RIFLES

Mark X Viscount

Bolt-action sporting rifle made in a variety of calibers, with 24" barrel, open sights and adjustable trigger. Magazine holds 3 or 5 cartridges. Manufactured in Yugoslavia. Blued, with walnut stock.

NIB	Exc.	V.G.	Good	Fair	Poor
450	300	250	200	175	125

Mark X Lightweight

As above, with 20" barrel and composition stock. Introduced in 1988.

NIB	Exc.	V.G.	Good	Fair	Poor
450	300	250	200	175	125

Mini Mark X

As above, with short action in .223-caliber only, 20" barrel, open sights and adjustable trigger. Five-shot magazine. Introduced in 1987.

NIB	Exc.	V.G.	Good	Fair	Poor
450	300	250	200	175	125

Mark X American Field

As above, with finely figured walnut stock, ebony fore-end tip, pistol-grip cap, sling swivels and recoil pad. Introduced in 1984.

NIB	Exc.	V.G.	Good	Fair	Poor
525	400	350	300	250	175

Whitworth Express Rifle

.375 H&H or .458 Win. Magnum bolt-action sporting rifle, with 24" barrel, express sights and 3-shot magazine. Blued, with walnut stock. Introduced in 1974.

NIB	Exc.	V.G.	Good	Fair	Poor
950	750	550	350	250	200

Whitworth Mannlicher Carbine

.243, .270, 7x57mm, .308 and .30-06 caliber bolt-action rifle, with 20" barrel, open sights, sling swivels and full length stock. Manufactured between 1984 and 1987.

NIB	Exc.	V.G.	Good	Fair	Poor
—	725	550	375	250	200

Cavalier

Bolt-action sporting rifle. Made in a variety of calibers, with modern style stock having rollover cheekpiece. Discontinued.

NIB	Exc.	V.G.	Good	Fair	Poor
—	500	400	350	200	150

Mannlicher Carbine

As above, with 20" barrel and full length stock. Discontinued.

NIB	Exc.	V.G.	Good	Fair	Poor
—	600	500	425	275	195

Continental Carbine

As above, with double-set triggers. Discontinued.

NIB	Exc.	V.G.	Good	Fair	Poor
—	625	525	450	300	225

Alaskan Model

Similar to Mark X in .375 H&H or .458 Win. Magnum, with 24" barrel. Discontinued in 1985.

NIB	Exc.	V.G.	Good	Fair	Poor
—	950	750	550	350	200

22-ATD

.22-caliber semi-automatic rifle, with 19.4" barrel, open sights and 11-shot magazine. Blued, with hardwood stock. Manufactured by Norinco. Introduced in 1987.

NIB	Exc.	V.G.	Good	Fair	Poor
195	125	95	65	50	40

HANDGUNS

Helwan Brigadier

9mm semi-automatic pistol, with 4.5" barrel, fixed sights and 8-shot magazine. Blued, with plastic grips. Introduced in 1988.

NIB	Exc.	V.G.	Good	Fair	Poor
375	275	200	175	125	100

FEG R-9

9mm semi-automatic pistol patterned after Browning 35, with 13-shot magazine. Blued, with walnut grips. Manufactured in 1986 and 1987.

NIB	Exc.	V.G.	Good	Fair	Poor
—	350	250	185	145	100

FEG PPH

.380-caliber double-action semi-automatic pistol, with 3.5" barrel and 6-shot magazine. Blued, with plastic grips.

NIB	Exc.	V.G.	Good	Fair	Poor
—	300	175	150	125	100

Mark II AP

Copy of Walther PP. Chambered for .380 ACP or .22 LR cartridge.

NIB	Exc.	V.G.	Good	Fair	Poor
300	175	125	100	75	50

Mark II APK

Copy of Walther PPK. Chambered for .380 ACP cartridge only.

NIB	Exc.	V.G.	Good	Fair	Poor
300	175	125	100	75	50

Mauser Parabellum Karabiner

9mm caliber semi-automatic carbine, with 11.75" barrel and detachable shoulder stock. Fitted in leather case. **NOTE:** Only 100 imported into U.S. This arm subject to BATFE registration.

NIB	Exc.	V.G.	Good	Fair	Poor
6500	5750	5000	4000	3000	2250

Mauser Parabellum Cartridge Counter

Reproduction of cartridge counter Luger. Fitted in leather case, with only 100 units imported into U.S.

NIB	Exc.	V.G.	Good	Fair	Poor
4000	3000	2500	2000	1500	1000

Virginian Dragoon

Single-action revolver in .357 Magnum, .41 Magnum, .44 Magnum or .45 Colt, with 5", 6", 7.5", 8.75" or 12" barrel, fixed or adjustable sights and 6-shot cylinder. Originally made in Switzerland, then in U.S.A. Discontinued in 1984. **NOTE:** Add 20 percent for Swiss manufacture; 15 percent for 12" barrel.

NIB	Exc.	V.G.	Good	Fair	Poor
—	325	275	200	150	100

Stainless Dragoon

As above in stainless steel.

NIB	Exc.	V.G.	Good	Fair	Poor
—	375	300	245	175	105

Virginian Dragoon Silhouette

Similar to stainless Virginia Dragoon, except in .357 or .44 Magnum, with 7.5", 8.375" or 10.5" barrel. Adjustable sights, target grips.

NIB	Exc.	V.G.	Good	Fair	Poor
500	425	350	300	250	150

Dragoon Deputy

Similar to Virginia Dragoon except in .357 or .44 Magnum. Blue finish, with case-hardened frame or stainless and 5" barrel.

NIB	Exc.	V.G.	Good	Fair	Poor
450	375	300	250	200	125

Virginian .22 Convertible

As above in .22-caliber, with 5.5" barrel.

NIB	Exc.	V.G.	Good	Fair	Poor
—	275	200	125	100	75

Virginian Stainless .22 Convertible

As above in stainless steel.

NIB	Exc.	V.G.	Good	Fair	Poor
—	295	225	165	100	80

INTERARMS/HIGH STANDARD
Houston, Texas

In 2000, High Standard Manufacturing Company of Houston, Texas resurrected the Interarms name. They began making several AK-style semi-automatic rifles in U.S.A. Following is a sampling of these models.

AK-47 (7.62x39mm)

NIB	Exc.	V.G.	Good	Fair	Poor
1000	850	700	500	400	250

AKM Series (7.62x39mm)

NIB	Exc.	V.G.	Good	Fair	Poor
550	450	375	300	225	150

AK-74 (5.45x39mm)

NIB	Exc.	V.G.	Good	Fair	Poor
600	500	400	325	275	200

INTERDYNAMICS OF AMERICA
Miami, Florida

KG-9

9mm caliber semi-automatic pistol, with 3" barrel and 36-shot magazine. Manufactured from 1981 to 1983. **NOTE:** Earliest models fire from open bolt. Valued at approximately 150 percent of values shown here.

NIB	Exc.	V.G.	Good	Fair	Poor
—	800	650	575	500	300

KG-99

As above, with barrel shroud. Manufactured from 1981 to 1984.

NIB	Exc.	V.G.	Good	Fair	Poor
—	800	650	575	500	300

KG-99 Stainless

As above in stainless steel. Manufactured in 1984.

NIB	Exc.	V.G.	Good	Fair	Poor
—	800	650	575	500	300

KG-99M

More compact version of above. Manufactured in 1984.

NIB	Exc.	V.G.	Good	Fair	Poor
—	800	650	575	500	300

INTRATEC USA, INC.
Miami, Florida

This manufacturer was in business from 1985 to 2000, under the names Intratec and Intratec USA, Inc.

TEC-9

9mm caliber semi-automatic pistol, with 5" shrouded barrel and 36-shot magazine. Introduced in 1985.

NIB	Exc.	V.G.	Good	Fair	Poor
450	350	295	200	150	100

TEC-9C

As above, with 16" barrel and folding stock. Manufactured in 1987.

NIB	Exc.	V.G.	Good	Fair	Poor
—	450	350	295	200	100

TEC-9M

As above, with 3" barrel and 20-shot magazine. Also made in stainless steel.

NIB	Exc.	V.G.	Good	Fair	Poor
450	350	295	200	150	100

TEC-22 "Scorpion"

Similar to above in .22-caliber, with 4" barrel and 30-shot magazine.

NIB	Exc.	V.G.	Good	Fair	Poor
325	225	175	100	75	50

TEC-38

.38-caliber over/under double-action derringer, with 3" barrels. Manufactured between 1986 and 1988.

NIB	Exc.	V.G.	Good	Fair	Poor
—	195	125	90	65	45

IRVING, W.
New York, New York

Single-Shot Derringer

.22-caliber spur trigger single-shot pistol, with 2.75" half octagonal barrel. Silver plated brass frame, blued barrel and rosewood grips. Barrel marked "W. Irving". Manufactured in 1860s. **NOTE:** .32-caliber variation has 3" barrel and worth approximately 40 percent more than values listed.

NIB	Exc.	V.G.	Good	Fair	Poor
—	—	1050	475	195	125

Pocket Revolver 1st Model

.31-caliber spur trigger percussion revolver, with 3" octagonal barrel, 6-shot cylinder and brass frame. Barrel marked "W. Irving". Approximately 50 made between 1858 and 1862.

NIB	Exc.	V.G.	Good	Fair	Poor
—	—	2500	925	275	175

Pocket Revolver 2nd Model

.31-caliber percussion revolver, with 4.5" round barrel, loading lever and brass or iron frame. Barrel marked "Address W. Irving. 20 Cliff St. N.Y.". Approximately 600 manufactured with brass frame; 1,500 with iron frame. **NOTE:** Brass-frame version will bring a premium of about 35 percent.

NIB	Exc.	V.G.	Good	Fair	Poor
—	—	1450	495	200	100

IRWINDALE ARMS, INC.
Irwindale, California

See—AMT

ISRAELI MILITARY INDUSTRIES
Israel

Civilian firearms manufactured by this firm have been and are being retailed by Action Arms Limited, Magnum Research and Mossberg.

ITHACA GUN CO.
Ithaca, New York

Material was supplied by Walter C. Snyder and is copyrighted in his name. Used with author's permission.

Ithaca Gun Company was founded by William Henry Baker, John VanNatta and Dwight McIntyre. Gun production started during latter half of 1883, at an industrial site located on Fall Creek, Ithaca, New York. Leroy Smith joined the company by 1885 and George Livermore joined the firm in 1887. By 1894, the company was under exclusive control of Leroy Smith and George Livermore. Many of the company's assets were purchased by Ithaca Acquisition Corporation in 1987 and moved to King Ferry, New York, where it operated until May, 1996. Now, dba, Ithaca Gun Company of Upper Sandusky, Ohio.

HAMMER MODELS

Ithaca Baker Model

First model produced by the company was designed by W.H. Baker and manufactured from 1883 through 1887. Offered in six grades; Quality A ($35) through Quality F ($200), in 10- or 12-gauge. All Ithaca-produced Baker models had exposed hammers. Grades above Quality B are seldom encountered and an expert appraisal is recommended.

Quality A

Courtesy Walter C. Snyder

NIB	Exc.	V.G.	Good	Fair	Poor
—	900	500	300	200	100

Quality B

NIB	Exc.	V.G.	Good	Fair	Poor
—	1850	1350	750	300	100

New Ithaca Gun

Introduced in 1888; discontinued during 1915. Like its predecessor, introduced in same seven grades, Quality A through Quality F. Later Quality F was discontinued. By 1900 a "condensed steel" barreled model named Quality X was introduced. New Ithaca Gun was produced in gauges 10-, 12-, 16- and very rarely 20-gauge. Lower grade models carried logo "New Ithaca Gun" usually within a banner on each side of frame. Like its predecessor, grades above Quality B are seldom encountered and an expert appraisal is recommended. 16-gauge guns command a 30 percent price premium. Extremely rare 20-gauge model requires an expert appraisal.

Quality A

Courtesy Walter C. Snyder

NIB	Exc.	V.G.	Good	Fair	Poor
—	1100	775	295	175	100

Quality AA

NIB	Exc.	V.G.	Good	Fair	Poor
—	1100	775	295	175	100

Quality B

NIB	Exc.	V.G.	Good	Fair	Poor
—	1300	875	450	225	100

Quality X

NIB	Exc.	V.G.	Good	Fair	Poor
—	1300	875	450	225	100

The "New Double Bolted Hammer Gun"

During 1915, Ithaca Gun Company replaced New Ithaca Gun, with model it referred to as "our new model two bolt hammer gun". New hammer gun had coil springs powering external hammers. The "two bolt" lock up was accomplished by a bottom bolt and top lever engagement, with rear nub of rib extension. Lower grade models were marked on both sides of frame, with a setter dog and logo "Ithaca Gun Co.". The 1915 catalog is last year hammer guns were advertised, but old records indicate a few were sold as late as 1919.

Grades offered were X, A, AA, B, C, D and E. The 1915 catalog advertised a price of $29 for a Quality A model and $150 for elaborately engraved Quality E. All grades were available in 10-, 12- and 16-gauge. Like the New Ithaca Gun, grades above Quality B are seldom encountered and an expert appraisal is recommended. 16-gauge guns command a 30 percent price premium. Extremely rare 20-gauge model requires an expert appraisal.

Quality A

NIB	Exc.	V.G.	Good	Fair	Poor
—	1300	875	350	225	100

Quality AA

NIB	Exc.	V.G.	Good	Fair	Poor
—	1600	1075	450	250	100

Quality B

NIB	Exc.	V.G.	Good	Fair	Poor
—	1600	1075	450	250	100

Quality X

NIB	Exc.	V.G.	Good	Fair	Poor
—	1600	1075	450	250	100

HAMMERLESS MODELS

First hammerless Ithaca gun was introduced in 1888. All Ithaca double guns were discontinued in 1948. Gauge and grade can usually be found on left front corner of water table of frame. Serial number usually found on right side of same water table on barrel flats and fore-end iron.

Crass Model

Crass Model, named after Ithaca's Frederick Crass who designed it, was introduced in 1888. Offered in Quality 1 through Quality 7. Quality 1P model with no engraving introduced in 1898. Crass Model underwent three major frame redesigns, before it was discontinued during 1901. Gun was available in 10-, 12- and 16-gauge. Automatic ejectors introduced in 1893. Available in any Quality gun at extra cost.

NOTE: 16-gauge guns will command a 20 percent price premium. Guns above Quality 4 are seldom encountered and an expert appraisal is necessary. Automatic ejectors add $250. Serial number range for Crass Model approximately 7000 to 50000.

Quality 1

NIB	Exc.	V.G.	Good	Fair	Poor
—	900	575	400	225	100

Quality 1-1/2

NIB	Exc.	V.G.	Good	Fair	Poor
—	900	575	400	225	100

Quality 1P

NIB	Exc.	V.G.	Good	Fair	Poor
—	900	575	400	225	100

Quality 2

Courtesy Walter C. Snyder

NIB	Exc.	V.G.	Good	Fair	Poor
—	1300	875	600	250	100

Quality 3

NIB	Exc.	V.G.	Good	Fair	Poor
—	1800	1300	775	325	100

Quality 4

NIB	Exc.	V.G.	Good	Fair	Poor
—	2250	1850	1075	325	100

Lewis Model

Chester Lewis, an Ithaca Gun employee, was credited with design of this gun that now bears his name. Gun was bolted through rib extension in addition to traditional under bolt. Available from 1901 through 1906 and offered in Qualities 1 through 7. Made in 10-, 12- and 16-gauge. After 1906, 20-gauge. Automatic ejectors were offered at an added cost. **NOTE:** Automatic ejectors add about $250 to grades below Quality 4. Serial number range for Lewis Model approximately 55000 to 123600.

Quality 1

NIB	Exc.	V.G.	Good	Fair	Poor
—	900	575	325	175	100

Quality 1 Special

Courtesy Walter C. Snyder

NIB	Exc.	V.G.	Good	Fair	Poor
—	900	575	325	175	100

Quality 1-1/2

NIB	Exc.	V.G.	Good	Fair	Poor
—	950	600	350	200	100

Quality 2

NIB	Exc.	V.G.	Good	Fair	Poor
—	1150	725	500	225	100

Quality 3

NIB	Exc.	V.G.	Good	Fair	Poor
—	1850	1500	850	425	100

Quality 4

NIB	Exc.	V.G.	Good	Fair	Poor
—	2700	2350	1900	475	100

Quality 5

NIB	Exc.	V.G.	Good	Fair	Poor
—	3700	3150	2100	725	300

Quality 6

NIB	Exc.	V.G.	Good	Fair	Poor
—	6300	4750	3200	775	300

Quality 7

NIB	Exc.	V.G.	Good	Fair	Poor
—	6300	4750	3200	775	300

Minier Model

Minier Model, named after Ithaca's David Minier, was introduced in 1906 and available through 1908. Offered in Qualities Field through 7 and any grade could be ordered with ejectors. Minier Model was first Ithaca gun to use coil springs to power internal hammers. Model was triple bolted, e.g., two fastenings at rib extension and under bolt. Offered in 10-, 12-, 16- and 20-gauge. **NOTE:** Automatic ejectors add $250 to guns below Quality 4. Serial number range for Minier Model approximately 130000 to 151000.

Field Grade

NIB	Exc.	V.G.	Good	Fair	Poor
—	1150	725	500	225	100

Quality 1

NIB	Exc.	V.G.	Good	Fair	Poor
—	1150	725	500	225	100

Quality 1 Special

NIB	Exc.	V.G.	Good	Fair	Poor
—	1150	725	500	225	100

Quality 1-1/2

NIB	Exc.	V.G.	Good	Fair	Poor
—	1150	725	500	225	100

Quality 2

NIB	Exc.	V.G.	Good	Fair	Poor
—	1350	700	475	225	100

Quality 3

Courtesy Walter C. Snyder

NIB	Exc.	V.G.	Good	Fair	Poor
—	2250	1200	575	450	100

Quality 4

Courtesy Amoskeag Auction Company

NIB	Exc.	V.G.	Good	Fair	Poor
—	2700	1325	875	450	100

Quality 5

NIB	Exc.	V.G.	Good	Fair	Poor
—	3700	3150	2100	725	300

Quality 6

NIB	Exc.	V.G.	Good	Fair	Poor
—	5250	4100	1550	725	300

Quality 7

NIB	Exc.	V.G.	Good	Fair	Poor
—	6800	4300	1700	800	300

Flues Model

Flues Model Ithaca gun, built on three-piece lock mechanism invented and patented by Emil Flues. Introduced in 1908, remained in production through

1926 when it was replaced by Ithaca New Double. Offered in 10-, 12-, 16-, 20- and 28-gauge. Enjoyed longest production life of any Ithaca double gun. Several grades offered beginning with Field Grade and ending with Sousa Special. Flues Model had same bolting system as used on Minier Model. Any grade could have been ordered, with automatic ejectors at an extra cost. Single-selective trigger made by Infallible Trigger Company, offered after 1914 and was first single trigger offered from this company. **NOTE:** Add $200 for factory-ordered single trigger; $200 for automatic ejectors on grades lower than Grade 4. Small gauges command a price premium. 20-gauge gun may command up to 50 percent price premium; 28-gauge Field Grade, perhaps as much as 200 percent. Serial number range for Flues approximately 175000 to 399000. Expert appraisals are recommended on higher-grade, small-gauge models, as they are seldom encountered.

Field Grade

Courtesy Walter C. Snyder

NIB	Exc.	V.G.	Good	Fair	Poor
—	1100	700	375	250	100

Grade 1

NIB	Exc.	V.G.	Good	Fair	Poor
—	1100	700	375	250	100

Grade 1 Special

NIB	Exc.	V.G.	Good	Fair	Poor
—	1100	700	375	250	100

Grade 1-1/2

NIB	Exc.	V.G.	Good	Fair	Poor
—	1250	850	500	350	100

Grade 2

NIB	Exc.	V.G.	Good	Fair	Poor
—	1350	900	575	400	100

Grade 3

NIB	Exc.	V.G.	Good	Fair	Poor
—	2300	1600	800	500	100

Grade 4

NIB	Exc.	V.G.	Good	Fair	Poor
—	2300	1600	800	500	100

Grade 5

NIB	Exc.	V.G.	Good	Fair	Poor
—	2800	2200	1650	600	200

Grade 6

Courtesy Walter C. Snyder

NIB	Exc.	V.G.	Good	Fair	Poor
—	11000	6000	2750	1100	300

Grade 7

NIB	Exc.	V.G.	Good	Fair	Poor
—	11500	7000	3000	1250	300

Sousa

NIB	Exc.	V.G.	Good	Fair	Poor
—	17000	12000	7500	3750	N/A

The New Ithaca Double

New Ithaca Double commonly referred to as NID, manufactured from 1926 to 1948. Has the distinction of being last double gun manufactured by factory. NID was bolted by a single rotary top bolt. External cocking indicators were standard on all NID models until about 1934, when they were eliminated from the design. Selective and non-selective single triggers and automatic ejectors, were optional at additional costs. Special variation of NID was introduced in 1932 to accommodate 10-gauge 3.5" Magnum ammunition and named appropriately, Magnum 10. All NID guns were available in Grades Field, 1, 2, 3, 4, 5, 7 and Sousa (renamed the $1,000 grade after 1936). Magnum 10-gauge and standard 10-, 12-, 16-, 20-, 28-gauge and .410 bore were offered. **NOTE:** Like most collectible double guns, smaller gauges command a price premium over 12-gauge model. 16-gauge Field Grade may command a 25 percent price premium; 20-gauge Field Grade may command up to a 50 percent price premium; 28-gauge and .410 caliber Field Grade models, perhaps as much as 250-300 percent. It is recommended that an expert opinion be sought for valuation of high-grade small-gauge models. Of late, Magnum 10-gauge model also commands a price premium. Few of these guns trade and advice of an expert appraiser is suggested. Add $150 for non-selective single trigger; $250 for single-selective trigger; $300 for ventilated rib; $300 for automatic ejectors for grades below Grade 4; $200 for beavertail forearm; $300 for Monte Carlo buttstock.

Field Grade

NIB	Exc.	V.G.	Good	Fair	Poor
—	1100	700	375	250	100

Grade 1

NIB	Exc.	V.G.	Good	Fair	Poor
—	1350	850	475	250	100

Grade 2

Courtesy Walter C. Snyder

NIB	Exc.	V.G.	Good	Fair	Poor
—	1650	900	725	350	100

Grade 3

NIB	Exc.	V.G.	Good	Fair	Poor
—	2600	1600	1075	425	100

Grade 4

NIB	Exc.	V.G.	Good	Fair	Poor
—	3250	2700	1600	475	100

Grade 5

NIB	Exc.	V.G.	Good	Fair	Poor
—	4300	3400	2200	775	200

Grade 7

NIB	Exc.	V.G.	Good	Fair	Poor
—	12000	7500	4250	1100	300

Sousa Grade

NIB	Exc.	V.G.	Good	Fair	Poor
—	28000	15000	8000	4000	800

ITHACA CLASSIC DOUBLES (1998-2003)

Special Field Grade

Side-by-side double offered in 16-, 20-, 28-gauge and .410 bore. Choice of matted rib barrel lengths of 26", 28" or 30". Ivory bead front sight. Action is case colored, with light line border engraving. Stock is feather crotch black walnut, with 22 lpi checkering. Choice of pistol-/straight-grip. Double trigger standard. Weight about: 20-gauge 5 lbs. 14 oz.; 28-gauge 5 lbs. 8 oz.; .410 bore 5 lbs. 5 oz.

NIB	Exc.	V.G.	Good	Fair	Poor
6200	4750	4000	1700	800	300

Grade 4E

Available in 16-, 20-, 28-gauge and .410 bore, with 26", 28" and 30" barrels. Has gold plated triggers, jeweled barrel flats and hand tuned locks. Black walnut stock has 28 lpi checkering, with fleur-de-lis pattern. Pistol-/straight-grip stock. Action is hand engraved, with three game scenes and bank note scroll. Case colored frame.

NIB	Exc.	V.G.	Good	Fair	Poor
8000	6000	3000	1750	775	300

Grade 7E

Has all gauges and barrel lengths of above gun. Action is hand engraved, with gold two tone inlays. Exhibition grade black walnut stock, with elaborate patterns. Custom built dimensions.

NIB	Exc.	V.G.	Good	Fair	Poor
11000	8750	7500	4250	1100	300

Sousa Grade

Available in same gauges and barrel lengths as above guns. Stocks with presentation grade black walnut and hand carved with 32 lpi checkering. Action hand engraved, with bank note scroll and gold inlays. Entire gun hand fitted and polished. Extremely limited availability. Special order only. In production from 1998 to 2003.

NIB	Exc.	V.G.	Good	Fair	Poor
30000	20000	15000	—	—	—

LEFEVER ARMS COMPANY, INC.

During 1921, Ithaca Gun under the name "The Lefever Arms Company, Inc." introduced a line of lower-cost boxlock guns. See Lefever Arms Company section of this book for prices concerning those guns.

WESTERN ARMS CORPORATION

During 1929, Ithaca Gun Company created Western Arms Corporation, which introduced a new low-cost double gun. That new double gun was named, The Long Range Double. Produced in 12-, 16-, 20-gauge and .410 bore. Model last made at start of World War II. **NOTE:** 20-gauge guns often command a 20 percent premium; .410 bore can command up to 250 percent premium.

The Long Range Double

This model had walnut stocks that were not checkered. **NOTE:** Add $100 for single trigger; $200 for automatic ejectors.

NIB	Exc.	V.G.	Good	Fair	Poor
—	550	450	200	150	N/A

The Long Range Double Deluxe

Usually made exclusively for Montgomery Ward Company. Sold by them under the name: Western Field Deluxe. Had line checkering pattern at grip and on splinter fore-end. Many of Ithaca produced Western Field Deluxe guns had automatic ejectors and that fact was stamped into right barrel. **NOTE:** Add $100 for single triggers; $200 for automatic ejectors.

NIB	Exc.	V.G.	Good	Fair	Poor
—	575	475	300	150	N/A

ITHACA SINGLE-BARREL TRAP GUNS

Ithaca Gun Company introduced a single-barrel trap gun in 1914. Based upon Emil Flues three piece lock design used for double gun, which become known as Flues Model Single-Barrel Trap. Flues Model was discontinued during 1922 and replaced that year by model designed by Ithaca's, Frank Knickerbocker, commonly referred to as "Knick". Knick Model discontinued in 1988, shortly after Ithaca Acquisition Corp. purchased assets of Ithaca Gun Company. For many years, Ithaca Single-Barrel Trap Gun was the gun of choice for many champion shooters.

Flues Model Single-Barrel Trap Gun (1914 to 1922)

Flues Model trap gun was introduced in 1914. Offered in Grades 4, 5, 6 and 7. Lower cost Victory grade introduced in 1919. Highest cost variety Sousa Special introduced in 1918. All Flues model trap guns were made within same serial number sequence as double guns, but do have letter "T" for Trap following serial number. All Flues Models, with exception of Victory Grade, were produced with an automatic ejector. Rubber anti-recoil pad was an option. Guns having a pre-1916 engraving pattern will command highest prices.

Courtesy Walter C. Snyder

Victory Grade

NIB	Exc.	V.G.	Good	Fair	Poor
—	1300	900	700	300	N/A

Grade 4E

NIB	Exc.	V.G.	Good	Fair	Poor
—	2350	1900	1300	400	N/A

Grade 5E

Courtesy Walter C. Snyder

NIB	Exc.	V.G.	Good	Fair	Poor
—	4200	3100	2550	600	N/A

Grade 6E

NIB	Exc.	V.G.	Good	Fair	Poor
—	6300	5250	3200	900	N/A

Grade 7E

NIB	Exc.	V.G.	Good	Fair	Poor
—	8350	6200	4100	1050	N/A

Sousa Grade

NIB	Exc.	V.G.	Good	Fair	Poor
—	16500	11000	9000	2500	N/A

Knick Model Single-Barrel Trap

Knick Model trap gun introduced during 1922. Based on design credited to Frank Knickerbocker. Design was simple and very serviceable. Had been in continuous production until 1988, when it was discontinued. Model available in Victory, 4, 5, 7 and Sousa Special Grades. Sousa was replaced by: $1,000 Grade in about 1936; which was replaced by $2,000 Grade by 1952; $2,500 Grade by 1960; $3,000 Grade by 1965; $5,000 Grade by 1974; finally, Dollar Grade in early 1980s, as cost of production increased. All Knick models were produced with automatic ejector and rubber anti-recoil pad.

Victory Grade

Courtesy William Hammond

NIB	Exc.	V.G.	Good	Fair	Poor
2500	1350	900	700	300	N/A

Grade 4E

Courtesy C. Hadley Smith

NIB	Exc.	V.G.	Good	Fair	Poor
3300	2450	1950	1100	500	N/A

Grade 5E

NIB	Exc.	V.G.	Good	Fair	Poor
5500	4400	3300	2750	875	N/A

Grade 7E

Courtesy Walter C. Snyder

NIB	Exc.	V.G.	Good	Fair	Poor
8800	5500	4450	3300	1100	N/A

Sousa Grade

NIB	Exc.	V.G.	Good	Fair	Poor
19000	11000	6600	4400	N/A	N/A

$1,000 to $2,500 Grades

Courtesy Walter C. Snyder

NIB	Exc.	V.G.	Good	Fair	Poor
16500	13500	8800	6500	2200	N/A

$3,000 through the Dollar Grade

NIB	Exc.	V.G.	Good	Fair	Poor
13500	11000	6500	5500	2200	N/A

Century Grade Trap (SKB)

12-gauge boxlock single-barrel shotgun, with 32" or 34" ventilated rib barrel. Automatic ejector. Blued, with walnut stock. Manufactured by SKB during 1970s.

NIB	Exc.	V.G.	Good	Fair	Poor
—	900	700	550	350	300

Century II (SKB)

An improved version of above model.

NIB	Exc.	V.G.	Good	Fair	Poor
—	950	700	600	450	350

ITHACA MODEL 66

Model 66 Supersingle—1963-1978

12-, 20-gauge or .410 bore lever action single-shot shotgun, with 24" barrel. Blued, with walnut stock. **NOTE:** Add 50 per premium for 20-gauge and .410 bore.

Courtesy C. Hadley Smith

NIB	Exc.	V.G.	Good	Fair	Poor
300	180	150	125	100	50

Model 66 Youth Grade

Special gun offered for youth market in 20-gauge and .410 bore.

NIB	Exc.	V.G.	Good	Fair	Poor
300	180	150	125	100	50

Model 66 Buck Buster (RS Barrel)

As above in 20-gauge, with Deerslayer 22" barrel fitted with rifle sights.

NIB	Exc.	V.G.	Good	Fair	Poor
325	250	200	150	125	75

Model 66 Vent Rib

NIB	Exc.	V.G.	Good	Fair	Poor
325	250	200	150	125	75

ITHACA AUTO & BURGLAR GUN/NFA, CURIO OR RELIC

Ithaca Auto & Burglar Gun, is a double-barreled 20-gauge smooth bore pistol. Manufactured by Ithaca Gun Company, Ithaca, New York, from 1922 to 1934. Total production approximately 4,500. Made by modifying Ithaca's standard field grade double-barrel shotgun, by shortening barrels and fitting receiver with a pistol-grip. Standard factory guns had blued 10" barrels, case-hardened receivers, with legend "Auto & Burglar Gun/ Ithaca Gun Co./Ithaca, New York" and figure of a pointing dog stamped on each side. Barrel length on 21 guns inspected varied to 10.25" (typically in increments divisible by .125"), apparently from inexact factory quality control. Ithaca set a $37.50 retail price when gun was in production, but some dealers sold it for $40 or more. Production halted when government ruled Ithaca Auto & Burglar Gun to be a "firearm" in "any other weapon" category under National Firearms Act (NFA) of 1934.

There are two variations, termed Model A and Model B. Model A utilizes so-called Flues frame (named after Emil Flues who designed it in 1908). Its distinctive grip has a curving butt and large spur. Model A designed for 2.5" shells and is not considered safe to fire using modern ammunition. Approximately 2,500 Model A Auto & Burglar Guns were manufactured from 1922 to 1925, when Flues model was discontinued.

Model B utilizes so-called NID frame (short for New Ithaca Double). Introduced in 1926 and discontinued in 1948. NID is designed for modern ammunition and 2.75" shells. Has cocking indicators and different pistol-grip that is perpendicular to barrel, which lacks distinctive spur. Some Model Bs have been observed with rosettes or "stars" engraved in each side of receiver. Their significance is unknown at this time, but they probably are decorations. Approximately 2,000 Model B Auto & Burglar Guns were manufactured from 1926 to 1934.

Model A

Serial numbered from 343336 to 398365

NIB	Exc.	V.G.	Good	Fair	Poor
—	2500	2000	1750	900	500

Model B

Serial numbered from 425000 to 464699

NOTE: Non-standard or special order guns command premiums of 100 percent or more. Original holsters (marked Auto and Burglar Gun/made by/ITHACA GUN CO./ithaca, n.y.) are extremely rare and worth $300 to $500 or more.

NIB	Exc.	V.G.	Good	Fair	Poor
—	2750	2200	2000	950	550

ITHACA MODEL 37 REPEATER

Ithaca Model 37 Repeater was introduced in 1937 in 12-gauge, 1938 in 16-gauge and 1939 in 20-gauge. It underwent very few design changes throughout its long life, which ended in 1987. Ithaca Acquisition Corp. acquired assets of Ithaca Gun Company during 1987, renaming the gun Model 87. Name has recently been changed again to M37, after assets of Ithaca Acquisition Corp. were purchased in May of 1996 by Ithaca Gun Company, LLC. All Model 37 guns were chambered only for 2.75 ammunition until 1983, when Magnum with 3" chamber was introduced to some configurations. Most Model 37 guns had blued metal and walnut stocks, with exception of Model 37 Field Grade series, which had matte finished metal and birch stocks. 16-gauge guns were discontinued in 1973. Ithaca Gun closed in April, 2005, but reopened in 2006 as Ithaca Guns USA of Upper Sandusky, Ohio.

NOTE: 20-gauge guns made before 1968 will generally command a price premium.

Model 37/Standard Grade—1937-1983

Guns made before 1968 will enjoy 15 percent price premium; those made before World War II 30 percent price premium.

Courtesy C. Hadley Smith

NIB	Exc.	V.G.	Good	Fair	Poor
—	350	200	175	125	75

Model 37S/Skeet Grade—1937-1953

Guns made before World War II will enjoy 50 percent price premium.

NIB	Exc.	V.G.	Good	Fair	Poor
—	600	400	350	250	100

Model 37T/Trap—1937-1953

Guns made before World War II will enjoy 50 percent price premium.

NIB	Exc.	V.G.	Good	Fair	Poor
—	600	400	350	250	100

Model 37T/Target—1954-1961

NIB	Exc.	V.G.	Good	Fair	Poor
—	600	400	350	250	100

Model 37R/Solid Rib—1940-1967

Guns made before World War II will enjoy 50 percent price premium.

Courtesy Walter C. Snyder

NIB	Exc.	V.G.	Good	Fair	Poor
—	400	275	225	200	75

Model 37 Military Marked (WWII)

One of the scarcest military shotguns. Built in three different configurations; 30" barrel, 20" barrel and 20" barrel with hand guard and bayonet lug (Trench Gun). Rare shotgun, proceed with caution. **NOTE:** Add $200 for government release papers; 150 percent for Trench Gun configuration.

Courtesy Richard M. Kumor, Sr.

NIB	Exc.	V.G.	Good	Fair	Poor
—	2000	1800	1500	—	—

Model 37RD/Deluxe Solid Rib—1954-1962

Courtesy C. Hadley Smith

NIB	Exc.	V.G.	Good	Fair	Poor
—	500	375	300	200	100

Model 37 Deerslayer—1959-1987

All Deerslayer models made before 1968 will enjoy 10 to 20 percent price premium.

Courtesy C. Hadley Smith

NIB	Exc.	V.G.	Good	Fair	Poor
—	300	250	200	125	75

Model 37 Deluxe Deerslayer—1959-1971

NIB	Exc.	V.G.	Good	Fair	Poor
—	300	250	225	125	75

Model 37 Super Deluxe Deerslayer—1959-1987

Courtesy C. Hadley Smith

NIB	Exc.	V.G.	Good	Fair	Poor
—	450	325	275	200	100

Model 37 Supreme Grade—1967-1987

NIB	Exc.	V.G.	Good	Fair	Poor
—	700	450	350	200	100

Model 37 Field Grade Standard—1983-1985

NIB	Exc.	V.G.	Good	Fair	Poor
—	350	200	150	125	75

Model 37 Field Grade Vent Rib—1983-1986

NIB	Exc.	V.G.	Good	Fair	Poor
—	350	250	200	125	75

Model 37 Basic Featherlight—1979-1983

Manufactured in 12-gauge only.

Courtesy Walter C. Snyder

NIB	Exc.	V.G.	Good	Fair	Poor
—	300	250	200	125	75

Model 37V/Vent Rib—1961-1983

Guns made before 1968 will enjoy 10 to 20 percent price premium.

NIB	Exc.	V.G.	Good	Fair	Poor
—	350	300	175	150	75

Model 37RV/Deluxe Vent Rib—1961-1966

Courtesy Walter C. Snyder

NIB	Exc.	V.G.	Good	Fair	Poor
—	750	500	300	200	75

Model 37D/Deluxe—1955-1977

Guns made before 1968 will enjoy 10 to 20 percent price premium.

Courtesy C. Hadley Smith

NIB	Exc.	V.G.	Good	Fair	Poor
—	400	250	175	125	75

Model 37DV/Deluxe Vent Rib—1961-1987

Guns made before 1968 will enjoy 10 to 20 percent price premium.

NIB	Exc.	V.G.	Good	Fair	Poor
—	450	300	200	150	100

Model 37 Magnum 3" Chamber—1978-1987

NIB	Exc.	V.G.	Good	Fair	Poor
—	400	300	225	125	75

Model 37 Field Grade Magnum—1984-1987

NIB	Exc.	V.G.	Good	Fair	Poor
—	300	225	175	125	75

Model 37 UltraLight—1978 to 1987

UltraLight had aluminum alloy frame and trigger plate. Barrels marked Ultra Featherlight. Serial number prefaced with the mark "ULT". Both 12- and 20-gauge offered.

NIB	Exc.	V.G.	Good	Fair	Poor
—	475	400	300	150	100

ITHACA GUN CO. • 587

Model 37 English UltraLight—1982-1987

Same as Model 37 UltraLight, with English-style straight-grip stock.

NIB	Exc.	V.G.	Good	Fair	Poor
—	500	450	350	150	100

Model 37 Camo

Introduced in 1985, with green or brown camouflage finish. Offered only in 12-gauge.

NIB	Exc.	V.G.	Good	Fair	Poor
—	350	300	200	150	100

Model 37 Bicentennial

Special model produced during 1976 to commemorate 200th year Anniversary of United States. Gun came with full-length trunk-style hard case and pewter belt buckle numbered to gun. Serial number was prefaced with "U.S.A." NOTE: Subtract 35 percent if original case and belt buckle are missing.

NIB	Exc.	V.G.	Good	Fair	Poor
650	500	300	200	125	75

Model 37 Ducks Unlimited Commemorative, Auction Grade

Special edition made during 1977. Serial number sequence 40-DU0001 to 40-DU1125.

NIB	Exc.	V.G.	Good	Fair	Poor
650	400	300	150	100	75

Model 37 Ducks Unlimited Commemorative, Trade Grade

Special edition made during 1977. Lower grade version of Auction Grade. Serial number preceded with the mark DU37040.

NIB	Exc.	V.G.	Good	Fair	Poor
450	400	350	200	N/A	N/A

Model 37 2500 Series Centennial

Commemorative Model 37 12-gauge shotgun, with silver-plated receiver and press checkered stocks. Manufactured in 1984.

NIB	Exc.	V.G.	Good	Fair	Poor
800	500	300	150	100	75

Model 37 Presentation Series Centennial

Commemorative Model 37 12-gauge shotgun. Gold-plated receiver and high grade hand checkered stocks. Manufactured from 1981 to 1986 and later on special order only.

NIB	Exc.	V.G.	Good	Fair	Poor
1500	800	500	150	100	—

Hi-Grade Ithaca Model 37 Guns

Ithaca Gun company offered custom engraving services from its in-house engraver, one of which was retained until about 1972, or through an outside contract engraver, who was usually William Mains. Many customers requested some degree of custom work and guns with various patterns turn up from time to time. Four standard engraving patterns offered to customers: Grade 1; Grade 2; Grade 3 and very elaborate $1,000 Grade pattern. Increasing production costs forced $1,000 Grade to become $2,000 Grade, $2,500 and finally $3,000 Grade over the years. **NOTE:** All factory engraved Model 37 guns are rare and require an expert appraiser to determine an accurate value.

$1,000 Grade

Model 37, with engraved receiver, gold inlays and well-figured walnut stock. Manufactured between 1940 and 1942.

NIB	Exc.	V.G.	Good	Fair	Poor
10000	5000	3000	2000	N/A	N/A

$2,000 Grade

Manufactured from 1946 to 1957.

NIB	Exc.	V.G.	Good	Fair	Poor
10000	5000	3000	2000	N/A	N/A

$3,000 Grade

Manufactured from 1958 to 1967.

NIB	Exc.	V.G.	Good	Fair	Poor
8000	4000	2500	1500	N/A	N/A

Model 37 Law Enforcement Weapons

Ithaca Gun Company entered the law enforcement market in 1962. Introduced Model 37 Military and Police (M&P) and Model 37DS Police special (DSPS). M&P Model styled after riot guns, made for various military contracts. DSPS styled after Ithaca Deerslayer. Both models offered with 8-shot capacity after 1968. Chrome finish was an available option after 1976. Both models usually had ring turned slide handles. Only those models available to general public, i.e. barrel lengths of 18" or longer, are listed. **NOTE:** Add 25 percent if marked with police department; 20 percent for 8-shot model in NIB or EXC. condition; additional 15 percent for chrome plated models in similar condition.

Military and Police (M&P)—1962-1986

NIB	Exc.	V.G.	Good	Fair	Poor
550	450	250	200	125	75

DS Police Special—1962-1986

NIB	Exc.	V.G.	Good	Fair	Poor
575	450	250	200	125	75

ITHACA MODEL 87 REPEATER

During 1987, many assets of bankrupt Ithaca Gun Company were purchased by Ithaca Acquisition Corporation. Manufacture of Model 37 resumed that summer, after the gun was renamed Model 87. Many models offered by the old company were continued. All Model 87 field guns were produced with ventilated ribs. All Deerslayer models continued rifle sights, used on Model 37 guns.

Model 87 Basic—1989-1994

Early models had birchwood stocks, later production had walnut. All had ring turned slide handles.

NIB	Exc.	V.G.	Good	Fair	Poor
350	300	250	175	125	75

Model 87 Magnum

12- or 20-gauge Magnum slide action shotgun, with 25" barrel. Fitted with screw-in choke tubes and ventilated rib, that is similar to Model 37. Blued, with walnut stock.

NIB	Exc.	V.G.	Good	Fair	Poor
400	350	300	225	150	100

Model 87 Field Grade—1987-1990

Stocks were walnut, with pressed checkering.

NIB	Exc.	V.G.	Good	Fair	Poor
325	250	200	175	125	75

Model 87 Camo—1987-1994

NIB	Exc.	V.G.	Good	Fair	Poor
300	250	200	175	125	75

Model 87 Turkey Gun—1987-1996

Courtesy C. Hadley Smith

NIB	Exc.	V.G.	Good	Fair	Poor
325	250	200	175	125	75

Model 87 Deluxe—1987-1996

Buttstocks and slide handle were walnut, with machine cut checkered pattern.

Courtesy C. Hadley Smith

NIB	Exc.	V.G.	Good	Fair	Poor
375	300	250	200	125	75

Model 87 Ultralite—1987-1990

All IAC manufactured Ultralite guns carry old Model 37 serial number.

Courtesy C. Hadley Smith

NIB	Exc.	V.G.	Good	Fair	Poor
500	350	250	175	125	75

Model 87 English—1993-1996

Hand checkered walnut stocks. Slide handle styled after pre-war Model 37 slide handle.

NIB	Exc.	V.G.	Good	Fair	Poor
400	350	250	175	125	75

Model 87 Ultralite Deluxe

NIB	Exc.	V.G.	Good	Fair	Poor
400	350	300	250	125	75

Model 87 Supreme Grade—1987-1996

High grade walnut stocks, with hand checkering. Metal had extra fine polish and finish.

Courtesy C. Hadley Smith

NIB	Exc.	V.G.	Good	Fair	Poor
1000	700	500	300	250	100

Model 87 Deerslayer Basic—1989-1996

Walnut oil-finish butt and slide handle stocks. Slide handle was classic ring turned style.

NIB	Exc.	V.G.	Good	Fair	Poor
300	275	250	200	125	75

Model 87 Deerslayer—1989-1996

Sometimes advertised as Model 87 Deerslayer Field. Buttstock and slide handle were walnut. Usually had pressed checkered pattern. Slide handle was beavertail style.

Courtesy C. Hadley Smith

NIB	Exc.	V.G.	Good	Fair	Poor
350	300	250	200	125	75

Model 87 Deluxe Deerslayer—1989-1996

Buttstock and slide handle were walnut, with machine-cut checkering pattern. Slide handle was beavertail.

NIB	Exc.	V.G.	Good	Fair	Poor
400	350	250	200	125	75

Model 87 Deerslayer II—1988-1996

Fixed rifle barrel and Monte Carlo buttstock. Small number of guns specially made with fast twist barrel to handle Brenneke ammunition. Marked "BRENNEKE" on receiver. **NOTE:** Brenneke-marked guns will command a 30 percent price premium.

Courtesy C. Hadley Smith

NIB	Exc.	V.G.	Good	Fair	Poor
550	450	350	200	125	75

Model 87 Home Protection and Law Enforcement

Ithaca Acquisition Corporation continued production of many law enforcement firearms produced by Ithaca Gun Company. Only those models available to general public are listed.

Military & Police—1987-1996

Generally produced with non-checkered walnut buttstock and ring turned slide handle, both of which were oil-finished. **NOTE:** Add 20 percent for 8-shot model in NIB or excellent condition; additional 15 percent for chrome plated models in similar condition.

NIB	Exc.	V.G.	Good	Fair	Poor
450	395	275	200	125	75

DS Police Special—1987-1996

Produced with either pressed checkered or non-checkered walnut buttstock and ring-turned slide handle, both lacquer finished. Metal usually finished with a commercial polished blue, but chrome-plated finish also available. **NOTE:** Add 20 percent for 8-shot model in NIB or excellent condition; add an additional 15 percent for chrome plated models in similar condition.

NIB	Exc.	V.G.	Good	Fair	Poor
450	395	275	200	125	75

NEW MODEL 37

During 1996, assets of bankrupt Ithaca Acquisition Corporation were purchased by a new company named Ithaca Gun Company, LLC. One of the first public actions of the new firm was to rename Model 87, Model 37. Before resuming production later that year, serial number of new Model 37 is prefaced with letter "M".

Model 37 Deerslayer II

Offered in 12- and 20-gauge. Fitted with 20" or 25" barrel, with rifled bores. Barrel fixed to receiver. Magazine capacity 5 rounds. Walnut stock. Weight about 7 lbs. In 2001 a 16-gauge version, with fixed rifled barrel was offered.

NIB	Exc.	V.G.	Good	Fair	Poor
950	800	650	475	300	200

Smooth Bore Deluxe

Offered in 12-, 16- or 20-gauge. Interchangeable barrels in 20" or 25" and smoothbore for deer. Walnut stock. Magazine capacity 5 rounds. Weight about 6.75 lbs. Discontinued.

NIB	Exc.	V.G.	Good	Fair	Poor
675	400	350	275	200	100

Rifled Deluxe

Same as above in 12- and 20-gauge only, with rifled barrels. Discontinued.

NIB	Exc.	V.G.	Good	Fair	Poor
675	400	350	275	200	100

Deerslayer III

Updated slug-only version of classic Model 37 pump-action shotgun, in 12- or 20-gauge. Fully rifled heavy fluted 26" barrel, with 1:28 twist. Bottom ejection. Fancy black walnut stock and fore-end. Blued barrel and receiver.

NIB	Exc.	V.G.	Good	Fair	Poor
1100	950	800	600	400	200

Model 37 28 Gauge

28-gauge pump action shotgun. Scaled down receiver, with traditional Model 37 bottom ejection and easy takedown. 26" or 28" barrel, black walnut stock and fore-end. Available in Fancy "A", Fancy "AA" and Fancy "AAA" grades, with increasingly elaborate receiver engraving and decoration. Special order only. Values shown are for "Fancy A" grade.

NIB	Exc.	V.G.	Good	Fair	Poor
1000	850	525	400	350	200

Model 37 Deluxe Field

Offered in 12-, 16- and 20-gauge. Interchangeable ventilated rib barrels 26", 28" or 30" (12-gauge only). Walnut stock. Magazine capacity 5 rounds. Weight about 7 lbs. Discontinued.

NIB	Exc.	V.G.	Good	Fair	Poor
625	475	375	250	150	100

Model 37 Deluxe Field English Style

Offered in 20-gauge only, with 24", 26" or 28" ventilated rib barrels. Walnut stock. Weight about 7 lbs. Magazine capacity 5 rounds. Discontinued.

NIB	Exc.	V.G.	Good	Fair	Poor
650	475	375	250	150	100

Model 37 Ultra Featherlight Grouse Special

Based on Classic Model 37, with bottom ejection. Features aluminum receiver and 24" ventilated rib barrel, with choke tubes. Straight-grip stock of American black walnut. Discontinued.

NIB	Exc.	V.G.	Good	Fair	Poor
650	525	395	275	150	100

Model 37 Ultra Featherlight Youth

Similar to above, with 22" barrel and 12.75" length of pull. Buttstock with ventilated recoil pad. Discontinued.

NIB	Exc.	V.G.	Good	Fair	Poor
600	475	375	250	150	100

Model 37 Sporting Clays

Features choice of 24", 26" or 28" wide ventilated rib barrels, with Briley choke tubes. Receiver has antiqued finish, with scroll engraving and high grade American black walnut. Discontinued.

NIB	Exc.	V.G.	Good	Fair	Poor
1350	1000	750	575	300	150

Model 37 Trap

Similar features as Sporting Clays, with 30" wide ventilated rib barrel.

NIB	Exc.	V.G.	Good	Fair	Poor
900	750	650	475	300	200

Model 37 Women's Endowment Shotgun

Offered in 16- or 20-gauge, with straight-grip stock. Length of pull designed for woman's height of 5'5". American walnut stock, with cut checkering. Discontinued.

NIB	Exc.	V.G.	Good	Fair	Poor
635	500	375	250	150	100

Model 37 Waterfowler

Available in 12-gauge only, with 28" steel shot barrel. Camo pattern stock. Weight about 7 lbs. Magazine capacity 5 rounds.

NIB	Exc.	V.G.	Good	Fair	Poor
850	700	600	500	275	200

Model 37 New Classic

Available in 12-, 16- or 20- gauge, with hand checkered walnut stock. Choice of pistol-/straight-grip. High polish bolt and other component parts. Sunburst recoil pad. Interchangeable ventilated rib barrels are 26" or 28". Weight about 7 lbs. Discontinued.

NIB	Exc.	V.G.	Good	Fair	Poor
810	625	475	375	250	150

Model 37 Turkeyslayer

First version of this model made from 1996 to 2004, with 22" barrel and camo stock. Offered in 12- or 20-gauge. Later model introduced in 2010, in 12-gauge only, with 24" fixed barrel, synthetic stock with matte black or camo finish. Available with laminated thumb-hole stock. Other features include Briley extended and ported extra-full turkey choke, lengthened forcing cone, Pachmayr Decelerator recoil pad, Tru-Glo fiber optic front sight. Weight: 7.6 lbs. with standard stock, 8.2 lbs with thumb-hole.

NIB	Exc.	V.G.	Good	Fair	Poor
800	650	550	400	275	200

Model 37 Home Defense

In 12- or 20-gauge, with 18.5" or 20" barrel, rifle sights and matte blue finish. Black synthetic or wood stock, 20" fixed barrel rifle sights. Magazine holds 8 rounds (12-gauge only); 5 rounds (12- or 20-gauge).

NIB	Exc.	V.G.	Good	Fair	Poor
700	600	500	400	275	200

Model 37 Hogslayer

In 12-gauge, with 20" rifled barrel and sights. Tubular magazine holds 8 rounds. Matte blued barrel, action and finish. Synthetic stock. Discontinued.

NIB	Exc.	V.G.	Good	Fair	Poor
450	400	355	300	250	200

MODEL 51

A 12- or 20-gauge semi-automatic shotgun, with 26", 28" or 30" ventilated rib barrels. Blued, with walnut stock. Manufactured from 1970 to 1985 as listed.

Model 51A Standard

Plain barrel. **NOTE:** Add $100 for ventilated rib.

Courtesy C. Hadley Smith

NIB	Exc.	V.G.	Good	Fair	Poor
—	400	325	250	150	75

Model 51A Magnum

3" chamber. **NOTE:** Add $100 for ventilated rib.

NIB	Exc.	V.G.	Good	Fair	Poor
—	425	350	275	175	75

Model 51A Waterfowler

Matte finished.

NIB	Exc.	V.G.	Good	Fair	Poor
—	425	350	275	175	75

Model 51A Deerslayer

Courtesy C. Hadley Smith

NIB	Exc.	V.G.	Good	Fair	Poor
—	325	275	225	150	75

Model 51A Turkey Gun

Courtesy C. Hadley Smith

NIB	Exc.	V.G.	Good	Fair	Poor
—	425	350	275	175	75

Model 51 Supreme Trap

NIB	Exc.	V.G.	Good	Fair	Poor
—	425	375	325	250	75

Model 51 Supreme Skeet

NIB	Exc.	V.G.	Good	Fair	Poor
—	450	400	350	275	200

Model 51 Ducks Unlimited Commemorative

NIB	Exc.	V.G.	Good	Fair	Poor
600	500	375	325	275	200

Model 51 Presentation

Engraved receiver.

NIB	Exc.	V.G.	Good	Fair	Poor
1500	1250	1000	750	500	300

MAG-10

A 10-gauge Magnum semi-automatic shotgun, manufactured in a variety of barrel lengths, styles and finishes. Manufactured from 1975 to 1986 as listed. **NOTE:** Market for Ithaca Mag-10s has declined somewhat, with success of 3.5" 12-gauge load. Apparently because most owners consider their Mag-10s as hunting weapons, not collectors' pieces. Nevertheless, NIB or Excellent+ examples still command fairly high prices, if right buyer can be found.

Standard Grade

NIB	Exc.	V.G.	Good	Fair	Poor
—	750	650	600	300	250

Standard Vent Rib Grade

NIB	Exc.	V.G.	Good	Fair	Poor
—	850	700	675	550	250

Deluxe Vent Rib Grade

NIB	Exc.	V.G.	Good	Fair	Poor
—	1000	775	750	600	250

Supreme Grade

NIB	Exc.	V.G.	Good	Fair	Poor
—	1100	850	800	700	250

Roadblocker—Military and Police Model

NIB	Exc.	V.G.	Good	Fair	Poor
—	750	650	600	300	250

Presentation Grade

Engraved, gold-inlaid, 200 made.

NIB	Exc.	V.G.	Good	Fair	Poor
1875	1500	1100	900	750	300

National Wild Turkey Federation

1985 manufacture.

NIB	Exc.	V.G.	Good	Fair	Poor
850	700	600	550	450	350

RIFLES

Model X5-C

.22-caliber semi-automatic rifle, with 7-shot magazine. 10-shot magazine available as an extra cost option. Blued, with walnut stock. Manufactured between 1958 and 1964.

NIB	Exc.	V.G.	Good	Fair	Poor
400	200	150	100	75	50

Model X5T Lightning

.22-caliber tubular feed auto-loading rifle, produced between 1959 and 1963. Some models stocked with curly maple stocks. **NOTE:** These guns will command a 25 percent price premium.

NIB	Exc.	V.G.	Good	Fair	Poor
450	175	150	100	75	50

Model X-15 Lightning

Similar to above. Manufactured between 1964 and 1966.

NIB	Exc.	V.G.	Good	Fair	Poor
450	175	150	100	75	50

Model 49 Saddlegun—1961-1979

.22-caliber lever action single-shot rifle, with 18.5" barrel, fixed sights, alloy receiver and hardwood stock. Offered chambered for .22 Magnum in 1962. **NOTE:** Deduct 20 percent for .22 LR.

Courtesy C. Hadley Smith

NIB	Exc.	V.G.	Good	Fair	Poor
350	220	175	100	50	25

Deluxe Grade

Fitted with gold plated trigger and hammer. Equipped with sling and sling swivels.

NIB	Exc.	V.G.	Good	Fair	Poor
400	250	200	125	50	25

Presentation Grade

High grade wood and engraved frame.

NIB	Exc.	V.G.	Good	Fair	Poor
425	300	250	200	50	25

Model 49R—1968-1971

Lever action .22-caliber tubular feed repeater. Magazine capacity 15 LR cartridges.

NIB	Exc.	V.G.	Good	Fair	Poor
350	250	200	150	50	25

Model 72 Saddlegun—1973-1979

.22- or .22 Magnum caliber lever action rifle, with 18.5" barrel. Tubular magazine, open sights and walnut stock. Made by Erma in Germany.

NIB	Exc.	V.G.	Good	Fair	Poor
300	250	225	200	100	25

LSA-55 or 65

Bolt-action sporting rifle, manufactured in a variety of calibers and barrel lengths, by Tikka of Finland. Imported between 1969 and 1977 in models listed.

LSA-55 Standard

NIB	Exc.	V.G.	Good	Fair	Poor
—	500	350	300	250	175

LSA-55 Deluxe

NIB	Exc.	V.G.	Good	Fair	Poor
—	600	375	325	275	200

LSA-55 Varmint Heavy Barrel

NIB	Exc.	V.G.	Good	Fair	Poor
—	600	400	350	300	225

LSA-55 Turkey Gun

12-gauge by .222 Remington caliber over/under combination rifle/shotgun, with 24.5" barrels, single trigger, exposed hammer and walnut stock. Manufactured in Finland by Tikka between 1970 and 1981.

NIB	Exc.	V.G.	Good	Fair	Poor
—	900	700	450	350	275

LSA-65 Long Action

NIB	Exc.	V.G.	Good	Fair	Poor
—	500	350	300	250	175

LSA-65 Deluxe

NIB	Exc.	V.G.	Good	Fair	Poor
—	600	375	325	275	200

HANDGUNS

Model 1911

First 1911 made by Ithaca since WWII. Chambered in .45 ACP, with hand-lapped carbon steel frame and slide. Checkered front strap, skeletonized hammer and trigger, checkered cocobolo grips and choice of adjustable Novak Combat or Bomar Target sights. Other features include stainless steel Match grade barrel bushing and full-length two-piece guide rod. Optional lockable canvas case. Introduced in 2011. Also available in Carry size, with 4.25" barrel. **NOTE:** Add $100 for case.

NIB	Exc.	V.G.	Good	Fair	Poor
1600	1300	1000	750	—	—

X-Caliber

.22- to .44 Magnum caliber single-shot pistol, with 10" or 15" barrels. Featuring dual firing pin system so that interchangeable barrels could be used. Model 20 is blued; Model 30 Teflon coated. Introduced in 1988. Made by Sterling Arms. **NOTE:** Add 20 percent premium for .44.

NIB	Exc.	V.G.	Good	Fair	Poor
600	475	300	225	175	125

IVER JOHNSON ARMS, INC.
Rockledge, Florida

This brand was resurrected in 2006, by Iver Johnson Arms, Inc., a new company based in Rockledge, Florida. This company manufactures several 1911-pattern pistols and imports a series of self-defense pump-action shotguns from Turkey. From 2006 to 2009, a four-barreled derringer, Frontier Four and two 1911-type pistols under Raven brand were manufactured.

Frontier Four Derringer

Four-barrel, stainless .22 LR single-action derringer, with unique rotating firing pin. Based on old Sharps derringer. Weight 5.5 oz. Introduced 2006. Discontinued.

NIB	Exc.	V.G.	Good	Fair	Poor
195	150	100	75	50	—

Eagle Target Series 1911 .45

All-steel 7+1 capacity 1911 .45 ACP, with 5" Government or 4.5" Commander barrel. Adjustable white outline rear sight and trigger. Polished blue. Introduced 2006. **NOTE:** Add $150 for LR model with accessory rail.

NIB	Exc.	V.G.	Good	Fair	Poor
650	550	425	315	250	150

Eagle Target Series 1911 .22 LR

Aluminum slide and frame, 15+1 capacity 1911 .22 LR, with 5" Government or 4.5" Commander barrel. Weight 19 oz. Adjustable white outline rear sight and trigger. Blued or stainless. Introduced 2006.

NIB	Exc.	V.G.	Good	Fair	Poor
600	500	400	300	200	100

Raven Series 1911 .45

All-steel 7+1 capacity 1911 .45 ACP, with 5" Government or 4.5" Commander barrel. Fixed sights. Matte blue, Parkerized or two-tone. Introduced 2006. Discontinued.

NIB	Exc.	V.G.	Good	Fair	Poor
550	425	315	250	150	100

Raven Series 1911 .22 LR

Aluminum slide and frame, 15+1 capacity 1911 in .22 LR, with 5" Government or 4.5" Commander barrel. Weight 19 oz. Fixed sights. Matte blued or stainless two-tone finish. Introduced 2006. Discontinued.

NIB	Exc.	V.G.	Good	Fair	Poor
550	425	315	250	150	100

1911A1

Several variations of Series 70 type 1911A1 are offered in .45 ACP and 9mm chamberings, in full-size, Commander-size and Officers models. Available in a wide variety of finishes, including matte blue, polished blue, O.D. Green, Coyote Tan, Pink, Zombie and others. Values are for standard blue finish. **NOTE:** Add 10 to 15 percent for special finishes.

NIB	Exc.	V.G.	Good	Fair	Poor
500	450	400	300	250	200

PAS Shotgun

Series of pump-action shotguns designed primarily for self-defense use. All are 12-gauge, with lightweight alloy black receivers, black polymer stocks with straight-/pistol-grip and choice of sighting systems and accessory rails. **NOTE:** Add 10 to 15 percent for pistol-grip stock and fiber-optic sights.

NIB	Exc.	V.G.	Good	Fair	Poor
260	220	180	150	120	90

IVER JOHNSON ARMS & CYCLE WORKS
Middlesex, New Jersey
See — AMAC

Established in 1883 in Fitchburg, Massachusetts. Company has produced a wide variety of firearms during its existence.

HANDGUNS

Trade Name Revolvers

Series of spur trigger revolvers made by Iver Johnson. Bearing only trade names such as Encore, Eclipse, Favorite, Tycoon and Eagle. In general value for these revolvers are listed.

NIB	Exc.	V.G.	Good	Fair	Poor
—	250	170	120	95	65

Safety Automatic Double-Action

.22, .32 CF or .38 CF caliber double-action revolver. Produced in a variety of barrel lengths with-/without exposed hammers. Manufactured between 1893 and 1950.

NIB	Exc.	V.G.	Good	Fair	Poor
—	250	170	120	95	65

Model 1900

.22- to .38-caliber double-action revolver, with 2.5", 4.5" or 6" barrel. Blued or nickel-plated. Rubber grips and no cartridge ejecting system. Manufactured between 1900 and 1947.

NIB	Exc.	V.G.	Good	Fair	Poor
—	250	170	120	95	65

Safety Cycle Automatic

Similar to Safety Automatic, with 2" barrel.

NIB	Exc.	V.G.	Good	Fair	Poor
—	250	170	120	95	65

Petite

.22 Short caliber double-action folding trigger revolver, with 1" barrel and 7-shot cylinder. Nickel-plated, with rubber grips. Introduced in 1909.

NIB	Exc.	V.G.	Good	Fair	Poor
—	350	250	200	150	100

Supershot Sealed 8

.22-caliber double-action revolver, with 6" barrel. Counterbored 8-shot cylinder. Blued, with rubber grips. Manufactured from 1919 to 1957.

NIB	Exc.	V.G.	Good	Fair	Poor
—	250	170	120	95	65

Protector Sealed 8

As above, with 2.5" barrel.

NIB	Exc.	V.G.	Good	Fair	Poor
—	250	170	120	95	65

Supershot 9

Similar to Supershot Sealed 8, with 9-shot un-counterbored cylinder. Manufactured between 1929 and 1949.

NIB	Exc.	V.G.	Good	Fair	Poor
—	250	170	120	95	65

Trigger Cocker Single-Action

.22-caliber single-action revolver, with 6" barrel and 8-shot counterbored cylinder. Blued, with walnut grips. Manufactured between 1940 and 1947.

NIB	Exc.	V.G.	Good	Fair	Poor
—	200	125	100	50	25

.22 Target Single-Action

As above, with adjustable sights and grips. Manufactured between 1938 and 1948.

NIB	Exc.	V.G.	Good	Fair	Poor
—	250	190	150	125	65

Model 844

.22-caliber double-action revolver, with 4.5" or 6" barrel. Adjustable sights and 8-shot cylinder. Manufactured in 1950s.

NIB	Exc.	V.G.	Good	Fair	Poor
—	225	140	100	80	40

Model 855

As above, with single-action and 6" barrel. Manufactured in 1950s.

NIB	Exc.	V.G.	Good	Fair	Poor
—	225	140	100	80	40

Model 55A Sportsmen Target

.22-caliber single-action revolver, with 4.75" or 6" barrel. Fixed sights and 8-shot cylinder. Blued, with walnut grips.

NIB	Exc.	V.G.	Good	Fair	Poor
—	200	125	100	75	35

Model 55S-A Cadet

.22- to .38-caliber single-action revolver, with 2.5" barrel and fixed sights. Blued, with plastic grips. Introduced in 1955.

NIB	Exc.	V.G.	Good	Fair	Poor
—	250	170	120	95	65

Model 57A Target

As above, with 4.5" or 6" barrel and adjustable sights. Manufactured between 1955 and 1975.

NIB	Exc.	V.G.	Good	Fair	Poor
—	175	110	85	60	35

Model 66 Trailsman

.22-caliber double-action revolver, with 6" barrel. Adjustable sights and 8-shot cylinder. Blued, with walnut grips. Manufactured between 1958 and 1975.

NIB	Exc.	V.G.	Good	Fair	Poor
—	125	75	65	50	25

Model 67 Viking

As above, with safety hammer.

NIB	Exc.	V.G.	Good	Fair	Poor
—	125	75	65	50	25

Model 67S Viking Snub

Same as above. Fitted with 2" barrel.

NIB	Exc.	V.G.	Good	Fair	Poor
—	125	75	65	50	25

Model 50

.22- or .22 Magnum single-action revolver, with 4.75" or 6" barrel and 8-shot cylinder. Fixed or adjustable sights. Also known as Sidewinder. Manufactured between 1961 and 1975.

NIB	Exc.	V.G.	Good	Fair	Poor
—	125	75	65	50	25

American Bulldog

.22- to .38-caliber double-action revolver, with 2.5" or 4" barrel. Adjustable sights. Blued or nickel-plated, with plastic grips. Manufactured between 1974 and 1976.

NIB	Exc.	V.G.	Good	Fair	Poor
—	175	100	75	50	25

Rookie

.38-caliber revolver, with 4" barrel and 5-shot cylinder. Blued or nickel-plated, with plastic grips.

NIB	Exc.	V.G.	Good	Fair	Poor
—	175	100	75	50	25

Cattleman Series

Manufactured by Aldo Uberti. Listed under that name in this book.

Model X300 Pony

.380 semi-automatic pistol, with 3" barrel and 6-shot magazine. Blued, with plastic grips. Introduced in 1975.

NIB	Exc.	V.G.	Good	Fair	Poor
—	275	195	165	135	85

Trailsman

.22-caliber semi-automatic pistol, with 4.5" or 6" barrel and 10-shot magazine. Blued, with plastic or walnut grips.

NIB	Exc.	V.G.	Good	Fair	Poor
—	275	195	165	135	85

TP22/TP25 Pistol

.22 or .25 ACP caliber double-action semi-automatic pistol, with 2.8" barrel and 7-shot magazine. Blued or nickel-plated, with plastic grips.

NIB	Exc.	V.G.	Good	Fair	Poor
—	275	195	165	135	85

RIFLES

Model X

Bolt action .22-caliber single-shot rifle. Fitted with 22" barrel, open sights and pistol-grip. Manufactured between 1927 and 1932.

NIB	Exc.	V.G.	Good	Fair	Poor
—	175	110	90	70	40

Model XA

As above, with Lyman receiver sight swivels, leather strap and ivory bead. Manufactured between 1927 and 1932.

NIB	Exc.	V.G.	Good	Fair	Poor
—	325	225	175	130	80

Model 2X

Fitted with 24" heavy barrel and adjustable sights. Manufactured between 1932 and 1955.

NIB	Exc.	V.G.	Good	Fair	Poor
—	400	300	250	150	100

Li'L Champ

Chambered for .22 LR cartridge. Bolt-action single-shot rifle. Weight about 3 lbs.

NIB	Exc.	V.G.	Good	Fair	Poor
—	125	85	70	50	30

Long Range Rifle

Single-shot bolt-action rifle, chambered for .50-caliber Browning cartridge. Fitted with 29" fluted barrel and adjustable trigger. Bipod. Comes supplied with 20 power Leupold scope. Limited production. Weight about 36 lbs. Manufactured between 1988 and 1993.

NIB	Exc.	V.G.	Good	Fair	Poor
—	4600	4000	3000	2500	1000

JJ 9mm Carbine

Copy of U.S. military M1. Blued finish and hardwood stock. Magazine is 20 rounds. Chambered for 9mm cartridge. Built between 1985 and 1986. **NOTE:** Add 10 percent for folding stock. Deduct 5 percent for plastic stock.

NIB	Exc.	V.G.	Good	Fair	Poor
—	500	400	250	175	100

Delta-786 Carbine

Similar to M1 carbine in 9mm only. Matte finish. Manufactured in 1989.

NIB	Exc.	V.G.	Good	Fair	Poor
—	500	400	250	175	100

Carbine .30 Caliber

Similar to M1 carbine and chambered for .30 carbine cartridge. Offered in various stock configurations. Built from 1985 to 1986; again in 1988 to 1993. **NOTE:** Add $50 for Paratrooper model. Deduct $75 for Johnson 5.7mm caliber. No premium for stainless steel.

NIB	Exc.	V.G.	Good	Fair	Poor
—	600	485	315	250	150

U.S. Carbine .22 Caliber

Same as above. Chambered for .22 LR or .22 Magnum cartridge. Built in 1985 and 1986; again in 1988. Fitted with 15-round magazine.

NIB	Exc.	V.G.	Good	Fair	Poor
—	350	295	225	150	75

Slide Action Targetmaster

Chambered for .22 LR or .22 Magnum cartridge. Has 15-round tubular magazine. Manufactured between 1985 and 1988; again in 1990.

NIB	Exc.	V.G.	Good	Fair	Poor
—	250	170	125	100	50

Wagonmaster Model EW .22 HBL Lever Action

Chambered for .22 LR or .22 Magnum cartridge. Fitted with hardwood stock. Blued finish. Grooved scope mounts. Built in 1985 and 1986; again between 1988 and 1990.

NIB	Exc.	V.G.	Good	Fair	Poor
—	250	175	130	100	50

Model IJ .22 HB Semi-Automatic (Trail Blazer)

Chambered for .22 LR only, with 10-round magazine. Manufactured only in 1985.

NIB	Exc.	V.G.	Good	Fair	Poor
—	225	130	100	60	40

SHOTGUNS

Champion

Single-barrel shotgun manufactured in a variety of gauges, as well as .44- or .45-caliber, with 26" to 32" barrels. External hammers and automatic ejectors. Blued, with walnut stock. Manufactured between 1909 and 1956.

NIB	Exc.	V.G.	Good	Fair	Poor
—	250	200	150	75	25

Matted Rib Grade

As above in 12-, 16- or 20-gauge, with matte rib barrel. Manufactured between 1909 and 1948.

NIB	Exc.	V.G.	Good	Fair	Poor
—	275	225	175	95	50

Trap Grade

As above in 12-gauge, with 32" ventilated rib barrel. Manufactured between 1909 and 1942.

NIB	Exc.	V.G.	Good	Fair	Poor
—	525	350	275	175	100

Hercules Grade

Boxlock double-barrel shotgun manufactured in a variety of gauges, with 26" to 32" barrels. Double triggers and extractors. Blued, with walnut stock.

NOTE: Add premium for these features:

Single trigger—25 percent Ejectors—25 percent

28-gauge—100 percent .410 bore—100 percent

20-gauge—50 percent 16-gauge—20 percent

Engraving—100 percent Vent rib—25 percent

NIB	Exc.	V.G.	Good	Fair	Poor
—	1350	1050	775	550	350

Skeeter Model

As above, but more finely finished. Discontinued in 1946.

NOTE: Add premium for these features:

Single trigger — 25 percent Ejectors — 25 percent

28-gauge — 100 percent .410 bore — 100 percent

20-gauge — 50 percent 16-gauge — 20 percent

Engraving — 100 percent Vent rib — 25 percent

NIB	Exc.	V.G.	Good	Fair	Poor
—	2250	1600	1050	750	300

Super Trap

12-gauge boxlock double-barrel shotgun, with 32" full choked barrels and extractors. Discontinued in 1942. **NOTE:** Add 50 percent for Miller single-selective trigger; 35 percent for non-selective single trigger.

NIB	Exc.	V.G.	Good	Fair	Poor
—	2650	2000	1350	850	350

Silver Shadow

12-gauge boxlock over/under shotgun, with 26" or 28" ventilated rib barrels. Double triggers and extractors. Blued, with walnut stock. Manufactured in Italy and imported by Iver Johnson. **NOTE:** Available with single trigger, which would increase values listed by approximately 25 percent.

NIB	Exc.	V.G.	Good	Fair	Poor
—	550	400	350	300	200

IXL
New York, New York

Pocket Revolver

.31-caliber double-action percussion revolver, with 4" octagonal barrel and 6-shot cylinder. Blued, with walnut grips. Barrel marked "IXL N.York". Approximately 750 made without hammer spurs and 150 with side mounted hammers during 1850s.

NIB	Exc.	V.G.	Good	Fair	Poor
—	—	—	1250	600	300

Navy Revolver

As above in .36-caliber. Approximately 100 made, with both center and side mounted hammers during 1850s.

NIB	Exc.	V.G.	Good	Fair	Poor
—	—	—	3250	1400	500

J

JACQUESMART, JULES
Liege, Belgium

Le Monobloc

6.35mm semi-automatic pistol, with 2" barrel and 6-shot magazine. Slide marked "Le Monobloc/Pistolet Automatique/Brevefte". Blued, with composition grips. Production ceased in 1914.

Courtesy James Rankin

NIB	Exc.	V.G.	Good	Fair	Poor
—	550	450	350	200	100

JACQUITH, ELIJAH
Brattleboro, Vermont

Revolving Under Hammer Rifle

Extremely rare .40-caliber percussion revolving rifle, with 34" round-octagonal barrel and 8-shot cylinder. Believed that approximately 25 of these rifles were made in 1838 and 1839. Barrel marked "E. Jaquith Brattleboro. Vt." Prospective purchasers should secure a qualified appraisal prior to acquisition.

NIB	Exc.	V.G.	Good	Fair	Poor
—	—	18000	7250	2200	2200

JAGER WAFFENFABIK
Suhl, Germany

Jager Semi-Automatic Pistol

7.65mm caliber semi-automatic pistol, with 3" barrel and 7-shot magazine. Largely made from steel stampings. Weight about 23 oz. Blued, with plastic grips. Slide marked "Jager-Pistole DRP Angem". Approximately 5,500 made prior to 1914. **NOTE:** Add 50 percent for Imperial proofed examples.

Courtesy Richard M. Kumor, Sr.

NIB	Exc.	V.G.	Good	Fair	Poor
—	500	375	325	175	100

JEFFERY, W. J. & CO. LTD.
London, England

Company produced high quality shotguns and rifles. Their products have been used by wealthy sportsmen for many years. They produced guns under their own banner and also as contractors for other distributors. They made guns sold by Army & Navy Department Store in London. Guns of this type were basically custom-ordered and as such are extremely hard to evaluate on a general basis. We supply estimated values for standard rifle models.

Single-Shot

Built on Farquharson Falling Block action. Chambered for many calibers up to .600 Nitro Express. Also a custom-order gun and barrel length was optional. Usually finish is blued with folding express sights. Select hand-checkered walnut stock. These were high quality firearms and values would be determined, for the most part, by options and embellishments on particular specimens. Individual appraisal is definitely advised. Caliber in which rifle is chambered will also have an effect on value. Obsolete calibers bring less and larger express calibers bring more.

NIB	Exc.	V.G.	Good	Fair	Poor
—	9000	6750	3750	21700	900

Boxlock Double Rifle

Boxlock chambered for many different calibers. Found with either top or underlever action and has folding express sights. Stock and forearm are select hand-checkered walnut and finish is usually blue. This was a custom-order proposition and values can be affected by many variables such as caliber options and embellishment. Damascus barreled hammer guns are worth approximately 50 percent less.

NIB	Exc.	V.G.	Good	Fair	Poor
—	22000	15250	10950	3850	2500

Sidelock Double Rifle

Has detachable sidelocks. Otherwise comparable to boxlock version.

NIB	Exc.	V.G.	Good	Fair	Poor
—	35000	22500	12250	7000	4000

JENISON, J. & CO.
Southbridge, Connecticut

Under Hammer Pistol

.28-caliber single-shot under hammer percussion pistol, with 4" half-octagonal barrel marked "J.Jenison & Co./Southbridge, Mass.". Blued, with maple or oak grip. Manufactured during 1850s.

NIB	Exc.	V.G.	Good	Fair	Poor
—	—	1550	850	400	200

JENKS-HERKIMER
New York
Manufacturer—E. Remington & Son

Jenks Carbine

Identical to "Mule Ear Carbine" listed in (JENKS CARBINE), except barrel length is 24.25" and lock fitted with Maynard tape primer. Lock marked "Remington's/Herkimer/N.Y." Barrel marked "W. Jenks/USN/RC/P/Cast Steel". Approximately 1,000 manufactured circa 1846.

NIB	Exc.	V.G.	Good	Fair	Poor
—	—	5000	4250	1750	750

JENKS-MERRILL
Baltimore, Maryland

An alteration of Jenks Carbine to a breech loading system developed by J.H. Merrill. Conventional sidelock marked "J. H. Merrill Balto./Pat. July 1858". Breech retains mark "Wm.Jenks/ USN". Approximately 300 altered between 1858 and 1860.

NIB	Exc.	V.G.	Good	Fair	Poor
—	—	9750	8500	3500	950

JENKS CARBINE
Springfield, Massachusetts
Manufacturer—N. P. Ames

Jenks "Mule Ear" Carbine

.54-caliber percussion side hammer carbine, with 24.5" round barrel and full length stock secured by two barrel bands. Lock case hardened, barrel browned and furniture of brass. Lock marked "N.P.Ames/Springfield/ Mass.". Barrel stamped "Wm.Jenks/USN" followed by inspector's initials. Buttstock carries an inspector's cartouche. Approximately 4,250 made between 1841 and 1846. Some marked "USR" for "U.S. Revenue Cutter Service". These would bring approximately 80 percent premium over values listed. However, prospective purchasers should secure a qualified appraisal prior to acquisition.

Courtesy Milwaukee Public Museum, Milwaukee, Wisconsin

NIB	Exc.	V.G.	Good	Fair	Poor
—	—	4500	3750	1500	600

Jenks Navy Rifle

As above, with 30" round barrel and full-length stock secured by three barrel bands. Approximately 1,000 made for U.S. Navy in 1841.

Courtesy Milwaukee Public Museum, Milwaukee, Wisconsin

NIB	Exc.	V.G.	Good	Fair	Poor
—	—	5000	4250	1750	750

JENNINGS
Windsor, Vermont
Manufacturer—Robbins & Lawrence
See—Winchester Repeating Arms

JENNINGS F. A., INC.
Carson City, Nevada

Distributor of arms manufactured by Calwestco in Chino, California and Bryco Firearms in Carson City, Nevada.

J-22

.22-caliber semi-automatic pistol, with 2.5" barrel and 6-shot magazine. Aluminum, finished in bright chrome, Teflon or satin nickel. Plastic or wood grips.

NIB	Exc.	V.G.	Good	Fair	Poor
150	90	75	65	50	35

Bryco Model 25

.25-caliber semi-automatic pistol, with 2.5" barrel and 6-shot magazine. Constructed and finished as above.

NIB	Exc.	V.G.	Good	Fair	Poor
150	90	75	65	50	35

Bryco Model 38

.22, .32 or .380 semi-automatic pistol, with 2.8" barrel and 6-shot magazine. Constructed and finished as above.

NIB	Exc.	V.G.	Good	Fair	Poor
150	90	75	65	50	35

Bryco Model 48

Similar to above, with redesigned trigger guard. Squared forward section. Introduced in 1988.

NIB	Exc.	V.G.	Good	Fair	Poor
150	90	75	65	50	35

JERICHO
Israeli Military Industries, Israel

Jericho

9mm or .41 Action Express double-action semi-automatic pistol, with 4.72" barrel, polygonal rifling, ambidextrous safety and fixed sights. Blued, with plastic grips.

NIB	Exc.	V.G.	Good	Fair	Poor
575	500	400	350	300	200

JIEFFCO
Liege, Belgium
See—Robar et Cie

JOHNSON, STAN, BYE & CO.
Worcester, Massachusetts

Established in 1871 by Martin Bye and Iver Johnson. Company primarily manufactured inexpensive pistols. In 1883 Johnson assumed full control of the company and renamed it Iver Johnson Arms Company.

Defender, Eagle, Encore, Eureka, Favorite, Lion, Smoker, and Tycoon

.22-, .32-, .38- or .44-caliber spur trigger revolver. Manufactured with various barrel lengths. Normally nickel-plated. Barrel marked with one of the above trade names.

NIB	Exc.	V.G.	Good	Fair	Poor
—	—	500	200	75	25

Eclipse

.22-caliber spur trigger single-shot pistol, with 1.5" barrel. Blued, with walnut grips.

NIB	Exc.	V.G.	Good	Fair	Poor
—	—	250	100	50	25

American Bulldog

.22-, .32-, or .38-caliber double-action revolver, with 3" barrel. Blued or nickel-plated. Walnut or composition grips.

NIB	Exc.	V.G.	Good	Fair	Poor
—	—	250	100	50	25

JOSLYN
Springfield, Massachusetts
Manufacturer—Springfield Armory

Joslyn Breechloading Rifle

First mass-produced true breechloading cartridge firearm. Manufactured in a national armory. Actions were supplied by Joslyn Firearms Company. Chambered for .56-50 rimfire cartridge. Has 35.5" round barrel and full-length stock that is held on by three barrel bands. Lock marked "U.S./Springfield" with "1864" at back. Barrel marked "B. F. Joslyn's Patent/Oct. 8th, 1861 / June 24th, 1862". Approximately 3,000 manufactured circa 1865. Probably issued to Union forces, but unknown if they saw action before end of Civil War.

NIB	Exc.	V.G.	Good	Fair	Poor
—	—	5500	3495	1950	500

Model 1855 Carbine

.54-caliber breech loading single-shot percussion carbine, with 22.5" barrel secured to fore-end by one barrel band. Blued case hardened, with brass mounts. Lock marked "A.H.Waters & Co./Milbury, Mass." and patent dates stamped on breech lever. Approximately 1,000 manufactured in 1855 and 1856.

NIB	Exc.	V.G.	Good	Fair	Poor
—	—	2750	2000	950	300

.50-70 Alteration

Approximately 1,600 Joslyn rifles re-chambered to fire .50-70 centerfire cartridge. Conversion consisted of rechambering and drilling a new firing pin hole after rimfire pin was sealed. No specific serial number range in which these conversions were done. Most of these weapons were eventually converted to smoothbores and sold in Africa. Original military specimens are extremely scarce.

NIB	Exc.	V.G.	Good	Fair	Poor
—	—	6000	4200	2500	750

Model 1855 Rifle

Similar to above in .58-caliber, with 38" barrel secured by three barrel bands. Several hundred made in 1856.

NIB	Exc.	V.G.	Good	Fair	Poor
—	—	4500	3250	1100	400

JOSLYN
Milbury, Massachusetts
Manufacturer—A. H. Waters

JOSLYN FIREARMS COMPANY
Stonington, Connecticut

Model 1862 Carbine

.52 rimfire breech-loading single-shot carbine, with 22" round barrel secured by one barrel band. Blued case hardened, with brass mounts. Lock marked "Joslyn Firearms Co./Stonington/Conn.", and patent date marked on barrel. Trigger plate 8" long and upper tang measures 4.5". Approximately 4,000 manufactured in 1862.

Courtesy Milwaukee Public Museum, Milwaukee, Wisconsin

NIB	Exc.	V.G.	Good	Fair	Poor
—	—	4500	3700	1500	400

Model 1864 Carbine

As above, with case hardened iron mounts, 7" trigger plate and 2" upper tang. Approximately 12,000 made in 1864 and 1865.

Courtesy Milwaukee Public Museum, Milwaukee, Wisconsin

NIB	Exc.	V.G.	Good	Fair	Poor
—	—	4200	3300	1100	400

Army Model Revolver

.44-caliber side hammer percussion revolver, with 8" octagonal barrel and 5-shot cylinder. Blued case hardened, with walnut grips. Barrel marked "B. F. Joslyn/Patd. May 4, 1858". Martially marked examples are worth a premium of approximately 25 percent over values listed.

First Model

With brass trigger guard and iron butt cap. Approximately 500 made in 1861.

NIB	Exc.	V.G.	Good	Fair	Poor
—	—	6000	4750	2000	650

Second Model

Fitted with iron trigger guard, without butt cap. Approximately 2,500 made in 1861 and 1862.

NIB	Exc.	V.G.	Good	Fair	Poor
—	—	5500	4250	1600	500

JURRAS, LEE
Prescott, Arizona
See—Auto Mag

While Jurras is best known for manufacturing last model of Auto Mag, he also produced the pistol listed sold by J. & G. Sales in Prescott, Arizona.

Howdah Pistol

.375-, .416-, .460-, .475-, .500-, .577-caliber single-shot pistol, with 12" barrel, adjustable sights and Nitex finish. Built on Thompson/Center Contender frame. Supposedly, approximately 100 produced.

NIB	Exc.	V.G.	Good	Fair	Poor
—	1750	1100	800	650	500

JUSTICE, P. S.
Philadelphia, Pennsylvania

Percussion Rifle

.58-caliber percussion rifle, with 35" round barrel secured by two barrel bands, browned barrel, polished lock and brass furniture. Lock marked "P.S. Justice/Philada.". Approximately 2,500 manufactured in 1861.

Courtesy Milwaukee Public Museum, Milwaukee, Wisconsin

NIB	Exc.	V.G.	Good	Fair	Poor
—	—	2300	1900	875	450

K.F.C. (KAWAGUCHIYA FIREARMS CO.)
Japan

E-1 Trap or Skeet Over/Under

12-gauge boxlock double-barrel shotgun, with 26" or 30" barrels, competition rib, single-selective trigger and automatic ejectors. Engraved, blued with walnut stock. Manufactured until 1986.

NIB	Exc.	V.G.	Good	Fair	Poor
—	950	800	700	500	300

E-2 Trap or Skeet Over/Under

As above, but more finely finished.

NIB	Exc.	V.G.	Good	Fair	Poor
—	1400	1250	1000	750	350

Field Grade Over/Under

As above, with narrow rib and 26" or 28" barrels. Discontinued in 1986.

NIB	Exc.	V.G.	Good	Fair	Poor
—	650	575	500	400	275

Model 250

12-gauge semi-automatic shotgun, with 26", 28" or 30" barrels fitted for choke tubes. Matte blued, with walnut stock. Manufactured from 1980 to 1986.

NIB	Exc.	V.G.	Good	Fair	Poor
—	350	300	275	200	100

KAHR ARMS
Worcester, Massachusetts

K9

Semi-automatic pistol chambered for 9mm cartridge. Ultra-compact size. Barrel length 3.5"; overall length 6"; width at slide .9". Magazine capacity 7 rounds. Available in blue or electroless nickel finish. Weight 25 oz. **NOTE:** Add $30 for blackened stainless steel slide; $130 for night sights; $250 for KP9 Gen2, with accessory rail, fiber optic sights, three magazines.

NIB	Exc.	V.G.	Good	Fair	Poor
550	425	325	250	150	75

Lady K9

Same as above, with lightened recoil spring.

NIB	Exc.	V.G.	Good	Fair	Poor
500	375	300	225	125	50

K9 Elite

Introduced in 2003. This 9mm features 3.5" barrel and polished stainless steel slide. Magazine capacity 7 rounds. Weight about 25 oz. **NOTE:** Add $110 for night sights.

NIB	Exc.	V.G.	Good	Fair	Poor
575	425	350	275	150	100

MK9 Elite

Introduced in 2003. This 9mm features 3" barrel and polished stainless steel slide. Magazine capacity 7 rounds. Weight about 24 oz. **NOTE:** Add 15 percent for laser grips or night sights.

NIB	Exc.	V.G.	Good	Fair	Poor
725	595	450	300	175	100

P9 Compact Polymer

Introduced in 1999. This 9mm features 3.5" barrel, with double-action-only trigger. Black polymer frame, with stainless steel slide. Overall length 6"; height 4.5"; weight about 18 oz. Magazine capacity 7 rounds.

NIB	Exc.	V.G.	Good	Fair	Poor
625	550	475	325	250	100

K9 Compact Polymer Covert

Same as above, with .5" shorter grip frame. Weight about 17 oz. Magazine capacity 6 rounds. Introduced in 1999.

NIB	Exc.	V.G.	Good	Fair	Poor
625	550	475	325	250	100

TP9

Introduced in 2004. This 9mm features black polymer frame, with matte stainless steel slide. Fitted with 4" barrel. Weight about 20 oz. **NOTE:** Add 15 percent for Novak night sights; $250 for TP9 Gen2, with accessory rail, fiber optic sights, three magazines; $350 for 6" barrel model, with Leupold Delta Point Reflex sight.

602 • KAHR ARMS

NIB	Exc.	V.G.	Good	Fair	Poor
625	550	475	325	250	100

TP40

Double-action-only semi-automatic pistol chambered in .40 S&W. Black polymer frame, matte stainless slide, 4" barrel, textured polymer grips, 6- or 7-round capacity depending on magazine. Drift-adjustable white bar-dot sights or Novak two-dot tritium sights. Introduced 2006.

NIB	Exc.	V.G.	Good	Fair	Poor
625	550	475	325	250	100

TP45

Similar design to TP9 and TP40 models, except chambered in .45 ACP. **NOTE:** Add $250 for TP45 Gen2, with accessory rail, fiber optic sights, three magazines; $350 for 6" barrel model, with Leupold Delta Point Reflex sight.

NIB	Exc.	V.G.	Good	Fair	Poor
625	550	475	325	250	100

PM9

9mm fitted with 3" barrel, blackened stainless steel slide and black polymer frame. Magazine capacity 6 rounds. Weight about 16 oz. Introduced in 2004. **NOTE:** Add 15 percent for night sights.

NIB	Exc.	V.G.	Good	Fair	Poor
700	600	475	325	250	100

PM9 Micro

Fitted with 3" barrel. Chambered for 9mm cartridge. Weight about 16 oz. Polymer frame and stainless steel slide. Introduced in 2002.

NIB	Exc.	V.G.	Good	Fair	Poor
700	600	400	300	200	100

CM Series

Chambered for 9mm, .40 S&W or .45 ACP. Similar to PM Series, with standard rifled barrel instead of polygonal. Fewer machined parts. Shipped with one magazine.

NIB	Exc.	V.G.	Good	Fair	Poor
465	425	375	325	300	250

CW380

Striker-fired .380 ACP micro-compact, with DA-only trigger, black polymer frame, matte stainless slide and fixed bar-dot sights. Introduced in 2013.

NIB	Exc.	V.G.	Good	Fair	Poor
385	345	300	275	—	—

K40

Similar to K9, but chambered for .40 S&W cartridge. Magazine capacity 6 rounds. Weight 26 oz. **NOTE:** Add 15 percent for night sights.

NIB	Exc.	V.G.	Good	Fair	Poor
750	650	450	350	250	150

K40 Elite

Introduced in 2003. This .40 S&W features 3.5" barrel and polished stainless steel slide. Magazine capacity 6 rounds, with beveled magazine well. Weight about 26 oz. **NOTE:** Add 15 percent for night sights; 10 percent nickel finish; 15 percent black titanium finish; 5 percent K40 stainless steel version.

NIB	Exc.	V.G.	Good	Fair	Poor
800	700	575	400	300	175

K40 Covert

Similar to K40, with .5" shorter grip frame and flush fitting 5-round magazine. Barrel length 3.5". Weight about 25 oz. Finish matte stainless steel.

NIB	Exc.	V.G.	Good	Fair	Poor
575	425	350	275	150	100

MK40

.40 S&W model fitted with 3" barrel. Overall length 5.4"; height 4". Finish matte stainless steel. Magazine capacity 5 rounds. Uses same magazines as K40 Covert. Introduced in 1999.

NIB	Exc.	V.G.	Good	Fair	Poor
700	600	400	300	200	100

MK40 Elite

Introduced in 2003. This .40 S&W features 3" barrel and polished stainless steel slide. Magazine capacity 5 rounds, with beveled magazine well. Weight about 25 oz. **NOTE:** Add 10 percent for night sights.

NIB	Exc.	V.G.	Good	Fair	Poor
750	625	525	425	225	150

P40

Similar to P9, but chambered for .40 S&W cartridge. Fitted with 3.5" match grade barrel. Matte stainless steel slide and black polymer frame. Supplied with two 6-round stainless steel magazines. Weight about 19 oz. Introduced in 2001. **NOTE:** Add $30 for blackened stainless steel slide; $130 for night sights.

NIB	Exc.	V.G.	Good	Fair	Poor
550	425	325	250	150	75

P45

Introduced in 2005. Chambered for .45 ACP cartridge, with polymer frame and stainless steel slide. Barrel length 3.5". Fixed sights. Magazine capacity 6 rounds. Height 4.8"; overall length 6.3"; slide width 1"; weight about 18.5 oz. **NOTE:** Add 15 percent for night sights.

NIB	Exc.	V.G.	Good	Fair	Poor
675	550	375	275	170	125

MK9

9mm model with double-action-only trigger. Barrel length 3"; overall length 5.5"; height 4"; weight about 22 oz. One 6-round and 7-round magazine, with grip extension standard. Fitted with specially designed trigger for shorter trigger stroke. **NOTE:** Add 15 percent for night sights or laser grips.

NIB	Exc.	V.G.	Good	Fair	Poor
700	600	400	300	200	100

CW9

9mm introduced in 2005. Features 3.5" barrel, polymer frame and stainless steel slide. Magazine capacity 7 rounds. Height 4.5"; overall length 6"; slide width .9".

NIB	Exc.	V.G.	Good	Fair	Poor
475	375	250	200	150	100

CW40

Semi-automatic with textured polymer grip. Chambered for .40 S&W and 6+1 capacity. Double-action, with 3.6" barrel. Adjustable rear sights. Weight 16.8 oz. Introduced 2006.

NIB	Exc.	V.G.	Good	Fair	Poor
500	375	300	225	125	50

Wilson Combat Kahr Pistols

Offered in both K9 and K40 models. Customized pistol by Wilson's Gun Shop. Features hard chrome frame, black slide, 30 lpi checkering on front strap, beveled magazine well and several other special features. Initial production for K40 is 50 pistols; K9 25 pistols.

NIB	Exc.	V.G.	Good	Fair	Poor
1300	1050	800	550	325	200

Model 1911PKZ

Model uses Auto-Ordnance 1911 pistols, re-engineered by Kahr Arms. Includes Parkerized finish, lanyard loop and U.S. Army roll mark on slide. Seven-round magazine standard. Introduced in 2001.

NIB	Exc.	V.G.	Good	Fair	Poor
475	375	250	—	—	—

Model 1911 Standard

Features blued finish plastic grips, with Thompson medallion and bullet logo on slide. Seven-round magazine. Introduced in 2001.

NIB	Exc.	V.G.	Good	Fair	Poor
450	325	250	200	150	100

Model 1911C

Similar to Standard Model, with 4.25" barrel.

NIB	Exc.	V.G.	Good	Fair	Poor
500	400	250	200	150	100

Model 1911WGS Deluxe

Model has blued finish, rubber wrap-around grips, with Thompson medallion high profile white dot sights and Thompson bullet logo on slide. Seven-round magazine. Introduced in 2001.

NIB	Exc.	V.G.	Good	Fair	Poor
575	475	425	300	225	125

P380 .380 ACP Pistol

DAO semi-automatic pocket pistol chambered in .380 ACP. Features include 2.5" Lothar Walther barrel, black polymer frame and grips, stainless steel slide 6+1 capacity. Overall length 4.9"; weight 11.3 oz. **NOTE:** Add 15 percent for night sights.

NIB	Exc.	V.G.	Good	Fair	Poor
625	500	400	295	175	75

CT45

Chambered for .45 ACP. Listed by manufacturer as part of its Value Series. Features include black polymer frame, matte stainless slide, 4" barrel and textured polymer grips. A double-action-only trigger-cocking system, with locked breech. Browning-type recoil lug, with no magazine disconnect. Overall length 6.6"; weight 24 oz. Similar models with virtually identical features include CT40 in .40 S&W (22 oz.) and CT9 in 9mm (18.5 oz.). Introduced in 2014.

NIB	Exc.	V.G.	Good	Fair	Poor
400	365	325	285	250	200

KASSNAR IMPORTS, INC.
Harrisburg, Pennsylvania

Standard Over/Under

12-, 20- or 28-gauge and .410 bore boxlock double-barrel shotgun, with 26" or 28" barrels. Ventilated ribs, single trigger and extractors. Blued, with walnut stock.

NIB	Exc.	V.G.	Good	Fair	Poor
350	275	225	200	150	100

Deluxe Over/Under

As above, with more finely figured stock.

NIB	Exc.	V.G.	Good	Fair	Poor
400	325	250	225	175	100

Standard Side-by-Side

20- or 28-gauge and .410 bore boxlock folding double-barrel shotgun, with 26" barrels. Double triggers and extractors. Blued, with walnut stock.

NIB	Exc.	V.G.	Good	Fair	Poor
250	200	175	150	100	75

Deluxe Side-by-Side

As above in .410 bore only, with more finely figured wood.

NIB	Exc.	V.G.	Good	Fair	Poor
300	250	200	175	125	75

KBI, INC.
Harrisburg, Pennsylvania

Company previously imported firearms from several manufacturers. These brands included Charles Daly handguns, shotguns and rifles, which are listed in the "D" section under Daly, Charles.

Kassnar PSP-25

.25-caliber semi-automatic pistol, with 2" barrel. Manufactured in Charlottesville, Virginia under license from Fabrique Nationale. Introduced in 1989.

NIB	Exc.	V.G.	Good	Fair	Poor
275	200	175	150	100	—

KEBERST INTERNATIONAL
Kendall International
Paris, Kentucky

Model 1A

.338 Lapua Magnum, .338-416 Rigby or .338-06 caliber bolt-action rifle, with 24" barrel having integral muzzle-brake. Fitted with 3-9 power Leupold telescope. Matte blued, with camouflaged composition stock. Manufactured in 1987 and 1988.

NIB	Exc.	V.G.	Good	Fair	Poor
—	3750	3000	2500	1800	900

KEL-TEC CNC INDUSTRIES
Cocoa, Florida

Kel-Tec PMR-30

Caliber .22 WMR, steel barrel and slide, glass reinforced Zytel grip frame. Slide cover, 30-round magazine, single-action trigger, ambidextrous manual safety, fiber optic sights and accessory rail. Fluted 4.3" barrel, with matte black finish. Weight 13.6 oz. New 2011.

NIB	Exc.	V.G.	Good	Fair	Poor
400	325	250	200	150	75

P-11

Semi-automatic pistol chambered for 9mm cartridge. Double-action-only. Barrel length 3.1"; overall length 5.6"; weight 14 oz. Magazine capacity 10 rounds. Standard model has blued slide, with black grip. Stainless steel and Parkerized finish are offered as well. **NOTE:** Add $100 for stainless steel; $40 for Parkerized finish; $60 for hard chrome.

NIB	Exc.	V.G.	Good	Fair	Poor
320	225	175	125	100	100

P-32

.32-caliber semi-automatic pistol fitted with 2.68" barrel. Double-action-only. Blued slide and frame. Magazine capacity 7 rounds. Overall length 5"; height 3.5"; weight about 6.6 oz. **NOTE:** Add $40 for Parkerized finish; $60 for hard chrome.

NIB	Exc.	V.G.	Good	Fair	Poor
305	225	175	125	100	100

P-3AT

Chambered for .380 cartridge. Fitted with 2.75" barrel. Blued finish. Magazine capacity 6 rounds. Weight about 7.3 oz. **NOTE:** Add $40 for Parkerized finish; $60 for hard chrome.

NIB	Exc.	V.G.	Good	Fair	Poor
310	225	175	125	100	50

P-40

Similar to P-11, but chambered for .40 S&W cartridge. Barrel length 3.3". Magazine capacity 9 rounds. Blued finish. Weight about 16 oz. **NOTE:** Add $40 for Parkerized finish; $60 for hard chrome.

NIB	Exc.	V.G.	Good	Fair	Poor
320	225	175	125	100	100

SUB-2000 Rifle

Introduced in 1996. Semi-automatic rifle chambered for 9mm or .40 S&W cartridge. Barrel length 16.1". Rifle can be folded closed, with overall length of 16". Different grip assembly can be fitted to this rifle allowing for use of different magazines. Weight about 4.6 lbs.

NIB	Exc.	V.G.	Good	Fair	Poor
375	295	175	125	75	50

SU-16

Semi-automatic gas operated rifle chambered for .223 cartridge. Fitted with 18" barrel. Rifle has several unique features: fore-end folds down to form a bipod; stock can store spare magazines; rifle folds into two parts for carry. Weight about 5 lbs. SU-16A, 18.5" barrel; SU-16B, 16" lightweight barrel; SU-16C, 16" barrel folding stock; SU-16CA, 16" standard barrel and stock.

NIB	Exc.	V.G.	Good	Fair	Poor
625	525	400	295	200	125

PLR-16

5.56mm NATO gas-operated semi-automatic AR-15-style long-range pistol. Windage-adjustable rear sight. Picatinny rail. Muzzle threaded for muzzle-brake. 9.2" barrel; weighs 51 oz.; 10-round or M-16 magazine. Blued finish polymer construction. Introduced 2006.

NIB	Exc.	V.G.	Good	Fair	Poor
650	550	425	325	200	100

RFB Rifle

Bullpup semi-automatic rifle, with 18", 24" or 32" barrel. Black laminated stock, third swivel for bipod. Forward ejection takes FAL-type magazines. Chambered in .308 Winchester. Introduced in 2007. **NOTE:** Price shown for sporter.

NIB	Exc.	V.G.	Good	Fair	Poor
1850	1600	—	—	—	—

KEMPER, SHRIVER & COMPANY
Nashville, Tennessee

Delivered rifles made from sporting arm parts to Ordnance Department at Nashville, from December 1861 to March 1862. In all, 150 arms were assembled. Overall length 48.5"; octagonal barrels shortened 33" and bored to .48-caliber; some fitted with saber bayonet lugs; stocks of military with brass furniture.

NIB	Exc.	V.G.	Good	Fair	Poor
—	—	4750	2000	1500	700

KENDALL, INTERNATIONAL
Paris, Kentucky

See—Keberst International

KENDALL, NICANOR
Windsor, Vermont

Under Hammer Pistol

.31- to .41-caliber under hammer percussion pistol, with 4" to 10" octagonal/round barrels marked "N.Kendall/Windsor,Vt." Browned or blued, with brass mounts and maple grips. Manufactured in 1850s.

NIB	Exc.	V.G.	Good	Fair	Poor
—	—	1950	600	200	125

KENO
Unknown

Derringer

.22-caliber single-shot spur trigger pistol, with 2.5" barrel, brass frame and walnut grips. Barrel blued or nickel-plated and marked "Keno".

NIB	Exc.	V.G.	Good	Fair	Poor
—	—	750	500	175	100

KERR
London, England

Kerr Revolver

.44-caliber double-action percussion revolver, with 5.5" barrel and 6-shot cylinder. Blued, with walnut grips. Frame marked "Kerr's Patent 648" and "London Armoury Bermondsey".

Courtesy Bonhams & Butterfields, San Francisco, California

NIB	Exc.	V.G.	Good	Fair	Poor
—	—	4250	2000	800	300

KESSLER ARMS CORPORATION
Silver Creek, New York

Bolt-Action Shotgun

12-, 16- or 20-gauge shotgun, with 26" or 28" barrels. Blued, with walnut stock. Manufactured between 1951 and 1953.

NIB	Exc.	V.G.	Good	Fair	Poor
—	125	75	50	30	20

Levermatic Shotgun

12-, 16- or 20-gauge lever-action shotgun, with 26" or 28" barrel. Blued, with walnut stock. Manufactured between 1951 and 1953. A nice low-end collectible.

NIB	Exc.	V.G.	Good	Fair	Poor
—	300	275	200	150	75

KETTNER, EDWARD
Suhl, Germany

Drilling

High-quality three-barreled firearm chambered for 12x12- or 16x16-gauge, over various metric rifle cartridges. Barrels 25" in length. Features are ejectors, selective triggers and pop-up rifle sights that appear when rifle barrel is selected. Gun is deep-relief engraved in German style and has a high-grade checkered walnut stock. Manufactured between 1922 and 1939.

NIB	Exc.	V.G.	Good	Fair	Poor
—	—	3200	1700	900	500

KIMBALL ARMS COMPANY
Detroit, Michigan

Semi-Automatic Pistol

.30-caliber carbine semi-automatic pistol, with 3.5" or 5" barrel. Blued, with plastic grips. Also believed to have been made in .22 Hornet and .357 Magnum, though few legitimate examples have been seen. Manufactured from 1955 to 1958. Approximately 238 made.

Courtesy James Rankin

NIB	Exc.	V.G.	Good	Fair	Poor
—	3000	2000	1500	1000	450

KIMBER MFG., INC.
Yonkers, New York

Kimber of Oregon was established in April, 1979 by Greg and Jack Warne. Company produced high quality rimfire and centerfire rifles until going out of business in early 1991. Kimber produced approximately 60,000 rifles during its operation. In April 1993, Greg Warne opened Kimber of America in Clackamas, Oregon. This new company presently manufactures the same high-quality rifles built on an improved Model 82 Sporter action and stock, but in rimfire only. In 1995, company expanded its product line to include centerfire rifles as well as a 1911 .45 ACP semi-automatic pistol line. In 1997, manufacturing operations were consolidated in the New York pistol factory and two factories in Oregon were closed. Guns may be found stamped "Kimber of America", "Kimber, Yonkers, NY" or "Kimber, Clackamas, Oregon".

DISCONTINUED MODELS

Model 82 Classic

.22 LR, .22 Magnum or .22 Hornet bolt-action rifle, with 22" barrel furnished without sights and 4- or 5-shot magazine. Blued, with walnut stock. Discontinued in 1988. **NOTE:** Add 10 percent for Model 82 Series rifles in .22 Magnum caliber; 15 percent for rifles chambered in .22 Hornet.

NIB	Exc.	V.G.	Good	Fair	Poor
950	800	600	550	450	350

Cascade

As above, with Monte Carlo-style stock.

NIB	Exc.	V.G.	Good	Fair	Poor
950	800	650	600	500	400

Custom Classic

As above in .218 Bee or .25-20.

NIB	Exc.	V.G.	Good	Fair	Poor
1500	1250	725	650	400	300

Mini Classic

Model 82 with 18" barrel. Manufactured in 1988.

NIB	Exc.	V.G.	Good	Fair	Poor
900	750	550	475	400	300

Deluxe Grade

Similar to Custom Classic. Introduced in 1989.

NIB	Exc.	V.G.	Good	Fair	Poor
1500	1250	650	550	450	350

Model 82A Government

.22-caliber bolt-action rifle, with 25" heavy barrel fitted with telescope mounts. Matte blued, with walnut stock. Introduced in 1987.

NIB	Exc.	V.G.	Good	Fair	Poor
675	550	450	375	300	200

Continental

Similar to Custom Classic, with 20" barrel, open sights and full length Mannlicher-style stock. Introduced in 1987.

NIB	Exc.	V.G.	Good	Fair	Poor
2000	1600	1250	950	400	300

Super Continental

As above, but more finely finished. Discontinued in 1988.

NIB	Exc.	V.G.	Good	Fair	Poor
2200	1750	1300	1000	600	300

Super America

Model 82 more finely finished. Discontinued in 1988.

NIB	Exc.	V.G.	Good	Fair	Poor
2000	1600	950	850	650	500

Super Grade

As above. Introduced in 1989.

NIB	Exc.	V.G.	Good	Fair	Poor
2200	1750	1300	1000	600	475

Centennial

Commemorative rifle moderately engraved. Including special match barrel, skeleton buttplate, hand-selected walnut stock and light engraving. Issued to commemorate 100th Anniversary of .22 LR cartridge. One hundred manufactured in 1987.

NIB	Exc.	V.G.	Good	Fair	Poor
4000	2800	2000	1750	1500	1150

Brownell

In 1986, 500 commemorative rifles were produced in honor of Leonard Brownell. Featuring a high-grade Mannlicher-style full-length walnut stock.

NIB	Exc.	V.G.	Good	Fair	Poor
2800	2250	1500	1200	600	500

MODEL 84 SERIES—DISCONTINUED MODELS

Bolt-action rifle manufactured in a variety of smallbore centerfire calibers, with 22" or 24" barrel and 5-shot magazine. Blued, with walnut stock. Variations are listed.

Classic

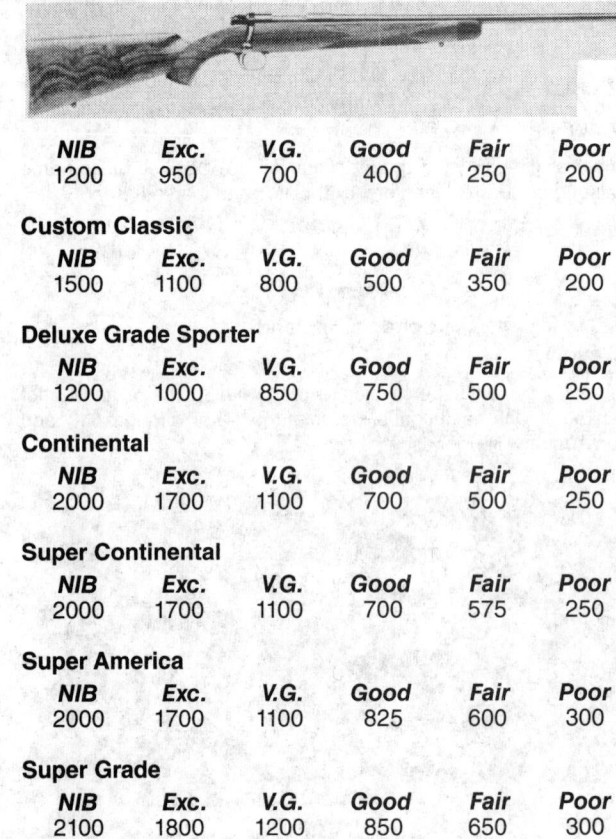

NIB	Exc.	V.G.	Good	Fair	Poor
1200	950	700	400	250	200

Custom Classic

NIB	Exc.	V.G.	Good	Fair	Poor
1500	1100	800	500	350	200

Deluxe Grade Sporter

NIB	Exc.	V.G.	Good	Fair	Poor
1200	1000	850	750	500	250

Continental

NIB	Exc.	V.G.	Good	Fair	Poor
2000	1700	1100	700	500	250

Super Continental

NIB	Exc.	V.G.	Good	Fair	Poor
2000	1700	1100	700	575	250

Super America

NIB	Exc.	V.G.	Good	Fair	Poor
2000	1700	1100	825	600	300

Super Grade

NIB	Exc.	V.G.	Good	Fair	Poor
2100	1800	1200	850	650	300

Ultra Varmint

As above, with 24" stainless steel barrel and laminated birchwood stock. Introduced in 1989.

NIB	Exc.	V.G.	Good	Fair	Poor
1500	1100	900	750	550	250

Super Varmint

As above, with walnut stock. Introduced in 1989.

NIB	Exc.	V.G.	Good	Fair	Poor
2000	1600	1200	850	650	300

Predator

.221 Fireball, .223 Rem., 6mm TCU, 7mm TCU or 6x45mm caliber single-shot bolt-action pistol. Based upon Model 84 action, with 14.75" barrel adopted for telescope. Blued, with walnut stock. Available in two grades as listed. Manufactured in 1987 and 1988 only.

Hunter Grade

NIB	Exc.	V.G.	Good	Fair	Poor
1800	1350	950	600	400	300

Super Grade

NIB	Exc.	V.G.	Good	Fair	Poor
2500	2000	1500	1000	500	400

MODEL 89 SERIES/BGR (BIG GAME RIFLES)

Bolt-action sporting rifle, produced in .257 Roberts to .505 Gibbs caliber, with 22" or 24" barrel. Blued, with walnut stock. Variations of this model are listed. **NOTE:** Rare calibers (.257 Roberts, 7x57, .375 H&H) will bring a premium of 25 percent or more.

Classic

NIB	Exc.	V.G.	Good	Fair	Poor
800	650	550	400	300	200

Custom Classic

NIB	Exc.	V.G.	Good	Fair	Poor
1000	850	650	450	350	250

Deluxe Grade

NIB	Exc.	V.G.	Good	Fair	Poor
1400	1150	900	650	450	250

Super America

NIB	Exc.	V.G.	Good	Fair	Poor
1800	1250	900	700	500	250

Super Grade

NIB	Exc.	V.G.	Good	Fair	Poor
1800	1250	900	700	500	250

African Grade

NOTE: Add 10 percent for .375 H&H or .505 Gibbs.

NIB	Exc.	V.G.	Good	Fair	Poor
5500	4250	3200	2400	1200	500

MODEL 82C SERIES—DISCONTINUED MODELS

In 1998 Model 82C series rifles went out of production.

Classic

Bolt-action rifle chambered for .22 LR cartridge. Receiver drilled and tapped for sights. Fitted with 22" barrel. Detachable magazine holds 4 rounds. Stock is plain, with standard grade Claro Walnut. Checkering is 18 lpi, with 4 point side panel pattern. Red rubber butt pad and polished steel pistol-grip cap are standard. Weight about 6.5 lbs. Reintroduced in 1989.

NIB	Exc.	V.G.	Good	Fair	Poor
900	650	500	400	—	—

Super America

Same as above. Fitted with AAA fancy grade Claro Walnut, with ebony tip and beaded cheekpiece. Hand checkering 22 lpi in a full-coverage pattern. Steel buttplate and pistol-grip cap are standard.

NIB	Exc.	V.G.	Good	Fair	Poor
2200	1500	1100	750	300	300

Custom Match

Bolt-action .22-caliber has 22" barrel. Stock AA French walnut, with full coverage checkering. Finish rust blued. Weight about 6.75 lbs.

NIB	Exc.	V.G.	Good	Fair	Poor
2000	1600	950	700	400	200

Custom Shop Super America (Basic)

Same as above. Furnished with a number of special order options that greatly affect value. Seek an independent appraisal before sale.

Stainless Classic Limited Edition

Introduced in 1996. Limited edition Model 82C chambered for .22 LR cartridge. Stainless steel barrel 22" long. A 4-shot magazine included. Production limited to about 600 rifles.

NIB	Exc.	V.G.	Good	Fair	Poor
1900	1750	1100	800	500	300

SVT (Short Varmint/Target)

First introduced in 1996, this .22-caliber rifle is a single-shot. Fitted with 18" stainless steel fluted barrel. Walnut stock is target style, with no checkering. Weight about 7.5 lbs.

NIB	Exc.	V.G.	Good	Fair	Poor
1350	1050	700	500	400	175

HS (Hunter Silhouette)

Introduced in 1997. Features 24" half-fluted barrel. Chambered for .22 LR cartridge. Stock American walnut, with high comb. Trigger fully adjustable. Four-round magazine standard. Weight about 7 lbs.

NIB	Exc.	V.G.	Good	Fair	Poor
1350	1050	700	500	400	175

Single-Shot Varmint

Chambered for .17 Rem. or .223 Rem. cartridge. Fitted with 25" stainless steel fluted barrel. Claro walnut stock, with varmint-style forearm. Weight about 7.5 lbs. In 1998, Model 84C series rifle went out of production.

NIB	Exc.	V.G.	Good	Fair	Poor
1500	1175	900	600	400	200

Sporterized Model 98 Swedish Mausers

These are reconditioned and reworked Mausers. Fitted with new match grade stainless steel fluted barrels in 24" or 26" depending on caliber. Stock is new synthetic checkered. Chambered in .257 Roberts, .270 Win., .280 Rem., .30-06, 7mm Rem. Magnum, .300 Win. Magnum, .338 Win. Magnum and .220 Swift with 25" barrel. **NOTE:** Suggested retail price: $535 for standard calibers; $560 for Magnum.

Sporterized Model 96 Swedish Mausers

Similar to above in terms of reworking and reconditioning. Chambered for these calibers:

.22-250 w/stainless steel heavy barrel fluted—Retail $500.

.243 Win.—$400 to $465 depending on finish.

6.5x55mm—$340 to $370 depending on finish.

7mm-08 Rem.—$415 to $465 depending on finish.

.308 Win.—$415 to $520 depending on finish and barrel configuration.

RECENT PRODUCTION MODELS

17 SERIES

Series of .17 Mach 2 rifles. Introduced in 2005. Features are similar to 22 Series.

Hunter

Fitted with 22" light sporter barrel. No sights. Checkered walnut stock, with black pad and clear stock finish. Magazine capacity 5 rounds. Weight about 6.5 lbs.

NIB	Exc.	V.G.	Good	Fair	Poor
900	700	500	375	250	125

SVT (Short Varmint/Target) (Centerfire)

Fitted with 18.25" stainless steel bull fluted barrel, with no sights. Checkered walnut stock, with black pad and oil finish. Magazine capacity 5 rounds. Weight about 7.9 lbs.

NIB	Exc.	V.G.	Good	Fair	Poor
1200	950	775	575	350	150

Pro Varmint

Features 20" stainless steel heavy sporter fluted barrel, with no sights. Stock gray laminate, with oil-finish and no checkering. Magazine capacity 5 rounds. Weight about 6.75 lbs.

NIB	Exc.	V.G.	Good	Fair	Poor
1150	875	675	500	325	150

Classic Varmint

Fitted with 20" heavy sporter fluted barrel, with no sights. Checkered walnut stock, with oil-finish. Magazine capacity 5 rounds. Weight about 6.5 lbs.

NIB	Exc.	V.G.	Good	Fair	Poor
1200	950	775	575	350	150

22 SERIES

In 1999, Kimber introduced a new line of bolt-action .22-caliber rimfire rifles. First deliveries were made early in 2000. Series built on a totally new design from bolt, to magazine, to barrel. All rifles in this series have 5-round magazine capacity. Line replaces Model 82-C series of rifles.

Classic

.22-caliber rifle fitted with 22" barrel. Fully adjustable trigger. Stock A grade Claro walnut, with 18 lpi checkering. Fitted with Model 70 style safety. Blued finish. Weight about 6.5 lbs.

NIB	Exc.	V.G.	Good	Fair	Poor
1200	950	775	575	350	150

Custom Classic

Fitted with 22" barrel, ebony fore-end tip, hand-rubbed oil-finish and 24 lpi checkering. Introduced in 2003. Weight about 6.5 lbs.

NIB	Exc.	V.G.	Good	Fair	Poor
1425	1100	850	675	450	150

Super America

Features 22" barrel, with fully adjustable trigger. Stock AAA grade Claro walnut, with 22 lpi wrap-around checkering and ebony fore-end tip. Black recoil pad. Weight about 6.5 lbs.

NIB	Exc.	V.G.	Good	Fair	Poor
1900	1400	1075	775	500	200

SVT (Short Varmint/Target)

Fitted with 18" fluted stainless steel barrel and gray laminated wood stock. High target comb. Weight about 7.5 lbs. In 2004, offered in Mach 2 .17-caliber.

NIB	Exc.	V.G.	Good	Fair	Poor
1150	875	675	500	325	150

Classic Varmint

Introduced in 2003. Features 20" barrel, with hand-rubbed oil-finish and 20 lpi checkering. Weight about 6.5 lbs. In 2004, available in Mach 2 .17-caliber.

NIB	Exc.	V.G.	Good	Fair	Poor
1150	875	675	500	325	150

Pro Varmint

Features heavy fluted 20" stainless steel barrel and gray laminated stock. No sights. Magazine capacity 5 rounds. Weight about 6.75 lbs. Introduced in 2004. Available in Mach 2 .17-caliber.

NIB	Exc.	V.G.	Good	Fair	Poor
1200	950	775	575	350	150

HS (Hunter Silhouette)

Fitted with 24" medium sporter match grade barrel, with match chambered and half fluting. Walnut stock, with 18 lpi checkering and Monte Carlo comb. Weight about 7 lbs.

NIB	Exc.	V.G.	Good	Fair	Poor
900	700	500	375	250	125

Youth

Introduced in 2002. This .22-caliber rifle fitted with 18.5" barrel. Checkered Claro walnut stock, with 12.25" lop. Weight about 5.25 lbs.

NIB	Exc.	V.G.	Good	Fair	Poor
850	675	495	300	200	100

Hunter

Lower-priced version of Classic.

NIB	Exc.	V.G.	Good	Fair	Poor
800	650	550	400	300	200

Custom Match Limited Edition

Introduced in 2004. Limited edition of 300 rifles. Features checkered French walnut stock of AAA wood and several custom features. Serial numbered from KAN25001-KAN25300.

NIB	Exc.	V.G.	Good	Fair	Poor
2850	2300	—	—	—	—

MODEL 84M SERIES

Classic

Introduced in 2001. Centerfire bolt-action rifle chambered for .243 Win., .260 Rem., 7mm-08 Rem. and .308 Win. In 2005, offered chambered for .22-250 cartridge. Fitted with 22" light sporter match grade barrel, Claro walnut stock with 20 lpi checkering and satin wood finish. Matted blue finish. Fitted with 1" Pachmayr Decelerator recoil pad. Weight about 5.75 lbs.

NIB	Exc.	V.G.	Good	Fair	Poor
1100	895	700	475	300	150

Montana

Essentially, a stainless steel version of Model 84M Classic with black synthetic stock. Weight about 5.25 lbs. Introduced in 2003.

NIB	Exc.	V.G.	Good	Fair	Poor
1200	950	775	575	350	150

Super America

First offered in 2003. Available in .243, .260 Rem., 7mm-08 Rem. and .308 Win. Fitted with 22" barrel. In 2005, offered chambered for .223 cartridge. Stock select walnut, with 24 lpi checkering. Fitted with ebony fore-end tip, cheekpiece and hand-rubbed oil-finish. Weight about 5.75 lbs., depending on caliber. Magazine capacity 5 rounds.

NIB	Exc.	V.G.	Good	Fair	Poor
1800	1350	1000	650	325	175

Pro Varmint

Introduced in 2004. Chambered for .22-250 Win. cartridge. Fitted with 24" stainless steel fluted barrel, with no sights. In 2005, offered in .204 Ruger and .223 calibers. Gray laminated stock. Magazine capacity 5 rounds. Weight 7.25 lbs.

NIB	Exc.	V.G.	Good	Fair	Poor
1075	800	575	400	300	150

Varmint

Similar to Classic, fitted with stainless steel 26" match grade barrel. Chambered for .22-250 Rem. cartridge. In 2005, offered in .204 Ruger caliber. Fitted with .5" solid recoil pad. Weight about 7.4 lbs.

NIB	Exc.	V.G.	Good	Fair	Poor
1000	750	500	375	300	150

SVT

Stock gray laminate, with Monte Carlo comb. Barrel length 18.25" in stainless steel and fluted. Chambered for .223 cartridge. Magazine capacity 5 rounds. Weight about 8.3 lbs.

NIB	Exc.	V.G.	Good	Fair	Poor
1200	950	775	575	350	150

LongMaster VT

Bolt-action rifle chambered for .22-250 cartridge. Fitted with 26" fluted stainless steel match grade barrel. Special laminated target stock. Weight about 10 lbs. No sights. Introduced in 2002.

NIB	Exc.	V.G.	Good	Fair	Poor
1200	950	775	575	350	150

LongMaster Classic

Same features as Model 84M Classic, with 24" fluted stainless steel barrel. Chambered for .308 Win. cartridge. In 2005, offered in .223-caliber. Checkered walnut stock. Weight about 7.25 lbs. Introduced in 2002.

NIB	Exc.	V.G.	Good	Fair	Poor
1200	950	775	575	350	150

LongMaster Pro

Introduced in 2003. Single-shot bolt-action rifle fitted with 24" fluted heavy barrel. Chambered for .308 Win. or .22-250 cartridge. Fitted with synthetic benchrest stock. Weight about 7.25 lbs.

NIB	Exc.	V.G.	Good	Fair	Poor
1350	1050	700	500	400	175

Light Police Tactical

Based on Model 84 action, with 24" medium weight fluted match barrel. Black laminated stock and third swivel for bipod. Chambered in .308 Win. or .223 Rem. Introduced in 2007.

NIB	Exc.	V.G.	Good	Fair	Poor
1200	1000	800	600	300	150

Model 84L Classic Rifle

Bolt-action rifle chambered in .270 Win. and .30-06. Features include 24" sightless matte blue sporter barrel; hand-rubbed A-grade walnut stock, with 20 lpi panel checkering; pillar and glass bedding; Mauser claw extractor; 3-position M70-style safety; 5-round magazine; adjustable trigger.

NIB	Exc.	V.G.	Good	Fair	Poor
1000	850	720	400	300	200

Model 84L Montana

Long-action variation of Model 84 action. Chambered in .25-06 Remington, .270 Winchester, .280 Ackley Improved and .30-06 Springfield. Capacity 4-rounds in blind magazine. Kevlar-reinforced carbon fiber stock. Match-grade barrel, chamber and trigger. Free-floating 24" barrel is both pillar and glass bedded. Model 70-type 3-position safety. Weight under 6 lbs. Introduced in 2011.

NIB	Exc.	V.G.	Good	Fair	Poor
1150	1000	850	600	300	200

MODEL 8400 SERIES

Series introduced in 2003. Features smallest action size compatible with WSM family of cartridges.

Classic

Fitted with select walnut stock with 20 lpi checkering. Chambered for WSM calibers: .270, 7mm, .300 and .325. Barrel length 24" with no sights. Magazine capacity 3 rounds. Weight about 6.6 lbs. **NOTE:** Add $140 for French walnut.

NIB	Exc.	V.G.	Good	Fair	Poor
1000	795	600	475	300	150

Montana

Features 24" stainless steel barrel, with no sights. Stock black synthetic, with no checkering. Same calibers as Classic. Weight about 6.25 lbs.

NIB	Exc.	V.G.	Good	Fair	Poor
1350	1050	700	500	400	175

Sonora

Features brown laminate stock and 24" barrel. Chambered in .25-06, 7mm Rem., .308 Win., .30-06 or .300 Win. Magnum. Discontinued 2011.

NIB	Exc.	V.G.	Good	Fair	Poor
1100	900	750	600	400	200

Caprivi

Medium-bore variation of Model 8400 with 3-leaf express sight, double cross-bolts, AA-Grade French walnut stock. Chambered in .375 H&H, .416 Rem. or .458 Lott.

NIB	Exc.	V.G.	Good	Fair	Poor
3000	2500	2000	1500	750	400

Talkeetna

Dangerous-game rifle in .375 H&H only. Kevlar stock, single-leaf express sight, 24" barrel.

NIB	Exc.	V.G.	Good	Fair	Poor
1850	1450	1100	900	500	300

Super America

Fitted with AAA walnut stock, with 24 lpi checkering. Cheekpiece and ebony fore-end tip are standard. Barrel length 24", with no sights. Chambered for same calibers as Classic. Weight about 6.6 lbs.

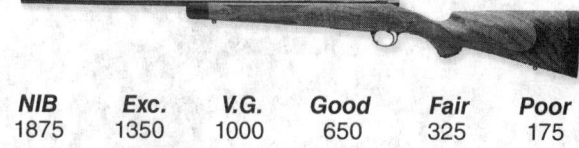

NIB	Exc.	V.G.	Good	Fair	Poor
1875	1350	1000	650	325	175

Classic Select Grade

Similar to 8400 Classic, with hand-rubbed oil-finished select stock of Claro or French walnut. Introduced 2006.

NIB	Exc.	V.G.	Good	Fair	Poor
1100	895	700	475	300	150

Tactical

24" heavyweight match barrel, stippled black McMillan stock, third swivel for bipod. Chambered in .308 Winchester. Introduced in 2007.

NIB	Exc.	V.G.	Good	Fair	Poor
1650	1200	800	550	300	150

Advanced Tactical

Similar to Model 8400 Tactical, with KimPro II Dark Earth finish, fully-adjustable stock and hard case. Introduced in 2007.

NIB	Exc.	V.G.	Good	Fair	Poor
1800	1350	1000	650	325	175

Advanced Tactical II

Similar to above, with improved and enhanced features. Chambered in 6.5 Creedmoor, .308 Win. or .300 Win. Magnum, with Manners folding stock and adjustable comb, match grade barrel with muzzle-brake, oversized bolt knob, upper and lower Picatinny rails and KimPro II Desert Tan finish.

NIB	Exc.	V.G.	Good	Fair	Poor
3600	3000	2400	1750	800	500

Patrol Rifle

Bolt-action tactical rifle chambered in .308 Win. Features include 20" 1:12 fluted sightless matte blue heavy barrel; black epoxy-coated laminated wood stock, with 20 lpi panel checkering; pillar and glass bedding; Mauser claw extractor; 3-position M70-style safety; 5-round magazine; adjustable trigger.

NIB	Exc.	V.G.	Good	Fair	Poor
1300	1100	850	500	350	200

AUGUSTA SHOTGUNS

Shotguns made in Italy for Kimber. Based on Boss-type action, each model fitted with H-Viz sights and Pachmayr Decelerator recoil pads. Back bored. Single-selective trigger and automatic ejectors. Introduced in 2002.

Sporting

Chambered for 12-gauge shell. Fitted with choice of barrel lengths from 28.5" to 32". Checkered walnut stock, with pistol-grip and schnabel forearm. Blued finish, with silver frame. Weight about 7.75 lbs.

NIB	Exc.	V.G.	Good	Fair	Poor
5000	4500	3000	1750	600	300

Field

Chambered for 12-gauge shell. Choice of barrel lengths from 26" to 27.5". Checkered with pistol-grip and beavertail forearm. Weight about 7 lbs.

NIB	Exc.	V.G.	Good	Fair	Poor
4750	3900	2650	1500	475	225

Trap

12-gauge offered in barrel lengths from 30" to 34". Beavertail forearm. Wide ramped ventilated rib. Weight about 7.75 lbs.

NIB	Exc.	V.G.	Good	Fair	Poor
5200	4700	3000	1750	600	300

Skeet

12-gauge gun. Choice of 26" or 27.5" barrels fitted with 11mm flat rib. Checkered walnut stock, with beavertail forearm. Weight about 7.5 lbs.

NIB	Exc.	V.G.	Good	Fair	Poor
5200	4700	3000	1750	600	300

VALIER SHOTGUNS

Side-by-side guns introduced into Kimber line in 2005.

Grade I

Lightweight properly-scaled side-by-side in 16- and 20-gauge. Double triggers and extractors. Choked IC and Mod. Color case-hardened receiver, straight stock and splinter fore-end. Hand checkered wood at 24 lpi. Chambered for: 2.75" shells 16-gauge; 3" shells 20-gauge.

NIB	Exc.	V.G.	Good	Fair	Poor
3300	2900	2300	1250	600	300

Grade II

Similar to Valier Grade I, with higher grade wood. Choice of color case blued or bone charcoal receiver in 20-gauge; bone charcoal only in 16-gauge. Automatic ejectors.

NIB	Exc.	V.G.	Good	Fair	Poor
4900	3500	2700	1500	700	300

MARIAS SHOTGUNS

Grade I

Single-trigger sidelock over/under, features scroll hand engraving and bone charcoal case colors, with 24 lpi checkered wood. Grade I available with 28" barrels and Prince of Wales stock in 12- and 20-gauge. Chambered for 3" shells. Automatic ejectors. Comes with 5 choke tubes.

NIB	Exc.	V.G.	Good	Fair	Poor
4600	3300	2300	1200	600	300

Grade II

Similar to Marias Grade I, with higher grade wood. Available in 12-gauge with PW stock or 20-gauge with PW or straight stock in 26", 28" or 30" barrels.

NIB	Exc.	V.G.	Good	Fair	Poor
4900	3500	2700	1500	700	300

CLASSIC .45 PISTOLS

CUSTOM SERIES

First introduced in 1996. A quality built American-made 1911 designed by Chip McCormick for Kimber. **NOTE:** In 2001, Kimber phased in a new safety system on its pistols: Kimber firing pin safety. Models with this new firing pin safety will bear designation "II" as part of their model name.

Custom

Barrel length 5", with black oxide finish fixed sights. Black synthetic grips. Magazine capacity 8 rounds. Weight about 38 oz. **NOTE:** Add $100 for night sights.

NIB	Exc.	V.G.	Good	Fair	Poor
850	750	650	475	300	150

Custom II

NOTE: Add $10 for walnut grips; $100 for night sights.

NIB	Exc.	V.G.	Good	Fair	Poor
825	675	500	375	250	125

Custom Heritage Edition

Chambered for .45 ACP cartridge. Fitted with 5" barrel. Magazine capacity 7 rounds. Checkered front strap, ambidextrous thumb safety, aluminum trigger, hand checkered rosewood grips, special edition markings on slide. Sights are low-profile fixed. Weight about 38 oz. Introduced in 2000.

NIB	Exc.	V.G.	Good	Fair	Poor
1150	950	700	495	300	150

Custom Stainless II

Similar to Custom in stainless steel. Made in .45 ACP, .38 Super, 9mm and .40 S&W. **NOTE:** Add $100 for night sights.

NIB	Exc.	V.G.	Good	Fair	Poor
1000	800	650	475	300	150

Stainless Limited Edition

Similar to Custom Stainless, except for black thumb release, black grip safety, black magazine release button and black barrel bushing. Limited to approximately 1,200 pistols.

NIB	Exc.	V.G.	Good	Fair	Poor
1200	950	775	575	350	150

Custom Target

Custom Target has same features as Custom, with addition of adjustable rear sight.

NIB	Exc.	V.G.	Good	Fair	Poor
825	675	500	375	250	125

Custom TLE II (Tactical Law Enforcement)

Introduced in 2003. Features Meprolight three-dot night sights and 30 lpi checkering on front strap. Magazine capacity 7 rounds. Weight about 38 oz. **NOTE:** Add $135 for stainless steel version offered in 2004.

NIB	Exc.	V.G.	Good	Fair	Poor
900	700	500	375	250	125

Custom TLE/RL II

Similar to TLE, with addition of an integral tactical rail. Weight about 39 oz. Introduced in 2004.

NIB	Exc.	V.G.	Good	Fair	Poor
1050	825	675	450	295	150

Stainless II

Chambered for .45 ACP or .40 S&W cartridge. Fitted with 5" barrel and fixed low profile sights. Both frame and slide are satin stainless steel. Magazine capacity: .45 ACP 7 rounds; .40 S&W 8 rounds. Weight about 38 oz.

NIB	Exc.	V.G.	Good	Fair	Poor
865	650	450	275	150	100

Stainless II (polished)

As above, chambered for .38 Super cartridge. Frame and slide are polished stainless steel. Magazine capacity 9 rounds. Weight about 38 oz. Introduced in 2005.

NIB	Exc.	V.G.	Good	Fair	Poor
1150	950	700	495	300	150

Stainless Ultra TLE II

1911-style semi-automatic pistol chambered in .45 ACP. Features include 7-round magazine; full length guide rod; aluminum frame with stainless slide; satin silver finish; checkered frontstrap; 3" barrel; tactical gray double diamond grips; tritium 3-dot night sights.

NIB	Exc.	V.G.	Good	Fair	Poor
1000	900	750	650	500	400

Stainless Target II

Chambered for .45 ACP or .38 Super cartridge, with slide and frame machined from stainless steel. Weight 38 oz.

NIB	Exc.	V.G.	Good	Fair	Poor
980	750	600	400	250	125

Stainless Target II 9mm/10mm

As above, chambered for 9mm or 10mm cartridge. Magazine capacity: 9mm 9-rounds; 10mm 8-rounds. Both pistols produced on a one-run basis only, with production in low hundreds. Introduced in 2003.

NIB	Exc.	V.G.	Good	Fair	Poor
1150	950	700	495	300	150

Stainless Target II (polished)

As above, chambered for .38 Super cartridge. Frame and slide are polished stainless steel. Magazine capacity 9 rounds. Weight about 38 oz. Introduced in 2005.

NIB	Exc.	V.G.	Good	Fair	Poor
1200	950	775	575	350	150

Stainless Target Limited Edition

Similar to Stainless Target, with black thumb safety, black grip safety, black slide release and black barrel bushing. Limited to approximately 700 pistols. Introduced in 1998.

NIB	Exc.	V.G.	Good	Fair	Poor
900	700	500	375	250	125

Custom Royal

Has all the features of Custom, plus high polish blue finish, hand checkered walnut grips and long guide rod.

NIB	Exc.	V.G.	Good	Fair	Poor
900	700	500	375	250	125

Custom Royal II

NIB	Exc.	V.G.	Good	Fair	Poor
1500	1100	750	400	250	125

Custom TLE/RL II Special Edition

.45 ACP pistol fitted with 5" barrel and fixed night sights. Steel frame and slide, with tactical accessory rail on frame. Black rubber grips. Black matte finish. Magazine capacity 7 rounds. Weight about 38 oz. Introduced in 2003.

NIB	Exc.	V.G.	Good	Fair	Poor
1150	950	700	495	300	150

Warrior

Introduced in 2005. Chambered for .45 ACP cartridge. Fitted with 5" barrel with night sights. Grips are Kimber G-10 Tactical, with lanyard loop. Accessory rail on frame. KimPro finish. Magazine capacity 7 rounds. Weight about 39 oz.

NIB	Exc.	V.G.	Good	Fair	Poor
1200	950	775	575	350	150

Desert Warrior

Similar to Warrior, with desert tan finish and lighter tan G10 tactical grips.

NIB	Exc.	V.G.	Good	Fair	Poor
1200	950	775	575	350	150

25th ANNIVERSARY LIMITED EDITIONS

Anniversary Custom

Introduced in 2004. Limited edition of 1,911 pistols. Chambered for .45 ACP cartridge. Select walnut grips. Serial numbered: KAPC0001-KAPC1911.

NIB	Exc.	V.G.	Good	Fair	Poor
850	650	450	275	150	100

Anniversary Gold Match

Limited to 500 pistols in .45 ACP. Serial numbered KAPG0001-KAPG0500.

NIB	Exc.	V.G.	Good	Fair	Poor
1200	950	775	575	350	150

Anniversary Match Pair Custom

Matched pair of Custom pistols in .45 ACP. Matching serial numbers and presentation case. Limited to 250 pairs.

NIB	Exc.	V.G.	Good	Fair	Poor
2500	2100	—	—	—	—

GOLD MATCH SERIES

Gold Match

All features of Custom Royal, plus BoMar adjustable sights and fancy checkered diamond grips.

NIB	Exc.	V.G.	Good	Fair	Poor
1200	950	775	575	350	150

Gold Match II

NIB	Exc.	V.G.	Good	Fair	Poor
1200	950	775	575	400	150

Stainless Gold Match

Similar to Gold Match, except slide and frame are stainless steel. Introduced in 1998.

NIB	Exc.	V.G.	Good	Fair	Poor
1200	950	775	575	350	150

Gold Team Match II

Introduced in 2003. This .45 ACP 5" barrel model features stainless steel slide and frame along with Kimber Tactical Extractor with loaded chamber indicator. Front strap checkered 30 lpi and grips are red, white and blue. USA Shooting Team logo. Weight about 38 oz.

NIB	Exc.	V.G.	Good	Fair	Poor
1350	1225	950	575	400	150

Team Match II .38 Super

As above, without external extractor. Limited production run. Introduced in 2003.

NIB	Exc.	V.G.	Good	Fair	Poor
1600	1300	1000	575	400	150

TEN II SERIES

In 2002, Polymer series pistols were upgraded to Ten II series. Added features: firing pin block safety; Kimber-made frame of improved dimensions; external extractor. Original Polymer pistol magazines of 10 and 14 rounds will interchange with newer Ten II Series pistols.

Polymer

Features polymer frame, with matte black oxide slide. Sights are McCormick low profile. Barrel length 5"; overall length 8.75"; weight about 34 oz. One 14-round magazine supplied with gun when new.

NIB	Exc.	V.G.	Good	Fair	Poor
700	600	550	395	200	100

Polymer Stainless

Similar to Polymer model, with stainless steel slide. Weight about 34 oz.

NIB	Exc.	V.G.	Good	Fair	Poor
750	650	550	425	225	125

Polymer Target

Introduced in 1998. Has matte black oxide slide, with adjustable sights and 14-round magazine. Weight about 34 oz.

NIB	Exc.	V.G.	Good	Fair	Poor
950	775	625	450	245	150

Polymer Stainless Target

Same as above, with stainless steel slide. Introduced in 1998.

NIB	Exc.	V.G.	Good	Fair	Poor
950	775	625	450	245	150

Polymer Pro Carry Stainless

Chambered for .45 ACP cartridge, with 4" barrel. McCormick Low Profile sights. Stainless steel slide, with black polymer frame. Weight about 32 oz. Magazine capacity 14 rounds. Introduced in 1999.

NIB	Exc.	V.G.	Good	Fair	Poor
750	675	550	395	200	100

Polymer Stainless Gold Match

Similar to Polymer Gold Match, with addition of stainless steel slide. Chambered for several calibers: .45 ACP; 9mm; .38 Super; .40 S&W. Weight about 34 oz.

NIB	Exc.	V.G.	Good	Fair	Poor
1000	850	775	575	350	150

Pro Carry Ten II

.45 ACP model features 4" bull barrel, with no barrel bushing. Stainless steel slide. Weight about 28 oz.

NIB	Exc.	V.G.	Good	Fair	Poor
850	675	550	395	200	100

Ultra Ten CDP II

Introduced in 2003. Features night sights and rounded edges. Fitted with 3" bull barrel. Chambered for .45 ACP. Weight about 24 oz.

NIB	Exc.	V.G.	Good	Fair	Poor
900	800	700	575	350	150

Gold Match Ten II

.45 ACP 5" barrel model has all standard features of Gold Match. Black polymer frame and blued steel slide. Magazine capacity 14 rounds. Weight about 34 oz.

NIB	Exc.	V.G.	Good	Fair	Poor
1200	950	775	575	350	150

BP Ten II

.45 ACP pistol has 5" barrel and 10-round magazine. Steel slide with polymer frame. Fixed sights. Black matte finish. Weight about 30 oz. Introduced in 2003.

NIB	Exc.	V.G.	Good	Fair	Poor
750	675	550	395	200	100

Pro BP Ten II

As above, with 4" barrel. Weight about 31 oz. Introduced in 2003.

NIB	Exc.	V.G.	Good	Fair	Poor
750	675	550	395	200	100

COMPACT SERIES

Compact

Steel frame and slide. Pistols fitted with 4" bull barrel and shortened grip (.4" shorter than full size). Offered in .45 ACP. Finish is matte black oxide. Grips are black synthetic. Overall length 7.7"; weight about 43 oz. Introduced in 1998.

NIB	Exc.	V.G.	Good	Fair	Poor
675	550	400	300	200	100

Compact Aluminum

Same appearance as Compact, with aluminum frame. Matte black finish. Weight about 28 oz. Introduced in 1998.

NIB	Exc.	V.G.	Good	Fair	Poor
675	550	400	300	200	100

Compact Stainless

Same as Compact model, with stainless steel slide and frame. Offered in both .45 ACP and .40 S&W. Introduced in 1998.

NIB	Exc.	V.G.	Good	Fair	Poor
850	675	550	395	200	100

Compact Stainless II

NIB	Exc.	V.G.	Good	Fair	Poor
900	675	500	375	250	125

Compact Stainless Aluminum

Offered in both .45 ACP and .40 S&W. Features 4" barrel, with stainless steel slide and aluminum frame. Weight about 28 oz. **NOTE:** Add $25 for .40 S&W.

NIB	Exc.	V.G.	Good	Fair	Poor
750	600	475	300	200	100

PRO CARRY

Pro Carry II

Introduced in 1998. This .45 ACP or .40 S&W model features full-size aluminum frame and 4" slide and bull barrel. Other features are match grade trigger, beveled magazine well, full-length guide rod, low-profile combat sights and 7-round magazine. Finish is matte black oxide. Weight about 28 oz. In 2005, was offered in 9mm.

NIB	Exc.	V.G.	Good	Fair	Poor
850	675	550	395	200	100

Pro Carry II Night Sights

As above fitted with night sights.

NIB	Exc.	V.G.	Good	Fair	Poor
750	675	600	425	250	150

Pro Carry Stainless

Same as Pro Carry, with stainless steel slide. **NOTE:** Add $50 for .38 Super

NIB	Exc.	V.G.	Good	Fair	Poor
850	700	550	395	200	100

Pro Carry Stainless Night Sights

As above fitted with night sights.

NIB	Exc.	V.G.	Good	Fair	Poor
950	750	625	450	275	175

Pro TLE/RL II

Introduced in 2005. Features .45 ACP, with 4" barrel and night sights. Slide and frame are steel, with steel finish. Accessory rail on frame. Magazine capacity 7 rounds. Weight about 36 oz.

NIB	Exc.	V.G.	Good	Fair	Poor
1150	950	700	495	300	150

Stainless Pro TLE/RL II

As above, with stainless steel frame and slide. Introduced in 2005.

NIB	Exc.	V.G.	Good	Fair	Poor
1250	925	750	525	350	175

Super Carry Pro

1911-style semi-automatic pistol, chambered in .45 ACP. Features include 8-round magazine; ambidextrous thumb safety; carry melt profiling; full length guide rod; aluminum frame with stainless slide; satin silver finish; super carry serrations; 4" barrel; micarta laminated grips; tritium night sights.

NIB	Exc.	V.G.	Good	Fair	Poor
1300	1125	950	500	300	200

Pro TLE II TFS

This TLE II variation is Threaded For Suppression (TFS). In .45 ACP with 4.5" barrel.

NIB	Exc.	V.G.	Good	Fair	Poor
1050	900	750	600	400	200

Sapphire Pro II

A 9mm limited edition model with 4" barrel, engraving accents on the bright blue polished stainless slide, G-10 grips and 3-dot night sights. Introduced in 2015.

NIB	Exc.	V.G.	Good	Fair	Poor
1500	1300	—	—	—	—

SUPER CARRY SERIES

Super Carry Custom HD

.45 Carry Pro pistols, feature stainless steel slide and frame, match-grade barrel and bushing, ambidextrous thumb safety, beavertail tang, directional serrations on slide, mainspring housing and front strap. Other features include night sights, 8-round magazine, rounded heel and "melt" treatment for easy carrying. Weight 38 oz., 5" barrel and KimPro finish. Super Carry Pro has 4" barrel, Ultra has 3" and 6-round magazine. Introduced in 2011.

NIB	Exc.	V.G.	Good	Fair	Poor
1400	1200	1000	750	300	200

Super Carry Ultra Plus

Combines full-size round-heel frame of Carry Pro, with short slide and 3" barrel of Carry Ultra. Lightweight alloy frame reduces weight to 25 oz., with 8-round magazine. Introduced in 2011.

NIB	Exc.	V.G.	Good	Fair	Poor
1350	1150	965	725	300	200

Solo Carry STS

Micro compact pistol designed for concealed carry. Single-action striker-fired 9mm, with stainless steel slide, alloy frame, 6-round magazine, ambidextrous thumb safety and magazine release. Weight 17 oz.; barrel length 2.7"; width 1.2"; overall length 5.5". Finish is KimPro or bright stainless. Introduced in 2011.

NIB	Exc.	V.G.	Good	Fair	Poor
650	535	450	400	300	200

ULTRA CARRY II SERIES

Ultra Carry

Chambered for .45 ACP or .40 S&W cartridge. Fitted with 3" barrel and McCormick low profile sights. Grips are black synthetic. Magazine capacity 7 rounds. Weight about 25 oz. Black oxide finish. Introduced in 1999. **NOTE:** Add $100 for night sights.

NIB	Exc.	V.G.	Good	Fair	Poor
765	600	475	350	200	100

Ultra Carry II

NIB	Exc.	V.G.	Good	Fair	Poor
800	625	500	375	225	125

Ultra Carry Stainless

Same as above, with stainless steel slide. **NOTE:** Add $25 for .40 S&W model; $100 for night sights.

NIB	Exc.	V.G.	Good	Fair	Poor
850	650	525	395	245	135

Ultra Carry Stainless II

NIB	Exc.	V.G.	Good	Fair	Poor
875	675	550	425	260	150

Micro Carry

Semi-automatic single-action in .380 ACP. Stainless steel slide with aluminum frame, 1911-style controls with ambidextrous thumb safety. Capacity 6+1. Low-profile 3-dot night sights. Crimson Trace laser grips available (CDP model). Introduced in 2013. **NOTE:** Add $200 for CT grips; $300 for Sapphire bright polished blue finish.

NIB	Exc.	V.G.	Good	Fair	Poor
600	500	450	400	375	—

Micro Raptor

Enhanced variation of Micro Carry, with match grade trigger, carry-melt treatment, Zebra wood grips with scale pattern and satin silver or black finish.

NIB	Exc.	V.G.	Good	Fair	Poor
875	750	600	450	350	300

Warrior SOC

Full-size 1911-style semi-automatic in .45 ACP. Stainless steel frame, slide, barrel and bushing. Tactical Wedge night sights, Crimson Trace Rail Master laser sights included. Tan/green KimPro finish, textured G-10 grips, lanyard ring.

NIB	Exc.	V.G.	Good	Fair	Poor
1400	1200	1050	850	600	—

Master Carry Series

Semi-automatic 1911-style pistol in .45 ACP. Offered in three sizes: Custom (5" barrel); Pro (4"); Carry (3"). Stainless frame on Custom; alumi-num on Pro and Carry. Crimson Trace laser grips included. Other features include 3-dot Tactical Wedge night sights, KimPro II finish, rounded heel grip. Introduced in 2013.

NIB	Exc.	V.G.	Good	Fair	Poor
1425	1225	1100	900	650	—

CUSTOM SHOP PISTOLS

Centennial Edition 1911

Highly artistic 1911-style semi-automatic pistol, chambered in .45 ACP. Features include color case-hardened steel frame; extended thumb safety; charcoal-blue finished steel slide; 5" match grade barrel; special serial number; solid smooth ivory grips; nitre blue pins; adjustable sights; presentation case. Edition limited to 250 units. Finished by Doug Turnbull Restoration.

NIB	Exc.	V.G.	Good	Fair	Poor
4000	3600	3200	—	—	—

Royal Carry

Limited edition of 600 pistols. Chambered for .45 ACP. Fitted with 4" barrel with night sights. Hand checkered rosewood grips. Steel slide and aluminum frame. High polish blue finish. Magazine capacity 7 rounds. Weight about 28 oz. Introduced in 1998.

NIB	Exc.	V.G.	Good	Fair	Poor
1000	800	650	475	300	150

Elite Carry

Introduced in 1998. Limited to 1,200 custom shop pistols. Chambered for .45 ACP, with 4" barrel and night sights. Frame aluminum, with black oxide finish. Slide steel, with stainless steel finish. Ambidextrous extended thumb safety, checkered front strap, match trigger and hand checkered rosewood grips. Magazine capacity 7 rounds. Weight about 28 oz.

NIB	Exc.	V.G.	Good	Fair	Poor
1000	800	650	475	300	150

Gold Guardian

Limited edition custom shop pistols to 300 units. Chambered for .45 ACP. Fitted with 5" barrel, with fixed night sights. Stainless steel slide and frame. Ambidextrous extended thumb safety, match grade barrel, extended magazine well, match trigger, special markings and serial number. Magazine capacity 8 rounds; weight about 38 oz. Introduced in 1998.

NIB	Exc.	V.G.	Good	Fair	Poor
1500	1200	950	575	400	150

Combat Carry

Chambered for .45 ACP or .40 S&W cartridge, with 4" barrel. Many custom features and special markings. Stainless steel slide and blued frame. Night sights standard. Weight about 28 oz. Introduced in 1999.

NIB	Exc.	V.G.	Good	Fair	Poor
1050	850	675	500	325	165

Gold Combat

Full-size pistol chambered for .45 ACP cartridge. Many custom features. Night sights standard. Special markings. Weight about 38 oz. Blued slide and frame. Introduced in 1999.

NIB	Exc.	V.G.	Good	Fair	Poor
1680	1250	925	700	350	175

Gold Combat II

NIB	Exc.	V.G.	Good	Fair	Poor
1730	1300	925	750	425	200

Gold Combat Stainless

Same as above, with stainless steel slide.

NIB	Exc.	V.G.	Good	Fair	Poor
1725	1300	925	750	425	200

Gold Combat Stainless II

NIB	Exc.	V.G.	Good	Fair	Poor
1680	1250	925	700	350	175

Super Match

Kimber's most accurate .45 ACP pistol. Fitted with 5" barrel and many special features. Adjustable sights. Weight about 38 oz. Stainless steel slide and frame, with two-tone finish. Introduced in 1999.

NIB	Exc.	V.G.	Good	Fair	Poor
1925	1500	900	600	350	175

Super Match II

NIB	Exc.	V.G.	Good	Fair	Poor
1985	1550	900	600	350	175

LTP II

Designed for limited pistol competition. Fitted with external extractor, 5" barrel with tungsten guide rod, flat top serrated slide with adjustable sights, extended and beveled magazine well holding 10 rounds. Front strap has 20 lpi checkering. Weight about 38 oz.

NIB	Exc.	V.G.	Good	Fair	Poor
2100	1575	925	625	375	200

Raptor II

Introduced in 2005. This .45 ACP features 5" barrel with night sights. Blued finished. Scale serrations on front strap and slide, with scaled zebra wood grips. Magazine capacity 8 rounds. Weight about 38 oz.

NIB	Exc.	V.G.	Good	Fair	Poor
1215	925	750	525	350	175

Pro Raptor II

Similar to Raptor II, except a 4" barrel. Weight about 35 oz. Introduced in 2005.

NIB	Exc.	V.G.	Good	Fair	Poor
1100	825	700	500	300	125

Grand Raptor II

.45 ACP pistol, with 5" match grade stainless steel barrel and adjustable night sights. Black aluminum trigger and rosewood grips. Slide serrations are lizard scale. Stainless steel frame. Slide is matte black and engraved with Custom Shop logo.

NIB	Exc.	V.G.	Good	Fair	Poor
1500	1200	950	575	400	150

Ultra Raptor II

.45 ACP model features 3" ramped match grade bushing-less bull barrel. Fixed night sights. Ambidextrous thumb safety. Lizard scale slide serrations. Introduced in 2005.

NIB	Exc.	V.G.	Good	Fair	Poor
1250	925	750	525	350	175

Ultra RCP II

Introduced in 2003. Features 3" barrel, aluminum frame and sight rail. Chambered for .45 ACP cartridge. Magazine capacity 7 rounds. Weight 26 oz. No longer in production.

NIB	Exc.	V.G.	Good	Fair	Poor
1300	975	795	550	370	195

Gold Combat RL II

Similar to above model, with premium trigger, KimPro finish and rosewood grips. Magazine capacity 8 rounds. Weight about 38 oz. Introduced in 2003.

NIB	Exc.	V.G.	Good	Fair	Poor
1775	1325	1100	700	425	245

Target Match

Limited edition of 1,000 pistols. Chambered for .45 ACP cartridge. Matte black frame, with adjustable sights. Match grade barrel and chamber. Solid aluminum trigger. Checkered front strap and underside of trigger guard. Special serial numbers: KTM0001-KTM1000. Introduced in 2005.

NIB	Exc.	V.G.	Good	Fair	Poor
1400	1050	875	650	395	175

Super America

Billed as Kimber's ultimate top-of-the-line custom 1911. Polished matte blue finish, scroll engraving, mammoth ivory grips, presentation case with matching sheath knife. Introduced 2007.

NIB	Exc.	V.G.	Good	Fair	Poor
3000	2250	1700	1000	600	225

CDP SERIES (Custom Defense Package)

Ultra CDP

Custom shop model features 3" barrel, night sights, hand checkered rosewood grips and numerous other features. Stainless steel slide and matte black frame. Chambered for .45 ACP cartridge. Magazine capacity 6 rounds. Weight about 25 oz. Introduced in 2000.

NIB	Exc.	V.G.	Good	Fair	Poor
1100	825	700	500	300	125

Ultra CDP II

Compact 1911-style semi-automatic pistol, chambered in .45 ACP. Features include 7-round magazine; ambidextrous thumb safety; carry "melt" profiling; full length guide rod; aluminum frame with stainless slide; satin silver finish; checkered front strap; 3" barrel; rosewood double diamond Crimson Trace laser grips; tritium 3-dot night sights.

NIB	Exc.	V.G.	Good	Fair	Poor
1550	1350	850	525	350	175

Compact CDP

Introduced in 2000. Features 4" bull barrel, night sights, hand checkered rosewood grips and other custom features. Stainless steel slide and matte black frame. Chambered for .45 ACP cartridge. Magazine capacity 6 rounds. Weight about 28 oz.

NIB	Exc.	V.G.	Good	Fair	Poor
1200	950	775	575	350	150

Compact CDP II

NIB	Exc.	V.G.	Good	Fair	Poor
1250	995	795	595	350	150

Pro CDP

Similar to Compact CDP, with full length grip. Magazine capacity 7 rounds. Weight about 28 oz. Introduced in 2000.

NIB	Exc.	V.G.	Good	Fair	Poor
1100	825	700	500	300	125

Pro CDP II

NIB	Exc.	V.G.	Good	Fair	Poor
1175	900	775	550	350	150

Custom CDP

.45 ACP full-size pistol fitted with 5" match grade barrel. Stainless steel slide, with front and rear beveled serrations. Matte black steel frame, with checkered rosewood grips. Night sights standard. Introduced in 2001.

NIB	Exc.	V.G.	Good	Fair	Poor
1200	950	775	575	350	150

Custom CDP II

NIB	Exc.	V.G.	Good	Fair	Poor
1250	1000	800	600	375	165

ECLIPSE II SERIES

Eclipse Custom II

Chambered for .45 ACP cartridge. Fitted with 5" barrel and match-grade bushing. Fixed night sights. Magazine capacity 8 rounds. Weight about 38 oz. Introduced in 2002. In 2005, offered in 10mm. **NOTE:** Add $110 for 10mm.

NIB	Exc.	V.G.	Good	Fair	Poor
1175	900	775	550	350	150

Eclipse Target II

Similar to Eclipse Custom II, with addition of adjustable night sights. Introduced in 2002.

NIB	Exc.	V.G.	Good	Fair	Poor
1200	950	775	575	350	150

Eclipse Ultra II

.45 ACP pistol with 3" barrel. Slide machined from stainless steel forging. Front strap checkering. Fixed night sights. Magazine capacity 7 rounds. Weight about 34 oz. Introduced in 2002.

NIB	Exc.	V.G.	Good	Fair	Poor
1100	825	700	500	300	125

Eclipse Pro II

Similar to Eclipse Ultra II. Features full-length grip frame and 4" barrel. Fixed night sights. Introduced in 2002.

NIB	Exc.	V.G.	Good	Fair	Poor
1100	825	700	500	300	125

Eclipse Pro Target II

Similar to Eclipse Pro, with adjustable night sights. Introduced in 2002.

NIB	Exc.	V.G.	Good	Fair	Poor
1190	950	725	525	325	150

TACTICAL SERIES

Series of pistols introduced in 2003. Each pistol has 30 lpi checkering on front strap and under trigger guard, Meprolight three-dot night sights, extended and beveled magazine well, magazines with extended bumper pads, laminated grips and match grade barrel and chamber.

KIMBER MFG., INC. • 627

Tactical Custom II

Chambered for .45 ACP cartridge. Fitted with 5" barrel. Magazine capacity 7 rounds. Weight about 31 oz.

NIB	Exc.	V.G.	Good	Fair	Poor
1250	1000	800	600	375	165

Tactical Pro II

Fitted with 4" barrel. Weight about 28 oz.

NIB	Exc.	V.G.	Good	Fair	Poor
1250	1000	800	600	375	165

Tactical Ultra II

Fitted with 3" barrel. Weight about 25 oz.

NIB	Exc.	V.G.	Good	Fair	Poor
1250	1000	800	600	375	165

COVERT SERIES

Custom Covert II

1911-style semi-automatic carry gun, chambered in .45 ACP. Aluminum frame finished in Desert Tan; steel slide in matte black. 5" barrel with 3-dot sights. Introduced in 2007.

NIB	Exc.	V.G.	Good	Fair	Poor
1500	1200	950	575	400	150

Pro Covert II

Similar to Custom Covert II, with 4" barrel. Introduced in 2007.

NIB	Exc.	V.G.	Good	Fair	Poor
1500	1200	950	575	400	150

Ultra Covert II

Similar to Pro Covert II, with 3" barrel. Introduced 2007.

NIB	Exc.	V.G.	Good	Fair	Poor
1300	975	795	550	370	195

AEGIS SERIES

Pro Aegis II

1911-style semi-automatic carry gun, chambered in 9mm Parabellum. Frame finished in matte aluminum; steel slide in matte black. 4" bull barrel with 3-dot sights. Introduced in 2007.

NIB	Exc.	V.G.	Good	Fair	Poor
1000	800	650	475	300	150

Custom Aegis II

Full-size 1911-style semi-automatic carry gun, chambered in 9mm Parabellum. Aluminum frame finished in matte aluminum; steel slide in matte black. 5" bull barrel with 3-dot sights. Introduced in 2007.

NIB	Exc.	V.G.	Good	Fair	Poor
1100	825	700	500	300	125

Ultra Aegis II

Similar to Pro Aegis II, with 4" barrel. Introduced in 2007.

NIB	Exc.	V.G.	Good	Fair	Poor
1100	825	700	500	300	125

Ultra Onyx II Special Edition

Limited edition model has a deep black Onyx PVD coating and custom engraving. In .45 or 9mm. Features include a rounded heel with ball-milled grooves on front strap, mainspring housing and thin Micarta grips. Barrel length 3", with Tritium night sights. Introduced in 2015.

NIB	Exc.	V.G.	Good	Fair	Poor
1500	1300	—	—	—	—

Model K6s

Kimber's first revolver, a double-action-only .357 Magnum with 6-shot cylinder, 2" barrel, fixed sights, stainless steel frame, barrel with smooth satin finish and rubber grips. Weight about 23 oz. Introduced in 2016.

NIB	Exc.	V.G.	Good	Fair	Poor
800	725	600	—	—	—

RIMFIRE SERIES

Rimfire Custom

Introduced in 2003. This .22-caliber pistol features 5" barrel, with fixed sights and 10-round magazine. Matte black or silver anodized finish. Weight about 23 oz.

NIB	Exc.	V.G.	Good	Fair	Poor
750	525	365	225	150	100

Rimfire Target

As above, with adjustable sights. In 2004, available in .17-caliber Mach 2.

NIB	Exc.	V.G.	Good	Fair	Poor
800	575	400	275	200	125

Rimfire Super

Introduced in 2004. Features serrated flat top slide, with flutes in upper corners, ambidextrous thumb safety, aluminum trigger and two-tone finish. Weight about 23 oz.

NIB	Exc.	V.G.	Good	Fair	Poor
1100	825	700	500	300	125

.22 LR Conversion Kit

Introduced in 1998. Kit features a complete upper assembly: slide, barrel, guide rod, shock buffer and 10-round magazine. Finish satin silver or satin blue. Will fit all Kimber 1911 .45 ACP models. In 2005, offered for .17 Mach 2 cartridge conversion.

NIB	Exc.	V.G.	Good	Fair	Poor
300	250	200	125	75	25

KING PIN
Unknown

Derringer

.22-caliber spur trigger brass constructed single-shot pistol, with 2.5" barrel and walnut grips. Believed to have been made during 1880s.

NIB	Exc.	V.G.	Good	Fair	Poor
—	—	675	200	100	50

KIRRIKALE, ENDUSTRISI
Ankara, Turkey

Kirrikale Pistol

7.65 or 9mm short caliber semi-automatic pistol, with 3.5" barrel and 6-shot magazine. Blued, with plastic grips. Slide marked "MKE"; and "Kirrikale Tufek Fb Cal.—". Imported by Firearms Center in Victoria, Texas and Mandall Shooting Supplies. An unauthorized copy of Walther PP, that was imported into U.S. briefly.

NIB	Exc.	V.G.	Good	Fair	Poor
450	350	275	225	150	100

KLEINGUENTHER/KDF, INC.
Kleinguenther Distinctive Firearms
Seguin, Texas

Condor

12-gauge boxlock over/under shotgun, with 28" barrels, ventilated ribs, single-selective trigger and automatic ejectors. Blued, with walnut stock. Manufactured in Italy.

NIB	Exc.	V.G.	Good	Fair	Poor
—	700	600	525	375	275

Brescia

A 12-gauge boxlock double-barrel shotgun, with 28" barrels, double triggers and extractors. Blued, with walnut stock. Manufactured in Italy.

NIB	Exc.	V.G.	Good	Fair	Poor
—	400	325	300	200	125

K-14 Insta Fire Rifle

Bolt-action sporting rifle, manufactured in a variety of calibers, with 24" or 26" barrels furnished without sights. Blued, with Monte Carlo-style walnut stock.

NIB	Exc.	V.G.	Good	Fair	Poor
—	1750	1350	1100	500	250

K-15

Similar to above, with 60-degree bolt angle and accurized barrel. Guaranteed to fire .5" group at 100 yards. Manufactured with a variety of optional features.

NIB	Exc.	V.G.	Good	Fair	Poor
—	1750	1350	1100	500	250

K-15 Pro-Hunter

As above, with matte blued or electroless nickel-plated and fiberglass stock.

NIB	Exc.	V.G.	Good	Fair	Poor
—	1750	1350	1100	500	250

K-15 Swat Rifle

7.62x54mm caliber bolt-action rifle, with 24" or 26" barrel. Furnished without sights. Parkerized finish and 4-shot magazine. Walnut stock.

NIB	Exc.	V.G.	Good	Fair	Poor
—	1800	1400	1150	700	350

K-15 Dangerous Game

As above in .411 KDF caliber.

NIB	Exc.	V.G.	Good	Fair	Poor
—	2500	2000	1300	1000	700

K-16

Bolt-action sporting rifle, manufactured in a variety of calibers, with 24" or 26" barrel. Furnished without sights, single stage adjustable trigger, accurized barrel and Dupont Rynite stock. Produced with a variety of optional features.

NIB	Exc.	V.G.	Good	Fair	Poor
—	1750	1350	1100	500	250

Titan Menor

.222- or .223-caliber bolt-action rifle, with 24" or 26" barrel. Furnished without sights. Monte Carlo-style or standard schnabel tipped walnut stock. Blued.

NIB	Exc.	V.G.	Good	Fair	Poor
—	1200	900	550	400	200

Titan II Standard

As above, with mid-sized action.

NIB	Exc.	V.G.	Good	Fair	Poor
—	1200	900	550	400	200

Titan II Magnum

As above, with long action. Discontinued in 1988.

NIB	Exc.	V.G.	Good	Fair	Poor
—	1350	1100	675	450	200

Titan .411 KDF Mag.

As above in .411 KDF, with 26" barrel having integral muzzle-brake. Blued or electroless nickel-plated, with walnut stock. Discontinued in 1988.

NIB	Exc.	V.G.	Good	Fair	Poor
—	2500	2000	1300	1000	700

K-22

.22-caliber bolt-action rifle, with 21" free floating barrel. Furnished without sights, adjustable trigger and 5-shot magazine. Also known as Mauser 201.

NIB	Exc.	V.G.	Good	Fair	Poor
—	500	400	300	175	100

Deluxe

NIB	Exc.	V.G.	Good	Fair	Poor
—	525	425	325	200	125

Deluxe Custom

NIB	Exc.	V.G.	Good	Fair	Poor
—	650	550	450	375	225

Deluxe Special Select

NIB	Exc.	V.G.	Good	Fair	Poor
—	1150	850	750	650	325

Model 2005

.22-caliber semi-automatic rifle, with 19.5" barrel, open sights and 5-shot magazine. Blued, with walnut stock. Also, available in deluxe model. Imported in 1986.

NIB	Exc.	V.G.	Good	Fair	Poor
250	175	150	100	75	50

Model 2107

.22- or .22-caliber Magnum bolt-action rifle, with 19.5" barrel, open sights and 5-shot magazine. Blued, with walnut stock.

NIB	Exc.	V.G.	Good	Fair	Poor
—	375	325	250	150	100

Model 2112

Deluxe version of Model 2107.

NIB	Exc.	V.G.	Good	Fair	Poor
—	400	325	275	175	125

KLIPZIG & COMPANY
San Francisco, California

Pocket Pistol

.41-caliber single-shot percussion pistol, with 2.5" barrel, German silver mounts and walnut stocks. Manufactured during 1850s early 1860s.

NIB	Exc.	V.G.	Good	Fair	Poor
—	—	1950	975	400	200

KNICKERBOCKER
Made by Crescent Fire Arms Co.

Knickerbocker Pistol NFA

Knickerbocker is a 14" double-barreled 20-gauge smooth bore pistol, manufactured by Crescent Fire Arms Co. of Norwich, Connecticut. On the basis of its hammerless design and dates of production of similarly designed firearms by Crescent, the Knickerbocker was probably manufactured sometime during early 1900s. Receiver is case-hardened and barrels are nickel-plated. Right side of receiver stamped "AMERICAN GUN CO./ NEW YORK U S A"; left side "KNICKERBOCKER". Probably was intended for law enforcement and/or defensive purposes and manufactured using the same techniques used to produce Ithaca Auto & Burglar Gun. Receiver fitted with checkered pistol-grip, resembling that of Model 1 and Model 2 smooth bore H&R Handy-Gun. Only known specimen of Knickerbocker bears serial number 200114. Knickerbocker was classified as "any other weapon" under NFA in 1934, because it was originally designed as "a so-called shotgun with a pistol grip"; because it is concealable (see Treasury Department ruling S.T. 772, dated August 6, 1934). Its rarity precludes being able to reliably estimate its value at this time.

Double-Barrel Shotgun

Knickerbocker was a popular Dutch name for a New Yorker. It was used as a brand on many hammerless sidelock doubles made by Crescent Fire-arms Co. Valued from $100 to $700 depending on model and condition.

KNIGHT RIFLES
Centerville, Iowa

Company was started in 1985, by Tony Knight. Company produces in-line blackpowder muzzle-loading rifles and a complete line of accessories.

Disc Magnum

Available in .50-caliber, with choice of blued or stainless steel 24" or 26" barrel. Adjustable rear sight. Checkered stock, with palm swell and rubber recoil pad. Stock offered in black or camo. Adjustable trigger. Weight about 8 lbs. **NOTE:** Add $50 for camo finish; $70 for stainless steel.

NIB	Exc.	V.G.	Good	Fair	Poor
450	350	300	250	200	150

Bighorn Magnum

Available in .50-caliber, with choice of 22" or 26" blued or stainless steel barrel. Adjustable rear sight. Checkered stock, with rubber recoil pad. Stock offered in black or camo. Adjustable trigger. Weight about 7.7 lbs. **NOTE:** Add $50 for camo finish; $70 for stainless steel.

NIB	Exc.	V.G.	Good	Fair	Poor
325	250	200	175	150	100

T-Bolt Magnum

Available in .50-caliber, with choice of blue or stainless steel 22" or 26" barrel. Adjustable rear sight. Composite stock, with rubber recoil pad. Stock available in camo. Adjustable trigger. Weight about 8 lbs. **NOTE:** Add $50 for camo finish; $70 for stainless steel.

NIB	Exc.	V.G.	Good	Fair	Poor
400	325	275	225	150	100

LK-93 Wolverine

Available in .50- or .54-caliber, with choice of 22" blued or stainless steel barrel. Adjustable rear sight. Composite skeleton or thumbhole stock. Stock available in black or camo. Adjustable trigger. Weight about 6.5 lbs. **NOTE:** Add $50 for camo finish; $70 for stainless steel; $40 for thumbhole stock.

NIB	Exc.	V.G.	Good	Fair	Poor
265	200	150	100	75	25

LK-93 Wolverine Youth

Same as above, with shorter length of pull. Offered in black stock only.

NIB	Exc.	V.G.	Good	Fair	Poor
275	225	175	125	100	75

American Knight

Available in .50-caliber, with 22" blued barrel. Adjustable rear sight. Black composite stock. Non-adjustable trigger. Weight about 6.3 lbs.

NIB	Exc.	V.G.	Good	Fair	Poor
200	150	100	75	50	25

MK-85 Hunter

Offered in .50- or .54-caliber, with blued finish and walnut stock.

NIB	Exc.	V.G.	Good	Fair	Poor
550	450	375	325	250	200

MK-85 Predator

Stainless steel version of Hunter model. Offered with composite stock or various camo finishes. **NOTE:** Add $50 for camo finish.

NIB	Exc.	V.G.	Good	Fair	Poor
650	525	450	300	250	200

MK-85 Stalker

Offered in .50- or .54-caliber, with a variety of stock options. Standard stock is composite. Blued finish. **NOTE:** Add $50 for camo finish.

NIB	Exc.	V.G.	Good	Fair	Poor
565	450	375	325	250	200

MK-85 Knight Hawk

Offered in .50- or .54-caliber, with black composite stock and stainless steel.

NIB	Exc.	V.G.	Good	Fair	Poor
750	600	500	400	300	200

MK-86 Shotgun

Available in 12-gauge, with 24" extra full choked barrel. Black composite stock, with blued finish.

NIB	Exc.	V.G.	Good	Fair	Poor
600	475	375	250	200	150

HK-94 Hawkeye Pistol

.50-caliber pistol fitted with 12" barrel. Overall length 20"; weight 52 oz. Offered in stainless steel or blued finish. First offered in 1993. Discontinued in 1998. **NOTE:** Add $70 for stainless steel.

NIB	Exc.	V.G.	Good	Fair	Poor
400	300	250	200	150	100

Rolling Block Rifle

Rolling Block black powder rifle, similar in design to old Remington Rolling Block. 209 primer ignition, .50-caliber barrel rifled for sabots. Finishes include blued/composite, stainless/camo and all-camo. Introduced in 2007. Values shown are for stainless.

NIB	Exc.	V.G.	Good	Fair	Poor
375	300	200	125	100	50

Long Range Hunter

.45-, .50- or .52-caliber bolt-action muzzle-loader, with 27" fluted stainless barrel. Said to shoot 4" 3-shot groups at 200 yards. Laminated stock. Introduced in 2007.

NIB	Exc.	V.G.	Good	Fair	Poor
525	400	300	200	100	50

KNIGHT'S ARMAMENT COMPANY
Titusville, Florida
(previously in Vero Beach, Florida)

STONER SR-15 RIFLES

SR-15 Match

Chambered for .223 Win. Fitted with target contour 20" free floating barrel. Two-stage match trigger. Flat top receiver. No sights. Weight about 7.9 lbs.

NIB	Exc.	V.G.	Good	Fair	Poor
1850	1400	1050	750	500	200

SR-15 M-5 Rifle

.223 fitted with 20" standard weight barrel, with two-stage target trigger. Hand guard employs RAS accessory system. Fitted with flip-up low profile rear sight. Weight about 7.6 lbs.

NIB	Exc.	V.G.	Good	Fair	Poor
1700	1250	950	700	400	200

SR-15 E3 URX Carbine

Similar to SR-15 M-5, with 16" barrel, telescoping buttstock and vertical fore-end grip. Introduced 2006.

NIB	Exc.	V.G.	Good	Fair	Poor
2100	1700	1250	950	500	200

SR-15 M-4 Carbine

Model includes RAS system and flip-up rear sight. Two-stage target trigger and 16" lightweight barrel. Weight about 6.8 lbs.

NIB	Exc.	V.G.	Good	Fair	Poor
1700	1250	950	700	400	200

STONER SR-25 RIFLES

SR-25 Match

Chambered for .308-caliber. Fitted with 24" target contour free floating barrel. Special rifling and twist rate. No sights. Weight about 10.75 lbs.

NIB	Exc.	V.G.	Good	Fair	Poor
3495	2600	1850	950	600	400

SR-25 Lightweight Match

.308 rifle fitted with 20" free floating barrel. No sights. Weight about 9.5 lbs.

NIB	Exc.	V.G.	Good	Fair	Poor
2995	2250	1500	900	550	350

SR-25 Stoner Carbine

Fitted with 16" free floating barrel and special short non-slip hand guard. Weight about 7.75 lbs.

NIB	Exc.	V.G.	Good	Fair	Poor
2995	2250	1500	900	—	—

SR-25 APC

Latest evolution of 7.62mm NATO carbine. Advanced Precision Carbine (APC) has 16" barrel with flash suppressor, ambidextrous bolt release, safety and magazine release. A drop-in two-stage trigger serves double duty for long or close range shooting. Introduced in 2014.

NIB	Exc.	V.G.	Good	Fair	Poor
4800	4000	3000	2200	900	400

SR-25 Competition Match

Chambered for .308 or .260 cartridge. Has 26" match barrel. Fitted with special forearm, which rotates in 15 degree increments. Trigger is adjustable two-stage, with extended trigger guard. Special bolt stop and charging handle. Adjustable buttstock. May be fitted with several extra cost options that will affect price.

NIB	Exc.	V.G.	Good	Fair	Poor
6000	4750	3000	1750	1000	600

SR-25 Mk11 Mod 0 Match Rifle

Introduced in 2004. Features heavy 20" free floating target grade barrel.

NIB	Exc.	V.G.	Good	Fair	Poor
5295	3900	2500	1650	100	475

SR-50 Rifle

Semi-automatic rifle chambered for .50 BMG cartridge. Magazine feed. Weight about 31 lbs.

NIB	Exc.	V.G.	Good	Fair	Poor
7000	5500	4000	3000	2000	750

KOHOUT & SPOLECNOST
Kdyne, Czechoslovakia

Mars

6.35 or 7.65mm caliber semi-automatic pistol. Larger caliber having grip safety. Blued, with plastic grips impressed with word "Mars". Slide marked "Mars 7.65 (or 6.35) Kohout & Spol. Kdyne". Manufactured between 1928 and 1945.

NIB	Exc.	V.G.	Good	Fair	Poor
—	350	250	200	150	100

Niva, PZK

Similar to above in 6.35mm caliber.

NIB	Exc.	V.G.	Good	Fair	Poor
—	350	250	200	150	100

KOLB, HENRY M.
Philadelphia, Pennsylvania

Revolvers listed were manufactured by Henry Kolb and Charles Foehl until 1912, when R.F. Sedgely replaced Foehl. Manufacture continued until approximately 1938.

Baby Hammerless

.22-caliber folding trigger double-action revolver, with enclosed hammer and 5-shot cylinder.

NIB	Exc.	V.G.	Good	Fair	Poor
—	300	200	150	100	50

New Baby Hammerless

Similar to above, with hinged barrel to facilitate loading.

NIB	Exc.	V.G.	Good	Fair	Poor
—	300	200	150	100	50

KOLIBRI/FREDERICH PFANNL
Rehberg, Austria

2.7mm

2.7mm semi-automatic pistol, with 7-round magazine. F.P. trademark on grips, Kolibri name at bottom of grips. Single cartridge may be worth as much as $75!

Courtesy James Rankin

NIB	Exc.	V.G.	Good	Fair	Poor
—	2500	1550	850	600	400

3mm

3mm semi-automatic pistol, with 6-round magazine. The 3mm version rarer of the two Kolibri pistols. F.P. trademark on grips.

Courtesy James Rankin

NIB	Exc.	V.G.	Good	Fair	Poor
—	2800	2000	1500	1000	600

KOMMER, THEODOR WAFFENFABRIK
Zella Mehlis, Germany

Model 1

6.35mm semi-automatic pistol, with 8-shot magazine. Blued, with plastic grips. Kommer name on both slide and frame, with T.K. trademark on grips. Manufactured during 1920s.

Courtesy James Rankin

NIB	Exc.	V.G.	Good	Fair	Poor
—	300	250	200	150	90

Model 2

6.35mm semi-automatic pistol, with 6-round magazine. Similar to Model 1906 Browning. Barrel length 2"; weight about 13 oz. Kommer name on slide. Late TH.K. trademark on grips. Manufactured in 1930s.

Courtesy James Rankin

NIB	Exc.	V.G.	Good	Fair	Poor
—	300	250	200	150	90

Model 3

6.35mm semi-automatic pistol, with 9-round magazine. Kommer name on slide. TH.K. trademark on grips. Same as Model 2, with extended grips straps for longer magazine.

Courtesy James Rankin

NIB	Exc.	V.G.	Good	Fair	Poor
—	300	250	200	150	90

Model 4

7.65mm caliber semi-automatic pistol, with 7-shot magazine. Without a grip safety. Similar to FN Model 1901. Barrel length 3"; weight about 20 oz. Slide marked "Waffenfabrik Kommer Zella Mehlis Kal. 7.65". Manufactured between 1936 and 1940.

Courtesy James Rankin

NIB	Exc.	V.G.	Good	Fair	Poor
—	375	325	275	175	100

KONGSBERG
Norway

Thumbhole Sporter

Introduced in 1993. This bolt-action rifle chambered for .22-250 and .308 Win. cartridges. Fitted with 23" heavy barrel. Stock is American walnut, with stippled thumbhole grip and wide fore-end. Cheekpiece is adjustable for height. Weight about 8.5 lbs. Available in both right-/left-hand configurations. **NOTE:** Add 10 percent for left-hand model.

NIB	Exc.	V.G.	Good	Fair	Poor
1575	1250	900	550	350	200

Classic Rifle

Also introduced in 1993. Chambered for a wide variety of calibers from .22-250 to .338 Win. Magnum. Fitted with 23" barrel for standard calibers; 26" barrel for Magnum calibers. European walnut stock, with straight comb. Hand checkered. Open sights. Weight about 7.5 lbs., depending on caliber. Offered in both right-/left-hand configurations. **NOTE:** Add 10 percent for left-hand model; 10 percent for Magnum calibers.

NIB	Exc.	V.G.	Good	Fair	Poor
995	800	650	375	225	125

KORRIPHILA
Germany

HSP

7.65mm Luger, .38 Special, 9mm Police, 9mm Luger, 9mm Steyr, 10mm ACP and .45 ACP caliber. Double-action semi-automatic pistol, with 4" barrel made of stainless steel.

NIB	Exc.	V.G.	Good	Fair	Poor
7500	6000	5000	2500	1250	550

HSP—Single-Action Only

NIB	Exc.	V.G.	Good	Fair	Poor
7500	6000	5000	2500	1250	550

Odin's Eye

Essentially same model as above. Same calibers, with choice of 4" or 5" barrel lengths. Frame and slide made of Damascus steel.

NIB	Exc.	V.G.	Good	Fair	Poor
14000	10000	7500	4000	1500	500

KORTH
Germany

Korth started business in Ratzegurg, Germany, in 1954.

Semi-Automatic Pistol

9mm caliber double-action semi-automatic pistol, with 4" barrel, adjustable sights and 13-shot magazine. Other calibers offered: .40 S&W, .357 SIG and 9x21. Optional 5" barrel also offered. Weight about 44 oz. Matte or polished blue, with walnut grips. Introduced in 1985.

NIB	Exc.	V.G.	Good	Fair	Poor
7000	5000	3750	2750	1300	650

Combat Revolver

.22 LR, .22 Magnum, .357 Magnum and 9mm caliber revolver, with 3", 4", 5.25" or 6" barrel and 6-shot cylinder. Barrels and cylinders are interchangeable. Matte or polished blue, with walnut grips.

NIB	Exc.	V.G.	Good	Fair	Poor
5000	3900	3000	1750	1150	700

Match Revolver

Built in same calibers as Combat revolver, with 5.25" or 6" barrel. Adjustable sight notch widths and rear sight. Machined trigger shoe. Adjustable match grips, with oiled walnut and matte finish.

NIB	Exc.	V.G.	Good	Fair	Poor
6250	5000	4000	2250	1500	1000

KRAG-JORGENSEN

This was the first bolt-action repeating rifle that used smokeless powder to be adopted by the U.S. government as a service rifle. Adopted as Model 1892, it was similar to the Denmark military rifle, which had been designed by Norwegians Ole Krag and Erik Jorgensen. Most unique part of this design was the side-mounted hinged magazine. With the exception of Model 1898 Practice Rifle, which was chambered for .22 rimfire — all Krag rifles were chambered for .30-40 Government cartridge. From 1892 to 1899, more than a dozen variations were made. Over the years many have been altered or "customized". Values shown here are for unmodified, original rifles. For more on Krag-Jorgensen, see Standard Catalog of Military Firearms 8th Edition (2016) by Phillip Petersen.

Model of 1892

1st Type, Serial number 1 — 1500

NIB	Exc.	V.G.	Good	Fair	Poor
—	20000	12500	6500	3000	900

2nd Type, Serial number 1501 — 24562

NIB	Exc.	V.G.	Good	Fair	Poor
—	10000	7500	4000	2000	600

Model 1892, altered to 1896

NIB	Exc.	V.G.	Good	Fair	Poor
—	1800	950	750	450	200

Model 1896

NOTE: Add 10 percent for carbine variation.

NIB	Exc.	V.G.	Good	Fair	Poor
—	2750	2000	1600	750	300

Model 1898

NOTE: Add a premium of 100 to 120 percent for carbine variation.

NIB	Exc.	V.G.	Good	Fair	Poor
—	1250	900	650	450	200

Model 1898 Practice Rifle (.22 rimfire)

NIB	Exc.	V.G.	Good	Fair	Poor
—	—	4500	2000	850	300

Model 1899 Carbine

NIB	Exc.	V.G.	Good	Fair	Poor
—	1850	1400	900	750	300

KRAUSER, ALFRED
Zella Mehlis, Germany

Helfricht or Helkra

6.35mm semi-automatic pistol, with 2" barrel. Produced in four models: fourth, with enclosed barrel. Blued, with composition grips. Manufactured from 1921 to 1929.

NIB	Exc.	V.G.	Good	Fair	Poor
—	475	400	350	250	150

KRICO
Stuttgart, West Germany

Sporting Rifle

.22 Hornet or .222-caliber bolt-action rifle, with 22", 24" or 26" barrels. Single-/double-set trigger, adjustable sights and 4-shot magazine. Blued, with walnut stock. Manufactured between 1956 and 1962.

NIB	Exc.	V.G.	Good	Fair	Poor
—	650	550	475	375	275

Sporting Carbine

As above, with 20" barrel and full length stock.

NIB	Exc.	V.G.	Good	Fair	Poor
—	675	575	500	400	300

Varmint Special Rifle

Sporting Rifle, with heavier barrel.

NIB	Exc.	V.G.	Good	Fair	Poor
—	650	550	475	375	275

Model 300

.22-caliber bolt-action rifle, with 23.5" barrel, 5-shot magazine and grooved receiver. Blued, with walnut stock. Imported prior to 1989.

NIB	Exc.	V.G.	Good	Fair	Poor
—	700	600	550	400	300

Model 302 and 304

Variations of above. Discontinued in 1986.

NIB	Exc.	V.G.	Good	Fair	Poor
—	700	600	550	400	300

Model 311 Smallbore

.22-caliber bolt-action rifle, with 22" barrel. Double-set triggers, adjustable sights and 5- or 10-shot magazine. Blued, with walnut stock. Not imported after 1988.

NIB	Exc.	V.G.	Good	Fair	Poor
—	325	275	225	150	100

Model 320

As above, with 19.5" barrel and full length stock. Discontinued in 1988.

NIB	Exc.	V.G.	Good	Fair	Poor
—	700	600	550	400	300

Model 340

.22-caliber bolt-action rifle, with 21" heavy barrel. Furnished without sights, adjustable trigger and 5-shot magazine. Blued, with walnut stock. Not imported after 1988.

NIB	Exc.	V.G.	Good	Fair	Poor
—	750	625	575	425	325

Model 340 Mini-Sniper

As above, with matte finish. Barrel fitted with muzzle-brake. Stock with raised cheekpiece, as well as ventilated hand guard.

NIB	Exc.	V.G.	Good	Fair	Poor
—	1000	850	750	500	400

Model 340 Kricotronic

Model 340 fitted with electronic trigger. Not imported after 1988.

NIB	Exc.	V.G.	Good	Fair	Poor
—	1450	1000	850	600	500

Model 360S Biathlon Rifle

Introduced in 1991. Features .22 LR straight pull bolt-action, with 5-round magazine. Fitted with 21.25" barrel and 17 oz. match trigger. Walnut stock, with high comb and adjustable buttplate. Fully adjustable match peep sight. Weight about 9.25 lbs.

NIB	Exc.	V.G.	Good	Fair	Poor
1950	1350	850	500	300	150

Model 360S2 Biathlon Rifle

Same as above, with black epoxy finished walnut stock, with pistol-grip. Weight 9 lbs.

NIB	Exc.	V.G.	Good	Fair	Poor
1500	1250	800	400	200	100

Model 400 Match

Chambered for .22 LR or .22 Hornet. Bolt-action rifle fitted with heavy match 23" barrel, double-set of match triggers and 5-round magazine. Match-style stock of European walnut. Weight about 8.8 lbs.

NIB	Exc.	V.G.	Good	Fair	Poor
900	775	650	500	300	150

Model 400 Sporter

.22 Hornet caliber bolt-action rifle, with 23.5" barrel, open sights and 5-shot magazine. Blued, with walnut stock. Not imported after 1988.

NIB	Exc.	V.G.	Good	Fair	Poor
—	750	625	550	425	325

Model 420

As above, with 19.5" barrel, double-set triggers and full-length stock. Discontinued in 1988.

NIB	Exc.	V.G.	Good	Fair	Poor
—	900	750	675	500	400

Model 440

Similar to Model 340. Not imported after 1988.

NIB	Exc.	V.G.	Good	Fair	Poor
—	950	800	700	500	375

Model 500 Kricotronic Match Rifle

Chambered for .22 LR. Bolt-action rifle fitted with 23.6" barrel and tapered bore. Walnut stock, with match-type adjustable buttplate. Electronic ignition system gives fastest lock time. Weight about 9.4 lbs.

NIB	Exc.	V.G.	Good	Fair	Poor
3900	3000	2400	1650	1000	400

Model 600 Sporter

.17 Rem. to .308 Win. caliber bolt-action rifle, with 23.5" barrel. Open sights and 3-shot magazine. Blued, with walnut stock. Not imported after 1988.

NIB	Exc.	V.G.	Good	Fair	Poor
—	1150	950	875	700	575

Model 600 Sniper Rifle

Bolt-action rifle chambered for .222, .223, .22-250, .243 and 308. Fitted with 25.6" heavy barrel, with flack hider. Stock walnut, with adjustable rubber buttplate. Magazine holds 4 rounds. Weight about 9.2 lbs.

NIB	Exc.	V.G.	Good	Fair	Poor
2900	2100	1500	1100	600	300

Model 600 Match Rifle

Chambered for same calibers as 600 Sniper, with addition of 5.6x50 Magnum. Fitted with 23.6" barrel. Match stock is vented in forearm for cooling. Wood is walnut, with cheekpiece. Weight about 8.8 lbs.

NIB	Exc.	V.G.	Good	Fair	Poor
1500	1100	750	600	300	150

Model 620

As above, with 20.5" barrel, double-set triggers and full-length stock.

NIB	Exc.	V.G.	Good	Fair	Poor
1500	1100	750	600	300	150

Model 640 Varmint Rifle

Similar to above in .22-250, .222- or .223-caliber, with 23.5" heavy barrel. Not imported after 1988.

NIB	Exc.	V.G.	Good	Fair	Poor
—	1250	1025	925	775	625

Model 640 Sniper Rifle

As above, with matte finish. Discontinued in 1988.

NIB	Exc.	V.G.	Good	Fair	Poor
1500	1100	750	600	300	150

Model 640 Deluxe Sniper Rifle

As above in .223- or .308-caliber, with 23" barrel, stippled stock and adjustable trigger. Not imported after 1988.

NIB	Exc.	V.G.	Good	Fair	Poor
—	1700	1250	1000	750	650

Model 700 Sporter

.270- or .30-06 caliber bolt-action rifle, with 23.5" barrel, single-set trigger and 3-shot magazine. Blued, with walnut stock. Discontinued in 1988.

NIB	Exc.	V.G.	Good	Fair	Poor
—	1050	850	750	600	500

Model 720

As above, with 20.5" barrel, double-set triggers and full-length stock. Discontinued in 1988.

NIB	Exc.	V.G.	Good	Fair	Poor
—	1200	900	750	600	500

Model 720 Limited Edition

As above in .270-caliber only, with gold-plated furniture and gold highlighted engraving. Not imported after 1988.

NIB	Exc.	V.G.	Good	Fair	Poor
—	2500	2000	1750	1400	900

KRIDER, J. H.
Philadelphia, Pennsylvania

Pocket Pistol

.41-caliber percussion pocket pistol, with 3" barrel, German silver furniture and walnut stock. Barrel marked "Krider Phila.". Manufactured during 1850s and 1860s.

NIB	Exc.	V.G.	Good	Fair	Poor
—	—	1750	700	300	150

Militia Rifle

.58-caliber percussion rifle, with 39" browned barrel. Full length stock secured by two barrel bands. Lock marked "Krider". Case-hardened and furniture of brass. Several hundred manufactured in 1861.

Courtesy Milwaukee Public Museum, Milwaukee, Wisconsin

NIB	Exc.	V.G.	Good	Fair	Poor
—	—	4550	2000	750	225

KRIEGHOFF, HEINRICH, GUN CO.
Ulm, Germany

Krieghoff-manufactured Lugers are listed in Luger section.

DRILLINGS AND COMBINATION GUNS

Plus Model

Three-barrel combination rifle/shotgun. Produced in a variety of gauges and calibers, with 25" barrels. Double triggers and automatic ejectors. Blued, with walnut stock. Introduced in 1988.

NIB	Exc.	V.G.	Good	Fair	Poor
6600	5250	4100	3500	2000	750

Trumpf Model

Combination rifle/shotgun. Produced in a variety of calibers and gauges, with 25" barrels and double triggers. Blued, with walnut stock.

NIB	Exc.	V.G.	Good	Fair	Poor
11000	7700	5100	3500	2000	750

Trumpf Dural

As above lightweight boxlock, with Duraluminum frame. **NOTE:** Add $1,850 for single trigger; $450 for free-floating barrel.

NIB	Exc.	V.G.	Good	Fair	Poor
11000	7700	5100	3500	2000	750

Neptun

Combination over/under rifle/shotgun, with sidelocks. Produced in a variety of gauges and calibers. Engraved, blued with walnut stock.

NIB	Exc.	V.G.	Good	Fair	Poor
15000	12000	10500	5000	2500	1500

Neptun Dural

As above lightweight boxlock, with Duraluminum frame.

NIB	Exc.	V.G.	Good	Fair	Poor
15000	12000	10500	5000	2500	1500

Neptun Primus

Neptun, with relief engraving and detachable sidelocks.

NIB	Exc.	V.G.	Good	Fair	Poor
20000	17000	14000	7500	3500	2000

Neptun Primus Dural

As above lightweight sidelock, with Duraluminum frame.

NIB	Exc.	V.G.	Good	Fair	Poor
20000	18000	14000	7500	3500	2000

Optima

Classic drilling combination of side-by-side shotgun barrels over a rifle barrel. Shotgun offered in 12- or 20-gauge; rifle barrel in .308 Win., .30-06 or several popular European cartridges. Features include twin-hammer action, with Universal trigger system, combination cocking device and a set trigger integrated in the front trigger. Values shown are for base model. Many options available.

NIB	Exc.	V.G.	Good	Fair	Poor
10000	8500	6500	5000	3000	900

DOUBLE RIFLES

Many optional engraving patterns available for these double rifles that may affect price. Consult an expert prior to sale.

Teck Over/Under

Boxlock over/under rifle manufactured in a variety of calibers, with 25" barrels. Double triggers, extractors and express sights. Blued, with walnut stock. **NOTE:** Add $1,500 for .458 Win. Magnum.

NIB	Exc.	V.G.	Good	Fair	Poor
9000	8250	6600	5000	2250	1500

Ulm Model

As above, with sidelocks.

NIB	Exc.	V.G.	Good	Fair	Poor
15000	12000	10500	7500	3000	2000

Ulm Primus

As above, with detachable sidelocks.

NIB	Exc.	V.G.	Good	Fair	Poor
23500	19500	16500	11500	7000	3000

Ultra

Boxlock over/under rifle offered with several different options. Same caliber or different caliber rifle barrels. Built on 20-gauge frame, with game scene engraving. Weight depends on caliber and combination of calibers, but between 6.5 lbs. and 8 lbs.

NIB	Exc.	V.G.	Good	Fair	Poor
7500	6100	4400	3000	1500	800

Classic

Side-by-side rifle with side plates. Offered in 7x65R to 9.3x74R calibers, with optional interchangeable 20-gauge shotgun barrel. Single trigger. Choice of standard stock with cheekpiece or classic Bavaria style. Weight about 7.25 to 8 lbs., depending on calibers.

NIB	Exc.	V.G.	Good	Fair	Poor
8800	6900	5000	3500	2000	800

Classic Big Five

Similar to Classic, but chambered for .375 H&H, .375 NE, .458 Win. Magnum, .416 Rigby, .470 NE and .500 NE 3". Double trigger, with hinged front trigger. Weight about 9.25 to 10 lbs., depending on caliber. Interchangeable barrels are optional.

NIB	Exc.	V.G.	Good	Fair	Poor
10900	82500	5100	3500	2000	750

SHOTGUNS

Model 32 Standard

12-, 20-, 28-gauge or .410 bore boxlock over/under shotgun, with 26.5" to 32" barrels. Single-selective trigger and automatic ejectors. Blued, with walnut stock. Discontinued in 1980. **NOTE:** Add 50 percent for 28-gauge or .410 two barrel set; 100 percent for four-barrel Skeet set.

NIB	Exc.	V.G.	Good	Fair	Poor
—	3000	2500	2000	1100	750

San Remo Grade

NIB	Exc.	V.G.	Good	Fair	Poor
—	5000	3750	1900	1400	1000

Monte Carlo Grade

NIB	Exc.	V.G.	Good	Fair	Poor
—	6250	4850	2750	1650	1250

Crown Grade

Courtesy Bonhams & Butterfields

NIB	Exc.	V.G.	Good	Fair	Poor
—	8700	6500	4300	2200	1500

Super Crown Grade

NIB	Exc.	V.G.	Good	Fair	Poor
18000	14700	10500	6850	3750	2000

Single Barrel Trap Gun

Model 32, with single 32" to 34" barrel.

NIB	Exc.	V.G.	Good	Fair	Poor
—	3950	3250	1700	1075	600

Teck Over/Under

Similar to Teck double rifle, but offered in 12- and 16-gauge.

NIB	Exc.	V.G.	Good	Fair	Poor
12000	10000	7500	4550	3000	1750

Teck Dural

Same as above, with lightweight aluminum frame.

NIB	Exc.	V.G.	Good	Fair	Poor
12000	10000	7500	4550	3000	1750

Ulm

Sidelock over/under offered in both 12- and 16-gauge.

NIB	Exc.	V.G.	Good	Fair	Poor
20000	16500	13000	8000	4500	3000

Ulm Dural

Lightweight version of above model.

NIB	Exc.	V.G.	Good	Fair	Poor
20000	16500	13000	8000	4500	3000

Ulm Primus

Deluxe version of Ulm series, with sidelocks and extensive engraving.

NIB	Exc.	V.G.	Good	Fair	Poor
30000	22250	16500	12000	7000	3500

Ulm Primus Dural

Lightweight version of above model.

NIB	Exc.	V.G.	Good	Fair	Poor
30000	22250	16500	12000	7000	3500

Ultra

Lightweight over/under gun offered in 12- or 20-gauge.

NIB	Exc.	V.G.	Good	Fair	Poor
—	6250	4850	2750	1650	1250

KS-5 Single Barrel Trap

Boxlock 12-gauge only trap gun, with 32" or 34" ventilated tapered rib barrel. Case-hardened frame, with satin gray finish. Barrel features adjustable point of impact. Offered with screw-in choke tubes. Weight about 8.6 lbs.

NIB	Exc.	V.G.	Good	Fair	Poor
8000	7500	5900	3650	1250	800

KS-5 Special

Same as above, with adjustable rib and comb.

NIB	Exc.	V.G.	Good	Fair	Poor
8250	7750	6100	3900	1500	1000

K-80 Trap

Boxlock 12-gauge shotgun built to trap dimensions. Offered in many variations. Available in over/under trap, with choice of 30" or 32" ventilated tapered step rib barrels. Single-barrel offered in 32" or 34" tapered step rib lengths. Single-barrels are adjustable for point of impact. Top single-barrel available in 34" length. Trap combos are also offered. All barrels offered with/without choke tubes. Checkered walnut stock offered in Monte Carlo or straight trap dimensions. Trap gun weight about 8.75 lbs. Prices listed for Standard Grade. **NOTE:** Add 70 percent for Bavaria Grade; 100 percent for Danube Grade; 200 percent for Gold Target Grade.

Over/Under Trap

NIB	Exc.	V.G.	Good	Fair	Poor
9800	8000	6000	4200	2500	1000

Unsingle Trap

NIB	Exc.	V.G.	Good	Fair	Poor
11000	9000	7200	5500	3000	1500

Top Single Trap

NIB	Exc.	V.G.	Good	Fair	Poor
11500	10000	8000	6000	3700	1850

Trap Combos

NIB	Exc.	V.G.	Good	Fair	Poor
13000	10700	9600	7400	4300	1900

K-20 Sporting and Field

Compact frame variation of K-80, chambered in 20- or 28-gauge and .410 bore. Barrels are 30" or 32", with five choke tubes and tapered flat rib. Checkered walnut stock, auto ejectors and single-selective trigger. Weight about 7.25 lbs. Available with extra sets of barrels in other two gauges.

NIB	Exc.	V.G.	Good	Fair	Poor
9000	8000	7000	4000	2200	1000

K-80 Sporting Clays

Same frame as trap model, with addition of lightweight alloy model available in 12-gauge only. Barrel lengths: standard weight 28", 30" or 32", with tapered flat rib; lightweight alloy 28" or 30" flat rib barrels. Select European walnut stock, with hand checkering and supplied with #3 Sporting stock, with schnabel forearm. Weight: standard weight 8.25 lbs.; lightweight alloy 7.75 lbs. Prices listed are for Standard Grade. **NOTE:** Add 70 percent for Bavaria Grade; 100 percent for Danube Grade; 200 percent for Gold Target Grade.

NIB	Exc.	V.G.	Good	Fair	Poor
9500	8000	7000	4000	2200	1000

K-80 Skeet

Offered in a number of variations. Standard and Lightweight skeet, with 28" or 30" tapered or parallel ribs; International skeet, with 28" parallel broadway rib; 4-barrel skeet set in 12-, 20-, 28-gauge and .410 bore, with 8mm rib. Stock hand checkered select European walnut, with choice of several skeet dimensions. Values listed are for Standard Grade. **NOTE:**

Add 70 percent for Bavaria Grade; 100 percent for Danube Grade; 200 percent for Gold Target Grade. Optional Engravings available by special order on NIB or Exc. conditions guns: Add $1500 Parcours; $2800 Parcours Special; $1100 Super Scroll; $2900 Gold Super Scroll; $4700 Custom Bavaria over Bavaria Grade price.

Standard Weight Skeet

NIB	Exc.	V.G.	Good	Fair	Poor
7500	6250	4950	3300	2200	1000

Lightweight Skeet

NIB	Exc.	V.G.	Good	Fair	Poor
7500	6250	4950	3300	2200	1000

International Skeet

NIB	Exc.	V.G.	Good	Fair	Poor
7500	6250	4950	3300	2200	1000

4 Barrel Set

NIB	Exc.	V.G.	Good	Fair	Poor
17000	10000	7600	4400	3300	2200

SIDE-BY-SIDE DOUBLES

Essencia Boxlock

High-grade model introduced in 2003. Has round-body receiver, with English-style scroll engraving and gold highlights. Offered in 12-, 16-, 20- and 28-gauge, with 28" or 30" barrels and fixed IC/M chokes. Straight-grip Turkish walnut checkered stock, single (non-selective) or double triggers and automatic ejectors. **NOTE:** Add $1000 for 28-gauge; $1000 for single trigger.

NIB	Exc.	V.G.	Good	Fair	Poor
22000	17500	15000	10000	3000	800

Essencia Sidelock

Also introduced in 2003. Back-action sidelock on three frame sizes, designed for different gauges. Offered in 12-, 16-, 20- and 28-gauge. Barrel lengths 18", 26.5" or 30", with fixed chokes or Briley choke tubes. Receiver is color case-hardened, with gold-inlayed engraving. Straight-/pistol-grip Turkish walnut checkered stock, single (non-selective) or double triggers and automatic ejectors. **NOTE:** Add $1000 for 28-gauge; $1000 for single trigger; $1500 for Briley choke tubes.

NIB	Exc.	V.G.	Good	Fair	Poor
27000	22500	18000	12000	4000	800

KRNKA, KAREL
Vienna, Austria

Karel Krnka was a talented firearms inventor, born in 1858. He began his career in firearms design as a member of the Austro-Hungarian army. He made many improvements to their service rifle design. After he left the military, he took the job of head engineer, with ill-fated and short-lived "Gatling Gun Company". This company ceased operations in 1890. Krnka then went to work for the patent office and remained there for a few years. In 1898, he became foreman of Roth Cartridge Company and worked with Roth on firearm designs until the death of Roth in 1909. After this, he became associated with Hertenberger Cartridge Company; and finally in 1922 he moved to Czechoslovakia, where he became a firearms designer for the firm of C.Z. He remained at this post until his death in 1926. He recorded his first firearm patent in 1888 for a mechanical repeater with a ring trigger. His best known innovations are the internal butt magazine, that is loaded by means of a stripper clip and rotating locked bolt, with internal firing pin. These designs were never actually turned into a mass-marketed pistol, but were major contributions in the development of a practical semi-automatic pistol design.

Model 1892

NIB	Exc.	V.G.	Good	Fair	Poor
—	—	8200	5500	2200	1050

KSN INDUSTRIES
Israel

Golan

Semi-automatic pistol introduced in 1996. Chambered for 9mm or .40 S&W cartridge. Double-action trigger, with ambidextrous controls. Barrel length 3.9". Magazine capacity: 10 rounds in U.S.; rest of the world 15 rounds 9mm, 11 rounds .40 S&W. Weight 29 oz.

NIB	Exc.	V.G.	Good	Fair	Poor
650	525	400	325	200	100

Kareen MK II

Single-action semi-automatic pistol, chambered for 9mm cartridge. Barrel length 4.5". Ambidextrous safety and rubber grips. Steel slide and frame. Weight about 34 oz.

NIB	Exc.	V.G.	Good	Fair	Poor
500	395	250	200	150	100

Kareen MK II—Compact

Same as above, with 3.9" barrel. Weight about 32 oz.

NIB	Exc.	V.G.	Good	Fair	Poor
575	425	325	250	200	150

GAL

Same as full size Kareen. Chambered for .45 ACP cartridge.

NIB	Exc.	V.G.	Good	Fair	Poor
575	425	325	250	200	150

KUFAHL, G. L.
Sommerda, Germany

Kufahl Needle-Fire Revolver

Designed and patented in Britain in 1852 by G.L. Kufahl, who tried unsuccessfully to interest a British company in producing it. He then went to the firm of Rheinmettal Dreyse, where a needle-fire gun was produced in 1838. This company manufactured his design. This revolver was chambered for a unique, totally consumed .30-caliber "cartridge". A lead projectile had the ignition percussion cap affixed to its base, with propellant powder in rear. Firing pin had to be long enough to penetrate the powder charge and hit the percussion cap. This does not sound efficient, but realize that these were the days before cartridges. This revolver has a 3.2" barrel and an unfluted cylinder that holds six shots. It is not bored all the way through, but is loaded from the front. Finish is blued, with a modicum of simple engraving and checkered wood grips that protrude all the way over the trigger. Markings are "Fv.V. Dreyse Sommerda".

NIB	Exc.	V.G.	Good	Fair	Poor
—	—	2950	1600	650	400

KYNOCH GUN FACTORY
Birmingham, England

Established by George Kynoch in approximately 1886. Company ceased operation in 1890.

Early Double Trigger Revolver

.45-caliber double trigger revolver, with 6" barrel, 6-shot cylinder and enclosed hammer. Blued, with walnut grips. Manufactured in 1885.

NIB	Exc.	V.G.	Good	Fair	Poor
—	—	1600	950	575	350

Late Double Trigger Revolver

Similar to above in .32-, .38- or .45-caliber. Cocking trigger enclosed within trigger guard. Approximately 600 made between 1890 and 1896.

NIB	Exc.	V.G.	Good	Fair	Poor
—	—	2100	1575	900	575

L

LAGRESE
Paris, France

Lagrese Revolver

Large ornate revolver chambered for .43 rimfire cartridge. Has 6.25" barrel, 6-shot fluted cylinder, no top strap, frame as well as grip straps are cast in one piece, with barrel screwed into frame. It is loaded through a gate and has double-action lock work. Outstanding feature about this well-made revolver is its extremely ornate appearance. There are more sweeps and curves than could be imagined. In general outline somewhat resembles the leMat, though with a single barrel. Engraved and blued, with well-figured curved walnut grips. Marked "Lagrese Bte a Paris". Manufactured in late 1860s.

NIB	Exc.	V.G.	Good	Fair	Poor
—	—	3500	2750	1300	875

LAHTI
Finland
See—Husqvarna

Lahti

Commercial version of Finnish L-35 9mm pistol. Pistols have barrel and trigger guard design of L-35, but barrel extension of Swedish M40. Produced in late 1950s.

Courtesy J.B. Wood

NIB	Exc.	V.G.	Good	Fair	Poor
—	1250	1000	800	550	300

LAKELANDER
Gulfport, Mississippi

Model 389 Premium

Bolt-action rifle chambered for .270 Win., .308 Win. and .30-06 calibers. Fitted with 22" lightweight barrel. Stock oil-finished walnut, with diamond checkering. Rosewood fore-end cap, black recoil pad and Monte Carlo buttstock. Weight about 7.6 lbs. Introduced in 1997.

NIB	Exc.	V.G.	Good	Fair	Poor
1750	1350	950	700	375	200

Model 389 Classic

Similar to 389 Premium above. Offered with traditional checkering and stock (less fancy walnut stock). Weight about 7.3 lbs. Introduced in 1997.

NIB	Exc.	V.G.	Good	Fair	Poor
1725	1325	925	675	350	150

Model 389 Match-Maker

Bolt-action chambered for .308 cartridge. Fitted with 21.7" barrel. Stock is target style, with adjustable chin support with benchrest-style buttpad. Weight about 8.4 lbs. Introduced in 1997. **NOTE:** Add $50 for Magnum calibers.

NIB	Exc.	V.G.	Good	Fair	Poor
2250	1850	1350	850	575	250

LAMB, H. C. & CO.
Jamestown, North Carolina

Muzzleloading Rifle

Chambered for .58-caliber and utilizes percussion ignition system. Has 33" barrel and full-length oak stock held on by two barrel bands. Ramrod mounted under barrel made of iron. All other trim is brass. A bayonet lug at muzzle. Rifle was made for Confederacy and workmanship was crude, as it was on most CSA weapons. Stock marked "H.C.Lamb & Co., N.C." Supposedly 10,000 rifles ordered, but approximately 250 manufactured between 1861 and 1863. Rarity of guns of Confederacy gives them a great deal of collector appeal.

Courtesy Milwaukee Public Museum, Milwaukee, Wisconsin

NIB	Exc.	V.G.	Good	Fair	Poor
—	—	35000	15000	2750	500

LAMES
Chiavari, Italy

Skeet or Trap Grade

Over/under shotgun chambered for 12-gauge, with 26" skeet-and-skeet barrels or 30" or 32" full-choked barrels. Has competition-style wide ventilated rib and automatic ejectors. Trigger single-selective and finish blued. Trap gun has Monte Carlo stock of checkered walnut. Both models feature recoil pads.

NIB	Exc.	V.G.	Good	Fair	Poor
—	700	575	475	375	200

California Trap Grade

Over/under similar to standard trap model, with separated barrels. All other features the same.

NIB	Exc.	V.G.	Good	Fair	Poor
—	775	650	575	475	225

Field Grade

Similar in design to standard trap model, with 3" chambers and barrel lengths of 26", 28" or 30". Field dimensioned stock. Features various choke combinations. Also available with separated barrels of California Trap for an additional 20 percent cost.

NIB	Exc.	V.G.	Good	Fair	Poor
—	475	450	350	250	150

LANBER ARMAS S.A.
Vizcaya, Spain

Model 2072 Slug

Fixed choke double-barrel slug gun, with 3" chambers and 20" barrel. Fiber-optic rifle sights. Weight about 6 lbs. Hard-to-find gun.

NIB	Exc.	V.G.	Good	Fair	Poor
900	800	650	475	300	200

Model 844 ST

12-gauge over/under shotgun, with 26" or 28" ventilated rib barrels. Chokes vary. Features single-selective trigger, extractors and engraved receiver, with blued finish and walnut stock. Manufactured until 1986.

NIB	Exc.	V.G.	Good	Fair	Poor
—	425	350	300	250	175

Model 844 MST

Similar to Model 844 ST except chambered for 3" Magnum. Has 30" Full and Modified choked barrels.

NIB	Exc.	V.G.	Good	Fair	Poor
—	525	450	300	250	175

Model 844 EST

Similar to others, but features automatic ejectors.

NIB	Exc.	V.G.	Good	Fair	Poor
—	575	425	350	300	200

Model 844 EST CHR

Has automatic ejectors and double triggers. All other features same as EST.

NIB	Exc.	V.G.	Good	Fair	Poor
—	550	400	325	275	175

Model 2004 LCH

Over/under chambered for 12-gauge. Features 28" ventilated rib barrels, with screw-in choke tubes. Single-selective trigger, automatic ejectors. Engraved boxlock action that is matte finished, with hand-checkered walnut stock. Discontinued in 1986.

NIB	Exc.	V.G.	Good	Fair	Poor
—	775	650	550	475	375

Model 2008 LCH and Model 2009 LCH

Trap and skeet versions of series. Basic differences in barrel lengths and stock dimensions.

Model 2008 LCH

NIB	Exc.	V.G.	Good	Fair	Poor
—	900	750	650	575	475

Model 2067

20-gauge over/under, with 3" chambers. Has 28" barrels, auto ejectors and oil-finished walnut stock. Weight about 6.6 lbs.

NIB	Exc.	V.G.	Good	Fair	Poor
775	650	550	450	375	200

Model 2077 Hunter Light

A 2.75" 12-gauge, with 26" barrels and lightweight alloy receiver. Weight about 6.2 lbs.

NIB	Exc.	V.G.	Good	Fair	Poor
850	725	575	475	400	200

Model 2087 Hunter

12-gauge comes with 3" chambers, auto ejectors, oil-finished walnut stock and 28" or 30" barrel. Weight about 7 lbs.

NIB	Exc.	V.G.	Good	Fair	Poor
775	650	550	450	375	200

Model 2097 Sporting

Sporting clays model in 12-gauge, with 3" chambers and 28" or 30" barrels. Weight about 7.7 lbs. **NOTE:** Add $50 for Sporting LUX.

NIB	Exc.	V.G.	Good	Fair	Poor
850	725	575	475	400	200

Model 2088 Rival I

Sporting clays model is 2.75" 12-gauge, with 28" barrels and case-hardened receiver. Weight about 7.6 lbs.

NIB	Exc.	V.G.	Good	Fair	Poor
1600	1300	850	600	400	200

Model 2089 Rival II

This 2.75" 12-gauge sporting clays has 30" barrels, one fixed and other threaded for choke tubes. Blued receiver. Weight about 7.9 lbs.

NIB	Exc.	V.G.	Good	Fair	Poor
1600	1300	850	600	400	200

Model 2070 Becada

This 3" 12-gauge developed for woodcock hunting. Features one fixed choke barrel; one barrel threaded for chokes. Barrel length 23"; weight about 6 lbs.

NIB	Exc.	V.G.	Good	Fair	Poor
850	725	575	475	400	200

Model 2531 Victoria I

12-gauge semi-automatic has 3" chamber and 28" barrel, with internal choke tube system. Stock oil-finished walnut. Receiver blued. Weight about 6.8 lbs.

NIB	Exc.	V.G.	Good	Fair	Poor
600	500	400	300	200	100

Model 2532 Victoria II

Similar to above. Available with 26" or 28" barrel.

NIB	Exc.	V.G.	Good	Fair	Poor
625	525	425	325	225	100

Model 2532 Victoria II EXT

Similar to above, with 24.5" barrel. External choke tube system.

NIB	Exc.	V.G.	Good	Fair	Poor
625	525	425	325	225	100

Model 2534

Lighter version of 2532. Weight about 6.4 lbs., with 26" barrel.

NIB	Exc.	V.G.	Good	Fair	Poor
625	525	425	325	225	100

Model 2533 Victoria LUX

Semi-automatic 3" 12-gauge. Features brushed silver finish scrollwork and gold mallard on receiver. Barrel 26" or 28". Weight about 6.8 lbs.

NIB	Exc.	V.G.	Good	Fair	Poor
650	550	450	350	250	100

Model 2533 Victoria LUX EXT

As above, with 24.5" barrel. External choke tube system.

NIB	Exc.	V.G.	Good	Fair	Poor
650	550	450	350	250	100

Model 2535 Victoria Slug

Dedicated slug gun has fiber-optic rifle sights atop 24" fixed cylinder barrel.

NIB	Exc.	V.G.	Good	Fair	Poor
650	550	450	350	250	100

LANCASTER, CHARLES
London, England

4-Barreled Pistol

Unique pistol for several reasons. Chambered for .476 rimfire cartridge and four 6.25" barrels. Bore has slightly twisted oval pattern that imparts a spin to bullet. Barrels are hinged at bottom and break downward for loading. Double-action type lockwork, with long difficult trigger pull. Pistol well made and caliber suitably heavy to insure stopping power. Primary goal was military; successful seeing action in Sudan campaigns of 1882 and 1885. This powerful weapon was also popular with big game hunters as a backup sidearm. Finish blued, with checkered walnut grips. Marked "Charles Lancaster (Patent) 151 New Bond St. London". Introduced in 1881. There are smaller-caliber versions of this pistol, with shorter barrels. They are not as well known as large-caliber version and values would be similar as their rarity would be balanced by desirability of large bore models.

NIB	Exc.	V.G.	Good	Fair	Poor
—	—	8000	5750	2500	1500

2-Barreled Pistol

Similar to 4 barreled version, with only two superposed barrels. Chambered for a variety of calibers from .320 to .577. Also chambered for 20-gauge and .410 bore. Advantage to 2 barreled pistol it is lighter and better balanced. The 2 barrel is less common than 4 barrel version.

Courtesy James Rankin

NIB	Exc.	V.G.	Good	Fair	Poor
—	—	6000	3750	1750	1000

4-Barreled Shotgun

Also produced a shotgun in 4 barrel configuration. Chambered for 12- or 16-gauge, with 28" barrels. Gun is as one would imagine, quite heavy and poorly balanced; not a great success.

NIB	Exc.	V.G.	Good	Fair	Poor
—	—	6250	4000	2000	1000

Bolt-Action Rifle

High-grade sporting rifle chambered for various different calibers. Barrel 24" in length; finish blued with classic-styled hand-checkered walnut stock. Discontinued in 1936.

NIB	Exc.	V.G.	Good	Fair	Poor
—	3500	1900	1250	800	600

LANG, J.
London, England

Percussion Pistol

Chambered for .60-caliber percussion. Single-barreled muzzle-loading pistol, with 3.25" barrel. Essentially a defensive weapon that was well made. Damascus barrels and ornate engraved hammer and frame.

NIB	Exc.	V.G.	Good	Fair	Poor
—	—	4510	3000	1100	600

Gas Seal Revolver

Chambered for .42-caliber percussion and 4.75" barrel. Unfluted cylinder holds 6 shots and spring-loaded to be forced into barrel when cocked, in order to obtain "Gas Seal" feature desired. Revolver was well made and finished. Lightly engraved, with case colored cylinder, blued barrel and frame. Grips are finely checkered walnut. Markings are "J.Lang 22 Cockspur St. London". This type of firearm was forerunner of later designs such as Russian Nagant. Manufactured in 1850s.

NIB	Exc.	V.G.	Good	Fair	Poor
—	—	3000	1500	1000	550

LANGENHAN, FRIEDRICH
Zella Mehlis, Germany

F.L. Selbstlader is not a manufacturer, but the German designation for self-loader used on pistols made by Friedrich Langenhan.

Army Model

Blowback-operated semi-automatic chambered for 7.65mm Auto Pistol cartridge. Has 4" barrel and detachable magazine that holds 8 rounds. Weight about 24 oz. Made with separate breech-block that is held into slide by a screw. This feature doomed pistol to eventual failure, when this screw became worn it could loosen when firing and allow breech-block to pivot upwards—and slide would then be propelled rearward and into the face of shooter. Produced with wood grips.

Courtesy James Rankin

NIB	Exc.	V.G.	Good	Fair	Poor
—	375	300	250	175	100

Open Model

Semi-automatic similar to Army Model, with some minor variations. Open window in frame. Checkered hard rubber grips, with "FL" logo on each side.

Courtesy James Rankin

NIB	Exc.	V.G.	Good	Fair	Poor
—	400	325	275	200	100

Closed Model

Similar to Open Model, with closed frame and other minor variations.

Courtesy James Rankin

NIB	Exc.	V.G.	Good	Fair	Poor
—	400	325	275	200	100

Model 2

Blowback-operated semi-automatic chambered for 6.35mm cartridge. Has 3" barrel and 8-round detachable magazine. Weight about 18 oz.

Fires by means of concealed hammer. Breech-block separate from rest of slide and held in place by a heavy crossbolt. Finish blued. Grips are molded checkered black plastic, with monogram "F.L." at top. Slide marked "Langenhan 6.35". Manufactured between 1921 and 1936.

Courtesy James Rankin

NIB	Exc.	V.G.	Good	Fair	Poor
—	375	300	250	200	100

Model 3

Similar to Model 2 except somewhat smaller. Barrel 2.25" in length. Butt only large enough to house a 5-round detachable magazine. Weight about 17 oz. Markings the same with addition of "Model 111" on slide. Manufactured until 1936.

NIB	Exc.	V.G.	Good	Fair	Poor
—	325	275	250	200	150

LAR MFG. CO.
West Jordan, Utah

Grizzly Mark I

.357 Magnum, .45 ACP, 10mm or .45 Win. Magnum semi-automatic pistol, with 5.4", 6.5", 8" or 10" barrel. Millett sights, ambidextrous safety and 7-shot magazine. Parkerized, blued or hard-chrome plated, with rubber grips. Available with cartridge conversion units, telescope mounts or compensator. Weight about 48 oz. Introduced in 1984.

NIB	Exc.	V.G.	Good	Fair	Poor
1400	150	950	700	400	200

Grizzly Mark II

As above, with fixed sights. Without ambidextrous safety. Manufactured in 1986.

NIB	Exc.	V.G.	Good	Fair	Poor
—	1300	1050	775	475	300

Grizzly Mark IV

Similar to Mark I. Chambered for .44 Magnum cartridge. Barrel lengths 5.4" or 6.5". Choice of blue or Parkerized finish.

NIB	Exc.	V.G.	Good	Fair	Poor
1500	1100	775	500	400	200

Grizzly Mark V

Same as above, but chambered for .50 AE cartridge. Empty weight 56 oz. **NOTE:** Add $200 for nickel finish.

NIB	Exc.	V.G.	Good	Fair	Poor
1950	1350	1000	650	425	200

Grizzly State Pistol

Limited edition of 50 Grizzly pistols. Serial numbers match order in which each state was admitted into the union. Each pistol features state outline, state seal and name of state engraved in gold. Supplied with cherrywood fitted case, with glass top. Chambered for .45 Win. Magnum cartridge.

NIB	Exc.	V.G.	Good	Fair	Poor
3000	—	—	—	—	—

Grizzly 50 Big Boar

Single-shot breech loading rifle chambered for .50-caliber BMG cartridge. Barrel 36" in length. Weight about 30 lbs. **NOTE:** Add $100 for Parkerized finish; $250 for nickel frame; $350 for full nickel finish.

NIB	Exc.	V.G.	Good	Fair	Poor
2350	2000	1550	1100	550	300

LARUE TACTICAL
Leander, Texas

OBR (Optimized Battle Rifle)

AR-style series available in 5.56 NATO (.223 Rem.) or 7.62 NATO (.308 Win.). In several variations and barrel lengths. Hand guard does not touch barrel at any point, resulting in a weapon that remains cool, even after high rates of fire. There is a continuous upper rail for day/night accessories, plus three 3" Picatinny rail sections to be attached anywhere on the hand guard. A two-point adjustable gas selector allows optimum function between suppressed and unsuppressed operation. Barrel lengths available are 12" (Class III model for LE/Military), 16.1", 18" and 20". Values shown are for 5.56 NATO models.

NIB	Exc.	V.G.	Good	Fair	Poor
1900	1600	1350	975	550	250

OBR (Optimized Battle Rifle) 7.62 NATO/.308 Win.

Same basic features as 5.56 version, with heavier frame for larger calibers. Barrel lengths 16", 18" or 20". Has proprietary XTRAXTN chamber for enhanced extraction, with wide range of loads and temperatures.

NIB	Exc.	V.G.	Good	Fair	Poor
2800	2400	1900	1400	750	300

LASALLE
France

Slide-Action Shotgun

Chambered for 12- or 20-gauge. Offered with 26", 28" or 30" barrel, with Improved-Cylinder, Modified or Full chokes. Receiver alloy anodized blue and ventilated rib barrel blued. Stock checkered walnut.

NIB	Exc.	V.G.	Good	Fair	Poor
—	275	225	200	150	100

Semi-Automatic Shotgun

Gas-operated semi-automatic shotgun chambered for 12-gauge only. Same barrel length and choke combinations as above. Receiver alloy and stock checkered walnut.

NIB	Exc.	V.G.	Good	Fair	Poor
—	325	250	200	175	100

LASERAIM ARMS
Little Rock, Arkansas

Series I

Offered in 10mm or .45 ACP. Single-action semi-automatic pistol. Fitted with 6" barrel with compensator. Adjustable rear sight. Stainless steel frame and barrel, with matte black Teflon finish. Introduced in 1993. Magazine capacity: 10mm 8-rounds; .45 ACP 7-rounds. Weight about 46 oz.

NIB	Exc.	V.G.	Good	Fair	Poor
650	550	400	300	200	100

Series II

Similar to Series I. Has no compensator. Fitted with 5" barrel. Stainless steel finish. Compact version has 3.375" barrel. Introduced in 1993. Weight: 43 oz. 5" barrel; 37 oz. compact version.

NIB	Exc.	V.G.	Good	Fair	Poor
625	525	375	275	175	100

Series III

Similar to Series II except offered with 5" barrel only. Dual port compensator. Introduced in 1994. Weight about 43 oz.

NIB	Exc.	V.G.	Good	Fair	Poor
650	550	400	300	200	100

LAURONA
Eibar, Spain

Company has manufactured quality shotguns in Spain since 1941, but there has not been a U.S. importer for many years. Last importer was Galaxy Imports of Victoria, Texas, which brought several models of over/under and side-by-side shotguns into the country from about 1967 to early 1990s. One of the unique features of standard Laurona over/under series was a double trigger system, with each trigger acting as a non-selective single trigger. One trigger fired bottom barrel first, then top barrel; other trigger fired top barrel first then bottom barrel. We thank Thomas Barker of Galaxy Imports for information and specifications in these listings.

Model 67

First over/under Laurona chambered for 12-gauge only. Double triggers and 28" ventilated rib barrels, with extractors. Boxlock action. Barrels are blued and stock checkered walnut in 20 lpi skip line checkering.

NIB	Exc.	V.G.	Good	Fair	Poor
—	400	250	150	75	50

Model 71

Similar to Model 67, with minor cosmetic changes and improvements to facilitate ease of manufacturing. Receiver bright chrome, with roll engraving depicting dogs on right side and birds on left. Imported and sold by Sears & Roebuck about 1973-1974. Earlier models had traditional solid center ribbed blued barrels; later models black chrome finished solid ribbed barrels.

NIB	Exc.	V.G.	Good	Fair	Poor
—	450	300	200	100	75

MODEL 82

Similar to Model 71, with auto-ejectors. Chambered for 12-gauge only. All barrels separated without center rib. Black chrome finish and hard chrome bores, with long forcing cones in chambers. Firing pins changed to traditional round type. Many internal parts improved for reliability. Checkering

changed from skip diamond to standard 20 lpi. In most respects 82 Models are representative of present-day Laurona over/under shotguns and will share most internal parts. **NOTE:** Super Models listed have nickel-finish receivers featuring delicate fine scroll engraving, with black chrome relief. All barrels have very durable rust-resistant black chrome finish.

Model 82 Game

Barrels are 28" with 2.75" or 3" chambers, long forcing cones, hard chrome bores, 5mm rib and chokes. Finish on barrels is black chrome, with nickel receiver with Louis XVI style engraving. Tulip fore-end, field-style stock, with plastic buttplate. Weight about 7 lbs.

NIB	Exc.	V.G.	Good	Fair	Poor
—	550	400	250	125	100

Model 82 Super Game

Similar to Model 82 Game except more elaborate and very delicate engraving

NIB	Exc.	V.G.	Good	Fair	Poor
—	600	500	300	125	100

Model 82 Trap Combi

Similar to Model 82 Game except for 28" or 29" barrels. Rib is 8mm. Trap stock fitted with rubber recoil pad. Weight about 7.4 lbs.

NIB	Exc.	V.G.	Good	Fair	Poor
—	700	500	350	300	200

Model 82 Trap Competition

Similar to Model 82 Trap Combi except for 13mm aluminum rib, with long white sight. Engraving consists of motifs on sides of receiver. Beavertail fluted fore-end and Monte Carlo Trap stock, with black rubber special Trap recoil pad. Weight about 8 lbs.

NIB	Exc.	V.G.	Good	Fair	Poor
—	700	500	300	250	200

Model 82 Super Trap (U only)

Similar to Model 82 Trap Competition except for special trap Pachmayr recoil pad, with imitation leather face. Engraving very delicate fine scroll. Weight 7 lbs. 12 oz.

NIB	Exc.	V.G.	Good	Fair	Poor
—	650	500	350	300	250

Model 82 Super Skeet

Similar to Model 82 Super Trap except fitted with 28" barrels, choked skeet with field-style buttstock and plastic buttplate. Weight about 7 lbs.

NIB	Exc.	V.G.	Good	Fair	Poor
—	650	500	300	250	200

Model 82 Pigeon Competition

Similar to Model 82 Trap Competition except fitted with 28" barrels. Recoil pad is special competition-style Pachmayr, with imitation leather face. Weight about 7 lbs. 13 oz.

NIB	Exc.	V.G.	Good	Fair	Poor
—	650	500	350	300	250

Model 82 Super Pigeon

Similar to Model 82 Super Trap except fitted with 28" barrels. Weight about 7 lbs. 9 oz.

NIB	Exc.	V.G.	Good	Fair	Poor
—	675	575	450	300	250

MODEL 83/84/85

NOTE: Super Game models listed were available with an extra set of 20-gauge multi-choke barrels in 26" or 28". Add $400 to Exc. value for these barrels. Models with cast-on stocks for left-hand shooters add $50 to Exc. value.

Model 84S Super Game

Similar to Model 82 Super Game except for new single-selective trigger which is designated by "S" in model number. Chambered for 12-gauge 3" Magnum, with 28" barrels and 8mm rib. Weight about 7 lbs.

NIB	Exc.	V.G.	Good	Fair	Poor
—	500	400	350	200	100

Model 83MG Super Game

Similar to Model 82 Super Game except this model was the advent of Laurona's new multi-choke. **CAUTION!** Laurona multi-choke is not compatible with any other brand of screw-in chokes because of black chrome plating on metric threads. Do not attempt to interchange with other guns. Barrel for this model in 12-gauge are 28" in length; 20-gauge 26" or 28". Both are chambered for 3" shell. Rib is 8mm. Weight about 7 lbs.

NIB	Exc.	V.G.	Good	Fair	Poor
—	700	450	350	200	100

Model 85MS Super Game

Similar to Model 83MG Super Game except for single-selective trigger. Chambered for 12- or 20-gauge 3" Magnum. Weight about 7 lbs.

NIB	Exc.	V.G.	Good	Fair	Poor
—	750	650	450	250	200

Model 84S Super Trap

Single-selective trigger with 29" barrels. Chambered for 2.75" shells, with long forcing cones. Aluminum rib is 13mm wide. Auto ejectors. Receiver nickel plated, with fine scroll engraving and black chrome relief. Beavertail forearm and choice of Monte Carlo or standard Trap stock. Weight about 7 lbs. 12 oz.

NIB	Exc.	V.G.	Good	Fair	Poor
—	1000	750	550	350	250

Model 85MS Super Trap

Similar to Model 82S Super Trap except multi-choke in bottom barrel with fixed choke on top barrel. Weight about 7 lbs. 12 oz.

NIB	Exc.	V.G.	Good	Fair	Poor
—	1100	900	700	500	300

Model 85MS Super Pigeon

Similar to Model 85MS Super Trap except with 28" barrels, fixed IM choke on top barrel and multi-choke on bottom barrel. Intended for live bird competition. Weight about 7 lbs. 4 oz.

NIB	Exc.	V.G.	Good	Fair	Poor
—	1100	900	800	600	300

Model 85MS Special Sporting

Similar to Model 85MS Super Pigeon except for field-style buttstock, with plastic buttplate. Intended for upland game. Weight about 7 lbs. 4 oz.

NIB	Exc.	V.G.	Good	Fair	Poor
—	1100	900	800	600	300

Model 84S Super Skeet

Similar to Model 85MS Special Sporting except choked skeet and skeet. Weight about 7 lbs.

NIB	Exc.	V.G.	Good	Fair	Poor
—	950	900	800	600	300

OVER/UNDER MODELS SILHOUETTE 300

Guns are basically same as Super series above with these exceptions: Readily identified by white and black chrome stripped receiver, with model engraved on side of receiver. Barrels are multi-choked on both bores and have 11mm steel ribs. **NOTE:** Two types of chokes were used. Some guns came with knurl head-type as in Super models and others were made with flush invector style. Later option for ease of changing chokes is knurl long choke, which is a flush-type with a knurl head added. Both later type chokes, flush and knurl long-type, can be used in early multi-choke models, with some extension showing.

Silhouette 300 Trap

Has barrels 29" with 2.75" chambers. Long forcing cones, with hard chrome bores and 11mm rib. Beavertail forearm and straight comb trap stock fitted with ventilated black rubber recoil pad are standard. Weight about 8 lbs.

NIB	Exc.	V.G.	Good	Fair	Poor
—	1100	800	500	200	100

Silhouette 300 Sporting Clays

Similar to Model 300 Trap except with 28" barrels. Some guns came with 3" chambers. Buttstock is field style, with plastic buttplate or hard rubber sporting clay pad. Weight about 8 lbs.

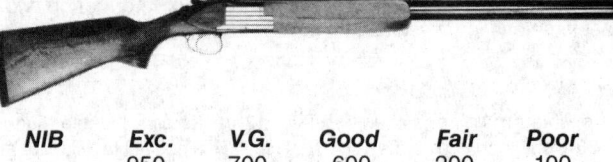

NIB	Exc.	V.G.	Good	Fair	Poor
—	950	700	600	200	100

Silhouette 300 Ultra Magnum

Similar to Model 300 Sporting Clays except with 3.5" chamber in 12-gauge for waterfowl hunting. Weight about 7 lbs. 8 oz.

NIB	Exc.	V.G.	Good	Fair	Poor
—	1000	800	500	275	150

SIDE-BY-SIDE SHOTGUNS

Models with "X" after model number were made after 1975 and finished with non-rusting black chrome on barrels and action, with hard chrome bores. Made in 12-, 16- and 20-gauge. Smaller gauges made on special order. Side-by-side shotguns were discontinued by Laurona after 1978 to concentrate on the over/under market.

Model 11

Boxlock action, with triple Greener-type round crossbolt. Independent firing pins bushed into face of the action. Barrels of "Bellota" steel. Made in 12-, 16- and 20-gauge.

NIB	Exc.	V.G.	Good	Fair	Poor
—	400	350	300	200	150

Model 13

Similar to Model 11, with Purdey-type bolting system. Extractor of double radius.

NIB	Exc.	V.G.	Good	Fair	Poor
—	400	350	300	200	150

Model 13X

Barrels and action finished in black chrome, with hard chrome bores.

NIB	Exc.	V.G.	Good	Fair	Poor
—	500	400	300	250	200

Model 13E

Similar to Model 13, with automatic ejectors.

NIB	Exc.	V.G.	Good	Fair	Poor
—	500	400	300	250	200

Model 13XE

Similar to Model 13E except black chrome finish and hard chrome bores.

NIB	Exc.	V.G.	Good	Fair	Poor
—	600	500	400	350	300

Model 15 Economic Pluma

Similar to Model 13 except first model has hard chrome bores.

NIB	Exc.	V.G.	Good	Fair	Poor
—	450	400	300	250	200

Model 15X

Similar to Model 15 except black chrome finish and hard chrome bores.

NIB	Exc.	V.G.	Good	Fair	Poor
—	500	400	300	250	200

Model 15E Economic Pluma

Similar to Model 15, with automatic ejectors.

NIB	Exc.	V.G.	Good	Fair	Poor
—	550	450	350	300	250

Model 15XE

Similar to Model 15E except black chrome finish and hard chrome bores.

NIB	Exc.	V.G.	Good	Fair	Poor
—	600	500	400	350	300

Model 52 Pluma

Boxlock action, with back of action scalloped and artistically engraved in fine English-style scroll. Churchill rib and double radius extractor. Hard chrome bores. Weight about 6 lbs.

NIB	Exc.	V.G.	Good	Fair	Poor
—	750	650	500	400	350

Model 52E Pluma

Similar to Model 52, with automatic ejectors. Weight about 6 lbs. 2 oz.

NIB	Exc.	V.G.	Good	Fair	Poor
—	850	750	600	500	450

SIDE-BY-SIDE SIDELOCKS

Model 103

Blued sidelock, with some light border engraving. Triple Purdey-type bolting system. Extractor of double radius. Barrels of special "Bellota" steel, with hard chrome bores. Made in 12-, 16- and 20-gauge.

NIB	Exc.	V.G.	Good	Fair	Poor
—	900	800	700	500	400

Model 103E

Similar to Model 103, with automatic ejectors.

NIB	Exc.	V.G.	Good	Fair	Poor
—	1000	800	700	600	500

Model 104X

Case colored sidelocks, with Purdey-type bolting system. Extractor with double radius. Fine double safety sidelocks. Gas relief vents. Articulated trigger. Hard chrome bores. Demi-block barrels of special "Bellota" steel. Black chrome barrels. Produced in 12-, 16- and 20-gauge, with smaller bores available on special order.

NIB	Exc.	V.G.	Good	Fair	Poor
—	1200	1000	800	700	600

Model 104XE

Same as Model 104X, with Holland automatic selective ejectors.

NIB	Exc.	V.G.	Good	Fair	Poor
—	1350	1100	900	800	700

Model 105X Feather

Same as Model 104X, with concave rib. Weight in 12-gauge about 6 lbs. 2 oz.

NIB	Exc.	V.G.	Good	Fair	Poor
—	1250	1000	800	700	600

Model 105XE Feather

Same as Model 105X, with Holland automatic selective ejectors.

NIB	Exc.	V.G.	Good	Fair	Poor
—	1400	1250	1000	800	750

Model 502 Feather

Fine sidelock, with Purdey-type bolting system. Very fine double safety sidelocks hand detachable. Gas relief vents. Holland automatic selective ejectors. Articulated trigger. Inside hard chromed Demi-block barrels of special "Bellota" steel. Outside Black Chrome finish. Fine English-style scroll engraving. Marble gray or Laurona Imperial finish. Churchill or concave type rib. Weight 12-gauge about 6.25 lbs. Offered in 12-, 16- and 20-gauge.

NIB	Exc.	V.G.	Good	Fair	Poor
—	2200	1800	1600	1500	1400

Model 801 Deluxe

Same as Model 502 Feather, but engraving is true deluxe Renaissance style. Fully handmade with Imperial finish. First grade walnut stock and forearm.

NIB	Exc.	V.G.	Good	Fair	Poor
—	4400	4000	3750	2750	2250

Model 802 Eagle

Same as Model 801 Deluxe, except highly artistic base relief hand engraving of hunting scenes.

NIB	Exc.	V.G.	Good	Fair	Poor
—	5000	4500	4000	3500	3250

LAW ENFORCEMENT ORDNANCE CORP.
Ridgeway, Pennsylvania

Striker 12

Semi-automatic shotgun designed for self-defense. Chambered for 12-gauge. Has 18.25" cylinder bored barrel. Unique feature about this gun is its 12-round drum magazine. Barrel is shrouded and stock folds. Fixed-stock model also available. Introduced primarily as a law enforcement tool. Original models had 12" barrels and were legal for law enforcement agencies and Class 3 licensed individuals only. Shotgun no longer imported into U.S. Shotgun now classified as a Class III weapon and subject to restrictions of BATFE. Be certain that the particular shotgun is transferable before purchase. If there are any questions contact BATFE before purchase. Striker 12 shotguns in excellent condition may sell for as much as $1500.

LAZZERONI ARMS COMPANY
Tucson, Arizona

Model 2000ST-F

This model, as with all Lazzeroni models, is chambered for company's own proprietary calibers. The 6.17 (.243) Spitfire, 6.53 (.257) Scramjet, 6.71 (.264) Phantom, 7.21 (.284) Tomahawk, 7.82 (.308) Patriot and 8.59 (.338) Galaxy. Fitted with 27" match grade barrel, with fully adjustable trigger and removable muzzle-brake. Conventional fiberglass stock.

NIB	Exc.	V.G.	Good	Fair	Poor
3700	3000	2200	1500	800	300

Model 2000ST-W

As above, fitted with black wood laminate stock. No longer offered.

NIB	Exc.	V.G.	Good	Fair	Poor
4800	3900	2700	1750	1000	350

Model 2000ST-FW

As above, fitted with conventional fiberglass stock and additional black wood laminate stock. No longer offered.

NIB	Exc.	V.G.	Good	Fair	Poor
5300	4250	3000	2000	1200	500

Model 2000ST-28

Model is 28" barrel variation of Model 2000 ST. Chambered for 7.82 Warbird cartridge. Introduced in 1999.

NIB	Exc.	V.G.	Good	Fair	Poor
5300	4250	3000	2000	1200	500

Model 2000SLR

Model has 28" extra-heavy fluted barrel, with conventional fiberglass stock. Chambered for 6.53 Scramjet, 7.21 Firehawk and 7.82 Warbird.

NIB	Exc.	V.G.	Good	Fair	Poor
3900	3100	2300	1600	900	400

Model 2000SP-F

Fitted with 23" match grade barrel and Lazzeroni thumbhole fiberglass stock. Chambered for all Lazzeroni calibers.

NIB	Exc.	V.G.	Good	Fair	Poor
3700	3000	2200	1500	800	300

Model 2000SP-W

Same as above, with black wood laminate thumbhole stock. No longer offered.

NIB	Exc.	V.G.	Good	Fair	Poor
4800	3900	2700	1750	1000	350

Model 2000SP-FW

Same as above, but supplied with two stocks: thumbhole fiberglass and black wood laminate. No longer offered.

NIB	Exc.	V.G.	Good	Fair	Poor
5300	4250	3000	2000	1200	500

Model 2000SA

Designed as a lightweight mountain rifle. Chambered for .308, .284 or .338 propriety calibers. Barrel length 24" and fluted except for .338-caliber. Offered in both right-/left-hand models. Stock has Monte Carlo cheekpiece. Weight about 6.8 lbs.

NIB	Exc.	V.G.	Good	Fair	Poor
4000	3100	2300	1600	900	400

Model 2000DG

Offered in Saturn and Meteor calibers only. Fitted with 24" barrel. Fibergrain stock finish, removable muzzle-brake and threaded muzzle protector are standard. Weight about 10 lbs.

NIB	Exc.	V.G.	Good	Fair	Poor
4400	3500	2700	1850	1050	450

Model 700ST

Built around a modified Remington 700 action. Fitted with 26" barrel. Chambered for all Lazzeroni long-action calibers except Saturn and Meteor. Weight about 8 lbs. Synthetic stock.

NIB	Exc.	V.G.	Good	Fair	Poor
2400	1850	1550	1200	900	200

Swarovski P.H. 3-12x50 Rifle

NIB	Exc.	V.G.	Good	Fair	Poor
1400	1150	925	600	400	150

Savage 16 LZ

Introduced in 2001. Features 24" stainless steel barrel, synthetic stock. Chambered for 7.82 Patriot and 7.21 Tomahawk cartridges. Weight about 6.8 lbs. Values shown include Cabela's 4.5-14x42mm scope.

NIB	Exc.	V.G.	Good	Fair	Poor
900	775	500	375	200	100

Sako TRG-S

Fitted with 26" stainless steel barrel and synthetic stock. Chambered for 7.82 Warbird and 7.21 Firebird cartridges. Weight about 7.9 lbs. Values shown include Burris 6-14x50mm mil-dot scope.

NIB	Exc.	V.G.	Good	Fair	Poor
1400	1150	925	600	400	150

Model 2005 Global Hunter

Features include precision CNC-machined 17R stainless steel receiver; stainless steel match-grade button-barrel; Jewel competition trigger; titanium firing pin; slim line graphite/composite stock; precision-machined aluminum-alloy floorplate/trigger guard assembly; Vais muzzle-brake; and Limbsaver recoil pad. Base price listed.

NIB	Exc.	V.G.	Good	Fair	Poor
6900	5900	4700	3250	1500	500

LE FORGERON
Liege, Belgium

Model 6020 Double Rifle

Boxlock-actioned side-by-side. Chambered for 9.3x74R cartridge. Has

25" barrels, with double triggers and automatic ejectors. Finish blued and pistol-grip stock is checkered walnut.

NIB	Exc.	V.G.	Good	Fair	Poor
—	6100	4950	4400	3300	1250

Model 6040

Simply Model 6020, with false sideplates. All other specifications the same.

NIB	Exc.	V.G.	Good	Fair	Poor
—	6900	5750	4950	3850	1500

Model 6030

Double rifle that has true sidelock action and engraved. Deluxe French walnut stock.

NIB	Exc.	V.G.	Good	Fair	Poor
—	11000	8800	8000	6100	2000

Boxlock Shotgun

Side-by-side double-barreled shotgun chambered for 20- or 28-gauge. Barrel lengths optional as are choke combinations. Has single-selective trigger and automatic ejectors. Engraved and blued, with deluxe French walnut stock. **NOTE:** Add 20 percent for false sideplates.

NIB	Exc.	V.G.	Good	Fair	Poor
—	5500	4400	3600	2500	1000

Sidelock Shotgun

Similar specifications to boxlock, except it has true sidelock action. Generally more deluxe in materials and workmanship.

NIB	Exc.	V.G.	Good	Fair	Poor
—	13000	12000	9350	7250	2500

LE FRANCAIS
Francais D'Armes et Cycles de St. Etienne
St. Etienne, France
See—Manufrance

Gaulois

8mm palm pistol designed by Brun-Latrige. Manufactured by Le Francais. Furnished with 5-round magazine.

Courtesy James Rankin

NIB	Exc.	V.G.	Good	Fair	Poor
—	—	950	550	400	300

Le Francais Model 28 (Type Armee)

Unique pistol chambered for 9mm Browning cartridge. A large pistol, with 5" barrel hinged with a tip-up breech. Blowback-operated semi-automatic pistol that has no extractor. Empty cases are blown out of breech by gas pressure. One feature about this pistol that is desirable, it's possible to tip barrel breech forward like a shotgun and load cartridges singly, while holding contents of magazine in reserve. Weapon has fixed sights and blued finish, with checkered walnut grips. Manufactured in 1928.

Courtesy James Rankin

NIB	Exc.	V.G.	Good	Fair	Poor
—	1250	950	750	500	200

Police Model (Type Policeman)

Blowback-operated double-action semi-automatic chambered for .25 ACP cartridge. Has 3.5" barrel and 7-round magazine. Same hinged barrel feature of Model 28. Blued, with fixed sights and Ebonite grips. Manufactured 1913 to 1914.

Courtesy James Rankin

NIB	Exc.	V.G.	Good	Fair	Poor
—	800	650	450	300	150

Officer's Model (Pocket Model)

Also referred to as "Staff Model". Blowback-operated semi-automatic chambered for .25 ACP cartridge. Has 2.5" barrel and concealed hammer. Fixed sights and finish blued. Grips are Ebonite. Manufactured between 1914 and 1938 in two variations: early and second type.

Courtesy James Rankin

Early variation Pocket

652 • LE MAT

NIB	Exc.	V.G.	Good	Fair	Poor
—	300	250	200	150	100

Target Model (Type Champion)

Chambered for 6.35mm cartridge and fitted with 6" barrel. Extended magazine base is for grip purposes, not additional cartridges.

Courtesy James Rankin

NIB	Exc.	V.G.	Good	Fair	Poor
—	900	700	550	400	275

LE MAT
Paris, France

LeMat

Somewhat unique background that makes it a bit controversial among collectors. Foreign-made firearm manufactured in Paris, France, as well as Birmingham, England. Designed and patented by an American, Jean Alexander Le Mat of New Orleans, Louisiana; purchased for use by Confederate States of America and used in Civil War. Curious firearm, as it is a huge weapon that has two barrels. Top 6.5" barrel chambered for .42-caliber percussion and supplied by 9-shot unfluted cylinder that revolves on a 5", .63-caliber smoothbore barrel that doubles as cylinder axis pin. These two barrels are held together by a front and rear ring. Rear sight is a notch in nose of hammer. Attached ramrod on side of top barrel. Weapon marked "Lemat and Girards Patent, London". Finish blued, with checkered walnut grips. Fewer than 3,000 manufactured. Approximately one-half were purchased by Confederate States of America. Made between 1856 and 1865.

Courtesy Milwaukee Public Museum, Milwaukee, Wisconsin

NIB	Exc.	V.G.	Good	Fair	Poor
—	—	30000	25000	7500	1750

Baby LeMat

Similar in appearance (though a good deal smaller in size) to standard model pistol. Chambered for .32-caliber percussion. Has 4.25" top barrel and .41-caliber smoothbore lower barrel. Cylinder is unfluted and holds 9 shots. Barrel marked "Systeme Le Mat Bte s.g.d.g. Paris". Has British proofmarks. Blued, with checkered walnut grips. Scarcest model Le Mat. Only an estimated 100 manufactured. Used by Confederate States of America in Civil War.

NIB	Exc.	V.G.	Good	Fair	Poor
—	—	28500	22000	1100	3300

LeMat Revolving Carbine

Chambered for centerfire, rimfire cartridges or percussion. Barrels are half round half octagon and 20" in length. Chambered for a variety of calibers, but usually in percussion .42-caliber, with .62-caliber smoothbore lower barrel.

Courtesy Little John's Auction Service, Inc., Paul Goodwin photo

NIB	Exc.	V.G.	Good	Fair	Poor
—	—	31500	25000	11000	3000

LE PAGE SA.
Liege, Belgium

Pinfire Revolver

Company was in business of revolver manufacture in 1850s. Produced a .40-caliber pinfire revolver, similar to Lefauchaux and other pinfires of the day. Barrel lengths vary and unfluted cylinder holds 6 shots. Pistols are double-action and sometimes found with ornate, but somewhat crude engraving. Finish is blued, with wood grips. Quality of these weapons is fair. They were serviceable, but ammunition created somewhat of a problem. Rather fragile and difficult to handle, with protruding primer pin to contend with.

NIB	Exc.	V.G.	Good	Fair	Poor
—	—	775	325	200	125

Semi-Automatic Pistol

Semi-automatic pistol, with open top slide and exposed hammer. Chambered for 6.35mm, 7.65mm, 9mm Short and 9mm Long cartridges. Large grip with finger grooves.

Courtesy James Rankin

NIB	Exc.	V.G.	Good	Fair	Poor
—	875	675	525	300	200

Pocket Pistol

Semi-automatic pistol in caliber 6.35mm. Checkered hard rubber grips, with crossed sword and pistol logo of Le Page on each side of grip.

Courtesy James Rankin

NIB	Exc.	V.G.	Good	Fair	Poor
—	325	275	225	175	75

LEBEAU COURALLY
Liege, Belgium

Company has been in business since 1865. Made more guns for royalty than any other gun company in the world. Prices listed are for guns without engraving. Other extra-cost options will affect price. All guns are built to order. Virtually no upper end for values to these infrequently-encountered guns. Values are certainly well in excess of $30,000 for any model in Very Good or better condition.

LEE FIREARMS CO.
Milwaukee, Wisconsin

Lee Single-Shot Carbine

Rare single-shot break-open carbine that pivots to right side for loading. Chambered for .44 rimfire cartridge. Has 21.5" barrel, with hammer mounted in center of frame. Carbine has walnut buttstock, but no forearm and marked "Lee's Firearms Co. Milwaukee, Wisc.". Approximately 450 manufactured between 1863 and 1865. Few surviving examples and one should be wary of fakes.

Courtesy Milwaukee Public Museum, Milwaukee, Wisconsin

NIB	Exc.	V.G.	Good	Fair	Poor
—	—	6500	2200	900	400

Lee Sporting Rifle

Similar to military carbine except it has a longer octagonal barrel. Barrel length varied and there were more of these manufactured. Survival rate appears to have been better than for carbine model.

Courtesy Milwaukee Public Museum, Milwaukee, Wisconsin

NIB	Exc.	V.G.	Good	Fair	Poor
—	—	1750	700	300	150

LEECH & RIGDON
Greensboro, Georgia

Leech & Rigdon Revolver

Confederate revolver patterned after 1851 Colt Navy. Chambered for .36-caliber percussion. Has 6-shot unfluted cylinder. The 7.5" barrel is part-octagonal and has a loading lever beneath it. Frame is open-topped; finish blued, with brass grip straps and walnut one-piece grips. Barrel marked "Leech & Rigdon CSA." Approximately 1,500 revolvers manufactured in 1863 and 1864. All contracted for/by Confederacy and considered to be prime acquisition for collectors. Beware of fakes!

Courtesy Jim and Caroline Cerny

NIB	Exc.	V.G.	Good	Fair	Poor
—	—	42000	27500	11000	2750

LEFAUCHAUX, CASIMER & EUGENE
Paris, France

Pinfire Revolver

Pinfire ignition system was invented by Casimir Lefauchaux in 1828, but not widely used until 1850s. Consists of smooth rimless case that contains powder charge and percussion cap. Pin protrudes from side of this case at rear and when struck by hammer is driven into cap, thereby igniting charge and firing weapon. Pistols for this cartridge are slotted at end of cylinder to allow pins to protrude and be struck by downward blow of hammer. This particular revolver chambered for .43-caliber and has 5.25" barrel. Cylinder holds 6 shots; finish blued, with checkered walnut grips. Manufactured after 1865. Selected for service by French military.

NIB	Exc.	V.G.	Good	Fair	Poor
—	—	—	575	250	125

LEFEVER, D. M., SONS & COMPANY
Syracuse, New York

In 1901, when Dan Lefever was forced out of Lefever Arms the company he had founded in 1884, he organized another company to produce a line of high-grade boxlock side-by-side doubles. He operated Lefever, D.M. & sons until his death in 1906, at which time the firm closed its doors. During this five-year period, approximately 1,200 shotguns were made in several grades. This makes them quite rare and difficult to evaluate. It is important to get an appraisal from a trusted source before buying or selling. Prices shown are average values.

Lefever Double-Barrel Shotgun

Side-by-side, double-barrel shotgun chambered for 12-, 16- or 20-gauge. Offered with various barrel lengths and choke combinations that were made to order. Features double triggers and automatic ejectors. Single-selective trigger was available as an option. Finish blued, with checkered walnut stock. Individual grades differ in amount of ornamentation and general quality of materials and workmanship utilized in their construction. Discontinued in 1906. There are an "Optimus" and "Uncle Dan" grade, which are top-of-the-line models, that features extremely high quality in materials and workmanship and a great deal of ornamentation. This firearm is extremely rare and seldom found in today's market. It is impossible to evaluate on a general basis. **NOTE:** For all models listed: add 50 percent for 20-gauge; 25 percent for single-selective trigger.

O Excelsior Grade—Extractors

NIB	Exc.	V.G.	Good	Fair	Poor
—	2750	2200	1750	950	700

Excelsior Grade—Auto Ejectors

NIB	Exc.	V.G.	Good	Fair	Poor
—	3250	2700	2100	1250	900

F Grade, No. 9

NIB	Exc.	V.G.	Good	Fair	Poor
—	3700	2950	2350	1500	1100

E Grade, No. 8

NIB	Exc.	V.G.	Good	Fair	Poor
—	4750	4200	3200	2400	1700

D Grade, No. 7

NIB	Exc.	V.G.	Good	Fair	Poor
—	5800	5000	4000	2750	2000

C Grade, No. 6

NIB	Exc.	V.G.	Good	Fair	Poor
—	8000	7000	6000	3000	2500

B Grade, No. 5

NIB	Exc.	V.G.	Good	Fair	Poor
—	8700	8000	7000	3500	3000

AA Grade, No. 4

NIB	Exc.	V.G.	Good	Fair	Poor
—	11500	10500	9000	4200	2750

LEFEVER ARMS CO.
Syracuse, New York

Founded by Dan Lefever (president), in 1884, who was a pioneer in the field of breech-loading firearms. He was referred to as "Uncle Dan" within the firearms industry. He was responsible for many improvements in double-barrel shotgun design. He developed the automatic hammerless system in late 1880s. He also developed a compensating action that allowed simple adjustments to compensate for action wear. In 1901, he was forced out of the company and organized another company—D.M. Lefever, Sons & Company—also in Syracuse. Dan Lefever died in 1906 and his new company went out of business. The original company was acquired by Ithaca in 1916. They continued to produce Lefever guns until 1948.

Sideplated Shotgun

Double-barrel side-by-side shotgun chambered for 10-, 12-, 16- or 20-gauge. Offered with 26", 28", 30" or 32" barrels, with various choke combinations. Barrels are Damascus or fluid steel. Damascus guns have become collectible and in better condition—very good to excellent—can bring nearly the same price as fluid-steel guns. Features a fractional sidelock, because hammers were mounted in frame and sears and cocking indicators were mounted on sideplates. After serial number 25,000, entire locking mechanism was frame mounted and only cocking indicators remained on sideplates. Double triggers are standard. Finish blued, with checkered walnut stock. A number of variations that differ in amount of ornamentation and quality of materials and workmanship utilized in their construction. Automatic ejectors are represented by the letter "E" after respective grade designation. Shotgun manufactured between 1885 and 1919. We strongly recommend that a qualified appraisal be secured if a transaction is contemplated. Also, an Optimus Grade and Thousand Dollar Grade offered. These are extremely high-grade, heavily ornamented firearms inlaid with precious metals. Extremely rare and evaluating them on a general basis is impossible. **NOTE:** All models listed: add 50 percent for 16-gauge; 100 percent for 20-gauge; 10 percent for single-selective trigger.

H Grade

NIB	Exc.	V.G.	Good	Fair	Poor
—	2500	1600	950	550	350

HE Grade

NIB	Exc.	V.G.	Good	Fair	Poor
—	3000	2000	1550	900	650

G Grade

NIB	Exc.	V.G.	Good	Fair	Poor
—	2800	1800	1200	700	425

GE Grade

NIB	Exc.	V.G.	Good	Fair	Poor
—	3500	2300	1800	1000	650

F Grade

NIB	Exc.	V.G.	Good	Fair	Poor
—	3200	2000	1550	900	650

FE Grade

NIB	Exc.	V.G.	Good	Fair	Poor
—	5000	3200	2200	1300	800

E Grade

NIB	Exc.	V.G.	Good	Fair	Poor
—	5500	3700	2400	1400	900

EE Grade

Courtesy Rock Island Auction Company

NIB	Exc.	V.G.	Good	Fair	Poor
—	10000	8000	3100	1850	1150

D Grade

NIB	Exc.	V.G.	Good	Fair	Poor
—	8500	6000	3000	1800	1100

DS Grade

NIB	Exc.	V.G.	Good	Fair	Poor
—	2100	1800	1000	700	500

DE Grade

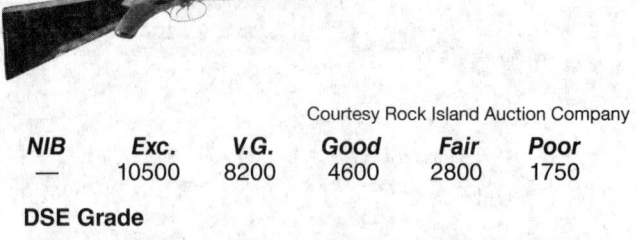

Courtesy Rock Island Auction Company

NIB	Exc.	V.G.	Good	Fair	Poor
—	10500	8200	4600	2800	1750

DSE Grade

NIB	Exc.	V.G.	Good	Fair	Poor
—	3500	2750	1800	1000	700

C Grade

NIB	Exc.	V.G.	Good	Fair	Poor
—	11000	8500	4200	2400	1500

CE Grade

NIB	Exc.	V.G.	Good	Fair	Poor
—	18000	12000	5650	3400	2100

B Grade

NIB	Exc.	V.G.	Good	Fair	Poor
—	28000	19500	7000	3200	2000

BE Grade

NIB	Exc.	V.G.	Good	Fair	Poor
—	32000	24000	10000	4000	2500

A Grade

NIB	Exc.	V.G.	Good	Fair	Poor
—	40000	34000	16000	6000	3700

AA Grade

NIB	Exc.	V.G.	Good	Fair	Poor
—	50000	40000	25000	8000	5000

LEFEVER ARMS COMPANY, INC. (ITHACA)
Syracuse, New York

During 1916, Ithaca Gun company purchased the gun making assets of Syracuse, New York based Lefever Arms Company. Between then and World War I, they continued to manufacture the same sideplate gun that had been made in Syracuse until about 1919, when they were discontinued. Prices for those guns are listed in Sideplated Shotgun section. During 1921, Ithaca Gun Company, under the name Lefever Arms Company, Inc., introduced a line of lower cost boxlock guns. Eventually, six different models were produced. Ithaca's Lefever guns were produced in 12-, 16- and 20-gauge and .410 bore. **NOTE:** 20-gauge guns often command a price premium of 50 percent; .410 bore gun may command up to 200 percent premium.

Nitro Special

Side-by-side double-barrel shotgun chambered for 12-, 16-, 20-gauge and .410 bore. Barrels were offered in lengths of 26" to 32", with various choke combinations. Features boxlock action, with double triggers and extractors standard. Finish blued, with case colored receiver and checkered walnut stock. Manufactured between 1921 and 1948. Incredible as it may seem, its price at introduction was $29. **NOTE:** Add 100+ percent for .410; $100 for single-selective trigger; $200 for automatic ejectors.

NIB	Exc.	V.G.	Good	Fair	Poor
—	600	400	250	200	100

Long Range Single-Barrel Trap and Field (Model 2)

Manufactured from 1927 to 1947. Model 2 was a single-barrel, with no rib. Like Nitro Special it had walnut stocks. Line cut checkered at grip area of buttstock and on fore-end.

NIB	Exc.	V.G.	Good	Fair	Poor
—	500	300	200	150	100

Single-Barrel Trap Ventilated Rib (Model 3)

Manufactured from 1927 to 1942. Model 3 was a single-barrel, with same ventilated rib used on "Knick" trap gun. Walnut stocks had line cut checkering at grip area of buttstock and on fore-end.

NIB	Exc.	V.G.	Good	Fair	Poor
—	1200	500	250	150	100

Double-Barrel Ventilated Rib Trap (Model 4)

Manufactured during 1929, but cataloged until 1939. Model 4 was a double-barrel, with ventilated rib barrel. Walnut stocks had line cut checkering at grip area of buttstock and on beavertail fore-end. Only about 200 units produced.

NIB	Exc.	V.G.	Good	Fair	Poor
—	2000	1200	1000	700	300

A Grade (Model 5)

Manufactured from 1936 to 1939. A Grade was a double-barreled gun. Walnut stocks had pointed checkering cut at grip area of buttstock and on splinter fore-end. Line engraving outlined its nicely sculptured frame. **NOTE:** Add $200 for single trigger; $200 for automatic ejectors; $300 for beavertail fore-end.

NIB	Exc.	V.G.	Good	Fair	Poor
—	900	600	400	300	100

Skeet Special (Model 6)

Manufactured from 1936 to 1939. A Grade was a double-barreled gun. Walnut stocks had pointed checkering cut at grip area of buttstock and on beavertail fore-end. Beavertail fore-end, single trigger, automatic ejectors, recoil pad and ivory center and front sight were standard. Frame was sculptured and line engraved like Model 5.

NIB	Exc.	V.G.	Good	Fair	Poor
—	1500	1200	1000	400	100

LEMAN, H. E.
Lancaster, Pennsylvania

Leman Militia Rifle

.58-caliber percussion muzzle-loader has 33" round barrel. Stock is full-length and held on by two barrel bands. Ramrod mounted under barrel. Trim is brass and barrel browned, with case colored lock. Lock marked "H.E.Leman/Lancaster, Pa." Approximately 500 manufactured between 1860 and 1864. Believed used by Pennsylvania State Militia in Civil War.

NIB	Exc.	V.G.	Good	Fair	Poor
—	—	4750	2000	750	300

LEONARD, G.
Charlestown, Massachusetts

Pepperbox

.31-caliber four-barreled pepperbox, with concealed hammer. Barrels 3.25" in length. Ring trigger used to cock weapon, while smaller trigger located outside ring is used to fire weapon. Barrels on this pistol do not revolve. Revolving striker inside frame that turns to fire each chamber. Barrels must be removed for loading and capping purposes. Frame is iron and blued, with engraving. Rounded grips are walnut. Barrel stamped "G. Leonard Jr. Charlestown". Fewer than 200 manufactured in 1849 and 1850.

NIB	Exc.	V.G.	Good	Fair	Poor
—	—	1850	725	300	150

LES, INC.
Skokie, Illinois

Rogak P-18

9mm caliber double-action semi-automatic pistol, with 5.5" barrel and 18-shot magazine. Stainless steel. Discontinued.

NIB	Exc.	V.G.	Good	Fair	Poor
—	380	350	295	200	150

LEW HORTON
Westborough, Massachusetts

This company is a full-line distributor of several major firearm manufacturers. They specialize in exclusive special editions of various models.

LEWIS MACHINE & TOOL COMPANY (LMT)
Milan, Illinois

Company founded in 1980 and manufactures a wide range of military-type rifles. Originally, the firm made weapons for law enforcement and government agencies in U.S., but now makes products for civilian community and foreign armed forces.

.308 Modular Weapon System (MWSE)

Gas piston operating system, with monolithic rail system with one-piece upper receiver, free floated cryogenically treated barrel which can quickly be changed to another size, two-stage trigger, 20-shot magazine.

NIB	Exc.	V.G.	Good	Fair	Poor
2500	2000	1550	1200	750	400

Defender Standard Model 16

Standard flattop upper receiver, with 16" chrome-lined 1:7"-twist barrel, standard semi-automatic bolt carrier group, tactical charging handle, Generation 1 collapsible buttstock.

NIB	Exc.	V.G.	Good	Fair	Poor
1200	1000	750	500	350	200

CQB Series

Piston operated with CQB/MRP (Close Quarter Battle/Monolithic Rail Platform) upper receiver, 16" chrome lined 5.56" barrel with SOPMOD buttstock and standard trigger group. Also offered in 6.8 SPC. **NOTE:** Add $200 for 6.8 SPC.

NIB	Exc.	V.G.	Good	Fair	Poor
1900	1650	1250	750	450	250

LIDDLE & KAEDING
San Francisco, California

Pocket Revolver

Manufactured by Forehand and Wadsworth, but stamped with above name. Company was a dealer in California and had nothing whatsoever to do with production of this revolver. Chambered for .32 rimfire cartridge. Has 3.25" octagonal barrel and 5-shot fluted cylinder. Frame is iron and finish blued, with walnut grips. Few hundred manufactured between 1880 and 1886. Dealer's name marked on top strap.

NIB	Exc.	V.G.	Good	Fair	Poor
—	—	575	450	200	75

LIEGEOISE D ARMES
Liege, Belgium

Side-by-Side Boxlock Shotgun

Double-barreled gun chambered for 12- and 20-gauge. Barrels 28" or 30" in length. Choke combinations are varied. Single trigger and automatic ejectors. Action moderately engraved. Finish blued, with checkered walnut stock.

NIB	Exc.	V.G.	Good	Fair	Poor
—	900	700	500	400	200

Liegeoise Pistol

Semi-automatic pistol in 6.35mm caliber.

Courtesy James Rankin

NIB	Exc.	V.G.	Good	Fair	Poor
—	250	200	175	125	75

LIGNOSE
Suhl, Germany

In 1921, Bergmann Industriewerke was incorporated into Aktiengesellschaft Lignose, Berlin, with a manufacturing division in Suhl.

Liliput Model I

Manufactured in caliber 6.35mm during 1920s.

NIB	Exc.	V.G.	Good	Fair	Poor
—	400	300	200	150	100

Lignose Model 2

Pocket Model in 6.35mm caliber.

Courtesy James Rankin

NIB	Exc.	V.G.	Good	Fair	Poor
—	450	400	350	250	150

Lignose Model 3

Same as Model 2, with 9-round magazine capacity.

NIB	Exc.	V.G.	Good	Fair	Poor
—	750	650	500	400	250

Einhand Model 2A

Unique design resembled Swiss Chylewski. Allows shooter to cock and fire this blowback-operated semi-automatic pistol with one hand (Einhand). Chambered for 6.35mm cartridge. Has 2" barrel. Magazine holds 6 shots. Finish blued, with molded horn grips marked "Lignose". Trigger guard on this pistol has a reverse curve that fits finger and moves backward to cock slide. Short-grip model without Einhard feature was Model 2; long grip model without Einhand was Model 3. First 9,000 to 10,000 examples (all four variations serial numbered in same series) were marketed under Bergmann name; only later Lignose. Manufactured in early 1920s by Bergman Company. Firm merged with Lignose under whose name it was produced.

Courtesy James Rankin

NIB	Exc.	V.G.	Good	Fair	Poor
—	750	650	500	400	250

Einhand Model 3A

Similar to Model 2A, with longer grip that houses 9-shot magazine. All other specifications same as Model 2A.

Courtesy Orvel Reichert

NIB	Exc.	V.G.	Good	Fair	Poor
—	850	700	650	500	300

LILLIPUT
See—Menz

LINDE A.
Memphis, Tennessee

Pocket Pistol

Company manufactured a small concealable firearm, patterned after Henry Deringer Philadelphia-type pistol. Chambered for .41-caliber percussion. Has 2.5" barrel, German silver mountings and walnut stock. Manufactured in 1850s.

NIB	Exc.	V.G.	Good	Fair	Poor
—	—	2150	875	300	150

LINDSAY, JOHN P.
Union Knife Company
Naugatuck, Connecticut

Union Knife Company manufactured Lindsay 2-shot pistols for inventor John P. Lindsay. There are three separate and distinct models listed.

2 Shot Belt Pistol

An oddity. Single-barreled .41-caliber percussion pistol, with double chamber that contains two powder charges and projectiles that are simultaneously fired by two separate hammers. Hammers are released by a single trigger that allows them to fall in proper sequence. 5.5" octagonal barrel contoured into a radical stepped-down shape and spur trigger. Frame is brass, with scroll engraving. Barrel blued and marked "Lindsay's Young America". Estimated to be fewer than 100 manufactured between 1860 and 1862.

NIB	Exc.	V.G.	Good	Fair	Poor
—	—	4400	1500	700	300

2 Shot Pocket Pistol

Smaller version of Belt Pistol. Chambered for same caliber, but has 4" barrel. Approximately 200 manufactured between 1860 and 1862.

Courtesy W. P. Hallstein III and son Chip

NIB	Exc.	V.G.	Good	Fair	Poor
—	—	3500	3000	1100	400

2 Shot Martial Pistol

Large version of Lindsay design. Chambered for .45-caliber smoothbore. Has 8.5" part-round part-octagonal barrel. Other respects similar to smaller models. Inventor tried to sell this pistol to the government, but was unsuccessful. Estimated 100 manufactured between 1860 and 1862.

NIB	Exc.	V.G.	Good	Fair	Poor
—	—	—	5400	2200	700

LINS, A. F.
Philadelphia, Pennsylvania

Pocket Pistol

Chambered for .41-caliber percussion. Copy of Henry Deringer pistol. Has 3" barrel, walnut stock and marked "A. Fred. Lins. Philada." Manufactured between 1855 and 1860.

NIB	Exc.	V.G.	Good	Fair	Poor
—	—	2100	1075	350	200

Rifled Musket

Single-shot muzzle-loading percussion rifle, chambered for .58-caliber. Has 39" barrel and full-length walnut stock held on by three barrel bands. Iron ramrod mounted under barrel. Mountings are iron. A bayonet lug combined with front sight. Lock marked "A. Fred. Lins/Philada." Rare weapon used by Union forces in Civil War. Approximately 200 manufactured in 1861 and 1862.

Courtesy Milwaukee Public Museum, Milwaukee, Wisconsin

NIB	Exc.	V.G.	Good	Fair	Poor
—	—	5500	2000	825	300

LITTLE SHARPS RIFLE MFG. CO.
Big Sandy, Montana

Little Sharps Rifle

Hand-built reproduction of single-shot Sharps rifle is 20 percent smaller than original. Chambered for a wide variety of calibers from .22 LR to .375 LSR. A number of extra cost options are available for this rifle. Price listed for basic model.

NIB	Exc.	V.G.	Good	Fair	Poor
3250	2750	2000	1500	900	500

LJUTIC INDUSTRIES
Yakima, Washington

Bi-Matic Semi-Automatic

Custom-built gas-operated semi-automatic shotgun, known for its low level of felt recoil. Chambered for 12-gauge. Has 26" to 32" barrels choked for skeet or trap. Stock specifications are to customer's order. **NOTE:** Add 15 percent for interchangeable chokes.

NIB	Exc.	V.G.	Good	Fair	Poor
2750	2100	1300	800	400	200

Dynatrap Single-Barrel

Single-shot trap gun chambered for 12-gauge. Has 33" ventilated rib full-choke barrel. Features push-button opener and manual extractor. Stock made to trap specifications. Many options affect value.

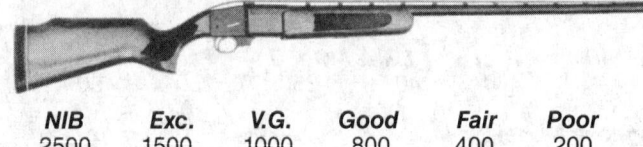

NIB	Exc.	V.G.	Good	Fair	Poor
2500	1500	1000	800	400	200

Model X-73 Single-Barrel

Similar features to Dynatrap, with high competition rib. Appraisal is recommended. **NOTE:** Add 15 percent for interchangeable chokes.

NIB	Exc.	V.G.	Good	Fair	Poor
2750	2100	1300	800	400	200

Mono Gun Single-Barrel

Chambered for 12-gauge. Has 34" ventilated rib barrel. Essentially a custom-order proposition that is available with standard, as well as release trigger. Many value-affecting options available. **NOTE:** Add 15 percent for interchangeable chokes.

NIB	Exc.	V.G.	Good	Fair	Poor
6500	5700	4200	3000	1000	—

LTX Model

Deluxe version of Mono Gun, with 33" medium-height ventilated rib. High-grade walnut stock, with fine hand checkering. Options raise values drastically.

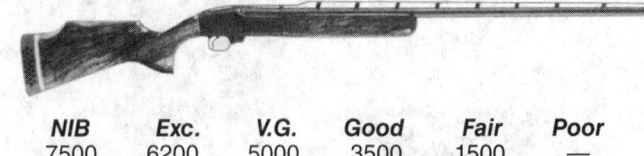

NIB	Exc.	V.G.	Good	Fair	Poor
7500	6200	5000	3500	1500	—

Space Gun

Unique single-barrel gun chambered for 12-gauge, with trap choking. Stock and forearm reminds one of a crutch in appearance, but allows shooter to have in-line control, with little felt recoil. Barrel, forearm and stock are all on one line. There is a recoil pad and high ventilated rib.

NIB	Exc.	V.G.	Good	Fair	Poor
3750	3000	2250	1500	900	200

Bi-Gun Over/Under

Over/under double chambered for 12-gauge. Has 30" or 32" ventilated rib barrels that are separated. Choking to trap specifications. Stock deluxe hand-checkered walnut.

NIB	Exc.	V.G.	Good	Fair	Poor
7250	6000	4000	1000	600	200

Bi-Gun Combo

Over/under Bi-Gun supplied with high ribbed single-barrel, in addition to separated over/under barrels.

NIB	Exc.	V.G.	Good	Fair	Poor
10000	7000	4000	2000	1000	200

LM-6 Super Deluxe

Over/under gun made to customer's specifications. Available in 12-gauge, with barrel lengths from 28" to 34". All other specifications are custom. **NOTE:** Add $7,000 for extra single-barrel.

NIB	Exc.	V.G.	Good	Fair	Poor
15000	11500	7500	5000	2500	1000

LLAMA
Philippines

Same firm that was founded in 1904 and produced several inexpensive revolvers and pistols prior to 1931. In 1931, company began to produce a semi-automatic pistol based on Colt Model 1911. They were of high quality and have been sold around the world. After Spanish civil war, company moved its facilities to Vitoria, Spain, where it continued to build handguns under Llama trade name. In 1980s, firm introduced a new line of pistols that were more modern in design and function. Llama pistol is still produced today. For Llama pistols built prior to 1936 slide marking reads: "GABILONDO Y CIA ELOEIBAR (ESPANA) CAL 9MM/.380IN LLAMA". For pistols built after 1936 slide marking reads: "LLAMA GABILONDO Y CIA ELOEIBAR (ESPANA) CAL 9MM .380". Current production Llama pistols will show a slide marking with either "LLAMA CAL..." or "GABILONDO Y CIA VITORIA (ESPANA)" and Llama logo. Llama pistols are now made in the Philippines, by Metro Arms and imported into the U.S. by Eagle Imports of Wanamassa, New Jersey.

SEMI-AUTOMATICS

Model I-A

7.65mm blowback design introduced in 1933. Magazine capacity 7 rounds. Barrel 3.62"; overall length 6.3"; weight about 19 oz.

NIB	Exc.	V.G.	Good	Fair	Poor
—	275	225	125	100	75

Model II

Chambered for 9mm Short. Introduced in 1933. Identical to Model I. Discontinued in 1936.

NIB	Exc.	V.G.	Good	Fair	Poor
—	265	200	150	125	100

Model III

Improved version of Model II. Introduced in 1936. Discontinued in 1954.

NIB	Exc.	V.G.	Good	Fair	Poor
—	275	225	175	125	100

Model III-A

Similar to Model III except chambered for .380 ACP. Addition of Colt-type grip safety. Introduced in 1955. Weight about 23 oz.

NIB	Exc.	V.G.	Good	Fair	Poor
—	300	250	195	125	100

Model IV

Chambered for 9mm Largo or .380 ACP. Not fitted with grip safety. Introduced in 1931. First of Llama designs.

NIB	Exc.	V.G.	Good	Fair	Poor
—	275	225	175	125	100

Model V

Same as Model IV, but intended for export to U.S. Stamped "made in Spain" on slide.

NIB	Exc.	V.G.	Good	Fair	Poor
—	275	225	175	125	100

Model VI

Chambered for 9mm Short, without a grip safety.

NIB	Exc.	V.G.	Good	Fair	Poor
—	275	225	175	125	100

Model VII

Introduced in 1932. Manufactured until 1954. Chambered for .38 Auto cartridge. No grip safety.

NIB	Exc.	V.G.	Good	Fair	Poor
—	400	300	225	150	100

Model VIII

Introduced in 1955. Chambered for .45 ACP, .38 Auto or 9mm Largo. Fitted with a grip safety. Barrel length 5"; overall length 8.5"; weight about 38 oz. Magazine capacity 7 rounds. **NOTE:** Many of these pistols marked ".38". Unclear whether these pistols were intended for use with .38 Super cartridge or with milder .38 Automatic. We do not recommend full-house Super loadings in these pistols.

NIB	Exc.	V.G.	Good	Fair	Poor
—	400	300	225	150	100

Model IX

Chambered for 7.65mm Para, 9mm Largo or .45 ACP. Has locked breech, with no grip safety. Built from 1936 to 1954.

NIB	Exc.	V.G.	Good	Fair	Poor
—	400	300	200	150	100

Model IX-A

Version of Model IX. Fitted with a grip safety and 5" barrel. Current production models chambered for .45 ACP only. Weight about 30 oz.

NIB	Exc.	V.G.	Good	Fair	Poor
—	400	300	200	150	100

Model IX-B

Version of Model IX series. Chambered in .45 ACP. Fitted with extended slide release, black plastic grips and target-type hammer. Offered in blue or satin chrome finish.

NIB	Exc.	V.G.	Good	Fair	Poor
400	300	250	175	125	100

Model IX-C

Last large-frame version of Model IX. Chambered for .45 ACP. Fitted with 5.125" barrel. Blade front sight, with adjustable rear. Magazine capacity 10 rounds. Weight about 41 oz.

NIB	Exc.	V.G.	Good	Fair	Poor
400	300	250	200	150	100

Model IX-D

Compact frame version, with 4.25" barrel. Chambered for .45 ACP cartridge. Stocks are black rubber. Fixed front sight, with adjustable rear. Introduced in 1995. Magazine capacity 10 rounds. Weight about 39 oz.

NIB	Exc.	V.G.	Good	Fair	Poor
450	350	250	200	150	100

Model X

First produced in 1935. Chambered for 7.65mm cartridge. No grip safety.

NIB	Exc.	V.G.	Good	Fair	Poor
—	295	225	150	100	75

Model X-A

Version similar to Model X, with a grip safety. Produced from 1954 to present.

NIB	Exc.	V.G.	Good	Fair	Poor
—	300	225	150	100	75

Model XI

Chambered for 9mm Parabellum. Different from previous models with longer curved butt, ring hammer and vertically grooved walnut grips. Magazine capacity 9 rounds. Barrel length 5". Discontinued in 1954.

NIB	Exc.	V.G.	Good	Fair	Poor
—	350	300	250	175	125

Model XI-B

Similar to Model XI, with spur hammer and shorter barrel.

NIB	Exc.	V.G.	Good	Fair	Poor
400	375	275	150	100	75

Model XII-B

Chambered for .40 S&W cartridge. Has compact frame.

NIB	Exc.	V.G.	Good	Fair	Poor
400	375	275	150	100	75

Model XV

Chambered for .22 LR and marked "Especial". Fitted with grip safety. Comes in several finishes and different grip styles. Barrel length 3.6"; overall length 6.5"; weight about 17 oz.

NIB	Exc.	V.G.	Good	Fair	Poor
—	325	275	195	125	100

Model XVI

Deluxe version of Model XV, with engraving, ventilated rib and adjustable sights.

NIB	Exc.	V.G.	Good	Fair	Poor
—	350	275	200	150	100

Model XVII "Especial"

Vest pocket-sized model chambered for .22 Short. Small version of Model XV, with finger-contoured grip.

NIB	Exc.	V.G.	Good	Fair	Poor
—	275	225	175	125	100

Model XVIII

Introduced in 1998. Chambered for .25 ACP cartridge. Offered with gold or chrome finish and stag grips.

NIB	Exc.	V.G.	Good	Fair	Poor
—	300	225	175	150	125

Model Omni

Chambered for .45 ACP or 9mm cartridge. Fitted with 4.25" barrel. Blued finish. Adjustable rear sight. Magazine capacity: 7 rounds .45 ACP; 13 rounds 9mm. Weight about 40 oz. Produced between 1984 and 1986.

NIB	Exc.	V.G.	Good	Fair	Poor
475	350	250	150	125	100

Model Max-I

Introduced in 1995. This 1911 design single-action features 9mm or .45 ACP chambers, with 4.25" or 5.125" barrel. Black rubber grips, with blade front sight and adjustable rear. Weight: 34 oz. compact model; 36 oz. Government model. As of 2016, this model is back in production. Made in the Philippines and imported by Eagle Imports. **NOTE:** Add $25 for compact model; $25 for duo-tone model.

NIB	Exc.	V.G.	Good	Fair	Poor
400	350	250	175	150	100

Previous Production Prior to 2006

NIB	Exc.	V.G.	Good	Fair	Poor
425	375	300	225	185	125

New Production

NIB	Exc.	V.G.	Good	Fair	Poor
500	435	375	300	250	200

Model Mini-Max

Chambered for 9mm, .40 S&W or .45 ACP. Furnished with 6-round magazine. Barrel length 3.5". Checkered rubber grips. Introduced in 1996. Weight about 35 oz. Choice of blue, duo-tone, satin chrome or stainless steel finish. As of 2016, this model is back in production. Made in the Philippines and imported by Eagle Imports. Values shown apply to old and new production. **NOTE:** Add $40 for satin chrome; $60 for stainless; $20 for duo-tone.

NIB	Exc.	V.G.	Good	Fair	Poor
400	375	275	150	100	75

Mini-Max Sub Compact

Semi-automatic chambered for 9mm, .40 S&W or .45 ACP. Fitted with 3.14" barrel. Overall length 6.5"; height 4.5". Skeletonized combat-style hammer. Grips are black polymer. Weight about 31 oz. Introduced in 1999. **NOTE:** Add $40 for satin chrome; $60 for stainless; $20 for duo-tone.

NIB	Exc.	V.G.	Good	Fair	Poor
400	375	275	150	100	75

Model Max-I with Compensator

Similar to Max-I, with addition of compensator. Introduced in 1996. Weight about 42 oz.

NIB	Exc.	V.G.	Good	Fair	Poor
450	400	300	175	125	95

Micro-Max

Chambered for .32 ACP or .380 cartridge. Operates on a straight blowback system, with single-action trigger. Black polymer grips. Barrel length 3.6"; overall 6.5"; height 4.37"; weight about 23 oz. Introduced in 1999. **NOTE:** Add $20 for satin chrome finish.

NIB	Exc.	V.G.	Good	Fair	Poor
400	375	275	150	100	75

Model 82

Large-frame double-action semi-automatic pistol. Features plastic grips, ambidextrous safety, 3-dot sights. Barrel length 4.25"; overall 8"; weight about 39 oz. Choice of blue or satin chrome finish.

NIB	Exc.	V.G.	Good	Fair	Poor
650	500	350	250	150	100

Model 87 Competition

Chambered for 9mm cartridge. Fitted with integral muzzle compensator. Has a number of competition features such as oversize safety, beveled magazine well, release and 14-round capacity. Offered between 1989 and 1993.

NIB	Exc.	V.G.	Good	Fair	Poor
1200	925	650	525	300	150

Compact Frame Semi-Automatic

9mm or .45 ACP caliber semi-automatic pistol, with 4.25" barrel and 7- or 9-shot detachable magazine. Blued. Introduced in 1986.

NIB	Exc.	V.G.	Good	Fair	Poor
350	300	225	150	100	75

Small Frame Semi-Automatic

.22, .32 ACP and .380 ACP caliber semi-automatic pistol, with 3.6875" barrel and 7-shot detachable magazine. Blued or satin chrome finish. **NOTE:** Add $75 for satin chrome.

NIB	Exc.	V.G.	Good	Fair	Poor
350	300	225	150	100	75

Large Frame Semi-Automatic

9mm, .38 Super or .45 ACP caliber semi-automatic pistol, with 5.25" barrel and 7- or 9-shot detachable magazine, depending on caliber. Blued or satin chrome. **NOTE:** Add $125 for satin chrome.

NIB	Exc.	V.G.	Good	Fair	Poor
450	400	300	175	125	100

Mugica

Eibar gun dealer, Jose Mugica, sold Llama pistols under his private trade name. They are marked "mugica-ebir-spain" on slide. These pistols do not seem to have any additional value over and above their respective Llama models. For the sake of clarification, Mugica models are listed with their Llama counterparts:

Mugica Model 101	Llama Model X
Mugica Model 101-G	Llama Model X-A
Mugica Model 105	Llama Model III
Mugica Model 105-G	Llama Model III-A
Mugica Model 110	Llama Model VII
Mugica Model 110-G	Llama Model VIII
Mugica Model 120	Llama Model XI

Tauler

In an arrangement similar to Mugica, a gun dealer in Madrid sold Llama pistols under his own brand name. Most of these pistols were sold in early 1930s to police and other government officials. Most common Llama mod-els were Models I to VIII. Slide inscriptions were in English and had name Tauler in them. No additional value is attached to this private trademark.

REVOLVERS

RUBY EXTRA MODELS

Revolvers produced in the 1950s, were copies of Smith & Wessons. Marked "RUBY EXTRA" on left side of frame. Top of grips had a Ruby medallion. Barrel address stamped: gabilondo y cia elgoeibar espana. Ruby Extra Models represent company's attempts to produce and sell a low-cost revolver.

Model XII

Chambered for .38 Long cartridge. Fitted with 5" barrel and squared butt.

NIB	Exc.	V.G.	Good	Fair	Poor
—	200	150	125	100	75

Model XIII

Chambered for .38 Special. Has a round butt with 4" or 6" ventilated rib barrel. 6" barreled gun fitted with adjustable sights and target grips.

NIB	Exc.	V.G.	Good	Fair	Poor
—	225	175	150	125	100

Model XIV

Offered in .22 LR or .32-caliber. Available in a wide choice of barrel lengths and sights.

NIB	Exc.	V.G.	Good	Fair	Poor
—	200	150	125	100	75

Model XXII Olimpico

Designed as .38 Special target revolver. Features adjustable anatomic grip and rear sight, ventilated rib barrel and a web that joins barrel to ejector shroud.

NIB	Exc.	V.G.	Good	Fair	Poor
—	275	225	150	125	100

Model XXIX Olimpico

Model XXII chambered for .22 LR.

NIB	Exc.	V.G.	Good	Fair	Poor
—	250	200	150	125	100

Model XXVI

Chambered for .22 LR. Features traditional grips and shrouded ejector rod.

NIB	Exc.	V.G.	Good	Fair	Poor
—	175	150	125	100	75

Model XXVII

Similar to above, with 2" barrel. Chambered for .32 Long cartridge.

NIB	Exc.	V.G.	Good	Fair	Poor
—	175	150	125	100	75

Model XXVIII

Chambered for .22 LR. Fitted with 6" barrel. Ramp front sight and adjustable rear.

NIB	Exc.	V.G.	Good	Fair	Poor
—	200	175	150	100	75

Model XXXII Olimpico

A .32 target revolver, with unusual cylinder and frame design.

NIB	Exc.	V.G.	Good	Fair	Poor
—	400	300	250	200	150

Martial

.22 or .38 Special caliber double-action revolver, with 6-round swingout cylinder, 4" or 6" barrel and adjustable sights. Blued, with checkered hardwood grips. Manufactured between 1969 and 1976. **NOTE:** Add $500 for engraved chrome; $600 for engraved blue; $1,000 to $3,000 for gold model.

NIB	Exc.	V.G.	Good	Fair	Poor
—	275	225	200	150	125

Comanche I

.22-caliber revolver fitted with 6" barrel and 9-shot cylinder. Rubber grips with adjustable sights. Choice of blue or stainless steel. Weight about 39 oz.

NIB	Exc.	V.G.	Good	Fair	Poor
240	175	125	100	75	50

Comanche II

As above in .38 Special caliber, with 6-shot cylinder. Choice of 3" or 4" barrel. Rubber grips and adjustable sights. Blue or stainless steel. Weight about 30 oz.

NIB	Exc.	V.G.	Good	Fair	Poor
225	175	125	100	75	50

Comanche III

As above in .357 Magnum, with 3", 4" or 6" barrel. Adjustable sights. Rubber grips. Blue or stainless steel. Weight about 30 oz. for 3" or 4" barrel; 39 oz. for 6". Introduced in 1975. **NOTE:** Add 20 percent for satin chrome.

NIB	Exc.	V.G.	Good	Fair	Poor
275	225	175	125	100	75

Super Comanche

As above in .357 or .44 Magnum, with 10" ventilated rib barrel and adjustable sights. Blued, with walnut grips. Weight about 47 oz.

NIB	Exc.	V.G.	Good	Fair	Poor
325	250	200	150	100	75

LOEWE, LUDWIG & CO.
Berlin, Germany
See—Borchardt

During 1870s and 1880s, this firm manufactured a close copy of Smith & Wesson Russian Model for the Russian government. They are marked "Ludwig Loewe Berlin" on top of barrel.

Loewe Smith & Wesson Russian Revolver

NIB	Exc.	V.G.	Good	Fair	Poor
—	—	1250	600	325	125

LOHNER, C.
Philadelphia, Pennsylvania

Pocket Pistol

.44-caliber single-shot percussion pistol, with 5" barrel, German silver mounts and walnut grip. Barrel marked "C. Lohner". Manufactured during 1850s.

NIB	Exc.	V.G.	Good	Fair	Poor
—	—	1600	675	250	125

LOMBARD, H. C. & CO.
Springfield, Massachusetts

Pocket Pistol

.22-caliber single-shot spur trigger pistol, with 3.5" octagonal barrel. Frame is silver plated, barrel blued and grips are of walnut. Barrel marked "H.C. Lombard & Co. Springfield, Mass."

NIB	Exc.	V.G.	Good	Fair	Poor
—	—	500	225	150	100

LONE STAR RIFLE COMPANY
Conroe, Texas

Company builds custom black-powder rifles. They are built on a rolling block design and offered in two basic configurations. There are a wide number of options that will affect the price of these rifles.

Sporting Rifle

Basic configuration that features straight-grip stock, with semi-crescent butt. Offered in a wide variety of calibers from .32-40 to .50-90. Barrel lengths and configurations, wood, triggers, sights, engraving, finishes, hammers and accessories will greatly affect the final price. Basic retail price: $2195.

Target Rifle

Basic configuration that features straight-grip stock, with semi-crescent butt. Offered in a wide variety of calibers from .32-40 to .50-90. Barrel lengths and configurations, wood, triggers, sights, engraving, finishes, hammers and accessories will greatly affect the final price. Basic retail price: $2195.

LORCIN ENGINEERING CO., INC.
Mira Loma, California

Company in business from 1989 to 1999.

Model L-25

.25-caliber semi-automatic pistol, with 2.5" barrel and 7-shot magazine. Weight 14.5 oz.; overall length 4.8". Introduced in 1989.

NIB	Exc.	V.G.	Good	Fair	Poor
125	100	75	40	30	20

Model LT-25

Same as above, with aluminum alloy frame. Introduced in 1989.

NIB	Exc.	V.G.	Good	Fair	Poor
125	100	75	40	30	20

Model L-22

Chambered for .22 LR cartridge, with 2.5" barrel. Magazine capacity 9 rounds. Introduced in 1989. Weight 16 oz.

NIB	Exc.	V.G.	Good	Fair	Poor
125	100	75	40	30	20

Model L-380

Semi-automatic pistol chambered for .380 ACP cartridge. Barrel length 3.5", with magazine capacity of 7 rounds. Introduced in 1992. Weight about 23 oz.

NIB	Exc.	V.G.	Good	Fair	Poor
125	100	75	40	30	20

Model L-380 10th Anniversary

Same as above, but frame and slide are plated in 24 karat gold. Limited edition model.

NIB	Exc.	V.G.	Good	Fair	Poor
125	100	75	40	30	20

Model L-32

Same as above, but chambered for .32 ACP cartridge. Introduced in 1992

NIB	Exc.	V.G.	Good	Fair	Poor
125	100	75	40	30	20

Model LH-380

Semi-automatic pistol chambered for .380 ACP cartridge. Barrel length 4.5" and magazine capacity 10 rounds. Offered in black, satin or bright chrome finishes.

NIB	Exc.	V.G.	Good	Fair	Poor
150	125	100	75	60	50

Model L-9mm

Same as above, but chambered for 9mm cartridge. Weight 36 oz.

NIB	Exc.	V.G.	Good	Fair	Poor
150	125	100	75	60	50

Derringer

Over/under pistol chambered for .38 Special, .357 Magnum and .45 ACP. Barrel length 3.5"; overall length 6.5".

NIB	Exc.	V.G.	Good	Fair	Poor
140	120	95	65	50	40

LOWELL ARMS CO.
See—Rollin White Arms Co.

LOWER, J. P.
See—Slotter & Co.

LUGERS
Various Manufacturers

Just before the turn of the 20th century, Georg Luger redesigned Borchardt semi-automatic pistol so that its mainspring was housed in rear of grip. Resulting pistol was to prove extremely successful and his name has become synonymous with the pistol despite the fact his name never appeared on it.

These companies manufactured Luger pattern pistols at various times.

1. DWM - Deutsch Waffen und Munitions - Karlsruhe, Germany

2. The Royal Arsenal of Erfurt Germany

3. Simson & Company - Suhl, Germany

4. Mauser - Oberndorf, Germany

5. Vickers Ltd. - England

6. Waffenfabrik Bern - Bern, Switzerland

7. Heinrich Krieghoff - Suhl, Germany

DEUTSCH WAFFEN UND MUNITIONS

1899/1900 Swiss Test Model

4.75" barrel, 7.65mm caliber. Swiss Cross in Sunburst stamped over chamber. Serial range runs to three digits. With fewer than 100 manufactured and only one known to exist, it is one of the rarest Lugers and first true Luger that was produced. Model is far too rare to estimate an accurate value.

1900 Swiss Contract

4.75" barrel, 7.65mm caliber. Swiss Cross in Sunburst stamped over chamber. Military serial number range is 2001-5000; commercial range 01-21250. Approximately 2,000 commercial and 3,000 military models manufactured. **NOTE:** Add 20 percent for wide trigger.

Swiss Cross & Sunburst

NIB	Exc.	V.G.	Good	Fair	Poor
—	8000	6750	4000	1500	1000

1900 Commercial

4.75" barrel, 7.65mm caliber. Area above chamber is blank. Serial range 01-19000. Approximately 5,500 manufactured for commercial sale in Germany or other countries. Some have "Germany" stamped on frame. Imported into the U.S. Some were even stamped after bluing.

Courtesy Gale Morgan

NIB	Exc.	V.G.	Good	Fair	Poor
—	8500	6000	3000	1000	650

1900 American Eagle

4.75" barrel, 7.65mm caliber. American Eagle crest stamped over chamber. Serial range between 2000-200000. Approximately 11,000-12,000 commercial models marked "Germany" and 1,000 military test models, without commercial import stamp. Serial numbers of military lots are between 6100-7100. **NOTE:** For these models add a premium of 40 to 50 percent, depending on condition.

NIB	Exc.	V.G.	Good	Fair	Poor
—	5500	4000	2000	850	600

1900 Test Eagle

NIB	Exc.	V.G.	Good	Fair	Poor
—	7500	5000	3000	2000	1500

1900 Bulgarian Contract

Old model 1900 Type, with no stock lug. Has 4.75" barrel and chambered for 7.65mm cartridge. Bulgarian crest stamped over chamber and safety marked in Bulgarian letters. Serial range 20000-21000, with 1,000 manufactured. Military test model and quite rare, as most were re-barreled to 9mm during the time they were used. Even with 9mm versions, approximately 10 are known to exist. Only variation to feature a marked safety before 1904.

Courtesy Gale Morgan

NIB	Exc.	V.G.	Good	Fair	Poor
—	12500	8500	4000	2500	1800

1900 Carbine

11.75" barrel, 7.65mm caliber. Carbines have a gracefully contoured and finely checkered walnut forearm and detachable shoulder stock. Rear sight on this extremely rare variation is a five-position sliding model located on rear link. Area above chamber is blank. Serial range is three digits or under. This may have been a prototype, as less than 100 were produced. Model far too rare to estimate an accurate value.

1902 Prototype

6" barrel, 7.65mm caliber. Serial numbers are in 10000 range, with capital B and chamber is blank. 6" barrel is of a heavy contour. Less than 10 manufactured. Rarity of this variation precludes estimating value.

1902 Commercial—"Fat Barrel"

Thick 4" barrel, 9mm caliber. Area above chamber is blank. Chambered for 9mm cartridge. Serial numbers fall within 22300-22400 and 22900-23500 range. Approximately 600 manufactured. Greater part of those noted were marked "Germany" for export purposes.

NIB	Exc.	V.G.	Good	Fair	Poor
—	13500	10500	6000	4000	1500

1902 American Eagle

As above, with an American Eagle stamped over chamber. Chambered for 9mm cartridge. Serial numbers fall within 22100-22300 and 22450-22900 range. Solely intended for export sales in U.S.A. and all are marked "Germany" on frame. Approximately 700 manufactured.

NIB	Exc.	V.G.	Good	Fair	Poor
—	16000	12000	7000	3750	1300

1902 American Eagle Cartridge Counter

As above, with "Powell Indicating Device" added to left grip. Slotted left grip, with a numbered window that allows visual access to number or rounds remaining in special "indicator magazines". There were 50 Lugers altered in this way at the request of U.S. Board of Ordinance, for U.S. Army evaluation. Serial numbers are 22401-22450. Be especially wary of fakes!

NIB	Exc.	V.G.	Good	Fair	Poor
—	45000	32000	20000	6000	3500

1902 Carbine

11.75" barrel, 7.65mm caliber. Sight has four positions and is silver-soldered to barrel. Stock and forearm were sold with this weapon. Serial range was 21000-22100, 23500-24900 and 50000 to 50100. Approximately 2,500 manufactured for commercial sale in and out of Germany.

Many were imported into United States, but none here have been noted with "Germany" export stamp. **NOTE:** Prices include matching stock. Add 15 percent for 50000 to 50100 serial numbers.

Courtesy Gale Morgan

NIB	Exc.	V.G.	Good	Fair	Poor
—	22500	17000	10000	3500	2500

1902 Presentation Carbine

11.75" barrel, 7.65mm caliber. Carbines have initials of owner gold-inlaid above chamber. Furnished with checkered walnut stock and forearm. Only four have been noted in 9000C serial number range. They have initials "GL" for Georg Luger on back of rear toggle. Too rare to estimate value.

1902/06 Carbine (Transitional)

11.75" barrel, 7.65mm caliber. Assembled from Model 1902 parts with new toggle assembly. Four-position sliding sight silver-soldered to barrel and checkered walnut stock and forearm. Approximately 100 manufactured in 23600 serial number range. **NOTE:** Prices include matching stock.

Paul Goodwin photo

NIB	Exc.	V.G.	Good	Fair	Poor
—	17000	14500	8000	5000	3000

1903 Commercial

4" barrel, 7.65mm caliber. Chamber area is blank. Approximately 50 manufactured for export to France. Serial numbered 25000-25050. Extractor on this model marked "CHARGE".

NIB	Exc.	V.G.	Good	Fair	Poor
—	17000	13000	5000	3200	2500

1904 Navy

6" thick barrel, 9mm caliber. Chamber area is blank and extractor marked "Geladen". Safety marked "Gesichert". Approximately 1,500 manufactured in one- to four-digit serial range, for military issue to German Navy. Toggle has a "lock" similar to 1900 types. **NOTE:** Advised that a professional appraisal be obtained before purchase.

NIB	Exc.	V.G.	Good	Fair	Poor
—	75000	50000	30000	6000	4500

1906 Navy Commercial

New model 1906 Type, with stock lug. Has 6" barrel and chambered for 9mm cartridge. Chamber is blank and extractor marked "Geladen". Safety marked "Gesichert" and some have "Germany" export stamp. Proper magazine has a wood bottom, with concentric circles on sides. Approximately 2,500 manufactured in 25050-65000 serial range. Produced for commercial sales in and outside of Germany.

NIB	Exc.	V.G.	Good	Fair	Poor
—	8000	5800	2700	1500	1000

1906 Commercial

4" barrel, 9mm caliber. Extractor marked "Geladen" and area of frame under safety in its lower position is polished and not blued. Chamber is blank. Approximately 4,000 manufactured for commercial sales. Some have "Germany" export stamp. Serial range is 26500-68000.

NIB	Exc.	V.G.	Good	Fair	Poor
—	5000	4000	1600	800	600

1906 Commercial (Marked Safety)

As above, with area of frame under safety in its lowest position marked "Gesichert". Barrel is 4.75" in length and chambered for 7.65mm cartridge. Approximately 750 manufactured, serial numbered 25050-26800.

NIB	Exc.	V.G.	Good	Fair	Poor
—	6500	5000	2000	800	600

1906 American Eagle

4" barrel, 9mm caliber. Chamber area has the American Eagle stamped on it. Extractor marked "Loaded". Frame under safety at its lowest point is polished and not blued. Has no stock lug. Approximately 3,000 manufactured for commercial sale in U.S.A., in serial range 25800-69000. They were supplied with "Caliber 9mm Magnum".

NIB	Exc.	V.G.	Good	Fair	Poor
—	6500	4000	1200	700	500

1906 American Eagle (Marked Safety)

4.75" barrel, 7.65mm caliber. Frame under safety at its lowest point marked "Gesichert". Approximately 750 manufactured in 25100-26500 serial number range.

Courtesy Gale Morgan

NIB	Exc.	V.G.	Good	Fair	Poor
—	7500	5500	2000	1200	800

1906 American Eagle 4.75" Barrel

As above, with polished bright safety area. Approximately 8,000 manufactured in 26500-69000 serial range.

NIB	Exc.	V.G.	Good	Fair	Poor
—	5000	3000	1100	700	450

1906 U.S. Army Test Luger .45 Caliber

5" barrel, .45 ACP caliber. Sent to United States for testing in 1907. Chamber is blank, extractor marked "Loaded". Frame is polished under safety lever. Trigger on this model has an odd hook at the bottom. Only five of these pistols were manufactured. Referred to as the "Million Dollar Luger", it is believed that no one has ever paid close to that price. One sold in the late '80s for $430,000. **BUYER CAUTION:** Perfect copies of this model have been made. See John Martz - Custom Lugers at the end of this Luger section.

1906 Swiss Commercial

4.75" barrel, 7.65mm caliber. Swiss Cross in Sunburst appears over chamber. Extractor marked "Geladen". Frame under safety is polished. No stock lug and proofmarks are commercial. Approximately 1,000 manufactured in 35000-55000 serial number range.

Courtesy Bonhams & Butterfields, San Francisco, California

NIB	Exc.	V.G.	Good	Fair	Poor
—	5800	4700	2500	1400	800

1906 Swiss Military

Swiss Commercial except with military proofmarks.

NIB	Exc.	V.G.	Good	Fair	Poor
—	5500	3800	2200	900	700

1906 Swiss Police Cross in Shield

As above, with shield replacing sunburst on chamber marking. There were 10,215 of both models combined. In 5000-15215 serial number range.

Courtesy Gale Morgan

NIB	Exc.	V.G.	Good	Fair	Poor
—	5200	4200	2000	1000	700

1906 Dutch Contract

4" barrel, 9mm caliber. No stock lug and chamber is blank. Extractor marked "Geleden" on both sides and safety marked "RUST", with a curved upward pointing arrow. Manufactured for military sales to Netherlands. Date will be found on barrel of most examples encountered. Dutch refinished their pistols on a regular basis and marked date on barrels. Approximately 4,000 manufactured, serial numbered between 1 and 4000.

Courtesy Gale Morgan

NIB	Exc.	V.G.	Good	Fair	Poor
—	5000	3500	1500	800	600

1906 Royal Portuguese Navy

4" barrel, 9mm caliber and no stock lug. Royal Portuguese Naval crest, an anchor under a crown, stamped above chamber. Extractor marked "CARREGADA" on left side. Frame under safety is polished. Approximately 1,000 manufactured with one- to four-digit serial numbers.

NIB	Exc.	V.G.	Good	Fair	Poor
—	11000	8000	6500	4000	2500

1906 Royal Portuguese Army (M2)

4.75" barrel, 7.65mm caliber. No stock lug. Chamber area has Royal Portuguese crest of Mannuel II stamped upon it. Extractor marked "CARREGADA". Approximately 5,000 manufactured, with one- to four-digit serial numbers.

Courtesy Gale Morgan

NIB	Exc.	V.G.	Good	Fair	Poor
—	4000	3200	1200	600	500

1906 Republic of Portugal Navy

4" barrel, 9mm caliber. No stock lug and extractor marked "CARREGADA". Made after 1910, when Portugal had become a republic. Anchor on chamber is under letters "R.P." Approximately 1,000 manufactured, with one- to four-digit serial numbers.

NIB	Exc.	V.G.	Good	Fair	Poor
—	10500	8000	5500	2500	1500

1906 Brazilian Contract

4.75" barrel, 7.65mm caliber. No stock lug and chamber area is blank. Extractor marked "CARREGADA" and frame under safety is polished. Approximately 5,000 manufactured for military sales to Brazil.

NIB	Exc.	V.G.	Good	Fair	Poor
—	3750	2900	1100	750	450

1906 Bulgarian Contract

4.75" barrel, 7.65mm caliber. No stock lug and extractor and safety are marked in cyrillic letters. Bulgarian crest stamped above chamber. Nearly all of the examples located have barrels replaced with 4", 9mm units. This was done after later 1908 model was adopted. Some were refurbished during Nazi era and these pistols bear Waffenamts and usually mismatched parts. Approximately 1,500 manufactured, with serial numbers of one- to four-digits.

NIB	Exc.	V.G.	Good	Fair	Poor
—	10000	7500	5000	3500	1500

1906 Russian Contract

4" barrel, 9mm caliber. No stock lug. Extractor and safety are marked with cyrillic letters. Crossed Nagant rifles are stamped over chamber. Approximately 1,000 manufactured, with one- to four-digit serial numbers; but few survive. An extremely rare variation and caution should be exercised if purchase is contemplated.

Courtesy Gale Morgan

NIB	Exc.	V.G.	Good	Fair	Poor
—	16000	12500	6500	4000	2500

1906 Navy 1st Issue

6" barrel, 9mm caliber. Safety and extractor are both marked in German. Chamber area is blank. There is a stock lug and unique two-position sliding Navy sight is mounted on rear toggle link. Approximately 12,000 manufactured for German Navy, with serial numbers of one- to five-digits. Wooden magazine bottom features concentric rings. **NOTE:** Many of these pistols had their safety changed so they were "safe" in lower position. Known as "1st issue altered". Value at approximately 20 percent less.

Courtesy Gale Morgan

NIB	Exc.	V.G.	Good	Fair	Poor
—	12500	7500	3000	1500	950

1906 Navy 2nd Issue

As above, but manufactured to be safe in lower position. Approximately 11,000, 2nd Issue Navies, manufactured with one- to five-digit serial numbers—some with an "a" or "b" suffix. Produced for sale to German Navy.

Courtesy Gale Morgan

NIB	Exc.	V.G.	Good	Fair	Poor
—	7000	4500	2500	1200	700

1908 Commercial

4" barrel, 9mm caliber. No stock lug and chamber area is blank. Extractor and safety are both marked in German and many examples are marked with "Germany" export stamp. Approximately 9,000 manufactured in 39000-71500 serial number range.

NIB	Exc.	V.G.	Good	Fair	Poor
—	5000	3500	750	600	450

1908 Bulgarian

Considered by many to be the most unique Luger manufactured. It has a 4" barrel, "DWM" logo over the chamber, no stock lug, Cyrillic lettered safety and extractor, Bulgarian crest on middle link and no lanyard loop

at rear of frame, but rather at lower end of rear grip strap. Nealy 10,000 manufactured, but few survived the heavy wartime use. Extremely rare in V.G. to Exc. condition.

NIB	Exc.	V.G.	Good	Fair	Poor
—	7500	5500	1500	1000	600

1908 Navy Commercial

6" barrel, 9mm caliber. Has a stock lug, no grip safety and characteristic two-position sliding sight mounted on rear toggle link. Chamber area is blank and safety and extractor are both marked. The "Germany" export stamp appears on some examples. Approximately 1,500 manufactured in 44000-50000 serial number range.

NIB	Exc.	V.G.	Good	Fair	Poor
—	8300	5000	2500	1750	1250

1908 Navy

As above, with "Crown M" military proof. May or may not have concentric rings on magazine bottom. Approximately 40,000 manufactured, with one- to five-digit serial numbers and "a" or "b" suffix. These Lugers are quite scarce, as many were destroyed during and after WWI.

NIB	Exc.	V.G.	Good	Fair	Poor
—	8000	5000	2000	1100	800

1914 Navy

Stamped with dates from 1914-1918 above chamber. Approximately 30,000 manufactured, with one- to five-digit serial numbers with an "a" or "b" suffix. They are scarce, as many were destroyed as a result of WWI. **WARNING:** Many counterfeit pistols reported. **NOTE:** Add 10 percent for 1916 date.

NIB	Exc.	V.G.	Good	Fair	Poor
—	6700	4700	2500	950	700

1908 Military 1st Issue

4" barrel, 9mm caliber. No stock lug. Extractor and safety are both marked in German. Chamber is blank. Approximately 20,000 manufactured, with one- to five-digit serial numbers—some with an "a" suffix.

NIB	Exc.	V.G.	Good	Fair	Poor
—	3500	2000	1000	500	350

1908 Military Dated Chamber (1910-1913)

As above, with date of manufacture stamped on chamber.

NIB	Exc.	V.G.	Good	Fair	Poor
—	2500	1700	800	500	350

1913 Commercial

As above, with grip safety. Approximately 1,000 manufactured, with serial numbers 71000-72000; but few have been noted and are considered to be quite rare.

NIB	Exc.	V.G.	Good	Fair	Poor
—	3200	2200	1300	850	600

1914 Military

As above, with stock lug. Chamber dated 1914 - 1918.

NIB	Exc.	V.G.	Good	Fair	Poor
—	2500	1700	600	500	350

1914 Artillery

8" barrel, 9mm caliber. Features a nine-position adjustable sight, which has a base that is an integral part of barrel. Has stock lug and furnished with military-style flat board stock and holster rig (see Accessories). Chamber dated from 1914-1918. Safety and extractor are both marked. Developed for artillery and machine gun crews; many thousands were manufactured, with one- to five-digit serial numbers—some have letter suffixes. Quite desirable from a collector's standpoint and is rarer than its production figures would indicate. After the war many were destroyed as the allies deemed them more insidious than other models, for some reason. **NOTE:** Add 100 percent to Models stamped with 1914 date. Complete matching rig adds considerably to value.

Courtesy Gale Morgan

NIB	Exc.	V.G.	Good	Fair	Poor
—	5000	3500	1700	1500	900

DWM Double Dated

4" barrel, 9mm cartridge. Date 1920 or 1921 stamped over original chamber date of 1910-1918, creating double-date nomenclature. These are arsenal-reworked WWI military pistols and were then issued to German military and/or police units within provisions of Treaty of Versailles. Many thousands of these Lugers were produced.

NIB	Exc.	V.G.	Good	Fair	Poor
—	2000	1000	550	400	300

1920 Police Rework

As above, except original manufacture date was removed before rework date was stamped. There were many thousands of these produced. **NOTE:** It is not unusual to find with one or two "Police Matched" magazines.

NIB	Exc.	V.G.	Good	Fair	Poor
—	1800	1200	500	350	300

1920 Commercial

Similar to above, with 3.5" to 6" barrels in 7.65mm or 9mm calibers. Marked "Germany" or "Made in Germany" for export. Others are unmarked and were produced for commercial sale inside Germany. Some of these pistols are military reworks, with markings and proofmarks removed; others were newly manufactured. Extractors and safety are both marked and chamber is blank. Serial number range one- to five-digits and letter suffixes often appear. **NOTE:** Add 15 percent for 9mm.

NIB	Exc.	V.G.	Good	Fair	Poor
—	2300	1300	950	450	350

1920 Commercial Navy

6" barrel, 9mm caliber. Some have a stock lug; others have been noted without. Chamber area is generally blank, but some have been found with 1914-1918 dates stamped on them. These were reworked by DWM from Military Navy Lugers after WWI for commercial sales. They are marked "Germany" or "Made in Germany" and were sold by Stoeger Arms, among others. Extractor and safety are both marked and unique Navy sight is on rear toggle link. No one knows exactly how many were produced, but they are quite scarce.

NIB	Exc.	V.G.	Good	Fair	Poor
—	9000	5000	2100	1100	850

1920 Commercial Artillery

8" barrel, 9mm caliber. Erfurt-manufactured pistols, as well as DWM-manufactured pistols, were reworked in this manner. Export markings "Germany" or "Made in Germany" are found on most examples. Number produced is not known, but examples are quite scarce.

NIB	Exc.	V.G.	Good	Fair	Poor
—	4500	3000	1100	700	450

1920 Long Barrel Commercial

10" to 24" barrels, 7.65mm or 9mm caliber. Extractor and safety are both marked and an artillery model rear sight is used. Often built to customer's specifications. They are rare and number manufactured is not known.

NIB	Exc.	V.G.	Good	Fair	Poor
—	5000	3450	1500	1000	800

1920 Carbine

11.75" barrel, 7.65mm caliber. Chamber is blank and extractor marked "Geleden" or "Loaded". Safety is not-marked. Carbine has checkered walnut forearm and stock. Most have "Germany" or "Made in Germany" export stamp. There were few of these carbines manufactured for commercial sales in and outside of Germany. Only two-digit serial numbers observed. **NOTE:** Prices include stock.

NIB	Exc.	V.G.	Good	Fair	Poor
—	14000	10500	5000	2500	1500

1920 Navy Carbine

Assembled from surplus Navy parts, with distinctive two position sliding navy sight on rear toggle link. Most are marked with export stamp and have naval military proofmarks still in evidence. Safety and extractor are marked and rarely one is found chambered for 9mm cartridge. Few were manufactured.

NIB	Exc.	V.G.	Good	Fair	Poor
—	19500	11000	5250	3000	1700

1920 Swiss Commercial

3.5" or 6" barrels, 7.65mm or 9mm caliber. Swiss Cross in Sunburst stamped over chamber and extractor marked "Geladen". Frame under safety is polished. There were a few thousand produced, with serial numbers in one- to five-digit range, sometimes with a letter suffix.

NIB	Exc.	V.G.	Good	Fair	Poor
—	4000	1800	1200	800	600

1923 Stoeger Commercial

3.5" to 24" barrels, 7.65mm or 9mm caliber. There is a stock lug. Chamber area is either blank or has the American Eagle stamped on it. Export stamp and "A.F.Stoeger Inc. New York" is found on right side of receiver. Extractor and safety are marked in German or English. This was model Stoeger registered with U.S. Patent office to secure Luger name and some examples will be so marked. There were less than 1,000 manufactured, with one- to five-digit serial numbers without a letter suffix. Individual appraisal must be secured on barrel lengths above 6". Be wary as fakes have been noted. Values given here are for shorter barreled models. **NOTE:** Add 25 percent for barrel lengths over 8"; 15 percent for three-line model.

Courtesy Gale Morgan

NIB	Exc.	V.G.	Good	Fair	Poor
—	6000	4500	1800	1000	700

Abercrombie & Fitch Commercial 100

Swiss Lugers were made for commercial sale in United States by "Abercrombie & Fitch Co. New York. Made in Switzerland". —in either one or two lines—stamped on top of barrel. Barrel is 4.75" in length and there were 49 chambered for 9mm and 51 chambered for 7.65mm cartridge. Has a grip safety and no stock lug. Swiss Cross in Sunburst stamped over chamber. Extractor is marked, but safety area is polished. Serial range is four digits—some with a letter suffix. This is a rare and desirable Luger. Be careful of fakes on models of this type and rarity.

NIB	Exc.	V.G.	Good	Fair	Poor
—	11000	8000	4500	3000	2000

1923 Commercial

7.5" barrel, 7.65mm caliber. Has a stock lug and chamber area is blank. Extractor and safety are both marked in German. Manufactured for commercial sales in and outside of Germany. Approximately 18,000 produced, with serial numbers in 73500-96000 range.

NIB	Exc.	V.G.	Good	Fair	Poor
—	2500	1800	800	600	450

1923 Commercial Safe & Loaded

As above, except extractor and safety are marked in English "Safe" & "Loaded". Approximately 7,000 manufactured in 73500-96000 serial number range.

Courtesy Gale Morgan

NIB	Exc.	V.G.	Good	Fair	Poor
—	3500	2200	1000	800	500

1923 Dutch Commercial & Military

4" barrel, 9mm caliber. Has a stock lug and chamber area is blank. Extractor marked in German and safety marked "RUST", with a downward pointing arrow. Sold commercially and to military in Netherlands. Approximately 1,000 manufactured in one- to three-digit serial range, with no letter suffix.

NIB	Exc.	V.G.	Good	Fair	Poor
—	4000	2800	1000	850	550

Royal Dutch Air Force

4" barrel, 9mm caliber. Marked with Mauser Oberndorf proofmark. Serial numbered in 10000 to 14000 range. Safety marked "RUST".

NIB	Exc.	V.G.	Good	Fair	Poor
—	5000	2900	1000	800	550

VICKERS LTD.

Vickers was not a manufacturer but an intermediary marketer.

1906 Vickers Dutch

4" barrel, 9mm caliber. No stock lug and uses a grip safety. Chamber is blank and extractor marked "Geleden". "Vickers Ltd." stamped on front toggle link. Safety marked "RUST", with an upward pointing arrow. Examples have been found with an additional date as late as 1933 stamped on barrel. Dates indicate arsenal refinishing and in no way detract from value of this variation. Arsenal reworks are matte-finished and originals are a higher-polished rust blue. Approximately 10,000 manufactured in 1-10100 serial-number range.

NIB	Exc.	V.G.	Good	Fair	Poor
—	3800	3000	1800	1200	750

ERFURT ROYAL ARSENAL

1908 Erfurt

4" barrel, 9mm caliber. No stock lug; year of manufacture from 1910-1913 stamped above chamber. Extractor and safety are both marked in German. "ERFURT" under a crown stamped on front toggle link. Many thousands produced as Germany was involved in WWI. Found in one- to five-digit serial range, sometimes with a letter suffix.

NIB	Exc.	V.G.	Good	Fair	Poor
—	2100	1350	600	400	350

1914 Erfurt Military

4" barrel, 9mm caliber. Has a stock lug and date of manufacture over chamber 1914-1918. Extractor and safety are both marked in German and front link marked "ERFURT" under a crown. Finish on this model is rough; as war progressed in 1917 and 1918 finish got worse. Many thousands produced with one- to five-digit serial numbers, some with letter suffixes.

NIB	Exc.	V.G.	Good	Fair	Poor
—	2000	1100	600	400	350

1914 Erfurt Artillery

8" barrel, 9mm caliber. Has a stock lug. Issued with a flat board-type stock and other accessories which will be covered in the section of this book dealing with same. Sight is a nine-position adjustable model. Chamber is dated 1914 and extractor and safety are both marked in German. "ERFURT" under a crown is stamped on front toggle link. A great many manufactured with one- to five-digit serial numbers, some with a letter suffix. Model similar to DWM Artillery, except finish is not as fine.

NIB	Exc.	V.G.	Good	Fair	Poor
—	3750	2200	1100	800	600

Double Date Erfurt

4" barrel, 9mm caliber. Area above chamber has two dates: original 1910-1918 and date of rework, 1920 or 1921. Extractor and safety are both marked in German. Model can be found with or without stock lug. "ERFURT" under a crown is stamped on front toggle link. Police or military unit markings are found on front of grip straps, more often than not. Thousands produced by DWM as well as Erfurt.

NIB	Exc.	V.G.	Good	Fair	Poor
—	1200	700	500	400	350

SIMSON & CO. SUHL, GERMANY

Simson was official rework firm for German army. Thanks to Edward Tinker for his contributions to this section.

Simson & Co. Rework

4" barrels, 9mm caliber. Chamber is blank, but some examples are dated 1917 or 1918. Forward toggle link stamped "SIMSON & CO. Suhl". Extractor and safety are marked in German. Most examples have stock lugs; some have been noted without them. Only difference between military and commercial models is proofmarks.

NIB	Exc.	V.G.	Good	Fair	Poor
—	2750	1650	900	600	500

Simson Grip Safety Rework

4" barrel, 9mm caliber. Grip safety was added. There is a stock lug. Chamber area is blank; extractor is marked but safety is not. Only a few of these commercial reworks manufactured. Caution should be taken to avoid fakes.

NIB	Exc.	V.G.	Good	Fair	Poor
—	3860	2600	1500	850	550

Simson Dated Military

4" barrel, 9mm caliber. There is a stock lug and year of manufacture from 1925-1926 stamped above chamber (below serial number 700). Extractor and safety both marked in German. Checkered walnut grips of Simson-made Lugers are noticeably thicker than others. This is an extremely rare variation. Few seem to have survived.

NIB	Exc.	V.G.	Good	Fair	Poor
—	5300	2600	1800	900	650

Simson S Code

4" barrel, 9mm caliber. Forward toggle link stamped with Gothic S, possibly for "Simson". It has a stock lug and area above chamber is blank. Extractor and safety are both marked. Grips are also thicker. Fewer than 12,000 manufactured, with one- to five-digit serial numbers—some with letter "a" suffix. Quite rare on today's market.

NIB	Exc.	V.G.	Good	Fair	Poor
—	6000	3250	1500	1000	750

EARLY NAZI ERA REWORKS MAUSER

Produced between 1930 and 1933. Normally marked with Waffenamt markings.

Deaths Head Rework

4" barrel, 9mm caliber. Has a stock lug; skull and crossbones are stamped, in addition to date of manufacture, on chamber area. Date was from 1914-1918. Extractor and safety are both marked. Waffenamt proof is present. Thought that this variation was produced for 1930-1933 era "SS" division of Nazi Party. Mixed serial numbers are encountered on this model and do not lower value. A rare Luger on today's market.

NIB	Exc.	V.G.	Good	Fair	Poor
—	3500	1900	950	600	450

Kadetten Institute Rework

4" barrel, 9mm caliber. Has a stock lug and chamber area stamped "K.I." above date 1933. This stood for Cadets Institute, an early "SA" and "SS" officers' training school. Extractor and safety are both marked and Waffenamt is present. Only a few hundred reworked and variation is quite scarce. Be wary of fakes.

NIB	Exc.	V.G.	Good	Fair	Poor
—	4500	2900	1100	800	600

Mauser Unmarked Rework

4" barrel, 9mm caliber. Entire weapon is void of identifying markings. Extensive refurbishing, removal of all markings, re-barreling, etc. Stock lug is present and extractor and safety are marked. Waffenamt proofmark is on right side of receiver. Number manufactured is not known.

NIB	Exc.	V.G.	Good	Fair	Poor
—	2500	1350	850	600	450

MAUSER MANUFACTURED LUGERS 1930-1942 DWM

Mauser Oberndorf

4" barrel, 9mm caliber. Has a stock lug, blank chamber area and marked extractor and safety. Early example of Mauser Luger. Front toggle link is still marked DWM. Leftover parts were intermixed with new Mauser parts in production of this pistol. One of the first Lugers to be finished with "Salt" blue process. Approximately 500 manufactured with one- to four-digit serial numbers, with letter "v" suffix. A rare variation.

NIB	Exc.	V.G.	Good	Fair	Poor
—	8000	6100	2000	1500	900

1934/06 Swiss Commercial Mauser

4.75" barrel, 7.65mm caliber. No stock lug, but has a grip safety. Swiss Cross in Sunburst stamped above chamber. Extractor and safety marked

1934 Mauser Swedish Contract

4.75" barrel, 9mm or 7.65mm caliber. Chamber dated 1938 or 1939. Extractor and safety are both marked in German. There is a stock lug. Front toggle link stamped with Mauser banner. Only 275 dated 1938; 25 dated 1939 in 9mm; 30 dated 1939 in 7.65mm. Serial number range is four-digits with letter "v" suffix.

NIB	Exc.	V.G.	Good	Fair	Poor
—	6000	3800	2000	1500	700

1934 Mauser Swedish Commercial

4" barrel, 7.65mm caliber. 1940 stamped over chamber; "Kal. 7.65" stamped on left side of barrel. Extractor and safety are both marked and Mauser banner stamped on front toggle link. There is a stock lug. Model is rare. Only a few hundred manufactured, with four-digit serial numbers with letter "w" suffix.

NIB	Exc.	V.G.	Good	Fair	Poor
—	4500	2950	1200	850	600

1934 Mauser German Contract

4" barrel, 9mm caliber. Chamber dated 1939-1942. Front toggle link stamped with Mauser banner. There is a stock lug. Extractor and safety are both marked. Grips are walnut or black plastic. Several thousand manufactured, with one- to five-digit serial numbers—some with letter suffixes. Purchased for issue to police or paramilitary units.

NIB	Exc.	V.G.	Good	Fair	Poor
—	4500	3200	1500	800	550

Austrian Bundes Heer (Federal Army)

4" barrel, 9mm caliber. Chamber is blank and there is a stock lug. Extractor and safety marked in German. Austrian Federal Army Proof stamped on left side of frame above trigger guard. Approximately 200 manufactured, with four-digit serial numbers and no letter suffix.

NIB	Exc.	V.G.	Good	Fair	Poor
—	4000	2350	1200	700	500

Mauser 2 Digit Date

4" barrel, 9mm caliber. Last two digits of year of manufacture—41 or 42—stamped over chamber. There is a stock lug and Mauser banner on front toggle link. Extractor and safety both marked. Proofmarks were commercial. Grips are walnut or black plastic. Approximately 2,000 manufactured for sale to Nazi political groups. They have one- to five-digit serial numbers; some have letter suffix.

NIB	Exc.	V.G.	Good	Fair	Poor
—	3500	2600	1500	900	650

Ku Luger (Prefix or suffix)

4" barrel, 9mm Luger. Probably manufactured by Mauser for German Luftwaffe in early 1940s. Serial number (on left side receiver area) has "Ku" prefix or suffix. Total production estimated at 5000 pieces.

Courtesy Gale Morgan

NIB	Exc.	V.G.	Good	Fair	Poor
—	4750	3000	1200	900	550

KRIEGHOFF MANUFACTURED LUGERS

1923 DWM/Krieghoff Commercial

4" barrel, 7.65mm or 9mm caliber. Chamber dated 1921 or left blank. There is a stock lug. Front toggle marked DWM, as they manufactured this Luger to be sold by Krieghoff. "Krieghoff Suhl" stamped on back above lanyard loop. Second "F" in Krieghoff was defective and all specimens have this distinctive die strike. Safety and extractor are marked in German. Only a few hundred manufactured, with four-digit serial numbers with letter "i" suffix.

NIB	Exc.	V.G.	Good	Fair	Poor
—	5000	3500	1700	900	500

DWM/Krieghoff Commercial

As above, but marked "Heinrich Krieghoff Waffenfabrik Suhl" on right side of frame. Some examples have "Germany" export stamp. Several hundred manufactured, with four-digit serial numbers with a letter suffix.

NIB	Exc.	V.G.	Good	Fair	Poor
—	4800	3650	2000	950	800

Krieghoff Commercial Inscribed Side Frame

4" or 6" barrel, 7.65mm or 9mm caliber. 1,000 were marked "Heinrich Krieghoff Waffenfabrik Suhl" on left side of frame and 500 were devoid of this marking. All have dagger and anchor trademark over "H.K. Krieghoff Suhl" on front toggle link. Extractor and safety are both marked. There is a stock lug and grips are of brown checkered plastic. Approximately 1,500 manufactured, with one- to four-digit serial numbers with "P" prefix.

NIB	Exc.	V.G.	Good	Fair	Poor
—	8500	6400	3000	2000	1000

S Code Krieghoff

4" barrel, 9mm caliber. Krieghoff trademark stamped on front toggle link and letter "S" stamped over chamber. There is a stock lug. Extractor and safety are both marked. Grips are wood on early manufactured pistols and brown checkered plastic on later examples. Approximately 4,500 manufactured for Luftwaffe, with one- to four-digit serial numbers.

NIB	Exc.	V.G.	Good	Fair	Poor
—	8500	5500	2000	950	750

Grip Safety Krieghoff

4" barrel, 9mm caliber. Chamber area is blank and front toggle link stamped with Krieghoff trademark. There is a stock lug and grip safety. Extractor marked "Geleden" and safety marked "FEUER" (fire) in the lower position. Grips are checkered brown plastic. Rare Luger and number produced is not known.

NIB	Exc.	V.G.	Good	Fair	Poor
—	9500	5900	3400	1700	900

36 Date Krieghoff

4" barrel, 9mm caliber. It has a stock lug and Krieghoff trademark on front toggle link. Safety and extractor are marked. Grips are brown plastic. Two-digit year of manufacture, 36, stamped over chamber. Approximately 700 produced in 3800-4500 serial number range.

NIB	Exc.	V.G.	Good	Fair	Poor
—	9000	6000	2600	1200	950

4 Digit Dated Krieghoff

As above, with date of production, 1936-1945, stamped above chamber. Approximately 9,000 manufactured within 4500-14000 serial number range. **NOTE:** Add 25 percent for 1942 or 1943 dates; 100 percent for 1944 or 1945.

Courtesy Gale Morgan

NIB	Exc.	V.G.	Good	Fair	Poor
—	7500	6000	3000	1500	750

2nd Series Krieghoff Commercial

4" barrel, 9mm caliber. There is a stock lug and Krieghoff trademark stamped on front link. Chamber area is blank. Extractor and safety are marked. Approximately 500 manufactured for commercial sales inside Germany. Date of manufacture is estimated at 1939-1940. This variation has dark finish that results from bluing without polishing surface, which was done during these years. Grips are coarsely checkered black plastic. Serial number range is one- to three-digits, with a "P" prefix.

NIB	Exc.	V.G.	Good	Fair	Poor
—	6500	4200	2200	1300	800

Post-War Krieghoff

4" barrel, 9mm caliber. There is a stock lug and chamber area is blank. Extractor and safety are marked. Serial numbers in one- to three-digit range are unusually large—about .1875 of an inch. There were 300 post-war Lugers produced for occupation forces. They were assembled from leftover parts and only 150 have Krieghoff trademark on front toggle link—second 150 have blank links.

NIB	Exc.	V.G.	Good	Fair	Poor
—	6000	3500	2000	750	650

Krieghoff Post-War Commercial

As above in 7.65mm caliber. Extractor not marked. Approximately 200 manufactured, with standard-sized two- or three-digit serial numbers. They were supposedly sold to occupation forces in PX stores.

NIB	Exc.	V.G.	Good	Fair	Poor
—	6500	3500	2200	700	550

East German Luger Rework, aka VOPO

Imported between 1996 and 1999, primarily by Miltex of La Plata, Maryland. These Russian reworked 9mm Luger pistols, were the first surplus Lugers imported to the United States since 1960s military surplus boom. Primarily captured by Soviet troops during WWII, these Lugers may be found with original matching or nonmatching numbers. Many were re-marked by the Russians, with examples having re-stamped matching numbers done by steel die or electro penciling. Issued to East German military and Volks Polizei (hence the People's Police, nickname VOPO), most had the walnut grips removed by the Russians, and were stored in barrels of oil to preserve them until they were reissued to the German Democratic Republic in 1946. It is believed they were removed from East German service by 1958. Black-lined hard rubber or plastic grips made both in Russia and Hungary were fitted to these pistols, as well as the more commonly encountered, East German-made brown checkered plastic grips that has a target-style design at the top. Many VOPO Lugers have Nazi Waffenampt "scrubbed" or a remaining Reich's Eagle with an obliterated swastika. Many are found with no German proofs at all. Snubbed by collectors at first, they now have a following and are a complete area of Luger collecting all to their own. Some re-barreled examples have an East German Crown over N marking on lower barrel, reflecting a replacement.

NIB	Exc.	V.G.	Good	Fair	Poor
—	1275	1100	875	600	300

LUGER ACCESSORIES
Detachable Carbine Stocks

Approximately 13" in length, with sling swivel and horn buttplate.

NIB	Exc.	V.G.	Good	Fair	Poor
—	6500	4500	3000	1000	700

Artillery Stock with Holster

Artillery stock is a flat board style, approximately 13.75" in length. There is a holster and magazine pouches, with straps attached. A desirable addition to Artillery Luger.

NIB	Exc.	V.G.	Good	Fair	Poor
—	3500	2500	1000	800	600

Navy Stock without Holster

As above, but 12.75" in length with metal disc inlaid on left side.

NIB	Exc.	V.G.	Good	Fair	Poor
—	4500	3000	1500	800	400

Ideal Stock/Holster with Grips

Telescoping metal tube stock, with attached leather holster. Used in conjunction with metal-backed set of plain grips that correspond to metal hooks on stock and allow attachment. This Ideal Stock is U.S. patented and is so marked.

NIB	Exc.	V.G.	Good	Fair	Poor
—	3500	2000	1500	700	450

Drum Magazine 1st Issue

A 32-round snail-like affair that is used with Artillery Luger. Also used with adapter in German 9mm sub-machine gun. 1st Issue has a telescoping tube that is used to wind the spring. There is a dust cover that protects interior from dirt.

NIB	Exc.	V.G.	Good	Fair	Poor
—	2500	2000	1500	550	300

Drum Magazine 2nd Issue

As above, with folding spring winding lever.

NIB	Exc.	V.G.	Good	Fair	Poor
—	2000	1700	1000	550	300

Drum Magazine Loading Tool

Tool slipped over magazine and allows spring to be compressed so cartridges could be inserted.

NIB	Exc.	V.G.	Good	Fair	Poor
—	1500	800	500	300	200

Drum Carrying Case

NIB	Exc.	V.G.	Good	Fair	Poor
—	500	350	125	100	50

LATE PRODUCTION MAUSER LUGERS MANUFACTURED DURING THE 1970S
P.08 Interarms

4" or 6" barrel, 7.65mm or 9mm caliber.

NIB	Exc.	V.G.	Good	Fair	Poor
1750	1250	550	400	350	300

Swiss Eagle Interarms

Swiss-style straight front grip strap and American Eagle crest over chamber. Chambered for 7.65mm or 9mm and offered with 4" or 6" barrel.

NIB	Exc.	V.G.	Good	Fair	Poor
1800	950	650	350	325	300

Cartridge Counter

Chambered for 9mm cartridge. Fitted with slotted grip to show cartridge count in magazine.

NIB	Exc.	V.G.	Good	Fair	Poor
2500	1600	1100	750	500	350

Commemorative Bulgarian

Bulgarian crest stamped over chamber. Only 100 produced.

NIB	Exc.	V.G.	Good	Fair	Poor
2200	1600	1100	750	500	350

Commemorative Russian

Crossed Nagant rifles stamped over chamber. Only 100 produced.

NIB	Exc.	V.G.	Good	Fair	Poor
2750	1600	1100	750	500	350

Modern Production Carbine

Splendid reproduction produced on limited basis. Workmanship is excellent. Carbine and stock furnished in case.

NIB	Exc.	V.G.	Good	Fair	Poor
6000	4500	4000	3200	2500	2000

JOHN MARTZ CUSTOM LUGERS
Martz Luger Carbine

16" barrel. Fewer than 100 manufactured.

NIB	Exc.	V.G.	Good	Fair	Poor
—	9000	7000	4500	2500	1000

.45 ACP or .357 SIG

6" barrel, .45 ACP caliber. Assembled from two Luger pistols that were split and welded together. Fewer than 100 manufactured.

NIB	Exc.	V.G.	Good	Fair	Poor
—	5500	4000	3000	—	—

Baby Luger 9mm & 7.65mm

Compact Luger pistol. Fewer than 300 produced.

Courtesy Gale Morgan

NIB	Exc.	V.G.	Good	Fair	Poor
—	4000	2500	1500	—	—

Baby Luger .380 ACP

As above in .380-caliber. Seven were manufactured.

Courtesy Gale Morgan

NIB	Exc.	V.G.	Good	Fair	Poor
—	8000	6000	4000	—	—

LUNA
Zella-Mehlis, Germany

Model 200 Free Pistol

.22-caliber Martini action single-shot pistol, with 11" barrel, adjustable sights and walnut grips. Manufactured prior to WWII.

NIB	Exc.	V.G.	Good	Fair	Poor
—	1850	1250	800	500	300

Model 300 Free Pistol

Single-shot target pistol chambered for .22 Short cartridge. Fitted with 11" barrel, set trigger, walnut stocks and forearm, with adjustable palm rest. Built about 1929 to 1939.

NIB	Exc.	V.G.	Good	Fair	Poor
—	1950	1250	800	500	300

Target Rifle

.22 or .22 Hornet caliber Martini action single-shot rifle, with 20" barrel, adjustable sights and walnut stock. Manufactured prior to WWII.

NIB	Exc.	V.G.	Good	Fair	Poor
—	1800	1350	850	500	250

LWRC INTERNATIONAL
Cambridge, Maryland

A manufacturer of AR-type rifles for military, law enforcement and civilian markets. All models a proprietary short-stroke, self-regulating, gas piston operating system that prevents the gases from contacting the bolt carrier or receiver. LWRC is acronym for Land Warfare Resources Corporation and previously stood for Leitner-Wise Rifle Company, Inc.

M6-A2

Standard carbine available in 5.56 NATO/.223 Rem., with 16.1" barrel (10.5" or 14.7" lengths for LE/Military) and in several AR configurations.

NIB	Exc.	V.G.	Good	Fair	Poor
2000	1700	1350	950	550	250

PSD-Pistol

Similar features as M6-A2, with 8" barrel and Magpul MIAD pistol-grip.

NIB	Exc.	V.G.	Good	Fair	Poor
1900	1600	1250	900	500	250

SIX8

Similar features to M6-A2, except chambered for 6.8 SPC II cartridge (6.8x43mm), a high-performance version of 6.8 Rem. SPC.

NIB	Exc.	V.G.	Good	Fair	Poor
2250	2000	1650	1200	600	300

REPR

Rapid Engagement Precision Rifle chambered for 7.62 NATO/.308 Win., with 16.1" or 20" barrel. Custom packages including one lower receiver, with two or more barreled uppers are available. Finish colors are black, Flat Dark Earth, Patriot Brown or O.D. Green.

NIB	Exc.	V.G.	Good	Fair	Poor
3100	2750	2150	1500	750	350

LYMAN
Middletown, Connecticut

Lyman In-Line

Introduced in 1998. In-line muzzle-loader offered in .50- or .54-caliber. Fitted with 22" barrel. Hardwood stock. **NOTE:** Add $80 for stainless steel version.

NIB	Exc.	V.G.	Good	Fair	Poor
300	250	200	125	75	50

Deerstalker Rifle

Available in .50- or .54-caliber percussion or flintlock. Fitted with 24" barrel and hardwood stock. **NOTE:** Add $80 for stainless steel version.

NIB	Exc.	V.G.	Good	Fair	Poor
375	250	200	150	100	50

Deerstalker Carbine

Same as above, with 21" barrel. Offered in .50-caliber only.

NIB	Exc.	V.G.	Good	Fair	Poor
375	250	200	150	100	50

Great Plains Rifle

Offered in .50- or .54-caliber flint or percussion. Barrel length 32". Hardwood stock. **NOTE:** Add $25 for flintlock version; $10 for left-hand rifles. Early models in Excellent condition are showing significant collector potential.

NIB	Exc.	V.G.	Good	Fair	Poor
525	400	300	175	125	100

Trade Rifle

Offered in .50- or .54-caliber, with 28" octagonal barrel and hardwood stock. Polished brass furniture. **NOTE:** Add $25 for flintlock rifle.

NIB	Exc.	V.G.	Good	Fair	Poor
300	250	200	125	75	50

Plains Pistol

Available in .50- or .54-caliber percussion.

NIB	Exc.	V.G.	Good	Fair	Poor
375	250	200	125	75	50

Model 1878 Sharps

Replica of famous single-shot in .45-70. Features tang-mounted aperture sight, globe front sight, checkered stock with a comfortable shotgun-style buttplate, laser-engraved sideplate and 30" barrel. Made in Italy by Pedersoli. Imported by Lyman beginning in 2014.

NIB	Exc.	V.G.	Good	Fair	Poor
1750	1450	1200	900	—	—

Little Sharps

Also known as Ideal Model, this smaller variation of original Sharps was chambered in a wide range of both rimfire and centerfire calibers. Made in Italy by Armi-Sport. Discontinued.

NIB	Exc.	V.G.	Good	Fair	Poor
1500	1200	850	650	500	350

M

M. B. ASSOCIATES-GYROJET
San Ramon, California

Established in 1960 by R. Maynard and Art Biehl. M. B. Associates produced Gyrojet pistols and carbines from 1962 to 1970. Basically a hand held rocket launcher, shooting a 12mm or 13mm spin stablized rocket cartridge, composed of four-part solid rocket fuel. Nose of the round was forced rearward onto a stationary firing pin, igniting fuel, expelling round and recocking for next shot. These were not very accurate and led to MBA's demise. Ammunition typically sells for $35 per round or more. By Dave Rachwal.

Mark I Model A Commemorative

13mm pistol cased with Goddard commemorative medal and 10 dummy rounds. Black anodized finish, with walnut grips.

NIB	Exc.	V.G.	Good	Fair	Poor
—	2195	1500	1200	900	500

Mark I Model B Commemorative

13mm pistol cased with commemorative Goddard medal and 10 dummy rounds. Black with walnut grips; or antique nickel with pearlite grips.

NIB	Exc.	V.G.	Good	Fair	Poor
—	1895	1695	1000	600	300

Mark I Model B

13mm pistol cardboard box. Black anodized, with walnut grips usually. Produced in many variations and finishes.

NIB	Exc.	V.G.	Good	Fair	Poor
—	995	800	650	400	200

Mark II Model C

12mm pistol. Black anodized, with walnut grips. Manufactured for 12mm round to conform with 1968 gun control act, because 13mm is .51-caliber and 12mm is .49-caliber.

NIB	Exc.	V.G.	Good	Fair	Poor
—	995	800	650	400	200

Mark I Model A Carbine

13mm black anodized finish, with walnut stock and carrying handle.

NIB	Exc.	V.G.	Good	Fair	Poor
—	2495	2195	1700	1000	600

Mark I Model B Carbine

13mm antique nickel finish, with walnut stock. Sporter carbine had flared muzzle and sleek lines.

NIB	Exc.	V.G.	Good	Fair	Poor
—	1495	800	900	400	200

M.O.A. CORP.
Dayton, Ohio

Maximum

Single-shot pistol. Manufactured in a variety of calibers from .22 rimfire to .454 Casull, with 8.5", 10" or 14" barrel, adjustable sights, stainless steel receiver, blued barrel and walnut grip. Introduced in 1986. **NOTE:** Add 100 percent for stainless steel barrel.

NIB	Exc.	V.G.	Good	Fair	Poor
800	600	475	325	250	125

Carbine

As above, with 18" barrel. Discontinued.

NIB	Exc.	V.G.	Good	Fair	Poor
1000	675	525	350	275	150

MAC
See—Ingram

MADSEN
Copenhagen, Denmark

Model 47

NIB	Exc.	V.G.	Good	Fair	Poor
—	700	525	400	275	125

MAGNUM RESEARCH, INC.
Minneapolis, Minnesota

See Also—Desert Eagle

BFR (Long Cylinder)

Single-action revolver, with long cylinder. Chambered for .22 Hornet, .30-30, .475/.480, .444, .45-70, .460 S&W and .45 LC/.410, with 7.5" or 10" barrel; .444 Marlin with 10" barrel. Also chambered for .500 S&W Magnum. Fitted with adjustable sights and stainless steel finish. Weight about 4 lbs. with 7.5" barrel. Introduced in 1998.

NIB	Exc.	V.G.	Good	Fair	Poor
900	775	500	350	200	100

BFR Little Max (Short Cylinder)

Single-action revolver has a standard cylinder chambered for .454 Casull (6.5", 7.5", or 10" barrel), .45 Long Colt (6.5" or 7.5" barrel), .22 Hornet (7.5" barrel) or .50 A.E (7.5" barrel). Weight about 3.5 lbs. with 7.5" barrel. Introduced in 1998. Discontinued.

NIB	Exc.	V.G.	Good	Fair	Poor
800	675	500	350	200	100

IMI SP-21

Semi-automatic double-action pistol. Chambered for 9mm, .40 S&W or .45 ACP cartridge. Barrel length 3.9". Magazine capacity 10 rounds for all calibers. Polymer frame, with steel slide and barrel. Weight about 26 oz. Made in Israel by Israel Military Industries. Discontinued.

Flashlight not included

NIB	Exc.	V.G.	Good	Fair	Poor
550	400	300	200	150	100

MAKAROV PISTOL

Makarov

The 9mm Makarov (9x18mm) caliber, 8-shot, semi-automatic, double-action, straight blowback pistol was adopted by the Soviet Union in 1951, to replace older 7.62x25mm Tokarev pistol. Production at Izhevsk factory continued through 1992, following the fall of the USSR. Makarov has a 3.68" barrel and mechanically similar to Walther PP/PPK series of pistols. Makarovs began to arrive in the U.S. in 1993, but due to the 1994 voluntary trade restriction of Russian military arms, importation was halted by 1995. All military versions have red-checkered plastic grips, with the circled star in the center. Makarov was licensed for production in China and Soviet satellites of East Germany and Bulgaria. Manufacture date and Izshevsk factory marking are found on the left frame, with serial number on both left slide flat and frame. Those dated in the 1950s are seldom seen. **NOTE:** Add 40 percent for those dated 1959 or earlier. The small quantity of Russian variants sold to East Germany in 1980s—some having German post-unification proof marks—will bring a 30 percent premium. These are also marked "Germany". Some imports marked with "Bulgaria" are known as "sneak" model that mistakenly entered the U.S. and will bring a 20 percent premium. Non-import marked specimens are highly desirable, especially if accompanied by military capture papers, and will raise prices considerably.

NIB	Exc.	V.G.	Good	Fair	Poor
—	700	600	550	400	200

Bulgarian Makarov

Manufactured under license from 1975 to 2007. Production was undertaken at the state factory Number 10 in Kazanlak (under Soviet supervision until 1976). After 1989, factory's name was changed to Arsenal or AD. Some specially made after the fall of communism, with Cerakote finish and red star grips for U.S. market. As the last licensed Makarov, many were sold to Slovenia after the Iron Curtain fell. As the most commonly encountered of all Makarov designed pistols, Bulgarian version is identified by Circle 10 on left frame along with serial numbers on this side as well. Manufacture dates consist of a coded numerical suffix adjacent to the serial number. Slovenian imported versions are usually in new, unfired condition, in cosmoline and if accompanied by holster and maintenance log book, values will increase by 40 percent. Those manufactured in the 1970s appear to fetch a higher price.

NIB	Exc.	V.G.	Good	Fair	Poor
—	575	450	375	275	200

East German Makarov

Similar to Russian made variant, however the blue finish is of a higher quality. Manufactured at Ernst Thaelmann state factory from 1958 (very rare) to 1965. Black plastic checkered grips are without the Soviet star. Identified by a "K100" in a rectangle on left frame adjacent to a small circle in a triangle. Serial number is on both left slide and frame, plus last two digits of manufacture year. Internal parts are serial numbered. A post-unification-made version produced with leftover parts marked SIMON SUHL/THUR is highly desirable and can bring a 50 percent premium, depending on condition. Often considered the "Colt" of Makarov pistols. It appears those with descreet import markings reap a far higher price.

NIB	Exc.	V.G.	Good	Fair	Poor
—	775	700	650	500	250

MALIN, F. E.
London, England

Boxlock and sidelock shotguns made by Malin were imported into United States for a number of years. As these arms were all essentially built to specific customer's requirements, values listed are rough estimates only.

Boxlock Basic Model

Features an Anson & Deeley action and high-grade walnut. All other specification were on custom-order basis. Gun should definitely be individually appraised as values will fluctuate greatly with options.

NIB	Exc.	V.G.	Good	Fair	Poor
4800	4000	3500	2500	1850	1000

Sidelock Basic Model

Features Holland & Holland-type detachable sidelock action. All other features (as on boxlock) were on a custom-order basis. This model should also be appraised individually.

NIB	Exc.	V.G.	Good	Fair	Poor
7000	6000	4750	3000	2500	1250

MALTBY, HENLEY AND CO.
New York, New York

Spencer Safety Hammerless Revolver

.32-caliber double-action revolver, with 3" barrel and 5-shot cylinder. Frame and barrel made of brass. Cylinder of steel. Barrel marked "Spencer Safety Hammerless Pat. Jan. 24, 1888 & Oct. 29, 1889". Several thousand manufactured during 1890s.

Courtesy Mike Stuckslager

NIB	Exc.	V.G.	Good	Fair	Poor
—	—	325	225	125	75

MANHATTAN FIREARMS COMPANY
Norwich, Connecticut
Newark, New Jersey

Bar Hammer Pistol

.31-, .34- or .36-caliber single-shot percussion pistol, with 2" or 4" barrel. Hammer marked "Manhattan F.A. Mfg. Co. New York". Blued, with walnut grips. Approximately 1,500 made during 1850s.

NIB	Exc.	V.G.	Good	Fair	Poor
—	—	1050	750	300	150

Shotgun Hammer Pistol

.36-caliber bar hammer single-shot percussion pistol, with 5.5" half octagonal barrel marked as above. Blued, with walnut grips. Approximately 500 made.

NIB	Exc.	V.G.	Good	Fair	Poor
—	—	1050	750	300	150

Pepperbox

.28- or .31-caliber double-action percussion pepperbox, with 3", 4" or 5" barrels and 5- or 6-shot barrel groups. Blued case-hardened, with walnut grips. Marked as above and also "Cast Steel". Major variations of this pistol are as follows:

Courtesy Milwaukee Public Museum, Milwaukee, Wisconsin

Three-shot with 3" Barrel
Manually rotated barrels.

NIB	Exc.	V.G.	Good	Fair	Poor
—	—	950	550	250	125

Five-shot with 3", 4", 5" Barrel
Automatically rotated barrels.

NIB	Exc.	V.G.	Good	Fair	Poor
—	—	1100	650	450	250

Six-shot with 3" or 4" Barrel
Automatic rotation.

NIB	Exc.	V.G.	Good	Fair	Poor
—	—	1100	650	450	250

Six-shot with 5" Barrel
Automatic rotation.

NIB	Exc.	V.G.	Good	Fair	Poor
—	—	1600	1200	550	350

Pocket Revolver

.31-caliber percussion revolver, with 4", 5" or 6" barrel and 5- or 6-shot cylinder. Blued case-hardened, with walnut grips. Barrel marked "Manhattan Firearms/Manufg. Co. New York" on 5-shot model, serial numbers from 1 to approximately 1,000; "Manhattan Firearms Mfg. Co. New York" on 6-shot model, frame marked "December 27, 1859".

Courtesy Milwaukee Public Museum, Milwaukee, Wisconsin

First Model—Five-Shot

NIB	Exc.	V.G.	Good	Fair	Poor
—	—	1200	600	450	150

Second Model—Six-Shot

NIB	Exc.	V.G.	Good	Fair	Poor
—	—	1200	600	450	150

London Pistol Company

As above marked "London Pistol Company". Approximately 200 manufactured between 1859 and 1861.

NIB	Exc.	V.G.	Good	Fair	Poor
—	—	1400	750	450	150

.36 Caliber Percussion Revolver

.36-caliber percussion revolver, with 4", 5" or 6.5" octagonal barrel and 5- or 6-shot cylinder. Blued case-hardened, with walnut grips. Approximately 78,000 made between 1859 and 1868. There were five variations.

Courtesy Milwaukee Public Museum, Milwaukee, Wisconsin

Model I

A 5-shot cylinder marked "Manhattan Firearms Mfg. Co. New York". Serial numbers from 1 through 4200. **NOTE:** Add 15 percent premium for 6" barreled version.

NIB	Exc.	V.G.	Good	Fair	Poor
—	—	1500	1050	550	150

Model II

As above, with 1859 patent date marked on barrel. Serial range 4200 to 14500.

NIB	Exc.	V.G.	Good	Fair	Poor
—	—	1650	1350	550	150

Model III

A 5-shot cylinder marked "Manhattan Firearms Co. Newark NJ", together with 1859 patent date. Serial numbers from 14500 to 45200.

NIB	Exc.	V.G.	Good	Fair	Poor
—	—	1575	1200	500	150

Model IV

As above, with modified recoil shield. Patent date March 8, 1864 added to barrel inscription. Serial numbers from 45200 to 69200.

NIB	Exc.	V.G.	Good	Fair	Poor
—	—	1600	1250	450	150

Model V

NIB	Exc.	V.G.	Good	Fair	Poor
—	—	1700	1350	550	200

.22 Caliber Pocket Revolver

.22-caliber spur trigger revolver, with 3" barrel and 7-shot cylinder. Blued silver plated, with walnut or rosewood grips. Approximately 17,000 made during 1860s. Fairly close copy of S&W No. 1.

Courtesy Milwaukee Public Museum, Milwaukee, Wisconsin

NIB	Exc.	V.G.	Good	Fair	Poor
—	—	550	300	250	100

Manhattan-American Standard Hero

.34-caliber single-shot percussion pistol, with 2" or 3" round barrel that unscrews for loading. Blued, brass frame, with walnut grips. Marked "A.S.T. Co./HERO". Made by American Standard Tool Company, Manhattan's successor. Approximately 30,000 manufactured between 1868 and 1873.

Manhattan Manufactured

Marked "HERO/M.F.A.Co.". Approximately 5,000 produced.

NIB	Exc.	V.G.	Good	Fair	Poor
—	—	625	550	250	100

American Standard Manufactured

Approximately 25,000 produced.

NIB	Exc.	V.G.	Good	Fair	Poor
—	—	625	500	225	100

MANN, FRITZ
Suhl, Germany

6.35mm Pocket Pistol

6.35mm caliber semi-automatic pistol, with 1.65" barrel and 5-shot magazine. Blued, with plastic grips having name "Mann" cast in them. Weighs only 9 oz. One of the smallest semi-automatic pistols ever manufactured. Made between 1920 and 1922.

NIB	Exc.	V.G.	Good	Fair	Poor
—	395	295	200	150	100

7.65mm Pocket Pistol

7.65mm or 9mm short semi-automatic pistol, with 2.35" barrel and 5-shot magazine. Blued, with plastic grips that have name "Mann" cast in them. Manufactured between 1924 and 1929.

NIB	Exc.	V.G.	Good	Fair	Poor
—	375	275	200	150	100

MANNLICHER PISTOL
Steyr, Austria
See—Steyr

MANNLICHER SCHOENAUER
Steyr, Austria

Military models and their history, technical data, descriptions and prices see *Standard Catalog of Military Firearms* under "Austria-Hungary". Currently imported Mannlicher models, see Steyr.

Model 1903 Carbine

6.5x54mm caliber bolt-action rifle, with 17.7" barrel. Rotary magazine capacity 5 rounds. Folding rear leaf sight, double-set triggers and full-length walnut stock. Discontinued prior to WWII.

NIB	Exc.	V.G.	Good	Fair	Poor
—	2200	1650	1300	1000	550

Model 1905 Carbine

As above chambered for 9x56mm cartridge. Discontinued prior to WWII.

NIB	Exc.	V.G.	Good	Fair	Poor
—	1850	1500	1000	750	550

Model 1908 Carbine

As above chambered for 7x57mm or 8x56mm cartridge. Discontinued prior to WWII.

NIB	Exc.	V.G.	Good	Fair	Poor
—	1950	1600	1000	750	550

Model 1910 Carbine

As above chambered for 9.5x57mm cartridge. Discontinued prior to WWII.

NIB	Exc.	V.G.	Good	Fair	Poor
—	1850	1500	1000	750	550

Model 1924 Carbine

As above chambered for .30-06 cartridge. Discontinued prior to WWII.

NIB	Exc.	V.G.	Good	Fair	Poor
—	2750	2250	1750	1000	550

High Velocity Rifle

As above in 7x64mm Brenneke, .30-06, 8x60Smm Magnum, 9.3x62mm and 10.75x68mm caliber, with 23.5" barrel and folding leaf sight. Half-length walnut stock. Discontinued prior to WWII. **NOTE:** Add 75 percent for Takedown Model.

NIB	Exc.	V.G.	Good	Fair	Poor
—	2750	2250	1750	1000	550

Model 1950

.257 Roberts, .270 Winchester and .30-06 caliber bolt-action rifle, with 24" barrel and 5-shot rotary magazine. Blued, with half length walnut stock. Manufactured between 1950 and 1952.

NIB	Exc.	V.G.	Good	Fair	Poor
2000	1600	1250	800	650	450

Model 1950 Carbine

As above, with 20" barrel and full-length stock.

NIB	Exc.	V.G.	Good	Fair	Poor
2200	1750	1250	800	650	450

Model 1950 6.5 Carbine

As above in 6.5x54mm Mannlicher Schoenauer caliber, with 18.5" barrel and full-length stock.

NIB	Exc.	V.G.	Good	Fair	Poor
2300	1900	1400	1000	650	300

Model 1952

Similar to above, with turned back bolt handle. Manufactured between 1952 and 1956.

NIB	Exc.	V.G.	Good	Fair	Poor
2400	2100	1850	1300	650	300

Model 1952 Carbine

Similar to Model 1950 carbine. Additionally in 7x57mm caliber. Manufactured between 1952 and 1956.

NIB	Exc.	V.G.	Good	Fair	Poor
2450	2100	1850	1300	650	300

Model 1952 6.5mm Carbine

As above in 6.5x54mm Mannlicher Schoenauer caliber, with 18.5" barrel. Manufactured between 1952 and 1956.

NIB	Exc.	V.G.	Good	Fair	Poor
2400	2000	1500	850	650	300

Model 1956 Rifle

.243 or .30-06 caliber bolt-action rifle, with 22" barrel and Monte Carlo-style stock. Manufactured between 1956 and 1960.

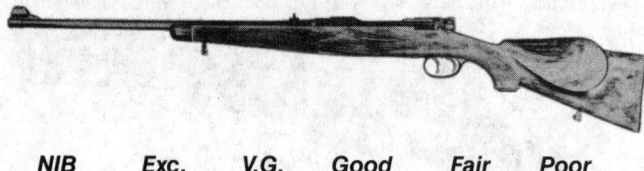

NIB	Exc.	V.G.	Good	Fair	Poor
2100	1900	1700	950	650	300

Model 1956 Carbine

As above, with 20" barrel and full-length stock. Manufactured between 1956 and 1960.

NIB	Exc.	V.G.	Good	Fair	Poor
2100	1900	1700	950	650	300

Model 1961 MCA Rifle

As above modified for easier use with telescopic sight.

NIB	Exc.	V.G.	Good	Fair	Poor
1750	1550	1250	1000	800	650

Model 1961 MCA Carbine

As above, with 20" barrel and half-length stock.

NIB	Exc.	V.G.	Good	Fair	Poor
1950	1650	1250	1100	700	600

Alpine Model

Variant of Model 1961 MCA was chambered in .243 Win. or .30-06. Featured engraving on the bolt handle and oak leaf carving on stock. Manufactured from 1965 to 1967.

NIB	Exc.	V.G.	Good	Fair	Poor
4000	3500	2850	2000	1000	300

Model M72 LM Rifle

Fitted with 23" fluted barrel, double-set or single trigger and full-length stock. Manufactured between 1972 and 1980.

NIB	Exc.	V.G.	Good	Fair	Poor
—	1300	1050	700	550	450

MANUFRANCE
St. Etienne, France
See—Le Francais

Auto Stand

.22-caliber semi-automatic pistol. Manufactured by Pyrenees and sold by Manufrance under trade name Auto Stand.

NIB	Exc.	V.G.	Good	Fair	Poor
—	250	225	200	150	100

Buffalo Stand

.22-caliber bolt-action pistol, with 12" barrel and adjustable sights. Blued, with walnut stock. Manufactured prior to 1914.

NIB	Exc.	V.G.	Good	Fair	Poor
—	250	225	200	150	100

Le Agent

8mm caliber double-action revolver, with 5" barrel. Blued, with walnut grips.

NIB	Exc.	V.G.	Good	Fair	Poor
—	200	100	175	150	75

Le Colonial

As above, with enclosed hammer.

NIB	Exc.	V.G.	Good	Fair	Poor
—	200	175	150	100	75

LeFrancais

Semi-automatic pistol chambered for 7.65mm cartridge. Built on blow-back design. 7.65mm pistols first built in 1950, discontinued 1959. Very few of these pistols are in U.S.

Courtesy J.B. Wood

NIB	Exc.	V.G.	Good	Fair	Poor
—	525	425	300	200	100

MANURHIN
Saint-Bonnet-le-Chateau, France

Company manufactured Walther PP and PPK models under license. These are marked "Manufacture de Machines du Haut-Rhin" on left front of slide and "Lic Excl. Walther" on left rear. These arms were imported into U.S.A. in early 1950s by Thalson Import Company of San Francisco, California and later by Interarms. Latter are marked "Mark 11" and "Made in France". Manurhin is now owned by Chapuis Armes. **NOTE:** All models add 15 percent for police markings.

Model PP

Similar to Walther Model PP, with revised safety. Discontinued.

NIB	Exc.	V.G.	Good	Fair	Poor
—	400	350	300	225	150

Model PPK/S

Similar to Walther Model PPK/S, with revised safety. Discontinued.

NIB	Exc.	V.G.	Good	Fair	Poor
—	400	350	300	225	150

Model PP Sports

Target version of PP. Chambered for .22-caliber shell. Available in various barrel lengths. Discontinued.

NIB	Exc.	V.G.	Good	Fair	Poor
—	400	350	300	225	150

Model 73 Defense Revolver

.38 Special or .357 Magnum caliber double-action swing-out cylinder revolver, with 2.5", 3" or 4" barrel having fixed sights. Blued, with walnut grips.

NIB	Exc.	V.G.	Good	Fair	Poor
1150	1000	850	750	500	350

Model 73 Gendarmerie

As above, with 5.5", 6" or 8" long barrel and adjustable sights.

NIB	Exc.	V.G.	Good	Fair	Poor
1250	1100	900	800	550	400

Model 73 Sport

Similar to above, with shortened lock time and target-style adjustable sights.

NIB	Exc.	V.G.	Good	Fair	Poor
1250	1100	900	800	550	400

Model 73 Convertible

As above, with interchangeable .22-, .32- or .38-caliber barrels and cylinders.

NIB	Exc.	V.G.	Good	Fair	Poor
2250	1850	1600	1400	950	750

Model 73 Silhouette

Similar to Model 73 Sport in .22 to .357 Magnum caliber, with 10" or 10.75" shrouded barrel. Form fitting walnut grips.

NIB	Exc.	V.G.	Good	Fair	Poor
1200	1050	850	750	500	350

MARATHON PRODUCTS, INC.
Santa Barbara, California

.22 First Shot

.22-caliber single-shot bolt-action rifle, with 16.5" barrel. Overall length 31". Blued, with walnut stock. Manufactured between 1985 and 1987.

NIB	Exc.	V.G.	Good	Fair	Poor
—	75	55	45	30	25

.22 Super Shot

As above, with 24" barrel. Manufactured between 1985 and 1987.

NIB	Exc.	V.G.	Good	Fair	Poor
—	75	55	45	30	25

.22 Hot Shot Pistol

.22-caliber bolt-action pistol, with 14.5" barrel. Blued, with walnut stock. Manufactured in 1986 and 1987.

NIB	Exc.	V.G.	Good	Fair	Poor
—	100	55	45	30	25

Centerfire Rifle

Bolt-action sporting rifle. Manufactured in a variety of calibers, with 24" barrel, open sights, adjustable trigger and 5-shot magazine. Blued, with walnut stock. Manufactured in 1985 and 1986.

NIB	Exc.	V.G.	Good	Fair	Poor
—	325	250	200	150	125

MARBLE'S ARMS & MFG. CO.
Gladstone, Michigan

Marble's Game Getter Gun—NFA, curio or relic

Marble's suspended sales of Game Getter in United States after Treasury Department ruled it was a "firearm" under NFA, but continued sales abroad. Retail price in 1934 was about $24 (12" or 15" barrels) to $26 (18" barrels). Bureau of Internal Revenue removed 18" barrel variation from NFA in a Letter Ruling dated March 1, 1939. Today, 12" and 15" barrel variations are controlled under NFA in "any other weapon" category. If shoulder stock is removed from a 12", 15" or 18" barreled Game Getter, however, ATF has ruled it to be a NFA "firearm" subject to a $200 transfer tax.

Model 1908

Serial numbered from A to M; then 001 to 10000.

NIB	Exc.	V.G.	Good	Fair	Poor
2750	2200	1600	1150	750	350

Model 1908 was available in two variations. Model 1908A has a flexible rear tang sight and Model 1908B has a filler block. Some confusion about serial numbering exists, because some Marble's factory representatives gave out incorrect information during 1960s and 1970s. According to some letters from this period, on Marble's factory letterhead, serial numbers began with number 700 and ended with 9999. Original factory records, however, disclose that Model 1908 was first shipped from factory in 1909, serial numbered with letters A through M, before beginning numerically with serial number 001 through 10000, when production ended in May, 1914. Serial number 001 was shipped from factory on March 3, 1909 and last Model 1908 was shipped on May 22, 1918.

Markings on Model 1908 are:

    Type I (serial 1 to about 4000)

    Type II (about serial 4000 to 9999)

LEFT SIDE:

MANUFACTURED BY THE
MARBLE SAFETY AXE CO.
GLADSTONE, MICH. U.S.A.
Marble Arms & Mfg. Co.

MANUFACTURED BY THE
MARBLE SAFETY AXE CO.
GLADSTONE, MICH. U.S.A.

SUCCESSOR

RIGHT SIDE:
Calibers 22 & 44
Patent Allowed

Calibers 22 & 44
Patent Allowed
Each of the markings on right side is enclosed within an elongated circle.

OTHER CHARACTERISTICS: Separate flat buttplate attached with two screws up to approximately serial number 1200; afterwards, a flattened buttplate was integrally formed from same round steel used to form skeleton stock. Early stocks have drop adjustment with a knurled collar .375" diameter by .1875" long; at approximately serial number 2500, collar was changed to .500" by .625" long. Hammer spur is curved down up to approximately serial number 2,000, then curve at hammer is up.

Model 1908 was originally designed for .22 Short, Long or LR and .44 shot and ball ammunition, but the most satisfactory load was long-cased .44-

40 that held shot in place with a disk and mouth crimp. The 1915 Marble's catalog stated Model 1908 was available for use with 2" .410 shotgun shell; chambering is slightly different from that of .44-40, but is seldom encountered. Production of Model 1908 was not resumed because of WWI.

Model 1921

NIB	Exc.	V.G.	Good	Fair	Poor
2100	1750	1250	900	500	250

To meet continuing demand for the extremely popular 1908, Marble's produced an entirely new gun in 1921. Grip, folding stock (made from cold-rolled sheet metal and nickel-plated) and other features were redesigned. Serial number range for Model 1921 is 10001 (shipped in October 1921) to 20076. Most production of Model 1921 apparently ended around the time of WWII; however, factory records disclose Marble's was exporting 15" barrel Model 1921s into Canada in 1955, where their registration was not required at that time. Marble's also assembled approximately 200 Model 1921s from parts circa 1960-61 and sold them (without holster) for $200 each.

Model 1921 was originally designed for 2" .410 shotgun shell, but Marble's changed the extractor marking on some guns to 2" or 2.5" to indicate factory rechambering for 2.5" shell, which has been reported to have started in 1924. However, change to a 2.5" chamber may not have been uniform, because both 2" and 2.5" marked guns have been observed in low (14000) and high (19000) serial number ranges. Lowest serial number with 2.5" marking observed so far is 14601. Range from approximately 14500 to 17000 have plastic rather than walnut grips, single-bladed rear sight rather than multiple-blade and blued rather than case-hardened hammer. Outside this range, only 19288 has 2" marking; and number 19692 is marked 2.5". No Model 1921 Game Getters are known to have been factory chambered for 3" .410 shell.

The markings on the Model 1921 are:

LEFT SIDE:

Marble's

Game Getter Gun

Marble Arms & Mfg.Co.

Gladstone, Mich.U.S.A.

RIGHT SIDE:

UPPER BARREL 22 S.L. LR.&N.R.A

LOWER BARREL .44GG & .410 2"

OTHER CHARACTERISTICS: Other barrel markings for Model 1921 in .410 are .410 2" and .410 2.5"; latter appears in serial number range from approximately 15000 to 16600 and in the low 19000 range.

NOTE: Boxed guns (wooden box, Model 1908; cardboard box, Model 1921) with accessories, or 18" barrel variations, nonstandard calibers (.25-20, .32-20, .38-40, etc.) command premiums of 50 to 200 percent or more; an original holster is $75 to $150. Two (2) new-in-box Model 1908 with 15" and 18" barrels sold for $2,700 and $3,600, respectively, in 1994. An original wooden Model 1908 box alone may sell for $500 to $900. All 18" barrel variations are rare.

Marble's Game Getter Pistol and other special-order or experimental Game Getters—NFA, curio or relic

Contemporary articles and advertisements in Hunter-Trader-Trapper and some early Marble's catalogs, state that a small number of Model 1908 Game Getters were originally manufactured (with rifled barrels) for .25-20, .32-20 and .38-40 cartridges. An illustrated advertisement in a 1910 issue of Hunter-Trapper-Trader states that 12", 15" and 18" barrel Game Getters were available for delivery in .25-20, .32-20 and .38-40 and that these firearms were designed as over/under rifles with rifled barrels. An article in October 1913 issue of Outdoor Life states that Marble's was manufacturing a Game Getter pistol, with 10" barrels and that any barrel length could be ordered.

Original factory records have confirmed the manufacture of foregoing Game Getters and clarified their designs. All original guns are thus correctly classified as experimental or special-order guns and all are extremely rare. Factory records disclose that about 20 each of Model 1908 were manufactured with .22/25-20 and .22/.32-20 over/under rifled barrels, but barrel lengths are not specified. No .22/.38-40 Model 1908 Game Getters are listed in factory records, but that may not have precluded a later factory alteration to that configuration. It is important to note that any Model 1908 Game Getter with over/under rifled barrels less than 18" in length is currently subject to registration under NFA as a short barreled rifle, with a $200 transfer tax. Under current law, if these firearms are not registered they are contraband and cannot be legally owned unless ATF administratively removes them from NFA as collector's items.

Factory records disclose that eight Model 1908 Game Getter pistols were manufactured and all were shipped to a Minneapolis hardware store. Two specimens have been located: serial number 3810, with a 8" .22/.44 smooth bore barrel, and serial number 3837, with a 10" .22/.44 smooth bore barrel. Inspection of serial numbers 3810 and 3837 (including removal of grips) reveal they were never fitted with shoulder stocks, because the portion of frame which would have accommodated the stock was never machined out to receive one. Under current law, an original Marble's Game Getter pistol is subject to registration under NFA as an "Any Other Weapon" with a $5 transfer tax. According to very incomplete factory records, a relatively small number—about a dozen—Model 1921 Game Getters were manufactured with .22/.38-40 rifled barrels, but barrel lengths are not specified. It is possible that other factory-original configurations exist, such as .22/.25-20 and others.

MARGOLIN
Tula, Soviet State Arsenal

Model MT Sports

Semi-automatic .22-caliber pistol, with no barrel weights. Not threaded for a compensator. Barrel length 7.5". Furnished with a black plastic case, with spare magazine and repair parts. Discontinued.

Courtesy Orvel Reichert

NIB	Exc.	V.G.	Good	Fair	Poor
—	600	500	400	300	200

Model MTS-1

.22 short semi-automatic pistol, with 5.9" barrel having an integral muzzle-brake (7.4" overall), adjustable walnut grips and 6-shot magazine. Normally accompanied by a wooden case, with cleaning accessories. Discontinued.

Courtesy Orvel Reichert

NIB	Exc.	V.G.	Good	Fair	Poor
—	1300	1025	800	450	350

Model MTS-2

As above in .22 LR, with 5.9" barrel. Discontinued.

Courtesy Orvel Reichert

NIB	Exc.	V.G.	Good	Fair	Poor
—	1200	900	600	400	350

MARIETTE BREVETTE
Liege, Belgium

A number of European manufacturers produced percussion pepperbox pistols based upon a patent issued to Mariette during 1840s and 1850s. These pistols have detachable barrels that are loaded at breech, double-action ring triggers and internally mounted hammers. Normally blued and foliate engraved.

4" Barrel Pepperbox

NIB	Exc.	V.G.	Good	Fair	Poor
—	—	2250	900	400	—

6" Barrel Pepperbox

NIB	Exc.	V.G.	Good	Fair	Poor
—	—	2250	900	400	

MARLIN FIREARMS CO.
Madison, North Carolina

Marlin, along with its subsidiaries Harrington & Richardson/NEF, are now owned by Freedom Group Family of Companies.

BALLARD RIFLES

Established by John Mahlon Marlin in 1863. Marlin manufactured pistols until 1875, when he began production of Ballard rifles. In 1881, he made his first lever-action repeating rifle for which his company became famous.

BALL & WILLIAMS BALLARDS

First Model

This model was the first Ballard produced. Introduced in 1861. Offered with 24" or 28" octagonal barrel. Frame case colored and barrel blued. Walnut stock is varnished. Major identifying feature of this model is inside extractor. This was the only Ballard that had this feature before Marlin began to manufacture the rifle in 1875. Barrel stamped "Ball & Williams/Worchester, Mass." and "Ballards Patent/Nov. 5, 1861". Approximately 100 manufactured. Serial numbered from 1-100.

NIB	Exc.	V.G.	Good	Fair	Poor
—	—	3000	2500	900	400

Military Rifle

There is not enough known about these rifles and probably never will be. Chambered most frequently for .44 and .54 rimfire cartridges and feature outside tangs and extractors. Offered with 30" round barrel and full-length forearm. There are three barrel bands and sling swivels. Government ordered only 35 of these for use in Civil War; if one was to be definitely authenticated as a genuine martial specimen, it would be quite valuable. Many of these rifles were marked "Kentucky" on top of receiver, because militia of that state armed its men with Ballard rifles and carbines. This marking was a sales aid used by the company and does not indicate militia ownership. Number manufactured is not known. Barrel markings are as on First Model.

NIB	Exc.	V.G.	Good	Fair	Poor
—	—	5000	2850	1250	300

Civil War Military Carbine

This model has a 22" part-round, part-octagonal barrel. Chambered for .44 rimfire cartridge. Has outside tang and extractor. Stock and forearm are walnut, with a barrel band sling swivel. Buttstock bears an oval cartouche surrounding inspector's marks "MM". These letters also appear stamped on major metal parts. Government ordered 1,509 for use in Civil War. Barrel was marked same as rifle.

NIB	Exc.	V.G.	Good	Fair	Poor
—	—	5500	3750	1500	500

Sporting Rifle

Chambered for .32, .38 and .44 rimfire cartridges. Octagonal barrel 24", 26" or 28" in length and blued. Frame is case colored. Stock and forearm are varnished walnut. A knob protrudes in front of frame to operate outside manual extractor. Crescent buttplate standard. Approximately 6,500 manufactured. Barrel markings same as on First Model.

NIB	Exc.	V.G.	Good	Fair	Poor
—	—	2000	1550	500	200

Sporting Carbine

Similar in appearance to Sporting Rifle, with 22" part-round part-octagonal barrel. Chambered for .44- and .54-caliber cartridge. Sling swivel is found on a barrel band in front. Knob on bottom activates outside extractor. Some encountered with "Kentucky" stamped on top, but this does not affect value. Markings are same as on previous models. There are no production figures available, but some estimate approximately 2,000 were manufactured.

NIB	Exc.	V.G.	Good	Fair	Poor
—	—	2200	1750	600	250

Dual Ignition System

This system allows use of rimfire cartridge or percussion method by simply turning striker on hammer from one position to the other. Features a percussion nipple mounted on breechblock and hammer marked "Patented Jan. 5, 1864". Patent was held by Merwin and Bray. This swivel system is usually found on sporting models and would increase value of weapon by 20 percent.

MERRIMACK ARMS CO. AND BROWN MANUFACTURING CO. (BALLARDS)

Values for Ballard rifles manufactured by these two firms are the same and specifications are similar. Identifying difference is markings "Merrimack Arms & Mfg. Co./Newburyport Mass." or "Brown Mfg. Co. Newburyport, Mass.". Merrimack produced approximately 3,000 of these rifles between 1867 and 1869 serial numbered in 18000-20000 range. Brown produced approximately 1,800 between 1869 and 1873 in 20000-22000 serial number range.

Sporting Rifle

Produced in .22- (rare), .32-, .38-, .44-, .46- and .52-caliber rimfire or percussion. Most encountered feature the dual ignition system and had nipple in breechblock. Round or octagonal barrel in 24", 26" or 28" lengths. Appearance and finish similar to Ball & Williams rifles; major difference is inside tang. Extractor was still outside mounted and manually activated. Exact production breakdown is unknown. There is no premium for dual ignition system on these later guns.

NIB	Exc.	V.G.	Good	Fair	Poor
—	—	1700	1250	450	200

Sporting Carbine

Quite similar in appearance to Sporting Rifle, with 22" part-round part-octagonal barrel.

NIB	Exc.	V.G.	Good	Fair	Poor
—	—	1800	1350	550	300

Military Rifle

Military Rifle similar to sporting version except, has a 30" round barrel and full-length forearm, with three barrel bands. Chambered for .44- and .52-caliber rimfire or percussion, with dual ignition system.

NIB	Exc.	V.G.	Good	Fair	Poor
—	—	2000	1500	650	300

Shotgun

Similar to Sporting Rifle in appearance. Chambered for 24-gauge, with 30" round barrel. A groove milled in top of frame to use as a sight. Buttplate is shotgun-style instead of usual crescent shape.

NIB	Exc.	V.G.	Good	Fair	Poor
—	—	1200	800	350	200

MARLIN-BALLARD RIFLES

Commencing in 1875, Ballard single-shot rifle was made by John Marlin for Schoverling and Daly. In 1881, business was incorporated and became Marlin Firearms Co. All Ballards made from then until 1891, when they were discontinued, were produced under this banner. Only real difference in rifles manufactured during these periods was in markings. Earlier rifles stamped "J.M. Marlin New Haven. Conn. U.S.A./Ballards Patent. Nov. 5, 1861"; post-1881 models stamped "Marlin Firearms Co. New Haven Ct. U.S.A./Patented Feb. 9, 1875/Ballards Patent Nov. 5, 1861".

Ballard Hunters Rifle

Resembles earlier Brown Manufacturing Company rifles. Utilizes many leftover parts acquired by Marlin. Chambered for .32, .38 and .44 rimfire and centerfire. Features John Marlin's unique reversible firing pin that allows same gun to use both rimfire and centerfire ammunition simply by rotating firing pin in breechblock. Model still had external ejector and bears J.M. Marlin markings. Approximately 500 manufactured in 1 to 500 serial range. Produced in 1875 and 1876.

NIB	Exc.	V.G.	Good	Fair	Poor
—	—	3700	2750	950	400

Ballard No. 1 Hunters Rifle

Model bears early J.M. Marlin marking only. Manufactured from 1876 until 1880. Discontinued before incorporation. Has 26", 28" and 30" barrel. Chambered for .44 rimfire or centerfire cartridge. Has reversible firing pin and new internal extractor. Production figures are not available. Serial number range between 500 and 4000.

NIB	Exc.	V.G.	Good	Fair	Poor
—	—	4500	3000	1000	400

Ballard No. 1-1/2 Hunters Rifle

Similar to No. 1. Chambered for .45-70, .40-63 and .40-65 cartridges. Does not have reversible firing pin. Barrel length 30" and 32". Manufactured between 1879 and 1883. Found with both early and later markings.

Courtesy Marlin Firearms Co.

NIB	Exc.	V.G.	Good	Fair	Poor
—	—	5200	3750	1500	500

Ballard No. 1-3/4 "Far West" Hunters Rifle

Model made by J. M. Marlin only. Similar to No. 1-1/2. Difference being addition of double-set triggers and a ring on opening lever. Manufactured in 1880 and 1881.

NIB	Exc.	V.G.	Good	Fair	Poor
—	—	6300	4750	2000	600

Ballard No. 2 Sporting Rifle

Chambered for .32, .38 rimfire or centerfire cartridges and .44 centerfire. Has reversible firing pin. Offered in 26", 28" and 30" barrel lengths. Features "Rocky Mountain" sights. Manufactured between 1876 and 1891. Found with both early and late markings.

Courtesy Milwaukee Public Museum, Milwaukee, Wisconsin

NIB	Exc.	V.G.	Good	Fair	Poor
—	—	3200	2000	650	200

Ballard No. 3 Gallery Rifle

Similar to No. 2 rifle. Chambered for .22 rimfire cartridge. Has a manually operated external extractor. Sights are same and a 24" barrel was offered in addition to 26", 28" and 30". Manufactured between 1876 and 1891.

NIB	Exc.	V.G.	Good	Fair	Poor
—	—	3200	2000	650	200

Ballard No. 3F Gallery Rifle

Deluxe version of No. 3. Has a pistol-grip stock, nickel-plated Schutzen-style buttplate and an opening lever like a repeating rifle. Features a 26" octagonal barrel and oil-finished stock. Manufactured in late 1880s. Quite scarce in today's market.

Courtesy Marlin Firearms Co.

NIB	Exc.	V.G.	Good	Fair	Poor
—	—	6500	4250	1750	500

Ballard No. 4 Perfection Rifle

Chambered for a number of centerfire calibers from .32-40 to .50-70. Barrel lengths from 26" to 30". Sights are "Rocky Mountain" type. Manufactured between 1876 and 1891.

Courtesy Rock Island Auction Company

NIB	Exc.	V.G.	Good	Fair	Poor
—	—	6500	4250	1750	500

Ballard No. 3-1/2 Target Rifle

Similar to No. 4 Perfection Rifle. Has a checkered stock, with shotgun-style buttplate, 30" barrel and tang peep sight with globe front sight. Chambered for .40-65 cartridge. Manufactured from 1880-1882.

NIB	Exc.	V.G.	Good	Fair	Poor
—	—	6500	4250	1750	500

Ballard No. 4-1/2 Mid Range Rifle

Variation of No. 4 Perfection model. Has a higher-grade checkered stock, with shotgun buttplate, 30" part-round part-octagonal barrel. Chambered for .38-40, .40-65 and .45-70 cartridges. Features a Vernier tang peep sight and globe front sight. Manufactured between 1878 and 1882.

NIB	Exc.	V.G.	Good	Fair	Poor
—	—	6750	4500	2000	500

Ballard No. 4-1/2 A-1 Mid Range Target Rifle

Deluxe version of No. 4-1/2" rifle. Features scroll engraving on frame, with "Ballard A-1" on left and "Mid-Range" on right. Chambered for .38-50 and .40-65 cartridge. Has a high-grade checkered stock, with horn fore-end tip. Sights are highest-grade Vernier tang sight and a spirit lever front sight. Shotgun or rifle-style butt was optional. Manufactured between 1878 and 1880.

Courtesy Milwaukee Public Museum, Milwaukee, Wisconsin

NIB	Exc.	V.G.	Good	Fair	Poor
—	—	9000	7250	3500	750

Ballard No. 5 Pacific Rifle

Model has a 30" or 32" medium to heavyweight barrel, with a ramrod mounted underneath. Chambered for many different calibers from .38-50 to .50-70. Features "Rocky Mountain" sights, crescent butt, double-set triggers and a ring-style opening lever. Manufactured between 1876 and 1891.

Courtesy Milwaukee Public Museum, Milwaukee, Wisconsin

NIB	Exc.	V.G.	Good	Fair	Poor
—	—	5500	4750	2000	500

Ballard No. 5-1/2 Montana Rifle

Similar to Pacific Rifle, with an extra heavyweight barrel. Chambered for .45 Sharps cartridge only. Features checkered steel shotgun-style buttplate. Manufactured from 1882-1884. Has late markings only.

Courtesy Milwaukee Public Museum, Milwaukee, Wisconsin

NIB	Exc.	V.G.	Good	Fair	Poor
—	—	15000	10000	5500	1250

Ballard No. 6 Schuetzen Off Hand Rifle

Model has a 30" or 32" octagonal barrel. Chambered for .40-65, .44-75 and .38-50 cartridges. Stock is of select walnut in high-combed Schuetzen style. Buttplate is nickel-plated. Receiver is not engraved. Sights are Vernier tang type on rear and a spirit lever front. Triggers are double-set. Opening lever has a ring and spur. Marked J.M. Marlin only. Manufactured between 1876 and 1880.

NIB	Exc.	V.G.	Good	Fair	Poor
—	—	—	6500	2500	500

Ballard No. 6 Schuetzen Rifle

Similar to Off Hand. Produced by later Marlin Firearms Company and was so marked. More deluxe version, with checkered stock, horn fore-end tip and a fully engraved receiver. Chambered for .32-40 and .38-55 cartridges. Manufactured between 1881 and 1891.

Courtesy Milwaukee Public Museum, Milwaukee, Wisconsin

NIB	Exc.	V.G.	Good	Fair	Poor
—	—	13000	8500	4500	1250

Ballard No. 6-1/2 Off Hand Mid Range Rifle

Chambered for .40-54 Everlasting cartridge only. Has 28" or 30" part-round part-octagonal barrel, Schuetzen-style stock, and plain non-engraved receiver. Manufactured between 1880 and 1882.

NIB	Exc.	V.G.	Good	Fair	Poor
—	20000	9500	5500	2500	500

Ballard No. 6-1/2 Rigby Off Hand Mid Range Rifle

Chambered for .38-50 and .40-65 cartridges. Features Rigby ribbed-style barrel in 26" and 28" lengths, with Vernier rear and globe front sights. High grade checkered walnut Schuetzen-style stock, with horn fore-end tip and pistol-grip cap. Buttplate nickel-plated. Opening lever of ring type, with single trigger. Extensively engraved receiver. Manufactured from 1880 to 1882.

Courtesy Marlin Firearms Co.

NIB	Exc.	V.G.	Good	Fair	Poor
—	—	14500	9000	5500	1250

Ballard No. 6-1/2 Off Hand Rifle

Chambered for .32-40 and .38-55 cartridges. Features barrel lengths 28" and 30". Checkered high-grade walnut Schuetzen-style stock, with nickel-plated buttplate. Fore-end tip and pistol-grip cap are of horn. Receiver engraved. Has single trigger, full-ring opening lever, Vernier tang rear sight and spirit lever front sight. Made by Marlin Firearms Company between 1883 and 1891. Found with later markings only.

NIB	Exc.	V.G.	Good	Fair	Poor
—	—	14000	9000	5500	1250

Ballard No. 7 "Creedmore A-1" Long Range Rifle

Model commonly chambered for .44-100 or .45-100 cartridges. Has 34" part-round part-octagonal barrel. High grade checkered pistol-grip stock, with a horn fore-end tip and shotgun-style butt. Sights are a special 1,300-yard Vernier tang rear and a spirit level front. Another sight base on heel of stock for mounting rear sight for ultra long-range shooting. Opening lever is similar to a repeating rifle. Single trigger featured. Receiver engraved and marked "Ballard A-1" on left and "Long Range" on right. Manufactured between 1876 and 1886. Found with both early and late markings.

Courtesy Milwaukee Public Museum, Milwaukee, Wisconsin

NIB	Exc.	V.G.	Good	Fair	Poor
—	—	15000	9700	5500	1250

Ballard No. 7 Long Range Rifle

Similar to "Creedmore A-1". Slightly less deluxe. Engraving less elaborate. Lettering on receiver is absent. Manufactured between 1883 and 1890. Found with later markings only.

Courtesy Marlin Firearms Co.

NIB	Exc.	V.G.	Good	Fair	Poor
—	—	13500	8000	4500	850

Ballard No. 7A-1 Long Range Rifle

Higher grade version of "Creedmore A-I", with fancier walnut and checkered straight stock. Better sights and deluxe engraving also featured. Manufactured between 1879 and 1883. Found with both markings.

Courtesy Marlin Firearms Co.

NIB	Exc.	V.G.	Good	Fair	Poor
—	—	16000	1000	5500	1250

Ballard No. 7A-1 Extra Grade Long Range Rifle

Highest grade version of No. 7 rifles. Features 34" "Rigby" -type ribbed round barrel. Usually a special-order rifle, with most features to customer specifications. Manufactured in limited numbers between 1879 and 1883. Found with both markings.

Courtesy Marlin Firearms Co.

NIB	Exc.	V.G.	Good	Fair	Poor
—	—	19500	11500	6500	1500

Ballard No. 8 Union Hill Rifle

Model has 28" and 30" part-round part-octagonal barrel. Chambered for .32-40 and .38-55 cartridges. Checkered pistol-grip stock, with nickel-plated buttplate; opening lever is fully enclosed ring as on repeaters. Double-set trigger and a tang peep, with globe front sight. Receiver not engraved. Manufactured between 1884 and 1890. Found only with late markings. This was one of the most popular rifles in Ballard line.

Courtesy Milwaukee Public Museum, Milwaukee, Wisconsin

NIB	Exc.	V.G.	Good	Fair	Poor
—	—	7000	4250	1750	500

Ballard No. 9 Union Hill Rifle

Similar to No. 8. Features a single trigger and better sights. Manufactured between 1884 and 1891. Has later markings only.

NIB	Exc.	V.G.	Good	Fair	Poor
—	—	7000	4250	1750	500

Ballard No. 10 Schuetzen Junior Rifle

Simply a heavier barreled version of No. 9. Barrel 32" long. Checkered pistol-grip stock is off-hand style. Rear sight Vernier Mid Range. Front sight spirit-level type. Popular model. Manufactured between 1885 and 1891. Found with later markings only.

NIB	Exc.	V.G.	Good	Fair	Poor
—	—	7000	4750	2000	650

MARLIN HANDGUNS

1st Model Derringer

First handgun produced by Marlin. Barrel 2.0625" long and pivots to side for loading. There is a plunger under the frame that is depressed to free barrel. This device is a Ballard patent. Chambered for .22 rimfire cartridge. No extractor. Frame brass and usually nickel-plated. Has two grooves milled beneath blued barrel. Grips are rosewood. Barrel stamped "J.M. Marlin, New Haven, Ct.". Approximately 2,000 manufactured between 1863 and 1867. Quite scarce on today's market.

NIB	Exc.	V.G.	Good	Fair	Poor
—	—	1350	750	300	100

O.K. Model Derringer

O.K. Model chambered for .22, .30 and .32 rimfire cartridges. Barrel 2.125" or 3.125" on .32 rimfire. No extractor. Functions as 1st Model. Frame plated brass, with flat sides. Barrel found blued or nickel-plated. Grips are rosewood. Markings same as on 1st Model, but located on right side of barrel. Top of barrel marked "O.K." Approximately 5,000 manufactured between 1863 and 1870.

NIB	Exc.	V.G.	Good	Fair	Poor
—	—	1350	750	300	100

Victor Model Derringer

Similar in appearance to "O.K.". Larger in size and chambered for .38-caliber rimfire cartridge. Barrel 2.6875" long; there was for the first time an extractor. Finish and function unchanged. Right side of barrel stamped "J.M. Marlin/New Haven, Ct./Pat. April 5.1870". "Victor" stamped on top of barrel. Approximately 4,000 manufactured between 1870 and 1881.

NIB	Exc.	V.G.	Good	Fair	Poor
—	—	1600	1250	500	150

Nevermiss Model Derringer

Made in three different sizes. Chambered for .22, .32 and .41 rimfire cartridges. Barrel 2.5" long and swings sideways for loading. Frame plated brass. Barrels blued or nickel-plated. Grips are rosewood. Frame grooved under barrels as on 1st model. There is an extractor. Barrel markings same as on "Victor", with top of barrel marked "Nevermiss". Approximately 5,000 manufactured between 1870 and 1881.

.22 Caliber Model

NIB	Exc.	V.G.	Good	Fair	Poor
—	—	1500	1150	500	100

.32 Caliber Model

NIB	Exc.	V.G.	Good	Fair	Poor
—	—	1200	750	350	100

.41 Caliber Model

Courtesy Marlin Firearms Co.

NIB	Exc.	V.G.	Good	Fair	Poor
—	—	3750	2500	1000	400

Stonewall Model Derringer

Identical to .41-caliber "Nevermiss". Top of barrel marked "Stonewall". Rarely encountered.

Courtesy Marlin Firearms Co.

NIB	Exc.	V.G.	Good	Fair	Poor
—	—	6000	4250	2000	750

O.K. Pocket Revolver

Solid-frame spur-trigger single-action revolver. Chambered for .22 rimfire short. Round barrel 2.25" and 7-shot cylinder is unfluted. Frame nickel-plated brass, with blue or nickel-plated barrel. Bird's-head grips are rosewood. Cylinder pin is removable and used to knock empty cases out of cylinder. Top of barrel marked "O.K." and "J.M. Marlin. New Haven, Conn. U.S.A.". Approximately 1,500 manufactured between 1870 and 1875.

Courtesy Marlin Firearms Co.

NIB	Exc.	V.G.	Good	Fair	Poor
—	—	700	500	200	75

Little Joker Revolver

Similar in appearance to "O.K." revolver. Some are reported to have engraving and ivory or pearl grips. Approximately 500 manufactured between 1871 and 1873.

Courtesy Marlin Firearms Co.

NIB	Exc.	V.G.	Good	Fair	Poor
—	—	500	500	350	125

J.M. MARLIN STANDARD POCKET REVOLVERS

In 1872, Marlin began production of its Smith & Wesson look-alike. Manhattan Firearms Company had developed a copy of Model 1 S&W .22 cartridge revolver. In 1868, company ceased business and revolvers were produced by American Standard Tool Company until their dissolution in 1873. In 1872, Marlin had entered into an agreement with this company to manufacture these revolvers, which were no longer protected by Rollin White patent after 1869. Marlin revolvers are similar to those made by American Standard. Only real difference being that Marlin grips are of bird's-head round configuration. A contoured grip frame and a patented pawl spring mechanism is utilized on Marlin revolvers.

Marlin XXX Standard 1872 Pocket Revolver

This is the first in a series of four Standard model revolvers. Chambered for .30-caliber rimfire. Earlier model has an octagonal 3.125" barrel; later, a round 3" barrel. There are round and octagonal barrel variations (with unfluted cylinders) and round barrel variations (with short and long fluted cylinders). All barrels are ribbed and tip up for loading. They have plated brass frames and barrels are nickel-plated. Bird's-head grips are of rosewood or hard rubber, bearing the monogram "M.F.A. Co." inside a star. There is a spur trigger. Markings "J.M. Marlin-New Haven Ct." appear on earlier octagonal barreled models. "U.S.A. Pat. July 1. 1873" was added to later round barreled models. All barrels are marked "XXX Standard 1872". Approximately 5,000 of all types manufactured between 1872 and 1887.

Octagon Barrel—Early Variation

NIB	Exc.	V.G.	Good	Fair	Poor
—	—	900	500	300	75

Round Barrel—Non-Fluted Cylinder

NIB	Exc.	V.G.	Good	Fair	Poor
—	—	800	400	275	75

Round Barrel—Short Fluted Cylinder

NIB	Exc.	V.G.	Good	Fair	Poor
—	—	750	350	200	75

Round Barrel—Long Fluted Cylinder

NIB	Exc.	V.G.	Good	Fair	Poor
—	—	750	450	150	75

Marlin XX Standard 1873 Pocket Revolver

Similar in appearance to XXX Standard 1872. Chambered for .22 Long rimfire and marked "XX Standard 1873". There are three basic variations: early octagonal barrel with non-fluted cylinder; round barrel with non-fluted cylinder; round barrel with fluted cylinder. Function and features same as described for "XXX Standard 1872". Approximately 5,000 manufactured between 1873 and 1887.

Early Octagon Barrel Model

Courtesy Marlin Firearms Co.

NIB	Exc.	V.G.	Good	Fair	Poor
—	—	900	600	200	100

Round Barrel—Fluted Cylinder

Courtesy Marlin Firearms Co.

NIB	Exc.	V.G.	Good	Fair	Poor
—	—	750	500	200	75

Round Barrel—Non-Fluted Cylinder

Courtesy Marlin Firearms Co.

NIB	Exc.	V.G.	Good	Fair	Poor
—	—	875	650	400	100

Marlin No. 32 Standard 1875 Pocket Revolver

Similar in appearance to "XXX Standard 1872". Chambered for .32 rimfire cartridge. 3" round barrel, with a rib. 5-shot cylinder fluted and in two different lengths to accommodate .32 Short or Long cartridge. Finish, function and most markings are same as on previous models, with exception of barrel top marking "No. 32 Standard 1875". Approximately 8,000 manufactured between 1875 and 1887.

Courtesy Marlin Firearms Co.

NIB	Exc.	V.G.	Good	Fair	Poor
—	—	675	450	200	75

Marlin 38 Standard 1878 Pocket Revolver

Different than its predecessors. Features a steel frame and flat bottom butt, with hard rubber monogram grips. Still a spur trigger and 3.25" ribbed round barrel that tipped up for loading. Chambered for .38 centerfire cartridge. Finish is full nickel plate. Top of barrel marked "38 Standard 1878". Approximately 9,000 manufactured between 1878 and 1887.

Courtesy Marlin Firearms Co.

NIB	Exc.	V.G.	Good	Fair	Poor
—	—	900	600	250	75

Marlin 1887 Double-Action Revolver

Last handgun Marlin produced and the only double-action. Chambered for .32- or .38-caliber centerfire cartridges. Break-open auto-ejector type. Fluted cylinder holds 6 shots in .32-caliber; 5 shots in .38-caliber. Round ribbed 3.25" barrel. Frame made of steel. Standard finish nickel-plated, with blued trigger guard. Many full-blued examples have been noted. Round butt grips are hard rubber. Top of barrel marked "Marlin Firearms Co. New Haven Conn. U.S.A./Patented Aug. 9 1887". Approximately 15,000 manufactured between 1887 and 1899.

Courtesy Marlin Firearms Co.

NIB	Exc.	V.G.	Good	Fair	Poor
—	—	800	500	200	75

EARLY PRODUCTION MARLIN RIFLES

Model 1881 Lever-Action Rifle

First Marlin lever-action rifle. Always been regarded as a high quality rifle. Capable of handling large calibers and well received by the shooting public. Chambered for .32-40, .38-55, .40-60, .45-70 and .45-85. The 24", 28" or 30" octagonal barrel is standard. Round barrels were offered and are scarce today. There is a tubular magazine beneath the barrel. Rear sight is buckhorn type, with a blade on front. Ejects its empty cartridges from top. Finish blued, with case colored hammer, lever and buttplate. Walnut stock is varnished. Approximately 20,000 manufactured between 1881 and 1892, but this is not easy to ascertain, as factory records on Marlin rifles are quite incomplete. **NOTE:** Add 200-300 percent premium for 1st Models prior to serial number 600; 15 percent premium for .45-70 caliber.

NIB	Exc.	V.G.	Good	Fair	Poor
—	4000	3000	2000	750	300

Lightweight Model

Thinner frame, lever and barrel. Caliber .32-40 and .38-55. Barrels 24" and 28" only.

NIB	Exc.	V.G.	Good	Fair	Poor
—	3500	2600	1750	600	300

Model 1888 Lever-Action Rifle

Chambered for .32-20, .38-40 and .44-40 cartridges. Shorter action was designed (chiefly by Lewis Hepburn) to handle pistol cartridges for which it was chambered. Standard barrel was octagonal, but round barrels were available as special-order items. Top ejecting action. Has buckhorn rear and blade front sight. Finish blued, with case colored hammer, lever and buttplate. Walnut stock varnished. Approximately 4,800 manufactured in 1888 and 1889. As with most of these fine old rifles, many special-order options were available that affect today's market value. Individual appraisal would be necessary for these special models, to ascertain both value and authenticity. **NOTE:** Add 40 percent premium for half octagon barrel; 20 percent premium for round barrel.

NIB	Exc.	V.G.	Good	Fair	Poor
—	3500	3000	2500	600	350

Model 1889 Lever-Action Rifle

Marlin's first side-eject solid-top rifle. Chambered for .25-20, .32-20, .38-40 and .44-40 cartridges. Features octagonal or round barrels in lengths from 24" to 32", lever latch and buckhorn rear and blade front sights. Finish blued, with case colored hammer, lever and buttplate. Plain walnut stock is varnished. Barrel stamped "Marlin Fire-Arms Co. New Haven Ct. U.S.A./Patented Oct.11 1887 April 2.1889". Many options were offered. Again one must urge individual appraisal on such variations. Values fluctuate greatly due to some seemingly insignificant variation. Approximately 55,000 manufactured between 1889 and 1899.

Production Model

24" barrel.

NIB	Exc.	V.G.	Good	Fair	Poor
—	1850	1700	1000	450	150

Short Carbine

15" barrel. 327 produced.

Courtesy Marlin Firearms Co.

NIB	Exc.	V.G.	Good	Fair	Poor
—	—	5000	2250	1000	500

Carbine 20" Barrel and Saddle Ring on Left Side of Receiver

Courtesy Marlin Firearms Co.

NIB	Exc.	V.G.	Good	Fair	Poor
—	—	2250	1250	500	250

Musket

30" barrel, with full-length stock. 68 made in .44-40.

NIB	Exc.	V.G.	Good	Fair	Poor
—	—	6500	3000	1250	650

Model 1891 Lever-Action Rifle

Marlin's first rifle designed to fire .22 rimfire; first repeating rifle to accept .22 Short, Long and LR cartridges interchangeably. Chambered for .32 rimfire and centerfire. The 24" octagonal barrel is standard, with buckhorn rear and blade front sights. Finish blued, with case colored hammer, lever and buttplate. Stock is plain walnut. First variation marked "Marlin Fire-Arms Co. New Haven, Ct. U.S.A./Pat'd Nov.19.1878. April 2.1889. Aug.12 1890" on barrel, with solid-topped frame marked "Marlin Safety". Second variation marked the same with "March 1,1892" added. Approximately 18,650 manufactured between 1891 and 1897.

1st Variation

.22 rimfire only. Side loading. Approximately 5,000 made.

NIB	Exc.	V.G.	Good	Fair	Poor
—	—	2500	1000	550	300

2nd Variation

.22 and .32 rimfire. .32 centerfire. Tube loading Model 1891. Later model tangs (3rd variation). **NOTE:** Add 20 percent for .22 rifle with "1891" stamped on tang. Deduct 50 percent for .32-caliber.

NIB	Exc.	V.G.	Good	Fair	Poor
—	—	1500	500	300	150

Model 1892 Lever-Action Rifle

Basically an improved version of Model 1891. Similar to second variation of 1891. Only notable exceptions were tang marking "Model 1892" and "Model 92" on later models. .22 rimfire was scarce in Model 1892. Approximately 45,000 manufactured between 1895 and 1916. There were many options. These special-order guns must be individually appraised to ascertain value and authenticity.

.22 Rimfire

NOTE: Add 20 percent for antique (pre-1898).

NIB	Exc.	V.G.	Good	Fair	Poor
—	—	1350	400	250	150

.32 Rimfire and Centerfire

NIB	Exc.	V.G.	Good	Fair	Poor
—	—	950	350	150	100

Model 1893 Lever-Action Rifle

First rifle Marlin designed for, then new, smokeless powder cartridges. Chambered for .25-36, .30-30, .32 Special, .32-40 and .38-55. Offered standard: round or octagonal barrel in lengths of 24" to 32"; buckhorn rear and blade front sights. Receiver, lever, hammer and buttplate are case colored. Rest is blued. Stock varnished walnut.

As with all early Marlins, many options were offered and when encountered, will drastically alter value of particular rifle. For this reason, we supply values for basic model and urge securing competent appraisal on non-standard specimens. Barrel on earlier guns marked "Marlin Fire-Arms Co. New Haven, Ct.U.S.A./ Patented Oct.11. 1887.April 2.1889. Aug.1.1893". In 1919, markings were changed to "The Marlin Firearms Corporation/ New Haven, Conn.U.S.A.Patented". Rifles manufactured after 1904 are marked "Special Smokeless Steel" on left side of barrel. Upper tang marked "Model 1893" on early guns; "Model 93" on later specimens. Approximately 900,000 manufactured between 1893 and 1935. Factory records are incomplete on Model 1893.

Antique Production (Pre-1898)

Courtesy Bonhams & Butterfields, San Francisco, California

NIB	Exc.	V.G.	Good	Fair	Poor
—	3000	2000	650	450	275

Modern Production 1899-1935

NOTE: Add 100 percent premium for musket. Deduct 50 percent for B model with blued receiver.

NIB	Exc.	V.G.	Good	Fair	Poor
—	2000	1100	550	350	225

Model 1894 Lever-Action Rifle

Similar to Model 1893, with a shorter action. Chambered for .25-20, .32-20, .38-40 and .44-40. Offered standard: 24" to 32" round or octagonal barrels with full-length magazine tubes; buckhorn rear and blade front sights. Finish is case colored receiver, lever, hammer and buttplate. Rest is blued. Walnut stock varnished. First versions marked "Marlin Fire-Arms Co., New Haven, Ct.U.S.A./Patented Oct.11, 1887. April 2,1889". Top of frame marked "Marlin Safety" and model designation is not stamped on tang. These early rifles were chambered for .38-40 and .44-40 only. Later rifles added patent date "Aug. 1, 1893"; "Model 1894" was stamped on tang. On latest versions this was shortened to "Model 94". Approximately 250,000 manufactured between 1894 and 1935. This model was produced with a great many options. Individual appraisal should be secured when confronted with these features.

Antique Production (Pre-1898)

NIB	Exc.	V.G.	Good	Fair	Poor
—	3500	2500	1850	750	350

Modern Production (1899-1935)

NOTE: Add 100 percent premium for musket; 25 percent premium saddle ring carbine; 30 percent premium "Baby" carbine.

NIB	Exc.	V.G.	Good	Fair	Poor
—	2800	2000	1200	600	250

Model 1895 Lever-Action Rifle

A large rifle designed to fire larger hunting cartridges. Chambered for .33 W.C.F., .38-56, .40-65, .40-70, .40-83, .45-70 and .45-90. Came standard with: round or octagonal barrels from 26" to 32" in length; bull-length magazine tube; buckhorn rear and blade front sights. Finish is case colored receiver, lever and hammer. Rest is blued. Varnished walnut stock. Barrel markings are same as Model 1894. Top tang marked "Model 1895". After 1896 "Special Smokeless Steel" was stamped on barrel. There were many options available and they have a big effect on value. Approximately 18,000 manufactured between 1895 and 1917.

Antique Production (Pre-1898)

NIB	Exc.	V.G.	Good	Fair	Poor
—	4000	3000	2200	1250	400

Modern Production (1899-1917)

NOTE: Add 75 to 100 percent for rare carbine variations.

NIB	Exc.	V.G.	Good	Fair	Poor
—	3600	2700	1800	800	300

Model 1897 Lever-Action Rifle

Improved version of Model 1892. Chambered for .22 rimfire only. Came standard with: 24", 26" or 28" round, octagonal or part-round, part-octagonal barrel; buckhorn rear and blade front sights; all were manufactured as takedown rifles. Case colored receiver, lever and hammer. Rest is blued. Walnut stock varnished. Approximately 125,000 manufactured between 1897 and 1917. In 1922, production began with designation changed to "Model 39" which is produced to this day. There were options offered with this rifle that have great effect on value. Take this into consideration and seek qualified appraisal.

Standard Production Rifle

NOTE: Add 40 percent for first year production antique.

NIB	Exc.	V.G.	Good	Fair	Poor
—	2200	1500	1100	650	200

Deluxe Rifle

Checkering and fancy pistol-grip stock.

NIB	Exc.	V.G.	Good	Fair	Poor
—	3000	2000	1500	850	300

POST 1900 PRODUCTION MARLIN RIFLES

Model 18

Slide-action model chambered for .22 rimfire cartridges. Offered standard with 20" round or octagonal barrel, open sights and straight walnut stock. Has an exposed hammer. Blued finish, with blued steel buttplate. There is a half-length tubular magazine. Stock features a quick takedown screw on top tang which was marked "Model 18". Manufactured between 1906 and 1909.

Courtesy Marlin Firearms Co.

NIB	Exc.	V.G.	Good	Fair	Poor
1500	1200	800	650	300	200

Model 20

Slide-action chambered for .22 rimfire cartridges. Offered standard with 24" octagonal barrel and open sight, with an exposed hammer. Only made as a "Takedown" receiver model. Blued, with straight walnut stock. Manufactured between 1907 and 1922.

NIB	Exc.	V.G.	Good	Fair	Poor
1500	1200	800	650	300	200

Model 25

Slide-action chambered for .22 Short only. Not a commercial success. Standard: 23" round or octagonal barrel; open sights. Called a takedown model, but only stock is removable—receiver does not separate. Has an exposed hammer, tubular magazine and straight walnut stock. Finish is blued. Manufactured in 1909 and 1910.

Courtesy Marlin Firearms Co.

NIB	Exc.	V.G.	Good	Fair	Poor
1600	1300	850	700	350	200

Model 27

Centerfire slide-action rifle. Chambered for .25-20 and .32-20 cartridges, also .25-caliber rimfire cartridge. Features 24" octagonal barrel, with two-thirds-length magazine tube that holds 7 shots. Has open sights, blued finish and straight walnut stock with crescent buttplate. Manufactured from 1910 to 1916. **NOTE:** Deduct 20 percent chambered for .25 rimfire.

NIB	Exc.	V.G.	Good	Fair	Poor
1500	1200	850	500	350	200

Model 27S

Similar to Model 27, with a sliding button on right side of receiver that permitted gun to be opened while a cartridge was in the chamber. Offered with a round (1913) or octagonal 24" barrel. The .25 rimfire cartridge was added in 1913 to those already available. introduced in 1910 and manufactured until 1932. **NOTE:** Deduct 20 percent chambered for .25 rimfire.

NIB	Exc.	V.G.	Good	Fair	Poor
1500	1200	850	500	350	200

Model 29

Slide action model identical to Model 20, with 23" round barrel and smooth walnut fore-end instead of a grooved one as found on Model 20. Manufactured between 1913 and 1916. **NOTE:** Deduct 20 percent chambered for .25 rimfire.

Courtesy Marlin Firearms Co.

NIB	Exc.	V.G.	Good	Fair	Poor
1500	1200	800	650	300	200

Model 32

First of hammerless slide-action rifles. Chambered for .22 rimfire. Has 24" octagonal barrel and half-length magazine tube. A takedown rifle, with adjustable sights and features "Ballard" rifling. Blued, with a pistol-grip walnut stock. Advent of WWI and need for Marlin to produce military arms, cut short production of this model. Manufactured in 1914 and 1915 only.

Courtesy Marlin Firearms Co.

NIB	Exc.	V.G.	Good	Fair	Poor
1800	1500	1200	850	400	300

Model 37

Slide-action model same as Model 29, with 24" round barrel and full-length magazine tube. Manufactured between 1913 and 1916.

Courtesy Marlin Firearms Co.

NIB	Exc.	V.G.	Good	Fair	Poor
1200	1000	700	600	300	200

Model 38

Hammerless slide-action introduced after end of WWI to replace Model 32. Similar in appearance. Features Rocky Mountain adjustable rear and ivory bead front sight instead of distinctive round Swebilius sight on Model 32. Manufactured between 1920 and 1930.

NIB	Exc.	V.G.	Good	Fair	Poor
1300	1100	850	650	300	200

Model 40

Slide-action identical to Model 27S centerfire. Barrel marked "Marlin-Rockwell". Top tang stamped "Marlin/Mod. 40". Rare, not many marked in this manner have been noted.

NIB	Exc.	V.G.	Good	Fair	Poor
1600	1300	850	500	350	200

Model 47

Similar to Model 20, with 23" round barrel and improved magazine tube. Has case colored receiver and checkered buttstock. Not offered for sale nor was it listed in Marlin's catalog, but offered free of charge to anyone purchasing four shares of Marlin stock for $100. One other fact about this model it was the first Marlin to be case colored with new cyanide method; this created a tiger-striped pattern that is peculiar to Model 47.

NIB	Exc.	V.G.	Good	Fair	Poor
—	1000	800	600	300	150

Model 1936, Rifle or Carbine

Lever-action model is a direct descendant of Model 1893. Chambered for .30-30 and .32 Special cartridge. Stock streamlined with a pistol-grip added and 20" round barrel. A barrel band and improved sights are utilized. Has a 7-shot tube magazine and semi-beavertail forearm. Receiver, lever and hammer are case colored. Rest is blued. Manufactured between 1936 and 1948. Designated Model 36 in 1937.

1st Variation (early 1936)

Variation has a slight "fish-belly" forearm, long tang, case colored receiver, lever and hammer, with no serial number prefix. These are rare.

NIB	Exc.	V.G.	Good	Fair	Poor
—	1200	850	400	175	125

2nd Variation (late 1936-1947)

Variation has thicker forearm, short tang and "B" serial number prefix.

NIB	Exc.	V.G.	Good	Fair	Poor
—	1000	650	300	150	100

Model 36 Rifle or Carbine (1937-1948)

First and Second variations of this lever-action both have case colored receiver and "C" serial number prefix. Second variation tapped for receiver sight.

NIB	Exc.	V.G.	Good	Fair	Poor
—	800	600	400	195	125

1st & 2nd Variations

NIB	Exc.	V.G.	Good	Fair	Poor
—	800	600	400	195	125

3rd Variation—Blued Receiver

NIB	Exc.	V.G.	Good	Fair	Poor
—	600	400	300	175	100

Model 36 Sporting Carbine

Similar to 1936 Carbine, with 20" barrel. Features two-thirds-length magazine tube and holds 6 shots instead of 7. Front sight is a ramp sight with hood.

NIB	Exc.	V.G.	Good	Fair	Poor
—	800	600	400	195	125

Model 36A-DL Rifle

Lever-action model similar to Model 36A, with deluxe checkered stock. Features sight swivels. Furnished with leather sling.

NIB	Exc.	V.G.	Good	Fair	Poor
1000	800	650	400	225	150

MODEL 336

Information on Model 336 provided by the late Doug Murray, author and publisher of The 336 (1983). **NOTE:** Beginning in 1980s, Marlin used "S" suffix on its model numbers (e.g., 336CS, 1895S, etc.) to designate models with new crossbolt safety. This suffix has now been dropped in most cases, even though safety remains.

Model 336 Carbine (R.C. Regular Carbine)

Introduced in 1948. Improved version of Model 36. Features a new-type round bolt chrome-plated, with improved extractor and redesigned cartridge carrier that improved feeding. Chambered for .30-30 and .32 Special cartridges. Has 20" tapered round barrel, with Ballard-type rifling. Finish blued, with receiver top matted to reduce reflections. Pistol-grip stock and semi-beavertail fore-end are of American walnut. Features Rocky Mountain-style rear and bead front sights. Hammer is lowered to facilitate scope mounting.

NIB	Exc.	V.G.	Good	Fair	Poor
—	475	325	175	125	100

Model 336C

Same as Model 336 Carbine. In 1951, catalog model designation was changed. In 1952, .35 Remington cartridge was added. In 1963, .32 Special was discontinued. This variation was discontinued in 1983.

NIB	Exc.	V.G.	Good	Fair	Poor
—	475	325	175	125	100

Model 336A

Similar to 336C, with 24" barrel and steel fore-end tip instead of a barrel band. Magazine tube is two-thirds-length and holds 6 shots. Introduced in 1948 and built until 1962. Reintroduced in 1973. Discontinued in 1980. In 1950, .35 Rem. was added. In 1960, .32 Special was discontinued.

NIB	Exc.	V.G.	Good	Fair	Poor
—	475	325	175	125	100

Model 336ADL

Differs from Model 336A. Has deluxe wood checkered stock and fore-end, quick detachable swivels, better grade finish and a sling.

NIB	Exc.	V.G.	Good	Fair	Poor
—	650	500	300	150	125

Model 336SC (Sporting Carbine)

Basically a 336A, with fore-end tip. Two-thirds magazine has 20" barrel instead of 24" found on 336A. **NOTE:** Add 25 percent for .219 Zipper.

NIB	Exc.	V.G.	Good	Fair	Poor
600	500	400	350	250	150

Model 336SD (Sporting Deluxe Carbine)

336 SC in a deluxe checkered stock version, with quick detachable swivels. Supplied with a sling. **NOTE:** Scarce model as only 4,392 were built.

NIB	Exc.	V.G.	Good	Fair	Poor
—	1000	750	400	200	125

Model 336 MicroGroove Zipper

Advertised as a fast-handling lever-action carbine. Chambered for .219 Zipper cartridges flat trajectory, varmint-type round. Has 20" heavy barrel, which was the feature that doomed it to failure as this was too short to coax maximum performance and accuracy from cartridge. "MicroGroove" rifling that was used did not yield long barrel life; model survived from 1955 through 1959, when it was discontinued. Externally similar to 336 SC. **NOTE:** First few thousand Zippers were made in standard weight barrels, not heavy weight. These are scarce and found in "M" prefix code number. Add 100 percent.

NIB	Exc.	V.G.	Good	Fair	Poor
1600	1000	800	600	300	150

Model 336T (Texan)

Straight-stock version of 336C. Chambered for .30-30 cartridge, with 20" barrel. Produced in .35 Rem. from 1953 to 1964; .44 Magnum from 1965 to 1967. Manufactured from 1953-1983.

NIB	Exc.	V.G.	Good	Fair	Poor
—	650	475	395	250	175

Model 336DT

Deluxe-stock version of "Texan", with map of Texas and a longhorn carved on butt. Manufactured between 1962 and 1964. Calibers: .30-30 and .35 Rem.

NIB	Exc.	V.G.	Good	Fair	Poor
—	700	550	425	275	175

Model 336 "Marauder"

Simply a 336T, with 16.25" barrel and slimmer fore-end. Chambered for .30-30 or .35 Rem. cartridges. Has a gold trigger. Drilled and tapped for both scope mounts and receiver sights. Manufactured in 1963 and 1964.

NIB	Exc.	V.G.	Good	Fair	Poor
—	750	675	550	300	150

Model 336 .44 Magnum

This is the 336 "Marauder", with 20" MicroGroove barrel chambered for .44 Magnum cartridge. Holds 10 shots. Introduced in 1963. Not very successful, because of feeding difficulties.

NIB	Exc.	V.G.	Good	Fair	Poor
—	600	450	295	150	100

Model 336 "Centennial"

In 1970, a 100th year medallion was embedded into the buttstock of 336 Carbines, 336 Texan and 444 Rifle.

NIB	Exc.	V.G.	Good	Fair	Poor
—	625	500	375	250	150

1970 100th Year Commemorative Matched Pair

Deluxe octagonal barreled .30-30, with engraved receiver and deluxe wood with an inlaid medallion, accompanied by a matching Model 339 .22 rimfire rifle. They are numbered the same and furnished in a deluxe luggage case. There were 1,000 sets manufactured in 1970. These are commemoratives. It should be noted that collectors usually will only show interest if they are new and unfired in original packaging. All accessories and brochures should be included for them to be worth top dollar. Once a commemorative has been used, it has no more value than as a shooter.

NIB	Exc.	V.G.	Good	Fair	Poor
2250	1750	1200	750	500	400

Model 336 "Zane Grey Century"

Introduced in 1972, 100th year anniversary birth of Zane Grey, famous Western author. Has 22" octagonal barrel chambered for .30-30. Stock is high grade walnut. Features brass buttplate and pistol-grip cap. Zane Grey medallion inlaid into receiver. Manufactured 10,000 in 1972. This is a commemorative rifle and must be new in box to generate top collector appeal.

NIB	Exc.	V.G.	Good	Fair	Poor
600	425	275	200	150	100

Model 336 Octagon

Introduced to utilize octagonal barrel making equipment that was on hand from manufacture of commemorative's. Essentially a 336T, with 22" tapered octagonal barrel chambered for .30-30 only. Features full-length magazine tube, slim fore-end with steel cap and classic-style hard rubber buttplate. Walnut stock is straight and lever square. Finish, including trigger, blued. Made in 1973 only.

NIB	Exc.	V.G.	Good	Fair	Poor
725	600	500	325	175	150

Model 336ER (Extra Range)

Introduced in 1983. Advertised as being chambered for .307 and .356 Winchester cartridges. .307 was never produced. .356 Winchester was supposed to add new capabilities to this classic rifle, but it never caught on with the shooting public. Discontinued in 1986 after only 2,441 Model ERs were manufactured. Has 20" barrel and 5-shot tube magazine.

NIB	Exc.	V.G.	Good	Fair	Poor
—	825	550	300	250	150

Model 336C

Current carbine model of this line. Has a hammer-block safety. Chambered for .30-30, .35 Remington and until 1988, .375 Winchester. Barrel 20" and magazine tube holds 6 shots. Pistol-grip stock and semi-beavertail forearm are American walnut. Has been manufactured since 1984. The 1983 model was known as 336C. Had no hammer-block safety. Weight about 7 lbs.

NIB	Exc.	V.G.	Good	Fair	Poor
475	350	225	200	175	150

Model 336SS

Similar to Model 336C in .30-30 only. Stainless steel barrel and receiver.

NIB	Exc.	V.G.	Good	Fair	Poor
525	400	250	200	150	100

Model 336LTS

Latest version of old "Marauder" carbine. Dubbed LTS or "Lightweight" instead of Marauder, as it was feared the latter designation would be inappropriate in today's society. Features 16.5" barrel, with full-length tube magazine that holds 5 shots. Walnut stock has straight-grip. Barrel band on forearm. Butt has rubber rifle pad. Introduced in 1988. Discontinued.

NIB	Exc.	V.G.	Good	Fair	Poor
675	450	300	250	200	150

Model 336 Cowboy

Similar to Model 336 CS. Available in both .30-30 and .38-55 calibers. Fitted with 24" tapered octagon barrel. Rear sight is Marble buckhorn. Tubular magazine holds 6 rounds. Straight-grip walnut stock has hard rubber buttplate. Weight about 7.5 lbs. First introduced in 1999.

NIB	Exc.	V.G.	Good	Fair	Poor
875	650	525	325	175	150

Model 336M

Introduced in 2000. Chambered for .30-30 cartridge. Features stainless steel receiver and barrel; all other parts are nickel plated. Barrel length 20". Magazine capacity 6 rounds. Checkered walnut stock has Mar-Shield finish. Rubber buttpad. Weight about 7 lbs. Marlin's first stainless steel rifle.

NIB	Exc.	V.G.	Good	Fair	Poor
675	550	425	275	175	125

Model 336CC

Chambered for .30-30 cartridge. Fitted with 20" barrel. Features Mossy Oak Break-Up camo finish. Adjustable rear sight. Weight about 7 lbs. Introduced in 2001.

NIB	Exc.	V.G.	Good	Fair	Poor
500	390	325	250	200	100

Model 336W

Similar to Model 336C in .30-30 only. Gold-plated trigger and hardwood stock. Available with factory-mounted 3x9 scope. **NOTE:** Add 10 percent for scope package.

NIB	Exc.	V.G.	Good	Fair	Poor
450	395	325	250	200	100

Model 336Y "Spike Horn"

Chambered for .30-30 cartridge. Fitted with 16.5" barrel. Features checkered walnut stock with pistol-grip. Magazine capacity 5 rounds. Adjustable rear sight. Weight about 6.5 lbs. Introduced in 2003.

NIB	Exc.	V.G.	Good	Fair	Poor
575	425	300	200	150	100

Model 336XLR

Lever-action chambered in .30-30 or .35 Remington, with 5-shot tubular magazine, 24" stainless steel barrel, along with stainless steel receiver, trigger, trigger guard plate, magazine tube, loading gate and lever. Full pistol-grip, swivel studs and Ballard-type rifling precision fluted bolt. Features solid top receiver with side-ejection, adjustable folding semi-buckhorn rear sight, ramp front sight, tapped for scope mount. Designed for Hornady LEVERevolution cartridges. Introduced 2006.

NIB	Exc.	V.G.	Good	Fair	Poor
725	600	475	350	225	175

Model 336BL

Lever-action chambered for .30-30. Features include 6-shot full length tubular magazine; 18" blued barrel with Micro-Groove rifling (12 grooves); big-loop finger lever; side ejection; blued steel receiver; hammer block safety; brown laminated hardwood pistol-grip stock with fluted comb; cut checkering; deluxe recoil pad; blued swivel studs.

NIB	Exc.	V.G.	Good	Fair	Poor
525	400	250	200	150	100

Model 30AS

Similar to 336 CS. Stock made of walnut-finished hardwood instead of genuine American walnut. Chambered for .30-30 only.

Marlin 30AS with scope

NIB	Exc.	V.G.	Good	Fair	Poor
395	285	200	175	125	100

Model 375

Introduced in 1980. Has 20" MicroGroove barrel. Chambered for .375 Winchester cartridge. Its appearance much the same as Model 336,

with walnut pistol stock and steel fore-end tip. Discontinued in 1983 after 16,315 manufactured.

NIB	Exc.	V.G.	Good	Fair	Poor
625	500	375	250	175	100

Model 444

Introduced in 1965. Chambered for .444 Marlin. Essentially a Model 336 action modified to accept larger cartridge. Has 24" round barrel that was cut back to 22" in 1971. Holds 5 shots total. When introduced, featured straight-grip Monte Carlo stock and semi-beavertail fore-end with barrel band. Another band holds the two-thirds-length magazine tube in place. In 1971 stock was changed to pistol-grip, without Monte Carlo comb.

NIB	Exc.	V.G.	Good	Fair	Poor
—	600	450	300	175	125

Model 444S

Introduced in 1972. Essentially, later 444 with steel fore-end tip instead of barrel bands.

NIB	Exc.	V.G.	Good	Fair	Poor
—	500	350	175	150	125

Model 444SS

In 1984, company added a crossbolt hammer-block safety to 444S and re-designated it 444SS.

NIB	Exc.	V.G.	Good	Fair	Poor
700	600	500	350	150	125

Model 444P Outfitter

Introduced in 1999. Chambered for .444 Marlin cartridge. Fitted with 18.5" ported barrel. Tubular magazine capacity 5 rounds. Walnut stock, with straight-grip. Ventilated recoil pad standard. Weight about 6.75 lbs. Discontinued 2002.

NIB	Exc.	V.G.	Good	Fair	Poor
725	600	425	335	275	200

Model 444XLR

Similar to Model 1895XLR. Chambered in .444 Marlin. Introduced 2006.

NIB	Exc.	V.G.	Good	Fair	Poor
625	500	375	250	175	100

Model 1894

Production of Model 336 in .44 Magnum was a frustrating experience. Action was simply too long for a short pistol case. In 1969, Marlin reintroduced Model 1894 chambered for .44 Magnum cartridge. Barrel 20". Full-length magazine tube holds 10 rounds. Features adjustable rear and ramp-type front sight. Finish blued, with matted receiver top. Walnut stock has straight-grip; fore-end a barrel band. From 1969 to 1971 there was a brass saddle ring.

NIB	Exc.	V.G.	Good	Fair	Poor
525	375	300	200	150	100

Model 1894 Octagon Barrel

Basically same as Model 1894, with 20" octagonal barrel. Steel fore-end tip instead of barrel band. Manufactured 2,957 in 1973 only.

NIB	Exc.	V.G.	Good	Fair	Poor
—	650	525	350	225	100

Model 1894 Sporter

Variation has 20" round barrel, half-length magazine tube that holds 6 shots. Hard rubber classic-style buttplate. Manufactured 1,398 in 1973 only.

NIB	Exc.	V.G.	Good	Fair	Poor
625	475	325	250	175	125

Model 1894P

Introduced in 2000. Chambered for .44 Magnum or .44 Special cartridges. Barrel length 16.25". Magazine capacity 8 rounds. Adjustable rear sight. Blued finish, with bead blasted receiver top. Drilled and tapped for scope mount. Weight about 5.75 lbs.

NIB	Exc.	V.G.	Good	Fair	Poor
600	450	375	300	150	100

Model 1894CS

Chambered for .38 Special and .357 Magnum cartridges. Features 18.5" round barrel, with full-length magazine tube and two barrel bands. Holds 9 shots. Walnut straight-grip stock. Manufactured between 1969 and 1984. In 1984, hammer-block crossbolt safety was added and model number was changed to 1894CS. All other specifications remained the same. Model is now known, again, as Model 1894C.

NIB	Exc.	V.G.	Good	Fair	Poor
—	525	375	275	125	100

Model 1894M

Similar to other 1894 rifles. Chambered for .22 Magnum cartridge. Features an outside loading tube magazine that holds 11 shots. Barrel 20". Steel fore-end tip instead of barrel band. Manufactured between 1983 and 1988. Only produced with crossbolt safety.

NIB	Exc.	V.G.	Good	Fair	Poor
—	550	450	325	275	150

Model 1894S

Introduced in 1984. Chambered for .41 Magnum and .44 Special/.44 Magnum cartridges. In 1988, .45 Colt chambering offered. Barrel 20".

Straight-grip stock. Fore-end has steel cap. Currently produced as Model 1894. Features hammer-block safety.

NIB	Exc.	V.G.	Good	Fair	Poor
550	450	375	275	175	125

Model 1894CL (Classic)

Introduced in 1988. Same basic rifle chambered for old .25-20 and .32-20 cartridges. Also chambered for .218 Bee. Barrel 22". Half-length magazine tube holds 6 shots. Walnut stock has no white spacers. Has black buttplate. Discontinued in 1993. **NOTE:** Collector interest has been growing since it was discontinued in 1993.

NIB	Exc.	V.G.	Good	Fair	Poor
750	550	450	300	250	150

Model 1894CL (Classic) New

Reintroduced in 2005. Chambered for .32-20 cartridge. Barrel 22", with open sights. Tubular magazine capacity 6 rounds. Checkered straight-grip walnut stock. Weight about 6 lbs. Discontinued.

NIB	Exc.	V.G.	Good	Fair	Poor
700	600	475	395	300	125

Model 1894 Century Limited

Anniversary edition of Marlin Model 1894. Limited to 2,500 rifles. Chambered in .44-40 caliber. Frame engraved and case colored. Fitted with 24" octagon barrel with 10-round magazine tube. Stock semi-fancy walnut with straight-grip and cut checkering, with brass crescent buttplate.

NIB	Exc.	V.G.	Good	Fair	Poor
1500	1200	800	600	400	300

Model 1894 Century Limited Employee Edition

Same as above. Limited to 100 rifles. Has finer grade wood. The Marlin man on horse logo inlaid in gold on right side of receiver.

NIB	Exc.	V.G.	Good	Fair	Poor
4000	3500	3000	—	—	—

Model 1894 Cowboy

Introduced in 1996. Lever-action features 24" tapered octagon barrel, with 10-round tubular magazine. Chambered for .45 Long Colt, a popular cartridge for "Cowboy Action Shooting". Straight-grip checkered stock. Flued steel forearm cap. Weight about 7.5 lbs.

NIB	Exc.	V.G.	Good	Fair	Poor
750	600	450	300	225	150

Model 1894 Cowboy 32

As above chambered for .32 H&R Magnum cartridge. Introduced in 2004.

NIB	Exc.	V.G.	Good	Fair	Poor
750	600	450	300	225	150

Model 1894 Cowboy II

Introduced in 1997. Same as Model 1894 Cowboy chambered for several cartridges. Available in .44-40, .357 Magnum .38 Special and .44 Magnum/.44 Special. Made with 20" or 24" barrel.

NIB	Exc.	V.G.	Good	Fair	Poor
650	525	300	225	150	100

Model 1894CP

Chambered for .375 Magnum cartridge. Fitted with 16.25" ported barrel. Tubular magazine holds 8 rounds. Checkered American black walnut stock. Adjustable semi-buckhorn rear sight. Receiver drilled and tapped for scope mount. Weight about 5.75 lbs. Introduced in 2001.

NIB	Exc.	V.G.	Good	Fair	Poor
626	575	450	300	225	100

Model 1894SS

Lever-action chambered for .44 Magnum and .44 Special cartridges. Barrel 20", with 10-round magazine. Stainless steel barrel and receiver. Checkered walnut stock, with straight-grip. Rubber buttpad. Weight about 6 lbs. Introduced in 2002.

NIB	Exc.	V.G.	Good	Fair	Poor
650	500	400	300	200	100

Model 1894PG

Introduced in 2003. Lever-action chambered for .44 Rem. Magnum cartridge. Fitted with 20" barrel. Checkered walnut stock, with pistol-grip. Magazine capacity 10 rounds. Adjustable rear sight. Blued finish. Weight about 6.5 lbs.

NIB	Exc.	V.G.	Good	Fair	Poor
575	450	300	225	150	100

Model 1894FG

Lever-action chambered for .41 Rem. Magnum cartridge. Fitted with 20" barrel. Checkered walnut stock, with pistol-grip. Magazine capacity 10 rounds. Weight about 6.5 lbs. Introduced in 2003.

NIB	Exc.	V.G.	Good	Fair	Poor
600	450	300	225	150	100

Model 1894 Cowboy

Fitted with 20" barrel. Chambered for .38 Special cartridge. Designed for Cowboy Action Shooting. Special hand-tuned parts. Magazine capacity 10 rounds. Walnut stock, with straight-grip. Case colored receiver, bolt, trigger plate and lever. Weight about 6 lbs. Introduced in 2002. In 2003, offered chambered for .45 Colt cartridge.

NIB	Exc.	V.G.	Good	Fair	Poor
825	750	600	500	300	150

Marlin 1894 Deluxe

Lever-action chambered in .44 Magnum/.44 Special. Features include 10-shot tubular magazine; squared finger lever; side ejection; richly polished deep blued metal surfaces; solid top receiver; hammer block safety; #1 grade fancy American black walnut straight-grip stock and fore-end; cut checkering; rubber rifle butt pad; Mar-Shield finish; blued steel fore-end cap; swivel studs; deep-cut Ballard-type rifling (6 grooves).

NIB	Exc.	V.G.	Good	Fair	Poor
600	500	400	325	250	150

Marlin 1894CSS

Lever-action chambered in .357 Magnum/.38 Special. Features include 9-shot tubular magazine; stainless steel receiver, barrel, lever, trigger and hammer; squared finger lever; side ejection; solid top receiver; hammer block safety; American black walnut straight-grip stock and fore-end; cut checkering; rubber rifle butt pad; Mar-Shield finish.

NIB	Exc.	V.G.	Good	Fair	Poor
725	600	450	350	300	200

Marlin 1894 CSBL

Chambered in .357/.38 Special, with 7-round capacity. Barrel 16.25", stock gray/black laminated. Other features include Marlin's Big Loop lever; stainless steel barrel, receiver, trigger guard plate and loading gate. Ghost ring sighting system, with mounting rail for optical sights. Introduced in 2011.

NIB	Exc.	V.G.	Good	Fair	Poor
800	725	600	500	400	300

Model 1895 and 1895SS

Model 1895 was reintroduced on Model 336 action, that had been modified to handle .45-70 cartridge. This was done to capitalize on nostalgia wave that descended on the country in early 1970s. Features 22" round barrel, with two-thirds-length magazine tube that holds 4 shots. Walnut stock had straight-grip until Model 1895S was released in 1980, when pistol-grip stock was used. In 1983, Model 1895SS with crossbolt hammer-block safety was added; currently produced in this configuration. **NOTE:** Add 25 percent for early "B" prefix guns below serial number 12000.

NIB	Exc.	V.G.	Good	Fair	Poor
600	500	325	200	150	100

Model 1895M

Similar to Model 1895. Chambered in .450 Marlin.

NIB	Exc.	V.G.	Good	Fair	Poor
600	500	325	200	150	100

Model 1895 Century Limited

Chambered for .45-70 cartridge. Features: 4-shot tubular magazine; 24" half round/half octagon barrel; semi-fancy walnut stock, with pistol-grip. Receiver French grayed and engraved with the Marlin man on one side and two bears on other. Weight about 7.5 lbs. Discontinued. 299 produced.

NIB	Exc.	V.G.	Good	Fair	Poor
1400	1200	900	600	400	200

Model 1895 Century Limited Employee Edition

Similar to above. Limited to 100 rifles. Company logo inlaid in gold on right side; left side has two cow elk and bull elk.

NIB	Exc.	V.G.	Good	Fair	Poor
3200	2700	2250	—	—	—

Model 1895G Guide Gun

Chambered for .45-70 Government cartridge. Has 18.5" ported barrel. Straight-grip walnut stock, with cut checkering and ventilated recoil pad. Adjustable rear sight. Weight about 6.75 lbs. Introduced in 1998.

NIB	Exc.	V.G.	Good	Fair	Poor
650	550	450	350	250	150

Model 1895GS Guide Gun

Introduced in 2001. This .45-70 rifle fitted with 18.5" ported barrel, with 4-round magazine. Stainless steel receiver and barrel. American black walnut stock, with cut checkering and ventilated recoil pad. Adjustable rear semi-buckhorn sight. Weight about 7 lbs. Early models had ported barrel, now discontinued.

NIB	Exc.	V.G.	Good	Fair	Poor
750	650	550	450	350	100

Model 1895 Cowboy

Chambered for .45-70 cartridge. Fitted with 26" tapered octagon barrel. Tubular magazine has 9-round capacity. Adjustable semi-buckhorn rear sight. American black stock, with cut checkering. Hard rubber butt. Weight about 8 lbs. Introduced in 2001.

NIB	Exc.	V.G.	Good	Fair	Poor
650	550	450	350	200	100

Model 1895XLR

Lever-action chambered in .45-70 Government or .450 Marlin; 4-shot tubular magazine; 24" stainless steel barrel; stainless steel receiver, trigger, trigger guard plate, magazine tube, loading gate and lever. Full pistol-grip, swivel studs and Ballard-type rifling precision fluted bolt. Features solid top receiver with side-ejection, adjustable folding semi-buckhorn rear sight, ramp front sight, tapped for scope mount. Designed for Hornady LEVERevolution cartridges. Introduced 2006.

NIB	Exc.	V.G.	Good	Fair	Poor
700	600	525	400	300	150

Model 1895MXLR

Similar to Model 1895XLR. Chambered in .450 Marlin. Introduced 2006.

NIB	Exc.	V.G.	Good	Fair	Poor
700	600	525	400	300	150

Model 1895 SBLR

Similar to Model 1895GS Guide Gun, with stainless steel barrel (18.5"), receiver, large loop lever and magazine tube. Black/gray laminated butt-stock and fore-end, XS ghost ring rear sight, hooded ramp front sight, receiver/barrel-mounted top rail for mounting accessory optics. Chambered in .45-70 Government. Overall length 42.5"; weight 7.5 lbs.

NIB	Exc.	V.G.	Good	Fair	Poor
875	700	600	525	400	150

Model 1895GBL

Lever-action chambered in .45-70 Government. Features include 6-shot full-length tubular magazine; 18.5" barrel, with deep-cut Ballard-type rifling (6 grooves); big-loop finger lever; side ejection; solid-top receiver; deeply blued metal surfaces; hammer block safety; pistol-grip two tone brown laminate stock, with cut checkering; ventilated recoil pad; Mar-Shield finish, swivel studs. Introduced 2010.

NIB	Exc.	V.G.	Good	Fair	Poor
550	500	425	350	250	150

Model 308MXLR

Similar to Model 1895MXLR. Chambered in proprietary .308 Marlin Express cartridge.

NIB	Exc.	V.G.	Good	Fair	Poor
700	600	525	400	300	150

Model 308MX

Similar to Model 308MXLR, with blued receiver and barrel.

NIB	Exc.	V.G.	Good	Fair	Poor
550	450	350	250	150	100

Model 338MXLR

Lever-action chambered for .338 Marlin Express. Features 24" stainless steel barrel; stainless steel receiver, lever and magazine tube; black/gray laminated checkered stock and fore-end; hooded ramp front sight and adjustable semi-buckhorn rear; drilled and tapped for scope mounts; receiver-mounted crossbolt safety. Overall length 42.5"; weight 7.5 lbs.

NIB	Exc.	V.G.	Good	Fair	Poor
700	600	525	400	300	150

Model 338MX

Similar to Model 338MXLR, with blued metal. Walnut stock and fore-end.

NIB	Exc.	V.G.	Good	Fair	Poor
550	450	350	250	150	100

Model 1897 Century Limited

Introduced in 1997. Chambered for .22-caliber cartridge. Commemorates 100th Anniversary of Model 1897. Fitted with 24" half round/half octagon barrel, with adjustable Marble rear sight and Marble front sight with brass bead. Blued receiver engraved and gold inlaid. Semi-fancy walnut stock. Hard rubber buttplate. Weight about 6.5 lbs.

NIB	Exc.	V.G.	Good	Fair	Poor
1150	950	700	550	300	200

Model 1897 Century Limited Employee Edition

Similar to above, with additional gold engraving on lever. Limited to 100 rifles.

NIB	Exc.	V.G.	Good	Fair	Poor
2000	1650	1250	—	—	—

Model 1897 Cowboy

.22-caliber lever-action rifle. Fitted with 24" tapered octagon barrel, with adjustable Marble buckhorn sight and Marble front sight with brass bead. Full-length tubular magazine holds 26 Shorts, 21 Longs and 19 LR cartridges. Walnut straight-grip stock, with hard rubber buttplate. Weight 7.5 lbs. Introduced in 1999.

NIB	Exc.	V.G.	Good	Fair	Poor
700	550	450	350	200	100

Model 1897 Annie Oakley

Introduced in 1998. This .22-caliber features 18.5" tapered octagon barrel, adjustable Marble rear sight and Marble front sight. Blued receiver roll engraved, with gold signature. Stock straight-grip, with blued end cap. Hard rubber buttplate. Weight about 5.5 lbs.

NIB	Exc.	V.G.	Good	Fair	Poor
1200	1000	750	600	400	200

Model 1897 Texan

Chambered for .22-caliber cartridge. Fitted with 20" octagon barrel; walnut stock with straight-grip. Magazine capacity 14 to 21 cartridges depending on type. Weight about 6 lbs. Introduced in 2002.

NIB	Exc.	V.G.	Good	Fair	Poor
700	600	400	300	200	125

Glenfield Lever-Action Rifles

Glenfield line of rifles were designed to be sold in large outlet chain stores. Simply cheaper versions that were to be sold for less money. Rifles functioned fine, but birch was used instead of walnut and pressed checkering instead of handcut. Manufactured under Glenfield name between 1964 and 1983. There are five models of Lever-Action Glenfields: 30, 30A, 30AS, 30GT and 36G. Chambered for .30-30 cartridge. Basic differences are slight and in most cases, merely cosmetic. They are good serviceable rifles, but have little or no collector interest or investment potential.

NIB	Exc.	V.G.	Good	Fair	Poor
295	250	200	150	125	100

Model 30AW

Lever-action chambered for .30-30 cartridge. Has 20" barrel and 6-round magazine tube. Stock walnut finished birch, with pistol-grip cap. Hard rubber buttplate. Introduced in 1998.

NIB	Exc.	V.G.	Good	Fair	Poor
300	250	200	150	125	100

MODEL 39

Originally evolved from Model 1891, invented by L.L. Hepburn. Model 1891 became Model 1892 and eventually developed into takedown Model 1897. Latter two were produced until 1915, when discontinued in favor of machine gun production for WWI. In 1922, when the company was sold to John Moran and became Marlin Firearms Corp., .22 rimfire lever-action was reintroduced as Model 39. Has been in production in one form or another ever since.

Model 39

Introduced in 1922. Model 39 was chambered for .22 rimfire, had 24" octagonal barrel and takedown receiver. Has full-length magazine tube which holds 25 Shorts, 20 Longs or 18 LR cartridges. Most Model 39s had a spring-loaded button outer magazine tube release. Very early variations had Model '97 type knurled latch release. As Model 39As were being phased in around 1939, many have more modern removable inner magazine tube. Has solid top frame and side ejection, Rocky Mountain rear and ivory bead front sight. Receiver, lever and hammer are case colored; barrel blued. Pistol-grip stock and steel-capped forearm are varnished walnut. Manufactured in this form between 1922 and 1938, with a number of options that could affect value and would warrant an individual appraisal. Model 39s with a "star" stamped on tang, were considered high grade guns by factory inspector and will command a premium in better condition examples. **NOTE:** Model 39s made prior to 1932 that have either no prefix or prefix S on serial number, should not be used with high-speed ammunition. Prefix HS indicates an improved bolt that is safe for this ammunition.

Standard Rifle

NIB	Exc.	V.G.	Good	Fair	Poor
—	4000	3000	2000	1000	750

Deluxe Rifle

Factory checkering, fancy wood and "star" stamp on tang.

NIB	Exc.	V.G.	Good	Fair	Poor
—	4500	3500	2200	1000	750

Model 39A

Improved version of Model 39. Has a heavier tapered round barrel, semi-beavertail forearm and redesigned pistol-grip stock. Rubber buttplate was replaced by one of a synthetic fiber; otherwise, specifications were similar to Model 39. Manufactured from 1939 to 1960. Several variations are listed.

Pre-war Variations (1939-1941)

Case colored receiver, no serial number prefix (1939) or "B" prefix (1940-1941).

NIB	Exc.	V.G.	Good	Fair	Poor
—	2200	1400	900	500	400

Post-war Variations (1945-1953)

Serial number prefixes up to letter "K". Ballard-type deep rifling. **NOTE:** Add 20 percent premium for C prefix 1st post-war variation, with figured wood.

NIB	Exc.	V.G.	Good	Fair	Poor
—	700	575	425	250	200

Post-war Variations (1954-1956)

Serial number prefixes L, M, N, with MicroGroove barrel.

NIB	Exc.	V.G.	Good	Fair	Poor
—	600	495	395	225	125

Golden 39A's" (1954-1963)

Gold trigger, MicroGroove rifling. Serial number prefixes L through W.

NIB	Exc.	V.G.	Good	Fair	Poor
—	550	450	325	195	125

Model 39A Mountie

Basically a carbine version of Model 39A. Features 20" tapered round barrel, straight-grip walnut stock and slimmed-down forearm. Manufactured between 1953 and 1960.

1st Variation

K prefix and 24" barrel, fat forearm. **NOTE:** Add 20 percent for slim forearm.

NIB	Exc.	V.G.	Good	Fair	Poor
—	600	450	300	200	100

Standard

NIB	Exc.	V.G.	Good	Fair	Poor
—	450	325	175	125	100

Model 39A 1960 Presentation Model

Released in 1960. Marlin's 90th Anniversary model. Similar to 39A. Has chrome-plated barrel and receiver, with high grade checkered walnut stock and fore-end. There is a squirrel carved on right side of buttstock. Produced 500 in 1960. This is a commemorative. Desirable to collectors only if NIB with all boxes and papers with which it was originally sold.

NIB	Exc.	V.G.	Good	Fair	Poor
1500	1200	800	650	300	200

Model 39M Mountie 1960 Presentation Model

Carbine version of 90th Anniversary model. Same as 39A, with 20" barrel and straight-grip stock. Manufactured 500 in 1960.

NIB	Exc.	V.G.	Good	Fair	Poor
1500	1200	800	650	300	200

Model 39ADL

Same as 90th Anniversary issue except blued instead of chrome-plated. Manufactured 3,306 between 1960 and 1963.

NIB	Exc.	V.G.	Good	Fair	Poor
1200	900	700	550	300	200

Model Golden 39A

Similar to 39A, with gold-plated trigger and sling swivels. Manufactured between 1960 and 1983.

NIB	Exc.	V.G.	Good	Fair	Poor
—	650	550	400	250	125

Model 39 Carbine

Slimmer lighter version of Model 39A. Features slimmer fore-end and thinner barrel. Manufactured 12,140 between 1963 and 1967.

NIB	Exc.	V.G.	Good	Fair	Poor
—	550	400	250	175	100

Model 39 Century Limited

Introduction of this model marked 100th Anniversary of the Marlin Company. Features 20" octagonal barrel, with semi-buckhorn rear and brass blade front sight. Stock is fancy walnut, with straight-grip, brass fore-end tip and buttplate. A medallion inlaid into right side of receiver. Brass plate on stock. Manufactured 34,197 in 1970. As a commemorative, needs to be as it came from the factory to command collector interest.

NIB	Exc.	V.G.	Good	Fair	Poor
950	550	300	150	125	100

Model 39A Article II

Commemorated National Rifle Association's 100th Anniversary in 1971. Has 24" octagonal barrel, high grade walnut pistol-grip stock, brass fore-end tip and buttplate. Right side of receiver has NRA's Second Amendment "Right to Keep and Bear Arms" medallion inlaid. Manufactured in 1971.

NIB	Exc.	V.G.	Good	Fair	Poor
750	450	300	150	125	100

Model 39M Article II

Same as Model 39A Article II, except a carbine version with 20" octagonal barrel and straight-grip stock. Manufactured 3,824 in 1971. As commemorative, NIB condition is essential to collector interest.

NIB	Exc.	V.G.	Good	Fair	Poor
775	475	325	175	150	100

Model 39A Octagon

Produced because the company had machinery and some leftover barrels from two commemorative models produced in 1970 and 1971. A regular production run that was meant to be used and was not a special issue. Has 24" tapered octagonal barrel. Chambered for .22 rimfire cartridges. Pistol-grip walnut stock, with steel fore-end tip. Manufactured 2,551 in 1972 and 1973. This was not a commercially successful model and discontinued for that reason.

NIB	Exc.	V.G.	Good	Fair	Poor
800	600	400	250	200	175

Model 39M Octagon

This is the 20" octagonal barreled carbine version, with straight-grip stock. Manufactured 2,140 in 1973.

NIB	Exc.	V.G.	Good	Fair	Poor
750	600	400	250	200	175

Model 39D

Essentially Model 39M carbine 20" barrel version, with pistol-grip stock. Manufactured in 1971; reintroduced in 1973. The 1971 version has white line spacers and pistol-grip caps; 1973 version has neither of these features.

NIB	Exc.	V.G.	Good	Fair	Poor
—	625	475	325	195	125

Golden 39A

Current production model of this extremely popular .22 rifle. Features hammer-block crossbolt safety and sling swivel studs. Similar in appearance to its predecessors. Takedown style.

NIB	Exc.	V.G.	Good	Fair	Poor
650	550	425	325	225	200

Model 39TDS

Similar to Model 39AS, with 20" carbine barrel and straight-grip stock. Replaced Model 39M. Introduced in 1988. Superseded by current Golden 39A, which is a takedown design.

NIB	Exc.	V.G.	Good	Fair	Poor
600	475	300	200	150	100

Model 39AWL

Limited edition of 2,000 rifles distributed solely through Wal-Mart. Fitted with 24.5" octagon barrel, select checkered walnut stock, gold filled engraving and stamped "Wildlife For Tomorrow".

NIB	Exc.	V.G.	Good	Fair	Poor
750	600	400	300	200	125

Model 56 Levermatic

Streamlined version of lever-action. Features short lever throw and one-piece walnut stock. Round 22" barrel. Chambered for .22 rimfire cartridges, with 7-shot detachable magazine. Open sights. Gold-plated trigger. Receiver made of aluminum after 1956. Manufactured 31,523 between 1955 and 1964.

NIB	Exc.	V.G.	Good	Fair	Poor
—	325	225	150	75	50

Model 56 "Clipper King" Levermatic

Same as Model 56, except specially packaged. Comes with 4X .22 scope. Name "Clipper King" stamped on barrel. Buttplate red hard rubber. Manufactured only 152 in 1959.

NIB	Exc.	V.G.	Good	Fair	Poor
—	350	250	175	100	75

Model 57 Levermatic

Similar to Model 56, with tube magazine and Monte Carlo stock. In 1960, Marlin went back to a steel receiver on this model. Manufactured 34,628 from 1959 to 1965.

NIB	Exc.	V.G.	Good	Fair	Poor
—	325	225	150	75	50

Model 57M Levermatic

Model 57 chambered for .22 Magnum cartridge. Manufactured 66,889 between 1959 and 1969.

NIB	Exc.	V.G.	Good	Fair	Poor
—	450	350	250	175	100

Model 62 Levermatic

Similar in appearance to Model 57, except chambered for centerfire .256 Magnum cartridge, with 4-shot magazine. In 1966, .30 carbine cartridge was added. This model has a 23" "MicroGroove" barrel, with open sights and walnut one-piece stock. First 4,000 Model 62s were shipped without serial numbers in violation of federal law. Company recalled rifles for numbering; and to this day, owner of a centerfire Model 62 can return rifle for numbering. Manufactured 15,714 between 1963 and 1969. **NOTE:** Add 15 percent for .256. From 1969 to 1972, first digit of serial number indicates year of manufacture. In 1973, system was changed by having first two digits subtracted from 100 to find year of production. For example: 2717793=100-27=1973.

NIB	Exc.	V.G.	Good	Fair	Poor
—	600	475	375	225	100

MISCELLANEOUS RIMFIRE RIFLES

Marlin Firearms Company produced a great many bolt-action rifles, both single-shot and repeaters, starting in 1930 and continuing today. These rifles were low-priced and designed primarily as utility rifles. They also manufactured many auto-loaders of the same type during these years. Glenfield name will also be found on these models, as many were produced to be marketed by large chain outlets. These rifles have limited value as collectibles at the present time, but no one can deny that they're durable accurate good-natured little rifles.

Model 70P "Papoose"

Semi-automatic takedown carbine. Chambered for .22 rimfire family of cartridges. Has 16.25" barrel and 7-shot detachable magazine. Supplied with 4X scope. Bright red case that will float if dropped overboard. Stock walnut-finished birch, with pistol-grip. Rubber buttplate. Introduced in 1986.

NIB	Exc.	V.G.	Good	Fair	Poor
275	200	150	100	75	50

Model 70PSS

Same as Model 70P above. Furnished with 10-round magazine. Finished in stainless steel, with synthetic stock. Automatic last shot bolt hold-open.

NIB	Exc.	V.G.	Good	Fair	Poor
245	175	125	100	85	60

Model 70HC

This is the Model 70 .22 rimfire semi-automatic that has been produced since 1983, with high-capacity 25-round "Banana" magazine.

NIB	Exc.	V.G.	Good	Fair	Poor
200	160	140	110	85	75

Model 9 Camp Carbine

Model has 16.5" barrel. Chambered for 9mm Parabellum pistol cartridge. Has 12- or 20-shot detachable magazine, walnut-finished hardwood pistol-grip stock and sandblasted matte-blued finish. Open sights. Receiver drilled and tapped for scope mounting. Introduced in 1985.

NIB	Exc.	V.G.	Good	Fair	Poor
625	500	395	250	175	125

Model 9N

Similar to Model 9mm Carbine. Furnished with nickel-plated metal parts.

NIB	Exc.	V.G.	Good	Fair	Poor
650	525	425	275	195	125

Model 45 Camp Carbine

Same as 9mm version. Chambered for .45 ACP cartridge. Has 7-shot detachable magazine. Very hot collectible.

NIB	Exc.	V.G.	Good	Fair	Poor
675	600	425	300	225	175

Model 922M

First offered in 1993. A semi-automatic .22 Win. Magnum rimfire rifle. Features 7-shot clip; 20.5" MicroGroove barrel; receiver sandblasted, drilled and tapped for scope mounting; Monte Carlo black walnut stock, with rubber rifle buff pad; adjustable rear sight and ramp front sight with hood. Weight 6.5 lbs.

NIB	Exc.	V.G.	Good	Fair	Poor
550	450	375	225	150	125

Model 995

Semi-automatic .22 LR only rifle features 7-shot clip, 18" MicroGroove barrel. Receiver grooved for scope mount and has a serrated non-glare top. Adjustable sights. Monte Carlo American black walnut stock, with checkered pistol-grip and forearm. White buttplate spacer standard. Weight 5 lbs. Introduced in 1979.

NIB	Exc.	V.G.	Good	Fair	Poor
175	110	80	70	60	40

Model 995SS

Same as above, with stainless steel finish. Black fiberglass stock. Introduced in 1995.

NIB	Exc.	V.G.	Good	Fair	Poor
195	125	100	85	60	50

Model 990L

Semi-automatic .22 LR Marlin features tubular 14-round magazine, with 22" MicroGroove barrel. Trigger gold plated. Receiver grooved for scope mount. Stock a two-tone brown birch Monte Carlo. Rubber rifle buttpad standard. Weight 5.75 lbs.

NIB	Exc.	V.G.	Good	Fair	Poor
150	120	100	80	65	50

Model 7000

First offered in 1997. A semi-automatic .22-caliber rifle, with 18" heavy barrel. Magazine holds 10 rounds. Black synthetic stock, with Monte Carlo comb and molded checkering. Receiver grooved for scope mount. No sights included. Weight about 6 lbs.

NIB	Exc.	V.G.	Good	Fair	Poor
200	150	125	100	75	50

Model 7000T

Target rifle fitted with an 18" barrel with recessed muzzle. No sights. Stock laminated red, white and blue with pistol-grip. Serrated rubber buttplate adjustable for length of pull, height and angle. Weight about 7.5 lbs. Introduced in 1999.

NIB	Exc.	V.G.	Good	Fair	Poor
425	375	325	275	150	100

Model 795

Similar to Model 7000 above, with 18" standard weight barrel. Weight about 5 lbs. Available with 4X scope. **NOTE:** Add $5 for scope.

NIB	Exc.	V.G.	Good	Fair	Poor
150	115	—	—	—	—

Model 795SS

As above, with stainless steel action and barrel. Black fiberglass stock. Weight about 4.5 lbs. Introduced in 2002.

NIB	Exc.	V.G.	Good	Fair	Poor
200	150	125	100	75	50

Model 60

Semi-automatic 14-shot .22-caliber LR. Features 22" MicroGroove barrel, with adjustable rear sight. Receiver grooved for scope mount. Stock birch, with Monte Carlo comb. Weight 5.5 lbs. Introduced in 1960.

NIB	Exc.	V.G.	Good	Fair	Poor
175	125	90	60	50	40

Model 60SS

Introduced in 1993. Similar to Model 60. Features stainless barrel, bolt and magazine tube. All other metal parts are nickel plated. Stock is two-tone black/gray laminated birch Monte Carlo.

NIB	Exc.	V.G.	Good	Fair	Poor
275	225	150	125	75	50

Model 60SN

Similar to Model 60SS, with black synthetic stock, molded checkering and swivel studs. Blued metal. Introduced in 2007. Available with factory-mounted 3x9 scope. **NOTE:** Add 10 percent for scope package.

NIB	Exc.	V.G.	Good	Fair	Poor
200	150	125	100	75	50

Model 60S-CF

Similar to Model 60SN, with carbon fiber-dipped black synthetic stock, giving it a – quote – "racy, high tech look". Woo-hoo!

NIB	Exc.	V.G.	Good	Fair	Poor
250	225	175	125	100	75

Model 60SB

Introduced in 1998. Features stainless steel 22" barrel, bolt and magazine tube. Stock birch, with Monte Carlo. Hard rubber buttplate.

NIB	Exc.	V.G.	Good	Fair	Poor
175	125	90	60	50	40

Model 60SSK

Similar to Model 60SB. Addition of black synthetic Monte Carlo stock, with checkering.

NIB	Exc.	V.G.	Good	Fair	Poor
195	195	150	125	100	75

Model 60C

Similar to Model 60, with Realtree camo finish. Introduced in 2000.

NIB	Exc.	V.G.	Good	Fair	Poor
195	195	150	125	100	75

Model 60DL

Introduced in 2004. Features Monte Carlo hardwood stock, with Walnu-tone walnut pattern finish. Full pistol-grip. Weight about 5.5 lbs.

NIB	Exc.	V.G.	Good	Fair	Poor
175	125	90	60	50	40

Model 60DLX

Semi-automatic rifle chambered for .22 LR. Features include 14-shot tubular magazine; side ejection; manual and automatic last-shot bolt hold-opens; receiver top with serrated non-glare finish; cross-bolt safety; steel charging handle; Monte Carlo American walnut-finished hardwood; full pistol-grip; tough Mar-Shield finish; 19" barrel with MicroGroove rifling. Limited availability.

NIB	Exc.	V.G.	Good	Fair	Poor
225	175	125	100	75	50

Model 2000

Bolt-action single-shot target rifle. Chambered for .22 LR. Barrel 22" long MicroGroove design, with match chamber and recessed muzzle. Rear sight fully adjustable target peep sight, with hooded front sight supplied with 10 aperture inserts. Stock Marlin blue fiberglass/Kevlar material, with adjustable buttplate. Aluminum forearm rail, with forearm stop and quick detachable swivel. Weight 8 lbs. Discontinued.

NIB	Exc.	V.G.	Good	Fair	Poor
650	500	400	325	250	200

Model 2000A

A 1996 version of Model 2000. Introduced in 1994. Features adjustable comb and ambidextrous pistol-grip. Marlin logo molded into side of buttstock. Weight about 8.5 lbs. Discontinued.

NIB	Exc.	V.G.	Good	Fair	Poor
750	600	500	375	300	250

Model 2000L

Introduced in 1996. Version of Model 2000. Features black/gray laminated stock. Fitted with heavy 22" barrel and match chamber; two-stage target trigger; rubber buttplate adjustable for length of pull, height and angle. Weight about 8 lbs. Discontinued.

NIB	Exc.	V.G.	Good	Fair	Poor
800	650	550	400	325	250

Model 880

Bolt-action clip-fed rifle. Chambered for .22 LR caliber. Clip is a 7-shot magazine. MicroGroove barrel is 22". Has adjustable folding rear sight and ramp front sight with hood. Weight 5.5 lbs. Introduced in 1988. Discontinued in 2004.

NIB	Exc.	V.G.	Good	Fair	Poor
160	135	110	90	75	50

Model 880SS

Introduced in 1994. This .22-caliber rifle features synthetic stock; stainless steel receiver and 22" barrel; 7-shot magazine standard. Discontinued in 2004.

NIB	Exc.	V.G.	Good	Fair	Poor
250	175	150	125	75	60

Model 880SQ

Similar to Model 880. Fitted with 22" heavy barrel and no sights. Introduced in 1996. Weight about 7 lbs. Discontinued in 2004.

NIB	Exc.	V.G.	Good	Fair	Poor
285	225	200	150	100	75

Model 881

Bolt-action .22-caliber rifle has tubular magazine that holds 25 Shorts, 19 longs and 17 LR. A 22" MicroGroove barrel has adjustable folding rear sight and ramp front sight with hood. Stock black walnut, with Monte Carlo. Rubber rifle buttpad, with sling swivels. Weight 6 lbs. First offered in 1988. Discontinued in 2004.

NIB	Exc.	V.G.	Good	Fair	Poor
175	150	125	100	80	60

Model 882SS

Bolt-action magazine rifle chambered for .22 Magnum cartridge. Stainless steel barrel and action, with black synthetic stock. Marlin "Fire Sights" installed. Introduced in 1998. Discontinued in 2004.

NIB	Exc.	V.G.	Good	Fair	Poor
225	175	150	100	75	50

Model 25N

Marlin promotional model. Bolt-action rifle chambered for .22 LR only. Seven-shot clip magazine, with 22" MicroGroove barrel. Receiver grooved for scope mount. Walnut finished birch stock. Weight 5.5 lbs.

NIB	Exc.	V.G.	Good	Fair	Poor
125	90	80	70	50	40

Model 25NC

Similar to above, with Mossy Oak Break-Up camo finish. Introduced in 2000.

NIB	Exc.	V.G.	Good	Fair	Poor
125	100	80	70	50	40

Model 25MN

Same as above chambered for .22 Win. Magnum rimfire cartridge. Weight 6 lbs.

NIB	Exc.	V.G.	Good	Fair	Poor
175	150	125	100	80	60

Model 25MNC

Similar to above, with Mossy Oak Break-Up camo finish. Weight about 6 lbs. Introduced in 2001.

NIB	Exc.	V.G.	Good	Fair	Poor
195	160	125	100	80	60

Model 17V

Introduced in 2002. Bolt-action rifle chambered for .17 Hornady Magnum rimfire cartridge. Fitted with 22" heavy barrel. Hardwood stock. No sights. Magazine capacity 7-round detachable magazine. Weight about 6 lbs.

NIB	Exc.	V.G.	Good	Fair	Poor
225	200	150	115	90	50

Model 17VS

As above, with stainless steel heavy barrel and action. Laminated stock. Weight about 7 lbs. Discontinued.

NIB	Exc.	V.G.	Good	Fair	Poor
285	225	200	150	100	75

Model 15YN "Little Buckaroo"

Marlin promotional model referred to as "Little Buckaroo". Bolt-action .22-caliber single-shot rifle for the beginner. Features MicroGroove 16.25" barrel, adjustable rear sight and receiver grooved for scope mount. Birch stock. Weight 4.25 lbs.

NIB	Exc.	V.G.	Good	Fair	Poor
125	100	75	60	50	40

Model 15N

Bolt-action rifle chambered for .22 Short, Long and LR. Fitted with adjustable rear sight. Full size birch stock interchangeable with Model 15YN. Weight about 4.25 lbs. Introduced in 1998.

NIB	Exc.	V.G.	Good	Fair	Poor
185	145	100	75	60	40

Model 15YS (Youth)

Single-shot bolt-action rifle, with shorter-than-standard length of pull. Barrel length 16.25". Hardwood stock. Weight about 4.25 lbs. Introduced in 2002.

NIB	Exc.	V.G.	Good	Fair	Poor
175	140	110	65	50	35

Model 81TS

Bolt-action rifle chambered for .22 Short, Long and LR cartridges. Fitted with 22" barrel and tubular magazine. Comes with black Monte Carlo synthetic stock. Adjustable rear sight. Weight about 6 lbs. Introduced in 1998. Discontinued in 2004.

NIB	Exc.	V.G.	Good	Fair	Poor
175	140	110	65	50	35

Model 882

Bolt-action rifle chambered for .22 Win. Magnum rimfire cartridge. A 7-shot clip standard. MicroGroove 22" barrel, with adjustable rear sight and ramp front sight with hood. Receiver grooved for scope mount. Black walnut stock, with Monte Carlo. Rubber rifle butt. Weight 6 lbs. Introduced in 1988. Discontinued in 2004.

NIB	Exc.	V.G.	Good	Fair	Poor
285	225	200	150	100	75

Model 882L

Same as above. Furnished with two-tone brown hardwood Monte Carlo stock. Weight 6.25 lbs. Discontinued in 2004.

NIB	Exc.	V.G.	Good	Fair	Poor
275	215	190	145	90	60

Model 882SS

Same as above. Furnished in stainless steel. Black fiberglass stock. Introduced in 1995. Discontinued in 2004.

NIB	Exc.	V.G.	Good	Fair	Poor
285	225	200	150	100	75

Model 882SSV

Variation of Model 882. Introduced in 1997. All in stainless steel. Chambered for .22 WMR cartridge. Fitted with nickel plated 7-round magazine and 22" barrel. Stock black synthetic, with molded checkering. Receiver grooved for scope mount. 1" brushed aluminum scope ring mounts included. Weight about 7 lbs. Discontinued in 2004.

NIB	Exc.	V.G.	Good	Fair	Poor
285	225	200	150	100	75

Model 83TS

Chambered for .22 Win. Magnum cartridge. Fitted with 22" barrel and 12-round tubular magazine. Adjustable rear sight. Bolt-action, with synthetic stock. Weight about 6 lbs. Introduced in 2001. Discontinued in 2004.

NIB	Exc.	V.G.	Good	Fair	Poor
250	200	165	145	100	75

Model 883

Bolt-action rifle. Chambered for .22 Win. Magnum cartridge, with 12-shot tubular magazine. Furnished with 22" MicroGroove barrel; adjustable rear sight, ramp front sight with hood; checkered American black walnut stock, with Monte Carlo. Weight 6 lbs. Introduced in 1988. Discontinued in 2004.

NIB	Exc.	V.G.	Good	Fair	Poor
285	225	200	150	100	75

Model 883N

Same as above. Furnished with stainless steel barrel, receiver, front breech bolt and striker. All other metal parts, except for sights, are nickel plated. Discontinued in 2004.

NIB	Exc.	V.G.	Good	Fair	Poor
285	225	200	150	100	75

Model 883SS

Introduced in 1993. Similar to Model 883, with all metal parts in stainless steel or nickel. Stock is two-tone brown birch Monte Carlo that is not checkered. Discontinued in 2004.

NIB	Exc.	V.G.	Good	Fair	Poor
275	215	190	145	90	60

Model 717M2

Introduced in 2005. Semi-automatic chambered for .17 Mach 2 cartridge. Laminated hardwood stock, with Monte Carlo comb. Fitted with 18" barrel and iron sights. Magazine capacity 7 rounds. Weight about 5 lbs.

NIB	Exc.	V.G.	Good	Fair	Poor
300	250	200	175	150	125

MODEL 900 SERIES

Bolt action rimfire series was introduced into Marlin line in 2004. Features T-900 fire control system. This is a trigger and safety system that features a wide serrated trigger and improved trigger pull. Safety activation also improved. The 900 series also features drilled and tapped receivers on all models.

Model 983T

Chambered for .22 WMR cartridge. Fitted with 22" barrel. Monte Carlo black fiberglass stock, with checkering. Adjustable sights. Tubular 12-round magazine. Weight about 6 lbs.

NIB	Exc.	V.G.	Good	Fair	Poor
285	225	200	150	100	75

Model 983S

As above, with laminated two-tone stock.

NIB	Exc.	V.G.	Good	Fair	Poor
285	225	200	150	100	75

Model 983

.22 WMR model features Monte Carlo stock of American black walnut, with full pistol-grip and checkering.

NIB	Exc.	V.G.	Good	Fair	Poor
285	225	200	150	100	75

Model 917

Bolt-action rifle chambered in .17 Hornady Magnum rimfire; 7-shot clip magazine; fiberglass-filled synthetic stock with full pistol-grip; swivel studs and molded-in checkering. Adjustable open rear sight, ramp front. 22" barrel. Introduced 2006.

NIB	Exc.	V.G.	Good	Fair	Poor
285	225	200	150	100	75

Model 917V

Chambered for .17 HMR cartridge. Fitted with 22" heavy barrel. Hardwood Monte Carlo stock, with full pistol-grip. No sights. Detachable magazine with 7-round capacity. Weight about 6 lbs.

NIB	Exc.	V.G.	Good	Fair	Poor
285	225	200	150	100	75

Model 917VR

Similar to Model 917, with fiberglass-filled synthetic stock. Introduced 2006.

NIB	Exc.	V.G.	Good	Fair	Poor
285	225	200	150	100	75

Model 917VS

As above, with gray/black laminated hardwood stock. No sights. Magazine nickel plated. Weight about 7 lbs. Scope bases included.

NIB	Exc.	V.G.	Good	Fair	Poor
285	225	200	150	100	75

Model 917VS-CF

Similar to Model 917VS, with carbon fiber-patterned stock.

NIB	Exc.	V.G.	Good	Fair	Poor
285	225	200	150	100	75

Model 917VSF

Chambered for .17 HMR cartridge. Fitted with 22" heavy stainless steel fluted barrel. No sights. Nickel magazine capacity 7 rounds. Laminated gray stock, with Monte Carlo comb. Weight about 6.75 lbs. Introduced in 2005.

NIB	Exc.	V.G.	Good	Fair	Poor
300	250	200	175	150	125

Model 917VT

Similar to above, with laminated brown thumbhole stock. Introduced 2008.

NIB	Exc.	V.G.	Good	Fair	Poor
350	300	250	175	145	110

Model 917VST

Similar to above, with laminated gray/black thumbhole stock. Introduced 2008.

NIB	Exc.	V.G.	Good	Fair	Poor
400	350	295	245	125	100

Model 917M2

Chambered for .17 Mach 2 cartridge. Fitted with 22" heavy barrel. Monte Carlo hardwood stock, with full pistol-grip. No sights. Scope bases included. Magazine capacity 7 rounds. Weight about 5.5 lbs.

NIB	Exc.	V.G.	Good	Fair	Poor
300	250	200	175	150	125

Model 917M2S

As above, with Monte Carlo gray/black laminated stock. Full pistol-grip. Stainless steel barrel and receiver. Nickel plated magazine.

NIB	Exc.	V.G.	Good	Fair	Poor
325	275	225	200	175	125

Model 982S

Chambered for .22 WMR cartridge. Fitted with 22" stainless steel barrel. Adjustable sights. Black fiberglass stock, with Monte Carlo. Full pistol-grip. Detachable 7-round nickel magazine. Weight about 6 lbs.

NIB	Exc.	V.G.	Good	Fair	Poor
285	225	200	150	100	75

Model 982L

As above, with gray/black laminated stock. Weight about 6.25 lbs.

NIB	Exc.	V.G.	Good	Fair	Poor
300	250	200	175	150	125

Model 982

Similar to 982S, with American black walnut checkered stock, with Monte Carlo. Full pistol-grip. Adjustable sights. Weight about 6 lbs.

NIB	Exc.	V.G.	Good	Fair	Poor
285	225	200	150	100	75

Model 982VS

As above, with black fiberglass Monte Carlo stock. Heavy 22" stainless steel barrel. Nickel plated 7-round magazine. No sights. Weight about 7 lbs.

NIB	Exc.	V.G.	Good	Fair	Poor
325	275	225	200	175	125

Model 982VS-CF

As above, with synthetic stock. Dipped carbon-fiber textured finish.

NIB	Exc.	V.G.	Good	Fair	Poor
325	275	225	200	175	125

Model 925M

As above, with hardwood stock. Full pistol-grip. Fitted with 22" standard weight barrel. Adjustable sights. Weight about 6 lbs.

NIB	Exc.	V.G.	Good	Fair	Poor
250	200	165	145	100	75

Model 925RM

Similar to Model 925M, with black fiberglass-filled synthetic stock.

NIB	Exc.	V.G.	Good	Fair	Poor
250	200	165	145	100	75

Model 925MC

As above, with Monte Carlo Mossy Oak Break-up camo stock. Weight about 6 lbs.

NIB	Exc.	V.G.	Good	Fair	Poor
285	225	200	150	100	75

Model 980V

Chambered for .22 LR cartridge. Fitted with 22" heavy barrel. Black fiberglass stock, with Monte Carlo. Full pistol-grip. No sights. Magazine capacity 7 rounds. Weight about 7 lbs.

NIB	Exc.	V.G.	Good	Fair	Poor
285	225	200	150	100	75

Model 980S

As above, with standard weight 22" barrel and 7-round nickel plated magazine. Stainless steel barrel and receiver. Adjustable sights. Weight about 6 lbs.

NIB	Exc.	V.G.	Good	Fair	Poor
285	225	200	150	100	75

Model 980S-CF

As above, with carbon fiber stock. Introduced in 2007.

NIB	Exc.	V.G.	Good	Fair	Poor
285	225	200	150	100	75

Model 981T

Chambered to handle interchangeably .22 Short, Long or LR cartridges in a tubular magazine. Black Monte Carlo fiberglass stock, with full pistol-grip. Adjustable sights. Fitted with standard weight 22" barrel. Weight about 6 lbs.

NIB	Exc.	V.G.	Good	Fair	Poor
285	225	200	150	100	75

Model 981TS

Bolt-action rifle chambered in .22 S/L/LR. Features include tubular magazine (holds 25 Short, 19 Long or 17 Long Rifle) cartridges; thumb safety; red cocking indicator; black fiberglass-filled synthetic stock, with full pistol-grip; molded-in checkering and swivel studs; 22" stainless steel barrel, with MicroGroove rifling (16 grooves). Adjustable semi-buckhorn folding rear sight, ramp front with high visibility orange front sight post; cutaway Wide-Scan hood. Receiver grooved for scope mount; drilled and tapped for scope bases.

NIB	Exc.	V.G.	Good	Fair	Poor
300	250	225	150	100	75

Model 925

Chambered for .22 LR cartridge. Fitted with 22" standard weight barrel. Adjustable sights. Monte Carlo hardwood stock. Full pistol-grip. Seven-round magazine. Weight about 5.5 lbs.

NIB	Exc.	V.G.	Good	Fair	Poor
225	175	150	125	95	75

Model 925R

As above, with factory-mounted 3x9 scope.

NIB	Exc.	V.G.	Good	Fair	Poor
250	200	165	145	100	75

Model 925C

As above, with Monte Carlo hardwood stock in Mossy Oak Break-up camo pattern. Adjustable sights.

NIB	Exc.	V.G.	Good	Fair	Poor
250	200	165	145	100	75

Model 915Y Compact

Single-shot .22 rimfire rifle, with 16.25" barrel. Hardwood stock, with impressed checkering. Iron sights.

NIB	Exc.	V.G.	Good	Fair	Poor
200	150	125	100	75	50

Model 915YS Compact

Similar to above, with stainless steel receiver and barrel. No checkering. Fiber optic sights.

NIB	Exc.	V.G.	Good	Fair	Poor
225	175	150	125	95	75

Model 322

Chambered for .222 cartridge. Has 24" medium-weight barrel, with MicroGroove rifling. Checkered walnut pistol-grip stock. Magazine holds 4 shots. Adjustable trigger. Sights are Sako products. Sako receiver fitted for Sako scope mounting bases. Non-Sako receivers were apparently also used. MicroGroove rifling in barrel was not successful for this caliber and accuracy fell off after as few as 500 shots—so this model was dropped and replaced. Serial numbers were Sako. Manufactured 5,859 between 1954 and 1959.

NIB	Exc.	V.G.	Good	Fair	Poor
600	550	450	350	300	200

Model 422

Successor to Model 322. Simply same rifle fitted with 24" featherweight stainless steel barrel. Named "Varmint King". Features Monte Carlo stock, with cheekpiece. Manufactured only 354 between 1956 and 1958.

NIB	Exc.	V.G.	Good	Fair	Poor
950	600	500	400	300	200

Model 455

Built on Fabrique Nationale Belgian Mauser action. Chambered for .308 and .30-06 cartridges. Stainless steel barrel made by Marlin, with 5-shot magazine. Bishop checkered walnut stock, with detachable sling swivels and leather sling. Rear sight Lyman 48; front ramp type, with detachable hood. Receiver drilled and tapped for scope mounts. Trigger adjustable Sako unit. Manufactured 1,079 in .30-06; only 59 in .308 between 1955 and 1959.

NIB	Exc.	V.G.	Good	Fair	Poor
—	700	595	425	300	200

Model MR-7

Introduced in 1996. American-made bolt-action centerfire rifle of a totally new design. Chambered for .25-06 (first offered in 1997), .243, .270 Win. .280, .308 or .30-06 cartridges. Fitted with 22" barrel. Has American black walnut stock; 4-shot detachable box magazine. Offered with or without sights. Weight about 7.5 lbs. Discontinued 1999.

NIB	Exc.	V.G.	Good	Fair	Poor
450	350	300	250	175	150

Model MR-7B

Similar to MR-7. Fitted with 4-round blind magazine; birch stock. Offered in .30-06 or .270; with or without sights. Introduced in 1998. Discontinued.

NIB	Exc.	V.G.	Good	Fair	Poor
375	300	250	175	150	100

Model XL7

Introduced in 2008. Centerfire bolt-action rifle, with adjustable Pro-Fire trigger system. 4+1 capacity. Chambered in .25-06, .270 and .30-06. Crowned precision-rifled 22" barrel that is joined to receiver with a pressure nut. Black synthetic stock, with raised cheekpiece. Soft-Tech recoil pad. No sights; drilled and tapped for mounts. **NOTE:** Add $50 for factory scope package.

NIB	Exc.	V.G.	Good	Fair	Poor
325	275	225	200	175	125

Model XL7C

Similar to above, with Realtree APG HD camo finish.

NIB	Exc.	V.G.	Good	Fair	Poor
350	300	250	175	145	110

Model XS7 Short-Action

Similar to Model XL7. Chambered in 7mm-08, .243 Win. and .308 Win. **NOTE:** Add $50 for factory scope package.

NIB	Exc.	V.G.	Good	Fair	Poor
325	275	225	200	175	125

Model XS7Y Youth Rifle

Similar to above, with smaller dimensions.

NIB	Exc.	V.G.	Good	Fair	Poor
325	275	225	200	175	125

Model XS7C Camo

Similar to above, with Realtree APG HD camo stock.

NIB	Exc.	V.G.	Good	Fair	Poor
350	300	250	175	145	110

Model XS7S

Bolt-action rifle similar to Model XS7, with stainless steel barrel, receiver and trigger group. Short action.

NIB	Exc.	V.G.	Good	Fair	Poor
375	325	275	175	150	100

Model XL7

Entry-level bolt action rifle chambered in .25-06 Rem., .270 Win., .30-06 Spr. Features include 4+1 magazine capacity; pillar bedded 22" barrel; Pro-Fire adjustable trigger system; 2-position safety; red cocking indicator; swivel studs; matte blue/black finish; black synthetic stock, with molded in checkering and Soft-Tech recoil pad. No sights.

NIB	Exc.	V.G.	Good	Fair	Poor
325	285	235	200	150	75

MARLIN PUMP SHOTGUNS

Model 1898

Made in 12-gauge, with exposed hammer. Has takedown receiver. Walnut pistol-grip stock and fore-end. 5-shot tube magazine. Barrel lengths from 26" to 32". Manufactured between 1898 and 1905.

Grade A

Variation has 30", 32" or 38" barrel. Full choke. Plainest grade.

Courtesy Marlin Firearms Co.

NIB	Exc.	V.G.	Good	Fair	Poor
—	475	425	325	125	75

Grade A Brush or Riot

Same shotgun, with 26" cylinder-bore barrel.

NIB	Exc.	V.G.	Good	Fair	Poor
—	425	375	250	150	100

Grade B

Same as Grade A, with special smokeless steel barrel. Checkered stock.

NIB	Exc.	V.G.	Good	Fair	Poor
—	675	550	350	150	100

Grade C

More deluxe version, with engraving. Fancier wood.

NIB	Exc.	V.G.	Good	Fair	Poor
—	1150	850	550	275	125

Grade D

Variation has Damascus barrel. Greatest amount of engraving.

NIB	Exc.	V.G.	Good	Fair	Poor
—	2100	1400	900	450	250

Model 16

Exactly the same as Model 1898, except chambered for 16-gauge only. Four grades are the same. Manufactured between 1903 and 1910.

Grade A

NIB	Exc.	V.G.	Good	Fair	Poor
—	500	450	400	250	150

Grade B

NIB	Exc.	V.G.	Good	Fair	Poor
—	650	550	400	200	100

Grade C

NIB	Exc.	V.G.	Good	Fair	Poor
—	1100	850	500	300	150

Grade D

NIB	Exc.	V.G.	Good	Fair	Poor
—	2000	1400	950	425	250

Model 17

An exposed-hammer gun, with a solid frame and straight-grip stock. Chambered for 12-gauge, with 30" or 32" barrel. Manufactured between 1906 and 1908.

NIB	Exc.	V.G.	Good	Fair	Poor
—	525	450	275	150	75

Model 17 Brush Gun

Variation similar to standard Model 17, with 26" cylinder-bore barrel.

NIB	Exc.	V.G.	Good	Fair	Poor
—	550	475	325	200	100

Model 17 Riot Gun

Variation has 20" cylinder-bore barrel.

NIB	Exc.	V.G.	Good	Fair	Poor
—	600	525	325	150	125

Model 19

A takedown gun chambered for 12-gauge. Basically an improved and lightened version of Model 1898. Available in same four grades. Manufactured in 1906 and 1907.

Grade A

NIB	Exc.	V.G.	Good	Fair	Poor
—	500	450	250	150	100

Grade B

NIB	Exc.	V.G.	Good	Fair	Poor
—	600	550	500	350	225

Grade C

NIB	Exc.	V.G.	Good	Fair	Poor
—	750	675	5550	425	300

Grade D

Courtesy Marlin Firearms Co.

NIB	Exc.	V.G.	Good	Fair	Poor
—	1850	1500	1050	400	200

Model 21 "Trap"

Basically same as Model 19, with straight-grip stock. 1907 catalog listed it as a Trap model. Manufactured in 1907 and 1908. Four grades similar to previous models.

Grade A

NIB	Exc.	V.G.	Good	Fair	Poor
—	450	450	300	200	100

Grade B

NIB	Exc.	V.G.	Good	Fair	Poor
—	600	550	350	200	100

Grade C

NIB	Exc.	V.G.	Good	Fair	Poor
—	750	675	500	350	200

Grade D

NIB	Exc.	V.G.	Good	Fair	Poor
—	1600	1300	1050	700	550

Model 24

Actually an improved version of Model 21. Has pistol-grip stock and exposed hammer. Features automatic recoil lock on slide; matte rib barrel. Otherwise, quite similar to its predecessor. Manufactured between 1908 and 1917.

Grade A

Courtesy Marlin Firearms Co.

NIB	Exc.	V.G.	Good	Fair	Poor
—	475	400	350	150	100

Grade B

NIB	Exc.	V.G.	Good	Fair	Poor
—	600	550	450	350	225

Grade C

NIB	Exc.	V.G.	Good	Fair	Poor
—	750	675	550	425	300

Grade D

NIB	Exc.	V.G.	Good	Fair	Poor
—	1600	1300	900	600	400

Marlin "Trap Gun"

Unique, in it has no numerical designation and simply known as "Trap Gun". A takedown gun, with interchangeable barrels from 16" to 32". Straight-grip buttstock, Quite similar in appearance to Model 24. Manufactured between 1909 and 1912.

NIB	Exc.	V.G.	Good	Fair	Poor
—	1000	700	525	350	200

Model 26

Similar to Model 24 Grade A, with solid frame. 30" or 32" barrels.

NIB	Exc.	V.G.	Good	Fair	Poor
—	525	450	325	125	100

Model 26 Brush Gun

Model has 26" cylinder-bored barrel.

NIB	Exc.	V.G.	Good	Fair	Poor
—	550	475	325	200	100

Model 26 Riot Gun

Variation has 20" cylinder-bored barrel.

NIB	Exc.	V.G.	Good	Fair	Poor
—	600	525	325	150	125

Model 28 Hammerless

First of the Marlin hammerless shotguns. A takedown 12-gauge, with barrels from 26" to 32" in length. Stock has pistol-grip. Comes in four grades like its predecessors. Manufactured between 1913 and 1922.

Grade A

NIB	Exc.	V.G.	Good	Fair	Poor
—	400	335	200	100	70

Grade B

NIB	Exc.	V.G.	Good	Fair	Poor
—	600	550	350	350	225

Grade C

NIB	Exc.	V.G.	Good	Fair	Poor
—	750	625	550	425	300

Grade D

Courtesy Marlin Firearms Co.

NIB	Exc.	V.G.	Good	Fair	Poor
—	1700	1200	800	600	300

Model 28TS Trap Gun

Variation same as Model 28, with 30" Full choke barrel. Matte rib and high-comb straight-grip stock. Manufactured in 1915.

NIB	Exc.	V.G.	Good	Fair	Poor
—	725	600	525	425	300

Model 28T Trap Gun

Variation is deluxe model similar to Model 28TS, with engraving, high-grade walnut and hand checkering. Manufactured in 1915.

NIB	Exc.	V.G.	Good	Fair	Poor
—	750	625	550	425	300

Model 30

Improved version of Model 16, 16-gauge shotgun. Features similar, with addition of improved takedown system and automatic recoil lock on slide. Manufactured between 1910 and 1914.

Grade A

NIB	Exc.	V.G.	Good	Fair	Poor
—	550	475	350	200	100

Grade B

NIB	Exc.	V.G.	Good	Fair	Poor
—	600	550	450	200	100

Grade C

NIB	Exc.	V.G.	Good	Fair	Poor
—	750	675	550	250	150

Grade D

NIB	Exc.	V.G.	Good	Fair	Poor
—	1400	1200	1000	700	550

Model 30 Field Grade

Similar to Model 30 Grade B, with 25" modified-choke barrel. Straight-grip stock. Manufactured in 1913 and 1914.

NIB	Exc.	V.G.	Good	Fair	Poor
—	450	375	250	150	100

Model 31

Smaller version of Model 28 Hammerless takedown. Chambered for 16- and 20-gauge. Barrel lengths 26" and 28". Available in usual four grades. Various different chokes. Manufactured between 1915 and 1922.

Grade A

Courtesy Marlin Firearms Co.

NIB	Exc.	V.G.	Good	Fair	Poor
—	500	450	350	150	100

Grade B

NIB	Exc.	V.G.	Good	Fair	Poor
—	600	550	450	250	150

Grade C

NIB	Exc.	V.G.	Good	Fair	Poor
—	750	675	550	300	150

Grade D

NIB	Exc.	V.G.	Good	Fair	Poor
—	1400	1200	1000	600	300

Model 42/42A

Originally listed as Model 42, but in the second year of production, designation was changed to /42A for no apparent reason than standardization of models. Similar to Model 24, except barrel markings are different. Still an exposed hammer takedown gun chambered for 12-gauge. Manufactured between 1922 and 1933.

NIB	Exc.	V.G.	Good	Fair	Poor
—	375	325	200	150	100

Model 43A

Hammerless model quite similar to Model 28, with different markings and less attention to finishing detail. Manufactured between 1923 and 1930.

NIB	Exc.	V.G.	Good	Fair	Poor
—	400	350	250	150	75

Model 43T

Same as Model 43A takedown hammerless, with 30" or 32" matte rib barrel. Straight-grip stock of high grade walnut, with non-gloss oil-finish. Fitted recoil pad. Manufactured between 1922 and 1930.

NIB	Exc.	V.G.	Good	Fair	Poor
—	500	450	350	200	100

Model 43TS

Custom-order version of Model 43T. Same in all respects, except stock could be ordered to any specifications shooter desired. Manufactured between 1922 and 1930.

NIB	Exc.	V.G.	Good	Fair	Poor
—	700	625	550	250	150

Model 44A

Similar to Model 31. Advertised as its successor. Hammerless takedown chambered for 20-gauge. Features improved bolt opening device located in trigger guard area instead of at the top of receiver. Shorter 4-shot magazine tube. Manufactured from 1922 until 1933.

Courtesy Marlin Firearms Co.

NIB	Exc.	V.G.	Good	Fair	Poor
—	475	400	275	150	100

Model 44S

Similar to Model 44A, with higher grade walnut stock. Featured hand-cut checkering.

NIB	Exc.	V.G.	Good	Fair	Poor
—	500	425	300	200	100

Model 49

12-gauge exposed-hammer takedown. Combines features of Model 42 and Model 24. Basically a lower-priced model that was never listed in

Marlin catalog. Part of Frank Kenna's money-raising program—anyone who purchased four shares of stock for $25 per share was given one, free of charge. Manufactured between 1925 and 1928.

NIB	Exc.	V.G.	Good	Fair	Poor
—	700	625	550	250	150

Model 53

Hammerless takedown 12-gauge that was not in production for long. Theorized that Model 53 was produced to use up old parts on hand when Model 43 was introduced. Manufactured in 1929 and 1980.

Courtesy Marlin Firearms Co.

NIB	Exc.	V.G.	Good	Fair	Poor
—	450	400	275	175	125

Model 63

Last of the slide-action shotguns produced by Marlin until Model 120 in 1971. Hammerless takedown 12-gauge. Replaced Model 43A in Marlin catalog. Had improvements over earlier guns, but its introduction during Depression did little to bolster sales. Offered free of charge to anyone purchasing four shares of Marlin stock at $25 per share. Manufactured between 1931 and 1933.

NIB	Exc.	V.G.	Good	Fair	Poor
—	500	450	350	200	100

Model 63T

Trap-grade version of Model 63. Has better grade hand-checkered stock. Fitted recoil pad and oil-finish. Manufactured between 1931 and 1933.

NIB	Exc.	V.G.	Good	Fair	Poor
—	600	525	450	200	125

Model 63TS

Variation same as Model 63T, except stock dimensions were custom-made to customer's specifications. Manufactured between 1931 and 1933.

NIB	Exc.	V.G.	Good	Fair	Poor
—	700	625	550	250	150

Premier Mark I

Made by Manufrance and called LaSalle. Marlin was able to purchase them, without barrels at a good enough price, for Marlin to barrel and market them under their own name. This model is 12-gauge only. Alloy receiver and seven interchangeable barrels in 26" to 30" lengths. Various chokes. Plain stock is French walnut. Biggest problem with this gun is that the lightweight (6 lbs.) produced severe recoil and less than enjoyable to shoot. In production from 1959 through 1963, with approximately 13,700 sold.

NIB	Exc.	V.G.	Good	Fair	Poor
—	325	225	175	150	100

Premier Mark II

Similar to Mark I, with light engraving. Checkered stock.

NIB	Exc.	V.G.	Good	Fair	Poor
—	325	225	175	150	100

Premier Mark IV

Similar to Mark II, with more engraving on receiver. **NOTE:** Add 10 percent for ventilated rib.

NIB	Exc.	V.G.	Good	Fair	Poor
—	325	225	175	150	100

Model 120

Styled to resemble Winchester Model 12. Advertised as an all steel and walnut shotgun. Offered with interchangeable barrels from 26" to 40". Various chokes were available. Checkered walnut stock, with fitted recoil pad. Tube magazine holds 5 shots, 4 in 3". Trap Model available (1973-1975); slug gun (1974-1984). Manufactured between 1971 and 1985. A really nice gun, if a bit heavy. **NOTE:** Add 10 percent for 36" "Long Tom" barrel.

NIB	Exc.	V.G.	Good	Fair	Poor
—	350	300	250	150	125

Model 778 (Glenfield)

Similar to Model 120, with walnut finished hardwood stock instead of walnut. Glenfield name stamped on it. Manufactured between 1979 and 1984.

NIB	Exc.	V.G.	Good	Fair	Poor
—	275	225	175	125	100

MARLIN OVER/UNDER & TOP-BREAK SHOTGUNS

Model 60 Single-Barrel Shotgun

Break-open exposed-hammer top lever-opening 12-gauge, with 30" or 32" full-choke barrel. Pistol-grip stock. Approximately 60 manufactured in 1923.

NIB	Exc.	V.G.	Good	Fair	Poor
—	400	350	250	150	75

Model 90 Over/Under Shotgun

Produced in response to a request from Sears Roebuck, that Marlin should manufacture an over/under shotgun for Sears to market in their stores. Guns produced for Sears have prefix 103 in their serial numbers and marked "Ranger" before WWII and "J.C. Higgins" after the war. Prior to 1945, they were not marked Marlin; after that date Sears requested that the company stamp their name on the guns. They were also produced as Marlin Model 90 during the same period. Chambered for 12-, 16- and 20-gauge, as well as .410 bore. The 16- and 20-gauge guns first offered in 1937, with 26" or 28" barrels. In 1939, .410 bore was first offered with 26" barrel and 3" chambers. Barrels are 26", 28" or 30", with various chokes. Action is boxlock with extractors. Guns made prior to 1950 were solid between the barrels; after that date there was a space between barrels. Can be found with double-/single triggers and checkered walnut stock. Ventilated rib offered as an option beginning in 1949. Be aware that this model was also available as a combination gun in .22 LR/.410, .22 Hornet/.410 and .218 Bee/.410. Approximately 34,000 Model 90s manufactured between 1937 and 1963. **NOTE:** Add 33 percent single trigger; 25 percent 20-gauge; 300 percent .410 bores; 300 percent premium combination guns. There are other rare gauge and barrel combinations that may affect value.

Marlin Model 90 Combination Gun

NIB	Exc.	V.G.	Good	Fair	Poor
—	550	425	350	275	200

MARLIN LEVER-ACTION SHOTGUNS

Model .410 Lever-Action Shotgun (Original)

Unique venture for Marlin Company—a lever-action shotgun based on Model 1893 action. Longer loading port, modified tube magazine that held 5 shots and smoothbore barrel chambered for .410 shot shell. Finish blued, with walnut pistol-grip stock and grooved beavertail fore-end. Hard rubber rifle-type buttplate. Available with 22" or 26" full-choke barrel. This gun was also part of the stock purchase plan and was given free of charge to anyone purchasing four shares at $25 per share. Also cataloged for sale. Manufactured between 1929 and 1932.

Courtesy Mike Stuckslager

NIB	Exc.	V.G.	Good	Fair	Poor
—	1600	1000	650	500	200

Model .410 Deluxe (Original)

Variation was never cataloged. Essentially same as standard version, with hand-checkered stock. Fore-end does not have grooves as found on standard model. Be wary of fakes!

NIB	Exc.	V.G.	Good	Fair	Poor
—	2200	1200	800	400	200

Model .410 (New)

Lever-action shotgun chambered for 2.5" .410 shot shell. Checkered walnut stock, fluorescent front sight. Based on Model 336 action. Discontinued.

NIB	Exc.	V.G.	Good	Fair	Poor
700	625	550	450	300	—

Model 410XLR 410 XLR

New in 2009. Latest Marlin .410 shotgun. Built on M1895 chassis. Chambered for 2.5" .410 shot shells. Receiver and barrel stainless. Stock laminated wood.

NIB	Exc.	V.G.	Good	Fair	Poor
750	675	575	450	300	—

MARLIN BOLT-ACTION SHOTGUNS

Model 50DL

Bolt-action 12-gauge shotgun. Available with 28" modified barrel, black synthetic stock. Ventilated recoil pad standard. Brass bead front sight. Weight about 7.5 lbs.

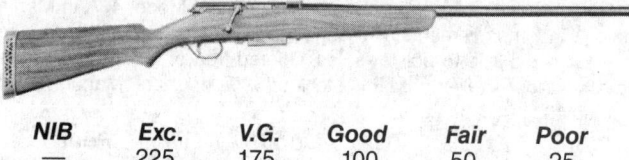

NIB	Exc.	V.G.	Good	Fair	Poor
300	275	225	150	125	100

Model 55

Chambered for 12-, 16- and 20-gauge, with full or adjustable choke. Barrels 26" or 28". Bolt-action, with 2-shot box magazine. Pistol-grip stock is plain. Manufactured between 1950 and 1965.

NIB	Exc.	V.G.	Good	Fair	Poor
—	225	175	100	50	25

Model 55 Swamp Gun

Simply Model 55, with 3" Magnum, 20" barrel. Adjustable choke. Manufactured between 1963 and 1965.

NIB	Exc.	V.G.	Good	Fair	Poor
—	300	250	175	75	50

Model 55 Goose Gun

Model 55, with 3" chamber, 36" Full choke 12-gauge barrel. Recoil pad and sling. Introduced in 1962.

NIB	Exc.	V.G.	Good	Fair	Poor
375	250	175	150	75	50

Model 55S Slug Gun

Model 55, with 24" cylinder-bore barrel. Rifle sights. Manufactured between 1974 and 1983.

NIB	Exc.	V.G.	Good	Fair	Poor
—	250	200	150	100	50

Model 5510 Goose Gun

Chambered for 3.5" 10-gauge. Has 34" Full choke barrel. Recoil pad and sling. Manufactured between 1976 and 1985.

NIB	Exc.	V.G.	Good	Fair	Poor
—	400	300	250	175	100

Model 55GDL

Bolt-action shotgun fitted with 36" full choke barrel. Reinforced black synthetic stock. Magazine holds two rounds. Ventilated recoil pad standard. First introduced in 1997. Weight about 8 lbs. Discontinued.

NIB	Exc.	V.G.	Good	Fair	Poor
350	325	275	200	150	100

Model 512 Slugmaster

Introduced in 1994. Bolt-action shotgun features rifled 21" barrel. Equipped with two-shot detachable magazine. Ventilated recoil pad. Special scope also provided. Weight about 8 lbs. Discontinued.

NIB	Exc.	V.G.	Good	Fair	Poor
350	325	275	200	150	100

Model 512DL Slugmaster

Introduced in 1997. Bolt-action features black synthetic stock, with fully rifled 21" barrel. Chambered for 12-gauge shell. A two-round magazine is standard. Adjustable rear sight, with ramp front sight. In 1998, furnished with "Fire Sights". Receiver drilled and tapped for scope mount. Weight about 8 lbs. Discontinued.

NIB	Exc.	V.G.	Good	Fair	Poor
395	250	200	150	125	100

Model 512P

Introduced in 1999. Similar to Model 512 DL, with addition of 21" fully rifled and ported barrel. Fire sights standard. Weight about 8 lbs. Discontinued.

NIB	Exc.	V.G.	Good	Fair	Poor
395	250	200	150	125	100

Model 25MG

Bolt-action .22 Win. Magnum shot shell only. Fitted with 22" smoothbore barrel. Has 7-round magazine. Hardwood stock. Weight about 6 lbs. First introduced in 1999.

NIB	Exc.	V.G.	Good	Fair	Poor
225	175	145	125	100	75

MODERN L.C. SMITH SHOTGUNS

Modern line of L.C. Smith shotguns made in Europe. Imported into USA under Marlin name from 2005 to 2009.

Model LC410-DB

Side-by-side .410 bore, with fleur-de-lis checkered walnut stock, single selective trigger, selective automatic ejectors, three choke tubes (IC, M, F) and 26" chrome-lined barrels, with solid rib and bead front sight. Case colored receiver has gold game bird embossed on side and bottom.

NIB	Exc.	V.G.	Good	Fair	Poor
1800	1750	1400	900	600	300

Model LC28-DB

Similar to above in 28-gauge.

NIB	Exc.	V.G.	Good	Fair	Poor
1900	1850	1500	1000	750	300

Model LC12-DB

12-gauge double barrel features 3" chambers, single trigger, selective automatic ejectors, three choke tubes (IC, M, F), 28" barrels, with solid rib and bead front sight. Walnut stock checkered. Has fluted comb, beavertail forearm and recoil pad. Case coloring on receiver and side plates.

NIB	Exc.	V.G.	Good	Fair	Poor
1400	1275	875	700	350	200

Model LC20-DB

Similar to above in 20-gauge.

NIB	Exc.	V.G.	Good	Fair	Poor
1600	1500	1100	800	400	200

Model LC12-OU

Over/under features 3" chambers, single selective trigger, selective automatic ejectors, automatic safety, three choke tubes (IC, M, F), 28" barrels, with ventilated rib and bead front sight. Checkered walnut stock, with fluted comb. Recoil pad. Case coloring on receiver and sideplates.

NIB	Exc.	V.G.	Good	Fair	Poor
950	825	600	450	300	200

Model LC20-OU

Similar to above in 20-gauge.

NIB	Exc.	V.G.	Good	Fair	Poor
950	825	600	450	300	200

MARLIN MODERN MUZZLE-LOADERS

Model MLS-50/54

Marlin in-line muzzle-loaders were introduced in 1997. They are stainless steel. Available in .50- or .54-caliber. Barrel 22" long. Adjustable Marble rear sight, ramp front sight with brass bead. Drilled and tapped for scope mount. Black synthetic stock, with molded checkering. Weight about 7 lbs. Discontinued. Not particularly easy to take down for cleaning.

NIB	Exc.	V.G.	Good	Fair	Poor
300	225	200	150	75	50

MAROCCHI ARMI
Brescia, Italy

Model 2000

12-gauge Magnum single-shot, with 28" barrel, exposed hammer and automatic ejector. Blued, with walnut stock.

NIB	Exc.	V.G.	Good	Fair	Poor
—	100	80	65	50	35

Field Master I

12-gauge over/under, with 26" or 28" ventilated rib barrels fitted for choke tubes, single trigger and automatic ejectors. Blued French case-hardened, with walnut stock.

NIB	Exc.	V.G.	Good	Fair	Poor
—	500	395	300	200	150

Field Master II

As above, with single-selective trigger.

NIB	Exc.	V.G.	Good	Fair	Poor
—	525	450	350	225	175

CONQUISTA SERIES

Grade I is standard grade, with special polished steel finish and machined engraved. Stock and forearm are select walnut, with hand checkered 20 lpi. Grade II has roll engraved game scenes. Stock is select figured walnut. Grade III is hand engraved by a master engraver featuring game scenes. Finely figured walnut stock.

Sporting Clays Model

Offered in 12-gauge, with 28", 30" or 32" ventilated rib barrels. Screw in chokes are standard. Adjustable trigger. Weight about 8 lbs.

Grade I

NIB	Exc.	V.G.	Good	Fair	Poor
1950	1700	1175	850	600	300

Grade II

NIB	Exc.	V.G.	Good	Fair	Poor
2350	1900	1475	950	700	350

Grade III

NIB	Exc.	V.G.	Good	Fair	Poor
3350	2850	1825	1150	800	400

Sporting Light—Grade I

Same as above, but slightly smaller dimensions. Available in 28" or 30" barrel length. Weight about 7.5 lbs.

NIB	Exc.	V.G.	Good	Fair	Poor
2050	1700	1175	850	600	300

Sporting Clays Left-Hand Model—Grade I

Same as Sporting Clays Model. Designed for left-handed shooter.

NIB	Exc.	V.G.	Good	Fair	Poor
2150	1700	1175	850	600	300

Lady Sport Model

Offered in 12-gauge only, with 28" or 30" ventilated rib barrels. Slightly smaller dimensions for women. Weight 7.75 lbs.

Grade I

NIB	Exc.	V.G.	Good	Fair	Poor
2150	1700	1175	850	600	300

Spectrum Grade—Colored Frame

NIB	Exc.	V.G.	Good	Fair	Poor
2100	1750	1200	850	600	300

Lady Sport Left-Handed

Same as above for left-handed shooters.

Grade I

NIB	Exc.	V.G.	Good	Fair	Poor
2100	1750	1200	850	600	300

Spectrum Grade

NIB	Exc.	V.G.	Good	Fair	Poor
2175	1800	1225	850	600	300

Trap Model

Built for competition shooter. Features 30" or 32" ventilated rib barrels. Trap dimension stock. Weight about 8.25 lbs.

Grade I

NIB	Exc.	V.G.	Good	Fair	Poor
2025	1750	1200	850	600	300

Grade II

NIB	Exc.	V.G.	Good	Fair	Poor
2400	1950	1500	1000	750	350

Grade III

NIB	Exc.	V.G.	Good	Fair	Poor
3400	2700	18900	1500	800	400

Skeet Model

Designed for competition shooter. Only 28" ventilated rib barrel offered as standard. Skeet dimension stock and chokes. Weight about 7.75 lbs.

Grade I

NIB	Exc.	V.G.	Good	Fair	Poor
2025	1750	1200	850	600	300

Grade II

NIB	Exc.	V.G.	Good	Fair	Poor
2425	1950	1525	1000	750	350

Grade III

NIB	Exc.	V.G.	Good	Fair	Poor
3400	2700	1900	1500	800	400

Classic Doubles Model 92

Offered in 12-gauge only, with 30" ventilated rib barrels. Adjustable trigger. Walnut stock, with 18 lpi checkering. Weight about 8.12 lbs.

NIB	Exc.	V.G.	Good	Fair	Poor
1650	1350	875	600	500	250

Model 99—Grade I

Over/under gun. Features silver-grayed receiver; boxlock action, with single-selective trigger; pistol-grip stock; schnabel forearm. Sporting models offered with 28", 30" or 32" barrels; trap with 30" or 32" barrels; skeet with 28" or 30" barrels. All barrels supplied with five extended choke tubes.

NIB	Exc.	V.G.	Good	Fair	Poor
3125	2350	1800	750	700	300

Model 99—Grade III

Has all the above features in addition to five flush-mounted choke tubes. Silver game scene engraved receiver.

NIB	Exc.	V.G.	Good	Fair	Poor
5200	3400	2200	950	800	300

MARS
See—Gabbet-Fairfax or Bergmann

MARSTON, S.W.
New York, New York

Double-Action Pepperbox

.31-caliber double-action percussion pepperbox, with 5" barrel group and ring trigger. Blued, with walnut grips. Manufactured between 1850 and 1855.

NIB	Exc.	V.G.	Good	Fair	Poor
—	—	2000	1125	600	250

2-Barrel Pistol

.31- or .36-caliber revolving barrel 2-shot pistol, with ring trigger. Barrel marked "J.Cohn & S.W.Marston-New York". Blued brass frame, with walnut grips. Manufactured during 1850s.

NIB	Exc.	V.G.	Good	Fair	Poor
—	—	2700	1250	450	200

MARSTON, W. W. & CO.
New York, New York

W.W. Marston & Company manufactured a variety of firearms, some of which are marked only with trade names: Union Arms Company, Phoenix Armory, Western Arms Company, Washington Arms Company, Sprague and Marston and Marston and Knox.

Double-Action Single-Shot Pistol

.31- or .36-caliber bar hammer percussion pistol, with 2.5" or 5" half octagonal barrel. Blued, with walnut grips. Manufactured during 1850s.

NIB	Exc.	V.G.	Good	Fair	Poor
—	—	650	325	150	100

Pocket Revolver

.31-caliber percussion revolver, with 3.25" to 7.5" barrel and 6-shot cylinder. Blued, with walnut grips. Approximately 13,000 manufactured between 1857 and 1862.

NIB	Exc.	V.G.	Good	Fair	Poor
—	—	1250	550	200	125

Navy Revolver

.36-caliber percussion revolver, with 7.5" or 8.5" octagonal barrel and 6-shot cylinder. Blued, with walnut grips. Manufactured between 1857 and 1862.

NIB	Exc.	V.G.	Good	Fair	Poor
—	—	3100	1400	600	200

Single-Action Pistol

.31- or .36-caliber percussion pistol, with 4" or 6" barrel. Blued, with walnut grips. Manufactured during 1860s.

NIB	Exc.	V.G.	Good	Fair	Poor
—	—	675	580	250	100

Breech-Loading Pistol

.36-caliber breech loading percussion pistol, with 4" to 8.5" half octagonal barrel. Brass or iron frame. Blued case-hardened, with walnut grips. Approximately 1,000 manufactured in 1850s.

Courtesy Milwaukee Public Museum, Milwaukee, Wisconsin

Brass Frame

NIB	Exc.	V.G.	Good	Fair	Poor
—	—	4400	3600	1650	500

Iron Frame

NIB	Exc.	V.G.	Good	Fair	Poor
—	—	3900	3000	1100	300

Double-Action Pepperbox

.31-caliber double-action 6-shot percussion pepperbox, with 4" or 5" barrel groups. Bar hammer. Blued case-hardened, with walnut grips. Manufactured during 1850s.

Courtesy Milwaukee Public Museum, Milwaukee, Wisconsin

NIB	Exc.	V.G.	Good	Fair	Poor
—	—	3200	2500	1150	300

3-Barrel Derringer

.22-caliber 3-barreled spur-trigger pocket pistol, with sliding knife blade mounted on left side of 3" barrel group. Blued silver-plated, with walnut grips. Barrel marked "Wm. W. Marston/New York City". Approximately 1,500 manufactured between 1858 and 1864.

Knife Blade Model

Courtesy Milwaukee Public Museum, Milwaukee, Wisconsin

NIB	Exc.	V.G.	Good	Fair	Poor
—	—	5575	4100	1650	400

Without Knife

Courtesy Milwaukee Public Museum, Milwaukee, Wisconsin

NIB	Exc.	V.G.	Good	Fair	Poor
—	—	2550	2000	775	200

3-Barrel Derringer .32 Caliber

Similar to above in .32-caliber, with 3" or 4" barrels. Not fitted with knife blade. Approximately 3,000 manufactured between 1864 and 1872.

Courtesy Milwaukee Public Museum, Milwaukee, Wisconsin

NIB	Exc.	V.G.	Good	Fair	Poor
—	—	3750	3000	825	200

MASQUELIER, S. A.
Liege, Belgium

Carpathe

.243, .270, .7x57mm, 7x65Rmm or .30-06 caliber single-shot rifle, with 24" barrel, adjustable trigger and sights. Blued, with engraved receiver. Walnut stock. Imported until 1986.

NIB	Exc.	V.G.	Good	Fair	Poor
—	3750	2950	1950	1250	750

Express

.270, .30-06, 8x57JRSmm or 9.3x74Rmm caliber over/under double-barrel rifle, with 24" barrels, single-selective trigger and automatic ejectors. Blued engraved, with walnut stock. Not imported after 1986.

NIB	Exc.	V.G.	Good	Fair	Poor
—	3800	2950	1950	1250	750

Ardennes

As above, but made on custom order only. Discontinued in 1986.

NIB	Exc.	V.G.	Good	Fair	Poor
—	8000	6000	3750	2500	1000

Boxlock Side-by-Side Shotgun

12-gauge boxlock double-barrel shotgun. Manufactured in a variety of barrel lengths, with single-selective trigger and automatic ejectors. Blued, with walnut stock. Imported prior to 1987.

NIB	Exc.	V.G.	Good	Fair	Poor
—	4750	3500	2500	1500	850

Sidelock Side-by-Side Shotgun

Similar to above, with detachable sidelocks. Finely engraved. Imported prior to 1987.

NIB	Exc.	V.G.	Good	Fair	Poor
—	14500	11750	7000	5000	1750

MASSACHUSETTS ARMS CO.
Chicopee Falls, Massachusetts

Wesson & Leavitt Dragoon

.40-caliber percussion revolver, with 7" round barrel, 6-shot cylinder and side-mounted hammer. Blued case-hardened, with walnut grips. Approximately 800 manufactured in 1850 and 1851.

Early Model with 6" Barrel

Approximately 30 made.

NIB	Exc.	V.G.	Good	Fair	Poor
—	—	8500	6600	275	750

Fully Marked 7" Barrel Standard Model

NIB	Exc.	V.G.	Good	Fair	Poor
—	—	8000	6050	2200	650

Wesson & Leavitt Belt Revolver

.31-caliber percussion revolver, with 3" to 7" round barrel and 6-shot cylinder. Similar in appearance to above. Approximately 1,000 manufactured in 1850 and 1851.

Courtesy Milwaukee Public Museum, Milwaukee, Wisconsin

NIB	Exc.	V.G.	Good	Fair	Poor
—	—	3000	1900	775	250

Maynard Primed Belt Revolver

Similar to above, with Maynard tape primer. Approximately 1,000 manufactured between 1851 and 1857.

Courtesy Milwaukee Public Museum, Milwaukee, Wisconsin

NIB	Exc.	V.G.	Good	Fair	Poor
—	—	3700	2750	880	250

Maynard Primed Pocket Revolver

Similar to above in .28- or .30-caliber, with 2.5" to 3.5" octagonal or round barrels. Approximately 3,000 made between 1851 and 1860.

Courtesy Milwaukee Public Museum, Milwaukee, Wisconsin

NIB	Exc.	V.G.	Good	Fair	Poor
—	—	1950	1400	625	200

Adams Patent Navy Revolver

As above in .36-caliber, with 6" octagonal barrel. Approximately 600 of the 1,000 made were purchased by U.S. government. **NOTE:** Those bearing inspection marks will bring approximately a 20 percent premium over values listed.

Courtesy Milwaukee Public Museum, Milwaukee, Wisconsin

NIB	Exc.	V.G.	Good	Fair	Poor
—	—	3750	2500	825	300

Single-Shot Pocket Pistol

.31-caliber single-shot percussion pistol, with 2.5" to 3.5" half octagonal barrel. Maynard tape primer. Barrel marked "Mass. Arms Co/Chicopee Falls" and primer door "Maynard's Patent Sept. 22, 1845". Blued case-hardened, with walnut grips. Manufactured in 1850s.

NIB	Exc.	V.G.	Good	Fair	Poor
—	—	4000	2750	925	300

MAYNARD CARBINE

Single-shot breechloader chambered for .35- or .50-caliber percussion. Round 20" barrel. Trigger guard is a lever that pivots barrel in break-open fashion when lowered. Finish blued, with case colored frame. Buttstock walnut and there is no fore-end. This carbine was designed by same Maynard who invented the tape primer system. There are two models—a 1st and 2nd. They were made for both sporting use and as a U.S. Martial carbine. 2nd Model was used considerably during Civil War.

1st Model

Marked "Maynard Patentee/May 27, 1851/June 17, 1856". Has iron patch-box; curved buttplate; Maynard tape primer system; tang sight. Later production fitted with a sling swivel. Approximately 400 of these carbines are U.S. marked. Total manufactured in late 1850s is unknown.

Courtesy Milwaukee Public Museum, Milwaukee, Wisconsin

U.S. Martially Marked

NIB	Exc.	V.G.	Good	Fair	Poor
—	—	6500	4050	2000	700

Commercial Model

NIB	Exc.	V.G.	Good	Fair	Poor
—	—	4000	3000	1250	400

2nd Model

Chambered for .50-caliber only. Does not have tape primer system or tang sight. There is no patchbox. Buttplate is not as curved as on 1st Model. Marked "Manufactured By/Mass. Arms Co./Chicopee Falls". Approximately 20,000 manufactured between 1860 and 1865. Used by Union forces during Civil War.

Courtesy Milwaukee Public Museum, Milwaukee, Wisconsin

NIB	Exc.	V.G.	Good	Fair	Poor
—	—	2500	2050	700	500

Maynard Patent Sporting Rifle

Sporting rifles bearing designations Model 1865, 1873 and 1882 were manufactured in a wide variety of calibers, gauges, stock styles, finishes and options.

Courtesy Milwaukee Public Museum, Milwaukee, Wisconsin

NIB	Exc.	V.G.	Good	Fair	Poor
—	—	2500	1650	660	200

MATEBA ARMS
Italy

AutoRevolver

Introduced in 2000. Chambered for .357 Magnum or .44 Magnum, with 4", 6" or 8" barrel. Features single-action trigger that has a reciprocating cylinder that fires from bottom chamber rather than top. Firing of the gun cocks hammer and cycles action for next round. Available with or without compensator. Offered in blue or nickel finish. Extra barrels available. Distributed in USA by American Western Arms (AWA). **NOTE:** Add $50 for nickel finish; $140 for extra barrel. Deduct $80 for guns without compensator.

NIB	Exc.	V.G.	Good	Fair	Poor
1600	1100	900	600	400	200

AutoRevolver Carbine

Similar in principle to a handgun, with 16" or 18" barrel. Walnut buttstock, pistol-grip and fore-end.

NIB	Exc.	V.G.	Good	Fair	Poor
1800	1300	1000	700	500	300

MATRA MANURHIN DEFENSE
Mulhouse, France

See—Manurhin

MAUNZ MFG., INC.
Maumee, Ohio

Manufacturer (1970s-1980s) of high-end law enforcement and competition rifles based primarily on M14 military rifle.

Model 77 Service Match Rifle

Semi-automatic rifle chambered in .308 Winchester. Other chamberings on custom order. 22" barrel standard; medium and heavy barrels available. Charcoal gray parkerized finish. Custom rifles had heavyweight Kevlar or graphite/fiberglass stocks covered in black gelcoat. Red/white/blue stocks were also produced. 300 produced.

NIB	Exc.	V.G.	Good	Fair	Poor
—	2500	2250	2000	1850	1500

Model 87 Maunz Match Rifle

Semi-automatic rifle chambered in .308 Winchester and 6.30 Maunz. Limited .338 and .45 Maunz chamberings on custom order. Sold only to Master competitors and American Shooters Union members.

NIB	Exc.	V.G.	Good	Fair	Poor
—	2500	2200	2000	1500	1200

Model 57 M1A

Semi-automatic rifle chambered in .30-06, .276 and .308 Winchester. Also .45 Maunz (rare). M1 Garand receiver, with M14 parts and National Match barrels. Custom-built glass-bedded stock. Approximately 200 made.

NIB	Exc.	V.G.	Good	Fair	Poor
—	1500	1250	1000	800	600

Model 67 Match Grade for Practice

Semi-automatic rifle chambered in .308 Winchester, 6.30 Maunz and .45 Maunz. Camp Perry stamped. Not allowed for Service Rifle competition. Combination of M1 Garand and M14 parts. Approximately 250 made.

NIB	Exc.	V.G.	Good	Fair	Poor
—	2000	1800	1500	1200	1500

MAUSER WERKE

Established in 1869 by Peter and Wilhelm Mauser, this company came under effective control of Ludwig Loewe and Company of Berlin in 1887. In 1896, latter company was reorganized under name Deutsches Waffen und Munition as it is better known, DWM. **NOTE:** Historical information, technical details, photos and prices on military Mausers see *Standard Catalog of Military Firearms, 7th Edition, Gun Digest Books 2013.*

Early Model 98 Sporting Rifles

Wide variety of commercial Model 98 Sporting Rifles were made. Most of which had 23.5" ribbed barrels, open sights, 5-shot magazines, single-/double-set triggers and full or semi-pistol-grip stocks.

Type A—Short Action

NIB	Exc.	V.G.	Good	Fair	Poor
—	10000	9000	7200	3500	1000

Type A—Medium Action

NIB	Exc.	V.G.	Good	Fair	Poor
—	7000	5000	4000	2000	1000

Type A—Long Action

NIB	Exc.	V.G.	Good	Fair	Poor
—	8000	6000	5000	2500	1000

Type B

NIB	Exc.	V.G.	Good	Fair	Poor
—	4800	3500	2300	1400	500

Type K

NIB	Exc.	V.G.	Good	Fair	Poor
—	7500	6500	4000	2000	700

Type M

NIB	Exc.	V.G.	Good	Fair	Poor
—	5500	5000	4000	2800	900

Type S

NIB	Exc.	V.G.	Good	Fair	Poor
—	5500	5000	4000	2800	900

MODEL 1896 BROOMHANDLE MAUSER PISTOL

Manufactured from 1896 to 1939. Model 1896 Pistol was produced in a wide variety of styles as listed. It is recommended that those considering purchase of any models listed should consult Breathed & Schroeders's *System Mauser* (Chicago 1967) as it provides detailed descriptions and photographs of various models. **NOTE:** Prices listed are for pistol only. A correct matching stock/holster will add approximately 40 percent to value of each category. Non-matching stock/holster will add $350 and $600 to prices.

"BUYER BEWARE" ALERT by Gale Morgan: I have personally seen English Crest, U.S. Great Seal, unheard-of European dealers, aristocratic Coats-of-Arms and Middle East Medallions beautifully photo-etched into magazine wells and rear panels of some really common wartime commercials, with price tags that have been elevated to $2,500 plus. They are quite eye-catching and if they are sold as customized/modified

Mausers, seller can price the piece at whatever the market will bear. However, if sold as a factory original—BUYER BEWARE.

Six-Shot Step-Barrel Cone Hammer

7.63mm semi-automatic pistol, with 5.5" barrel, fixed rear sight and checkered walnut grips. Marked "Ruecklauf Pistole System Mauser, Oberndorf am/Neckar 1896". Very few were manufactured. Too rare to price.

Twenty-Shot Step-Barrel Cone Hammer

As above, with 20-shot extended magazine and tangent rear sight. Engraved "system mauser" on top of chamber. Too rare to price.

System Mauser 10-Shot Cone Hammer

As above, with fixed or tangent rear sight. Step barrel (pictured) is very rare as is tapered barrel. Magazine capacity 10 rounds.

Courtesy Joe Schroeder

NIB	Exc.	V.G.	Good	Fair	Poor
—	25000	17000	12000	8000	7000

Six-Shot Standard Cone Hammer

Similar to above, with no step in barrel, 6-shot magazine and marked "Waffenfabrik Mauser, Oberndorf A/N" over the chamber. May have fixed, or rarely, tangent rear sight.

Courtesy Joe Schroeder

NIB	Exc.	V.G.	Good	Fair	Poor
—	15000	12000	6750	4500	3000

Twenty-Shot Cone Hammer

As above, with extended magazine holding 20 cartridges. May have panels or flat sides.

Courtesy Joe Schroeder

NIB	Exc.	V.G.	Good	Fair	Poor
—	40000	35000	20000	10000	7000

Standard Cone Hammer

As above, with 10-shot magazine and 23-groove grips. Price includes matching stocks.

Courtesy Rock Island Auction Company

NIB	Exc.	V.G.	Good	Fair	Poor
—	8000	5000	2000	1400	800

Fixed Sight Cone Hammer

Similar to standard Cone Hammer, except fixed integral sight is machined into barrel extension.

Courtesy Joe Schroeder

NIB	Exc.	V.G.	Good	Fair	Poor
—	8000	5500	3500	2000	1000

Turkish Contract Cone Hammer

As above, but sight marked in Farsi and bearing crest of Sultan Abdul-Hamid II on frame. Approximately 1,000 were made.

Courtesy Gale Morgan

Courtesy Joe Schroeder

NIB	Exc.	V.G.	Good	Fair	Poor
—	15000	12000	8500	5000	2000

Early Transitional Large Ring Hammer

Variation has same characteristics of "Standard Cone Hammer", except hammer has larger open ring.

Courtesy Wallis & Wallis, Lewes, Sussex, England

NIB	Exc.	V.G.	Good	Fair	Poor
—	5500	4000	2500	1150	800

Model 1899 Flat Side—Italian Contract

Similar to above, with 5.5" barrel, adjustable rear sight and frame sides milled flat. Left flat of chamber marked with "DV" proof. Approximately 5,000 manufactured in 1899.

Courtesy Joe Schroeder

NIB	Exc.	V.G.	Good	Fair	Poor
—	6000	4000	2000	1200	900

Early Flat Side

Similar to above, except with "pinned" rear sight. Without Italian markings.

NIB	Exc.	V.G.	Good	Fair	Poor
—	5000	3500	2800	1000	750

Late Flat Side

Similar to above, with an integral pin mounted adjustable rear sight. Often marked with dealer's names such as "Von Lengerke & Detmold, New York".

NIB	Exc.	V.G.	Good	Fair	Poor
—	4000	3200	2000	1000	750

Flat Side Bolo

Similar to above, with 3.9" barrel, fixed sights. Checkered walnut grips. Very rare.

NIB	Exc.	V.G.	Good	Fair	Poor
—	7500	6000	4000	3000	2000

Early Large Ring Hammer Bolo

As above, with milled frame, adjustable rear sight. Grooved wood or hard rubber grips cast with a floral pattern. 10-shot magazine.

NIB	Exc.	V.G.	Good	Fair	Poor
—	4700	3700	2000	1500	1000

Shallow-Milled Panel Model

Full size. Similar to above, with 5.5" barrel. Either 23-groove walnut or checkered hard rubber grips. Shallow frame panels.

NIB	Exc.	V.G.	Good	Fair	Poor
—	3800	2700	1000	750	500

Deep-Milled Panel Model

As above, with deeper milled panels on sides of receiver.

NIB	Exc.	V.G.	Good	Fair	Poor
—	4500	3000	2000	1000	750

Late Large Ring Hammer Bolo

Similar to Early Large Ring Hammer Bolo, with late style adjustable rear sight.

Courtesy Joe Schroeder

NIB	Exc.	V.G.	Good	Fair	Poor
—	4000	3000	2000	1000	750

Six-Shot Large Ring Bolo

Similar to above Large Ring Bolo, with 6-shot magazine. May be equipped with fixed or tangent sights.

Courtesy James Rankin

NIB	Exc.	V.G.	Good	Fair	Poor
—	8900	6500	5000	3000	1800

Early Small Ring Hammer Model, Transitional

Model 96, with early long extractor, hammer with small-diameter hole and 5.5" barrel. Grips have 34 grooves.

Courtesy Joe Schroeder

NIB	Exc.	V.G.	Good	Fair	Poor
—	3200	2000	1500	1000	500

Early Small Ring Hammer Bolo Model

As above, with 3.9" barrel. Wood or hard rubber grips cast with a floral pattern. Serial numbers in 40,000 range.

NIB	Exc.	V.G.	Good	Fair	Poor
—	4500	3000	2000	1500	600

Six-Shot Small Ring Hammer Model

As above, with 27-groove walnut grips.

NIB	Exc.	V.G.	Good	Fair	Poor
—	8500	6500	3000	1800	1000

Standard Pre-war Commercial

Model 96, with 5.5" barrel, late-style adjustable rear sight and 34-groove walnut grips or checkered hard rubber grips. Often found with dealers markings such as "Von Lengerke & Detmold".

Courtesy Joe Schroeder

NIB	Exc.	V.G.	Good	Fair	Poor
—	3500	2500	1200	650	300

9mm Export Model

As above in 9mm Mauser, with 34-groove walnut grips.

NIB	Exc.	V.G.	Good	Fair	Poor
—	3750	2250	1500	1000	700

Mauser Banner Model

Standard pre-war features, except chamber stamped with Mauser Banner trademark and 32-groove walnut grips. Approximately 10,000 were manufactured.

Courtesy Joe Schroeder

NIB	Exc.	V.G.	Good	Fair	Poor
—	4500	3200	2300	1100	600

Persian Contract

Persian rampant lion on left rear panel. Prospective purchasers should secure a qualified appraisal prior to acquisition. Serial numbers in 154000 range.

NIB	Exc.	V.G.	Good	Fair	Poor
—	4700	4000	2700	1400	1000

Standard Wartime Commercial

Identical to pre-war Commercial Model 96, except it has 30-groove walnut grips. Rear of hammer stamped "NS" for new safety. Many also bear German or Austrian military acceptance proofs.

Courtesy Gale Morgan

NIB	Exc.	V.G.	Good	Fair	Poor
—	2500	1750	1000	500	350

9mm Parabellum Military Contract

As above in 9mm Parabellum caliber, with 24-groove grips. Stamped with large "9" filled with red paint. **NOTE:** Add 20 percent to full rig.

NIB	Exc.	V.G.	Good	Fair	Poor
—	3500	2500	1000	700	450

1920 Rework

Model 96 modified to barrel length of 3.9" and in 7.63mm Mauser or 9mm Parabellum caliber. Often encountered with police markings.

Late Post-war Bolo Model

As above, with Mauser Banner trademark stamped on left rear panel.

Courtesy Gale Morgan

Courtesy Joe Schroeder

NIB	Exc.	V.G.	Good	Fair	Poor
—	1750	1000	500	400	350

Luger Barreled 1920 Rework

Similar to above. Fitted with Luger 4" barrel or a sighted Luger barrel-band, 12- or 23-groove walnut grips and 9mm caliber.

Courtesy Gale Morgan

NIB	Exc.	V.G.	Good	Fair	Poor
—	2500	1200	700	500	450

Early Post-war Bolo Model

Model 96 in 7.63mm caliber, with 3.9" barrel, adjustable rear sight and 22-groove walnut grips.

NIB	Exc.	V.G.	Good	Fair	Poor
—	3000	2100	1000	400	200

Courtesy James Rankin

NIB	Exc.	V.G.	Good	Fair	Poor
—	3000	2000	1000	400	200

French Gendarme Model

Standard Model 96 fitted with 3.9" barrel. Checkered hard rubber grips. Although reputed to have been made under a French contract, no record of that has been found to date.

Courtesy James Rankin

NIB	Exc.	V.G.	Good	Fair	Poor
—	4500	3000	1000	600	350

Early Model 1930

7.63mm caliber Model 96, with 5.2" barrel, grooved side rails, 12-groove walnut grips and late-style safety. **NOTE:** Add 25 percent with correct stocks.

NIB	Exc.	V.G.	Good	Fair	Poor
—	3000	2000	1700	800	500

Late Model 1930

Similar to above, except for solid receiver rails.

NIB	Exc.	V.G.	Good	Fair	Poor
—	3500	2200	1700	800	400

Model 1930 Removable Magazine

Similar to above, with detachable magazine. Prospective purchasers should secure a qualified appraisal prior to acquisition. Too rare to price.

CARBINE MODELS

Cone Hammer Flat Side Carbine

7.63mm caliber carbine, with 11.75" full length "rib" barrel, early adjustable sight, flat frame and detachable buttstock. Prospective purchasers should secure a qualified appraisal prior to acquisition. Too rare to price. **NOTE:** Watch for fakes.

Large Ring Hammer Transitional Carbine

Similar to above, with milled frame panels. Prospective purchasers should secure a qualified appraisal prior to acquisition.

NIB	Exc.	V.G.	Good	Fair	Poor
—	25000	18000	11000	5000	3000

Large Ring Hammer Flatside Carbine

Similar to above, with 14.5" barrel. Prospective purchasers should secure a qualified appraisal prior to acquisition.

NIB	Exc.	V.G.	Good	Fair	Poor
—	23000	17000	10000	5000	3000

Small Ring Hammer Carbine

Similar to above, with hammer having a smaller diameter hole at its tip. Prospective purchasers should secure a qualified appraisal prior to acquisition. Some late carbines were chambered for 9mm export.

NIB	Exc.	V.G.	Good	Fair	Poor
—	21000	18000	15000	6000	4000

CHINESE COPIES

Chinese Marked, Handmade Copies

Crude copies of Model 96 and unsafe to fire.

NIB	Exc.	V.G.	Good	Fair	Poor
—	500	400	350	250	175

Taku-Naval Dockyard Model

Approximately 6,000 very good quality copies of Model 96 were made at Taku-Naval Dockyard. In several variations, both flat and paneled sides.

NIB	Exc.	V.G.	Good	Fair	Poor
—	3500	2000	1000	600	400

Shansei Arsenal Model

Approximately 8,000 Model 96 pistols were manufactured in .45 ACP caliber. Copies of Model 96 were made by Unceta (Astra) and Zulaica y Cia (Royal) and marketed by the firm of Beistegui Hermanos. These copies are covered in their own sections of this text. **NOTE:** Within past several years, a large quantity of Model 96 pistols exported to or made in China have been imported into United States. It has been reported that some newly made copies of Shansei .45 were recently exported from China. Proceed with caution.

Courtesy Gale Morgan

NIB	Exc.	V.G.	Good	Fair	Poor
—	5000	3500	2250	1500	1300

MAUSER POCKET PISTOLS

Model 1910

6.35mm (.25 ACP) caliber pistol, with 3" barrel, 9-shot magazine. Checkered walnut or (scarce) hard rubber wrap-around grip. Early examples (below serial 60,000 or so) have a pivoting take-down latch above trigger guard and are identified as "Sidelatch" models by collectors. Later production Models 1910s are often identified as Model 1910/14. Manufactured from 1910 to 1934.

Sidelatch Model

NIB	Exc.	V.G.	Good	Fair	Poor
—	1200	900	600	300	300

Later Production (Model 1910/14)

NIB	Exc.	V.G.	Good	Fair	Poor
—	550	300	200	150	100

Model 1914

Larger version of Model 1910. Chambered for 7.65mm Browning (.32 ACP), with 3.5" or (rarely) 4.5" barrel. Very early examples up to serial 2500 or so had a contoured hump on slide and are called "Humpbacks" by collectors; these bring a considerable premium. Model 1914s with police or military markings bring a small premium. Manufactured between 1914 and 1934.

Model 1914 "Humpback"

NIB	Exc.	V.G.	Good	Fair	Poor
—	4000	3000	1750	800	400

Model 1914 (later)

NIB	Exc.	V.G.	Good	Fair	Poor
—	475	300	200	150	100

Model 1912/14

While Mauser's pocket pistols were very successful on the commercial market, Mauser was also trying to develop a larger caliber pistol for military use. Most successful of these was Model 1912/14, though only about 200 were ever made. A few of these did reach commercial market and it's likely the pistol would have continued in production had WWI not broken out. Higher serial numbered guns were slotted for Model 1896-style holster stock. Few of these also had tangent sights. **NOTE:** Add 50 percent for shoulder stock.

NIB	Exc.	V.G.	Good	Fair	Poor
—	38000	30000	22000	10000	5000

Model WTP I

Mauser's first post-WWI new design. First vest pocket pistol, with 2.5" barrel and 6-shot magazine. Grips were plastic wrap-around, with one, two or three grip screws depending on production period. Production ended in late 1930s, when WTP II was introduced.

NIB	Exc.	V.G.	Good	Fair	Poor
—	750	500	400	250	150

Model WTP II

WTP II was a much more compact design than its predecessor, with 2" barrel and separate grip panels instead of Mauser's usual wrap-around grip. Production was limited by the outbreak of WWII, so WTP II is much scarcer than WTP I. Under French occupation, at least several hundred WTP II's were assembled and sold; these can be identified by their very low electric penciled serial numbers and lack of German proofing. Brings a slight premium over pre-war German manufactured pistols.

Courtesy Gale Morgan

NIB	Exc.	V.G.	Good	Fair	Poor
—	1250	900	700	350	200

Model 1934

In response to competition from Walther and others, in 1934 Mauser spruced up its aging 1910/14 and 1914 pistols with a new high-polish finish and form-fitting swept back grips. Nickel finish was offered, but is very rare (50 percent premium, but beware of re-nickeled blued guns). The 7.65mm pistols became popular with both military and police, but those so marked can bring a considerable premium.

Courtesy Orvel Reichert

Courtesy Orvel Reichert

Courtesy Gale Morgan

6.35mm

NIB	Exc.	V.G.	Good	Fair	Poor
—	525	325	250	200	125

7.65mm Commercial

NIB	Exc.	V.G.	Good	Fair	Poor
—	450	325	250	200	125

7.65mm Eagle L proofed

NIB	Exc.	V.G.	Good	Fair	Poor
—	675	450	300	250	150

7.56mm Large Eagle over M (Navy)

NIB	Exc.	V.G.	Good	Fair	Poor
—	1200	750	450	300	200

MODEL HSc

HSc was a totally new design. Chambered for 7.65mm Browning. Featuring double-action lockwork and partially concealed external hammer. Introduced just as WWII broke out. HSc was produced through the war for both commercial sale and military use. Serials started at 700,000 and first 1500 or so had grip screws located near bottom of grip and bring a large premium. Finish deteriorated as war progressed. Some HSc pistols were even produced under French occupation after the war ended. **NOTE:** Add 20 percent for Waffenamt markings; 50 percent for Navy marked front straps.

Low Grip Screw Model

As above, with screws that attach grip located near bottom of grip. Highly-polished blue checkered walnut grips. Early address without lines and has Eagle N proof. Some have been observed with Nazi Kreigsmarine markings. Approximately 2,000 were manufactured.

NIB	Exc.	V.G.	Good	Fair	Poor
—	8000	5000	1800	750	650

Early Commercial Model

Highly polished blued finish, checkered walnut grips, standard Mauser address on slide and Eagle N proofmark. Floorplate of magazine stamped with Mauser Banner.

NIB	Exc.	V.G.	Good	Fair	Poor
—	750	500	350	175	125

Transition Model

As above, but not as highly finished.

NIB	Exc.	V.G.	Good	Fair	Poor
—	525	400	300	150	100

Early Nazi Army Model

Courtesy Orvel Reichert

NIB	Exc.	V.G.	Good	Fair	Poor
—	650	550	400	200	125

Late Nazi Army Model

NIB	Exc.	V.G.	Good	Fair	Poor
—	450	375	250	150	100

Early Nazi Navy Model

NIB	Exc.	V.G.	Good	Fair	Poor
—	1350	1000	750	400	300

Wartime Nazi Navy Model

NIB	Exc.	V.G.	Good	Fair	Poor
—	1100	800	650	400	200

Early Nazi Police Model

NIB	Exc.	V.G.	Good	Fair	Poor
—	600	500	425	250	175

Wartime Nazi Police Model

NIB	Exc.	V.G.	Good	Fair	Poor
—	500	400	350	250	175

Wartime Commercial Model

As above, without acceptance markings on trigger guard.

NIB	Exc.	V.G.	Good	Fair	Poor
—	425	350	300	200	125

French Manufactured Model

Blued or Parkerized, with walnut or plastic grips. Trigger guard marked on left side with monogram "MR".

NIB	Exc.	V.G.	Good	Fair	Poor
—	375	275	225	150	100

Model HSc Post-war Production

In late 1960s, Mauser resumed production of HSc in both 7.65mm and 9mm Browning short (.380). Five thousand post-war HSc pistols were specially marked with an American eagle and bring a slight premium over standard marked pistols. In 1980s, Mauser licensed HSc production to Gamba in Italy, which produced an enlarged frame version of HSc, with a double-column magazine. In both German and Italian production, .380s bring about a 20 percent premium over .32s.

Mauser Production (.32)

NIB	Exc.	V.G.	Good	Fair	Poor
—	525	450	300	175	125

Gamba Production

In recent years Mauser has licensed several firms other than Gamba to produce pistols bearing Mauser trademark, such as Browning Hi Power knockoff made in Hungary. In 1999, Mauser was bought by SIG-Sauer and a new large caliber Mauser pistol was announced.

NIB	Exc.	V.G.	Good	Fair	Poor
—	600	475	325	200	100

MAUSER RIFLES—RECENT PRODUCTION

In February 1999, SIGARMS announced acquisition of Mauser line of small arms. Current production is in Isny, Germany. Some Mauser rifles were imported and distributed by SIGARMS and later Briley Manufacturing, located in Houston, Texas. Beginning in 2009, Mauser rifles are imported by Mauser USA, San Antonio, Texas.

Model 2000

.270, .308 or .30-06 caliber bolt-action rifle, with 24" barrel, open sights and 5-shot magazine. Blued, with checkered walnut stock. Manufactured between 1969 and 1971 by Heym.

NIB	Exc.	V.G.	Good	Fair	Poor
—	600	450	300	200	150

Model 3000

As above, with 22" barrel, no sights and Monte Carlo-style stock. Manufactured from 1971 to 1974 by Heym.

NIB	Exc.	V.G.	Good	Fair	Poor
—	600	450	300	200	150

Model 3000 Magnum

As above in 7mm Rem. Magnum, .300 Win. Magnum and .375 H&H Magnum caliber, with 26" barrel and 3-shot integral magazine. Blued, with checkered walnut stock. Produced by Heym.

NIB	Exc.	V.G.	Good	Fair	Poor
—	675	525	375	250	200

Model 4000

Similar to Model 3000 in .222- or .223-caliber, with folding open sights. Produced by Heym.

NIB	Exc.	V.G.	Good	Fair	Poor
—	550	400	250	200	150

Model 225

.243 to .300 Weatherby Magnum caliber bolt-action rifle, with 24" or 26" barrel, no sights, adjustable trigger and 3- or 5-shot magazine. Blued, with walnut stock.

NIB	Exc.	V.G.	Good	Fair	Poor
1400	1250	1000	750	600	500

Model ES340

.22-caliber single-shot bolt-action rifle, with 25.5" barrel, open sights and walnut stock. Manufactured before WWII.

NIB	Exc.	V.G.	Good	Fair	Poor
—	300	250	225	175	125

Model DSM34

Similar to above, with 25" barrel and full-length walnut stock. Manufactured prior to WWII.

NIB	Exc.	V.G.	Good	Fair	Poor
—	325	275	250	200	150

Model MS420B

Similar to above, with 25" barrel and 5-shot magazine. Manufactured before WWII.

NIB	Exc.	V.G.	Good	Fair	Poor
—	375	325	300	275	200

Model ES350

.22-caliber single-shot bolt-action rifle, with 27.5" barrel. Checkered pistol-grip walnut stock. Manufactured before WWII.

NIB	Exc.	V.G.	Good	Fair	Poor
—	450	400	375	350	275

Model M410

Similar to above, with 23.5" barrel and 5-shot magazine. Manufactured before WWII.

NIB	Exc.	V.G.	Good	Fair	Poor
—	375	325	300	275	200

Model M420

As above, with 25.5" barrel.

NIB	Exc.	V.G.	Good	Fair	Poor
375	325	300	275	200	

Model EN310

.22-caliber single-shot bolt-action rifle, with 19.75" barrel, open sights and plain walnut stock. Manufactured before WWII.

NIB	Exc.	V.G.	Good	Fair	Poor
—	250	225	200	150	100

Model EL320

As above, with 23.5" barrel. Checkered walnut stock.

NIB	Exc.	V.G.	Good	Fair	Poor
—	275	250	225	175	125

Model KKW

.22-caliber single-shot bolt-action rifle, with 26" barrel, ladder rear sight and full-length walnut stock. Manufactured prior to WWII.

NIB	Exc.	V.G.	Good	Fair	Poor
—	400	350	300	225	150

Model MS350B

.22-caliber bolt-action rifle, with 26.75" barrel, adjustable rear sight and 5-shot magazine. Blued, with walnut stock.

NIB	Exc.	V.G.	Good	Fair	Poor
—	475	400	350	275	200

Model ES340B

Similar to above in single-shot form.

NIB	Exc.	V.G.	Good	Fair	Poor
—	375	300	250	175	100

Model MM41OBN

.22-caliber bolt-action rifle, with 23.5" barrel, adjustable sights and 5-shot magazine. Blued, with walnut stock.

NIB	Exc.	V.G.	Good	Fair	Poor
—	400	350	300	200	125

Model MS420B

As above, with 26.75" barrel and target-style stock.

NIB	Exc.	V.G.	Good	Fair	Poor
—	400	350	300	200	125

Model 107

Bolt-action rifle chambered for .22 LR. Barrel length 21.6". Box magazine has 5-shot capacity. Beechwood checkered Monte Carlo stock is full size, with pistol-grip plastic buttplate. Rear sight adjustable. Metal finish blue. Weight about 5 lbs.

NIB	Exc.	V.G.	Good	Fair	Poor
265	225	180	150	125	100

Model 201 Standard

Features 21" medium heavy free-floating barrel. Receiver accepts all rail mounts. Drilled and tapped for scope mount. Magazine capacity 5-shot. Chambered for .22 LR or .22 WMR cartridge. Beechwood stock is hand checkered, with plastic buttplate. Monte Carlo stock fitted with cheekpiece. Weight about 6.5 lbs.

NIB	Exc.	V.G.	Good	Fair	Poor
600	500	350	200	150	100

Model 66 Standard

Centerfire bolt-action rifle. Fitted with European walnut hand-checkered oil-finished half stock design. Rosewood fore-ends and pistol-grip caps are standard. Fitted with rubber recoil pad and 1" quick disconnect sling swivels. Interchangeable 24" barrels in standard calibers: .243 Win., .270, .308, .30-06, 5.6x57, 6.5x57, 7.64 and 9.3x62. Weight about 7.5 lbs.

NIB	Exc.	V.G.	Good	Fair	Poor
1700	1450	1100	700	550	350

Model 66 Magnum

Same as above. Chambered for 7mm Rem. Magnum, .300 and .338 Win. Magnum, 6.5x68, 8x86S, 9.3x64. Fitted with 26" barrel. Weight about 7.9 lbs.

NIB	Exc.	V.G.	Good	Fair	Poor
1800	1550	1200	800	600	400

Model 66 Safari

Same as above. Chambered for .375 H&H and .458 Win. Magnum. Fitted with 26" barrel. Weight about 9.3 lbs.

NIB	Exc.	V.G.	Good	Fair	Poor
2600	2000	1250	850	650	400

Model 66 Stuzen

Same as Standard Model 66. Fitted with a full stock. Barrel length 21". Calibers same as Standard. Weight about 7.5 lbs.

NIB	Exc.	V.G.	Good	Fair	Poor
2500	2100	1500	800	600	400

IDF Mauser Rifle Model 66SP

Bolt-action rifle chambered for .308 Win. cartridge. Adjustable trigger for pull and travel. Barrel length 27". Specially designed stock has broad fore-end and thumbhole pistol-grip. Cheekpiece adjustable as is recoil pad. Supplied with case. This rifle is military issue. Fewer than 100 imported into U.S. by Springfield Armory.

NIB	Exc.	V.G.	Good	Fair	Poor
2250	1575	1100	850	650	400

Model 77

Fitted with a 24" barrel. Bolt-action rifle chambered for .243, .270, 6.5x57, 7x64, .308 and .30-06 calibers. Detachable box magazine. Set trigger. Walnut stock, with cheekpiece. Hand checkering. Weight about 7.25 lbs.

NIB	Exc.	V.G.	Good	Fair	Poor
1250	950	800	650	450	200

Model 77 Ultra

Fitted with a 20" barrel. Chambered for 6.5x57, 7x64 and .30-06 calibers. Weight about 7.5 lbs.

NIB	Exc.	V.G.	Good	Fair	Poor
1250	950	800	650	450	200

Model 77 Mannlicher

Similar to Ultra Model, with full-length Mannlicher stock. Set trigger. Weight about 7.5 lbs.

NIB	Exc.	V.G.	Good	Fair	Poor
1250	950	800	650	450	200

Model 77 Big Game

Chambered for .375 H&H Magnum cartridge. Fitted with a 26" barrel. Weight about 8.5 lbs.

NIB	Exc.	V.G.	Good	Fair	Poor
1100	900	750	600	500	200

Model 86-SR

Introduced in 1993. Bolt-action .308 is sometimes referred to as "Specialty Rifle". Fitted with a laminated wood and special match thumbhole or fiberglass stock, with adjustable cheekpiece. Stock has rail in fore-arm and adjustable recoil pad. Magazine capacity 9 rounds. Finish a non-glare blue. Barrel length with muzzle-brake 28.8". Many special features are found on this rifle from adjustable trigger weight to silent safety. Mauser offers many options on this rifle that will affect price. Weight about 11 lbs.

NIB	Exc.	V.G.	Good	Fair	Poor
9500	7500	5000	3500	1800	1000

Model 93 SR

Introduced in 1996. A tactical semi-automatic rifle chambered for .300 Win. Magnum or .338 Lapua cartridge. Barrel length 25.5"; overall length 48.4". Barrel fitted with a muzzle-brake. Magazine capacity: 6 rounds .300; 5 rounds .338-caliber. Weight about 13 lbs.

NIB	Exc.	V.G.	Good	Fair	Poor
10000	9000	7500	5000	3500	1500

Model 96

Bolt-action rifle chambered for .25-06, .270 Win., 7x64, .308 or .30-06 cartridge. Fitted with a 22" barrel (24" Magnum calibers) and has a 5-round top loading magazine. Receiver drilled and tapped. Checkered walnut stock. No sights. Weight about 6.25 lbs.

NIB	Exc.	V.G.	Good	Fair	Poor
700	600	500	300	125	100

Model 98 Standard

Built on classic Mauser square-bridge action, this model has been offered in most popular calibers, including most big Magnums for dangerous game. Features include an extra-select hand-checkered walnut stock. This is a custom rifle, with limited production. Values shown are for standard calibers.

NIB	Exc.	V.G.	Good	Fair	Poor
8000	6500	5000	3500	2500	700

Model 99 Standard

Bolt-action centerfire sporting rifle. Offered with two stock designs: classic with straight oil-finish stock or high luster with cheekpiece and schnabel fore-end and Monte Carlo with rosewood fore-end tip and pistol-grip cap. Chambered for standard calibers: .243, .25-06, .270, .308, .30-06, 5.6x57, 6.5x57, 7x57, 7x64. Barrel length 24"; weight about 8 lbs.

NIB	Exc.	V.G.	Good	Fair	Poor
900	700	600	500	400	300

Model 99 Magnum

Same as above. Chambered for Magnum calibers: 7mm Rem. Magnum, .257 Wby., .270 Wby., .300 Wby., .300 and .338 Win. Magnum, 8x68S and 9.3x64. Fitted with 26" barrel. Weight about 8 lbs.

NIB	Exc.	V.G.	Good	Fair	Poor
950	750	650	550	400	300

M03

Offered in several variants and grades. Chambered in a wide range of popular calibers from .222 Remington to .375 H&H Magnum. Built on traditional Mauser square-bridge action. Features include barrel interchangeability and manual cocking system, with safety/cocking lever at rear of bolt. Made by Blaser. Values shown are for basic model, with synthetic stock. Higher grade wood and various levels of engraving are available. **NOTE:** Add $500 for checkered walnut stock.

NIB	Exc.	V.G.	Good	Fair	Poor
4000	3400	2800	2000	1000	400

M12

Modern Mauser design, with solid steel construction, checkered walnut or synthetic stock with Prince of Wales pistol-grip, three-position safety, detachable magazine and short 60-degree bolt lift. Offered in .22-250, .243, .270, 6.5x55, 7x64, 7mm Rem. Magnum, .308, .30-06, .300 Win. Magnum, 8x57JS, 9.3x62, .338 Win. Magnum. Several variations are available, with barrel lengths of 19", 22" or 24.5" with or without sights. Introduced in 2013. **NOTE:** Add $300 for walnut stock.

NIB	Exc.	V.G.	Good	Fair	Poor
1375	1150	900	750	500	300

CURRENT MAUSER PRODUCTION PISTOLS

Model 80 SA

Single-action semi-automatic pistol. Based on Browning Hi-Power design. Chambered for 9mm Parabellum cartridge. Barrel length 4.66"; magazine capacity 14 rounds; weight about 35 oz.

NIB	Exc.	V.G.	Good	Fair	Poor
550	475	295	175	125	100

Model Compact DA

Same as above, with double-action trigger. Shorter barrel 4.13". Weight about 33 oz.

NIB	Exc.	V.G.	Good	Fair	Poor
340	320	250	175	125	100

Model 90 DA

Similar to Model 80, with double-action trigger.

NIB	Exc.	V.G.	Good	Fair	Poor
550	475	295	175	125	100

Model M2 (Imported by SIG ARMS)

Introduced in 2000. Chambered for .45 ACP, .40 S&W or .357 SIG cartridges. Has an aluminum alloy frame and steel slide. Action is an enclosed hammerless striker-fired design. Barrel length 3.5". Fixed sights. Weight about 29 oz. Magazine capacity: 8 rounds .45 ACP; 10 rounds .40 S&W and .357 SIG.

NIB	Exc.	V.G.	Good	Fair	Poor
475	400	300	200	150	100

MAVERICK ARMS, INC.
Subsidiary of O. F. Mossberg & Sons, Inc.
Eagle Pass, Texas

Model 88

12-gauge Magnum slide-action shotgun, with 28" or 30" barrels, anodized receiver, composition stock. Introduced in 1989.

NIB	Exc.	V.G.	Good	Fair	Poor
250	150	125	100	75	50

Model 88 Slug Pump Shotgun

12-gauge Magnum pump-action shotgun, with interchangeable cylinder-bore barrel. Black synthetic stock; forearm blued metal finish; 6-shot magazine. **NOTE:** Add $20 for rifled 24" barrel, with adjustable rifle sights.

NIB	Exc.	V.G.	Good	Fair	Poor
295	200	100	75	60	50

Model 88 Six-Shot Security Model

12-gauge Magnum pump-action shotgun, with 6-shot magazine. Interchangeable 18.5" cylinder-bore fixed choke barrel; rugged black synthetic stock and forearm; blued metal finish; brass front sight bead, are also included. **NOTE:** Add 5 percent for 8-shot Security Model, with 20" cylinder-bore fixed choke barrel; 10 percent for heat shield.

NIB	Exc.	V.G.	Good	Fair	Poor
295	200	100	75	60	50

Model HS-12

A 12-gauge over/under shotgun offered in several variations. Field model has 28" barrels, with improved-cylinder and modified choke tubes, selective single trigger, extractors and synthetic stock; Tactical model has an 18.5" barrel and Picatinny rails. **NOTE:** Add $50 for this model.

NIB	Exc.	V.G.	Good	Fair	Poor
400	375	325	250	200	100

MAYNARD/PERRY
Keen, Walker & Co.
Danville, Virginia

Brass Framed Carbine

Overall length 40"; barrel length 22.5"; caliber .54. Browned blued barrel, brass frame and walnut stock. Manufactured in 1861 and 1862. Fewer than 300 produced.

NIB	Exc.	V.G.	Good	Fair	Poor
—	—	33000	14000	8000	1500

McMILLAN & CO. INC., G.
(Later: Harris/McMillan Gunworks, Harris Gunworks)
Phoenix, Arizona

Competition Model

Custom order bolt-action rifle in .308, 7mm-08 and .300 Win. Magnum caliber. Barrel length, stock type and dimensions to customer's specifications. Introduced in 1988.

NIB	Exc.	V.G.	Good	Fair	Poor
1700	1500	1150	800	600	300

Model 86 Sniper's Rifle

Custom order rifle in .308 Win. or .300 Win. Magnum calibers, with synthetic stock. Choice of scope systems. Introduced in 1988.

NIB	Exc.	V.G.	Good	Fair	Poor
3250	2700	1900	1100	600	300

Model 86 System

As above, with Ultra scope mounting system, bipod and fitted case. Introduced in 1988.

NIB	Exc.	V.G.	Good	Fair	Poor
3700	3250	2300	1800	850	550

Model 87 Long Range Sniper's Rifle

Large stainless steel, single-shot bolt-action rifle in .50 BMG caliber. Featuring 29" barrel, with an integral muzzle-brake. Camouflaged synthetic stock. Weight 21 lbs. Accurate to 1,500 meters. Introduced in 1988.

NIB	Exc.	V.G.	Good	Fair	Poor
6000	5200	4000	2750	1000	500

Model 87 System

As above, with bipod and 20X Ultra scope mounting system. Fitted case. Introduced in 1988.

NIB	Exc.	V.G.	Good	Fair	Poor
6500	5700	4400	3150	1200	600

Signature Model

Bolt-action sporting rifle. Manufactured in a variety of calibers up to .375 H&H, with 22" or 24" stainless barrel. Composition stock and 3- or 4-shot magazine. Introduced in 1988.

NIB	Exc.	V.G.	Good	Fair	Poor
2200	1750	1250	800	600	300

Signature Stainless

Same as above, with barrel and action made of stainless steel. Fiberglass stock. Left-/right-hand model. .416 Rigby also offered in this configuration. Introduced in 1990.

NIB	Exc.	V.G.	Good	Fair	Poor
2500	2050	1650	1000	750	400

Signature Alaskan

Introduced in 1989. Offered in .270, .280 Rem., .30-06, 7mm Rem. Magnum, .300 Win. Magnum, .300 Wby. Magnum, .358 Win. Magnum, .340 Wby. Magnum, .375 H&H. Match grade barrel from 22" to 26" in length. Single leaf rear sight, barrel band front sight.

NIB	Exc.	V.G.	Good	Fair	Poor
3000	2700	2000	1500	950	500

Signature Titanium Mountain

Offered in calibers from .270 Win. to 7mm Rem. Magnum. Match grade barrel produced from titanium. Stock is graphite. Weight about 6.5 lbs.

NIB	Exc.	V.G.	Good	Fair	Poor
3500	3000	2500	1800	950	500

Signature Varminter

Available in calibers .223, .22-250, .220 Swift, .243, 6mm Rem., .25-06, 7mm-08, .308. Barrel lengths from 22" to 26". Heavy barrel configuration, with hand bedded fiberglass stock. Field bipod is standard. Introduced in 1989.

NIB	Exc.	V.G.	Good	Fair	Poor
2500	2000	1500	900	600	400

Talon Safari

Bolt-action rifle offered in various calibers from .300 Win. Magnum to .458 Win. Magnum. Stainless steel 24" barrel, 4-round magazine, fiberglass stock. Introduced in 1989. Weight about 10 lbs.

NIB	Exc.	V.G.	Good	Fair	Poor
3750	3250	2200	6500	950	500

Talon Sporter

Offered in calibers from .25-06 to .416 Rem. Magnum. 24" barrel with no sights. Built on pre-1964 Winchester Model 70 action. Choice of walnut or fiberglass stock. Weight about 7.5 lbs.

NIB	Exc.	V.G.	Good	Fair	Poor
2500	2000	1750	1250	600	250

Model 300 Phoenix Long Range Rifle

Introduced in 1992. Chambered for .300 Phoenix cartridge. Fitted with 28" barrel. No sights. Fiberglass stock. Weight about 12.5 lbs.

NIB	Exc.	V.G.	Good	Fair	Poor
3000	2500	2050	1450	600	350

Model 40 Sniper

Bolt-action rifle chambered for .308 cartridge. Introduced in 1990. Fitted with 24" match grade heavy weight barrel. No sights. Weight about 9 lbs.

NIB	Exc.	V.G.	Good	Fair	Poor
2500	2000	1500	1150	500	300

Model 92 Bullpup

Single-shot rifle chambered for .50-caliber BMG. Fitted with 26" barrel. No sights. Fiberglass bullpup stock. First introduced in 1995.

NIB	Exc.	V.G.	Good	Fair	Poor
4500	3750	2800	2200	1000	500

Model 93 SN

Bolt-action rifle chambered for .50 BMG. Fitted with 29" barrel with muzzle-brake. Magazine holds 10 rounds. No sights. Weight about 21.5 lbs. Folding fiberglass stock. Introduced in 1995.

NIB	Exc.	V.G.	Good	Fair	Poor
4750	4250	3500	2450	1450	750

McMillan LRHR

Long Range Hunting Rifle, designed for precision shooting. Custom made benchrest tolerances in a long or short action. Chambered in .243 Win., .308 Win., 7mm Rem., .300 Win. and .338 Lapua Magnum. Action is pillar bedded. Barrel lengths: 24", 26" or 27", depending on caliber. McMillan A-3 fiberglass stock is standard.

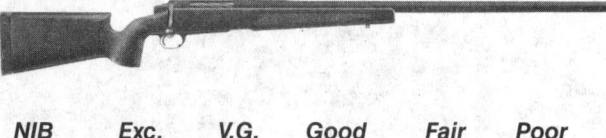

NIB	Exc.	V.G.	Good	Fair	Poor
4750	4000	3000	2500	—	—

McMILLAN FIREARMS
Phoenix, Arizona

A manufacturer of custom rifles including hunting, tactical and hybrid models.

Legacy

Built on McMillan G31 short action in .223, .243, .260 Rem., .308 Win. or .300 WSM, with 22" or 24" match-grade barrel. Walnut, graphite or laminate stock. Machined one-piece aluminum hinged floorplate. Various options available.

NIB	Exc.	V.G.	Good	Fair	Poor
5500	4700	3700	2500	800	300

Heritage

Built on G31 long action in 6.5-284, .284 Win., 7mm Rem. Magnum, .30-06, .300 Win. Magnum, with 24" or 26" match-grade barrel. Other features similar to Legacy model.

NIB	Exc.	V.G.	Good	Fair	Poor
5600	4800	3800	2600	900	300

TAC-Series

Available in .308 Win., .300 Win. Magnum, .338 Lapua or .416 Barret with medium heavy free-floating contour or fluted barrel. Muzzle-brake is optional. A-3 or A-5 fiberglass tactical stock available in various colors with adjustable cheekpiece and length of pull. Detachable 5-shot magazine or hinged floorplate.

NIB	Exc.	V.G.	Good	Fair	Poor
5000	4200	3200	2000	900	300

TAC-50 A1

Chambered in .50 BMG with 29" match-grade free floating fluted Navy contour barrel with Picatinny rail, threaded muzzle and muzzle-brake. McMillan TAC-50 stock has an adjustable cheekpiece and A1 bipod. Detachable magazine holds 5 rounds.

NIB	Exc.	V.G.	Good	Fair	Poor
9000	8000	7000	—	—	—

MEAD & ADRIANCE
St. Louis, Missouri

Company retailed a variety of single-shot percussion pistols, most of which were manufactured by Ethan Allen of Grafton, Massachusetts. In general, value for pistols marked "Mead & Adriance" are listed.

Single-Shot Pistols

NIB	Exc.	V.G.	Good	Fair	Poor
—	—	2500	1650	550	250

MENDENHALL, JONES & GARDNER
Greensboro, North Carolina

Muzzle Loading Rifle

.58-caliber percussion rifle, with 33" barrel. Full-length walnut stock secured by two barrel bands. Finished in white, with lock marked "M.J.&G.,N.C.".

NIB	Exc.	V.G.	Good	Fair	Poor
—	—	39000	33000	14000	5000

MENZ, AUGUST
Suhl, Germany

Established prior to WWI to manufacture Beholla pistols. Company was purchased by Lignose in 1937.

Menta

Identical to Beholla, which is listed separately.

NIB	Exc.	V.G.	Good	Fair	Poor
—	350	250	200	150	100

Liliput

4.25mm caliber semi-automatic pistol, with 2" barrel and 6-shot magazine. Overall length 3.5"; weight 10 oz. Slide marked "Liliput Kal. 4.25". Also manufactured in 6.35mm caliber; overall length 4". Blued, with composition grips.

NIB	Exc.	V.G.	Good	Fair	Poor
—	800	600	450	300	200

Menz Model II

As above in 7.65mm caliber.

NIB	Exc.	V.G.	Good	Fair	Poor
—	400	300	250	200	125

Menz VP Model

Similar to Model II in 6.35mm caliber, with 2.35" barrel, 6-shot magazine. Fitted with a cocking indicator.

NIB	Exc.	V.G.	Good	Fair	Poor
—	400	300	250	200	125

Model III

A total redesign. Quality is much better than previous Menz pistols. Has a closed-top slide, fixed barrel, exposed hammer. Similar to Model 1910 Browning. Produced until 1937.

NIB	Exc.	V.G.	Good	Fair	Poor
—	450	350	300	250	150

MERCURY
Liege, Belgium

Model 622 VP

.22-caliber semi-automatic rifle, with 20" barrel, open sights and 7-shot magazine. Blued, with walnut stock. Manufactured by Robar & Son.

NIB	Exc.	V.G.	Good	Fair	Poor
—	325	275	250	200	125

MERCURY(2)
Eibar, Spain

Double-Barreled Shotgun

10-, 12- or 20-gauge Magnum boxlock double-barrel shotgun, with 28" or 32" barrels, double triggers and extractors. Blued, with walnut stock. **NOTE:** Add 75 percent for 10-gauge.

NIB	Exc.	V.G.	Good	Fair	Poor
—	325	250	225	175	125

MERIDEN FIREARMS CO.
Meriden, Connecticut

Pocket Pistol

.32- or .38-caliber double-action revolver. Manufactured in a variety of barrel lengths, with exposed or enclosed hammer. Nickel-plated with rubber grips. Barrel marked "Meriden Firearms Co. Meriden, Conn. USA." Manufactured between 1895 and 1915.

NIB	Exc.	V.G.	Good	Fair	Poor
—	—	375	200	75	50

Double-Barrel Shotguns

From 1905-1918 Meriden Fire Arms Co., successor to A.J. Aubrey, made 12-, 16- and 20-gauge sidelock double-barrel shotguns. These were better quality hammer and hammerless side-by-sides fitted with twist laminated Damascus and steel barrels in grades A to G. Some of these guns were beautifully engraved by same artisans who worked for Parker Bros. and other Connecticut gunmakers. Prices in 1910 ranged from $40 to $250, but they represented great value for the money, as they were superior to the popular Crescent guns which they closely resembled. Current values depend on model, grade, gauge and condition. Difficult to find examples in excellent condition as these were sold by Sears to customers who put them to hard use. In good condition their current values range from $250 for plain Janes to $3,500 or more for top grades, of which few specimens are known.

Single-Barrel Shotguns and Rifles

Meriden Fire Arms Co. also made many single-barrel shotguns and rifles. Current values are determined by growing collector interest and condition.

MERKEL, GEBRUDER
Suhl, Germany

Merkel brothers began manufacturing rifles and shotguns in Suhl, Germany in 1898. Company is best known for its over/under and side-by-side shotguns, but has also produced double-barreled express rifles, drillings with various rifle/shotgun combinations, falling block single-shot rifles and bolt-action rifles. Many experts consider Merkels to be equal in quality to some of the better Italian and English guns. Because of the company's long and complex history, including years during which it operated behind the Iron Curtain, there are many un-catalogued models that may be encountered. Merkel firearms are imported by Merkel USA, a subsidiary of Steyr Arms in Trussville, Alabama.

SIDE-BY-SIDE SHOTGUNS

Model 8

Self-cocking Deeley boxlock action, with cocking indicators. Locking mechanism is a Greener cross-bolt, with double-barrel locking lug. Triggers are single-selective or double. Safety is automatic and tang mounted. Has an extractor. Offered in 12- and 16-gauge with 28" solid rib barrels; 20-gauge with 26.75" barrels. Available with straight-/pistol-grip oil-finished walnut stock. Receiver case colored, with light scroll engraving. Weight about: 12- and 16-gauge 6.8 lbs.; 20-gauge 6 lbs.

NIB	Exc.	V.G.	Good	Fair	Poor
1500	1150	900	600	500	400

Model 117/117E

Offered in 12- and 16-gauge, with various barrel lengths. Featured a boxlock action, with double triggers and extractors. Ejectors were available under "E" designation. Boxlock action body was scrupled at rear with fine line scroll engraving.

NIB	Exc.	V.G.	Good	Fair	Poor
—	6000	4350	1950	1000	500

Model 118/118E

Offered in 12- and 16-gauge. Similar to above model, with slightly more engraving and better wood. Some engraving coverage on breech end of barrels.

NIB	Exc.	V.G.	Good	Fair	Poor
—	7100	4900	2800	1200	650

Model 124/125

Similar to above models, but supplied with extractors for Model 124 and ejectors for Model 125. Both models have more engraving coverage with game scenes. Finer checkering and fancy wood is seen on this model.

Model 124

NIB	Exc.	V.G.	Good	Fair	Poor
—	5400	4350	2500	1500	700

Model 125

NIB	Exc.	V.G.	Good	Fair	Poor
—	6000	4600	3500	2000	1000

Model 130

One of Merkel's highest grade side-by-side shotguns. Featured sidelock action, extra fancy wood, fine line checkering and full coverage game scene engraving.

NIB	Exc.	V.G.	Good	Fair	Poor
—	25500	17500	10000	3200	300

Model 126

Similar to Model 130. Fitted with removable sidelocks.

NIB	Exc.	V.G.	Good	Fair	Poor
—	18500	15500	82700	4500	300

Model 170

Offered in 12-gauge only, with automatic ejectors. Boxlock action engraved, with fine full coverage scroll.

NIB	Exc.	V.G.	Good	Fair	Poor
—	6000	4900	3900	2500	300

Model 127

Merkel's finest side-by-side shotgun. Sidelock action featured full coverage fine line scroll engraving of the best quality.

NIB	Exc.	V.G.	Good	Fair	Poor
—	25000	19500	14500	6000	300

Model 47E

Same as above. Fitted with ejectors. Offered in 12-, 16- or 20-gauge. Supplied with fitted luggage case.

NIB	Exc.	V.G.	Good	Fair	Poor
4000	3400	2300	1200	600	200

Model 147

Same as Model 8. Silver/grayed receiver, with fine engraved hunting scenes, engraved border and screws. Discontinued.

NIB	Exc.	V.G.	Good	Fair	Poor
3700	3250	2300	1100	600	200

Model 147E

Same as above. Fitted with ejectors. Offered in 12-, 16-, 20- or 28-gauge. Supplied with fitted luggage case.

NIB	Exc.	V.G.	Good	Fair	Poor
6000	5000	4250	3250	1200	400

Model 147EL

Similar to Model 147E, with fancy walnut stock. Supplied with fitted luggage case.

NIB	Exc.	V.G.	Good	Fair	Poor
6500	5500	4650	3600	1300	400

Model 122

Features same specifications as above models, but has false sideplates. Fitted with ejectors. Receiver is silver/gray, with fine engraved hunting scenes on false sideplates, engraved border and screws.

NIB	Exc.	V.G.	Good	Fair	Poor
4000	3500	3000	1900	950	300

Model 47SL

Same as above, with scroll engraving in place of hunting scenes.

NIB	Exc.	V.G.	Good	Fair	Poor
8200	6100	4400	3000	1750	300

Model 147SL

Features true H&H style sidelocks, with cocking indicators. Gauge and barrel lengths as above. Stock fancy walnut. Weight: 20-gauge 6.4 lbs.; 28-gauge about 6.1 lbs.

NIB	Exc.	V.G.	Good	Fair	Poor
10000	7000	5500	3850	2250	300

Model 147SSL

Similar to Model 147SL. Fitted with removable sideplates. Fancy walnut stock. Supplied with fitted luggage case.

NIB	Exc.	V.G.	Good	Fair	Poor
8800	6500	5200	3000	2500	300

Models 247S/347S

Same as Model 147S, with different types of engraving.

Model 247S

Large scroll engraving.

NIB	Exc.	V.G.	Good	Fair	Poor
7700	5800	4400	2500	2000	300

Model 347S

Medium scroll engraving.

NIB	Exc.	V.G.	Good	Fair	Poor
7100	6100	4950	3850	2250	300

Model 447SL

Small scroll engraving. **NOTE:** Add $1,200 wood upgrade; $1,400 custom stock dimensions; $900 left-hand stocks.

NIB	Exc.	V.G.	Good	Fair	Poor
9900	7300	6000	4400	2700	300

Model 280

Boxlock gun chambered for 28-gauge shell. Fitted with 28" barrels choked Improved Cylinder and Modified. Double triggers with ejectors. Straight-grip walnut stock. Scroll engraving, with case colored receiver. Weight about 5.2 lbs.

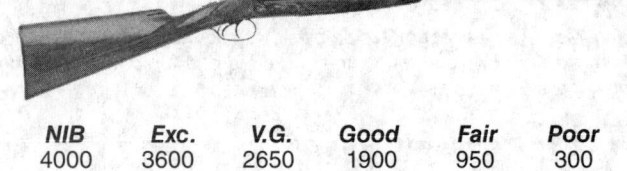

NIB	Exc.	V.G.	Good	Fair	Poor
4000	3600	2650	1900	950	300

Model 280EL

Features Anson & Deely boxlock action, with engraved hunting scenes on a silver/gray action. Double triggers. Fancy walnut, with straight-grip stock. Offered in 28-gauge, with 28" barrels. Fitted luggage case standard. Weight about 5.2 lbs. First imported in 2000.

NIB	Exc.	V.G.	Good	Fair	Poor
6500	5500	3850	2500	1500	300

Model 280SL

Similar to Model 280EL, with English-style scroll engraving on H&H style sidelocks. Choice of pistol-/straight-grip fancy walnut stock. Fitted luggage case standard. First imported in 2000.

NIB	Exc.	V.G.	Good	Fair	Poor
10500	9000	7500	5000	2000	500

Model 360

Boxlock model same as Model 280, but chambered for .410 bore. Straight-grip walnut stock. Scroll engraving on case colored receiver. Barrel is 28" choke Modified and Full. Weight about 5.2 lbs.

NIB	Exc.	V.G.	Good	Fair	Poor
4200	3600	2650	1400	800	300

Model 360EL

Same as Model 280EL, but chambered for .410 shell. Fitted with 28" barrels. Fancy walnut. Fitted case. Weight about 5.5 lbs. First imported in 2000.

NIB	Exc.	V.G.	Good	Fair	Poor
7000	5700	4100	2750	1300	300

Model 360SL

Same as Model 360EL, with English-style scroll engraving on H&H style sidelocks. Choice of pistol-/straight-grip stock. First imported in 2000.

NIB	Exc.	V.G.	Good	Fair	Poor
10500	8100	5900	3750	1600	300

Model 280/360 Two Barrel Set

Set consists of 28 gauge 28" barrel; .410 bore 28" barrel, with scroll engraving. Oil-finish walnut stock. Double triggers. Straight-grip stock.

NIB	Exc.	V.G.	Good	Fair	Poor
6500	6000	5000	3750	1600	500

Model 280/360EL Two Barrel Set

Set consists of 28-gauge 28" barrel; .410 bore 28" barrel, with engraved hunting scenes. Fancy walnut stock. Double triggers. Straight-grip stock. First imported in 2000.

NIB	Exc.	V.G.	Good	Fair	Poor
9500	8000	6000	3750	1600	500

Model 280/360SL Two Barrel Set

Same as above, with English-style scroll engraving. Choice of pistol-/straight-grip stock. First imported in 2000.

NIB	Exc.	V.G.	Good	Fair	Poor
15500	11500	8000	5500	3500	500

Model 1620

Boxlock side-by-side gun chambered for 16-gauge shell. Fitted with 28" barrels; double triggers; barrel chokes Improved Cylinder and Modified; ejectors; straight-grip walnut stock, with oil-finish; case colored receiver; light scroll engraving; fitted luggage case. Weight about 6.1 lbs. **NOTE:** Add $2,300 two-barrel set. Second set 20-gauge 28" barrels.

NIB	Exc.	V.G.	Good	Fair	Poor
4200	3600	2500	1800	1000	300

Model 1620E

Similar to Model 1620, with fine engraved hunting scenes on silver/gray receiver.

NIB	Exc.	V.G.	Good	Fair	Poor
5000	4000	3000	2000	1000	300

Model 1620EL

As above, with high-grade walnut straight-grip stock and deeply engraved hunting scenes. **NOTE:** Add $2,900 two-barrel set. Second set 20-gauge 28" barrels.

NIB	Exc.	V.G.	Good	Fair	Poor
6000	5000	3850	2200	1100	300

Model 1620SL

Similar to 1620 models above, with grayed sidelocks with deeply engraved hunting scenes. High-grade walnut stock, with oil-finish. Weight 6.6 lbs. **NOTE:** Add $3,800 two-barrel set. Second set 20-gauge 28" barrels.

NIB	Exc.	V.G.	Good	Fair	Poor
11000	8400	6100	3750	1800	500

Model 1622

Introduced in 2006. This 16-gauge boxlock side-by-side features full sideplates; case-hardened receiver with cocking indicators; ejectors; single-selective or double triggers; pistol-grip or English style stock. Fixed IC and Mod. chokes. **NOTE:** Add 50 percent for 2-barrel set. Second set 20-gauge 28" barrels.

NIB	Exc.	V.G.	Good	Fair	Poor
4000	3200	2550	1700	1400	300

Model 1622E

Similar to 1622, with fine engraved hunting scenes on silver/gray receiver.

NIB	Exc.	V.G.	Good	Fair	Poor
7500	5700	4100	2750	1300	300

Model 1622EL

Similar to Model 1622E, with luxury grade wood. **NOTE:** Add 30 percent for 2-barrel set. Second set 20-gauge 28" barrel.

NIB	Exc.	V.G.	Good	Fair	Poor
8800	6500	5200	3000	2500	300

OVER/UNDER SHOTGUNS

Model 102E

Was Merkel's standard over/under boxlock model. Offered in 12-gauge 28" barrels; 16-gauge 26" barrels. Both fitted with double triggers, semi-pistol-grip and ejectors.

NIB	Exc.	V.G.	Good	Fair	Poor
—	1800	1450	1100	650	400

Model 103E

Similar to standard, with more English scroll engraving coverage and better wood. Was offered in 12-, 16- and 20-gauge.

NIB	Exc.	V.G.	Good	Fair	Poor
—	2450	1650	1350	950	600

Model 204E

Essentially a Model 203E, with finer engraving. Discontinued prior to 1939.

NIB	Exc.	V.G.	Good	Fair	Poor
—	6600	4900	3300	2200	1750

Model 301E

Boxlock model with scalloped action. Chambered for 12-, 16-, 20-, 24-, 28- and 32-gauge. Engraving is an English scroll. Trigger guard is horn. Double triggers. Pistol-grip is standard. Produced prior to 1939.

NIB	Exc.	V.G.	Good	Fair	Poor
—	4900	4000	2500	2000	1850

Model 302E

Similar to Model 301E. Fitted with sideplates. Full-coverage engraving features game scenes. Produced prior to WWII.

NIB	Exc.	V.G.	Good	Fair	Poor
—	13250	11000	8250	4400	2000

Model 303 Luxus

Over/under Merkel is custom built to customer's specifications. Each gun is unique. Should be appraised by a knowledgeable individual who is familiar with quality European shotguns.

NIB	Exc.	V.G.	Good	Fair	Poor
22000	18500	15000	—	—	—

Model 304E

Pre-war model was highest grade in Merkel's over/under shotgun line. Sidelock gun with full coverage scroll engraving of the highest quality. Fine line checkering and extra fancy wood make this gun difficult to appraise due to its rarity.

Model 400E

Higher grade over/under fitted with Kersten crossbolt, finer engraving and fancy wood. Merkel offered this grade in 12-, 16-, 20-, 24-, 28- and 32-gauge, with choice of barrel lengths. Produced prior to 1939.

NIB	Exc.	V.G.	Good	Fair	Poor
—	1950	1450	1000	600	400

Model 401E

Similar to model above, with full coverage game scene engraving.

NIB	Exc.	V.G.	Good	Fair	Poor
—	2750	2000	1350	800	600

Model 200E

Action on this model is a self-cocking Blitz, where hammers are attached to trigger plates. Locking mechanism is a Kersten double crossbolt lock, with release. Trigger may be single-selective or double. Manual safety is mounted on tang. Fitted with coil spring ejectors. Offered in 12- and 16-gauge with 28" solid rib barrels; 20-gauge with 26.75" barrels. Oil-finished stock offered with straight-/pistol-grip. Receiver case colored, with engraved border and screws. Weight: 12-gauge 7 lbs.; 16-gauge 6.8 lbs.; 20-gauge 6.4 lbs.

NIB	Exc.	V.G.	Good	Fair	Poor
2900	2200	1650	1000	800	500

Model 200ES

Features a Blitz action, with cocking indicators and Kersten double cross bolt lock, with release. Trigger is single-selective, with tang-mounted manual safety. Coil spring ejectors are standard. Offered in 12-gauge only, with 26.75" or 28" ventilated rib barrel. Walnut stock has skeet dimensions, with pistol-grip. Receiver silver/gray, with 112 coverage scroll engraving, engraved borders and screws. Weight about 7.3 lbs.

NIB	Exc.	V.G.	Good	Fair	Poor
4400	3600	2750	2200	1500	1000

Model 200ET

Same as Model 200ES in trap configuration. Ventilated rib barrel length offered is 30".

NIB	Exc.	V.G.	Good	Fair	Poor
4700	3850	3000	2250	1750	1000

Model 200SC (Sporting Clays)

Introduced in 1995. Offered in 12-gauge only, with 3" chambers and 30" barrels with ventilated rib. Fitted with a single-selective trigger adjustable for length of pull. Special walnut oil-finished stock, with 26 lpi checkering. Pistol-grip and Pachmayr Sporting Clays recoil pad standard. Weight about 7.6 lbs. **NOTE:** Add $500 with Briley choke tubes.

NIB	Exc.	V.G.	Good	Fair	Poor
7200	6000	3300	1500	900	450

Model 201E

Same as Model 200E, with silver/gray receiver with fine engraved hunting scenes, engraved border and screws.

NIB	Exc.	V.G.	Good	Fair	Poor
3700	3100	2500	1650	1000	750

Model 201ES

Same as Model 200SC, with full coverage scroll engraving.

NIB	Exc.	V.G.	Good	Fair	Poor
4950	4050	3300	2500	2000	1000

Model 201ET

Same as Model 210ES. Fitted with 30" barrel and trap stock dimensions.

NIB	Exc.	V.G.	Good	Fair	Poor
4950	4100	3300	2750	2000	1000

Model 202E

Same basic specifications as Model 201E. Fitted with false sideplates with cocking indicators.

NIB	Exc.	V.G.	Good	Fair	Poor
8200	5500	3850	2500	1500	1000

Model 203E

Has true H&H style sidelocks, with cocking indicators. Sideplates are removable with cranked screw. Gauge selection and barrel are same as those listed above. Silver/gray receiver has English-style large scroll engraving. Discontinued.

NIB	Exc.	V.G.	Good	Fair	Poor
13500	10400	8250	5000	2500	1000

Model 303E

Same as Model 203E, with detachable sidelock plates with integral retracting hook. Model 303E has medium scroll work engraving and H&H type ejectors.

NIB	Exc.	V.G.	Good	Fair	Poor
18700	16500	13400	7500	5000	2500

Model 303EL

Features H&H style sidelocks that are quick detachable without tools. Receiver engraved with hunting scenes. Offered in 12-, 20- and 28-gauge. Double triggers. Fancy walnut stock, with pistol-/straight-grip. Weight about: 12-gauge 7 lbs.; 20-gauge 6.4 lbs.; 28-gauge 6.4 lbs. Fitted luggage case standard.

NIB	Exc.	V.G.	Good	Fair	Poor
26000	18700	13000	7500	5000	2500

Model 2000EL

Features Kersten crossbolt lock; scroll engraving on silver/gray receiver; modified Anson & Deely boxlock action. Offered in 12-, 20- or 28-gauge with ejectors, single-selective or double triggers, fancy wood and choice of pistol-/straight-grip stock. Weight about: 12-gauge 7 lbs.; 20-gauge 6.4 lbs.; 28-gauge 6.4 lbs.

NIB	Exc.	V.G.	Good	Fair	Poor
6000	5100	3600	2200	1500	750

Model 2000EL Sporter

Similar to above model. Fitted with 30" barrels 12-gauge; 28" barrels 20- and 28-gauge.

NIB	Exc.	V.G.	Good	Fair	Poor
6000	5200	3600	2200	1500	750

Model 2000CL

Introduced in 2005. Chambered for 12-, 20- or 28-gauge, with 28" barrels choked Improved Cylinder and Modified. Scroll engraved receiver, with case colors. Single-selective trigger, with auto ejectors. High grade wood, with semi-pistol-grip and straight-grip.

NIB	Exc.	V.G.	Good	Fair	Poor
7700	5800	3750	2200	1500	750

Model 2000CL Sporter

As above in 12-gauge, 30" barrels with ventilated rib; 20- and 28-gauge, 28" barrels with solid rib. Pistol-grip stock. Introduced in 2005.

NIB	Exc.	V.G.	Good	Fair	Poor
8100	6100	3750	2200	1500	750

Model 2001EL

Similar to Model 2000, with finely engraved hunting scenes. Offered in 12-, 20-, 28-gauge.

NIB	Exc.	V.G.	Good	Fair	Poor
9000	7500	4950	2900	2000	1000

Model 2001EL Sporter

Same as above, with 30" barrels 12-gauge; 28" barrels 20- and 28-gauge.

NIB	Exc.	V.G.	Good	Fair	Poor
11000	7300	5300	3600	2000	1000

Model 2002EL

Features finely engraved hunting scenes, with arabesque style. Offered in 12-, 20-, 28-gauge.

NIB	Exc.	V.G.	Good	Fair	Poor
11000	8800	6000	4400	2200	1200

Model 2016EL

16-gauge gun, with 28" barrels, single non-selective trigger and ejectors. Fixed chokes. Checkered walnut stock, with semi-pistol-grip. Scroll engraving on case colored receiver. Weight about 6.6 lbs.

NIB	Exc.	V.G.	Good	Fair	Poor
8750	7000	5000	3000	1500	750

Model 2016EL Two Barrel Set

As above, with extra set of 20-gauge 28" barrels with fixed chokes.

NIB	Exc.	V.G.	Good	Fair	Poor
12000	10500	8000	5000	3000	1000

Model 2116EL

16-gauge model similar to above, with game scene engraving on case colored receiver.

NIB	Exc.	V.G.	Good	Fair	Poor
10500	8500	6750	5000	2000	1000

Model 2116EL Two Barrel Set

As above, with extra set of 20-gauge 28" barrels with fixed chokes.

NIB	Exc.	V.G.	Good	Fair	Poor
14500	12000	9000	7000	2900	2000

PRE-WAR SINGLE-SHOT AND BOLT-ACTION RIFLES

Merkel built special single-shot and bolt-action rifles. Produced prior to WWII. Seldom seen in United States. Buyer should exercise caution and seek expert assistance prior to sale.

Model 180

Top-lever single rifle, with double under lugs built on boxlock action. Stock is .750 with pistol-grip. Commonly referred to as a stalking rifle. Offered in a variety of European calibers. Rare Merkel.

NIB	Exc.	V.G.	Good	Fair	Poor
—	3300	2400	1650	1000	500

Model 183

Top-lever model features H&H type sidelock action, with sidelock on left side and removable sideplate on right side. Fitted with straight-grip stock, full-length forearm with sling swivels, fine line checkering and fancy wood. Rare rifle.

NIB	Exc.	V.G.	Good	Fair	Poor
—	8300	5500	3850	2000	1200

Model 190

Merkel's version of a Sporting rifle built on Mauser action. Offered in a variety of European calibers. Special order rifles that will be seen in a variety of configurations.

NIB	Exc.	V.G.	Good	Fair	Poor
6000	5000	3500	2000	1100	650

DOUBLE RIFLES, COMBINATION GUNS, DRILLINGS

Model 410E

Merkel's base boxlock model with ejectors. Produced prior to WWII.

NIB	Exc.	V.G.	Good	Fair	Poor
—	2500	1950	1350	750	500

Model 411E

Similar to above, with addition of a small coverage of scroll engraving.

NIB	Exc.	V.G.	Good	Fair	Poor
—	2750	2200	1650	1100	600

Model 300

Boxlock hammerless four barrel shotgun/rifle combination. Shotgun barrels were 12-, 16- or 20-gauge; while top rifle barrel was .22 rimfire with bottom rifle barrel .30-30 or .25-35. Probably any combination of rifle and shotgun could be used as this was a special order gun. Very rare.

Model 311E

Combination gun has additional English scroll engraving.

NIB	Exc.	V.G.	Good	Fair	Poor
—	8600	7200	5500	2250	1250

Model 312E

Fitted with sideplates and game scene engraving.

NIB	Exc.	V.G.	Good	Fair	Poor
—	10400	9000	7500	4000	2000

Model 313E

Model has sidelocks, with fine full coverage scroll engraving. Expert appraisal is recommended due to this model's rarity and unique features.

NIB	Exc.	V.G.	Good	Fair	Poor
18000	13000	11750	8800	4400	2000

Model 314E

Sidelock model is also rare and unique. Expert appraisal is recommended prior to sale. Extra barrels will frequently be seen with this model.

Model 128E

Side-by-side double rifle is a droplock design, with scroll and game scene engraving. Wood is Circassian walnut, with fine line checkering. Offered in a variety of European calibers.

Model 132E

Similar to Model 128E, with full coverage scroll engraving and fancy wood.

Model 140-1

Features Greener crossbolt scroll engraving, with case-hardened receiver. Extractors and double triggers, with pistol-grip stock are standard. Offered in a wide variety of European and American calibers.

NIB	Exc.	V.G.	Good	Fair	Poor
6500	5200	4100	2900	2000	1000

Model 140-1.1

Same as above, with finely engraved hunting scenes.

NIB	Exc.	V.G.	Good	Fair	Poor
7400	6100	4400	2900	2000	1000

Model 140-2

Double rifle has an Anson & Deely boxlock action. Double triggers. Barrel length 23.6". Chambered for .375 H&H, .416 Rigby and .470 NE. Pistol-grip stock, with cheekpiece on oil-finish walnut. Weight about 10.7 lbs. depending on caliber.

NIB	Exc.	V.G.	Good	Fair	Poor
11500	8250	6000	3750	2200	1500

Model 140-2.1

Similar to one above. Engraved with African game scenes.

NIB	Exc.	V.G.	Good	Fair	Poor
13400	9300	6600	3750	2200	1500

Model 150-1

Features an arabesque engraving on silver/gray receiver. Extractors, double triggers and pistol-grip are standard.

NIB	Exc.	V.G.	Good	Fair	Poor
8250	6600	5100	3000	2000	900

Model 150-1.1

Same as above, with finely engraved hunting scenes.

NIB	Exc.	V.G.	Good	Fair	Poor
9500	7700	6000	3500	2500	1000

Model 160S Luxus Double Rifle

Double rifle is part of Luxus series. Features highest quality sidelock action, wood and fittings. Offered in .222 Rem., 5.6x5OR Magnum, .243, 6.5x57R, 7x57, 7x65, .3006, .30R Blaser, 8x57IRS, 8x57RS, .308 Win.

and 9.3x74R. Weight about 8 lbs. An expert appraisal should be sought prior to sale, due to unique nature of this model.

NIB	Exc.	V.G.	Good	Fair	Poor
15000	12500	8500	5750	4300	1200

Model 160S-2.1

Same as above, with finely engraved hunting scenes. Chambered for .470 Nitro Express. Weight about 11 lbs.

NIB	Exc.	V.G.	Good	Fair	Poor
28500	20750	16500	12000	7500	1500

Model 211E Rifle/Shotgun Combination

Over/under model features gray metal boxlock action, with hunting scenes. Top barrel available in 12-, 16- or 20-gauge; bottom barrel offered in .22 Hornet, 5.6R Magnum, 5.6R, .222 Rem., .243 Win., 6.5x55, 6.5x57R, 7x57R, 7x65R, .30-06, 8x57IRS, 9.3x74R and .375 H&H Magnum. Barrel has a solid rib. Trigger is single-selective. Select walnut stock is hand checkered. Weight about 7 lbs.

NIB	Exc.	V.G.	Good	Fair	Poor
6600	4950	3850	2250	1500	700

Model 210E Rifle/Shotgun Combination

Same as above. Features scroll engraved case-hardened receiver. Discontinued.

NIB	Exc.	V.G.	Good	Fair	Poor
6900	5500	4400	2750	1200	700

Model 211E Rifle/Shotgun Combination

Similar to above, with finely engraved hunting scenes.

NIB	Exc.	V.G.	Good	Fair	Poor
8300	6600	4900	3000	1500	750

Model 213E Rifle/Shotgun Combination

Combination gun features sidelocks, with English style large scroll engraving on silver/gray receiver. Fitted with double triggers and pistol-grip with cheekpiece.

NIB	Exc.	V.G.	Good	Fair	Poor
13000	10000	8200	5500	1900	900

Model 313E Rifle/Shotgun Combination

Same as above, with finer scroll engraving and fancy wood.

NIB	Exc.	V.G.	Good	Fair	Poor
19000	15000	8250	6500	2000	1000

Model 220E Over/Under Double Rifle

Boxlock design with Kersten double crossbolt, scroll engraved case-hardened receiver, Blitz action, double triggers and pistol-grip stock with cheekpiece.

NIB	Exc.	V.G.	Good	Fair	Poor
10000	6600	4950	3800	1700	825

Model 221E Over/Under Double Rifle

Similar to above, with game scene engraving on silver/gray receiver.

NIB	Exc.	V.G.	Good	Fair	Poor
12500	9350	6300	4500	2300	900

Model 223E Over/Under Double Rifle

Fitted with sidelocks. Features English-style arabesque engraving in large scrolls on silver/gray receiver.

NIB	Exc.	V.G.	Good	Fair	Poor
16000	14000	11000	8000	4200	1000

Model 240-1

Boxlock double rifle and shotgun. Chambered for 7x65R, .30R Blaser, 6.5x57R, 8x57IRS, 9.3x74R, .30-06 and .308 Win. Shotgun barrels are 20-gauge, with 23.6" barrels and double triggers. Ejectors. Scroll engraving. Walnut stock, with pistol-grip and cheekpiece. Weight about 10 lbs.

NIB	Exc.	V.G.	Good	Fair	Poor
8000	6300	5000	4000	3000	1300

Model 240-1.1

As above, with hunting scene engraving on grayed receiver.

NIB	Exc.	V.G.	Good	Fair	Poor
9100	7100	6000	5000	4000	1500

Model 323E Over/Under Double Rifle

Similar to above, with finer engraving.

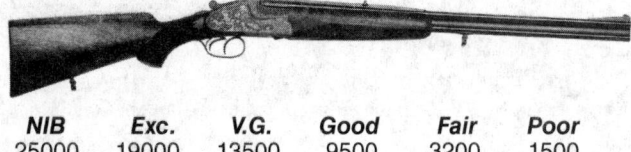

NIB	Exc.	V.G.	Good	Fair	Poor
25000	19000	13500	9500	3200	1500

Model 95K Drilling

Three-barrel shotgun/rifle combination. Top two barrels are chambered for 12-, 16- or 20-gauge; bottom barrel available in rifle calibers from .22 Hornet to .375 H&H Magnum. Action is a boxlock design, with scroll engraving on borders and screws. Stock is select grade walnut, with raised comb, pistol-grip with cap, cheekpiece and plastic butt-plate. Weight about 7.7 lbs. Discontinued

NIB	Exc.	V.G.	Good	Fair	Poor
9400	7400	4700	3000	2000	1000

Model 96K

Similar to above, with scroll engraving on case-hardened frame.

NIB	Exc.	V.G.	Good	Fair	Poor
9800	7800	5000	3700	2200	1000

Model 96K—Engraved

Same as above, with finely engraved hunting scenes. Arabesque engraving on silver/gray receiver.

NIB	Exc.	V.G.	Good	Fair	Poor
11000	8500	5500	4000	2700	1100

K-SERIES STALKING RIFLES

K1 (K3) Jagd

Introduced in 2003. Single-shot break-open rifle. Chambered for .243, 270, 7x57R, .308 Win., .30-06, 7mm Rem. Magnum, .300 Win. Magnum and 9.3x74R cartridge. Fitted with 23.6" barrel. Hunting scene engraving. Weight about 5.4 lbs. This model's name was changed in 2012 to K3 Jagd. **NOTE:** Add $400 premium for full-length Mannlicher stock.

NIB	Exc.	V.G.	Good	Fair	Poor
3200	2750	1900	1600	1100	600

K2 (K4)

High-grade variation of K1/K3 series with octagon barrel, deep-relief hand engraved hunting scenes, hand carved high-grade walnut stock. Higher grade versions were made in 2005 and 2006 with values of up to 100 percent of those shown here.

NIB	Exc.	V.G.	Good	Fair	Poor
12500	11000	9000	6500	—	—

POST-WAR BOLT-ACTION RIFLES

KR-1 Premium

Short-stroke bolt-action rifle. Chambered for .243, .308 or .30-06 and 7mm Rem. Magnum and .300 Win. Magnum calibers. Barrel length for standard calibers 20" or 22"; Magnum calibers 22" or 24". Checkered walnut stock, with hog-back comb. Magazine capacity 3 rounds. Single-set trigger. Interchangeable barrels. Arabesque engraving on bolt housing and trigger plate. Select walnut stock, with Bavarian cheekpiece. Weight about 6.4 lbs. depending on caliber and barrel length. Introduced in 2005. **NOTE:** Add $200 for Magnum calibers.

NIB	Exc.	V.G.	Good	Fair	Poor
3000	2200	1600	1000	500	200

KR-1 Weimar

As above, with rounded bolt housing. Hand chiselled engraving, with game scenes. Trigger and lockbolt head are gold titanium nitride plated. Select walnut stock, with rosewood forearm tip and Bavarian double fold cheekpiece. Introduced in 2005. **NOTE:** Add $200 for Magnum calibers.

NIB	Exc.	V.G.	Good	Fair	Poor
10000	8800	7100	5500	3000	600

RX Helix

Straight-pull bolt-action takedown rifle, with a universal-length action that accommodates calibers from .222 Rem. to .300 Win. Magnum. Two-piece stock is No. 2-grade checkered walnut. Interchangeable barrels are available in many calibers. Introduced in 2013. Values shown are for standard model. Several higher-grade versions are available at prices up to $10,000.

NIB	Exc.	V.G.	Good	Fair	Poor
3350	2800	2100	1600	800	300

Helix Explorer

Explorer model has synthetic stock and most features of RX Helix.

NIB	Exc.	V.G.	Good	Fair	Poor
2550	2000	1500	1250	500	200

SEMI-AUTOMATIC RIFLES

SR1 Semi-Auto

Gas-operated semi-automatic rifle chambered in .223 Rem., .308 Win., .30-06 and .300 Win. Magnum, plus several European calibers. Features include a free-floating 20" barrel, checkered walnut stock and fore-end, Battue rib rear sight with adjustable front. Stock has adjustable drop and cast off.

NIB	Exc.	V.G.	Good	Fair	Poor
1750	1500	1100	800	400	200

MERRILL, JAMES H.
Baltimore, Maryland

Merrill Rifle

Single-shot breech loading rifle. Chambered for .54-caliber. Utilizes percussion ignition system. Breech opens for loading by lifting and pulling back on a lever. Barrel 33" in length. Full-length walnut stock held on by two barrel bands. Mountings and patch box are brass; lock is case colored, with browned barrel. Lock marked "J.H. Merrill Balto./Pat. July 1858". There are military acceptance marks on stock. Approximately 775 of these rifles manufactured and purchased by government for use during Civil War. Made in 1864 and 1865.

Courtesy Milwaukee Public Museum, Milwaukee, Wisconsin

NIB	Exc.	V.G.	Good	Fair	Poor
—	—	7800	6350	2750	750

Merrill Carbine

Similar in appearance to rifle, except barrel length is 22"; stock only half-length with one barrel band. There are some variations that are quite subtle in appearance, but which have a considerable effect on values. We recommend that an independent appraisal be secured. Values given are for standard 1st and 2nd Types. Approximately 15,000 total manufactured. Most were used in Civil War.

1st Type

No eagle stamped on lock. Breech lever is flat.

Courtesy Milwaukee Public Museum, Milwaukee, Wisconsin

NIB	Exc.	V.G.	Good	Fair	Poor
—	—	3750	2750	1500	500

2nd Type

Eagle stamped on lock. Stock has no patch box. Breech lever has a round tip.

Courtesy Milwaukee Public Museum, Milwaukee, Wisconsin

NIB	Exc.	V.G.	Good	Fair	Poor
—	—	4250	3000	1750	600

MERRILL, LATROBE & THOMAS
S. Remington—Maker
Ilion, New York

Carbine

.58-caliber breech loading percussion carbine. Overall length 38"; barrel 21". Lock marked "S. Remington/ Ilion, N.Y."; barrel "Merrill, Latrobe &

Thomas/Baltimore, Md./Patent Applied For". Approximately 170 made in 1855.

NIB	Exc.	V.G.	Good	Fair	Poor
—	—	45000	35000	12500	700

MERRILL
Fullerton, California

Sportsman

Single-shot pistol manufactured in a variety of calibers. Either 9" or 12" octagonal barrel having a wide ventilated rib, adjustable sights and integral telescope mounts. Blued, with walnut grips. **NOTE:** Add $100 Interchangeable barrels; $25 wrist support.

NIB	Exc.	V.G.	Good	Fair	Poor
—	700	575	325	175	125

MERRIMACK ARMS
See—Brown Manufacturing Co.

MERWIN & BRAY
Worcester, Massachusetts

Company marketed a number of firearms produced by various manufacturers under its own name.

Merwin & Bray Pocket Pistol

.32-caliber spur trigger single-shot pistol, with 3.5" barrel. Blued silver-plated, with walnut grips. Barrel marked "Merwin & Bray New York".

NIB	Exc.	V.G.	Good	Fair	Poor
—	—	—	300	150	75

MERWIN HULBERT & CO.
New York, New York

Merwin Hulbert & Co., New York City, founder Joseph Merwin, had previously been involved in Merwin & Bray. Merwin Hulbert & Co. or its principals were also involved in Phoenix Rifle, Evans Rifle Company, American Cartridge Company and Hopkins & Allen of Norwich, CT. Most Merwin Hulbert revolvers will be marked with Hopkins & Allen name, in addition to Merwin Hulbert. They were made for a fairly brief period, with most production apparently taking place during 1870s & early 1880s.

There has been some confusion over a classification system for MH revolvers. System adopted here is based on distinctions listed in Art Phelps' book, The Story of Merwin Hulbert & Co. Firearms. We believe this is the first time Phelps system has been adapted to a list format.

LARGE-FRAME MERWIN HULBERT SIXGUNS

There has been a marked increase in interest in Merwin Hulbert & Co. over the past decade, with many coming to recognize them as one of the pre-eminent makers of large-frame revolvers used in the American West. Total production of large-frame revolvers has been estimated at a few thousand by some sources. However, frequency with which they are encountered suggests possibly greater production.

MH used a unique system of opening, loading & unloading their revolvers which was supposed to allow selective ejection of spent shells, leaving remaining cartridges in place. A latch on bottom of frame is pushed toward rear of gun and barrel and cylinder are rotated to right (clockwise, as viewed from rear of revolver) 90 degrees. Barrel and cylinder are then pulled forward, far enough to allow empty brass to fall free. This system required exceptional quality machining and some modern authorities are on record as considering Merwin Hulbert to have the finest workmanship of all revolvers of that era.

All are .44-caliber 6-shot large-frame revolvers. Beyond that, to fully identify a large-frame Merwin Hulbert, you must specify the following:

1. MODEL DESIGNATION — First Model has an open top and scoop flutes, round barrel and two small screws above trigger guard. Second Model similar to first, except with only one screw above trigger guard. Third Model has a top-strap with standard flutes and a round barrel. Fourth Model is similar to third, except it has a ribbed barrel. Open-top 1st and 2nd Models seem to be more sought after. 4th Model is rare and will bring a premium from a serious Merwin collector.

2. FRONTIER ARMY or POCKET ARMY — Frontier Army models have a square butt and were made in 1st through 4th models. Pocket Army models have a bird's-head butt, with a pointed extension with lanyard hole and are found in 2nd or 3rd Model configuration. Generally, Frontier Army will bring more than Pocket Army.

3. SINGLE-ACTION or DOUBLE-ACTION — Topstrap models 3rd and 4th were manufactured in both single- and double-action. Single-action models tend to bring more.

4. BARREL LENGTH — Standard barrel length on Frontier Army 1st, 2nd & 3rd Models is 7", with 5.5" barrel common on 4th Model. Standard barrel length on Pocket Army was a more "pocket-sized" 3.5". However somewhat ironically, bird's-head butt models marked "Pocket Army" were also produced with full length 7" barrels. Generally, these longer barrels will bring a bit more than shorter ones.

5. CALIBER — Most common is .44-40 (designated "Winchester Calibre 1873"). Merwins were also chambered for .44 Merwin Hulbert (somewhat similar to S&W .44 American cartridge) and .44 Russian. Less common calibers may bring a small premium from serious Merwin collectors.

6. FOREIGN COPIES — Merwin Hulbert design was relatively widely copied during the period of use, particularly in Spain. It seems that much of this production may have gone to Mexico and some found their way to U.S. Although these Spanish copies may bear markings such as "System Merwin Hulbert" or other usage of words "Merwin Hulbert", they generally will not be found with Hopkins & Allen marking. Spanish firms making Merwin copies included Orbea Hermanos and Anitua y Charola. These Spanish copies may bring half or less of what an original Merwin will bring and it can sometimes take a fairly experienced eye to tell the difference.

7. ENGRAVING — Special order engraving was available and it was usually executed in a distinctive and colorful "punch dot" style, which has come to be associated with Merwins (although it is occasionally encountered on other makes of firearms). For a long time, this style was somewhat dismissed as a bit crude and lacking in artistry. However, a new appreciation of Merwin engraving has emerged and factory engraved pieces will bring a significant premium. Often, a panel scene depicts an animal, object or landmark. These panel scenes have an almost "folk art" quality to them and will enhance value further. Engraved Merwins are sometimes encountered with engraving filled with colored enamel, quite rare, and if original, this will bring a further premium.

8. FINISH — Vast majority were nickel plated. Original blued guns will bring a premium.

Courtesy Supica's Old Town Station

Top: Open Top Pocket Army. Bottom: Topstrap Double-Action Pocket Army

First Model Frontier Army, .44 Open Top

Two screws, square butt, 7" barrel.

NIB	Exc.	V.G.	Good	Fair	Poor
—	—	5500	3000	1500	500

Second Model Frontier Army, .44 Open Top

One screw, square butt, 7" barrel.

NIB	Exc.	V.G.	Good	Fair	Poor
—	—	4500	2750	1000	500

Second Model Pocket Army, .44 Open Top

Bird's-head butt. 3.5" barrel standard, 7" will bring a premium.

NIB	Exc.	V.G.	Good	Fair	Poor
—	—	3500	2000	700	400

Third Model Frontier Army, Single-Action, .44 Topstrap

Square butt, 7" barrel.

NIB	Exc.	V.G.	Good	Fair	Poor
—	—	3750	2250	800	450

Third Model Frontier Army, Double-Action, .44 Topstrap

Square butt, 7" barrel.

NIB	Exc.	V.G.	Good	Fair	Poor
—	—	3250	1750	700	400

Third Model Pocket Army, Single-Action, .44 Topstrap

Bird's-head butt. 3.5" barrel standard, 7" will bring a premium.

NIB	Exc.	V.G.	Good	Fair	Poor
—	—	3250	1750	700	400

Third Model Pocket Army, Double-Action, .44 Topstrap

Bird's-head butt. 3.5" barrel standard, 7" will bring a premium.

NIB	Exc.	V.G.	Good	Fair	Poor
—	—	3000	1600	650	400

Fourth Model Frontier Army, Single-Action, .44 Topstrap

Ribbed barrel, scarce. 5.5" barrel seems to be most common, also offered in 7" and 3.5".

NIB	Exc.	V.G.	Good	Fair	Poor
—	—	5000	2750	800	550

Fourth Model Frontier Army, Double-Action, .44 Topstrap

Ribbed barrel. Barrel lengths as above.

NIB	Exc.	V.G.	Good	Fair	Poor
—	—	4750	2500	750	550

SMALL-FRAME MERWIN HULBERT POCKET REVOLVERS

.32 & .38 centerfire revolvers were manufactured with unique Merwin Hulbert twist-open system, like large frame revolvers. They were often advertised as chambered for .32 MH & Co. or .38 MH & Co. cartridges, but it appears as if these cartridges may have been essentially the same as .32 S&W and .38 S&W rounds. Of course, Merwin Hulbert revolvers were manufactured for original lower pressure black-powder loadings of these cartridges. Saw-handled grip frames were standard, although some were manufactured with distinctive Pocket Army type pointed "skullcrusher" bird's-head grip frames. These will generally bring a premium. Most common barrel length for most models is 3.5", with 5.5" barrels somewhat scarcer in most models and 2.75" barrels quite scarce and worth a premium. A number of police departments purchased small frame Merwin Hulbert revolvers in late 19th century. Department marked guns will bring a premium.

Terminology alert—note that .44-caliber "Pocket Army" model is a large-frame and listed in section above.

.22 Merwin Hulbert revolver is the only one not to use MH twist-open system. It is, instead, a tip-up revolver closely resembling S&W Model One.

First Pocket Model Single-Action

Spur-trigger, cylinder pin exposed at front of frame, round loading aperture in recoil shield (no loading gate), five-shot .38, scarce.

NIB	Exc.	V.G.	Good	Fair	Poor
—	—	1250	800	300	175

Second Pocket Model Single-Action

Spur-trigger, cylinder pin exposed, sliding loading gate, five-shot .38.

NIB	Exc.	V.G.	Good	Fair	Poor
—	—	1000	650	285	150

Third Pocket Model Single-Action Spur-Trigger

Enclosed cylinder pin, sliding loading gate, five-shot .38.

NIB	Exc.	V.G.	Good	Fair	Poor
—	—	950	600	225	125

Third Pocket Model Single-Action w/Trigger Guard

Five-shot .38.

NIB	Exc.	V.G.	Good	Fair	Poor
—	—	1000	675	285	150

Double-Action Pocket Model, Small Frame

.32-caliber five-shot. Patent marked folding hammer spur will bring a small premium.

NIB	Exc.	V.G.	Good	Fair	Poor
—	—	800	550	185	125

Double-Action Pocket Model, Medium Frame

Usually .38 five-shot. Scarce, .32 seven-shot will bring 25- to 50 percent premium. Patent marked folding hammer spur will bring a small premium.

NIB	Exc.	V.G.	Good	Fair	Poor
—	—	900	900	225	150

Tip-Up .22 Spur-Trigger

.22 rimfire, S&W patent infringement, looks similar to S&W Model. One Third Issue. Scarce. "Made by Merwin Hulbert & Co. for Smith & Wesson" marking will bring a small premium.

NIB	Exc.	V.G.	Good	Fair	Poor
—	—	1000	650	275	175

MERWIN HULBERT RIFLES

Very similar in design to Hopkins & Allen single-shot breech loaders. Advertised in .22 and .32 rimfire, as well as .32 WCF, .38 WCF and .44 WCF. May have been offered in .32-40 and .38-55 chamberings. A 20-gauge shotgun barrel was offered separately for these rifles. Features included set trigger, rebounding hammer, pistol-grip stock and takedown. Seldom encountered, Merwin Hulbert name on these should bring a premium over standard Hopkins & Allen single-shot rifles. A small frame "Merwin Hulbert & Co's. Junior" rifle was also offered, chambered for .22 rimfire.

METROPOLITAN ARMS CO.
New York, New York

Established in February 1864, company manufactured copies of Colt Model 1851 and 1861 Navy Revolvers, as well as copies of Colt Model 1862 Police Revolver. Two of the firm's principle officers were Samuel and William Syms (formerly of Blunt & Syms) and it is believed that they were responsible for production. Curiously although, most Metropolitan pistols were produced during 1864 to 1866 period. Company itself was not dissolved until 1920.

1851 Navy Revolver

.36-caliber percussion revolver, with 7.5" octagonal barrel and 6-shot cylinder. Blued case-hardened, with walnut grips. Barrel marked "Metropolitan Arms Co. New York". Approximately 6,000 made during 1860s. Those bearing H.E. Dimick markings are worth considerably more than standard marked examples.

Standard Navy Model

NIB	Exc.	V.G.	Good	Fair	Poor
—	—	—	4100	1400	500

H.E. Dimick Navy Model

NIB	Exc.	V.G.	Good	Fair	Poor
—	—	—	8000	3000	850

1861 Navy Revolver

.36-caliber percussion revolver, with 7.5" round barrel and 6-shot cylinder. Loading lever of rack-and-pinion type. Blued case-hardened, with walnut grips. Barrel marked "Metropolitan Arms Co. New York". Approximately 50 made in 1864 and 1865.

NIB	Exc.	V.G.	Good	Fair	Poor
—	—	—	8000	3300	950

Police Revolver

.36-caliber percussion revolver, with 4.5", 5.5" or 6.5" round barrels and fluted 5-shot cylinder. Blued case-hardened, with walnut grips. Barrel normally marked "Metropolitan Arms Co. New York", although examples have been noted without any markings. Approximately 2,750 made between 1864 and 1866.

NIB	Exc.	V.G.	Good	Fair	Poor
—	—	2400	1650	650	250

MIIDA
Marubeni America Corp.
Japan

Model 612

12-gauge boxlock over/under shotgun, with 26" or 28" ventilated rib barrels, single-selective trigger, automatic ejectors. Blued, with walnut stock. Imported between 1972 and 1974.

NIB	Exc.	V.G.	Good	Fair	Poor
—	900	750	600	400	250

Model 612 Skeet

As above, with 27" Skeet choked barrels. Some engraving. Imported between 1972 and 1974.

NIB	Exc.	V.G.	Good	Fair	Poor
—	900	750	600	400	250

Model 2100 Skeet

Similar to Model 612, with more engraving coverage.

NIB	Exc.	V.G.	Good	Fair	Poor
—	950	800	650	450	300

Model 2200 Trap or Skeet

As above, with 30" trap or 27" skeet bored barrels. More finely engraved. Imported between 1972 and 1974.

NIB	Exc.	V.G.	Good	Fair	Poor
—	1100	850	700	450	300

Model 2300 Trap or Skeet

More finely finished Model 2200. Imported from 1972 until 1974.

NIB	Exc.	V.G.	Good	Fair	Poor
—	1200	900	750	500	300

Model GRT Trap or GRS Skeet

12-gauge boxlock shotgun. Fitted with false sideplates, 27" skeet or 29" Full choked barrels, single-selective trigger, automatic ejector. Imported between 1972 and 1974.

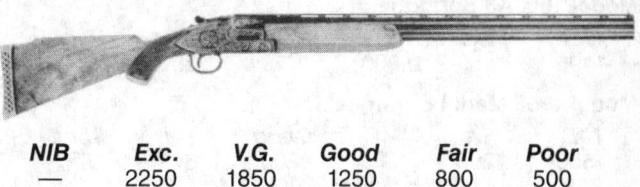

NIB	Exc.	V.G.	Good	Fair	Poor
—	2250	1850	1250	800	500

MILLER ARMS
Sturgis, South Dakota

Miller rifle models are made by Dakota Arms, which is now part of the Remington group. **NOTE:** There are a large number of extra costs options available for these rifles.

Standard Rifle

Single-shot falling block rifle. Fitted with 26" round barrel. Chambered for centerfire cartridges up to .375-caliber. Stock is checkered XXX walnut, with pistol-grip. Quarter rib scope base. Weight depends on caliber.

NIB	Exc.	V.G.	Good	Fair	Poor
5000	4000	3000	2000	700	350

Low Boy

Features 24" half round/half octagon barrel. All other features as above.

NIB	Exc.	V.G.	Good	Fair	Poor
5000	4000	2250	1300	700	350

Model F

Similar to standard rifle, with addition of 26" octagon barrel, tang sight. Globe front sight. All calibers to .45-110.

NIB	Exc.	V.G.	Good	Fair	Poor
5500	4750	3000	2200	1300	500

MILTECH
Los Altos, California

Company rebuilds and refinishes selected military firearms. All firearms are thoroughly inspected for safety and are considered safe to shoot. All firearms have their original receivers and markings. These rifles are not stamped with Miltech name, but do have a unique Miltech pine crate serial numbered to gun as standard. Company will verify it did the rebuild if asked. All guns come with manual, sling and other selected accessories depending on model.

German Mauser Model 98k

NIB	Exc.	V.G.	Good	Fair	Poor
1495	1150	900	750	550	300

M1 Garand

NOTE: Add $225 for International Harvester and Winchester.

NIB	Exc.	V.G.	Good	Fair	Poor
1595	1200	850	700	500	300

M1D Garand

NIB	Exc.	V.G.	Good	Fair	Poor
2950	2500	1900	1350	700	400

M1 Carbine

NOTE: Add $200-300 for Rockola and Winchester.

NIB	Exc.	V.G.	Good	Fair	Poor
1295	1050	800	575	375	200

Model 1941 Johnson

NIB	Exc.	V.G.	Good	Fair	Poor
5000	4000	3000	2000	1000	500

Model 1903 Springfield

NIB	Exc.	V.G.	Good	Fair	Poor
1495	1150	900	750	550	300

Model 1903A3 Springfield

NIB	Exc.	V.G.	Good	Fair	Poor
1495	1150	900	750	550	300

Model 1903 Mark I Springfield

NIB	Exc.	V.G.	Good	Fair	Poor
1550	1225	975	800	575	325

Model 1917 U.S. Enfield

NIB	Exc.	V.G.	Good	Fair	Poor
1495	1150	900	750	550	300

MINNEAPOLIS F. A. CO.
Minneapolis, Minnesota

Palm Pistol

.32-caliber radial cylinder pistol, with 1.75" barrel. Manufactured by Ames Manufacturing Company (see Ames entry). Nickel-plated, with hard rubber grips. Sideplates marked "Minneapolis Firearms Co." and "The Protector". Several thousand sold during 1890s.

NIB	Exc.	V.G.	Good	Fair	Poor
—	—	2250	1850	950	300

MIROKU B. C.
Miroku, Japan

Firearms produced by this manufacturer have been imported and marketed by a variety of companies such as Charles Daly, Browning, Winchester and SKB.

MITCHELL ARMS, INC.
Santa Ana, California

Importer and distributor of foreign-made firearms. Company no longer in business. However, some Mitchell models were available under Brolin Arms through 1998. Brolin Arms was no longer in business as of 1999. Company also imported Yugoslavian-manufactured semi-automatic AK-47 rifles in 7.62x39mm, as well as 7.62x54mm.

RIFLES

Galil

.22 or .22 Magnum caliber copy of Galil rifle. Introduced in 1987.

NIB	Exc.	V.G.	Good	Fair	Poor
500	400	300	150	125	100

MAS

.22 or .22 Magnum caliber copy of French MAS Bullpup Service Rifle. Introduced in 1987.

NIB	Exc.	V.G.	Good	Fair	Poor
400	325	200	150	125	100

AK-22

.22 or .22 Magnum caliber copy of AK-47 rifle. Introduced in 1985.

NIB	Exc.	V.G.	Good	Fair	Poor
400	300	250	125	100	75

M-16

.22 rimfire copy of Colt AR-15. Introduced in 1987.

NIB	Exc.	V.G.	Good	Fair	Poor
325	250	150	125	100	75

PPSH-30/50

.22 or .22 Magnum caliber copy of PPSH Submachine gun.

NIB	Exc.	V.G.	Good	Fair	Poor
375	325	225	150	75	60

HANDGUNS

Trophy II

Semi-automatic pistol chambered for .22 LR cartridge. Offered in 7.25" fluted or 5.5" bull barrel. Barrels are interchangeable. Trigger adjustable for weight and pull. Walnut grips, with thumb rest standard.

NIB	Exc.	V.G.	Good	Fair	Poor
400	325	275	200	150	100

Citation II

Similar to Trophy II, with matte satin finish.

NIB	Exc.	V.G.	Good	Fair	Poor
375	300	250	200	150	100

Sharpshooter II

Stainless steel target pistol, with 5.5" bull barrel to which barrel weights can be added. Fully adjustable rear sight. Checkered walnut grips standard.

NIB	Exc.	V.G.	Good	Fair	Poor
325	275	225	200	150	100

Olympic I.S.U.

Competition pistol features 6.75" barrel, with integral stabilizer. Rear sight adjustable as is trigger. Barrel weights adjustable and removable.

NIB	Exc.	V.G.	Good	Fair	Poor
525	475	400	300	200	100

Victor II

.22-caliber pistol built from stainless steel. Has interchangeable barrels in 4.5" or 5.5" lengths. Barrels have full length ventilated ribs, checkered walnut grips with thumb rest. Gold plated trigger is adjustable.

NIB	Exc.	V.G.	Good	Fair	Poor
450	375	325	250	175	125

Victor II with Weaver Rib

NIB	Exc.	V.G.	Good	Fair	Poor
525	450	375	275	175	125

High Standard Collectors' Association Special Editions

Limited run of Mitchell's version of High Standard pistol, with special roll marking on slide "High Standard / Collectors Association / Special Edition" and a special serial number series with HSCA prefix. Manufactured by Pastucek Industries, Fort Worth, Texas.

Trophy II

5.5" barrel. See standard Mitchell guns for rest of description.

NIB	Exc.	V.G.	Good	Fair	Poor
420	325	—	—	—	—

Victor II

4.5" barrel. See standard Mitchell guns for rest of description.

NIB	Exc.	V.G.	Good	Fair	Poor
450	325	—	—	—	—

Citation II

7.25" barrel. See standard Mitchell guns for rest of description.

NIB	Exc.	V.G.	Good	Fair	Poor
400	300	—	—	—	—

Three Gun Set

Includes Trophy II, Olympic ISU and Victor II. Eleven sets manufactured.

NIB	Exc.	V.G.	Good	Fair	Poor
1400	1100	—	—	—	—

Six Gun Set

Includes 5.5" Trophy II, 6.75" Olympic II, 4.5" Victor II, Sharpshooter II, Citation II and 4.5" Sport King II. Nineteen sets manufactured.

NIB	Exc.	V.G.	Good	Fair	Poor
2450	1975	—	—	—	—

Skorpion

.32-caliber semi-automatic pistol, with 4.75" barrel. Either 20- or 30-shot magazine. Blued, with plastic grips. Imported from Yugoslavia in 1987 and 1988 only.

NIB	Exc.	V.G.	Good	Fair	Poor
—	600	500	425	350	175

Spectre

9mm caliber semi-automatic pistol, with 8" shrouded barrel. Either 30- or 50-shot magazine. Blued, with plastic grips. Also produced with 18" barrel and folding buttstock. Imported from Yugoslavia in 1987 and 1988.

NIB	Exc.	V.G.	Good	Fair	Poor
—	600	500	425	350	175

MITCHELL'S MAUSERS
Fountain Valley, California

Black Arrow

.50-caliber bolt-action rifle, with 5-round box magazine. Fitted with recoil compensator, iron sights, bipod.

NIB	Exc.	V.G.	Good	Fair	Poor
6000	5000	4000	2700	1600	500

Centurion

Double-action revolver, with 4" or 6" barrel. Chambered for .357 Magnum cartridge. Blued or stainless steel.

NIB	Exc.	V.G.	Good	Fair	Poor
695	550	400	300	200	100

Valkyrie

Chambered for .44 Magnum cartridge. Choice of 4" or 6" barrel. Blued or stainless steel.

NIB	Exc.	V.G.	Good	Fair	Poor
895	700	500	400	300	200

Gold Series '03

Chambered for 9mm, .40 S&W or .45 ACP cartridge. Built on Model 1911 Government Model. Blued or stainless steel.

NIB	Exc.	V.G.	Good	Fair	Poor
795	600	450	325	250	150

Escalade

Slide-action shotgun chambered for 12-gauge shell. Fitted with 18.5" barrel; 28" ventilated rib barrel; 22" barrel with Turkey choke. Turkish walnut stock. Blued.

NIB	Exc.	V.G.	Good	Fair	Poor
395	300	250	200	150	100

Sabre

Semi-automatic 12-gauge shotgun. Choice of 22" or 28" ventilated rib barrel. Blued.

NIB	Exc.	V.G.	Good	Fair	Poor
495	400	350	300	250	150

Mauser M98 North American

Bolt-action rifle fitted with Mauser 98 action. Offered in most standard hunting calibers. **NOTE:** Add $2,000 for Magnum calibers.

NIB	Exc.	V.G.	Good	Fair	Poor
7000	6000	4500	2275	1500	400

Mauser M98 Varmint

As above chambered for .22-250 or .220 Swift.

NIB	Exc.	V.G.	Good	Fair	Poor
6000	5000	3500	1775	1000	300

Mauser M98 African/Alaskan

Chambered for heavy calibers up to .500 Jeffery.

NIB	Exc.	V.G.	Good	Fair	Poor
8000	7500	6500	2500	1500	500

MK ARMS, INC.
Irvine, California

Model 760

9mm caliber semi-automatic carbine, with 16" shrouded barrel, fixed sights and 14-, 24- or 36-shot magazine. Parkerized with folding stock. Introduced in 1983.

NIB	Exc.	V.G.	Good	Fair	Poor
950	700	575	400	250	125

MKE
Ankara, Turkey
Kirrikale

7.65mm or 9mm short semi-automatic pistol, with 4" barrel and 7-shot magazine. Unauthorized copy of Walther PP. Blued, with plastic grips.

NIB	Exc.	V.G.	Good	Fair	Poor
450	375	275	225	150	100

MODESTO SANTOS CIA.
Eibar, Spain
Action, Corrientes, and M.S.

6.35mm or 7.65mm caliber semi-automatic pistol of low quality. Marked on slide "Pistolet Automatique Model 1920". Blued, with composition grips having monogram "M.S." cast in them. Manufactured between 1920 and 1935.

NIB	Exc.	V.G.	Good	Fair	Poor
—	275	175	125	75	50

Action

6.35mm or 7.65mm semi-automatic pistol. Marked on slide "Pistolet Automatique Modele 1920". Often found bearing trade name "Corrientes" as well as maker's trademark "MS".

NIB	Exc.	V.G.	Good	Fair	Poor
—	275	175	115	80	60

MONTENEGRAN-GASSER
See—Gasser, Leopold

MOORE'S PATENT FIREARMS CO.
Brooklyn, New York

In 1866, this company became known as National Arms Company.

No. 1 Derringer

.41-caliber spur trigger all metal pistol, with 2.5" barrel. Blued or silver-plated. Approximately 10,000 manufactured between 1860 and 1865. Also marketed as No. 1 Derringer by Colt Company after they purchased National Arms Company in 1870.

Courtesy Milwaukee Public Museum, Milwaukee, Wisconsin

1st Variation Marked "Patent Applied For"

NIB	Exc.	V.G.	Good	Fair	Poor
—	—	3200	2500	1100	400

2nd Variation Marked "D. Moore Patented Feb. 19 1861"

NIB	Exc.	V.G.	Good	Fair	Poor
—	—	2200	1500	700	250

Standard Model Marked "Moore's Pat F.A. Co."

NIB	Exc.	V.G.	Good	Fair	Poor
—	—	1200	850	350	150

National Arms Co. Production.

Courtesy Milwaukee Public Museum, Milwaukee, Wisconsin

NIB	Exc.	V.G.	Good	Fair	Poor
—	—	1250	875	385	150

Iron Model

NIB	Exc.	V.G.	Good	Fair	Poor
—	—	1300	1100	550	250

Pocket Revolver

.32 teat fire caliber spur trigger revolver, with round 3.25" barrel and 6-shot cylinder. Blued or silver plated, with walnut grips. Approximately 30,000 manufactured between 1864 and 1870.

NIB	Exc.	V.G.	Good	Fair	Poor
—	—	800	550	275	100

Belt Revolver

.32 rimfire caliber revolver, with 4", 5" or 6" octagonal barrel and 7-shot cylinder. Barrel and cylinder blued. Brass frame sometimes silver-plated, with walnut grips. Barrel marked "D. Moore Patent Sept. 18, 1860". Several thousand manufactured between 1861 and 1863.

Courtesy Milwaukee Public Museum, Milwaukee, Wisconsin

Courtesy Rudolph R. Massenzi

Belt Revolver and holster belonging to Capt. Henry Kellogg, Illinois 33rd during American Civil War.

NIB	Exc.	V.G.	Good	Fair	Poor
—	—	1450	950	350	150

MORGAN & CLAPP
New Haven, Connecticut

Single-Shot Pocket Pistol

.22- or .23-caliber spur trigger single-shot pistol, with 3.5" octagonal barrel. Blued silver-plated frame, with walnut grips. Barrel marked "Morgan & Clapp New Haven". Active 1864 to 1867.

NIB	Exc.	V.G.	Good	Fair	Poor
—	—	1150	650	250	100

MORINI
Italy

C-80 Standard

.22-caliber single-shot pistol, with free floating 10" barrel, match sights. Adjustable frame and grips. Discontinued in 1989.

NIB	Exc.	V.G.	Good	Fair	Poor
—	1100	800	675	550	250

CM-80 Super Competition

As above, with trigger adjustable from 5 to 120 grams pressure, Plexiglass front sight, polished finish. Discontinued in 1989.

NIB	Exc.	V.G.	Good	Fair	Poor
—	1200	900	750	650	300

Model 84E Free Pistol

Introduced in 1995. Competition single-shot pistol features 11.4" barrel chambered for .22 LR. Adjustable electronic trigger and sights. Weight about 44 oz.

NIB	Exc.	V.G.	Good	Fair	Poor
1650	1150	900	700	500	200

MORRONE
Hope Valley, Rhode Island

See—Rhode Island Arms Company

MORSE
Greenville, South Carolina
State Armory

Morse Carbine

Overall length 40"; barrel length 20"; caliber .50 (other calibers are known to have been made on an experimental basis). Round barrel blued; frame brass; stock walnut or beechwood. Approximately 1,000 manufactured during Civil War.

Courtesy Milwaukee Public Museum, Milwaukee, Wisconsin

NIB	Exc.	V.G.	Good	Fair	Poor
—	—	27000	23000	7500	1500

MOSSBERG, O. F. & SONS, INC.
North Haven, Connecticut

Founded by Oscar F. Mossberg in 1892 at Fitchburg, Massachusetts. Company for a time was located at Chicopee Falls, Massachusetts and since 1962 has been in North Haven, Connecticut. Oldest family-owned firearms manufacturer in America.

HANDGUNS

Brownie

.22-caliber four-barreled pocket pistol, with revolving firing pin. Resembles a semi-automatic. Manufactured from 1906 to approximately 1940. Premium for in box with papers.

NIB	Exc.	V.G.	Good	Fair	Poor
750	450	325	300	225	150

Model 715P

AR-style semi-automatic .22 LR pistol. Has 25-round magazine, 6" barrel with A2-style muzzle-brake, full-length Picatinny top rail and short ventilated quad-rail fore-end and pistol-grip synthetic stock. Adjustable front and rear sights or 1x30mm red dot sight. **NOTE:** Add $40 for Red Dot Combo model; $100 for Duck Commander, with Realtree Max-5 camo finish.

NIB	Exc.	V.G.	Good	Fair	Poor
275	235	210	180	150	125

RIFLES

Model K

.22-caliber slide-action rifle, with 22" barrel, tubular magazine, internal hammer and takedown system. Blued, with walnut stock. Discontinued in 1931.

NIB	Exc.	V.G.	Good	Fair	Poor
—	350	250	150	75	50

Model M

As above, with 24" octagonal barrel. Manufactured from 1928 and 1931.

NIB	Exc.	V.G.	Good	Fair	Poor
—	350	250	150	75	50

Model L

.22-caliber Martini-style single-shot takedown rifle, with 24" barrel. Manufactured from 1927 to 1932.

NIB	Exc.	V.G.	Good	Fair	Poor
—	600	475	350	175	100

Beginning in 1930, Mossberg company manufactured a variety of utilitarian single-shot and repeating bolt-action rifles. Later they introduced a similar line of semi-automatic rifles. As these arms were intended for extensive use and were low-priced, values for them may be categorized as listed.

Bolt-Action Rifles

Model10	Model 20	Model 340B
Model 14	Model 25	Model 340K
Model 140B	Model 25A	Model 340M
Model 140K	Model 26B	Model 341
Model 142A	Model 26C	Model 342K
Model 142K	Model 30	Model 346B
Model 144	Model 320B	Model 346K
Model 144LS	Model 320K	Model 352K
Model 146B	Model 321K	

Model 140B

NIB	Exc.	V.G.	Good	Fair	Poor
400	300	200	100	75	50

Semi-Automatic Rifles

Model 50	Model 151M	Model 351C
Model 51	Model 152	Model 351K
Model 51M	Model 152K	
Model 151K	Model 350K	Model 432

Model 51M

NIB	Exc.	V.G.	Good	Fair	Poor
350	300	200	150	100	50

Targo Smoothbore Series

Early 1940s, Mossberg produced a series of bolt-action .22 rimfire rifles, with smoothbore barrels. Rifles were mainly designed for clay target game called Targo, in which shooters used .22 LR shot ammunition. Game never achieved much popularity. Rifled barrel section several inches long could be attached to muzzle, which allowed use of standard ammunition. Some models came with a smoothbore attachment that extended length of barrel. Other accessories included clay target launcher that attached to barrel, case designed for rifle and supply of small clay targets. There were several model variations: single shot (Model 26T), two repeater models with 7-round magazines (42T and 42TR) and fourth version with an extended 15-round clip (B42T). Most of these rifles were produced from 1940-1942 and again in late '40s, after WWII. Two models were introduced briefly in early 1960s, Model 320TR single shot and 340TR repeater. **NOTE:** Add 50 percent for original case and all original accessories; 20 percent for Model 26T or B42T0 rarest models of this series.

NIB	Exc.	V.G.	Good	Fair	Poor
500	425	350	250	200	100

Model 400 Palomino

.22-caliber lever-action rifle, with 22" barrel, open sights and tubular magazine. Also made with 18.5" barrel. Blued, with walnut stock. Manufactured from 1959 to 1964.

NIB	Exc.	V.G.	Good	Fair	Poor
350	300	200	150	100	50

Model 702 Plinkster

Introduced in 2004. This .22-caliber semi-automatic rifle fitted with 18" barrel and adjustable sights. Detachable 10-round magazine. Blued finish. Choice of black synthetic, hardwood, synthetic thumb-hole, solid pink, pink camo or Mossy Oak New Break-up camo finish stock. Weight about 4 lbs. Also available as scope package (add 10 percent). Tiger maple or carbon fiber stock and chromed barrel and receiver. By 2008, a variety of color and stock options, including a modern synthetic version of Mossberg's old flip-down fore-end and thumb-hole stocks had been added to line. These will bring more or less than values listed, according to local demand.

NIB	Exc.	V.G.	Good	Fair	Poor
175	145	110	75	50	25

Model 702 International Plinkster

Features 21" chrome barrel, with iron sights. Black synthetic stock. Weight about 4.5 lbs. **NOTE:** Add $75 for muzzle-brake.

NIB	Exc.	V.G.	Good	Fair	Poor
195	160	125	90	65	40

Flex 22 Tactical

Based on action of Model 702, with tactical features including pistol-grip, adjustable stock, muzzle-brake, top mounted rail and 25-round magazine.

NIB	Exc.	V.G.	Good	Fair	Poor
325	275	225	175	150	125

Model 817 Varmint

Introduced in 2008. Offered by Mossberg International features 21" free-floating blued or brushed chrome barrel, hardwood or black synthetic stock, factory Weaver mounts, detachable box magazine and .17 HMR chambering.

NIB	Exc.	V.G.	Good	Fair	Poor
175	150	125	100	75	50

Tactical .22

AR-styled rimfire auto-loading rifle, with 18" free-floating barrel. Matte blue finish. Matte black synthetic stock, with fixed or adjustable length of pull. Magazine capacity 10 or 25 rounds. Quad fore-end for unlimited mounting opportunities of optical or light systems. Peep rear and front post sight are standard.

NIB	Exc.	V.G.	Good	Fair	Poor
235	200	160	120	100	80

Blaze

Semi-automatic rifle chambered for .22 LR, with polymer stock, 16.5" barrel. Choice of adjustable iron sights or Dead Ringer Holographic Green Dot sight with four reticle configurations. Capacity: 10- or 25-round magazine. Finish: black or camo (Kryptec Highlander, Muddy Girl or Wild Fire). Introduced in 2015. **NOTE:** Add $65 for Green Dot sight model; $60 for camo finish.

NIB	Exc.	V.G.	Good	Fair	Poor
175	150	125	90	60	50

Blaze-47

Semi-automatic rifle chambered for .22 LR, with 10- or 25-round magazine. Design is patterned after AK-47 profile, with 16.5" barrel, fiber optic adjustable rear and raised front sight, synthetic or wood stock. Synthetic stock adjustable for length of pull. Introduced in 2015. **NOTE:** Add $50 for wood stock.

NIB	Exc.	V.G.	Good	Fair	Poor
300	250	200	150	125	100

Model 715T Flat-Top

AR-style semi-automatic chambered for .22 LR, with 10- or 25-round magazine, 6-position stock with adjustable length of pull, black or Moonshine Muddy Girl finish. Barrel length 16.25"; weight 5.5 lbs. Choice of mounted front and adjustable rear sights or 30mm Red Dot sight. **NOTE:** Add $50 for Moonshine Muddy Girl finish (shown).

NIB	Exc.	V.G.	Good	Fair	Poor
335	300	250	200	165	120

Model 100 ATR (All-Terrain Rifle)

Introduced in 2005. Bolt-action rifle chambered for .270 or .30-06 calibers. Fitted with 22" barrel. No sights. Choice of black synthetic, synthetic walnut or camo stock. Matte blue or all-weather finish. Weight about 7 lbs.; .243, 308. Also available as 3X9 scope package. **NOTE:** Add 10 percent for scope; $40 for all-weather finish.

NIB	Exc.	V.G.	Good	Fair	Poor
360	300	250	200	150	100

Model 100 ATR Night Train

Similar to above, with black synthetic stock, factory-mounted 4x16 scope, bipod and .308 Winchester chambering. Introduced 2008.

NIB	Exc.	V.G.	Good	Fair	Poor
375	325	275	225	165	125

Model 100 ATR Super Bantam

Similar to Model 100 ATR. Chambered only in .243 and .308. No sights. Synthetic black stock adjustable for length of pull. Introduced in 2007.

NIB	Exc.	V.G.	Good	Fair	Poor
360	300	250	200	150	100

Model 800

Bolt-action rifle manufactured in a variety of calibers, with 22" barrel and folding leaf rear sight. Blued, with walnut stock. Introduced in 1967.

NIB	Exc.	V.G.	Good	Fair	Poor
400	325	200	150	100	75

Model 800D

As above, with comb stock, rosewood fore-end tip and pistol-grip cap. Manufactured from 1970 to 1973.

NIB	Exc.	V.G.	Good	Fair	Poor
400	300	250	200	150	100

Model 800V

As above, with 24" heavy barrel not fitted with sights. Introduced in 1968.

NIB	Exc.	V.G.	Good	Fair	Poor
400	300	225	150	100	75

Model 800M

As above, with Mannlicher-style stock.

NIB	Exc.	V.G.	Good	Fair	Poor
500	375	250	200	150	100

Model 800SM

As above, with 4X scope.

NIB	Exc.	V.G.	Good	Fair	Poor
550	425	275	225	150	100

Model 801 Half-Pint Plinkster

Entry-level .22 LR single-shot rifle, with removable magazine plug to allow insertion of 10-round magazine. 16" barrel, hardwood stock, adjustable open sights. Overall weight 4 lbs. Introduced 2008.

NIB	Exc.	V.G.	Good	Fair	Poor
150	125	100	75	50	25

Model 802 Plinkster

Bolt-action rifle chambered in .22 LR, with 18" steel barrel. Black synthetic stock with schnabel. Available with 4X scope package (add 10 percent). Introduced 2006.

NIB	Exc.	V.G.	Good	Fair	Poor
150	125	100	75	50	25

Model 817 Plinkster

Similar to Model 802 Plinkster. Chambered in .17 HMR. Introduced in 2007.

NIB	Exc.	V.G.	Good	Fair	Poor
175	150	125	100	75	50

Model 810

.270 to .338 Win. Magnum caliber bolt-action rifle, with 22" or 24" barrel. Fitted with folding rear sight. Blued, with Monte Carlo-style stock. Introduced in 1970.

NIB	Exc.	V.G.	Good	Fair	Poor
—	275	250	200	150	100

Model 472C

.30-30 or .35 Rem. caliber lever-action rifle, with 20" barrel, open sights and tubular magazine. Blued, with walnut stock. Introduced in 1972.

NIB	Exc.	V.G.	Good	Fair	Poor
—	250	195	150	100	75

Model 472P

As above, with pistol-grip stock. Not fitted with saddle ring.

NIB	Exc.	V.G.	Good	Fair	Poor
—	250	195	150	100	75

Model 472 One in Five Thousand

As above, with etched receiver, brass buttplate, saddle ring and barrel band. Total 5,000 made in 1974.

NIB	Exc.	V.G.	Good	Fair	Poor
—	400	350	300	200	150

Model 479 PCA

Similar to Model 472C in .30-30 caliber, with 20" barrel. Blued, with walnut stock.

NIB	Exc.	V.G.	Good	Fair	Poor
—	250	195	150	100	75

Model 479 RR (Roy Rogers)

As above, with gold-plated trigger, barrel band and "Roy Rogers" signature. Total 5,000 made in 1983.

NIB	Exc.	V.G.	Good	Fair	Poor
—	325	250	200	150	100

Model 464 Lever-Action Centerfire

Side-loading top-ejecting lever rifle, with button-rifled 20" barrel, blued finish and hardwood stock. Straight-/pistol-grip stock. Tang-mounted thumb safety. Chambered in .30-30.

NIB	Exc.	V.G.	Good	Fair	Poor
—	400	350	300	200	150

Model 464 Lever-Action Rimfire

Rimfire version of above, with 18" barrel.

NIB	Exc.	V.G.	Good	Fair	Poor
—	375	300	250	200	150

SSi-One Sporter

Introduced in 2000. Single-shot rifle chambered for .223, .243, 270 Win., .308 and .30-06 cartridges. Fitted with 24" barrel, without sights. Matte blue finish. Checkered walnut stock. Weight about 8 lbs. Interchangeable barrels including 12-gauge.

NIB	Exc.	V.G.	Good	Fair	Poor
475	370	300	225	175	125

SSi-One Varmint

Similar to single-shot model above. Fitted with 24" bull barrel chambered for .22-250 cartridge. Walnut stock. Weight about 10 lbs. Introduced in 2000. Interchangeable barrels.

NIB	Exc.	V.G.	Good	Fair	Poor
475	370	300	225	175	125

SSi-One Slug

Single-shot model similar to other SSi-One guns. Fitted with 24" fully rifled 12-gauge barrel. Walnut stock. Weight about 8 lbs. Interchangeable barrels. Introduced in 2000.

NIB	Exc.	V.G.	Good	Fair	Poor
500	400	325	250	200	150

SSi-One Turkey

Same as above, with 24" smoothbore barrel. Will handle 3.5" Magnum 12-gauge shells. Weight about 7.5 lbs. Introduced in 2001.

NIB	Exc.	V.G.	Good	Fair	Poor
500	400	325	250	200	150

Model 1500

.223 to .338 Win. Magnum bolt-action rifle, with 22" or 24" barrel, 5- or 6-shot magazine and various sights. Blued, with hardwood or walnut stock. Manufactured by Howa in Japan. Also known as Smith & Wesson Model 1500. Offered in 1986 and 1987.

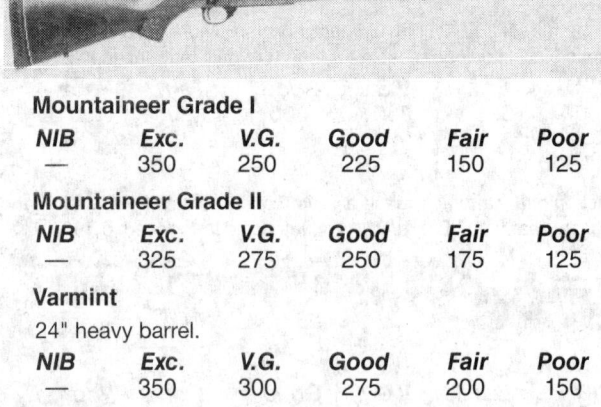

Mountaineer Grade I

NIB	Exc.	V.G.	Good	Fair	Poor
—	350	250	225	150	125

Mountaineer Grade II

NIB	Exc.	V.G.	Good	Fair	Poor
—	325	275	250	175	125

Varmint

24" heavy barrel.

NIB	Exc.	V.G.	Good	Fair	Poor
—	350	300	275	200	150

Model 1550

As above in .243, .270 or .30-06 caliber. Offered in 1986 and 1987.

NIB	Exc.	V.G.	Good	Fair	Poor
—	325	275	250	175	125

Model 1700 LS

Similar to above in same calibers, with 22" barrel not fitted for sights. Machine jeweled bolt and knurled bolt handle. Blued, with walnut stock. Schnabel fore-end. Offered in 1986 and 1987.

NIB	Exc.	V.G.	Good	Fair	Poor
—	400	350	275	200	150

Mossberg 4x4

Bolt-action centerfire rifle. Chambered in .25-06, .270, .30-06, 7mm Rem. Magnum, .300 Win. Magnum, .338 Win. Magnum. Barrel length 22" (iron sight) or 24" (sightless). Detachable box magazine, two-position safety. Walnut, laminated or black synthetic stock, with lightening cutouts in butt and fore-end. Scope package also available. Introduced in 2007.

NIB	Exc.	V.G.	Good	Fair	Poor
475	375	300	225	175	125

Mossberg 4X4 Classic Stock Synthetic

Similar to above, with black synthetic stock. Marinecote metal surfaces.

NIB	Exc.	V.G.	Good	Fair	Poor
—	450	350	275	200	125

Mossberg 4X4 Scoped Combo

Similar to above, with matte blue finish and 3x9 scope. Various stock compositions, including laminate.

NIB	Exc.	V.G.	Good	Fair	Poor
—	450	350	275	200	125

Mossberg 4X4 Classic Walnut Stock

Similar to above, with checkered walnut stock.

NIB	Exc.	V.G.	Good	Fair	Poor
—	500	450	350	225	150

Patriot

Bolt action chambered in .22-250 Rem., .243 Win., .25-06, .270 Win., 7mm-08 Rem., 7mm Rem. Magnum, .308 Win., .30-06, .300 Win. Magnum, .338 Win. Magnum and .375 Ruger. Features include 22" fluted barrel, adjustable trigger, choice of fiber-optic iron sights or scope base. Finish is matte black or Marinecote. Available with black synthetic, laminate or walnut stock, as shown in photo. Also available with Mossy Oak camo finish. Introduced in 2015. **NOTE:** Add $50 for walnut stock; $75 for camo.

NIB	Exc.	V.G.	Good	Fair	Poor
335	300	275	200	175	125

Patriot Vortex Scoped Combo

As above, but includes Vortex Crossfire II 3-9x40mm scope featuring Dead-Hold BDC reticle

NIB	Exc.	V.G.	Good	Fair	Poor
470	400	325	250	200	150

Patriot Night Train I

Tactical variation chambered in .308 Win. with 4-16x50mm scope, Picatinny rails, adjustable bipod and black synthetic or OD green stock. Night Train II and III models in .308 Win. or .300 Win. Magnum have suppressor-ready threaded barrels with SilencerCo muzzle-brake and neoprene cheek-raising kit with interchangeable insert pads. **NOTE:** Add $150 for Night Train 2 or 3.

NIB	Exc.	V.G.	Good	Fair	Poor
550	500	450	350	300	250

Model MMR Hunter

AR-15 style semi-automatic carbine in .223/5.56 NATO, with 20" free-floated barrel, start SE-1 pistol-grip, fixed A-2 stock, round aluminum hand guard, flattop receiver. Available in black, Mossy Oak Brush or Mossy Oak Treestand camo. Available in several other variations including Tactical model

NIB	Exc.	V.G.	Good	Fair	Poor
885	790	700	600	450	300

Model MVP Flex

Bolt-action centerfire in .223/5.56 or .308/7.62 NATO. Feeds from any AR-15 or AR-10 magazine. Synthetic FLEX system stock. Barrel 18.5" or 20" with or without threaded muzzle and flash hider (on 18.5" model). Also available in Predator/Varmint variation with target-style laminated stock; Patrol Model with 16.25" barrel in .223, .308 or .300 Blackout. **NOTE:** Deduct 10 percent for Predator/Varmint; 25 percent for Patrol model.

NIB	Exc.	V.G.	Good	Fair	Poor
850	700	625	500	400	300

SHOTGUNS

Mossberg manufactured a variety of shotguns that were sold at low to moderate prices. Values for these arms are approximately all the same.

Miscellaneous Bolt-Action Shotguns

Model 73	Model 185K	Model 390K
Model 173	Model 190D	Model 390T
Model 173Y	Model 190K	Model 395K
Model 183D	Model 195D	Model 395S
Model 183K	Model 195K	Model 395T
Model 183T	Model 385K	
Model 185D	Model 385T	

NIB	Exc.	V.G.	Good	Fair	Poor
—	150	125	90	65	35

Model 695

Introduced in 1969. Bolt-action shotgun chambered for 12-gauge shell. Barrel length 22" with rifled or plain bore. Finish matte blue. In 1997, offered with 22" plain ported barrel with rifled bore. Magazine capacity 3 rounds. Weight about 7.5 lbs.

NIB	Exc.	V.G.	Good	Fair	Poor
275	225	175	150	125	100

Model 695 Camo

Introduced in 2000. Same as standard Model 695, with addition of Woodlands camo finish.

NIB	Exc.	V.G.	Good	Fair	Poor
375	325	275	250	195	150

Model 200K

12-gauge slide-action shotgun, with 28" barrel and Mossberg select choke. Blued, with composition slide handle. Walnut stock. Manufactured from 1955 to 1959.

NIB	Exc.	V.G.	Good	Fair	Poor
—	150	125	100	75	50

MODEL 500 SERIES

12-, 20-gauge or .410 bore slide-action shotgun. Manufactured in a variety of barrel lengths and styles as listed.

Model 500 Regal

NIB	Exc.	V.G.	Good	Fair	Poor
—	250	200	150	100	75

Model 500 Field Grade

NIB	Exc.	V.G.	Good	Fair	Poor
285	250	200	150	100	75

Model 500 Steel Shot

Chrome bore.

NIB	Exc.	V.G.	Good	Fair	Poor
—	300	250	200	125	100

Model 500 Slugster

Crown grade, iron sights.

NIB	Exc.	V.G.	Good	Fair	Poor
—	275	250	200	150	100

Model 500 Camper

18.5" barrel, camo case.

NIB	Exc.	V.G.	Good	Fair	Poor
—	295	275	225	175	100

Model 500 Hi-Rib Trap

NIB	Exc.	V.G.	Good	Fair	Poor
—	275	250	200	150	100

Model 500 Super Grade

NIB	Exc.	V.G.	Good	Fair	Poor
—	300	275	225	175	100

Model 500 Pigeon Grade

NIB	Exc.	V.G.	Good	Fair	Poor
—	375	300	250	200	125

Model 500 Pigeon Grade Trap

NIB	Exc.	V.G.	Good	Fair	Poor
—	450	375	300	250	175

Model 500 Persuader

Riot gun, 18.5" barrel 12-gauge; 20" barrel 20-gauge (added 2008).

NIB	Exc.	V.G.	Good	Fair	Poor
300	275	225	175	100	75

Model 500 Mariner

Marinecote finish.

NIB	Exc.	V.G.	Good	Fair	Poor
400	325	225	200	150	125

Model 500 Cruiser

Pistol-grip only.

NIB	Exc.	V.G.	Good	Fair	Poor
375	300	250	200	125	100

Model 500 Muzzleloader Combo

NIB	Exc.	V.G.	Good	Fair	Poor
350	325	275	225	200	150

Model 500 Bantam

Introduced in 1996. Slightly smaller overall than full-size guns. Chambered for 20-gauge shell. Fitted with 22" shotgun barrel; 24" rifled ventilated rib barrel. Walnut stock. Weight about 6.9 lbs.

NIB	Exc.	V.G.	Good	Fair	Poor
275	225	200	150	125	100

Model 500 Super Bantam Field

Introduced in 2005. Features 20-gauge 3" chamber, with 22" ventilated rib barrel with choke tubes. Blued finish. Synthetic stock, with adjustable length of pull. Weight about 5.25 lbs.

NIB	Exc.	V.G.	Good	Fair	Poor
315	275	175	125	100	75

Model 500 Super Bantam Turkey

20-gauge 3" model has 22" ventilated rib ported barrel, with extra full choke. Synthetic camo stock. Adjustable stock for length of pull. Weight about 5.25 lbs. Introduced in 2005.

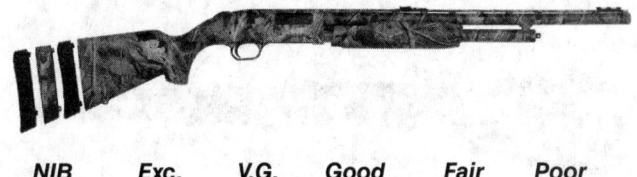

NIB	Exc.	V.G.	Good	Fair	Poor
375	325	250	175	150	100

Model 500 Super Bantam Slug

20-gauge model features full rifled 24" ported barrel, with adjustable sights. Synthetic stock, with blue or camo finish. Weight about 5.25 lbs. Introduced in 2005. In 2008, a version with an integrated scope base was added to this series.

NIB	Exc.	V.G.	Good	Fair	Poor
375	325	250	175	150	100

Model 500 Super Bantam Combo

Introduced in 2005. Features 22" ventilated rib barrel, with choke tubes; 24" fully rifled ported barrel. Camo finish, with adjustable length of pull synthetic stock. Weight about 5.25 lbs.

NIB	Exc.	V.G.	Good	Fair	Poor
400	325	275	200	150	125

Model 500 Bullpup

12-gauge slide-action Bullpup shotgun, with 18.5" or 20" shrouded barrel. Matte black finish, with composition stock. Introduced in 1986. Discontinued. Values shown are for 6-shot version. **NOTE:** Add 25 percent for 8-shot.

NIB	Exc.	V.G.	Good	Fair	Poor
600	500	375	250	150	100

Model 500 Slug Gun Viking Grade

Introduced in 1996. A 12-gauge with 24" rifled barrel; iron sights; green synthetic stock. **NOTE:** In 1997, Mossberg introduced ported barrels on some of its slug models. These ported barrels will be seen on rifled barrels only.

NIB	Exc.	V.G.	Good	Fair	Poor
300	275	225	175	100	75

Model 500 Grand Slam Turkey

12- or 20-gauge 3" gun. Introduced in 2004. Offered with 20" ventilated rib barrel; adjustable fiber optic sights; ported Extra Full choke tube. Available in Realtree Hardwood or Mossy Oak Break-Up camo pattern. Weight about: 7 lbs. 12-gauge; 6.75 lbs. 20-gauge.

NIB	Exc.	V.G.	Good	Fair	Poor
375	325	250	175	150	100

Model 500 Flyway Series

Introduced in 2005. A 12-gauge 3.5", with 28" ventilated rib barrel with fiber optic front sight. Choke tubes. Advantage camo synthetic stock. Weight about 7.5 lbs.

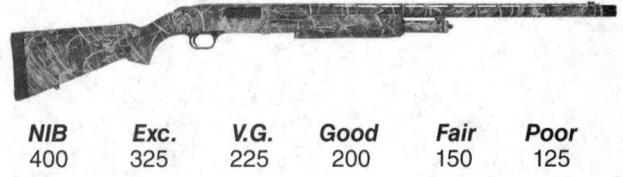

NIB	Exc.	V.G.	Good	Fair	Poor
400	325	225	200	150	125

Model 500 FLEX

Introduced in 2012, this variant of Model 500 series features FLEX TLS (Tool-less Locking System), which allows user a simple method of changing stocks, fore-ends and recoil pad. Chambered for 12- or 20-gauge and offered in Hunting and Tactical variations. Also available in combo models with two barrels, one for hunting and one for home security: Deer/Security Combo; Turkey/Security Combo; Waterfowl/Security Combo. Duck Commander has fiber optic sight, Realtree Max-5 camo finish on stock and fore-end, OD Green finish on metal parts, special engraving of Duck Commander logo on synthetic stock.

Flex Hunting

NIB	Exc.	V.G.	Good	Fair	Poor
500	425	350	285	225	200

Flex Tactical

NIB	Exc.	V.G.	Good	Fair	Poor
550	475	400	325	275	225

Flex Deer/Security Combo

NIB	Exc.	V.G.	Good	Fair	Poor
700	600	475	350	300	225

Flex Turkey/Security; Waterfowl/Security

NIB	Exc.	V.G.	Good	Fair	Poor
600	500	400	325	275	225

Flex Duck Commander

NIB	Exc.	V.G.	Good	Fair	Poor
650	550	450	400	300	200

Model 500 Combo

500 series has a total of nine combination sets available to choose from. They are combination of shotgun barrels and rifled barrels for different hunting applications. Offered in both 12- and 20-gauge sets of same gauge only.

NIB	Exc.	V.G.	Good	Fair	Poor
400	325	275	225	175	125

Model 500 USA

Introduced in 1997. Similar to military model. Has Parkerized finish, with heavy-duty sling swivels. Fitted with plain 20" barrel choked Cylinder. Stock black synthetic. Magazine capacity 6 rounds. Weight about 7.2 lbs.

NIB	Exc.	V.G.	Good	Fair	Poor
250	200	175	150	125	100

Model 500 HS (Home Security)

Chambered for .410 shell. Fitted with 18.5" barrel. Magazine capacity 5 rounds. Synthetic stock and blue finish. **NOTE:** In 1999, Mossberg offered a .50 muzzle-loader 24" fully rifled barrel that will fit directly onto any six-shot Model 500.

NIB	Exc.	V.G.	Good	Fair	Poor
350	325	275	225	200	150

Model 500 Rolling Thunder

Home Defense/Tactical is a 3" 12-gauge. Featuring pistol-grip, 23" barrel with heat shield and recoil-reducing stabilizer and 6-round capacity.

NIB	Exc.	V.G.	Good	Fair	Poor
400	325	275	225	175	125

Model 500 Tactical Cruiser "Door Buster"

Similar to above, with serrated muzzle. A TALO exclusive.

NIB	Exc.	V.G.	Good	Fair	Poor
525	425	325	225	175	125

Model 500 Tactical

An 8-shot pump has 20" barrel and ghost ring sights. Black synthetic pistol-grip stock can be adjusted to provide 10.75" to 14.625" length of pull. Weight 6.25 lbs. Capacity 7+1. Matte blue finish.

NIB	Exc.	V.G.	Good	Fair	Poor
480	440	400	370	320	280

Model 500 ATI Scorpion

Top-of-the-line tactical Model 500 outfitted with various features from Advanced Technology International Co. (ATI). Including 6-position stock with adjustable cheek, Scorpion rear pad and grip, ATI Halo Heatshield, two 2" accessory rails and removable top rail, and three add-a-shell units that mount in nine different positions on the gun. Model 500 features include an ambidextrous safety, dual extractors, twin action bars and anti-jam elevator. Introduced in 2016, with limited availability only through a Talo Group distributor.

NIB	Exc.	V.G.	Good	Fair	Poor
600	500	—	—	—	—

Model 500 Magpul

This variation of Model 500 Tactical shotgun features Magpul SGA stock, with adjustable length of pull and interchangeable cheek riser. Barrel 18.5" with 6-shot capacity; 20" with 8-shots. Introduced in 2014.

NIB	Exc.	V.G.	Good	Fair	Poor
500	425	375	300	250	200

Model 500 JIC (Just In Case)

Survival model is a 3" 12-gauge. Featuring pistol-grip, 18.5" barrel and weatherproof pack tube. Three different models available with different finishes and accessory packages. **NOTE:** Add 15 percent for nickel finish; 10 percent for JIC II with black finish in black nylon case.

NIB	Exc.	V.G.	Good	Fair	Poor
375	325	250	175	150	100

Model 505 Youth

Offered in 20-gauge or .410 bore. Fitted with 20" ventilated rib barrel with choke tubes 20-gauge; fixed modified choke .410 bore. Wood stock, with recoil pad. Blued finish. Weight about 5.25 lbs.

NIB	Exc.	V.G.	Good	Fair	Poor
315	275	175	125	100	75

Model 510 Mini Shotgun

Compact pump-action shotgun. Based on Model 500 action. Chambered in 3" 20-gauge and .410 bore. Features include 18.5" ventilated rib barrel with interchangeable (20-gauge) or fixed (.410 bore) choke, black synthetic stock, inserts to adjust length of pull from 10.5" to 11.5" and 4-shot capacity. Weight 5 lbs.

NIB	Exc.	V.G.	Good	Fair	Poor
315	275	175	125	100	75

MODEL 535 SERIES

Model 535 ATS (All Terrain Shotgun) Field

Introduced in 2005. This 12-gauge 3.5" model features 28" ventilated rib barrel with choke tubes. Blued finish, with checkered wood stock and pistol-grip. Weight about 6.75 lbs.

NIB	Exc.	V.G.	Good	Fair	Poor
375	325	250	175	150	100

Model 535 ATS Turkey

As above, with 22" ventilated rib barrel with extra full choke. Fiber optic front sight. Synthetic stock, with matte blue or camo finish. Weight about 6.5 lbs. Introduced in 2005. **NOTE:** Add $55 for camo finish.

NIB	Exc.	V.G.	Good	Fair	Poor
375	325	250	175	150	100

Model 535 ATS Waterfowl

Fitted with 28" ventilated rib barrel with choke tubes. Fiber optic front sight. Synthetic stock, with matte blue or camo finish. Weight about 6.75 lbs. Introduced in 2005. **NOTE:** Add $55 for camo finish.

NIB	Exc.	V.G.	Good	Fair	Poor
375	325	250	175	150	100

Model 535 ATS Slugster

Fitted with fully rifled 24" ventilated rib barrel with adjustable sights. Choice of matte blue or camo finish. Synthetic stock. Weight about 7 lbs.

NIB	Exc.	V.G.	Good	Fair	Poor
375	325	250	175	150	100

Model 535 ATS Combos

Set offered in several different configurations: Field/Deer 28" and 24"; Turkey/Deer 22" and 24"; Turkey/Slug/Waterfowl 22" and 28". Weight from 6.5 to 7 lbs. depending on barrel length. Introduced in 2005. **NOTE:** Add $55 for camo finish.

NIB	Exc.	V.G.	Good	Fair	Poor
475	400	350	225	150	175

MODEL 590 SERIES

Model 590 Special Purpose

Fitted with 20" shrouded barrel, bayonet lug, Parkerized or blued finish. Speed feed stock. Ghost ring sights. Introduced in 1987. Weight about 7.25 lbs.

NIB	Exc.	V.G.	Good	Fair	Poor
325	275	200	175	125	100

Model 590 Mariner

Marinecote finish.

NIB	Exc.	V.G.	Good	Fair	Poor
425	350	275	225	150	100

Model 590DA

12-gauge introduced in 2000. Features 6-round tubular magazine and 18.5" barrel. Choice of plain bead sight or ghost ring. Choke is fixed Modified. Weight about 7 lbs. A 14" barreled model also offered, but NFA rules apply. **NOTE:** Add $50 for ghost ring sights.

NIB	Exc.	V.G.	Good	Fair	Poor
500	400	300	200	150	100

Model 590 Bullpup

Model 500 with 20" barrel and 9-shot magazine. Introduced in 1989. Discontinued.

NIB	Exc.	V.G.	Good	Fair	Poor
600	500	400	250	200	125

Model 590A1 Blackwater

A 12-gauge pump with 3" chamber, 20" long heavy-walled barrel, measures 41" overall. Ghost ring/AR-style sights. Length of pull 13.875". Features synthetic Speedfeed stock and Parkerized finish. Thumb safety atop receiver. Capacity 8+1 rounds; weight 7.25 lbs. Blackwater logo etched on receiver.

NIB	Exc.	V.G.	Good	Fair	Poor
585	500	425	350	300	150

Model 590 Tri Rail

Pump chambered for 3" 12-gauge loads. Features protective heat shield on 20" barrel. Overall length 40.875". Has synthetic Speedfeed stock. Bead front sight. Tri-Rail fore-end, with removable side rails and integral bottom rail. Extended magazine gives an 8+1 capacity. Matte blue finish. Length of pull 13.8". Weight 7.25 lbs.

NIB	Exc.	V.G.	Good	Fair	Poor
540	490	440	390	300	150

Model 590 A1

Features adjustable aluminum stock and ghost ring sights. Heavy-walled barrel 20" long. Length of pull can be adjusted between 10.5" and 14.25".

Weight 7.5 lbs. Capacity 8+1. Parkerized finish.

NIB	Exc.	V.G.	Good	Fair	Poor
480	420	325	250	200	125

MODEL 835 SERIES

Model 835 Ulti-Mag

12-gauge Magnum slide-action shotgun. Features 24" or 28" ventilated rib barrel fitted for choke tubes; 6-shot magazine; composition camo or walnut stock; barrel is ported. Introduced in 1988. In 1998, offered with Shadow Grass camo pattern on both stock and barrel. In 1999, offered with Woodland camo. Weight 7.3 to 7.7 lbs. In 2000, offered with Realtree Hardwoods camo finish.

Woodland Camo

NIB	Exc.	V.G.	Good	Fair	Poor
425	350	275	225	150	100

Model 835 Ulti-Mag Viking Grade

Introduced in 1996. Features 12-gauge 3.5" Magnum chamber. Green synthetic stock. Modified choke tube. Furnished with 28" ventilated rib barrel.

NIB	Exc.	V.G.	Good	Fair	Poor
300	250	200	175	125	100

Model 835 Ulti-Mag Crown Grade

Features checkered walnut stock, with fluted comb. Chambered for 12-gauge with 3.5" chamber. Offered in 24" or 28" ventilated rib barrels, with blued or camo finish. Weight about 7.3 to 7.7 lbs.

NIB	Exc.	V.G.	Good	Fair	Poor
375	300	225	200	150	100

Model 835 Ulti-Mag Crown Grade Combo Model

Same as above. Offered with 28" ventilated rib barrel; 24" rifled barrel. Iron sights.

NIB	Exc.	V.G.	Good	Fair	Poor
425	325	250	225	175	150

Model 835 Ulti-Mag Grand Slam Turkey

Introduced in 2004. This 12-gauge 3.5" features 20" ventilated rib over-bored barrel, with Extra Full ported choke tube. Magazine capacity 6 rounds 2.75" shells; 5 rounds 3"; 4 rounds 3.5". Adjustable fiber optic sights. Available in Realtree Hardwoods camo or Mossy Oak Break-Up. Weight about 7.25 lbs.

NIB	Exc.	V.G.	Good	Fair	Poor
400	325	275	225	175	125

Model 835 Ulti-Mag Thumbhole Turkey

New in 2006. Dedicated pump-action 12-gauge turkey. Features thumb-hole stock and overbored barrel. Chambered for 3.5" shells. X-Factor ported choke tube. Barrel 20". Adjustable fiber-optic front and rear sights. Weight about 7.75 lbs. Available in Mossy Oak New Break-Up camo or Realtree Hardwoods Green camo.

NIB	Exc.	V.G.	Good	Fair	Poor
475	400	325	250	200	125

Model 835 Ulti-Mag Tactical Turkey

Same as above, with extended pistol-grip stock that is adjustable for length of pull from 10.75" to 14.5".

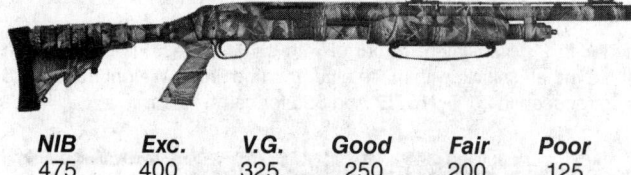

NIB	Exc.	V.G.	Good	Fair	Poor
475	400	325	250	200	125

Model 835 Wild Turkey Federation

As above, with Wild Turkey Federation medallion inlaid in stock. Introduced in 1989.

NIB	Exc.	V.G.	Good	Fair	Poor
475	400	325	250	200	125

Model 835 American Field

12-gauge has checkered walnut stock, 28" ventilated rib barrel with Modified choke tube. Weight about 7.7 lbs.

NIB	Exc.	V.G.	Good	Fair	Poor
300	275	225	200	150	100

Model 835 Ulti-Mag Duck Commander

Same features as 835 Ulti-Mag slide-action series, with addition of Max-5 Realtree camo, premium Tru-Glo/Tru-Bead dual color front fiber optic sight, logo of Duck Commander TV show engraved on stock and American flag bandana. Introduced in 2014.

NIB	Exc.	V.G.	Good	Fair	Poor
625	550	400	325	250	150

MODEL 935 MAGNUM SERIES

Introduced in 2004.

Model 935 Magnum Waterfowl Camo

12-gauge 3.5" semi-automatic. Available with 26" or 28" ventilated rib overbored barrel, with fiber optic bead and choke tubes. Offered with Mossy Oak Break-Up or Advantage Max-4 camo pattern. Magazine capacity 5 rounds 3"; 4 rounds 3.5". Weight about 7.75 lbs.

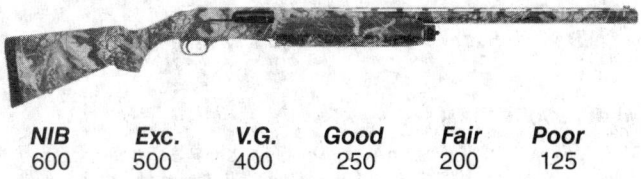

NIB	Exc.	V.G.	Good	Fair	Poor
600	500	400	250	200	125

Model 935 Magnum Slugster

Similar to above, with 24" fully rifled barrel and sights, Realtree AP camo overall.

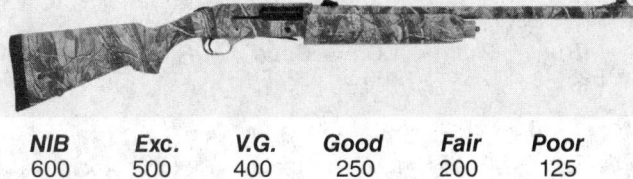

NIB	Exc.	V.G.	Good	Fair	Poor
600	500	400	250	200	125

Model 935 Magnum Turkey/Deer Comb

Similar to above, with interchangeable 24" Turkey barrel. Mossy Oak New Break-up camo overall.

NIB	Exc.	V.G.	Good	Fair	Poor
700	600	500	350	275	150

Model 935 Magnum Turkey Camo

12-gauge 3.5" model features 24" ventilated rib overbored barrel with adjustable fiber optic sights. Ultra Full choke tube. Offered in Mossy Oak Break-Up or Hardwoods HD-Green. Weight about 7.75 lbs.

NIB	Exc.	V.G.	Good	Fair	Poor
600	500	400	250	200	125

Model 935 Magnum Turkey Pistol Grip

Similar to above, with full pistol-grip stock.

NIB	Exc.	V.G.	Good	Fair	Poor
625	525	425	275	225	150

Model 935 Magnum Waterfowl Synthetic

12-gauge 3.5" gun features 26" or 28" ventilated rib overbored barrel with choke tubes. Fiber optic bead. Matte black finish, with black synthetic stock. Weight about 7.75 lbs.

NIB	Exc.	V.G.	Good	Fair	Poor
550	450	350	250	150	125

Model 935 Magnum Turkey Synthetic

As above, with 24" ventilated rib overbored barrel with Ultra Full choke tube. Weight about 7.75 lbs.

NIB	Exc.	V.G.	Good	Fair	Poor
550	450	350	250	150	125

Model 935 Magnum Waterfowl/Turkey Combo

Similar to above, with 24" Turkey; 28" Waterfowl barrels. Mossy Oak New Break-up finish overall.

NIB	Exc.	V.G.	Good	Fair	Poor
800	650	500	400	250	150

Model 935 Grand Slam Turkey

12-gauge 3.5" model features 22" ventilated rib overbored barrel with Extra Full ported choke tube. Adjustable fiber optic sights. Offered in Realtree Hardwoods Green or Mossy Oak Break-Up camo pattern. Camo sling included. Weight about 7.5 lbs.

NIB	Exc.	V.G.	Good	Fair	Poor
650	550	450	275	225	150

Model 935 Magnum

Chambered for 12-gauge 3.5" Magnum. Semi-automatic model offered in waterfowl or turkey versions, with several camo options and barrel lengths. **NOTE:** Add $100 for full camo coverage; $150 for Grand Slam model with ported barrel; $200 for pistol-grip stock.

NIB	Exc.	V.G.	Good	Fair	Poor
600	515	425	350	250	150

Model 935 Duck Commander

Same features as 935 Magnum semi-automatic series, with addition of Max-5 Realtree camo, premium Tru-Glo/Tru-Bead dual color front fiber optic sight, logo of Duck Commander TV show engraved on stock and American flag bandana. Introduced in 2014.

NIB	Exc.	V.G.	Good	Fair	Poor
825	750	600	450	300	200

MODEL 930 SERIES

12-gauge 3" chamber semi-automatic shotgun series. Introduced in 2005.

Model 930 Field

12-gauge 3" gun fitted with 26" or 28" ventilated rib barrels with choke tubes. Barrel is ported. Checkered walnut stock, with recoil pad. Magazine capacity 5 rounds. Blued finish. Weight about 7.75 lbs.

NIB	Exc.	V.G.	Good	Fair	Poor
525	425	325	225	175	125

Model 930 Turkey

Fitted with synthetic stock and 24" ventilated rib ported barrel. Chokes are extra full extended tubes. Offered with matte blue or camo finish. Weight about 7.5 lbs. **NOTE:** Add $100 for camo finish.

NIB	Exc.	V.G.	Good	Fair	Poor
500	400	300	200	150	100

Model 930 Turkey Pistol Grip

Similar to above, with full pistol-grip stock, matte black or Mossy Oak Obsession camo finish overall.

NIB	Exc.	V.G.	Good	Fair	Poor
650	550	450	275	225	150

Model 930 Waterfowl

Fitted with 28" ventilated rib ported barrel with choke tubes. Choice of matte blue or camo finish. Weight about 7.75 lbs. **NOTE:** Add $100 for camo finish.

NIB	Exc.	V.G.	Good	Fair	Poor
500	400	300	200	150	100

Model 930 Pro Waterfowl

Similar to 930 Waterfowl. Upgraded features including ported barrel, fiber optic front sight, Mossy Oak Shadow Grass Blades camo and Stock Drop System that provides drop-at-comb adjustment.

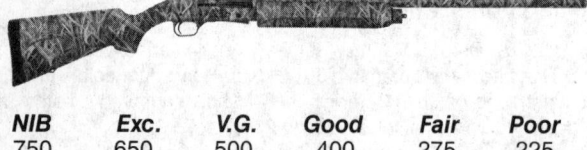

NIB	Exc.	V.G.	Good	Fair	Poor
750	650	500	400	275	225

Model 930 Pro Sporting

Designed for clay target shooting in 12-gauge, with 28" ported barrel, ventilated rib, HiViz sights and Briley extended choke tubes. Special sporting clays stock, with adjustable drop. Designed in collaboration with professional shooting instructors Gil and Vicki Ash. Introduced in 2016.

NIB	Exc.	V.G.	Good	Fair	Poor
900	800	650	500	—	—

Model 930 Slugster

Features 24" ventilated rib ported barrel, with plain or Monte Carlo synthetic stock. Matte blue or camo finish. Weight about 7.5 lbs. **NOTE:** Add $100 for camo finish.

NIB	Exc.	V.G.	Good	Fair	Poor
525	425	325	225	175	125

Model 930 Tactical

3" 12-gauge has 18.5" barrel and cylinder bore. Synthetic stock, with matte black finish. **NOTE:** Add $75 for ventilated heat shield.

NIB	Exc.	V.G.	Good	Fair	Poor
500	400	300	200	150	100

Model 930 Road Blocker

Similar to above, with muzzle-brake.

NIB	Exc.	V.G.	Good	Fair	Poor
525	425	325	225	175	125

Model 930 SPX

Billed as "home security" model, 3" 12-gauge SPX has 7-round magazine tube, 18.5" barrel, Picatinny rail, ghost ring rear sight and fiber-optic front. **NOTE:** Deduct 10 percent for white dot sights.

NIB	Exc.	V.G.	Good	Fair	Poor
500	400	300	225	150	125

Model 930 Home Security/Field Combo

Combo unit with 18.5" Cylinder bore barrel; 28" ported Field barrel; black synthetic stock; matte black finish.

NIB	Exc.	V.G.	Good	Fair	Poor
600	500	400	300	200	150

MODEL 3000 SERIES

Model 3000

12- or 20-gauge slide-action shotgun. Manufactured in a variety of barrel lengths and styles. Blued, with walnut stock. Also known as Smith & Wesson Model 3000.

NIB	Exc.	V.G.	Good	Fair	Poor
—	325	250	175	125	75

Model 3000 Waterfowl

As above, with matte finish. Fitted with sling swivels and accompanied by a camouflage sling. Produced in 1986.

NIB	Exc.	V.G.	Good	Fair	Poor
—	350	275	200	150	100

Model 3000 Law Enforcement

As above, with 18.5" or 20" cylinder-bore barrel. Manufactured in 1986 and 1987.

NIB	Exc.	V.G.	Good	Fair	Poor
—	375	275	200	150	100

MODEL 1000 SERIES

Model 1000

12- or 20-gauge semi-automatic shotgun. Manufactured in a variety of barrel lengths and styles. Receiver of an aluminum alloy and blued. Also known as Smith & Wesson Model 1000. Offered in 1986 and 1987.

NIB	Exc.	V.G.	Good	Fair	Poor
—	300	250	200	150	100

Model 1000 Slug

As above, with 22" barrel fitted with rifle sights. Offered in 1986 and 1987.

NIB	Exc.	V.G.	Good	Fair	Poor
—	325	250	200	125	100

Model 1000 Super Series

As above, with steel receiver. Self-regulating gas system that allows use of standard or Magnum shells.

NIB	Exc.	V.G.	Good	Fair	Poor
—	375	300	250	150	100

Model 1000 Super Waterfowl

Matte finish.

NIB	Exc.	V.G.	Good	Fair	Poor
—	375	300	250	150	100

Model 1000 Super Slug

Rifle sights.

NIB	Exc.	V.G.	Good	Fair	Poor
—	375	300	250	150	100

Model 1000 Super Trap

30" high rib barrel.

NIB	Exc.	V.G.	Good	Fair	Poor
—	395	325	275	175	125

Model 1000 Super Skeet

25" barrel.

NIB	Exc.	V.G.	Good	Fair	Poor
—	395	325	275	175	125

MODEL 9200 SERIES

Has a variety of configurations. A 12-gauge semi-automatic, with walnut or camo synthetic stock. Barrel lengths 22" to 28". Weight 7 to 7.7 lbs.

Model 9200 Viking Grade

NIB	Exc.	V.G.	Good	Fair	Poor
350	300	275	200	100	75

Model 9200 USST Crown Grade

NIB	Exc.	V.G.	Good	Fair	Poor
400	350	300	200	100	75

Model 9200 Combos

NIB	Exc.	V.G.	Good	Fair	Poor
475	425	350	250	150	100

Model 9200 Special Hunter

28" ventilated rib barrel, with synthetic stock.

NIB	Exc.	V.G.	Good	Fair	Poor
475	425	350	250	150	100

Model 9200 Deer Combo

NIB	Exc.	V.G.	Good	Fair	Poor
475	425	350	250	150	100

Model 9200 Turkey Camo

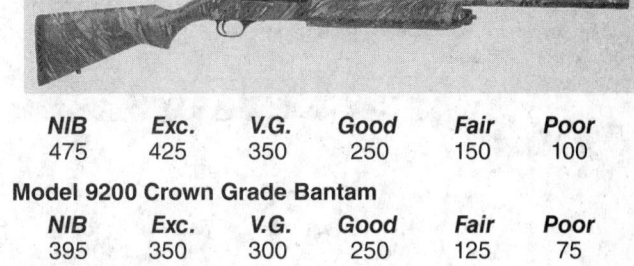

NIB	Exc.	V.G.	Good	Fair	Poor
475	425	350	250	150	100

Model 9200 Crown Grade Bantam

NIB	Exc.	V.G.	Good	Fair	Poor
395	350	300	250	125	75

Model 9200 Jungle Gun

12-gauge auto-loader fitted with plain 18.5" barrel with bead sight. Barrel choked Cylinder. Chambers are 2.75". Magazine capacity 5 rounds. Parkerized finish. Synthetic stock.

NIB	Exc.	V.G.	Good	Fair	Poor
525	450	325	200	150	125

Model SA-20

Synthetic-stocked matte black 20-gauge autoloader. Chambered for 3" shells. Has 26" or 28" ventilated rib barrel. Comes with five choke tubes. Weight about 6 lbs. Bantam model has 1" shorter length of pull and 24" barrel. Weight about 5.6 lbs. Introduced in 2008.

NIB	Exc.	V.G.	Good	Fair	Poor
400	350	300	200	100	75

Model SA-20 Tactical

Mossberg's SA-20 Tactical Autoloader in 20-gauge only. Easy-Load elevator facilitates fast one-handed reloading. Top-mounted Picatinny-style rail accommodates optical sights, while magazine tube rail allows mounting lights, lasers and other accessories. Ghost ring rear and fiber optic front sights. Gas-operated action. Capacity 4+1. Cylinder-bore barrel 20" long. Available with conventional black synthetic or synthetic pistol-grip stock. Weight about 6 lbs.

NIB	Exc.	V.G.	Good	Fair	Poor
480	440	400	370	320	280

Model 5500 MKI I

12-gauge semi-automatic shotgun. Supplied with 26" barrel 2.75" shells; 28" barrel 3" shells. Blued, with walnut stock. Introduced in 1989.

NIB	Exc.	V.G.	Good	Fair	Poor
300	235	200	175	150	125

RESERVE SERIES

Introduced in 2005 and 2008. Over/under and side-by-side guns in 12-, 20-, 28-gauge and .410 bore. Made in Turkey.

Silver Reserve Field Over/Under

Ventilated rib barrels offered in: 12-gauge 28"; 20-gauge 26" or 28"; 28-gauge 26"; .410 bore 26". All gauges have choke tubes except .410 with fixed chokes. Steel silvered receiver, with scroll engraving and game scenes in gold. Checkered walnut stock, with recoil pad. Single trigger. Weight 6 lbs. to 7.7 lbs. depending on gauge. **NOTE:** Add 20 percent for 28-gauge and .410 bore.

NIB	Exc.	V.G.	Good	Fair	Poor
600	500	300	200	150	100

Silver Reserve Sporting Over/Under

As above in 12-gauge only, with 28" ventilated 10mm rib barrels with choke tubes and ported barrels. Weight about 7.7 lbs.

NIB	Exc.	V.G.	Good	Fair	Poor
700	600	425	300	225	125

Silver Reserve II Field

This series replaced the original Silver Reserve over/under models in 2012. New features include wrap-around engraving on receiver, satin finished select-grade checkered walnut stock. Choice of automatic ejectors or extractors.

NIB	Exc.	V.G.	Good	Fair	Poor
650	550	425	300	250	200

Silver Reserve II Sport

Competition model in 12-gauge only with 28" ported barrels, extended choke tubes and fiber optic front sight. Super Sport has wider rib, dual bead sights and stock with ajustable comb. **NOTE:** Add $200 for Super Sport.

NIB	Exc.	V.G.	Good	Fair	Poor
800	700	550	400	300	250

Silver Reserve Side-by-Side

New in 2008. Blued barrels lengths: 12-gauge 26" or 28"; 20- and 28-gauge 26". Stock and fore-end select black walnut, with satin finish. Receiver satin-finished silver, with scroll engraving. Bores chrome-plated. All models come with five choke tubes. Weight: 7.2 lbs. 12-gauge; 6.4 to 6.5 lbs. 20- and 28-gauge.

NIB	Exc.	V.G.	Good	Fair	Poor
850	750	600	450	250	150

Onyx Reserve Sporting Side-by-Side

Similar to Silver Reserve Sporting, with blued receiver.

NIB	Exc.	V.G.	Good	Fair	Poor
800	700	575	400	225	150

Silver Reserve II Field

This model replaced the Silver Reserve Field in 2012. Upgraded walnut stock has satin finish, silver receiver has more elaborate engraving than earlier model. In 12-, 20- or 28-gauge.

NIB	Exc.	V.G.	Good	Fair	Poor
900	800	675	500	350	250

MOUNTAIN ARMS
Ozark, Missouri

Wildcat

Similar to Rau Arms Wildcat (q.v.) and Garcia Bronco, with plastic stock inserts. Takedown model offered as well. Estimated 6,243 produced 1971-1978. First several thousand bore Rau Arms label.

NIB	Exc.	V.G.	Good	Fair	Poor
225	175	125	100	65	35

MOUNTAIN RIFLES, INC.
Palmer, Alaska

Mountaineer

Bolt-action rifle introduced in 1997. Built on Remington action with Model 70 style bolt release. Factory muzzle-brake installed with open sights. Timney trigger standard. Stock fiberglass. Finish Parkerized. Chambered for many different calibers from .223 Rem. to .416 Rem., including Dakota and Weatherby cartridges. Weight starts about 6 lbs. depending on caliber. Several options that will affect price. Left-hand offered as an option.

NIB	Exc.	V.G.	Good	Fair	Poor
2195	1750	1400	1100	750	300

Super Mountaineer

Similar to Mountaineer, but bolt is fluted and hollow. Barrel is match grade stainless steel, with muzzle-brake. Kevlar/Graphite stock. Wide variety of calibers. Weight starts about 4.25 lbs. depending on caliber.

NIB	Exc.	V.G.	Good	Fair	Poor
2895	2350	1900	1500	1000	400

Pro Mountaineer

Built on Winchester Model 70 action. Premium match grade barrel, with muzzle-brake. Model 70 trigger. Stainless steel matte finish. Kevlar/Graphite stock. Wide variety of calibers. Weight starts about 6 lbs.

NIB	Exc.	V.G.	Good	Fair	Poor
2895	2350	2350	1900	1500	400

Pro Safari

Built on MRI action with controlled feed. Premium match grade barrel. Timney trigger. Matte blue finish. Exhibition grade walnut stock, with custom bottom metal. Weight starts about 7 lbs. depending on caliber. Caliber from .223 to .458 Lott.

NIB	Exc.	V.G.	Good	Fair	Poor
4495	3500	2300	1750	1200	500

Ultra Mountaineer

Built on MRI action, with premium match grade barrel and muzzle-brake. Timney trigger. Parkerized finish. Kevlar/Graphite stock. Calibers from .223 to .505 Gibbs. Weight begins at 5 lbs. depending on caliber. **NOTE:** Add $500 for Rigby-length calibers.

NIB	Exc.	V.G.	Good	Fair	Poor
2995	2500	2200	1900	1500	400

MUGICA, JOSE
Eibar, Spain

See—Llama

Trade name found on Llama pistols that were manufactured by Gabilondo.

MURFEESBORO ARMORY
Murfeesboro, Tennessee

Established in 1861 by William Ledbetter. Made copies of U.S. Model 1841 Rifle complete with patchbox and double strapped nose cap. Barrel bands pinned to stock. Between 270 and 390 made from October 1861 through March 1862. Overall length 48.75"; barrel length 33"; .54-caliber. Unmarked except for serial number on various parts including barrel.

NIB	Exc.	V.G.	Good	Fair	Poor
—	—	27500	16500	6600	2000

MURPHY & O'CONNEL
New York, New York

Pocket Pistol

.41-caliber single-shot percussion pocket pistol, with 3" barrel, German silver mounts. Walnut stock. Manufactured during 1850s.

NIB	Exc.	V.G.	Good	Fair	Poor
—	—	3500	2950	1100	450

MURRAY, J. P.
Columbus, Georgia

Percussion Rifle

.58-caliber percussion rifle, with 33" barrel, full stock and brass mounts. Also made with 23.5" to 24" barrel as a carbine. Lock marked "J.P. Murray/Columbus Ga.". Several hundred manufactured between 1862 and 1864.

NIB	Exc.	V.G.	Good	Fair	Poor
—	—	50000	33000	14000	1500

MUSGRAVE
Republic of South Africa

RSA NR I Single-Shot Target Rifle

.308-caliber single-shot bolt-action rifle, with 26" barrel, match sights, adjustable trigger. Target-style stock made of walnut. Manufactured between 1971 and 1976.

NIB	Exc.	V.G.	Good	Fair	Poor
—	550	425	300	225	125

Valiant NR6

.243, .270, .308, .30-06 and 7mm Rem. Magnum caliber bolt-action sporting rifle, with 24" barrel, open sights. English-style stock. Imported from 1971 to 1976.

NIB	Exc.	V.G.	Good	Fair	Poor
—	450	350	275	175	125

Premier NR5

As above, with 26" barrel. Pistol-grip Monte Carlo-style stock. Discontinued in 1976.

NIB	Exc.	V.G.	Good	Fair	Poor
—	550	450	325	225	150

MUSKETEER RIFLES
Firearms International/Garcia
Washington, D.C.

Sporter

.243 to .300 Win. Magnum caliber bolt-action rifle, with 24" barrel without sights. Monte Carlo-style stock. Imported between 1963 and 1972. **NOTE:** Add 20 percent for Magnum chamberings.

NIB	Exc.	V.G.	Good	Fair	Poor
—	500	375	275	195	120

Deluxe Sporter

As above, with adjustable trigger. More finely figured walnut stock.

NIB	Exc.	V.G.	Good	Fair	Poor
—	550	400	300	200	125

Carbine

Sporter, with 20" barrel.

NIB	Exc.	V.G.	Good	Fair	Poor
—	500	375	275	195	120

N

NATIONAL ARMS CO.
Brooklyn, New York
See—Moore's Patent Firearms Co.

Successor to Moore's Patent Firearms Company in 1865. Purchased by Colt Company in 1870.

Large Frame Teat-Fire Revolver

.45 teat fire caliber revolver with 7.5" barrel and 6-shot cylinder. Blued or silver-plated with walnut grips. Barrel marked "National Arms Co. Brooklyn". Exact number made is unknown. Estimated fewer than 30.

NIB	Exc.	V.G.	Good	Fair	Poor
—	—	24500	19000	6050	850

No. 2 Derringer

.41-caliber spur trigger pocket pistol with 2.5" barrel. Blued or silver-plated with walnut grips. Later manufactured by Colt Company as their No. 2 Derringer.

Courtesy Rock Island Auction Company

NIB	Exc.	V.G.	Good	Fair	Poor
—	—	1750	1300	550	150

NAVY ARMS COMPANY
Martinsburg, West Virginia

Founded in 1957 by the late Val Forgett, Jr. Over the years, this company has imported many black-powder and modern surplus firearms and replicas. Many of the models imported are classified as curios and relics. In 2012, Navy Arms now operated by Val Forgett III, temporarily suspended the importation side of the business. Presently the company is working with Winchester and Turnbull Manufacturing Co. on marketing a series of Winchester Model 1873 rifles. Shown on these following pages are examples of the many firearms that have been imported by Navy Arms.

SHOTGUNS
Model 83

12- or 20-gauge Magnum over/under shotgun. Manufactured in a variety of barrel lengths and styles, with double triggers and extractors. Blued, engraved, with walnut stock. Introduced in 1985.

NIB	Exc.	V.G.	Good	Fair	Poor
500	400	275	200	175	100

Model 93

As above, with automatic ejectors.

NIB	Exc.	V.G.	Good	Fair	Poor
575	475	300	250	200	100

Model 95

As above, with single trigger and screw-in choke tubes.

NIB	Exc.	V.G.	Good	Fair	Poor
600	500	350	250	200	100

Model 96 Sportsman

As above in 12-gauge only, with gold-plated receiver.

NIB	Exc.	V.G.	Good	Fair	Poor
600	500	350	250	200	100

Model 100

12-, 20-, 28-gauge or .410 bore over/under boxlock shotgun, with 26" ventilated rib barrels, single trigger and extractors. Blued, chrome-plated, with walnut stock. Introduced in 1989. NOTE: Add 20 percent for .410.

NIB	Exc.	V.G.	Good	Fair	Poor
450	350	200	150	100	75

Model 100 Side-by-Side

12- or 20-gauge Magnum boxlock double-barrel shotgun, with 27.5" barrels, double triggers and extractors. Blued, with walnut stock. Imported between 1985 and 1987.

NIB	Exc.	V.G.	Good	Fair	Poor
—	475	350	250	200	100

Model 150

As above, with automatic ejectors.

NIB	Exc.	V.G.	Good	Fair	Poor
—	495	375	300	225	125

Model 105

12- or 20-gauge and .410 bore folding single-barrel shotgun, with 26" or 28" blued barrel, chrome-plated engraved receiver and hardwood stock. Introduced in 1985.

NIB	Exc.	V.G.	Good	Fair	Poor
125	80	75	65	50	35

Model 105 Deluxe

As above, with ventilated rib barrel. Checkered walnut stock.

NIB	Exc.	V.G.	Good	Fair	Poor
150	100	85	75	60	45

REPLICA LONG GUNS

Harpers Ferry Flint Rifle

Copy of 1803 rifle in original .54-caliber. Features rust blued 35" barrel. Weight 8.5 lbs.

NIB	Exc.	V.G.	Good	Fair	Poor
600	475	350	300	200	100

Harpers Ferry "Journey of Discovery" Rifle

Similar to Harpers Ferry Flint Rifle above, with oil-finished walnut stock and brass fittings. Brass patchbox engraved "Lewis and Clark's 'Journey of Discovery'; 1803 to 1806". Introduced in 2003.

NIB	Exc.	V.G.	Good	Fair	Poor
775	600	475	275	175	100

Brown Bess Musket

Replica copy of second model used between 1760 and 1776. Bright finish on metal and one-piece walnut stock, with polished brass locks. Barrel length 42"; weight 9.5 lbs.

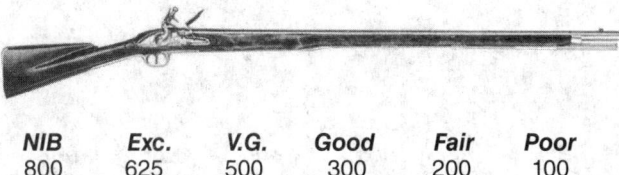

NIB	Exc.	V.G.	Good	Fair	Poor
800	625	500	300	200	100

Brown Bess Carbine

Same as above. Fitted with 30" barrel. Weight 7.75 lbs.

NIB	Exc.	V.G.	Good	Fair	Poor
800	625	500	300	200	100

1777 Charleville Musket

Copy of French flintlock in .69-caliber. Fittings are steel, with brass front sight and flashpan. Barrel length 44.625"; weight about 8.75 lbs

NIB	Exc.	V.G.	Good	Fair	Poor
900	700	550	400	300	150

1777 Standard Charleville Musket

Same as above, with polished steel barrel and select walnut stock.

NIB	Exc.	V.G.	Good	Fair	Poor
900	700	550	400	300	150

1816 M.T. Wickham Musket

Furnished in .69-caliber, with steel ramrod and button head. Brass flashpan and walnut stock standard.

NIB	Exc.	V.G.	Good	Fair	Poor
600	550	450	350	250	200

1808 Springfield Musket

A U.S. copy of 1763 Charleville musket, with 1808 Springfield markings. Barrel length 44"; weight 8.75 lbs.

NIB	Exc.	V.G.	Good	Fair	Poor
950	800	600	400	200	100

Pennsylvania Long Rifle

Offered in percussion or flintlock ignition. Choice of .32- or .45-caliber. Has octagonal 40.5" rust blued barrel, polished lock, double-set triggers and brass furniture on walnut stock. Weight 7.5 lbs.

Percussion

NIB	Exc.	V.G.	Good	Fair	Poor
450	375	250	200	150	100

Flintlock

NIB	Exc.	V.G.	Good	Fair	Poor
475	400	275	225	150	100

Kentucky Rifle

Offered in percussion or flintlock ignition. Has blue steel barrel, case colored lockplate and polished brass patchbox inletted into walnut stock. Available in .45- or 50-caliber. Barrel length 35"; weight 6 lbs. 14 oz.

Percussion

NIB	Exc.	V.G.	Good	Fair	Poor
475	325	200	150	100	75

Flintlock

NIB	Exc.	V.G.	Good	Fair	Poor
495	335	225	150	100	75

Mortimer Flintlock Rifle

Offered in .54-caliber, with rust blued barrel, walnut stock with cheekpiece and checkered straight-grip. Has external safety and sling swivels. Barrel length 36"; weight 9 lbs. Optional shotgun barrel. Made by Pedersoli. **NOTE:** Add $240 for optional shotgun barrel.

NIB	Exc.	V.G.	Good	Fair	Poor
900	750	600	500	450	150

Tryon Creedmoor Rifle

.45-caliber features heavy blued 33" octagonal barrel, hooded front sight, adjustable tang sight, double-set triggers, sling swivels and walnut stock. Weight about 9.5 lbs.

NIB	Exc.	V.G.	Good	Fair	Poor
800	600	525	450	400	150

Standard Tryon Rifle

Same as above, without target sights.

NIB	Exc.	V.G.	Good	Fair	Poor
700	500	350	300	250	200

Deluxe Tryon Rifle

Same as above, with polished and engraved lock and patchbox.

NIB	Exc.	V.G.	Good	Fair	Poor
750	525	375	325	250	200

Parker-Hale Whitworth Rifle

Replica of British sniper rifle in .451-caliber. Used by Confederates during Civil War. Round 36" barrel. Features globe front sight and ladder rear. Walnut stock hand checkered. Weight 9 lbs. 10 oz. **NOTE:** Add $150 for limited edition telescope.

NIB	Exc.	V.G.	Good	Fair	Poor
850	675	600	450	300	150

Parker-Hale Volunteer Rifle

.451-caliber rifle, with hand checkered walnut stock. Fitted with 32" barrel, with globe front sight and ladder rear. Weight 9.5 lbs.

NIB	Exc.	V.G.	Good	Fair	Poor
825	650	550	400	300	150

Parker-Hale 3 Band Volunteer Rifle

Same basic specifications as Whitworth rifle. Furnished with Alexander Henry rifling.

NIB	Exc.	V.G.	Good	Fair	Poor
750	650	600	400	250	50

Rigby Target Rifle

1880s replica chambered for .451-caliber. Fitted with adjustable front sight and vernier tang sight. Lock, breech plug, trigger guard, buttplate and escutcheons are case colored. Barrel length 32"; weight 7 lbs. 12 oz.

NIB	Exc.	V.G.	Good	Fair	Poor
700	500	450	300	200	100

1861 Springfield Rifle

.58-caliber replica. Fitted with 1855-style hammer. Barrel length 40"; weight 10 lbs. 4 oz.

NIB	Exc.	V.G.	Good	Fair	Poor
550	425	350	300	200	100

Model 1873 Springfield Officer's Trapdoor

Features single-set trigger, case colored breechblock, deluxe walnut stock, adjustable rear peep sight with Beech front sight. Chambered for .45-70 cartridge. Fitted with 26" round barrel. Weight about 8 lbs. Introduced in 2003.

NIB	Exc.	V.G.	Good	Fair	Poor
900	750	495	350	300	200

1862 C.S. Richmond Rifle

Confederate rifle is .58-caliber. Faithful reproduction of those produced at Richmond Armory. Barrel length 40"; weight 10 lbs. 4 oz.

NIB	Exc.	V.G.	Good	Fair	Poor
550	425	350	300	200	100

J.P. Murray Carbine

Confederate cavalry .58-caliber carbine. Has case colored lock and brass furniture on walnut stock. Barrel length 23.5"; weight 8 lbs. 5 oz.

NIB	Exc.	V.G.	Good	Fair	Poor
495	325	250	200	150	100

1863 Springfield Rifle

Exact replica of famous Springfield Musket. Barrel length 40", with 3 barrel bands. All metal parts are finished bright. Weight 9.5 lbs.

NIB	Exc.	V.G.	Good	Fair	Poor
550	425	350	300	200	100

1841 Mississippi Rifle

Also known as "Yager" rifle. Offered in .54- or .58-caliber. Barrel length 33"; weight 9.5 lbs.

NIB	Exc.	V.G.	Good	Fair	Poor
450	325	250	200	150	100

Zouave Rifle

Civil War replica is .58-caliber. Polished brass hardware and blued 33" barrel. Weight 9 lbs.

NIB	Exc.	V.G.	Good	Fair	Poor
450	325	250	200	150	100

Parker-Hale 1861 Musketoon

Made by Gibbs Rifle Company using 130-year-old gauges for reference. This .577-caliber replica features 24" barrel, with folding ladder military sight. Stock is walnut and lock case colored. All furniture polished brass. Weight 7.5 lbs.

NIB	Exc.	V.G.	Good	Fair	Poor
400	325	250	200	150	100

Navy Arms Musketoon

Same as above. Manufactured in Italy.

NIB	Exc.	V.G.	Good	Fair	Poor
400	325	250	200	150	100

Parker-Hale 1858 Two Band Musket

.577-caliber model based on 1858 Enfield naval pattern. Fitted with military sight graduated to 1,100 yards. Case colored lock. Walnut stock with brass fittings. Barrel length 33"; weight 8.5 lbs.

NIB	Exc.	V.G.	Good	Fair	Poor
550	425	350	300	200	100

Navy Arms 1858 Two Band Musket

Same as above. Built in Italy.

NIB	Exc.	V.G.	Good	Fair	Poor
450	325	250	200	150	100

Parker-Hale Three Band Musket

Replica based on design produced between 1853 and 1863. Rear sight based on an 1853 model graduated to 900 yards. Fitted with case colored lock. Walnut stock with brass furniture. Barrel length 39"; weight 9 lbs.

NIB	Exc.	V.G.	Good	Fair	Poor
600	475	400	300	200	100

Navy Arms Three Band Musket

Same as above. Produced in Italy.

NIB	Exc.	V.G.	Good	Fair	Poor
475	350	300	250	200	100

Navy Arms Revolving Carbine

Fitted with 20" barrel. Chambered for .357 Magnum, .44-40 or .45 Colt cartridge. Has revolving 6-shot cylinder. Straight-grip stock with brass buttplate and trigger guard. Action based on Remington Model 1874 revolver. Introduced in 1968, discontinued 1984.

NIB	Exc.	V.G.	Good	Fair	Poor
600	500	400	300	200	100

1859 Sharps Infantry Rifle

.54-caliber copy of three band Sharps. Barrel length 30". Case-hardened receiver and patchbox. Blued barrel and walnut stock. Weight about 8.5 lbs.

NIB	Exc.	V.G.	Good	Fair	Poor
1150	800	600	400	300	150

1859 Berdan Sharps Rifle

Similar to 1859 Sharps, with double-set triggers.

NIB	Exc.	V.G.	Good	Fair	Poor
1200	850	650	450	325	150

1873 Sharps No. 2 Creedmore

Chambered for .45-70 cartridge. Fitted with 30" round barrel. Polished nickel receiver. Target-grade rear tang sight and globe front, with inserts. Checkered walnut stock, with pistol-grip. Weight about 10 lbs. Introduced in 2002.

NIB	Exc.	V.G.	Good	Fair	Poor
1425	1000	750	550	375	200

Sharps #2 Silhouette Rifle

Identical to standard No. 2, with full octagon barrel. Weight about 10.5 lbs. Introduced in 2003.

NIB	Exc.	V.G.	Good	Fair	Poor
1325	1000	750	550	375	200

Sharps #2 Sporting Rifle

Same as No. 2 standard rifle, with case colored receiver. Introduced in 2003.

NIB	Exc.	V.G.	Good	Fair	Poor
1425	1000	750	550	375	200

1873 Sharps Quigley

Chambered for .45-70 cartridge. Fitted with heavy 34" octagon barrel. Case-hardened receiver with military patchbox. Open sights. Weight about 13 lbs. Introduced in 2002.

NIB	Exc.	V.G.	Good	Fair	Poor
1600	1250	900	625	395	225

1874 Sharps Infantry Rifle

Fitted with 30" round barrel. Chambered for .45-70 cartridge. Blued barrel, with case-hardened receiver. Walnut stock, with 3 barrel bands. Weight about 8.5 lbs.

NIB	Exc.	V.G.	Good	Fair	Poor
1150	800	600	400	300	150

1874 Sharps Sniper Rifle

Same as 1874 Infantry rifle, with double-set triggers.

NIB	Exc.	V.G.	Good	Fair	Poor
1200	850	650	450	325	150

Sharps Cavalry Carbine

Breech-loading .54-caliber carbine, with 22" blued barrel. Military-style sights, walnut stock and saddle bar with ring are standard. Weight 7 lbs. 12 oz.

NIB	Exc.	V.G.	Good	Fair	Poor
1050	800	600	400	300	150

Sharps Cavalry Carbine Cartridge Model

Same as above. Chambered for .45-70 Government cartridge.

NIB	Exc.	V.G.	Good	Fair	Poor
1150	800	600	400	300	150

1874 Sharps Plains Rifle

Features case colored receiver, blued barrel and checkered walnut stock. Offered in .44-70 or .54-caliber percussion. Barrel length 28.5"; weight 8 lbs. 10 oz.

NIB	Exc.	V.G.	Good	Fair	Poor
1150	800	600	400	300	150

1874 Sharps Sporting Rifle

Similar to above. Features full pistol-grip, 32" medium weight octagonal barrel, double-set triggers and case colored frame. Weight about 10.75 lbs.

NIB	Exc.	V.G.	Good	Fair	Poor
1325	1000	750	550	375	200

1874 Sharps Buffalo Rifle

Chambered for .45-70 or .45-90 cartridge. Fitted with 28" heavy octagon barrel. Buttstock checkered. Weight about 12 lbs.

NIB	Exc.	V.G.	Good	Fair	Poor
1325	1000	750	550	375	200

1874 Sharps No. 3 Long Range Rifle

Built by Pedersoli. Fitted with 34" medium weight octagon barrel, globe target front sight and match grade rear tang sight. Double-set trigger. Case-hardened frame. Walnut stock. Weight about 11 lbs.

NIB	Exc.	V.G.	Good	Fair	Poor
2000	1600	1200	900	750	400

1873 Winchester Rifle

Replica features case colored receiver, blued octagon 24" barrel and walnut stocks. Offered in .44-40 or .45 Long Colt. Weight about 8 lbs. 4 oz.

NIB	Exc.	V.G.	Good	Fair	Poor
900	725	600	500	400	200

1873 Winchester Carbine

Same specifications as rifle. Fitted with 19" round barrel, blued receiver and saddle ring. Weight 7 lbs. 4 oz.

NIB	Exc.	V.G.	Good	Fair	Poor
900	725	600	500	400	200

1873 Winchester Sporting Rifle

Features 24.25" octagonal barrel, case colored receiver and checkered pistol-grip. Offered in .44-40 or. 45 Long Colt. Weight about 8 lbs. 14 oz.

NIB	Exc.	V.G.	Good	Fair	Poor
950	750	650	525	400	200

1873 Sporting Long Range Rifle

Similar to Winchester Sporting Rifle. Chambered for .44-40 cartridge. Fitted with 30" octagon barrel. Long-range rear tang sight. Weight about 7.5 lbs. Introduced in 2002.

NIB	Exc.	V.G.	Good	Fair	Poor
1075	850	750	625	500	250

1873 Border Model

Introduced in 2000. Features 20" blued octagon barrel, with buckhorn rear sight. Magazine capacity 10 rounds. Walnut checkered pistol-grip stock, with oil-finish. Chambered for .357 Magnum, .44-40 or .45 Colt cartridge.

NIB	Exc.	V.G.	Good	Fair	Poor
975	800	700	550	450	225

Winchester/Turnbull Model 1873 Rifle

Available exclusively from Navy Arms, this is a faithful reproduction of the "Gun That Won The West". Chambered in .45 Colt or .357 Magnum, with a Turnbull color case-hardened frame, deluxe checkered American walnut stock and fore-end, 20" or 24.250" octagonal barrel, semi-buckhorn rear and gold bead front sight. Introduced in 2014.

NIB	Exc.	V.G.	Good	Fair	Poor
2250	1800	1600	1200	900	450

Winchester/Turnbull Model 1892 Coyote Killer

Like Model 1873 rifle created by Winchester and Turnbull, this Model 1892 has a Grade 1 American walnut checkered stock and fore-end, bone-charcoal color case-hardened frame, Marble's semi-buckhorn rear and gold bead front sight mounted on a full octagonal barrel. Chambered in .44 Magnum or .45 Colt. Barrel length 20"; weight 6 lbs. Introduced in 2016.

NIB	Exc.	V.G.	Good	Fair	Poor
2250	1800	—	—	—	—

Lightning Deluxe

Replica of slide-action Colt Lightning Rifle of the 1880s, made by Davide Pedersoli in Italy, with enhancements by Turnbull Restoration and Mfg. Co. Chambered in .357 Magnum or .45 Colt. Features include hand-selected and expertly checkered Grade 1 American walnut stock and fore-end, bone-charcoal color case-hardened receiver, high-polish full octagonal barrel in 20" or 24". Sights are semi-buckhorn rear and gold bead dovetail front. Introduced in 2016.

NIB	Exc.	V.G.	Good	Fair	Poor
2250	1800	—	—	—	—

Lightning Slide Action

Standard model of Deluxe model, made by Pedersoli. Imported from 2010 to 2012. Same features with standard walnut stock and case colored finish.

NIB	Exc.	V.G.	Good	Fair	Poor
1000	850	700	550	450	300

1866 "Yellowboy" Rifle

Features brass receiver, 24" octagon barrel and walnut stocks. Weight 8.5 lbs.

NIB	Exc.	V.G.	Good	Fair	Poor
850	675	525	450	300	150

1866 "Yellowboy" Carbine

Same as above. Fitted with 19" round barrel and saddle ring. Weight 7 lbs. 4 oz.

NIB	Exc.	V.G.	Good	Fair	Poor
850	675	525	450	300	150

1866 "Yellowboy" Short Rifle

Introduced in 2000. Features 20" barrel with buckhorn rear sight. Walnut stock with oil-finish. Receiver is yellow brass. Chambered for .38 Special, .44-40 or .45 Colt cartridge. Magazine capacity 10 rounds.

NIB	Exc.	V.G.	Good	Fair	Poor
850	675	525	450	300	150

Iron Frame Henry

Replica of famous and rare .44-40 Iron Frame Henry. Features case colored frame. Barrel length 24"; weight 9 lbs.

NIB	Exc.	V.G.	Good	Fair	Poor
925	750	650	500	400	200

Blued Iron Frame Henry

Same as above. Furnished with highly polished blued receiver.

NIB	Exc.	V.G.	Good	Fair	Poor
925	750	650	500	400	200

Military Henry

Based on brass frame military version of Henry rifle. Furnished with sling swivels mounted on left side. Buttplate fitted with trap door. Caliber .44-40; barrel length 24"; weight 9 lbs. 4 oz.

NIB	Exc.	V.G.	Good	Fair	Poor
900	725	625	500	400	200

Henry Carbine

Brass frame carbine version. Features 22" barrel. Chambered for .44-40 cartridge. Weight 8 lbs. 12 oz.

NIB	Exc.	V.G.	Good	Fair	Poor
875	700	600	500	400	200

Henry Trapper

Replica not based on actual Henry. Fitted with unique 16.5" barrel. Brass frame model. Weight 7 lbs. 7 oz. Chambered for .44-40 cartridge.

NIB	Exc.	V.G.	Good	Fair	Poor
875	700	600	500	400	200

1892 Rifle

Lever-action rifle chambered for .357 Magnum, .44-40, .45 Colt or .32-20 cartridge. Octagon 24.25" barrel. Walnut stock, crescent butt and blued or case colored receiver. Weight about 6.25 lbs.

NIB	Exc.	V.G.	Good	Fair	Poor
525	425	350	300	250	200

1892 Short Rifle

Same as above, with 20" octagon barrel. Weight about 6.25 lbs.

NIB	Exc.	V.G.	Good	Fair	Poor
525	425	350	300	250	200

1892 Carbine

Similar to short rifle. Fitted with 20" round barrel. Saddle ring on left side of receiver. Weight about 5.75 lbs.

NIB	Exc.	V.G.	Good	Fair	Poor
450	350	300	250	200	150

1892 Brass Frame Carbine

Same as above, with polished brass receiver.

NIB	Exc.	V.G.	Good	Fair	Poor
450	350	300	250	200	150

1892 Brass Frame Rifle

Same as carbine, with polished brass receiver.

NIB	Exc.	V.G.	Good	Fair	Poor
525	425	350	300	250	200

No. 2 Creedmoor Target Rifle

Reproduction of Remington No. 2 Creedmoor. Features case colored receiver, tapered 30" octagonal barrel, hooded front sight, Creedmoor tang sight and walnut stock, with checkered pistol-grip. Furnished in .45-70 Government. Weight 9 lbs.

NIB	Exc.	V.G.	Good	Fair	Poor
900	725	625	500	400	200

Rolling Block Buffalo Rifle

Replica of Remington Buffalo rifle. Fitted with 26" or 30" octagonal or half octagonal barrel, case colored receiver, blade front sight and notch rear, brass trigger guard and walnut stocks. Tang drilled and tapped for tang sight.

NIB	Exc.	V.G.	Good	Fair	Poor
750	600	475	300	200	100

Half Octagon Barrel Model

NIB	Exc.	V.G.	Good	Fair	Poor
750	600	475	300	200	100

"John Bodine" Rolling Block Rifle

Chambered for .45-70 cartridge. Fitted with 30" octagon barrel. Double-set triggers. Match-grade rear tang sight. Weight about 12 lbs. Introduced in 2002.

NIB	Exc.	V.G.	Good	Fair	Poor
1550	1150	800	575	350	200

1885 High Wall

Chambered for .45-70 cartridge. Fitted with 30" medium heavy octagon barrel. Case colored receiver, target sights and walnut stocks. Also available with 28" round barrel. **NOTE:** Deduct $100 for Buckhorn sights; $60 for 28" barrel.

NIB	Exc.	V.G.	Good	Fair	Poor
900	725	600	500	400	200

1873 Springfield Infantry Rifle

Copy of Trapdoor Springfield. Chambered for .45-70. Fitted with 32.5" barrel. Walnut stock. Case-hardened breechlock. Weight about 8.25 lbs.

NIB	Exc.	V.G.	Good	Fair	Poor
975	800	600	500	400	200

1873 Springfield Cavalry Carbine

Same as above, with 22" barrel. Weight about 7 lbs.

NIB	Exc.	V.G.	Good	Fair	Poor
875	700	600	500	400	200

Ithaca/Navy Hawken Rifle

Offered in .50- or .54-caliber percussion. Features 31.5" rust blued octagon barrel. Percussion lockplate case colored. Rest of hardware blued, with exception of nose cap and escutcheons. Weight about 9 lbs. 13 oz.

NIB	Exc.	V.G.	Good	Fair	Poor
350	300	250	200	150	100

Hawken Rifle

Features case colored lock, 28" blued octagon barrel, adjustable sights, double-set triggers and hooked breech. Polished brass furniture and patchbox are mounted on walnut stock. Weight about 8.5 lbs.

NIB	Exc.	V.G.	Good	Fair	Poor
300	200	175	125	95	60

Hawken Hunter Rifle

Offered in .50-, .54- or .58-caliber. Features blued hardware, adjustable sights, case colored lock and hooked breech. Walnut stock hand checkered, with cheekpiece. Rubber recoil pad standard. Barrel length 28".

NIB	Exc.	V.G.	Good	Fair	Poor
295	190	150	100	75	60

Hawken Hunter Carbine

Same as above. Fitted with 22.5" barrel. Weight about 6 lbs. 12 oz.

NIB	Exc.	V.G.	Good	Fair	Poor
295	190	150	100	75	60

Kodiak MKIV Double Rifle

Built in Europe by Pedersoli. Chambered for .45-70 cartridge. Features walnut stock, with cheekpiece and hand checkering. Barrel length 24", with adjustable sights. Engraved sideplates are polished bright. Sling swivels standard. Weight 10.2 lbs.

NIB	Exc.	V.G.	Good	Fair	Poor
4500	3350	2500	1500	600	400

Mortimer Flintlock or Percussion Shotgun

Replica of 12-gauge English Mortimer. Features waterproof pan, roller frizzen (flintlock only), external safety. All parts case colored. Barrel length 36"; weight 7 lbs.

NIB	Exc.	V.G.	Good	Fair	Poor
975	800	600	500	400	200

Fowler Shotgun

12-gauge side-by-side, with straight-grip stock. Features hooked breech and 28" blued barrels. Sideplates are engraved and case colored. Double triggers and checkered walnut stock standard. Weight 7.25 lbs.

NIB	Exc.	V.G.	Good	Fair	Poor
550	395	300	250	200	100

Navy Arms Steel Shot Magnum

Same as above in 10-gauge. Weight 7 lbs. 9 oz.

NIB	Exc.	V.G.	Good	Fair	Poor
575	400	295	125	100	75

T&T Shotgun

Turkey and trap have straight-grip stock and 28" barrel choked Full and Full. Locks are case colored and engraved. Checkered walnut stock. Weight 7.5 lbs.

NIB	Exc.	V.G.	Good	Fair	Poor
550	395	300	250	200	100

Japanese Tanegashima Matchlock

A .50-caliber, with 41" barrels. Weight 8.5 lbs.

NIB	Exc.	V.G.	Good	Fair	Poor
1150	800	600	400	300	150

HANDGUNS

Le Page Pistol

.44-caliber percussion pistol. Has 10.25" tapered octagon barrel, adjustable single-set trigger. Lock, trigger guard and buttcap engraved. Hand checkered walnut stocks. Weight 36 oz.

NIB	Exc.	V.G.	Good	Fair	Poor
450	375	300	250	200	100

Single Cased Set

NIB	Exc.	V.G.	Good	Fair	Poor
580	530	475	400	300	150

Double Cased Set

NIB	Exc.	V.G.	Good	Fair	Poor
995	875	750	600	400	200

Flintlock

Same as above, with flintlock ignition. Weight 41 oz.

NIB	Exc.	V.G.	Good	Fair	Poor
470	425	350	250	150	100

Smoothbore Flintlock Pistol

Same as above, with smoothbore.

NIB	Exc.	V.G.	Good	Fair	Poor
470	425	350	250	150	100

Smoothbore Flintlock Pistol Single Cased Set

NIB	Exc.	V.G.	Good	Fair	Poor
800	700	600	400	300	150

Smoothbore Flintlock Pistol Double Cased Set

NIB	Exc.	V.G.	Good	Fair	Poor
1395	1275	1050	600	400	200

Kentucky Pistol

Percussion replica of a pistol developed in 1840s. Has 10.125" blued barrel, case colored lock, brass furniture and trigger guard, with walnut stock. Weight 32 oz.

NIB	Exc.	V.G.	Good	Fair	Poor
295	225	200	125	85	60

Single Cased Set

NIB	Exc.	V.G.	Good	Fair	Poor
350	275	225	175	125	75

Double Cased Set

NIB	Exc.	V.G.	Good	Fair	Poor
550	450	350	250	150	100

Flintlock Pistol

Same as above, with flintlock ignition.

NIB	Exc.	V.G.	Good	Fair	Poor
225	175	150	100	75	60

Flintlock Pistol Single Cased Set

NIB	Exc.	V.G.	Good	Fair	Poor
350	275	225	175	125	75

Flintlock Pistol Double Cased Set

NIB	Exc.	V.G.	Good	Fair	Poor
550	450	350	275	175	100

Harpers Ferry Pistol

Has .58-caliber rifled 10" barrel. Case-hardened lock and walnut stock. Weight about 39 oz.

NIB	Exc.	V.G.	Good	Fair	Poor
300	250	200	150	100	75

Pistol Single Cased Set

NIB	Exc.	V.G.	Good	Fair	Poor
350	275	225	175	125	100

LE MAT PISTOLS
18th Georgia Le Mat Pistol

9-shot .44-caliber percussion revolver has 7.625" blued barrel and engraved cylinder. Engraved banner on left side of frame reads "DEO VIN-

DICE". Hammer and trigger case colored. Stock checkered walnut. Comes with Le Mat mould and velvet draped French fitted case. Weight 55 oz.

NIB	Exc.	V.G.	Good	Fair	Poor
795	625	500	400	300	150

Beauregard Le Mat Pistol

Replica of Cavalry model. Comes cased.

NIB	Exc.	V.G.	Good	Fair	Poor
1000	800	650	550	350	200

Navy Le Mat

Features knurled pin barrel release and spur barrel selector.

NIB	Exc.	V.G.	Good	Fair	Poor
795	625	500	400	300	150

Army Le Mat

Features knurled pin barrel release and cross pin barrel selector.

NIB	Exc.	V.G.	Good	Fair	Poor
795	625	500	400	300	150

Cavalry Le Mat

Features lanyard ring, spur trigger, lever type barrel release and cross pin barrel selector.

NIB	Exc.	V.G.	Good	Fair	Poor
795	625	500	400	300	150

Starr Double-Action Model 1858 Army

Double-action revolver chambered for .44-caliber. Fitted with 6" barrel. Blued finish. Weight about 48 oz.

NIB	Exc.	V.G.	Good	Fair	Poor
350	250	200	150	100	75

Starr Single-Action Model 1863 Army

Fitted with 8" barrel. Chambered for .44-caliber. Blued finish and walnut stock. Weight about 48 oz.

NIB	Exc.	V.G.	Good	Fair	Poor
350	250	200	150	100	75

1862 New Model Police

Replica based on Colt .36-caliber pocket pistol of the same name. Features half fluted and re-dated cylinder. Case colored frame and loading gate. Polished brass trigger guard and backstrap. Barrel length 5.5"; weight 26 oz.

NIB	Exc.	V.G.	Good	Fair	Poor
300	250	175	150	100	75

1862 New Model Book-Style Cased Set

NIB	Exc.	V.G.	Good	Fair	Poor
350	250	200	150	100	75

Paterson Revolver

Replica is 5-shot .36-caliber. Cylinder scroll engraved with stagecoach scene. Hidden trigger drops down when hammer is cocked. Barrel length 9"; weight 43 oz.

NIB	Exc.	V.G.	Good	Fair	Poor
475	425	350	250	150	100

Engraved Paterson Revolver

Features hand engraving with silver inlays.

NIB	Exc.	V.G.	Good	Fair	Poor
575	475	350	250	200	100

1851 Navy

Colt replica offered in .36- or .44-caliber. Naval battle scene engraved in cylinder. Octagon 7.5" barrel. Trigger guard and backstrap polished brass. Walnut grips are hand rubbed. Weight 32 oz. **NOTE:** Add $100 for optional shoulder stock.

NIB	Exc.	V.G.	Good	Fair	Poor
350	250	200	150	100	75

Single Cased Set

NIB	Exc.	V.G.	Good	Fair	Poor
375	275	225	150	100	75

Double Cased Set

NIB	Exc.	V.G.	Good	Fair	Poor
550	450	375	275	200	100

1851 Navy Conversion

Replica of Colt 1851 Navy cartridge conversion. Offered in .38 Special or .38 Long Colt. Choice of 5.5" or 7.5" barrels. Weight about 40 oz.

NIB	Exc.	V.G.	Good	Fair	Poor
475	425	350	250	150	100

Augusta 1851 Navy Pistol

Available with 5" or 7.5" barrel. Engraved with "A" coverage.

NIB	Exc.	V.G.	Good	Fair	Poor
350	250	200	150	100	75

Model 1851 Navy Frontiersman

Introduced in 2003. Features 5" .36-caliber barrel. Receiver, loading lever and hammer case colored. Barrel and cylinder charcoal blued. Fitted with German silver backstrap and walnut grips.

NIB	Exc.	V.G.	Good	Fair	Poor
350	250	200	150	100	75

Reb Model 1860 Pistol

Replica of Confederate Griswold and Gunnison revolver. Features blued round 7.5" barrel. Brass frame, trigger guard and backstrap. Offered in .36- or .44-caliber. Weight 44 oz.

NIB	Exc.	V.G.	Good	Fair	Poor
165	150	125	90	75	35

Reb 1860 Sheriff's Model

Same as above. Fitted with 5" barrel. Weight 40 oz.

NIB	Exc.	V.G.	Good	Fair	Poor
165	150	125	90	75	35

1847 Walker Dragoon

Replica of rare Colt .44-caliber revolver. Barrel and cylinder blued. Frame and loading lever case colored. Barrel length 9"; weight 75 oz.

NIB	Exc.	V.G.	Good	Fair	Poor
400	325	275	250	200	100

Single Cased Set

NIB	Exc.	V.G.	Good	Fair	Poor
450	375	325	250	200	100

Single Deluxe Cased Set

NIB	Exc.	V.G.	Good	Fair	Poor
525	425	350	300	200	100

1860 Army Pistol

.44-caliber features case colored frame and loading lever. Blued barrel, cylinder and backstrap. Trigger guard brass. Cylinder engraved with battle scene. Barrel length 8"; weight 41 oz.

NIB	Exc.	V.G.	Good	Fair	Poor
350	250	200	150	100	75

Single Cased Set

NIB	Exc.	V.G.	Good	Fair	Poor
375	275	225	150	100	75

Double Cased Set

NIB	Exc.	V.G.	Good	Fair	Poor
550	450	375	275	200	100

1860 Army Conversion

Chambered for .38 Special or .38 Long Colt. Fitted with 5.5" or 7.5" barrel. Blued finish. Walnut grips. Weight about 40 oz.

NIB	Exc.	V.G.	Good	Fair	Poor
475	425	350	250	150	100

1858 New Model Remington-Style Pistol

Replica has solid frame as did original. Frame and 8" barrel blued. Trigger guard brass. Walnut grips standard. Weight 40 oz.

NIB	Exc.	V.G.	Good	Fair	Poor
350	250	200	150	100	75

Single Cased Set

NIB	Exc.	V.G.	Good	Fair	Poor
375	275	225	150	100	75

Double Cased Set

NIB	Exc.	V.G.	Good	Fair	Poor
550	450	375	275	200	100

Stainless Steel 1858 New Model Army

Same as above in stainless steel. Weight 40 oz.

NIB	Exc.	V.G.	Good	Fair	Poor
375	275	225	150	100	75

Single Cased Set

NIB	Exc.	V.G.	Good	Fair	Poor
375	275	225	150	100	75

Double Cased Set

NIB	Exc.	V.G.	Good	Fair	Poor
550	450	375	275	200	10

Brass Framed 1858 New Model Army

Version features highly polished brass frame. Barrel length 7.75".

NIB	Exc.	V.G.	Good	Fair	Poor
165	150	125	90	75	35

Single Cased Set

NIB	Exc.	V.G.	Good	Fair	Poor
250	200	150	100	75	60

Double Cased Set

NIB	Exc.	V.G.	Good	Fair	Poor
395	325	300	250	200	100

1858 Target Model

Same as above. Features patridge front sight and adjustable rear. Barrel length 8".

NIB	Exc.	V.G.	Good	Fair	Poor
300	225	175	125	75	50

Deluxe 1858 New Model Army

Replica built to exact dimensions as original. Barrel length 8", with adjustable front sight. Trigger guard silver plated. Action tuned for competition. Weight 46 oz.

NIB	Exc.	V.G.	Good	Fair	Poor
400	325	250	200	150	100

Spiller and Burr Pistol

.36-caliber pistol, with 7" blued octagon barrel. Frame brass, with walnut grips. Weight 40 oz.

NIB	Exc.	V.G.	Good	Fair	Poor
350	250	200	150	100	75

Single Cased Set

NIB	Exc.	V.G.	Good	Fair	Poor
375	275	225	150	100	75

Double Cased Set

NIB	Exc.	V.G.	Good	Fair	Poor
550	450	375	275	200	100

Rogers and Spencer

Features 7.5" blued barrel and frame. Offered in .44-caliber. Walnut grips. Weight 48 oz.

NIB	Exc.	V.G.	Good	Fair	Poor
375	275	225	150	100	75

"London Gray" Rogers and Spencer Pistol

Same as above, with burnished satin chrome finish.

NIB	Exc.	V.G.	Good	Fair	Poor
375	275	225	150	100	75

Rogers and Spencer Target Model

Same as standard. Fitted with adjustable target sights.

NIB	Exc.	V.G.	Good	Fair	Poor
375	275	225	150	100	75

1861 Navy Conversion

Replica of cartridge conversion 1861 Navy. Chambered for .38 Special or .38 Long Colt. Fitted with 5.5" or 7.5" barrel. Weight about 40 oz.

NIB	Exc.	V.G.	Good	Fair	Poor
475	425	350	250	150	100

1872 Colt Open Top

Features 5.5" or 7.5" barrel. Case-hardened frame. Blued barrel and cylinder. Silver-plated brass trigger guard and backstrap. Walnut grips. Chambered for .38-caliber cartridge. Weight about 40 oz.

NIB	Exc.	V.G.	Good	Fair	Poor
500	375	225	175	150	125

1873 Colt-Style Single-Action Army

Replica features case colored frame and hammer. Blued round barrel in

3", 4.75", 5.5" or 7.5" lengths. Trigger guard and cylinder blued. Offered in .44-40, .45 Long Colt, .357 Magnum and .32-20.

NIB	Exc.	V.G.	Good	Fair	Poor
500	375	225	175	150	125

Model 1873 SAA Stainless Gunfighter

Introduced in 2003. Same as standard 1873. Features all stainless steel construction. Offered in .45 Colt and .357 Magnum caliber. Choice of 4.75", 5.5" or 7.5" barrel. Weight about 45 oz. depending on barrel length.

NIB	Exc.	V.G.	Good	Fair	Poor
525	400	250	195	150	125

Economy Model 1873 S.A.A.

Same as above, with brass trigger guard and backstrap.

NIB	Exc.	V.G.	Good	Fair	Poor
325	250	200	150	125	100

Nickel 1873 S.A.A.

NIB	Exc.	V.G.	Good	Fair	Poor
525	400	250	195	150	125

1873 U.S. Cavalry Model

.45 Long Colt features U.S. arsenal stampings, case colored frame and walnut grips. Barrel length 7.5"; weight 45 oz.

NIB	Exc.	V.G.	Good	Fair	Poor
500	375	225	175	150	125

1873 Pinched Frame Model

Replica of "pinched" frame 1873. "U" shape rear sight notch. Chambered for .45 Colt, with 7.5" barrel.

NIB	Exc.	V.G.	Good	Fair	Poor
500	375	225	175	150	125

1873 Flat Top Target

Features windage adjustable rear sight on flat top frame. Spring loaded front sight. Barrel length 7.5". Offered in .45 Colt. Weight about 40 oz. Introduced in 1998.

NIB	Exc.	V.G.	Good	Fair	Poor
500	375	225	175	150	125

Deputy Single-Action Army

Similar to Model 1873, with bird's-head grip. Barrel lengths 3", 3.5", 4" and 4.75". Chambered for .44-40 and .45 Colt.

NIB	Exc.	V.G.	Good	Fair	Poor
400	325	250	200	150	100

Shootist Model S.A.A.

Reproduction of Colt 1873. Parts are interchangeable with originals. Blued barrel, cylinder, trigger guard and backstrap. Case-hardened frame and hammer. Walnut grips. Offered in 4.75", 5.5" and 7.5" barrel lengths. Chambered for .357 Magnum, .44-40 or .45 Colt.

NIB	Exc.	V.G.	Good	Fair	Poor
500	375	225	175	150	125

Scout Small Frame Revolver

Identical to Colt 1873 SAA, with smaller dimensions. Offered in .38 Special. Choice of 4.75" or 5.5" barrel. Weight about 30 oz. Introduced in 2003.

NIB	Exc.	V.G.	Good	Fair	Poor
400	325	250	200	150	100

Deluxe 1873 Colt Revolver

Chambered for .32-20 cartridge. Features bright charcoal blue barrel, with case colored frame and hammer. Walnut grips. Fitted with 5.5" barrel. Limited production. Weight about 41 oz.

NIB	Exc.	V.G.	Good	Fair	Poor
500	375	225	175	150	125

Bisley Model

Features famous Bisley grip. Barrel lengths 4.75", 5.5" and 7.5". Chambered for .44-40 or .45 Colt.

Bisley Flat Top Target

Similar to Bisley, with 7.5" barrel. Flat top frame, with adjustable front sight and windage adjustable rear. Chambered for .44-40 or .45 Colt. Weight about 40 oz.

NIB	Exc.	V.G.	Good	Fair	Poor
500	375	225	175	150	125

1875 Remington-Style Revolver

Frame case colored. All other parts blued except brass trigger guard. Available in .44-40 or .45 Long Colt. Furnished with walnut grips. Barrel length 7.5"; weight 41 oz.

NIB	Exc.	V.G.	Good	Fair	Poor
525	400	250	195	150	125

1890 Remington-Style Revolver

Modified version of 1875 model. Offered in .44-40 or .45 Long Colt. Web under barrel has been eliminated. Blued 5.5" steel barrel and frame. Lanyard loop on bottom of walnut grips. Weight 39 oz.

NIB	Exc.	V.G.	Good	Fair	Poor
500	375	225	175	150	125

TOP BREAK REVOLVERS

Model 1875 Schofield—Wells Fargo 5" barrel

NIB	Exc.	V.G.	Good	Fair	Poor
500	375	225	175	150	125

Model 1875 Schofield—Cavalry 7" barrel

Reproduction of S&W Model 3 top break revolver in .44-40 or .45 Long Colt. Cavalry model has 7" barrel; Wells Fargo model 5". Weight about 39 oz.

NIB	Exc.	V.G.	Good	Fair	Poor
750	650	525	450	350	125

Model 1875 Schofield—Deluxe

Charcoal blue finish with gold inlays and "A" style hand engraving. Available in Cavalry or Wells Fargo model. Special order only.

NIB	Exc.	V.G.	Good	Fair	Poor
750	650	525	450	350	125

Model 1875 Schofield—B Engraved

Available in Cavalry or Wells Fargo model. Grade "B" is style engraved, with 35 percent coverage. Special order only.

NIB	Exc.	V.G.	Good	Fair	Poor
1700	1400	1000	800	500	300

Model 1875 Schofield—C Engraved

Available in Cavalry or Wells Fargo in "C" style engraving, with 50 percent coverage. Special order only.

NIB	Exc.	V.G.	Good	Fair	Poor
1400	1100	800	600	350	200

Model 1875 Founder's Model

Introduced in 2003 to honor Val Forgett, Sr. and Aldo Uberti. Features charcoal blued barrel and cylinder. Color case-hardened receiver, backstrap, trigger guard and trigger. Grip white ivory polymer. Limited production. Special serial number prefix of "VF".

NIB	Exc.	V.G.	Good	Fair	Poor
1150	950	800	675	550	275

Model 1875 Schofield—Hideout

Short-barrel variation of Schofield. Fitted with 3.5" barrel. Chambered for .44-40 or .45 Colt cartridge. Weight about 38 oz.

NIB	Exc.	V.G.	Good	Fair	Poor
750	650	525	450	350	125

New Model Russian

Built around single-action Smith & Wesson Model 3. Chambered for .44 Russian cartridge. Fitted with 6.5" barrel. Case colored spur trigger guard, latch and hammer. Blued frame, barrel and cylinder. Walnut grips. Weight about 40 oz. Introduced in 1999.

NIB	Exc.	V.G.	Good	Fair	Poor
750	650	525	450	350	125

MILITARY SURPLUS ARMS

SKS Type 56 w/Scope Rail

Semi-automatic gas operated rifle. Chambered for 7.62x39 cartridge. Has 10-round clip. Fitted with scope rail on left side of receiver. Barrel length 20.5"; weight 8 lbs.

NIB	Exc.	V.G.	Good	Fair	Poor
400	325	250	200	150	100

Standard SKS Type 56

Same as above, without scope rail.

NIB	Exc.	V.G.	Good	Fair	Poor
400	325	250	200	150	100

Standard SKS Type 56 With Scope and Bipod

As above, with 2.75 power Type 89 scope and RPK style folding bipod.

NIB	Exc.	V.G.	Good	Fair	Poor
400	325	250	200	150	100

SKS "Cowboy's Companion" Carbine

Barrel length version 16.5". Weight 7 lbs. 8 oz.

NIB	Exc.	V.G.	Good	Fair	Poor
400	325	250	200	150	100

Military Version

Military version of "Cowboy's Companion". Fitted with short cruciform folding bayonet.

NIB	Exc.	V.G.	Good	Fair	Poor
400	325	250	200	150	100

SKS "Hunter" Carbine

Checkered composite Monte Carlo stock, with full length pull. Comes with 5-round magazine.

NIB	Exc.	V.G.	Good	Fair	Poor
400	325	250	200	150	100

TT-Olympia Pistol

Reproduction of Walther target pistol. Chambered for .22 LR. Barrel length 4.625"; weight 27 oz.

NIB	Exc.	V.G.	Good	Fair	Poor
275	200	150	125	100	50

TU-90 Pistol

Based on Tokagypt pistol. Features wrap-around grip, with thumb rest. Barrel length 4.5"; weight 30 oz.

NIB	Exc.	V.G.	Good	Fair	Poor
250	190	115	75	50	40

TU-111 Mauser

Replica of Mauser 111 9mm pistol, with 5.250" barrel and 10- or 20-shot magazine. Made in China, with limited importation into U.S. in early '90s.

NIB	Exc.	V.G.	Good	Fair	Poor
1000	800	650	500	350	150

TU-KKW Training Rifle

Based on 98 Mauser. Chambered for .22 LR cartridge. Fitted with military sights, bayonet lug, cleaning rod and take down disc. Comes with detachable 5-round box magazine. Barrel length 26"; weight 8 lbs.

NIB	Exc.	V.G.	Good	Fair	Poor
325	275	200	150	100	60

TU-KKW Sniper Trainer

Same as above, with 2.75 power Type 89 scope. Quick detachable mounting system.

NIB	Exc.	V.G.	Good	Fair	Poor
375	325	275	200	150	100

TU-33/40 Carbine

Based on WWII Mauser G 33/40 mountain carbine. Chambered for .22 LR or 7.62x39 cartridge. Barrel length 20.75"; weight 7.5 lbs.

NIB	Exc.	V.G.	Good	Fair	Poor
325	275	200	150	100	—

JW-15 Rifle

Bolt-action design based on BRNO Model 5 action. Chambered for .22 LR. Features adjustable sights, sling swivels, detachable 5-round magazine. Top of receiver dovetailed for easy scope mounting. Barrel 24" long; weight 5 lbs. 12 oz.

NIB	Exc.	V.G.	Good	Fair	Poor
100	80	70	60	50	35

Martini Target Rifle

.444 or .45-70 caliber single-shot Martini-action rifle, with 26" or 30" octagonal barrel, tang sight and walnut stock. Offered between 1972 and 1984.

NIB	Exc.	V.G.	Good	Fair	Poor
—	625	500	400	300	150

Parker-Hale Sniper Rifle

See—Parker-Hale.

RPKS-74

5.56mm or 7.62x39mm caliber semi-automatic rifle, with 19" barrel. Patterned after Russian AK series rifles.

NIB	Exc.	V.G.	Good	Fair	Poor
550	450	375	275	200	10

No. 5 Enfield Jungle Carbine

Replica chambered for .303 British cartridge. Fitted with cupped buttplate and flashider. Barrel length 20.5". Magazine capacity 10 rounds. Weight about 7 lbs.

NIB	Exc.	V.G.	Good	Fair	Poor
375	325	275	200	150	100

Classic Colt Handguns

Few American manufacturers today can say they've been around for almost two centuries, and have impacted the course of history during that timespan. Colt is one of those few brands that have stood the test of time, and its name and rampant horse logo have become synonymous with American innovation, precision and rugged dependability.

Just the Colt name is immediately associated with handguns – even for those with zero interest in firearms. Since 1837, Colt's revolvers and pistols have been carried by pioneering settlers throughout our nation's expansion; relied upon by soldiers defending freedom in combat all over the globe; counted on by law enforcement personnel daily to keep the peace; and used by everyday citizens for self-defense and safe, enjoyable shooting.

The following assortment of original Colt handguns are fine examples of the company's evolution and history. Each one has been set up for auction by Lock, Stock & Barrel Investments, an online auction company that specializes in firearms, firearms paraphernalia, military and war memorabilia, and reloading equipment. Well known as shooting and collectible firearms experts, LSB has two locations in California, and is always eager to work with new customers on purchases and consignments.

All photos courtesy of www.LSBauctions.com.

Colt 1855 Sidehammer Model 2 Pocket Revolver

.28 Caliber, 3½-inch barrel, Made in 1856.

The "Root," as it was also known, was the only solid-frame revolver ever manufactured by Colt. Several .28- or .31-caliber variations were manufactured from 1855-1870. This piece sold at auction for $2,106.

Colt 1873 Single Action Army

.45 Colt, 7½-inch barrel, Made in 1874.

This historic Colt bears the inspection marks of Orville Ainsworth and the serial number 4591, which place it as issued to Lt. Col. George Armstrong Custer's 7th Cavalry Regiment. To add to its history, the accompanying period holster bears the marks "JSC," for J.S. Collins, a saddlemaker who became the Secretary of the Sioux Indian Commission from 1875-1877. Circumstances and speculation may very well place them both at the Battle of the Little Bighorn on June 25-26, 1876.

Colt 2nd Generation Single Action Army

.45 Colt, 7½-inch barrel, Made in 1956.

Television and film Westerns revived the popularity of the Single Action Army after World War II, and Colt responded by introducing the iconic revolver's 2nd Generation. Many collectors and shooters believe the 2nd Generations are the best made of all Single Action Army models. They were offered in .38 Special, .357 Magnum, .44 Special and .45 Colt.

Colt Model 1860 Army

.44 Caliber, 8-inch barrel, Made in 1864.

This particular Model 1860 was manufactured during the Civil War, and has seen quite a bit of use since then. Some of the case coloring is still visible, as is the faint engraving of the Ormsby Naval Battle on the cylinder. Model 1860s were the primary sidearms of Union officers during the Civil War, and were popular with enlisted men and civilians that could afford to own one.

Colt 1st Generation Single Action Army Bisley

.38-40 W.C.F., 7½-inch barrel, Made in 1909.

The long grip, wide hammer spur, wide trigger and slotted front blade sight are some of the Bisley target model's distinguishing features. Its silver-plated finish, customized mother-of-pearl grips and fancy holster rig must have been prized by the original owner, C.A. MacMillan, according to the accompanying factory letter.

Colt Model .357 Magnum – Serial Number: 4

.38 Special/.357 Magnum, 4-inch barrel, Made in 1954

Introduced as a deluxe edition of the Colt Trooper, the Model .357 Magnum featured a bull barrel, smooth cylinder latch, wide target hammer, and grooved back and trigger. It also had a solid machined steel front blade sight, while the rear sight was an early variation of the Colt Accro Adjustable Sight. The pistol shown here is serial number 4, so it was the fifth model made out of 15,000 total.

The legendary Python revolver was introduced in 1955 and subsequently overshadowed the fine Model .357 Magnum.

Colt Model 1900 Sight Safety

.38 Auto, 6-inch barrel, Made From 1900-1903.

Though the Model 1900 was somewhat clumsy and unbalanced, and its unique safety not the most ergonomic, the pistol was reliable in function for military trials. Colt sold 200 to each the Navy and Army for testing, and 3,300 were sold on the civilian market. A large number of Model 1900 sight safeties were later converted to a Model 1902 type.

Colt Model 1905 With Shoulder Stock

.45 Rimless, 5-inch barrel, Made 1906.

The Colt Model 1905 is very important to Colt's handgun history as it was initially chambered for a .45 Rimless cartridge, then was the first to be chambered in .45 ACP; and its developement led to the Model 1907 and eventually the legendary 1911. Around 6,300 were manufactured from 1905-1911, it has a seven-shot magazine and no safety. Less than 500 were made to accept the shoulder stock that doubled as its holster – making this piece quite rare indeed.

Colt Model 1911

.45 ACP, 5-inch barrel, Made in 1913

There is no question that the Mode[l]
1911 has served American soldier[s]
well since its earliest days. The
original owner of the pistol show[n]
here was World War I veteran Sgt
Myles Aylward. He carried it throug[h]
his service in the Great War, an[d]
it was kept by his family i[n]
memory of his servic[e]
to his country

Colt Model 1911 Comba[t]
Commander, Series 7[0]

.45 ACP, 4¼-inch barrel, Made in 1974

Colt's Combat Commander was [a]
shorter, lighter version of the full-siz[e]
1911, and remained very popular wit[h]
military, law enforcement and civilia[n]
personnel because of those feature[s]
This model retained its factory bo[x]
owner's manual and thre[e]
magazines to make it [a]
definite head-turner

Colt Model 1932 New Service Shooting Master

.38 Special, 6-inch barrel, Made in 1934.

With a tall Partridge-style front sight and adjustable rear sight – both from King Gun Sight Company, and a heavy, slightly tapered barrel, Colt attempted to cater to target shooters of the time. Though, it didn't prove as popular as the company had hoped. But Colt collectors today would find this revolver to be a prize in such excellent condition.

Colt Model 1903 Pocket Hammerless

.32 ACP, 3¾-inch barrel, Made in 1928.

Another collaboration between John Browning and Colt produced the popular Model 1903, which was manufactured between 1903 and 1945. Its natural pointing and concealable design made it popular on both sides of the law. The NYPD and Shanghai Municipal Police both adopted it, and infamous criminals Al Capone and John Dillinger were both known to favor the pistol.

Colt Diamondback

.22 LR, 6-inch barrel, Made in 1981.

Colt's Diamondback revolver was manufactured from 1966 to 1986 and was offered in .38 Special and .22 LR for target shooters. Its ventilated rib, adjustable target sights and wide hammer fit the bill perfectly for many shooters. Engraved at the Colt Custom Gun Shop by Jan L. Gwinnell in 1981, this beautiful Diamondback and its case would make many a collector quite happy.

Colt Model 1911A1

.45 ACP, 5-inch barrel, Made in 1942.

This was the personal sidearm of U.S. Marine Colonel Dean Wilker. The yellow tag shown is from the armory at El Toro Marine Air Station, Calif., where Col. Wilker retired in 1974 after serving in WWII, Korea and Vietnam. He was stationed at El Toro a number of times and was commanding officer at the helicopter station in Santa Ana from 1971 to 1972. Another great example of a Colt with a very interesting history.

Colt Police Positive

.32 New Police Caliber, 4-inch barrel, Made in 1907.

The Police Positive was externally the same as the New Police model, with the addition of a positive lock feature and two new chamberings – .38 New Police and .38 Smith & Wesson. The Police Positive was manufactured from 1905 to 1947. Exquisite engraving, bone grips and a custom oak case set this revolver apart from the masses.

Colt Model 1903 General Officer's Pistol

.32 ACP, 3¾-inch barrel. Marked "U.S. PROPERTY," this pistol was issued to U.S. Air Force Lt. Colonel Charles A. Glover as his personal sidearm during his military service. With a leather holster and brass Air Force belt buckle, this Colt would make a wonderful addition to any military collection.

Colt Model 1911A1 and Model 1917

.45 ACP. This pair of Colt's belonged to WWII U.S. Navy hero, Commander H.H. Greer and his father. The 1911A1 is a commercial gun shipped in 1937 to Greer. The gun is accompanied by the original sales receipt showing delivery to Greer. Commander Greer's father's WWI Colt Model 1917 is also included. Both guns are listed by serial number on an accompanying New York state carry permit from shortly after the war.

Colt Woodsman Target, First Series

.22 LR, 6⅝-inch barrel, Made in 1940.

Colt Woodsmans have been highly sought after by shooters and collectors for many years for their simple, accurate, dependable design. This Woodsman is in excellent condition and includes a factory box, instruction sheet, bore brush and test target.

Colt Woodsman Match Target, First Series

.22 LR, 6⅝-inch barrel, Made in 1940.

A heavy barrel, Partridge-style front sight, fully adjustable rear sight and one-piece wraparound walnut "Elephant Ear" grips made this model Woodsman a top choice for target shooters. And with only 11,000 produced, it becomes more collectible every year.

Colt New Service Model

.45 Colt, 7½-inch barrel, Made in 1907.

For a nearly 110-year-old revolver, this Colt is in pretty darn good condition. The rugged frame, good trigger and variety of calibers offered made the New Service so popular that it was made from 1898 to 1944 – one of the longest runs of any Colt double action.

Colt Banker's Special

.38 S&W, 2-inch barrel, Made in 1941.

Introduced in 1926, this easily concealable revolver was designed with bank employees in mind. The U.S. Postal Service also equipped their railway mail clerks with the potent little wheelgun. 35,000 were made from 1926 to 1943.

Colt Python

.38 Special/.357 Magnum, 2½-inch barrel, Made in 1974.

Often described as the Cadillac of Colt double-action revolvers, the Colt Python only gathers more collector interest with each passing year. So a short-barrel, polished-nickel version with its original serialized box is a truly rare find these days.

Colt Python

.357 Magnum, 6-inch barrel, Made in 1978.

The cover gun of this 27th Edition of *Standard Catalog of Firearms* was beautifully engraved by master engraver Howard Dove, known as the Official Engraver to the Colt Collector's Association. Gold inlayed patriotic images cover the **barrel, frame** and **cylinder**, while the **grips are** two-piece wraparound bone adorned **with** gold. A completely **exquisite** display of firearm artistry.

No. 6 Enfield Jungle Carbine

Reproduction chambered for .303 British cartridge, with 20.5" barrel and flashider. Weight about 7 lbs. 10 round magazine.

NIB	Exc.	V.G.	Good	Fair	Poor
375	325	275	200	150	100

Ishapore 2A No. 1 MK III Rifle

Refinished rifle with 25" barrel. Chambered for .308 Win. cartridge. Magazine capacity 12 rounds. Weight about 9.3 lbs.

NIB	Exc.	V.G.	Good	Fair	Poor
350	250	200	150	100	75

2A Tanker Carbine

Replica with short 20" barrel. Chambered for .308 Win. Magazine capacity 12 rounds. Weight about 8.7 lbs.

NIB	Exc.	V.G.	Good	Fair	Poor
375	325	275	200	150	100

MK III Tanker Carbine

Similar to above. Chambered for .303 British cartridge. Magazine capacity 10 rounds.

NIB	Exc.	V.G.	Good	Fair	Poor
375	325	275	200	150	100

Lithgow No. 1 MK III Rifle

Rifles in unissued condition. Barrel length 25". Chambered for .303 British cartridge. Magazine capacity 10 rounds. Weight about 9 lbs.

NIB	Exc.	V.G.	Good	Fair	Poor
400	325	250	200	150	100

No. 1 MK III Enfield Rifle

Standard MK III S.M.L.E. rifles that have been refinished. Barrel length 25.25". Magazine capacity 10 rounds of .303 British cartridge. Weight about 9 lbs.

NIB	Exc.	V.G.	Good	Fair	Poor
375	325	275	200	150	100

No. 4 Tanker Carbine

Cut-down version of No. 4 MK I Enfield. Barrel length 20.5". Chambered for .303 British cartridge. Magazine capacity 10 rounds. Weight about 8.2 lbs.

NIB	Exc.	V.G.	Good	Fair	Poor
350	250	200	150	100	75

No. 4 MK I Enfield Rifle

Reconditioned rifle. Barrel length 25". Magazine capacity 10 rounds of .303 British cartridge. Weight about 8.6 lbs.

NIB	Exc.	V.G.	Good	Fair	Poor
350	250	200	150	100	75

Savage No. 4 MK I Rifle

Chambered for .303 British cartridge, with 25" barrel. Stocks are unissued. Magazine capacity 10 rounds. Weight about 8.7 lbs.

NIB	Exc.	V.G.	Good	Fair	Poor
375	325	275	200	150	100

Luger

.22-caliber semi-automatic pistol, with 4", 6" or 8" barrel, fixed sights and 10-shot magazine. Blued, with walnut grips. Manufactured in U.S.A. - 1986 and 1987.

NIB	Exc.	V.G.	Good	Fair	Poor
—	325	275	225	175	125

Grand Prix Silhouette Pistol

.30-30, .44 Magnum, 7mm Special and .45-70 caliber single-shot pistol, with 13.75" barrel. Adjustable sights and aluminum heat-disbursing rib. Matte-blued, walnut grips and forearm. Manufactured in 1985.

NIB	Exc.	V.G.	Good	Fair	Poor
—	450	375	295	225	150

NEAL, W.
Bangor, Maine

Under Hammer Pistol

.31-caliber under hammer percussion pistol, with 5" to 8" barrels. Iron frame and walnut grip. Barrel marked "Wm. Neal/Bangor, Me.".

NIB	Exc.	V.G.	Good	Fair	Poor
—	—	1350	1000	450	150

NEPPERHAN FIREARMS CO.
Yonkers, New York

Pocket Revolver

.31-caliber percussion revolver, with 3.5" to 6" barrels and 5-shot cylinder. Blued case-hardened, with walnut grips. Barrel marked "Nepperhan/Fire Arms Co" and on some additionally "Yonkers New York". Latter worth a slight premium over values listed. Approximately 5,000 made during 1860s.

NIB	Exc.	V.G.	Good	Fair	Poor
—	—	1400	1000	385	200

NESIKA BAY PRECISION, INC.
Sturgis, South Dakota

Hunting Rifles

Offered in a number of different calibers. Several stock options to choose from. All rifles fitted with adjustable trigger.

NIB	Exc.	V.G.	Good	Fair	Poor
4000	2900	2300	1500	750	400

Varmint Rifles

Offered in a variety of calibers, barrel lengths and weights. Single shot or repeater.

NIB	Exc.	V.G.	Good	Fair	Poor
3500	2900	2300	1500	750	400

Urban Tactical Rifle

Chambered for .308 cartridge. Fitted with 20" fluted barrel. Detachable box magazine. Weight about 10 lbs. **NOTE:** Add $100 for .300 Win. Magnum; 5-10 percent for Heavy Tactical version.

NIB	Exc.	V.G.	Good	Fair	Poor
5800	4800	3500	2700	800	500

NEW ENGLAND FIREARMS CO.
Madison, North Carolina

Formerly located in Gardner, Massachusetts, New England Firearms (NEF) is part of the Freedom Group of gun companies headquartered in Madison, NC. Some models have been marketed under both the NEF brand and H&R 1871. After 2007, the NEF brand has been seen only on imported models.

Model R22

.22 Magnum or .32 H&R Magnum double-action revolver, with 2.5", 4" or 6" barrel. Cylinder 6- or 9-shot. Blued or nickel-plated, with walnut grips. Introduced in 1988.

NIB	Exc.	V.G.	Good	Fair	Poor
150	100	80	70	60	40

Excell

Introduced in 2005. Chambered for 12-gauge 3" shell. Fitted with 28" ventilated rib barrel, with choke tubes. Checkered black synthetic stock. Magazine capacity 5 rounds. Weight about 7 lbs.

NIB	Exc.	V.G.	Good	Fair	Poor
450	375	295	225	150	100

Excell Waterfowl

As above, with Realtree Advantage Wetlands camo finish. Introduced in 2005.

NIB	Exc.	V.G.	Good	Fair	Poor
475	400	325	250	175	125

Excell Turkey

Fitted with 22" barrel with choke tubes and fiber optic front sight. Realtree Advantage Hardwoods camo finish. Weight 7 lbs. Introduced in 2005.

NIB	Exc.	V.G.	Good	Fair	Poor
475	400	325	250	175	125

Excell Combo

Has black synthetic stock and two barrels: 28" ventilated rib with choke tubes; 24" rifled barrel. Weight about 7 lbs. depending on barrel length. Introduced in 2005.

NIB	Exc.	V.G.	Good	Fair	Poor
500	425	345	260	185	135

Pardner

12-, 16-, 20-gauge or .410 bore single-shot shotgun, with 24", 26" or 28" barrel. Blued, with walnut stock. Introduced in 1987.

NIB	Exc.	V.G.	Good	Fair	Poor
150	100	80	70	60	40

Pardner Youth

Similar to above. Offered only in 20-, 28-gauge and .410 bore. Fitted with 26" barrel. Weight between 5 and 6 lbs.

NIB	Exc.	V.G.	Good	Fair	Poor
150	100	80	70	60	40

Special Purpose

Similar model offered only in 10-gauge. Available in several different configurations: 10-gauge with hardwood stock 28" barrel; camo model with 28" barrel or 32" barrel choked Modified; black matte finish model with 24" barrel with screw-in turkey Full choke. Weight about 9.5 lbs.

Special Purpose Turkey Gun

NIB	Exc.	V.G.	Good	Fair	Poor
250	175	125	100	75	50

Pardner Pump Turkey

Chambered for 12-gauge 3" shell. Fitted with 22" barrel with turkey choke tube. Magazine capacity 5 rounds. Weight about 7.5 lbs. Introduced in 2005.

NIB	Exc.	V.G.	Good	Fair	Poor
275	225	175	125	100	75

Pardner Pump Walnut Shotgun

12- or 20-gauge pump-action shotgun, with American walnut furniture, 26" or 28" ventilated rib barrel, 3" chamber and screw-in choke tube. Weight 7.5 lbs.

NIB	Exc.	V.G.	Good	Fair	Poor
—	275	225	175	125	100

Pardner Pump Synthetic Shotgun

Similar to above, with black synthetic buttstock and fore-end.

NIB	Exc.	V.G.	Good	Fair	Poor
—	225	175	150	100	75

Pardner Pump Field Shotgun

Similar to above, with Realtree APG HD camo finish.

NIB	Exc.	V.G.	Good	Fair	Poor
—	275	225	175	125	100

Pardner Pump Compact Field Shotgun

Similar to above, with 1.25" shorter length of pull and 21" barrel.

NIB	Exc.	V.G.	Good	Fair	Poor
—	225	175	150	100	75

Pardner Pump Compact Walnut Shotgun

Similar to Pardner Pump Walnut, with 1.25" shorter length of pull and 21" barrel. Weight 6.25 lbs.

NIB	Exc.	V.G.	Good	Fair	Poor
—	225	175	150	100	75

Pardner Pump Compact Synthetic Shotgun

Similar to above, with black synthetic buttstock and fore-end.

NIB	Exc.	V.G.	Good	Fair	Poor
—	225	175	150	100	75

Pardner Pump Combo

Introduced in 2005. Features two 12-gauge 3" barrels. One 28" with ventilated rib and choke tubes other 22" rifled slug barrel. Walnut stock. Weight about 7.5 lbs. depending on barrel length.

NIB	Exc.	V.G.	Good	Fair	Poor
275	225	175	125	100	75

Pardner Pump Protector

Similar to Pardner Pump, with matte black finish throughout. Synthetic buttstock and fore-end. Also available with carbon fiber dipped stock.

NIB	Exc.	V.G.	Good	Fair	Poor
—	225	175	150	100	75

Survivor

Based on single-shot break-action design. Rifle or shotgun fitted with synthetic stock, with integral storage compartments. Offered in .410/.45 Colt, 12- and 20-gauge, .223 Rem. and .357 Magnum. Barrel length 22". Weight about 6 lbs.

NIB	Exc.	V.G.	Good	Fair	Poor
200	175	150	125	100	75

Handi-Rifle (aka Handi-Gun)

.22 Hornet, .223, .243, .270, .280, .30-30, .44 Magnum or .45-70 caliber version of above. A 22" barrel fitted with open sights. Blued, with walnut stock. Introduced in 1989. In 2003, offered in stainless steel. In 2004, .22-250, .25-06 and .204 calibers added. In 2005, .500 S&W added.

NIB	Exc.	V.G.	Good	Fair	Poor
275	200	150	125	100	75

Tracker

Single-shot break-open shotgun. Offered in 12- and 20-gauge, with rifled or cylinder bore barrel both 24" long. Equipped with adjustable rifle sights. Weight about 6 lbs.

NIB	Exc.	V.G.	Good	Fair	Poor
150	125	100	75	60	50

Super Light Rifle

Single-shot rifle chambered for .22 Hornet or .223 Rem. Fitted with 20" light weight barrel. Choice of scope mount, no sights or adjustable rear sight and ramp front sight. Black polymer stock, with semi-beavertail fore-end. Weight about 5.5 lbs.

NIB	Exc.	V.G.	Good	Fair	Poor
175	125	100	75	60	50

Huntsman

Blackpowder gun, with break-open action. Hardwood pistol-grip stock. Fitted with 24" barrel. Chambered for .45- or .50-caliber slug. Recoil pad. Weight about 6.5 lbs. Introduced in 2002. In 2003, offered in stainless steel.

NIB	Exc.	V.G.	Good	Fair	Poor
175	125	100	75	60	50

Tracker II

Combination two-barrel set. Blackpowder and 12-gauge slug barrel. Case colored frame. Hardwood stock.

NIB	Exc.	V.G.	Good	Fair	Poor
275	225	175	125	100	—

Handi-Rifle Combo

Combination two-barrel set. .50 blackpowder and .243 Win. barrel. Hardwood stock. No iron sights.

NIB	Exc.	V.G.	Good	Fair	Poor
275	225	175	125	100	—

Sportster

Single-shot .22-caliber Short/LR or .22 WMR rifle, with 20" barrel. No iron sights. Black polymer Monte Carlo stock, with matte black metal finish. Scope mount rail. Weight about 5.5 lbs.

NIB	Exc.	V.G.	Good	Fair	Poor
175	125	100	75	60	50

Sportster Youth

As above, with standard stock. Weight about 5.25 lbs.

NIB	Exc.	V.G.	Good	Fair	Poor
175	125	100	75	60	50

Sportster .17 HMR

Single-shot chambered for .17 HMR cartridge. Fitted with 22" heavy varmint barrel. No iron sights. Black polymer Monte Carlo stock, with matte black metal finish. Weight about 7 lbs.

NIB	Exc.	V.G.	Good	Fair	Poor
175	125	100	75	60	50

Sportster .17 M2

As above chambered for .17 Mach2 cartridge. Introduced in 2005.

NIB	Exc.	V.G.	Good	Fair	Poor
175	125	100	75	60	50

Sportster SL

Semi-automatic rifle chambered for .22 LR cartridge. Fitted with 19" barrel. Walnut finished hardwood stock, with Monte Carlo and pistol-grip. Adjustable sights. 10-round magazine. Weight about 5.5 lbs. Introduced in 2004.

NIB	Exc.	V.G.	Good	Fair	Poor
150	125	100	75	60	50

Sportster Versa-Pack

Two-barrel set: 22" .410 barrel; other 20" .22-caliber barrel. Hardwood stock, with straight-grip. Iron sights. Weight about 5.5 lbs.

NIB	Exc.	V.G.	Good	Fair	Poor
250	175	125	100	75	50

Sidekick Muzzleloader

Introduced in 2004. Features break-open action, side lever release chambered for .50-caliber ball. Barrel length 24" or 26". American hardwood stock, with pistol-grip and recoil pad. Black matte finish or stainless steel. Adjustable fiber optic sights. Weight about 6.5 lbs. **NOTE:** Add $70 for stainless steel.

NIB	Exc.	V.G.	Good	Fair	Poor
200	165	125	100	75	50

NEW ULTRA LIGHT ARMS
Granville, West Virginia

Previously known as Ultra Light Arms, this manufacturer makes a variety of bolt-action rifles fitted with Douglas barrels of varying lengths, custom triggers and reinforced graphite stocks. Values listed are for base models. **NOTE:** Forbes Rifles, LLC makes a production-grade version of Model 24B rifle. See that listing.

Model 20 (Short Action)

Weight 4.5 lbs., with 22" barrel. Composte stock, with choice of colors or camo finish. Adjustable trigger. No sights. Offered in left-/right-hand.

NIB	Exc.	V.G.	Good	Fair	Poor
3100	2750	2500	1850	900	500

Model 20 RF Rimfire

Weight about 4.5 lbs., with 22" barrel. Stock synthetic, with choice of colors or camo finish. No sights. Adjustable trigger. Available as single-shot or repeater.

NIB	Exc.	V.G.	Good	Fair	Poor
1450	1300	1100	600	450	250

Model 20 Hunter's Pistol

Bolt-action repeating pistol designed with serious hunter in mind. Offered in various popular calibers, with 14" high-quality Douglas heavy barrel. Has 5-shot magazine. Matte blued, with reinforced graphite Kevlar stock. Introduced in 1987.

NIB	Exc.	V.G.	Good	Fair	Poor
1250	1000	800	625	500	300

Model 24 (Long Action)

Weight about 5.25 lbs., with 22" barrel.

NIB	Exc.	V.G.	Good	Fair	Poor
3100	2750	2500	1850	900	500

Model 28 Magnum

Weight about 5.75 lbs., with 24" barrel.

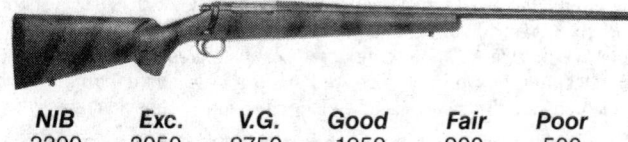

NIB	Exc.	V.G.	Good	Fair	Poor
3300	3050	2750	1950	900	500

Model 40 Magnum

Weight about 7.5 lbs., with 26" barrel.

NIB	Exc.	V.G.	Good	Fair	Poor
3300	3050	2750	1950	900	500

Model 90

Muzzle-loading rifle built with .45- or .50-caliber barrel. Graphite stock. Williams sights. Barrel length 28". Adjustable trigger. Weight about 6 lbs.

NIB	Exc.	V.G.	Good	Fair	Poor
950	750	600	475	350	200

Model 290

Blackpowder model with 209 Primer ignition, .45- or .50-caliber, 24" button-rifled barrel, Timney trigger, Kevlar stock with recoil pad, sling swivels, scope mount.

NIB	Exc.	V.G.	Good	Fair	Poor
1200	1100	900	750	650	300

NEWBURY ARMS CO.
Catskill, New York
Albany, New York

Pocket Pistol

.25-caliber spur trigger pocket pistol, with 4" octagonal barrel. Blued, silver-plated with walnut grips.

NIB	Exc.	V.G.	Good	Fair	Poor
—	—	2400	2050	875	200

Pocket Revolver

.26-caliber double-action percussion revolver, with 5" barrel and C-shaped exposed trigger. Blued, with iron or brass frame and walnut grips. Barrel marked "Newbury Arms Co. Albany". Produced in limited numbers between 1855 and 1860.

NIB	Exc.	V.G.	Good	Fair	Poor
—	—	7800	6900	3000	750

NEWCOMB, H. G.
Natchez, Mississippi

Pocket Pistol

.41-caliber percussion pocket pistol, with 2.5" barrel, German silver mounts and walnut stock. Manufactured in 1850s.

NIB	Exc.	V.G.	Good	Fair	Poor
—	—	2400	1850	700	250

NEWTON ARMS CO.
Buffalo, New York

Also known as Buffalo Newton Rifle Company and Charles Newton Rifle Company. In operation from 1913 to 1932.

NOTE: Any rifles listed chambered for a Newton caliber, will bring a premium over standard calibers of about 25 percent.

Newton-Mauser Rifle

.256 Newton caliber bolt-action rifle, with 24" barrel and double-set triggers. Blued, with walnut stock. Manufactured circa 1914.

NIB	Exc.	V.G.	Good	Fair	Poor
—	—	1300	850	500	300

Standard Rifle First Type

.22, .256, .280, .30, .33 and .35 Newton as well as .30-06 caliber bolt-action rifle, with 24" barrel. Open or aperture sights and double-set triggers. Blued, with walnut stock. Manufactured between 1916 and 1918.

Courtesy Amoskeag Auction Company, Inc.

NIB	Exc.	V.G.	Good	Fair	Poor
—	2500	2150	1500	900	400

Standard Rifle Second Model

.256, .30, or .35 Newton as well as .30-06 caliber bolt-action rifle as above, with Enfield-style bolt handle. Manufactured after 1918.

NIB	Exc.	V.G.	Good	Fair	Poor
—	2500	2150	1500	900	400

Buffalo Newton Rifle

As above marked "Buffalo Newton Rifle Company".

NIB	Exc.	V.G.	Good	Fair	Poor
—	2000	1650	1000	600	300

NICHOLS & CHILDS
Conway, Massachusetts

Percussion Belt Revolver

.34-caliber percussion revolver, with 6" round barrel and 6-shot cylinder. Blued or browned, with walnut grips. Estimated fewer than 25 made in 1838.

NIB	Exc.	V.G.	Good	Fair	Poor
—	—	1450	1175	4900	1250

Revolving Percussion Rifle

.36- or .40-caliber percussion rifle, with 22", 26" or 30" barrel and 5-, 6-, 7- or 9-shot cylinder. Blued or browned, with walnut stock and patchbox. Believed approximately 150 made between 1838 and 1840.

NIB	Exc.	V.G.	Good	Fair	Poor
—	—	25000	16500	6600	2000

NIGHTHAWK CUSTOM
Berryville, Arkansas

Custom Talon/Talon II

1911-style semi-automatic with 5" (Talon) or 4.25" (Talon II) barrel and fixed or adjustable sights. Several other barrel lengths/finishes available.

NIB	Exc.	V.G.	Good	Fair	Poor
2750	2200	1550	1200	700	300

Custom Predator

1911-style semi-automatic with 4.25"or 5" barrel and fixed or adjustable sights. Several other barrel lengths/finishes available.

NIB	Exc.	V.G.	Good	Fair	Poor
3000	2400	1850	1400	750	300

GRP

Global Response Pistol. 1911-style semi-automatic, with 4.25" or 5" barrel and fixed or adjustable sights. Several other barrel lengths/finishes available.

NIB	Exc.	V.G.	Good	Fair	Poor
2750	2200	1550	1200	700	300

Heinie Signature Series

Competition, Government Recon or Officer Compact configurations, all chambered in 9mm. 5" barrel except for Compact which is 4.25". Heinie Slant Pro sights. Recon has accessory rail. Many custom features.

NIB	Exc.	V.G.	Good	Fair	Poor
3100	2700	2100	1600	1000	350

Lady Hawk

Medium-frame 1911-style pistol in 9mm or .45 ACP with 4.25" match-grade barrel, titanium blue Perma Kote finish with hard chrome controls. Sights are Heinie Straight-Eight Slant Pro. Ultra thin chain link front and backstrap for reduced grip circumference.

NIB	Exc.	V.G.	Good	Fair	Poor
3100	2700	2100	1600	1000	350

Falcon

Full-size 1911 design with Coyote Tan, black or OD Green finish, dimpled grip, front and rear cocking serrations, Heinie Ledge rear sight. Chambered in 9mm, 10mm or .45 ACP

NIB	Exc.	V.G.	Good	Fair	Poor
3000	2500	2000	1500	800	350

Bob Marvel Custom 1911

Features Nighthawk/Marvel Everlast Recoil System, which allows a shooter to go at least 10,000 rounds before a spring change is necessary. Felt recoil and muzzle flip are also reduced. Other features include fully adjustable sights that have been recessed into the slide and dehorned, hand stippling on top of slide and a one-piece mainspring housing/magwell.

NIB	Exc.	V.G.	Good	Fair	Poor
3500	2850	2150	1650	800	340

T3

Compact 1911-style pistol, with Officers-size frame and Commander-size slide and barrel. All steel frame and slide, horizontally slanted serrations on mainspring housing and rear of slide, blue or stainless finish. Other features include Heinie Slant-Pro Straight Eight night sights, custom lightweight aluminum trigger and extended mag well. Designed by renowned custom pistolsmith Bob Marvel. Chambered in 9mm, .40 S&W or .45 ACP. Compact T4 model has similar features to T3, with 3.8" barrel and ultra-thin grips. Available in 9mm only.

NIB	Exc.	V.G.	Good	Fair	Poor
3100	2600	2000	1450	800	300

Hi-Power

Nighthawk's customized Browning Hi-Power 9mm. Upgrades including stippled frame and trigger guard, select cocobolo checkered grips, extended beavertail, Heinie slant pro rear sight, gold bead front and contoured magazine well. Introduced in 2016.

NIB	Exc.	V.G.	Good	Fair	Poor
2700	2300	1650	—	—	—

War Hawk Series

Available in full-size or compact models, with 5" barrel on Government model frame or 4.25" on Officer's size. Among the custom-style features are front and rear multi-faceted slide serrations, one-piece machined and checkered mainspring housing/mag well, high-cut front strap, lightweight aluminum match trigger, G10 Hyena Brown grips, red fiber optic front sight, Jardine Hook rear sight and War Hawk engraved logo on slide. Numerous upgrades available. Introduced in 2015.

NIB	Exc.	V.G.	Good	Fair	Poor
3500	3000	2650	1800	900	400

Kestrel

Chambered in .45 ACP. Designed for concealed carry. Based on a full-size frame, with a compact "Commander" size 4.25" barrel. Custom features including Heinie Straight Eight night sights, match-grade crowned and recessed barrel, reduced frame circumference and ultra-thin Nighthawk Alumagrips. Introduced in 2016.

NIB	Exc.	V.G.	Good	Fair	Poor
3250	2850	—	—	—	—

VIP

Very Impressive Pistol (VIP) is the top-of-the-line from Nighthawk. Features the company's finest customizations including a classic antique nickel finish, hand engraving throughout, ivory grips, 14k gold bead front sight, custom vertical front strap, mainspring serrations and a handsome cocobolo presentation case. Introduced in 2016.

NIB	Exc.	V.G.	Good	Fair	Poor
7200	6400	—	—	—	—

NOBLE
Haydenville, Massachusetts

In business between 1946 and 1971. Company manufactured a variety of plain utilitarian firearms. In general, these arms are all worth approximately the same, that is, less than $200 in excellent condition. Noble firearms represent an attractive opportunity for beginning collectors, as most can be had very inexpensively.

RIFLES

Model 10

.22-caliber bolt-action single-shot rifle, with 24" barrel. Pistol-grip stock with no checkering. Open sights. Produced in late 1950s.

NIB	Exc.	V.G.	Good	Fair	Poor
—	75	60	50	40	30

Model 20

.22-caliber bolt-action rifle. Fitted with 22" barrel. Open sights. Produced from late 1950s to early 1960s.

NIB	Exc.	V.G.	Good	Fair	Poor
—	75	60	50	40	30

Model 33

.22-caliber slide-action rifle. Fitted with 24" barrel and tubular magazine. Tenite stock. Produced from late 1940s to early 1950s.

NIB	Exc.	V.G.	Good	Fair	Poor
—	80	70	60	50	40

Model 33A

Same as above, with wood stock.

NIB	Exc.	V.G.	Good	Fair	Poor
—	75	60	50	40	30

Model 222

Single-shot bolt-action rifle chambered for .22-caliber cartridge. Plain pistol-grip stock.

NIB	Exc.	V.G.	Good	Fair	Poor
—	85	75	60	50	40

Model 235

Rather dopey but kinda cute .22-caliber slide-action rifle, with 24" barrel. Tubular magazine. Plain pistol-grip stock and grooved slide handle.

NIB	Exc.	V.G.	Good	Fair	Poor
—	200	125	75	60	50

Model 275

.22-caliber lever-action rifle, with tubular magazine. Fitted with 24" barrel. Plain stock has semi-pistol grip.

NIB	Exc.	V.G.	Good	Fair	Poor
—	175	100	80	60	50

SHOTGUNS

Model 40

Hammerless slide-action shotgun chambered for 12-gauge shell. Fitted with tubular magazine, 28" barrel with multi choke. Plain pistol stock, with grooved slide handle.

NIB	Exc.	V.G.	Good	Fair	Poor
—	125	100	85	70	50

Model 50

Same as above, without multi choke.

NIB	Exc.	V.G.	Good	Fair	Poor
—	115	90	80	65	50

Model 60

Hammerless slide-action shotgun in 12- or 16-gauge. Tubular magazine. Fitted with 28" barrel with adjustable choke. Plain pistol-grip stock, with grooved slide handle.

NIB	Exc.	V.G.	Good	Fair	Poor
—	175	150	125	100	75

Model 65

Same as above, without adjustable choke.

NIB	Exc.	V.G.	Good	Fair	Poor
—	150	125	100	75	60

Model 66CLP

Offered in 12- or 16-gauge. Slide-action shotgun fitted with 28" plain barrel and keyed lock fire control system.

NIB	Exc.	V.G.	Good	Fair	Poor
—	160	140	110	85	70

Model 66RCLP

Similar to above, with 28" ventilated rib barrel. Checkered pistol-grip stock. Adjustable choke standard.

NIB	Exc.	V.G.	Good	Fair	Poor
—	200	175	150	125	100

Model 66RLP

Same as above, without adjustable choke.

NIB	Exc.	V.G.	Good	Fair	Poor
—	175	150	125	100	75

Model 66XL

Similar to above, with plain barrel. Checkering only on slide handle.

NIB	Exc.	V.G.	Good	Fair	Poor
—	150	125	100	75	60

Model 70CLP

Similar to Model 66 series. Offered in .410 bore, with 26" barrel and adjustable choke. Both buttstock and slide handle checkered.

NIB	Exc.	V.G.	Good	Fair	Poor
—	175	150	125	100	75

Model 70RCLP

Variation fitted with 26" ventilated rib barrel.

NIB	Exc.	V.G.	Good	Fair	Poor
—	200	175	150	125	100

Model 70RLP

Has ventilated rib barrel. No adjustable choke.

NIB	Exc.	V.G.	Good	Fair	Poor
—	175	150	125	100	75

Model 70XL

This version has no adjustable choke. Fitted with 26" ventilated rib barrel. Stock checked.

NIB	Exc.	V.G.	Good	Fair	Poor
—	125	100	80	70	60

Model 602RCLP

Hammerless slide-action shotgun chambered for 20-gauge shell. Fitted with 28" ventilated barrel and adjustable choke. Checkered pistol-grip stock, with slide handle.

NIB	Exc.	V.G.	Good	Fair	Poor
—	225	200	175	125	100

Model 602CLP

Same as above, with plain barrel.

NIB	Exc.	V.G.	Good	Fair	Poor
—	175	150	125	100	75

Model 602RLP

Same as Model RCLP, without addition of adjustable choke device.

NIB	Exc.	V.G.	Good	Fair	Poor
—	200	175	150	125	100

Model 602XL

Same as above, with only slide handle checkered.

NIB	Exc.	V.G.	Good	Fair	Poor
—	150	125	100	75	60

Model 662

20-gauge slide-action shotgun. Has plain aluminum barrel, with checkered pistol-grip and slide handle. Receiver is made from aluminum. Produced in late 1960s.

NIB	Exc.	V.G.	Good	Fair	Poor
—	200	175	150	125	100

Model 80

Semi-automatic inertia-operated shotgun. Chambered for .410 shell. Fitted with 26" barrel, plain pistol stock with slotted forearm. Produced in early to mid 1960s.

NIB	Exc.	V.G.	Good	Fair	Poor
—	250	200	150	125	100

Model 166L

12-gauge slide-action shotgun, with key lock system. Fitted with 24" barrel bored for rifled slug. Lyman peep rear sight with post front. Checkered pistol and slide handle.

NIB	Exc.	V.G.	Good	Fair	Poor
—	250	200	150	125	100

Model 420

Box lock design side-by-side shotgun, with double triggers. Offered in 12-, 16-, 20-gauge and .410 bore. Barrel length 28" for all gauges; except .410 is 26". Lightly engraved frame. Checkered walnut stock and splinter forearm.

NIB	Exc.	V.G.	Good	Fair	Poor
—	300	250	200	150	100

Model 450E

Similar to Model 420, with addition of automatic ejectors. Not offered in .410 bore. Checkered pistol-grip stock, with beavertail forearm. Produced in late 1960s.

NIB	Exc.	V.G.	Good	Fair	Poor
—	350	275	225	175	125

NORINCO
Peoples Republic of China
China North Industries Corp.

Norinco is a state-owned conglomerate in China. Exported firearms to United States from 1988 to 1995. Importation of Norinco firearms was banned in conjunction with 1994 Crime Bill and various trade sanctions against China, with the exception of several shotguns that were marketed between 1999 and 2002.

ATD .22

.22-caliber semi-automatic rifle, with 19.4" barrel and 11-shot magazine located in butt. Blued, with hardwood stock. Importation began in 1987.

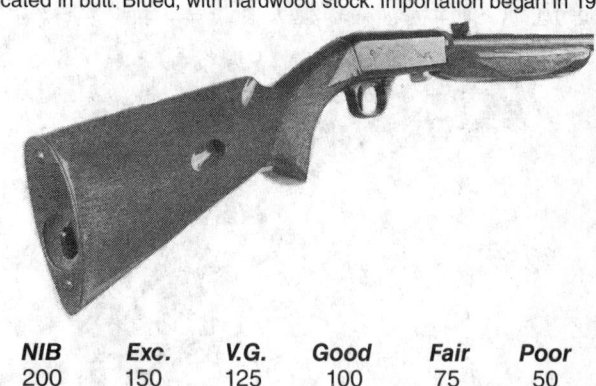

NIB	Exc.	V.G.	Good	Fair	Poor
200	150	125	100	75	50

EM-321

.22-caliber slide-action rifle, with 19.5" barrel and 10-shot tubular magazine. Blued, with hardwood stock. Introduced in 1989.

NIB	Exc.	V.G.	Good	Fair	Poor
150	100	85	75	65	50

Model HL-12-203 Shotgun

12-gauge boxlock over/under shotgun, with 30" ventilated rib barrels fitted for choke tubes. Single trigger and automatic ejectors. Blued, with hardwood stock. Introduced in 1989.

NIB	Exc.	V.G.	Good	Fair	Poor
400	325	275	225	175	125

Model HL-12-102 Shotgun

12-gauge slide-action shotgun, with 28" barrel and 3-shot magazine. Blued, with hardwood stock. Introduced in 1989.

NIB	Exc.	V.G.	Good	Fair	Poor
275	225	200	175	125	100

Model 97 Hammer Pump

Similar in appearance to Winchester Model 1897 shotgun. Fitted with 20" barrel with cylinder choke. Hardwood stock.

NIB	Exc.	V.G.	Good	Fair	Poor
375	275	200	150	100	75

Type 54-1 Tokarev

7.62x25mm caliber semi-automatic pistol, with 4.6" barrel, fixed sights and 8-shot magazine. Blued, with plastic grips. Imported in 1989.

NIB	Exc.	V.G.	Good	Fair	Poor
—	300	250	200	100	80

1911 A1

Steel-framed clone of 1911 .45 A1 semi-automatic. Very popular with competition shooters as a platform for custom guns. No longer imported.

NIB	Exc.	V.G.	Good	Fair	Poor
—	400	350	200	100	80

Model 213 Pistol

Copy of Browning P-35 semi-automatic pistol. Sold in 1988 only.

NIB	Exc.	V.G.	Good	Fair	Poor
—	250	200	150	100	75

Type 59 Makarov

.380 or 9mm Makarov caliber double-action semi-automatic pistol, with 3.5" barrel and 8-shot magazine. Blued, with plastic grips.

NIB	Exc.	V.G.	Good	Fair	Poor
—	275	250	225	175	125

SKS Rifle

7.62x39mm caliber semi-automatic rifle, with 20.5" barrel. Folding bayonet and 10-shot fixed or 30-shot detachable magazine. Blued, with hardwood stock. Importation began in 1988.

NIB	Exc.	V.G.	Good	Fair	Poor
—	400	300	225	150	100

Type 84S AK

Similar to AKS service rifle in 5.56mm caliber, with 16" barrel and 30-shot magazine.

NIB	Exc.	V.G.	Good	Fair	Poor
900	800	700	550	350	200

Type 84S-1

As above, with under-folding metal stock.

NIB	Exc.	V.G.	Good	Fair	Poor
1050	900	750	575	375	225

Type 84S-3

As above, with composition stock.

NIB	Exc.	V.G.	Good	Fair	Poor
1000	850	700	600	400	225

NORTH & COUCH
New York, New York

Animal Trap Gun

.28- or .30-caliber percussion pepperbox, with 1.75" or 2.12" barrel group. Hammer made with-/without spur. Marked "North & Couch, Middletown, Conn." or "North & Couch New York". Manufactured during 1860s.

Disk Hammer Model

NIB	Exc.	V.G.	Good	Fair	Poor
—	—	2200	1850	700	300

Spur Hammer Model

NIB	Exc.	V.G.	Good	Fair	Poor
—	—	3000	2750	900	350

NORTH AMERICAN ARMS
Provo, Utah

Mini-Revolver

.22 or .22 Magnum caliber spur trigger revolver, with 1" or 2.5" barrel and 5-shot cylinder. Stainless steel, with plastic or laminated rosewood grips. Introduced in 1975. Made in styles listed.

Standard Rimfire Version

NIB	Exc.	V.G.	Good	Fair	Poor
225	175	150	—	125	100

2 Cylinder Magnum Convertible Version

NIB	Exc.	V.G.	Good	Fair	Poor
275	200	175	—	145	125

Viper Belt Buckle Version

NIB	Exc.	V.G.	Good	Fair	Poor
225	175	150	—	125	100

Magnum Version

NIB	Exc.	V.G.	Good	Fair	Poor
250	200	175	—	150	100

Standard 3 Gun Set

NIB	Exc.	V.G.	Good	Fair	Poor
725	575	400	—	300	225

Deluxe 3 Gun Set

NIB	Exc.	V.G.	Good	Fair	Poor
800	650	475	—	375	275

Cased .22 Magnum

NIB	Exc.	V.G.	Good	Fair	Poor
350	250	200	—	150	125

Companion

.22-caliber cap-and-ball mini revolver. Has 1.125" barrel. Overall length 4.6"; weight about 5 oz.

NIB	Exc.	V.G.	Good	Fair	Poor
200	165	150	125	100	75

Super Companion

Same as above, with longer cylinder. Has 1.62" barrel. Weight about 7 oz.

NIB	Exc.	V.G.	Good	Fair	Poor
200	165	150	125	100	75

Black Widow

Five-shot fixed-sight revolver, with 2" or 4" barrel and oversize black rubber grips. Chambered for .22 LR or .22 Win. Magnum stainless steel. Weight about 8.8 oz. **NOTE:** Add $20 for adjustable sights.

NIB	Exc.	V.G.	Good	Fair	Poor
280	225	175	125	100	75

Mini-Master

Similar to Black Widow, with 2" or 4" barrel. Choice of .22 LR or .22 Win. Magnum stainless steel. Weight about 10.7 oz. **NOTE:** Add $20 for adjustable sights.

NIB	Exc.	V.G.	Good	Fair	Poor
280	225	175	125	100	75

"The Earl" Single-Action Revolver

Single-action mini-revolver patterned after 1858-style Remington percussion revolver. Chambered in .22 Magnum, with .22 LR accessory cylinder. Features include 4" octagonal barrel, spur trigger, 5-shot cylinder, faux loading lever that serves as cylinder pin release, wood grips, fixed notch rear sight and barleycorn front. Overall length 7.75". Weight 6.8 oz.

.22 Magnum only

NIB	Exc.	V.G.	Good	Fair	Poor
290	225	175	125	100	75

.22 convertible

NIB	Exc.	V.G.	Good	Fair	Poor
325	275	200	150	125	100

Sidewinder

A 5-shot swing-out cylinder model in .22 Magnum or .22 LR. Stainless steel, with walnut grips and 4" barrel

NIB	Exc.	V.G.	Good	Fair	Poor
300	260	200	150	120	90

Single-Action Revolver

Polished stainless steel single-action revolver. Chambered for .45 Win. Magnum and .450 Magnum Express cartridge. Has 7.5" barrel and 5-shot cylinder. Transfer bar safety and grips are walnut. Discontinued in 1988. Available with two cylinders. **NOTE:** Add $200 for extra cylinder.

NIB	Exc.	V.G.	Good	Fair	Poor
—	1200	950	700	400	250

Guardian

Semi-automatic double-action-only pocket pistol. Chambered in .32 ACP, .32 NAA or .25 NAA. Magazine capacity 6 rounds. Barrel length 2.2"; overall length 4.4"; weight empty 13.5 oz. Introduced in 1998. **NOTE:** Add 25 percent for Crimson Trace laser grips.

NIB	Exc.	V.G.	Good	Fair	Poor
400	300	225	175	150	125

Guardian .380

Similar to above. Chambered for .380 cartridge. Barrel length 2.5". Magazine capacity 6 rounds. Weight about 19 oz. **NOTE:** Add 25 percent for Crimson Trace laser grips.

NIB	Exc.	V.G.	Good	Fair	Poor
450	350	250	195	175	150

NORTH AMERICAN ARMS CORP.
Toronto, Canada

Brigadier

.45 ACP caliber semi-automatic pistol, with 5" barrel, 8-shot magazine and alloy frame. Weight 4.5 lbs. Produced in limited quantity between 1948 and 1951. Rarely if ever seen. **NOTE:** Value should be in excess of $5000 in Excellent or better condition.

NORTH AMERICAN SAFARI EXPRESS
Liege, Belgium
See—Francotte

Trade name used by Francotte on their double rifles imported and distributed by Armes De Chasse of Chads Ford, Pennsylvania.

NORTON ARMAMENT CORPORATION
Mt. Clemens, Michigan
See—Budischowsky

Firm manufactured Budischowsky Model TP-70 semi-automatic pistols prior to 1979. After that date, these arms were made by American Arms and Ammunition Company. Values below are for early Michigan production. **NOTE:** Deduct 15 percent for later Florida and Utah production.

NIB	Exc.	V.G.	Good	Fair	Poor
—	500	375	250	125	100

NORWICH PISTOL CO.
Norwich, Connecticut

Established in 1875 by New York retailer Maltby, Curtis & Company. This firm manufactured a wide variety of inexpensive spur trigger revolvers that were sold under these trade names: America, Bulldozer, Challenge, Chieftain, Crescent, Defiance, Hartford Arms, Maltby Henley, Metropolitan Police, Nonpariel, Norwich Arms, Parole, Patriot, Pinafore, Prairie King, Protector, Spy, True Blue, U.M.C. Winfield Arms. Company ceased operations in 1881. Value for any of its arms listed is approximate.

NIB	Exc.	V.G.	Good	Fair	Poor
—	—	300	200	75	50

NOSLER CUSTOM
Bend, Oregon

Nosler Custom Model 48 Sporter

Bolt-action centerfire rifle. Chambered in various calibers, 24" barrel, round top receiver, onyx gray composite stock. Introduced 2007. Price shown includes scope. Limited edition series has high grade walnut stock, double square bridge action, with integral scope bases. Only 500 made. **NOTE:** Add 50 percent for limited edition model.

NIB	Exc.	V.G.	Good	Fair	Poor
2850	2600	2100	1350	800	500

Nosler Model 48 Professional

Custom made on Nosler action, with glass-bedded Aramid Fiber reinforced composite stock. Match-grade hand-lapped stainless steel barrel. Custom three-pound trigger, two-position safety, choice of fixed or detachable magazine. Available in most popular calibers from .22-250 to 9.3x62mm.

NIB	Exc.	V.G.	Good	Fair	Poor
2500	2100	1850	1200	600	350

Nosler Custom Rifle (Limited Edition)

Built on Nosler action, with integral scope bases, hand-lapped stainless steel barrel, glass bedded American walnut stock with 20 lpi checkering. Comes with choice of three VX-3 Leupold scopes with matching serial number and custom reticle designed for different chamberings. Limited to 500 rifles per series. Offered in .300 WSM, .280 Ackley Improved, .338 Win. Magnum.

NIB	Exc.	V.G.	Good	Fair	Poor
4000	3750	3200	2600	—	—

Nosler Varmageddon

AR-15 style semi-automatic in .223 Rem. Features include 18" Noveske stainless barrel, with 1/2 x 28 muzzle threads, low profile gas block, Noveske backup iron sights, forged Vltor upper receiver. Comes with Leupold CDS VX3 4.5-14x50 scope and mounts, Harris bi-pod, soft case and two boxes of Nosler Varmageddon ammo. Made for Nosler by Noveske Rifleworks. New in 2013

NIB	Exc.	V.G.	Good	Fair	Poor
2100	1850	1600	1400	—	—

NOWLIN MANUFACTURING COMPANY
Claremore, Oklahoma

Match Classic

This 1911 pistol has a wide range of features. Can be chambered in 9mm, .38 Super, 9x23, .40 S&W and .45 ACP. Has 5" barrel, adjustable trigger, checkered main spring housing, hardwood grips, front and rear cocking serrations. Price listed for basic pistols. Options will greatly affect price.

NIB	Exc.	V.G.	Good	Fair	Poor
1600	1250	800	600	400	250

Compact Carry

Similar to Match Classic, with exception of 4" barrel on full-size frame. Again, options will greatly affect price.

NIB	Exc.	V.G.	Good	Fair	Poor
1495	1100	700	500	300	200

Match Master

These hand-built pistols offered choice of S.T.I., Caspian Hi-Cap or Nowlin STD Government frames. Available in 9mm, 9x23, .38 Super, .40 S&W and .45 ACP. Many special features included in standard pistol. Many extra cost options are available. **NOTE:** Add $140 for hard chrome finish.

NIB	Exc.	V.G.	Good	Fair	Poor
2400	1750	1200	800	600	300

O

O.D.I.
Midland Park, New Jersey

Viking

.45-caliber double-action semi-automatic pistol, with 5" barrel and 7-shot magazine. Stainless steel, with teak grips. Manufactured in 1981 and 1982.

NIB	Exc.	V.G.	Good	Fair	Poor
700	625	375	300	200	100

Viking Combat

As above, with 4.25" barrel.

NIB	Exc.	V.G.	Good	Fair	Poor
700	625	375	300	200	100

O.K.
Unknown

See—Marlin

OBREGON
Mexico City, Mexico

This is a .45-caliber semi-automatic pistol, with 5" barrel. Similar to Colt M1911A1, with combination side and safety latch on left side of frame. Breech is locked by rotating barrel, instead of Browning swinging link. This unusual locking system results in a tubular front end appearance to pistol. Originally designed for Mexican military, it was not adopted as such and only about 1,000 pistols were produced and sold commercially. Pistol is 8.5" overall; weight about 40 oz. Magazine holds seven cartridges. A rare pistol; independent appraisal suggested prior to sale.

NIB	Exc.	V.G.	Good	Fair	Poor
—	3750	2300	1850	1550	800

O'CONNELL, DAVID
New York, New York

Pocket Pistol

.41-caliber percussion pocket pistol, with 2.5" barrel, German silver mounts and walnut stock. Manufactured during 1850s.

NIB	Exc.	V.G.	Good	Fair	Poor
—	—	3650	3000	1025	300

O'DELL, STEPHEN
Natchez, Mississippi

Pocket Pistol

.34- to .44-caliber percussion pocket pistol, with 2" to 4" barrel, German silver mounts and walnut stock. Manufactured during 1850s.

NIB	Exc.	V.G.	Good	Fair	Poor
—	—	6750	6000	2500	950

OHIO ORDNANCE INC.
Chardon, Ohio

Model 1918A3 Self-Loading Rifle

Semi-automatic version of famed Browning Automatic Rifle. Chambered for .30-06 cartridge. Has a 20-round magazine. Introduced in this configuration in 1996. **NOTE:** Add $200 for .308 or 8mm caliber guns. Deduct 10 percent for bakelite stock.

NIB	Exc.	V.G.	Good	Fair	Poor
3800	3300	2500	1850	1500	750

Colt Browning Water Cooled Gun

Introduced in 2001. Semi-automatic version of famous Browning Model 1928 belt-fed machine gun. Features .30-06 or 7.65 Argentine caliber belt-fed gun, with tripod, wooden ammo box, water hose, water can and one 250 cloth belt. **NOTE:** Add $200 for .308 or 8mm caliber guns.

NIB	Exc.	V.G.	Good	Fair	Poor
3700	3300	2500	1850	1500	750

1919A4

Semi-automatic version of air-cooled belt-fed .30-caliber 1919 machine gun. Chambered for .308/7.62 NATO.

NIB	Exc.	V.G.	Good	Fair	Poor
3250	2800	2000	1250	1100	500

OJANGUREN Y VIDOSA
Eibar, Spain

This typical Eibar company produced mediocre firearms from early 1920s. Forced out of business during Spanish Civil War.

Apache (Model 1920)

Typical Eibar Browning copy chambered for 6.35mm cartridge. Low quality associated with most Spanish arms of this era. Slide marked "Pistole Browning Automatica Cal. 6.35 Apache". Finish is blued. Plastic grips have a head with a beret and word "Apache" molded into them.

NIB	Exc.	V.G.	Good	Fair	Poor
—	250	175	125	75	50

7.65mm

As above chambered for 7.65mm cartridge.

Courtesy James Rankin

NIB	Exc.	V.G.	Good	Fair	Poor
—	275	225	190	100	75

Ojanguren

Trade name this company used to cover line of revolvers they produced in 1930s. Produced two in .32-caliber and two chambered for .38 Special cartridge. Similar in appearance and barrel lengths of 3" or 6". Finishes are blued, with plastic grips. One of the .38-caliber models "Legitimo Tanque" is a reasonably well-made gun that was popular with Spanish target shooters. These guns have little collector or practical value and are all priced alike.

NIB	Exc.	V.G.	Good	Fair	Poor
—	175	125	100	75	50

Tanque

Blowback-operated semi-automatic chambered for 6.35mm cartridge. Has a 1.5" barrel and is actually an original design, which was rarely found on Eibar guns of this period. Has an oddly shaped slide and barrel is retained by means of a screw in front of frame. It has a 6-shot magazine and slide marked "6.35 Tanque Patent". Plastic grips have a tank molded into them and word "Tanque", as well as letters "O&V".

NIB	Exc.	V.G.	Good	Fair	Poor
—	175	125	100	75	50

OLD WEST GUN CO.
Houston, Texas

See—Cimarron Arms

An importer of reproduction firearms primarily manufactured by Aldo Uberti of Italy. In 1987, this company purchased the inventory of Allen Firearms and subsequently changed their name to Cimarron Arms.

OLYMPIC ARMS, INC.
Olympia, Washington

This company has been in business since the 1950s, first as a barrel maker and later as a manufacturer of bolt-action and AR-style rifles. In the 1980s, company bought Safari Arms, a manufacturer of 1911-style pistols. Many of these models remained in production under the Safari name until 2004, when they were changed to the Olympic brand. In 2014, the company announced that all handgun production was being discontinued.

PISTOLS

Black Widow

.45-caliber semi-automatic pistol, with 3.9" barrel and 6-shot magazine. Nickel-plated, with ivory Micarta grips with a spider engraved on them.

NIB	Exc.	V.G.	Good	Fair	Poor
700	575	450	350	300	200

Enforcer

.45-caliber semi-automatic pistol, with 3.8" barrel and 6-shot magazine. Parkerized, anodized or nickel-plated, with rubber grips. Weight about 36 oz.

NIB	Exc.	V.G.	Good	Fair	Poor
900	750	600	450	300	200

Match Master

As above, with 5" barrel and 7-shot magazine. Weight about 40 oz.

NIB	Exc.	V.G.	Good	Fair	Poor
650	500	400	350	300	200

Match Master 6"

Same as above, with 6" barrel and slide. Weight about 44 oz.

NIB	Exc.	V.G.	Good	Fair	Poor
675	550	400	350	300	200

Cohort

Fitted with 4" bull barrel. Full size frame. Magazine capacity 7 rounds. Weight about 38 oz.

NIB	Exc.	V.G.	Good	Fair	Poor
800	650	500	400	300	200

Safari G.I.

Built on Match Master frame, with 5" barrel and fixed sights. Finish is flat black Parkerized. Checkered walnut grips.

NIB	Exc.	V.G.	Good	Fair	Poor
600	450	400	350	300	200

Schuetzen Pistol Works Big Deuce

Made in Olympic Arms specialty shop called, Schuetzen Pistol Works. Marked "Schuetzen Pistol Works" on slide and "Safari Arms" on frame. Introduced in 1995. Semi-automatic pistol chambered for .45 ACP cartridge. Fitted with 6" barrel, smooth walnut grips and a number of other custom features. Magazine capacity 7 rounds. Weight about 40 oz. Black slide, with stainless steel frame.

NIB	Exc.	V.G.	Good	Fair	Poor
950	800	700	500	275	150

Schuetzen Pistol Works Crest

Similar to above model with same markings. This version features .45 ACP pistol, with 4.5", 5" or 5.5" barrel. Checkered walnut grips. Offered in both right-/left-hand configurations. Stainless steel finish. Introduced in

1993. Weight about 39 oz. depending on barrel length. **NOTE:** Left-hand model will bring a small premium.

NIB	Exc.	V.G.	Good	Fair	Poor
800	650	500	400	275	150

Schuetzen Pistol Works Griffon

Similar to above specialty models. This version fitted with 5" barrel and smooth walnut grips. Magazine capacity 10 rounds. Stainless steel finish. Numerous custom features. Introduced in 1995.

NIB	Exc.	V.G.	Good	Fair	Poor
1300	1150	975	650	400	200

Schuetzen Pistol Works Carrier

Special built model along the lines of Detonics Score Master, with adjustable sights.

NIB	Exc.	V.G.	Good	Fair	Poor
700	600	500	400	250	150

Black-Tac

Semi-automatic .45 ACP pistol treated with "black-tac" process – advantages of hard chrome without its drawbacks such as embrittlement.

NIB	Exc.	V.G.	Good	Fair	Poor
800	650	500	400	275	150

Constable

Semi-automatic pistol chambered for .45 ACP, with 4" barrel, 5.75" sight radius, 7+1 capacity, weight 35 oz. Introduced 2006.

NIB	Exc.	V.G.	Good	Fair	Poor
950	800	700	500	275	150

Custom Street Deuce

Semi-automatic chambered for .45 ACP, with 5.2" bull barrel, 7" sight radius, 7+1 capacity, weight 38 oz. Many options. Introduced 2006.

NIB	Exc.	V.G.	Good	Fair	Poor
1300	1150	975	650	400	200

Custom Journeyman

Semi-automatic chambered for .45 ACP, with 4" bull barrel, 6" sight radius, 6+1 capacity, weight 35 oz. Many options. Introduced 2006.

NIB	Exc.	V.G.	Good	Fair	Poor
1100	800	675	500	300	150

Trail Boss

Semi-automatic pistol in Westerner line chambered for .45 ACP, with 6" barrel, 8" sight radius, 7+1 capacity, weight 43 oz. Introduced 2006.

NIB	Exc.	V.G.	Good	Fair	Poor
950	800	700	500	275	150

Westerner

Semi-automatic pistol chambered for .45 ACP, with 5" barrel, 7" sight radius, 7+1 capacity, weight 39 oz. Introduced 2006.

NIB	Exc.	V.G.	Good	Fair	Poor
950	800	700	500	275	150

Model OA-93-PT

Similar to OA-93-CAR, with F8R hand guard, vertical grip, post-ban muzzle-brake and detachable stock.

NIB	Exc.	V.G.	Good	Fair	Poor
1100	800	675	500	300	150

Wolverine

Polymer-frame ventilated rib replica of old "ray gun" .22 Whitney Wolverine semi-automatic pistol. Cool, baby!

NIB	Exc.	V.G.	Good	Fair	Poor
300	265	250	200	150	100

RIFLES

SGW Ultra Match (PCR-1)

Match grade copy of AR-15, with 20" or 24" barrel. Not fitted with carrying handle. Weight about 10 lbs.

NIB	Exc.	V.G.	Good	Fair	Poor
1250	1000	800	500	400	200

Model PCR-2

Similar to above, with 16" match grade barrel, post front and E2 rear sight. Weight about 8.2 lbs.

NIB	Exc.	V.G.	Good	Fair	Poor
1300	1050	850	550	450	225

Model PCR-3

Same as above, with forged T-12 upper receiver.

NIB	Exc.	V.G.	Good	Fair	Poor
1300	1050	850	550	450	225

Model PCR-4

Fitted with 20" steel barrel. Post front sight and A-1 style rear sight. Weight about 8.5 lbs.

NIB	Exc.	V.G.	Good	Fair	Poor
900	725	575	450	350	150

Model PCR-5

Similar to above, with 16" barrel. Weight about 7 lbs.

NIB	Exc.	V.G.	Good	Fair	Poor
900	725	575	450	350	150

Model PCR-6

AR-15 style rifle chambered for 7.62x39 Russian caliber. Fitted with 16" barrel. Post front sight and A-1 style rear sight. Weight about 7 lbs.

NIB	Exc.	V.G.	Good	Fair	Poor
900	725	575	450	350	150

Model PCR-7 "Eliminator"

Shortened version of PCR-4. Fitted with 16" barrel, A2: hand guard, stock and pistol-grip. Weight about 7.6 lbs.

NIB	Exc.	V.G.	Good	Fair	Poor
900	725	575	450	350	150

Model PCR-Service Match

.223-caliber rifle has 20" stainless steel match barrel. Fitted with post front sight and E-2 style rear sight. Weight about 8.7 lbs.

NIB	Exc.	V.G.	Good	Fair	Poor
1100	800	675	500	300	150

Ultra CSR Tactical Rifle

Bolt-action rifle chambered for .308 Win. cartridge. Barrel length 26". Magazine capacity 5 rounds. Tactical-style stock is black synthetic, with aluminum bedding block. Comes complete with scope rings and Harris bipod in a hardcase. Weight about 9.4 lbs.

NIB	Exc.	V.G.	Good	Fair	Poor
1100	800	675	500	300	150

Model CAR-97

Chambered for .223 cartridge or optional 9mm, .40 S&W or .45 ACP pistol cartridges. Fitted with 16" barrel and non-collapsible CAR-style stock. Overall length 34"; weight about 7 lbs. **NOTE:** Add $50 for pistol cartridge conversion.

NIB	Exc.	V.G.	Good	Fair	Poor
900	725	575	450	350	150

Model OA-96

Model has 6" barrel with pistol-grip only, no buttstock. The 30-round magazine is pinned and cannot be detached. Break-open-action allows loading with stripper clips. Overall length 15.75"; weight about 4.2 lbs. BATFE approved.

NIB	Exc.	V.G.	Good	Fair	Poor
1100	800	675	500	300	150

Model OA-98

Similar to OA-93, with lightening holes on grip mount and magazine. Fitted with 6" barrel. No vertical grip. Weight about 3 lbs. No buttstock.

NIB	Exc.	V.G.	Good	Fair	Poor
1100	800	675	500	300	150

UM-1P

Gas-operated .223 semi-automatic target rifle based on AR-15 chassis. Features include 24" stainless steel bull barrel, anodized finish, pistol-grip with bottom swell, Picatinny rail, Harris bipod and competition trigger.

NIB	Exc.	V.G.	Good	Fair	Poor
900	725	575	450	350	150

UM-1

Similar to UM-1P, with 20" stainless steel bull barrel, standard pistol-grip, no bipod.

NIB	Exc.	V.G.	Good	Fair	Poor
900	725	575	450	350	150

SM-1P

Tricked-out AR-15 in .223 with 20" stainless steel barrel, free-floating sleeve hand guard, carry handle upper or Picatinny rail flattop, pneumatic recoil buffer, Bob Jones interchangeable sight system, competition trigger and Maxhard receivers.

NIB	Exc.	V.G.	Good	Fair	Poor
1300	1050	850	550	450	225

SM-1

Similar to SM-1P, with standard receivers, trigger and sights. No pneumatic recoil buffer.

NIB	Exc.	V.G.	Good	Fair	Poor
1000	700	575	450	300	150

ML-1

Similar to SM-1, with 16" barrel, flash hider, 6-position collapsible buttstock and free-floating aluminum tube hand guard.

NIB	Exc.	V.G.	Good	Fair	Poor
1000	700	575	450	300	150

ML-2

Similar to ML-1, with flat-top upper receiver. Picatinny rails, standard buttstock and bull barrel.

NIB	Exc.	V.G.	Good	Fair	Poor
1000	700	575	450	300	150

Model K8

Similar to ML-2, with 20" barrel and extended aluminum tube hand guard.

NIB	Exc.	V.G.	Good	Fair	Poor
1000	700	575	450	300	150

Model K8-MAG

Similar to K8, with 24" bull barrel and chambered in .223 WSM, .243 WSM or .25 WSM.

NIB	Exc.	V.G.	Good	Fair	Poor
1000	700	575	450	300	150

K3B

Features include 16" chrome-moly barrel with flash-hidefully adjustable rear sight, 6-position collapsible buttstock and carbine-length hand guard.

NIB	Exc.	V.G.	Good	Fair	Poor
900	725	575	450	350	150

K3B-M4

Similar to K3B, with M4S fiberite hand guard with heatshield. Overall length 32.25".

NIB	Exc.	V.G.	Good	Fair	Poor
900	725	575	450	350	150

K3B-CAR

Similar to K3B, with 30.5" overall length.

NIB	Exc.	V.G.	Good	Fair	Poor
900	725	575	450	350	150

K3B-FAR

Similar to K3B, with Featherweight barrel. Weight 5.84 lbs.

NIB	Exc.	V.G.	Good	Fair	Poor
900	725	575	450	350	150

K4B

Similar to K3B, with 20" barrel and rifle-length fiberite hand guard.

NIB	Exc.	V.G.	Good	Fair	Poor
900	725	575	450	350	150

K4B-A4

Similar to K4B, with ventilated FIRSH rifle-length hand guard.

NIB	Exc.	V.G.	Good	Fair	Poor
950	775	600	475	375	175

LTF

Features include 16" chrome-moly barrel, free-floating FIRSH hand guard with Picatinny rails, ACE FX skeleton stock, ERGO pistol-grip and multiple-aperture flipup sight system.

NIB	Exc.	V.G.	Good	Fair	Poor
1100	800	675	500	350	150

LT-M4

Similar to LTF, with 16" stainless steel barrel.

NIB	Exc.	V.G.	Good	Fair	Poor
1100	800	675	500	350	150

K16

Similar to K8, with 16" bull chrome-moly barrel.

NIB	Exc.	V.G.	Good	Fair	Poor
800	625	475	400	300	125

GI-16

Basic AR-15-inspired semi-automatic rifle chambered in .223. 16" chrome-moly barrel, with flash-hider, 6-position collapsible buttstock, carbine-length hand guard and rear sight adjustable for windage only.

NIB	Exc.	V.G.	Good	Fair	Poor
900	725	575	450	350	150

Plinker Plus

Similar to GI-16, with standard buttstock.

NIB	Exc.	V.G.	Good	Fair	Poor
800	625	475	400	250	100

Plinker Plus 20

Similar to Plinker Plus, with 20" barrel and rifle-length hand guard.

NIB	Exc.	V.G.	Good	Fair	Poor
850	675	525	425	300	125

K7 Eliminator

Similar to K4B, with 16" barrel, extended hand guard and sight radius of 20" barreled models.

NIB	Exc.	V.G.	Good	Fair	Poor
900	725	575	450	350	150

K30

Similar to GI-16 chambered in .30 Carbine. Includes mag well insert to accept military-spec magazines.

NIB	Exc.	V.G.	Good	Fair	Poor
900	725	575	450	350	150

K9/K10/K40/K45

Similar to K30. Chambered respectively for 9mm Parabellum, 10mm, .40 S&W and .45ACP. Models use converted surplus military magazines.

NIB	Exc.	V.G.	Good	Fair	Poor
900	725	575	450	350	150

K9-GL/K40-GL

Similar to K9 and K40. Accepts standard Glock pistol magazines.

NIB	Exc.	V.G.	Good	Fair	Poor
900	725	575	450	350	150

Model OA-93-CAR

Features include OA-93 FT recoil-reducing upper, 16" chrome-moly barrel, with Phantom flash hider and side-folding buttstock.

NIB	Exc.	V.G.	Good	Fair	Poor
1000	700	575	450	300	150

Model OA-93-PT

Similar to OA-93-CAR, with F8R hand guard, vertical grip, post-ban muzzle-brake and detachable stock.

NIB	Exc.	V.G.	Good	Fair	Poor
1000	700	575	450	300	150

Olympic Arms Gamestalker

Sporting AR-style rifle chambered in .223, .243, .25 WSSM and .300 OSSM. Features include forged aluminum upper and lower; flat top receiver with Picatinny rail; gas block front sight; 22" stainless steel fluted barrel; free-floating slotted tube hand guard; camo finish overall; ACE FX skeleton stock. Price: $1,359.

OMEGA
Springfield Armory
Geneseo, Illinois

Omega Pistol

High-grade target-type pistol patterned after Colt Model 1911 pistol, with marked improvements. Chambered for .38 Super, 10mm and .45 ACP cartridges. Barrel 5" or 6" in length and has polygonal rifling. Barrels furnished ported or plain and feature a lockup system that eliminates barrel link and bushing associated with normal Browning design. Has a dual extractor system, adjustable sights and Pachmayr grips. Introduced in 1987.

NIB	Exc.	V.G.	Good	Fair	Poor
900	725	575	450	350	150

Over/Under Shotgun

12-, 20-, 28-gauge and .410 bore boxlock over/under shotgun, with 26" or 28" ventilated rib barrels, single trigger and extractors. Blued, with walnut stock.

NIB	Exc.	V.G.	Good	Fair	Poor
—	450	300	200	150	125

Side-by-Side Shotgun

20-, 28-gauge and .410 bore boxlock double-barrel shotgun, with 26" barrels, double triggers and extractors. Blued, with hardwood stock.

NIB	Exc.	V.G.	Good	Fair	Poor
—	350	250	150	100	75

Single Barreled Shotgun

12-, 20-gauge and .410 bore single-barrel shotgun. Manufactured in a variety of barrel lengths and fitted with an extractor. Blued, with hardwood stock.

NIB	Exc.	V.G.	Good	Fair	Poor
—	125	85	65	50	35

OMEGA FIREARMS CO.
Flower Mound, Texas

Bolt-Action Rifle

A .25-06 to .358 Norma Magnum bolt-action rifle, with 22" or 24" barrel, octagonal bolt, adjustable trigger and rotary magazine. Blued, with two-piece walnut or laminated stock. Discontinued circa 1975.

NIB	Exc.	V.G.	Good	Fair	Poor
—	800	650	550	424	200

OPUS SPORTING ARMS, INC.
Long Beach, California

Opus One

A .243, .270 or .30-06 caliber bolt-action rifle, with 24" barrel, well figured walnut stock and ebony pistol-grip cap as well as fore-end tip. Built on Model 70 Winchester action. Manufactured in 1987 and 1988.

NIB	Exc.	V.G.	Good	Fair	Poor
—	2250	1600	1150	700	350

Opus Two

As above in 7mm Rem. Magnum and .300 Win. Magnum.

NIB	Exc.	V.G.	Good	Fair	Poor
—	2500	1750	1250	750	350

Opus Three

As above in .375 H&H and .458 Win. Magnum.

NIB	Exc.	V.G.	Good	Fair	Poor
—	3000	2000	1500	900	500

ORBEA & CIA
Eibar, Spain

Pocket Pistol

6.35mm semi-automatic pistol, with 2.5" barrel. Blued, with plastic grips. Slide marked "Orbea y Cia Eibar Espana Pistola Automatica Cal. 6.35". Manufactured about 1918 to 1936.

NIB	Exc.	V.G.	Good	Fair	Poor
—	250	175	125	75	50

ORTGIES, HEINRICH & CO.
Erfurt, Germany

Ortgies Pistol

6.35mm or 7.65mm semi-automatic pistol, with 2.75" or 3.25" barrel. Blued, with walnut grips. Slide marked "Ortgies & Co. Erfurt". After 1921, these pistols were manufactured by Deutsche Werke. **NOTE:** Deduct $100 for 6.35 mm.

NIB	Exc.	V.G.	Good	Fair	Poor
—	550	300	175	125	85

ORVIS
Sunderland, Vermont

Importer and retailer of sporting goods including foreign manufactured firearms. Orvis sells some of these side-by-side and over/under guns under its own name. Most are made by Beretta, Arrieta or other Italian manufacturers. Values approximate those of similar models made by gunmakers.

OSBORN, S.
Canton, Connecticut

Under Hammer Pistol

.34-caliber under hammer percussion pistol, with 7" half octagonal barrel, brass mounts and walnut grip. Barrel marked "S. Osborn/Canton, Conn."

NIB	Exc.	V.G.	Good	Fair	Poor
—		800	550	250	125

OSGOOD GUN WORKS
Norwich, Connecticut

Duplex Revolver

.22-caliber spur trigger revolver, with two super-imposed barrels: upper most .22-caliber; lower .32-caliber. Cylinder with eight .22 chambers. Hammer fitted with movable firing pin so pistol can be used as a revolver or single shot, with .32-caliber barrel. Blued or nickel-plated, with hard rubber grips. Barrel marked "Osgood Gun Works-Norwich Conn." and "Duplex". An unknown quantity manufactured during 1880s.

Courtesy Milwaukee Public Museum, Milwaukee, Wisconsin

NIB	Exc.	V.G.	Good	Fair	Poor
—	—	1600	875	350	100

OVERTON, JOHN
Nashville, Tennessee

Formerly armorer at Harpers Ferry Armory. He delivered 81 rifles copying U.S. Model 1841, with saber bayonet lug on right side of barrel. Unmarked externally but are serial numbered internally. Overall length ca. 48.75"; barrel length 33"; .54-caliber.

NIB	Exc.	V.G.	Good	Fair	Poor
—	—	18500	14000	5500	2000

OWA
Osterreiche Werke Anstalt
Vienna, Austria

OWA Pocket Pistol

6.35mm semi-automatic pistol, with 2" barrel. "OWA" logo cast in grips. Blued, with plastic grips. Manufactured between 1920 and 1925.

Courtesy Orvel Reichert

NIB	Exc.	V.G.	Good	Fair	Poor
—	400	325	200	150	1000

P.38
GERMAN WWII SERVICE PISTOL

NOTE: For history, technical data, descriptions, photos and prices see: Standard Catalog of Military Firearms.

WALTHER COMMERCIAL

Commercial version of P.38 is identified by commercial proofmarks of a crown over N or an eagle over N. Production started around serial number 1000 and went through 26659. First of commercial pistols and a high-quality well made gun, with complete inscription on left slide. Few of these early pistols were equipped with checkered wooden grips. Quality decreased as war progressed. Many variations of these commercial models and values can range up to more than $30,000. Suggested these pistols be appraised and evaluated by an expert. For post-war Walther P.38 pistols, see Walther section.

Few of Walther Commercial Model variations are listed.

MOD HP

H Prefix w/rectangular firing pin

NIB	Exc.	V.G.	Good	Fair	Poor
—	3200	2000	950	750	450

Early w/High Gloss Blue

NIB	Exc.	V.G.	Good	Fair	Poor
—	3000	1750	750	600	400

.30 caliber, extremely rare

NIB	Exc.	V.G.	Good	Fair	Poor
—	28000	—	—	—	—

Early w/High Gloss Blue & Alloy Frame

NIB	Exc.	V.G.	Good	Fair	Poor
—	10000	6500	3500	2000	1000

Croatian Contract
100 built, 6 known

NIB	Exc.	V.G.	Good	Fair	Poor
—	10000	—	—	—	—

Late w/Military Blue Finish
NOTE: Add $500 for "Eagle/359" on right side.

NIB	Exc.	V.G.	Good	Fair	Poor
—	2000	1400	750	550	350

MOD P38—Late with Military Blue
1800 produced.

NIB	Exc.	V.G.	Good	Fair	Poor
—	2700	1750	750	600	400

"ac45" Zero Series
1200 made.

NIB	Exc.	V.G.	Good	Fair	Poor
—	2800	1750	750	600	400

WALTHER MILITARY

ZERO SERIES

First Issue

NIB	Exc.	V.G.	Good	Fair	Poor
—	9500	8000	6000	3500	1500

Second Issue

NIB	Exc.	V.G.	Good	Fair	Poor
—	8000	6750	5250	2000	1000

Third Issue

NIB	Exc.	V.G.	Good	Fair	Poor
—	3500	2200	1250	800	500

480 CODE

NIB	Exc.	V.G.	Good	Fair	Poor
—	7000	5000	3250	1750	1000

"AC" CODES

This variation follows 480 code.

"AC" (no date)

NIB	Exc.	V.G.	Good	Fair	Poor
—	9000	7500	5000	3000	2000

"AC40"

Added

NIB	Exc.	V.G.	Good	Fair	Poor
—	3800	2500	1750	1000	600

Standard

NIB	Exc.	V.G.	Good	Fair	Poor
—	3000	2000	1200	700	500

"AC41"

1st Variation

NIB	Exc.	V.G.	Good	Fair	Poor
—	2200	1100	700	500	350

2nd Variation

NIB	Exc.	V.G.	Good	Fair	Poor
—	2000	1000	700	450	300

3rd Variation

NIB	Exc.	V.G.	Good	Fair	Poor
—	1500	800	600	400	300

"AC42"

1st Variation
NOTE: Add $800 for "byf" Mauser code

NIB	Exc.	V.G.	Good	Fair	Poor
—	1300	550	400	350	275

2nd Variation

NIB	Exc.	V.G.	Good	Fair	Poor
—	1100	500	400	300	250

"AC43"

1st Variation

NIB	Exc.	V.G.	Good	Fair	Poor
—	900	450	300	250	200

2nd Variation

NIB	Exc.	V.G.	Good	Fair	Poor
—	900	450	300	250	200

Single Line Slide

NIB	Exc.	V.G.	Good	Fair	Poor
—	1200	550	450	350	250

"AC44"

NOTE: Add $300 for FN frame (Eagle/140).

NIB	Exc.	V.G.	Good	Fair	Poor
—	800	450	300	250	200

"AC45"

NOTE: Add $200 for pistols with Czech barrels; barrel code "fnh".

1st Variation

NIB	Exc.	V.G.	Good	Fair	Poor
—	800	450	300	250	200

2nd Variation

NIB	Exc.	V.G.	Good	Fair	Poor
—	950	500	325	300	250

3rd Variation

NIB	Exc.	V.G.	Good	Fair	Poor
—	750	400	300	250	200

MAUSER MILITARY

"byf42"

NIB	Exc.	V.G.	Good	Fair	Poor
—	2200	1200	700	500	300

"byf43"

NIB	Exc.	V.G.	Good	Fair	Poor
—	950	550	300	250	200

"byf44"

NOTE: Add $100 for dual tone finish (combination of blue/gray components).

NIB	Exc.	V.G.	Good	Fair	Poor
—	950	550	300	250	200

AC43/44—FN slide

NIB	Exc.	V.G.	Good	Fair	Poor
—	2200	1200	725	550	400

"SVW45"

German Proofed

NIB	Exc.	V.G.	Good	Fair	Poor
—	2900	2000	1300	550	400

French Proofed

NIB	Exc.	V.G.	Good	Fair	Poor
—	650	400	300	250	200

"SVW46"— French Proofed

NIB	Exc.	V.G.	Good	Fair	Poor
—	800	500	400	350	300

MAUSER "POLICE" P.38

"byf/43"

NIB	Exc.	V.G.	Good	Fair	Poor
—	2500	1700	1200	800	500

"byf/44"

NIB	Exc.	V.G.	Good	Fair	Poor
—	2500	1700	1200	800	500

"ac/43"

NIB	Exc.	V.G.	Good	Fair	Poor
—	5000	3500	2000	1250	800

"ac/44"

NIB	Exc.	V.G.	Good	Fair	Poor
—	5000	3500	2000	1250	800

"svw/45"

NIB	Exc.	V.G.	Good	Fair	Poor
—	6000	4500	2500	1600	1000

SPREEWERKE MILITARY

"cyq"

Eagle /211 on frame

2 known.

NIB	Exc.	V.G.	Good	Fair	Poor
—	5000	—	—	—	—

1st Variation

NIB	Exc.	V.G.	Good	Fair	Poor
—	1400	1000	750	600	500

Standard Variation

NOTE: Add $250 if "A" or "B" prefix.

NIB	Exc.	V.G.	Good	Fair	Poor
—	800	400	275	250	200

Zero Series

NOTE: Add $250 for AC43 or AC44 marked "FN" slide.

NIB	Exc.	V.G.	Good	Fair	Poor
—	1250	550	400	350	275

POST-WAR PISTOLS

Standard Slides

NIB	Exc.	V.G.	Good	Fair	Poor
—	400	250	200	175	150

Single Line Code (Rare)

NIB	Exc.	V.G.	Good	Fair	Poor
—	1000	550	350	250	200

Manurhin

NIB	Exc.	V.G.	Good	Fair	Poor
—	400	300	200	175	150

P.A.F.
Pretoria Small Arms Factory
Pretoria, South Africa

P.A.F. Junior

.22- or .2 caliber semi-automatic pistol, with 2" barrel and 6-shot magazine. Blued, with plastic grips. Slide marked "Junior Verwaardig in Suid Afrika Made in South Africa". Manufactured during 1950s.

NIB	Exc.	V.G.	Good	Fair	Poor
—	350	250	125	100	70

PAGE-LEWIS ARMS CO.
Chicopee Falls, Massachusetts

Model A Target

.22-caliber single-shot lever-action rifle, with 20" barrel and open sights. Blued, with walnut stock. Manufactured from 1920 to 1926.

NIB	Exc.	V.G.	Good	Fair	Poor
—	300	225	175	125	100

Model B Sharpshooter

As above, with 24" barrel and longer fore-end.

NIB	Exc.	V.G.	Good	Fair	Poor
—	300	225	175	125	100

Model C Olympic

As above, with 24" barrel and improved sights.

NIB	Exc.	V.G.	Good	Fair	Poor
—	375	275	200	150	100

Challenge Model 49

Single-shot .22 LR boy's rifle. Manufactured cira 1925-1930. Stamped on top of barrel "Page Lewis Arms Co., Chicopee Falls, Mass USA/22 LR" Model 49. 22" long barrel, fixed front and rear sights.

NIB	Exc.	V.G.	Good	Fair	Poor
—	150	100	75	50	35

PALMER
Windsor, Vermont
E. G. Lamson & Co.

Palmer Bolt-Action Carbine

.50-caliber single-shot bolt-action carbine, with 20" round barrel, walnut half stock and full sidelock. Blued and case-hardened. Receiver marked "Wm. Palmer / Patent / Dec.22, 1863" and lock "G.Lamson & Co./ Windsor, Vt." Approximately 1,000 made in 1865.

NIB	Exc.	V.G.	Good	Fair	Poor
—	3000	2250	1500	700	250

PARA USA (PARA-ORDNANCE)

Previously known as Para-Ordnance of Scarborough, Ontario, Canada. In 2009, company relocated to Pineville, North Carolina. In January, 2012, assets of Para USA were purchased by Freedom Group, parent company of Remington, Marlin, Bushmaster and several other companies. On Feb. 9, 2015, Remington Outdoor Company (formerly Freedom Group) announced that the Para USA trademark was being discontinued and its handgun models would be integrated into the Remington brand and manufactured in a new facility in Huntsville, Alabama.

Para Elite Series

In 2013, Para USA introduced a new family of 1911-style pistols in a wide range of models. Caliber: .45 ACP, 9mm (Elite LS Hunter only). Capacity: 6, 7 or 8 rounds; 9 rounds (9mm LS Hunter). Barrel: 3", 4" or 5" (.45 models), 6" (9mm LS Hunter). Pro Model has Ed Brown mag well, HD extractor, checkered front strap and mainspring housing, Trijicon sights. **NOTE:** Add $250 for Pro Model; $200 LS Hunter.

NIB	Exc.	V.G.	Good	Fair	Poor
850	785	650	500	—	—

Para 1911 100th Anniversary

Classic 1911 styling to commemorate centennial of design. Caliber .45 ACP, military-style thumb and grip safeties, solid muzzle bushing and hammer. Three-dot sights. Weight 39 oz., 5" barrel, Covert Black finish. Smooth cocobolo grips. Comes with one 7- and 8-round magazine.

NIB	Exc.	V.G.	Good	Fair	Poor
925	775	665	500	350	200

Model P14.45

Similar in appearance to Colt Government model. This .45 ACP semi-automatic pistol features 5" barrel, flared ejection port, combat style hammer, beveled magazine well and 13-round magazine. Overall length 8.5"; weight 40 oz. for steel and stainless steel version; 31 oz. for alloy frame model. Finish black except for stainless steel model. **NOTE:** Add $50 for steel frame; $45 for stainless steel; $30 for duo-tone.

NIB	Exc.	V.G.	Good	Fair	Poor
700	550	500	400	300	200

Model P14.45 Limited

Similar to above. Extra features such as full length recoil guide, beavertail grip safety, adjustable rear sight, competition hammer, lowered ejection port, front and rear slide serrations and trigger overtravel stop. Match grade barrel. Choice of black carbon steel or stainless steel finish. Weight about 40 oz.

NIB	Exc.	V.G.	Good	Fair	Poor
1200	900	725	575	400	200

Model P14.45 LDA/P14.45 LDA Stainless

Essentially same as P14.45, with double-action trigger. Offered in black carbon steel only. Weight about 40 oz. First introduced in 1999. **NOTE:** Add $50 for stainless steel.

NIB	Exc.	V.G.	Good	Fair	Poor
800	600	400	350	225	150

Model P16.40

Essentially same as Model 14.45, except chambered for .40 S&W cartridge. Magazine capacity 15 rounds. **NOTE:** Add $50 for steel frame; $45 for stainless steel; $30 for duo-tone.

NIB	Exc.	V.G.	Good	Fair	Poor
800	600	400	350	225	150

Model P16.40 Limited

Similar to above. Extra features such as full length recoil guide, beavertail grip safety, adjustable rear sight, competition hammer, lowered ejection port, front and rear slide serrations and trigger overtravel stop. Match grade barrel. Black carbon steel finish.

NIB	Exc.	V.G.	Good	Fair	Poor
1200	900	725	575	400	200

Model P16.40 LDA

Double-action version of P16.40 in black carbon steel only. First offered in 1999.

NIB	Exc.	V.G.	Good	Fair	Poor
800	600	400	350	225	150

Model P13.45

Introduced in 1994. This .45 ACP model features 4.25" barrel, with 13-round magazine. Grip .25" longer than 12.45 model. Offered in light alloy, carbon or stainless steel. Overall length 7.75"; height 5.25"; weight about 36 oz. in steel version, 28 oz. in alloy version. **NOTE:** Add $50 for steel frame; $45 for stainless steel; $30 for duo-tone.

NIB	Exc.	V.G.	Good	Fair	Poor
600	450	350	300	200	100

Model P13.45/P12.45 Limited

Similar to above, with extra features such as full length recoil guide, beavertail grip safety, adjustable rear sight, competition hammer, lowered ejection port, front and rear slide serrations and trigger overtravel stop. Match grade barrel. Black carbon steel finish.

P13.45

NIB	Exc.	V.G.	Good	Fair	Poor
800	600	400	350	225	150

Model P12.45 LDA/P12.45 LDA

Fitted with 3.5" barrel and 12-round magazine. Features double-action trigger. Finish black. Weight about 34 oz. Introduced in 2000. **NOTE:** Add $50 for stainless steel.

NIB	Exc.	V.G.	Good	Fair	Poor
750	600	450	300	200	100

Model P12.45/P12.40

Similar to Model P14 but in a smaller package. Introduced in 1993. Has all the same features as Model P14. Magazine capacity 11 rounds. Available in alloy, steel or stainless steel. Weight 24 oz. in alloy; 33 oz. in steel. P12.40 is same model chambered for .40 S&W cartridge. **NOTE:** Add $50 for steel frame; $45 for stainless steel; $30 for duo-tone.

NIB	Exc.	V.G.	Good	Fair	Poor
800	600	400	350	225	150

Model P10.45/P10.40/P10.9

Introduced in 1996. At the time, was smallest semi-automatic .45 ACP in production. Overall length 6.5"; height 4.5". Magazine capacity 10 rounds. Barrel length 3.5". Offered in stainless steel, duo-tone or black alloy finish. Chambered for .40 S&W and 9mm cartridge. Weight about 31 oz. for stainless; 24 oz. for alloy. **NOTE:** Add $50 for steel frame; $45 for stainless steel; $30 for duo-tone.

NIB	Exc.	V.G.	Good	Fair	Poor
600	450	350	300	0	100

Model P10.45 Limited

Similar to above. Extra features such as full length recoil guide, beavertail grip safety, adjustable rear sight, competition hammer, lowered ejection port, front and rear slide serrations and trigger overtravel stop. Match grade barrel. Black carbon steel finish.

NIB	Exc.	V.G.	Good	Fair	Poor
650	500	400	300	200	100

Model P18.9

Chambered for 9mm cartridge. Fitted with 5" barrel. Finish stainless steel. Rear sight adjustable; dovetail front sight. Magazine capacity 18 rounds (10 rounds for US and Canada). Weight about 40 oz.

NIB	Exc.	V.G.	Good	Fair	Poor
775	625	500	350	200	125

Model P18.9 LDA

Double-action version of P18-9. Offered in black carbon steel only. Introduced in 1999.

NIB	Exc.	V.G.	Good	Fair	Poor
775	625	500	350	200	125

Model C7.45 LDA (Para Companion)

.45 ACP pistol fitted with 3.5" barrel. Stainless steel slide and frame. Low profile fixed sights. Magazine capacity 7 rounds. Weight about 32 oz.

NIB	Exc.	V.G.	Good	Fair	Poor
700	550	400	300	200	100

Model C6.45 LDA (Para Carry)

Similar to above, with 3" barrel and 6-round magazine. Weight about 30 oz.

NIB	Exc.	V.G.	Good	Fair	Poor
750	575	550	375	200	100

Model Stealth Carry

Introduced in 2005. Chambered for .45 ACP cartridge. Fitted with 3" barrel with Novak adjustable sights. LDA trigger. Black slide, frame and polymer grips. Magazine capacity 6 rounds. Weight about 30 oz.

NIB	Exc.	V.G.	Good	Fair	Poor
850	675	550	425	300	150

Model Para CCW

Introduced in 2003. This .45 ACP model features 4.25" barrel, with stainless steel receiver and frame. Magazine capacity 7 rounds. Fitted with LDA trigger system. Weight about 34 oz.

NIB	Exc.	V.G.	Good	Fair	Poor
900	800	650	500	350	125

Model Para Companion Carry Option

Similar to CCW above. Fitted with 3.5" barrel. Weight about 32 oz. Introduced in 2003.

NIB	Exc.	V.G.	Good	Fair	Poor
775	575	400	300	200	100

Model Tac-Four

.45 ACP model features LDA trigger system. Fitted with 4.25" barrel and stainless steel slide and frame. Early models shipped with two pre-ban

13-round magazines. Later models will ship with two 10-round magazines. Weight about 36 oz. Introduced in 2003.

NIB	Exc.	V.G.	Good	Fair	Poor
900	800	650	500	350	125

Model Tac-Four LE

Same as above. Shipped with two 13-round magazines to certified law enforcement only, back in the ban days.

NIB	Exc.	V.G.	Good	Fair	Poor
900	800	650	500	350	125

PARA PXT SERIES PISTOLS

In 2004, company introduced new extractor called Power Extractor (PXT). Company also added a number of new finishes and features for its PXT line. All Para pistols have integral ramp barrels that are of match grade quality. All pistols have full-length guide rod, match trigger, flared ejection port, extended slide lock safety, beavertail grip safety, cocobolo stocks with gold medallion and high-visibility low-mount dovetail three-dot sights.

Para introduced five finishes:

1. Sterling—All stainless steel, black slide with polished sides.

2. Stealth—Black slide, black frame with black fire controls.

3. Black Watch—Black slide, green frame with green fire controls on hi-cap models and black controls on single-stack models.

4. Regal—Black slide, black frame with stainless steel fire controls.

5. Spec Ops—Green slide, green frame with black fire controls.

SINGLE ACTION, SINGLE STACK MODELS

Model LTC

This .45 ACP pistol has 4.25" ramped match barrel, with steel receiver and Regal finish. Fixed 3-dot sights. Cocobolo wood grips, with gold medallion. Magazine capacity 7 rounds. Weight about 37 oz.

NIB	Exc.	V.G.	Good	Fair	Poor
775	575	400	300	200	100

Model LTC Alloy

As above, with alloy frame. Weight about 28 oz.

NIB	Exc.	V.G.	Good	Fair	Poor
775	575	400	300	200	100

Model LTC Stainless

Same as Model LTC, with stainless steel frame and slide. Weight about 35 oz. Introduced in 2005.

NIB	Exc.	V.G.	Good	Fair	Poor
800	625	500	400	150	125

Hawg 9

Chambered for 9mm cartridge. Fitted with 3" ramped barrel. Alloy receiver and steel slide. Fixed 3-dot sights. Black slide, frame and polymer stocks. Stainless steel fire controls. Weight about 24 oz.; 12-shot magazine. Introduced in 2005.

NIB	Exc.	V.G.	Good	Fair	Poor
800	625	500	400	150	125

Hawg 7

Caliber .45 ACP, single-action trigger, stainless steel slide, alloy frame with Griptor grooves, extended thumb and grip safeties, fiber optic front and 2-dot rear sights, 7-round magazine. Weight 32 oz., 3.5" barrel with Covert Black finish. Introduced in 2011.

NIB	Exc.	V.G.	Good	Fair	Poor
800	675	550	400	300	200

Model OPS

.45 ACP pistol fitted with 3.5" barrel. Has stainless steel frame and slide. Low mount fixed sights. Cocobolo grips. Magazine capacity 7 rounds. Weight about 32 oz. Introduced in 2005.

NIB	Exc.	V.G.	Good	Fair	Poor
850	675	550	425	300	150

Model 1911

.45 ACP model has 5" barrel, with steel receiver and Regal finish. Magazine capacity 7 rounds. Weight about 39 oz.

NIB	Exc.	V.G.	Good	Fair	Poor
775	575	400	300	200	100

1911 SSP

7+1 capacity .45 ACP 1911-style semi-automatic, with 5" barrel. Competition triggers and hammers. Fixed sights. Cocobolo grip panels. Weight 39 oz.

NIB	Exc.	V.G.	Good	Fair	Poor
925	800	675	500	400	175

GI Expert LTC

Caliber .45 ACP, single-action trigger, Commander-length stainless slide on alloy frame, extended grip safety, competition trigger, fiber optic front and 2-dot rear sights. Weight 28 oz., 4.25" barrel with Covert Black finish. Magazine capacity 8-rounds.

NIB	Exc.	V.G.	Good	Fair	Poor
750	635	500	400	300	200

1911 Wild Bunch

Designed for SASS Traditional and Modern "Wild Bunch" shooting matches. Class 1911 features. Caliber .45 ACP, traditional thumb and grip safeties, hammer, solid trigger, recoil system, 7-round magazine, plain sights and barrel without integral ramp. Weight 39 oz., 5" barrel with Covert Black finish. Introduced in 2011.

NIB	Exc.	V.G.	Good	Fair	Poor
685	585	475	400	300	200

HIGH CAPACITY, SINGLE ACTION MODELS

Warthog

Introduced in 2004. This .45 ACP pistol fitted with 3" barrel. Receiver is alloy. Black slide and frame, with stainless steel fire controls. Overall length 6.5"; height 4.5". Magazine capacity 10 rounds. Weight about 24 oz. In 2005, chambered for 9mm cartridge.

NIB	Exc.	V.G.	Good	Fair	Poor
925	800	675	500	400	175

Stainless Warthog

Stainless .45 ACP with 10+1 capacity. Barrel 3", weight 31 oz. Fixed 3-dot sights and plastic grips. Introduced 2006.

NIB	Exc.	V.G.	Good	Fair	Poor
875	675	575	400	300	150

Stealth Warthog

Chambered for .45 ACP cartridge. Fitted with 3" ramped barrel. Black alloy slide, frame and fire controls. Tritium night sights. Extended slide lock, beavertail grip and firing pin. Weight about 24 oz. Introduced in 2004.

NIB	Exc.	V.G.	Good	Fair	Poor
850	675	550	425	300	150

Slim Hawg

.45 ACP pistol with 6+1 capacity. Single-stack single-action 1911. Barrel 3", weight 30 oz. Stainless construction, checkered wood grips. Fixed 3-dot sights. Introduced 2006.

NIB	Exc.	V.G.	Good	Fair	Poor
850	675	550	425	300	150

Lite Hawg 9

Double-stack 12+1 capacity single-action 9mm in non-reflective black finish. Barrel 3", weight 31.5 oz. Fixed 3-dot sights. Introduced 2006.

NIB	Exc.	V.G.	Good	Fair	Poor
850	675	550	425	300	150

P12.45

.45 ACP model fitted with 3.5" barrel. Has stainless steel receiver and finish. Magazine capacity 10 or 12 rounds. Weight about 34 oz.

NIB	Exc.	V.G.	Good	Fair	Poor
800	625	500	400	150	125

P13.45

.45 ACP pistol has 4.25" barrel, with stainless steel receiver and Spec Ops finish. Magazine capacity 10 or 13 rounds. Weight about 36 oz.

NIB	Exc.	V.G.	Good	Fair	Poor
750	575	550	375	200	100

Midnight Blue P14-45

Double-stack 14+1 single-action .45 ACP in non-reflective black. 5" barrel, fixed 3-dot sights and black plastic grips. Introduced 2006.

NIB	Exc.	V.G.	Good	Fair	Poor
750	575	550	375	200	100

Hi-Cap LTC

Introduced in 2005. Chambered for .45 ACP cartridge. Fitted with 4.25" barrel with low mount fixed sights. Slide and frame are green, with black fire controls. Black polymer grips. Magazine capacity 14 rounds. Weight about 37 oz.

NIB	Exc.	V.G.	Good	Fair	Poor
850	675	550	425	300	150

Stealth P14.45

.45 ACP model fitted with 5" barrel. Has steel receiver with Stealth finish. Magazine capacity 10 or 14 rounds. Weight about 40 oz.

NIB	Exc.	V.G.	Good	Fair	Poor
850	675	550	425	300	150

P14.45

As above, with stainless steel receiver and finish.

NIB	Exc.	V.G.	Good	Fair	Poor
925	800	675	500	400	175

14.45 Tactical

Based upon classic Para-Ordnance 14.45 high-capacity 1911 design in .45 ACP. Stainless steel slide and frame, with 14-round double-stack magazine. Custom features include Ed Brown National Match barrel, bushing, slide stop and checkered mainspring housing; Dawson Precision mag well; ambidextrous thumb safeties; extended grip tang and accessory rail. Sights are adjustable rear and fiber optic front. Covert Black finish. Weight 42 oz., barrel length 5". PXT Tactical model same except for single-stack frame, 8-round magazine, 4.25" barrel and weight of 36 oz.

NIB	Exc.	V.G.	Good	Fair	Poor
1350	1150	875	650	350	200

P18.45

Chambered for 9mm Parabellum cartridge. Fitted with 5" barrel. Receiver and finish stainless steel. Magazine 10 or 18 rounds. Weight about 40 oz.

NIB	Exc.	V.G.	Good	Fair	Poor
850	675	525	375	200	125

HIGH CAPACITY, SINGLE ACTION, LIMITED MODELS

S12.45 Limited

.45 ACP pistol has 3.5" barrel, with stainless steel receiver and Sterling finish. Magazine capacity 10 or 12 rounds. Weight about 34 oz. Introduced in 2005.

NIB	Exc.	V.G.	Good	Fair	Poor
925	800	675	500	400	175

S13.45 Limited

.45 ACP pistol with 4.25" barrel. Stainless steel receiver and Sterling finish. Spurless hammer. Magazine capacity 10 or 13 rounds. Weight about 36 oz.

NIB	Exc.	V.G.	Good	Fair	Poor
925	800	675	500	400	175

Stealth S14.45 Limited

.45 ACP pistol fitted with 5" barrel. Has steel receiver with Stealth finish. Magazine capacity 10 or 14 rounds. Weight about 40 oz.

NIB	Exc.	V.G.	Good	Fair	Poor
925	800	675	500	400	175

S14.45 Limited

As above, with stainless steel receiver and Sterling finish.

NIB	Exc.	V.G.	Good	Fair	Poor
1000	795	600	450	275	225

Long Slide Limited

Lengthened barrel and slide for competition or hunting. Caliber .435 ACP. Weight 41 oz., barrel length 6". Front and rear slide serrations, ambidextrous thumb safeties, extended grip safety, adjustable rear and fiber optic front sight, 14-round magazine and stainless finish. Introduced in 2011.

NIB	Exc.	V.G.	Good	Fair	Poor
1200	1025	825	650	450	300

Stealth S16.40 Limited

Chambered for .40 S&W cartridge. Fitted with 5" barrel. Receiver steel with Stealth finish. Magazine capacity 10 or 16 rounds. Weight about 40 oz.

NIB	Exc.	V.G.	Good	Fair	Poor
1100	950	750	500	400	175

S16.40 Limited

As above, with stainless steel receiver and Sterling finish.

NIB	Exc.	V.G.	Good	Fair	Poor
925	800	675	500	400	175

18.9 Limited

Chambered for 9mm Parabellum. Features include stainless steel slide and frame with dual grasping grooves, 18-round magazine, adjustable rear and fiber optic front sight, ambidextrous thumb safeties, extended grip tang and competition trigger. Weight 40 oz., barrel length 5". Finish bright stainless.

NIB	Exc.	V.G.	Good	Fair	Poor
1100	875	750	575	350	200

Todd Jarrett .40 USPSA P-16

Limited edition 16+1 (or 10+1) .40 S&W custom competition pistol, with adjustable rear and fiber optic front sight. 5" barrel, weight 40 oz. Covert non-reflective black or sterling finish.

NIB	Exc.	V.G.	Good	Fair	Poor
1500	1250	900	675	450	200

Todd Jarrett .45 USPSA

Limited edition 8+1 .45 ACP caliber custom competition pistol, with adjustable rear and fiber optic front sight. 5" barrel, weight 39 oz. Covert non-reflective black or stainless finish.

NIB	Exc.	V.G.	Good	Fair	Poor
1500	1250	900	675	450	200

LDA, DOUBLE ACTION, SINGLE STACK

CARRY OPTION

Companion II

Caliber .45 ACP, Light Double Action (LDA) trigger, Commander-length stainless slide on full-size stainless frame, extended grip safety, fiber optic front sight and 8-round magazine. Weight 35 oz., 4.25" barrel, with Covert Black finish. Introduced in 2011.

NIB	Exc.	V.G.	Good	Fair	Poor
775	650	550	400	300	200

Carry Model

.45 ACP model has 3" barrel and stainless steel receiver and finish. Magazine capacity 6 rounds. Weight about 30 oz.

NIB	Exc.	V.G.	Good	Fair	Poor
925	800	675	500	400	175

Stealth Carry

Similar to above, with Stealth finish and Novak adjustable sights.

NIB	Exc.	V.G.	Good	Fair	Poor
925	800	675	500	400	175

CCO (Companion Carry Option)

.45 ACP model fitted with 3.5" barrel. Receiver and finish stainless steel. Magazine capacity 7 rounds. Weight about 32 oz.

NIB	Exc.	V.G.	Good	Fair	Poor
850	700	575	400	300	125

CCW

Similar to above, with 4.45" barrel. Weight about 34 oz.

NIB	Exc.	V.G.	Good	Fair	Poor
850	700	575	400	300	125

DOUBLE ACTION ONLY, SINGLE STACK MODELS

Black Watch Companion

.45 ACP pistol fitted with 3.5" barrel. Receiver stainless steel with black watch finish. Magazine capacity 7 rounds. Weight about 32 oz.

NIB	Exc.	V.G.	Good	Fair	Poor
850	675	525	375	200	125

TAC-S

Chambered for .45 ACP cartridge, with 4.45" barrel. Steel receiver and Spec Ops finish. Magazine capacity 7 rounds. Weight about 35 oz.

NIB	Exc.	V.G.	Good	Fair	Poor
750	575	550	375	200	100

Black Watch SSP

.45 ACP pistol has 5" barrel, with steel receiver and Black Watch finish. Fixed 3-dot sights. Match trigger. Cocobolo wood grip, with gold medallion. Magazine capacity 7 rounds. Weight about 39 oz.

NIB	Exc.	V.G.	Good	Fair	Poor
750	575	550	375	200	100

SSP

Similar to above, with stainless steel receiver and finish.

NIB	Exc.	V.G.	Good	Fair	Poor
800	625	500	400	150	125

LDA, DOUBLE ACTION, SINGLE STACK

LIMITED MODELS

Stealth Limited

.45 ACP pistol has 5" barrel, with adjustable sights. Receiver steel with Stealth finish. Magazine capacity 7 rounds. Weight about 40 oz.

NIB	Exc.	V.G.	Good	Fair	Poor
850	700	575	400	300	125

Limited

.45 ACP model has 5" barrel. Stainless steel receiver with Sterling finish. Magazine capacity 7 rounds. Weight about 40 oz. Adjustable sights.

NIB	Exc.	V.G.	Good	Fair	Poor
925	800	675	500	400	175

LDA, DOUBLE ACTION, HIGH CAPACITY CARRY OPTION SERIES

Carry 12

.45 ACP pistol with 3.5" barrel. Fitted with night sights. Receiver and finish stainless steel. Magazine capacity 10 or 12 rounds. Weight about 34 oz.

NIB	Exc.	V.G.	Good	Fair	Poor
850	700	575	400	300	125

Tac-Four

.45 ACP model fitted with 4.35" barrel. Stainless steel receiver with Spec Ops finish. Magazine capacity 10 or 13 rounds. Sights are 3-dot. Weight about 36 oz.

NIB	Exc.	V.G.	Good	Fair	Poor
850	700	575	400	300	125

Tac-Five

Light double-action 9mm with 18+1 capacity. 5" barrel, weight 37.5 oz., stainless finish, adjustable rear sight, plastic grips.

NIB	Exc.	V.G.	Good	Fair	Poor
850	700	575	400	300	125

LDA, DOUBLE ACTION, HIGH CAPACITY MODELS

Stealth Hi-Cap .45

.45 ACP pistol has 5" barrel, with steel receiver and Stealth finish. Spurless hammer. Sights are 3-dot. Magazine capacity 10 or 14 rounds. Weight about 40 oz.

NIB	Exc.	V.G.	Good	Fair	Poor
800	625	500	400	150	125

Hi-Cap .45

Similar to above, with stainless steel receiver and finish.

NIB	Exc.	V.G.	Good	Fair	Poor
800	625	500	400	150	125

Colonel

.45 ACP pistol fitted with 4.25" barrel, with low mount fixed sights. Slide and frame are green, with black fire controls. Black polymer grips. Magazine capacity 14 rounds. Weight about 37 oz. Introduced in 2005.

NIB	Exc.	V.G.	Good	Fair	Poor
800	625	500	400	150	125

Hi-Cap .40

Chambered for .40 S&W cartridge. Fitted with 5" barrel and 3-dot sights. Stainless steel receiver and finish. Magazine capacity 10 or 16 rounds. Weight about 40 oz.

NIB	Exc.	V.G.	Good	Fair	Poor
800	625	500	400	150	125

Stealth Hi-Cap 9

9mm pistol fitted with 5" barrel with 3-dot sights. Steel receiver with Stealth finish. Magazine capacity 10 or 18 rounds. Weight about 40 oz.

NIB	Exc.	V.G.	Good	Fair	Poor
800	625	500	400	150	125

Hi-Cap 9

Similar to above, with stainless steel receiver and finish.

NIB	Exc.	V.G.	Good	Fair	Poor
850	700	575	400	300	125

Covert Black Nite-Tac

Introduced in 2005. This .45 ACP pistol fitted with 5" barrel and covert black finish. Low mount fixed sights. Magazine capacity 14 rounds. Weight about 40 oz.

NIB	Exc.	V.G.	Good	Fair	Poor
850	700	575	400	300	125

Nite-Tac

As above, with stainless steel frame and slide. Introduced in 2005.

NIB	Exc.	V.G.	Good	Fair	Poor
800	625	500	400	150	125

Nite-Tac .40

.40 S&W 16+1 capacity double-action duty pistol, with fixed sights. 5" barrel, weight 40 oz., stainless finish.

NIB	Exc.	V.G.	Good	Fair	Poor
800	625	500	400	150	125

Nite-Tac 9

9mm 18+1 double-action duty pistol, with fixed sights. 5" barrel, weight 40 oz., stainless finish.

NIB	Exc.	V.G.	Good	Fair	Poor
800	625	500	400	150	125

LDA, DOUBLE ACTION, HIGH CAPACITY, LIMITED

Hi-Cap Limited .40

.40 S&W pistol has 5" barrel with 3-dot sights. Stainless steel receiver with Sterling finish. Magazine capacity 16 rounds. Weight about 40 oz.

NIB	Exc.	V.G.	Good	Fair	Poor
1000	875	725	575	400	200

Stealth Hi-Cap Limited 9

Chambered for 9mm cartridge. Fitted with 5" barrel with 3-dot sights. Receiver steel with Stealth finish. Magazine capacity 18 rounds. Weight about 40 oz.

NIB	Exc.	V.G.	Good	Fair	Poor
1000	875	725	575	400	200

Hi-Cap Limited 9

As above, with stainless steel receiver and Sterling finish.

NIB	Exc.	V.G.	Good	Fair	Poor
1200	975	825	650	450	225

Stealth Hi-Cap Ltd .45

.45 ACP pistol has 5" barrel with 3-dot sights and spurless hammer. Receiver steel with Stealth finish. Magazine capacity 10 or 14 rounds. Weight about 40 oz.

NIB	Exc.	V.G.	Good	Fair	Poor
1000	875	725	575	400	200

Hi-Cap Limited .45

Similar to above, with stainless steel receiver and Sterling finish.

NIB	Exc.	V.G.	Good	Fair	Poor
1100	975	825	650	450	225

TTR RIFLE SERIES

Para's Tactical Target Rifle based on AR platform, with 16.5" barrel, 30-round magazine. Chambered in .223 Rem./5.56x45 NATO. Flat Top upper receiver, full-length Picatinny rail, short or long-rail forearm, adjustable buttstock. Delayed impingement gas system, front and rear flip-up sights. Accepts all M16 and AR-15 magazines. Manufactured 2009 - 2011.

NIB	Exc.	V.G.	Good	Fair	Poor
1950	1700	1450	1100	900	400

PARDINI
Italy

Standard Target Pistol

.22-caliber semi-automatic pistol, with 4.7" barrel, adjustable rear sight and trigger. Blued, with two sizes of walnut grips. One suitable for use by ladies. Introduced in 1986.

NIB	Exc.	V.G.	Good	Fair	Poor
1450	1200	975	800	600	350

Rapidfire Pistol

Similar to above in .22 Short, with alloy bolt, 4.6" barrel and enclosed grip. Weight about 43 oz. Introduced in 1995.

NIB	Exc.	V.G.	Good	Fair	Poor
1450	1200	975	800	600	350

Centerfire Pistol

Similar to standard model in .32 S&W caliber. Introduced in 1986.

NIB	Exc.	V.G.	Good	Fair	Poor
1450	1200	975	800	600	350

Free Pistol

.22-caliber single-shot pistol, with 9.8" barrel, adjustable sights and grip. Furnished with barrel weights. Weight about 35 oz. Introduced in 1995.

NIB	Exc.	V.G.	Good	Fair	Poor
1550	1300	1050	900	700	450

PARKER-HALE LTD.
Birmingham, England

S&W Victory Conversion

.22-caliber double-action revolver, with 4" barrel and 6-shot cylinder. Blued, with walnut grips. Alteration of Smith & Wesson Victor model.

NIB	Exc.	V.G.	Good	Fair	Poor
—	295	200	150	100	75

Model 1200

.22-250 to .300 Win. Magnum bolt-action rifle, with 24" barrel and open sights. Blued, with walnut stock.

NIB	Exc.	V.G.	Good	Fair	Poor
700	550	450	400	350	250

Model 1100 Lightweight

As above, with 22" barrel and 4-shot magazine. Introduced in 1985.

NIB	Exc.	V.G.	Good	Fair	Poor
600	475	400	300	250	200

Model 81 Classic

.22-250 to 7mm Rem. Magnum bolt-action rifle, with 24" barrel and open sights. Blued, with walnut stock. Introduced in 1985.

NIB	Exc.	V.G.	Good	Fair	Poor
875	750	600	500	400	350

Model 81 African

As above in .375 H&H caliber. Introduced in 1986.

NIB	Exc.	V.G.	Good	Fair	Poor
1750	1200	1100	700	500	350

Model 84 Target

Similar to Model 81 in .308-caliber. Has adjustable rear sights and cheekpiece.

NIB	Exc.	V.G.	Good	Fair	Poor
1300	1000	800	600	450	250

Model 85 Sniper

As above, with scope and bipod.

NIB	Exc.	V.G.	Good	Fair	Poor
3250	2500	975	—	—	—

Model 640E Shotgun

12-, 16- or 20-gauge boxlock double-barrel shotgun. Manufactured in a variety of barrel lengths with double triggers and extractors. Blued French case-hardened, with walnut stock. Introduced in 1986.

NIB	Exc.	V.G.	Good	Fair	Poor
575	450	400	300	250	200

Model 640A

As above, with pistol-grip, beavertail fore-end and single trigger. Introduced in 1986.

NIB	Exc.	V.G.	Good	Fair	Poor
675	550	500	400	300	200

Model 645E

As above, but more finely finished and engraved.

NIB	Exc.	V.G.	Good	Fair	Poor
700	550	500	400	300	200

Model 670E

Sidelock double-barrel shotgun made on special order. Introduced in 1986.

NIB	Exc.	V.G.	Good	Fair	Poor
3000	2500	1850	1200	750	400

Model 680E—XXV

As above, with case-hardened lockplates and 25" barrels.

NIB	Exc.	V.G.	Good	Fair	Poor
3000	2500	1850	1200	750	400

BLACKPOWDER REPRODUCTIONS

1853 Enfield Rifle Musket

Three band version in .577-caliber. Barrel length 39". Rear sight graduated to 900 yards. Weight about 9 lbs.

NIB	Exc.	V.G.	Good	Fair	Poor
600	475	375	250	175	75

1858 Enfield Naval Pattern Rifle

Naval version with two bands in .577-caliber. Barrel length 33". Walnut stock, with brass furniture. Rear sight adjustable to 1100 yards. Weight about 8.5 lbs.

NIB	Exc.	V.G.	Good	Fair	Poor
550	425	325	200	125	50

1861 Enfield Artillery Carbine Musketoon

Artillery version in .577-caliber, with 24" barrel. Walnut stock, with brass furniture. Rear sight adjustable to 600 yards. Weight about 7.5 lbs.

NIB	Exc.	V.G.	Good	Fair	Poor
550	425	325	200	125	50

Whitworth Military Target Rifle

Model in .451-caliber. Barrel length 36". Weight about 9.9 lbs.

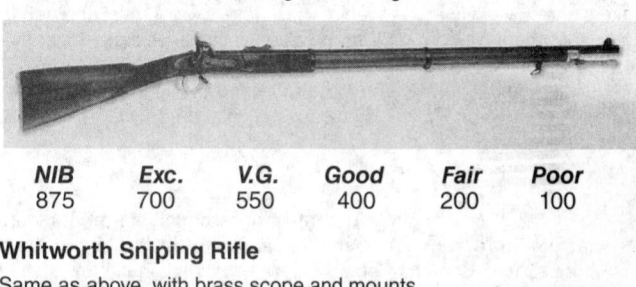

NIB	Exc.	V.G.	Good	Fair	Poor
875	700	550	400	200	100

Whitworth Sniping Rifle

Same as above, with brass scope and mounts.

NIB	Exc.	V.G.	Good	Fair	Poor
1400	1050	800	550	300	150

Volunteer Percussion Target Rifle

Rifle in .451-caliber. Fitted with 33" barrel. Two banded design, with walnut stock and brass furniture. Adjustable rear sight. Weight about 9.5 lbs.

NIB	Exc.	V.G.	Good	Fair	Poor
850	650	550	400	200	100

PARKER
Springfield, Massachusetts

4-Shot Pistol

.33-caliber percussion pistol, with 4" half-octagonal barrel and 4-shot sliding chamber. Marked "Albert Parker/Patent Secured/Springfield, Mass." Original finish unknown, with walnut grips. Prospective purchasers are advised to secure a qualified appraisal prior to acquisition.

NIB	Exc.	V.G.	Good	Fair	Poor
—	—	15000	13500	6000	2000

PARKER BROS.
Meriden, Connecticut

Perhaps best known of all American shotgun manufacturers. Established by Charles Parker shortly after the Civil War. This company has produced a wide variety of shotguns in a number of different styles over the years. In early 1930s, company was purchased by Remington Arms Company.

Parker shotguns are among the most collectible of American-made shotguns. Both beginner and veteran collectors should be aware that originality and condition are absolutely critical in establishing such high values for these shotguns. There are numerous upgraded and refinished guns that are represented as original. Beware that such misrepresentations exist, because refinished and upgraded Parker guns should sell for as much as 50 to 75 percent below the price of an original gun. Extreme caution should be exercised and we would recommend that an expert be consulted. Even the most advanced collectors may benefit from such consultations. Also, prices indicated for guns in excellent condition may fluctuate drastically, especially in high grade or small bore guns, due to their extreme rarity.

In addition, uncommon extras such as single triggers, ventilated ribs, beavertail forearms, straight-grip stocks and skeleton steel buttplates may add substantial value to an individual gun. Extra sets of factory barrels that were installed at the time of delivery will add an average of 30 percent premium. This premium will increase with grade and gauge; higher the grade and smaller the gauge, higher the premium.

Letters of authenticity are available. These letters are a must in order for any Parker gun to attain maximum value. Contact: Research Committee, Parker Gun Collectors Association, P.O. Box 126502, Harrisburg, PA 17112. Letter is $40 for members of PCGA and $100 for non-members. Much information on Parker shotguns is accessible on PGCA website: www.parkerguns.org.

VH

12-, 16-, 20-, 28-gauge or .410 bore boxlock double-barrel shotgun. Manufactured in a variety of barrel lengths with double triggers and extractors. Blued case-hardened receiver, with walnut stock. Only 2,297 guns had single triggers; only 3,983 had straight-grip stocks. Approximately 78,659 were made: 10-gauge—20, 12-gauge—51,901, 16-gauge—14,446, 20-gauge—10,406, 28-gauge—1,417, .410 bore—469. Also made with automatic ejectors and known as Model VHE. The E suffix was used on all models to denote automatic ejectors. **NOTE:** Add 40 percent VHE; 60 percent 20-gauge; 500 percent 28-gauge and .410 bore.

Courtesy Bonhams & Butterfields

NIB	Exc.	V.G.	Good	Fair	Poor
—	5500	4500	3500	2750	1850

PH

Similar to above, with a small amount of scroll engraving. Slightly better grade of walnut. Approximately 1,339 were made: 10-gauge—798, 12-gauge—839, 16-gauge—208, 20-gauge—204, 28-gauge—5, .410 bore—4. **NOTE:** Add 40 percent PHE (ejectors); 60 percent 20-gauge; extremely rare 28-gauge and .410 bore models, prices can command a 1000 percent premium.

Courtesy Bonhams & Butterfields

NIB	Exc.	V.G.	Good	Fair	Poor
—	6000	5000	4000	3200	2000

GH

Similar to above, with a modest amount of scroll and game scene engraving. Barrels marked "Parker Special Steel". Only about 430 G grades were built with straight-grip stocks. Approximately 4,291 were made: 8-gauge—11, 10-gauge—63, 12-gauge—2,501, 16-gauge—607, 20-gauge—990, 28-gauge—91, .410 bore—28. **NOTE:** Add 35 percent GHE (ejectors); 15 percent 16-gauge; 50 percent 20-gauge; 300 percent 28-gauge; 500 percent .410 bore.

NIB	Exc.	V.G.	Good	Fair	Poor
—	7500	6500	5000	4000	2500

DH

As above, but more finely finished. Engraving coverage more profuse. Most modern D grade guns were fitted with Titanic barrels. Only about 280 were built with Parker single triggers; about 280 built with ventilated ribs. Approximately 9,346 were made: 8-gauge—10, 10-gauge—45, 12-gauge—6,330, 16-gauge—1,178, 20-gauge—1,536, 28-gauge—187, .410 bore—60. **NOTE:** Add 35 percent DHE (ejectors); 15 percent 16-gauge; 50 percent 20-gauge; 300 percent 28-gauge; 500 percent .410 bore.

Courtesy Bonhams & Butterfields

NIB	Exc.	V.G.	Good	Fair	Poor
—	8800	7500	5500	4500	3000

CH

As above, with more scroll and game scene engraving coverage. Marked with Acme steel barrels. Only about 93 C grades had straight-grip stocks. Approximately 697 were made: 8-gauge—2, 10-gauge—9, 12-gauge—410, 16-gauge—105, 20-gauge—149, 28-gauge—16, .410 bore—6. **NOTE:** Add 35 percent CHE (ejectors); 10 percent 16-gauge; 40 percent 20-gauge; 400 percent 28-gauge; 700 percent .410 bore.

NIB	Exc.	V.G.	Good	Fair	Poor
—	17000	15000	11000	8000	4000

BH

As above, but offered in a variety of different styles of engraved decoration. Only about 66 guns had straight-grip stocks, 29 had beavertail fore-ends, 20 were built with ventilated ribs and 57 had single triggers. Approximately 512 were made: 10-gauge—2, 12-gauge—317, 16-gauge—71, 20-gauge—109, 28-gauge—13. **NOTE:** Prospective purchasers are advised to secure qualified appraisal prior to acquisition. Add 35 percent BHE (ejectors); 15 percent 16-gauge; 50 percent 20-gauge; 300 percent 28-gauge.

NIB	Exc.	V.G.	Good	Fair	Poor
—	22000	18500	14000	12000	5000

AH

As above, but highly engraved with finely figured walnut stocks. Most had Acme steel barrels. About 42 A grade guns were built with straight-grip stocks. Approximately 167 were made: 10-gauge—1, 12-gauge—92, 16-gauge—23, 20-gauge—44, 28-gauge—6, .410 bore—1. **NOTE:** Add 30 percent AHE (ejectors); 25 percent 16-gauge; 75 percent 20-gauge; 300 percent 28-gauge; .410 bore "priceless" as only one is believed to have been made.

Courtesy Bonhams & Butterfields

NIB	Exc.	V.G.	Good	Fair	Poor
—	36000	32000	20000	15000	5000

AAH

As above, with Whitworth or Peerless barrels. Not made in .410 bore. Engraving is more extensive and of first quality. Only 1 AA grade has ventilated rib, 10 were built with single trigger and 95 had straight-grip stocks. Approximately 238 were made: 10-gauge—2, 12-gauge—185, 16-gauge—19, 20-gauge—27, 28-gauge—5. **NOTE:** Due to rarity of this grade, prospective purchasers are advised to secure qualified appraisal prior to acquisition. Add 30 percent AAHE (ejectors); 35 percent 16-gauge; 75 percent 20-gauge; 250 percent 28-gauge.

NIB	Exc.	V.G.	Good	Fair	Poor
—	55000	45000	37500	20000	3000

A-1 Special

As above, but made strictly on special order. Not manufactured in .410 bore. Two A-1 Specials were built with ventilated rib, 7 had single triggers, 3 had beavertail fore-ends and 24 were built with straight-grip stocks. Approximately 79 were made: 12-gauge—55, 16-gauge—6, 20-gauge—11, 28-gauge—7. **NOTE:** Add 35 percent 16-gauge; 75 percent 20-gauge; 400 percent 28-gauge.

Courtesy Bonhams & Butterfields

NIB	Exc.	V.G.	Good	Fair	Poor
—	100000	80000	65000	35000	5000

Single-Barrel Trap

12-gauge single-shot, with 30", 32" or 34" barrel. Automatic ejector and walnut stock. Produced in a variety of grades as listed. Prospective purchasers are advised to secure a qualified appraisal prior to acquisition.

S.C. Grade

NIB	Exc.	V.G.	Good	Fair	Poor
—	9000	8500	6500	3500	1500

S.B. Grade

NIB	Exc.	V.G.	Good	Fair	Poor
—	11000	10000	8000	5000	2000

S.A. Grade

NIB	Exc.	V.G.	Good	Fair	Poor
—	15000	14000	12000	8000	5000

S.A.A. Grade

NIB	Exc.	V.G.	Good	Fair	Poor
—	35000	30000	25000	15000	5000

S.A-1 Special Grade

NIB	Exc.	V.G.	Good	Fair	Poor
—	40000	35000	30000	15000	5000

Under Lifter Hammer Gun

Side hammer double-barrel shotgun. Manufactured in a variety of gauges, with barrel release located in front of trigger guards. Damascus barrels, case-hardened locks, blued furniture with walnut stocks. Manufactured during 1870s and later.

NIB	Exc.	V.G.	Good	Fair	Poor
—	6000	3200	1500	800	600

Trojan

12-, 16- or 20-gauge boxlock double-barrel shotgun. Manufactured in a variety of barrel lengths, with double triggers and extractors. Only 27 Trojans were built with single triggers. Blued case-hardened receiver, with walnut stock. Approximately 33,000 were made: 12-gauge—21,977, 16-gauge—6,573, 20-gauge—5450. **NOTE:** Add 20 percent 16-gauge; 40 percent 20-gauge;

NIB	Exc.	V.G.	Good	Fair	Poor
—	3800	3000	2000	1000	600

PARKER FIELD & SONS
London, England

Gas Seal Revolver

.42-caliber percussion revolver, with 6" barrel and 6-shot cylinder. Blued case-hardened, with walnut grips. Manufactured during 1860s.

NIB	Exc.	V.G.	Good	Fair	Poor
—	—	2500	1950	900	450

PARKER GUN

Parker Gun, a division of Remington Arms Company, offers a current production of this classic shotgun. Made by Connecticut Shotgun Manufacturing Co., the AAHE Grade is offered only in 28-gauge. This made-to-order gun is priced from $49,000 and must be ordered directly from Remington, P.O. Box 700, Madison, NC 27025.

PARKER REPRODUCTIONS
Japan

Company had exact reproductions of Parker D, DHE, B and A-1 Special shotguns made in Japan. They are of the finest quality and workmanship. Styles of engraving and features of these shotguns correspond exactly to original Parker Arms. Following values are a starting point.

DHE Grade

Side-by-side shotgun offered in 12-, 20- and 28-gauge. Barrel lengths 26" or 28" with solid matte rib. Stocks are select walnut, with choice of pistol-/straight-grip. Choice splinter or beavertail forearms offered. Single-/double triggers available. Receiver case colored and scroll engraved with game scenes to match original Parker DHE grade. Weight:

12-gauge 6.75 lbs.; 20-gauge 6.5 lbs.; 28-gauge 5.3 lbs.

12 Gauge

NOTE: Add 30 percent 20-gauge; 40 percent 28-gauge.

NIB	Exc.	V.G.	Good	Fair	Poor
4000	3000	2400	1800	1200	400

16/20 Combination

Introduced in 1993. Limited to 500 sets. Offered with 28" barrels only. This set features 16-gauge barrel on 20-gauge frame. Weight 6.25 lbs.

NIB	Exc.	V.G.	Good	Fair	Poor
11000	8900	7500	3500	2000	650

28 Gauge

NIB	Exc.	V.G.	Good	Fair	Poor
6000	4250	3000	2000	1400	400

28 Gauge/.410 Bore Combination

NOTE: Add $990 for additional barrel; $170 for beavertail forearm. D Grade three-barrel sets are offered in 16/20/20 combinations for additional $2300.

NIB	Exc.	V.G.	Good	Fair	Poor
15000	12000	9000	7500	3000	1000

DHE Grade Steel-Shot Special

Offered in 12-gauge only, with 28" barrels. Fitted with 3" chambers and special chrome lined barrels. Weight 7 lbs.

NIB	Exc.	V.G.	Good	Fair	Poor
6000	5000	3950	2200	1200	400

BHE Grade Limited Edition

Features engraving similar to original Parker BHE Grade. Fancy walnut stocks with fine line checkering was standard. Offered in 12-, 20- and 28-gauge. A 28-gauge/.410 bore combination was also offered. Only 100 shotguns in this grade produced in 1989. **NOTE:** Add 20 percent for 20-gauge; 150 percent for 28-gauge or .410 bore.

NIB	Exc.	V.G.	Good	Fair	Poor
8500	6500	5000	2250	900	450

2-Barrel Set

NIB	Exc.	V.G.	Good	Fair	Poor
25000	22000	15000	10000	6000	3000

A-1 Special

Introduced in 1988. Grade featured fine scroll engraving and presentation French walnut, with custom checked pattern. Stock was hand carved with fleur-de-lis and features 32 lpi checkering. Grip cap was rosewood and gold or gold initial plate on straight-grip guns. Gold wire was used on breech end on barrels. Serial numbers were in gold relief as were the word "SAFE" and "L" and "R" on models with selective single trigger. Barrel flats and frame water table were jeweled. This grade offered in 12-, 16-, 20- and 28-gauge, with a few early guns sold with 28-gauge/.410 bore combinations. Furnished with English-style oak-and-leather case, with canvas and leather cover, engraved snap caps and engraved oil bottle.

12 or 20 Gauge

NIB	Exc.	V.G.	Good	Fair	Poor
13000	11500	9000	6500	5000	700

28 Gauge

NIB	Exc.	V.G.	Good	Fair	Poor
16000	14000	9500	7000	3500	600

28 Gauge & .410 Combination

NIB	Exc.	V.G.	Good	Fair	Poor
30000	26000	20000	12000	7000	4000

16 Gauge and 20 Gauge Combination

NIB	Exc.	V.G.	Good	Fair	Poor
35000	32000	24000	15000	7500	4000

A-1 Special Custom Engraved

A custom A-1 Special hand-engraved to each individual customer's specifications. Only limited number of these shotguns were built. Initial price in 1989 was $10,500. Sky's the limit on a gun of this sort.

PEABODY
Providence, Rhode Island
Providence Tool Company

For historical information, photos and data on Peabody military rifles see Standard Catalog of Military Firearms.

Peabody Rifle and Carbine

.43 Spanish, .443, .45 Peabody, .45-70, .50 or .50-70 caliber single-shot rifle, with 33" or 20" (carbine) barrel. Full-length or half stock. Receiver marked "Peabody's Patent July 22, 1862 / Manf'd by Providence Tool Co. Prov. R.I." Blued, with walnut stock. Produced in large quantities during 1860s and 1870s.

Courtesy Milwaukee Public Museum, Milwaukee, Wisconsin

NIB	Exc.	V.G.	Good	Fair	Poor
—	—	1950	900	300	100

Sporting Rifle

As above in sporting configuration. Barrels 26" or 28". Frame marked, "Peabody's Patent, July 22, 1862 / Manf'd by Providence Tool Co., Prov. R.I.". Blued case-hardened, with walnut stock. Manufactured approximately 1866 to 1875.

NIB	Exc.	V.G.	Good	Fair	Poor
—	—	5500	3000	1100	400

PEABODY-MARTINI SPORTING RIFLES

Creedmoor

.40-90 or .44-100 caliber Martini-action single-shot rifle, with 32" round/octagonal barrel, butt-mounted vernier rear sight, combination wind gauge and spirit level front sight. Receiver marked, "Peabody & Martini Patents" and barrel "Manufactured by the Providence Tool Co. Providence R.I. U.S.A.". Blued case-hardened, with walnut stock.

Courtesy Milwaukee Public Museum, Milwaukee, Wisconsin

NIB	Exc.	V.G.	Good	Fair	Poor
—	—	8250	3850	1650	550

Creedmoor Mid-Range

Similar to above in .40-70 or .40-90 caliber, with 28" round/octagonal barrel, vernier tang sight and wind gauge front. Blued case-hardened, with walnut stock.

NIB	Exc.	V.G.	Good	Fair	Poor
—	—	6600	3700	1400	400

What Cheer

Creedmoor, without pistol-grip.

NIB	Exc.	V.G.	Good	Fair	Poor
—	—	6600	3600	1350	400

What Cheer Mid-Range

Mid-Range Creedmoor, without pistol-grip.

NIB	Exc.	V.G.	Good	Fair	Poor
—	—	5500	3100	1100	300

Kill Deer

.45-70 caliber single-shot Martini-action rifle, with 28" or 30" round/octagonal barrels, adjustable tang rear sight and globe front. Blued case-hardened, with walnut stock.

NIB	Exc.	V.G.	Good	Fair	Poor
—	—	8250	4700	1650	500

PEAVY, A. J.
South Montville, Maine

Knife-Pistol

.22-caliber single-shot knife pistol. Constructed of steel and brass, with folding trigger. Sideplates marked "A.J. Peavy Pat. Sept. 5, '65 & Mar. 27, '66". Produced between 1866 and 1870.

NIB	Exc.	V.G.	Good	Fair	Poor
—	—	6000	4700	1900	500

PECARE & SMITH
New York, New York

Pepperbox

.28-caliber 4-/1-shot percussion pepperbox, with folding trigger and 4" barrel group enclosed within an iron casing. Blued silver-plated frame, with walnut grips. Barrel casing marked "Pecare & Smith". Manufactured during 1840s and early 1850s.

NIB	Exc.	V.G.	Good	Fair	Poor
—	—	4800	3000	1300	350

Ten-Shot Pepperbox (rare)

NIB	Exc.	V.G.	Good	Fair	Poor
—	—	9500	6600	2750	600

PEDERSEN, JOHN D.
Denver, Colorado & Jackson, Wyoming

Pedersen Rifle

NIB	Exc.	V.G.	Good	Fair	Poor
—	15000	7500	5000	2500	500

Pedersen Carbine

NIB	Exc.	V.G.	Good	Fair	Poor
—	17500	8500	6000	3000	—600

PEDERSEN CUSTOM GUNS
North Haven, Connecticut

Division of O.F. Mossberg Company. Operated between 1973 and 1975.

Model 4000 Shotgun

Mossberg Model 500 slide-action shotgun. In 12-, 20-gauge or .410 bore, with 26", 28" or 30" ventilated rib barrels. Blued engraved, with walnut stock. Manufactured in 1975.

NIB	Exc.	V.G.	Good	Fair	Poor
—	400	350	250	200	100

Model 4000 Trap

Chambered for 12-gauge only, with 30" Full choke barrel. Monte Carlo stock, with factory recoil pad.

NIB	Exc.	V.G.	Good	Fair	Poor
—	500	400	300	200	100

Model 4500

As above, with reduced amount of engraving.

NIB	Exc.	V.G.	Good	Fair	Poor
—	425	325	225	175	100

Model 4500 Trap

Same as Model 4000 Trap, with less engraving.

NIB	Exc.	V.G.	Good	Fair	Poor
—	400	350	250	200	100

Model 1500

12-gauge Magnum over/under shotgun, with 26", 28" or 30" ventilated rib barrels, single-selective trigger and automatic ejectors. Blued, with walnut stock. Weight about 7.5 lbs. depending on barrel length. Manufactured between 1973 and 1975.

NIB	Exc.	V.G.	Good	Fair	Poor
—	900	775	550	300	200

Model 1500 Skeet

Similar to above. Fitted with 27" barrels, skeet-style stock and chokes.

NIB	Exc.	V.G.	Good	Fair	Poor
—	950	825	600	350	200

Model 1500 Trap

Fitted with Monte Carlo-style stock. Choice of 30" or 32" barrels.

NIB	Exc.	V.G.	Good	Fair	Poor
—	950	825	600	350	200

Model 1000

As above in two grades of decoration. Manufactured between 1973 and 1975.

Grade I

NIB	Exc.	V.G.	Good	Fair	Poor
—	1750	1250	800	500	200

Grade II

NIB	Exc.	V.G.	Good	Fair	Poor
—	1500	1000	750	400	200

Model 1000 Magnum

Chambered for 12-gauge 3" shell. Fitted with 30" barrels.

Grade I

NIB	Exc.	V.G.	Good	Fair	Poor
—	1600	1200	800	500	200

Grade II

NIB	Exc.	V.G.	Good	Fair	Poor
—	1400	1100	750	400	200

Model 1000 Skeet

Offered in 12-gauge only, with 26" or 28" barrels. Skeet-style stock and chokes.

Grade I

NIB	Exc.	V.G.	Good	Fair	Poor
—	1750	1250	800	400	200

Grade II

NIB	Exc.	V.G.	Good	Fair	Poor
—	1500	1000	750	400	200

Model 1000 Trap

Chambered for 12-gauge. Fitted with 30" or 32" barrels. Trap-style Monte Carlo stock.

Grade I

NIB	Exc.	V.G.	Good	Fair	Poor
—	1600	1200	800	500	200

Grade II

NIB	Exc.	V.G.	Good	Fair	Poor
—	1400	1100	750	400	200

Model 2000

12- or 20-gauge boxlock double-barrel shotgun, with 26", 28" or 30" barrels. Single-selective trigger and automatic ejectors. Produced in two grades of decoration. Manufactured in 1973 and 1974.

Grade I

NIB	Exc.	V.G.	Good	Fair	Poor
—	2000	1500	1000	600	200

Grade II

NIB	Exc.	V.G.	Good	Fair	Poor
—	1750	1250	800	400	200

Model 2500

12- or 20-gauge boxlock double-barrel shotgun, with 26" or 28" barrels. Double triggers and automatic ejectors. Blued, with walnut stock.

NIB	Exc.	V.G.	Good	Fair	Poor
—	400	300	250	150	200

Model 3000

Mossberg Model 810 bolt-action rifle. Manufactured in .270 to .338 Win. Magnum caliber, with 22" or 24" barrel with open sights. Produced in three grades.

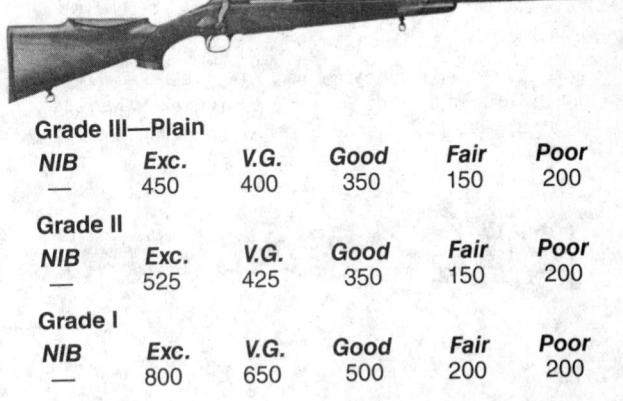

Grade III—Plain

NIB	Exc.	V.G.	Good	Fair	Poor
—	450	400	350	150	200

Grade II

NIB	Exc.	V.G.	Good	Fair	Poor
—	525	425	350	150	200

Grade I

NIB	Exc.	V.G.	Good	Fair	Poor
—	800	650	500	200	200

Model 4700

Mossberg Model 472 lever-action in .30-30 or .35 Rem. caliber, with 24" barrel and 5-shot tubular magazine. Blued, with walnut stock.

NIB	Exc.	V.G.	Good	Fair	Poor
—	450	375	275	175	100

PEDERSOLI, DAVIDE
Brescia, Italy

Davide Pedersoli & Co. was founded in 1957 by the late Davide Pedersoli. In nearly half-century since, Pedersoli has established itself as a manufacturer of extremely high-quality replica and modern firearms. Pedersoli products are frequently marked with importer's or retailer's name (e.g., Dixie Gun Works or Cabela's) rather than Pedersoli brand, usually at widely varying discounts. Many muzzle-loading rifles and pistols are available in kit form at reduced prices. **NOTE:** Rapidly-fluctuating currency markets can result in values for newly-imported Pedersoli guns being 10-15 percent higher than values listed below.

HANDGUNS

Mang In Graz Pistol

Recreation of single-shot .38- or .44-caliber percussion pistol. Made circa 1850 by Martin Mang. **NOTE:** Add 10 percent for target; 20 percent for deluxe.

NIB	Exc.	V.G.	Good	Fair	Poor
1100	750	500	400	300	150

Kuchenreuter Pistol

Recreation of single-shot .38- or .44-caliber percussion pistol. Made circa 1854 by Bartholomaus Kuchenreuter of Steinweg, Germany. **NOTE:** Add 20 percent for deluxe.

NIB	Exc.	V.G.	Good	Fair	Poor
1350	900	600	500	400	200

Mortimer Pistol

Recreation of single-shot .44-caliber pistol. First made circa 1810 by H. W Mortimer & Son of London. Smooth or rifled barrel. Percussion and flint versions available. **NOTE:** Add 10 percent for match model; 20 percent for deluxe.

NIB	Exc.	V.G.	Good	Fair	Poor
895	755	525	375	250	100

LePage Dueller

Recreation of single-shot .31-, .36- or .44-caliber dueling pistol. Made by Henry LePage circa 1840. Percussion and flint versions available. .**NOTE:** Add 20 percent for deluxe.

NIB	Exc.	V.G.	Good	Fair	Poor
895	755	525	375	250	100

Charles Moore Dueling Pistol

Recreation of single-shot .36- or .44-caliber dueling pistol. Made by Charles Moore of London circa 1800. Percussion and flint versions available. **NOTE:** Add 10 percent for target model.

NIB	Exc.	V.G.	Good	Fair	Poor
600	450	300	200	100	50

Carleton Underhammer Pistol

Recreation of saw-handled .36-caliber underhammer percussion pistol. circa 1850.

NIB	Exc.	V.G.	Good	Fair	Poor
750	600	450	300	150	75

Remington Pattern Target Revolver

Replica of Remington "1858-style" .44-caliber percussion revolver.

NIB	Exc.	V.G.	Good	Fair	Poor
450	350	250	100	75	50

Rogers & Spencer Target Percussion Target Revolver

Replica of .44-caliber Rogers and Spencer revolver, that didn't quite make it in time for Civil War.

NIB	Exc.	V.G.	Good	Fair	Poor
425	325	250	100	75	50

Kentucky Pistol

Recreation of single-shot .45-, .50- and .54-caliber pistol of American colonial era. Flint and percussion versions available. **NOTE:** Add 50 percent for "Silver Star" models.

NIB	Exc.	V.G.	Good	Fair	Poor
300	250	225	150	100	50

Bounty Pistol

Similar to Kentucky Pistol standard version, with 16" barrel. .45- or .50-caliber only.

NIB	Exc.	V.G.	Good	Fair	Poor
300	250	225	150	100	50

Navy Moll Pistol

Similar to Kentucky pistol, with brass trim. Flint and percussion versions available. .45-caliber.

NIB	Exc.	V.G.	Good	Fair	Poor
425	325	250	100	75	50

Harper's Ferry Pistol

Recreation of .58-caliber flintlock pistol procured for U. S. Navy in 1806.

NIB	Exc.	V.G.	Good	Fair	Poor
425	325	250	100	75	50

Queen Anne Pistol

Recreation of English 17th-century cannon-barrel flintlock pistol. .50-caliber smoothbore barrel. Steel or brass construction.

NIB	Exc.	V.G.	Good	Fair	Poor
375	295	225	75	50	25

An IX Pistol

Recreation of .69-caliber Napoleonic flintlock cavalry pistol of 1803. Brass trim.

NIB	Exc.	V.G.	Good	Fair	Poor
500	400	300	200	100	50

An XIII Pistol

Simplified 1806 version of An IX pistol.

NIB	Exc.	V.G.	Good	Fair	Poor
500	400	300	200	100	50

Remington Rider Derringer

Recreation of Remington Rider single-shot .177 percussion parlor pistol. Available in white or with case-hardened gold-toned or engraved/silvered finish. Pricing for basic model.

NIB	Exc.	V.G.	Good	Fair	Poor
175	150	100	75	50	25

Derringer Liegi

Recreation of circa 1850 screw-barrel percussion pocket pistol, with folding trigger and bag grip. .44-caliber. **NOTE:** Add 10 percent for engraved model.

NIB	Exc.	V.G.	Good	Fair	Poor
175	150	100	75	50	25

Zimmer Pistol

Recreation of circa 1850 single-shot percussion parlor pistol. .177-caliber; fluted grip with butt cap. Discontinued.

NIB	Exc.	V.G.	Good	Fair	Poor
500	400	300	200	100	50

Saloon Pistol

Recreation of circa 1850 single-shot percussion parlor pistol. .36- or .177-caliber. Discontinued.

NIB	Exc.	V.G.	Good	Fair	Poor
500	400	300	200	100	50

RIFLES

Swivel-Breech Rifle

Muzzle-loading over/under rotating percussion rifle in .45-, .50- or .54-caliber. Browned barrel, walnut stock. Discontinued.

NIB	Exc.	V.G.	Good	Fair	Poor
700	625	500	350	175	100

Bristlen A. Morges Target Rifle

Recreation of 1850-vintage percussion target rifle made by Marc Bristlen of Morges, Switzerland. Schuetzen-style buttplate, double triggers, false muzzle. Shoots .35- or .45-caliber elongated conical. **NOTE:** Add 20 percent for deluxe model.

NIB	Exc.	V.G.	Good	Fair	Poor
1350	900	600	500	400	200

Waadtlander Target Rifle

Similar to Bristel A. Morges target rifle. Rifled for .45-caliber round ball. **NOTE:** Add 20 percent for deluxe version.

NIB	Exc.	V.G.	Good	Fair	Poor
1350	900	600	500	400	200

Swiss Rifle

Similar to Waadtlander Target Rifle in flintlock, with 29.5" barrel.

NIB	Exc.	V.G.	Good	Fair	Poor
1350	900	600	500	400	200

Wurttemberg Mauser

Replica of 1857 Mauser military percussion rifle. Shoots .54 Minie ball. Designed for 100m target shooting.

NIB	Exc.	V.G.	Good	Fair	Poor
1000	850	700	575	400	125

Gibbs Rifle

Recreation of 1865-vintage long-range percussion rifle made by George Gibbs of London. Shoots elongated .40- or .45-caliber conicals.

NIB	Exc.	V.G.	Good	Fair	Poor
1350	900	600	500	400	200

Tryon Rifle

Recreation of noteworthy American percussion plains rifle circa 1850.

.45-, .50- or .54-caliber. **NOTE:** Add 10 percent for Creedmore; 20 percent for deluxe target.

NIB	Exc.	V.G.	Good	Fair	Poor
750	600	450	300	150	75

Mortimer Rifle

Recreation of arms made circa 1850 by H. W Mortimer & Son of London. Percussion and flint versions available. Various configurations including Whitworth, Vetterli and 12-gauge fowler.

NIB	Exc.	V.G.	Good	Fair	Poor
1050	875	600	500	400	175

Indian Trade Musket

Recreation of 18th-century flintlock smoothbore fusil as typified by colonial and early 19th-century trading companies.

NIB	Exc.	V.G.	Good	Fair	Poor
825	750	650	500	400	175

Frontier Rifle

Recreation of typical American hunting rifle circa 1800-1840. .32-, .36-, .45-, .50- and .54-caliber versions available in flintlock and percussion. Various barrel lengths.

NIB	Exc.	V.G.	Good	Fair	Poor
750	600	450	300	150	75

Kentucky Rifle

Recreation of Pennsylvania-style rifle circa 1800. .32-, .45- and .50-caliber percussion or flintlock. **NOTE:** Add 35 percent for "Silver Star" model.

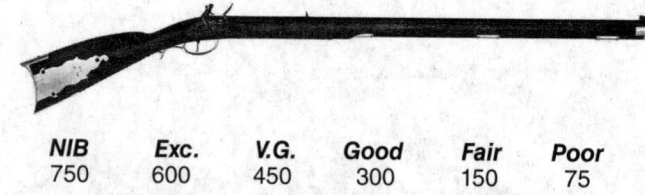

NIB	Exc.	V.G.	Good	Fair	Poor
750	600	450	300	150	75

Alamo Rifle

Recreation of long rifle used in Mexican War of 1840s. Double triggers; .32-, .45- or .50-caliber.

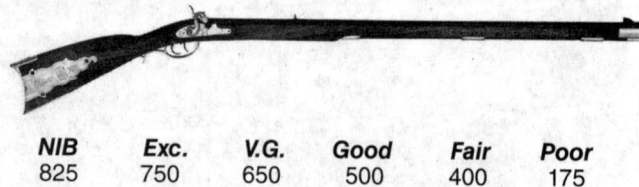

NIB	Exc.	V.G.	Good	Fair	Poor
825	750	650	500	400	175

Cub

Scaled-down Pennsylvania-type rifle in .36-, .45- or .50-caliber. Percussion or flint. **NOTE:** Add 25 percent for flint.

NIB	Exc.	V.G.	Good	Fair	Poor
550	425	350	250	200	100

Country Hunter

Exceedingly simple half-stock .50-caliber percussion or flintlock rifle.

NIB	Exc.	V.G.	Good	Fair	Poor
500	425	350	250	200	100

Jager Rifle

Massive, decidedly Germanic .54-caliber percussion or flintlock rifle based on Teutonic hunting arms, circa 1750-1850.

NIB	Exc.	V.G.	Good	Fair	Poor
950	875	700	550	375	200

Leger 1763 Charleville Musket

Recreation of Revolution-era .69-caliber smoothbore flintlock musket.

NIB	Exc.	V.G.	Good	Fair	Poor
1050	875	600	500	400	175

Revolutionnaire 1777 Musket

Similar to Charleville musket in detail. Patterned after muskets used in French Revolution.

NIB	Exc.	V.G.	Good	Fair	Poor
1050	875	600	500	400	175

Corrige An IX

Similar to Revolutionnaire 1777 musket. Differing in details of frizzen, etc.

NIB	Exc.	V.G.	Good	Fair	Poor
1050	875	600	500	400	175

An IX Dragoon Musket

Similar to Corrige An IX musket, with 40.5" cavalry-length barrel.

NIB	Exc.	V.G.	Good	Fair	Poor
1050	875	600	500	400	175

Austrian 1798 Flintlock Musket

Similar to 1777 musket, with Austrian modifications in barrel bands, bayonet mount, etc.

NIB	Exc.	V.G.	Good	Fair	Poor
1050	875	600	500	400	175

Prussian 1809 Flintlock Musket

Similar to French 1777 musket in .75-caliber with "Potsdam" markings.

NIB	Exc.	V.G.	Good	Fair	Poor
1050	875	600	500	400	175

Brown Bess Flintlock Musket

Recreation of legendary .75-caliber smoothbore musket. Used by British troops before, during and after American Revolutionary War.

NIB	Exc.	V.G.	Good	Fair	Poor
950	875	700	550	375	200

Springfield 1795 Musket

Recreation of America's first indigenous military arm, .69-caliber smoothbore.

NIB	Exc.	V.G.	Good	Fair	Poor
950	875	700	550	375	200

Harper's Ferry 1816 Musket

Recreation of U.S. martial .69-caliber smoothbore flintlock musket.

NIB	Exc.	V.G.	Good	Fair	Poor
950	875	700	550	375	200

Rocky Mountain Hawken

Faithful recreation of legendary plains rifle, .54-caliber.

NIB	Exc.	V.G.	Good	Fair	Poor
850	695	550	400	250	125

Springfield 1861 Rifle

Recreation of .58-caliber percussion rifle. Used in American Civil War.

NIB	Exc.	V.G.	Good	Fair	Poor
950	875	700	550	375	200

Kodiak Combination Gun

Percussion side-by-side rifle/shotgun combination, with 12-gauge smoothbore barrel and .50-, .54- and .58-caliber rifled barrel.

NIB	Exc.	V.G.	Good	Fair	Poor
1100	850	600	425	300	200

Kodiak Double Rifle

Side-by-side double percussion rifle in .50-, .54-, .58- and .72-caliber. Sights regulated to 75 yards.

NIB	Exc.	V.G.	Good	Fair	Poor
1200	950	700	475	325	200

Rolling Block Rifle

Replica of famous Remington rolling block single-shot rifle, circa 1867-1890. Various centerfire chamberings and configurations including Baby carbine. Prices shown are for standard version in .45-70.

NIB	Exc.	V.G.	Good	Fair	Poor
950	875	700	550	375	200

1859 Sharps Cavalry Carbine

Replica of Sharps percussion carbine with 22" barrel, patchbox and elevator sight; .54-caliber. Available as Infantry Rifle with 30" barrel.

NIB	Exc.	V.G.	Good	Fair	Poor
895	825	775	675	475	200

1862 Robinson Confederate Sharps

Similar to 1859 Sharps carbine, with different barrel band, receiver details and rear sight.

NIB	Exc.	V.G.	Good	Fair	Poor
800	675	575	400	300	125

Sharps 1863 Sporting Rifle

Replica of Sharps sporting rifle, with 32" barrel, set trigger and sculpted fore-end; .45- or .54-caliber. .45-caliber version rifled for elongated conicals.

NIB	Exc.	V.G.	Good	Fair	Poor
850	725	625	450	350	150

1874 Sharps

High-quality replica of first Sharps chambered for metallic cartridges. Chamberings include .45-70, .45-90, .45-110, .45-120, .50-70 and .50-90. Several variations available including Sporting Standard Sporting, Cavalry Rifle, Cavalry Carbine, Sporting Deluxe, Sporting Extra Deluxe, Silhouette Standard, Silhouette Deluxe, Boss, Business Rifle, Buffalo, Billy Dixon, Long Range, Quigley, Creedmore #2 and Competition Standard. Prices given are for Standard Sporting model.

NIB	Exc.	V.G.	Good	Fair	Poor
1100	850	600	425	300	200

1873 Trapdoor Springfield

Replica of famous single-shot cartridge rifle chambered in .45-70. Several variations available including Standard Rifle, Standard Carbine, Officer's Model and Long Range Model. Prices given are for Standard Rifle. **NOTE:** Add 30 percent for deluxe models.

NIB	Exc.	V.G.	Good	Fair	Poor
1100	850	600	425	300	200

Kodiak Mark IV Express Rifle

Side-by-side double rifle chambered for .45-70 cartridge.

NIB	Exc.	V.G.	Good	Fair	Poor
4500	3750	3000	2000	900	300

Pedersoli Lightning Rifle

Updated replica of Model 1883 Colt Lightning Magazine Rifle. Pump action with magazine disconnector. Chambered for .44-40 and .45 Colt.

NIB	Exc.	V.G.	Good	Fair	Poor
1100	850	600	425	300	200

SHOTGUNS

Double Percussion Shotgun

Side-by-side muzzle-loading shotgun in 10-, 12- and 20-gauge. Interchangeable chokes. Camo models available. Prices given are for basic version in 12-gauge.

NIB	Exc.	V.G.	Good	Fair	Poor
650	550	475	300	175	125

Coach Shotgun

Side-by-side 12-gauge percussion shotgun, with 20" barrels. Discontinued.

NIB	Exc.	V.G.	Good	Fair	Poor
600	525	450	275	150	125

Mortimer Shotgun

Recreation of 12-gauge Fowlers. Made circa 1830-1850 by H. W Mortimer & Son of London. Percussion and flint versions available.

NIB	Exc.	V.G.	Good	Fair	Poor
1100	850	600	425	300	200

MODERN MUZZLELOADERS

Denali

In-line .50-caliber muzzle-loader, with lever-operated break-open action. Walnut/blue or camo/blue finish. **NOTE:** Add 15 percent for camo.

NIB	Exc.	V.G.	Good	Fair	Poor
380	350	275	200	100	50

Brutus 94

In-line .50-caliber muzzle-loader. Blued/composite, blued/synthetic or stainless/blued/walnut finish. **NOTE:** Add 15 percent for camo.

NIB	Exc.	V.G.	Good	Fair	Poor
350	300	200	125	100	75

Brutus Ovation

In-line .50-caliber muzzle-loader, with interchangeable barrels. Developed in cooperation with Mid-Western Outdoor Specialties and so marked. One-piece stock. Blued/hardwood or blued/camo finish. **NOTE:** Add 15 percent for camo.

NIB	Exc.	V.G.	Good	Fair	Poor
350	300	200	125	100	75

Rolling Block Percussion Rifle

.50-caliber muzzle-loading version of Remington rolling block rifle. Blued/hardwoods or blued/camo finish.

NIB	Exc.	V.G.	Good	Fair	Poor
350	300	200	125	100	75

PERAZZI
Brescia, Italy

Company founded in 1957. During 1970s, Ithaca and Winchester imported and sold Perazzi shotguns. Perazzi has now taken over its own importation and distribution in United States, with creation of Perazzi USA, Inc. Many shooters consider Perazzi to be finest currently produced shotgun in the world. Perazzi has an extensive variety of models to choose from. In addition, each model may be available in different grades. These grades are based on type of finish, engraving and wood quality. Vast majority of Perazzi shotguns that are sold in this country are Standard Grade guns. According to Perazzi USA, these Standard Grade guns account for approximately 98 percent of North American sales. Therefore, it is unlikely that shooter or collector will encounter high-grade Perazzi guns. It should be pointed out that in some models no Extra Grade or Extra Gold Grade shotguns have ever been sold in United States. For benefit of reader, an approximate description of each grade follows. It is a general description, because Perazzi customer may order practically any combination of finishes or engraving patterns he or she desires. Use this list as a general guide. It is suggested that anyone wanting to know more about Perazzi guns buy a copy of Karl Lippard's book, Perazzi Shotguns. He can be reached at P.O. Box 60719, Colorado Springs, CO.

OUT-OF-PRODUCTION SHOTGUNS

NOTE: Very high premiums on early SCO and higher grades.

COMP 1-SB TRAP (Standard Grade)

Single-barrel trap gun in 12-gauge only, with 32" or 34" ventilated rib barrel.

NIB	Exc.	V.G.	Good	Fair	Poor
—	2500	1750	1000	750	500

COMP 1-TRAP (Standard Grade)

Over/under version of above model.

NIB	Exc.	V.G.	Good	Fair	Poor
—	4800	4000	3000	2250	500

Light Game Model (Standard Grade)

Offered in 12-gauge, with 27.5" ventilated rib barrel. Trigger group not detachable. Produced between 1972 and 1974.

NIB	Exc.	V.G.	Good	Fair	Poor
—	6250	4750	3000	1400	500

MT-6 Model (Standard Grade)

Offered in 12-gauge, with tapered ventilated rib. Trigger group not removable. Discontinued in 1983.

NIB	Exc.	V.G.	Good	Fair	Poor
—	3800	3000	2000	1000	400

MX3

Discontinued in 1988. Available in 12-gauge only for single-barrel trap, over/under trap, combination trap, skeet and sporting configurations. **NOTE:** Add 50 percent for Combination Trap Guns.

Standard Grade

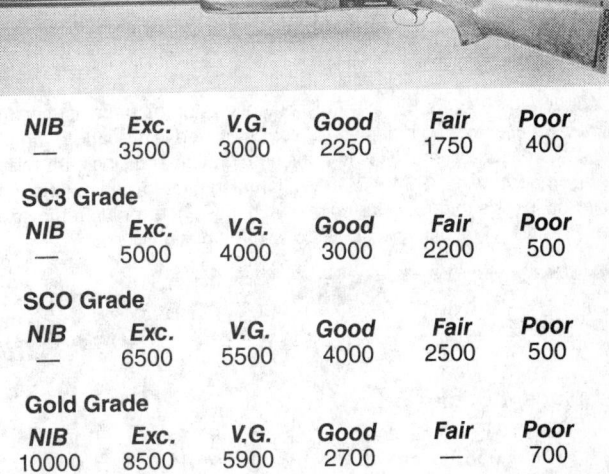

NIB	Exc.	V.G.	Good	Fair	Poor
—	3500	3000	2250	1750	400

SC3 Grade

NIB	Exc.	V.G.	Good	Fair	Poor
—	5000	4000	3000	2200	500

SCO Grade

NIB	Exc.	V.G.	Good	Fair	Poor
—	6500	5500	4000	2500	500

Gold Grade

NIB	Exc.	V.G.	Good	Fair	Poor
10000	8500	5900	2700	—	700

Grand American Special

Introduced in 1988. Features high ramped rib similar to MX3 model. Fore-end was grooved. Discontinued in 1991. Offered in these trap configurations: single-barrel, combination and over/under.

Standard Grade

NIB	Exc.	V.G.	Good	Fair	Poor
—	5250	4250	3500	2000	700

SC3 Grade

NIB	Exc.	V.G.	Good	Fair	Poor
—	6500	5250	4500	3000	700

SCO Grade

NIB	Exc.	V.G.	Good	Fair	Poor
—	8000	6500	5500	3750	700

Gold Grade

NIB	Exc.	V.G.	Good	Fair	Poor
—	10000	7500	6000	4000	700

SCO Grade w/Sideplates

NIB	Exc.	V.G.	Good	Fair	Poor
—	13500	10000	7500	6000	700

Gold Grade w/Sideplates

NIB	Exc.	V.G.	Good	Fair	Poor
—	15000	12000	8500	6500	700

SHO Model

Over/under sidelock model available in 12-gauge only, in both Type 1 and Type 2 configurations. Type 1 does not have rebounding firing pins and worth approximately 50 percent less than; Type 2 models that are fitted with rebounding firing pins. No parts available in this country or at the factory for Type 1 guns. An expert appraisal recommended for this model due to its unique features.

SHO model features silver finish with fine scroll engraving, with game scenes to customer's specifications. Select walnut stock built to customer's dimensions, with fine line checkering. Custom built shotgun. Special order only. Sky's the limit.

DHO Model

Side-by-side shotgun offered in 12-gauge only. Has full sidelocks and silver receiver finish. Scroll and game scene engraving of same quality as SHO Model. Fancy walnut stock, with fine line checkering. An expert appraisal recommended for this model due to its unique features. Special order only. Sky's the limit.

DHO Extra Gold

Available in any gauge and barrel length combination. Only finest presentation walnut and checkering. Totally custom built shotgun. Special order only. Sky's the limit.

RECENT PRODUCTION SHOTGUNS

MX9

Introduced in 1993. Features removable inserts on rib to adjust point of impact; walnut stock with adjustable comb. Offered in 12-gauge with 32" or 34" barrel. Screw-in chokes in trap configuration and single-barrels in Trap/Combo models. Competition version also offered with unique ventilated rib inserts to correct for point of impact. Trigger group removable. Available in several different grades of ornamentation.

Standard Grade

NIB	Exc.	V.G.	Good	Fair	Poor
—	6500	5000	3500	1800	700

SC3 Grade

NIB	Exc.	V.G.	Good	Fair	Poor
—	11500	6000	5000	3000	700

SCO Grade

NIB	Exc.	V.G.	Good	Fair	Poor
—	18000	8000	7000	3500	7000

Standard Grade Trap Combo

NIB	Exc.	V.G.	Good	Fair	Poor
—	9500	6500	5000	3500	900

MX10

Introduced in 1993. Single-Barrel Trap models feature different method of rib height and pattern adjustment. Has adjustable stock. Available in 12-gauge with 32" or 34" barrels. Trap/Combo models offered in 12-gauge with 29.5" or 31.5" over/under barrels with 32" or 34" single-barrel. Chokes are fixed. Competition models offered in 12- and 20-gauge with choice of 29.5" or 31.5" barrel for 12-gauge and 29.5" barrel for 20-gauge. Ventilated rib height adjustable as is comb position on stock. Trigger removable.

Standard Grade

NIB	Exc.	V.G.	Good	Fair	Poor
—	8250	7000	6000	4300	700

SC3 Grade

NIB	Exc.	V.G.	Good	Fair	Poor
—	10000	8500	7000	5200	700

SCO Grade

MX 10 Competition model

NIB	Exc.	V.G.	Good	Fair	Poor
—	13500	11000	8500	6750	700

Standard Grade Combo Model

NIB	Exc.	V.G.	Good	Fair	Poor
—	15000	13000	10500	5000	700

TM1 Special Standard Grade

Basic single-barrel Perazzi. Trap model offered in 12-gauge, with 32" or 34" barrel. Trigger adjustable.

NIB	Exc.	V.G.	Good	Fair	Poor
—	4000	2000	1250	850	700

TMX Special

Similar to TM1 Special, with select walnut.

Standard Grade

NIB	Exc.	V.G.	Good	Fair	Poor
—	5000	4200	2700	1900	700

SCO Grade

NIB	Exc.	V.G.	Good	Fair	Poor
—	8000	6000	5000	2100	700

TM9

Top-single model with sculpted nickel or blue frame. **NOTE:** Add $1200 for TM9X model with adjustable rib and comb, in V.G. or or better condition.

NIB	Exc.	V.G.	Good	Fair	Poor
6800	5500	3700	2500	2000	800

MX8 Special

Features low contour ventilated rib, adjustable trigger and grooved fore-end. **NOTE:** Some SCO engraving patterns on early models have sold in $30,000 to $45,000 price range, depending on engraver. Get an expert appraisal. Beware of counterfeits.

Standard Grade

NIB	Exc.	V.G.	Good	Fair	Poor
—	5500	4000	3000	2000	700

SC3 Grade

NIB	Exc.	V.G.	Good	Fair	Poor
—	7500	5500	3800	2500	700

SCO Grade

NIB	Exc.	V.G.	Good	Fair	Poor
—	13000	10500	8000	5000	700

Standard Grade Trap Combo

NIB	Exc.	V.G.	Good	Fair	Poor
—	7500	5000	3500	2000	700

MX8/20

First introduced in 1993. Features removable trigger group. Available in 20-gauge only. Choice of 27.5", 28.375", 29.5" flat ventilated rib barrels. Choice of fixed or screw-in chokes on sporting model. Stock custom made to customer's dimensions, with beavertail fore-end.

Standard Grade

NIB	Exc.	V.G.	Good	Fair	Poor
10000	8500	6500	4800	2000	—

SC3 Grade

NIB	Exc.	V.G.	Good	Fair	Poor
16000	14500	12000	7500	3000	—

SCO Grade

NIB	Exc.	V.G.	Good	Fair	Poor
30000	24000	17500	12000	5000	—

MX8/20-8/20C

Introduced in 1993. Offered in 20-gauge, with 26" or 27.625" ventilated rib barrels. Trigger group removable. Stock is high-grade walnut custom made to customers' specifications. Fore-end is round. MX8/20 supplied with fixed chokes; MX8/20C has 5 screw-in choke tubes. **NOTE:** Add $400 for MX8/20C values.

Standard Grade

NIB	Exc.	V.G.	Good	Fair	Poor
10500	9000	7000	5000	2250	—

SC3 Grade

NIB	Exc.	V.G.	Good	Fair	Poor
16500	13500	10000	8000	4000	—

SCO Grade

NIB	Exc.	V.G.	Good	Fair	Poor
32000	25000	20000	14000	7000	—

MX7 Standard Grade

Introduced in 1993. Over/under trap offered in 12-gauge, with 29.5" or 31.5" over/under barrels with 32" or 34" single-barrel. Has a non-renewable trigger group feathering fixed coil spring trigger mechanism. Trigger is selective and works in conjunction with safety catch. Ventilated rib is ramped on Combo Trap model. Walnut stock custom made to customer's dimensions.

NIB	Exc.	V.G.	Good	Fair	Poor
—	4500	3200	2500	1750	700

MX7C Standard Grade

Introduced in 1993. Offered in 12-gauge, with non-renewable trigger group. Has coil spring mechanism, fully selective in conjunction with safety. Offered in 27.5", 29.5" or 31.5" flat ventilated rib barrels. Screw-in chokes are standard. Walnut stock custom made to customer's dimensions. Fore-end is beavertail.

NIB	Exc.	V.G.	Good	Fair	Poor
—	5500	4000	3000	2000	700

DB81 Special

Offered in 12-gauge only. Features high ramped ventilated rib. Trigger adjustable, with internal selector. Barrel lengths 29.5" or 31.5".

NOTE: Add $1,000 for two fore-ends and two triggers for Trap/Combo models.

Standard Grade

NIB	Exc.	V.G.	Good	Fair	Poor
—	8700	6500	5200	2500	700

SC3 Grade

NIB	Exc.	V.G.	Good	Fair	Poor
—	11000	8000	7000	3500	700

SCO Grade

NIB	Exc.	V.G.	Good	Fair	Poor
—	17500	12500	10000	6500	700

COMPETITION MODELS

Competition versions are over/under shotguns in trap, skeet, pigeon and sporting models. Stock dimensions based on particular model chosen. Trap models feature trap stock dimensions and forearm designed for that purpose. Other models have their own particular specifications. However, prices are based on a common style referred to by Perazzi as Competition. Thus, all models within this group are priced the same regardless of specific type.

Mirage Special Standard Grade

Features adjustable trigger. Available in 12-gauge, with choice of 27.5", 28.375", 29.5" or 31.5" ventilated rib barrels.

NIB	Exc.	V.G.	Good	Fair	Poor
—	5500	3750	2500	1100	700

Mirage Special Sporting Standard Grade

Similar to Mirage Special, with external trigger selection and screw-in chokes. Offered in 12-gauge only. Choice of 27.5", 28.375" or 29.5" ventilated rib barrels.

NIB	Exc.	V.G.	Good	Fair	Poor
—	4500	3250	2500	1100	700

Mirage Special Sporting Classic Standard Grade

Features same basic specifications as Mirage Special Sporting. Addition of scroll border on receiver and trigger guard. Wood is slightly higher quality. Offered in 12-gauge only, with 27.5", 28.375" or 29.5" ventilated rib barrels.

NIB	Exc.	V.G.	Good	Fair	Poor
—	4500	3250	2500	1100	700

Mirage MX8 Sporting Standard Grade

NIB	Exc.	V.G.	Good	Fair	Poor
—	5800	4250	3000	1500	700

SCO Model

Similar to MX8. Offered only in 12-gauge. Barrel lengths from 27.5" to 31.5". Trigger adjustable instead of removable.

NIB	Exc.	V.G.	Good	Fair	Poor
—	10500	6000	4500	3000	700

Mirage Special 4-Gauge Set

Similar to Mirage Special in appearance and specifications. Fitted with four barrel sets with 27.62" barrels in 12-, 20-, 28-gauge and .410 bore. **NOTE:** Add $2,000 for 28.37" barrels; $3,000 for 29.5" barrels.

Standard Grade

NIB	Exc.	V.G.	Good	Fair	Poor
—	—	10000	7000	4500	700

SC3 Grade

NIB	Exc.	V.G.	Good	Fair	Poor
—	21000	15000	10000	7500	700

SCO Grade

NIB	Exc.	V.G.	Good	Fair	Poor
—	28000	19000	12500	8500	700

MX12/12C

Offered in 12-gauge only, with 26.75" or 27.5" ventilated rib barrels. Single-selective trigger nonrefillable. Walnut stock fitted with schnabel fore-end. Receiver has light-scroll engraved border. MX12 supplied with fixed chokes; MX12C fitted with 5 screw-in choke tubes. **NOTE:** Add $400 to MX12 prices to get MX12C values.

Standard Grade

NIB	Exc.	V.G.	Good	Fair	Poor
11000	9000	6800	4500	2000	1000

SC3 Grade

NIB	Exc.	V.G.	Good	Fair	Poor
18000	15000	12000	9000	5000	1200

SCO Grade

NIB	Exc.	V.G.	Good	Fair	Poor
30000	26000	20000	15000	10000	3000

MX20/20C

Offered in 20-gauge. Features non-removable trigger group. Frame smaller than 12-gauge. Offered with 26" or 27.5" ventilated rib barrels. MX20 has fixed chokes; MX20C supplied with 5 screw-in choke tubes. **NOTE:** Add $400 to MX20 prices to get MX20C values.

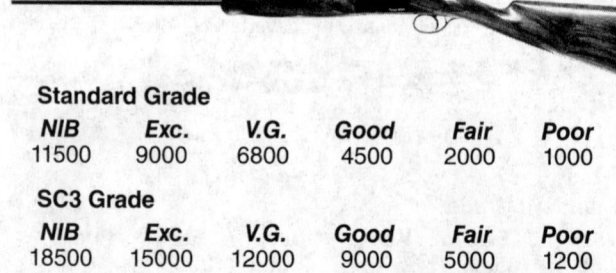

Standard Grade

NIB	Exc.	V.G.	Good	Fair	Poor
11500	9000	6800	4500	2000	1000

SC3 Grade

NIB	Exc.	V.G.	Good	Fair	Poor
18500	15000	12000	9000	5000	1200

SCO Grade

NIB	Exc.	V.G.	Good	Fair	Poor
32000	25000	20000	13500	7000	3000

MX28 and MX410

Introduced in 1993, these two models feature a non-removable trigger group and special small frame for each. MX28: .28-gauge weight about 5.5 lbs.; MX410: .410 bore weight slightly less. Both supplied with fixed chokes, flat ribs, custom made stocks and round fore-ends. Each model offered with choice of 26" or 27.5" barrels. Both MX28 and MX410 are priced the same.

Standard Grade

NIB	Exc.	V.G.	Good	Fair	Poor
21000	16000	12000	9000	6000	1000

SCO Grade

NIB	Exc.	V.G.	Good	Fair	Poor
42000	36000	29000	20000	10000	3000

MX-2000

In 12-, 20-, 28-gauge or .410 bore in several grades and styles. Standard features include fixed or removable trigger group, choke tubes or fixed chokes, fixed or adjustable ventilated rib and comb. Prices shown are for Game, Sporting, Pigeon, Skeet and Trap models. **NOTE:** Add 50 percent for Gold grades, which have higher levels of engraving, gold inlays and wood.

NIB	Exc.	V.G.	Good	Fair	Poor
8750	7750	6000	4200	3000	1000

MX-2005

This un-single model has a 34" barrel with extra-high 5-notch adjustable rib, removable trigger group and adjustable comb.

NIB	Exc.	V.G.	Good	Fair	Poor
8500	7500	5500	4000	2800	1000

PERRY & GODDARD
Renwick Arms Co.
New York, New York

Derringer

.44-caliber single-shot spur trigger pistol, with 2" octagonal barrel. Blued or silver-plated, with walnut or gutta-percha grips. Barrel may be swiveled so either end can serve as chamber and marked "Double Header/ E.S. Renwick". Produced in limited quantities during 1860s.

NIB	Exc.	V.G.	Good	Fair	Poor
—	—	21000	9400	1500	500

PERRY PATENT FIREARMS CO.
Newark, New Jersey

Perry Single-Shot Pistol

.52-caliber breech-loading percussion pistol, with 6" round barrel. Blued, with walnut grips. Barrel marked "Perry Patent Firearms Co./Newark, N.J." Approximately 200 made between 1854 and 1856 in two styles.

1st Type

Long contoured trigger guard opening lever.

NIB	Exc.	V.G.	Good	Fair	Poor
—	—	4950	1900	500	200

2nd Type

S curved shorter trigger guard. Automatic primer feed that protrudes from butt.

NIB	Exc.	V.G.	Good	Fair	Poor
—	—	4700	1650	500	200

Perry Carbine

.54-caliber breech-loading percussion carbine, with 20.75" barrel and half-length walnut stock secured by one barrel band. Blued, with case-hardened lock. Approximately 200 were made.

Courtesy Milwaukee Public Museum, Milwaukee, Wisconsin

NIB	Exc.	V.G.	Good	Fair	Poor
—	27500	13000	8250	3600	1000

PERUGINI & VISINI
Brescia, Italy

Arms by this maker were imported by W.L. Moore of Westlake Village, California.

Liberty Model

Side-by-side 12-, 20-, 28-gauge and .410 bore shotgun, with 28" barrels. Anson & Deeley action with double Purdy lock. Blued overall, with checkered walnut stock.

NIB	Exc.	V.G.	Good	Fair	Poor
7500	6000	4500	2500	1250	750

Classic Model

12- or 20-gauge double-barrel shotgun, with H&H-style sidelock and double Purdy lock. Barrels are 28". Single trigger and automatic ejectors. Sidelocks and mounts engraved and blued. Well figured checkered walnut stock.

NIB	Exc.	V.G.	Good	Fair	Poor
15000	11500	9500	4000	2000	1000

Bolt-Action Rifle

Mauser-type bolt-action rifle. Available in a variety of chamberings, with 24" or 26" barrels. Sights not furnished. Well figured checkered walnut stock.

NIB	Exc.	V.G.	Good	Fair	Poor
6500	4250	3000	1500	900	500

Deluxe Bolt-Action Rifle

As above, with first quality walnut stocks and case.

NIB	Exc.	V.G.	Good	Fair	Poor
7500	5000	3500	1500	1000	600

Eagle Single-Shot

Anson & Deeley single-shot rifle. Fitted with 24" or 26" barrels, open sights, automatic ejector and adjustable trigger. Stock of checkered walnut.

NIB	Exc.	V.G.	Good	Fair	Poor
7500	4250	4000	1500	1000	600

Boxlock Express Rifle

Anson & Deeley action double-barrel rifle. Chambered for .444 Marlin or 9.3x74R cartridges. Barrel length 24". Fitted with express sights. Double triggers and automatic ejectors. Receiver case-hardened. Barrels and mounts blued. Checkered walnut stock.

NIB	Exc.	V.G.	Good	Fair	Poor
7000	5500	3750	2000	1500	500

Magnum Over/Under

Anson & Deeley action over/under rifle. Available in .375 H&H and .458 Win. Magnum. Barrels are 24" and fitted with express sights. Double triggers and automatic ejectors. Receiver and barrels blued. Stock checkered walnut.

NIB	Exc.	V.G.	Good	Fair	Poor
7000	5500	3750	2000	1500	500

Super Express Rifle

H&H-style sidelock double-barrel rifle, with 24" barrel. Fitted with express sights. Available in a variety of chamberings. Receiver and sidelocks case-hardened or bright finish. Fully engraved. Checkered walnut stock.

NIB	Exc.	V.G.	Good	Fair	Poor
20000	17500	13000	10000	6500	1000

Victoria Side-by-Side Rifle

Similar to Boxlock Express Rifle. Chambered for .30-06, 7x65R or 9.3x74R cartridges. Barrels were 24" or 26". Double triggers and automatic ejectors. Blued, with minimal engraving. Stock checkered walnut.

NIB	Exc.	V.G.	Good	Fair	Poor
6500	5250	4000	3000	1500	750

Selous Side-by-Side Rifle

First quality double-barrel express rifle, with 24" or 26" barrels. Fully detachable H&H-style sidelocks, double triggers and automatic ejectors. Fully engraved, with well figured checkered walnut stocks.

NIB	Exc.	V.G.	Good	Fair	Poor
22500	17500	12500	6000	3000	1500

PETTINGILL C. S.
New Haven, Connecticut
Rogers, Spencer & Co.
Willowvale, New York

Pocket Revolver

Hammerless double-action .31-caliber percussion revolver, with 4" octagonal barrel. Frame of brass or iron. Blued barrel. Grips of oil-finished walnut. First and Second Models marked "Pettingill's Patent 1856" as well as "T.K. Austin". Third Model marked "Pettengill Patent 1856" and "Raymond and Robitaille Patented 1858". Approximately 400 manufactured in late 1850s early 1860s.

1st Model
Brass frame.

NIB	Exc.	V.G.	Good	Fair	Poor
—	—	2750	2000	1100	400

2nd Model
Iron frame.

NIB	Exc.	V.G.	Good	Fair	Poor
—	—	1650	1000	660	200

3rd Model
Iron frame and improved action.

NIB	Exc.	V.G.	Good	Fair	Poor
—	—	1400	800	450	200

Navy Revolver

As above in .34-caliber, with 4.5" barrel and 6-shot cylinder. Frame of iron, blued overall and grips of walnut. Marked "Pettengill's Patent 1856" and "Raymond & Robitaille Patented 1858". Approximately 900 manufactured in late 1850s early 1860s.

Courtesy Milwaukee Public Museum, Milwaukee, Wisconsin

NIB	Exc.	V.G.	Good	Fair	Poor
—	—	3500	1900	775	250

Army Revolver

As above in .44-caliber. Fitted with 7.5" barrel. Frame of iron case-hardened, octagonal barrel blued, grips of oil-finished walnut. Early production marked as Navy models, while later production examples marked "Petingill's Patent 1856, pat'd July 22, 1856 and July 27, 1858". Believed 3,400 made in 1860s. **NOTE:** Some examples will be found with government inspector's marks and worth approximately 25 percent more.

Courtesy Milwaukee Public Museum, Milwaukee, Wisconsin

NIB	Exc.	V.G.	Good	Fair	Poor
—	—	4950	2250	1650	500

PFANNL, FRANCOIS
Krems, Austria

Erika

4.25mm semi-automatic pistol, with hinged barrel assembly. Barrel length 1.5" or 2.25". Grips marked "Erika". Approximately 3,500 made between 1912 and 1926.

NIB	Exc.	V.G.	Good	Fair	Poor
—	3000	2500	1750	900	500

PGM PRECISION
France

Model PGM

Highly sophisticated semi-automatic rifle. Designed and built on modular component system. Barrel change is fast. Available calibers .308 Win., .300 Savage, 7mm-08, .243 and .22-250. Match grade barrel length 23.4". Fully adjustable trigger and buttstock. Adjustable bipod. Five-round magazine standard. Weight about 13 lbs.

NIB	Exc.	V.G.	Good	Fair	Poor
13500	9000	7000	3500	1750	1000

PHILLIPS & RODGERS INC.
Huntsville, Texas

Medusa Model 47

Introduced in 1996. Unique multi-caliber revolver. Designed to chamber, fire and extract almost any cartridge. Using 9mm, .357 or .38 cartridges—total of about 25 different calibers. Barrel length 2.5", 3", 4", 5" or 6". Rubber grips and interchangeable front sights. Finish is matte blue. Rarely if ever encountered. Discontinued.

NIB	Exc.	V.G.	Good	Fair	Poor
1100	850	550	450	275	150

Ruger 50 Conversion

Conversion executed on a new revolver converts .44 Magnum Ruger into .50 Action Express. Stainless steel or blue, with 5-shot cylinder. Barrel length 6.5".

NIB	Exc.	V.G.	Good	Fair	Poor
1000	800	550	450	275	150

PHOENIX
Lowell, Massachusetts

Pocket Pistol

Rare .25 ACP semi-automatic pistol, with 2.25" barrel and 6-round magazine. Receiver and slide blued. Grips are hard rubber. Manufactured during 1920s.

NIB	Exc.	V.G.	Good	Fair	Poor
—	950	700	350	200	100

PHOENIX ARMS
Ontario, California

HP22

Pocket-size semi-automatic pistol chambered for .22 LR cartridge. Barrel length 3"; magazine capacity 11 rounds. Offered in bright chrome or polished blue finish. Black checkered grips. Top of gun fitted with ventilated rib. Overall length 4.1"; weight about 20 oz.

NIB	Exc.	V.G.	Good	Fair	Poor
175	125	90	65	40	25

HP25

Same as above. Chambered for .25 ACP cartridge. Magazine capacity 10 rounds.

NIB	Exc.	V.G.	Good	Fair	Poor
175	125	90	65	40	25

HP22/HP25 Target

Conversion kit to convert HP22/HP25 into target pistol. Kit includes extended ventilated rib barrel and convertible 10-round magazine. Finish blue or nickel.

NIB	Exc.	V.G.	Good	Fair	Poor
100	75	60	40	30	25

Raven

Small pocket-size semi-automatic pistol chambered for .25 ACP cartridge. Magazine capacity 6 rounds. Barrel length 2.4", with fixed sights. Offered in 3 finishes: bright chrome, satin nickel or polished blue. Grips ivory, pink pearl or black. Overall length 4.8"; weight about 15 oz.

NIB	Exc.	V.G.	Good	Fair	Poor
175	125	90	65	40	25

PHOENIX ARMS CO.
Liege, Belgium

See—Robar and de Kirkhave

PICKERT, FRIEDRICH
Arminius Waffenfabrik
Zella-Mehlis, Germany

Firm produced revolvers bearing trade name "Arminius". Revolvers manufactured by Pickert are of double-action type, with or without exposed hammers. Some models fitted with ejectors, while others have removable cylinders. Calibers and barrel lengths vary. After WWII, trade name was acquired by Hermann Wiehauch.

Arminius 7.65mm

Five-shot concealed hammer revolver in 7.65mm caliber. Arminius head on grips.

Courtesy James Rankin

NIB	Exc.	V.G.	Good	Fair	Poor
—	350	225	175	125	90

Arminius Single-Shot Target Pistol

Single-shot target pistol chambered for .22-caliber cartridge. Some built under name PICKERT. Arminius name seen on frame.

Courtesy James Rankin

NIB	Exc.	V.G.	Good	Fair	Poor
—	900	700	600	400	300

Pickert Revolver

Similar to Arminius revolver, with half-round half-octagon barrel. Chambered for 7.54mm cartridge.

Courtesy James Rankin

NIB	Exc.	V.G.	Good	Fair	Poor
—	275	225	175	150	100

PIEPER, HENRI & NICOLAS
Liege, Belgium

Originally founded by Henri Pieper in 1859. Company was reorganized in 1898, when his son Nicolas assumed control. Firm perhaps best known for a series of semi-automatic pistols that are listed below. Pieper also manufactured a bewildering variety of drillings, combination guns, cape guns, rook rifles, salon rifles and even volley guns. These guns must be evaluated on their own merits and their value strictly a function of what the market will bear.

Pieper Model 1907

6.35 or 7.65mm semi-automatic pistol. Featuring hinged barrel assembly 2.5" in length. Receiver and barrel blued. Grips hard rubber with firm's trademark cast in them. Model 1907 variation does not have hinged barrel assembly. Model 1908 also known as "Basculant"; Model 1918 as "Demontant".

Courtesy Orvel Reichert

NIB	Exc.	V.G.	Good	Fair	Poor
—	250	150	125	100	75

Model 1908/Basculant

Tipping barrel pistol chambered for 6.35mm Auto cartridge. Similar in appearance to Model 1907, with several improvements. Front end of barrel retained by a pivot bolt. Recoil spring rod had a hook that engaged lug on slide.

Courtesy Orvel Reichert

NIB	Exc.	V.G.	Good	Fair	Poor
—	275	175	150	125	100

Pieper Bayard Revolver

In competition with Nagant gas seal revolver, Henri Pieper developed a superior design. Revolvers of this type have 5" barrels and chambered for 8mm cartridges. First model had automatic ejection system; second utilized swing-out cylinder. Standard finish blued. Checkered hard rubber grips.

NIB	Exc.	V.G.	Good	Fair	Poor
—	1000	750	500	250	100

Legia

Patterned after that of Browning. Chambered for 6.35mm cartridge. Standard magazine holds 6 rounds; 10-round available.

NIB	Exc.	V.G.	Good	Fair	Poor
—	250	150	125	100	75

Bayard

6.35, 7.65 or 9mm short semi-automatic pistol, with 2.5" barrel. Standard magazine capacity 6 rounds. Slide stamped "Anciens Etablissement Pieper Liege, Belgium".

NIB	Exc.	V.G.	Good	Fair	Poor
—	250	150	125	100	75

PIETTA, F.LLI
Gussago, Italy

This is a manufacturer of current and replica firearms, best known for its single-action revolvers. These models are imported by Cimarron, Taylor's and Co., Heritage, Cabela's, Dixie Gun Works and Navy Arms. Refer to these importers under their individual listings.

PILSEN, ZBROVKA
Pilsen, Czechoslovakia

Pocket Pistol

Essentially a Model 1910 Browning semi-automatic pistol, without grip safety. Pistol was 7.65mm caliber and had 3.5" barrel, with 6-round magazine. Slide marked "Akciova Spolecnost drive Skodovny zavody Zbrovka Plzen". Standard finish blued. Grips hard rubber. Manufactured during 1920s.

NIB	Exc.	V.G.	Good	Fair	Poor
—	300	200	150	125	100

PIOTTI
Brescia, Italy

Italian gun making firm located in Gardone Val Trompia in province of Brescia. Shotguns are hand crafted and limited to a few each year. Each gun made to individual specifications. Many consider them one of the best double shotguns made in the world today. Actions are Anson & Deeley boxlock or Holland & Holland sidelock. Several features offered on these shotguns at no additional cost: type of stock and forearm, barrel length and chokes, rib, action shape and finish.

Other features are considered extra cost options and will affect value of gun. These are: single triggers, detachable sidelocks, automatic safety, recoil pads, upgraded wood, engraving and multi-gauge sets. With exception of a few grades, Piotti guns are available in 10-, 12-, 16-, 20-, 28-gauge and .410 bore. Depending on gauge, barrel lengths are from 25" to 32".

Model Piuma (BSEE)

Firm's standard boxlock offering. Available in 12-gauge to .410 bore. Features ejectors and scalloped frame. Fine scroll and rosette engraving standard. **NOTE:** Around serial number 9000 or 1989, Piotti began building Model BSEE to same standards as King Model. Therefore, guns below serial number 9000 deduct about 40 percent from prices listed.

NIB	Exc.	V.G.	Good	Fair	Poor
14250	10500	7500	6000	4000	700

Westlake Model

Piotti's second quality model. Features case colored receiver, with gold line work. Offered in 12-, 16- and 20-gauge. Discontinued in 1989.

NIB	Exc.	V.G.	Good	Fair	Poor
13000	10500	8000	6000	3500	700

Over/Under Gun

Features King 2 engraving, which has light border scroll with 10 percent coverage. Custom engraving patterns available at extra charge.

NIB	Exc.	V.G.	Good	Fair	Poor
44750	33500	25000	17500	10000	1000

Model King No. I

Features sidelock with fine line scroll engraving, with full coverage. Gold crown inlaid on top lever prior to 1989. H&H or Purdey-style engraving. Select walnut, with hand checkering standard. Chambered from 10-gauge to .410 bore.

NIB	Exc.	V.G.	Good	Fair	Poor
33000	25000	18000	12500	8000	2700

Monte Carlo Model

Less expensive version of King Model. Had H&H or Purdey-style engraving. Discontinued in 1989. Upgraded and became part of King Model. This occurred around serial number 9000.

NIB	Exc.	V.G.	Good	Fair	Poor
14000	10000	7000	6000	3500	700

Model King Extra

Similar to King No. 1, with addition of a number of engraving styles from English to game scenes with gold inlays. Because of the wide variety of engraving patterns offered, it is advisable to secure a qualified appraisal before purchase.

Model Lunik

Fitted with H&H sidelocks. Engraving is Renaissance-style relief cut scroll. Gold crown inlaid on top lever. Offered in gauges from 10- to .410 bore.

NIB	Exc.	V.G.	Good	Fair	Poor
33000	25000	18000	12000	7000	1700

Model Monaco

Sidelock model features all the best Piotti has to offer. Extra attention paid to hand work and fitting. Only finest European hardwoods used. Available in 10-gauge to 410 bore. Offered with three different types of engraving designated No. 1, No. 2 and No. 4.

No. 1 or No. 2

NIB	Exc.	V.G.	Good	Fair	Poor
42000	35000	28000	19500	12000	2000

No. 3

NIB	Exc.	V.G.	Good	Fair	Poor
46000	40000	32000	22000	13000	2000

No. 4

NIB	Exc.	V.G.	Good	Fair	Poor
56000	45000	36000	28000	—	—

PLAINFIELD MACHINE CO.
Dunelien, New Jersey

Super Enforcer

Cut-down version of U.S. M1 Carbine, with 12" barrel and pistol-grip. Finish blued. Stocks walnut.

NIB	Exc.	V.G.	Good	Fair	Poor
—	600	475	375	225	100

M1 Carbine

Commercial reproduction of U.S. M1 Carbine. Finish blued. Walnut stock.

NIB	Exc.	V.G.	Good	Fair	Poor
—	400	350	225	150	100

M1 Paratrooper Carbine

As above, with telescoping wire buttstock and walnut fore-end.

NIB	Exc.	V.G.	Good	Fair	Poor
—	475	375	275	200	125

PLAINFIELD ORDNANCE CO.
Middlesex, New Jersey

Stainless steel .22-caliber semi-automatic pistol, with 10-shot magazine and 1" barrel. Also available in .25 ACP. Conversion kits were available.

Model 71

Conversion Kit

NIB	Exc.	V.G.	Good	Fair	Poor
—	50	40	30	25	20

.22 or .25 Caliber Pistol

NIB	Exc.	V.G.	Good	Fair	Poor
—	175	125	100	75	50

Model 72

As above, with alloy frame.

NIB	Exc.	V.G.	Good	Fair	Poor
—	175	125	100	75	50

PLANT'S MANUFACTURING CO.
New Haven, Connecticut

Army Model Revolver

Large single-action revolver. Chambered for .42-caliber cup-primed cartridge that loads from front of cylinder. Barrel length 6" and octagonal form with rib. Frame made of brass or iron. Finish blued, with walnut or rosewood grips. Interchangeable percussion cylinders also made for these revolvers. If present, values would be increased approximately 30 percent. Revolver was marketed by Merwin & Bray. Approximately 1,500 of 1st and 2nd Models manufactured; 10,000 of 3rd Model in 1860s.

1st Model Brass Frame

Marked "Plant's Mfg. Co. New Haven, Ct." on barrel, "M & B" on side of frame and "Patented July 12, 1859" on cylinder. Approximately 100 manufactured.

NIB	Exc.	V.G.	Good	Fair	Poor
—	—	2750	1025	700	150

1st Model Iron Frame

As above, with iron frame. Approximately 500 made.

NIB	Exc.	V.G.	Good	Fair	Poor
—	—	2750	1025	700	300

2nd Model Rounded Brass Frame

Distinguished by markings "Merwin & Bray, New York" on frame and patent date "July 21, 1863". Approximately 300 made.

NIB	Exc.	V.G.	Good	Fair	Poor
—	—	3600	1400	700	300

2nd Model Iron Frame

As above, with iron frame.

NIB	Exc.	V.G.	Good	Fair	Poor
—	—	2500	825	500	300

3rd Model

As above, with flat brass frame.

Courtesy Milwaukee Public Museum, Milwaukee, Wisconsin

NIB	Exc.	V.G.	Good	Fair	Poor
—	—	1900	1300	450	150

Pocket Revolver

Similar to Army model described above except chambered for .30-caliber cartridges. Barrel length 3.5", 5-shot cylinder. Frame normally silver plated, barrel and cylinder blued and grips of rosewood or walnut. Model encountered with a variety of retailer's markings: Eagle Arms Co., New York, "Reynolds, Plant & Hotchkiss, New Haven, Ct.", and "Merwin & Bray Firearms Co., N.Y." Approximately 20,000 were made.

Courtesy Milwaukee Public Museum, Milwaukee, Wisconsin

NIB	Exc.	V.G.	Good	Fair	Poor
—	—	1100	600	250	100

POINTER
Hopkins & Allen
Norwich, Connecticut

Single-Shot Derringer

Unmarked Hopkins & Allen single-shot pistol stamped "Pointer" on barrel. Barrel length 2.75", caliber .22, frame of nickel-plated brass. Barrel swings sideways for loading. Bird's-head walnut grips. Believed about 2,500 made between 1870 and 1890.

NIB	Exc.	V.G.	Good	Fair	Poor
—	—	450	375	250	100

POLY-TECHNOLOGIES, INC./POLY-TECH
China

SKS

Semi-automatic rifle. Chambered for 7.62x39mm cartridge, with 20.5" barrel and 10-shot fixed magazine. Based on Soviet Siminov carbine. Finish blued. Stock and hand guard made of Chinese hardwood.

NIB	Exc.	V.G.	Good	Fair	Poor
425	375	200	150	100	50

AKS-762

Semi-automatic version of Chinese-type 56 Assault rifle. Chambered for 7.62x39mm cartridge, with 16.5" barrel. Furnished with 20-round magazine and Chinese bayonet. Finish blued. Stock is hardwood. **NOTE:** Add $250 folding stock model; 15 percent for milled receiver.

NIB	Exc.	V.G.	Good	Fair	Poor
950	800	675	500	350	200

AK-47/S

Chambered for 7.62x39 cartridge. **NOTE:** Add $350 folding stock model; $15 with Soviet-style bayonet.

NIB	Exc.	V.G.	Good	Fair	Poor
1350	1150	850	750	600	400

M-14/S

Reproduction of U.S. M14 rifle. Chambered for 7.62mm cartridge, with 22" barrel and 20-round magazine. Finish blued. Stock is hardwood.

NIB	Exc.	V.G.	Good	Fair	Poor
1000	875	675	500	350	200

POND, LUCIUS, W.
Worcester, Massachusetts

Pocket Revolver

Single-action spur trigger .32-caliber revolver, with octagonal barrels of 4", 5" or 6" length. Barrel top strap and cylinder pivot upwards for loading. Made with brass or iron frames. A screwdriver fitted in butt. Revolvers were an infringement of Rollin White's patent, they were discontinued. Some revolvers found with inscription "Manuf'd. for Smith & Wesson Pat'd. April 5, 1855". These examples worth approximately 20 percent more than values listed.

Courtesy Milwaukee Public Museum, Milwaukee, Wisconsin

Brass Framed Revolver

NIB	Exc.	V.G.	Good	Fair	Poor
—	—	1100	875	350	100

Iron Framed Revolver

NIB	Exc.	V.G.	Good	Fair	Poor
—	—	1000	775	300	75

Separate Chamber Revolver

To avoid Rollin White patent, this revolver chambered for .22- or .32-caliber rimfire cartridges that fit into separate steel chamber inserts that can be removed from front of cylinder for loading. The .22-caliber version has 3.5" octagonal barrel with 7-round unfluted cylinder; .32-caliber version has 4", 5" or 6" octagonal barrel and 6-shot unfluted cylinder. Frames are silver-plated brass. Barrels and cylinders blued. Grips of walnut. Standard markings include "L.W. Pond, Worcester, Mass." and patent dates. Approximately 2,000 manufactured in .22-caliber; 5,000 in .32-caliber between 1863 and 1870.

.22 Caliber Version

NIB	Exc.	V.G.	Good	Fair	Poor
—	—	1750	1400	550	150

.32 Caliber Version

NIB	Exc.	V.G.	Good	Fair	Poor
—	—	1750	1400	550	150

PORTER, P. W.
New York, New York

Turret Revolver

Extremely rare 9-shot vertical cylinder .41-caliber percussion revolver, with 5.25" round barrel. Trigger guard is also a lever that turns cylinder and cocks hammer. Automatic primer system also fitted to this revolver. Manufactured during 1850s in an unknown quantity.

NIB	Exc.	V.G.	Good	Fair	Poor
—	—	23500	19500	8800	100

Turret Rifle

9-shot vertical cylinder .44-caliber rifle, with 26" or 28" octagonal barrel. Only markings are "Address P.W. Porter/New York". Four variations of this rifle known. The 22" barreled carbine would command 25 percent premium. Approximately 1,250 manufactured during 1850s.

1st Model with Canister Magazine

Fitted with a 30-shot round canister magazine over turret. Made in Tennessee and extremely rare. Most often canisters are not encountered and values reflect this. Approximately 25 made.

NIB	Exc.	V.G.	Good	Fair	Poor
—	—	37500	30000	13500	2000

2nd Model (New York)

NIB	Exc.	V.G.	Good	Fair	Poor
—	—	15000	12000	5125	1000

3rd Model (New York)

Model has screw-off cover over magazine.

NIB	Exc.	V.G.	Good	Fair	Poor
—	—	13000	1050	5200	1000

4th Model (New York)

As above, without automatic primer magazine. Nipples are exposed.

NIB	Exc.	V.G.	Good	Fair	Poor
—	—	10500	8800	4150	750

PRAHA ZBROJOVKA
Prague, Czechoslovakia

Established in 1918 by A. Novotny. Company ceased operations in 1926.

VZ2L

7.65mm semi-automatic pistol. Patterned after Model 1910 Browning, without grip safety. Barrel length 3.5", magazine capacity 6 rounds, grips of wood. Slide marked "Zbrojowka Praga Praha".

NIB	Exc.	V.G.	Good	Fair	Poor
—	400	250	200	150	100

Praga 1921

6.35mm semi-automatic pistol, with slide of stamped steel cut with a finger groove at front. Folding trigger. Barrel 2" in length. Slide marked "Zbrojowka Praga Praha Patent Cal 6.35". Grips of molded plastic, with name "Praga" cast in them. A dangerous feature of this pistol is that it is striker-fired with no hammer. Intended to be carried fully loaded and cocked in the pocket with absolutely no safety of any kind. I do not recommend this. Folding trigger does not spring out until slide is drawn back slightly by using finger groove in front of it.

NIB	Exc.	V.G.	Good	Fair	Poor
—	375	225	200	150	100

PRAIRIE GUN WORKS
Winnipeg, Manitoba, Canada

M-15

Lightweight mountain rifle chambered for .22-250, 6mm-284, .25-284, 6.5-284, 7mm-08, .308 Win. and most short calibers. Built on Remington 700 action, with 20" lightweight barrel. Stock is Kevlar and comes in green, black or gray. Barrel length usually 20". Weight about 4.75 lbs.

NIB	Exc.	V.G.	Good	Fair	Poor
2600	2200	1750	1200	800	500

M-18

Similar to above. Chambered for long action calibers. Fitted with barrel lengths from 22" to 24". Weight about 5.25 lbs.

NIB	Exc.	V.G.	Good	Fair	Poor
2600	2200	1750	1200	800	500

PRANDELLI & GASPARINI
Brescia, Italy

Boxlock Side-by-Side Shotgun

Good quality double-barrel 12- or 20-gauge shotgun, with 26" or 28" barrels. Single-selective trigger, automatic ejectors and Anson & Deeley action. Blued, stock of select walnut.

NIB	Exc.	V.G.	Good	Fair	Poor
—	2500	1750	1100	700	450

Sidelock Side-by-Side Shotgun

Similar to above, with full sidelocks.

NIB	Exc.	V.G.	Good	Fair	Poor
—	3500	2650	1500	900	500

Boxlock Over/Under Shotgun

Over/under double-barrel 12- or 20-gauge shotgun, with 26" or 28" barrels, single triggers and automatic ejectors. Blued, with select walnut stock.

NIB	Exc.	V.G.	Good	Fair	Poor
—	2750	1850	1200	900	350

Sidelock Over/Under Shotgun

As above, with full sidelocks.

NIB	Exc.	V.G.	Good	Fair	Poor
—	3000	2500	1800	950	450

PRATT, GEORGE
Middletown, Connecticut

Trap Gun

Doubled-barreled stationary burglar alarm or animal trap gun. Chambered for .38-caliber centerfire. Barrel 4" in length. All components are made of cast iron, with galvanized finish. Barrels and action mounted on round base, which can turn 360 degrees. Patent date "Dec. 18, 1883" marked on gun. Many manufactured between 1880 and early 1890s.

NIB	Exc.	V.G.	Good	Fair	Poor
—	—	1800	1200	500	150

PRATT, H.
Roxbury, Massachusetts

Under Hammer Pistol

.31-caliber percussion single-shot pistol, with 8.5" octagonal barrel. Frame marked "H. Pratt's/ Patent". Manufactured during 1850s.

NIB	Exc.	V.G.	Good	Fair	Poor
—	—	1700	1350	650	200

PRECISION SMALL ARMS
Aspen, Colorado

PSA-25

Semi-automatic pistol chambered for .25 ACP. Barrel length 2.13"; magazine capacity 6 rounds. Frame and slide steel alloy. Weight 9.5 oz.; overall length 4.11". Grips black polymer. Standard finish black oxide. Modeled after Browning Baby. **NOTE:** Add $50 brushed chrome finish; $75 stainless steel.

NIB	Exc.	V.G.	Good	Fair	Poor
525	400	300	225	150	75

Featherweight Model

Same as above, with aluminum frame. Chrome slide with gold-plated trigger.

NIB	Exc.	V.G.	Good	Fair	Poor
1000	850	700	475	250	100

Diplomat Model

Black oxide, with gold highlights and ivory grips.

NIB	Exc.	V.G.	Good	Fair	Poor
1000	850	700	500	400	200

Montreaux Model

Gold plated with ivory grips.

NIB	Exc.	V.G.	Good	Fair	Poor
825	750	600	450	300	200

Renaissance Model

Same as above, with hand engraved steel frame and slide. Antique stain chrome finish.

NIB	Exc.	V.G.	Good	Fair	Poor
2600	2100	1600	1200	700	300

Imperiale

Inlaid gold filigree over blue, with scrimshawed ivory grips.

NIB	Exc.	V.G.	Good	Fair	Poor
3300	2750	2100	1500	850	350

PREMIER
Italy and Spain

Trade name used by various retailers on shotguns manufactured in Italy and Spain that were imported during late 1950s and early 1960s.

Regent Side-by-Side Shotgun

Double-barrel shotgun, with 26" to 30" barrels. Available in all standard gauges. Receiver blued, stock of walnut. Normally found with pistol-grip and beavertail fore-end.

NIB	Exc.	V.G.	Good	Fair	Poor
—	450	250	200	150	100

Regent Magnum

As above chambered for 3.5" 10-gauge Magnum cartridge. Barrels 32" in length and choked Full and Full.

NIB	Exc.	V.G.	Good	Fair	Poor
—	500	300	250	200	150

Brush King

Identical to Regent Model, except fitted with 22" Modified and Improved Cylinder barrels. Straight-grip English-style stock.

NIB	Exc.	V.G.	Good	Fair	Poor
—	500	375	250	200	150

Ambassador Model

More ornate version of Regent Model.

NIB	Exc.	V.G.	Good	Fair	Poor
—	600	450	300	250	175

Presentation Custom Grade

Custom-order shotgun, with game scenes and gold and silver inlays.

NIB	Exc.	V.G.	Good	Fair	Poor
—	2500	1750	1250	850	400

PRESCOTT, E. A.
Worcester, Massachusetts

Percussion Pocket Revolver

.31-caliber percussion spur trigger revolver, with 4" or 4.25" octagonal barrel and 6-shot cylinder. Frame brass. Grips walnut. Believed approximately 100 manufactured during 1860 and 1861.

NIB	Exc.	V.G.	Good	Fair	Poor
—	—	3700	2500	1125	200

Pocket Revolver

.22- or .32-caliber spur trigger revolver, with 3" or 4" barrel. .22-caliber version has 7-shot cylinder; .32 caliber 6-shot cylinder. Standard markings "E.A. Prescott Worcester Mass. Pat. Oct. 2, 1860". Approximately 1,000 manufactured between 1862 and 1867.

NIB	Exc.	V.G.	Good	Fair	Poor
—	—	1050	825	350	100

Navy Revolver

Single-action revolver fitted with conventional trigger. Chambered for .38 rimfire cartridges, with 7.25" octagonal barrel. Unfluted cylinder holds 6 shots. Frame silver-plated brass or blued iron; barrel and cylinder blued, with walnut grips. Barrel marked "E.A. Prescott, Worcester, Mass. Pat. Oct. 2, 1860". Believed several hundred manufactured between 1861 and 1863. Iron frame model will bring a small premium.

Courtesy Milwaukee Public Museum, Milwaukee, Wisconsin

NIB	Exc.	V.G.	Good	Fair	Poor
—	—	1850	1400	550	200

Army Revolver

Similar in appearance to Navy model, with larger frame. Chambered for .44-caliber rimfire cartridge. Fitted with 9" octagon barrel, with extractor rod and loading gate on right side of frame. Very rare.

NIB	Exc.	V.G.	Good	Fair	Poor
—	—	24500	19500	8800	600

Belt Revolver

Although similar in appearance to early Smith & Wesson revolvers, Prescott has a solid frame. Available in .22- or .32-caliber: .22-caliber has 3" barrel; .32-caliber 5.75" barrel. Markings are identical found on Pocket Revolver. Approximately 300 manufactured between 1861 and 1863.

NIB	Exc.	V.G.	Good	Fair	Poor
—	—	1150	825	325	100

PRETORIA
Pretoria, South Africa

See—P.A.F.

PRINZ
Germany

Grade 1 Bolt-Action Rifle

High quality bolt-action rifle. Chambered for .243, .30-06, .308, 7mm Rem. Magnum or .300 Win. Magnum cartridges. Barrel length 24", double-set triggers available. Finish blued. Stock oil-finished select walnut. Introduced in 1989.

NIB	Exc.	V.G.	Good	Fair	Poor
1200	950	700	450	325	150

Grade 2 Bolt-Action Rifle

As above, with rosewood fore-end tip. Pistol-grip cap.

NIB	Exc.	V.G.	Good	Fair	Poor
1300	1075	750	475	350	175

Tip Up Rifle

High quality single-shot rifle. Available in a variety of American cartridges. Barrel length 24". Not furnished with sights. Finish blued, stock of select walnut.

NIB	Exc.	V.G.	Good	Fair	Poor
3000	2250	1700	1135	850	300

Model 85 "Princess"

Combination 12-gauge shotgun and rifle, with 24" or 26" barrels, double triggers and automatic ejectors. Finish blued, stock of select walnut.

NIB	Exc.	V.G.	Good	Fair	Poor
3500	2850	2100	1650	1000	300

PROFESSIONAL ORDNANCE, INC.
Ontario, California

Company was purchased by Bushmaster.

Carbon-15 Pistol—Type 97

Introduced in 1996. Semi-automatic pistol built on carbon fiber upper and lower receiver. Chambered for 5.56 cartridge. Has 7.25" fluted stainless steel barrel. Ghost ring sights are standard. Magazine is AR-15 compatible. Quick detach compensator. Furnished with 10-round magazine. Weight about 46 oz. **NOTE:** Pistol has several options that will affect value.

NIB	Exc.	V.G.	Good	Fair	Poor
925	700	550	425	300	150

Carbon-15 Rifle—Type 97

Similar to above. Fitted with 16" barrel, quick detachable buttstock and compensator, Weaver type mounting base. Overall length 35"; weight about 3.9 lbs.

NIB	Exc.	V.G.	Good	Fair	Poor
950	725	600	500	350	150

Carbon-15 Rifle—Type 97S

Introduced in 2000. Rifle incorporated several new features. Fore-grip is double walled and insulated with a sheet of ultra-lightweight alumina silica ceramic fiber. Recoil buffer has been increased in size by 30 percent for less recoil. New ambidextrous safety has been added. New multi carry silent sling with Hogue grip standard. Weight about 4.3 lbs.

NIB	Exc.	V.G.	Good	Fair	Poor
1285	950	700	550	375	150

Carbon-15 Pistol—Type 21

Introduced in 1999. Features light profile stainless steel 7.25" barrel. Ghost ring sights are standard. Optional recoil compensator. A 30-round magazine standard until supplies are exhausted. Weight about 40 oz.

NIB	Exc.	V.G.	Good	Fair	Poor
925	700	550	425	300	150

Carbon-15 Rifle—Type 21

Fitted with 16" light profile stainless steel barrel. Quick detachable stock, weaver mounting base. Introduced in 1999. Weight about 3.9 lbs.

NIB	Exc.	V.G.	Good	Fair	Poor
1150	900	650	500	325	125

PROTECTION
Unknown

Protection Pocket Revolver

.28-caliber percussion spur-trigger revolver, with 3.25" octagonal barrel and 6-shot cylinder. Roll engraved with police arrest scene. Frame brass. Grips walnut. Cylinder marked "Protection". Approximately 1,000 manufactured during late 1850s early 1860s.

1st Model

Roll engraved cylinder.

NIB	Exc.	V.G.	Good	Fair	Poor
—	—	1500	1150	450	100

2nd Model

Plain cylinder above serial no. 650.

NIB	Exc.	V.G.	Good	Fair	Poor
—	—	1300	950	350	100

PTK INTERNATIONAL, INC.
Atlanta, Georgia

See—Poly-Technologies, Inc.

PULASKI ARMORY
Pulaski, Tennessee

Founded in 1861, this firm produced rifles for State of Tennessee. Overall length 48.5" to 49.5"; round barrels 32.5" to 33.25"; caliber .54. Resembles U.S. Model 1841 Rifles without patchbox. Had single screw sporting locks, with diamond-shaped ferrules. Usually marked on barrel "PULASKI T. C.S.A. 61". Production estimated about 300.

NIB	Exc.	V.G.	Good	Fair	Poor
—	—	16500	10000	5000	1500

PUMA

Model 92 Rifle

Copy of Winchester lever-action rifle. Fitted with 24" octagon barrel. Chambered for .44 Magnum, .357 Magnum, .454 Casull or .45 Colt cartridge. Offered in a variety of finishes: stainless steel; blued; blued and brass; blued and case colored. Fitted with crescent butt and hardwood stock. **NOTE:** Add $50 for stainless steel.

NIB	Exc.	V.G.	Good	Fair	Poor
550	425	350	275	200	100

Model 92 Carbine

Also available with 20" round barrel. Chambered as above, plus .454 Casull and .480 Ruger. Fitted with a shotgun butt. **NOTE:** Add $50 for stainless steel.

NIB	Exc.	V.G.	Good	Fair	Poor
550	425	350	275	200	100

Model 92 Trapper

Introduced in 2004. Features 16" barrel, with large-loop lever and saddle ring. Available in all calibers noted above.

NIB	Exc.	V.G.	Good	Fair	Poor
550	425	350	275	200	100

PPS22

New in 2009. A .22 LR version of Soviet PPSh sub-machine gun. Comes with one 50-round drum magazine.

NIB	Exc.	V.G.	Good	Fair	Poor
575	475	350	275	200	100

PURDEY, J. & SONS LTD.
London, England

Perhaps the finest manufacturer of shotguns, double-barrel and bolt-action rifles in the world. Virtually all their products are made on special order and impossible to establish general values. Prospective purchasers are advised to seek qualified guidance prior to acquisition of any arms made by this maker. Prices listed are for standard guns with no extras. Below, are approximate base prices for new custom shotguns and rifles based on the exchange rate between English pound and U.S. dollar as of September, 2014. Prices do not include VAT, which is approximately 20 percent. These guns are made to order to buyer's specifications and can be made in any gauge or caliber.

CURRENT PRODUCTION

Hammerless Ejector Side-by-Side Game Gun

Available in 12-, 16-, 20-, 28-gauge and .410 bore. Engraved sidelocks.

NIB	Exc.	V.G.	Good	Fair	Poor
136,500	—	—	—	—	—

Hammerless Ejector Over/Under Gun

Offered in 12-, 16-, 20-, 28-gauge and .410 bore, with sidelocks.

NIB	Exc.	V.G.	Good	Fair	Poor
149,750	—	—	—	—	—

Double-Barreled Rifle

Custom made side-by-side double rifle with sidelocks. **NOTE:** Up to .375 bore size: $190,000; .375 to .500 bore size: $190,000; .500 bore size and up: $201,650.

OLDER MANUFACTURED SHOTGUNS AND RIFLES

Best Quality Game Gun

NOTE: Add 50 percent for 20-gauge; 80 to 100 percent for 28-gauge or .410 bore.

NIB	Exc.	V.G.	Good	Fair	Poor
40000	35000	27500	20000	8000	—

Best Quality Heavy Duck Gun

NIB	Exc.	V.G.	Good	Fair	Poor
24000	20000	12500	7500	5000	—

Best Quality Over/Under

NOTE: Add 50 percent for 20-gauge; 100 percent for 28-gauge.

NIB	Exc.	V.G.	Good	Fair	Poor
50000	42000	32000	25000	9000	—

Double Rifle

.300 H&H

NIB	Exc.	V.G.	Good	Fair	Poor
—	55000	47500	40000	25000	—

.375 H&H

NIB	Exc.	V.G.	Good	Fair	Poor
—	70000	60000	50000	35000	—

.470 N.E.

NIB	Exc.	V.G.	Good	Fair	Poor
—	90000	75000	65000	45000	—

.600 N.E.

NIB	Exc.	V.G.	Good	Fair	Poor
—	100000	85000	70000	55000	—

PYRENEES
Hendaye, France

Founded in 1923, this company has produced a variety of models. Most popular of which was "Unique" series. Prior to 1939, a variety of trade names were marked on their products such as these: Superior, Capitan, Cesar, Chantecler, Chimere Renoir, Colonial, Prima, Rapid Maxima, Reina, Demon, Demon-marine, Ebac, Elite, Gallia, Ixor, Le Majestic, St. Hubert, Selecta, Sympathique, Touriste, Le Sanspariel, Le Tout Acier, Mars, Perfect, Triomphe Francais, Unis & Vindex. Following 1939, this company's products are simply stamped "Unique".

NOTE: During World War II, production at this company was taken over by the Nazis. Consequently, the various models listed will be found with German inspection marks. These arms are worth approximately 25 percent more than values listed.

Model 10 Unique

6.35mm semi-automatic pistol similar to Model 1906 Browning. Slide marked "Le Veritable Pistolet Francais Unique". Introduced in 1923.

NIB	Exc.	V.G.	Good	Fair	Poor
—	295	195	165	100	75

Model 11

As above, with grip safety and loaded chamber indicator.

NIB	Exc.	V.G.	Good	Fair	Poor
—	325	225	195	150	100

Model 12

As above, without loaded chamber indicator.

NIB	Exc.	V.G.	Good	Fair	Poor
—	295	195	165	100	75

Model 13

As above, with 7-shot magazine.

NIB	Exc.	V.G.	Good	Fair	Poor
—	295	195	165	100	75

Model 14

As above, with 9-shot magazine.

NIB	Exc.	V.G.	Good	Fair	Poor
—	295	195	165	100	75

Model 15

As above in 7.65mm caliber. Introduced in 1923.

NIB	Exc.	V.G.	Good	Fair	Poor
—	295	195	165	100	75

Model 16

As above, with 7-shot magazine.

Courtesy Orvel Reichert

NIB	Exc.	V.G.	Good	Fair	Poor
—	295	195	165	100	75

Model 17

As above, with 9-shot magazine.

Courtesy Orvel Reichert

NIB	Exc.	V.G.	Good	Fair	Poor
—	325	225	195	150	100

Model 18

7.65mm caliber semi-automatic pistol. Patterned after Model 1920 Browning, without grip safety.

NIB	Exc.	V.G.	Good	Fair	Poor
—	295	195	165	100	75

Model 19

As above, with 7-shot magazine.

NIB	Exc.	V.G.	Good	Fair	Poor
—	295	195	165	100	75

Model 20

As above, with 9-shot magazine.

NIB	Exc.	V.G.	Good	Fair	Poor
—	325	225	195	150	100

Model 21

As above chambered for 9mm short cartridge.

NIB	Exc.	V.G.	Good	Fair	Poor
—	325	225	195	150	100

POST-WAR UNIQUE

Model BCF66

9mm short semi-automatic pistol, with 3.5" barrel, open top slide and external hammer. Slide marked "Armes Unique Hendaye BP France". Blued finish. Plastic grips.

NIB	Exc.	V.G.	Good	Fair	Poor
—	295	195	165	100	75

Model C

Virtually identical to Model 17 listed above. Slide marked "7.65 Court 9 coups Unique". Blued finish. Plastic grips with trademark "PF" in a circle cast into them.

NIB	Exc.	V.G.	Good	Fair	Poor
—	250	175	150	125	75

Model F

Identical to Model C, except chambered for 9mm Short cartridges. Magazine capacity 8 rounds.

NIB	Exc.	V.G.	Good	Fair	Poor
—	295	195	165	100	75

Model D

.22-caliber semi-automatic pistol, with barrels ranging from 4" to 7.5" in length. The 7.5" barreled version fitted with muzzle-brake. Magazine capacity 10 rounds. Finish blued, plastic grips.

NIB	Exc.	V.G.	Good	Fair	Poor
—	275	225	200	150	125

Model DES/VO

Identical to Model D, but chambered for .22 Short cartridges.

NIB	Exc.	V.G.	Good	Fair	Poor
—	275	225	200	150	125

Model L

Similar to Model D, except chambered for .22, .32 ACP and 9mm Short cartridges. Available with steel or alloy frame.

NIB	Exc.	V.G.	Good	Fair	Poor
—	295	195	165	100	75

Model DES 69

As above, with better quality sights, special trigger and improved grips.

NIB	Exc.	V.G.	Good	Fair	Poor
—	325	225	195	150	100

Model 2000

Courtesy John J. Stimson, Jr.

NIB	Exc.	V.G.	Good	Fair	Poor
1250	950	775	500	350	150

QUACKENBUSH
Herkimer, New York

Quackenbush Safety Cartridge Rifle

Single-shot takedown boy's rifle. Chambered for .22 rimfire cartridges in .22 Short or .22 Long. Barrel length 18". Weight about 4.5 lbs. All metal parts nickel-plated. Breech swings to side for loading. Stock of walnut. Manufactured between 1886 and about 1920. Approximately 50,000 produced. Quackenbush also made nickel-plated nutcrackers. Who'd'a thought?

NIB	Exc.	V.G.	Good	Fair	Poor
—	—	800	650	300	150

Junior Safety Rifle

Same as above, with skeleton stock. Built between 1893 and 1920. About 7,000 guns manufactured. Weight about 4 lbs.

NIB	Exc.	V.G.	Good	Fair	Poor
—	—	950	600	200	100

Bicycle Rifle

Chambered for .22 cartridge. Fitted with 12" barrel. Skeleton wire pistol-grip.

NIB	Exc.	V.G.	Good	Fair	Poor
—	—	1300	750	350	150

QUINABAUG MFG. CO.
Southridge, Massachusetts

Under Hammer Pistol

.31-caliber percussion under hammer pistol, with barrels from 3" to 8" in length. Frame of blued iron, grips of walnut or maple. Top of frame marked "Quinabaug Rifle M'g Co. Southbridge, Mass." Barrels are normally marked "E. Hutchings & Co. Agents". Manufactured during 1850s.

NIB	Exc.	V.G.	Good	Fair	Poor
—	—	1900	1400	600	200

R

R. G. INDUSTRIES
Miami, Florida
Rohm Gmbh
Sontheim/Brenz, Germany

An importer of inexpensive handguns of dubious quality that ceased operations in 1986.

RG-25

A .25-caliber semi-automatic pistol. Available blued or chrome-plated finish.

NIB	Exc.	V.G.	Good	Fair	Poor
—	75	65	50	25	0

RG-16

A double-barrel .22-caliber chrome-plated derringer.

NIB	Exc.	V.G.	Good	Fair	Poor
—	75	65	50	20	0

RG-17

As above, except chambered for. 38 Special cartridge.

NIB	Exc.	V.G.	Good	Fair	Poor
—	75	70	60	25	0

RG-14

A .22-caliber double-action revolver, with 4" barrel and 6-shot cylinder. Blued finish, plastic grips.

NIB	Exc.	V.G.	Good	Fair	Poor
—	75	70	60	25	0

RG-30

A .22 LR or Magnum double-action revolver. Blued finish, plastic grips.

NIB	Exc.	V.G.	Good	Fair	Poor
—	75	65	50	25	0

RG-40

A .38 Special double-action revolver, with swing-out cylinder. Blued finish, plastic grips.

NIB	Exc.	V.G.	Good	Fair	Poor
—	75	70	60	25	0

RG-57

A .357 or .44 Magnum double-action revolver, with 6-shot cylinder. Blued finish, checkered wood grips.

NIB	Exc.	V.G.	Good	Fair	Poor
—	75	70	60	25	0

RG-63

A .22-caliber double-action revolver resembling Colt Model 1873.

NIB	Exc.	V.G.	Good	Fair	Poor
—	75	70	60	25	0

RG-66

A .22 or .22 Magnum single-action revolver patterned after Colt Model 1873.

NIB	Exc.	V.G.	Good	Fair	Poor
—	90	70	50	25	0

RG-66T

As above, with adjustable sights.

NIB	Exc.	V.G.	Good	Fair	Poor
—	90	70	50	25	0

RG-74

A .22-caliber double-action revolver, with swing-out cylinder.

NIB	Exc.	V.G.	Good	Fair	Poor
—	75	65	55	25	0

RG-88

A .357 Magnum double-action revolver, with swing-out cylinder.

NIB	Exc.	V.G.	Good	Fair	Poor
—	75	65	55	25	0

R.E.
Valencia, Spain

Initials "R.E." stand for "Republica Espana". This copy of Spanish Army Model 1921, also known as Astra 400, was produced between 1936 and 1939 during Spanish Civil War by the Republican forces. This variation can be identified by "RE" monogram on butt and the absence of any manufacturer's stampings.

NIB	Exc.	V.G.	Good	Fair	Poor
—	475	325	250	175	100

RADOM
Radom, Poland

For history, technical data, descriptions, photos and prices see the Standard Catalog of Military Firearms.

VIS-35 Reissue

An exact copy of original VIS-35 pistol. Limited to 100 pistols, with fewer than that number imported into U.S. Importer, "Dalvar of USA" is stamped on barrel. **NOTE:** Deduct 50 percent for "non-eagle" version.

NIB	Exc.	V.G.	Good	Fair	Poor
2300	2000	1500	1100	600	300

FB P-64

Polish semi-automatic, straight blowback pistol in 9mm Makarov caliber. Produced from 1964 to 1983. P-64 replaced older Polish-made PW wz.33, a licensed Tokarev copy, and was manufactured by Fabrika Broni in Radom, Poland. This 6-shot pistol has a 3.3" barrel and is very similar in size to the Walther PPK. Also similar mechanically, but no external slide latch is present, as empty magazine locks the slide in the open position. Major drawback is its heavy felt recoil, replaced in 1984. Huge quantities have been imported to the United States from the late 2000s until recently. Features a blue finish, plastic wrap-around grips, marked "P-64" and "9mm" on left slide flat. Serial number and date of manufacture on right side.

NIB	Exc.	V.G.	Good	Fair	Poor
—	275	240	225	200	150

FB P-83

Superbly made replacement for older P-64, the P-83 is an 8-shot 9mm Makarov caliber, straight blowback semi-automatic pistol, with large comfortable lined wrap-around rubber grips. Also known as Vanad pistol, it is dimensionally similar to the Russian Makarov. (Vanad is a reference to vanadium, an alloy used to strengthen steel). Produced at the Polish Fabrika Broni factory. Has a 3.5" barrel, with a unique take-down system by which the trigger guard slides forward, as opposed to being pulled down as required on most Makarov-size pistols. P-83 was used by Polish forces in the Yugoslav and Iraq Wars, and is still a reserve issue item in Polish military and police forces. Imported to the United States beginning in late 2000s.

NIB	Exc.	V.G.	Good	Fair	Poor
—	395	350	300	275	225

RANDALL FIREARMS CO.
Sun Valley, California

This company was in operation from 1983 to 1985. It was the first manufacturer to mass-produce 1911-type pistols in stainless steel. Also, the first to make a mirror-image left-hand variation. Many models were offered, most in .45 ACP or 9mm. Records show only two samples were chambered in .38 Super. Total production of Randall Firearms Co. was almost 10,000 pistols.

Model A111

Caliber .45 Auto; barrel length 5"; round-slide top, right-hand with fixed sights. Total production: 3,431. **NOTE:** Add a premium of $100 for Exc. thru Good prices for original box.

Photo by Steve Comus

Randall matched set, serial-number RFOO010C. Made for the TV series "Magnum PI".

NIB	Exc.	V.G.	Good	Fair	Poor
1050	950	650	400	350	200

Model A121

Caliber .45 Auto; barrel length 5"; flat-slide top, right-hand with fixed sights. Total production: 1,067. **NOTE:** Add a premium of $100 for Exc. thru Good prices for original box.

NIB	Exc.	V.G.	Good	Fair	Poor
1150	1000	800	425	375	200

Model A131

Caliber .45 Auto; barrel length 5"; flat-slide top, right-hand with Millet sights. Total production: 2,083. **NOTE:** Add a premium of $100 for Exc. thru Good prices for original box.

Photo by Larry Gray

Randall A131/SO in .451 Detonics Magnum with Randall memorabilia.

NIB	Exc.	V.G.	Good	Fair	Poor
1300	1050	875	550	400	200

Model A112

Caliber 9mm; barrel length 5"; round-slide top, right-hand with fixed sights. Total production: 301. **NOTE:** Add a premium of $100 for Exc. thru Good prices for original box.

NIB	Exc.	V.G.	Good	Fair	Poor
1350	950	900	575	425	200

Model A122

Caliber 9mm; barrel length 5"; flat-slide top, right-hand with fixed sights. Total production: 18. **NOTE:** Add a premium of $100 for Exc. thru Good prices for original box.

NIB	Exc.	V.G.	Good	Fair	Poor
1900	1600	1350	800	540	300

Model A211

Caliber .45 Auto; barrel length 4.25"; round-slide top, right-hand with fixed sights. Total production: 922. **NOTE:** Add a premium of $100 for Exc. thru Good prices for original box.

NIB	Exc.	V.G.	Good	Fair	Poor
1150	1000	800	425	375	200

Model A231

Caliber .45 Auto; barrel length 4.25"; flat-slide top, right-hand with Millet sights. Total production: 574. **NOTE:** Add a premium of $100 for Exc. thru Good prices for original box.

NIB	Exc.	V.G.	Good	Fair	Poor
1350	950	900	575	425	200

Model A212

Caliber 9mm; barrel length 4.25"; round-slide top, right-hand with fixed sights. Total production: 76. **NOTE:** Add a premium of $100 for Exc. thru Good prices for original box.

NIB	Exc.	V.G.	Good	Fair	Poor
1450	1050	925	650	500	300

Model A232

Caliber 9mm; barrel length 4.25"; flat-slide top, right-hand with Millet sights. Total production: 5. **NOTE:** Add a premium of $100 for Exc. thru Good prices for original box.

NIB	Exc.	V.G.	Good	Fair	Poor
2400	1900	1565	—	—	—

Model A311

Caliber .45 Auto; barrel length 4.25"; round-slide top, right-hand with fixed sights. Total production: 361. **NOTE:** Add a premium of $100 for Exc. thru Good prices for original box.

Photo by Steve Comus

A311B black oxide LeMay special order by Soldier of Fortune magazine for field testing in El Salvador.

NIB	Exc.	V.G.	Good	Fair	Poor
1700	1375	1150	900	700	300

Model A331 Curtis LeMay

Caliber .45 Auto; barrel length 4.25"; flat-slide top, right-hand with Millet sights. Total production: 293.

NIB	Exc.	V.G.	Good	Fair	Poor
1800	1475	1250	950	735	300

Model A312

Caliber 9mm; barrel length 4.25"; round-slide top, right-hand with fixed sights. Total production: 2. **NOTE:** Add a premium of $100 for Exc. thru Good prices for original box.

NIB	Exc.	V.G.	Good	Fair	Poor
3750	3300	2575	—	—	—

Model A332

Caliber 9mm; barrel length 4.25"; flat-slide top, right-hand with Millet sights. Total production: 9. **NOTE:** Add a premium of $100 for Exc. thru Good prices for original box.

NIB	Exc.	V.G.	Good	Fair	Poor
2250	1775	1450	1000	750	300

Model B111

Caliber .45 Auto; barrel length 5"; round-slide top, left-hand with fixed sights. Total production: 297. **NOTE:** Add a premium of $100 for Exc. thru Good prices for original box.

NIB	Exc.	V.G.	Good	Fair	Poor
1900	1550	1200	975	700	300

Model B121

Caliber .45 Auto; barrel length 5"; flat-slide top, left-hand with fixed sights. Total production: 110. **NOTE:** Add a premium of $100 for Exc. thru Good prices for original box.

NIB	Exc.	V.G.	Good	Fair	Poor
2250	1775	1450	1000	750	300

Model B122

Caliber 9mm; barrel length 5"; flat-slide top, left-hand with fixed sights. Total production: 2.

NIB	Exc.	V.G.	Good	Fair	Poor
4000	3500	2675	—	—	—

Model B123

Caliber .38 Super; barrel length 5"; flat-slide top, left-hand with fixed sights. Total production: 2.

NIB	Exc.	V.G.	Good	Fair	Poor
4000	3500	2675	—	—	—

Model B131

Caliber .45 Auto; barrel length 5"; flat-slide top, left-hand with Millet sights. Total production: 225. **NOTE:** Add a premium of $100 for Exc. thru Good prices for original box.

Photo by Steve Comus

B131/SO left-hand service model with custom Chuck Stapel knife.

NIB	Exc.	V.G.	Good	Fair	Poor
2075	1700	1400	875	700	300

Model B311

Caliber .45 Auto; barrel length 4.25"; round-slide top, left-hand with fixed sights. Total production: 52. **NOTE:** Add a premium of $100 for Exc. thru Good prices for original box.

Photo by Steve Comus

Randall left-hand B311 with original box. Few left-hand Randalls were shipped in boxes. Most were shipped in Randall pistol rugs.

NIB	Exc.	V.G.	Good	Fair	Poor
2250	1775	1450	1000	750	300

Model B312

Caliber 9mm; barrel length 4.25"; round-slide top, left-hand with fixed sights. Total production: 9. **NOTE:** Add a premium of $100 for Exc. thru Good prices for original box.

Photo by Steve Comus

Randall B312 left-hand 9mm LeMay, one of the most sought-after of the B-series guns.

Photo by Steve Comus

Randall B312 with factory 45 ACP conversion unit. Only one of these factory units were made.

NIB	Exc.	V.G.	Good	Fair	Poor
3750	3300	2575	—	—	—

Model B331

Caliber .45 Auto; barrel length 4.25"; flat-slide top, left-hand with Millet sights. Total production: 45. **NOTE:** Add a premium of $100 for Exc. thru Good prices for original box.

NIB	Exc.	V.G.	Good	Fair	Poor
2500	2050	1675	1100	600	300

Model C311

Caliber .45 Auto; barrel length 4.25"; round-slide top, right-hand with fixed sights. Total production: 1.

NIB	Exc.	V.G.	Good	Fair	Poor
4250	—	—	—	—	—

Model C332

Caliber 9mm; barrel length 4.25"; flat-slide top, right-hand with Millet sights. Total production: 4.

NIB	Exc.	V.G.	Good	Fair	Poor
1900	1550	1200	975	700	300

Model B321 SET

Photo by Steve Comus

Randall B321 of the B321 set, serial-number REK1.

NIB	Exc.	V.G.	Good	Fair	Poor
24500	—	—	—	—	—

Model A111/111 Matched Set

Serial numbers: RFOOOOOC, RFOO001C, RFOO010-C, RFOO024C.

NIB	Exc.	V.G.	Good	Fair	Poor
9200	—	—	—	—	—

Austrian Randall

Total production: 5. Due to the rarity, values for this model are very speculative. An expert appraisal is advised.

Photo by Christopher Todd

Close-up view of Austrian proof marks.

RANDALL MAGAZINES

.45 LeMay—Right-Hand

NIB	Exc.	V.G.	Good	Fair	Poor
100	90	80	80	—	—

.45 LeMay—Dogleg Right-Hand

NIB	Exc.	V.G.	Good	Fair	Poor
80	70	70	70	—	—

.45 LeMay—Left-Hand

NIB	Exc.	V.G.	Good	Fair	Poor
150	130	125	125	—	—

.45 LeMay—Dogleg Left-Hand

NIB	Exc.	V.G.	Good	Fair	Poor
140	130	120	120	—	—

.45 Service—Right-Hand

NIB	Exc.	V.G.	Good	Fair	Poor
60	45	40	40	—	—

.45 Service—Left-Hand

NIB	Exc.	V.G.	Good	Fair	Poor
125	115	100	100	—	—

9mm Service—Right-Hand

NIB	Exc.	V.G.	Good	Fair	Poor
125	115	100	100	—	—

9mm Service—Left-Hand

NIB	Exc.	V.G.	Good	Fair	Poor
200	175	150	150	—	—

RANGER ARMS, INC.
Gainesville, Texas

.22 Rifle

Bolt-action rifle produced in .22 LR. Checkered walnut Monte Carlo stock. Manufactured early 1970s.

NIB	Exc.	V.G.	Good	Fair	Poor
—	200	150	100	75	50

Statesman

Bolt-action rifle produced in various centerfire calibers, with 22" barrel, no sights and checkered walnut stock. Standard finish blued. Manufactured early 1970s.

NIB	Exc.	V.G.	Good	Fair	Poor
—	900	750	600	350	200

Statesman Magnum

As above, chambered for Magnum calibers, with 24" barrel.

NIB	Exc.	V.G.	Good	Fair	Poor
—	950	800	650	375	200

Senator

As above, with a better finish.

NIB	Exc.	V.G.	Good	Fair	Poor
—	1000	850	700	525	250

Senator Magnum

As above, chambered for Magnum cartridges.

NIB	Exc.	V.G.	Good	Fair	Poor
—	1150	900	750	575	250

Governor

As above, with better walnut and finer lined checkering.

NIB	Exc.	V.G.	Good	Fair	Poor
—	1300	1050	800	600	300

Governor Magnum

As above, chambered for Magnum cartridges.

NIB	Exc.	V.G.	Good	Fair	Poor
—	1540	1200	950	750	300

RAPTOR ARMS CO.
Shelton, Connecticut

Raptor Bolt-Action Rifle

Economy-class rifle introduced in 1997. Chambered for .270-, .30-06, .243-, .25-06 and .308-calibers. Fitted with 22" barrel and black synthetic checkered stock. An upgrade model was available with wooden stock. Adjustable trigger. Weight about 7.5 lbs.

NIB	Exc.	V.G.	Good	Fair	Poor
275	225	175	125	100	75

Peregrine Bolt-Action Rifle

Similar to above, with checkered hardwood stock. Special order.

NIB	Exc.	V.G.	Good	Fair	Poor
275	225	175	125	100	75

RAST & GASSER
See—Gasser

RAU ARMS CORP.
El Dorado, Kansas

Wildcat

Single-shot pivoting-barrel .22 rimfire rifle. Skeletonized stock, with walnut or mahogany inset. Fore-end acts as extractor. Similar in overall look to FIE/Garcia Bronco in .22 only. Mfg. 1969-1970, with 2500-3000 produced. Later produced by Mountain Arms. See that listing.

Model 500

Blued, with walnut stock insert.

NIB	Exc.	V.G.	Good	Fair	Poor
300	200	150	100	75	45

Model 600 Deluxe

Chrome finish, with mahogany stock insert.

NIB	Exc.	V.G.	Good	Fair	Poor
325	225	175	125	95	50

RAVELL
Barcelona, Spain

Maxim Double Rifle

H&H-styled sidelock double-barrel rifle. Available in .375 H&H or 9.3x74R, with 23" barrels having express sights. Double triggers and automatic ejectors. Sidelocks and mounts engraved. Stock of well figured walnut. Normally fitted with a recoil pad.

NIB	Exc.	V.G.	Good	Fair	Poor
4500	3500	2750	1850	1250	850

RAVEN ARMS
Industry, California

P-25

A .25-caliber semi-automatic pistol, with 2.75" barrel and 6-round magazine. Available with blued, chrome or nickel-plated finish and walnut grips. Manufacture ceased in 1984.

NIB	Exc.	V.G.	Good	Fair	Poor
—	100	75	50	35	25

MP-25

As above, with die-cast frame and imitation ivory grips.

NIB	Exc.	V.G.	Good	Fair	Poor
110	80	55	45	35	25

READ & WATSON
Danville, Virginia

During 1862 and 1863, Read & Watson produced approximately 900 altered Hall rifles for State of Virginia. These arms were made from Hall rifles issued to the state prior to the Civil War. Original breech loading mechanisms were removed and a brass breech piece or receiver was secured in their place. New buttstocks were fitted and original Hall furniture was reused. Carbines have an overall length of 42.125"; barrel length 26"; in .52-caliber. Position and style of serial numbers varies.

NIB	Exc.	V.G.	Good	Fair	Poor
—	—	18500	15500	7100	1000

RECORD-MATCH ANSCHUTZ
Zelia-Mehlis, Germany

Model 210 Free Pistol

Single-shot .22-caliber target pistol using Martini falling block action. Barrel length 11", set trigger and adjustable sights. Blued finish, with checkered walnut grips and fore-end. Manufactured during 1930s.

NIB	Exc.	V.G.	Good	Fair	Poor
—	1500	1200	1000	825	400

Model 210A

As above, with a lightweight alloy frame.

NIB	Exc.	V.G.	Good	Fair	Poor
—	1425	1125	975	775	350

Model 200 Free Pistol

As above, without a set trigger.

NIB	Exc.	V.G.	Good	Fair	Poor
—	1125	1050	875	550	300

REEDER, GARY CUSTOM GUNS
Flagstaff, Arizona

Company offers complete guns as listed below. It also offers custom options built on customer guns as well. An extensive number of custom options is available on any of these models. Prices listed below reflect the standard for that particular model. Retail prices only are listed below due to lack of active secondary market for these limited edition guns. Reeder is a custom manufacturer, or re-stylist, working primarily with Ruger frames. Only a representative sampling of his works is presented here and values are estimates only. Since many of Reeder's guns are made to custom specs, their value is largely a matter of finding the right buyer.

Arizona Ranger Classic

Built on a Ruger Vaquero frame. Chambered for .45 Long Colt cartridge. Fitted with choice of 4.5", 5.5", or 7.5" barrel. Blue or stainless steel finish. Special engraving, with Stag grips.

NIB	Exc.	V.G.	Good	Fair	Poor
1400	1225	975	—	—	—

Badlands Classic

Built on a Ruger Vaquero frame. Chambered for .45 Long Colt cartridge, with an extra .45 ACP cylinder. Fitted with 4.5" barrel. Special engraving. Pearl grips.

NIB	Exc.	V.G.	Good	Fair	Poor
1400	1225	975	—	—	—

Black Widow

Chambered for .44 Magnum cartridge. Fitted with 4.625" barrel, with black Chromex finish. Round butt, with black Cape Buffalo grips. Engraved with Black Widow on each side of cylinder. Built on a Ruger Super Blackhawk.

NIB	Exc.	V.G.	Good	Fair	Poor
1300	1075	850	—	—	—

Black Widow II

Similar to Black Widow. Chambered for .45 Long Colt cartridge. Barrel length 4.5".

NIB	Exc.	V.G.	Good	Fair	Poor
1350	1125	900			

Cowboy Classic

Built on a Ruger Vaquero frame. Chambered for .45 Long Colt, with 6.75" barrel. Stainless steel or black Chromix finish. Ivory polymer or pearlite grips. Special engraving.

NIB	Exc.	V.G.	Good	Fair	Poor
1350	1125	900	—	—	—

Cowtown Classic

Built on a Ruger Vaquero frame. Chambered for .45 Long Colt, with 7.5" barrel. Special engraving. Walnut grips.

NIB	Exc.	V.G.	Good	Fair	Poor
1350	1125	900	—	—	—

Gamblers Classic

Built on a Ruger Vaquero frame. Chambered for .45 Long Colt, with 2.5" barrel. Stainless steel or black Chromix finish. Choice of black or white pearl grips. No ejector rod. Special engraving.

NIB	Exc.	V.G.	Good	Fair	Poor
1350	1125	900	—	—	—

Lone Star Classic

Built on a Ruger Vaquero frame. Chambered for .45 Long Colt cartridge, with 7.5" barrel. Stainless steel finish. Special engraving and walnut grips, with five notches.

NIB	Exc.	V.G.	Good	Fair	Poor
1350	1125	900	—	—	—

Long Rider Classic

Built on a Ruger Vaquero frame. Chambered for .45 Long Colt cartridge, with 4.5", 5.5" or 7.5" barrel. Special engraving with black Chromix finish. Gunfighter grip, with simulated pearl or ivory.

NIB	Exc.	V.G.	Good	Fair	Poor
1350	1125	900	—	—	—

Texas Ranger Classic

Built on a Ruger Vaquero frame. Chambered for .45 Long Colt cartridge, with 4.5", 5.5" or 7.5" barrel. Stainless steel finish. Special engraving. Simulated pearl gunfighter grips.

NIB	Exc.	V.G.	Good	Fair	Poor
1350	1125	900	—	—	—

Trail Rider Classic

Built on a Ruger Vaquero frame. Chambered for .45 Long Colt cartridge, with 7.5" barrel. Black Chromix finish. Special engraving. Simulated pearl grips.

NIB	Exc.	V.G.	Good	Fair	Poor
1350	1125	900	—	—	—

Tombstone Classic

Built on a Ruger Vaquero frame. Chambered for .45 Long Colt cartridge, with 3.5" barrel. Black Chromix finish. Special engraving. Simulated pearl or ivory bird's-head grips.

NIB	Exc.	V.G.	Good	Fair	Poor
1350	1125	900	—	—	—

Doc Holliday Classic

Built on a Ruger Vaquero frame. Chambered for .45 Long Colt cartridge, with 3.5" barrel. Stainless steel or black Chromix finish. Special engraving. Simulated pearl gambler grips.

NIB	Exc.	V.G.	Good	Fair	Poor
1350	1125	900	—	—	—

Night Rider

Built on a Ruger Vaquero frame. Chambered for .44-40 cartridge, with 7.5" barrel. Black Chromix finish. Special engraving. Stag grips.

NIB	Exc.	V.G.	Good	Fair	Poor
1350	1125	900	—	—	—

Ultimate Vaquero

Built on a Ruger Vaquero frame. Chambered for .45 Long Colt cartridge, with 4" barrel. Stainless steel or black Chromix finish. Special engraving. Simulated pearl gambler grips.

NIB	Exc.	V.G.	Good	Fair	Poor
1350	1125	900	—	—	—

Ultimate Bisley

Built on a Ruger Vaquero frame. Chambered for .45 Long Colt or .44 Magnum cartridge, with 4.5", 5.5", 6.5" or 7.5" barrel. Black Chromix finish. Special engraving. Simulated pearl or ivory Bisley grips.

NIB	Exc.	V.G.	Good	Fair	Poor
1350	1125	900	—	—	—

Long Colt Hunter

Built on a Ruger Blackhawk frame. Chambered for .45 Long Colt cartridge, with 5.5" or 7.5" barrel. Stainless steel finish. Adjustable rear sight and gold bead front. Special engraving. Ebony grips.

NIB	Exc.	V.G.	Good	Fair	Poor
1350	1125	900	—	—	—

Long Colt Hunter II

Built on a Ruger Redhawk frame. Chambered for .45 Long Colt or .44 Magnum cartridge, with 5" barrel. Stainless steel finish. Special engraving. Wooden gunfighter grips.

NIB	Exc.	V.G.	Good	Fair	Poor
1350	1125	900	—	—	—

African Hunter

Built on a Ruger Bisley or Super Blackhawk frame. Chambered for .475 or .500 Linebaugh cartridge, with 6" barrel. Available with/without muzzle-brake. Adjustable rear sight and interchangeable front. Stainless steel or black Chromix finish. Special engraving. Ebony grips.

NIB	Exc.	V.G.	Good	Fair	Poor
1350	1125	900	—	—	—

Ultimate 41

Built on a Ruger Blackhawk frame. Chambered for .41 Magnum or .41 GNR cartridge, with 4.5", 5.5" or 7.5" barrel. Unfluted cylinder. Stainless steel finish. Adjustable rear sights. Special engraving. Ebony grips.

NIB	Exc.	V.G.	Good	Fair	Poor
1500	1295	950	—	—	—

Coyote Classic

Built on a Ruger frame. Chambered for .22 Hornet, .22 K Hornet, .218 Bee, .218 Mashburn Bee, .17 Ackley Bee, .17 Ackley Hornet, .256 Win. and .25-20, with 8" barrel. Adjustable rear sight drilled and tapped for scope mount. Black Chromix or stainless steel finish. Special engraving. Laminated cherry grips.

NIB	Exc.	V.G.	Good	Fair	Poor
1350	1125	900	—	—	—

Classic Hunter

Built on a Ruger Vaquero frame. Chambered for .475 Linebaugh cartridge, with heavy 6" barrel. Black Chromix finish. Special engraving. Laminated ironwood, cherry or walnut gunfighter grips.

NIB	Exc.	V.G.	Good	Fair	Poor
1500	1295	950	—	—	—

Alaskan Grizzly

Built on a Ruger Vaquero frame. Chambered for .475 or .500 Linebaugh cartridge, with customer's choice of barrel. Black Chromix or stainless steel finish. Special engraving. Horn or black laminated gunfighter grips.

NIB	Exc.	V.G.	Good	Fair	Poor
1350	1125	900	—	—	—

Ultimate Back Up 2

Built on a Ruger Blackhawk or Super Blackhawk frame. Chambered for .475 or .500 Linebaugh cartridge, with 3.5" ported barrel. Stainless steel finish. Special engraving. Laminated wood or Buffalo horn grips.

NIB	Exc.	V.G.	Good	Fair	Poor
1500	1295	950	—	—	—

Montana Hunter

Built on a Ruger Blackhawk or Super Blackhawk frame. Chambered for .45 Long Colt or .44 Magnum cartridge, with customer's choice of barrel. Stainless steel finish. Special engraving. Laminated gunfighter grips.

NIB	Exc.	V.G.	Good	Fair	Poor
1350	1125	900	—	—	—

Alaskan Survivalist

Built on a Ruger Redhawk frame. Chambered for .45 Long Colt or .44 Magnum cartridge, with 3" barrel. Adjustable rear sight. Stainless steel finish. Special engraving. Ebony round butt grips.

NIB	Exc.	V.G.	Good	Fair	Poor
1350	1125	900	—	—	—

American Hunter

Built on a Winchester Model 94 big bore frame. Chambered for .444 Marlin cartridge. Black Chromix finish. Ghost ring rear sight. Special engraving. Checkered walnut stock.

NIB	Exc.	V.G.	Good	Fair	Poor
1350	1125	900	—	—	—

Alaskan Classic

Built on a Marlin Model 1895 frame. Chambered for .45-70 cartridge. Barrel length 16.5". Black Chromix finish. Ghost ring rear sight. Special engraving. Checkered walnut stock.

NIB	Exc.	V.G.	Good	Fair	Poor
1500	1295	950	—	—	—

Buffalo Hunter

Built on a Marlin Model 1895 frame. Chambered for .475 GNR cartridge. Barrel length 18". Full length magazine tube. Black Chromix finish. Peep rear sight. Special engraving. Checkered walnut stock.

NIB	Exc.	V.G.	Good	Fair	Poor
1500	1295	950	—	—	—

Kodiak Hunter

Built on a Contender frame. Chambered for .50 Action Express or .454 Casull cartridge. Barrel length 10". Black Chromix finish. Adjustable rear sight, with barrel band front sight. Special engraving. Walnut grips.

NIB	Exc.	V.G.	Good	Fair	Poor
1350	1125	900	—	—	—

Ultimate Encore

Built on a Thompson/Center frame. Chambered for a variety of big bore cartridges. Fitted with 15" barrel, with muzzle-brake. Black Chromix finish. Ghost ring rear sight. Special engraving.

NIB	Exc.	V.G.	Good	Fair	Poor
1350	1125	900	—	—	—

Ultimate 44

Built on customer's Ruger Hunter. Features: extra long five-shot cylinder; Bisley hammer and trigger; special grip frame, with laminated cherry grips; Magna-Ported barrel; sling swivels and action job. Game scene engraving.

NIB	Exc.	V.G.	Good	Fair	Poor
1500	1295	950	—	—	—

Southern Comfort

Built on customer's Blackhawk or Super Blackhawk Ruger. Revolver features five-shot cylinder. Chambered for .454 Casull cartridge. Tear drop hammer, special set back trigger, special grip frame and light engraving. Barrel length to customer's choice.

NIB	Exc.	V.G.	Good	Fair	Poor
1500	1295	950	—	—	—

Professional Hunter

A number of special features, from extended frame to 5-shot cylinder. Choice of calibers from .224 GNR to .500 Maximum. Fitted with 8" barrel, with heavy taper. Limited production.

NIB	Exc.	V.G.	Good	Fair	Poor
2750	2295	1650	—	—	—

Ultimate 480

Built on customer's Ruger Blackhawk or Super Blackhawk frame. Chambered for .480 cartridge. Cylinder has five rounds. Heavy barrel to customer's length. Special grip. Blued or stainless steel.

NIB	Exc.	V.G.	Good	Fair	Poor
1400	1195	875	—	—	—

Ultimate 500

Chambered for .500 S&W cartridge. Fitted with heavy 5-shot cylinder. Barrel length of customer's choice. Black or ivory Micarta grips. Engraved games scenes and other special features.

NIB	Exc.	V.G.	Good	Fair	Poor
2750	2295	1650	—	—	—

Classic 45

Chambered for .45 Colt, .45 ACP or .45 Schofield cartridge, without full moon clips. Fitted with 6-shot unfluted cylinder. Special set back trigger, Bisley hammer, Super Blackhawk or Blackhawk stainless steel frame and other special features.

NIB	Exc.	V.G.	Good	Fair	Poor
1350	1125	900	—	—	—

Big 5 Classic

Single-shot rifle built on customer's Ruger No. 1 rifle. Chambered for .500 Jeffery cartridge. Fitted with heavy barrel to customer's length and muzzle-brake. Tuned action. Buttstock weight added. Game scene engraved.

NIB	Exc.	V.G.	Good	Fair	Poor
2200	1725	1150	—	—	—

The BMF

Features 4" barrel. Chambered for .500 Maximum cartridge and Magna-Ported. Bisley grip. Satin stainless steel finish, with black Micarta grips. Game scene engraved.

NIB	Exc.	V.G.	Good	Fair	Poor
2750	2295	1650	—	—	—

Double Duce

Ruger Single Six revolver. Fitted with 8-shot cylinder and 8" barrel for .22 WMR cartridge. Longer grip frame, with red cherry grips. Game scene engraved.

NIB	Exc.	V.G.	Good	Fair	Poor
1350	1125	900	—	—	—

Ultimate Black Widow

Built on customer's Blackhawk, Bisley or Super Blackhawk Ruger. Chambered for .475 or .500 Linebaugh. Heavy duty 5-shot cylinder. Barrel length to customer's choice. Bisley grip, with black Micarta grips. Black Chromix finish.

NIB	Exc.	V.G.	Good	Fair	Poor
1350	1125	900	—	—	—

REFORM
August Schuler
Suhl, Germany

Reform Pistol

A 6.35 or .25 ACP four barreled double-action pistol. Constructed so that barrel unit rises upward when trigger is pulled. Superficially resembles a

semi-automatic pistol. Blued, with hard rubber grips. Manufactured between 1906 and about 1913.

NIB	Exc.	V.G.	Good	Fair	Poor
—	1750	1200	950	600	375

REID, JAMES
New York, New York

Model 1 Revolver

Spur trigger .22-caliber revolver, with 3.5" octagonal barrel and 7-shot unfluted cylinder. Blued, with walnut grips. Barrel marked "J. Reid, New York". Approximately 500 manufactured between 1862 and 1865.

NIB	Exc.	V.G.	Good	Fair	Poor
—	—	1175	950	375	100

Model 2 Revolver

As above in .32-caliber. Barrel marked "Address W.P. Irving, 20 Cliff Street. N.Y." or "James P. Fitch. N.Y." Approximately 1,300 manufactured between 1862 and 1865.

NIB	Exc.	V.G.	Good	Fair	Poor
—	—	1175	950	385	100

Model 3 Revolver

Similar to above, with grip angle sharpened. Chambered for .32 rim-fire cartridge, with 4.75" barrel. Cylinder chambers are threaded so that percussion nipples can be inserted. Barrel marked "J. Reid N.Y. City". Approximately 300 made between 1862 and 1865.

NIB	Exc.	V.G.	Good	Fair	Poor
—	—	1550	1375	550	200

Model 4 Revolver

As above, with barrel lengths varying from 3.75" to 8". Approximately 1,600 manufactured between 1862 and 1865.

NIB	Exc.	V.G.	Good	Fair	Poor
—	—	1550	1375	550	200

"My Friend" Knuckle Duster

A 7-shot .22-caliber revolver. Constructed entirely of metal, without a barrel. Frame of silver-plated brass or blued iron. Marked "My Friend Patd. Dec. 26, 1865". Grip is formed with a finger hole so that the pistol can be used as a set of brass knuckles.

Courtesy W.P. Hallstein III and son Chip

Brass Frame

NIB	Exc.	V.G.	Good	Fair	Poor
—	1550	1200	800	500	200

Iron Frame

NIB	Exc.	V.G.	Good	Fair	Poor
—	2800	2250	800	500	250

.32 Caliber Knuckle Duster

As above in .32-caliber. Approximately 3,400 manufactured between 1869 and 1884.

Brass Frame

NIB	Exc.	V.G.	Good	Fair	Poor
—	1800	1500	800	600	200

Iron Frame

NIB	Exc.	V.G.	Good	Fair	Poor
—	2800	2250	1300	800	250

.41 Caliber Knuckle Duster

As above in .41-caliber. Marked "J. Reid's Derringer". Approximately 300 manufactured between 1875 and 1878.

NIB	Exc.	V.G.	Good	Fair	Poor
—	18500	15000	9000	6500	1500

Model No. 1 Knuckle Duster

As above with 3" barrel. Approximately 350 made between 1875 and 1880.

Courtesy W.P. Hallstein III and son Chip

NIB	Exc.	V.G.	Good	Fair	Poor
—	3350	2750	1300	850	250

Model No. 2 Knuckle Duster

As above with 1.75" barrel. Approximately 150 made between 1875 and 1880.

NIB	Exc.	V.G.	Good	Fair	Poor
—	3950	3000	1700	1250	500

Model No. 3 Derringer

A .41-caliber revolver, with 3" octagonal barrel and 5-shot fluted cylinder. Frame silver-plated. Blued barrel and cylinder. Approximately 75 made between 1880 and 1884.

NIB	Exc.	V.G.	Good	Fair	Poor
—	2900	2500	1200	950	350

Model No. 4 Derringer

As above, with brass frame and walnut grips. Marked "Reid's Extra". Approximately 200 made during 1883 and 1884.

NIB	Exc.	V.G.	Good	Fair	Poor
—	1800	1500	1000	700	250

New Model Knuckle Duster

Similar to Model 2, with 2" barrel and 5-shot cylinder. Barrel marked "Reid's New Model .32 My Friend". Approximately 150 made in 1884.

NIB	Exc.	V.G.	Good	Fair	Poor
—	1800	1500	1050	650	250

REISING ARMS CO.
Hartford, Connecticut

Standard Model

A .22-caliber semi-automatic pistol, with hinged 6.5" barrel and 10-round magazine. Standard finish blued, however, nickel-plated versions are known. Slide marked with company's name and patent dates. Bakelite grips impressed with a bear's head and motto "Reising, It's A Bear". Manufactured in both New York City and Hartford during 1920s. CAUTION: High-velocity ammunition should not be used in these pistols.

New York Manufacture

NIB	Exc.	V.G.	Good	Fair	Poor
—	900	750	500	300	100

Hartford Manufacture

NIB	Exc.	V.G.	Good	Fair	Poor
—	450	350	275	175	100

REMINGTON ARMS COMPANY, INC.
Madison, North Carolina

Founded in 1816 by Eliphalet Remington. Company has distinction of being oldest firearms manufacturing firm in United States. Since 1856, it has been known by four different names: between 1856 and 1888, E. Remington & Sons; 1888-1910, Remington Arms Company; 1910-1925, Remington Arms U.M.C. Company (Union Metallic Cartridge Company); and 1925 to present, Remington Arms Company.

1st Model Remington-Beals Revolver

A .31-caliber 5-shot percussion revolver, with 3" octagonal barrel. Cylinder turning mechanism mounted on left outside frame. Blued case-hardened, silver-plated, brass trigger guard and gutta-percha grips. Barrel marked, "F. Beal's Patent, June 24, '56 & May 26, '57"; frame "Remington's Ilion, N.Y.". Approximately 5,000 manufactured in 1857 and 1858.

NIB	Exc.	V.G.	Good	Fair	Poor
—	4500	3000	2500	500	300

2nd Model Remington-Beals Revolver

Spur trigger .31-caliber 5-shot percussion revolver, with 3" octagonal barrel. Blued case-hardened, with squared gutta-percha grip. Barrel marked "Beals Patent 1856 & 57, Manufactured by Remingtons Ilion, N.Y.". Approximately 1,000 manufactured between 1858 and 1860.

NIB	Exc.	V.G.	Good	Fair	Poor
—	6000	5000	4500	2500	1000

3rd Model Remington-Beals Revolver

A .31-caliber 5-shot percussion revolver, with 4" octagonal barrel. Loading lever mounted beneath barrel. Blued case-hardened, with gutta-percha grips. Barrel marked "Beals Pat. 1856, 57, 58" and also "Manufactured by Remingtons, Ilion, N.Y.". Approximately 1,500 manufactured in 1859 and 1860.

NIB	Exc.	V.G.	Good	Fair	Poor
—	4500	4000	3350	1150	500

Remington-Rider Revolver

Double-action .31-caliber percussion revolver, with 3" barrel and 5-shot cylinder. Most of these revolvers were blued but a few were nickel-plated case-hardened, with gutta-percha grips. This model also encountered altered to .32 rimfire. Barrel marked "Manufactured by Remingtons, Ilion, N.Y., Riders Pt. Aug. 17, 1858, May 3, 1859". Approximately 20,000 manufactured between 1860 and 1873. **NOTE:** Cartridge variation worth approximately 20 percent less than original percussion version.

NIB	Exc.	V.G.	Good	Fair	Poor
—	2500	1400	1100	675	300

Remington-Beals Army Revolver

A .44-caliber percussion revolver, with 8" barrel and 6-shot cylinder. Blued case-hardened, with walnut grips. Barrel marked "Beals Patent Sept. 14, 1858 Manufactured by Remington's Ilion, New York". Approximately 2,500 manufactured between 1860 and 1862. **NOTE:** Martially marked example extremely rare and would be worth approximately 35 percent additional.

NIB	Exc.	V.G.	Good	Fair	Poor
—	6500	4750	2500	1500	500

Remington-Beals Navy Revolver

Similar in appearance to Remington-Beals Army Revolver in .36-caliber, with 7.5" octagonal barrel. First examples of this model were fitted with a loading lever that would not allow cylinder pin to be completely removed. These examples are worth approximately 80 percent more than standard model. Approximately 1,000 of these revolvers were purchased by the United States government and martially marked examples are worth approximately 40 percent more than values listed below. Manufactured from 1860 to 1862. Total production of approximately 15,000.

Courtesy Wallis & Wallis, Lewes, Sussex, England

NIB	Exc.	V.G.	Good	Fair	Poor
—	6500	4750	2500	1500	500

1861 Army Revolver

A .44-caliber percussion revolver, with 8" octagonal barrel and 6-shot cylinder. Loading lever cut with a slot so that cylinder pin can be drawn forward without lever being lowered. Blued case-hardened, with walnut grips. Barrel marked "Patented Dec. 17, 1861 Manufactured by Remington's, Ilion, N.Y.". Some examples were converted to .46-caliber rimfire cartridge and would be worth approximately 25 percent more than original martially marked standard percussion model. Approximately 12,000 manufactured in 1862. This model also known as "Old Army Model".

Paul Goodwin photo

NIB	Exc.	V.G.	Good	Fair	Poor
—	7000	4750	2000	1000	500

1861 Navy Revolver

As above in .36-caliber, with 7.25" octagonal barrel. Blued case-hardened, with walnut grips. Also found altered to .38 metallic cartridge. Cartridge examples are worth approximately 35 percent less than percussion versions. Approximately 8,000 manufactured in 1862. **NOTE:** Add 25 percent for martial.

Paul Goodwin photo

NIB	Exc.	V.G.	Good	Fair	Poor
—	7200	6200	4500	2000	1000

New Model Army Revolver

A .44-caliber 6-shot percussion revolver, with 8" octagonal barrel. Blued case-hardened, with walnut grips. Barrel marked "Patented Sept. 14, 1858 E. Remington & Sons, Ilion, New York, U.S.A. New Model". Approximately 132,000 made between 1863 and 1873.

Standard Model—Military Version

NIB	Exc.	V.G.	Good	Fair	Poor
—	7000	5750	3750	1800	400

Civilian Model—No Government Inspector's Markings

NIB	Exc.	V.G.	Good	Fair	Poor
—	6000	5000	3000	1000	400

.44 or .46 Cartridge Conversion

Courtesy Milwaukee Public Museum, Milwaukee, Wisconsin

NIB	Exc.	V.G.	Good	Fair	Poor
—	4800	3000	1400	875	400

New Model Navy Revolver

As above in .36-caliber, with 7.23" octagonal barrel. Approximately 22,000 made between 1863 and 1875.

Courtesy Milwaukee Public Museum, Milwaukee, Wisconsin

Military Version

NIB	Exc.	V.G.	Good	Fair	Poor
—	7000	6000	4000	1900	900

Civilian Version

NIB	Exc.	V.G.	Good	Fair	Poor
—	5200	4000	2400	1000	400

.38 Cartridge Conversion—1873 to 1888

NIB	Exc.	V.G.	Good	Fair	Poor
—	4200	2400	1000	450	300

New Model Single-Action Belt Revolver

As above with 6.5" barrel. Blued or nickel-plated case-hardened, with walnut grips. Sometimes encountered altered to .38 cartridge. Cartridge examples are worth approximately 25 percent less than values listed below. Approximately 3,000 made between 1863 and 1873. **NOTE:** Blued models will command a premium.

Paul Goodwin photo

NIB	Exc.	V.G.	Good	Fair	Poor
—	4800	3000	1500	1000	500

Remington-Rider Double-Action Belt Revolver

Double-action .36-caliber percussion revolver, with 6.5" octagonal barrel marked "Manufactured by Remington's, Ilion, N.Y. Rider's Pt. Aug. 17, 1858, May 3, 1859". Blued or nickel-plated case-hardened, with walnut grips. Also found converted to cartridge and such examples would be worth approximately 20 percent less than values listed below. Several hundred of this model were made with fluted cylinders and are worth a premium of about 25 percent. Approximately 5,000 made between 1863 and 1873.

Courtesy Milwaukee Public Museum, Milwaukee, Wisconsin

NIB	Exc.	V.G.	Good	Fair	Poor
—	4500	2750	1500	900	400

New Model Police Revolver

A .36-caliber percussion revolver, with octagonal barrels ranging from 3.5" to 6.5" and 5-shot cylinder. Blued or nickel-plated case-hardened, with walnut grips. Also found converted to cartridge and such examples would be worth approximately 20 percent less than values listed below. Approximately 18,000 manufactured between 1863 and 1873. **NOTE:** Blued models will command a premium.

Paul Goodwin photo

NIB	Exc.	V.G.	Good	Fair	Poor
—	4200	3000	2000	800	300

New Model Pocket Revolver

A .31-caliber spur trigger percussion revolver, with octagonal barrels ranging from 3" to 4.5" in length and 5-shot cylinder. Blued or nickel-plated case-hardened, with walnut grips. Barrel marked "Patented Sept.

14, 1858, March 17, 1863 E. Remington & Sons, Ilion, New York U.S.A. New Model.". Approximately 25,000 manufactured between 1863 and 1873. **NOTE:** Add 15 percent for blued models.

1st Version

Brass frame and trigger.

NIB	Exc.	V.G.	Good	Fair	Poor
—	4200	3200	1800	1300	300

2nd Version

Iron frame, brass trigger.

NIB	Exc.	V.G.	Good	Fair	Poor
—	—	2750	1400	900	300

3rd Version

Iron frame, iron trigger.

NIB	Exc.	V.G.	Good	Fair	Poor
—	—	2400	1200	800	300

.32 Cartridge Conversion

NIB	Exc.	V.G.	Good	Fair	Poor
—	—	2200	1000	600	300

Remington-Rider Derringer

Small silver-plated brass single-shot .17-caliber percussion pistol, with 3" round barrel. Barrel marked "Rider's Pt. Sept. 13, 1859". Approximately 1,000 manufactured between 1860 and 1863. Beware of fakes.

NIB	Exc.	V.G.	Good	Fair	Poor
—	—	6900	3300	975	300

Zig-Zag Derringer

A 6-shot .22-caliber revolving barrel pocket pistol, with barrels 3.25" in length. Barrels are cut with zigzag grooves, which are part of the revolving mechanism. Trigger formed as a ring that when moved forward and rearward turns the barrels and cocks the internal hammer. Barrel group marked "Elliot's Patent Aug. 17, 1858 May 29, 1860" as well as "Manufactured by Remington's Ilion, N.Y.". Approximately 1,000 manufactured in 1861 and 1862.

Paul Goodwin photo

NIB	Exc.	V.G.	Good	Fair	Poor
—	5000	3600	1650	650	300

Remington-Elliot Derringer

A 5-shot .22-caliber or 4-shot .32-caliber pepperbox pistol, with a revolving firing pin. Blued or nickel-plated, with hard rubber grips. Barrel group marked "Manufactured by E. Remington & Sons, Ilion, N.Y. Elliot's Patents May 19, 1860 - Oct.1, 1861". Approximately 25,000 manufactured between 1863 and 1888.

5-shot .22 caliber

NIB	Exc.	V.G.	Good	Fair	Poor
—	5000	3600	1500	750	200

4-shot .32 caliber

Courtesy W.P. Hallstein III and son Chip

NIB	Exc.	V.G.	Good	Fair	Poor
—	5000	3600	1500	750	200

Vest Pocket Pistol

A .22-caliber single-shot pistol, with 3.25" barrel. Blued or nickel-plated, with walnut grips. Barrel marked "Remington's Ilion, N.Y. Patent Oct. 1, 1861". Early examples have been noted without any barrel markings. Approximately 25,000 manufactured from 1865 to 1888. **NOTE:** Add 35 percent premium for blued models.

Paul Goodwin photo

NIB	Exc.	V.G.	Good	Fair	Poor
—	3000	2000	1000	400	200

Large-Bore Vest Pocket Pistol

As above in .30-, .32- or .41-caliber, with barrel lengths of 3.5" or 4". Blued or nickel-plated, with walnut or rosewood grips. Barrel markings as above, except for the addition of patent date, November 15, 1864. Smaller caliber versions are worth approximately 20 percent more than .41-caliber. Approximately 10,000 manufactured from 1865 to 1888. **NOTE:** Add 35 percent premium for blued models.

NIB	Exc.	V.G.	Good	Fair	Poor
—	3300	2200	1200	350	150

Remington-Elliot Single-Shot Derringer

A .41-caliber single-shot pistol, with 2.5" round barrel. Blued or nickel-plated, with walnut, ivory or pearl grips. Barrel marked "Remingtons, Ilion, N.Y. Elliot Pat. Aug. 27, 1867". Approximately 10,000 manufactured between 1867 and 1888. **NOTE:** Add 35 percent premium for blued models. For all variations of Remington Over/Under Derringer below, examine closely for broken or cracked barrel hinge and subtract from value accordingly.

NIB	Exc.	V.G.	Good	Fair	Poor
—	3500	2500	1200	400	125

REMINGTON OVER/UNDER DERRINGERS

Double-barrel .41-caliber pocket pistol, with 3" round barrels that pivot upward for loading. There is a lock bar to release barrels on the right side of frame. Firing pin raises and lowers automatically to fire each respective barrel. It has a spur trigger and bird's-head grip. Finish blued or nickel-plated and featured with walnut, rosewood or checkered hard rubber grips. Examples with factory pearl or ivory grips would be worth a small premium. Approximately 150,000 manufactured between 1866 and 1935.

Early Type I

Manufactured without an extractor, this type marked "E." Remington & Sons, Ilion, N.Y." on one side and "Elliot's Patent Dec. 12, 1865" on other side of barrel rib. Only a few hundred manufactured in 1866. **NOTE:** Add 25 percent premium for blued models.

NIB	Exc.	V.G.	Good	Fair	Poor
—	10000	8000	5000	4000	3000

Type I Mid-Production

As above fitted with an extractor. Manufactured in late 1860s. **NOTE:** Add 25 percent premium for blued models.

NIB	Exc.	V.G.	Good	Fair	Poor
—	6000	5000	4000	2500	1200

Type I Late Production

Fitted with an automatic extractor and marked on top of barrel rib. Manufactured from late 1860s to 1888. **NOTE:** Add 25 percent premium for blued models.

NIB	Exc.	V.G.	Good	Fair	Poor
—	4500	3400	2200	1000	200

Type II

Marked "Remington Arms Co., Ilion, N.Y." on barrel rib. Manufactured between 1888 and 1911. **NOTE:** Add 25 percent premium for blued models.

NIB	Exc.	V.G.	Good	Fair	Poor
—	5000	4000	3000	2000	1000

Type III

Marked "Remington Arms - U.M.C. Co., Ilion, N.Y." on barrel rib. Manufactured between 1912 and 1935. **NOTE:** Add 40 percent if there is no "L" in the serial number. For Type III models, blue or nickel prices are the same.

NIB	Exc.	V.G.	Good	Fair	Poor
—	3500	2500	1500	800	500

Remington-Rider Magazine Pistol

A 5-shot .32-caliber magazine pistol, with spur trigger and 3" octagonal barrel. Magazine located beneath barrel and can be loaded from front. Blued nickel-plated or case-hardened, with walnut, pearl or ivory grips. Barrel marked "E. Remington & Sons, Ilion, N.Y. Riders Pat. Aug. 15, 1871". Approximately 10,000 manufactured between 1871 and 1888. **NOTE:** Add 50 percent premium for blued finish.

Courtesy William F. Krause

NIB	Exc.	V.G.	Good	Fair	Poor
—	3000	1950	825	350	150

Model 1865 Navy Rolling Block Pistol

Spur trigger single-shot rolling block .50-caliber rimfire cartridge pistol, with 8.5" round barrel. Blued case-hardened, with walnut grips and fore-end. Barrel marked "Remingtons, Ilion N.Y. U.S.A. Pat. May 3d Nov. 15th, 1864 April 17th, 1866". Examples bearing military inspection marks are worth approximately 25 percent more than values listed below. Examples are also found altered to centerfire cartridge and these are worth approximately 10 percent less than values listed below. Approximately 6,500 manufactured between 1866 and 1870.

NIB	Exc.	V.G.	Good	Fair	Poor
—	6000	4500	3000	1000	400

Model 1867 Navy Rolling Block Pistol

A .50-caliber single-shot rolling block pistol, with 7" round barrel. Blued case-hardened, with walnut grips and fore-end. Majority of these pistols were purchased by the United States government. Civilian examples without inspection marks are worth approximately 30 percent more than values listed.

NIB	Exc.	V.G.	Good	Fair	Poor
—	6000	4500	3000	1000	400

Model 1871 Army Rolling Block Pistol

A .50-caliber rolling block single-shot pistol, with 8" round barrel. Blued case-hardened, with walnut grips and fore-end. Distinguishing feature is a rearward extension at top of the grip and a squared butt. Approximately 6,000 manufactured between 1872 and 1888. Engraved ivory-stocked versions, as pictured below, will bring considerable premiums.

NIB	Exc.	V.G.	Good	Fair	Poor
—	3500	2350	1800	875	400

Remington-Smoot No. 1 Revolver

A .30-caliber spur trigger revolver, with 2.75" octagonal barrel and 5-shot fluted cylinder. Blued or nickel-plated, with walnut or hard rubber grips.

Barrel rib marked "E. Remington & Sons, Ilion, N.Y. Pat. W. S. Smoot Oct. 21, 1873". Examples dating from beginning of production are found with a revolving recoil shield. Such examples would command approximately 300 percent premium over values listed. **NOTE:** Add 50 percent premium for blued finish.

NIB	Exc.	V.G.	Good	Fair	Poor
—	2000	1650	1100	675	250

Remington-Smoot No. 2 Revolver

As above in .32-caliber. Approximately 20,000 manufactured between 1878 and 1888. **NOTE:** Add 50 percent premium for blued finish.

NIB	Exc.	V.G.	Good	Fair	Poor
—	1800	875	600	275	100

Remington-Smoot No. 3 Revolver

Two variations of this spur trigger .38-caliber revolver exist. One with rounded grip and no barrel rib; other with squared back, squared butt grip with barrel rib. Centerfire versions are also known and are worth approximately 10 percent more than values listed below. Blued or nickel-plated, with hard rubber grips. Approximately 25,000 manufactured between 1878 and 1888. **NOTE:** Add 50 percent premium for blued finish.

Paul Goodwin photo

NIB	Exc.	V.G.	Good	Fair	Poor
—	1700	650	550	325	100

New No. 4 Revolver

A .38- or .41-caliber spur trigger revolver, with 2.5" barrel and no ejector rod. Blued or nickel-plated, with hard rubber grips. Barrel marked "E. Remington & Sons, Ilion, N.Y.". Approximately 10,000 manufactured between 1877 and 1888. **NOTE:** Add 50 percent premium for blued finish.

Paul Goodwin photo

NIB	Exc.	V.G.	Good	Fair	Poor
—	1700	775	475	225	100

Remington Iroquois Revolver

A .22-caliber spur trigger revolver, with 2.25" barrel and 7-shot cylinder. Blued or nickel-plated, with hard rubber grips. Barrel marked "Remington, Ilion, N.Y." and "Iroquois". Some examples will be found without Remington markings. Approximately 10,000 manufactured between 1878 and 1888. **NOTE:** Add 50 percent premium for blued finish.

NIB	Exc.	V.G.	Good	Fair	Poor
—	2000	1100	825	385	150

Model 1875 Single-Action Revolver

A .44 Rem., .44-40 or .45-caliber single-action revolver, with 7.5" barrel. Blued or nickel-plated case-hardened, with walnut grips. Some examples found fitted with a lanyard ring at butt. Barrel marked "E. Remington & Sons Ilion, N.Y. U.S.A.". Approximately 25,000 manufactured between 1875 and 1889. **NOTE:** Add 40 percent for blued version.

Courtesy Milwaukee Public Museum, Milwaukee, Wisconsin

NIB	Exc.	V.G.	Good	Fair	Poor
—	14000	10000	6000	3000	1000

Model 1890 Single-Action Revolver

A .44-40 caliber single-action revolver, with 5.5" or 7.5" barrel and 6-shot cylinder. Blued or nickel-plated, with hard rubber grips bearing monogram "RA" at top. Barrel marked "Remington Arms Co., Ilion, N.Y.". Approximately 2,000 manufactured between 1891 and 1894. Beware of fakes. **NOTE:** Add 40 percent for blued version.

Paul Goodwin photo

NIB	Exc.	V.G.	Good	Fair	Poor
—	15000	10000	6000	3000	1000

Model 1891 Target Rolling Block Pistol

A .22, .25 Stevens or .32 S&W caliber single-shot rolling block pistol, with 10" half octagonal barrel fitted with target sights. Blued case-hardened, with walnut grips and fore-end. Barrel marked "Remington Arms Co. Ilion, N.Y."; frame "Remingtons Ilion N.Y. U.S.A. Pat. May 3 Nov. 15, 1864 April 17, 1866 P S". An extremely rare pistol, with slightly more than 100 manufactured between 1892 and 1898. Prospective purchasers are advised to secure a qualified appraisal prior to acquisition.

Paul Goodwin photo

NIB	Exc.	V.G.	Good	Fair	Poor
—	4000	3700	2750	1200	500

Model 1901 Target Rolling Block

As above, except bridge block thumb piece has been moved out of the line of sight and rear sight mounted on frame instead of barrel. Approximately 735 manufactured between 1901 and 1909.

Paul Goodwin photo

NIB	Exc.	V.G.	Good	Fair	Poor
—	4000	3650	2750	1200	500

Mark III Signal Pistol

A 10-gauge spur trigger flare pistol, with 9" round barrel. Frame of brass and barrel of iron finished matte black, with walnut grips. Barrel marked "The Remington Arms - Union Metallic Cartridge Co., Inc. Mark III, Remington Bridgeport Works Bridgeport, Connecticut U.S.A.". Approximately 25,000 manufactured between 1915 and 1918.

Paul Goodwin photo

NIB	Exc.	V.G.	Good	Fair	Poor
—		725	375	110	55

Model 51

A .32- or .380-caliber semi-automatic pistol, with 3.5" barrel. Magazines capable of holding 7 or 8 cartridges depending on caliber. Blued, with hard rubber grips having legend "Remington UMC" in a circle at top. Slide marked "The Remington Arms - Union Metallic Cartridge Co., Inc. Remington Ilion Wks. Ilion, N.Y. U.S.A. Pedersen's Patents Pending". Later versions carried a 1920 and 1921 patent date. Early examples have 9 grooves on slide; later models 15 grooves, with frame marked "Remington Trademark". Early variations are worth approximately 10 percent more than values listed below; .32-caliber examples are worth approximately 25 percent additional. Approximately 65,000 manufactured between 1918 and 1934.

Courtesy Orvel Reichert

NIB	Exc.	V.G.	Good	Fair	Poor
—	750	575	350	125	75

Model 53

Built in 1917 for U.S. government test in .45 ACP. Similar to Model 51, except for size and an external hammer. Tested by US Army and Navy. Overall length 8.25"; weight about 35 oz.; magazine capacity 7 rounds. Too rare to price.

Courtesy James Rankin

1911R1 SERIES

Model 1911R1

Combines traditional 1911 features with modern touches. Caliber .45 ACP. Carbon steel slide and frame, traditionally styled trigger, hammer, recoil system, walnut grips, 7-round magazine, thumb and grip safeties. Dovetailed front and rear sights, with white dots, lowered and flared ejection port. Weight 38.5 oz., 5" barrel and Satin Black Oxide or stainless finish. Model 1911 Enhanced has match-grade barrel and bushing, front cocking serrations, extended thumb safety and beavertail tang, textured grips, adjustable rear and fiber optic front sights and lightweight trigger and hammer. Introduced 2010. **NOTE:** Add $50 for stainless finish. A Commander version available with 4.25" barrel.

NIB	Exc.	V.G.	Good	Fair	Poor
600	525	435	350	200	150

Model 1911R1 Centennial

Same features as 1911R1, with special Centennial engravings on slide, Centennial serial number range, dovetailed brass-bead front and black serrated rear sight. Custom grips with Remington medallions.

NIB	Exc.	V.G.	Good	Fair	Poor
1100	925	800	600	—	—

Model 1911R1 Centennial Limited Edition

Same features as above, plus uniquely engraved slide with gold banner, custom charcoal blued finish, 24-karat gold front sight, smooth exhibition grade walnut grips. Each Limited Edition model is hand assembled and comes in a custom wood presentation case. Introduced in 2011. Production scheduled for only 300 units.

NIB	Exc.	V.G.	Good	Fair	Poor
2000	1900	1800	—	—	—

Model 1911R1 Enhanced

Same features and dimensions as other 1911R1 models, with custom enhancements. In .45 ACP, with 8-round magazine. Adjustable rear sight and fiber optic front. Hardwood checkered grips. Front and rear slide serrations, with checkered mainspring housing. Aluminum anodized trigger. Match grade barrel and bushing. Carbon steel frame and slide, with

satin black oxide finish. Custom carrying case. Introduced 2012; stainless version 2013. **NOTE:** Add $150 for optional threaded barrel; $50 for stainless finish.

NIB	Exc.	V.G.	Good	Fair	Poor
875	775	675	550	400	350

Model 1911R1 Carry

Same general specifications as other 1911R1 models. Added features include: all sharp edges have been dehorned; Novak combat sights, with tritium front sight; Cocobolo checkered grips; Beavertail grip safety, with checkered memory bump; rear slide serrations, with checkered mainspring housing and front strap; aluminum anodized trigger; match grade barrel and bushing; carbon steel frame and slide, with satin black oxide finish. Custom carrying case. 8+1 capacity. Introduced 2013.

NIB	Exc.	V.G.	Good	Fair	Poor
1150	1000	900	700	450	350

Remington-UMC Commemorative 1911

Limited edition replica of Remington manufactured military 1911 made in 1918 and 1919. This edition limited to 4,000 units made in 2014.

NIB	Exc.	V.G.	Good	Fair	Poor
2400	2000	1600	—	—	—

Model R51

Sub-compact 9mm with double-action only operation, 3.4" barrel, low-profile fixed sights, grip safety, ambidextrous magazine release and 7+1 capacity. Introduced in 2014. **NOTE:** In July of 2014, Remington stopped production of R51 and announced a recall of the pistol due to reports of functioning problems. Anyone who purchased an early production R51 may return it to Remiington and receive a new one, along with two additional magazines and a custom Pelican case. To find out if your R51 is subject to the recall, contact Remington at (800) 243-9700. You will be asked to provide your name, address, telephone number and serial number of your pistol. Production of R51 resumed in August of 2016, with what Remington describes as a perfected design. Among updated features are a fast re-set polymer trigger, a more aggressive extractor and an enhanced recoil spring. MSRP is $448.00.

NIB	Exc.	V.G.	Good	Fair	Poor
400	350	300	275	200	150

Model RM380

Mini-compact double-action only pistol chambered in .380 ACP with 6+1 capacity and 2.9" stainless steel barrel. Slide is all steel and frame aluminum. Overall length 5.27"; weight empty 12.2 oz.; height 3.86"; width .94". Other features include a fully functional slide stop and ambidextrous magazine release. Introduced in 2015.

NIB	Exc.	V.G.	Good	Fair	Poor
385	335	300	275	—	—

RIFLES

Model 1841 "Mississippi Rifle"

A .54-caliber percussion rifle, with 33" barrel. Full stock secured by two barrel bands. Lock case-hardened marked (Remington's Herkimer N.Y.). Barrel browned and furniture of brass. Stock fitted with brass patchbox on right side. Approximately 20,000 manufactured between 1846 and 1855.

Paul Goodwin photo

NIB	Exc.	V.G.	Good	Fair	Poor
—	—	2000	1750	750	400

Model 1861 U.S. Rifle Musket

A .58-caliber percussion rifle, with 40" barrel. Full length stock secured by three barrel bands. Lock marked "Remington's Ilion, N.Y.". Finished in white, with walnut stock. Approximately 40,000 manufactured between 1864 and 1866.

Paul Goodwin photo

NIB	Exc.	V.G.	Good	Fair	Poor
—	4500	3000	1250	500	200

Model 1863 Zouave Rifle

A .58-caliber percussion rifle, with 33" barrel. Full length stock secured by two barrel bands. Lock case-hardened marked "Remington's Ilion N.Y.". Barrel blued and furniture of brass. Approximately 12,500 manufactured between 1862 and 1865.

Paul Goodwin photo

NIB	Exc.	V.G.	Good	Fair	Poor
—	6000	4000	2250	1500	500

Breech-Loading Carbine

A .46 or .50 rimfire single-shot rolling block carbine, with 20" barrel. Blued case-hardened, with walnut stock. Tang marked "Remington's Ilion, N.Y. Pat. Dec. 23, 1863 May 3 & Nov. 16, 1864". The .50-caliber version worth approximately 15 percent more than .46-caliber. Approximately 15,000 .50-caliber variations were made, most of which were sold to France. Approximately 5,000 carbines were made in .46-caliber. Manufactured from 1864 to 1866.

Paul Goodwin photo

NIB	Exc.	V.G.	Good	Fair	Poor
—	—	3750	1500	500	200

Revolving Rifle

A .36- or. 44-caliber revolving rifle, with 24" or 28" octagonal barrels and 6-shot cylinder. Trigger guard formed with scrolled finger extension at rear. Blued case-hardened, with walnut stock. These rifles are also encountered converted to cartridge and would be worth approximately 20 percent less than percussion values listed below. Barrel marked "Patented Sept. 14, 1858 E. Remington & Sons, Ilion, New York, U.S.A. New Model". The .44-caliber model will bring a premium of about 15 percent and is rare. Approximately 1,000 manufactured between 1866 and 1879.

Courtesy Buffalo Bill Historical Center, Cody, Wyoming

NIB	Exc.	V.G.	Good	Fair	Poor
—	6000	5000	2500	1500	500

NIB	Exc.	V.G.	Good	Fair	Poor
—	20000	11500	8000	5500	900

Remington-Beals Rifle

A .32- or .38-caliber sliding barrel single-shot rifle, with octagonal barrels of 24", 26" or 28" length. Barrel can be moved forward by lowering trigger guard/lever. This model found with frames made of brass or iron, the latter being worth approximately 20 percent more than values listed below. Walnut stock. Barrel marked "Beals Patent June 28, 1864 Jan. 30, 1866 E. Remington & Sons, Ilion, New York.". Approximately 800 manufactured between 1866 and 1888. Few examples are known to have been factory engraved. Prospective purchasers are advised to secure a qualified appraisal prior to acquisition.

Courtesy Milwaukee Public Museum, Milwaukee, Wisconsin

NIB	Exc.	V.G.	Good	Fair	Poor
—	2500	1500	950	400	150

U.S. Navy Rolling Block Carbine

NIB	Exc.	V.G.	Good	Fair	Poor
—	4500	4000	2750	1000	350

Model 1867 Navy Cadet Rifle

Paul Goodwin photo

NIB	Exc.	V.G.	Good	Fair	Poor
—	4000	3500	1400	700	350

Rolling Block Military Rifles

NIB	Exc.	V.G.	Good	Fair	Poor
—	—	900	750	400	100

NO. 1 ROLLING BLOCK SPORTING RIFLE

Standard No. 1 Sporting Rifle

Single-shot rolling block rifle. Produced in a variety of calibers from .40-50 to .50-70 centerfire, as well as .32, .44 and .46 rimfire. Standard octagonal barrel lengths were 28" or 30".

Courtesy Milwaukee Public Museum, Milwaukee, Wisconsin

Long-Range Creedmoor Rifle

A .44-90, .44-100 or .44-105 caliber rolling block rifle, with 34" half-octagonal barrel, long-range vernier tang sights and globe front. Blued case-hardened, with walnut stock and checkered pistol-grip. Rifle was available with a number of optional features. A qualified appraisal should be secured if those features are in doubt. Produced from 1873 to 1890.

Courtesy Bonhams & Butterfields, San Francisco, California

NIB	Exc.	V.G.	Good	Fair	Poor
—	12500	10000	7000	3500	1500

Mid-Range Target Rifle

As above, except chambered for .40-70, .44-77, .45-70 or .50-70 caliber, with 28" or 30" half-octagonal barrels. Produced from 1875 to 1890.

NIB	Exc.	V.G.	Good	Fair	Poor
—	—	6000	2750	1750	300

Short-Range Rifle

As above, chambered for cartridges between .38- and .44-caliber, with 26" or 30" round or octagonal barrels. Open rear sight, with Beach front sight. Walnut stock is checkered. Produced from 1875 to 1890.

NIB	Exc.	V.G.	Good	Fair	Poor
—	—	5000	2750	1675	250

Black Hills Rifle

As above in .45-60 caliber, with 28" round barrel. Fitted with open sights and plain straight-grip stock. Produced from 1877 to 1882.

NIB	Exc.	V.G.	Good	Fair	Poor
—	—	5000	2750	1675	250

Shotgun

As above in 16-gauge, with 30" or 32" Damascus or fluid steel barrels. Produced from 1870 to 1892.

NIB	Exc.	V.G.	Good	Fair	Poor
—	2800	1650	1200	750	150

Baby Carbine

As above, with 20" thin round barrel. Chambered for .44-40 cartridge. Fitted with a saddle ring on left side of frame. Blued case-hardened, with walnut stock and carbine buttplate. Manufactured from 1892 to 1902.

NIB	Exc.	V.G.	Good	Fair	Poor
—	8000	4250	2250	900	200

Model 1-1/2 Sporting Rifle

Lightweight variation of above, using 1.25" wide No. 1 rolling block action. Chambered for rimfire cartridges from .22 to .38 Extra Long, as well as centerfire cartridges from .32-20 to .44-40. Medium weight octagonal barrels from 24" to 28" in length, with open rear and blade-type front sight. Blued case-hardened, with walnut stock. Several thousand manufactured between 1888 and 1897.

Paul Goodwin photo

NIB	Exc.	V.G.	Good	Fair	Poor
—	4000	3000	950	400	100

Model 2 Sporting Rifle

As above using No. 2 action. Chambered for various cartridges from .22- to .38-caliber, with 24" or 26" octagonal barrels. Blued case-hardened, with walnut stock. Produced with a number of optional features that affect its value. Prospective purchasers are advised to secure a qualified appraisal prior to acquisition. Manufactured from 1873 to 1910.

Paul Goodwin photo

NIB	Exc.	V.G.	Good	Fair	Poor
—	3200	2200	700	250	100

No. 4 Rolling Block Rifle

Built on lightweight No. 4 action. Available in .22, .25 Stevens or .32-caliber, with 22.5" or 24" octagonal barrel. Blued case-hardened, with walnut stock. Takedown version was also made and these are worth approximately 10 percent more than values listed. Approximately 50,000 manufactured between 1890 and 1933.

NIB	Exc.	V.G.	Good	Fair	Poor
—	1300	1000	400	200	75

No. 4 S Military Rifle

At the request of United States Boy Scouts in 1913, Remington Company designed a military style rifle having a 28" barrel and full length fore-end secured by one barrel band. A short upper hand guard was also fitted and a bayonet stud is found at the muzzle. In 1915, designation of this model was changed from "Boy Scout" to "Military Model". Approximately 15,000 manufactured between 1913 and 1923.

Paul Goodwin photo

NIB	Exc.	V.G.	Good	Fair	Poor
—	—	2250	950	400	275

No. 5 Rolling Block Rifle

Built on No. 5 action, this rifle was designed for smokeless cartridges. Made in a variety of barrel lengths, calibers and in a carbine version. Blued case-hardened, with walnut stock.

NIB	Exc.	V.G.	Good	Fair	Poor
—	—	2250	800	350	100

No. 5 Sporting or Target Rifle

Chambered for .30-30, .303 British, 7mm, .30 U.S., .32-40, .32 U.S. and .38-55 cartridges. Offered with 28" or 30" round barrels. Features a plain straight-grip stock, with half-length fore-end. Has open rear sights and was available with double-set triggers that would add approximately 10 percent to value. Manufactured between 1898 and 1905.

NIB	Exc.	V.G.	Good	Fair	Poor
—	—	5750	2250	850	300

Model 1897

A 7x57mm and .30 U.S. caliber full stock rolling block rifle. Model 1902 is of identical form, except it was fitted with an automatic ejector. Manufactured from 1897 to 1902.

Paul Goodwin photo

NIB	Exc.	V.G.	Good	Fair	Poor
—	2800	1250	550	250	100

Carbine

As above fitted with 20" round barrel and half-length fore-end secured by one barrel band.

NIB	Exc.	V.G.	Good	Fair	Poor
—	—	1750	750	350	100

No. 6 Falling Block Rifle

Lightweight small rifle designed expressly to be used by young boys. Chambered for .22 rimfire cartridge, as well as .32 Short or Long. Also produced with smoothbore barrel to be used with shot cartridges. Round barrel 20" in length. Has a takedown action, with barrel held on by a knurled knob underneath the frame. It is a lightweight rolling block, with a thin operating knob on the breech. Finish is blued overall. Early models featured case colored frame and these versions would be worth approximately 10 percent additional. Has a straight-grip walnut stock, with a small forearm. Over 250,000 manufactured between 1902 and 1903.

Paul Goodwin photo

NIB	Exc.	V.G.	Good	Fair	Poor
—	750	475	300	100	75

No. 7 Rolling Block Rifle

Readily identifiable by its accentuated checked pistol-grip. Available in .22 or .25-10 Stevens caliber, with 24", 26" or 28" half octagonal barrels. Fitted with a tang mounted aperture rear sight. Blued case-hardened, with walnut stock. Approximately 1,000 manufactured between 1903 and 1911.

NIB	Exc.	V.G.	Good	Fair	Poor
—	7500	6000	4000	2000	500

REMINGTON-HEPBURN RIFLES

Remington-Hepburn No. 3 Rifle

Lever activated falling block single-shot rifle designed by Lewis Hepburn. Available in a variety of calibers from .22 Win. centerfire to .50-90 Sharps. Octagonal or round barrels 26", 28" or 30" length. Blued case-hardened, with walnut stock. Available with a variety of optional features that affect value considerably. Prospective purchasers are advised to secure a qualified appraisal prior to acquisition. Approximately 10,000 manufactured between 1883 and 1907.

NIB	Exc.	V.G.	Good	Fair	Poor
—	8000	6500	4000	1200	300

Remington-Hepburn No. 3 Match Rifle

As above fitted with a high comb buttstock and nickel-plated Schuetzen buttplate. Manufactured in various calibers from .25-20 Stevens to .40-65, with 30" half octagonal barrels. Model was made in two versions: "A Quality" with plain stock, tang mounted rear sight and a Beach front sight; "B Quality" with checkered walnut stock having a cheek rest, checkered fore-end, vernier rear sight and combination wind gauge and spirit level front sight. Double-set triggers were also available and these would add approximately 10 percent to values listed below. Approximately 1,000 manufactured between 1883 and 1907.

A Quality

Paul Goodwin photo

NIB	Exc.	V.G.	Good	Fair	Poor
—	9000	7500	4750	1800	350

B Quality

Paul Goodwin photo

NIB	Exc.	V.G.	Good	Fair	Poor
—	10000	8250	5000	1900	500

Remington-Hepburn No. 3 Long-Range Creedmoor Rifle

As above in .44-caliber, with 32" or 34" half-octagonal barrel. Long-range vernier rear sight, combination wind gauge and spirit level front sight. Deluxe checkered walnut stock and rubber shotgun buttplate. Produced with a number of optional features that affect value. Prospective purchasers are advised to secure a qualified appraisal prior to acquisition. Manufactured from 1880 to 1907.

Paul Goodwin photo

NIB	Exc.	V.G.	Good	Fair	Poor
—	12000	8500	4750	1800	350

Remington-Hepburn No. 3 Mid-Range Creedmoor Rifle

As above chambered for .40-65 cartridge. Fitted with 28" barrel.

NIB	Exc.	V.G.	Good	Fair	Poor
—	10000	6500	3000	950	350

Remington-Hepburn No. 3 Long-Range Military Rifle

Rare variation chambered for .44-20 Rem. cartridge. Has round 34" barrel and full-length forearm held on by two barrel bands. Blued case colored finish. Stock is walnut. There are two basic versions: plain grade, has uncheckered straight-grip stock, with military-type sights; fancy grade, features high-grade checkered pistol-grip stock, with full-length checkered fore-end, vernier tang sight, wind gauge and spirit lever front sight. A few manufactured in the 1880s.

Paul Goodwin photo

Plain Grade

NIB	Exc.	V.G.	Good	Fair	Poor
—	9000	6000	3000	1200	400

Fancy Grade

NIB	Exc.	V.G.	Good	Fair	Poor
—	11000	8000	4000	1500	600

Remington-Hepburn No. 3 Schuetzen Match Rifle

As above instead of side lever the action is raised or lowered by means of lever on the trigger guard. Chambered for various popular cartridges. Offered with 30" or 32" part-octagonal heavy barrel. Features vernier tang sight, with hooded front sight. Standard with double-set triggers and palm rest. Finish blued and case colored, with high-grade checkered walnut stock and fore-end. Has ornate Swiss-type Schuetzen buttplate. Also known as "Walker-Hepburn Rifle". There were two versions available. One, standard breech-loader with Remington Walker-marked barrel; the other, a muzzle-loading variation fitted with a removable false muzzle. This version was supplied with brass bullet starter and other accessories. Prospective purchasers are advised to secure a qualified appraisal prior to acquisition.

Breechloading Version

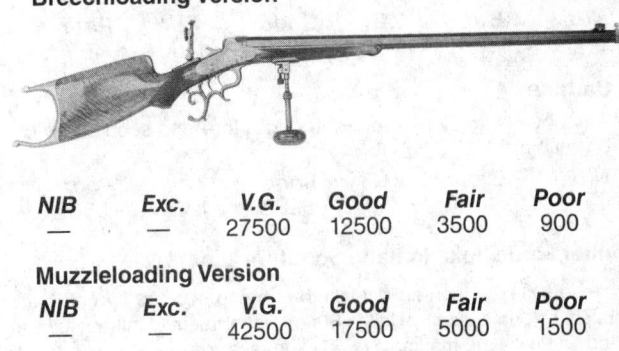

NIB	Exc.	V.G.	Good	Fair	Poor
—	—	27500	12500	3500	900

Muzzleloading Version

NIB	Exc.	V.G.	Good	Fair	Poor
—	—	42500	17500	5000	1500

Remington-Hepburn No. 3 High-Power Rifle

Model No. 3 also available in a variety of smokeless cartridges: .30-30, .30-40, .32 Special, .32-40 and .38-55. Standard barrel lengths were 26", 28" or 30". Produced from 1900 to 1907.

NIB	Exc.	V.G.	Good	Fair	Poor
—	4000	2500	1750	650	250

REMINGTON-KEENE MAGAZINE RIFLE

Bolt-action rifle chambered for .40, .43 and .45-70 centerfire cartridges, with 22", 24.5", 29.25" or 32.5" barrels. Readily identifiable by exposed hammer at end of the bolt. Blued case-hardened hammer and furniture, with walnut stock. Receiver marked "E. Remington & Sons, Ilion, N.Y." together with patent dates 1874, 1876 and 1877. Magazine on this rifle was located beneath the barrel. Receiver fitted with a cut-off so that rifle could be used as a single-shot. Approximately 5,000 manufactured between 1880 and 1888 in variations listed.

Sporting Rifle

24.5" barrel.

Remington-Keene Repeating Sporting Rifle Fancy Grade

NIB	Exc.	V.G.	Good	Fair	Poor
—	3450	2000	750	350	150

Army Rifle

Barrel length 32.5". Full-length stock secured by two barrel bands.

Courtesy Milwaukee Public Museum, Milwaukee, Wisconsin

NIB	Exc.	V.G.	Good	Fair	Poor
—	—	—	3500	950	450

Navy Rifle

As above, with 29.25" barrel.

NIB	Exc.	V.G.	Good	Fair	Poor
—	—	—	4500	1750	450

Carbine

As above, with 22" barrel. Half-length fore-end secured by one barrel band.

NIB	Exc.	V.G.	Good	Fair	Poor
—	—	5750	3250	1250	350

Frontier Model (aka Indiana Scout Carbine)

As above, with 24" barrel. Half-length fore-end secured by one barrel band. Those purchased by United States Department of Interior for arming Indian Police are marked "U.S.I.D." on receiver.

NIB	Exc.	V.G.	Good	Fair	Poor
—	—	—	5250	2500	850

REMINGTON-LEE RIFLES

Remington-Lee Magazine Rifle

Designed by James Paris Lee. Rifles of this type were originally manufactured by Sharps Rifle Company in 1880. Remington Company began production of this model in 1881, after Sharps Company ceased operations. Approximately 100,000 Lee magazine rifles manufactured between 1880 and 1907. Their variations are listed.

Courtesy Milwaukee Public Museum, Milwaukee, Wisconsin

Remington-Lee Model 1879 Sharps Mfg.

Barrel length 28", with full-length stock secured by two barrel bands. Barrel marked "Sharps Rifle Co. Bridgeport, Conn." and "Old Reliable" in rectangular cartouche. Approximately 300 made prior to 1881.

NIB	Exc.	V.G.	Good	Fair	Poor
—	—	4750	3000	2000	600

Remington-Lee Model 1879 U.S. Navy Model

NIB	Exc.	V.G.	Good	Fair	Poor
—	4000	2800	1600	750	250

Remington-Lee Model 1879 Sporting Rifle

Barrel length 28" or 30"; .45-70 or .45-90 caliber. Checkered pistol-grip stock, with sporting-style fore-end. Markings on receiver as above. Approximately 450 made.

NIB	Exc.	V.G.	Good	Fair	Poor
—	—	2500	1750	700	250

Remington-Lee Model 1879 Military Rifle

Identical to Navy model, except chambered for .43 Spanish cartridge. Limited number were produced in .45-70 caliber. Spanish versions are worth approximately 25 percent less than values listed below. Approximately 1,000 made. Majority of these rifles were for export.

NIB	Exc.	V.G.	Good	Fair	Poor
—	3200	2200	1250	500	150

Remington-Lee Model 1882 Army Contract

NIB	Exc.	V.G.	Good	Fair	Poor
—	4000	2800	1250	750	300

Remington-Lee Model 1885 Navy Contract

NIB	Exc.	V.G.	Good	Fair	Poor
—	4000	2800	1750	750	300

Remington-Lee Model 1882 & 1885 Military Rifles

Barrel length 32". Full-length stock secured by two barrel bands. Chambered for .42 Russian, .43 Spanish, .45 Gardner or .45-70 cartridges. Values for those rifles not in .45-70 caliber would be approximately 25 percent less than those listed. Approximately 10,000 Model 1882 rifles made; 60,000 Model 1885 rifles. Two models can be differentiated by the cocking piece on the bolt of Model 1885 is larger. Majority of these rifles made for foreign contracts and commercial sales.

NIB	Exc.	V.G.	Good	Fair	Poor
—	3500	3000	2500	1200	300

Remington-Lee Model 1882 & 1885 Sporting Rifle

As above chambered for .45-70 and .45-90 caliber, with 26" or 30" octagonal barrels and walnut sporting stocks. Approximately 200 made.

NIB	Exc.	V.G.	Good	Fair	Poor
—	3200	2700	2000	900	250

Remington-Lee Model 1882 & 1885 Carbine

As above, with 24" barrel and half-length fore-end secured by one barrel band. Prospective purchasers are advised to secure a qualified appraisal prior to acquisition.

NIB	Exc.	V.G.	Good	Fair	Poor
—	3200	2700	2000	900	250

Remington-Lee Model 1899

Designed for use with smokeless and rimless cartridges. Marked on receiver "Remington Arms Co. Ilion, N.Y. Patented Aug. 26th 1884 Sept. 9th 1884 March 17th 1885 Jan 18th 1887". Produced from 1889 to 1907 in variations listed.

Military Rifle

NIB	Exc.	V.G.	Good	Fair	Poor
—	3000	2000	1000	400	200

Military Carbine

NIB	Exc.	V.G.	Good	Fair	Poor
—	3200	2200	1250	500	250

Remington-Lee Sporting Rifle

As above, with 24", 26" or 28" round or octagonal barrel. Half-length sporting stock, with checkered pistol-grip. Approximately 7,000 manufactured.

NIB	Exc.	V.G.	Good	Fair	Poor
—	3000	2400	2000	900	250

Remington Lebel Bolt-Action Rifle

NIB	Exc.	V.G.	Good	Fair	Poor
—	—	750	450	150	100

Remington Mosin-Nagant Bolt-Action Rifle

NIB	Exc.	V.G.	Good	Fair	Poor
—	—	600	300	100	75

U.S. Model 1917 Magazine Rifle

NIB	Exc.	V.G.	Good	Fair	Poor
—	—	1250	600	150	100

Remington-Whitmore Model 1874

Sidelock double-barrel shotgun, combination shotgun/rifle or double-barrel rifle, with 28" or 30" fluid steel barrels. Also available with Damascus barrels. Barrels released by pushing forward the top lever. Blued case-hardened, with straight-/semi-pistol-grip walnut stock. Barrels marked "A. E. Whitmore's Patent Aug. 8, 1871, April 16, 1872". Rib between barrels marked "E. Remington & Sons, Ilion, N.Y.". Several thousand manufactured between 1874 and 1882.

Shotgun

NIB	Exc.	V.G.	Good	Fair	Poor
—	—	1750	850	450	100

Combination Gun (Rare)

NIB	Exc.	V.G.	Good	Fair	Poor
—	—	4250	3200	1500	300

Double Rifle

Very rare.

NIB	Exc.	V.G.	Good	Fair	Poor
—	—	9000	4250	1500	500

Model 1882 Shotgun

Sidelock double-barrel 10- or 12-gauge shotgun, with 28" or 30" fluid steel or Damascus barrels. Blued case-hardened, with checkered pistol-grip stock and hard rubber buttplate. Barrels are marked "E. Remington & Sons, Ilion, N.Y." and lock marked "Remington Arms Co.". Has a conventional top lever that moves to the side. Offered with optional engraving. Such models should be individually appraised. Approximately 7,500 manufactured between 1882 and 1889.

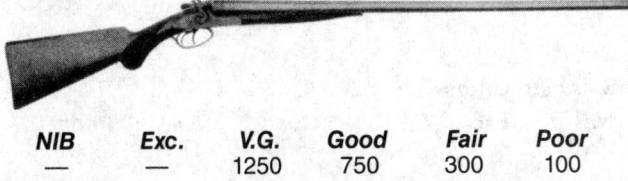

NIB	Exc.	V.G.	Good	Fair	Poor
—	—	1250	750	300	100

Model 1883 through 1889 Shotgun

Sidelock 10-, 12- or 16-gauge double-barrel shotgun, with fluid steel or Damascus barrels 28" to 32" in length. Models 1883, 1885, 1887 and 1889 are all somewhat alike, varying only in form of their hammers and internal mechanisms. Blued case-hardened checkered pistol-grip stock, with a grip cap. Available in a variety of styles including highly engraved models that should be individually appraised. Approximately 30,000 manufactured between 1883 and 1909.

NIB	Exc.	V.G.	Good	Fair	Poor
—	—	1800	1100	800	200

Model 1893 (No. 9)

Single-barrel hammer gun in 10-, 12-, 16-, 20-, 24- and 28-gauge. Barrel lengths from 28" to 34". Case colored frame, with hard rubber buttplate.

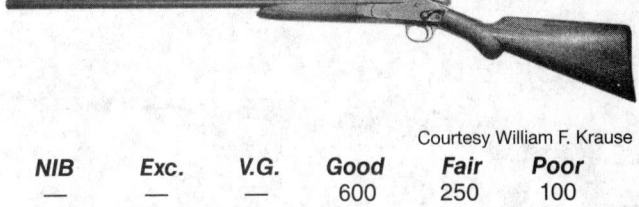

Courtesy William F. Krause

NIB	Exc.	V.G.	Good	Fair	Poor
—	—	—	600	250	100

Hammerless Shotgun Model 1894

Boxlock 10-, 12- or 16-gauge double shotgun, with fluid steel or Damascus barrels 26" to 32" in length. Blued case-hardened, with pistol-grip stock. Available in a variety of styles. It is advised that highly engraved examples should be individually appraised. **NOTE:** Add 25 percent premium for fluid steel barrels.

NIB	Exc.	V.G.	Good	Fair	Poor
—	1750	1250	750	300	100

Model 1900 Shotgun

As above in 12- and 16-gauge only. Same cautions apply to highly engraved examples.

NIB	Exc.	V.G.	Good	Fair	Poor
—	1500	1000	600	250	100

Model 8 Rifle

A .25, .30, .32 or .35 Rem. semi-automatic rifle. Featuring 22" barrel, with open sights. Barrel covered by a full-length tube that encloses the recoil spring. Blued, with walnut stock. Approximately 60,000 made between 1906 and 1936 in styles listed. **NOTE:** Add 35 percent for .25 Rem. Some collectors will pay and demand, prices substantially in excess of those listed below for Grades C, D and E

Standard Grade

Courtesy Remington Arms

NIB	Exc.	V.G.	Good	Fair	Poor
1400	1200	800	550	250	125

Model 8A

Checkered stock.

NIB	Exc.	V.G.	Good	Fair	Poor
1600	1300	900	600	300	150

Model 8C

NIB	Exc.	V.G.	Good	Fair	Poor
3000	2500	1500	900	500	300

8D Peerless

Light engraving.

NIB	Exc.	V.G.	Good	Fair	Poor
6000	5000	3500	1750	800	400

8E Expert

NIB	Exc.	V.G.	Good	Fair	Poor
7500	6000	4000	2250	1100	450

8F Premier

Heavily engraved.

Paul Goodwin photo

NIB	Exc.	V.G.	Good	Fair	Poor
10000	8500	7500	3750	1600	700

Model 81 Woodsmaster

Improved variation of Model 8. Chambered for same calibers (but not .25 apparently) as well as .300 Savage cartridge. Produced from 1936 to 1950 in styles listed. **NOTE:** Add 300 percent for police model, with detachable 15-round magazine.

Standard Grade

NIB	Exc.	V.G.	Good	Fair	Poor
1100	900	750	500	250	125

Model 81A

NIB	Exc.	V.G.	Good	Fair	Poor
1200	1000	850	500	250	125

81D Peerless

Engraved.

NIB	Exc.	V.G.	Good	Fair	Poor
7500	6000	4000	2250	1100	450

81F Premier

Heavily engraved.

NIB	Exc.	V.G.	Good	Fair	Poor
10000	8500	7500	3750	1600	700

Model 12 or 12A

A .22-caliber slide-action rifle, with 22" round or octagonal barrel having open sights. Blued, with walnut stock. Manufactured from 1909 to 1936 in styles listed.

Model 12A

NIB	Exc.	V.G.	Good	Fair	Poor
1200	1050	900	600	225	150

Model 12B

.22 Short Gallery Model.

NIB	Exc.	V.G.	Good	Fair	Poor
2000	1800	1200	900	400	150

Model 12C

24" octagon barrel.

NIB	Exc.	V.G.	Good	Fair	Poor
1400	1150	950	650	300	175

12C N.R.A. Target

Limited production.

NIB	Exc.	V.G.	Good	Fair	Poor
2400	2100	1400	1000	500	300

Model 12CS

.22 Remington Special.

NIB	Exc.	V.G.	Good	Fair	Poor
1500	1250	1000	800	400	175

12D Peerless

Light engraving.

NIB	Exc.	V.G.	Good	Fair	Poor
7000	6000	5000	3000	1500	750

12E Expert

NIB	Exc.	V.G.	Good	Fair	Poor
8500	7200	6000	3500	2000	1000

12F Premier

Heavily engraved.

Paul Goodwin photo

NIB	Exc.	V.G.	Good	Fair	Poor
10000	9000	5250	3150	1500	800

Model 121 and/or 121A

A .22-caliber slide-action rifle, with 24" round barrel. Blued, with walnut stock. Manufactured from 1936 to 1954 in styles listed.

Standard Grade

NIB	Exc.	V.G.	Good	Fair	Poor
1000	850	650	500	175	100

121D Peerless

Engraved.

NIB	Exc.	V.G.	Good	Fair	Poor
6500	5000	3750	1800	1000	500

121F Premier

Heavily engraved.

NIB	Exc.	V.G.	Good	Fair	Poor
9000	7500	5250	3150	1500	800

Model 121S

.22 WRF.

NIB	Exc.	V.G.	Good	Fair	Poor
1200	1050	900	600	350	250

121SB—Smoothbore

There are four different variations of this smoothbore rifle. Seek expert advice before a sale.

NIB	Exc.	V.G.	Good	Fair	Poor
1500	1350	1100	650	400	300

Model 14 or 14A

A .25, .30, .32 or .35 Rem. caliber slide-action rifle, with 22" round barrel and open sights. Blued, plain walnut stock. Manufactured from 1912 to 1936. **NOTE:** Add 85 percent for .25 Remington.

NIB	Exc.	V.G.	Good	Fair	Poor
—	900	750	500	300	200

Model 14R

As above, with 18.5" barrel.

NIB	Exc.	V.G.	Good	Fair	Poor
—	1500	800	500	300	200

Model 14-1/2

As above, except chambered for .38-40 or .44-40 cartridge, with 22.5" barrel. Carbine with 18.5" barrel, known as Model 14-1/2R, would be worth approximately 10 percent more than values listed. Manufactured from 1912 to 1922.

NIB	Exc.	V.G.	Good	Fair	Poor
—	2000	1250	700	350	250

Model 16

A .22-caliber (Rem. Automatic, not interchangeable with anything else) semi-automatic rifle, with 22" barrel and open sights. Blued, with walnut stock. Later production examples were known as Model 16A. Manufactured from 1914 to 1928. **NOTE:** Peerless and Premier Grades have engraving and higher grades of walnut. Add 400 percent premium for Peerless grade; 700 percent for Premier grade.

Courtesy Remington Arms

NIB	Exc.	V.G.	Good	Fair	Poor
1500	1100	900	600	400	200

Model 141

A .30, .32 or .35 Rem. caliber slide-action rifle, with 24" barrel having open sights. Blued, with plain walnut stock. Later production versions were known as Model 141A. Manufactured from 1936 to 1950.

Courtesy Remington Arms

NIB	Exc.	V.G.	Good	Fair	Poor
1000	800	650	500	250	175

Model 141 Special Grade

This model has a higher-grade checkered walnut stock and fore-end. **NOTE:** Add 200 percent premium for engraved Peerless Grade; 300 percent for Premier Grade with more elaborate engraving.

NIB	Exc.	V.G.	Good	Fair	Poor
1800	1600	1200	900	600	300

Model 25

A .25-20 or .32-20 caliber slide-action rifle, with 24" barrel having open sights. Blued, with walnut stock. Later production examples were known as Model 25A. Carbine version with an 18" barrel as Model 25R. Manufactured from 1923 to 1936. **NOTE:** Add 100 percent for rifles with 18" barrels.

NIB	Exc.	V.G.	Good	Fair	Poor
—	1000	750	400	250	200

Model 24

Designed by John M. Browning. Semi-automatic rifle in .22-caliber, with 19" barrel and open sights. Blued, with walnut pistol-grip stock. Later production versions known as Model 24A. Produced from 1922 to 1935.

Courtesy Wallis & Wallis, Lewes, Sussex, England

NIB	Exc.	V.G.	Good	Fair	Poor
1200	1000	600	400	200	100

Model 241 Speedmaster

A .22-caliber takedown semi-automatic rifle, with 24" barrel and open sights. Blued, with walnut stock. Later production versions known as Model 241A. Approximately 56,000 made between 1935 and 1949 in styles listed.

NIB	Exc.	V.G.	Good	Fair	Poor
1200	800	650	550	350	200

Model 241

Courtesy Remington Arms

NIB	Exc.	V.G.	Good	Fair	Poor
750	550	400	250	200	150

241D Peerless

Engraved.

NIB	Exc.	V.G.	Good	Fair	Poor
6500	5000	3750	1800	1000	500

241E Expert

NIB	Exc.	V.G.	Good	Fair	Poor
8000	7500	4000	2250	1200	800

241F Premier

Heavily engraved.

NIB	Exc.	V.G.	Good	Fair	Poor
10000	9000	5250	3150	1500	800

Model 550A

A .22 Short, Long or LR caliber semi-automatic rifle, with 24" barrel and open sights. Blued, with walnut pistol-grip stock. Approximately 220,000 made between 1941 and 1971.

NIB	Exc.	V.G.	Good	Fair	Poor
—	350	275	150	100	75

Model 550P

As above, with aperture rear sight.

NIB	Exc.	V.G.	Good	Fair	Poor
—	375	300	175	125	100

Model 550-2G

As above, except fitted with shell deflector and screw eye for securing it to a shooting gallery counter.

NIB	Exc.	V.G.	Good	Fair	Poor
500	400	375	225	135	75

Model 30A "Express"

Sporting rifle using U.S. Model 1917 Enfield bolt-action. Chambered for various Rem. cartridges as well as 7x57mm and .30-06 cartridges. Barrel length 22". Checkered walnut stock. Carbine model fitted with 20" barrel was known as Model 30R. Manufactured from 1921 to 1940.

Courtesy Remington Arms

NIB	Exc.	V.G.	Good	Fair	Poor
—	950	700	475	175	100

Model 30S

As above chambered for .257 Roberts, 7x57 and .30-06 cartridges. Barrel 24", with Lyman receiver sight. Select checkered walnut stock. Manufactured from 1930 to 1940.

NIB	Exc.	V.G.	Good	Fair	Poor
—	1300	975	495	250	150

Model 41A "Targetmaster"

A bolt-action rimfire rifle chambered for .22-caliber Short, Long and LR. Barrel 27", with open rear sight and bead front. Pistol-grip stock is plain. Produced from 1936 to 1940.

NIB	Exc.	V.G.	Good	Fair	Poor
—	300	200	150	100	50

Model 41AS

Same as above. Chambered for .22 Rem. Special or .22 WRF cartridge.

NIB	Exc.	V.G.	Good	Fair	Poor
—	275	175	125	100	75

Model 41P

Same as Model 41A, with addition of rear peep sight and hooded front.

NIB	Exc.	V.G.	Good	Fair	Poor
—	325	225	175	125	50

Model 41SB

Same as Model 41A, except used with .22 shot cartridge. Barrel is smoothbore.

NIB	Exc.	V.G.	Good	Fair	Poor
—	350	275	195	150	75

Miscellaneous Remington Bolt Action Rimfires, 1930-1970

From 1930 to 1970, Remington Company produced a variety of single-shot and repeating .22-caliber rifles. Values for these are much the same, consequently, they are listed for reference only.

Model 33	Model 341 A	Model 510 P
Model 33 NRA	Model 341 P	
Model 34	Model 341 SB	
Model 34 NRA	Model 510	Model 510 SB

Courtesy Remington Arms

Model 510

NIB	Exc.	V.G.	Good	Fair	Poor
300	250	200	125	75	50

Model 37

A .22-caliber bolt-action magazine target rifle, with heavy 28" barrel. Featuring target-sights and telescope bases. Blued, with walnut target style stock. Manufactured from 1937 to 1940.

Courtesy Remington Arms

NIB	Exc.	V.G.	Good	Fair	Poor
1200	1000	600	400	300	250

Model 37-1940

As above, with improved lock, trigger pull and redesigned stock. Manufactured from 1940 to 1954.

Courtesy Remington Arms

NIB	Exc.	V.G.	Good	Fair	Poor
1300	1100	750	500	300	200

Model 504

This .22-caliber bolt action rifle was introduced in 2004. Barrel 20", with no sights. American walnut stock, with checkering and pistol-grip. Satin blue metal finish. 6-round flush mounted detachable magazine. Receiver drilled and tapped for scope mounts. Weight about 6 lbs. Discontinued 2006. Also was chambered in .17 Mach 2 and .17 HMR.

NIB	Exc.	V.G.	Good	Fair	Poor
650	550	400	300	200	100

Model 504 Custom

Introduced in 2005. Features fancy walnut stock.

NIB	Exc.	V.G.	Good	Fair	Poor
1500	1300	1000	650	300	200

Model 504-T LS HB

Introduced in 2005. Features 20" heavy barrel, with blued finish. Chambered for .22 LR or .17 HMR cartridge. Brown laminate stock, with Monte Carlo comb. Weight about 8.5 lbs.

NIB	Exc.	V.G.	Good	Fair	Poor
800	675	475	275	250	150

Model 541 S Custom

A .22-caliber bolt-action magazine rifle, with 24" barrel. Blued, with scroll engraved receiver. Checkered walnut stock having a rosewood pistol-grip cap and fore-end tip. Manufactured from 1972 to 1984.

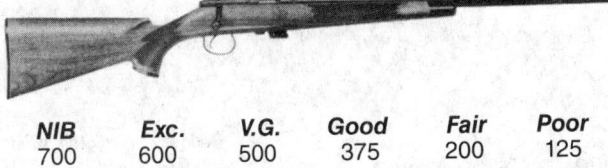

NIB	Exc.	V.G.	Good	Fair	Poor
700	600	500	375	200	125

Model 541T

As above, drilled and tapped for telescopic sights. Introduced in 1986.

NIB	Exc.	V.G.	Good	Fair	Poor
375	275	200	175	125	75

Model 541T Heavy Barrel

Same as standard 541-T, with exception of 24" heavy barrel. First introduced in 1993.

NIB	Exc.	V.G.	Good	Fair	Poor
450	350	300	250	200	125

Model 547

High-quality magazine-fed .17 or .22 rimfire sporter, with walnut stock, crowned muzzle, tuned trigger and other goodies. Suspiciously similar to defunct Model 504. Dealer exclusive for 2007.

NIB	Exc.	V.G.	Good	Fair	Poor
1000	775	600	400	275	200

Model 511 Scoremaster

A .22-caliber bolt-action magazine sporting rifle, with 22" barrel. Blued, with walnut stock. Six-round magazine.

NIB	Exc.	V.G.	Good	Fair	Poor
375	325	250	175	125	75

Model 512

Bolt-action .22 rimfire repeater identical to 511, except with tubular magazine located beneath the barrel. Capacity is 15 LR, 17 Long and 22 Short cartridges. Manufactured from 1940 to 1962. All 500 series models (510, 511, 512, 513 and 521) feature a red cocking indicator at rear of bolt.

NIB	Exc.	V.G.	Good	Fair	Poor
400	350	275	200	150	100

Model 513 TR Matchmaster

A .22-caliber bolt-action magazine target rifle, with heavy 27" barrel and Redfield aperture rear sight. Blued, with target-style walnut stock. Manufactured from 1940 to 1969.

NIB	Exc.	V.G.	Good	Fair	Poor
500	400	300	200	150	100

Model 513 S

As above, with Marble sights and checkered walnut sporting-style stock. Manufactured from 1941 to 1956.

NIB	Exc.	V.G.	Good	Fair	Poor
950	800	700	475	375	225

Model 514

Bolt-action single-shot .22 rimfire rifle manufactured from 1948 to 1971. Total of 770,932 were made, with standard barrels and sights. Another 5,617 were made with Routledge Bore barrels, which were meant for use only with .22 LR Shot loads and came with a shotgun-style bead front sight. These rifles have 24" smoothbore barrel, with bore diameter of .22" that opens up to .40 for the last 12". Routledge Bore Model 514 was never in Remington catalog and available only on special order. Design originated with Michigan trap shooter and gunsmith Fred Routledge in 1938. **NOTE:** Add $100 for Routledge barrel.

NIB	Exc.	V.G.	Good	Fair	Poor
300	250	200	125	75	50

Model 521 TL Jr.

A .22-caliber bolt-action magazine target rifle, with heavy 25" barrel and Lyman sights. Blued, with target-style walnut stock. Manufactured from 1947 to 1969.

NIB	Exc.	V.G.	Good	Fair	Poor
400	350	250	175	125	75

Model 760

Slide-action sporting rifle chambered for various popular centerfire cartridges from .222 up to .35 Rem. cartridge, with 22" round barrel and open sights. Features detachable box magazine. Blued, with checkered walnut pistol-grip stock. Manufactured between 1952 and 1982. Examples of this rifle chambered for .222, .223, .244 and .257 Roberts are worth a premium of 100 to 200 percent over other calibers. Produced in styles listed.

Standard Model

NIB	Exc.	V.G.	Good	Fair	Poor
—	500	395	275	195	150

Carbine

18.5" barrel.

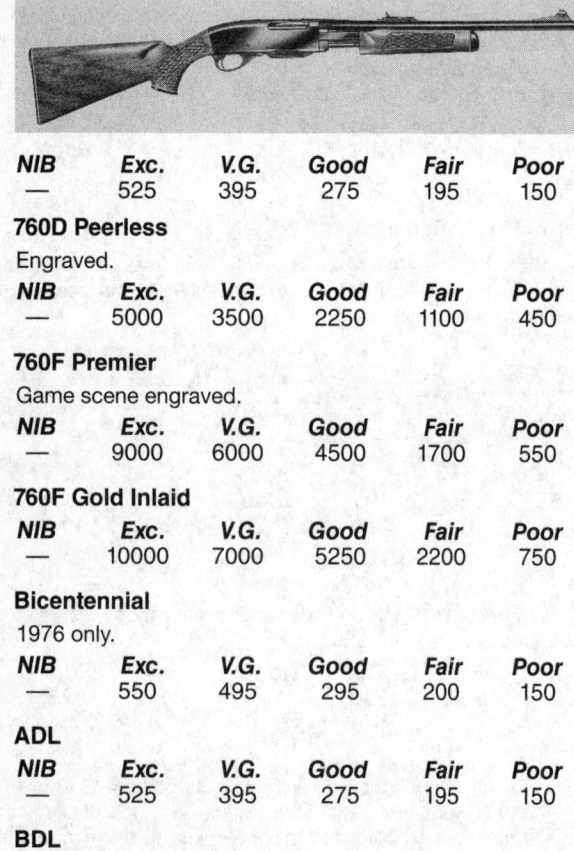

NIB	Exc.	V.G.	Good	Fair	Poor
—	525	395	275	195	150

760D Peerless

Engraved.

NIB	Exc.	V.G.	Good	Fair	Poor
—	5000	3500	2250	1100	450

760F Premier

Game scene engraved.

NIB	Exc.	V.G.	Good	Fair	Poor
—	9000	6000	4500	1700	550

760F Gold Inlaid

NIB	Exc.	V.G.	Good	Fair	Poor
—	10000	7000	5250	2200	750

Bicentennial

1976 only.

NIB	Exc.	V.G.	Good	Fair	Poor
—	550	495	295	200	150

ADL

NIB	Exc.	V.G.	Good	Fair	Poor
—	525	395	275	195	150

BDL

Basketweave checkering.

NIB	Exc.	V.G.	Good	Fair	Poor
—	525	395	275	195	150

Model 552A Speedmaster

A .22-caliber semi-automatic rifle, with 23" barrel and open sights. Blued, with pistol-grip walnut stock. Manufactured from 1959 to 1988.

NIB	Exc.	V.G.	Good	Fair	Poor
300	250	225	150	75	50

Model 552 BDL

As above, with more fully figured stock and impressed checkering. Introduced in 1966. This is the only U.S.-made .22 semi-automatic that functions with Short, Long and LR ammunition.

Courtesy Remington Arms

NIB	Exc.	V.G.	Good	Fair	Poor
550	475	400	300	200	100

Model 552 BDL Deluxe Speedmaster NRA Edition

Introduced in 2005. Features walnut stock, with checkering and high gloss finish. Blued receiver and barrel, with NRA logos etched on both sides of receiver.

NIB	Exc.	V.G.	Good	Fair	Poor
520	400	300	195	125	95

Model 572 Fieldmaster

A .22-caliber slide-action rifle, with 21" barrel and open sights. Blued, with walnut stock. Manufactured from 1955 to 1988.

Courtesy Remington Arms

NIB	Exc.	V.G.	Good	Fair	Poor
350	300	225	150	75	50

Model 572 BDL

As above, with more fully figured walnut stock and impressed checkering. Introduced in 1966.

NIB	Exc.	V.G.	Good	Fair	Poor
550	475	400	300	200	100

Model 572SB

Same as Model 572, with a smoothbore barrel. Chambered for .22 LR shot cartridge.

NIB	Exc.	V.G.	Good	Fair	Poor
325	275	200	125	75	60

Model 572 BDL Smoothbore

Similar to Model 572, with unrifled barrel for use with shot cartridges. Introduced as a special production item in 2007.

NIB	Exc.	V.G.	Good	Fair	Poor
650	575	400	350	110	85

Model 580

A .22-caliber single-shot bolt-action rifle, with 24" barrel, open sights and Monte Carlo-style stock. Blued. Manufactured from 1968 to 1978.

Courtesy Remington Arms

NIB	Exc.	V.G.	Good	Fair	Poor
—	250	200	150	75	50

Model 580 BR

Same as above, with 1" shorter buttstock.

NIB	Exc.	V.G.	Good	Fair	Poor
250	200	150	175	75	50

Model 580 SB

Same as Model 580, with smoothbore barrel for .22 LR shot cartridges.

NIB	Exc.	V.G.	Good	Fair	Poor
300	250	175	125	75	50

Model 581

A .22-caliber bolt-action magazine rifle. Blued, with 24" barrel and walnut stock. Manufactured from 1967 to 1983.

NIB	Exc.	V.G.	Good	Fair	Poor
300	250	175	125	75	50

Model 581 Left-Hand

Same as above. Built for left-handed shooter.

NIB	Exc.	V.G.	Good	Fair	Poor
295	250	175	125	75	50

Model 581-S

As above, fitted with 5-round detachable magazine. Introduced in 1986.

NIB	Exc.	V.G.	Good	Fair	Poor
300	250	175	125	75	50

Model 582

As above, fitted with tubular magazine in place of detachable box magazine. Manufactured from 1967 to 1983.

Courtesy Remington Arms

NIB	Exc.	V.G.	Good	Fair	Poor
300	250	175	125	75	50

Model 591

A 5mm rimfire Magnum bolt-action rifle, with 24" barrel and Monte Carlo-style stock. Approximately 20,000 made between 1970 and 1973.

NIB	Exc.	V.G.	Good	Fair	Poor
450	300	225	175	125	75

Model 592

As above, with tubular magazine. Approximately 7,000 made.

NIB	Exc.	V.G.	Good	Fair	Poor
450	300	225	175	125	75

Model 740

Semi-automatic rifle, with 22" barrel and detachable box magazine. Chambered in .244 Rem., .280 Rem., .308 or .30-06. Blued, with plain walnut stock. Also available with 18.5" barrel that would be worth approximately 10 percent more than values listed below. Manufactured from 1955 to 1960. **NOTE:** Add 30 percent premium for .244 Rem.

NIB	Exc.	V.G.	Good	Fair	Poor
—	300	225	200	150	100

ADL

As above, with a checkered walnut pistol-grip stock.

NIB	Exc.	V.G.	Good	Fair	Poor
—	350	250	225	150	100

BDL

As above, with a more finely figured walnut stock.

NIB	Exc.	V.G.	Good	Fair	Poor
—	400	275	250	150	100

Peerless Grade

Higher grade wood, scroll engraving.

NIB	Exc.	V.G.	Good	Fair	Poor
3600	2800	2000	—	—	—

Premier Grade

Best grade walnut, extensive engraving throughout. **NOTE:** Add $2000 for gold inlays.

NIB	Exc.	V.G.	Good	Fair	Poor
7000	6000	3000	—	—	—

Model 742

A 6mm Rem., .243, .280, .30-06 or .308-caliber semi-automatic rifle, with 22" barrel and 4-shot magazine. Also available with 18" barrel in calibers .308 and .30-06 that are worth approximately 10 percent more than values listed below. Blued, with checkered walnut stock. Manufactured from 1960 to 1980.

Courtesy Remington Arms

NIB	Exc.	V.G.	Good	Fair	Poor
—	350	275	250	150	100

BDL Standard Grade
As above, with Monte Carlo-style stock and basketweave checkering.

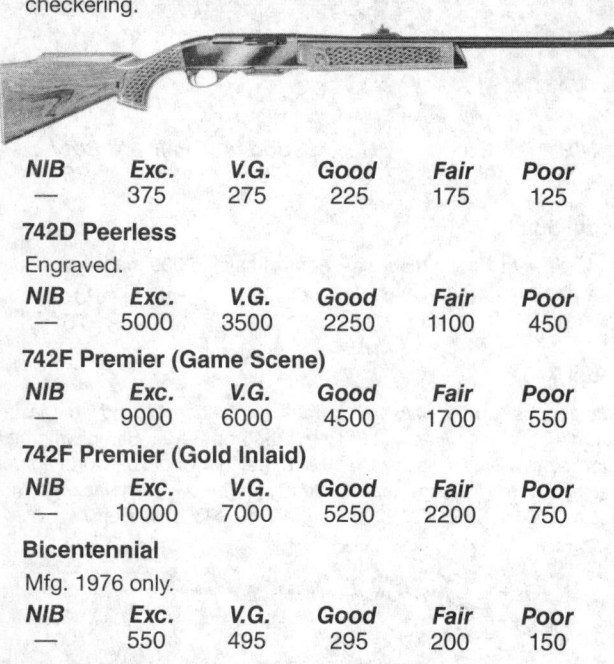

NIB	Exc.	V.G.	Good	Fair	Poor
—	375	275	225	175	125

742D Peerless
Engraved.

NIB	Exc.	V.G.	Good	Fair	Poor
—	5000	3500	2250	1100	450

742F Premier (Game Scene)

NIB	Exc.	V.G.	Good	Fair	Poor
—	9000	6000	4500	1700	550

742F Premier (Gold Inlaid)

NIB	Exc.	V.G.	Good	Fair	Poor
—	10000	7000	5250	2200	750

Bicentennial
Mfg. 1976 only.

NIB	Exc.	V.G.	Good	Fair	Poor
—	550	495	295	200	150

Model 76 Sportsman
A .30-06 slide-action rifle, with 22" barrel and 4-shot magazine. Blued, with walnut stock. Manufactured from 1985 to 1987.

NIB	Exc.	V.G.	Good	Fair	Poor
—	325	225	175	125	75

Model 7600
Variation of the above. Chambered for a variety of cartridges from 6mm Rem. to .35 Whelen, with 22" barrel and detachable magazine. Also available with 18.5" barrel. Blued, with checkered walnut stock. In 1996, fine line engraving on receiver was offered as standard.

Model 7600 with engraving

Close-up of engraving on Model 7600

Courtesy Remington Arms

Standard Grade

NIB	Exc.	V.G.	Good	Fair	Poor
750	600	500	300	150	100

7600D Peerless
Engraved.

NIB	Exc.	V.G.	Good	Fair	Poor
—	5000	3500	2250	1100	450

7600F Premier
Game scene engraved.

NIB	Exc.	V.G.	Good	Fair	Poor
—	9000	6000	4500	1700	550

Premier
Gold inlaid.

NIB	Exc.	V.G.	Good	Fair	Poor
—	10000	7000	5250	2200	750

Synthetic
Same as standard grade Model 7600, with black synthetic stock. A .30-06 carbine version is also available. Introduced in 1998.

NIB	Exc.	V.G.	Good	Fair	Poor
510	375	275	200	150	100

Special Purpose
Same configuration as standard Model 7600. Equipped with a special finish on both the wood and metal that is non-reflective. First offered in 1993.

NIB	Exc.	V.G.	Good	Fair	Poor
600	475	350	225	150	100

7600P Patrol
Introduced in 2002. Chambered for .308 cartridge. Fitted with 16.5" barrel. Synthetic stock, with matte black finish. Parkerized finish on metal. Wilson Combat rear ghost ring sights, with AO front sight. Weight about 7 lbs.

NIB	Exc.	V.G.	Good	Fair	Poor
600	475	350	225	150	100

Buckmasters ADF (American Deer Foundation)
Introduced in 1997. Built only for that year. Chambered for .30-06 cartridge and is a limited edition item. Fitted with 22" barrel and special fine line engraved receiver.

NIB	Exc.	V.G.	Good	Fair	Poor
600	475	350	225	150	100

Model Six

Centerfire slide-action rifle, with 22" barrel and 4-shot detachable magazine. Blued, with walnut stock. Manufactured from 1981 to 1987. Chambered in 6mm Rem., .243 Win., .270 Win., .308 Win., .30-06. Discontinued in 1987. **NOTE:** Add 50 percent for 6mm Rem.

NIB	Exc.	V.G.	Good	Fair	Poor
750	600	450	350	200	125

Model 7615 Tactical Pump Carbine

Pump-action rifle based on Model 7600 action. Chambered in .223 Rem., with 16.5" barrel. Folding synthetic stock. Introduced in 2007.

NIB	Exc.	V.G.	Good	Fair	Poor
600	475	350	225	150	100

Model 7615 Special Purpose Synthetic

Similar to Model 7615 Tactical, with fixed stock and Picatinny rail. Dealer exclusive for 2007.

NIB	Exc.	V.G.	Good	Fair	Poor
625	500	375	250	175	125

Model 7615 Camo Hunter

Similar to Model 7615 Tactical, with fixed buttstock and entirely camo-finished except for action parts and trigger guard assembly. Introduced in 2007.

NIB	Exc.	V.G.	Good	Fair	Poor
650	525	400	265	195	150

Model 7615 Ranch Carbine

Similar to Model 7615 Tactical, with fixed walnut buttstock and fore-end. 18.5" barrel. No iron sights. Drilled and tapped for scope mounts. Introduced in 2007.

NIB	Exc.	V.G.	Good	Fair	Poor
625	500	375	250	175	125

Model 74 Sportsman

A .30-06 caliber semi-automatic rifle, with 22" barrel and 4-shot detachable magazine. Blued, with walnut stock. Manufactured from 1985 to 1987.

NIB	Exc.	V.G.	Good	Fair	Poor
—	350	250	175	125	75

Model Four

As above, with select Monte Carlo-style stock. Manufactured from 1982 to 1987.

NIB	Exc.	V.G.	Good	Fair	Poor
—	500	400	350	275	175

Model 7400

A semi-automatic rifle with 22" barrel. Chambered for .243, .270, .280, .30-06, .308 and .35 Whelen. Blued with checkered walnut stock. Average weight about 7.5 lbs. Introduced in 1982. In 1996, offered with fine line engraving on receiver as standard.

NIB	Exc.	V.G.	Good	Fair	Poor
600	475	350	250	200	100

Synthetic

Similar to Model 7400, with black non-reflective synthetic stock. A .30-06 carbine also offered. Introduced in 1998.

NIB	Exc.	V.G.	Good	Fair	Poor
550	400	300	200	150	100

Weathermaster

Introduced in 2003. Semi-automatic features weather-resistant black synthetic stock and matte nickel-plated receiver, barrel and magazine. Barrel length 22", with iron sights. Chambered for .30-06 or .270 Win. cartridges. Weight about 7.5 lbs.

NIB	Exc.	V.G.	Good	Fair	Poor
650	525	400	300	200	100

Carbine

Same as above, with 18.5" barrel. Chambered for .30-06 cartridge.

NIB	Exc.	V.G.	Good	Fair	Poor
550	400	300	200	150	100

Special Purpose

Same configuration as standard Model 7400. Equipped with special finish on both the wood and metal that is non-eflective. First offered in 1993.

NIB	Exc.	V.G.	Good	Fair	Poor
450	350	300	250	200	100

Buckmasters ADF (American Deer Foundation)

Introduced in 1997. Built only in that year as a limited model. Chambered for .30-06 cartridge. Fitted with 22" barrel. Special fine line engraving and polished blue finish. American walnut stock, with Monte Carlo and cut checkering. Weight is 7.5 lbs.

Close-up detail on engraving for Model 7400 Buckmasters ADF

NIB	Exc.	V.G.	Good	Fair	Poor
600	500	400	300	200	100

Model 7400 Custom Grade

Custom Shop model available in three levels of engraving, gold inlay, wood grade and finish, metal work finish, recoil pad/buttplate and dimensions. Each gun should be individually appraised prior to sale.

F Grade

NIB	Exc.	V.G.	Good	Fair	Poor
—	9000	6000	4500	1700	550

F Grade with Gold Inlay

NIB	Exc.	V.G.	Good	Fair	Poor
—	10000	7000	5250	2200	750

Model 750 Woodsmaster

This model replaced the 7400 family of semi-automatic rifles in 2006. Features include an improved gas-operating system and lower profile. Standard model has walnut stock; rifle version has 22" barrel; carbine has 18.5" barrel.

NIB	Exc.	V.G.	Good	Fair	Poor
875	725	600	450	300	200

Model 750 Synthetic

Similar to Model 750 Woodsmaster, with black synthetic stock and fore-end. Introduced in 2007.

NIB	Exc.	V.G.	Good	Fair	Poor
625	550	400	300	225	125

Model R-15 VTR Predator Rifle

AR-style rifle chambered for .223 Rem. or .204 Ruger. Supplied with one 5-shot magazine, but accepts AR-style higher-cap magazines. 22" fluted barrel; fixed stock. Finish: Advantage MAX-12 HD overall.

NIB	Exc.	V.G.	Good	Fair	Poor
1100	900	695	500	250	125

Model R-15 VTR Predator Carbine

Similar to above, with 18" barrel.

NIB	Exc.	V.G.	Good	Fair	Poor
1100	900	695	500	250	125

Model R-15CS VTR Predator Carbine

Similar to above, with collapsible buttstock.

NIB	Exc.	V.G.	Good	Fair	Poor
1145	950	750	550	275	150

Model R-15 Hunter

Similar to R-15 in .30 Rem. AR or .450 Bushmaster, 22" barrel, Realtree AP HD camo.

NIB	Exc.	V.G.	Good	Fair	Poor
1200	975	750	550	275	150

Model R-15 VTR Byron South Edition

.223, 18" barrel, Advantage MAX-1 HD camo.

NIB	Exc.	V.G.	Good	Fair	Poor
1200	975	750	550	275	150

Model R-15 VTR SS Varmint

As above, with 24" stainless steel barrel.

NIB	Exc.	V.G.	Good	Fair	Poor
1200	975	750	550	275	150

Model R-15 VTR Thumbhole

Similar to R-15 Hunter, with thumbhole stock.

NIB	Exc.	V.G.	Good	Fair	Poor
1300	1075	850	595	295	150

Model R-15 MOE

Semi-automatic .223 (AR-15 type), with AAC 51 Tooth Brakeout flash hider, Magpul Grip and trigger guard, competition two-stage trigger finished in Mossy Oak Brush camo. Available with: 16" barrel with collapsible stock and mid-length fore-end; 18" carbine with fixed stock and Dissipator fore-end; 18" barrel carbine with collapsible stock and Dissipator fore-end; 22" barrel rifle with fixed stock and Dissipator fore-end. Introduced 2013.

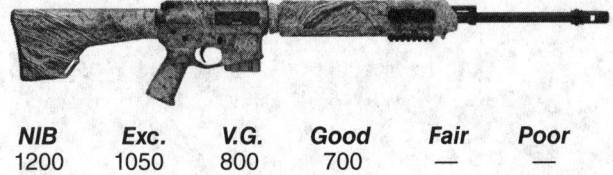

NIB	Exc.	V.G.	Good	Fair	Poor
1200	1050	800	700	—	—

Model R-25 Modular Repeating Rifle

Enhanced AR-style semi-automatic rifle. Chambered in .243, 7mm-08 and .308 Win. Features include 20" chrome-moly barrel, single-stage trigger, four-round magazine, aluminum alloy upper and lower Mossy Oak Treestand camo finish overall. Overall length 38.25"; weight 7.75 lbs.

NIB	Exc.	V.G.	Good	Fair	Poor
1500	1250	900	700	300	200

Model R-25 GII

The next generation R-25. Features include a downsized but stronger rifle with a matched pair of forged, anodized, Teflon-coated upper and lower receivers. Also, a lighter bolt carrier and improved extractor/ejector system, free-floated barrel and Hogue rubber pistol-grip. Introduced in 2015.

NIB	Exc.	V.G.	Good	Fair	Poor
1550	1300	950	—	—	—

REMINGTON'S "NYLON SERIES" .22 RIFLES

Model 10 Nylon

Bolt-action single shot. Approximately 10,700 (approx. 2000 smoothbore and only 200 of those with 24" barrel) produced from 1962-1964. Mohawk brown nylon stock, with white accents, chrome spoon style bolt handle, safety engages upon cocking, .22 Short, Long and LR. Available in both rifled and smoothbore versions (smoothbore barrels are marked "smoothbore") and barrel lengths of 19.5" and 24". **NOTE:** Add 100 percent+ for 24" versions; 100 percent+ for NIB.

Courtesy Remington Arms

10 (model)

NIB	Exc.	V.G.	Good	Fair	Poor
—	700	600	500	300	200

10 (SB)

NIB	Exc.	V.G.	Good	Fair	Poor
—	1000	800	700	500	450

Model 11 Nylon

Bolt-action repeater, 6- or 10-round metal box magazine. Approximately 22,500 produced from 1962-1964. Mohawk brown nylon stock, with white accents, chrome spoon style bolt handle, manual right side safety. .22 Short, Long or LR. Barrel lengths 19.5" and 24". **NOTE:** Add 100 percent for 24" version.

NIB	Exc.	V.G.	Good	Fair	Poor
—	475	375	300	275	175

Model 12 Nylon

Bolt-action repeater, 14-round external tubular magazine under the barrel. Approximately 27,600 produced from 1962-1964. Mohawk brown nylon stock, with white accents, chrome spoon style bolt handle, manual right side safety. .22 Short, Long or LR. Barrel lengths 19.5" and 24". **NOTE:** Add 100 percent for 24" version.

NIB	Exc.	V.G.	Good	Fair	Poor
—	475	375	300	275	175

Model 66 Nylon

Semi-automatic, 19.5" barrel, 14-round tubular magazine fed through buttplate. In excess of 1,000,000 produced from 1959-1987. Seven different variations of style and color were sold. Non-serialized prior to 1968 gun control act of 1968. An "A" prefix was added to serialization in 1977.

66 (MB) "Mohawk" Brown

Blued metal parts, dark chocolate brown stock with white accents, .22 LR ONLY. 1959-1987. Approx. 678,000.

NIB	Exc.	V.G.	Good	Fair	Poor
400	350	300	150	125	100

66 (SG) "Seneca" Green

Blued metal parts, dark olive green stock (often confused with MB in artificial light) with white accents, .22 LR ONLY, 1959-1962. Approx. 45,000.

NIB	Exc.	V.G.	Good	Fair	Poor
600	550	450	325	275	175

66 (AB) "Apache" Black

Bright chrome plated metal parts, black stock with white accents, .22 LR ONLY. 1962-1983. Approx. 220,000.

NIB	Exc.	V.G.	Good	Fair	Poor
600	500	425	350	250	125

66 (BD) "Black Diamond"

Blued metal parts, black stock with black diamonds in fore-end. Remainder of accents are white, .22 LR ONLY, 1978-1987. Approx. 56,000.

NIB	Exc.	V.G.	Good	Fair	Poor
450	425	375	300	250	150

66 (GS) "Gallery Special"

Blued metal parts, dark brown stock with white accents. Barrel marked .22 SHORT. Distinguished by shell deflector over ejection port and loop on fore-end for counter chain. 1961-1981. Approx. 6500.

NIB	Exc.	V.G.	Good	Fair	Poor
1300	1200	950	700	450	300

66 (AN) "150th Anniversary Rifle"

Blued metal parts, dark brown stock with white accents, .22 LR ONLY. Distinguished by 150th Anniversary stamping on left side of receiver cover. 1966 ONLY. Approx. 4000.

NIB	Exc.	V.G.	Good	Fair	Poor
750	700	600	450	300	250

66 (BI) "Bicentennial Rifle"

Blued metal parts, dark brown stock with white accents, .22 LR ONLY. Distinguished by eagle and 1776/1976 stamping on left side of receiver cover. 1976 ONLY. Approx. 10,000.

NIB	Exc.	V.G.	Good	Fair	Poor
700	600	500	325	275	200

Model 76 Nylon

Only lever-action repeater Remington ever produced. 19.5" barrel, 14-round tubular magazine, fed through buttplate. Produced from 1962-1964 in three different variations.

76 (MB) "Trailrider"

Blued metal parts, dark brown stocks with white accents. Approximately 25,300 produced.

NIB	Exc.	V.G.	Good	Fair	Poor
—	1700	600	500	375	250

76 (AB) "Trailrider"

Bright chrome metal parts, black stock with white accents. Approximately 1600 produced.

NIB	Exc.	V.G.	Good	Fair	Poor
—	2000	800	700	500	400

76 (not cataloged)

Blued metal parts, black stock with white accents. Production numbers do not exist.

NIB	Exc.	V.G.	Good	Fair	Poor
—	1800	675	600	400	300

Model 77 Nylon

Known as 77 (MB): Semi-automatic, 19.5" barrel, 5-round plastic box magazine. Blued metal parts, dark brown stock with white accents. .22 LR ONLY. 1970-1971. Approx. 15,300 produced. This model was replaced by Model 10C in 1972. **NOTE:** Add 100 percent for NIB.

NIB	Exc.	V.G.	Good	Fair	Poor
—	500	375	300	200	150

Model 10C Nylon

Known as 10C. Identical copy of 77 (MB), except box magazine capacity was increased to 10 rounds. 1972-1978. Approx. 128,000 produced. **NOTE:** Add 50 percent for NIB.

NIB	Exc.	V.G.	Good	Fair	Poor
—	325	275	225	175	100

Model 77 Apache Nylon

Known as "APACHE 77". Semi-automatic, 19.5" barrel, 10-round plastic box magazine. Metal parts coated with black "teflon-like" finish, bright green stock with swirls of orange, brown and black (highly variable), not to be confused with the 66 (SG). Rifle was contracted as an "exclusive" run, marketed by K-Mart. Number manufactured is hazy, but estimates run from 54,000 to over 100,000. Produced from 1987-1989. **NOTE:** Add 100 percent for NIB.

NIB	Exc.	V.G.	Good	Fair	Poor
—	350	250	200	140	120

Model 522 Viper

Introduced in 1993. A new Remington .22 rimfire caliber semi-automatic design. Black stock made from synthetic resin, while receiver is made from a synthetic as well. Features 20" barrel and 10-shot detachable clip. Weight 4.6 lbs.

NIB	Exc.	V.G.	Good	Fair	Poor
160	120	100	80	60	40

MODEL 597 SERIES
Model 597

Introduced in 1997. Automatic .22 LR rimfire rifle features carbon steel barrel, with alloy receiver. All metal has a non-reflective matte black finish. Stock is dark gray synthetic. Barrel length 20". Weight about 5.5 lbs.

NIB	Exc.	V.G.	Good	Fair	Poor
225	150	100	70	50	25

Sporter

Introduced in 1998. This version of Model 597 has a blued finish, with hardwood stock and beavertail-style forearm. Magazine capacity 10 rounds.

NIB	Exc.	V.G.	Good	Fair	Poor
225	150	100	70	50	25

Stainless Sporter

Same as Model 597SS. Fitted with hardwood stock. Introduced in 2000.

NIB	Exc.	V.G.	Good	Fair	Poor
275	200	150	100	75	25

LSS

This version of Model 597 is similar to above, with addition of a laminated stock and stainless steel finish.

NIB	Exc.	V.G.	Good	Fair	Poor
300	225	175	125	100	50

SS

This version is also chambered for .22 LR. Has a stainless steel barrel on an alloy receiver. Stock is gray synthetic, with beavertail style forearm. Magazine capacity 10 rounds. Weight about 5.5 lbs. Introduced in 1998.

NIB	Exc.	V.G.	Good	Fair	Poor
240	175	125	100	75	25

HB

Introduced in 2001. Features 20" carbon steel heavy barrel. Chambered for .22 LR cartridge. Fitted with brown laminated stock. No sights. Weight about 6 lbs.

NIB	Exc.	V.G.	Good	Fair	Poor
275	225	165	125	75	25

HB Magnum

Same as model above. Chambered for .22 Win. Magnum cartridge. Introduced in 2001.

NIB	Exc.	V.G.	Good	Fair	Poor
425	325	200	165	125	50

Magnum

Features 20" carbon steel barrel, alloy receiver and black synthetic stock. Chambered for .22 Win. Magnum cartridge. Weight about 6 lbs.

NIB	Exc.	V.G.	Good	Fair	Poor
350	250	200	150	100	50

Magnum LS

Chambered for .22 Magnum. Receiver and barrel blued, with gray laminated hardwood stock and beavertail-style forearm. Magazine capacity 10 rounds. Introduced in 1998. In 2003, also offered chambered for .17 HMR cartridge.

NIB	Exc.	V.G.	Good	Fair	Poor
375	275	195	145	100	50

Custom Target

Available on special order from Custom Shop. Chambered for .22 LR cartridge. Has 20" stainless steel heavy target barrel, without sights. Stock green laminated-wood targetstyle, with pistol-grip. Trigger custom tuned. Weight about 7.5 lbs. Introduced in 1998.

NIB	Exc.	V.G.	Good	Fair	Poor
600	475	400	275	200	150

Custom Target Magnum

Similar to model above. Chambered for .22 Win. Magnum. Weight about 8 lbs. Introduced in 1998. Special order item only.

NIB	Exc.	V.G.	Good	Fair	Poor
750	600	500	375	250	175

LSS

Similar to Model 597, with laminated stock, stainless barrel and 3-9X scope. Dealer exclusive for 2007.

NIB	Exc.	V.G.	Good	Fair	Poor
275	200	150	100	75	25

Synthetic Scope Combo

"Package rifle" similar to Model 597, with 3-9X scope included. Introduced in 2007.

NIB	Exc.	V.G.	Good	Fair	Poor
300	225	175	125	100	50

TVP (Target/Varmint/Plinker)

Ultra-funky .22 LR autoloader built on Model 597 chassis. Features include bolt-guidance system, with twin tool-steel guide rails; laminated skeletonized wood stock; non-glare matte finish; 10-shot metal detachable magazine; last-shot hold-open bolt for added safety. Scope rail. Introduced in 2008.

NIB	Exc.	V.G.	Good	Fair	Poor
530	465	395	275	175	125

Yellow Jacket

Similar to above, with yellow and black laminated stock.

NIB	Exc.	V.G.	Good	Fair	Poor
500	395	225	150	100	75

Blaze Camo

Model 597, with synthetic stock molded in screamin' blaze orange and black.

NIB	Exc.	V.G.	Good	Fair	Poor
275	225	165	125	75	25

Pink Camo

Similar to above, with pink – yes pink – and black camo-pattern stock.

NIB	Exc.	V.G.	Good	Fair	Poor
275	225	165	125	75	25

FLX

Similar to Model 597 Blaze/Pink camo, with FLX Digital Camo stock.

NIB	Exc.	V.G.	Good	Fair	Poor
275	225	165	125	75	25

AAC

Same features as other 597 models, except it has 16.5" barrel that will accept AAC flash hider, muzzle-break or suppressor. Staggered-stack magazine holds 10 rounds. Weight 5.5 lbs.

NIB	Exc.	V.G.	Good	Fair	Poor
195	165	140	115	100	75

VTR - Quad Rail

Semi-automatic rifle chambered in .22 LR. Styled to resemble AR. Features include matte blued finished; black synthetic stock; 16" barrel; Pardus A2-style collapsible pistol-grip stock; quad-rail free-floated tube; 10-round magazine.

NIB	Exc.	V.G.	Good	Fair	Poor
400	360	325	275	210	150

VTR A-2 Fixed Stock

Similar to VTR - Quad Rail, with fixed A2-style stock. Standard hand guard, with quad rail.

NIB	Exc.	V.G.	Good	Fair	Poor
400	360	325	275	210	150

VTR Collapsible Stock

Similar to VTR A-2 Fixed Stock, with Pardus A2-style collapsible pistol-grip stock.

NIB	Exc.	V.G.	Good	Fair	Poor
400	360	325	275	210	150

VTR A-TACS Camo

Semi-automatic rifle chambered in .22 LR. Styled to resemble AR. Features include ATACS camo finish overall; 16" barrel; Pardus A2-style collapsible pistol-grip stock; round hand guard without rails; receiver-mounted optics rail; 10-round magazine.

NIB	Exc.	V.G.	Good	Fair	Poor
525	465	425	350	275	185

Model Five

.22 rimfire bolt-action sporter. Calibers .22 LR, .22 WMR, .17 HMR; five-shot detachable magazine; barrel 22" blued, with iron sights; receiver blued for scope mounts; stock laminated walnut, with QD swivels. Introduced 2006. **NOTE:** Add 10 percent for .22 WMR.

NIB	Exc.	V.G.	Good	Fair	Poor
300	250	175	125	75	25

MODEL 40X SERIES

Target Rifle

A .22-caliber rimfire single-shot bolt-action rifle, with heavy 28" barrel. Fitted with Redfield Olympic sights or telescopic sight bases. Blued, with walnut target style stock having a hard rubber butt-plate. Manufactured from 1955 to 1964.

Courtesy Remington Arms

NIB	Exc.	V.G.	Good	Fair	Poor
875	750	550	425	350	300

Sporter

As above, with 24" barrel, 5-shot magazine. Walnut sporting style stock. Fewer than 700 made between 1969 and 1980.

Courtesy Remington Arms

NIB	Exc.	V.G.	Good	Fair	Poor
4500	3750	3000	2250	1000	500

Centerfire Target

Chambered for .222, .222 Magnum, .308 or .30-06 centerfire cartridges. Manufactured from 1961 to 1964.

NIB	Exc.	V.G.	Good	Fair	Poor
1100	950	700	500	300	200

40XB Rangemaster Centerfire

Features stainless steel barrel, receiver and bolt. Receiver drilled, tapped and fitted with 27.25" heavy target barrel. Trigger fully adjustable. Choice of walnut or synthetic stock. Starting in 1998, offered with a special laminated thumbhole stock. Offered in calibers from .222 to .300 Win. Magnum. Rifle built to order in Custom Shop. Made since 1964. **NOTE:** Add $300 for thumbhole stock.

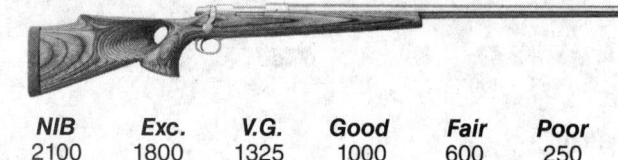

NIB	Exc.	V.G.	Good	Fair	Poor
2100	1800	1325	1000	600	250

40XB BR

A bench rest Custom Shop version of above model. Has 22" stainless heavy barrel. Chambered for .22 BR Rem. Adjustable trigger. Built to order.

NIB	Exc.	V.G.	Good	Fair	Poor
1200	1000	850	600	450	200

40XB Tactical Rifle

First offered in 2003. Bolt-action rifle features Teflon coated stainless steel 27.25" barrel. Chambered for .308 Win. cartridge. Fitted with H.S. Precision tactical stock, with vertical pistol-grip. Remington 40-X trigger.

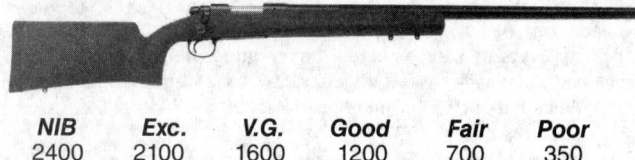

NIB	Exc.	V.G.	Good	Fair	Poor
2400	2100	1600	1200	700	350

40XS Tactical

Bolt-action rifle chambered in .308 Win. or .338 Lapua Magnum. Features include 416 stainless steel Model 40-X 24" 1:12 barreled action; black polymer coating; McMillan A3 series stock, with adjustable length of pull and comb; adjustable trigger and all-steel trigger guard; Harris bipod, with quick adjust swivel lock; Leupold Mark IV 3.5-10x40mm long range M1 scope with Mil Dot reticle; Badger Ordnance all-steel Picatinny scope rail and rings. **NOTE:** Deduct 50 percent if without Leupold scope, Harris Bipod, Badger Ordnance Picatinny rail.

NIB	Exc.	V.G.	Good	Fair	Poor
4000	3600	3000	2000	—	—

40XR KS Sporter

Rimfire model in .22 LR or .22 WMR. Sporter contoured 24" barrel, Kevlar stock, no sights. Magazine capacity 5+1. Made from 1994 to 2000.

NIB	Exc.	V.G.	Good	Fair	Poor
1300	1000	850	600	450	350

40XR Custom Sporter

From Remington Custom Shop, high-grade version of 40X rimfire, with specifications made to order. In .22 LR or .22 WMR. Limited production.

NIB	Exc.	V.G.	Good	Fair	Poor
4200	3750	3200	2400	1500	500

Model XR-100 Rangemaster

Introduced in 2005. Features 26" barrel. Chambered for .204 Ruger, .223 or .22-250 calibers. Black laminate stock, with thumbhole and ventilated forearm. Adjustable trigger. Blued finish. Weight about 9.12 lbs.

NIB	Exc.	V.G.	Good	Fair	Poor
880	675	500	395	275	150

Model XC KS

Custom Shop position rifle, with 24" stainless steel heavy barrel. Chambered for .223 Rem. and .308 Win. cartridges. Kevlar stock, with palm rail. Weight about 11 lbs.

NIB	Exc.	V.G.	Good	Fair	Poor
2650	2225	1850	1400	800	400

Model 673 Guide Rifle

Introduced in 2003. Bolt-action rifle features 22" ventilated rib barrel. Chambered for 6.5mm Rem. Magnum, .308, .300 RUM or .350 Rem. Magnum cartridge. Adjustable rear sight. Stock is dark and light tan laminate, with checkering. Magazine capacity three rounds. Weight about 7.5 lbs. Discontinued 2006. Slight premium for .300 RUM.

NIB	Exc.	V.G.	Good	Fair	Poor
650	525	400	300	200	150

Model 720A

A .257 Roberts, .270 or .30-06 bolt-action sporting rifle, with 22" barrel and 5-shot integral magazine. Blued, with checkered walnut stock. Approximately 2,500 manufactured from 1941 to 1944. Another 1,000 or so were made in 1942 for the U.S. Navy, mostly in .30-06 with a few in .270 and .257 Roberts. **NOTE:** Add 100 percent for .270; 150 percent for .257 Roberts.

Courtesy Remington Arms

NIB	Exc.	V.G.	Good	Fair	Poor
1400	1200	1000	700	300	200

Model 721

A .264 Magnum, .270, .280 or .30-06 bolt-action rifle, with 24" barrel and 4-shot magazine. Blued, with plain walnut stock. Manufactured from 1948 to 1962.

Courtesy Remington Arms

Standard Version

NIB	Exc.	V.G.	Good	Fair	Poor
500	450	350	200	150	100

ADL

Checkered stock.

NIB	Exc.	V.G.	Good	Fair	Poor
550	475	375	250	200	125

BDL

High grade stock.

NIB	Exc.	V.G.	Good	Fair	Poor
600	500	400	300	250	150

Model 721A Magnum

.300 H&H or .264 Win.

NIB	Exc.	V.G.	Good	Fair	Poor
650	550	400	350	275	150

Model 722

Short-action variation of Model 721. Chambered for .222 Rem., .222 Rem. Magnum, .243 Win., .244 Rem., .257 Roberts, .300 Savage, .308 Win. BDL models featured high-grade select walnut stocks; ADL had checkered stocks. Made from 1948 to 1962. **NOTE:** Add 25 percent for BDL; 10 percent for ADL; 25 percent for .222 Rem. Magnum, .243, .257 or .308 chamberings.

NIB	Exc.	V.G.	Good	Fair	Poor
550	450	350	200	150	100

Model 725 ADL

Short-lived but well-made model. Offered in .222 Rem., .243 Win., .244 Rem., .270 Win., .280 Rem., and .30-06 Springfield. 4-round magazine capacity (5 in .222). Adjustable open rear sight, hooded ramp front. Checkered walnut stock, with Monte Carlo comb, sling swivels. Barrel length: 22" (24" .222). Weight about 7 lbs. Made from 1958 to 1961. **NOTE:** Add $150 for .280 Rem. if NIB or Exc.

Courtesy Remington Arms

NIB	Exc.	V.G.	Good	Fair	Poor
900	800	525	275	225	150

Model 725 Kodiak

A .375 H&H Magnum or .458 Win. Magnum bolt-action sporting rifle, with 26" barrel, muzzle-brake, open sights and 3-shot magazine. Blued, with checkered walnut stock. Manufactured in 1961. Very limited production.

NIB	Exc.	V.G.	Good	Fair	Poor
5000	4000	3000	2000	1000	300

Model 78 Sportsman

Centerfire bolt-action sporting rifle, with 22" barrel and 4-shot magazine. Blued, with walnut stock. Introduced in 1985. Calibers: .223, .243, .270, .308, .30-06.

NIB	Exc.	V.G.	Good	Fair	Poor
335	275	225	200	150	100

Model 600

Centerfire bolt-action sporting rifle, with 18.5" ventilated rib barrel and checkered walnut stock. Manufactured from 1964 to 1967. Calibers: .222 Rem., .223 Rem., 6mm Rem., .243, .308, .35 Rem. **NOTE:** Add 100 percent for .223 Rem.

Courtesy Remington Arms

NIB	Exc.	V.G.	Good	Fair	Poor
650	550	450	350	225	150

Model 600 Mohawk

As above, with plain barrel. Chambered only for .222 Rem., .243 Win. or .308 Win. cartridges. Manufactured from 1971 to 1979.

NIB	Exc.	V.G.	Good	Fair	Poor
—	450	375	225	175	125

Model 600 Magnum

As above, chambered for 6.5mm Rem. Magnum and .350 Rem. Magnum cartridges. Stock of laminated walnut and beechwood. Manufactured from 1965 to 1967.

NIB	Exc.	V.G.	Good	Fair	Poor
—	1000	750	600	450	200

Model 660

Improved version of Model 600. Manufactured from 1968 to 1971. **NOTE:** Add 100 percent for .223 Rem.

NIB	Exc.	V.G.	Good	Fair	Poor
700	600	425	350	250	200

Model 660 Magnum

As above, chambered for 6.5mm Rem. Magnum or .350 Rem. Magnum cartridges. Fitted with laminated stock.

NIB	Exc.	V.G.	Good	Fair	Poor
—	1000	750	600	450	200

MODEL 700 SERIES

Model 700 ADL

Centerfire bolt-action sporting rifle, with 20", 22" or 24" barrel, open sights and 4-shot magazine. Blued, with checkered Monte Carlo-style walnut stock. Introduced in 1962. Available in most popular calibers from .222 Rem. to .300 Win. Magnum.

NIB	Exc.	V.G.	Good	Fair	Poor
425	325	250	200	150	100

Model 700 ADL Synthetic

Features black matte metal finish, with 22" or 24" barrel on Magnums. Synthetic stock is black with checkering, recoil pad and sling swivel studs. Receiver drilled and tapped for scope. Offered in .243, .270, .30-06 and 7mm Rem. Magnum. In 1998, available in .223 Rem. and .300 Win. Magnum.

Courtesy Remington Arms

NIB	Exc.	V.G.	Good	Fair	Poor
350	300	250	200	150	100

Model 700 ADL Synthetic Youth

Introduced in 1998. Has a shortened synthetic stock, with 13" lop. Offered in .243- and .308-calibers.

NIB	Exc.	V.G.	Good	Fair	Poor
400	300	250	200	150	100

Model 700 BDL

Same as above, with hinged floorplate, cut checkering, black fore-end tip and pistol-grip cap. Offered in a wide variety of calibers from .17 Rem. to .338 Rem. Ultra Magnum. Weights between 7.25 lbs. to 7.62 lbs. depending on caliber and barrel length. Introduced in 1962 as an upgraded variation of 700 ADL

Courtesy Remington Arms

NIB	Exc.	V.G.	Good	Fair	Poor
500	450	400	350	300	150

Model 700 BDL LH (Left-Hand)

Offered in selected calibers for left-hand shooters. They are: .270 Win., 7mm Rem. Magnum, .30-06 and .300 Rem. Ultra Magnum.

NIB	Exc.	V.G.	Good	Fair	Poor
600	500	450	325	250	150

Model 700 BDL (DM)

Same as above, with detachable magazine. Introduced in 1995.

NIB	Exc.	V.G.	Good	Fair	Poor
715	525	400	300	225	150

Model 700 BDL LSS

Introduced in 1996. Has synthetic stock and stainless steel bolt, floor plate, trigger guard and sling swivels. Action and barrel are stainless steel as well. In 1997, .260 Rem. cartridge was also available.

Courtesy Remington Arms

NIB	Exc.	V.G.	Good	Fair	Poor
600	475	400	350	300	200

Model 700 BDL SS DM—Magnum Rifle

Introduced in 1996. Fitted with factory installed muzzle-brake on its Magnum calibers: 7mm Rem. Magnum, .300 Win. Magnum, .300 Wthby. Magnum, .338 Win. Magnum and .338 Rem. Ultra Magnum. Weight about 7.5 lbs. In 1997, 7mm STW cartridge was added.

Courtesy Remington Arms

NIB	Exc.	V.G.	Good	Fair	Poor
775	650	500	300	200	150

Model 700 BDL SS Short Action

Fitted with a stainless steel 24" barrel. Chambered for 7mm Rem. Ultra Magnum and .300 Rem. Ultra Magnum. Black synthetic stock. No sights. Weight about 7.325 lbs. Introduced in 2003.

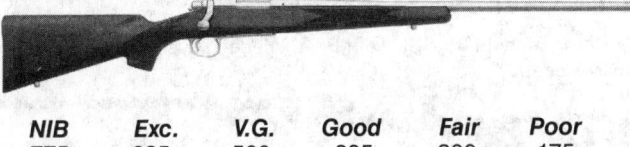

NIB	Exc.	V.G.	Good	Fair	Poor
775	625	500	395	300	175

Model 700 BDL SS Camo Special Edition (RMEF)

Special edition rifle for Rocky Mountain Elk Foundation. Fitted with 24" barrel. Chambered for .300 Rem. Ultra Magnum cartridge. Camo stock, with stainless steel receiver and barrel. Weight about 7.5 lbs. Introduced in 2001. In 2002, 7mm Rem. Ultra Magnum chambering was added for one year only. In 2003, .300 Rem. Ultra Magnum was offered.

NIB	Exc.	V.G.	Good	Fair	Poor
835	650	500	395	300	175

Model 700 50th Anniversary Edition

Introduced in 2012. A recreation of original M700 BDL of 1962. Satin finished walnut stock has a cheek piece, cut fleur-de-lis checkering, white-line spacers, black fore-end grip caps and recoil pad. Laser engraving on floorplate commemorates the 50th Anniversary. Barrel length 24". Chambered for 7mm Rem. Magnum, the cartridge that was introduced with Model 700 BDL.

NIB	Exc.	V.G.	Good	Fair	Poor
1250	1000	850	—	—	—

Model 700 EtronX

Introduced in 2000. Features new technology that electronically discharges the round resulting in nearly instant ignition. LED located on top of grip that shows safe or fire and chamber status. Also, a low battery indicator and malfunction indicators as well. Fitted with 26" stainless steel fluted barrel. Stock is fiberglass and graphite reinforced with Kevlar. Chambers are .220 Swift, .22-250 Rem. and .243 Win. cartridges. Aver-

age weight about 8.88 lbs. Gun was a flopperoo, but is now considered an almost-prime collectible. Discontinued 2004.

NIB	Exc.	V.G.	Good	Fair	Poor
1450	1300	1150	700	500	300

Model 700 Sendero

Model 700 configuration chambered for .25-06, .270, 7mm Rem. Magnum, .300 Win. Magnum. Fitted with synthetic stock and 26" heavy barrel.

NIB	Exc.	V.G.	Good	Fair	Poor
600	475	400	300	200	150

Model 700 Sendero SF

Introduced in 1996. Features stainless steel fluted barrel. Synthetic stock, with full length bedding. Weight about 8.5 lbs. Chambered for same calibers as standard Sendero above, except for .270. In 1997, 7mm STW cartridge was made available. In 2003, 7mm Rem. Ultra Magnum and .300 Rem. Ultra Magnum were added.

Courtesy Remington Arms

NIB	Exc.	V.G.	Good	Fair	Poor
900	800	600	450	350	200

Model 700 Sendero SF-II

Similar to Sendero SF, with HS Precision synthetic stock. Chambered in .264 WM, 7mm RM, 7mm RUM, .300 WM and .300 RUM. Introduced 2006.

NIB	Exc.	V.G.	Good	Fair	Poor
1150	985	835	700	500	300

Model 700 Sendero Composite

Introduced in 1999. Features a composite barrel of graphite fiber, with stainless steel liner. Stock is synthetic. Calibers available are .25-06, 7mm STW and .300 Win. Magnum. Barrel length 26". Weight just under 8 lbs.

NIB	Exc.	V.G.	Good	Fair	Poor
1400	1250	975	700	475	300

Model 700 Mountain Rifle

As above, with tapered 22" blued lightweight barrel. Checkered walnut stock. Introduced in 1986.

NIB	Exc.	V.G.	Good	Fair	Poor
425	325	250	200	150	100

Model 700 KS Mountain Rifle

As above, with lightweight Kevlar stock. Introduced in 1986.

NIB	Exc.	V.G.	Good	Fair	Poor
750	700	600	500	400	300

Model 700 Mountain Rifle (DM)

Introduced in 1995. Same as standard Mountain Rifle, with detachable magazine. In 1998, available in .260 Rem. caliber.

Courtesy Remington Arms

NIB	Exc.	V.G.	Good	Fair	Poor
780	575	425	300	250	175

Model 700 Safari Grade

As Model 700BDL. Chambered for 8mm Rem. Magnum, .375 H&H, 8mm Rem. Magnum, .416 Rem. Magnum or .458 Win. Magnum cartridges. 24" barrel and 3-shot magazine. Blued, with finely figured walnut checkered stock. Model KS Safari Grade was fitted with Kevlar stock and would be worth approximately 20 percent more than values listed. Introduced in 1962.

NIB	Exc.	V.G.	Good	Fair	Poor
1500	1300	1000	700	400	300

Model 700 RS

As above chambered for .270 Win., .280 Rem. or .30-06 cartridges. 22" barrel and 4-shot magazine. Blued, with DuPont Rynite stock. Manufactured during 1987 and 1988.

NIB	Exc.	V.G.	Good	Fair	Poor
—	550	425	350	250	150

Model 700 FS

As above, with Kevlar stock.

NIB	Exc.	V.G.	Good	Fair	Poor
—	550	475	400	300	200

Model 700 BDL European

First available in 1993. Features oil-finish stock, with Monte Carlo comb and raised cheekpiece. Checkering is fine line. In addition, rifle has hinged floorplate, sling swivel studs, hooded ramp front sight and adjustable rear sight. Offered in these calibers: .243, .207, .280, 7mm-08, 7mm Magnum, .30-06 and .308.

NIB	Exc.	V.G.	Good	Fair	Poor
675	400	350	300	250	200

Model 700 BDL Stainless Synthetic

Offered in 1993. Features stainless steel receiver, barrel and bolt. Synthetic stock has straight comb, raised cheekpiece and hinged floor plate. Metal finished in a black matte non-reflective finish. Available in 14 calibers from .223 to .338 Win. Magnum. All barrel lengths regardless of caliber are 24".

NIB	Exc.	V.G.	Good	Fair	Poor
750	600	500	300	200	150

Model 700 BDL Stainless Synthetic (DM)

Same as above, with detachable magazine. Introduced in 1995.

Courtesy Remington Arms

NIB	Exc.	V.G.	Good	Fair	Poor
800	650	525	350	200	150

Model 700 CDL

Introduced in 2004. Features classic-style checkered walnut stock, with black fore-end tip and grip cap. Hinged floor plate. Chambered for .243, .270, 7mm-08, 7mm Rem. Magnum, 7mm Rem. Ultra Magnum, .30-06, .300 Win. Magnum and .300 Rem. Ultra Magnum. Standard calibers are fitted with 24" barrel; Magnum calibers have 26" barrel. Weight about 7.5 lbs. depending on caliber.

NIB	Exc.	V.G.	Good	Fair	Poor
740	550	400	295	200	125

Model 700 CDL Boone and Crockett

Similar to Model 700 CDL, with B&C laser-engraved barrel. Dealer exclusive for 2007.

NIB	Exc.	V.G.	Good	Fair	Poor
750	560	400	295	200	125

Model 700 CDL SF Ltd.

Similar to Model 700 CDL, with engraved floorplate and stainless fluted barrel. Chambered in .30-06 and .17 Rem. Fireball. 2006 "Centennial" model commemorates centennial of .30-06 cartridge, introduced in 2006 for one year only. Beginning in 2006, Remington produced this model only in one caliber each year, as follows: .17 Rem. Fireball (2007); .260 Rem. (2008); .257 Roberts (2009); .280 Rem. (2010); 6mm Rem. (2011); 7mm Rem. Magnum (2012); .300 Win. Magnum (2013); .223 Rem. (2014); .22-250 (2015); .35 Whelen (2016).

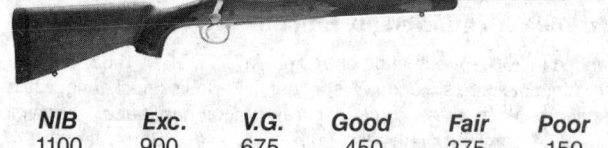

NIB	Exc.	V.G.	Good	Fair	Poor
1100	900	675	450	275	150

Model 700 Mountain Rifle Stainless Synthetic

Same as Mountain Rifle, with stainless steel receiver, bolt and barrel. Offered in .25-06 Rem., .270, .280 and .30-06. All calibers supplied with 22" barrel. In 1998, available in .260 Rem. caliber.

NIB	Exc.	V.G.	Good	Fair	Poor
830	600	450	300	225	150

Model 700 LSS Mountain Rifle

Introduced in 1999. Fitted with two-tone laminated stock, with black fore-end tip and cheekpiece. Stainless steel barrel and action. Offered in .260 Rem., 7mm-08 Rem., .270 Win. and .30-06. Barrel length 22". Weight about 6.5 lbs.

NIB	Exc.	V.G.	Good	Fair	Poor
830	625	450	300	200	100

Model 700 Titanium

Introduced in 2001. Features titanium receiver drilled and tapped for scope mounts. Fitted with 22" stainless steel barrel. Chambered for both Long and Short calibers. Synthetic stock. Weight about 5.25 lbs. In 2002, .308 Win. chambering added.

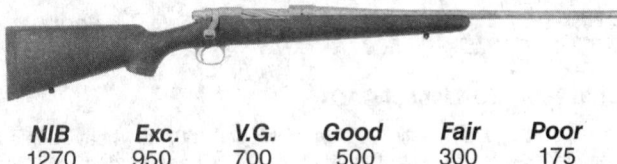

NIB	Exc.	V.G.	Good	Fair	Poor
1270	950	700	500	300	175

Model 700 Varmint Special Synthetic

Stock on this model reinforced with DuPont Kevlar fiberglass and graphite. Offered with heavy barrel. All metal has fine matte black finish. Barrel rests on a machined aircraft-grade aluminum bedding stock. Receiver drilled and tapped for scope mounts. Offered in .22-250, .223 and .308 calibers. In 1993, .220 Swift was added. This model was later dropped from the product line. In 2000, it was reintroduced in all calibers above, except .220 Swift.

NIB	Exc.	V.G.	Good	Fair	Poor
600	475	400	350	300	200

Model 700 VS SF (Varmint Synthetic Stainless Fluted)

Introduced in 1994. Features stainless steel barrel, receiver and action. Fitted with 26" heavy varmint barrel that has a spherical concave crown contour. Six flutes reduce barrel weight and help cooling. Synthetic stock made from fiberglass reinforced with graphite is standard. Stock is dark gray. Offered in .223, .220 Swift, .22-250 and .308 calibers. The .243 Win. cartridge added in 1997. Weight about 8.375 lbs. In 1998, barrel was fluted and ported.

NIB	Exc.	V.G.	Good	Fair	Poor
800	650	500	400	300	150

Model 700 Varmint Special Wood

Same as above, but furnished with walnut stock. Offered in these calibers: .222, .22-250, .223, 6mm, .243, 7mm-08 and .308.

NIB	Exc.	V.G.	Good	Fair	Poor
825	675	525	400	300	150

Model 700 Varmint Laminated Stock (VLS)

Same as above, but furnished with special laminated stock. Introduced in 1995. The 7mm-08 Rem. cartridge was added in 1997. In 1998, a beavertail fore-end was added, as well as .260 Rem. and 6mm Rem. calibers.

Courtesy Remington Arms

Model 700 VLS with beavertail forearm

NIB	Exc.	V.G.	Good	Fair	Poor
750	575	425	300	250	150

Model 700 VS Composite (Varmint Synthetic Composite)

Fitted with a graphite fiber composite barrel. Chambered for .223 Rem., .22-250 or .308 cartridges. Stock synthetic. Barrel length 26". Weight 7.9 lbs. Introduced in 1999.

NIB	Exc.	V.G.	Good	Fair	Poor
1675	1250	950	600	425	300

Model 700 LV SF (Light Varmint)

Introduced in 2004. Features black synthetic stock, with 22" stainless steel fluted barrel. Chambered for .17 Rem., .221 Rem. Fireball, .223 and .22-250. Weight about 6.75 lbs.

NIB	Exc.	V.G.	Good	Fair	Poor
950	700	475	300	225	125

Model 700 VS SF II

Introduced in 2005. Features varmint synthetic stock, with stainless steel action and stainless fluted barrel. Chambered for .204 Ruger, .220 Swift, .223 and .22-250. Barrel length 26". Weight about 8.5 lbs.

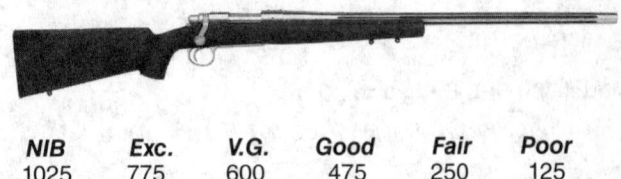

NIB	Exc.	V.G.	Good	Fair	Poor
1025	775	600	475	250	125

Model 700 VSF

Chambered for .17 Rem. Fireball, .204 Ruger, .220 Swift, .223 or .22-250. Fitted with 26" blued fluted heavy barrel. Tan synthetic stock. Weight about 8.5 lbs. Introduced in 2005.

NIB	Exc.	V.G.	Good	Fair	Poor
930	700	475	300	225	125

Model 700 LSS LH (Laminated Stock SS Left-Hand)

Introduced in 1998. Features stainless steel barreled action, with satin finish. Stock similar to BDL style, with Monte Carlo comb and cheekpiece, with hinged floor plate. Barrel 24", with no sights. Offered in .270, .30-06, 7mm Rem. Magnum and .300 Win. Magnum.

NIB	Exc.	V.G.	Good	Fair	Poor
700	550	400	300	250	150

Model 700 SPS

Introduced in 2005. Features an improved synthetic stock, RS recoil pad and hinged floorplate. Chambered for Short, Standard and Long action calibers. Supplied with sling swivels studs. Matte blue finish. Weight about 7.5 lbs. depending on caliber and barrel length.

NIB	Exc.	V.G.	Good	Fair	Poor
575	450	300	200	150	100

Model 700 SPS Synthetic Left hand

Similar to Model 700 SPS, but configured for left-handed shooters.

NIB	Exc.	V.G.	Good	Fair	Poor
575	450	300	200	150	100

Model 700 SPS Varmint

Varmint version of Model 700 SPS, with 26" heavy-contour barrel. Synthetic stock, with weight-reducing cuts in fore-end. Available in a variety of chamberings from .17 Rem. Fireball to .308 Win. Introduced in 2007.

NIB	Exc.	V.G.	Good	Fair	Poor
575	450	300	200	150	100

Model 700 SPS Dangerous Game

Similar to 700 SPS, but chambered in .375 H&H Magnum. A TALO exclusive.

NIB	Exc.	V.G.	Good	Fair	Poor
675	550	400	275	200	150

Model 700 SPS Stainless

As above, with matte stainless steel barrel and action. No Ultra Magnum calibers offered in this configuration. Introduced in 2005.

NIB	Exc.	V.G.	Good	Fair	Poor
610	475	350	225	150	100

Model 700 SPS DM

Same as Model SPS, with detachable magazine. Matte blue finish. Introduced in 2005.

NIB	Exc.	V.G.	Good	Fair	Poor
575	450	300	200	150	100

Model 700 SPS Youth

Offered in both Long and Short action calibers. Features barrel lengths of 20" and 22" depending on caliber. Weight about 7 lbs. Introduced in 2005.

NIB	Exc.	V.G.	Good	Fair	Poor
525	425	275	175	125	100

Model 700 SPS Tactical

Similar to Model 700 Police, with 20" barrel and calibers .223 and .308. Laser-engraved tactical barrel. Dealer exclusive for 2007.

NIB	Exc.	V.G.	Good	Fair	Poor
800	675	500	375	250	175

Model 700 SPS Tactical AAC

Special Purpose Synthetic version of Model 700. 20" heavy-contour hammer-forged barrel, with threaded muzzle. Chambered in .308 Win. Hogue Overmolded Ghillie Green pillar-bedded stock, with semi-beavertail forearm, Super-Cell recoil pad. Remington X-Mark Pro externally adjustable trigger. Black oxide finish. Weight 7.5 pounds.

NIB	Exc.	V.G.	Good	Fair	Poor
650	550	475	400	300	200

Model 700 VTR A-TACS Camo with Scope

Bolt action rifle chambered in .223 and .308 Win. Features include ATACS camo finish overall; triangular contour 22" barrel has an integral muzzle-brake; black overmold grips; 1:9 (.223-caliber) or 1:12 (.308) twist; factory-mounted scope.

NIB	Exc.	V.G.	Good	Fair	Poor
875	750	625	550	380	225

Model 700 XCR

Introduced in 2005. Features stainless steel action and barrel, synthetic stock, rubber grip and forearm panels, hinged floorplate and RS recoil pad. Chambered for .270 Win., .280 Rem., 7mm Ultra Magnum, .30-06, .300 WSM and .300 Win. Magnum cartridges. Barrel lengths 24" and 26" depending on caliber. Weight around 7.5 lbs. depending on caliber. **NOTE:** Add $25 for Magnum calibers.

NIB	Exc.	V.G.	Good	Fair	Poor
865	650	500	375	295	125

Model 700 XCR (Rocky Mountain Elk Foundation)

As above, with camo stock, engraved floorplate and 7mm Rem. Magnum caliber. Introduced in 2005.

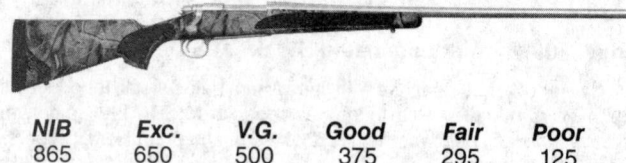

NIB	Exc.	V.G.	Good	Fair	Poor
865	650	500	375	295	125

Model 700 XCR II RMEF Limited Edition

Reintroduction of Rocky Mountain Elk Foundation rifle in .257 Wthby. Magnum. Features include 26" barrel, with Black TriNyte finish and nickel floor plate. Realtree AP-HD stock, with Hogue Overmolded Grip Panels, X-Mark Pro externally adjustable trigger and SuperCell recoil pad. Introduced in 2013.

NIB	Exc.	V.G.	Good	Fair	Poor
1075	950	800	—	—	—

Model 700 SPS Tactical II

Available in .223 Rem., .300 Black Out or .308 Win. Threaded muzzle, with 16.5" heavy barrel: 1/2 x 28 on .223 Rem., 5/8 x 24 on .300 Black Out and .308 Win. Hogue Chillie Green Overmolded stock and X-Mark Pro trigger. Introduced 2013.

NIB	Exc.	V.G.	Good	Fair	Poor
700	600	500	450	—	—

Remington 700 XCR II

Bolt-action rifle chambered in .25-06 Rem., .270 Win., .280 Rem., 7mm Rem. Magnum, 7mm Rem. Ultra Magnum, .300 WSM, .300 Win Magnum, .300 Rem. Ultra Magnum, .338 Win. Magnum, .338 Rem. Ultra Magnum, .375 H&H, .375 Rem. Ultra Magnum, .30-06 Springfield. Features include black TriNyte corrosion control system coating; coated stainless steel barrel and receiver; olive drab green Hogue overmolded synthetic stock; SuperCell recoil pad; X-Mark Pro Trigger System; 24" or 26" barrel depending on chambering.

NIB	Exc.	V.G.	Good	Fair	Poor
825	735	600	500	350	200

Remington 700 XCR II - Bone Collector Edition

Similar to Remington 700 XCR II, with Realtree AP HD camo stock.

NIB	Exc.	V.G.	Good	Fair	Poor
900	785	675	550	380	225

Model 700 Classic

Limited edition model. Furnished with a straight comb, satin finished walnut stock, sling swivel studs and hinged magazine floorplate. Series began in 1981. Each year Remington offered Model 700 Classic in a special chambering, concluding the series in 2005. **NOTE:** Add 25 percent for .250 Savage, .257 Roberts, 6.5x55 or 7x57.

Courtesy Remington Arms

A list of chamberings by year.

1981—7MM Mauser	1994—6.5X55
1982—.257 Roberts	1995—.300 Win. Mag.
1983—.300 H&H Mag.	1996—.375 H&H Mag.
1984—.250-3000	1997—.280 Rem.
1985—.350 Rem. Mag.	1998—8mm Rem. Mag.
1986—.264 Win. Mag.	1999—.17 Remington
1987—.338 Win. Mag.	2000—.223 Remington
1988—.35 Whelen	2001—7mm-08
1989—.300 Wthby. Mag.	2002—.221 Rem. Fireball
1990—.25-06 Rem.	2003—.300 Savage
1991—7mm Wthby. Mag.	2004—8mm Mauser
1992—.220 Swift	2005—.308 Winchester
1993—.222 Rem.	

NIB	Exc.	V.G.	Good	Fair	Poor
900	700	600	500	350	250

Model 700 Custom

Special order rifle available in American, English or California walnut. Stock can be fitted to customer's own dimensions. Engraving available as is a large selection of calibers. Model 700 Custom rifles should be priced individually and an appraisal should be obtained.

Model 700 Custom "C" Grade

Introduced in 2003. Custom Shop bolt-action rifle. Fitted with fancy walnut Monte Carlo stock and rosewood fore-end tip and grip cap. Offered in all standard calibers. Barrel length 24" for all calibers, except Ultra Magnums which are 26".

NIB	Exc.	V.G.	Good	Fair	Poor
2700	2200	1700	1200	600	250

AWR (Alaskan Wilderness Rifle)

Built in Custom Shop to order. Features blind magazine and stainless steel components on black matte synthetic stock. Fitted with 24" barrel. All metal parts finished in a black satin. Offered in .300 Wthby. Magnum, 7mm Rem. Magnum, .300 Win. Magnum, .338, and .375 calibers. In 1998, 7mm STW was added. Weight about 6.75 lbs.

NIB	Exc.	V.G.	Good	Fair	Poor
1400	1100	850	700	350	200

APR (African Plains Rifle)

Custom Shop model features hinged floorplate, 26" barrel and blue metal finish. Stock laminated Monte Carlo style, with cheekpiece. Fitted with black rubber recoil pad. Offered in same calibers as Model 700 AWR. Weight about 7.75 lbs.

NIB	Exc.	V.G.	Good	Fair	Poor
2400	2000	1500	1000	500	250

ABG (African Big Game)

Custom Shop rifle fitted with laminated stock, matte finished receiver, barrel and 3-round detachable magazine. Chambered for .375 Rem. Ultra Magnum, .375 H&H, .416 Rem. Magnum and .458 Win. Magnum. Introduced in 2001. Many extra cost options are offered for Custom Shop firearms.

NIB	Exc.	V.G.	Good	Fair	Poor
2750	2350	1800	1250	750	350

Model 700 Safari KS Stainless

New addition to Remington line in 1993. Safari KS Stainless has a special reinforced Kevlar stock in a non-reflective gray finish. Checkering is 18 lpi. Offered in these calibers: .375 H&H Magnum, .416 Rem. Magnum and .458 Win. Magnum.

NIB	Exc.	V.G.	Good	Fair	Poor
2200	1800	1500	900	600	300

Model 700 Police

Chambered for .223 cartridge. Fitted with 26" heavy barrel (1-9" twist), black synthetic stock and Parkerized finish.

NIB	Exc.	V.G.	Good	Fair	Poor
850	675	500	395	200	125

Model 700 Police DM

Same as above. Chambered for .308 Win. (1-12" twist) or .300 Win. Magnum (1-10" twist). Detachable magazine standard. **NOTE:** Add $20 for .300 Win. Magnum.

NIB	Exc.	V.G.	Good	Fair	Poor
850	675	500	395	200	125

Model 700 Police Lightweight Tactical

Chambered for .308 Win. cartridge. Fitted with 20" fluted barrel (1-12" twist). Stock is slim composite Kevlar, with dual front swivel studs. Parkerized finish. Detachable magazine. Weight about 7.5 lbs. Introduced in 1998.

NIB	Exc.	V.G.	Good	Fair	Poor
700	550	400	300	200	125

Model 700 XCR Tactical Long Range Rifle

Chambered in .223 Rem., .300 Lapua and .338 WM. Crowned stainless varmint contour 26" barrel. Olive drab Bell & Carlson synthetic stock. Coated overall with TriNyte Corrosion Control finish. Introduced in 2007. **NOTE:** Add 50 percent for .338 Lapua.

NIB	Exc.	V.G.	Good	Fair	Poor
925	800	675	500	300	150

Model 700 XCR Compact Tactical

Similar to above, with Black TriNyte PVD coating OD green stock; hinged floorplate magazine; dual front swivel studs and rear stud; free-floating 20" barrel with LTR-style fluting; 40-X externally adjustable trigger; tactical-style 1 in 9" (.223-caliber) or 1 in 12" twist (.308-caliber). Chambered in .223 and .308.

NIB	Exc.	V.G.	Good	Fair	Poor
1400	1150	875	650	475	200

Model 700 Target Tactical Rifle

Bolt-action rifle chambered in .308 Win. Features include: 26" triangular counterbored barrel, with 1: 11-1/2 rifling; textured green Bell & Carlson varmint/tactical stock, with adjustable comb and length of pull; adjustable trigger; satin black oxide finish on exposed metal surfaces; hinged floorplate; SuperCell recoil pad; matte blue on exposed metal surfaces. Overall length 45.75". Weight 11.75 lbs.

NIB	Exc.	V.G.	Good	Fair	Poor
1800	1550	1175	850	675	300

Model 700 Tactical Chassis

Variation of M700 Tactical rifle built on a MDT TAC21 Chassis. Magpul fully adjustable stock and pistol-grip. 24" or 26" free-floating barrel. Chambered in .308 Win., .300 Win. Magnum or .338 Lapua. Features include a full-length MIL-STN-1914 accessory rail, stainless steel barreled action with black Cerakote finish, target tactical bolt handle, AAC 51-T muzzle-brake and X-Mark Pro adjustable trigger. Introduced in 2014.

NIB	Exc.	V.G.	Good	Fair	Poor
2500	2100	1700	—	—	—

Model 700 VTR Varmint-Tactical Rifle

Bolt-action rifle chambered in .17 Rem. Fireball, .204 Ruger, .22-250, .223 Rem., .243 Win. and .308 Win. Features include: 22" triangular counterbored barrel; olive drab overmolded or Digital Tiger TSP Desert Camo stock ,with ventilated semi-beavertail fore-end; tactical-style dual swivel mounts for bipod; matte blue on exposed metal surfaces. Overall length 41.625". Weight 7.5 lbs.

NIB	Exc.	V.G.	Good	Fair	Poor
750	625	500	375	200	125

Model 700 VTR Desert Recon

Similar to above, with Digital Desert Camo stock. Chambered for .223 and .308 Win. only.

NIB	Exc.	V.G.	Good	Fair	Poor
750	625	500	375	200	125

Model 700 XHR Extreme Hunting Rifle

Bolt-action rifle chambered in .243 Win., .25-06, .270 Win., 7mm-08, 7mm Rem. Magnum, .300 Win. Magnum, 7mm Rem. Ultra Magnum, .30-06 and .300 Rem. Ultra Magnum. Features include: 24", 25" or 26" triangular Magnum-contour counterbored barrel; adjustable trigger; synthetic stock finished in Realtree AG HD camo; satin black oxide finish on exposed metal surfaces; hinged floorplate; SuperCell recoil pad. Overall length 41.625" to 46.5". Weight 7.25 lbs. to 7.625 lbs.

NIB	Exc.	V.G.	Good	Fair	Poor
850	675	500	395	200	125

Model 700 SPS Buckmasters Edition

Similar to Model 700 SPS, with engraved floorplate and camo stock. Also available in Youth model. Chambered in .243 only. Introduced in 2007.

NIB	Exc.	V.G.	Good	Fair	Poor
500	450	400	350	300	150

Model 700 Alaskan Ti

Lightweight (6.25 lbs.) version of Model 700, with titanium receiver, 24" fluted stainless barrel and Bell & Carlson synthetic stock. Chambered in a variety of Long, Short and Super-Short cartridges. Introduced in 2007.

NIB	Exc.	V.G.	Good	Fair	Poor
1750	1350	1050	775	500	200

Model 700 LSS 50th Anniversary of .280 Remington

Similar to Model 700 LSS, in .280 Rem. Dealer exclusive for 2007.

NIB	Exc.	V.G.	Good	Fair	Poor
800	675	500	375	250	175

Model 700 VL SS Thumbhole

Similar to Model 700 VS Composite, with brown laminated thumbhole stock and stainless steel barrel. Introduced in 2007.

NIB	Exc.	V.G.	Good	Fair	Poor
900	750	500	300	200	125

Model 700 Tactical Weapons System

This set designed for law enforcement use. Features Model 700 Police chambered for .308 Win. cartridge, 24" barrel (1-12" twist) and detachable magazine. Furnished with Leupold VARI X III scope, with rings and base; Harris 1A2 bipod, sling, lens covers and case.

NIB	Exc.	V.G.	Good	Fair	Poor
2500	2000	1650	1150	800	500

Model 710

Introduced in 2001. Chambered for .270 Win. or .30-06 cartridge. Fitted with 22" barrel and dark gray synthetic stock. Detachable box magazine. Supplied with pre-mounted Bushnell Sharpshooter 3-9x scope. Barrel finish ordnance gray steel, with matte finish. Weight about 7.12 lbs. In 2004, 7mm Rem. Magnum and .300 Win Magnum chamberings were added. In 2005, receiver was extruded solid steel. Calibers: .243, 7mm RM, .300 WM.

NIB	Exc.	V.G.	Good	Fair	Poor
375	285	225	195	150	100

Model 710 Youth

Similar to Model 710, with 20" barrel and 39.5" overall length. Chambered in .243 Win. Introduced 2006.

NIB	Exc.	V.G.	Good	Fair	Poor
375	285	225	195	150	100

Model 783

Bolt-action repeater in .270 Win., 7mm Rem. Magnum, .308 Win., .30-06. Cylindrical receiver, with barrel attached via external nut, injection molded synthetic stock, pillar bedded action, detachable box magazine, recoil pad and Crossfire trigger. New for 2013.

NIB	Exc.	V.G.	Good	Fair	Poor
400	365	330	300	250	200

Model 788

Centerfire bolt-action sporting rifle, with 22" or 24" barrel and plain walnut stock. An 18" barrel carbine was also manufactured and worth approximately 10 percent more than values listed below. Manufactured from 1967 to 1983. **NOTE:** Add 30 percent premium for .44 Magnum; 25 percent for .30-30; 20 percent premium for 7mm-08 caliber; 40 percent premium for left-hand models in 6mm and .308.

NIB	Exc.	V.G.	Good	Fair	Poor
—	500	425	375	300	250

Model Seven

Centerfire bolt-action sporting rifle, with 18.5" barrel and 4- or 5-shot magazine. Blued, with checkered walnut stock. Chambered for .17 Rem., .222 Rem., .223 Rem., .243 Rem., 6mm Rem., .260 Rem., 7mm-08 Rem. and .308 Win. Introduced into Remington product line in 1982.

NIB	Exc.	V.G.	Good	Fair	Poor
600	475	325	275	200	100

Model Seven FS

As above, with Kevlar stock. Introduced in 1987.

NIB	Exc.	V.G.	Good	Fair	Poor
600	525	450	375	275	150

Model Seven Synthetic

Updated Synthetic short-action series in .223 Rem., .243 Win., .260 Rem., 7mm-08 Rem. and .308 Win. 20" satin blue carbon steel barrel and matte black stock. Externally adjustable X-Mark Pro trigger is standard. No sights furnished. Weight 6.5 lbs. Compact version has 18" barrel, chambered in .243 or 7mm-08 only.

NIB	Exc.	V.G.	Good	Fair	Poor
585	500	425	365	300	200

Model Seven SS (Stainless Synthetic)

Introduced in 1994. Features stainless steel barrel, receiver and bolt with matte finish. Fitted with 20" barrel and hinged floorplate. Synthetic stock is textured black. Available in .243, 7mm-08 and .308. In 1997, .260 Rem. cartridge was also offered. Weight about 6.25 lbs.

NIB	Exc.	V.G.	Good	Fair	Poor
625	450	350	300	200	150

Model Seven LSS

Has stainless steel barrel and action. Fitted with satin finished laminated stock. Chambered for .22-250, .243, and 7mm-08 Rem. Weight about 6.5 lbs. Introduced in 2000.

NIB	Exc.	V.G.	Good	Fair	Poor
625	500	375	300	200	100

Model Seven LS

Offers a laminated stock, with carbon steel blued barrel. Calibers: .22-250, .243, .260 Rem., 8mm-08 Rem. and .308 Win. Weight about 6.5 lbs. Introduced in 2000.

NIB	Exc.	V.G.	Good	Fair	Poor
625	500	375	300	200	100

Model Seven MS

First introduced in 1993. Available through Remington Custom Shop. Features 20" barrel, with Mannlicher stock made from select grain wood and laminated for strength. Available in most short-action calibers including .222 Rem., .223 Rem., .22-250, .243 Win., 6mm Rem., .250 Savage, .257 Roberts, .260 Rem., 7mm-08, .308 Win., .35 Rem., .350 Rem. Magnum. **NOTE:** Add 20 percent for .250 Savage, .257 Roberts, .35 Rem.

NIB	Exc.	V.G.	Good	Fair	Poor
2600	2250	1650	1100	600	400

Model Seven AWR

Alaskan Wilderness Model has black synthetic stock, stainless steel action and 22" barrel with black matte Teflon finish. Weight 6.125 lbs. Detachable 3-shot magazine. Available from Remington Custom Shop from 2002 - 2008. Chambered only in 6.8 Rem. SPC, 7mm Rem. SAUM or .300 Rem. SAUM. Replaced by Model Seven AWR II in 2008. Came with 20" or 22" stainless steel barrel, Bell & Carlson olive green fiberglass stock and hinged floorplate. Chamberings include .260 Rem., .270 WSM, 7mm-08, 7mm Rem. SAUM, .308 Win., .300 WSM, .300 Rem. SAUM and .350 Rem. Magnum. **NOTE:** Add 10 percent for AWR II.

NIB	Exc.	V.G.	Good	Fair	Poor
2400	1800	1500	500	350	250

Model Seven Youth

First offered in 1993. A youth version of standard Model 7. Buttstock is 1" shorter than standard. Available in 6mm, .243 and 7mm-08. In 1998, available in .260 Rem. caliber.

NIB	Exc.	V.G.	Good	Fair	Poor
600	495	350	225	175	100

Model Seven CDL

Similar to Model Seven, with satin walnut, satin blue finish, sightless barrel and Limbsaver recoil pad. Introduced 2006.

NIB	Exc.	V.G.	Good	Fair	Poor
775	625	550	400	275	150

Model Seven XCR Camo

Similar to Model Seven LSS, with camo stock, fluted barrel and weather-resistant coating. Chambered in .243, 7mm-08, .308, .270 WSM and .300 WSM. Introduced in 2007.

NIB	Exc.	V.G.	Good	Fair	Poor
775	650	500	395	275	175

Model Seven 25th Anniversary Version

Similar to Model Seven in 7mm-08 only, with 25th Anniversary medallion inset at pistol-grip cap area. High-sheen blued finish on receiver bolt and 22" standard-contour barrel. X-Mark Pro Trigger and SuperCell recoil pad. Introduced 2008.

NIB	Exc.	V.G.	Good	Fair	Poor
950	700	550	350	250	150

Model Seven Predator

Similar to Model Seven, with full coverage in Mossy Oak Brush camo; fluted Magnum contour 22" barrel; synthetic stock as on Model Seven XCR; X-Mark Pro Trigger. Chambered in .17 Rem. Fireball, .204, .223, .22-250 and .243.

NIB	Exc.	V.G.	Good	Fair	Poor
800	650	500	395	275	175

Model 770

Package rifle similar to Model 710, with redesigned bolt assembly and magazine catch. Chambered in .243, .270, 7mm-08, .308, .30-06 and .300 WM. Available in Youth model. Chambered in .243 only. Introduced in 2007. In 2008, a version with stainless steel barrel and receiver and full camo finish was introduced. A 3-9X Bushnell scope is included. **NOTE:** Add $75 for camo finish.

NIB	Exc.	V.G.	Good	Fair	Poor
400	300	225	175	100	50

Model 770 Youth

Similar to Model 770, with shorter stock and barrel.

NIB	Exc.	V.G.	Good	Fair	Poor
375	275	200	165	90	50

Model 715 Sportsman

Similar to Model 770. Dealer exclusive for 2007.

NIB	Exc.	V.G.	Good	Fair	Poor
375	275	200	165	90	50

Model 798

Long-action sporting rifle built on reworked 98 Mauser action. Calibers: .243, .308, .30-06, .270, .300 WM, .375 H&H, .458 WM. Barrel 22" or 24" blued sightless. Stock brown laminated, with recoil pad. Claw extractor, 2-position safety, hinged floorplate. **NOTE:** Add 10 percent for Magnum chamberings; 30 percent for .375 and .458. Introduced 2006.

NIB	Exc.	V.G.	Good	Fair	Poor
575	400	300	200	125	100

Model 798 Stainless Laminate

Similar to Model 798, with laminated stock and stainless barrel. Chambered in .243, .25-06, .270, .30-06, 7mm Magnum, .300 WM and .375 H&H Magnum. Introduced in 2007. **NOTE** Add 25 percent for .375.

NIB	Exc.	V.G.	Good	Fair	Poor
650	475	350	250	175	125

Model 798 SPS

Similar to Model 798, with blued barrel and black synthetic stock. Introduced 2008.

NIB	Exc.	V.G.	Good	Fair	Poor
575	400	300	200	125	100

Model 798 Safari

Similar to Model 798. Chambered in .375 H&H or .458 Win. Magnum. Introduced 2008.

NIB	Exc.	V.G.	Good	Fair	Poor
850	700	575	400	325	250

Model 799

Similar to Model 798, but short-action without recoil pad. Calibers .22 Hornet, .222 Rem., .22-250, .223, 762X39. Introduced 2006.

NIB	Exc.	V.G.	Good	Fair	Poor
525	400	300	200	125	100

Model 1816 Commemorative Flint Lock Rifle

Introduced in 1995. Features .50-caliber 39" octagonal barrel. Stock is hand finished extra fancy curly maple. Built for one year only. Special order only.

NIB	Exc.	V.G.	Good	Fair	Poor
1825	1200	850	700	500	300

Remington No. 1 Rolling Block Mid-Range

Classic rifle reintroduced into Remington line in 1997. Features 30" half octagon, half-round barrel. Chambered for .45-70 Government cartridge. Designed for use with black powder and lead cast bullets. Receiver is case colored. All barrel, receiver and metalwork markings match original rifle. Rear tang-mounted vernier sight and front globe sight, with interchangeable inserts. Single-set trigger is standard. Steel buttplate. Weight about 9.75 lbs.

NIB	Exc.	V.G.	Good	Fair	Poor
2200	1900	1500	1200	700	400

Remington Mid-Range Sporter Rolling Block

Introduced in 1998. Features 30" round barrel, with pistol-grip sporter stock. Adjustable rear sight. Chambered for .30-30, .444 Marlin and .45-70 Government. A number of extra cost options are available, including barrels, sights, fancy wood, etc. Prices listed below are for standard model.

NIB	Exc.	V.G.	Good	Fair	Poor
1800	1600	1350	900	600	350

Model SPR18 Single Shot Rifle

Break-action rifle, with silvertone receiver and fluted barrel. Calibers .223, .243, .270, .30-06, .308. Weight 6.75 lbs. Imported. Introduced 2005.

NIB	Exc.	V.G.	Good	Fair	Poor
260	225	175	150	100	75

Model SPR22 Double Rifle

Top-lever operated break-action SXS double rifle in .30-06 and .45-70. Double triggers, tang safety. Barrels can be regulated via jackscrew. Imported. Introduced 2005.

NIB	Exc.	V.G.	Good	Fair	Poor
1000	850	700	600	450	300

Model SPR94 Combo Gun

Over/under rifle/shotgun. Combinations .410/.22 rimfire, .410/.17HMR, .410/.22WMR, 12-gauge/.223, 12-gauge/.30-06, 12-gauge/.308. Double triggers, tang safety. Imported. Introduced 2005.

NIB	Exc.	V.G.	Good	Fair	Poor
850	700	600	450	300	200

Model 412

Compact single-shot chambered for .22 LR. 19.5" blued barrel, hardwood stock. Introduced 2006.

NIB	Exc.	V.G.	Good	Fair	Poor
165	125	100	75	50	25

MODERN MUZZLELOADERS

Model 700 ML

Introduced in 1996. An in-line design and first built on a modern action. Chambered for .50- or .54-caliber bullet. Fitted with synthetic stock and rubber recoil pad. Barrel length 24". Weight about 7.75 lbs. Camo stock option added in 1997. Discontinued 2006.

Courtesy Remington Arms

NIB	Exc.	V.G.	Good	Fair	Poor
350	250	200	150	100	75

Model 700 ML Custom

Introduced in 1997. Similar to above featuring satin metal finish and gray laminated thumbhole stock, with roll-over cheekpiece. Discontinued.

NIB	Exc.	V.G.	Good	Fair	Poor
550	425	350	275	200	100

Model 700 MLS

Same as above, with stainless steel barrel and action. Discontinued.

Courtesy Remington Arms

NIB	Exc.	V.G.	Good	Fair	Poor
400	300	250	200	150	100

Model 700 MLS Custom

Similar to above model, with satin stainless steel finish and two-toned gray laminated thumbhole stock, with roll-over cheekpiece. Introduced in 1997. Discontinued.

NIB	Exc.	V.G.	Good	Fair	Poor
600	475	375	325	225	125

Model 700 ML Youth

Similar to Model ML. Shortened stock, with 13" lop and rubber recoil pad. Discontinued.

NIB	Exc.	V.G.	Good	Fair	Poor
370	300	250	200	150	100

Model 700 Ultimate Muzzle Loader

This model introduces the Ultimate Muzzle Loader (UML) ignition system. It uses a unique brass case containing a Remington 9.5 large-Magnum rifle primer that is push fed into the breech plug, creating a gas seal in the flash hole of the primer. This can handle up to a 200-grain Magnum powder charge for velocities over 2,400 fps. Features include .50-caliber fluted stainless barrel and laminate or Bell & Carlson synthetic stock. Introduced in 2014.

NIB	Exc.	V.G.	Good	Fair	Poor
1075	925	750	550	300	200

Genesis Muzzleloaders

Fixed-breech hammer-fired muzzle-loaders manufactured in a variety of configurations. Imported. Manufactured from 2006 to 2008.

NIB	Exc.	V.G.	Good	Fair	Poor
200	180	160	135	110	85

SHOTGUNS

Model 11

12-, 16- or 20-gauge semi-automatic shotgun, with barrels ranging in length from 26" to 32". Designed by John M. Browning. Produced under license from Fabrique Nationale. Blued, with checkered walnut stock. Approximately 300,000 made from 1911 to 1948. **NOTE:** Add 30 percent for solid or ventilated rib to listed values.

NIB	Exc.	V.G.	Good	Fair	Poor
—	800	650	500	400	300

11B Special

Engraved.

NIB	Exc.	V.G.	Good	Fair	Poor
—	1400	1100	600	500	400

11C Trap

NIB	Exc.	V.G.	Good	Fair	Poor
—	1600	1300	950	450	225

11D Tournament

NIB	Exc.	V.G.	Good	Fair	Poor
—	2200	1600	1000	600	450

11E Expert

Engraved.

NIB	Exc.	V.G.	Good	Fair	Poor
—	4500	3250	2700	1500	300

11F Premier

Heavily engraved.

No. 11F "Premier" Grade

NIB	Exc.	V.G.	Good	Fair	Poor
—	9000	7000	5000	3500	500

11R

20" barrel riot gun.

NIB	Exc.	V.G.	Good	Fair	Poor
—	1000	850	700	500	400

Model 10A

A 12-, 16- or 20-gauge slide-action shotgun, with barrels ranging from 26" to 32". Takedown blued, with plain walnut stock. Manufactured from 1907 to 1929.

Courtesy Remington Arms

NIB	Exc.	V.G.	Good	Fair	Poor
—	375	300	250	200	100

Model 17

A 20-gauge slide-action shotgun, with barrels from 26" to 32". Takedown blued, with plain walnut stock. Approximately 48,000 made from 1917 to 1933. **NOTE:** Add 25 percent for ventilated rib.

Courtesy Remington Arms

NIB	Exc.	V.G.	Good	Fair	Poor
—	395	300	250	175	100

Model 29

As above, chambered for 12-gauge cartridge. Approximately 24,000 manufactured from 1929 to 1933. **NOTE:** Add 40 percent for 32" barrels; 25 percent for ventilated rib.

NIB	Exc.	V.G.	Good	Fair	Poor
—	450	350	300	200	175

Model 31

A 12-, 16- or 20-gauge slide-action shotgun, with barrels from 26" to 32". Magazine capacity 2 or 4 rounds. Takedown blued, with walnut stock. Approximately 160,000 made from 1931 to 1949. **NOTE:** Add 50 percent for 32" barrel; 40 percent for early models with checkered stocks; 25 percent for solid or ventilated rib; 25 percent for early banded barrels.

NIB	Exc.	V.G.	Good	Fair	Poor
—	450	325	275	200	125

MODEL 870 SERIES

Model 870 Wingmaster

A 12-, 16- or 20-gauge slide-action shotgun, with 26", 28" or 30" barrels and 5-shot tubular magazine. Blued, with plain walnut stock. Manufactured from 1950 to 1963. **NOTE:** Add 10 percent for ventilated rib.

NIB	Exc.	V.G.	Good	Fair	Poor
—	350	225	200	150	100

Model 870 Field Wingmaster

As above, with checkered walnut stock and screw-in choke tubes. Introduced in 1964. In 1980, 16-gauge was dropped as an offering, but was later reinstated (see below).

NIB	Exc.	V.G.	Good	Fair	Poor
550	450	300	225	150	100

Model 870 Field Wingmaster 16 Gauge

In 2002, 16-gauge was reintroduced into the Wingmaster line. Offered with 26" or 28" ventilated rib barrel and choke tubes. Walnut stock, with blued finish. Weight about 7 lbs. Offered in 16-gauge in other configurations listed.

NIB	Exc.	V.G.	Good	Fair	Poor
600	475	375	250	200	100

Model 870 Wingmaster NRA Edition

A 12-gauge 3" gun, with 28" ventilated rib barrel and choke tubes. Walnut stock, with checkering. Blued receiver, with NRA logos on both sides. Introduced in 2005.

NIB	Exc.	V.G.	Good	Fair	Poor
550	450	300	225	150	100

Model 870 Wingmaster Jr.

Introduced in 2005. Features a 20-gauge gun, with 18.75" ventilated rib barrel and choke tubes. Checkered walnut stock, with recoil pad. Blued finish. Weight about 6 lbs.

NIB	Exc.	V.G.	Good	Fair	Poor
550	450	300	225	150	100

Model 870 Field Wingmaster Small Bores

Introduced in 1999. Now offered in both 28-gauge and .410 bore. Checkered walnut stock. High polish blue finish. Both guns are fitted with 25" barrels. 28-gauge has RemChokes while .410 comes with fixed Modified chokes. Weight about 6 lbs. Price listed is for .410 bore. **NOTE:** Add $50 for 28-gauge.

Wingmaster 28 gauge

NIB	Exc.	V.G.	Good	Fair	Poor
1075	925	750	550	300	200

Model 870 Magnum

As above chambered for 12- or 20-gauge. 3" Magnum shells. Introduced in 1964. Choke tubes introduced in 1987.

NIB	Exc.	V.G.	Good	Fair	Poor
575	425	300	225	150	100

Model 870 Express

As above for 3", 12-gauge shells, with 28" ventilated rib and one choke tube. Parkerized, with matte finished stock. Introduced in 1987.

NIB	Exc.	V.G.	Good	Fair	Poor
330	250	200	150	100	75

Model 870 Express Synthetic

NIB	Exc.	V.G.	Good	Fair	Poor
330	250	200	150	100	75

Model 870 Express Synthetic Youth

NIB	Exc.	V.G.	Good	Fair	Poor
300	250	200	150	100	75

Model 870 Express Jr. NWTF Edition

20-gauge model fitted with 18.75" ventilated rib barrel, with choke tubes. Synthetic stock has camo finish. Metal matte black. Weight about 6 lbs. Introduced in 2005.

NIB	Exc.	V.G.	Good	Fair	Poor
320	250	200	150	100	75

Model 870 Express Super Magnum

Introduced in 1998. Similar to 870 Express, but chambered for 3.5" 12-gauge. Offered in walnut stock, with blued 28" barrel. Matte black synthetic, with 26" or 28" barrel or various camo finishes. Also available as a combo, with extra 20" rifled deer barrel. **NOTE:** Add $100 for camo; 20 percent for combo with deer barrel. Introduced in 1998.

NIB	Exc.	V.G.	Good	Fair	Poor
425	330	225	175	125	100

Model 870 Express Super Magnum Fall Flight

Chambered for 12-gauge, with 2.75", 3" or 3.5" shells. Fitted with 30" ventilated rib barrel and choke tubes. Skyline Fall Flight camo finish. Weight about 7.75 lbs. Introduced in 2005.

NIB	Exc.	V.G.	Good	Fair	Poor
475	375	275	225	175	150

Model 870 Express Synthetic Super Mag Turkey-Waterfowl Camo

Pump action shotgun. Chambered in 12-gauge, 2.75" to 3.5" shells. Features include full Mossy Oak Bottomland camo coverage; 26" barrel with HiViz fiber-optics sights; Wingmaster HD Waterfowl and Turkey Extra Full RemChokes; SuperCell recoil pad; drilled and tapped receiver.

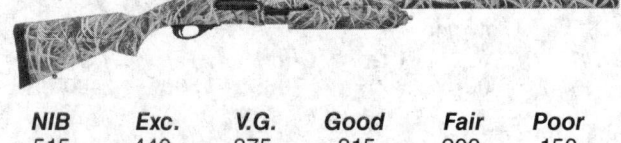

NIB	Exc.	V.G.	Good	Fair	Poor
515	440	375	315	200	150

Model 870 Super Mag Turkey-Predator Camo with Scope

Pump action shotgun chambered in 12-gauge, 2.75" to 3.5" shells. Features include 20" barrel; TruGlo red/green selectable illuminated sight mounted on pre-installed Weaver-style rail; black padded sling; Wingmaster HD Turkey/Predator RemChoke; full Mossy Oak Obsession camo coverage; ShurShot pistol-grip stock, with black overmolded grip panels; TruGlo 30mm Red/Green Dot Scope pre-mounted.

NIB	Exc.	V.G.	Good	Fair	Poor
575	500	425	350	200	150

Model 870TA Trap

As above, with competition ventilated rib and checkered stock. Produced in 12-gauge only. Discontinued in 1986.

NIB	Exc.	V.G.	Good	Fair	Poor
500	400	300	200	150	100

Model 870TB Trap

As above, with 28" or 30" Full choke, ventilated rib barrel and trap-style walnut stock. Manufactured from 1950 to 1981.

NIB	Exc.	V.G.	Good	Fair	Poor
—	450	325	275	200	125

Model 870TC Trap

As above, with finely figured walnut stock and screw-in choke tubes.

NIB	Exc.	V.G.	Good	Fair	Poor
575	475	400	350	250	150

Model 870 Express Deer Gun

Fitted with 20" fully rifled barrel, iron sights and Monte Carlo stock. Also offered with 20" IC rifle sighted barrel. Available in 12-gauge only.

NIB	Exc.	V.G.	Good	Fair	Poor
370	275	200	150	125	100

Model 870 Express Deer/Turkey Combo

This 3" 12-gauge has a 21" barrel threaded for RemChokes for turkey hunting and 23" rifled slug barrel, with cantilever scope mount for deer hunting. Receiver and barrel are matte black; synthetic stock is Mossy Oak Break-Up camo.

NIB	Exc.	V.G.	Good	Fair	Poor
625	500	425	350	250	150

Model 870 Express Left-Hand

Left-hand version of Express model fitted with 28" ventilated rib barrel. Checkered hardwood stock. Black matte finish.

NIB	Exc.	V.G.	Good	Fair	Poor
360	275	200	150	100	75

Model 870 Express Synthetic Turkey Camo

12-gauge pump action shotgun chambered for 2.75" and 3" shells. Features include 21" ventilated rib bead-sighted barrel; standard Express finish on barrel and receiver; Turkey Extra Full RemChoke; synthetic stock with integrated sling swivel attachment.

NIB	Exc.	V.G.	Good	Fair	Poor
445	385	325	275	200	150

Model 870 Express Super Magnum Turkey

This 12-gauge gun will handle 2.75", 3" or 3.5" shells. Fitted with 23" ventilated rib barrel, black synthetic stock and matte black metal finish. Weight about 7.25 lbs. Introduced in 1999.

NIB	Exc.	V.G.	Good	Fair	Poor
390	290	200	150	100	75

Model 870 Express Synthetic Deer

Fitted with 20" fully rifled barrel, with adjustable rifle sights. Black synthetic stock, with Monte Carlo comb and matte black finish. Weight about 7 lbs. Introduced in 1999.

NIB	Exc.	V.G.	Good	Fair	Poor
370	275	200	150	100	75

Model 870 Express Compact Deer

20-gauge; similar to Model 870 Express Synthetic Deer, with smaller dimensions.

NIB	Exc.	V.G.	Good	Fair	Poor
425	300	200	150	100	75

Model 870 Express Compact Pink Camo

20-gauge; similar to Model 870 Express, with pink camo synthetic stock.

NIB	Exc.	V.G.	Good	Fair	Poor
370	275	200	150	100	75

Model 870 Express Compact Synthetic

Similar to above, with matte black synthetic stock.

NIB	Exc.	V.G.	Good	Fair	Poor
370	275	200	150	100	75

Model 870 Express Compact Camo

Similar to above, with camo buttstock and for-end.

NIB	Exc.	V.G.	Good	Fair	Poor
395	295	215	150	100	75

Model 870 Express Compact Jr.

Similar to above, with shorter barrel and lop.

NIB	Exc.	V.G.	Good	Fair	Poor
370	275	200	150	100	75

Model 870 Express Combos

Offered in both 12- and 20-gauge, with 26" ventilated rib modified barrel and 20" fully rifled deer barrel.

NIB	Exc.	V.G.	Good	Fair	Poor
500	395	250	200	150	100

Model 870 Express Youth Gun

Available in 20-gauge only. Built for children. Has 13" length of pull and 21" ventilated rib barrel. Sold with Modified RemChoke tube.

NIB	Exc.	V.G.	Good	Fair	Poor
330	250	200	150	125	100

Model 870 Express Turkey

Furnished in 12-gauge, with 21" ventilated rib barrel. Extra-full Rem-Choke Turkey tube.

NIB	Exc.	V.G.	Good	Fair	Poor
345	250	175	150	125	100

Model 870 Express Camo Turkey

Similar to Express Turkey, with complete coverage of camo stock. Metal is matte black.

NIB	Exc.	V.G.	Good	Fair	Poor
400	300	225	150	100	75

Model 870 20 Gauge Express Youth Camo Turkey

Similar to Model 870 Express Camo. In 20-gauge, with shortened stock (13" lop).

NIB	Exc.	V.G.	Good	Fair	Poor
400	300	225	150	100	75

Model 870 Express Small Game

Offered in 20-gauge or .410 bore. Has a non-reflective metal and wood finish. The .410 bore furnished with 25" ventilated rib Full choke barrel; 20-gauge available with 26" or 28" ventilated rib barrel, with Modified RemChoke tube.

NIB	Exc.	V.G.	Good	Fair	Poor
225	200	175	150	125	100

Model 870 Express HD (Home Defense)

Introduced in 1995. Features 18" 12-gauge barrel, with cylinder barrel and front bead sight. Weight about 7.25 lb.

Courtesy Remington Arms

NIB	Exc.	V.G.	Good	Fair	Poor
345	250	175	150	125	100

Model 870 Classic Trap

Introduced in 2000. Features special fine line engraving, with gold inlays. Stock is select walnut, with Monte Carlo comb, 30" barrel, with contoured ventilated rib. Ventilated recoil pad, with white-line spacers. Choke tubes. Weight about 8 lbs.

NIB	Exc.	V.G.	Good	Fair	Poor
675	550	450	300	200	—

Model 870 Special Field

Pump-action shotgun available in 12- or 20-gauge. Features English-style straight-grip stock, 21" ventilated rib barrel and slim shortened slide handle. Weight: 12-gauge 7 lbs.; 20-gauge 6.25 lbs. Comes with a set of RemChoke tubes.

NIB	Exc.	V.G.	Good	Fair	Poor
650	550	375	250	150	100

Model 870 Rifle Deer Gun

New 20-gauge model introduced in 1994. Features fully rifled 20" barrel. Has a new scope rail design that is more rigid. Finish blue and Monte Carlo stock walnut. Equipped with recoil pad and checkering.

NIB	Exc.	V.G.	Good	Fair	Poor
450	400	350	300	200	100

Model 870 Brushmaster Deer Gun

12-gauge slide-action shotgun. Fitted with 20" RemChoke plain barrel and Monte Carlo stock. Available for left-/right-hand shooters.

NIB	Exc.	V.G.	Good	Fair	Poor
350	300	250	200	150	100

Model 870 Express Youth Turkey Camo

Similar to model above. Chambered for 20-gauge shell. Finished with Realtree Camo. Weight about 6 lbs.

NIB	Exc.	V.G.	Good	Fair	Poor
400	300	225	150	125	100

Model 870 Youth Deer Gun

Chambered for 20-gauge shell. Fitted with 21" full choked barrel. Realtree Camo finish. Magazine capacity 4 rounds. Weight about 6 lbs.

NIB	Exc.	V.G.	Good	Fair	Poor
350	300	250	200	150	100

Model 870 Security

Offered in 12-gauge only. This personal protection shotgun has 18.5" Cylinder-choked plain barrel, with front bead sight.

NIB	Exc.	V.G.	Good	Fair	Poor
350	300	250	200	150	100

Model 870 SPS-Camo

Offered in 12-gauge only. Choice of 26" or 28" ventilated rib barrel, with RemChoke tubes. Wood and metal are finished in brown camo color. Introduced in 2001.

NIB	Exc.	V.G.	Good	Fair	Poor
600	425	325	225	175	125

Model 870 SPS Super Magnum Camo

Chambered for 12-gauge shells, with chambers that will handle both 3" and 3.5" Magnum, as well as all 2.75" shells. Barrel 23", with ventilated rib and RemChokes. Finish Mossy Oak camo. Weight about 7.25 lbs. Introduced in 1999.

NIB	Exc.	V.G.	Good	Fair	Poor
600	425	325	225	175	125

Model 870 SPS-BG Camo

First time available in 1993. Features 12-gauge 20" plain barrel, with IC and Turkey Super Full RemChoke tubes. Wood and metal are finished in brown camo color.

NIB	Exc.	V.G.	Good	Fair	Poor
400	300	225	175	125	100

Model 870 SPS Fully Rifled Deer Gun

20-gauge model features 18.5" fully rifled heavy barrel, with no sights. Receiver has cantilever scope mount. Black synthetic stock. Black matte finish. Weight about 8 lbs. Magazine capacity 4 rounds. Introduced in 2004.

NIB	Exc.	V.G.	Good	Fair	Poor
500	375	250	175	125	100

Model 870 SPS Super Slug Deer Gun

Features 23" fully rifled modified contour barrel which is equipped with a barrel mounted cantilever scope mount. Stock is black synthetic. Weight about 8 lbs. Introduced in 1999.

NIB	Exc.	V.G.	Good	Fair	Poor
600	425	325	250	175	100

Model 870 SPS-T

12-gauge model comes standard with 21" ventilated rib barrel, RemChoke tubes in IC and Turkey Super Full, black synthetic stock and black matte finish.

NIB	Exc.	V.G.	Good	Fair	Poor
575	475	400	350	250	150

Model 870 SPS-T Camo

Same as above, with exception of 21" ventilated rib barrel. IC and Turkey Super Full RemChoke tubes. Both wood and metal are finished in green camo color.

NIB	Exc.	V.G.	Good	Fair	Poor
600	425	325	250	175	100

Model 870 SPS-T Youth Turkey Camo

Finished in Mossy Oak Break-Up. Chambered for 12-gauge shell. Fitted with 20" Super Full choke. Weight about 7.125 lbs. Introduced in 2001.

NIB	Exc.	V.G.	Good	Fair	Poor
565	450	325	250	175	125

Model 870 SPS-T Super Magnum Camo

This 12-gauge model will handle 2.75", 3" and 3.5" shells. Fitted with 23" barrel and RemChokes. Finish Mossy Oak camo. Weight about 7.25 lbs. Introduced in 1999.

NIB	Exc.	V.G.	Good	Fair	Poor
615	425	325	250	175	125

Model 870 SPS-T Camo NWTF 25th Anniversary

Fitted with 21" barrel that has special fiber optic sighting system. NWTF logo on left side of receiver. Introduced in 1998.

NIB	Exc.	V.G.	Good	Fair	Poor
600	450	325	250	175	125

Model 870 SPS-T Super Mag

Similar to Model 870 SP-T Thumbhole, with pistol-grip stock and ventilated rib barrel.

NIB	Exc.	V.G.	Good	Fair	Poor
630	450	350	275	200	150

Model 870 SPS-T/20

20-gauge turkey gun features 3" chamber, 23" ventilated rib barrel, R3 recoil pad and full coverage in Mossy Oak New Break-Up camo. Drilled and tapped for scope mount.

NIB	Exc.	V.G.	Good	Fair	Poor
550	450	325	250	195	150

Model 870 SPS-T Camo

Chambered for 20-gauge 3" shell. Fitted with 20" barrel and full choke. Stock is Mossy Oak camo. Fiber optic front sight. Weight about 6 lbs. Introduced in 2003.

NIB	Exc.	V.G.	Good	Fair	Poor
600	450	325	250	175	125

Model 870 SP-T Super Magnum Thumbhole

12-gauge 3.5" gun fitted with 23" barrel and choke tubes. Mossy Oak Obsession finish. Open sights, with fiber-optic front sight. Weight about 8 lbs. Introduced in 2005.

NIB	Exc.	V.G.	Good	Fair	Poor
650	500	350	250	175	125

Model 870 Dale Earnhardt Limited Edition

12-gauge with 28" ventilated rib barrel and choke tubes. Checkered walnut stock. Receiver engraved with Earnhardt's likeness and gold signature. High polish blue finish. Weight about 8 lbs. Introduced in 2005.

NIB	Exc.	V.G.	Good	Fair	Poor
650	500	350	250	175	125

Model 870 Marine Magnum

This 12-gauge shotgun has a nickel finish on the inside and outside of receiver and barrel. Synthetic stock checkered. The 18" barrel is bored cylinder. Fitted with 7-round magazine. Sling swivel studs are standard.

NIB	Exc.	V.G.	Good	Fair	Poor
560	325	275	225	175	125

Model 870 SPS

Offered in 12-gauge only. Synthetic stock and black matte finish. Barrel 26" or 28", with ventilated rib and RemChoke tubes.

NIB	Exc.	V.G.	Good	Fair	Poor
325	275	225	175	125	100

Model 870 SPS-Deer

Available with 20" rifle and plain barrel. This 12-gauge shotgun has black synthetic stock and black matte finish. First introduced in 1993.

NIB	Exc.	V.G.	Good	Fair	Poor
550	450	325	250	195	150

Model 870 Police

This model comes in a wide variety (21) of 12-gauge configurations. Fitted with barrel from 14" (Class III), 18" or 20". Most with Parkerized finish, although some variations have blued finish. Wood, folding, Speedfeed or synthetic stock. Rifle or bead sights. Some configurations with ghost ring and tritium night sights. Some variations have 7- or 8-round magazine extensions, depending on barrel length.

NIB	Exc.	V.G.	Good	Fair	Poor
650	525	400	300	225	125

Model 870 Tac-2 SpecOps Stock

Tactical 3" 12-gauge. Available with Knoxx pistol-grip or folding stock. Barrel 18", with fixed Cylinder choke. Magazine capacity 6 shells. Weight 7 lbs.

NIB	Exc.	V.G.	Good	Fair	Poor
615	425	325	250	175	125

Model 870 Tac-3 Speedfeed IV

Tactical 3" 12-gauge, with pistol-grip stock and 20" barrel. Extended 7-round magazine. Weight 7.5 lbs.

NIB	Exc.	V.G.	Good	Fair	Poor
600	450	325	250	175	125

Model 870 Tac-3 Folder

As above, with Knoxx Spec-Ops folding stock. Weight 7 lbs.

NIB	Exc.	V.G.	Good	Fair	Poor
600	450	325	250	175	125

Model 870 Express Tactical A-TACS Camo

Pump action shotgun chambered for 2.75" and 3" 12-gauge. Features include full A-TACS digitized camo; 18.5" barrel; extended ported Tactical RemChoke; SpeedFeed IV pistol-grip stock with SuperCell recoil pad; fully adjustable XS ghost ring sight rail with removable white bead front sight; 7-round capacity with factory-installed 2-shot extension; drilled and tapped receiver; sling swivel stud.

NIB	Exc.	V.G.	Good	Fair	Poor
600	525	450	375	275	185

Model 870 Custom Grade

Custom Shop model available in three levels of engraving, gold inlay, wood grade and finish, metal work finish, recoil pad/buttplate and dimensions.

D Grade

NIB	Exc.	V.G.	Good	Fair	Poor
3000	200	1100	—	—	—

F Grade

NIB	Exc.	V.G.	Good	Fair	Poor
6000	4000	2250	—	—	—

F Grade with Gold Inlay

NIB	Exc.	V.G.	Good	Fair	Poor
10000	7500	5000	—	—	—

Model 870 SP-T Thumbhole

Introduced in 2005. This 3.5" 12-gauge is designed specifically for turkey hunting. Full coverage in Mossy Oak Obsession camo and thumbhole stock. The 23" barrel features fiber-optic adjustable rifle sights and is drilled and tapped for scope mounting. Includes R3 recoil pad, sling, swivels and Turkey Super Full choke tube.

NIB	Exc.	V.G.	Good	Fair	Poor
615	425	325	250	175	125

Model 870 Special Purpose Thumbhole

Laminated stock 12-gauge slug gun, with 3" chamber and 23" fully rifled cantilever barrel.

NIB	Exc.	V.G.	Good	Fair	Poor
525	475	350	275	200	150

Model 870 XCS Marine Magnum

New in 2007, this weather-resistant 870 is a 3" 12-gauge, with full black TriNyte coverage, 18" fixed Cylinder barrel and 7-round capacity. Weight 7.5 lbs.

NIB	Exc.	V.G.	Good	Fair	Poor
675	495	400	300	200	125

Model 870 SPS MAX Gobbler

Dedicated turkey gun is a 3.5" 12-gauge. Featuring length-adjustable Knoxx SpecOps stock, 23" barrel, fiber-optic rifle sights, Turkey Super Full choke tube and full coverage in Realtree APG camo. Drilled and tapped for Weaver style mount. Weight 8 lbs.

NIB	Exc.	V.G.	Good	Fair	Poor
650	550	425	350	225	150

Model 870 20 Gauge Lightweight Magnum

Fixed-choke, high-gloss 3" version of Model 870 Wingmaster, with impressed checkering. Introduced mid-1980s. Also chambers 2.75" shells. Discontinued.

NIB	Exc.	V.G.	Good	Fair	Poor
550	450	325	250	195	150

Model 870 Wingmaster 100th Anniversary

Commemorative Edition 12-gauge celebrating 100 years of Remington pump shotguns (dating from introduction of Model 10 in 1908). Introduced in 2008. Offered only for one year. Gold-inlaid logos on both sides of receiver and "B" Grade American walnut stock, with high-gloss finish. Includes three choke tubes.

NIB	Exc.	V.G.	Good	Fair	Poor
875	600	475	350	200	125

Model 870 American Classic

Part of Remington American Classic series honoring some of the great models of the 20th century. Inaugurating this line in 2014, is this special edition Model 870 pump action and a comparable Model 1100 semi-automatic. Features include a higher B-grade walnut stock, gold filled engraving and ventilated recoil pad, with white outline as was found on the originals.

NIB	Exc.	V.G.	Good	Fair	Poor
1000	850	700	600	400	300

Model 870 with Claro Walnut

This 2008 upgrade to 870 Wingmaster. Features semi-fancy claro walnut stock and fore-end. Available in 3" 12- and 20-gauge, with 28" and 26" barrels, respectively. Three choke tubes included.

NIB	Exc.	V.G.	Good	Fair	Poor
875	600	475	350	200	125

Model 870 Express Magnum ShurShot Cantilever

This 3" 12-gauge has a 23" fully rifled barrel, with cantilever scope mount. Matte black finish. Weight about 7.75 lbs.

NIB	Exc.	V.G.	Good	Fair	Poor
550	450	325	250	195	150

Model 870 SPS ShurShot Synthetic Super Slug

Pump-action shotgun based on 870 platform. Chambers 12-gauge 2.75" and 3" shells interchangeably. Extra-heavy (1" dia.) 25.5" fully rifled barrel pinned to receiver. SuperCell recoil pad. Drilled and tapped for scope mounts, with Weaver rail included. Matte black metal surfaces, Mossy Oak Treestand ShurShot buttstock and fore-end. Overall length 47". Weight 7.875 lbs.

NIB	Exc.	V.G.	Good	Fair	Poor
550	450	325	250	195	150

Model 870 Express Super Magnum Waterfowl

Introduced in 2008. This dedicated waterfowl gun is completely finished in Mossy Oak Duck Blind camo. The 3.5" 12-gauge has 28" barrel, HiViz single bead sight. Includes one choke tube. Weight about 7.5 lbs.

NIB	Exc.	V.G.	Good	Fair	Poor
350	300	250	200	150	100

Model 870 Express Magnum ShurShot Turkey

Turkey-dedicated model has matte black finish, with ShurShot pistol-grip/thumbhole stock. Fore-end finished in Mossy Oak Obsession camo. The 3" 12-gauge has 21" barrel. Includes a Turkey Extra Full choke tube. Weight about 7.5 lbs.

NIB	Exc.	V.G.	Good	Fair	Poor
500	400	325	250	175	100

Model 870 SPS ShurShot Turkey

New in 2008. This 12-gauge chambered for shells up to 3.5". Features Remington's ShurShot pistol-grip/thumbhole stock. Fully covered in Realtree's APG HD camo. Has 23" non-ventilated rib barrel outfitted with fiber-optic rifle-type sights and includes an extended Turkey RemChoke. Weight about 7.5 lbs.

NIB	Exc.	V.G.	Good	Fair	Poor
625	495	400	300	200	125

Model 870 Express Tactical

Similar to Model 870, in 12-gauge only (2.75" and 3" interchangeably) with 18.5" barrel, Tactical RemChoke extended/ported choke tube, black synthetic buttstock and fore-end, extended magazine tube, gray powder-coat finish overall. 38.5" overall length. Weight 7.5 lbs.

NIB	Exc.	V.G.	Good	Fair	Poor
575	465	325	250	195	150

Model 870 Express Tactical with Ghost Ring Sights

Similar to Model 870 Express Tactical, with top-mounted accessories rail and XS ghost ring rear sight.

NIB	Exc.	V.G.	Good	Fair	Poor
625	495	400	300	200	125

Model 870 Tactical Desert Recon

Tactical version 870 features Digital Tiger desert camo on synthetic stock and fore-end. Olive-drab powder-coated barrel and receiver. Available with 18" (6-round mag. capacity) or 20" (7-round mag. capacity) barrel. Speedfeed I (shell holding) or Speedfeed IV (pistol-grip) stock. **NOTE:** Add 10 percent for Speedfeed IV stock.

NIB	Exc.	V.G.	Good	Fair	Poor
625	495	400	300	200	125

Model 887 Nitro Mag Pump Shotgun

Pump-action shotgun based on Model 870. Chambers 2.75", 3" and 3.5" 12-gauge shells interchangeably. Black matte ArmorLokt rustproof coating throughout. SuperCell recoil pad. 28" barrel, with solid rib. Hi-Viz front sight, with interchangeable light tubes. Black synthetic stock, with contoured grip panels.

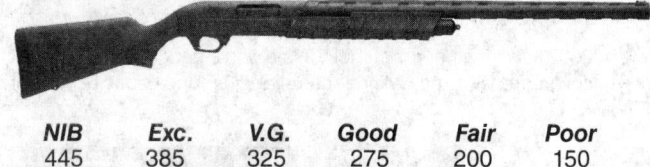

NIB	Exc.	V.G.	Good	Fair	Poor
445	385	325	275	200	150

Model 887 Nitro Mag Waterfowl

Similar to above, with Advantage Max-4 camo overall.

NIB	Exc.	V.G.	Good	Fair	Poor
450	400	350	300	200	100

Model 887 Bone Collector Edition

Pump-action shotgun chambered in 12-gauge, 2.75" to 3.5" shells. Features include ArmorLokt rustproof coating; synthetic stock and fore-end; 26" barrel; full camo finish; integral swivel studs; SuperCell recoil pad; solid rib and HiViz front sight. Bone Collector logo.

NIB	Exc.	V.G.	Good	Fair	Poor
560	475	400	335	250	150

Model 887 Nitro Mag Camo Combo

Pump-action shotgun chambered in 12-gauge, 2.75" to 3.5" shells. Features include 22" turkey barrel, with HiViz fiber-optic rifle sights and 28" waterfowl, with HiViz sight; extended Waterfowl and Super Full Turkey RemChokes are included; SuperCell recoil pad; synthetic stock and fore-end, with specially contoured grip panels; full camo coverage.

NIB	Exc.	V.G.	Good	Fair	Poor
625	535	460	385	325	200

Model 887 Nitro Mag Tactical

Pump-action shotgun chambered in 12-gauge, 2.75" to 3.5" shells. Features include 18.5" barrel, with ported extended tactical RemChoke; 2-shot magazine extension; barrel clamp, with integral Picatinny rails; ArmorLokt coating; synthetic stock and fore-end, with specially contour grip panels.

NIB	Exc.	V.G.	Good	Fair	Poor
450	400	350	275	200	150

Model 48 Sportsman

A 12-, 16- or 20-gauge semi-automatic shotgun, with 26", 28" or 32" barrels and 3-shot tubular magazine. Blued. with checkered walnut stock.

Approximately 275,000 made from 1949 to 1959. **NOTE:** Add 20 percent for ventilated rib.

NIB	Exc.	V.G.	Good	Fair	Poor
—	325	300	250	175	100

Model 11-48

As above, with addition of 28-gauge and .410 bore. Approximately 425,000 made from 1949 to 1968. **NOTE:** Add 20 percent for 20-gauge; 100 percent for 28-gauge or .410 bore.

NIB	Exc.	V.G.	Good	Fair	Poor
—	300	250	200	150	75

Model 58 Sportsman

A 12-, 16- or 20-gauge semi-automatic shotgun, with 26", 28" or 30" barrels and 3-shot tubular magazine. Receiver is scroll engraved and blued. Checkered walnut stock. Approximately 270,000 made from 1956 to 1963. **NOTE:** Add 50 percent for skeet model.

NIB	Exc.	V.G.	Good	Fair	Poor
—	300	250	200	150	75

Model 878 Automaster

As above in 12-gauge only. Approximately 60,000 made from 1959 to 1962.

NIB	Exc.	V.G.	Good	Fair	Poor
—	350	250	175	125	75

MODEL 1100 SERIES

A 12-, 16-, 20-, 28-gauge or .410 bore semi-automatic shotgun, with barrels from 26" to 30". Fitted with choke tubes after 1987. Blued, with checkered walnut stock. Manufactured beginning in 1963. **NOTE:** Smaller bore versions are worth approximately 20 percent more than values listed.

NIB	Exc.	V.G.	Good	Fair	Poor
550	450	350	200	150	100

Model 1100 Classic Field

Introduced in 2003. Chambered for 16-gauge shell. Fitted with choice of 26" or 28" ventilated rib barrel, with RemChoke tubes. Checkered wal-

nut stock, with pistol-grip. High polish blue finish. Magazine capacity 4 rounds. Weight about 7 to 7.25 lbs. depending on barrel length.

NIB	Exc.	V.G.	Good	Fair	Poor
800	600	450	300	200	100

Model 1100 Small Game

Available in 20-, 28-gauge or .410 bore. Fitted with 25" ventilated rib barrels. 28-gauge and .410 have fixed chokes, while 20-gauge has RemChoke tubes.

NIB	Exc.	V.G.	Good	Fair	Poor
500	450	400	350	250	150

Model 1100 Youth Gun

Offered in 20-gauge only, with 21" ventilated rib 2.75" barrel. Stock has special 13" length of pull. Gun supplied with a set of RemChoke tubes.

NIB	Exc.	V.G.	Good	Fair	Poor
600	400	350	300	200	150

Model 1100 Youth Synthetic

Fitted with 21" ventilated rib barrel, this 20-gauge gun has a 1" shorter length of pull than standard. Matte black finish. Black synthetic stock. Weight about 6.5 lbs. Introduced in 1999.

NIB	Exc.	V.G.	Good	Fair	Poor
575	400	300	225	150	100

Model 1100 Youth Synthetic Camo

Same as model above, with Realtree camo finish and chambered for 20-gauge 3" Magnum shells. Weight about 6.75 lbs. Introduced in 1999.

NIB	Exc.	V.G.	Good	Fair	Poor
695	475	325	225	175	100

Model 1100 Tournament Skeet

Offered in 20-, 28-gauge and .410 bore. The 28-gauge and .410 come with 25" Skeet choked ventilated rib barrels; 20-gauge supplied with 26" Skeet choked ventilated rib barrel.

Courtesy Remington Arms

NIB	Exc.	V.G.	Good	Fair	Poor
800	650	500	400	250	150

Model 1100 Tournament Skeet, 12 Gauge

Introduced in 2003. Fitted with 26" light contour ventilated rib barrel. Stock semi-fancy walnut. Receiver rolled-marked "tournament skeet". Supplied with extended choke tubes and gold-plated trigger. Weight about 7.75 lbs.

NIB	Exc.	V.G.	Good	Fair	Poor
650	500	400	300	200	100

Model 1100 Classic Trap

Features 30" low-profile ventilated rib barrel. Stock semi-fancy walnut, with Monte Carlo comb and ventilated recoil pad. Receiver has fine line engraving, with gold inlays. Trigger is gold. Weight about 8.25 lbs.

NIB	Exc.	V.G.	Good	Fair	Poor
850	725	600	475	350	200

Model 1100 Sporting 12

Introduced in 2000. This 12-gauge features 28" low profile ventilated rib barrel. Stock walnut, with cut checkering and Sporting Clays-style recoil pad. Gold trigger and fine line engraving on receiver. Weight about 8 lbs.

NIB	Exc.	V.G.	Good	Fair	Poor
725	650	475	400	300	150

Model 1100 Sporting 20

High grade walnut stock, with glass finish and recoil pad. Fitted with 28" barrel, with target sights. Interchangeable chokes. Introduced in 1998.

NIB	Exc.	V.G.	Good	Fair	Poor
700	625	425	400	300	150

Model 1100 Sporting 28

Introduced in 1996. Chambered for 28-gauge shell. Fitted with interchangeable chokes and 25" ventilated rib barrel. Stock is walnut, with Tournament grade checkering and recoil pad.

Courtesy Remington Arms

NIB	Exc.	V.G.	Good	Fair	Poor
825	700	575	475	350	200

Model 1100 Competition Master

Introduced in 2003. Features 12-gauge gun chambered for 2.75" shell. Fitted with 22" ventilated rib barrel, with RemChokes and fiber optic front sight. Has gray synthetic stock, with matte black finish on receiver and barrel. Magazine extension has 8-round capacity. Receiver mounted ammo carrier for seven extra shells. Weight about 8 lbs. Designed for practical shooting competition.

NIB	Exc.	V.G.	Good	Fair	Poor
725	600	425	400	300	150

Model 1100 Competition

Introduced in 2005. Chambered for 12-gauge shells, with 2.75" chamber. Fitted with 30" target style barrel, with 10mm ventilated rib. Extended choke tubes. Receiver nickel plated. Stock semi-fancy American walnut, with checkering and high gloss finish. Adjustable comb offered as option. Weight about 8 lbs. **NOTE:** Add $175 for adjustable comb model.

NIB	Exc.	V.G.	Good	Fair	Poor
950	775	650	525	350	175

Model 1100 LT-20

20-gauge model features choice of 26" or 28" ventilated rib barrels, with RemChoke tubes. Blue finish and walnut Monte Carlo stock. Recoil pad and cut checkering are standard. Weight 6.75 to 7 lbs. depending on barrel length.

NIB	Exc.	V.G.	Good	Fair	Poor
600	450	400	300	200	150

Model 1100 LT-20 "Limited"

20-gauge lightweight Model 1100 Field gun. Stock 1" shorter than standard and 23" barrel for youthful beginner shooters of smaller stature.

NIB	Exc.	V.G.	Good	Fair	Poor
675	525	475	375	275	200

Model 1100 1 OF 3000

Remington announced Model 1100 Limited Edition "One of Three Thousand", in September, 1980. High grade gun, with positive cut checkered fancy American walnut wood, fitted rosewood grip cap, thin brown butt pad, 14K gold trimmed and etched with hunting scenes on receiver. All metal parts including receiver, barrel, bolt and magazine cap have a high-luster finish. Available only in 1980.

NIB	Exc.	V.G.	Good	Fair	Poor
2000	1600	1000	800	400	250

Model 1100 Special Field

In 12-, 20-gauge or .410 bore. Shorter variation of standard 1100. Barrel length was originally 21" (1983-1993); changed to 23" from (1994 to 1999) when model was discontinued. Ventilated rib on all models. **NOTE:** Add 20 percent for .410 bore.

NIB	Exc.	V.G.	Good	Fair	Poor
600	500	400	350	300	150

Model 1100 TBMC Trap Gun

12-gauge, with 30" ventilated rib barrel in Full or Modified trap chokes. Featured a figured and checkered stock and fore-end. Had a rubber recoil pad. Monte Carlo style stock was optional. A left-hand version was also available. Due to a shortage of American walnut, in mid-year, Remington began fitting some Model 1100 and Model 870 Field Grade shotguns with lightweight mahogany stocks and fore-ends.

NIB	Exc.	V.G.	Good	Fair	Poor
725	650	475	400	300	150

Model 1100 LT-20 Deer Gun

Same as above, with 21" barrel, adjustable sights and improved cylinder choke. Satin finish with American walnut stock. Weight about 6.5 lbs.

NIB	Exc.	V.G.	Good	Fair	Poor
525	450	400	300	200	150

Model 1100 LT-20 Synthetic

Same as above, with synthetic stock and recoil pad.

NIB	Exc.	V.G.	Good	Fair	Poor
550	375	325	275	200	150

Model 1100 LT-20 Magnum

20-gauge Model 1100 chambered for 3" 20-gauge shell. Fitted with 28" ventilated rib barrel, with interchangeable chokes. Checkered walnut stock. Weight about 7 lbs.

NIB	Exc.	V.G.	Good	Fair	Poor
575	395	400	300	200	150

Model 1100 LT-20 Synthetic Camo NWTF 25th Anniversary

Fitted with 21" barrel and special fiber optic sighting system. NWTF logo on left side of receiver. Introduced in 1998.

NIB	Exc.	V.G.	Good	Fair	Poor
650	525	450	300	250	125

Model 1100 Synthetic

Introduced in 1995. Furnished with black synthetic stock, with black matte metal finish. Available in both 12- and 20-gauge. Weight about 6.75 to 7 lbs. depending on barrel length. In 2003, offered chambered for 16-gauge shell.

Courtesy Remington Arms

NIB	Exc.	V.G.	Good	Fair	Poor
550	450	350	250	200	100

Model 1100 Synthetic Deer Gun

Same as above, with 21" fully rifled barrel with cantilever rail for scope mounting. Furnished with 2.75" chamber. Stock black synthetic, with checkering and Monte Carlo-style cheekpiece. Recoil pad standard.

NIB	Exc.	V.G.	Good	Fair	Poor
525	450	400	300	200	150

Model 1100 Competition Synthetic

Super-tuned for competitive shooters. Overbored 30" barrel, with lengthened forcing cones. Optimized for 2.75" target loads and light field loads.

Receiver and all internal parts have nickel-Teflon finish. Synthetic stock has SuperCell recoil pad. 12-gauge only. Weight 8.25 lbs.

NIB	Exc.	V.G.	Good	Fair	Poor
900	800	675	525	400	250

Model 1100 Custom Grade

Custom Shop model available in three levels of engraving, gold inlay, wood grade and finish, metal work finish, recoil pad/buttplate and dimensions. Each gun should be individually appraised prior to sale.

D Grade

NIB	Exc.	V.G.	Good	Fair	Poor
3000	200	1100	—	—	—

F Grade

NIB	Exc.	V.G.	Good	Fair	Poor
6000	4000	2250	—	—	—

F Grade with Gold Inlay

NIB	Exc.	V.G.	Good	Fair	Poor
10000	7500	5000	—	—	—

Model 1100 G3

Introduced in 2006. Updated 1100 features Realwood high gloss semi-fancy stock and fore-end. Available in 12- and 20-gauge, with 26" or 28" barrel. Chambered for 3" shells. Includes 5 ProBore chokes for 12-gauge; 5 Remchokes for 20-gauge. R3 recoil pad and high-grade travel case. Left-handed version added in 2008.

NIB	Exc.	V.G.	Good	Fair	Poor
825	600	450	300	225	150

Model 1100 Tactical Speedfeed IV

All-black 2.75" 12-gauge has 18" barrel, with fixed Improved Cylinder choke and Speedfeed IV stock. Extended 6-round magazine. Weight 7.5 lbs.

NIB	Exc.	V.G.	Good	Fair	Poor
825	600	450	300	225	150

Model 1100 Tactical Standard Stock

Tactical 2.75" 12-gauge has 22" barrel threaded for RemChokes. Extended 8-round magazine.

NIB	Exc.	V.G.	Good	Fair	Poor
825	600	450	300	225	150

Model 1100 Premier Sporting

Introduced in 2008. A dedicated sporting clays gun. Comes in 12-, 20-, 28-gauge and .410 bore, with 2.75" chamber (3" in .410). Polished nickel receiver, with fine-line embellishments and gold accents. Stock and fore-end are semi-fancy American walnut, with high-gloss finish. Full line of Briley choke tubes and Premier Sporting hard case are included. Weight about: 8 lbs. 12-gauge; 7 lbs. 20-gauge; 6.5 lbs. 28-gauge and .410 bore. **NOTE:** Add 5 percent for 28-gauge and .410 bore.

NIB	Exc.	V.G.	Good	Fair	Poor
1150	1000	850	675	475	300

Model 1100 50th Anniversary Limited Edition

Model 1100s most popular semi-automatic shotgun in the world. To commemorate 50 years of service to shooters, this Limited Edition model has machine-cut engraved receiver, with gold fill and high-grade walnut stock. White diamond grip cap and white line spacer recall the style of stock in 1963. In 12-gauge only, with 28" ventilated rib barrel. Introduced 2013, with limited production.

NIB	Exc.	V.G.	Good	Fair	Poor
1800	1600	1400	—	—	—

Model 1100 American Classic

Part of Remington American Classic series honoring some of the great models of the 20th century. Inaugurating this line in 2014 is this special edition Model 1100 semi-automatic and comparable Model 870 pump-action. Features include higher B-grade walnut stock, gold filled engraving and ventilated recoil pad with white outline, as was found on the originals.

NIB	Exc.	V.G.	Good	Fair	Poor
1450	1200	—	—	—	—

MODEL 11-87 SERIES

Model 11-87 Premier

A 3" 12-gauge semi-automatic shotgun, with 26" to 32" ventilated rib barrels having screw-in choke tubes. Blued, with checkered walnut stock. Weight about 7.75 lbs. Introduced in 1987. In 1999, offered in a left-hand version.

Model 11-87 Premier left-hand model

NIB	Exc.	V.G.	Good	Fair	Poor
700	600	450	300	200	150

Model 11-87 Premier 20 Gauge

Introduced in 1999. Built on a small frame receiver. Will chamber both 2.75" and 3" shells. Available in both 26" and 28" ventilated rib barrels, with twin beads. Barrels are built for RemChokes. Stock walnut, with gloss finish. Weight about 7 lbs.

NIB	Exc.	V.G.	Good	Fair	Poor
675	575	425	300	225	125

Model 11-87 Dale Earnhardt Tribute

Introduced in 2003 to honor Dale Earnhardt. This 12-gauge fitted with 28" ventilated rib barrel and walnut stock with checkering. Engraved on receiver is a likeness of Earnhardt, his signature and scroll work inlayed in gold. Serial numbers start with "DE3." Weight about 7.75 lbs.

NIB	Exc.	V.G.	Good	Fair	Poor
675	575	425	300	225	125

Model 11-87 Upland Special

Offered in 12- or 20-gauge, with 23" barrel and twin bead sights. Chambered for 3" shells. Stock walnut, with straight-grip. Choke tubes standard. Weight about: 7.25 lbs. 12-gauge; 6.5 lbs. 20-gauge. Introduced in 2000.

NIB	Exc.	V.G.	Good	Fair	Poor
725	600	450	300	225	125

Model 11-87 Premier Cantilever Scope Mount Deer Gun

Semi-automatic has a Monte Carlo stock. Option of barrel-mounted scope (not included). Optional with fully rifled barrel 21" long, with 1-in-35" twist. Also available in 21" non-rifled barrel, with Rifled and IC RemChoke tubes. Available in 12-gauge only. Sling swivel studs and camo are standard.

NIB	Exc.	V.G.	Good	Fair	Poor
800	675	400	300	200	150

Model 11-87 Premier Trap

Available in right-/left-hand models. Straight or Monte Carlo comb. 2.75" chamber, 30" ventilated rib overbored barrel and special Rem. Trap choke tubes. Model set up to handle 12-gauge target loads only.

NIB	Exc.	V.G.	Good	Fair	Poor
525	475	425	300	200	150

Model 11-87 Premier SC (Sporting Clays)

Features special target stock, with 3.16" length of pull longer than standard and .250" higher at heel. Butt pad is radiused at heel and rounded at toe. Receiver top, barrel and rib have a fine matte finish on the blueing. Ventilated rib is a medium wide 8mm, with stainless steel mid bead and Bradley-style front bead sight. Gun supplied new with these RemChoke tubes: Skeet, Improved Skeet, Improved Cylinder, Modified and Full. Supplied from factory with a two-barrel custom fitted hard case.

Courtesy Remington Arms

Remington Model 11-87 Sporting Clays with nickel-plated receiver and ported barrel

NIB	Exc.	V.G.	Good	Fair	Poor
750	600	450	350	200	150

Model 11-87 SC NP (Sporting Clays Nickel-Plated)

Same as above, with nickel-plated receiver.

NIB	Exc.	V.G.	Good	Fair	Poor
800	650	500	400	300	200

Model 11-87 SPS-BG Camo

12-gauge fitted with rifle sighted 21" barrel, with brown camo finish on stock and metal parts. Introduced in 1993.

NIB	Exc.	V.G.	Good	Fair	Poor
525	475	425	300	200	150

Model 11-87 SPS-T Camo

Same as above, but supplied with 21" ventilated rib barrel with IC and Turkey Super Full RemChoke tubes. Camo finish is green. Introduced in 1993.

NIB	Exc.	V.G.	Good	Fair	Poor
550	450	350	250	200	150

Model 11-87 SPS

12-gauge furnished with 26" or 28" ventilated rib barrel, with IC Mod. and Full RemChoke tubes. Stock black synthetic material and metal finished in black matte. In 1997, a camo version was introduced.

NIB	Exc.	V.G.	Good	Fair	Poor
500	400	300	250	200	150

Model 11-87 SPS-Deer

Same as above, with 21" rifled sighted barrel. First introduced in 1993.

NIB	Exc.	V.G.	Good	Fair	Poor
525	475	425	300	200	150

Model 11-87 Waterfowl

12-gauge gun fitted with 28" ventilated rib barrel with choke tubes and Hi-Viz sights. Camo pattern is Mossy Oak Shadow-grass. Weight about 8.25 lbs. Introduced in 2004.

NIB	Exc.	V.G.	Good	Fair	Poor
925	700	600	500	350	175

Model 11-87 SPS-T

Same as above, with 21" ventilated rib barrel with IC and Turkey Super Full RemChoke tubes. In 1997, a camo version was introduced.

NIB	Exc.	V.G.	Good	Fair	Poor
525	475	425	300	200	150

Model 11-87 SPS-T Camo NWTF 25th Anniversary

Model has 21" barrel, with special fiber optic sighting system. NWTF logo on left side of receiver. Introduced in 1998.

NIB	Exc.	V.G.	Good	Fair	Poor
700	595	425	300	200	150

Model 11-87 SP Super Magnum

Introduced in 2000. Chambered for 12-gauge 3.5" Magnum shell. Fitted with 26" or 28" ventilated rib barrel. Walnut stock, with flat finish. Recoil pad. Matte black finish. Weight about 8.25 lbs.

NIB	Exc.	V.G.	Good	Fair	Poor
675	500	350	300	125	100

Model 11-87 SPS Super Magnum

Same as above, with black synthetic stock. Introduced in 2000. Weight about 8.25 lbs.

NIB	Exc.	V.G.	Good	Fair	Poor
675	500	350	300	125	100

Model 11-87 SPS-T Super Magnum (NWTF Edition)

Introduced in 2005. Features 12-gauge 3.5" chamber, 23" barrel with choke tubes and iron sights. Mossy Oak Obsession camo stock, with Monte Carlo comb. Weight about 8 lbs.

NIB	Exc.	V.G.	Good	Fair	Poor
950	775	650	525	350	175

Model 11-87 Police

Offered chambered for 12-gauge shells. Features synthetic stock, 18" barrel with bead rifle or ghost ring sights and 7-shot magazine extension. **NOTE:** Add $20 for rifle sights; $60 for ghost ring sights.

NIB	Exc.	V.G.	Good	Fair	Poor
675	500	350	300	125	100

Model 11-87 Custom Grade

Custom Shop model available in three levels of engraving, gold inlay, wood grade and finish, metal work finish, recoil pad/buttplate and dimensions.

D Grade

NIB	Exc.	V.G.	Good	Fair	Poor
3000	200	1100	—	—	—

F Grade

NIB	Exc.	V.G.	Good	Fair	Poor
6000	4000	2250	—	—	—

F Grade with Gold Inlay

NIB	Exc.	V.G.	Good	Fair	Poor
10000	7500	5000	—	—	—

Model 11-87 Sportsman Synthetic

Introduced in 2005. Features black synthetic stock, with choice of 12- or 20-gauge 3" chambers; 26" or 28" barrels with Mod. choke tube. Weight about 7.75 to 8.25 lbs. depending on gauge and barrel length.

NIB	Exc.	V.G.	Good	Fair	Poor
675	500	350	300	125	100

Model 11-87 Sportsman Super Magnum

In 2008, Remington added this 3.5" version of 11-87 Sportsman. Has 28" barrel. Weight 8.25 lbs.

NIB	Exc.	V.G.	Good	Fair	Poor
750	625	550	400	300	200

Model 11-87 Sportsman Rifled

A 12-gauge 3" gun, with 21" rifled barrel with cantilever scope mount. Black synthetic stock, with black metal finish. Weight about 8.5 lbs. Introduced in 2005.

NIB	Exc.	V.G.	Good	Fair	Poor
675	500	350	300	125	100

Model 11-87 Sportsman Youth

A 20-gauge 3" gun, with 21" ventilated rib barrel and choke tubes. Black synthetic stock. Length of pull 13". Weight about 6.5 lbs. Introduced in 2005.

NIB	Exc.	V.G.	Good	Fair	Poor
600	450	400	300	200	150

Model 11-87 Sportsman Compact Synthetic

Similar to Model 11-87 black synthetic, with reduced overall dimensions.

NIB	Exc.	V.G.	Good	Fair	Poor
700	595	500	350	225	150

Model 11-87 Sportsman Youth Camo

Same as above, with full coverage in Mossy Oak Break-Up camo.

NIB	Exc.	V.G.	Good	Fair	Poor
750	625	550	400	300	175

Model 11-87 Sportsman NRA Edition

This 12-gauge 3" model fitted with 28" ventilated rib barrel, with choke tubes. Synthetic stock, with Mossy Oak New Break-Up camo. NRA logo on left side of matte black receiver. Introduced in 2005.

NIB	Exc.	V.G.	Good	Fair	Poor
675	500	350	300	125	100

Model 11-87 SP Thumbhole

Laminated thumbhole stock 12-gauge slug gun, with 3" chamber and 21" fully rifled cantilever barrel.

NIB	Exc.	V.G.	Good	Fair	Poor
700	595	500	350	225	150

Model 11-87 SPS-T Super Magnum

Similar to above, with pistol-grip stock and ventilated rib barrel.

NIB	Exc.	V.G.	Good	Fair	Poor
750	625	550	400	300	200

Model 11-87 SP-T Thumbhole

This 12-gauge with 3.5" chamber is made specifically for turkey hunting. Camouflaged in Mossy Oak Obsession, with R3 recoil pad and thumb-hole stock. The 23" barrel has fiber-optic adjustable rifle sights and drilled and tapped for scope mounting. Includes a Turkey Super Full choke tube and sling/swivels. Introduced 2006.

NIB	Exc.	V.G.	Good	Fair	Poor
750	625	550	400	300	200

Model 11-87 Sportsman Camo

New in 2007. Camo version of Sportsman comes in 12- and 20-gauge, with 26" or 28" barrel. Finished in Mossy Oak Break-Up camo.

NIB	Exc.	V.G.	Good	Fair	Poor
750	625	550	400	300	200

Model 11-87 Sportsman Camo Rifled

Camo 12-gauge slug gun, with 21" barrel and cantilever scope mount.

NIB	Exc.	V.G.	Good	Fair	Poor
750	625	550	400	300	200

Model 11-87 Sportsman Camo Youth

Youth model in 20-gauge, with shorter length of pull. Introduced in 2007. Weight about 6.5 lbs.

NIB	Exc.	V.G.	Good	Fair	Poor
700	595	500	350	225	150

Model 11-87 Sportsman Field

Semi-automatic shotgun chambered in 12- and 20-gauge, 2.75" and 3" shells. Features include 26" (20-gauge) or 28" (12-gauge) barrel; ventilated rib; RemChokes (one supplied); satin-finished walnut stock and fore-end with fleur-de-lis pattern; dual sights; nickel-plated bolt and trigger.

NIB	Exc.	V.G.	Good	Fair	Poor
680	575	435	350	225	150

Model 11-87 Sportsman Super Mag Synthetic

Semi-automatic shotgun chambered in 12-gauge, 3.5" shells. Features include black matte synthetic stock and fore-end; rubber overmolded grip panels on stock and fore-end; black padded sling; HiViz sights featuring interchangeable light pipe; 28" ventilated rib barrel; SuperCell recoil pad; RemChoke.

NIB	Exc.	V.G.	Good	Fair	Poor
730	650	550	425	250	175

Model 11-87 Sportsman Super Mag Shurshot Turkey

Similar to above, with ambidextrous ShurShot pistol-grip stock; full Realtree APG HD coverage; 23" barrel with fully adjustable TruGlo rifle sights. Wingmaster HD Turkey Choke included.

NIB	Exc.	V.G.	Good	Fair	Poor
875	750	625	500	300	175

Model 11-87 SPS Super Magnum Waterfowl

This 3.5" 12-gauge finished in Mossy Oak Duck Blind camo. Has 30" barrel and includes three chokes. Weight 8.25 lbs.

NIB	Exc.	V.G.	Good	Fair	Poor
950	775	650	525	350	175

Model 11-87 Sportsman Super Mag ShurShot Turkey

New in 2008. Specialized turkey shotgun, with ShurShot stock is a 3.5" chamber 12-gauge with 23" non-ventilated rib barrel. Comes with fiber-optic rifle-type sights and synthetic stock and fore-end. Gun fully covered in Realtree APG HD camo. Weight about 7.6 lbs.

NIB	Exc.	V.G.	Good	Fair	Poor
800	695	550	450	300	175

Model 11-87 Sportsman Super Magnum Waterfowl

Full coverage in Mossy Oak Duck Blind camo. Shell-holding Speedfeed stock and three choke tubes.

NIB	Exc.	V.G.	Good	Fair	Poor
850	725	595	475	325	195

Model 11-87 Sportsman ShurShot Cantilever

Dedicated slug gun in 3" 12-gauge features 23" fully rifled barrel, with cantilever scope mount. Is matte black, with synthetic stock and fore-end finished in Realtree Hardwoods HD camo. Weight about 8 lbs.

NIB	Exc.	V.G.	Good	Fair	Poor
850	725	595	475	325	195

Model 11-96 Euro Lightweight

Introduced in 1996. Based on Model 11-87 action. Two ventilated rib barrel lengths are offered: 26" and 28" supplied with three RemChokes. Fine line engraving on receiver and checkered Claro walnut stocks are standard. Blued finish. Weight about 7 lbs. Made for one year only.

NIB	Exc.	V.G.	Good	Fair	Poor
1000	875	625	500	325	200

Model SP-10

A 3.5" 10-gauge semi-automatic shotgun, with 26" or 30" ventilated rib barrels having screw-in choke tubes. Matte blued, with checkered walnut stock.

NIB	Exc.	V.G.	Good	Fair	Poor
1500	1275	950	775	600	300

Model SP-10 Magnum Camo

Introduced in 1993. This 10-gauge semi-automatic designed for turkey or deer hunter. Available with 26" or 30" ventilated rib barrel or 22" deer barrel. Additional barrel option is 23" ventilated rib barrel, with camo finish. All barrels are fitted with RemChoke tubes.

NIB	Exc.	V.G.	Good	Fair	Poor
1550	1325	1000	825	625	325

Model SP-10 Magnum Camo NWTF 25th Anniversary

A special fiber optic sighting system. "NWTF" logo on left side of receiver. Barrel length 23". Introduced in 1998.

NIB	Exc.	V.G.	Good	Fair	Poor
1550	1325	1000	825	625	325

Model SP-10 Synthetic

Features black synthetic stock, with 26" barrel. Chambered for 10-gauge shells. Matte black metal finish. Choke tubes standard. Introduced in 2000. Weight about 10 lbs.

NIB	Exc.	V.G.	Good	Fair	Poor
1300	1150	900	775	575	300

Model SP-10 RC/VT

This 10-gauge introduced in 2005. Fitted with 26" ventilated rib barrel, with choke tubes. Mossy Oak Obsession finish. Weight about 10.75 lbs.

NIB	Exc.	V.G.	Good	Fair	Poor
1300	1150	900	775	575	300

Model SP-10 Custom Grade

Custom Shop model available in three levels of engraving, gold inlay, wood grade and finish, metal work finish, recoil pad/buttplate and dimensions. Limited production or activity on used gun market. Price estimates for NIB models start at $2000 to $3000 and vary depending on quality of custom features.

Model SP-10 Magnum Waterfowl

New in 2007. A synthetic stock 3.5" 10-gauge waterfowl specific model, with Mossy Oak Duck Blind camo finish and 26" barrel. Includes three Briley ported choke tubes. Weight about 10.9 lbs.

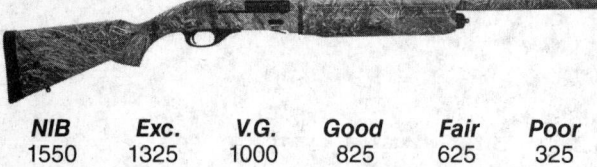

NIB	Exc.	V.G.	Good	Fair	Poor
1550	1325	1000	825	625	325

Model SP-10 Magnum Thumbhole Camo

Special turkey model features synthetic thumbhole stock and complete Mossy Oak Obsession camo finish. Barrel is 23". Briley ported Turkey choke included. Weight 10.9 lbs.

NIB	Exc.	V.G.	Good	Fair	Poor
1650	1500	1200	900	675	350

Model 105CTi

New in 2006. Ultralight gas-operated 12-gauge autoloader. Features advanced recoil reduction and bottom feed and ejection. Available with 26" or 28" barrel. Satin finish walnut stock. Chambered for 3" shells. Includes three ProBore chokes. Weight about 7 lbs. Discontinued in 2009.

NIB	Exc.	V.G.	Good	Fair	Poor
1175	950	800	600	475	275

Versa Max

Versa Max gas-operated semi-automatic shoots everything from 2.75" target loads to 3.5" Magnums. Synthetic stock in black and camo finishes is fully adjustable for length-of-pull, drop-of-comb and cast. 12-gauge only; 26" and 28" barrels; 7.7 lbs. Introduced in 2011. Also available with Wood-Tech stock finish, Realtree and Mossy Oak camo, Tactical model and special-finish "Zombie" models. Values shown are for standard synthetic stock model. **NOTE:** Add $250 for camo finishes or Tactical model; $175 for Wood-Tech or Zombie finishes

NIB	Exc.	V.G.	Good	Fair	Poor
1200	1100	1000	850	600	300

Model V3 Field Sport

Latest generation of Remington semi-automatic shotgun operates on Versaport gas system. Handles all ammo from 2.75" target loads to 3" Magnums. Barrel length 26" or 28". Stock choice: black, camo synthetic or American walnut satin-finished, all with adjustable length of pull. Introduced in 2015. **NOTE:** Add $100 for camo or walnut stock.

NIB	Exc.	V.G.	Good	Fair	Poor
750	675	500	—	—	—

Model 32

A 12-gauge over/under shotgun, with 26", 28" or 30" separated barrels and single-selective trigger. Approximately 15,000 made from 1932 to 1942. **NOTE:** Add 10 percent for solid or ventilated rib.

Standard Grade

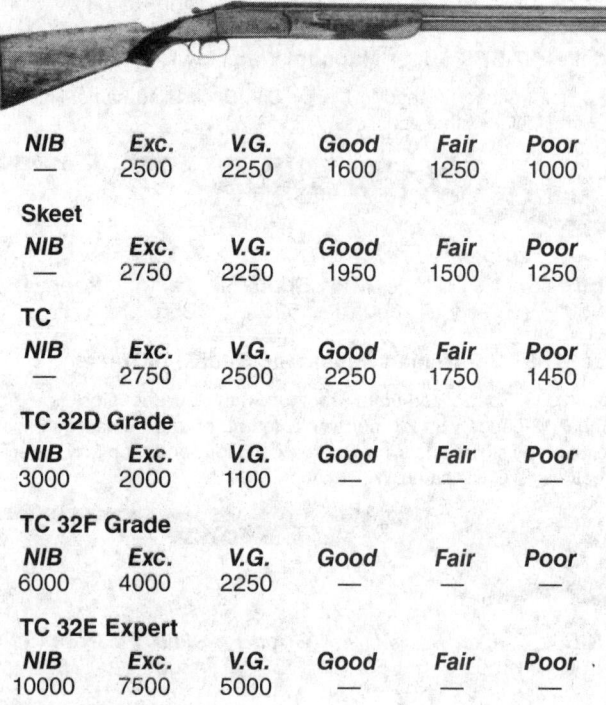

NIB	Exc.	V.G.	Good	Fair	Poor
—	2500	2250	1600	1250	1000

Skeet

NIB	Exc.	V.G.	Good	Fair	Poor
—	2750	2250	1950	1500	1250

TC

NIB	Exc.	V.G.	Good	Fair	Poor
—	2750	2500	2250	1750	1450

TC 32D Grade

NIB	Exc.	V.G.	Good	Fair	Poor
3000	2000	1100	—	—	—

TC 32F Grade

NIB	Exc.	V.G.	Good	Fair	Poor
6000	4000	2250	—	—	—

TC 32E Expert

NIB	Exc.	V.G.	Good	Fair	Poor
10000	7500	5000	—	—	—

Model 3200

A 12-gauge over/under shotgun, with 26", 28" or 30" separated ventilated rib barrels, single-selective trigger and automatic ejector. Blued, with checkered walnut stock. Manufactured from 1972 to 1984.

Field Grade

NIB	Exc.	V.G.	Good	Fair	Poor
—	800	725	600	450	300

Magnum

3" chambers.

NIB	Exc.	V.G.	Good	Fair	Poor
—	1000	850	750	550	300

Skeet

NIB	Exc.	V.G.	Good	Fair	Poor
—	1200	995	800	600	300

4-Gauge Set

NIB	Exc.	V.G.	Good	Fair	Poor
—	5500	4750	3500	2450	1500

Trap

NIB	Exc.	V.G.	Good	Fair	Poor
—	1200	995	800	600	300

Special Trap

Deluxe wood.

NIB	Exc.	V.G.	Good	Fair	Poor
—	1350	1150	750	700	300

Competition Trap

Engraved.

NIB	Exc.	V.G.	Good	Fair	Poor
—	2750	2000	1350	950	300

Premier

Heavily engraved.

NIB	Exc.	V.G.	Good	Fair	Poor
—	5500	4750	3900	—	—

"One of One Thousand"

1,000 produced.

NIB	Exc.	V.G.	Good	Fair	Poor
—	3500	3000	2500	—	—

Model 300 Ideal

This 12-gauge over/under shotgun was introduced in 2000. Offered with choice of 26", 28" or 30" barrels. Single-selective trigger and automatic ejectors. Metal finish blue. Stock walnut, with semi-gloss finish. Solid black recoil pad. Weight about 7.62 lbs. for 28" barrels. Dropped from production in 2001.

NIB	Exc.	V.G.	Good	Fair	Poor
1650	1400	1150	700	575	300

Model 90-T Single-Barrel Trap

Offered in 12-gauge only. Single-barrel trap shotgun fitted with 32" or 34" overbored Full choke barrel.

NIB	Exc.	V.G.	Good	Fair	Poor
3600	2500	1450	1100	600	300

Model 90-T Single-Barrel Trap (High Rib)

Same as described above, with exception of an adjustable high rib for shooters who prefer a more open target picture and higher head position.

NIB	Exc.	V.G.	Good	Fair	Poor
3600	2500	1450	1100	600	300

Model 332

Reintroduction in 2002 of famous Remington Model 32. Features mechanical set trigger, automatic ejectors, with choice of ventilated rib barrel lengths in 26", 28" and 30". Checkered walnut stock. Black oxide metal finish. Chambered for 12-gauge, with 3" chambers. Weight about 7.75 lbs. depending on barrel length.

NIB	Exc.	V.G.	Good	Fair	Poor
1250	900	750	600	400	250

Remington Peerless

Introduced in 1993. New Remington over/under shotgun offered in 12-gauge only. Available in 26", 28" and 30" ventilated rib barrel lengths. Fitted with RemChoke tubes (IC, M, F). Sideplates are removable. Stock American walnut. Production stopped in 1998.

NIB	Exc.	V.G.	Good	Fair	Poor
1250	900	750	600	400	250

Model 396 Sporting

Introduced in 1996. Over/under shotgun designed for sporting clay shooting. Offered in 12-gauge only, with 30" barrels. Chokes are interchangeable RemChoke system. Fancy American stock, with satin finish. Scroll engraving on receiver and blue finish. Weight about 8 lbs.

Courtesy Remington Arms

NIB	Exc.	V.G.	Good	Fair	Poor
2150	1700	1150	875	500	300

Model 396 Skeet

Same as above, with choice of 28" or 30" barrels.

Courtesy Remington Arms

NIB	Exc.	V.G.	Good	Fair	Poor
2150	1700	1150	875	500	300

Model 396 Custom Grade

Custom Shop model available in three levels of engraving, gold inlay, wood grade and finish, metal work finish, recoil pad/buttplate, and dimensions. Each gun should be individually appraised prior to sale. Limited production or activity on used gun market. Price estimates for NIB models start at $2000 to $3000 and vary depending on quality of custom features.

PREMIER SERIES OVER/UNDERS

Introduced in 2006. Italian-made over/unders in Premier Series. Feature premium figured walnut stocks, schnabel fore-ends, ProBore chokes, 3" chambers (2.75" in 28-gauge). Includes a hardside case.

STS Competition

This 12-gauge with 28", 30" or 32" overbored barrels has an engraved nickel-plated receiver and high-gloss finished stock. Weight about 7.8 lbs. **NOTE:** Add 15 percent for adjustable-stock model.

NIB	Exc.	V.G.	Good	Fair	Poor
1500	1300	950	700	550	300

Field Grade

Available in 12-, 20- and 28-gauge, with satin finish and nickel receiver. Barrel length 26" or 28". Includes three flush chokes. Weight about: 6.5 lbs. 20- and 28-gauge; 7.5 lbs. 12-gauge.

NIB	Exc.	V.G.	Good	Fair	Poor
1400	1200	900	650	500	300

Upland Grade

As above, with oil-finish stock. Case colored receiver, with gold game bird scene.

NIB	Exc.	V.G.	Good	Fair	Poor
1450	1250	900	675	525	300

RGS

Special Conservation Gun of the Year, in 2007, for Ruffed Grouse Society. A 20-gauge, with 26" barrels, satin oil-finished stock and satin black oxide receiver. Includes five choke tubes. Weight 6.5 lbs.

NIB	Exc.	V.G.	Good	Fair	Poor
1650	1400	1150	700	575	300

Remington Parker AAHE Double

Built to order. Side-by-side double is exact in every respect to original Parker Brothers shotguns. Made from 1860s to 1937 and again until 1942, after Remington purchased the company. In 2006, Remington partnered with Connecticut Shotgun Mfg. Co., to build high-grade AAHE model. Offered in 28-gauge only, with many options including stock dimensions and engraving patterns. Prices start at $49,000.

BOLT-ACTION HANDGUNS

Model XP-100

A .221 Rem. Fireball or .223 Rem. caliber bolt-action single-shot pistol. Available with or without 14.5" ventilated rib barrel and adjustable sights. Blued, with nylon stock. Introduced in 1963. Discontinued.

NIB	Exc.	V.G.	Good	Fair	Poor
800	600	375	300	225	175

Model XP-100 Silhouette

As above chambered for 7mm Rem. or .35 Rem. cartridges. Fitted with 15" barrel drilled and tapped for a telescope. Discontinued.

NIB	Exc.	V.G.	Good	Fair	Poor
725	525	325	250	200	125

Model XP-100 Custom

Custom-made version of above, with 15" barrel. Nylon or walnut stock. Available in .223 Rem., .250 Savage, 6mm Benchrest, 7mm Benchrest, 7mm-08 or .35 Rem. calibers. Introduced in 1986. Discontinued.

NIB	Exc.	V.G.	Good	Fair	Poor
950	800	650	550	425	300

Model XP-100 Hunter

Features laminated wood stock, 14.5" drilled and tapped barrel and no sights. Offered in these calibers: .223 Rem., 7mm BR Rem., 7mm-08 Rem., and .35 Rem. Discontinued.

NIB	Exc.	V.G.	Good	Fair	Poor
800	675	375	300	250	175

Model XP-100R Repeater

Introduced in 1998. Chambered for .22-250, .223, .260 and .35 Rem. cartridges. Fitted with 14.5" barrel that is drilled and tapped for sights. Receiver drilled and tapped for scope mounts. Fiberglass stock. Weight about 4.5 lbs. Manufactured 1998. Discontinued.

NIB	Exc.	V.G.	Good	Fair	Poor
950	800	500	450	225	200

SPARTAN GUNWORKS BY REMINGTON

Imported firearms introduced into Remington line in 2004; discontinued 2009.

Model SPR 210

Side-by-side with single-selective trigger and auto ejectors. Boxlock receiver is nickel. Fitted with 26" or 28" barrels, with choke tubes in 12- and 20-gauge. Fixed chokes in 28-gauge and .410 bore. Also offered with 20" barrel, with choke tubes and blued receiver. Checkered walnut stock, with recoil pad. Weight about 6.75 lbs. depending on gauge and barrel length. **NOTE:** Add $30 for 28-gauge and .410 bore.

NIB	Exc.	V.G.	Good	Fair	Poor
475	400	350	225	175	100

Model SPR 220

Double trigger model, with 20" barrels and choke tubes. Extractors. Nickel or blued receiver. Walnut stock, with recoil pad. Weight about 6.25 lbs.

NIB	Exc.	V.G.	Good	Fair	Poor
425	375	300	200	150	100

Model SPR 310

An over/under gun chambered for 12-, 20-, 28-gauge and .410 bore. Choice of 26" or 28" ventilated rib barrels, with choke tubes; or 26" bar-

rels for 28-gauge and .410 bore. Single selective trigger and auto ejectors. Checkered walnut stock, with recoil pad. Weight about 7.5 lbs.

NIB	Exc.	V.G.	Good	Fair	Poor
475	400	350	225	175	125

Model SPR 310S

Chambered for 12- and 20-gauge 3" shell. Fitted with 29.5" (12-gauge) or 28.5" (20-gauge) ported barrels with choke tubes. Checked walnut stock, with recoil pad. Weight about 7.5 lbs.

NIB	Exc.	V.G.	Good	Fair	Poor
700	600	475	350	275	200

Model SPR 100/Sporting

Single-shot chambered for 12-, 20-gauge or .410 bore. Fitted with 29.5" (12-gauge), 28.5" (20-gauge) or 26" (.410) barrel. Single trigger, with ejectors or extractors. Youth model offered with 24" barrel chambered for .410 bore. Checkered walnut stock, with recoil pad. Weight about 6.25 lbs. **NOTE:** Add $40 for Sporting models.

NIB	Exc.	V.G.	Good	Fair	Poor
250	175	125	100	75	50

Model SPR 18

Single-shot rifle chambered for .223, .243, .270 or .30-06 calibers. Nickel receiver. Fitted with 23.5" barrel, with iron sights. Checkered walnut stock, with recoil pad. Weight about 6.75 lbs.

NIB	Exc.	V.G.	Good	Fair	Poor
275	200	150	125	95	75

Model SPR 22

Side-by-side double rifle chambered for .30-06 or .45-70 calibers. Fitted with 23.5" barrels. Blued receiver and checkered walnut stock, with recoil pad. Weight about 7.5 lbs.

NIB	Exc.	V.G.	Good	Fair	Poor
1000	825	700	575	400	250

Model SPR 94

Features an over/under rifle/shotgun combination. Chambered for .410/17HMR, .410/.22WMR, 12-/.223, 12-/.30-06 or 12-/.308. Fitted with

24" barrel, with iron sights. Checkered walnut stock, with recoil pad. Blued receiver. Weight about 8 lbs. depending on combination. **NOTE:** Add 30 percent for centerfire models.

NIB	Exc.	V.G.	Good	Fair	Poor
375	300	225	150	100	75

REMINGTON CUSTOM SHOP

Remington Custom Shop builds a number of specialty rifles and shotguns as well as specific custom guns for its customers. Remington will build a wide number of special features from special wood type, finish and styling options to engraving. These special order features add considerably to the cost of a gun and will affect its price. Custom Shop can be reached at 315-895-3288 for current prices and availability.

REMINGTON 180TH ANNIVERSARY LIMITED EDITION RIFLES AND SHOTGUNS

Remington manufactured 180 each of these firearms to commemorate the founding of the company in 1816:

Model 700, Model 7600, Model 7400, Model 870, and Model 11-87.

These firearms featured fine line hand engraving, with gold embellishments. Rifles were chambered for .30-06 cartridge, with 22" barrels; shotguns were chambered for 12-gauge shell, with 26" ventilated rib barrels with RemChokes. All guns had blue finishes, with high gloss semi-fancy walnut stocks. Any estimate about current values would be quite speculative. If sold in a five-gun set, each should have matching serial numbers. Suggested retail price for the five-gun set was $6,925 in 1996. Individual guns carried these suggested retail prices:

Model 700	180th Anniversary	Commemorative—$1,372
Model 7400	180th Anniversary	Commemorative—$1,372
Model 7600	180th Anniversary	Commemorative—$1,332
Model 870	180th Anniversary	Commemorative—$1,305
Model 11-87	180th Anniversary	Commemorative—$1,465

RENETTE, GASTINNE
Paris, France

SHOTGUNS

Model 105

Anson & Deeley action 12- or 20-gauge double-barrel shotgun. Available in a variety of barrel lengths, with double triggers and automatic ejectors. Blued case-hardened, with checkered walnut stock.

NIB	Exc.	V.G.	Good	Fair	Poor
—	4000	3200	2500	1700	300

Model 98

As above, except more finely finished.

NIB	Exc.	V.G.	Good	Fair	Poor
—	5200	4500	3500	2800	300

Model 202

A 12- or 20-gauge sidelock double-barrel shotgun. Made only on custom order. French case-hardened. Blued, with checkered walnut stock.

NIB	Exc.	V.G.	Good	Fair	Poor
—	9000	7000	5000	3450	300

Model 353

Custom manufactured double-barrel shotgun, with detachable sidelocks. Highly finished.

NIB	Exc.	V.G.	Good	Fair	Poor
—	35000	30000	1700	8000	500

RIFLES

Type G Rifle

A .30-06, 9.3x74R or .375 H&H double-barrel rifle, with 24" barrels, express sights, double triggers and automatic ejectors. Engraved. Blued, with checkered walnut stock.

NIB	Exc.	V.G.	Good	Fair	Poor
—	5500	3700	3000	2000	650

Type R Deluxe

As above, engraved with hunting scenes and more finely figured walnut stock.

NIB	Exc.	V.G.	Good	Fair	Poor
—	7000	5000	3400	2900	750

Type PT President

As above, inlaid in gold with extremely well figured walnut stock.

NIB	Exc.	V.G.	Good	Fair	Poor
—	8000	6400	4000	3500	950

Mauser Bolt-Action

Custom-made bolt-action rifle built on a Mauser action. Choice of calibers and stock styles. Base price listed.

NIB	Exc.	V.G.	Good	Fair	Poor
—	11000	9000	6500	3000	750

Deluxe Mauser Bolt-Action

Same as above, with fancy wood and other options.

NIB	Exc.	V.G.	Good	Fair	Poor
—	20000	14000	9000	6500	1250

RENWICK ARMS CO.
See—Perry & Goddard

REPUBLIC ARMS, INC.
Chino, California

This company was in business from 1997 to 2001. The Republic Patriot pistol may still be available from Cobra Enterpises.

RAP 440

Pistol chambered for .40 S&W or 9mm cartridges. A double-/single-action operation. Fitted with 3.75" barrel. Magazine capacity 7 rounds. Grips are two-piece black plastic. Weight about 32 oz. Sights are three dot, with fixed ramp front and windage adjustable rear. Introduced in 1998. Imported by TSF of Fairfax, Virginia.

NIB	Exc.	V.G.	Good	Fair	Poor
550	450	300	200	150	100

Republic Patriot

Double-action-only .45 ACP caliber pistol, with 3" barrel and fixed sights. Black polymer frame, with checkered grips and stainless steel slide. Magazine capacity 6 rounds. Weight about 20 oz. Introduced in 1997.

NIB	Exc.	V.G.	Good	Fair	Poor
325	250	200	150	100	75

RETOLAZA HERMANOS
Eibar, Spain

Brompetier

Folding trigger 6.35mm or 7.65mm caliber double-action revolver, with 2.5" barrel. Safety mounted on left side of frame. Manufactured until 1915.

NIB	Exc.	V.G.	Good	Fair	Poor
—	250	125	85	70	45

Gallus or Titan

A 6.35mm semi-automatic pistol. Normally marked "Gallus" or "Titan". Blued, with plastic grips.

NIB	Exc.	V.G.	Good	Fair	Poor
—	275	150	100	75	50

Liberty, Military, Retolaza, or Paramount

A 6.35mm or 7.65mm semi-automatic pistol, with 3" barrel and 8-shot magazine. Slide marked with any of the trade names listed above.

NIB	Exc.	V.G.	Good	Fair	Poor
—	275	150	100	75	50

Puppy

Folding trigger .22-caliber double-action revolver, with 5-shot cylinder. Trade name "Puppy" stamped on barrel.

NIB	Exc.	V.G.	Good	Fair	Poor
—	175	125	75	50	25

Stosel

A 6.35mm semi-automatic pistol. Marked on slide "Automatic Pistol Stosel No. 1 Patent". Blued, with plastic grips.

NIB	Exc.	V.G.	Good	Fair	Poor
—	275	150	100	75	50

Titanic

A 6.35mm semi-automatic pistol, with 2.5" barrel. Slide marked "1913 Model Automatic Pistol Titanic Eibar". Blued, with plastic grips.

NIB	Exc.	V.G.	Good	Fair	Poor
—	275	150	100	75	50

REUNIES
Liege, Belgium

Dictator

A 6.35mm semi-automatic pistol, with 1.5" barrel and 5-shot magazine. Name "Dictator" together with company's details stamped on slide. Features bolt of tubular form, front end of which is hollow and encloses the barrel breech. Manufactured from 1909 to about 1925.

NIB	Exc.	V.G.	Good	Fair	Poor
—	275	150	100	75	50

Texas Ranger or Cowboy Ranger

Patterned after Colt Model 1873 revolver. A .38 Special caliber, barrel 5.5" and marked with company's details. Legends: "Cowboy Ranger" or "Texas Ranger". Manufactured from 1922 to 1931.

NIB	Exc.	V.G.	Good	Fair	Poor
—	350	200	100	75	50

REUTH, F.
Hartford, Connecticut

Animal Trap Gun

Cast iron .28- to .50-caliber percussion trap gun. Single-/double-barrel 3.5" or 5" in length. Firearm fires a barbed arrow and is triggered by a cord attached to an animal trap or bait. Barrels marked "F. Reuth's Patent, May 12, 1857". Several hundred made between 1858 and 1862.

NOTE: Single-barrel model more common than double-barrel and worth approximately 20 percent less.

NIB	Exc.	V.G.	Good	Fair	Poor
—	—	2000	1650	550	150

REXIO DE ARMAS (COMANCHE)
Argentina

RS 22

A 9-shot revolver chambered for .22 LR cartridge. Choice of blued or stainless steel frame. Fixed or adjustable sights. Barrel lengths 4" or 6". Fitted with rubber grips. **NOTE:** Add $30 for stainless steel.

NIB	Exc.	V.G.	Good	Fair	Poor
235	175	150	125	75	50

RS 22M

Same as above, chambered for .22 Win. Magnum cartridge. **NOTE:** Add $30 for stainless steel.

NIB	Exc.	V.G.	Good	Fair	Poor
235	175	150	125	75	50

RJ 22

Chambered for .22 LR cartridge. Fitted with 3", 4" or 6" barrel. Checkered walnut or synthetic grips. Adjustable rear sight. Blued finish.

NIB	Exc.	V.G.	Good	Fair	Poor
175	125	95	75	50	25

RJ 38

Same as above, chambered for .38 Special cartridge.

NIB	Exc.	V.G.	Good	Fair	Poor
175	125	95	75	50	25

RS 357

Same as above, chambered for .357 Magnum cartridge. Offered with 3", 4" or 6" barrels. **NOTE:** Add $30 for stainless steel.

NIB	Exc.	V.G.	Good	Fair	Poor
235	175	125	95	75	50

Outfitter Single-Shot

Break-down single pistol. Chambered for .45 Colt/.410 .22 LR or .22 Win. Magnum. Blued 10" barrel, with synthetic grip. Weight about 43 oz.

NIB	Exc.	V.G.	Good	Fair	Poor
200	150	—	—	—	—

Outfitter Single-Shot Compact

Same as above, with 6" barrel in .22 Win. Magnum or .45 Colt/.410.

NIB	Exc.	V.G.	Good	Fair	Poor
200	150	125	95	75	50

RHEINMETALL
Sommerda, Germany

Dreyse 6.35mm Model 1907

A 6.35mm semi-automatic pistol, with 2" barrel. Manual safety and 6-shot magazine. Weight about 14 oz. Slide marked "Dreyse". Blued, with hard rubber grips having trademark "RFM" molded in them. Patent for this design issued in 1909 to Louis Schmeisser.

Courtesy James Rankin

NIB	Exc.	V.G.	Good	Fair	Poor
—	400	250	200	150	100

Dreyse 7.65mm Model 1907

As above, chambered for 7.65mm cartridge. Barrel 3.6", with 7-shot magazine. Weight about 25 oz. Blued, with horn grips.

Courtesy Orvel Reichert

NIB	Exc.	V.G.	Good	Fair	Poor
—	300	200	150	125	75

Dreyse 9mm

As above, chambered for 9mm cartridge. Barrel 5", with 8-shot magazine. Weight about 37 oz. Slide marked "Rheinische Metallwaaren Und Maschinenfabrik, Sommerda". Blued, with hard rubber grips. Manufactured prior to 1916 and in small numbers.

Courtesy James Rankin

NIB	Exc.	V.G.	Good	Fair	Poor
—	4500	3750	2500	1500	750

Rheinmetall 32

A 7.65mm semi-automatic pistol, with 3.65" barrel and 8-shot magazine. Slide marked "Rheinmetall ABT. Sommerda". Blued, with walnut grips. Overall length 6.5"; weight about 23.5 oz. Production began in 1920.

Courtesy James Rankin

NIB	Exc.	V.G.	Good	Fair	Poor
—	350	225	175	125	90

Rheinmetall 9mm

A 9mm version of Rheinmetall. Built in 1935 to compete with 9mm Parabellum German military pistols of that time. It was unsuccessful.

Courtesy James Rankin

NIB	Exc.	V.G.	Good	Fair	Poor
—Too Rare To Price—		—	—	—	—

Dreyse Light Rifle or Carbine

Model 1907 in caliber 7.65 Browning. Fitted with a fixed stock and 6-round magazine.

Courtesy James Rankin

NIB	Exc.	V.G.	Good	Fair	Poor
—	1850	1400	1150	700	300

RHODE ISLAND ARMS CO.
Hope Valley, Rhode Island

Morrone

A 12- or 20-gauge over/under boxlock shotgun, with 26" or 28" barrels, single trigger and automatic ejectors. Blued, with straight-/pistol-grip walnut checkered stock. 450 made in 12-gauge; 50 in 20-gauge. Manufactured from 1949 to 1953.

NIB	Exc.	V.G.	Good	Fair	Poor
—	1700	1200	850	600	350

RICHLAND ARMS CO.
Blissfield, Michigan

This company, which ceased operation in 1986, imported a variety of Spanish-made shotguns.

Model 41 Ultra Over/Under

A 20-, 28-gauge or .410 bore double-barrel shotgun, with 26" or 28" ventilated rib barrels, single non-selective trigger and automatic ejectors. French case-hardened receiver and checkered walnut stock.

NIB	Exc.	V.G.	Good	Fair	Poor
—	300	250	200	150	100

Model 747 Over/Under

As above in 20-gauge only, with single-selective trigger.

NIB	Exc.	V.G.	Good	Fair	Poor
—	425	350	300	250	175

Model 757 Over/Under

Greener-style boxlock 12-gauge double-barrel shotgun, with 26" or 28" ventilated rib barrels, double triggers and automatic ejectors. Finished as Model 747.

NIB	Exc.	V.G.	Good	Fair	Poor
—	300	250	200	175	125

Model 787 Over/Under

As above, fitted with screw-in choke tubes.

NIB	Exc.	V.G.	Good	Fair	Poor
—	450	375	325	275	200

Model 808 Over/Under

A 12-gauge double-barrel shotgun, with 26", 28" or 30" ventilated rib barrels, single trigger and automatic ejectors. Blued, with checkered walnut stock. Manufactured in Italy from 1963 to 1968.

NIB	Exc.	V.G.	Good	Fair	Poor
—	425	350	300	250	175

Model 80 LS

A 12-, 20-gauge or .410 bore single-barrel shotgun, with 26" or 28" barrels. Blued, with checkered walnut stock.

NIB	Exc.	V.G.	Good	Fair	Poor
—	175	125	100	80	60

Model 200

Anson & Deeley-style 12-, 16-, 20-, 28-gauge or .410 bore double-barrel shotgun, with 22", 26" or 28" barrels, double triggers and automatic ejectors. Blued, with checkered walnut stock.

NIB	Exc.	V.G.	Good	Fair	Poor
—	350	300	250	200	125

Model 202

As above, with an extra set of interchangeable barrels. Imported from 1963 to 1985.

NIB	Exc.	V.G.	Good	Fair	Poor
—	325	275	225	175	100

Model 711 Magnum

As above, chambered for 3" shells and fitted with 30" or 32" barrels.

NIB	Exc.	V.G.	Good	Fair	Poor
—	350	300	250	200	150

Model 707 Deluxe

As above, more finely finished and fitted with well figured walnut stocks.

NIB	Exc.	V.G.	Good	Fair	Poor
—	350	300	250	200	150

RICHMOND ARMORY
Richmond, Virginia

Carbine

This weapon was manufactured for use by Confederate States of America and is extremely collectible. This muzzle-loading carbine chambered for .58-caliber percussion. Has a 25" round barrel and full-length stock that is held on by two barrel bands. Manufactured from parts that were captured at Harper's Ferry Armory in 1861. Locks are marked "Richmond, VA" and dated from 1861 to 1865. There are sling swivels in front of trigger guard and on the front barrel band; a third swivel is on the underside of buttstock. Quantity manufactured is not known. Made between 1861 and 1865.

Courtesy Milwaukee Public Museum, Milwaukee, Wisconsin

NIB	Exc.	V.G.	Good	Fair	Poor
—	—	28500	22000	8250	1000

Musketoon

Weapon similar to the carbine, except barrel is 30" in length and front sight is also the bayonet lug. There is no sling swivel on buttstock. Manufactured between 1861 and 1865.

NIB	Exc.	V.G.	Good	Fair	Poor
—	—	24000	19000	7700	1000

Rifled Musket

Also similar to the Carbine, with 40" barrel and full-length stock held on by three barrel bands. Front sling swivel is on the middle barrel band instead of front band. Manufactured between 1861 and 1865.

Courtesy Milwaukee Public Museum, Milwaukee, Wisconsin

NIB	Exc.	V.G.	Good	Fair	Poor
—	—	30000	22000	8250	1000

RIEDL RIFLE CO.
Westminster, California

Single-Shot Rifle

Company produced custom order dropping block single-shot rifles in a variety of calibers and barrel lengths. Rifles were normally fitted only with telescopic or target sight bases. Blued, with checkered walnut stock. Premium for African or Magnum chamberings.

NIB	Exc.	V.G.	Good	Fair	Poor
—	1750	1500	1250	750	400

RIFLESMITH INC.
Sheridan, Montana
See—Axtell Rifle Co.

RIGBY, JOHN & CO., LTD.
London, England

This company was established in the 18th century in U.K. and has produced a wide variety of firearms over the years. It traces its roots back to 1735 in Dublin, where the company was known for its percussion dueling pistols. A branch was opened in London in 1865, where some of the world's finest double rifles were made for more than 130 years, many of them made to order. In 1997, a group of investors acquired the company and moved it to Paso Robles, California, where a limited number of Rigby models were manufactured for several years. In 2010, an investor group from Texas bought the company and returned it to London, where Paul Roberts of J. Roberts and Sons was contracted to make rifles. The L&O Group, which owns Mauser, Blaser and Sauer, purchased the company in 2013. It was relocated to a new facility in Pensbury Place, London in 2014.

RIFLES

MAGAZINE RIFLES, CURRENT PRODUCTION

Magazine Rifle

Utilizing a Mauser action, this rifle is available in a number of calibers, barrel lengths and 3- or 5-shot magazine. Checkered walnut stock.

Courtesy Faintich Auction Service, Paul Goodwin photo

NIB	Exc.	V.G.	Good	Fair	Poor
—	12500	10000	7000	4000	1000

Big Game Rifle

Available on a single-/double square bridge Mauser action in .375 H&H, .416 Rigby or .450 Rigby calibers. Classic features of original Rigby rifles include 3-position wing safety, express sights, quarter rib, extractor and Turkish walnut stock, with traditional checkering pattern. Barreled actions are built in Germany by Mauser, as was done with original Rigby rifles a century ago. Higher-grade wood, engraving and color case-hardening are available. Deluxe model has premium finish and features; Vintage model traditional stock and specifications. **NOTE:** Prices shown are based on BP=USD exchange rate in July, 2016 and do not include British VAT. Add 20 percent for Deluxe or Vintage model.

NIB	Exc.	V.G.	Good	Fair	Poor
8000	7000	6000	—	—	—

London Best Rifle

Bespoke magazine rifle custom made to buyer's specifications in any caliber, with highest grade walnut and engraving. Price starts about $125,000 based on exchange rate as of July, 2016.

African Express

Utilizing a square bridge Mauser action. Chambered for .375 H&H, .404 Gibbs, .416 Rigby, .458 Win. Magnum, .505 Gibbs cartridges. Barrel lengths vary from 20" to 24"; 4-shot magazine standard.

NIB	Exc.	V.G.	Good	Fair	Poor
—	25000	20000	15000	10000	2000

Single-Shot Rifle

Utilizing a Farquharson falling block action, this rifle is chambered for a variety of cartridges. Has a 24" barrel. Receiver finely engraved and blued. Stock of well figured walnut.

NIB	Exc.	V.G.	Good	Fair	Poor
—	8000	7000	5500	2500	600

Second Quality Boxlock Double Rifle

Double-barrel rifle chambered for cartridges from .275 Magnum to .577 Nitro Express, with 24" to 28" barrel. Fitted with express sights, double triggers and automatic ejectors. Blued, with light engraving. Checkered walnut stock.

NIB	Exc.	V.G.	Good	Fair	Poor
—	20000	17000	11000	5500	900

Best Quality Boxlock Double Rifle

As above, but more finely engraved. Better quality walnut stocks.

NIB	Exc.	V.G.	Good	Fair	Poor
—	30000	22500	15000	7500	1000

Best Quality Sidelock Double Rifle

As above, but fitted with full sidelocks. Best bouquet engraving. Finely figured walnut stocks.

NIB	Exc.	V.G.	Good	Fair	Poor
—	50000	42500	33000	15000	1500

SHOTGUNS

Sidelock Double

Offered in all gauges, with choice of barrel lengths, chokes, stock dimensions, grip and fore-end styles. Double triggers and automatic ejectors. Prices shown are for Sandringham Grade. Regal Grade has higher grade wood and engraving. Made in London prior to 1998. **NOTE:** Add 20 percent for Regal Grade; 30 percent for 20-gauge; 40 percent for 28-gauge or .410 bore.

NIB	Exc.	V.G.	Good	Fair	Poor
9000	7500	6000	4500	3000	1000

Boxlock Double

Same features and options as above, except boxlock action. Prices shown are for Chatsworth Grade. Sackville Grade has higher grade wood and engraving. Made in London prior to 1998. **NOTE:** Add 30 percent for Sackville Grade; 20 percent for 20-gauge; 30 percent for 28-gauge or .410 bore.

NIB	Exc.	V.G.	Good	Fair	Poor
4500	3700	2800	2000	1500	500

RIGDON, ANSLEY & CO.
Augusta, Georgia

1851 Colt Navy Type

A .36-caliber percussion revolver, with 7.5" barrel and 6-shot cylinder. Blued, with walnut grips. Initial production examples marked "Augusta, GA. C.S.A."; later models "C.S.A." Approximately 1,000 manufactured in 1864 and 1865.

Courtesy Milwaukee Public Museum, Milwaukee, Wisconsin

Early Production Model

NIB	Exc.	V.G.	Good	Fair	Poor
—	—	70000	61000	27500	2000

Standard Production Model

NIB	Exc.	V.G.	Good	Fair	Poor
—	—	63500	4950	1925	1500

RIPOMANTI, GUY
St. Etienne, France

Side-by-Side Shotgun

High-grade shotgun offered on a strictly made-to-order basis. There is a boxlock model that begins at $8,500; a sidelock that is priced from $22,500. These prices rise depending on options and embellishments desired. These guns are rarely seen on the used-gun market.

Side-by-Side Double Rifles

Extremely high-grade and basically made to order. They are rarely encountered on today's market. They have been imported since 1988. They range in price from $11,000 up.

Over/Under Double Rifle

Boxlock action over/under chambered for 9.3x74R cartridge. Barrels are 23.5" and have express sights. There are double triggers and automatic ejectors. Highly engraved and features high-grade hand-checkered walnut stock.

NIB	Exc.	V.G.	Good	Fair	Poor
12500	9750	7750	5000	4000	900

RIVERSIDE ARMS CO.
Chicopee Falls, Massachusetts

See—Stevens, J. Arms Co.

Double-Barrel Shotguns

Brand name used by J. Stevens Arms Co. on many good quality double-barrel shotguns. Value depends on model, gauge and condition. From $100 to $1,600. See also Stevens.

Courtesy William Hammond

RIZZINI, BATTISTA
Bresica, Italy

NOTE: There are a number of extra cost options for Rizzini guns that can greatly affect price. Extra barrels and upgraded wood are such options.

SHOTGUNS

Aurum Light

Over/under model features 24.5" to 27.5" ventilated rib barrel. Figured oil-finish walnut stock, with hand checkering and pistol-grip. Game scene engraved receiver. Auto ejectors and single-selective trigger. Weight about 6 lbs. Made in 12-, 16-, 20-, 28-gauge and .410 bore. **NOTE:** Add $500 for 28-gauge or .410 bore.

Courtesy William Larkin Moore & Co.

NIB	Exc.	V.G.	Good	Fair	Poor
3000	2600	2000	1500	900	500

Artemis Classic

Features engraved sideplates with game scenes. Offered in 12-, 16-, 20-, 28-gauge and .410 bore. Barrel lengths from 24" to 27.5". Auto ejectors and single-selective trigger. Figured walnut stock, with hand checkering and pistol-grip. Weight about 6 lbs.

Courtesy William Larkin Moore & Co.

NIB	Exc.	V.G.	Good	Fair	Poor
3200	2700	2300	1900	1000	500

Artemis Deluxe

Similar to standard Artemis, with addition of gold inlaid game scenes and fancy walnut stock. Cased.

NIB	Exc.	V.G.	Good	Fair	Poor
6000	4200	3500	2500	1250	600

Artemis EL

Features sideplates, with hand engraved English scroll and game scenes. Extra fancy walnut stock. Cased.

NIB	Exc.	V.G.	Good	Fair	Poor
18000	13500	10000	8000	6000	900

Upland EL

NIB	Exc.	V.G.	Good	Fair	Poor
4000	3500	3000	2500	1250	600

S780 Emel

Boxlock model offered in 12-, 16-, 20-, 28-gauge or .410 bore. Barrel lengths from 24" to 27.5". Hand engraved receiver, with game scenes.

Auto ejectors and single-selective trigger. Fancy walnut stock, with hand checkering. Leather case. Weight about: 12-gauge 6.8 lbs.; smaller gauges 6 lbs.

NIB	Exc.	V.G.	Good	Fair	Poor
13500	11000	8750	7000	4250	900

S782 Emel Field Classic

Similar to S792, with addition of hand engraved gold inlaid game scenes.

NIB	Exc.	V.G.	Good	Fair	Poor
15000	13000	10000	8750	5700	900

S790 Emel Field

Similar to S780, with exception of thistle-leaf style engraving pattern.

NIB	Exc.	V.G.	Good	Fair	Poor
10500	8000	6500	5000	4250	900

S792 Emel Field

Features sideplates engraved with English scroll and game scenes. Extra select walnut stock. Available in 12-, 16-, 20-, 28-gauge and .410 bore. Barrel lengths from 24" to 27.5".

NIB	Exc.	V.G.	Good	Fair	Poor
11000	9750	8000	6750	5000	900

Premier Sporting

Offered in 12- or 20-gauge. Choice of barrel lengths from 27.5" to 31.5". Blued boxlock action, with auto ejectors and single-selective trigger. Select walnut stock, with hand checkering and oil-finish. Pistol-grip stock and beavertail fore-end. Weight about 7.5 lbs.

NIB	Exc.	V.G.	Good	Fair	Poor
3000	2750	2100	1600	900	500

Sporting EL

NIB	Exc.	V.G.	Good	Fair	Poor
3750	2800	2200	1750	975	600

S790 EL Sporting

Offered in 12-gauge only. Barrels from 27.5" to 31.5". Boxlock action, with chrome plate. Auto ejectors and single-selective trigger. Fancy walnut pistol-grip stock. Weight about 7.5 lbs.

NIB	Exc.	V.G.	Good	Fair	Poor
7500	6250	5000	3750	2900	800

Rizzini Omnium

Model represents entry level of Rizzini over/unders, but it has features not found on comparably priced guns. These include jeweled monoblocs, braised ribs, precisely regulated trigger and blued or coin finish. Other features are interchangeable choke tubes, checkered walnut stock with schnabel fore-end, ventilated rib, automatic ejectors and scroll engraving. In 12- or 20-gauge, with frame sizes appropriate to gauge. **NOTE:** Add $200 for Omnium Light, with coin finish.

NIB	Exc.	V.G.	Good	Fair	Poor
2250	1875	1550	1000	750	300

EXPRESS RIFLES

Express 90 L

Over/under chambered for 7x65R, 8x57JRS, 9.3x74R, .30-06, .308 Win., .444 Marlin. Barrel length 16". Boxlock action, with case colored receiver. Auto ejectors and single trigger. Pistol-grip walnut stock, with Bavarian cheekpiece. Hand checkered oil-finish stock. Weight about 8 lbs.

NIB	Exc.	V.G.	Good	Fair	Poor
4750	4250	3500	2500	1750	800

Express 92 EL

Same calibers as above. Sideplates engraved with English scroll and game scenes. Extra select walnut stock, with pistol-grip and round cheekpiece.

NIB	Exc.	V.G.	Good	Fair	Poor
11000	9500	8000	5500	2500	900

RIZZINI, FRATELLI
Brescia, Italy

Early guns were manufactured with Antonio Zoli. As a result, these were off-the-shelf guns of lower prices. These early guns were imported by Abercombie and Fitch of New York. Some of these guns will be stamped with A&F address on the barrel. These side-by-side guns have a boxlock action.

NOTE: At the present time, this Italian gun company builds about 24 shotguns a year. Each gun is highly individualized for the customer. Company produces only two models. These are listed to give the reader some idea of the value of one of these models. None of these models includes the cost of engraving. Multi barrel set and multi gauge sets are extra.

Rizzini models with serial numbers above #1709 have their own patented action, and prices listed reflect that action. Guns listed have a H&H style action and should deduct approximately 30 percent from prices listed.

Lusso Grade
12 gauge

NIB	Exc.	V.G.	Good	Fair	Poor
3200	2850	2200	1600	900	400

20 gauge

NIB	Exc.	V.G.	Good	Fair	Poor
3700	3250	2800	2200	1500	550

28 gauge and .410 bore

NIB	Exc.	V.G.	Good	Fair	Poor
4000	3600	3000	2500	1700	600

Extra Lusso Grade—Scalloped receiver
12 gauge

NIB	Exc.	V.G.	Good	Fair	Poor
4800	4150	3250	2700	1500	700

20 gauge

NIB	Exc.	V.G.	Good	Fair	Poor
5450	4600	3500	2900	1650	700

28 gauge

NIB	Exc.	V.G.	Good	Fair	Poor
5850	4900	3750	3250	1900	700

.410 bore

NIB	Exc.	V.G.	Good	Fair	Poor
6250	5250	3900	3500	2350	750

Model R-1

Available in 12-gauge to .410 bore. Barrels from 25" to 30", single-/double trigger, pistol-/straight-grip, rib, barrel length and chokes are standard items. Features H&H sidelock action.

12, 16, or 20 gauge

NIB	Exc.	V.G.	Good	Fair	Poor
85000	72000	57500	40000	—	—

28 gauge or .410 bore

NIB	Exc.	V.G.	Good	Fair	Poor
90000	76000	62000	45000	—	—

Model R-2

Has a boxlock action and removable inspection plate on the bottom of frame. Stock and forearm fitted with Turkish Circassian walnut. Offered in 12-gauge to .410 bore.

NIB	Exc.	V.G.	Good	Fair	Poor
17000	14000	1000	7500	5000	700

NOTE: Engraving extras for above models will add $8,700 for English scroll pattern and $22,000 for Fracassi style engraving. Other types of engraving are offered. Extra set of barrels in same gauge add 15 percent.

ROBAR AND de KIRKHAVE
Liege, Belgium
Model 1909-1910

A 6.35mm or 7.65mm caliber semi-automatic pistol, with 3" barrel. Barrel located under the recoil spring housing. Slide marked "Pistolet Automatique Jieffeco Depose Brevete SGDG". Blued, with plastic grips. Manufactured from 1910 to 1914. Copy of Browning Model 1900.

Courtesy James Rankin

NIB	Exc.	V.G.	Good	Fair	Poor
—	500	400	300	200	100

Model 1911

Semi-automatic pistol in caliber 6.35mm. Same as Model 1909-1910. Slide serrations have been added at the muzzle.

Courtesy James Rankin

NIB	Exc.	V.G.	Good	Fair	Poor
—	500	400	300	200	100

Model 1912

Semi-automatic pistol in caliber 7.65mm. Similar to Model 1909-1910. Slide serrations have been added at the muzzle.

Courtesy James Rankin

NIB	Exc.	V.G.	Good	Fair	Poor
—	500	400	300	200	100

Melior Model 1907

Semi-automatic pistol in calibers 6.35mm and 7.65mm. Barrel located under the recoil spring housing.

Courtesy James Rankin

NIB	Exc.	V.G.	Good	Fair	Poor
—	500	400	300	200	100

Melior Model 1913-1914

Semi-automatic pistol in caliber 6.35mm and 7.65mm. Same as Model 1907, with slide serrations at the muzzle.

NIB	Exc.	V.G.	Good	Fair	Poor
—	500	400	300	200	100

Melior Pocket Model

Semi-automatic pistol in 6.35mm caliber. Nearly identical to Jieffeco's made by the same company, Robar. Manufactured in 1920s and imported into U.S. by Phoenix Arms Company, Mass. Phoenix name appears on the pistol. Model resembles the FN Browning Model 1910.

Courtesy James Rankin

NIB	Exc.	V.G.	Good	Fair	Poor
—	350	250	175	125	75

Melior Vest Pocket Model

Semi-automatic pistol in caliber 6.35mm, with open-top slide. Blue finish, with black checkered rubber grips. Robar logo "ROC" on each grip.

Courtesy James Rankin

NIB	Exc.	V.G.	Good	Fair	Poor
—	300	250	200	150	100

Melior Model .22 Long Rifle

Semi-automatic pistol chambered for .22 LR cartridge. Very similar in appearance to Pocket Model, with no squeeze grip safety.

Courtesy James Rankin

NIB	Exc.	V.G.	Good	Fair	Poor
—	500	400	300	200	100

Melior Model .22 Target

Semi-automatic in .22 LR caliber. Barrel is detachable so that various lengths may be used. Knurled nut at front of the slide allows for barrel changes.

Courtesy James Rankin

NIB	Exc.	V.G.	Good	Fair	Poor
—	500	400	300	200	100

New Model Jieffeco (7.65mm)

In the 1920s, Robar and de Kirkhave introduced a New Model, Jieffeco. Similar to FN Browning Model 1910. At this time, the right to import Jieffeco into the U.S. was arranged with Davis Warner Arms Corp., New York, whose company name was used on the pistol. Model is a semi-automatic pistol in caliber 7.65mm. On the slide is "Pistolet Automatique Jieffeco Repose".

Courtesy James Rankin

NIB	Exc.	V.G.	Good	Fair	Poor
—	350	250	175	125	75

New Model Jieffeco (6.35mm)

Similar to 7.65mm model, this compact variation is chambered in 6.35mm or .25 ACP. On the slide is "Pistolet Automatique Jieffeco Made in Liege, Belgium. Davis Warmer Arms Corporation, New York".

Courtesy James Rankin

NIB	Exc.	V.G.	Good	Fair	Poor
—	350	250	175	125	75

Mercury

As above in .22-caliber. Imported by Tradewinds of Tacoma, Washington. Slide marked "Mercury Made in Belgium". Blue or nickel-plated. Manufactured from 1946 to 1958.

NIB	Exc.	V.G.	Good	Fair	Poor
—	200	150	125	100	75

ROBAR COMPANIES
Phoenix, Arizona

This company has been building precision rifles, shotguns and pistols since 1983.

Robar Patriot Tactical Shotgun

Built on a Remington Model 870. Features 18" barrel, express sights, seamless extended magazine tube, side-saddle shell carrier, Wolff springs, etc.. Roguard/NP3 finish.

NIB	Exc.	V.G.	Good	Fair	Poor
765	600	500	400	300	100

Robar Spec Ops Tactical Shotgun

Similar to model above. Fitted with tactical ghost ring night sights, safety and sling.

NIB	Exc.	V.G.	Good	Fair	Poor
990	800	700	600	400	100

Robar Elite Tactical Shotgun

Features a number of special options: Robar choke with forcing cone; modified bolt; Pachmayr pad; etc.

NIB	Exc.	V.G.	Good	Fair	Poor
1700	1350	1000	875	600	300

Robar MK I Tactical Rifle

Built on Remington Model 700 action, with 24" heavy factory barrel. Chambered for .308 or .223 cartridge. Fitted with gray Choate Ultimate sniper stock, Robar bipod and adjustable trigger. Roguard/MP3 finish.

NIB	Exc.	V.G.	Good	Fair	Poor
3400	2900	2250	1600	900	300

Robar MK II Tactical Rifle

As above, chambered for .308 cartridge only. Special trigger job and special hand finish of internal parts and chamber.

NIB	Exc.	V.G.	Good	Fair	Poor
3400	2900	2250	1600	900	300

Robar SR60 Precision Rifle

Fully accurized Remington Model 700 action, with bench rest quality barrel and chamber. Custom stock, with hand bedding and pillars. Choice: .308 with 20" or 24" barrel; .223 with 24" barrel.

NIB	Exc.	V.G.	Good	Fair	Poor
3900	3500	2900	2200	1400	500

ROBBINS & LAWRENCE
Windsor, Vermont

Pepperbox

A .28- or .31-caliber percussion 5 barrel pistol, with barrel groups measuring 3.5" or 4.5" in length. Ring trigger, blued iron frame with simple scroll engraving. Browned barrels are marked "Robbins & Lawrence Co. Windsor, VT. Patent. 1849". Barrel groups for this pistol were made in two types: fluted in both calibers; ribbed in .31-caliber only. Approximately 7,000 made between 1851 and 1854.

NIB	Exc.	V.G.	Good	Fair	Poor
—	—	2700	2200	650	200

ROBERTS DEFENSE
Oshkosh, Wisconsin

This manufacturer of 1911-type semi-automatic pistols started production in 2013. All models are chambered in .45 ACP and are hand fitted throughout the entire assembly process.

Operator Series

Offered in full- or Commander-size, with forged steel frame and true Picatinny rail. Dark Ops model has black nitride frame and slide. Desert Ops model has Flat Dark Earth Ceracote frame and black nitride slide.

NIB	Exc.	V.G.	Good	Fair	Poor
1400	1200	975	700	350	200

Recon Series

In full-size Commander or Officer frame sizes, with 3.5", 4.25" or 5" barrel lengths. Models have a lightweight alloy frame, black finish and fiber optic front sights.

NIB	Exc.	V.G.	Good	Fair	Poor
1275	1050	900	550	300	200

Super Grade Custom Series

These models come in all three frame sizes. Choice of all stainless or stainless frame, with black nitride slide. Grips are checkered wood. All components are of match grade quality.

NIB	Exc.	V.G.	Good	Fair	Poor
1325	1120	925	500	300	200

ROBERTSON
Philadelphia, Pennsylvania

Pocket Pistol

A .41-caliber single-shot percussion derringer. Barrels ranging in length from 3" to 4.5". Barrel marked "Robertson, Phila.".

NIB	Exc.	V.G.	Good	Fair	Poor
—	—	2000	1650	500	200

ROBINSON, ORVIL
See—Adirondack Arms Company

ROBINSON, S.C.
Richmond, Virginia

From December, 1862 through March 1, 1863, S.C. Robinson produced copies of the Sharps carbine. These arms had an overall length of 38.5", with .52-caliber barrels 21.5" long. Lockplates were marked "S.C. ROBINSON/ARMS MANUFACTORY/RICHMOND VA/1862" along with the serial number. Barrels were marked forward of the rear sight "S.C. ROBINSON/ARMS MANUFACTORY", as well as "RICHMOND VA/1862" to rear of the sight. Total number made estimated to be slightly more than 1,900.

In March, 1863, Robinson factory was taken over by Confederate States Government. Carbines produced after that date are only stamped with the serial number on their lockplates and "RICHMOND VA" on their barrels. Total number made in excess of 3,400.

Robinson Sharps

NIB	Exc.	V.G.	Good	Fair	Poor
—	—	37000	30000	9300	1500

Confederate Sharps

NIB	Exc.	V.G.	Good	Fair	Poor
—	—	32000	27500	8250	1500

ROBINSON ARMAMENT CO.
Salt Lake City, Utah

Super VEPR

Semi-automatic rifle made in Russia. Chambered for .308, .223 or 7.62x39mm cartridge. Uses an RPK-type receiver. Chrome lined 21.65" barrel. Walnut thumbhole stock. Black oxide finish. Weight about 8.5 lbs.

NIB	Exc.	V.G.	Good	Fair	Poor
1200	800	675	500	400	200

M-96 Expeditonary Rifle

Chambered for .223 or 7.62x39mm cartridge. Can use AK or AR magazines. Quick-change barrel. Adjustable gas operating system. Can interchange calibers without tools. Built in U.S.A.

NIB	Exc.	V.G.	Good	Fair	Poor
1750	1400	1100	800	575	300

M-96 Carbine

As above, with shorter barrel.

NIB	Exc.	V.G.	Good	Fair	Poor
1750	1400	1100	800	575	300

M-96 Top Fed

Same specifications as rifle, but magazine is fitted to top of receiver.

NIB	Exc.	V.G.	Good	Fair	Poor
1900	1550	1175	900	625	350

ROCK ISLAND ARMORY
(TRADE NAME OF ARMSCOR)
Pahrump, Nevada

Arms Corp. of the Philippines manufactures firearms under both Armscor and Rock Island brand names. For Armscor models, see that listing.

M1911-A1 FSP

Full-size 1911-pattern pistol in 9mm, .38 Super or .45 ACP. Blue, Duracoat, stainless or two-tone finish, front and rear slide serrations, rubber grips, standard or night sights. In standard or high-capacity variations. FS Match Model has fiber optic front sight, bobbed hammer, checkered walnut grips. Also available in compact version (CSP), with 3.5" barrel. **NOTE:** Add $200 for FS Match; $100 for Meprolight night sights.

NIB	Exc.	V.G.	Good	Fair	Poor
425	375	325	300	250	225

TCM

1911-style series chambered for .22 TCM cartridge. Centerfire round based on necked-down 9mm case, with .223 bullet. In standard, mid-size or target variations. Introduced 2013.

NIB	Exc.	V.G.	Good	Fair	Poor
750	675	600	500	—	—

M2011-A1

High capacity or single-stack configurations in .45 ACP or high-capacity 9mm. Features include fiber optic front and adjustable white-dot rear sights, combat hammer, extended grip and thumb safeties and tactical accessory rail.

NIB	Exc.	V.G.	Good	Fair	Poor
600	525	450	400	300	225

MAPP

Single-/double-action design based on CZ-75 series. In 9mm with 16-shot magazine, 3.5" or 4" barrel, Picatinny rail, adjustable rear sight, ambidextrous safety.

NIB	Exc.	V.G.	Good	Fair	Poor
450	400	350	300	250	225

TCM Rifle

Bolt-action model made in 9mm or .22 TCM, with removable 17-shot box magazine, synthetic stock, skeletonized trigger, Parkerized finish and fixed or adjustable sights.

NIB	Exc.	V.G.	Good	Fair	Poor
750	675	500	400	300	200

Pro Match Ultra Big Rock

A 10mm model with 6" barrel, choice of single-stack or high-capacity magazine. **NOTE:** Add $150 for high-capacity model. Introduced in 2015.

NIB	Exc.	V.G.	Good	Fair	Poor
1000	850	725	500	300	200

ROCK RIVER ARMS, INC.
Colona, Illinois

This manufacturer of AR-style rifles and carbines, also made a series of 1911-pattern pistols for several years. In 2012, the decision was made to concentrate on the AR product line. All 1911 models listed in the following pages are discontinued.

PISTOLS

Elite Commando

Built on a National Match frame, with 4" National Match slide with double serrations and lowered ejection port (5" barrel optional). Front strap is 30 lpi. Night sights standard. Aluminum trigger and many more custom features. Checkered cocobolo grips. Guaranteed 2.5" groups at 50 yards. Chambered for .45 ACP cartridge.

NIB	Exc.	V.G.	Good	Fair	Poor
1725	1300	950	775	500	300

Standard Match

Many of the same features as above model, without night sights. Also chambered for .45 ACP cartridge.

NIB	Exc.	V.G.	Good	Fair	Poor
1025	750	600	450	300	200

National Match Hardball

Similar features as above models, with adjustable rear Bomar sight and dovetail front. Chambered for .45 ACP cartridge.

NIB	Exc.	V.G.	Good	Fair	Poor
1500	1100	825	675	500	300

Bullseye Wadcutter

Features Rock River slide scope mount. Guaranteed to shoot 1.5" groups at 50 yards. Chambered for .45 ACP.

NIB	Exc.	V.G.	Good	Fair	Poor
1650	1250	925	750	525	325

Basic Limited Match

Similar to Bullseye Wadcutter, with Bomar adjustable rear sight and dovetail front. Chambered for .45 ACP.

NIB	Exc.	V.G.	Good	Fair	Poor
1700	1300	950	750	525	325

Limited Match

Match pistol comes standard with many custom features. Guaranteed to shoot 1.5" groups at 50 yards. Chambered for .45 ACP.

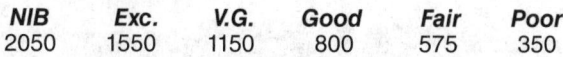

NIB	Exc.	V.G.	Good	Fair	Poor
2050	1550	1150	800	575	350

Hi-Cap Basic Limited

Model gives the customer a choice of STI, SVI, Para-Ordnance or Entreprise frames. Many special features. Chambered for .45 ACP. **NOTE:** Add $200 for Para-Ordnance or Entreprise frames.

NIB	Exc.	V.G.	Good	Fair	Poor
1895	1500	1200	800	575	300

Ultimate Match Achiever

An IPSC-style pistol, with scope and three port muzzle compensator. Many special features. Chambered for .38 Super cartridge.

NIB	Exc.	V.G.	Good	Fair	Poor
2250	1750	1150	800	575	350

Match Master Steel

Bianchi-style pistol, with scope and three port muzzle-brake. Chambered for .38 Super Cartridge.

NIB	Exc.	V.G.	Good	Fair	Poor
2350	1850	1200	850	600	375

Basic Carry

Introduced in 2005. This .45 ACP model features 5" match barrel, checkered front strap, lowered and flared ejection port, Novak rear sight, dehorned for carry and rosewood grips. Many other special features.

NIB	Exc.	V.G.	Good	Fair	Poor
1525	1150	825	675	500	300

Pro Carry

Similar to Basic Carry, with 4.25", 5" or 6" barrel. Choice of Heinie or Novak tritium sights and polished finish; guaranteed to shoot 2.5" group at 50 yards with select ammunition. Other options available.

NIB	Exc.	V.G.	Good	Fair	Poor
1795	1400	1100	675	500	250

Tactical Pistol

This .45 ACP pistol fitted with a 5" slide, with front serrations and match grade barrel. Heine or Novak rear sight, checkered front strap, tactical mag catch and safety. Dehorned for carry. Rosewood grips. Introduced in 2005. **NOTE:** Add $200 for Black "T" finish.

NIB	Exc.	V.G.	Good	Fair	Poor
1925	1450	1200	800	575	300

Limited Police Competition 9mm

9mm model features 5" slide, with double serrations. Three position rear sight and dovetail front. Checkered front strap. Deluxe blued finish and grips. Many other special features. Introduced in 2005. **NOTE:** Add $200 for Black "T" finish.

NIB	Exc.	V.G.	Good	Fair	Poor
2310	1750	1150	800	575	350

Unlimited Police Competition 9mm

Similar to above, with additional special features such as 6" slide. Introduced in 2005. **NOTE:** Add $200 for Black "T" finish.

NIB	Exc.	V.G.	Good	Fair	Poor
2310	1750	1150	800	575	350

RIFLES

CAR A2

These are AR-15-style rifles. Chambered for .223 cartridge. Fitted with 16" barrel, with CAR hand guards. Two stage trigger. Choice of A2 or non-collapsible buttstock and black or green furniture. Weight about 7 lbs. **NOTE:** Add $25 for non-collapsible buttstock.

NIB	Exc.	V.G.	Good	Fair	Poor
925	750	600	500	375	200

CAR A2M

Same as above, with mid-length hand guard. **NOTE:** Add $25 for non-collapsible buttstock.

NIB	Exc.	V.G.	Good	Fair	Poor
925	750	600	500	375	200

CAR A4

Similar to models above, with flattop receiver and CAR hand guard. **NOTE:** Add $25 for non-collapsible buttstock.

NIB	Exc.	V.G.	Good	Fair	Poor
925	750	600	500	375	200

CAR A4M

Flattop receiver with mid-length hand guard. **NOTE:** Add $25 for non-collapsible buttstock.

NIB	Exc.	V.G.	Good	Fair	Poor
925	750	600	500	375	200

Standard A2

AR-15-style rifle fitted with 20" barrel. Chambered for .223 cartridge. Two stage trigger. Fixed stock and full-length hand guard. Weight about 8.2 lbs.

NIB	Exc.	V.G.	Good	Fair	Poor
925	750	600	500	375	200

National Match A2

Features .22 Wylde chamber, with 20" Wilson air-gauged match stainless steel barrel. A2 receiver. Two stage trigger. Free float high temp thermo mold hand guard. Match sights. Weight about 9.7 lbs.

NIB	Exc.	V.G.	Good	Fair	Poor
1265	950	800	650	500	300

Standard A4 Flattop

Same as Standard A2, with flattop receiver.

NIB	Exc.	V.G.	Good	Fair	Poor
925	750	600	500	375	200

Varmint Rifle

Flattop model fitted with 24" stainless steel barrel, without sights. Chambered for .223 cartridge. Fixed stock. Two-stage trigger. Weight about 9.5 lbs.

NIB	Exc.	V.G.	Good	Fair	Poor
1050	875	600	475	375	200

Varmint EOP (Elevated Optical Platform)

Chambered for .223 Wylde. Fitted with Wilson air-gauged bull stainless steel barrel. Choice of 16", 18", 20" and 24" barrel lengths. Free float aluminum hand guard. National Match two stage trigger. Weight about: 8.2 lbs with 16" barrel; 10 lbs with 24" barrel. **NOTE:** Add $10 for each barrel length over 16".

NIB	Exc.	V.G.	Good	Fair	Poor
1050	875	600	475	375	200

Advanced Tactical Hunter

Chambered for 5.56/.223 Rem. Carbine-style adjustable stock, 18" cryogenically treated stainless steel barrel with tactical muzzle-brake. Half-quad free-floating mid-length hand guard, winter designed trigger guard, two-stage trigger. Numerous options. Introduced in 2011.

NIB	Exc.	V.G.	Good	Fair	Poor
1100	1000	850	700	400	250

NM A2-DCM Legal

Fitted with 20" stainless steel barrel. National Match sleeve and specially selected upper and lower to ensure tight fit. Special high temp hand guards. Two-stage trigger. National Match sights. Weight about 9 lbs.

NIB	Exc.	V.G.	Good	Fair	Poor
1200	1000	825	600	450	200

Government Model

Chambered for .223 cartridge. Fitted with 16" Wilson chrome barrel with A2 flash hider. National Match two stage trigger. A4 upper receiver. Flip-up rear sight. EOTech M951 light system. Surefire M73 Quad Rail hand guard, and 6 position tactical CAR stock. Weight about 8.2 lbs.

NIB	Exc.	V.G.	Good	Fair	Poor
2310	1750	1150	800	575	350

Tactical CAR A4

.223-caliber rifle has 16" Wilson chrome barrel, with A2 flash hider. A4 upper receiver, with detachable carry handle. Two stage National Match trigger. R-4 hand guard. Six position tactical CAR stock. Weight about 7.5 lbs.

NIB	Exc.	V.G.	Good	Fair	Poor
950	800	650	500	350	200

Elite CAR A4

As above, with mid-length hand guard. Weight about 7.7 lbs.

NIB	Exc.	V.G.	Good	Fair	Poor
950	800	650	500	350	200

Tactical CAR UTE (Universal Tactical Entry) 2

.223-caliber rifle has 16" Wilson chrome barrel, with A2 flash hider. R-2 hand guard. Upper receiver is a UTE2, with standard A4 rail height. Two stage trigger and 6 position CAR tactical stock. Weight about 7.5 lbs.

NIB	Exc.	V.G.	Good	Fair	Poor
950	800	650	500	350	200

Elite CAR UTE 2

As above, with mid-length hand guard. Weight about 7.7 lbs.

NIB	Exc.	V.G.	Good	Fair	Poor
950	800	650	500	350	200

Entry Tactical

.223 model features 16" Wilson chrome barrel, with R-4 profile. A4 upper receiver, with detachable carry handle. National Match two stage trigger. Six position tactical CAR stock. R-4 hand guard. Weight about 7.5 lbs.

NIB	Exc.	V.G.	Good	Fair	Poor
950	800	650	500	350	200

TASC Rifle

Features 16" Wilson chrome barrel, with A2 flash hider. A2 upper receiver, with windage and elevation rear sight. R-4 hand guard. A2 buttstock. Weight about 7.5 lbs.

NIB	Exc.	V.G.	Good	Fair	Poor
925	750	600	500	375	200

LAR-15 Lightweight

Features a chrome moly 16" lightweight barrel, with carbon fiber hand guard in several variants, 6-position tactical stock, low profile gas block. In 5.56 NATO/.223. Weight 5.6 to 6 lbs. Introduced in 2015.

NIB	Exc.	V.G.	Good	Fair	Poor
1100	950	800	550	350	250

LAR-15 X-1 Rifle

Featuring .223 Wylde chamber, a hybrid chamber designed to better accept both 5.56 NATO and .223 Rem. ammo. Forged upper and lower receivers, 18" fluted stainless barrel with Rock River Beast or Hunter muzzle-brake and low profile gas block are other features. Buttstock is RRA A2 or CAR, with Hogue Rubber pistol-grip and RRA's TRO-XL extended length free float rail hand guard. The X-1 Rifle is available in other variations and chamberings, including 6.5 SPCII, .458 Socom and 7.62 NATO.

X-1 .223 Wylde

NIB	Exc.	V.G.	Good	Fair	Poor
1250	1000	700	550	350	200

X-1 6.8 SPCII, .300 AAC or .458 Socom

NIB	Exc.	V.G.	Good	Fair	Poor
1350	1150	900	650	400	300

X-1 7.62 NATO

NIB	Exc.	V.G.	Good	Fair	Poor
1500	1300	1050	800	450	200

Texas Rifle

In 5.56 NATO or .223 Rem. Wylde chamber. Rock River Texas XL free-float hand guard in Magpul FDE, Barret Bronze or Burnt Bronze finish. Two-stage trigger, winter trigger guard, directionally tuned and ported muzzle-brake. Has a mid-length gas system and low-profile gas block. Hand guard has full-length rail with 2.5" rail at 3, 6 and 9 o'clock. A2 or CAR stock, Hogue pistol-grip. Introduced in 2015.

NIB	Exc.	V.G.	Good	Fair	Poor
1500	1250	1000	—	—	—

LAR 47 X-1

Chambered for 7.62x39mm cartridge. This model has an 18" fluted barrel, muzzle-brake, extended free-floating rail, Operator A2 or CAR stock, with Hogue pistol-grip. Introduced in 2015.

NIB	Exc.	V.G.	Good	Fair	Poor
1400	1200	900	700	450	300

ROGERS & SPENCER
Utica, New York

Army Revolver

.44-caliber 6-shot percussion revolver, with 7.5" octagonal barrel. Barrel marked "Rogers & Spencer/Utica, N.Y." Blued case-hardened hammer, with walnut grips bearing inspector's mark "RPB". Approximately 5,800 made between 1863 and 1865.

Courtesy Milwaukee Public Museum, Milwaukee, Wisconsin

NIB	Exc.	V.G.	Good	Fair	Poor
—	—	3500	2500	1000	550

ROGUE RIFLE COMPANY
Prospect, Oregon

See—Chipmunk Rifles

ROGUE RIVER RIFLEWORKS
Paso Robles, California

Boxlock Double Rifle

These rifles are custom fitted and available in any barrel length or caliber from .22 Hornet to .577 NE. Anson & Deeley boxlocks. Choice of finish, fore-end, engraving, wood and various other options. Each rifle should be appraised individually before a sale. Prices listed are for basic rifle, with no extras.

NIB	Exc.	V.G.	Good	Fair	Poor
17500	15000	12000	9500	5000	900

Sidelock Double Rifle

These rifles are custom fitted and available in any barrel length or caliber from .22 Hornet to .577 NE. Holland & Holland pattern sidelocks. Choice of finish, fore-end, engraving, wood and various other options. Each rifle should be appraised individually before a sale. Prices listed are for basic rifle, with no extras.

NIB	Exc.	V.G.	Good	Fair	Poor
50000	42500	30000	17000	7500	900

ROHM GMBH
Sonthein/Brenz, Germany

This company produced a variety of small handguns that were imported into the United States prior to the Gun Control Act of 1968. These included several types of double-action and single-action revolvers, .25 semi-automatics and derringers. Most of these were marketed under the RG name. In early 1970s, the company established a manufacturing facility in Miami. Most of these same models were made there, until the company went out of business in 1986. These firearms were low-priced, utility models and there is little collector's interest. Values would be in the $100 to $125 range, or less.

ROHRBAUGH
Bayport, New York

The Rohrbaugh company closed its doors in 2014.

R9/R9S

Introduced in 2004. A very small pistol made in 9mm or .380 ACP. Offered with-/without sights. Magazine capacity 6 rounds. Barrel length 2.9"; height 3.7"; length 5.2"; slide width .812"; weight about 12.8 oz. Values shown are for basic model.

NIB	Exc.	V.G.	Good	Fair	Poor
1200	950	775	600	400	200

380/380S

NIB	Exc.	V.G.	Good	Fair	Poor
—	950	775	600	400	200

ROMERWERKE
Suhl, Germany
Romer

A .22-caliber semi-automatic pistol, with 2.5" or 6.5" barrel and 7-shot magazine. Barrels are interchangeable and marked "Kal. .22 Long Rifle"; slide marked "Romerwerke Suhl". Blued, with plastic grips. Manufactured between 1924 and 1926.

NIB	Exc.	V.G.	Good	Fair	Poor
—	625	500	450	325	225

RONGE, J. B.
Liege, Belgium
Bulldog

A .32-, .380- or .45-caliber double-action revolver, with 3" barrel. Unmarked except for monogram "RF" on grips. Various trade names have been noted on these revolvers and are believed to have been applied by retailers. Manufactured from 1880 to 1910.

NIB	Exc.	V.G.	Good	Fair	Poor
—	250	150	100	75	50

ROSS RIFLE CO.
Quebec, Canada

Designed by Sir Charles Ross, this controversial straight-pull action rifle was made in a wide range of commercial and military variations from 1903 to 1917. In recent years, some models have become quite collectible. Models listed are a sampling of the many different variations. **NOTE:** Some models should not be fired before they are checked by a gunsmith familiar with the Ross design.

Mark I

Barrel length 28"; .303-caliber. "Harris Controlled Platform Magazine" can be depressed by external lever to facilitate loading.

Courtesy Buffalo Bill Historical Center, Cody, Wyoming

NIB	Exc.	V.G.	Good	Fair	Poor
—	1800	1500	1000	600	400

Mark I Carbine

As above, with 22" barrel.

NIB	Exc.	V.G.	Good	Fair	Poor
—	1600	1200	800	500	300

Mark II

As above, with modified rear sight.

NIB	Exc.	V.G.	Good	Fair	Poor
—	2000	1600	1100	650	400

Mark III (Military)

Introduced in 1910, with improved lockwork and stripper clip guides. **NOTE:** Mark III and Model 1910 (M10) rifles can be very dangerous to fire if bolt has been taken apart and incorrectly reassembled. DO NOT FIRE one of these rifles without having it examined by a gunsmith who is totally familiar with the Ross design.

Courtesy Buffalo Bill Historical Center, Cody, Wyoming

NIB	Exc.	V.G.	Good	Fair	Poor
—	1900	1550	1050	600	400

Mark III/M-10 Sporter Rifle

.280 Ross or .303-caliber straight-pull sporting rifle, with 24" barrel and open sights. Blued, with checkered walnut stock. **NOTE:** Mark III and Model 1910 (M10) rifles can be very dangerous to fire if bolt has been taken apart and incorrectly reassembled. DO NOT FIRE one of these rifles without having it examined by a gunsmith who is totally familiar with the Ross design.

Courtesy Buffalo Bill Historical Center, Cody, Wyoming

.280 Ross Caliber

NIB	Exc.	V.G.	Good	Fair	Poor
—	2000	1600	1100	600	400

.303 British Caliber

NIB	Exc.	V.G.	Good	Fair	Poor
—	1600	1250	850	400	300

ROSSI, AMADEO
São Leopoldo, Brazil

Rossi handguns are manufactured under license by Taurus.

SHOTGUNS

Overland Shotgun

An exposed hammer sidelock 12-, 20-gauge or .410 bore double-barrel shotgun, with 26" or 28" barrels and double triggers. Manual extractors. Blued, with walnut stock. Discontinued in 1988.

NIB	Exc.	V.G.	Good	Fair	Poor
250	225	200	150	100	75

Squire Shotgun

A 12-, 20-gauge or .410 bore double-barrel shotgun, with 20", 26" or 28" barrels, double triggers and manual ejectors. Blued, with walnut stock.

NIB	Exc.	V.G.	Good	Fair	Poor
350	300	250	200	150	100

Field Grade Shotgun

Single-shot tip-open gun, with oil-finish hardwood stock, low profile hammer and pistol-grip. No checkering. Offered in 12-, 20-gauge or .410 bore. Barrel length 28"; weight about; 5.25 lbs. 12- and 20-gauge; 4 lbs. .410 bore.

NIB	Exc.	V.G.	Good	Fair	Poor
115	75	50	25	—	10

Youth Model Shotgun

Same as above, with shorter length of pull and 22" barrel. Offered in 20-gauge and .410 bore only. Weight about: 5 lbs. 20-gauge; 3.75 lbs. .410 bore.

NIB	Exc.	V.G.	Good	Fair	Poor
115	75	50	25	—	10

Matched Pair Combo Guns

Model matches single-barrel shotgun, with .22 LR barrel. Offered in 12-/.22, 20-/.22 and .410/.22. Adjustable sights on rifle barrel. Blued finish.

NIB	Exc.	V.G.	Good	Fair	Poor
165	125	100	65	50	25

Stainless Matched Pair Combo Guns

Similar to above, with stainless barrel/receiver. Introduced 2008.

NIB	Exc.	V.G.	Good	Fair	Poor
200	165	125	100	75	50

Trifecta

Similar to Matched Pair, with black synthetic stock and blued barrel; includes easily interchangeable .243 Win. or .44 Magnum, .22 Long Rifle and 20-gauge barrels.

NIB	Exc.	V.G.	Good	Fair	Poor
300	250	200	150	100	75

Turkey Gun

Introduced in 2008. A specialized version of Roosi's 12-gauge single-shot shotgun. Features 3.5" chamber, fiber optic sights, drilled and tapped barrel, included scope mount base and removable Briley Extended Turkey Choke.

NIB	Exc.	V.G.	Good	Fair	Poor
200	165	125	100	75	50

Rossi Circuit Judge

Revolving shotgun chambered in .410 bore (2.5" or 3") .45 Colt. Based on Taurus Judge handgun. Features include 18.5" barrel; fiber optic front sight; 5-round cylinder; hardwood Monte Carlo stock.

NIB	Exc.	V.G.	Good	Fair	Poor
600	—	—	—	—	—

RIFLES

Model 62

Copy of Winchester Model 62 rifle. Round or octagonal 16.5" or 23" barrels. Blued or stainless steel, with walnut stock. Imported from 1988 to 1998.

NIB	Exc.	V.G.	Good	Fair	Poor
200	165	125	100	75	50

Model 59

As above, in .22 Magnum caliber.

NIB	Exc.	V.G.	Good	Fair	Poor
250	200	150	110	85	60

Model 92

Copy of Winchester Model 1892. Chambered for .357 Magnum, .44 Magnum, .45 Colt or .44-40. Barrels 16" or 20". Blued, with walnut stock. Engraved version of this model worth approximately 20 percent more than the values listed. **NOTE:** Add $75 for stainless steel version introduced in 1997.

NIB	Exc.	V.G.	Good	Fair	Poor
475	350	295	225	175	100

Model 92 Rifle

Introduced in 1997. Fitted with 24" half-octagon barrel and brass blade front sight. Magazine capacity 13 rounds of .45 Colt. Weight about 6.8 lbs.

NIB	Exc.	V.G.	Good	Fair	Poor
500	375	325	250	200	125

Rossi Rio Grande

Variation of Model 92. Chambered for .45-70 plus .410-bore shotshell. Side ejection and hammer extension allow a scope to be mounted easily. Scope-mounting rail is atop the receiver. Barrel is 20", with adjustable rear open sight, bead front. Hardwood stock with recoil pad. Cross bolt safety.

NIB	Exc.	V.G.	Good	Fair	Poor
500	400	350	275	200	100

Model 92 Large Loop

Has 16" barrel. Chambered for .44 Magnum or .45 Colt cartridge. Weight about 5.5 lbs. Finish is blue. Introduced in 1997.

NIB	Exc.	V.G.	Good	Fair	Poor
475	350	295	225	175	100

Model 65

Similar to Model 92. Chambered for .44 Special or .44 Magnum cartridge. Barrel length 20". Blued, with walnut stock. Introduced in 1989.

NIB	Exc.	V.G.	Good	Fair	Poor
500	375	325	250	200	125

Single-Shot Rifle

Offered in a variety of configurations. Chambered for .22 LR, .22 Magnum, .357 Magnum, .44 Magnum, .45 Colt, .223 Rem., .243-calibers. Fitted with 23" barrel, wood stock and choice of matte blue or stainless steel finish. Weight varies from 4.75 lbs. to 6.25 lbs. depending on caliber. **NOTE:** Add $30 for stainless steel; $10 for .357 and .44; $30 for .223 or .243.

NIB	Exc.	V.G.	Good	Fair	Poor
225	175	125	100	75	50

Single Shot Rifle—Heavy Barrel

Chambered for .223, .243, .22-250. Fitted with 23" heavy barrel and plain wood stock. Matte blue finish. Weight about 7 lbs. Introduced in 2005.

NIB	Exc.	V.G.	Good	Fair	Poor
230	175	125	100	75	50

Muzzleloading Rifle

Rifle has .50-caliber bore. Fitted with 23" barrel. Hardwood stock, with recoil pad. Weight about 6.3 lbs. Introduced in 2003. Blue or stainless steel. **NOTE:** Add $35 for matte stainless steel finish.

NIB	Exc.	V.G.	Good	Fair	Poor
165	130	100	75	50	25

Muzzleloader Matched Pair

A .50-caliber muzzle-loader, with an extra 20-gauge, .243 or .270 barrel. All matched pairs come with blued finish. Price listed for 20-gauge barrel. **NOTE:** Add $40 for .243; $150 for .270.

NIB	Exc.	V.G.	Good	Fair	Poor
250	200	150	100	75	50

Rossi Blued Synthetic Matched Pair

Single-shot combo outfit consisting of interchangeable rifle and shotgun barrels. Synthetic stock, blued barrel and receiver. Combinations include 12- or 20-gauge/.22LR, .22 WMR, .17 HMR, .223, .243, .270, .308, .30-06 and .410 bore/.22 LR or .410 bore/.17 HMR. Youth and full-size versions available.

NIB	Exc.	V.G.	Good	Fair	Poor
250	200	150	100	75	50

Rossi Stainless Synthetic Matched Pair

Single-shot combo outfit consisting of interchangeable rifle and shotgun barrels. Synthetic stock, stainless barrel and receiver. Combinations include 12- or 20-gauge/.22LR, .22 WMR, .17 HMR, .223, .243, .270, .308, .30-06 and .410 bore/.22 LR or .410 bore/.17 HMR. Youth and full-size versions available.

NIB	Exc.	V.G.	Good	Fair	Poor
275	225	165	115	90	50

Rossi Wizard

Single-shot rifle chambered in 23 different rimfire/centerfire/shotshell/muzzle-loading configurations. Features include drop-barrel action; quick tool-less barrel interchangeability; fiber optic front sight; adjustable rear sight, with barrel-mounted optics rail; hardwood or camo Monte Carlo stock.

NIB	Exc.	V.G.	Good	Fair	Poor
225	200	175	150	110	80

Rossi Ranch Hand

Based upon Rossi's R92 lever-action rifle. Calibers: .38/.357, .44 Magnum or .45 Colt. Barrel length 12"; overall length 24"; weight 4.9 lbs. (empty). Large loop lever 6-round tubular magazine, shortened hardwood buttstock. Open buckhorn rear sight, bead front. Blue or case-hardened carbon steel receiver, with saddle ring.

NIB	Exc.	V.G.	Good	Fair	Poor
450	400	325	250	200	100

HANDGUNS

Model 51

A .22-caliber double-action revolver, with 6" barrel, adjustable sights and 6-shot cylinder. Blued, with walnut grips. Imported prior to 1986.

NIB	Exc.	V.G.	Good	Fair	Poor
—	150	100	75	50	40

Model 511 Sportsman

As above, with 4" barrel. Made of stainless steel, with walnut grips. Introduced in 1986.

NIB	Exc.	V.G.	Good	Fair	Poor
225	200	150	125	100	75

Model 461

A 6-round revolver chambered for .357 Magnum cartridge. Fitted with 2" barrel. Rubber grips and blued finish. Weight about 26 oz.

NIB	Exc.	V.G.	Good	Fair	Poor
300	225	195	150	125	75

Model 462

Same as above, with stainless steel finish.

NIB	Exc.	V.G.	Good	Fair	Poor
350	275	225	165	140	90

Model 68S

This new version introduced in 1993. Features a shrouded ejector rod and fixed sights. Chambered for .38 Special cartridge. Offered with 2" or 3" barrel. Grips wood or rubber. Finish blue or nickel. Weight about 23 oz.

NIB	Exc.	V.G.	Good	Fair	Poor
175	150	125	100	75	60

Model 69

As above in .32 S&W caliber, with 3" barrel and 6-shot cylinder. Imported prior to 1986.

NIB	Exc.	V.G.	Good	Fair	Poor
—	125	100	75	50	40

Model 70

As above in .22-caliber, with 3" barrel and 6-shot cylinder. Imported prior to 1986.

NIB	Exc.	V.G.	Good	Fair	Poor
—	125	100	75	50	40

Model 84

Stainless steel .38 Special caliber double-action revolver, with ribbed 3" or 4" barrel. Blued, with walnut grips. Imported in 1985 and 1986.

NIB	Exc.	V.G.	Good	Fair	Poor
—	175	150	125	100	75

Model 851

As above, with 3" or 4" ventilated rib barrel and adjustable sights.

NIB	Exc.	V.G.	Good	Fair	Poor
200	175	150	125	100	75

Model 68

A .38 Special double-action revolver, with 2" or 3" barrel and 5-shot cylinder. Blued or nickel-plated, with walnut grips.

NIB	Exc.	V.G.	Good	Fair	Poor
225	175	150	125	100	75

Model 31

A .38 Special caliber double-action revolver, with 4" barrel and 5-shot cylinder. Blued or nickel-plated, with walnut grips. Imported prior to 1986.

NIB	Exc.	V.G.	Good	Fair	Poor
225	175	150	125	100	75

Model 677

First introduced in 1997. Chambered for .357 Magnum cartridge. Matte blue finish, with 2" barrel and black rubber grips. Weight about 26 oz.

NIB	Exc.	V.G.	Good	Fair	Poor
300	250	200	150	125	100

Model 88S

Introduced in 1993. This improved model has the same features of Model 68, with addition of a stainless finish. Chambered for .38 Special cartridge. Fitted with 2" or 3" barrel. Available with wood or rubber grips. Cylinder holds 5 cartridges. Weight about 22 oz.

NIB	Exc.	V.G.	Good	Fair	Poor
325	275	225	165	140	100

Model 351

Chambered for .38 Special +P cartridge. Fitted with 2" barrel and rubber grips. 5-round cylinder. Blued finish. Weight about 24 oz.

NIB	Exc.	V.G.	Good	Fair	Poor
300	250	200	150	125	100

Model 352

Same as above, with stainless steel finish.

NIB	Exc.	V.G.	Good	Fair	Poor
325	275	225	165	140	100

Model 951

A .38 Special caliber double-action revolver, with 3" or 4" ventilated rib barrel and 6-shot cylinder. Blued, with walnut grips. Introduced in 1985.

NIB	Exc.	V.G.	Good	Fair	Poor
300	250	200	150	125	100

Model 971

As above in .357 Magnum caliber, with solid ribbed 4" barrel and enclosed ejector rod. Adjustable sights. Blued, with walnut grips. Introduced in 1988.

NIB	Exc.	V.G.	Good	Fair	Poor
300	250	200	150	125	100

Model 971 Comp

Introduced in 1993. Similar to Model 971, with the addition of a compensator on 3.25" barrel. Overall length 9"; weight 32 oz. Chambered for .357 Magnum cartridge.

NIB	Exc.	V.G.	Good	Fair	Poor
335	265	200	150	125	100

Model 971 Comp Stainless

As above, but constructed of stainless steel with checkered black rubber grips. Introduced in 1989.

NIB	Exc.	V.G.	Good	Fair	Poor
350	275	225	150	125	100

Model 972

Revolver; 6-shot polished stainless double-action .357 Magnum. Adjust-

able rear sight and red insert on front sight. 6" barrel, rubber grip, 35 oz. Uses Taurus security system. Introduced 2006.

NIB	Exc.	V.G.	Good	Fair	Poor
375	295	250	150	125	100

Model 877

Introduced in 1996. This 6-shot revolver chambered for .357 Magnum cartridge. Fitted with 2" heavy barrel. Stainless steel, with black rubber grips. Weight about 26 oz.

NIB	Exc.	V.G.	Good	Fair	Poor
350	275	225	150	125	100

Model 89

As above in .32 S&W caliber, with 3" barrel.

NIB	Exc.	V.G.	Good	Fair	Poor
325	275	225	165	140	100

Model 971 VRC (vented rib compensator)

Introduced in 1996. Features choice of 2.5", 4" or 6" ventilated rib barrel, with integral compensator. Stainless steel, with black rubber grips. Weight from 30- to 39 oz. depending on barrel length.

NIB	Exc.	V.G.	Good	Fair	Poor
375	295	250	150	125	100

Model 988 Cyclops

Introduced in 1997. Chambered for .357 Magnum cartridge. Fitted with four recessed compensator ports on each side of muzzle. Offered in 6" or 8" barrel lengths. 6-shot double-action revolver. Weight about: 44 oz. 6" model; 51 oz. 8" model. Stainless steel finish.

Cyclops with scope mounted

NIB	Exc.	V.G.	Good	Fair	Poor
525	475	350	275	200	150

Model 720

Double-action revolver chambered for .44 Special. Features 5-round cylinder and 3" barrel. Overall length 8"; weight about 27.5 oz. Finish stainless steel.

NIB	Exc.	V.G.	Good	Fair	Poor
525	475	350	275	200	150

ROTH-SAUER

See—Sauer, J. P. & Son

ROTTWEIL

Rottweil, West Germany

Model 650

A 12-gauge over/under shotgun, with 28" ventilated rib barrels, screw-in choke tubes, single-selective trigger and automatic ejectors. Receiver engraved and case-hardened. Checkered stock of well figured walnut. Imported prior to 1987.

NIB	Exc.	V.G.	Good	Fair	Poor
—	900	700	550	425	150

Model 72

A 12-gauge over/under shotgun, with 28" ventilated rib barrels, screw-in choke tubes, single-selective trigger and automatic ejectors. Blued, with well figured checkered walnut stock. Imported prior to 1988.

NIB	Exc.	V.G.	Good	Fair	Poor
—	2200	1550	975	650	350

Model 72 American Skeet

As above, with 26.75" ventilated rib barrel, single-selective trigger and automatic ejectors. Receiver also engraved. Imported prior to 1988.

NIB	Exc.	V.G.	Good	Fair	Poor
—	2200	1550	975	650	350

Model 72 Adjustable American Trap

As above, with 34" ventilated rib barrel adjustable to point of impact. Imported prior to 1987.

NIB	Exc.	V.G.	Good	Fair	Poor
—	2200	1550	975	650	350

Model 72 American Trap

As above, without the barrel being adjustable to point of impact.

NIB	Exc.	V.G.	Good	Fair	Poor
—	2100	1450	875	550	300

Model 72 International Skeet

As above, with 26.75" ventilated rib barrels choked Skeet. Imported prior to 1988.

NIB	Exc.	V.G.	Good	Fair	Poor
—	2100	1450	875	550	300

Model 72 International Trap

As above, with 30" high ventilated rib barrels that are choked Improved, Modified and Full. Imported prior to 1988.

NIB	Exc.	V.G.	Good	Fair	Poor
—	2100	1450	875	550	300

ROYAL AMERICAN SHOTGUNS

Woodland Hills, California

Model 100

A 12- or 20-gauge over/under shotgun, with 26", 28" or 30" ventilated rib barrels, double triggers and extractors. Blued, with walnut stock. Imported from 1985 to 1987.

NIB	Exc.	V.G.	Good	Fair	Poor
—	550	375	250	175	150

Model 100AE

As above, with single trigger and automatic ejectors.

NIB	Exc.	V.G.	Good	Fair	Poor
—	650	475	275	200	175

Model 600

A 12-, 20-, 28-gauge or .410 bore double-barrel shotgun, with 25", 26", 28" or 30" ventilated rib barrels, double triggers and extractors. Blued, with walnut stock. Imported from 1985 to 1987.

NIB	Exc.	V.G.	Good	Fair	Poor
—	600	425	300	200	175

Model 800

A 28-gauge or .410 bore detachable sidelock double-barrel shotgun, with 24", 26" or 28" barrels, double triggers and automatic ejectors. Blued French case-hardened, with English-style walnut stock. Imported from 1985 to 1987.

NIB	Exc.	V.G.	Good	Fair	Poor
—	1550	1200	900	675	400

RUBY ARMS COMPANY
Guernica, Spain

Ruby

A 6.35mm or 7.35mm caliber semi-automatic pistol, with 3.5" barrel and 6-shot magazine. Slide marked "Ruby". Blued, with plastic grips.

NIB	Exc.	V.G.	Good	Fair	Poor
—	275	175	125	75	50

RUGER
See—Sturm, Ruger Co.

RUPERTUS, JACOB
Philadelphia, Pennsylvania

Navy Revolver

This model equally as rare as Army model. Chambered for .36-caliber percussion. Otherwise, quite similar in appearance to Army model. Approximately 12 manufactured in 1859. Both of these revolvers were manufactured for test purposes and were not well-received by the military, so further production was not accomplished.

NIB	Exc.	V.G.	Good	Fair	Poor
—	—	15000	11750	5500	1250

Pocket Model Revolver

Smaller version of Army and Navy model. Chambered for .25-caliber percussion. It has no loading lever but has a 3.125" octagonal barrel. Approximately 12 manufactured in 1859.

NIB	Exc.	V.G.	Good	Fair	Poor
—	—	11000	8250	3600	950

Double-Barrel Pocket Pistol

A .22-caliber double-barrel pistol, with 3" round barrels and a spur trigger. Hammer fitted with a sliding firing pin. Blued, with walnut grips.

NIB	Exc.	V.G.	Good	Fair	Poor
—	—	2400	1900	850	200

Army Revolver

An extremely rare revolver. Chambered for .44-caliber percussion. Has a 7.25" octagon barrel, with an integral loading lever that pivots to the side instead of downward. Hammer is mounted on the side and there is a pellet priming device located on the backstrap. There is only one nipple on the breech that lines up with top of the cylinder. Cylinder is unfluted and holds 6-shots. Finish is blued, with walnut grips; frame marked "Patented April 19, 1859". There were less than 12 manufactured in 1859. It would behoove one to secure a qualified independent appraisal if a transaction were contemplated.

Courtesy Greg Martin Auctions

NIB	Exc.	V.G.	Good	Fair	Poor
—	—	28500	12000	5500	1500

Single-Shot Pocket Pistol

A .22, .32, .38 or .41 rimfire single-shot pistol, with half-octagonal barrels ranging in length from 3" to 5". Barrel marked "Rupertus Pat'd. Pistol Mfg. Co. Philadelphia". Blued, with walnut grips. Approximately 3,000 made from 1870 to 1885. **NOTE:** The .41-caliber variety is worth approximately 200 percent more than the values listed.

NIB	Exc.	V.G.	Good	Fair	Poor
—	—	900	650	225	75

Spur Trigger Revolver

A .22-caliber revolver, with 2.75" barrel and unfluted 7-shot cylinder. Top strap marked "Empire Pat., Nov. 21, 71". Blued or nickel-plated, with walnut grips. Also made in .32 and .32 rimfire, with 5-shot semi-fluted cylinder. A larger model in .41 rimfire with 5-shot semi-fluted cylinder was made with top strap marked "Empire 41". Made during 1870s and 1880s. **NOTE:** Add 20 percent for .41-caliber.

NIB	Exc.	V.G.	Good	Fair	Poor
—	—	450	250	175	100

RWS
Dynamit Nobel
Nurenberg, Germany

Model 820 S

A .22-caliber target rifle, with 24" heavy barrel and adjustable aperture sights. Trigger is fully adjustable. Three-position adjustable match stock, with stippled pistol-grip and fore-end. Discontinued in 1986.

NIB	Exc.	V.G.	Good	Fair	Poor
1650	1275	975	625	450	250

Model 820 SF

As above, with a heavier barrel. Discontinued in 1986.

NIB	Exc.	V.G.	Good	Fair	Poor
1700	1350	1000	550	400	250

Model 820 K

Offhand "Running Boar" model of above, with lighter barrel. Furnished without sights. Discontinued in 1986.

NIB	Exc.	V.G.	Good	Fair	Poor
1700	1350	1000	550	400	250

S

S.A.E.
Miami, Florida

S.A.E. was an importer of Spanish shotguns, some of very fine quality. Most notable of these is the S.A.E. line of Sarasqueta shotguns from Eibar, Spain. Not all S.A.E. shotguns are marked with the maker's name.

Model 210S

A 12-, 20-gauge or .410 bore double-barrel shotgun, with 26" or 28" barrels. Double triggers and manual extractors. Blued French case-hardened, with checkered walnut stock. Imported in 1988.

NIB	Exc.	V.G.	Good	Fair	Poor
—	475	395	300	225	150

Model 340X

Holland & Holland-style sidelock 10- or 20-gauge double-barrel shotgun, with 26" barrels. Double triggers and automatic ejectors. Blued case-hardened, with checkered English style walnut stock. Imported in 1988.

NIB	Exc.	V.G.	Good	Fair	Poor
—	850	675	500	400	200

Model 209E

As above, except also chambered for .410 bore cartridges and more finely engraved. Imported in 1988.

NIB	Exc.	V.G.	Good	Fair	Poor
—	1100	850	700	550	250

Model 70

A 12- or 20-gauge over/under shotgun, with 26" ventilated rib barrels, screw-in choke tubes, single trigger and automatic ejectors. Modestly engraved receiver is blued or French case-hardened. Stock of finely figured walnut. Imported in 1988.

NIB	Exc.	V.G.	Good	Fair	Poor
—	500	375	250	200	100

Model 66C

12-gauge over/under shotgun, with 26" or 30" ventilated rib barrels choked for skeet or trap, single trigger and automatic ejectors. Boxlock action fitted with false sideplates, which are engraved and gold inlaid. Blued, with checkered Monte Carlo-style stock and beavertail forearm. Imported in 1988.

NIB	Exc.	V.G.	Good	Fair	Poor
—	1100	850	700	575	300

S.E.A.M.
Eibar, Spain

This retailer sold a number of pistols produced by the firm of Urizar, prior to 1935.

Praga

A 7.65-caliber semi-automatic pistol marked "Praga Cal 7.65" on the slide. Blued, with plastic grips impressed with trademark "S.E.A.M.".

NIB	Exc.	V.G.	Good	Fair	Poor
—	275	175	125	90	65

S.E.A.M.

A 6.35mm semi-automatic pistol, with 2" barrel. Slide marked "Fabrica de Armas SEAM". Blued, with black plastic grips having trademark "SEAM" cast into them.

NIB	Exc.	V.G.	Good	Fair	Poor
—	250	175	125	90	65

Silesia

As above in 7.65mm caliber, with 3" barrel. Slide stamped with "Silesia".

NIB	Exc.	V.G.	Good	Fair	Poor
—	250	175	125	90	65

S.W.D., INC.
Atlanta, Georgia

Cobray M-11

A 9mm semi-automatic pistol, with 32-round magazine. Parkerized finish.

NIB	Exc.	V.G.	Good	Fair	Poor
—	550	495	400	275	100

M-11 Carbine

As above, with 16.25" barrel enclosed in a shroud. Fitted with a telescoping wire stock.

NIB	Exc.	V.G.	Good	Fair	Poor
—	800	650	550	275	100

Terminator

A 12- or 20-gauge single-shot shotgun, with 18" cylinder bored barrel. Parkerized finish. Said to be exceptionally rare, but attracts little interest.

NIB	Exc.	V.G.	Good	Fair	Poor
—	150	80	70	60	50

SABATTI
See—European American Armory Corp.

SACKET, D. D.
Westfield, Massachusetts

Under Hammer Pistol

A .34- or .36-caliber single-shot percussion pistol, with half octagonal 3" or 4" barrel marked "D. D. Sacket/Westfield/Cast Steel". Manufactured during 1850s.

NIB	Exc.	V.G.	Good	Fair	Poor
—	—	1550	1200	550	165

SAFARI ARMS
Phoenix, Arizona

In operation from 1978 to 1987. Company was purchased by Olympic Arms of Olympia, Washington, in 1987. The models listed were produced by that company under the Safari name until 2004, when most were rebranded under Olympic Arms.

Enforcer

A .45-caliber semi-automatic pistol, with 3.9" barrel and 5-shot magazine. Patterned after Colt Model 1911. Blued, Armaloy, electroless nickel-plate or Parkerized finish, with checkered walnut or neoprene grips.

NIB	Exc.	V.G.	Good	Fair	Poor
700	600	500	400	350	150

Match Master

As above, with 5" barrel.

NIB	Exc.	V.G.	Good	Fair	Poor
700	600	500	400	350	150

Black Widow

As above, with ivory Micarta grips etched with a black widow.

NIB	Exc.	V.G.	Good	Fair	Poor
700	600	500	400	350	150

Model 81

As above, without grip etching. Also offered in .38-caliber.

NIB	Exc.	V.G.	Good	Fair	Poor
800	700	600	500	400	200

Model 81L

As above, with 6" barrel.

NIB	Exc.	V.G.	Good	Fair	Poor
850	750	650	550	450	200

Ultimate Unlimited

Bolt-action single-shot pistol, with 15" barrel. Chambered for a variety of cartridges. Blued, with laminated stock.

NIB	Exc.	V.G.	Good	Fair	Poor
850	750	650	550	450	200

Survivor I Conversion Unit

Conversion unit lifted to Model 1911 frame that alters that pistol to a bolt-action carbine. Barrel length 16.25", caliber .223, folding stock.

NIB	Exc.	V.G.	Good	Fair	Poor
300	275	250	200	150	100

Counter Sniper Rifle

A .308-caliber bolt-action target rifle, with heavy 26" barrel and 20-round detachable magazine. Matte blued, with colored composite stock.

NIB	Exc.	V.G.	Good	Fair	Poor
1200	1050	850	650	450	200

SAIGA
Izhevsk, Russia

A series of AK type rifles and shotguns manufactured in Russia by Izhmash.

RIFLES

Model IZ-114, AZ-132

Kalashnikov-type semi-automatic rifle chambered in .223 Rem. (IZ-114) or 7.62x39mm (IZ-132). Black synthetic or wood stock and forearm, 16" or 20.5" barrel. Imported by several companies including EAA, U.S. Sporting Goods and others.

NIB	Exc.	V.G.	Good	Fair	Poor
550	450	300	225	200	150

Model AZ-139

Same as above, except in .308 Win. and 22" barrel.

NIB	Exc.	V.G.	Good	Fair	Poor
750	650	500	300	250	150

Model 100

Hunting style semi-automatic rifle, with synthetic stock in .223, 7.62x39, .308 or .30-06. Magazine capacity 3 or 10 rounds.

NIB	Exc.	V.G.	Good	Fair	Poor
685	600	500	350	250	150

SGL 21/31

Russian-made series with stamped receivers, Warsaw or NATO stock in Desert Sand, OD Green or Plum finish. Black polymer folding stock available. Features include bayonet lug, double-stage trigger, scope rail. Chambered for 7.62x39mm (21) or 5.45x39mm (31). **NOTE:** Add $400 for SGL 31.

NIB	Exc.	V.G.	Good	Fair	Poor
800	700	550	400	300	200

SHOTGUNS

Model 109

Semi-automatic shotgun based on AK-47 design. In 12-, 20-gauge or .410 bore. Black synthetic stock and forearm, 5- or 10-shot magazine. **NOTE:** Add $75 for .410 bore.

NIB	Exc.	V.G.	Good	Fair	Poor
750	625	500	375	250	200

SAKO
Riihimaki, Finland

NOTE: Arms produced by this company prior to 1972 are worth approximately 25 percent more than arms of the same type produced thereafter. Prices for fair and poor condition reflect worth of the action. In 2000, Beretta Holding Co. purchased Sako and distributes product line through Beretta U.S.A.

Standard Sporter

Bolt-action magazine rifle produced in a wide variety of calibers, with varying barrel lengths, etc. Blued, with checkered walnut stocks.

NIB	Exc.	V.G.	Good	Fair	Poor
—	750	650	450	400	300

Deluxe Model

As above, with engraved floorplate and checkered Monte Carlo-style stock. Featuring rosewood pistol-grip cap and fore-end tip.

NIB	Exc.	V.G.	Good	Fair	Poor
—	900	750	600	450	400

Finnbear

As above, with a long action available in a variety of large bore calibers. Fitted with 20" or 23.5" barrel. Blued, with checkered stock. For .458 Win. Magnum (only 20 produced), values double. **NOTE:** Add 15 percent for other Magnum chamberings or Deluxe version; 20 percent for Mannlicher Carbine version.

NIB	Exc.	V.G.	Good	Fair	Poor
—	1000	850	650	400	300

Forester

As above, with a shorter action suitable for use with intermediate cartridges. **NOTE:** Add 20 percent for Mannlicher Carbine version.

NIB	Exc.	V.G.	Good	Fair	Poor
—	1000	850	650	400	300

Vixen

As above, with a short action. **NOTE:** Add 20 percent for Mannlicher Carbine version.

NIB	Exc.	V.G.	Good	Fair	Poor
—	1000	850	650	400	300

FN Action

Manufactured from 1950 to 1957. This model utilized a Fabrique Nationale manufactured receiver. Chambered for .270 Win. and .30-06 cartridges. Otherwise, as above.

NIB	Exc.	V.G.	Good	Fair	Poor
—	800	600	475	400	300

FN Magnum Action

As above, with a long action for .300 and .375 H&H.

NIB	Exc.	V.G.	Good	Fair	Poor
—	900	700	550	400	300

Anniversary Model

A 7mm Rem. Magnum bolt-action rifle, with 24" barrel. Blued, checkered walnut stock. A total of 1,000 manufactured. As with any commemorative firearm, this model should be NIB to realize its full resale potential.

NIB	Exc.	V.G.	Good	Fair	Poor
2500	850	750	450	400	300

Finnwolf

A 4-shot lever-action rifle produced in .243- and .308-calibers. Blued, checkered walnut stock. Manufactured from 1962 to 1974.

NIB	Exc.	V.G.	Good	Fair	Poor
—	1400	1200	750	450	300

Finnfire

Bolt-action rifle chambered for .22 LR cartridge. Fitted with 22" barrel and choice of iron or no sights. European walnut stock. A 5-shot detachable magazine is standard. Weight about 5.25 lbs.

Courtesy Stoeger

NIB	Exc.	V.G.	Good	Fair	Poor
1150	950	700	575	400	300

Finnfire Heavy Barrel

Same as above, with a heavy barrel.

Courtesy Stoeger

NIB	Exc.	V.G.	Good	Fair	Poor
1150	950	700	575	400	300

Finnfire Hunter

Introduced in 2000. Bolt-action model chambered for .22 LR cartridge. Fitted with 22" barrel and Sako 75 style select walnut stock. Weight about 5.75 lbs.

NIB	Exc.	V.G.	Good	Fair	Poor
1150	950	700	575	400	300

Finnfire Sporter

Chambered for .22 LR cartridge and built on P94S action. Has a walnut stock, with adjustable cheekpiece and buttplate spacer system that allows for length of pull and buttplate angle adjustment. Trigger is adjustable. Introduced in 1999.

NIB	Exc.	V.G.	Good	Fair	Poor
1150	950	700	575	400	300

Sako Quad Combo

Introduced in 2005. Bolt-action rifle features four interchangeable barrels in four different rimfire calibers. Black synthetic stock. Detachable 5-round magazine. Included barrels are: .22 Long Rifle; .22 WMR; .17 HMR; .17 Mach 2. All 22" in length. Blued finish. Weight about 5.75 lbs. **NOTE:** NIB price for rifles with only one barrel is $948. Extra barrels are $260 each.

NIB	Exc.	V.G.	Good	Fair	Poor
1450	1300	1075	800	500	300

Hunter

Offered in three action lengths: short; medium; long. Short action calibers available are: .17 Rem., .222, .223 in 21.25" barrel. Medium action calibers are: .22-250, .243, .308 and 7mm-08 in 21.75" barrel. Long action calibers are: .25-06, .270 Win., .280 Rem., .30-06 for 22" barrel length. In 24" barrel the long action calibers are: 7mm Rem. Magnum, .300 Win. and .300 Wby. Magnum, .338 and .375 Win. Magnum and .416 Rem. Magnum. In 1996, .270 Wthby Magnum, 7mm Wthby Magnum and .340 Wthby were added to the long action calibers. Available in left-handed version for all but short action calibers. Adjustable trigger is standard. Checkered European walnut stock. Weight for short action 6.25 lbs.; medium action 6.5 lbs.; long action 7.75 to 8.25 depending on caliber.

Medium Action

NIB	Exc.	V.G.	Good	Fair	Poor
1200	1050	875	600	500	300

Short Action

NOTE: Add 10 percent to Medium Action prices for .222 Rem. and .223 Rem.; 20 percent to Medium Action prices for .17 Rem.

Long Action

NOTE: Add 10 percent for long action calibers in .300 and .338 Win. Magnum; 20 percent for .375 H&H Magnum; 25 percent for .416 Rem. Magnum.

NIB	Exc.	V.G.	Good	Fair	Poor
1400	1175	1000	750	600	300

Carbine

As above, with 18.5" barrel. Produced with medium or long-length action.

NIB	Exc.	V.G.	Good	Fair	Poor
1200	1050	875	600	500	300

Long Range Hunting Rifle

Similar to long action Hunter. Fitted with 26" fluted barrel. Chambered for .25-06, .270 Win., 7mm Rem. Magnum and .300 Win. Magnum. Intro-duced in 1996. **NOTE:** Add 10 percent to medium action prices for .222 Rem. and .223 Rem.; 20 percent to medium action prices for .17 Rem.

NIB	Exc.	V.G.	Good	Fair	Poor
1500	1300	1050	875	650	300

Laminated Model

Features laminated checkered hardwood stock made up of 36 layers. Solid recoil pad is standard as are quick detachable sling swivels. Available in both medium and long action calibers. Medium action calibers are: .22-250, .243, .308 and 7mm-08 with 21.75" barrel; weight of 6.5 lbs. Long action calibers are: .25-06, .270, .280, .30-06 with 22" barrel; weight of 7.75 lbs. Offered with 24" barrels are: 7mm Rem. Magnum, .300, .338 Win. Magnum and .375 H&H ; weight 7.75 lbs.

Medium Action

NOTE: Add 10 percent to prices for .222 Rem. and .223 Rem.; 20 percent for .17 Rem.

NIB	Exc.	V.G.	Good	Fair	Poor
1200	1050	875	600	500	300

Long Action

NOTE: Add 10 percent for long action calibers in .300 and .338 Win. Magnum; 20 percent for .375 H&H Magnum; 25 percent for .416 Rem. Magnum.

NIB	Exc.	V.G.	Good	Fair	Poor
1400	1175	1000	750	600	300

FiberClass

Features a black plain fiberglass stock. Offered in long action calibers only. The .25-06, .270, .280 and .30-06 are fitted with 22" barrels; weight 7.25 lbs. The 7mm Rem. Magnum, .300 Win. Magnum, .338 Win. Magnum and .375 H&H are fitted with 24" barrel; weight 7.25 lbs. The .416 Rem. Magnum has a 24" barrel; weight 8 lbs. **NOTE:** Add 10 percent for long action calibers in .300 and .338 Win. Magnum; 20 percent for .375 H&H Magnum; 25 percent for .416 Rem. Magnum.

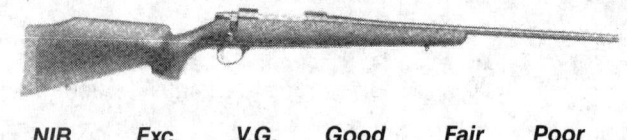

NIB	Exc.	V.G.	Good	Fair	Poor
1050	800	600	500	400	400

FiberClass Carbine

As above, with a fiberglass stock.

NIB	Exc.	V.G.	Good	Fair	Poor
1050	800	600	500	400	400

Carbine

Features a Mannlicher-style stock, with two-piece forearm. Has a checkered walnut stock, with oil-finish. Offered in both medium and short actions, all with 18.5" barrels. Medium action .243 and .308; weight 6 lbs.; long action calibers .270 and .30-06; weight 7.25 lbs.; .338 Win. Magnum and .375 H weight 7.75 lbs. **NOTE:** Add 10 percent for long action calibers in .338 Win. Magnum; 20 percent for .375 H&H Magnum.

Medium Action

NIB	Exc.	V.G.	Good	Fair	Poor
1200	1050	875	600	500	300

Long Action

NOTE: Add 10 percent for long action calibers in .338 Win. Magnum; 20 percent for .375 H&H Magnum.

NIB	Exc.	V.G.	Good	Fair	Poor
1200	1050	875	600	500	300

Varmint-Heavy Barrel

Checkered walnut stock features an extra wide beavertail forearm, with oil-finish. Offered in both short and medium action. All are fitted with 23" heavy barrel weighing 8.5 lbs. Short action calibers are: .17 Rem., .222 and .223; medium action calibers are: .22-250, .243, .308 and 7mm-08.

Short Action

NOTE: Add 10 percent for .222 and .223 Rem.; 20 percent for .17 Rem.

NIB	Exc.	V.G.	Good	Fair	Poor
1200	1050	875	600	500	300

Medium Action

NIB	Exc.	V.G.	Good	Fair	Poor
1200	1050	875	600	500	300

PPC Bench Rest/Varmint

Similar to Varmint but single-shot. Fitted with 23.75" barrel. Weight 8.75 lbs. Available in short action special calibers .22 PPC and 6mm PPC.

NIB	Exc.	V.G.	Good	Fair	Poor
1350	1150	975	650	500	300

Classic Grade

Hand-checkered select walnut stock, with matte lacquer finish is featured on this grade. Offered in medium and long action. Long action rifles are offered in left-hand model. Medium action caliber is .243 Win., with 21.75" barrel; weight 6 lbs. Long action calibers: .270, .30-06 and 7mm Rem. Magnum. with 24" barrels; weight about 7.5 lbs.

NIB	Exc.	V.G.	Good	Fair	Poor
1200	1050	875	600	500	300

Deluxe Grade

Features a high grade European walnut stock, with hand cut basket weave checkering. Fore-end tip and grip are fitted with rosewood. English-style recoil pad is standard. Long action models are offered in left-hand configuration. Like the Hunter model short, medium and long actions are available in the same calibers, barrel lengths and weights..

Medium Action

NIB	Exc.	V.G.	Good	Fair	Poor
1400	1175	1000	750	600	300

Short Action

NOTE: Add 10 percent for .222 and .223 Rem.; 20 percent for .17 Rem.

Long Action

NOTE: Add 10 percent for long action calibers in .300 and .338 Win. Magnum; 20 percent for .375 H&H Magnum; 25 percent for .416 Rem. Magnum; $100 for left-hand models.

NIB	Exc.	V.G.	Good	Fair	Poor
1400	1175	1000	750	600	300

Super Grade/Super Deluxe

Similar to Deluxe Grade. Offered with fancy walnut stock and oak-leaf carving. Floor plate and trigger guard are engraved. Pistol-grip cap has inlaid silver plate. Offered in same actions and calibers as Hunter and Deluxe Grades.

Medium Action

NIB	Exc.	V.G.	Good	Fair	Poor
2500	1750	1200	750	625	300

Short Action

NOTE: Add 10 percent for .222 and .223 Rem.

Long Action

NOTE: Add 10 percent for long action calibers in .300 and .338 Win. Magnum; 20 percent for .375 H&H Magnum; 25 percent for .416 Rem. Magnum.

NIB	Exc.	V.G.	Good	Fair	Poor
2500	1750	1200	750	625	300

Safari Grade

As above, chambered for .300 Win. Magnum, .338 Win. Magnum or .375 H&H cartridges.

NIB	Exc.	V.G.	Good	Fair	Poor
2700	2500	1900	1100	800	400

MODEL 75 SERIES

Introduced in March 1997. Based on a new design by Sako. Each of the five different action sizes is manufactured for a specific range of calibers. Its action, barrel and stocks are all redesigned components. Offered in a variety of configurations and calibers. Sako actions are offered separately in carbon steel, white and stainless steel.

Model 75 Hunter

Available in five different action sizes for calibers from .17 Rem. to .416 Rem. Magnum. Weight varies from 6.37 lbs. to 9 lbs. Barrel lengths from 22" to 24.37". Choice of checkered walnut stock or black synthetic stock. All Hunter models are sold without sights as standard, but open sights are an option. Magazine is detachable except for .300 Rem. Ultra Magnum and .416 Rem. Magnum. Single-set trigger is an option. In 2003, a left-hand model was offered in .270 Win and .30-06. In 2004, .270 WSM and .300 WSM calibers were added. **NOTE:** Add $30 for long action calibers from .270 to .416.

NIB	Exc.	V.G.	Good	Fair	Poor
1425	1050	700	500	400	300

Model 75 Stainless Synthetic

Same as above, but available with synthetic stock and stainless steel barrel and action. Offered in calibers from .22-250 to .375 H&H. **NOTE:** Add $30 for long action calibers.

NIB	Exc.	V.G.	Good	Fair	Poor
1500	1100	750	600	400	300

Model 75 Deluxe

Features all the elements of Hunter model. Plus, special checkering on select walnut stock with special black finish. All models have a hinged floor plate. In 2004, .270 WSM and .300 WSM calibers were added. Weight about 7.75 lbs. **NOTE:** Add $100 for long action calibers.

NIB	Exc.	V.G.	Good	Fair	Poor
1600	1050	800	700	500	400

Model 75 Big Game Deluxe

Similar to M75 Deluxe, except chambered for .416 Rem. Magnum cartridge. Fitted with iron sights.

NIB	Exc.	V.G.	Good	Fair	Poor
1600	1050	800	700	500	400

Model 75 Varmint

Chambered for .17 Rem., .222 Rem., .223 and .22-250, all with 24" heavy barrels. In 1999, Sako added .22 PPC and 6mm PPC calibers. Other calibers are .260 Rem., .308 and .204 Ruger. Weight about 8.4 lbs. Walnut stock.

NIB	Exc.	V.G.	Good	Fair	Poor
1250	950	750	600	450	400

Model 75 Varmint Set Trigger

As above, with single-set trigger. Introduced in 2005.

NIB	Exc.	V.G.	Good	Fair	Poor
1550	1100	875	700	500	400

Model 75 Varmint Stainless

Introduced in 1999. Similar to Varmint 75, with stainless steel barrel. Magazine is detachable, but can be loaded through the ejection port. Trigger is adjustable. Offered in all calibers as the standard Model 75 Varmint. Weights vary from about 8 lbs. to 8.6 lbs. Stock is laminated.

NIB	Exc.	V.G.	Good	Fair	Poor
1200	1050	875	600	500	300

Model 75 Varmint Stainless Set Trigger

As above, with stainless steel barrel and receiver. Laminated stock. Weight about 9 lbs. Introduced in 2005.

NIB	Exc.	V.G.	Good	Fair	Poor
1400	1175	1000	750	600	300

Model 75 Finnlight

Introduced in 2001. Bolt-action rifle features short, medium and long action calibers. Stainless steel barrel lengths from 20.25" to 22.5" depending on caliber. Barrels are fluted. Synthetic stock. Weight about 6.5 lbs. depending on caliber. In 2003, offered in .300 WSM caliber.

NIB	Exc.	V.G.	Good	Fair	Poor
1300	1075	900	650	500	300

Model 75 Grey Wolf

Bolt-action rifle chambered for a wide variety of calibers from .223 to 7mm WSM. Stainless steel barrel 22.5" or 24.3" depending on caliber, without sights. Gray stock laminated and checkered. Rubber recoil pad. Detachable magazine. Weight about 7.75 lbs. depending on caliber. Introduced in 2005.

NIB	Exc.	V.G.	Good	Fair	Poor
1400	1175	1000	750	600	300

Model 75 Custom Deluxe

Introduced in 2003. Features an oil-finished premium-grade walnut stock, with a special fine-line checkering pattern. Factory recoil pad. Chambered for .270 Win or .30-06 cartridges.

NIB	Exc.	V.G.	Good	Fair	Poor
3250	2500	1900	1100	800	400

Model 75 Custom Single Shot

Introduced in 2004. Single-shot model chambered for .308 cartridge. Fitted with 23.625" heavy fluted stainless steel barrel, without sights. Checkered laminated stock, with beavertail forearm. Weight about 9 lbs.

NIB	Exc.	V.G.	Good	Fair	Poor
3250	2500	1900	1100	550	400

Model 75 Super Deluxe

A special order rifle. Advise obtaining an expert opinion before a sale. Prices listed are for the base rifle.

NIB	Exc.	V.G.	Good	Fair	Poor
2500	2100	1600	1275	600	400

Model 78

A .22 or .22 Hornet bolt-action rifle, with 22" barrel. Blued, with checkered walnut stock. Discontinued in 1986.

NIB	Exc.	V.G.	Good	Fair	Poor
—	850	675	500	375	250

Model 2700 Finnsport

A .270 to .300 Win. Magnum bolt-action rifle, with 22" barrel. Blued, checkered walnut stock. Discontinued in 1985.

NIB	Exc.	V.G.	Good	Fair	Poor
—	900	750	600	475	200

Safari 80th Anniversary Model

Limited edition rifle. Built on Sako 75 Magnum long action. Chambered for .375 H&H cartridge. Match grade heavy barrel. Select grade walnut stock, with straight comb and ebony fore-end tip. Quarter rib. Equipped with Swarovski PV-1 1.25x24 scope. Engraved floor plate. Supplied with hand-made leather case, with cleaning accessories. Limited to 80 rifles worldwide. Serial numbers 200101 to 200180.

NIB	Exc.	V.G.	Good	Fair	Poor
15950	12500	8500	—	—	—

Sako 85 Hunter

Bolt-action centerfire rifle. Chambered in short and long calibers ranging from .223 Rem. to .375 H&H Magnum. Controlled round feeding. Checkered walnut stock. Satin blued sightless 22.4375", 22.875" or 24.375" barrel. Introduced in 2007. **NOTE:** Add 30 percent premium for .375.

NIB	Exc.	V.G.	Good	Fair	Poor
1100	900	775	600	475	300

Sako 85 Stainless Synthetic

Similar to Sako 85 Hunter, with stainless steel receiver and barrel. Introduced 2007, discontinued 2008.

NIB	Exc.	V.G.	Good	Fair	Poor
1200	1000	875	650	525	350

Sako 85 Synthetic

Similar to 85 Hunter, with coated black synthetic stock and black matte metal finish. Chambered in 6.5x55, .270 Win., .308 Win., .30-06. Introduced in 2014.

NIB	Exc.	V.G.	Good	Fair	Poor
1500	1250	950	650	400	250

Sako 85 Finnlight

Similar to Sako 85 Stainless Synthetic, with recoil pad and ultra-lightweight synthetic stock. Chambered in long and short cartridges ranging from .243 to .300 Win. Magnum. Introduced 2007.

NIB	Exc.	V.G.	Good	Fair	Poor
1550	1100	875	700	500	400

Sako 85 Varmint

Similar to Sako 85 Hunter, with recoil pad and 7.5 oz. set trigger. Chambered in .204 Ruger, .243, .22-250 or .308. Introduced 2007.

NIB	Exc.	V.G.	Good	Fair	Poor
1300	1075	900	650	500	300

Sako 85 Laminated SS Varmint

Similar to Sako 85 Varmint, with laminated stock and stainless steel barrel. Introduced 2007.

NIB	Exc.	V.G.	Good	Fair	Poor
1400	1175	1000	750	600	300

A-7 American Bolt-Action Rifle

Bolt-action rifle chambered in .22-250, .243 Win., .25-06, .260 Rem., .270 Win., .270 WSM, .300 WSM, .30-06, .300 WM, .308 Win., .338 Federal, .7mm Rem. Magnum, 7mm-08. Features include blued or stainless barrel (22.4375" standard, 24.375" Magnum) and receiver, black composite stock with sling swivels and recoil pad, two-position safety, adjustable trigger, detachable 3+1 box magazine. Weight 6.3 lbs. to 6.13 lbs.

NIB	Exc.	V.G.	Good	Fair	Poor
850	725	575	400	300	200

A-7 Big Game Roughtech

Same features as A-7 American, with Roughtech synthetic pistol-grip stock and fluted or heavy barrel. Chambered in .270 Win., 7mm Rem. Magnum, .308 Win., 30-06, .300 Win. Magnum.

NIB	Exc.	V.G.	Good	Fair	Poor
1000	875	700	550	400	250

A-7 Long Range Roughtech

Similar to Big Game Roughtech, with 26" barrel and wide fore-end. Chambered in .25-06, 7mm Rem. Magnum, .308 Win., .300 Win. Magnum. Introduced in 2016.

NIB	Exc.	V.G.	Good	Fair	Poor
1250	1000	900	—	—	—

A-7 Tecomate

Chambered in .270 WSM (23" barrel) or .300 WSM (24.25") barrel. Magazine capacity 4 rounds. Features a new Bell & Carlson Medalist composite stock. Integral aluminum bedding system CNC produced from aircraft quality 6061-T6 aluminum. Flat bottom receiver. Stainless action. Introduced in 2011.

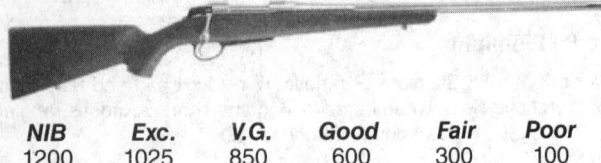

NIB	Exc.	V.G.	Good	Fair	Poor
1200	1025	850	600	300	100

Sako Classic Deluxe

High grade version of Model 85. Oil-finished walnut stock, with palm swell and cheekpiece, pronounced pistol-grip, rosewood pistol and fore-end tip. Barrel band for sling swivel. Free-floating barrel. All metal parts are highly polished and blued. Medium or long action depending upon caliber. Adjustable trigger. Open sights are available. Five cartridges available to include .270 Win., 7x64, .30-06, .370 Sako Magnum and .375 H&H. Introduced in 2011.

NIB	Exc.	V.G.	Good	Fair	Poor
3450	3100	2600	2000	1600	500

Sako 85 Bavarian

Available in full length (shown) or carbine style. Offered in most standard calibers, plus 6.5x55 Swedish. Comes with set trigger and adjustable express sights. Stock is oil-finished high-grade checkered walnut, with rosewood grip and fore-end caps. Carbine has full-length Mannlicher-style stock, with Bavarian-style comb and cheekpiece. **NOTE:** Add 15 percent for Carbine model.

NIB	Exc.	V.G.	Good	Fair	Poor
1950	1750	1400	1000	750	250

Sako 85 Kodiak

Weatherproof design has stainless steel barrel and action. Gray laminated stock reinforced with two crossbolts. Free-floating bull barrel in 21", 22.5" or 24.3" lengths. Offered in calibers from .22-250 to .375 H&H.

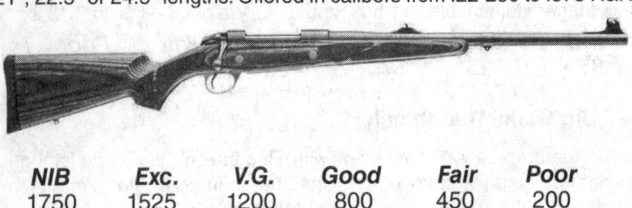

NIB	Exc.	V.G.	Good	Fair	Poor
1750	1525	1200	800	450	200

Sako Black Bear Series

Model 85 variation available in short and medium actions only. Short action chambered in .308 Win. or .338 Federal; medium action in .30-06, 8x57 JS, 9.3x62 and 9.3x66 (.370) Sako. Controlled feeding, detachable magazine, single-stage adjustable trigger. Black injection molded stock, with Soft Touch areas around pistol-grip and fore-end. Open sights are available. Scope can be mounted to integral Sako mounting system on receiver. Bull barrel, free-floating and hammer forged. Brown Bear model has similar features, but with brown laminated hardwood stock. Chambered in .338 Win. Magnum or .375 H&H. Introduced in 2011.

NIB	Exc.	V.G.	Good	Fair	Poor
1600	1350	1100	950	600	300

TRG-S

Features a unique cold-forged receiver. Stock is special reinforced polyurethane Monte Carlo, without checkering. Recoil pad has spacer for adjustable length of pull. Trigger is adjustable. Detachable magazine holds 5 rounds. Offered in a variety of calibers from .243 to .375 H&H. Non-Magnum calibers fitted with 22" barrel; weight 7.75 lbs.; Magnum calibers fitted with 24" barrel; weight 7.75 lbs. In 1996, .270 Withby Magnum, 7mm Withby Magnum, .340 Withby Magnum and 6.5x55S were added.

NIB	Exc.	V.G.	Good	Fair	Poor
1000	850	675	500	350	250

TRG-21

Receiver similar to TRG-S, with polyurethane stock featuring a unique design. Chambered for .308 cartridge. Trigger is adjustable for length and two-stage pull; also for horizontal or vertical pitch. Has several options that would affect price; muzzle-brake, one-piece scope mount, bipod, quick detachable sling swivels and military nylon sling. Offered in .308 Win. only. Fitted with 25.75" barrel; weight 10.5 lbs.

NIB	Exc.	V.G.	Good	Fair	Poor
2500	2000	1500	1000	600	400

TRG-22

Similar to TRG-21. Meets exact specifications to comply with Finish military requirements. Chambered for .308 cartridge. Introduced in 2000. Offered in both green and black finish. Weight about 10.25 lbs. **NOTE:** Add $2,250 for folding stock version.

NIB	Exc.	V.G.	Good	Fair	Poor
3000	2400	1850	1250	800	500

TRG-41

Exactly the same as TRG-21, except chambered for .338 Lapua Magnum cartridge.

NIB	Exc.	V.G.	Good	Fair	Poor
3000	2500	2000	—	—	—

TRG-42

Similar to TRG-41. Meets exact specifications to comply with Finish military requirements. Chambered for .338 Lapua or .300 Win. Magnum cartridge. Introduced in 2000. Weight about 11.25 lbs.

NIB	Exc.	V.G.	Good	Fair	Poor
4000	3000	2000	—	—	—

SAM, INC.
Special Service Arms Mfg., Inc.
Reston, Virginia

Model 88 Crossfire

Semi-automatic combination 12-gauge/.308-caliber shotgun/rifle, with 7-shot shotgun magazine and 20-shot rifle magazine. Barrel length 20". Matte black finish, with composition stock. This weapon can be fired in either mode by means of a selector switch mounted on receiver.

NIB	Exc.	V.G.	Good	Fair	Poor
1900	1500	1175	800	550	300

SAMCO GLOBAL ARMS, INC.
Miami, Florida

This firm imports a variety of military surplus firearms, that under current law, are marked with the importer's name.

SARASQUETA, FELIX
Eibar, Spain

Merke

A 12-gauge over/under double-barrel shotgun, with 22" or 27" ribbed and separated barrels, non-selective trigger and manual extractors. Blued, checkered walnut stock. Imported in 1986 only.

NIB	Exc.	V.G.	Good	Fair	Poor
—	500	375	200	150	100

SARASQUETA, J. J.
Eibar, Spain

Model 107E

A 12-, 16- or 20-gauge boxlock double-barrel shotgun, with a variety of barrel lengths, double triggers and automatic ejectors. Blued, with checkered walnut stock. Discontinued in 1984.

NIB	Exc.	V.G.	Good	Fair	Poor
—	425	300	275	225	100

Model 119E

As above, with a more finely figured walnut stock.

NIB	Exc.	V.G.	Good	Fair	Poor
—	525	400	375	325	150

Model 130E

As above, but engraved.

NIB	Exc.	V.G.	Good	Fair	Poor
—	950	700	600	450	250

Model 131E

As above, with considerably more engraving.

NIB	Exc.	V.G.	Good	Fair	Poor
—	1350	900	800	650	350

Model 1882 E LUXE

As above, with a single-selective trigger and gold inlays. Silver inlaid version is sold for approximately 10 percent less.

NIB	Exc.	V.G.	Good	Fair	Poor
—	1750	1250	900	650	350

SARASQUETA, VICTOR
Eibar, Spain

Model 3

A 12-, 16- or 20-gauge boxlock or sidelock double-barrel shotgun. Available in a variety of barrel lengths, with double triggers and automatic ejectors. Blued, with checkered straight stock. Sidelock version is worth approximately 20 percent more than values listed. Basic Model 3 was offered in a variety of grades featuring different amounts of engraving and better quality wood. These shotguns are listed under the model designations of 4 to 12E.

NIB	Exc.	V.G.	Good	Fair	Poor
—	650	500	450	350	300

Model 4
NIB	Exc.	V.G.	Good	Fair	Poor
—	1200	1000	875	600	300

Model 4E (Auto-ejectors)
NIB	Exc.	V.G.	Good	Fair	Poor
—	1600	1400	1100	800	400

Model 203
NIB	Exc.	V.G.	Good	Fair	Poor
—	700	600	525	425	325

Model 203E
NIB	Exc.	V.G.	Good	Fair	Poor
—	900	750	625	475	375

Model 6E
NIB	Exc.	V.G.	Good	Fair	Poor
—	1400	1250	875	525	425

Model 7E

NIB	Exc.	V.G.	Good	Fair	Poor
—	1500	1350	1000	750	475

Model 10E

NIB	Exc.	V.G.	Good	Fair	Poor
—	2600	2100	1650	950	750

Model 11E

NIB	Exc.	V.G.	Good	Fair	Poor
—	3000	2600	2000	1150	850

Model 12E

NIB	Exc.	V.G.	Good	Fair	Poor
—	3200	2850	2200	1300	1000

SARDIUS
Israel

SD-9

A 9mm double-action semi-automatic pistol, with 3" barrel and 6-shot magazine. Matte black finish, with composition grips. Imported since 1988.

NIB	Exc.	V.G.	Good	Fair	Poor
425	300	250	200	150	100

SARSILMAZ
Mercan/Istanbul, Turkey

Professional

CZ-75-style compensated semi-automatic in white chrome finish chambered for 9mm. Single-action with adjustable trigger, laser engraving. 16- or 18-round capacity. 42.3 oz.; 5.1" barrel. MSRP: $437.

K2

CZ-75-style double-action semi-automatic in white chrome or blued. Chambered for 9mm. 16- or 18-round capacity. 35.3 oz.; 4.6" barrel. Plastic grips.

NIB	Exc.	V.G.	Good	Fair	Poor
—	300	225	175	125	50

Kama Sport

CZ-75-style semi-automatic 9mm in white chrome or blued. Double-action with 3.9" compensated barrel, laser engraving. 15+1 or 17+1 capacity. 35.4 oz. Plastic grips.

NIB	Exc.	V.G.	Good	Fair	Poor
—	325	250	195	135	50

Kama

CZ-75-style semi-automatic 9mm in white chrome or blued. Double-action with 4.3" compensated barrel, laser engraving. 15+1 or 17+1 capacity. 35.4 oz.; 7.7". Plastic grips.

NIB	Exc.	V.G.	Good	Fair	Poor
—	300	225	175	125	50

Kilinc 2000 Mega

CZ-75-style semi-automatic 9mm in white chrome or blued. Double-action with 4.7" barrel. 16- or 18-round capacity. 35 oz. Plastic grips. Fixed sights.

NIB	Exc.	V.G.	Good	Fair	Poor
—	300	225	175	125	50

Kilinc 2000 Light

CZ-75-style semi-automatic 9mm in white chrome, blued or camo. Double-action with 4.7" barrel, laser engraving. 15+1 or 17+1 capacity. 35.4 oz. Plastic grips.

NIB	Exc.	V.G.	Good	Fair	Poor
—	300	225	175	125	50

Hancer 2000/2000 Light

CZ-75-style semi-automatic 9mm in white chrome or blued. Double-action with 3.9" barrel, laser engraving. 13+1 capacity. 33.5 oz. (25.4 oz. Light model). Plastic grips.

NIB	Exc.	V.G.	Good	Fair	Poor
—	300	225	175	125	50

Bernardelli

CZ-75-style double-action semi-automatic in 9mm. Black/white or blued finish. The 15+1 model has a 4.7" barrel, 27 oz., Plastic grips. The 13+1 model has a 3.9" barrel; 26.7 oz. Plastic grips, fixed sights.

NIB	Exc.	V.G.	Good	Fair	Poor
—	300	225	175	125	50

SAUER & SON, J. P.
Suhl and Eckernfoerde, Germany

Oldest firearms manufacturing firm in Germany. Founded in 1751 in Suhl. During this period the company produced high quality handguns and long guns. In 1938, it introduced a new double-action semi-automatic pistol, Sauer 38H. Pistol had the first decocking lever ever used on a mass produced pistol. In

1951, company relocated to Eckernfoerde where it continued to produce high quality firearms. **NOTE:** Model 90 Supreme and Model 202 have been imported by SIGARMS Inc.

Bolt-Action Rifle

Mauser action sporting rifle. Chambered for a variety of cartridges, with 22" or 24" barrel featuring a raised rib. Double-set triggers, express sights. Blued, with checkered walnut stock. Manufactured prior to WWII.

NIB	Exc.	V.G.	Good	Fair	Poor
—	1250	900	6500	400	300

Model 200

Bolt-action rifle chambered for a variety of cartridges. Short or medium length actions, 24" barrels, set trigger, 4-round magazine. Blued, checkered walnut stock. Discontinued 1987. **NOTE:** Add $235 for extra barrels.

NIB	Exc.	V.G.	Good	Fair	Poor
1350	1050	700	500	425	350

Model 200 Lightweight

As above, with an alloy receiver. Discontinued in 1987.

NIB	Exc.	V.G.	Good	Fair	Poor
—	1100	900	550	325	250

Model 200 Lux

As above, with finely figured walnut stock, rosewood pistol-grip cap and fore-end tip. Gold-plated trigger and machine jewelled bolt. Imported prior to 1988.

NIB	Exc.	V.G.	Good	Fair	Poor
—	1200	950	700	475	400

Model 200 Carbon Fiber

Fitted with a carbon composition stock. Imported in 1987 and 1988.

NIB	Exc.	V.G.	Good	Fair	Poor
—	1300	1100	800	500	400

Model 202 Supreme

Bolt-action rifle with a barrel change feature. Fitted with adjustable two-stage trigger, quick-change fluted barrel, black rubber recoil pad and removable box magazine. Stock is select American claro walnut, with high gloss finish and rosewood fore-end and grip cap. Buttstock has a Monte Carlo comb and cheekpiece. Offered in .243, .270, .308, .30-06 calibers; barrel length 23.6"; weight about 7.7 lbs. Supreme Magnum series available in 7mm Magnum, .300 Win. Magnum, .375 H&H Magnum calibers; barrel length 26"; weight about 8.4 lbs.

NIB	Exc.	V.G.	Good	Fair	Poor
2700	2000	1350	1000	750	400

Model 202 Takedown

A true takedown model. Introduced in 2003. Chambered for .300 Win. Magnum and .375 H&H. Other calibers will be offered in the future. Fancy Turkish walnut stock, with Monte Carlo and rosewood fore-end tip. Base price listed.

NIB	Exc.	V.G.	Good	Fair	Poor
5700	4400	2900	2000	1200	400

Model S202 Wolverine

Similar to Model 202 Supreme above, with 25.6" barrel, beavertail fore-end and adjustable cheekpiece. Chambered in various varmint calibers.

NIB	Exc.	V.G.	Good	Fair	Poor
—	2300	1950	1500	1050	400

Model S202 Highland

Similar to Model 202 Supreme above, with 20" barrel, schnabel fore-end and easily-detachable buttstock. Chambered in .308 Win. and various European cartridges.

NIB	Exc.	V.G.	Good	Fair	Poor
—	2500	1950	1500	1050	400

Model S202 Forest

Carbine-style version of Model 202 Highland above. Intended specifically for drive hunts. Has standard fore-end and 25.6" barrel. Chambered in various varmint calibers.

NIB	Exc.	V.G.	Good	Fair	Poor
—	2500	1950	1500	1050	400

Model S202 Hardwood

Similar to Model 202 Highland above. Oddly enough, with a synthetic stock with orange inserts. Chambered in .308 Win. and various European cartridges.

NIB	Exc.	V.G.	Good	Fair	Poor
—	2300	1950	1500	1050	400

Model S202 Match

Target version of Model 202, with 26.8" match barrel, wide fore-end. Chambered in .300 Win. Magnum and 6.5x55 Swedish.

NIB	Exc.	V.G.	Good	Fair	Poor
—	2500	1950	1500	1050	400

Model S202 Outback

Similar to Model 202 Hardwood above, with lightweight construction and plain black synthetic stock

NIB	Exc.	V.G.	Good	Fair	Poor
—	2500	1950	1500	1050	400

Model S202 Team Sauer

Classically-styled sporter version of Model 202, with heavy medium or Magnum-weight barrel. Walnut Monte Carlo stock. Chambered in various European and American long-action cartridges from 6.5x55 Swedish up to .300 Win. Magnum.

NIB	Exc.	V.G.	Good	Fair	Poor
—	1950	1600	1250	800	400

Model 90

Bolt-action rifle produced in a number of calibers and in all action lengths, with 23" or 26" barrels. Detachable magazine. Blued, with checkered walnut stock.

NIB	Exc.	V.G.	Good	Fair	Poor
—	1300	1100	675	500	300

Model 90 Stutzen

As above, with a full-length Mannlicher-style stock. Imported prior to 1990.

NIB	Exc.	V.G.	Good	Fair	Poor
—	1350	1150	725	550	350

Model 90 Safari

Model 90 made for use with .458 Win. Magnum cartridge. Fitted with a 24" barrel. Imported from 1986 to 1988. **NOTE:** Model 90 Series of bolt-action rifles was available in a deluxe version that differed with grade of workmanship and materials utilized. This deluxe series would be worth approximately 60 percent additional.

NIB	Exc.	V.G.	Good	Fair	Poor
—	2300	2000	1250	900	400

Model 90 Supreme

Similar to above, with gold-plated trigger, machine jewelled bolt and finely figured checkered walnut stock. Introduced in 1987.

NIB	Exc.	V.G.	Good	Fair	Poor
—	2500	2200	1425	1000	400

SSG-3000

See entry in SIG-Sauer section.

SG 550 Sniper

NOTE: For other current Sauer rifles see SIGARMS.

NIB	Exc.	V.G.	Good	Fair	Poor
5500	4750	3875	2700	2000	500

SHOTGUN/RIFLE COMBINATIONS

Luftwaffe M30 Survival Drilling

Double-barrel 12-gauge by 9.3x74R combination shotgun/rifle, with 28" barrels. Blued, with checkered walnut stock and marked with Nazi inspection. Stampings on stock and barrel breech. Normally furnished with an aluminum case. **NOTE:** Add 50 percent to prices for case.

NIB	Exc.	V.G.	Good	Fair	Poor
20000	15000	9500	6000	3250	1500

Model 3000 Drilling

Chambered for a variety of gauges and calibers. Built upon a boxlock action, with a Greener crossbolt. Action is lightly engraved. Blued, checkered walnut stock.

NIB	Exc.	V.G.	Good	Fair	Poor
5500	3700	2750	2000	1500	1250

Model 54 Combo

Combination rifle/shotgun. Chambered for a variety of gauges and calibers, with an action as above. Discontinued in 1986.

NIB	Exc.	V.G.	Good	Fair	Poor
—	3000	2250	1750	1400	1200

SHOTGUNS

Model 60

A 12-, 16- or 20-gauge double-barrel boxlock shotgun. Produced in a variety of barrel lengths, with double triggers and manual extractors. Blued, with checkered walnut stock. Produced prior to WWII.

NIB	Exc.	V.G.	Good	Fair	Poor
—	1300	950	725	550	400

Royal Model

A 12- or 20-gauge boxlock double-barrel shotgun, with 26", 28" or 30" barrels. Single-selective triggers, with automatic ejectors. Frame is scalloped. Blued, with checkered walnut stock. Manufactured from 1955 to 1977.

NIB	Exc.	V.G.	Good	Fair	Poor
—	1500	1250	1000	750	500

Grade I Artemis

A 12-gauge sidelock double-barrel shotgun, with 28" barrels, single-selective trigger and automatic ejector. Engraved, blued with checkered walnut stock. Manufactured from 1966 to 1977.

NIB	Exc.	V.G.	Good	Fair	Poor
—	5000	4250	3500	2500	2000

Grade II Artemis

As above, but more finely finished.

NIB	Exc.	V.G.	Good	Fair	Poor
—	6500	5750	4750	3500	3000

Model 66

A 12-gauge sidelock double-barrel shotgun, with 26", 28" or 30" barrel. Single-selective trigger and automatic ejectors. Blued, checkered walnut stock. Produced in three different grades that have different degrees of engraving. Produced from 1966 to 1975.

Grade I

NIB	Exc.	V.G.	Good	Fair	Poor
—	2000	1800	1500	1150	800

Grade II

NIB	Exc.	V.G.	Good	Fair	Poor
—	3000	2800	2500	2150	1800

Grade III

NIB	Exc.	V.G.	Good	Fair	Poor
—	3750	3500	2850	2500	2000

PISTOLS

Written and compiled by our very good friend Jim Cate.

Bär Pistol

Invented by Burkard Behr and made by Sauer. This was Sauer's first modern small pistol. It has stacked barrels (over/under configuration) that allow the shooter to fire two shots, rotate the barrel and then fire two more shots before loading. It was first patented in Germany in 1897 and in the USA in 1899. It shoots the 7mm Bär cartridge only. (DO NOT ATTEMPT TO FIRE THE .25 ACP/6.35mm CARTRIDGE IN THIS PISTOL.) It was made from 1897 to 1911 or 1912. Some pistols have Bakelite grips; some have diamond-pattern checkered wood grips. A case extractor rod screws into the bottom of the frame. No trigger guard. **NOTE:** Add $150 for original box and instructions.

NIB	Exc.	V.G.	Good	Fair	Poor
—	1250	800	450	275	–

Roth-Sauer Model

Very first automatic pistol produced by J.P. Sauer & Son. Designed by Karl Krinka for George Roth. Available only in 7.65 Roth-Sauer caliber. A locked breech design, beautifully finished and extremely well made. Later this design was modified and became the Roth-Steyr military pistol, which was adopted by Austria in 1907. A difficult-to-find pistol.

NIB	Exc.	V.G.	Good	Fair	Poor
—	2500	1800	900	500	300

SAUER MODEL 1913 FIRST SERIES

First Series, which incorporates an extra safety button on the left side of frame near trigger. Rear sight is simply a milled recess in the cocking knob itself. Serial number range runs from 1 to approximately 4750. First series is found only in 7.65mm caliber. All were for commercial sales as far as can be determined. Some were tested by various militaries, no doubt.

A. European variation—all slide legends are in the German language.

B. English Export variation—slide legends are marked, J.P. Sauer & Son, Suhl - Prussia, "Sauer's Patent" Pat'd May 20 1912.

Both were sold in thick paper cartons or boxes, with the color being a reddish purple with gold colored letters, etc. Examples of the very early European variation are found with the English language brochure or manual as well as an extra magazine, cleaning brush and grease container. These were shipped to England or the U.S. prior to Sauer producing the English Export variation. **NOTE:** Original box with accessories and manual: Add $500 if complete and in very good to excellent condition.

A. European variation:

NIB	Exc.	V.G.	Good	Fair	Poor
—	1500	900	650	400	250

B. English Export variation

NIB	Exc.	V.G.	Good	Fair	Poor
—	1800	1200	800	500	300

SAUER MODEL 1913 SECOND SERIES

Extra safety button eliminated. Rear sight acts as cocking knob retainer.

Commercial variation

Normal European/German slide markings are normally found; however it has been called to my attention that there are English Export pistols in this SECOND SERIES. They have the English markings on the slide which are similar to those found on FIRST SERIES Model 1913. This is applicable to both the 7.65mm and 6.35mm Model 1913/19 pistols. These are exceptional scarce pistols and should command at least a 50 percent premium, perhaps more due to their rarity. This commercial variation had factory manuals printed in English, Spanish and German which came with the cardboard boxed pistols. **NOTE:** With the original Sauer box, accessories and manual: Add $300 if in very good to excellent condition.

Caliber 7.65mm variation

NIB	Exc.	V.G.	Good	Fair	Poor
—	525	425	300	250	100

Caliber 7.65 variation with all words in English (i.e Son, Prussia, etc.)

NIB	Exc.	V.G.	Good	Fair	Poor
—	800	575	450	300	200

Police Variations

These will be standard German Commercial configuration, but always having Zusatzsicherung (additional safety) added to pistol. Safety is found between regular safety lever and top of left grip. Police used both calibers 7.65mm and 6.35mm, but 7.65mm was predominant. After early part of 1930s, 6.35mm was not available to police departments. Thus, 6.35mm police marked Sauer is rather scarce in relation to 7.65mm caliber. Few in 7.65mm are dated 1920 on left side of frame and were used by auxiliary policemen in Bavaria. Normal police property markings are on front or rear grip straps. Most were originally issued with at least two magazines and police accepted holster. Mags were usually numbered and holsters are found with and without pistol numbers. **NOTE:** Add 10 percent for one correctly numbered magazine; 20 percent if found with both correctly numbered magazines; 30 percent if found with correct holster and magazines.

Caliber 6.35mm police marked with Zusatzsicherung

NIB	Exc.	V.G.	Good	Fair	Poor
—	550	375	275	200	75

Caliber 7.65mm police marked without Zusatzsicherung

NIB	Exc.	V.G.	Good	Fair	Poor
—	575	325	275	175	125

Caliber 7.65mm police marked with Zusatzsicherung

NIB	Exc.	V.G.	Good	Fair	Poor
—	575	400	275	175	125

R.F.V. (Reich Finanz Verwaltung)

This Sauer variation is rarely found in any condition. R.F.V. markings and property number could be 1 to 4 digits. This variation is found in both calibers. Used by the Reich's Customs and Finance department personnel.

Caliber 6.35mm R.F.V. marked pistols

NIB	Exc.	V.G.	Good	Fair	Poor
—	1000	750	500	350	250

Caliber 7.65mm R.F.V. marked pistols

NIB	Exc.	V.G.	Good	Fair	Poor
—	750	600	400	300	200

Imperial Military Variations

Normal German commercial variations of the time period. Either Imperial Eagle acceptance marking applied on front of trigger guard and having small Imperial Army inspector's acceptance marking (crown over a scriptic letter) on right side of frame close to Nitro proof; or just Imperial Army inspector's marking alone. Usually pistols are found in 40000 to 85000 range. However, quantity actually of Imperial Military accepted is quite low even though thousands were privately purchased by officer corps. There are examples in 6.35mm which are Imperial Military accepted, but these are very scarce. **NOTE:** Add 30 percent for 6.35mm.

Caliber 7.65mm Imperial Military accepted pistols

NIB	Exc.	V.G.	Good	Fair	Poor
—	1500	750	350	275	150

SAUER MODEL 1913 THIRD SERIES

This series has an extra safety (Zusatzsicherung) noted on left side of frame to left of the grip. This device blocked the trigger-bar internally. These were sold commercially. A few were exported with GERMANY noted on them and to a very few police departments. Police examples will have grip-strap markings including property number of the pistol.

Caliber 7.65mm Commercial with Zusatzsicherung

NIB	Exc.	V.G.	Good	Fair	Poor
1750	850	650	400	275	150

Police with Zusatzsicherung and police grip-strap markings

NIB	Exc.	V.G.	Good	Fair	Poor
2500	1500	900	500	300	150

POST WWI AND WWII VARIATIONS

Paramilitary marked Sauer pistols of the 1925-35 period

Very few Model 1913 pistols would have been marked by paramilitary groups or organizations of this period. Usually this marking is no more than a series of numbers above another series of numbers, such as 23 over 12. These are found usually on the left side of frame next to left grip. Most of these numbers are indicative of property numbers assigned to a particular pistol belonging to a particular SA Group, Stahlhelm or right-wing organization such as Red Front (early communist). Any pistol of this type should be examined by an expert to determine if it is an original example.

NIB	Exc.	V.G.	Good	Fair	Poor
—	1500	800	500	200	100

Norwegian police usage, post WWII

After the war was over, many surplus German weapons were put back into use by the government of Norway. Germans had occupied this country and large numbers of weapons remained when the fighting ended. This included a large number of surplus Sauer pistols being utilized by the police (POLITI) forces. Most of the Sauers that were used by the Politi, which have been imported into the U.S. have been Model 1913; however, there were a number of Model 1930 pistols which reached our country as well. All examples, regardless of model, have the word POLITI stamped on the slide as well as a rampant lion on a shield under a crown marking. Following this is the property number. This number is also stamped into the left side of the frame. Most saw much usage during the post-war period. All are in 7.65mm caliber.

NIB	Exc.	V.G.	Good	Fair	Poor
—	500	400	200	150	100

Model 19 in 6.35mm

This particular pistol must be divided into three (3) sub-variations. This variation appears to be in a serial number range of its own. First sub-variation appears to run from 1 to 40000. It is highly doubtful if this quantity was manufactured. Second sub-variation incorporates a Zusatzsicherung or Additional Safety which can be seen between the normal safety lever and top of the left grip. It locked the trigger bar when in use. This second range appears to run from approximately serial number 40000 to 51000 which probably was continuous in the number produced. Lastly, third sub-variation examples were manufactured during or after 1926. Trigger guard has a different shape; slide has a greater area of vertical milled finger grooves; added Additional safety (Zusatzsicherung) now acts as the hold open device as well. These are found up to approximately 57000. Then a few examples of the first sub-variation are found from 57000 up to about 62500. This was, no doubt, usage of remaining parts. **NOTE:** Any commercial pistol could be special ordered with a factory nickel finish, special grip material (pearl, wood, etc.) as well as different types of engraving. It would be in your best interest to have these pistols examined by an expert.

Caliber 6.35mm first sub-variation

NIB	Exc.	V.G.	Good	Fair	Poor
—	450	375	250	150	75

Caliber 6.35mm second sub-variation

NIB	Exc.	V.G.	Good	Fair	Poor
—	475	375	250	150	75

Caliber 6.35mm third sub-variation

NIB	Exc.	V.G.	Good	Fair	Poor
—	650	500	500	200	100

Caliber 6.35mm English export variation

NIB	Exc.	V.G.	Good	Fair	Poor
—	1000	700	500	300	200

1926 Export Model

This variation's name comes from actual Sauer factory records found in the Suhl Archive. An interim pistol produced during 1926 to early 1929 period. Found only in 7.65mm caliber. This was an advancement of the normal 1913 design, which included changes in: (1) safety lever's design that became a slide hold open device as well; (2) shape of the frame was altered in that the trigger guard became more streamlined and the rear of frame was shortened and serrations were added to the slide as well as cocking knob. These are found in 162000 to 169000 range in relatively small clusters. Two to four thousand are presumed to have been manufactured. A scarce Sauer pistol! To date, none have been seen in nickel.

NIB	Exc.	V.G.	Good	Fair	Poor
2500	950	700	500	300	150

W.T.M.-Westentaschen Model—Vest Pocket Model

Several variations of vest pocket pistols were manufactured. First was called Model 1920 by the Sauer firm. We usually refer to it as Model 1924. Pistol, as well as all other W.T.M. examples, were designed to carry in your pocket. Quite small in size and found only in 6.35mm or .25 ACP caliber. Later in 1928, an updated version became available and was referred to as Model 1928. These differed in internal parts design and slide configuration. Bottom of grip marked "Cal.6.35.28.". Last version appeared in 1933 and still utilized same grips, but trigger and other small parts differed. All three were available in blue or nickel finish, engraving and fancy grip material. Very few Model 1933 had stainless steel (NIROSTA marked) barrels.

Model 1920

Serrations on front and rear of slide.

NIB	Exc.	V.G.	Good	Fair	Poor
1000	600	500	300	200	75

Model 1928

"Cal. 6.35.28" on black Bakelite grips.

NIB	Exc.	V.G.	Good	Fair	Poor
1100	800	500	350	200	75

Model 1933

Different type of trigger. Found in 253000 to early 254000 serial number range. **NOTE:** Add $200 factory nickel; $250 factory engraving; $250 exotic grip material; $500 factory paper box with cleaning brush, extra magazine and brochure; $750 in original factory imitation leather covered metal presentation case with accessories; $500 NIROSTA marked stainless barrel.

NIB	Exc.	V.G.	Good	Fair	Poor
1500	1000	600	400	275	150

MODEL 1930 VARIATIONS

Dutch Models

These different types of Dutch pistols will have JOH MUNTS - AMSTERDAM on left side of slide. Grips are usually mottled gray color. Sauer manufactured different pistols for Dutch police, Navy, Army, Department of Finance, S.M.N. (Steam Ships Netherlands) and possibly other agencies. **NOTE:** Accessories: cleaning rod, brush, aluminum oil bottle and manuals, add accordingly.

Dutch Police

First variation manufactured w/o adjustable front sight and lanyard loop.

NIB	Exc.	V.G.	Good	Fair	Poor
—	950	800	400	250	125

Amsterdam Police

Manufactured w/o adjustable sight, but having lanyard loop.

NIB	Exc.	V.G.	Good	Fair	Poor
1500	1300	1050	800	450	200

Navy

Made w/o adjustable sight. Anchor & Crown marked on rear grip strap.

NIB	Exc.	V.G.	Good	Fair	Poor
1500	1300	1050	800	450	200

S.M.N.

Found with and w/o adjustable front sights, no lanyard loop. S.M.N. marked horizontally near bottom of rear grip strap.

NIB	Exc.	V.G.	Good	Fair	Poor
1500	1300	1050	800	450	200

Department of Finance

Found with and w/o adjustable front sight, no lanyard loop. DF over date-1933 on rear grip strap.

NIB	Exc.	V.G.	Good	Fair	Poor
—	1500	1300	500	250	150

1930 Commercial Model

These pistols were for sale in Germany and other countries through normal commercial outlets. Very few are factory nickeled, engraved or both; some are with NIROSTA marked barrels and a very few were made in Duralumin or Dural. Standard caliber was 7.65mm, but a very limited number were made in .22 LR (.22 Long). Standard grip material is black Bakelite. Most of the regular pistols were purchased by military officers, some went to paramilitary groups such as the SA. **NOTE:** Add $100 for any variation listed with nickel finish; $500 for engraving; $600 for both nickel and engraving; $750 for nickel, engraving and with a fancy grip material (pearl or ebony, etc.).

Standard Commercial

NIB	Exc.	V.G.	Good	Fair	Poor
1500	1300	1050	800	450	200

Standard Commercial with NIROSTA marked barrel, 7.65mm

NIB	Exc.	V.G.	Good	Fair	Poor
2000	1450	1100	800	450	200

Standard Commercial in .22 LR (.22 Long)

NIB	Exc.	V.G.	Good	Fair	Poor
—	3500	2000	1500	500	300

Duralumin (Dural) Variation, 7.65mm

NIB	Exc.	V.G.	Good	Fair	Poor
—	3500	2750	2000	1200	450

BEHORDEN MODEL

Behorden (Authority) Model is different from Model 1930. It has a trigger safety and a loaded indicator provided.

Behorden Commercial

These are normally found with a high polished blued finish. Were available with a nickel finish, engraving, or both, as well as fancy grip material and NIROSTA marked barrel. Regular caliber is 7.65mm, but a very few are known in .22 LR that are probably proto-type pistols. **NOTE:** Add $100 for nickel finish; $250 for engraving; $350 for both; $500 with nickel, engraving and a fancy grip material; $500 for NIROSTA marked stainless barrel; 300 percent for .22-caliber.

NIB	Exc.	V.G.	Good	Fair	Poor
1850	900	550	400	350	200

Late Behorden Commercial

These are actually Model 1930 pistols found in 220000 to 223000 serial number range. They do not have trigger safety and/or indicator pin.

NIB	Exc.	V.G.	Good	Fair	Poor
—	600	450	300	200	125

Duralumin Model (Dural)

Frame and slide are made of Duralumin material. These are rare pistols! **NOTE:** Add $250 for stainless barrel.

Blue Anodized Variation

Found with and w/o NIROSTA marked barrels.

NIB	Exc.	V.G.	Good	Fair	Poor
7500	5000	3500	2500	1500	850

Nonanodized Variation

Found with and w/o NIROSTA marked barrels.

NIB	Exc.	V.G.	Good	Fair	Poor
7000	4000	3500	2500	1500	850

Presentation Examples of Anodized and Nonanodized Variations

Please consult an expert for pricing.

Police Models

Examples will be found with police acceptance on the left side of trigger guard. In a few cases on the front or rear grip straps. Black Bakelite grips are standard.

Sunburst K Police Acceptance

Non-adjustable front sight (a round blade).

NIB	Exc.	V.G.	Good	Fair	Poor
—	900	700	450	275	200

Sunburst K Police Acceptance

Adjustable front sight.

NIB	Exc.	V.G.	Good	Fair	Poor
—	900	700	450	300	225

Diamond in Sunburst Police Acceptance

All known are with the adjustable front sight.

NIB	Exc.	V.G.	Good	Fair	Poor
—	2000	1500	800	400	225

Grip Strap Marked Variations

(Having abbreviations of a city and property number of the pistol on grip strap.) Very few of these are known. Examples are S.Mg. 52, Sch. 78, etc.

NIB	Exc.	V.G.	Good	Fair	Poor
—	1250	700	400	250	150

MODEL 36/37

These very few pistols are all prototype Sauer pistols which preceded Model 38. They are in 210,000 range. Please consult an expert to determine value! EXTREMELY RARE.

MODEL 38 AND 38-H (H MODEL) VARIATIONS

Model 38

This pistol started at 260000. Crown N Nitro proofed, has cocking/decocking lever, loaded indicator pin and is double-action. High polish blue in 7.65mm (standard production pistol); found without thumb safety on slide; with pinned mag release. VERY RARE.

One Line Slide Legend Variation (pinned magazine release button - no screw)

Crown N proofs. Approximately 250 produced. Extremely rare!

NIB	Exc.	V.G.	Good	Fair	Poor
—	3800	3000	2000	600	300

Two Line Slide Legend Variation (pinned magazine release button - no screw)

C/N proofs, blued, with pinned magazine release (about 850 produced) VERY RARE. **NOTE:** Add $250 factory nickel; $1000 engraving; $500 NIROSTA marked barrel.

NIB	Exc.	V.G.	Good	Fair	Poor
—	2600	2000	1500	500	275

Two Line Slide Legend Variation (magazine release button - with screw)

C/N proofs, blued, magazine release button retained by a screw. RARE. **NOTE:** Add $250 factory nickel; $350 factory chrome; $1000 engraving; $500 NIROSTA marked barrel.

NIB	Exc.	V.G.	Good	Fair	Poor
—	2500	1500	900	500	275

SA der NSDAP Gruppe Thuringen Marked Variation

Blued, C/N proofs, with magazine release button held by a screw. VERY RARE.

NIB	Exc.	V.G.	Good	Fair	Poor
—	5500	4500	2500	650	275

Model 38 pistols converted to H Models by Sauer factory

Currently fewer than 30 known examples in collections. Thumb safety levers were added. Unique milling on left side of slide determines these pistols in 262xxx, 263xxx and 264xxx ranges. Includes SA der NSDAP Gruppe Thringen marked pistols.

NIB	Exc.	V.G.	Good	Fair	Poor
—	3500	2000	1000	450	—

Model 38-H or H Model

This model has a thumb safety on the slide, CROWN N NITRO proof, high polish blued finish, a cocking/decocking lever, double-action. Found in 7.65mm caliber as the standard production pistol. This model is found only with two line slide legend or logo. Type 1, variation 2.

Standard Commercial Variation

NOTE: Add $100 for factory nickel (factory chromed has not been identified); $1000 for factory engraving; $250 for exotic grip material; $500 for NIROSTA marked stainless barrel.

NIB	Exc.	V.G.	Good	Fair	Poor
—	1200	900	600	300	175

SA der NSDAP Gruppe Thuringia Variation

Same as Standard above. Having SA markings on slide, with blued finish. VERY RARE. NOTE: Add $1200 for SA marked Akah holster in excellent condition.

NIB	Exc.	V.G.	Good	Fair	Poor
—	4500	3500	2500	900	400

L.M. Model

(Leicht Model-lightweight model); frame and slide made of DURAL (Duralumin), in the 264800 range, with thumb safety and regular black Bakelite grips. EXTREMELY RARE.

NIB	Exc.	V.G.	Good	Fair	Poor
—	6500	5000	3000	1500	850

Flash Light Model

Only four known examples of this variation. Battery flash light attached by four screws to pistol. Carried by SS night patrol at the Reich's chancellory in Berlin. No specific markings, but known serial numbers are 266814, 266842, 266845.

NIB	Exc.	V.G.	Good	Fair	Poor
—Too Rare To Price—	—	—	—	—	—

Police Accepted Variation

Found with Police Eagle C acceptance on left trigger guard and having Crown N proofs. RARE.

NIB	Exc.	V.G.	Good	Fair	Poor
—	3000	2500	1850	500	175

TYPE TWO MODEL 38-H (H MODEL)

There are no Model 38 pistols in Type Two description, only H Model with thumb safety. These begin at serial number 269100 and have Eagle N Nitro proofs, with blued high polish finish and black Bakelite grips. Normal caliber is 7.65mm.

H Model - Type Two

Standard Commercial

NOTE: Add $1500 boxed examples complete with factory manual, clean ring rod, all accessories, extra magazine, etc.; $250 factory nickel; $350 factory chrome; $1000 factory engraving.

NIB	Exc.	V.G.	Good	Fair	Poor
3500	1500	850	600	300	200

.22 Caliber Variation

Slide and magazines marked CAL. .22 LANG. (Some with steel frame and slides; some with Dural frames and slides.) Found in 269900 range. Very Rare.

NIB	Exc.	V.G.	Good	Fair	Poor
—	10500	6000	3000	1000	600

Jager Model

Special order pistol in .22-caliber. Similar in appearance to Walther's 1936 Jagerschafts pistol. Very rare.

NIB	Exc.	V.G.	Good	Fair	Poor
—	12500	7500	4000	1000	400

Police Eagle C and Eagle F Acceptance Variations

First Eagle N (post January 1940) police accepted pistols. Found in 270000 to 276000 ranges. NOTE: Add 50 percent for E/F.

NIB	Exc.	V.G.	Good	Fair	Poor
—	1850	1000	600	325	200

German Military Variation Double Eagle 37

First official military accepted range of 2,000 pistols. In a range found between 271000 to 273000. Two Eagle 37 military acceptance marks found on trigger guard.

NIB	Exc.	V.G.	Good	Fair	Poor
—	3850	2500	1300	700	300

Second Military Variation

Pistols found with high polish finish. Have only one Eagle 37 acceptance mark. Letter H found on all small parts.

NIB	Exc.	V.G.	Good	Fair	Poor
—	1850	1450	800	400	200

Police Eagle C Acceptance

This variation includes remainder of high polish blued police accepted pistols. **NOTE:** Add $50 matching magazine; $200 both matching mags and correct police holster; $300 both matching mags and correct matching numbered police accepted and dated holster.

NIB	Exc.	V.G.	Good	Fair	Poor
—	1500	1000	600	275	175

TYPE THREE 38-H MODEL (H MODEL)

Terminology used because the change of exterior finish of Sauer pistols. Due to urgency of the war, order was received not to polish exterior surfaces of pistols, as had been done previously. Also a change in formulation of grip's material. Later in this range there will be found stamped parts, zinc triggers and magazine bottoms, etc. used to increase pistol's production. Type Three has a full slide legend.

H Model - Type Three

Military Accepted

One Eagle 37 Waffenamt mark.

NIB	Exc.	V.G.	Good	Fair	Poor
—	850	650	400	275	150

Commercial

Only Eagle N Nitro proof marks. **NOTE:** See Type Two Commercial. Prices apply here also.

NIB	Exc.	V.G.	Good	Fair	Poor
3000	800	500	400	250	150

Police Accepted with the Police Eagle C Acceptance

NOTE: See Type Two Police. Prices apply here also.

NIB	Exc.	V.G.	Good	Fair	Poor
—	850	650	350	250	150

TYPE FOUR 38-H MODEL (H MODEL)

Continuation of pistol as described in Type Three, except J.P. Sauer & Sohn, Suhl legend is dropped from slide and only CAL. 7.65 is found on left side. Word PATENT may or may not appear on right side. Many are found with a zinc trigger.

H Model - Type Four

Military Accepted

NIB	Exc.	V.G.	Good	Fair	Poor
—	850	650	400	275	150

Commercial

Having only Eagle N Nitro proofs. **NOTE:** See Type Two Commercial info. Prices apply here also.

NIB	Exc.	V.G.	Good	Fair	Poor
3500	900	600	400	250	150

Police Accepted with the Police Eagle C Acceptance

NOTE: See Type Two Price info. Prices apply here also.

NIB	Exc.	V.G.	Good	Fair	Poor
—	850	650	450	300	150

Eigentum NSDAP SA Gruppe Alpenland Slide Marked Pistols

Unique pistols found in 456000 and 457000 serial number ranges. Has thumb safety levers on slides.

NIB	Exc.	V.G.	Good	Fair	Poor
4500	3500	3000	2000	600	400

NSDAP SA Gruppe Alpenland Slide Marked Pistols

Unique pistols found in 465000 serial number range. Has thumb safety levers on slide.

NIB	Exc.	V.G.	Good	Fair	Poor
4500	3500	3000	2000	600	400

Himmler Presentation Pistols

These desirable pistols have high polish finish with DEM SCHARFSCHUTZEN - H. HIMMLER on left side of slide (with no other markings) and J.P. SAUER & SON over CAL. 7.65 on right side (opposite of normal). Pistols came in imitation leather cover metal cases, with cloth interiors having a cleaning brush, extra magazine and cartridges. Very rare pistols! Extremely rare if cased! Only 12 are known presently.

NIB	Exc.	V.G.	Good	Fair	Poor
40000	38500	25000	18000	5000	1500

Model 38

To speed up production even more thumb safety (Handsicherung-Hammer safety) was eliminated. Side continues to be marked only with CAL. 7.65. Frame's serial number changes from right side to left at 472000, with overlaps up to 489000.

Military Accepted

One Eagle 37 Waffenamt mark.

NIB	Exc.	V.G.	Good	Fair	Poor
—	700	500	400	250	175

Commercial

Only the Eagle N Nitro proofs. **NOTE:** See Type Two Commercial info. Prices apply here also.

NIB	Exc.	V.G.	Good	Fair	Poor
2000	900	500	350	250	175

Police Accepted with Police Eagle C Acceptance

NIB	Exc.	V.G.	Good	Fair	Poor
—	700	500	400	300	200

Police Accepted with Police Eagle F Acceptance

NIB	Exc.	V.G.	Good	Fair	Poor
—	1250	800	600	325	200

TYPE FIVE MODEL 38 & H MODEL PISTOLS

Two different basic variations of Type Five Sauer pistols. May or may not have thumb safety lever on slide. Main criteria is whether frame is factory numbered as per normal and follows chronological sequence of those pistols in preceding model. After frames were used which were already numbered and finished upon arrival of U.S. Army, last variation came about. Neither variation has any Nitro proof marks. **NOTE:** There are some pistols which have post-war Russian Crown N Nitro proofs. Russians assembled or refurbished a very few pistols after U.S. Army left Suhl after the war. Several have been found with newly made barrels in 7.65mm, with C/N proof. Hard to find Sauer!

First Variation

Factory numbered sequential frames starting on or near serial number 506800. Slides and breech blocks may or may not match.

NIB	Exc.	V.G.	Good	Fair	Poor
—	600	500	300	225	100

Second Variation

Started with serial number 1; made from mostly rejected parts, generally have notched trigger guards, may or may not be blued, no Nitro proofs, slides may or may not have factory legends, etc. Approximately 300 assembled. Definitely rare Sauer pistols.

NIB	Exc.	V.G.	Good	Fair	Poor
—	1000	800	500	300	150

SAVAGE & NORTH
Middletown, Connecticut

Figure 8 Revolver

A .36-caliber percussion revolver with 7" octagonal barrel and 6-shot cylinder. Barrel marked "E. Savage, Middletown. CT./H.S. North. Patented June 17, 1856". Four models of this revolver are: (1) with a rounded brass frame and mouths of the chamber fitting into the end of barrel breech; (2) with a rounded iron frame and modified loading lever that is marked

"H.S. North, Patented April 6, 1858"; (3) with a flat-sided brass frame having a round recoil shield; (4) with an iron frame. Approximately 400 manufactured between 1856 and 1859.

First Model

Courtesy Bonhams & Butterfields

First Model Figure 8 Revolver

NIB	Exc.	V.G.	Good	Fair	Poor
—	—	16500	7250	1500	500

Second Model

NIB	Exc.	V.G.	Good	Fair	Poor
—	—	9900	3850	850	400

Third Model

NIB	Exc.	V.G.	Good	Fair	Poor
—	—	9900	3850	850	400

Fourth Model

NIB	Exc.	V.G.	Good	Fair	Poor
—	—	11000	4400	1000	450

SAVAGE ARMS CORPORATION
Utica, New York
Westfield, Massachusetts

Model 1895

A Savage .303-caliber lever-action rifle with 26" or 30" barrel and 5-shot rotary magazine. Identifiable by hole in breechbolt. Barrel marked "Savage Repeating Arms Co. Utica, N.Y. U.S.A. Pat. Feb. 7, 1893, July 25, 1893. CAL. .303". Blued, with walnut stock. Approximately 8,000 manufactured between 1895 and 1899. **NOTE:** Add 100 percent for carbine version.

Courtesy Rock Island Auction Company

NIB	Exc.	V.G.	Good	Fair	Poor
—	6000	5000	3750	2000	900

Model 1899-A 22" Barrel Short Rifle

Chambered for .303, .30-30, .25-35, .32-40, .38-55. Serial number range from 10000 to 220000. Produced from 1899 to 1922. Same cocking indicator as 1899-A rifle. **NOTE:** Add 50 percent for .25-35, .32-40, and .38-55 calibers.

NIB	Exc.	V.G.	Good	Fair	Poor
—	1600	100	600	300	100

Model 1899-A 26" Round Barrel Rifle

A .25-35, .30-30, .303 Savage, .32-40 or .38-55, .300 Savage caliber lever-action rifle with 26" barrel marked "Savage Arms Company, Utica, N.Y. Pat. Feb. 7, 1893, July 25.'93, Oct.3.'99 .CAL.30". Manufactured between 1899 and 1926/27. Blued, with walnut stock. Serial number range 10000 to 300000. Block cocking indicator on bolt to s/n 90000 then changed to pin indicator on tang. **NOTE:** Add 50 percent for .25-35, .32-40, and .38-55 calibers.

Courtesy Rock Island Auction Company

NIB	Exc.	V.G.	Good	Fair	Poor
—	1500	1000	600	250	100

Model 1899-B 26" Octagon Barrel Rifle

In calibers .303, .30-30, .25-35, .32-40, .38-55. Manufactured between 1899 and 1915. Serial number range 10000 to 175000. Same cocking indicator as 1899-A rifle. **NOTE:** Add 50 percent for .25-35, .32-40, and .38-55 calibers.

Courtesy Rock Island Auction Company

NIB	Exc.	V.G.	Good	Fair	Poor
—	1900	1300	800	350	150

Model 1899-C 26" Half Octagon Barrel Rifle

In calibers .303, .30-30, .25-35, .32-40, .38-55. Manufactured between 1899 and 1915. Serial number range 10000 to 175000. Same cocking indicator as 1899-A rifle. **NOTE:** Add 50 percent for .25-35, .32-40, and .38-55 calibers.

Courtesy Rock Island Auction Company

NIB	Exc.	V.G.	Good	Fair	Poor
—	2300	1700	1100	400	150

Model 1899-D Military Musket

Chambered for .303 Savage only, with 28" barrel. Fitted with full military stocks. Produced from 1899 to 1915. Several hundred produced for Canadian Home Guard during WWI. These will have rack number on buttplate.

NIB	Exc.	V.G.	Good	Fair	Poor
7500	6500	5000	3700	1000	400

Model 1899-F Saddle Ring Carbine

Fitted with 20" barrel only in calibers .303, .30-30, .25-35, .32-40, .38-55. Built from 1899 to 1919 in serial number range 19000 to 200000. Same cocking indicator as 1899-A rifle. Earliest style with barrel band is rarest variation. **NOTE:** Add 100 percent for .25-35, .32-40 and .38-55 calibers; 200 percent for barrel band carbine.

Courtesy Rock Island Auction Company

NIB	Exc.	V.G.	Good	Fair	Poor
—	2400	1600	1000	700	350

Model 1899-CD Deluxe Rifle

In calibers .303, .30-30, .25-35, .32-40, .38-55. Serial number range 50000 to 175000. Built from 1905 to 1917. Same cocking indicator as 1899-A rifle. Standard Deluxe 1899 rifle with 26" round, octagon or half octagon barrel with pistol-grip stock and checkering. Takedown barrel or short 22" barrel. **NOTE:** Add 30 percent for .25-35, .32-40, and .38-55 calibers.

NIB	Exc.	V.G.	Good	Fair	Poor
—	3000	2200	1600	600	250

Model 1899-H Featherweight Rifle

Chambered for .303, .30-30, .25-35, and .22 HP Savage in 20" barrel. Serial number range 50000 to 220000. Built from 1905 to 1919. Revolutionary .22 HP cartridge introduced in this model in 1912. Most 1899-Hs are found with takedown barrels. **NOTE:** Add 50 percent for .25-35; 25 percent for .22 HP.

Paul Goodwin photo

NIB	Exc.	V.G.	Good	Fair	Poor
—	1900	1400	700	300	100

Model 1899 .250-3000 Savage Rifle

Deluxe Model 1899 was developed to introduce Charles Newton designed .250-3000 Savage cartridge. Fitted with 22" featherweight takedown barrel, pistol-grip, checkered perch belly stock, unique checkered trigger. Built from 1914 to 1921. Serial number range 146500 to 237500.

NIB	Exc.	V.G.	Good	Fair	Poor
—	1800	1500	800	350	100

Model 99-B 26"/24" Standard Weight Takedown

Chambered for .303, .30-30, and .300 Savage. Serial number range 200000 to 344000. Produced from 1920 to 1934. In 1926 a new 24" barrel with ramp front sight was introduced.

NIB	Exc.	V.G.	Good	Fair	Poor
—	1200	900	500	300	100

Model 99-C 22" Standard Weight Short Rifle

Chambered for .303, .30-30, and .300 Savage. Serial number range 238000 to 290000. Built from 1922 to 1926. This model looks like a shortened 26" rifle but with a heavily crowned muzzle.

NIB	Exc.	V.G.	Good	Fair	Poor
—	1100	800	500	200	100

Model 99-D 22" Standard Weight Takedown Rifle

Chambered for .303, .30-30, and .300 Savage. Serial number range 238000 to 290000. Built from 1922 to 1926. Same heavily crowned muzzle as 99-C.

NIB	Exc.	V.G.	Good	Fair	Poor
—	1200	900	500	200	100

Model 99-E Lightweight Rifle

Chambered for .22 HP, .30-30, .303, .250-3000, and .300 Savage. Manufactured between 1922 and 1934. Serial number range 238000 to 344000. In 1926 new ramp front sight introduced. **NOTE:** Add 25 percent for .22 Hi Power and .250-3000 calibers.

NIB	Exc.	V.G.	Good	Fair	Poor
—	1450	950	600	300	100

Model 99-F Lightweight Takedown Rifle

As above, but in lightweight takedown barrels in 20", 22" and 24". Chambered for .22 HP, .30-30, .303, .250-3000 and .300 Savage. These were tapered lightweight barrels. Manufactured between 1920 and 1940. Serial number range 200000 to 398000. In 1926, new ramp front sight introduced. Early versions look similar to Model 1899-H featherweight. In 1938, checkered stocks offered. Rare option. **NOTE:** Add 50 percent for .22 HP and .250-3000; 75 percent for 1938 checkered stocks.

NIB	Exc.	V.G.	Good	Fair	Poor
—	1700	1200	700	300	100

Model 99-G Deluxe Takedown Pistol Grip Rifle

Calibers and barrel lengths as above, with pistol-grip checkered stock. Manufactured between 1922 and 1941. Serial number range 238000 to 407000. No takedown Model 99s made after 1941. **NOTE:** Add 50 percent for .22 Hi Power; 25 percent for .250-3000.

NIB	Exc.	V.G.	Good	Fair	Poor
—	1950	1400	800	300	100

Model 99-H Carbine/Barrel Band Carbine

Fitted with 20" or 22" barrels. Chambered for .30-30, .303, .250-3000 and .300 Savage. Serial number range 220000 to 400000. Built between 1923 and 1940. Distinctive plain stocks with no flat pads on side of buttstock. Curved carbine style butt-plate. In 1931, barrel band added to fore-end, then commonly called "barrel band carbine". In 1935, flat pads added to buttstock sides, plus front ramp sight. **NOTE:** Add 50 percent for 1935 barrel band carbine; 25 percent for .250-3000 and .300 Savage.

NIB	Exc.	V.G.	Good	Fair	Poor
—	1200	800	500	200	100

Combination Cased Set .300 Savage/.410 Barrel

Fitted with 22" or 24" barrels, with .410 barrels and .300 Savage in Model 99-F, 99-G or 99-K configuration. In black fitted case. Serial number range 240000 to 350000. Built from 1922 to 1934. BE AWARE: barrel address on .410 barrel matches that on the rifle barrel; and .410 barrel takes up correctly on the receiver; and case fits the .410 barrel and receiver.

NIB	Exc.	V.G.	Good	Fair	Poor
—	4000	2500	1500	800	300

Model 99-A 24" Featherweight Rifle

Fitted with 24" barrel, with new 1926 ramp front sight. Chambered for .303, .30-30 or .300 Savage. Serial number range 290000 to 370000. Built from 1926 to 1937. Buttplate older 1899 crescent style.

NIB	Exc.	V.G.	Good	Fair	Poor
—	900	700	5500	250	75

Model 99-K Deluxe Engraved Rifle

Premier Savage Model 99, with engraved receiver. Fitted with checkered pistol-grip stock of select American walnut and takedown frame. Hand honed and fitted. Chambered for .22 HP, .30-30, .303, .250-3000 and .300 Savage. Barrels 22" or 24". Serial number range 285000 to 398000. Manufactured between 1926 and 1940. **NOTE:** Add 30 percent for .22-caliber Hi Power. Some of these models found with cased set with .410 barrel, add $700 for V.G. case and barrels.

Courtesy Rock Island Auction Company

NIB	Exc.	V.G.	Good	Fair	Poor
3500	3000	2500	1400	600	200

Model 99-R Heavy Stocked Rifle

Features heavy pistol-grip checkered stock, with rounded fore-end tip. Barrels 22" or 24". Chambered for .250-3000, .303, .300 Savage, .308, .243 and .358-calibers. Serial number range 340000 to 1060000. Manufactured between 1932 and 1960. **NOTE:** Add 50 percent for .358; 100 percent for rare uncataloged .30-30. Approximately 10 made for A.F. Stoeger of N.Y.C. for N.Y. State Police in 1935 in serial number range 348600. Most of these are found with Redfield No. 102 side peep sight and .250" rack number stamped in stock below pistol-grip.

Courtesy Rock Island Auction Company

NIB	Exc.	V.G.	Good	Fair	Poor
—	1300	800	550	200	100

Model 99-RS Special Sights

As above, with Lyman aperture rear tang sight. In 1940, changed to Redfield micrometer tang sight. First model fitted with Savage quick release sling swivels. No .30-30 calibers made in this model. Manufactured between 1932 and 1942. **NOTE:** Add 50 percent for .358.

Courtesy Rock Island Auction Company

NIB	Exc.	V.G.	Good	Fair	Poor
—	1500	1000	600	350	200

Model 99-EG Standard Weight Rifle

Produced with plain uncheckered pistol-grip stock until 1940. Available in .22 Hi Power, .250 Savage, .30-30, .303 Savage, .300 Savage, .308, .243 and .358. Serial number range 350000 to 1060000. Manufactured between 1935 and 1960. **NOTE:** Add 20 percent for pre-1940 uncheckered stocks; 100 percent for rifles chambered .22 Hi Power and .358.

Courtesy Rock Island Auction Company

NIB	Exc.	V.G.	Good	Fair	Poor
—	900	650	400	200	75

Model 99-T Deluxe Featherweight Rifle

Classic short barrel deluxe Model 99, with semi-beavertail fore-end and distinct long checkering pattern. Fitted with 20" or 22" barrels. Chambered for .250-3000, .30-30, .303, .22 HP or .300 Savage. Serial number range 350000 to 400000. Manufactured between 1935 and 1940. **NOTE:** Add 100 percent for .22 Hi Power caliber; 20 percent for .250-3000.

Courtesy Rock Island Auction Company

NIB	Exc.	V.G.	Good	Fair	Poor
2000	1750	1200	800	450	200

Model 99-F Featherweight Rifle

First Savage made with model designation visible on outside. Located at rear on right side of barrel. True featherweight with slender 22" barrel, lightweight stocks with butt end hollowed out. Chambered for .250-3000, .300 Savage, .308, .243, .284 and .358-calibers. Built from 1955 to 1973. **NOTE:** Add 75 percent for .284 and .358-calibers; 50 percent for .250 Savage.

NIB	Exc.	V.G.	Good	Fair	Poor
1200	1000	800	500	250	75

Model 99-DL Deluxe Monte Carlo Rifle

Deluxe version of Model 99EG. Available in .243, .250 Savage, .300 Savage, .284, .358 and .308-calibers. Monte Carlo-style stock. Manufactured between 1960 and 1973. **NOTE:** Add 75 percent for .358 and .284-calibers.

NIB	Exc.	V.G.	Good	Fair	Poor
900	800	550	350	200	100

Model 99-E Economy Rifle

Ugly duckling of Savage line. Model 99-E lacked many standard features such as left side cartridge counter, tang sight holes, walnut stocks and capped pistol-grip. Fitted with 20", 22" or 24" barrels. Chambered for .250-3000, .300 Savage, .243 and .308-calibers. Built from 1960 to 1984. **NOTE:** Model 99-E was last original rotary magazine. Production discontinued in 1984 for Model 99.

NIB	Exc.	V.G.	Good	Fair	Poor
850	750	575	375	150	50

Model 99-C Clip Magazine Rifle

Recent production model in .22-250, .243, .284 Win., 7mm-08 or .308-caliber. Barrel 22" and open sights. Blued, with walnut stock. Features clip magazine, first modification to Model 99 in 66 years. Introduced in 1965. Dropped from production and reintroduced in 1995 in .243 and .308-calibers. Weight about 7.75 lbs. **NOTE:** Add 50 percent for .22-250, .284 and 7mm-08.

NIB	Exc.	V.G.	Good	Fair	Poor
850	550	400	250	150	50

Model 99-DE Citation Grade Rifle

Premier Savage with engraved receiver. Nickel-like finish and impressed checkering on select walnut stocks. Marked 99-M. Offered in .243, .284 and .308-calibers, with 22" barrel only. Manufactured between 1965 and 1970. **NOTE:** Add 30 percent for .284-caliber.

NIB	Exc.	V.G.	Good	Fair	Poor
1750	1600	1200	700	400	200

Model 99-PE Presentation Grade Rifle

Presentation grade Model 99, with engraved receiver. Hand checkered finely figured walnut stock. Mountain lion on right side of receiver and elk on left side. Chambered for .243, .284 and .308-caliber, with 22" barrel. Manufactured between 1965 and 1970. **NOTE:** Add 30 percent for .284-caliber.

NIB	Exc.	V.G.	Good	Fair	Poor
2500	2000	1500	800	500	300

Model 1895 Anniversary Edition

A .308-caliber reproduction of Model 1895, with 24" octagonal barrel. Engraved receiver, walnut stock with schnabel fore-end. Brass crescent buttplate, brass medallion inlaid in stock. Manufactured 9,999 in 1970.

NIB	Exc.	V.G.	Good	Fair	Poor
950	775	600	450	300	200

Model 99-A Saddle Gun

Variation of original Model 99A, with 20" or 22" barrel. Chambered for .243, .250 Savage, .300 Savage, .308 and .375-caliber. Serial number range in new "A" series on left side. Manufactured between 1971 and 1982. **NOTE:** Add 25 percent for .375-caliber.

NIB	Exc.	V.G.	Good	Fair	Poor
1200	800	500	400	300	200

Model 99-.358 and 99-.375 Brush Guns

Similar to Model 99-A straight-grip saddle gun, but in .358 and .375 Win. (1980) calibers. Has plain grooved fore-end, rubber recoil pad. Serial number range in new "A" series on left side. Built from 1977 to 1980. **NOTE:** Add 25 percent for .358 Win. caliber.

NIB	Exc.	V.G.	Good	Fair	Poor
1200	800	500	400	300	200

Model 99-CD Deluxe Clip Model

North American classic rifle, with distinct stocks of checkered walnut. Long grooved fore-end, deep shaped pistol-grip, Monte Carlo stock with cheekpiece. Fitted with 22" barrel. Chambered for .250-3000, .308 or .243. Serial number range in new "A" series on left side. Built from 1975 to 1980.

NIB	Exc.	V.G.	Good	Fair	Poor
1100	850	600	400	300	200

Model 99-CE (Centennial Edition)

Introduced in 1995. Limited edition to 1,000 rifles. Serial numbers from AS0001 to AS1000. Chambered for .300 Savage cartridge. Engraved receiver with gold inlays. Select American walnut stock, with Monte Carlo comb.

Courtesy Savage Arms

NIB	Exc.	V.G.	Good	Fair	Poor
1600	1300	900	750	500	250

Model 1903

A .22-caliber slide-action rifle, with 24" octagon barrel having open sights. Blued, with walnut stock. Manufactured between 1903 and 1922. **NOTE:** Late model rifles have updated slide handle. Pistol-grip stock in same style as Model 1914.

Courtesy Rock Island Auction Company

NIB	Exc.	V.G.	Good	Fair	Poor
600	500	400	250	150	100

Model 1903 Gallery Model

Same general specifications as Model 1903, except for a mechanical counter attached to record shots fired.

NIB	Exc.	V.G.	Good	Fair	Poor
700	600	500	350	150	100

Model 1903 Factory Engraved Models

NOTE: These models are seldom seen. Secure a qualified appraisal prior to sale. **NOTE:** Add premiums as shown.

Grade EF

Grade "B" checkering, fancy English walnut stock, Savage 22B front sights, 21B rear sight. **NOTE:** Add 50 percent.

Expert Grade

Fancy American walnut stock, Grade "A" engraving, Grade "B" checkering, standard sights. **NOTE:** Add 150 percent.

Grade GH

Plain American walnut stock, Grade "A" checkering, 22B front sight, 21B rear sight. **NOTE:** Add 50 percent.

Gold Medal Grade

Plain American walnut stock, animal ornamentation on receiver, Grade "A" checkering, standard sights. **NOTE:** Add 60 percent.

Model 1909

As above, with 20" barrel. Manufactured between 1909 and 1915.

NIB	Exc.	V.G.	Good	Fair	Poor
700	600	500	350	150	100

Model 1911

Produced from 1911 to 1915, in .22 Short only. Bolt-action repeater. American walnut stock. Shotgun steel buttplate, bead front sight with adjustable open rear sight. Tubular magazine loaded through buttstock, capacity 20 rounds. Weight about 4 lbs.

NIB	Exc.	V.G.	Good	Fair	Poor
—	475	425	225	125	100

Model 1912

A .22-caliber semi-automatic rifle, with 20" barrel, open sights and in takedown form. Magazine capacity 7 rounds. Blued, with walnut stock. Manufactured between 1912 and 1916. Weight about 4.5 lbs.

NIB	Exc.	V.G.	Good	Fair	Poor
900	750	500	300	125	90

Model 6

Similar to above, with 24" barrel and tubular magazine. Walnut stock checkered prior to 1938; plain after 1965.

NIB	Exc.	V.G.	Good	Fair	Poor
—	350	300	200	125	50

Model 7

As above, with detachable magazine. Manufactured between 1938 and 1954.

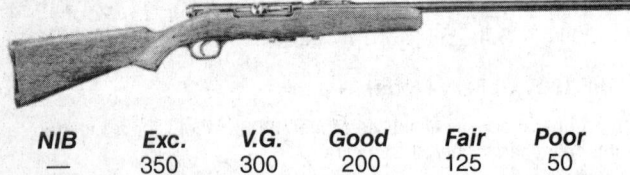

NIB	Exc.	V.G.	Good	Fair	Poor
—	350	300	200	125	50

Model 1914

As above, with 24" octagonal barrel. Manufactured between 1914 and 1926.

NIB	Exc.	V.G.	Good	Fair	Poor
—	350	300	200	125	50

Model 25

A .22-caliber slide-action rifle, with 24" octagonal barrel, open sights and tubular magazine. Blued, with plain walnut stock. Manufactured between 1925 and 1929.

Courtesy Rock Island Auction Company

NIB	Exc.	V.G.	Good	Fair	Poor
—	450	350	250	200	125

Model 29

Similar to above, with 22" octagonal barrel, later changed to round on post-war rifles. Checkered walnut stock, later changed to plain on post-war rifles. Manufactured between 1929 and 1967.

NIB	Exc.	V.G.	Good	Fair	Poor
—	450	325	200	150	100

Model 170

A .30-30 or .35 Rem. caliber slide-action rifle, with 22" barrel and 3-shot tubular magazine. Blued, with walnut stock. Manufactured between 1970 and 1981.

NIB	Exc.	V.G.	Good	Fair	Poor
—	550	400	250	175	100

Model 1904

A .22-caliber single-shot bolt-action rifle, with 18" barrel and walnut stock. Manufactured between 1904 and 1931. **NOTE:** After 1915 this model became known as Model 04.

NIB	Exc.	V.G.	Good	Fair	Poor
—	200	150	100	75	50

Model 1905

As above, with 24" barrel. Manufactured between 1905 and 1919.

NIB	Exc.	V.G.	Good	Fair	Poor
—	200	150	100	75	50

Model 1905 Style "B"

Same as Model 1905 Target, with shotgun buttplate.

NIB	Exc.	V.G.	Good	Fair	Poor
—	375	300	200	150	50

Model 1905 Special Target Rifle

Same as Model 1905 Target Rifle, except for hand checkered fancy American walnut stock.

NIB	Exc.	V.G.	Good	Fair	Poor
—	450	325	250	150	100

Model 19 NRA

A .22-caliber bolt-action rifle, with 25" barrel, detachable magazine and full-length military-style stock. Approximately 50,000 manufactured between 1919 and 1937.

NIB	Exc.	V.G.	Good	Fair	Poor
—	395	250	175	100	75

Model 19L

As above, with Lyman receiver sight. Manufactured between 1933 and 1942.

NIB	Exc.	V.G.	Good	Fair	Poor
—	425	275	225	200	150

Model 19M

As above, with 28" barrel. Fitted with telescope sight bases. Manufactured between 1933 and 1942.

NIB	Exc.	V.G.	Good	Fair	Poor
—	395	250	175	100	75

Model 19H

Model 19 chambered for .22 Hornet. Manufactured between 1933 and 1942.

NIB	Exc.	V.G.	Good	Fair	Poor
—	600	475	350	300	200

Model 3

A .22-caliber single-shot bolt-action rifle, with 24" barrel, open sights and walnut stock. Manufactured between 1933 and 1952.

NIB	Exc.	V.G.	Good	Fair	Poor
—	200	150	100	75	50

Model 4

Similar to above, with 24" barrel and 5-shot magazine. Produced from 1932 to 1964.

NIB	Exc.	V.G.	Good	Fair	Poor
—	200	150	100	75	50

Model 4M

As above, in .22 Magnum. Produced from 1960 to 1964.

NIB	Exc.	V.G.	Good	Fair	Poor
—	225	175	110	75	50

Model 5

Model 4, with a tubular magazine. Manufactured between 1933 and 1964.

NIB	Exc.	V.G.	Good	Fair	Poor
—	200	150	100	75	50

Model 1920

A .250-3000 or .300 Savage bolt-action rifle, with 22" or 24" barrel, open sights and 5-shot magazine. Blued, with walnut stock and schnabel fore-end. Manufactured between 1920 and 1929. An improved version introduced in 1926, that was heavier and had a Lyman #54 peep sight.

NIB	Exc.	V.G.	Good	Fair	Poor
—	1000	600	465	300	200

Model 1922

A variation of Model 19 NRA, with sporting-style stock and schnabel fore-end. Fitted with 23" round barrel. Chambered for .22-caliber cartridge. Superceded Model 23; looks like Model 23 Sporter. Introduced in 1922, discontinued 1923. Very rare.

NIB	Exc.	V.G.	Good	Fair	Poor
—	750	600	475	300	200

Model 23A

Bolt-action .22 LR rifle introduced in 1923. Features 5-round detachable box magazine and 23" barrel with open sights. Large loading port on left side of receiver permitted easy single-shot loading. Plain stock, with pistol-grip and schnabel fore-end. A varnish wood finish was applied to this model. Production stopped in 1933.

NIB	Exc.	V.G.	Good	Fair	Poor
—	350	275	150	125	100

Model 23AA

An improved version of Model 23A. Introduced in 1933. Features better speed lock, redesigned stock with oil-finish. Receiver tapped for No. 15 Savage extension peep sight. Weight about 6 lbs. Production ceased in 1942.

NIB	Exc.	V.G.	Good	Fair	Poor
—	395	295	200	150	125

Model 23B

Similar to Model 23A, except chambered for .25-20 cartridge. Barrel length 25", forearm a full 1.5" wide beavertail. Receiver tapped for peep sight, magazine capacity 4 rounds. Production from 1923 to 1940.

NIB	Exc.	V.G.	Good	Fair	Poor
—	375	325	250	200	100

Model 23C

Same configuration as Model 23B, with exception of caliber .32-20. Manufactured from 1923 to 1946.

NIB	Exc.	V.G.	Good	Fair	Poor
—	375	325	250	200	100

Model 23D

Same configuration as Model 23B, only chambered for .22 Hornet cartridge. Manufactured from 1932 to 1948.

NIB	Exc.	V.G.	Good	Fair	Poor
—	375	325	250	200	100

Model 40 (Old Model)

Similar to above, in .250-3000, .300 Savage, .30-30 and .30-06 caliber. Manufactured between 1928 and 1940.

NIB	Exc.	V.G.	Good	Fair	Poor
—	425	350	295	250	175

Model 45 Super

Similar to Old Model 40, with Lyman receiver sight and checkered walnut stock. Manufactured between 1928 and 1940.

NIB	Exc.	V.G.	Good	Fair	Poor
—	400	350	300	200	150

Model 35

A .22-caliber bolt-action rifle, with 22" barrel, open sights and 5-shot magazine. Blued, with Monte Carlo-style hardwood stock.

NIB	Exc.	V.G.	Good	Fair	Poor
—	175	150	125	75	50

Model 46

As above, with a tubular magazine. Manufactured between 1969 and 1973.

NIB	Exc.	V.G.	Good	Fair	Poor
—	175	150	125	75	50

Model 340

A .22 Hornet, .222 Rem., .223 or .30-30 caliber bolt-action rifle, with 22" or 24" barrel. Open sights and 4- or 5-shot magazine. Blued, with plain walnut stock. Manufactured between 1950 and 1985.

NIB	Exc.	V.G.	Good	Fair	Poor
—	375	325	250	200	100

Model 342

As above, in .22 Hornet caliber. Manufactured between 1950 and 1955.

NIB	Exc.	V.G.	Good	Fair	Poor
—	375	325	250	200	100

MODEL 110 SERIES

Model 110 Sporter

Bolt-action rifle manufactured in a variety of calibers. Barrel 22", open sights and 4-shot magazine. Blued, with walnut stock. Manufactured between 1958 and 1963.

NIB	Exc.	V.G.	Good	Fair	Poor
400	325	250	175	125	100

Model 110-M

Similar to above, in 7mm Magnum to .338 Win. Magnum. Manufactured between 1963 and 1969.

NIB	Exc.	V.G.	Good	Fair	Poor
400	325	275	200	150	125

Model 110-D

Similar to Model 110, in .22-250 to .338 Win. Magnum, with detachable magazine. Manufactured between 1966 and 1988.

NIB	Exc.	V.G.	Good	Fair	Poor
400	300	250	200	150	100

Model 110-P Premier Grade

As above, with finely figured walnut stock, rosewood fore-end tip and pistol-grip cap. Manufactured between 1964 and 1970.

NIB	Exc.	V.G.	Good	Fair	Poor
650	575	450	325	250	200

Model 110-PE

As above, with an engraved receiver, magazine floorplate and trigger guard. Manufactured between 1968 and 1970.

NIB	Exc.	V.G.	Good	Fair	Poor
900	800	700	500	400	300

Model 110-F

DuPont Rynite stock and sights. Discontinued.

NIB	Exc.	V.G.	Good	Fair	Poor
450	400	350	300	250	200

Model 110-FX

As above without sights. Discontinued.

NIB	Exc.	V.G.	Good	Fair	Poor
400	350	300	250	200	150

Model 110-FP

Composite stock and 24" heavy barrel. In 2003, Savage AccuTrigger was added. Discontinued.

NIB	Exc.	V.G.	Good	Fair	Poor
600	450	325	225	150	150

Model 110-G

Checkered hardwood stock and sights. Discontinued.

NIB	Exc.	V.G.	Good	Fair	Poor
425	325	275	225	175	125

Model 110-GX

As above without sights. Discontinued.

NIB	Exc.	V.G.	Good	Fair	Poor
400	300	250	200	150	100

Model 110-CY

Compact version of Model 110 series. Shorter length of pull on a walnut stock and 22" barrel. Overall length 42.5"; weight about 6.5 lbs. Chambered in .223, .243, .270, .300 Savage and .308-calibers. Discontinued.

NIB	Exc.	V.G.	Good	Fair	Poor
400	300	250	200	150	100

Model 110-FP Tactical

Offered in calibers from .223 Rem. to .300 Win. Magnum. Bolt-action rifle has 24" heavy barrel with recessed muzzle. Synthetic stock is black, as are all other surfaces. Available in both right-/left-hand versions. Weight about 8.5 lbs. Discontinued.

NIB	Exc.	V.G.	Good	Fair	Poor
600	450	325	225	150	150

Model 110-FP Duty

Introduced in 2002. Chambered for .308 cartridge. Features 24" free-floating barrel, with open sights. Black synthetic stock. Third swivel stud for bipod. Matte blue finish. Magazine capacity 4 rounds. Weight about 8.5 lbs. Discontinued.

NIB	Exc.	V.G.	Good	Fair	Poor
600	450	300	250	200	100

Model 110-FP-LE1

Similar to Model 110FP-Duty (.308), with 20" barrel. No sights. Weight about 8.25 lbs. Introduced in 2002, discontinued.

NIB	Exc.	V.G.	Good	Fair	Poor
500	375	275	225	175	100

Model 110-FP-LE2

Same as above, but fitted with 26" barrel. Weight about 8.75 lbs. Introduced in 2002, discontinued.

NIB	Exc.	V.G.	Good	Fair	Poor
500	375	275	225	175	100

Model 110-Fiftieth Anniversary

Short-action rifle commemorating 50th Anniversary of Model 10. Chambered in .300 Savage, with 22" barrel. 1000 numbered rifles, high-luster blued barrel and action, unique checkering pattern on select walnut stock, high-grade hinged floorplate, scroll pattern on receiver, 24-karat gold plated double-barrel bands, 24-karat gold plated AccuTrigger, embossed recoil pad.

NIB	Exc.	V.G.	Good	Fair	Poor
1000	750	600	475	300	200

Model 110 BA Law Enforcement Rifle

Bolt-action rifle chambered for .300 Win. Magnum and .338 Lapua Magnum. Features include: aluminum stock; Savage's innovative three-dimensional bedding system; interchangeable buttstocks; pistol-grips; three-sided accessory rail; 5-round detachable magazine; high-efficiency muzzle-brake; Magpul PRS adjustable stock; 26" carbon steel barrel.

NIB	Exc.	V.G.	Good	Fair	Poor
1900	1650	1400	1100	700	300

MODEL 111 SERIES

Model 111 Classic Hunter Series

All models under this series are fitted with a classic American designed straight comb stock with pistol-grip. Chambered in 13 different calibers from .223 Rem. to .338 Win. Magnum. Weights vary with caliber and stock type, but range from 6.365 to 7 lbs. Models are fitted with a detachable or internal magazine. All Hunter series rifles are drilled and tapped for scope mounts.

Model 111G

Top loading, with walnut stock and recoil pad. Chambered for .25-06, .270, .30-06, 7mm Rem. Magnum and .300 Win. Magnum. Fitted with 22" or 24" barrel, depending on caliber with iron sights. Weight about 7 lbs.

NIB	Exc.	V.G.	Good	Fair	Poor
495	375	275	200	150	100

Model 111GCNS

A long action model as above, with 22" or 24" barrel depending on caliber with no sights. Introduced in 2005.

NIB	Exc.	V.G.	Good	Fair	Poor
515	400	325	250	175	100

Model 111GC

Detachable magazine with walnut stock and recoil pad. Discontinued.

Savage Model 111 GC

NIB	Exc.	V.G.	Good	Fair	Poor
450	350	300	250	200	150

Model 111GL

Same as Model 111G, with left-hand action.

NIB	Exc.	V.G.	Good	Fair	Poor
485	350	250	200	150	100

Model 111F

Top loading, with graphite stock. Chambered for .25-06, .270, .30-06, 7mm Rem. Magnum, .300 Win. Magmum and .338 Win. Magnum. Fitted with 22" or 24" barrel, with iron sights. Weight about 6.75 lbs.

NIB	Exc.	V.G.	Good	Fair	Poor
485	350	250	200	150	100

Model 111FL

As above, with left-hand action.

NIB	Exc.	V.G.	Good	Fair	Poor
485	350	250	200	150	100

Model 111FC

Detachable magazine with graphite stock. Discontinued.

NIB	Exc.	V.G.	Good	Fair	Poor
450	350	300	250	200	150

Model 111FCNS

Introduced in 2005. Chambered for .25-06, .270, .30-06, 7mm Rem. Magnum, .300 Win. Magnum and .338 Win. Magnum. Fitted with 22" or 24" barrel, no sights. Black synthetic stock. Weight about 6.75 lbs., depending on caliber.

NIB	Exc.	V.G.	Good	Fair	Poor
505	375	275	—	—	—

Model 111FXP3

Top loading, with graphite stock and 3x9 scope. Rings, bases and sling.

NIB	Exc.	V.G.	Good	Fair	Poor
515	400	350	300	200	150

Model 111FCXP3

Same as above, with detachable magazine.

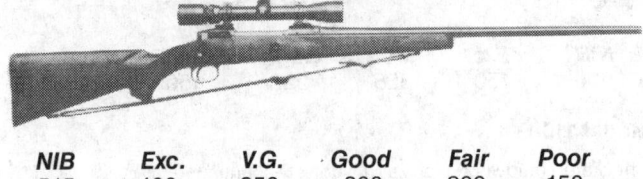

NIB	Exc.	V.G.	Good	Fair	Poor
515	400	350	300	200	150

Model 111FAK

Blued steel barrel, composite stock, muzzle-brake. Discontinued.

NIB	Exc.	V.G.	Good	Fair	Poor
450	350	300	250	200	150

MODEL 112 SERIES

Model 112BT / 112BT-S (Long Action)

Introduced for the first time in 1994. A competition grade rifle. Chambered for .223 Rem. and .308 Win. Features 26" heavy stainless steel barrel, fitted to an alloy steel receiver. In 1995, .300 Win. Magnum was added and referred to as Model 112BT-S. Barrel finish black. Stock laminated, with ambidextrous palm swell and adjustable cheek rest. Weight about 11 lbs.

Savage Model 112 BT

NIB	Exc.	V.G.	Good	Fair	Poor
1025	850	700	500	300	250

Model 112 Series Varmint Rifles

Series of varmint rifles feature 26" barrels. Offered with composite or laminated wood stocks. All Model 112s are top loading. Drilled and tapped for scope mounting. Available in .223, .22-250 and .220 Swift. Configuration weight about: 10.5 lbs. BV; 9 lbs. FV.

Model 112BVSS (Long Action)

Laminated wood stock, with high comb and ambidextrous palm swell. Fitted with stainless steel barrel, bolt and trigger guard. In 1996, .300 Win. Magnum, 7mm Rem. Magnum, .308 Win., .30-06 and .25-06 were added.

NIB	Exc.	V.G.	Good	Fair	Poor
720	550	400	275	200	150

Model 112BVSS-S

Same as above, but single-shot.

NIB	Exc.	V.G.	Good	Fair	Poor
600	450	325	225	150	150

Model 112FVSS

Fitted with stainless steel barrel and composite stock. In 1995, a stainless steel "fluted" barrel and several new calibers were added: 300 Win.

Magnum, 7mm Rem. Magnum, .25-06 Rem. In 2003, Savage AccuTrigger was added.

NIB	Exc.	V.G.	Good	Fair	Poor
475	400	350	300	200	150

Model 112FVSS-S

Single-shot version of above model.

NIB	Exc.	V.G.	Good	Fair	Poor
475	400	350	300	200	150

Model 112FV

Similar to above, with a blued barrel.

NIB	Exc.	V.G.	Good	Fair	Poor
375	300	250	200	150	100

Model 112BT—Competition Grade

A competition rifle introduced in 1996. Features 26" blackened stainless steel barrel and custom target style laminated stock, with adjustable cheek rest. Chambered for .223 or .308 cartridges. Weight about 11 lbs. Barrel is pillar bedded.

NIB	Exc.	V.G.	Good	Fair	Poor
950	850	700	500	300	250

MODEL 114 SERIES

Model 114C—Classic

Introduced in 2000. Features select grade oil-finished walnut stock, with cut checkering. No sights. Chambered for .270 and .30-06, with 22" barrel; 7mm Magnum and .300 Win. Magnum, with 24" barrel.

NIB	Exc.	V.G.	Good	Fair	Poor
615	450	325	225	—	—

Model 114CE—Classic European

Introduced in 1996. Chambered for .270 Win., .30-06, 7mm Rem. Magnum and .300 Win. Magnum. Barrel lengths 22" or 24", depending on caliber. Oil-finished stock, with skip line checkering and cheekpiece. Schnabel type fore-end tip. Rubber recoil pad and pistol-grip cap are standard. High luster blue finish. Weight about 7.12 lbs. Discontinued.

Courtesy Savage Arms

NIB	Exc.	V.G.	Good	Fair	Poor
550	475	400	350	300	150

Model 114CU

Has select grade walnut oil-finished stock. Finish, high polish blue and bolt has laser etched Savage logo. Detachable magazine standard. Receiver drilled and tapped for scope mount. Offered in .270, .30-06, 7mm Rem. Magnum and .300 Win. Magnum. Weight about 7.125 lbs. Discontinued.

NIB	Exc.	V.G.	Good	Fair	Poor
500	425	325	250	200	150

Model 114U—Ultra

Introduced in 1999. Features high gloss walnut stock, with custom checkering. Blued finish is high luster, with laser-etched Savage logo on bolt body. Chambered for .270 Win., .30-06, 7mm-08 Rem. and .300 Win. Magnum. Barrel length 22" or 24". Weight about 7 lbs.

NIB	Exc.	V.G.	Good	Fair	Poor
500	425	325	250	200	150

MODEL 116 SERIES

This series of rifles feature graphite stocks and stainless steel barreled actions. An adjustable muzzle-brake also included. All rifles in 116 series are drilled and tapped for scope mounts.

Model 116FCSAK (Long Action)

Features a detachable box magazine. Fluted 22" barrel. Offered in .270, .30-06, 7mm Rem. Magnum, .300 Win. Magnum and .338 Win. Magnum. Weight about 6.5 lbs.

NIB	Exc.	V.G.	Good	Fair	Poor
660	500	375	250	175	175

Model 116FSAK (Long Action)

Same as above, with on-off choice for muzzle-brake given to shooter. AccuTrigger added in 2004.

NIB	Exc.	V.G.	Good	Fair	Poor
600	450	325	225	175	175

Model 116BSS

Introduced in 2001. Features laminated stock. Chambered for .270 Win., .30-06, 7mm Rem. Magnum, .300 Win. Magnum and .300 Rem. Ultra Magnum. Fitted with 24" or 26" stainless steel barrel. No sights. Weight about 7.5 lbs. Discontinued.

NIB	Exc.	V.G.	Good	Fair	Poor
625	500	365	225	175	175

Model 116FSS (Long Action)

Standard configuration for 116 series. Features top-loading action, with 22" or 24" barrel. No muzzle-brake. Weight about 6.75 lbs. Offered in 7 calibers from .223 to .338 Win. Magnum. AccuTrigger added in 2004.

NIB	Exc.	V.G.	Good	Fair	Poor
550	475	375	300	200	150

Model 116FCS

Same as above, with stainless steel removable box magazine.

NIB	Exc.	V.G.	Good	Fair	Poor
550	475	375	300	200	150

Model 116FSK—Kodiak (Long Action)

Features top loading action, with 22" barrel and muzzle-brake. Weight about 7.25 lbs.

NIB	Exc.	V.G.	Good	Fair	Poor
575	495	385	300	200	150

Model 116SE—Safari Express

Introduced in 1994. Features select grade walnut stock, with ebony tip and deluxe checkering. Offered in .300 Win. Magnum, .338 Win. Magnum and .458-calibers. In 1995, .425 Express cartridge added. In 2000, stainless steel action and barrel, with adjustable muzzle-brake. Weight about 8.5 lbs. Discontinued.

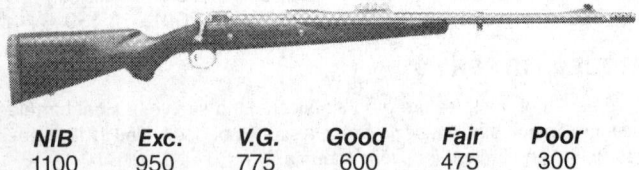

NIB	Exc.	V.G.	Good	Fair	Poor
1100	950	775	600	475	300

Model 116US

Introduced in 1995. Features stainless steel action and barrel, high gloss American walnut stock, with ebony tip and custom checkering. Offered in .270 Win., .30-06, 7mm Rem. Magnum and .300 Win. Magnum. Barrel 22" or 24". Discontinued.

NIB	Exc.	V.G.	Good	Fair	Poor
600	500	400	300	250	200

MODEL 12 SERIES VARMINT

Introduced in 1998, this series features short action heavy barrel line of rifles designed for long-range shooting.

Model 12BVSS

Features 26" fluted stainless steel barrel, recessed crown and brown laminated stock, with beavertail fore-end. Chambered for .223, .22-250 and .308. Magazine capacity 4 rounds. Weight about 9.5 lbs. Introduced in 1998. In 2003, Savage AccuTrigger added.

NIB	Exc.	V.G.	Good	Fair	Poor
720	550	400	275	200	100

Model 12BVSS-S

Same as above, in single-shot version. Chambered for .223 and .22-250. Weight 9 lbs. In 2003, Savage AccuTrigger added.

NIB	Exc.	V.G.	Good	Fair	Poor
720	550	400	275	200	150

Model 12BVSS-SXP

Introduced in 2003. Single-shot chambered for .223 Rem. or .22-250 Rem. Fitted with 26" stainless steel fluted barrel. Savage AccuTrigger. Stock target-style heavy prone laminate. Weight about 12 lbs.

NIB	Exc.	V.G.	Good	Fair	Poor
675	525	400	275	200	150

Model 12BTCSS

Similar to Model 12BVSS, with laminated thumbhole Monte Carlo stock. Short action and detachable box magazine.

NIB	Exc.	V.G.	Good	Fair	Poor
725	550	400	275	200	100

Model 12FVSS

Stainless steel 26" fluted barrel and synthetic stock. Offered in .223, .22-250 and .308-calibers. Weight about 9 lbs. Introduced in 1998. A left-hand version also offered. In 2003, Savage AccuTrigger added.

NIB	Exc.	V.G.	Good	Fair	Poor
600	500	375	250	200	100

Model 12FVSS-S

Same as above, in single-shot configuration. Chambered for .223 or .22-250. Weight about 9 lbs. In 2003, Savage AccuTrigger added. Discontinued.

NIB	Exc.	V.G.	Good	Fair	Poor
550	450	325	225	175	100

Model 12FV (Short Action)

Similar to other 12 Series rifles, with blued action and 26" non-fluted barrel. Synthetic stock. Chambered for .223 or .22-250. Weight about 9 lbs. Introduced in 1998. In 2003, Savage AccuTrigger added.

NIB	Exc.	V.G.	Good	Fair	Poor
575	495	385	300	200	150

Model 12FLV

As above, with left-hand action. Introduced in 2005.

NIB	Exc.	V.G.	Good	Fair	Poor
575	495	385	300	200	150

Model 12VSS—Varminter (Short Action)

Introduced in 2000. Features Choate adjustable black synthetic stock. Heavy fluted stainless steel barrel. Box magazine holds 4 rounds. Chambered for .223 or .22-250. Weight about 15 lbs. In 2003, Savage AccuTrigger added.

NIB	Exc.	V.G.	Good	Fair	Poor
700	525	375	275	200	100

Model 12 Varminter Low Profile

Introduced in 2004. Chambered for .223 Rem. or .22-250. Fitted with 26" heavy fluted stainless steel barrel, with no sights. Low-profile laminated stock, with extra wide beavertail forearm. Adjustable trigger. Available as a repeater or single-shot. Weight about 10 lbs.

NIB	Exc.	V.G.	Good	Fair	Poor
600	500	375	250	200	100

Model 12 LRPV Long Range Precision Varminter

Similar to Model 12 FVSS, with 30" stainless bull barrel and various accurizing refinements. Chambered in .204 Ruger, .223 Rem. and .22-250. Introduced in 2007. Available in single-shot and 4+1 repeating versions.

NIB	Exc.	V.G.	Good	Fair	Poor
850	700	575	425	300	150

Model 12 Varminter Low Profile

Single-shot and 4+1 repeating versions. Chambered in .22 Hornet, .204, .223, .22-250 and .243. Laminated stock. Fluted 26" barrel. Left-hand version available.

NIB	Exc.	V.G.	Good	Fair	Poor
950	800	650	500	350	175

Model 12 FCV Varmint Rifle

New Model 12 FCV varmint rifle, includes AccuStock with beavertail fore-end, AccuTrigger, detachable box magazine and heavy fluted barrel.

NIB	Exc.	V.G.	Good	Fair	Poor
675	600	525	450	300	150

Model 12 F-Class Target Rifle

International-class target rifle chambered in 6.5x284 Norma. Ventilated fore-end, laminated "under-hold" target stock, oversize bolt knob, AccuTrigger, 30" stainless barrel. Also available in Model 12F/TR version, with conventional buttstock and elevated cheekpiece. Introduced in 2007.

NIB	Exc.	V.G.	Good	Fair	Poor
1200	1000	750	600	475	200

Model 12 Long Range Precision

Target series rifle with target style AccuTrigger, HS Precision fiberglass matte black stock. Fluted 26" barrel. Detachable magazine with 4-round capacity. Weight 11 lbs.; overall length 46.25". Chambered for .243 Win., .260 Rem. or 6.5 Creedmoor.

NIB	Exc.	V.G.	Good	Fair	Poor
925	825	700	550	400	250

Model 12 Palma

Target rifle designed for Palma Trophy Match competition in .308 Win.

Single-shot, with 30" stainless steel heavy barrel, laminated adjustable stock and Savage AccuTrigger.

NIB	Exc.	V.G.	Good	Fair	Poor
1800	1525	1250	900	500	250

MODEL 40 VARMINT HUNTER

Model 40 Varmint Hunter

Introduced in 2004. Chambered for .22 Hornet or .223 Rem. Fitted with 24" heavy barrel, with no sights. Laminated stock, with wide beavertail forearm. Blued. Single-shot. Weight about 7.75 lbs. **NOTE:** Add $30 for .223 Rem.

NIB	Exc.	V.G.	Good	Fair	Poor
400	300	250	200	150	100

MODEL 10 SERIES

Model 10FP—Tactical (Short Action)

Short action chambered for .223- or .308-calibers. Fitted with 24" barrel. Black synthetic stock. Drilled and tapped for scope mount. Weight about 8 lbs. Introduced in 1998. In 2003, Savage AccuTrigger added. Premium for Choate or McMillan stock.

NIB	Exc.	V.G.	Good	Fair	Poor
545	450	325	225	150	100

Model 10FLP

Same as above, in left-hand. In 2003, Savage AccuTrigger added.

NIB	Exc.	V.G.	Good	Fair	Poor
550	450	325	225	150	100

Model 10FM—Sierra

Introduced in 1998. Features 20" barrel chambered for .223, .243 or .308. In 2002, .300 WSM caliber added. Black synthetic stock. Magazine capacity 4 rounds. Weight about 6 lbs. Discontinued.

NIB	Exc.	V.G.	Good	Fair	Poor
500	400	300	150	125	100

Model 10FCM—Sierra

Introduced in 2005. Features 20" light barrel, with detachable magazine. Chambered for .243, 7mm-08 Rem., .308, .270 and .300 WSM. Black synthetic stock. Weight about 6.25 lbs.

NIB	Exc.	V.G.	Good	Fair	Poor
550	450	325	225	150	100

Model 10FCM—Scout Rifle

Chambered for 7mm-08 Rem. or .308 Win. Fitted with 20" barrel, removable ghost ring rear sight, one-piece scope mount and other special features. Weight about 6.2 lbs. Introduced in 1999; discontinued 2005; reintroduced 2007.

NIB	Exc.	V.G.	Good	Fair	Poor
545	450	325	225	150	100

Model 10GY Youth

Similar to Model 10FM. Features shortened hardwood stock. Fitted with 22" barrel and open sights. Chambered for .223, .243 or .308. Weight about 6.25 lbs. Introduced in 1998.

NIB	Exc.	V.G.	Good	Fair	Poor
450	325	225	165	125	100

Model 10 Predator Hunter

Similar to Model 10FCM. Overall camo finish, 22" medium-contour barrel and AccuTrigger. Chambered in .204 Ruger, .22-250 and .223. Introduced in 2007. **NOTE:** Savage Predator line of rifles now includes a version with new AccuStock, Savage launched in 2009. This version has AccuStock, AccuTrigger, detachable box magazine and medium-contour fluted barrel. Stock finished in Realtree Advantage Max 1 and metal is matte black. MSRP is $945.

NIB	Exc.	V.G.	Good	Fair	Poor
600	475	350	275	200	100

Model 10XP Predator

Package rifle with factory-mounted scope. Entirely covered in camo finish. Barrel 22". Chambered in .204, .223 and .22-250. Introduced in 2008.

NIB	Exc.	V.G.	Good	Fair	Poor
650	500	395	300	225	125

Model 10XP Predator Hunter Bolt-Action Rifle Package

Bolt-action rifle similar to Model 10. Chambered in .223, .204, .22-250 or .243 Win. Includes 4-12x40 scope, 22" barrel, Accu-Trigger, choice of Realtree Snow or Mossy Oak Brush camo overall.

NIB	Exc.	V.G.	Good	Fair	Poor
725	575	425	325	250	150

LAW ENFORCEMENT SERIES

Model 10FP-LE1

Chambered for .308 Win. cartridge. Fitted with 20" heavy barrel, with no

sights. Black synthetic stock. AccuTrigger. Weight about 8.25 lbs. Introduced in 2003.

NIB	Exc.	V.G.	Good	Fair	Poor
550	450	325	225	150	100

Model 10FP-LE1A

As above, chambered for .223 Rem. and .308. Black synthetic Choate adjustable stock, with accessory rail. Weight about 10.75 lbs. Introduced in 2003.

NIB	Exc.	V.G.	Good	Fair	Poor
650	500	395	300	225	125

Model 10FP-LE2B

Bolt-action chambered for .308 Win. Fitted with McMillan fiberglass tactical stock. Barrel 26", with no sights. AccuTrigger. Matte blue finish. Weight about 10 lbs. Introduced in 2003.

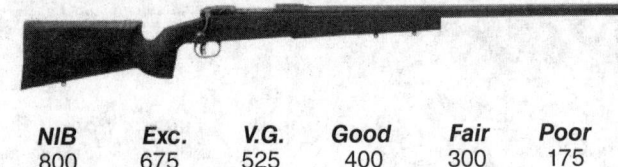

NIB	Exc.	V.G.	Good	Fair	Poor
800	675	525	400	300	175

Model 10FP-LE2

Introduced in 2003. Features 26" barrel. Chambered for .308 Win. Fitted with black synthetic stock. AccuTrigger. Weight about 8.75 lbs.

NIB	Exc.	V.G.	Good	Fair	Poor
650	500	395	300	225	125

Model 10FP-LE2A

Chambered for .223 or .308. Fitted with 26" heavy barrel, with no sights. Black synthetic Choate adjustable stock, with accessory rail. Weight about 11.25 lbs. Introduced in 2003.

NIB	Exc.	V.G.	Good	Fair	Poor
725	575	425	325	250	150

Model 10FPXP-LEA

This item is a package of both rifle and scope with accessories. Features Model 10FP, with 26" barrel and black synthetic stock. Leupold 3.5-10x40 black matte scope, with Mil Dot scope covers and one-piece base. Harris bipod and heavy duty aluminum case. Weight about 10.5 lbs. Introduced in 2003.

NIB	Exc.	V.G.	Good	Fair	Poor
1950	1450	1100	700	450	300

Model 10FPXP-LE

As above, with Choate adjustable stock and accessory rail. Weight about 11.25 lbs. Introduced in 2003.

NIB	Exc.	V.G.	Good	Fair	Poor
1805	1350	1000	600	350	200

Model 10FCP-HS Precision

Similar to Model 110FP-LE1, with one-piece HS Precision synthetic target stock and detachable box magazine. Introduced in 2007.

NIB	Exc.	V.G.	Good	Fair	Poor
650	500	395	300	225	125

Model 10FCP Choate

Similar to Model 10FP-LE1, with Choate synthetic stock. Introduced in 2007.

NIB	Exc.	V.G.	Good	Fair	Poor
675	535	395	300	225	125

Model 10FCP McMillan

Similar to Model 10FP-LE1, with synthetic McMillan precision stock. Introduced in 2007.

NIB	Exc.	V.G.	Good	Fair	Poor
1100	900	725	575	400	200

Model 10FPXP-HS Precision

Similar to Model 10FPXP-LEA, with HS Precision Tactical Stock. Introduced 2006.

NIB	Exc.	V.G.	Good	Fair	Poor
1725	1500	1250	800	600	300

Model 10FP-HS

Similar to Model 10FP-LE1, with HS Precision Tactical stock. Introduced 2006.

NIB	Exc.	V.G.	Good	Fair	Poor
950	800	625	475	300	200

Model 10 Precision Carbine

Similar to Model 10, with 20" medium contour barrel, synthetic camo Accu-Stock. Chambered in .223 or .308.

NIB	Exc.	V.G.	Good	Fair	Poor
800	675	525	400	300	175

Model 10FLCP

Similar to Model 10 FCP, in left-hand configuration, with standard or AccuStock.

NIB	Exc.	V.G.	Good	Fair	Poor
800	675	525	400	300	175

Model 10 BAS Law Enforcement Bolt-Action Rifle

Bolt-action repeater based on Model 10 action. Has 24" fluted heavy barrel with muzzle-brake, M4-style collapsible buttstock, pistol-grip with palm swell, all-aluminum AccuStock, Picatinny rail for mounting optics. Chambered in .308 Win.

NIB	Exc.	V.G.	Good	Fair	Poor
1600	1350	1000	750	500	300

Model 10 BAT-S

Similar to above, with multi-adjustable buttstock.

NIB	Exc.	V.G.	Good	Fair	Poor
1700	1400	1075	800	550	325

MODEL 10 SERIES MUZZLELOADER

Model 10ML-II

Fitted with .50-caliber 24" barrel, with adjustable sights. Synthetic stock. Blued finish. Weight about 7.75 lbs.

NIB	Exc.	V.G.	Good	Fair	Poor
530	375	300	200	150	100

Model 10MLSS-II

As above in stainless steel.

NIB	Exc.	V.G.	Good	Fair	Poor
590	375	325	200	150	100

Model 10ML-II Camo

Introduced in 2002. Has camo stock finish, with blued barrel and action.

NIB	Exc.	V.G.	Good	Fair	Poor
570	425	300	200	150	100

Model 10MLSS-II Camo

Has camo stock finish, with stainless steel barrel and action. Introduced in 2002.

NIB	Exc.	V.G.	Good	Fair	Poor
625	475	350	200	150	100

Model 10MLBSS-II

Features brown laminate stock, with stainless steel action and barrel. Weight 8.75 lbs. Introduced in 2002.

NIB	Exc.	V.G.	Good	Fair	Poor
665	500	375	200	150	100

Model 10ML-IIXP

Introduced in 2002. Has blued action and barrel, with synthetic stock. Fitted with 3-9x40mm scope. Weight 9.25 lbs.

NIB	Exc.	V.G.	Good	Fair	Poor
570	425	300	200	150	100

Model 10MLSS-IIXP

Same as above, with stainless steel barrel and action.

NIB	Exc.	V.G.	Good	Fair	Poor
625	475	350	200	150	100

MODEL 11 SERIES

Model 11F

Features short action chambered for .223, .22-250, .243 or .308. Barrel 22", with open sights. Black synthetic stock. Weight about 6.75 lbs. Introduced in 1998.

NIB	Exc.	V.G.	Good	Fair	Poor
485	350	250	175	125	100

Model 11FCNS

Introduced in 2005. Chambered for .22-250, .243, 7mm-08, .308, .270 WSM, .7mm WSN and .300 WSM. Barrel 22" or 24", without sights. Detachable box magazine. Black synthetic stock. Weight about 6.5 lbs.

NIB	Exc.	V.G.	Good	Fair	Poor
500	375	250	175	125	100

Model 11 Lightweight Hunter

Chambered for five standard cartridges, plus 6.5 Creedmoor. Lightweight at 5.5 lbs. Satin-finished American walnut wood stock. AccuTrigger, detachable box magazine, matte blue barrel and action with spiral fluted bolt. Barrel 20".

NIB	Exc.	V.G.	Good	Fair	Poor
750	650	500	400	250	150

Model 11G

Chambered for .223, .243, .22-250 or .308. Fitted with 22" barrel. Wood stock has fancy checkered pattern, black recoil pad and gold medallion. Fitted with open sights. Weight about 6.75 lbs. Introduced in 1998.

NIB	Exc.	V.G.	Good	Fair	Poor
500	375	250	175	125	100

Model 11BTH

Laminated thumbhole-stock version of Model 11. Chambered in .204, .223, .22-250 and .22 Hornet. Blued 22" barrel.

NIB	Exc.	V.G.	Good	Fair	Poor
625	475	350	200	150	100

Model 11GCNS

Introduced in 2005. Chambered for .22-250, .243, 7mm-08, .308, .270 WSM, 7mm WSM and .300 WSM. Fitted with 22" or 24" barrel, without sights. Checkered walnut stock. Detachable box magazine. Weight about 6.75 lbs.

NIB	Exc.	V.G.	Good	Fair	Poor
525	400	300	200	150	100

Model 11FYCAK

Short-action youth model chambered in .243, 7mm-08 and .308. Blue 22" barrel, with muzzle-brake. No sights. Stock black composite. Weight 6.5 lbs.; overall length 41.5". Introduced 2006.

NIB	Exc.	V.G.	Good	Fair	Poor
515	400	300	200	125	100

Model 111FYCAK

Similar to Model 11FYCAK, but long-action chambered for .25-06, .270 and .30-06. Introduced 2006.

NIB	Exc.	V.G.	Good	Fair	Poor
515	400	300	200	125	100

Model 111FHNS

Similar to Model 111FCNS, with hinged floorplate. Introduced 2006.

NIB	Exc.	V.G.	Good	Fair	Poor
515	400	300	200	125	100

Model 11FCXP3

Similar to Model 111FCXP3, in short-action. Introduced 2006.

NIB	Exc.	V.G.	Good	Fair	Poor
515	400	300	200	125	100

Model 11FYCXP3

Similar to Model 11FCXP3, in youth version chambered in .243 Win.

NIB	Exc.	V.G.	Good	Fair	Poor
450	325	250	175	150	100

MODEL 14 SERIES

Model 14 Classic

Short-action chambered for .22-250, .243, .270 WSM, 7mm-08, .300 WSM and .308. Barrel polished blue 22" or 24", without sights. Stock select lacquered walnut, with contrasting fore-end. Introduced 2006. Also available in American Classic version with optional left-hand action.

NIB	Exc.	V.G.	Good	Fair	Poor
600	500	400	300	200	100

Model 14 Left Hand

Similar to above in left-hand. Chambered in .250 and .300 Savage only. Suggested retail price: $779.

Model 114 Classic

Similar to Model 14 Classic, in long-action. Chambered for .270, 7mm RM and .300 WM. Introduced 2006. Also available in American Classic version with optional left-hand action.

NIB	Exc.	V.G.	Good	Fair	Poor
625	475	350	200	150	100

Model 14 Euro Classic

Similar to Model 14 Classic, with iron sights. Introduced 2006.

NIB	Exc.	V.G.	Good	Fair	Poor
625	475	350	200	150	100

Model 114 Euro Classic

Similar to Model 114 Classic, with iron sights. Introduced 2006.

NIB	Exc.	V.G.	Good	Fair	Poor
625	475	350	200	150	100

Model 14 / 114 American Classic Stainless

Traditional design has an oil-finished American walnut stock. Features wrap-around checkering, black fore-end tip and no Monte-Carlo. Available in short-/long-action versions. Short action chambered for .243 or .308 Win.; long action .270 Win., .30-06 and 7mm Rem. Magnum. All with 22" barrel. Introduced in 2011.

NIB	Exc.	V.G.	Good	Fair	Poor
825	750	650	500	350	150

MODEL 16 SERIES

Model 16FSS

Short action with top-loading design. Magazine capacity 4 rounds. Chambered for .223, .243 or .308. Fitted with 22" stainless steel barrel. Black synthetic stock. Introduced in 1998.

NIB	Exc.	V.G.	Good	Fair	Poor
550	425	325	250	200	100

Model 16FLSS

Same as above, with left-hand action.

NIB	Exc.	V.G.	Good	Fair	Poor
550	425	325	250	200	100

Model 16FCSAK

Introduced in 2005. Chambered for .243, 7mm-08 Rem., .308, .270 WSM, 7mm WSM and .300 WSM. Fitted with 22" or 24" barrel. Detachable box magazine. Black synthetic stock. Weight about 7.5 lbs.

NIB	Exc.	V.G.	Good	Fair	Poor
660	500	400	300	200	100

Model 16FCSS

Chambered for .22-250, .243, 7mm-08 Rem., .308, .270 WSM, 7mm WSM and .300 WSM. Fitted with 22" or 24" barrel. Detachable box magazine. Black synthetic stock. Weight about 6.5 lbs. Introduced in 2005.

NIB	Exc.	V.G.	Good	Fair	Poor
570	425	375	250	175	125

Model 16BSS

Introduced in 2002. Features short action chambered for 7mm RSUM, .300 RSUM and .300 WSM cartridges. Fitted with 24" stainless steel barrel, drilled and tapped for scope mounts. Laminated stock with cut checkering. Weight about 7.75 lbs. Discontinued.

NIB	Exc.	V.G.	Good	Fair	Poor
640	475	400	300	200	100

Model 16FHSAK

Similar to Model 116FHSAK, but short-action only. Introduced 2006.

NIB	Exc.	V.G.	Good	Fair	Poor
600	475	350	200	150	100

Model 16FHSS

Similar to Model 16FSS, with hinged floorplate. Introduced 2006.

NIB	Exc.	V.G.	Good	Fair	Poor
600	475	350	200	150	100

Long Range Precision Varminter

Single-shot bolt-action chambered in .204 Ruger, .223 or .22-250. Features include AccuTrigger and oversized bolt handle. Composite stock, sightless stainless steel fluted barrel. Weight 11.25 lbs. Introduced 2006.

NIB	Exc.	V.G.	Good	Fair	Poor
900	750	600	450	300	200

Model 112 Varmint, Low Profile

Long action bolt rifle chambered for .25-06 (4) and .300 WM (3). Stock brown laminated, with recoil pad. Barrel 26" sightless stainless steel bull. Weight 11.25 lbs.

NIB	Exc.	V.G.	Good	Fair	Poor
600	475	350	200	150	100

Model 25 Lightweight Varminter

Short action rifle chambered in .204 and .223. Medium-contour fluted barrel, with recessed target crown, free-floating sleeved barrel, dual pillar bedding, three locking lugs, 60-degree bolt lift, AccuTrigger adjustable from 2.5 to 3.25 lbs., detachable box magazine. Weight 8.25 lbs.

NIB	Exc.	V.G.	Good	Fair	Poor
575	450	325	250	150	100

Model 25 Lightweight Varminter Thumbhole

Similar to above, with thumbhole stock.

NIB	Exc.	V.G.	Good	Fair	Poor
650	525	400	325	275	125

Model 25 Classic Sporter

Short action rifle chambered in .204 and .223. Free-floating sleeved barrel, dual pillar bedding, three locking lugs, 60-degree bolt lift, AccuTrigger adjustable from 2.5 to 3.25 lbs. Detachable box magazine. Satin lacquer American walnut stock, with contrasting fore-end tip and wrap-around checkering.

NIB	Exc.	V.G.	Good	Fair	Poor
600	475	350	200	150	100

Model 25 Walking Varminter

Chambered for .204 Ruger, .22 Hornet, .222 Rem., .223 Rem. and 5.7x28mm. Features 22" barrel sleeved for rigidity. Triple pillar bedding and Weaver scope bases. Has three-lug bolt, with 60-degree throw to allow mounting of a large diameter. AccuTrigger standard. Center feed detachable magazine and synthetic stock.

NIB	Exc.	V.G.	Good	Fair	Poor
475	425	350	250	200	150

Savage Edge Bolt Action Rifle

Entry level bolt-action repeating rifle. Chambered in .223, .22-250, .243 Win., 7mm-08, .308 Win., .25-06, .270 Win. and .30-06. Features include 22" matte black barrel, synthetic black stock, 4-round capacity detachable box magazine, drilled and tapped for scope mounts. Also available in camo finish (Edge Camo); XP variation (with 3x9 scope); Camo XP (with camo finish and scope). In 2011, name of this model was changed to Axis. **NOTE:** Add 15 percent for camo stock; 20 percent for scope.

NIB	Exc.	V.G.	Good	Fair	Poor
300	265	225	200	150	100

Axis Series and Edge

Comes in Long or Short action. Offered in 8-cartridge choices from .223 Rem. to .30-06 Springfield. Stainless action, natural color. Detachable box magazine. Right-hand action only. Synthetic stock, with camo or black matte finish. Drilled and tapped for scope mounts. Also available with 3-9x40 mounted scope. Previously called "The Edge". **NOTE:** Add 15 percent for camo stock; 20 percent for scope; 30 percent for pillar bedded hardwood stock (Axis II XP); 50 percent for stainless.

NIB	Exc.	V.G.	Good	Fair	Poor
325	285	250	200	150	125

RIMFIRE RIFLES

NOTE: As of 2006, virtually all Savage rimfire rifles (with exception of 30G and semi-automatics) were equipped with AccuTrigger as a standard feature.

Model 60

A .22-caliber semi-automatic rifle, with 20" barrel, open sights and tubular magazine. Blued, with Monte Carlo-style walnut stock. Manufactured between 1969 and 1972.

NIB	Exc.	V.G.	Good	Fair	Poor
—	100	80	70	50	35

Model 64G

Introduced in 1996. Semi-automatic .22 long rifle has 20.25" barrel and 10-shot detachable magazine. Finish is blue. Monte Carlo stock, with checkered pistol-grip. Bead front sight, with adjustable open rear sight standard. Weight about 5.5 lbs.

NIB	Exc.	V.G.	Good	Fair	Poor
160	125	90	60	50	40

Model 64GXP

As above, with unmounted 4x15mm scope.

NIB	Exc.	V.G.	Good	Fair	Poor
170	125	100	80	60	50

Model 64BTV

Similar to Model 64, with laminated thumbhole stock.

NIB	Exc.	V.G.	Good	Fair	Poor
170	125	100	80	60	50

Model 64F

Introduced in 1997. Features black synthetic stock, with blue finish. Chambered for .22 LR. Fitted with 20.25" barrel. Weight about 5.5 lbs.

NIB	Exc.	V.G.	Good	Fair	Poor
140	120	90	65	50	25

Model 64FSS

Similar to above, with stainless steel action and barrel. Introduced in 2002.

NIB	Exc.	V.G.	Good	Fair	Poor
200	150	110	75	50	25

Model 64FV

Introduced in 1998. Features heavy 21" target barrel, with no sights. Black synthetic stock standard. Chambered for .22 LR cartridge. Weight about 6 lbs. Discontinued.

NIB	Exc.	V.G.	Good	Fair	Poor
150	125	90	65	50	25

Model 64FVXP

Similar to Model 64FV, with scope package. Introduced 2006.

NIB	Exc.	V.G.	Good	Fair	Poor
190	150	110	75	50	25

Model 64FVSS

Similar to Model FV, with stainless steel action and barrel. Introduced in 2002. Discontinued.

NIB	Exc.	V.G.	Good	Fair	Poor
225	175	125	100	75	50

Model 64FXP

A package model that offers a .22 LR gun, with 20.25" barrel. Detachable 10-round magazine. Open sights and 4x15mm scope. Introduced in 1998. Weight about 5.25 lbs.

NIB	Exc.	V.G.	Good	Fair	Poor
150	125	90	65	50	25

Model 88

As above, with hardwood stock. Manufactured between 1969 and 1972.

NIB	Exc.	V.G.	Good	Fair	Poor
—	100	80	70	50	35

Model 90 Carbine

As above, with 16.5" barrel and carbine-style stock. Fore-end secured by one barrel band. Discontinued.

NIB	Exc.	V.G.	Good	Fair	Poor
—	100	80	70	50	35

Model A-17

Semi-automatic rifle chambered for .17 HMR (Hornady Magnum Rimfire) cartridge operating on a delayed blowback system. Removable rotary magazine has a capacity of 10 rounds. Barrel length 22"; weight 5.4 lbs. Receiver drilled and tapped for scope mounts and bases are included. Features include famous Savage AccuTrigger and a push-button crossbolt safety located in front of trigger guard. Stock is injection-molded polymer, with a matte black finish. Sporter model has a gray laminate stock; Target Thumbhole model has a heavy barrel, gray laminate thumbhole stock and oversized bolt handle. Introduced in 2016. **NOTE:** Add $75 for Sporter model; $130 for Target Thumbhole variant.

NIB	Exc.	V.G.	Good	Fair	Poor
400	350	—	—	—	—

Model 93G

Introduced in 1996. Bolt-action repeating rifle chambered for .22 WMR cartridge. Fitted with 20.75" barrel, with 5-shot magazine. Walnut-stained hardwood stock, with cut checkering. Open sights standard. Weight about 5.75 lbs. In 2001, offered in left-hand version (Model 93GL).

NIB	Exc.	V.G.	Good	Fair	Poor
195	150	100	75	60	50

Model 93FS

This .22 WMR model features stainless steel finish, with 20.75" barrel and black synthetic stock. Five-round magazine. Front bead sight and sporting rear. Introduced in 1997. Weight about 5.5 lbs. Discontinued.

NIB	Exc.	V.G.	Good	Fair	Poor
195	150	100	75	60	50

Model 93 Classic

Similar to Model 93G, with sporter-weight barrel. Oil-finished premium walnut stock. AccuTrigger. Introduced in 2007.

NIB	Exc.	V.G.	Good	Fair	Poor
475	375	325	200	150	100

Model 93 Classic Thumbhole

Similar to above, with thumbhole stock.

NIB	Exc.	V.G.	Good	Fair	Poor
515	400	300	200	125	100

Model 93XP

.22 WMR package gun, with 22" barrel and factory-mounted 3x9 scope. Overall finish in Mossy Oak Brush camo.

NIB	Exc.	V.G.	Good	Fair	Poor
400	325	250	150	100	75

Model 93FVSS

Features 21" heavy barrel chambered for .22 WMR cartridge. Recessed target muzzle and stainless steel barreled action. Equipped with black synthetic stock. Magazine capacity 5 rounds. Weight about 6 lbs. Introduced in 1998.

NIB	Exc.	V.G.	Good	Fair	Poor
275	200	150	100	70	50

Model 93BTVS

Similar to Model 93FVSS, with laminated thumbhole stock. Introduced in 2007.

NIB	Exc.	V.G.	Good	Fair	Poor
400	325	250	150	100	75

Model 93F

Similar to above, with blued finish. Synthetic stock, with open sights. Weight about 5 lbs. Introduced in 1998.

NIB	Exc.	V.G.	Good	Fair	Poor
185	125	95	65	50	25

Model 93R17-F

Bolt-action rifle chambered for .17 HMR cartridge. Fitted with 20.75" barrel, no sights. Black synthetic stock. Magazine capacity 5 rounds. Blued finish. Weight about 5 lbs. Introduced in 2003.

NIB	Exc.	V.G.	Good	Fair	Poor
225	175	125	100	75	50

Model 93R17-BVSS

Similar to above, with 21" stainless steel barrel, no sights and laminated hardwood stock. Weight about 6 lbs. Introduced in 2003.

NIB	Exc.	V.G.	Good	Fair	Poor
325	250	190	125	75	50

Model 93R17-FSS

This .17 HMR caliber rifle has 20.75" stainless steel barrel, no sights and black synthetic stock. Weight about 5 lbs. Introduced in 2003.

NIB	Exc.	V.G.	Good	Fair	Poor
250	180	130	100	75	50

Model 93R17-Camo

As above, with Realtree Hardwoods camo stock. Weight about 5 lbs. Introduced in 2003.

NIB	Exc.	V.G.	Good	Fair	Poor
250	180	130	100	75	50

Model 93R17-FVSS

As above, with 21" stainless steel heavy barrel. Weight about 6 lbs. Introduced in 2003.

NIB	Exc.	V.G.	Good	Fair	Poor
275	210	150	125	75	50

Model 93R17-GV

This .17 HMR model has walnut finished hardwood checkered stock. Heavy 21" barrel, no sights. Blued finish. Weight about 6 lbs. Introduced in 2003. Left-hand model available.

NIB	Exc.	V.G.	Good	Fair	Poor
230	175	125	100	75	50

Model 93R17-GVXP

Similar to Model 93R17-GV, with scope package. Introduced 2006.

NIB	Exc.	V.G.	Good	Fair	Poor
250	180	130	100	75	50

Model 93R17-FXP

Similar to Model 93R17-F, with scope package. Introduced 2006.

NIB	Exc.	V.G.	Good	Fair	Poor
250	180	130	100	75	50

Model 93FVSS-XP

Similar to Model 93FVSS, with scope package. Introduced 2006.

NIB	Exc.	V.G.	Good	Fair	Poor
300	225	150	125	75	50

Model 93FSS

Similar to discontinued Model 93FS, with no sights and AccuTrigger. Introduced 2006.

NIB	Exc.	V.G.	Good	Fair	Poor
275	210	150	125	75	50

Model 93FV

Similar to Model 93F, with AccuTrigger. Introduced 2006.

NIB	Exc.	V.G.	Good	Fair	Poor
250	180	130	100	75	50

Model 93R17-BTVS

Similar to Model 93R17-BVSS, with laminated thumbhole stock. Introduced 2006.

NIB	Exc.	V.G.	Good	Fair	Poor
350	295	245	195	150	100

Model 93R17-BLTVS

Similar to above, in left-hand. Suggested retail price: $441.

Model 93R17-BV

Similar to Model 93R17-GV, with brown laminated stock. Wide beavertail fore-end. Introduced 2006.

NIB	Exc.	V.G.	Good	Fair	Poor
350	295	245	195	150	100

Model 93R17 Classic

Similar to Model 93R17, with sporter-weight barrel and oil-finished premium walnut stock. AccuTrigger. Introduced in 2007.

NIB	Exc.	V.G.	Good	Fair	Poor
450	345	295	200	135	100

Model Mark II BRJ

Similar to Mark II Model 93. Features spiral fluting pattern on heavy barrel, blued finish and Royal Jacaranda wood laminate stock. In .22 LR, .22 WMR or .17 HMR.

NIB	Exc.	V.G.	Good	Fair	Poor
400	350	300	250	200	100

Model Mark II TRR-SR

Similar to Mark II Model 93. Features heavy barrel, matte finish and tactical-style wood stock.

NIB	Exc.	V.G.	Good	Fair	Poor
475	425	350	300	250	150

Model CUB-G (Mini-Youth)

Introduced in 2003. Single-shot bolt-action rifle chambered for .22-caliber cartridge. Barrel length 16". Walnut-stained hardwood stock is proportionally scaled down. Weight about 3.3 lbs. In 2005, offered in .17 HM2.

NIB	Exc.	V.G.	Good	Fair	Poor
155	125	100	75	50	25

Model CUB-T

Similar to Model CUB-G, with laminated thumbhole stock. Introduced in 2007.

NIB	Exc.	V.G.	Good	Fair	Poor
235	195	145	100	75	50

Model B Mag

Bolt-action rimfire chambered for .17 Win. Super Magnum (.17 WSM) cartridge. New compact action design, with rear locking lugs and cock-on-close bolt. AccuTrigger is user-adjustable without special tools. Features include: center-feed rotating 8-round magazine, black synthetic stock, matte black finish, 22" carbon steel barrel. New in 2013.

NIB	Exc.	V.G.	Good	Fair	Poor
315	275	225	—	—	—

Model 30G "Stevens Favorite"

Based on Stevens Favorite model. Lever-action single-shot .22-caliber rifle. Fitted with 21" half octagonal barrel. Walnut stock with schnabel fore-end. Blued finish. Weight about 4.25 lbs. Introduced in 1999. Additional calibers added are .22 WMR and .22 Hornet. **NOTE:** Add $35 for .22WMR; $60 for .22 Hornet.

NIB	Exc.	V.G.	Good	Fair	Poor
325	275	225	150	100	50

Model 30G "Favorite" Takedown

Introduced in 2004. Has a takedown feature. Offered in: .17 HMR with 21" full octagon barrel, sights and scope base included; .22 LR with 21" half octagon barrel and sights. **NOTE:** Add $65 for .17 HMR model.

NIB	Exc.	V.G.	Good	Fair	Poor
325	275	225	150	100	50

MARK I & II SERIES

Introduced in 1996. This series of .22-caliber rifles feature both single-shot and repeating models. They are available in both right-/left-hand models.

Mark I-G

Bolt-action single-shot rifle chambered for .22 Short, Long or Long Rifle cartridges. Fitted with 20.75" barrel. Cut checkered walnut finished stock. Bead front sight and open adjustable rear sight. Offered in both right-/left-hand models. Weight about 5.5 lbs.

NIB	Exc.	V.G.	Good	Fair	Poor
150	100	80	70	60	50

Mark I-FVT

Similar to Mark I-G, with synthetic stock, rear peep sight and hooded front sight. Introduced 2006.

NIB	Exc.	V.G.	Good	Fair	Poor
200	150	100	80	70	60	—

Mark I-GY (Youth Model)

Same as above, with 19" barrel and shorter buttstock. Weight about 5 lbs.

MARK I GY

NIB	Exc.	V.G.	Good	Fair	Poor
150	100	80	70	60	50

Mark I-GSB Smoothbore

This version of Mark I is a smoothbore model made for .22-caliber shot cartridges. Barrel length 20.75". Weight about 5.5 lbs.

NIB	Exc.	V.G.	Good	Fair	Poor
150	100	80	70	60	50

Mark II-G

Bolt-action repeater with 10-shot magazine. Chambered for .22 LR cartridge. Checkered walnut finished stock. Open sights. Barrel length 20.75". Offered in both right-/left-hand versions. Weight about 5.5 lbs.

NIB	Exc.	V.G.	Good	Fair	Poor
170	125	90	70	60	50

Mark II-GY (Youth Model)

Same as above, with 19" barrel and shorter stock.

NIB	Exc.	V.G.	Good	Fair	Poor
170	125	90	70	60	50

Mark II-GXP

Same as Mark II-G, but includes an unmounted 4x15mm scope. Discontinued.

NIB	Exc.	V.G.	Good	Fair	Poor
130	100	80	70	60	50

Mark II-FSS

Stainless steel .22-caliber rifle, with 20.75" barrel and 10-round magazine. Receiver dovetailed for scope mounting. Stock black synthetic. Weight about 5 lbs.

NIB	Exc.	V.G.	Good	Fair	Poor
210	150	110	75	65	45

Mark II-LV

Fitted with 21" heavy barrel, in .22-caliber. Laminated hardwood stock, with cut checkering. Blue finish and 10-round magazine. Weight about 6.5 lbs. Introduced in 1997. Discontinued.

NIB	Exc.	V.G.	Good	Fair	Poor
200	150	110	75	65	45

Mark II-F

Has the standard Mark II barreled action, with black synthetic stock. Detachable 10-round magazine standard. Weight about 5 lbs. Introduced in 1998. In 2006, .17 Hornady Mach 2 added.

NIB	Exc.	V.G.	Good	Fair	Poor
150	110	80	70	65	45

Mark II-FXP

Similar to Mark II-F, with 4x15mm scope. Weight about 5.25 lbs. Introduced in 1998.

NIB	Exc.	V.G.	Good	Fair	Poor
155	110	80	70	65	45

Mark II Camo

Similar to Mark II-F, with forest camo synthetic stock. Introduced 2006.

NIB	Exc.	V.G.	Good	Fair	Poor
200	165	135	100	75	50

Mark II-FV

Introduced in 1998. Features 21" heavy barrel, with blue alloy steel receiver. Stock black synthetic. Detachable magazine capacity 5 round. Weight about 6 lbs. In 2006, .17 Hornady Mach 2 added.

NIB	Exc.	V.G.	Good	Fair	Poor
215	150	110	80	60	45

Mark II-FVXP

Similar to Mark II-FV, with scope package. Introduced 2006.

NIB	Exc.	V.G.	Good	Fair	Poor
250	195	150	125	75	50

Mark II-FVT

Similar to Mark II-FV, with rear peep sight and hooded front. Introduced 2006.

NIB	Exc.	V.G.	Good	Fair	Poor
315	250	195	145	100	75

Mark II-BV

Features 21" stainless steel bull barrel, without sights. Brown laminate stock. Chambered in .22 LR. Introduced 2006.

NIB	Exc.	V.G.	Good	Fair	Poor
300	225	175	150	100	75

Mark II BTV

Similar to above, with laminated thumbhole ventilated stock. AccuTrigger. Blued receiver and bull barrel.

NIB	Exc.	V.G.	Good	Fair	Poor
375	325	250	150	125	100

Mark II BVTS

Similar to above, with stainless barrel and receiver. Available in right-/left-hand (BTVLS) configuration. Suggested retail price: $393 (standard); $441 (left-hand).

NIB	Exc.	V.G.	Good	Fair	Poor
395	350	265	165	140	125

Mark II Classic

Similar to Mark II-FV, with sporter-weight barrel. Oil-finished premium walnut stock. AccuTrigger. Introduced in 2007. **NOTE:** Add $50 for thumbhole stock.

NIB	Exc.	V.G.	Good	Fair	Poor
395	350	295	225	150	100

MODEL 900 SERIES

First offered in 1996. Series consists of .22-caliber rimfire target rifles in various configurations. All available in both right-/left-hand versions.

Model 900B—Biathlon

Features hardwood stock, with 5-round magazine, carrying and shooting rails, butt hook and hand stop. Barrel 21" and comes with snow cover. Receiver sight are peep variety. Front sight has 7 aperture inserts as standard. Weight about 8.25 lbs.

NIB	Exc.	V.G.	Good	Fair	Poor
475	400	350	300	2175	125

Model 900 TR—Target

Has one-piece hardwood stock, with shooting rail and hand stop. Rear sight adjustable peep and front sight has 7 aperture inserts. Barrel length 25". Five-shot magazine standard. Weight about 8 lbs.

NIB	Exc.	V.G.	Good	Fair	Poor
400	325	275	225	150	100

Model 900S—Silhouette

Version features 21" heavy barrel, with recessed target style crown. Fitted with one-piece silhouette-style stock, with high comb and satin walnut finish. Receiver drilled and tapped for scope mount. Weight about 8 lbs.

NIB	Exc.	V.G.	Good	Fair	Poor
400	325	275	225	150	100

Model 24

External hammer combination rifle/shotgun, with 24" barrels. Blued, with walnut stock. Manufactured from 1950 to 1965 in a variety of styles. Standard chambering .22 by .410.

NIB	Exc.	V.G.	Good	Fair	Poor
550	500	400	325	250	150

Model 24S

Similar to above, except has side-mounted operating lever. Available with 20-gauge lower barrel.

NIB	Exc.	V.G.	Good	Fair	Poor
450	375	325	250	200	150

Model 24MS

Similar to above, except rifle barrel chambered for .22 WMR.

NIB	Exc.	V.G.	Good	Fair	Poor
600	525	425	350	275	175

Model 24DL

Satin chrome, with checkered stock.

NIB	Exc.	V.G.	Good	Fair	Poor
—	450	375	325	175	125

Model 24 Field—Lightweight Version

NIB	Exc.	V.G.	Good	Fair	Poor
—	450	375	275	150	100

Model 24C

Nickel finish.

NIB	Exc.	V.G.	Good	Fair	Poor
—	450	375	275	150	100

Model 24VS

.357 Magnum or .357 Maximum/20 gauge, nickel finish.

NIB	Exc.	V.G.	Good	Fair	Poor
675	575	450	400	300	200

Model 24F

DuPont Rynite stock.

NIB	Exc.	V.G.	Good	Fair	Poor
500	400	325	250	150	100

Model 2400

Combination 12-gauge by .222- or .308-caliber over/under rifle/shotgun, with 23.5" barrels and Monte Carlo-style stock. Made by Valmet. Imported between 1975 and 1980.

NIB	Exc.	V.G.	Good	Fair	Poor
—	700	575	450	350	275

Model 389

Over/under design with 12-gauge 3" Magnum shotgun barrel over rifle barrel. Chambered for .222 Rem. or .308 Win. Double triggers, hammerless action, checkered walnut stock. Made in 1988 and 1989.

NIB	Exc.	V.G.	Good	Fair	Poor
800	700	600	450	350	200

Model 42

Over/under design with .22 Long Rifle or WMR rifle barrel over .410 shotgun barrel. Separated barrels, with black synthetic stock and sling swivels. Opens with lever in front of trigger guard. New in 2013

NIB	Exc.	V.G.	Good	Fair	Poor
400	350	300	—	—	—

SAVAGE SHOTGUNS

Model 411 Upland Sporter

SEE—Stevens.

Model 420

A 12-, 16- or 20-gauge boxlock over/under shotgun with 26", 28" or 30" barrels. Double triggers and extractors. Manufactured between 1937 and 1943.

Courtesy Nick Niles, Paul Goodwin photo

NIB	Exc.	V.G.	Good	Fair	Poor
—	500	400	300	200	150

Model 420 with Single Trigger

NIB	Exc.	V.G.	Good	Fair	Poor
—	500	400	300	200	150

Model 430

As above, with checkered walnut stock and solid barrel rib. Produced from 1937 to 1943.

NIB	Exc.	V.G.	Good	Fair	Poor
—	550	450	350	200	150

Model 430 with Single Trigger

NIB	Exc.	V.G.	Good	Fair	Poor
—	600	450	300	200	150

Model 320

This is a side-by-side model.

NIB	Exc.	V.G.	Good	Fair	Poor
—	800	650	500	400	300

Model 412

.410 bore adapter.

NIB	Exc.	V.G.	Good	Fair	Poor
—	80	60	50	40	30

Model 412F

.410 bore adapter.

NIB	Exc.	V.G.	Good	Fair	Poor
—	50	45	40	35	25

Model 220

A 12-, 16-, 20-gauge or .410 bore boxlock single-barrel shotgun, with 26" to 32" barrels. Blued, with walnut stock. Manufactured between 1938 and 1965.

NIB	Exc.	V.G.	Good	Fair	Poor
—	100	80	70	50	35

Model 210F

Introduced in 1996. Bolt-action shotgun has 24" rifled barrel for slugs. Chambered for 3" 12-gauge shell. No sights. Magazine holds 2 rounds. Weight about 7.5 lbs.

NIB	Exc.	V.G.	Good	Fair	Poor
575	500	425	350	200	125

Model 210F Slug Warrior Camo

As above, with camo stock.

NIB	Exc.	V.G.	Good	Fair	Poor
595	525	450	375	225	150

Model 210FT

Introduced in 1997. A 12-gauge bolt-action shotgun, with camouflage finish. Chambered for 3" shells. Fitted with 24" barrel. 2-round magazine. Weight about 7.5 lbs. Drilled and tapped for scope mounting.

NIB	Exc.	V.G.	Good	Fair	Poor
575	500	425	350	200	125

Model 720

A 12- or 16-gauge semi-automatic shotgun, with 26" to 32" barrels. Blued, with walnut stock. Manufactured between 1930 and 1949.

NIB	Exc.	V.G.	Good	Fair	Poor
—	450	375	275	225	100

Model 726 Upland Sporter

As above, with 2-shot magazine. Manufactured between 1931 and 1949.

NIB	Exc.	V.G.	Good	Fair	Poor
—	450	375	275	225	100

Model 740C Skeet

Model 726, with 24.5" barrel. Features a Cutts compensator and skeet-style stock. Manufactured between 1936 and 1949.

NIB	Exc.	V.G.	Good	Fair	Poor
—	450	375	275	225	100

Model 745

Model 720, in 12-gauge with alloy receiver and 28" barrel. Manufactured between 1940 and 1949.

NIB	Exc.	V.G.	Good	Fair	Poor
—	450	375	275	225	100

Model 755

A 12- or 16-gauge semi-automatic shotgun, with 26" to 30" barrels. Blued, with walnut stock. Also available with Savage Super Choke. Manufactured between 1949 and 1958.

NIB	Exc.	V.G.	Good	Fair	Poor
—	295	225	175	125	75

Model 775

As above, with alloy receiver. Manufactured between 1950 and 1966.

NIB	Exc.	V.G.	Good	Fair	Poor
—	295	225	175	125	75

Model 750

A 12-gauge semi-automatic shotgun, with 26" or 28" barrel. Model 750SC fitted with Savage Super Choke; Model 750AC with Poly Choke. Blued, with walnut stock. Manufactured between 1960 and 1967.

NIB	Exc.	V.G.	Good	Fair	Poor
—	295	225	175	125	75

Model FA-1

Savage Fox semi-automatic shotgun, imported from Japan in 1981 and 1982. Marked KTG. Offered in 12-gauge only, with 28" or 30" ventilated rib barrels. Walnut stock, with cut checkering. Magazine capacity 4 rounds. Weight about 7.5 lbs.

NIB	Exc.	V.G.	Good	Fair	Poor
—	350	300	250	200	150

Model FP-1

Similar to above, with 3" chambers and 5-round magazine.

NIB	Exc.	V.G.	Good	Fair	Poor
—	350	300	250	200	150

Model 21

Slide-action shotgun built between 1920 and 1928. Chambered for 12-gauge, with 26", 28", 30" or 32" barrel. Walnut pistol-grip stock and slide handle. Takedown. Almost identical to famous Winchester Model 12. Offered in a number of different configurations including standard grade, Trap grade, Tournament grade and Riot Model. About 13,000 built.

NIB	Exc.	V.G.	Good	Fair	Poor
—	450	375	275	225	100

Model 28

Slide-action shotgun is an improved version of Model 21. Manufactured from 1928 to 1934. There are several variations including: Model 28-A standard grade; Model 28-B standard grade with raised matted rib; Model 28-C; Riot; Model 28-D Trap grade; in 1931, Model 28-3 an improved version with checkering and roll marked game scenes on receiver.

NIB	Exc.	V.G.	Good	Fair	Poor
—	450	375	275	225	100

Model 30

A 12-, 16-, 20-gauge and .410 bore slide-action shotgun, with 26" to 30" ventilated rib barrels. Blued, with walnut stock. Manufactured between 1958 and 1978.

NIB	Exc.	V.G.	Good	Fair	Poor
—	300	195	150	100	75

Model 242

A .410 bore boxlock double-barrel over/under shotgun, with 26" barrels, single trigger, extractors and exposed hammer. Manufactured between 1977 and 1981.

Courtesy Nick Niles, Paul Goodwin photo

NIB	Exc.	V.G.	Good	Fair	Poor
—	550	475	350	225	125

Model 550

A 12- or 20-gauge boxlock side-by-side double-barrel shotgun, with 26", 28" or 30" barrels. Single triggers and automatic ejectors. Blued, with hardwood stock. Manufactured between 1971 and 1973. Barrels built by Valmet.

Courtesy Nick Niles, Paul Goodwin photo

NIB	Exc.	V.G.	Good	Fair	Poor
—	500	400	300	200	150

Model 440

An Italian made 12- or 20-gauge boxlock over/under shotgun, with 26", 28" or 30" ventilated rib barrels. Single-selective trigger and extractors. Blued, with walnut stock. Manufactured between 1968 and 1972.

NIB	Exc.	V.G.	Good	Fair	Poor
—	600	500	400	300	200

Model 440A

Courtesy Nick Niles, Paul Goodwin photo

NIB	Exc.	V.G.	Good	Fair	Poor
—	600	500	400	300	200

Model 440B-T

NIB	Exc.	V.G.	Good	Fair	Poor
—	800	650	500	350	250

Model 444 Deluxe

As above, with more finely figured stock and automatic ejectors. Imported between 1969 and 1972.

NIB	Exc.	V.G.	Good	Fair	Poor
—	550	475	400	300	225

Model 444

NIB	Exc.	V.G.	Good	Fair	Poor
—	600	500	400	300	200

Model 444B

NIB	Exc.	V.G.	Good	Fair	Poor
—	700	550	400	300	250

Model 440T

A 12-gauge Model 440, with 30" barrels and trap-style stock. Imported between 1969 and 1972.

NIB	Exc.	V.G.	Good	Fair	Poor
—	600	500	400	300	200

Model 330

A Valmet manufactured 12- or 20-gauge over/under shotgun, with 26", 28" or 30" barrels. Single-selective trigger and extractors. Blued, with walnut stock. Imported between 1970 and 1978.

Courtesy Nick Niles, Paul Goodwin photo

NIB	Exc.	V.G.	Good	Fair	Poor
—	800	650	500	350	250

Model 333

As above, with ventilated rib and automatic ejectors. Imported between 1973 and 1980.

NIB	Exc.	V.G.	Good	Fair	Poor
—	700	550	400	300	200

Model 333T

As above, with 30" barrel and trap-style stock. Imported between 1972 and 1980.

NIB	Exc.	V.G.	Good	Fair	Poor
—	800	650	500	350	250

Model 312 Field Over/Under

NIB	Exc.	V.G.	Good	Fair	Poor
—	800	600	450	300	200

Model 312 Trap

NIB	Exc.	V.G.	Good	Fair	Poor
—	700	600	550	350	200

Model 312 Sporting Clay

NIB	Exc.	V.G.	Good	Fair	Poor
—	800	600	450	300	200

Model 320 Field

NIB	Exc.	V.G.	Good	Fair	Poor
—	800	600	450	300	200

(SAVAGE) FOX B MODELS

Fox Model B was introduced about 1939, by Savage, for the hunter who wanted better fit and finish than offered by Stevens brand Model 530. Made in many variations until 1988. **NOTE:** Values shown are for 12-gauge. Add 15 percent for 16-gauge; 50 percent for 20-gauge; 100 percent for .410 bore.

Fox Model B—Utica, NY

NIB	Exc.	V.G.	Good	Fair	Poor
700	600	500	375	250	200

Fox Model B—Chicopee Falls, Mass. (later Westfield, Mass.)

Courtesy Nick Niles, Paul Goodwin photo

NIB	Exc.	V.G.	Good	Fair	Poor
600	500	375	250	200	125

Fox Model B—Single Trigger

NIB	Exc.	V.G.	Good	Fair	Poor
750	625	500	375	250	200

Fox Model BDL

NIB	Exc.	V.G.	Good	Fair	Poor
750	625	500	375	250	200

Fox Model BDE

Courtesy Nick Niles, Paul Goodwin photo

NIB	Exc.	V.G.	Good	Fair	Poor
650	550	400	300	200	150

Fox Model BSE

Courtesy Nick Niles, Paul Goodwin photo

NIB	Exc.	V.G.	Good	Fair	Poor
750	625	500	375	250	200

Fox Model BE

NIB	Exc.	V.G.	Good	Fair	Poor
800	700	600	475	300	200

Milano

Italian-made over/under available in 12-, 20-, 28-gauge and .410-bore. On frames scaled to match. All with 28" barrels and 3" chambers. Single-selective trigger. Three choke tubes (fixed IC and Mod. on .410-bore). Automatic ejectors.

NIB	Exc.	V.G.	Good	Fair	Poor
1400	1000	800	700	350	250

PISTOLS

Elbert Searle was granted a patent on an automatic pistol which utilized the bullet's torque to twist barrel into a locking position with slide. Patent also featured a double-row staggered magazine which increased capacity over ordinary pistols. Patent was sold to Savage and first Savage automatic pistol Model 1907 was produced. **NOTE:** Savage automatic pistols with original cardboard box will bring between $50 and $100 premium. Instruction pamphlet, cleaning brush or other advertising material is present, price will escalate.

Model 1907

A .32 or .380 semi-automatic pistol, with 3.75" or 4.25" barrel and 9- or 10-shot magazine. Blued, with hard rubber rectangular grips. This model is often incorrectly termed Model 1905 or Model 1910. **NOTE:** The .380-caliber worth approximately 30 percent more than values listed.

NIB	Exc.	V.G.	Good	Fair	Poor
—	525	350	250	150	100

Model 1907 Portugese Contract

Similar to commercial guns, with a lanyard ring same as French contract model. Original Portugese pistols will have Portugese Crest on grips.

Only about 1,150 of these pistols were produced. Very rare. Proceed with caution.

NIB	Exc.	V.G.	Good	Fair	Poor
—	1700	1250	950	600	300

Model 1915 Hammerless

Similar to Model 1907, except fitted with grip safety and internal hammer. Approximately 6,500 pistols produced in .32-caliber and 3,900 in .380-caliber. Manufactured between 1915 and 1917. Rarest of regular-production Savage automatic pistols.

Courtesy Orvel Reichert

.32 Caliber

NIB	Exc.	V.G.	Good	Fair	Poor
—	1250	900	500	400	200

.380 Caliber

NIB	Exc.	V.G.	Good	Fair	Poor
—	1800	1350	1000	500	300

Model 1917

As above, with external hammer and without grip safety. Form of grip frame widened in kind of trapezoidal shape. Manufactured between 1917 and 1928. **NOTE:** Add $100 for .380.

Model 1917 with watch fob for salesmen samples

NIB	Exc.	V.G.	Good	Fair	Poor
—	600	475	300	250	200

Model 6.35mm

A small number of .25-caliber Savage pistols manufactured between 1915 and 1919. Perhaps less than 25 were built. There are two major variations of this pistol. First, wide or 10-serrations grip; second 27-serrations grip variation. This change occured around 1917. Magazine capacity was 6 to 7 rounds. Very rare.

Courtesy Bailey Brower, Jr., Copyright 2005, Bailey Brower, Jr.

NIB	Exc.	V.G.	Good	Fair	Poor
—	8000	7000	4000	2500	1000

Model 1907 Test Pistol

Manufactured in 1907 in .45 ACP. Pistol was tested in U.S. Army trials. About 290 pistols produced for these trials. Double-stack magazine held 8 rounds.

Courtesy Bailey Brower, Jr., Copyright 2005, Bailey Brower, Jr

NIB	Exc.	V.G.	Good	Fair	Poor
—	13500	11000	9500	6000	4000

Model 1910 Test Pistol

A modified Model 1907, with heavier slide that was not concave like Model 1907. A total of nine Model 1910s built. Too Rare To Price

NIB	Exc.	V.G.	Good	Fair	Poor
—	—	—	—	—	—

Model 1911 Test Pistol

This example was completely modified with a longer and thinner grip. Checkered wood grips were attached by friction instead of screws. Slide release was modified. A full grip safety was added. Heavier serrated hammer (cocking lever) was added. Four of these pistols were built. Serial #1 has never been located. Too rare to price.

Model 101

.22-caliber single-shot pistol, resembling a revolver with 5.5" barrel. Blued, with hardwood grips. Made in Chicopee Falls or Westfield, Mass. Manufactured between 1960 and 1968.

NIB	Exc.	V.G.	Good	Fair	Poor
—	225	175	125	100	75

500 HANDGUN SERIES

Introduced in 1998. This line of short action handguns feature left-hand bolt and right-hand ejection. All are fitted with an internal box magazine, composite stock and 14" barrel.

Model 501F—Sport Striker

This handgun fitted with a left-hand bolt and 10" free floating barrel. Detachable clip holds 10 rounds of .22 LR cartridges. Drilled and tapped for scope mount. Weight about 4 lbs. Introduced in 2000.

NIB	Exc.	V.G.	Good	Fair	Poor
350	295	250	175	150	100

Model 501FXP

Introduced in 2002. Similar to above, but fitted with 1.25-4x28mm scope with soft case.

NIB	Exc.	V.G.	Good	Fair	Poor
375	325	265	195	165	110

Model 502F—Sport Striker

Same as 501F, but chambered for .22 WMR cartridge. Magazine capacity 5 rounds. Introduced in 2000.

NIB	Exc.	V.G.	Good	Fair	Poor
375	325	265	195	165	110

Model 503F—Sport Striker

Same as Model 502F-Sport Striker, but chambered for .17 HMR cartridge. Blued finish. Weight about 4 lbs. Introduced in 2003.

NIB	Exc.	V.G.	Good	Fair	Poor
375	325	265	195	165	110

Model 503FSS—Sport Striker

As above, with stainless steel action and barrel.

NIB	Exc.	V.G.	Good	Fair	Poor
395	350	290	210	180	125

Model 510F Striker

Blued barrel action. Chambered for .22-250, .243 or .308-calibers. Weight about 5 lbs.

NIB	Exc.	V.G.	Good	Fair	Poor
475	400	350	295	175	150

Model 516FSS

Similar to model above, with stainless steel barreled action.

NIB	Exc.	V.G.	Good	Fair	Poor
495	425	365	310	195	150

Model 516FSAK

Features stainless steel barreled action, with adjustable muzzle-brake.

NIB	Exc.	V.G.	Good	Fair	Poor
525	450	395	345	225	165

Model 516FSAK Camo

As above, with Realtree Hardwood camo stock. Chambered for .300 WSM cartridge. Weight about 5.5 lbs. Introduced in 2002.

NIB	Exc.	V.G.	Good	Fair	Poor
600	525	450	300	235	75

Model 516BSS

Fitted with laminated thumbhole stock, left-hand bolt for right-hand ejection, 14" barrel. Chambered for .223, .243, 7mm-08 Rem., .260 Rem. and .308 Win. calibers. Magazine capacity 2 rounds. Weight about 5 lbs. Introduced in 1999.

NIB	Exc.	V.G.	Good	Fair	Poor
600	525	450	300	235	75

Model 516BSAK

Similar to model above. Chambered for .223 or .22-250 cartridges. The 14" barrel fitted with an adjustable muzzle-brake. Introduced in 1999.

NIB	Exc.	V.G.	Good	Fair	Poor
600	525	450	300	235	75

SAVAGE REVOLVING FIREARMS CO.
Middletown, Connecticut

Navy Revolver

A .36-caliber double-action percussion revolver, with 7" octagonal barrel and 6-shot cylinder. Frame marked "Savage R.F.A. Co./H.S. North Patented June 17, 1856/Jan. 18, 1859, May 15, 1860". Approximately 20,000 manufactured between 1861 and 1865. About 12,000 purchased by U.S. Government.

Courtesy Greg Martin Auctions

NIB	Exc.	V.G.	Good	Fair	Poor
—	—	4250	1750	700	500

SCATTERGUN TECHNOLOGIES
Formerly—Nashville, Tennessee
Berryville, Arkansas

NOTE: In 1999, Scattergun Technologies was purchased by Wilson Combat and became a division of Wilson Combat.

TR-870

This model is based on Remington Model 870 slide-action shotgun. Offered in a wide variety of configurations with different features. Standard model fitted with 18" barrel and chambered for 12-gauge shell. Stock is composite, with recoil pad. Tactical fore-end has flashlight built in. Ghost ring rear sight. Front sight has tritium insert. Six-round shell carrier on left side of receiver. Introduced in 1991. Weight for standard model about 9 lbs. Prices listed are for standard model.

NIB	Exc.	V.G.	Good	Fair	Poor
1000	800	650	550	300	200

WILSON COMBAT CURRENT PRODUCTION MODELS

NOTE: Add $100 to all models with Armor-Tuff finish

Standard Model

Based on Remington 12-gauge 3" 870 Magnum. This model fitted with 18" cylinder bore barrel. Adjustable ghost ring rear sight, with tritium front. Seven-round extended magazine. Side saddle shell carrier. Synthetic stock. Tactical sling standard. Parkerized finish. Fitted with SUREFIRE tactical light.

NIB	Exc.	V.G.	Good	Fair	Poor
1150	850	625	500	400	300

Border Patrol Model

Similar to Standard Model, without tactical light. A 14" barrel is offered. All NFA rules apply to purchase of short barrel shotgun.

NIB	Exc.	V.G.	Good	Fair	Poor
875	650	475	300	200	150

Professional Model

Features all Standard Model components. Fitted with a 14" barrel. Magazine capacity 6 rounds. All NFA rules apply to purchase of short barrel shotgun.

NIB	Exc.	V.G.	Good	Fair	Poor
1175	875	650	500	400	300

Entry Model

Has all features of Standard Model. Fitted with 12.5" barrel. Magazine capacity 5 rounds. All NFA rules apply to purchase of short barrel shotgun.

NIB	Exc.	V.G.	Good	Fair	Poor
950	700	600	500	400	300

K-9 Model

Built on Remington 12-gauge 3" 11-87 Magnum semi-automatic. Fitted with ghost ring rear sights and tritium front. Extended magazine holds 7 rounds. Barrel 18". Synthetic stock, with side saddle shell carrier. Parkerized finish.

NIB	Exc.	V.G.	Good	Fair	Poor
1075	800	700	600	500	350

SWAT Model

Similar to K-9 model. Fitted with tactical light and 14" barrel. All NFA rules apply to purchase of short barrel shotgun.

NIB	Exc.	V.G.	Good	Fair	Poor
1350	1000	800	650	550	400

SCCY INDUSTRIES
South Daytona, Florida

SCCY CPX

Hammer-fired double-action-only compact 9mm pistol, with black polymer frame. Stainless steel slide and barrel. Black or matte stainless finish. Available with/without thumb safety. Introduced 2012.

NIB	Exc.	V.G.	Good	Fair	Poor
280	250	230	185	150	100

SCCY CPX-3

Ultra compact model chambered for .380 ACP. Magazine capacity 10 rounds, plus one in the chamber. CPX-3 utilizes a unique and exclusive Quad-Lock system that provides improved barrel stability and accuracy. Introduced in 2016.

NIB	Exc.	V.G.	Good	Fair	Poor
295	265	225	200	150	100

SCHALK, G. S.
Pottsville, Pennsylvania

Rifle Musket

A .58-caliber percussion rifle, with 40" round barrel. Full length stock secured by three barrel bands. Barrel marked "G. Schalk Poftsville 1861". Finished in white, with walnut stock. Approximately 100 manufactured.

Courtesy Milwaukee Public Museum, Milwaukee, Wisconsin

NIB	Exc.	V.G.	Good	Fair	Poor
—	—	6900	3300	750	500

SCHALL & CO.
New Haven, Connecticut

Manufactured the Fiala repeating pistol for Fiala. Later, after Fiala's bankruptcy, Schall provided parts, repair service and produced repeating pistols with the Schall name. Marketed by Schall between 1930 and 1935.

Repeating Pistol

A .22-caliber pistol, with 10-shot magazine. Tapered 6.5" barrel, with fixed sights and blued finish. Rear sight much simpler than those on Fiala. Grips are wood, with ribs running lengthwise. Typically marked "schall & co./new haven, conn usa" but guns exist with no markings. **NOTE:** Original Fiala pistols had 7.5" barrels, but not so the Schalls (a fact revealed to us by our friend Jack in Florida).

Courtesy Dr. Jon Miller

NIB	Exc.	V.G.	Good	Fair	Poor
—	500	425	325	190	170

SCHMIDT, HERBERT
Ostheim, West Germany

Model 11, Liberty 11, and Eig Model E-8

A .22-caliber double-action revolver, with 2.5" barrel and 6-shot cylinder. Blued, with plastic grips.

NIB	Exc.	V.G.	Good	Fair	Poor
—	125	80	60	40	25

Model 11 Target

As above, with 5.5" barrel and adjustable sights.

NIB	Exc.	V.G.	Good	Fair	Poor
—	150	120	75	45	30

Frontier Model or Texas Scout

.22-caliber revolver, with 5" barrel and 6-shot cylinder. Blued, with plastic grips.

NIB	Exc.	V.G.	Good	Fair	Poor
—	125	80	60	40	25

SCHMIDT & COMPANY, E.
Houston, Texas

Pocket Pistol

A .45-caliber percussion single-shot pistol, with 2.5" barrel. German silver mounts and walnut stock. Barrel marked "E. Schmidt & Co. Houston". Manufactured between 1866 and 1870.

NIB	Exc.	V.G.	Good	Fair	Poor
—	—	9000	4400	1000	350

SCHNEIDER & CO.
Memphis, Tennessee

Pocket Pistol

A .41-caliber single-shot percussion pocket pistol, with 3.5" octagonal barrel. Iron or German silver mounts. Walnut stock. Lock marked "Schneider & Co./Memphis, Tenn." Manufactured 1859 and 1860.

NIB	Exc.	V.G.	Good	Fair	Poor
—	—	4500	1850	650	300

SCHNEIDER & GLASSICK
Memphis, Tennessee

Pocket Pistols

A .41-caliber percussion pocket pistol, with 2.5" barrel. German silver mounts and walnut stock. Barrel marked "Schneider & Glassick, Memphis, Tenn." Manufactured 1860 to 1862.

NIB	Exc.	V.G.	Good	Fair	Poor
—	—	7000	5250	2500	800

SCHOUBOE
See—Dansk Rekylriffel Syndikat

SCHUERMAN ARMS, LTD.
Scottsdale, Arizona

Model SA40

Introduced in 2004. Bolt-action rifle chambered for a wide variety of calibers from Short action to Long Magnum. Offered in both right-/left-hand models. Barrel lengths from 20" to 26" in stainless steel. No sights. Stock laminated fiberglass sporter style. Retail prices start at $5440. **NOTE:** There are a number of extra costs options that may be ordered with this model. These options will affect price.

SCHULER, AUGUST
Suhl, Germany

Reform

A 6.35mm caliber four-barreled pocket pistol, with 2.5" barrels. Barrel unit rises as trigger is pulled. Blued, with walnut or hard rubber grips. Manufactured between 1907 and 1914.

NIB	Exc.	V.G.	Good	Fair	Poor
—	850	750	650	450	300

SCHULTZ & LARSEN
Ofterup, Denmark

Model 47 Match Rifle

A .22-caliber single-shot bolt-action rifle, with 28" barrel. Adjustable sights and trigger. Blued, with ISU-style stock.

NIB	Exc.	V.G.	Good	Fair	Poor
—	800	650	550	400	250

Model 61 Match Rifle

As above, fitted with a palm rest.

NIB	Exc.	V.G.	Good	Fair	Poor
—	1000	850	750	600	300

Model 62 Match Rifle

Similar to above. Manufactured for centerfire cartridges.

NIB	Exc.	V.G.	Good	Fair	Poor
—	1250	900	750	650	350

Model 54 Free Rifle

Similar to above, with 27" barrel and ISU stock.

NIB	Exc.	V.G.	Good	Fair	Poor
—	950	800	700	550	300

Model 68 DL

A .22-250 to .458 Win. Magnum bolt-action rifle, with 24" barrel. Adjustable trigger. Well figured walnut stock.

NIB	Exc.	V.G.	Good	Fair	Poor
—	850	700	600	450	200

SCHWARZLOSE, ANDREAS
Berlin, Germany

Military Model 1898 (Standart)

Semi-automatic pistol, with 6.5" barrel. Rotary locked bolt, 7-shot magazine and adjustable rear sight. Chambered for 7.63x25mm Borchardt cartridge. Weight about 28 oz. Blued, with walnut grips. Pistol was neither a commercial or military success, and fewer than 500 were made. (CAUTION: Although the 7.63x25mm Mauser cartridge will chamber, it's too powerful for this firearm).

NIB	Exc.	V.G.	Good	Fair	Poor
—	24000	20000	12000	5500	3000

SEARS, ROEBUCK & CO. BRAND
Chicago, Illinois

Double-Barrel Shotguns

Between 1892 and 1988, the world's largest mail order house carried a huge inventory of sporting doubleguns, including any foreign and domestic brands whose makers did not object to Sears' famous price discounts. To increase sales volume, however, Sears also created its own brands which they supported with innovative design, extravagant advertising claims, unbeatable pricing and excellent quality control. These doubles, like many other firearm products handled by Sears, were listed in its very detailed semi-annual catalog from about 1892, when the company first offered doubleguns, until about 1988 when social and political pressures made the company stop handling firearms.

Sears marketing people gave birth to and successfully exploited many house and private brands which we no longer associate with Sears at all. In fact, many of these brands clearly rollmarked on guns are now unfamiliar to many collectors. Frequently seen and important in the market segment which many might describe as affordable doubles are some of the most often seen Sears trade names or brands. Listed in chronological order: T. Barker, S.R. & Co., Triumph, Thomas Barker, Sam Holt, Chicago Long Range Wonder, American Bar Lock, Meriden Fire Arms Co., Norwich, A. J. Arbrey Gun Co., New England, Gladiator, Berkshire, Ranger, Eastern Arms Co., J.C. Higgins, Sears, and Ted Williams. These guns were of good quality but sold at bargain prices which gave them tremendous appeal. They were made for Sears to Sears' specifications by a number of American firms and a few foreign ones as well, all of which produced excellent shotguns under their own names. Among the best-known American companies were J. Stevens, Savage Arms, A.H. Fox, High Standard, N.R. Davis, Crescent Firearms, Ithaca, A. Fyrberg, Colton Mfg. Co., Marlin, Hunter Gun Co., Baker Gun Co., and probably a few others. Among the foreign makers were AYA, H. Pieper, Janssen, SKB, Rossi, CBC, and A. Zoli.

Sears customers were not aware of this, but they did trust Sears name and bought many millions of these shotguns over nearly 100 years that Sears was in the business. Today these guns are becoming recognized as interesting and valuable collectibles in their own special niche. Their values range from $100 to $3,500 or more depending on make, model, decoration, if any, and relative rarity.

SEAVER, E.R.
New York, New York

Pocket Pistol

A .41-caliber percussion pocket pistol, with 2.5" barrel. German silver mounts. Walnut stock.

NIB	Exc.	V.G.	Good	Fair	Poor
—	—	2300	1825	975	400

SECURITY INDUSTRIES
Little Ferry, New Jersey

Model PSS

A .38 Special double-action revolver, with 2" barrel. Fixed sights and 5-shot cylinder. Stainless steel, with walnut grips. Manufactured between 1973 and 1978.

NIB	Exc.	V.G.	Good	Fair	Poor
—	250	150	125	100	75

Model PM357

As above, with 2.5" barrel. In .357 Magnum caliber. Manufactured between 1975 and 1978.

NIB	Exc.	V.G.	Good	Fair	Poor
—	300	200	175	150	100

Model PPM357

As above, with 2" barrel. Hammer without a finger spur. Manufactured between 1975 and 1978.

NIB	Exc.	V.G.	Good	Fair	Poor
—	300	200	175	150	100

SEDCO INDUSTRIES, INC.
Lake Elsinore, California

Company in business from 1988 to 1990.

Model SP22

A .22-caliber semi-automatic pistol, with 2.5" barrel. Blackened or nickel-plated, with plastic grips. Introduced in 1989.

NIB	Exc.	V.G.	Good	Fair	Poor
125	90	65	50	35	25

SEDGELY, R. F., INC.
Philadelphia, Pennsylvania

R.F. Sedgely produced specialized bolt-action rifles using Model 1903 Springfield action. As these arms were for the most part custom order pieces, it is impossible to provide standardized values. It should be noted that his prime engraver was Rudolph J. Kornbrath. Sedgely also made a .22-caliber hammerless pistol.

SEECAMP, L. W. CO., INC.
Milford, Connecticut

LWS .25 ACP Model

A .25-caliber semi-automatic pistol, with 2" barrel. Fixed sights and 7-shot magazine. Stainless steel, with plastic grips. Approximately 5,000 manufactured between 1982 and 1985.

NIB	Exc.	V.G.	Good	Fair	Poor
500	400	300	200	150	100

LWS .32 ACP Model

A .32-caliber double-action semi-automatic pistol, with 2" barrel and 6-shot magazine. Matte or polished stainless steel, with plastic grips.

NIB	Exc.	V.G.	Good	Fair	Poor
525	450	400	350	200	150

Matched Pair

Matched set of the above, with identical serial numbers. Total of 200 sets made, prior to 1968.

NIB	Exc.	V.G.	Good	Fair	Poor
—	900	800	700	500	350

LWS .380 Model

Same as .32-caliber, but chambered for .380 cartridge. Essentially same weight and dimensions as .32-caliber pistol. Introduced in 1999.

NIB	Exc.	V.G.	Good	Fair	Poor
900	650	500	400	300	100

SEMMERLING
Waco, Texas

See—American Derringer Corporation

SERBU FIREARMS
Tampa, Florida

BFG-50 Rifle

A .50-caliber single-shot bolt-action rifle. Fitted with 29.5" barrel. Also offered with 36" barrel. Parkerized finish. Weight about 22 lbs.

NIB	Exc.	V.G.	Good	Fair	Poor
2195	1600	1275	1000	700	350

BFG-50 Carbine

As above, fitted with 22" barrel. Weight about 17 lbs.

NIB	Exc.	V.G.	Good	Fair	Poor
2195	1600	1275	1000	700	350

BFG-50A

A gas operated semi-automatic takedown rifle, with 25" barrel. Parkerized finish. Magazine capacity 10 rounds. Weight about 25 lbs.

NIB	Exc.	V.G.	Good	Fair	Poor
6700	5200	400	2750	1700	500

SHARPS ARMS CO., C.
Big Timber, Montana

Company was founded in 1975 in Richland, Washington and moved to Big Timber, Montana, in 1980. It also produced custom-built rifles, including Model 1877 Sharps and others, to individual customer specifications. Models listed are standard production, without extras.

Model 1874 Sharps Hartford Sporting Rifle

Chambered for a number of popular blackpowder calibers. Fitted with 26", 28" or 30" tapered octagon barrel and double-set triggers. American walnut stock, with Hartford semi-cresent steel butt. Silver nose cap. Case colored receiver, with blued barrel. Optional sights. Weight about 10 lbs.

NIB	Exc.	V.G.	Good	Fair	Poor
2300	1775	1350	1200	800	500

Model 1874 Bridgeport Sporting Rifle

As above, with Bridgeport checkered steel butt. Schnabel-style fore-end.

NIB	Exc.	V.G.	Good	Fair	Poor
2300	1775	1350	1200	1000	500

Model 1875 Carbine—Hunters Rifle

Offered in a variety of calibers from .38-55 to .50-70. Fitted with choice of tapered round military-style barrels. Lengths 22", 24" or 26". Full buckhorn and silver blade sights. Semi-cresent military-style butt, with slender fore-end. Case colored receiver and blued barrel. Double-set triggers.

NIB	Exc.	V.G.	Good	Fair	Poor
2300	1775	1350	1200	1000	500

Model 1874 Boss Gun

Features engraved receiver, XXX fancy walnut, 34" #1 heavy tapered octagon barrel, long range tang sight, buckhorn rear sight globe with post front sight, and Hartford nose cap. Calibers offered from .38-55 to .50-100. Weight about 13.5 lbs. with 34" #1 barrel. **NOTE:** Add $750 for Grade II; $1,500 for Grade III.

NIB	Exc.	V.G.	Good	Fair	Poor
4395	3250	2250	1500	1000	500

Model 1875 Target & Sporting Rifle

Offered in a variety of calibers. Fitted with 30" heavy tapered round barrel. American walnut stock, with pistol-grip. Case colored receiver, with blued barrel. Single trigger. Price listed without sights.

NIB	Exc.	V.G.	Good	Fair	Poor
1500	1300	1075	900	775	400

Model 1875 Classic Rifle

Features a receiver with octagon top. Tapered octagon barrel lengths from 26" to 30". American walnut stock, with straight-grip and crescent butt. Single trigger. German steel nose cap. Case colored receiver, with blued barrel. Weight about 9.5 lbs. with 30" barrel. Priced without sights.

NIB	Exc.	V.G.	Good	Fair	Poor
1500	1300	1075	900	775	400

Model 1885 High Wall Sporting Rifle

Offered with 26", 28" or 30" tapered octagon barrel. Calibers from .22 to .45-120. Single trigger. American walnut stock, with straight-grip and oil-finish. Checkered steel butt plate. Schnabel fore-end. Priced without sights. Weight about 9.25 lbs. with 30" barrel.

NIB	Exc.	V.G.	Good	Fair	Poor
2200	1750	1450	1195	750	400

Model 1885 High Wall Classic Rifle

As above, with crescent butt. Stock with cheek rest. Silver inlay in fore-end.

NIB	Exc.	V.G.	Good	Fair	Poor
2200	1750	1450	1195	750	400

SHARPS RIFLE COMPANY
Glenrock, Wyoming

SRC 25-45 Rifle

This AR-pattern rifle is chambered for .25-45 Sharps cartridge, a proprietary round based on a .223 case necked up to .257. The "45" refers to length of the .223 case in millimeters. (Factory ammo with a Speer 87-grain bullet and Federal cases with the correct head stamp is available from Sharps Rifle Co.). Rifle uses AR-15 magazines and available in several configurations. Price shown is for base model. Introduced in 2015.

NIB	Exc.	V.G.	Good	Fair	Poor
1100	1000	—	—	—	—

SHARPS RIFLE MANUFACTURING COMPANY
Hartford, Connecticut

First Sharps rifles to be manufactured were made by A.S. Nippes of Mill Creek, Pennsylvania. Later they were made by Robbins & Lawrence of Windsor, Vermont. It wasn't until 1855, that Sharps established his own factory in Hartford, Connecticut. After his death in 1874, the company was reorganized as Sharps Rifle Company and remained in Hartford until 1876 when it moved to Bridgeport, Connecticut. It effectively ceased operations in 1880. The following descriptions are just a brief guide and are by no means exhaustive.

Model 1849

Breechloading .44-caliber percussion rifle, with 30" barrel having a wooden cleaning rod mounted beneath it. Breech activated by the trigger guard lever. There is an automatic disk-type capping device on right side of receiver. Finish blued and case colored. Stock is walnut, with a brass patchbox, buttplate and fore-end cap. Marked "Sharps Patent 1848". Approximately 200 manufactured in 1849 and 1850 by A.S. Nippes Company.

NIB	Exc.	V.G.	Good	Fair	Poor
—	—	23000	18000	7500	1500

Model 1850

As above, with Maynard priming mechanism mounted on breech. Marked "Sharps Patent 1848" on breech; barrel "Manufactured by A.S. Nippes Mill Creek, Pa." Priming device marked "Maynard Patent 1845". Approximately 200 manufactured in 1850. Also known as 2nd Model Sharps.

NIB	Exc.	V.G.	Good	Fair	Poor
—	—	21000	15000	6000	1200

Model 1851 Carbine

Single-shot breechloading percussion rifle, in .36-, .44- or .52-caliber. A 21.75" barrel and Maynard tape priming device. Blued and case-hardened, with walnut stock. Forearm held on by a single-barrel band. Buttplate and barrel band are brass. Military versions feature brass patchbox. Tang marked "C. Sharps Patent 1848"; barrel "Robbins & Lawrence";

priming device "Edward Maynard Patentee 1845". Approximately 1,800 carbines and 180 rifles manufactured by Robbins & Lawrence in Windsor, Vermont, in 1851. **NOTE:** Those bearing U.S. inspection marks are worth approximately 75 percent more than values listed.

Courtesy Milwaukee Public Museum, Milwaukee, Wisconsin

NIB	Exc.	V.G.	Good	Fair	Poor
—	—	12000	9500	4250	1000

Model 1852

Similar to above, with Sharps' Patent Pellet Primer. Barrel marked "Sharps Rifle Manufg. Co. Hartford, Conn.". Blued, case-hardened brass furniture and walnut stock. Manufactured in carbine, rifle, sporting rifle and shotgun form. Approximately 4,600 carbines and 600 rifles made between 1853 and 1855.

Military Carbine

Courtesy Bonhams & Butterfields

NIB	Exc.	V.G.	Good	Fair	Poor
—	—	9000	6750	3000	750

Military Rifle

NIB	Exc.	V.G.	Good	Fair	Poor
—	—	12500	9750	4000	1000

Sporting Rifle

NIB	Exc.	V.G.	Good	Fair	Poor
—	—	6500	4250	1750	500

Shotgun

NIB	Exc.	V.G.	Good	Fair	Poor
—	—	4700	3250	1250	500

Model 1853

As above, without spring retainer for lever hinge being mounted in the fore-stock. Approximately 10,500 carbines and 3,000 rifles made between 1854 and 1858.

Military Carbine

Courtesy Milwaukee Public Museum, Milwaukee, Wisconsin

NIB	Exc.	V.G.	Good	Fair	Poor
—	—	8500	6250	2750	750

Military Rifle

NIB	Exc.	V.G.	Good	Fair	Poor
—	—	12000	9500	4000	1000

Sporting Rifle

Courtesy Bonhams & Butterfields

NIB	Exc.	V.G.	Good	Fair	Poor
—	—	4500	2750	1250	450

Shotgun

Courtesy Bonhams & Butterfields

NIB	Exc.	V.G.	Good	Fair	Poor
—	—	4300	2500	1000	450

Model 1855

As above, in .52-caliber. Fitted with Maynard tape primer marked "Edward Maynard Patentee 1845". Approximately 700 made between 1855 and 1856.

NIB	Exc.	V.G.	Good	Fair	Poor
—	—	14500	10500	4250	1000

Model 1855 U.S. Navy Rifle

As above, with 28" barrel, full-length stock and bearing U.S. Navy inspection marks. Approximately 260 made in 1855.

Courtesy Milwaukee Public Museum, Milwaukee, Wisconsin

NIB	Exc.	V.G.	Good	Fair	Poor
—	—	13000	10500	4000	1000

Model 1855 British Carbine

Model 1855 with British inspection marks. Approximately 6,800 made between 1855 and 1857.

Courtesy Milwaukee Public Museum, Milwaukee, Wisconsin

NIB	Exc.	V.G.	Good	Fair	Poor
—	—	8750	6250	3000	850

SHARPS STRAIGHT BREECH MODELS

Model 1859 Carbine

Similar to above models, with breech opening cut on an almost vertical angle.

22" Barrel, Brass Mountings

Courtesy Milwaukee Public Museum, Milwaukee, Wisconsin

NIB	Exc.	V.G.	Good	Fair	Poor
—	—	7700	6250	2500	500

Iron Mountings

Courtesy Milwaukee Public Museum, Milwaukee, Wisconsin

NIB	Exc.	V.G.	Good	Fair	Poor
—	—	—	3250	1500	500

Model 1863 Carbine

Courtesy Mike Stuckslager

NIB	Exc.	V.G.	Good	Fair	Poor
—	—	5000	3250	1500	500

Model 1863 Rifle

Without bayonet lug.

NIB	Exc.	V.G.	Good	Fair	Poor
—	—	4500	3750	1500	500

Model 1865 Rifle

Without bayonet lug.

NIB	Exc.	V.G.	Good	Fair	Poor
—	—	4200	3250	1000	500

Model 1865 Carbine

NIB	Exc.	V.G.	Good	Fair	Poor
—	—	4500	3750	1750	500

Model 1859 Rifle

30" Barrel

NIB	Exc.	V.G.	Good	Fair	Poor
—	—	5500	4250	2000	800

36" Barrel

NIB	Exc.	V.G.	Good	Fair	Poor
—	—	5500	4250	2000	800

Sporting Rifle

As above, with octagonal barrels, set triggers and finely figured walnut stocks. Model 1853 Sporting rifle was built as a special order, about 32 produced. Model 1863 Sporting Rifle was also built on special order, about 16 produced. No two of this model are alike. All reside in museums or collections.

Coffee-Mill Model

Some Sharps' carbines were fitted with coffee-mill style grinding devices set into their buttstocks. **CAUTION:** These arms are exceptionally rare and extreme caution should be exercised prior to purchase. FAKES EXIST.

Courtesy Milwaukee Public Museum, Milwaukee, Wisconsin

NIB	Exc.	V.G.	Good	Fair	Poor
—	—	65000	42500	15000	5000

Metallic Cartridge Conversions

In 1867, approximately 32,000 Model 1859, 1863 and 1865 Sharps were altered to .52-70 rimfire and centerfire caliber.

Courtesy Mike Stuckslager

NIB	Exc.	V.G.	Good	Fair	Poor
—	—	5500	4250	2000	600

Model 1869

A .40-50 to .50-70 caliber model produced in a military form, with 26", 28" or 30" barrels; as a carbine with 21" or 24" barrels and in a sporting version with various barrel lengths. Fore-end stock fitted with a pewter tip. Approximately 650 made.

Carbine

.50-70, saddle ring on frame.

NIB	Exc.	V.G.	Good	Fair	Poor
—	—	5500	4250	1750	500

Military Rifle

.50-70, 30" barrel with three barrel bands.

NIB	Exc.	V.G.	Good	Fair	Poor
—	—	6500	5250	2000	800

Sporting Rifle

26" barrel, .44-77 and .50-70.

NIB	Exc.	V.G.	Good	Fair	Poor
—	—	8000	6500	3000	950

Model 1870 Springfield Altered

Chambered for .50-70 caliber. Fitted with 35.5" barrel, with two barrel bands. Walnut stock. Case-hardened lock and breechlock. Buttplate stamped "US". Also built for Army trials with 22" barrel converted to centerfire.

First Type

Most common, straight breech.

Courtesy Bonhams & Butterfields

NIB	Exc.	V.G.	Good	Fair	Poor
—	—	5000	3750	1750	500

Second Type

Model 1874 action, serial #1 to 300.

NIB	Exc.	V.G.	Good	Fair	Poor
—	—	8000	6000	2750	750

Carbine

22" barrel converted to centerfire.

NIB	Exc.	V.G.	Good	Fair	Poor
—	—	10500	8250	5000	1250

Model 1874

Manufactured in a variety of calibers, barrel lengths and stock styles. Barrel markings are of three forms: initially, "Sharps Rifle Manufg. Co. Hartford, Conn." ; then, "Sharps Rifle Co. Hartford, Conn." ; finally "Sharps Rifle Co. Bridgeport, Conn." As of 1876 "Old Reliable" was stamped on barrels. This marking usually found on Bridgeport-marked rifles only. Major styles of this model are listed.

Military Carbine

.50-70, 21" barrel (460 made).

NIB	Exc.	V.G.	Good	Fair	Poor
—	—	7950	5500	2750	750

Military Rifle

In .45-70 and .50-70 centerfire caliber, with 30" barrel. Full-length fore-end secured by three barrel bands. Approximately 1,800 made.

Courtesy Dennis Callender

NIB	Exc.	V.G.	Good	Fair	Poor
—	—	7500	5000	2250	750

Hunter's Rifle

In .40, .44, .45-70 and .50-70 caliber, with 26", 28" or 30" round barrels. Open sights. Approximately 600 manufactured.

NIB	Exc.	V.G.	Good	Fair	Poor
—	—	8000	6250	2750	800

Business Rifle

In .40-70 and .45-75 Sharps caliber, with 26", 28" or 30" round barrel. Adjustable sights and double-set triggers. Approximately 1,600 manufactured.

Courtesy Mike Stuckslager

NIB	Exc.	V.G.	Good	Fair	Poor
—	—	7750	6000	3250	1000

Sporting Rifle

Offered in a variety of calibers, barrel lengths weights and styles, stock styles. Approximately 6,000 manufactured.

Courtesy Milwaukee Public Museum, Milwaukee, Wisconsin

NIB	Exc.	V.G.	Good	Fair	Poor
—	—	15000	8500	4000	1500

Creedmoor Rifle

With a checkered pistol-grip stock, vernier sights, combination wind gauge and spirit level front sight, set trigger and shotgun style butt. Approximately 150 made.

NIB	Exc.	V.G.	Good	Fair	Poor
—	—	24000	17500	8500	2000

Mid-Range Rifle

Similar to above, with crescent buttplate. Approximately 180 made.

Courtesy Bonhams & Butterfields

NIB	Exc.	V.G.	Good	Fair	Poor
—	—	22500	15000	6500	1500

Long-Range Rifle

As above, with 34" octagonal barrel. Approximately 425 manufactured.

NIB	Exc.	V.G.	Good	Fair	Poor
—	—	23000	16500	6000	1500

Schuetzen Rifle

Similar to above, with checkered pistol-grip stock and fore-end. Large Schuetzen style buttplate, double-set triggers and vernier tang sight. Approximately 70 manufactured.

Courtesy Bonhams & Butterfields

NIB	Exc.	V.G.	Good	Fair	Poor
—	—	22500	15000	6500	2000

Model 1877

Similar to Model 1874. In .45-70 caliber, with 34" or 36" barrel. Barrel marked "Sharps Rifle Co. Bridgeport, Conn. Old Reliable". Approximately 100 manufactured in 1877 and 1878.

NIB	Exc.	V.G.	Good	Fair	Poor
—	—	30000	10000	5000	2000

MODEL 1878 SHARPS-BORCHARDT

An internal hammer breechloading rifle. Manufactured from 1878 to about 1880. Frame marked "Borchardt Patent Sharps Rifle Co. Bridgeport Conn. U.S.A.". **NOTE:** Be advised that actions on Borchardt Sporting Rifles are worth a minimum of $750. Military actions are not as difficult to locate as Sporting actions. For the sake of continuity, rifles in poor condition but with usable actions are priced at the minimum of $750.

Carbine

Approximately 385 made in .45-70 caliber, with 24" barrel. Fore-end secured by one barrel band.

Courtesy Milwaukee Public Museum, Milwaukee, Wisconsin

NIB	Exc.	V.G.	Good	Fair	Poor
—	—	4700	3750	1500	750

Military Rifle

Approximately 12,000 made in .45-70 caliber, with 32.25" barrels. Full stocks secured by two barrel bands.

Courtesy Bonhams & Butterfields

NIB	Exc.	V.G.	Good	Fair	Poor
—	—	3000	1250	900	750

Sporting Rifle

Approximately 1,600 made in .45-70 caliber, with 30" round or octagonal barrels.

NIB	Exc.	V.G.	Good	Fair	Poor
—	—	6000	2500	800	750

Hunter's Rifle

Approximately 60 made in .40-caliber, with 26" barrels. Plain walnut stocks.

NIB	Exc.	V.G.	Good	Fair	Poor
—	—	4500	1750	1000	750

Business Rifle

Approximately 90 made, with 28" barrels in .40-caliber.

NIB	Exc.	V.G.	Good	Fair	Poor
—	—	4500	2000	1000	750

Officer's Rifle

Approximately 50 made in .45-70 caliber, with 32" barrels. Checkered walnut stocks.

NIB	Exc.	V.G.	Good	Fair	Poor
—	—	7500	3750	1500	750

Express Rifle

Approximately 30 made in .45-70 caliber, with 26" barrels. Set triggers and checkered walnut stocks.

Courtesy Little John's Auction Service, Inc., Paul Goodwin photo

NIB	Exc.	V.G.	Good	Fair	Poor
—	—	12500	6000	2000	800

Short-Range Rifle

Approximately 155 made in .40-caliber, with 26" barrels. Venier rear sights, wind gauge front sight. Checkered walnut stock.

Courtesy Little John's Auction Service, Inc., Paul Goodwin photo

NIB	Exc.	V.G.	Good	Fair	Poor
—	—	7500	3750	1000	800

Mid-Range Rifle

Similar to above, with 30" barrel. Approximately 250 manufactured.

Courtesy Little John's Auction Service, Inc., Paul Goodwin photo

NIB	Exc.	V.G.	Good	Fair	Poor
—	10000	7000	4000	2000	900

Long-Range Rifle

Similar to above, with different sights. Approximately 230 manufactured.

Courtesy Amoskeag Auction Company

NIB	Exc.	V.G.	Good	Fair	Poor
—	—	16000	6500	2500	900

C. Sharps & Company and Sharps & Hankins Company Breechloading, Single-Shot Pistol

A .31-, .34- or .36-caliber breechloading percussion pistol, with 5" or 6.5" round barrels. Blued case-hardened, with walnut stock.

Courtesy Buffalo Bill Historical Center, Cody, Wyoming

NIB	Exc.	V.G.	Good	Fair	Poor
—	—	7000	5000	2000	600

Pistol-Grip Rifle

A .31- or .38-caliber breechloading percussion rifle resembling above. Manufactured in a variety of barrel lengths. Blued case-hardened, with walnut stock having German silver mounts.

Courtesy Bonhams & Butterfields

NIB	Exc.	V.G.	Good	Fair	Poor
—	—	6800	4750	2500	750

Percussion Revolver

A .25-caliber percussion revolver, with 3" octagonal barrel and 6-shot cylinder. Blued, with walnut grips. Barrel marked "C. Sharps & Co., Phila. Pa.". Approximately 2,000 manufactured between 1857 and 1858.

NIB	Exc.	V.G.	Good	Fair	Poor
—	—	4250	3000	1250	500

4-Shot Pepperbox Pistols

Between 1859 and 1874, these companies manufactured 4 barrel cartridge pocket pistols in a variety of calibers, barrel lengths and finishes. Barrels slide forward for loading. Major models are listed.

Courtesy Buffalo Bill Historical Center, Cody, Wyoming

Model 1

Manufactured by C. Sharps & Co., in .22 rimfire caliber.

NIB	Exc.	V.G.	Good	Fair	Poor
—	—	800	600	250	100

Model 2

As above, in .30 rimfire caliber.

NIB	Exc.	V.G.	Good	Fair	Poor
—	—	800	600	250	100

Model 3

Manufactured by Sharps & Hankins. Marked "Address Sharps & Hankins Philadelphia Penn." on frame. Caliber .32 Short rimfire.

NIB	Exc.	V.G.	Good	Fair	Poor
—	—	950	750	300	150

Model 4

Similar to above in .32 Long rimfire, with rounded bird's-head grip.

Courtesy John J. Stimson, Jr.

NIB	Exc.	V.G.	Good	Fair	Poor
—	—	950	750	300	150

Model 1861 Navy Rifle

A .52 Sharps & Hankins caliber breechloading single-shot rifle, with 32.75" barrel. Full stock secured by three barrel bands. Blued case-hardened, with walnut stock. Approximately 700 made in 1861 and 1862.

Courtesy Milwaukee Public Museum, Milwaukee, Wisconsin

NIB	Exc.	V.G.	Good	Fair	Poor
—	—	5000	300	2000	700

Model 1862 Navy Carbine

A .24-caliber breechloading carbine, with 24" leather covered barrel. Case-hardened, with walnut stock. Frame marked "Sharps & Hankins Philada.". Approximately 8,000 manufactured between 1861 and 1862.

Courtesy Milwaukee Public Museum, Milwaukee, Wisconsin

NIB	Exc.	V.G.	Good	Fair	Poor
—	—	5000	3500	2000	700

Short Cavalry Carbine

Similar to above, with 19" blued barrel. Approximately 500 manufactured.

NIB	Exc.	V.G.	Good	Fair	Poor
—	—	5000	3500	2000	700

Army Model

Similar to above, with 24" barrel that does not have a leather covering. Approximately 500 purchased by the Army.

NIB	Exc.	V.G.	Good	Fair	Poor
—	—	4750	3000	1750	700

SHATTUCK, C. S.
Hatfield, Massachusetts

Double-Barrel Shotguns

In addition to single-barrel shotguns, Shattuck made about 1,000 hammerless doubles.

Courtesy Nick Niles

NIB	Exc.	V.G.	Good	Fair	Poor
—	1000	500	400	300	200

Boom

A .22-caliber spur trigger revolver, with 2" octagonal barrel and 6-shot cylinder. Nickel-plated, with rosewood or walnut grips. Barrel marked "Boom" and "Pat. Nov. 4. 1879". Manufactured during 1880s.

NIB	Exc.	V.G.	Good	Fair	Poor
—	—	400	150	100	75

Pocket Revolver

A .32-caliber spur trigger revolver, with 3.5" octagonal barrel and 5-shot cylinder. Nickel-plated, with hard rubber grips. Barrel marked "C. S. Shattuck Hatfield, Mass. Pat. Nov. 4, 1879". Manufactured during 1880s.

NIB	Exc.	V.G.	Good	Fair	Poor
—	—	500	200	150	100

SHAW & LEDOYT
Stafford, Connecticut

Under Hammer Pistol

A .31-caliber under hammer percussion pistol, with 2.5" to 3.5" half-octagonal barrel. Blued, with brass mounted walnut grip. Frame marked "Shaw & LeDoyt/Stafford. Conn.". Manufactured during 1850s.

NIB	Exc.	V.G.	Good	Fair	Poor
—	—	1750	1300	550	150

SHAWK & McLANAHAN
St. Louis, Missouri

Navy Revolver

A .36-caliber percussion revolver, with 8" round barrel and 6-shot cylinder. Blued, with brass frame and walnut grips. Marked "Shawk & McLanahan, St. Louis, Carondelet, Mo.". Produced in limited quantities prior to 1860.

Courtesy Little John's Auction Service, Inc., Paul Goodwin photo

NIB	Exc.	V.G.	Good	Fair	Poor
—	—	15000	12000	5500	2000

SHERIDAN PRODUCTS, INC.
Racine, Wisconsin

Knockabout/Model D

A .22-caliber single-shot pistol, with 5" barrel. Fixed sights. Blued, with plastic grips. Manufactured between 1953 and 1960.

NIB	Exc.	V.G.	Good	Fair	Poor
—	350	225	175	100	50

SHILEN RIFLES, INC.
Ennis, Texas

Model DGA Bench Rest Rifle

Centerfire single-shot bolt-action rifle, with 26" barrel. Fiberglass or walnut stock.

NIB	Exc.	V.G.	Good	Fair	Poor
—	1750	1400	1100	850	500

Model DGA Sporter

A .17 Rem. to .308 Win. caliber bolt-action sporting rifle, with 24" barrel without sights. Blued, with walnut stock.

NIB	Exc.	V.G.	Good	Fair	Poor
—	1750	1400	1100	850	500

Model DGA Varminter

As above, in varmint calibers with 25" barrel.

NIB	Exc.	V.G.	Good	Fair	Poor
—	1750	1400	1100	850	500

Model DGA Silhouette Rifle

As above, in .308 Win. only.

NIB	Exc.	V.G.	Good	Fair	Poor
—	1750	1400	1100	850	500

SHILOH RIFLE MFG. CO., INC.
Big Timber, Montana

Established in Farmingdale, New York, in 1976, this company moved to Big Timber, Montana, in 1983 with the name Shiloh Products. Changed its name to Shiloh Rifle Manufacturing Co. in that same year. In 1985, the company began marketing its products factory direct. In 1991, Robert, Phyllis and Kirk Bryan purchased the company. Those interested in Sharps reproduction rifles manufactured by this company are advised to contact them in Big Timber. **NOTE:** Company will build a rifle to customers' specifications. It is, therefore, possible that many of these rifles have special-order features that are not reflected in the base model price. Since Shiloh is in effect a custom (or at least semi-custom) manufacturer, rifles listed here are representative but not inclusive.

Model 1863 Military Rifle

A .54-caliber percussion rifle, with 30" barrel, single-/double-set triggers. Full-length walnut stock secured by three barrel bands.

NIB	Exc.	V.G.	Good	Fair	Poor
1900	1650	1100	900	700	500

Model 1863 Sporting Rifle

As above, with 30" octagonal barrel, sporting sights and half-length stock.

NIB	Exc.	V.G.	Good	Fair	Poor
1800	1550	1050	850	600	450

Model 1863 Military Carbine

Model 1863, with 22" round barrel. Carbine stock secured by one barrel band.

NIB	Exc.	V.G.	Good	Fair	Poor
1900	1650	1100	900	700	500

Model 1862 Confederate Robinson

As above, with 21.5" barrel, brass buttplate and barrel band.

NIB	Exc.	V.G.	Good	Fair	Poor
1900	1650	1100	900	700	500

Model 1874 Creedmoor Target Rifle

Furnished with 32" half-round half-octagon barrel. Extra-fancy wood stock with pistol-grip, no cheek rest and shotgun butt. Single trigger. No sights.

NIB	Exc.	V.G.	Good	Fair	Poor
2700	2250	1700	1300	800	500

Model 1874 Buffalo Rifle (Quigley)

Offered in .45-70 or .45-110, with 34" heavy octagon barrel. Mid-range tang sight, with globe front sight. Semi-buckhorn rear sight. Double-set triggers. Military buttstock, with patchbox. No cheek rest. Straight-grip stock.

NIB	Exc.	V.G.	Good	Fair	Poor
3300	2750	2100	1700	1200	500

Model 1874 Long Range Express Rifle

Manufactured in a variety of calibers, with 34" octagonal barrel, double-set triggers, vernier rear sight and globe front.

NIB	Exc.	V.G.	Good	Fair	Poor
2200	1750	1450	1195	750	400

Model 1874 Montana Roughrider Rifle

As above, with octagonal or half-octagonal barrels from 24" to 34".

NIB	Exc.	V.G.	Good	Fair	Poor
2200	1750	1450	1195	750	400

Saddle Rifle

As above, with 26" barrel. Shotgun butt.

NIB	Exc.	V.G.	Good	Fair	Poor
2200	1750	1450	1195	750	400

No. 1 Sporter Deluxe Rifle

Similar to above, with 30" octagonal barrel.

NIB	Exc.	V.G.	Good	Fair	Poor
2200	1750	1450	1195	750	400

No. 3 Standard Sporter

As above, with military-style stock.

NIB	Exc.	V.G.	Good	Fair	Poor
2200	1750	1450	1195	750	400

Business Rifle

As above, with heavy 28" barrel.

NIB	Exc.	V.G.	Good	Fair	Poor
2200	1750	1450	1195	750	400

Model 1874 Military Rifle

Model 1874, with 30" round barrel, military sights. Full-length stocks secured by three barrel bands.

NIB	Exc.	V.G.	Good	Fair	Poor
2200	1750	1450	1195	750	400

Model 1874 Carbine

Similar to above, with 24" round barrel.

NIB	Exc.	V.G.	Good	Fair	Poor
2000	1550	1150	750	500	300

Jaeger

Model 1874, with 26" half-octagonal barrel, open sights and pistol-grip stock with shotgun butt.

NIB	Exc.	V.G.	Good	Fair	Poor
2200	1750	1450	1195	750	400

Hartford Model

Reproduction of Sharps Hartford Model.

NIB	Exc.	V.G.	Good	Fair	Poor
2200	1750	1450	1195	750	400

Model 1874 Military Carbine

Similar to Military Rifle, with 22" round barrel.

NIB	Exc.	V.G.	Good	Fair	Poor
2200	1750	1450	1195	750	400

SIG-HAMMERLI
Lenzburg, Switzerland

Model P240 Target Pistol

A .32 S&W Long Wadcutter or .38 Midrange caliber semi-automatic pistol, with 5.9" barrel. Adjustable rear sight and trigger. 5-shot magazine. Blued, with adjustable walnut grips. Imported prior 1987.

Courtesy John J. Stimson, Jr.

NIB	Exc.	V.G.	Good	Fair	Poor
—	1300	1150	950	750	600

.22 Conversion Unit

Barrel, slide and magazine used to convert the above to .22-caliber.

NIB	Exc.	V.G.	Good	Fair	Poor
—	500	450	400	300	200

Model P208S

Semi-automatic target pistol chambered for .22 LR cartridge. Barrel length 5.9", with adjustable sights. Sight radius 8.2". Trigger has adjustable pull weight, travel, slack weight and creep. Grips are stippled walnut, with adjustable palm shelf. Weight about 37 oz. empty.

NIB	Exc.	V.G.	Good	Fair	Poor
1900	1600	1300	1100	750	500

Model P280

Semi-automatic pistol chambered for .22 LR cartridge or .32 S&W Long Wadcutter. Single-action-only. Barrel length 4.6", with sight radius of 8.7". Adjustable sights. Trigger adjustable for pull weight, take-up, let-off and creep. Stippled walnut grip, with adjustable palm shelf. Weight: 35 oz. .22-caliber; 42 oz. .32-caliber. Magazine capacity: .22-caliber 6 rounds; .32-caliber 5 rounds.

NIB	Exc.	V.G.	Good	Fair	Poor
1200	10000	800	650	500	300

Model P160/162

.22 LR single-shot pistol designed for international free pistol competition. Barrel length 11.3", with sight radius of 14.6". Trigger fully adjustable as are sights. Stippled walnut grips, with adjustable palm shelf and rake angle. Model 160 has a mechanical trigger; Model 162 fitted with an electric trigger.

NIB	Exc.	V.G.	Good	Fair	Poor
2300	2000	1700	1250	800	400

Trailside PL 22

Introduced in 1999. Semi-automatic pistol chambered for .22 LR cartridge. Barrel length 4.5" or 6", with fixed sights. Synthetic grips. Two-tone finish. Magazine capacity 10 rounds. Weight about: 28 oz. with 4.5" barrel; 30 oz. with 6" barrel. **NOTE:** Add $90 for 6" barrel.

NIB	Exc.	V.G.	Good	Fair	Poor
575	500	375	295	200	100

Trailside PL 22 Target

Similar to PL 22, with addition of adjustable sights and walnut grips. Introduced in 1999. **NOTE:** Add $25 for 6" barrel.

NIB	Exc.	V.G.	Good	Fair	Poor
595	525	400	325	225	125

Trailside Competition

Introduced in 2004. This .22-caliber model features 6" barrel, with adjustable competition grip and sights. Counterweights and two-tone finish. Magazine capacity 10 rounds. Weight about 36 oz.

NIB	Exc.	V.G.	Good	Fair	Poor
800	675	500	425	300	150

SIG
Neuhausen, Switzerland

P 210

Pistol introduced in 1947. Standard issue sidearm of Swiss military from 1949 to 1975. Also issued to Danish Army as Model M49. Chambered in 9mm Parabellum, 7.65 (.30 Luger) and .22 Long Rifle, with 8-round magazine. A .22 conversion kit also available for centerfire models. Short-recoil operated single-action pistol, with frame-mounted manual safety and 4.75" barrel. Several variations of original P210 were imported into U.S. from 1950s until about 1987, with limited importation of a few more models until 2007. Upgraded and improved version introduced in 2011 as P210 Legend. See listing under SIG Sauer. **NOTE:** Add premium of 40 to 50 percent for .22 LR conversion kit.

P210 Danish Army Model M49

NIB	Exc.	V.G.	Good	Fair	Poor
3000	2500	2000	1500	800	400

P 210-1

Fixed sights, walnut grips, polished finish. Imported until 1986.

NIB	Exc.	V.G.	Good	Fair	Poor
2600	2200	1700	1100	500	350

P 210-2

Fixed sights, plastic or wood grips, matte finish. Imported 1987 to 2002.

NOTE: Add 50 percent premium for West German Police model, with loaded chamber indicator.

NIB	Exc.	V.G.	Good	Fair	Poor
2000	1600	1000	750	400	300

P 210-5

Adjustable sights, extended frame and barrel (5"), wood or rubber grips, matte finish, adjustable trigger. Push-button magazine release. Limited importation from 1997 to 2007.

NIB	Exc.	V.G.	Good	Fair	Poor
2250	1850	1650	1000	600	400

P 210-6

As above, with 4.75" barrel.

NIB	Exc.	V.G.	Good	Fair	Poor
2250	1850	1650	1000	600	400

P210-7

In .22 LR caliber. Fewer than 500 made.

NIB	Exc.	V.G.	Good	Fair	Poor
3500	2900	2400	1600	1000	400

P210-8

Special order target model, with adjustable sights, wood grips, heavy frame. Available from 2001 to 2003 only. Limited importation.

NIB	Exc.	V.G.	Good	Fair	Poor
3800	3200	2650	1800	1000	400

SIGARMS/SIG-SAUER
Eckernforde, Germany
Neuhausen, Switzerland
Exeter, New Hampshire

In 1985, SIG established a U.S. presence by opening SIG Arms in Exeter, New Hampshire. Name was changed to Sig-Sauer in 2007. Most current SIG firearms are manufactured in U.S., but some are imported from Switzerland or Germany. Since 2000, SIG has been owned by Luke and Ortmeier Group, which also owns Blaser, Mauser and J.P. Sauer.

PISTOLS

P210

Model reintroduced into U.S. in 2001. Based on Swiss military version first built in 1949. Designed primarily as a target pistol. Furnished in four different variations. All variations chambered for 9mm cartridge. **NOTE:** Older P210 models imported before 1968 without importer stamps and pistols built during late 1940s and early 1950s, may bring a premium to collectors. Be aware that extra barrels, conversion kits and other special order features will add additional value.

P210 Legend

Updated variation of P210. Features include side-mounted magazine release, improved and extended beavertail, black Nitron finish and choice of fixed or adjustable sights. Available only in 9mm. Introduced in 2011. Made in Germany. **NOTE:** Add $200 for adjustable sights.

NIB	Exc.	V.G.	Good	Fair	Poor
2000	1850	1500	1100	700	400

P220

High-quality double-action semi-automatic pistol chambered for .38 Super, .45 ACP and 9mm Parabellum. Has 4.41" barrel and fixed sights. Features decocking lever that was found originally on Sauer Model 38H. Two versions of this pistol—one with bottom magazine release (commonly referred to as European model); other with release on side (commonly referred to as American model), as on Model 1911 Colt. Frame is lightweight alloy, matte-finished and available in blue, nickel or K-Kote finish. Black plastic grips. .45 ACP magazine capacity 7 rounds, weight 25.7 oz.; .38 Super magazine capacity 9 rounds, weight 26.5 oz.; 9mm magazine holds 9 rounds, overall weight 26.5 oz. Manufactured from 1976 and still in production. The 9mm and .38 Super versions are no longer in production. Prices listed are for guns with standard blue finish. **NOTE:** Add $40 K-Kote finish; $40 nickel slide; $100 stainless steel. In 2004, a blued version with tactical rail was offered.

P220 with tactical rail

NIB	Exc.	V.G.	Good	Fair	Poor
825	600	400	300	200	150

P220 .22

As above chambered for .22 LR cartridge.

NIB	Exc.	V.G.	Good	Fair	Poor
500	400	300	200	150	100

P220 ST

As above chambered for .45 ACP cartridge. Features stainless steel frame and slide, with tactical rail. Also includes a SIGARMS tactical knife and aluminum carrying case. Weight about 39 oz.

NIB	Exc.	V.G.	Good	Fair	Poor
875	700	550	425	300	150

P220 Sport

Introduced in 1999. This .45 ACP pistol similar to P220. Addition of 5.5" barrel, with stainless steel compensator. Frame and slide are stainless steel. Magazine capacity 7 rounds. Weight about 44 oz.

NIB	Exc.	V.G.	Good	Fair	Poor
1400	1250	1000	775	500	300

P220R SAO

An 8+1 or 10+1 capacity single-action semi-automatic. Chambered for .45 ACP. Polymer grip and Nitron finish, 4.4" barrel, weight 30.4 oz., 5-lb. trigger. Picatinny rail. Introduced 2006.

NIB	Exc.	V.G.	Good	Fair	Poor
750	600	475	350	200	150

P220R DAK

Semi-automatic with 8+1 or 10+1 capacity. Chambered for .45 ACP. Polymer grip and Nitron finish, 4.4" barrel, weight 30.4 oz., 7.5-lb. trigger. Picatinny rail. Introduced 2006.

NIB	Exc.	V.G.	Good	Fair	Poor
875	700	600	475	350	200

P220 SAS

An 8+1 capacity double-action semi-automatic. Chambered for .45 ACP. Fixed sights, wood grips, 4.4" barrel, weight 30.4 oz., 6.5-lb. trigger. Introduced 2006.

NIB	Exc.	V.G.	Good	Fair	Poor
1000	875	725	600	400	200

P220 Carry SAS

An 8+1 capacity double-action semi-automatic. Chambered for .45 ACP. Fixed sights, wood grips, 3.9" barrel, weight 30.4 oz., 6.5-lb. trigger. Introduced 2006.

NIB	Exc.	V.G.	Good	Fair	Poor
900	795	700	550	400	200

P220 Carry

An 8+1 or 10+1 capacity single-/double-action semi-automatic. Chambered for .45 ACP. Fixed sights, polymer grips, 3.9" barrel, weight 30.4 oz. Introduced 2006.

NIB	Exc.	V.G.	Good	Fair	Poor
875	725	600	450	350	200

P220R Equinox

An 8+1 or 10+1 capacity single-/double-action semi-automatic. Chambered for .45 ACP. Fixed sights, wood grips, 4.4" barrel, weight 30.4 oz. Introduced 2006.

NIB	Exc.	V.G.	Good	Fair	Poor
1200	1050	750	600	450	300

P220R Carry Equinox

An 8+1 or 10+1 capacity single-/double-action semi-automatic. Chambered for .45 ACP. Fixed sights, wood grips, 3.9" barrel, weight 30.4 oz. Introduced 2006.

NIB	Exc.	V.G.	Good	Fair	Poor
875	700	575	450	350	200

P220 Langdon Edition

.45 ACP pistol introduced in 2004. Features 4.4" barrel, Nill wood grips, fiber optic sight, competition rear sight, front serrations, short trigger and other special features. Two-tone finish. Magazine capacity 8 rounds. Weight about 41 oz. Manufactured 500.

NIB	Exc.	V.G.	Good	Fair	Poor
1300	1050	800	600	450	250

P220 Combat

Similar to P220, with sand-colored alloy slide and steel frame. Threaded barrel for suppressor. Capacity 8+1 or 10+1. Designed for SOCOM sidearm trials. Introduced in 2007.

NIB	Exc.	V.G.	Good	Fair	Poor
1100	950	750	600	400	200

P220 Match

Similar to P220, with 5"barrel. Adjustable sights. Introduced 2007.

NIB	Exc.	V.G.	Good	Fair	Poor
950	800	675	500	300	150

P220 Super Match

Super-accurized version of P220 Match, with single-action only trigger, beavertail safety and custom wood grips. Limited edition.

NIB	Exc.	V.G.	Good	Fair	Poor
1200	975	850	600	400	200

P220 Compact

Similar to P220, with 3.9" barrel and 6+1 capacity. Single-action only or single-/double-action. Various finishes, grip and sight options.

NIB	Exc.	V.G.	Good	Fair	Poor
950	800	675	500	375	200

P220 Elite

Similar to P220, with SIG's new Short Reset Trigger (SRT). Beavertail safety, front cocking serrations, front strap checkering, SIGLITE\xa8 Night Sights and custom wood grips. Introduced in 2008. Also available in single-action only model.

NIB	Exc.	V.G.	Good	Fair	Poor
950	800	675	500	375	200

P220 Elite Stainless

Similar to above in stainless. Introduced 2008.

NIB	Exc.	V.G.	Good	Fair	Poor
1250	1100	875	650	450	200

P220 Carry Elite Stainless

Compact version of above, with 3.9" barrel; chambered in .45 ACP; 8-round capacity. Introduced 2008.

NIB	Exc.	V.G.	Good	Fair	Poor
1250	1100	875	650	450	200

P220 Platinum Elite

Fine-tuned enhanced version of P220 Elite, with front cocking serrations, front strap checkering, SIGLITE Adjustable Combat Night Sights and custom aluminum grips.

NIB	Exc.	V.G.	Good	Fair	Poor
1000	825	700	550	400	200

P220 Extreme

Two-tone black Nitron/stainless finish, with front slide serrations, Siglite night sights, Hogue G10 grips

NIB	Exc.	V.G.	Good	Fair	Poor
1000	850	750	600	450	350

P224

Sub-compact variation of P220/229 series, with double-stack magazine, steel slide, alloy frame, black wood grips and Siglite night sights. In 9mm, .357 Sig or .40 S&W. Available with DA/SA or DAK trigger. Introduced in 2012

NIB	Exc.	V.G.	Good	Fair	Poor
1000	875	675	500	400	250

P225

Similar to Model P220, except chambered for 9mm cartridge. More compact pistol, with 3.86" barrel. Has 8-shot detachable magazine and adjustable sights. Finish is matte blue, K-Kote or electroless nickel plate, with black plastic grips. Overall length 7.1"; height 5.2"; weight 26.1 oz. No longer in production. **NOTE:** Add $70 K-Kote finish; $70 nickel slide.

NIB	Exc.	V.G.	Good	Fair	Poor
625	575	500	400	200	150

P225 Limited

This 9mm 3.9" model features Novak low-carry rear sight, three magazines, SIG-Sauer range bag. Introduced in 2004. Weight about 26 oz.

NIB	Exc.	V.G.	Good	Fair	Poor
800	625	500	395	275	150

P225-A

Reintroduction of P225 model. Several changes include an enhanced Short Reset Trigger and single-stack frame size. Chambered in 9mm, with 8-round magazine. Introduced in 2016. **NOTE:** Add $100 for Night Sights.

NIB	Exc.	V.G.	Good	Fair	Poor
875	800	—	—	—	—

P226

Full size high-capacity pistol, with 4.41" barrel. Chambered for 9mm or .40 S&W cartridge. In 1996, available chambered for .357 SIG cartridge, with 15- or 20-round detachable magazine and high-contrast sights. Blued, electroless nickel plated or polymer finish (known as K-Kote). Overall length 7.7"; height 5.5"; weight 26.5 oz. Introduced in 1983. In 2003, available with integral rail system on frame. In 2004, offered with optional Crimson Trace laser grips. **NOTE:** Add $50 for K-Kote finish; $50 for nickel slide; $125 for Crimson Trace laser grips.

NIB	Exc.	V.G.	Good	Fair	Poor
825	600	550	450	300	200

P226BR .22

Similar to above in .22 LR. **NOTE:** Add $125 for Crimson Trace laser grips.

NIB	Exc.	V.G.	Good	Fair	Poor
550	475	350	250	175	100

P226 Navy Seal

Special limited edition 9mm pistol fitted with 4.4" barrel. Special serial numbers from "nsw0001" and above. Black finish.

NIB	Exc.	V.G.	Good	Fair	Poor
1400	900	750	550	400	300

P226 ST

Similar to P226, with stainless steel frame and slide. Offered in 9mm, .40 S&W and .357 SIG. Barrel length 4.4". Magazine capacity 10 rounds. Weight about 39 oz. Features include reverse two-tone finish, 3-dot sights and Hogue rubber grips. Very limited production in 2004 and 2005.

NIB	Exc.	V.G.	Good	Fair	Poor
1000	850	700	575	400	200

P226 Sport Stock

Introduced in 2002, this 9mm pistol features heavy match barrel and adjustable rear sight. Hand tuned. Specifications same as P226 ST. Available by special order only.

NIB	Exc.	V.G.	Good	Fair	Poor
1600	1450	1200	950	700	300

P226 Sport

Introduced in 2001. Similar to other SIG Sport models. Chambered for 9mm Luger cartridge. Stainless steel slide and frame. Adjustable target sights and competition barrel weight.

NIB	Exc.	V.G.	Good	Fair	Poor
1350	1175	1000	850	700	300

JP226 Jubilee Pistol

Variation is a special limited edition of P226. Each gun carries a special serial number prefixed JP. Grips are hand carved select European walnut. Slide and frame covered with solid gold wire inlays. Trigger, hammer, decocking lever, slide catch lever and magazine catch are all gold plated. Each pistol comes in custom fitted hard case of full leather. No longer imported into U.S. Fewer than 250 imported between 1991 and 1992.

NIB	Exc.	V.G.	Good	Fair	Poor
1795	1500	1200	900	700	400

P226R DAK

Introduced in 2005. Features double-action-only DAK trigger system, with double strike capability. Chambered for 9mm, .357 SIG or .40 S&W cartridge. Barrel 4.4". Fixed sights. Magazine capacity 10, 12 or 15 rounds. Weight about: 32 oz. 9mm; 34 oz. .357 SIG or .40 S&W.

NIB	Exc.	V.G.	Good	Fair	Poor
900	775	600	450	300	200

P226 X-Five

Single-action model chambered for 9mm or .40 S&W cartridge. Fitted with 5" barrel. Adjustable rear sight and trigger pull. Slide has front cocking serrations. Checkered wood Nill grips. Magazine capacity: 19 rounds 9mm; 14 rounds .40 S&W. Stainless steel finish. Weight about 47 oz.

NIB	Exc.	V.G.	Good	Fair	Poor
1700	1525	1275	900	550	300

P226 Tactical

9mm pistol has 4.98" extended threaded barrel. Fixed sights. Alloy frame. Magazine capacity 15 rounds. Weight about 32 oz. Black finish. Ellett Brothers exclusive. Introduced in 2005.

NIB	Exc.	V.G.	Good	Fair	Poor
900	795	600	450	300	150

P226 SAS

Double-action semi-automatic, with 12+1 capacity. Chambered for .40 S&W. Fixed sights, wood grips, 4.4" barrel, weight 34 oz., 6.5-lb. trigger. Introduced 2006.

NIB	Exc.	V.G.	Good	Fair	Poor
875	750	600	475	300	150

P226R Equinox

An 10+1 or 12+1 capacity single-/double-action semi-automatic. Chambered for .40 S&W. Fixed sights, wood grips, 4.4" barrel, weight 34 oz. Introduced 2006.

NIB	Exc.	V.G.	Good	Fair	Poor
1175	1025	875	700	550	350

P226 SCT

All black Nitron finished P226. Featuring front cocking serrations, SI-GLITE Rear Night Sight, TRUGLO tritium fiber optic front sight. Comes with four newly designed 20-round magazines for 9mm; or four 15-round magazines for .40 S&W.

NIB	Exc.	V.G.	Good	Fair	Poor
950	825	700	575	400	200

P226 Elite

Introduced in 2008. Similar to P226, with redesigned short-reset trigger and improved ergonomics. Chambered in 9mm, .40 S&W and .357 SIG. Model P226 Enhanced Elite has same features as P226 Elite, with addition of ergonomic one-piece reduced-reach polymer grips.

NIB	Exc.	V.G.	Good	Fair	Poor
1050	900	825	675	450	250

P226 Elite Stainless

Similar to above in stainless steel.

NIB	Exc.	V.G.	Good	Fair	Poor
1100	1000	900	750	475	275

P226 Platinum Elite

Fine-tuned enhanced version of P226 Elite, with front cocking serrations, front strap checkering, SIGLITE Adjustable Combat Night Sights and custom aluminum grips.

NIB	Exc.	V.G.	Good	Fair	Poor
1250	1175	950	775	500	300

Mosquito

Model essentially a P226 reduced to 90 percent of its original size. Double-/single-action trigger fitted with 3.98" barrel. Chambered for .22 Long Rifle cartridge. Polymer frame with Picatinny rail. Fixed sights. Magazine capacity 10 rounds. Weight about 24.5 oz. Black finish. Introduced in 2005.

NIB	Exc.	V.G.	Good	Fair	Poor
325	300	250	200	150	100

P226 SAO

Single-action only variation of Model P226. Made in Germany. Introduced 2013.

NIB	Exc.	V.G.	Good	Fair	Poor
1100	1000	850	600	450	350

P226 Legion

Similar to P226 SAO. Has custom G-10 grips, SIG X-Ray High Visibility Night Sights, enhanced checkering on front strap and trigger guard, reduced and contoured beavertail and Legion Gray finish. Introduced in 2016.

NIB	Exc.	V.G.	Good	Fair	Poor
1250	1000	—	—	—	—

P226 MK25 Navy Model

A 9mm semi-automatic model, with black Nitron or Flat Dark Earth finish, Picatinny rail and night sights. Added touch of an anchor engraved on the slide.

NIB	Exc.	V.G.	Good	Fair	Poor
1000	900	750	500	400	250

P227

A .45 ACP chambered semi-automatic, with a slender double-stack 10-round magazine. Comes in several variations, with 3.9" or 4.4" barrel. Edges are dehorned and models available with/without a Picatinny rail. SIGLITE Night Sights are standard. **NOTE:** Add $100 for Equinox model, with wood grips.

NIB	Exc.	V.G.	Good	Fair	Poor
950	850	725	450	375	200

P228

Compact version of P226 fitted with 3.86" barrel. Chambered for 9mm cartridge. Available in blue, K-Kote or nickel finish, with black grips. Overall length 7.1"; height 5.4"; weight 26.1 oz. Made from 1990 to 1997; reintroduced 2004 to 2006. **NOTE:** Add $50 K-Kote finish; $50 nickel slide.

NIB	Exc.	V.G.	Good	Fair	Poor
725	600	475	350	200	150

P228 (New Model)

Reintroduced in 2013. Black Nitron or stainless two-tone finish. Standard single-/double-action operation, SIGLITE Night Sights, two 15-round magazines.

NIB	Exc.	V.G.	Good	Fair	Poor
1000	850	700	500	400	350

P229

Similar to P228 except chambered for .40 S&W cartridge. Has blackened stainless steel slide and lightweight aluminum alloy frame. Slide slightly larger to accommodate more powerful cartridge. In 1996, 9mm chamber also offered. Overall length 7.1"; height 5.4"; weight 27.54 oz. Magazine capacity 12 rounds. Introduced in 1992. In 1994, a new caliber for this model was introduced: .357 SIG developed by Federal. Magazine capacity 12 rounds.

NIB	Exc.	V.G.	Good	Fair	Poor
800	675	550	400	250	150

P229 Nickel

Same as standard P229. with full nickel finish over stainless steel slide and alloy frame. Weight about 27.5 oz. Introduced in 1998.

NIB	Exc.	V.G.	Good	Fair	Poor
850	525	600	450	275	175

P229 Stainless

Introduced in 2005. Same features as standard P229 except for stainless steel slide and frame. Weight about 41 oz. Magazine capacity 12 rounds.

NIB	Exc.	V.G.	Good	Fair	Poor
900	775	600	475	300	150

P229 Sport

Chambered for .357 SIG cartridge. Fitted with 4.8" barrel, with muzzle compensator. Adjustable target sights. Both frame and slide are stainless steel. Magazine capacity 10 rounds. Weight about 41 oz. Introduced in 1998.

NIB	Exc.	V.G.	Good	Fair	Poor
1500	1350	1175	950	600	400

P229 Limited

.40 S&W pistol features 3.9" barrel with fixed sights. Stainless steel slide with Nitron finish. Scroll engraving on top of slide, high polished 24 kt gold accents on trigger, hammer, magazine catch and grip screws. Hardwood grips.

NIB	Exc.	V.G.	Good	Fair	Poor
950	825	675	500	350	200

P229 Combo

Chambered for .40 S&W cartridge and fitted with 3.9" barrel. Fixed sights. Black Nitron finish. Spare barrel chambered for .357 SIG included. Magazine capacity 10 rounds. Weight about 30 oz. Introduced in 2004.

NIB	Exc.	V.G.	Good	Fair	Poor
900	775	625	450	300	175

P229 Elite

Features ergonomic beavertail grip, front cocking serrations, front strap checkering, SIGLITE Night Sights, custom wood grips and new Short Reset Trigger (SRT). Available in 9mm and .40 S&W. P229 Enhanced Elite has same features as P229 Elite, with addition of ergonomic one-piece reduced-reach polymer grips.

NIB	Exc.	V.G.	Good	Fair	Poor
1100	900	825	675	450	250

P229 Platinum Elite

Fine-tuned enhanced version of P229 Elite, with front cocking serrations, front strap checkering, SIGLITE Adjustable Combat Night Sights and custom aluminum grips.

NIB	Exc.	V.G.	Good	Fair	Poor
1100	900	800	695	475	300

1911 C3

Compact 1911-style autoloader features 7+1 capacity, two-tone finish, custom rosewood grips and 4.2" barrel. Alloy frame gives an unloaded weight of just under 30 oz.

NIB	Exc.	V.G.	Good	Fair	Poor
900	775	600	475	300	150

1911 Platinum Elite

1911-style 8+1 autoloader in .45 ACP, 5"barrel, Nitron frame, aluminum grips. Introduced in 2008.

NIB	Exc.	V.G.	Good	Fair	Poor
1100	950	800	675	500	300

1911 Platinum Elite Carry

Compact version of above, with 4.5" barrel. Introduced in 2008.

NIB	Exc.	V.G.	Good	Fair	Poor
1250	1025	875	750	575	350

1911-22

Same dimensions as standard 1911 pistol. Caliber .22 LR, alloy frame and slide, 10-round magazine, blowback operated, extended thumb safety, extended beavertail grip safety, magazine disconnect safety, skeletonized hammer and trigger. Weight 18 oz. Nitron finish.

NIB	Exc.	V.G.	Good	Fair	Poor
340	285	235	200	165	100

1911 Scorpion

Caliber .45 ACP, stainless steel slide and frame, 8-round magazine, extended thumb safety, extended beavertail grip safety, skeletonized hammer and flat trigger, checkered front strap and mainspring housing, Low-Mount night sights and accessory rail. Frame and slide has Cerkote desert tan finish, grips are Hogue G10 Magwell with Piranha texture.

NIB	Exc.	V.G.	Good	Fair	Poor
975	850	700	500	300	150

Model GSR

.45 ACP pistol introduced in 2004. Fitted with 5" barrel. Single-action only. Offered with white stainless steel frame and slide or blued frame and slide. Also offered with black Nitron finish. Tac rail standard. Hand fitted. Magazine capacity 8 rounds. Weight about 39 oz.

NIB	Exc.	V.G.	Good	Fair	Poor
1000	850	675	500	300	150

1911 STX

From SIG SAUER Custom Shop. This is a two-tone non-railed 1911, with Nitron slide over a natural stainless frame. Frame and slide are carefully machined and handfitted and de-horned for comfortable carry. Other features include match-grade barrel, extended ambidextrous thumb safety, beavertail safety with speed bump, checkered front strap and mainspring housing. Custom wood grips.

NIB	Exc.	V.G.	Good	Fair	Poor
1000	850	675	500	300	150

1911 TACOPS TB

Tactical Operations model has an integral accessory rail, ambidextrous safety, Ergo XT grips, low profile night sights and threaded barrel.

NIB	Exc.	V.G.	Good	Fair	Poor
1000	850	675	500	300	150

REVOLUTION SERIES

Revolution

All-stainless frames and slides in four configurations. Novak Night Sights, Rose- or Diamond Wood custom grips. Stainless or Nitron finish. 8+1 capacity, 45 ACP, single-action, 5" barrel, 40.3 oz. Introduced 2006.

NIB	Exc.	V.G.	Good	Fair	Poor
900	775	600	475	300	150

Revolution Custom STX

Single-action .45 ACP stainless semi-automatic with 8+1 capacity. Adjustable combat night sights and custom wood grip panels, 5" barrel, 40.6 oz. Introduced 2006.

NIB	Exc.	V.G.	Good	Fair	Poor
1100	950	800	675	500	300

Revolution TTT

Stainless semi-automatic with 8+1 capacity. Single-action .45 ACP. Adjustable combat night sights and custom wood grip panels, 5" barrel, 40.3 oz. Introduced 2006.

NIB	Exc.	V.G.	Good	Fair	Poor
1000	850	675	575	425	300

Revolution XO

Single-action .45 ACP stainless semi-automatic with 8+1 capacity. Polymer grip panels. 8.65" LOA, 5" barrel, 40.3 oz. Introduced 2006.

NIB	Exc.	V.G.	Good	Fair	Poor
900	775	600	475	300	150

Revolution Target

Single-action .45 ACP stainless semi-automatic with 8+1 capacity. Adjustable target night sights. Custom wood grip panels, 5" barrel, 40.3 oz. Stainless or Nitron finish. Introduced 2006.

NIB	Exc.	V.G.	Good	Fair	Poor
950	825	650	495	325	150

Revolution Carry

Single-action .45 ACP stainless semi-automatic with 8+1 capacity. Fixed sights. Custom wood grip panels, 4" barrel, 35.4 oz. Stainless or Nitron finish. Introduced 2006.

NIB	Exc.	V.G.	Good	Fair	Poor
900	775	600	475	300	150

Revolution Compact

Stainless semi-automatic single-action .45 ACP with 6+1 capacity. Fixed sights. Custom wood grip panels, 4" barrel, 30.3 oz. Stainless or Nitron finish. Introduced 2006.

NIB	Exc.	V.G.	Good	Fair	Poor
950	825	650	495	325	150

Revolution Compact SAS

Dehorned version of Revolution Compact.

NIB	Exc.	V.G.	Good	Fair	Poor
950	825	650	495	325	150

Revolution Compact C3

Similar to Revolution Compact, with black anodized alloy frame and stainless or Nitron-finished slide.

NIB	Exc.	V.G.	Good	Fair	Poor
950	825	650	495	325	150

Revolution Custom Compact RCS

Stainless semi-automatic single-action .45 ACP with 6+1 capacity. Fixed sights. Custom wood grip panels, 4" barrel, 30.3 oz. Stainless or Nitron finish. Introduced 2006.

NIB	Exc.	V.G.	Good	Fair	Poor
950	825	650	495	325	150

P229R DAK

Introduced in 2005. Features double-action only DAK trigger system, with double strike capability. Chambered for 9mm, .357 SIG or .40 S&W cartridge, with 4.4" barrel. Fixed sights. Magazine capacity 10, 12 or 15 rounds. Weight about: 32 oz. 9mm; 34 oz. .357 SIG or .40 S&W.

NIB	Exc.	V.G.	Good	Fair	Poor
850	525	600	450	275	175

P229 SCT

All black Nitron finished P229 featuring front cocking serrations, SI-GLITE Rear Night Sight, TRUGLO tritium fiber optic front sight. Comes with four newly designed 17-round magazines for 9mm; or four 14-round magazines for .40 S&W.

NIB	Exc.	V.G.	Good	Fair	Poor
1100	950	800	675	500	300

P238

Compact .380 single-action with 1911-style controls, but no grip safety. Offered in many grip and finish variations. Ambidextrous safety available. **NOTE:** Add $100 for rosewood grips or Hogue rubber grips; $50 for ambidextrous safety.

NIB	Exc.	V.G.	Good	Fair	Poor
635	550	450	400	300	200

P938

Slightly larger version of P238. Chambered in 9mm. Other features similar to P238. Available with several grip and finish options.

NIB	Exc.	V.G.	Good	Fair	Poor
700	620	515	450	350	225

P239

Introduced in 1996. Chambered for 9mm, .40 S&W or .357 SIG cartridge. Double-/single-action or double-action only. Barrel 3.6" long.

Overall length 6.6"; weight 25 oz. Fitted with a single column magazine: 7 rounds .357 SIG; 8 rounds 9mm. **NOTE:** All of the above SIG pistols from P220 to P239 are available with "SIGLITE" Night Sights. Add $80 for these optional sights.

NIB	Exc.	V.G.	Good	Fair	Poor
725	600	475	350	200	150

P239 Limited

This .40 S&W features a rainbow titanium slide. Trigger, hammer, grip screws and control levers also rainbow titanium. Magazine capacity 7 rounds. Weight about 27 oz. Introduced in 2004.

NIB	Exc.	V.G.	Good	Fair	Poor
725	600	475	350	200	150

P230

Semi-automatic compact pocket-type pistol. Chambered for .22 LR, .32 ACP, .380 ACP and 9mm Ultra. Has 3.62" barrel. 10-, 8- or 7-round magazine. Weight between 16.2 oz. and 20.8 oz. Finish blued or stainless, with black plastic grips. Manufactured from 1976. In 1996, a two-tone finish was offered. No longer in production. **NOTE:** Add $85 for stainless steel finish; $35 for stainless steel slide.

NIB	Exc.	V.G.	Good	Fair	Poor
450	375	300	250	200	150

P232

Improved model of P230. Incorporates numerous changes to improve function and reliability. Basic features, operation and dimensions remain the same as P230.

NIB	Exc.	V.G.	Good	Fair	Poor
450	375	300	250	200	150

P232 (1998 Model)

In 1998, this model has as standard features night sights and Hogue grips, with an all stainless steel finish. Chambered for .380 ACP. Has 7-round magazine. Weight about 21 oz.

NIB	Exc.	V.G.	Good	Fair	Poor
500	375	300	250	200	150

P232 Limited

This .380 pistol features a black finish, night sights and satin nickel accents. Hogue rubber grips with finger grooves. Magazine capacity 7 rounds. Weight about 28 oz. Introduced in 2004.

NIB	Exc.	V.G.	Good	Fair	Poor
575	450	375	250	200	100

P245 Compact

Introduced in 1999. Chambered for .45 ACP cartridge. Fitted with 3.9" barrel. Magazine capacity 6 rounds. Overall length 7.3"; weight about 28 oz. Available finishes are blue and K-Kote. SIGLITE Night Sights also available.

NIB	Exc.	V.G.	Good	Fair	Poor
775	650	500	375	250	150

P245 Custom Shop

Introduced in 2004. This .45 ACP pistol limited to 75 guns. Features Teflon-impregnated nickel slide, frame, trigger, hammer, etc. Hand-tuned

action. Target crowned barrel. Novak low-carry sights, limited edition markings. Weight about 27 oz.

NIB	Exc.	V.G.	Good	Fair	Poor
2100	1700	1450	1000	600	350

SIG P250

Modular pistol comes in full, compact (shown) and sub-compact size. Offered in 9mm, .357 SIG, .380 ACP (sub-compact only), .40 S&W and .45 ACP. Double-stack magazine capacity 17 rounds (9mm & .380), 14 rounds (.357 & .40), 10 rounds (.45). Design allows shooter to change calibers, grip size and model size. Double-action only operation. Features include an accessory rail, Nitron slide finish, contrast or SIGLITE Night Sights. A compact .22 rimfire version is available, with similar features. **NOTE:** Add $80 for night sights. Deduct $50 for .22 rimfire version.

NIB	Exc.	V.G.	Good	Fair	Poor
425	385	350	300	250	175

P290

New micro-compact pistol for concealed carry. Caliber 9mm Parabellum is double-action only, with stainless steel slide, polymer frame, 6-round magazine, three-dot sights and removable grip panels. Weight 20.5 oz., barrel length 2.9". Finish is Nitron or two-tone stainless. Available with detachable laser sight. **NOTE:** Add $70 for laser sight.

NIB	Exc.	V.G.	Good	Fair	Poor
450	400	375	325	275	200

P320

Double-action only semi-automatic available in 9mm or .40 S&W. Barrel length 4.7". Double-stack magazine capacity 14 rounds (.40); 17 rounds (9mm). Other features include SIGLITE Night Sights, interchangeable grip panels and black Nitron finish.

NIB	Exc.	V.G.	Good	Fair	Poor
600	525	450	350	300	200

SIG PRO SERIES

SP2340

Introduced in 1998. Chambered for .357 SIG or .40 S&W cartridge. Built on a polymer frame with accessory rails on the dust cover. Barrel length 3.9". Standard finish blue. Weight about 28 oz. Comes with two sets of interchangeable grips and two 10-round magazines. Available in single-/double-action or double-action only.

SP2340 with laser sights

NIB	Exc.	V.G.	Good	Fair	Poor
650	525	450	375	300	150

SP2009

Similar to SP2340. Chambered for 9mm cartridge. Weight about 25 oz. Magazine capacity 10 rounds.

NIB	Exc.	V.G.	Good	Fair	Poor
500	425	350	225	175	100

SP2022

Chambered for 9mm, .357 SIG or .40 S&W cartridges. Fitted with 3.85" barrel, with fixed sights. Polymer frame. Black finish. Weight about 27 to 30 oz. Magazine capacity 10 or 12 rounds, depending on caliber.

NIB	Exc.	V.G.	Good	Fair	Poor
575	450	325	250	200	150

SHOTGUNS

Model SA3 Hunter

Introduced in 1997. Over/under shotgun chambered for 20-gauge shell. Fitted with 26" or 28" barrels. Single-selective trigger and automatic ejectors. Stock figured walnut, with pistol-grip. Receiver polished steel, with engraved game scenes. Weight about 6.8 lbs.

NIB	Exc.	V.G.	Good	Fair	Poor
1200	1050	750	600	400	300

Model SA3 Sporting

12-gauge over/under introduced in 1998. Features 28" or 29.5" barrel, with wide 11mm rib. Front and mid-target sights. Both barrels and action blued. Walnut stock, with pistol-grip and recoil pad. Weight about 7.3 lbs.

NIB	Exc.	V.G.	Good	Fair	Poor
1675	1250	1000	700	500	400

Model SA5 Sporting

Introduced in 1998. This 12-gauge fitted with choice of 28" or 29.5" barrels. Single-selective trigger and automatic ejectors are standard. Barrels fitted with 10mm rib. Receiver polished steel, with engraved clay target on each side. Weight about 7.6 lbs.

NIB	Exc.	V.G.	Good	Fair	Poor
2500	2000	1500	1100	750	500

AURORA SERIES

These shotguns were first imported and introduced into SIG product line in 2000. They are made in Italy by B. Rizzini. All guns in this series are over/under guns.

Aurora TR Field Shotguns

All the TR field guns offered in 12-, 20-, 28-gauge and .410 bore. All have single triggers and ejectors. Barrel lengths 26" or 28". Weights vary:7 lbs. 12-gauge; to 6 lbs. .410. Select walnut stock, with oil-finish. Cut checkering of 20 lpi. Choke tubes on 12- and 20-gauge; fixed chokes on 28-gauge and .410 bore.

TR 20U

Features a boxlock action, with case-hardened frame. No engraving. Straight-grip stock.

Aurora TR 20U 28 gauge

NIB	Exc.	V.G.	Good	Fair	Poor
2000	1750	1475	1200	900	400

TR 20

Features a boxlock action, with nickel finish and no engraving. Pistol-grip.

Aurora TR 20 .410 bore

NIB	Exc.	V.G.	Good	Fair	Poor
1850	1500	1325	1000	750	300

TR 30

Features case-hardened action, with side plates. No engraving. Pistol-grip.

Aurora TR 30 12 gauge

NIB	Exc.	V.G.	Good	Fair	Poor
2225	1850	1550	1375	1000	400

TR 40 Silver

Features silver action and side plates with gold inlaid game scenes. Pistol-grip.

NIB	Exc.	V.G.	Good	Fair	Poor
2575	2100	1550	1200	950	450

TR 40 Gold

Features case-hardened action and side plates with gold inlaid game scenes. Pistol-grip.

NIB	Exc.	V.G.	Good	Fair	Poor
2675	2000	1450	1100	800	500

New Englander

Introduced in 2000 jointly by SIG and L.L. Bean. This over/under chambered in 12- and 20-gauge. Choice of 26" or 28" barrels. Single-selective trigger, auto ejectors, choke tubes all standard. L.L. Bean logo inlaid in gold on receiver. Select turkish walnut stock, with oil-finish. Prince of Wales-style pistol-grip and rubber recoil pad.

NIB	Exc.	V.G.	Good	Fair	Poor
1995	1500	1200	900	700	350

TT 25 Competition

Offered in 12- and 20-gauge, with 28" to 32" barrels for 12-gauge; 28" or 30" barrels for 20-gauge. Choke tubes. Single-selective auto ejectors are standard. Wide competition ventilated rib. Pistol-grip on select walnut stock, with 20 lpi checkering. Weight about: 12-gauge 7.25 lbs.; 20-gauge 6.75 lbs.

Aurora TT 25 12 gauge

NIB	Exc.	V.G.	Good	Fair	Poor
1995	1500	1200	900	700	350

TT45

Similar to TT25, with addition of case-hardened receiver and side plates with engraving and gold inlay game scenes.

NIB	Exc.	V.G.	Good	Fair	Poor
3275	2795	2200	1775	1300	450

RIFLES

SIG AMT

Semi-automatic rifle chambered for .308 cartridge. Fitted with 19" barrel and wooden buttstock and forearm. Folding bipod standard. Box magazine capacity 5, 10 or 20 rounds. Weight about 10 lbs. Built from 1960 to 1974.

NIB	Exc.	V.G.	Good	Fair	Poor
4500	3800	3100	2500	1500	1000

SIG PE-57

Similar to above. Chambered for 7.5x55 Swiss cartridge.

NIB	Exc.	V.G.	Good	Fair	Poor
4500	3800	3000	2500	1500	1000

SIG 550

Semi-automatic rifle chambered for .223 cartridge. Fitted with 18" barrel.

NIB	Exc.	V.G.	Good	Fair	Poor
9000	7000	5500	3000	1800	1000

SIG 551

Same as above. Fitted with 16" barrel.

NIB	Exc.	V.G.	Good	Fair	Poor
10500	9500	7500	4000	2000	1000

SSG 2000

High-grade bolt-action sniping-type rifle. Chambered for .223, 7.5mm Swiss, .300 Wthby. Magnum and .308 Win. Has a 24" barrel and 4-round box magazine. Furnished without sights. Finish matte blue, with thumb-hole-style stippled walnut stock with adjustable cheekpiece. Discontinued in 1986.

NIB	Exc.	V.G.	Good	Fair	Poor
8000	6000	3500	2700	1500	—

SSG 3000

Chambered for .308 Win. cartridge. Fitted with 23.4" barrel and ambidextrous McMillian Tactical stock. Magazine capacity 5 rounds. Overall length 46.5"; weight about 12 lbs. Model comes in three different packages.

Level I

Base model with no bipod or scope, but with carrying case.

NIB	Exc.	V.G.	Good	Fair	Poor
2550	2000	1600	1350	950	600

Level II

At this level a Leupold Vari-X III 3.5-10x40mm Duplex scope and Harris bipod, with carrying case.

NIB	Exc.	V.G.	Good	Fair	Poor
3500	2750	2300	1700	1200	600

Level III

Supplied with Leupold Mark 4 M1-10x40mm Mil-Dot Scope, with Harris bipod and carrying case.

NIB	Exc.	V.G.	Good	Fair	Poor
4500	3500	2700	2400	1500	700

Conversion Kit—.22 LR

In 2001, a .22-caliber conversion was offered for SSG 3000 rifle. Kit includes a heavy contured barrel bolt and 5-round magazine.

NIB	Exc.	V.G.	Good	Fair	Poor
750	—	—	—	—	—

Model SHR 970

Introduced in 1998. Bolt-action rifle chambered for .25-06 Rem., .270, .280 Rem., .30-06 or .308 cartridges. Has a 22" barrel. Receiver drilled and tapped for scope mounts. Detachable box magazine. Stock black synthetic or walnut. Barrels are interchangeable. Weight about 7.2 lbs. **NOTE:** Add $30 for walnut stock.

NIB	Exc.	V.G.	Good	Fair	Poor
725	650	575	400	300	200

Model SHR 970 Magnum

Same as above, but chambered for 7mm Rem. Magnum or .300 Win. Magnum. Barrel length 24". Weight about 7.4 lbs. **NOTE:** Add $30 for walnut stock.

NIB	Exc.	V.G.	Good	Fair	Poor
775	725	625	450	350	250

Model SHR 970 Tactical

Introduced in 2000. Features a McMillan stock, non-reflective metal coating, heavy fluted contoured barrel, integral muzzle-brake. Chambered for .308 Win. or .300 Win. Magnum cartridges. Receiver drilled and tapped for scope mount. Stock has a fitted rubber recoil pad.

NIB	Exc.	V.G.	Good	Fair	Poor
1400	1200	1000	775	600	400

Model 202 Standard

Bolt-action rifle features synthetic or Turkish walnut stock. Bolt is jeweled. Detachable 3-round box magazine. Offered in standard calibers from .22-250 to .30-06 and Magnum calibers from 7mm Rem. Magnum to .375 H&H Magnum. Barrel length 24" for standard calibers; 26" for Magnum calibers. Weight about 7.5 lbs.

NIB	Exc.	V.G.	Good	Fair	Poor
1650	1200	975	750	600	400

Model 202 Lightweight

Features a black synthetic stock, fluted barrel. Chambered for .22-250, .243, .25-06, .270 or .30-05 calibers. Barrel length 24". Magazine capacity 3 rounds. Alloy receiver and quick change barrel system are standard. Weight about 6.5 lbs. Introduced in 2001.

NIB	Exc.	V.G.	Good	Fair	Poor
1600	1150	925	700	550	350

Model 202 Varmint

Chambered for .22-250, .243 or .25-06 cartridge. Fitted with 26" fluted bull barrel. Stock Turkish walnut, with adjustable cheekpiece. Three-round detachable box magazine. Quick change barrel system. Weight about 9.5 lbs.

NIB	Exc.	V.G.	Good	Fair	Poor
1600	1150	925	700	550	350

Model 202 Supreme

Bolt-action model chambered for .243, .25-06, 6.5x55 Swedish, .270 Win., .308 Win. or .30-06. Fitted with 24" barrel. Synthetic or walnut stock. Magazine capacity 3 rounds. Weight about 7.7 lbs. No sights. **NOTE:** Add $50 for walnut stock.

NIB	Exc.	V.G.	Good	Fair	Poor
1800	1650	1400	1100	800	400

Model 202 Supreme Magnum

As above, but chambered for 7mm Rem. Magnum, .300 Win. Magnum, .300 Wby. Magnum or .375 H&H Magnum. Magazine capacity 3 rounds. Synthetic or walnut stock. Weight about 8.4 lbs. **NOTE:** Add $50 for walnut stock.

NIB	Exc.	V.G.	Good	Fair	Poor
1875	1725	1475	1150	850	450

SIG 556

Generally similar to SIG 556, but made in USA. Chambered in 5.56 NATO. Collapsible stock, 16" mil-spec barrel, Picatinny rail and all the trendy tactical goodies. Introduced 2006.

NIB	Exc.	V.G.	Good	Fair	Poor
1200	1000	850	750	500	400

SIG 556 SWAT

Features a 16" military grade cold hammer forged barrel. Chambered in 5.56mm NATO, with a twist rate of 1 in 7". High performance flash suppressor, vented tactical quad rail forearm machined from aircraft grade aluminum alloy and hard coat anodized for durability, quad rail with four Picatinny rails, Picatinny equipped receiver. Rifle comes standard with flip-up combat front and rear sight system. Trigger housing machined from an aircraft grade aluminum alloy forging, with a hard-coat anodized finish designed to survive extreme conditions. Rifle comes equipped with a smooth two-stage trigger, ambidextrous safety and designed to accept standard AR magazines.

NIB	Exc.	V.G.	Good	Fair	Poor
1500	1300	1100	950	875	600

SIG 556 HOLO

Similar to above, with holographic sight. Without quad rail and other features.

NIB	Exc.	V.G.	Good	Fair	Poor
1550	1350	1100	900	800	400

SIG 556 DMR

Sniper version of SIG 556 SWAT, with bipod and other accurizing features.

NIB	Exc.	V.G.	Good	Fair	Poor
1650	1500	1350	1000	850	500

SIG516 Gas Piston Rifle

AR-style rifle chambered in 5.56 NATO. Features include 14.5", 16", 18" or 20" chrome-lined barrel; free-floating aluminum quad rail fore-end with four M1913 Picatinny rails; threaded muzzle with standard (0.5x28TPI) pattern; aluminum upper and lower receiver is machined; black anodized finish; 30-round magazine; flattop upper; various configurations available.

NIB	Exc.	V.G.	Good	Fair	Poor
1100	950	800	650	500	300

SIG716 Tactical Patrol Rifle

AR-10 type rifle chambered in 7.62 NATO/.308 Win. Features include gas-piston operation with 3 round-position (4-position optional) gas valve; 16", 18" or 20" chrome-lined barrel with threaded muzzle and nitride finish; free-floating aluminum quad rail fore-end with four M1913 Picatinny rails; telescoping buttstock; lower receiver machined from 7075-T6 Aircraft grade aluminum forging; upper receiver machined from 7075-T6 aircraft grade aluminum with integral M1913 Picatinny rail.

NIB	Exc.	V.G.	Good	Fair	Poor
1900	1750	1500	1250	900	450

SIG M400

A true AR platform tactical rifle with 16" Nitride treated barrel, 7075-T6 aircraft grade aluminum forged lower receiver and direct-impingement operating system with rotating locking bolt. Offered in a wide range of variations, with many options. Values shown are for standard (Classic) model.

NIB	Exc.	V.G.	Good	Fair	Poor
1100	975	800	600	400	250

SIG MCX

AR-15 variant in 5.56 NATO, 7.62x39 or .300 AAC Blackout. Has a SIG SAS folding stock, SIG grip, mil-spec AR trigger, aluminum KeyMod hand guard and 16" barrel. Modular design allows easy caliber interchangeability. Also offered in pistol version. Introduced in 2015.

NIB	Exc.	V.G.	Good	Fair	Poor
1750	1350	1000	800	400	250

Sauer SSG 3000

Imported by SIG-Sauer from 2000 to 2012. A 5-round bolt-action sniper rifle chambered in .308 Win. Heavy-contoured hammer forged barrel fitted with flash suppressor/muzzle-brake to provide greater accuracy, with reduced muzzle signature. Both barrel and receiver feature black oxide finish to eliminate glare. Short, smooth 60 degree bolt throw allows for rapid operation. Like safety release bolt action is quiet. Massive six-lug lockup system used to give greater strength and accuracy. Pistol-grip and fully adjustable stock give shooter a custom fit. Trigger adjustable for trigger position, trigger take up, let-off point and trigger pull weight. Receiver features dovetail that will accept a wide range of sighting systems, including factory available M1913 rail. Price include Leupold Vari-X III 3.5-10x40 scope.

NIB	Exc.	V.G.	Good	Fair	Poor
4000	3550	2700	2000	1200	600

SIG 50

Bolt-action tactical rifle chambered for .50 BMG cartridge. Designed for ultra long-range tactical applications. Match-grade trigger set for 3.5 lbs. Stock has adjustable cheekpiece, pistol-grip and length of pull. Barrel 29" heavy fluted with muzzle-brake. Full length machined rails allow mounting of accessories. Fluted bolt, heavy duty steel bipod, Duracoat coating. Weight 23.5 lbs. Introduced in 2011.

NIB	Exc.	V.G.	Good	Fair	Poor
8300	7400	6350	—	—	—

SILMA
Italy

STANDARD MODELS

Model 70 EJ

Over/under chambered for 12- or 20-gauge shell, with 28" ventilated rib barrels and choke tubes. Single-selective trigger and auto ejectors. Checkered walnut stock. Weight about: 12-gauge 7.6 lbs.; 20-gauge 6.9 lbs. Silver engraved receiver.

12 Gauge

NIB	Exc.	V.G.	Good	Fair	Poor
950	800	675	495	300	200

20 Gauge

NIB	Exc.	V.G.	Good	Fair	Poor
875	725	600	400	265	150

DELUXE MODELS

Model 70 EJ

Chambered for 12-, 20-, 28-gauge or .410 bore shell. Fitted with 28" ventilated rib barrels. Checkered select walnut stock, with deluxe engraved receiver. Weight: 7.6 lbs. 12-gauge; 6.9 lbs. smaller gauges.

12 Gauge

NIB	Exc.	V.G.	Good	Fair	Poor
1050	750	600	475	350	200

20 Gauge

NIB	Exc.	V.G.	Good	Fair	Poor
950	700	550	425	300	175

28 and .410 Gauge

NIB	Exc.	V.G.	Good	Fair	Poor
1075	800	650	525	400	250

Superlight

Offered in 12- or 20-gauge, with 28" barrels and choke tubes. Checkered select walnut stock. Receiver made from alloy steel. Weight about: 12-gauge 6.7 lbs.; 6.3 lbs. 20-gauge.

NIB	Exc.	V.G.	Good	Fair	Poor
1100	825	675	550	425	275

Clays Model

Designed for sporting clays. Chambered for 12-gauge 3" shell. Fitted with 28" barrel, choke tubes and wide ventilated rib. Checkered select walnut stock.

NIB	Exc.	V.G.	Good	Fair	Poor
1300	975	775	625	500	400

SIMPLEX
Unknown

Simplex

German design based on Bergmann-Mars pistol. An 8mm caliber semi-automatic pistol, with 2.6" barrel. Front mounted 5-round magazine. Blued, with hard rubber grips having trade name "Simplex" cast in them. Manufactured from 1901 to around 1906. Early samples may have come from Germany; later pistols are thought to have been produced in Belgium.

NIB	Exc.	V.G.	Good	Fair	Poor
—	1650	1050	550	400	200

SIMPSON, R. J.
New York, New York

Pocket Pistol

A .41-caliber single-shot percussion pocket pistol, with 2.5" barrel. German silver mounts and walnut stock. Manufactured during 1850s and 1860s.

NIB	Exc.	V.G.	Good	Fair	Poor
—	—	2400	1750	700	300

SIMSON & COMPANY
Suhl, Germany

See—Luger

NOTE: Models listed and pictured are taken from a mid-1930s Simson catalog. Because the company was Jewish-owned, Nazis took control in mid-1930s changing the name to "Berlin Suhler Waffen". Prices are estimates.

SHOTGUNS

Model 235

Side-by-side shotgun chambered for 12- or 16-gauge, with Anson & Deely action. Scalloped frame, with scroll engraving. Walnut stock, with pistol-grip. Double triggers.

Courtesy Jim Cate

NIB	Exc.	V.G.	Good	Fair	Poor
—	900	700	550	400	350

Model 73

Similar to above, with more scroll engraving coverage.

Courtesy Jim Cate

NIB	Exc.	V.G.	Good	Fair	Poor
—	950	750	600	400	350

Model 74

Features deep cut game scene engraving. Select walnut stock, with fine-line checkering.

Courtesy Jim Cate

NIB	Exc.	V.G.	Good	Fair	Poor
—	1100	800	600	450	350

Model 74E

Same as above, with automatic ejectors.

Courtesy Jim Cate

NIB	Exc.	V.G.	Good	Fair	Poor
—	1200	850	650	450	350

Model 76

Side-by-side fitted with game scene engraved side plates. Offered in 12- or 16-gauge.

Courtesy Jim Cate

NIB	Exc.	V.G.	Good	Fair	Poor
—	1400	1100	800	550	400

Model 76E

As above, with automatic ejectors.

Courtesy Jim Cate

NIB	Exc.	V.G.	Good	Fair	Poor
—	1500	1200	850	550	400

PISTOLS

Model 1922

A 6.35mm semi-automatic pistol, with 2" barrel and 6-shot magazine. Slide marked "Selbstlade Pistole Simson DRP" and "Waffenfabrik Simson & Co Suhl". Blued, with black plastic grips.

NIB	Exc.	V.G.	Good	Fair	Poor
—	600	475	400	300	100

Model 1927

Similar to above, with slimmer frame. Stamped with trademark of three overlapping triangles having letter "S" enclosed.

NIB	Exc.	V.G.	Good	Fair	Poor
—	600	475	400	300	100

SIRKIS INDUSTRIES, LTD.
Ramat-Gan, Israel

SD9

A 9mm double-action semi-automatic pistol, with 3" barrel, fixed sights and 7-shot magazine. Blued, with plastic grips. Also known as Sardius.

NIB	Exc.	V.G.	Good	Fair	Poor
—	325	275	225	175	100

Model 35 Match Rifle

A .22-caliber single-shot bolt-action rifle, with 26" free-floating barrel, adjustable rear sight and trigger. Blued, with walnut stock.

NIB	Exc.	V.G.	Good	Fair	Poor
—	600	550	500	400	200

Model 36 Sniper's Rifle

A 7.62x54mm caliber semi-automatic rifle, with 22" barrel. Matte blued, with composition stock.

NIB	Exc.	V.G.	Good	Fair	Poor
—	675	600	550	450	200

SKB ARMS COMPANY
Omaha, Nebraska

This respected Japanese manufacturer began making shotguns for U.S. market in 1960s. Made various models for Browning, Weatherby and other American brands. In 1970s, SKB began marketing many models under its own name. End of 2009, SKB factory closed its doors. Final inventory was purchased by G. U. Inc. of Omaha, Nebraska. As of mid 2013, G.U. Inc. began importing several shotgun models from Turkey under the SKB brand. Approximately 1967 to 1977, Ithaca imported a series of over/under and side-by-side shotguns from SKB. These models were virtually identical to other SKB-made guns and had the same model numbers. Values shown in this section also apply to Ithaca guns.

SIDE-BY-SIDE GUNS

Model 100

Boxlock 12- or 20-gauge double-barrel shotgun, with 25" to 30" barrels. Single-selective trigger and automatic ejectors. Blued, with walnut stock. Imported prior to 1981. Discontinued.

NIB	Exc.	V.G.	Good	Fair	Poor
1200	1000	900	800	550	400

Model 150

As above, with some engraving. A beavertail forearm and figured walnut stock. Imported from 1972 to 1974.

NIB	Exc.	V.G.	Good	Fair	Poor
1250	1000	900	800	550	400

Model 200

As above, with French case-hardened and scalloped receiver. Discontinued.

NIB	Exc.	V.G.	Good	Fair	Poor
1300	1150	900	675	500	400

Model 200E

As above, with English-style stock. Imported prior to 1989.

NIB	Exc.	V.G.	Good	Fair	Poor
1350	1200	850	650	450	350

Model 280

Same as Model 200, but fitted with straight-grip stock. Discontinued.

NIB	Exc.	V.G.	Good	Fair	Poor
1400	1200	850	650	450	350

Model 300

As above, with more engraving. Figured walnut stock. Discontinued.

NIB	Exc.	V.G.	Good	Fair	Poor
1450	1250	900	700	475	350

Model 385

Similar to Model 300, but chambered for 12-, 20- or 28-gauge shell. Scroll engraved frame, with semi-fancy walnut pistol-/straight-grip stock. Limited quantities imported. Weight about 7 lbs. Discontinued.

NIB	Exc.	V.G.	Good	Fair	Poor
1800	1600	1475	1100	700	400

Model 385 2 Barrel Set

Same as above, with 20- and 28-gauge set of 26" or 28" barrels. Discontinued.

NIB	Exc.	V.G.	Good	Fair	Poor
2600	2500	2250	1300	900	500

Model 385 Sporting Clays

Chambered for 12-, 20- or 28-gauge. Fitted with 28" barrel. Pistol-grip stock. Weight about 7 lbs. Discontinued. **NOTE:** Add $900 for extra set of 20- or 28-gauge barrels.

NIB	Exc.	V.G.	Good	Fair	Poor
1850	1750	1475	1100	700	400

Model 400E

As above, with engraved false sideplates and English-style stock. Imported prior to 1990.

NIB	Exc.	V.G.	Good	Fair	Poor
1750	1600	1400	900	700	400

Model 480E

As above, with French case-hardened receiver and more finely figured walnut stocks. Discontinued.

NIB	Exc.	V.G.	Good	Fair	Poor
1800	1650	1475	1100	700	400

Model 485

Features engraved sideplate boxlock action. Chambered for 12-, 20- or 28-gauge, with 26" or 28" barrels. Choke tubes. Weight about 7.7 lbs. Discontinued.

NIB	Exc.	V.G.	Good	Fair	Poor
2750	2100	1500	900	650	300

Model 485 2 Barrel Set

Same as above, with extra set of barrels in 20/28-gauge combinations with 26" barrels. Choice of pistol-/straight-grip stock. Discontinued.

NIB	Exc.	V.G.	Good	Fair	Poor
3900	3000	1850	1500	1200	500

OVER/UNDER GUNS

MODEL 85TSS SERIES

This series, introduced in 2004, features a low-profile boxlock action. Fitted with an inertia trigger (12- and 20-gauge), mechanical on 28-gauge and .410 bore. Single-selective trigger, with manual safety. Silver nitride finish. Barrels have automatic ejectors, ventilated rib and choke tubes. Pigeon porting is optional. Stocks are American walnut, with matte finish. Fitted with Pachmayr recoil pad. Adjustable comb stock is optional.

Close-up of adjustable comb

Model 85TSS Sporting Clays

Chambered for 12-, 20-, 28-gauge and .410 bore. Features 28", 30" or 32" barrels on 12-gauge; 28" or 30" barrels on small bore guns. Choke tubes. Fixed or adjustable comb. Choice of multiple barrel sets. Weight about: 12 gauge 8.5 lbs.; 7.5 lbs. smaller bore guns. **NOTE:** Add $175 for adjustable comb; $1,200 for two- barrel sets; $2,800 for three-barrel 20-, 28-gauge and .410 sets.

NIB	Exc.	V.G.	Good	Fair	Poor
1875	1600	1425	1075	800	450

Model 85TSS Trap

This 12-gauge 3" trap model fitted with 30" or 32" backbored barrels, with adjustable 12mm rib. Fixed or adjustable comb, with-/without Monte Carlo. Weight about 8.75 lbs. **NOTE:** Add $175 for adjustable comb.

NIB	Exc.	V.G.	Good	Fair	Poor
1875	1600	1425	1075	800	450

Model 85TSS Trap Unsingle

A single-barrel trap gun, with 32" or 34" adjustable rib barrel. Standard comb or Monte Carlo, with-/without adjustable comb. Weight about 9 lbs. **NOTE:** Add $175 for adjustable comb.

NIB	Exc.	V.G.	Good	Fair	Poor
2100	1900	1625	1250	1000	500

Model 85TSS Trap Unsingle Combo

Features 32" or 34" single-barrel and 30" or 32" over/under barrels. Barrel rib adjustable. Monte Carlo or standard stock, with-/without adjustable comb. **NOTE:** Add $175 for adjustable comb.

NIB	Exc.	V.G.	Good	Fair	Poor
3175	2500	2250	1875	1300	600

Model 85TSS Skeet

Offered in 12-, 20-, 28-gauge and .410 bore. 12-gauge offered with 28", 30" or 32" backbored barrels, with 9.5mm rib; small gauges offered with 28" or 30" backbored barrels, with 8.5mm rib. Weight about: 12-gauge 8.35 lbs.; 7.5 lbs. smaller gauges. Fixed or adjustable comb. **NOTE:** Add $175 for adjustable comb; $2,800 for three-barrel set.

NIB	Exc.	V.G.	Good	Fair	Poor
2100	1900	1625	1250	1000	500

Model 500

A 12-, 20-, 28-gauge or .410 bore over/under shotgun, with 26", 28" or 30" ventilated rib barrels. Blued, with walnut stock. Imported from 1966 to 1979.

NIB	Exc.	V.G.	Good	Fair	Poor
850	700	575	400	325	200

Model 505 Field

The 505 Series also produced in sporting clays, trap and skeet configurations. Valued at approximately 10 percent additional.

NIB	Exc.	V.G.	Good	Fair	Poor
1270	950	700	500	350	250

Model 505 3-Gauge Skeet Set

As above, with 3 sets of barrels.

NIB	Exc.	V.G.	Good	Fair	Poor
2500	1800	1400	975	650	650

Model 585

Similar to Model 505, but offered in 12-, 20-, 28-gauge and .410 bore. Barrel lengths 26" or 28". Weight: 7.25 lbs. small bores; 8 lbs. 12-gauge.

NIB	Exc.	V.G.	Good	Fair	Poor
1550	1200	950	650	400	300

Model 585 Gold Package

Has all the features of 585 series, with addition of a gold-plated trigger, gold-plated game scenes and schnabel fore-end. Blued or silver receiver.

NIB	Exc.	V.G.	Good	Fair	Poor
1600	1250	975	675	425	300

Model 585 Skeet

Offered in 12-, 20- or 28-gauge and .410 bore, with 28" barrels. Skeet stock and beavertail forearm. Black recoil pad. Weight about 8 lbs. 12-gauge.

NIB	Exc.	V.G.	Good	Fair	Poor
1600	1250	975	675	425	300

Model 585—3 Barrel Skeet Set

Fitted with 20-, 28-gauge and .410 bore barrels. Skeet choked.

NIB	Exc.	V.G.	Good	Fair	Poor
2500	2250	1875	1300	600	400

Model 585—3 Barrel Skeet Set Gold Package

Same as above, with engraving. Silver or blued receiver.

NIB	Exc.	V.G.	Good	Fair	Poor
2600	2350	1875	675	600	400

Model 585 Youth/Ladies

Similar to 585, with shortened length of pull to 13.5". Weight about: 6.6 lbs. 20-gauge; 7.5 lbs. 12-gauge.

NIB	Exc.	V.G.	Good	Fair	Poor
1525	1300	975	700	350	200

Model 585 Youth Gold Package

Same as above, with gold trigger, gold-plated game scenes and schnabel fore-end. Silver or blued receiver.

NIB	Exc.	V.G.	Good	Fair	Poor
1625	1375	1025	750	400	200

Model 585 Upland

Similar to 585 series, except for straight-grip stock. Offered in 12-, 20-, 28-gauge, all with 26" barrels. Weight about: 7.75 lbs. 12-gauge; 6.75 lbs. 20-, 28-gauge.

NIB	Exc.	V.G.	Good	Fair	Poor
1525	1300	975	700	350	200

Model 585 Upland Gold Package

This model has additional gold package features of gold trigger, gold game scenes and schnabel fore-end. Silver or blued receiver.

NIB	Exc.	V.G.	Good	Fair	Poor
1600	1375	1025	750	350	225

Model 600

Similar to Model 585, with silver-plated receiver.

NIB	Exc.	V.G.	Good	Fair	Poor
1000	875	650	500	350	200

Model 600 Magnum

As above, chambered for 3", 12-gauge cartridges. Imported from 1969 to 1972.

NIB	Exc.	V.G.	Good	Fair	Poor
—	900	675	525	375	200

Model 600 Trap Gun

As above, with 30" or 32" barrels trap choked, with high comb walnut stock.

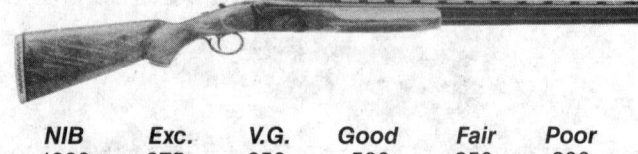

NIB	Exc.	V.G.	Good	Fair	Poor
1000	875	650	500	350	200

Model 600 Skeet Gun

As above, chambered for 12-, 20-, 28-gauge or .410 bore cartridges, with 26" or 28" barrels that are skeet choked.

NIB	Exc.	V.G.	Good	Fair	Poor
1000	875	650	500	350	200

Model 600 Skeet Combo Set

As above, with an extra set of three interchangeable barrels. Furnished with a carrying case.

NIB	Exc.	V.G.	Good	Fair	Poor
2900	2550	2100	1650	1200	600

Model 605

Similar to Model 600, with engraved and French case-hardened receiver. **NOTE:** 605 Series also available in trap or skeet configurations. Values are similar.

NIB	Exc.	V.G.	Good	Fair	Poor
1250	950	700	500	400	400

Model 605 3-Gauge Skeet Set

As above, with three extra sets of barrels.

NIB	Exc.	V.G.	Good	Fair	Poor
2900	2550	2100	1650	1200	600

Model 680E

Similar to Model 600, with engraved receiver and English-style stock. Imported from 1973 to 1976.

NIB	Exc.	V.G.	Good	Fair	Poor
1400	1100	850	600	500	250

Model 685

Over/under shotgun offered in 12-, 20-, 28-gauge and .410 bore. Barrel lengths 26" or 28", with choke tubes. Engraved receiver has a silver finish, with gold inlays. Walnut stock is semi-fancy.

NIB	Exc.	V.G.	Good	Fair	Poor
1400	1100	850	600	500	250

Model 700 Trap Gun

Similar to Model 600 Trap, with a wider rib. Additional engraving. Figured walnut stock. Imported from 1969 to 1975.

NIB	Exc.	V.G.	Good	Fair	Poor
1600	1250	975	675	425	300

Model 700 Skeet Gun

As above, with skeet chokes.

NIB	Exc.	V.G.	Good	Fair	Poor
1700	1350	1050	775	500	350

Model 785

Offered in 12-, 20-, 28-gauge and .410 bore. This over/under features 26" or 28" barrels, with choke tubes. Single trigger, ejectors and checkered walnut stock. Silver receiver is scroll engraved. Weight about: 8 lbs. 12-gauge; 7.25 lbs. small bores.

NIB	Exc.	V.G.	Good	Fair	Poor
1800	1500	900	750	500	300

Model 785—2 Barrel Set

These two barrel sets are in combination 12/20, 20/28 and 28/.410 bore, with 26" and 28" barrels.

NIB	Exc.	V.G.	Good	Fair	Poor
2900	2650	2200	1775	1200	600

Model 785 Sporting Clays

Chambered for 12-, 20-, 28-gauge. Barrels lengths from 28" to 32" in 12 gauge; 28" in 20- and 28-gauge. Recoil pad standard. **NOTE:** Add $900 for Sporting Clays set.

NIB	Exc.	V.G.	Good	Fair	Poor
2250	1750	1150	1400	900	500

Model 785 Skeet

Offered in 12-, 20-, 28-gauge and .410 bore, with 28" barrels. Recoil pad standard.

NIB	Exc.	V.G.	Good	Fair	Poor
2250	1750	1150	1400	900	500

Model 785 3-Gauge Skeet Set

Furnished with 12-, 20-, 28-gauge barrel, all 28" in length. Weight about 7.3 lbs.

NIB	Exc.	V.G.	Good	Fair	Poor
4400	3250	2500	1700	1200	600

Model 785 Trap

Offered in 12-gauge, with-/without Monte Carlo stock. Barrel lengths 30" or 32". Ventilated recoil pad standard.

NIB	Exc.	V.G.	Good	Fair	Poor
2250	1750	1150	1400	900	500

Model 785 Trap Combo

Features 30" or 32" over/under barrels, with a single 32" or 34" barrel. Standard stock or Monte Carlo.

NIB	Exc.	V.G.	Good	Fair	Poor
3050	2250	1250	100	700	375

Model 800 Trap Gun

As above, with trap chokes and more engraving. Imported from 1969 to 1975.

NIB	Exc.	V.G.	Good	Fair	Poor
2000	1000	850	650	550	250

Model 800 Skeet Gun

As above in 12- or 20-gauge, with 26" or 28" skeet choked barrels. Imported from 1969 to 1975.

NIB	Exc.	V.G.	Good	Fair	Poor
2000	1000	850	650	550	250

Model 880 Crown Grade

A false sidelock 12-, 20-, 28-gauge or .410 bore boxlock double-barrel shotgun, with single-selective trigger and automatic ejectors. Engraved sideplates and receiver are French case-hardened. Figured walnut stock is checkered. Imported prior to 1981.

NIB	Exc.	V.G.	Good	Fair	Poor
1900	1700	1350	1100	900	450

Model 885

A false sidelock 12-, 20-, 28-gauge or .410 bore boxlock shotgun. Similar to Model 800.

NIB	Exc.	V.G.	Good	Fair	Poor
1600	1250	1050	900	700	300

Model 5600

Over/under gun offered in 12-gauge only, in trap or skeet configurations.

NIB	Exc.	V.G.	Good	Fair	Poor
1000	825	700	500	400	200

Model 5700

Similar to above, with light scroll engraving on receiver. Figured walnut stock.

NIB	Exc.	V.G.	Good	Fair	Poor
1500	1250	1000	700	400	250

Model 5800

Similar to Model 5600, with more engraving coverage on receiver. Fancy walnut stock. **NOTE:** Add 100 percent premium for Custom Deluxe model.

NIB	Exc.	V.G.	Good	Fair	Poor
2200	1850	1300	900	500	300

GC 7

This over/under series was last produced by SKB. Three versions offered: Game Bird, Clays and Trap. Game Bird and Clays made in 12-, 20-, 28-gauge and .410 bore, with Trap only in 12-gauge. All models made on a low-profile boxlock action, with Greener-type crossbolt, automatic ejectors and single-selective trigger. Barrels are 26" to 34", with lengthened forcing cones and Briley choke tubes. Each series made in three grades, with escalating levels of engraving and wood quality. Prices shown for Grade I. **NOTE:** Add 20 to 30 percent for Grade II; 40 to 50 percent for Grade III. Multi-barrel sets can bring up to 100 percent premium.

Game Bird

NIB	Exc.	V.G.	Good	Fair	Poor
1500	1200	900	750	500	400

Clays and Trap

NIB	Exc.	V.G.	Good	Fair	Poor
1600	1300	1000	800	600	400

Model 7300

12- or 20-gauge slide-action shotgun. Blued, with walnut stock. Imported prior to 1981.

NIB	Exc.	V.G.	Good	Fair	Poor
—	300	250	200	150	100

Model 7900

As above, but skeet choked.

NIB	Exc.	V.G.	Good	Fair	Poor
400	300	250	200	150	100

Model 300

A 12- or 20-gauge semi-automatic shotgun, with 26", 28" or 30" barrels. Blued, with walnut stock. Imported from 1968 to 1972. **NOTE:** Add 20 percent for ventilated rib barrel.

NIB	Exc.	V.G.	Good	Fair	Poor
—	450	395	350	300	200

Model 1300

Redesigned version of Model 300, with ventilated rib barrel and screw-in choke tubes. Imported since 1988.

NIB	Exc.	V.G.	Good	Fair	Poor
450	400	350	300	200	150

Model XL 900 MR

A 12-gauge semi-automatic shotgun, with 26" to 30" ventilated rib barrels. Etched alloy receiver. Checkered walnut stock. Imported prior to 1981.

NIB	Exc.	V.G.	Good	Fair	Poor
—	475	425	375	325	200

Model 1900

As above, but also chambered for 20-gauge shells. Available with 22", 26" or 28" ventilated rib barrels. Screw-in choke tubes. Blued, with walnut stock.

NIB	Exc.	V.G.	Good	Fair	Poor
500	425	375	300	250	175

Model 3000

Similar to above, with modified receiver design. Imported prior to 1990.

NIB	Exc.	V.G.	Good	Fair	Poor
—	475	400	350	250	150

POST 2013 PRODUCTION

Model 200 Field

Side-by-side made in 20-, 28-gauge and .410 bore, with oil-finished hand checkered Turkish walnut stock. Prince of Wales pistol-grip and beavertail fore-end. Sculpted and hand-engraved boxlock receiver has bison bone charcoal case-hardening. Other features include single-selective trigger, automatic ejectors, bright blue finish and five interchangeable choke tubes. Imported from Turkey. **NOTE:** Add $150 for 28-gauge or .410 bore.

NIB	Exc.	V.G.	Good	Fair	Poor
1750	1500	1225	900	450	200

Model 200 Sporting

Same general features as 200 Field grade. Also available in 12-gauge. Barrel lengths 28" or 30" in all gauges and have a raised ventilated rib. **NOTE:** Add $100 for 28-gauge or .410 bore.

NIB	Exc.	V.G.	Good	Fair	Poor
2100	1825	1500	1100	500	250

Model 250 Field

Same features as 200 Field, except has engraved decorative sideplates.

NIB	Exc.	V.G.	Good	Fair	Poor
2200	1850	1700	1300	550	300

Model 590

Over/under in 12- or 20-gauge, with features similar to Model 200 side-by-side series. Imported from Turkey.

NIB	Exc.	V.G.	Good	Fair	Poor
1100	900	750	600	300	200

Model 90 TSS

Over/under in 12- or 20-gauge, with features designed for trap, skeet or sporting clays. Features include a stock with adjustable comb and length of pull. High ventilated rib. Skeet has fixed stock. Imported from Turkey. **NOTE:** Deduct $250 for skeet model.

NIB	Exc.	V.G.	Good	Fair	Poor
1500	1300	1050	800	450	200

Model 7000 SL

A true side-lock model featuring H&H 7-pin removable sidelocks, with safety sears. Premium grade Turkish walnut stock, with extensive fine-line hand checkering on grip, butt and fore-end. Special order only. Made in Turkey.

NIB	Exc.	V.G.	Good	Fair	Poor
5800	5200	4500	—	—	—

Century III

Single-barrel trap gun in 12-gauge, with 30" or 32" ventilated rib barrel, fixed or adjustable Grade II walnut stock, lengthened forcing cone, competition choke tube system, laser engraving. Made in Turkey. **NOTE:** Add $150 for adjustable stock.

NIB	Exc.	V.G.	Good	Fair	Poor
1000	850	700	500	350	200

Model IS300

Semi-automatic in 12-gauge only. Operates on an inertia-recoil action. Available with synthetic, camo or oil-finished walnut stock. Back-bored barrels and competition choke tube system. Made in Turkey. **NOTE:** Deduct $75 for synthetic stock.

NIB	Exc.	V.G.	Good	Fair	Poor
600	500	400	300	200	100

SLOTTER & CO.
Philadelphia, Pennsylvania

Pocket Pistol

A .41-caliber percussion pocket pistol, with 2.5" to 3.5" barrel. German silver mounts and walnut stock. Marked "Slotter & Co. Phila.". Manufactured during 1860s.

NIB	Exc.	V.G.	Good	Fair	Poor
—	—	3000	2200	950	250

SMITH, L. C.
Syracuse, New York
Hunter Arms Company
Fulton, New York

One of the finest American-made double-barrel shotguns and very collectible in today's market. It was manufactured between 1880 and 1888 in Syracuse, New York; and between 1890 and 1945 in Fulton, New York, by Hunter Arms Company. In 1945, Marlin Firearms Company acquired Hunter Arms, and the L.C. Smith was made until 1951. In 1968, L.C. Smith was resurrected for five years, and production ceased in 1973. Marlin brought the L.C. Smith brand to market with models imported from Italy from 2004 to 2010. Values given are approximate for standard production models; and we strongly feel that competent, individual appraisals should be secured, especially on the rarer and higher grade models, if a transaction is contemplated.

Values given are for fluid steel, hammerless guns only. Damascus-barreled guns have become collectible if they are in very good or better condition, and values are approximately the same as for the fluid steel models. Damascus guns in less than good condition are worth considerably less.

Early Hammerless Shotguns

Models listed were manufactured between 1890 and 1913. They are chambered for 10-, 12-, 16- and 20-gauge. Produced with various barrel lengths and choke combinations. Feature full sidelock actions. Difference in models and their values is based on degree of ornamentation and quality of materials and workmanship utilized in their construction. General values furnished are for 10-, 12- or 16-gauge only.

NOTE: Add 50 percent for 20-gauge; 25 percent premiun for 10- and 16-gauge; $250 for single-selective trigger; 30 percent for automatic ejectors.

00 Grade

60,000 manufactured.

NIB	Exc.	V.G.	Good	Fair	Poor
—	2050	1800	1300	650	400

0 Grade

30,000 manufactured.

NIB	Exc.	V.G.	Good	Fair	Poor
—	2150	1900	1400	700	450

No. 1 Grade

10,000 manufactured.

NIB	Exc.	V.G.	Good	Fair	Poor
—	3150	2600	1950	800	550

No. 2 Grade

13,000 manufactured.

NIB	Exc.	V.G.	Good	Fair	Poor
—	3500	2900	1625	900	700

No. 3 Grade

4,000 manufactured.

NIB	Exc.	V.G.	Good	Fair	Poor
—	4250	3400	2275	1000	750

Pigeon Grade

1,200 manufactured.

NIB	Exc.	V.G.	Good	Fair	Poor
—	8500	7500	5000	3000	1500

No. 4 Grade

500 manufactured.

NIB	Exc.	V.G.	Good	Fair	Poor
—	10000	9000	7000	4500	2400

A-1 Grade

700 manufactured, all damascus, no 20-gauge.

NIB	Exc.	V.G.	Good	Fair	Poor
—	8000	7000	5000	3000	1500

No. 5 Grade

500 manufactured.

NIB	Exc.	V.G.	Good	Fair	Poor
—	12000	11000	8000	6500	3000

Monogram Grade

100 manufactured.

NIB	Exc.	V.G.	Good	Fair	Poor
—	18000	15000	11000	7500	4500

A-2 Grade

200 manufactured.

NIB	Exc.	V.G.	Good	Fair	Poor
—	25000	21000	16000	10000	6000

A-3 Grade

20 manufactured. Too rare to generalize a value.

Later Production Hammerless Shotguns

These were manufactured at Fulton, New York, between 1914 and 1951. They are side-by-side double-barrel shotguns. Chambered for 12-, 16-, 20-gauge and .410 bore. Offered with various barrel lengths and choke combinations. Feature a full sidelock action. Available with double-/single triggers, extractors and automatic ejectors. Finishes are blued and case colored, with checkered walnut stocks that are straight, semi-pistol-grip or pistol-grip configurations. Various models differ as to degree of ornamentation and quality of materials and workmanship utilized in their construction. These are highly collectible American shotguns. Because these guns were manufactured as late as 1951, mint original specimens and even unfired new in box guns will be offered for sale occasionally. These guns are worth considerably more than excellent condition guns and more than ever an individual, expert authentication and appraisal is recommended if a transaction is anticipated.

NOTE: Values supplied are for 12-gauge only. Add 25 percent premium for 16-gauge; 50 percent premium for 20-gauge; 200 percent premium for .410 bore (field grade); 300 to 400 percent for higher grades; $250 for single-selective triggers; 30 percent premium for automatic ejectors.

Courtesy Milwaukee Public Museum, Milwaukee, Wisconsin

Field Grade

Courtesy William Hammond

L.C. Smith 12 gauge and .410 bore Field Grade

NIB	Exc.	V.G.	Good	Fair	Poor
—	2500	1600	1125	700	350

Specialty Grade

Courtesy William Hammond

NIB	Exc.	V.G.	Good	Fair	Poor
—	5000	4000	3000	2000	1000

Skeet Special Grade

Courtesy William Hammond

NIB	Exc.	V.G.	Good	Fair	Poor
—	4500	3500	2700	1800	900

Premier Skeet Grade

NIB	Exc.	V.G.	Good	Fair	Poor
—	5200	4200	3000	2000	1000

Eagle Grade

NIB	Exc.	V.G.	Good	Fair	Poor
—	8000	7000	5500	4000	2000

Crown Grade

With this grade, automatic ejectors became standard equipment. The .410 bore is extremely rare in this model and non-existent in higher grades. There were only six manufactured, and they cannot be generally evaluated.

Courtesy William Hammond

12 and 20 gauge Crown Grades

NIB	Exc.	V.G.	Good	Fair	Poor
—	12000	10000	7500	5000	3000

Ideal Grade

With this grade, automatic ejectors became standard equipment. The .410 is extremely rare in this model and non-existent in higher grades. There were only six manufactured, and they cannot be generally evaluated.

NIB	Exc.	V.G.	Good	Fair	Poor
—	3200	2500	1700	900	500

Trap Grade

With this grade, automatic ejectors became standard equipment. The .410 is extremely rare in this model and non-existent in higher grades. There were only six manufactured, and they cannot be generally evaluated.

NIB	Exc.	V.G.	Good	Fair	Poor
—	4000	3000	2500	1500	1000

Monogram Grade

There were two higher grades offered: Premier Grade and Deluxe Grade. They are extremely rare, and there have not been enough transactions to generally evaluate them. This version is offered standard, with automatic ejectors and single-selective trigger.

NIB	Exc.	V.G.	Good	Fair	Poor
—	18000	15000	10000	6000	3500

HUNTER ARMS BOXLOCKS

These shotguns are inexpensive high quality boxlocks. Built with quality equal to Field Grade L.C. Smith. Receiver, fore-end iron, trigger guard and triggers are all machined from forgings. Durability of these guns has proven to be excellent.

Fulton Model

Utility side-by-side boxlock shotgun, chambered for 12-, 16-, 20-gauge and .410 bore. Offered with various barrel lengths and choke combinations. Has double triggers and extractors, with non-selective single trigger option. Values given are for 12-gauge only. **NOTE:** Add 50 percent premium for 20-gauge; 250 percent premium for .410 bore; 25 percent for 16-gauge; $150 for single trigger.

NIB	Exc.	V.G.	Good	Fair	Poor
—	1150	925	600	425	150

Fulton Special

Slightly higher grade version of Fulton Model. Featuring modest engraving and pointed checkering. **NOTE:** Add 50 percent premium for 20-gauge; 25 percent for 16-gauge; $200 for single trigger.

Courtesy William Hammond

NIB	Exc.	V.G.	Good	Fair	Poor
—	1400	1050	750	500	200

Hunter Special

Similar to Fulton Model, but features L.C. Smith rotary locking bolt. **NOTE:** Add 75 percent premium for 20-gauge; 300 percent premium for .410 bore; 25 percent for 16-gauge.

Courtesy William Hammond

NIB	Exc.	V.G.	Good	Fair	Poor
—	1100	950	750	500	200

Single Barrel Trap Guns

High quality break-open single-shot trap guns, chambered for 12-gauge only. Feature 32" or 34" ventilated rib barrels that are full-choked. Have boxlock actions and are standard with automatic ejectors. Finish blued and case colored. Checkered walnut stock, with recoil pad. Various models differ in amount of ornamentation and quality of materials and workmanship utilized in their construction. A total of approximately 2,650 manufactured between 1917 and 1951. Although these firearms are actually rarer and just as high in quality as their side-by-side counterparts, they are simply not as collectible as the side-by-side variations.

NOTE: Only two Premier Grade and three Deluxe Grade trap guns manufactured. This rarity makes it unrealistic to give an estimate of values. Beware of fakes.

Olympic Grade

NIB	Exc.	V.G.	Good	Fair	Poor
—	3000	2200	1500	900	500

Specialty Grade

NIB	Exc.	V.G.	Good	Fair	Poor
—	4500	3500	2000	1000	800

Crown Grade

NIB	Exc.	V.G.	Good	Fair	Poor
—	9000	6700	4500	2500	1500

Monogram Grade

NIB	Exc.	V.G.	Good	Fair	Poor
—	16000	10000	7500	5000	2500

1968 Model

Side-by-side double-barrel shotgun. Chambered for 12-gauge, with 28" ventilated rib barrel, choked Full and Modified. Features sidelock action, with double triggers and extractors. Finish blued and case colored, with checkered walnut stock. Offered by Marlin between 1968 and 1973. These are less desirable than earlier models because of manufacturing expedients used. Investment cast receiver rather than machined forgings were used. Cyanide case-hardening replaced bone charcoal hardening and aluminum ventilated ribs were used. A thin brown polymer layer was used to create the fit between lock plates and buttstock, which is a departure from traditional fitting.

NIB	Exc.	V.G.	Good	Fair	Poor
1750	1475	1100	850	450	300

1968 Deluxe Model

Similar to 1968 Model, but features a Simmons floating rib and beavertail-type forearm. Manufactured by Marlin between 1971 and 1973.

NIB	Exc.	V.G.	Good	Fair	Poor
2200	1800	1350	1100	700	400

L.C. SMITH 2005-2009 (MARLIN)

These L.C. Smith models were made in Italy or Spain and imported into the U.S. under the Marlin name. See listings under Marlin section.

SMITH, OTIS
Rockfall, Connecticut

This company manufactured a line of single-action spur-trigger revolvers that are chambered for .22, .32, .38 and .41 rimfire cartridges. Pistols have varying barrel lengths. Cylinder access pin is retained by a button on the left side of frame. Cylinder usually holds five-shots. Finishes are blued or nickel-plated, with bird's-head grips. Quality was considered to be mediocre.

Model 1883 Shell-Ejector

Single-action break-open self ejecting revolver, with ribbed 3.5" barrel. Chambered for .32 centerfire. Has a 5-shot fluted cylinder and spur trigger. Quite well made. Finish is nickel-plated, with black plastic grips.

NIB	Exc.	V.G.	Good	Fair	Poor
—	—	500	275	100	75

Model 1892

Double-action concealed-hammer revolver. Chambered for .38 centerfire cartridge. Has a 4" barrel. For the first time, a conventional trigger and trigger guard. It is gateloaded and has a solid frame. Nickel-plated, with black plastic grips. Also appeared under Maltby, Henley & Company banner marked "Spencer Safety Hammerless" or "Parker Safety Hammerless". Otis Smith Company ceased operations in 1898.

NIB	Exc.	V.G.	Good	Fair	Poor
—	—	500	275	100	75

SMITH & WESSON
Springfield, Massachusetts

SMITH & WESSON ANTIQUE HANDGUNS

NOTE: A surprising number of pistols are still found in their original boxes, even for older models. This can add 100 percent to the value of the pistol.

Model 1, 1st Issue Revolver

This was the first metallic-cartridge arm produced by Smith & Wesson. It is a small revolver that weighs about 10 oz. Chambered for .22 Short rimfire cartridge. Octagonal barrel 3.25" long. Holds 7 cartridges. Barrel and non-fluted cylinder pivot upward upon release of the latch under the frame. Has a square butt with rosewood grips. Oval brass frame is silver-plated. Barrel and cylinder are blued. Barrel is stamped with company name and address; patent dates also appear. Sides of frame are rounded on the 1st issue. Other characteristics which distinguish the more valuable 1st issue from later issues include a perfectly round side plate and a hinged hammer spur. Smith & Wesson manufactured approximately 11,000 of these revolvers between 1857 and 1860. Since this was the first of its kind, it is not difficult to understand the need for the number of variations within this model designation. Many small improvements were made on the way to the next model. These variations are as follows:

1st Type

Serial range 1 to low 200s. Revolving recoil shield, bayonet type catch on frame. **NOTE:** Rarity makes valuation speculative.

NIB	Exc.	V.G.	Good	Fair	Poor
—	—	15000	10000	8000	1000

2nd Type

Serial range low 200s to 1130. Improved recoil plate.

NIB	Exc.	V.G.	Good	Fair	Poor
—	—	10000	6000	2500	500

3rd Type

Serial range 1130 to low 3000s. Bayonet catch dropped for spring-loaded side catch.

Courtesy Jim Supica, Old Town Station

NIB	Exc.	V.G.	Good	Fair	Poor
—	7500	5500	4000	2500	500

4th Type

Serial range low 3000s to low 4200s. Recoil shield made much smaller.

NIB	Exc.	V.G.	Good	Fair	Poor
—	3000	2250	1800	1250	300

5th Type

Serial range low 4200s to low 5500s. Has 5-groove rifling instead of 3.

NIB	Exc.	V.G.	Good	Fair	Poor
—	3000	2250	1800	1250	300

6th Type

Serial range low 5500s to end of production 11670. A cylinder ratchet replaced revolving recoil shield.

NIB	Exc.	V.G.	Good	Fair	Poor
—	2000	1600	1400	1000	250

Model 1, 2nd Issue

Similar in appearance to 1st Issue, this 2nd Issue variation has several notable differences that make identification rather simple. Sides of frame on 2nd Issue are flat not rounded as on 1st Issue. Sideplate is irregular in shape—not round like on 1st Issue. Barrel was 3.1875" in length. Barrel is stamped "Smith & Wesson" while cylinder is marked with three patent dates: April 3, 1858, July 5, 1859 and December 18, 1860. There have been 2nd Issue noted with full silver or nickel-plating. Smith & Wesson manufactured approximately 115,000 of these revolvers between 1860 and 1868. Serial numbers started around 11000 where 1st Issue left off and continued to 126400. Approximately 4,400 revolvers marked "2D Quality" on barrels. These revolvers were slightly defective and were sold at a lesser price. They will bring approximately 100 percent premium on today's market.

Courtesy Mike Stuckslager

NIB	Exc.	V.G.	Good	Fair	Poor
—	900	750	600	250	100

Model 1, 3rd Issue

This is a redesigned version of its fore-runners. Another .22 Short rimfire 7-shot revolver, this model has a fluted cylinder and round barrel with a raised rib. This variation was manufactured totally from wrought iron. Three patent dates are stamped on top of ribbed barrel as is "Smith & Wesson". Features bird's-head type grips of rosewood and fully blued nickel-plated or two-toned. Frame nickel, barrel and cylinder blued. There are two barrel lengths offered: 3.25" and 2.6875". Shorter barrel introduced in 1872. Serial numbering began with #1 and continued to 131163. They were manufactured between 1868 and 1882. Model 1, 3rd Issue was last of tip-up style produced by Smith & Wesson.

Courtesy Mike Stuckslager

Shorter Barreled Version
Rare.

NIB	Exc.	V.G.	Good	Fair	Poor
—	1500	1350	800	400	100

Longer Barreled Version

NIB	Exc.	V.G.	Good	Fair	Poor
—	750	500	275	200	100

Model 1-1/2 1st Issue (1-1/2 Old Model)

This model was the first of .32-caliber Rimfire Short revolvers that S&W produced. It is a larger version of Model 1, but is physically similar in appearance. Model 1-1/2 was offered with 3.5" octagonal barrel. Has a 5-shot non-fluted cylinder and square butt with rosewood grips. In 1866, a 4" barrel version was produced for a short time. Estimated about 200 were sold. Finish blued or nickel-plated. Serial numbering, on this model, ran from 1 to 26300; interestingly to note, S&W had most of the parts for this revolver manufactured on contract by King & Smith of Middletown, Connecticut. Smith & Wesson merely assembled and finished them. They were produced between 1865 and 1868. **NOTE:** Add 50 percent premium for 4" barrel variation.

Courtesy Mike Stuckslager

NIB	Exc.	V.G.	Good	Fair	Poor
—	795	650	400	200	100

Model 1-1/2 2nd Issue (1-1/2 New Model)

Factory referred to this model as New Model 1-1/2 and it is an improved version of 1st Issue. Somewhat similar in appearance with a few notable exceptions. Barrel is 2.5" or 3.5" in length, round with a raised rib. Grip is of bird's-head configuration and 5-shot cylinder is fluted. Chambered for .32 Long rimfire cartridge. Cylinder stop located in the top frame instead of bottom. Finish and grip material are the same as 1st Issue. Approximately 100,700 manufactured between 1868 and 1875.

Courtesy Mike Stuckslager

3.5" Barrel

Courtesy Mike Stuckslager

NIB	Exc.	V.G.	Good	Fair	Poor
900	800	650	375	175	100

2.5" Barrel

Rare. Watch for fakes.

NIB	Exc.	V.G.	Good	Fair	Poor
2500	1500	1100	600	350	100

Model 1-1/2 Transitional Model

Approximately 650 of these were produced by fitting 1st Issue cylinders and barrels to 2nd Issue frames. They also have 1st Model octagon barrels, with 2nd Model bird's-head grips. These revolvers fall into serial number range 27200-28800.

NIB	Exc.	V.G.	Good	Fair	Poor
—	—	3000	1500	800	300

Model 2 Army or Old Model

Similar in appearance to Model 1, 2nd Issue, this revolver was extremely successful from a commercial standpoint. Released just in time for commencement of hostilities in the Civil War. Smith & Wesson had, in this revolver, the only weapon able to fire self-contained cartridges and be easily carried as a backup by soldiers going off to war. This resulted in a backlog of more than three years, before the company finally stopped taking orders. Chambered for .32 Long rimfire cartridge, has a 6-shot non-fluted cylinder and 4", 5" or 6" barrel lengths. Has a square butt with rosewood grips and blued or nickel-plated. Approximately 77,155 manufactured between 1861 and 1874. Rare.

Courtesy Mike Stuckslager

5" or 6" Barrel

Standard barrel.

NIB	Exc.	V.G.	Good	Fair	Poor
—	2450	1500	950	450	300

4" Barrel

Rare, use caution. **NOTE:** A slight premium for early two-pin model. For rare 8" model add 800 percent.

NIB	Exc.	V.G.	Good	Fair	Poor
—	—	6000	3650	1500	500

.32 Single-Action (so-called "1-1/2 Frame" Centerfire)

This model represented the first .32 S&W centerfire caliber top-break revolver that automatically ejected spent cartridges upon opening. Similar in appearance to Model 1-1/2 2nd Issue. This model has a 5-shot fluted cylinder and bird's-head grip of wood or checkered hard rubber. Offered with barrel lengths of 3", 3.5", 6", 8" and 10". The 8" and 10" barrel are rare and were not offered until 1887. This model pivots downward on opening. Features a rebounding hammer that made the weapon much safer to fully load. Approximately 97,599 manufactured between 1878 and 1892.

Courtesy W.P. Hallstein III and son Chip

Early Model w/o Strain Screw—Under #6500

Courtesy Mike Stuckslager

NIB	Exc.	V.G.	Good	Fair	Poor
—	1200	600	300	175	75

Later Model with Strain Screw

Courtesy Mike Stuckslager

NIB	Exc.	V.G.	Good	Fair	Poor
—	1000	450	300	150	75

8" or 10" Barrel

Very rare; use caution.

NIB	Exc.	V.G.	Good	Fair	Poor
—	—	4500	2500	800	400

.38 Single-Action 1st Model (Baby Russian)

This model is sometimes called "Baby Russian". A top break automatic-ejecting revolver, chambered for .38 S&W centerfire cartridge. Offered with 3.25" or 4" round barrel. Raised rib has a 5-shot fluted cylinder and finished in blue or nickel plating. A 5" barrel was added as an option a short time later. Butt is rounded, with wood or checkered hard rubber grips inlaid with S&W medallion. It has a spur trigger. Approximately 25,548 manufactured in 1876 and 1877, of which 16,046 were nickel; 6,502 blued.

Courtesy Mike Stuckslager

NIB	Exc.	V.G.	Good	Fair	Poor
—	2000	1200	900	350	150

.38 Single-Action 2nd Model

With the exception of an improved and shortened extractor assembly and availability of additional barrel lengths of 3.25", 4", 5", 6", 8" and 10", with 8" and 10" barrel lengths being the most rare, this model is quite similar in appearance to 1st Model. Approximately 108,225 manufactured between 1877 and 1891.

Courtesy Mike Stuckslager

8" and 10" Barrel

Very rare, use caution.

NIB	Exc.	V.G.	Good	Fair	Poor
—	—	4000	2250	950	500

3.25", 4", 5", and 6" Barrel Lengths

Small premium for 5" or 6" lengths.

NIB	Exc.	V.G.	Good	Fair	Poor
—	700	350	225	175	75

.38 Single-Action 3rd Model

This model differs from first two models because it is fitted with a trigger guard. Chambered for .38 S&W centerfire cartridge. Has a 5-shot fluted cylinder and is a top break design with automatic ejection upon opening. Barrel lengths are 3.25", 4" and 6". Finish blued or nickel-plated. Butt is rounded, with checkered hard rubber grips featuring S&W medallions. Approximately 26,850 manufactured between 1891 and 1911.

Courtesy Mike Stuckslager

NIB	Exc.	V.G.	Good	Fair	Poor
—	2000	1300	1000	600	200

.38 Single-Action Mexican Model

This extremely rare model is quite similar in appearance to 3rd Model Single-Action. Notable differences are flat hammer sides, with no outward flaring of spur. Spur trigger assembly was not made integrally with the frame, but a separate part added to it. One must exercise extreme caution as S&W offered a kit that would convert the trigger guard assembly of Third Model to spur trigger of Mexican Model. This, coupled with the fact that both models fall within the same serial range, can present a real identification problem. Another feature of Mexican Model is absence of a half cock. The exact number of Mexican Models manufactured between 1891 and 1911 is unknown, but estimated that the number is small.

NIB	Exc.	V.G.	Good	Fair	Poor
—	3950	3650	1500	950	400

.32 Double-Action 1st Model

This is one of the rarest of all S&W revolvers. There were only 30 manufactured. It also has a straight-sided sideplate that weakened the revolver frame. Perhaps this was the reason that so few were made. This model was the first break-open double-action automatic-ejecting .32 that S&W produced. Features a 3" round barrel with raised rib, 5-shot fluted cylinder and round butt with plain uncheckered black hard rubber grips. Finish blued or nickel-plated. All 30 of these revolvers were manufactured in 1880. **NOTE:** Rarity makes valuation speculative.

NIB	Exc.	V.G.	Good	Fair	Poor
—	—	12000	7500	4000	1000

.32 Double-Action 2nd Model

This revolver is chambered for .32 S&W cartridge. Has 3" round barrel with a raised rib. The 5-shot cylinder is fluted. Finish blued or nickel-plated. It is a top break design with a round butt. Grips are checkered or floral-embossed hard rubber, with S&W monogram. This model has an oval sideplate, eliminating the weakness of 1st Model. Approximately 22,142 manufactured between 1880 and 1882.

Courtesy Mike Stuckslager

NIB	Exc.	V.G.	Good	Fair	Poor
—	700	350	225	175	75

.32 Double-Action 3rd Model

This model incorporates internal improvements that are not evident in appearance. Most notable identifiable difference between this model and its predecessors is in the surface of the cylinder. Flutes are longer; there is only one set of stops instead of two; free groove is no longer present. Approximately 21,232 manufactured in 1882 and 1883.

Courtesy Mike Stuckslager

NIB	Exc.	V.G.	Good	Fair	Poor
—	625	350	225	175	75

.32 Double-Action 4th Model

This model is quite similar in appearance to 3rd Model, except the trigger guard is oval in shape instead of squared back as in previous models. There were also internal improvements. Approximately 239,600 manufactured between 1883 and 1909. **NOTE:** Add 50 percent premium for revolvers built before 1898.

Courtesy Mike Stuckslager

NIB	Exc.	V.G.	Good	Fair	Poor
—	575	300	200	125	65

.32 Double-Action 5th Model

Only difference between this model and its predecessors, is that this model has the front sight machined as an integral part of barrel rib. On other models, sight was pinned in place. Approximately 44,641 manufactured between 1909 and 1919.

Courtesy Mike Stuckslager

NIB	Exc.	V.G.	Good	Fair	Poor
—	500	375	250	125	100

SAFETY HAMMERLESS

This model was a departure from what was commonly being produced at this time. Some attribute the Safety Hammerless design to D.B. Wesson's hearing that a child had been injured by cocking and firing one of the company's pistols. This story has never been proven. Nevertheless, concealed hammer and grip safety make this an ideal pocket pistol for those needing concealability in a handgun. This is a small revolver chambered for .32 S&W and .38 S&W cartridges. It has a 5-shot fluted cylinder. Offered with 2", 3" and 3.5" round barrel, with raised rib. Butt is rounded and has checkered hard rubber grips, with S&W logo. Finish blue or nickel plated. Revolver is a top break automatic-ejecting design; 1st Model has latch for opening located in the rear center of top strap instead of at the sides. Latch is checkered for a positive grip. This model is commonly referred to as "Lemon Squeezer", because the grip safety must be squeezed as it is fired.

Courtesy Mike Stuckslager

.32 Safety Hammerless (aka .32 New Departure or .32 Lemon Squeezer) 1st Model

Push button latch serial number 1- 91417. Built 1888-1902. **NOTE:** Add 50 percent premium for revolvers built before 1898.

NIB	Exc.	V.G.	Good	Fair	Poor
—	475	275	165	100	50

.32 Safety Hammerless 2nd Model

T-bar latch pinned front sight. Serial number 91418-169999. Built 1902 to 1909.

Courtesy Mike Stuckslager

NIB	Exc.	V.G.	Good	Fair	Poor
—	450	275	165	100	50

.32 Safety Hammerless 3rd Model

T-bar latch integral forged front sight. Serial number 170000-242981. Built 1909 to 1937. **NOTE:** Add 200 percent for 2" barrel Bicycle Model.

NIB	Exc.	V.G.	Good	Fair	Poor
—	450	325	265	150	50

.38 Double-Action 1st Model

Similar in appearance to .32 1st Model. Having a straight cut side-plate, but chambered for .38 S&W cartridge. Grips are checkered. Manufactured 4,000 in 1880.

NIB	Exc.	V.G.	Good	Fair	Poor
—	1200	650	400	250	75

.38 Double-Action 2nd Model

Similar in appearance to .32 2nd Model, but chambered for .38 S&W cartridge. Approximately 115,000 manufactured between 1880 and 1884.

Courtesy Mike Stuckslager

NIB	Exc.	V.G.	Good	Fair	Poor
—	550	375	225	200	100

.38 Double-Action 3rd Model

Essentially the same in appearance as .32 Model, but chambered for .38 S&W cartridge. Also offered with 3.25", 4", 5", 6", 8" and 10" barrel. There were numerous internal changes in this model, similar to .32 Double-Action 3rd Model. Approximately 203,700 manufactured between 1884 and 1895.

8" and 10" Barrel
Rare, use caution.

Courtesy Mike Stuckslager

NIB	Exc.	V.G.	Good	Fair	Poor
—	—	2500	1500	800	200

Standard Barrel

NIB	Exc.	V.G.	Good	Fair	Poor
—	550	450	325	200	75

.38 Double-Action 4th Model

This is .38 S&W version of 4th Model. Identical in outward appearance to 3rd Model. Relocation of sear was the main design change in this model.

Approximately 216,300 manufactured between 1895 and 1909. **NOTE:** Add 20 percent premium for revolvers built before 1898.

NIB	Exc.	V.G.	Good	Fair	Poor
—	495	230	225	150	75

.38 Double-Action 5th Model

This model same as .32, except chambered for .38 S&W cartridge. Approximately 15,000 manufactured between 1909 and 1911.

Courtesy Mike Stuckslager

NIB	Exc.	V.G.	Good	Fair	Poor
—	525	385	225	150	75

.38 Double-Action Perfected

A unique top-break, with both a barrel latch similar to other top-breaks and thumbpiece similar to hand ejectors. Also the only top-break where trigger guard is integral to the frame, rather than a separate piece. Produced from 1909 to 1911 in their own serial number range. About 59,400 built.

NIB	Exc.	V.G.	Good	Fair	Poor
900	600	525	295	165	85

.38 Safety Hammerless 1st Model

Z-bar latch. Serial number range 1 to 5250. Made 1887 only. **NOTE:** Add 50 percent for 6" barrel. RARE!

NIB	Exc.	V.G.	Good	Fair	Poor
1200	900	600	425	250	100

.38 Safety Hammerless 2nd Model

Push button latch protrudes above frame. Serial number 5251-42483. Built 1887-1890.

Courtesy Mike Stuckslager

NIB	Exc.	V.G.	Good	Fair	Poor
—	500	350	250	175	100

.38 Safety Hammerless 3rd Model

Push button latch flush with frame. Serial number 42484-116002. Built 1890-1898.

NIB	Exc.	V.G.	Good	Fair	Poor
—	475	355	225	165	100

.38 Safety Hammerless Army Test Revolver

Approximately 100 sold to U.S. government in 1890. They have 3rd Model features, but in 2nd Model serial number range 41333-41470. Fitted with 6" barrels and marked "US". **CAUTION:** Be wary of fakes. **NOTE:** Rarity makes valuation speculative.

NIB	Exc.	V.G.	Good	Fair	Poor
—	—	10000	7500	4000	—

.38 Safety Hammerless 4th Model

Produced in .38 S&W only. The only difference in 4th Model and 3rd Model is adoption of standard T-bar type of barrel latch as found on most of the top break revolvers. ".38 S&W Cartridge" was also added to the left side of barrel. Approximately 104,000 manufactured between 1898 and 1907. Serial number range 116003 to 220000.

Courtesy Mike Stuckslager

NIB	Exc.	V.G.	Good	Fair	Poor
—	450	335	275	110	50

.38 Safety Hammerless 5th Model

Last of the "Lemon Squeezers". Only appreciable difference between this model and 4th Model is the front sight blade on 5th Model is an integral part of the barrel, not a separate blade pinned onto the barrel. Approximately 41,500 manufactured between 1907 and 1940. Serial number range 220001 to 261493. **NOTE:** Add 50 percent for 2" barrel version.

Courtesy Mike Stuckslager

NIB	Exc.	V.G.	Good	Fair	Poor
—	500	395	275	110	50

Model 3 American 1st Model

This model represented a number of firsts for Smith & Wesson Company. It was first of the top break automatic ejection revolvers. Also first Smith & Wesson in a large caliber (chambered for .44 S&W American cartridge as well as .44 Henry rimfire on rare occasions). Also known as 1st Model American. This large revolver offered with an 8" round barrel with a raised rib as standard. Barrel lengths of 6" and 7" were also available. It has a 6-shot fluted cylinder and square butt with walnut grips. Blued or nickel-plated. Interesting to note, this model appeared three years before Colt's Single-Action Army and perhaps, more than any other model, was associated with the historic American West. Only 8,000 manufactured between 1870 and 1872.

Standard Production Model

NOTE: Add 25 percent for "oil hole" variation found on approximately first 1,500 guns; 50 percent for unusual barrel lengths other than standard 8". Original "Nashville Police" marked guns worth a substantial premium.

NIB	Exc.	V.G.	Good	Fair	Poor
—	—	7000	3500	1500	500

Transition Model

Serial number range 6466-6744. Shorter cylinder (1.423"). Improved barrel catch.

NIB	Exc.	V.G.	Good	Fair	Poor
—	—	6000	3000	1500	500

U.S. Army Order

Serial number range 125-2199. One thousand produced with "U.S." stamped on top of barrel. "OWA" on left grip.

NIB	Exc.	V.G.	Good	Fair	Poor
—	—	17500	7500	3000	500

.44 Rimfire Henry Model

Only 200 produced throughout serial range. **NOTE:** Rarity makes valuation speculative.

NIB	Exc.	V.G.	Good	Fair	Poor
—	—	12000	6000	3000	500

Model 3 American 2nd Model

An improved version of 1st Model. Most notable difference is larger diameter trigger pivot pin and frame protrusions above trigger to accommodate it. Front sight blade on this model is made of steel instead of nickel silver. Several internal improvements were also incorporated into this model. This model commonly known as American 2nd Model. The 8" barrel length was standard. Approximately 20,735 manufactured, including 3,014 chambered for .44 rimfire Henry, between 1872 and 1874. **NOTE:** There have been 5.5", 6", 6.5" and 7" barrels noted; but they are extremely scarce and would bring a 40 percent premium over standard 8" model. Use caution when purchasing these short barrel revolvers.

Courtesy Buffalo Bill Historical Center, Cody, Wyoming

.44 Henry Rimfire

NIB	Exc.	V.G.	Good	Fair	Poor
—	—	6500	3250	1500	500

Standard 8" Model, .44 American Centerfire

NIB	Exc.	V.G.	Good	Fair	Poor
—	6750	5000	3000	1250	500

Model 3 Russian 1st Model

Quite similar in appearance to American 1st and 2nd Model revolvers. S&W made several internal changes to this model to satisfy the Russian government. Markings on this revolver are distinct. Caliber for which it's chambered .44 S&W Russian, is different. Approximately 20,000 Russian-Contract revolvers. Serial number range 1-20000. They are marked in Russian Cyrillic letters. Russian double-headed eagle stamped on rear portion of barrel, with inspector's marks underneath it. All contract guns have 8" barrels and lanyard swivels on the butt. These are rarely encountered, as most were shipped to Russia. Commercial run of this model numbered approximately 4,655. Barrels are stamped in English and include the words "Russian Model". Some are found with 6" and 7" barrels, as well as standard 8". There were also 500 revolvers that were rejected from the Russian contract series and sold on the commercial market. Some of these are marked in English; some, Cyrillic. Some have the Cyrillic markings ground off and English restamped. Manufactured from 1871 to 1874.

Russian Contract Model, Cyrillic Barrel Address

NIB	Exc.	V.G.	Good	Fair	Poor
—	—	7000	3500	2000	500

Commercial Model

NIB	Exc.	V.G.	Good	Fair	Poor
—	—	5000	2750	1250	500

Rejected Russian Contract Model

NIB	Exc.	V.G.	Good	Fair	Poor
—	—	5000	2750	1250	500

Model 3 Russian 2nd Model

This revolver was known as "Old Model Russian". This is a complicated model to understand as there are many variations within the model designation. Serial numbering is quite complex as well and values vary greatly due to relatively minor model differences. Before purchasing this model, it would be advisable to secure competent appraisal as well as to read reference materials solely devoted to this firearm. Chambered for .44 S&W Russian, as well as .44 Henry rimfire cartridge. It has a 7" barrel and a round butt featuring a projection on the frame that fits into the thumb web. Grips are walnut and finish blue or nickel-plated. Trigger guard has a reverse curved spur on the bottom. Approximately 85,200 manufactured between 1873 and 1878.

Courtesy Jim Supica, Old Town Station

Commercial Model

6,200 made, .44 S&W Russian, English markings.

NIB	Exc.	V.G.	Good	Fair	Poor
—	—	3250	1500	850	400

.44 Rimfire Henry Model

500 made.

NIB	Exc.	V.G.	Good	Fair	Poor
—	—	4750	2250	1000	500

Russian Contract Model

70,000 made; rare, as most were shipped to Russia. Cyrillic markings; lanyard swivel on butt.

NIB	Exc.	V.G.	Good	Fair	Poor
—	—	3500	1750	950	500

1st Model Turkish Contract

.44 rimfire Henry, special rimfire frames, serial-numbered in own serial number range 1-1000.

NIB	Exc.	V.G.	Good	Fair	Poor
—	—	6000	3750	1750	500

2nd Model Turkish Contract

Made from altered centerfire frames from regular commercial serial number range. 1,000 made. Use caution with this model.

NIB	Exc.	V.G.	Good	Fair	Poor
—	—	4500	2250	1000	500

Japanese Govt. Contract

Five thousand made between 1-9000 serial number range. Japanese naval insignia, an anchor over two wavy lines, found on butt. Barrel is Japanese proofed and words "Jan.19, 75 REISSUE July 25, 1871" are stamped on barrel, as well.

NIB	Exc.	V.G.	Good	Fair	Poor
—	—	3500	1700	950	500

Model 3 Russian 3rd Model

This revolver is also known as "New Model Russian". Factory referred to this model as Model of 1874 or Cavalry Model. Chambered for .44 S&W Russian and .44 Henry rimfire cartridge. Barrel is 6.5" and round butt is the same humped-back affair as 2nd Model. Grips are walnut and finish blue or nickel-plated. Most notable differences in appearance between this model and 2nd Model are shorter extractor housing under the barrel and integral front sight blade instead of pinned-on one found on previous models. This is another model that bears careful research before attempting to evaluate. Minor variances can greatly affect values. Secure detailed reference materials and qualified appraisal. Approximately 60,638 manufactured between 1874 and 1878.

Commercial Model

.44 S&W Russian. Marked "Russian Model" in English. Made 13,500.

NIB	Exc.	V.G.	Good	Fair	Poor
—	—	9000	5000	2500	500

.44 Henry Rimfire Model

NIB	Exc.	V.G.	Good	Fair	Poor
—	—	4500	2700	900	500

Turkish Model

5,000 made from altered centerfire frames. Made to fire .44 Henry rimfire. "W" inspector's mark on butt. Fakes have been noted; be aware.

NIB	Exc.	V.G.	Good	Fair	Poor
—	—	4500	2700	900	500

Japanese Contract Model

1,000 made. Has Japanese naval insignia, an anchor over two wavy lines, stamped on butt.

NIB	Exc.	V.G.	Good	Fair	Poor
—	—	3100	1950	850	500

Russian Contract Model

Barrel markings are in Russian Cyrillic. Approximately 41,100 produced.

NIB	Exc.	V.G.	Good	Fair	Poor
—	—	3100	1950	850	500

Model 3 Russian 3rd Model (Loewe & Tula Copies)

German firm of Ludwig Loewe produced a copy of this model that is nearly identical to the S&W. This German revolver was made under Russian contract, as well as for commercial sales. Contract model has different Cyrillic markings than S&W and letters "HK" as inspector's marks. Commercial model has markings in English. Russian arsenal at Tula also produced a copy of this revolver with a different Cyrillic dated stamping on barrel.

Courtesy Mike Stuckslager

Loewe

NIB	Exc.	V.G.	Good	Fair	Poor
—	—	2900	1750	700	400

Tula

NIB	Exc.	V.G.	Good	Fair	Poor
—	—	3350	2000	800	400

Model 3 Schofield 1st Model

"US" Contract

3,000 issued.

NIB	Exc.	V.G.	Good	Fair	Poor
—	15000	7500	4250	2250	500

Civilian Model

No "US" markings, 35 made, Very Rare. **NOTE:** Use caution. UNABLE TO PRICE. At least double the military model values. Expert appraisal needed.

Model 3 Schofield 2nd Model

No "US" markings, 35 made, Very Rare.

"US" Contract

4,000 issued.

NIB	Exc.	V.G.	Good	Fair	Poor
—	10500	6500	4000	2250	500

Civilian Model

646 made.

NIB	Exc.	V.G.	Good	Fair	Poor
—	12000	7000	4000	2000	500

Model 3 Schofield—Surplus Models

After the government dropped Schofield as an issue cavalry sidearm, remaining U.S. inventory of these revolvers was sold off as military surplus. Many were sold to National Guard units and remainder were sold to Bannerman's or to Schuyler, Hartley & Graham, two large gun dealers who then resold the guns to supply the growing need for guns on the Western frontier. Schuyler, Hartley & Graham sold a number of guns to Wells Fargo Express Co. These weapons were nickel-plated and had barrels shortened to 5", as were many others sold during this period. Beware of fakes when contemplating purchase of Wells Fargo revolvers.

Wells Fargo & Co. Model

NIB	Exc.	V.G.	Good	Fair	Poor
—	—	8000	4000	2000	500

Surplus Cut Barrel—Not Wells Fargo

NIB	Exc.	V.G.	Good	Fair	Poor
—	—	3500	2000	1200	500

New Model No. 3 Single-Action

Always interested in perfecting Model 3 revolver D.B. Wesson redesigned and improved old Model 3 in hopes of attracting more sales. Russian contracts were almost filled, so the company decided to devote the effort necessary to improve on this design. In 1877, this project was undertaken. Extractor housing was shortened; cylinder retention system was improved; shape of grip was changed to a more streamlined and attractive configuration. This New Model has a 3.5", 4", 5", 6", 6.5", 7", 7.5" or 8" barrel length, with 6-shot fluted cylinder. The 6.5" barrel and .44 S&W Russian chambering is the most often encountered variation of this model, but the factory considered the 3.5" and 8" barrels as standard and these were kept in stock as well. New Model No. 3 was also chambered for .32 S&W, .32-44 S&W, .320 S&W Rev. Rifle, .38 S&W, .38-40, .38-44 S&W, .41 S&W, .44 Henry rimfire, .44 S&W American, .44-40, .45 S&W Schofield, .450 Rev., .45 Webley, .455 MkI and .455 MkII. They are blued or nickel-plated and have checkered hard rubber grips, with S&W logo molded into them, or walnut grips. There are many sub-variations within this model designation and the potential collector should secure detailed reference material that deals with this model. Approximately 35,796 of these revolvers manufactured between 1878 and 1912. Nearly 40 percent were exported to fill contracts with Japan, Australia, Argentina, England, Spain and Cuba. There were some sent to Asia, as well. Proofmarks of these countries will establish their provenance, but will not add appreciably to standard values.

Standard Model

6.5" barrel, .44 S&W Russian.

Courtesy Mike Stuckslager

NIB	Exc.	V.G.	Good	Fair	Poor
—	5000	3700	2000	1000	500

Japanese Naval Contract

Largest foreign purchaser of this model. More than 1,500 produced, with anchor insignia stamped on frame.

Courtesy Mike Stuckslager

NIB	Exc.	V.G.	Good	Fair	Poor
—	—	3700	2000	1000	500

Japanese Artillery Contract

This variation numbered in 25000 serial range. They are blued, with 7" barrel and lanyard swivel on butt. Japanese characters are stamped on extractor housing.

NIB	Exc.	V.G.	Good	Fair	Poor
—	—	5000	2500	1250	500

Maryland Militia Model

Variation is nickel-plated, has 6.5" barrel and chambered for .44 S&W Russian cartridge. Butt stamped "U.S." and inspector's marks "HN" and "DAL" under date 1878 appear on revolver. There were 280 manufactured between serial numbers 7126 and 7405. **NOTE:** Rarity makes valuation speculative.

NIB	Exc.	V.G.	Good	Fair	Poor
—	—	10000	6000	3000	500

Argentine Model

Essentially not a factory contract, but a sale through Schuyler, Hartley and Graham. They are stamped "Ejercito/Argentino" in front of trigger guard. Order amounted to some 2,000 revolvers between serial numbers 50 and 3400.

NIB	Exc.	V.G.	Good	Fair	Poor
—	—	7000	3500	1750	500

Australian Contract

This variation is nickel-plated and chambered for .44 S&W Russian cartridge. Marked with Australian Colonial Police Broad Arrow on the butt. There were 250 manufactured with 7" barrels and detachable shoulder stocks. Stock has Broad Arrow stamped on lower tang. There were also 30 manufactured with 6.5" barrels, without the stocks. They all are numbered in 12000-13000 serial range.

Courtesy Mike Stuckslager

Revolver with Stock and Holsters

NOTE: Deduct 40 percent for no stock.

NIB	Exc.	V.G.	Good	Fair	Poor
—	—	8000	4750	2750	500

Turkish Model

Essentially the New Model No. 3 chambered for .44 rimfire Henry cartridge. Stamped with letters "P", "U" and "AFC" on various parts of the revolver. Barrels are all 6.5"; finish blued, with walnut grips. Lanyard swivels are found on the butt. There were 5,461 manufactured. Serial numbered in their own range starting at 1 through 5461, between 1879 and 1883.

Courtesy Mike Stuckslager

NIB	Exc.	V.G.	Good	Fair	Poor
—	—	7000	3500	1750	500

New Model No. 3 Target Single-Action

Similar in appearance to standard New Model No. 3, but was the company's first production target model. It has a 6.5" round barrel, with a raised rib and 6-shot fluted cylinder. Finished in blue or nickel-plated. Grips are walnut or checkered hard rubber, with S&W logo molded into them. Chambered in .32 S&W or .38 S&W. Company referred to these models as .32-44 Target or .38-44 Target, depending on caliber. Designation of .44 referred to the frame size, i.e. a .32 caliber built on a .44 caliber frame. This model was offered with a detachable shoulder stock as an option. These stocks are extremely scarce on today's market. Approximately 4,333 manufactured between 1887 and 1910. **NOTE:** Add 50 percent for shoulder stock.

Courtesy Mike Stuckslager

NIB	Exc.	V.G.	Good	Fair	Poor
—	—	3100	1350	850	400

New Model No. 3 Frontier Single-Action

Another model similar in appearance to standard New Model No. 3. It has a 4", 5" or 6.5" barrel. Chambered for .44-40 Win. Centerfire cartridge. Because the original New Model No. 3 cylinder was 1.4375" in length, this would not accommodate the longer .44-40 cartridge. Cylinder on No. 3 Frontier was changed to 1.5625" in length. Later the company converted 786 revolvers to .44 S&W Russian and sold them to Japan. This model is blued or nickel-plated and has checkered grips of walnut or hard rubber. They are serial numbered in their own range from 1 through 2072. Manufactured from 1885 until 1908. This model was designed to compete with Colt Single-Action Army, but was not successful.

Courtesy Mike Stuckslager

.44-40—Commercial Model

NIB	Exc.	V.G.	Good	Fair	Poor
—	—	5000	2500	1250	500

Japanese Purchase Converted to .44 S&W Russian

NIB	Exc.	V.G.	Good	Fair	Poor
—	—	4000	2000	1000	500

New Model No. 3—.38 Winchester

This variation was the last of New Model No. 3s to be introduced. Offered in .38-40 Win. as a separate model from 1900 until 1907. Finish blue or nickel-plate. Grips are checkered hard rubber or walnut. Barrel lengths of 4" or 6.5" were offered. This model was not at all popular, as only 74 were manufactured in their own serial range 1 through 74. Today's collectors are extremely interested in this extremely rare model. **NOTE:** Rarity makes valuation speculative.

Courtesy Mike Stuckslager

NIB	Exc.	V.G.	Good	Fair	Poor
—	—	14000	8000	4000	500

.44 Double-Action 1st Model

A top break revolver that automatically ejects the spent cartridge cases upon opening. Barrel latch is located at top and rear of cylinder; pivot in front and at the bottom. Also known as "The D.A. Frontier" or "The New Model Navy". Chambered for .44 S&W Russian. Built on a modified Model 3 frame. Found on rare occasions chambered for .38-40 and .44-40 Win. Barrel lengths are 4", 5", 6" and 6.5" round, with a raised rib. A 3.5" barrel was produced on this model by special request. Collectors should be aware that the barrel for this model and New Model No. 3 were interchangeable and the factory did in fact use barrels from either model. Serial number on rear of the barrel should match number on the butt, cylinder and barrel latch. Cylinder holds 6-shots and is fluted. It has double sets of stop notches and long free grooves between the stops. It is serial numbered in its own range, beginning at 1. Approximately 54,000 manufactured between 1881 and 1913.

Courtesy Bonhams & Butterfields, San Francisco, California

Standard .44 S&W Russian

NIB	Exc.	V.G.	Good	Fair	Poor
—	4000	2000	1300	700	400

Model .44 Double-Action Wesson Favorite

Favorite is basically a lightened version of 1st Model D.A. .44. Barrel is thinner and offered in 5" length only. There are lightening cuts in the frame between trigger guard and cylinder; cylinder diameter was smaller and there is a groove milled along the barrel rib. Favorite chambered for .44 S&W Russian cartridge. Has a 6-shot fluted cylinder, with same double-cylinder stop notches and free grooves as 1st Model Double-Action .44. Company name and address, as well as patent dates, are stamped into edge of the cylinder instead of on barrel rib. Serial-numbered in the same range, between 9000 and 10100. Revolver was most often nickel-plated, but also offered blued. Grips are walnut or checkered hard rubber, with S&W logo molded in. Approximately 1,000 manufactured in 1882 and 1883. Use caution when purchasing a blued model. **NOTE:** Rarity makes valuation speculative. Add 25 percent for blued finish.

NIB	Exc.	V.G.	Good	Fair	Poor
—	—	9000	5000	2500	500

Model .44 Double-Action Frontier

Chambered for .44-40 cartridge. This is a separate model from .44 Double-Action 1st Model. It has a longer 19/16" cylinder like the later .44 double-action 1st Model's. Produced from 1886 to 1916 with their own serial number range. Approximately 15,340 built.

NIB	Exc.	V.G.	Good	Fair	Poor
—	4000	2000	1200	750	400

Model .38 Winchester Double-Action

Similar to .44 Double-Action 1st Model, except for chamber. Fitted with long cylinder. Approximately 276 produced, in their own serial number range, from 1900 to 1910.

NIB	Exc.	V.G.	Good	Fair	Poor
—	—	5500	3000	1250	500

1st Model Single-Shot

This unusual pistol combines frame of .38 Single-Action 3rd Model, with a single-shot barrel. This model is a top break and functions exactly as revolver models do. Barrel length 6", 8" or 10". Chambered for .22 LR, .32 S&W and .38 S&W. Finish blue or nickel plated, with square butt. Grips are checkered hard rubber extension types for a proper target hold. This pistol is considered quite rare on today's market, as only 1,251 manufactured between 1893 and 1905.

.22 L.R.

NIB	Exc.	V.G.	Good	Fair	Poor
—	2000	1500	1000	600	400

.32 S&W

NIB	Exc.	V.G.	Good	Fair	Poor
—	2200	1750	1275	700	500

.38 S&W

NIB	Exc.	V.G.	Good	Fair	Poor
—	2500	1900	1400	750	500

2nd Model Single-Shot

2nd Model Single-Shot has a frame with the recoil shield removed. Chambered for .22 LR only. Offered with 10" barrel. Finish blue or nickel plated. Grips are checkered hard rubber extension types. Approximately 4,617 manufactured between 1905 and 1909.

Courtesy Mike Stuckslager

NIB	Exc.	V.G.	Good	Fair	Poor
—	1500	1100	650	350	175

3rd Model Single-Shot

Basic difference between this model and 2nd Model is that this pistol could be fired double-action as well as single-action. Frame came from double-action perfected model. Manufactured 6,949 between 1909 and 1923.

Courtesy Mike Stuckslager

NIB	Exc.	V.G.	Good	Fair	Poor
—	2000	1400	1200	600	300

Straight Line Single-Shot

Unique pistol that very much resembles a semi-automatic. Barrel is 10" in length and pivots to left for loading. Chambered for .22 LR cartridge. Finished in blue, with walnut grips inlaid with S&W medallions. Hammer is straight-line in function and does not pivot. Manufactured 1,870 between 1925 and 1936.

Courtesy Bonhams & Butterfields, San Francisco, California

NIB	Exc.	V.G.	Good	Fair	Poor
—	3200	2500	1500	750	400

.32 Hand Ejector Model of 1896 or .32 Hand Ejector 1st Model

This model was the first time S&W made a revolver with a swing-out cylinder. Interestingly, there is no cylinder latch; but the action opens by pulling forward on the exposed portion of the cylinder pin. This frees the spring tension and allows the cylinder to swing free. Another novel feature of this model is the cylinder stop location, which is located in the top of the frame over the cylinder. Chambered for .32 S&W Long cartridge, has a 6-shot fluted cylinder and offered with 3.25", 4.25" and 6" long barrels. Available with a round or square butt, has checkered hard rubber grips and is blued or nickel-plated. Factory installed target sights were available by special order. Company name, address and patent dates are stamped on the cylinder instead of barrel. Approximately 19,712 manufactured between 1896 and 1903.

Courtesy Mike Stuckslager

NIB	Exc.	V.G.	Good	Fair	Poor
900	650	425	350	200	150

Hand Ejector Model of 1903

Quite different from its predecessor. Cylinder locks front and back; cylinder stop located in bottom of frame and familiar sliding cylinder latch found on left side of frame. Barrel lengths 3.25", 4.25" and 6". The 6-shot cylinder is fluted. Chambered for .32 S&W Long. Offered blued or nickel-plated. Round butt grips are checkered hard rubber. Approximately 19,425 manufactured in 1903 and 1904; serial number range 1 to 19425.

Courtesy Mike Stuckslager

NIB	Exc.	V.G.	Good	Fair	Poor
—	1500	1100	800	400	250

.32 Hand Ejector Model of 1903 1st Change

Differs internally from model of 1903. Serial number range 19426 to 51126, is really the only way to differentiate the two. Approximately 31,700 manufactured between 1904 and 1906.

NIB	Exc.	V.G.	Good	Fair	Poor
—	1750	1300	800	500	300

.32 Hand Ejector Model of 1903 2nd Change

Produced from 1906 to 1909. Serial number range 51127 to 95500. Total of 44,373 manufactured.

.32 Hand Ejector Model of 1903 3rd Change

Produced from 1909 to 1910. Serial number range 95501 to 96125. Total of 624 manufactured.

.32 Hand Ejector Model of 1903 4th Change

Produced in 1910. Serial number range 96126 to 102500. Total of 6,374 manufactured.

.32 Hand Ejector Model of 1903 5th Change

Produced from 1910 to 1917. Serial number range 102500 to 263000. Total of 160,500 manufactured.

.32 Hand Ejector Third Model

Produced from 1911 to 1942. Serial number range 263001 to 536684. Total of 273,683 manufactured.

NIB	Exc.	V.G.	Good	Fair	Poor
—	650	500	375	250	150

K-32 Hand Ejector First Model

One of the rarest pre-war K-frame revolvers. Chambered for .32 S&W Long cartridge. Less than 100 were made between 1936 and 1941. After WWII, this model was part of the K-22/K-32/K-38 Masterpiece series of 6" barreled target-sighted revolvers. Due to its rarity, an expert appraisal is essential.

NIB	Exc.	V.G.	Good	Fair	Poor
—	18000	13500	9000	3500	800

.22 Ladysmith 1st Model

Designed primarily as a defensive weapon for women. Small size and caliber made it ideal for that purpose. Chambered for .22 Long cartridge. Has 7-shot fluted cylinder. Barrel lengths 3" and 3.5". Weight 9.625 oz. Blued or nickel-plated. Round butt, with checkered hard rubber grips. Checkered cylinder-latch button on left side of frame. Approximately 4,575 manufactured between 1902 and 1906.

NIB	Exc.	V.G.	Good	Fair	Poor
—	2500	1700	1100	650	450

.22 Ladysmith 2nd Model

Essentially, quite similar in appearance to 1st Model. Difference being in pull-forward cylinder-latch located under the barrel, replacing button on left side of frame. New method allowed lockup front and back for greater action strength. Barrel length 2.25" was dropped; caliber and finishes the same. Approximately 9,374 manufactured between 1906 and 1910; serial number range 4576 to 13950.

Courtesy Mike Stuckslager

NIB	Exc.	V.G.	Good	Fair	Poor
—	2300	1500	900	500	300

.22 Ladysmith 3rd Model

Quite different in appearance to 2nd Model. Features square butt and smooth walnut grips, with inlaid S&W medallions. Barrel lengths remained the same, with addition of 2.25" and 6" variation. Under barrel cylinder lockup was not changed, nor caliber and finishes. Approximately 12,200 manufactured between 1910 and 1921; serial number range 13951 to 26154. **NOTE:** Add 50 percent premium for 2.25" and 6" barrel lengths.

Courtesy W.P. Hallstein III and son Chip

NIB	Exc.	V.G.	Good	Fair	Poor
—	2300	1500	900	500	300

K-22 Outdoorsman/Masterpiece

Pre-war version of K-22 K-frame, 6" barreled revolver. Chambered for .22 Short, Long and Long Rifle. Walnut grips, adjustable rear sight, ribbed barrel. Manufactured from 1931 to 1940. In 1940, name was changed to K-22 Masterpiece and an improved adjustable rear sight was added. S&W short action was another improvement. Only about 1,000 K-22 Masterpieces manufactured in 1940. **NOTE:** Add 100 percent premium for 1940 manufacture in 682,420 - 696,952 serial number range.

NIB	Exc.	V.G.	Good	Fair	Poor
2500	2000	1600	1000	500	300

.38 Hand Ejector Military & Police 1st Model or Model of 1899

Early swing-out cylinder revolver. No front lockup for action. Release on left side of frame. Chambered for .38 S&W Special and .32 Win. Centerfire cartridge (.32-20). Has 6-shot fluted cylinder. Offered with 4", 5", 6", 6.5" or 8" barrel in .38-caliber; 4", 5" and 6.5" in .32-20 caliber. Finish blued or nickel-plated; grips checkered walnut or hard rubber. Manufactured between 1899 and 1902: 20,975 in .38-caliber serial number range 1 to 20975; 5,311 in .32-20 caliber serial number range 1 to 5311.

Courtesy Mike Stuckslager

NIB	Exc.	V.G.	Good	Fair	Poor
—	1750	1300	800	500	300

Commercial Model

NIB	Exc.	V.G.	Good	Fair	Poor
—	1500	1200	800	450	350

U.S. Navy Model

Produced 1,000 in 1900. .38 S&W, 6" barrel, blued with checkered walnut grips. "U.S.N." stamped on butt. Serial number range 5000 to 6000.

NIB	Exc.	V.G.	Good	Fair	Poor
—	3500	2600	1500	750	400

U.S. Army Model

Produced 1,000 in 1901. Same as Navy Model except marked "U.S.Army/Model 1899" on butt. "K.S.M." and "J.T.T." on grips. Serial number range 13001 to 14000.

NIB	Exc.	V.G.	Good	Fair	Poor
—	3500	2600	1500	750	400

.38 Hand Ejector M&P 2nd Model or Model of 1902

The 2nd Model similar in appearance to 1st Model. Major difference is the addition of the front lockup under the barrel and ejector rod was increased in diameter. Barrel lengths: .38 S&W were 4", 5", 6" or 6.5"; .32-20 available in 4", 5" or 6.5". Both calibers offered in round butt only configuration. Approximately 12,827 manufactured in .38 S&W in 1902 and 1903; serial number range 20976 to 33803. In .32-20 caliber 4,499 were produced; serial number range 5312 to 9811. **NOTE:** Add 250 percent for U.S. Navy Model.

NIB	Exc.	V.G.	Good	Fair	Poor
—	1200	900	500	250	100

.38 Hand Ejector M&P 2nd Model, 1st Change

Built between 1903 and 1905. This variation represents change to the square butt, which made for better shooting control and standardized frame shape. Both .38 S&W and .32-20 were available in 4", 5" or 6.5" barrel lengths. Manufactured 28,645 .38-caliber, serial number range 33804 to 62449; and 8,313 .32-20s, serial number 9812 to 18125.

NIB	Exc.	V.G.	Good	Fair	Poor
—	1100	800	400	250	100

.38 Hand Ejector Model of 1905

A continuation of .38 M&P Hand Ejector series. Built from 1905 to 1906. Available in 4", 5", 6" and 6.5" barrels, for both .38 and .32-20 calibers. Finished in blue or nickel, with round or square butt. The .38-caliber serial number range 62450 to 73250, about 10,800 produced. The .32-20 caliber serial number range spans 18126 to 22426, or 4,300 produced. **NOTE:** Prices for the following four variations will be the same as those noted above.

NIB	Exc.	V.G.	Good	Fair	Poor
—	1200	950	650	400	150

1st Change

Produced from 1906 to 1908. Similar to original model of 1905, with regard to barrel lengths, finish and butt styles. The 1st change in .38-caliber was produced in serial number range 73251 to 120000, with 46,749 sold. In .32-20 caliber serial number range was 22427 to 33500, with 11,073 sold.

2nd Change

Produced from 1908 to 1909. Only internal changes were made to this model. Best approach to differentiate this model is by serial number. The .38-caliber serial number range from 120001 to 146899, with 26,898 produced. In .32-20 caliber serial number range between 33501 to 45200, with 11,699 produced.

3rd Change

Produced from 1909 to 1915. The 3rd Change variation available only in 4" or 6" barrel lengths, for both .38 and .32-20. The .38-caliber serial number range between 146900 to 241703, with 94,803 sold.

Courtesy Mike Stuckslager

4th Change

Last variation was also the longest production run. Produced from 1915 to 1942. Barrel lengths: .38-caliber available in 2", 4", 5" or 6"; while .32-20 caliber offered in 4", 5" or 6". The .38-caliber serial number range from 241704 to 1000000; while .32-20 caliber produced from 1915 to 1940, serial number range from 65701 to 144684.

Courtesy Mike Stuckslager

.22-32 Hand Ejector

This is a very interesting model from a collector's point of view. Phillip B. Bekeart, a San Francisco firearms dealer, requested that S&W manufacture a .22-caliber target-grade revolver on the heavier .32 frame. He believed in his idea so passionately, that he immediately ordered 1,000 guns for himself. This initial order is found within serial number range 1 to 3000 and are known to collectors as the authentic Bekearts. Remainder of the extensive production run are simply .22-32 Hand Ejectors. Chambered for .22 LR cartridge and a 6-shot fluted cylinder, with 6" barrel. Finish blue, with square butt and checkered extension-type walnut grips. There were only 292 revolvers of his initial order delivered to Mr. Bekeart, but the first 1,000 pistols are considered to be True Bekearts. Production number of each respective pistol is stamped into the base of the extended wooden grips. S&W went on to manufacture several hundred thousand of these revolvers between 1911 and 1953.

Courtesy Mike Stuckslager

Bekeart Model

Serial number range 138226 to 139275, in .32 Hand Ejector series. Production number stamped on butt. Professional appraisal should be secured.

NIB	Exc.	V.G.	Good	Fair	Poor
—	1500	1400	900	700	250

Standard Model

NIB	Exc.	V.G.	Good	Fair	Poor
—	1200	800	600	500	250

.22-32 Kit Gun (Pre WWII)

Same features as Standard Model, except for a smaller grip frame and 4" barrel.

NIB	Exc.	V.G.	Good	Fair	Poor
3500	3000	2400	1600	600	250

.44 Hand Ejector 1st Model

Also known by collectors as ".44 Triple Lock" or "The New Century". Triple Lock nickname came from a separate locking device located on extractor rod shroud that is used in addition to usual two locks. Chambered for .44 S&W Special cartridge or .44 S&W Russian. On a limited basis, also chambered in .44-40, .45 Colt, .455 Mark II and .38-40. Fluted cylinder holds 6-shots. Barrel offered in standard lengths of 5" or 6.5". Limited quantity of 4" barrels produced. Finish blued or nickel-plated; grips checkered walnut with gold S&W medallion on later models. Approximately 15,375 manufactured between 1908 and 1915. **NOTE:** Add 100 percent premium for factory target sights.

Courtesy Mike Stuckslager

.44 S&W Special

NIB	Exc.	V.G.	Good	Fair	Poor
3000	2800	1500	1000	600	400

Other Calibers (Rare)

NIB	Exc.	V.G.	Good	Fair	Poor
7500	6000	4000	2500	1500	800

.44 Hand Ejector 2nd Model

Quite similar in appearance to 1st Model. Major difference, elimination of third or triple lock device and heavy ejector rod shroud. Other changes are internal and not readily apparent. Standard in .44 S&W Special chambering, but offered rarely in .38-40, .44-40 and .45 Colt. Specimens have been noted with adjustable sights in 6.5" barrel lengths. Standard barrel lengths 4", 5" and 6.5". Approximately 17,510 manufactured between 1915 and 1937, serial number range 15376 to 60000. **NOTE:** Add 50 percent premium for factory target sights.

.44 S&W Special

NIB	Exc.	V.G.	Good	Fair	Poor
—	2500	1900	1200	600	300

.38-40, .44-40 or .45 Colt

Very few factory models were made in these calibers. Values shown are speculative. Use caution and consult an expert appraiser.

NIB	Exc.	V.G.	Good	Fair	Poor
—	5000	4000	2800	1000	500

.44 Hand Ejector 3rd Model or Model of 1926

Similar in appearance to 2nd Model, but brought back the heavy ejector rod shroud of 1st Model, without triple lock device. Barrel lengths 4", 5" and 6.5". The .44 Hand Ejector Model, manufactured between 1926 and 1949. **NOTE:** Add 50 percent premium for factory target sights.

Courtesy Mike Stuckslager

.44 S&W Special

NIB	Exc.	V.G.	Good	Fair	Poor
—	3500	2400	2000	1000	500

.44-40 or .45 Colt

Very few factory models made in these calibers. Values shown are speculative. Use caution and consult an expert appraiser.

NIB	Exc.	V.G.	Good	Fair	Poor
—	5500	4500	3000	1000	500

.45 Hand Ejector U.S. Service Model of 1917

WWI was on the horizon and it seemed certain that the United States would become involved. S&W people began to work with Springfield Armory to develop a hand ejector model that would fire .45-caliber Government cartridge. This was accomplished in 1916 by the use of half-moon clips. New revolver is quite similar to .44 Hand Ejector in appearance. It has a 5.5" barrel, blued finish with smooth walnut grips and a lanyard ring on the butt. Designation "U.S.Army Model 1917" is stamped on the butt. After the war broke out, the government was not satisfied with S&W's production and actually took control of the company for the duration of the war. This was the first time that the company was not controlled by a Wesson. Factory records indicate that there were 163,476 Model 1917s manufactured between 1917 and 1919, the WWI years. After the war, sale of these revolvers continued on a commercial and contract basis until 1949, when this model was finally dropped from the S&W product line.

Military Model

NIB	Exc.	V.G.	Good	Fair	Poor
—	1500	1200	1000	400	200

Brazilian Contract

25,000 produced for Brazilian government in 1938. Brazilian crest stamped on sideplate.

NIB	Exc.	V.G.	Good	Fair	Poor
—	1100	800	500	250	125

Commercial Model

High gloss blue and checkered walnut grips.

Courtesy Mike Stuckslager

NIB	Exc.	V.G.	Good	Fair	Poor
—	2000	1500	1000	475	300

.455 Mark II Hand Ejector 1st Model

Designed the same as .44 Hand Ejector 1st Model, with no caliber stamping on the barrel. Barrel length 6.4". Of the 5,000 revolvers produced, only 100 sold were commercial guns, rest were military. Produced between 1914 and 1915. Commercial model worth a premium.

NIB	Exc.	V.G.	Good	Fair	Poor
—	1400	1150	700	400	200

.455 Mark II Hand Ejector 2nd Model

Similar to first model, without an extractor shroud. Barrel length also 6.5". Serial number range 5000 to 74755. Manufactured from 1915 to 1917.

NIB	Exc.	V.G.	Good	Fair	Poor
—	1300	1050	600	350	175

S&W .35 Automatic Pistol

Production of .35 Automatic was S&W's first attempt at an auto-loading pistol. As was always the case, company strived for maximum safety and dependability. Has a 3.5" barrel and 7-shot detachable magazine. Chambered in .35 S&W Automatic, a one-time-only cartridge, that eventually proved to be the major downfall of this pistol from a commercial standpoint. There were two separate safety devices—a revolving cam on the backstrap and a grip safety on the front strap that had to be fully depressed simultaneously while squeezing the trigger. Finish blue or nickel-plated; grips are walnut, with S&W inlaid medallions. Magazine release slides from side to side and is checkered, expensive to manufacture, and destined to be modified. Approximately 8,350 manufactured.

NIB	Exc.	V.G.	Good	Fair	Poor
—	750	450	300	200	150

S&W .32 Automatic Pistol

In 1921, it became apparent to the powers that controlled S&W that .35-caliber automatic was never going to be a commercial success. Harold Wesson, the new president, began to redesign the pistol to accept the .32 ACP, a commercially accepted cartridge, and to streamline the appearance to be more competitive with other pistols on the market, notably Colt's. This new pistol used as many parts from older models as possible for economy's sake. Pivoting barrel was discontinued, as was the cam-type safety in the rear grip strap. A magazine disconnector and a reduced-strength recoil spring to ease cocking were employed. Barrel length kept at 3.5" and 7-shot magazine was retained. Finish is blued only and grips are smooth walnut. Manufactured only 957, between 1924 and 1936. They are eagerly sought by collectors.

Courtesy James Rankin

NIB	Exc.	V.G.	Good	Fair	Poor
—	2500	1750	1100	700	500

SMITH & WESSON MODERN HANDGUNS

With development of Hand Ejector Models and swing-out cylinders, Smith & Wesson opened the door to a number of new advancements in the revolver field. New system allowed for a solid frame, making weapon much stronger than old top break design. Company also developed different basic frame sizes and gave them letter designations. I frame, which later developed into slightly larger J frame, was used for .22-32 and small concealable .38 revolvers. Medium K frame used for .38 duty-/target-type weapons. N frame was heavy-duty frame used for larger .357-, .44- and .45-caliber revolvers. Hand ejector went through many evolutionary changes over the years. Beginning in 1959, all S&W models were given numerical designations — Model 10, Model 14, etc. Models are cataloged here by their numerical designations, brief description given and current values offered. Important to note that S&W revolvers we see marketed by the company today have undergone many changes in reaching its present configuration. Early models featured five screws in their construction, not counting grip screw. Four screws fastening sideplate and another through front of trigger guard that retained cylinder stop plunger. First change involved elimination of top sideplate screw and five-screw Smith & Wesson became four-screw. Later the frame was changed to eliminate cylinder stop plunger screw and three-screw was created. Some models offered with flat cylinder latch that was serrated instead of familiar checkering. In 1978, method of attaching barrel to frame was changed and familiar pin was eliminated. At the same time, recessed cylinder commonly found on Magnum models was also eliminated. All these factors have a definite affect on value and collectability of a particular S&W handgun.

NOTE: Pre-model number designations are listed in parentheses after model number. Premium up to 100 percent can apply to some of these handguns if accompanied by original box, and if both gun and box are in excellent or better condition. See Performance Center pages at end of Smith & Wesson section for many special and limited editions of these handguns.

Courtesy Smith & Wesson

Model 10 (.38 Military & Police)

This model has been in production in one configuration or another since 1899. It was always the mainstay of S&W line. Originally known as .38 Military and Police Model. Model 10 is built on the K, or medium frame, and was always meant as a duty gun. Offered with 2", 3", 4", 5" or 6" barrel. Currently only 4" and 6" are available. Round or square butt, chambered for .38 Special. Offered in blue or nickel-plate, with checkered walnut grips. Model designation stamped on yoke on all S&W revolvers. This model, with many other modern S&W pistols, underwent several engineering changes. These changes may affect value of the pistol, and an expert should be consulted. Dates of these changes are as follows:

10-NONE-1957		10-2-1961		10-4-1962	
10-1-1959		10-3-1961		10-5-1962	
10-6-1962					

NIB	Exc.	V.G.	Good	Fair	Poor
500	300	200	150	125	90

Victory Model

Manufactured during WWII. Model 10, with sandblasted and parkerized finish, lanyard swivel and smooth walnut grips. Serial number has a V prefix. Available only in 2" and 4" barrel lengths. Victory Model discontinued April 27, 1945, with serial number VS811119. **NOTE:** Add 75 percent premium for top strap marked Navy; 100 percent premium for Navy variation with both top strap and side plate marked; 125 percent premium for Navy variation marked "N.Y.M.I."; unknown premium amount for revolvers marked "U.S.G.C." or "U.S.M.C.". Exercise caution.

NIB	Exc.	V.G.	Good	Fair	Poor
750	625	500	400	300	200

Model 11 (.38/200 British)

First produced in 1947, S&W received many contracts for this service pistol. Nicknamed .38/200 British Service Revolver. S&W sold many of these models throughout 1950s and 1960s. Several rare variations of this model will greatly affect its value. Consult an expert if special markings and barrel lengths are encountered.

NIB	Exc.	V.G.	Good	Fair	Poor
1200	900	600	500	400	300

Model 12 (.38 Military & Police Airweight)

Model 12 was introduced in 1952. Starting serial number C223999. Merely a Model 10, with lightweight alloy frame and cylinder. In 1954, alloy cylinder was replaced with one of steel that added an additional 4 oz. in weight. Discontinued in 1986. **NOTE:** Add 40 percent for aluminum cylinder.

NIB	Exc.	V.G.	Good	Fair	Poor
—	700	500	250	125	100

USAF M-13 (Aircrewman)

Manufactured in early 1950s, for U.S. Air Force on Model 12 K-frame. Chambered in .38 Special and have an alloy frame and cylinder. They were to be carried by pilots and other flight-crew members for emergency use. Air Force ultimately rejected the model, because of problems encountered with the alloy cylinder, and most were destroyed. Because of this, Aircrewman is one of the rarest modern-day Smith & Wesson revolvers. Serial numbers in C247000 to C406000 range. It is not known how many still exist. Genuine model is seldom seen for sale. Numerous fakes have been documented, so it is strongly suggested that a knowledgeable S&W expert be consulted for an appraisal. A few "Baby" Aircrewman 5-shot revolvers were made on S&W J-frame, and it is believed that fewer than 15 of these guns still exist. Because of the rarity of these two models and few actual transactions that have occurred in recent years, it is not possible to list meaningful values.

Model 13 (.357 Military & Police)

Simply Model 10 M&P. Chambered for .357 Magnum. Fitted with a heavy barrel. Introduced in 1974.

NIB	Exc.	V.G.	Good	Fair	Poor
525	425	350	275	175	125

Model 14 (K-38 Masterpiece)

Also known as "K-38". In 1957, "Model 14" stamped on yoke. Offered in 6" barrel, with adjustable sights. In 1961, single-action version with faster lock time offered. Discontinued in 1981. **NOTE:** Add 25 percent for single-action.

NIB	Exc.	V.G.	Good	Fair	Poor
700	625	500	400	300	200

Model 15 (K-38 Combat Masterpiece)

Also known as "Combat Masterpiece". Produced at request of law enforcement officers who wanted "K-38" fitted with a 4" barrel. Production in 1950; discontinued 1987.

NIB	Exc.	V.G.	Good	Fair	Poor
750	675	550	450	300	200

Model 16 (K-32 Masterpiece)

Also known as "K-32" until 1957. Identical in appearance to Model 14, except chambered for .32 S&W. Model 16 did not enjoy the commercial popularity like Model 14, and was dropped from the line in 1973. Only 3,630 K-32s/Model 16s were sold between 1947 and 1973. Reintroduced in 1990 in .32 Magnum; discontinued 1993. **NOTE:** Add 25 percent for 1946—1957 production (no Model 16 marking).

Courtesy Mike Stuckslager

NIB	Exc.	V.G.	Good	Fair	Poor
2750	2200	1800	1200	400	200

Model 16 (.32 Magnum)

Reintroduced in 1990, in .32 Magnum; discontinued 1993.

NIB	Exc.	V.G.	Good	Fair	Poor
1250	800	450	200	150	100

K-32 Combat Masterpiece

S&W produced a limited number of 4" barreled K-32 revolvers. Never given a number designation, as they were discontinued before 1957 when the numbering system began.

NIB	Exc.	V.G.	Good	Fair	Poor
2600	2000	1500	900	350	300

Model 17 (K-22)

Numerical designation S&W placed on "K-22" in 1957. Target model .22 rimfire revolver has always been popular since its introduction in 1946. Offered in 4", 6" and 8.375" barrel lengths, with all target options. The 8.375" barrel dropped from product line in 1993. Finish blued, with checkered walnut grips.

Courtesy Mike Stuckslager

NIB	Exc.	V.G.	Good	Fair	Poor
800	700	650	500	375	275

Model 17 Plus

Introduced in 1996. New version of old Model 17. Has a 10-round cylinder for its .22 LR cartridges. Features 6" full lug barrel, with Patridge front sight and adjustable rear. Hammer is semi-target style and trigger a smooth combat style. Finish matte black and grips are Hogue black rubber. Drilled and tapped for scope mounts. Weight about 42 oz. Discontinued.

NIB	Exc.	V.G.	Good	Fair	Poor
650	475	300	175	125	100

Model 617 Plus

Identical to Model 17, but furnished with stainless steel frame and cylinder.

NIB	Exc.	V.G.	Good	Fair	Poor
575	400	250	200	150	100

Model 647

Introduced in 2003. Chambered for .17 HMR cartridge. Fitted with 8.375" barrel, with full lug. Six-round cylinder capacity. Stainless steel finish. Adjustable rear sight. Hogue rubber grips. Fitted with a target trigger and hammer. Drilled and tapped for scope. Weight about 52.5 oz. Discontinued.

NIB	Exc.	V.G.	Good	Fair	Poor
775	525	375	225	175	100

Model 648

Identical to Model 617, but chambered for .22 Magnum rimfire cartridge.

NIB	Exc.	V.G.	Good	Fair	Poor
675	500	375	225	175	100

Model 648 (New Model)

Introduced in 2003. Medium frame revolver chambered for .22 WMR cartridge. Fitted with 6" full lug barrel. Pinned Patridge front sight and adjustable rear. New extractor system. Drilled and tapped for scope mount. Stainless steel finish. Weight 45 oz.

NOTE: On "K Frame" Target Models:

1. Factory eliminated upper corner screw from side plate in 1955. The 5-screw became a 4-screw. Change occurred around serial number K260000.
2. Model number designations were stamped on yoke in 1957.

NIB	Exc.	V.G.	Good	Fair	Poor
700	525	395	250	200	125

Model 18 (K-22 Combat Masterpiece)

Model designation for 4" barrel "Combat Masterpiece". Chambered for .22 rimfire.

NIB	Exc.	V.G.	Good	Fair	Poor
—	675	475	300	200	125

Model 19 (.357 Combat Magnum)

Introduced in 1954 at the urging of Bill Jordan, a competition shooter with U.S. Border Patrol. He went on to become a respected gun writer. Built on "K-Frame" and was first medium frame revolver chambered for powerful .357 Magnum cartridge. Since its inception, Model 19 has been one of S&W's most popular revolvers. First revolver to be introduced as a three-screw model. Originally offered with 4" heavy barrel with extractor shroud; 6" became available in 1963. Finish blued or nickel plated. Grips are checkered walnut. Goncalo Alves target stocks first appeared in 1959. In 1968, a 2.5" round butt version was introduced. Model 19 has been basis for two commemorative's—Texas Ranger/with Bowie Knife and Oregon State Police/with Belt Buckle. No longer in production.

Combat Magnum (Pre-Model 19, 1954-1958)

NOTE: Add 50 percent for nickel finish.

NIB	Exc.	V.G.	Good	Fair	Poor
1800	1500	1100	850	500	300

Model 19, 19-1

NOTE: Add 40 percent for nickel finish.

NIB	Exc.	V.G.	Good	Fair	Poor
1200	950	750	500	300	200

Model 19-2, 19-3

NIB	Exc.	V.G.	Good	Fair	Poor
650	550	450	375	300	200

Oregon State Police Cased with Buckle

NIB	Exc.	V.G.	Good	Fair	Poor
900	—	—	—	—	—

Texas Ranger Cased with Knife

NIB	Exc.	V.G.	Good	Fair	Poor
700	—	—	—	—	—

Model 20 (.38/.44 Heavy Duty)

Known as ".38/.44 Heavy Duty" before the change to numerical designations. This model was brought out in 1930, in response to requests from law enforcement personnel for a more powerful sidearm. This model, along with .38-44 S&W Special cartridge, was an attempt to solve this problem. Manufactured with a standard 5" long barrel, but has been noted rarely as short as 3.5" and as long as 8.375". Built on large N-frame. Blued or nickel-plated, with checkered walnut grips. Eventually the popularity of .357 Magnum made Model 20 superfluous, and was discontinued in 1966. Post-war production was about 20,000 revolvers. **NOTE:** Add 50 percent for pre-war.

Courtesy Mike Stuckslager

NIB	Exc.	V.G.	Good	Fair	Poor
1250	1000	850	600	450	200

Model 21 (1950 Military)

Known as "1950 Military" and "4th Model .44 Hand Ejector", before Model 21 designation was applied in 1957. Chambered for .44 Special cartridge and equipped with fixed sights. Built on N frame and is quite rare. Manufactured only 1,200 in 16 years of production. Discontinued 1966.

NIB	Exc.	V.G.	Good	Fair	Poor
2800	2500	1800	950	650	500

Model 21 Thunder Ranch

Limited edition variation is a 4" barreled .44 Special, with gold-plated logo of legendary Arizona shooting school on the frame.

NIB	Exc.	V.G.	Good	Fair	Poor
800	650	500	400	300	200

Model 696

Introduced in 1997. Features 3" underlug barrel. Chambered for .44 Special. Fitted on an L-frame. Capacity 5 rounds. Grips are Hogue black rubber. Finish stainless steel. Weight about 48 oz.

NIB	Exc.	V.G.	Good	Fair	Poor
850	725	600	450	300	—

Model 22 (1950 .45 Military)

Known as "1950 .45 Military" before 1957. Actually introduced in 1951. Similar in appearance to Model 21, except hambered for .45 Auto Rim or .45 ACP cartridge. Half-moon clips are used with the latter. Manufactured 3,976 between 1951 and 1966. Beginning serial number S85,000.

NIB	Exc.	V.G.	Good	Fair	Poor
1850	1550	1350	950	650	500

Model 23 (.38-44 Outdoorsman)

The ".38-44 Outdoorsman" was model name of this N-frame revolver before the 1957 designation change. Simply Model 20, with adjustable sights. Introduced in 1931, as a heavy-duty sporting handgun with hunters in mind. S&W produced 4,761 of these pre-war revolvers. Features 6.5" barrel. Blued finish. First S&W to have the new checkered walnut "Magna" grips. After 1949, this revolver was thoroughly modernized and had the later ribbed barrel. A total of 8,365 manufactured before it was discontinued in 1966; 6,039 were of the modernized configuration. **NOTE:** Add 50 percent for pre-war production.

Courtesy Mike Stuckslager

NIB	Exc.	V.G.	Good	Fair	Poor
1700	1500	1200	600	250	200

Model 22 – Thunder Ranch .45 ACP

Limited edition six-shot single-/double-action chambered for .45 ACP. Blued, with 4" tapered barrel. Weight 37.5 oz. Cocobolo grips engraved with Thunder Ranch insignia. Fixed sights. Serial numbers begin with TRR0000.

NIB	Exc.	V.G.	Good	Fair	Poor
—	850	675	500	250	200

Model 24 (.44 Target Model of 1950)

Introduced as .44 Target Model of 1950. Simply the N-frame Model 21, with adjustable target sights. Quite popular with long-range handgunning devotees and their leader, Elmer Keith. Introduction of .44 Magnum in 1956, began the death knell of Model 24. Finally discontinued in 1966. S&W produced a total of 5,050 Model 24s. Reintroduced in 1983 and 1984—and then was dropped again. **NOTE:** Add 25 percent for 4" barrel; 40 percent for 5". Deduct 60 percent for 1983-84 model.

NIB	Exc.	V.G.	Good	Fair	Poor
2500	2000	1600	1000	650	500

Model 25 (.45 Target Model of 1950)

Prior to model designation change in 1957. this model was known as .45 Target Model of 1955. An improved version of 1950 Target .45. Features a heavier barrel 4", 6.5" or 8" in length, with blued or nickel-plated finish. All target options were offered. Chambered for .45 ACP or .45 Auto-rim cartridges. Later chambered for .45 Colt as Model 25-5. **NOTE:** Add 100 percent premium for .45 Colt.

NIB	Exc.	V.G.	Good	Fair	Poor
1750	1550	1350	950	650	500

Model 25-3 125th Anniversary with Case

NIB	Exc.	V.G.	Good	Fair	Poor
1300	—	—	—	—	—

Model 25-2

Discontinued modern version of Model 25. Chambered in .45 ACP. The 6.5" barrel is shortened to 6". Available in a presentation case.

NIB	Exc.	V.G.	Good	Fair	Poor
900	775	650	400	300	150

Model 25 Mountain Gun

Introduced in 2004. This .45 Colt N-frame round butt model features 4" tapered barrel, with black blade front sight and adjustable rear. Cocobolo wood grips. Blued finish. Weight about 40 oz.

NIB	Exc.	V.G.	Good	Fair	Poor
750	625	500	425	300	150

Model 625-2

Stainless steel version of Model 25-2. Fitted with a 5" barrel. Pachmayr SK/GR gripper stocks as standard. Designed for pin shooting. Weight about 45 oz.

NIB	Exc.	V.G.	Good	Fair	Poor
750	625	500	425	300	150

Model 625 IDPA

As above, but fitted with 4" barrel, Patridge front sight and adjustable rear. Hogue grips. Introduced in 2002. Weight about 43 oz.

NIB	Exc.	V.G.	Good	Fair	Poor
1000	850	700	575	400	200

Model 625 JM (Jerry Miculek)

Introduced in 2005. Chambered for .45 ACP cartridge. Fitted with a 4" full lug barrel, with Patridge front sight and adjustable rear. Capacity 6 rounds. Wood grips. Weight about 43 oz.

NIB	Exc.	V.G.	Good	Fair	Poor
750	625	500	425	300	150

Model 625 Mountain Gun

First time offered in 1996. Chambered for .45 Colt cartridge. Fitted with 4" tapered barrel, with ramp front sight and adjustable rear. Frame drilled and tapped for scope mount.

NIB	Exc.	V.G.	Good	Fair	Poor
650	500	400	300	200	125

Model 610

Introduced in 1998. Chambered for 10mm cartridge. Fitted with a 6.5" full-lug barrel and unfluted cylinder. Hogue grips are standard. Adjustable rear sight. Interchangeable front sight. Weight about 52 oz.

NIB	Exc.	V.G.	Good	Fair	Poor
750	625	500	425	300	150

Model 26 (1950 .45 Target)

Numerical designation of 1950 .45 Target Model. This large N-frame revolver is basically the same as Model 25, but has a lighter, thinner barrel. This caused its unpopularity among competitive shooters who wanted a heavier revolver. This brought about Model 25 and the demise of Model 26, in 1961. Manufactured only 2,768. Model 26 also has two additional variations and are marked 26-1 and 26-2.

NIB	Exc.	V.G.	Good	Fair	Poor
3500	2500	1800	1000	500	200

Factory Registered .357 Magnum

In early 1930s, a gun writer named Phillip B. Sharpe, became interested in the development of high performance loads to be used in then-popular .38-44 S&W revolvers. He repeatedly urged S&W to produce a revolver especially made to handle these high pressure loads. In 1934, S&W asked Winchester to produce a new cartridge that would create the ballistics that Sharpe was seeking. This new cartridge was made longer than standard .38 Special case, so that it could not inadvertently be fired in an older gun. S&W never felt that this would be a commercially popular venture and from the onset visualized ".357 Magnum" as a strictly deluxe hand-built item. They were to be individually numbered, in addition to serial number, and registered to the new owner. New Magnum was to be the most expensive revolver in the line. This gun went on the market in 1935, and the first one was presented to FBI Director, J. Edgar Hoover. The gun was to become a tremendous success. S&W could only produce 120 per month, and this did not come close to filling orders. The ".357 Magnum", as it was designated, continued as one of the company's most popular items.

Factory Registered Model was built on the N-frame. It could be custom ordered with any barrel length from 3.5" up to 8.375". Finish is blue and grips are checkered walnut. This model was virtually hand-built and test targeted. A certificate of registration was furnished with each revolver. Registration number was stamped on the yoke of revolver, with the prefix "Reg.". This practice of numbering and registering each revolver ceased in 1938, after 5,500 were produced.

NOTE: For top dollar, all accessories and registration letter must be present.

Courtesy Mike Stuckslager

NIB	Exc.	V.G.	Good	Fair	Poor
13500	10000	8500	5000	2000	500

Pre-war .357 Magnum

Same as Factory Registered Model, without certificate and individual numbering. Approximately 1,150 manufactured between 1938 and 1941. Production ceased for WWII weapons production.

NIB	Exc.	V.G.	Good	Fair	Poor
8000	6500	5000	3500	1500	500

Model 27 (.357 Magnum)

In 1948, after the end of WWII, production of this revolver commenced. New rebound slide operated hammer block and short throw hammer were utilized. Barrel lengths offered were 3.5", 5", 6", 6.5" and 8.375". In 1957, model designation was changed to Model 27. In 1975, target trigger, hammer and Goncalo Alves target grips were made standard. Some additional variations may be of interest to the collector. Around serial number SI71584, the three-screw sideplate model was first produced. In 1960, designation -1 was added to model indicating change to a left-hand thread to extractor rod. In 1962, cylinder stop was changed which disposed the need for a plunger spring hole in front of trigger guard. Change was indicated by a -2 behind model number. **NOTE:** Add $1,000 premium for pre-1957 production; $100 for early 4-screw model; 25 percent for 2.5 or 5" barrel

NIB	Exc.	V.G.	Good	Fair	Poor
800	700	600	450	350	300

Model 627

Special edition stainless steel version of Model 27. Offered with a 5.5" barrel. Manufactured in 1989 only. Approximately 4,500 produced.

NIB	Exc.	V.G.	Good	Fair	Poor
650	450	350	300	200	150

Model 627 Pro Series

Introduced in 2008. An eight-shot .357 revolver, with stainless steel frame, adjustable sights, 4" barrel and various accurizing refinements.

NIB	Exc.	V.G.	Good	Fair	Poor
—	900	675	495	300	150

Model 28 (Highway Patrolman)

Model 27 revolver was extremely popular among law enforcement officers. Many police agencies were interested in purchasing such a weapon—except for cost. In 1954, S&W produced a new model called at the time, "Highway Patrolman". Had all desirable performance features of deluxe Model 27, but lacked cosmetic features that drove up price. Finish matte blue; rib sandblasted instead of checkered or serrated; grips standard checkered walnut. Barrel lengths 4" and 6.5". On late models, 6.5" barrel reduced to 6", as on all S&Ws. Designation changed to Model 28 in 1957. S&W discontinued Model 28 in 1986. **NOTE:** Add 25 percent premium for pre-Model 28. For top dollar, all accessories and registration letter must be present.

NIB	Exc.	V.G.	Good	Fair	Poor
700	625	500	400	325	250

Model 29 (.44 Magnum)

Early 1950s, handgun writers under leadership of Elmer Keith, were in the habit of loading .44 Special cartridge to high performance levels and firing them in existing .44 Hand Ejectors. They urged S&W to produce a revolver strong enough to consistently fire these heavy loads. In 1954, Remington at the request of S&W, produced .44 Magnum cartridge. Cases with .357 Magnum were longer so that they would not fit in chambers of older guns. First .44 Magnum became available for sale in early 1956. First 500 were made with 6.5" barrel; 4" became available later that year. In 1957, model designation was changed to 29 and 8.375" barrel was introduced. Available in blue or nickel-plate. Came standard with all target options. Offered in a fitted wood case. Model 29 is considered by many knowledgeable people to be the finest revolver S&W has ever produced. Older Model 29 revolvers are in a different collector category than most modern S&W revolvers. Early four-screw models can be worth 100 percent premium in excellent condition. These early models were produced from 1956 to 1958. Approximately 6,500 were sold. One must regard these revolvers on a separate basis and have them individually appraised for proper valuation. In 1993, 4" barrel dropped from production.

NIB	Exc.	V.G.	Good	Fair	Poor
2500	2000	1400	1000	400	250

Early 5-Inch Barrel Model 29

Rarest of Model 29s. Total of 500 manufactured in 1958. Collectors are cautioned to exercise care before purchasing one of these rare Model 29 variations.

NIB	Exc.	V.G.	Good	Fair	Poor
9800	8800	7000	5000	4000	2800

Model 629

Simply a stainless steel version of Model 29. Chambered for .44 Magnum. In 2002, offered with HiViz sights.

NIB	Exc.	V.G.	Good	Fair	Poor
700	550	400	300	200	125

Model 629 Classic

This model has additional features that standard Model 629 does not have. Such as: chamfered cylinder, full lug barrel, interchangeable front sights, Hogue combat grips, drilled and tapped frame to accept scope mounts.

NIB	Exc.	V.G.	Good	Fair	Poor
700	550	400	300	200	125

Model 629 Classic DX

Has all of the features of the Model 629 Classic. Introduced in 1991. Plus: two sets of grips and five interchangeable front sights. Available in 6.5" or 8.375" barrel. A 5" barrel option offered in 1992; dropped in 1993.

NIB	Exc.	V.G.	Good	Fair	Poor
750	600	500	400	300	200

Model 629 Mountain Gun

Limited edition 6-shot revolver. Introduced in 1993. Features 4" barrel chambered for .44 Magnum. Built on large N-frame. Made from stainless steel and drilled and tapped for scope mounts. Equipped with Hogue round butt rubber mono-grip. Standard sights are a pinned black ramp front sight and adjustable black rear blade. Weight about 40 oz. Reintroduced in 1999.

NIB	Exc.	V.G.	Good	Fair	Poor
675	450	400	350	300	150

Model 629 Backpacker

A 1994 variation of Model 629. Built on N-frame, with round butt. Cylinders are fluted and chamfered. Barrel length 3", with adjustable rear sight. Finish is stainless steel and Hogue rubber grips are standard. Weight about 40 oz.

NIB	Exc.	V.G.	Good	Fair	Poor
750	600	500	400	300	200

Model 629 Classic Powerport

Introduced in 1996. Offers an integral compensator, with 6.5" full lug barrel. Patridge front sight is pinned and rear sight fully adjustable. Frame drilled and tapped for scope mounts. Synthetic Hogue combat-style grips are standard. Weight about 52 oz.

NIB	Exc.	V.G.	Good	Fair	Poor
700	550	400	300	200	125

Model 31 (.32 Regulation Police)

Same as Model 30, with a square butt. It was known as .32 Regulation Police before 1957. Discontinued.

NIB	Exc.	V.G.	Good	Fair	Poor
—	425	300	200	150	100

Model 31 (.32 Regulation Police Target)

Target model of Regulation Police. RARE! Only 196 of these special variations were produced in 1957. All specifications same as Model 31, except for addition of adjustable sights.

NIB	Exc.	V.G.	Good	Fair	Poor
—	1500	925	750	525	300

Model 32 (.38/.32 Terrier)

Known as Terrier prior to 1957, was introduced in 1936. Essentially a .38 Regulation Police chambered for .38 S&W, with 2" barrel and round butt. Like Model 30 and 31, this revolver was originally built on I-frame, which was changed to J-frame in 1960. The -1 behind model number signifies this change. Offered in blue or nickel-plate. Has a 5-shot cylinder, fixed sights and checkered walnut grips. Discontinued in 1974. **NOTE:** A limited production version with alloy frame and steel cylinder was produced as Model 032. Add 30 percent for this model.

NIB	Exc.	V.G.	Good	Fair	Poor
—	425	300	200	150	100

Model 33 (.38 Regulation Police)

Simply the .38 Regulation Police, with a square butt and 4" barrel. Chambered for .38 S&W. Factory referred to this model as .38-.32 revolver. Also built on small I-frame and later changed to J-frame in 1960. Discontinued in 1974.

Courtesy Mike Stuckslager

NIB	Exc.	V.G.	Good	Fair	Poor
—	425	300	200	150	100

Model 34 (.22/.32 Kit Gun)

Introduced in 1936 as .22-32 Kit Gun. Has a 2" or 4" barrel, round or square butt and adjustable sights. Underwent several modifications before it reached its present form. S&W modernized this revolver in 1953, with addition of a coil mainspring and micro-click sights. Model 34 is built on this improved version. Revolver is a .32 Hand Ejector chambered for .22 rimfire. Built on I-frame until 1960, when changeover to improved J-frame occurred. The -1 behind model number indicates this variation. Offered blued or nickel-plate.

Courtesy Mike Stuckslager

NIB	Exc.	V.G.	Good	Fair	Poor
550	425	300	250	175	100

1946-1952 Production

NIB	Exc.	V.G.	Good	Fair	Poor
1200	1000	850	600	300	200

1953-1991 Production

NIB	Exc.	V.G.	Good	Fair	Poor
700	550	450	350	250	200

Model 35 (.22/.32 Target)

A square-butt, 6" barreled version of .22/32 Hand Ejector. Known prior to 1957 as .22/32 Target. Underwent same changes as Model 34. Discontinued in 1973.

Courtesy Mike Stuckslager

NIB	Exc.	V.G.	Good	Fair	Poor
1000	800	600	400	275	100

AIRLITE SERIES (TITANIUM CYLINDER—ALUMINUM ALLOY FRAME)

Model 317 AirLite

This 8-round revolver introduced in 1997. Chambered for .22 LR cartridge. Fitted with 2" barrel, serrated ramp front sight and fixed rear. Dymondwood boot grips. Produced from carbon, stainless steel and aluminum alloy on a J-frame. Weight about 9.9 oz.

NIB	Exc.	V.G.	Good	Fair	Poor
550	400	375	295	175	100

Model 317 AirLite Kit Gun

This version of Model 317 was introduced in 1998. Fitted with a 3" barrel, with adjustable rear sight. Choice of Dymondwood grips or Uncle Mike's Combat grips. Weight about 12 oz. In 2001, offered with HiViz green dot front sight.

NIB	Exc.	V.G.	Good	Fair	Poor
700	550	425	300	200	150

Model 317 AirLite Ladysmith

Features a 2" barrel and Dymondwood grips. Display case standard. Weight about 10 oz.

NIB	Exc.	V.G.	Good	Fair	Poor
700	550	425	300	200	150

Model 331 AirLite

Chambered for .32 H&R Magnum cartridge on a J-frame. Barrel length 1.875". Exposed hammer offers single-/double-action. Frame aluminum, as is barrel shroud and yoke. Cylinder is titanium. Barrel has a stainless steel liner. Matte finish. Because the revolver is made from aluminum and titanium, it has a two-tone appearance because of the two different materials. Choice of wood or rubber boot grips. Capacity 6 rounds. Weight about: 12 oz. with rubber grip; 11.2 oz. with wood grip. Introduced in 1999.

NIB	Exc.	V.G.	Good	Fair	Poor
700	550	425	300	200	150

Model 332 AirLite

Similar to Model 331 above, with a concealed hammer and double-action configuration. Weight: 12 oz. with rubber grips; 11.3 oz. with wood grips.

NIB	Exc.	V.G.	Good	Fair	Poor
700	550	425	300	200	150

Model 337 AirLite

This model has an aluminum frame, exposed hammer and titanium cylinder. Front sight is black and pinned. Smooth trigger. Cylinder capacity five rounds. Chambered for .38 Special +P ammo. Barrel length 1.875". Wood or rubber grips. Weight about: 11.2 oz. with wood grips; 12 oz. with rubber grips. Introduced in 1999.

NIB	Exc.	V.G.	Good	Fair	Poor
600	450	325	250	175	100

Model 342 AirLite

Similar to Model 340, with double-action-only concealed hammer. Weight: 11.3 oz. with wood grips; 12 oz. with rubber grips. Introduced in 1999.

NIB	Exc.	V.G.	Good	Fair	Poor
700	550	425	300	200	150

Model 325PD

Introduced in 2004. This 6-round large frame revolver chambered for .45 ACP cartridge. Fitted with 2.75" barrel. Wooden grips and HiViz sights. Black oxide finish. Weight about 21.5 oz.

NIB	Exc.	V.G.	Good	Fair	Poor
900	775	600	450	300	150

Model 337 Kit Gun

Similar to Model 337. Fitted with 3" barrel. Adjustable rear sight. Weight about 13.5 oz. In 2001, offered with HiViz green dot front sight.

NIB	Exc.	V.G.	Good	Fair	Poor
650	475	325	250	175	100

Model 337 PD

Similar to Model 337, with matte black finish over aluminum frame. Hogue Bantam grips. Weight 10.7 oz. Introduced in 2000.

NIB	Exc.	V.G.	Good	Fair	Poor
600	450	325	250	175	100

Model 340

Introduced in 2001. Hammerless model features Scandium alloy frame. Fitted with 1.875" barrel. Chambered for .357 Magnum cartridge, with 5-round cylinder. Matte stainless gray finish. Pinned black front sight. Hogue Bantam grips standard. Weight about 12 oz.

NIB	Exc.	V.G.	Good	Fair	Poor
700	550	425	300	200	150

Model 340 PD

Same as Model 340, with gray/black finish. Introduced in 2001.

NIB	Exc.	V.G.	Good	Fair	Poor
750	500	375	275	200	150

Model 342 PD

Similar to Model 337, with matte black finish over aluminum frame. Hogue Bantam grips. Weight about 10.8 oz. Introduced in 2000.

NIB	Exc.	V.G.	Good	Fair	Poor
700	550	425	300	200	150

Model 351PD

This 7-shot revolver chambered for .22 Magnum cartridge. Fitted with 1.875" barrel. Black oxide finish. Rubber grips. HiViz sights. Weight about 10.6 oz.

NIB	Exc.	V.G.	Good	Fair	Poor
625	475	350	225	175	75

Model 360

This J-frame model features a Scandium alloy frame, with exposed hammer and 5-shot cylinder. Fixed sights on a 1.875" barrel. Matte stainless gray finish. Weight about 12 oz. Introduced in 2001.

NIB	Exc.	V.G.	Good	Fair	Poor
700	550	425	300	200	150

Model 360 Kit Gun

This version of M360 is fitted with 3.125" barrel, HiViz green dot front sight and adjustable rear. Weight about 14.5 oz. Introduced in 2001.

NIB	Exc.	V.G.	Good	Fair	Poor
700	550	425	300	200	150

Model 386

Introduced in 2001. This L-frame model features 6-shot cylinder chambered for .357 Magnum cartridge. Fitted with 3.125" barrel, HiViz green dot front sight and adjustable rear. Scandium alloy frame, with matte stainless gray finish. Weight about 18.5 oz. Hogue Batam grips.

NIB	Exc.	V.G.	Good	Fair	Poor
800	675	500	400	300	200

Model 386 PD

Same as above, with gray/black finish and 2.5" barrel, red ramp front sight and adjustable rear. Weight about 17.5 oz.

NIB	Exc.	V.G.	Good	Fair	Poor
800	675	500	400	300	200

Model 386 Sc/S

Single-/double-action L-frame revolver in .38/.357 Magnum. 7-shot cylinder, 2.5" barrel, Patridge front sight, adjustable rear, Scandium/alloy frame, matte black finish, rubber grips. Introduced 2007.

NIB	Exc.	V.G.	Good	Fair	Poor
750	600	475	350	250	175

Model 386 XL Hunter

Single-/double-action L-frame revolver chambered in .357 Magnum. Features 6" full-lug barrel, 7-round cylinder, Hi-Viz fiber optic front sight, adjustable rear, Scandium frame, stainless steel cylinder, black matte finish, synthetic grips.

NIB	Exc.	V.G.	Good	Fair	Poor
750	625	550	465	350	150

Model 396 Mountain Lite

L-frame revolver chambered for .44 Special cartridge. Fitted with 5-round titanium cylinder and aluminum alloy frame. Barrel length 3". Has green HiViz front sight and adjustable rear. Introduced in 2000. Weight about 19 oz.

NIB	Exc.	V.G.	Good	Fair	Poor
750	600	475	350	250	175

Model 242

Medium frame revolver chambered for .38 Special +P cartridge. Semi-concealed hammer and 2.5" barrel. Pinned black ramp front sight. Black rubber boot grips. Seven-round cylinder. Matte alloy and titanium finish. Weight about 19 oz. Introduced in 1999. Discontinued.

NIB	Exc.	V.G.	Good	Fair	Poor
550	450	300	225	175	75

Model 296

Also a medium frame revolver chambered for .44 Special cartridge. Fitted with 2.5" barrel. Concealed hammer. Cylinder capacity 5 rounds. Weight about 19 oz. Introduced in 1999.

NIB	Exc.	V.G.	Good	Fair	Poor
700	550	425	300	200	150

Model 586

Six-/seven-shot double-action revolver (L-frame). Chambered for .357 Magnum cartridge. It will also chamber and fire .38 Special cartridges. Available with 2.5", 3", 4", 5", 6" and 8.375" barrel lengths. Blued frame and cylinder, adjustable sights, walnut Magna or rubber grips.

NIB	Exc.	V.G.	Good	Fair	Poor
550	425	300	200	150	100

Model 686

Six-/seven-shot double-action revolver (L-frame). Chambered for .357 Magnum cartridge. It will also chamber and fire .38 Special cartridges. Available with 2.5", 3", 4", 5", 6" and 8.375" barrel lengths. Stainless steel frame and cylinder, adjustable sights, walnut Magna or rubber grips. Introduced in 1980. Performance Center also made a limited number of 686s in .38 Super for competitive shooters. **NOTE:** Add 50% for Super.

NIB	Exc.	V.G.	Good	Fair	Poor
700	550	425	300	200	150

Model 329PD

Chambered for .44 Magnum cartridge. Fitted with a 4" barrel. Large Scandium frame, with matte black finish. Orange dot front sight and ad-justable rear. Cylinder capacity 6 rounds. Wood or rubber grips. Weight about 26.5 oz. Introduced in 2003.

NIB	Exc.	V.G.	Good	Fair	Poor
800	675	500	400	300	200

Model 610 (2007 Reintroduction)

This N-frame model chambered for 10mm cartridge. Fitted with a variety of barrel lengths. Adjustable rear sight. Six-round non-fluted cylinder. Hogue rubber combat grips. Stainless steel finish. Weight about 50 oz. for 4" model. Reintroduced in 2007.

NIB	Exc.	V.G.	Good	Fair	Poor
750	600	475	350	250	175

Model 36 (.38 Chief's Special)

Known as Chief's Special. Introduced in 1950. Built on J-frame. Chambered for .38 Special cartridge. Holds 5-shots. Has a 2" or 3" barrel. Initially offered in a round butt. In 1952, a square-butt version was released. Finished in blue or nickel-plate, with checkered walnut grips. A 3" heavy barrel was first produced in 1967, and became standard in 1975. The 2" barrel dropped from production in 1993.

NIB	Exc.	V.G.	Good	Fair	Poor
575	375	275	200	150	100

Model 36LS (.38 Ladysmith)

Similar to Model 36, with exception only offered with 2" barrel. Rosewood grips and soft carrying case, standard. Weight 20 oz.

NIB	Exc.	V.G.	Good	Fair	Poor
625	450	300	200	150	100

Model 36 (Chief's Special Target)

Since 1955, a limited number of Chief's Specials with adjustable sights have been manufactured. Offered with 2" or 3" barrels, round or square butts and blue or nickel-plated. Between 1957 and 1965, these target models were stamped Model 36 on the yoke. Revolvers manufactured between 1965 and model discontinuance in 1975, were marked Model 50. This is a very collectible revolver. A total of 2,313 of these special target models were sold in various model designations. Some are more rare than others.

Courtesy W.P. Hallstein III and son Chip

NIB	Exc.	V.G.	Good	Fair	Poor
—	775	575	300	200	125

Model 37

Introduced in 1952 as Chief's Special Airweight. Initially had an alloy frame and cylinder. In 1954, following many complaints regarding damaged revolvers, cylinders were made of steel. Barrel lengths, finishes and grip options on Airweight are the same as on standard Chief Special. In 1957, Model 37 designation was adopted. These early alloy frame and cylinder revolvers were designed to shoot only standard velocity .38 Special cartridges. Use of high velocity ammunition was not recommended by the factory. **NOTE:** All 1998 and later production models were rated for +P ammunition.

NIB	Exc.	V.G.	Good	Fair	Poor
575	375	275	200	150	100

Model 637

Same as model above, with aluminum frame and stainless steel finish. **NOTE:** Current production models are now rated for +P ammunition.

NIB	Exc.	V.G.	Good	Fair	Poor
575	375	275	200	150	100

Model 637 Carry Combo

As above, but supplied with Kydex carry holster. Introduced in 2004.

NIB	Exc.	V.G.	Good	Fair	Poor
575	375	275	200	150	100

Model 637 Power Port Pro Series

Aluminum J-frame revolver, with stainless steel cylinder. Chambered for .38 Special (5-shots). 2.125" ported black stainless barrel. Introduced 2008. Dealer sets pricing.

NIB	Exc.	V.G.	Good	Fair	Poor
575	375	275	200	150	100

Model 637CT

Same as Model 637, with Crimson Trace lasergrips.

NIB	Exc.	V.G.	Good	Fair	Poor
650	575	375	275	200	100

Model 38 (Airweight Bodyguard)

Introduced in 1955 as Airweight Bodyguard. This was a departure from S&W's usual procedure in that the alloy-framed version came first. Chambered for .38 Special and available with 2" barrel standard. Although a 3" barrel was offered, it is rarely encountered. Frame of Bodyguard is extended to conceal and shroud the hammer, but at the same time allows hammer to be cocked by the thumb. This makes this model an ideal pocket revolver, as it can be drawn without catching on clothing. Available blue or nickel-plated, with checkered walnut grips. **NOTE:** All 1998 and later production models were rated for +P ammunition.

NIB	Exc.	V.G.	Good	Fair	Poor
525	350	225	175	125	100

Model 638

Same as model above, with aluminum frame and stainless steel finish. **NOTE:** Current production models now rated for +P ammunition.

NIB	Exc.	V.G.	Good	Fair	Poor
475	375	300	225	175	125

Model 49 (Bodyguard)

Introduced in 1959. Identical in configuration to Model 38, except frame is made of steel.

NIB	Exc.	V.G.	Good	Fair	Poor
—	575	450	300	250	200

Model 649 (Bodyguard Stainless)

Stainless steel version of Model 49. Introduced in 1985. Also available in .357 Magnum. As of 1998, offered in .38 Special-only version.

NIB	Exc.	V.G.	Good	Fair	Poor
500	350	225	200	175	125

Model 40 (aka Model 42) Centennial

Introduced in 1952 as Smith & Wesson's 100th Anniversary and appropriately called "Centennial Model". A Safety Hammerless design. Built on J-frame. Features a fully concealed hammer and grip safety. Chambered for .38 Special cartridge. Offered with 2" barrel blued or nickel plate. Grips are checkered walnut. Centennial discontinued in 1974.

Courtesy Mike Stuckslager

NIB	Exc.	V.G.	Good	Fair	Poor
625	550	375	225	150	100

Model 42—Airweight Centennial

Identical in configuration to Model 40, except furnished with an aluminum alloy frame. Discontinued in 1974. Editors Note: First 37 Model 42s were manufactured with aluminum alloy cylinders. They weigh 11.250 oz., compared to 13 oz. for standard model. Balance of Model 42 production was with steel cylinders. **NOTE:** Add 300 percent for extremely rare aluminum alloy cylinder variation.

NIB	Exc.	V.G.	Good	Fair	Poor
450	400	325	200	150	100

Model 640 Centennial

Stainless steel version of Model 40. Furnished with 2" or 3" barrel. Both frame and cylinder are stainless steel. The 3" barrel no longer offered as of 1993. As of 1998, also offered in .38 Special-only version.

NIB	Exc.	V.G.	Good	Fair	Poor
500	375	250	200	150	100

Model 640 Centennial .357 Magnum

Introduced in 1995. This version of Model 640 chambered for .357 cartridge. Fitted with 2.125" barrel. Stainless steel, with a fixed notch rear sight and pinned black ramp front sight. Length 6.75". Weighs 25 oz.

NIB	Exc.	V.G.	Good	Fair	Poor
525	400	250	200	150	100

Model 642 Centennial Airweight

Identical to Model 640, with exception of a stainless steel cylinder and aluminum alloy frame. Furnished with 2" or 2.5" barrel. Discontinued in 1992. Replaced by Model 442, which was introduced in 1993. This model reintroduced in 1996. **NOTE:** Current production models now rated for +P ammunition.

NIB	Exc.	V.G.	Good	Fair	Poor
450	300	250	200	150	100

Model 642CT (Crimson Trace)

As above, fitted with Crimson Trace laser grips. Weight about 15 oz. Introduced in 2004.

NIB	Exc.	V.G.	Good	Fair	Poor
650	575	375	275	200	100

Model 642LS Ladysmith

Similar to Model 642. Fitted with smooth combat wood grips and softside carry case. **NOTE:** Current production models now rated for +P ammunition.

NIB	Exc.	V.G.	Good	Fair	Poor
575	450	325	275	175	100

Model 642 PowerPort Pro Series

Similar to Model 642, with gray aluminum frame and black stainless ported barrel. Dealer sets pricing. Introduced 2008.

NIB	Exc.	V.G.	Good	Fair	Poor
575	450	325	275	175	100

Model 631

Chambered for .32 Magnum cartridge. Fitted with 2" (fixed sights); 4" (adjustable sights) barrel. Stainless steel finish. Weight 22 oz., with 23" barrel. Produced in 1990.

NIB	Exc.	V.G.	Good	Fair	Poor
650	575	375	275	200	100

Model 631 Lady Smith

Similar to above model, with rosewood grips and laser etched. Fitted with 2" barrel.

NIB	Exc.	V.G.	Good	Fair	Poor
650	575	375	275	200	100

Model 632 Centennial

Similar to other Centennial models, but chambered for .32 H&R Magnum cartridge. Standard with 2" barrel, stainless steel cylinder and aluminum alloy frame. Dropped from product line in 1993.

NIB	Exc.	V.G.	Good	Fair	Poor
650	575	375	275	200	100

Model 632 PowerPort Pro Series

J-frame revolver chambered in .327 Federal Magnum. Six-shot cylinder, 3" full-lug ported barrel with full-length extractor. Pinned, serrated front sight, adjustable rear. Synthetic grips. Stainless steel frame and cylinder.

NIB	Exc.	V.G.	Good	Fair	Poor
775	650	495	350	250	175

Models 637 CT/638 CT/642 CT

Similar to Models 637, 638 and 642, with Crimson Trace Laser Grips. Suggested retail price $920.

Model 042 Centennial Airweight

Produced in 1992, but not catalogued. Chambered for .38 Special. Fitted with 2" barrel. Frame is alloy. Marked "MOD 042". No grip safety. Blued finish. Weight about 16 oz. Supposedly a reworked Model 642 "blemish gun" distributed through a national wholesaler.

NIB	Exc.	V.G.	Good	Fair	Poor
650	575	375	275	200	100

Model 442 Centennial Lightweight

This 5-shot revolver chambered for .38 Special. Equipped with 2" barrel, aluminum alloy frame and carbon steel cylinder. Has a fully concealed hammer. Weight 15.8 oz. Front ramp sight serrated and rear sight a fixed square notch. Rubber combat grips from Michael's of Oregon are standard. Finish blue/black or satin nickel. Introduced in 1993. **NOTE:** Current production models now rated for +P ammunition.

NIB	Exc.	V.G.	Good	Fair	Poor
400	300	250	200	150	100

Model 442/642/640/632 Pro Series

Double-action only J-frame, with concealed hammers. Chambered in .38 Special +P (442 & 642), .357 Magnum (640) or .327 Federal (632). Features include 5-round cylinder, matte stainless steel frame, fixed sights or dovetail night sights (632, 640), synthetic grips, cylinder cut for moon clips (442, 642, 640). Suggested retail price $640 (standard) to $916 (night sights).

Model 438

J-frame double-action-only revolver chambered in .38 Special +P. Five-shot cylinder, 1.87" barrel, fixed front and rear sights, synthetic grips. Aluminum alloy frame, stainless steel cylinder. Matte black finish throughout.

NIB	Exc.	V.G.	Good	Fair	Poor
575	450	325	275	175	100

Model 940

Styled like other Centennial models. Chambered for 9mm Parabellum cartridge. Has stainless steel cylinder and frame. Furnished with 2" or 3" barrel. The 3" barrel version dropped from production in 1993.

NIB	Exc.	V.G.	Good	Fair	Poor
700	550	425	300	200	150

Model 43 (.22/.32 Kit Gun Airweight)

Built on J-frame. Chambered for .22 rimfire. Offered in round or square butt, with checkered walnut grips. Has 3.5" barrel, adjustable sights and blued or nickel-plated. Frame made of aluminum alloy. Except for this, identical to Model 34 or .22/.32 Kit Gun. This model has a rare 2" barrel configuration as well as .22 WRM. Introduced in 1954; discontinued in 1974.

Courtesy Mike Stuckslager

NIB	Exc.	V.G.	Good	Fair	Poor
650	575	375	275	200	100

Model 51 (.22/.32 Kit Gun Magnum)

Simply Model 34, chambered for .22 Win. Magnum rimfire. First introduced in 1960, beginning with serial number 52637. Available in both round and square butt, with round butt variation having a total production of only 600. Model 51 discontinued in 1974.

NIB	Exc.	V.G.	Good	Fair	Poor
—	675	400	250	200	125

Model 651

Stainless steel version of Model 51. .22 Magnum Kit Gun manufactured between 1983 and 1987.

NIB	Exc.	V.G.	Good	Fair	Poor
—	675	400	250	200	125

Model 73

Produced in about 1973. Built on a special "C" size frame. Cylinder holds 6 rounds. Chambered for .38 Special cartridge. Fitted with 2" barrel. Total of 5,000 built. All but 20 were destroyed. An extremely rare S&W revolver. Marked "MOD 73" on yoke.

Courtesy Jim Supica, Old Town Station

NIB	Exc.	V.G.	Good	Fair	Poor
8500	—	—	—	—	—

Model 45 (Post Office)

A special purpose K-frame Military & Police Model. Chambered for .22 rimfire. Designed as a training revolver for police departments and U.S. Postal Service. Manufactured in limited quantities between 1948 and 1957. In 1963, production abruptly began and ended again. There were 500 of these revolvers released on a commercial basis, but they are rarely encountered.

NIB	Exc.	V.G.	Good	Fair	Poor
1250	800	650	450	300	100

Model 48 (K-22 Masterpiece Magnum)

Introduced in 1959. Identical to Model 17 or K-22, except chambered for .22 WRM cartridge. Offered in 4", 6" and 8.375" barrel lengths. Blued finish. Discontinued in 1986.

NIB	Exc.	V.G.	Good	Fair	Poor
700	500	275	225	150	100

Model 53 (Magnum Jet)

Introduced in 1961. Chambered for .22 Jet, a Remington cartridge. Barrel lengths 4", 6" and 8.375". Finish blued. Sights were adjustable. Furnished with cylinder inserts that would allow .22 rimfire cartridges to be fired. Frame had two firing pins. Approximately 15,000 produced before it was discontinued in 1974. Price includes guns with individual chambered inserts. **NOTE:** Add $150 for auxiliary .22 LR cylinder.

NIB	Exc.	V.G.	Good	Fair	Poor
1500	750	450	350	250	200

Model 57

Introduced in 1964. Chambered for .41 Magnum cartridge. Built on N-frame. Offered in 4", 6" and 8.375" barrel lengths. Blued frame and adjustable sights. Model designations are: 57-1 1982; 57-2 1988; 57-3 1990; 57-4 1993. **NOTE:** Add 25 percent for nickel finish; 100 percent premium for pre-1969 model with "S" serial number prefix.

NIB	Exc.	V.G.	Good	Fair	Poor
750	600	500	400	300	200

Model 657

A stainless steel version of Model 57. Introduced in 1980. Still in production. In 2001, this model reintroduced again with 7.5" barrel, with pinned front sight and adjustable rear sight. Hogue rubber combat grips. Weight about 52 oz.

NIB	Exc.	V.G.	Good	Fair	Poor
670	525	425	295	200	150

Model 56 (KXT-38 USAF)

Introduced in 1962. A 2" heavy barrel built on the K-frame. Chambered for .38 Special. Marked "U.S." on backstrap. Total of 15,205 produced. Discontinued in 1964. Most were reportedly destroyed by the Air Force.

NIB	Exc.	V.G.	Good	Fair	Poor
5500	4250	3000	2000	1250	800

Model 58

Chambered for .41 Magnum and fitted with fixed sights. Offered in blued or nickel finish, with 4" barrel. Checkered walnut grips are standard. Introduced in 1964.

NIB	Exc.	V.G.	Good	Fair	Poor
1100	650	450	300	225	125

Model 547

Introduced in 1980. Chambered for 9mm cartridge. Offered with 3" or 4" barrel. Finish is blued. Discontinued.

NIB	Exc.	V.G.	Good	Fair	Poor
650	475	375	275	200	125

Model 460 XVR

Introduced in 2005. Chambered for .460 S&W Magnum, which has the highest muzzle velocity of any production handgun. Fitted with 8.375" barrel, with interchangeable compensators. Frame size extra large. Capacity 5 rounds. Adjustable sights, with Hi-Viz front sight. Finger groove grips. Satin stainless finish. Weight about 72.5 oz. **NOTE:** Add $135 for 4" barrel model.

NIB	Exc.	V.G.	Good	Fair	Poor
1300	1000	800	600	400	300

Model 460V

X-frame double-action trigger and 5" barrel in .460 S&W Magnum caliber. Also accepts .454 Casull and .45 Colt. Sorbothane recoil-reducing grip, interchangeable muzzle compensator. 5-shot, stainless with satin finish. Weight 62.5 oz. Introduced 2006.

NIB	Exc.	V.G.	Good	Fair	Poor
1000	875	750	600	400	300

Model 500

Introduced in 2003. Chambered for .500 S&W Magnum cartridge. Fitted with 8.375" barrel, with compensator. Built on the X-frame. Cylinder holds 5 rounds. Stainless steel frame and barrel. Interchangeable front blade sight and adjustable rear. K-frame size Hogue grips. Weight about 72.5 oz. In 2004, offered with a 4" barrel, with compensator. Weight about 56 oz. Introduced in 2008, 6.5" model. **NOTE:** Add $135 for 4" barrel model.

S&W Model 500 with 4" barrel

NIB	Exc.	V.G.	Good	Fair	Poor
1000	875	750	600	400	300

Model 60

Introduced in 1965. Similar to Model 36, but in stainless steel. Offered with a 2" barrel, with fixed sights, walnut grips and smooth trigger. The 3" barrel version comes with a full underlug, adjustable sights, serrated trigger and rubber grips. Weight about: 2" version 20 oz.; 3" version 25 oz. In 1996, this model offered chambered for .357 Magnum cartridge, with a 2.125" barrel. Weight about 23 oz. This model also offered in .38 Special-only. **NOTE:** Add 50 percent for 2" Model 60s with adjustable sights.

2" Barrel

NIB	Exc.	V.G.	Good	Fair	Poor
450	350	300	200	125	100

3" Barrel

NIB	Exc.	V.G.	Good	Fair	Poor
475	375	350	250	150	100

5" Barrel

Introduced in 2005.

NIB	Exc.	V.G.	Good	Fair	Poor
550	475	375	295	200	125

Model 60LS (LadySmith)

Chambered for .38 Special, with 2" barrel and stainless steel frame and cylinder. A slightly smaller version of Model 60, made for small hands. New version offered in 1996, chambered for .357 Magnum cartridge.

NIB	Exc.	V.G.	Good	Fair	Poor
450	350	300	200	125	100

Model 60 with Hi-Viz Sight

Similar to Model 60, with light-gathering Hi-Viz red dot front sight and adjustable rear. Introduced 2007.

NIB	Exc.	V.G.	Good	Fair	Poor
525	400	300	225	175	100

Model 60 Pro Series

Similar to Model 60, in .38/.357 with night front sights, "high-hold" enforcing walnut grips, 3" barrel and matte stainless finish. Introduced 2008.

NIB	Exc.	V.G.	Good	Fair	Poor
650	475	375	275	200	125

Model 63

Introduced in 1977. Simply Model 34 made of stainless steel.

NIB	Exc.	V.G.	Good	Fair	Poor
500	375	250	225	200	150

Model 64 (Military & Police Stainless)

Stainless steel version of Model 10 M&P. Introduced in 1970. Model 64-1 variation introduced in 1972 and is heavy barrel version.

NIB	Exc.	V.G.	Good	Fair	Poor
500	325	275	225	175	125

Model 65 (.357 Military & Police Heavy Barrel Stainless)

Stainless steel version of Model 13 M&P .357 Magnum. Introduced in 1974.

NIB	Exc.	V.G.	Good	Fair	Poor
425	300	275	225	175	125

Model 66 (.357 Combat Magnum Stainless)

Released in 1970. Stainless steel version of Model 19 or Combat Magnum. Chambered for .357 Magnum. Has adjustable sights, square butt with checkered walnut grips and initially offered with a 4" barrel. In 1974, a 2.5" barrel, round butt version was made available. Also available in a 6" barrel, with all target options until discontinued in 1993. Reintroduced in 2014.

NIB	Exc.	V.G.	Good	Fair	Poor
575	400	250	200	150	125

Model 67 (.38 Combat Masterpiece Stainless)

Introduced in 1972. Stainless steel version of Model 15, with 4" barrel. Chambered for .38 Special cartridge. Model designation changes are as follows: {None} 1972 to 1977; {-1} 1977 to 1988; {-2} 1988 to 1993; {-3} 1993 to present.

NIB	Exc.	V.G.	Good	Fair	Poor
500	300	250	200	150	100

Model 69

Built on the L-frame. A five-shot .44 Magnum, with 4.25" barrel and stainless finish. Sights are Smith & Wesson's classic white-outline adjustable rear and red-ramp front. Grips are synthetic, with finger grooves. Introduced in 2014.

NIB	Exc.	V.G.	Good	Fair	Poor
725	625	500	385	275	200

Model 650

Introduced in 1983. Stainless steel model built on a J-frame, with 3" heavy barrel. Chambered for .22 WRM. Has a round butt and fixed sights. Discontinued in 1988.

NIB	Exc.	V.G.	Good	Fair	Poor
600	450	250	175	125	100

Model 651

This J-frame model introduced in 1983. Chambered for .22 WRM. Fitted with a 4" barrel. Stainless steel finish and adjustable sights. Designation changes are: {None} 1983 to 1988; {-1} 1988 to 1990; {-2} 1988 to 1990.

NIB	Exc.	V.G.	Good	Fair	Poor
575	400	250	200	150	100

Model 686 Powerport

Introduced in 1995. This version of Model 686 features 6" full lug barrel, with integral compensator. Frame drilled and tapped for scope mounts. Hogue grips are furnished as standard.

NIB	Exc.	V.G.	Good	Fair	Poor
650	550	450	400	300	200

Model 686 Plus Mountain Gun

Fitted with 4" tapered barrel and chambered for .357 Magnum cartridge. Has adjustable rear sights. Hogue rubber grips are standard. Stainless steel finish. Weight about 44 oz.

NIB	Exc.	V.G.	Good	Fair	Poor
650	475	450	400	300	200

Model 686 Magnum Plus

Offered for the first time in 1996. Features a 7-shot cylinder and available with 2.5", 4" or 6" barrel lengths. Fitted with red ramp front sight and fully adjustable rear. Frame drilled and tapped for scope mounts. Hogue synthetic grips are standard. Stainless steel is satin finished. Weight about 45 oz.

NIB	Exc.	V.G.	Good	Fair	Poor
625	500	450	400	300	200

Model 686—5" Barrel

A .357 Magnum stainless steel model. Fitted with a 5" barrel, with HiViz front sight and adjustable rear. Cylinder holds 7 rounds. Cocobolo wood grips. Weight about 41 oz. Introduced in 2004.

NIB	Exc.	V.G.	Good	Fair	Poor
575	475	395	300	200	100

Model 686 Plus

Single-/double-action L-frame revolver in .38/.357 Magnum. 7-shot cylinder, 3" barrel, Patridge front sight, adjustable rear, stainless finish, rubber grips. Introduced 2007.

NIB	Exc.	V.G.	Good	Fair	Poor
600	550	450	400	300	200

Model 686 Plus Pro Series

Single-/double-action L-frame revolver chambered in .357 Magnum. Features include 5" barrel, with tapered underlug, 7-round cylinder, satin stainless steel frame and cylinder, synthetic grips, interchangeable and adjustable sights. From S&W Performance Center.

NIB	Exc.	V.G.	Good	Fair	Poor
750	650	500	400	300	200

Model 929

Built on the N-frame, this is an 8-shot 9mm revolver. Used by Smith & Wesson competitive shooter Jerry Miculek. Barrel length 6.5". Adjustable rear and Patridge front sight. From S&W Performance Center.

NIB	Exc.	V.G.	Good	Fair	Poor
975	800	650	500	400	250

Model M986

From S&W Performance Center, this 9mm is built on the L-frame, with 7-shot cylinder. Designed for use with moon clips. Barrel length 5". Sights are adjustable rear and Patridge style front.

NIB	Exc.	V.G.	Good	Fair	Poor
975	800	650	500	400	250

Model M&P R8

An 8-shot .357/.38 Special revolver, built on Smith & Wesson's N-frame. Has a 5" barrel and Scandium alloy frame. Weight 36 oz. Sights are adjustable V-notch rear and interchangeable-dot front. Other features include an accessory rail and synthetic grips, with finger grooves. From S&W Performance Center.

NIB	Exc.	V.G.	Good	Fair	Poor
1125	975	800	600	350	250

Model 619

Chambered for .357 Magnum cartridge. Fitted with 4" two-piece semi-lug barrel, with fixed sights. Stainless steel frame and barrel. Capacity 7 rounds. Medium frame. Weight about 37.5 oz. Rubber grips. Introduced in 2005.

NIB	Exc.	V.G.	Good	Fair	Poor
575	475	395	300	200	100

Model 620

Similar to model above, with a 4" barrel, with adjustable rear sight and red ramp front. Weight about 37.9 oz. Introduced in 2005.

NIB	Exc.	V.G.	Good	Fair	Poor
600	550	450	400	300	200

Model 3 Schofield

Reintroduction of famous Schofield revolver in 2000. Single-action top-break model chambered for .45 S&W cartridge. Barrel length 7". Frame and barrel are blue while hammer and trigger are case-hardened. Sights are fixed rear notch and half moon post front. Walnut grips. Weight 40 oz. In 2002, offered in 7" nickel version as well as 5" blue and 5" nickel configuration.

NIB	Exc.	V.G.	Good	Fair	Poor
1750	1400	1050	800	500	300

HERITAGE SERIES REVOLVERS

These revolvers are built by S&W Performance Center and produced for Lew Horton Distributing Co. Each model similar in appearance to original, but has modern internal features. These handguns are produced in limited runs from 100 units to 350 units.

Model 1917

Chambered for .45 ACP cartridge. Fitted with a 5.5" heavy tapered barrel. High-profile front blade sight, with fixed rear. Checkered service grips, with lanyard ring. Offered in blue, case colored or military finish. Shipped in a S&W collectible box. **NOTE:** Add $60 for case color finish.

NIB	Exc.	V.G.	Good	Fair	Poor
900	775	600	450	300	150

Model 15

Chambered for .38 S&W Special. Fitted with 4" barrel. Grips are S&W checkered target. Adjustable rear sight. Offered in nickel or color case-hardened.

NIB	Exc.	V.G.	Good	Fair	Poor
800	675	550	400	250	125

Model 15 McGivern

Similar to above model, but fitted with 5" barrel and checkered diamond grips. Engraved sideplate of McGivern's speed record. Blue finish.

NIB	Exc.	V.G.	Good	Fair	Poor
900	775	600	450	300	150

Model 17

Chambered for .22-caliber cartridge. Fitted with 6" barrel, Patridge front sight and adjustable rear. Four-screw sideplate. Diamond checkered S&W walnut grips. Blue or case colored finish. **NOTE:** Add $30 for case colored finish.

NIB	Exc.	V.G.	Good	Fair	Poor
800	675	550	400	250	125

Model 24

Chambered for .44 Special cartridge. Fitted with a 6.5" tapered barrel. McGivern gold-bead front sight, with adjustable rear. Four-screw sideplate, chamfered charge holes, checkered diamond grips. **NOTE:** Add $60 for case colored finish.

NIB	Exc.	V.G.	Good	Fair	Poor
900	775	600	450	300	150

Model 25

Similar to Model 24, but chambered for .45 Colt cartridge. Blue or case colored finish. **NOTE:** Add $30 for case colored finish.

NIB	Exc.	V.G.	Good	Fair	Poor
900	775	600	450	300	150

Model 29

Similar to Model 24 and Model 25, but chambered for .44 Magnum cartridge. Oversized wood grips. Blue or nickel finish. Was to be produced in 2002 only. Serial numbers begin with "DBW2005".

NIB	Exc.	V.G.	Good	Fair	Poor
900	775	600	450	300	150

CLASSIC SERIES

Model 14 Classic

Recreation of vintage Model 14 revolver, chambered in .38 Special +P. Six-shot cylinder, 6" barrel with pinned Patridge front sight and micro-adjustable rear. Carbon steel frame. Cylinder with blued finish. Weight 34.5 oz.

NIB	Exc.	V.G.	Good	Fair	Poor
800	675	525	400	275	150

Model 14 Classic (nickel)

Same as above, with nickel finish. Discontinued.

NIB	Exc.	V.G.	Good	Fair	Poor
900	775	600	500	375	200

Model 15 Classic

Identical to Model 14 Classic, except with 4" barrel.

NIB	Exc.	V.G.	Good	Fair	Poor
800	675	525	400	275	150

Model 17 Masterpiece Classic

Recreation of K-22 Masterpiece in .22 LR. Blue finish, 6" barrel, adjustable rear sight and wood grips.

NIB	Exc.	V.G.	Good	Fair	Poor
850	725	550	400	275	150

Model 36 Classic

Replica of vintage Model 36 Chief's Special in .38 Special. Five-shot cylinder. Carbon steel frame, 1.875" or 3" barrel, fixed sights. Blued, case colored or nickel finish. Altamont wood grips. Introduced 2007.

NIB	Exc.	V.G.	Good	Fair	Poor
600	500	400	250	150	100

Model 21 Classic

Replica of vintage Model 21 N-frame revolver in .44 Special. Six-shot cylinder. Carbon steel frame, 4" barrel, fixed sights. Blued, case colored or nickel finish. Altamont wood grips. Introduced 2007.

NIB	Exc.	V.G.	Good	Fair	Poor
900	750	525	400	275	150

Model 22 Classic

Replica of vintage Model 22 N-frame revolver in .45 ACP. Six-shot cylinder. Carbon steel frame, 4" barrel, fixed sights. Blued, case colored or nickel finish. Altamont wood grips. Introduced 2007.

NIB	Exc.	V.G.	Good	Fair	Poor
900	750	525	400	275	150

Model 22 of 1917 Classic

Similar to Model 22 Classic, without ejector rod shroud and with lanyard ring on butt. Replica of U.S. Army WWI-era revolver. Introduced 2007.

NIB	Exc.	V.G.	Good	Fair	Poor
900	700	525	400	275	150

Model 24 Classic

In .44 Special, with 6.5" barrel. Wood grips, with square butt and adjustable rear sight.

NIB	Exc.	V.G.	Good	Fair	Poor
850	725	550	400	275	150

Model 25 Classic

Identical to Model 24 Classic, except chambered for .45 Colt.

NIB	Exc.	V.G.	Good	Fair	Poor
850	725	550	400	275	150

Model 27 Classic

Reintroduction of vintage Model 27. Available in blue or bright nickel finish. 6.5" barrel, walnut grips. Introduced 2008. **NOTE:** Add 25 percent for 75th Anniversary Model.

NIB	Exc.	V.G.	Good	Fair	Poor
900	700	525	400	275	150

Model 29 Classic

Replica of original (1956) Model 29 N-frame revolver in .44 Magnum. Six-shot cylinder. Carbon steel frame, 6.5" barrel, fixed sights. Blued or nickel finish, with/without engraving. Altamont wood grips. Introduced 2007.

NIB	Exc.	V.G.	Good	Fair	Poor
900	775	600	500	375	200

Model 10 Classic

Single-/double-action K-frame revolver chambered in .38 Special. Features include bright blue steel frame and cylinder, checkered wood grips, 4" barrel, adjustable Patridge-style sights.

NIB	Exc.	V.G.	Good	Fair	Poor
600	500	450	375	275	150

Model 40/42 Centennial Classic

Recreation of 5-shot J-frame model. Designed for double-action-only operation, with fully concealed hammer and grip safety. Model 40 has a steel frame; weight 19 oz. Model 42 has an alloy frame; weight 13 oz.

NIB	Exc.	V.G.	Good	Fair	Poor
650	550	450	375	300	200

Model 48 Classic

Single-/double-action K-frame revolver chambered in .22 Magnum Rimfire (.22 WMR). Features include bright blue steel frame and cylinder, checkered wood grips, 4" or 6" barrel, adjustable Patridge-style sights.

NIB	Exc.	V.G.	Good	Fair	Poor
750	625	500	400	275	150

MILITARY & POLICE (M&P) REVOLVER SERIES

M&P 340

Double-action-only revolver built on Centennial (hammerless) J-frame. .357 Magnum/.38 Special; 5-shot cylinder; 1.87" barrel with fixed night sights. Matte black finish on Scandium/alloy frame. Introduced 2007.

NIB	Exc.	V.G.	Good	Fair	Poor
700	575	400	250	150	100

M&P 340CT

Similar to above, with Crimson Trace Laser grips. Introduced 2007.

NIB	Exc.	V.G.	Good	Fair	Poor
825	700	600	500	350	175

M&P 360

Double-action-only revolver built on Chief's Special (hammered) J-frame. .357 Magnum/.38 Special; 5-shot cylinder; 1.87" barrel with fixed night sights. Matte black finish on Scandium/alloy frame. Introduced 2007.

NIB	Exc.	V.G.	Good	Fair	Poor
700	575	400	250	150	100

M&P R8

Double-action-only revolver built on large N-frame. .357 Magnum/.38 Special; 8-shot cylinder; 5" barrel, with adjustable Patridge sights with interchangeable inserts. Matte black finish on Scandium/alloy frame. Introduced 2007.

NIB	Exc.	V.G.	Good	Fair	Poor
1100	850	600	500	375	200

Governor

Built on S&W L-frame. This 6-shot revolver can fire .410 shotshells, .45 Colt and .45 ACP (with moon clips) ammunition. Scandium alloy frame, stainless steel cylinder, Tritium night sight, internal security lock and Hogue synthetic grips. Barrel length 2.75"; weight 29.6 oz.; overall length 8.5". Matte black finish. Available with Crimson Trace Laser grips. Introduced in 2011. **NOTE:** Add $200 for Crimson Trace Laser grips.

NIB	Exc.	V.G.	Good	Fair	Poor
650	525	425	365	250	150

SEMI-AUTOMATIC PISTOLS

NOTE: Pistols with S&W factory-installed night sights add $100 to NIB and Exc. prices; S&W factory engraving add $1,000 for Class C (1/3 coverage); $1,250 for Class B (2/3 coverage); $1,500 for Class A (full coverage). See Performance Center section at the end of S&W section for special and limited edition version of many of these models.

Model 39

First double-action semi-automatic pistol produced in the United States. Introduced in 1957. Had an alloy frame and chambered for 9mm Parabellum or .30 Luger. Barrel was 4". Finish blued or nickel, with checkered walnut grips. Rear sight was adjustable. Magazine capacity 8 rounds. Discontinued in 1982. The .30 Luger model is very rare and was mostly sold in Europe. **NOTE:** Add 150 percent for .30 Luger.

NIB	Exc.	V.G.	Good	Fair	Poor
600	450	250	200	150	100

Model 39 Steel Frame

A total of 927 steel frame Model 39s produced. RARE; use caution.

NIB	Exc.	V.G.	Good	Fair	Poor
2500	2000	1500	1200	750	500

Model 59

Introduced in 1971. Similar to Model 39, with a wide grip to hold a double column magazine of 14 rounds. Furnished with black checkered plastic grips. Discontinued in 1982.

NIB	Exc.	V.G.	Good	Fair	Poor
575	500	350	200	150	100

Model 439

Introduced in 1979. Improved version of Model 39. Furnished with adjustable rear sight. Discontinued in 1988.

NIB	Exc.	V.G.	Good	Fair	Poor
600	450	350	325	250	100

Model 639

Stainless steel version of Model 439. Introduced in 1984; discontinued 1988.

NIB	Exc.	V.G.	Good	Fair	Poor
600	450	350	325	250	100

Model 459

Improved-sight version of 15-shot Model 59 9mm pistol. Introduced in 1979; discontinued 1987.

NIB	Exc.	V.G.	Good	Fair	Poor
600	450	350	325	250	100

Model 659

Stainless steel version of Model 459 9mm pistol. Features ambidextrous safety and all other options of Model 459. Introduced in 1982; discontinued 1988.

NIB	Exc.	V.G.	Good	Fair	Poor
550	425	350	300	250	150

Model 539

Yet, another version of Model 439 9mm pistol. Incorporates all features of Model 439, with a steel frame instead of aluminum alloy. Introduced in 1980; discontinued 1983.

NIB	Exc.	V.G.	Good	Fair	Poor
525	400	350	300	250	200

Model 559

This variation of Model 459 9mm pistol, has a steel frame instead of aluminum alloy. Identical in all other respects.

NIB	Exc.	V.G.	Good	Fair	Poor
475	400	350	300	250	200

Model 469

Model 469 brought out in answer to the need for a more concealable high-capacity pistol. Essentially a "Mini" version of Model 459. Chambered for 9mm Parabellum. Detachable 12-round magazine, with finger-grip extension and shortened frame. Barrel 3.5" long; hammer bobbed and does not protrude; safety ambidextrous. Finish matte blue, with black plastic grips. Introduced in 1983; discontinued 1988.

NIB	Exc.	V.G.	Good	Fair	Poor
450	375	325	275	200	150

Model 669

Stainless steel version of Model 469 9mm pistol. All features of Model 469 are incorporated. Model 669 manufactured from 1986 to 1988.

NIB	Exc.	V.G.	Good	Fair	Poor
475	425	350	300	250	200

Model 645

Model 645 is a large-framed, stainless steel double-action pistol. Chambered for .45 ACP cartridge. Has a 5" barrel, adjustable sights and detachable 8-shot magazine. Offered with fixed or adjustable sights. Ambidextrous safety. Grips are molded black nylon. Manufactured between 1985 and 1988.

NIB	Exc.	V.G.	Good	Fair	Poor
600	450	375	325	250	150

Model 745—IPSC

Similar in outward appearance to Model 645, but quite a different pistol. A single-action semi-automatic chambered for .45 ACP cartridge. Frame made of stainless steel. Slide of blued carbon steel. Barrel 5". Detachable magazine holds 8 rounds. Sights are fully adjustable target types. Grips checkered walnut. Introduced in 1986; discontinued 1990.

NIB	Exc.	V.G.	Good	Fair	Poor
775	600	500	400	350	250

TARGET PISTOLS

Model 41

NOTE: Add up to $500 (depending on condition) for full set of steel and aluminum barrel weights; $750 (depending on condition) for .22 Short conversion kit; 400 percent for military marked pistols.

Courtesy John J. Stimson, Jr.

Model 41 barrel types

NIB	Exc.	V.G.	Good	Fair	Poor
1100	850	600	500	325	150

Model 41 (New Model)

Restyled in 1994. Featuring recontoured hardwood stocks, Millet adjustable rear sight, drilled and tapped barrel for scope mounting.

NIB	Exc.	V.G.	Good	Fair	Poor
775	600	500	400	350	250

Model 41-1

Introduced in 1960. Chambered for .22 Short rimfire only. Developed for International Rapid Fire competition. In appearance quite similar to Model 41, except slide and frame made of aluminum alloy in order to lighten it to function with .22 Short cartridge. Not a commercial success like Model 41, so it was discontinued after fewer than 1,000 were manufactured.

Courtesy John J. Stimson, Jr.

Model 41-1 .22 Short with optional weights

NIB	Exc.	V.G.	Good	Fair	Poor
2200	1800	1500	1000	500	300

Model 41 Fiftieth Anniversary Edition

Similar to original Model 41, but machine-engraved with Class A+ coverage. Gold plated borders. Glass-topped presentation case. Introduced 2008. Serial Number Range: FYA0001 - FYA0500.

NIB	Exc.	V.G.	Good	Fair	Poor
1600	1400	1200	900	600	400

Model 46

Lower-cost version of Model 41. Developed for the Air Force in 1959. Appearance essentially same as Model 41, with 7" barrel. Later a 5" barrel introduced and finally in 1964, a heavy 5.5" barrel. This economy target pistol never had the popularity the more expensive Model 41 had. Discontinued in 1968, after approximately 4,000 were manufactured.

Courtesy Mike Stuckslager

NIB	Exc.	V.G.	Good	Fair	Poor
1100	900	800	650	400	200

Model 61 Escort

In 1970, Model 61 was introduced as the only true pocket automatic that S&W produced. Chambered for .22 LR cartridge, with 2.5" barrel and

5-round magazine. Offered blued or nickel finish, with black checkered plastic grips. Dropped from product line in 1974.

NIB	Exc.	V.G.	Good	Fair	Poor
300	225	200	150	100	75

Model 52A

Introduced in 1961. Chambered in .38 AMU caliber for Army marksmanship training. Army rejected the 87 pistols built, so they were released to the public. Letter "A" stamped behind model designation. RARE find. Use caution.

NIB	Exc.	V.G.	Good	Fair	Poor
3750	3000	2500	2000	1200	500

Model 52 (.38 Master)

Introduced in 1961 as a target pistol. Chambered for .38 Special mid-range wadcutter cartridge. Similar in appearance to Model 39, but single-action-only by virtue of a set screw. Fitted with 5" barrel and 5-round magazine. Blued finish, with checkered walnut grips. About 3,500 produced in this configuration. Discontinued in 1963.

NIB	Exc.	V.G.	Good	Fair	Poor
1000	800	600	500	400	300

Model 52-1

In 1963, this variation featured a true single-action design. Produced until 1971.

NIB	Exc.	V.G.	Good	Fair	Poor
850	725	450	350	300	200

Model 52-2

Introduced in 1971, with a coil spring-style extractor. Discontinued in 1993.

NIB	Exc.	V.G.	Good	Fair	Poor
750	600	475	400	300	200

Model 2214 (The Sportsman)

Semi-automatic pistol chambered for .22 LR. Designed for casual use. Fitted with a 3" barrel. Magazine capacity 8 rounds. Slide blued carbon steel. Frame is alloy. Introduced in 1990; discontinued 1997.

NIB	Exc.	V.G.	Good	Fair	Poor
250	200	150	125	100	50

Model 2206

This .22 LR pistol offered with 4.5" or 6" barrel. Magazine capacity 12 rounds. Adjustable rear sight. Stainless steel frame and slide.

NIB	Exc.	V.G.	Good	Fair	Poor
300	250	175	125	100	50

Model 2206 TGT (Target)

Introduced in 1995. Features selected 6" barrel, bead blasted sighting plane and polished flat side surfaces. Patridge front sight and Millet adjustable rear are standard. Serrated trigger, with adjustable trigger stop and 10-round magazine.

NIB	Exc.	V.G.	Good	Fair	Poor
350	300	250	200	150	100

Model 422 Field

Introduced in 1987. This .22 LR pistol has 4.5" or 6" barrel, with an alloy frame and steel slide. Magazine capacity 10 rounds. Fixed sights and black plastic grips. Finish matte blue.

NIB	Exc.	V.G.	Good	Fair	Poor
350	275	225	125	100	50

Model 422 Target

Same as Field model, with adjustable sights and checkered walnut grips.

NIB	Exc.	V.G.	Good	Fair	Poor
350	275	225	125	100	50

Model 622 Field

Stainless steel version of Model 422 Field.

NIB	Exc.	V.G.	Good	Fair	Poor
400	300	225	150	125	75

Model 622 Target

Stainless steel version of Model 422 Target.

NIB	Exc.	V.G.	Good	Fair	Poor
400	300	225	150	125	75

Model 622VR

Redesigned in 1996. This .22-caliber model features 6" ventilated rib barrel. Fitted with matte black trigger and new trigger guard. Front sight serrated ramp style, with adjustable rear. Weight about 23 oz. Grips are black polymer.

NIB	Exc.	V.G.	Good	Fair	Poor
375	275	200	150	100	75

Model 22A Sport

Introduced in 1997. Features 4", 5.5" or 7" barrel. Chambered for .22 LR cartridge. Magazine capacity 10 rounds. Rear sight adjustable. Grips: two-piece polymer; or two-piece Soft Touch. Frame and slide aluminum alloy and stainless steel. Finish blue. Weight about: 28 oz. 4" model; 32 oz. 5.5" model; 33 oz. 7" model. Prices quoted are for 4" model. In 2001, furnished with Hi-Viz green dot front sight. In 2008, full-camo version introduced. **NOTE:** Add $40 for full-camo version.

NIB	Exc.	V.G.	Good	Fair	Poor
290	200	150	100	75	50

Model 22S Sport

Also introduced in 1997. Similar to above model, with 5.5" and 7" barrel on stainless steel frames. Weight about 41 oz. and 42 oz. respectively. In 2001, furnished with Hi-Viz green dot front sight.

NIB	Exc.	V.G.	Good	Fair	Poor
300	225	175	150	100	50

Model 22A Target

This .22-caliber target pistol has a 10-round magazine. Adjustable rear sight. Target grips, with thumb rest. Bull barrel 5.5". Finish blue. Weight about 39 oz. Introduced in 1997.

NIB	Exc.	V.G.	Good	Fair	Poor
290	200	150	100	75	45

Model 22S Target

Same as above, with stainless steel frame and slide. Weight about 48 oz.

NIB	Exc.	V.G.	Good	Fair	Poor
300	225	175	150	100	50

Model 22A Camo

Introduced in 2004. This .22 LR model features Mossy Oak Break-Up finish. Weight about 39 oz.

NIB	Exc.	V.G.	Good	Fair	Poor
325	250	175	150	100	50

SW22 Victory

A new .22 LR target pistol design, with removable and interchangeable match barrel, fiber-optic adjustable sights, Picatinny rail, textured grips with finger grooves and all stainless construction. Magazine capacity 10 rounds. Two magazines are included. Optional Krytek Highlander camo finish. Available with threaded barrel. Introduced in 2016. **NOTE:** Add $50 for Krytek finish; $20 for threaded barrel.

NIB	Exc.	V.G.	Good	Fair	Poor
350	315	—	—	—	—

Model 3904

In 1989, S&W redesigned the entire line of 9mm semi-automatic handguns. The 3904 is chambered for 9mm Parabellum. Has an 8-shot detachable magazine and 4" barrel with a fixed bushing. Frame is alloy. Trigger guard squared for two-hand hold. Magazine well beveled and grips are one-piece wrap-around made of Delrin. Three-dot sighting system is employed. Discontinued.

NIB	Exc.	V.G.	Good	Fair	Poor
450	400	325	300	275	225

Model 3906

Stainless steel version of Model 3904. Features are the same. Introduced in 1989; discontinued.

NIB	Exc.	V.G.	Good	Fair	Poor
450	400	325	300	275	225

Model 3914

Offered as a slightly smaller alternative to Model 3904. This 9mm pistol has 3.5" barrel, 8-round magazine, blued carbon steel slide and alloy frame.

NIB	Exc.	V.G.	Good	Fair	Poor
525	450	400	350	300	250

Model 3913

Similar to Model 3914, but features a stainless steel slide and alloy frame.

NIB	Exc.	V.G.	Good	Fair	Poor
525	450	400	350	300	250

Model 3914LS

Redesigned Model 3914 that has a more modern appearance. LS refers to LadySmith. Chambered for 9mm cartridge. All other features same as Model 3914, including blued carbon slide and alloy frame.

NIB	Exc.	V.G.	Good	Fair	Poor
525	450	400	350	300	200

Model 3913LS

Identical to Model 3914LS, with exception of stainless steel slide.

NIB	Exc.	V.G.	Good	Fair	Poor
525	450	400	350	300	200

Model 3954

Similar to Model 3914, but offered in double-action-only. Discontinued in 1993.

NIB	Exc.	V.G.	Good	Fair	Poor
525	450	400	350	300	200

Model 915

Introduced in 1993. Chambered for 9mm cartridge. Features 4" barrel, matte blue finish, fixed rear sight and wrap-around rubber grips. Overall length 7.5"; weight about 28 oz.

NIB	Exc.	V.G.	Good	Fair	Poor
400	350	250	200	150	100

Model 5904

A full high capacity 15-shot version of Model 3904. Introduced in 1989. Features slide mounted decocking lever and 4" barrel. Blued carbon steel slide and alloy frame. Discontinued.

NIB	Exc.	V.G.	Good	Fair	Poor
525	450	375	325	275	200

Model 5903

Same caliber and features as Model 5904 and Model 5906, but furnished with stainless steel slide and alloy frame.

NIB	Exc.	V.G.	Good	Fair	Poor
525	450	400	350	300	250

Model 5906

Stainless steel version of Model 5904. Both slide and frame are stainless steel.

NIB	Exc.	V.G.	Good	Fair	Poor
525	450	375	275	200	—

Model 5906 Special Edition

Double-action semi-automatic pistol chambered for 9mm, with 15-round magazine. Frame and slide have a special machine finish. Grips are one-piece wrap-around Xenoy. Front sight is a white dot post. Rear sight a Novak L-Mount Carry, with two white dots. Manual safety/decocking lever and firing pin safety. Introduced in 1993.

NIB	Exc.	V.G.	Good	Fair	Poor
575	450	350	300	250	150

Model 5926

S&W offers a 9mm pistol similar to 5906, with frame mounted decocking lever. Both slide and frame are stainless steel. Discontinued in 1993.

NIB	Exc.	V.G.	Good	Fair	Poor
525	450	375	300	250	150

Model 5946

This 9mm pistol offers the same features as Model 5926, but in a double-action-only model. Hammer configuration is semi-bobbed instead of serrated.

NIB	Exc.	V.G.	Good	Fair	Poor
525	450	400	350	300	250

Model 5967

A 9mm model with M5906 frame and M3914 slide. Has stainless steel frame and blued slide. Novak Lo-Mount fixed sights. Introduced in 1990 and sold through Lew Horton.

NIB	Exc.	V.G.	Good	Fair	Poor
600	475	400	350	300	250

Model 6904

Concealable shortened version of Model 5904. Has 12-shot magazine, fixed sights, bobbed hammer and 3.5" barrel.

NIB	Exc.	V.G.	Good	Fair	Poor
525	450	400	350	300	250

Model 6906

Stainless steel slide and alloy frame, but otherwise similar to M6904.

NIB	Exc.	V.G.	Good	Fair	Poor
525	450	400	350	300	200

Model 6946

Double-action version of Model 6906.

NIB	Exc.	V.G.	Good	Fair	Poor
525	450	400	350	300	200

Model 4003

Chambered for .40 S&W cartridge. Fitted with 4" barrel, 11-round magazine, serrated hammer. Stainless steel slide and alloy frame.

NIB	Exc.	V.G.	Good	Fair	Poor
575	500	400	350	300	200

Model 4004

Identical to Model 4003, except for blue carbon steel slide and alloy frame. Discontinued in 1993.

NIB	Exc.	V.G.	Good	Fair	Poor
575	500	400	350	300	200

Model 4006

Identical to Model 4003, except both slide and frame are stainless steel. This adds 8 oz. to weight of pistol.

NIB	Exc.	V.G.	Good	Fair	Poor
575	500	400	350	300	200

Model 4026

Similar to Model 4006, except has a frame-mounted decocking lever.

NIB	Exc.	V.G.	Good	Fair	Poor
575	500	400	350	300	200

Model 4046

Similar to Model 4006, with double-action-only configuration.

NIB	Exc.	V.G.	Good	Fair	Poor
575	500	400	350	300	250

Model 4013

Compact version of 4000 series. This .40-caliber model features 3.5" barrel, 8-round magazine, stainless steel slide and alloy frame.

NIB	Exc.	V.G.	Good	Fair	Poor
575	500	400	350	300	200

Model 4014

Identical to Model 4013, except for a blued carbon steel slide and alloy frame.

NIB	Exc.	V.G.	Good	Fair	Poor
575	500	400	350	300	200

Model 4053

Identical to Model 4013, except offered in double-action-only configuration.

NIB	Exc.	V.G.	Good	Fair	Poor
575	500	400	350	300	200

Model 4054

Same as Model 4053, except for a blued carbon steel slide and alloy frame. Dropped from S&W product line in 1992.

NIB	Exc.	V.G.	Good	Fair	Poor
575	500	400	300	250	200

Model 411

Introduced in 1993 as a no frills model. Features alloy frame, 4" barrel, matte blue finish, fixed sights and wrap-around rubber grips. Chambered for .40 S&W cartridge, with 11-round magazine. Overall length 7.5"; weight about 29 oz.

NIB	Exc.	V.G.	Good	Fair	Poor
400	350	300	250	200	150

Model 1006

Full-size 10mm pistol, with 5" barrel and 9-round magazine. Choice of fixed or adjustable sights. Both slide and frame are stainless steel.

NIB	Exc.	V.G.	Good	Fair	Poor
675	550	400	350	300	200

Model 4056 TSW

A double-action-only pistol chambered for .40 S&W cartridge. Fitted with 3.5" barrel, with white dot sights. Curved backstrap. Stainless steel and alloy frame. Stainless steel finish. Magazine capacity 9 rounds. Introduced in 1997. Weight about 36 oz.

NIB	Exc.	V.G.	Good	Fair	Poor
700	575	400	325	250	150

Model 1066

Slightly smaller version of Model 1006. Furnished with 4.25" barrel. Discontinued in 1993.

NIB	Exc.	V.G.	Good	Fair	Poor
675	550	400	350	300	200

Model 1076

Identical to Model 1066, except for frame-mounted decocking lever.

NIB	Exc.	V.G.	Good	Fair	Poor
675	550	400	350	300	200

Model 1086

Similar to Model 1066, but offered in double-action-only. Discontinued in 1993.

NIB	Exc.	V.G.	Good	Fair	Poor
650	525	375	300	250	200

Model 1026

Similar to Model 1006, with 5" barrel and frame mounted decocking lever.

NIB	Exc.	V.G.	Good	Fair	Poor
675	550	400	350	300	200

Model 4506

Newly designed double-action .45 ACP pistol. All stainless steel. Has 5" barrel, 8-shot detachable magazine and wrap-around black Delrin grips. Discontinued.

NIB	Exc.	V.G.	Good	Fair	Poor
550	475	400	350	300	250

Model 4505

Identical to Model 4506, except with blued slide and frame.

NIB	Exc.	V.G.	Good	Fair	Poor
550	475	400	350	300	250

Model 4516

Compact version of full size .45-caliber S&W automatics. Furnished with 3.75" barrel and 7-round magazine. Chambered in .45-caliber. Has stainless slide and frame. Discontinued in 1991; reintroduced in 1994.

NIB	Exc.	V.G.	Good	Fair	Poor
550	475	425	375	300	250

Model 4536

Compact version and similar to Model 4616. Offered with decock lever on frame.

NIB	Exc.	V.G.	Good	Fair	Poor
550	475	400	350	300	250

Model 4546

Full size version of Model 4506. Offered in double-action-only.

NIB	Exc.	V.G.	Good	Fair	Poor
550	475	400	350	300	250

Model 4040PD

When introduced in 2003, this was the first Scandium frame S&W pistol. Chambered for .40 S&W cartridge. Fitted with 3.5' barrel. White dot front sight, with Novak Lo Mount rear. Matte black finish. Magazine capacity 7 rounds. Soft rubber grips. Weight about 25.6 oz.

NIB	Exc.	V.G.	Good	Fair	Poor
700	575	400	325	250	150

Model SW1911

Introduced in 2003. Full size pistol chambered for .45 ACP and 9mm Parabelluum cartridges. Fitted with 5" barrel. White dot front sight and

Novak Lo-Mount rear. Stainless steel frame and slide. Checkered black rubber grips. Magazine capacity 8 rounds (9 in 9mm). Weight about 39 oz. In 2005, offered with wood grips and black oxide finish.

NIB	Exc.	V.G.	Good	Fair	Poor
965	750	600	500	375	200

Model SW1911 Adjustable

As above, fitted with adjustable sights. Introduced in 2004.

NIB	Exc.	V.G.	Good	Fair	Poor
850	700	600	500	375	200

Model SW1911Sc

This .45 ACP model fitted with Commander size slide and Scandium frame. Fixed sights. Checkered wood grips. Black oxide finish. Weight about 28 oz. Introduced in 2004.

NIB	Exc.	V.G.	Good	Fair	Poor
900	750	650	550	400	250

Model 1911 PD

This .45 ACP model offered with 4.25" or 5" barrel, with Novak low mount sights. Wood grips. Frame alloy, with black finish. Magazine capacity 8

rounds. Weight about: 28 oz. 4.25" model; 29.5 oz. 5" model.

NIB	Exc.	V.G.	Good	Fair	Poor
850	700	600	500	375	200

Model SW1911 E Series

Full-size 1911-style pistol in .45 ACP caliber. Stainless steel frame and slide, with "fish scale" scalloped slide serrations front and rear. Other features include checkered front strap, mainspring housing, oversized extractor, enlarged ejection port, titanium firing pin and laminated textured wood grips. Available with Crimson Trace Laser grips. Introduced in 2011. **NOTE:** Add 20 percent for Crimson Trace Laser grips; 30 percent for integral accessory rail.

NIB	Exc.	V.G.	Good	Fair	Poor
800	685	575	450	300	150

Model SW1911 DK (Doug Koenig)

Introduced in 2005. This .45 ACP model fitted with 5" stainless steel barrel. Adjustable rear sight, with black blade front. Frame stainless steel, with black carbon steel slide. Wood grips. Magazine capacity 8 rounds. Weight about 41 oz.

NIB	Exc.	V.G.	Good	Fair	Poor
850	700	600	500	375	200

Model SW1911 Pro Series

Similar to Model SW1911, with Novak fiber optic sights, skeletonized trigger and various tactical/performance enhancements. Introduced 2008. Available in .45 ACP or 9mm.

NIB	Exc.	V.G.	Good	Fair	Poor
1100	950	800	600	375	250

Model SW1911 Pro Sub-Compact

Chopped 1911-style semi-automatic pistol. Chambered for .45 ACP. 7+1 capacity, 3" barrel. Wood grips, Scandium frame with stainless steel slide, matte black finish throughout. Overall length 6.9"; weight 26.5 oz.

NIB	Exc.	V.G.	Good	Fair	Poor
950	800	600	400	300	250

TSW SERIES (Tactical Smith & Wesson)

This series is an upgrade of older S&W pistol series, many of which have been discontinued. These pistols come with traditional double-action trigger or double-action-only trigger. All TSW pistols have an equipment rail for mounting lights or lasers. All are marked "TACTICAL S&W" on slide.

3913/3953 TSW

Chambered for 9mm cartridge. Fitted with 3.5" barrel. White dot front sight and Novak Lo-Mount rear. Aluminum alloy frame. Magazine capacity 7 rounds. Weight about 25 oz. Stainless steel finish. The 3913 is traditional double-action; while 3953 double-action-only.

NIB	Exc.	V.G.	Good	Fair	Poor
650	525	475	400	325	125

4013/4053 TSW

Chambered for .40 S&W cartridge. Fitted with 3.5" barrel. White dot front sight and Novak Lo-Mount rear sight. Aluminum alloy frame and stainless steel slide. Magazine capacity 9 rounds. Weight about 27 oz. The 4013 is traditional double-action; while 4053 double-action-only.

NIB	Exc.	V.G.	Good	Fair	Poor
650	525	475	400	325	125

4513/4553 TSW

Chambered for .45 ACP cartridge. Fitted with 3.75" barrel. White dot front sight and Novak Lo-Mount rear. Aluminum alloy frame with stainless steel slide. Magazine capacity 7 rounds. Weight about 29 oz. The 4513 is traditional double-action; while 4553 double-action-only. **NOTE:** Deduct $50 for double-action-only model 4553.

NIB	Exc.	V.G.	Good	Fair	Poor
650	525	475	400	325	125

5903/5906/5943/5946 TSW

These pistols chambered for 9mm cartridge. Fitted with 4" barrel. Fixed sights standard (5903, 5906, 5943, 5946); optional, adjustable and night sights (5906). Offered in traditional double-action (5903, 5906); while double-action-only (5943, 5946). Magazine capacity 10 rounds. Weight about 38 oz. Stainless steel finish. **NOTE:** Add $100 for night sights; $50 for adjustable sights.

NIB	Exc.	V.G.	Good	Fair	Poor
650	525	475	400	325	125

4003/4006/4043/4046 TSW

These models come in the same configurations as 5903 group, except chambered for .40 S&W cartridge. Magazine capacity 10 rounds. Weight about 28 oz. **NOTE:** Add $100 for night sights; $50 for adjustable sights.

NIB	Exc.	V.G.	Good	Fair	Poor
650	525	475	400	325	125

4563/4566/4583/4586 TSW

Similar to above, but chambered for .45 ACP cartridge. Fitted with 4.25" barrel. Same configurations as above. Weight about 31 oz. **NOTE:** Add $100 for night sights; $50 for adjustable sights.

NIB	Exc.	V.G.	Good	Fair	Poor
650	525	475	400	325	125

CHIEF'S SPECIAL SERIES

CS9

Chambered for 9mm cartridge. Fitted with 3" barrel. Has stainless steel slide and aluminum alloy frame. Also available in blued finish. Hogue wrap-around grips standard. Fixed sights. Magazine capacity 7 rounds. Weight about 21 oz.

NIB	Exc.	V.G.	Good	Fair	Poor
550	395	315	250	200	125

CS45

Similar to model above, but chambered for .45 ACP cartridge. Barrel length 3.25". Magazine capacity 6 rounds. Weight about 24 oz.

NIB	Exc.	V.G.	Good	Fair	Poor
575	400	315	250	200	125

CS40

This Chief's Special model chambered for .40 S&W cartridge. Barrel length 3.25". Magazine capacity 7 rounds. Weight about 24 oz.

NIB	Exc.	V.G.	Good	Fair	Poor
550	395	315	250	200	125

CS40 Two-Tone

Same as above, with alloy frame and black slide. Limited edition. Introduced in 2000.

NIB	Exc.	V.G.	Good	Fair	Poor
575	400	315	250	200	125

SIGMA SERIES

SW40F

New pistol introduced in 1994. A departure from traditional S&W pistol. Features stainless steel barrel, carbon steel slide and polymer frame. Offered in .40 S&W and 9mm calibers, with 15- and 17-round capacities.

NIB	Exc.	V.G.	Good	Fair	Poor
450	400	350	300	250	200

Compact SW9C

Same as above, with barrel and slide .5" shorter than full size Sigma. Offered in both .40 S&W and 9mm.

NIB	Exc.	V.G.	Good	Fair	Poor
450	400	350	300	250	200

SW9M

Introduced in 1996. Chambered for 9mm cartridge. Fitted with 3.25" barrel. Magazine capacity 7 rounds. Frame is polymer and slide carbon steel. Height 4.5"; overall length 6.25"; weight 18 oz.

NIB	Exc.	V.G.	Good	Fair	Poor
450	400	350	300	250	200

SW9V

Chambered for 9mm cartridge. Fitted with 4" barrel and 10-round magazine. A traditional double-action. White dot sights are standard. Grips integral to the frame. Stainless steel slide. Satin stainless finish, with gray or black frame. Weight about 25 oz. Introduced in 1997.

NIB	Exc.	V.G.	Good	Fair	Poor
450	400	350	300	250	200

SW9P

Same as Model SW9V, with a ported barrel. Introduced in 2001.

NIB	Exc.	V.G.	Good	Fair	Poor
450	400	350	300	250	200

SW9G

Same as standard SW9, with black Melonite stainless steel slide and NATO green polymer frame. Introduced in 2001.

NIB	Exc.	V.G.	Good	Fair	Poor
450	400	350	300	250	200

SW40V

Same as above, but chambered for .40 S&W cartridge. Weight 25 oz. Introduced in 1997.

NIB	Exc.	V.G.	Good	Fair	Poor
450	400	350	300	250	200

SW40P

Same as Model SW40V, with a ported barrel. Introduced in 2001.

NIB	Exc.	V.G.	Good	Fair	Poor
450	400	350	300	250	200

SW40G

Same as standard SW40, with black Melonite stainless steel slide and NATO green polymer frame. Introduced in 2001.

NIB	Exc.	V.G.	Good	Fair	Poor
450	400	350	300	250	200

SW380

Introduced in 1995. Chambered for .380 ACP cartridge. Barrel length 3"; overall length 5.8"; weight 14 oz. Magazine capacity 6 rounds.

NIB	Exc.	V.G.	Good	Fair	Poor
325	275	200	150	100	75

ENHANCED SIGMA SERIES

Introduced in 1999. Series features shorter trigger pull, slide stop guard, redesigned extractor and ejector. Ejection port is lower. Also fitted with an accessory groove. Checkering pattern is more aggressive.

SW9E

Chambered for 9mm cartridge. Has a 4" barrel, with Tritium sights. Stainless steel slide, with black Melonite finish. Magazine capacity 10 rounds. Weight about 25 oz.

NIB	Exc.	V.G.	Good	Fair	Poor
375	300	225	175	150	75

SW40E

Similar to above, but chambered for .40 S&W cartridge. Weight about 24 oz.

NIB	Exc.	V.G.	Good	Fair	Poor
375	300	225	175	150	75

SW9VE

Chambered for 9mm cartridge. Fitted with a 4" barrel. Fixed sights and stainless steel slide. Weight about 25 oz.

NIB	Exc.	V.G.	Good	Fair	Poor
375	300	225	175	150	75

SW9VE Allied Forces

Similar to SW9VE, with black Melonite slide. Adopted by Afghanistan internal security and border forces. Introduced 2007. **NOTE:** Add 75 percent for "Disaster Ready Kit" (case and emergency supplies).

NIB	Exc.	V.G.	Good	Fair	Poor
575	425	300	225	150	75

SW40VE

Similar to above, but chambered for .40 S&W cartridge. Weight about 24 oz.

NIB	Exc.	V.G.	Good	Fair	Poor
375	300	225	175	150	75

SW40VE Allied Forces

Similar to SW9VE Allied Forces in .40 S&W. Introduced 2007. **NOTE:** Add 75 percent for "Disaster Ready Kit" (case and emergency supplies).

NIB	Exc.	V.G.	Good	Fair	Poor
575	425	300	225	150	75

SW99

Features a polymer frame designed and manufactured in Germany by Walther. Slide and barrel manufactured by S&W in the U.S. Chambered for 9mm or .40 S&W cartridge. Fitted with 4" barrel on 9mm; 4.125" barrel on .40 S&W. Adjustable rear sights. Decocking slide-mounted lever. Barrel and slide stainless steel, with black Melonite finish. Trigger traditional double-action. Magazine capacity 10 rounds. Weight about 25 oz. Introduced in 1999.

NIB	Exc.	V.G.	Good	Fair	Poor
400	350	300	225	150	75

SW99 Compact

Introduced in 2003. Similar to full size SW99, with 3.5" barrel and shorter grip frame. Chambered for both 9mm or .40 S&W cartridge. Stainless steel barrel and slide, with polymer frame. Magazine capacity: 10 rounds 9mm; 8 rounds .40 S&W. Weight about 23 oz.

NIB	Exc.	V.G.	Good	Fair	Poor
400	350	300	225	150	75

SW99 .45 ACP

Same as SW99, but chambered for .45 ACP cartridge. Magazine capacity 9 rounds. Weight about 26 oz. Introduced in 2003.

NIB	Exc.	V.G.	Good	Fair	Poor
500	400	325	250	150	100

SW990L Compact

Introduced in 2005. Chambered for 9mm or .40 S&W cartridge. Barrel length 3.5". Adjustable rear sight, with dot front. Polymer frame. Stainless steel slide, with Melonite finish. Plastic grips. Magazine capacity: 10 rounds 9mm; 8 rounds .40 S&W. Weight about 23 oz.

NIB	Exc.	V.G.	Good	Fair	Poor
475	400	300	225	150	100

SW990L Full Size

Similar to above, but chambered for 9mm, .40 S&W and .45 ACP cartridges. Barrel lengths: 4" for 9mm; 4.125" for .40 S&W model; 4.25" for .45 ACP. Magazine capacity: 16 rounds 9mm; 12 rounds .40 S&W. Weight about 25 oz. Introduced in 2005. **NOTE:** Add $40 for .45 ACP model.

NIB	Exc.	V.G.	Good	Fair	Poor
500	400	325	250	150	100

410

First introduced in 1996. Features an alloy frame, with carbon steel slide. Chambered for .40 S&W cartridge. Barrel length 4". Magazine capacity 10 rounds. Overall length 7.5". Weight about 29 oz.

NIB	Exc.	V.G.	Good	Fair	Poor
450	400	325	250	150	100

410 Two-Tone

Same as Model 410, with alloy finish frame and black slide. Limited edition.

NIB	Exc.	V.G.	Good	Fair	Poor
475	400	325	250	150	100

410S

Introduced in 2003. Stainless steel version of Model 410. Weight about 28 oz.

NIB	Exc.	V.G.	Good	Fair	Poor
475	400	300	250	150	100

457

Introduced in 1996. This .45 ACP model features 3.75" barrel, with rounded trigger guard and double-action. Fitted with single side decocker. Magazine capacity 7 rounds. Overall length 7.25"; weight about 29 oz. Frame is alloy and slide carbon steel. Finish matte black.

NIB	Exc.	V.G.	Good	Fair	Poor
500	400	325	250	150	100

457S

Same as above in stainless steel. Weight about 29 oz. Introduced in 2003.

NIB	Exc.	V.G.	Good	Fair	Poor
500	400	325	250	150	100

908

Introduced in 1996. An economy compact pistol. Chambered for 9mm cartridge. Fitted with 3.5" barrel. Traditional double-action. Fixed rear sight. Magazine capacity 8 rounds. Overall length 6.875"; weight about 26 oz.

NIB	Exc.	V.G.	Good	Fair	Poor
450	400	325	225	150	100

908S

Same as Model 908 in stainless steel. Weight about 24 oz. Introduced in 2003.

NIB	Exc.	V.G.	Good	Fair	Poor
475	425	350	250	150	100

908S Carry Combo

Introduced in 2004. Same as above, with addition of Kydex carry holster.

NIB	Exc.	V.G.	Good	Fair	Poor
500	400	325	250	150	100

909

Introduced in 1995. Chambered for 9mm cartridge. Blue carbon steel slide, aluminum alloy frame and is double-action. Single column magazine and curved backstrap.

NIB	Exc.	V.G.	Good	Fair	Poor
405	350	250	150	100	75

910

Also introduced in 1995. Same as above, with double-column magazine and straight backstrap.

NIB	Exc.	V.G.	Good	Fair	Poor
400	300	200	150	100	75

910S

Introduced in 2003. Stainless steel version of Model 910. Weight about 28 oz.

NIB	Exc.	V.G.	Good	Fair	Poor
400	325	250	150	100	75

MILITARY & POLICE (M&P) SEMI-AUTO SERIES

M&P 9mm

Full-size (M&P) semi-automatic chambered in 9mm. Double-action-only (DAO), striker-fired operation. Capacity 17+1, 4.25" barrel, 6.5 lb. trigger, weight 24.25 oz. Picatinny rail and polymer frame. Optional tritium low-light sights. Introduced 2006.

NIB	Exc.	V.G.	Good	Fair	Poor
500	425	300	225	150	75

M&P 9-JG

Similar to above, with interchangeable palmswell grip panels, including two pink ones. Dealer sets pricing. Introduced 2008.

NIB	Exc.	V.G.	Good	Fair	Poor
475	425	300	225	150	75

M&P 9 Pro Series

Similar to M&P9 and M&P40, with green fiber optic sights and interchangeable palmswell grip panels. Black Melonite finish. Introduced 2008.

NIB	Exc.	V.G.	Good	Fair	Poor
600	475	350	250	150	75

M&P 9L

Similar to M&P9, with 5" barrel. Introduced 2008.

NIB	Exc.	V.G.	Good	Fair	Poor
575	425	300	225	150	75

M&P 40

Full-size semi-automatic chambered in .40 S&W. First of new M&P series. Capacity 15+1, 4.25" barrel, .5 lb. trigger, weight 24.25 oz. Polymer frame and Picatinny rail. Optional tritium low-light sights. Introduced 2006.

NIB	Exc.	V.G.	Good	Fair	Poor
475	425	300	225	150	75

M&P .357 SIG

Full-size (M&P) semi-automatic chambered in .357 Magnum. Capacity 15+1, 4.25" barrel, 6.5 lb. trigger, weight 24.25 oz. Polymer frame and Picatinny rail. Optional tritium low-light sights. Introduced 2006.

NIB	Exc.	V.G.	Good	Fair	Poor
575	425	300	225	150	75

M&P 45

Semi-automatic similar to M&P40 in .45 ACP. Black or Dark Earth Brown finish. Introduced 2007.

NIB	Exc.	V.G.	Good	Fair	Poor
575	425	300	225	150	75

M&P 45 with Thumb Safety

Similar to above, with ambidextrous thumb safety. Introduced 2008.

NIB	Exc.	V.G.	Good	Fair	Poor
585	435	310	235	160	75

M&P 9c

Semi-automatic compact similar to M&P9, with 3.5" barrel, short grip frame and 10+1 or 12+1 capacity. Black Melonite finish. Introduced 2007.

NIB	Exc.	V.G.	Good	Fair	Poor
475	425	300	225	150	75

M&P 40c

Semi-automatic compact similar to M&P9c in .40 S&W. Black Melonite finish. Introduced 2007.

NIB	Exc.	V.G.	Good	Fair	Poor
475	425	300	225	150	75

M&P 357c

Semi-automatic compact similar to M&P40c in .357 SIG. Black Melonite finish. Introduced 2007.

NIB	Exc.	V.G.	Good	Fair	Poor
575	425	300	225	150	75

M&P Shield

Sub-compact version of M&P series in 9mm or .40 S&W. Barrel 3.1", weight 19 oz. Available in two grip lengths, with one additional round in longer magazine. Capacity: 7 or 8 rounds 9mm; 6 or 7 rounds .40 S&W. Introduced in 2012

NIB	Exc.	V.G.	Good	Fair	Poor
400	350	300	250	200	175

M&P 45 Shield

.45 ACP model of the Shield. Has all features of 9mm and .40 S&W versions, plus a more aggressive grip texture, front cocking serrations, 3.3" barrel and weighs about 1.5 oz. more—20.5 oz. Magazine capacity 6+1 or 7+1, with both magazines provided. Available with/without thumb safety. Introduced in 2016.

NIB	Exc.	V.G.	Good	Fair	Poor
415	375	—	—	—	—

M&P BG380

Sub-compact, hammer-fired model chambered for .380 ACP cartridge. (BG) stands for Bodyguard, which should not be confused with Bodyguard .38 S&W J-frame revolver. Barrel length 2.75"; overall length 5.25"; unloaded weight listed at 12.3 oz. Available with/without thumb safety. Also offered with integrated Crimson Trace Red Laser or Crimson Trace Green Laserguard. **NOTE:** Add $80 for Red Laser; $140 for Green Laserguard.

NIB	Exc.	V.G.	Good	Fair	Poor
335	300	265	225	200	175

M&P VTAC

Caliber 9mm Parabellum/.40 S&W. Magazine capacity: 19 (9mm); 17 (.40). Stainless steel slide. Polymer frame, with Flat Dark Earth finish. Striker fired double-action-only ambidextrous slide release. Reversible magazine catch. Weight 24 oz. Barrel 4.25", with VTAC Warrior night sights.

NIB	Exc.	V.G.	Good	Fair	Poor
665	550	475	400	300	150

M&P 22

Rimfire version of M&P pistol. Striker-fired, with aluminum alloy slide and polymer frame. Magazine capacity 10 or 12 rounds. Ambidextrous thumb safety and slide release. Reversible magazine catch. Weight 24 oz. Barrel length 4.1". Introduced in 2011.

NIB	Exc.	V.G.	Good	Fair	Poor
375	325	275	225	150	100

SMITH & WESSON COMMEMORATIVES
(REFERENCE ONLY)

Smith & Wesson has, over the years, built many special edition handguns. These guns have been to commemorate some important national or regional event or group. S&W has also built a large number of special edition handguns for certain distributors, such as Lew Horton which is listed. There are well over 200 special production guns not reflected in this pricing guide. Not even S&W has all of the information on these guns and with many the number is so small that a market price would not be possible to establish. Listed are a number of S&W Commemoratives that we do have information on. Due to the difficulty in determining value, only the original retail price is listed. Remember, to receive full value for these guns, they must be NIB unfired with unturned cylinders.

Model 14 Texas Ranger Comm.

Introduced in 1973. Supplied with 4" barrel and cased. Edition limited to 10,000. 8,000 of these had knives. Serial numbers TR 1 to TR 10000. Original Retail Introductory Price: $250.00

Model 25-3 S&W 125th Anniversary Comm.

Introduced in 1977. Limited edition of 10,000. Serial numbers SW0000 to SW10000. Deluxe models marked 25-4. Original Retail Introductory Price: $350.00

Model 26-4 Georgia State Police Comm.

Introduced in 1988/1989. Supplied with 5" barrel. Total production of 802 guns. Known Serial numbers BBY00354 to BBY0434. Original Retail Introductory Price: $405.00

Model 27 .357 50th Anniversary Comm.

Introduced in 1985. Supplied with 5" barrel and cased. Limited edition to 2,500 guns. Serial numbers REG0001 to REG2500. Originai Retail Introductory Price: N/A

Model 29-3 Elmer Keith Comm.

Introduced in 1986. Supplied with 4" barrel. Gun etched in gold. Limited edition of 2,500 guns. Serial numbers EMK0000 to EMK0100 for Deluxe models and EMK 010 to EMK2500 for standard model. Original Retail Introductory Price: $850.00

Model 544 Texas Wagon Train 150th Anniversary Comm.

Introduced in 1986. Limited to 7801 guns. Serial numbers TWT0000 to TWT7800. Original Issue Introductory Price: N/A

Model 586 Mass. State Police Comm.

Introduced in 1986. Fitted with 6" barrel. Limited to 631 guns. Serial numbers with ABT-AUC prefix. Original Retail Introductory Price: N/A

Model 629-1 Alaska 1988 Iditarod Comm.

Introduced in 1987. Limited to 545 guns. Serial numbers from AKI0001 to AKI0545. Original Retail Introductory Price: N/A

Model 745 IPSC Comm.

Introduced in 1986. Limited to 5362 guns. Serial numbers DVC0000 to DVC5362. Original Retail Introductory Price: N/A

Model 4516-1 U.S. Marshall Comm.

Introduced in 1990. Limited to 500 guns. Serial numbers USM0000 to USM0499. Original Retail Introductory Price: $599.95

Model SW1911 PD Gunsite Commemorative

Honors Lt. Col. Jeff Cooper's Gunsite Training Academy. Scandium alloy single-action .45 ACP, with 4.25" barrel and 8+1 capacity. Fixed sights. 28 oz. Introduced 2006.

NIB	Exc.	V.G.	Good	Fair	Poor
950	700	600	500	350	175

Model SW1911 – Rolling Thunder Commemorative

Limited edition commemorates American POW-MIAs. Rolling Thunder and POW-MIA logos in imitation bonded ivory grips. Chambered for .45 ACP. Blued, 8+1 capacity, 5" barrel, 38.5 oz. Introduced 2006.

NIB	Exc.	V.G.	Good	Fair	Poor
950	700	600	500	350	175

SMITH & WESSON PERFORMANCE

CENTER HANDGUNS (REFERENCE ONLY)

The role of Smith & Wesson's Performance Center has changed, since it was established in 1990. What was once a specialized tune-up and competition one-off production department, has now become a separate facility in providing specialized and limited handguns to the public, often with distributors participation. Change came about 1991, when Performance Center initiated its own limited edition designs. These editions are generally limited between 300 and 600 pistols for each model. Performance Center, in fact, has its own distinct product line. Performance Center pistols are made in its own shop using its own designers. One of these distributors that has played a major role in offering these special guns to the public is Lew Horton Distribution Company.

.40 S&W Tactical

Limited edition semi-automatic handgun offered exclusively by Lew Horton through Performance Center. Special pistol fitted with 5" match-grade barrel, hand fit spherical barrel bushing, custom tuned action, special trigger job, oversized frame and slide rails, wrap-around straight backstrap grip. Replaceable front and Novak rear sights. Special serial numbers. Offered in 1992. Limited to 200 units. Suggested Retail Introductory Price: $1,500.

.40 S&W Compensated

Similar to .40 S&W Tactical, but furnished with 4.625" barrel and single chamber compensator. Also a Lew Horton/Performance pistol. Production of 250 units. Offered in 1992. Suggested Retail Introductory Price: $1,700

.40 S&W Performance Action Pistol

Offered in limited quantities in 1990. This Performance Center .40 S&W semi-automatic pistol was used by the Smith & Wesson shooting team. Frame and barrel are stainless steel with blued carbon steel slide, two port compensator, two fitted and numbered 13-round magazines, 5.25" match grade barrel, extended frame beavertail, square combat trigger guard, oversize magazine release button, spherical barrel bushing, wrap-around straight backstrap grip, extended magazine funnel and BoMar adjustable rear sight. Action is tuned for accuracy and precision. Suggested Retail Introductory Price: N/A

Model 681 Quadport

A Lew Horton revolver limited to 300 guns, with special serial numbers. This 7-shot revolver has a 3" underlug quadport barrel. Action is tuned, cylinders are chamfered and trigger has an overtravel stop. Sights are fixed combat type. Suggested Retail Introductory Price: $675

Model 686 Competitor

Introduced by Lew Horton and Performance Center for 1993. Limited edition revolver features a match grade barrel and unique under barrel weight system. Action has been custom tuned and receiver is drilled and tapped for scope mounts. Charge holes are chambered, ejector rod housing is enclosed and grip is an extended competition type. Special serial numbers. Suggested Retail Introductory Price: $1,100

Model 686 Hunter

Similar to Model 686 Competitor. Also a limited edition Lew Horton revolver. Chambered for .357 Magnum. Features under barrel weight system, internal scope mount and custom tuned action. Special serial numbers. Suggest Retail Introductory Price: $1,154

Model 686 Carry Comp 4

Offered in limited quantities by Lew Horton and Performance Center in 1992. This new design features unique single chamber integral barrel compensator. Front is windage adjustable and action is custom tuned. Chambered for .357 Magnum cartridge. Special serial numbers. Suggested Retail Introductory Price: $1,000

Model 686 Carry Comp 3

The 1993 Lew Horton limited edition version of Model 686 Carry Comp 4" model, with a 3" barrel. Same features apply to both models. Suggested Retail Introductory Price: $1,000

Model 686 Plus

This Lew Horton model features a 7-round cylinder, with chamfered charge holes for use with full moon clips for both .38 Special and .357 Magnum cartridges. Fitted with a tapered 6" barrel, with countersunk muzzle. Gold bead front sight and adjustable rear. Altamont wood grips are standard. Stainless steel finish. Weight about 44 oz. Suggested Retail Introductory Price: $930

Model 686 - .38 Super

Introduced in 2003. This 6-round revolver chambered for .38 Super cartridge. Fitted with a 4" barrel, with tapered lug. Interchangeable red ramp front sight and adjustable rear. Stainless steel, with glass bead finish. Cocobolo grips. Weight about 37 oz. Distributed by Bangers. Suggested Retail Introductory Price: N/A

Model 629 Hunter

Introduced in 1992 by Lew Horton and Performance Center. Limited edition revolver features a new design that utilizes a 6" under barrel weight system, special integral barrel compensator. Action has been custom tuned. Receiver has an integral scope mount. Chambered for .44 Magnum. Special finger groove grips are standard. Special serial numbers. Suggested Retail Introductory Price: $1,234

Model 629 Hunter II

Another Lew Horton/Performance Center limited edition revolver. Features 2x Nikon scope, with steel see-through rings. Barrel is Mag-Na-Ported and incorporates Performance Center's under barrel weight arrangement. Action is custom tuned. Supplied with a ballistic nylon range carry bag. Special serial numbers. Suggested Retail Introductory Price: $1,234

Model 629 Comped Hunter

Offered through RSR. Features 6" barrel, with 4-port detachable compensator. Cylinder unfluted. Sights are adjustable. Fitted with Altamount wood grips. Tuned action. Stainless steel. Weight about 59 oz. Suggested Retail Introductory Price: $1,100

Model 629 12" Hunter/7.5" Hunter

Introduced in 2000. This Lou Horton revolver fitted with a 12" barrel, with Patridge front sight and Wilson silhouette adjustable rear. Hogue Combat grips. Finish glassbead stainless steel. Comes with a Waller 21" gun rug. Weight about 65 oz. A 7.5" version introduced in 2008. Suggested Retail Introductory Price: $1,025

Model 629 Magnum Hunter Trail Boss

Exclusive to RSR. Limited edition chambered for .44 Magnum cartridge. Fitted with 3" barrel. Stainless steel finish. Suggested Retail Introductory Price: $733

Model 629 Compensated Hunter

Chambered for .44 Magnum cartridge. Fitted with 7.5" barrel, with compensator. Barrel also has a removable stainless steel scope mount. Open sights fitted with adjustable orange ramp front and adjustable rear. Rosewood grips. 6-round cylinder. Weight 52 oz. Talo exclusive. Introduced in 2001. Suggested Retail Introductory Price: $1190

Model 629 Stealth Hunter

Fitted with 7.5" ported barrel. Chambered for .44 Magnum cartridge. 6-round cylinder. Finish is black-T and NATO green. Red ramp Millett front sight and adjustable rear. Hogue rubber combat grips standard. Furnished with lockable aluminum case. Weight about 56 oz. Introduced in 2001. Camfour Distributor exclusive. Suggested Retail Introductory Price: $1,025

Model 629 Extreme

Chambered for .44 Magnum cartridge. Fitted with a 12" barrel, with sling swivel. Bomar sights. Rubber grips. Suggested Retail Introductory Price: $1,025

Model 629 Carry Comp

Introduced in 1992 by Lew Horton and Performance Center. Limited edition revolver chambered for .44 Magnum cartridge. Features an integral ported 3" barrel, fluted cylinder, radiused charge holes, dovetail front and fixed groove rear sight. Fitted with a rubber combat grip. Action is custom by Performance Center. Special serial numbers. Suggested Retail Introductory Price: $1,000

Model 629 Carry Comp II

Limited edition 1993 offering by Lew Horton and Performance Center. Similar to 1992 Model 629 Carry Comp, except this 1993 model has a special unfluted cylinder and fully adjustable rear sight. Special serial numbers. Suggested Retail Introductory Price: $1,000

Model 629 Comped Hunter

Chambered for .44 Magnum cartridge. Built with a 7.5" barrel, with a tapered full length lug and compensator. Front sight is drift adjustable orange ramp and adjustable rear. Stainless steel, with glass bead finish. Removable scope mount. Rosewood grips. Weight about 52 oz. Introduced in 2003. Suggested Retail Introductory Price: $1,100

Model 610

Introduced in 1998 by Lew Horton. Features a 3" full lug barrel. Chambered for 10mm cartridge. Nonfluted cylinder, red ramp front sight and white outline rear. Rosewood grips. Limited to 300 revolvers. Suggested Retail Introductory Price: $740

Model 640 Carry Comp

Introduced in 1991 by Lew Horton and Performance Center. Chambered for .38 S&W Special, with a strengthened action to handle +P loads. Fitted with heavy 2.625" barrel, with unique integral barrel compensator. Front sight replaceable and adjustable for windage. Rear sight a fixed groove. Custom trigger job and custom tuned action are also part of the package. Special serial numbers. Suggested Retail Introductory Price: $750

Model 640 .357 Quadport

Introduced in 1996. Similar to model above, but chambered for .357 Magnum cartridge and quadported. Limited to 190 revolvers. Special serial numbers. Suggested Retail Introductory Price: $675

Model 460 Airweight

Chambered for .38 Special cartridge. Fitted with 2" Mag-Na-Ported barrel and 5-shot cylinder. Fixed sights. Eagle Secret Service grips. Weight about 16 oz. Limited to 450 revolvers. Introduced in 1994. Suggested Retail Introductory Price: $580

Model 625 Light Hunter

Large frame revolver chambered for .45 Colt. Fitted with 6" Mag-Na-Ported barrel, with integral Weaver-style base. Stainless steel finish and black Hogue rubber grips. Drift adjustable Millet front and fully adjustable rear sight. Offered in limited quantities. Introduced in 1997 by RSR. Suggested Retail Introductory Price: $580

Model 625

Introduced in 1998. Chambered for .45 ACP or .45 Colt cartridge. Fitted with a 3" full lug barrel, fluted cylinder and rosewood grips. Limited to 150 revolvers in each chambering. Suggested Retail Introductory Price: $755

Model 625 V-Comp

Chambered for .44 Magnum cartridge. Fitted with a 4" barrel and removable three-port compensator. Front sight is a red ramp, with black adjustable rear. Hogue wood combat grips. Furnished with aluminum case. Weight about 43 oz. Finish stainless steel. Distributed by RSR. Introduced in 1999. Suggested Retail Introductory Price: $1,000

Model 625—5.25

Introduced in 2001. Features special Jerry Miculek Hogue laminated combat grip. Chambered for .45 ACP cartridge. Fitted with 5.25" barrel. Stainless steel finish. Interchangeable gold bead front sight and adjustable rear. Weight about 42 oz. Camfour exclusive. Suggested Retail Introductory Price: N/A

Model 627—8 Shot

Chambered for .357 Magnum cartridge. Has an 8-round capacity. Drilled and tapped, with adjustable sights on a 5" tapered and contoured barrel. Tuned action. Hogue wood grips. Satin stainless steel finish. Weight about 44 oz. A Lew Horton exclusive. Introduced in 1997. Suggested Retail Introductory Price: $1,160

Model 627 Defensive—8 Shot

Chambered for .357 Magnum. Fitted with an 8-round unfluted cylinder recessed for full moon clips. Barrel length 2.625". Adjustable rear sight and drift adjustable front. Wooden eagle boot grips. Weight about 38 oz. Introduced in 1999. Furnished with aluminum case. Suggested Retail Introductory Price: $1,025

Model 651

A limited edition revolver by RSR. Chambered for .22 WMR cartridge. Fitted with a 2" barrel and boot grips. Stainless steel finish. Suggested Retail Introductory Price: $492

"Shorty-Forty" .40 S&W

Introduced in 1992. Available exclusively from Lew Horton. Limited edition Performance Center pistol features light alloy frame, oversize slide rails and spherical barrel bushing. Match grade barrel is joined to a custom tuned action. Special serial numbers. Suggested Retail Introductory Price: $950

Model 647 Varminter

Introduced in 2003. Chambered for .17 HMR cartridge. Fitted with a 12" fluted barrel, with removable black Patridge front sight and adjustable rear. Integral scope mount on barrel. 6-round cylinder. Stainless steel finish. Weight about 54 oz. Suggested Retail Introductory Price: $1,100

Model 500 Magnum Hunter

Introduced in 2003. Chambered for .500 S&W cartridge. Fitted with a 10.5" barrel, with compensator. Sling swivel studs and sling are standard. Orange dovetail ramp front sight and adjustable rear. Stainless steel, with glass bead finish. Hogue rubber grips. Weight about 82 oz. Suggested Retail Introductory Price: $1390

Model 460XVR

Built for serious handgun hunters. Chambered for .460 S&W Magnum. Stainless steel cylinder, frame and barrel. 5-round capacity. Adjustable rear and removable Partridge front sight. Other features include sling swivels, dual accessory rails and synthetic grips. Weight a hefty 79.2 oz. Fluted 12" barrel, with compensator. Reintroduced in 2011, by Performance Center. Suggested Retail Introductory Price: $1,619.

"Shorty Forty" Mark III

Offered in 1995. A Lew Horton exclusive features low-mount adjustable sights, hand-fitted titanium barrel bushing, checkered front strap. Action as been hand honed. Sold with two magazines: one 11 rounds; other 9 rounds. Suggested Retail Introductory Price: $1,000

Shorty .45

Introduced by Lew Horton in 1996. This .45 ACP pistol has a hand-fitted titanium barrel bushing, oversize frame and slide rails, match grade barrel, checkered front strap, hand honed double-action and special serial numbers. Suggested Retail Introductory Price: $1,095

Shorty Nine

Lew Horton exclusive limited to 100 units. Features hand-fitted titanium barrel bushing, oversize slide rails, action job, low mount adjustable sights, checkered front strap, match grade barrel and two tone finish. Furnished with two 12-round magazines. Suggested Retail Introductory Price: $1,000

9 Recon

A RSR exclusive introduced in 1999. Chambered for 9mm cartridge. Fitted with 3.5" barrel. Rear sight Novak Lo-Mount. Hogue wrap-around rubber grips. Slide black carbon steel, with alloy frame. Magazine capacity 12 rounds. Weight about 27 oz. Suggested Retail Introductory Price: $1,178

Performance Center .45 Limited

A Lew Horton full-size single-action pistol. Hand-fitted titanium barrel bushing, fitted slide lock, match grade barrel, adjustable sights, oversize magazine well, tuned action and checkered front strap. Suggested Retail Introductory Price: $1,400

45 Recon

Another RSR pistol. Chambered for .45 ACP cartridge. An enhanced version of "Shorty 45". The 4.25" barrel is ported, with Novak Lo-Mount sights. Hogue wrap-around rubber grips. Stainless steel slide and barrel, with aluminum frame. Weight about 28 oz. Magazine capacity 7 rounds. Matte black finish. Furnished with aluminum case. Suggested Retail Introductory Price: $1,221

Shorty .356 TSW

This new cartridge also available in another Lew Horton/Performance Center limited edition pistol with 4" barrel. Features a steel frame and hand-fitted slide, with spherical barrel bushing. Double-action custom tuned by Performance Center. Magazine holds 12 rounds. Similar in appearance to "Shorty-Forty". Offered in 1993. Special serial numbers. Suggested Retail Introductory Price: $1,000

Model .356 TSW "Limited" Series

A Lew Horton gun. Chambered for new .356 TSW caliber (TSW stands for Team Smith & Wesson). A new caliber, actually 9mm x 21.5mm cartridge, with ballistics of around 1,235 fps with 147-grain bullet. Designed as a low-end .357 competition pistol. Built for the competitive shooter (IPSC) it features a 15-round magazine and distinctive profile and markings. Single-action trigger is adjustable for reach while slide, frame and barrel are custom fitted. Comes with a spherical barrel bushing and adjustable BoMar sights. Frame grip is checked 20 lpi. Magazine well is extended as is magazine release. Magazine is fitted with a pad. Suggested Retail Introductory Price: $1,350

Model 5906 Performance Center

Introduced in 1998. This 9mm pistol features front slide serrations, ambidextrous decocker, titanium coated barrel bushing, match grade barrel and Novak Lo-Mount sights. Sold with one 15- and 10-round magazine. Stainless steel finish. Suggested Retail Introductory Price: $1,200

Model 845 of 1998

This .45 ACP caliber model has a 5" match grade barrel, with hand-lapped rails on frame and slide. Patridge front sight and adjustable Bomar rear. Single-action trigger tuned. Slide has front serrations. Magazine capacity 8 rounds. Stainless steel finish. Limited to 150 pistols. Suggested Retail Introductory Price: $1,500

Model .45 CQB Combat

Introduced in 1998. This Lew Horton model features a 4" match grade barrel. Novak Lo-Mount sights. Double-action trigger, with ambidextrous decocker. Available in both matte black and stainless steel finish. Matte black model has alloy frame; weight about 30 oz. Stainless steel version has stainless frame; weight about 38 oz. Suggested Retail Introductory Price: $1,200

Model 945

A single-action-only pistol chambered for .45 ACP cartridge. Fitted with a 5" match grade barrel and Bomar adjustable rear sight. Grips checkered black/silver wood laminate, with matte stainless steel slide and frame. Magazine capacity 8 rounds. Empty weight about 44 oz. Introduced in 1998. Suggested Retail Introductory Price: $1,600

Model 945 Black Model

Performance Center Model features 3.25" barrel, with black stainless steel slide. Frame aluminum. Novak Lo-Mount sights. Hogue checkered wood laminate grips. Furnished with two 6-round magazines and locking aluminum gun case. Weight about 24 oz. Exclusive with RSR. Suggested Retail Introductory Price: $1,550

Model 945-40

This PC model fitted with a 3.75" barrel chambered for .40 S&W cartridge. Novak Lo-Mount sights and Hogue checkered wood laminate grips are standard. Furnished with two 7-round magazines and locking aluminum case. Clear glass bead finish. Exclusive with Sports South. Suggested Retail Introductory Price: $1,275

Model 945 Micro

Similar to Model 945 Black Model, with stainless steel finish. Exclusive with Camfour Distributor. Suggested Retail Introductory Price: $1,300

Model SW945

This .45 ACP pistol fitted with a 5" barrel, with Wilson Combat adjustable rear sight. Scalloped slide serrations both front and rear. Checkered wood grips. Many special features. Weight about 40.5 oz. Suggested Retail Introductory Price: $2,085

Model SW1911

Chambered for .45 ACP cartridge. Fitted with a 5" barrel, with adjustable rear sight. Checkered wood grips. Many special features. Scalloped slide serrations front and rear. Black Melonite finish. Magazine capacity 8 rounds. Weight about 41 oz. Also offered in a stainless steel version for $160 less. Suggested Retail Price: $2,270

Model SW1911 DK

Chambered for .38 Super cartridge. Fitted with a 5" barrel, with adjustable rear sight. Smooth wood grips, with DK logo. Stainless steel finish, with scalloped serrations at rear of slide. Many special features. Magazine capacity 10 rounds. Weight about 41.5 oz. Introduced in 2005. Suggested Retail Price: $2,320

Model SW1911 Tactical Rail

One of Tactical Rail Series for SWAT Teams and tactical applications. Picatinny rail and fixed sights. Blued or stainless. Single-action .45 ACP, with 5" barrel and 8+1 capacity. Weight 39 oz. Introduced 2006. MSRP: $1,057

Model 66 .357 Magnum F-Comp

Performance Center revolver designed as a carry gun. Furnished with 3" ported barrel and full underlug. Thumbpiece has been cut down to accommodate all speed loaders. Charge holes are countersunk. K-frame action has been custom tuned. Rear sight is a fully adjustable black blade, while front sight features a Tritium dot night sight. Furnished with a round butt combat-style rubber grip. Stainless steel finish. Weight about 35 oz. A Lew Horton special limited edition of 300 units. **NOTE:** In 2003, this revolver was produced for all S&W stocking dealers. Suggested Retail Introductory Price: $800

Model 66

A RSR exclusive. Chambered for .357 Magnum cartridge. Fitted with 3" barrel. Red ramp front sight. Stainless steel finish. Limited edition. Suggested Retail Introductory Price: $490

Model 681 Quad Port

Chambered for .357 Magnum cartridge. Fitted with a 3" barrel, with quadporting. Fixed rear sight. Seven-round cylinder with moon clips. Two sets of grips are standard: Hogue Bantam and checkered wood laminate. Stainless steel finish. Weight about 35 oz. Camfour exclusive. A 4" barrel version also available. Suggested Retail Introductory Price: $850

Model 25

This PC model is a reintroduction of original Model 25. Chambered for .45 Colt cartridge. Fitted with a tapered 6" barrel, with pinned gold bead Patridge front sight. Four screw frame. Furnished with locking aluminum case. Weight about 42 oz. Sports South exclusive.

NIB	Exc.	V.G.	Good	Fair	Poor
900	750	650	550	375	—

Model 657

Lew Horton/Performance Center revolver fitted with a 3" full lug barrel. Chambered for .41 Magnum cartridge. Fluted cylinder, with red ramp front sight and white outline rear. Rosewood grips. Limited to 150 revolvers in 1998. Suggested Retail Introductory Price: $720

Model 657 Classic

Offered in limited quantities of 350 units. This Lew Horton/Performance Center revolver features an unfluted cylinder and 6.5" barrel on a drilled and tapped N-frame. Chambered for .41 Magnum cartridge. Fitted with adjustable rear sight. Special serial numbers. Suggested Retail Introductory Price: $550

Model 657 Defensive

Introduced in 1999 by Lew Horton. This .41 Magnum revolver fitted with 2.625" barrel, with drift adjustable Millet front sight and fully adjustable rear sight. Stainless steel finish, with 6-shot unfluted cylinder. Hogue combat grips. Weight about 40 oz. Furnished with aluminum case. Suggested Retail Introductory Price: $1,025

Model 657 Hunter

Introduced in 1995. A RSR Wholesale Guns exclusive. Fitted with an integral weaver base, Mag-Na-Ported 6" barrel with Millet red ramp front sight and adjustable rear. Stainless steel finish, special serial numbers, chamfered charge holes and adjustable trigger stop. Limited to 500 guns. Suggested Retail Introductory Price: $1,000

Model 19 .357 Magnum K-Comp

Same gun as F-Comp, but furnished with black matte finish. Sold through stocking dealers on an unlimited basis. Suggested Retail Introductory Price: $800

Model 60 Carry Comp

Introduced in the summer of 1993. This J-frame revolver fitted with a 3" full underlug barrel, with integral compensator. Charge holes are radiused for quick loading. Action tuned by Performance Center. Pistol rated for +P ammunition. Grips are fancy wood contoured for speed loaders. This Lew Horton revolver limited to 300 guns. Special serial numbers. Suggested Retail Introductory Price: $795

Paxton Quigley Model 640

Performance Center offering restricted to 300 revolvers. Built around Model 640. Limited edition handgun has a 2" compensated barrel, windage adjustable front sight, specially tuned action and tapestry soft gun case. Each gun has a distinct serial number range. Suggested Retail Introductory Price: $720

Model 640 Centennial Powerport

Introduced in 1996. A Lew Horton exclusive. Fitted with a 2.125" barrel, with integral compensator. Front sight is a black blade, with Tritium insert and rear is a fixed notch. Cylinder holds five .357 or .38 rounds. Stainless steel, with Pachmayr decelerator compact grips. Overall length 6.75"; weight about 25 oz. Limited to 300 units. Suggested Retail Introductory Price: $675

Model 327 Carry

Introduced in 2004. This 8-shot model chambered for .357 Magnum cartridge. Barrel length 2", with dovetail .260 orange ramp. Scandium alloy frame, with stainless steel barrel, titanium cylinder and shroud. Black oxide finish except for gray cylinder. Cocobolo wood grips. Weight about 21 oz. Suggested Retail Price: $1,226

Model 940 Centennial .356

Offered exclusively from Lew Horton. This J-frame revolver chambered for new .356 cartridge. Has a 2" compensated barrel. It will also fire 9mm cartridge. Features a tuned action, radius hammer and trigger. Special serial numbers. Suggested Retail Introductory Price: $760

Model 13 .357

A Lew Horton exclusive. Features a 3" barrel with 4 Mag-Na-Ports, a bobbed hammer for double-action-only, chambered charge holes, beveled cylinder, contoured grip and thumb latch for speed loader clearance, overtravel trigger stop and FBI grips. Limited to 300 guns. Suggested Retail Introductory Price: $730

Model 845 Single-Action

Offered by Lew Horton. Chambered for .45 ACP. Designed for the competitive shooter. Adjustable reach trigger precision fitted slide, frame and barrel are some of the special features. Barrel bushing spherical and front sight dovetailed. Magazine well extended as is magazine release and safety. Both front and rear sight are adjustable. Suggested Retail Introductory Price: $1,470

Model 952

Chambered for 9mm cartridge. This semi-automatic has a 5" barrel. Stainless steel frame and slide. Adjustable rear sight. Checkered wood grips. Magazine capacity 9 rounds. Weight about 41 oz. Suggested Retail Introductory Price: $2,030

Model 1911

This .45 ACP PC model features a 5" barrel, micro-click adjustable black rear sight and dovetail black front. Checkered wine laminate grips. Stainless steel frame and slide, with black oxide finish. Magazine capacity 8 rounds. Weight about 41 oz. Introduced in 2004. Suggested Retail Price: $2,270

SMITH & WESSON LONG ARMS

.320 Revolving Rifle Model

Model is rare and unique—prize to a S&W collector. Revolving Rifle chambered for .320 S&W Revolving Rifle cartridge. Has a 6-shot fluted cylinder. Offered with 16", 18" and 20" barrel. Only 76 rifles are nickel-plated and remainder of production are blued. Butt rounded, with red hard rubber checkered grips and forearm of the same material. Detachable shoulder stock, with black hard rubber buttplate featuring S&W logo. Rifle furnished in a leather carrying case, with accessories. As fine a firearm as this was, it was a commercial failure for S&W; they finally came to the realization the public did not want a revolving rifle. They manufactured only 977 of them between 1879 and 1887. **NOTE:** Values are for a complete unit. Deduct 40 percent without stock. Add 10 percent for 16" or 20" barrels.

NIB	Exc.	V.G.	Good	Fair	Poor
—	12000	9000	6000	2000	1500

Model A Rifle

Bolt-action with 23.75" barrel, chambered for .22-250, .243, .270, .308, .30-06, 7mm Magnum and .300 Win. Magnum. Folding rear sight. Checkered Monte Carlo stock, with contrasting rosewood fore-end tip. Pistol-grip cap. Manufactured for S&W by Husqvarna of Sweden, from 1969 to 1972.

NIB	Exc.	V.G.	Good	Fair	Poor
400	325	275	200	150	100

Model B

As above, with schnabel fore-end and 20.75" barrel.

NIB	Exc.	V.G.	Good	Fair	Poor
425	350	295	200	150	100

Model C

As above, with cheekpiece.

NIB	Exc.	V.G.	Good	Fair	Poor
425	350	295	225	175	125

Model D

As above, with Mannlicher-style stock.

NIB	Exc.	V.G.	Good	Fair	Poor
700	600	400	350	250	150

Model 1500 Series

Bolt-action series of hunting rifles made for S&W by Howa of Japan in 1983 and 1984. Calibers included .222 Rem., .223 Rem., .22-250 Rem., .243 Win., .25-06 Rem., .270 Win., 7mm Rem. Magnum, .308 Win., .30-06 and .300 Win. Magnum. Offered in several variations with blue or stainless receiver, plain or checkered wood stock (Deluxe model). Barrel lengths 22", except 24" for Magnum calibers. Heavy barrel varmint version was available. Model 1700 Classic Hunter was similar, except for a removable magazine and schnabel fore-end. **NOTE:** Add 10 percent for Deluxe or Varmint model; 15 percent for Model 1700.

NIB	Exc.	V.G.	Good	Fair	Poor
450	400	350	300	250	150

I-Bolt Rifle

Bolt-action hunting rifle made in the U.S.A. by S&W, from 2008 to 2009. Calibers .25-06, .270 Win., .30-06, 7mm Rem. Magnum and .300 Win. Magnum. Offered with wood, synthetic or camo stock. Blue or stainless finish. Integral Picatinny rail. **NOTE:** Add 10 percent for camo stock.

NIB	Exc.	V.G.	Good	Fair	Poor
475	425	365	300	250	150

M&P 15 Military and Police Tactical Rifle

Gas-operated semi-automatic built along lines of AR-15. Caliber 5.56mm NATO. Magazine capacity 30. Barrel 16" 1:9. Stock 6-position telescoping composite. Weight 6.74 lbs. unloaded. Sights adjustable front and rear. Variants: M&P15A & M&P15T (no carry handle; folding battle sight). Introduced 2006.

NIB	Exc.	V.G.	Good	Fair	Poor
1200	950	800	675	450	200

M&P 15 PC

Generally similar to M&P rifle, with accurized tubular floated barrel, 2-stage match trigger, 20" matte stainless barrel. No sights. Introduced 2007.

NIB	Exc.	V.G.	Good	Fair	Poor
1750	1300	950	800	550	250

M&P 15 Sport

More economical addition to M&P rifle line. Chambered for 5.56 NATO, with black anodized upper and lower receiver of 7075 T6 aluminum. Polymer hand guard, 16" 4140 steel barrel. Adjustable sights, single-stage trigger, chrome-lined gas key and bolt carrier. Flash suppressor compensator. Introduced in 2011.

NIB	Exc.	V.G.	Good	Fair	Poor
665	550	475	400	300	150

M&P 15PC Camo

AR-style semi-automatic rifle chambered for .223 Rem./5.56 NATO. A2 configuration, 10-round magazine. No sights, but integral front and rear optics rails. Two-stage trigger, aluminum lower, stainless 20" barrel with 1:8 twist. Finished in Realtree Advantage Max-1 camo. Overall length 38.5"; weight 8.2 lbs.

NIB	Exc.	V.G.	Good	Fair	Poor
1500	1075	875	750	500	275

M&P 15VTAC Viking Tactics

AR-style semi-automatic rifle chambered in .223 Rem./5.56 NATO. Six-position CAR stock. 16" barrel. Surefire flash-hider and G2 light with VTAC light mount; VTAC/JP hand guard; JP single-stage match trigger and speed hammer; three adjustable Picatinny rails; VTAC padded two-point adjustable sling. Overall length 35" extended; 32" collapsed. Weight 6.5 lbs. 30-round magazine.

NIB	Exc.	V.G.	Good	Fair	Poor
1750	1300	950	800	550	250

M&P 15 Piston Rifle

Similar to AR-derived M&P15, with gas piston. Chambered in 5.56 NATO. Features adjustable gas port, optional Troy quad mount hand guard, chromed bore/gas key/bolt carrier/chamber, 6-position telescoping or MagPul MOE stock, flattop or folding MBUS sights, aluminum receiver, alloy upper and lower, black anodized finish, 30-round magazine, 16" barrel with birdcage. Suggested Retail Price: $1531 (standard hand guard); $1692 (Troy quad mount hand guard).

M&P 15 300 Whisper

Chambered for .300 Whisper cartridge. Comes with/without suppressor. Stock and fore-end in Realtree APG camo.

NIB	Exc.	V.G.	Good	Fair	Poor
950	850	700	500	400	300

M&P 15R

This variation chambered for Russian 5.45x39mm cartridge. Made from 2008 to 2011.

NIB	Exc.	V.G.	Good	Fair	Poor
900	800	750	500	300	200

M&P 15-22

.22 LR rimfire verson of AR-derived M&P tactical autoloader. Features include blowback action, 15.5" or 16" barrel, 6-position telescoping or fixed stock, quad mount Picatinny rails, plain barrel or compensator, alloy upper and lower, matte black finish, 10- or 25-round magazine.

NIB	Exc.	V.G.	Good	Fair	Poor
450	400	350	250	200	175

M&P 10

AR-style rifle chambered for 7.62 NATO/.308 Win., with 18" barrel. Features ambidextrous safety, magazine catch and gas block with integral Picatinny accessory rail.

NIB	Exc.	V.G.	Good	Fair	Poor
1375	1125	950	700	400	250

Model 916

Series of slide-action shotguns made in U.S.A. by S&W, from 1972 to 1981. Made in 12-, 16- and 20-gauge in various barrel lengths, with fixed chokes. Ventilated rib or plain barrel. Offered in both solid-frame and take-down versions. **NOTE:** Add 10 percent for ventilated rib; 10 percent for take-down model.

NIB	Exc.	V.G.	Good	Fair	Poor
200	180	150	120	100	75

Model 3000

Slide-action shotgun made in Japan by Howa, for S&W. Imported from 1982 to about 1989. In 12- or 20-gauge, with 3" chamber, checkered wood stock and fore-end. Fixed chokes or choke tubes. Standard barrel lengths 26", 28" or 30". Also offered in 18" or 20" in police model; 22" in a slug gun with rifle sights. **NOTE:** Add 10 percent for choke tubes.

NIB	Exc.	V.G.	Good	Fair	Poor
350	320	280	225	180	100

Model 1000

Series of gas-operated semi-automatic shotguns patterned after Rem. Model 1100. Offered in 12- or 20-gauge, with barrel lengths from 22" to 30" with fixed chokes or interchangeable tubes. Checkered walnut stock and fore-end. Engraved aluminum receiver. Available in several variations including waterfowl, trap and skeet models. **NOTE:** Add 25 percent for waterfowl; 50 percent for trap.

NIB	Exc.	V.G.	Good	Fair	Poor
400	350	285	220	150	100

Model 1012/1020

Series of gas-operated semi-automatics imported by S&W from Turkey, from 2007 to 2009. Available in 12-gauge (1012) or 20-gauge (1020), with barrel lengths from 24" to 30" and five choke tubes. Stock adjustable for length and drop. Satin finished walnut or black synthetic stock or total camo coverage. **NOTE:** Add 20 percent for camo coverage; 30 percent for 3.5" 12-gauge model.

NIB	Exc.	V.G.	Good	Fair	Poor
500	425	385	325	250	200

Elite Gold & Silver Series

Elite Gold side-by-side in 20-gauge only, with quality double-gun features. Grade III checkered walnut stock, with English-style straight-/pistol-grip. Choice of single/double triggers. Automatic ejectors, color case-hardened frame, fixed chokes of IC/M or M/F. Barrel lengths 26" or 28". Weight about 6.5 lbs. Elite Silver an over/under in 12-gauge only. Features similar to Elite Gold, except has five choke tubes, single trigger and recoil pad. Weight about 7.5 lbs. Both of these models imported from Turkey, from 2007 to 2010.

NIB	Exc.	V.G.	Good	Fair	Poor
1800	1500	1100	800	500	250

SMITH AMERICAN ARMS COMPANY
Springfield, Massachusetts

Smith Carbine

A .50-caliber breechloading percussion carbine, with 21.75" round barrel having an octagonal breech. Blued case-hardened, with walnut stock. Barrel marked "Address/Poultney & Trimble/Baltimore, USA" and frame "Smith's Patent/June 23, 1857" as well as "American Arms Co./Chicopee Falls". Approximately 30,000 manufactured, most of which were purchased by the United States government. Sales agents were Poultney & Trimble of Baltimore, Maryland.

NIB	Exc.	V.G.	Good	Fair	Poor
—	—	2750	1200	500	200

SNAKE CHARMER
Sporting Arms Manufacturing, Inc.
Little Field, Texas

Snake Charmer

A .410 bore single-shot shotgun, with 18.5" barrel. Stainless steel, with composition stock.

NIB	Exc.	V.G.	Good	Fair	Poor
200	125	100	75	50	25

SNEIDER, CHARLES E.
Baltimore, Maryland

Two-Cylinder Revolver

A .22-caliber spur trigger revolver, with 2.75" octagonal barrel and twin 7-shot cylinders that can be pivoted. Barrel marked "E. Sneider Pat. March 1862". Produced in limited quantities during 1860s.

NIB	Exc.	V.G.	Good	Fair	Poor
—	—	14000	11000	5500	1250

SODIA, FRANZ
Ferlach, Austria

A wide variety of double-barrel shotguns, drillings and combination shotgun/rifles are made by this maker.

SOKOLOVSKY CORP. SPORT ARMS
Sunnyvale, California

.45 Automaster

A .45-caliber stainless steel semi-automatic pistol, with 6" barrel fitted with Millet adjustable sights and 6-shot magazine. Approximately 50 pistols have been made since 1984.

NIB	Exc.	V.G.	Good	Fair	Poor
4850	3800	2750	2000	1500	500

SPALDING & FISHER
Worcester, Massachusetts

Double Barreled Pistol

A .36-caliber percussion double-barrel pocket pistol, with 5.5" barrels, blued iron frame and walnut grips. Top of barrels marked "Spalding & Fisher". Produced during 1850s.

NIB	Exc.	V.G.	Good	Fair	Poor
—	—	1350	925	400	100

SPANG & WALLACE
Philadelphia, Pennsylvania

Pocket Pistol

A .36-caliber percussion pocket pistol, with 2.5" to 6" barrel, German silver furniture and checkered walnut stock. Barrel marked "Spang & Wallace/Phila.". Manufactured during late 1840s and early 1850s.

Courtesy Bonhams & Butterfields

NIB	Exc.	V.G.	Good	Fair	Poor
—	—	2850	1500	750	200

SPENCER
Boston, Massachusetts

Spencer Carbine

One of the most popular firearms used by Union forces during the Civil War. Chambered for a metallic rimfire cartridge known as "No. 56". It's actually a .52-caliber and made with a copper case. Barrel is 22" in length. Finish blued, with a carbine-length walnut stock held on by one barrel band. There is a sling swivel at the butt. Approximately 50,000 manufactured between 1863 and 1865.

Courtesy Bonhams & Butterfields, San Francisco, California

NIB	Exc.	V.G.	Good	Fair	Poor
—	—	7500	5000	2500	500

Military Rifle—Navy Model

Similar to the carbine, with 30" round barrel and full-length walnut stock held on by three barrel bands. Features an iron fore-end tip and sling swivels. Civil War production consisted of two models. A Navy model manufactured between 1862 and 1864 (approximately 1,000 of these so marked).

NIB	Exc.	V.G.	Good	Fair	Poor
—	—	10000	7500	5000	1000

Military Rifle—Army Model

Approximately 11,450 produced for the Army during the Civil War. Similar to Navy model, except front sight doubles as a bayonet lug. Manufactured in 1863 and 1864.

Courtesy Milwaukee Public Museum, Milwaukee, Wisconsin

NIB	Exc.	V.G.	Good	Fair	Poor
—	—	8000	6000	2500	600

Springfield Armory Post-war Alteration

After conclusion of the Civil War, approximately 11,000 carbines were refurbished and rechambered for .50-caliber rimfire. Barrels were sleeved and a device known as "Stabler cut-off" was added to convert the arm to single-shot function. Often they were refinished and restocked. Inspector's marks "ESA" will be found in an oval cartouche on left side of the stock. These alterations took place in 1867 and 1868.

NIB	Exc.	V.G.	Good	Fair	Poor
—	—	5250	3950	1700	500

Model 1865 Contract

Manufactured by Burnside Rifle Company in 1865. Similar to Civil War-type carbine and marked "By Burnside Rifle Co./Model 1865". Approximately 34,000 manufactured. Old records show that 30,500 were purchased by the United States government and 19,000 of these had "Stabler cut-off" device.

Courtesy Wallis & Wallis, Lewes, Sussex, England

NIB	Exc.	V.G.	Good	Fair	Poor
—	—	5300	3250	1250	500

SPENCER ARMS CO.
Windsor, Connecticut
Slide-Action Shotgun

From 1882 to 1889, they manufactured the first successful slide action repeating shotgun. Designed by Christopher M. Spencer, who also designed Civil War era Spencer military carbines. Shotgun came in both solid and take-down, in 10- and 12-gauge. In 1890, Francis Bannerman & Sons of New York, bought patents and machinery and moved the operation to Brooklyn, New York. They produced what is known as Spencer Bannerman models from 1890 to 1907. Later Bannerman models are worth 50 percent less than Spencer models. **NOTE:** Add 20 percent premium for take-down model; 10 percent premium for 10-gauge models.

NIB	Exc.	V.G.	Good	Fair	Poor
—	—	1000	600	200	125

SPENCER REVOLVER
Maltby, Henley & Company
New York, New York

Safety Hammerless Revolver

A .32-caliber hammerless double-action revolver, with a 3" barrel. Frame and barrel made of brass, cylinder of steel and grips of walnut. Barrel marked "Spencer Safety Hammerless Pat. Jan. 24, 1888 & Oct. 29, 1889". Manufactured by Norwich Pistol Company circa 1890.

NIB	Exc.	V.G.	Good	Fair	Poor
—	—	500	225	150	100

SPHINX
Sphinx Engineering SA
Porrentru, Switzerland
Imported by Sile Distributors Inc.

AT-380

Semi-automatic pistol is a small .380-caliber in double-action-only. Magazine capacity 11 rounds. Offered in stainless steel, blued or two-tone finish. Barrel 3.27"; overall length 6.03". Sights are fixed and grips are black checkered plastic. Weight 25 oz.

NIB	Exc.	V.G.	Good	Fair	Poor
600	550	400	300	200	100

AT-2000 SERIES PISTOLS

A series number applied to several different variations of the same basic design. Based on CZ 75 pistol. AT-2000 is a semi-automatic pistol, offered in 9mm and .40 S&W. Barrel lengths are different depending on variation, but AT-2000 can be converted from double-action to double only in just a matter of minutes.

AT-2000S/SDA

Chambered for 9mm or .40 S&W cartridge. Barrel length 4.53". Overall length 8.12". Magazine capacity: 15 rounds for 9mm; 13 rounds for .40 S&W. Available in double-action (S) or double-action-only (SDA). Offered with two-tone or all blued finish. Weight 35 oz.

NIB	Exc.	V.G.	Good	Fair	Poor
1500	1150	875	675	600	300

AT-2000P/PDA

Slightly smaller of the AT-2000S. Magazine capacity: 13 rounds for 9mm; 11 rounds for .40 S&W. Features the same, except barrel length 3.66". Overall length 7.25"; weight 31 oz.

NIB	Exc.	V.G.	Good	Fair	Poor
1500	1150	875	675	600	300

AT-2000PS

This version, sometimes referred to as Police Special, features shorter barrel of AT-2000P model on the larger AT-2000S frame. Barrel length 3.66". Magazine capacity: 15 rounds for 9mm; 13 rounds for .40 S&W.

NIB	Exc.	V.G.	Good	Fair	Poor
1500	1150	875	675	600	300

AT-2000H/HDA

Smallest version of AT-2000 series. Magazine capacity: 10 rounds for 9mm; 8 rounds for .40 S&W. Barrel length 3.34"; overall length 6.78"; weight 26 oz.

NIB	Exc.	V.G.	Good	Fair	Poor
1500	1150	875	675	600	300

AT-2000C

This is the competitor model. Features a competition slide, dual port compensator, match barrel and Sphinx scope mount. Offered in double-/single-action. Available in 9mm, 9x21 and .40 S&W.

NIB	Exc.	V.G.	Good	Fair	Poor
2200	1600	1200	800	600	400

AT-2000CS

Same as above model. Fitted with BoMar adjustable sights.

NIB	Exc.	V.G.	Good	Fair	Poor
2250	1650	1250	850	650	425

AT-2000GM

Grand Master model. Features are similar to AT-2000C. Offered in single-action-only.

NIB	Exc.	V.G.	Good	Fair	Poor
3000	2550	2100	1750	1250	500

AT-2000GMS

Same as above. Fitted with BoMar adjustable sights.

NIB	Exc.	V.G.	Good	Fair	Poor
3050	2600	2150	1800	1300	525

3000

16+1 autoloader chambered in 9mm or .45 ACP. Stainless steel frame and slide, manual safety, single/double/decocking action. Weight 40.56 oz. Also available in compact version.

NIB	Exc.	V.G.	Good	Fair	Poor
2000	1650	1150	500	300	200

SPIES, A. W.
New York, New York

Pocket Pistol

A .41-caliber percussion pocket pistol, with 2.5" barrel, German silver furniture and checkered walnut stock. Produced during 1850s.

NIB	Exc.	V.G.	Good	Fair	Poor
—	—	1950	1775	900	300

SPILLER & BURR
Atlanta, Georgia

Navy Revolver

A .36-caliber percussion revolver, with 6" or 6.5" octagonal barrel and 6-shot cylinder. Barrel and cylinder blued. Frame of brass, with walnut grips. Some pistols are marked "Spiller & Burr" while others are simply marked "C.S.". Approximately 1,450 made between 1862 and 1865. .

NIB	Exc.	V.G.	Good	Fair	Poor
—	—	45000	22500	15500	1500

SPITFIRE
JSL (Hereford) Ltd.
Hereford, England

Semi-automatic pistol is a design based on CZ 75. This is a hand-built pistol designed by John Slough and built from a solid block of steel. Stainless steel frame and slide are cut with spark erosion and diamond grinding. Barrels are built and bored in the same factory. This is primarily a competition pistol. Manufactured 1992-1994.

Standard Model (G1)

Chambered for 9x21, 9mm Parabellum or .40 S&W cartridges. Uses locked breech concept. Trigger system single-/double-action. Fitted with an ambidextrous safety. Barrel 3.7"; overall length 7.1". Magazine capacity 9mm is 15 rounds. Sights are fixed. Empty weight 35 oz. Finish stainless steel. Comes supplied with presentation box, two magazines and allen key. Discontinued.

NIB	Exc.	V.G.	Good	Fair	Poor
1300	900	700	500	300	200

Master Model

Similar to Standard Model, without sights. Fitted with a stainless steel bridge mount to take an Aimpoint sight. Also has a dual port compensator. Supplied with presentation box and two magazines. Discontinued.

NIB	Exc.	V.G.	Good	Fair	Poor
2100	1750	1250	800	400	200

Squadron Model

This model has a Standard Model frame, adjustable rear sight slide, adjustable rear sight slide with compensator, Master Model slide and barrel with stainless steel bridge mount and Aimpoint sight, four magazines, screwdriver, allen key, oil bottle, spare springs, cleaning kit, and fitted leather case. Discontinued.

NIB	Exc.	V.G.	Good	Fair	Poor
6000	4800	2100	900	450	200

Sterling Model (G2)

Chambered for 9x21, 9mm Parabellum or .40 S&W cartridges. Features same as Standard Model, except it has adjustable sights. Discontinued.

NIB	Exc.	V.G.	Good	Fair	Poor
1400	1000	800	600	300	200

Super Sterling (G7)

Also chambered for 9x21, 9mm Parabellum and .40 S&W. Features single port compensator and 4.3" barrel. Overall length 8.25". Weight about 36 oz. Discontinued.

NIB	Exc.	V.G.	Good	Fair	Poor
1600	1200	900	700	350	200

Competition Model (G3)

Chambered for 9x21, 9mm Parabellum or .40 S&W cartridge. Features tapered slide rib, adjustable rear sight, dual pod compensator, match hammer, adjustable trigger stop with presentation box. Barrel 5.27", with compensator. Weight 40 oz. Discontinued.

NIB	Exc.	V.G.	Good	Fair	Poor
1800	1400	1000	800	400	200

Battle of Britain Commemorative

A limited edition of 1,056 Spitfires in 9mm Parabellum. Each one represents one of the Spitfire aircraft. Stainless steel slide has inscription "Battle of Britain-50th Anniversary". Grips are checkered walnut, log book of history of that particular aircraft and a wooden presentation box with engraved plaque. Discontinued.

NIB	Exc.	V.G.	Good	Fair	Poor
1950	1400	1000	800	400	200

Westlake Britarms

This is a .22 LR Match pistol. Barrel length 5.77", sight base 8.42", magazine capacity 5 rounds. Weight about 47 oz. Trigger adjustable for length, front and rear trigger stops, adjustable palm rest on contoured wood grips, take-down barrel design with removable weight. Limited importation.

NIB	Exc.	V.G.	Good	Fair	Poor
1850	1400	1000	800	400	200

SPRINGFIELD ARMORY

Springfield Armory was our country's first federal armory, beginning in 1777 in Springfield, Massachusetts, at a site chosen by George Washington. For almost two centuries, it was the primary facility for the manufacturer of firearms for the armed forces of the United States, until its closing in 1968. For information on the many models made at Springfield Armory, please refer to Standard Catalog of Military Firearms, now in its 8th Edition, published by Gun Digest Books, a division of F&W Media. Current manufacturer and importer of modern rifles and handguns, Springfield Armory, Inc. of Geneseo, Illinois, is not associated with the historic military armory of the same name.

SPRINGFIELD ARMORY INC.
Geneseo, Illinois

RIFLES

M1 Garand Rifle

A .270 (discontinued), .308 or .30-06 caliber semi-automatic rifle, with 24" barrel and 8-shot magazine. Patterned directly after U.S. M1 Rifle.

Courtesy Milwaukee Public Museum, Milwaukee, Wisconsin

NIB	Exc.	V.G.	Good	Fair	Poor
—	1000	825	550	400	300

Iwo Jima M1 Garand

Similar to standard M1 Model, but shipped in reproduction WWII-era crate with signed decorative lithograph. Introduced 2006.

NIB	Exc.	V.G.	Good	Fair	Poor
1600	1300	1000	800	400	200

M1A Basic Rifle

Chambered for .308 Win. Fitted with a painted black fiberglass stock. Barrel length 22", without flash suppressor. Front sights are military square post and rear military aperture (battle sights). Magazine capacity 5, 10 or 20 box. Weight 9 lbs.

NIB	Exc.	V.G.	Good	Fair	Poor
1250	1000	850	650	400	250

D-Day M1 Garand Limited Edition

Introduced in 2005. Chambered for .30-06 cartridge. Fitted with 24" barrel. Military style sights. Two-stage military trigger. Limited to 1,944 rifles, each with a military-style wooden crate. Each side of the buttstock has stamped memorials to D-Day.

NIB	Exc.	V.G.	Good	Fair	Poor
1600	1200	925	675	425	250

M1A Standard Rifle

Chambered for .308 Win. or .243 cartridge. Fitted with 22" barrel, with adjustable rear sight and walnut stock, with fiberglass hand guard. Comes equipped with 20-round box magazine. Weight 9 lbs.

NIB	Exc.	V.G.	Good	Fair	Poor
1500	1100	850	650	400	250

M1A-A1 Bush Rifle

Chambered for .308 or .243 cartridge. Choice of walnut stock, black fiberglass or folding stock (no longer produced). Fitted with 18.25" barrel. Weight 8.75 lbs. **NOTE:** Add $250 for folding stock.

NIB	Exc.	V.G.	Good	Fair	Poor
1400	1100	850	650	400	250

M1A Scout Squad Rifle

This .308 model fitted with an 18" barrel. Choice of fiberglass or walnut stock. Military sights. Supplied with 10-round magazine. Weight about: fiberglass stock 9 lbs.; walnut stock 9.3 lbs.

NIB	Exc.	V.G.	Good	Fair	Poor
1800	1100	750	550	300	175

M1A National Match

Chambered for .308 as standard or choice of .243 cartridge. Fitted with medium weight National Match 22" glass bedded barrel and walnut stock. Special rear sight adjustable to half minute of angle clicks. Weight 10.06 lbs.

NIB	Exc.	V.G.	Good	Fair	Poor
2050	1400	1000	700	500	250

M1A Super Match

This is Springfield's best match grade rifle. Chambered for .308 as standard and also .243 cartridge. Fitted with special oversize heavy walnut stock, heavy Douglas match glass bedded barrel and special rear lugged receiver. Special rear adjustable sight. Weight 10.125 lbs. **NOTE:** Add $165 for walnut stock and Douglas barrel; $600 for black McMillan stock and Douglas stainless steel barrel; $600 for Marine Corp. camo stock and Douglas stainless steel barrel; $535 for adjustable walnut stock and Douglas barrel; $900 for adjustable walnut stock and Krieger barrel.

NIB	Exc.	V.G.	Good	Fair	Poor
2500	1850	1350	900	600	300

M1A Model 25 Carlos Hathcock

Introduced in 2001. Features match trigger, stainless steel heavy match barrel, McMillan synthetic stock with adjustable cheek pad, Harris Bi-pod and other special features. Chambered for .308 cartridge. Weight about 12.75 lbs. A special logo bears his signature.

NIB	Exc.	V.G.	Good	Fair	Poor
4650	3450	2500	1750	800	400

M21 Law Enforcement/Tactical Rifle

Similar to Super Match. Addition of a special stock, with rubber recoil pad and height adjustable cheekpiece. Available as a special order only. Weight 11.875 lbs.

NIB	Exc.	V.G.	Good	Fair	Poor
3000	2600	2000	1500	650	350

M1A SOCOM 16

This M1A1 rifle features 16.25" barrel, with muzzle-brake. Black fiberglass stock, with steel buttplate. Forward scout-style scope mount. Front sight post has tritium insert. Weight about 9 lbs. Introduced in 2004.

NIB	Exc.	V.G.	Good	Fair	Poor
1575	1250	875	650	400	250

M1A SOCOM II

Introduced in 2005. Features full length top rail and short bottom rail for accessories. Weight about 11 lbs.

NIB	Exc.	V.G.	Good	Fair	Poor
1700	1450	950	700	450	300

M1A SOCOM Urban Rifle

Similar to SOCOM, with black and white camo stock. Introduced in 2005.

NIB	Exc.	V.G.	Good	Fair	Poor
1725	1475	950	700	450	300

IDF Mauser Rifle Model 66SP

Bolt-action rifle chambered for .308 Win. cartridge. Adjustable trigger for pull and travel. Barrel length 27". Specially designed stock has broad fore-end and thumbhole pistol-grip. Cheekpiece adjustable as is recoil pad. Supplied with case. Rifle is military issue. Fewer than 100 imported into the U.S.

NIB	Exc.	V.G.	Good	Fair	Poor
2200	1750	950	700	450	300

SAR-48

This is pre-ban version of SAR-4800.

NIB	Exc.	V.G.	Good	Fair	Poor
1400	1200	850	600	500	250

SAR-4800

Semi-automatic gas operated rifle, similar in appearance to FN-FAL/LAR rifle. Chambered for .308 Win. cartridge. Fitted with 21" barrel. Has a fully adjustable rear sight. Weight about 9.5 lbs. No longer imported.

NIB	Exc.	V.G.	Good	Fair	Poor
1600	1200	800	600	400	250

SAR-8

Semi-automatic rifle similar in appearance to HK-91. Chambered for .308 Win. Recoil operated delayed roller-lock design. Barrel length 18". Rear sight is fully adjustable. Weight about 8.7 lbs. No longer imported.

NIB	Exc.	V.G.	Good	Fair	Poor
950	750	600	400	300	200

SAR-8 Tactical

Similar to above model. Fitted with a heavy barrel. Introduced in 1996. No longer imported. Fewer than 100 imported into U.S.

NIB	Exc.	V.G.	Good	Fair	Poor
1450	1100	750	600	400	300

M6 Scout

A .22, .22 Magnum or .22 Hornet and .410 bore over/under combination shotgun rifle, with 18" barrel. Black anodized finish, with synthetic stock. Discontinued. US-made version commands a premium over Czech-made. Values shown are for US-made version. **NOTE:** Add 30 percent for Hornet.

NIB	Exc.	V.G.	Good	Fair	Poor
600	450	295	200	100	50

M6 Scout—Stainless Steel

Same as above in stainless steel. First introduced in 1996; discontinued.

NIB	Exc.	V.G.	Good	Fair	Poor
625	475	325	225	150	75

PISTOLS

M6 Scout Pistol

As above, with 10" barrel and no folding stock. Parkerized or stainless steel finish. Weight about 28 oz. Introduced in 2002. Discontinued. **NOTE:** Add $30 for stainless steel.

NIB	Exc.	V.G.	Good	Fair	Poor
575	425	295	200	100	50

Model 1911-A1

A 9mm, .38 Super or .45-caliber copy of Colt Model 1911-A1 semi-automatic pistol. Blued or Parkerized. Introduced in 1985.

NIB	Exc.	V.G.	Good	Fair	Poor
625	425	375	350	300	250

Model 1911-A1 Service Model

Introduced in 2003. This .45 ACP pistol has a 5" barrel, with Bo-Mar adjustable three-dot rear sight. Also a number of special features such as extended mag well, titanium firing pin and beavertail grip safety. Stainless steel magazine capacity 7 rounds. Black stainless steel finish. Weight about 35 oz.

NIB	Exc.	V.G.	Good	Fair	Poor
925	750	600	500	400	200

Model 1911-A1 Service Mil-Spec

Chambered for .45 ACP cartridge. Fitted with a 5" barrel. Fixed sights. Matte stainless steel finish. Black plastic grips. Weight about 36 oz. Introduced in 2003.

NIB	Exc.	V.G.	Good	Fair	Poor
610	475	375	350	300	250

Model 1911-A1 Service Model Lightweight

This .45 ACP pistol has a 5" barrel, with lightweight alloy frame and bi-tone finish. Novak Lo-Mount sights. A large number of special features. Checkered cocobolo grips. Magazine capacity 7 rounds. Weight about 30 oz. Introduced in 2003.

NIB	Exc.	V.G.	Good	Fair	Poor
875	700	600	500	400	200

Model 1911-A1 Stainless

Similar to standard Model 1911, but chambered for .45 ACP cartridge. Offered in stainless steel. Equipped with three-dot sights, beveled magazine well and checkered walnut grips. Weight about 39.2 oz. **NOTE:** Add $50 for Bomar sights.

NIB	Exc.	V.G.	Good	Fair	Poor
900	750	625	400	350	200

Model 1911-A1 Factory Comp

Chambered for .45 ACP or .38 Super. Fitted with a three chamber compensator. Rear sight is adjustable. Extended thumb safety and Videcki speed trigger are standard features. Also, checkered walnut grips, beveled magazine well and Commander hammer are standard. Weight 40 oz. **NOTE:** Factory Comp pistols chambered for .38 Super may bring a small premium.

NIB	Exc.	V.G.	Good	Fair	Poor
1050	925	750	600	500	300

Model 1911-A1 Factory Comp High Capacity

Same as above, with 13-round magazine.

NIB	Exc.	V.G.	Good	Fair	Poor
1050	925	750	600	500	300

Model 1911-A2 S.A.S.S.

Single-shot pistol built on Model 1911 frame. Available in two barrel lengths; 10.75" and 14.9". Offered in .22 LR, .223, 7mm-08, 7mmBR, .357 Magnum, .308 and .44 Magnum calibers. This conversion kit is available for those wishing to use it on their own Model 1911 pistol frames.

NIB	Exc.	V.G.	Good	Fair	Poor
500	400	325	275	200	100

Model 1911-A1 Defender

Chambered for .45 ACP cartridge. Fitted with a tapered cone dual port compensator, reversed recoil plug, full length recoil spring guide, fully adjustable rear sight, serrated front strap, rubberized grips and Commander-style hammer. Capacity 8-round magazine. Finish is bi-tone. Weight 40.16 oz.

NIB	Exc.	V.G.	Good	Fair	Poor
875	700	600	500	400	200

Model 1911-A1 Loaded Defender Lightweight

As above, with loaded features: precision fit frames, slides and barrels, flat serrated mainspring housing, lowered and flared ejection port, Delta lightweight hammer, loaded chamber indicator, titanium firing pin, carry bevel treatment, ambidextrous thumb safety, high hand beavertail grip safety, dovetail front sight, Novak or adjustable rear sight and adjustable speed trigger.

NIB	Exc.	V.G.	Good	Fair	Poor
950	775	675	550	450	250

Model 1911-A1 Compact

Available in blue or bi-tone, this .45 ACP fitted with 4.5" barrel and compact compensator. Equipped with Commander-style hammer and three-dot sights. Walnut grips are standard. Comes with 7-round magazine. Weight 37.2 oz. **NOTE:** Add $40 for stainless steel.

NIB	Exc.	V.G.	Good	Fair	Poor
900	750	625	400	350	200

Lightweight Compact Comp

Fitted with 4.5" barrel and single port compensator. Magazine holds 8 rounds of .45 ACP. Frame is alloy. Weight 30 oz.

NIB	Exc.	V.G.	Good	Fair	Poor
900	750	625	400	350	200

Model 1911-A1 Compact Mil-Spec

Same as standard blued steel Compact model, with Parkerized finish.

NIB	Exc.	V.G.	Good	Fair	Poor
850	700	575	350	300	200

Model 1911-A1 Long Slide

Features 6" barrel, 3-dot fixed sights, checkered wooden grips and 8-round magazine capacity. Finish stainless steel. Weight about 38 oz. Introduced in 1997.

NIB	Exc.	V.G.	Good	Fair	Poor
950	775	675	550	450	250

Model 1911-A1 Loaded Long Slide

As above, with loaded features: precision fit frames, slides and barrels, flat serrated mainspring housing, lowered and flared ejection port, Delta lightweight hammer, loaded chamber indicator, titanium firing pin, carry bevel treatment, ambidextrous thumb safety, high hand beavertail grip safety, dovetail front sight, Novak or adjustable rear sight and adjustable speed trigger.

NIB	Exc.	V.G.	Good	Fair	Poor
1100	950	775	600	475	350

Model 1911-A1 Champion

This .45 ACP pistol has a shortened slide, barrel and reduced size frame. Fitted with 4" barrel, 8-round magazine, Commander hammer, checkered walnut grips and special 3-dot sights. Weight 33.4 oz.

NIB	Exc.	V.G.	Good	Fair	Poor
795	650	500	400	295	150

Model 1911-A1 Champion Mil-Spec

Same as above, with Parkerized finish.

NIB	Exc.	V.G.	Good	Fair	Poor
700	600	400	350	225	125

Model 1911-A1 Stainless Champion

Same as above, but offered in stainless steel. Weight about 33.4 oz.

NIB	Exc.	V.G.	Good	Fair	Poor
850	700	575	350	300	200

Model 1911-A1 Loaded Champion Stainless

As above, with loaded features: precision fit frames, slides and barrels, flat serrated mainspring housing, lowered and flared ejection port, Delta lightweight hammer, loaded chamber indicator, titanium firing pin, carry bevel treatment, ambidextrous thumb safety, high hand beavertail grip safety, dovetail front sight, Novak or adjustable rear sight and adjustable speed trigger.

NIB	Exc.	V.G.	Good	Fair	Poor
1000	875	700	575	500	300

Champion Compact

Includes same features as Champion, with shortened grip frame length and 7-round magazine. Weight 32 oz.

NIB	Exc.	V.G.	Good	Fair	Poor
850	700	575	350	300	200

Model 1911 Loaded Champion Lightweight

A lightweight aluminum frame, with Novak night sights. Checkered rubber grips. Finish OD Green and Black Armory Kote. Weight about 28 oz. Introduced in 2004.

NIB	Exc.	V.G.	Good	Fair	Poor
850	700	575	350	300	200

Ultra Compact 1911-A1

Features a 3.5" barrel, with 7.125" overall length. Has a stainless steel frame, beveled mag well, speed trigger, match grade barrel and walnut grips. Weight 31 oz.

NIB	Exc.	V.G.	Good	Fair	Poor
850	700	575	350	300	200

Ultra Compact Lightweight MD-1

Same as above in .380-caliber, with alloy frame. Weight 24 oz.

NIB	Exc.	V.G.	Good	Fair	Poor
700	600	400	350	225	125

Ultra Compact 1911-A1 Mil-Spec

Same as Ultra Compact Model, with Parkerized or blued finish.

NIB	Exc.	V.G.	Good	Fair	Poor
750	650	450	350	225	125

V10 Ultra Compact 1911-A1

Same as Ultra Compact 1911-A1, but fitted with a compensator built into barrel and slide.

NIB	Exc.	V.G.	Good	Fair	Poor
900	750	625	400	350	200

V10 Ultra Compact 1911-A1 Mil-Spec

Same as above, with Parkerized finish.

NIB	Exc.	V.G.	Good	Fair	Poor
850	700	575	350	300	200

Model 1911-A1 High Capacity

Chambered in .45 ACP (10-rounds) or 9mm (16-rounds). Standard features include Commander hammer, walnut grips and beveled magazine well. Blued finish. Weight 42 oz. In 1997, offered in stainless steel and Parkerized finish. **NOTE:** Add $40 for stainless steel. Deduct $25 for Parkerized finish.

NIB	Exc.	V.G.	Good	Fair	Poor
650	525	400	300	200	100

Compact High Capacity

Same as above, with 11-round magazine.

NIB	Exc.	V.G.	Good	Fair	Poor
650	525	400	300	200	150

Ultra Compact High Capacity

This .45 ACP model offered in three different 3.5" barrel variations: stainless steel, Parkerized and ported. Standard magazine capacity 10 rounds. Weight about 31 oz. **NOTE:** Add $60 for stainless steel; $100 for ported models.

NIB	Exc.	V.G.	Good	Fair	Poor
700	600	400	350	225	125

Micro Compact—Parkerized

Chambered for .45 ACP cartridge. Fitted with 3" bull barrel. Aluminum frame, with steel slide. Novak night sights. Cocobolo grips. Offered with Parkerized finish. Weight about 24 oz. Magazine capacity 6 rounds. Introduced in 2002.

NIB	Exc.	V.G.	Good	Fair	Poor
850	700	575	350	300	200

Micro Compact—Stainless

As above, with stainless steel frame and slide. Novak tritium night sights. Weight about 24 oz. Introduced in 2003.

NIB	Exc.	V.G.	Good	Fair	Poor
900	750	625	400	350	200

Micro Compact—O.D. Green

As above, with Armory Kote Green finish. Pearce grips. Introduced in 2003.

NIB	Exc.	V.G.	Good	Fair	Poor
900	750	625	400	350	200

Micro Compact—Black Stainless

As above, with black stainless steel finish and Slimline cocobolo grips. Weight about 32 oz. Introduced in 2003.

NIB	Exc.	V.G.	Good	Fair	Poor
900	750	625	400	350	200

Micro Compact Lightweight

Similar to other Micro models, but fitted with an aluminum frame and Novak night sights. Cocobolo wood grips. Bi-Tone finish. Equipped with XML Mini Light. Introduced in 2004. Weight about 24 oz.

NIB	Exc.	V.G.	Good	Fair	Poor
900	750	625	400	350	200

Loaded Micro Compact Lightweight

As above, with loaded features: precision fit frames, slides and barrels, flat serrated mainspring housing, lowered and flared ejection port, Delta lightweight hammer, loaded chamber indicator, titanium firing pin, carry bevel treatment, ambidextrous thumb safety, high hand beavertail grip safety, dovetail front sight, Novak or adjustable rear sight and adjustable speed trigger. Introduced in 2005.

NIB	Exc.	V.G.	Good	Fair	Poor
1000	975	775	600	475	300

Model 1911-A1 Mil-Spec Operator

Chambered for .45 ACP. Fitted with 5" barrel. Features Picatinny rail system on frame. Fixed sights. Magazine capacity 7 rounds. Parkerized finish.

NIB	Exc.	V.G.	Good	Fair	Poor
900	750	625	400	350	200

Model 1911-A1 Loaded Operator

Introduced in 2002. Features an integral Picatinny rail on the frame. Chambered for .45 ACP cartridge. Fitted with a 5" barrel. Novak night sights. Parkerized finish. Magazine capacity 7 rounds.

NIB	Exc.	V.G.	Good	Fair	Poor
1150	950	700	500	375	250

Combat Commander

Copy of Colt Model 1911-A1 Combat Commander. Chambered for .45 ACP only. Introduced in 1988.

NIB	Exc.	V.G.	Good	Fair	Poor
600	500	400	350	225	125

Trophy Match

This model has special features such as fully adjustable target sights, match grade 5" barrel and special wide trigger. Weight about 36 oz. Available in blue, stainless steel or bi-tone finish. In 1997, offered chambered for 9mm cartridge. Values would be the same for both .45 ACP and 9mm models. **NOTE:** Add $40 for stainless steel.

NIB	Exc.	V.G.	Good	Fair	Poor
1000	975	775	600	475	300

Loaded Leatham Trophy Match

Introduced in 2005. This .40 S&W pistol fitted with a 5" barrel, with fully adjustable target sights. Black Polymer grips. Dawson magazine well, tuned trigger, match barrel and bushing, checkered front strap and other special features. Black finish. Weight about 39 oz.

NIB	Exc.	V.G.	Good	Fair	Poor
1200	1075	900	700	575	300

1911 GI SERIES

Full Size

Chambered for .45 ACP cartridge. Fitted with a 5" barrel. Old style fixed sights. Standard checkered brown plastic grips. Lanyard loop on mainspring housing. Stainless steel frame and slide. Magazine capacity 7 rounds. Weight about 36 oz. Introduced in 2004. Also offered with Parkerized, OD Green or stainless steel finish. **NOTE:** Add $30 for stainless steel. Deduct $45 for Parkerized or OD finish.

NIB	Exc.	V.G.	Good	Fair	Poor
560	450	375	325	250	125

Full Size High-Capacity

As above, with 10-round magazine. Weight about 38 oz. Introduced in 2005.

NIB	Exc.	V.G.	Good	Fair	Poor
600	500	425	375	295	175

Champion

A scaled-down version of full-size model above. Fitted with 4" fully supported barrel and low-profile military sights. Also has double diamond walnut grips. Black or Parkerized finish. Weight about 34 oz. Introduced in 2004.

NIB	Exc.	V.G.	Good	Fair	Poor
600	500	425	375	295	175

Champion Lightweight

Introduced in 2005. This .45 ACP model fitted with a 4" barrel, with fully supported ramp. Low profile military sights. Checkered walnut grips. Weight about 28 oz.

NIB	Exc.	V.G.	Good	Fair	Poor
600	500	425	375	295	175

Micro-Compact

As above, but fitted with a 3" fully supported and ramped barrel. Magazine capacity 6 rounds. Weight about 32 oz. Introduced in 2004.

NIB	Exc.	V.G.	Good	Fair	Poor
600	500	425	375	295	175

P9 SERIES

A double-action 9mm, .45 ACP or .40 S&W pistol based on Czech CZ 75 design. Incorporates several design features including: stainless steel trigger, sear safety mechanism, extended sear safety lever, redesigned back strap, lengthened beavertail grip area and new high strength slide stop. Discontinued in 1993.

P9 Standard

Standard pistol fitted with 4.7" barrel, low profile target sights and ribbed slide. Magazine capacity: 9mm 16 rounds; .45 ACP 10 rounds; .40 S&W 12 rounds. Offered in blue or stainless finish. Weight about 35 oz.

NIB	Exc.	V.G.	Good	Fair	Poor
600	500	425	375	295	175

P9 Factory Comp.

Competition pistol fitted with triple port compensator, extended magazine release, adjustable rear sight, slim competition wood grips and bi-tone finish. Weight 34 oz. Dropped from Springfield product line in 1993.

NIB	Exc.	V.G.	Good	Fair	Poor
700	600	400	350	225	125

P9 Ultra (IPSC Approved)

Competition pistol features longer slide and barrel, 5". Special target sights, rubberized competition grips. Engraved with IPSC logo. Available in bi-tone finish only. Weight 34.5 oz. Dropped from production in 1993.

NIB	Exc.	V.G.	Good	Fair	Poor
775	575	425	350	250	200

Super Tuned Champion

Introduced in 1997. Features 4" barrel chambered for .45 ACP cartridge and Novak fixed Lo-Mount sights. Tuned and polished extractor and ejector. Polished feed ramp and barrel throat. Magazine capacity 7 rounds. Choice of blued or Parkerized finish. Weight about 36 oz.

NIB	Exc.	V.G.	Good	Fair	Poor
850	700	575	350	300	200

Super Tuned V10

Similar to model above, with 3.5" barrel. Finish is bi-tone or stainless steel. Weight about 33 oz. Introduced in 1997. **NOTE:** Add $100 for stainless steel.

NIB	Exc.	V.G.	Good	Fair	Poor
1000	895	700	600	400	250

Super Tuned Standard

Features a 5" barrel, with stainless steel finish. Weight about 39 oz. Has all other super tune features. Introduced in 1997.

NIB	Exc.	V.G.	Good	Fair	Poor
1000	895	700	600	400	250

Range Officer

A 1911 pistol ready to compete out of the box. Caliber: .45 ACP and 9mm. Barrel 5" with blue finish, forged steel slide and frame, 7-round magazine. Other features include adjustable rear sight, match grade barrel and bushing, checkered mainspring housing, lightweight Delta hammer, extended thumb safety and beavertail grip tang. Weight 40 oz.

NIB	Exc.	V.G.	Good	Fair	Poor
800	675	550	450	350	200

Tactical Response Pistol (TRP)

This .45 ACP pistol fitted with a 5" barrel and choice of stainless steel or Black Armory Kote finish. Fully checkered front strap and mainspring housing. Novak Lo-Mount sights. Magazine capacity 8 rounds. Weight about 37 oz.

NIB	Exc.	V.G.	Good	Fair	Poor
1360	1150	850	600	400	250

TRP Champion

Same as above, with 3.9" barrel and Black Armory Kote finish. Weight about 33 oz.

NIB	Exc.	V.G.	Good	Fair	Poor
1175	950	800	600	400	200

TRP Pro

Fitted with a 5" barrel and many special features including Novak Lo-Mount tritium sights. Magazine capacity 7 rounds. Meets specifications for FBI SWAT team. Weight 36 oz.

NIB	Exc.	V.G.	Good	Fair	Poor
2000	1750	1200	900	675	300

TRP Operator

This model has all the features of TRP series, with addition of an integral light rail on the frame. Fitted with a 5" barrel. Adjustable night sights. Introduced in 2002. **NOTE:** Add $60 for night sights; $100 for OD Green frame and slide.

NIB	Exc.	V.G.	Good	Fair	Poor
1350	1025	800	600	400	250

Lightweight Operator

Blued semi-automatic .45 ACP, with 5" bull barrel. Fixed sights, 5 to 6 lb. trigger pull, Cocobolo grips. Weight 31 oz. Picatinny rail. Introduced 2006.

NIB	Exc.	V.G.	Good	Fair	Poor
850	700	575	350	300	200

Lightweight Champion Operator

Similar to above, with 4" bull barrel. Introduced 2006.

NIB	Exc.	V.G.	Good	Fair	Poor
850	700	575	350	300	200

Enhanced Micro Pistol (EMP)

Tiny little 1911-style semi-automatic chambered in 9mm Parabellum or .40 S&W. Short-/single-action design, 7-shot capacity, 3" bull barrel, fixed sights. Stainless frame that is .125" shorter than company's Compact models. Premium for night sights and other refinements.

NIB	Exc.	V.G.	Good	Fair	Poor
1175	950	800	600	400	200

XD PISTOLS

These pistols are fitted with a polymer frame, grip safety, chamber indicator and raised firing pin indicator. Offered in black or OD Green finish.

XD 4"

Chambered for 9mm, .40 S&W, .357 SIG or .45 GAP cartridges. Barrel length 4". Magazine capacity: 9mm 15 rounds; .40 S&W 12 rounds; .357 SIG 12 rounds; .45 GAP 9 rounds. Weight about 23 oz. **NOTE:** Add $60 for night sights; $100 for OD Green frame and slide.

NIB	Exc.	V.G.	Good	Fair	Poor
550	450	350	250	175	125

XD 4" Bi-Tone

Offered in 9mm or .40 S&W. This 4" pistol has a black polymer frame and stainless steel slide. Magazine capacity 10 rounds. Weight about 26 oz. Introduced in 2003.

NIB	Exc.	V.G.	Good	Fair	Poor
585	495	375	275	200	150

XD V-10 Ported 4"

Similar to XD, with 4" ported barrel chambered for 9mm, .40 S&W or .357 SIG. Black finish. Weight about 26 oz.

NIB	Exc.	V.G.	Good	Fair	Poor
550	450	350	250	175	125

XD 5" Tactical

Fitted with 5" barrel. Chambered for 9mm, .40 S&W, .357 SIG and .45 ACP. From 2005 to 2007, also offered .45 GAP. Magazine capacity: 9mm 15 rounds; .40 S&W or .357 SIG 12 rounds; .45 ACP 10 rounds; .45 GAP 9 rounds. Weight from 26 to 31 oz. Offered in black or O.D. Green finish.

NIB	Exc.	V.G.	Good	Fair	Poor
600	450	350	250	200	150

XD 5" Tactical Pro

Introduced in 2003. Features Robar NP3 finish, fiber optic front sight and fixed rear. Frame built with an oversized beavertail frame extension of a higher grip. Chambered for 9mm, .357 SIG., 40 S&W and .45 GAP cartridge. Magazine capacity: 9mm 15 rounds; .40 S&W and .357 SIG 12 rounds; .45 GAP 9 rounds. Weight about 31 oz.

NIB	Exc.	V.G.	Good	Fair	Poor
875	750	600	500	375	250

XD 5" Bi-Tone Tactical

Introduced in 2005. Chambered for .45 GAP cartridge. Fitted with a 5" barrel. Black polymer frame and stainless steel slide. Magazine capacity 9 rounds. Weight about 31 oz.

NIB	Exc.	V.G.	Good	Fair	Poor
600	500	400	300	200	125

XD Sub-Compact

Introduced in 2003. This polymer pistol chambered for 9mm or .40 S&W cartridge. Fitted with a 3" barrel, with light rail on the dust cover. Grip safety and safe action trigger. Magazine capacity 10 rounds. Weight about 20 oz. Fixed sights. **NOTE:** Add $60 for night sights; $70 for XML Mini light.

NIB	Exc.	V.G.	Good	Fair	Poor
550	450	350	250	175	125

XD 45 ACP

Polymer semi-automatic in black, green or bi-tone. Holds 13+1 .45 ACP. Imported from Croatia. Fixed sights. Service model: 4" barrel, weight 30 oz. Tactical model: 5" barrel, weight 32 oz. Picatinny rail. Introduced 2006.

NIB	Exc.	V.G.	Good	Fair	Poor
585	495	375	275	200	150

XD(M)

Enhanced variation of XD series, with interchangeable backstraps, improved magazine release and disassembly design. Offered in 9mm, .40 S&W or .45 ACP, with 4.5" barrel. Three-dot sights with night sights available. Black or two-tone polymer frame, Ultra Safety Assurance trigger, striker fired, grip safety, ambidextrous magazine releases, accessory rail, loaded chamber and cocked striker indicators. Weight about 27 oz. empty. Also available in Competition model (9mm only), with 5.25" barrel with lightening cut on top of slide

NIB	Exc.	V.G.	Good	Fair	Poor
650	525	400	300	200	100

XDM-3.8

Sub-compact model chambered in 9mm Parabellum (19+1) and .40 S&W (16+1). Features include 3.8" steel full-ramp barrel; dovetail front and rear 3-dot sights (tritium and fiber-optics sights available); polymer frame; stainless steel slide with slip-resistant slide serrations; loaded chamber indicator; grip safety. Black, bi-tone or stainless steel finish. Overall length 7", weight 27.5 oz. (9mm).

NIB	Exc.	V.G.	Good	Fair	Poor
650	525	400	300	200	100

XD-S

Designed for concealed carry, this member of XD polymer-frame series is a single-stack 9mm or .45 ACP, with 3.3" or 4" barrel. Sights are fiber optic front and dovetail rear. Magazine capacity: 9mm 7 rounds; .45 ACP 5 rounds.

NIB	Exc.	V.G.	Good	Fair	Poor
500	435	350	300	250	200

XD Mod. 2

This model has the same features as other XD models, with several enhancements. These include improved gripping textures, re-contoured slimmer frame and slide, higher position grip safety and no-snag trigger guard. In 9mm, .40 S&W or .45 ACP, with 3", 3.3", 4" or 5" barrel. **NOTE:** Add $25 for .45-caliber, available only with 3.3" barrel.

NIB	Exc.	V.G.	Good	Fair	Poor
500	425	350	285	225	200

LEATHAM LEGEND SERIES

This series introduced in 2003. Identified with a unique series marking, serial number and certificate of authenticity. Two sets of grips will come with each pistol: one cocobolo with lazer engraved signature of Rob Leatham; the other a black micarta double diamond slimline grip. Custom aluminum case is standard for this series.

TGO 1

A full custom pistol from Springfield Custom Shop, with Nowlin Match Grade throated barrel and bushing. Robar bi-tone finish, Bomar low-mount adjustable sights and a number of other custom features. Chambered for .45 ACP cartridge. Weight about 38 oz. Four magazines are standard.

NIB	Exc.	V.G.	Good	Fair	Poor
2400	1875	1500	—		

TGO 2

Similar to TGO 1, but hand-built by Springfield Armory.

NIB	Exc.	V.G.	Good	Fair	Poor
1900	1500	1200	—		—

TGO 3

An enhanced high-end production model, with lightweight aluminum slide. Bi-tone finish. Weight about 30 oz.

NIB	Exc.	V.G.	Good	Fair	Poor
1295	1025	800	—		—

SPRINGFIELD CUSTOM SHOP

This specialty shop was formed to build custom pistols to customer's own specifications. When these one-of-a-kind pistols are encountered, it is advisable for shooter or collector to get an independent appraisal. Springfield Custom also offers standard custom and Racegun packages that are readily available and in stock. These pistols are commercially available.

Custom Carry

Chambered for the following cartridges: .45 ACP, 9mm Parabellum, .38 Super, 10mm, .40 S&W, 9mmx21. Fitted with fixed 3-dot sights, speed trigger, match barrel and bushing, extended thumb safety, beveled magazine well, Commander hammer, polished feed ramp and throated barrel, tuned extractor, lowered and flared ejection port, fitted slide to frame, full length spring guide rod and walnut grips. Supplied with two magazines and plastic carrying case.

NIB	Exc.	V.G.	Good	Fair	Poor
1600	1450	1075	800	500	300

Basic Competition Model

Chambered for .45 ACP. Features a variety of special options for the competition shooter. Special BoMar sights, match trigger, custom slide to frame fit, polished feed-ramp and throated barrel are just some of the features.

NIB	Exc.	V.G.	Good	Fair	Poor
1800	1600	1275	1050	650	400

N.R.A. PPC

Designed to comply with NRA rules for PPC competition. Chambered for .45 ACP cartridge, with match grade barrel and chamber. Polished feedramp, throated barrel, recoil buffer system, walnut grips and fully adjustable sights. Sold with a custom carrying case.

NIB	Exc.	V.G.	Good	Fair	Poor
1600	1450	1075	800	500	300

Trophy Master Expert Limited Class

Chambered for .45 ACP. Adjustable BoMar rear sight, match barrel, polished ramp and throated barrel, extended ambidextrous thumb safety, beveled and polished magazine well, full length recoil spring guide, match trigger, Commander hammer, lowered and flared ejection port, tuned extractor, fitted slide to frame, extended slide release, flat mainspring housing, Pachmayr wrap-around grips, two magazines with slam pads and plastic carrying case.

NIB	Exc.	V.G.	Good	Fair	Poor
2100	1750	1300	950	600	400

Expert Pistol

Similar to above model, with progressive triple port compensator.

NIB	Exc.	V.G.	Good	Fair	Poor
2200	1850	1400	1000	650	400

Bureau Model 1911-A1

Introduced in 1998. Features 5" match barrel, speed trigger, lowered and flared ejection port, beavertail grip safety, Lo-Mount Novak night sights, front strap checkering, Black T finish and special serial numbers with FBI prefix. Bureau Model markings on slide.

NIB	Exc.	V.G.	Good	Fair	Poor
2100	1750	1300	950	600	400

Springfield Formula "Squirtgun"

Chambered for .45 ACP, .38 Super, 9mmx19, 9mmx21, 9mmx23. Fitted with a high capacity 20-round frame, customer specifications sights, hard chrome frame and slide, triple chambered tapered cone compensator, full recoil spring guide and reverse plug, shock butt, lowered and flared ejection port, fitted trigger, Commander hammer, polished feed ramp and throated barrel, flat checkered mainspring housing, extended ambidextrous thumb safety, tuned extractor, checkered front strap, bottom of trigger guard checkered, rear of slide serrated, cocking sensations on front of slide, built in beveled magazine well and checkered wood grips.

NIB	Exc.	V.G.	Good	Fair	Poor
3500	2950	2500	2000	1400	700

Bullseye Wadcutter

Chambered for .45 ACP, .38 Super, 10mm and .40 S&W. Slide fitted with BoMar rib. Standard features include full length recoil spring guide rod, speed trigger, Commander hammer, lowered and flared ejection port, tuned extractor, fitted slide to frame, beveled magazine well, checkered front strap, checkered main spring housing, removable grip scope mount, match barrel and bushing, polished feed ramp and throated barrel, walnut grips and two magazines with slam pads.

NIB	Exc.	V.G.	Good	Fair	Poor
1800	1600	1275	1050	650	400

Trophy Master Distinguished Pistol

Chambered for the following cartridges: .45 ACP, .38 Super, 10mm, .40 S&W, 9mmx21. Special BoMar adjustable rear sight with hidden rear leaf, triple port compensator on match barrel, full length recoil spring guide rod and recoil spring retainer, shock butt, lowered and flared ejection port, fitted speed trigger, Commander hammer, polished feed ramp and throated barrel, flat checkered magazine well and mainspring housing matched to beveled magazine well, extended ambidextrous thumb safety, tuned extractor, checkered front strap, flattened and checkered trigger guard, serrated slide top and compensator, cocking sensations on front of slide, checkered walnut grips, two magazines with slam pads and carrying case.

NIB	Exc.	V.G.	Good	Fair	Poor
2450	1900	1350	1000	650	500

Distinguished Limited Class

Similar to above model, but built to comply with USPSA "Limited Class" competition rules. This model has no compensator.

NIB	Exc.	V.G.	Good	Fair	Poor
2695	2000	1500	1000	650	500

CMC Formula "Squirtgun"

Chambered for .45 ACP, .38 Super, 9mmx19, 9mmx21, 9mmx23. Has a 20-round magazine and modular frame. All other features same as Trophy Master.

NIB	Exc.	V.G.	Good	Fair	Poor
2750	2000	1200	800	400	200

National Match Model

As above, with National Match barrel and bushing, adjustable sights and checkered walnut grips. Introduced in 1988.

NIB	Exc.	V.G.	Good	Fair	Poor
1535	1150	850	600	400	300

Competition Grade

As above, hand-tuned Match-grade trigger, low-profile combat sights, ambidextrous safety and Commander-type hammer. Furnished with Pachmayr grips. Introduced in 1988.

NIB	Exc.	V.G.	Good	Fair	Poor
1600	1200	900	650	400	350

A Model Master Grade Competition Pistol

Similar to Custom Carry Gun, with National Match barrel and bushing. Introduced in 1988.

NIB	Exc.	V.G.	Good	Fair	Poor
1700	1500	1250	850	400	350

Model B-1 Master Grade Competition Pistol

Specially designed for USPSA/IPSC competition. Introduced in 1988.

NIB	Exc.	V.G.	Good	Fair	Poor
2000	1750	1250	850	400	350

High Capacity Full-House Race Gun

Built with all available race gun options. Offered in .45 ACP, 9x25 Dillon, .38 Super and custom calibers on request.

NIB	Exc.	V.G.	Good	Fair	Poor
3085	2300	1700	1200	700	400

Night Light Standard

Introduced in 1996. Limited edition from Springfield, distributor Lew Horton. Full size Model 1911A1 pistol chambered for .45 ACP. Has a lightweight frame and slide, with Millett night sights with Hogue rubber wrap-around grips. Fitted with extended beavertail safety. Weight 29 oz.

NIB	Exc.	V.G.	Good	Fair	Poor
620	500	400	300	200	100

Night Light Compact

This model also introduced by Lew Horton in 1996. Similar to above model, but fitted with 4.25" barrel and lightweight frame and slide. Weight 27 oz.

NIB	Exc.	V.G.	Good	Fair	Poor
620	500	400	300	200	100

Night Compact

Same as above, with steel frame and slide.

NIB	Exc.	V.G.	Good	Fair	Poor
620	500	400	300	200	100

Omega

A .38 Super, 10mm Norma or .45-caliber semi-automatic pistol, with 5" or 6" polygon rifled barrel, ported or unported, adjustable sights and Pachmayr grips. Patterned somewhat after Colt Model 1911. Introduced in 1987. **NOTE:** Add $400 for Caliber Conversion Units.

NIB	Exc.	V.G.	Good	Fair	Poor
650	500	350	250	200	125

XD Custom Pro

This pistol was built in the Custom Shop and available in service and tactical sizes. Calibers offered include 9mm, .357 SIG, .40 S&W, .40 GAP and .45 ACP. Among some of the special features are high hand frame relief, overtravel stop, low-mount Bomar sights, extended magazine release, National Match barrel and special finish. Discontinued.

NIB	Exc.	V.G.	Good	Fair	Poor
1500	1100	825	675	500	300

XD Carry Pro

This model offered in sub-compact, service and tactical sizes. In sub-compact size the following calibers are offered: 9mm and .40 S&W. Many special features as listed above.

NIB	Exc.	V.G.	Good	Fair	Poor
750	550	400	300	200	100

SPRINGFIELD ARMS COMPANY
Springfield, Massachusetts

Belt Model

A .31-caliber percussion revolver, with 4", 5" or 6" round barrels, centrally mounted hammer and etched 6-shot cylinder. Made with/without a loading lever. Early production versions marked "Jaquith's Patent 1838" on frame; later production marked "Springfield Arms" on top strap. Approximately 150 made.

NIB	Exc.	V.G.	Good	Fair	Poor
—	—	2600	1925	875	200

Warner Model

As above, but marked "Warner's Patent Jan. 1851". Approximately 150 made.

NIB	Exc.	V.G.	Good	Fair	Poor
—	—	3200	2750	1325	250

Double Trigger Model

As above, with two triggers, one which locks the cylinder. Approximately 100 made in 1851.

NIB	Exc.	V.G.	Good	Fair	Poor
—	—	2750	2200	875	200

Pocket Model Revolver

A .28-caliber percussion revolver with 2.5" round barrel, centrally mounted hammer, no loading lever and etched 6-shot cylinder. Marked "Warner's Patent Jan. 1851" and "Springfield Arms Company". Blued case-hardened, with walnut grips. Early production examples do not have a groove on cylinder and have a rounded frame. Approximately 525 made in 1851.

Courtesy Milwaukee Public Museum, Milwaukee, Wisconsin

NIB	Exc.	V.G.	Good	Fair	Poor
—	—	1750	1250	585	150

Ring Trigger Model

As above, fitted with a ring trigger that revolved the cylinder. Approximately 150 made in 1851.

Courtesy Milwaukee Public Museum, Milwaukee, Wisconsin

NIB	Exc.	V.G.	Good	Fair	Poor
—	—	1725	1275	550	200

Double Trigger Model

As above, with two triggers set within a conventional trigger guard. Forward trigger revolves the cylinder. Approximately 350 made in 1851.

NIB	Exc.	V.G.	Good	Fair	Poor
—	—	1625	1275	550	200

Late Model Revolver

As above, except cylinder is automatically turned when hammer is cocked. Top strap marked "Warner's Patent/James Warner, Springfield, Mass.". Approximately 500 made in 1851.

NIB	Exc.	V.G.	Good	Fair	Poor
—	—	1300	875	325	100

Dragoon

A .40-caliber percussion revolver with 6" or 7.5" round barrel. Some fitted with/without loading levers. Top strap marked "Springfield Arms Company". Blued with walnut grips. Approximately 110 made in 1851.

NIB	Exc.	V.G.	Good	Fair	Poor
—	—	10000	8800	3850	950

Navy Model

A .36-caliber percussion revolver with 6" round barrel, centrally mounted hammer and 6-shot etched cylinder. Top strap marked "Springfield Arms Company". Blued case-hardened, with walnut grips. This model manufactured in two variations: one with a single trigger; other with a double trigger, the forward one which locks the cylinder. Both variations had loading levers. Approximately 250 made in 1851.

NIB	Exc.	V.G.	Good	Fair	Poor
—	—	6000	4250	1650	500

Double-Barrel Shotguns

Springfield Arms Co. was bought by Stevens, who used the Springfield brand name on many good quality single-/double-barrel shotguns. Values range from $100 to $1,600 depending on model, gauge and condition. See also Stevens.

SQUIBBMAN
SEE—Squires Bingham Mfg. Co., Inc.

SQUIRES BINGHAM MFG. CO., INC.
Rizal, Philippine Islands

Firearms produced by this company are marketed under the trademark Squibbman.

Model 100D

A .38 Special caliber double-action swingout cylinder revolver, with 3", 4" or 6" ventilated rib barrel, adjustable sights, matte black finish and walnut grips.

NIB	Exc.	V.G.	Good	Fair	Poor
—	175	100	80	60	40

Model 100DC

As above, without ventilated rib.

NIB	Exc.	V.G.	Good	Fair	Poor
—	200	100	80	60	40

Model 100

As above, with tapered barrel and uncheckered walnut grips.

NIB	Exc.	V.G.	Good	Fair	Poor
—	200	100	80	60	40

Thunder Chief

As above in .22 or .22 Magnum caliber with heavier ventilated rib barrel, shrouded ejector and ebony grips.

NIB	Exc.	V.G.	Good	Fair	Poor
—	225	125	100	80	60

SSK INDUSTRIES
Bloomingdale, Ohio
SSK-Contender

Custom-made pistol available in 74 different calibers from .178 Bee to .588 JDJ. Built on Thompson/Center action.

NIB	Exc.	V.G.	Good	Fair	Poor
1250	1050	875	600	550	300

SSK-XP100

Custom-made pistol utilizing Rem. XP100 action. Available in a variety of calibers and sight configurations.

NIB	Exc.	V.G.	Good	Fair	Poor
1400	1225	900	625	575	400

.50 Caliber XP100

As above, with integral muzzle-brake and reinforced composition stock.

NIB	Exc.	V.G.	Good	Fair	Poor
1750	1500	1250	1000	750	450

STAFFORD, T. J.
New Haven, Connecticut

Pocket Pistol

A .22-caliber single-shot spur trigger pistol, with 3.5" octagonal barrel marked "T.J. Stafford New Haven Ct.". Silver-plated brass frame. Walnut or rosewood grips.

Courtesy W.P. Hallstein III and son Chip

NIB	Exc.	V.G.	Good	Fair	Poor
—	—	775	600	250	100

Large Frame Model

As above in .38 rimfire caliber, with 6" barrel.

NIB	Exc.	V.G.	Good	Fair	Poor
—	—	1050	850	400	200

STAG ARMS
New Britain, Connecticut

NOTE: All Stag rifles are available in left hand configuration. Prices are approximately $25 - $40 higher than right handed models listed here.

Stag-15 Model 1 Pre-Ban

Basic M-4 Carbine pattern. Cal. 5.56mm/.223. 16" M-4 barrel, with flash hider and bayonet lug. A2 upper receiver, with adjustable rear sight. Six-position collapsible buttstock.

NIB	Exc.	V.G.	Good	Fair	Poor
950	800	675	500	350	200

Stag-15 Model 2 Pre-Ban

As above, with flattop upper receiver. Includes MI ERS flip type rear sight assembly.

NIB	Exc.	V.G.	Good	Fair	Poor
950	800	675	500	350	200

Stag-15 Model 2 T

As above, with A.R.M.S. sight system and Samson MRFS-C four sided hand guard.

NIB	Exc.	V.G.	Good	Fair	Poor
1050	900	775	600	400	250

Stag-15 Model 3 Pre-Ban

M-4 type carbine featuring flattop receiver and gas block, with Picatinny rails. Six-position collapsible buttstock.

NIB	Exc.	V.G.	Good	Fair	Poor
950	800	675	500	350	200

Stag-15 Model 4 Pre-Ban

A-2 type rifle featuring 20" barrel. Flash hider and bayonet lug.

NIB	Exc.	V.G.	Good	Fair	Poor
950	800	675	500	350	200

Stag 6.8 Model 5 Pre-Ban

Cal. 6.8 SPC. 16" barrel. Flattop receiver, with Picatinny rail. Six-position collapsible buttstock. 25-round magazine.

NIB	Exc.	V.G.	Good	Fair	Poor
1050	900	775	600	400	250

Stag-15 Model 6 Pre-Ban Super Varminter

24" heavy barrel. No flash hider. Flattop receiver, with Picatinny rail. Two-stage trigger. Free float round hand guard. A2 type fixed stock.

NIB	Exc.	V.G.	Good	Fair	Poor
1050	900	775	600	400	250

Stag-8T

AR/M4-style in .223 Rem./5.56 NATO, with 16" chrome-lined barrel. Adjustable gas piston action, synthetic pistol-grip, Diamondhead VRS-T aluminum hand guard and flip-up front and rear sights.

NIB	Exc.	V.G.	Good	Fair	Poor
1000	900	800	500	400	300

STALCAP, ALEXANDER T.F.M.
Nashville, Tennessee

First in business during 1850s, Stalcap received a contract in 1862, to modify sporting arms for military use. Overall length 50.875" to 51.75"; octagonal barrels 35.25" - 36" turned round at muzzle for socket bayonets; .54-caliber. Rifles assembled with sporting locks, new stocks and brass furniture. At least 102 rifles were delivered in 1862. These arms are unmarked.

NIB	Exc.	V.G.	Good	Fair	Poor
—	—	6500	4250	2000	1000

STANDARD ARMS CO.
Wilmington, Delaware

Model G

Chambered for .25 Rem., .30 Rem. and .35 Rem., with 22" barrel. Open sights. Integral box magazine and closable gas port that allowed rifle to be used as a slide action. Blued, with walnut stock. Produced in limited quantities, circa 1910. A notorious jamamatic. Bronze alloy buttplate and fore-end.

NIB	Exc.	V.G.	Good	Fair	Poor
—	750	600	450	250	150

Model M

Manually-operated pump-only version of Model G.

NIB	Exc.	V.G.	Good	Fair	Poor
—	900	725	550	300	150

STAR, BONIFACIO ECHEVERRIA
Eibar, Spain

SEE—Echeverria

STARR, EBAN T.
New York, New York

Single-Shot Derringer

A .41-caliber single-shot pistol, with pivoted 2.75" round barrel. Hammer mounted on right side of frame. Trigger formed in the shape of a button located at front of the frame. Frame marked "Starr's Pat's May 10, 1864". Brass frame silver-plated. Barrel blued or silver-plated, with checkered walnut grips. Manufactured from 1864 to 1869.

Courtesy Milwaukee Public Museum, Milwaukee, Wisconsin

NIB	Exc.	V.G.	Good	Fair	Poor
—	—	2300	1850	825	200

Four Barreled Pepperbox

A .32-caliber 4 barreled pocket pistol, with 2.75" to 3.25" barrels. Frame marked "Starr's Pat's May 10, 1864". Brass frames, silver-plated. Barrel blued, with plain walnut grips. Produced in six variations.

Courtesy Milwaukee Public Museum, Milwaukee, Wisconsin

First Model

Fluted breech. Barrel release mounted on right side of frame.

NIB	Exc.	V.G.	Good	Fair	Poor
—	—	3900	2750	875	200

Second Model

Flat breech.

NIB	Exc.	V.G.	Good	Fair	Poor
—	—	2500	1925	650	200

Third Model

Rounded breech, with visible firing-pin retaining spring.

NIB	Exc.	V.G.	Good	Fair	Poor
—	—	2350	1650	550	150

Fourth Model

Rounded breech, without visible springs.

NIB	Exc.	V.G.	Good	Fair	Poor
—	—	2100	1650	550	150

Fifth Model

A larger more angular grip.

NIB	Exc.	V.G.	Good	Fair	Poor
—	—	1950	1400	450	150

Sixth Model

Frame length increased in size.

NIB	Exc.	V.G.	Good	Fair	Poor
—	—	2100	1650	550	150

STARR ARMS COMPANY
New York, New York

1858 Navy Revolver

A .36-caliber double-action percussion revolver, with 6" barrel and 6-shot cylinder. Blued case-hardened, with walnut grips. Frame marked "Starr

Arms Co. New York". Approximately 3,000 made between 1858 and 1860.

Courtesy Milwaukee Public Museum, Milwaukee, Wisconsin

Standard Model

NIB	Exc.	V.G.	Good	Fair	Poor
—	—	4100	3250	1100	350

Martially Marked (JT)

NIB	Exc.	V.G.	Good	Fair	Poor
—	—	5100	4250	1750	700

1858 Army Revolver

A .44-caliber double-action percussion revolver, with 6" barrel and 6-shot cylinder. Blued case-hardened, with walnut grips. Frame marked "Starr Arms Co. New York". Approximately 23,000 manufactured.

NIB	Exc.	V.G.	Good	Fair	Poor
—	6200	4300	2500	1100	300

1863 Army Revolver

Similar to above, but single-action with 8" round barrel. Approximately 32,000 manufactured between 1863 and 1865.

Courtesy Milwaukee Public Museum, Milwaukee, Wisconsin

NIB	Exc.	V.G.	Good	Fair	Poor
—	6750	4700	3250	1500	350

Percussion Carbine

A .54-caliber breechloading percussion carbine, with 21" round barrel secured by one barrel band. Blued case-hardened, with walnut stock. Lock marked "Starr Arms Co./Yonkers, N.Y.".

Courtesy Milwaukee Public Museum, Milwaukee, Wisconsin

NIB	Exc.	V.G.	Good	Fair	Poor
—	—	3500	2750	1250	400

Cartridge Carbine

Similar to above in .52 rimfire caliber. Approximately 5,000 manufactured.

Courtesy Milwaukee Public Museum, Milwaukee, Wisconsin

NIB	Exc.	V.G.	Good	Fair	Poor
—	—	3750	2500	1000	350

STEEL CITY ARMS, INC.
Pittsburgh, Pennsylvania

Double Deuce

A .22-caliber stainless steel double-action semi-automatic pistol, with 2.5" barrel, 7-shot magazine and plain rosewood grips. Introduced in 1984.

Courtesy J.B. Wood

NIB	Exc.	V.G.	Good	Fair	Poor
—	300	250	200	150	100

STENDA WAFFENFABRIK
Suhl, Germany

Pocket Pistol

A 7.65mm semi-automatic pistol similar to "Beholla", "Leonhardt" and "Menta". Stenda took over production of Beholla pistol design at the end of WWI. Only major difference in Stenda design was elimination of Beholla's worst feature, the pin that went through slide and retained the barrel. Replaced by a sliding catch that anchored it in place and unlocked the slide so barrel could be removed without the need of a vise and drift pin. Stenda pistol can be identified by the fact there are no holes through the slide and there is a catch on the frame above the trigger. Finish blued with plastic grips; slide marked "Waffenfabrik Stendawerke Suhl". Approximately 25,000 made before production ceased in 1926.

NIB	Exc.	V.G.	Good	Fair	Poor
—	450	275	225	165	100

STERLING ARMAMENT LTD.
London, England

Parapistol MK 7 C4

A 9mm semi-automatic pistol, with 4" barrel. Detachable 10-round magazine. Black wrinkled paint finish, with plastic grips.

NIB	Exc.	V.G.	Good	Fair	Poor
600	475	400	300	200	100

Parapistol MK 7 C8

As above, with 7.8" barrel.

NIB	Exc.	V.G.	Good	Fair	Poor
625	500	400	300	200	100

Sterling MK 6

A semi-automatic copy of Sterling submachine gun, with 16.1" barrel, folding metal stock and side mounted magazine. Finished as above.

NIB	Exc.	V.G.	Good	Fair	Poor
1500	950	750	500	300	200

Sterling AR 180

Copy of Armalite Model AR18, 5.56mm rifle. Finished with black wrinkled paint, or more rarely, blued.

NIB	Exc.	V.G.	Good	Fair	Poor
1100	750	600	500	350	200

STERLING ARMS CORPORATION
Gasport, New York

Model 283 Target 300

Similar in appearance to Hi-Standard semi-automatic pistols. Chambered for .22 LR cartridge. Offered with 4", 4.5" or 8" barrels. Rear sight adjustable. Magazine holds 10 rounds. Grips are black plastic. Weight about 36 oz.

NIB	Exc.	V.G.	Good	Fair	Poor
300	250	175	100	75	60

Model 284 Target 300L

Similar to above, except for 4.5" or 6" tapered barrel, with barrel band.

Courtesy John J. Stimson, Jr.

NIB	Exc.	V.G.	Good	Fair	Poor
325	275	175	100	75	60

Model 285 Husky

Similar to Model 283, with fixed sights. Offered with 4.5" barrel only.

NIB	Exc.	V.G.	Good	Fair	Poor
300	250	175	100	75	60

Model 286 Trapper

Similar to Model 284, except for fixed sights.

NIB	Exc.	V.G.	Good	Fair	Poor
300	250	175	100	75	60

Model 287 PPL .380

Pocket-size semi-automatic pistol, chambered for .380 ACP cartridge. Fitted with a 1" barrel. Overall length 5.25". Magazine holds 6 rounds. Weight about 22 oz.

NIB	Exc.	V.G.	Good	Fair	Poor
225	175	125	75	50	25

Model PPL .22

Small pocket pistol similar to Model 287. Chambered for .22 LR cartridge. Barrel 1" long. Weight about 24 oz.

NIB	Exc.	V.G.	Good	Fair	Poor
275	225	150	75	60	50

Model 300

Similar to Model 287, but chambered for .25 ACP cartridge. Has a 2.25" barrel, with 6-round magazine. Overall length 5". Weight about 14 oz.

NIB	Exc.	V.G.	Good	Fair	Poor
250	225	150	75	50	40

Model 300S

Stainless steel version of Model 300.

NIB	Exc.	V.G.	Good	Fair	Poor
265	235	165	75	50	40

Model 302

Identical to Model 300, except chambered for .22 LR cartridge.

NIB	Exc.	V.G.	Good	Fair	Poor
250	225	150	75	50	40

Model 302S

Same as above in stainless steel.

NIB	Exc.	V.G.	Good	Fair	Poor
265	235	165	75	60	50

Model 400

Double-action semi-automatic pistol. Chambered for .380 ACP cartridge, with 3.5" barrel. Magazine holds 7 rounds. Overall length 6.5". Weight about 24 oz.

NIB	Exc.	V.G.	Good	Fair	Poor
300	275	200	125	100	75

Model 400S

Stainless steel version of Model 400.

NIB	Exc.	V.G.	Good	Fair	Poor
325	300	2255	125	100	75

Model 402

Similar to Model 400, except chambered for .22 LR cartridge.

NIB	Exc.	V.G.	Good	Fair	Poor
250	225	150	75	60	40

Model X-Caliber

Single-shot .22 LR, .22 WMR, .357 Magnum or .44 Magnum pistol. Interchangeable barrels from 8" and 10". Adjustable rear sight. Finger groove grips. **NOTE:** Deduct 50 percent for rimfire.

NIB	Exc.	V.G.	Good	Fair	Poor
450	400	300	225	150	100

STEVENS ARMS CO., J.
Chicopee Falls, Massachusetts

In 1864, this firm began doing business as J. Stevens & Company. In 1888, it was incorporated as J. Stevens Arms & Tool Company. It operated as such until 1920, when it was taken over by Savage Arms Company. It has operated as an independent division in this organization since. This company produced a great many firearms—most that were of an affordable nature. They are widely collected. One interested in them should take advantage of literature available on the subject.

Vest Pocket Pistol

Single-shot pocket pistol. Chambered for .22 and .30 rimfire cartridges. The .22-caliber version is rarely encountered and would be worth approximately 25 percent more than values illustrated. Has a 2.75" part-octagonal barrel that pivots upward for loading, external hammer and spur-type trigger. Frame nickel-plated or blued, with blued barrel. Odd shaped flared-grips are made of rosewood. First models marked "Vest Pocket Pistol" only. Later models have barrels marked "J. Stevens & Co. Chicopee Falls, Mass.". Approximately 1,000 manufactured between 1864 and 1876.

Courtesy Milwaukee Public Museum, Milwaukee, Wisconsin

NIB	Exc.	V.G.	Good	Fair	Poor
—	5000	3450	2300	1300	1000

Pocket Pistol

A more conventional-appearing single-shot pocket pistol. Chambered for .22 or .30 rimfire cartridges. Has a 3.5" part-octagonal barrel that pivots upward for loading. Features plated brass frame, with blued or nickel-plated barrel and rosewood two-piece grips. Barrel marked "J. Stevens & Co. Chicopee Falls, Mass.". Approximately 15,000 manufactured between 1864 and 1886.

Courtesy Milwaukee Public Museum, Milwaukee, Wisconsin

NIB	Exc.	V.G.	Good	Fair	Poor
—	700	500	250	125	100

Gem Pocket Pistol

Single-shot derringer-type pocket pistol. Chambered for .22 or .30 rimfire cartridges. Has a 3" part-octagonal barrel that pivots to side for loading, nickel-plated brass frame, with blued or plated barrel and bird's-head grips made of walnut or rosewood. Barrel marked "Gem". Stevens name or address does not appear on this firearm. Approximately 4,000 manufactured between 1872 and 1890.

NIB	Exc.	V.G.	Good	Fair	Poor
—	1100	900	600	425	300

.22 or .41 Caliber Derringer

Single-shot pocket pistol. Chambered for .22- or .41-caliber rimfire cartridge. Has a 4" part-octagonal barrel that pivots upward for loading, spur trigger and external hammer. Frame plated brass, with blued barrel. Walnut bird's-head grips. Firearm completely unmarked except for serial number. Approximately 100 manufactured in 1875.

.22 Caliber

NIB	Exc.	V.G.	Good	Fair	Poor
—	6500	6000	5000	3000	1500

.41 Caliber

NIB	Exc.	V.G.	Good	Fair	Poor
—	6200	5600	4000	2500	1400

No. 41 Pistol

Single-shot pocket pistol. Chambered for .22 and .30 Short cartridges. Has a 3.5" part-octagonal barrel that pivots upward for loading. Features external hammer and spur-type trigger. Has an iron frame, with firing pin mounted in recoil shield. Blued or nickel-plated, with square-butt walnut grips. Approximately 90,000 manufactured between 1896 and 1916.

Courtesy Rock Island Auction Company

NIB	Exc.	V.G.	Good	Fair	Poor
—	500	425	300	250	135

Single-Shot Pistol

Single-shot pistol chambered for .22 or .30 rimfire cartridges. Has a 3.5" part-octagonal barrel that pivots upward for loading. Quite similar in appearance to original pocket pistol. Plated brass frame and blued or nickel-plated barrel, with walnut square-butt grips. Barrel marked "J. Stevens A&T Co.". Approximately 10,000 manufactured between 1886 and 1896.

NIB	Exc.	V.G.	Good	Fair	Poor
—	550	400	300	200	150

Tip Up Rifles

Series of rifles produced by Stevens beginning in 1870s through 1895. There are a number of variations, but are all quite similar in appearance. They feature a distinctive sloped frame made of iron and nickel-plated. Most frames are similar in size, but there is a slightly lighter frame used on "Ladies Model" rifles. These Tip Up rifles are chambered for various calibers from .22 rimfire to .44 centerfire cartridges. Offered barrel lengths of 24", 26", 28" or 30". Actions are nickel-plated, as well as trigger guards and buttplates. Barrels blued, and two-piece stocks are of walnut. Offered with various buttplates and sights. A shotgun version is also offered. There are a number of variations that differ only slightly. Model numbers are not marked on rifles. We suggest securing a qualified appraisal if in doubt. Major variations and their values are as follows:

Courtesy Milwaukee Public Museum, Milwaukee, Wisconsin

Ladies Model—.22 or .25 Rimfire Only, 24" or 26" Barrel

NIB	Exc.	V.G.	Good	Fair	Poor
—	3750	3200	2400	1500	700

Tip Up Rifle—Without Fore-end

NIB	Exc.	V.G.	Good	Fair	Poor
—	750	650	500	250	200

Tip Up Rifle—With Fore-end, Swiss-Type Buttplate

NIB	Exc.	V.G.	Good	Fair	Poor
—	1250	1000	600	400	250

Tip Up Shotgun—All Gauges, 30" or 32" Barrel

NIB	Exc.	V.G.	Good	Fair	Poor
—	600	500	300	150	100

Ideal Single-Shot Rifle

This excellent rifle manufactured by Stevens between 1896 and 1933. A single-shot falling-block type action that is activated by a trigger guard action lever. Produced in many popular calibers from .22 rimfire up to .30-40. Also manufactured in a number of special Stevens calibers. Offered with various barrel lengths in many different grades, from plain Spartan starter rifles up to some extremely high-grade Schuetzen-type target rifles, with all available options. In 1901, Harry Pope of Hartford, Connecticut, went to work for Stevens and brought his highly respected barrel to Stevens Company. He remained an employee for only two years and firearms produced during this period have the name "Stevens-Pope" stamped on top of barrel in addition to other factory markings. Rifles marked in this manner and authenticated, would be worth an approximate 50 percent premium if they are in very good to excellent condition. Due to numerous variations and options offered, we strongly recommend securing a qualified appraisal, especially on higher-grade Ideal series rifles, before a purchase.

No. 44

This version chambered for various calibers. Offered with 24" or 26" barrel. Has an open rear sight, with Rocky Mountain-type front sight. Finish blued and case colored, with walnut stock. Approximately 100,000 manufactured between 1896 and 1933.

NIB	Exc.	V.G.	Good	Fair	Poor
—	1300	1080	700	400	225

No. 44-1/2

Similar in appearance to No. 44, but features an improved action. Barrel lengths up to 34" and will be found with Stevens-Pope barrel. Manufactured between 1903 and 1916.

Courtesy J.B. Barnes

NIB	Exc.	V.G.	Good	Fair	Poor
—	2175	1950	1500	1000	725

No. 044-1/2

This version also known as "English Model" rifle. Similar to No. 44-1/2, except it has a shotgun butt and tapered barrel. There were a number of options offered that would affect the value. Manufactured between 1903 and 1916.

Courtesy Mike Stuckslager

NIB	Exc.	V.G.	Good	Fair	Poor
—	2175	1950	1500	1000	725

No. 45

This version also known as "Range Rifle". Chambered for various calibers from .22 rimfire to .44-40. Identifying features are Beach sights, with additional vernier tang sight and Swiss-type buttstock. Offered with 26" or 28" part-octagonal barrel. Manufactured between 1896 and 1916. Values listed are for standard version. **NOTE:** Deduct 25 percent for .44 action.

NIB	Exc.	V.G.	Good	Fair	Poor
—	2375	2150	1600	1100	825

No. 46

Same as No. 45, with fancy wood stock. Manufactured from 1896 to 1902. Built in No. 44 action-only.

NIB	Exc.	V.G.	Good	Fair	Poor
—	2700	2375	1900	1500	1100

No. 47

This version similar to No. 45, with pistol-grip buttstock. **NOTE:** Deduct 25 percent for .44 action.

NIB	Exc.	V.G.	Good	Fair	Poor
—	5400	4750	3600	3000	1200

No. 48

Same as No. 47, with fancy wood checkered stock. Manufactured from 1896 to 1902. Built in No. 44 action-only. A very rare model.

NIB	Exc.	V.G.	Good	Fair	Poor
—	6000	5100	4200	3000	2000

No. 49

Also known as "Walnut Hill Rifle". A high grade target rifle chambered for many calibers between .22 rimfire and .44-40. Offered with 28" or 30" part-octagonal barrel that is medium-/heavy-weight. Furnished with globe front sight and vernier tang sight. Blued, with case colored frame. Has a high-grade checkered varnished walnut stock, that has a high comb. Features a pistol-grip, cheekpiece, Swiss-type buttplate and loop-type trigger guard lever that resembles that of a lever-action rifle. Receiver engraved. There were a number of options available that would increase value when present. We recommend an appraisal when in doubt. Manufactured between 1896 and 1916.

Courtesy J.B. Barnes

NIB	Exc.	V.G.	Good	Fair	Poor
—	8000	7500	4500	3000	2000

Model 50

Identical to Model 49, but offered with higher-grade walnut stock. A very rare model.

Courtesy J.B. Barnes

NIB	Exc.	V.G.	Good	Fair	Poor
—	9200	8600	5200	3500	2400

Model 51

This version also known as "Schuetzen Rifle". Quite similar to No. 49, except it features double-set triggers, higher-grade walnut stock, wooden insert in trigger guard action lever and heavy Schuetzen-type buttplate. There were many options available on this model. We recommend securing an appraisal when in doubt. Manufactured between 1896 and 1916.

Courtesy J.B. Barnes

NIB	Exc.	V.G.	Good	Fair	Poor
—	15000	13000	8250	5000	2500

No. 52

Also known as "Schuetzen Junior". Similar to No. 51, except it features more engraving and higher-grade walnut stock. Manufactured between 1897 and 1916.

Courtesy J.B. Barnes

NIB	Exc.	V.G.	Good	Fair	Poor
—	15000	13000	8250	5000	2500

No. 53

Same as No. 51, except for addition of a fancy wood stock and palm rest. Produced from 1896 to 1902. Offered only with No. 44 action. A rare rifle.

NIB	Exc.	V.G.	Good	Fair	Poor
—	13000	10000	8000	5000	2500

No. 54

Similar to No. 52, except it has double-set triggers, palm rest and heavy Swiss-style buttplate. Offered with 30" or 32" part-octagonal heavy barrel. This was Stevens' top-of-the-line rifle. Offered with many options. An appraisal should be secured if in doubt. Manufactured between 1897 and 1916. **NOTE:** Prices are based on No. 44-1/2 action. A No. 44 action will bring 20 percent less than the prices listed.

NIB	Exc.	V.G.	Good	Fair	Poor
—	19500	17500	12500	9000	5500

No. 55

This version is one of Stevens' Ideal Ladies Models. Chambered for smaller rimfire calibers between .22 Short and .32 Long rimfire. Features 24" or 26" part-octagonal barrel, with vernier tang sight. Finish blued and case colored, with checkered pistol-grip walnut stock that features Swiss-type buttplate. Lighter weight rifle manufactured between 1897 and 1916.

NIB	Exc.	V.G.	Good	Fair	Poor
—	7000	5500	3750	2200	1100

No. 56

Ladies' Model rifle similar to No. 55, except chambered for centerfire cartridges. Has a higher-grade walnut stock. It was made on improved No. 44-1/2 action. Manufactured between 1906 and 1916.

Courtesy J.B. Barnes

NIB	Exc.	V.G.	Good	Fair	Poor
—	7500	6000	4250	2400	1200

No. 404

This version chambered for .22 rimfire cartridge only. Features 28" round barrel, with globe front sight and Lyman No. 42 receiver sight. Finish blued and case colored. Walnut straight-grip stock, with semi-beavertail fore-end. Features shotgun-type buttplate. Manufactured between 1910 and 1916.

NIB	Exc.	V.G.	Good	Fair	Poor
—	1300	1075	875	750	600

No. 414

Also known as "Armory Model". Chambered for .22 LR cartridge only. Built on No. 44 action. Features 26" round barrel. Has Rocky Mountain front sight, with Lyman receiver sight at rear. Finish blued and case colored, with straight-grip walnut stock. Fore-end held on by single barrel band. Manufactured between 1912 and 1932.

Courtesy Mike Stuckslager

NIB	Exc.	V.G.	Good	Fair	Poor
—	1000	750	550	300	275

No. 417 Walnut Hill Model

Heavy single-shot lever action target rifle. Chambered for .22 LR, .22 Short or .22 Hornet cartridges. Weight about 10.5 lbs. Produced from 1932 to 1940.

NIB	Exc.	V.G.	Good	Fair	Poor
—	1625	1300	850	600	400

No. 417 1/2 Walnut Hill Model

A sporting version of Model 417. Weight about 8.5 lbs. Manufactured from 1932 to 1940.

NIB	Exc.	V.G.	Good	Fair	Poor
—	1725	1400	950	700	450

No. 418 Walnut Hill Jr.

A light single-shot lever action target rifle. Chambered for .22 LR or .22 Short. Weight about 6.5 lbs. Manufactured from 1932 to 1940.

NIB	Exc.	V.G.	Good	Fair	Poor
—	975	800	550	300	200

No. 418 1/2 Walnut Hill Jr.

Similar to Model 418, but chambered for .25 rimfire or .22 WRF cartridges. Also fitted with sporting sights. Manufactured from 1932 to 1940.

NIB	Exc.	V.G.	Good	Fair	Poor
—	975	800	550	300	200

BOY'S RIFLES

Stevens Company produced an extensive line of smaller, single-shot rifles chambered for small calibers. Intended primarily for use by young shooters. These firearms have become quite collectible and are considered a field of specialty by many modern collectors. **NOTE:** There are many variations that were available with a number of options that would affect their value. We supply information and values for the major variations, but would recommend securing a qualified appraisal if in doubt.

"FAVORITE" RIFLES

This series of rifles chambered for .22, .25 and .32 rimfire. Has a 22" blued part-octagonal barrel, with case colored frame. A take-down type action, with interchangeable barrel feature. Available with optional sights and buttplates. Approximately 1,000,000 manufactured between 1893 and 1939. The variations are listed.

Courtesy Buffalo Bill Historical Center, Cody, Wyoming

1st Model Favorite

This version chambered for .22 or .25 rimfire cartridge. Has a removable sideplate on right side of receiver, not found on any other variation. Approximately 1,000 manufactured between 1893 and 1894.

NIB	Exc.	V.G.	Good	Fair	Poor
—	1300	875	700	500	350

No. 17

This is standard plain version, with open sights.

NIB	Exc.	V.G.	Good	Fair	Poor
—	600	435	325	175	125

No. 20

This version chambered for .22 or .32 rimfire shot cartridges. Has a smoothbore barrel and no rear sight.

NIB	Exc.	V.G.	Good	Fair	Poor
—	650	475	350	175	125

No. 21

Known as "Bicycle Rifle". Features 20" barrel, with open sights standard. Furnished with canvas carrying case that would be worth approximately a 30 percent premium. Manufactured between 1898 and 1903.

NIB	Exc.	V.G.	Good	Fair	Poor
—	800	625	375	170	110

No. 21 Ladies Model

This version bears same model number as "Bicycle Rifle", but has 24" barrel and high grade checkered walnut stock, with Swiss buttplate. Features vernier tang sight. Manufactured between 1910 and 1916.

NIB	Exc.	V.G.	Good	Fair	Poor
—	7000	5500	3750	2200	1100

No. 16

This version known as "Crack Shot". Chambered for .22 or .32 rimfire cartridges, with 20" round barrel. Rolling-block-type action, with thumb lever on side. Utility-type rifle with open sights. Blued and case colored finish. Plain two-piece walnut stock, with rubber buttplate. Barrel marked "Crack Shot" along with standard Stevens' barrel address markings. Manufactured between 1900 and 1913.

NIB	Exc.	V.G.	Good	Fair	Poor
—	600	500	350	225	100

No. 16-1/2

Similar to No. 16, except chambered for .32 rimfire shot cartridge, with smoothbore barrel. Manufactured between 1900 and 1913.

NIB	Exc.	V.G.	Good	Fair	Poor
—	625	525	375	250	125

No. 23—Sure Shot

This version chambered for .22 rimfire cartridge. Has a 20" round barrel that pivots to right for loading and a barrel release on the frame. Blued and case colored, with plain walnut buttstock and no fore-end. Manufactured between 1894 and 1897.

NIB	Exc.	V.G.	Good	Fair	Poor
—	2700	2375	1500	1000	600

No. 15

Also known as "Maynard Junior". Chambered for .22 rimfire cartridge. Has an 18" part-octagonal barrel. Action similar to Civil War Maynard rifle, with trigger guard activating lever. Finish all blued, with board-type buttstock and no forearm. Barrel marked "Stevens Maynard, J. R." in addition to standard Stevens' barrel address. Manufactured between 1902 and 1912.

Courtesy Mike Stuckslager

NIB	Exc.	V.G.	Good	Fair	Poor
—	600	500	350	225	100

No. 15-1/2

A smoothbore version of No. 15.

NIB	Exc.	V.G.	Good	Fair	Poor
—	625	525	375	250	125

No. 14

Also known as "Little Scout". Utility take-down rifle. Blued, with one-piece board-type stock. Features rolling-block-type action. Manufactured between 1906 and 1910.

NIB	Exc.	V.G.	Good	Fair	Poor
—	550	425	300	225	100

No. 14-1/2

Similar to No. 14, except has a two-piece stock. Also marked "Little Scout". Manufactured between 1911 and 1941.

NIB	Exc.	V.G.	Good	Fair	Poor
—	500	375	200	150	100

No. 65

Also known as "Little Krag". Single-shot bolt-action rifle chambered for .22 rimfire cartridge. One-piece stock and 20" round barrel marked "Little Krag". Quite scarce. Manufactured between 1903 and 1910.

NIB	Exc.	V.G.	Good	Fair	Poor
—	600	500	350	200	100

No. 12

Also known as "Marksman". Chambered for .22, .25 and .32 rimfire cartridges. Has a 22" barrel that pivots upward for loading. Activated by an S-shaped trigger guard lever. Manufactured between 1911 and 1930.

Courtesy Mike Stuckslager

NIB	Exc.	V.G.	Good	Fair	Poor
—	550	425	300	225	100

No. 26

Also known as "Crack Shot". Has a rolling block-type action. Chambered for .22 or .32 rimfire cartridges. Offered with 18" or 20" round barrel. Blued and has a two-piece stock. Manufactured between 1912 and 1939.

Courtesy Mike Stuckslager

NIB	Exc.	V.G.	Good	Fair	Poor
—	550	425	300	225	100

No. 26-1/2

Smoothbore version of No. 26.

NIB	Exc.	V.G.	Good	Fair	Poor
—	550	500	350	250	100

No. 11—Junior

Single-shot rolling block rifle chambered for .22 rimfire cartridge. Has 20" blued barrel and board-type stock, without buttplate. Last model offered in Boy's Rifle series. Manufactured between 1924 and 1931.

NIB	Exc.	V.G.	Good	Fair	Poor
—	550	425	300	225	100

Model 71

Reintroduced version of "Stevens Favorite". Chambered for .22 LR cartridge. Has a 22" octagonal barrel. Finish blued and case colored, with plain walnut stock that has an inlaid medallion and a crescent buttplate. There were 10,000 manufactured in 1971.

NIB	Exc.	V.G.	Good	Fair	Poor
400	300	175	125	100	75

Model 72

Reintroduced version of "Crack Shot". Features single-shot, falling block action. Chambered for .22 rimfire cartridge. Has 22" octagon barrel, with open sights. Blued and case colored, with straight walnut stock. Introduced in 1972.

NIB	Exc.	V.G.	Good	Fair	Poor
400	300	175	125	100	75

Model 70

Slide-action rifle chambered for .22 rimfire cartridge. Also known as "Visible Loading Rifle". Features 20" round barrel, with 3/4-length tubular magazine. Finish blued and case colored, with walnut stock. Features open sights, but available with other options. Offered as No. 70-1/2, 71, 71-1/2, 72 and 72-1/2. These different model numbers denote various sight combinations. Otherwise, they are identical. Manufactured between 1907 and 1932.

NIB	Exc.	V.G.	Good	Fair	Poor
—	450	350	225	100	75

No. 80

Slide-action repeating rifle chambered for .22 rimfire cartridge. Has 24" round barrel, with tubular magazine. Features open sights and blued, with walnut stock. Manufactured between 1906 and 1910.

NIB	Exc.	V.G.	Good	Fair	Poor
—	500	350	225	175	100

High Power Rifle

A series of lever-action hunting rifles chambered for .25, .300, .32 and .35 Rem. centerfire cartridges. Features 22" round barrel, with tubular magazine. Finish blued, with walnut stock. Available in four variations: No. 425, No. 430, No. 435 and No. 440. These designations denote increased ornamentation and high quality materials and workmanship used in construction. Approximately 26,000 manufactured between 1910 and 1917.

No. 425

NIB	Exc.	V.G.	Good	Fair	Poor
—	1150	900	600	300	200

No. 430

NIB	Exc.	V.G.	Good	Fair	Poor
—	1300	1000	650	400	300

No. 435

NIB	Exc.	V.G.	Good	Fair	Poor
—	1750	1400	1000	600	400

No. 440

NIB	Exc.	V.G.	Good	Fair	Poor
—	3350	3000	2400	1600	850

SPORTING PISTOLS

Beginning in 1869, Stevens Company produced a series of single-shot break-open target and sporting pistols that pivot upward for loading. Chambered for .22 and .25 rimfire cartridges, as well as various centerfire cartridges from .32 Short Colt to .44 Russian. These pistols were made with various barrel lengths and have spur trigger or conventional trigger with a guard. They are all single-actions, with exposed hammers. Finishes are nickel-plated frames, with blued barrels and walnut grips. Variations and their values are listed.

Six-inch Pocket Rifle

This version chambered for .22 rimfire cartridge. Has a 6" part-octagonal barrel, with open sights. Barrel marked "J. Stevens & Co. Chicopee Falls, Mass.". Approximately 1,000 manufactured between 1869 and 1886.

NIB	Exc.	V.G.	Good	Fair	Poor
—	750	500	400	350	200

No. 36

This version known as "Stevens-Lord" pistol. Chambered for various rimfire and centerfire calibers up to .44 Russian. Offered with 10" or 12" part-octagonal barrel. Features a firing pin in the frame, with a bushing. Has a conventional trigger, with spurred trigger guard. Features standard Stevens barrel address. Named after Frank Lord, a target shooter well-known at this time. Approximately 3,500 manufactured from 1880 to 1911.

Courtesy J.B. Barnes

NIB	Exc.	V.G.	Good	Fair	Poor
—	1750	1400	1000	650	400

First Issue Stevens-Conlin

Chambered for .22 or .32 rimfire cartridges. Has a 10" or 12" part-octagonal barrel. Features a plated brass frame, with blued barrel and checkered walnut grips with a weighted buttcap. Has a spur trigger with/without a trigger guard. Named after James Conlin, owner of a shooting gallery located in New York City. Approximately 500 manufactured between 1880 and 1884.

Courtesy J.B. Barnes

NIB	Exc.	V.G.	Good	Fair	Poor
—	2700	2300	1700	900	500

Second Issue Stevens-Conlin No. 38

Similar to First Issue, with conventional trigger, spurred trigger guard and fully adjustable rear sight. Approximately 6,000 manufactured between 1884 and 1903.

NIB	Exc.	V.G.	Good	Fair	Poor
—	1850	1625	1200	800	450

No. 37

Also known as "Stevens-Gould". Named after a 19th century firearms writer. Resembles No. 38, without spur on the trigger guard. Approximately 1,000 manufactured between 1889 and 1903.

Courtesy J.B. Barnes

NIB	Exc.	V.G.	Good	Fair	Poor
—	2600	2200	1300	850	450

No. 35

Chambered for .22 rimfire, .22 Stevens-Pope and .25 Stevens cartridges. Offered with 6", 8", 10" or 12.25" part-octagonal barrel. Firing pin has no bushing. Features an iron frame that is blued or plated, with a blued barrel. Plain walnut grips, with a weighted buttcap. Featured open sights. Approximately 43,000 manufactured between 1923 and 1942. **NOTE:** Longer barrels worth a premium.

NIB	Exc.	V.G.	Good	Fair	Poor
—	450	325	275	175	100

No. 35 Target

Similar to No. 35, but has a better quality trigger guard and sights. Approximately 35,000 manufactured between 1907 and 1916.

NIB	Exc.	V.G.	Good	Fair	Poor
—	500	400	325	200	100

No. 35 Off-Hand/Auto-Shot Shot Gun

Stevens No. 35 is a .410 bore pistol manufactured by J. Stevens Arms Co., Chicopee Falls, Massachusetts. It was available with an 8" or 12.25" smoothbore barrel, for 2.5" shells only. In two variations: Off-Hand Shot Gun (1923 to 1929); and Auto-Shot (1929 to 1934). Total production is unknown because the .410 and .22 rimfire variations of No. 35 share the same serial number range. Researcher Ken Cope estimates total Auto-Shot production was approximately 2,000, and Off-Hand production at 20,000 to 25,000. Production was halted after the government ruled the .410 Stevens to be a "firearm" in the "any other weapon" category under the NFA in 1934, when its retail price was about $12. Stevens does not possess the same collector appeal as other .410 smoothbore pistols, because (1) its relatively light weight makes it an uncomfortable shooter, and (2) the gun is not well made. **NOTE:** 8" barrel commands a 25 to 50 percent premium.

No. 35 Off-Hand Shot Gun

Serial range from 1 to 43357.

Courtesy John J. Stimson, Jr.

NIB	Exc.	V.G.	Good	Fair	Poor
—	400	250	200	100	75

No. 35 Auto-Shot

NIB	Exc.	V.G.	Good	Fair	Poor
—	450	300	200	125	100

No. 43

This version also called "Diamond". Produced in two distinct variations called First Issue and Second Issue. First Issue has a brass frame; Second Issue an iron frame and no firing pin bushing. Otherwise, they are quite similar and would be valued the same. They are chambered for .22 rimfire cartridge. Offered with 6" or 10" part-octagonal barrel. Frames nickel-plated or blued, with blued barrels and square-butt walnut grips. Approximately 95,000 manufactured between 1886 and 1916. **NOTE:** Add 25 percent premium for 10" barrels.

Paul Goodwin photo

NIB	Exc.	V.G.	Good	Fair	Poor
—	600	400	250	150	75

No. 10 Target Pistol

This version was a departure from its predecessors. Very much resembles a semi-automatic pistol, but in reality a single-shot. Chambered for .22 rimfire cartridge. Has an 8" round barrel that pivots upward for loading and a blued steel frame, with checkered rubber grips. Instead of the usual exposed hammer, this version has a knurled cocking piece that extends through rear of the frame. Approximately 7,000 manufactured between 1919 and 1933.

Courtesy John J. Stimson, Jr.

NIB	Exc.	V.G.	Good	Fair	Poor
—	400	300	200	150	100

POCKET RIFLES

This series of pistols similar to target and sporting pistols, except that these were produced with detachable shoulder stocks that bear the same serial number as the pistol with which they were sold. They are sometimes referred to as "Bicycle Rifles". The collector interest in these weapons is quite high; but it would behoove one to be familiar with the provisions of the Gun Control Act of 1968 when dealing in or collecting this variation—as when the stock is attached, they can fall into the category of a short-barreled rifle. Some are considered to be curios and relics, and others have been totally declassified; but some models may still be restricted. We strongly recommend securing a qualified, individual appraisal on these highly collectible firearms if a transaction is contemplated. **NOTE:** Values supplied include the matching shoulder stock. If the stock number does not match the pistol, the values would be approximately 25 percent less; and with no stock at all, 50 percent should be deducted.

Old Model Pocket Rifle

Chambered for .22 rimfire cartridge. Has an 8" or 10" part-octagonal barrel, a spur trigger and an external hammer on which the firing pin is mounted. Extractor is spring-loaded. A plated brass frame, blued barrel and walnut or rosewood grips. Shoulder stock nickel-plated or black. Barrel marked "J. Stevens & Co. Chicopee Falls, Mass.". Approximately 4,000 manufactured between 1869 and 1886.

NIB	Exc.	V.G.	Good	Fair	Poor
—	900	700	550	325	200

Reliable Pocket Rifle

Chambered for .22 rimfire cartridge. Appearance is quite similar to Old Model. Basic difference is the extractor operates as part of the pivoting barrel mechanism instead of being spring-loaded. Barrel marked "J. Stevens A&T Co.". Approximately 4,000 manufactured between 1886 and 1896.

NIB	Exc.	V.G.	Good	Fair	Poor
—	800	625	500	400	300

No. 42 Reliable Pocket Rifle

Similar to first issue Reliable, except it has an iron frame, with the firing pin mounted in it without a bushing. Shoulder stock is shaped differently. Approximately 8,000 manufactured between 1896 and 1916.

NIB	Exc.	V.G.	Good	Fair	Poor
—	700	575	475	350	250

First Issue New Model Pocket Rifle

This version is first of the medium-frame models, with a frame width of 1". All of its predecessors have a .625" wide frame. Chambered for .22 and .32 rimfire cartridges. Offered with barrel lengths of 10", 12", 15" or 18" that are part-octagonal in configuration. External hammer has the firing pin mounted on it. Has a plated brass frame, blued barrel and walnut or rosewood grips. Shoulder stock is nickel-plated and fitted differently than the small-frame models, in that there is a dovetail in the butt and top leg is secured by a knurled screw. Barrel marked "J. Stevens & Co. Chicopee Falls, Mass.". Approximately 8,000 manufactured between 1872 and 1875.

Courtesy Mike Stuckslager

NIB	Exc.	V.G.	Good	Fair	Poor
—	1100	1000	650	500	400

Second Issue New Model Pocket Rifle

Similar to First Issue, except firing pin is mounted in the frame with a bushing. Approximately 15,000 manufactured between 1875 and 1896.

Paul Goodwin photo

NIB	Exc.	V.G.	Good	Fair	Poor
—	975	850	600	500	350

Vernier Model

Similar to Second Issue, except it features a vernier tang sight located on back strap. Approximately 1,500 manufactured between 1884 and 1896.

Courtesy Rock Island Auction Company

NIB	Exc.	V.G.	Good	Fair	Poor
—	1200	900	650	525	300

No. 40

Similar to its medium-frame predecessors, except it has a longer grip frame and a conventional trigger, with trigger guard. Approximately 15,000 manufactured between 1896 and 1916.

Courtesy Rock Island Auction Company

NIB	Exc.	V.G.	Good	Fair	Poor
—	975	850	650	400	300

No. 40-1/2

Similar to No. 40, with a vernier tang sight mounted on the back strap. Approximately 2,500 manufactured between 1896 and 1915.

NIB	Exc.	V.G.	Good	Fair	Poor
—	1100	975	700	550	400

No. 34 (Hunter's Pet)

This is first of the heavy-frame pocket rifles that featured a 1.25" wide frame. Also known as "Hunter's Pet". Chambered for many popular cartridges from .22 rimfire to .44-40 centerfire. Offered with part-octagonal 18", 20", 22" or 24" barrel. Has a nickel-plated iron frame and blued barrel. Detachable stock is nickel-plated and grips are walnut. Few produced with a brass frame; and if located, these would be worth twice the value indicated. Firing pin mounted in the frame, with the bushing and features a spur trigger. Approximately 4,000 manufactured between 1872 and 1900.

NIB	Exc.	V.G.	Good	Fair	Poor
—	1250	1050	700	450	350

No. 34-1/2

Similar to No. 34, except it features a vernier tang sight mounted on the back strap. Approximately 1,200 manufactured between 1884 and 1900.

NIB	Exc.	V.G.	Good	Fair	Poor
—	1425	1250	900	650	450

BOLT-ACTION UTILITY RIFLES

Stevens Company produced a number of inexpensive, utilitarian, bolt-action rifles. These were both single-shot and repeaters. They have been popular over the years as starter rifles for young shooters. Their values are quite similar and are listed for reference purposes only.

Model 053—Single-Shot
Model 056—5-Shot Magazine
Model 066—Tube Magazine
Model 083—Single-Shot
Model 084—5-Shot Magazine
Model 086—Tube Magazine
Model 15—Single-Shot
Model 15Y—Single-Shot
Model 419—Single-Shot
Model 48—Single-Shot
Model 49—Single-Shot
Model 50—Single-Shot
Model 51—Single-Shot
Model 52—Single-Shot
Model 53—Single-Shot
Model 56—5-Shot Magazine
Model 66—Tube Magazine

NIB	Exc.	V.G.	Good	Fair	Poor
—	—	200	100	70	50

Model 416

Target rifle chambered for .22 LR cartridge. Has 24" heavy barrel, with aperture sights. Features 5-round detachable magazine. Blued, with target-type walnut stock.

NIB	Exc.	V.G.	Good	Fair	Poor
—	450	350	200	150	100

Model 322

Bolt-action sporting rifle chambered for .22 Hornet cartridge. Has a 20" barrel, with open sights and detachable box magazine. Finish blued, with plain walnut stock.

NIB	Exc.	V.G.	Good	Fair	Poor
—	175	125	100	75	50

Model 322-S

This version features an aperture rear sight.

NIB	Exc.	V.G.	Good	Fair	Poor
—	225	125	100	75	50

Model 89

Single-shot Martini-type falling-block rifle, chambered for .22 LR cartridge. Has an 18.5" barrel and trigger guard loop-lever activator. Finish blued, with straight walnut stock. Introduced in 1976; discontinued.

NIB	Exc.	V.G.	Good	Fair	Poor
—	125	80	70	60	40

Model 87M

Designed to look like M1 Garand. Chambered for .22 rimfire cartridge.

Courtesy Richard M. Kumor, Sr.

NIB	Exc.	V.G.	Good	Fair	Poor
—	600	500	375	225	150

Model 987

Blowback-operated semi-automatic rifle, chambered for .22 LR cartridge. Has a 20" barrel, with 15-round tubular magazine. Finish blued, with hardwood stock.

NIB	Exc.	V.G.	Good	Fair	Poor
—	150	100	75	50	25

ECONOMY LINE (SAVAGE, 2006)

Model 200

Long-/short-action bolt rifle, chambered in .223, .22-250, .243, 7MM-08, .308, .25-06, .270, .30-06, 7mm RM or .300 WM. Gray checkered synthetic stock and 22" (short-action) or 24" (long-action) blued sightless barrel. Introduced 2006.

NIB	Exc.	V.G.	Good	Fair	Poor
325	275	225	175	125	100

Model 200XP Long or Short Action Package Rifle

Similar to above, with 4x12 scope.

NIB	Exc.	V.G.	Good	Fair	Poor
375	300	250	200	150	125

Model 200XP Camo

Similar to above, with camo stock.

NIB	Exc.	V.G.	Good	Fair	Poor
400	325	275	225	175	150

Cadet Mini-Youth

Similar to Savage Cub .22 rimfire. Introduced 2006.

NIB	Exc.	V.G.	Good	Fair	Poor
200	150	125	100	75	50

Model 315 Youth

Similar to Cadet Mini-Youth, with sightless barrel. Introduced 2006.

NIB	Exc.	V.G.	Good	Fair	Poor
200	150	125	100	75	50

Model 310

Five-shot bolt-action repeater chambered for .17 HMR. Detachable box magazine, synthetic stock, blued 20.75" sightless barrel. Introduced 2006.

NIB	Exc.	V.G.	Good	Fair	Poor
200	150	125	100	75	50

Model 310 Heavy Barrel

Similar to Stevens Model 310, with 21" bull barrel. Introduced 2006.

NIB	Exc.	V.G.	Good	Fair	Poor
225	175	150	115	75	50

Model 300

Clip-fed bolt-action repeater chambered for .22 rimfire. Gray synthetic stock and 20.75" blued barrel. Also available with scope package (add 10 percent). Introduced 2006.

NIB	Exc.	V.G.	Good	Fair	Poor
200	150	125	100	75	50

Model 305

Similar to Model 310. Chambered in .22 WMR. Introduced 2006.

NIB	Exc.	V.G.	Good	Fair	Poor
225	175	150	115	75	50

MISCELLANEOUS SINGLE-SHOT SHOTGUNS

This company manufactured a number of single-barrel break-open single-shot shotguns. They were chambered for various gauges, with various length barrels and chokes. They are quite similar in appearance and were designed as inexpensive utility-grade weapons. There is little or no collector interest in them at this time and their values are similar. They are listed for reference purposes only.

Model 89	Model 102	Model 140
Model 90	Model 104	Model 160
Model 93	Model 105	Model 165
Model 94	Model 106	Model 170
Model 94A	Model 107	Model 180
Model 94C	Model 108	Model 944
Model 95	Model 110	Model 958
Model 97	Model 120	Model 970
Model 100	Model 125	

Model 107

NIB	Exc.	V.G.	Good	Fair	Poor
—	150	100	75	50	25

Model 182

Single-shot break-open shotgun, chambered for 12-gauge. Offered with 30" or 32" trap choked barrels. Features hammerless action, with an automatic ejector and lightly engraved receiver. Finish blued, with checkered trap-grade stock.

NIB	Exc.	V.G.	Good	Fair	Poor
—	175	125	100	75	50

Model 185

This version features a half-octagonal barrel, with automatic ejector and checkered walnut stock. **NOTE:** Deduct 25 percent for Damascus barrel.

NIB	Exc.	V.G.	Good	Fair	Poor
—	175	125	100	75	50

Model 190

A 12-gauge hammerless gun, with an automatic ejector. Lightly engraved, with a half-octagonal barrel. **NOTE:** Deduct 25 percent for Damascus barrel.

NIB	Exc.	V.G.	Good	Fair	Poor
—	175	125	100	75	50

Model 195

Another deluxe version that features engraving, half-octagonal barrel and high-grade checkered walnut stock. **NOTE:** Deduct 25 percent for Damascus barrel.

NIB	Exc.	V.G.	Good	Fair	Poor
—	350	250	200	150	100

Model 240

Over/under model features a boxlock frame, with exposed hammers.

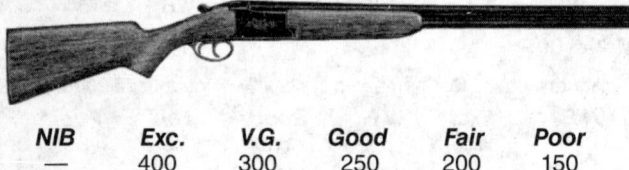

NIB	Exc.	V.G.	Good	Fair	Poor
—	400	300	250	200	150

Model .22/.410

Over/under .22/.410 combo gun, with Tenite stock. Manufactured 1939-1950.

NIB	Exc.	V.G.	Good	Fair	Poor
—	350	300	250	175	100

DOUBLE-BARREL SHOTGUNS

STEVENS BRAND

Firm of J. Stevens and its successors, produced a number of utility-grade side-by-side double-barrel shotguns, between 1877 and 1988. Chambered for 10-, 12-, 16- or 20-gauge and .410 bore. Stevens shotguns in 10-gauge and .410 bore will normally bring a premium as do guns with single triggers and ejectors. They have various-length barrels and choke combinations. Feature double triggers and extractors, except where noted. A complete list of Stevens brand models, including the three in-house brands, Riverside, Springfield and Super Value, are listed.

Model 1877—Hammer Boxlock

NIB	Exc.	V.G.	Good	Fair	Poor
—	575	450	350	250	200

Model 250—Hammer Sidelock

NIB	Exc.	V.G.	Good	Fair	Poor
—	575	450	350	250	200

Model 225—Hammer Boxlock

Courtesy Nick Niles, Paul Goodwin photo

NIB	Exc.	V.G.	Good	Fair	Poor
—	575	450	350	250	200

Model 260—Hammer Sidelock

NIB	Exc.	V.G.	Good	Fair	Poor
—	575	450	350	250	200

Model 270—Hammer Sidelock

NIB	Exc.	V.G.	Good	Fair	Poor
—	575	450	350	250	200

Model 280—Hammer Sidelock

NIB	Exc.	V.G.	Good	Fair	Poor
—	575	450	350	250	200

Model 325—Hammerless Boxlock

NIB	Exc.	V.G.	Good	Fair	Poor
—	450	400	350	250	200

Model 350—Hammerless Boxlock

NIB	Exc.	V.G.	Good	Fair	Poor
—	450	400	350	250	200

Model 360—Hammerless Boxlock

NIB	Exc.	V.G.	Good	Fair	Poor
—	450	400	350	250	200

Model 370—Hammerless Boxlock

NIB	Exc.	V.G.	Good	Fair	Poor
—	450	400	350	250	200

Model 380—Hammerless Boxlock

NIB	Exc.	V.G.	Good	Fair	Poor
—	575	450	350	250	200

Model 235—Hammer Boxlock

NIB	Exc.	V.G.	Good	Fair	Poor
—	450	400	350	250	200

Model 335 (Early)—Hammerless Boxlock

Courtesy Nick Niles, Paul Goodwin photo

NIB	Exc.	V.G.	Good	Fair	Poor
—	450	400	350	250	200

Model 335 (Late)—Hammerless Boxlock

NIB	Exc.	V.G.	Good	Fair	Poor
—	450	400	350	250	200

Model 255—Hammer Sidelock

NIB	Exc.	V.G.	Good	Fair	Poor
—	450	400	350	250	200

Model 265—Hammer Sidelock

Courtesy Nick Niles, Paul Goodwin photo

NIB	Exc.	V.G.	Good	Fair	Poor
—	450	400	350	250	200

Model 355—Hammerless Boxlock

NIB	Exc.	V.G.	Good	Fair	Poor
—	800	575	450	350	250

Model 365—Hammerless Boxlock

Courtesy Nick Niles, Paul Goodwin photo

NIB	Exc.	V.G.	Good	Fair	Poor
—	925	625	500	400	300

Model 375 (London Proofs)—Hammerless Boxlock

NIB	Exc.	V.G.	Good	Fair	Poor
—	1500	950	700	450	350

Model 375 (U.S.)—Hammerless Boxlock

NIB	Exc.	V.G.	Good	Fair	Poor
—	1100	700	575	400	300

Model 385 (London Proofs)—Hammerless Boxlock

NIB	Exc.	V.G.	Good	Fair	Poor
—	1650	1050	700	450	350

Model 385 (U.S.)—Hammerless Boxlock

NIB	Exc.	V.G.	Good	Fair	Poor
—	1200	850	575	450	300

Model 345—Hammerless Boxlock

Courtesy Nick Niles, Paul Goodwin photo

NIB	Exc.	V.G.	Good	Fair	Poor
—	575	450	350	250	200

Model 330—Hammerless Boxlock

Stevens Model 330 early fork-type cocking lever

NIB	Exc.	V.G.	Good	Fair	Poor
—	450	400	350	250	200

Model 515—Hammerless Boxlock

NIB	Exc.	V.G.	Good	Fair	Poor
—	625	525	450	350	300

Model 515—Single Trigger Hammerless Boxlock

NIB	Exc.	V.G.	Good	Fair	Poor
—	750	575	450	350	300

Model 500—Skeet Hammerless Boxlock

Courtesy Nick Niles, Paul Goodwin photo

NIB	Exc.	V.G.	Good	Fair	Poor
—	1250	925	800	700	400

Model 530—Hammerless Boxlock

NIB	Exc.	V.G.	Good	Fair	Poor
—	450	400	350	250	200

Model 530M—Tenite Hammerless Boxlock

NIB	Exc.	V.G.	Good	Fair	Poor
—	450	400	350	250	200

Model 530M—Tenite Single Trigger Hammerless Boxlock

NIB	Exc.	V.G.	Good	Fair	Poor
—	750	575	450	350	300

Model 530A—Hammerless Boxlock

Courtesy Nick Niles, Paul Goodwin photo

NIB	Exc.	V.G.	Good	Fair	Poor
—	450	400	350	250	200

Model 530A—Single Trigger Hammerless Boxlock

NIB	Exc.	V.G.	Good	Fair	Poor
—	525	450	350	300	250

Model 311—Tenite Hammerless Boxlock

Stevens Model 311

Courtesy Nick Niles

NIB	Exc.	V.G.	Good	Fair	Poor
—	450	400	350	250	200

Model 331—Single Trigger Hammerless Boxlock

NIB	Exc.	V.G.	Good	Fair	Poor
—	525	400	300	250	200

Model 311—Tenite Single Trigger Hammerless Boxlock

NIB	Exc.	V.G.	Good	Fair	Poor
—	575	500	450	350	300

Model 311A—Hammerless Boxlock

NIB	Exc.	V.G.	Good	Fair	Poor
—	525	450	350	250	200

Model 311C—Hammerless Boxlock

Courtesy Nick Niles, Paul Goodwin photo

NIB	Exc.	V.G.	Good	Fair	Poor
—	400	350	250	200	150

Model 311D—Hammerless Boxlock

Courtesy Nick Niles, Paul Goodwin photo

NIB	Exc.	V.G.	Good	Fair	Poor
—	450	400	350	250	200

Model 311E—Hammerless Boxlock

NIB	Exc.	V.G.	Good	Fair	Poor
—	600	450	400	300	250

Model 311F—Hammerless Boxlock

NIB	Exc.	V.G.	Good	Fair	Poor
—	450	400	350	250	200

Model 311H—Hammerless Boxlock

NIB	Exc.	V.G.	Good	Fair	Poor
—	450	400	350	250	200

Model 311H—Vent Rib Hammerless Boxlock

Courtesy Nick Niles, Paul Goodwin photo

NIB	Exc.	V.G.	Good	Fair	Poor
—	500	450	350	300	250

Model 311J/R—Hammerless Boxlock

Courtesy Nick Niles, Paul Goodwin photo

NIB	Exc.	V.G.	Good	Fair	Poor
—	400	350	250	200	150

Model 311J/R—Solid Rib Hammerless Boxlock

NIB	Exc.	V.G.	Good	Fair	Poor
—	400	350	250	200	150

Model 311H—Waterfowler Hammerless Boxlock

NIB	Exc.	V.G.	Good	Fair	Poor
—	700	575	450	350	250

Model 240—.410 Over/Under Hammer Tenite

NIB	Exc.	V.G.	Good	Fair	Poor
—	575	450	350	250	200

RIVERSIDE BRAND

Model 215—Hammer Boxlock

Courtesy Nick Niles, Paul Goodwin photo

NIB	Exc.	V.G.	Good	Fair	Poor
—	750	525	400	250	200

Model 315 (Early)—Hammerless Boxlock

NIB	Exc.	V.G.	Good	Fair	Poor
—	575	450	350	250	200

Model 315 (Late)—Hammerless Boxlock

NIB	Exc.	V.G.	Good	Fair	Poor
—	575	450	350	250	200

SUPER VALUE BRAND

Model 511—Hammerless Boxlock

NIB	Exc.	V.G.	Good	Fair	Poor
—	525	400	300	200	150

Model 511—Sunken Rib Hammerless Boxlock

NIB	Exc.	V.G.	Good	Fair	Poor
—	575	450	350	200	150

SPRINGFIELD BRAND

Model 215—Hammer Boxlock

NIB	Exc.	V.G.	Good	Fair	Poor
—	575	450	350	250	150

Model 311—Hammerless Boxlock

Courtesy Nick Niles, Paul Goodwin photo

NIB	Exc.	V.G.	Good	Fair	Poor
—	575	450	350	250	150

Model 315—Hammerless Boxlock

Courtesy Nick Niles, Paul Goodwin photo

NIB	Exc.	V.G.	Good	Fair	Poor
—	575	450	350	250	200

Model 3150—Hammerless Boxlock

NIB	Exc.	V.G.	Good	Fair	Poor
—	700	575	400	250	200

Model 3151—Hammerless Boxlock

NIB	Exc.	V.G.	Good	Fair	Poor
—	850	700	450	350	250

Model 3151—Single Trigger Hammerless Boxlock

NIB	Exc.	V.G.	Good	Fair	Poor
—	950	800	575	450	300

Model 311—Single Trigger Hammerless Boxlock

NIB	Exc.	V.G.	Good	Fair	Poor
—	800	700	575	450	300

Model 5151—Hammerless Boxlock

Courtesy Nick Niles, Paul Goodwin photo

NIB	Exc.	V.G.	Good	Fair	Poor
—	575	450	350	250	200

Model 5151—Single Trigger Hammerless Boxlock

NIB	Exc.	V.G.	Good	Fair	Poor
—	700	525	400	300	200

Model 311—New Style Hammerless Boxlock

Courtesy Nick Niles, Paul Goodwin photo

NIB	Exc.	V.G.	Good	Fair	Poor
—	575	450	350	250	150

Model 311—New Style Tenite Hammerless Boxlock

NIB	Exc.	V.G.	Good	Fair	Poor
—	575	450	350	250	150

Model 511—Sunken Rib Hammerless Boxlock

NIB	Exc.	V.G.	Good	Fair	Poor
—	575	450	350	250	150

Model 511—Hammerless Boxlock

NIB	Exc.	V.G.	Good	Fair	Poor
—	525	400	300	200	150

Model 511A—Hammerless Boxlock

NIB	Exc.	V.G.	Good	Fair	Poor
—	525	400	300	200	150

STEVENS/SAVAGE SHOTGUNS

Model 411 Upland Sporter

Introduced in 2003. Side-by-side shotgun chambered for 12- or 20-gauge and .410 bore. The 12-gauge fitted with 28" barrels; 20-gauge and .410 have 26" barrels. Single trigger with ejectors. False sideplates are laser engraved. European walnut stock, with pistol-grip and splinter fore-end. Weight about 6.75 to 6.5 lbs. depending on gauge. **NOTE:** Add 50 percent for 20-gauge and .410 bore models.

NIB	Exc.	V.G.	Good	Fair	Poor
550	425	350	300	200	125

STEVENS DATE CODE

Collectors will find a date code stamped on every double-barrel shotgun in Stevens brands, produced between March 1949 and December 1968. Usually, it's behind the hinge pin or ahead of trigger guard on bottom of the frame. It will appear as a small circle containing a number and letter. Letters correspond to years shown in the following table. Significance of the numbers is not known.

DATE CODES			
A-1949	B-1950	C-1951	D-1952
E-1953	F-1954	G-1955	H-1956
I-1957	J-1958	K-1959	L-1960
M-1961	N-1962	P-1963	R-1964
S-1965	T-1966	U-1967	V-1968
W-1969	X-1970		

BOLT-ACTION SHOTGUNS

Stevens Company produced a number of bolt-action shotguns that are single-shot or repeaters. Chambered for 20-gauge or .410 bore. Blued, with walnut stocks. Values for these utility-grade shotguns are similar.

Model 237—Single-Shot	Model 39—Tube Magazine
Model 258—Clip Fed	Model 58—Clip Fed
Model 37—Single-Shot	Model 59—Tube Magazine
Model 38—Clip Fed	

Model 58

Model 59

NIB	Exc.	V.G.	Good	Fair	Poor
—	125	100	75	50	35

SLIDE-ACTION UTILITY-GRADE SHOTGUNS

J. Stevens Arms Company also produced a series of utility-grade slide-action shotguns. Chambered for various gauges, barrel lengths and chokes. Finishes blued, with walnut stocks. Values are similar and listed for reference purposes.

Model 67	Model 77-AC	Model 520	Model 621
Model 67-VR	Model 77-M	Model 522	Model 820
Model 77	Model 77-SC	Model 620	

NIB	Exc.	V.G.	Good	Fair	Poor
—	225	150	125	100	75

Model 620 U.S. Marked Trench Gun

NOTE: Add $150 for bayonet.

Courtesy Richard M. Kumor Sr.

NIB	Exc.	V.G.	Good	Fair	Poor
—	3000	2500	1650	1200	750

Model 124

Manually-operated bolt-action shotgun, chambered for 12-gauge. Has 28" barrel, with various chokes. Blued and brown plastic Tenite stock. An odd duck: looks like a semi-automatic and is often mistaken for such.

NIB	Exc.	V.G.	Good	Fair	Poor
—	225	175	75	65	50

Model 67

Slide-action shotgun chambered for 12- or 20-gauge and .410 bore. Has 3" chambers. Offered with various barrel lengths and choke tubes, with 5-shot tube magazine. Features blued steel receiver, with walnut stock. Discontinued in 1989.

NIB	Exc.	V.G.	Good	Fair	Poor
—	250	175	150	100	75

Model 675

Slide-action shotgun chambered for 12-gauge, with 24" ventilated rib barrel and iron sights. Finish blued, with hardwood stock and recoil pad. Manufactured in 1987 and 1988.

NIB	Exc.	V.G.	Good	Fair	Poor
—	275	240	200	150	100

Model 69-RXL

Matte-finished riot version of Model 67 series slide-action shotgun. Has 18.25" cylinder-bore barrel and furnished with a recoil pad. Discontinued in 1989.

NIB	Exc.	V.G.	Good	Fair	Poor
—	250	175	150	100	75

Model 350 Pump Shotgun

Pump-action shotgun chambered for 2.75" and 3" 12-gauge. Features include all-steel barrel and receiver; bottom-load and -eject design; black synthetic stock; 5+1 capacity. Price: $267 (Field Model w/28" barrel, screw-in choke); $241 (Security Model w/18" barrel, fixed choke); $307 (Combo Model with Field and Security barrels); $254 (Security Model with 18.25" barrel w/ghost ring rear sight).

STEYR
Steyr, Austria

STEYR & MANNLICHER PISTOLS

By: Joseph Schroeder: Not all Mannlicher pistols made by Steyr. Many pistols made by Steyr were not designed by Mannlicher. However, since by far greatest number of Mannlicher's pistols were made by Steyr we believe it will be appropriate to include all of Ferdinand Ritter von Mannlicher's pistols along with other Steyr designs under this heading.

Schoenberger

Considered by many to be first "commercial" semi-automatic pistol. Only about two dozen were made in 1892. Steyr-made 8mm Schoenberger was based on patents granted to Laumann in 1890-91. Had a magazine in front of trigger guard. Too rare to price.

Mannlicher Model 1894

Mannlicher's first "successful" self-loading pistol. Model 1894 had a blow-forward action and double-action lockwork. Earliest examples were made in Austria, probably by Steyr, in 7.6mm. Greatest number made by SIG in 1896-97 for Swiss army tests. These 100 pistols had shorter barrel, smaller frame and in 6.5mm. Prices are for Swiss examples. **NOTE:** Add 20 percent for 7.6mm pistols.

Courtesy Rock Island Auction Company

NIB	Exc.	V.G.	Good	Fair	Poor
—	18000	12000	6600	5500	3000

Mannlicher Model 1896/03

Most confusing of Mannlicher's pistols. Earliest examples, which have fixed magazine and ribbed barrel, may have been made by Steyr and are very rare. Later versions, with removable box magazine, have been called "Model 1896/03" and "Model 1901", and made as both pistol and pistol-carbine, possibly in Switzerland. Chambered for 7.65mm Mannlicher cartridge, which is really a 7.65mm Borchardt. Prices listed are for standard later model pistol or pistol-carbine (12" barrel, tangent sight); double prices for early pistol or late model pistol with detachable holster stock.

Courtesy Joseph Schroeder

NIB	Exc.	V.G.	Good	Fair	Poor
—	8250	5500	3850	2750	1500

Mannlicher Model 1899

Earliest version of Mannlicher's final semi-automatic pistol design. Only about 250 made by Dreyse in Soemmerda, Germany. Chambered for tapered case 7.63mm Mannlicher cartridge. Distinguished by large safety lever on left side, take-down screw under barrel and Dreyse markings.

Courtesy Joseph Schroeder

NIB	Exc.	V.G.	Good	Fair	Poor
—	9400	7150	4950	3850	2000

Mannlicher Model 1901

Marked "WAFFENFABRIK Steyr" on left side and "SYSTEM MANNLI-CHER" on right. Model 1901 distinguished by its checkered grips, rear

sight located on rear of barrel, 8-round fixed magazine. Serial numbers to little over 1000.

Courtesy Joseph Schroeder

NIB	Exc.	V.G.	Good	Fair	Poor
—	4000	3500	1750	900	700

Mannlicher Model 1905

Improved version of Model 1901. Longer grip holding 10 rounds, grooved wooden grips, rear sight on rear of breechblock and "MODEL 1905" added to right side. Later production moved all markings to left side so Argentine crest could be placed on right side. Prices listed for original commercial Model 1905, NOT a re-blued Argentine contract with crest ground off. **NOTE:** Deduct 60 percent for reworked examples.

Courtesy Joseph Schroeder

NIB	Exc.	V.G.	Good	Fair	Poor
—	2425	1875	1350	800	400

Argentine Contract

NIB	Exc.	V.G.	Good	Fair	Poor
—	2750	2250	1650	900	500

Roth Steyr Model 1907

Based on patents granted to Karel Krnka and Georg Roth. The 8mm Model 1907 had rotating barrel locking system and was first self-loading pistol adopted by Austro-Hungarian Army. **NOTE:** Add 20 percent for early Steyr examples without large pin visible on right side of frame, or for those made in Budapest instead of Steyr. Slight premium for correct stripper clips.

Courtesy Joseph Schroeder

NIB	Exc.	V.G.	Good	Fair	Poor
—	1250	750	600	350	250

Steyr Model 1908 Pocket Pistol

Based on Belgian patents of Nicholas Pieper. These .25- and .32-caliber pocket pistols featured tipping barrels built by Steyr under license from Pieper in Liege. Production suspended during WWI, but may have resumed after war ended. Prices for either caliber.

NIB	Exc.	V.G.	Good	Fair	Poor
—	385	275	165	100	75

Steyr Hahn Model 1911 Commercially Marked

NOTE: Military versions of this model see Standard Catalog of Military Firearms.

NIB	Exc.	V.G.	Good	Fair	Poor
—	2200	1650	1220	875	450

Steyr Model SP

Steyr's first post WWII pistol. Model SP was a beautifully made .32 ACP. Being double-action-only and more expensive than most of its contemporaries, was not competitive and discontinued in early 1960s. Fewer than 1,000 made. Slide marked "STEYR-DAIMLER-PUCH A.G. MOD. SP KAL. 7.65mm".

Courtesy Joseph Schroeder

NIB	Exc.	V.G.	Good	Fair	Poor
—	950	825	550	385	200

Steyr Model GB

GB introduced in mid-1970s as a 9mm Parabellum military pistol. Large in size, with 18-round magazine capacity. Other features included polygon rifling and gas trap around barrel to delay breech opening. Initially produced as Rogak P-18 by L.E.S. of Morton Grove, Illinois. Discontinued due in part to quality control problems. Just over 2,000 made. Later production by Steyr as GB was to much higher standards, but GB never achieved much popularity and discontinued in 1988.

Rogak P-18

NIB	Exc.	V.G.	Good	Fair	Poor
—	425	350	250	175	125

Steyr GB

NIB	Exc.	V.G.	Good	Fair	Poor
—	800	675	525	400	200

RIFLES

Following Steyr/Mannlicher guns were imported by GSI Inc. Trussville, Alabama. **NOTE:** Earlier models see Mannlicher Schoenauer.

SPORTER SERIES

Series includes rifles that are lightweight and have reduced overall length. All Sporter models have interchangeable 5-round rotary magazine. Stock is oil-finished walnut in Mannlicher full stock design or half stock version. In both stock configurations an oval European cheekpiece is standard. Rifles offered in four different action lengths: SL (super light), L (light), M (medium) or S (Magnum). Also available with single-/double-set triggers.

Model M72 L/M

.243, .270, 7x57mm, 7x64mm, .308 or .30-06 caliber bolt-action rifle, with 23" fluted barrel and single-/double-set triggers. Blued, checkered walnut stock. Manufactured from 1972 to 1980.

NIB	Exc.	V.G.	Good	Fair	Poor
—	1325	1025	750	550	450

Model SL

Features super light action. Offered with 20" barrel in full stock version or 23.0625" barrel in half stock version. Rubber buttpad standard. Model does not have fore-end tip on its half stock variation. Offered in following calibers: .222 Rem., .222 Rem. Magnum, .223 and 5.6x50 Magnum. Weight about: 6.2 lbs. full stock; 6.3 lbs. half stock.

NIB	Exc.	V.G.	Good	Fair	Poor
2000	1650	1000	750	500	300

Model SL Carbine

As above, with 20" fluted barrel. Mannlicher-style stock.

NIB	Exc.	V.G.	Good	Fair	Poor
1950	1750	1050	800	550	350

Varmint Model

Features heavy 26" barrel. Chambered for .222 Rem., .223, 5.6x57, .243 Win., .308 Win. and .22-250. Fore-end of stock is ventilated. Grip enlarged and textured. Choice of single-/double-set triggers. Recoil pad standard. Weight about 8 lbs.

NIB	Exc.	V.G.	Good	Fair	Poor
1950	1750	1050	800	550	350

Model L

Rifle has light action. Offered in same stock configuration and barrel lengths as Model SL. Calibers are: 5.6x57, .243 Win., .308, .22-250 and 6mm Rem. Weight about: 6.3 lbs. full stock; 6.4 lbs. half stock.

NIB	Exc.	V.G.	Good	Fair	Poor
1850	1650	1000	750	500	300

Luxus Series

Luxury model offers choice of full or half stock variations in select walnut, with fine line checkering. Pistol-grip is steeply angled. Luxus rifles fitted with swept back European cheekpiece. Single-set trigger standard. Box magazine holds 3 rounds. Optional engraving and stock carving may be encountered on these models, that will dramatically affect price. Luxus rifles available with light, medium or Magnum length actions.

Luxus Model L

Same dimensions and barrel lengths as Sporter version. Calibers are: 5.6x57, .243 Win., .308, .22-250 and 6mm Rem.

NIB	Exc.	V.G.	Good	Fair	Poor
2400	2000	1100	800	600	350

Luxus Model M

Same dimensions and barrel lengths as Sporter Model M. Available in these calibers: 6.5x57, .270 Win., 7x64, .30-06, 9.3x 62, 6.5x55, 7.5 Swiss, 7x57 and 8x57JS.

NIB	Exc.	V.G.	Good	Fair	Poor
2400	2000	1100	800	600	350

Luxus Model S

Same as Sporter Model S. Offered in following calibers: 6.5x68, 7mm Rem. Magnum, .300 Win. Magnum and 8x68S.

NIB	Exc.	V.G.	Good	Fair	Poor
2400	2000	1100	800	600	350

Model M

Features medium action. Same barrel and stock configurations as other two models listed above. Exception, has no buttpad and does have fore-end tip on its half stock variation. Available in these calibers: 6.5x57, .270 Win., 7x64, .30-06, 9.3x62, 6.5x55, 7.5 Swiss, 7x57 and 8x57JS. Weight about: 6.8 lbs. full stock; 7 lbs. half stock.

NIB	Exc.	V.G.	Good	Fair	Poor
2500	2100	1200	900	600	300

Professional Model M

Fitted with medium weight action. Features black synthetic checkered stock. Comes fitted with ventilated rubber recoil pad. Offered with 20" or 23.6" barrel. Available with single-/double-set trigger. Available in these

calibers: 6.5x57, .270 Win., 7x64, .30-06, 9.3x62, 6.5x55, 7.5 Swiss, 7x57 and 8x57JS. Weight about 7.25 lbs.

NIB	Exc.	V.G.	Good	Fair	Poor
1500	1200	950	700	600	300

Model S/T

Similar to above in heavy barreled version. Offered in these calibers: 9.3x64, .375 H&H and .458 Win. Magnum. Optional buttstock magazine available. Weight about 9 lbs.

NIB	Exc.	V.G.	Good	Fair	Poor
2100	1900	1400	1100	800	500

Tropical Rifle

As above, with 26" heavy barrel. Chambered for .375 H&H and .458 Win. Magnum. Not imported after 1985.

NIB	Exc.	V.G.	Good	Fair	Poor
—	2000	1750	1100	650	450

Model MIII Professional

Introduced in 1995. Economy version of Model M Professional. Fitted with 23.5" barrel, black synthetic stock and choice of single-/double-set triggers. Offered in .25-06, .270 Win., .30-06 and 7x64 calibers. Weight about 7.5 lbs. **NOTE:** Add $100 for checkered walnut stock.

NIB	Exc.	V.G.	Good	Fair	Poor
1000	800	600	400	300	200

STEYR SBS (SAFE BOLT SYSTEM)

Series introduced in 1997. Features a newly designed bolt. Offered in two distinct models: SBS Forester and SBS ProHunter.

SBS ProHunter

Model has 23.6" barrel, 4-round magazine and single adjustable trigger. Offered in .243 Win., .25-06, .270 Win., 7mm-08, .308 Win., .30-06, 7mm Rem. Magnum, .300 Win. Magnum and several European calibers. Weight about 7.5 lbs. Furnished with black synthetic stock, recoil pad and buttspacers. Introduced in 1999. **NOTE:** Add $150-$300 for custom metric calibers; $30 for 7mm Magnum and .300 Win. Magnum calibers.

NIB	Exc.	V.G.	Good	Fair	Poor
750	650	575	400	300	150

SBS ProHunter Stainless Steel

Same as ProHunter model, with stainless steel action and barrel. Introduced in 2000. **NOTE:** Add $150-$300 for custom metric calibers; $30 for 7mm Magnum and .300 Win. Magnum calibers.

NIB	Exc.	V.G.	Good	Fair	Poor
900	750	675	500	400	250

SBS ProHunter Camo

Same as standard ProHunter, with camo synthetic stock. **NOTE:** Add $150-$300 for custom metric calibers; $30 for 7mm Magnum and .300 Win. Magnum calibers.

NIB	Exc.	V.G.	Good	Fair	Poor
1000	850	700	575	400	200

SBS ProHunter Camo Stainless Steel

Same as above, with stainless steel action and barrel. **NOTE:** Add $150-$300 for custom metric calibers; $30 for 7mm Magnum and .300 Win. Magnum calibers.

NIB	Exc.	V.G.	Good	Fair	Poor
1050	900	750	600	475	250

SBS ProHunter Mountain Rifle

Chambered for .243, .25-06, .270 and 7mm-08 calibers. Fitted with 20" barrel and no sights. Receiver engraved "Mountain Rifle". Synthetic stock with recoil pad standard. Weight 7.25 lbs. Introduced in 1999.

NIB	Exc.	V.G.	Good	Fair	Poor
1000	850	700	575	400	200

SBS ProHunter Mountain Stainless Steel

Same as ProHunter Mountain, with stainless steel action and barrel. Introduced in 2000.

NIB	Exc.	V.G.	Good	Fair	Poor
1050	900	750	600	425	200

SBS ProHunter Mountain Camo

Same as ProHunter, with camo synthetic stock. Introduced in 2000.

NIB	Exc.	V.G.	Good	Fair	Poor
1150	1000	850	700	475	250

SBS ProHunter Mountain Camo Stainless Steel

Same as above, with stainless steel action and barrel. Introduced in 2000.

NIB	Exc.	V.G.	Good	Fair	Poor
1150	1000	850	700	475	250

SBS ProHunter (Youth/Ladies)

Fitted with walnut stock and buttspacers (to create shorter length of pull). Extra thick recoil pad. Chambered for .243, 7mm-08 and .308. Weight about 7.25 lbs. Introduced in 1999.

NIB	Exc.	V.G.	Good	Fair	Poor
1000	850	700	575	400	200

SBS ProHunter Compact

Same as above, with black synthetic stock. Offered with stainless steel action and barrel. **NOTE:** Add $80 for stainless steel.

NIB	Exc.	V.G.	Good	Fair	Poor
1000	850	700	575	400	200

SBS ProHunter 376 Steyr

Chambered for .376 Steyr cartridge. Fitted with 20" barrel and iron sights. Synthetic stock, with special thick pad. Weight about 8 lbs. Introduced in 1999.

NIB	Exc.	V.G.	Good	Fair	Poor
1200	950	800	675	400	200

SBS Forester

Same as Pro Hunter model. Furnished with walnut stock and recoil pad. **NOTE:** Add $150-$300 for custom metric calibers; $30 for 7mm Rem. Magnum and .300 Win. Magnum.

NIB	Exc.	V.G.	Good	Fair	Poor
850	725	625	500	400	200

SBS Classic American

Features 23.6" barrel, single adjustable trigger, stain finish walnut stock with recoil pad. Offered in calibers from .243 to .300 Win. Magnum. Weight about 7.2 lbs. Introduced in 2000. **NOTE:** Add $150-$300 for custom metric calibers; $30 for 7mm Magnum and .300 Win. Magnum calibers.

NIB	Exc.	V.G.	Good	Fair	Poor
1500	1100	850	650	500	300

SBS Classic Mannlicher

Offered in same calibers as above, except for 7mm Rem. Magnum and .300 Win. Magnum. Fitted with 25.6" barrel. Walnut stock is full Mannlicher style, with recoil pad. Fitted with open sights. Weight about 7.2 lbs. Introduced in 2000.

NIB	Exc.	V.G.	Good	Fair	Poor
2300	2000	1600	1000	675	400

SBS Forester Mountain Rifle

Walnut stock with 20" barrel and no sights. Chambered for a variety of calibers including .243, .25-06, .270, 7mm-08, .308, .30-06 and 6.5x55. Receiver engraved "Mountain Rifle". Introduced in 1999.

NIB	Exc.	V.G.	Good	Fair	Poor
850	725	625	500	400	200

Mannlicher SBS European—Half Stock

Fitted with 23.6" barrel and iron sights. Chambered for wide variety of American and European calibers from .243 to 9.3x62. European style figured walnut stock. Adjustable trigger. Recoil pad. Weight about 7.5 lbs.

NIB	Exc.	V.G.	Good	Fair	Poor
2795	2200	1750	1200	700	400

Mannlicher SBS European—Half Stock Carbine

Same as above, with 20" barrel.

NIB	Exc.	V.G.	Good	Fair	Poor
2795	2200	1750	1200	700	400

Mannlicher SBS European—Full Stock

Same as above, with full European stock covering 20" barrel.

NIB	Exc.	V.G.	Good	Fair	Poor
2895	2300	1800	1250	750	450

Mannlicher SBS Magnum European—Half Stock

Chambered for 7mm Rem. Magnum, .300 Win. Magnum, 6.5x68 and 8x68S calibers. Fitted with 25.6" barrel and iron sights. Walnut stock. Weight about 7.75 lbs.

NIB	Exc.	V.G.	Good	Fair	Poor
2895	2300	1800	1250	750	450

Steyr Scout—Jeff Cooper Package

Developed by Col. Jeff Cooper. Chambered for .308 Win. cartridge. Fitted with 19" fluted barrel. Stock is gray synthetic, with removable buttspacers and folding bi-pod. Magazine capacity 5 rounds, with optional 10-round magazines available. Weight about: 7 lbs. w/scope; 6.3 lbs. w/o scope. Adjustable single trigger. Factory-installed Leupold M8 2.5x28mm scope. Introduced in 1998.

NIB	Exc.	V.G.	Good	Fair	Poor
2600	2000	1600	1100	650	400

Steyr Scout Package

Similar to Jeff Cooper Package, without Jeff Cooper logo. Stock black synthetic. Offered in .223 Rem., .243 Win., 7mm-08 as well as .308 and .375 Steyr calibers.

NIB	Exc.	V.G.	Good	Fair	Poor
2100	1800	1550	1000	700	400

Scout

Same as above but rifle only.

NIB	Exc.	V.G.	Good	Fair	Poor
2100	1800	1550	1000	700	400

Steyr Scout Tactical

Model has 19.25" fluted barrel. Chambered for .223 or .308 Win. cartridge. Integral bipod. Emergency ghost ring sights. **NOTE:** Add $100 for stainless steel.

NIB	Exc.	V.G.	Good	Fair	Poor
2050	1500	1000	800	750	425

PRECISION/TACTICAL RIFLES

Model SSG-PI

Features black synthetic stock. Originally designed as military sniper rifle. Fitted with cocking indicator, single-/double-set trigger, 5-round rotary magazine or 10-round. Receiver milled to NATO specifications for Steyr ring mounts. Barrel length 26". Weight about 9 lbs. Offered in .308 Win. **NOTE:** Originally called SSG 69.

NIB	Exc.	V.G.	Good	Fair	Poor
1700	1300	1000	800	600	400

SSG-PII Police Rifle

Version of SSG, with heavier 26" barrel. Larger knob-style bolt handle. Weight about 10.11 lbs.

NIB	Exc.	V.G.	Good	Fair	Poor
1700	1300	1000	800	600	400

SSK-PIIK Police Kurz

Similar to above, with 20" heavy barrel. Weight about 10 lbs.

NIB	Exc.	V.G.	Good	Fair	Poor
1700	1300	1000	800	600	400

SSG-PII & PIIK McMillan

Fitted with McMillan A-3 stock, adjustable cheekpiece and removable buttspacers. Special forearm rail.

NIB	Exc.	V.G.	Good	Fair	Poor
2300	1750	1350	950	750	500

SSG-PIV

Similar to PIIK, with 16.75" heavy barrel and removable flash hider. Barrel is threaded. Weight about 9.11 lbs.

NIB	Exc.	V.G.	Good	Fair	Poor
2500	2000	1500	1000	750	500

Match

NIB	Exc.	V.G.	Good	Fair	Poor
3000	2500	2000	1500	800	500

SSG 08

Bolt-action chambered in .308 Win., .300 Win. Magnum and .338 Lapua Magnum. Barrel length 20" to 23.6", with muzzle-brake. Fully adjustable aluminum folding stock and pistol-grip, Versa-Pod and optics rail.

NIB	Exc.	V.G.	Good	Fair	Poor
5000	4000	3200	2500	2000	500

SSG Carbon Fiber

Features an innovative carbon-fiber stock made from a chipped-carbon sheet molding compound similar to that used in Formula One cars and jet fighters. Material is lighter and much stronger than steel. Stock has an adjustable cheek piece and butt plate, heavy bipod and integral adjustable rear elevation pod. Barreled action with 20" barrel and muzzle-brake. Safe Bolt system are the same as on other SSG rifles. Introduced in 2015.

NIB	Exc.	V.G.	Good	Fair	Poor
3300	3000	—	—	—	—

Match UIT

Designed as an international target rifle. Features special shaped pistol-grip, adjustable trigger for length of pull and pressure. Enlarged bolt handle and non-glare barrel. Chambered for .308 Win. cartridge.

NIB	Exc.	V.G.	Good	Fair	Poor
3900	3500	3000	2000	1500	1000

JAGD Match

Introduced in 1995. Features 20" or 23.5" barrel with sights. Stock is laminated. Full stock version offered on 20" barrel; half stock on 23.5" barrel. Available in a variety of configurations, with calibers from .222 Rem. to .458 Win. Magnum.

NIB	Exc.	V.G.	Good	Fair	Poor
1750	1250	900	500	350	200

SBS TACTICAL SERIES

SBS Tactical

Fitted with black synthetic stock, 20" barrel with no sights. Chambered for .308 cartridge. Removable buttspacers. Black bolt body. Receiver engraved "SBS Tactical". Introduced in 1999. Weight about 7.25 lbs. **NOTE:** Add $100 for stainless steel (introduced 2000).

NIB	Exc.	V.G.	Good	Fair	Poor
1150	950	700	550	300	200

SBS Tactical Heavy Barrel

Also has black synthetic stock. Fitted with 26" heavy barrel and no sights. Black bolt body. Receiver engraved "SBS Tactical HB". Weight about 8 lbs. Introduced in 1999. Offered with 20" barrel called "HBC". Both barrel lengths chambered for .308 cartridge.

NIB	Exc.	V.G.	Good	Fair	Poor
1250	1050	800	650	300	200

SBS Tactical Heavy Barrel Carbine

Features 20" heavy barrel, no sights, matte blue finish. Chambered for .308 caliber. Introduced in 2000.

NIB	Exc.	V.G.	Good	Fair	Poor
1150	950	700	550	300	200

SBS Tactical McMillan

Fitted with 26" barrel chambered for .308 cartridge. Has McMillan A-3 stock. Oversize bolt handle. Weight about 9.8 lbs. Introduced in 1999.

NIB	Exc.	V.G.	Good	Fair	Poor
1600	1250	950	750	60	400

SBS CISM Rifle

Chambered for .308 cartridge and fitted with 19.7" heavy barrel. Stock is laminated wood, with black lacquer finish. Stock has forearm rail, with handstop adjustable buttplate and cheekpiece. Trigger is adjustable. Weight about 10.25 lbs. Introduced in 1999.

NIB	Exc.	V.G.	Good	Fair	Poor
3295	2500	1950	1600	1200	700

SBS Tactical Elite Heavy Barrel

Introduced in 2000. Features 26" heavy barrel, no sights, matte blue finish, Zytel stock with adjustable cheekpiece and buttplate. Full length Picatinny mounting rail. Magazine capacity 5 or 10 rounds. Chambered for .308 cartridge. **NOTE:** Add $100 for stainless steel; $1,000 for ZF optics.

NIB	Exc.	V.G.	Good	Fair	Poor
2400	1750	1400	1000	700	400

SBS Tactical Elite Heavy Barrel Carbine

Same as Tactical Elite Heavy Barrel. Fitted with 20" heavy barrel. Introduced in 2000.

NIB	Exc.	V.G.	Good	Fair	Poor
2400	1750	—	—	—	—

Steyr AUG

5.56mm semi-automatic Bullpup rifle, with 20" barrel incorporating Swarovski 1.5x telescopic sight. Green carbon composite stock. Weight about 8.5 lbs. Recommend independent local appraisals.

NIB	Exc.	V.G.	Good	Fair	Poor
3700	3100	2500	1600	1300	650

Steyr AUG—Police Model

Same as above, with black stock and 16" barrel.

NIB	Exc.	V.G.	Good	Fair	Poor
3700	3100	2500	1600	1300	650

Steyr AUG Special Receiver

Receiver only. Special flattop with Stanag mounting.

NIB	Exc.	V.G.	Good	Fair	Poor
3700	3100	2500	1600	1300	650

Steyr USR

Post-ban version of AUG. Fitted with Swarovski 1.5x scope and gray synthetic stock.

NIB	Exc.	V.G.	Good	Fair	Poor
3700	3100	2500	1600	1300	650

Steyr Zephyr

.22-caliber rimfire bolt-action carbine. Has 5-round detachable magazine, dovetailed receiver for scope rings. Fitted with full stock. Made from 1953 to 1968.

NIB	Exc.	V.G.	Good	Fair	Poor
—	1800	1475	1150	800	400

PISTOLS

Model SPP

Introduced in 1993, this is a 9mm semi-automatic pistol. Made from synthetic materials and operates on a delayed blowback rotating barrel system. Magazine capacity 15 or 30 rounds. Barrel length 5.9"; overall length 12.75"; weight about 42 oz. Due to its appearance and design, this pistol was banned from importation into U.S. shortly after its introduction. Because of this circumstance, price of this pistol may fluctuate widely.

NIB	Exc.	V.G.	Good	Fair	Poor
1000	900	750	600	500	400

Model M

Chambered for .40 S&W, 9mm or .357 SIG cartridge. Semi-automatic pistol has polymer frame and 3 user selectable safety systems. Loaded chambered indicator. Triangle/Trapezoid sights. Limited access lock with key. Weight about 28 oz. Magazine capacity 10 rounds. Introduced in 1999.

NIB	Exc.	V.G.	Good	Fair	Poor
500	400	325	275	235	200

Model M-A1

Updated version of Model M, with redesigned grip frame and Picatinny rail. Striker-fired DA-only pistol in 9mm, .357 SIG and .40 S&W. Magazine capacity: 15 for 9mm, 12 for .40 and .357 SIG. 3.5" or 4" barrel (S-A1).

NIB	Exc.	V.G.	Good	Fair	Poor
500	400	325	275	235	200

STEYR HAHN
See—Steyr

STEYR MANNLICHER
See—Steyr

STI INTERNATIONAL
Georgetown, Texas

LS9 & LS40

Single-stack pistol chambered for 9mm or .40 S&W cartridge. Fitted with 3.4" barrel and short grip. Heine Low Mount sights. Rosewood grips. Matte blue finish. Magazine capacity: 7 rounds 9mm; 6 rounds .40 S&W. Weight about 28 oz.

NIB	Exc.	V.G.	Good	Fair	Poor
850	675	550	400	300	200

BLS9 & BLS40

Same as above, with full length grip. Magazine capacity: 9 rounds 9mm; 8 rounds .40 S&W.

NIB	Exc.	V.G.	Good	Fair	Poor
825	650	525	375	275	200

Ranger

Chambered for .45 ACP cartridge. Fitted with 3.9" barrel, with a short grip. Fixed STI sights. Blued frame, with stainless steel slide. Weight about 29 oz.

NIB	Exc.	V.G.	Good	Fair	Poor
950	775	600	500	400	200

Ranger II

Chambered for .45 ACP cartridge. Fitted with 4.15" ramped bull barrel. Slide is flattop, with rear serrations and chamfered fore-end. Ambidextrous safety and high rise grip safety. Adjustable rear sight. Blued lower frame. Weight about 39 oz.

NIB	Exc.	V.G.	Good	Fair	Poor
925	800	675	525	400	200

Trojan

Chambered for .45 ACP, .40 Super, .40 S&W and 9mm cartridge. Fitted with a 5" barrel. Rosewood grips. Matte blue finish. 8-round magazine capacity. Weight about 36 oz. **NOTE:** Add $275 for .40 Super with .45 ACP conversion; $250 for Trojan with 6" slide.

NIB	Exc.	V.G.	Good	Fair	Poor
1150	925	750	600	500	300

Tactical 4.15

Chambered for 9mm, .40 S&W or .45 ACP cartridge. Fully supported ramped 4.15" bull barrel. Frame has tactical rail. Slide has rear serrations. Fixed rear sight. Aluminum magazine well. Black polycoat finish. Weight about 34.5 oz.

NIB	Exc.	V.G.	Good	Fair	Poor
1750	1475	1150	900	650	350

Tactical

As above, with 5" barrel. Flat blue finish. Weight about 39 oz.

NIB	Exc.	V.G.	Good	Fair	Poor
1750	1475	1150	900	650	350

Trubor

Chambered for 9mm "major", 9x23 or .38 Super cartridges. Steel frame fully supported and ramped one piece, with bull barrel and integral com-

pensator. Slide has front and rear serrations. Sights are C-More or OK Red Dot reflix. Blued finish. Weight about 42.5 oz. with scope.

NIB	Exc.	V.G.	Good	Fair	Poor
2500	2100	1600	1200	900	500

Lawman

This .45 ACP pistol has a 5" ramped barrel, with match grade bushing. Aluminum trigger. Series 70 grip safety. Novak 3 dot sights. Checkered walnut grips. Polymer finish, with brown slide over tan frame. Weight about 36 oz.

NIB	Exc.	V.G.	Good	Fair	Poor
1200	975	825	675	500	250

Xcaliber Single Stack

Chambered for .450 SMC cartridge. Fitted with a 6" slide. Adjustable rear sight. Weight about 38 oz. Blue finish. Single-stack magazine. Discontinued.

NIB	Exc.	V.G.	Good	Fair	Poor
1475	1275	1050	775	500	350

Xcaliber Double Stack

Same as Xcaliber Single Stack, except it has a double-stack magazine. Discontinued.

NIB	Exc.	V.G.	Good	Fair	Poor
1800	1600	1175	900	600	400

Executive

Chambered for .40 S&W cartridge. Fitted with a 5" ramped bull barrel. Adjustable rear sight. Gray synthetic grip and hard chrome slide. Weight about 39 oz. Double-stack magazine.

NIB	Exc.	V.G.	Good	Fair	Poor
2350	2000	1650	1100	725	400

VIP

Chambered for .45 ACP cartridge. Fitted with a 3.9" ramped bull barrel. Stainless steel flattop slide. Fixed rear sight. 10-round magazine capacity. Weight about 25 oz.

NIB	Exc.	V.G.	Good	Fair	Poor
1400	1100	800	650	400	250

Edge

Chambered for 9mm, 10mm, .40 S&W and .45 ACP cartridge, with 5" ramped bull barrel. Dual-stack magazine. Bomar style sights. Blue finish. Weight about 39 oz.

NIB	Exc.	V.G.	Good	Fair	Poor
1800	1400	1000	700	500	300

Eagle

Chambered for customer's choice of caliber. Fitted with 5" ramped bull barrel. Fixed sights. Blued frame and stainless steel slide. Weight about 30 oz.

NIB	Exc.	V.G.	Good	Fair	Poor
1700	1200	900	600	400	250

Duty One

Chambered for 9mm, .40 S&W or .45 ACP cartridges. 5" bull barrel is fully supported and ramped. Steel frame, with single-stack magazine. Front strap checkering and tactical rail. Grips are rosewood. Slide has front and rear serrations. Adjustable sights. Finish flat blue. Weight about 38 oz.

NIB	Exc.	V.G.	Good	Fair	Poor
1100	900	750	500	400	250

Duty CT

1911-style steel frame single-stack, with integral tactical rail and rosewood grips. 5" slide/barrel, fixed 2-dot tritium rear sight. Weight 36.6 oz. Also available in 4.15" commander size. Blued.

NIB	Exc.	V.G.	Good	Fair	Poor
1100	900	750	500	400	250

Competitor

Chambered for .38 Super cartridge. Fitted with 5.5" ramped bull barrel, with compensator and C-More scope. Stainless steel slide. Weight about 44 oz. with scope and mount. Discontinued.

NIB	Exc.	V.G.	Good	Fair	Poor
2350	2000	1650	1100	725	400

Grandmaster

Custom built to customer's specifications in 9mm "major", 9x23 and .38 Super.

NIB	Exc.	V.G.	Good	Fair	Poor
2800	2500	2000	1500	850	500

Rangemaster

Fitted with 5" fully supported and ramped bull barrel. Chambered for 9mm or .45 ACP cartridge. Has a full length dust cover, checkered front strap, mainspring housing and square trigger guard. Front and rear slide serrations. Adjustable sights. Rose grips. Polished blue finish. Weight about 38 oz.

NIB	Exc.	V.G.	Good	Fair	Poor
1500	1350	1100	800	500	250

Rangemaster II

Single-stack blued variation of Rangemaster. Chambered for 9mm, .40 S&W, .45 ACP. 5" slide/barrel. Weight 37 oz. Introduced 2006.

NIB	Exc.	V.G.	Good	Fair	Poor
1300	1125	900	600	400	200

Targetmaster

As above, with 6" barrel.

NIB	Exc.	V.G.	Good	Fair	Poor
1650	1250	900	650	400	250

Stinger

Chambered for 9mm or .38 Super cartridge. Fitted with 3.9" barrel, with compensator. Sights are OKO or C-More on STI mount. Blued finish. Weight about 38 oz.

NIB	Exc.	V.G.	Good	Fair	Poor
2775	2275	1850	1450	900	500

Hawk 4.3

This pistol modeled on 1911 design. Equipped with 4.3" barrel, with steel slide. Frame made from polymer. Features an increased magazine capacity while retaining the 1911 grip thickness. Chambered for .38 Super, .45 ACP, .40 S&W, 10mm and 9x25 calibers. Built primarily for competition shooting. Discontinued.

NIB	Exc.	V.G.	Good	Fair	Poor
1700	1200	900	600	400	250

Night Hawk 4.3

Chambered for .45 ACP only, with 4.3" bull barrel. A host of special features: narrow tactical safety, front and rear slide serrations and extended dust cover. Tritium sights optional. Blued finish. Weight 33 oz. Discontinued.

NIB	Exc.	V.G.	Good	Fair	Poor
1925	1600	1300	1050	750	400

Falcon 3.9

Similar to above model. Fitted with 3.9" barrel. Weight about: 30 oz. w/ steel frame; 25 oz. w/aluminum frame. Discontinued.

NIB	Exc.	V.G.	Good	Fair	Poor
1925	1600	1300	1050	750	400

Sparrow 5.0

Chambered for .22 LR cartridge only. Fitted with 5" bull barrel, with fixed sights. Weight about 30 oz. Discontinued.

NIB	Exc.	V.G.	Good	Fair	Poor
925	800	675	525	400	200

Edge 5.1

Chambered for .40 S&W only, with 5" bull barrel and many special features. BoMar front and rear sights. Weight 39 oz.

NIB	Exc.	V.G.	Good	Fair	Poor
1800	1400	1000	700	500	300

Eagle 5.1

Similar to Model 2011 Hawk, but furnished with 5" barrel. Comes standard with BoMar adjustable sights.

NIB	Exc.	V.G.	Good	Fair	Poor
1925	1600	1300	1050	750	400

Eagle 5.5

Similar to above model. Furnished with 5.5" barrel, with compensator.

NIB	Exc.	V.G.	Good	Fair	Poor
2395	1950	1600	1200	850	500

Eagle 6.0

Chambered for 9mm, .38 Super, .40 S&W or .45 ACP cartridges. Fitted with a 6" bull barrel. Many special features. BoMar front and rear sights. Blued finish. Weight about 42 oz.

NIB	Exc.	V.G.	Good	Fair	Poor
1925	1600	1300	1050	750	400

Hunter 6.0

Chambered for 10mm cartridge only. Fitted with a 6" bull barrel. Heavy extended frame. Many special features. Leupold 2x scope. Blued finish. Weight with scope 51 oz.

NIB	Exc.	V.G.	Good	Fair	Poor
2350	1900	1600	1200	850	500

Special Edition

Chambered for 9mm, .40 S&W or .45 ACP cartridge. Fitted with a fully supported and ramped 5" bull barrel. Hi-Rise grip. Sights are Dawson fiber optic, with adjustable rear. Slide has Saber Tooth serrations and custom engraving. Finish is 24 karat gold on all steel parts except barrel. Weight about 38 oz.

NIB	Exc.	V.G.	Good	Fair	Poor
2900	2500	1975	1600	1200	500

I.P.S.C. 30th Anniversary

Similar to Special Edition. Hard chrome upper, with color inlays and blued lower.

NIB	Exc.	V.G.	Good	Fair	Poor
2775	2400	1700	1400	950	450

TruSight

Semi-automatic pistol chambered for 9mm, .40 S&W, .45 ACP. Double-stack magazine. Steel frame, 4.15" slide/barrel. Dawson fiber optic front sight, adjustable rear. Weight 36.1 oz. Blued, with multiple options. IPSC, USPSA approved. Introduced 2006.

NIB	Exc.	V.G.	Good	Fair	Poor
1800	1575	1200	900	600	350

Legacy

Chambered for .45 ACP single-stack. 5" slide/barrel, LOA 8.5", weight 38 oz. with adjustable rear sight. Cocobola smooth grips. IDPA, USPSA approved. Introduced 2006.

NIB	Exc.	V.G.	Good	Fair	Poor
1500	1300	1050	750	600	300

GP6

Polymer framed single-/double-action pistol, with ambidextrous safeties and fized three-dot sight system. Chambered in 9mm Parabellum.

NIB	Exc.	V.G.	Good	Fair	Poor
650	500	375	250	175	75

Sentinel Premier

Top-of-the-line ISPC and IDPA competition 1911, with Dawson Precision/STI "Perfect Impact" style white outline tritium adjustable sights and STI Tritium competition front; forged steel government length standard-width frame; and many other refinements. Sentinel Premier comes standard with case, owner's manual and one Wilson Combat Elite Tactical magazine.

NIB	Exc.	V.G.	Good	Fair	Poor
1700	1500	1300	1000	800	450

Limited Edition 20th Anniversary

1911-style semi-automatic pistol. Chambered in 9x19, .38 Super, .40 S&W and .45 ACP to commemorate 20th Anniversary. Features include ambidextrous thumb safeties and knuckle relief high-rise beavertail grip safety; gold TiN (or Titanium Nitride) coating; full length steel bar stock slide, with custom serrations specific to this model; 5" fully ramped and supported bull barrel; STI adjustable rear sight and Dawson fiber optic front sight. STI will only build 200 of these pistols and serial numbers reflect this (1 of 200, 2 of 200, etc.)

NIB	Exc.	V.G.	Good	Fair	Poor
3200	2900	2600	—	—	—

Duty One

1911-style semi-automatic pistol. Chambered in .45 ACP. Features include government size frame, with integral tactical rail and 30 lpi checkered front strap; milled tactical rail on dust cover of the frame; ambidextrous thumb safeties; high rise beavertail grip safety; lowered and flared ejection port; fixed rear sight; front and rear cocking serrations; 5" fully supported STI International ramped bull barrel.

NIB	Exc.	V.G.	Good	Fair	Poor
1300	1100	850	700	300	200

Apeiro

1911-style semi-automatic pistol. Chambered in 9x19, .40 S&W and .45 ACP. Features include Schuemann "Island" barrel; patented modular steel frame, with polymer grip; high capacity double-stack magazine; stainless steel ambidextrous thumb safeties and knuckle relief high-rise beavertail grip safety; unique sabertooth rear cocking serrations; 5" fully ramped fully supported "island" bull barrel, with sight milled in to allow faster recovery to point of aim; custom engraving on polished sides of (blued) stainless steel slide; stainless steel magwell; STI adjustable rear sight and Dawson fiber optic front sight; blued frame.

NIB	Exc.	V.G.	Good	Fair	Poor
2200	1850	1500	1200	800	400

Eclipse

Compact 1911-style semi-automatic pistol. Chambered in 9x19, .40 S&W and .45 ACP. Features include slide with rear cocking serrations, oversized ejection port; 2-dot tritium night sights recessed into the slide; high-capacity polymer grip; single sided blued thumb safety; bobbed high-rise blued knuckle relief beavertail grip safety; 3" barrel. Also comes with alloy frame as Escort model.

NIB	Exc.	V.G.	Good	Fair	Poor
1625	1400	1185	900	600	300

DVC Open

Top-of-the-line competition pistol, with slide cuts to decrease weight, increase cycle rate and alleviate muzzle jump. Titanium Nitride finished barrel and improved compensator, new sear and trigger mechanism, special texturing and improved ergonomics. In .38 Super or 9mm, with 10- or 20-round magazine, 5" barrel, polished hard chrome finish, C-More 6 MOA dot sight. Weight 48 oz. Introduced in 2015.

NIB	Exc.	V.G.	Good	Fair	Poor
3600	3200	2700	—	—	—

DVC Limited

Competition model designed for Limited Division. Similar to DVC Open model, with fiber optic front and adjustable rear sights. Chambered in 9mm or .40 S&W. Introduced in 2015

NIB	Exc.	V.G.	Good	Fair	Poor
2700	2200	1800	—	—	—

Texican Single Action Revolver

SAA-styled revolver chambered in .38 Special and .45 Colt. Features include 4.75" or 6.5" (.45) or 5.25" barrel (.38), competition sights, springs, triggers and hammers; color case-harden and blued finish standard.

NIB	Exc.	V.G.	Good	Fair	Poor
1100	935	775	600	300	200

FPI 2260 Rifle

Chambered for .22 Long Rifle cartridge. Aluminum receiver, with adjustable trigger and quick magazine release. Integral scope mount.

NIB	Exc.	V.G.	Good	Fair	Poor
1000	850	675	500	300	150

Sporting Competition Rifle

AR-style semi-automatic rifle. Chambered in 5.56 NATO. Features include 16" 410 stainless 1:8 barrel; mid-length gas system; Nordic Tactical Compensator and JP Trigger group; custom STI Valkyrie hand guard and gas block; flattop design with Picatinny rail; anodized finish with black Teflon coating. Also available in Tactical configuration.

NIB	Exc.	V.G.	Good	Fair	Poor
1175	1000	825	650	350	250

STOCK, FRANZ
Berlin, Germany

Stock

A .22, 6.35mm or 7.65mm semi-automatic pistol, with an open topped slide. Frame marked "Franz Stock Berlin". Blued, with black composition grips impressed with the name "Stock" at the top. Manufactured from 1918 to early 1930s.

Courtesy J.B. Wood

NIB	Exc.	V.G.	Good	Fair	Poor
—	525	400	300	250	150

STOCKING & CO.
Worcester, Massachusetts

Pepperbox

A .28 or .316 barreled percussion pepperbox revolver, with barrel lengths from 4" to 6". Hammer fitted with a long cocking piece at the rear and trigger guard may or may not be made with a spur at the rear. Blued, with walnut grips. Barrel group marked "Stocking & Co., Worcester". Manufactured between 1846 and 1854.

NIB	Exc.	V.G.	Good	Fair	Poor
—	—	1950	1650	600	200

Single-Shot Pistol

A .36-caliber single-shot percussion pistol. Same pattern as Pepperbox, with 4" half octagonal barrel. Marked as above. Manufactured from 1849 to 1852.

NIB	Exc.	V.G.	Good	Fair	Poor
—	—	1200	850	350	100

STOEGER, A. F./STOEGER INDUSTRIES

First guns shown, pistols, were imported many years ago to South Hackensack, New Jersey. All the rest have been imported by Stoeger Industries in: Accokeek, Maryland

HANDGUNS

.22 Luger

A .22-caliber simplified copy of German Model P.08 semi-automatic pistol, with 4.5" or 5.5" barrel and aluminum frame. Word "Luger" is roll engraved on right side of the frame. Blued, with checkered brown plastic grips. Made by Erma.

NIB	Exc.	V.G.	Good	Fair	Poor
—	350	275	200	150	100

Target Luger

As above, with adjustable target sights. Made by Erma.

NIB	Exc.	V.G.	Good	Fair	Poor
—	375	295	225	175	125

Luger Carbine

As above, with an 11" barrel, walnut fore-end and checkered walnut grips. Furnished with a red velvet lined black leatherette case. Manufactured during 1970s. Made by Erma.

NIB	Exc.	V.G.	Good	Fair	Poor
—	1100	775	500	350	150

American Eagle Luger

Identical to German design. Chambered for 9mm, with 7-round magazine and fitted with a 4" barrel. Checkered walnut grips. Stainless steel. Weight about 32 oz.

NIB	Exc.	V.G.	Good	Fair	Poor
1100	975	650	450	300	100

American Eagle Navy Model

Same as above, with a 6" barrel.

NIB	Exc.	V.G.	Good	Fair	Poor
1200	1075	700	450	300	100

Cougar

Double-action semi-automatic offered in 9mm. .40 S&W or .45 ACP. Manufactured in Turkey and based on Beretta model of the same name. Traditional DA/SA design, with ambidextrous safety/decocking lever, white dot sights and Picatinny rail (.45 only). Also made in compact variation.

NIB	Exc.	V.G.	Good	Fair	Poor
425	375	325	275	200	150

Pro Series 95

Target pistol in .22 LR, with 5.5" or 7.25" barrel, adjustable trigger and sights. Imported by Stoeger in 1995 and 1996. **NOTE:** Add $75 for bull barrel.

NIB	Exc.	V.G.	Good	Fair	Poor
450	400	350	300	250	150

SHOTGUNS

Model 2000

Semi-automatic shotgun chambered for 12-gauge shell. Fitted with 26", 28" or 30" ventilated rib barrel. Single trigger, with screw-in chokes. Weight about 7 lbs. Introduced in 2001.

NIB	Exc.	V.G.	Good	Fair	Poor
500	400	300	200	150	75

Model 2000 Deluxe

Same as above, with high grade walnut stock and etched receiver. Gold trigger.

NIB	Exc.	V.G.	Good	Fair	Poor
625	500	400	300	250	125

Model 2000 Camo

As above, with Advantage Timber HD camo stock.

NIB	Exc.	V.G.	Good	Fair	Poor
500	400	300	200	150	75

Model 2000 Slug

Chambered for 12-gauge shell, with 3" chamber. Barrel length 24". Fitted with a black synthetic stock. Smooth bore barrel. Adjustable rifle-type

sights. Optional field-style barrels in 24", 26" or 28". Weight about 6.7 lbs. Introduced in 2003.

NIB	Exc.	V.G.	Good	Fair	Poor
450	350	250	175	125	50

Model 2000 Synthetic

As above, with 24", 26" or 28" ventilated rib barrel. Black synthetic stock. Weight about 6.8 lbs. Introduced in 2003.

NIB	Exc.	V.G.	Good	Fair	Poor
500	400	300	200	150	75

Model 3000

Semi-automatic chambered for 2.75" and 3" loads. Minimum recommended load 3-dram, 1.125 oz. Magazine capacity 4+1. Inertia-driven action based on Benelli operating system. Barrel 26" or 28" with 3 choke tubes. Finish black synthetic or camo (Realtree APG or Max-4). Introduced in 2013. **NOTE:** Add $75 for camo finish.

NIB	Exc.	V.G.	Good	Fair	Poor
475	400	350	285	235	200

Model 3500

12-gauge auto-loader comes with 24", 26" or 28" barrel. Fitted with ventilated stepped rib and fiber-optic front sight. Inertia operation. Weight 7.5 lbs. Alloy receiver drilled and tapped. Includes Weaver-style scope base. All M3500s come supplied with five choke tubes (Extra-full turkey, Full, Modified, Improved Cylinder and Cylinder). Shim kit provides drop and cast adjustment. Threaded steel recoil reducer (included) can be installed in buttstock to help manage felt recoil from heavy Magnum loads. Available in three different finishes: matte black synthetic, Realtree APG or Realtree Max-4. **NOTE:** Add 20 percent for total camo coverage.

NIB	Exc.	V.G.	Good	Fair	Poor
535	450	385	325	250	200

Coach Gun

Side-by-side gun chambered for 12- or 20-gauge and .410 shell. Fitted with 20" barrels, with double triggers. Improved Cylinder and Modified fixed chokes. Weight about 7 lbs. **NOTE:** Add $50 for nickel finish.

NIB	Exc.	V.G.	Good	Fair	Poor
400	275	225	175	125	75

Silverado Coach Gun

Offered in 12-, 20-gauge and .410 bore, with straight-/pistol-grip stock. Matte nickel finish. Straight stock version offered in 12- and 20-gauge only. Weight about 6.5 lbs.

NIB	Exc.	V.G.	Good	Fair	Poor
450	320	250	175	125	75

Coach Gun Supreme

Similar to above, but offered with blue, stainless or nickel receiver. Introduced in 2004. **NOTE:** Add $10 for stainless; $30 for nickel.

NIB	Exc.	V.G.	Good	Fair	Poor
450	320	250	175	125	75

Uplander

Side-by-side shotgun chambered for 12-, 16-, 20-, 28-gauge and .410 bore. Choice of 26" or 28" barrels. Fixed chokes. Double triggers. Weight about 7.25 lbs.

NIB	Exc.	V.G.	Good	Fair	Poor
375	275	175	125	100	75

Uplander Special

As above, with straight-grip and oil-finish stock. Offered in 12-, 20- or 28-gauge. Weight about 7.3 lbs.

NIB	Exc.	V.G.	Good	Fair	Poor
395	300	200	150	100	75

Uplander Supreme

Same as above, with select wood and screw-in chokes.

NIB	Exc.	V.G.	Good	Fair	Poor
425	350	250	175	125	100

Uplander English

This variation fitted with a straight-grip stock. Chambered for 20-gauge or .410 bore. Fitted with 24" barrels. Weight about 7 lbs. Also available with a short stock.

NIB	Exc.	V.G.	Good	Fair	Poor
395	300	200	150	100	75

Uplander Youth

Offered in 20-gauge or .410 bore. Features 13" LOP, with 22" barrels choked Improved Modified and Modified. Weight about 6.75 lbs.

NIB	Exc.	V.G.	Good	Fair	Poor
375	275	175	125	100	75

Condor

Over/under shotgun chambered in 12-, 16-, 20-gauge and .410 bore. Available with 26" and 28" barrels in all gauges; 26" barrel in .410 bore. Single trigger. Blued finish. 16-gauge chambered for 2.75" shells; all others have 3" chambers. Weights run from 6 lbs. to 7.4 lbs. depending on bore.

NIB	Exc.	V.G.	Good	Fair	Poor
375	275	175	125	100	75

Condor Special

Similar to standard Condor, with matte stainless receiver. Rubbed oil-finish stock. Introduced in 2003.

NIB	Exc.	V.G.	Good	Fair	Poor
475	375	295	200	125	100

Condor Combo

Introduced in 2004. Features a two-barrel set of 12- and 20-gauge. Barrel length: 12-gauge 28"; 20-gauge 26". Choke tubes. Offered in 3 grades: Field, Special and Supreme.

Field

NIB	Exc.	V.G.	Good	Fair	Poor
500	400	300	200	100	75

Special

NIB	Exc.	V.G.	Good	Fair	Poor
650	500	400	275	175	125

Supreme

NIB	Exc.	V.G.	Good	Fair	Poor
775	650	500	300	200	150

Condor Supreme Deluxe

Similar to above model, with cut checkering and high polish blue. Offered in 12- and 20-gauge, with 26" or 28" barrels as well as 24" barrels for 20-gauge. Automatic ejectors.

NIB	Exc.	V.G.	Good	Fair	Poor
500	400	300	200	100	75

Condor Competition

These 3" 12- and 20-gauge over/unders feature 30" barrels, AA Grade wood and adjustable combs. Three choke tubes. Weight about: 7.3 lbs. 20-gauge; 7.8 lbs. 12-gauge.

NIB	Exc.	V.G.	Good	Fair	Poor
650	500	400	275	175	125

Condor Competition Combo

As above, with 12- and 20-gauge barrels.

NIB	Exc.	V.G.	Good	Fair	Poor
775	650	500	300	200	150

Condor Outback

New in 2007. Outback comes in 12- and 20-gauge. Chambered for 3" shells. Finish A Grade satin walnut stock, with blued barrels and receiver or matte black walnut stock, with polished barrels and receiver. Barrels are 20", with rifle sights. Includes two choke tubes. **NOTE:** Add $40 for black/nickel finish.

NIB	Exc.	V.G.	Good	Fair	Poor
375	275	175	125	100	75

Single Barrel Classic Youth

Available in 20-gauge or .410 bore, with 13" length of pull and 22" ventilated rib barrel. Straight-grip stock. Weight about 5 lbs.

NIB	Exc.	V.G.	Good	Fair	Poor
125	100	75	50	25	10

Single Barrel Classic

As above, with standard length of pull. Available in 12-, 20-gauge or .410 bore. Barrel length: 12-gauge 26" or 28"; 20-gauge 26"; .410 bore 24". Open pistol-grip. Weight about 5.5 lbs.

NIB	Exc.	V.G.	Good	Fair	Poor
125	100	75	50	25	10

Single Barrel Special

As above, with stainless steel frame. Offered in 12-, 20-gauge or .410 bore. Weight about 5.5 lbs.

NIB	Exc.	V.G.	Good	Fair	Poor
125	100	75	50	25	10

P-350

Pump-action 12-gauge shotgun introduced in 2005. All versions are chambered for 3.5" shells. Available with 24", 26" or 28" barrel in matte black synthetic or Advantage Timber camo finish; 26" or 28" barrel in Max-4 camo finish. Comes with 5 choke tubes. Weight about 6.8 lbs. Also available is a Defense model, with 18.5" barrel and fixed cylinder bore. **NOTE:** Add 15 percent for camo models.

NIB	Exc.	V.G.	Good	Fair	Poor
275	225	175	125	100	50

P-350 Camo

Pump-action 12-gauge chambered for 3.5" shells. Has a 24", 26" or 28" barrel and matte black, Max-4, Timber or APG finish. Also some pistol-grip stock offerings with 24" barrels. Includes five choke tubes. Weight about 6.8 lbs. **NOTE:** Add $20 for pistol-grip stock; $75 for camo finish.

NIB	Exc.	V.G.	Good	Fair	Poor
350	275	225	150	125	75

P-350 Defense

Same as above in matte black finish, with 18.5" fixed cylinder choke barrel. **NOTE:** Add $20 for pistol-grip stock.

NIB	Exc.	V.G.	Good	Fair	Poor
300	225	175	125	100	50

STREET SWEEPER
Atlanta, Georgia

Street Sweeper

A 12-gauge semi-automatic double-action shotgun, with 18" barrel and 12-shot rotary drum magazine. Matte black finish. Introduced in 1989. **NOTE:** This firearm is now on the restricted list as a Class III weapon and subject to NFA rules. This model requires registration with BATFE to avoid federal penalties. Make sure the shotgun is transferable prior to sale.

NIB	Exc.	V.G.	Good	Fair	Poor
2195	—	—	—	—	—

STURDIVANT, LEWIS G.
Talladega, Alabama

Received contract from the state of Alabama for 2,000 "Mississippi" or "Enfield" rifles. Two hundred and eighty were received on this contract. These arms resemble U.S. Model 1841 Rifles without patchboxes. Overall length 48.5"; barrel length 33"; .577-caliber. Unmarked.

STURM, RUGER & CO.
Southport, Connecticut

SEMI-AUTOMATIC RIMFIRE PISTOLS

Standard Model "Red Eagle Grips"

Blowback semi-automatic, with fixed exposed 4.75" barrel. Receiver tubular, with round bolt. There is a 9-shot detachable magazine. Sights are fixed. Finish blued. Black hard rubber grips on this first model feature a red Ruger eagle or hawk medallion on the left side. Approximately 25,600 manufactured before Alexander Sturm's death in 1951, but this model may be seen as high as 35000 serial number range. Because variations of this model exist, an expert opinion should be sought before a final price is established. **NOTE:** Factory verified plated pistols will bring between $2,500 and $5,000 depending on condition. Approximately 890 pistols were shipped in a wooden "salt cod" box. Add a premium of $3000 if NIB; $1000 to $2000 if good to excellent condition.

NIB	Exc.	V.G.	Good	Fair	Poor
750	550	450	325	250	150

Standard Model

Identical to Red Eagle, except after Sturm's death grip medallions were changed from red to black. Produced from 1952-1982 in 4.75" and 6" barrels. There are a great many variations of this pistol, but a book dealing with this pistol alone should be consulted as differences in variations are subtle and valuation of these variations is definitely a matter for individual appraisal.

NIB	Exc.	V.G.	Good	Fair	Poor
450	400	300	250	200	100

Standard Model—Marked "Hecho en Mexico"

Early in 1957, Ruger shipped 250 sets of parts to Armanex in Mexico. Armanex fabricated barrels for the sets of parts and then finished and assembled 250 pistols—200 with 4.75" barrel and 50 with 6.5" barrel. Due to the rarity of these pistols, an expert examination and appraisal is recommended.

NIB	Exc.	V.G.	Good	Fair	Poor
1750	1500	1200	850	600	400

Mark I Target Model

Success of Ruger Standard Model, led quite naturally to a demand for a more accurate target model. In 1951, a pistol that utilized the same frame and receiver with a 6.875" target-type barrel and adjustable sights was introduced. Early target models number 15000 to 16999 and 25000 to 25300 have Red Eagle grips. In 1952, a 5.25" tapered barrel model was introduced, but was soon discontinued. In 1963, popular 5.5" bull barrel model was introduced. These models enjoyed well deserved success. Manufactured from 1951-1982.

Red Eagle 6-7/8" barrel

NIB	Exc.	V.G.	Good	Fair	Poor
750	675	500	350	250	150

Black or Silver Eagle 6-7/8" barrel

NOTE: Add 35 percent for original hinged box; $75-$100 with factory supplied muzzle-brake; 50 percent for other Mark I Target models under serial number 72500 in original hinged box.

NIB	Exc.	V.G.	Good	Fair	Poor
450	400	300	250	200	125

5-1/4" Tapered Barrel Model

NOTE: Add 50 percent if in original 5.25" marked hinged box.

NIB	Exc.	V.G.	Good	Fair	Poor
875	750	600	400	300	200

5-1/2" Bull Barrel Model

NIB	Exc.	V.G.	Good	Fair	Poor
450	400	300	250	200	125

Rollmarked with U.S. on Top of Frame

These pistols will have .0625" or .125" high serial numbers. **NOTE:** Add 25 percent if pistol has .125" high serial numbers.

NIB	Exc.	V.G.	Good	Fair	Poor
—	875	700	550	400	300

Stainless Steel 1 of 5,000

This model is a special commemorative version of first standard with "Red Eagle" grips. Made of stainless steel and rollmarked with Bill Ruger's signature on it. Pistol is encased in a wood "salt cod" case.

NIB	Exc.	V.G.	Good	Fair	Poor
395	350	300	225	175	125

MARK II .22 CALIBER PISTOL SPECIFICATIONS

Supplied in .22 LR, with various barrel weights and lengths. Magazine capacity 10 rounds. Trigger grooved, with curved finger surface. High speed hammer provides fast lock time. Grips are sharply checkered and made of black gloss Delrin material. Stainless steel models have a brushed satin finish. **NOTE:** Beginning in 2004, all Ruger adjustable sight .22 pistols were drilled and tapped for an included Weaver-type scope base adapter.

STANDARD MODEL MARK II

Generally an improved version of first Ruger pistol. There is a hold-open device. Magazine holds 10 rounds. Introduced in 1982.

NIB	Exc.	V.G.	Good	Fair	Poor
350	250	150	125	100	75

Model MK450

Introduced in 1999, to commemorate 50th Anniversary of first Ruger rimfire pistol. Fitted with 4.75" barrel, with fixed sights. Chambered for .22 LR cartridge. Pistol-grips have a red Ruger medallion and Ruger crest on the barrel. Furnished in a red case. Weight about 35 oz. Production limited to one year.

NIB	Exc.	V.G.	Good	Fair	Poor
385	350	250	175	125	75

Model MK6

Same as above, with 6" barrel. Weight 37 oz.

NIB	Exc.	V.G.	Good	Fair	Poor
350	275	225	125	100	75

Model KMK4

Same as Mark II Standard, except made of stainless steel.

NIB	Exc.	V.G.	Good	Fair	Poor
375	300	200	150	125	100

Model KMK6

Same as above, with 6" barrel. Weight about 37 oz. **NOTE:** In 1997, Ruger produced 650 of Model MK6, with special features for "Friends of the NRA" auction of the same year. These guns have high polish blueing, faux ivory grip panels, gold inlaid National Rifle Association inscription and gold inlaid number of "1 of 650" to "650 of 650".

NIB	Exc.	V.G.	Good	Fair	Poor
375	300	200	150	125	100

Target Model

Model incorporates the same improvements as Mark II Standard. Offered with 5.5" bull, 6.875" tapered and 10" heavy barrel. A 5.25" tapered barrel was added in 1990, but discontinued in 1994. Blued finish. This model has adjustable target sights. Introduced in 1982. **NOTE:** In 1989, approximately 2,000 5.5" bull barrel Mark II pistols, with blue barreled receivers and stainless steel grip frames were produced by Ruger on order from a Ruger distributor. They exist in the 215-25xxx to 215-43xxx serial number range.

NIB	Exc.	V.G.	Good	Fair	Poor
400	350	300	225	175	125

Stainless Steel Target Model

Same as blued version, but made of stainless steel.

NIB	Exc.	V.G.	Good	Fair	Poor
450	400	350	300	250	200

Government Model

Similar to blue Mark II Target, with 6.875" bull barrel. Civilian version of a training pistol that the military is purchasing from Ruger. Only difference is this model does not have U.S. markings. **NOTE:** Add 150 to 175 percent premium for models with "U.S." marking. An expert examination and appraisal is suggested.

NIB	Exc.	V.G.	Good	Fair	Poor
450	325	225	200	150	100

Stainless Steel Government Model

Stainless steel version of Government Model. **NOTE:** Same with U.S. markings. These are found in serial number range of 210-00001 to 210-18600. Only a couple dozen are in civilian hands.

NIB	Exc.	V.G.	Good	Fair	Poor
475	350	250	225	175	125

Competition Model KMK678GC

Competition model features a stainless steel frame, with checkered laminated hardwood thumb rest grips, heavy 6.875" bull barrel factory drilled and tapped for scope mount, Partridge type front sight undercut to prevent glare and adjustable rear sight. Weight 45 oz. **NOTE:** In 1997, Ruger produced 204 of these pistols in blue instead of stainless steel for one of their distributors. They are very scarce. In 1995, Ruger produced a similar blued pistol (1,000 total: 500 each with or without scope rings) with 5.5" slab side barrels. These are not marked "Competition Target Model" like the previously described variation.

NIB	Exc.	V.G.	Good	Fair	Poor
400	325	275	200	125	100

Bull Barrel Model MK4B

Introduced in 1996. This bull barrel variation has a blued finish, with 4" barrel. Grips are checkered composition. Weight about 38 oz.

NIB	Exc.	V.G.	Good	Fair	Poor
400	325	275	200	125	100

RUGER 22/45 MODEL

This .22 LR caliber pistol has same grip angle and magazine latch as Model 1911 .45 ACP. Semi-automatic action is stainless steel and grip frame is made from Zytel, a fiberglass reinforced lightweight composite material. Front sight Patridge-type. Available in several different configurations. A 4" tapered barrel and standard model sights; 5.25" tapered barrel with target sights; 5.5" bull barrel with target sights. The 5.25" barrel was discontinued in 1994.

KP4

Features 4.75" standard weight barrel, with fixed sights. Weight 28 oz.

NIB	Exc.	V.G.	Good	Fair	Poor
300	275	250	200	125	75

KP514

Furnished with a target tapered barrel 5.25" in length. Comes with adjustable sights. Weight 38 oz. Discontinued.

NIB	Exc.	V.G.	Good	Fair	Poor
300	200	175	150	100	75

KP512

Equipped with 5.5" bull barrel, with adjustable sights. Weight 42 oz. **NOTE:** In 1995, Ruger produced 500 22/45s with stainless steel 6.875" Government type barreled receivers for one of their distributors. They appear around 220-59xxx serial number range. In 1997, another Ruger distributor succeeded in contracting Ruger to make a similar 22/45 only in blue, with 6.875" slab side bull barrels. Approximately 1,000 were produced, with serial numbers extending to 220-87xxx serial number range.

NIB	Exc.	V.G.	Good	Fair	Poor
300	200	175	150	100	75

P4

A limited number, about 1,000, of this variation were produced in 1995. A 4" bull barrel on a P frame. Introduced into the product line as a production pistol in 1997. Weight about 31 oz.

NIB	Exc.	V.G.	Good	Fair	Poor
350	200	150	100	75	50

22/45 Threaded Barrel

Variation of Model 22/45, with muzzle threaded to accept various accessories. Muzzle capped to protect threads, receiver and barrel drilled and tapped to accept accessory rails. Weight 32 oz.; 4.5" barrel, with blue finish.

NIB	Exc.	V.G.	Good	Fair	Poor
375	325	285	200	135	100

P512

This variation of the stainless steel version has a blued receiver, with P-style frame.

NIB	Exc.	V.G.	Good	Fair	Poor
350	250	150	100	75	60

22/45 Lite

Lightened version of standard 22/45 model, with 4.4" barrel. Weight 23 oz. Introduced in 2012.

NIB	Exc.	V.G.	Good	Fair	Poor
425	375	300	225	150	100

MARK III .22 CALIBER PISTOL

SPECIFICATIONS

Mark III series was introduced in 2004. Series features a newly designed magazine release button located on left side of the frame. Mark III pistols also have a visible loaded chamber indicator, an internal lock, magazine disconnect, re-contoured sights and ejection port.

Standard Pistol

Introduced in 2005. This .22-caliber pistol fitted with 4.75" or 6" barrel. Fixed rear sight. Blued finish. Magazine capacity 10 rounds. Black checkered grips. Weight about 35 oz.

NIB	Exc.	V.G.	Good	Fair	Poor
300	250	185	150	100	75

Hunter

This .22-caliber pistol fitted with 6.88" target crowned fluted stainless steel barrel. Adjustable rear sight, with Hi-Viz front. Checkered Cocobolo grips. Drilled and tapped for scope mount. Supplied with green case, scope base adapter and 6 interchangeable LitePipes for front sight. Weight about 41 oz. Introduced in 2005. **NOTE:** Add 50 percent for Crimson Trace laser-grips (limited edition for 2008).

NIB	Exc.	V.G.	Good	Fair	Poor
575	500	400	325	225	125

Competition

This .22-caliber model features 6.88" flat sided heavy barrel, with adjustable rear sight and Patridge front. Stainless steel finish. Checkered wood grips. Weight about 45 oz. Introduced in 2005.

NIB	Exc.	V.G.	Good	Fair	Poor
535	425	350	275	175	100

Mark III 22/45 Standard Pistol

This .22-caliber pistol has a grip frame similar to Colt 1911 pistol. The 4" bull barrel is flat sided. Blued steel frame. Fixed sights. Magazine capacity 10 rounds. Grips are checkered black polymer. Weight about 29 oz.

NIB	Exc.	V.G.	Good	Fair	Poor
300	225	175	125	100	75

Mark III 22/45 Stainless

Similar to above, with stainless barrel, aluminum upper receiver, Zytel polymer frame.

NIB	Exc.	V.G.	Good	Fair	Poor
425	375	325	250	175	125

Mark III 512 Pistol

This .22 LR pistol has 5.5" bull barrel and adjustable rear sight. Steel frame blued. Checkered black synthetic grips. Weaver-style scope base adapter included. Magazine capacity 10 rounds. Weight about 41 oz.

Ruger® Mark III Pistol
MKIII512

NIB	Exc.	V.G.	Good	Fair	Poor
350	300	225	175	125	100

Mark III 22/45 Hunter

Similar to 22/45 .22 pistol, with Mark III-style improvements. 6.875" or 4.5" fluted barrel, HiViz front sight, with six interchangeable inserts. Blued or stainless finish. Pricing is for stainless model. Introduced in 2007.

NIB	Exc.	V.G.	Good	Fair	Poor
465	395	300	225	150	100

Mark III 22/45RP Pistol

Semi-automatic pistol chambered in .22 LR. Features include polymer frame with grip panels that recreate feel of 1911; 1911-style controls including magazine button, manual safety and bolt stop locations as classic 1911 pistol; slim polymer grip frame with serrated front strap and checkered back strap; blued alloy steel 5.5" bull barrel with fixed front sight and micro-adjustable rear sight; adjustable sights drilled/tapped for Weaver mounts. Weight 31 oz. Offered in several variations including 22/45 Lite with weight of 23 oz., 4.4" stainless steel threaded barrel. Introduced in 2013.

NIB	Exc.	V.G.	Good	Fair	Poor
425	375	300	265	235	200

Charger

A 10" barrel pistol version of 10/22 .22 LR rifle. Black matte finish, black laminated stock (other colors available), bipod and Weaver-style mounts. Includes one 10-round magazine. Introduced in 2008; discontinued 2012.

NIB	Exc.	V.G.	Good	Fair	Poor
375	300	225	175	125	100

Charger — New Model

New variation of Charger design offers improved ergonomics, new features and new BX-15 magazine. Take-down model has all features of standard model plus quick disconnect feature found on 10/22 Take-down rifle. Choice of brown or Green Mountain laminate stock. Introduced in 2015. **NOTE:** Add $100 for Green Mountain.

NIB	Exc.	V.G.	Good	Fair	Poor
250	225	200	—	—	—

OLD MODEL SINGLE-ACTION REVOLVERS (PRE-TRANSFER BAR)

Single Six Revolver

A .22 rimfire 6-shot single-action revolver. First offered with 5.5" barrel length and fixed sight. In 1959, additional barrel lengths were offered in 4.625", 6.5" and 9.5". Based in appearance on Colt Single-Action Army, but internally a new design that features coil springs instead of old-style flat leaf springs. Also features a floating firing pin and is generally a stronger action than what was previously available. Early model had a flat loading gate and was made this way from 1953-1957, when the contoured gate became standard. Early models had checkered hard rubber grips; changed to smooth varnished walnut by 1962. Black eagle grip medallions were used from the beginning of production to 1971, when a silver eagle grip medallion replaced it. No "Red Eagle" single-sixes were ever produced. Manufactured from 1953-1972.

Flat Gate Model

60,000 produced.

NOTE 1: Be aware that revolvers serial numbered under 2000 will bring a premium of 25 percent to 125 percent depending on condition, low serial number and color of cylinder frame—bright reddish purple the most desirable.

NOTE 2: Values cited below are for unconverted examples and for converted examples with original parts present.

Courtesy John C. Dougan

NIB	Exc.	V.G.	Good	Fair	Poor
900	700	500	450	225	150

Contoured Gate Model

Introduced 1957. There were 258 5.5" barrel factory engraved pistols in this model. Add a 25 percent premium for 3-screw models. **NOTE:** Be aware that 4.625" and 9.5" barrel lengths will bring a premium. Add $3,500 to $6,000 for factory engraved and cased models.

NIB	Exc.	V.G.	Good	Fair	Poor
700	600	500	350	200	125

SINGLE SIX ENGRAVED SERIES

Between 1954 and 1958, 250 Single Sixes were engraved by the factory. They are known as RSSE models, for Ruger Single Six Engraved. These are extremely rare and among the most collectible of all Ruger firearms. A total of 22 revolvers were sent to Spain for engraving and 238 were engraved by Charles Jerred in the U.S. (See the article "Fancy Rugers" elsewhere in this book for some history and photographs of these beautiful sixguns.) Due to the rarity of these models and the fact that most are in the hands of collectors, values shown here are quite speculative. Whether buying or selling, an appraisal by a knowledgeable Ruger expert would be required.

Spanish Engraved (serial no. 7 and 8; and 5100 to 5119)

NIB	Exc.	V.G.	Good	Fair	Poor
22500	20000	16000	—	—	—

All Blue Jerred Engraved

NIB	Exc.	V.G.	Good	Fair	Poor
18000	15000	12000	—	—	—

Standard Jerred Engraved

NIB	Exc.	V.G.	Good	Fair	Poor
10000	8500	6500	—	—	—

Single Six Convertible

Similar to Single Six, but furnished with an extra .22 rimfire Magnum cylinder. **NOTE:** Barrel lengths in 4.625" and 9.5" will bring a premium.

NIB	Exc.	V.G.	Good	Fair	Poor
650	550	450	375	225	150

Single Six .22 Magnum Model

Similar to Single Six, except chambered for .22 rimfire Magnum and frame was so marked. Offered in 6.5" barrel length only. Manufactured for three years. An extra long rifle cylinder was added later in production. Serial numbers are in 300000-340000 range.

NIB	Exc.	V.G.	Good	Fair	Poor
600	500	400	350	200	125

Lightweight Single Six

Similar to Single Six, with aluminum alloy frame and 4.625" barrel. Variation produced between 1956 and 1958. Serial number range 200000-212000. Approximately first 6,500 produced with alloy cylinders and steel chamber inserts. **NOTE:** An "S" will be found following the serial number or on bottom of frame. Individual evaluation and appraisal recommended. These are factory seconds and are verifiable. **NOTE:** Add 25 to 40 percent for original Lightweight Single-Six boxes.

Courtesy Know Your Ruger Single-Action Revolvers 1953-63
Blacksmith Corp.

Courtesy Know Your Ruger Single-Action Revolvers 1953-63
Blacksmith Corp.

Silver Anodized Frame with Aluminum Cylinder Model with Martin Hardcoat Finish

NIB	Exc.	V.G.	Good	Fair	Poor
1500	1100	900	750	500	300

Black Anodized Aluminum Frame and Cylinder Model

NIB	Exc.	V.G.	Good	Fair	Poor
1100	950	700	600	350	250

Black Anodized Frame with Blue Steel Cylinder Model

NIB	Exc.	V.G.	Good	Fair	Poor
950	800	600	500	300	200

Silver Anodized Aluminum Frame with Blue Steel Cylinder and "S" Marking

Only a few hundred pistols, in this variation, were produced by the factory with an "S" suffix.

NIB	Exc.	V.G.	Good	Fair	Poor
1600	1200	900	750	500	300

Super Single Six

Introduced in 1964. Single Six with adjustable sights. Prices listed for pistols with 5.5" and 6.5" barrels. **NOTE:** Listed models are factory verifiable.

Courtesy Know Your Ruger Single-Actions: The Second Decade.
Blacksmith Corp.

NIB	Exc.	V.G.	Good	Fair	Poor
600	500	400	350	200	125

4-5/8" Barrel

200 built.

NIB	Exc.	V.G.	Good	Fair	Poor
1750	1500	1200	900	500	250

Nickel-Plated Model

Approximately 100 built.

NIB	Exc.	V.G.	Good	Fair	Poor
2350	1900	1600	1200	600	300

Bearcat (Old Model)

Scaled-down version of single-action. Chambered for .22 rimfire. Has 4" barrel and unfluted roll engraved cylinder. Frame is alloy and has a brass colored anodized alloy trigger guard. Finish is blue and grips are plastic impregnated wood until 1963, thereafter, walnut with eagle medallions were used. Manufactured from 1958-1970. **NOTE:** Add $150 to $200 premium for a serial number under 30000; $350 for black anodized trigger guard; 20 percent for alphabet prefix serial number.

Courtesy Know Your Ruger Single-Actions: The Second Decade.
Blacksmith Corp.

NIB	Exc.	V.G.	Good	Fair	Poor
450	350	300	265	225	175

Super Bearcat (Old Model)

Similar to Bearcat, with a steel frame. Later models a blued steel trigger guard and grip frame. Early examples still used brass. Manufactured from 1971 to 1974.

Courtesy W.P. Hallstein III and son Chip

NIB	Exc.	V.G.	Good	Fair	Poor
575	500	395	275	225	175

Flattop—.357 Magnum

Success of Single Six led to production of a larger version chambered for .357 Magnum cartridge. This model is a single-action, with 6-shot fluted cylinder and flattop strap with adjustable "Micro sight". Barrel length 4.625", 6.5" and 10". Finish blue, with checkered hard rubber grips on early examples and smooth walnut on later ones. Approximately 42,600 manufactured between 1955 and 1962.

4-5/8" Barrel

NIB	Exc.	V.G.	Good	Fair	Poor
1200	1000	600	350	250	200

6-1/2" Barrel

NIB	Exc.	V.G.	Good	Fair	Poor
1000	850	600	450	350	250

10" Barrel

NIB	Exc.	V.G.	Good	Fair	Poor
2800	2500	1000	850	750	600

Blackhawk Flattop .44 Magnum

In 1956, the .44 Magnum was introduced and Ruger jumped on the bandwagon. Similar in appearance to .357, but has a slightly heavier frame and larger cylinder. Available in 6.5", 7.5" and 10" barrel. Manufactured from 1956-1963. Approximately 29,700 manufactured.

6-1/2" Barrel

NIB	Exc.	V.G.	Good	Fair	Poor
1250	800	600	450	350	250

7-1/2" Barrel

NIB	Exc.	V.G.	Good	Fair	Poor
1325	950	700	600	450	300

10" Barrel

NIB	Exc.	V.G.	Good	Fair	Poor
3000	2000	1200	800	700	400

Blackhawk

Similar to "Flattop", but rear sight is protected by two raised protrusions—one on each side. Available chambered for .30 Carbine, .357 Magnum, .41 Magnum or .45 Colt cartridge. Barrel lengths: 4.625" or 6.5" in .357 Magnum and .41 Magnum; 4.625" or 7.5" in .45 Colt; 7.5" only in .30 Carbine. Finish blue and grips are walnut, with Ruger medallions. Produced from 1962 to 1972. Note that "Old Style" Blackhawk (i.e., pre-transfer bar) is a popular platform for custom revolvers, so prices may exceed those shown depending on circumstances. **NOTE:** Add 20 percent for .41 Magnum; 50 percent for .45 Colt; 35 percent for .30 Carbine. Original verified factory brass grip frame will add at least $800 to above prices. It was available chambered for .357 Magnum or .41 Magnum (4.625" or 6.5" barrel), or .45 Colt (4.625" or 7.5" barrel). The .41 Magnum with factory installed brass frame will bring $1000 to $2500 depending on condition.

Courtesy Know Your Ruger Single-Action Revolvers 1953-63.
Blacksmith Corp.

NIB	Exc.	V.G.	Good	Fair	Poor
700	500	350	200	150	125

Blackhawk Convertible

Same as Blackhawk, with an extra cylinder to change or convert calibers. The .357 Magnum has a 9mm cylinder; .45 Colt a .45 ACP cylinder. **NOTE:** The 4.625" barrel will bring a slight premium. Non-prefix serial numbered .357/9mm Blackhawks will bring a premium.

.357/9mm

NIB	Exc.	V.G.	Good	Fair	Poor
750	650	450	300	200	150

.45 L.C./.45 ACP

NIB	Exc.	V.G.	Good	Fair	Poor
1250	1100	800	600	400	200

Super Blackhawk Old Model

The formidable recoil of .44 Magnum cartridge was difficult to handle in a revolver, with a small grip such as found on Blackhawk. So, it was decided to produce a larger-framed revolver, with increased size in grip. Rear of trigger guard was squared off and cylinder was left unfluted to increase mass. Offered with 7.5" barrel; 600 6.5" barrel Super Blackhawks were produced by factory error. This model is blued and has smooth walnut grips with medallions. First of these revolvers were offered in a fitted wood case and are rare today. Super Blackhawk was made from 1959-1972. **NOTE:** Pistols with verified factory installed brass grip frame, each example should be appraised. Add $250 for pistols with brass grip frames.

NIB	Exc.	V.G.	Good	Fair	Poor
800	600	400	300	200	150

Early Model in Wood Presentation Case

NIB	Exc.	V.G.	Good	Fair	Poor
1200	1000	750	475	400	300

In Fitted White Cardboard Case

NIB	Exc.	V.G.	Good	Fair	Poor
1800	1600	1000	950	875	675

Long Grip Frame in Wood Case

300 guns built.

NIB	Exc.	V.G.	Good	Fair	Poor
2000	1800	1150	1050	800	675

Factory Verified 6-1/2" Barrel

Approximately 600 guns built in 23000-25000 serial number range.

NIB	Exc.	V.G.	Good	Fair	Poor
1500	1300	950	700	450	375

Hawkeye Single-Shot

Shooting public wanted a small-caliber high-velocity handgun. Smith & Wesson Model 53, chambered for .22 Jet, appeared in 1961; cartridge created extraction problems for a revolver. Ruger solved this problem with introduction of Hawkeye—a single-shot that looked like a six shooter. In place of the cylinder was a breech block that cammed to the side for loading. This pistol was excellent from an engineering and performance standpoint, but was not a commercial success. Hawkeye chambered for .256 Magnum, a bottleneck cartridge and 8.5" barrel and adjustable sights. Finish blued, with walnut medallion grips. Barrel tapped at the factory for a 1" scope base. Pistol is quite rare as only 3,300 were produced in 1963 and 1964.

Courtesy John C. Dougan

NIB	Exc.	V.G.	Good	Fair	Poor
2500	1900	1400	850	600	500

EDITOR'S COMMENT: All the above single-action Ruger pistols, fitted with factory optional grips, will bring a premium regardless of model. This premium applies to pistols manufactured from 1954 to 1962 only. Optional grips premium is: Ivory $800; Stag $400.

NEW MODEL SINGLE-ACTION REVOLVERS

Ruger firm in 1973, completely modified their single-action lockwork to accommodate a hammer block or transfer bar. This hammer block or transfer bar prevented accidental discharge, should a revolver be dropped. In doing so, the company circumvented a great deal of potential legal problems and made collectibles out of previous models.

Super Single Six Convertible (New Model)

Similar in appearance to old model, but has the new hammer block safety system. Frame has two pins instead of three screws. Opening the loading gate frees cylinder stop for loading. Barrel lengths are 4.625", 5.5", 6.5" and 9.5". Sights are adjustable and finish blued. Grips are walnut, with a medallion. An interchangeable .22 Magnum cylinder is supplied. Introduced in 1973 and currently in production.

NIB	Exc.	V.G.	Good	Fair	Poor
450	350	250	200	175	125

Stainless Steel Single Six Convertible

Same as standard blued model, but made from stainless steel. Offered with 4.625", 6.5" and 9.5" barrel. **NOTE:** Add 40 percent premium for pre-warning pistols (1973-1976) with 4.625" or 9.5" barrel; 100 percent premium, at least, to NIB prices for pistols with 4.625" barrels with "made in the 200th year of American Liberty" rollmark on the barrel.

NIB	Exc.	V.G.	Good	Fair	Poor
475	400	300	250	225	175

New Model Single Six (.22 LR only) "Star" Model

Produced in blue and stainless for one year only in 4.625", 5.5", 6.5" and 9.5" barrel lengths. Very low production on this model.

Blue Variation 5.5" or 6.5" Barrel

NIB	Exc.	V.G.	Good	Fair	Poor
450	400	350	300	275	200

9.5" Barrel—Rare

NIB	Exc.	V.G.	Good	Fair	Poor
550	500	450	400	350	250

4.62" Barrel—Very Rare

NIB	Exc.	V.G.	Good	Fair	Poor
800	750	450	400	350	250

Stainless Variation 5.5" or 6.5" Barrel

NIB	Exc.	V.G.	Good	Fair	Poor
450	350	275	225	175	150

9.5" Barrel

NIB	Exc.	V.G.	Good	Fair	Poor
600	500	400	300	225	175

4.62" Barrel—Rare

NIB	Exc.	V.G.	Good	Fair	Poor
650	550	500	400	300	200

Fixed Sight New Model Single Six

First made as drift adjustable rear sight (500 each in 4.625", 5.5" and 6.5" blue); and now a catalogued item as a pinched frame style fixed rear sight. Barrel lengths offered in 5.5" and 6.5" lengths. Finish blued or glossy stainless steel. Rear sight fixed. Weights between 32 and 38 oz. depending on barrel length and cylinder.

Blued Finish

NIB	Exc.	V.G.	Good	Fair	Poor
325	295	250	165	125	100

Stainless Steel

NIB	Exc.	V.G.	Good	Fair	Poor
395	300	250	200	150	125

Colorado Centennial Single Six

A stainless steel grip frame and balance blued. Walnut grips, with medallion insert. Barrel 6.5". Furnished with a walnut case with a centennial medal insert. Manufactured 15,000 in 1975.

NIB	Exc.	V.G.	Good	Fair	Poor
500	400	300	200	125	100

Model "SSM" Single Six

Single Six chambered for .32 H&R Magnum cartridge. First 800 pistols marked with "SSM" on cylinder frame and will bring a slight premium. Sold from 1984 to 1997. Adjustable sights.

NIB	Exc.	V.G.	Good	Fair	Poor
700	525	375	225	150	125

New Model Single Six .32 H&R

Introduced in 2000. Revolver chambered for .32 H&R Magnum cartridge. Fitted with 4.625" barrel. Offered in blue or stainless steel. Short (.250" shorter) simulated ivory grips. Vaquero-style frame, with fixed sights. Values shown are for stainless. **NOTE:** Deduct 25 percent for blued.

NIB	Exc.	V.G.	Good	Fair	Poor
525	400	300	225	175	125

New Model Single Six 50th Anniversary Model

Introduced in 2003. Features 4.625" barrel, with blued finish. Top of barrel rollmarked "50 YEARS OF SINGLE SIX 1953 TO 2003". Comes standard with both .22 LR and .22 WMR cylinders. Cocobolo grips, with red Ruger medallion. Packaged in a red plastic case, with special "50 Year" label. Offered only in 2003.

NIB	Exc.	V.G.	Good	Fair	Poor
425	350	300	225	175	125

New Model Super Single Six

Chambered for .22 LR and a separate cylinder for .22 WMR cartridge. Barrel lengths 4.625", 5.5", 6.5" and 9.5". Rosewood grips. Adjustable or fixed sights. Blued finish, except optional stainless steel on 5.5" or 6.5" revolvers. Weight about 35 oz. depending on barrel length. **NOTE:** Add $80 for stainless steel model.

NIB	Exc.	V.G.	Good	Fair	Poor
375	325	275	225	175	125

New Model Super Single Six, .17 HMR

As above, with 6.5" barrel. Chambered for .17 HMR cartridge. Weight about 35 oz. Introduced in 2003.

NIB	Exc.	V.G.	Good	Fair	Poor
400	350	275	225	175	125

New Model Single Six Hunter Convertible

Chambered for .17 HMR/.17 Mach 2. Fitted with 7.5" barrel, with adjustable rear sight. Stainless steel finish, with black laminate grips. Integral barrel rib machined for scope rings. Weight about 45 oz. Introduced in 2005.

NIB	Exc.	V.G.	Good	Fair	Poor
675	500	400	300	250	175

Single-Ten

10-shot version of Single-Six, with 5.5" barrel and walnut Gunfighter grips. Other features include satin stainless finish and Williams adjust-

able fiber optic sights. Introduced in late 2011. A 9-shot variation with 6.5" barrel introduced in 2013 as Single-Nine.

NIB	Exc.	V.G.	Good	Fair	Poor
525	450	385	300	220	150

Single-Nine

Identical to Single Ten, except chambered for .22 Win. Magnum rimfire. Has 9-round cylinder.

NIB	Exc.	V.G.	Good	Fair	Poor
525	450	385	300	220	150

Single Seven

Distributor exclusive model (from Lipsey's) is chambered for .327 Federal Magnum cartridge, with a 7-round cylinder. Stainless revolver has 5.5" barrel, adjustable sights and wood grips. Introduced in 2015.

NIB	Exc.	V.G.	Good	Fair	Poor
565	500	425	—	—	—

Buckeye Special

Built in 1989 and 1990. Chambered for .38-40, 10mm, .32-20 or .32 H&R cartridges.

NIB	Exc.	V.G.	Good	Fair	Poor
750	600	400	275	200	125

New Model Blackhawk

Similar in appearance to old model Blackhawk. Offered in same calibers and barrel lengths. Has transfer bar safety device. Introduced in 1973. Chambered in .30 Carbine, .357 Magnum, .41 Magnum and .45 Colt. Various barrel lengths.

NIB	Exc.	V.G.	Good	Fair	Poor
500	425	300	200	150	125

New Model Blackhawk Flattop

The .44 Special Blackhawk became a reality in 2010. Made only in Flattop design, with blue finish and 4.625" or 5.5" barrel.

NIB	Exc.	V.G.	Good	Fair	Poor
500	425	300	200	150	120

New Model Blackhawk Bisley

Based on Colt Bisley frame, with adjustable sights and longer grip frame. Chambered in .44 Magnum or .45 Colt, with 7.5" barrel, blue finish, alloy frame and hardwood grips.

NIB	Exc.	V.G.	Good	Fair	Poor
700	600	475	375	300	250

50th Anniversary New Model Blackhawk NVB34-50

Introduced in 2005. Features smaller original size XR-3 grip, smaller main frame with checkered hard rubber grips. Adjustable rear sight. Special commemorative gold roll mark on top of barrel. Chambered for .357 Magnum and fitted with 4.625" barrel. Weight about 45 oz. All Blackhawk revolvers now feature this new/old smaller main frame.

NIB	Exc.	V.G.	Good	Fair	Poor
575	425	300	200	150	125

Stainless Steel Blackhawk (New Model)

New Model Blackhawk made from stainless steel. To date offered in .357, .44, .45 L.C. and .327 Federal calibers.

NIB	Exc.	V.G.	Good	Fair	Poor
600	500	420	300	200	150

Blackhawk Convertible (New Model)

Same as Blackhawk, with interchangeable conversion cylinders—.357 Magnum/9mm and .45 Colt/.45 ACP. Prices listed are for blued model.

NIB	Exc.	V.G.	Good	Fair	Poor
465	350	250	175	150	125

.45 ACP & .45 Long Colt Convertible (1998)

NIB	Exc.	V.G.	Good	Fair	Poor
550	450	350	275	225	150

Stainless Model .357/9mm

300 guns built.

NIB	Exc.	V.G.	Good	Fair	Poor
925	700	600	500	375	250

Fiftieth Anniversary .44 Magnum Flattop New Model Blackhawk

Six-shot single-action .44 Magnum (also accepts .44 Special), with 6.5" barrel and adjustable rear sight. Weight 47 oz. Recreation of original .44 Flattop Blackhawk. Blued, with checkered rubber grips. Gold color-filled rollmark on top of barrel. Introduced 2006.

NIB	Exc.	V.G.	Good	Fair	Poor
750	625	525	400	350	300

Model SRM Blackhawk .357 Maximum

This is the New Model Blackhawk, with 7.5" or 10.5" barrel. Chambered for .357 Maximum and intended for silhouette shooting. This model experienced problems with gas erosion in the forcing cone and under the top strap and was removed from production in 1984. Approximately 9200 were manufactured.

NIB	Exc.	V.G.	Good	Fair	Poor
—	675	575	400	275	250

Super Blackhawk (New Model)

Similar in appearance to Old Model, but has the transfer bar safety device. Manufactured from 1973 to present. Commenced at serial number 81-00001.

NIB	Exc.	V.G.	Good	Fair	Poor
600	550	450	325	250	175

Super Blackhawk Stainless Steel

Same as blued version, but made of stainless steel. In 1998, offered in 4.625" or 7.5" barrels, with hunter grip frame. Laminated grip panels. **NOTE:** Add $50 for hunter grip frame and laminated grip panels.

NIB	Exc.	V.G.	Good	Fair	Poor
650	600	500	350	250	175

Super Blackhawk Hunter

Introduced in 2002. This .44 or .41 Magnum features 7.5" barrel, with integral full-length solid rib for scope mounts. Stainless steel. Adjustable rear sight. Scope rings included. Weight about 52 oz.

NIB	Exc.	V.G.	Good	Fair	Poor
800	700	500	350	250	175

50th Anniversary Matched Set .357 and .44 Magnum

Matched pair of Ruger New Blackhawks, one in .44 and the other in .357, commemorating 50th Anniversary of Ruger Blackhawk revolver. Gold-filled rollmarked 6.5" and 4.625" barrels, respectively. Includes presentation case. Production limited. Introduced 2007.

NIB	Exc.	V.G.	Good	Fair	Poor
1350	1150	900	775	600	400

Bisley Model

This model has the modified features found on famous old Colt Bisley Target model—the flattop frame, fixed or adjustable sights and longer grip frame that has become the Bisley trademark. Bisley is available chambered for .22 LR, .32 H&R Magnum, .357 Magnum, .41 Magnum, .44 Magnum and .45 Long Colt. Barrel lengths 6.5" and 7.5"; cylinders fluted or unfluted and roll engraved. Finish a satin blue, and grips are smooth Goncalo Alves with medallions. Bisley was introduced in 1986. **NOTE:** Approximately 750 stainless grip frame .22-caliber Bisleys were made. These will demand a premium. Add $100 for stainless; $125 for convertible stainlesss.

.22 LR and .32 H&R Magnum

NOTE: Add $100 for .32 Magnum Bisley.

NIB	Exc.	V.G.	Good	Fair	Poor
425	375	225	200	150	125

.357 Magnum, .41 Magnum, .44 Magnum, .45 Colt

NIB	Exc.	V.G.	Good	Fair	Poor
700	600	475	300	200	125

Shootists Bisley

Produced in 1994, for Shootist organization in memory of Tom Ruger. Chambered for .22 cartridge, these revolvers were limited to 52 total produced. Stainless steel and fitted with 4.625" barrels. Barrels marked, "IN MEMORY OF OUR FRIEND TOM RUGER THE SHOOTIST 1994". Some of these revolvers, but not all, have name of the owner engraved on backstrap. **NOTE:** Due to this model's rarity, values are speculative.

Courtesy Jim Taylor

NIB	Exc.	V.G.	Good	Fair	Poor
2500	2000	1200	1000	—	—

Old Army Percussion Revolver

A .45-caliber percussion revolver, with 5" or 7.5" barrel. Has 6-shot cylinder, with blued finish and walnut grips. Beginning in 1994, this model offered with fixed sights. Weight about 46 oz. All models now discontinued. **NOTE:** Add $450 for pistols with original factory installed brass grip frame; 20 percent for 5.5" model.

NIB	Exc.	V.G.	Good	Fair	Poor
575	475	375	250	175	150

Old Army Stainless Steel

Same as blued version, except made of stainless steel. **NOTE:** Add 200 percent for stainless 200th Year model.

NIB	Exc.	V.G.	Good	Fair	Poor
650	525	400	275	225	150

Ruger Vaquero

Single-action pistol introduced in 1993. Voted handgun of the year by the shooting industry. Fixed sight version of New Model Blackhawk. Available in stainless steel or blued, with case colored frame. Offered in three different barrel lengths: 4.62", 5.5" and 7.5". Chambered for .45 Long Colt. In 1994, .44-40 and .44 Magnum calibers were added to Vaquero line. Capacity 6 rounds. Weight between 39 and 41 oz. depending on barrel length. Discontinued; superseded by New Vaquero. **NOTE:** Add 25 percent for Vaqueros with 4.625" barrel chambered for .44 Magnum in both blue and stainless are un-catalogued.

NIB	Exc.	V.G.	Good	Fair	Poor
500	425	325	200	150	100

Ruger Bisley Vaquero

Introduced in 1997. Features 5.5" barrel chambered for .44 Magnum or .45 Long Colt. Grips are smooth rosewood. Finish blued, with case colored frame. Blade front sight and notch rear. Weight about 40 oz. Discontinued.

NIB	Exc.	V.G.	Good	Fair	Poor
600	500	425	325	225	150

Ruger Vaquero Bird's-head

Introduced in 2001. Features bird's-head grip. Chambered for .45 Long Colt cartridge. Fitted with 5.5" barrel. Offered in stainless steel and blued finish. Weight about 40 oz. Discontinued. **NOTE:** In 2002, offered with 3.75" barrel and black Micarta grips. In 2003, offered chambered for .357 Magnum cartridge. Simulated ivory grips also offered.

NIB	Exc.	V.G.	Good	Fair	Poor
650	550	400	300	175	125

"Cowboy Pair"

Matched pair of engraved and consecutively serial-numbered New Vaquero revolvers in .45 Colt. Includes lined wood collector case. Production limited to 500 sets. Introduced 2007.

NIB	Exc.	V.G.	Good	Fair	Poor
3500	3000	2500	1350	1000	600

Ruger New Vaquero

Introduced in 2005. Features slimmer pre-1962 XR-3 style grip frame, with color case finish. Cylinder frame is mid-size. Cylinder is beveled. Ejector rod head is crescent shaped. Chambered for .357 Magnum or .45 Colt. Barrel lengths 4.625", 5.5" and 7.5" (not in .357). Choice of case colored finish or stainless steel. Black checkered grips. Weight about 37 oz.

NIB	Exc.	V.G.	Good	Fair	Poor
575	475	400	300	200	100

SASS Vaquero Set

Two high-gloss stainless Vaqueros in .357 and/or .45 Colt, with consecutive serial numbers. SASS (Single Action Shooting Society) prefixes.

NIB	Exc.	V.G.	Good	Fair	Poor
1500	1400	1250	1000	—	—

Ruger New Model Bisley Vaquero

Similar to New Vaquero, with Bisley-style hammer and grip frame. Chambered in .357 and .45 Colt. Features include 5.5" barrel, simulated ivory grips, fixed sights, 6-shot cylinder. Overall length 11.12". Weight: 45 oz. **NOTE:** Add 15 percent for stainless steel finish.

NIB	Exc.	V.G.	Good	Fair	Poor
565	425	325	225	165	150

New Ruger Bearcat (Super Bearcat)

This old favorite was reintroduced in 1994. Furnished with .22 LR and .22 WMR cylinder. Barrel length 4", with fixed sights. Grips walnut. Offered with blued finish. **NOTE:** There was a factory recall on Magnum cylinders. Bearcats with both cylinders are very rare.

Blue

NIB	Exc.	V.G.	Good	Fair	Poor
425	325	250	175	125	100

Stainless Steel

NIB	Exc.	V.G.	Good	Fair	Poor
450	350	275	200	150	125

Convertible (Recalled)

NIB	Exc.	V.G.	Good	Fair	Poor
1100	1000	900	650	400	200

Adjustable Sights (Lipsey's Exclusive)

NIB	Exc.	V.G.	Good	Fair	Poor
565	500	425	375	325	275

New Model Super Bearcat

Reintroduced in 2002, this .22-caliber features stainless steel or blued finish, 4" barrel with fixed sights and rosewood grips. Weight about 24 oz. **NOTE:** Add $50 for stainless steel.

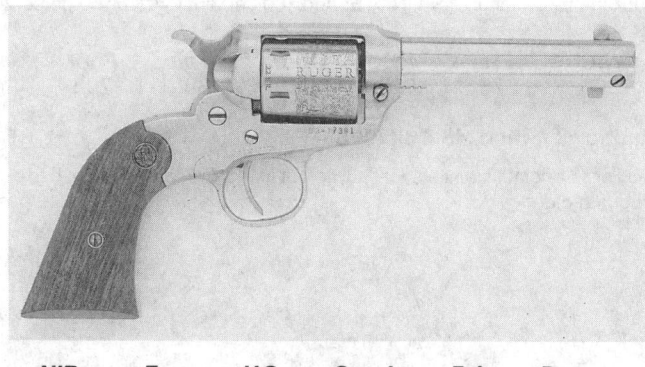

NIB	Exc.	V.G.	Good	Fair	Poor
425	325	250	175	125	100

Fiftieth Anniversary New Bearcat

Gussied-up version of New Bearcat (.22 LR only). Commemorating 50th Anniversary of original Bearcat. Blued finish, with gold-filled anniversary script, gold-colored trigger guard. Special box with anniversary booklet. Manufactured in 2008 only.

NIB	Exc.	V.G.	Good	Fair	Poor
700	600	500	—	—	—

DOUBLE-ACTION REVOLVERS

Security Six

This revolver, also known as Model 117, chambered for .357 Magnum cartridge. Has 2.75", 4" or 6" barrel. Features adjustable sights, with blue or stainless finish and a square butt, with checkered walnut grips. Manufactured between 1970 and 1985. Early guns with fixed sights and square butt were also marked "Security-Six". Later termed "Service-Six" and so marked. Prices listed only for adjustable sight and square butt "Security-Six" models. **NOTE:** Fixed sight guns marked "Security-Six" and round butt "Security-Sixes", with adjustable sights are worth a premium.

NIB	Exc.	V.G.	Good	Fair	Poor
450	400	350	295	200	150

Speed Six

Known as: Model 207 chambered for .357 Magnum; Model 208 chambered for .38 Special; Model 209 chambered for 9mm. Has 2.75" or 4" barrel, fixed sights, round butt with checkered walnut grips and was blued. Some with factory bobbed hammers. Introduced in 1973; discontinued. **NOTE:** Add 200 percent for military (lanyard ring) and .38 S&W (not .38 Special) marked models.

NIB	Exc.	V.G.	Good	Fair	Poor
400	350	300	250	200	150

Models 737, 738, 739

These are designations for stainless steel versions of Speed-Six. Same revolver except for material used in manufacture. **NOTE:** Add $150 for 739.

NIB	Exc.	V.G.	Good	Fair	Poor
500	425	350	300	225	125

GP-100

Chambered for .327 Federal or .357 Magnum/.38 Special. Available with fixed or adjustable sights. Barrel lengths 3", 4" or 6". Frame designed for constant use of heavy Magnum loads. Rear sight has a white outline. Front sight features interchangeable colored inserts. Finish blued. Grips are a new design made of rubber, with smooth Goncalo Alves inserts. Introduced in 1986.

NIB	Exc.	V.G.	Good	Fair	Poor
550	400	325	250	150	100

GP-100 Stainless

Same as GP-100, except material used is stainless steel.

NIB	Exc.	V.G.	Good	Fair	Poor
600	450	375	300	200	150

GP-100 Match Champion

This .357 Magnum has a slab-sided half-lug 4.2" barrel. Novak Lo-Mount rear and green fiber-optic front sights. Stainless finish. Hogue hardwood grips, with stippled sides. Introduced in 2014. **NOTE:** Add $40 for fixed sights.

NIB	Exc.	V.G.	Good	Fair	Poor
550	450	325	225	150	125

Redhawk

Large frame double-action revolver. Chambered for .357 and .41 Magnums until 1992; .44 Magnum until discontinued in 2009. Barrel lengths 5.5" and 7.5". Finish blued and grips are smooth walnut. Redhawk introduced in 1979. **NOTE:** Add 100 percent for .357; 50 percent for .41.

NIB	Exc.	V.G.	Good	Fair	Poor
650	500	425	350	250	150

Redhawk Stainless Steel

Same as blued version, except constructed of stainless steel. Chambered for .357 Magnum until 1985; .41 Magnum until 1992; and currently for .44 Magnum. In 1998, offered chambered for .45 Long Colt cartridge. Barrel lengths 4", 5.5" and 7.5". Temporarily discontinued in 2013, but back in production in 2014. **NOTE:** Add 100 percent for .357; 50 percent for .41.

NIB	Exc.	V.G.	Good	Fair	Poor
800	675	525	400	300	200

Redhawk 4-Inch .45 Colt (2008)

Similar to original stainless Redhawk, but in .45 Colt only, with 4" barrel. Hogue molded grips.

NIB	Exc.	V.G.	Good	Fair	Poor
800	700	600	450	300	200

NIB	Exc.	V.G.	Good	Fair	Poor
585	500	450	400	350	300

SP-101

Similar in appearance to GP-100, but has a smaller frame. Chambered for .22 LR (6-shot), .38 Special (5-shot), .357 Magnum (5-shot), 9mm (5-shot). Grips are all black synthetic. Sights adjustable for windage. Barrel lengths 2" or 3". Construction of stainless steel. Introduced in 1989. 6" barrel available for .22-caliber. .327 Federal Magnum chambering added 2008. **NOTE:** Add $100 for Crimson Trace lasergrips (limited edition for 2008).

NIB	Exc.	V.G.	Good	Fair	Poor
525	425	300	200	150	125

SP-101 Spurless-Hammer

Introduced in 1993. Features SP-101, without exposed hammer spur. Available in two calibers: .38 Special; .357 Magnum, with 2.25" barrel. Double-action revolver has fixed sights. Holds 5 rounds. Weight about 26 oz.

Redhawk .45 ACP/.45 Colt

An all stainless steel model, with 4.2" barrel, checkered hardwood grips, adjustable rear and red ramp front sights. Chambered for both .45 ACP and .45 Colt ammunition. Uses half-moon clips, three included. Introduced in 2016.

NIB	Exc.	V.G.	Good	Fair	Poor
950	800	—	—	—	—

Super Redhawk

A more massive version of Redhawk. Weight 53 oz. Offered with 7.5" or 9.5" barrel. Made of stainless steel, with brushed or dull gray finish. Barrel rib milled to accept Ruger scope-ring system. Grips are combination rubber and Goncalo Alves-type found on GP-100. Introduced in 1987. In 1999, offered in .454 Casull cartridge, with 7.5" or 9.5" barrel. In 2001, offered in .480 Ruger caliber in 7.5" or 9.5" barrel. Also available in .44 Magnum. **NOTE:** Add $200 for .454 Casull or .480 Ruger caliber. Revolvers chambered for .454 Casull also accept .45 Long Colt cartridges.

NIB	Exc.	V.G.	Good	Fair	Poor
740	550	400	275	200	150

Super Redhawk Alaskan

Chambered for .454 Casull and .45 Colt interchangeable or .480 Ruger cartridge. Barrel length 2.5", with adjustable rear sight. Cylinder capacity 6 rounds. Stainless steel finish. Hogue Tamer rubber grips. Weight about 42 oz. Introduced in 2005. .44 Magnum chambering added 2007.

NIB	Exc.	V.G.	Good	Fair	Poor
850	700	500	375	250	200

Police Service-Six

Also known as: Model 107 chambered for .357 Magnum; Model 108 chambered for .38 Special; Model 109 chambered for 9mm. Barrel 2.75" or 4". A few 6" barrel Service-Sixes also produced and these are worth a premium. Has fixed sights and square butt, with checkered walnut grips. Finish blued. 9mm discontinued in 1984; other two calibers in 1988. **NOTE:** Add 60 percent for 9mm.

NIB	Exc.	V.G.	Good	Fair	Poor
425	350	300	200	150	100

Model 707 and 708

Designation for stainless versions of Police Service-Six. Not produced in 9mm and only 4" barrel offered. Discontinued in 1988.

NIB	Exc.	V.G.	Good	Fair	Poor
450	375	300	200	150	100

LCR Lightweight Compact Revolver

Polymer-frame compact revolver chambered in .22 LR, 9mm, .38 Special and .357 Magnum. Features include 5-shot stainless steel cylinder finished in Advanced Target Gray, 1.875" stainless steel barrel, fixed sights, Hogue or Crimson Trace grips, matte black frame. Overall length 6.5". Weight 13 oz. **NOTE:** Add $75 for .357 Magnum; $200 for Crimson Trace Lasergrips.

NIB	Exc.	V.G.	Good	Fair	Poor
425	350	250	200	150	100

LCRX

Same basic design as LCR model, except for visible external hammer. Available with 1.875" or 3" barrel (shown), with Crimson Trace Lasergrips. **NOTE:** Add $60 for 9mm or .357; $280 for Lasergrips.

NIB	Exc.	V.G.	Good	Fair	Poor
465	400	350	300	250	175

SEMI-AUTOMATIC CENTERFIRE HANDGUNS

P-85

This model was Ruger's entry into wonder-nine market. While it was announced in 1985, it was 1987 before it went into production. P-85 was first of a series of "P" model Ruger pistols, which remained in production through 2013. Also, first Ruger firearm manufactured at Prescott, Arizona plant. A very successful moderately priced double-action high-capacity 9mm pistol, at a time when law enforcement and much of the civilian market was embracing this type of pistol. Original model had a matte black finish, black synthetic grips, alloy frame and steel slide. Other features were 4.5" barrel, fixed three-dot sights and ambidextrous safety. **NOTE:** As of 2013, all P-series pistols had been discontinued.

NIB	Exc.	V.G.	Good	Fair	Poor
400	360	300	275	200	150

KP85

Same as matte black version, except receiver assembly made of stainless steel.

NIB	Exc.	V.G.	Good	Fair	Poor
425	375	325	295	200	150

KP89X

Introduced in 1993. Features stainless steel convertible safety model, which comes with both 9mm and .30 Luger barrels. Barrels are interchangeable, without the use of tools. Magazine capacity 15 rounds. Less than 6,000 produced.

NIB	Exc.	V.G.	Good	Fair	Poor
500	400	345	245	200	150

P89

Introduced in 1991. Semi-automatic pistol chambered for 9mm cartridge. Blued finish and 15-round magazine. Safety is a manual ambidextrous lever type. Barrel 4.5". Empty weight about 36 oz.

NIB	Exc.	V.G.	Good	Fair	Poor
425	350	300	225	150	100

KP89

Same configuration as P89, but furnished with stainless steel finish. Introduced in 1991.

NIB	Exc.	V.G.	Good	Fair	Poor
450	375	325	250	150	100

P89DC

Features a blued finish. Chambered for 9mm Parabellum cartridge. Fitted with a decock-only lever (no manual safety). After decocking, the gun can be fired by a double-action pull of the trigger.

NIB	Exc.	V.G.	Good	Fair	Poor
425	375	350	250	200	150

KP89DC

Stainless steel version of P89DC, with decock only.

NIB	Exc.	V.G.	Good	Fair	Poor
450	375	325	250	150	100

KP89DAO

Chambered for 9mm cartridge. Stainless steel double-action-only version of above model.

NIB	Exc.	V.G.	Good	Fair	Poor
450	375	325	250	150	100

KP90

Chambered for .45 ACP cartridge. Stainless steel. Magazine holds 7 rounds. Fitted with a manual safety. Introduced in 1991.

NIB	Exc.	V.G.	Good	Fair	Poor
500	450	375	285	225	150

KP90DC

Stainless steel version of KP90, with decock-only system. Chambered for .45 ACP cartridge.

NIB	Exc.	V.G.	Good	Fair	Poor
500	450	375	285	225	150

P90

Same as above model, with blued finish. Introduced in 1998.

NIB	Exc.	V.G.	Good	Fair	Poor
475	425	350	275	225	150

KP91DC

Features stainless steel finish. Chambered for .40 S&W cartridge. Magazine capacity 11 rounds. Has a decock-only system. Introduced in 1992; discontinued.

NIB	Exc.	V.G.	Good	Fair	Poor
475	375	325	295	200	150

KP91DAO

Chambered for .40 S&W, with stainless steel finish. Features double-action-only system. Discontinued.

NIB	Exc.	V.G.	Good	Fair	Poor
475	375	325	295	200	150

P93D

Blued version, with ambidextrous decocker and 3.9" barrel. Introduced in 1998.

NIB	Exc.	V.G.	Good	Fair	Poor
400	300	250	200	150	100

KP93DC

Introduced in 1993, as a compact stainless steel model. Chambered for 9mm cartridge. Magazine capacity 15 rounds. Available in decock-only configuration. Barrel length 3.9". Weight about 24 oz. empty.

NIB	Exc.	V.G.	Good	Fair	Poor
475	425	350	275	225	150

KP93DAO

Double-action-only version of KP93 compact series.

NIB	Exc.	V.G.	Good	Fair	Poor
475	425	350	275	225	150

KP94

Introduced in 1994. This model is smaller than full-size "P" series and compact P93 pistols. Offered in 9mm or .40 S&W calibers. Has an aluminum alloy frame and stainless steel slide. Barrel length 4.25". Magazine capacity: 9mm 15 rounds; .40 S&W 11 rounds. Weight about 33 oz. Offered in double-action-only and traditional double-action. Decock-only model also available.

NIB	Exc.	V.G.	Good	Fair	Poor
415	350	300	250	200	150

KP94DC

Similar to model above in decock only.

NIB	Exc.	V.G.	Good	Fair	Poor
415	350	300	250	200	150

P94

Blued version of KP94. Introduced in 1998.

NIB	Exc.	V.G.	Good	Fair	Poor
400	300	250	200	150	100

KP94DAO

Same as KP94, but in double-action-only.

NIB	Exc.	V.G.	Good	Fair	Poor
400	350	300	250	200	150

KP944

Chambered for .40 S&W cartridge. Has a stainless steel tapered slide, 11-round magazine and manual safety. Models made after September, 1994 have a 10-round magazine.

NIB	Exc.	V.G.	Good	Fair	Poor
450	400	350	275	225	150

KP944DC

Same as above, with decock-only system.

NIB	Exc.	V.G.	Good	Fair	Poor
450	400	350	275	225	150

KP944DAO

Same as model above in double-action-only.

NIB	Exc.	V.G.	Good	Fair	Poor
450	400	350	275	225	150

P95

Introduced in 1996. This 9mm pistol features 3.9" barrel, polymer frame and stainless steel slide. Decocker only. Fixed 3-dot sights are standard. Overall length 7.3". Empty weight about 29 oz. In 2001, offered with a manual safety and blued finish.

NIB	Exc.	V.G.	Good	Fair	Poor
450	350	300	225	150	100

KP95DC

Same as matte black version of P95, only in stainless steel. Has a de-cock-only lever.

NIB	Exc.	V.G.	Good	Fair	Poor
450	350	300	225	150	100

P95DAO

Same as above in double-action-only.

NIB	Exc.	V.G.	Good	Fair	Poor
450	350	300	225	150	100

KP95DAO

Same as model above in double-action-only. In 2001, offered with a manual safety and blued finish.

NIB	Exc.	V.G.	Good	Fair	Poor
450	350	300	225	150	100

KP97D

Introduced in 1999. Decock-only model chambered for .45 ACP cartridge. Has a stainless steel slide. Magazine capacity 7 rounds. Fixed sights. Weight about 27 oz.

NIB	Exc.	V.G.	Good	Fair	Poor
450	350	300	225	150	100

KP97DAO

Same specifications as model above in double-action-only. Introduced in 1999.

NIB	Exc.	V.G.	Good	Fair	Poor
450	350	300	225	150	100

KP345

Introduced in 2004. This .45 ACP model features 4.2" stainless steel barrel and slide, fixed sights, internal lock, loaded chamber indicator, magazine disconnect and new cam block design to reduce recoil. Black polymer checkered grips. Magazine capacity 8 rounds. Weight about 29 oz. Available with ambidextrous safety or decocker.

NIB	Exc.	V.G.	Good	Fair	Poor
550	425	300	250	175	125

KP345PR

Similar to model above, but fitted with Picatinny-style rail under forward portion of the frame. Introduced in 2004.

NIB	Exc.	V.G.	Good	Fair	Poor
550	425	300	250	175	125

SR9 / SR40

Introduced in 2008. Ruger's first striker-fired semi-automatic pistol. Chambered in 9mm Parabellum or .40 S&W. Double-action-only, with 4.14" barrel, 17+1 capacity. Available in three finish configurations: stainless steel slide with matte black frame; blackened stainless slide with matte black frame; blackened stainless slide with matte black frame. Also available in compact version, with 3.5" barrel (SR9c, SR40c). **NOTE:** Ruger recalled all early-production SR9 pistols with a "330" serial number prefix because of a potential safety issue. SR40 has a 15-round magazine.

NIB	Exc.	V.G.	Good	Fair	Poor
450	350	300	225	150	100

SR45

Slightly larger variation of SR40. Chambered for .45 ACP, with 10-round magazine, 4.5" barrel.

NIB	Exc.	V.G.	Good	Fair	Poor
475	425	375	300	250	200

9E

An economy priced variation of SR9, with fixed (drift adjustable) sights.

NIB	Exc.	V.G.	Good	Fair	Poor
385	350	300	265	225	150

SR22

Polymer-frame semi-automatic in .22 Long Rifle. Barrel length 3.5", overall length 6.4". Weight unloaded 17.5 oz. Features include Picatinny accessory rail, interchangeable grips and adjustable sights. Thumb safety/decocking lever and magazine release are all ambidextrous. **NOTE:** Add $25 for threaded barrel or silver anodized finish.

NIB	Exc.	V.G.	Good	Fair	Poor
350	300	275	225	150	100

LCP (Lightweight Compact Pistol)

Introduced in 2008. Ruger's first true pocket pistol. Chambered in .380 (6+1 capacity), with 2.75" barrel. Double-action-only. Glass-filled nylon frame, with steel barrel. Black matte finish.

NIB	Exc.	V.G.	Good	Fair	Poor
325	285	235	185	125	100

LCP Crimson Trace

Similar to above, with Crimson Trace Lasergrips.

NIB	Exc.	V.G.	Good	Fair	Poor
475	425	350	275	225	150

LC9

Sub-compact 9mm pistol designed for concealed carry. Magazine capacity 7 rounds; barrel length 3.12"; weight 17.1 oz. Steel slide, glass-filled nylon receiver, double-action-only trigger, hammer-fired operation. Three-dot sights, loaded-chamber indicator, manual safety, magazine disconnect and slide stop. **NOTE:** Add $100 for Crimson Trace LG-431 laser sight.

NIB	Exc.	V.G.	Good	Fair	Poor
385	335	285	200	150	100

LC380

Variation of LC9. Chambered for .380 ACP cartridge. Dimensions identical to LC9. New 2013.

NIB	Exc.	V.G.	Good	Fair	Poor
350	300	250	200	150	125

American Pistol

This is a full-size semi-automatic striker-fired pistol. Chambered in 9mm or .45 ACP, with a Browning-type locked breech action. A patent-pending barrel cam controls rearward movement of the slide, reducing felt recoil and muzzle flip. The frame is glass-filled nylon, with integral grips and three grip inserts to adjust to the shooter's preference. The slide is stainless steel, with a black nitride finish. Magazine capacity (17 rounds) 9mm; (10) .45 ACP. In addition to the central trigger safety, which is depressed when trigger is pulled, the pistol is available with/without an external thumb safety. Weight about 31 oz. unloaded. Sights are Novak three-dots and are adjustable for windage. Introduced in 2016.

NIB	Exc.	V.G.	Good	Fair	Poor
500	450	—	—	—	—

SR 1911

Caliber .45 ACP, stainless steel slide and frame, 8-round magazine, extended thumb safety, grip tang and magazine release, Novak Lo-Mount 3-dot sights, checkered mainspring housing and hardwood grips. Standard 1911 dimensions and controls. Introduced in 2011. A Commander-size model with 4.25" barrel introduced in 2013.

NIB	Exc.	V.G.	Good	Fair	Poor
725	600	500	400	350	200

SR 1911 LW Cmdr.

Lightweight version of Commander-size SR 1911. A two-tone model, with black matte anodized aluminum frame and stainless slide. Introduced in 2015.

NIB	Exc.	V.G.	Good	Fair	Poor
780	700	600	500	400	300

SEMI-AUTOMATIC RIFLES

10/22 Standard Carbine With Walnut Stock

This model has an 18.5" barrel and chambered for .22 LR. A 10-shot detachable rotary magazine and folding rear sight. Stock is smooth walnut, with a barrel band and carbine-style buttplate. Rifle enjoys a fine reputation for accuracy and dependability and considered an excellent value. Introduced in 1964. **NOTE:** Deduct $20 for Birch stock.

NIB	Exc.	V.G.	Good	Fair	Poor
275	225	125	100	75	50

10/22 Standard Carbine Stainless Steel

Same as above, with stainless steel barrel and receiver.

NIB	Exc.	V.G.	Good	Fair	Poor
300	250	150	125	100	75

10/22 Magnum

Introduced in 1999. Chambered for .22 Magnum cartridge. Barrel length 18.5". Folding rear sight and gold bead front. Hardwood stock. Weight about 5.5 lbs. Discontinued.

NIB	Exc.	V.G.	Good	Fair	Poor
950	800	700	500	350	200

10/22 Sporter (Finger Groove Old Model)

Similar to Standard Carbine, except it has a Monte Carlo stock, finger-groove fore-end and no barrel band. Manufactured between 1966 and 1971. **NOTE:** Add 300 percent for factory hand checkering.

NIB	Exc.	V.G.	Good	Fair	Poor
650	575	450	350	250	200

10/22 Deluxe Sporter

Same as Sporter, with checkered stock and better buttplate. Introduced in 1971.

NIB	Exc.	V.G.	Good	Fair	Poor
325	250	150	125	100	75

10/22 International Carbine

Similar to Standard Carbine, with full-length Mannlicher-style stock. Manufactured between 1966 - 1971. Fairly rare on today's market. **NOTE:** Add 50 percent for factory hand checkering.

NIB	Exc.	V.G.	Good	Fair	Poor
—	1100	625	450	300	250

10/22 International Carbine (New Model)

This 1994 model is a reintroduction of older version. Offered in blued or stainless steel finish. Barrel length 18.5". Magazine capacity 10 rounds. Hardwood stock had no checkering when first introduced. Shortly afterwards, factory began checkering these stocks. Weight about 5.2 lbs. Discontinued.

NIB	Exc.	V.G.	Good	Fair	Poor
465	300	225	—	—	—

10/22T

Introduced in 1996. Target version of 10/22 line. Has laminated American hardwood stock, with blued heavy barrel and hammer-forged spiral finish. Comes standard without sights. Barrel length 20". Weight about 7.25 lbs.

NIB	Exc.	V.G.	Good	Fair	Poor
450	350	275	200	150	100

10/22TNZ

This target model features 20" stainless steel barrel and receiver, with laminated thumbhole stock. No sights. Weight about 7 lbs. Introduced in 2001.

NIB	Exc.	V.G.	Good	Fair	Poor
500	375	275	200	150	100

10/22 Canadian Centennial

In 1966 and 1967, approximately 4,500 10/22 Sporters were built for the Canadian Centennial. First 2,000 sold with Rem. Model 742 in .308-caliber, with matching serial numbers. Ruger Sporter may be checkered or uncheckered. Two-gun set boxed separately or together.

Two Gun Set

NIB	Exc.	V.G.	Good	Fair	Poor
700	—	—	—	—	—

10/22 Only

NIB	Exc.	V.G.	Good	Fair	Poor
450	—	—	—	—	—

10/22 Laminated Stock Carbine

Produced in varying quantities since 1986, these models are becoming quite collectible. Stocks range in color from dark green to gray and various shades of brown. Because there are so many different variations, each should be individually appraised. Prices listed are for blued carbine models. **NOTE:** Add about $40 to NIB price for stainless steel.

NIB	Exc.	V.G.	Good	Fair	Poor
250	200	175	150	125	100

10/22 Laminated Stock Sporter

This model has a tree bark laminated stock.

NIB	Exc.	V.G.	Good	Fair	Poor
325	275	225	175	150	100

10/22 Laminated Stock International

Stainless steel model was an exclusive Wal-Mart product. A few of this model produced in blue.

Blue

NIB	Exc.	V.G.	Good	Fair	Poor
400	325	250	200	150	100

Stainless Steel

NIB	Exc.	V.G.	Good	Fair	Poor
350	275	225	175	125	100

10/22 All Weather

Fitted with stainless steel barrel, action and synthetic stock. Introduced in 1997. In 2001, offered with blued finish. **NOTE:** Deduct $40 for blued model.

NIB	Exc.	V.G.	Good	Fair	Poor
300	225	175	125	100	70

10/22 Carbine 40th Anniversary

Blued, with hardwood stock. Equipped with 40th Anniversary clear magazine, with red rotor. Original scope base adapter. Nickel-silver medallion inlaid on right side of buttstock.

NIB	Exc.	V.G.	Good	Fair	Poor
280	225	175	125	100	75

10/22 50th Anniversary

In 2013 early 2014, Ruger staged a contest for 10/22 fans to design a 50th Anniversary Model. Winning entry became a production model in mid 2014. Has 18.5" stainless barrel, black composite stock with adjustable comb and length of pull, ghost ring adjustable sights and grooved fore-end. MRSP at its 2014 introduction was $379

NIB	Exc.	V.G.	Good	Fair	Poor
300	275	—	—	—	—

10/22 Compact Rifle 10/22 CRR

Similar to 10/22 standard rifle, with 16.25" blued barrel, shorter hardwood stock, fiber optic sights and 34.5" overall length. Introduced 2006.

NIB	Exc.	V.G.	Good	Fair	Poor
275	225	175	125	100	75

K10/22T Ruger 10/22 Target Stainless

Similar to 10/22 Target, with stainless steel barrel and laminated stock.

NIB	Exc.	V.G.	Good	Fair	Poor
495	425	350	275	200	150

10/22-T

Similar to 100/22 Target Stainless, with blued steel barrel and receiver. Introduced in 2007.

NIB	Exc.	V.G.	Good	Fair	Poor
450	350	275	200	150	100

10/22RPFCARH (Lipsey's Distributor's Special)

Similar to 10/22, but covered throughout with RealTree Hardwoods HD camo finish. Introduced 2008.

NIB	Exc.	V.G.	Good	Fair	Poor
275	225	175	125	100	75

10/22VLEH Target Tactical

Semi-automatic rimfire chambered in .22 LR. Features include precision-rifled cold hammer-forged spiral-finished 16.125" crowned match barrel; Hogue® OverMolded® stock; 10/22T target trigger; precision-adjustable bipod for steady shooting from bench; 10-round rotary magazine. Weight 6.875 lbs.

NIB	Exc.	V.G.	Good	Fair	Poor
485	400	350	300	225	150

10/22 Takedown

Barrel and fore-end separate from rest of rifle. Features same as other 10/22 models. Comes with nylon carry bag. **NOTE:** Add $20 for threaded 16.6" barrel and flash suppressor.

NIB	Exc.	V.G.	Good	Fair	Poor
365	320	280	235	225	200

Model 10/17

Introduced in 2004. Chambered for .17 HMR cartridge. Fitted with 20" barrel. Magazine capacity 9 rounds. Weight about 6.5 lbs. Discontinued.

NIB	Exc.	V.G.	Good	Fair	Poor
600	475	300	200	150	100

SR-22 Rifle

AR-style semi-automatic rifle. Chambered in .22 LR, based on 0/22 action. Features include all-aluminum chassis replicating AR-platform dimensions between sighting plane; buttstock height and grip; Picatinny rail optic mount includes 6-position telescoping M4-style buttstock (on Mil-Spec diameter tube); Hogue Monogrip pistol-grip; buttstocks and grips interchangeable with any AR-style compatible option; round mid-length hand guard mounted on a standard-thread AR-style barrel nut; precision-rifled cold hammer forged 16.125" alloy steel barrel capped with an SR-556/Mini-14 flash suppressor.

NIB	Exc.	V.G.	Good	Fair	Poor
535	460	385	325	250	150

Model 44 Carbine

A short 18.5" barreled gas-operated carbine. Chambered for .44 Magnum cartridge. Has a 4-shot non-detachable magazine, folding rear sight and plain walnut stock. Handy deer hunting carbine. Manufactured between 1961 - 1985.

NIB	Exc.	V.G.	Good	Fair	Poor
550	450	350	300	200	150

Deerstalker Model

Same as Model 44 Carbine, with "Deerstalker" stamped on it. Manufactured in 1961 - 1962 only.

NIB	Exc.	V.G.	Good	Fair	Poor
950	800	600	400	300	200

Model 44 RS

This is Model 44, with sling swivels and aperture sight. **NOTE:** "Liberty" marked 44RS carbines are extremely rare and will bring a premium.

NIB	Exc.	V.G.	Good	Fair	Poor
—	600	550	350	200	150

Model 44 Sporter (Finger Groove Old Model)

This version has Monte Carlo stock, finger-groove fore-end and no barrel band. Manufactured until 1971. **NOTE:** Factory hand checkered models will bring at least 75 percent premium.

NIB	Exc.	V.G.	Good	Fair	Poor
—	750	600	400	250	200

Model 44 International Carbine

This version features a full-length Mannlicher-style stock. Discontinued in 1971 and quite collectible. **NOTE:** Factory hand checkered models will bring at least 50 percent premium.

NIB	Exc.	V.G.	Good	Fair	Poor
—	800	600	425	350	275

Model 44 25th Anniversary Model

This version lightly engraved. Has a medallion in the stock. Only made in 1985, the last year of production.

NIB	Exc.	V.G.	Good	Fair	Poor
550	400	350	300	250	200

Model 99/44 Deerfield Carbine

While chambered in .44 Magnum, this model is not related to .44 Carbine, but a variation of Mini-14. In production from 2000 to 2006. Fitted with 18.5" barrel, this gas-operated rifle has a hardwood stock and 4-round magazine. Adjustable rear sight. Blued finish. Weight about 6.2 lbs. This rifle will not cycle .44 Special ammo. Discontinued.

NIB	Exc.	V.G.	Good	Fair	Poor
700	525	400	275	200	150

Mini-14

Paramilitary-style carbine chambered for .223 Rem. and on a limited basis for .222 cartridge. Has an 18.5" barrel and gas-operated. Detachable magazines originally offered held 5, 10 or 20 rounds. High-capacity magazines are now discontinued. Prices for them are what the market will bear. Mini-14 has a military-style stock and aperture sight. Introduced in 1975. 20-round magazine added 2009.

NIB	Exc.	V.G.	Good	Fair	Poor
600	500	400	275	200	150

Mini-14 Stainless Steel

Same as Mini-14, except constructed of stainless steel.

NIB	Exc.	V.G.	Good	Fair	Poor
650	550	450	300	200	150

Mini-14 Target

Acccurized version of Mini-14, with matte stainless barrel and receiver, black laminated thumbhole stock, adjustable harmonic dampener. No sights. Also available with non-thumbhole synthetic stock. Introduced in 2007.

NIB	Exc.	V.G.	Good	Fair	Poor
1025	900	775	600	400	250

Mini-14 Ranch

Similar to standard Mini-14, with folding rear sight and receiver milled to accept Ruger scope-ring system. Rings are supplied with rifle. 6.8 Rem. chambering also available. **NOTE:** Models chambered in .222-caliber will bring a premium.

NIB	Exc.	V.G.	Good	Fair	Poor
750	625	500	375	225	175

Mini-14 Stainless All-Weather Ranch

Introduced in 1999. Has all the features of stainless steel Ranch, with addition of black polymer stock. Weight about 6.5 lbs.

NIB	Exc.	V.G.	Good	Fair	Poor
810	600	450	300	200	150

Mini-14 NRA

Ruger Mini-14 NRA, with two 20-round magazines, gold-tone medallion in grip cap and special serial number sequence (NRA8XXXXX). Produced in 2008 only. Also available with 5-round magazine.

NIB	Exc.	V.G.	Good	Fair	Poor
1000	700	575	—	—	—

Mini-14 ATI Stock

Tactical version of Mini-14, with 6-position collapsible stock or folding stock, grooved pistol-grip, multiple Picatinny optics/accessories rails. Suggested retail price: $872.

NIB	Exc.	V.G.	Good	Fair	Poor
675	550	425	300	200	150

Mini-14 Tactical

Similar to Mini-14, with 16.12" barrel with flash hider, black synthetic stock, adjustable sights. Also chambered for .300 Blackout.

NIB	Exc.	V.G.	Good	Fair	Poor
850	700	600	450	325	250

SR-556

AR-style semi-automatic chambered in 5.56 NATO. Feature include two-stage piston; quad rail hand guard; Troy Industries sights; black synthetic fixed or telescoping buttstock; 16.12" 1:9 steel barrel with birdcage; 10- or 30-round detachable box magazine; black matte finish overall. The 6.8 PPC was added in 2010, but discontinued after one year.

NIB	Exc.	V.G.	Good	Fair	Poor
1850	1550	1250	900	600	250

AR-556

An M4-style direct-impingement Modern Sporting Rifle. It's American-made and affordable. Features include forged 7075-T6 aluminum upper and lower receivers, cold hammer-forged chrome-moly steel barrel, telescoping 6-position stock, enlarged trigger guard, milled F-height gas block with post front sight and 30-round Magpul magazine. Introduced in 2015.

NIB	Exc.	V.G.	Good	Fair	Poor
650	500	400	300	225	150

SR-762

Same basic AR-style design of SR-556, but modified to handle 7.62 NATO (.308 Win.) cartridge.

NIB	Exc.	V.G.	Good	Fair	Poor
1900	1550	1300	900	500	250

Mini-Thirty

Brought out by Ruger in 1987. Similar in appearance to standard Mini-14. Supplied with Ruger scope rings. Chambered in 7.63x39; 6.8mm added in 2007.

NIB	Exc.	V.G.	Good	Fair	Poor
550	450	300	250	200	150

Mini-Thirty Stainless with Synthetic Stock

NIB	Exc.	V.G.	Good	Fair	Poor
700	550	450	300	200	150

GB Model

This model has a factory-installed folding stock, flash suppressor and bayonet lug. Designed and sold by Ruger to law enforcement agencies. A number have come on the civilian market through surplus sales and police trade-ins. With the assault rifle hysteria, prices of this model have fluctuated wildly in some areas. Now that Ruger has discontinued the folding stock and high-capacity magazines, this could become even less predictable. Note that this is a semi-automatic and totally different than the full-auto version of this weapon available only through Class 3 dealers.

NIB	Exc.	V.G.	Good	Fair	Poor
—	1350	1100	650	400	300

PC4/PC9 Carbine

Semi-automatic carbine chambered for 9mm (PC9) or .40 S&W (PC4) cartridges. Fitted with 16.25" barrel and black synthetic stock. Post front sight, with adjustable rear. Receiver sight is also offered. Detachable magazine has 10-round capacity. Weight about 6.4 lbs. Introduced in 1998; discontinued. **NOTE:** Add $30 for receiver sight.

NIB	Exc.	V.G.	Good	Fair	Poor
625	450	325	225	150	100

SINGLE-SHOT RIFLES

In 2013 Ruger announced that beginning in 2014, each variation of No. 1 rifle would be chambered in a different caliber each year. In 2014, Light Sporter was made only in .280 Rem., Varminter in .220 Swift, RSI International in .257 Roberts, Medium Sporter in 9.3x62 and Tropical in .450/400 Nitro Express 3". In 2015, Light Sporter chambered in 7mm-08 Rem., Varminter in .223 Rem., RSI International 6.5x55, Standard in .257 Wby., Tropical in .375 H&H and Medium Sporter in .30-06. Firearms distributor Lipsey's is the exclusive source for all currently manufactured No. 1 rifles. It is unknown how this limiting of caliber choices will affect values of Ruger No. 1s in the future. In 2016, Lipsey's announced these variations of Ruger No. 1: Light Sporter (1-A) .275 Rigby (7x57 Mauser), 24" bbl.; Standard Rifle (1-B) .257 Wby. or 6.5 Creedmoor, 28" bbl.; Medium Sporter (1-S) .35 Whelen, 24" bbl. or .44 Magnum, 20" bbl.; Varmint (1-V) .243 Win., 26" bbl. All models have walnut stocks. MSRP from $1,449 to $1,499.00.

No. 1 Light Sporter (1-A)

Features open sights, barrel band on lightweight barrel and Alexander Henry-style forearm. Offered with 22" barrel in many popular calibers. Weight 7.25 lbs.

NIB	Exc.	V.G.	Good	Fair	Poor
1050	900	750	550	350	200

No, 1 Light Standard (1-AB)

Similar to Light Sporter 1-A, with 22" sightless blued barrel.

NIB	Exc.	V.G.	Good	Fair	Poor
900	800	650	450	300	200

No. 1 Standard (1-B)

Furnished with no sights, medium barrel, semi-beavertail forearm and quarter rib with 1" Ruger scope rings. Weight 8 lbs. Introduced in 1966. Chambered in most popular calibers at various times. **NOTE:** Add 25 to 50 percent premium for rare calibers like .257 Roberts, 6.5 Rem. Magnum, 7x57 Mauser.

NIB	Exc.	V.G.	Good	Fair	Poor
965	725	550	375	250	200

No. 1 Standard Stainless (1-B-BBZ)

In production from 2000 to 2010. Chambered in most popular calibers from .204 Ruger to .458 Win. Gray laminate stock. Barrel lengths from 22" to 26".

NIB	Exc.	V.G.	Good	Fair	Poor
995	750	550	375	250	200

No. 1 Tropical (1-H)

Fitted with open sights. Barrel band on heavy barrel, with Alexander Henry-style forearm. Weight 9 lbs. **NOTE:** In 2001: offered with stainless steel finish and black laminated stock in .375 H&H. Added in 2003: .458 Lott and .405 Win. cartridges; In 2008: .450/.400 Nitro Express; In 2009: .416 Ruger. Few 24" heavy barrel 1-H rifles chambered for .45-70 Government cartridge up to 1976. These bring substantial premium and should be appraised individually. **NOTE:** Add 100 percent for .404 Jeffery caliber; 250 percent for .45-70.

NIB	Exc.	V.G.	Good	Fair	Poor
1050	900	750	550	350	200

No. 1 International (1-RSI)

This No. 1 rifle features a lightweight barrel, with full length forearm and open sights. Weight 7.25 lbs.

NIB	Exc.	V.G.	Good	Fair	Poor
1100	950	800	600	400	250

No. 1 Medium Sporter (1-S)

Equipped with open sights, barrel band on medium weight barrel and Alexander Henry-style forearm. Weight 8 lbs. In 2001, offered in stainless steel and black laminated stock in .45-70 caliber. Chambered in a wide range of calibers including .218 Bee to .480 Ruger. Added in 2009, .300 H&H, .338 Ruger Compact Magnum, .375 Ruger, .460 S&W Magnum, .480Ruger/.475 Linebaugh. **NOTE:** In 1999, a 50th Anniversary No. 1 Medium Sporter Model in .45-70 with engraving and high grade walnut stock offered. Add 100 percent premium for this model.

NIB	Exc.	V.G.	Good	Fair	Poor
1000	850	700	500	300	200

No. 1 Special Varminter (1-V)

Model furnished with no sights, heavy barrel, target scope blocks with 1" Ruger scope rings and semi-beavertail forearm. Weight about 9 lbs.

NIB	Exc.	V.G.	Good	Fair	Poor
1100	950	800	600	400	250

No. 1 Stainless Varminter (1-V-BBZ)

Introduced in 2000. Features laminated wood stock and stainless steel finish. Chambered for .22-250. Fitted with 24" barrel. Weight about 9 lbs.

NIB	Exc.	V.G.	Good	Fair	Poor
995	750	550	375	250	200

No. 3 Carbine

A less elaborate inexpensive version of No.1. Action the same, except lever is less ornate in appearance and lacks the locking bar. Unchecked-ered stock is a military carbine style, with barrel band. Similar in appearance to Model 44 and 10/22. This serviceable rifle chambered for .45-70, when released in 1972. Later chamberings added .22 Hornet, .30-40 Krag, .223, .44 Magnum and .375 Win. Barrel 22" long. Folding rear sight. Discontinued in 1987. **NOTE:** Add 25 percent premium for .44 Magnum or .375 Win.

NIB	Exc.	V.G.	Good	Fair	Poor
—	625	500	300	200	125

BOLT-ACTION RIFLES

Ruger introduced Model 77R in 1968. It filled the need for a good quality reasonably priced bolt-action hunting rifle, and has been a commercial success. There are certain variations of this rifle that collectors actively seek. One should avail oneself of specialized literature on this model and secure individual appraisals on rare variations, as differences are slight and beyond the scope of this book.

Model 77-R/RS

Introduced in 1968. Offered with 22", 24" or 26" barrel. Model 77 chambered for most calibers from .22-250 through .458 Win. Magnum. Action is a modified Mauser-type, finished in blue with checkered walnut stock and red rubber buttplate. Available milled for Ruger scope rings or in round-top style that allows mounting of any popular scope ring system. Designated 77R when supplied with rings only; and 77RS when supplied with rings and sights. This model replaced by Model 77 MK II.

NIB	Exc.	V.G.	Good	Fair	Poor
500	400	350	300	250	200

Model 77-RS

NOTE: Add $400 for 6.5 Rem., .284, .350 Rem.

NIB	Exc.	V.G.	Good	Fair	Poor
550	450	400	300	250	200

Model 77 Flat Bolt

This is an example of the slight variations that make this model collect-ible. Essentially same rifle, with knob on bolt handle flattened. Only produced in this configuration until 1972. Watch for fakes and read specialized material. Calibers such as 6.5 Rem. Magnum, .284 and .350 Rem. Magnum will bring a premium especially in RS model. Non-prefixed rifles exist in calibers and configurations other than those advertised by Ruger. These should be individually appraised. **NOTE:** Add $400 for 6.5 Rem., .284, .350 Rem.

NIB	Exc.	V.G.	Good	Fair	Poor
—	650	500	400	350	275

Model 77 RL & RLS

This variation similar to standard model, except it features an ultralight 20" barrel and black forearm tip. Also available in 18.5" carbine version, with sights designated RLS. Chambered for .22-250, .243, .257, .270, .250-3000, .308 and .30-06. Weight only 6 lbs.

NIB	Exc.	V.G.	Good	Fair	Poor
550	450	375	325	275	225

Model 77V Varmint

Similar to standard Model 77, except it has a 24" heavy barrel that is drilled and tapped for target-scope bases and wider beavertail forearm. Chambered for .22-250, .243, 6mm, .25-06, .280 and .308. Also chambered for .220 Swift in a 26" heavyweight barrel.

NIB	Exc.	V.G.	Good	Fair	Poor
500	400	350	300	250	200

Model 77 RSI

This version of Model 77 has a full-length Mannlicher-style stock. Was chambered for .22-250, .250-3000, .243, .270, 7mm-08, .308 and .30-06.

NIB	Exc.	V.G.	Good	Fair	Poor
700	600	500	300	275	200

Model 77 RS African

A heavier-barreled version, with steel trigger guard and floorplate. Earlier versions were stocked with fine-quality Circassian walnut. Chambered for .458 Win. Magnum. **NOTE:** Fewer than 50 rifles chambered for .416 Taylor cartridge and produced up to 1976. Selling prices range from $3,000 to $5,000 and should be individually appraised. **NOTE:** Add $100 for early models with Circassian walnut stocks.

NIB	Exc.	V.G.	Good	Fair	Poor
700	550	400	350	300	250

Model 77/17

Introduced in 2003. Chambered for .17 HMR cartridge. Fitted with 22" barrel, with no sights. Walnut stock, with blued finish. Magazine capacity 9 rounds. Weight about 6 lbs.

NIB	Exc.	V.G.	Good	Fair	Poor
700	600	475	375	250	150

Model 77/17 Synthetic

As above, with black synthetic stock and blued finish.

NIB	Exc.	V.G.	Good	Fair	Poor
625	475	350	250	175	125

Model 77/17 Varmint

As above, with black laminate stock and 24" stainless steel heavy barrel, with no sights. Weight about 7 lbs.

NIB	Exc.	V.G.	Good	Fair	Poor
685	500	375	265	195	145

Model 77/17RM2

Introduced in 2005. Chambered for .17 Mach 2 caliber. Fitted with 20" barrel, with no sights. Walnut stock, with checkering. Blued finish. Weight about 6.5 lbs. Discontinued.

NIB	Exc.	V.G.	Good	Fair	Poor
625	475	350	250	175	125

Model 77/17RM2 Stainless Steel

As above, with stainless steel finish and black laminate stock. Weight about 7.25 lbs. Introduced in 2005; discontinued.

NIB	Exc.	V.G.	Good	Fair	Poor
745	625	500	400	275	150

Model 77/22

A high quality, .22 rimfire (LR and WMR) rifle designed for the serious shooter. Has a 20" barrel and 10-shot detachable rotary magazine. Made of steel and stock with checkered walnut. Available with sights, scope rings or both as an extra-cost ($20) option. Introduced in 1984. Early guns without 77/22 rollmark on the receiver will bring a premium.

NIB	Exc.	V.G.	Good	Fair	Poor
700	600	475	375	250	150

Model 77/22 Synthetic Stock

This version is quite similar to standard 77/22, with black matte-finished synthetic stock.

NIB	Exc.	V.G.	Good	Fair	Poor
625	450	350	250	200	150

Model 77/22 Stainless Steel/Synthetic Stock

Same as blued version, except made of stainless steel.

NIB	Exc.	V.G.	Good	Fair	Poor
750	650	500	400	275	150

Model 77/22 Varmint

Introduced in 1993. Features stainless steel finish, laminated wood stock, heavy 20" varmint barrel with no sights. Scope rings are included as standard. Chambered for .22 LR or Win. Magnum rimfire.

NIB	Exc.	V.G.	Good	Fair	Poor
650	525	425	300	250	150

Model 77/22M

Simply 77/22 chambered for .22 Magnum cartridge. Finish is blue. Magazine capacity 9 rounds.

NIB	Exc.	V.G.	Good	Fair	Poor
700	600	475	375	250	150

Model 77/22M Stainless Steel

Same as blued 77/22M, only constructed of stainless steel.

NIB	Exc.	V.G.	Good	Fair	Poor
750	650	500	400	275	150

Model 77/22—.22 Hornet

Introduced in 1994. This version of 77/22 series chambered for .22 Hornet cartridge. Furnished with/without sights. Barrel 20". Has 6-round detachable rotary magazine. Stock checkered walnut, with sling swivels. Weight about 6 lbs. Also available chambered for .17 Hornet.

NIB	Exc.	V.G.	Good	Fair	Poor
725	625	500	375	250	150

Model K77/22VHZ

Introduced in 1995. This .22 Hornet variation features stainless steel heavyweight barrel and laminated American hardwood stock. Offered without sights.

NIB	Exc.	V.G.	Good	Fair	Poor
685	525	425	300	250	150

Model 77R MKII

Introduced in 1992. A basic Model 77 rifle. Features blued metal parts and no sights. Available in 15 different calibers from .223 to .338 Win. Magnum. Barrel lengths from 22" to 24" depending on caliber. Comes from factory with scope bases and rings. Weight about 7 lbs.

NIB	Exc.	V.G.	Good	Fair	Poor
715	525	375	250	200	150

Model 77RP MKII

Also introduced in 1992 and differs from Model 77R. Added stainless steel barrel, receiver and synthetic stock. Available in 10 calibers. In 1998, added the .25-06 caliber.

NIB	Exc.	V.G.	Good	Fair	Poor
715	525	375	250	200	150

Model 77RS MKII

Blued version of basic rifle, with addition of open sights. Available in 9 calibers from .243 Win. to .458 Win. Magnum.

NIB	Exc.	V.G.	Good	Fair	Poor
760	600	450	350	250	175

Model 77RSP MKII

Stainless version of basic rifle, with addition of synthetic stock and open sights. Available in 6 calibers: .243, .270, 7MM Rem. Magnum, .30-06, .300 Win. Magnum, .338 Win. Magnum. Introduced in 1993.

NIB	Exc.	V.G.	Good	Fair	Poor
500	400	350	300	250	175

Model 77RSI MKII

Also introduced in 1993. Features blued barrel and full-length walnut stock. Offered in .243-, .270-, .30-06-, .308-calibers, all with 18" barrel.

NIB	Exc.	V.G.	Good	Fair	Poor
820	600	450	350	250	175

Model 77RL MKII

This model features a short action in six calibers from .223 to .308, all with 20" barrel. Weight about 6 lbs. Introduced in 1992.

NIB	Exc.	V.G.	Good	Fair	Poor
770	575	425	300	200	150

Model 77LR MKII

A left-handed rifle furnished in long action calibers: .270, 7mm Rem. Magnum, .30-06, .300 Win. Magnum. Introduced in 1992.

NIB	Exc.	V.G.	Good	Fair	Poor
770	575	425	300	200	150

Model 77RLP MKII

Introduced in 1999. Similar to RL model above, with all-weather synthetic stock. Weight about 6.5 lbs.

NIB	Exc.	V.G.	Good	Fair	Poor
715	525	400	275	200	150

Model 77VT MKII

A target rifle introduced in 1993. Furnished with no sights, heavy laminated wood stock with beavertail fore-end and adjustable trigger. Barrel,

bolt and action are stainless steel. Weight about 9.75 lbs. Furnished in eight calibers from .223 to .308.

NIB	Exc.	V.G.	Good	Fair	Poor
820	650	475	350	250	175

Model 77RBZ MKII

Features a stainless steel barrel and action. Fitted with laminated hardwood stock. No sights. Weight about 7.25 lbs. Offered in a wide variety of calibers from .223 to .338 Win. Magnum. Introduced in 1997.

NIB	Exc.	V.G.	Good	Fair	Poor
600	500	400	300	225	175

Model 77RSBZ MKII

Same as above, but fitted with open sights. Introduced in 1997.

NIB	Exc.	V.G.	Good	Fair	Poor
800	650	475	350	250	125

Model 77CR MKII Compact Rifle

Introduced in 2001. Features 16.5" barrel, with 4-round magazine. Chambered for .223 Rem., .243 Win., .260 Rem. and .308 Win. cartridges. Blued model fitted with walnut stock; stainless steel model with black laminated stock. Weight about 5.75 lbs. **NOTE:** Add $50 for stainless steel model (M77CRBBZ).

NIB	Exc.	V.G.	Good	Fair	Poor
650	550	400	275	200	150

Model 77 Express MKII

Introduced in 1992. Features select Circassian walnut straight comb checkered (22 lpi) stock. Buttstock fitted with a rubber recoil pad; pistol-grip with metal grip cap. Barrel length 22" features blade front sight and V-notch rear express. Receiver machined for scope mounts, which are included. Available in these calibers: .270, .30-06, 7mm Rem. Magnum, .300 Win. Magnum, .338 Win. Magnum. Weight about 7.5 lbs.

NIB	Exc.	V.G.	Good	Fair	Poor
1200	850	650	550	400	200

Model 77 Magnum MKII RSM

Similar in all respects to Model 77 Express MKII, except offered in these calibers: .375 H&H, .416 Rigby and .458 Lott. Weight about: 9.25 lbs. for .375; 10.25 lbs. for.416 and .458 Lott.

NIB	Exc.	V.G.	Good	Fair	Poor
1975	1500	1100	750	525	350

M77 MKII Frontier Rifle

Bolt-action rifle based on M77 MKII chassis. Introduced in 2005, this variation is configured for scout-style scope mount system. Chambered in .243, .308, 7mm-08, .300 WSM, .325 WSM, .338 Federal. Gray laminated stock, 16.5" blued or stainless barrel. Stainless barrel and action model introduced 2006. In 2008, added .338 Federal and .358 Win. Frontier Rifle discontinued in 2008. **NOTE:** Add 15 percent for stainless barrel; 10 percent for stainless barrel and action.

NIB	Exc.	V.G.	Good	Fair	Poor
600	500	400	300	225	175

Guide Gun

Compact variation of Model 77 Mark II, with 20" barrel, muzzle-brake, barrel band, express-style sights and integral scope mounts. Chambered in .30-06, .300 Win. Magnum, .300 RCM, .338 Win. Magnum, .338 RCM, .375 H&H or .416 Ruger. Green Mountain laminated hardwood stock, with adjustable length of pull. Introduced in 2013.

NIB	Exc.	V.G.	Good	Fair	Poor
1075	950	800	650	500	300

Gunsite Scout

Based on Ruger M77 rifle design. 16.5" barrel and forward mounted Picatinny rail for intermediate eye relief scopes. Chambered in .308 Win., with 10-round detachable magazine, integral scope mounts with rings and flash suppressor. Adjustable ghost ring rear sight and ramp front. Black/gray laminated stock, with checkering and soft rubber recoil pad with spacers.

NIB	Exc.	V.G.	Good	Fair	Poor
850	750	600	450	300	200

Model 77/44RS

Bolt-action chambered for .44 Magnum cartridge. Features 18.5" barrel, with open sights. Stock American walnut, with rubber buttpad and checkering on forearm and pistol-grip. Detachable rotary magazine has 4 round capacity. Weight about 6 lbs. Introduced in mid-1997. Discontinued in 2004, reintroduced in 2009, with synthetic or Next GI Vista camo stock. **NOTE:** Deduct $100 for older model with wood stock.

NIB	Exc.	V.G.	Good	Fair	Poor
750	650	500	400	275	150

Model 77/44RSP

Introduced in 1999. Has matte stainless steel barrel and action. Black synthetic stock. Chambered for .44 Magnum cartridge. Weight about 6 lbs.

NIB	Exc.	V.G.	Good	Fair	Poor
575	465	375	250	175	125

Model 77/357

Rotary magazine rifle similar to 77/44RS, except chambered for .357 Magnum/.38 Special rounds.

NIB	Exc.	V.G.	Good	Fair	Poor
700	600	450	385	250	200

HAWKEYE SERIES

Few exceptions Hawkeye Series introduced in 2007. Replaced Ruger's M77 Mark II line. In 2010, Hawkeye series began being offered in left-hand versions.

HM77R Hawkeye

Slimmed-down version of M77. American walnut stock, blued barrel, Mauser-style controlled feed extractor, soft red rubber recoil pad, stainless steel bolt, new LC6 trigger, engraved solid steel floorplate. Chambered in .25-06, 7mm-08, 7mm Magnum, .308, .30-06, .300 Win Magnum, .338 Win Magnum. Left-hand and laminate-stock versions available. Introduced in 2007.

NIB	Exc.	V.G.	Good	Fair	Poor
650	550	400	225	175	125

M77 Hawkeye Ultra-Light

Similar to Hawkeye, with lightweight 20" blued barrel. Chambered in .223, .243 Win., .257 Roberts, .270 Win., .308 Win. and .30-06.

NIB	Exc.	V.G.	Good	Fair	Poor
700	600	450	300	225	175

M77 Hawkeye All-Weather Ultra-Light

Similar to above, with black synthetic stock. Matte stainless barrel and receiver. Chambered in .204, .223, .243 Win., .270 Win. and .30-06.

NIB	Exc.	V.G.	Good	Fair	Poor
600	500	400	300	225	175

M77 Hawkeye Compact

Similar to M77 Hawkeye Ultra-Light, with 16.5" barrel and smaller overall dimensions. Chambered in .223, .243 Win., .260 Rem., 7mm-08, .308 Win., 6.8 SPC and 7.62x39.

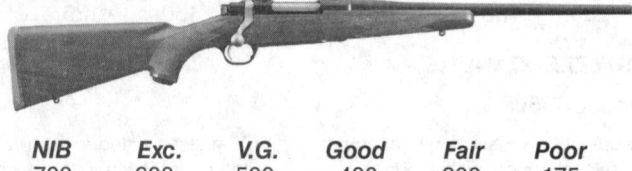

NIB	Exc.	V.G.	Good	Fair	Poor
700	600	500	400	300	175

M77 Hawkeye Laminate Compact

Similar to above, with black laminate stock. Matte stainless barrel and receiver.

NIB	Exc.	V.G.	Good	Fair	Poor
650	525	425	300	250	150

M77 Hawkeye All-Weather

All-weather version of HM77R Hawkeye, with synthetic stock and stainless barrel. Same chamberings as HM77R, with .338 Federal and .358 Win. as well. Introduced 2007. Left-hand introduced 2008.

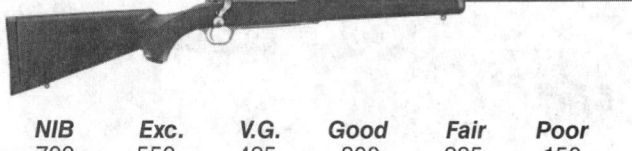

NIB	Exc.	V.G.	Good	Fair	Poor
700	550	425	300	225	150

M77PRCM Hawkeye Compact Magnum

Similar to Hawkeye, with .500" shorter synthetic stock. Stainless steel barrel and receiver. Chambered for .416 Ruger, .375 Ruger, .300 Ruger Compact Magnum, .338 Ruger Compact Magnum. Introduced 2008.

NIB	Exc.	V.G.	Good	Fair	Poor
775	675	550	450	325	195

M77RCM Hawkeye Compact Magnum

Similar to above, with blued barrel and walnut stock. Introduced 2008.

NIB	Exc.	V.G.	Good	Fair	Poor
800	700	575	475	350	200

M77 Hawkeye Magnum Hunter

Stainless model offered only in .300 Win. Magnum. Features include Green Hogue stock, 24" barrel with removable muzzle-brake and LC6 trigger.

NIB	Exc.	V.G.	Good	Fair	Poor
950	800	600	400	250	150

M77 Hawkeye Alaskan

Similar to M77 All-Weather, with iron sights, Diamond black finish, stainless or matte blued barrel/receiver and Hogue stock. Chambered in .375 Ruger or .416 Ruger. Introduced 2007. Left-hand introduced 2008.

NIB	Exc.	V.G.	Good	Fair	Poor
1000	850	700	500	300	200

M77 Hawkeye African

Similar to M77 All-Weather, with checkered walnut stock and express-style sights. Chambered in .223 Rem., 9.3x62, .300 Win. Magnum, .338 Win. Magnum, .375 Ruger, .416 Ruger. Introduced 2007. Left-hand introduced 2008.

NIB	Exc.	V.G.	Good	Fair	Poor
1050	875	750	550	300	200

M77 Hawkeye Tactical

Similar to M77 Hawkeye, with 20" matte blue heavy barrel, overmolded Hogue synthetic stock. Chambered in .223, .243 Win. and .308 Win.

NIB	Exc.	V.G.	Good	Fair	Poor
875	750	625	500	300	200

M77 Hawkeye Predator

Similar to M77 Hawkeye, with 24" matte stainless barrel. Green-toned Green Mountain laminate stock. Chambered in .204, .223 and .22-250.

NIB	Exc.	V.G.	Good	Fair	Poor
850	650	525	425	300	200

M77 Hawkeye International

Similar to Hawkeye, with 18.5" barrel and full-length Mannlicher-style stock. Chambered in .243, .270, .308 Win. and .30-06.

NIB	Exc.	V.G.	Good	Fair	Poor
825	725	600	475	350	225

M77 Hawkeye Varmint Target

Chambered in .204 Ruger, .223 Rem., 22-250, 6.5 Creedmoor and .308 Win. Features heavy contour 26" barrel, black laminate target-type stock and adjustable two-stage trigger.

NIB	Exc.	V.G.	Good	Fair	Poor
850	700	550	400	250	150

American Rifle

Budget-price bolt-action in .223 Rem., .22-250, .243, .270 Win., 7mm-08, .308, .30-06. Features 4-shot rotary magazine, black composite stock and matte black finish. Includes tang safety, adjustable trigger and free-floating hammer-forged barrel. Introduced in 2012. Available with factory mounted Redfield Revolution 3-9x scope. Added in 2016, American Rifle Magnum model chambered in 7mm Rem. Magnum or .300 Win. Magnum. **NOTE:** Add $200 for scope; $200 for Magnum model.

NIB	Exc.	V.G.	Good	Fair	Poor
400	350	300	250	225	200

American Rifle Compact

Chambered in .223, .22-250, .243, 7mm-08 and .308 Win., with 18" barrel. Shorter stock, with 12.5" length of pull.

NIB	Exc.	V.G.	Good	Fair	Poor
400	350	300	250	150	125

American Rifle All-Weather Stainless

Same features as standard model, with stainless steel barrel and action. Also offered in Compact model. Introduced in 2014.

NIB	Exc.	V.G.	Good	Fair	Poor
500	425	350	300	225	150

American Rifle Predator

This model has Moss Green composite stock and scope rail atop receiver. Calibers are .204 Ruger, .223 Rem., .22-250, .243, 6.5 Creedmoor and .308. Introduced in 2015.

NIB	Exc.	V.G.	Good	Fair	Poor
435	400	325	275	225	150

Amrican Rifle Ranch

Chambered for 5.56 NATO/.223 or .300 Blackout. Has a Flat Dark Earth composite stock, scope rail and 16.6" barrel. Introduced in 2015.

NIB	Exc.	V.G.	Good	Fair	Poor
435	400	325	275	225	150

Ruger Precision Rifle

A totally new model designed specifically for extra long-range shooting. Calibers are: .243 Win., 26" bbl.; 6.5 Creedmoor, 24" bbl.; .308 Win., 20" bbl. Multi-magazine interface functions with M110, SR25, DPMS and Magpul style magazines. Action features three-lug bolt, with dual cocking cams and oversized handle. Receivers are precision machined: upper from 4140 chrome-moly steel; lower from an aero-space aluminum forging. Ruger Precision MSR stock has a soft rubber buttpad. Left-folding stock hinge accepts any AR-style stock. Weight from 9.7 to 11 lbs., depending on barrel length. Introduced in 2015.

NIB	Exc.	V.G.	Good	Fair	Poor
1150	1000	—	—	—	—

American Rimfire Rifle

In 2014, a rimfire version of American Rifle was introduced. Similar features as centerfire model. Available in full-size version, with 22" barrel; compact model, with 18" barrel.

NIB	Exc.	V.G.	Good	Fair	Poor
280	235	200	175	150	125

MUZZLELOADERS

Model 77/50RS

An in-line percussion rifle chambered for .50-caliber. Fitted with a 22" barrel and open sights. Stock is birch, with rubber buttplate and no checkering. Blued finish. Weight about 6.5 lbs. Introduced in mid-1997; discontinued.

NIB	Exc.	V.G.	Good	Fair	Poor
425	325	225	175	125	100

Model 77/50RSO

Similar to model above, with straight-grip checkered walnut stock and curved buttplate. Introduced in 1998.

NIB	Exc.	V.G.	Good	Fair	Poor
475	350	250	200	125	100

Model 77/50RSBBZ

Introduced in 1998. Features all specifications of Model 77/50RS, with addition of black/gray laminated stock and stainless steel finish.

NIB	Exc.	V.G.	Good	Fair	Poor
500	375	275	225	125	100

Model 77/50RSP

This model has a stainless steel barrel and action. Fitted with black synthetic stock and pistol-grip. Weight about 6.5 lbs. Introduced in 1999.

NIB	Exc.	V.G.	Good	Fair	Poor
575	400	300	200	125	100

LEVER-ACTION RIFLES

Model 96/17

Introduced in 2003. Chambered for .17 HMR cartridge. Fitted with an 18.5" barrel. Magazine capacity 9 rounds. Hardwood stock and open sights. Weight about 5.25 lbs. Discontinued.

NIB	Exc.	V.G.	Good	Fair	Poor
600	500	400	300	150	125

Model 96/22

Introduced into Ruger line in 1996. Chambered for .22 LR. Stock American hardwood. Barrel length 18.5". Magazine capacity 10 rounds. Open sights are standard. Weight about 5.25 lbs. Discontinued.

NIB	Exc.	V.G.	Good	Fair	Poor
500	400	325	200	150	125

Model 96/22M

Same as above, but chambered for .22 WMR cartridge. Magazine capacity 9 rounds. Discontinued.

NIB	Exc.	V.G.	Good	Fair	Poor
600	500	400	300	200	125

Model 96/44

Same as .22-caliber, except chambered for .44 Magnum cartridge. Magazine capacity 4 rounds. Weight about 5.875 lbs. Discontinued.

NIB	Exc.	V.G.	Good	Fair	Poor
750	600	500	300	200	125

SHOTGUNS

Red Label Early Production

Red Label over/under shotgun introduced in 1977. Only in 20-gauge, with 12-gauge version added in 1982; 28-gauge in 1995. Original Red Label had blue finish on both receiver and barrels. Fixed chokes, with 26" or 28" ventilated rib barrels and bead front sight. Interchangeable choke tubes were offered as a option in 1988 and became standard in 1990. Stainless receiver with blued barrel became optional in 1985 and then standard starting in 1989. General features include single selective mechanical trigger, selective automatic ejectors and checkered American walnut stock, with pistol-grip or English-type straight-grip. Streamlined box-lock action has no exposed pins or screws. Weights ranged from 7 to 8 lbs. Red label was in production through 2011. After a hiatus of a couple years and a few minor changes, it returned to Ruger catalog in 2014.

NIB	Exc.	V.G.	Good	Fair	Poor
1500	1200	950	750	400	250

Red Label 2014 Model

This model returned to Ruger line in 2014 with a few changes, mostly on the inside. The 2014 model, in 12-gauge only, has a one-piece cast receiver, compared to two pieces welded together in older version. Locking lugs do not protrude through receiver and there are no side ribs between barrels. After being back in production for only about a year, at the end of 2014 Red Label was discontinued for the second time, and perhaps forever.

NIB	Exc.	V.G.	Good	Fair	Poor
1200	1000	800	600	—	—

Red Label Sporting Clays

Introduced in 1994. Offered in 20-gauge, with 3" chambers and 30" barrels. Walnut stock has checkering and pistol-grip. Weight about 7 lbs.

Courtesy compliments of Bill Ruger, John C. Dougan

NIB	Exc.	V.G.	Good	Fair	Poor
1600	1300	1050	800	400	200

Red Label All-Weather

Offered in 12-gauge only, with 26", 28" or 30" barrels. Fitted with black synthetic stock and pistol-grip. Weight about 7.5 lbs. Introduced in 1999.

NIB	Exc.	V.G.	Good	Fair	Poor
1300	875	650	400	300	250

Red Label Series — Hand Engraved

This series of hand-engraved Red Labels was first catalogued in 1996, with three different engraving coverages. A total of 375 were produced by several prominent engravers, between 1997 and 2000.

Grade 1

NIB	Exc.	V.G.	Good	Fair	Poor
2400	2000	1500	1200	—	—

Grade 2 (1/3 coverage)

NIB	Exc.	V.G.	Good	Fair	Poor
2600	2200	1700	1400	—	—

Grade 3 (2/3 coverage)

NIB	Exc.	V.G.	Good	Fair	Poor
3000	2500	2000	1700	—	—

Red Label Engraved

Features scroll engraved receiver, with gold inlaid game bird appropriate to gauge. 12-gauge pheasant; 20-gauge grouse; 28-gauge woodcock. Walnut stock. Other specifications same as standard Red Label shotguns. Introduced in 2000 and made until 2011. Premium for 28-gauge.

NIB	Exc.	V.G.	Good	Fair	Poor
1800	1500	1200	900	500	300

Red Label All-Weather Engraved

Introduced in 2000. Features scroll engraved receiver, with gold inlaid duck. Offered in 12-gauge only, with 26", 28" or 30" barrel.

NIB	Exc.	V.G.	Good	Fair	Poor
1675	1325	1075	750	500	300

Woodside Over/Under

Introduced in 1995. Features Circassian walnut stock, with pistol-/straight-grip. Available in 12- or 20-gauge, with barrel lengths 26", 28" or 30". Screw-in chokes are standard. **NOTE:** Woodside shotgun also available in three different engraving patterns. Discontinued 2002.

NIB	Exc.	V.G.	Good	Fair	Poor
1500	1300	950	650	300	250

Trap Model

Introduced in 2000. A 12-gauge single-barrel trap gun, with 34" barrel choked Full and Modified. Fitted with mechanical trigger and auto ejector. Stock select walnut, with adjustable cheekpiece and buttplate. Receiver engraved. Weight about 9 lbs.

NIB	Exc.	V.G.	Good	Fair	Poor
3800	3000	2500	1800	900	500

Gold Label Side-by-Side

Introduced in 2002. Chambered for 12-gauge 3" shell. Offered with 28" barrels and choke tubes. Choice of pistol-/straight-grip checkered walnut stock. Ejectors and single trigger. Weight about 6.33 lbs. Discontinued 2008.

NIB	Exc.	V.G.	Good	Fair	Poor
3500	3000	2300	1600	900	450

SUNDANCE INDUSTRIES, INC.
North Hollywood, California

This company was in business from 1989 to 2002.

Model D-22M

A .22 or .22 Magnum caliber double-barrel over/under pocket pistol, with 2.5" barrels and aluminum alloy frame. Blackened finish or chrome-plated, with simulated pearl or black grips. Introduced in 1989.

NIB	Exc.	V.G.	Good	Fair	Poor
—	225	175	125	100	75

Model BOA

Introduced in 1991. Semi-automatic pistol chambered for .25 ACP cartridge. Fitted with 2.5" barrel, with fixed sights. Grip safety. Choice of black or chrome finish. Magazine capacity 7 rounds. Weight about 16 oz.

NIB	Exc.	V.G.	Good	Fair	Poor
125	100	80	70	50	25

Model A-25

Similar to BOA, without grip safety.

NIB	Exc.	V.G.	Good	Fair	Poor
125	100	80	70	50	25

Model Laser 25

Similar to Model BOA, with grip safety. Equipped with a laser sight. Laser activated by squeezing grip safety. Weight with laser 18 oz. Introduced in 1995.

NIB	Exc.	V.G.	Good	Fair	Poor
220	175	125	100	75	50

Sundance Point Blank

An over/under derringer chambered for .22 LR cartridge. Fitted with 3" barrel and double-action trigger. Enclosed hammer. Matte black finish. Weight about 8 oz. Introduced in 1994.

NIB	Exc.	V.G.	Good	Fair	Poor
95	80	70	50	25	10

SUPER SIX LTD.
Fort Atkinson, Wisconsin

Bison Bull

Massive single-action .45-70 revolver, with blued carbon steel (Bison Bull) or engraved molybdenum bronze (Golden Bison Bull) frame. Adjustable sights, 10.5" barrel, 17.5" overall length, weight 6 lbs. Introduced in 2006. Value shown for blued version. **NOTE:** Add 350 percent for engraved version.

NIB	Exc.	V.G.	Good	Fair	Poor
1200	1050	900	775	600	500

SUTHERLAND, S.
Richmond, Virginia

Pocket Pistol

A .41-caliber percussion single-shot pistol, with round barrels of 2.5" to 4" in length. German silver mounts and walnut stock. Lock normally marked "S. Sutherland" or "S. Sutherland/Richmond". Manufactured during 1850s.

NIB	Exc.	V.G.	Good	Fair	Poor
—	—	2950	2200	800	300

SYMS, J. G.
New York, New York

Pocket Pistol

A .41-caliber single-shot percussion pistol, with 1.5" to 3.5" barrels. German silver mounts and walnut stock. Lock normally marked "Syms/New York". Manufactured during 1850s.

NIB	Exc.	V.G.	Good	Fair	Poor
—	—	2600	2150	825	300

SYREN SHOTGUNS
Cambridge, Maryland

Syren Tempio

These shotguns are marketed primarily to women. Made by Caesar Guerini and Fabarm in Italy and have features that are found on better grades of over/unders. Gauges are 12, 20 and 28, with .410 available in a combo with 28- or 20-/28-gauges. Barrel lengths are 28", 30" or 32" (Sporting), with choke tubes, choice of manual or automatic safety, deluxe grade walnut stock, coin finished receiver with roses and scroll engraving. Field and Light model weight 5.25 to 6 lbs.; Sporting model from 7.5 to 8 lbs. Introduced in 2015. **NOTE:** Add $300 for Sporting model.

NIB	Exc.	V.G.	Good	Fair	Poor
3300	2800	2500	1600	800	300

XLR5 Sporter

Semi-automatic designed for lighter target loads. Stock designed for female anatomy, with smaller pistol-grip, Monte Carlo comb, optimized cast, pitch and length of pull. Made by Fabarm. Introduced in 2014.

NIB	Exc.	V.G.	Good	Fair	Poor
1750	1400	1000	800	400	200

T

TACONIC FIREARMS LTD.
Cambridge, New York

M98 Ultimate Hunter

Bolt-action rifle based on M98 Mauser action. Available in calibers from .22-250 to .358 Win. Stainless steel and barrel length 22". Titanium grip cap. Stock is XXX English walnut, with cheekpiece and oil-finish. Ebony fore-end tip. Scope bases are integral to receiver. Prices listed are for standard rifle. There is an extensive list of options which will greatly affect price. For example, an optional quarter rib will add $1000 to the base price of gun. Value speculative.

NIB	Exc.	V.G.	Good	Fair	Poor
6000 — 10000					

TALLASSEE
Tallassee, Alabama

Carbine

A .58-caliber single-shot percussion carbine, with 25" round barrel and full-length stock secured by two barrel bands. Fitted with sling swivels. Barrel and lock finished in bright brass furniture and walnut stock. Lock marked "C.S./Tallassee/ Ala.". Approximately 500 of these carbines manufactured in 1864. Very Rare.

Courtesy Milwaukee Public Museum, Milwaukee, Wisconsin

NIB	Exc.	V.G.	Good	Fair	Poor
—	—	100000	70000	40000	10000

TANFOGLIO
Valtrompia, Italy

Products of this company, which was established in late 1940s, have been imported into the United States by various companies including Eig Corporation, F.I.E. of Hialeah, Florida and Excam.

Sata

A .22 or 6.35mm caliber semi-automatic pistol, with 3" barrel. Slide marked "Pistola SATA Made in Italy"; grips "SATA". Blued, with black plastic grips.

NIB	Exc.	V.G.	Good	Fair	Poor
—	250	175	125	90	75

Titan

A 6.35mm caliber semi-automatic pistol, with 2.5" barrel and external hammer. Slide marked "Titan 6.35"; on U.S. imported examples "EIG". Blued, with plastic grips.

NIB	Exc.	V.G.	Good	Fair	Poor
—	250	175	125	90	75

Super Titan

Similar in design to above, with larger frame. In .380 ACP. Walnut grips.

NIB	Exc.	V.G.	Good	Fair	Poor
—	265	195	150	125	95

TA 90 or TZ-75

A 9mm caliber semi-automatic pistol, with 4.75" barrel and 15-shot magazine. Blued or chrome-plated, with walnut or rubber grips. Those imported by Excam were known as Model TA 90, while those imported by F.I.E. are known as Model TZ-75.

NIB	Exc.	V.G.	Good	Fair	Poor
450	400	350	300	250	200

TA 90B

As above, with a 3.5" barrel, 12-shot magazine and Neoprene grips. Introduced in 1986.

NIB	Exc.	V.G.	Good	Fair	Poor
450	400	350	300	250	200

TA 90 SS

As above, with a ported 5" barrel, adjustable sights and two-tone finish. Introduced in 1989.

NIB	Exc.	V.G.	Good	Fair	Poor
650	600	500	450	400	300

TA 41 AE

As above, in .41 Action Express caliber. Introduced in 1989.

NIB	Exc.	V.G.	Good	Fair	Poor
500	450	400	350	300	250

TA 41 SS

As above, with ported 5" barrel, adjustable sights and two-tone finish. Introduced in 1989.

NIB	Exc.	V.G.	Good	Fair	Poor
650	600	500	450	400	300

TA 76

A .22-caliber single-action revolver, with 4.75" barrel and 6-shot cylinder. Blued or chrome-plated, with brass back strap and trigger guard. Walnut grips.

NIB	Exc.	V.G.	Good	Fair	Poor
100	90	80	65	50	25

TA 76M Combo

As above, with 6" or 9" barrel. Interchangeable .22 Magnum caliber cylinder.

NIB	Exc.	V.G.	Good	Fair	Poor
110	100	90	75	60	35

TA 38SB

A .38 Special caliber over/under double-barrel pocket pistol, with 3" barrels and hammer block safety. Blued, with checkered nylon grips. Discontinued in 1985.

NIB	Exc.	V.G.	Good	Fair	Poor
—	100	90	80	60	40

TANNER, ANDRE
Switzerland

Model 300 Free Rifle

A 7.5mm Swiss or .308-caliber single-shot rifle. Varying length barrels having adjustable target sights and adjustable trigger. Walnut stock fitted with palm rest and adjustable cheekpiece. Blued.

NIB	Exc.	V.G.	Good	Fair	Poor
4750	3750	3000	2500	1500	750

Model 300S

As above, with 10-shot magazine. Not fitted with a palm rest. Discontinued in 1988.

NIB	Exc.	V.G.	Good	Fair	Poor
4500	3500	2750	2250	1250	750

Model 50F

As above in .22-caliber, with thumbhole stock. Discontinued in 1988.

NIB	Exc.	V.G.	Good	Fair	Poor
3750	3000	2500	1750	900	500

TARPLEY J. & F. AND E. T. GARRETT & CO.
Greensboro, North Carolina

Carbine

A .52-caliber breech-loading single-shot percussion carbine, with 22" round barrel and plain walnut buttstock. Blued, with case-hardened frame. Tang marked "J H Tarpley's./Pat Feb 14./1863". Over 400 of these carbines manufactured.

NIB	Exc.	V.G.	Good	Fair	Poor
—	—	80000	65000	30000	10000

TAURUS INTERNATIONAL MFG. CO.
Porto Alegre, Brazil

PISTOLS

PT-92C

This 9mm model is a large capacity semi-automatic pistol, with 4.25" barrel. Drift adjustable 3-dot combat rear sight. Magazine holds 13 rounds in a double column. Choice of blued, stain nickel or stainless steel finish. Brazilian hardwood grips are standard. Weight 31 oz.

NIB	Exc.	V.G.	Good	Fair	Poor
450	325	275	220	160	100

PT-92

Slightly larger and heavier version of PT-92C. Has 5" barrel, with drift adjustable 3-dot combat rear sight. Magazine capacity 15 rounds. Model is 1" longer overall than above model. Weight 34 oz. Also available in blued, nickel and stainless steel. **NOTE:** Add $20 for stainless steel; $50 for blue with gold finish; $60 for stainless steel with gold accents; $250 for blued or stainless steel .22 LR conversion kit.

NIB	Exc.	V.G.	Good	Fair	Poor
400	300	225	150	100	75

PT-99

Similar in appearance and specifications to PT-92. This version has additional feature of fully adjustable 3-dot rear sight. **NOTE:** Add $20 for stainless steel finish.

NIB	Exc.	V.G.	Good	Fair	Poor
425	325	250	150	100	75

PT-92AF

A 9mm caliber double-action semi-automatic pistol, with 4.92" barrel, exposed hammer and 15-shot magazine. Blued or nickel-plated, with plain walnut grips.

NIB	Exc.	V.G.	Good	Fair	Poor
400	350	300	250	200	150

PT-100

Similar to other full-size Taurus semi-automatics, except chambered for .40 S&W cartridge. Supplied with 5" barrel, with drift adjustable rear sight. Magazine capacity 11 rounds. Also available in blued, nickel or stainless steel. Weight 34 oz. **NOTE:** Add $50 for Special Edition, blued steel with gold fixtures and rosewood grips; $110 for blued steel with gold fixtures and pearl grips.

NIB	Exc.	V.G.	Good	Fair	Poor
500	400	300	200	150	100

PT-101

Same as model above, but furnished with fully adjustable rear 3-dot combat sight.

NIB	Exc.	V.G.	Good	Fair	Poor
450	350	300	250	150	100

Deluxe Shooter's Pak

Offered by Taurus as a special package. Consists of pistol, with extra magazine in a fitted custom hard case. Available for these models: PT-92, PT-99, PT-100 and PT-101. **NOTE:** Add about 10 percent to prices of these models for this special feature.

PT-138

Introduced in 1998. This polymer frame pistol chambered for .380 cartridge. Fitted with 4" barrel in blue or stainless steel. Weight about 16 oz. Magazine capacity 10 rounds.

Blue

NIB	Exc.	V.G.	Good	Fair	Poor
350	250	200	175	125	100

Stainless Steel

NIB	Exc.	V.G.	Good	Fair	Poor
375	275	225	175	125	100

PT-908

Semi-automatic double-action pistol chambered for 9mm Parabellum cartridge. Fitted with 3.8" barrel, with drift adjustable rear 3-dot combat sight. Magazine capacity 8 rounds in a single column. Available in blued, satin nickel or stainless steel. Stocks are black rubber. Weight 30 oz. Introduced in 1993.

NIB	Exc.	V.G.	Good	Fair	Poor
375	325	275	225	150	100

PT-911

Introduced in 1997. Chambered for 9mm cartridge. Fitted with 4" barrel. Magazine capacity 10 rounds. Choice of blue or stainless steel. Weight about 28 oz. Black rubber grips are standard. **NOTE:** Add $20 for stainless steel.

NIB	Exc.	V.G.	Good	Fair	Poor
450	350	275	225	175	125

PT-111

Chambered for 9mm cartridge. Fitted with 3.25" barrel. Magazine is 10 rounds. Weight about 19 oz. **NOTE:** Add $15 for matte stainless steel finish; $80 for night sights.

NIB	Exc.	V.G.	Good	Fair	Poor
375	300	250	175	125	100

PT-140

Chambered for .40 S&W cartridge. Fitted with 3.25" barrel. Magazine capacity 10 rounds. Weight about 19 oz. **NOTE:** Add $15 for matte stainless steel finish; $80 for night sights.

NIB	Exc.	V.G.	Good	Fair	Poor
350	300	265	180	125	100

PT-140 Millennium

Chambered for .40 S&W cartridge. Fitted with 3.25" barrel. Features polymer frame and blue or stainless steel slide. Fixed sights. Magazine capacity 10 rounds. Weight about 19 oz. **NOTE:** Add $75 for night sights.

Blue

NIB	Exc.	V.G.	Good	Fair	Poor
345	315	225	150	100	75

Stainless Steel

NIB	Exc.	V.G.	Good	Fair	Poor
375	325	250	175	100	75

PT-145 Millennium

Similar to PT-140. Chambered for .45 ACP cartridge. Barrel length 3.27". Weight about 23 oz. Magazine capacity 10 rounds. **NOTE:** Add $75 for night sights.

Blue

NIB	Exc.	V.G.	Good	Fair	Poor
345	315	225	150	100	75

Stainless Steel

NIB	Exc.	V.G.	Good	Fair	Poor
375	325	250	175	100	75

Millennium Pro

Introduced in 2003. This pistol is third generation series in Millennium line. Features captured dual spring and guide assembly, re-engineered magazine release and internal firing pin lock. Larger 3-dot sighting system, positive slide serrations, internal magazine base extension and enlarged external safety with positive click are other improvements.

NIB	Exc.	V.G.	Good	Fair	Poor
365	300	200	150	100	75

Millennium G2

Moderately priced concealed-carry 9mm model, with thin profile and melted edges. Available in two compact models, PT111 and PT140. Features include high profile sights, accessory rail and textured grips. Double-/single-action operation. Introduced in 2014.

NIB	Exc.	V.G.	Good	Fair	Poor
275	250	225	200	150	125

Model 609TI-PRO

Similar to Millennium Pro, with titanium slide. Chambered in 9mm Parabellum. Features include 13+1 capacity, 3.25" barrel, checkered polymer grips, Heinie Straight-8 sights. Overall length 6.125"; weight 19.7 oz.

NIB	Exc.	V.G.	Good	Fair	Poor
500	450	325	225	175	125

PT-400/400SS

Chambered for .400 CorBon cartridge. Fitted with 4.25" ported barrel, with fixed sights. Magazine capacity 8 rounds. Offered in blue or stainless steel. Rubber grips. Weight about 30 oz.

Blue

NIB	Exc.	V.G.	Good	Fair	Poor
375	300	200	150	100	75

Stainless Steel

NIB	Exc.	V.G.	Good	Fair	Poor
420	325	225	150	100	75

PT-132

Chambered for .32 ACP cartridge. Fitted with 3.25" barrel. Magazine capacity 10 rounds. Weight about 20 oz. **NOTE:** Add $15 for matte stainless steel finish.

NIB	Exc.	V.G.	Good	Fair	Poor
325	275	200	150	100	75

PT-58

Introduced in 1988. Chambered for .380 ACP cartridge. Fitted with 4" barrel, with drift adjustable rear sight. Conventional double-action design. Available in blued, satin nickel or stainless steel. Fitted with Brazilian hardwood grips. Weight 30 oz.

NIB	Exc.	V.G.	Good	Fair	Poor
300	250	200	150	100	75

PT-145

Chambered for .45 ACP cartridge. Fitted with 3.25" barrel. Magazine capacity 10 rounds. Weight about 23 oz. **NOTE:** Add $15 for matte stainless steel finish; $80 for night sights.

NIB	Exc.	V.G.	Good	Fair	Poor
325	275	250	200	150	100

PT-45

Introduced in 1994. Semi-automatic double-action pistol. Chambered for .45 ACP cartridge. Barrel is 3.75" in length. Magazine capacity 8 rounds. Offered in blued or stainless steel, with grips of Brazilian hardwood. Fixed sights are standard. Overall length 7.1"; weight about 30 oz.

Blue

NIB	Exc.	V.G.	Good	Fair	Poor
350	275	200	150	100	75

Stainless Steel

NIB	Exc.	V.G.	Good	Fair	Poor
400	325	250	200	150	100

PT-745B/SS

Chambered for .45 ACP cartridge. Fitted with 3.25" barrel. Fixed sights. Polymer grips. Blue or stainless steel. Magazine capacity 6 rounds. Weight about 21 oz. Introduced in 2004. **NOTE:** Add $15 for stainless steel.

NIB	Exc.	V.G.	Good	Fair	Poor
375	315	275	225	125	175

PT-640B/SS

Similar to above. Chambered for .40 S&W cartridge. Magazine capacity 10 rounds. Weight about 24 oz. Introduced in 2004. **NOTE:** Add $15 for stainless steel.

NIB	Exc.	V.G.	Good	Fair	Poor
375	315	275	225	125	175

PT-24/7-45B

This .45 ACP pistol fitted with 4.25" barrel and fixed sights. Ribbed grips. Blued receiver. Magazine capacity 12 rounds. Weight about 27 oz. Introduced in 2004. **NOTE:** Add $15 for stainless steel slide.

NIB	Exc.	V.G.	Good	Fair	Poor
400	300	285	225	150	100

PT-24/7 G2

Double-/single-action semi-automatic pistol. Chambered in 9mm Parabellum (15+1), .40 S&W (13+1), and .45 ACP (10+1). Features include blued or stainless finish; "Strike Two" capability; new trigger safety; low-profile adjustable rear sights for windage and elevation; ambidextrous magazine release; 4.2" barrel; Picatinny rail; polymer frame; polymer grip with metallic inserts and three interchangeable backstraps. Also offered in compact model, with shorter grip frame and 3.5" barrel.

NIB	Exc.	V.G.	Good	Fair	Poor
425	350	300	250	175	125

PT-24/7-PRO Standard

4" barrel; stainless, duotone or blued finish.

NIB	Exc.	V.G.	Good	Fair	Poor
400	300	285	225	150	100

PT-24/7-PRO Compact

3.2" barrel; stainless, titanium or blued finish.

NIB	Exc.	V.G.	Good	Fair	Poor
400	300	285	225	150	100

PT-24/7-PRO Long Slide

5.2" barrel; matte stainless, blued or stainless finish.

NIB	Exc.	V.G.	Good	Fair	Poor
400	300	285	225	150	100

PT-24/7-9B

As above, but chambered for 9mm cartridge. Magazine capacity 17 rounds. Weight about 27 oz. Introduced in 2005. **NOTE:** Add $15 for stainless steel slide.

NIB	Exc.	V.G.	Good	Fair	Poor
400	300	285	225	150	100

PT-24/7-40B

As above, but chambered for .40 S&W cartridge. Magazine capacity 15 rounds. Weight about 27 oz. Introduced in 2005. **NOTE:** Add $15 for stainless steel slide.

NIB	Exc.	V.G.	Good	Fair	Poor
400	300	285	225	150	100

PT-24/7LS-9SS-17

Full-size stainless semi-automatic chambered for 9mm. Long grip and slide. Capacity 17+1. Single-/double-action. 5" barrel. Weight 27.2 oz. Fixed 2-dot rear sight. In short grip 10+1 capacity. Introduced in 2006; discontinued 2010.

NIB	Exc.	V.G.	Good	Fair	Poor
425	345	295	245	175	125

PT-24/79SSC-17

Compact stainless semi-automatic chambered for 9mm. Short grip and slide. Capacity 15+1. Single-/double-action. 3.5" barrel. Weight 27.2 oz. Fixed 2-dot rear sight. In short grip 10+1 capacity. Introduced in 2006; discontinued 2010.

NIB	Exc.	V.G.	Good	Fair	Poor
400	300	285	225	150	100

PT-24/7PLS-9SSPTi-17

Full-size semi-automatic chambered for 9mm. Capacity 17+1 or 10+1. Single-/double-action. Titanium slide, 4" barrel. Weight 27.2 oz. Introduced in 2006.

NIB	Exc.	V.G.	Good	Fair	Poor
400	300	285	225	150	100

PT-24/7 OSS

Introduced in 2007. Available in .45 ACP, .40 S&W and 9mm Parabellum. 12+1 capacity (.45), single-/double-action. Ambidextrous decock and safety, match grade barrel, polymer frame with steel upper. Claimed to exceed all requirements set by United States Special Operations Command. Developed to compete in SOCOM pistol trials. **NOTE:** Add 5 percent for stainless.

NIB	Exc.	V.G.	Good	Fair	Poor
425	345	295	245	175	125

PT-24/7PLS-9SSCTi-17

Compact semi-automatic chambered for 9mm. Capacity 17+1. Single-/double-action. Titanium slide, 3.3" barrel. Weight 25.4 oz. Introduced in 2006.

NIB	Exc.	V.G.	Good	Fair	Poor
425	345	295	245	175	125

PT-24/7PLS

Similar to above, with 5" barrel. Chambered in 9mm Parabellum, .38 Super and .40 S&W.

NIB	Exc.	V.G.	Good	Fair	Poor
425	345	295	245	175	125

2045 Large Frame Pistol

Similar to Taurus Model 24/7, but chambered in .45 ACP only. Features include polymer frame, blued or matte stainless steel slide, 4.2" barrel, ambidextrous "memory pads" to promote safe finger position during loading, ambi three-position safety/decocker. Picatinny rail system, fixed sights. Overall length 7.34". Weight 31.5 oz.

NIB	Exc.	V.G.	Good	Fair	Poor
450	375	325	250	175	125

809-B 9mm

Introduced in 2008. Basically a Model 24/7 OSS, with an exposed hammer. 17+1 capacity, black Tenifer finish.

Ambidextrous Three-Position Safety and Decocker

17+1 Rounds

NIB	Exc.	V.G.	Good	Fair	Poor
550	425	350	275	200	150

800 Series Compact

Compact double-/single-action semi-automatic pistol chambered in 9mm (12+1), .357 SIG (10+1) and .40 cal. (10+1). Features include 3.5" barrel; external hammer; loaded chamber indicator; polymer frame; blued or stainless slide.

NIB	Exc.	V.G.	Good	Fair	Poor
485	410	350	275	200	150

PT191140B

1911-style .40-caliber semi-automatic. Blued steel. 5" barrel, 8+1 capacity. Weight 32 oz. Fixed Heinie two-dot straight-eight sight. Blue or stainless. Introduced in 2006. **NOTE:** Add 10 percent for stainless.

NIB	Exc.	V.G.	Good	Fair	Poor
675	550	425	300	200	125

PT1911

Blued or stainless 1911-style single-action in .45 ACP. 8+1 capacity. LOA 8.5". Weight 32 oz. 5" barrel, fixed Heinie two-dot straight-eight sight. Numerous options. Introduced in 2006. **NOTE:** Add 10 percent for alloy frame and Picatinny rail versions (added 2007); 10 percent for stainless.

NIB	Exc.	V.G.	Good	Fair	Poor
675	550	425	300	200	125

Model 1911B-9

Similar to above, but chambered in 9mm Parabellum (9+1).

NIB	Exc.	V.G.	Good	Fair	Poor
675	550	425	300	200	125

Model 1911B-38

Similar to above, but chambered in .38 Super.

NIB	Exc.	V.G.	Good	Fair	Poor
675	550	425	300	200	125

Model 1911HC

Similar to Taurus Model 1911, with 12+1 capacity; .45 ACP only.

NIB	Exc.	V.G.	Good	Fair	Poor
725	600	475	375	250	150

PT-745GB

Blued semi-automatic in .45 GAP, with 7+1 capacity. 3.25" barrel, fixed sights, weight 22 oz., polymer grip plates. Introduced in 2006.

NIB	Exc.	V.G.	Good	Fair	Poor
375	300	225	175	125	100

PT745B/SS-LS

Blued or stainless semi-automatic in .45 ACP. 4.25" barrel, weight 23.3 oz. 7+1 capacity, polymer grip plates. Introduced in 2006.

NIB	Exc.	V.G.	Good	Fair	Poor
375	300	225	175	125	100

PT917B20

9mm blued or stainless semi-automatic, with 20+1 capacity. Fixed sights, 4" barrel, weight 31.8 oz. Introduced in 2006.

NIB	Exc.	V.G.	Good	Fair	Poor
375	300	225	175	125	100

PT609Ti-13

This 9mm semi-automatic has titanium finish plus 13+1 capacity, 3.25" barrel. Fixed sights, weight 19.2 oz. Introduced in 2006.

NIB	Exc.	V.G.	Good	Fair	Poor
500	425	300	225	150	100

PT138BP12 Millennium Pro

Blued or stainless SA/DA semi-automatic in .380 ACP, with 12+1 capacity. Fixed sights, 3.25" barrel, weight 18.7 oz. Introduced in 2006. Also available in .32 ACP and .40 S&W.

NIB	Exc.	V.G.	Good	Fair	Poor
400	300	285	225	150	100

PT-38B/SS

Chambered for .38 Super cartridge. Fitted with 4.25" barrel, with fixed sights. Grips are checkered rubber. Blued or stainless steel. Magazine capacity 10 rounds. Weight about 30 oz. Introduced in 2004. **NOTE:** Add $15 for stainless steel.

NIB	Exc.	V.G.	Good	Fair	Poor
425	345	295	245	175	125

PT-38SSSPRL

Introduced in 2005. Chambered for .38 Super cartridge. Fitted with 4.25" barrel. Magazine capacity 10 rounds. Finish is stainless steel and gold. Weight about 30 oz. **NOTE:** Deduct $60 for stainless steel only.

NIB	Exc.	V.G.	Good	Fair	Poor
475	400	300	225	150	100

738 TCP Compact Pistol

Lightweight DAO semi-automatic pistol. Chambered for .380 ACP. Features include 3.35" barrel; polymer frame; blued (738B), stainless (738SS) or titanium (738Ti) slide; concealed hammer; low-profile fixed sight; ambi safety; loaded chamber indicator. Capacity 6+1 (standard magazine) or 8+1 (extended magazine). Overall length 5.195". Weight 9 oz. (titanium slide) to 10.2 oz.

NIB	Exc.	V.G.	Good	Fair	Poor
300	275	250	225	150	100

709 "Slim"

Semi-automatic pistol chambered in 9mm Parabellum. Features include streamlined profile, 3.25" barrel, 7+1 capacity, fixed sights, checkered polymer grips, choice of blued (709B) or stainless (709SS) slide. Single-/double-action. Overall length 6.25". Weight 10 oz.

NIB	Exc.	V.G.	Good	Fair	Poor
400	300	285	225	150	100

638 Pro Compact

Caliber .380 ACP, steel slide, polymer frame, 15-round magazine. Barrel length 3.2". Single-action trigger has integral safety. Other features include ambidextrous thumb safety, accessory rail, adjustable rear sight and loaded chamber and cocked striker indicators. Taurus Security System. Weight 28 oz. Blue or matte stainless finish.

NIB	Exc.	V.G.	Good	Fair	Poor
410	350	300	250	200	150

DT Hybrid

Caliber 9mm Parabellum/.40 S&W, steel slide, polymer/steel frame, 3.2" barrel. Magazine capacity 13 rounds, 11 for .40. Single-action trigger has Strike Two capability. Integral trigger safety, manual safety and Taurus Security System. Ambidextrous magazine release, adjustable rear sight and loaded-chamber indicator. Weight 24 oz. Finish blue or matte stainless.

NIB	Exc.	V.G.	Good	Fair	Poor
465	400	350	285	200	150

917

Lightweight compact semi-automatic chambered in 9mm Parabellum. Matte blue or stainless finish, 17+1 or 20+1 capacity. Introduced in 2007.

NIB	Exc.	V.G.	Good	Fair	Poor
400	300	285	225	150	100

PT-945C

Introduced in 1995. This .45 ACP double-action pistol features 4" barrel, with 8-round magazine. Grips are black rubber. Sights are drift adjustable 3-dot combat style. Weight about 30 oz. Offered in blue or stainless steel, with or without ported barrel.

Blue

NOTE: Add $45 for blued finish with gold accents and ported barrel; $35 for ported barrel and blue finish; $40 for ported barrel.

NIB	Exc.	V.G.	Good	Fair	Poor
450	350	250	200	150	100

Stainless Steel

NOTE: Add $40 for ported barrel with stainless steel finish or stainless steel finish with gold accents.

NIB	Exc.	V.G.	Good	Fair	Poor
475	400	300	250	150	100

PT-945S

Same as above, but chambered for .45 Super cartridge. Introduced in 1998.

Blue

NIB	Exc.	V.G.	Good	Fair	Poor
450	350	250	200	150	100

Stainless Steel

NIB	Exc.	V.G.	Good	Fair	Poor
475	375	275	225	150	100

PT-940

Similar to PT-945, except chambered for .40 S&W cartridge. Fitted with a 4" barrel. Magazine capacity 10 rounds. Choice of blue or stainless steel. Black rubber grips. Weight about 28 oz. Introduced in 1997. **NOTE:** Add $20 for stainless steel.

NIB	Exc.	V.G.	Good	Fair	Poor
425	315	265	200	125	75

PT-938

Chambered for .380 ACP cartridge. Fitted with 3" barrel. Black rubber grips. Choice of blue or stainless steel. Weight about 27 oz. Introduced in 1997.

NIB	Exc.	V.G.	Good	Fair	Poor
365	300	245	175	80	50

922 Sport

Introduced in 2003. Semi-automatic .22-caliber pistol features lightweight polymer frame. Single-/double-action trigger. Barrel length 6". Magazine capacity 10 rounds. Adjustable sights. Weight about 25 oz. **NOTE:** Add $15 for matte stainless steel finish.

NIB	Exc.	V.G.	Good	Fair	Poor
310	250	175	150	100	75

PT-22

Semi-automatic double-action-only pistol. Features 2.75" barrel, with fixed sights and manual safety. Chambered for .22 LR cartridge. Magazine capacity 8 rounds. Stocks are Brazilian hardwood. Finish available in blue, blue with gold trim, nickel or two-tone. Weight 12.3 oz. **NOTE:** Add $50 for Special Edition blued steel, with gold fixtures and rosewood grips; $110 for blued steel, with gold fixtures and pearl grips.

NIB	Exc.	V.G.	Good	Fair	Poor
250	175	250	75	60	50

PT-922

.22-caliber pistol has 6" barrel, with fiber optic adjustable sights. Polymer grips. 10-round magazine. Blued finish. Weight about 29 oz. Introduced in 2004.

NIB	Exc.	V.G.	Good	Fair	Poor
365	300	245	175	80	50

PT-25

Similar in appearance to PT-22. Chambered for .25 ACP cartridge. Magazine capacity 9 rounds. Fitted with 2.75" barrel. Offered in blue, blue with gold trim, two-tone finish or nickel. **NOTE:** Add $50 for Special Edition blued steel, with gold fixtures and rosewood grips; $110 for blued steel, with gold fixtures and pearl grips.

NIB	Exc.	V.G.	Good	Fair	Poor
250	175	125	75	60	50

22PLY/25PLY Small Polymer Frame Pistols

Similar to Taurus Models PT-22 and PT-25, with lightweight polymer frame. Features include .22 LR (22PLY, 9+1) or .25 ACP (25PLY, 8+1) chambering, 2.33" tip-up barrel, matte black finish, extended magazine with finger lip manual safety. Overall length 4.8". Weight 10.8 oz.

NIB	Exc.	V.G.	Good	Fair	Poor
225	200	175	—	—	—

Taurus Curve

Unique .380 semi-automatic, designed to fit contours of the body for more confort and security when carry concealed. Magazine capacity 6+1, weight 10.2 oz., barrel length 2.5". Other dimensions: overall length 5.2"; height 3.7"; width 1.18". Introduced in 2015.

NIB	Exc.	V.G.	Good	Fair	Poor
335	300	250	200	175	150

REVOLVERS

Model 17MB2/MSS2

This 8-shot revolver chambered for .17 HMR cartridge. Fitted with 1.75" barrel, with fixed sights. Blued or stainless steel. Hard rubber grips. Weight about 22 oz. Introduced in 2004. **NOTE:** Add $45 for stainless steel.

NIB	Exc.	V.G.	Good	Fair	Poor
360	280	225	175	150	100

Model 73

A .32 S&W Long double-action swing-out cylinder revolver, with 3" barrel and 6-shot cylinder. Blued or nickel plated, with walnut grips.

NIB	Exc.	V.G.	Good	Fair	Poor
250	195	150	125	100	75

Model 80

Full-size 6-round .38 Special. with 3" or 4" heavy tapered barrel. Supplied with fixed sights. Offered with blued or stainless steel (offered new in 1993) finish. Brazilian hardwood grips are standard. Weight 30 oz. **NOTE:** Add $45 for stainless steel

NIB	Exc.	V.G.	Good	Fair	Poor
285	195	135	110	85	700

Model 82

Nearly identical to Model 80. Has 3" or 4" heavy solid rib barrel in place of heavy tapered barrel. Weight 34 oz. **NOTE:** Add $40 for stainless steel.

NIB	Exc.	V.G.	Good	Fair	Poor
285	195	135	110	85	70

Model 82B4

Chambered for .38 Special +P cartridge. Fitted with 4" heavy solid rib barrel. Cylinder holds 6 rounds. Rubber grips. Fixed sights. Blue finish. Weight about 37 oz.

NIB	Exc.	V.G.	Good	Fair	Poor
295	250	200	125	100	75

Model 82SS4

Same as above, with stainless steel finish. Weight about 37 oz.

NIB	Exc.	V.G.	Good	Fair	Poor
315	265	185	125	100	75

Model 827B4

Chambered for .38 Special +P cartridge. Fitted with 4" heavy barrel, with solid rib. Cylinder is 7 shots. Rubber grips. Blued finish. Weight about 37 oz. Fixed sights.

NIB	Exc.	V.G.	Good	Fair	Poor
300	250	200	150	100	75

Model 827SS4

Same as above, with stainless steel finish. Weight about 35 oz.

NIB	Exc.	V.G.	Good	Fair	Poor
350	300	250	175	125	75

Model 83

Similar to Model 82, except for fully adjustable rear sight and Patridge-type front sight. Offered with 4" barrel only, with blued or stainless steel (new for 1993) finish. Weight 34 oz.

NIB	Exc.	V.G.	Good	Fair	Poor
300	250	200	150	100	75

Model 86

Similar to Model 83, with exception of 6" barrel, target hammer, adjustable trigger and blue-only finish. Weight 34 oz.

NIB	Exc.	V.G.	Good	Fair	Poor
325	275	225	175	125	75

Model 85

Double-action revolver chambered for .38 Special. Available in 2" or 3" heavy solid rib barrel fitted with ejector shroud. Sights are fixed. Blued finish and stainless steel (new for 1993) are offered, with Brazilian hardwood grips. Weight 21 oz. with 2" barrel. Beginning in 1996, model was furnished with Uncle Mike's Boot Grips. **NOTE:** Add $50 for Special Edition blued steel, with gold fixtures and rosewood grips; $110 for blued steel, with gold fixtures and pearl grips.

NIB	Exc.	V.G.	Good	Fair	Poor
300	225	175	125	100	75

Model 85 Stainless

As above in stainless steel. Beginning in 1996, furnished with Uncle Mike's Boot Grips.

NIB	Exc.	V.G.	Good	Fair	Poor
350	275	225	200	150	100

Model 85CH

Same as above, but offered in 2" or 3" barrel with shrouded hammer. Double-action-only. **NOTE:** Add $50 for stainless steel; $25 for ported barrel on 2" models.

NIB	Exc.	V.G.	Good	Fair	Poor
300	225	175	125	100	75

Model 85 UL

Double-action revolver built on small aluminum frame. Chambered for .38 Special cartridge. Fitted with 2" barrel. Choice of blue or stainless steel finish. Weight about 17 oz. Introduced in 1997. **NOTE:** Add $50 for

Special Edition blued steel, with gold fixtures and rosewood grips; $110 for blued steel, with gold fixtures and pearl grips; $30 for stainless steel.

NIB	Exc.	V.G.	Good	Fair	Poor
325	250	195	150	125	100

Model 85 Hy-Lite Magnesium

Similar to Model 85. Weight only 13.8 oz. Gray alloy frame and Hy-Lite sights. Introduced in 2007.

NIB	Exc.	V.G.	Good	Fair	Poor
375	300	250	200	175	125

Model 85 Ultra-Lite Gray

Similar to Model 85, with lightweight magnesium frame. Fixed or fiber-optic front sight. Introduced in 2007.

NIB	Exc.	V.G.	Good	Fair	Poor
375	300	250	200	175	125

Model 85 Ultra-Lite Titanium

Similar to Model 85, with titanium cylinder and barrel shroud. Introduced in 2007.

NIB	Exc.	V.G.	Good	Fair	Poor
475	400	275	200	175	125

Model 85 View

Variant of Model 85 series of 5-shot .38-Special revolvers. Sideplate on right side of frame made of clear Lexan polycarbon thermoplastic, showing inner working's of the revolver's mechanism. Rest of frame is aluminum, with silver or pink finish. Cylinder and barrel are of titanium. Introduced in 2014, but sales were poor, production was limited and model was discontinued. It was announced in 2015, that the View would be replaced by Moded 85 "No-View", same design but with a blue aluminum sideplate. Values shown apply to either model.

NIB	Exc.	V.G.	Good	Fair	Poor
500	425	385	—	—	—

Model 850

Chambered for .38 Special cartridge. Fitted with 2" barrel, with fixed sights. Hammerless with 5-round cylinder. Rubber grips. Weight about 23 oz. Choice of blue or stainless steel. **NOTE:** Add $50 for stainless steel.

NIB	Exc.	V.G.	Good	Fair	Poor
375	300	250	200	175	125

Model 850 Ultra-Lite Blue

Similar to Model 850, with lightweight alloy frame. Introduced 2007.

NIB	Exc.	V.G.	Good	Fair	Poor
375	300	250	200	175	125

Model 850 Ultra-Lite Stainless Steel

Similar to Model 850 Ultra-Lite Blue, with stainless finish. Introduced in 2007.

NIB	Exc.	V.G.	Good	Fair	Poor
375	300	250	200	175	125

Model 605

Similar to Model 650, with ultra-lightweight frame. Blue or stainless finish. Weight 23 oz. Introduced in 2007.

NIB	Exc.	V.G.	Good	Fair	Poor
375	300	250	200	175	125

Taurus Polymer Protector

Single-/double-action revolver chambered in .38 Special +P. Features include 5-round cylinder; polymer frame; faux wood rubber-feel grips; fixed sights; shrouded hammer with cocking spur; blued finish; 2.5" barrel. Weight 18.2 oz.

NIB	Exc.	V.G.	Good	Fair	Poor
380	320	275	230	200	150

Model 650

Same as Model 850, but chambered for .357 Magnum cartridge. **NOTE:** Add $50 for stainless steel.

NIB	Exc.	V.G.	Good	Fair	Poor
375	300	250	200	175	125

Taurus 405 Revolver

Chambered for .40 S&W, with steel cylinder, alloy frame, 5-round capacity, 2" barrel. Taurus Security System and Ribber (ribbed) grips. Weight 29 oz. Blue or matte stainless finish. Available in .44 Special as Model 445, with weight of 22 oz. **NOTE:** Add 15 percent for stainless finish.

NIB	Exc.	V.G.	Good	Fair	Poor
385	325	275	235	200	150

Model 851 and 651 Revolvers

Small-frame SA/DA revolvers similar to Taurus Model 85, with Centennial-style concealed-hammer frame. Chambered in .38 Special +P (Model 851) or .357 Magnum (Model 651). Features include five-shot cylinder; 2" barrel; fixed sights; blue, matte blue, titanium or stainless finish; Taurus security lock. Overall length 6.5". Weight 15.5 oz. (titanium) to 25 oz. (blued and stainless).

NIB	Exc.	V.G.	Good	Fair	Poor
400	300	285	225	150	100

Model 94

Double-action revolver chambered for .22 LR cartridge. Swing-out cylinder holds 9 rounds. Available with heavy solid rib, 3" or 4" barrel. In 1996, a 5" barrel option was added in both blue and stainless steel. Ramp front sight with fully adjustable rear. Offered in blued or stainless steel, with Brazilian hardwood grips. Weight 25 oz. with 4" barrel.

Blue

NIB	Exc.	V.G.	Good	Fair	Poor
350	275	225	200	150	100

Stainless Steel

NIB	Exc.	V.G.	Good	Fair	Poor
375	300	250	225	175	125

Model 94 UL

Introduced in 1997. Built on small aluminum frame, with 2" barrel. Chambered for .22 LR cartridge. Choice of blue or stainless steel. Weight about 14 oz.

NIB	Exc.	V.G.	Good	Fair	Poor
400	300	285	225	150	100

Model 941

Similar in appearance to Model 94. This version chambered for .22 WMR. Available with choice of 3" or 4" heavy solid rib barrel. In 1996, a 5" barrel option was added that holds 8 rounds. Ramp front sight, with fully adjustable rear. Available in blued or stainless steel. Brazilian hardwood grips. Weight 27.5 oz.

Blue

NIB	Exc.	V.G.	Good	Fair	Poor
350	250	175	125	100	75

Stainless Steel

NIB	Exc.	V.G.	Good	Fair	Poor
375	275	200	150	100	75

Model 941 UL

Same as standard Model 941, with aluminum frame and 2" barrel. Weight about 18 oz. Introduced in 1997.

NIB	Exc.	V.G.	Good	Fair	Poor
400	300	285	225	150	100

Model 96

Full-size .22 LR revolver, with 6" heavy solid rib barrel. Fully adjustable rear sight, with target hammer and adjustable target trigger. Cylinder holds 6 rounds. Available in blued only, with Brazilian hardwood grips. Weight 34 oz.

NIB	Exc.	V.G.	Good	Fair	Poor
300	250	200	150	125	100

Model 741

Double-action revolver chambered for .32 H&R Magnum cartridge. Features 3" or 4" heavy solid rib barrel, with fully adjustable rear sight. Swing-out cylinder holds 6 rounds. Available in blued or stainless steel (introduced in 1993), with Brazilian hardwood grips. Weight 30 oz. **NOTE:** Add $40 for stainless steel.

NIB	Exc.	V.G.	Good	Fair	Poor
200	175	150	125	100	75

Model 761

Similar to Model 741. This version has 6" barrel, target hammer and adjustable target trigger. Available blued only. Weight 34 oz.

NIB	Exc.	V.G.	Good	Fair	Poor
350	250	175	125	100	75

Model 65

Double-action revolver chambered for .357 Magnum cartridge. Offered with 2.5" (introduced in 1993) or 4" heavy solid rib barrel, with ejector shroud. Fitted with fixed sights. Brazilian hardwood grips. Available blued or stainless steel. Weight 34 oz. with 4" barrel. **NOTE:** Add $40 for stainless steel.

NIB	Exc.	V.G.	Good	Fair	Poor
325	225	150	125	100	75

Model 605

Introduced in 1995. Revolver chambered for .357 Magnum cartridge. Fitted with 2.25" or 3" heavy barrel. Offered in blue or stainless steel. Weight 25 oz.

Blue

NIB	Exc.	V.G.	Good	Fair	Poor
325	225	150	125	100	75

Stainless Steel

NIB	Exc.	V.G.	Good	Fair	Poor
375	275	200	150	100	75

Model 605 Custom (B2C)

Same as above. Offered with 2.25" compensated barrel.

Blue

NIB	Exc.	V.G.	Good	Fair	Poor
400	300	285	225	150	100

Stainless Steel

NIB	Exc.	V.G.	Good	Fair	Poor
450	350	300	250	150	100

Model 605CHB2/SS2

Chambered for .357 Magnum cartridge. Fitted with 2.25" solid rib barrel and 5-shot cylinder. Offered with concealed hammer. Weight about 24 oz.

Blue

NIB	Exc.	V.G.	Good	Fair	Poor
350	250	175	125	100	75

Stainless Steel

NIB	Exc.	V.G.	Good	Fair	Poor
375	275	200	150	100	75

Model 605CHB2C/SS2C

Same as above, with concealed hammer and ported barrels.

Blue

NIB	Exc.	V.G.	Good	Fair	Poor
350	250	175	125	100	75

Stainless Steel

NIB	Exc.	V.G.	Good	Fair	Poor
375	275	200	150	100	75

Model 66

Similar to Model 65. Offered with 2.5", 4" or 6" barrel, with fully adjustable rear sight. Blued or stainless steel. Weight 35 oz. with 4" barrel. The 2.5" barrel introduced in 1993.

NIB	Exc.	V.G.	Good	Fair	Poor
225	200	175	150	125	100

Model 66CP

Similar to Model 66. Features compensated heavy solid rib 4" or 6" ejector shroud barrel. Introduced in 1993. Weight 35 oz.

NIB	Exc.	V.G.	Good	Fair	Poor
250	225	200	150	125	100

Model 66B4/SS4

Chambered for .357 Magnum cartridge, with 4" solid rib barrel and 7-shot cylinder. Adjustable sights. Rubber grips. Weight about 38 oz.

Blue

NIB	Exc.	V.G.	Good	Fair	Poor
350	275	225	150	125	100

Stainless Steel

NIB	Exc.	V.G.	Good	Fair	Poor
400	325	275	225	150	100

Model 607

Introduced in 1995. This .357 Magnum features 4" or 6.5" integral compensated barrel in blue or stainless steel. The 6.5" barrel fitted with a ventilated rib.

Blue

NIB	Exc.	V.G.	Good	Fair	Poor
325	275	225	200	150	100

Stainless Steel

NIB	Exc.	V.G.	Good	Fair	Poor
400	350	300	200	150	100

Model 606

Introduced in 1997. This 6-round model chambered for .357 Magnum cartridge. Fitted with 2" solid rib barrel, with ramp front sight and notched rear. Available in double-/single-action or double-action-only. Offered in blue or stainless steel. Rubber grips are standard. Weight about 29 oz. A number of variations offered on this model. **NOTE:** Add $50 for stainless steel.

NIB	Exc.	V.G.	Good	Fair	Poor
375	275	200	150	100	75

Model 608

Introduced in 1996. Revolver chambered for .357 Magnum cartridge. Cylinder bored for 8 rounds. Offered in 4" and 6.5" barrel lengths, with integral compensator. Front sight serrated ramp, with red insert and rear is adjustable. Offered in both blued and stainless steel versions. Weight about 51.5 oz. with 6.5" barrel.

Blue

NIB	Exc.	V.G.	Good	Fair	Poor
425	325	250	200	150	100

Stainless Steel

NIB	Exc.	V.G.	Good	Fair	Poor
450	350	300	200	150	100

Model 689

Chambered for .357 Magnum cartridge. Features heavy ventilated rib barrel in 4" or 6" lengths. Fully adjustable rear sight is standard. Offered in blued or stainless steel. Weight 37 oz. In 1998, fitted with 7-round cylinder.

NIB	Exc.	V.G.	Good	Fair	Poor
375	275	200	150	100	75

Model 617

Chambered for .357 Magnum cartridge, with 7-round cylinder. Fitted with 2" barrel. Choice of blue or stainless steel finish. Some variations offered a ported barrel. Introduced in 1998.

Blue

NIB	Exc.	V.G.	Good	Fair	Poor
400	325	275	225	175	125

Stainless Steel

NIB	Exc.	V.G.	Good	Fair	Poor
400	325	275	225	175	125

Ported Barrel

NIB	Exc.	V.G.	Good	Fair	Poor
425	325	250	200	150	100

Model 617 CHB2/SS2

Chambered for .357 Magnum cartridge. Features concealed hammer, 2" solid rib barrel and fixed sights.

Blue

NIB	Exc.	V.G.	Good	Fair	Poor
350	275	225	175	125	100

Stainless Steel

NIB	Exc.	V.G.	Good	Fair	Poor
425	325	250	200	150	100

Model 627 Tracker

Chambered for .357 Magnum cartridge. Has 7-round cylinder. The 4" barrel is ported, with heavy underlug. Adjustable rear sight. Matte stainless steel finish. Introduced in 2000.

NIB	Exc.	V.G.	Good	Fair	Poor
450	325	275	225	175	125

Model 669

Chambered for .357 Magnum cartridge. Features 4" or 6" heavy solid rib barrel, with full shroud. Fully adjustable rear sight. Available with blued or stainless steel finish. Brazilian hardwood grips are standard. Weight 37 oz. with 4" barrel. **NOTE:** Add $60 for stainless steel.

NIB	Exc.	V.G.	Good	Fair	Poor
375	275	200	150	100	75

Model 669CP

Variation of Model 669 was introduced in 1993. Features 4" or 6" compensated barrel. Fully adjustable rear sights are standard. Offered with blue or stainless steel finish. Weight 37 oz. In 1998, fitted with 7-round cylinder. **NOTE:** Add $60 for stainless steel.

NIB	Exc.	V.G.	Good	Fair	Poor
425	325	250	200	150	100

Model 415

Chambered for .41 Magnum cartridge. Fitted with 2.5" ported barrel. Fixed sights. Rubber grips. Matte stainless steel finish. Weight about 30 oz.

NIB	Exc.	V.G.	Good	Fair	Poor
450	350	300	200	150	100

Model 431

Chambered for .44 Special cartridge. This double-action revolver furnished with 3" or 4" heavy solid rib barrel, with ejector shroud. Cylinder capacity 5 rounds. Fixed sights are standard. Choice of blued or stainless steel finish. Weight 35 oz. **NOTE:** Add $60 for stainless steel.

NIB	Exc.	V.G.	Good	Fair	Poor
450	350	300	200	150	100

Model 817 (Ultra-Lite)

Chambered for .357 Magnum cartridge. Fitted with 7-shot cylinder and 2" solid rib barrel. Features an alloy frame. Stainless steel or blued finish. Some models are ported. Weight about 21 oz. **NOTE:** Add $20 for ported barrels.

Blue

NIB	Exc.	V.G.	Good	Fair	Poor
350	275	225	175	125	100

Stainless Steel

NIB	Exc.	V.G.	Good	Fair	Poor
390	325	275	225	175	100

Model 441

Similar to Model 431. Furnished with 3" or 4" plus 6" barrel. Comes standard with fully adjustable rear sight. Cylinder capacity 5 rounds. Blued or stainless steel finish. Weight 40.25 oz. with 6" barrel. **NOTE:** Add $60 for stainless steel.

NIB	Exc.	V.G.	Good	Fair	Poor
395	300	240	150	125	100

Model 444 Multi

Features 4" barrel, with adjustable sights. Chambered for .44 Magnum cartridge. Cylinder holds 6 rounds. Frame is alloy, with titanium cylinder. Grips have cushion inset. Weight about 28 oz. Introduced in 2004.

NIB	Exc.	V.G.	Good	Fair	Poor
575	475	375	300	275	200

Model 905I-B1/SS1

Introduced in 2003. Revolver chambered for 9mm pistol cartridge. Barrel length 2". Cylinder capacity 5 rounds. Weight about 21 oz. Blue or stainless steel finish. **NOTE:** Add $45 for matte stainless steel finish.

NIB	Exc.	V.G.	Good	Fair	Poor
385	325	250	175	100	75

Model 951SH2

Chambered for 9mm cartridge. Fitted with 2" barrel, with adjustable sights. Cylinder holds 5 rounds. Titanium frame and finish. Rubber grips. Weight about 16 oz.

NIB	Exc.	V.G.	Good	Fair	Poor
475	350	265	200	150	100

Model 907SH2

9mm revolver has 7-shot cylinder, 2" barrel, with fixed sights and rubber grips. Titanium frame and finish. Weight about 17 oz. Introduced in 2004.

NIB	Exc.	V.G.	Good	Fair	Poor
475	350	265	200	150	100

Model 907B2/SS2

Chambered for 9mm cartridge. Fitted with 2" barrel, with fixed sights. Rubber grips. Ultra light alloy frame in blue or stainless steel. Weight about 18.5 oz. Introduced in 2004. **NOTE:** Add $45 for stainless steel.

NIB	Exc.	V.G.	Good	Fair	Poor
390	300	250	200	150	100

RAGING BULL SERIES

Model 218 Raging Bee

Introduced in 2002. Chambered for .218 Bee cartridge. Fitted with 10" ventilated rib barrel, with adjustable sights. Cylinder holds 8 rounds. Matte stainless steel finish.

NIB	Exc.	V.G.	Good	Fair	Poor
900	775	600	475	350	200

Model 22H Raging Hornet

Chambered for .22 Hornet cartridge. Has 10" barrel, with base mount and adjustable sights. Matte stainless steel finish. Cylinder holds 8 rounds. Rubber grips.

NIB	Exc.	V.G.	Good	Fair	Poor
750	675	550	400	300	200

Model 30C Raging Thirty

Chambered for .30 Carbine cartridge. Fitted with 10" ventilated rib barrel, with adjustable sights. Cylinder holds 8 rounds. Supplied with full moon clips. Matte stainless steel finish. Introduced in 2002.

NIB	Exc.	V.G.	Good	Fair	Poor
750	675	550	400	300	200

Model 416 Raging Bull

Model has 6.5" ventilated rib ported barrel, with adjustable sights. Chambered for .41 Magnum cartridge. Matte stainless steel finish. Introduced in 2002. Cylinder holds 6 rounds.

NIB	Exc.	V.G.	Good	Fair	Poor
625	500	400	300	225	100

Model 454 Raging Bull

Chambered for .454 Casull. Built on a large frame, with 5-round capacity. Barrel lengths 5", 6.5" or 8.375"; fitted with ventilated rib and integral compensator. Sights are adjustable. Finish blue or stainless steel. Black rubber or walnut grips. Weight 53 oz. with 6.5" barrel.

Blue

NIB	Exc.	V.G.	Good	Fair	Poor
700	650	575	450	325	175

Stainless Steel

NIB	Exc.	V.G.	Good	Fair	Poor
750	675	550	400	300	200

Black Stainless Steel

NIB	Exc.	V.G.	Good	Fair	Poor
750	675	550	400	300	200

Model 500 Magnum Raging Bull

Introduced in 2004. Chambered for .500 Magnum cartridge. Ventilated barrel length 10", with adjustable sights. Cushion inset grips. Stainless steel finish. Weight about 72 oz.

NIB	Exc.	V.G.	Good	Fair	Poor
900	775	600	475	350	200

Model 500MSS2 Raging Bull

Stainless .500 S&W Magnum, with 5-shot capacity, 2.25" barrel, soft rubber grips. Weight 68 oz. Adjustable rear sight, single-/double-action. Introduced in 2006.

NIB	Exc.	V.G.	Good	Fair	Poor
900	775	600	475	350	200

Model 44/444

Introduced in 1994. Heavy frame revolver chambered for .44 Magnum cartridge. Choice of three barrel lengths: 4" with solid rib; 6.5" and 8.375" with ventilated rib. All Model 44s have a built in compensator. Front sight is a serrated ramp, with adjustable rear. Blued or stainless finish. Weight 53 oz. for 6.5" barrel.

Blue

NIB	Exc.	V.G.	Good	Fair	Poor
—	425	300	200	150	100

Stainless Steel

NIB	Exc.	V.G.	Good	Fair	Poor
600	475	375	250	200	125

TRACKER SERIES

Model 17

Introduced in 2002. Features 6.5" or 12" ventilated rib barrel. Chambered for .17 HMR cartridge. Adjustable sights. Matte stainless steel finish. Cylinder holds 7 rounds. Weight about: 41 oz. for 6.5"; 50 oz. for 12".

NIB	Exc.	V.G.	Good	Fair	Poor
375	300	225	175	125	100

Model 970

Chambered for .22 LR cartridge. Fitted with 6.5" ventilated rib heavy barrel, with adjustable sights. Matte stainless steel finish. Rubber grips. Cylinder holds 7 rounds. Introduced in 2002.

NIB	Exc.	V.G.	Good	Fair	Poor
300	200	165	125	100	75

Model 971

Same as Model 970, but chambered for .22 Magnum cartridge. Introduced in 2002.

NIB	Exc.	V.G.	Good	Fair	Poor
300	200	165	125	100	75

Tracker .22/.22 Mag.

Same as Model 971, except chambered for .22 LR, with interchangeable .22 WMR cylinder. Both cylinders hold 9 rounds. Weight: 38 to 44 oz., with 4.5" or 6" barrel. Blue or matte stainless finish. **NOTE:** Add 10 percent for stainless.

NIB	Exc.	V.G.	Good	Fair	Poor
465	400	350	285	200	150

Model 425 Tracker

Chambered for .41 Magnum cartridge. Features 4" heavy underlug ported barrel. Adjustable rear sight. Cylinder chambered for 5 rounds. Matte stainless steel finish. Introduced in 2000.

NIB	Exc.	V.G.	Good	Fair	Poor
425	325	250	200	150	100

Model 44 Tracker

.44 Magnum revolver has 4" barrel, with adjustable sights and Ribber (ribbed) grips. 5-shot cylinder. Stainless steel finish. Weight about 34 oz. Introduced in 2004.

NIB	Exc.	V.G.	Good	Fair	Poor
425	325	250	200	150	100

Tracker .45

Similar to other Tracker models, but chambered in .45 ACP (via full-moon clips), with 5-shot cylinder. 4" barrel, with Picatinny rail. Stainless steel frame and cylinder. Introduced in 2007.

NIB	Exc.	V.G.	Good	Fair	Poor
450	350	275	225	175	125

Model 445

Small frame revolver chambered for .44 Special cartridge. Fitted with 2" barrel, with ramp front sight and notched rear. Cylinder holds 5 rounds. Black rubber grips. Offered in blue or stainless steel. Weight about 28 oz. Factory barrel porting, add $20, is optional. Introduced in 1997. **NOTE:** Add $50 for stainless steel.

NIB	Exc.	V.G.	Good	Fair	Poor
425	325	250	200	150	100

Model 450

Chambered for .45 Long Colt cartridge. Features 2" heavy solid rib barrel, with 5-shot cylinder and fixed sights. Ported barrel. Rubber grips. Stainless steel finish. Weight about 28 oz. **NOTE:** Add $30 for Ultra Lite model.

NIB	Exc.	V.G.	Good	Fair	Poor
450	350	275	225	175	125

Model 455

Introduced in 2002. Chambered for .45 ACP cartridge. Choice of 2", 4" or 6.5" barrels. Adjustable sights on 4" and 6.5" barrels. Matte stainless steel finish. Rubber grips. Supplied with full moon clips.

NIB	Exc.	V.G.	Good	Fair	Poor
450	350	275	225	175	125

Model 460

Chambered for .45 Long Colt cartridge. Fitted with 4" or 6.5" ventilated rib barrel, with adjustable sights. Matte stainless steel finish. Introduced in 2002.

NIB	Exc.	V.G.	Good	Fair	Poor
450	350	275	225	175	125

Model 45

Chambered for .45 Long Colt. Fitted with choice of 6.5" or 8.375" heavy ventilated rib barrels. Cylinder holds 6 rounds. Rubber grips, ported barrels and adjustable sights are standard. Weight about 53 oz. with 6.5" barrel.

Blue

NIB	Exc.	V.G.	Good	Fair	Poor
450	350	275	225	175	125

Stainless Steel

NIB	Exc.	V.G.	Good	Fair	Poor
—	375	300	225	200	125

Model 627

Chambered for .357 Magnum cartridge. Fitted with 4" ported or 6.5" ventilated rib ported barrel, with adjustable sights. Rubber grips. Matte stainless steel finish. Introduced in 2002. **NOTE:** Add $200 for titanium model.

NIB	Exc.	V.G.	Good	Fair	Poor
425	350	275	225	150	100

Tracker 10mm 10TSS4

Matte stainless 10mm, with 4" barrel and fixed sights. Five-shot, rubber grip. Weight 34.8 oz. Introduced in 2006.

NIB	Exc.	V.G.	Good	Fair	Poor
500	400	295	250	175	125

Tracker 10SS8

10mm 6-shot matte stainless, with 6.5" (54.5 oz.) or 8.375" (59.5 oz.) barrel. Fixed sights, rubber grips. Introduced in 2006.

NIB	Exc.	V.G.	Good	Fair	Poor
500	400	295	250	175	125

Tracker 4510TKR

Shoots 2.5" .410 bore shells or .45 Colt. Holds 5 shots. Stainless or blued, 2.25" or 6.5" barrel, rubber grip. Single-/double-action, 9.1" LOA. Weight 32 oz. Introduced in 2006.

NIB	Exc.	V.G.	Good	Fair	Poor
500	400	295	250	175	125

Tracker 590 5mm

Double-action 9-shot stainless steel revolver. Chambered in 5mm Rem. Magnum Rimfire. Introduced in 2008. Discontinued 2011.

NIB	Exc.	V.G.	Good	Fair	Poor
400	350	300	225	200	150

JUDGE SERIES

Judge

Stainless steel or lightweight alloy-frame version of Tracker Model 4410. Chambered in 3" .410/.45 Colt (4510TKR-3MAG) or 2.5" .410/.45 Colt (4510TKR-3UL) with 3" (3" Magnum) or 2.5" barrel (2.5"). Introduced in 2007.

MAGNUM Stopping-Power
Fires both .410 GA 3-inch Magnum or 2.5-inch Shotshells and .45 Colt Ammunition

NIB	Exc.	V.G.	Good	Fair	Poor
525	425	300	265	195	150

Model 4510TKR-SSR

Similar to Judge, with ported barrel and tactical rail.

NIB	Exc.	V.G.	Good	Fair	Poor
600	525	425	300	265	175

Judge Public Defender Polymer

Single-/double-action revolver chambered in .45 Colt/.410. Features include 5-round cylinder; polymer frame; Ribber rubber-feel grips; fiber-optic front sight; adjustable rear sight; blued or stainless cylinder; shrouded hammer with cocking spur; blued finish; 2.5" barrel. Weight 27 oz.

NIB	Exc.	V.G.	Good	Fair	Poor
550	450	375	300	250	150

Judge Public Defender Ultra-Lite

Single-/double-action revolver chambered in .45 Colt/.410. Features include 5-round cylinder; lightweight aluminum frame; Ribber rubber-feel grips; fiber-optic front sight; adjustable rear sight; blued or stainless cylinder; shrouded hammer with cocking spur; blued finish; 2.5" barrel. Weight 20.7 oz.

NIB	Exc.	V.G.	Good	Fair	Poor
600	500	425	325	250	150

Raging Judge Magnum

Single-/double-action revolver chambered for .454 Casull, .45 Colt, 2.5" and 3" .410. Features include 3" or 6" barrel; fixed sights with fiber-optic front; blued or stainless steel finish; ventilated rib for scope mounting (6" only); cushioned Raging Bull grips.

NIB	Exc.	V.G.	Good	Fair	Poor
825	700	550	400	350	200

Raging Judge Magnum Ultra-Lite

Single-/double-action revolver chambered for .454 Casull, .45 Colt, 2.5" and 3" .410. Features include 3" or 6" barrel; aluminum alloy frame; fixed sights with fiber-optic front; blued or stainless steel finish; cushioned Raging Bull grips. Weight: 41.4 oz. (3" barrel).

NIB	Exc.	V.G.	Good	Fair	Poor
875	725	575	425	350	200

NIB	Exc.	V.G.	Good	Fair	Poor
900	775	600	475	350	200

SILHOUETTE SERIES

Model 17-12

Chambered for .17 HMR cartridge. Fitted with 12" ventilated rib silhouette barrel. Adjustable sights. Cylinder holds 7 rounds. Matte stainless steel finish. Introduced in 2002.

NIB	Exc.	V.G.	Good	Fair	Poor
700	600	475	350	200	150

Model 66

Chambered for .357 Magnum cartridge. Fitted with 12" barrel, with adjustable sights. Choice of blue or stainless steel finish. Rubber grips. Introduced in 2002. **NOTE:** Add $60 for stainless steel.

NIB	Exc.	V.G.	Good	Fair	Poor
525	425	300	265	195	150

Model 980

Chambered for .22 LR cartridge. Fitted with 12" target barrel, with adjustable sights. Cylinder holds 7 rounds. Matted stainless steel finish. Rubber grips. Introduced in 2002.

NIB	Exc.	V.G.	Good	Fair	Poor
375	350	300	250	200	150

Model 981

Same as Model 980, but chambered for .22 Magnum cartridge.

NIB	Exc.	V.G.	Good	Fair	Poor
375	350	300	250	200	150

Model 217

Chambered for .218 Bee cartridge. Fitted with 12" ventilated rib barrel, with adjustable sights. Cylinder holds 7 rounds. Matte stainless steel finish. Introduced in 2002.

TITANIUM SERIES

Introduced in 1999. This series of revolvers features titanium barrels, with stainless steel bore liners, titanium frames and cylinders. Hammers, triggers, latches, ejector rod and other small parts are made from case-hardened chrome moly steel. All Taurus Titanium revolvers have factory porting and rated for +P ammunition. Rubber grips are standard. Three different finishes are offered: Bright Spectrum blue, Matte Spectrum blue and Matte Spectrum gold.

Model 85Ti

Chambered for .38 Special. Fitted with 2" barrel, with 5-shot cylinder. Fixed sights.

NIB	Exc.	V.G.	Good	Fair	Poor
525	425	300	200	150	100

Model 731Ti

Chambered for .32 H&R Magnum. Fitted with 2" barrel, with 6-shot cylinder. Fixed sights.

NIB	Exc.	V.G.	Good	Fair	Poor
525	425	300	200	150	100

Model 617Ti

Chambered for .357 Magnum. Fitted with 2" barrel and 7-shot cylinder. Fixed sights. Weight about 20 oz.

NIB	Exc.	V.G.	Good	Fair	Poor
600	525	425	300	265	175

Model 627Ti

Features 7-round cylinder chambered for .357 Magnum cartridge. Fitted with ported 4" barrel, with adjustable sights. Gray finish. Weight about 28 oz. depending on barrel length.

NIB	Exc.	V.G.	Good	Fair	Poor
700	600	475	350	200	150

Model 415Ti

Chambered for .41 Magnum. Fitted with 2.5" barrel, with 5-shot cylinder. Fixed sights. Weight about 21 oz.

NIB	Exc.	V.G.	Good	Fair	Poor
600	475	350	250	150	125

Model 425Ti

Chambered for .41 Magnum cartridge. Has a 5-round cylinder, ported 4" barrel, with adjustable rear sight. Gray finish. Introduced in 2000.

NIB	Exc.	V.G.	Good	Fair	Poor
600	475	350	250	150	125

Model 450Ti

Chambered for .45 Long Colt. Fitted with 2" barrel, with 5-shot cylinder. Fixed sights. Weight about 19 oz.

NIB	Exc.	V.G.	Good	Fair	Poor
600	475	350	250	150	125

Model 445Ti

Chambered for .44 Special. Fitted with 2" barrel, with 5-shot cylinder. Fixed sights. Weight about 20 oz.

NIB	Exc.	V.G.	Good	Fair	Poor
600	475	350	250	150	125

Model UL/Ti

Chambered for .38 Special. Has Titanium cylinder and alloy frame. Fitted with 2" unported barrel. Cylinder is 5 shot. Fixed sights.

NIB	Exc.	V.G.	Good	Fair	Poor
525	425	300	200	150	100

GAUCHO SERIES

S/A-45, B/S/SM

Chambered for .45 Colt cartridge. Fitted with 5.5" barrel, with fixed sights. Checkered wood grips. Blued or stainless steel finish. Weight about 37 oz. Introduced in 2004. Discontinued. **NOTE:** Add $15 for stainless steel.

NIB	Exc.	V.G.	Good	Fair	Poor
400	325	275	225	175	125

S/A-45, S/S/CH

Chambered for .45 Colt cartridge. Fitted with 5.5" barrel, with fixed sights. Choice of Sundance stainless steel finish or case-hardened blued finish. Weight about 37 oz. Introduced in 2004. Discontinued.

NIB	Exc.	V.G.	Good	Fair	Poor
400	325	275	225	175	125

S/A-357-B, S/SM, S/S, CHSA

Single-action 6-shot chambered for .357/.38-caliber. Barrel lengths 4.75" (36.2 oz.), 5.5" (36.7 oz.), 7.5" (37.7 oz.). Fixed sights. Blued matte stainless, polished stainless or blued/case-hardened receiver. Introduced in 2006. Discontinued. **NOTE:** Add $15 for stainless steel.

NIB	Exc.	V.G.	Good	Fair	Poor
400	325	275	225	175	125

S/A-44-40-B, S/SM, S/S, CHSA

Single-action 6-shot chambered for .44-40 caliber. Barrel lengths 4.75" (36.2 oz.), 5.5" (36.7 oz.), 7.5" (37.7 oz.). Fixed sights. Blued matte stainless, polished stainless or blued/case-hardened receiver. Introduced in 2006. Discontinued.

NIB	Exc.	V.G.	Good	Fair	Poor
450	375	300	225	175	125

S/A-45-B12, S/SM12, S/S12, CHSA12

Single-action Buntline-style 6-shot revolver chambered for .45 Colt. Barrel length 12" (41.5 oz.). Fixed sights. Blued matte stainless, polished stainless or blued/case-hardened receiver. Introduced in 2006. Discontinued. **NOTE:** Add $15 for stainless steel.

NIB	Exc.	V.G.	Good	Fair	Poor
450	375	300	250	195	100

RIFLES

Model 62

Introduced in 2000. Replica of Winchester Model 62 .22-caliber rifle. Fitted with 23" barrel and adjustable rear sight. Magazine capacity 13 rounds. Weight about 5 lbs. Hardwood stock. In 2003, offered in .22 WMR and .17 HMR calibers. Discontinued. **NOTE:** Add 15 percent for stainless.

NIB	Exc.	V.G.	Good	Fair	Poor
350	300	225	175	125	75

Model 62 Carbine

Same as above, with 16.5" barrel. Magazine capacity 12 rounds. Weight about 4.5 lbs. Introduced in 2000. In 2003, offered in .22 WMR and .17 HMR calibers. Discontinued. **NOTE:** Add 10 percent for stainless.

NIB	Exc.	V.G.	Good	Fair	Poor
350	300	225	175	125	75

Model 62 Upstart

Similar to Model 62 above, with shorter buttstock. Introduced in 2002. Discontinued.

NIB	Exc.	V.G.	Good	Fair	Poor
350	300	225	175	125	75

Model 72

Same as Model 62, but chambered for .22 Magnum cartridge. Discontinued. **NOTE:** Add $15 for stainless steel.

NIB	Exc.	V.G.	Good	Fair	Poor
350	300	225	175	125	75

Model 72 Carbine

Same as Model 62 Carbine, but chambered for .22 Magnum cartridge. Discontinued. **NOTE:** Add $15 for stainless steel.

NIB	Exc.	V.G.	Good	Fair	Poor
350	300	225	175	125	75

Model 63

Copy of Winchester Model 63 in takedown. Chambered for .22 LR cartridge. Fitted with 23" round barrel, with adjustable rear sight. Offered in blue or stainless steel. Introduced in 2002. In 2003, offered chambered for .17 HMR and .22 WMR. Discontinued.

NIB	Exc.	V.G.	Good	Fair	Poor
300	245	200	150	100	75

Model 62LAR Lever Rifle

Lever-action rifle chambered in .22 LR. 23" blued barrel, walnut-finish hardwood stock. Introduced 2006. Discontinued.

NIB	Exc.	V.G.	Good	Fair	Poor
300	250	200	150	125	100

Model 62LAR-SS

Similar to Model 62LAR in stainless steel. Introduced 2006. Discontinued.

NIB	Exc.	V.G.	Good	Fair	Poor
350	300	225	175	150	125

Thunderbolt

Slide-action rifle a knockoff of Colt Lightning rifle. Chambered for .45 Colt cartridge and .38/.357 Magnum. Fitted with 26" barrel, with adjustable sights. Blued or stainless steel finish. Stocks are hardwood. Weight about 8.125 lbs. Introduced in 2004. Discontinued. **NOTE:** Add $50 for stainless steel or bright "Sundance" stainless finish.

NIB	Exc.	V.G.	Good	Fair	Poor
550	450	325	250	175	150

CT9G2

Semi-automatic carbine, with hybrid aluminum/polymer construction. Reinforced steel frame. Lower receiver made with high-strength polymer reinforced with steel. Upper receiver has flat top Picatinny rail. Two-position safety lever. Adjustable rear sight, fixed front. Ambidextrous slide catch. Available in 9mm, .40 S&W, .45 ACP. Taurus Security System installed. Introduced in 2011. Discontinued.

NIB	Exc.	V.G.	Good	Fair	Poor
700	600	500	—	—	—

TAYLOR, L.B.
Chicopee, Massachusetts

Pocket Pistol

A .32-caliber spur trigger single-shot pocket pistol, with 3.5" octagonal barrel marked "L. B. Taylor & Co. Chicopee Mass.". Silver-plated brass frame, blued barrel and walnut grips. Manufactured during late 1860s and early 1870s.

NIB	Exc.	V.G.	Good	Fair	Poor
—	—	1150	875	385	100

TAYLOR'S & CO., INC.
Winchester, Virginia

HANDGUNS

Napoleon Le Page Pistol (Model 551)

Percussion French-style duelling pistol. Chambered for .45-caliber. Fitted with 10" octagon barrel. Walnut stock, silver plated buttcap and trigger guard. Double-set triggers. Made by Uberti.

NIB	Exc.	V.G.	Good	Fair	Poor
450	375	300	250	200	100

Kentucky Pistol (Model 550)

Chambered for .45-caliber ball. Fitted with 10" barrel. Bird's-head grip, with brass ramrod thimbles and case-hardened sidelock. Made by Uberti.

NIB	Exc.	V.G.	Good	Fair	Poor
295	225	200	125	85	60

Colt Model 1847 Walker (Model 500A)

Fitted with 9" round barrel. Chambered for .44-caliber. Has 6-round engraved cylinder. Steel frame and backstrap. Brass trigger guard. One-piece walnut grips. Made by Uberti.

NIB	Exc.	V.G.	Good	Fair	Poor
400	325	275	250	200	100

Colt Model 1851 Navy

Offered with brass or steel frame. Brass backstrap and trigger guard. Chambered for .36-caliber. Fitted with 7.5" barrel. Cylinder holds 6 rounds. One-piece walnut grip. Brass frame model made by Armi San Marco; steel frame by F.LLI Pietta.

Brass Frame (Model 210)

NIB	Exc.	V.G.	Good	Fair	Poor
295	225	200	125	85	60

Steel Frame (Model 245)

NIB	Exc.	V.G.	Good	Fair	Poor
350	250	200	150	100	75

Remington Model 1858

A .44-caliber brass or steel frame. Brass trigger guard model, with 8" octagon barrel. Cylinder holds 6 rounds. Two-piece walnut grips. Brass frame made by F. LLI Pietta; steel frame by Armi San Marco.

Brass Frame (Model 410)

NIB	Exc.	V.G.	Good	Fair	Poor
295	225	200	125	85	60

Steel Frame (Model 430)

NIB	Exc.	V.G.	Good	Fair	Poor
350	250	200	150	100	75

Colt Model 1848 Baby Dragoon (Models 470, 471, 472)

Chambered for .31-caliber. Fitted with 5-round cylinder. Barrel length 4". Choice of blued or white steel frame. Brass backstrap and trigger guard. One-piece walnut grip. Made by Uberti.

NIB	Exc.	V.G.	Good	Fair	Poor
350	250	200	150	100	75

Starr Model 1858 (Model 510, 511)

Offered in double-/single-action. Chambered for .44-caliber. Fitted with 6" round barrel. Made by F. LLI Pietta.

NIB	Exc.	V.G.	Good	Fair	Poor
350	250	200	150	100	75

Colt Model 1860 Army

Features 8" round barrel except for Sheriff's model which is 5.5". Choice of brass or steel frame. Brass backstrap and trigger guard. Chambered for .44-caliber. One-piece walnut grip. Brass frame model made by Armi San Marco; steel frame by Uberti. **NOTE:** Half-fluted cylinder model also offered.

Brass Frame (Model 300)

NIB	Exc.	V.G.	Good	Fair	Poor
295	225	200	125	85	60

Steel Frame (Model 310, 312, 315)

NIB	Exc.	V.G.	Good	Fair	Poor
350	250	200	150	100	75

Colt Dragoon (Models 485A, 490A, 495A)

Offered in 1st, 2nd and 3rd models each. Fitted with 7.5" barrel. Chambered for .44-caliber. Steel frame, brass backstrap and trigger guard. The 2nd and 3rd models have square cylinder stop. Loading lever inverted on 3rd model. All have one-piece walnut grip. Made by Uberti. **NOTE:** Add $15 for 3rd model.

NIB	Exc.	V.G.	Good	Fair	Poor
350	250	200	150	100	75

Colt Model 1861 Navy (Model 210)

Chambered for .36-caliber. Fitted with 7.5" round barrel. Cylinder 6 rounds. Brass frame, backstrap and trigger guard. One-piece walnut grip. Made by Uberti.

NIB	Exc.	V.G.	Good	Fair	Poor
295	225	200	125	85	60

Colt Model 1862 Police (Model 315B)

Fitted with 6.5" round barrel. Chambered for .36-caliber. Case-hardened frame, with brass backstrap and trigger guard. Made by Uberti.

NIB	Exc.	V.G.	Good	Fair	Poor
350	250	200	150	100	75

Colt Model 1862 Pocket (Model 315C)

Similar to above model, but fitted with 6.5" octagonal barrel. Made by Uberti.

NIB	Exc.	V.G.	Good	Fair	Poor
350	250	200	150	100	75

Remington Model 1863 Pocket (Model 435)

Chambered for .31-caliber ball. Fitted with 3.5" barrel. Cylinder 5 rounds. Frame, backstrap and trigger guard are brass. Walnut grip. Made by Armi San Marco.

NIB	Exc.	V.G.	Good	Fair	Poor
295	225	200	125	85	60

Colt Model 1873 Cattleman (Models 700, 701, 702)

Famous replica made in several different configurations. Offered in barrel lengths of 4.75", 5.5" and 7.5". Calibers are: .45 Colt, .44-40, .44 Special, .38-40, .357 Magnum and .45 ACP. Frame case-hardened, with steel backstrap. One-piece walnut grip. Made by Uberti. **NOTE:** Add $80 for dual cylinder; $80 for nickel finish.

NIB	Exc.	V.G.	Good	Fair	Poor
500	375	225	175	150	125

Colt Model 1873 Bird's-head (Models 703A, 703B, 703C)

Same as above. Offered with bird's-head grip.

NIB	Exc.	V.G.	Good	Fair	Poor
500	375	225	175	150	125

Colt Model 1873 "Outfitter"

Chambered for .45 Colt or .357 Magnum cartridge. Fitted with 4.75", 5.5" or 7.5" barrel. Stainless steel finish. Walnut grips.

NIB	Exc.	V.G.	Good	Fair	Poor
500	375	225	175	150	125

HARTFORD ARMORY MODELS

Introduced to Taylor product line in 2004. Company produces revolvers made entirely in U.S. Each gun comes with a lifetime warranty. All Hartford Armory revolvers come in a numbered wooden case, with brass snap caps and plaque.

Remington Model 1875

Offered in these calibers: .38/.357, .44-40, .44 Special/Magnum or .45 Colt. Barrel lengths 5.75" or 7.5". Walnut grips. Armory dark blue finish.

NIB	Exc.	V.G.	Good	Fair	Poor
900	800	700	600	450	300

Remington Model 1890

Offered in .38/.357, .44-40, .44 Special/Magnum or .45 Colt. Choice of 5.5" or 7.5" barrel. Armory dark blue finish. Walnut grips.

NIB	Exc.	V.G.	Good	Fair	Poor
900	800	700	600	450	300

1911-A1 Model

Replica of famous 1911-A1 .45 ACP semi-automatic. Imported by Taylor's from Armscor in the Phillipines. Basic model has 5" barrel, blue finish, flat or arched mainspring housing and several optional grip choices: checkered or smooth walnut or cocobolo wood, with/without diamond design. There is also a Tactical model in 9mm, 10mm or .45 ACP, with Picatinny rail, fiber optic front sight, extended beavertail, ambidextrous safety and combat hammer. Compact Tactical also offered with 3.625" barrel. **NOTE:** Add $20 to $40 for Tactical models, based on overall condition.

NIB	Exc.	V.G.	Good	Fair	Poor
435	400	350	200	150	100

RIFLES

Kentucky Rifle

Offered in flintlock or percussion. Rifle is .40-caliber. Fitted with 3.5" barrel. One-piece stock, with brass fixtures.

Flintlock (Model 183)

NIB	Exc.	V.G.	Good	Fair	Poor
495	335	225	150	100	75

Percussion (Model 182)

NIB	Exc.	V.G.	Good	Fair	Poor
475	325	200	150	100	75

Model 1842 U.S. Percussion Musket (Model 125)

Offered as a smoothbore or rifled musket, with 42" .69-caliber barrel. Finish is white. One-piece walnut stock.

Smoothbore

NIB	Exc.	V.G.	Good	Fair	Poor
450	325	250	200	150	100

Rifled with Rear Sight (Model 126)

NIB	Exc.	V.G.	Good	Fair	Poor
450	325	250	200	150	100

Model 1855 U.S. Percussion Musket (Model 116)

Has .58-caliber 40" barrel, with rear sight. One-piece walnut stock. White satin finish.

NIB	Exc.	V.G.	Good	Fair	Poor
500	375	225	175	150	125

Model 1853 3-Band Enfield Musket (Model 120)

Rifled musket has 39" .58-caliber barrel. Blued finish. One-piece walnut stock. Brass buttplate, nosecap and trigger guard.

NIB	Exc.	V.G.	Good	Fair	Poor
475	350	300	250	200	100

Model 1858 2-Band Enfield Musket (Model 121)

Similar to above, with .58-caliber 33" barrel.

NIB	Exc.	V.G.	Good	Fair	Poor
475	350	300	250	200	100

Model 1861 Springfield Musket (Model 110)

Has 40" .58-caliber barrel, with one-piece walnut stock. White satin finish.

NIB	Exc.	V.G.	Good	Fair	Poor
550	425	350	300	200	100

Model 1862 C.S. Richmond Musket (Model 115)

Fitted with 40" .58-caliber barrel, with three barrel bands. Brass buttplate and nosecap. White satin finish. One-piece walnut stock.

NIB	Exc.	V.G.	Good	Fair	Poor
550	425	350	300	200	100

Model 1863 Remington Zouave (Model 140)

Fitted with 33" barrel. Chambered for .58-caliber ball. One-piece walnut stock. Blued finish, brass buttplate, nosecap, trigger guard, patchbox and barrel bands.

NIB	Exc.	V.G.	Good	Fair	Poor
450	325	250	200	150	100

Henry Rifle

Lever-action rifle chambered for .44-40 or .45 Colt cartridge. Fitted with 24.25" octagon barrel. Walnut stock. Open sights.

Brass Frame (Model 198)

NIB	Exc.	V.G.	Good	Fair	Poor
1200	900	750	600	400	200

Iron Frame (Model 199)

NIB	Exc.	V.G.	Good	Fair	Poor
1275	975	800	650	400	200

Winchester Model 1866 (Model 201)

Chambered for .44-40 or .45 Colt cartridge. Fitted with 24.25" octagon barrel. Brass frame. Open sights. Made by Uberti.

NIB	Exc.	V.G.	Good	Fair	Poor
900	700	575	400	300	175

Winchester Model 1866 Yellowboy Carbine (Model 202)

Same as above, with 19" round barrel and additional .38 Special caliber. Made by Uberti.

NIB	Exc.	V.G.	Good	Fair	Poor
950	700	525	450	300	150

Winchester Model 1873 (Model 200)

Lever-action chambered for .44-40 or .45 Colt cartridge. Fitted with 24.25" octagon barrel. Made by Uberti.

NIB	Exc.	V.G.	Good	Fair	Poor
900	725	600	500	400	200

Winchester Model 1873 Carbine (Model 200B)

Chambered for .45 Long Colt cartridge. Fitted with 19" barrel. Magazine capacity 10 rounds. Walnut stock. Case colored frame.

NIB	Exc.	V.G.	Good	Fair	Poor
900	725	600	500	400	200

Winchester Model 1873 Sporting Rifle (Model 200C)

Chambered for .45 Long Colt cartridge. Fitted with 30" octagon barrel. Checkered walnut stock, with pistol-grip. Case colored frame. Blued barrel.

NIB	Exc.	V.G.	Good	Fair	Poor
900	725	600	500	400	200

Winchester Model 1885 High Wall (Model 203)

Offered with 30" or 32" barrels. Chambered for .45-70 cartridge. Walnut stock.

NIB	Exc.	V.G.	Good	Fair	Poor
900	725	600	500	400	200

Winchester Model 1885 Low Wall Sporting Rifle (Model 204)

Single-shot rifle chambered for .22 LR, .32-20 or .38-40 cartridge. Checkered walnut stock.

NIB	Exc.	V.G.	Good	Fair	Poor
900	725	600	500	400	200

Winchester Model 92

Introduced in 2004. Lever-action rifle chambered for .32-20, .32 H&R Magnum, .357 Magnum, .38 Special, .38-40, .44-40, .44 S&W or .45 Colt. Barrel length 20" or 24" octagon. Takedown feature. Hardwood stock, with blued barrel finish and case colored frame.

NIB	Exc.	V.G.	Good	Fair	Poor
725	625	450	300	250	200

Sharps Model 1859 Infantry (Model 151)

Rifle fitted with 30" round barrel. Chambered for .54-caliber cartridge. One-piece walnut, with 3 barrel bands. Adjustable rear sight.

NIB	Exc.	V.G.	Good	Fair	Poor
1150	800	600	400	300	150

Sharps Model 1859 Berdan Military (Model 152)

.54-caliber rifle fitted with 30" round barrel. One-piece walnut stock, with 3 barrel bands. Adjustable rear sight. Fitted with double-set triggers.

NIB	Exc.	V.G.	Good	Fair	Poor
1150	800	600	400	300	150

Sharps Model 1859 Cavalry (Model 153)

Model has 22" round barrel, with adjustable rear sight. Chambered for .54-caliber. Walnut stock fitted with patchbox.

NIB	Exc.	V.G.	Good	Fair	Poor
1150	800	600	400	300	150

Sharps Model 1863 Cavalry (Model 154)

Similar to Model 1859 Cavalry, without patchbox.

NIB	Exc.	V.G.	Good	Fair	Poor
1150	800	600	400	300	150

Sharps Model 1863 Sporting Rifle (Model 131)

.54-caliber model offered with 30" or 32" octagon barrel. Single-/double-set triggers. Walnut stock. **NOTE:** Add $20 for double-set trigger.

NIB	Exc.	V.G.	Good	Fair	Poor
1150	800	600	400	300	150

Sharps Model 1874 Sporting Rifle (Model 138)

Offered with a variety of features. Available in .45-70 with choice of: 30" or 32" octagon barrel; single trigger or double-set triggers. Also available with Hartford-style pewter fore-end tip. In this configuration, available in .45-70, .40-65, .45-90 or .45-120 calibers. Checkered stock, with patchbox optional. **NOTE:** Add $125 for Hartford-style fore-end tip; $250 for checkered stock with patchbox.

NIB	Exc.	V.G.	Good	Fair	Poor
895	700	545	400	315	175

Sharps Model 1874 Deluxe Sporting Rifle (Model 155)

This .45-70 caliber model features hand checkered walnut stock, with oil-finish. Receiver in white, with standard scroll engraving. **NOTE:** Add $800 for Deluxe Model 1874, with gold inlay.

NIB	Exc.	V.G.	Good	Fair	Poor
1800	1350	1050	775	595	200

Sharps Model 1874 Infantry Rifle (Model 157)

This .45-70 caliber model features 30" round barrel, with 3 barrel bands. One-piece walnut stock, with patchbox. Adjustable rear sight. Single trigger.

NIB	Exc.	V.G.	Good	Fair	Poor
1325	1000	750	550	375	200

Sharps Model 1874 Berdan Rifle (Model 158)

Similar to above, with double-set trigger.

NIB	Exc.	V.G.	Good	Fair	Poor
1325	1000	750	550	375	200

Sharps Model 1874 Cavalry (Model 159)

This .45-70 caliber model fitted with 22" round barrel. Adjustable rear sight.

NIB	Exc.	V.G.	Good	Fair	Poor
1150	800	600	400	300	150

Spencer Model 1865 Carbine (Model 160)

Lever-action model chambered in calibers: .56-50, .44 Russian or .45 Schofield. Fitted with 20" round barrel. Walnut stock. Case-hardened receiver. Blued barrel. Made by Armi Sport.

NIB	Exc.	V.G.	Good	Fair	Poor
1200	1050	875	750	500	400

Spencer Model 1865 Rifle

As above, with 30" barrel and three barrel bands. Chambered for .56-50 cartridge.

NIB	Exc.	V.G.	Good	Fair	Poor
1200	1050	875	750	500	400

SHOTGUNS

1878 Coach Gun

Classic side-by-side hammer gun, with double triggers and 20" barrels. Chambered for 3" 12-gauge shells. Features include checkered stock, with pistol-grip and color case-hardened frame.

NIB	Exc.	V.G.	Good	Fair	Poor
800	700	550	400	250	150

1887 Lever Action

Replica of Winchester lever-action 12-gauge Model 1887 shotgun. Made with 18.5", 22" or 28" barrel. Color case-hardened frame.

NIB	Exc.	V.G.	Good	Fair	Poor
1000	825	650	500	250	150

TERRIER ONE
Terrier One

A .32-caliber double-action swing-out cylinder revolver, with 2.25" barrel and 5-shot cylinder. Nickel-plated, with checkered walnut grips. Manufactured from 1984 to 1987.

NIB	Exc.	V.G.	Good	Fair	Poor
—	100	75	50	30	25

TERRY, J. C.
New York City, New York
Pocket Pistol

A .22-caliber spur trigger single-shot pocket pistol, with 3.75" round barrel. Back strap marked "J.C. Terry/Patent Pending". Silver-plated brass frame, blued barrel and rosewood or walnut grips. Manufactured in late 1860s.

NIB	Exc.	V.G.	Good	Fair	Poor
—	—	1300	950	475	100

TEXAS CONTRACT RIFLES

Three contractors produced rifles for the State of Texas during 1862 and 1863. One of these patterns has a sporting back-action lock, Enfield barrel bands, an overall length of 47.375", heavy 32" long barrel of .58-caliber. Total deliveries by all contractors amounted to 1,464 rifles. Quality of these arms was decidedly inferior and often complained about.

TEXAS GUNFIGHTERS
Ponte Zanano, Italy
Shootist Single-Action

A .45 Long Colt caliber single-action revolver, with 4.75" barrel. Nickel-plated, with one-piece walnut grips. Made by Aldo Uberti. Introduced in 1988.

NIB	Exc.	V.G.	Good	Fair	Poor
400	350	250	200	150	75

1-of-100 Edition

As above, with one-piece mother-of-pearl grips. Fitted in a case, with an additional set of walnut grips. 100 were made in 1988.

NIB	Exc.	V.G.	Good	Fair	Poor
450	375	295	225	175	100

TEXAS LONGHORN ARMS, INC.
Richmond, Texas
Jezebel

A .22 or .22 Magnum single-shot pistol, with 6" barrel. Stainless steel, with walnut stock and fore-end. Introduced in 1987.

NIB	Exc.	V.G.	Good	Fair	Poor
750	675	600	550	500	350

Texas Border Special

A .44 Special or .45 Colt caliber single-action revolver, with 3.5" barrel and Pope-style rifling. Blued case-hardened, with one-piece walnut grips.

NIB	Exc.	V.G.	Good	Fair	Poor
1500	1250	1000	800	600	300

Mason Commemorative

As above in .45 Colt, with 4.75" barrel and Mason's insignia. Gold inlaid. Introduced in 1987.

NIB	Exc.	V.G.	Good	Fair	Poor
1500	1250	1000	800	600	300

South Texas Army

As above, with 4.75" barrel. Chambered for .357 Magnum cartridge. Fitted with conventional one-piece walnut grips.

NIB	Exc.	V.G.	Good	Fair	Poor
1500	1250	1000	800	600	300

West Texas Target

As above, with 7.5" barrel and flattop frame. Caliber .32-20, in addition to calibers noted above.

NIB	Exc.	V.G.	Good	Fair	Poor
1500	1250	1000	800	600	300

Grover's Improved Number Five

Similar to above in .44 Magnum, with 5.5" barrel. Serial Numbered K1 to K1200. Introduced in 1988.

NIB	Exc.	V.G.	Good	Fair	Poor
2300	1350	800	—	—	—

Texas Sesquicentennial Commemorative

As above, engraved in style of Louis D. Nimschke. One-piece ivory grips and fitted case.

NIB	Exc.	V.G.	Good	Fair	Poor
2500	2000	1500	900	750	400

THAMES ARMS CO.
Norwich, Connecticut

A .22-, .32- or .38-caliber double-action top break revolver, with varying barrels lengths. Normally marked "Automatic Revolver", which refers to cartridge ejector. Nickel-plated, with walnut grips.

NIB	Exc.	V.G.	Good	Fair	Poor
—	500	200	100	75	50

THIEME & EDELER
Eibar, Spain

Pocket Pistol

A 7.65mm caliber semi-automatic pistol, with 3" barrel marked "T E". Blued, with black plastic grips. Manufactured prior to 1936.

NIB	Exc.	V.G.	Good	Fair	Poor
—	250	150	100	75	50

THOMPSON
See—Auto Ordnance Corp.

THOMPSON/CENTER ARMS
Springfield, Massachusetts

Thompson/Center Arms Co. was founded in Rochester, New York in 1965 by K.W. Thompson and Warren Center. Company's first gun was a break-open, single-shot pistol, known as Contender. More than 400,000 were produced between 1967 and 2000, when the original model was discontinued. In 2007, Thompson/Center became a division of Smith & Wesson and production was moved to Springfield, Massachusetts.

CONTENDER

Standard version offered with 10" octagon barrel. Later with 10" Bull barrel, 10" ventilated rib barrel, 14" Super models, 14" Super with ventilated rib, 16" Super models and 16" Super models with ventilated rib. Stainless steel finish available on all models except 10" octagon barrel. Action on these handguns is a single-shot break open design. Unless otherwise stated, barrels are blued. Competitor grip is walnut, with rubber insert mounted on back of grip. Finger groove grip is also available made from walnut, with finger notching and thumb rest. Fore-end is American black walnut in various lengths and designs depending on barrel size. Stainless steel models have rubber grips, with finger grooves. Standard sights are Patridge rear, with ramp front. An adjustable rear sight was offered as an option. Barrels with ventilated ribs were furnished with fixed rear sight and bead front. **NOTE:** Early frames with no engraving, called flatsides, and those with eagle engraving bring between $2,000 and $2,500 on collector market.

NOTE: Barrel interchangeability is acceptable for blued barrels and frames, with stainless steel barrels and frames. DO NOT interchange Alloy II barrels and frames with blued or stainless steel components.

10" Octagon Barrel Model

First Contender design. Offered in .22 LR only. Supplied with adjustable rear sight and mounting holes for scope. Grips are Competitor or rubber. Weight about 44 oz.

NIB	Exc.	V.G.	Good	Fair	Poor
375	300	250	200	150	100

10" Bull Barrel Model

Comes standard with adjustable rear sight, mounting holes for scope mounts and Competitor grips for blued models; rubber grips on stainless steel. Offered in these calibers as complete pistols: .22 LR, .22 LR Match, .22 Win. Magnum (blued only), .22 Hornet, .223, 7mm T.C.U. (blued only), .30-30, .32-20 (blued only), .357 Magnum, .357 Rem. Max (blued only), .44 Magnum, .45 Colt, .410 bore. In 1994, Thompson/Center introduced .300 Whisper cartridge to its Contender product line. Weight about 50 oz.

NIB	Exc.	V.G.	Good	Fair	Poor
375	300	250	200	150	100

10" Vent Rib Model

Features a raised ventilated rib. Chambered for .45 Long Colt/.410 bore. Fixed rear sight and bead front. Detachable choke screws into the muzzle for use with .410 shell. Furnished with Competitor or rubber grips.

NIB	Exc.	V.G.	Good	Fair	Poor
370	320	270	220	150	100

Super 14" Model

Features a 14" bull barrel. Furnished with adjustable rear sight and ramp front. Drilled and tapped for scope mounts. Competitor or rubber grips offered. Available in blued or stainless steel finish. Furnished in these calibers in a complete pistol only: .22 LR, .22 LR Match, .17 Rem. (blued only), .22 Hornet, .222 Rem. (blued only), .223 Rem., 7mm T.C.U. (blued only), 7-30 Waters, .30-30, .357 Rem. Max (blued only), .35 Rem., .375 Win. (blued only), .44 Magnum (blued only). Weight about 56 oz.

NIB	Exc.	V.G.	Good	Fair	Poor
400	360	300	250	200	150

Super 14" Vent Rib Model

Similar to 10" ventilated rib model. Chambered for .45 Long Colt/.410 bore. Furnished with 14" ventilated rib barrel.

NIB	Exc.	V.G.	Good	Fair	Poor
475	385	325	275	215	150

Super 16" Model

Fitted with 16.25" tapered barrel and two position adjustable rear sight. Drilled and tapped for scope mount. Furnished with Competitor or rubber grips. Choice of blued or stainless steel finish. Available in these calibers as complete pistols only: .22 LR, .22 Hornet, .223 Rem., 7-30 Waters, .30-30, .35 Rem., .45-70 Government. Weight about 56 oz.

NIB	Exc.	V.G.	Good	Fair	Poor
370	320	275	215	150	100

Super 16" Vent Rib Model

Chambered for .45 Long Colt/.410 bore. Offered for the first time in 1993. All other features same as other Contender .45/.410 bore pistols.

NIB	Exc.	V.G.	Good	Fair	Poor
390	350	300	250	175	125

Contender Hunter Model

Designed for handgun hunting. Offered in two barrel lengths 12" and 14", fitted with compensator and 2.5 power scope. There are no iron sights fitted. Nylon carrying sling and soft leather carrying case are standard. Offered in these calibers: 7-30 Waters, .30-30 Win., .35 Rem., .45-70 Government, .44 Magnum, .223 Rem. and .375 Win. Fitted with Competitor grips. Offered in blued or stainless steel finish. Weight about 64 oz.

NIB	Exc.	V.G.	Good	Fair	Poor
575	500	400	300	200	100

G2 CONTENDER SERIES

Introduced in 2003. A second generation Contender that features a slightly different look: simplified internal design that allows re-cocking the hammer, without having to break open the action; different shaped grips that give more clearance between grip and finger guard. These G2 firearms will accept previously manufactured Contender barrels and fore-ends, but not grips.

G2 Contender

Chambered for .22 Hornet, .357 Magnum, .44 Magnum, .45 Colt/.410 in 12" barrels. Chambered for .17 HMR, .22 LR, .22 Hornet, .223 Rem., 7-30 Waters, .30-30, .44 Magnum, .45 Colt/.410, .45-70 in 14" barrels. Adjustable sights. Drilled and tapped for scope mounts. Walnut grips. Weight about: 3.5 lbs. for 12" barrel gun; 3.75 lbs. for 14" barrel. In 2004, .204 Ruger and .375 JDJ calibers added.

NIB	Exc.	V.G.	Good	Fair	Poor
560	450	375	300	250	175

G2 Contender Rifle

Fitted with 23" barrel, with no sights. Chambered for .17 HMR, .22 LR, .223 Rem., .30-30, .45-70. Walnut stock, with blued finish. Weight about 5.4 lbs. In 2004, .375 JDJ and .204 Ruger calibers added.

NIB	Exc.	V.G.	Good	Fair	Poor
600	500	400	325	275	200

G2 Contender Shotgun

Chambered for .410 bore shell. Fitted with 24" ventilated rib barrel. Walnut stock. Weight about 5.4 lbs. Introduced in 2004.

NIB	Exc.	V.G.	Good	Fair	Poor
600	500	400	325	275	200

CONTENDER CARBINE MODEL

Built from same design as Contender Model. Features completely interchangeable barrels. Chambered for 12 different cartridges from .22 LR to .35 Rem. A .410 bore shotgun barrel is also offered. Standard model has 21" barrel stocked with walnut; stainless steel models a composite stock in fitted walnut is also available. All are drilled and tapped for scope mounts. Available in blued or stainless steel.

Standard 21" Carbine

Fitted with 21" plain barrel and walnut stocks. Offered in these calibers as a complete gun only: .22 LR, .22 LR Match (blued only), .17 Rem. (blued only), .22 Hornet, .223 Rem., 7-30 Waters, .30-30, .35 Rem. (blued only), .375 Win. (blued only). Weight 5.3 lbs.

NIB	Exc.	V.G.	Good	Fair	Poor
500	400	350	300	250	200

21" Carbine .410 Bore

Same as above, with ventilated rib barrel and screw-in choke.

NIB	Exc.	V.G.	Good	Fair	Poor
475	375	300	250	200	100

16" Youth Model Carbine

Special walnut buttstock, with 12" length of pull and 16.25" barrel. Short buttstock can be replaced with standard buttstock. Blued or stainless steel finish. Complete guns offered in same calibers as 21" Carbine, with exception of .375 Win. and addition of .45 Long Colt/.410 bore with ventilated rib barrel.

NIB	Exc.	V.G.	Good	Fair	Poor
475	375	300	250	200	100

ENCORE SERIES

Encore Pistol

Introduced in 1996. Single-shot pistol will feature 10.625", 15" or 24" barrels chambered for .30-06, .308 Win., 7mm-08 Rem., .223 Rem., .22-250 Rem., .44 Magnum, 7mmBR. This new handgun is designed for use with higher pressure cartridges. Barrels will not interchange with Contender. Weight about: 56 oz. for 10.625" barrel gun; 4 lbs. 15" barrel; 6.75 lbs. 24" barrel. **NOTE:** Add $60 for stainless steel frame and barrels.

NIB	Exc.	V.G.	Good	Fair	Poor
550	450	375	300	250	175

HotShot Youth Rifle

Single-shot dropping-barrel rifle chambered in .22 LR. Features include crowned 19" steel barrel, exposed hammer, synthetic fore-end and buttstock, peep sight (receiver drilled and tapped for optics), three stock pattern options (black, Realtree AP and pink AP). Overall weight 3 lbs., 11.5" length of pull.

NIB	Exc.	V.G.	Good	Fair	Poor
195	165	125	100	75	50

Encore Rifle

Similar to Encore pistol, with longer barrels and walnut stock and forearm. A wide variety of calibers offered from .22-250 to .300 Win. Magnum. Barrel lengths from 24" to 26". Heavy barrels offered in 7mm Rem. Magnum, .300 Win. Magnum and .22-250, with no sights. Weight about: 6 lbs. 12 oz. for 7mm-08 with 24" barrel. Introduced in 1997. In 1998, .260 Rem., .280 Rem., .45-70 Government cartridges added. In 1999, blued and stainless steel frames and barrels were offered. In 2003, .375 H&H Magnum with 26" barrel without sights was offered. In 2004, .280 Rem., .204 Ruger, .405 Win. were added. **NOTE:** Add about $60 for stainless steel frame and barrels.

NIB	Exc.	V.G.	Good	Fair	Poor
650	550	425	300	225	175

Encore Katahdin Carbine

Fitted with heavy 18" barrel, with integral muzzle-brake. Offered in .444 Marlin, .450 Marlin and .45-70 Government calibers. Blued finish, with composite stock and adjustable fiber optic sights. Weight about 6.75 lbs. Introduced in 2002.

NIB	Exc.	V.G.	Good	Fair	Poor
650	550	425	300	225	175

Encore Katahdin Turkey Gun

A 12-gauge 3" chamber gun, with 20" barrel and screw-in Turkey Chokes. Open sights. Realtree Hardwoods HD camo composite stock. Weight about 6 lbs. Introduced in 2005.

NIB	Exc.	V.G.	Good	Fair	Poor
750	575	450	325	225	200

Encore Shotgun 20 Gauge

Introduced in 1998. Fitted with 26" 20-gauge ventilated rib barrel. Walnut stock and fore-end. Choke tubes are standard.

NIB	Exc.	V.G.	Good	Fair	Poor
650	550	425	300	225	175

Encore Camo Shotgun 12 Gauge

Features 24" smoothbore barrel, with screw-in Turkey Choke, camo stock and metal pattern. Blued frame, with composite stock. Introduced in 2002.

NIB	Exc.	V.G.	Good	Fair	Poor
750	575	450	325	225	200

Encore Shotgun 12 Gauge

Features 3" chamber and 26" ventilated rib barrel, with bead front sight. Blued, with walnut stock. Weight about 6.6 lbs. Introduced in 2004.

NIB	Exc.	V.G.	Good	Fair	Poor
750	575	450	325	225	200

Encore Rifled Shotgun 20 Gauge

Introduced in 2000. Features 26" rifled shotgun barrel chambered for 20-gauge shell. Adjustable rear sight. Walnut stock and blued finish.

NIB	Exc.	V.G.	Good	Fair	Poor
650	550	425	300	225	175

Encore Rifled Shotgun 12 Gauge

Introduced in 2002. Fitted with 24" rifled barrel, with adjustable fiber optic sights. Blued, with walnut stock.

NIB	Exc.	V.G.	Good	Fair	Poor
650	550	425	300	225	175

Encore Turkey Gun

Introduced in 2005. Chambered for 20-gauge shell, with 3" chamber. Barrel 26", with open sights and screw-in Turkey Chokes. Realtree Hardwoods HD camo composite stock.

NIB	Exc.	V.G.	Good	Fair	Poor
650	550	425	300	225	175

PRO HUNTER SERIES

Pro Hunter

Similar to Encore rifle, with plain or fluted barrel. Various finish and stock options. Barrels interchange with standard Encore barrels. Muzzle-loading and pistol versions available. Introduced 2007.

NIB	Exc.	V.G.	Good	Fair	Poor
650	500	400	275	200	100

Pro Hunter Predator Rifle

Contender-style break-action single-shot rifle. Chambered in .204 Ruger, .223 Rem., .22-250, .308 Win. Features include 28" deep-fluted interchangeable barrel, composite buttstock and fore-end with non-slip inserts in cheekpiece, pistol-grip and fore-end. Max 1 camo finish overall. Overall length 42.5". Weight 7.75 lbs.

NIB	Exc.	V.G.	Good	Fair	Poor
750	650	500	400	300	250

Pro Hunter Turkey Gun

Contender-style break-action single-shot shotgun. Chambered in 12- or 20-gauge and 3" shells. Features include 24" barrel, with interchangeable choke tubes (Extra Full supplied), composite buttstock and fore-end with non-slip inserts in cheekpiece, pistol-grip and fore-end. Adjustable fiber optic sights, Sims recoil pad, AP camo finish overall. Overall length 40.5". Weight 6.5 lbs.

NIB	Exc.	V.G.	Good	Fair	Poor
750	650	525	400	250	150

Pro Hunter Katahdin

Chambered in .45-70, .460 S&W or .500 S&W. This break-action single-shot has 20" interchangeable fluted barrel, Flex-Tech stock with textured and grooved grip surfaces. Adjustable rear and fiber optic front sights.

NIB	Exc.	V.G.	Good	Fair	Poor
700	600	485	—	—	—

ICON SERIES

Icon

Bolt-action centerfire rifle chambered in .22-250, .243, .308, .30 Thompson-Center. Barrel length 22" (iron sight) or 24" (sightless). Detachable box magazine, Introduced in 2007.

NIB	Exc.	V.G.	Good	Fair	Poor
900	800	675	525	300	200

Icon Classic Long Action Rifle

Similar to Icon, with long-action design. Chambered for .270, .30-06, .300 Win. Magnum and 7mm Rem. Magnum.

NIB	Exc.	V.G.	Good	Fair	Poor
1000	850	700	600	400	200

Icon Weathershield Medium Action Rifle

Similar to Icon, with stainless steel barrel and receiver. Black synthetic or Realtree AP Camo stock.

NIB	Exc.	V.G.	Good	Fair	Poor
1000	850	700	600	400	200

VENTURE SERIES

Venture Medium Action Rifle

Bolt-action rifle chambered in .204, .22-250, .223, .243, 7mm-08, .308 and 30TC. Features include 24" crowned medium weight barrel, classic styled composite stock with inlaid traction grip panels, adjustable 3.5 to 5 lb. trigger along with drilled and tapped receiver (bases included). 3+1 detachable nylon box magazine. Overall length 43.5". Weight 7 lbs.

NIB	Exc.	V.G.	Good	Fair	Poor
500	400	325	250	175	100

Venture Predator PDX Rifle

Bolt-action rifle chambered in .204, .22-250, .223, .243, .308. Similar to Venture Medium action, with heavy deep-fluted 22" barrel and Max-1 camo finish overall. Overall length 41.5". Weight 8 lbs.

NIB	Exc.	V.G.	Good	Fair	Poor
600	500	425	350	275	200

Venture Weather Shield

Advanced Weather Shield finish for durability. Classic styled composite stock, with Hogue Overmolded Grip panels. T/C large bolt design for smooth operation. 60 degree bolt lift. Receiver drilled and tapped, with bases included. Magazine capacity, 3+1. Available in short-/long-action models for most standard, Magnum and WSM cartridges.

NIB	Exc.	V.G.	Good	Fair	Poor
525	450	380	325	225	150

Dimension

Bolt-action rifle available in 10 calibers from .204 Ruger to .300 Win. Magnum. Barrel lengths 22" or 24". Synthetic stock has competition cheekpiece. Other features are an aluminum receiver, free-floated barrel and choice of right-/left-hand action. Introduced in 2012.

NIB	Exc.	V.G.	Good	Fair	Poor
600	525	450	400	350	200

OTHER RIFLES

Model R55

Semi-automatic rifle chambered for .17 Mach 2 cartridge. Fitted with 20" match grade barrel, with adjustable sights. Black composite or laminated hardwood stock. Receiver blued or stainless steel. Magazine capacity 5 rounds. Weight about 5.5 lbs. Introduced in 2005. **NOTE:** Add $65 for black composite stock.

NIB	Exc.	V.G.	Good	Fair	Poor
550	450	375	300	250	175

TCR 87 Hunter Model

Single-shot top lever rifle. Chambered for cartridges from .22 LR to .308 Win. Fitted with 23" barrel. Finish blue, with walnut stock. Discontinued as a regular production rifle in 1993.

NIB	Exc.	V.G.	Good	Fair	Poor
650	550	425	300	225	175

T/C 22 LR Classic

Introduced in 2000. A semi-automatic rifle chambered for .22 LR cartridge. Fitted with 22" match grade barrel. Walnut stock, with Monte Carlo comb. Adjustable rear sight. Magazine capacity 8 rounds. Weight about 5.5 lbs.

NIB	Exc.	V.G.	Good	Fair	Poor
450	350	275	225	175	100

.22 Classic Benchmark

An updated version of Classic, with 18" heavy barrel and no sights. Wood laminated target stock. Magazine capacity 10 rounds. Weight about 6.8 lbs. Introduced in 2003.

NIB	Exc.	V.G.	Good	Fair	Poor
475	375	300	250	200	100

Silver Lynx

This .22-caliber semi-automatic rifle introduced in 2004. Fitted with a 20" stainless steel barrel. Black composite stock, with Monte Carlo comb. Magazine capacity 5 rounds. Weight about 5.5 lbs.

NIB	Exc.	V.G.	Good	Fair	Poor
400	300	225	150	100	75

BLACKPOWDER FIREARMS

System 1

Introduced in 1997. This concept features complete muzzle-loading system, with interchangeable barrels. Offered with .32-, .50-, .54-, .58-caliber and 12-gauge shotgun barrels, with walnut stock and blued finish; or stainless steel, with synthetic stock. Barrel lengths 26". Weight about 7.5 lbs. Sights adjustable. **NOTE:** Add $30 for synthetic stock and stainless steel.

NIB	Exc.	V.G.	Good	Fair	Poor
350	300	225	175	125	75

Thunder Hawk

Introduced in 1993. Features .50-caliber caplock in-line ignition, with 21" round barrel. Rear sight adjustable and ramp front. Stock is plain American black walnut, with rubber recoil pad. Trigger adjustable. In 1994, available in stainless steel. Weight 6.75 lbs.

NIB	Exc.	V.G.	Good	Fair	Poor
225	200	175	150	100	75

Thunder Hawk Shadow

Introduced in 1996. Features in-line ignition in .50- or .54-caliber, with 24" round barrel. Comes standard with black checkered composite stock. Weight about 7 lbs. In 1997, offered with camouflage stock and blued finish.

NIB	Exc.	V.G.	Good	Fair	Poor
300	250	200	150	100	75

Grey Hawk

Stainless steel composite stock rifle is a .50-caliber cap-lock, with 24" round barrel. Utilizes a hooked breech system. Lock is a heavy-duty coil spring, with floral engraving pattern. Adjustable rear sight and bead front are standard. Weight about 7 lbs.

NIB	Exc.	V.G.	Good	Fair	Poor
225	200	175	150	100	75

Hawken Caplock Rifle

Available in .45-, .50- and .54-caliber. Rifle has 28" octagonal barrel and hooked breech system. Triggers are fully adjustable and can function as double-set or single-stage. Adjustable sights, with bead front are standard. Trim is solid brass. Stock select American walnut, with cheekpiece. Weight about 8.5 lbs.

NIB	Exc.	V.G.	Good	Fair	Poor
300	250	200	150	100	75

Hawken Flintlock Rifle

Offered in .50-caliber, with 28" octagonal barrel. All other features same as above.

NIB	Exc.	V.G.	Good	Fair	Poor
310	260	200	150	100	75

Hawken Custom/Elite

Introduced in 1994. Model is .50-caliber traditional cap-lock rifle, with double-set triggers and crescent butt. Select American walnut stock, with no patchbox. Finish is high luster blue.

NIB	Exc.	V.G.	Good	Fair	Poor
400	350	275	175	100	75

Omega 45/Omega 50

Muzzle-loader chambered for .45- or .50-caliber. Fitted with 28" round barrel. Adjustable sights. Composite or laminated stock. Weight about 7 lbs. Introduced in 2002. **NOTE:** Add $50 for stainless steel; $60 for Realtree camo stock.

NIB	Exc.	V.G.	Good	Fair	Poor
535	425	325	250	150	75

Omega Pivoting Breech Rifle

Introduced in 2004. Rifle has 28" stainless steel fluted barrel bored for .50-caliber slug. Laminated wood thumbhole stock. Fiber optic sights. Weight about 7 lbs.

NIB	Exc.	V.G.	Good	Fair	Poor
400	350	275	175	100	75

Renegade Caplock Rifle

Offered in .50- or .54-caliber, with 26" octagonal barrel. Adjustable triggers can function as double-set or single-stage. Adjustable sights, with blued trim. Walnut stock. Offered in right-/left-hand models. Weight about 8 lbs.

NIB	Exc.	V.G.	Good	Fair	Poor
460	350	250	150	100	75

Renegade Flintlock

Available in .50-caliber and right-hand only. Other features same as Caplock model.

NIB	Exc.	V.G.	Good	Fair	Poor
460	350	250	150	100	755

Big Boar Rifle

Hooked breech model features .58-caliber, with 26" octagonal barrel. Single trigger and adjustable sights are standard. Trim is blued steel. American walnut stock, with rubber pad. Weight about 7.75 lbs.

NIB	Exc.	V.G.	Good	Fair	Poor
550	400	300	250	200	100

High Plains Sporter

A .50-caliber caplock, with 24" round barrel. Lock is case colored. Choice of adjustable open sights or tang sight. Trim is blued. Stock is walnut, with rubber recoil pad, pistol-grip and sling swivel studs. Weight about 7 lbs.

NIB	Exc.	V.G.	Good	Fair	Poor
275	250	200	150	100	75

Tree Hawk

Available in caplock .50-caliber or 12-gauge. .50 caliber carbine has 21" barrel and offered in camo colors; 12 gauge shotgun fitted with 27" barrel and also comes in camo colors. Weight about 6.75 lbs.

Rifle

NIB	Exc.	V.G.	Good	Fair	Poor
275	250	200	150	100	75

Shotgun

NIB	Exc.	V.G.	Good	Fair	Poor
275	250	200	150	100	75

White Mountain Carbine

Available in .45-, .50- or .54-caliber caplock or .50 flintlock. Fitted with 20.5" octagon barrel. Lock is case colored and trim blued. Stock is walnut, with rubber recoil pad. Weight about 6.5 lbs. Discontinued.

NIB	Exc.	V.G.	Good	Fair	Poor
400	350	275	175	100	75

Black Mountain Magnum

Introduced in 1999. Features 26" round barrel, with walnut or composite stock. Chambered for .50-, .54-caliber or 12-gauge, with 27" round barrel. All models are caplock. Blued finish. Discontinued.

NIB	Exc.	V.G.	Good	Fair	Poor
400	350	275	175	100	75

Pennsylvania Hunter

Offered in .50-caliber caplock or flintlock. Fitted with octagon/round barrel in 31.5" or 21.5". Fully adjustable sights, walnut stock and blued trim are standard. Rifle weight about 7.5 lbs.; carbine about 6.5 lbs. Discontinued.

Rifle

NIB	Exc.	V.G.	Good	Fair	Poor
400	325	250	200	150	100

Carbine

NIB	Exc.	V.G.	Good	Fair	Poor
400	325	250	200	150	100

Pennsylvania Match Rifle

Similar to Pennsylvania Hunter Rifle, except equipped with tang peep sight and globe front sight. Discontinued.

NIB	Exc.	V.G.	Good	Fair	Poor
—	450	375	300	250	175

New Englander Rifle

Offered in .50- or .54-caliber caplock, with walnut stock and 26" round barrel. Adjustable sights. Weight about 7 lbs. 15 oz. A 12" barrel is optional. Discontinued. **NOTE:** Add $150 for interchangeable shotgun barrel.

NIB	Exc.	V.G.	Good	Fair	Poor
350	275	200	150	100	75

New Englander Shotgun

Same as above, with 27" barrel in 12-gauge, with screw in full choke. Weight about 6 lbs. 8 oz. Discontinued.

NIB	Exc.	V.G.	Good	Fair	Poor
350	275	200	150	100	75

New Englander Composite

Offered with composite stock. The .50- or .54-caliber rifle has 24" barrel and 12-gauge shotgun has 27" barrel. Discontinued.

Rifle

NIB	Exc.	V.G.	Good	Fair	Poor
350	275	200	150	100	75

Shotgun

NIB	Exc.	V.G.	Good	Fair	Poor
350	275	200	150	100	75

Scout Carbine

Muzzle-loading carbine of .50- or .54-caliber, with in-line ignition system. Offered with walnut or composite stock (first offered in 1993). Fitted with 21" round barrel. Adjustable rear sight and fixed blade front. Brass barrel band and trigger guard on walnut stock; blued barrel band and trigger guard on composite stock. Weight about 7 lbs. 4 oz. Discontinued.

Walnut Stock

NIB	Exc.	V.G.	Good	Fair	Poor
325	275	200	150	100	75

Composite Stock

NIB	Exc.	V.G.	Good	Fair	Poor
250	225	175	150	100	75

Scout Rifle

Similar to Scout Carbine, with 24" stepped half-round, half-octagonal barrel. Weight about 8 lbs. Discontinued.

Walnut Stock

NIB	Exc.	V.G.	Good	Fair	Poor
425	350	275	225	150	100

Composite Stock

NIB	Exc.	V.G.	Good	Fair	Poor
400	325	250	200	150	100

Scout Pistol

Same design as Scout carbine. Single-action pistol available in .45-, .50- or .54-caliber. Fitted with 12" barrel, adjustable rear sight and blued finish, with brass trigger guard. Black walnut grips. Weight 4 lbs. 6 oz. Discontinued.

NIB	Exc.	V.G.	Good	Fair	Poor
250	225	200	175	100	75

Fire Hawk Deluxe

Introduced in 1996. An in-line muzzle-loader. Offered in .50- or .54-caliber, with blued or stainless steel barrel. Semi-fancy checkered walnut stock has a cheekpiece. Round barrel is 24" long. Adjustable rear leaf sight, with ramp style front bead. Weight about 7 lbs.

NIB	Exc.	V.G.	Good	Fair	Poor
400	325	250	200	125	100

Fire Hawk

Similar to Deluxe Fire Hawk, with standard American walnut stock or composition stock.

NIB	Exc.	V.G.	Good	Fair	Poor
300	250	200	150	100	75

Thumbhole Stock

NIB	Exc.	V.G.	Good	Fair	Poor
325	275	225	175	100	75

Camo Stock

NIB	Exc.	V.G.	Good	Fair	Poor
325	275	225	175	100	75

Bantam

NIB	Exc.	V.G.	Good	Fair	Poor
275	225	175	125	100	75

.32 & .58 caliber models

NIB	Exc.	V.G.	Good	Fair	Poor
300	250	200	150	100	75

Fire Storm

Offered as a percussion or flintlock. Fitted with 26" barrel chambered for .50-caliber. Black composite stock. Adjustable fiber optics rear sight. Weight about 7 lbs. Introduced in 2000.

NIB	Exc.	V.G.	Good	Fair	Poor
375	300	225	150	100	75

Black Diamond

An in-line muzzle-loading rifle, with removable breech plug. Fitted with 22.5" .50-caliber barrel. Stock is Rynite. Choice of blue or stainless steel. Introduced in 1998. Discontinued. **NOTE:** Add $50 for stainless steel.

NIB	Exc.	V.G.	Good	Fair	Poor
325	275	225	175	100	75

Black Diamond XR

This .45- or .50-caliber muzzle-loader is fitted with 26" round barrel. Offered with blued finish, camo or stainless steel. Weight about 6.75 lbs. Introduced in 2002. Discontinued.

NIB	Exc.	V.G.	Good	Fair	Poor
375	300	225	150	100	75

Triumph

.50-caliber toggle-breech inline muzzle-loader, with only four moving parts. Blued/synthetic, Weathershield/synthetic or Weathershield/stainless finish. Introduced 2007.

NIB	Exc.	V.G.	Good	Fair	Poor
425	350	275	225	150	100

Impact Muzzleloading Rifle

.50-caliber single-shot rifle. Features include 209 primer ignition, sliding hood to expose removable breechplug, synthetic stock adjustable from 12.5" to 13.5", 26" blued 1:28 rifled barrel, adjustable fiber optic sights, aluminum ramrod, camo composite stock, QLA muzzle system. Weight 6.5 lbs. **NOTE:** Add $20 for camo stock.

NIB	Exc.	V.G.	Good	Fair	Poor
200	175	140	100	80	50

NorthWest Explorer Muzzleloading Rifle

.50-caliber single-shot rifle. Features include dropping block action, #11 percussion cap ignition, 28" blued or Weathershield 1:48 rifled barrel, adjustable fiber optic sights, aluminum ramrod, black or camo composite stock with recoil pad, QLA muzzle system. Weight 7 lbs. **NOTE:** Add $60 for Realtree Hardwoods camo stock.

NIB	Exc.	V.G.	Good	Fair	Poor
280	235	200	175	125	75

G2 Contender Muzzleloader

A 209x45 24" muzzle-loader barrel. Will interchange with G2 Contender rifle barrels. Weight about 5.5 lbs.

NIB	Exc.	V.G.	Good	Fair	Poor
600	500	400	325	275	200

G2 Contender Muzzeloader .50 caliber

In .50-caliber, with 24" barrel. Weight about 6.5 lbs. Introduced in 2005.

NIB	Exc.	V.G.	Good	Fair	Poor
600	500	400	325	275	200

Encore 209x50 Mag Rifle

Muzzle-loading rifle chambered for .50-caliber. Fitted with 26" barrel. Designed to handle Magnum loads up to 150 grains of FFG black powder. Blued or stainless steel finish. Introduced in 1998. **NOTE:** Add $75 for stainless steel; $140 for Realtree camo stock

NIB	Exc.	V.G.	Good	Fair	Poor
650	500	400	275	200	100

Encore 209x50 Mag Carbine

Similar to above model. Fitted with 20" ported barrel. Realtree camo stock. Weight about 6.75 lbs. Introduced in 2004.

NIB	Exc.	V.G.	Good	Fair	Poor
650	500	400	275	200	100

Encore 209x50 Pistol

Model features 15" barrel chambered for .50-caliber. Walnut stock and blued finish. Weight about 16 oz. Introduced in 2000.

NIB	Exc.	V.G.	Good	Fair	Poor
550	450	375	300	250	175

THUNDER FIVE
MIL Inc.
Piney Flats, Tennessee

Thunder-Five

Five shot double-action revolver, with 2" rifled barrel, matte finish, ambidextrous hammer block safety, Pachmayr grips, chambered in .45 Long Colt/.410 shotgun.

NIB	Exc.	V.G.	Good	Fair	Poor
575	425	345	250	200	150

TIKKA
Tikkakoski, Finland

RIFLES

Whitetail Hunter

Features hand checkered walnut stock, with matte lacquer finish. Furnished without sights, but receiver is grooved. Magazine is detachable box type. Three action lengths are offered: short, medium and long. In short action caliber choices are: .17 Rem., .223, .22-250, .243 and .308 with 22.4" barrels and weight 7 lbs.; medium action: .270 and .30-06 with 22.4" barrels and weight 7.3 lbs.; long action: 7mm Rem. Magnum, .300

and .338 Win. Magnum with 24.4" barrel and weight 7.5 lbs.

NIB	Exc.	V.G.	Good	Fair	Poor
725	600	500	400	200	150

Whitetail Hunter Deluxe

Similar to standard model above, but furnished with cheekpiece, select walnut stock, rosewood pistol-grip cap and fore-end tip. Metal surfaces are a highly polished blue. Same calibers as offered above.

NIB	Exc.	V.G.	Good	Fair	Poor
875	700	600	400	200	150

Whitetail/Battue Rifle

Rifle originally designed for the French market. Barrel 20.5" long and fitted with a raised quarter rib. Walnut is checkered, with rubber recoil pad standard. Black fiberglass stock is offered as an option. In a medium action only caliber is .308. In a long action calibers are: .270, .30-06, 7mm Rem. Magnum, .300 and .338 Win. Magnum. All models weigh about 7 lbs. In 2000, offered in a left-hand model. **NOTE:** Add $50 for stainless steel finish; $20 for Magnum calibers; $60 for left-hand model.

NIB	Exc.	V.G.	Good	Fair	Poor
650	500	400	275	200	100

Varmint/Continental Rifle

Features 23.5" heavy barrel, without sights. Checkered walnut stock has a wide fore-end. Offered in .17 Rem., .223, .22-250, .243 and .308. Weight about 8.5 lbs.

NIB	Exc.	V.G.	Good	Fair	Poor
725	600	500	400	200	150

Long Range Hunting

Same as above in .25-06, .270, .7mm Magnum and .300 Win. Magnum. Fitted with 26" heavy barrel.

NIB	Exc.	V.G.	Good	Fair	Poor
725	600	500	400	200	150

Sporter

Introduced in 1998. Features a select walnut stock, adjustable cheekpiece, adjustable buttplate, adjustable trigger. Comes without open sights. Detachable 5-round magazine. Chambered for .223, .22-250 and .308-calibers.

NIB	Exc.	V.G.	Good	Fair	Poor
950	825	675	500	395	200

T3 Hunter

Introduced in 2003. This bolt-action rifle features a hand-forged barrel and adjustable trigger. Offered in standard and Magnum calibers from .223 to .338 Win. Magnum. Walnut stock with recoil pad. Detachable magazine holds three rounds for all calibers except .223 (four). No sights. Barrel lengths are 22.5" and 24.25" for standard and Magnum calibers respectively. Weight about 6.75 lbs.

NIB	Exc.	V.G.	Good	Fair	Poor
750	625	500	400	200	150

T3 Lite

As above, with a black synthetic stock and blued finish. Introduced in 2003.

NIB	Exc.	V.G.	Good	Fair	Poor
675	550	425	325	150	100

T3 Lite Stainless

As above, with stainless steel barrel and synthetic stock.

NIB	Exc.	V.G.	Good	Fair	Poor
725	600	500	400	200	150

T3 Big Boar

Bolt-action rifle chambered for .308, .30-06 or .300 WSM cartridges. Fitted with 19" barrel with no sights. Black synthetic stock, with recoil pad. Blued finish. Magazine capacity 3 rounds. Weight about 6 lbs. Introduced in 2005.

NIB	Exc.	V.G.	Good	Fair	Poor
725	600	500	400	200	150

T3 Super Varmint

Bolt-action model chambered for .223 Rem., .22-250 Rem. or .308 cartridge. Stainless steel receiver and barrel, with Picatinny rail on receiver. Barrel length 23.3". Black synthetic stock has adjustable comb. Adjustable trigger. Detachable magazine. Introduced in 2005.

NIB	Exc.	V.G.	Good	Fair	Poor
1575	1350	1100	750	575	300

T3 Varmint

Chambered for .223, .22-250 and .308 cartridges. Fitted with 23.3" barrel with no sights. Synthetic stock, with blued finish. Adjustable trigger. Rubber recoil pad. **NOTE:** Add $70 for stainless steel version.

NIB	Exc.	V.G.	Good	Fair	Poor
850	725	575	400	295	150

T3 Tactical

Introduced in 2004. Rifle chambered for .223 or .308 cartridge. Fitted with 20" barrel with muzzle-brake. Black synthetic varmint-style stock, with adjustable cheekpiece. Detachable magazine capacity 5 rounds. Picatinny rail on receiver top.

NIB	Exc.	V.G.	Good	Fair	Poor
1500	1350	1050	850	575	350

Tikka Target

Bolt-action rifle chambered for .223, .22-250, 7mm-08 Rem., .308 Win. and 6.5x55 Swedish Mauser cartridge. Fitted with 23.25" barrel. Adjustable walnut target stock. Trigger is adjustable for weight. No sights. Weight about 9 lbs.

NIB	Exc.	V.G.	Good	Fair	Poor
950	825	675	500	395	200

SHOTGUNS/DOUBLE RIFLES

(FORMERLY VALMET)

Tikka, Valmet and Sako have been merged into one company, SAKO Ltd. These firearms are now manufactured in Italy under the brand name Tikka. Parts are interchangeable between Valmet guns made in Finland and Tikka guns made in Italy.

412S Shotgun

Over/under shotgun available in 12-gauge only, with 26" or 28" barrels. Stock is checkered European walnut. Weight about 7.25 lbs.

NIB	Exc.	V.G.	Good	Fair	Poor
950	800	650	500	300	200

412S Shotgun/Rifle

Same as above, with 12-gauge barrel and choice of .222 or .308 barrel. Barrel length 24". Weight 8 lbs.

NIB	Exc.	V.G.	Good	Fair	Poor
1000	850	700	500	300	200

412S Double Rifle

Same as above, with 24" over/under rifle barrel in 9.3x74R. Weight about 8.5 lbs.

NIB	Exc.	V.G.	Good	Fair	Poor
1150	950	750	500	300	200

412S Sporting Clays

Introduced in 1993. Offered in 12-gauge, with 28" barrels and choke tubes.

NIB	Exc.	V.G.	Good	Fair	Poor
1000	850	700	500	300	200

512S Field Grade

Introduced in 2000. Over/under gun chambered for 12-gauge 3" shell. Fitted with 26" or 28" choke tube barrels. **NOTE:** Add $650 per set for shotgun/rifle barrel sets.

NIB	Exc.	V.G.	Good	Fair	Poor
1125	850	750	500	300	200

512S Sporting Clays

This 12-gauge 3" model fitted with 30" barrel and choke tubes.

NIB	Exc.	V.G.	Good	Fair	Poor
1175	900	750	500	300	200

TIMBER WOLF

See—Action Arms Ltd.

TIPPING & LAWDEN

Birmingham, England

Thomas Revolver

A .320, .380 or .450 double-action revolver, with 4.5" barrel and 5-shot cylinder. Utilizing a cartridge extraction system, designed by J. Thomas of Birmingham. in which barrel and cylinder may be moved forward. Manufactured from 1870 to 1877.

NIB	Exc.	V.G.	Good	Fair	Poor
—	—	1400	950	400	175

TIPPMAN ARMS

Fort Wayne, Indiana

Model 1917

A .22-caliber semi-automatic one-half scale reproduction of Browning Model 1917 water-cooled machine gun. Barrel length 10". A tripod was sold with this model. Manufactured in 1986 and 1987.

NIB	Exc.	V.G.	Good	Fair	Poor
5750	5250	—	—	—	—

Model 1919 A-4

A .22-caliber semi-automatic one-half scale reproduction of Browning Model 1919 A-4 machine gun. Barrel length 11". Furnished with a tripod. Manufactured in 1986 and 1987.

NIB	Exc.	V.G.	Good	Fair	Poor
3000	2750	—	—	—	—

Model .50 HB

A .22 Magnum caliber semi-automatic one-half scale reproduction of Browning .50-caliber machine gun. Barrel length 18.25". Furnished with a tripod. Manufactured in 1986 and 1987.

NIB	Exc.	V.G.	Good	Fair	Poor
6000	5500	—	—	—	—

TISAS (TRABZON GUN INDUSTRY CORP.)

Trabzon, Turkey

Fatih 13

Beretta-style autopistol clone chambered in .32 ACP. Introduced 1994.

NIB	Exc.	V.G.	Good	Fair	Poor
300	225	150	125	75	50

Kanuni 16

Single-/double-action autopistol chambered in 9mm Parabellum, with 15- or 17-shot capacity. Black, chrome or chrome/gold finish. Introduced 1999.

NIB	Exc.	V.G.	Good	Fair	Poor
325	225	150	125	75	50

Kanuni S

Lightweight version of Kanuni 16. Black, chrome or chrome/black finish. Introduced 2000.

NIB	Exc.	V.G.	Good	Fair	Poor
325	225	150	125	75	50

Zigana M16

Single-/double-action autopistol chambered in 9mm Parabellum, with 15- or 17-shot capacity and 5" barrel. Introduced 2000.

NIB	Exc.	V.G.	Good	Fair	Poor
395	300	225	195	150	75

Zigana K

Compact version of Zigana M16, with 4" barrel. Introduced 2002.

NIB	Exc.	V.G.	Good	Fair	Poor
395	300	225	195	150	75

Zigana T

Longer (5.5") barrel version of Zigana M16. Introduced 2002.

NIB	Exc.	V.G.	Good	Fair	Poor
395	300	225	195	150	75

Zigana Sport

Compensated version of Zigana K, with 4.5" barrel. Introduced 2005.

NIB	Exc.	V.G.	Good	Fair	Poor
395	300	225	195	150	75

Zigana C45

Similar to Zigana M16. Chambered in .45 ACP, with 4.75" barrel. Introduced 2005.

NIB	Exc.	V.G.	Good	Fair	Poor
395	300	225	195	150	75

Zigana F

"Meltdown" version of Zigana M16, with radiused edges and improved ergonomics. Introduced 2007.

NIB	Exc.	V.G.	Good	Fair	Poor
395	300	225	195	150	75

TOBIN ARMS MANUFACTURING CO.
Norwich, Connecticut and Windsor, Ontario, Canada

Tobin Arms Manufacturing Co. operated from about 1905 to 1925 making an exposed hammer double and two hammerless models in four grades. The "Simplex" was cleverly designed (based on a patent by C.M. Wollam) side plated double-barrel internal hammer shotgun which resembled the Hopkins and Allen guns of that time. Some may have been private branded. Most of the Tobin doubles were made in Norwich, Conn. and are so marked. After 1909, operations were transferred to Windsor, Ont., Canada. Some guns will be found with that address. Tobin guns are not often seen by collectors and are highly prized because of their relative rarity and they were considered good guns by top dealers such as C.J. Godfrey Co. of New York City and Iver Johnson Sporting Goods of Boston. Values depend on condition and range from $200 in poor condition to $1000 and up for engraved versions in good to very good condition.

NOTE: Tobin also manufactured a .22 rimfire single-shot rifle apparently during the period 1910-1925. These are rather scarce and their value is estimated to be in the $500 - $700 range, depending on condition.

A rough timeline of Tobin Arms Manufacturing Company follows:

1903: founded by Frank M. Tobin in Norwich, CT.

1904-1909: manufactured hammer and hammerless sidelock shotguns (12ga. and 16ga.) in Norwich, Connecticut, USA

1909: purchased by a group of Canadian Investors and moved to Woodstock, ON, CAN

1910-1923/25: manufactured shotguns and rifles (entire product list unknown)

1923/25: purchased by sporting goods distributor G.B.Crandall

1923/25-1951: G.B.Crandall continued production until 1951 (possibly under the name GB Crandall)

Thanks to Jack of Florida for furnishing us with this information!

TODD, GEORGE H.
Montgomery, Alabama

Rifled Musket

A .58-caliber single-shot percussion rifle, with 40" barrel and full length stock secured by three barrel bands. Barrel and lock finished in bright brass furniture and walnut stock. Lock marked "George H. Todd/ Montgomery, Ala." TOO RARE TO PRICE.

TOKAREV
USSR

Russian Tokarev

Russian Tula Tokarev or TT-33, replaced earlier TT-30 in 1934 and remained in service into the late 1950s, despite its supposed replacement by the Makarov in 1951. An 8-shot semi-automatic pistol in 7.62x25mm caliber. Has a 4.6" barrel, with a short-recoil tilting barrel system. Tokarev was manufactured at Izshevsk arsenal until 1952. Probably has seen service with more countries, both communist and third world, than any other military handgun. Only safety feature on this pistol is placing the hammer at half-cock. Blued finish, hard rubber lined grips with communist star and CCCP (USSR) marked between the star points. Serial number with star and year of production is found on rear left frame. Top of slide also numbered. Take-down latch located on right frame. Russian Tokarev has recently become highly collectible, especially WWII dated examples. **NOTE:** Add 40 percent premium for pistols with wartime wooden grips.

NIB	Exc.	V.G.	Good	Fair	Poor
—	950	800	675	575	300

Chinese Licenses Tokarev

China received tooling to manufacture the Tokarev in 1950, and began production of their own copy at Number 66 Shenyang factory. Introduced as Type 51, which used a combination of Russian and Chinese made parts, it was practically identical to its Russian Counterpart. Replaced by Type 54 (in 1954), it differed by virtue that its construction was completely indigenous without borrowed Russian components. Markings on Type 51 and 54 have serial number, a star and production year on rear left frame, with Chinese written model number on right side, as well as stamped on upper top rear of the slide. As with the Russian version, they have become highly collectible in recent times given their affiliation with both Korean and Vietnam wars. Surviving Type 51 pistols are normally in very rough shape, but reap high prices, as much as 50 percent over those shown, which represent the more common Type 54. These were never imported into the United States and the majority are war-time bring backs. Again, the presence of capture papers greatly enhance values.

NIB	Exc.	V.G.	Good	Fair	Poor
—	750	675	600	475	300

Polish Licensed Tokarev

From 1947 to 1959, Poland manufactured the PW wz.33 at FB factory Number 11 in Radom. This was their copy of Russian Tokarev built under Soviet license. Mechanically identical to TT-33, its hard rubber grips do not have the star in a circle and are straight lined. Production year and Number 11 in a circle are marked on slide top, with serial number and year marked on left frame. Imported to United States in the 1990s, BATF demanded that all Tokarev-type imports be installed with a trigger block safety. Thus, importers were responsible in assuring installation of this prior to the pistols entering U.S. Most import outlets have since sold out of these pistols. Collectors feel it destroys originality, which is true, not to mention the addition of import markings which reduce value as well. Polish Tokarev imports have a rotating thumb or bar safety on left frame (depending on the importer), which some owners have removed and replaced with a dummy pin to restore originality. Those Polish Takarev variants picked up in Vietnam or elsewhere, without this feature, will increase prices 50 to 60 percent higher.

NIB	Exc.	V.G.	Good	Fair	Poor
—	395	325	300	225	200

M48 Hungarian Tokarev

Perhaps the rarest of all Eastern European Tokarev pistols is the Hungarian Model 48. Manufactured at the Femaru factory in Budapest from 1949 to about 1958. Never imported to United States and very few have been found on the world market making it quite scarce. Those made from 1949 to 1956 have "Rakosi" crest (the Hungarian premier at the time); those from late 1956 to possibly 1958 having "Kadar" crest. Lined hard rubber grips on M48 have Hungarian communist emblem in the center. Serial numbers and manufacture year on left frame.

NIB	Exc.	V.G.	Good	Fair	Poor
—	2500	1850	1500	1200	600

Romanian Licensed Tokarev

Manufactured at Cugir Romania arms factory, TTC or Tulskiye Tokarev Cugir was produced from 1952 to 1959. Remained the standard Romanian service pistol until the Romanian revolution of 1989. Huge quantities of TTC have been imported to United States in the last 15 years and are still available from distributors as of this writing. Lined hard rubber grips have "RPR" between the star points which is *Republika Populus Romana* or Peoples Republic of Romania. Much like the Polish version, TTC has BATF-required supplemental trigger safety. It is believed none were ever exported to other nations such as North Vietnam, thus their appearance in the United States was an all time first. However, an example found without the import safety or markings would yield a great price. Serial number located on left frame and upper slide. Interestingly, the narrow finger grips at the slide's rear are similar to a Colt 1911, and not the line and oval type of Russian TT-33. Most offered for sale from dealers at the present include a brown leather holster.

NIB	Exc.	V.G.	Good	Fair	Poor
—	300	275	250	200	150

Pakistani TT-33 Tokarev

Since 1941, Badar & Brother have produced sporting arms and some military ordnance as well. Though not a Com Bloc country, Pakistan used the Tokarev until sometime in the recent 15 years. B&B manufactured a very high quality copy of which a thousand or more were imported to United States through TGI in Knoxville, Tennessee from 2008 to 2009 time frame. They have since sold out from distributors and are identical to Russian version. This model likely holds the distinction of being the newest Tokarev manufactured. Those imported were available in original 7.62x25 or 9mm Luger. Finished in a matte-like blue finish, they were neatly boxed and came with a manual and spare magazine. Regarding the required BATF supplemental safety, the B&B Tokarev has a very efficient thumb safety installed on rear left side of frame. Far more efficient and cosmetically appealing than those installed on aforementioned Polish and Romanian import.

NIB	Exc.	V.G.	Good	Fair	Poor
700	650	600	550	500	300

Yugoslavian M-57A Licensed Tokarev

This version of Tokarev was manufactured by Crvena Zastava in Serbia from 1957 to 1992. A redesigned variant of the Tokarev. Frame was extended with a longer grip to allow use of a 9-shot magazine. Has a clamp-retained firing pin assembly versus cross pin retainer found on standard Tokarev design. A matted sight ramp on the slide top was also added to reduce glare. M-57 Tokarev pistols began to be imported to United States in the 1990s. Listed as M-57A, because of the addition to U.S.-required supplemental safety, which is a flat, frame mounted type that slides along the upper left grip. Those that have the communist crest, with six pointed flame and Roman numerals, are of interest to collectors as they are pre-1980s production and will enhance values up to 40 percent. Serial number is located on right frame and slide flat, with M-57 marked on left slide. Zastava continues to produce this pistol in 9mm Luger and lists as M-70A.

NIB	Exc.	V.G.	Good	Fair	Poor
—	500	450	400	375	275

TOMISKA, ALOIS
Pilsen, Czechoslovakia

Little Tom

A 6.35mm or 7.65mm caliber semi-automatic pistol, with 2.5" barrel. Slide marked "Alois Tomiska Plzen Patent Little Tom". Grips inlaid with a medallion bearing the monogram "AT". Blued, with checkered walnut grips. Manufactured from 1908 to 1918. Subsequently produced by Wiener Waffenfabrik.

NIB	Exc.	V.G.	Good	Fair	Poor
—	550	425	350	250	125

TORKELSON ARMS CO.
Harfield, Warren, and Worcester, Massachusetts

Double-Barrel Shotguns

Reinhard T. Torkelson's company made double-barrel boxlock side-by-side hammerless shotguns, in four models at several locations between 1885 and 1910. He worked with Iver Johnson at Fitchburg, Mass. and also built guns carrying Lovell (Boston) name. His "New Worcester" marked guns are quite common. They were sold by Sears and other large and well known houses.

NIB	Exc.	V.G.	Good	Fair	Poor
—	600	300	200	150	100

TRADEWINDS
Tacoma, Washington
Model H-170

A 12-gauge semi-automatic shotgun, with 26" or 28" ventilated rib barrel and 5-shot tubular magazine. Blued anodized alloy receiver and walnut stock.

NIB	Exc.	V.G.	Good	Fair	Poor
—	300	250	225	150	100

Model 260-A

A .22-caliber semi-automatic rifle, with 22.5" barrel, open sights and 5-shot magazine. Blued, with walnut stock.

NIB	Exc.	V.G.	Good	Fair	Poor
—	200	175	125	100	75

Model 311-A

A .22-caliber bolt-action rifle, with 22.5" barrel, open sights and 5-shot magazine. Blued, with walnut stock.

NIB	Exc.	V.G.	Good	Fair	Poor
—	175	150	100	75	50

Model 5000 "Husky"

A centerfire bolt-action rifle, with 24" barrel, adjustable sights and 4-shot magazine. Blued, with walnut stock.

NIB	Exc.	V.G.	Good	Fair	Poor
—	350	300	275	200	100

TRADITIONS
Old Saybrook, Connecticut

These shotguns were imported from Italy until 2007. They were made by Fausti Stefano and Emil Rizzini. Since 2011, Traditions has imported only black-powder firearms and accessories.

OVER/UNDER SHOTGUNS

Hunter

Introduced in 2001. Features 12- or 20-gauge chambers, 26" or 28" ventilated rib barrels with fixed chokes. Single-selective trigger. Extractors. Checkered walnut stock. Blued frame and barrels. Black rubber recoil pad. Weight about: 7.25 lbs. 12-gauge; 6.75 lbs. 20-gauge.

NIB	Exc.	V.G.	Good	Fair	Poor
650	525	400	300	225	150

Field I

Offered in 12-, 20-, 28-gauge and .410 bore. Barrel lengths 26". Fixed chokes. Single-selective trigger and extractors. Coin finish engraved receiver. Checkered walnut stock. Black rubber recoil pad. Weight similar to Hunter model; .410 bore about 6.5 lbs.

NIB	Exc.	V.G.	Good	Fair	Poor
575	450	375	275	200	125

Field II

Similar to Field I, with additional choice of 16-gauge with 28" barrels. Also features screw-in chokes and automatic ejectors.

NIB	Exc.	V.G.	Good	Fair	Poor
750	625	500	375	250	125

Field II Combo

Features 20-gauge and .410 bore two barrel set. Both barrels are 26", with fixed chokes. Checkered walnut stock. Weight about 6 lbs. Introduced in 2004.

NIB	Exc.	V.G.	Good	Fair	Poor
1400	1200	950	800	500	300

Field III Gold

Similar to other Field series of guns, but offered in 12-gauge only with 26" or 28" barrels. Select oil-finish walnut stock. Engraved receiver, with gold pheasants and woodcock.

NIB	Exc.	V.G.	Good	Fair	Poor
1100	950	800	675	500	250

Upland II

Offered in both 12- and 20-gauge, with 26" barrels in 12-gauge; 24" or 26" barrels in 20-gauge. Straight-grip walnut stock. Engraved blued receiver. Schnabel fore-end. Choke tubes. Single-selective trigger and auto ejectors. Weight about: 12-gauge 7.25 lbs.; 20-gauge 6.25 lbs.

NIB	Exc.	V.G.	Good	Fair	Poor
800	650	500	350	275	150

Upland III

Introduced in 2001. Features 12-gauge, with 26" ventilated rib barrels. High grade checkered walnut stock, with hand engraved gold receiver. Schnabel fore-end. Single-selective trigger and auto ejectors standard. Screw-in chokes. Black rubber recoil pad. Weight about 7.25 lbs.

NIB	Exc.	V.G.	Good	Fair	Poor
1400	1200	950	800	500	300

Sporting Clay II

This 12-gauge gas operated model has 28" or 30" ventilated rib ported barrels. Screw-in extended choke tubes. Checkered walnut stock, with blued receiver and barrels. Weight about 8 lbs.

NIB	Exc.	V.G.	Good	Fair	Poor
900	775	650	475	300	150

Sporting Clay III

Features 12- or 20-gauge, with 28" or 30" ventilated rib barrels. High grade checkered walnut stock. Choke tubes. Weight about: 8.5 lbs.

12-gauge; 8.25 lbs. 20-gauge. **NOTE:** Add $200 for 20-gauge.

NIB	Exc.	V.G.	Good	Fair	Poor
1400	1200	950	800	500	300

Waterfowl II

Introduced in 2001. This 12-gauge fitted with 28" ventilated rib barrels and 3.5" chambers. Finish on stock and barrels is Advantage Wetlands camo. Blued engraved receiver. Recoil pad. Single-selective trigger, with auto ejectors. Weight about 7.25 lbs.

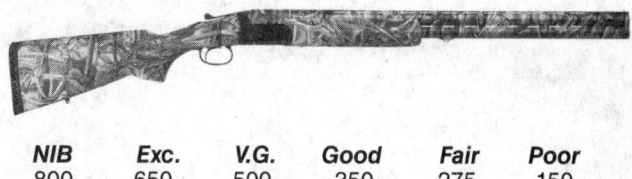

NIB	Exc.	V.G.	Good	Fair	Poor
800	650	500	350	275	150

Turkey II

Offered in 12-gauge, with choice of 24" or 26" ventilated rib barrels. Mossy Oak Break-Up camo finish, with blued receiver. X-Full choke. Single-selective trigger and auto ejectors. Weight about 7 lbs.

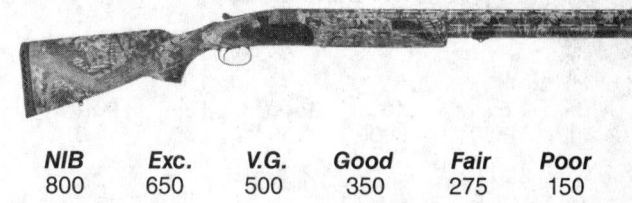

NIB	Exc.	V.G.	Good	Fair	Poor
800	650	500	350	275	150

Mag Hunter II

This 12-gauge features 28" barrels, with 3.5" chambers. Engraved blued receiver, with walnut stock or blued receiver, with Realtree Max-4 finish. Rubber recoil pad. Single-selective trigger, with auto ejectors. Screw-in chokes. Weight about 7 lbs. **NOTE:** Add 10 percent for camo model.

NIB	Exc.	V.G.	Good	Fair	Poor
900	765	650	500	350	175

Real 16

16-gauge gun fitted with 26" ventilated rib barrels. Checkered walnut stock. Choke tubes. Single trigger, with auto ejectors. Receiver is game scene engraved. Weight about 6.75 lbs. Introduced in 2004.

NIB	Exc.	V.G.	Good	Fair	Poor
1100	950	800	675	500	250

Real 16 Gold

As above, with gold-filled birds on receiver.

NIB	Exc.	V.G.	Good	Fair	Poor
1400	1200	950	800	500	300

Gold Wing II Silver

Chambered for 12-gauge 3" shell. Fitted with 28" ventilated rib barrels, with choke tubes. Single trigger and auto ejectors. Receiver engraved with game scenes. High grade walnut stock, with oil-finish. Weight about 7.5 lbs.

NIB	Exc.	V.G.	Good	Fair	Poor
1500	1300	1100	850	675	300

Gold Wing III

As above, with case colored receiver with gold inlays.

NIB	Exc.	V.G.	Good	Fair	Poor
2000	1750	1400	1050	800	400

Gold Wing III Silver

As above, with silver receiver with gold inlays.

NIB	Exc.	V.G.	Good	Fair	Poor
2100	1850	1500	1150	875	450

Gold Wing SL III

As above, with case colored side plates and gold inlays.

NIB	Exc.	V.G.	Good	Fair	Poor
2200	1950	1575	1225	950	450

Gold Wing SL III Silver

As above, with silver side plates and gold inlays.

NIB	Exc.	V.G.	Good	Fair	Poor
2300	2050	1675	1300	1000	500

SIDE-BY-SIDE SHOTGUNS

Elite I DT

Offered in 12-, 20-, 28-gauge and .410 bore. All gauges fitted with 26" barrels, with fixed chokes. Double triggers and extractors. Walnut stock. Weight about 6 lbs. **NOTE:** Add $60 for 28-gauge and .410 bore models.

NIB	Exc.	V.G.	Good	Fair	Poor
750	600	400	300	200	100

Elite I ST

Same as above, with single-selective trigger.

NIB	Exc.	V.G.	Good	Fair	Poor
900	750	550	425	300	150

Elite Hunter

Introduced in 2001. Features 12- or 20-gauge, with 26" barrels with screw-in chokes. Walnut stock, with beavertail fore-end. Single non-selective trigger. Weight about 6.5 lbs.

NIB	Exc.	V.G.	Good	Fair	Poor
950	800	600	475	350	200

Elite Field III ST

Introduced in 2001. Offered in 28-gauge or .410 bore, with 26" barrels. High grade walnut stock, with straight-grip. Fixed chokes. Engraved receiver with gold. Weight about 6.25 lbs.

NIB	Exc.	V.G.	Good	Fair	Poor
2000	1750	1400	1050	800	400

Uplander II Silver

Chambererd for 12-gauge 28" barrels; 20-gauge 26" barrels. Choke tubes. Silver receiver, with light scroll engraving. Checkered stock, with high grade walnut. Straight-grip. Single trigger and auto ejectors. Weight about 6.75 lbs.

NIB	Exc.	V.G.	Good	Fair	Poor
2100	1850	1500	1150	875	450

Uplander III Silver

As above, with more extensive engraving with gold inlays.

NIB	Exc.	V.G.	Good	Fair	Poor
2700	2350	1950	1600	900	500

Uplander V Silver

As above, with sideplates, extensive engraving and gold inlays.

NIB	Exc.	V.G.	Good	Fair	Poor
3000	2650	2200	1800	1100	600

SEMI-AUTOMATIC SHOTGUNS

ALS Field

Introduced in 2001. Offered in both 12- and 20-gauge, with 24", 26" or 28" ventilated rib barrels. Walnut stock, with black pad. Blued receiver and barrels. Screw-in chokes. Weight about 6.25 lbs.

NIB	Exc.	V.G.	Good	Fair	Poor
450	350	225	175	125	100

ALS Hunter

Same as above, with synthetic stock with 26" or 28" barrels.

NIB	Exc.	V.G.	Good	Fair	Poor
450	350	225	175	125	100

ALS Waterfowl

This 12-gauge has Advantage Wetlands camo. Fitted with 28" barrel, with screw-in chokes. Weight about 6.5 lbs.

NIB	Exc.	V.G.	Good	Fair	Poor
500	400	300	225	175	100

ALS Turkey

Same as above, with 21" barrel and Mossy Oak Break-up camo. Weight about 6 lbs.

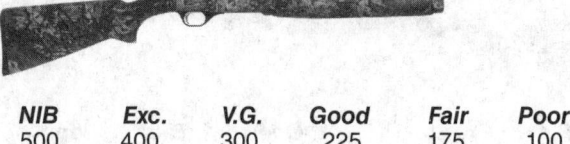

NIB	Exc.	V.G.	Good	Fair	Poor
500	400	300	225	175	100

TRANTER, WILLIAM
Birmingham, England

William Tranter produced a variety of revolvers on his own. A number of other makers produced revolvers based upon his designs. Consequently, "Tranter's Patent" is to be found on revolvers made by such firms as Deane, Adams and Deane, etc.

Model 1872

A .38-caliber double-action revolver, with 6" octagonal barrel and 6-shot cylinder. Blued, with walnut grips.

Courtesy Wallis & Wallis, Lewes, Sussex, England

NIB	Exc.	V.G.	Good	Fair	Poor
—	—	2200	975	400	200

Model 1878

A .450-caliber double-action revolver, with 6" octagonal barrel. Blued, with walnut grip. Manufactured from 1878 to 1887.

NIB	Exc.	V.G.	Good	Fair	Poor
—	—	2750	1350	500	250

TRIPLETT & SCOTT/MERIDEN MANUFACTURING COMPANY
Meriden, Connecticut

Repeating Carbine

A .50-caliber carbine, with 22" or 30" round barrel and 7-shot magazine located in the butt. Loaded by turning barrel until it comes in line with the magazine. Blued case-hardened, with walnut stock. Approximately 5,000 made in 1864 and 1865. **NOTE:** Add 20 percent for even scarcer 22" barrel version.

Courtesy Milwaukee Public Museum, Milwaukee, Wisconsin

NIB	Exc.	V.G.	Good	Fair	Poor
—	—	3500	1500	500	200

TRISTAR SPORTING ARMS
N. Kansas City, Missouri

In 2000, Tristar bought American Arms. American Arms no longer exists, but some of its models will appear under Tristar name. For American Arms firearms built prior to sale, see that section.

SILVER SERIES

Series of over/under guns that were produced by Spanish company Zabala.

Silver Sporting

Offered in 12-gauge, with 28" or 30" barrels. Single-selective trigger, auto ejectors, choke tubes, ported barrels with target rib. Checkered walnut stock, with pistol-grip and recoil pad.

NIB	Exc.	V.G.	Good	Fair	Poor
800	675	525	400	200	125

Specialty Magnums

A 12-gauge Magnum chambered for 3.5" shell. Fitted with 28" barrel. Choke tubes. Checkered black walnut stock, with pistol-grip. In 2003, a camo finish was offered. **NOTE:** Add $85 for camo finish.

NIB	Exc.	V.G.	Good	Fair	Poor
645	500	400	300	200	100

Silver Hunter

Offered in both 12- and 20-gauge, with 26" or 28" ventilated rib barrels. Single-selective trigger, choke tubes, engraved receiver with silver finish. Checkered walnut stock, with pistol-grip.

NIB	Exc.	V.G.	Good	Fair	Poor
625	500	400	300	200	100

Silver II

As above, with fixed chokes for 16-, 28-gauge and .410 bore models.

NIB	Exc.	V.G.	Good	Fair	Poor
670	525	425	325	225	125

Silver Classic

Offered in 12- and 20-gauge, with 28" ventilated rib barrels and choke tubes. Frame case colored and scroll engraved. Single-selective trigger and ejectors. Weight about 6.75 lbs.

NIB	Exc.	V.G.	Good	Fair	Poor
800	650	500	400	300	175

BASQUE SERIES

Series of side-by-side shotguns. Introduced in 2003. Produced in Spain by Zabala.

Brittany Sporting

Offered in 12- and 20-gauge, with 28" barrels, 3" chambers and choke tubes. Action is boxlock, with sideplates scroll engraved with case coloring. Semi-fancy checkered walnut stock, with oil-finish and pistol-grip. Semi-beavertail fore-end. Single-selective trigger and ejectors. Weight about 6.75 lbs.

NIB	Exc.	V.G.	Good	Fair	Poor
850	750	600	400	300	150

Brittany

Features boxlock action, with case colored frame with scroll engraving. Straight-grip walnut stock, with semi-beavertail fore-end. Offered in 12-, 16-, 20-, 28-gauge and .410 bore, with 3" chambers and choke tubes. Weight 6.2 - 7.4 lbs. depending on gauge.

NIB	Exc.	V.G.	Good	Fair	Poor
900	800	650	450	300	200

Brittany Classic

Enhanced Brittany model. Features fancy walnut wood and rounded pistol-grip, cut checkering, engraved case colored frame and auto selective ejectors. Available in 12-, 16-, 20-, 28-gauge and .410 bore, all with 3" chambers and 27" barrels. Weight about 6.7 lbs. in 12-gauge and slightly less in sub-gauges.

NIB	Exc.	V.G.	Good	Fair	Poor
1050	875	700	575	400	200

York

Side-by-side, with blued engraved receiver and 3" chambers. Comes in 12- and 20-gauge, with 26" or 28" barrels. Walnut pistol-grip stock and rubber recoil pad.

NIB	Exc.	V.G.	Good	Fair	Poor
625	500	400	300	200	100

Hunter Lite

Over/under with silver alloy engraved frame, 3" chambers, extractors, choke tubes and walnut pistol-grip stock and forearm. Weight: 20-gauge with 26" barrels 5.4 lbs.; 12-gauge with 28" barrels 6 lbs.

NIB	Exc.	V.G.	Good	Fair	Poor
450	325	225	175	100	75

Hunter

Similar to Hunter Lite, with blued steel frame.

NIB	Exc.	V.G.	Good	Fair	Poor
450	325	225	175	100	75

Field Hunter

Based on Hunter, this model includes selective auto ejectors and five choke tubes.

NIB	Exc.	V.G.	Good	Fair	Poor
575	450	325	250	150	100

Gentry/Gentry Coach

Offered in 12-, 16-, 20-, 28-gauge and .410 bore in Gentry and 12- and 20-gauge in Gentry Coach. Barrel lengths are 28" for Gentry (26" for 28-gauge and .410 bore) and 20" for Gentry Coach. Boxlock action, with engraved antique silver finish. Walnut stock, with pistol-grip. Choke tubes. Single-selective trigger. Weight about 6.5 lbs. depending on gauge.

NIB	Exc.	V.G.	Good	Fair	Poor
750	625	500	400	250	100

Derby Classic

Features sidelock frame and action that is engraved and case colored. Offered in 12-gauge, with fixed chokes in Modified and Full. Fitted with 28" barrel. Double trigger and automatic ejectors. Weight about 7.75 lbs.

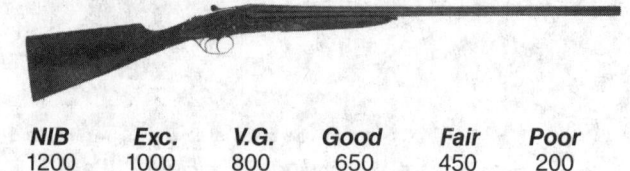

NIB	Exc.	V.G.	Good	Fair	Poor
1200	1000	800	650	450	200

TSA SERIES

These gas-operated semi-automatics are available in 12- and 20-gauge, with barrels from 24" to 26" depending on model.

TSA Field

Walnut fore-end and pistol-grip stock, 3" chamber, 3 choke tubes and magazine-cut-off feature. Weight about 5.7 lbs. in 20-gauge; 6.5 lbs.

in 12-gauge depending on barrel length. 20-gauge available in youth model.

NIB	Exc.	V.G.	Good	Fair	Poor
375	325	275	175	125	75

TSA Synthetic and Synthetic Mag

Same features as TSA Field Model, with non-glare black synthetic stock and fore-end. Also available with complete Realtree Max-4 coverage. Mag model has 3.5" chamber.

NIB	Exc.	V.G.	Good	Fair	Poor
375	325	275	175	125	75

300 SERIES

Tristar 300 series over/under guns were imported from Turkey.

Model 333

This over/under gun available in 12- or 20-gauge, with 26", 28" or 30" barrels in 12-gauge. Hand engraved frame. Fitted with 3" chambers and choke tubes. Single-selective triggers and auto ejectors. Fancy Turkish walnut stock. Weight about: 7.75 lbs. 12-gauge; 7.5 lbs. 20-gauge.

NIB	Exc.	V.G.	Good	Fair	Poor
650	600	425	325	225	150

Model 333SC

Similar to above model, with addition of 11mm sporting rib, recoil pad, forcing cones and ported barrels. Extended choke tubes.

NIB	Exc.	V.G.	Good	Fair	Poor
700	650	475	375	250	175

Model 333SCL

Same features as Model 333SC, with special stock.

NIB	Exc.	V.G.	Good	Fair	Poor
700	650	475	375	250	175

Model 333L

Same features as Model 333, with a special stock designed for women. Length of pull shorter, with special Monte Carlo comb.

NIB	Exc.	V.G.	Good	Fair	Poor
650	600	425	325	225	150

Model 330

This over/under has a standard Turkish walnut stock, with etched engraved frame. Offered in 12- and 20-gauge. Single trigger, with extractors and fixed chokes.

NIB	Exc.	V.G.	Good	Fair	Poor
450	325	225	175	100	75

Model 330D

Same as model above, with addition of selective auto ejectors.

NIB	Exc.	V.G.	Good	Fair	Poor
500	400	300	225	175	100

Model 300

Features an underlug action lock, with double triggers and extractors. Frame is etched. Offered in 12-gauge only, with 26" or 28" barrels with fixed chokes.

NIB	Exc.	V.G.	Good	Fair	Poor
450	325	225	175	100	75

Model 311

Side-by-side gun in 12- or 20-gauge, with 26" or 28" barrels with choke tubes. Standard Turkish walnut. Blued frame.

NIB	Exc.	V.G.	Good	Fair	Poor
500	400	300	225	175	100

Model 311R

Same as above, with 20" barrel choked Cylinder and Cylinder.

NIB	Exc.	V.G.	Good	Fair	Poor
500	400	300	225	175	100

EMILIO RIZZINI (Old Nova Series)

Gun line no longer imported. Tristar Nova series were imported from Italy.

TR-L

Offered in 12- or 20-gauge, with choice of 28" or 30" ventilated rib barrels. Choke tubes standard. Standard grade walnut, with pistol-grip. Action is silver finish boxlock, with auto ejectors and single-selective trigger. Weight about 7.5 lbs. Stock dimensions are made for a smaller shooter. Introduced in 1998.

NIB	Exc.	V.G.	Good	Fair	Poor
1000	850	700	575	400	200

TR-SC

Similar to Nova L. Offered in 12-gauge only, with standard stock dimensions. Semi-fancy walnut stock, with pistol-grip. Black sporting clays-style recoil pad. Weight between 7.5 and 8 lbs. depending on barrel length. Introduced in 1998.

NIB	Exc.	V.G.	Good	Fair	Poor
1000	850	700	575	400	200

TR-I

Offered in 12- and 20-gauge, with 26" or 28" barrels with fixed chokes. Walnut stock, with hand checkering and pistol-grip. Beavertail fore-end. Boxlock action is blue, with single-selective trigger and extractors. Weight about 7.5 lbs. Introduced in 1998.

NIB	Exc.	V.G.	Good	Fair	Poor
650	600	425	325	225	150

TR-II (Nova II)

Same as above, but fitted with automatic ejectors.

NIB	Exc.	V.G.	Good	Fair	Poor
700	650	475	375	250	175

TR-Mag

Similar to the Nova I. Chambered for 10- and 12-gauge with 3.5" shell. Choice of 24" or 28" ventilated rib barrels, with choke tubes. Non-reflective non-glare blue finish. Introduced in 1998. **NOTE:** Add $175 for 12-gauge with ejectors; $350 for 10-gauge gun.

NIB	Exc.	V.G.	Good	Fair	Poor
750	650	475	375	250	175

TTR-Royal

Offered in 12-, 20- or 28-gauge, with 28" ported choke tube barrels, straight-grip semi-fancy walnut stock and auto ejectors. Silver receiver, with gold engraving.

NIB	Exc.	V.G.	Good	Fair	Poor
1300	1250	1100	875	600	300

TR-Class SL

Top-of-the-line model, with sculptured frame and engraved side plates. Offered in 12-gauge only.

NIB	Exc.	V.G.	Good	Fair	Poor
1775	1500	1250	1000	750	500

411 SERIES

Shotguns are made in Italy by R.F.M. Luciano Rota.

Model 411

Side-by-side double imported from Italy. Introduced in 1998. Chambered for 12-, 20-gauge and .410 bore, with choice of 26" or 28" barrels with choke tubes or fixed chokes. Boxlock action, with engraving and case coloring. Double triggers and extractors. Standard walnut stock, with pistol-grip and splinter forearm. Weight between 6 and 6.5 lbs.

NIB	Exc.	V.G.	Good	Fair	Poor
850	675	500	375	250	150

Model 411R

Offered in 12- or 20-gauge, with 20" barrel. Fixed cylinder chokes. Extractors. Weight about: 6.5 lbs. 12-gauge; 6 lbs. 20-gauge.

NIB	Exc.	V.G.	Good	Fair	Poor
750	650	475	375	250	175

Model 411D

Similar to Model 411, with engraved case colored finish on receiver, auto ejectors, single trigger and straight-grip stock. Weight about: 28-gauge 6.25 lbs.; 12 gauge 7 lbs.

NIB	Exc.	V.G.	Good	Fair	Poor
1050	875	700	575	400	200

Model 411F

Same as Model 411D, with silver engraved receiver.

NIB	Exc.	V.G.	Good	Fair	Poor
1600	1400	1050	800	600	400

PHANTOM SERIES

Shotguns made in Turkey by Eqsilah. Discontinued in favor of new redesigned gun found under Diana Series.

Phantom Field

Gas-operated semi-automatic shotgun. Chambered for 12-gauge and 2.75" or 3" shell. Fitted with 24", 26" or 28" barrel. Checkered walnut stock, with pistol-grip. Screw-in chokes. Five-round magazine. **NOTE:** Add $75 for Magnum models.

NIB	Exc.	V.G.	Good	Fair	Poor
425	325	275	200	150	100

Phantom Synthetic

Same as above, with synthetic stock. **NOTE:** Add $75 for Magnum models.

NIB	Exc.	V.G.	Good	Fair	Poor
395	300	225	195	150	75

Phantom HP

Same features as Phantom Field, except with synthetic stock, 19" barrel and swivel studs.

NIB	Exc.	V.G.	Good	Fair	Poor
395	300	225	195	150	75

BREDA SERIES

Semi-automatic shotguns are made in Italy by Breda. Guns first imported by Tristar in 2003.

Ermes

Chambered for 12-gauge 3" shell. Fitted with 26" or 28" ventilated rib barrel. Inertia operated recoil system. Checkered walnut stock, with pistol-grip. Choice of black, nickel, gold or silver alloy receiver finish. Receiver engraved with hunting scenes. Adjustable stock spacers. Weight about 7.75 lbs.

Gold

NIB	Exc.	V.G.	Good	Fair	Poor
1935	1500	1250	1075	800	400

Silver

NIB	Exc.	V.G.	Good	Fair	Poor
1725	1350	1100	900	650	300

Nickel

NIB	Exc.	V.G.	Good	Fair	Poor
1650	1200	1050	750	500	300

Black

NIB	Exc.	V.G.	Good	Fair	Poor
1260	975	750	600	500	250

Astra 20

A 20-gauge, with 26" ventilated rib barrel. Black receiver. Walnut with pistol-grip and solid rubber recoil pad. Furnished with five choke tubes. Weight about 6 lbs.

NIB	Exc.	V.G.	Good	Fair	Poor
1140	900	750	600	465	200

Mira Sporting

Semi-automatic shotgun is gas-operated. Chambered for 12-gauge shell, with 3" chamber. Fitted with 30" ventilated rib barrel, with 10mm wide rib. Checkered walnut stock, with pistol-grip. Weight about 7 lbs.

NIB	Exc.	V.G.	Good	Fair	Poor
875	700	550	400	300	200

Mira Camo

As above, with 28" barrel and camo finish.

NIB	Exc.	V.G.	Good	Fair	Poor
875	700	550	400	300	200

CD DIANA SERIES

Shotguns made in Turkey by Eqsilah. This line replaced Phantom Series. First imported by Tristar in 2003.

CD Diana Field

Gas-operated semi-automatic shotgun. Chambered for 12-gauge 3" shell. Fitted with 26", 28" or 30" ventilated rib barrel. Checkered walnut stock, with pistol-grip. Choke tubes. Magazine cutoff. Weight about 7 lbs. depending on barrel length.

NIB	Exc.	V.G.	Good	Fair	Poor
425	325	275	200	150	100

CD Diana Synthetic

As above, with black synthetic stock. Also offered with 3.5" chamber. Weight about 6.75 lbs. **NOTE:** Add $90 for 3.5" Magnum model.

NIB	Exc.	V.G.	Good	Fair	Poor
400	300	250	200	150	100

CD Diana Slug

12-gauge gun fitted with 24" rifled slug barrel, with open adjustable sights. Black synthetic stock. Weight about 6.75 lbs.

NIB	Exc.	V.G.	Good	Fair	Poor
425	325	275	200	150	100

CD Diana Camo Mag

Similar to models above, with camo stock and barrel. Choice of 24" or 28" barrel, with 3.5" chamber. Weight about 6.75 lbs.

NIB	Exc.	V.G.	Good	Fair	Poor
575	450	350	225	175	100

Pee Wee

Single-shot bolt-action rifle chambered for .22 LR cartridges. Stock is walnut and about 1/2 the size of an adult rifle. Weight about 2.75 lbs. Open sights. Finish is blue.

NIB	Exc.	V.G.	Good	Fair	Poor
200	150	100	75	50	25

HANDGUNS

Model C-100

Compact model based on CZ75 design. DA/SA operation. Chambered in 9mm or .40 S&W, with 11- and 15-round magazine capacities, respectively. Blue or chrome finish, with 3.9" barrel, checkered polymer grips and fixed sights. Introduced in 2013.

NIB	Exc.	V.G.	Good	Fair	Poor
400	360	320	285	—	—

Model L-120

Full-size model based on CZ75 design in 9mm only. Similar features to those found on C-100, except with 4.7" barrel, 17-round magazine capacity. Available in chrome finish.

NIB	Exc.	V.G.	Good	Fair	Poor
400	360	320	285	—	—

TROCAOLA (TAC)
Eibar, Spain

Break-Top Revolvers

This maker produced a variety of .32-, .38- and .44-caliber top break revolvers between 1900 and 1936. These pistols can be identified by the monogram "TAC" stamped on left side of the frame. **NOTE:** Add 50 percent premium for .44 models.

NIB	Exc.	V.G.	Good	Fair	Poor
—	275	175	125	100	75

TRYON, EDWARD K. & COMPANY
Philadelphia, Pennsylvania

Pocket Pistol

A .41-caliber single-shot percussion pocket pistol, with 2" or 4" barrel, German silver mounts and walnut stock. Lock marked "Tryon/Philada". Manufactured during 1860s and 1870s.

NIB	Exc.	V.G.	Good	Fair	Poor
—	—	2550	1900	750	200

TUCKER SHERARD & COMPANY
Lancaster, Texas

Dragoon

A .44-caliber percussion revolver, with 7.75" round barrel. Fitted with loading lever and 6-shot cylinder. Barrel marked "Clark, Sherard & Co., Lancaster, Texas". Cylinder etched in two panels, with crossed cannons and legend "Texas Arms". Approximately 400 revolvers of this type were made between 1862 and 1867. Prospective purchasers are advised to secure a qualified appraisal prior to acquisition.

NIB	Exc.	V.G.	Good	Fair	Poor
—	—	60000	55000	22000	13000

TUFTS & COLLEY
New York, New York

Pocket Pistol

A .44-caliber single-shot percussion pocket pistol, with 3.5" barrel, German silver mounts and walnut stock. Lock marked "Tufts & Colley"; barrel "Deringer/Pattn.". Manufactured during 1860s.

NIB	Exc.	V.G.	Good	Fair	Poor
—	—	2450	1900	825	200

TURBIAUX, JACQUES
Paris, France
See—Ames

TURNER, THOMAS
Redding, England

Pepperbox

A .476 double-action percussion pepperbox having 6 barrels. Blued case-hardened, with walnut grips. Left side of frame engraved in an oval "Thomas Turner, Redding".

Courtesy Bonhams & Butterfields, San Francisco, California

NIB	Exc.	V.G.	Good	Fair	Poor
—	—	5500	1900	975	400

TYLER ORDNANCE WORKS
Tyler, Texas

This company produced 56 Austrian rifles, 508 Enfield rifles, 423 Hill rifles and 1,009 Texas rifles during the Civil War. **NOTE:** These rifles are very rare.

Tyler Texas Rifle

A .57-caliber single-shot rifle, with 27" barrel and full stock secured by two barrel bands. Lock marked "Texas Rifle/Tyler/Cal. .57".

NIB	Exc.	V.G.	Good	Fair	Poor
—	—	62500	44000	16500	12000

Hill Rifle

A .54-caliber single-shot percussion rifle, with 27" barrel and full stock secured by two brass barrel bands. Iron trigger guard and buttplate. Lock marked "Hill Rifle/Tyler/Tex/ Cal. .54".

NIB	Exc.	V.G.	Good	Fair	Poor
—	—	58000	40000	15000	12000

U

U.S. ARMS CO.
Riverhead, New York
See—United Sporting Arms, Inc.

U.S. M1 CARBINE
Various Manufacturers

For history, technical data, descriptions, photos and prices, see Standard Catalog of Military Firearms under United States Rifles. Prices listed are for rifles in original, unaltered condition. **NOTE:** Rifles that have been refinished or restored deduct about 50 percent.

Inland

NIB	Exc.	V.G.	Good	Fair	Poor
2000	1800	1200	600	425	350

Underwood

NIB	Exc.	V.G.	Good	Fair	Poor
2000	1800	1250	550	400	275

S.G. Saginaw

NIB	Exc.	V.G.	Good	Fair	Poor
2000	1800	1400	700	450	375

IBM

NIB	Exc.	V.G.	Good	Fair	Poor
2200	1900	1500	1000	500	250

Quality Hardware

NIB	Exc.	V.G.	Good	Fair	Poor
2000	1700	1100	525	375	250

National Postal Meter

NIB	Exc.	V.G.	Good	Fair	Poor
2100	1800	1100	575	375	250

Standard Products

NIB	Exc.	V.G.	Good	Fair	Poor
2150	1900	1200	600	425	250

Rockola

NIB	Exc.	V.G.	Good	Fair	Poor
2400	2000	1400	750	475	350

SG Grand Rapids

NIB	Exc.	V.G.	Good	Fair	Poor
2400	2000	1400	600	425	350

Winchester

NIB	Exc.	V.G.	Good	Fair	Poor
2500	2200	1700	1100	600	375

Irwin Pedersen

NIB	Exc.	V.G.	Good	Fair	Poor
4200	3500	2500	1300	800	500

M1 Carbine Cutaway

NIB	Exc.	V.G.	Good	Fair	Poor
—	2500	1500	900	600	500

M1 Carbine Sniper with infra red conversion

NIB	Exc.	V.G.	Good	Fair	Poor
—	1450	1000	800	400	300

U.S. M1 A1 Paratrooper Model

NIB	Exc.	V.G.	Good	Fair	Poor
—	4500	3500	2500	1250	750

U.S. ORDNANCE
Reno, Nevada

Models listed are machined to military specifications and semi-automatic only.

M-60

7.62mm belt-fed semi-automatic weapon. Modeled after famous machine gun used in Vietnam. Fitted with 22" barrel. Weight about 24 lbs.

NIB	Exc.	V.G.	Good	Fair	Poor
10000	8900	7000	5500	4000	2500

M-60E3

Shorter more lightweight version of standard M-60. Fitted with 17" barrel. Weight about 18 lbs.

NIB	Exc.	V.G.	Good	Fair	Poor
8900	7000	5500	4000	3000	1750

Browning Model 1919

Belt-fed model chambered for 7.62mm/.30-06 cartridges. Fitted with 23" barrel. Weight about 30 lbs. Prices listed are for gun only. **NOTE:** Add $125 for A6 stock, bipod and carry handle; $450 for A4 tripod.

Model 1919 with A4 tripod

NIB	Exc.	V.G.	Good	Fair	Poor
2800	2400	1900	1500	1200	900

Vickers

Chambered for .303 cartridge and belt-fed. Weight about 40 lbs. Prices listed are for gun only. **NOTE:** Add $500 for tripod.

NIB	Exc.	V.G.	Good	Fair	Poor
4800	4000	3000	2200	1700	900

U.S. REPEATING ARMS CO.
See—Winchester

UBERTI, ALDO/UBERTI USA
Ponte Zanano, Italy

Company manufactures high-grade reproductions of famous Western-style American firearms. Their products have been imported over the years by a number of different companies. They produce both blackpowder guns and cartridge firearms that are included in this section. This Italian manufacturer builds high quality firearms of the American West. Featured are Colt, Winchester and Remington. Each importer stamps its name on the firearm in addition to Uberti address. In 2000, Beretta Holding Company purchased Uberti.

Paterson Revolver

Exact copy of famous and rare Colt pistol. Offered in .36-caliber, with engraved 5-shot cylinder. Barrel is 7.5" long and octagonal forward of lug. Frame and backstrap are case-hardened steel. Grips are one-piece walnut. Overall length 11.5"; weight about 2.5 lbs.

NIB	Exc.	V.G.	Good	Fair	Poor
400	300	200	125	100	75

Walker Colt Revolver

Faithful reproduction of famous and highly sought-after Colts. Caliber .44; round barrel 9" long. Frame case-hardened steel. Trigger guard brass. 6-shot cylinder engraved with fighting dragoon scene. Grip one-piece walnut. Overall length 15.75"; weight a hefty 70 oz.

NIB	Exc.	V.G.	Good	Fair	Poor
500	400	300	200	125	100

Colt Whitneyville Dragoon

Transition Walker, reduced version of Model 1847 Walker. Fitted with 7.5" barrel. Chambered for .44-caliber.

NIB	Exc.	V.G.	Good	Fair	Poor
475	375	200	125	100	75

Colt 1st Model Dragoon Revolver

Shorter version of Walker. Evolved directly from that original design. A 6-shot .44-caliber, with 7.5" barrel. Frame color case-hardened steel. Backstrap and trigger guard brass. Grips one-piece walnut. Overall length 13.5"; weight about 63 oz.

NIB	Exc.	V.G.	Good	Fair	Poor
400	300	250	125	100	75

Colt 2nd Model Dragoon Revolver

Differs from 1st model in that cylinder bolt slot is square instead of oval.

NIB	Exc.	V.G.	Good	Fair	Poor
400	300	250	125	100	75

Colt 3rd Model Dragoon Revolver

Model varies from 2nd model as follows:

a: Loading lever taper is inverted.

b: Loading lever latch hook is different shape.

c: Loading lever latch.

d: Backstrap steel and trigger guard brass oval.

e: Frame is cut for shoulder stock.

NIB	Exc.	V.G.	Good	Fair	Poor
350	225	175	125	100	75

Colt Model 1849 Wells Fargo

No loading lever. Chambered for .31-caliber cartridge. Barrel is octagonal. Frame colored case-hardened steel. Backstrap and trigger guard brass. Cylinder engraved and holds 5 rounds. Grip one-piece walnut. Overall length 9.5"; weight 34 oz.

NIB	Exc.	V.G.	Good	Fair	Poor
325	200	150	125	100	75

Pocket Revolver

Same as Wells Fargo, with addition of loading lever.

NIB	Exc.	V.G.	Good	Fair	Poor
325	200	150	125	100	75

Colt Model 1848 Baby Dragoon

Similar is appearance to Model 1849, with 4" tapered octagonal barrel and square back trigger guard. No loading lever. Weight about 23 oz.

NIB	Exc.	V.G.	Good	Fair	Poor
325	200	150	125	100	75

Model 1851 Navy Colt

Chambered for .36-caliber, with engraved 6-shot cylinder. Tapered octagonal barrel 7.5". Frame case colored steel. Backstrap and oval trigger guard brass. Grips one-piece walnut. Overall length 13"; weight about 44 oz.

NIB	Exc.	V.G.	Good	Fair	Poor
400	300	250	125	100	75

Model 1861 Navy Colt

Sometimes referred to as "New Navy". Similar in appearance to Model 1851. Offered in two variations: military version has steel backstrap, trigger guard and cut for shoulder stock; civilian version has brass backstrap, trigger guard and not cut for shoulder stock.

Military Model

NIB	Exc.	V.G.	Good	Fair	Poor
400	300	250	125	100	75

Civilian Model

NIB	Exc.	V.G.	Good	Fair	Poor
400	300	250	125	100	75

Colt Model 1860 Army

Chambered for .44-caliber ball. Fitted with round tapered 8" barrel. Revolver has 6-shot engraved cylinder. Grips one-piece walnut. Overall length 13.75"; weight about 42 oz.

Military

Steel backstrap, brass trigger guard and cut for shoulder stock.

NIB	Exc.	V.G.	Good	Fair	Poor
400	300	250	125	100	75

Fluted Cylinder Military

NIB	Exc.	V.G.	Good	Fair	Poor
400	300	250	125	100	75

Civilian

Brass backstrap and trigger guard. Not cut for shoulder stock.

NIB	Exc.	V.G.	Good	Fair	Poor
400	300	250	125	100	75

Colt Model 1862 Police Revolvers

Chambered for .36-caliber. Fitted with round tapered barrel in 4.5", 5.5" or 6.5" and 5-shot fluted cylinder. Frame color case-hardened steel. Backstrap and trigger guard brass. Grips one-piece walnut. Weight about 25 oz.

NIB	Exc.	V.G.	Good	Fair	Poor
400	300	250	125	100	75

Colt Model 1862 Pocket Navy Revolver

Similar to Model 1862 Police. Fitted with 5-shot engraved non-fluted cylinder. Barrel lengths 4.5", 5.5" and 6.5". Weight about 27 oz.

NIB	Exc.	V.G.	Good	Fair	Poor
400	300	250	125	100	75

Colt Model 1868 Army Thuer Conversion

NIB	Exc.	V.G.	Good	Fair	Poor
450	325	225	175	150	100

Remington Model 1858 New Army .44 Caliber

Chambered for .44-caliber and fitted with tapered octagonal 8" barrel. Cylinder holds 6-shots. Frame blued steel. Trigger guard brass. Grips two-piece walnut. Overall length 13.75"; weight about 42 oz.

NIB	Exc.	V.G.	Good	Fair	Poor
300	200	150	125	100	75

Remington Model 1858 New Army .36 Caliber

Similar to above. Fitted with 7.375" tapered octagonal barrel. Weight about 40 oz.

NIB	Exc.	V.G.	Good	Fair	Poor
400	300	250	125	100	75

Remington Model 1858 New Army .44 Caliber Target

Version fitted with fully adjustable rear sight and ramp front.

NIB	Exc.	V.G.	Good	Fair	Poor
425	325	275	150	125	75

Remington Model 1858 New Army .44 Caliber Stainless Steel

All parts stainless steel.

NIB	Exc.	V.G.	Good	Fair	Poor
425	325	275	150	125	75

Remington Model 1858 New Army .44 Cal. SS Target

Same as Target Model. All parts stainless steel.

NIB	Exc.	V.G.	Good	Fair	Poor
450	325	250	200	125	75

Remington Model 1858 Target Revolving Carbine

Chambered for .44-caliber and fitted with 18" octagon barrel. Frame blued steel. Trigger guard brass. Stock select walnut. Overall length 35"; weight about 4.4 lbs.

NIB	Exc.	V.G.	Good	Fair	Poor
425	300	200	150	100	75

1875 Remington "Outlaw"

Replica of original Remington cartridge pistol. Chambered for .357 Magnum, .44-40, .45 ACP, .45 ACP/.45 L.C. conversion and .45 Colt. Frame case colored steel. Trigger guard brass. Offered with 7.5" round barrel blued or nickel-plated. Two-piece walnut grips. Overall length 13.75"; weight about 44 oz.

NIB	Exc.	V.G.	Good	Fair	Poor
450	325	250	200	125	75

Remington Model 1875 Frontier

Introduced in 2005. Features 5.5" barrel chambered for .45 Colt cartridge. Case colored frame with blued barrel, backstrap and trigger guard. Two-piece walnut grips. Weight about 40 oz.

NIB	Exc.	V.G.	Good	Fair	Poor
500	375	250	175	150	100

Remington Model 1890 Police

A 5.5"-barreled replica of original Remington Pistol. Chambered for .357 Magnum, .44-40, .45 ACP, .45 ACP/.45 L.C. conversion and .45 Colt. Frame case colored steel. Trigger guard brass. Available blued or nickel-plate. Grips two-piece walnut and fitted with grip ring. Overall length 11.75"; weight about 41 oz.

NIB	Exc.	V.G.	Good	Fair	Poor
500	375	250	175	150	100

Model 1871 Rolling Block Pistol

Single-shot target pistol chambered for .22 LR, .22 Magnum, .22 Hornet, .222 Rem., 223 Rem., .45 Long Colt or .357 Magnum. Has blued 9.5" half-octagonal half-round barrel. Case colored receiver. Walnut grip and forearm. Trigger guard brass. Overall length 14"; weight about 44 oz.

NIB	Exc.	V.G.	Good	Fair	Poor
500	375	250	175	150	100

Model 1871 Rolling Block Carbine

Similar to pistol, with 22.5" half-octagonal half-round barrel. Full-length walnut stock. Trigger guard and buttplate brass. Overall length 35.5"; weight about 4.8 lbs.

NIB	Exc.	V.G.	Good	Fair	Poor
650	525	400	275	200	125

Henry Rifle

Brass-framed reproduction of famous Winchester/Henry Rifle. Chambered for .44-40 or .45 Colt cartridge and basically only departure from being a true and faithful copy. Octagonal barrel 24.25" on rifle model; 22.25" on carbine model. Also two Trapper models offered: 18.5" barrel and 16.5" version. High-quality rifle and amazingly close to original in configuration. Three grades of engraving available. Weights are rifle 9.2 lbs.; carbine 9 lbs.; 18.5" trapper 7.9 lbs.; 16.5" trapper 7.4 lbs. Finish can be steel, standard blued or charcoal blue. **NOTE:** Add $350 Grade A; $450 Grade B; $600 Grade C.

NIB	Exc.	V.G.	Good	Fair	Poor
900	700	550	450	350	200

Winchester Model 1866

Faithful replica of Winchester 1866. Chambered for .22 LR, .22 Magnum, .38 Special, .44-40 and .45 Long Colt. Rifle version has brass frame and 24.25" tapered octagon barrel. Frame finish brass, with walnut stock. Weight about 8 lbs.

NIB	Exc.	V.G.	Good	Fair	Poor
800	650	550	450	350	200

1866 Yellowboy Carbine

Similar to standard rifle. Offered with 19" round tapered barrel.

NIB	Exc.	V.G.	Good	Fair	Poor
700	600	500	450	350	200

Winchester Model 1873 Carbine

Reproduction of Winchester 1873. Chambered for .357 Magnum, .45 Long Colt and .44-40. Case colored steel receiver, lever and round 19" tapered barrel. Stock and forearm walnut. Overall length 38.25"; weight about 7.4 lbs.

NIB	Exc.	V.G.	Good	Fair	Poor
900	700	500	450	350	200

Winchester Model 1873 Rifle

Similar to Carbine, with 24.25" octagonal barrel. Overall length 43.25"; weight about 8.2 lbs. **NOTE:** Extra barrel lengths from 20" to 30" in .45 L.C. and .44-40 also offered at extra cost.

NIB	Exc.	V.G.	Good	Fair	Poor
950	750	600	450	350	200

Winchester 1873 Short Sporting Rifle

As above fitted with 20" octagon barrel.

NIB	Exc.	V.G.	Good	Fair	Poor
950	800	600	450	350	200

Winchester 1873 Half-Octagon Rifle

Same as above, with 24.25" half octagon barrel. Stock has checkered pistol-grip.

NIB	Exc.	V.G.	Good	Fair	Poor
1000	800	600	450	350	200

Winchester 1873 Musket

Chambered for .44-40 or .45 Long Colt cartridge. Fitted with 30" barrel, full stock and three barrel bands. Magazine capacity 14 rounds. Weight about 9 lbs.

NIB	Exc.	V.G.	Good	Fair	Poor
1000	800	600	450	350	200

Model 1885 High Wall Single-Shot Carbine

Chambered for .38-55, .30-30, .44-40, .45 Colt, .40-65 or .45-70, with 28" barrel. Walnut stock.

NIB	Exc.	V.G.	Good	Fair	Poor
825	600	450	350	250	200

Model 1885 High Wall Single-Shot Rifle

Same as above, with 30" barrel.

NIB	Exc.	V.G.	Good	Fair	Poor
900	675	500	400	300	200

Model 1885 High Wall Single-Shot Rifle Pistol Grip

Fitted with 30" or 32" barrel and checkered pistol-grip stock. Same calibers as above.

NIB	Exc.	V.G.	Good	Fair	Poor
1000	800	600	450	350	200

Winchester 1885 Low Wall Sporting Rifle

Version of Low Wall Winchester. Chambered for .22 Hornet, .30-30, .44 Magnum or .45 Colt cartridges. Fitted with 30" octagon barrel. Walnut stock with pistol-grip. Weight about 7.5 lbs. Introduced in 2004.

NIB	Exc.	V.G.	Good	Fair	Poor
950	800	600	450	350	200

Winchester 1885 Low Wall Schuetzen

As above chambered for .45 Colt cartridge. Fitted with palm rest and Swiss butt. Weight about 7.75 lbs. Introduced in 2004.

NIB	Exc.	V.G.	Good	Fair	Poor
1200	950	800	600	450	350

Hawken Santa Fe

Based on famous original rifle. Reproduction bored for .54-caliber. Fitted with 32" octagon barrel, double-set trigger and case-hardened lock plate standard. Stock ferrule and wedge plates are German silver. Walnut stock with cheekpiece. Overall length 50"; weight about 9.5 lbs. Available in kit form.

NIB	Exc.	V.G.	Good	Fair	Poor
350	300	250	200	150	100

Cattleman

Single-action revolver patterned closely after Colt Single-Action Army. Chambered in various popular calibers: .357 Magnum, .44-40, .44 Special, .45 ACP, .45 L.C./.45 ACP convertible and .45 Colt. Offered with barrel lengths of 4.75", 5.5" and 7.5". Also with modern or black powder-type frame. Brass or steel backstraps. Finish blued, with walnut grips. Sheriff's Model with 3" barrel and no ejector rod chambered for .44-40 and .45 Colt also available and valued the same. Weight about 38 oz. for 5.5" barrel gun.

NIB	Exc.	V.G.	Good	Fair	Poor
400	275	225	150	100	75

Cattleman .22

Rimfire model chambered for .22 LR, with cylinder capacity of 6 or 12 rounds. Traditional SAA barrel lengths of 4.75", 5.5" or 7". Blue finish, with color case-hardened frame. Choice of steel or brass trigger guard and backstrap. **NOTE:** Add $50 for 12-round cylinder capacity.

NIB	Exc.	V.G.	Good	Fair	Poor
400	325	275	200	150	125

Cattleman Flattop Target Model

Similar to standard Cattleman, with adjustable rear sight.

NIB	Exc.	V.G.	Good	Fair	Poor
435	350	275	225	175	125

Cattleman Gunfighter NM

Chambered for .45 Colt cartridge. Fitted with 4.75", 5.5" or 7.5" barrel. Black checkered grip, with matte blued finish. Weight about 37 oz. Introduced in 2005.

NIB	Exc.	V.G.	Good	Fair	Poor
400	275	225	150	100	75

Cattleman Cody NM

As above, with nickel finish and ivory-style grips.

NIB	Exc.	V.G.	Good	Fair	Poor
500	375	250	175	150	100

Cattleman Frisco NM

As above, with charcoal blued barrel and case colored frame. Pearl grips.

NIB	Exc.	V.G.	Good	Fair	Poor
500	375	250	175	150	100

Cattleman El Patron CMS

Designed for Cowboy Mounted Shooter (CMS) competition. Caliber .357 Magnum or .45 Colt. Steel cylinder, frame and barrel, 6-round capacity, single-action trigger, low profile hammer, fixed sights and wood grips. Weight 36.8 oz. Barrel 3.5" or 4", with blue/case-hardened or stainless finish. **NOTE:** Add 25 percent for stainless finish.

NIB	Exc.	V.G.	Good	Fair	Poor
525	425	350	300	225	150

Bisley

Chambered for .32-20, .38 Special, .357 Magnum, .38-40, .44-40 and .44 Special. Fitted with 4.75", 5.5" or 7.5" barrel. Case-hardened frame, with two-piece walnut grips.

NIB	Exc.	V.G.	Good	Fair	Poor
435	350	275	225	175	125

Flattop

As above, with adjustable rear sight.

NIB	Exc.	V.G.	Good	Fair	Poor
435	350	275	225	175	125

Buntline Carbine

Version has 18" barrel. Fitted with permanently mounted shoulder stock, with brass buttplate and sling swivel. Chambered for .44-40, .45 Long Colt, .357 Magnum and .44 Magnum. Offered with fixed or adjustable sights.

NIB	Exc.	V.G.	Good	Fair	Poor
450	400	350	300	250	200

Buckhorn Buntline

Version chambered for .44 Magnum. Has 18" round barrel and cut for attaching shoulder stock. Steel backstrap and trigger guard. Overall length 23"; weight about 57 oz. **NOTE:** Add 25 percent for detachable shoulder stock.

NIB	Exc.	V.G.	Good	Fair	Poor
400	325	300	250	200	100

Buckhorn Target

Same as above. Fitted with adjustable rear sight and ramp front. Has flat upper frame.

NIB	Exc.	V.G.	Good	Fair	Poor
450	350	300	250	200	100

Phantom

Similar to Buckhorn. Chambered for .44 and .357 Magnum. Round 10.5" barrel. Frame blued, with blued steel backstrap. One-piece walnut grips, with anatomic profile. Adjustable sight. Weight about 53 oz.

NIB	Exc.	V.G.	Good	Fair	Poor
400	275	225	150	100	75

New Thunderer Model

Designed and imported exclusively by Cimarron Arms, for single-action shooting competition. Fitted with bird's-head grip with hard rubber. Chambered for .357 Magnum, .44 Special, .44 WCF and .45 Colt. Offered in barrel lengths of 3.5" and 4.75". Finish in nickel or blued, with case colored frame.

4 3/4" WITH EJECTOR

3 1/2" WITH EJECTOR

NIB	Exc.	V.G.	Good	Fair	Poor
450	350	300	250	200	100

1873 Stallion

Scaled-down version chambered for .22 LR/.22 Magnum. Blued, with case colored frame. Features one-piece walnut grips.

NIB	Exc.	V.G.	Good	Fair	Poor
350	295	250	200	150	100

Tornado

Five-shot revolver chambered for .454 Casull. Fitted with 4.75", 5.5" or 7.5" with ported barrel. Sandblasted nickel finish. Weight about 47 oz.

NIB	Exc.	V.G.	Good	Fair	Poor
1000	900	750	600	500	400

No. 3 Schofield Revolver

Patterned after original S&W revolver. Chambered for .44-40 or .45 Colt cartridge. Fitted with 3.5", 5" or 7" barrel. Weight with 7" barrel about 40 oz.

NIB	Exc.	V.G.	Good	Fair	Poor
800	700	600	475	325	200

No. 3 New Model Russian

Chambered for .44 Russian cartridge. Fitted with 6" or 7" barrel.

NIB	Exc.	V.G.	Good	Fair	Poor
900	800	700	575	400	300

Inspector Model

Double-action revolver built on same general lines as Colt Detective. Cylinder holds 6 cartridges. Chambered for .38 Special. Offered in barrel lengths with fixed sights: 2", 2.125", 2.5", 3", 4", 6". Also offered in 4" or 6" barrel lengths with adjustable sights. Grips are walnut. Finish blued or chrome. With 3" barrel weight about 24 oz.

NIB	Exc.	V.G.	Good	Fair	Poor
275	200	150	125	100	75

UGARTECHEA, ARMAS
Eibar, Spain

This company makes side-by-side boxlock and sidelock shotguns in a variety of models.

SIDELOCK MODELS

Upland Classic Model 75 EX

Available in 12-, 16-, 20- or 28-gauge, with automatic ejectors. Double or non-selective single trigger. Double trigger models feature hinged front trigger. English style scroll engraving, with case-hardened or coin finished receiver. **NOTE:** Add $300 for 28-gauge; $800 for higher grade hand rubbed wood.

NIB	Exc.	V.G.	Good	Fair	Poor
3100	2750	2000	1800	1200	800

Upland Classic Model 110

Available in 12-, 16-, 20- or 28-gauge and .410 bore. Round body design, with other features similar to Model 75 EX. **NOTE:** Add $300 for 28-gauge; $400 for .410 bore.

NIB	Exc.	V.G.	Good	Fair	Poor
4000	3400	2500	2000	1500	1000

Custom Grade Models

This series of sidelock guns are made on special order. Many custom options including barrel lengths, stock dimensions and upgraded wood. Higher grades feature increasing levels of engraving. Values for excellent condition models range from $4,000 to $10,000.

BOXLOCK MODELS

Upland Classic Grade I Model 30

Basic boxlock model offered in all gauges, with double triggers, extractors, splinter fore-end and straight-grip stock. **NOTE:** Add $200 for 28-gauge; $300 for .410 bore.

NIB	Exc.	V.G.	Good	Fair	Poor
1700	1300	1000	800	500	300

Upland Classic Grade III Model 40 NEX

Similar to Model 30, with automatic ejectors, double or non-selective single trigger, engraved receiver. **NOTE:** Add $300 for 28-gauge; $500 for .410 bore.

NIB	Exc.	V.G.	Good	Fair	Poor
2400	2000	1400	1200	900	500

UHLINGER, WILLIAM P.
Philadelphia, Pennsylvania

Pocket Revolver

.32-caliber spur trigger revolver, with 2.75" or 3" octagonal barrel and unfluted 6-shot cylinder. Blued, with rosewood or walnut grips. Manufactured during late 1860s early 1870s. Uhlinger-manufactured pistols will often be found with retailer's names on them, such as D.D. Cone, Washington, D.C.; J.P. Lower; W.L. Grant.

Long Cylinder (1-3/16")

NIB	Exc.	V.G.	Good	Fair	Poor
—	—	800	600	250	100

Short Cylinder (1")

NIB	Exc.	V.G.	Good	Fair	Poor
—	—	650	425	175	75

.32 Rimfire Model (5", 6", or 7" Barrel)

NIB	Exc.	V.G.	Good	Fair	Poor
—	—	800	600	250	100

ULTIMATE
See—Camex-Blaser USA, Inc.

ULTRA LIGHT ARMS
See—New Ultra Light Arms

UMAREX USA
Fort Smith, Arkansas

Umarex Colt Tactical Rimfire M4 Ops Carbine

Blowback semi-automatic rifle styled to resemble Colt M16. Chambered in .22 LR. Features include 16.2" barrel; front sight adjustable for elevation; adjustable rear sight; alloy lower; adjustable telestock; flattop receiver with removable carry handle; 10- or 30-round detachable magazine.

NIB	Exc.	V.G.	Good	Fair	Poor
500	425	365	300	225	150

Umarex Colt Tactical Rimfire M4 Carbine

Blowback semi-automatic rifle styled to resemble Colt M4. Chambered in .22 LR. Features include 16.2" barrel; front sight adjustable for elevation; adjustable rear sight; alloy lower; adjustable telestock; flattop receiver with optics rail; 10- or 30-round detachable magazine.

NIB	Exc.	V.G.	Good	Fair	Poor
550	465	400	335	250	165

Umarex Colt Tactical Rimfire M16 Rifle

Blowback semi-automatic rifle styled to resemble Colt M16. Chambered in .22 LR. Features include 21.2" barrel; front sight adjustable for elevation; adjustable rear sight; alloy lower; fixed stock; flattop receiver; removable carry handle; 10- or 30-round detachable magazine.

NIB	Exc.	V.G.	Good	Fair	Poor
500	425	365	300	225	150

Umarex Colt Tactical Rimfire M16 SPR Rifle

Blowback semi-automatic rifle styled to resemble Colt M16 SPR. Chambered in .22 LR. Features include 21.2" barrel; front sight adjustable for elevation; adjustable rear sight; alloy lower; fixed stock; flattop receiver with optics rail; removable carry handle; 10- or 30-round detachable magazine.

NIB	Exc.	V.G.	Good	Fair	Poor
575	485	425	360	275	185

Umarex H&K 416-22

Blowback semi-automatic rifle styled to resemble H&K 416. Chambered in .22 LR. Features include metal upper and lower receivers; RIS - rail interface system; retractable stock; pistol-grip with storage compartment; on-rail sights; rear sight adjustable for wind and elevation; 16.1" barrel; 10- or 20-round magazine. Also available in pistol version with 9" barrel.

NIB	Exc.	V.G.	Good	Fair	Poor
575	485	425	360	275	185

Umarex H&K MP5 A5

Blowback semi-automatic rifle styled to resemble H&K MP5. Chambered in .22 LR. Features include metal receiver; compensator; bolt catch; NAVY pistol-grip; on-rail sights; rear sight adjustable for wind and elevation; 16.1" barrel; 10- or 25-round magazine. Also available in pistol version with 9" barrel and SD-type fore-end.

NIB	Exc.	V.G.	Good	Fair	Poor
450	375	300	250	200	150

UNCETA
See—Astra-Unceta SA

UNION
Unknown

Pocket Pistol

.22-caliber spur trigger single-shot pistol, with 2.75" barrel marked "Union". Nickel-plated, with walnut grips.

NIB	Exc.	V.G.	Good	Fair	Poor
—	—	650	400	100	75

UNION FIRE ARMS COMPANY
Toledo, Ohio

Company was incorporated in 1902 and used names of Union Fire Arms, Union Arms Company, Illinois Arms Company (made for Sears) and Bee Be Arms Company. In 1917, company was either bought up or absorbed by Ithaca Gun Company.

NOTE: Union Fire Arms Company (or Union Firearms Company, as it is sometimes known) slide action shotguns are not commonly seen. Though not widely collected, they seem to attract considerable interest as oddities, much as Spencer/Bannerman slide action shotguns do. Values given below are approximate; as always, true value lies in eyes of buyer, not seller.

Double Barrel Shotguns

Union's predecessor, Colton Manufacturing Co. (1894-1902), made a double for Sears. Cleverly designed with coil mainspring striker locks set into sideplates. Union double in 12- and 16-gauge, with steel or Damascus barrels derived from it, but was a traditional hammerless sidelock side-by-side well-made gun (1902-1913) and also sold by Sears. Values depend on grade and condition. Union also offered, about 1905, an unusual boxlock hammer gun Model 25 in 12-gauge only. Employs external hammers, but they are mounted within frame and spurs protrude in front of topsnap opener. These guns are hard to find and values range from $300 to $1,200 depending on condition. Produced with steel twist or Damascus barrels only in plain grade.

Courtesy Nick Niles

NIB	Exc.	V.G.	Good	Fair	Poor
—	1300	525	4050	300	200

Model 24

Slide action Model 25 Peerless, was a fancy version of Model 24 and Model 25A, which was a trap model. Manufactured from 1902 to 1913 in 12- or 16-gauge, with 24", 26", 28" or 32" steel or Damascus barrels. Gun had unique double trigger. Front trigger cocked and decocked an internal firing pin and back trigger fired the gun. Gun is marked on left side of frame and pump release is on right side. Model had one serious drawback, the slide that extracted a spent shell extended back over comb of stock. This often hit shooter's thumb knuckle and caused injury. In 1907, Union redesigned their slide by reducing its length and shielding it behind a steel plate that covered rear half of opening. These are Model 24, 25 and 25A improved versions. Approximately 17,000 of all models combined were made.

NIB	Exc.	V.G.	Good	Fair	Poor
—	—	750	300	200	100

Model 50

Manufactured 1911 to 1913. Basically redesign of Model 24. Main distinguishing feature of Model 50 was the frame sloped down to meet comb of stock. Double trigger system was replaced by single trigger. Came in 12- or 16-gauge, with 26", 28", 30" or 32" Krupp steel barrel. Fewer than 3,000 made.

NIB	Exc.	V.G.	Good	Fair	Poor
—	—	850	400	300	200

Model 22

Essentially a no frills Model 23. Same barrel length and steel options. Plain walnut stock and no engraving. Fewer than 10,000 Model 22 and 23s made.

NIB	Exc.	V.G.	Good	Fair	Poor
—	—	300	100	75	50

Model 23

Manufactured between 1902 and 1913. Hammerless double with-/without automatic ejectors. Some engraving, came in both single/double trigger models. This was their top grade gun. Came in 12- and 16-gauge, with 28", 30" or 32" steel twist or Damascus barrels.

NIB	Exc.	V.G.	Good	Fair	Poor
—	—	450	150	125	100

Diamond Grade

Manufactured between 1905 and 1910. Unique octagonal breech in 12-gauge only, with 30" steel laminated or Damascus barrel. Premium grade single-shot. Few were made.

NIB	Exc.	V.G.	Good	Fair	Poor
—	—	450	200	100	50

Model 18

Manufactured 1906 to 1913. Came in 12- or 16-gauge, with 30", 32", 34" or 36" steel barrel. Plain single-shot. Very few made.

NIB	Exc.	V.G.	Good	Fair	Poor
—	—	200	75	50	25

Reifngraber

.32 or .38 S&W caliber gas operated semi-automatic pistol, with 3" barrel. Blued, with walnut grips. Approximately 100 were manufactured.

NIB	Exc.	V.G.	Good	Fair	Poor
—	—	2250	1100	500	350

Automatic Revolver

.32 S&W caliber. Similar to Webley Fosbery semi-automatic revolver, with 3" barrel. Blued, with walnut or hard rubber grips. Cylinder has zig-zag grooves.

NIB	Exc.	V.G.	Good	Fair	Poor
—	—	3250	1250	500	250

UNIQUE
Hendaye, France
See—Pyrenees

UNITED SPORTING ARMS, INC.
Tucson, Arizona

Blued Guns (Seville, etc.)

NIB	Exc.	V.G.	Good	Fair	Poor
N/A	500	450	350	—	—

Blue Silhouette (10.5" barrels)
NOTE: Add $100 stainless; $250 stainless long-frame models (calibers .357 Maximum/Super Magnum and .357 USA/Super Magnum).

NIB	Exc.	V.G.	Good	Fair	Poor
N/A	600	550	500	—	—

Silver Sevilles

NIB	Exc.	V.G.	Good	Fair	Poor
N/A	550	475	400	—	—

Stainless Steel Guns

NIB	Exc.	V.G.	Good	Fair	Poor
N/A	600	525	450	—	—

Tombstone Commemorative

NIB	Exc.	V.G.	Good	Fair	Poor
1000	750	625	525	—	—

Quik-Kit Stainless Steel
NOTE: Add $200 for each barrel and cylinder for Quik-Kit guns with extra barrel and cylinder; 20 percent if El Dorado Arms (either N.Y. or N.C.); 10 percent for 1.5" barrel Sheriff's Model; 20 percent for 10.5" barrel; 20 percent for bird's-head grip frame; 20 percent if brass grip frame. Deduct 10 percent if United Sporting Arms, Hauppauge, N.Y.; 20 percent if United Sporting Arms, Post Falls, ID.

NIB	Exc.	V.G.	Good	Fair	Poor
1500	1250	800	—	—	—

Quik-Kit Blued

NIB	Exc.	V.G.	Good	Fair	Poor
1200	1000	650	—	—	—

UNITED STATES ARMS
Otis A. Smith Company
Rockfall, Connecticut

Single-Action Revolver
.44 rimfire and centerfire single-action revolver, with 7" barrel and integral ejector. Hammer nose fitted with two firing pins so rimfire or centerfire cartridges can be used interchangeably. Barrel marked "United States Arms Company - New York"; top strap "No. 44". Blued, with hard rubber or rosewood grips. Manufactured in limited quantities. Circa 1870 to 1875.

NIB	Exc.	V.G.	Good	Fair	Poor
—	—	4750	3250	1250	500

UNITED STATES FIRE ARMS MFG.
(Formerly United States Patent Firearms Mfg. Co.)
Hartford, Connecticut

Company produced a wide variety of high quality replica handguns and rifles from 1992 until 2012.

Single-Action Army Revolver
Offered in wide variety of calibers including .22 rimfire, .32 WCF, .38 S&W, .357 Magnum, .38-40, .41 Colt, .44 Russian, .44-40, .45 Colt and .45 ACP. Barrel lengths 4.75", 5.5", 7.5", with/without ejector. Modern cross pin frame available for additional $10. Prices listed for standard grips and finish, Armory bone case finish and Dome blue finish.

NIB	Exc.	V.G.	Good	Fair	Poor
975	900	800	675	525	300

Single-Action Army Revolver Pre-War
As above, with pre-war "P" frame.

NIB	Exc.	V.G.	Good	Fair	Poor
1395	1150	950	700	550	300

Shooting Master
Large-frame model in .357 Magnum, with 7.5" barrel, U.S. hard rubber grips, blue finish and enlarged trigger guard. Adjustable rear sight, 6-round cylinder. Introduced in 2011. Also available in .327 Federal, with 8-shot cylinder (Sparrowhawk model).

NIB	Exc.	V.G.	Good	Fair	Poor
1300	1100	950	800	525	250

Flattop Target Model
Offered with same calibers as Single-Action Army above. Barrel lengths 4.75", 5.5" and 7.5". Grips two-piece hard rubber. Prices listed for standard finish. Introduced in 1997.

NIB	Exc.	V.G.	Good	Fair	Poor
1665	1450	1200	900	675	400

Rodeo
Single-action revolver offered in .45 Colt, .44-40, .44 Special, .32-20, .38-40 and .38 Special calibers. Choice of 4.75" or 5.50" barrel. Satin blue finish, with bone case hammer. "US" hard rubber grips standard.

NIB	Exc.	V.G.	Good	Fair	Poor
625	550	450	350	250	175

Rodeo II

Similar to Rodeo, with matte nickel finish and burl wood grips.

NIB	Exc.	V.G.	Good	Fair	Poor
575	475	350	275	225	200

Buntline

Features all blued finish, with 16" barrel. Chambered for .45 Colt cartridge.

NIB	Exc.	V.G.	Good	Fair	Poor
2300	1750	1475	1100	700	450

Buntline Special

Fitted with 16" barrel. Chambered for .45 Colt cartridge. Supplied with nickel stock. Limited edition. Cased.

NIB	Exc.	V.G.	Good	Fair	Poor
2895	2250	1750	1475	1100	700

China Camp Cowboy Action Gun

Chambered for .45 Colt cartridge, but other calibers available from .32 WCF to .44 WCF. Barrel lengths 4.75", 5.5" and 7.5". Special action job. Two-piece hard rubber grips standard. Finish is silver steel.

NIB	Exc.	V.G.	Good	Fair	Poor
1395	1150	950	700	550	300

Henry Nettleton Revolver

Exact reproduction of U.S. Government inspector model, produced in Springfield Armory. Offered in 5.5" and 7.5" models. Introduced in 1997. Discontinued.

NIB	Exc.	V.G.	Good	Fair	Poor
1575	1450	1200	900	600	350

.22 Plinker

Chambered for .22 cartridge. Fitted with choice of barrel lengths: 4.75", 5.5" or 7.5". Extra .22 WMR cylinder included.

NIB	Exc.	V.G.	Good	Fair	Poor
975	875	725	550	300	150

.22 Target

As above, with adjustable rear sight and replaceable front sight blade.

NIB	Exc.	V.G.	Good	Fair	Poor
1665	1450	1200	900	675	400

Gunslinger

Offered in .45 Colt, .44 Special, .44 WCF, .38 Special, .38 WCF or .32 WCF. Choice of 4.75", .5.5" or 7.5" barrel. Cross pin frame. Hard rubber grips. Aged bluing finish. Black style frame optional. **NOTE:** Add $135 for black powder frame.

NIB	Exc.	V.G.	Good	Fair	Poor
1145	1025	800	625	500	250

Custer Battlefield Gun

Replica of 1873 revolver used during height of Indian Wars, including Custer's Last Stand. Limited edition with cartouche of Ordnance Sub-inspector Orville W. Ainsworth; serial range 200 - 14,343. Six-shot 7.5" barrel. Antique Patina aged blue. One-piece walnut stock.

NIB	Exc.	V.G.	Good	Fair	Poor
1625	1450	1200	900	675	400

Hunter

Revolver chambered for .17 HMR cartridge. Fitted with 7.5" barrel, with adjustable rear sight and replaceable front sight blade. Finish matte blue. Discontinued.

NIB	Exc.	V.G.	Good	Fair	Poor
975	875	725	550	300	150

Sheriff's Model

Chambered for wide variety of calibers from .45 Colt to .32 WCF. Choice of 2.5", 3", 3.5" or 4" barrel. No ejector. **NOTE:** Add $250 for nickel finish.

NIB	Exc.	V.G.	Good	Fair	Poor
975	875	725	550	300	150

Omni-Potent Bird's-Head Model

Chambered for .45 Colt, .45 ACP, .44 Special, .44 WCF, .38 Special, .38 WCF or .32 WCF cartridges. Offered with bird's-head grips. Available with 3.5", 4" or 4.75" barrel lengths.

NIB	Exc.	V.G.	Good	Fair	Poor
1625	1450	1200	900	675	400

Omni-Potent Snubnose

As above, with 2", 3" or 4" barrel without ejector.

NIB	Exc.	V.G.	Good	Fair	Poor
1475	1300	1050	800	575	400

Omni-Potent Target

Choice of 4.75", 5.5" or 7.5" barrel, with adjustable rear sight and re-placeable front blade sight.

NIB	Exc.	V.G.	Good	Fair	Poor
1395	1150	950	700	550	300

Bisley Model

Based on famous Bisley model. Reproduction features barrel lengths of 4.75", 5.5", 7.5" and 10". The .45 Colt caliber is standard, but .32 WCF, .38 S&W, .44 S&W, .41 Colt, .38 WCF, .44 WCF are optional. Introduced in 1997. **NOTE:** Add $60 for 10" models.

NIB	Exc.	V.G.	Good	Fair	Poor
1575	1450	1200	900	600	350

Target

As above, with adjustable rear sight and replaceable blade front sight.

NIB	Exc.	V.G.	Good	Fair	Poor
1625	1450	1200	900	675	400

Pony Express

Features 5.50" engraved barrel and frame, with special finish. Ivory grips etched with pony express rider. Custom gun.

NIB	Exc.	V.G.	Good	Fair	Poor
3895	3500	2950	2200	1500	700

Sears 1902 Colt

Replica of Sears 1902 Colt SAA. Fitted with 5.50" barrel, pearl grips, full coverage engraving with gold line work on cylinder and barrel. Custom gun.

NIB	Exc.	V.G.	Good	Fair	Poor
8995	7500	6000	500	4000	1000

Model 1910

Stylized version of early Colt Model 1910 .45 ACP pistol.

NIB	Exc.	V.G.	Good	Fair	Poor
1895	1700	1550	1200	900	500

Model 1911 Army or Navy

Faithful version of early Colt Model 1911 military model.

NIB	Exc.	V.G.	Good	Fair	Poor
1700	1500	1100	900	500	350

Ace .22 LR

Recreation of 1911-style Colt Ace .22 LR, with 10+1 capacity. Walnut grips. Introduced 2006.

NIB	Exc.	V.G.	Good	Fair	Poor
1850	1650	1100	900	500	350

Super .38

1911-style semi-automatic. Blued finish; chambered for .38 Super Automatic with 9+1 capacity. Walnut grips. Introduced 2006.

NIB	Exc.	V.G.	Good	Fair	Poor
1800	1600	1200	900	500	350

RIFLES

Cowboy Action Lightning

Copy of Colt Lightning rifle. Chambered for .44-40, .45 Colt or .38 WCF cartridge. Fitted with 26" round barrel. Walnut stock with crescent butt. Magazine capacity 15 rounds. Introduced fall of 2003. Discontinued.

NIB	Exc.	V.G.	Good	Fair	Poor
1625	1450	1200	900	675	400

Cowboy Action Carbine

As above, with 20" round barrel. Magazine capacity 12 rounds. Discontinued.

NIB	Exc.	V.G.	Good	Fair	Poor
1625	1450	1200	900	675	400

Lightning Magazine Rifle

Premium version of Cowboy Action Lightning. Features choice of 26" round-/half-round or octagon barrel. Checkered American walnut forearm, with non-checkered stock with oil-finish. Many extra cost options are offered for this model. Discontinued. **NOTE:** Add $200 for half round barrel. Fancy wood, pistol-grip, finish and engraving offered for this rifle.

NIB	Exc.	V.G.	Good	Fair	Poor
1625	1450	1200	900	675	400

Lightning Magazine Carbine

As above, with 20" round barrel. Discontinued.

NIB	Exc.	V.G.	Good	Fair	Poor
1625	1450	1200	900	675	400

Lightning Baby Carbine

Fitted with 20" special round tapered barrel. Lightweight carbine forearm with border line. Discontinued.

NIB	Exc.	V.G.	Good	Fair	Poor
1995	1825	1600	1250	950	650

UNITED STATES REVOLVER ASSOCIATION

See—Harrington & Richardson Arms Co.

UNITED STATES SMALL ARMS CO.
Chicago, Illinois

Huntsman Model Knife Pistol

Made from approximately 1918-1930. Too Rare To Price.

UNIVERSAL FIREARMS
Hialeah, Florida/Jacksonville, Arkansas

Universal merged with Iver-Johnson in 1985 and relocated to Arkansas in 1986. Universal operated out of Florida from late 1950s to 1985.

Model 7312

12-gauge over/under shotgun. Separated 30" ventilated rib barrels, single-selective trigger and automatic ejectors. Case-hardened receiver engraved. Blued, with walnut stock. Imported from Italy.

NIB	Exc.	V.G.	Good	Fair	Poor
—	1250	900	450	300	175

Model 7412

As above, with extractors. Imported from Italy.

NIB	Exc.	V.G.	Good	Fair	Poor
—	1000	750	400	250	150

Model 7712

As above, with 26" or 28" barrels, non-selective single trigger and extractors. Imported from Italy.

NIB	Exc.	V.G.	Good	Fair	Poor
—	550	400	350	250	100

Model 7812

As above, with more detailed engraving and automatic ejectors. Imported from Italy.

NIB	Exc.	V.G.	Good	Fair	Poor
—	700	550	450	350	150

Model 7912

As above, with gold wash frame and single-selective trigger. Imported from Italy.

NIB	Exc.	V.G.	Good	Fair	Poor
—	1350	1000	750	600	300

Model 7112

12-gauge double-barrel boxlock shotgun, with 26" or 28" barrels, double triggers and extractors. Blued case-hardened, with walnut stock. Imported from Italy.

NIB	Exc.	V.G.	Good	Fair	Poor
—	450	300	250	200	100

Double Wing

10-, 12-, 20-gauge or .410 bore boxlock double-barrel shotgun, with 26", 28" or 30" barrels, double triggers and extractors. Blued, with walnut stock. Imported from Italy. Premium for 10-gauge and .410 bore.

NIB	Exc.	V.G.	Good	Fair	Poor
—	450	300	250	200	100

Model 7212

12-gauge single-barrel trap shotgun, with 30" ventilated rib, ported barrel and automatic ejector. Engraved case-hardened receiver and walnut stock. Imported from Italy.

NIB	Exc.	V.G.	Good	Fair	Poor
—	1200	850	650	450	300

Model 1000 Military Carbine

Copy of U.S. M1 Carbine, with 18" barrel. Blued, with birch wood stock.

NIB	Exc.	V.G.	Good	Fair	Poor
—	400	250	200	100	75

Model 1003

As above, with 16", 18" or 20" barrel.

NIB	Exc.	V.G.	Good	Fair	Poor
—	350	200	150	100	75

Model 1010

As above but nickel-plated.

NIB	Exc.	V.G.	Good	Fair	Poor
—	375	225	175	125	100

Model 1015

As above but gold-plated.

NIB	Exc.	V.G.	Good	Fair	Poor
—	400	250	200	150	125

Model 1005 Deluxe

As above, with polished blue finish and Monte Carlo-style stock.

NIB	Exc.	V.G.	Good	Fair	Poor
—	375	225	150	100	75

Model 1006 Stainless

As Model 1000 in stainless steel.

NIB	Exc.	V.G.	Good	Fair	Poor
—	450	300	225	125	100

Model 1020 Teflon

As above, with black or gray Dupont Teflon-S finish.

NIB	Exc.	V.G.	Good	Fair	Poor
—	375	225	175	125	100

Model 1256 Ferret

Model 1000 in .256 Win. Magnum caliber.

NIB	Exc.	V.G.	Good	Fair	Poor
—	350	200	175	125	100

Model 3000 Enforcer

Pistol version of Model 1000, with 11.25" barrel and 15- or 30-shot magazines. Prices for blued models. **NOTE:** Add 20 percent nickel finish; 40 percent gold-plated; 30 percent stainless steel; 20 percent Teflon-S.

NIB	Exc.	V.G.	Good	Fair	Poor
—	375	225	200	150	100

Model 5000 Paratrooper

Model 1000, with 16" or 18" barrel and folding stock. In stainless steel known as Model 5006.

NIB	Exc.	V.G.	Good	Fair	Poor
—	400	250	200	125	100

1981 Commemorative Carbine

Limited production version of Model 1000 cased with accessories. Produced in 1981.

NIB	Exc.	V.G.	Good	Fair	Poor
500	350	250	200	100	75

Model 2200 Leatherneck

.22-caliber version of U.S. M1 Carbine, with 18" barrel and blowback action. Blued, with birch wood stock.

NIB	Exc.	V.G.	Good	Fair	Poor
—	300	175	150	100	75

URIZAR, TOMAS
Eibar, Spain

Celta, J. Cesar, Premier, Puma, and Union

6.35mm semi-automatic pistol, with 3" barrel. Slide marked with trade names listed above. Blued, with black plastic grips cast with a wild man carrying a club.

NIB	Exc.	V.G.	Good	Fair	Poor
—	250	150	125	90	75

Dek-Du

5.5mm folding trigger double-action revolver, with 12-shot cylinder. Later versions made in 6.35mm. Manufactured from 1905 to 1912.

NIB	Exc.	V.G.	Good	Fair	Poor
—	225	125	100	75	50

Express

6.35mm semi-automatic pistol, with 2" barrel. Slide marked "The Best Automatic Pistol Express". Blued, with walnut grips. A 7.65mm variety exists with 4" barrel.

NIB	Exc.	V.G.	Good	Fair	Poor
—	225	125	100	75	50

Imperial

6.35mm caliber semi-automatic pistol, with 2.5" barrel. Model actually made by Aldazabal. Manufactured circa 1914.

NIB	Exc.	V.G.	Good	Fair	Poor
—	225	125	100	75	50

Le Secours or Phoenix

7.65mm semi-automatic pistol marked with either trade names listed above.

NIB	Exc.	V.G.	Good	Fair	Poor
—	225	125	100	75	50

Princeps

6.35mm or 7.65mm semi-automatic pistol. Marked on slide "Made in Spain Princeps Patent".

NIB	Exc.	V.G.	Good	Fair	Poor
—	225	125	100	75	50

Venus

7.65mm semi-automatic pistol, with grips having trade name "Venus" cast in them.

NIB	Exc.	V.G.	Good	Fair	Poor
—	225	125	100	75	50

USAS 12 DAEWOO PRECISION IND., LTD.
South Korea

USAS 12

12-gauge semi-automatic shotgun, with 18.25" cylinder-bored barrel. 10-shot box or 20-shot drum magazine. Parkerized with composition stock. Model no longer imported.

WARNING: As of May 1, 2001, this firearm must be registered with ATF and transfer tax of $200 paid. This firearm classified as a destructive device. Unregistered guns will be considered contraband after this date. Persons in possession will be in violation of federal law. Value speculative.

USELTON ARMS INC.
Goodlettsville, Tennessee

NOTE: Values shown for basic models. Sky's the limit.

Compact Classic

Chambered for .45 ACP cartridge, with 5" barrel. Checkered rosewood grips. Low-profile sights. Black and gray finish. Magazine capacity 7 rounds. Weight about 32 oz.

NIB	Exc.	V.G.	Good	Fair	Poor
1995	1700	1500	1100	800	500

Ultra Compact Classic

1911-style semi-automatic in .45-caliber, with fixed sights. Barrel 4.25", weight 34 oz., trigger pull 3-4 lb., 7+1 capacity. Rosewood or imitation ivory grips. Introduced 2006.

NIB	Exc.	V.G.	Good	Fair	Poor
1995	1700	1500	1100	800	500

Compact Classic Companion

Chambered for .357 Sig or .40 S&W cartridge. Fitted with 5" barrel. Low-profile sights. Black or polymer ivory grips. Stainless or gray finish. Magazine capacity 7 rounds. Weight about 32 oz.

NIB	Exc.	V.G.	Good	Fair	Poor
2250	1900	1700	1250	900	600

Carry Classic

Chambered for .45 ACP cartridge. Fitted with 4.25" barrel, with low-profile sights. Rosewood or polymer ivory grips. Gray and black finish. Magazine capacity 7 rounds. Weight about 34 oz.

NIB	Exc.	V.G.	Good	Fair	Poor
1995	1700	1500	1100	800	500

Ultra Carry

.45 ACP model features Damascus slide and titanium frame. Fitted with 3" barrel, with low-profile sights. Magazine capacity 7 rounds. Weight about 27 oz. **NOTE:** Also offered in titanium and stainless for $2350; stainless and black for $1850.

NIB	Exc.	V.G.	Good	Fair	Poor
3250	2900	2500	2000	1500	800

Tactical 1911

Chambered for .45 ACP cartridge. Fitted with 5" barrel, with Caspian adjustable sights. Rubber grips and moly coat finish. Magazine capacity 8 rounds. Weight about 40 oz.

NIB	Exc.	V.G.	Good	Fair	Poor
2200	1975	1600	1200	1000	500

Classic National Match

.45 ACP pistol has 5" barrel, with Caspian adjustable sights. Black aluma grips and finish. Magazine capacity 8 rounds. Weight about 40 oz. **NOTE:** Add $300 for compensator.

NIB	Exc.	V.G.	Good	Fair	Poor
2200	1975	1600	1200	1000	500

UZI ISRAELI MILITARY INDUSTRIES
See—Vector Arms, Inc.

Uzi Carbine Model A

Chambered for 9mm cartridge. Fitted with 16" barrel, with 25-round magazine. Gray Parkerized finish. Built from 1980 to 1983.

NIB	Exc.	V.G.	Good	Fair	Poor
1600	1450	1200	800	600	450

Uzi Carbine Model B

9mm, .41 Action Express or .45-caliber semi-automatic carbine, with 16.1" barrel. Magazines 20-, 25- or 32-shot box. A 50-shot drum magazine available in 9mm caliber. Black Parkerized finish. Plastic grips and folding stock. Strongly suggested that buyer or seller seek qualified local appraisal. First produced in 1983. Model no longer imported as of 1989.

NIB	Exc.	V.G.	Good	Fair	Poor
1500	1350	1100	750	550	400

Uzi Mini-Carbine

As above in 9mm or .45-caliber, with 19.75" barrel. No longer imported.

NIB	Exc.	V.G.	Good	Fair	Poor
2250	1600	1150	800	600	400

Uzi Pistol

As above in 9mm or .45 ACP, with 4.5" barrel, pistol-grip, no rear stock and 20-shot magazine. No longer imported.

NIB	Exc.	V.G.	Good	Fair	Poor
850	700	550	450	350	250

UZI EAGLE PISTOLS

As of 1999, these pistols no longer imported into U.S.

Full Size Model

Introduced in 1997. Double-action pistol chambered for 9mm and .40 S&W cartridge. Barrel length 4.4"; overall length 8.1". Tritium night sights standard.

NIB	Exc.	V.G.	Good	Fair	Poor
550	425	350	275	200	150

Short Slide Model

Introduced in 1997. Double-action pistol chambered for 9mm, .40 S&W and .45 ACP cartridge. Barrel length 3.7"; overall length 7.5". Tritium night sights standard.

NIB	Exc.	V.G.	Good	Fair	Poor
600	475	400	325	250	200

Compact Model

Introduced in 1997. Double-action pistol chambered for 9mm, .40 S&W and .45 ACP cartridge. Barrel length 3.5"; overall length 7.2". Tritium night sights standard. Magazine capacity: 8 rounds .45 ACP; 10 rounds other calibers. Double-action-only an option for this model.

NIB	Exc.	V.G.	Good	Fair	Poor
600	475	400	325	250	200

Polymer Compact Model

Introduced in 1997. Double-action pistol chambered for 9mm and .40 S&W cartridge. Barrel length 3.5"; overall length 7.2". Tritium night sights standard.

NIB	Exc.	V.G.	Good	Fair	Poor
550	425	350	275	200	150

V

VALKYRIE ARMS, LTD.
Olympia, Washington

Valkyrie Arms filed for bankruptcy in early 2008.

Browning 1919 A4 .30 Caliber

Semi-automatic version of famous Browning machine gun. Chambered for .30-06 or .308 cartridge. Comes equipped with tripod, pintle, T&E, belly linker and 200 links. An A6 configuration available. Introduced in1996.

NIB	Exc.	V.G.	Good	Fair	Poor
2850	2000	1500	1100	750	600

U.S. M3-A1

Re-creation of famous "grease gun" in semi-automatic. Barrel length 16.5". Supplied with three 30-round magazines. **NOTE:** Add $50 for dummy suppressor; $300 plus transfer tax of $200 for real suppressor. All NFA rules and state laws must be followed for suppressors.

NIB	Exc.	V.G.	Good	Fair	Poor
1500	1250	1000	750	500	300

DeLisle Carbine

Copy of famous World War II commando carbine used by British forces. Chambered for .45 ACP. Integral suppressor. All NFA rules must be followed. Only 167 original WWII carbines were produced. **NOTE:** Deduct $300 for dummy suppressor.

NIB	Exc.	V.G.	Good	Fair	Poor
1575	1250	1000	750	500	300

VALMET, INC.
Jyvaskyla, Finland

M-62S

Semi-automatic copy of Finnish M-62 service rifle in 7.62x39 caliber. Patterned after Russian AK47. Fitted with walnut or tubular steel stock. Manufactured after 1962.

NIB	Exc.	V.G.	Good	Fair	Poor
—	3000	2800	2300	900	750

M-71S

As above in 5.56mm caliber. Available with composition stock.

NIB	Exc.	V.G.	Good	Fair	Poor
—	1350	1000	850	650	450

Model 76s

As above in 5.56mm, 7.62x39mm or 7.62x51mm. Barrel 16.75" or 20.5".

5.56mm

NIB	Exc.	V.G.	Good	Fair	Poor
—	1750	1500	1250	750	600

7.62x39mm

NIB	Exc.	V.G.	Good	Fair	Poor
—	3000	2750	2500	2000	1250

Model 78

As above in 7.62x51mm, 7.62x39 or .223, with 24.5" barrel, wood stock and integral bipod.

NIB	Exc.	V.G.	Good	Fair	Poor
—	2150	1700	1300	850	600

Model 212 Lion

12-gauge over/under shotgun, with 26", 28" or 30" barrels, single-selective trigger and extractors. Blued, with walnut stock. Manufactured from 1947 to 1968. Amazingly similar to Savage Model 330 over/under. Values shown for standard field grade.

NIB	Exc.	V.G.	Good	Fair	Poor
—	750	625	500	400	300

Model 412 Combination Gun

12-gauge .30-06 over/under combination gun. Built on frame of 12-gauge Lion shotgun. Discontinued.

NIB	Exc.	V.G.	Good	Fair	Poor
—	1900	1475	1200	1050	700

VALTRO
Italy

1998 A1

Model 1911 clone chambered for .45 ACP. Fitted with match grade 5" barrel. Many special features include checkered front strap, beavertail grip safety, deluxe wood grips, serrated slide front and back, beveled magazine well. Weight about 40 oz. Introduced in 1998.

NIB	Exc.	V.G.	Good	Fair	Poor
2250	1950	1600	1275	800	500

Tactical 98 Shotgun

Chambered for 12-gauge. Fitted with 18.5" or 20" ported barrel. Pistol-grip or standard stock. Extended magazine with 5- or 7-rounds. Ghost ring sights.

NIB	Exc.	V.G.	Good	Fair	Poor
—	900	750	675	500	325

PM5

Slide-action shotgun chambered for 12-gauge 3" shell. Barrel length 20" choked Cylinder. Box-fed magazine. Value shown for pre-ban model.

NIB	Exc.	V.G.	Good	Fair	Poor
—	—				

VARNER SPORTING ARMS, INC.
Marietta, Georgia

Company made several over/under shotguns and rifle/shotgun combinations for Savage Company. These are no longer being imported into this country. Rifles listed are all patterned after Stevens Favorite model.

Hunter

.22-caliber single-shot rifle, with 21.5" half-octagonal takedown barrel fitted with an aperture rear sight. Blued, with well-figured walnut stocks. Introduced in 1988.

NIB	Exc.	V.G.	Good	Fair	Poor
375	300	250	200	150	100

Hunter Deluxe

As above, with case-hardened receiver and more finely figured stock.

NIB	Exc.	V.G.	Good	Fair	Poor
500	400	350	250	175	125

Presentation Grade

As above, with target hammer and trigger. Hand checkered stock.

NIB	Exc.	V.G.	Good	Fair	Poor
575	475	425	350	250	200

No. 1 Grade
Engraved.

NIB	Exc.	V.G.	Good	Fair	Poor
650	550	500	450	350	200

No. 2 Grade

NIB	Exc.	V.G.	Good	Fair	Poor
775	650	600	500	400	200

No. 3 Grade

NIB	Exc.	V.G.	Good	Fair	Poor
1100	850	700	550	350	200

VECTOR ARMS, INC.
North Salt Lake, Utah

Mini Uzi

Smaller version of full size Uzi. Chambered for 9mm cartridge only. Fitted with 18" barrel.

Pre-Ban

NIB	Exc.	V.G.	Good	Fair	Poor
—	2000	1700	1400	1050	700

Post-Ban

NIB	Exc.	V.G.	Good	Fair	Poor
—	1500	1250	1050	700	500

Uzi

Semi-automatic pre-ban Uzi carbine, with 18" barrel. Chambered for 9mm cartridge. Receiver built by Group Industries of Louisville, Kentucky, prior to May 1986. Receiver fixed parts manufacturing and receiver assembly by Vector Arms. Only 97 of these semi-automatic receivers manufactured. **NOTE:** Add $200 for .45 ACP or .22-caliber conversion kit.

Pre-Ban

NIB	Exc.	V.G.	Good	Fair	Poor
—	1500	1250	1050	700	500

Post-Ban

NIB	Exc.	V.G.	Good	Fair	Poor
—	1200	1050	800	675	500

VEKTOR
Pretoria, South Africa

Company made a variety of handguns and rifles for U.S. market until 2001. Now only manufactures firearms for South African military and law enforcement.

HANDGUNS

Model Z88

Semi-automatic pistol chambered for 9mm cartridge. Has 5" barrel and fixed sights. Weight about 35 oz. Blue finish. Magazine capacity 15 rounds or 10 in U.S. Clone of Beretta 92.

NIB	Exc.	V.G.	Good	Fair	Poor
600	475	350	250	175	100

Model SP1 Service Pistol

Chambered for 9mm cartridge. Fitted with 4.625" barrel. Fixed sights. Weight 35 oz. Blue finish. Magazine capacity 15 rounds or 10 in U.S. **NOTE:** Add $30 for anodized or nickel finish.

NIB	Exc.	V.G.	Good	Fair	Poor
600	475	350	250	175	100

Model SP1 Sport

Similar to SP1. Features 5" barrel, with three-chamber compensator. Blue finish. Weight about 38 oz.

NIB	Exc.	V.G.	Good	Fair	Poor
725	575	450	350	275	175

Model SP1 Tuned Sport

Model has three-chamber compensator on 5" barrel. Adjustable straight trigger and LPA 3-dot sighting system. Nickel finish. Weight about 38 oz.

NIB	Exc.	V.G.	Good	Fair	Poor
1200	950	800	575	400	300

Model SP1 Target

9mm model fitted with 6" barrel with adjustable straight trigger. LPA 3-dot sighting system. Weight about 40.5 oz. Two-tone finish.

NIB	Exc.	V.G.	Good	Fair	Poor
1200	950	800	575	400	300

Model SP1 Compact (General's Model)

Compact version of 9mm pistol fitted with 4" barrel. Fixed sights. Blue finish. Magazine capacity 15 rounds or 10 in U.S. Weight about 31.5 oz.

NIB	Exc.	V.G.	Good	Fair	Poor
650	525	400	300	200	75

Model SP2

Full size service pistol chambered for .40 S&W cartridge. Fitted with 4.625" barrel. Fixed sights. Magazine capacity 11 rounds or 10 in U.S. Blued finish. Weight about 35 oz.

NIB	Exc.	V.G.	Good	Fair	Poor
650	525	400	300	200	75

Model SP2 Compact (General's Model)

Compact .40 S&W pistol, with 4" barrel. Magazine capacity 11 rounds or 10 in U.S. Weight about 31.5 oz. Blue finish. Fixed sights.

NIB	Exc.	V.G.	Good	Fair	Poor
650	525	400	300	200	75

Model SP2 Competition

Chambered for .40 S&W cartridge. Fitted with 5.875" barrel. Features enlarged safety levers and magazine catch. Frame has been thickened for scope mount. Beavertail grip and straight trigger. Weight about 42 oz.

NIB	Exc.	V.G.	Good	Fair	Poor
1000	750	600	450	325	200

Model SP1 Ultra Sport

Designed for IPSC open-class competition. Barrel length 6", with 3" chamber compensator. Chambered for 9mm cartridge. Optical scope mount, with Weaver rails. Magazine capacity 19 rounds or 10 in U.S. Weight about 41.5 oz. Priced with Lynx scope.

NIB	Exc.	V.G.	Good	Fair	Poor
2150	1800	1575	1200	800	500

Model SP2 Ultra Sport

Same as above chambered for .40 S&W cartridge. Magazine capacity 14 rounds or 10 in U.S.

NIB	Exc.	V.G.	Good	Fair	Poor
2150	1800	1575	1200	800	500

Model SP2 Conversion Kit

Made for SP2, this is a 9mm conversion kit that consists of 9mm barrel, recoil spring and 9mm magazine.

NIB	Exc.	V.G.	Good	Fair	Poor
200	150	100	75	50	25

Model CP-1 Compact

Chambered for 9mm cartridge. Fitted with 4" barrel. Polymer frame and fixed sights. Weight about 25 oz. Magazine capacity 13 rounds standard, 12 rounds compact or 10 rounds in U.S. Offered with black or nickel slide. **NOTE:** This model was recalled in 2000 due to safety concerns.

NIB	Exc.	V.G.	Good	Fair	Poor
475	375	250	150	100	50

RIFLES

Vektor H5 Pump-Action Rifle

Pump-action rifle chambered for .233 cartridge. Fitted with thumbhole stock and 22" barrel. Magazine capacity 5 rounds.

NIB	Exc.	V.G.	Good	Fair	Poor
850	725	600	475	300	200

Vektor 98

Built on Mauser action. Chambered for a variety of calibers from .243 to .375 H&H. Fitted with one-piece walnut stock, with hand checkering. Magazine capacity 5 rounds. Open sights on Magnum calibers only.

NIB	Exc.	V.G.	Good	Fair	Poor
1200	950	800	575	400	300

Vektor Lyttelton

Numerous special features. Fitted with classic walnut stock and wrap-around checkering. Fixed sights. Calibers offered from .243 to .375 H&H.

NIB	Exc.	V.G.	Good	Fair	Poor
1595	1400	1100	800	575	300

VENUS WAFFENWERKE
Zella Mehlis, Germany

Venus

6.35mm, 7.65mm or 9mm semi-automatic pistol, with 3.5" barrel. Slide marked "Original Venus Patent"; grips bear monogram "OW". Designed by Oskar Will. Blued plastic grips. Manufactured from 1912 to 1914.

NIB	Exc.	V.G.	Good	Fair	Poor
—	700	550	400	250	100

VERNEY-CARRON
St. Etienne, France

Concours

12-gauge over/under boxlock shotgun, with 26" or 28" ventilated rib barrels, single-selective triggers, automatic ejectors and profuse engraving. Blued French case-hardened, with checkered walnut stock. First imported in 1978.

NIB	Exc.	V.G.	Good	Fair	Poor
—	1450	900	700	600	300

Skeet Model

As above, with 28" Skeet-choked barrel and pistol-grip stock.

NIB	Exc.	V.G.	Good	Fair	Poor
—	1600	1050	700	600	300

Snake Charmer II

.410 single-barrel break-action shotgun, with stainless steel barrel and receiver. Black ABS stock. Overall length 29".

NIB	Exc.	V.G.	Good	Fair	Poor
—	175	150	100	75	50

VERONA
Italy

HUNTING SHOTGUNS

Model SX401/S

12- or 20-gauge 3" semi-automatic. Offered with 26" or 28" ventilated rib barrel, with choke tubes. Checkered Turkish walnut stock. Weight about 6.75 lbs.

NIB	Exc.	V.G.	Good	Fair	Poor
800	600	475	350	150	100

Model SX405/S/L

As above, with black composite stock. Weight about 6.5 lbs.

NIB	Exc.	V.G.	Good	Fair	Poor
700	600	550	300	100	75

Model SX405W/H/SW/SH

12-gauge 3" Magnum semi-automatic gun. Choice of 26" or 28" ventilated rib barrel, with wetland or hardwood camo pattern. Weight about 6.5 lbs.

NIB	Exc.	V.G.	Good	Fair	Poor
800	600	475	350	150	100

LX501

Over/under shotgun chambered for 12-, 20-, 28-gauge and .410 bore. Single-selective trigger. Ejectors. Blued steel receiver. Walnut stock, with machine checkering. Offered with 28" ventilated rib barrels. Screw-in chokes for 12- and 20-gauge. Fixed chokes for 28-gauge and .410 bore. Chambers are 3" for all gauges except 28-gauge. Weight between 6.25 lbs. and 6.75 lbs. depending on gauge. **NOTE:** Add $30 for 28-gauge and .410 bore.

NIB	Exc.	V.G.	Good	Fair	Poor
1000	875	600	400	300	225

LX692G

Also offered in 12-, 20-, 28-gauge and .410 bore, with 28" ventilated rib barrels. Receiver fitted with sideplate. Gold inlaid hunting scenes on three sides. Matte finish walnut stock, with schnabel forearm, hand-cut checkering. Weight between 7.25 lbs. and 7.75 lbs. depending on gauge. **NOTE:** Add $40 for 28-gauge; $25 for .410 bore.

NIB	Exc.	V.G.	Good	Fair	Poor
1250	1100	875	725	500	300

LX692G-20/28

Same as above. Features 20-gauge, with extra set of 28-gauge barrels. Choke tubes standard. Weight about 7.5 lbs. with 20-gauge barrels.

NIB	Exc.	V.G.	Good	Fair	Poor
2000	1800	1500	1200	900	500

Model LX1001 Express Combo

Over/under gun features two sets of barrels; one for 20-gauge 2.75"; other .223, .243, .270, .308 or .30-06. The 20-gauge barrels are 28" ventilated rib and rifle are 22". Checkered walnut stock, with oil-finish. Engraved receiver.

NIB	Exc.	V.G.	Good	Fair	Poor
2580	2300	1975	1600	900	600

LX702G

Offered in 12- or 20-gauge, with 28" barrel chambered for 3" shells. Features case colored receiver, with side plates. Receiver engraved on three sides with gold inlaid upland bird hunting scenes. Full-figured Turkish walnut, with hand checkering and oil-finish. Single-selective trigger, black recoil pad, ejectors and schnabel forearm. Weight about: 12-gauge 7 lbs.; 20-gauge 6 lbs.

NIB	Exc.	V.G.	Good	Fair	Poor
1375	1200	950	700	500	350

SIDE-BY-SIDE SHOTGUNS

Model SS662GL

Side-by-side offered in 20- or 28-gauge, with 28" barrels choked Modified and Full. Double triggers. Engraved receiver. Checkered walnut stock, with straight-grip. Weight about 6 lbs. Made by Bernardelli. **NOTE:** Add 20 percent for 28-gauge.

NIB	Exc.	V.G.	Good	Fair	Poor
2200	2000	1750	1400	1000	500

Model SS772GL

As above, with slightly more engraving. **NOTE:** Add 20 percent for 28-gauge.

NIB	Exc.	V.G.	Good	Fair	Poor
2450	2200	1850	1550	1175	550

SPORTING/COMPETITION SHOTGUNS

LX680

Chambered for 12- or 20-gauge shells, with 2.75" chambers. Single-selective trigger, ejectors, lightly engraved steel receiver. Walnut stock, with beavertail firearm and hand-cut checkering. Ventilated recoil pad standard. Fitted with 28" barrels, with ventilated rib between barrels. Choke tubes. Weight about 6.5 lbs. depending on gauge.

NIB	Exc.	V.G.	Good	Fair	Poor
1075	900	700	525	375	250

LX692GS

Similar to above, with sideplates and gold inlaid hunting scenes.

NIB	Exc.	V.G.	Good	Fair	Poor
1425	1300	1050	750	500	350

LX680C S&T

Over/under features 28" or 30" 11mm ventilated rib barrels on 12-gauge frame. Single-selective trigger, ejectors. Matte finish Turkish walnut stock, with hand-cut checkering, beavertail forearm, wider comb. Lightly engraved steel receiver. Ventilated rib between barrels. Choke tubes. Weight about 7.75 lbs. depending on barrel length. 28" barrel designated as Skeet/Sporting; 30" Trap.

NIB	Exc.	V.G.	Good	Fair	Poor
1175	1000	800	600	425	275

LX692GC S&T

Same as above, with sideplates and gold inlaid game scenes.

NIB	Exc.	V.G.	Good	Fair	Poor
1550	1400	1150	850	600	350

LX702GC S&T

Features case colored receiver and sideplates, with gold inlaid birds. Offered in 12-gauge only. Choice of 28" or 30" barrels. Weight about 7.5 lbs.

NIB	Exc.	V.G.	Good	Fair	Poor
1625	1475	1175	800	600	350

Model SX801/L

Semi-automatic 12-gauge 2.75" shotgun. Fitted with 28" or 30" ventilated rib ported barrels, with choke tubes and Hi-Viz sights. Walnut stock, with Monte Carlo or adjustable comb. Weight about 6.75 lbs.

NIB	Exc.	V.G.	Good	Fair	Poor
865	700	575	400	275	200

Model SX801G/GL

As above, with higher grade walnut stock.

NIB	Exc.	V.G.	Good	Fair	Poor
1060	900	725	600	450	200

Model LX980CS

12-gauge 2.75" over/under gun. Fitted with 30" ported barrels, with extended choke tubes. Removable trigger assembly. Black receiver. Checkered select walnut stock. Weight about 7.5 lbs.

NIB	Exc.	V.G.	Good	Fair	Poor
3525	3200	2500	2000	1550	600

Model LX980GCS/GCT

As above, with 30" or 32" ported barrels. Select walnut stock has adjustable comb. Weight about 7.5 lbs.

NIB	Exc.	V.G.	Good	Fair	Poor
3775	3400	2800	2250	1700	650

VICKERS, LTD.
Crayford/Kent, England

Jubilee

.22-caliber single-shot Martini-action rifle, with 28" barrel, adjustable sights and pistol-grip walnut stock. Blued. Manufactured prior to WWII.

NIB	Exc.	V.G.	Good	Fair	Poor
—	1000	700	550	375	200

Empire

As above, with 27" or 30" barrel and straight stock.

NIB	Exc.	V.G.	Good	Fair	Poor
—	1000	700	550	375	200

VICTOR EJECTOR
See—Crescent F. A. Co.

VICTORY ARMS CO., LTD.
Northhampton, England

Model MC5

9mm, .38 Super, .41 Action Express, 10mm or .45-caliber semi-automatic pistol, with 4.25", 5.75" or 7.5" barrel, 10-, 12- or 17-shot magazine, decocking lever and Millett sights. Interchangeable barrels were available. Introduced in 1989.

NIB	Exc.	V.G.	Good	Fair	Poor
500	400	300	250	200	150

VIRGINIAN
See—Interarms

VOERE
Kufstein, Austria

In 1987, this company was purchased by Mauser-Werke. Voere actions are used in rifles made and sold by KDF, Inc. (Kleinguenther), of Seguin, Texas. Values for older-production rifles are listed.

Model 1007

Bolt-action rifle chambered for .22 LR cartridge. Fitted with 18" barrel, open sights, beechwood stock. Introduced in 1984; discontinued 1991.

NIB	Exc.	V.G.	Good	Fair	Poor
450	375	300	200	150	75

Model 1013

Bolt-action rifle chambered for .22 WMR cartridge. Fitted with 18" barrel. Magazine capacity 8 rounds. Open sight with adjustable rear. Military-style stock oil-finished. Double-set triggers.

NIB	Exc.	V.G.	Good	Fair	Poor
650	575	500	375	250	125

Model 2107

.22 LR bolt-action rifle has 19.5" barrel, with Monte Carlo stock. 8-round magazine. Weight about 6 lbs.

NIB	Exc.	V.G.	Good	Fair	Poor
650	575	500	375	250	125

Model 2107 Deluxe

Bolt-action rifle chambered for .22 LR cartridge. Checkered stock, with raised cheekpiece. Discontinued in 1988.

NIB	Exc.	V.G.	Good	Fair	Poor
650	575	500	375	250	125

Model 2114S

Semi-automatic rifle chambered for .22 LR cartridge. Fitted with 18" barrel. Magazine capacity 15 rounds. Open sight. Stock is beechwood. Single-stage trigger. No longer in production.

NIB	Exc.	V.G.	Good	Fair	Poor
450	375	300	200	150	75

Model 2115

Similar to above, with checkered stock. Weight about 5.75 lbs. Discontinued in 1995.

NIB	Exc.	V.G.	Good	Fair	Poor
500	425	350	250	200	100

Model 2150

Bolt-action centerfire rifle chambered for calibers from .22-250 to .338 Win. Magnum. Fitted with 22" barrels (24" on Magnums). Open sights with adjustable rear. Checkered walnut stock with oil-finish. Built on M98 Mauser action. Weight about 8 lbs. depending on caliber. Discontinued in 1995.

NIB	Exc.	V.G.	Good	Fair	Poor
—	1500	1200	850	550	300

Model 2155

Similar to Model 2150, with no sights and double-set triggers. Discontinued in 1995.

NIB	Exc.	V.G.	Good	Fair	Poor
—	1650	1350	1000	700	225

Model 2165

Similar to above, with open sights, walnut stock with Bavarian cheekpiece and schnabel forearm. Rosewood grip cap. Discontinued.

NIB	Exc.	V.G.	Good	Fair	Poor
—	1650	1350	1000	700	225

Model 2185

Semi-automatic centerfire rifle chambered for 7x64, .308 and .30-06 cartridges. Fitted with 20" barrel, open sights and adjustable rear. Checkered walnut stock. Available with full stock as well. **NOTE:** Add $100 for Mannlicher stock.

NIB	Exc.	V.G.	Good	Fair	Poor
—	1500	1200	950	850	400

Model 2185 Match

Same as Model 2185 except for 5-round magazine, hooded front sight, laminated stock with adjustable cheekpiece. Discontinued in 1994.

NIB	Exc.	V.G.	Good	Fair	Poor
4000	3400	2750	1150	650	400

Model Titan

Centerfire bolt-action rifle chambered in calibers from .243 to .375 H&H. Fitted with 24" or 26" barrels depending on caliber. No sights. Checkered Monte Carlo walnut stock with oil-finish. Discontinued in 1988.

NIB	Exc.	V.G.	Good	Fair	Poor
—	1200	1000	775	500	350

Model Titan Menor

Bolt-action rifle chambered for .222 Rem. and .223 Rem. Fitted with 23.5" barrel and 3-round magazine. No sights. Checkered Monte Carlo walnut stock, with rosewood grip cap. Introduced in 1986, dropped 1988.

NIB	Exc.	V.G.	Good	Fair	Poor
—	1000	800	600	400	250

Model VEC-91 Series

Bolt-action rifle that fires caseless 5.7mm ammo. Adjustable rear sight on 20" barrel. Checkered walnut stock with cheekpiece. Electronic trigger. Limited importation into U.S. from 1991 to about 2008. Seldom seen for sale on used gun market, in part due to expensive case-less ammunition.

NIB	Exc.	V.G.	Good	Fair	Poor
2000	1600	1450	1000	—	—

VOLCANIC ARMS COMPANY
New Haven, Connecticut
See—Winchester Repeating Arms Co.

VOLQUARTSEN CUSTOM
Carroll, Iowa

Company started in 1973 and began specializing in Ruger 10/22 aftermarket conversions. In 1997, the company began producing its own receivers. **NOTE:** Volquartsen offers beaucoup options on a wide variety of rifles. Values shown below are for more-or-less base models.

SEMI-AUTO RIFLES

Rifles are based on Ruger 10/22 design. Chambered for .22 LR or .22 WMR cartridge.

Standard

Fitted with 18.5" stainless steel barrel. Hogue rubber stock or brown laminated. No sights. Integral Weaver rail.

NIB	Exc.	V.G.	Good	Fair	Poor
1350	1200	950	700	550	300

Lightweight

Has 16.5" carbon-fiber barrel. Rubber or laminated stock. Integral Weaver rail.

NIB	Exc.	V.G.	Good	Fair	Poor
1370	1220	975	725	550	300

Deluxe

Has 20" stainless steel fluted and compensated barrel. Laminated or rubber stock.

NIB	Exc.	V.G.	Good	Fair	Poor
1360	1200	950	700	550	300

SIGNATURE SERIES

Fitted with 20" stainless steel fluted and compensated barrel. Engraved receiver, trigger guard and rings. Comes with Nikon 3.3x10 Titanium scope. Fancy walnut stock.

NIB	Exc.	V.G.	Good	Fair	Poor
2500	2200	1650	1200	600	300

VG-1

Has 20" stainless steel fluted and compensated barrel. Fitted with green McMillan fiberglass stock. Finish is black epoxy powder coating. Offered in .22 WMR only.

NIB	Exc.	V.G.	Good	Fair	Poor
1900	1700	1400	1150	900	500

Fusion Takedown Model

This semi-automatic has quick-change barrels in three different calibers: .17 HMR, .22 WMR and .22 LR.

One barrel: .22 LR

NIB	Exc.	V.G.	Good	Fair	Poor
1375	1125	950	700	350	150

One barrel: .17 WMR or .22 WMR

NIB	Exc.	V.G.	Good	Fair	Poor
1575	1265	1050	800	400	200

All three barrels included

NIB	Exc.	V.G.	Good	Fair	Poor
1775	1450	1100	900	450	250

Evolution Model

Centerfire model in .204 Ruger or .223 Rem. Gas-operated action. Stainless steel receiver has integral Picatinny rail. Laminate or laminate thumbhole stock in gray or brown. **NOTE:** Add $100 for thumbhole stock.

NIB	Exc.	V.G.	Good	Fair	Poor
2200	1825	1350	1100	500	300

VX-2500

Features 20" stainless steel fluted and compensated barrel. Fitted with VX-2500 stock, with aluminum forearm. Designed for benchrest shooting.

NIB	Exc.	V.G.	Good	Fair	Poor
2000	1750	1500	1200	900	500

VX-5000

Fitted with 18" carbon-fiber lightweight barrel, with compensator. Comes standard with VX-5000 stock, with aluminum fore-end.

NIB	Exc.	V.G.	Good	Fair	Poor
2200	1950	1700	1400	1000	600

PISTOLS

Pistols based on Ruger MK II design.

Black Cheetah Pistol

Special order only.

Compact

Fitted with 3.5" bull barrel and Hogue Monogrip. Adjustable rear sight and target front. Stainless steel finish. Weight about 42 oz.

NIB	Exc.	V.G.	Good	Fair	Poor
1000	850	700	525	400	300

Deluxe

Fitted with 5" to 10" special heavy barrel depending on customer's requirements. Adjustable rear sight and target front. Target grips. Stainless steel finish.

NIB	Exc.	V.G.	Good	Fair	Poor
1250	1000	900	700	575	450

Masters

Features 6.5" barrel, with aluminum alloy-finned underlug. Top rib has front blade sight with an adjustable rear. Rib cut to accommodate optics. Integral compensator. Weight about 56 oz.

NIB	Exc.	V.G.	Good	Fair	Poor
1600	1350	1200	900	650	500

Olympic

Designed for NRA or UIT competitive shooting. Has 7.5" match barrel, with unique gas chamber for recoil-free shooting. Target front sight and adjustable rear. Weight about 36 oz.

NIB	Exc.	V.G.	Good	Fair	Poor
1750	1450	1300	1000	650	500

Stingray

Fitted with 7.5" match-grade barrel, with radial flutes. Compensator standard. Supplied with Ultra Dot red dot optic or TL rear. Weight about 56 oz.

NIB	Exc.	V.G.	Good	Fair	Poor
1600	1350	1200	900	650	500

Terminator

Fitted with 7.5" match barrel, with integral compensator. Weaver-style or .375" tip-off scope mounting system. **NOTE:** Add $150 for Ultra Dot optics.

NIB	Exc.	V.G.	Good	Fair	Poor
1600	1350	1200	900	650	500

Ultra-Lite Match

NIB	Exc.	V.G.	Good	Fair	Poor
1600	1350	1200	900	650	500

V-6

V-6 has 6" ventilated rib triangular-shaped match barrel, with full-length underlug. Adjustable rear sight and target front. Rubber target grips. Weight about 36 oz.

WALCH, JOHN
New York, New York

Navy Revolver

A .36-caliber superimposed load percussion revolver, with 6" octagonal barrel and 6-shot cylinder. Fitted with 12 nipples, two hammers and two triggers. Barrel marked "Walch Firearms Co. NY." and "Patented Feb. 8, 1859". Blued, with walnut grips.

NIB	Exc.	V.G.	Good	Fair	Poor
—	—	13000	9000	4000	950

Pocket Revolver

A spur trigger .31-caliber 10-shot percussion revolver, with brass or iron frame and walnut grips. Iron frame version worth approximately 50 percent more than brass variety.

Courtesy Greg Martin Auctions

NIB	Exc.	V.G.	Good	Fair	Poor
—	—	5000	2750	1000	300

WALDMAN
Germany

Waldman

A 7.65mm semi-automatic pistol, with 3.5" barrel and 8-shot magazine. Slide marked "1913 Model Automatic Pistol" and some examples are marked "American Automatic Pistol". Blued, with checkered walnut grips inlaid with a brass insert marked "Waldman".

NIB	Exc.	V.G.	Good	Fair	Poor
—	300	225	200	150	100

WALLIS & BIRCH
Philadelphia, Pennsylvania

Pocket Pistol

A .41-caliber single-shot percussion pocket pistol, with 2.5" or 3" barrel, German silver furniture and walnut stock. Barrel marked "Wallis & Birch Phila.". Produced during 1850s.

NIB	Exc.	V.G.	Good	Fair	Poor
—	—	4050	2250	800	250

WALTHER, CARL
Zella Mehilis and Ulm/Donau, Germany

Model 1

A 6.35mm semi-automatic pistol. Barrel lengths 2" to 6". Blued, with checkered hard rubber grips. Walther logo on each grip. Introduced in 1908.

Courtesy James Rankin

NIB	Exc.	V.G.	Good	Fair	Poor
—	1000	700	400	200	200

Model 2

A 6.35mm semi-automatic pistol, with a knurled bushing at the muzzle that retains the mainspring. There are two variations: fixed rear sight; pop-up rear sight. Blued, with checkered hard rubber grips. Walther logo on each grip. Introduced in 1909.

Courtesy James Rankin

Fixed Sights

NIB	Exc.	V.G.	Good	Fair	Poor
—	800	600	300	200	150

Pop Up Sights

NIB	Exc.	V.G.	Good	Fair	Poor
—	1800	1000	600	400	300

Model 3

7.65mm semi-automatic pistol having a smooth barrel bushing. Blued, with checkered hard rubber grips. Walther logo on each grip. Introduced in 1910.

Courtesy James Rankin

NIB	Exc.	V.G.	Good	Fair	Poor
4000	3000	2000	1000	400	200

Model 4

A 7.65mm semi-automatic pistol larger than preceding models. Many variations of this model produced. Blued, with checkered hard rubber grips. Walther logo on each grip. Introduced in 1910.

Courtesy James Rankin

NIB	Exc.	V.G.	Good	Fair	Poor
700	600	500	400	275	150

Model 5

A 6.35mm semi-automatic pistol that is almost identical to Model 2. Fixed sights. Blued, with checkered hard rubber grips. Walther logo on each grip.

Courtesy James Rankin

NIB	Exc.	V.G.	Good	Fair	Poor
600	500	400	300	200	150

Model 6

9mm semi-automatic pistol. Largest of Walther numbered pistols. Approximately 1,500 manufactured. Blued, with checkered hard rubber grips. Walther logo on each grip. Sometimes seen with plain checkered wood grips. Introduced in 1915.

NIB	Exc.	V.G.	Good	Fair	Poor
9000	7500	5000	3000	1500	700

Model 7

A 6.35mm semi-automatic pistol in the same style as Model 4. Blued, with checkered hard rubber grips. Walther logo on each side. Introduced in 1917.

Courtesy James Rankin

NIB	Exc.	V.G.	Good	Fair	Poor
800	700	500	300	200	150

Model 8

A 6.35mm semi-automatic pistol. Finish is blue, silver or gold. Most were unengraved, but three types of engraving coverage were available from the factory: slide only, slide and frame and complete coverage overall. Grips are checkered hard rubber, with WC logo on one grip and 6.35mm on opposite side. Ivory grips are seen with many of the engraved models. Introduced in 1920 and produced until 1944. **NOTE:** Add $500 for factory case.

Courtesy James Rankin

Blue, Silver or Gold Finish

NIB	Exc.	V.G.	Good	Fair	Poor
—	750	600	300	200	150

Engraved Slide

NIB	Exc.	V.G.	Good	Fair	Poor
—	1000	700	500	300	200

Engraved Slide and Frame

NIB	Exc.	V.G.	Good	Fair	Poor
—	2500	2000	1100	450	300

Engraved, Complete Coverage

NIB	Exc.	V.G.	Good	Fair	Poor
—	4000	3500	1400	500	300

Model 9

A 6.35mm semi-automatic pistol. Smaller than Model 8. Built as Model 1, with exposed barrel. Same finishes and engraving as Model 8. Introduced in 1921; produced until 1944. All values same as Model 8.

Courtesy James Rankin

Sport Model 1926/ Walther Hammerless Target 22/ Walther Standard Sport/ Walther 1932 Olympia/ Sport Model Target/ Special Stoeger Model

All of these .22 LR caliber semi-automatic pistols are the same target pistol. Introduced by Walther in 1926. A well-made pistol, with a barrel length between 6" to 16". Has one-piece checkered wrap-around wood grips. There was also a .22 Short version of Olympia model produced for rapid fire Olympic shooting. There was also a torpedo-shape target weight available for shooters. **NOTE:** Add $200 for target weight; $500 for case.

Courtesy Orvel Reichert

NIB	Exc.	V.G.	Good	Fair	Poor
—	1800	1300	900	500	300

Walther 1936 Olympia

Semi-automatic target pistol in .22-caliber resembled earlier 1932 Olympia, but with many improvements. There were four standard models produced with many variations of each one. These variations included many barrel lengths, both round and octagon. There were duraluminum slides, frames and triggers. Various weight configurations as many as four separate weights to one gun. One-piece wrap-around checkered wood grips in different configurations for the individual shooter. Produced until 1944. **NOTE:** Prices are for Standard Model. Add $500 for Pentathlon or Hunter; $300 for Rapid Fire; $750 for weights. The four models were:

1. Funfklamph Pentathlon
2. Jagerschafts—Hunter
3. Sport or Standard Model
4. Schnellfeur—Rapid Fire

Courtesy John J. Stimson, Jr.

Olympia without weights

NIB	Exc.	V.G.	Good	Fair	Poor
2000	1500	1300	750	475	250

Model MP

A 9mm semi-automatic pistol that was the forerunner of Model AP and P.38 series. Found in variations that resemble a large Model PP or P.38. Blued finish, with one-piece wrap-around checkered wood grips.

Courtesy James Rankin

NIB	Exc.	V.G.	Good	Fair	Poor
—	35000	30000	25000	20000	15000

Model AP

A 9mm semi-automatic pistol that was the forerunner of Model P.38. A hammerless pistol in various barrel lengths. Sometimes with duraluminum frames and some with stocks. Blued finish, with one-piece wrap-around checkered wood grips. **NOTE:** Add $4000 with stock.

NIB	Exc.	V.G.	Good	Fair	Poor
—	28000	25000	20000	15000	10000

Model PP

Semi-automatic pistol in .22-, .25-, .32- and .380-caliber. Introduced in 1928. First successful commercial double-action pistol. Manufactured in finishes of blue, silver and gold, with three different types of engraving. Grips generally two-piece black or white plastic, with Walther banner on each grip. Grips in wood or ivory are seen, but usually on engraved guns. Many variations of Model PP and numerous NSDAP markings seen on pre-1946 models that were produced during Nazi regime. All reflect various prices.

.22 Caliber

NIB	Exc.	V.G.	Good	Fair	Poor
1200	800	600	350	250	150

.25 Caliber

NIB	Exc.	V.G.	Good	Fair	Poor
8000	6500	5000	3000	1500	700

.32 Caliber, High Polished Finish

Courtesy James Rankin

NIB	Exc.	V.G.	Good	Fair	Poor
1000	850	650	325	225	175

.32 Caliber, Milled Finish

NIB	Exc.	V.G.	Good	Fair	Poor
800	700	500	250	200	125

.380 Caliber

NIB	Exc.	V.G.	Good	Fair	Poor
2000	1600	1300	800	475	350

.32 Caliber, with Duraluminum Frame

NIB	Exc.	V.G.	Good	Fair	Poor
1000	900	700	550	400	200

.32 Caliber, with Bottom Magazine Release

NIB	Exc.	V.G.	Good	Fair	Poor
1500	1400	1000	600	400	200

.32 Caliber, with Verchromt Finish

NIB	Exc.	V.G.	Good	Fair	Poor
3000	2800	2500	1200	700	400

.32 Caliber, Allemagne Marked

NIB	Exc.	V.G.	Good	Fair	Poor
950	850	700	550	325	250

.32 Caliber, A. F. Stoeger Contract

NIB	Exc.	V.G.	Good	Fair	Poor
2700	2500	1750	1050	700	400

.32 Caliber, with Waffenampt Proofs, High Polished Finish

NIB	Exc.	V.G.	Good	Fair	Poor
1700	1500	1200	600	275	150

.32 Caliber, with Waffenampt Proofs, Milled Finish

NIB	Exc.	V.G.	Good	Fair	Poor
900	700	500	325	250	150

.32 Caliber, in Blue Finish and Full Coverage Engraving

NOTE: Add $500 for ivory grips; $700 for leather presentation cases; $1000 for .380-caliber.

NIB	Exc.	V.G.	Good	Fair	Poor
—	5000	4000	3000	1200	700

.32 Caliber, in Silver Finish and Full Coverage Engraving

NOTE: Add $500 for ivory grips; $700 for leather presentation cases; $1000 for .380-caliber.

NIB	Exc.	V.G.	Good	Fair	Poor
—	5500	4500	3000	1200	700

.32 Caliber, in Gold Finish and Full Coverage Engraving

NOTE: Add $500 for ivory grips; $700 for leather presentation cases; $1000 for .380-caliber.

NIB	Exc.	V.G.	Good	Fair	Poor
—	5800	5000	3500	1500	700

.32 Caliber, Police Eagle/C Proofed, High Polished Finish

NIB	Exc.	V.G.	Good	Fair	Poor
1600	1200	800	375	250	150

.32 Caliber, Police Eagle/C and Police Eagle/F Proofed, Milled Finish

NIB	Exc.	V.G.	Good	Fair	Poor
1000	900	600	375	275	150

.32 Caliber, NSKK Marked on the Slide

NOTE: Add $1,000 with proper NSKK DRGM AKAH holster.

NIB	Exc.	V.G.	Good	Fair	Poor
3500	3000	2700	850	550	300

.32 Caliber, NSDAP Gruppe Markings

NOTE: Add $1,000 with proper SA DRGM AKAH holster.

NIB	Exc.	V.G.	Good	Fair	Poor
2700	2500	2000	1000	500	300

.32 Caliber, PDM Marked with Bottom Magazine Release

NIB	Exc.	V.G.	Good	Fair	Poor
2400	2000	1500	1100	475	300

.32 Caliber, RJ Marked

NIB	Exc.	V.G.	Good	Fair	Poor
1400	900	700	475	400	150

.32 Caliber, RFV Marked, High Polished or Milled Finish

NIB	Exc.	V.G.	Good	Fair	Poor
1400	900	700	475	400	150

.32 Caliber, RBD Munster Marked

NIB	Exc.	V.G.	Good	Fair	Poor
2500	2200	1750	1200	650	400

.32 Caliber, RpLt Marked

NIB	Exc.	V.G.	Good	Fair	Poor
1650	1500	1200	700	375	200

.32 Caliber, Statens Vattenfallsverk Marked

NIB	Exc.	V.G.	Good	Fair	Poor
1650	1500	1200	700	375	200

.32 Caliber, AC Marked

NIB	Exc.	V.G.	Good	Fair	Poor
800	700	500	300	250	150

.32 Caliber, Duraluminum Frame

NIB	Exc.	V.G.	Good	Fair	Poor
1000	900	700	500	400	150

.380 Caliber, Bottom Magazine Release and Waffenamt Proofs

NIB	Exc.	V.G.	Good	Fair	Poor
2400	2000	1500	700	500	300

Model PPK

Semi-automatic pistol in .22-, .25-, .32- and .380-caliber. Introduced six months after Model PP in 1929. A more compact version of Model PP, with one less round in magazine. One-piece wrap-around checkered plastic grips in brown, black and white. Walther banner on each side of grips. Model PPK will be found with same types of finishes as Model PP, as well as same styles of engraving. Grips in wood or ivory are seen with some of the engraved models. As with Model PP, there are many variations of Model PPK and numerous NSDAP markings seen on pre-1946 models that were produced during the Nazi regime. All reflect various prices.

Courtesy James Rankin

.22 Caliber

NIB	Exc.	V.G.	Good	Fair	Poor
1900	1700	1500	750	325	175

.25 Caliber

NIB	Exc.	V.G.	Good	Fair	Poor
8500	6000	4000	1850	1000	500

.32 Caliber, High Polished Finish

NIB	Exc.	V.G.	Good	Fair	Poor
1400	950	750	450	250	150

.32 Caliber, Milled Finish

NIB	Exc.	V.G.	Good	Fair	Poor
1300	900	700	400	250	150

.380 Caliber

Courtesy Orvel Reichert

NIB	Exc.	V.G.	Good	Fair	Poor
4250	3000	2500	1600	750	375

.32 Caliber, with Duraluminum Frame

NIB	Exc.	V.G.	Good	Fair	Poor
2000	1500	1300	600	400	200

.32 Caliber, Marked Mod. PP on Slide

NIB	Exc.	V.G.	Good	Fair	Poor
6000	5000	4000	2500	1500	1000

.32 Caliber, with Panagraphed Slide

NIB	Exc.	V.G.	Good	Fair	Poor
2000	1200	750	450	300	200

.32 Caliber, with Verchromt Finish

NIB	Exc.	V.G.	Good	Fair	Poor
3800	2800	2500	1200	700	350

.32 Caliber, in Blue Finish and Full Coverage Engraving

NOTE: Add $1,000 for ivory grips; $1,000 for leather presentation cases; $1,000 for .380-caliber.

NIB	Exc.	V.G.	Good	Fair	Poor
—	5000	3500	2500	1200	700

.32 Caliber, in Silver Finish and Full Coverage Engraving

NOTE: Add $1,000 for ivory grips; $1,000 for leather presentation cases; $1,000 for .380-caliber.

NIB	Exc.	V.G.	Good	Fair	Poor
—	6000	4000	3000	1500	700

.32 Caliber, in Gold Finish and Full Coverage Engraving

NOTE: Add $1,000 for ivory grips; $1,000 for leather presentation cases; $1,000 for .380-caliber.

NIB	Exc.	V.G.	Good	Fair	Poor
—	6500	5500	3500	1500	700

.32 Caliber, Czechoslovakian Contract

NIB	Exc.	V.G.	Good	Fair	Poor
2000	1850	1500	1000	550	300

.32 Caliber, Allemagne Marked

NIB	Exc.	V.G.	Good	Fair	Poor
1150	1000	800	600	400	250

.32 Caliber, with Waffenampt Proofs and a High Polished Finish

NIB	Exc.	V.G.	Good	Fair	Poor
2400	1900	1600	900	400	250

.32 Caliber, with Waffenampt Proofs and a Milled Finish

NIB	Exc.	V.G.	Good	Fair	Poor
1700	1500	1300	750	300	175

.32 Caliber, Police Eagle/C Proofed, High Polished Finish

NIB	Exc.	V.G.	Good	Fair	Poor
1500	1200	1000	500	300	175

.32 Caliber, Police Eagle/C Proofed. Milled Finish

NIB	Exc.	V.G.	Good	Fair	Poor
1100	900	700	375	275	175

.32 Caliber, Police Eagle/F Proofed, Duraluminum Frame, Milled Finish

NIB	Exc.	V.G.	Good	Fair	Poor
1600	1300	1000	550	350	225

.22 Caliber, Late War, Black Grips

NIB	Exc.	V.G.	Good	Fair	Poor
2400	1800	1500	600	450	300

.32 Caliber, Party Leader Grips, Brown

NIB	Exc.	V.G.	Good	Fair	Poor
8000	6000	5500	3000	2250	2000

.32 Caliber, Party Leader Grips, Black

NOTE: Add $1,500 with proper Party Leader DRGM AKAH holster.

NIB	Exc.	V.G.	Good	Fair	Poor
8000	6000	5500	3200	2550	2500

.32 Caliber, RZM Marked

NIB	Exc.	V.G.	Good	Fair	Poor
3000	2400	1700	800	400	300

.32 Caliber, PDM Marked with Duraluminum Frame and Bottom Magazine Release

NIB	Exc.	V.G.	Good	Fair	Poor
3500	3200	2800	1300	750	450

.32 Caliber, RFV Marked

NIB	Exc.	V.G.	Good	Fair	Poor
3000	2500	2000	1150	650	400

.32 Caliber, DRP Marked

NIB	Exc.	V.G.	Good	Fair	Poor
2800	2400	1800	1200	450	275

.32 Caliber, Statens Vattenfallsverk

NIB	Exc.	V.G.	Good	Fair	Poor
1700	1500	1200	700	450	300

WALTHER POST-WORLD WAR II

Manufactured by the firm of: Manufacture de Machines du Haut Rhin at Mulhouse, France under license by Walther.

Model PP—Some with Duraluminum Frames

.22 Caliber

NIB	Exc.	V.G.	Good	Fair	Poor
850	750	600	400	275	175

.32 Caliber

NIB	Exc.	V.G.	Good	Fair	Poor
600	500	375	350	275	175

.380 Caliber

NIB	Exc.	V.G.	Good	Fair	Poor
850	750	600	400	275	175

Model PP—All Three Calibers Finished In Blue, Silver and Gold with Full Coverage Engraving

Blue

NIB	Exc.	V.G.	Good	Fair	Poor
—	1900	1500	900	600	300

Silver

NIB	Exc.	V.G.	Good	Fair	Poor
—	1900	1500	900	600	300

Gold

NIB	Exc.	V.G.	Good	Fair	Poor
—	1900	1500	900	600	300

Model PP Mark II

These Walthers were manufactured under license by Walther and produced by Manurhin Company. Sold exclusively by Interarms, Alexandria, Virginia. Mark IIs were the same pistols as those above and have the same types of finish and engraving as well as the same value.

Model PP Manurhin

Manurhin Company manufactured with Manurhin logo and inscription. Usually "Licensed by Walther" somewhere on the pistol. Same pistols as those above. Bearing same types of finish and engraving and having the same values.

Model PP Sport, Manurhin

Same gun as Model PP, with different barrel lengths running from 5.75" to 7.75". Basically a target .22-caliber, with adjustable rear sights for elevation and windage. Front sight also adjustable. There is a barrel bushing at the muzzle that attaches front sight to the barrel. Grips are contoured checkered plastic and squared at the bottom of grips or in the shape of an inverted bird's-head.

NIB	Exc.	V.G.	Good	Fair	Poor
—	900	600	450	375	275

Model PP Sport C, Manurhin

Same gun as Model PP Sport, but in single-action with a spur hammer. Has front and rear adjustable sights and squared target grips in checkered black, brown and plastic. Blued and silver finish.

NIB	Exc.	V.G.	Good	Fair	Poor
—	900	600	450	375	275

Model PP Sport, Walther

A .22-caliber Sport was manufactured by Manurhin, but sold by Walther with Walther logo and inscription. Same gun as Model PP Sport, Manurhin. Only sold for a period of two years.

Walther PP Sport

Courtesy John J. Stimson, Jr.

NIB	Exc.	V.G.	Good	Fair	Poor
—	900	600	450	375	275

Model PP 50th Anniversary Commemorative Model

In .22- or .380-caliber. Blued, with gold inlays. Hand-carved grips, with oak leaves and acorns. Walther banner carved into each side of grips. Wood presentation case.

NIB	Exc.	V.G.	Good	Fair	Poor
—	1500	1000	750	500	300

Model PPK—Some with Duraluminum Frames

.22 Caliber

NIB	Exc.	V.G.	Good	Fair	Poor
—	750	600	400	275	175

.32 Caliber

NIB	Exc.	V.G.	Good	Fair	Poor
—	550	400	350	275	175

.380 Caliber

NIB	Exc.	V.G.	Good	Fair	Poor
—	750	600	400	275	175

Model PPK—All Three Calibers Finished In Blue, Silver and Gold With Full Coverage Engraving

Blue

NIB	Exc.	V.G.	Good	Fair	Poor
—	1900	1500	750	450	300

Silver

NIB	Exc.	V.G.	Good	Fair	Poor
—	1900	1500	750	450	300

Gold

NIB	Exc.	V.G.	Good	Fair	Poor
—	1900	1500	750	450	300

Model PPK Mark II

These Walthers were manufactured under license by Walther and produced by Manurhin Company. Sold exclusively by Interarms, Alexandria, Virginia. Mark IIs were the same pistols as those above and have the same types of finish and engraving as well as the same value.

Model PPK Manurhin

Manurhin Company manufactured with Manurhin logo and inscription. Usually "Licensed by Walther" somewhere on the pistol. Same pistols as above. Bearing same types of finish and engraving and having the same value.

Courtesy James Rankin

Model PPK 50th Anniversary Commemorative Model

In .22- or .380-caliber. Blued, with gold inlays. Hand-carved grips, with oak leaves and acorns. Walther banner carved into each side of grips. Wood presentation case.

NIB	Exc.	V.G.	Good	Fair	Poor
—	2100	1800	1250	1000	500

Model PPK American

In 1986, Model PPK was licensed by Walther Company to be manufactured in the United States. Finish stainless steel in .380-caliber.

NIB	Exc.	V.G.	Good	Fair	Poor
—	500	375	300	200	150

Model PPK/S

This Walther originally manufactured in Germany in .22-, .32- and .380-caliber. For sale in U.S. market after introduction of United States Gun Control Act of 1968. Basically a Model PP, with cut-off muzzle and slide. Has two-piece black checkered plastic grips as seen on Model PP. Finished in blue, nickel, dull gold and verchromt. Prices shown for .380 model. **NOTE:** Add 15 percent for .22. Deduct 15 percent for .32.

NIB	Exc.	V.G.	Good	Fair	Poor
600	525	450	400	350	250

Model PPK/S American

Manufactured in United States. Same as German Model PPK/S. Caliber .380. Pistol finished in blue or stainless steel.

NIB	Exc.	V.G.	Good	Fair	Poor
—	500	375	300	200	150

Model TP

A Walther manufactured semi-automatic pistol in .22- and .25-calibers. Patterned after earlier Model 9. Finish is blue. Silver black plastic checkered grips, with Walther banner medallions in each grip.

NIB	Exc.	V.G.	Good	Fair	Poor
—	900	700	500	375	250

Model TPH

A Walther manufactured semi-automatic pistol in .22- and .25-caliber. Double-action pistol, with duraluminum frame. Finished in blue or silver.

Two-piece black checkered plastic grips. Full coverage engraving available. **NOTE:** Add $300 for engraved model.

NIB	Exc.	V.G.	Good	Fair	Poor
—	650	500	450	350	250

Model TPH American

Double-action semi-automatic pistol produced in both .22- and .25-caliber. Licensed by Walther and manufactured in the United States. Produced in stainless steel. Has two-piece black plastic checkered grips.

NIB	Exc.	V.G.	Good	Fair	Poor
—	400	300	200	150	100

Model PP Super

A .380 and 9x18 caliber double-action semi-automatic manufactured by Walther. Similar in design to Model PP, with P.38 type of mechanism. Finish is blue. Grips are wrap-around black checkered plastic or a type of molded wood colored plastic.

Courtesy Orvel Reichert

NIB	Exc.	V.G.	Good	Fair	Poor
—	750	500	350	250	150

Model P.38

Following WWII, P.38 was reintroduced in a variety of calibers, with 5" barrel and alloy or steel frame.

.22 Caliber

NIB	Exc.	V.G.	Good	Fair	Poor
1200	850	650	500	350	200

Other Calibers

NIB	Exc.	V.G.	Good	Fair	Poor
750	600	500	400	300	200

Steel-Framed (Introduced 1987)

Factory-engraved versions of P.38 pistol were blued, chrome, silver or gold-plated. We suggest that a qualified appraisal be secured when contemplating purchase.

NIB	Exc.	V.G.	Good	Fair	Poor
1400	1250	1000	750	500	400

Model P.38K

As above, with 2.8" barrel. Front sight mounted on the slide. Imported between 1974 and 1980.

NIB	Exc.	V.G.	Good	Fair	Poor
—	900	650	450	300	200

Model P.38 II

NIB	Exc.	V.G.	Good	Fair	Poor
—	800	550	350	250	200

Model P.38 IV

Redesigned version of above, with 4.5" barrel and 8-shot magazine. Fitted with a decocking lever and adjustable sights. Imported prior to 1983.

NIB	Exc.	V.G.	Good	Fair	Poor
—	900	650	450	300	200

RECENT AND CURRENT PRODUCTION

In 1999, Carl Walther Gmbh of Germany and Smith & Wesson entered into a joint agreement to manufacture and distribute Walther-branded firearms and accessories into U.S., beginning August 1, 1999. In 2012, Walther established Walther Arms, Inc. in Fort Smith, Arkansas to import and sell all Walther products in U.S.A., beginning in 2013.

Model PP Limited Edition

Introduced in 2000. Limited edition of 100 pistols: chambered in .380 ACP; 50 in .32 ACP. Finish high-polish blue. Slide marked "LAST EDITION 1929-1999". Supplied with a special case, with certificate and video of the history of Walther.

NIB	Exc.	V.G.	Good	Fair	Poor
1350	1100	900	700	500	300

Model PPK/E—Walther USA

Introduced in 2000. Chambered for .380 or .32 ACP cartridges. Later in that year .22 LR. Has a double-action trigger. Produced in Hungary by Walther. Barrel length 3.4". Magazine capacity: 7 rounds .380; 8 rounds for .32 ACP and .22 LR. Blued finish and plastic grips.

NIB	Exc.	V.G.	Good	Fair	Poor
400	325	250	195	125	75

Model PPK

Chambered for .380 ACP or .32 ACP cartridge. Fitted with 3.35" barrel. Offered in blue or stainless steel. Black plastic grips. Fixed red-dot sights. Magazine capacity: 6 rounds .380 ACP; 7 rounds .32 ACP. Weight about 21 oz.

NIB	Exc.	V.G.	Good	Fair	Poor
550	425	300	250	175	75

Model PPK/S

Same as PPK, with .25" longer grip. Magazine capacity: 7 rounds .380 ACP; 8 rounds .32 ACP. Weight about 23 oz. Offered in blue, stainless steel and two-tone finish. In 2013, .22 LR version reintroduced with magazine capacity of 10 rounds. **NOTE:** Deduct 15 percent for .22 LR.

NIB	Exc.	V.G.	Good	Fair	Poor
550	425	300	250	175	75

Model PPS

Striker-fired compact DAO semi-automatic pistol. Chambered in .40 S&W (6 rounds) or 9mm Parabellum (7 rounds). Features include polymer frame and grip, decocker button, loaded chamber indicator, 3.2" stainless steel barrel, integral Weaver-style accessory rail, black Tenifer finish overall.

NIB	Exc.	V.G.	Good	Fair	Poor
625	535	450	350	250	150

Seventy-fifth Anniversary PPK

Blued, with wood grips. Machine engraving. Available in .380 ACP with 6+1 capacity. Special SN beginning with 0000PPK. Shipped with glass-top display case. Single-/double-action 3.3" barrel. Weight 20.8 oz. Windage adjustable rear sight. Introduced 2006.

NIB	Exc.	V.G.	Good	Fair	Poor
800	700	600	400	—	—

Model P5

A 9mm semi-automatic pistol, with double-action firing mechanism. One of the first Walthers to have a decocker lever. Finish is a combination of black matte and high polish. Has black plastic checkered grips.

NIB	Exc.	V.G.	Good	Fair	Poor
1350	1000	750	500	300	200

Model P5, Compact

A shorter version of standard Model P5.

NIB	Exc.	V.G.	Good	Fair	Poor
1450	1100	850	600	375	250

Model P5 One Hundred Year Commemorative

Blued, with gold inlays. Hand-carved grips, with oak leaves and acorns. Walther banner carved into each side of grips.

NIB	Exc.	V.G.	Good	Fair	Poor
2750	1950	1600	1000	750	400

Model P88

A 9mm semi-automatic in double-action, with ambidextrous decocking lever. Fifteen-shot magazine and two-piece black checkered plastic grips. Combination of high polish and black matte finish.

NIB	Exc.	V.G.	Good	Fair	Poor
1700	1525	1275	975	700	400

Model P88 Compact

Shorter version of standard Model P88.

NIB	Exc.	V.G.	Good	Fair	Poor
1600	1425	1135	850	600	400

Model P99

Introduced in 1997. Single-/double-action design, with 4" barrel and polymer frame. Chambered for 9mm or .40 S&W cartridge. Magazine capacity 10 rounds (16 rounds 9mm; 12 rounds .40 S&W for law enforcement). Front sight interchangeable. Rear sight windage adjustable. Finish blue tenifer. Total length 7". Weight about 25 oz.

NIB	Exc.	V.G.	Good	Fair	Poor
800	700	550	450	300	200

Model P99 Compact AS/QA

Chambered for 9mm or .40 S&W cartridges, with double-action trigger. Quick action striker fired. Barrel length 3.5", with fixed sights. Magazine capacity: 10 rounds 9mm; 8 rounds .40 S&W. Weight about 19 oz.

NIB	Exc.	V.G.	Good	Fair	Poor
675	575	400	325	200	175

Model P990

Double-action-only version of P99.

NIB	Exc.	V.G.	Good	Fair	Poor
675	550	400	325	200	175

Model P99 QPQ

Similar to P99, with silver tenifer finish.

NIB	Exc.	V.G.	Good	Fair	Poor
750	625	475	375	275	250

Model P990 QPQ

Double-action-only version of P99 QPQ.

NIB	Exc.	V.G.	Good	Fair	Poor
750	625	475	375	275	250

Model P99 QA

Similar to P99, with constant short trigger pull about 6.5 lbs. Offered in both 9mm and .40 S&W calibers. Introduced in 2000.

NIB	Exc.	V.G.	Good	Fair	Poor
675	575	400	325	200	175

Model P99 Military

Similar to P99, with military finish.

NIB	Exc.	V.G.	Good	Fair	Poor
675	575	400	325	200	175

Model P99 La Chasse DU

Features laser-engraving on blue tenifer slide.

NIB	Exc.	V.G.	Good	Fair	Poor
750	625	475	375	275	250

Model P99 La Chasse

Features hand-engraving on gray tenifer slide.

NIB	Exc.	V.G.	Good	Fair	Poor
1675	1350	1100	750	500	300

Model P99 Commemorative

Limited edition P99 that features a high polish blue slide, with a special serial number and marking "COMMEMORATIVE FOR THE YEAR 2000". Offered in both 9mm and .40 S&W caliber. Each handgun comes with a special certificate and video of the history of Walther.

NIB	Exc.	V.G.	Good	Fair	Poor
750	625	475	375	275	250

PPQ

Caliber: 9mm Parabellum or .40 S&W. Steel slide polymer frame, with interchangeable backstraps. Magazine capacity: 15/12 (9mm); 17/14 (.40). Other features include front slide serrations, Quick Defense Trigger with integral safety, ambidextrous slide, magazine release, adjustable rear sight and loaded-chamber indicator. Finish matte black. Weight 24.5 oz., barrel length 4".

NIB	Exc.	V.G.	Good	Fair	Poor
525	475	425	380	325	200

PPQ .45

Similar to PPQ model, except chambered for .45 ACP. Has 4.25" barrel, polygonal rifling, ambidextrous controls, front and rear serrations on slide, combat 3-dot sights. Introduced in 2015.

NIB	Exc.	V.G.	Good	Fair	Poor
600	525	485	425	—	—

PPQ M2

Similar to PPQ model, with several improvements. Also available in .45 ACP.

NIB	Exc.	V.G.	Good	Fair	Poor
550	500	450	400	350	300

Model PPX

Polymer frame hammer-fired DA-only pistol, in 9mm or .40 S&W. Features include loaded-chamber viewpoint, ambidextrous slide stop, reversible mag release, Picatinny rail, two drop safeties and firing pin block. Black or stainless finish. New 2013. **NOTE:** Add $50 for stainless.

NIB	Exc.	V.G.	Good	Fair	Poor
400	350	300	275	250	200

CCP

Single-stack 9mm pistol. Designed for concealed carry, with 3.5" barrel, 8-round capacity, adjustable sights and manual thumb safety. Operates with Walther's Softcoil gas-delayed blowback system. Available with an all-black Cerakote finish or two-tone with stainless steel slide. Introduced in 2014.

NIB	Exc.	V.G.	Good	Fair	Poor
400	350	300	250	200	150

Model P22 Standard

Introduced in 2002. This .22-caliber pistol chambered for LR cartridge. Barrel length 3.4". Polymer frame, with double-action trigger. Adjustable rear sight. Magazine capacity 10 rounds. Weight about 20 oz. **NOTE:** In 2003, offered with military black slide and green frame or silver slide with black frame. Carbon fiber-framed model also available at about same price as standard models. Barrels are interchangeable on both P22 pistols.

NIB	Exc.	V.G.	Good	Fair	Poor
400	325	250	200	150	75

Model P22 Target

Similar to standard P22 model, with 5" barrel and weight. Weight about 21 oz.

NIB	Exc.	V.G.	Good	Fair	Poor
425	350	275	225	175	75

TARGET PISTOLS

Model FP

A .22 LR caliber single-shot target pistol that fires electrically. Has micro-adjustable electric firing system, with micrometer sights. Contoured wooden grips that are adjustable. Barrel 11.7". Finish blued.

NIB	Exc.	V.G.	Good	Fair	Poor
—	2000	1600	1000	500	400

Model GSP

Semi-automatic target pistol in .22 LR and .32-caliber. Has 4.5" barrel, 5-shot magazine and contoured wood target grips. Blued finish. Sold with attache-style extra-barrel case and accessories.

Courtesy John J. Stimson, Jr.

NIB	Exc.	V.G.	Good	Fair	Poor
—	1600	1200	750	650	300

Model GSP-C

Almost same pistol as Model GSP, but in .32-caliber S&W wadcutter.

NIB	Exc.	V.G.	Good	Fair	Poor
—	1500	1100	750	650	300

Model OSP

A .22 Short semi-automatic target pistol. Similar to Model GSP. Made for rapid fire target shooting. Blued finish, with contoured wood grips.

Custom engraved OSP

NIB	Exc.	V.G.	Good	Fair	Poor
—	1800	1200	750	650	300

Free Pistol

.22-caliber single-shot target pistol, with 11.7" barrel, micrometer sights, adjustable grips and electronic trigger. Blued.

NIB	Exc.	V.G.	Good	Fair	Poor
1900	1600	1200	900	700	550

Model R99

This 6-shot revolver chambered for .357 Magnum cartridge. Barrel length 3". Weight about 28 oz. Offered in blue or stainless steel. Introduced in 1999. Said to be a close ringer for S&W M19, but with different grips.

NIB	Exc.	V.G.	Good	Fair	Poor
1500	1300	1100	950	700	500

Model SP22-M1

.22 LR autoloader, with aluminum frame and 4" barrel.

NIB	Exc.	V.G.	Good	Fair	Poor
400	325	350	150	100	75

Model SP22-M2

Similar to above, with 6" barrel.

NIB	Exc.	V.G.	Good	Fair	Poor
400	325	250	150	100	75

Model SP22-M3

Similar to above, with match-grade barrel and adjustable trigger.

NIB	Exc.	V.G.	Good	Fair	Poor
475	400	325	200	150	100

Model SP22-M4

Similar to above, with wooden free-style grip assembly.

NIB	Exc.	V.G.	Good	Fair	Poor
750	675	550	400	250	150

RIFLES

Model B

A .30-06 caliber bolt-action rifle, with 22" barrel, 4-shot magazine and single-/double-set triggers. Double-set triggers are worth approximately 20 percent more than values listed. Blued, with walnut stock.

NIB	Exc.	V.G.	Good	Fair	Poor
—	775	700	450	250	175

Olympic Single-Shot

A .22-caliber bolt-action rifle, with 26" barrel, adjustable target sights and walnut stock. Fitted with palm rest and adjustable buttplate. Blued.

NIB	Exc.	V.G.	Good	Fair	Poor
—	1150	950	800	500	400

Model V

A .22-caliber single-shot bolt-action rifle, with 26" barrel and adjustable sights. Blued, with plain walnut stock. Manufactured before WWII.

NIB	Exc.	V.G.	Good	Fair	Poor
—	550	450	300	200	150

Model V Champion

As above, with checkered walnut stock.

NIB	Exc.	V.G.	Good	Fair	Poor
—	600	500	350	250	200

Model KKM International Match

A .22-caliber single-shot bolt-action rifle, with 28" barrel and adjustable sights. Blued, with walnut stock. Fitted for palm rest and adjustable buttplate. Manufactured after WWII.

NIB	Exc.	V.G.	Good	Fair	Poor
—	1550	1275	850	450	350

Model KKM-S

As above, with adjustable cheekpiece.

NIB	Exc.	V.G.	Good	Fair	Poor
—	1625	1350	850	500	400

Model KKW

As above, with military-style stock.

NIB	Exc.	V.G.	Good	Fair	Poor
—	1250	975	600	250	175

Model KKJ Sporter

A .22-caliber bolt-action rifle, with 22.5" barrel and 5-shot magazine. Blued, with checkered walnut stock. Available with double-set triggers and their presence would add approximately 20 percent to values listed. Manufactured after WWII.

NIB	Exc.	V.G.	Good	Fair	Poor
—	900	800	550	350	300

Model KKJ-MA

As above, in .22 Magnum rimfire.

NIB	Exc.	V.G.	Good	Fair	Poor
—	850	750	550	350	300

Model KKJ-HO

As above, in .22 Hornet.

NIB	Exc.	V.G.	Good	Fair	Poor
—	950	850	650	450	350

Model SSV Varmint

A .22-caliber bolt-action single-shot rifle, with 25.5" barrel not fitted with sights. Monte Carlo-style stock. Blued. Manufactured after WWII.

NIB	Exc.	V.G.	Good	Fair	Poor
—	700	600	475	375	300

Model UIT BV Universal

As above, with adjustable target sights. Walnut stock fitted with a palm rest and adjustable buttplate.

NIB	Exc.	V.G.	Good	Fair	Poor
1750	1500	1250	900	650	500

Model UIT Match

As above, with stippled pistol-grip and fore-end. Also available with an electronic trigger that would add approximately $50 to values listed.

NIB	Exc.	V.G.	Good	Fair	Poor
1350	1100	800	600	450	400

GX 1

As above, with adjustable Free Rifle stock.

NIB	Exc.	V.G.	Good	Fair	Poor
2250	2000	1750	1250	850	700

Prone Model 400

Target rifle in .22-caliber, with prone position stock.

NIB	Exc.	V.G.	Good	Fair	Poor
800	700	600	450	350	300

Model KK/MS Silhouette

A .22-caliber bolt-action rifle, with 25.5" front-weighted barrel furnished without sights. Thumbhole stock, with adjustable buttplate. Introduced in 1984.

NIB	Exc.	V.G.	Good	Fair	Poor
1300	1100	850	700	550	400

Running Boar Model 500

As above, with 23.5" barrel.

NIB	Exc.	V.G.	Good	Fair	Poor
1550	1350	950	750	600	450

Model WA-2000

A .300 Win. Magnum or .308-caliber bolt-action sporting rifle. Produced on custom order. Imported prior to 1989.

NIB	Exc.	V.G.	Good	Fair	Poor
30000	25000	20000	—	—	—

Model G22

A .22-caliber rifle, with 20" barrel and adjustable sights. Features cocking indicator, integrated lock, slide safety and multi function rail. Black or green finish. Weight about 6 lbs. Also sold as a package.

NIB	Exc.	V.G.	Good	Fair	Poor
450	350	225	175	125	100

Package A1 with Walther rifle scope

NIB	Exc.	V.G.	Good	Fair	Poor
500	400	275	225	175	150

Package A2 with laser

NIB	Exc.	V.G.	Good	Fair	Poor
500	400	275	225	175	150

Package A3 with Walther rifle scope & laser

NIB	Exc.	V.G.	Good	Fair	Poor
500	400	275	225	175	150

Package A4 with Walther PS22 red-dot sight

NIB	Exc.	V.G.	Good	Fair	Poor
500	400	275	225	175	150

SHOTGUNS

Model SF

A 12- or 16-gauge boxlock double-barrel shotgun. Fitted with double triggers and extractors. Blued, with checkered walnut stock fitted with sling swivels.

NIB	Exc.	V.G.	Good	Fair	Poor
—	1150	900	750	600	450

Model SFD

As above, with stock having a cheekpiece.

NIB	Exc.	V.G.	Good	Fair	Poor
—	1150	900	750	600	450

WALTHER MANURHIN
Mulhouse, France

Manurhin-manufactured Walther pistols are listed in Walther section under their respective model headings.

WARNANT, L. AND J.
Ognee, Belgium

Revolver

Modeled after pistols manufactured by Smith & Wesson. Warnants produced a variety of revolvers in .32-, .38- or .45-caliber, between 1870 and 1890.

NIB	Exc.	V.G.	Good	Fair	Poor
—	—	250	175	100	50

Semi-Automatic Pistol

A 6.35mm semi-automatic pistol, with 2.5" barrel and 5-shot magazine. Slide marked "L&J Warnant Bte 6.35mm". Blued, with black plastic grips bearing monogram "L&JW". Manufactured after 1908.

NIB	Exc.	V.G.	Good	Fair	Poor
—	350	200	150	100	75

1912 Model

A 7.65mm caliber semi-automatic pistol, with 3" barrel and 7-shot magazine. Slide marked "L&J Warnant Brevetes Pist Auto 7.65mm". Manufactured prior to 1915.

NIB	Exc.	V.G.	Good	Fair	Poor
—	350	200	150	100	75

WARNER, CHAS.
Windsor Locks, Connecticut

Pocket Revolver

A .31-caliber percussion revolver, with 3" round barrel and 6-shot unfluted cylinder. Cylinder marked "Charles Warner. Windsor Locks, Conn.". Blued, with walnut grips. Approximately 600 made between 1857 and 1860.

NIB	Exc.	V.G.	Good	Fair	Poor
—	—	1625	1300	500	100

WARNER, JAMES
Springfield, Massachusetts

Revolving Carbines

A variety of revolving carbines were made by this maker. Nearly all of which are .40-caliber, with octagonal barrels measuring 20" to 24" in length. Most commonly encountered variations are listed.

Manually Revolved Grooved Cylinder

Fitted with two triggers, one of which is a release so that cylinder can be manually turned. Not fitted with a loading lever. Top strap marked "James Warner/Springfield, Mass.". Approximately 75 made in 1849.

Courtesy Milwaukee Public Museum, Milwaukee, Wisconsin

NIB	Exc.	V.G.	Good	Fair	Poor
—	—	7500	4700	2200	500

Retractable Cylinder Model

This version has a cylinder that fits over the breech and it must be retracted before it can be manually rotated. Cylinder release is a button located in front of the trigger. It is marked "James Warner/Springfield Mass" and with an eagle over letters "U.S.". Cylinder is etched and there is no loading lever. Has a walnut stock, with patchbox and no forearm. Approximately 25 manufactured in 1849.

NIB	Exc.	V.G.	Good	Fair	Poor
—	—	9500	6900	3000	800

Automatic Revolving Cylinder

Cylinder is automatically turned when hammer is cocked. Fitted with loading lever. Marked "Warner's Patent/Jan. 1851" and "Springfield Arms Co.". Approximately 200 made during 1850s.

Courtesy Milwaukee Public Museum, Milwaukee, Wisconsin

NIB	Exc.	V.G.	Good	Fair	Poor
—	—	7500	4700	1900	500

Belt Revolver

A .31-caliber double-action percussion revolver, with 4" or 5" round barrel and 6-shot etched cylinder. Blued, with walnut grips. No markings appear on this model except serial number. Manufactured in 1851.

Courtesy Milwaukee Public Museum, Milwaukee, Wisconsin

NIB	Exc.	V.G.	Good	Fair	Poor
—	—	2100	1650	675	100

Pocket Revolver

A .28-caliber percussion revolver, with 3" octagonal barrel and 6-shot cylinder. Barrel marked "James Warner, Springfield, Mass., USA". Blued, with walnut grips. Approximately 500 were made.

NIB	Exc.	V.G.	Good	Fair	Poor
—	—	1050	725	275	100

Second Model

As above, with 3" or 4" barrel marked "Warner's Patent 1857".

Courtesy Wallis & Wallis, Lewes, Sussex, England

NIB	Exc.	V.G.	Good	Fair	Poor
—	—	1100	750	325	100

Third Model

As above, in .31-caliber.

NIB	Exc.	V.G.	Good	Fair	Poor
—	—	1000	650	300	100

Single-Shot Derringer

A .41-caliber rimfire single-shot pocket pistol, with 2.75" round barrel, brass frame and walnut grips. As this model is unmarked, it can only be identified by the large breechblock which lifts upward and to the left for loading.

NIB	Exc.	V.G.	Good	Fair	Poor
—	—	22500	19000	7250	1000

Pocket Revolver

A .30-caliber rimfire revolver, with 3" barrel and 5-shot cylinder. Barrel marked "Warner's Patent 1857". Blued or nickel-plated, with walnut grips. Approximately 1,000 made during late 1860s.

NIB	Exc.	V.G.	Good	Fair	Poor
—	—	975	600	165	75

WARNER ARMS CORPORATION
Brooklyn, New York and Norwich, Connecticut

Established in 1912, this firm marketed revolvers, rifles, semi-automatic pistols and shotguns made for them by other companies (including N.R. Davis & Sons, Ithaca Gun Company and so forth). In 1917, the company was purchased by N.R. Davis & Company. See also Davis-Warner. The arms marketed by Warner prior to 1917 are listed.

SHOTGUNS

Single Trigger Hammerless Utica Special Double-Barrel

In 12-gauge, with 28", 30" or 32" barrels.

Double Trigger Hammerless Double-Barrel

In 12- or 16-gauge, with 28", 30" or 32" barrels.

Grade X, SF, XT, SFT, XD and XDF Hammer Guns

In 12-, 16- or 20-gauge, with 28", 30" or 32" barrels.

Field Grade Hammer Gun

In 12- or 16-gauge, with 28" or 30" barrels.

Boxlock Hammerless

In 12- or 16-gauge, with 28", 30" or 32" barrels.

RIFLES

Number 522

A .22-caliber single-shot rifle, with 18" barrel.

Number 532

A .32-caliber single-shot rifle, with 18" barrel.

REVOLVERS

Double-Action

.32- and .38-caliber, with 4" or 5" barrels.

Double-Action Hammerless

.32- and .38-caliber, with 4" or 5" barrels.

SEMI-AUTOMATIC PISTOLS

"Faultless": Warner-Schwarzlose Model C, .32 ACP

NIB	Exc.	V.G.	Good	Fair	Poor
—	—	500	300	200	100

WEATHERBY
Paso Robles, California

Company was founded by Roy Weatherby in 1945 in South Gate, California. His original rifles were custom guns made to order on Mauser actions. In 1956, he contracted with both Sako and Schultz & Larsen to manufacture complete rifles, while he continued to make custom guns in California. In 1958, Weatherby introduced his Mark V action, which was designed to handle high pressures of his proprietary cartridges. Mark V action was made in U.S. with rifles assembled and finished in Weatherby shop in South Gate. Mark V featured a very modern stock design with glossy finish, high comb for scope use and contrasting grip and fore-end caps. Beginning in 1959, rifles were made in what was then West Germany. In 1972, production was moved to Japan, where rifles were made until 1995. Since that year, Weatherby rifles have all been made in U.S. Barreled action for Mark V is made by ATEK in Brainerd, Minnesota and action for Vanguard is made by Howa in Japan. Both Mark V and Vanguard are assembled in Paso Robles, California, Weatherby shop. For many years, Weatherby shotguns were made in Japan or Italy. Current models are made in Turkey.

Mark V

Deluxe bolt-action repeating rifle. Chambered for various popular standard calibers, as well as the full line of Weatherby cartridges from .240 Wby. Magnum to .300 Wby. Magnum. Furnished with 24" or 26" barrel, without sights. Has 3- or 5-round magazine, depending on caliber, deluxe high-polish blued finish, with select skip-line checkered walnut stock with rosewood forearm tip and pistol-grip cap. Available with a left-hand action.

NIB	Exc.	V.G.	Good	Fair	Poor
1200	1050	800	600	500	250

Mark V Deluxe

Stepped-up version of classic Mark V. Features include deluxe Claro walnut Monte Carlo stock, with rosewood fore-end, 26" or 28" high-polish blued sightless barrel. Chambered in .257, .270, 7mm, .300, .30-378, .340, .378, .416 and .460 Wby. Magnum. Also available in short-action model in .22-250, .243 Win., .240 Wby., .25-06, .270 Win., 7mm-08, .280 Rem., .308 Win., .30-06. **NOTE:** Add 25 percent for .30-378 Wby. Magnum.

NIB	Exc.	V.G.	Good	Fair	Poor
2400	2000	1300	1075	800	350

Mark V Sporter

Introduced in 1993. Identical to Mark V Deluxe, without custom features. Metal is a low luster finish. Stock is Claro walnut, with high gloss finish. Monte Carlo comb, with raised cheekpiece and black 1" recoil pad are standard features. Available in Weatherby calibers from .257 through .340 plus .270 Win., .30-06, 7mm Rem. Magnum, .300 Win. Magnum, .338 Win. Magnum. Weight 8 to 8.5 lbs. depending on caliber.

NIB	Exc.	V.G.	Good	Fair	Poor
1100	950	800	650	500	300

Mark V .375 Weatherby Magnum

This version was manufactured in Germany only. Chambered for currently obsolete .375 Wby. Magnum cartridge. This version has become very collectible.

NIB	Exc.	V.G.	Good	Fair	Poor
5000	3500	3000	2500	2000	1500

Mark V .378 Weatherby Magnum

Chambered for .378 Wby. Magnum cartridge. Furnished with 26" barrel only. **NOTE:** Add 50 percent for German guns in this caliber.

NIB	Exc.	V.G.	Good	Fair	Poor
2300	1825	1550	1200	850	500

Mark V .416 Weatherby Magnum

Extremely powerful rifle suitable for hunting the biggest game. Introduced in 1989.

NIB	Exc.	V.G.	Good	Fair	Poor
2400	1825	1550	1200	850	500

Mark V .460 Weatherby Magnum

Said to be the most powerful commercial rifle available in the world, with the possible exception of some of the recently-reintroduced British nitro chamberings. Available with 24" or 26" heavy barrel, with an integral recoil-reducing muzzle-brake. Has a custom reinforced stock. **NOTE:** Add 100 percent for German guns in this caliber.

NIB	Exc.	V.G.	Good	Fair	Poor
2500	2200	1850	1500	1000	600

Mark V Dangerous Game Rifle

Introduced in 2001. Features: synthetic stock, with Monte Carlo; 24" or 26" barrel, with barrel band; hooded front sight depending on caliber. Chambered for .378-, .416- and .460-Wby. Magnum. Adjustable trigger. Weight between 8.74 and 9.5 lbs. depending on caliber. In 2003, .458 Lott was offered.

NIB	Exc.	V.G.	Good	Fair	Poor
2500	2200	1850	1500	1000	600

Mark V Euromark

Features hand-checkered oil-finished Claro walnut stock, with ebony fore-end tip and pistol-grip cap. Has satin blued finish. Introduced in 1986.

NIB	Exc.	V.G.	Good	Fair	Poor
1500	1300	1050	800	575	350

Mark V Fluted Stainless

Introduced late in 1996. Features a fluted stainless steel barrel. Chambered for .257 Wby. Magnum to .300 Wby. Magnum calibers as well as 7mm Rem. Magnum and .300 Win. Magnum. Stock is synthetic, with raised comb and checkered stock. Weight varies depending on caliber.

NIB	Exc.	V.G.	Good	Fair	Poor
1200	1050	800	600	500	250

Mark V Fluted Synthetic

Similar to above model, with blued carbon steel action and barrel. Synthetic stock. Introduced late in 1996.

NIB	Exc.	V.G.	Good	Fair	Poor
1000	850	650	450	400	200

Mark V SLS

Features stainless steel barreled action, with laminated wood stock. Fitted with 1" black recoil pad. Chambered for calibers: .257 through .340 Wby. Magnum; 7mm Rem. Magnum, .300; .338 Win. Magnum; .375 H&H Magnum. Weight about 8.25 lbs. depending on caliber. Introduced in late 1996.

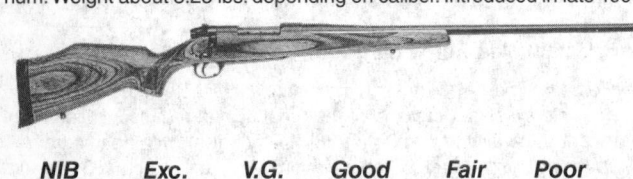

NIB	Exc.	V.G.	Good	Fair	Poor
1200	1050	800	600	500	250

Mark V Varmint

Chambered for .22-250 and .224 Wby. cartridge. Offered with 24" or 26" heavy barrel. **NOTE:** Add 50 percent for German built.

NIB	Exc.	V.G.	Good	Fair	Poor
975	800	750	550	450	400

Mark V Lazermark

This version had a laser-carved pattern on the stock and forearm in place of usual checkering. Introduced in 1985.

NIB	Exc.	V.G.	Good	Fair	Poor
2000	1750	1500	1100	600	300

Mark V Fibermark Composite

This version has a matte blue finish. Furnished with synthetic black wrinkle-finished stock. Chambered for calibers .22-250 to .375 H&H. Barrel lengths 24" to 26" depending on caliber.

NIB	Exc.	V.G.	Good	Fair	Poor
1250	1000	800	550	400	250

Mark V Ultramark

Custom-finished version, with glass-bedded action and special high-polish blue. Action hand-honed. Walnut stock features basket weave checkering. Introduced in 1989.

NIB	Exc.	V.G.	Good	Fair	Poor
2400	2000	1650	1200	800	500

Mark V Accumark

Introduced in 1995. Features Mark V Magnum action. Trigger preset at factory for 3.5 lbs. of pull. Fully adjustable for sear engagement at let-off weight. Action metal black oxide coated, with bead blast matte finish. Stainless steel barrel 26" in length, with low luster brushed finish. Weight about 8 lbs. Offered in all Weatherby calibers from .240 to .340 Wby. Magnum, plus 7mm Rem. Magnum, 7mm STW and .300 Win. Magnum.

NIB	Exc.	V.G.	Good	Fair	Poor
6000	5000	3700	3000	1200	600

NIB	Exc.	V.G.	Good	Fair	Poor
1700	1100	950	800	500	300

Mark V Accumark RC

Upgraded model with Range Certified (RC) guarantee to deliver sub-MOA 3-shot groups with Weatherby ammo. Chambered in all Weatherby Magnums up to .340, plus .270 Win., 7mm Rem., .308 Win., .30-06, .300 Win. Magnum and .338 Lapua. Button rifled free floated barrel, with target crown, T-6 bedding block, tuned/adjustable trigger.

NIB	Exc.	V.G.	Good	Fair	Poor
2100	1500	1250	1000	600	400

35th Anniversary Commemorative Mark V

Specially embellished rifle commemorated 35th Anniversary of the company. There were 1,000 produced in 1980. As with all commemoratives, it must be NIB with all furnished materials to be worth top dollar.

NIB	Exc.	V.G.	Good	Fair	Poor
1500	1300	1000	750	500	350

40th Anniversary Commemorative Mark V

Similar to 35th Anniversary model. Only 200 manufactured in 1985.

NIB	Exc.	V.G.	Good	Fair	Poor
1500	1300	1000	750	500	350

50th Anniversary Commemorative Mark V

Chambered only in .300 Wby. Magnum, with high-grade walnut Monte Carlo stock. Limited manufacture in 1995.

NIB	Exc.	V.G.	Good	Fair	Poor
2000	1500	1200	750	500	350

70th Anniversary Commemorative Mark V

Limited to 70 rifles in 2015. Chambered in .257 Wby. Magnum, with 24" barrel, high-grade checkered Claro walnut stock with rosewood grip and fore-end caps. Special engraved floorplate. Comes with custom leather case and commemorative knife.

NIB	Exc.	V.G.	Good	Fair	Poor
5400	4800	—	—	—	—

1984 Olympic Commemorative Mark V

Specially embellished Mark V rifle has gold-plated accents. Exhibition-grade walnut stock, with a star inlay. There were 1,000 manufactured in 1984. A commemorative rifle and must be NIB to bring premium value.

NIB	Exc.	V.G.	Good	Fair	Poor
1600	1300	1050	750	500	350

Safari Grade Mark V

Custom-order version available chambered from .300 Wby. Magnum through .460 Wby. Magnum. Available with a number of custom options. Ordered with an 8- to 10-month delivery delay.

Crown Grade Mark V

Weatherby's best-grade rifle. Available on a custom-order basis only. Features an engraved receiver and barrel, with exhibition-grade hand-checkered walnut stock. Also furnished with an engraved scope mount.

NIB	Exc.	V.G.	Good	Fair	Poor
8000	7000	5500	4000	1500	500

Mark V Super Varmint Master (SVM)

Introduced in 2000. Features 26" stainless steel barrel. Stock is laminated, with Monte Carlo comb. Fully adjustable trigger. Chambered for .220 Swift, .223 Rem., .22-250, .243 Win., 7mm-08 and .308 Win. Also offered in single-shot configuration. Weight about 8.5 lbs.

NIB	Exc.	V.G.	Good	Fair	Poor
1675	1400	1200	900	600	350

Mark V Special Varmint Rifle (SVR)

Introduced in 2003. Features 22" Krieger heavy barrel, Monte Carlo composite stock, black recoil pad and matte black finish. Adjustable trigger is standard. Available in .223 Rem. and .22-250. Weight about 7.25 lbs.

NIB	Exc.	V.G.	Good	Fair	Poor
1100	1000	800	700	500	300

MARK V LIGHTWEIGHT RIFLES

Mark V Synthetic Lightweight

Chambered in calibers from .22-250 to .308 Win.. Fitted with 24" barrel. Synthetic stock, with Monte Carlo comb. Magazine capacity 5 rounds. Weight about 6.5 lbs. Carbine version offered, with 20" barrel in .243, 7mm-08 and .308. Weight about 6 lbs.

NIB	Exc.	V.G.	Good	Fair	Poor
900	750	600	475	350	250

Mark V Stainless Lightweight

Similar to model above, with stainless steel barrel and action. Weight about 6.5 lbs. Carbine version also available.

NIB	Exc.	V.G.	Good	Fair	Poor
1100	950	800	650	525	300

Mark V Sporter Lightweight

Chambered for calibers ranging from .22-250 to .308 Win.. Fitted with 24" barrel. Stock is Claro walnut, with Monte Carlo comb. Weight about 6.75 lbs.

NIB	Exc.	V.G.	Good	Fair	Poor
1050	900	750	600	475	250

Mark V Accumark Lightweight

Chambered for calibers from .22-250 to .300 Wby. Fitted with 24" barrel. Magazine capacity 5 rounds. Special laminated synthetic stock. Weight about 7 lbs. Introduced in 1998.

NIB	Exc.	V.G.	Good	Fair	Poor
1250	1000	900	800	650	400

Mark V Ultra Lightweight

Similar to above model, with lightened components. Calibers begin with .243 and go to .300 Wby. Fitted with 24" or 26" barrel depending on caliber. Weight about 5.75 lbs. Introduced in 1998. In 2000, offered in a left-hand version. In 2001, available chambered for .338-06 A-Square cartridge.

NIB	Exc.	V.G.	Good	Fair	Poor
1450	1200	950	700	450	300

Mark V Deluxe Lightweight

Offered in calibers from .22-250 to .30-06. Fitted with 24" barrel, hand select walnut Monte Carlo stock, with rosewood fore-end tip and pistol-grip cap. Fine line checkering. Weight about 6.75 lbs. Introduced in 1999.

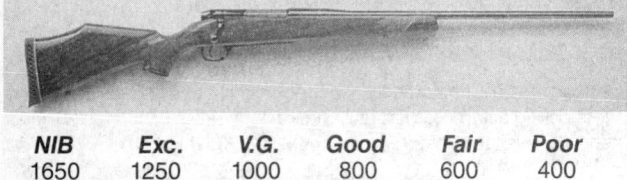

NIB	Exc.	V.G.	Good	Fair	Poor
1650	1250	1000	800	600	400

Mark V SPM (Super Predator Master)

Introduced in 2001. Features 24" blackened stainless steel fluted barrel. Chambered for .223 Rem., .22-250 Rem., .243 Win., 7mm-08 Rem. and .308 Win. cartridges. Fully adjustable trigger. Synthetic stock. Weight about 6.5 lbs. Right-hand only.

NIB	Exc.	V.G.	Good	Fair	Poor
1600	1300	1050	750	500	350

Mark V SBGM (Super Big Game Master)

Features 24" blackened stainless steel barrel Krieger fluted barrel (26" for Magnum calibers). Fully adjustable trigger. Tan composite stock, with raised comb Monte Carlo. Pachmayr Decelerator recoil pad. Offered in a wide variety of calibers from .240 Wby. Magnum to .300 Wby. Magnum. Weight about 5.75 lbs.; 6.75 lbs. for Magnum rifles. Introduced in 2002. **NOTE:** Add $60 for Magnum calibers.

NIB	Exc.	V.G.	Good	Fair	Poor
1650	1250	1000	800	600	400

Mark V Arroyo

Offered in 15 calibers from .240 Wby. Magnum to .340 Wby. Magnum. Features include fully adjustable trigger, stainless fluted barrel (22", 24" 26" depending on caliber), composite stock with palm swell and laminate raised comb, KUIU Clas camo. Accubrake available on some calibers. From Weatherby Custom Shop. Introduced in 2015.

NIB	Exc.	V.G.	Good	Fair	Poor
2400	2000	1500	1200	600	300

Mark V Outfitter

Chambered in all Weatherby calibers from .240 to .300, including 6.5-300 Wby. Magnum plus .270 Win., .308 Win. and .30-06. Features similar to Arroyo, with lighter weight (5.5 to 6.75 lbs.). Carbon Fiber stock has High Desert camo finish. From Weatherby Custom Shop. Introduced in 2015.

NIB	Exc.	V.G.	Good	Fair	Poor
2400	2000	1500	1200	600	300

Mark V Tacmark

Tactical rifle with 28" No. 3 contour fluted free-floating barrel. Chambered in .30-378 Wby. Magnum, .338 Lapua Magnum or .338-378 Wby. Magnum. Equipped with Accubrake. Fully adjustable stock, LXX adjustable trigger, detachable 5-round magazine. From Weatherby Custom Shop. Introduced in 2016.

NIB	Exc.	V.G.	Good	Fair	Poor
3000	2500	2000	—	—	—

THREAT RESPONSE RIFLE SERIES

These rifles are based on Mark V action.

TRR

Chambered for .223 or .308 Win. cartridge. Fitted with 22" heavy-contour black Krieger barrel. Black composite stock, with raised comb Monte Carlo. Flat-bottom forearm. Fully adjustable trigger. Recoil pad. Introduced in 2002.

NIB	Exc.	V.G.	Good	Fair	Poor
1250	1000	900	800	650	400

TRR Magnum

As above chambered for .300 Win. Magnum, .300 Wby. Magnum, .30-378 Wby. Magnum or .338-378 Wby. Magnum. Barrel length 26". **NOTE:** Add $150 for .30-378 and .338-378 calibers.

NIB	Exc.	V.G.	Good	Fair	Poor
1450	1200	950	700	450	300

TRR Magnum Custom

Has all the features of TRR Magnum, with addition of a fully adjustable stock. **DO NOT** use this model until company performs a safety upgrade to the bolt. Rifle can accidentally discharge without the bolt being fully engaged. Affected rifles bear serial numbers from one of these series on the receiver: 00001 through 03810; V00001 through V80966; VX00001 through VX44065; VS00001 through VS23699; VL00001 through VL46984; W00001 through W0099; NV0001 through NV0099. For more information contact Weatherby at 800-227-2018. **NOTE:** Add $150 for .30-378 or .338-378 calibers.

NIB	Exc.	V.G.	Good	Fair	Poor
2500	2200	1900	1600	1250	500

TRR RC (Range Certified)

Features laminated stock, with three-position buttstock, 26" Kreiger barrel with Accubrake and fully adjustable hand-tuned trigger. Offered in .300 Win. Magnum, .300 Wby. Magnum, .30-378 Wby., .338 Lapua and .338/378 Wby.

NIB	Exc.	V.G.	Good	Fair	Poor
3500	3000	2400	1700	800	350

VANGUARD

Vanguard (early production)

This was Weatherby's Japanese-manufactured economy rifle. Chambered for various popular standard American cartridges from .22-50 to .300 Win. Magnum cartridge. Bolt-action repeater, with 24" barrel furnished without sights. Has 3- or 5-shot magazine; finish is polished blue, with select checkered walnut stock with rosewood fore-end tip and pistol-grip cap. Discontinued in 1988.

NIB	Exc.	V.G.	Good	Fair	Poor
—	1100	925	750	600	350

Vanguard VGS

Satin-finish version. Discontinued in 1988.

NIB	Exc.	V.G.	Good	Fair	Poor
—	1000	825	650	500	300

Vanguard VGL

Lightweight carbine version has 20" barrel. Discontinued in 1988.

NIB	Exc.	V.G.	Good	Fair	Poor
—	900	725	550	400	250

Fiberguard

This version has matte-blued finish, with green fiberglass stock. Discontinued in 1988.

NIB	Exc.	V.G.	Good	Fair	Poor
—	750	575	400	300	200

Vanguard Classic I

Chambered for various popular standard calibers. Has 24" barrel and 3- or 5-shot magazine. Satin blue finish. Select checkered oil-finished walnut stock. Introduced in 1989.

NIB	Exc.	V.G.	Good	Fair	Poor
700	600	500	400	300	200

Vanguard Classic II

A more deluxe version, with higher-grade walnut stock.

NIB	Exc.	V.G.	Good	Fair	Poor
725	625	525	425	325	225

Vanguard VGX Deluxe

This version has high-gloss Monte Carlo-type stock and high-polished blued finish. Introduced in 1989.

NIB	Exc.	V.G.	Good	Fair	Poor
800	700	600	500	400	300

Vanguard Weatherguard

This version has wrinkle-finished black synthetic stock. Introduced in 1989. In 2003, offered in stainless steel. **NOTE:** Add $120 for stainless steel.

NIB	Exc.	V.G.	Good	Fair	Poor
650	500	400	300	225	175

Vanguard Synthetic

Features upgraded composite stock, with Monte Carlo comb, a ring/base scope mounting system and 24" barrel. Calibers from .223 Rem. to .338 Win. Magnum, including .257 Wby. Weight about 7.75 lbs. Introduced in 2004.

NIB	Exc.	V.G.	Good	Fair	Poor
400	350	300	250	175	100

Vanguard Stainless

Similar to Vanguard Synthetic, with stainless steel barrel and receiver.

NIB	Exc.	V.G.	Good	Fair	Poor
575	500	450	350	275	125

Vanguard Sporter

Similar to model above, with figured walnut stock, rosewood fore-end tip and fine line checkering. Chambered for calibers from .270 to .338 Win. Magnum. Barrel length 24". Weight about 8 lbs. Introduced in 2004. Also available with detachable magazine.

NIB	Exc.	V.G.	Good	Fair	Poor
550	450	350	250	175	100

Vanguard Sporter SS

Similar to Vanguard Sporter, with stainless steel barrel and receiver.

NIB	Exc.	V.G.	Good	Fair	Poor
675	575	475	375	275	125

Vanguard Varmint Special

Chambered in .223, .22-250 or .308. Blued #3 contour heavy crowned 22" barrel. Adjustable trigger. Synthetic tan composite stock, with black spiderweb pattern. Introduced 2006.

NIB	Exc.	V.G.	Good	Fair	Poor
575	475	375	275	195	125

Vanguard Synthetic Package

Introduced in 2004. Features 24" barrel, with adjustable trigger. Chambered for a variety of calibers from .223 Rem. to .338 Win. Magnum. Supplied with Bushnell Banner 3-9x40 scope, sling and hard case. Weight about 7.75 lbs.

NIB	Exc.	V.G.	Good	Fair	Poor
650	550	350	275	225	150

Vanguard Sub-MOA Matte or Stainless

Introduced in 2005. Features a guarantee to shoot .99" at 100 yards. Calibers from .223 Rem. to .338 Win. Magnum. Barrel length 24", with Monte Carlo Fiberguard stock. Adjustable trigger. Weight about 7.75 lbs. Also available in stainless steel. **NOTE:** Add $120 for stainless steel.

NIB	Exc.	V.G.	Good	Fair	Poor
800	700	600	500	300	200

Vanguard Sub-MOA Varmint

Similar to Vanguard Varmint Special, with ventilated beavertail fore-end. Chambered in .204, .223, .22-250 and .308. Introduced 2006.

NIB	Exc.	V.G.	Good	Fair	Poor
925	800	650	500	300	200

Vanguard Compact

Chambered for ..223, 22-250, .243 or .308. Fitted with 20" barrel and scaled-down hardwood stock, with shorter length of pull. Also included is a full size composite stock. Weight about 6.75 lbs. Introduced in 2005.

NIB	Exc.	V.G.	Good	Fair	Poor
550	450	350	250	175	100

Vanguard Youth Compact

Similar to above, with synthetic stock. Introduced 2008.

NIB	Exc.	V.G.	Good	Fair	Poor
550	450	350	250	175	100

Vanguard Deluxe

Similar to Vanguard, but features 24" polished blued barrel, glossy select Monte Carlo walnut stock, with rosewood fore-end and adjustable trigger. Chambered in .270, .30-06, .257 Wby. Magnum and .300 Wby. Magnum. Introduced 2006.

NIB	Exc.	V.G.	Good	Fair	Poor
750	650	550	450	325	225

VANGUARD SERIES 2

Vanguard Series 2 Back Country

All Vanguard Series 2 rifles guaranteed to shoot 3-shot group of less than 1" at 100 yds. when used with specified Weatherby factory or premium ammunition. Available in .240, .257 and .300 Wby. Magnum, plus .270 Win., .30-06, .300 Win. Magnum. Features include match-grade adjustable trigger, fluted 24" barrel, pillar-bedded Monte Carlo composite stock, with spiderweb accents, Pachmayr Decelerator recoil pad, Cera-Kote Tactical Grey finish. Average weight 6.75 lbs.

NIB	Exc.	V.G.	Good	Fair	Poor
1250	1100	950	800	500	350

Vanguard Series 2 Sporter

Classic Weatherby look. Monte Carlo A-grade turkish walnut stock, with raised comb, rosewood fore-end and fine-line diamond point checkering. Other features similar to Back Country model. Chambered in most popular calibers from .223 to .338 Win. Magnum, including .257 and .300 Wby. Magnums. Deluxe model has higher grade wood, with high gloss finish. **NOTE:** Add $300 for deluxe model.

NIB	Exc.	V.G.	Good	Fair	Poor
750	650	525	400	300	250

Vanguard Series 2 Synthetic

Available in a wide range of calibers from .223 to .338 Win. Magnum, including .240, .257 and .300 Wby. Magnums. Composite Griptonite stock. Barrel is 24" No. 2 contour. Weight 7.25 to 7.5 lbs. Blue or stainless finish. Also offered in youth model, with 20" barrel. **NOTE:** Add $100 for stainless. Deduct 10 percent for youth model.

NIB	Exc.	V.G.	Good	Fair	Poor
600	525	450	375	300	250

Vanguard Series 2 Varmint Special

Similar to Synthetic model in .223, .22-250 and .308 Win., with semi-heavy No. 3 contour 20" barrel. Weight about 8.75 lbs.

NIB	Exc.	V.G.	Good	Fair	Poor
750	650	525	400	300	250

Weathermark

Introduced in 1993. Features checkered composite stock, with matte blue metal finish. Available in Weatherby calibers from .257 through .340 and .270 Win., 7mm Rem. Magnum, .30-06, .300 and .338 Win. Magnum. Weight 7.5 lbs.

NIB	Exc.	V.G.	Good	Fair	Poor
550	450	350	250	175	100

Weathermark Alaskan

Similar to Weathermark, with checkered composite stock. Barreled action is electroless nickel, with non-glare finish. Muzzle-brake optional. Available in same calibers as Weathermark. Weight 7.7 lbs.

NIB	Exc.	V.G.	Good	Fair	Poor
750	650	550	450	325	225

WBY-X

Series of colorful and stylized bolt-actions built on Vanguard Series 2 design. Moderately priced and offer most of the features of other Weatherby rifles. All variations feature composite stocks, with camo finishes. Most models are offered in popular calibers from .223 Rem. to .300 Win. Magnum. Introduced in 2014.

NIB	Exc.	V.G.	Good	Fair	Poor
650	600	500	350	250	200

Mark XXII

Semi-automatic rifle chambered for .22 LR cartridge. Two versions—with detachable magazine; with tubular magazine. Has 24" barrel, with adjustable sights. Select checkered walnut stock, with rosewood forearm tip and pistol-grip cap. Originally produced in Italy and later manufactured in Japan. Introduced in 1965; discontinued 1989. **NOTE:** Premium for Italian guns.

Mark XXII Clip Model

Mark XXII Tube Model

NIB	Exc.	V.G.	Good	Fair	Poor
800	650	500	350	225	200

Mark XXII Bolt Action

Based on Anschutz design. Available in .22 Long Rifle or .17 HMR. Classic Mark V-style high-gloss walnut Monte Carlo stock, with precision cut checkering, rosewood fore-end tip and grip cap. Target-grade barrel is 23", weight 6.5 lbs. Fully adjustable single-stage trigger. Introduced in 2007. **NOTE:** Add 10 percent for .17 HMR.

NIB	Exc.	V.G.	Good	Fair	Poor
1250	1000	800	600	400	300

CUSTOM RIFLES

NOTE: Weatherby custom rifles offered with many different options that will affect price. Consult an expert prior to sale.

Weatherby Custom Grade engraving patterns

Vanguard Sage Country Custom

Introduced in 2008. Similar to Vanguard Synthetic, with injection-molded Desert Camo stock. Available in a variety of chamberings from .223 to .338 Win. Magnum.

NIB	Exc.	V.G.	Good	Fair	Poor
600	500	400	300	225	175

Vanguard Back Country Custom

Introduced in 2008. Lightweight version of Vanguard Synthetic, with fluted barrel, textured stock and overall weight of 6.75 lbs. Available in a variety of chamberings from .257 Wby. Magnum to .300 Wby. Magnum.

NIB	Exc.	V.G.	Good	Fair	Poor
950	850	725	625	425	200

Classic Custom

Features oil-finished French walnut stock, with 20 lpi checkering, ebony fore-end tip, metal grip cap and skeltonized steel buttplate. All metal work is matte blue. Calibers are all Weatherby from .257 Wby. Magnum to .340 Wby. Magnum.

NIB	Exc.	V.G.	Good	Fair	Poor
5100	4600	3500	2250	900	500

Safari Grade Custom

Features oil-finish French walnut stock, with Monte Carlo comb and fleur-de-lis checkering. Ebony fore-end tip and pistol-grip cap. Damascened bolt and follower, with checkered bolt handle. Quarter rib. Engraved floorplate "Safari Custom". Calibers from .257 Wby. Magnum to .460 Wby. Magnum.

NIB	Exc.	V.G.	Good	Fair	Poor
5300	4800	3700	2450	1050	550

Crown Custom

Features hand-carved walnut stock, with buttstock inlay, damascened bolt and follower with checkered bolt handle. Engraved barrel, receiver and trigger guard. Floorplate engraved with gold inlays.

NIB	Exc.	V.G.	Good	Fair	Poor
7500	6250	5000	3000	1500	750

Royal Custom

Introduced in 2002. Features Monte Carlo hand-checkered stock of fancy Claro walnut, with high-gloss finish. Engraved receiver, bolt sleeve and floorplate. Barrel length 26". Available in a wide variety of calibers.

NIB	Exc.	V.G.	Good	Fair	Poor
5300	4800	3700	2450	1050	550

Outfitter Custom

Features Bell & Carlson synthetic stock, with custom camo and Pachmayr pad. Lightweight stainless steel fluted barrel. Titanium nitride finish on all metalwork.

NIB	Exc.	V.G.	Good	Fair	Poor
2250	1700	1400	1100	700	400

Outfitter Krieger Custom

Features Bell & Carlson synthetic stock, with custom camo and Pachmayr pad. Custom Krieger stainless steel fluted barrel. Titanium nitride finish on all metalwork.

NIB	Exc.	V.G.	Good	Fair	Poor
3500	3000	2500	2000	1300	600

Chris Kyle Limited Edition

From Weatherby Custom Shop, this special limited edition rifle is in honor of Navy Seal Sniper Chris Kyle, who died in 2013. A portion of the proceeds from the sale of this rifle are donated to the Kyle family. Chambered in .300 Win. Magnum. Has a hand-laminated composite stock, with raised comb and Kryptek Highlander camo pattern. Other features include a fully adjustable trigger, fluted and free-floated stainless steel barrel, Pachmayr Decelerator pad and Chris Kyle frog logo on floorplate

NIB	Exc.	V.G.	Good	Fair	Poor
3500	3000	2700	2500	—	—

SEMI-AUTO & PUMP SHOTGUNS

PA-08 PUMP-ACTION SERIES

Weatherby introduced this line of pump-action shotguns in 2008. All models come in 12-gauge, with 3" chambers and have chrome-lined barrels. Knoxx stock models reduced recoil and are adjustable in length.

PA-08 Upland

Has a walnut stock and fore-end, with low-lustre finish. Matte black metal work. Available with 26" or 28" barrel. Includes three choke tubes.

NIB	Exc.	V.G.	Good	Fair	Poor
325	275	225	175	125	75

PA-08 Knoxx Strutter X

Strutter models feature synthetic stock and 24" ventilated rib barrel. Three choke tubes included. **NOTE:** Add 15 percent for Apparition Excel camo pattern.

NIB	Exc.	V.G.	Good	Fair	Poor
425	375	325	250	175	100

PA-08 Knoxx HD

Home defense model. Features 18" non-ventilated rib barrel and cylinder choke.

NIB	Exc.	V.G.	Good	Fair	Poor
425	375	325	250	175	100

PA-08 Field/Slug Combo

Features both 28" field barrel for hunting birds and 24" rifled slug barrel for deer. Field barrel is chrome lined and has a ventilated rib. Integral choke system features Briley thread pattern and comes with improved cylinder, Modified and Full-choked tubes. The 8-groove Slug barrel has a Weaver-compatible cantilevered scope mount base. Matte black finish. Weight about 6.75 lbs. Introduced in 2011.

NIB	Exc.	V.G.	Good	Fair	Poor
430	380	340	300	270	220

PA-459 Turkey Camo

Pump gun features Mothwing Camo's Spring Mimicry pattern on stock and fore-end. The 12-gauge gun has 19" barrel, 13.5" length of pull and overall length of 40". Weight about 6.5 lbs. Integral Picatinny rail allows mounting optical sights or other accessories. Rail has a clamp-style LPA ghost ring rear sight adjustable for windage and elevation.

NIB	Exc.	V.G.	Good	Fair	Poor
450	390	360	320	290	250

Centurion

Gas-operated semi-automatic shotgun chambered for 12-gauge. Offered with various barrel lengths and chokes. Has a checkered walnut stock. Manufactured between 1972 and 1981.

NIB	Exc.	V.G.	Good	Fair	Poor
450	400	300	250	200	150

Centurion Deluxe

This version is slightly engraved. Features ventilated rib barrel and higher-grade wood.

NIB	Exc.	V.G.	Good	Fair	Poor
500	400	325	275	225	175

Model 82

Gas-operated semi-automatic shotgun. Chambered for 12-gauge, with 2.75" or 3" chambers. Has various barrel lengths, with ventilated ribs and screw-in choke tubes. Features an alloy receiver and deluxe checkered walnut stock. Also available as the Buckmaster, with 22" open-choked barrel. Introduced in 1983.

NIB	Exc.	V.G.	Good	Fair	Poor
500	450	400	350	300	250

Model SAS Field

Introduced in 1999. Gas-operated semi-automatic features high-grade Claro walnut stock, with black pistol-grip cap. Fine-line checkering. Chambered for 12- or 20-gauge. Fitted with 26", 28" or 30" ventilated rib barrels in 12-gauge; 26" or 28" in 20-gauge. Weight: 7.5 lbs. 12-gauge; 7 lbs. 20-gauge, depending on barrel lengths., Fitted with Briley choke tubes.

NIB	Exc.	V.G.	Good	Fair	Poor
700	550	450	325	250	200

Model SAS Camo

Offered with Shadowgrass or Superflauge camo stocks. Available in 12-gauge only, with 3" chambers. Shadowgrass offered with 26" or 28" barrels; Superflauge with 24" or 26" barrels. Weight about 7.5 lbs.

Shadow Grass

NIB	Exc.	V.G.	Good	Fair	Poor
750	600	500	375	300	225

Superflauge

NIB	Exc.	V.G.	Good	Fair	Poor
750	600	500	375	300	225

Model SAS Slug Gun

Features 22" rifled barrel chambered for 3" 12-gauge shell. Barrel has cantilever base for scope mounts. Walnut stock has raised Monte Carlo comb. Sling swivel studs. Weight about 7.25 lbs. Introduced in 2003.

NIB	Exc.	V.G.	Good	Fair	Poor
750	600	500	375	300	225

Model SAS Sporting Clays

This 12-gauge gun fitted with 28" or 30" ventilated rib ported barrel. Walnut stock, with pistol-grip. Choke tubes standard. Weight about 7.5 lbs. Introduced in 2002.

NIB	Exc.	V.G.	Good	Fair	Poor
800	650	550	425	350	250

Model SAS Synthetic

Features black synthetic stock chambered for 12- or 20-gauge barrels as above. Introduced in 2000.

NIB	Exc.	V.G.	Good	Fair	Poor
525	450	375	300	250	175

SA-08 Upland

This semi-automatic was new in 2008. Features walnut stock, with oil-finish. Available in 12- and 20-gauge, with 3" chambers and 28" or 26" barrels. Three choke tubes included.

NIB	Exc.	V.G.	Good	Fair	Poor
650	550	450	250	175	150

SA-08 Youth

As above in 20-gauge, with 26" barrel only. Shorter 12.5" length of pull.

NIB	Exc.	V.G.	Good	Fair	Poor
550	425	300	250	175	150

SA-08 Entré Rios

Entré Rios autoloader has a scaled-down frame for 28-gauge. Features include a select cut-checkered walnut stock and high-gloss finish on barrel and receiver. Comes equipped with Skeet Improved cylinder and Modified choke tubes. Weight 5.25 lbs. Available with 26" or 28" barrel.

NIB	Exc.	V.G.	Good	Fair	Poor
600	500	425	365	310	200

SA-459 TR

Gas-operated autoloader features a bolt with an oversized hourglass design that's easily located in the dark. Comes equipped with a new TR accessory rail for mounting tactical lights or laser sights. Also has a fully adjustable LPA-style ghost ring sight. Pistol-grip buttstock has rubber-textured grip. Available in 12- or 20-gauge. Barrel length 18.5"; weight 7 lbs.

NIB	Exc.	V.G.	Good	Fair	Poor
625	550	400	325	250	150

Element Deluxe

Available in 12-, 20- or 28-gauge. Inertia-operated action, with chrome plated bolt, drop-out trigger system, AA-grade American walnut stock. Barrel 26" or 28", with ventilated rib, fiber optic front sight and three choke tubes. Also available as Element Synthetic with synthetic stock, rubberized pistol-grip and fore-end inserts; Element Waterfowler with Realtree Max-5 camo pattern. Introduced in 2015. **NOTE:** Add $50 for 28-gauge.

NIB	Exc.	V.G.	Good	Fair	Poor
900	750	600	450	300	200

OLDER MODEL PUMP SHOTGUNS

Patrician

Slide-action shotgun chambered for 12-gauge. Offered with various barrel lengths and choke combinations. Has a ventilated rib barrel, blued finish and checkered walnut stock. Manufactured between 1972 and 1981.

NIB	Exc.	V.G.	Good	Fair	Poor
400	350	325	300	250	175

Patrician Deluxe

Slightly engraved version, with fancier-grade walnut.

NIB	Exc.	V.G.	Good	Fair	Poor
450	425	400	350	275	200

Model 92

Slide-action shotgun chambered for 12-gauge, with 2.75" or 3" chambers. Offered with 26", 28" or 30" ventilated rib barrels, with screw-in choke tubes. Features a short twin-rail slide action and engraved alloy receiver. Finish is blued, with deluxe checkered walnut stock. A Buckmaster model with 22" open-choke barrel and rifle sights is also available.

NIB	Exc.	V.G.	Good	Fair	Poor
350	300	250	200	175	125

SIDE-BY-SIDE GUNS

These shotguns are built in Spain.

Athena SBS

Introduced in 2002. Features a case colored boxlock receiver, with false sideplates with scroll engraving. Offered in 12- or 20-gauge, with 26" or 28" barrels. Choke tubes. Turkish walnut stock, with straight-grip and recoil pad. Checkering is 22 lpi. Single trigger and ejectors. Weight about 7 lbs.

NIB	Exc.	V.G.	Good	Fair	Poor
1550	1200	1000	750	500	400

Athena D'Italia

Introduced in 2005. Chambered for 12-, 20- or 28-gauge. Fitted with 28" barrels for 12-gauge; 26" barrels for 20- and 28-gauge. Receiver has silver sideplates, with scroll engraving. Checkered walnut stock, with straight-grip. Weight about 7 lbs. **NOTE:** Add $135 for 28-gauge.

NIB	Exc.	V.G.	Good	Fair	Poor
2840	2100	1600	1100	750	500

Athena D'Italia PG

Introduced in 2006. Offered in same configurations as D'Italia. Identical in action and frame to D'Italia, with rounded pistol-grip stock and single gold trigger. Laser-cut checkering at 20 lpi. Introduced 2006. Pricing is for 12- and 20-gauge. **NOTE:** Add $200 for 28-gauge.

NIB	Exc.	V.G.	Good	Fair	Poor
3200	2500	2000	1500	1050	500

Athena D'Italia Deluxe

Renaissance floral engraving, with Bolino style game scene. AAA Fancy Turkish walnut, with 24 lpi hand checkering adorn this straight-grip stock model. Available in 12-, 20- and 28-gauge, with 26" or 28" barrels with fixed IC and Mod. chokes. Single trigger. Introduced 2006.

NIB	Exc.	V.G.	Good	Fair	Poor
7000	6000	4750	3000	2200	600

Orion SBS

Lower cost alternative to Athena. Turkish walnut stock, with pistol-grips and 18 lpi checkering. Case colored boxlock receiver. Offered in 12-, 20-, 28-gauge and .410 bore. Choke tubes except for .410 bore. Choice of 26" or 28" barrels. Weight about 7 lbs. Introduced in 2002.

NIB	Exc.	V.G.	Good	Fair	Poor
1750	1100	900	650	475	300

OVER/UNDER GUNS

Regency Field Grade

This is an over/under double-barrel shotgun chambered for 12- or 20-gauge. Has various length ventilated rib barrels and boxlock action, with engraved false sideplates. Features single-selective trigger and automatic ejectors. Finish blued, with checkered walnut stock. Imported from Italy between 1972 and 1980. Also offered as a trap grade with same value.

NIB	Exc.	V.G.	Good	Fair	Poor
1500	1200	1000	700	400	300

Olympian

Similar to Regency, with less engraving. Not imported after 1980. Skeet and trap as well as a field-grade model were available. Values were similar.

NIB	Exc.	V.G.	Good	Fair	Poor
1000	800	650	500	350	225

Orion Upland

This 12- or 20-gauge features Claro walnut stock, with rounded pistol-grip and slim forearm. Plain blued receiver. Choice of 26" or 28" ventilated rib barrel, with 3" chambers. Multi-choke system. Introduced in 1999.

NIB	Exc.	V.G.	Good	Fair	Poor
1200	1000	800	600	450	300

Orion Grade I

An over/under double-barrel shotgun chambered for 12- or 20-gauge, with 3" chambers. Offered with 26" or 28" ventilated rib barrels, with screw-in chokes. Has single-selective trigger and automatic ejectors. Boxlock action features no engraving. Finish blued, with checkered walnut stock. Introduced in 1989; discontinued in 2002; reintroduced in 2015. (see New Production)

NIB	Exc.	V.G.	Good	Fair	Poor
1200	1000	800	650	450	300

Orion Grade I — New Production

Same description as above. Reintroduced in 2015.

NIB	Exc.	V.G.	Good	Fair	Poor
950	800	650	—	—	—

Orion Grade II Skeet

Supplied with Claro walnut checkered stock, with full pistol-grip and rosewood grip cap. Receiver matte blue, with scroll engraving. Barrel has matte ventilated rib, with side vents and mid-point head with white bead front sight. Special ventilated recoil pad. Offered in 12- and 20 gauge, with 26" barrels. Fixed Skeet chokes are standard. Weight: 12 gauge 7.5 lbs.; 20-gauge 7.25 lbs.

NIB	Exc.	V.G.	Good	Fair	Poor
950	800	700	600	400	200

Orion Grade II Sporting Clays

Similar to Classic model, with full pistol-grip and rosewood grip cap. Receiver silver gray, with scroll engraving. Claro walnut stock is checkered, with high-gloss finish. Offered in 12-gauge, with 28" to 30" ventilated rib barrels. Supplied with five screw-in choke tubes.

NIB	Exc.	V.G.	Good	Fair	Poor
1300	1050	800	600	400	200

Orion Grade II Double Trap

Features an integral multi-choke tube. Monte Carlo stock has rosewood pistol-grip cap, with diamond shaped inlay. Receiver blue, with scroll engraving. Available with 30" or 32" ventilated rib barrels. Weight 8 lbs.

NIB	Exc.	V.G.	Good	Fair	Poor
950	800	700	550	400	200

Orion Grade II Single Trap

Similar to Double Trap. Furnished with single 32" barrel. Weight 8 lbs.

NIB	Exc.	V.G.	Good	Fair	Poor
950	800	700	550	400	200

Orion Grade II

This version is lightly engraved. Has a high-gloss finish. Otherwise, similar to Grade I.

NIB	Exc.	V.G.	Good	Fair	Poor
1200	1050	925	800	600	250

Orion Grade II Classic Field

Introduced in 1993. Features rounded pistol-grip and slim forearm design. Walnut stock is oil-finished. Receiver blued, with game scene engraving. Solid recoil pad is standard. Available in 12-, 20- and 28-gauge, with ventilated rib barrel lengths from 26" to 30" depending on gauge. Screw-in choke tubes standard. Weight 6.5 lbs. to 8 lbs. depending on gauge.

NIB	Exc.	V.G.	Good	Fair	Poor
950	800	700	550	400	200

Orion Grade II Classic Sporting Clays

Introduced in 1993. Has rounded pistol-grip, with slender forearm and oil-finished stock. Receiver blued, with scroll engraving. A stepped competition matte ventilated rib, with additional side vents is supplied. Recoil pad has a special radius heel. Offered in 12-gauge with 28" barrel. Furnished with five screw-in choke tubes. Weight 7.5 lbs.

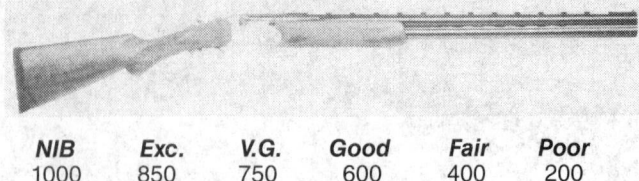

NIB	Exc.	V.G.	Good	Fair	Poor
1000	850	750	600	400	200

Orion Super Sporting Clays (SSC)

Introduced in 1999. This 12-gauge features walnut stock, with sporter-style pistol-grip and cast off. Barrel lengths 28", 30" or 32", with 3" chambers and 12mm grooved rib. Barrels are also ported and backbored. Comes with five choke tubes. Weight about 8 lbs.

NIB	Exc.	V.G.	Good	Fair	Poor
1750	1400	1150	925	750	350

Orion Grade III

This version has a game scene engraved coin-finished receiver and higher-grade walnut. Introduced in 1989.

NIB	Exc.	V.G.	Good	Fair	Poor
1400	1100	850	650	500	300

Orion Grade III Classic Field

New for 1993. Features a rounded pistol-grip and slim forearm, with oil-finish Claro walnut with fine line checkering. Receiver silver gray, with scroll engraving and gold game bird overlays. Available in 12-gauge with 28" ventilated rib barrels; 20-gauge with 26" ventilated rib barrels. Screw-in choke tubes standard.

NIB	Exc.	V.G.	Good	Fair	Poor
1600	1400	1000	750	500	300

Orion Grade III Classic English Field

Features English-style straight-grip stock. Choice of 12-gauge with 28" barrel; 20-gauge with 26" or 28" barrels. Receiver is engraved. Stock is oil-finished hand-checkered. Weight about: 12-gauge 7 lbs.; 20-gauge 6.5 lbs. Introduced in 1996.

NIB	Exc.	V.G.	Good	Fair	Poor
1450	1200	925	800	600	250

Orion D'Italia

Engraved silver-finish metalwork and fineline 20 lpi checkering. Turkish walnut stock, with high-gloss finish. Available in 12-gauge with 28" barrel; 20-gauge with 26" barrel.

NIB	Exc.	V.G.	Good	Fair	Poor
1750	1500	1200	900	750	400

Athena Grade III Classic Field

Offered in 12- or 20-gauge. Features hand select Claro walnut stock, with oil-finish. Pistol-grip is rounded. Silver-gray sideplates feature a rose and scroll engraving pattern, with gold overlaid hunting scenes. Available with 26" or 28" ventilated rib barrels, with multi-choke system. Weight about: 7.5 lbs. 12-gauge; 7 lbs. 20-gauge. Introduced in 1999. In 2001, a 28-gauge version offered with 26" or 28" barrels.

NIB	Exc.	V.G.	Good	Fair	Poor
1700	1500	1250	900	600	350

Athena Grade IV

An over/under double-barrel shotgun chambered for 12-, 20-, 28-gauge and .410 bore. Has 3" chambers. Offered with various barrel lengths, with ventilated ribs and screw-in choke tubes. Has a boxlock action, with Greener crossbolt single-selective trigger and automatic ejectors. Engraved false sideplates and satin nickel-plated action. Barrels blued, with select checkered walnut stock. Introduced in 1989.

NIB	Exc.	V.G.	Good	Fair	Poor
2100	1700	1500	1100	750	450

Athena Grade V Classic Field

Introduced in 1993. Features rounded pistol-grip, with slender forearm. High-grade Claro walnut stock is oil-finished, with fine line checkering. Receiver has a side plate that is silver/gray, with rose and scroll engraving. Ventilated rib barrels also have side vents. An Old English recoil pad is supplied. Offered in 12-gauge with 26", 28" or 30" barrels; 20-gauge with 26" and 28" barrels. Choke tubes are standard. Weatherby Athena Master skeet tube set: 12-gauge 28" skeet shotgun, plus two each 20-, 28-gauge and .410 bore fitted full-length Briley tubes with integral extractors. Packed in custom fitted aluminum case (not shown). **NOTE:** Add 50 percent for Master Skeet Set.

NIB	Exc.	V.G.	Good	Fair	Poor
2800	2400	1800	1400	900	500

Competition Model Athena

A trap or skeet version, with stock dimensions designed for skeet or trap. Competition-type ribs.

NIB	Exc.	V.G.	Good	Fair	Poor
1650	1400	1150	1000	750	600

HANDGUNS

Mark V – CFP (Compact Firing Platform)

Bolt-action handgun, with 5+1 capacity. 16" barrel, adjustable trigger, composite stock. Available in .223, .22-250, .243 and 7mm-08. Weight 5.25 lbs. Introduced 2006.

NIB	Exc.	V.G.	Good	Fair	Poor
1300	1050	800	600	400	200

Mark V Accumark CFP

Similar to Accumark rifle. Features synthetic stock of Kevlar and fiberglass, with matte black gel-coat finish. Offered in .223 Rem., .22-250, .243 Win., 7mm-08 and .308 Win. calibers. Fluted barrel length is 15". Weight about 5 lbs. Introduced in 2000.

NIB	Exc.	V.G.	Good	Fair	Poor
1050	800	600	400	225	150

WEAVER ARMS
Escondido, California

Nighthawk Assault Pistol

A 9mm semi-automatic pistol, with 10" or 12" barrel, alloy receiver and ambidextrous safety. Blackened with plastic grips. Introduced in 1987.

NIB	Exc.	V.G.	Good	Fair	Poor
550	450	400	350	300	150

Nighthawk Carbine

As above, with 16.1" barrel, retractable shoulder stock, 25-, 32-, 40- or 50-shot magazine. Introduced in 1984.

NIB	Exc.	V.G.	Good	Fair	Poor
600	500	450	350	300	150

WEBLEY & SCOTT, LTD.
Birmingham, England

Established in 1860, this firm has produced a wide variety of firearms over the years and has been known as Webley & Scott, Ltd. since 1906. This old English gunmaker traces its history as far back as 1790, when the company began, by making bullet moulds. In 1878, the British Bulldog revolver was developed and in 1887, the Webley model became the official sidearm of the British Defense Forces until 1964. Webley & Scott's history with shotguns goes back to the 1860s, when the company patented the first successful sidelock. Currently the company imports a line of quality shotguns from Turkey.

Model 1872 Royal Irish Constabulary

A .450 double-action revolver, with 3.25" barrel, 5-shot cylinder and rotating ejector. Also offered with 2.5" and 3.5" barrels. Blued, with checkered walnut grips.

NIB	Exc.	V.G.	Good	Fair	Poor
—	1000	750	475	250	150

Model 1880 Metropolitan Police

As above, with 2.5" barrel and 6-shot cylinder.

NIB	Exc.	V.G.	Good	Fair	Poor
—	1000	750	475	250	150

Model 1878 Webley-Pryse

Chambered for .455 and .476 Eley cartridge. **NOTE:** Add 200 percent premium for revolvers chambered for .577. Deduct 50 percent for revolvers chambered for cartridges below .442.

NIB	Exc.	V.G.	Good	Fair	Poor
—	2100	1500	950	550	300

New Model 1883 R.I.C.

Similar to Model 1880. Chambered in .455-caliber, with 4.5" barrel. Also made with 2.5" barrel.

NIB	Exc.	V.G.	Good	Fair	Poor
—	900	750	425	250	100

Model 1884 R.I.C. Naval

As above, with brass frame and oxidized finish. Octagon barrel length 2.75".

NIB	Exc.	V.G.	Good	Fair	Poor
—	2250	1650	1225	600	500

British Bulldog

Similar to New Model 1883 R.I.C. Blued checkered walnut grips. Those engraved on the backstrap "W.R.A. Co." were sold through Winchester Repeating Arms Company's New York sales agency and are worth a considerable premium over values listed. Manufactured from 1878 to 1914. **NOTE:** Add a premium for U.S. dealer markings, see model description.

NIB	Exc.	V.G.	Good	Fair	Poor
—	900	550	325	200	150

Pug

Similar to British Bulldog, but somewhat smaller. Interesting in that it has a manual safety. Chambered in .450, .442, and possibly others as well.

NIB	Exc.	V.G.	Good	Fair	Poor
—	800	500	325	200	150

Model 1878 Army Express Revolver

A .455-caliber double-action revolver, with 6" barrel and integral ejector. Blued, with one-piece walnut grips. **NOTE:** Add 100 percent premium for single-action version; 25 percent for .45 Long (.45 Colt) markings.

NIB	Exc.	V.G.	Good	Fair	Poor
—	2100	1500	850	500	350

Webley Kaufmann Model 1880

Top-break hinged-frame double-action revolver. Chambered for .450 centerfire cartridge, with 5.75" barrel. Curved bird's-head butt. Blued, with walnut grips.

NIB	Exc.	V.G.	Good	Fair	Poor
—	2300	1000	800	600	300

Webley-Green Model

Double-action top-break revolver. Chambered for .455 cartridge, with 6" ribbed barrel and 6-shot cylinder. The cylinder flutes are angular and not rounded in shape. Blued, with checkered walnut squared butt grips with a lanyard ring on the butt. Introduced in 1882. Manufactured until 1896. Also known as "WG" model.

NIB	Exc.	V.G.	Good	Fair	Poor
—	1900	1350	700	500	200

Mark I

A .442, .455 or .476 double-action top-break revolver, with 4" barrel and 6-shot cylinder. Blued, with checkered walnut grips. Manufactured from 1887 to 1894.

Courtesy Faintich Auction Services, Inc., Paul Goodwin photo

NIB	Exc.	V.G.	Good	Fair	Poor
—	950	550	375	250	150

Mark II

As above, with a larger hammer spur and improved barrel catch. Manufactured from 1894 to 1897.

NIB	Exc.	V.G.	Good	Fair	Poor
—	925	550	350	225	100

Mark III

As above, with internal improvements. Introduced in 1897.

NIB	Exc.	V.G.	Good	Fair	Poor
—	975	600	325	200	75

Mark IV

As above, with .455-caliber 3", 4", 5" or 6" barrel. Also available in: .22-caliber 6" barrel; .32-caliber 3" barrel; .38-caliber 3", 4" or 5" barrel.

Courtesy Faintich Auction Services, Inc., Paul Goodwin photo

NIB	Exc.	V.G.	Good	Fair	Poor
—	900	575	375	200	75

Mark IV Target

Chambered for .22-caliber cartridge. Fitted with 6" barrel, with target sights.

Courtesy Rock Island Auction Company

NIB	Exc.	V.G.	Good	Fair	Poor
—	1450	1000	800	500	300

Mark V

Similar to Mark IV, with 4" or 6" barrel. Manufactured from 1913 to 1915.

Courtesy Faintich Auction Services, Inc., Paul Goodwin photo

NIB	Exc.	V.G.	Good	Fair	Poor
—	1000	695	395	250	150

Mark VI

Similar to Mark V in design, with smaller frame, 4" or 6" barrel and modified grip. Chambered for .38/200 (.38 S&W). Pricing is for commercial version. **NOTE:** Deduct 40 percent for WAR FINISH-marked examples.

Courtesy Faintich Auction Services, Inc., Paul Goodwin photo

NIB	Exc.	V.G.	Good	Fair	Poor
—	800	600	375	225	150

Mark VI .22 Rimfire

Standard-size Mark V. Chambered for .22 rimfire cartridge. Used as a training pistol. Manufactured in 1918. Quite scarce.

Courtesy Faintich Auction Services, Inc., Paul Goodwin photo

NIB	Exc.	V.G.	Good	Fair	Poor
—	850	650	450	350	200

WEBLEY SEMI-AUTOMATIC PISTOLS

Webley-Fosbery Automatic Revolver

Recoil forces top half of this unusual pistol back to cock the hammer, while a stud in the frame cams the cylinder around to bring a fresh chamber into position. Early examples under serial number 75 or so, appear to be hand-made as no two seem to be identical; these bring a 100 percent premium over late-model pistols. Other low-number guns, under serial number 300 or so, also differ in appearance from later production and bring 25 percent premium. Early production was all in .455 Webley with 6-round cylinder; a .38 ACP version with 8-round cylinder was introduced about 1903, but is much scarcer than the .455.

Courtesy Joseph Schroeder

.455 Caliber

NIB	Exc.	V.G.	Good	Fair	Poor
—	9000	4500	3000	2000	1250

.38 Caliber

NIB	Exc.	V.G.	Good	Fair	Poor
—	10000	7250	4500	3000	2000

Model 1904

Made experimentally in both .38 ACP and .455-calibers. Highest serial numbered 1904 known in 30s. Very few seem to have survived. A later Webley experimental Model 1906 made in .45 for the U.S. Army trial, but apparently never submitted. Either model is too rare to price.

Courtesy Joseph Schroeder

Model 1905

Webley's first commercial semi-automatic pistol was this compact .32-caliber. Earliest Model 1905s have a diagonal machined flat on the slide and a hammer-mounted safety; these bring about 50 percent pre-mium. Model 1905 was replaced by Model 1908, after about 20,000 were made.

Courtesy Joseph Schroeder

NIB	Exc.	V.G.	Good	Fair	Poor
—	1200	1000	750	400	250

Model 1907

The 1907 is a .25-caliber pistol, with an outside hammer. One of Web-ley's most popular handguns. Remained in production until WWII. Over 50,000 made.

Courtesy Joseph Schroeder

NIB	Exc.	V.G.	Good	Fair	Poor
—	800	600	400	200	100

Model 1908

Model 1908 is a slight redesign of Model 1905. Webley's most popular self-loading pistol. Remained in production until WWII. Examples bear-ing a crown and letters "MP" were made for Metropolitan Police and bring a slight premium.

NIB	Exc.	V.G.	Good	Fair	Poor
—	650	550	350	175	125

Model 1909

Model 1909 is a modified and enlarged version of Model 1908. Cham-bered for 9mm Browning Long cartridge. Never popular and manufac-ture ended in 1914, with just under 1,700 made. Its most unusual feature was the slide release on top of the slide.

Courtesy J.B. Wood

NIB	Exc.	V.G.	Good	Fair	Poor
—	1475	850	500	300	200

Model 1910 .380

Simply a Model 1908 modified to accept .380 cartridge. Never very pop-ular. Under 2,000 sold.

Courtesy Joseph Schroeder

NIB	Exc.	V.G.	Good	Fair	Poor
—	1500	875	525	—	—

Model 1910 .38 ACP

Webley's first locked-breech pistol. Based closely on experimental Model 1906 design. Chambered for .38 ACP cartridge. There are two models, both with internal hammers; one with a grip safety and later without. Total production for both under 1,000, so both are rare.

Courtesy Joseph Schroeder

NIB	Exc.	V.G.	Good	Fair	Poor
—	2250	1500	900	500	350

Model 1911

Model 1911 is a single-shot .22-caliber training version of Model 1908. Developed specifically for Metropolitan Police. Features "blow open" ac-tion that ejects fired cartridge, but remains open for reloading. Bottom of frame is slotted for attaching a shoulder stock. Stocks are quite rare and will add more than 100 percent to value of the pistol.

Courtesy Joseph Schroeder

NIB	Exc.	V.G.	Good	Fair	Poor
—	1750	1400	1100	800	300

Model 1912

A perceived need for a hammerless version of Model 1907, led to the introduction of Model 1912. It actually does have an internal hammer, but recoil spring is two coils in the slide instead of large V-spring under the right grip frame, found in all other Webley semi-automatic pistols. Not as popular as Model 1907. Production totaled almost 15,000 vs. over 50,000 for hammer model.

NIB	Exc.	V.G.	Good	Fair	Poor
—	1200	1000	750	400	200

Model 1913

Model 1913 was the result of years of development in conjunction with the British government. Finally adopted in 1913, as Model 1913 MK1N for Royal Navy issue. Same breech-locking system as Model 1910, but has an external hammer. Chambered for .455 Webley Self-Loading cartridge. About 1,000 Model 1913s were sold commercially and serial-numbered along with smaller-caliber pistols. In 1915, a variation of Model 1913, with butt slotted for a shoulder stock, adjustable rear sight and hammer safety adopted for use by Royal Horse Artillery. Shoulder stocks are very rare. Double values listed for RHA model. All militaries were numbered in their own series; about 10,000 made in both variations.

NIB	Exc.	V.G.	Good	Fair	Poor
—	1950	1200	800	500	300

(RHA model)

Courtesy Joseph Schroeder

NIB	Exc.	V.G.	Good	Fair	Poor
—	5000	4000	3000	1000	600

Model 1922

Model 1922 was a redesign of Model 1909, in hopes of military adoption. Grip safety was replaced by a manual safety mounted on the slide; grip angle was changed; lanyard ring added to the butt. Unfortunately for Webley, its only official use was by the Union Defense Force of South Africa (1,000 pistols). South African guns are marked with a large "U" with an arrow in it. **NOTE:** Add 20 percent premium for South African marked guns.

NIB	Exc.	V.G.	Good	Fair	Poor
—	3000	2500	2000	1000	600

Model 2000 O/U

This 12-gauge features 3" chambers, five choke tubes, select grade oil-finished Turkish walnut stock, color case-hardened receiver, automatic ejectors and single trigger.

NIB	Exc.	V.G.	Good	Fair	Poor
400	350	300	250	200	150

Model 2000 SxS

Side-by-side model, with similar features and quality as 2000 over/under.

NIB	Exc.	V.G.	Good	Fair	Poor
400	350	300	250	200	150

Model 3000 Sidelock Series

This higher grade model features true sidelocks. The 7-pin design and two independent firing mechanisms are mounted on the sideplate and carefully inletted into the stock and mated with the receiver. Stock is a grade 2.5 walnut, hand checkered and oil-finished. The 3000 series is made in over/under and side-by-side configurations.

NIB	Exc.	V.G.	Good	Fair	Poor
5000	4000	3200	2500	1200	500

WEIHRAUCH, HANS HERMANN
Melrichstadt, West Germany

Model HW 60M

A .22-caliber single-shot bolt-action rifle, with 26.75" barrel. Adjustable sights. Blued, with walnut stock.

NIB	Exc.	V.G.	Good	Fair	Poor
800	650	550	400	350	250

Model HW 66

A .22 Hornet or .222 Rem. bolt-action rifle, with stainless steel 26" barrel. Single-/double-set triggers. Blued, with walnut stock.

NIB	Exc.	V.G.	Good	Fair	Poor
700	550	500	350	300	200

Model HW-3

Double-action solid-frame swing-out cylinder revolver. Chambered for .22 LR or .32 S&W Long cartridge. Barrel length 2.75". Cylinder holds 7- or 8-cartridges. Blued, with walnut grips. In America, known as Dickson Bulldog; in Europe as Gecado.

NIB	Exc.	V.G.	Good	Fair	Poor
—	100	75	50	35	25

Model HW-5

As above, with 4" barrel. Sold in United States under trade name "Omega".

NIB	Exc.	V.G.	Good	Fair	Poor
—	100	75	50	35	25

Model HW-7

As above in .22-caliber, with 6" barrel and 8-shot cylinder. Sold in United States as "Herter's Guide Model". Also available with target sights and thumbrest grips as Model HW-7S.

NIB	Exc.	V.G.	Good	Fair	Poor
—	100	75	50	35	25

Model HW-9

These pistols all carry Arminius trademark, bearded head wearing a winged helmet. Model number will be found on cylinder crane; caliber on barrel; words "Made in Germany" on the frame.

NIB	Exc.	V.G.	Good	Fair	Poor
—	100	75	50	35	25

WEISBURGER, A.
Memphis, Tennessee

Pocket Pistol

A .41-caliber percussion single-shot pocket pistol, with 2.5" barrel. German silver furniture and walnut stock. Manufactured during 1850s.

NIB	Exc.	V.G.	Good	Fair	Poor
—	—	6500	5100	3250	1800

WESSON, EDWIN
Hartford, Connecticut

Dragoon

A .45-caliber percussion revolver, with 7" round barrel and 6-shot unfluted cylinder. Barrel blued, frame case-hardened. Walnut grips fitted with a brass buttcap. Manufactured in 1848 and 1849.

NIB	Exc.	V.G.	Good	Fair	Poor
—	—	13500	9500	5000	1750

WESSON, FRANK
Worcester & Springfield, Massachusetts

Manual Extractor Model

A .22-caliber spur trigger single-shot pistol, with 4" octagonal barrel and thin brass frame. Barrel release located in front of the trigger. No markings. Approximately 200 made in 1856 and 1857.

NIB	Exc.	V.G.	Good	Fair	Poor
—	—	1400	950	400	100

First Model Small Frame

As above, with 3", 3.5" or 6" half-octagonal barrel. Blued, with rosewood or walnut grips. Barrel marked "Frank Wesson Worcester Mass/Pat'd Oct. 25, 1859 & Nov. 11, 1862". Serial numbered from 1 to 2500.

NIB	Exc.	V.G.	Good	Fair	Poor
—	—	900	575	225	75

Second Type

As above, with flat sighted frame and circular sideplate.

NIB	Exc.	V.G.	Good	Fair	Poor
—	—	900	575	225	75

First Model Medium Frame

As above in .30 or .32 rimfire, with 4" half-octagonal barrel and iron frame. Approximately 1,000 made between 1859 and 1862.

NIB	Exc.	V.G.	Good	Fair	Poor
—	—	950	600	225	75

Medium Frame Second Model

As above, with a longer spur trigger and slightly wider frame at the barrel hinge. Manufactured from 1862 to 1870.

NIB	Exc.	V.G.	Good	Fair	Poor
—	—	950	600	225	75

Small Frame Pocket Rifle

A .22-caliber spur trigger single-shot pistol, with 6" half-octagonal barrel and narrow brass frame. Adopted for use with a detachable skeleton shoulder stock. Barrel marked "Frank Wesson Worcester, Mass.". Manufactured from 1865 to 1875, with approximately 5,000 made. **NOTE:** Add 100 percent for matching shoulder stock. Prices for pistol only.

NIB	Exc.	V.G.	Good	Fair	Poor
—	—	1500	925	350	100

Medium Frame Pocket Rifle

As above in .22, .30 or .32 rimfire, with 10" or 12" half-octagonal barrel. Approximately 1,000 made from 1862 to 1870. **NOTE:** Add 100 percent for matching shoulder stock. Prices for pistol only.

NIB	Exc.	V.G.	Good	Fair	Poor
—	—	1000	650	200	75

Model 1870 Small Frame Pocket Rifle

As above in .22-caliber, with 10", 12", 15", 18" or 20" half-octagonal barrel that rotates to side for loading. Made with brass or iron frame. Has a half cocked notch on the hammer. **NOTE:** Add 100 percent for matching shoulder stock. Prices for pistol only.

NIB	Exc.	V.G.	Good	Fair	Poor
—	—	1000	650	200	75

1870 Medium Frame Pocket Rifle First Type

As above, with slightly larger frame. Chambered for .32 rimfire. Approximately 5,000 made from 1870 to 1893. **NOTE:** Add 100 percent for matching shoulder stock. Prices for pistol only.

NIB	Exc.	V.G.	Good	Fair	Poor
—	—	1000	650	200	75

1870 Medium Frame Pocket Rifle Second Type

As above, with an iron frame and push-button half cocked safety. **NOTE:** Add 100 percent for matching shoulder stock. Prices for pistol only

NIB	Exc.	V.G.	Good	Fair	Poor
—	—	900	475	175	75

1870 Medium Frame Pocket Rifle Third Type

As above, with three screws on left side of the frame. **NOTE:** Add 100 percent for matching shoulder stock. Prices for pistol only.

NIB	Exc.	V.G.	Good	Fair	Poor
—	—	900	475	175	75

1870 Large Frame Pocket Rifle First Type

As above in .32, .38, .42 or .44 rimfire, with octagonal barrel from 15" to 24" in length. Barrel marked "Frank Wesson Worcester, Mass Patented May 31, 1870". Fewer than 250 made between 1870 and 1880. **NOTE:** Add 100 percent for matching shoulder stock. Prices for pistol only.

NIB	Exc.	V.G.	Good	Fair	Poor
—	—	2750	1500	550	200

1870 Large Frame Pocket Rifle Second Type

As above, with sliding extractor. **NOTE:** Add 100 percent for matching shoulder stock. Prices for pistol only.

NIB	Exc.	V.G.	Good	Fair	Poor
—	—	2750	1500	550	200

Small Frame Superposed Pistol

A .22-caliber spur trigger over/under pocket pistol, with 2" or 2.5" octagonal barrels that revolve. Approximately 3,500 made between 1868 and 1880. On occasion, found with a sliding knife blade mounted on side of the barrels. **NOTE:** Add 25 percent for sliding knife blade mounted.

NIB	Exc.	V.G.	Good	Fair	Poor
—	—	3000	1750	850	250

Medium Frame Superposed Pistol

As above in .32 rimfire, with 2.5" or 3.5" barrels. Like the smaller version, occasionally found with a sliding knife blade mounted on side of the barrels. Manufactured from 1868 to 1880. **NOTE:** Add 25 percent for sliding knife blade mounted.

First Type Marked "Patent Applied For"

NIB	Exc.	V.G.	Good	Fair	Poor
—	—	2500	1250	400	100

Second Type Marked "Patent December 15, 1868"

NIB	Exc.	V.G.	Good	Fair	Poor
—	—	2450	1200	400	100

Third Type Full-Length Fluted Barrels

Courtesy W.P. Hallstein III and son Chip

NIB	Exc.	V.G.	Good	Fair	Poor
—	—	2750	1500	450	150

Large Frame Superposed Pistol

As above in .41 rimfire, with 3" octagonal barrel. Fitted with a sliding knife blade. Approximately 2,000 made from 1868 to 1880.

Courtesy W.P. Hallstein III and son Chip

NIB	Exc.	V.G.	Good	Fair	Poor
—	—	4200	2750	1250	400

No. 1 Long Range Rifle

A .44-100 or .45-100 caliber single-shot dropping block rifle, with 34" octagonal barrel. Blued, with checkered walnut stock. Barrel marked "F. Wesson Mfr. Worcester, Mass. Long Range Rifle Creedmoor". Manufactured in 1876.

NIB	Exc.	V.G.	Good	Fair	Poor
—	—	12500	4500	2000	500

No. 2 Mid-Range or Hunting Rifle

Similar to above, with firing pin located in a bolster on right side of the receiver. Trigger guard has a rear finger loop. Standard barrel lengths 28",
32" and 34"; and marked "F. Wesson Maker Worcester, Mass.". The 32" and 34" barrels are occasionally marked "Long Range Rifle Creedmoor". Approximately 100 made.

Courtesy Buffalo Bill Historical Center, Cody, Wyoming

NIB	Exc.	V.G.	Good	Fair	Poor
—	—	7250	3750	1750	500

No. 2 Sporting Rifle

A .38-100, .40-100 or .45-100 caliber single-shot dropping barrel-action rifle. Barrels ranging from 28" to 34" in length. Approximately 25 made.

Courtesy Buffalo Bill Historical Center, Cody, Wyoming

NIB	Exc.	V.G.	Good	Fair	Poor
—	—	8250	3750	1750	500

Military Carbine

Fitted with 24" barrel, with sling swivels. Chambered for .44-caliber rimfire cartridge. Approximately 4,500 manufactured. **NOTE:** Add 100 percent for martially marked examples.

NIB	Exc.	V.G.	Good	Fair	Poor
—	—	6000	2500	1100	500

WESSON & LEAVITT
Chicopee Falls, Massachusetts

Revolving Rifle

A .40-caliber percussion revolving rifle, with 16" to 24" round barrel and 6-shot cylinder. Blued, with walnut stock. Approximately 25 made in 1849.

NIB	Exc.	V.G.	Good	Fair	Poor
—	—	13000	7500	3500	950

Dragoon

A .40-caliber percussion revolver, with 6.25" or 7" round barrel and 6-shot cylinder. Marked "Mass. Arms Co./Chicopee Falls". Approximately 30 made with 6.25" barrel; and 750 with 7" barrel. Manufactured in 1850 and 1851.

Courtesy Milwaukee Public Museum, Milwaukee, Wisconsin

NIB	Exc.	V.G.	Good	Fair	Poor
—	—	9000	4750	2000	500

WESSON FIREARMS, DAN
Norwich, New York

Also See—Wesson Firearms Co., Inc., separate listing.

In 1996, assets of the Wesson Firearms Co. was purchased by New York International Corp. Full production of new models occurred in 1997. These firearms are laser marked on the barrel or frame with: "NYI" in an oval and below "DAN WESSON

FIREARMS"; on the next line "NORWICH, NEW YORK USA". In April 2005, Dan Wesson Firearms was acquired by CZ-USA. Production continues at the Norwich, New York facility.

NEW GENERATION SMALL-FRAME SERIES

NOTE: The "7" prefix denotes stainless steel frame and barrel. For models listed, add between 4 and 9 percent depending on barrel length and for stainless steel.

Model 22/722

A 6-shot revolver chambered for .22-caliber cartridge. Interchangeable barrel lengths 2.5", 4", 5.6", 8" and 10". Adjustable rear sight and interchangeable front. Hogue finger groove rubber grips. Weight: 36 oz.—2.5" barrel; 58 oz.—10" barrel.

NIB	Exc.	V.G.	Good	Fair	Poor
485	375	300	250	200	145

Model 22M/722M

Same as above, but chambered for .22 Win. Magnum cartridge.

NIB	Exc.	V.G.	Good	Fair	Poor
525	400	300	225	175	145

Model 32/732

Same as above, but chambered for .32 H&R cartridge.

NIB	Exc.	V.G.	Good	Fair	Poor
550	425	325	250	195	165

Model 3220/73220

Same as above, but chambered for .32-20 cartridge.

NIB	Exc.	V.G.	Good	Fair	Poor
550	425	325	250	195	165

Model 15/715

Same as above, but chambered for .38 Special and .357 Magnum cartridges.

NIB	Exc.	V.G.	Good	Fair	Poor
525	400	300	225	175	145

Model 715 (Current Production)

Made from 100 percent stainless steel. Chambered in .357 Magnum. Traditional double-action, with dual cylinder lockup, 6-round capacity, fully adjustable rear sight, transfer bar ignition. Interchangeable barrel, with ventilated rib. Includes barrel wrench kit. Weight 46 oz., 6" barrel, bright stainless finish. Reintroduced in 2011.

NIB	Exc.	V.G.	Good	Fair	Poor
975	850	700	500	350	200

NEW GENERATION LARGE-FRAME SERIES

NOTE: The "7" prefix denotes stainless steel frame and barrel. For models listed, add between 4 and 9 percent depending on barrel length and for stainless steel.

Model 41/741

A large-frame revolver, with 6-shot cylinder. Interchangeable barrels 4", 6", 8" and 10". Adjustable rear sight, with interchangeable front. Hogue finger groove rubber grips standard. Weight from 49 oz. for 4" barrel to 69 oz. for 10" barrel.

NIB	Exc.	V.G.	Good	Fair	Poor
575	475	350	225	175	125

Model 44/744

Same as above, but chambered for .44 Magnum cartridge.

NIB	Exc.	V.G.	Good	Fair	Poor
575	475	350	225	175	125

Model 45/745

Same as above, but chambered for .45 Colt cartridge.

NIB	Exc.	V.G.	Good	Fair	Poor
600	500	375	250	200	125

Model 360/7360

Same as above, but chambered for .357 Magnum cartridge.

NIB	Exc.	V.G.	Good	Fair	Poor
575	475	350	225	175	125

Model 460/7460

Same as above, but chambered for .45 ACP, .45 Auto Rim, .45 Super, .45 Win. Magnum or .460 Rowland cartridges.

NIB	Exc.	V.G.	Good	Fair	Poor
750	625	500	400	300	200

NEW GENERATION SUPERMAG-FRAME SERIES

NOTE: The "7" prefix denotes stainless steel frame and barrel. For models listed, add between 4 and 9 percent depending on barrel length and for stainless steel.

Model 40/740

A 6-shot revolver chambered for .357 Magnum, .357 Super Magnum/Maximum cartridges. Interchangeable barrels 4", 6", 8" or 10" lengths. Adjustable rear sight and interchangeable front. Hogue finger groove rubber grips standard. Weight from 51 oz. for 4" barrel to 76 oz. for 10" barrel.

NIB	Exc.	V.G.	Good	Fair	Poor
1300	1125	850	675	400	250

Model 414/7414

Same as above, but chambered for .414 Super Magnum cartridge.

NIB	Exc.	V.G.	Good	Fair	Poor
1300	1125	850	675	400	250

Model 445/7445

Same as above, but chambered for .445 Super Magnum cartridge.

NIB	Exc.	V.G.	Good	Fair	Poor
1500	1325	1050	875	550	350

NEW GENERATION COMPENSATED SERIES

NOTE: The "7" prefix denotes stainless steel frame and barrel. For models listed, add between 4 and 9 percent depending on barrel length and for stainless steel.

Model 15/715

A 6-shot revolver chambered for .357 Magnum cartridge. Interchangeable barrels 4", 6" or 10" lengths. Barrels have an integral compensator. Adjustable rear sight and interchangeable front. Hogue finger groove rubber grips.

NIB	Exc.	V.G.	Good	Fair	Poor
575	450	325	250	175	100

Model 41/741

Same as above, but chambered for .41 Magnum cartridge.

NIB	Exc.	V.G.	Good	Fair	Poor
675	550	425	350	250	125

Model 44/744

Same as above, but chambered for .44 Magnum cartridge.

NIB	Exc.	V.G.	Good	Fair	Poor
675	550	425	350	250	125

Model 45/745

Same as above, but chambered for .45 Colt cartridge.

NIB	Exc.	V.G.	Good	Fair	Poor
675	550	425	350	250	125

Model 360/7360

Same as above, but chambered for .357 Magnum on large frame.

NIB	Exc.	V.G.	Good	Fair	Poor
675	550	425	350	250	125

Model 445/7445 (Alaskan Guide)

Chambered for .445 SuperMag cartridge. Fitted with 4" heavy ported barrel. Special matte black coating over stainless steel. Introduced in 2002.

NIB	Exc.	V.G.	Good	Fair	Poor
1000	800	675	500	375	250

Model 460/7460

Same as above, but chambered for .45 ACP, .45 Auto Rim, .45 Super, .45 Win. Magnum or .460 Rowland cartridges.

NIB	Exc.	V.G.	Good	Fair	Poor
825	650	500	375	200	125

STANDARD SILHOUETTE SERIES

NOTE: All Standard Silhouette series revolvers are stainless steel.

Model 722 VH10

A 6-shot revolver chambered for .22-caliber cartridge. Interchangeable barrel system. Choice of fluted or non-fluted cylinders. Patridge front sight and adjustable rear. Hogue finger groove rubber grips standard. Lightweight slotted 8" shroud.

NIB	Exc.	V.G.	Good	Fair	Poor
825	650	500	375	200	125

Model 7360 V8S

Same as above, but chambered for .357 Magnum cartridge.

NIB	Exc.	V.G.	Good	Fair	Poor
825	650	500	375	200	125

Model 741 V8S

Same as above, but chambered for .41 Magnum cartridge with 8" slotted shroud.

NIB	Exc.	V.G.	Good	Fair	Poor
825	650	500	375	200	125

Model 741 V10S

Same as above, with 10" slotted shroud.

NIB	Exc.	V.G.	Good	Fair	Poor
925	750	600	475	300	175

Model 744 V8S

Chambered for .44 Magnum cartridge. Fitted with 8" slotted shroud.

NIB	Exc.	V.G.	Good	Fair	Poor
825	650	500	375	200	125

Model 744 V10S

Same as above, but fitted with 10" slotted shroud.

NIB	Exc.	V.G.	Good	Fair	Poor
925	750	600	475	300	175

Model 740 V8S

Chambered for .357 Super Magnum. Fitted with 8" slotted shroud.

NIB	Exc.	V.G.	Good	Fair	Poor
925	750	600	475	300	175

Model 7414 V8S

Chambered for .414 Super Magnum. Fitted with 8" slotted shroud.

NIB	Exc.	V.G.	Good	Fair	Poor
925	750	600	475	300	175

Model 7445 V8S

Chambered for .445 Super Magnum. Fitted with 8" slotted shroud.

NIB	Exc.	V.G.	Good	Fair	Poor
925	750	600	475	300	175

Dan Wesson VH8

.445 Super Magnum revolver designed for barrel interchangeability. Also fires standard .44-caliber rounds. Stainless; 6-shot; 8" barrel; weight 4.1 lb. Single-/double-action. Introduced 2006.

NIB	Exc.	V.G.	Good	Fair	Poor
1100	950	775	600	450	275

SUPER RAM SILHOUETTE SERIES

NOTE: All Super Ram Silhouette series revolvers are stainless steel.

Model 722 VH10 SRS1

Chambered for .22-caliber cartridge. Fitted with 10" slotted shroud. Interchangeable barrel system. Adjustable Bomar rear sight; Bomar SRS-1 hood front sight. Fluted or non-fluted cylinders. Hogue finger groove rubber grips.

NIB	Exc.	V.G.	Good	Fair	Poor
925	750	600	475	300	175

Model 7360 V8S SRS1

Same as above, but chambered for .357 Magnum cartridge. Fitted with 8" slotted shroud.

NIB	Exc.	V.G.	Good	Fair	Poor
1100	950	775	600	450	275

Model 741 V8S SRS1

Same as above, but chambered for .41 Magnum cartridge. Fitted with 8" slotted shroud.

NIB	Exc.	V.G.	Good	Fair	Poor
1100	950	775	600	450	275

Model 741 V10S SRS1

Same as above, but fitted with 10" slotted shroud.

NIB	Exc.	V.G.	Good	Fair	Poor
1100	950	775	600	450	275

Model 744 V8S SRS1

Same as above, but chambered for .44 Magnum cartridge. Fitted with 8" slotted shroud.

NIB	Exc.	V.G.	Good	Fair	Poor
1100	950	775	600	450	275

Model 744 V10S SRS1

Same as above, but fitted with 10" slotted shroud.

NIB	Exc.	V.G.	Good	Fair	Poor
1100	950	775	600	450	275

Model 740 V8S SRS1

Same as above, but chambered for .357 Super Magnum. Fitted with 8" slotted shroud.

NIB	Exc.	V.G.	Good	Fair	Poor
1200	1050	875	700	550	300

Model 7414 V8S SRS1

Same as above, but chambered for .414 Super Magnum. Fitted with 8" slotted shroud.

NIB	Exc.	V.G.	Good	Fair	Poor
1200	1050	875	700	550	300

Model 7445 V8S SS1

Same as above, but chambered for .445 Super Magnum. Fitted with 8" slotted shroud.

NIB	Exc.	V.G.	Good	Fair	Poor
1200	1050	875	700	550	300

PISTOL PACK SERIES

This series consists of a Dan Wesson revolver of customer's choice, with adjustable rear sight and four barrel assemblies in small-frame calibers (2.5", 4", 6" and 8"); large frame and supermag frame have three barrel assemblies (4", 6" and 8"). Also included is a cleaning kit, wrench kit, extra exotic wood grips, instruction manual and fitted hard case. Choice of blue or stainless steel finish ("7" prefix).

Model 22/722

Chambered for .22 LR.

NIB	Exc.	V.G.	Good	Fair	Poor
1200	1050	875	700	550	300

Model 32/732

Chambered for .32 H&R Magnum.

NIB	Exc.	V.G.	Good	Fair	Poor
2000	1700	1300	1000	550	300

Model 3220/73220

Chambered for .32-20.

NIB	Exc.	V.G.	Good	Fair	Poor
2000	1700	1300	1000	550	300

Model 15/715

Chambered for .357 Magnum.

NIB	Exc.	V.G.	Good	Fair	Poor
1200	1050	875	700	550	300

Model 41/741

Chambered for .41 Magnum.

NIB	Exc.	V.G.	Good	Fair	Poor
2000	1700	1300	1000	650	350

Model 44/744

Chambered for .44 Magnum.

NIB	Exc.	V.G.	Good	Fair	Poor
2000	1700	1300	1000	650	350

Model 45/745

Chambered for .45 Colt.

NIB	Exc.	V.G.	Good	Fair	Poor
2000	1700	1300	1000	650	350

Model 460/7460

Chambered for .45 ACP, .45 Auto Rim, .45 Super, .45 Win. Magnum or .460 Rowland cartridges.

NIB	Exc.	V.G.	Good	Fair	Poor
1450	1250	1050	850	650	350

Model 40/740

Chambered for .357 Maximum.

NIB	Exc.	V.G.	Good	Fair	Poor
1650	1300	1150	950	750	450

Model 414/7414

Chambered for .414 Super Magnum.

NIB	Exc.	V.G.	Good	Fair	Poor
1650	1300	1150	950	750	450

Model 445/7445

Chambered for .445 Super Magnum.

NIB	Exc.	V.G.	Good	Fair	Poor
1650	1300	—	—	—	—

HUNTER PACK SERIES

Hunter Pack comes with a Dan Wesson revolver of customer's choice, with adjustable rear sight and two 8" barrel assemblies, one with open sights; one drilled and tapped with Burris or Weaver mount installed. Extra set of exotic wood grips, wrench kit, cleaning kit and manual. Offered in blue or stainless steel ("7" prefix).

Model 22/722

Chambered for .22 LR.

NIB	Exc.	V.G.	Good	Fair	Poor
1200	950	—	—	—	—

Model 32/732

Chambered for .32 H&R Magnum.

NIB	Exc.	V.G.	Good	Fair	Poor
1200	950	—	—	—	—

Model 3220/73220

Chambered for .32-20.

NIB	Exc.	V.G.	Good	Fair	Poor
1200	1050	875	700	550	300

Model 15/715

Chambered for .357 Magnum.

NIB	Exc.	V.G.	Good	Fair	Poor
1200	1050	875	700	550	300

Model 41/741

Chambered for .41 Magnum.

NIB	Exc.	V.G.	Good	Fair	Poor
1450	1250	1050	850	650	350

Model 44/744

Chambered for .44 Magnum.

NIB	Exc.	V.G.	Good	Fair	Poor
1450	1250	1050	850	650	350

Model 45/745

Chambered for .45 Colt.

NIB	Exc.	V.G.	Good	Fair	Poor
1450	1250	1050	850	650	350

Model 460/7460

Chambered for .45 ACP, .45 Auto Rim, .45 Super, .45 Win. Magnum or .460 Rowland cartridges

NIB	Exc.	V.G.	Good	Fair	Poor
1450	1250	1050	850	650	350

Model 40/740

Chambered for .357 Maximum.

NIB	Exc.	V.G.	Good	Fair	Poor
1650	1300	1150	950	750	450

Model 414/7414

Chambered for .414 Super Magnum.

NIB	Exc.	V.G.	Good	Fair	Poor
1650	1300	1150	950	750	450

Model 445/7445

Chambered for .445 Super Magnum.

NIB	Exc.	V.G.	Good	Fair	Poor
1650	1300	1150	950	750	450

PISTOLS

Pointman Major

Semi-automatic pistol chambered for .45 ACP cartridge. Many special features including interchangeable front sight and adjustable rear, Jarvis match barrel, beveled magazine well and others. Stainless steel slide and frame. Rosewood checkered grips. Slide serrations both front and rear. High sighting rib, with interchangeable sights. Introduced in 2000.

NIB	Exc.	V.G.	Good	Fair	Poor
1200	1050	800	625	500	300

Pointman Seven

Many of the same features as Pointman Major, with blued slide and frame. No sighting rib.

NIB	Exc.	V.G.	Good	Fair	Poor
1100	950	700	525	400	300

Pointman Minor

Same as above, except blued slide and frame. No match barrel.

NIB	Exc.	V.G.	Good	Fair	Poor
1100	950	700	525	400	300

Pointman Seven Stainless

Same as above, with stainless steel frame and slide.

NIB	Exc.	V.G.	Good	Fair	Poor
1200	1050	800	625	500	300

Pointman Nine

Full-size 1911-style in 9mm, with 9+1 capacity. Front and rear slide serrations, adjustable rear sight, fiber optic front.

NIB	Exc.	V.G.	Good	Fair	Poor
1300	1100	850	600	450	300

Pointman Guardian

Fitted with 4.25" barrel and match trigger group. Adjustable rear sight, plus many other special features. Blued frame and slide, with sighting rib.

NIB	Exc.	V.G.	Good	Fair	Poor
1200	1050	800	625	500	300

Pointman Guardian Duce

Same as above, with blued steel slide and stainless steel frame.

NIB	Exc.	V.G.	Good	Fair	Poor
825	675	525	400	300	175

Pointman Major Australian

Introduced in 2002. Features fully adjustable Bomar-style target sight. Unique slide top configuration that features a rounded radius, with lengthwise sight serrations. Slide has Southern Cross engraved on right side. Chambered for .45 ACP cartridge only.

NIB	Exc.	V.G.	Good	Fair	Poor
1200	1050	800	625	500	300

Pointman Hi-Cap

This .45 ACP pistol fitted with 5" barrel. Blued carbon alloy wide-body frame, with 10-round magazine. Fixed rear target sight. Extended thumb safety as well as other special features.

NIB	Exc.	V.G.	Good	Fair	Poor
1100	950	700	525	400	300

Pointman Dave Pruitt Signature Series

Fitted with 5" match-grade barrel, with rounded top slide with bead blast matte finish. Chevron-style cocking serrations. Fixed rear sight, with tactical/target ramp front. Many special features.

NIB	Exc.	V.G.	Good	Fair	Poor
1100	950	700	525	400	300

RZ-10

10mm single-action semi-automatic, with 8+1 capacity, 5" barrel, fixed sights. Weight 2.4 lbs. Introduced 2006.

NIB	Exc.	V.G.	Good	Fair	Poor
1100	950	700	525	400	300

RZ-45 Heritage

Same as discontinued RZ-10, except in .45 ACP. The RZ refers to "Razorback", which is based on serrated Clark-style target rib machined onto the top of the slide. Introduced in 2010.

NIB	Exc.	V.G.	Good	Fair	Poor
1100	950	700	525	400	200

Guardian

Designed for concealed carry, with Bobtail frame. Calibers .38 Super, 9mm or .45 ACP, with steel slide, alloy frame, Novak Lo-Mount night sights, extended thumb and grip safeties, 8- or 9-round magazine and stippled Shadow grips. Weight 28.8 ozs., 4.3" barrel and black Duty finish.

NIB	Exc.	V.G.	Good	Fair	Poor
1300	1100	850	600	450	300

Valkyrie

In .45 ACP. This model has what is essentially a 4.5" Commander size barrel, with an Officer's model slide. Features include Black Duty finish, fixed tritium night sights and slim-line G10 grips. Introduced in 2015.

NIB	Exc.	V.G.	Good	Fair	Poor
1750	1400	1000	850	400	250

ECO

Officer-size model, with 3.5" barrel in 9mm or .45 ACP. Features aluminum frame and steel slide, night sights, G10 grips, Duty Black finish.

NIB	Exc.	V.G.	Good	Fair	Poor
1400	1100	900	700	450	350

Valor

Full-size 1911-style in 9mm or .45 ACP, with black ceramic coated or matte stainless finish. Slimline G10 grips, Heinie Ledge Straight-Eight Night Sights. Valor Commander identical, except for 4.25" barrel.

NIB	Exc.	V.G.	Good	Fair	Poor
1675	1350	1050	800	500	400

Elite Series — Havoc

Designed for Open IPSC/USPSA competition. In .38 Super or 9mm, with 5" barrel with compensator and C-More red dot sights. A 4.5" barrel was previously offered.

NIB	Exc.	V.G.	Good	Fair	Poor
3500	3000	2500	1700	900	500

PATRIOT SERIES

Patriot Marksman

Introduced in 2002. This .45 ACP pistol has 5" match grade barrel. Fixed sights. Many special features such as beveled mag well, lowered and flared ejection port, checkered wood grips. Magazine capacity 8 rounds. Weight about 38 oz.

NIB	Exc.	V.G.	Good	Fair	Poor
795	650	525	400	300	175

Patriot Expert

As above, but fitted with Bomar target-style adjustable rear sight.

NIB	Exc.	V.G.	Good	Fair	Poor
900	750	625	500	400	225

RIFLES

Coyote Target

Chambered for .22 LR or .22 Magnum cartridge. Fitted with 18.375" heavy bull barrel. Receiver drilled and tapped for scope mount. Hardwood stock, with high comb and flat-bottom fore-end. Magazine capacity 6 or 10 rounds. **NOTE:** Unknown whether Dan Wesson Coyote rifles were ever actually produced; we suspect not. Values shown are based on 2002 suggested retail prices.

NIB	Exc.	V.G.	Good	Fair	Poor
275	—	—	—	—	—

Coyote Classic

Also chambered for .22 LR or .22 Magnum cartridge. Fitted with 22.75" barrel, with open sights. Drilled and tapped for scope mount. Checkered hardwood stock. Magazine capacity 6 or 10 rounds. Introduced in 2002.

NIB	Exc.	V.G.	Good	Fair	Poor
235	—	—	—	—	—

WESSON FIREARMS CO., INC.
Palmer, Massachusetts

The Company was founded in 1968 by Daniel B. Wesson, great-grandson of D.B. Wesson co-founder of Smith & Wesson. This line of handguns is unique for its barrel/shroud interchangeability. Dan Wesson revolvers have established themselves as champion metallic silhouette competition guns. Company offers a comprehensive line of handguns for almost every use and will also custom build a handgun to customer specifications. Dan Wesson Arms was restructured on January 4, 1991 and identified as Wesson Firearms Company, Inc. Wesson handguns made after this date will be stamped with this new corporate name. In 1995, the company declared bankruptcy. (See WESSON FIREARMS, DAN)

Model 11

A .357 Magnum caliber double-action swing-out cylinder revolver, with interchangeable 2.5", 4" or 6" barrels. 6-shot cylinder. Blued, with walnut grips. Manufactured in 1970 and 1971. **NOTE:** Add 25 percent per barrel for extra barrels.

NIB	Exc.	V.G.	Good	Fair	Poor
300	275	150	125	100	75

Model 12

As above, with adjustable target sights.

NIB	Exc.	V.G.	Good	Fair	Poor
350	27	200	175	125	100

Model 14

As above, with recessed barrel locking nut. Furnished with a spanner wrench. Manufactured from 1971 to 1975.

NIB	Exc.	V.G.	Good	Fair	Poor
350	250	175	150	100	75

Model 15

As above, with adjustable target sights.

NIB	Exc.	V.G.	Good	Fair	Poor
375	275	200	175	125	100

Model 8

As above, in .38 Special caliber.

NIB	Exc.	V.G.	Good	Fair	Poor
325	225	150	125	100	75

Model 9

As Model 15, with adjustable sights. In .38 Special caliber. Manufactured from 1971 to 1975.

NIB	Exc.	V.G.	Good	Fair	Poor
350	275	200	175	125	100

.22 CALIBER REVOLVERS

Model 22

Double-action target revolver chambered for .22 LR cartridge. Available in 2", 4", 6" and 8" barrel length. Choice of shroud: standard rib; ventilated rib; ventilated heavy rib. All variations feature adjustable rear sight and red ramp interchangeable front. Target grips. Offered in bright blue or stainless steel finish. For revolvers with standard barrel assembly weights are: 2"—36 oz.; 4"—40 oz.; 6"—44 oz.; 8"—49 oz.

Model 722

Same as above, with stainless steel finish.

Model 22M

Same as above, but chambered for .22 Magnum with blued finish.

Model 722M

Same as above, but chambered for .22 Magnum. Stainless steel finish. **NOTE:** Add 10 percent for stainless steel finish.

Standard Rib Shroud

NIB	Exc.	V.G.	Good	Fair	Poor
375	300	200	150	100	75

Ventilated Rib Shroud

NIB	Exc.	V.G.	Good	Fair	Poor
400	325	225	150	100	75

Ventilated Heavy Rib Shroud

NIB	Exc.	V.G.	Good	Fair	Poor
425	330	240	200	125	100

P22 Pistol Pac

This model is also a target revolver similar to Model 22 and its variations. Chambered for .22 LR or .22 Magnum. Offered with three types of barrel shrouds: standard; ventilated; or ventilated heavy. Available in blued or stainless steel finish. Principal feature of Pistol Pac is the three barrel assemblies in 2.5", 4", 6" and 8", with extra grips, four additional front sights and a fitted carrying case. **NOTE:** Add 10 percent for stainless steel finish.

Standard Rib Shroud

NIB	Exc.	V.G.	Good	Fair	Poor
750	550	400	350	300	150

Ventilated Rib Shroud

NIB	Exc.	V.G.	Good	Fair	Poor
800	600	500	450	350	150

Ventilated Heavy Rib Shroud

NIB	Exc.	V.G.	Good	Fair	Poor
800	600	500	450	350	150

HP22 Hunter Pac

Chambered for .22 Magnum cartridge. Set includes ventilated heavy 8" shroud, ventilated 8" shroud only with Burris scope mounts and Burris scope in 1.5x4X variable or fixed 2X, barrel changing tool and fitted carrying case. Finish blued or stainless steel. **NOTE:** Hunter Pacs are a special order item and should be evaluated at the time of sale.

.32 CALIBER REVOLVERS

Model 32

A target revolver chambered for .32 H&R Magnum cartridge. Offered in 2", 4", 6" or 8" barrel lengths, with choice of rib shrouds. All variations are fitted with adjustable rear sight and red ramp interchangeable front. Target grips. Available in blued or stainless steel finish. Weights depend on barrel length and shroud type, but are between 35 and 53 oz.

Model 732

Same as above, with stainless steel finish.

Model 322

Same as above, but chambered for .32-20 cartridge with blued finish.

Model 7322

Same as above, but chambered for .32-20 cartridge. Stainless steel finish. **NOTE:** Add 10 percent for stainless steel finish.

Standard Rib Shroud

NIB	Exc.	V.G.	Good	Fair	Poor
475	325	200	150	100	75

Ventilated Rib Shroud

NIB	Exc.	V.G.	Good	Fair	Poor
500	350	225	150	100	75

Ventilated Heavy Rib Shroud

NIB	Exc.	V.G.	Good	Fair	Poor
525	375	250	150	100	75

P32 Pistol Pac

Offers same calibers, barrel shrouds and finishes as above models. In a set consisting of 2", 4", 6" and 8" barrels, extra grips, four additional sights and fitted case. **NOTE:** Add 10 percent for stainless steel finish.

Standard Rib Shroud

NIB	Exc.	V.G.	Good	Fair	Poor
1200	1000	650	500	400	300

Ventilated Rib Shroud

NIB	Exc.	V.G.	Good	Fair	Poor
1200	1000	650	500	400	300

Ventilated Heavy Rib Shroud

NIB	Exc.	V.G.	Good	Fair	Poor
1200	1000	650	500	400	300

329HP32 Hunter Pac

Chambered for .32 H&R Magnum or .32-20 cartridge. Set includes ventilated heavy 8" shroud, ventilated 8" shroud only with Burris scope mounts and Burris scope in 1.5x4X variable or fixed 2X, barrel changing tool and fitted carrying case. Finish blued or stainless steel. **NOTE:** Hunter Pacs are a special order item and should be evaluated at the time of sale.

.357 MAGNUM AND .38 CALIBER REVOLVERS

Model 14

Double-action service revolver chambered for .357 Magnum cartridge. Available with 2", 4" or 6" barrel, with service shroud. Has fixed sights, service grip. Offered in blued or stainless steel finish.

Model 714

Same as above, with stainless steel finish.

Model 8

Same as above, but chambered for .38 Special cartridge with blued finish.

Model 708

Same as above, but chambered for .38 Special. Stainless steel finish. **NOTE:** Add 10 percent for stainless steel finish.

NIB	Exc.	V.G.	Good	Fair	Poor
400	350	250	125	100	75

P14/8 Pistol Pac

This set consists of 2", 4" and 6" barrel, with service shroud and fixed sights. Has an extra grip, with fitted carrying case. P14 chambered for .357 Magnum; P8 chambered for .38 Special.

NIB	Exc.	V.G.	Good	Fair	Poor
800	700	600	500	400	300

Model 15

Designed as a double-action target revolver. Chambered for .357 Magnum cartridge. Available with 2", 4", 6", 8" and 10" barrel lengths, with standard rib shroud. Features adjustable rear sight and red ramp interchangeable front. Target grips. Offered with blued finish. Weights according to barrel length: 2"—32 oz.; 4"—36 oz.; 6"—40 oz.; 8"—44 oz.; 10"—50 oz.

Model 715

Same as above, with stainless steel finish.

Model 9

Same as above, but chambered for .38 Special cartridge with blued finish.

Model 709

Same as above, with stainless steel finish. **NOTE:** Add 10 percent for stainless steel finish.

Standard Rib Shroud

NIB	Exc.	V.G.	Good	Fair	Poor
800	700	600	500	400	300

Ventilated Rib Shroud

NIB	Exc.	V.G.	Good	Fair	Poor
800	700	600	500	400	300

Ventilated Heavy Rib Shroud

NIB	Exc.	V.G.	Good	Fair	Poor
800	700	600	500	400	300

330HP15 Hunter Pac

Chambered for .357 Magnum cartridge. Set includes ventilated heavy 8" shroud, ventilated 8" shroud only with Burris scope mounts and Burris scope in 1.5x4X variable or fixed 2X, barrel changing tool and fitted carrying case. Finish blued or stainless steel. **NOTE:** Hunter Pacs are a special order item and should be evaluated at the time of sale.

331 Model 40/Supermag

A target revolver chambered for .357 Maximum cartridge. Has an adjustable rear sight and red ramp interchangeable front, ventilated rib shroud and target grip. Barrel lengths 4", 6", 8" or 10". Ventilated slotted shroud available in 8" only. In 1993, a compensated barrel assembly "CBA" was added to the product line as a complete gun. Finish blued. Weighs about 64 oz. with ventilated rib shroud barrel. **NOTE:** Add 20 percent for Model 740 in stainless steel; 10 percent for stainless steel finish; $30 for .357 Supermag with compensated barrel assembly.

Ventilated Rib Shroud

NIB	Exc.	V.G.	Good	Fair	Poor
1100	950	750	600	450	300

Ventilated Slotted Shroud—8" barrel only

NIB	Exc.	V.G.	Good	Fair	Poor
1100	950	750	600	450	300

Ventilated Heavy Rib Shroud

NIB	Exc.	V.G.	Good	Fair	Poor
1100	950	750	600	450	300

332 HP40 Hunter Pac

Chambered for .357 Supermag cartridge. Set includes ventilated heavy 8" shroud, ventilated 8" shroud only with Burris scope mounts and Burris scope in 1.5x4X variable or fixed 2X, barrel changing tool and fitted carrying case. Finish blued or stainless steel. **NOTE:** Hunter Pacs are a special order item and should be evaluated at the time of sale.

Model 375

Also known as .375 Supermag. Chambered for .357 Maximum cartridge based on .375 Win. cartridge. Offered in 6", 8", 10" ventilated, ventilated heavy or ventilated slotted rib barrels. Sights are interchangeable and adjustable. Available in bright blue finish only. Weighs about 64 oz. with ventilated rib shroud barrel.

Ventilated Rib Shroud

NIB	Exc.	V.G.	Good	Fair	Poor
1100	950	750	600	450	300

Ventilated Heavy Rib Shroud

NIB	Exc.	V.G.	Good	Fair	Poor
1100	950	750	600	450	300

Ventilated Slotted Shroud—8" barrel only

NIB	Exc.	V.G.	Good	Fair	Poor
1100	950	750	600	450	300

P15/9 Pistol Pac

A set with 2", 4", 6" and 8" barrels. Chambered for .357 or .38 Special, with standard rib shroud, four additional sights, extra grip and carrying case. P15 chambered for .357 Magnum; P9 chambered for .38 Special. **NOTE:** Add 10 percent for stainless steel finish.

Standard Rib Shroud

NIB	Exc.	V.G.	Good	Fair	Poor
800	700	600	500	400	300

Ventilated Rib Shroud

NIB	Exc.	V.G.	Good	Fair	Poor
800	700	600	500	400	300

Ventilated Heavy Rib Shroud

NIB	Exc.	V.G.	Good	Fair	Poor
800	700	600	500	400	300

354HP375 Hunter Pac

Chambered for .375 Supermag cartridge. Set includes ventilated heavy 8" shroud, ventilated 8" shroud only with Burris scope mounts and Burris scope in 1.5x4X variable or fixed 2X, barrel changing tool and fitted carrying case. Finish blued or stainless steel. **NOTE:** Hunter Pacs are a special order item and should be evaluated at the time of sale.

.41, .44 MAGNUM AND .45 LONG COLT REVOLVERS

Model 44

A target double-action revolver chambered for .44 Magnum. Has 4", 6", 8" or 10" barrels, with ventilated rib shrouds. Other features include adjustable rear sight and red ramp interchangeable front. Target grips. Finish bright blue. Weights according to barrel length: 4"—40 oz.; 6"—56 oz.; 8"—64 oz.; 10"—69 oz.

Model 744

Same as above, with stainless steel finish.

301 Model 41

Same as above, but chambered for .41 Magnum with blued finish.

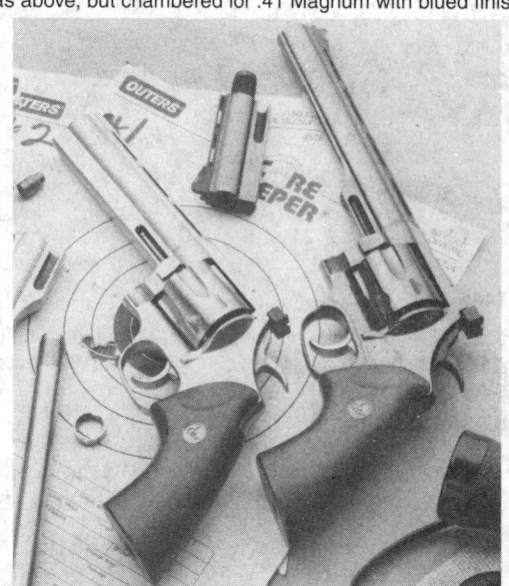

302 Model 741

Same as above, with stainless steel finish.

Model 45

Same as above, but chambered for .45 Long Colt with bright blue finish.

Model 745

Same as above, with stainless steel finish. **NOTE:** Add 10 percent for stainless steel finish.

Ventilated Rib Shroud

NIB	Exc.	V.G.	Good	Fair	Poor
1000	850	550	450	300	200

Ventilated Heavy Rib Shroud

NIB	Exc.	V.G.	Good	Fair	Poor
1000	850	550	450	300	200

P44/P41/P45 Pistol Pac

This set features 6" and 8" barrel assembly, with ventilated rib shroud, extra grip, two additional front sights and fitted carrying case. Chambered for .41 Magnum, .44 Magnum or .45 Long Colt. **NOTE:** Add 10 percent for stainless steel finish.

Ventilated Rib Shroud

NIB	Exc.	V.G.	Good	Fair	Poor
1000	850	550	450	300	200

Ventilated Heavy Rib Shroud

NIB	Exc.	V.G.	Good	Fair	Poor
1000	850	550	450	300	200

357HP41/44 Hunter Pac

Chambered for .41 or .44 Magnum cartridge. Set includes ventilated heavy 8" shroud, ventilated 8" shroud only with Burris scope mounts and Burris scope in 1.5x4X variable or fixed 2X, barrel changing tool and fitted carrying case. Finish blued or stainless steel. **NOTE:** Hunter Pacs are a special order item and should be evaluated at the time of sale.

359 Model 445

Double-action target revolver chambered for .445 Supermag cartridge. Barrel lengths and shrouds offered: 8" with ventilated slotted rib; 8" ventilated heavy slotted rib; 10" ventilated slotted rib. Barrel lengths also available in 4", 6", 8" and 10", with ventilated rib or ventilated heavy rib shrouds. In 1993, a compensated barrel assembly "CBA" was added to the product line as a complete gun. Fitted with adjustable rear sights and red ramp interchangeable front. Target grips. Finish bright blue. Typical weight with 8" ventilated rib shroud barrel about 62 oz.

Model 7445

Same as above, with stainless steel finish. **NOTE:** Add 10 percent for stainless steel finish; $30 for .44 Magnum and .445 Supermag, with compensated barrel assembly.

Ventilated Rib Shroud

NIB	Exc.	V.G.	Good	Fair	Poor
1100	950	750	600	450	300

Ventilated Heavy Rib Shroud

NIB	Exc.	V.G.	Good	Fair	Poor
1100	950	750	600	450	300

Model 7445 Alaskan Guide Special

A limited edition model (only 500 produced). Chambered for .445 Supermag cartridge. Features 4" ventilated heavy compensated shroud barrel assembly, synthetic grips and matte black titanium nitride finish. Overall barrel length 5.5"; weight 56 oz.

NIB	Exc.	V.G.	Good	Fair	Poor
950	700	600	350	200	100

HP455 Hunter Pac

Chambered for .445 Supermag cartridge. Set includes ventilated heavy 8" shroud, ventilated 8" shroud only with Burris scope mounts and Burris scope in 1.5x4X variable or fixed 2X, barrel changing tool and fitted carrying case. Finish blued or stainless steel. **NOTE:** Hunter Pacs are a special order item and should be evaluated at the time of sale.

FIXED BARREL HANDGUNS

Model 38P

A 5-shot double-action revolver designed for .38 Special cartridge. Barrel 2.5", with fixed sights. Choice of wood or rubber grips. Finish is blued. Weight 24.6 oz.

NIB	Exc.	V.G.	Good	Fair	Poor
350	225	150	125	100	75

Wesson Firearms Silhouette .22

A 6-shot .22 LR single-action only revolver, with 10" barrel. Fitted with compact-style grips, narrow notch rear sight. Choice of ventilated or ventilated heavy rib shroud. Finish blued or stainless steel. Weight with shroud: 55 oz. ventilated rib; 62 oz. ventilated heavy rib. **NOTE:** Add 10 percent for stainless steel finish.

Ventilated Rib Shroud

NIB	Exc.	V.G.	Good	Fair	Poor
495	325	275	200	150	100

Ventilated Heavy Rib Shroud

NIB	Exc.	V.G.	Good	Fair	Poor
495	350	285	200	150	100

Model 738P

Same as above, with stainless steel finish.

NIB	Exc.	V.G.	Good	Fair	Poor
525	350	285	200	150	100

Model 45/745 Pin Gun

This model uses a .44 Magnum frame, with 5" barrel and two-stage compensator. Choice of ventilated or ventilated heavy rib shroud. Chambered for .45 ACP, with/without half moon clips. Finish blued or stainless steel. Weight 54 oz. **NOTE:** Add 10 percent for stainless steel finish.

Ventilated Rib Shroud

NIB	Exc.	V.G.	Good	Fair	Poor
1100	950	750	600	450	300

Ventilated Heavy Rib Shroud

NIB	Exc.	V.G.	Good	Fair	Poor
1100	950	750	600	450	300

Model 14/714 Fixed Barrel Service

Same features as .357 Magnum Model 14, without interchangeable barrels. Barrel length 2.5" or 4", with fixed sights. Offered in blued or stainless steel. Weight with barrels: 2.5"—30 oz.; 4"—34 oz. **NOTE:** Add 10 percent for stainless steel finish.

NIB	Exc.	V.G.	Good	Fair	Poor
275	235	150	125	100	75

Model 15/715 Fixed Barrel Target

Same as .357 Magnum Model 15, with target sights and grips. Fixed barrel lengths 3" or 5". Available in blued or stainless steel. Weight with barrels: 3"—37 oz.; 5"—42 oz. **NOTE:** Add 10 percent for stainless steel finish.

NIB	Exc.	V.G.	Good	Fair	Poor
300	250	160	125	100	75

WESTERN ARMS

See—Bacon Arms Co.

WESTERN ARMS CORPORATION

See—Ithaca Gun Co.

WESTERN FIELD
Montgomery Ward

"Western Field" is the trade name used by Montgomery Ward & Company on arms that they retail. See Firearms Trade Names list at the end of this book.

WESTLEY RICHARDS & CO., LTD.
Birmingham, England

A wide variety of firearms have been produced by this company since its founding. Presently, it produces boxlock and sidelock double-barrel shotguns of both side-by-side and over/under form, bolt-action rifles and double-barrel rifles. Prospective purchasers are advised to secure individual appraisals prior to acquisition.

B Model SxS Boxlock, Pre-WWII

NOTE: Add 50 percent for 20-gauge; 80 percent for 28-gauge.

NIB	Exc.	V.G.	Good	Fair	Poor
5000	4250	3500	2800	—	—

Best Quality Sidelock, Current Model

Deluxe Sidelock

NIB	Exc.	V.G.	Good	Fair	Poor
30000	26500	22500	17500	—	—

Magazine Rifle

NIB	Exc.	V.G.	Good	Fair	Poor
12500	10000	8500	7250	—	—

Boxlock Double Rifle

NIB	Exc.	V.G.	Good	Fair	Poor
39000	33000	26500	22000	—	—

Best Quality Over/Under Shotgun, Current Model

NIB	Exc.	V.G.	Good	Fair	Poor
55000	47500	40000	32000	—	—

WHITE, ROLLIN
Lowell, Massachusetts

Pocket Pistol

A .32 or .38 rimfire spur trigger single-shot pistol, with 3" or 5" octagonal barrel. Brass or iron frames, with walnut grips. The .38-caliber version with 5" barrel was not produced in large quantities, therefore worth approximately 25 percent more than values listed. Barrels marked "Rollin White Arms Co., Lowell, Mass.".

NIB	Exc.	V.G.	Good	Fair	Poor
—	—	900	750	350	150

Pocket Revolver

A .22-caliber spur trigger revolver, with 3.25" octagonal barrel and 7-shot cylinder. Brass frame silver-plated, barrel blued and grips of walnut. Revolver marked in a variety of ways including: "Rollin White Arms Co., Lowell, Mass."; "Lowell Arms Co., Lowell, Mass."; or "Made for Smith & Wesson by Rollin White Arms Co., Lowell, Mass.". Approximately 10,000 made during late 1860s.

NIB	Exc.	V.G.	Good	Fair	Poor
—	—	775	600	250	75

WHITNEY ARMS COMPANY
ELI WHITNEY, SR./P. & E.W. BLAKE/ELI WHITNEY, JR.

As the United States' first major commercial arms maker, Eli Whitney's New Haven plant, which began production in 1798 and continued under family control for the next 90 years, was one of the more important American arms manufactories of the 19th century. Its products, accordingly, are eminently collectible. Moreover, during its 90 years of operation, Whitney clan produced a number of unusual arms, some exact copies of regulation U.S. martial longarms, others variations and derivatives of U.S. and foreign longarms, a variety of percussion revolvers and finally a variety of single-shot and repeating breechloading rifles in an attempt to capture a portion of the burgeoning market in these cartridge arms during the post-Civil War period. Contrary to the prevailing myth, Eli Whitney Sr., who also invented the cotton gin, did NOT perfect a system of interchangeability of parts in the arms industry. His contributions in this line were more as a propagandist for the concept that was brought to fruition by others, notably Simeon North and John Hall.

Eli Whitney, Sr. Armory Muskets, 1798-1824. 1798 U.S. Contract Muskets, Types I-IV

On January 14, 1798, Eli Whitney Sr., having convinced the U.S. War Department that he could mass-produce interchangeable musket parts, was awarded a contract for 10,000 muskets following the "Charlesville" (French M1766) pattern, then also being copied at the newly opened Springfield Armory and most of the U.S. musket contractors. Whitney's 1798 contract muskets measure between 58.875" and 57.75" in overall length, with longer arms delivered earlier. The .69-caliber smoothbore barrels measure approximately 44", though most are shy of that length by anywhere from .0625" to a maximum of 1.25". Lockplates are flat with a beveled edge and marked "U.STATES" in a curve on the pointed tail, with a perched eagle with down folded wings over "NEW HAVEN" forward of the cock. Four differences in material and manner of attachment of the pan distinguish subtypes: first delivery of 500 muskets in September, 1801 had an integral faceted iron pan (Type I); second delivery of 500 muskets in June, 1802 also had faceted iron pans, but were detachable (Type II); 1,000 muskets delivered in September, 1802 and March, 1803 had faceted detachable pans, but these were made of brass instead of iron (Type III); final 8,000 muskets delivered between 1803 and 1809, had detachable brass pans with a rounded bottom that Whitney copied from French M1777 musket (Type IV) and a rounded cock,

also copied from French M1777 musket. Generally speaking, due to the limited production of Types I - III, they should command a higher price; prices are given for the more common Type IV 1798 contract musket. It should be noted however, that about 1804 Whitney delivered 112 Type IV muskets to Connecticut's "1st Company of Governor's Foot Guards". Although similar to Type IV musket, these 112 arms are distinguished by the absence of "U.STATES" on the tail of the lock and addition of the name "CONNECTICUT" to left sideplate. Such an arm should demand a considerable premium over usual Type IV musket.

NIB	Exc.	V.G.	Good	Fair	Poor
—	—	7500	4500	2000	500

Whitney Connecticut, New York, and U.S. 1812 Contract Muskets

In 1808, Whitney received a contract from the state of New York for 2,000 muskets. In 1810, he received a second contract from the same source for an additional 2,000 muskets, all of which were eventually delivered by mid-1813. In the interim, in 1809, state of Connecticut contracted with Whitney to deliver 700 muskets per year over the next three years. With the outbreak of the War of 1812, in July, 1812, a contract was let to Eli Whitney for 15,000 muskets (later extended by another 3,000 muskets), conforming to the pattern he had made for the state of New York, but with 42" long barrels. All of these contract muskets shared most of the same features. Overall length was 58". The .69-caliber smoothbore barrel was nominally 42", though the two state contracts did not rigidly enforce that dimension. Lockplate of these muskets bore inscription "NEW HAVEN" within a curving scroll forward of the cock. Like Type III 1798 U.S. contract muskets, lockplates incorporated a detachable round-bottomed brass pan and a round faced cock. Stock was distinguished by having a low, virtually nonexistent comb similar to that of 1816 musket pattern. New York state contract muskets are distinguished by having the state ownership mark "SNY" on axis of barrel near the breech. (It should be noted that first 1,000 muskets delivered under U.S. 1812 contract were also delivered to New York, but these have the mark across the breech at right angles to axis of the barrel). Connecticut contract muskets are distinguishable by having state-ownership mark "S.C." (for "state of Connecticut" on barrel and top of the comb of the stock). On Connecticut muskets in better condition, Connecticut coat of arms (a shield with three clusters of grape vines) should also be visible struck into the wood on left side of the musket opposite the lock. Verifiable Connecticut and New York contract muskets should bring a premium over U.S. contract muskets.

NIB	Exc.	V.G.	Good	Fair	Poor
—	—	6000	3250	1500	500

Whitney (and P. & E.W. Blake) U.S. M1816/1822 Contract Muskets

U.S. M1816/1822 muskets manufactured at Whitney's Armory were identical to those produced at U.S. Armories at Springfield and Harpers Ferry. Overall length was 57.75". The 42" long, .69-caliber smoothbore barrels were finished with a browning solution until 1831; after that date metal was left in polished "bright". Stock and lock reflect Whitney's earlier attempts to impart his design elements into the U.S. patterns. Stock had low comb of his M1812 musket and lock incorporated rounded cock and round bottomed brass pan that he had championed from French M1777 musket. Lock markings varied during the period that this arm was produced, though all were marked on the pointed tail with a vertical stamp: "NEW HAVEN" arced around date (1825-1830), or in three vertical lines: "NEW / HAVEN / (date: 1831-1842)". Those made between 1825 and 1830, under direct supervision of Whitney's nephews, bore two line mark "U.S. / P. & E.W. BLAKE" forward of cock; those made from 1830 to 1837 bear "U.S" over "E. WHITNEY" with a crossed arrow and olive branch between; after 1837, crossed arrow and olive branch motif was eliminated in favor of the simple two lines. In addition to Whitney Armory's federal contracts, Whitney executed at least one contract with the state of South Carolina in mid-1830s for an estimated 800 to 2,000 muskets. Basically identical in configuration to federal contract muskets, South Carolina muskets were distinguished by the substitution of "S.C." for "U.S." over "E. WHITNEY" stamp on the lockplate. They also bear state ownership mark "So. CAROLINA" on top of the barrel. Due to their relative rarity and Confederate usage (especially if altered to percussion by means of a brazed bolster), South Carolina contract arms should bring a considerable premium.

NIB	Exc.	V.G.	Good	Fair	Poor
—	—	6500	3500	1500	500

Whitney Armory U.S. M1816/M1822 Muskets, Flintlock or Altered to Percussion and Adapted with "Sea Fencible" Heavy Buttplates

A number of Whitney U.S. M1816/M1822 muskets were delivered to Commonwealth of Massachusetts under terms of the 1808 Militia Act. Many of these were subsequently altered to percussion at Watertown Arsenal near Boston for the state after 1850. At some time in their career, both flintlock arms and those that had been altered to percussion were adapted to a heavy brass buttplate, with a peculiar knob at its heel. In the process, buttstock was usually narrowed to conform to width of the new buttplate, because many of the muskets encountered with this buttplate bore the inspection mark of Samuel Fuller ("SF/V" within a lozenge), these arms were initially considered to have been made for the Massachusetts "Sea Fencible" organizations formed during and after the War of 1812. That appellation, however, has been dismissed, although the exact purpose of the new buttplate and date of its application are not known. These buttplates are usually (but not necessarily) found on Whitney contract muskets and invariably are marked with Massachusetts state ownership mark "MS" on the barrel as well as rack numbers on tang of the buttplate itself. Despite the unknown purpose of these arms, they command a considerable premium over standard flintlock or altered to percussion Whitney muskets.

NIB	Exc.	V.G.	Good	Fair	Poor
—	—	6500	3500	1250	400

Whitney Armory U.S. M1816/M1822 Muskets, Altered to Percussion

From 1850 through 1856, many of the contract muskets in store at U.S. arsenals were altered from flintlock to percussion by means of "Belgian" or "cone-in barrel" method. System of alteration involved removal of flintlock battery from the lock, filling in the screw holes from those parts, substituting a percussion hammer for the cock, plugging the vent, removing the breech plug so as to "upset" the upper right-hand side top of barrel, drilling and threading the "upset" section for a cone, reinserting breech plug and screwing in a new percussion cone. The percussioned musket was effective, but the barrel was considerably weakened by this process. While some were rifled during the American Civil War, most saw service in that conflict as smoothbores. As a general rule, muskets so altered generally command about one-third the price of the arm in original flintlock. Exceptions are those with state ownership marks (eg. "OHIO" in the stock), with regimental marks, or with so-called "Sea Fencible" buttplate.

Whitney Armory Muskets, 1825-1842

Eli Whitney died in 1825. Although he had a son destined to take over the family business, Eli Whitney Jr. was only 5 years old when his father passed away and could not assume legal possession until he turned 21 in 1842. In the interim, company was administered by senior Whitney's trustees, Henry Edwards and James Goodrich, while the plant itself was run by Whitney's nephews, Philo and Eli Whitney Blake. During their control of the factory, three contracts were fulfilled for the U.S. government: one awarded in August, 1822 for 15,000 muskets (delivered between 1826 and 1830); second awarded in March, 1830 for 8,750 muskets (delivered between 1831 and 1836); final contract in January, 1840 for 3,000 muskets (delivered between 1840 and 1842). An additional 6,750 were delivered under annual allotments granted by the War Department between 1835 and 1839, over and above contracts for distribution to states under the 1808 Militia Act. Although the 1840 contract had originally called for U.S. M1840 muskets, in April of that year, the contract was altered so that Whitney's plant could continue to deliver what it had delivered consistently from 1824, the U.S. M1816/1822 flintlock musket.

Eli Whitney, Jr. Armory Rifles and Rifle-Muskets, 1842-1865

Upon reaching the age of 21 in 1842, Eli Whitney Jr. assumed command of his late father's gun making empire. Although he realized that the armory required updating to meet improved tolerances adopted by the U.S. War Department, he also realized that a profit might be made in turning out arms of lesser standards for independent sale to militia or the states. As a result, younger Whitney's product line included not only several of the regulation U.S. longarms, but also a number of "good and serviceable" militia arms, including:

Whitney U.S. M1841 Contract Rifle (unaltered)

Between 1842 and 1855, Eli Whitney Jr. received five contracts from the U.S. War Department to manufacture newly adopted U.S. M1841 percussion rifle: 7,500 in October, 1842 (delivered between 1844 and 1847); 7,500 in March, 1848, subsequently extended to 10,000 in January, 1849 (delivered between 1849 and 1853) 5,000 (previously contracted for by Edward K. Tryon) in October, 1848 (delivered contiguous with 1848 contract for 10,000); 5,000 in 1853 (delivered between 1853 and 1855); and 100 in 1855 (delivered that year). All except the final 1,100 delivered in 1855 conformed to the model made at Harpers Ferry, and of those 1,100, the only difference of 500 of them was the ramrod. This rifle was 49" in length overall, having a 33" long browned barrel, with .54-caliber rifled (7-groove) bore. Barrel bears stamp of inspection at the breech, usually "U S /(inspectors' initials) / P", while the left flat (after mid-1848 for Whitney rifles) should also bear stamping "STEEL" to indicate the barrel had been rolled from "cast steel". Furniture is brass, buttplate bearing stamped letters "U S". Lockplate is flat with a beveled edge and bears horizontal two line inscription "E. WHITNEY" / "U S" forward of the hammer and vertical two line inscription "N. HAVEN" / (date) on the tail. (Date also appears on breech plug tang). As originally made, M1841 rifle was not adapted for a bayonet, though several modifications were made to the rifle between 1855 and 1862 to affect that adaptation.

NIB	Exc.	V.G.	Good	Fair	Poor
—	—	7500	4750	1750	500

Whitney U.S. M1841/1855 Contract Rifle, Adapted to Saber Bayonet and Long Range Sights

Before the final 600 rifles (of 2,600 made in 1855) left the factory, U.S. War Department contracted with Whitney to bring them up to the standards of modified U.S. M1841 rifle then being produced or adapted at Harpers Ferry Armory. Adaptation was two fold. First, a long range rear "ladder" style rear sight having a 2..25" base was soldered to top of the barrel; then a .5" long bayonet lug with 1" guide was brazed to right side of the barrel, 2.5" from muzzle. To permit disassembly, old front band was removed and replaced with a shortened version. A new ramrod (also applied to 500 rifles without this adaptation) having an integral iron head cupped for newly adopted "Minie ball" replaced flat brass headed ramrod to complete the process; rifle remained in .54-caliber with 7-grooves. Neither was the front sight modified. Bayonets were furnished by Ames Manufacturing Company on a separate contract. Rifles so adapted at Whitney Armory are among the rarer variants of U.S. M1841 line and prices reflect that rarity.

NIB	Exc.	V.G.	Good	Fair	Poor
—	—	7500	4750	1750	650

Whitney U.S. M1841 Contract Rifles, Adapted to Saber Bayonets and Long Range Rear Sights (Colt 1862 Adaptation)

A large number of unaltered U.S. M1841 rifles remained on hand in U.S. Arsenals when the Civil War broke out. Primarily those of Whitney's and Robbins & Lawrence's manufacture. To upgrade these rifles, revolver maker, Samuel Colt arranged to purchase 10,500 and adapt them to bayonets and long-range sights. Sight that he affixed consisted of two leaf rear sight he had been using on his revolving rifles, with one leaf

flopping forward and one flopping backward from the 100 yard block. Saber bayonet lug he attached consisted of a blued clamping ring with integral .5" long lug attached that could fasten to barrel so the lug projected from the right side. These lugs were numbered both to bayonet and rifle's barrel, the number appearing on lower surface of barrel just behind the location of clamping ring. Colt also bored the rifles up to .58-caliber, leaving some with 7-grooves but re-rifling others with 3 wide grooves. An estimated half of the 10,200 rifles so modified by Colt were of Whitney's earlier production. Due to the Colt association, rifles so modified usually command slightly higher prices than other Civil War adaptations for saber or socket bayonets.

NIB	Exc.	V.G.	Good	Fair	Poor
—	—	7500	4750	1750	650

Whitney South Carolina Contract M1841 Rifle

To meet perceived needs of South Carolina, during anti-slavery debates following Mexican War Annexation, Whitney produced a variant of U.S. M1841 rifle for that state, delivering only 274 in 1849. Markings of this rifle differed only in having letters "S C" on the plate beneath "E. WHITNEY" stamp. Because South Carolina had previously contracted for 1,000 variant M1841 rifles from William Glaze & Co. in 1853 which accepted a socket bayonet, Whitney provided 274, 1849 dated rifles with that provision also, although the lug was located under the barrel instead of atop it. Because the socket bayonet dominated the forward 3" of the barrel, front sight was relocated to top of upper strap of the front band. Rifles from this contract are exceedingly rare.

NIB	Exc.	V.G.	Good	Fair	Poor
—	—	10000	6500	3250	950

Whitney "Good & Serviceable" M1841 Derivatives

From parts or entire rifles rejected from his federal contracts for U.S. M1841 rifles, between 1848 and 1860, Eli Whitney Jr. assembled a number of rifles similar in overall characteristics to federal contract rifles, but differing both in quantity and number of minor details. At least four variations were produced between 1855 and 1862 and sold to various states or independent militia companies. Distinguishing characteristics of these four are:

Type I: M1841 rifle adapted to saber bayonet, but not to long range sights. A .5" long saber bayonet lug (with/without 1" guide) brazed to right side of the barrel; long front band replaced with short double strapped band left over from 1855 contract. Some of this type (without 1" guide) are known with "OHIO" state ownership marks and are thought to be from among 420 purchased by the state in 1861 from Schuyler, Hartley & Graham. Examples are known with lockplate dated 1855, without any date or "US" stamp below "E. WHITNEY".

Type II: M1841 rifle adapted to saber bayonet and Sharps long range sight. These rifles also bear .5" brazed saber bayonet lug (with 1" guide) and short front band, but they also have Sharps M1853 "ladder" rear sight added in lieu of standard notched iron block. Moreover, rifles in this configuration lack the brass patchbox lid and its underlying cavity for implements and greased patches.

Type III: M1841 rifle adapted to socket bayonet and Sharps long range sight. These late-production (1859-1860) derivatives of M1841 rifle are adapted to Sharps long-range sight used on Type II rifles but have a patchbox. Unlike standard production, however, it is covered with an iron lid and hinge. Trigger guard strap is also iron. Lock plates delete both date from tail and "US" under "E. WHITNEY". An iron stud is added below barrel near muzzle for a socket bayonet, necessitating relocation of brass blade front sight to upper strap of the forward band. Probably fewer than 100 of this configuration were made, making it the most desirable of derivative M1841 rifles.

Type IV: M1841 rifle unadapted using modified parts. Rifles of this configuration use same markings as Type III rifles, but delete entirely the patchbox and its lid (like Type II rifles). Trigger guard strap is iron and lock screws seem to be the same as Whitney used for his Whitney short Enfield derivative rifles. It is suspected that these rifles were purchased from New York dealers and sold to Georgia during the secession crisis of 1860-1861, thereby enhancing their collector's value, though in general Whitney M1841 derivative rifles are equal in pricing:

NIB	Exc.	V.G.	Good	Fair	Poor
—	—	6500	3250	1250	500

Whitney M1842 Rifled Musket Derivative

Using rejected U.S. M1842 barrels sold at auction by Springfield Armory, Whitney assembled approximately 2,000 .69-caliber rifled muskets that he exchanged with the state of New Hampshire in 1858 for a number of old flintlock muskets owned by that state. These rifled muskets exhibit a number of anomalies from U.S. M1842 musket, although overall length (57.75") and barrel length (42") remain the same as that musket, the bores are rifles with 7 narrow grooves. In addition to dates and inspection marks placed at Springfield, usually bear state ownership mark "NEW HAMPSHIRE" on top of barrel. In finishing these rifled muskets, Whitney utilized a number of parts from other gun makers, including Sharps M1853 "ladder" style carbine rear sights, bands from Robbins & Lawrence P1853 Enfield rifle-musket contract and internal lock parts remaining from his M1841 rifles. Parts that are unique to these arms include iron nosecap and flat lockplate. Lockplates are unmarked, but barrels usually show a letter/number code common to Whitney's production during this period. Despite a production of approximately 2,000 muskets, survival rate for this type of arm is quite low.

NIB	Exc.	V.G.	Good	Fair	Poor
—	—	6500	3250	1250	400

Whitney P1853 "Long Enfield" Rifle-Musket Derivative

Having secured a number of bands and other furniture from Robbins & Lawrence contract for P1853 Enfield rifle-muskets, about 1859 Whitney developed a derivative of that arm that combined those bands with a 40" barrel in .58-caliber and rifled with 7-grooves that basically resembled the configuration of U.S. M1855 rifle-musket, a copy of which Whitney was also making. The 56" long rifle-musket that resulted was sold to state militia companies and two states: Maryland purchasing 2,000; and Georgia contracting for 1,700 (of which 1,225 were delivered). Although several components of furniture were from Robbins & Lawrence contract, nosecap was pewter (Enfield style), iron buttplate and brass trigger guard (bow/iron strap) were of a style peculiar to Whitney' Enfield series. Rear sight resembled ladder pattern of U.S. M1855 rifle-musket. Unique flat and unbeveled lockplate simply bears one line stamp "E. WHITNEY" forward of the hammer.

NIB	Exc.	V.G.	Good	Fair	Poor
—	—	6500	3250	1250	600

Whitney P1853 "Short Enfield" Rifle Derivative

At the same time Whitney developed his "Long Enfield" Rifle-Musket Derivative, he also prepared a short version of it, similar to British P1856 sergeant's rifle. Having an overall length of 49", rifle version had 33" long barrel in .58-caliber and rifled with 7-grooves like the rifle-musket. Furniture was basically same as rifle-musket as well, with a pewter nosecap, iron buttplate and combination brass bow and iron strap trigger guard (although some variants are known with all brass P1853 trigger guards). Two iron bands were from Robbins & Lawrence contract salvage, as were brass lock screw washers. Unique flat and unbeveled lockplate are same style used on "Long Enfield" Rifle-Musket Derivative and is similarly marked "E. WHITNEY" forward of the hammer. In manufacture of this rifle, four variants evolved as follows:

Type I: Buttstock incorporated an oval iron patchbox; front and rear sights were standard U.S. M1841 configuration and no provision was made for a saber bayonet.

Type II: Buttstock continued to incorporate an oval iron patchbox; rear sight was now the long range "ladder" type on a 2.3125" base as used on "Long Enfield" Rifle-Musket Derivative. Front sight was an iron block, with integral blade. A .5" long saber bayonet lug was added to right side of the barrel.

Type III: Oval iron patchbox was deleted from the buttstock. Front and rear sights remain as in Type II, as does bayonet lug.

Type IV. Identical to Type III, with a new single leaf rear sight on a 1.25" long base.

Total production of these rifles is estimated to have been between 800 and 1,000, with approximately half that number going to southern states. Prices should not vary between the four types; however, confirmed Confederate usage will increase the value significantly.

NIB	Exc.	V.G.	Good	Fair	Poor
—	—	8500	4250	2000	600

Whitney M1855 Rifle Derivative

At the same time Whitney advertised his Enfield derivative series of rifle-muskets and rifles, he also indicated the availability of a short rifle with saber bayonet. This rifle combined rejected barrels (made at Harpers Ferry in 1858 for U.S. M1855 rifles), with rejected unmilled Maynard tape primer lockplates that had been shaved of their top "hump", marked forward of hammer with single line stamp, "E. WHITNEY". Buttplate and trigger guard also conform to U.S. M1855 rifle, but bands are brass remaining from Whitney's M1841/1855 rifle contract. Early in production, these rifles used round brass lock screw washers following M1855 pattern; later production used winged brass lock screw washers that Whitney inherited from Robbins & Lawrence P1853 rifle-musket contract, which he used on his Enfield series derivatives. At least two patterns of saber bayonet were used on this rifle.

NIB	Exc.	V.G.	Good	Fair	Poor
—	—	7000	3500	1250	500

Whitney M1855 Rifle-Musket Derivative

In 1861, Whitney accepted a U.S. contract to produce 40,000 U.S. "M1855" rifle-muskets. What Whitney had in mind under this contract and what the War Department demanded were two different arms. Whitney's product was similar to U.S. M1855 rifle-musket, but differed in a number of respects. The 40" barrel was .58-caliber, but rifled with 7- rather than 3-grooves and adapted to English P1853 socket bayonet he had been using on his Enfield derivative rifle-muskets. Initial rear sight, while similar to U.S. M1855 type, was slightly shorter having a 2.3125" base. (On later production, Whitney substituted a shorter 1.25" long base, with a single pierced leaf sight). Nosecap was made of pewter and followed Enfield pattern rather than being malleable iron of U.S. M1855 pattern. On later production, Whitney also substituted brass winged lock screw washers from his Enfield derivative series. Lockplates for these arms were drawn from complete Maynard locks made at the federal armories in 1858 and 1859, but later rejected for flaws. Upon these plates Whitney stamped "E. WHITNEY / N. HAVEN", as on his early Connecticut contract M1861 derivative rifle-muskets. Except for the letter/number code, the barrels are unmarked. Examples are known whose stocks bear indications of issue to 8th Connecticut Infantry during the Civil War, suggesting Whitney may have sold the few made to Connecticut under his first state contract. Arms with these regimental marks should command a premium over unmarked arms.

NIB	Exc.	V.G.	Good	Fair	Poor
—	—	7000	3500	1250	500

Whitney M1861 Connecticut Contract Rifle-Musket Derivative

In 1861 and 1862, Eli Whitney Jr. entered into two contracts with his home state of Connecticut for respectively 6,000 and 8,000 rifle-muskets, generally conforming to U.S. M1861 rifle-musket. A number of exceptions to U.S. model, however, were permitted. On the first contract, 40" barrels were in .58-caliber, but were made with 7-groove rifling instead of 3-groove; on the second contract, arms were made with 3-groove rifling. Nosecaps for both contracts were of U.S. M1855/1861 pattern, but were cast in pewter instead of malleable iron. An exception was also permitted in the rear sights, which initially were same 1.25" long base with pierced single leaf that Whitney had used on his Type IV short Enfield derivative rifles, though later the base was changed to conform to the pattern adopted for U.S. M1861 rifle-musket, but still retaining the single leaf. Lockplates were M1861-style marked forward of the hammer "E. WHITNEY / N. HAVEN" on early production and with an eagle surmounting a panoply of flags and trophies over "WHITNEYVILLE" on later production. Barrels bore typical Whitney letter/number code and were adapted to Enfield pattern socket bayonets rather than U.S. M1855 socket bayonets. Later production occasionally bears inspection letters "G.W.Q.".

NIB	Exc.	V.G.	Good	Fair	Poor
—	—	6000	2750	1150	400

Whitney "High Humpback" Lockplate M1861 Rifle-Musket Derivative

With the completion of his Connecticut contracts, Whitney combined excess parts from its production with some of the unmilled and unshaved lockplates that he still had on hand from his M1855 Rifle Derivatives. The 56" long rifle-muskets that resulted have 40" barrels in .58-caliber, with 3-groove rifling and a rear sight that conforms to U.S. M1861 pattern that Whitney began making in 1863. Flat beveled unmilled lockplates bear two line stamp "E. WHITNEY / N. HAVEN" that Whitney had used on his M1855 rifle-musket derivative and on early M1861 Connecticut contract rifle-muskets, but showing considerable wear, to the extent that the second line is often incomplete or missing entirely. Photograph evidence indicates that the 21st Connecticut Infantry received some of these rifle-muskets. They are often mistaken as a southern purchase, which artificially raises the asking prices.

NIB	Exc.	V.G.	Good	Fair	Poor
—	—	7000	3250	1250	500

Whitney "Manton" M1861 Rifle-Musket Derivative

In order to dispose of some of his inferior arms from the second Connecticut state contract, Whitney assembled at least 1,300 bearing a fictitious Old English lock stamp "Manton" forward of hammer and date "1862" on its tail. In most respects, this arm resembled U.S. M1861 rifle-musket complete with 3-groove rifling in .58-caliber 40" barrel with typical Whitney letter/number code near the muzzle (often marked "G.W.Q." on its left flat). Nosecaps, in typical Whitney style, were cast from pewter instead of being formed from malleable iron. Rear sight closely follows M1861 pattern, but lacks the step on its side walls since it utilized a simple pierced leaf instead of compound double leaf of M1861 rifle-musket. These arms were disposed of in the New York City market after 1863 Draft Riot and issued to New York National Guard.

NIB	Exc.	V.G.	Good	Fair	Poor
—	—	8250	4250	2000	600

Whitney "Direct Vent" M1861 Rifle-Musket Derivatives

In his continued efforts to dispose of surplus and rejected parts from his Connecticut and federal contracts, Whitney devised in 1863 a rifle-musket generally conforming to M1861 rifle-musket except in two notable features. The bolster, instead of projecting considerably away from the barrel and having a clean-out screw was relatively short and flat faced. Process of making this bolster eliminated one production sequence, since it was not possible to drill the hole for the cone directly to the barrel. To accommodate the new cone position, lockplates were made flat without the bevel and inletted flush with the stock. Lockplates bear eagle surmounting the panoply of flags and trophies over "WHITNEYVILLE" stamp forward of hammer and are known with "1863" on the tail or without any date. Rear sight same as used on "Manton" rifle-musket derivative. Arms with barrels than 40", 39" and 30" exist, all in .58-caliber with 3-groove rifling; however, shortest of these may be post-war modifications for cadet use. Quantities made are not known, but surviving examples suggest limited production, probably to use faulty parts from 1863 federal contract.

NIB	Exc.	V.G.	Good	Fair	Poor
—	—	7000	3250	1250	400

Whitney U.S. M1861 Contract Rifle-Musket

In October 1863, Whitney secured a contract with U.S. War Department to produce 15,000 U.S. M1861 rifle-muskets. Arms manufactured under this contract conform in all respects to Springfield Model adopted in 1861. The 40" barrel in .58-caliber and rifled with 3-grooves; rear sight conforms to two-leaf model with stepped side walls. Nosecap is M1861 style and made of malleable iron. Socket bayonets furnished with them conform to U.S. M1855/M1861 pattern. Marks include "US" on buttplate and standard inspection marks on barrel and stock. Lockplate marked with eagle surmounting letters "US" forward of hammer and "WHITNEYVILLE" on forward projection of plate; date, "1863" or "1864" stamped on tail of plate.

NIB	Exc.	V.G.	Good	Fair	Poor
—	—	7000	3250	1250	400

Whitney U.S. Navy Contract Rifle

In July 1861, Whitney entered a contact with U.S. Navy to produce 10,000 rifles of "Plymouth Pattern". So called after U.S. Navy warship, whereupon the first Harpers Ferry trial rifles had been developed. New Navy rifle borrowed many of its characteristics from French M1846 "carbine a tige". Overall length 50" with 34" long barrel bearing a saber bayonet lug, with guide extending nearly to the muzzle on its right side. Bore was .69-caliber, rifled with 3 broad lands and grooves. Rear sight copied French M1846 and M1859 styles, i.e. it has an elevating ladder but no sidewalls. On early production, sights are serially numbered to rifle's serial number (appearing on breech plug tang). Barrels bear standard U.S. inspection marks on left quarter flat and production date ("1863" or "1864") on top of barrel near the breech. Two lock markings have been encountered. Earlier production uses flat beveled plate marked with date "1863" on its tail and an eagle surmounting a panoply of flags and trophies over name "WHITNEYVILLE". In later (after serial no. 3,000) lock's tail is marked "1864" and stamping forward of hammer matches that on U.S. M1861 Whitney contract rifle-muskets, i.e. a small eagle over "U S" and "WHITNEYVILLE" in forward projection of the plate. Inspector's initials (F.C.W.) appear on barrel and in a cartouche on the stock.

NIB	Exc.	V.G.	Good	Fair	Poor
—	—	8250	4250	1750	600

The Whitney Arms Company, 1865-1888

With closing of the American Civil War, Eli Whitney Jr. again turned his eyes to manufacture inexpensive arms from parts remaining on hand from his Civil War contracts. Extra barrels were turned into inexpensive muzzle-loading shotguns and a few breech-loading designs were toyed with. Following Remington's example, Whitney soon realized that a substantial profit could be made in the production of single-shot martial arms for foreign governments. The result was a series of breech-loading arms that copied many salient features of the Remington line, including a direct copy, after the expiration of Remington's patent, for "rolling block" mechanism. Not until late 1870s, did Whitney acquire the rights to several patents that led to the production of a lever-action repeating rifle. During the post-war period revolver production, which had begun with evasions of Colt's patents a decade prior to the Civil War, mushroomed with production of small spur-trigger rimfire cartridge revolvers. Despite the variety of arms produced, by 1883 Whitney was considering the sale of his company. Business reverses over the next five years necessitated the sale to Winchester in 1888. Primarily interested in securing patent rights for Whitney's lever-action series of rifles, Winchester closed the plant and moved its machinery to New Haven. After 90 years of production, Whitneyville Armory ceased to exist.

Single Barreled Percussion Shotgun

Firearm manufactured by Whitney out of surplus .58-caliber rifle barrels that were opened up and converted to smoothbore .60-caliber shotgun barrels. Offered in lengths 28" to 36" and marked "Whitney Arms Co., Whitneyville, Conn. Homogeneous Wrought Steel". Finish blued, with varnished walnut stocks that are crudely checkered. Approximately 2,000 manufactured between 1866 and 1869. These guns are rarely encountered on today's market.

NIB	Exc.	V.G.	Good	Fair	Poor
—	—	1300	950	400	150

Double-Barreled Percussion Shotgun

Specifications for this version are similar to single-barrel, except there are two side-by-side barrels with double locks, hammers and double triggers. They are slightly more common than single-barreled version.

NIB	Exc.	V.G.	Good	Fair	Poor
—	—	1300	950	400	150

Swing-Breech Carbine

Single-shot breech-loading carbine chambered for .46-caliber rimfire cartridge. Has 22" round barrel, with button-released breech-block that swings to the side for loading. Finish blued, with walnut stock. Fewer than 50 manufactured in 1866.

NIB	Exc.	V.G.	Good	Fair	Poor
—	—	6000	3250	1750	600

Whitney-Cochran Carbine

Single-shot breech-loading carbine chambered for .44 rimfire cartridge. Has 28" round barrel, with lever-activated breech-block that raises upward for loading. Manufactured under license from J.W. Cochran. Finish blued, with walnut stock. There is a saddle ring on left side of the frame. Marked "Whitney Arms Co. - Whitneyville, Conn.". Produced for 1867 Government Carbine Trials. Fewer than 50 manufactured in 1866 and 1867.

Courtesy Milwaukee Public Museum, Milwaukee, Wisconsin

NIB	Exc.	V.G.	Good	Fair	Poor
—	—	7000	3500	1500	600

Excelsior

Single-shot rifle chambered for .38, .44 or .50 rimfire cartridges. Found with various length octagonal or round barrels. Finish blued, with walnut stock. Forearm held on by one barrel band. Breech-block pivots downward for loading. There is a center-mounted hammer. Marked "Whitney Arms Co. Whitneyville Conn.". Shorter barreled carbine versions have a saddle ring on the frame. Approximately 200 manufactured between 1866 and 1870.

NIB	Exc.	V.G.	Good	Fair	Poor
—	—	6700	2750	1150	400

Whitney-Howard Lever Action (Thunderbolt)

Single-shot breech-loader chambered for .44 rimfire cartridge. Also been noted as a shotgun chambered for 20-gauge smoothbore, with barrels from 30" to 40" in length. Rifle version barrel lengths from 22" to 28". Breech-block opened by means of a combination lever and trigger guard. Also a carbine version with barrel lengths of 18.5" and 19". Approximately 2,000 manufactured totally between 1866 and 1870.

Shotgun

Courtesy Buffalo Bill Historical Center, Cody, Wyoming

NIB	Exc.	V.G.	Good	Fair	Poor
—	—	1400	650	300	100

Rifle

Courtesy Milwaukee Public Museum, Milwaukee, Wisconsin

NIB	Exc.	V.G.	Good	Fair	Poor
—	—	1600	900	450	150

Carbine

Courtesy Milwaukee Public Museum, Milwaukee, Wisconsin

NIB	Exc.	V.G.	Good	Fair	Poor
—	—	2000	1250	500	200

Whitney Phoenix

Little is known about the origin of this model. Built on a patent issued to Whitney in 1874. There are a number of variations that are all marked "Phoenix, Patent May 24, 74". Whitney name is not marked on any of the versions. They are all single-shot breech-loaders, with breech-block that lifts to the right side and upward for loading. Barrels are all blued, with case colored or blued receivers and walnut stocks. Approximately 25,000 manufactured totally between 1867 and 1881. Models and values listed.

Courtesy Milwaukee Public Museum, Milwaukee, Wisconsin

Gallery Rifle

Chambered for .22 rimfire caliber. Has 24" half-octagonal barrel. Production quite limited.

NIB	Exc.	V.G.	Good	Fair	Poor
—	—	3250	1500	600	200

Shotgun

Smoothbore version chambered for 10-, 12-, 14-, 16- or 22-gauge. Barrels between 26" and 32" in length. Approximately 5,000 manufactured.

NIB	Exc.	V.G.	Good	Fair	Poor
—	—	1100	600	250	100

Military Rifle

Chambered for .433-, .45- or .50-caliber centerfire cartridges. Has 35" round barrel, with full-length two-piece walnut stock held on by three barrel bands. Approximately 15,000 manufactured. Many were sent to Central or South America.

NIB	Exc.	V.G.	Good	Fair	Poor
—	—	5750	3000	1250	400

Schuetzen Rifle

Target-shooting version chambered for .38, .40 or .44 centerfire cartridges. Has 30" or 32" octagonal barrel, with Schuetzen-type walnut stock; forearm features hand checkering; nickel-plated Swiss-style buttplate; adjustable sights, with a spirit level. Model noted with double-set triggers. Few were manufactured.

NIB	Exc.	V.G.	Good	Fair	Poor
—	—	6000	3250	1250	400

Civilian Carbine

Chambered for .44-caliber centerfire. Has 24" round barrel; finish blued, with case colored frame; walnut stock; forearm held on by one barrel band. Military-type sights, buttplate and saddle ring mounted on the frame. Approximately 500 manufactured.

Courtesy Milwaukee Public Museum, Milwaukee, Wisconsin

NIB	Exc.	V.G.	Good	Fair	Poor
—	—	4800	2500	850	400

Military Carbine

Chambered for .433, .45 or .50 centerfire cartridges. Has 20.5" round barrel. Manufactured for Central and South America. Very rarely encountered on today's market.

Courtesy Milwaukee Public Museum, Milwaukee, Wisconsin

NIB	Exc.	V.G.	Good	Fair	Poor
—	—	5000	2750	1000	400

Whitney-Laidley Model I Rolling Block

Whitney acquired manufacturing rights for this model from inventors T. Laidley and C.A. Emery, who had received the patent in 1866. Whitney immediately started modifying the action to become competitive with Remington Rolling Block. Approximately 50,000 manufactured totally between 1871 and 1881. There are a number of variations of this model.

Military Carbine

Approximately 5,000 manufactured. Chambered for .433, .45 or .50 centerfire cartridges. Has 20.5" round barrel, with military-type sights. Saddle ring on receiver. Finish blued, with case colored frame and walnut stock. Most of them shipped to Central or South America.

NIB	Exc.	V.G.	Good	Fair	Poor
—	—	3500	1750	700	250

Civilian Carbine

Chambered for .44, .46 rimfire or .44 centerfire. Has 18.5" or 19.5" barrel. Blued, with case colored frame. Stock is walnut. Nickel-plated version also available. Approximately 1,000 manufactured.

NIB	Exc.	V.G.	Good	Fair	Poor
—	—	2800	1750	700	250

Military Rifle

Chambered the same as Military Carbine. Has 32.5" or 35" round barrel, with full-length two-piece stock held on by three barrel bands. Finish blued, with case colored receiver and walnut stock. Approximately 30,000 manufactured. Most of them shipped to Central or South America.

Courtesy Milwaukee Public Museum, Milwaukee, Wisconsin

NIB	Exc.	V.G.	Good	Fair	Poor
—	—	3950	2000	800	300

Gallery Rifle

A .22-caliber sporting-rifle version, with 24" octagonal barrel. Finish similar to Military Rifle. Approximately 500 manufactured.

NIB	Exc.	V.G.	Good	Fair	Poor
—	—	3400	1750	700	250

Sporting Rifle

Chambered for .38, .40, .44, .45 or .50 centerfire, as well as .32, .38 or .44 rimfire. Features barrel lengths from 24" to 30" in round or octagonal configurations. Finish similar to Military Rifle. Approximately 5,000 manufactured.

NIB	Exc.	V.G.	Good	Fair	Poor
—	—	3950	2000	750	300

Creedmoor No. 1 Rifle

Chambered for .44-caliber cartridge. Has 32" or 34" round/octagonal barrel; blued finish, with case colored frame; hand checkered select walnut stock and forearm. Features vernier adjustable sights, with a spirit level. Marked "Whitney Creedmoor". Fewer than 100 manufactured.

NIB	Exc.	V.G.	Good	Fair	Poor
—	—	11500	6250	2750	850

Creedmoor No. 2 Rifle

Similar to No. 1 Rifle, except chambered for .40-caliber cartridge, with 30" or 32" barrel.

NIB	Exc.	V.G.	Good	Fair	Poor
—	—	9500	4250	1750	500

Whitney-Remington Model 2 Rolling Block

When Remington's patent for Rolling Block action expired, Whitney was quick to reproduce the action labeling it his "New Improved System". Essentially quite similar to Remington's Rolling Block and is easily recognized when compared with Model 1 because it has only two parts — hammer and breech-block. Frame is also rounded. Tang on this model marked "Whitney Arms Company, New Haven Ct USA". Approximately 50,000 totally manufactured between 1881 and 1888. There are a number of variations listed.

Shotgun

Smoothbore version chambered for 12-, 14-, 16- or 20-gauge. Barrel lengths between 26" and 30", also 20" have been noted.

NIB	Exc.	V.G.	Good	Fair	Poor
—	—	1300	650	250	100

Military Carbine

Chambered for .433 and .45 centerfire cartridges. Has 20.5" barrel; blued, with case colored receiver; walnut stock. Approximately 5,000 manufactured. Most of them sent to South or Central America.

NIB	Exc.	V.G.	Good	Fair	Poor
—	—	3400	1750	700	300

Civilian Carbine

Chambered for .44 rimfire or centerfire cartridge, with 18.5" round barrel. Finish similar to Military Carbine. Approximately 2,000 manufactured.

NIB	Exc.	V.G.	Good	Fair	Poor
—	—	3100	1600	600	250

Military Rifle

Chambered for .433, .45 or .50 centerfire cartridge. Has 32.5" or 35" barrel. Finish similar to Military Carbine. Approximately 39,000 manufactured.

Courtesy Buffalo Bill Historical Center, Cody, Wyoming

NIB	Exc.	V.G.	Good	Fair	Poor
—	—	3950	2000	750	300

No. 1 Sporting Rifle

Chambered for various popular sporting cartridges. Barrel lengths from 26" to 30" in round/octagonal configuration. Finish blued, with case colored receiver and varnished walnut stock. Many options available that could radically affect value. A qualified appraisal would be advisable. Approximately 3,000 manufactured.

NIB	Exc.	V.G.	Good	Fair	Poor
—	—	4850	2500	1000	400

No. 2 Sporting Rifle

Smaller version of No. 1 Rifle. Chambered for .22 rimfire or .32, .38, .44-40 centerfire cartridges. Again, a qualified appraisal would be helpful as many options can affect value.

NIB	Exc.	V.G.	Good	Fair	Poor
—	—	3400	1750	700	250

Whitney-Burgess-Morse Rifle

Lever-action repeating rifle chambered for .45-70 Government cartridge. There are three variations. All have a magazine tube mounted beneath the barrel. Blued finishes and walnut stocks. Barrels marked "G. W. Morse Patented Oct. 28th 1856". Tang marked "A. Burgess Patented Jan. 7th, 1873, Patented Oct 19th 1873". Approximately 3,000 totally manufactured between 1878 and 1882. Variations are listed.

Sporting Rifle

This version has 28" octagonal/round barrel; magazine tube holds 9 rounds. A number of options available that can increase value drastically. We recommend a competent individual appraisal. Value given is for a standard model.

NIB	Exc.	V.G.	Good	Fair	Poor
—	—	6500	3250	1250	400

Military Rifle

Has 33" round barrel, with full-length forearm held on by two barrel bands; 11-round tubular magazine; bayonet lug and sling swivels. Features military sights. Also found chambered for .43 Spanish and .42 Russian cartridges. Approximately 1,000 manufactured.

NIB	Exc.	V.G.	Good	Fair	Poor
—	—	8000	4250	2000	700

Carbine

Has 22" round barrel, with full-length forearm held on by one barrel band; 7-round tubular magazine; saddle ring attached to the frame. Approximately 500 manufactured.

NIB	Exc.	V.G.	Good	Fair	Poor
—	—	9000	4750	2250	750

Whitney-Kennedy Rifle

Lever-action repeating rifle manufactured in two sizes. Has a magazine tube mounted under barrel; blued finish, with case colored lever; stock is walnut. Barrel marked "Whitney Arms Co New Haven, Conn. U.S.A.". Occasionally the word "Kennedy" is marked after the Whitney name. There are two major variations. One features a standard-type action lever; the other, same "S" shaped lever that is found on Burgess model. This version would be worth approximately 10 percent additional. As with many rifles of this era, there were many options available that will affect values. We strongly recommend securing a qualified appraisal for all, but the standard models, if a transaction is contemplated. Approximately 15,000 manufactured between 1879 and 1886. Variations of Whitney-Kennedy and their values are listed.

Courtesy Buffalo Bill Historical Center, Cody, Wyoming

Small Frame Sporting Rifle

Chambered for .32-20, .38-40 and .40-40 cartridges. Has 24" round/octagonal barrel. Examples will be noted with full-/half-length tubular magazine.

NIB	Exc.	V.G.	Good	Fair	Poor
—	—	5000	2750	1200	500

Large Frame Sporting Rifle

Chambered for .40-60, .45-60, .45-75 and .50-90 cartridges. Barrel lengths 26" or 28". **NOTE:** Add 20 percent for uncommon .50-caliber version.

NIB	Exc.	V.G.	Good	Fair	Poor
—	—	6000	3000	1350	500

Military Rifle

Large-frame model chambered for .40-.60, .44-.40 and .45-60 cartridges. Has 32.25" round barrel; 11- or 16-round tubular magazine; full-length walnut fore-end held on by two barrel bands. Features bayonet lug and sling swivels. Approximately 1,000 manufactured. Most of them shipped to Central or South America.

NIB	Exc.	V.G.	Good	Fair	Poor
—	—	6400	3750	1750	550

Military Carbine

Built on small-/large-frame action. Chambered for .38-40, .44-40, .40-60 or .45-60 cartridges. Has 20" or 22" round barrel; 9- or 12-round tubular magazine, depending on caliber; short fore-end held on by a single barrel band. Approximately 1,000 manufactured. Most of them sent to Central or South America.

Courtesy Buffalo Bill Historical Center, Cody, Wyoming

NIB	Exc.	V.G.	Good	Fair	Poor
—	—	6400	3750	1750	550

Hooded Cylinder Pocket Revolver

An unusual revolver chambered for .28-caliber percussion. Has a manually rotated 6-shot hooded cylinder that has etched decorations. Octagonal barrel in lengths of 3" to 6". A button at the back of frame unlocks cylinder so it can be rotated. Finish blued, with brass frame and two-piece rounded walnut grips. Marked "E. Whitney N. Haven Ct.". Approximately 200 manufactured between 1850 and 1853.

NIB	Exc.	V.G.	Good	Fair	Poor
—	—	5750	3250	1500	600

Two Trigger Pocket Revolver

Conventional-appearing pocket revolver, with a manually rotated cylinder. A second trigger located in front of conventional trigger guard that releases the cylinder so it can be turned. Chambered for .32-caliber percussion. Has 3" to 6" octagonal barrel; 5-shot unfluted cylinder that is etched; brass frame and remainder blued, with squared walnut two-piece grips. Iron-frame version also available, but only 50 produced. Approximately 650 totally manufactured between 1852 and 1854. **NOTE:** Add 60 percent for iron-frame version.

Courtesy Milwaukee Public Museum, Milwaukee, Wisconsin

NIB	Exc.	V.G.	Good	Fair	Poor
—	—	2750	2000	850	300

NIB	Exc.	V.G.	Good	Fair	Poor
—	—	5400	3750	1500	550

Whitney-Beals Patent Revolver

An unusual ring-trigger pocket pistol made in three basic variations.

Courtesy Milwaukee Public Museum, Milwaukee, Wisconsin

First Model

Chambered for .31-caliber percussion. Octagon 2" to 6" barrels. Brass frame and 6-shot cylinder. Marked "F. Beals/New Haven, Ct.". Only 50 manufactured.

NIB	Exc.	V.G.	Good	Fair	Poor
—	—	5000	3500	1500	450

.31 Caliber Model

Has an iron frame and 7-shot cylinder. Octagon 2" to 6" barrels. Marked "Address E. Whitney/Whitneyville, Ct.". Approximately 2,300 manufactured.

NIB	Exc.	V.G.	Good	Fair	Poor
—	—	2500	1500	600	200

.28 Caliber Model

Except for caliber, this model similar to .31 Caliber Model. Approximately 850 manufactured.

NIB	Exc.	V.G.	Good	Fair	Poor
—	—	2750	1750	700	300

Whitney 1851 Navy

A faithful copy of 1851 Colt Revolver. Virtually identical. There is a possibility that surplus Colt parts were utilized in construction of this revolver. Approximately 400 manufactured in 1857 and 1858.

NIB	Exc.	V.G.	Good	Fair	Poor
—	—	9000	4250	1750	650

WHITNEY NAVY REVOLVER

Single-action revolver chambered for .36-caliber percussion. Has standard octagonal barrel length of 7.5"; iron frame; 6-shot unfluted cylinder that is roll engraved. Finish blued, with case colored loading lever. Two-piece walnut grips. Barrel marked "E. Whitney/N. Haven" or "Eagle Co.". There are a number of minor variations on this revolver. We strongly urge a competent appraisal if contemplating a transaction. There were 33,000 total manufactured between 1858 and 1862.

Courtesy Wallis & Wallis, Lewes, Sussex, England

First Model

Nearly entire production of First Model marked "Eagle Co.". Reason for this marking unknown. Four distinct variations of this model.

First Variation

Has no integral loading-lever assembly. Has a thin top strap. Only 100 manufactured.

Second Variation

Similar to First Variation, with an integral loading lever. Approximately 200 manufactured.

NIB	Exc.	V.G.	Good	Fair	Poor
—	—	5000	3000	1200	400

Third Variation

Similar to Second Variation, with 3-screw frame instead of 4-screws. Loading lever also modified. Approximately 500 manufactured.

NIB	Exc.	V.G.	Good	Fair	Poor
—	—	4800	2500	1000	300

Fourth Variation

Has rounded frame and safety notch between nipples on rear of the cylinder. Examples noted marked "E. Whitney/N. Haven". Approximately 700 manufactured.

NIB	Exc.	V.G.	Good	Fair	Poor
—	—	4800	2500	1000	300

Second Model

First Variation

Features more robust frame, with brass trigger guard. Barrel marked "E. Whitney/N. Haven". Cylinder pin secured by a wing nut; has an integral loading lever. Approximately 1,200 manufactured.

NIB	Exc.	V.G.	Good	Fair	Poor
—	—	3750	2000	900	300

Second Variation

Has six improved safety notches on rear of cylinder. Approximately 10,000 manufactured.

NIB	Exc.	V.G.	Good	Fair	Poor
—	—	3200	1750	750	250

Third Variation

Improved Colt-type loading-lever latch. Approximately 2,000 manufactured.

NIB	Exc.	V.G.	Good	Fair	Poor
—	—	3200	1750	750	250

Fourth Variation

Similar to Third Variation, except cylinder marked "Whitneyville". Approximately 10,000 manufactured.

NIB	Exc.	V.G.	Good	Fair	Poor
—	—	3200	1750	750	250

Fifth Variation

Has a larger trigger guard. Approximately 4,000 manufactured.

NIB	Exc.	V.G.	Good	Fair	Poor
—	—	3200	1750	750	250

Sixth Variation

Has larger trigger guard. 5-groove rifling instead of usual 7-groove. Approximately 2,500 manufactured.

NIB	Exc.	V.G.	Good	Fair	Poor
—	—	3200	1750	750	250

WHITNEY POCKET REVOLVER

Single-action revolver chambered for .31-caliber percussion. Has 3" to 6" octagonal barrels; 5-shot unfluted cylinder that is roll engraved and marked "Whitneyville". Frame iron, with blued finish and case colored integral loading lever. Grips two-piece walnut. Development of this model, as far as models and variations go, is identical to that described in Navy Model designation. Values are different and we list them for reference. Again, we recommend securing a qualified appraisal if a transaction is contemplated. Approximately 32,500 manufactured from 1858 to 1862.

First Model

First Variation

NIB	Exc.	V.G.	Good	Fair	Poor
—	—	3750	2000	900	300

Second Variation

NIB	Exc.	V.G.	Good	Fair	Poor
—	—	2200	1250	500	200

Third Variation

NIB	Exc.	V.G.	Good	Fair	Poor
—	—	1900	1000	400	150

Fourth Variation

NIB	Exc.	V.G.	Good	Fair	Poor
—	—	1900	1000	400	150

Fifth Variation

NIB	Exc.	V.G.	Good	Fair	Poor
—	—	1900	1000	400	150

Second Model

First Variation

NIB	Exc.	V.G.	Good	Fair	Poor
—	—	1700	900	400	100

Second Variation

NIB	Exc.	V.G.	Good	Fair	Poor
—	—	1700	900	400	100

Third Variation

NIB	Exc.	V.G.	Good	Fair	Poor
—	—	1700	900	400	100

Fourth Variation

NIB	Exc.	V.G.	Good	Fair	Poor
—	—	1700	1000	425	125

New Model Pocket Revolver

Single-action spur-triggered pocket revolver. Chambered for .28-caliber percussion. Has 3.5" octagonal barrel; 6-shot roll engraved cylinder. Features iron frame, with blued finish and two-piece walnut grips. Barrel marked "E. Whitney/N. Haven". Approximately 2,000 manufactured between 1860 and 1867.

Courtesy Milwaukee Public Museum, Milwaukee, Wisconsin

NIB	Exc.	V.G.	Good	Fair	Poor
—	—	2000	1250	500	200

Rimfire Pocket Revolver

Spur-trigger single-action solid-frame pocket revolver. Produced in three frame sizes, depending on caliber. Chambered for .22, .32 and .38 rimfire cartridges. Frame brass and found in a variety of finishes- nickel-plated or blued, or a combination thereof. Bird's-head grips are rosewood or hard rubber; ivory or pearl grips are sometimes encountered and will bring a slight premium in value. Octagon barrels 1.5" to 5" and marked "Whitneyville Armory Ct. USA". Also noted with trade names "Monitor", "Defender" or "Eagle". Commonly referred to as Model No. 1, No. 1.5, Model 2 or Model 2.5. Values for all are quite similar. Approximately 30,000 manufactured of all types between 1871 and 1879.

Courtesy Milwaukee Public Museum, Milwaukee, Wisconsin

NIB	Exc.	V.G.	Good	Fair	Poor
—	—	750	500	200	75

WHITNEY FIREARMS COMPANY
Hartford, Connecticut

Wolverine

A .22-caliber semi-automatic pistol, with 4.75" barrel. Blued or nickel-plated, with plastic grips and aluminum alloy frame. This pistol readily distinguishable by its streamlined form. Approximately 13,000 examples made with blue finish; 900 with nickel-plated finish. Some slides marked "Wolverine Whitney Firearms Inc., New Haven, Conn USA"; others "Whitney" only. Wolverine-marked pistols are considered more rare. Pistol produced in two locations: New Haven, Connecticut; and Hartford, Connecticut. Manufactured from 1955 to 1962. Now being reproduced by Olympic Arms. Pricing is for original version.

Blue Finish

Blued pistols most often have brown or black grips.

NIB	Exc.	V.G.	Good	Fair	Poor
750	550	400	350	250	200

Nickel-Plated

Nickeled pistols most often have white plastic grips.

NIB	Exc.	V.G.	Good	Fair	Poor
2000	1800	1500	1250	800	500

WHITWORTH
See—Interarms

WICHITA ARMS, INC.
Wichita, Kansas

Classic Rifle

Single-shot bolt-action rifle. Produced in a variety of calibers, with 21" octagonal barrel. Offered with Canjar adjustable triggers. Blued, with checkered walnut stock.

NIB	Exc.	V.G.	Good	Fair	Poor
3000	2500	2250	1850	1250	1000

Varmint Rifle

As above, with round barrel.

NIB	Exc.	V.G.	Good	Fair	Poor
2000	1750	1500	1250	1000	800

Silhouette Rifle

As above, with 24" heavy barrel, gray composition stock and 2-oz. Can-jar trigger.

NIB	Exc.	V.G.	Good	Fair	Poor
2200	1900	1700	1000	850	650

Wichita International Pistol

Single-shot pivoted barrel target pistol. Produced in a variety of calibers from .22 to .357 Magnum, with 10.5" or 14" barrel. Fitted with adjustable sights or telescopic sight mounts. Stainless steel, with walnut fore-stock and grips.

NIB	Exc.	V.G.	Good	Fair	Poor
800	650	400	350	300	200

Wichita Classic Pistol

Bolt-action single-shot pistol. Chambered for a variety of calibers up to .308, with left-hand action and 11.25" barrel. Blued, with walnut stock.

NIB	Exc.	V.G.	Good	Fair	Poor
3000	2500	2250	1850	1250	1000

Wichita Classic Engraved

As above, but embellished.

NIB	Exc.	V.G.	Good	Fair	Poor
5000	4250	3500	2500	2000	1500

Wichita Silhouette Pistol

As above in 7mm HMSA or .308, with 15" barrel. Walnut stock made so pistol-grip is located beneath forward end of bolt.

NIB	Exc.	V.G.	Good	Fair	Poor
1100	950	750	600	500	400

Wichita MK40

As above, with 13" barrel, multi-range sights and composition or walnut stock. Standard finish blued. Also made in stainless steel.

NIB	Exc.	V.G.	Good	Fair	Poor
1100	950	750	600	500	400

WICKLIFFE RIFLES
Triple S Development
Wickliffe, Ohio/Austinburg, Ohio

NOTE: Wickliffe Rifle Company has been reorganized as a maker of custom single-shot rifles. Values below are for original Wickliffe guns.

Model 76

Single-shot falling-block rifle. Produced in a variety of calibers from .22 Hornet to .45-70. Barrels: 22" lightweight; or 26" heavyweight. Blued, with walnut stock. Introduced in 1976; discontinued.

NIB	Exc.	V.G.	Good	Fair	Poor
—	1200	1000	750	550	300

Model 76 Deluxe

As above, with nickel-silver pistol-grip cap, machine jeweled breech-block and more finely figured walnut stock. Introduced in 1976.

NIB	Exc.	V.G.	Good	Fair	Poor
—	1450	1250	900	700	450

Traditionalist

Model 76 in .30-06 or .45-70 caliber, with 24" barrel having open sights. Checkered walnut buttstock. Introduced in 1979.

NIB	Exc.	V.G.	Good	Fair	Poor
—	1200	1000	750	550	300

Stinger

Similar to Model 76. Chambered for .22 Hornet or .223 Rem., with 22" barrel. Fitted with Burris 6X power telescope. Blued, with checkered Monte Carlo-style stock. Introduced in 1979.

NIB	Exc.	V.G.	Good	Fair	Poor
—	1200	1000	750	550	300

Stinger Deluxe

As above, with a superior grade finish and more finely figured walnut stock.

NIB	Exc.	V.G.	Good	Fair	Poor
—	1250	1050	800	575	300

WIENER WAFFENFABRIK
Vienna, Austria

Little Tom

A 6.35mm or 7.65mm double-action semi-automatic pistol, with 2.5" barrel. Slide marked "Wiener Waffenfabrik Patent Little Tom" and caliber. Blued, with walnut or plastic grips inlaid with a medallion bearing company's trademark. Approximately 10,000 made from 1919 to 1925.

Little Tom—7.65mm

Paul Goodwin photo

NIB	Exc.	V.G.	Good	Fair	Poor
—	500	450	400	250	175

WILDEY FIREARMS CO., INC.
Cheshire, Connecticut
Newburg, New York
Warren, Connecticut

Wildey Auto Pistol

Gas-operated rotary-bolt double-action semi-automatic pistol. Chambered for .357 Peterbuilt, .45 Win. Magnum or .475 Wildey Magnum cartridges, with 5", 6", 7", 8" or 10" ventilated rib barrels. Gas-operated action is adjustable and features a single-shot cutoff. Rotary-bolt has three heavy locking lugs. Constructed of stainless steel, with adjustable sights and wood grips. Values of this rarely encountered pistol are based not only on condition, but caliber—as well as serial-number range. Earlier-numbered guns being worth a good deal more than later production models. All Wildey models are no longer in production.

Cheshire, Connecticut, Address

Produced in .45 Win. Magnum only. Serial numbered from No. 1 through 2489. **NOTE:** Serial numbers above 200 would be worth approximately $200 less respectively in each category of condition.

Serial No. 1 through 200

NIB	Exc.	V.G.	Good	Fair	Poor
2000	1500	1200	950	750	500

Survivor Model

Manufactured in Brookfield, Connecticut. **NOTE:** Add $100 for 12" barrel; $500 for 14" barrel; $1,100 for 18" Silhouette model.

NIB	Exc.	V.G.	Good	Fair	Poor
1500	1000	750	550	450	300

Hunter Model

As above, with matte stainless steel finish.

NIB	Exc.	V.G.	Good	Fair	Poor
1775	1250	900	700	600	450

Pin Gun

Gas-operated auto-loading pistol for competition shooting. In polished or matte stainless, with muzzle-brake. Variety of calibers and barrel lengths (7", 8", 10", 12", 14"). Weight 4.09 lb. (8" barrel).

NIB	Exc.	V.G.	Good	Fair	Poor
2000	1500	1200	950	750	500

Wildey Carbine

Features 18" barrel, with forearm. Calibers from .44 Auto Magnum to .475 Wildey Magnum. Choice of polished or matte stainless steel. **NOTE:** Add $ 225 for matte stainless finish.

NIB	Exc.	V.G.	Good	Fair	Poor
2500	2000	1550	1000	750	500

Presentation Model

As above, but engraved. Fitted with hand-checkered walnut grips.

NIB	Exc.	V.G.	Good	Fair	Poor
3000	2500	1950	1400	900	600

JAWS Viper

Jordanian Arms & Weapons System manufactured in Jordan. Semi-automatic chambered for 9mm, .40 S&W, 45 ACP. Barrels: 4.4" and 5". 10-round magazine. Stainless finish, with rubberized grip. .

NIB	Exc.	V.G.	Good	Fair	Poor
—	725	500	375	250	150

WILKINSON ARMS CO.
Covina, California

Diane

A .25-caliber semi-automatic pistol, with 2.25" barrel and 6-shot magazine. Blued, with plastic grips.

NIB	Exc.	V.G.	Good	Fair	Poor
—	400	325	200	150	100

Terry Carbine

A 9mm caliber semi-automatic carbine, with 16.25" barrel, adjustable sights and 30-shot magazine. Matte blued, with black composition or maple stock.

NIB	Exc.	V.G.	Good	Fair	Poor
—	675	450	325	200	125

WILLIAMSON
New York, New York

Derringer

A .41-caliber single-shot pocket pistol, with 2.5" sliding barrel. Blued, with silver-plated furniture. Checkered walnut grip. Barrel marked "Wil-

liamson's Pat. Oct. 2, 1866 New York". Fitted with an auxiliary percussion cap chamber adaptor. Manufactured from 1866 to about 1870.

NIB	Exc.	V.G.	Good	Fair	Poor
—	—	—	1250	500	100

WILSON, J. P.
Ilion, New York

Percussion Alarm Gun

Unusual little device chambered for .22-caliber percussion. Consists of approximately 1" rectangular brass block, with a chamber bored into it that accepts a black-powder charge. No provision for a projectile. There is a spring retained arm on top, which works as a hammer. As the device is activated by a door or a window, hammer snaps closed striking a percussion cap that causes the charge to fire, thereby creating an alarm notifying that the perimeter has been breached. Marked "J. P. Wilson/ Patented Feb. 8, 1859/Ilion, NY".

NIB	Exc.	V.G.	Good	Fair	Poor
—	—	1200	850	350	100

WILSON COMBAT
Berryville, Arkansas

Wilson began making custom 1911-style pistols using Colt slides and frames in 1977. Company produces a wide range of quality components for 1911 pistols, such as slides, triggers, safeties, barrels, etc. Models listed are for complete factory-built-and-assembled guns. These factory-built pistols are sold with a lifetime warranty, even to subsequent buyers. Pistols listed are divided into two categories. Semi-custom pistols are off-the-shelf guns available through participating dealers. Custom pistols are special order guns. Models listed below are representative, not inclusive.

POLYMER FRAME PISTOLS

Tactical Carry (KZ-45)

Chambered for .45 ACP cartridge. Fitted with 5" stainless steel match barrel. Numerous special features such as night sights, front and rear slide serrations. Frame stainless steel and reinforced polymer. Magazine capacity 10 rounds. Finish black polymer. Weight about 31 oz. Introduced in 1999; discontinued.

NIB	Exc.	V.G.	Good	Fair	Poor
1050	900	750	600	500	300

KZ 9mm

Polymer-frame 1911 chambered for 9mm. Full size 16+1 capacity, with 5" barrel; weight 33 oz. Compact size 14+1 capacity, with 4.1" barrel; weight 31 oz. Introduced 2006; discontinued.

NIB	Exc.	V.G.	Good	Fair	Poor
1500	1350	1200	900	750	300

Spec-Ops 9

An upgraded model based on discontinued KZ-9. Like KZ-9, it has a polymer frame and 16-round magazine. Chambering 9mm only. Barrel 4.5"; weight unloaded 29.6 oz.

NIB	Exc.	V.G.	Good	Fair	Poor
1950	1500	1200	900	450	200

ADP 9mm

Polymer frame. Capacity 11 rounds; weight 19.5 oz.; overall length 6.3"; barrel 3.75". Introduced 2006.

NIB	Exc.	V.G.	Good	Fair	Poor
675	525	400	300	200	125

SEMI-CUSTOM PISTOLS

Model 1996A2

Introduced in 1996. Offered in a number of different configurations which affect price. Base pistol chambered for .45 ACP cartridge. Has snagfree sights and blue finish. Barrel length 5"; magazine capacity 8 rounds; weight about 38 oz. There are numerous special features on the standard pistol. **NOTE:** Add $70 for tritium night sights; $125 for Wilson adjustable sights; $275 for nights sights, ambi safety, hard chrome frame; $325 for Wilson adjustable sights, ambi safety, hard chrome frame.

NIB	Exc.	V.G.	Good	Fair	Poor
1450	1150	1000	800	625	300

Protector

Fitted to a 5" slide, with match barrel adjustable sights and numerous other special features. Weight about 38 oz. Black polymer finish on slide and frame. Introduced in 1996. **NOTE:** Add $100 for stainless steel.

NIB	Exc.	V.G.	Good	Fair	Poor
1795	1450	1150	900	650	400

Protector Compact

Same as above, with 4.25" match-grade barrel. Weight about 34 oz. Introduced in 1996.

NIB	Exc.	V.G.	Good	Fair	Poor
1795	1450	1150	900	650	400

Sentinel Ultra Compact

This .45 ACP pistol fitted with 3.6" heavy tapered cone hand-fitted barrel, night sights, high-ride beavertail and numerous special features. Magazine capacity 6 rounds. Weight about 29 oz. Finish black polymer.

NIB	Exc.	V.G.	Good	Fair	Poor
2100	1675	1300	950	700	450

Tactical

This .45 ACP pistol fitted with 5" tapered cone hand-fitted barrel. Cocking serrations on front and rear of slide. High-ride beavertail safety and other special features. Night sights are standard. Cocobolo grips. Weight about 38 oz. Finish is black polymer. Magazine capacity 8 rounds. Introduced in 1999.

NIB	Exc.	V.G.	Good	Fair	Poor
1825	1450	1100	900	700	400

Classic

This model has a 5" barrel, adjustable sights, hard chrome finish on frame and other special features. Weight about 38 oz. Introduced in 1996. **NOTE:** Add $100 for stainless steel.

NIB	Exc.	V.G.	Good	Fair	Poor
1895	1500	1200	900	700	400

Service Grade Target

Chambered for .45 ACP cartridge. Features 5" stainless steel match hand-fitted barrel, with full length guide rod. Front and rear cocking serrations. Magazine well is beveled and grips are cocobolo. Numerous other special features. Weight about 38 oz. Finish black polymer. Magazine capacity 8 rounds.

NIB	Exc.	V.G.	Good	Fair	Poor
1825	1450	1150	850	650	350

Beretta/Wilson 92G Brigadier Tactical

Limited production model features all-steel Beretta and Wilson Combat parts. These include steel ambidextrous decocker-only levers, enhanced slide, modified M9A1 style checkered frame, with accessory rail and rounded trigger guard. Other features are Wilson Combat G10 grips, steel guide rod, Trijicon tritium front sight and Wilson Combat rear. Chambered in 9m, with 15+1 round capacity. Weight empty 36 oz.; loaded 43 oz. Available only from Wilson Combat or its dealers.

NIB	Exc.	V.G.	Good	Fair	Poor
1150	1000	800	550	400	350

Custom Carry Revolver

Built on Smith & Wesson .357 Magnum Model 66. Features 2.5" barrel, with adjustable night sights. Cylinder chambered and grip is black nylon, with smooth stainless steel finish. Weight about 30 oz.

NIB	Exc.	V.G.	Good	Fair	Poor
1175	950	800	650	500	300

.22 Classic Rimfire Pistol

Chambered for .22-caliber rimfire cartridge. Fitted with 5" barrel. Hard chrome frame and black anodized slide. Weight less than standard .45-caliber pistol. Introduced in 1996.

NIB	Exc.	V.G.	Good	Fair	Poor
1125	975	800	625	500	250

CUSTOM-BUILT PISTOLS

Wilson Custom pistols bear Wilson Combat or Wilson Custom label on right side of frame on the dust cover. Full custom guns are typically built on a Colt, Springfield Armory, Norinco, STI, Strayer Voight or Wilson Combat gun.

Combat Classic Super Grade (Tactical Super Grade)

Fitted with 5" match-grade hand-fit stainless steel barrel. Adjustable sights, high ride beavertail safety, contoured magazine well and polymer slide with hard chrome frame. Weight about 45 oz. In 9mm, .38 Super, .40 S&W, 10mm and .45 ACP.

NIB	Exc.	V.G.	Good	Fair	Poor
3595	2850	2300	1900	1500	600

Tactical Super Grade Compact

Similar to above model, with 4.1" match grade barrel. Magazine capacity 7 rounds. Weight about 40 oz. Introduced in 2003. Available in 9mm, .38 Super, .45 ACP.

NIB	Exc.	V.G.	Good	Fair	Poor
4475	3900	3200	2500	1850	650

Wilson X-TAC

Caliber .45 ACP, steel frame and slide, 8-round magazine, special XTAC-pattern slide serrations. Texturing on front strap and mainspring housing, stainless match-grade barrel and bushing, extended thumb safety, beavertail tang, G10 grips and contoured mag well. Weight 38.1 oz., 5" barrel with black Parkerized finish.

NIB	Exc.	V.G.	Good	Fair	Poor
2000	1700	1450	1150	750	300

CQB Light-Rail Lightweight

Calibers: 9mm Parabellum, .38 Super, .45 ACP. Compact size with 4" barrel, steel slide, alloy round butt frame. Weight 27.34 oz. Comes with one 7- and two 8-round magazines, fiber optic front sight, integral accessory rail, G10 grips, extended thumb safety, beavertail tang, checkered front strap and mainspring housing. Several other sizes and variations available in CQB series.

NIB	Exc.	V.G.	Good	Fair	Poor
2300	1976	1650	1300	850	300

Ultralight Carry Series

Full-size 1911, with aluminum frame and steel slide. Chambered in 9mm Parabellum, .38 Super or .45 ACP. Stainless fluted 5" barrel. Comes with one 7- and two 8-round magazines. Other features include countersunk slide stop, integral accessory rail, contoured mag well, G10 grips, extended thumb safety, beavertail tang, checkered front strap and mainspring housing. Weight 26.5 oz. Several Armor-Tuff finish options including black, O.D., silver, tan or two-tone. Compact model has 4" barrel (all calibers), Sentinel 3.6" barrel (9mm only).

NIB	Exc.	V.G.	Good	Fair	Poor
3400	3000	2500	2000	1200	400

Stealth Defense System

Built with a 4.25" slide and match-grade stainless steel barrel. Features night sights, checkered front strap and mainspring housing, with numerous special features. Black polymer finish. Weight about 34 oz. Offered in 9mm, .38 Super, .40 S&W, .45 ACP.

NIB	Exc.	V.G.	Good	Fair	Poor
2895	2250	1700	1300	900	400

Defensive Combat Pistol

This .45 ACP pistol built with 5" match-grade stainless steel barrel, night sights and numerous special features. Finish black polymer. Weight 38 oz.

NIB	Exc.	V.G.	Good	Fair	Poor
2395	1850	1250	1000	600	300

Classic Master Grade

This .45 ACP pistol fitted with 5" stainless steel hand-fitted match-grade barrel. Numerous special features such as ultralight hammer, ambidextrous safety, etc. Finish stainless steel frame and black polymer slide. Weight about 38 oz. Magazine capacity 8 rounds.

NIB	Exc.	V.G.	Good	Fair	Poor
2895	2250	1700	1300	900	400

Tactical Elite

Similar to other Wilson pistols, with addition of a special tactical heavy tapered cone barrel.

NIB	Exc.	V.G.	Good	Fair	Poor
2895	2250	1700	1300	900	400

Defensive Combat Pistol Deluxe

Has 5" match-grade stainless steel barrel and numerous special features. Fitted with adjustable sights. Weight about 38 oz. Finish black polymer.

NIB	Exc.	V.G.	Good	Fair	Poor
2595	2000	1350	1050	700	300

Professional Model Pistol

Introduced in 2004. This .45 ACP pistol features 4.1" stainless steel match barrel, tactical combat sights with tritium inserts. Many custom features. Magazine capacity 8 rounds. Offered in gray/black, green/black or all-black finish. Weight about 35 oz.

NIB	Exc.	V.G.	Good	Fair	Poor
1215	1650	1375	1100	750	450

Competition Pistols

Wilson Combat offers custom-built pistols to customer's specifications. An expert appraisal is recommended prior to sale.

TACTICAL RIFLES

UT-15 Urban Tactical

Semi-automatic rifle fitted with 16.25" fluted barrel, with tactical muzzle-brake. Flattop receiver. Aluminum hand guard. Chambered for .223 cartridge. Parkerized finish. Accepts all M-16/AR-15 magazines. Weight about 6.5 lbs. **NOTE:** Add $100 for Armor-Tuff finish.

NIB	Exc.	V.G.	Good	Fair	Poor
1900	1700	1450	1100	900	500

Tactical Hunter LW 6.8

Chambered for Remington 6.8 SPC, with 15-round magazine. Stainless lightweight match-grade 16" or 18" barrel. Forged upper and lower receivers. Enhanced bolt and carrier, with NP3 coating. Wilson Combat Quadrail, Accu-Tac flash hider. Armor Tuff polymer finish in black, gray or tan. Collapsible stock.

NIB	Exc.	V.G.	Good	Fair	Poor
2000	1700	1450	1150	750	300

TPR-15 Tactical Precision Rifle

Fitted with match-grade 18" fluted barrel. Free-floating aluminum hand guard. Chambered for .223 cartridge. Weight about 6.5 lbs. Parkerized finish. **NOTE:** Add $100 for Armor-Tuff finish.

NIB	Exc.	V.G.	Good	Fair	Poor
2500	2300	1950	1300	1100	600

M-4T Tactical Carbine

Features 16.25" M-4 style heavy barrel, with muzzle-brake. Flattop receiver. Chambered for .223 cartridge. Parkerized finish. Weight about 6.5 lbs. **NOTE:** Add $100 for Armor-Tuff finish.

NIB	Exc.	V.G.	Good	Fair	Poor
1900	1700	1450	1100	900	500

TL-15 Tactical Lightweight

Introduced in 2002. Flattop model features match-grade 16.25" lightweight barrel, with muzzle-brake. Aluminum hand guard and fixed buttstock. Chambered for .223 cartridge. Black Mil-Spec finish. **NOTE:** Add $100 for Armor-Tuff finish.

NIB	Exc.	V.G.	Good	Fair	Poor
1900	1700	1450	1100	900	500

Super Sniper

Fitted with 20" stainless steel match grade barrel, with 1 in 8 twist. Flattop receiver. Offered in Parkerized or Armor-Tuff finish. **NOTE:** Add $100 for Armor-Tuff finish.

NIB	Exc.	V.G.	Good	Fair	Poor
2350	2100	1800	1500	1150	600

WINCHESTER REPEATING ARMS
New Haven, Connecticut

Prices given here are, for the most part, standard guns without optional features that were so often furnished by the factory. These optional or extra-cost features are too numerous to list and can affect price of shotgun or rifle to an enormous degree. In some cases, these options are one of a kind. Collectors and those interested in Winchester firearms have the benefit of some original factory records. These records are now stored in Cody Firearms Museum, Buffalo Bill Historical Center, P.O. Box 1000, Cody, Wyoming (307) 587-4771. For a $25 fee, museum will provide factory letters containing original specifications of certain Winchester models using original factory records. **CAUTION:** Buyers should confirm by Cody letter any special-order feature on any Winchester within the Cody record range before paying a premium for a scarce feature.

Hunt Repeating Rifle

Walter Hunt described his repeating rifle as Volition Repeater. Hunt was granted U.S. patent #6663 in August 1849 for his repeating rifle. That paved the way for future generations of Winchester repeating rifles. Hunt's rifle design was unique and innovative as was his patent #5701 for a conical lead bullet that was to be fired in his rifle. This ingenious bullet had a hole in its base filled with powder and closed by a disc with an opening in the middle to expel the ignition from an independent priming source that used priming pellets made of fulminate of mercury. Rifle actually worked, but only the patent model was built; it is now in the Cody Firearms Museum.

Jennings

Second in the evolutionary line of Winchester rifles is the Jennings. Made by Robbins & Lawrence of Windsor, Vermont, this rifle incorporated the original concept of the Hunt design, with additional improvements utilized by Lewis Jennings. Jennings rifle is important not only as a link in the chain of repeating-rifle development, but also because it introduced Benjamin Henry Tyler to the concept of the tubular magazine lever-action repeating rifle. Jennings rifle was built in three separate and distinct models. While total production of the three types was contracted for 5,000 guns, it is probable that only about 1,000 were actually produced.

First Model

First Model Jennings was built in .54-caliber breech-loading single-shot configuration, with ring trigger, oval trigger guard and 26" barrel. A ramrod was fixed to underside of barrel as well. This variation was made from 1850 to 1851.

Courtesy Milwaukee Public Museum, Milwaukee, Wisconsin

NIB	Exc.	V.G.	Good	Fair	Poor
—	—	35000	25000	7000	1500

Second Model

Second Model Jennings was produced by adopting improvements made by Horace Smith. Second Model is a breech-loading repeating rifle, with an under barrel magazine tube and 26" barrel. Frame is sculpted, unlike First Model. Ring trigger is still present, but trigger guard was removed as part of the design change. Caliber remained .54 and rifle fitted with 25" barrel. Second Model produced in 1851 and 1852.

Courtesy Milwaukee Public Museum, Milwaukee, Wisconsin

NIB	Exc.	V.G.	Good	Fair	Poor
—	—	30000	20000	5000	1200

Third Model

Third Model represents an attempt by investors to use remaining parts and close out production. The .54-caliber Third Model was a muzzle-loading rifle, with a ramrod mounted under the 26.5" barrel. Same frame as used on First Model, but trigger was more of the conventional type. Trigger guard had a bow in the middle giving this model a distinctive appearance. This variation was produced in 1852 and marks the end of early conceptual period in repeating rifle development.

NIB	Exc.	V.G.	Good	Fair	Poor
—	—	23500	9500	4500	1500

Smith & Wesson Volcanic Firearms

An interesting connection in the evolution of lever-action repeating firearm, is found in the production of a small group of pistols and rifles built in Norwich, Connecticut, by Horace Smith and Daniel Wesson under the firm name of Smith & Wesson. Company built two types of Volcanic pistols. One was a large-frame model, with 8" barrel chambered in .41-caliber. About 500 large-frames were built. The other was a small-frame version, with 4" barrel chambered in .31-caliber. About 700 small-frames were built. In both variations the barrel, magazine and frame were blued. Smith & Wesson also produced a lever-action repeating rifle. These rifles are exceedingly rare, with fewer than 10 having been built. They were chambered for .528-caliber and fitted with 23" barrels. Because of the small number of rifles built, no value is offered.

Courtesy Buffalo Bill Historical Center, Cody, Wyoming

4" Pistol

NIB	Exc.	V.G.	Good	Fair	Poor
—	—	—	11000	4000	1000

8" Pistol

Courtesy Buffalo Bill Historical Center, Cody, Wyoming

NIB	Exc.	V.G.	Good	Fair	Poor
—	—	—	13000	6000	1500

Volcanic Firearms (Volcanic Repeating Arms Company)

With the incorporation of Volcanic Repeating Arms Company, a new and important individual was introduced who would have an impact on the American arms industry for the next 100 years: Oliver F. Winchester. This new company introduced the Volcanic pistol using improvements made by Horace Smith and Daniel Wesson. Volcanic firearms are marked on the barrel, "THE VOLCANIC REPEATING ARMS CO. PATENT NEW HAVEN, CONN. FEB. 14, 1854". Volcanic was offered as a .38-caliber breech-loading tubular magazine repeater, with blued barrel and bronze frame. These pistols were available in three barrel lengths.

Courtesy Milwaukee Public Museum, Milwaukee, Wisconsin

6" Barrel

NIB	Exc.	V.G.	Good	Fair	Poor
—	—	—	7000	3500	1500

8" Barrel

NIB	Exc.	V.G.	Good	Fair	Poor
—	—	—	7000	3500	1500

16" Barrel

NOTE: A few Volcanic pistols were produced with detachable shoulder stocks. These are considered quite rare. For original guns with this option, prices listed should be increased by 25 percent.

Courtesy Buffalo Bill Historical Center, Cody, Wyoming

NIB	Exc.	V.G.	Good	Fair	Poor
—	—	—	14000	5500	2500

Volcanic Firearms (New Haven Arms Company)

In 1857, New Haven Arms Company was formed to continue production of the former Volcanic Repeating Arms Company. Volcanic firearms continued to be built, but were now marked on the barrel, "NEW HAVEN, CONN. PATENT FEB. 14, 1854". Volcanic pistols produced by New Haven Arms Company were built in .30-caliber and used the same basic frame as original Volcanic. These pistols were produced in 3.5" and 6" barrel lengths.

3-1/2" Barrel

NIB	Exc.	V.G.	Good	Fair	Poor
—	—	6500	5000	2500	1500

6" Barrel

NIB	Exc.	V.G.	Good	Fair	Poor
—	—	7500	5750	3000	1500

Lever Action Carbine

New Haven Arms introduced, for the first time, a Volcanic rifle that featured a full-length slotted magazine tube, with spring-activated thumb piece follower that moved along the entire length of the magazine tube. Rifles were chambered for .38-caliber and offered in 16", 20", 24" barrel lengths.

Courtesy Buffalo Bill Historical Center, Cody, Wyoming

16" Barrel

NIB	Exc.	V.G.	Good	Fair	Poor
—	40000	26000	16000	6000	2000

20" Barrel

NIB	Exc.	V.G.	Good	Fair	Poor
—	45000	23000	19000	8000	3000

24" Barrel

Courtesy Little John's Auction Service, Inc., Paul Goodwin photo

NIB	Exc.	V.G.	Good	Fair	Poor
—	55000	37000	22500	10000	3000

Henry Rifle

With the development of B. Tyler Henry's improvements in metallic rimfire cartridge and his additional improvements in Volcanic frame, direct predecessor to Winchester lever-action repeater was born. New cartridge was .44-caliber rimfire. Henry rifle featured 24" octagon barrel, with tubular magazine holding 15 shells. Rifle had no forearm. Furnished with walnut buttstock and two styles of buttplates: early rounded heel crescent shape seen on guns produced from 1860 to 1862; later sharper heel crescent butt found on guns built from 1863 to 1866. Early models produced from 1860 to 1861 were fitted with an iron frame; later models built from 1861 to 1866 were fitted with brass frames. About 14,000 Henry rifles were made during entire production period; only about 300 were iron frame rifles.

Courtesy Bonhams & Butterfields, San Francisco, California

Iron Frame Rifle

Courtesy Bonhams & Butterfields, San Francisco, California

NIB	Exc.	V.G.	Good	Fair	Poor
—	—	120000	65000	30000	13000

Brass Frame Rifle

NIB	Exc.	V.G.	Good	Fair	Poor
—	—	53000	37500	17500	9000

Martially Inspected Henry Rifles

Beginning in 1863, Federal Government ordered 1,730 Henry Rifles for use in Civil War. Most of these government-inspected rifles fall into serial number range 3000 to 4000, while balance are close to this serial-number range. They are marked "C.G.C." for Charles G. Chapman, government inspector. These Henry rifles were used under actual combat conditions and for that reason it is doubtful there are any rifles that would fall into excellent condition category. Therefore, no price is given. **NOTE:** There are many counterfeit examples of these rifles. It is strongly advised that an expert in this field be consulted prior to sale.

NIB	Exc.	V.G.	Good	Fair	Poor
—	—	100000	60000	35000	20000

Winchester's Improvement Carbine

Overall length 43.5"; barrel length 24"; caliber .44 rimfire. Walnut stock with brass buttplate; receiver and magazine cover/fore-end of brass; barrel and magazine tube blued. Magazine loading port is exposed by sliding the fore-end forward. This design was protected by O.F. Winchester's British Patent Number 3285 issued December 19, 1865. Unmarked except for internally located serial numbers. Approximately 700 manufactured in December 1865 and early 1866. The majority of these were sold to Maximilian of Mexico. Prospective purchasers are strongly advised to secure an expert appraisal prior to acquisition.

NIB	Exc.	V.G.	Good	Fair	Poor
—	35000	27500	19500	13000	9000

Model 1866

In 1866, New Haven Arms Company changed its name to Winchester Repeating Arms Company. First firearm to be built under Winchester name was Model 1866. This first Winchester was a much-improved version of Henry. New magazine tube, developed by Nelson King Winchester's plant superintendent, was a vast improvement over slotted magazine tube used on Henry and its predecessor. Old tube allowed dirt to enter through slots and was weakened because of it. King's patent, assigned to Winchester, featured a solid tube that was much stronger and reliable. His patent also dealt with an improved loading system. Rifle now featured loading port on right side of receiver, with spring-loaded cover. Frame continued to be made from brass. Model 1866 was chambered for .44-caliber Flat Rimfire or .44-caliber Pointed Rimfire. Both cartridges could be used interchangeably.

Barrel on Model 1866 marked with two different markings. First, which is seen on early guns up to serial number 23000 reads, "HENRY'S PATENT-OCT. 16, 1860 KING'S PATENT-MARCH 29, 1866". Second marking reads, "WINCHESTER'S-REPEATING-ARMS. NEW HAVEN, CT. KING'S-IMPROVEMENT-PATENTED MARCH 29, 1866 OCTOBER 16, 1860". There are three basic variations of Model 1866:

1. Sporting Rifle: round or octagon barrel. Approximately 28,000 produced.

2. Carbine: round barrel. Approximately 127,000 produced.

3. Musket: round barrel. Approximately 14,000 produced.

Rifle and musket held 17 cartridges; carbine capacity 13. Unlike Henry, Model 1866s were fitted with walnut forearm. Model 1866 discontinued in 1898, with approximately 170,000 guns produced. Model 1866 sold in various special order configurations such as: barrels longer or shorter than standard, including engraved guns. Prices listed represent only standard-model 1866s. Guns with special-order features, an independent appraisal from an expert is highly recommended.

Courtesy Bonhams & Butterfields, San Francisco, California

First Model Rifle

First style has both Henry and King patent dates stamped on barrel. Flat-loading port cover and two-screw upper tang. Perhaps most distinctive feature of First Model is rapid drop at top rear of receiver near hammer. Often referred to as "Henry Drop", a reference to same receiver drop found on Henry rifle. First Models will be seen up through 15000 serial number range.

NIB	Exc.	V.G.	Good	Fair	Poor
—	85000	45000	20000	13000	4000

First Model Carbine

NIB	Exc.	V.G.	Good	Fair	Poor
—	40000	26000	17000	11000	3000

Second Model Rifle

Second style differs from the first most noticeably in its single-screw upper tang and a flare at the front of receiver to meet the forearm. Second Model also has a more gradual drop at rear of the receiver than First Model. Second style Model 1866 appears through serial number 25000.

NIB	Exc.	V.G.	Good	Fair	Poor
—	40000	25000	12500	7500	4000

Second Model Carbine

NIB	Exc.	V.G.	Good	Fair	Poor
—	30000	20000	9500	6750	3500

Third Model Rifle

Third style's most noticeable characteristic is more moderately curved receiver shape at rear of frame. Serial number now stamped in block numerals behind trigger, thus allowing numbers to be seen for the first time without removing stock. Barrel marking stamped with Winchester address. Third Model found between serial numbers 25000 and 149000. For the first time, musket version was produced in this serial-number range.

NIB	Exc.	V.G.	Good	Fair	Poor
—	30000	20000	8000	5000	3000

Third Model Carbine

NIB	Exc.	V.G.	Good	Fair	Poor
—	30000	20000	9500	5500	3500

Third Model Musket

NIB	Exc.	V.G.	Good	Fair	Poor
—	30000	20000	9500	5500	3500

Fourth Model Rifle

Fourth style has even less pronounced drop at top rear of frame. Serial number stamped in script on lower tang under lever. Fourth Model seen between serial number 149000 and 170100. Late guns having iron buttplate instead of brass.

NIB	Exc.	V.G.	Good	Fair	Poor
—	35000	20000	9500	5500	3500

Fourth Model Carbine

NIB	Exc.	V.G.	Good	Fair	Poor
—	35000	20000	9500	5500	3500

Fourth Model Musket

NIB	Exc.	V.G.	Good	Fair	Poor
—	35000	20000	9500	5500	3500

Model 1866 Iron Frame Rifle Musket

Overall length 54.5"; barrel length 33.25"; caliber .45 centerfire. Walnut stock, with case-hardened furniture; barrel burnished bright; receiver case-hardened. Finger lever catch mounted within a large bolster at rear of the lever. Unmarked, except for serial numbers that appear externally on receiver and often buttplate tang. Approximately 25 made during early autumn of 1866. Value speculative.

Model 1866 Iron Frame Swiss Sharpshooters Rifle

As above, in .41-Swiss caliber. Fitted with Scheutzen style stock supplied by the firm of Weber Ruesch in Zurich. Marked Weber Ruesch, Zurich on barrel and serial numbered externally. Approximately 400 to 450 manufactured in 1866 and 1867.

Model 1867 Iron Frame Carbine

Overall length 39.25"; barrel length 20"; caliber .44 rimfire. Walnut stock, with case-hardened furniture; barrel and magazine tube blued; receiver case-hardened. Finger lever catch mounted within rear curl of the lever. Unmarked, except for serial numbers that appear externally on receiver and often buttplate tang. Approximately 20 manufactured. Prospective purchasers are strongly advised to secure an expert appraisal prior to acquisition.

Model 1868 Iron Frame Rifle Musket

Calibers .45, .455 and .47 centerfire; overall length 49.5" (.455-cal.), 50.5" or 53" (.45- and .47-cal.); barrel length 29.5" (.455-cal.), 30.25" or 33" (.45- and .47-cal.). Walnut stock, with case-hardened or burnished bright furniture (.45- and .47-cal.); barrel burnished bright; receiver case-hardened or burnished bright (.45- and .47-cal.). Finger lever catch mounted on lower receiver tang. Rear of finger lever machined with a long flat extension on its upper surface. Unmarked, except for serial number. Approximately 30 examples made in .45- and .455-caliber; 250 in .47-caliber.

Model 1868 Iron Frame Carbine

Overall length 40"; barrel length 20"; caliber .44 centerfire. Walnut stock, with case-hardened furniture; barrel and magazine tube blued; receiver case-hardened. Finger lever catch as above. Unmarked, except for serial numbers (receiver and buttplate tang). Approximately 25 manufactured.

Model 1873

This Winchester rifle was one of the most popular lever-actions the company ever produced. This is the "gun that won the West" and with good reason. Chambered for the more powerful centerfire cartridge, .44-40. Compared to .44 Henry, this cartridge was twice as good. With the introduction of single-action Colt pistol in 1878, chambered for the same cartridge, the individual had the convenience of a pistol for protection and accuracy of the Winchester for food and protection. The .44-40 was the standard cartridge for Model 1873. Three additional cartridges were offered, but were not as popular as .44-40. The .38-40 first offered in 1879 and .32-20 introduced in 1882. In 1884, offered in .22-caliber rimfire, with a few special order guns built in .22 extra long rimfire. Approximately 19,552 .22-caliber Model 1873s were produced. Early model 1873s were fitted with an iron receiver until 1884, when a steel receiver was introduced.

Model 1873 was offered in three styles:

1. Sporting Rifle: 24" round, octagon or half-octagon barrel. Equipped standard with a crescent iron buttplate, straight-grip stock and capped forearm.

2. Carbine: 20" round barrel. Furnished standard with a rounded iron buttplate, straight-grip stock and carbine style fore-end fastened to barrel with a single barrel band.

3. Musket: 30" round barrel. Standard musket furnished with a nearly full-length forearm fastened to barrel with three barrel bands. Buttstock has a rounded buttplate.

Upper tang was marked with model designation and serial number was stamped on lower tang. Caliber stampings on Model 1873 are found on the bottom of the frame and on breech end of barrel. Winchester discontinued Model 1873 in 1919, after producing about 720,000 guns. Winchester Model 1873 was offered with a large number of extra-cost options that greatly affects the value of this gun. For example, Winchester built two sets of special Model 1873s: 1-of-100 and 1-of-1000. Winchester sold only eight 1-of-100 Model 1873s; and 136 of 1-of-1000 guns that were built. In recent years, some of these special guns were sold at auction and brought prices well in excess of $100,000. Prices listed here are for standard guns only. For Model 1873 with special features, it is best to secure an expert appraisal. Model 1873s with case colored receivers will bring a premium.

Courtesy Bonhams & Butterfields, San Francisco, California

First Model Rifle

Primary difference between the various styles of Model 1873, is found in appearance and construction of the dust cover. First Model has a dust cover held in place with grooved guides on either side. A checkered oval finger grip is found on top of the dust cover. Latch that holds lever firmly in place is anchored into the lower tang with visible threads. On later First Models, these threads are not visible. First Models appear from serial number 1 to about 31000.

NIB	Exc.	V.G.	Good	Fair	Poor
—	22000	18000	10000	3000	1400

First Model Carbine

NIB	Exc.	V.G.	Good	Fair	Poor
—	26000	20000	12000	4000	2500

First Model Musket

NIB	Exc.	V.G.	Good	Fair	Poor
—	16000	12000	7000	2500	1000

Second Model Rifle

Dust cover on Second Model operates on one central guide secured to receiver with two screws. Checkered oval finger grip is still used, but on later Second Model this is changed to a serrated finger grip on rear of the dust cover. Second Models are found in 31000 to 90000 serial number range.

NIB	Exc.	V.G.	Good	Fair	Poor
—	12000	8000	4000	2000	1250

Second Model Carbine

NIB	Exc.	V.G.	Good	Fair	Poor
—	20000	13000	7000	3000	1000

Second Model Musket

NIB	Exc.	V.G.	Good	Fair	Poor
—	5000	4000	2000	1250	900

Third Model Rifle

Central guide rail is still present on Third Model, but is now integrally machined as part of the receiver. Serrated rear edges of dust cover are still present on Third Model.

NIB	Exc.	V.G.	Good	Fair	Poor
—	6000	4000	2000	1000	750

Third Model Carbine

NIB	Exc.	V.G.	Good	Fair	Poor
—	12500	8000	5000	2000	800

Third Model Musket

NIB	Exc.	V.G.	Good	Fair	Poor
—	12000	10000	8000	4500	2500

Model 1873 .22 Rimfire Rifle

Winchester's first .22-caliber rifle and first .22-caliber repeating rifle made in America, was introduced in 1884 and discontinued in 1904. Its drawback was the small caliber. General preference during this period of time was for larger-caliber rifles. Winchester sold a little more than 19,000 .22-caliber Model 1873s.

NIB	Exc.	V.G.	Good	Fair	Poor
—	10000	6500	3000	1700	750

Model 1876

Winchester's Model 1876, sometimes referred to as Centennial Model, was company's response to the public's demand for a repeater rifle capable of handling larger and more potent calibers. Many single-shot rifles were available at this time to shoot more powerful cartridges. Winchester redesigned earlier Model 1873 to answer this need. Principal changes made to Model 1873, were a larger and stronger receiver to handle more powerful cartridges. Both the carbine and musket had their forearms extended to cover the full length of the magazine tube. Carbine barrel was increased in length from 20" to 22"; musket barrel from 30 to 32". Model 1876 was the first Winchester to be offered with a pistol-grip stock on its special Sporting Rifle. Model 1876 was available in these calibers: .45-77 W.C.F., .50-95 Express, .45-60 W.C.F., .40-60 W.C.F.

Model 1876 was offered in four different styles:

1. Sporting Rifle: 28" round, octagon or half-octagon barrel. Fitted with a straight-grip stock, with crescent iron buttplate. A special sporting rifle was offered with a pistol-grip stock.
2. Express Rifle: 26" round, octagon or half-octagon barrel. Same sporting rifle stock was used.
3. Carbine: 22" round barrel, with full-length forearm secured by one barrel band and straight-grip stock.
4. Musket: 32" round barrel, with full-length forearm secured by one barrel band and straight-grip stock.

Stamped on barrel is Winchester address with King's patent date. Caliber marking is stamped on bottom of receiver near magazine tube and breech end of barrel. Winchester also furnished Model 1876 in 1-of-100 and 1-of-1000 special guns. Only eight 1-of-100 1876s were built; and 54 1-of-1000 1876s. As with their Model 1873 counterparts, these rare guns often sell in the $75,000 range or more. Approximately 64,000 Model 1876s were built by Winchester between 1876 and 1897. As with other Winchesters prices given are for standard guns.

First Model Rifle

As with Model 1873, primary difference in model types lies in the dust cover. First Model has no dust cover. Seen between serial number 1 and 3000.

NIB	Exc.	V.G.	Good	Fair	Poor
—	20000	17500	12000	2750	1000

First Model Carbine

NIB	Exc.	V.G.	Good	Fair	Poor
—	19000	16000	10000	2500	1000

First Model Musket

NIB	Exc.	V.G.	Good	Fair	Poor
—	25000	20000	12000	5000	1500

Second Model Rifle

Second Model has a dust cover, with guide rail attached to receiver with two screws. On early Second Model, an oval finger guide is stamped on top of dust cover; while later models have a serrated finger guide along rear edge of dust cover. Second Models range from serial numbers 3000 to 30000.

NIB	Exc.	V.G.	Good	Fair	Poor
—	11000	7500	4000	2000	1000

Second Model Carbine

NIB	Exc.	V.G.	Good	Fair	Poor
—	20000	17500	12000	6000	2000

Second Model Musket

NIB	Exc.	V.G.	Good	Fair	Poor
—	20000	15000	8000	1750	1000

Second Model Northwest Mounted Police Carbine

Folding rear sight is graduated in meters instead of yards. **NOTE:** Deduct 50 percent from prices if factory records do not confirm NWMP use. A Model 1876 NWMP in excellent condition is very rare. Proceed with caution.

Courtesy Little John's Auction Service, Inc., Paul Goodwin photo

NIB	Exc.	V.G.	Good	Fair	Poor
—	15000	9000	4500	2000	1250

Third Model Rifle

Dust cover guide rail on Third Model is integrally machined as part of receiver, with serrated rear edge on dust cover. Third Model will be seen from serial numbers 30000 to 64000.

NIB	Exc.	V.G.	Good	Fair	Poor
—	14000	10000	6000	3000	1500

Third Model Carbine

NIB	Exc.	V.G.	Good	Fair	Poor
—	20000	17500	12000	6000	2000

Third Model Musket

NIB	Exc.	V.G.	Good	Fair	Poor
—	14000	10000	7500	4000	1000

Winchester Hotchkiss Bolt-Action Rifle

This model is also known as Hotchkiss Magazine Gun or Model 1883. Designed by Benjamin Hotchkiss in 1876. Winchester acquired manufacturing rights to this rifle in 1877. In 1879, the first guns were delivered for sale. Hotchkiss rifle was a bolt-action firearm designed for military and sporting use. First bolt-action rifle made by Winchester. Furnished in .45-70 Government, although the 1884 Winchester catalog lists a .40-65 Hotchkiss as being available. No evidence exists that such a chamber was ever actually furnished.

Model 1883 was available in three different styles:

1. Sporting Rifle: 26" round, octagon or half-octagon barrel. Fitted with a rifle-type stock that included a modified pistol-grip or straight-grip stock.

2. Carbine: 24" or 22.5" round barrel, with military-style straight-grip stock.

3. Musket: 32" or 28" round barrel, with almost full-length military-style straight-grip stock.

Winchester produced Model 1883 until 1899, having built about 85,000 guns.

Courtesy Bonhams & Butterfields, San Francisco, California

First Model Sporting Rifle

This model has safety and turn button magazine cut-off located above trigger guard on the right side. Sporting Rifle furnished with 26" round or octagon barrel; carbine a 24" round barrel, with saddle ring on left side of stock; musket a 32" round barrel, with two barrel bands, steel forearm tip and bayonet attachment under the barrel. Serial number range between 1 and about 6419.

NIB	Exc.	V.G.	Good	Fair	Poor
—	2000	1650	1250	800	400

First Model Carbine

NIB	Exc.	V.G.	Good	Fair	Poor
—	5500	2500	1500	900	500

First Model Musket

NIB	Exc.	V.G.	Good	Fair	Poor
—	2000	1650	1250	800	400

Second Model Sporting Rifle

Second Model Sporting Rifle remains unchanged from First Model, with these exceptions. Safety located on top left side of receiver; and magazine cutoff located on top right side of receiver to rear of the bolt handle. Carbine has a 22.5" round barrel, with nickeled forearm cap; musket now a 28" barrel. Serial number range runs from 6420 to 22521.

Courtesy Milwaukee Public Museum, Milwaukee, Wisconsin

NIB	Exc.	V.G.	Good	Fair	Poor
—	1750	1400	900	600	300

Second Model Carbine

NIB	Exc.	V.G.	Good	Fair	Poor
—	1750	1400	900	600	300

Second Model Musket

NIB	Exc.	V.G.	Good	Fair	Poor
—	4500	2250	1000	750	500

Third Model Sporting Rifle

Third Model is easily identified by two-piece stock separated by the receiver. Specifications for sporting rifle remain the same as before; while carbine is now fitted with a 20" barrel, with saddle ring and bar on left side of the frame; and musket remains unchanged from Second Model, except with the two-piece stock. Serial numbers range from 22552 to 84555.

NIB	Exc.	V.G.	Good	Fair	Poor
—	1650	1250	800	500	300

Third Model Carbine

NIB	Exc.	V.G.	Good	Fair	Poor
—	1650	1250	800	500	300

Third Model Musket

NIB	Exc.	V.G.	Good	Fair	Poor
—	1650	1250	800	500	300

Model 1885 (Single-Shot)

Model 1885 marks an important development between Winchester and John M. Browning. The Single-Shot rifle was first, of many, Browning patents that Winchester would purchase and provide the company with opportunities to diversify its firearms line. Model 1885 was the first single-shot rifle built by Winchester. The company offered more calibers in this model than any other. A total of 45 centerfire calibers were offered from .22 extra long to 50-110 express; as well as 14 rimfire calibers from .22 B.B. cap to .44 flat Henry. Numerous barrel lengths, shapes and weights were available; as were stock configurations, sights and finishes. These rifles were also available in solid frame and take-down styles. One could almost argue that each of the 139,725 Model 1885s built are unique. Model 1885 was manufactured between 1885 and 1920. Many collectors of Winchester Single-Shot specialize in nothing else. For this reason, it is difficult to provide pricing that will cover most of the Model 1885s that collectors will encounter. However, prices given here are for standard guns in standard configurations.

Model 1885 was offered in two basic frame types:

A. High Wall was the first frame type produced, and is so called because frame covers breech and hammer except for the hammer spur.

B. Breech and hammer are visible on Low Wall frame, with its low sides. This frame type was first introduced around 5000 serial number range.

Both High Wall and Low Wall were available in two type frame profiles; Thickside and Thinside. Thickside frame has flat sides that do not widen out to meet the stock. Thickside is more common on Low Wall rifle and rare on High Wall. Thinside frame has shallow milled sides that widen out to meet the stock. Thinside frames are common on High Wall rifle and rare on Low Wall.

1. Standard High Wall rifle was available with octagon or round barrel, with length determined by caliber. Buttstock and forearm were plain walnut, with crescent buttplate and blued frame.

2. Standard Low Wall rifle featured round or octagon barrel, with length determined by caliber. Plain walnut stock and forearm, with crescent buttplate.

3. High Wall musket most often had a 26" round barrel. Chambered for .22-caliber cartridge. Larger calibers were available as were different barrel lengths. Featured an almost full length forearm fastened to barrel with a single barrel band and rounded buttplate.

4. Low Wall musket is most often referred to as Winder Musket, named after distinguished marksman, Colonel C.B. Winder. Features a Lyman receiver sight and made in .22-caliber.

5. High Wall Schuetzen rifle was designed for serious target shooting. Available with numerous extras, including 30" octagon barrel; medium weight without rear sight seat; fancy walnut checkered pistol-grip Schuetzen-style buttplate; checkered forearm; double-set triggers; spur finger lever; adjustable palm rest.

6. Low Wall carbine was available in 15", 16", 18" and 20" round barrels. Carbine featured a saddle ring on left side of the frame and a rounded buttplate.

7. High Wall shotgun in 20-gauge, with 26" round barrel, straight-grip stock and shotgun style rubber buttplate.

NOTE: Add 25 percent premium for case colored frames over guns with blued frames. Calibers .50-110 and .50-100 will bring a premium depending on style and configuration.

CALIBER NOTE: As stated above, it is difficult to provide pricing on specific rifles, especially calibers, because of the wide range of variables. However, collectors may find it useful to know the most common rimfire calibers were .22 Short, .22 WCF and .22 Long in that order, with .22 Long Rifle a distant fourth. Most common centerfire calibers were .32 WCF and .32-40. Other popular centerfire calibers were .38-55, .25-20, .44 WCF, .32 Long WCF and .45-70. There were a number of chamberings that are extremely rare (one of each built). It is strongly recommended that research is done prior to a sale.

Courtesy Bonhams & Butterfields, San Francisco, California

Standard High Wall Rifle

Courtesy Bonhams & Butterfields, San Francisco, California

Deluxe High Wall

NIB	Exc.	V.G.	Good	Fair	Poor
—	5000	3500	2200	1500	950

Standard Low Wall Rifle

Courtesy Bonhams & Butterfields, San Francisco, California

NIB	Exc.	V.G.	Good	Fair	Poor
—	1800	1500	1400	1200	900

High Wall Musket

NIB	Exc.	V.G.	Good	Fair	Poor
—	1600	1300	1000	700	425

Low Wall Musket (Winder Musket)

Courtesy Buffalo Bill Historical Center, Cody, Wyoming

NIB	Exc.	V.G.	Good	Fair	Poor
—	1400	1200	800	500	300

High Wall Schuetzen Rifle

NIB	Exc.	V.G.	Good	Fair	Poor
—	10000	7000	3000	1850	1000

Low Wall Carbine

NIB	Exc.	V.G.	Good	Fair	Poor
—	7500	5000	3500	2750	1500

High Wall Shotgun

Courtesy Buffalo Bill Historical Center, Cody, Wyoming

NIB	Exc.	V.G.	Good	Fair	Poor
—	4500	3000	2250	1250	850

Model 1886

Based on a John Browning patent, Model 1886 was one of the finest and strongest lever-actions ever utilized in a Winchester rifle. Winchester introduced Model 1886, in order to take advantage of the more powerful centerfire cartridges of the time. Most popular caliber was .45-70 Government.

Model 1886 Rifles and Carbines were furnished with black walnut stocks, case-hardened frames, blued barrels and magazine tubes. In 1901, Winchester discontinued the use of case-hardened frames on all its rifles and used blued frames instead. For this reason, case-hardened rifles will bring a premium. Winchester provided a large selection of extra cost options on Model 1886. Rifles with these options, a separate evaluation should be made by a reliable source. Produced about 160,000 from 1886 to 1935. **NOTE:** A new record price for a single firearm was established in April 2016, when a very special Winchester Model 1886 rifle sold for $1.265 million. The historic rifle with serial number 1, had been presented to U.S. Army Captain Henry Lawton following his capture of Apache leader Geronimo in September of 1886. In near mint original condition, the rifle was sold at auction by Rock Island Auction Co. to an anonymous bidder.

Rifle was available in 10 different chambers:

.45-70 U.S. Government	.50-110 Express
.45-90 W.C.F.	.40-70 W.C.F.
.40-82 W.C.F.	.38-70 W.C.F.
.40-65 W.C.F.	.50-100-450
.38-56 W.C.F.	.33 W.C.F.

Model 1886s were available in several different configurations:

1. Sporting Rifle: 26" round, octagon and half-octagon barrel; full or half magazine; straight-grip stock, with plain forearm.

2. Fancy Sporting Rifle: 26" round or octagon barrel; half or full magazine; fancy checkered walnut pistol-grip, with checkered forearm.

3. Takedown Rifle: 24" round barrel; full or half magazine, with straight-grip stock fitted with shotgun rubber buttplate and plain forearm.

4. Extra Lightweight Takedown Rifle: 22" round barrel; full or half magazine, with straight-grip stock fitted with shotgun rubber buttplate and plain forearm.

5. Extra Lightweight Rifle: 22" round barrel; full or half magazine, with straight-grip stock fitted with a shotgun rubber buttplate and plain forearm.

6. Carbine: 22" round barrel; full or half magazine, with straight-grip stock and plain forearm.

7. Musket: 30" round barrel; musket-style forearm, with one barrel band. Military-style sights. About 350 Model 1886 Muskets were produced.

NOTE: Add 20 percent premium for .50 Express; 20 percent premium for case colored. Prices are influenced by caliber, with larger calibers bringing a premium.

Sporting Rifle

Courtesy Bonhams & Butterfields, San Francisco, California

NIB	Exc.	V.G.	Good	Fair	Poor
—	15000	15000	7500	5000	2500

Fancy Sporting Rifle

NIB	Exc.	V.G.	Good	Fair	Poor
—	25000	14500	8000	6000	3000

Takedown Rifle—Standard

NIB	Exc.	V.G.	Good	Fair	Poor
—	12500	900	4200	2000	700

Extra Lightweight Takedown Rifle—.33 caliber

NIB	Exc.	V.G.	Good	Fair	Poor
—	9000	5000	2000	750	400

Extra Lightweight Takedown Rifle—Other Calibers

NIB	Exc.	V.G.	Good	Fair	Poor
—	8750	6000	1800	1250	500

Extra Lightweight Rifle—.33 caliber

NIB	Exc.	V.G.	Good	Fair	Poor
—	6000	4000	1800	1000	500

Extra Lightweight Rifle—Other Calibers

NIB	Exc.	V.G.	Good	Fair	Poor
—	7000	5500	3000	950	500

Carbine

Carbine barrels are 22". Few were Trappers, with 20" barrels.
NOTE: Add 50 percent if Trapper.

Courtesy Bonhams & Butterfields, San Francisco, California

NIB	Exc.	V.G.	Good	Fair	Poor
—	19000	11000	7500	4500	2000

Musket

NIB	Exc.	V.G.	Good	Fair	Poor
—	19000	15000	9000	3500	1500

Model 71

When Winchester dropped Model 1886 from its line in 1935, the company replaced its large-bore lever-action rifle with Model 71. Chambered for .348-caliber. Model 71 is similar in appearance to Model 1886, with some internal parts strengthened to handle the powerful .348 cartridge. Frames and barrels were blued on all models of this rifle. Model 71 was produced from 1935 to 1957, with about 47,000 built.

Model 71 was available in three basic configurations:

1. Standard Rifle: 24" round barrel; 3/4 magazine; plain walnut pistol-grip stock; semi-beavertail forearm.

2. Standard Rifle (Carbine): 20" round barrel; 3/4 magazine; plain walnut pistol-grip stock; semi-beavertail forearm.

3. Deluxe Rifle: 24" round barrel; 3/4 magazine; checkered walnut pistol-grip stock; checkered semi-beavertail forearm.

4. Deluxe Rifle (Carbine): 20" round barrel; 3/4 magazine; checkered walnut pistol-grip stock; checkered semi-beavertail forearm.

NOTE: Add 10 percent for bolt peep sight; 20 percent premium for pre-war models (pre-war Model 71s have a longer tang than post-war equivalent).

Standard Rifle

NIB	Exc.	V.G.	Good	Fair	Poor
—	1500	1200	800	400	300

Standard Rifle (Carbine)

NIB	Exc.	V.G.	Good	Fair	Poor
—	3250	2000	1600	1200	650

Deluxe Rifle

NIB	Exc.	V.G.	Good	Fair	Poor
—	3500	3050	800	525	425

Deluxe Rifle (Carbine)

NIB	Exc.	V.G.	Good	Fair	Poor
—	4100	3500	2000	1250	700

Model 1892

Model 1892 was an updated successor to Model 1873, using a scaled down version of Model 1886 action. Chambered for popular smaller cartridges of the day, namely .25-20, .32-20, .38-40, .44-40 and rare .218 Bee. Built between 1892 and 1932, with slightly more than 1 million sold. Carbine model continued to be offered until 1941.

Model 1892 was available in several different configurations:

1. Sporting Rifle: solid frame or take-down (worth 20 percent extra premium); 24" round, octagon or half-octagon barrel; 1/2, 3/3 or full magazines; plain straight-grip walnut stock, with capped forearm.

2. Fancy Sporting Rifle: solid frame or take-down (worth 20 percent extra premium); 24" round, octagon or half-octagon barrel; 1/2, 3/3 or full magazines; checkered walnut pistol-grip stock; checkered capped forearm.

3. Carbine: 20" round barrel; full or half magazine; plain walnut straight-grip stock, with one barrel band forearm. Carbines offered only with solid frames.

4. Trapper's Carbine: 18", 16", 15" or 14" round barrel, with same dimensions of standard carbine. Federal law prohibits possession of rifles with barrel lengths shorter then 16". Model 1892 Trapper's Carbine can be exempted from this law, as a curio and relic, with federal permit providing trapper is an original trapper and left the factory with the short trapper barrel.

5. Musket: 30" round barrel, with full magazine. Almost full length forearm held by two barrel bands. Buttstock plain walnut, with straight-grip.

NOTE: Add 10 percent premium for Antique Winchester Model 1892s (pre-1898 manufacture).

Sporting Rifle

Courtesy Bonhams & Butterfields, San Francisco, California

NIB	Exc.	V.G.	Good	Fair	Poor
—	5000	3500	1250	700	350

Fancy Sporting Rifle

Courtesy Bonhams & Butterfields, San Francisco, California

NIB	Exc.	V.G.	Good	Fair	Poor
—	12000	7500	4000	2500	1000

Carbine

Courtesy Bonhams & Butterfields, San Francisco, California

NIB	Exc.	V.G.	Good	Fair	Poor
—	3500	2500	1700	1200	600

Trapper's Carbine

NOTE: Add 20 percent for 15" barrel; 50 percent for carbines chambered for .25-20 cartridge.

Courtesy Bonhams & Butterfields, San Francisco, California

NIB	Exc.	V.G.	Good	Fair	Poor
—	12000	8500	4000	2500	1250

Musket

NIB	Exc.	V.G.	Good	Fair	Poor
—	—	9500	4500	2500	1500

Model 1894

Based on a John M. Browning patent, Model 1894 was the most successful centerfire rifle Winchester ever produced. This model is still in production. Values given here reflect those rifles produced before 1964, or around serial number 2550000. Model 1894 was the first Winchester developed especially for the smokeless powder. Chambered for these cartridges: .32-40, .38-55, .25-35 Win., .30-30 Win. and .32 Win. Special. All Model 1894s were furnished with blued frames and barrels. Case-hardened frames were available as an extra-cost option. Case colored Model 1894s are rare and worth a considerable premium, perhaps as much as 1,000 percent. Guns with extra-cost options should be evaluated by an expert to determine proper value. Between 1894 and 1963, approximately 2,550,000 Model 1894s were sold.

Model 1894s were available in several different configurations:

1. Sporting Rifle: 26" round, octagon or half-octagon barrel; solid frame or take-down; full, 2/3 or 1/2 magazines; plain walnut straight-/pistol-grip stock; crescent buttplate; plain capped forearm.

2. Fancy Sporting Rifle: 26" round, octagon or half-octagon barrel; solid frame or take-down; full, 2/3 or 1/2 magazines; fancy walnut checkered straight-/pistol-grip stock; crescent buttplate; checkered fancy capped forearm.

3. Extra Lightweight Rifle: 22" or 26" round barrel; half magazine; plain walnut straight-grip stock; shotgun buttplate; plain capped forearm.

4. Carbine: 20" round barrel; plain walnut straight-grip stock; carbine style buttplate; forearm was plain walnut uncapped, with one barrel band; solid frame only. Carbines made prior to 1925, were fitted with a saddle ring on left side of receiver. Worth a premium over carbines without a saddle ring.

5. Trappers Carbine: 18", 16", 15" or 14" round barrel. Buttstock, forearm and saddle ring specifications same as standard carbine.

NOTE: Add 10 percent premium for Antique Winchester Model 1894s (pre-1898 manufacture); 100 percent premium for First year production guns, October 1894 to December 1894, documented by the Cody Museum; 25 percent for carbines chambered .25-35 or .38-55 cartridge. Deduct 35 percent for carbines without saddle rings. Values are for guns with saddle rings.

First Model Sporting Rifle

Very early model. Incorporates a screw entering receiver over the loading port from outside. RARE.

NIB	Exc.	V.G.	Good	Fair	Poor
—	7000	4000	2000	1250	500

Sporting Rifle

NOTE: Add 20 percent for take-down versions.

Courtesy Bonhams & Butterfields, San Francisco, California

NIB	Exc.	V.G.	Good	Fair	Poor
—	4000	3000	1500	850	450

Fancy Sporting Rifle

NOTE: Add 20 percent for take-down versions. Fancy Sporting Rifles were also engraved at customer's request. Check factory where possible and proceed with caution. Factory engraved Model 1894s are extremely valuable.

Courtesy Bonhams & Butterfields, San Francisco, California

NIB	Exc.	V.G.	Good	Fair	Poor
—	12000	7500	3500	2000	900

Extra Lightweight Rifle

Courtesy Bonhams & Butterfields, San Francisco, California

NIB	Exc.	V.G.	Good	Fair	Poor
—	5000	3500	1500	1000	450

Carbine

NIB	Exc.	V.G.	Good	Fair	Poor
—	3000	2000	600	400	200

Trapper's Carbine

NOTE: Add 30 percent for carbines chambered .25-35 or .38-55 calibers.

Courtesy Bonhams & Butterfields, San Francisco, California

NIB	Exc.	V.G.	Good	Fair	Poor
—	6500	4250	2500	1500	700

Model 53

A slightly more modern version of Model 1892. Offered in these calibers: .25-20, .32-20 and .44-40. Available in only one style: Sporting Rifle; 22" round barrel; half magazine; straight-/pistol-grip plain walnut stock, with shotgun butt. Available in solid frame or take-down, with blued frame and barrel. Produced from 1924 to 1932, with about 25,000 built. **NOTE:** Add 25 percent for take-down model; 60 percent for rifles chambered for .44-40 cartridge. Deluxe model was made with high-grade checkered stock. A few of these rifles were fitted with stainless steel barrels in early 1930s. If the black paint on these barrels is in good condition, they will bring a substantial premium.

NIB	Exc.	V.G.	Good	Fair	Poor
—	3000	2000	1000	500	300

Deluxe Model

NIB	Exc.	V.G.	Good	Fair	Poor
—	4000	3200	2400	1500	750

Model 55

A continuation of Model 1894, except in a simplified version. Available in same calibers as Model 1894. This rifle could be ordered only with a 24" round barrel; plain walnut straight-grip stock, with plain fore-end and shotgun butt. Frame and barrel were blued, with solid or take-down features. Produced between 1924 and 1932, with about 21,000 sold. Serial numbers were numbered separately until about serial number 4500; then numbered in Model 1894 sequence. **NOTE:** .25-35 calibers will bring up to 100 percent premium in V.G. or better condition. Add 20 percent premium for models with solid frames.

NIB	Exc.	V.G.	Good	Fair	Poor
—	2250	1500	900	500	300

Model 64

An improved version of Model 55. Features larger magazine, pistol-grip stock and forged front sight ramp. Trigger pull was also improved. Frame and barrel were blued. Chambered for .25-35 Win., .30-30 Win., .32 Win. Special and .219 Zipper added in 1938 (discontinued in Model 64 in 1941). Serial numbers were concurrent with Model 1894. Built between 1933 and 1957. Approximately 67,000 were sold. Reintroduced in 1972, discontinued in 1973. Values listed are for early version only. For 1972 model, see POST-1963 RIFLES section. **NOTE:** Add 150 percent for Deluxe model. Rifles chambered in .219 Zipper or .25-35 calibers are very rare. Add 400 percent for .219 Zipper; 200 percent for .25-35; 10 percent for bolt peep sight. Model 64s in .219 Zipper left factory with these sights as original equipment.

Bonhams & Butterfields, San Francisco, California

NIB	Exc.	V.G.	Good	Fair	Poor
—	1200	900	500	300	200

Carbine

20" barrel.

NIB	Exc.	V.G.	Good	Fair	Poor
—	2800	2000	1200	800	500

Model 65

Continuation of Model 53. Offered in three calibers: .25-20, .32-20 and .218 Bee. Had several improvements over Model 53, namely magazine capacity increased to 7 cartridges, forged ramp for front sight and lighter trigger pull. Available only in solid blued frame, with blued barrel and plain walnut pistol-grip stock. About 5,700 built between 1933 and 1947. **NOTE:** Add 50 percent for Deluxe model with high-grade checkered walnut stock; 10 percent for bolt peep sight. Model 65s in .218 Bee left factory with bolt peep sights as original equipment.

NIB	Exc.	V.G.	Good	Fair	Poor
—	5000	4000	2000	1000	500

Model 1895

Model 1895 was the first non-detachable box magazine rifle offered by Winchester. Built on a John M. Browning patent. Introduced by Winchester to meet the demand for a rifle that could handle new high-power, smokeless hunting cartridges of the period. Model 1895 was available in these calibers: .30-40 Krag, .38-72 Win., .40-72 Win., .303 British, .35 Win., .405 Government, 7.62 Russian, .30-03 and .30-06. Rifle gained fame as a favorite hunting rifle of Theodore Roosevelt. Because of its box magazine, Model 1895 has a distinctive look like no other Winchester lever-action rifle. Model 1895 was produced from 1895 to 1931, with about 426,000 sold.

Model 1895 was available in several different configurations:

1. Sporting Rifle: 28" or 24" (depending on caliber) round barrel; plain walnut straight-grip stock; plain fore-end. First 5,000 rifles manufactured with flat-sided receivers; and balance of production built with receiver sides contoured. After serial-number 60000, a take-down version was available.

2. Fancy Sporting Rifle: 28" round barrel; fancy walnut checkered straight-grip stock and forearm. Rifles with serial numbers below 5000 had flat sided frames.

3. Carbine: 22" round barrel; plain walnut straight-grip stock; military-style hand guard fore-end. Some carbines furnished with saddle rings on left side of receiver.

4. Musket:

A. Standard Musket - 28" round barrel; plain walnut straight-grip stock; musket style fore-end; two barrel bands.

B. U.S. Army N.R.A. Musket - 30" round barrel; Model 1901 Krag-Jorgensen rear sight; stock similar to standard musket. This musket could be used for "Any Military Arm" matches under the rules of National Rifle Association.

C. N.R.A. Musket Models 1903 and 1906 - 24" round barrel; special buttplate. Also eligible for all matches under "Any Military Arm" sponsored by NRA. This musket was fitted with the same stock as listed above.

D. U.S. Army Musket - 28" round barrel; chambered for .30-40 Krag; equipped with-/without knife bayonet. These muskets were furnished to U.S. Army for use during Spanish-American War and are "US" marked on receiver.

E. Russian Musket - similar to standard musket, but fitted with clip guides in the top of receiver, with bayonet. Approximately 294,000 Model 1895 Muskets were sold to Imperial Russian Government between 1915 and 1916. First 15,000 Russian Muskets had 8" knife bayonets, balance fitted with 16" bayonets.

NOTE: Add 10 percent premium for rifles built before 1898.

Sporting Rifle

NOTE: Add 100 percent premium for flat-side rifles; additional 15 percent for take-down rifles.

Flat-side rifle

NIB	Exc.	V.G.	Good	Fair	Poor
—	5000	3000	1200	700	300

Fancy Sporting Rifles

NOTE: Add 100 percent premium for flat-side rifles; additional 15 percent for take-down rifles.

NIB	Exc.	V.G.	Good	Fair	Poor
—	7000	5000	1500	1100	500

Carbine

Courtesy Bonhams & Butterfields, San Francisco, California

NIB	Exc.	V.G.	Good	Fair	Poor
—	5500	3250	1550	900	300

Standard Musket

NIB	Exc.	V.G.	Good	Fair	Poor
—	3200	1800	1000	600	300

U.S. Army N.R.A. Musket

NIB	Exc.	V.G.	Good	Fair	Poor
—	4500	2000	1200	800	400

N.R.A. Musket, Model 1903 and 1906

NIB	Exc.	V.G.	Good	Fair	Poor
—	5500	2500	1200	800	400

U.S. Army Musket

NIB	Exc.	V.G.	Good	Fair	Poor
—	5000	3000	1500	850	450

Russian Musket

NIB	Exc.	V.G.	Good	Fair	Poor
—	4000	2500	1000	500	250

Breechloading Double-Barrel Shotgun

Winchester imported an English-made shotgun sold under the Winchester name between 1879 and 1884. Available in 10- and 12-gauge, with 30" or 32" Damascus barrels. Sold in five separate grades referred to as "classes". Lowest grade was "D" and best grade called "Match Grade". They were marked on the sidelocks. Center rib was stamped "Winchester Repeating Arms Co., New Haven, Connecticut, U.S.A.". Prices shown are for "D" grade. About 10,000 of these guns were imported by Winchester. **NOTE:** Add 10 percent for "C" grade; 20 percent for "B" grade; 30 percent for "A" grade.

Class A, B, C, and D

NIB	Exc.	V.G.	Good	Fair	Poor
—	2500	2250	1250	850	500

Match Gun

NIB	Exc.	V.G.	Good	Fair	Poor
—	5000	4000	1800	850	500

Model 1887 Shotgun

Winchester enjoyed a great deal of success with its imported English shotgun, so the company decided to manufacture a shotgun of its own. In 1885, Winchester purchased the patent for a lever-action shotgun designed by John M. Browning. By 1887, Winchester had delivered the first Model 1887 Shotgun in 12-gauge. Shortly thereafter, in 10-gauge. Both gauges offered with 30" or 32" Full choked barrels, with 30" standard on 12-gauge; 32" on 10-gauge. In 1898, a Riot Gun was offered in 10- and 12-gauge, with 20" barrels choked Cylinder. Both variations offered with plain walnut pistol-grip stocks and fore-end. Frame was case-hardened and barrel blued. Between 1887 and 1901, Winchester sold approximately 65,000 Model 1887 shotguns.

Standard Shotgun

Courtesy Milwaukee Public Museum, Milwaukee, Wisconsin

NIB	Exc.	V.G.	Good	Fair	Poor
—	2750	1500	850	500	300

Riot Shotgun

Courtesy Bonhams & Butterfields, San Francisco, California

NIB	Exc.	V.G.	Good	Fair	Poor
—	3000	2000	950	600	400

Model 1901 Shotgun

A redesign of Model 1887 Shotgun. Offered in 10-gauge only, with 32" barrel choked Full, Modified or Cylinder. Barrel was reinforced to withstand the new smokeless powder loads. Frame blued instead of casehardened. Stock was plain walnut, with a modified pistol and plain forearm. Built between 1901 and 1920. About 65,000 guns sold.

NIB	Exc.	V.G.	Good	Fair	Poor
—	3000	2200	1200	400	250

Model 1893

First slide-action repeating shotgun built by Winchester. Featured an exposed hammer and side ejection. Based on a John M. Browning patent, this model was not altogether satisfactory. Action proved to be too weak to handle smokeless loads, even though the gun was designed for blackpowder. Offered in 12-gauge, with 30" or 32" barrels choked Full. Other chokes were available on special order and will command a premium. Stock was plain walnut, with a modified pistol-grip grooved slide handle and hard rubber buttplate. Receiver and barrel blued. Produced between 1893 and 1897, selling about 31000 guns.

Courtesy Bonhams & Butterfields, San Francisco, California

NIB	Exc.	V.G.	Good	Fair	Poor
—	1000	700	600	325	250

Model 1897

Model 1897 replaced Model 1893. Similar to Model 1893, the new model had several improvements such as stronger frame, chamber made longer to handle 2.75" shells, frame top was covered to force complete side ejection, stock made longer and with less drop. Available in 12- or 16-gauge, with 12-gauge in solid or take-down styles; 16-gauge in take-down only. Available with barrel lengths of 20", 26", 28", 30" and 32" in practically all choke options from Full to Cylinder. Model 1897 was a great seller for Winchester. During its 60-year production span, 1,025,000 guns were sold.

Model 1897 could be ordered in several different configurations:

1. Standard Gun: 12- or 16-gauge; 30" barrel 12-gauge and 28" barrel 16-gauge; plain walnut modified pistol-grip stock; grooved slide handle; steel buttplate standard.

2. Trap Gun: 12- or 16-gauge; 30" barrel 12-gauge and 28" barrel 16-gauge; fancy walnut stock; oil-finish checkered pistol-/straight-grip stock; checkered slide handle. Marked "TRAP" on bottom of frame.

3. Pigeon Gun: 12- or 16-gauge; 28" barrel on both gauges; straight-/pistol-grip stock; receiver hand engraved.

4. Tournament Gun: 12-gauge only; 30" barrel; select walnut checkered straight-grip stock; checkered slide handle; top of receiver matted to reduce glare.

5. Brush Gun: 12- or 16-gauge; 26" barrel; cylinder choke has a slightly shorter magazine tube than standard gun; plain walnut modified pistol-grip stock; grooved slide handle.

6. Brush Gun, Take-down: same as above with take-down feature; standard length magazine tube.

7. Riot Gun: 12-gauge; 20" barrel bored to shoot buckshot; plain walnut modified pistol-grip stock; grooved slide handle; solid frame or take-down.

8. Trench Gun: same as Riot Gun, but fitted with barrel hand guard and bayonet.

NOTE: Add 100 percent for 16-gauge guns in excellent, very good and good condition.

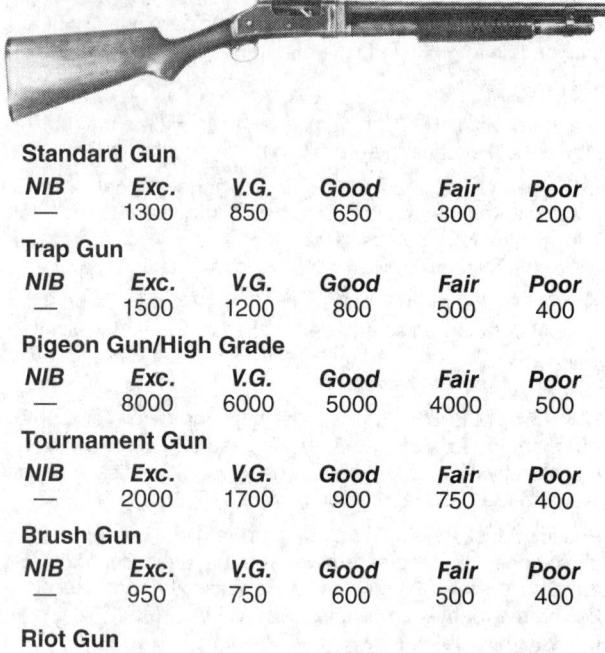

Standard Gun

NIB	Exc.	V.G.	Good	Fair	Poor
—	1300	850	650	300	200

Trap Gun

NIB	Exc.	V.G.	Good	Fair	Poor
—	1500	1200	800	500	400

Pigeon Gun/High Grade

NIB	Exc.	V.G.	Good	Fair	Poor
—	8000	6000	5000	4000	500

Tournament Gun

NIB	Exc.	V.G.	Good	Fair	Poor
—	2000	1700	900	750	400

Brush Gun

NIB	Exc.	V.G.	Good	Fair	Poor
—	950	750	600	500	400

Riot Gun

Courtesy Bonhams & Butterfields, San Francisco, California

NIB	Exc.	V.G.	Good	Fair	Poor
—	2500	1750	1000	600	400

Trench Gun

NOTE: Add 100 percent for 16-gauge in excellent, very good and good condition; 100 percent for military markings.

Courtesy Bonhams & Butterfields, San Francisco, California

NIB	Exc.	V.G.	Good	Fair	Poor
—	7500	4000	2000	1200	600

Winchester-Lee Straight Pull Rifle

U.S. Navy Musket

NIB	Exc.	V.G.	Good	Fair	Poor
—	2500	2000	1500	700	500

Commercial Musket

NIB	Exc.	V.G.	Good	Fair	Poor
—	2500	2000	1500	700	500

Sporting Rifle

Courtesy Amoskeag Auction Company

NIB	Exc.	V.G.	Good	Fair	Poor
—	2500	2000	1500	700	500

Model 1890

Model 1890 was the first slide-action rifle ever produced by Winchester. Designed by John and Matthew Browning. Chambered for .22 Short, Long and Winchester Rimfire cartridges (WRF cartridge was developed by Winchester specifically for Model 1890) not on an interchangeable basis. In 1919, .22 LR cartridge was offered as well. This rifle was slide-action top ejecting, with an 18" under barrel magazine tube. All Model 1890s were furnished standard with plain walnut straight stocks, with crescent buttplate and 12 groove slide handle. One of Winchester's best selling small caliber firearms and in worldwide use. Winchester offered many extra-cost options for this rifle that will greatly affect value. Secure an expert appraisal before proceeding. Produced from 1890 to 1932, with approximately 775,000 guns sold.

Model 1890 came in three separate and distinct variations that greatly affect value:

1. First Model: solid frame; 24" octagon barrel; case-hardened frame; fixed rear sight. Approximately 15,552 First Model guns produced. Their distinctive feature is concealed locking lugs and solid frame. Serial numbered on lower tang only. Built from 1890 to 1892.

2. Second Model (take-down): 24" octagon barrel; case-hardened frame; adjustable rear sight. Serial numbered from 15553 to 112970 (on lower tang only). These Second Model guns feature same concealed locking lugs, with added take-down feature. A Deluxe version was offered, with fancy walnut checkered straight-/pistol-grip stock and grooved slide handle.

2A. Second Model (blued frame variation): same as above, with blued frame. Serial numbered from 112971 to 325250 (on lower tang until 232328, then on bottom front end of receiver). These blued frame Second Models are much more numerous than case-hardened variety. A Deluxe version was offered, with fancy walnut checkered straight-/pistol-grip stock and grooved slide handle.

3. Third Model (take-down): 24" octagon barrel; blued frame; adjustable rear sight. Serial numbered from 325251 to as high as 853000 (numbered on both lower tang and bottom front of receiver). Distinctive feature of Third Model is locking cut made on the front top of receiver to allow breech bolt to lock externally. A Deluxe version was offered, with fancy walnut checkered stock, straight-/pistol-grip with grooved slide handle.

NOTE: Add 25 percent premium for Third Models chambered for .22 LR.

First Model—Standard Grade

NIB	Exc.	V.G.	Good	Fair	Poor
—	9000	5000	2500	1250	750

Second Model—Case Hardened Frame Standard

Courtesy Bonhams & Butterfields, San Francisco, California

NIB	Exc.	V.G.	Good	Fair	Poor
—	6000	3500	2000	1000	500

Deluxe

NIB	Exc.	V.G.	Good	Fair	Poor
—	10000	7000	3500	2000	1000

Second Model—Blued Frame Standard

NIB	Exc.	V.G.	Good	Fair	Poor
—	2500	1700	1500	750	250

Deluxe

NIB	Exc.	V.G.	Good	Fair	Poor
—	7500	5500	3000	1500	750

Third Model Standard

NIB	Exc.	V.G.	Good	Fair	Poor
—	2000	1400	900	450	250

Deluxe

NIB	Exc.	V.G.	Good	Fair	Poor
—	6500	4000	2000	1000	750

Model 1906

In 1906, Winchester decided to offer a lower-cost version of Model 1890. Model 1906 used same receiver, but fitted with 20" round barrel and plain gumwood straight-grip stock. When first introduced, it sold for two-thirds the price of Model 1890. For the first two years, it was chambered for .22 Short cartridge only. In 1908, it was modified to shoot .22 Short, Long and LR cartridges interchangeably. This modification ensured Model 1906's success. Between 1906 and 1932, about 800,000 were sold. All Model 1906s were take-down variety.

Model 1906 available in three important variations:

1. .22 Short Only: 20" round barrel; straight-grip gumwood stock; smooth slide handle. These were built from serial number 1 to around 113000.

2. Standard Model 1906: 20" round barrel; straight-grip gumwood stock; 12 groove slide handle. Serial numbered from 113000 to 852000.

3. Model 1906 Expert: 20" round barrel; pistol-grip gumwood stock; fluted smooth slide handle. Expert was available from 1918 to 1924. Offered in three different finishes: regular blued; half nickel (receiver, guard and bolt); full nickel (receiver, guard, bolt and barrel).

.22 Short Only

Courtesy Bonhams & Butterfields, San Francisco, California

NIB	Exc.	V.G.	Good	Fair	Poor
—	2500	1750	750	500	200

Standard

Courtesy Bonhams & Butterfields, San Francisco, California

NIB	Exc.	V.G.	Good	Fair	Poor
2000	1500	750	400	400	200

Expert

Prices are for half nickel. **NOTE:** Add 10 percent for blued guns; 100 percent for full nickel.

Courtesy Bonhams & Butterfields, San Francisco, California

NIB	Exc.	V.G.	Good	Fair	Poor
—	2500	1850	950	500	300

Model 61

Winchester developed Model 61 in an attempt to keep pace with its competitors' hammerless .22 rifles. Featured 24" round or octagonal barrel and could be ordered by customer in a variety of configurations. Collector interest is high, because of the fairly large number of variations. Model 61 is often considered a companion to Winchester Model 12 and Model 42 shotguns. Model 61 was fitted with plain walnut pistol-grip stock, with grooved slide handle. All Model 61s were take-down variety. Pre-war models will have a short slide handle. Manufactured between 1932 and 1963. Approximately 342,000 guns were sold.

Following is a list of chamber and barrel variations found in this model:

1. 24" round barrel; .22 Short, Long, LR.

2. 24" octagonal barrel; .22 Short only; add 150 percent.

3. 24" octagonal barrel; .22 LR only; add 150 percent.

4. 24" octagonal barrel; .22 WRF only; add 100 percent.

5. 24" round barrel; .22 LR shot only; add 200 percent.

5A. 24" round barrel; shot only Routledge bore; add 200 percent.

6. 24" round barrel; .22 WRF only; add 125 percent.

7. 24" round barrel; .22 LR only; add 50 percent.

8. 24" round barrel; .22 Win. Magnum; add 50 percent.

9. 24" round barrel; .22 Short only; add 100 percent.

Pre-war

NOTE: Add 50 percent premium (depending on caliber) for single caliber; 75 percent premium for octagon barrel; 250 percent premium for .22 LR shot only.

NIB	Exc.	V.G.	Good	Fair	Poor
3000	2200	1600	800	400	200

Post-war

Courtesy Bonhams & Butterfields, San Francisco, California

NIB	Exc.	V.G.	Good	Fair	Poor
2000	1400	1200	600	300	250

Magnum

NOTE: This variation produced from 1960 to 1963.

NIB	Exc.	V.G.	Good	Fair	Poor
2800	2400	1600	775	600	400

Model 62 and 62A

Model 1890 and Model 1906 were dropped from the Winchester product line in 1932. Model 62 was introduced to take their place. An updated version of earlier slide-action .22 rifles. Fitted with 23" round barrel and capable of shooting .22 Short, Long and LR cartridges interchangeably.

Winchester offered a Gallery version of Model 62, that was chambered for .22 Short only. Some of these Gallery guns have "Winchester" stamped on left side of receiver. Model 62 Gallery rifles have a triangular loading port on the loading tube that standard models did not have. A change in the breech bolt mechanism brought about a change in the name designation from Model 62 to Model 62A. This occurred around serial number 98000. Letter "A" now appears behind the serial number. This model stayed in production until 1958. Collectors will concede a premium for guns built prior to WWII, with small slide handles. Stock was plain walnut, with straight-grip and grooved slide handle. Both receiver and barrel were blued. All Model 62 and 62As were take-down. Approximately 409,000 guns were sold.

Pre-war

NOTE: Barrels marked with Model 62 are worth more than barrels marked with Model 62A by approximately 15 percent. Gallery models will bring a premium of 300 percent.

NIB	Exc.	V.G.	Good	Fair	Poor
2200	1500	850	400	250	150

Post-war

Courtesy Bonhams & Butterfields, San Francisco, California

NIB	Exc.	V.G.	Good	Fair	Poor
1500	1100	600	500	225	125

Model 62 Gallery

.22 Short only, with triangular loading port & "WINCHESTER" stamped on side of receiver. **NOTE:** Model 62 with "WINCHESTER" stamped on side of receiver is more desirable than one without this stamping. Deduct 10 percent for Gallery rifles without this stamping.

NIB	Exc.	V.G.	Good	Fair	Poor
3200	2000	1000	650	400	200

Model 1903

First semi-automatic rifle produced by Winchester was designed by T.C. Johnson. Offered in a take-down version only. Available in a 20" round barrel. Chambered for .22 Win. Automatic Rimfire. This ammunition is no longer produced, and when found is very expensive. Tubular magazine located in buttstock and holds 10-cartridges. Manufactured from 1903 to 1932, with about 126,000 sold.

Available in two different configurations:

1. Standard Rifle: 20" round barrel; plain walnut straight-grip stock; plain fore-end; steel crescent butt standard.

2. Deluxe Rifle: 20" round barrel; fancy checkered walnut pistol-grip stock; checkered forearm.

Standard

NIB	Exc.	V.G.	Good	Fair	Poor
—	1500	1000	600	200	100

Deluxe

NOTE: First 5,000 guns built without safeties; first 15,000 guns furnished with bronze firing pins instead of steel. Add 30 percent premium for early Model 1903s.

Courtesy Bonhams & Butterfields, San Francisco, California

NIB	Exc.	V.G.	Good	Fair	Poor
—	2500	2000	1200	500	250

Model 63

Model 63 took the place of Model 1903. In 1933, Winchester attempted to solve the problem of having to use a special .22-caliber cartridge to operate the blowback system. It is a very high quality semi-automatic rifle. Many collectors and shooters considered it the best rimfire semi-automatic rifle ever produced. Chambered for .22 LR cartridge. Available in a 20" barrel for the first four years or until about serial number 9800. Thereafter, offered with a 23" round barrel for remainder of the production period. Fitted with a plain walnut pistol-grip stock and forearm. Tubular magazine was located in the buttstock that came with a steel buttplate. Last 10,000 Model 63s were sold with a grooved receiver top to make the addition of a scope easier. Manufactured between 1933 and 1958, with about 175,000 guns sold. **NOTE:** Add 20 percent premium for grooved top receivers.

20" Barrel

Courtesy Bonhams & Butterfields, San Francisco, California

NIB	Exc.	V.G.	Good	Fair	Poor
2750	1400	800	500	400	250

23" Barrel

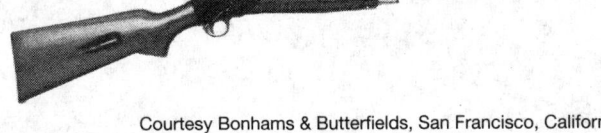

Courtesy Bonhams & Butterfields, San Francisco, California

NIB	Exc.	V.G.	Good	Fair	Poor
2200	1600	900	600	400	200

Model 1905

Model 1905 was a larger version of Model 1903. Developed by T.C. Johnson to handle more powerful centerfire cartridges. Chambered for .32 Win. Self-Loading and .35 Self-Loading cartridges. Loading by means of a detachable box magazine. Available in take-down only. First Winchester semi-automatic rifle to fire centerfire cartridges. Produced from 1905 to 1920, with about 30,000 rifles sold.

Offered in two different styles:

1. Sporting Rifle: 22" round barrel; plain walnut straight-grip (changed to pistol-grip in 1908) stock; plain fore-end.
2. Fancy Sporting Rifle: 22" round barrel; fancy walnut checkered pistol-grip stock; checkered fore-end.

Sporting

NIB	Exc.	V.G.	Good	Fair	Poor
—	700	550	350	175	125

Fancy Sporting

NIB	Exc.	V.G.	Good	Fair	Poor
—	900	750	500	200	150

Model 1907

Model 1907 was an improved version of Model 1905. Chambered for new .351 Win. Self-Loading cartridge. Outward appearance same as Model 1905, except for 20" round barrel. First introduced in 1937. Discon-

tinued in 1957, after selling about 59,000 guns. **NOTE:** Post-WWII Model 1907s command a premium over values shown below.

Available in three different styles:

1. Sporting Rifle: 20" round barrel; plain walnut pistol-grip stock; plain fore-end. Discontinued in 1937.
2. Fancy Sporting Rifle: 20" round barrel; fancy walnut checkered pistol-grip stock; checkered fore-end.
3. Police Rifle: 20" round barrel; plain walnut pistol-grip stock; beavertail fore-end. This version fitted with a leather sling, with/without knife bayonet.

Sporting

NIB	Exc.	V.G.	Good	Fair	Poor
—	750	500	350	175	125

Fancy Sporting

NIB	Exc.	V.G.	Good	Fair	Poor
—	850	650	450	200	150

Police

NIB	Exc.	V.G.	Good	Fair	Poor
—	950	750	575	300	250

Model 1910

Similar to Model 1907, but action made stronger to handle new Winchester .401 Self-Loading cartridge. Specifications for this model same as Model 1907. Built between 1907 and 1936. About 21,000 sold.

Sporting

Courtesy Bonhams & Butterfields, San Francisco, California

NIB	Exc.	V.G.	Good	Fair	Poor
—	900	750	550	400	200

Fancy Sporting

NIB	Exc.	V.G.	Good	Fair	Poor
—	1000	800	600	450	250

Model 55 (Rimfire Rifle)

Not to be confused with lever-action model. This .22-caliber rifle was a semi-automatic (auto-ejecting, actually) single-shot, with 22" round barrel. Fitted with plain walnut pistol-grip one-piece stock and fore-end. Safety goes on when each cartridge is inserted into chamber. This model was not serial numbered. Produced from 1957 to 1961. About 45,000 sold.

NIB	Exc.	V.G.	Good	Fair	Poor
—	400	350	225	150	75

Model 74

Semi-automatic chambered for .22 Short or .22 LR. Has a tubular magazine in the buttstock and a 24" round barrel. Bolt on this rifle was designed to be easily removed for cleaning or repair. Stock was plain walnut pistol-grip, with semi-beavertail fore-end. Gallery Special was offered, chambered for .22 Short and fitted with a steel shell deflector. This Gallery model was also available with chrome trimmings, at extra cost.

Sporting

Courtesy C.H. Wolfersberger

NIB	Exc.	V.G.	Good	Fair	Poor
—	400	300	225	150	100

Gallery Special—.22 Short Only

NOTE: Add 50 percent premium for Gallery models with chrome trimmings.

NIB	Exc.	V.G.	Good	Fair	Poor
—	800	600	325	225	150

Model 77

Built on blow-back design for semi-automatic rifles. Chambered for .22 LR. Features 22" round barrel, detachable box magazine or under barrel tubular magazine. Has a trigger guard made of nylon, plain walnut pistol-grip stock, with semi-beavertail fore-end and composition buttplate. Built between 1955 and 1963. Winchester sold about 217,000 of these rifles. **NOTE:** Add 10 to 20 percent premium for Models with tubular magazines.

NIB	Exc.	V.G.	Good	Fair	Poor
—	500	375	250	175	75

Model 100

Gas-operated semi-automatic chambered for .243-, .308- and .284-caliber cartridges. First commercial Winchester self-loading centerfire rifle made since Winchester Model 1905, Model 1907 and Model 1910. These models were produced until 1936-37. Winchester did produce the M1 Carbine during WWII. Available in a rifle version, with 22" round barrel; carbine version, with 19" barrel. Both furnished with a detachable box magazine. Stock was a one-piece design, with pistol-grip offered in hand-cut checkering or pressed basket weave checkering. Rifles introduced in 1960; carbine in 1967. Model 100 last produced in 1973. About 263,000 sold.

Rifle

NOTE: Prices given are for .308-caliber; add 15 percent for .243; 20 percent for .284; 15 percent premium for Pre-1964 models.

NIB	Exc.	V.G.	Good	Fair	Poor
—	600	475	350	250	200

Carbine

Only about 53,000 carbines made; about 1 for every 5 rifles. **NOTE:** Add 25 percent premium for .243; 100 percent for .284.

NIB	Exc.	V.G.	Good	Fair	Poor
—	675	525	400	325	225

Model 88

A modern short-stroke lever-action chambered for .243-, .308-, .284- and .358-calibers. Available in a rifle version, with 22" round barrel; carbine version, with 19" round barrel. Carbine model was not chambered for .358 cartridge. Both furnished with a detachable box magazine. Stock was a one-piece design, with pistol-grip offered in hand-cut checkering or pressed basket weave checkering after 1964. Rifle introduced in 1955; carbine in 1968. Both versions discontinued in 1973, with about 283,000 sold.

Rifle

NOTE: Add 50 percent for .243; 100 percent for .284; 300 percent for .358 Win.

1955-1963 Rifle Production

NIB	Exc.	V.G.	Good	Fair	Poor
1200	1000	800	600	400	350

1964-1973 Rifle Production

NIB	Exc.	V.G.	Good	Fair	Poor
1000	900	700	500	300	250

Carbine

Only 28,000 carbines built; about 1 for every 10 rifles. Rarely encountered. **NOTE:** Add 25 percent for .243; 100 percent for .284.

NIB	Exc.	V.G.	Good	Fair	Poor
—	1300	1150	900	650	300

Model 99 or Thumb Trigger

A modification of Model 1902, without a traditional trigger. Rifle was fired by depressing trigger with the thumb, which was part of the sear and extractor located behind the bolt. Chambered for .22 Short and Long until 1914, when it was also chambered for .22 Extra Long. All cartridges could be shot interchangeably. Stock was same as Model 1902, walnut stained gumwood, without trigger or trigger guard. This model was not serial numbered. Built between 1904 and 1923. Winchester sold about 76,000 rifles.

Courtesy Bonhams & Butterfields, San Francisco, California

NIB	Exc.	V.G.	Good	Fair	Poor
—	2400	2000	1000	700	500

Model 1900

Single-shot bolt-action .22-caliber rifle based on a John M. Browning design. Furnished with an 18" round barrel. Chambered for .22 Short and Long interchangeably. One-piece plain gumwood straight-grip stock, without a buttplate. Rifle was not serial numbered. Produced from 1899 to 1902. About 105,000 sold.

Courtesy Buffalo Bill Historical Center, Cody, Wyoming

NIB	Exc.	V.G.	Good	Fair	Poor
—	2000	1000	450	300	200

Model 1902

Also a single-shot, this model was the same general design as Model 1900, with several improvements. Special shaped metal trigger guard was added; shorter trigger pull; steel buttplate; rear peep sight; barrel was made heavier at the muzzle. Chambered for .22 Short and Long cartridges until 1914, when .22 Extra Long was added. In 1927, .22 Extra Long was dropped in favor of the more popular .22 LR. All of these cartridges were interchangeable. One-piece plain walnut stained gumwood stock, with straight-grip (metal trigger guard added a pistol-grip feel) and steel buttplate, which was changed to composition in 1907. This model was not serial numbered. About 640,000 sold between 1902 and 1931, when it was discontinued.

NIB	Exc.	V.G.	Good	Fair	Poor
—	1000	750	400	225	125

Model 1904

A slightly more expensive version of Model 1902. Featured 21" round barrel, one-piece plain gumwood straight-grip stock (metal trigger guard added a pistol-grip feel), with a small lip on the fore-end. Chambered for .22 Short and Long until 1914, when .22 Extra Long was added. In 1927, .22 LR cartridge was added in place of Extra Long. This model was not serial numbered. Produced between 1904 and 1931. About 303,000 rifles were sold.

NIB	Exc.	V.G.	Good	Fair	Poor
—	900	675	350	200	100

Model D Military Rifle

Overall length 46.375"; barrel length 26"; caliber 7.62mm. Walnut stock with blued barrel, receiver, magazine housing and furniture. Receiver ring over barrel breech stamped with serial number and Winchester proofmark. Total of 500 Model D rifles shipped to Russia for trial in March 1917. Value Speculative.

Imperial Bolt-Action Magazine Rifle (Model 51)

Designed by T.C. Johnson. Approximately 25 of these rifles made during 1919 and 1920, in two different styles and three calibers. Take-down variation has an overall length 42.25"; barrel length 22" and made in .27, .30-06 and .35 Newton calibers. Solid frame version identical in form, dimensions and calibers. Sight configurations and markings vary. Value Speculative.

Model 43

Introduced in 1949. Chambered for .218 Bee, .22 Hornet, .25-20 Win. and .32-20 Win. A bolt-action, with detachable box magazine. Fitted with 24" round barrel and front sight ramp forged integrally with barrel. Not drilled and tapped for scope blocks except for a few late rifles. Produced from 1949 to 1957, with about 63,000 sold. **NOTE:** Add 50 percent premium for rifles chambered .25-20 and .32-20. Deduct 40 percent for rifles with non-factory drilled and tapped scope holes.

Available in two styles:

1. Standard Rifle: 24" round barrel; plain walnut pistol-grip stock and fore-end; 1" sling swivels are standard.
2. Special Rifle: 24" round barrel; select walnut checkered pistol-grip stock and fore-end. Furnished with open sporting rear sight or Lyman 57A micrometer receiver sight.

Standard

NIB	Exc.	V.G.	Good	Fair	Poor
—	800	700	550	300	200

Special or Deluxe

NIB	Exc.	V.G.	Good	Fair	Poor
—	1500	1200	800	450	175

Model 47

Single-shot bolt-action rifle chambered for .22 Short, Long and LR interchangeably. Furnished with 25" round barrel, plain walnut pistol-grip stock and fore-end. Bolt, bolt handle and trigger are chrome plated. Has a special bolt, with a post on the underside. This moves into the safety

position when bolt is closed. This model was not serial numbered. Produced between 1948 and 1954. About 43,000 sold. **NOTE:** Add 10 percent premium for factory peep sight.

Courtesy Buffalo Bill Historical Center, Cody, Wyoming

NIB	Exc.	V.G.	Good	Fair	Poor
—	450	350	250	200	150

Target Rifle

Fitted with 28" round standard weight or heavyweight barrel. Plain walnut modified pistol-grip stock, with correct bolt.

NIB	Exc.	V.G.	Good	Fair	Poor
—	750	600	450	250	150

Model 52

One of the finest small-caliber well-made quality-built bolt-action rifles ever built. Model 52 was Winchester's answer to the increased demand for a military-style target rifle following WWI. Chambered for .22 LR cartridge. Designed by T.C. Johnson.

Model 52 was built in several different configurations over its production life:

1. Model 52: with finger groove in fore-end; one barrel band. Produced from 1920 to 1929.
2. Model 52 Target Rifle: same as above, without finger groove in fore-end; has first speed lock. Made from 1929 to 1932.
3. Model 52A Target Rifle: same as above, with addition of reinforced receiver and locking lug. Made from 1932 to 1935.
4. Model 52B Target Rifle: same as above, with addition of adjustable sling swivel and single-shot adapter. Made from 1935 to 1947.
5. Model 52C Target Rifle: same as above, with addition of an easily adjustable vibration-free trigger mechanism. Made from 1947 to 1961.
6. Model 52D Target Rifle: single-shot, with free-floating barrel; new design stock, with adjustable hand-stop channel.
7. Model 52 Bull Gun: same as target rifle; fitted with extra heavyweight barrel. Made from 1939 to 1960. Bull barrel measures 1.125" at receiver juncture; heavyweight measures 1". Both barrels measure .875" at muzzle.
8. Model 52 International Match: free-style stock, with thumbhole; adjustable buttstock and fore-end; introduced in 1969. International Prone model, with no thumbhole or adjustable buttplate and fore-end; introduced in 1975. Both discontinued in 1980.
9. Model 52 Sporter: 24" round barrel; select walnut checkered pistol-grip stock, with cheekpiece; fore-end, with black plastic tip; pistol-grip furnished with hard-rubber grip cap. Model 52 Sporter introduced in 1934, discontinued in 1958. It went through same improvements as Target Rifle, thus designation Model 52A Sporter, etc.

Standard

NIB	Exc.	V.G.	Good	Fair	Poor
—	1250	1000	750	250	300

Target

Courtesy Rock Island Auction Company

NIB	Exc.	V.G.	Good	Fair	Poor
—	1750	1500	1150	900	350

Target—Speed Lock

NIB	Exc.	V.G.	Good	Fair	Poor
—	1700	1400	1050	900	350

Model 52A Target Heavy Barrel—Rare

NIB	Exc.	V.G.	Good	Fair	Poor
—	1700	1400	1050	900	350

Model 52B Target Heavy & Standard Barrel

NIB	Exc.	V.G.	Good	Fair	Poor
—	1500	1300	950	700	300

Model 52B Target Bull Barrel

NIB	Exc.	V.G.	Good	Fair	Poor
—	1700	1400	1050	900	350

Model 52C Target

Courtesy Amoskeag Auction Company

NIB	Exc.	V.G.	Good	Fair	Poor
—	1700	1400	1050	800	500

Model 52D Target

Courtesy Amoskeag Auction Company

NIB	Exc.	V.G.	Good	Fair	Poor
—	1800	1500	1300	1050	500

Model 52B Bull Gun

NIB	Exc.	V.G.	Good	Fair	Poor
—	1800	1500	1300	1050	500

Model 52C Bull Gun

NIB	Exc.	V.G.	Good	Fair	Poor
—	1800	1500	1300	1050	500

International Match - Free Style

Approximately 300 manufactured.

NIB	Exc.	V.G.	Good	Fair	Poor
—	3550	2900	2050	1200	600

International Match - Prone

NOTE: Post-WWII Model 1907s command a premium over values shown below.

NIB	Exc.	V.G.	Good	Fair	Poor
—	1600	1350	1150	800	600

Model 52A Sporter

NIB	Exc.	V.G.	Good	Fair	Poor
4000	3600	2750	2000	1500	500

Model 52B Sporter

NIB	Exc.	V.G.	Good	Fair	Poor
4500	3900	3200	2400	1850	600

Model 52C Sporter

NIB	Exc.	V.G.	Good	Fair	Poor
5000	4100	3400	2300	1800	900

Model 54

Model 54 was to centerfire cartridges what Model 52 was to rimfire cartridges. Model 54 was also a quality-made bolt-action rifle, with non-detachable box magazine. Chambered for a variety of calibers: .270, .30-06, .30-30, 7mm, 7.65, 9.mm, .250-3000, .22 Hornet, .220 Swift and .257 Roberts. This was Winchester's first bolt-action rifle built for heavy, high velocity ammunition. Introduced in 1925, discontinued in 1936. About 50,000 sold. **NOTE:** Rare calibers are 7mm, 7.65mm and 9mm, which bring considerable premiums (in some cases as much as 250 percent) over standard calibers. Popular calibers such as .22 Hornet, .220 Swift, .30-30 and .257 Roberts will also bring a premium. Proceed with caution on Model 54s with rare caliber markings.

Model 54 was available in several different styles:

1. Standard Rifle: 24" or 20" round barrel (except .220 Swift which was 26"); plain walnut checkered pistol-grip stock and fore-end.

2. Carbine: 20" round barrel; plain walnut pistol-grip stock, with finger groove on each side of fore-end.

3. Sniper's Rifle: 26" round heavyweight barrel; plain walnut pistol-grip stock and fore-end.

4. N.R.A. Rifle: 24" round barrel; select walnut checkered pistol-grip stock and fore-end.

5. Super Grade Rifle: 24" round barrel; select walnut checkered pistol-grip stock, with cheekpiece; checkered fore-end, with black plastic tip; pistol-grip capped with hard rubber cap; Super Grade was equipped with 1" detachable sling swivels.

6. Target Rifle: 24" round heavyweight barrel; plain walnut checkered pistol-grip stock and fore-end.

7. National Match Rifle: 24" round barrel; plain walnut special target stock and fore-end.

Standard

NIB	Exc.	V.G.	Good	Fair	Poor
—	1300	1100	800	600	425

Carbine

NIB	Exc.	V.G.	Good	Fair	Poor
—	1400	1200	900	700	475

Sniper's Rifle

NIB	Exc.	V.G.	Good	Fair	Poor
—	1800	1500	1200	1000	550

N.R.A.

NIB	Exc.	V.G.	Good	Fair	Poor
—	1800	1500	1200	1000	550

Super Grade

NIB	Exc.	V.G.	Good	Fair	Poor
—	2400	1950	1600	1350	600

Target

NIB	Exc.	V.G.	Good	Fair	Poor
—	1800	1500	1200	1000	550

National Match

NIB	Exc.	V.G.	Good	Fair	Poor
—	1800	1500	1200	1000	550

Model 56

Designed to be a medium-priced bolt-action rimfire rifle. Featured a detachable box magazine. Chambered for .22 Short or .22 LR cartridges. Introduced in 1926, discontinued in 1929. About 8,500 rifles sold. **NOTE:** Add 50 percent premium for rifles chambered .22 Short only.

Model 56 offered in two styles:

1. Sporting Rifle: 22" round barrel; plain walnut pistol-grip stock and fore-end. Both styles had a distinctive lip on fore-end tip

2. Fancy Sporting Rifle: 22" round barrel; fancy walnut checkered pistol-grip stock and fore-end.

Sporting

NIB	Exc.	V.G.	Good	Fair	Poor
—	1500	1000	750	525	400

Fancy Sporting

Very rare, use caution.

NIB	Exc.	V.G.	Good	Fair	Poor
—	3000	2000	1500	900	750

Model 57

Model 57 was close in appearance to Model 56, with addition of a heavier stock, target sights and swivel bows attached to stock. Chambered for .22 Short or .22 LR. Featured 22" round barrel, with detachable box magazine. Stock was plain walnut pistol-grip and fore-end. Introduced in 1927, discontinued in 1936. About 19,000 sold. **NOTE:** Add 20 percent premium for web sling.

NIB	Exc.	V.G.	Good	Fair	Poor
—	950	700	450	325	250

Model 58

This model was an attempt by Winchester to market a low-priced .22-caliber rimfire rifle in place of its Models 1902 and 1904. Single-shot bolt-action cocked by pulling firing pin head to the rear. Had an 18" round barrel. Chambered for .22 Short, Long and LR interchangeably. One-piece plain wood stock, with straight-grip. This model was not serial numbered. Introduced in 1928, discontinued in 1931. About 39,000 sold.

NIB	Exc.	V.G.	Good	Fair	Poor
—	800	700	450	300	200

Model 59

Essentially a Model 58, with addition of a pistol-grip stock and 23" round barrel. Introduced in 1930 and dropped the same year. Total sales about 9,000 guns.

NIB	Exc.	V.G.	Good	Fair	Poor
—	1000	800	550	400	200

Model 60 and 60A

This rifle used the same action as Model 59. First introduced in 1931 furnished with a 23" round barrel, which was changed to 27" in 1933. Several other mechanical improvements were included; perhaps most noticeable were the chrome-plated bolt, bolt handle and trigger. Plain wood stock, with pistol-grip. In 1933, Model 60A was added which was the same rifle but in a target configuration. Front sight was a square top military blade, with Lyman 55W receiver sight. Model 60 discontinued in 1934: about 166,000 sold. Model 60A dropped in 1939: about 6,100 sold.

Courtesy Buffalo Bill Historical Center, Cody, Wyoming

Model 60

NIB	Exc.	V.G.	Good	Fair	Poor
—	375	250	200	150	100

Model 60A

NIB	Exc.	V.G.	Good	Fair	Poor
—	500	425	300	200	100

Model 67

Winchester again upgraded and improved Model 60, with an expansion of styles offered to the shooting public. Standard chamber was .22 Short, Long and LR interchangeably, with WRF added in 1935. Model 67s were not serial numbered for domestic sales, but numbered for foreign sales. Introduced in 1934, discontinued in 1963. About 384,000 sold. Many were fitted at the factory with telescopes. Bases were mounted on the rifle and scope was packed separately.

Model 67 was available in several different styles:

1. Sporting Rifle: 27" round barrel; stock similar to Model 60.

2. Smoothbore Rifle: 27" barrel; chambered for .22 Long shot or .22 LR shot.

3. Junior Rifle: 20" round barrel; shorter stock.

4. Rifle with miniature target boring: 24" round barrel; chambered for .22 LR shot.

Courtesy Buffalo Bill Historical Center, Cody, Wyoming

Sporting

NIB	Exc.	V.G.	Good	Fair	Poor
—	450	350	250	175	100

Smoothbore

Courtesy Buffalo Bill Historical Center, Cody, Wyoming

NIB	Exc.	V.G.	Good	Fair	Poor
—	800	600	400	250	200

Junior

NIB	Exc.	V.G.	Good	Fair	Poor
—	500	350	275	200	125

Miniature Target

Marked "for shot only". Has beads instead of standard iron rifle sights.

NIB	Exc.	V.G.	Good	Fair	Poor
—	1200	900	700	400	300

Model 677

Looked the same as Model 67, but manufactured without iron sights. Therefore, will have no sight cuts in the barrel. Furnished with 2-3/4 power scopes or 5-power scopes. This model was not serial numbered. Introduced in 1937; discontinued in 1939. **NOTE:** Add 100 percent premium for rifles chambered .22 WRF.

NIB	Exc.	V.G.	Good	Fair	Poor
—	2400	1800	1100	600	300

Model 68

Another takeoff on Model 67. Differed only in sight equipment offered. Fitted with a peep sight. First sold in 1934, dropped in 1946. Sales about 101,000. **NOTE:** Add 50 percent for factory scopes and no sights; 400 percent for factory scopes and no sights chambered .22 WRF.

Courtesy C.H. Wolfersberger

With Scope

NIB	Exc.	V.G.	Good	Fair	Poor
—	900	775	450	300	200

Without Scope

NIB	Exc.	V.G.	Good	Fair	Poor
—	300	225	150	100	75

Model 69 and 69A

Designed by Winchester to answer the demand for a medium-priced hunting and target .22 rimfire bolt-action rifle. Had a detachable box magazine. Many offered with factory-installed telescopes in 2-3/4 and 5-power. Plain walnut pistol-grip stock and fore-end. This model was not serial numbered. Model 69A introduced in 1937. Featured an improved cocking mechanism. Model 69 Introduced in 1935, dropped in 1963. About 355,000 sold. **NOTE:** Add 25 percent for Target Model; 35 percent for grooved receiver.

NIB	Exc.	V.G.	Good	Fair	Poor
—	475	400	350	200	100

Model 697

Similar in appearance to Model 69, except equipped exclusively for a telescope. Winchester offered 2-3/4 or 5-power scope, with bases attached at the factory and scope packed separately. Built between 1937 and 1941, with small sales. This model was not serial numbered. **NOTE:** Add 50 percent for factory scopes with no sights.

NIB	Exc.	V.G.	Good	Fair	Poor
—	2000	1200	800	600	400

Model 70

Considered by many to be the finest bolt-action rifle ever built in the United States. Pre-1964 Model 70 is highly sought after by shooters and collectors alike. Its smooth strong action has no peer. Often referred to as "The Riflemen's Rifle". Model 70 is an updated and improved version of Model 54. Features a hinged floorplate, new speed locks, new safety design that does not interfere with telescope, manually releasable bolt stop, more attractive buttstock and fore-end, and forged steel trigger guard. Like many Winchesters, Model 70 was available with several extra-cost options that should be evaluated by an expert. Values listed are given for pre-1964 Model 70s, with serial numbers from 1 to 581471. Standard calibers offered for Model 70 are these in order of rarity: .300 Savage, .35 Rem., .458 Win Magnum, 7mm, .358 Win., .250-3000 Savage, .300 Win Magnum, .338 Win. Magnum, .375 H&H Magnum, .257 Roberts, .220 Swift, .22 Hornet, .264 Win. Magnum, .300 H&H Magnum, .308 Win., .243 Win., .270 WCF, .30-06.

Model 70 was available in several different styles:

1. Standard Grade: 24" round barrel (except 26" round barrel for .220 Swift and .300 H&H Magnum—25" round barrel for .375 H&H Magnum after 1937); plain walnut checkered pistol stock and fore-end. Built from 1936 to 1963.

2. Standard Grade Carbine: 20" round barrel; chambered for .22 Hornet, .250-3000, .257 Roberts, .270, 7mm and .30-06; same stock as Standard Grade. Built from 1936 to 1946.

3. Super Grade Rifle: same barrel and calibers as Standard Grade; select checkered walnut capped pistol-grip stock, with cheekpiece; checkered fore-end, with plastic tip. Built from 1936 to 1960.

4. Featherweight: 22" round barrel; chambered for .243, .264, .270, .308, .30-06 and .358; fitted with aluminum trigger guard, buttplate and floor plate. Later versions with plastic buttplate. Built from 1952 to 1963.

5. Featherweight Super Grade: same as above, except not chambered for .358 cartridge; fitted with Super Grade stock. Built from 1952 to 1963.

6. National Match: same as Standard Grade, but fitted with target type stock and telescope bases; chambered for .30-06 only. Discontinued in 1960.

7. Target: 24" round medium-weight barrel; same stock as National Match; in .243 and .30-06 calibers. Discontinued in 1963.

8. Varmint: 26" round heavy barrel; heavier varmint stock; chambered for .243 and rare .220 Swift. Built from 1956 to 1963.

9. Westerner: 26" round barrel; Standard Grade stock; chambered for .264 Win. Magnum. Built from 1960 to 1963. Fitted with solid rubber pad for early production; vented pad for later guns.

10. Alaskan: 25" round barrel; Standard Grade stock; chambered for .338 Win. Magnum and .375 H&H Magnum. Built from 1960 to 1963. Fitted with solid rubber pad marked Winchester for early production; vented pad marked Winchester for later guns.

11. Bull Gun: 28" round barrel; same stock as National Match; chambered for .30-06 and .300 H&H Magnum. Built from 1936 to 1963.

Prices for Model 70 are, in many cases, based on caliber of rifle; more rare the caliber, more premium the gun will command. Beware of fakes. There are some unscrupulous individuals who specialize in faking Model 70s, including chambering them to rare calibers. Many pre-1964 Model 70s are still available in new condition in original box, with all the papers. **NOTE:** Add 25 to 50 percent if box is serial numbered to gun. Use caution prior to purchase of NIB guns due to fake boxes and papers.

PRICING NOTE: Asterisk (*) signifies value of rifle with respect to a usable action. Model 70 unaltered receivers bring $500 regardless of condition of barrel and stock. If receiver is unusable then rifle is worth the value of its usable parts, i.e. less than $500.

For Model 70s with "X" or "D" prefix, add a collector premium of 10 percent. These letters indicate that there were two rifles mistakenly stamped with the same serial number.

Standard Rifle .30-06 Springfield (1937-1963)

Pre-War

NIB	Exc.	V.G.	Good	Fair	Poor
—	2200	1600	1100	500*	500*

Post-War

NIB	Exc.	V.G.	Good	Fair	Poor
—	1450	1200	800	500*	500*

.270 Win. (1937-1963)

Pre-War

NIB	Exc.	V.G.	Good	Fair	Poor
—	2200	1900	1000	500*	500*

Post-War

NIB	Exc.	V.G.	Good	Fair	Poor
—	1550	1400	900	500*	500*

.243 Win. (1955-1963)

NIB	Exc.	V.G.	Good	Fair	Poor
—	2750	2200	1100	500*	500*

.300 H&H Magnum (1937-1963)

Pre-War

NIB	Exc.	V.G.	Good	Fair	Poor
—	3100	2500	1700	1000	500*

Post-War

NIB	Exc.	V.G.	Good	Fair	Poor
—	2650	2000	1400	850	500*

.264 Win. Magnum (1959-1963)

NIB	Exc.	V.G.	Good	Fair	Poor
—	2500	2000	1400	850	500*

.22 Hornet (1937-1958)

Pre-War

NIB	Exc.	V.G.	Good	Fair	Poor
—	3000	2400	2000	1000	500*

Post-War

NIB	Exc.	V.G.	Good	Fair	Poor
—	2750	2000	1500	750	500*

.220 Swift (1937-1963)

Pre-War

NIB	Exc.	V.G.	Good	Fair	Poor
—	3000	2400	1750	900	500*

Post-War

NIB	Exc.	V.G.	Good	Fair	Poor
—	2500	1750	1200	650	500*

.257 Roberts (1937-1959)

Pre-War

NIB	Exc.	V.G.	Good	Fair	Poor
—	3200	2500	1500	950	500*

Post-War

NIB	Exc.	V.G.	Good	Fair	Poor
—	2900	2100	1400	750	500*

.375 H&H Magnum (1937-1963)

Pre-War

NIB	Exc.	V.G.	Good	Fair	Poor
—	4300	3700	2200	1350	500*

Post-War

NIB	Exc.	V.G.	Good	Fair	Poor
—	3200	2500	1800	1000	500*

.338 Win. Magnum (1959-1963)

NIB	Exc.	V.G.	Good	Fair	Poor
—	3150	2550	1550	900	500*

.300 Win. Magnum (1962-1963)

NIB	Exc.	V.G.	Good	Fair	Poor
—	2650	2250	1200	750	500*

.250-3000 Savage (1937-1949)

NIB	Exc.	V.G.	Good	Fair	Poor
—	4750	3500	2500	1200	500*

7mm (1937-1949)

NIB	Exc.	V.G.	Good	Fair	Poor
—	5900	4800	2700	1700	700

.35 Rem. (1944-1947)

NOTE: Very rare. Only 404 manufactured.

NIB	Exc.	V.G.	Good	Fair	Poor
—	12000	10000	5000	3000	2000

.300 Savage (1944-1954)

NOTE: Very rare. Only 362 manufactured.

NIB	Exc.	V.G.	Good	Fair	Poor
—	12500	10500	5000	3000	2000

.458 Win. Magnum African

Built in Supergrade only, 1956-1963.

NIB	Exc.	V.G.	Good	Fair	Poor
—	7400	5350	4200	2750	1350

Featherweight

NOTE: Add 100 percent for .358 Win.; 25 percent for .264- and .270-calibers.

NIB	Exc.	V.G.	Good	Fair	Poor
—	2200	1450	1075	700	450

Super Grade

Features higher grade wood, with black fore-end tip, grip cap, cheekpiece and hand checkering. Made from 1937 to 1960 in all calibers. Prices shown are for standard calibers; .30-06 and .270 Win. **NOTE:** Add 50 to 100 percent for other chamberings (depending on condition) to prices listed by caliber.

NIB	Exc.	V.G.	Good	Fair	Poor
—	4400	3800	2200	1000*	1000*

Featherweight Super Grade

NIB	Exc.	V.G.	Good	Fair	Poor
—	5400	4300	3200	1650	1000

Standard Grade Carbine

NOTE: Add 100 percent for Super Grade rifles.

NIB	Exc.	V.G.	Good	Fair	Poor
—	2900	2000	1400	950	650

National Match

NIB	Exc.	V.G.	Good	Fair	Poor
—	3400	2550	1850	950	600

Target

NIB	Exc.	V.G.	Good	Fair	Poor
—	2450	2100	1150	750	550

Varmint

NOTE: Add 40 percent premium for .220 Swift.

NIB	Exc.	V.G.	Good	Fair	Poor
—	2350	1950	950	600	375*

Bull Gun

NIB	Exc.	V.G.	Good	Fair	Poor
—	3900	3200	2450	850	600

Model 72

Bolt-action rifle with tubular magazine. Chambered for .22 Short, Long and LR cartridges interchangeably. Early rifles available with 2-3/4 or 5-power telescopes, but majority furnished with open or peep sights. This model was not serial numbered. Built between 1938 and 1959. About 161,000 sold. **NOTE:** Add 100 percent premium for Gallery Special: 200 percent for factory scopes and no sights (depending on condition); 25 percent premium for peep sights; 20 percent for Model 72A with grooved receiver.

Available in two different configurations:

1. Sporting Rifle: 25" round barrel; chambered for .22 Short, Long and LR cartridges; one-piece plain walnut pistol-grip stock and fore-end.

2. Gallery Special: 25" round barrel; chambered for .22 Short only; stock same as Sporting Rifle.

Courtesy C.H. Wolfersberger

NIB	Exc.	V.G.	Good	Fair	Poor
—	425	350	275	200	125

Model 75

This model discontinued in 1958, with about 89,000 sold.

Available in two styles:

1. Sporting Rifle: 24" round barrel; chambered for .22 LR; select walnut checkered pistol-grip stock and fore-end; furnished with open rear sights or Lyman 57E receiver sight.

2. Target Rifle: 28" round barrel; chambered for .22 LR; plain walnut pistol-grip stock and fore-end; furnished with Winchester 8-power telescope or a variety of target sights.

Sporter

NIB	Exc.	V.G.	Good	Fair	Poor
—	1500	1000	800	500	350

Target

NIB	Exc.	V.G.	Good	Fair	Poor
—	900	700	600	500	200

Model SXR Super X Rifle

Gas-operated semi-automatic patterned after Browning BAR ShortTrac and LongTrac. Caliber and capacity: .30-06 (4), .300WM (3), .270 WSM (3), .300 WSM (3). Barrel: 22" (.30-06), 24" Magnum calibers. Weight 7.25 lbs. Stock two-piece checkered walnut. Introduced 2006.

NIB	Exc.	V.G.	Good	Fair	Poor
600	500	400	325	250	125

SHOTGUNS

Model 12

Designed by T.C. Johnson. First slide-action hammerless shotgun built by Winchester. Model 12 enjoyed great success in its 68-year history, with over two million sold. A high quality, well-made shotgun that is still in use in the hunting and shooting fields across the country. All Model 12s were of take-down variety. Dropped from regular product line in 1963, but a special model was produced in the Custom Shop until 1979. In 1972, Winchester resurrected Model 12 in its regular production line in 12-gauge only, with ventilated rib. This reintroduced Model 12 was dropped in 1980. Prices listed are for guns made prior to 1964 or with serial numbers below 1968307. Shotgun will be seen in many different combinations of gauges, barrel lengths, ribs and stocks, all of which determine value. The more rare a particular combination, higher the price. Buyer is urged to be extremely cautious before purchasing the more rare combinations, such as 28-gauge. Best advice is to seek assistance from an expert and get as many opinions as possible. Prices listed are for guns in standard configurations. **NOTE:** Following applies to all Model 12s: Add 10 percent for 16-gauge; 50 percent for 20-gauge; 600 percent for 28-gauge; 20 percent for solid rib; 30 percent for Winchester Special ventilated rib; 40 percent for milled rib; 20 percent for 32" barrels; 30 percent premium for original box and papers.

Model 12 was offered in several different styles:

1. Standard Grade: 12-, 16-, 20- and 28-gauge; plain, solid or ventilated rib round barrels; standard lengths 26", 28", 30", 32"; plain walnut pistol-grip stock; grooved slide handle. Built from 1912 to 1963.

2. Featherweight: same as above; lightweight alloy trigger guard. Built between 1959 and 1962.

3. Riot Gun: 12-gauge only; 20" round choked cylinder; stock same as Standard Grade. Built between 1918 and 1963.

4. Trench Gun: chambered for 12-gauge only; 20" round barrel; ventilated hand guard over barrel; fitted with bayonet lug; all metal surfaces "Parkerized"; these shotguns should be U.S. marked as a military firearm. Introduced in 1918 and built for U.S. Armed Forces on special order.

5. Skeet Grade: chambered for 12-, 16-, 20- and 28-gauge; 26" round barrel; solid or ventilated rib; select walnut checkered pistol stock; special checkered extension slide handle (longer than standard). Built from 1933 to 1963.

6. Trap Grade: chambered for 12-gauge only; 30" round barrel; solid or ventilated rib; select walnut pistol-/straight-grip stock; checkered extension slide handle. Built from 1914 to 1963.

7. Heavy Duck Gun: chambered in 12-gauge only; 30" or 32" round barrel; plain, solid or ventilated rib; plain walnut pistol-grip stock; fitted with Winchester solid red rubber recoil pad; plain grooved slide handle. Built from 1935 to 1963.

8. Pigeon Grade: chambered for 12-, 16-, 20- and 28-gauge; standard barrel lengths; choice of ribs; special order shotgun; will be seen in many different variations; most were factory engraved. Built from 1914 to 1963.

Courtesy Bonhams & Butterfields, San Francisco, California

Standard Grade—12 gauge

NIB	Exc.	V.G.	Good	Fair	Poor
—	850	700	600	500	200

Featherweight

NIB	Exc.	V.G.	Good	Fair	Poor
—	800	700	600	575	200

Riot Gun

NIB	Exc.	V.G.	Good	Fair	Poor
—	2400	1700	900	700	250

Trench Gun

NIB	Exc.	V.G.	Good	Fair	Poor
—	7500	6000	4000	1500	1000

Skeet Grade

NIB	Exc.	V.G.	Good	Fair	Poor
—	2200	1700	900	600	350

Trap Grade

NIB	Exc.	V.G.	Good	Fair	Poor
—	2000	1500	800	550	400

Heavy Duck Gun

NOTE: Add 25 percent premium for solid ribs.

NIB	Exc.	V.G.	Good	Fair	Poor
—	1150	900	350	425	300

Pigeon Grade

NIB	Exc.	V.G.	Good	Fair	Poor
—	3750	2300	1600	750	500

Model 25

Similar in appearance to Model 12. Does not have take-down feature. All guns were solid frame. Furnished in 12-gauge, with 26" or 28" plain round barrel and walnut pistol-grip stock, and grooved slide handle. This was an attempt by Winchester to introduce a less expensive version of Model 12. Introduced in 1949, dropped from product line in 1954. About 88,000 sold.

NIB	Exc.	V.G.	Good	Fair	Poor
—	700	550	400	250	100

Model 20

In order to utilize the expanded production facilities left over from WWI, Winchester introduced a series of three different models of single-shot shotguns; Model 20 was the first of three introduced in 1920. Has a visible hammer and top lever frame. First Winchester to have this type of breakdown action. Chambered for .410, 2.5" shell. Barrel is 26" round choked Full, plain walnut pistol-grip stock with hard rubber buttplate. Fore-end has a small lip on the front end. Dropped from product line in 1924. About 24,000 sold.

Courtesy C.H. Wolfersberger

NIB	Exc.	V.G.	Good	Fair	Poor
—	750	500	350	200	150

Model 36

Second of the single-shot shotguns to be introduced in 1920. Features a bolt-action that is cocked by pulling firing pin head to the rear. Fitted with an 18" round barrel. Chambered for 9mm Long Shot, Short Shot and Ball interchangeably. Plain gumwood straight-grip stock, with special metal pistol-grip trigger guard. Winchester referred to this model as "Garden Gun" for use against birds and pests around the house and barn. This model was not serial numbered. Dropped from product line in 1927. About 20,000 sold.

NIB	Exc.	V.G.	Good	Fair	Poor
—	1000	775	475	300	225

Model 41

Third of the low-priced single-shot shotguns to be introduced in 1920. Like Model 36, Model 41 was a bolt-action arrangement, but of much stronger construction and design. Features a 24" round barrel. Chambered for .410, 2.5" shell. Plain walnut pistol-grip stock and fore-end. Straight-grip stock furnished at no extra charge. This model was not serial numbered. Discontinued in 1934. About 22,000 sold.

Courtesy C.H. Wolfersberger

NIB	Exc.	V.G.	Good	Fair	Poor
—	600	500	350	300	200

MODEL 21

Winchester's finest effort with regard to quality, reliability and strength. Developed in late 1920s, introduction of this fine side-by-side shotgun was delayed by the company's financial troubles. When Winchester was purchased by the Olin family, Model 21 was assured the attention it richly deserved due to John M. Olin's love for the gun. Despite Model 21 being offered as a production gun it was, in fact, a hand-built custom-made shotgun. Almost each Model 21 built has a personality of its own, because each shotgun is slightly different with regard to chokes, barrel lengths, stock dimensions and embellishments. Introduced in 1931. From 1931 to 1959, Model 21 was considered a production line gun. About 30,000 were sold. In 1960, when Custom Shop was opened, Model 21 was built there using the same procedures. Sales during Custom Shop era were about 1,000 guns. Winchester changed the name of some Model 21 styles, but production methods stayed the same. In 1981, Winchester sold its firearms division to U.S. Repeating Arms Company, including the right to build Model 21. Again, production procedures stayed the same as did many of the former employees. U.S. Repeating Arms expanded and changed some of the style designations for Model 21. Production discontinued in about 1991. No sales figures are available for this time period. Collectors and shooters will be given the price breakdown for all three eras of production separately. **NOTE:** Fewer than 50 .410 Model 21s were built between 1931 and 1959 in all grades. Number of 28-gauge Model 21s built is unknown, but probably no greater than .410 bore.

Model 21—1931 to 1959

Model 21 was available in several different styles and configurations:

1. Standard Grade: chambered in 12-, 16-, 20-gauge; barrel lengths 26", 28", 30", 32"; matted or ventilated rib; select walnut checkered pistol-/straight-grip stock; checkered beavertail fore-end. Built from 1931 to 1959.

2. Tournament Grade: same as above; special dimension stock; marked "TOURNAMENT" on bottom of trigger plate. Built from 1933 to 1934.

3. Trap Grade: same as above; slightly better-grade wood; stock made to customers' dimensions; marked "TRAP" on trigger plate. Built from 1932 to 1959.

4. Skeet Grade: same as above; addition of 28-gauge; stock furnished with checkered butt; marked "SKEET" on trigger plate. Built from 1936 to 1959.

5. Duck Gun: chambered for 12-gauge; 3" Magnum shells; 30" or 32" barrels; Standard Grade stock, except for shorter length of pull; marked "DUCK" on trigger plate. Built from 1940 to 1952.

6. Magnum Gun: chambered for 12- or 20-gauge; 3" Magnum shells; same stock as Duck Gun; not marked on trigger plate. Built from 1953 to 1959.

7. Custom Built/Deluxe Grade: chambered for 12-, 16-, 20-, 28-gauge and .410 bore; barrel lengths from 26" to 32"; stock built to customers specifications using fancy walnut; marked "CUSTOM BUILT" on top of rib or "DELUXE" on trigger plate; these grades are frequently, but not always engraved. Built from 1933 to 1959.

NOTE: Some early Model 21s furnished with double triggers, extractors and splinter fore-ends. This combination reduces price of the gun regardless of grade. Deduct about 25 percent.

Standard Grade - 12 gauge

NIB	Exc.	V.G.	Good	Fair	Poor
—	6000	5000	3750	2400	2000

Standard Grade - 16 gauge

NIB	Exc.	V.G.	Good	Fair	Poor
—	8500	6700	5650	4700	4200

Standard Grade - 20 gauge

NIB	Exc.	V.G.	Good	Fair	Poor
—	9500	7500	6500	5100	4700

Tournament Grade - 12 gauge

NIB	Exc.	V.G.	Good	Fair	Poor
—	6500	5200	4150	3500	3300

Tournament Grade - 16 gauge

NIB	Exc.	V.G.	Good	Fair	Poor
—	8500	7200	6000	5000	4500

Tournament Grade - 20 gauge

NIB	Exc.	V.G.	Good	Fair	Poor
—	10000	8200	7200	6000	4800

Trap Grade - 12 gauge

NIB	Exc.	V.G.	Good	Fair	Poor
—	6800	5300	4250	3800	3600

Trap Grade - 16 gauge

NIB	Exc.	V.G.	Good	Fair	Poor
—	8500	7300	6100	5300	4900

Trap Grade - 20 gauge

NIB	Exc.	V.G.	Good	Fair	Poor
—	9000	7500	6550	5800	5300

Skeet Grade - 12 gauge

NIB	Exc.	V.G.	Good	Fair	Poor
—	6500	5000	3950	3400	3200

Skeet Grade - 16 gauge

NIB	Exc.	V.G.	Good	Fair	Poor
—	8200	7200	6000	4900	4400

Skeet Grade - 20 gauge

NIB	Exc.	V.G.	Good	Fair	Poor
—	9500	7800	6600	5000	4500

Duck/Magnum Gun

NOTE: Add 30 percent for 20-gauge Magnum. Factory ventilated ribs command a premium of about $1,800 on 12-gauge; $2,500 on 16- and 20-gauge. Model 21s with factory furnished extra barrels will bring an additional premium of about $2,500. Refinished and restored Model 21s are in a somewhat unique category of American-made collectible shotguns. A gun that has been professionally refinished by a master craftsman will bring approximately 90 percent value of factory original guns.

NIB	Exc.	V.G.	Good	Fair	Poor
—	6500	5100	4450	4000	3800

Custom Built/Deluxe Grade

Prices paid for guns of this grade are determined by gauge, barrel and choke combinations, rib type, stock specifications and engraving. Expert appraisal is recommended. It is best to secure a factory letter from Cody Firearms Museum. With respect to such a letter, it is important to note that these records are incomplete and may be inaccurate in a few cases. Records for Model 21s built during 1930s may be missing. Special-order guns may have incomplete records. In such cases, a written appraisal from an authoritative collector or dealer may be helpful.

12 gauge

NIB	Exc.	V.G.	Good	Fair	Poor
—	8000	7000	5750	4500	4000

16 gauge

NIB	Exc.	V.G.	Good	Fair	Poor
—	9000	8000	6750	5500	4500

20 gauge

NIB	Exc.	V.G.	Good	Fair	Poor
—	10500	8500	7250	6000	5000

.410 Bore

NIB	Exc.	V.G.	Good	Fair	Poor
—	50000	40000	31000	26000	22000

Custom Shop Model 21s—1960 to 1981

When Winchester moved production of Model 21 into the Custom Shop, a number of styles were greatly reduced.

There were now three distinct styles:

1. Custom Grade: chambered in 12-, 16-, 20-, 28-gauge and .410 bore; barrel lengths 26" to 32"; matted rib; fancy walnut checkered pistol-/straight-grip stock; checkered fore-end; pistol-grip guns furnished with steel grip cap; a small amount of scroll engraving was provided on frame of this grade.

2. Pigeon Grade: same chambers and barrel lengths as above; choice of matted or ventilated rib; leather-covered recoil pad; style "A" carving on stock and fore-end; gold engraved pistol-grip cap; frame engraved with 21-6 engraving pattern.

3. Grand American Grade: same chambers and barrel lengths as Pigeon Grade; addition of "B" carving on stock and fore-end; 21-6 engraving with gold inlays; extra set of interchangeable barrels with extra fore-end; all enclosed in a leather trunk case.

EDITOR'S COMMENT: According to Ned Schwing's excellent book, "Winchester's Finest, The Model 21", there were only eight 28-gauge and five .410-bore models made during the Custom Shop production era from 1960 to 1981. Any price estimates would be highly speculative.

Custom Grade—12 Gauge

NOTE: Add $4,000 for 16-gauge; $5,000 for 20-gauge.

NIB	Exc.	V.G.	Good	Fair	Poor
—	10000	8500	7300	6000	5200

Pigeon Grade—12 Gauge

NOTE: Add $6,000 for 16-gauge; $5,000 for 20-gauge.

NIB	Exc.	V.G.	Good	Fair	Poor
—	19000	16500	12500	10000	8000

Grand American—12 Gauge

NOTE: Add $15,000 for 16-gauge (extremely rare); $5,000 for 20-gauge.

NIB	Exc.	V.G.	Good	Fair	Poor
—	32000	25000	17500	14000	13000

ENGRAVED MODEL 21s

Winchester catalogued a number of special-order engraving patterns which ranged from a small amount of scroll (#1) to full-coverage game scene and scroll (#6). In addition, there were a few guns engraved on special order to the customer's request. Engraved guns are extremely rare. Value added will vary with rarity of gauge and date of manufacture. The following table represents value added for various standard engraving patterns on 12-gauge guns for "Custom Shop" (1960-1982) and "Pre-Custom Shop" (1932-1959) periods. However, it is advisable to seek the opinion of an authorative collector or dealer prior to a sale.

Engraving Pattern	Pre-Custom Shop	CustomShop
#1	30 percent	20 percent
#2	40 percent	30 percent
#3	60 percent	45 percent
#4	70 percent	50 percent
#5	90 percent	70 percent
#6	100 percent	80 percent

Custom Shop Model 21s—1982 to 1993

When U.S. Repeating Arms Company took over production of Model 21, Pigeon Grade was dropped from the line. Grand American Grade was retained with all the features of its predecessor, with the addition of a small-bore set featuring 28-gauge and .410 bore set of barrels. Two new grades were introduced in 1983: Standard Custom Grade and Special Custom Built. In addition to these grades, the factory would undertake to build for its customers whatever was desired. Due to the unique nature of these guns, it is advised that an expert appraisal be sought to establish a value. While the changeover from Winchester to U.S. Repeating Arms was a transfer of business assets, craftsmen and personnel remained the same. Collectors are reluctant to assign the same values to U.S. Repeating Arms Model 21s as those produced by Winchester. No official production figures are available for U.S.R.A. Model 21s, but the number is most likely small, perhaps around 200 guns.

Standard Custom Built

NIB	Exc.	V.G.	Good	Fair	Poor
9000	7000	6000	5000	4500	4000

Grand American

NIB	Exc.	V.G.	Good	Fair	Poor
19000	14000	10500	8500	6000	5000

Grand American Small Gauge Set—28 or .410 bore

NIB	Exc.	V.G.	Good	Fair	Poor
62500	46500	37500	27000	22000	20000

CURRENT MODEL 21 PRODUCTION

In 1995, Connecticut Shotgun Mfg. Co. purchased the assets of Winchester Model 21 Custom Shop. Beginning in 2002, Winchester licensed CSMC to build Model 21s on a custom-order basis in a wide variety of grades and models, made to the buyer's specifications. For more information, see listing for Connecticut Shotgun Mfg. Co. in this edition.

Model 24

Model 24 was Winchester's attempt to develop a medium-priced double-barrel shotgun. Like Model 21, it was a toplever break-down model available in 12-, 16-, 20-gauge and in various barrel lengths from 26" to 30". Offered in Standard model only, with double triggers, raised matted rib, plain walnut pistol-/straight-grip stock with semi-beavertail fore-end. Introduced in 1939; discontinued in 1957. About 116,000 sold. **NOTE:** Add 10 percent for 16-gauge; 25 percent for 20-gauge.

NIB	Exc.	V.G.	Good	Fair	Poor
—	750	500	400	250	200

Model 37

Developed to keep pace with Winchester's competitors in the low-price single-barrel exposed-hammer shotgun market. Available in 12-, 16-, 20-, 28-gauge and .410 bore, with barrel lengths from 26" to 30". Stock was plain walnut, with pistol-grip and semi-beavertail fore-end. This model was not serial numbered. Introduced in 1936, it stayed in the company line until 1963. Sold slightly over 1,000,000 guns. **NOTE:** Add 15 percent premium for so-called "red letter" (red-filled "W" on bottom of receiver).

Courtesy C.H. Wolfersberger

12 gauge

NIB	Exc.	V.G.	Good	Fair	Poor
—	400	350	300	250	100

16 gauge

NIB	Exc.	V.G.	Good	Fair	Poor
—	450	400	350	300	75

20 gauge

NIB	Exc.	V.G.	Good	Fair	Poor
—	600	525	500	425	100

28 gauge

NIB	Exc.	V.G.	Good	Fair	Poor
—	2000	1600	1150	850	450

.410 bore

NOTE: Add 50 percent premium for 32" barrels in 12- and 16-gauge. Use caution for 28-gauge. Many fakes are seen for sale.

NIB	Exc.	V.G.	Good	Fair	Poor
—	1000	850	500	300	100

Youth Model

26" Modified choke barrel. Win. red factory pad. 20-gauge only.

NIB	Exc.	V.G.	Good	Fair	Poor
—	600	550	450	350	125

Model 42

Commentary and values by Bud Bugni.

First slide-action shotgun ever developed exclusively for .410 bore. Invented by William Roemer. It was in effect, at least in outward appearance, a miniature Model 12. This shotgun was quality-built, fast-handling, racy looking that many refer to as "Everybody's Sweetheart". First American .410 bore chambered for new 3" shell as well as 2.5". Offered in several different configurations throughout its production. These configurations will greatly influence value:

1. Standard Grade: 26" or 28" plain or solid rib barrel; plain walnut pistol-grip stock; grooved slide handle; fitted with composition buttplate; straight-grip offered on special order basis, but is extremely rare. Built from 1933 to 1963.

2. Skeet Grade: 26" or 28" plain, solid or ventilated rib barrel; select walnut checkered pistol-/straight-grip stock; checkered extension slide handle; offered in Full, Modified, Improved Cylinder, Cylinder as well as Skeet chokes. Built from 1933 to 1963.

3. Trap Grade: 26" or 28" plain or solid rib barrel; fancy walnut special checkered pistol-/straight-grip stock; special checkered extension slide handle; checkering pattern has one closed diamond on each side of pistol-grip; straight-grip diamond located on underside of grip; extension slide handle has two uncut diamonds on each side. Most were stamped "TRAP" on bottom of receiver under serial number. Built from 1934 to 1939.

4. Deluxe Grade: continuation of Trap Grade; available with ventilated rib in 1954; some early models stamped "DELUXE" on bottom of receiver. This stamping is seldom seen and probably discontinued around 1949. Built from 1940 to 1963.

5. Pigeon Grade: same as Deluxe Grade, but engraved with pigeon on lower magazine tube. Very few of this grade built by Winchester and majority were done in late 1940s. Authentic Pigeon Grade 42s appear to have been built between 1945 and 1949. Some estimate less than 50 produced. Rare Model 42. Seek an expert opinion before sale.

As of late, I have heard horror stories from sincere, honest, decent folks who have purchased misrepresented guns from unscrupulous sellers or sellers who simply do not know their products. In some cases there are no return privileges, or buyer was unable to authenticate his purchase in a timely manner. This often has resulted in a heavy financial loss and that's a dish served cold. Contributors are listed in Standard Catalog of Firearms. These knowledgeable and dedicated people are eager to assist readers, or refer them to sources who can.—Bud Bugni

NOTE: Engraved Model 42s will occasionally be seen. Collectors are urged to seek expert advice on these rare and expensive guns. Model 42 produced from 1933 to 1963. About 164,000 were sold. Factory service and repair for this model was discontinued in February of 1972.

EXTRA BARRELS: Winchester offered extra interchangeable barrels for its Model 42s, at customer's request beginning in 1934. These extra sets of barrels are a rare option. Both barrels should have same barrel markings and matching serial numbers before originality can be considered. Values are difficult to determine, but as a general rule, add 60 percent to price of a Model 42 if it has factory-original extra barrel sets.

EDITOR'S COMMENT: Contrary to traditional views, Winchester did install factory ventilated ribs on its Model 42. Former employees and factory drawings substantiate this fact. However, subject of what is a factory rib and what is not has been covered in great detail in an excellent book on Model 42. Seek expert advice before selling or purchasing any Model 42 with ventilated rib.

NOTE: Pigeon Grade Model 42s, with documentation on expert authentication, add 100 percent. Must be individually appraised. Proceed with caution.

CUTTS COMPENSATOR GUNS: Approximately 66 original Cutts Compensator guns were produced in the Winchester factory, making this one of the rarest options on Model 42. New information reveals that Cutts Compensators were available on Model 42 as early as 1950. This offering appeared in Winchester retail price list dated December 15, 1950. Considering this, since ventilated ribs were not offered on M42 until 1954, one may see an original "Cutts Gun" with plain or solid rib barrel minus a choke mark. **NOTE:** Add 25 percent for original Cutts guns; deduct 50 percent for non-original Cutts guns.

Standard Grade

NOTE: Add 50 percent for Standard Grade with solid ribs; 25 percent for pre-war.

NIB	Exc.	V.G.	Good	Fair	Poor
3000	1950	1150	900	700	400

Skeet Grade—Solid Rib

NOTE: Add 25 percent chambered for 2.5" shells; 30 percent for pre-war. Deduct 25 percent for Skeet Grade with no rib.

NIB	Exc.	V.G.	Good	Fair	Poor
6500	5000	4250	3500	1950	1250

Skeet Grade—Ventilated Rib

NOTE: Add 25 percent chambered for 2.5" shells.

NIB	Exc.	V.G.	Good	Fair	Poor
7500	6000	4750	3500	2200	1250

Trap Grade - Plain or Solid Rib

NIB	Exc.	V.G.	Good	Fair	Poor
—	12500	10500	9500	5500	3000

Deluxe Grade—Solid Rib

NIB	Exc.	V.G.	Good	Fair	Poor
12000	9500	8500	6000	3500	1250

Deluxe Grade—Ventilated Rib

NIB	Exc.	V.G.	Good	Fair	Poor
14000	12000	10950	7500	4800	2400

Model 1911

Winchester's first self-loading shotgun. Developed by T.C. Johnson, in order to keep pace with Remington Auto-Loading Shotgun Model 11, which was developed by John M. Browning, with help from T.C. Johnson. Because of the delays involved in developing a brand new design, Model 1911 was introduced on October 7, 1911. This shotgun was a recoil operated mechanism, had a tubular magazine and take-down feature. Available in two styles:

1. Plain Model 1911: 26" or 28" barrel; 12-gauge; Choked Full, Modified or Cylinder; plain birch laminated pistol-grip stock and fore-end; hard rubber buttplate.

2. Fancy Model 1911: same as above, with fancy birch laminated stock.

Because of the hurry in getting this model ready for production, the shotgun demonstrated design weakness and never proved satisfactory. Discontinued in 1925. About 83,000 guns sold.

Plain

NIB	Exc.	V.G.	Good	Fair	Poor
—	650	375	300	250	200

Fancy

NIB	Exc.	V.G.	Good	Fair	Poor
—	800	500	400	300	250

Model 40

Represents Winchester's second attempt to build a self-loading long recoil-operated repeating shotgun. This shotgun was a hammerless tubular magazine gun, without the hump at rear of the receiver. Available in 12-gauge only, with barrel lengths from 28" to 30". Standard Grade had plain walnut pistol-grip stock and fore-end; Skeet Grade fitted with select walnut checkered pistol-grip stock and checkered fore-end. Model 40 suffered from the same design problems as Model 11. Introduced in 1940; discontinued in 1941. About 12,000 sold.

Standard Grade

NIB	Exc.	V.G.	Good	Fair	Poor
—	650	500	400	275	200

Skeet Grade

NIB	Exc.	V.G.	Good	Fair	Poor
—	950	600	500	300	250

Model 50

Company's third attempt to produce a satisfactory self-loading repeating shotgun. Winchester went to the short recoil system, utilizing a floating chamber design. This model begins with serial number 1000. Successful model and built between 1954 and 1961. About 200,000 sold. **NOTE:** Add 10 percent for 20-gauge; 20 percent for ventilated rib on Standard Grade.

Available in several different styles:

1. Standard Grade: 12-, 20-gauge; plain or ventilated rib; lengths from 26" to 30"; plain walnut checkered pistol-grip stock and fore-end.

2. Skeet Grade: 12-, 20-gauge; 26" ventilated rib barrel; walnut checkered pistol-grip stock and fore-end.

3. Trap Grade: 12-gauge; 30" ventilated rib barrel; walnut checkered Monte Carlo stock and fore-end.

4. Pigeon Grade: 12-, 20-gauge; barrel lengths to customers' specifications; fancy walnut checkered stock and fore-end; made on special orders only.

5. Featherweight: lighter version of all the above, except Trap Grade.

Standard Grade

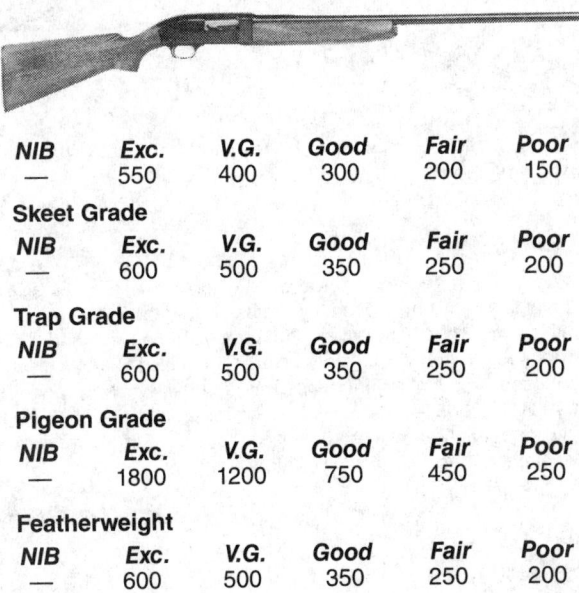

NIB	Exc.	V.G.	Good	Fair	Poor
—	550	400	300	200	150

Skeet Grade

NIB	Exc.	V.G.	Good	Fair	Poor
—	600	500	350	250	200

Trap Grade

NIB	Exc.	V.G.	Good	Fair	Poor
—	600	500	350	250	200

Pigeon Grade

NIB	Exc.	V.G.	Good	Fair	Poor
—	1800	1200	750	450	250

Featherweight

NIB	Exc.	V.G.	Good	Fair	Poor
—	600	500	350	250	200

Model 59

Fourth and final pre-1964 Winchester self-loading shotgun. Featured a steel and fiberglass barrel, with aluminum alloy receiver. Available in 12-gauge only. Barrel lengths from 26" to 30", with a variety of chokes. In 1961, Winchester introduced "Versalite" choke tube. This gave shooter a choice of Full, Modified or Improved Cylinder chokes in the same barrel. Sold about 82,000 Model 59s between 1960 and 1965. **NOTE:** Also made in 10-gauge (very rare), 20-gauge and 14-gauge. If any of these very low production or prototype guns are encountered, use extreme caution and seek an expert appraisal. Add 40 percent premium for barrels with three Versalite chokes and wrench; 20 percent premium for original box and papers.

Available in two different styles:

1. Standard Grade: plain walnut checkered pistol-grip stock and fore-end.

2. Pigeon Grade: select walnut checkered pistol-grip and fore-end.

Standard Grade

Courtesy Bonhams & Butterfields, San Francisco, California

NIB	Exc.	V.G.	Good	Fair	Poor
—	650	550	450	350	250

Pigeon Grade

NIB	Exc.	V.G.	Good	Fair	Poor
—	2500	2000	1200	600	300

POST-1963 RIFLES

Model 121

A single-shot bolt-action rifle chambered for .22 rimfire cartridge. Has a 20.75" barrel, with open sights. Finish blued, with plain walnut stock. Manufactured between 1967 and 1973. A youth model, with a shorter stock was designated 121Y and valued the same.

Courtesy Buffalo Bill Historical Center, Cody, Wyoming

NIB	Exc.	V.G.	Good	Fair	Poor
—	225	150	100	60	40

Model 131

Bolt-action repeater chambered for .22 rimfire cartridge. Has a 20.75" barrel, with open sights and 7-round detachable magazine. Finish blued, with plain walnut stock. Manufactured between 1967 and 1973. A tubular magazine version was designated Model 141 and valued the same.

NIB	Exc.	V.G.	Good	Fair	Poor
—	250	175	100	60	40

Model 310

Single-shot bolt-action rifle chambered for .22 rimfire cartridge. Features 22" barrel, with open sights. Finish blued, with checkered walnut stock. Manufactured between 1972 and 1975.

Courtesy Buffalo Bill Historical Center, Cody, Wyoming

NIB	Exc.	V.G.	Good	Fair	Poor
—	250	150	125	100	75

Model 320

Bolt-action repeating rifle. Similar in configuration to Model 310 single-shot. Has a 5-round detachable box magazine. Manufactured between 1972 and 1974.

NIB	Exc.	V.G.	Good	Fair	Poor
—	400	300	250	175	125

Model 250

Lever-action repeating rifle, with a hammerless action. Chambered for .22 rimfire cartridge. Has a 20.5" barrel, with open sights and tubular magazine. Finish blued, with checkered pistol-grip stock. Manufactured between 1963 and 1973.

NIB	Exc.	V.G.	Good	Fair	Poor
—	200	125	80	60	40

Model 250 Deluxe

This version similar to Model 250. Furnished with select walnut and sling swivels. Manufactured between 1965 and 1971.

NIB	Exc.	V.G.	Good	Fair	Poor
—	275	195	125	100	75

Model 255

Simply Model 250 chambered for .22 WMR cartridge. Manufactured between 1964 and 1970.

NIB	Exc.	V.G.	Good	Fair	Poor
—	225	150	100	70	50

Model 255 Deluxe

This version offered with select walnut and sling swivels. Manufactured between 1965 and 1973.

NIB	Exc.	V.G.	Good	Fair	Poor
—	375	250	175	125	75

Model 490

A blowback-operated semi-automatic rifle chambered for .22 LR cartridge. Has a 22" barrel, with open sights and 5-round detachable magazine. Finish blued, with checkered stock. Manufactured between 1975 and 1980.

NIB	Exc.	V.G.	Good	Fair	Poor
—	350	225	165	100	75

Model 270

Slide-action rifle chambered for .22 rimfire cartridge. Has a 20.5" barrel and tubular magazine. Finish blued, with checkered walnut stock. Manufactured between 1963 and 1973.

NIB	Exc.	V.G.	Good	Fair	Poor
—	350	225	165	100	75

Model 63 (1997)

Introduced in 1997. A re-creation of famous Model 63 .22-caliber automatic. Fitted with a 23" barrel and 10-round tubular magazine. Receiver top grooved for scope mounting.

Grade I

NIB	Exc.	V.G.	Good	Fair	Poor
800	525	—	—	—	—

High Grade

Engraved receiver with gold accents and select walnut stock.

NIB	Exc.	V.G.	Good	Fair	Poor
1050	850	700	575	400	300

Wildcat

Bolt-action repeater styled after Mosin-Nagant military sporter. Caliber: .22 LR. Magazine: 5- and 10-round detachable. Stock: checkered walnut with schnabel. Barrel: 21" blued. Weight: 4.5 lbs. Imported. Introduced 2006. Sporter and Target/Varmint versions available. **NOTE:** Add 5 percent for Target/Varmint.

NIB	Exc.	V.G.	Good	Fair	Poor
240	175	150	125	95	50

Model 94

Post-1964 lever-action carbine. Chambered for .30-30, 7-30 Waters and .44 Magnum cartridges. Offered with 20" or 24" barrel. Has a 6- or 7-round tubular magazine, depending on barrel length. Round barrel offered with open sights. Forearm held on by a single-barrel band. Finish blued, with straight-grip walnut stock. In 1982, modified to angle ejection to simplify scope mounting. Introduced as a continuation of Model 94 line, in 1964. In 2003, a top-tang safety was installed and .480 Ruger caliber was added. Model 94 series discontinued in 2006. Premium for unusual chamberings such as 7-30 Waters, etc.

NIB	Exc.	V.G.	Good	Fair	Poor
800	600	425	300	200	100

Model 94 Traditional—CW

As above, with checkered walnut stock. Chambered for .30-30, .44 Magnum and .480 Ruger cartridge. **NOTE:** Add $20 for .44 Magnum; $70 for .480 Ruger.

NIB	Exc.	V.G.	Good	Fair	Poor
850	575	450	325	225	125

Model 94 Ranger

Chambered for .30-30 cartridge. Fitted with a 20" barrel. Weight about 6.25 lbs. In 2003, a top-tang safety was installed.

NIB	Exc.	V.G.	Good	Fair	Poor
—	450	300	225	150	100

Model 94 Ranger Compact

Introduced in 1998. Features 16" barrel, with 12.5" lop. Chambered for .30-30 or .357 Magnum. Furnished with black recoil pad. Post-style front sight, with adjustable rear sight. Hardwood stock. Weight about 5.87 lbs

NIB	Exc.	V.G.	Good	Fair	Poor
—	475	325	250	150	100

Model 94 Black Shadow

Features black synthetic stock, with non-glare finish and black recoil pad. Offered in .30-30, .44 Magnum or .444 Marlin. Fitted with a 20" barrel. Weight about 6.5 lbs. Introduced in 1998.

NIB	Exc.	V.G.	Good	Fair	Poor
600	475	375	250	225	175

Model 94 Deluxe

Checkered stock.

NIB	Exc.	V.G.	Good	Fair	Poor
850	675	550	400	300	200

Model 94 Win-Tuff

Laminated stock.

NIB	Exc.	V.G.	Good	Fair	Poor
500	400	275	225	165	125

Model 94 XTR

Select checkered walnut stock. Discontinued 1988.

NIB	Exc.	V.G.	Good	Fair	Poor
—	700	450	350	250	175

Model 94 XTR Deluxe

Fancy checkering.

NIB	Exc.	V.G.	Good	Fair	Poor
—	725	475	375	275	200

Model 94 Trapper

Chambered for .30-30, .357 Magnum, .44 Magnum or .45 Colt cartridge. Barrel 16". In 2003, a top-tang safety was installed.

NIB	Exc.	V.G.	Good	Fair	Poor
750	575	450	350	250	150

Model 94 Antique Carbine

Gold-plated saddle ring.

NIB	Exc.	V.G.	Good	Fair	Poor
—	800	600	475	350	200

Model 94 Wrangler

.32 Win. Special.

NIB	Exc.	V.G.	Good	Fair	Poor
—	900	725	525	400	250

Model 94 Wrangler II

Loop lever.

NIB	Exc.	V.G.	Good	Fair	Poor
700	525	425	300	150	—

Model 94 Legacy 20-inch

Chambered for .30-30 Win. Fitted with a 20" barrel and half pistol-grip stock. Walnut buttstock and forearm are cut checkered. Weight 6.5 lbs. In 2003, a top-tang safety was installed.

NIB	Exc.	V.G.	Good	Fair	Poor
900	750	600	475	300	200

Model 94 Legacy 24-inch

Introduced in 2005. Features 24" round barrel, with full length magazine. Checkered walnut stock, with semi-pistol-grip. Chambered for .30-30, .357 Magnum, .44 Rem. Magnum or .45 Colt cartridge. Drilled and tapped for scope mount. Blued finish. Weight about 6.75 lbs.

NIB	Exc.	V.G.	Good	Fair	Poor
900	750	600	475	300	200

Model 94 Legacy 26-inch

Similar to model above, but offered in both round and octagon barrel; blue or case colored receiver. Marbles' tang sight. Chambered for .30-30 or .38-

55 calibers. Weight about 7 lbs. Introduced in 2005. Premium for .38-55.
NOTE: Add $55 for case colored receiver; $100 for octagon barrel.

NIB	Exc.	V.G.	Good	Fair	Poor
1100	875	750	575	400	300

Model 94 XTR Big Bore

This version chambered for .307, .356 or .375 Win. cartridges. Features angle-ejection; blued, with walnut Monte Carlo-type stock; recoil pad. Round barrel length 20". Has 6-round tubular magazine. Introduced in 1978. **NOTE:** Deduct 12.5 percent for .375 Win.

NIB	Exc.	V.G.	Good	Fair	Poor
1050	900	775	575	400	300

Model 94 Centennial Limited Editions

Introduced in 1994. These models celebrate 100-year Anniversary of Winchester Model 1894. Offered in three grades, these models are limited production. Grade I limited to 12,000 rifles; High Grade limited to 3,000 rifles; Custom High Grade only 94 produced. Each Limited model has different grades of select walnut and engraving coverage. All are chambered for .30-30 Win. cartridge.

Grade I

NIB	Exc.	V.G.	Good	Fair	Poor
1200	1000	900	700	575	400

High Grade

NIB	Exc.	V.G.	Good	Fair	Poor
1900	1300	1075	900	750	600

Custom High Grade

NIB	Exc.	V.G.	Good	Fair	Poor
4750	3900	2500	1000	750	450

Model 94 Heritage—Limited 1 of 1000

Introduced in 2002. Limited to 1,000 rifles. Fitted with half round/half octagon 26" barrel. Engraved #3 pattern, with gold plate. Fancy walnut stock. Chambered for .38-55 cartridge.

NIB	Exc.	V.G.	Good	Fair	Poor
5000	4000	3000	1750	1200	600

Model 94 Heritage—Custom 1 of 100

Similar to above, with finer wood. Engraved #2 pattern, with gold. Limited to 100 rifles. Introduced in 2002.

NIB	Exc.	V.G.	Good	Fair	Poor
7500	—	—	—	—	—

Model 94 Trails End

Chambered for .357 Magnum, .44 Magnum and .45 Colt. Offered with standard-size loop lever or Wrangler-style loop. Introduced in 1997. **NOTE:** Add $500 to NIB for .25-35 Win.

NIB	Exc.	V.G.	Good	Fair	Poor
1375	1050	825	600	450	300

Model 94 Trails End Octagon

As above, with 20" octagon barrel. Choice of blued or case colored receiver. Crescent butt. Weight about 6.75 lbs. Introduced in 2004. **NOTE:** Add $60 for case colored receiver.

NIB	Exc.	V.G.	Good	Fair	Poor
1395	1100	850	600	450	300

Model 94 Trails End Hunter

Offered in .25-35 Win., .30-30 Win. or .38-55 Win. Fitted with 20" round or octagon barrel. Plain walnut stock. Blued finish on round barrel; case colored on octagon barrel. Weight about 6.5 lbs. Introduced in 2005. **NOTE:** Add $290 for octagon barrel.

NIB	Exc.	V.G.	Good	Fair	Poor
1375	1050	825	600	450	300

Model 94 Timber Carbine

Introduced in 1999. Chambered for .444 Marlin cartridge. Barrel is 17.75" long and ported. Hooded front sight. Magazine capacity 5 rounds. Weight about 6 lbs. Finish blue. Walnut stock. In 2004, chambered for .450 Marlin cartridge.

NIB	Exc.	V.G.	Good	Fair	Poor
1000	850	700	600	400	300

Model 94 Timber Scout

Introduced in 2005. Features an 18" barrel. Chambered for .30-30 Win. or .44 Rem. Magnum cartridges. Quick detachable scope mount attached to barrel for long eye relief. Plain walnut stock, with pistol-grip. Blued finish. Weight about 6 lbs. Scope not included.

NIB	Exc.	V.G.	Good	Fair	Poor
900	750	600	475	300	200

Model 94 Pack Rifle

Lever-action model features an 18" barrel. Chambered for .30-30 or .44 Magnum. Has a plain walnut stock, with pistol-grip. Magazine is 3/4-style; 4-round capacity for .30-30; 5-round for .44 Magnum. Open sights. Weight about 6.25 lbs. Introduced in 2000.

NIB	Exc.	V.G.	Good	Fair	Poor
900	750	600	475	300	200

Model 1894 Custom Grade

Lever-action rifle chambered in .30-30. Features include 24" half round/half octagon deeply blued barrel; buckhorn rear sight with Marbles gold bead front; Grade IV/V walnut stock and fore-end with a rich high gloss finish; deep scroll engraving on both sides of blued receiver. Commemorates 200th Anniversary of Oliver F. Winchester's birth. An early Winchester Repeating Arms crest graces left side of receiver, with right side bearing the words "Two Hundred Years, Oliver F. Winchester" and dates "1810 - 2010" in gold. Barrel is deeply polished, with signature of Oliver F. Winchester in gold on top of the bolt. Sold individually in limited quantities and in 500 sets with High Grade.

NIB	Exc.	V.G.	Good	Fair	Poor
1800	1550	1300	—	—	—

Model 1894 High Grade

Lever-action rifle chambered in .30-30. Features include 24" half round/half octagon deeply blued barrel; buckhorn rear sight with Marbles gold bead front; silver nitride receiver; Grade II/III high gloss walnut stock and fore-end with a rich high gloss finish; delicate scroll work, with Oliver F. Winchester's signature in gold on top of the bolt. Left side of receiver bears an early Winchester Repeating Arms crest; on right side are the words "Two Hundred Years, Oliver F. Winchester" and dates "1810 - 2010". Sold individually in limited quantities and in 500 sets with the Custom Grade.

NIB	Exc.	V.G.	Good	Fair	Poor
1300	1100	900	—	—	—

Model 71

A true reproduction of the original. Drilled and tapped for a receiver sight. Polished blue 24" round barrel. Oil-finished American walnut stock, fore-end cap, no checkering. Marble gold bead front sight and buckhorn rear. Chambered for original .348 WCF caliber only. Introduced in 2011.

NIB	Exc.	V.G.	Good	Fair	Poor
1300	1100	—	—	—	—

Model 94 Short Rifle

Latest incarnation of famous Model 94 Carbine, with 20" round barrel and straight-grip walnut stock. Rifle-styled fore-end has black grip cap and full-length magazine. Receiver drilled and tapped for scope mounts, with hammer extension included. Marble gold bead front sight, semi-buckhorn rear. Overall length 38"; weight 6.75 lbs. Chambered in .30-30 or .38-55.

NIB	Exc.	V.G.	Good	Fair	Poor
1150	1000	800	500	300	250

Model 94 Sporter

Reminiscent of original Model 1894 Rifle. This new model for 2011, has a 24" half round/half octagon blued barrel; satin oil-finished American walnut stock; steel crescent buttplate; double-line border checkering pattern. Blue receiver drilled and tapped for optical sights. Gold bead front sight and buckhorn rear. Hammer extension included. Available in .30-30 or .38-55 Win.

NIB	Exc.	V.G.	Good	Fair	Poor
1175	1000	850	—	—	—

Model 94 150th Commemorative

To commemorate 150-years of Winchester, this classic lever-action rifles features a 24" octagon barrel, with gold band and Winchester 150th Anniversary gold script engraving. Other special features are Ulrich-style engraved silver nitride receiver sideplates, crescent buttplate and fore-end cap. Iron sights are semi-buckhorn adjustable rear and Marble's gold bead front. Straight-grip stock has classic cut spade-style checkering and high polish oil-finish. Chambered for classic .30-30 Win., with 8-round magazine. Introduced in 2016.

NIB	Exc.	V.G.	Good	Fair	Poor
2500	2000	—	—	—	—

Model 1886 Short Rifle

Reintroduced version of famed Model 1886, with Grade I American walnut stock. Blue steel fore-end cap; crescent buttplate; barrel 24"; full-length tubular magazine holds 6 cartridges. Chambered in .45-70 Government. Elegant satin finish on all wood and no checkering. Deep blue receiver, barrel and lever. Top-tang safety. Adjustable rear buckhorn sight and fine gold Marble front.

NIB	Exc.	V.G.	Good	Fair	Poor
1125	975	825	—	—	—

Model 1892 Carbine

New version of rifle made famous by actor John Wayne. Chambered for .357 Magnum, .44 Rem. Magnum or .45 Colt. American walnut stock, with straight-grip. Round 21" barrel. Receiver and lever deeply polished and blued. Full-length magazine. Front and rear iron sights.

NIB	Exc.	V.G.	Good	Fair	Poor
950	800	700	—	—	—

MODEL 9400 SERIES

Model 9410

Introduced in 2001. Features .410 shotgun in a lever-action configuration. Barrel length 24" smoothbore, with Cylinder or Invector chokes. Chambered is 2.5". Magazine capacity 9 rounds. Tru-glo front sight. Weight about 6.75 lbs. In 2003, a top-tang safety was installed.

NIB	Exc.	V.G.	Good	Fair	Poor
1450	1100	900	750	600	400

Model 9410 Semi-Fancy

As above, with semi-fancy walnut stock and checkering. Introduced in 2004.

NIB	Exc.	V.G.	Good	Fair	Poor
1600	1200	975	825	650	400

Model 9410 Packer

Introduced in 2002. Features 20" barrel, with 3/4 magazine and pistol-grip stock. Weight about 6.5 lbs.

NIB	Exc.	V.G.	Good	Fair	Poor
1000	850	700	600	400	300

Model 9410 Packer Compact

Introduced in 2003. Features reduced length of pull to 12.5". Fitted with Invector chokes. Weight about 6.25 lbs.

NIB	Exc.	V.G.	Good	Fair	Poor
1000	850	700	600	400	300

Model 9410 Ranger

Same as standard or traditional Model 9410, with hardwood stock without checkering. Weight about 6.75 lbs. Fitted with top-tang safety. Introduced in 2003.

NIB	Exc.	V.G.	Good	Fair	Poor
900	750	575	450	300	250

Model 9422

Introduced in 1972. Chambered for .22 rimfire and .22 rimfire Magnum cartridges. Fitted with a 20.5" barrel, front ramp sight with hood and adjustable semi-buckhorn rear. Tubular magazine holds 21 Shorts, 17 Longs and 15 LR cartridges. Magnum version holds 11 cartridges. Weight about 6.25 lbs. Two-piece American walnut stock, with no checkering. Between 1972 and 1992, approximately 750,000 were produced.

NIB	Exc.	V.G.	Good	Fair	Poor
850	675	525	375	225	125

Model 9422 XTR

Deluxe lever-action take-down rifle chambered for .22 rimfire cartridge. Round 20.5" barrel and tubular magazine. Finish blued, with checkered high-gloss straight-grip walnut stock. Introduced in 1978. **NOTE:** Add $100 for .22 Magnum version.

NIB	Exc.	V.G.	Good	Fair	Poor
1000	850	700	600	400	300

Model 9422 XTR Classic

Similar to standard Model 9422 XTR. Features 22.5" barrel; satin-finished plain pistol-grip walnut stock. Manufactured between 1985 and 1987.

NIB	Exc.	V.G.	Good	Fair	Poor
1100	925	750	650	450	325

Model 9422 WinTuff

Features uncheckered laminated wood stock that is brown in color. Chambered for .22 rimfire and .22 Win. Magnum rimfire. Weight 6.25 lbs. Other features same as standard Model 9422.

NIB	Exc.	V.G.	Good	Fair	Poor
850	675	525	375	225	125

Model 9422 WinCam

Chambered only for .22 Win. Magnum rimfire. Laminated stock is a green color. Weight 6.25 lbs.

NIB	Exc.	V.G.	Good	Fair	Poor
850	675	525	375	225	125

Model 9422 Trapper

Introduced in 1996. Features 16.5" barrel. Overall length 33"; weight 5.5 lbs.

NIB	Exc.	V.G.	Good	Fair	Poor
850	675	525	375	225	125

Model 9422 High Grade

This variation features a specially engraved receiver and fancy wood stock. Barrel length 20.5"; weight about 6 lbs.

NIB	Exc.	V.G.	Good	Fair	Poor
1000	850	700	600	400	300

Model 9422 25th Anniversary Rifle

Introduced in 1997. Features 20.5" barrel. Limited quantities.

Grade I

Engraved receiver.

NIB	Exc.	V.G.	Good	Fair	Poor
1000	850	700	600	400	300

High Grade

Engraved receiver, with silver border.

NIB	Exc.	V.G.	Good	Fair	Poor
1450	1100	900	750	600	400

Model 9422 Legacy

Has a checkered walnut semi-pistol-grip stock. Shoots .22-caliber LR, L or S cartridges. Fitted with a 16" barrel. Weight about 6 lbs. Introduced in 1998.

NIB	Exc.	V.G.	Good	Fair	Poor
850	675	525	375	225	125

Model 9422 Large Loop & Walnut

Introduced in 1998. Features walnut stock, with a large loop lever. Large loop offered on .22 LR, L or S. Standard lever on .22 WMR. Fitted with 16" barrel. Weight about 6 lbs.

NIB	Exc.	V.G.	Good	Fair	Poor
900	750	575	450	300	250

Model 9422 High Grade Series II

Features high-grade walnut stock, with cut checkering. Receiver engraved with dogs and squirrels. Fitted with 16" barrel. Weight about 6 lbs. Introduced in 1998.

NIB	Exc.	V.G.	Good	Fair	Poor
1450	1100	900	750	600	400

Model 9417 Traditional

Introduced in 2003. Chambered for .17 HMR cartridge. Fitted with 20.5" barrel. Adjustable sights. Checkered walnut stock, with straight-grip. Weight about 6 lbs.

NIB	Exc.	V.G.	Good	Fair	Poor
1200	975	850	675	400	300

Model 9417 Legacy

Similar to model above. Fitted with 22.5" barrel. Plain walnut stock, with checkered pistol-grip. Weight about 6 lbs. Introduced in 2003.

NIB	Exc.	V.G.	Good	Fair	Poor
1200	975	850	675	400	300

MODEL 9422 TRIBUTE SERIES

As of 2005, Model 9422 production will end. These final production Model 9422s, will be limited to a total production of 9,422 rifles. Each rifle will have Winchester Horse and Rider on one side and Model 9422 tribute logo on the other side.

Traditional Tribute

Features 20.5" barrel, with high grade checkered walnut stock. Blued receiver, with high-relief silver inlay on both sides of receiver.

NIB	Exc.	V.G.	Good	Fair	Poor
1400	1200	975	825	650	300

Legacy Tribute

Similar to model above, with semi-pistol-grip. Barrel 22.5".

NIB	Exc.	V.G.	Good	Fair	Poor
1500	1300	1075	925	650	300

Custom Traditional Tribute

Fitted with 20.5" barrel and high grade checkered walnut stock. High-relief scroll engraved receiver, with gold logos on both sides. Limited to 222 rifles.

NIB	Exc.	V.G.	Good	Fair	Poor
2600	2200	1650	1200	800	500

Special Edition Traditional Tribute

Has checkered walnut straight-grip stock. Engraved blued receiver. Barrel 20.5". Engraved logos on both sides of receiver.

NIB	Exc.	V.G.	Good	Fair	Poor
1200	975	850	675	400	300

Special Edition Legacy Tribute

Has checkered semi-pistol-grip stock. Blued receiver, with engraved logos on both sides. Barrel 22.5".

NIB	Exc.	V.G.	Good	Fair	Poor
1200	975	850	675	400	300

Model 64 (Post-'64)

A post-1964 version of lever-action Model 64. Chambered for .30-30 cartridge. Has 24" round barrel, with open sights and 5-round 2/3-length tubular magazine. Finish blued, with plain walnut pistol-grip stock. Manufactured between 1972 and 1974.

NIB	Exc.	V.G.	Good	Fair	Poor
—	800	650	550	375	250

Model 1885 Low Wall

Introduced in fall of 1999. Single-shot model chambered for .22 LR or .17 Mach 2 cartridge. Fitted with 24.5" half octagon barrel, with leaf rear sight. Drilled and tapped for tang sight. Crescent steel buttplate. Walnut stock. Weight about 8 lbs. Limited to 2,400 rifles.

Grade I

NIB	Exc.	V.G.	Good	Fair	Poor
1050	900	750	600	500	300

High Grade

NIB	Exc.	V.G.	Good	Fair	Poor
1300	1050	875	750	600	400

Model 1885 High Wall Hunter

Single-shot patterned after original Model 1885, designed by John Browning. Calibers: .223, .22-250, .270 WSM, 7mm WSM, .300 WSM, .325 WSM. Stock checkered walnut. Blued sightless 28" octagon barrel, with Pachmayr pad. Weight 8.5 lbs.

NIB	Exc.	V.G.	Good	Fair	Poor
1100	925	750	650	450	325

Model 1885 .30-06 Centennial High Wall Hunter

Similar to Model 1885 High Wall Hunter, with premium wood and gold inlay on receiver. Commemorates centennial of .30-06 cartridge. Introduced 2006.

NIB	Exc.	V.G.	Good	Fair	Poor
1300	1125	875	750	550	325

Model 1885 Low Wall Classic

Single-shot rifle chambered for .17 HMR cartridge. Fitted with 24" octagon barrel. Checkered walnut stock, with straight-grip and schnabel fore-end. Adjustable sights. Weight about 8 lbs. Introduced in 2003. In 2005, .17 Mach 2 caliber was offered.

NIB	Exc.	V.G.	Good	Fair	Poor
1100	925	750	650	450	325

Model 1885 Low Wall 17 Mach 2

Similar to Model 1885 High Wall, with low-profile receiver, crescent buttplate and 24" barrel. Chambered for .17 Mach 2 rimfire cartridge. Introduced 2006.

NIB	Exc.	V.G.	Good	Fair	Poor
1050	900	750	600	500	300

Model 1892

Introduced in mid-1997. Chambered for .357 Magnum, .44-40 and .45 Colt cartridges. Features straight-grip, full magazine and crescent buttplate.

Grade I

2,500 rifles, with engraved receiver.

NIB	Exc.	V.G.	Good	Fair	Poor
900	800	700	550	450	325

High Grade

1,000 rifles, with gold accents.

NIB	Exc.	V.G.	Good	Fair	Poor
1500	1300	1075	925	650	300

Model 1892 Short Rifle

Fitted with 20" barrel. Chambered for .45 Colt, .357 Magnum, .44 Magnum and .44-40 cartridges. Walnut stock, with blued barrel and receiver. Weight about 6.25 lbs. Introduced in 1999.

NIB	Exc.	V.G.	Good	Fair	Poor
1200	975	850	675	400	300

Model 1892 Carbine

Similar to 1892 Short Rifle, with satin-finished stock, full-length 10-shot magazine with barrel band. Introduced in 2011. Also available with large-loop lever.

NIB	Exc.	V.G.	Good	Fair	Poor
1000	850	700	500	350	200

John Wayne Model 1892 High Grade

Features silver-nickel receiver, with engraved portrait of actor on receiver. Banners on sides of receiver have silver-nickel engraving "John Wayne-American 1907-2007" and "Courage, Strength, Grit". In .44-40 caliber, with 18.5" barrel, large-loop lever, adjustable rear sight, blue hammer and trigger. Custom Grade has checkered stock, gold engraving, blue receiver. Limited editions with 4,000 High Grade and 1,000 Custom Grade. Manufactured 2007-2009. **NOTE:** Add $1000 for Custom Grade.

NIB	Exc.	V.G.	Good	Fair	Poor
1750	1650	1550	—	—	—

Model 1886

Introduced to Winchester line in 1997. This was a non-cataloged item. Features 26" octagon barrel, semi-pistol-grip and crescent buttplate.

Grade I

2,500 rifles, with blued receiver.

NIB	Exc.	V.G.	Good	Fair	Poor
1050	900	750	600	500	300

High Grade

1,000 rifles, with gold accents on receiver.

NIB	Exc.	V.G.	Good	Fair	Poor
1500	1300	1075	925	650	300

Model 1886 Take Down Classic

Introduced in 1999. Chambered for .45-70 cartridge. Features 26" barrel, with take-down feature. Walnut stock, with pistol-grip and crescent butt. Magazine capacity 8 rounds. Weight about 9.25 lbs.

NIB	Exc.	V.G.	Good	Fair	Poor
1300	1125	875	750	550	325

Model 1886 Extra Light

Similar to Model 1886 Classic. Fitted with 22" round tapered barrel and half magazine. Chambered for .45-70 cartridge. Shotgun butt. Weight about 7.25 lbs. Limited edition. Introduced in 2000.

Grade I (3,500)

NIB	Exc.	V.G.	Good	Fair	Poor
1100	925	750	650	450	325

High Grade (1,000)

NIB	Exc.	V.G.	Good	Fair	Poor
1500	1300	1075	925	650	300

Model 1886 Deluxe

Features case-hardened frame and full octagonal 24" barrel. Chambered in .45-70. Introduced in 2015.

NIB	Exc.	V.G.	Good	Fair	Poor
1500	1375	1000	—	—	—

Model 1895 Limited Edition

Introduced in 1995. Reproduction of famous Model 1895. Offered in .30-06 caliber, with 24" barrel. Magazine capacity 4 rounds. Weight about 8 lbs. Available in two grades, each limited to 4,000 rifles. Reintroduced in 2010, in .30-40 Krag caliber.

Grade I

NIB	Exc.	V.G.	Good	Fair	Poor
1050	900	750	600	500	300

High Grade

NIB	Exc.	V.G.	Good	Fair	Poor
1500	1300	1075	925	650	300

Model 1895—Limited Edition for the year 2000

Same as above, but chambered for .405 Win. cartridge. Introduced in 2000.

Grade I

NIB	Exc.	V.G.	Good	Fair	Poor
1100	925	750	650	450	325

High Grade

NIB	Exc.	V.G.	Good	Fair	Poor
1500	1300	1075	925	650	300

Model 1895 Saddle Ring Carbine

Patterned after original Model 1895 carbine. Features include blued 22" barrel, ladder-style rear sight, D&T for Lyman side mount, saddle ring on left side of receiver, rollmarked .30 Gov't 06. Chambered in .30-06 only. Commemorates centennial of .30-06 cartridge. Introduced 2006. No longer in production.

NIB	Exc.	V.G.	Good	Fair	Poor
1200	975	850	675	400	300

Model 1895 Theodore Roosevelt Safari Centennial High Grade

Lever-action rifle patterned after original Winchester Model 1895. Chambered in .405 Win. Commemorates Theodore Roosevelt's 1909 African Safari. Blued round 24" barrel, 4-round box magazine, checkered walnut fore-end and buttstock, with inlaid "TR" medallion. Engraved and silvered receiver. Weight 8 lbs.

NIB	Exc.	V.G.	Good	Fair	Poor
1600	1375	1075	925	650	300

Custom Grade

Similar to above, with jeweled hammer, fancier wood and engraving, gold-filled highlights and numerous accessories. Production limited to 1000 sets.

NIB	Exc.	V.G.	Good	Fair	Poor
3000	2500	1950	1575	1200	700

Model 73

Winchester's latest incarnation of what some historians call "The Gun That Won the West", and offered in several variations. Chambered in .357 Magnum, .44-40 or .45 Colt. Short Rifle has 20" barrel, straight-grip stock; Sporter 24" round/octagonal barrel, with/without pistol-grip (shown). Reintroduced in 2015. **NOTE:** Add $250 for color case-hardened receiver.

Short Rifle

NIB	Exc.	V.G.	Good	Fair	Poor
1100	950	800	—	—	—

Sporter

NIB	Exc.	V.G.	Good	Fair	Poor
1550	1400	1250	—	—	—

Model 1866 150th Commemorative

Only a limited number will be made to commemorate 150th Anniversary of the founding of Winchester Repeating Arms. Among the features are a custom grade V/VI walnut straight-grip stock, with satin finish and crescent buttplate. Full octagon 24" barrel, with gold band and special 150th Anniversary script and scroll engraving. Sights are ladder-style rear, with blade front. Chambered for .44-40 (WCF) caliber, with 13-round magazine. Introduced in 2016.

NIB	Exc.	V.G.	Good	Fair	Poor
3000	2600	—	—	—	—

Model 1873 150th Commemorative

This "Gun That Won the West" commemorates 150-years of Winchester. Features include grade V/VI walnut stock, scroll engraving with gold accents, adjustable tang sight, crescent buttplate and fore-end cap. Full octagon 24" barrel, with gold band and special 150th Anniversary script. Sights are tang-mounted rear peep and adjustable semi-buckhorn, with gold bead front. Chambered for .44-40 (WCF) caliber, with 13-round magazine. Introduced in 2016.

NIB	Exc.	V.G.	Good	Fair	Poor
3000	2600	—	—	—	—

Model 52B Sporting Rifle: 1993-1997 Production

A 1993 limited-edition rifle (6,000 guns). Faithful reproduction of famous Winchester Model 52 Sporter. Equipped with 24" barrel, adjustable trigger and "B" style cheekpiece. Reissued in 1997. Limited to 3,000 rifles. Made by Miroku in Japan.

NIB	Exc.	V.G.	Good	Fair	Poor
1000	850	700	500	350	300

Model XPR

Totally new bolt-action design. Based on some aspects of Model 70, combined with modern manufacturing methods for a more affordable price. Offered in .270 Win., .30-06, .300 Win. Magnum and .338 Win. Magnum. Features include a polymer stock, detachable box magazine and matte black finish. Available with Mossy Oak Break-Up Country finish. Introduced in 2015. **NOTE:** Add $50 for Mossy Oak Break-Up Country finish.

NIB	Exc.	V.G.	Good	Fair	Poor
465	420	375	—	—	—

POST-1963 MODEL 70

These post-Model 70 rifles were fitted with: redesigned actions; bolt with free-floating barrels; new style stocks with impressed checkering. In 1994, U.S. Repeating Arms reintroduced pre-1964 Model 70 action on many of its Model 70 rifles. At the present time, this new action does not affect values but may do so in the future depending on shooter reaction. In October of 2007, Winchester Repeating Arms announced that pre-'64-style Model 70 would once again be produced – this time at the FN plant in Columbia, So. Carolina.

Model 70—Standard Grade

Bolt-action sporting rifle chambered for various popular calibers such as .22-250, .222 Rem., .243 Win., .270 Win., .30-06 and .308 Win. Features 22" barrel, with open sights and 5-round integral box magazine. Finish blued, with Monte Carlo-type stock furnished with sling swivels. Manufactured between 1964 and 1971.

NIB	Exc.	V.G.	Good	Fair	Poor
—	600	475	325	175	110

Model 70 Varmint

Chambered for .22-25, .222 Rem. and .243 Win. cartridges. Fitted with 24" heavyweight barrel, with no sights. Magazine capacity 5 rounds. Weight about 9.75 lbs. Built from 1964 to 1971.

NIB	Exc.	V.G.	Good	Fair	Poor
—	600	450	300	150	100

Model 70 Westerner

Chambered for .264 Win. Magnum and .300 Win. Magnum cartridges. Open sights; 24" barrel; ventilated recoil pad. Weight about 7.25 lbs. Built from 1964 to 1971.

NIB	Exc.	V.G.	Good	Fair	Poor
—	650	475	325	175	110

Model 70 African

Chambered for .458 Win. Magnum cartridge. Fitted with 22" barrel, with open sights. Magazine capacity 3 rounds. Weight about 8.5 lbs. Built from 1964 to 1971.

NIB	Exc.	V.G.	Good	Fair	Poor
—	925	750	485	275	175

Model 70 Magnum

Chambered for 7mm Rem. Magnum, .300 Win. Magnum and .375 H&H cartridges. Barrel length 24"; weight about 7.75 lbs. Built from 1964 to 1971.

NIB	Exc.	V.G.	Good	Fair	Poor
—	750	585	375	225	175

Model 70 Deluxe

Built from 1964 to 1971. Features Monte Carlo stock, with hand checkering and ebony fore-end tip. Offered in .243, .270, .30-06, .300 Win. Magnum. Barrel 22"; Magnum 24". Weight about 7.5 lbs.

NIB	Exc.	V.G.	Good	Fair	Poor
—	750	575	350	175	125

Model 70 Mannlicher

Full-length Mannlicher-type stocked version of Model 70 bolt-action rifle. Chambered for .243, .270, .308 and .30-06 cartridges. Introduced in 1969. Features 19" barrel, with open sights. Finish blued. Discontinued in 1972. Only 2,401 produced. Excellent quality.

NIB	Exc.	V.G.	Good	Fair	Poor
—	975	825	625	425	310

Model 70 Target Rifle

Chambered for .308 or .30-06 cartridges. Offered with 24" heavy barrel, without sights. Furnished with bases for a target scope. Finish blued, with heavy walnut target stock and palm rest. Weight about 10.25 lbs.

NIB	Exc.	V.G.	Good	Fair	Poor
—	875	775	575	375	260

Model 70 International Match Army

Chambered for .308 cartridge. Has 24" heavy barrel furnished without sights and adjustable trigger. Blued, with target-type heavy stock that has an accessory rail and adjustable butt.

NIB	Exc.	V.G.	Good	Fair	Poor
—	950	850	600	400	300

Model 70A

Utility version of bolt-action post-1963 Model 70. Furnished without a hinged floorplate. Finish blued, with walnut stock. Manufactured between 1972 and 1978.

NIB	Exc.	V.G.	Good	Fair	Poor
—	500	400	350	300	125

Model 670

Economy-grade version of Model 70. Hardwood stock, iron sights, non-hinged floorplate, 22" blued barrel. Manufactured from 1967 to 1973.

NIB	Exc.	V.G.	Good	Fair	Poor
—	450	400	300	250	100

Model 70 XTR Featherweight

Built after the takeover by U.S.R.A. Company. Bolt-action sporting rifle chambered for various calibers from .22-250 up to .30-06 cartridges. Has 22" barrel that is furnished without sights and 5-round integral magazine.. Features short-/medium-length action. Finish blued, with checkered walnut stock. Introduced in 1981.

NIB	Exc.	V.G.	Good	Fair	Poor
—	725	625	450	325	265

Model 70 Fiftieth Anniversary

Commemorative version of post-1963 Model 70 bolt-action rifle. Chambered for .300 Win. Magnum. Offered with 24" barrel; engraved; high-gloss blued; deluxe checkered walnut stock. There were 500 manufactured in 1987. In order to realize collector potential, it must be NIB with all supplied materials.

NIB	Exc.	V.G.	Good	Fair	Poor
1500	1400	1200	900	500	300

Model 70 XTR Super Express

Heavy-duty version of post-1963 Model 70. Chambered for .375 H&H and .458 Win. Magnum cartridges. Offered with 22" or 24" heavy barrel and 3-round integral box magazine. Has extra recoil lugs mounted in the stock. Blued, with select straight-grain walnut stock. Recoil pad standard.

NIB	Exc.	V.G.	Good	Fair	Poor
1100	925	750	650	450	325

Model 70 XTR Varmint

Chambered for .22-250, .223 and .243 cartridges. Has 24" heavy barrel furnished without sights and 5-round magazine. Blued, with heavy walnut stock. Introduced in 1972.

NIB	Exc.	V.G.	Good	Fair	Poor
650	550	400	250	200	100

Model 70 Winlight

Offered in various calibers between .270 and .338 Win. Magnum. Features matte blue finish; fiberglass stock. Offered with 22" or 24" barrel; 3- or 4-round magazine. Introduced in 1986.

NIB	Exc.	V.G.	Good	Fair	Poor
700	550	400	250	200	100

Model 70 Ranger

Utility-grade bolt-action rifle. Chambered for .270 Win., .30-06 and 7mm Rem. Magnum cartridges. Offered with 22" or 24" barrel, open sights and 3- or 4-round box magazine. Finish blued, with plain hardwood stock.

NIB	Exc.	V.G.	Good	Fair	Poor
450	300	275	225	150	100

Model 70 Featherweight

Bolt-action rifle chambered in .22-250, .243, 7mm-08, .308, .270 WSM, 7mm WSM, .300 WSM, .325 WSM, .25-06, .270, .30-06, 7mm Rem. Magnum, .300 Win. Magnum, .338 Win. Magnum. Blued 22" barrel (24" Magnum), satin-finished checkered Grade I walnut stock, controlled round feeding. Capacity 5 rounds (short action); 3 rounds (long action). Weight 6.5 to 7.25 lbs. Pachmayr Decelerator pad. No sights, but drilled and tapped for scope mounts. Values shown are for long action. In 2003, a left-hand model offered. **NOTE:** Add $35 for left-hand; $60 for stainless steel. Deduct 15 percent for short action.

NIB	Exc.	V.G.	Good	Fair	Poor
850	650	450	375	225	125

Model 70 Featherweight Classic All-Terrain

Introduced in 1996. Features weather-resistant stainless steel barrel and action, with fiberglass/graphite black synthetic stock. Offered in .270 Win., .30-06, 7mm Rem. Magnum, .330 Win. Magnum. Weight about 7.25 lbs. Also offered with BOSS system. **NOTE:** Add $100 for BOSS.

NIB	Exc.	V.G.	Good	Fair	Poor
950	650	450	325	225	125

Model 70 Featherweight Super Short

Introduced in 2003. Features shorter receiver to handle .223 WSSM and .243 WSSM cartridges. Fitted with 22" barrel, checkered walnut stock and solid recoil pad. Weight about 6 lbs.

NIB	Exc.	V.G.	Good	Fair	Poor
770	600	500	400	300	200

Model 70 Classic Laredo

First offered in 1996. Features heavy 26" barrel, with pre-1964 action on a gray synthetic stock. Chambered for 7mm Rem. Magnum and .300 Win. Magnum. Beavertail forearm. Finish matte blue. In 1997, offered chambered for 7mm STW cartridge. In 1998, offered with fluted barrel. **NOTE:** Add $100 for BOSS; $125 for fluted barrel.

NIB	Exc.	V.G.	Good	Fair	Poor
750	650	550	500	400	300

Model 70 Classic Compact

Introduced in 1998. Scaled-down version of Featherweight. Length of pull 12.5"; 20" barrel. Chambered for .243, .308 and 7mm-08 calibers. Checkered walnut stock. Weight about 6.5 lbs.

NIB	Exc.	V.G.	Good	Fair	Poor
750	650	550	500	400	300

Model 70 Classic Sporter LT

Introduced in 1999. Chambered for a wide variety of calibers from .25-06 to .338 Win. Magnum. Fitted with 24" or 26" barrel, depending on caliber and no sights. Walnut stock, with buttpad. Blued finish. Offered in left-hand models from .270 to .338 Win. Magnum. Weight about 8 lbs. **NOTE:** Add $30 for left-hand models.

NIB	Exc.	V.G.	Good	Fair	Poor
750	650	550	500	400	300

Model 70 Classic Safari Express

Chambered for .375 H&H Magnum, .416 Rem. Magnum and .458 Win. Magnum. Fitted with 24" barrel. Magazine capacity 4 rounds. Walnut stock, with open sights. Left-hand model offered in .375 H&H. Weight about 8.5 lbs. Introduced in 1999. **NOTE:** Add $30 for .375 H&H left-hand.

NIB	Exc.	V.G.	Good	Fair	Poor
1350	1100	900	650	500	300

Model 70 Super Grade

Another U.S.R.A. rifle that features select walnut stock, claw-controlled round feed, single reinforced cross bolt, 24" barrel shipped with bases and rings. Buttstock has a straight comb, with classic cheekpiece and deep-cut checkering. Available in .270, .30-06, 7mm Rem. Magnum,

.300 Win. Magnum, .338 Win. Magnum, .270 WSM, .300 WSM. Weight about 7.75 lbs.

NIB	Exc.	V.G.	Good	Fair	Poor
1500	1300	1075	925	650	300

Model 70 RMEF Super Grade

As above, with stainless steel action and barrel. Chambered for .300 Win. Magnum cartridge. Fitted with 26" barrel. Checkered walnut stock, with solid recoil pad. Weight about 8 lbs. Introduced in 2003. Special RMEF (Rocky Mountain Elk Foundation) emblem on grip cap. Limited production.

NIB	Exc.	V.G.	Good	Fair	Poor
1600	1400	1175	975	650	300

Model 70 RMEF Super Grade III

Chambered for .325 WSM or .300 WSM calibers. Fitted with 24" stainless steel barrel, without sights. Super Grade walnut checkered stock, with shadowline cheekpiece. Weight about 7.75 lbs. RMEF grip cap medallion. Introduced in 2005.

NIB	Exc.	V.G.	Good	Fair	Poor
1200	950	875	650	500	300

Model 70 Classic Super Grade III

Similar to above, but chambered for a variety of short action calibers including WSM. Fitted with 24" barrel, except .300 Win. Magnum and .338 Win. Magnum have 26" barrels. No sights. Weight about 7.75 to 8 lbs., depending on caliber. Introduced in 2005.

NIB	Exc.	V.G.	Good	Fair	Poor
1400	1100	875	650	500	300

Model 70 Super Express

A U.S.R.A. version of post-1963 XTR Super Express. Specifications same as earlier model. Weight 8.5 lbs. Introduced in 1993.

NIB	Exc.	V.G.	Good	Fair	Poor
1500	1200	1075	975	650	300

Model 70 Heavy Varmint

Introduced by U.S.R.A. in 1993. Features fiberglass/graphite stock, with heavy 26" stainless steel barrel. Offered in .223, .22-250, .243 and .308. In 1997, offered in .222 Rem. cartridge. Weight about 10.75 lbs.

NIB	Exc.	V.G.	Good	Fair	Poor
750	575	500	425	375	200

Model 70 Heavy Varmint—Fluted Barrel

Introduced in 1997. Similar to above Varmint, with addition of fluted barrel. Calibers same as Heavy Varmint.

NIB	Exc.	V.G.	Good	Fair	Poor
825	625	500	475	350	250

Model 70 Stainless

All-metal parts are stainless steel, including barrel, with synthetic stock. Available with 24" barrel. Chambered for .270, .30-06, 7mm Rem. Magnum, .300 Win. Magnum and .338 Win. Magnum. Weight about 7.5 lbs. Currently in production. In 2001, offered in .300 Win. Short Magnum (WSM).

NIB	Exc.	V.G.	Good	Fair	Poor
850	650	450	375	225	125

Model 70 Classic Laminated Stainless

Introduced in 1998. Features laminated stock, with stainless steel barrel and action. Offered in .270, .30-06, 7mm Rem. Magnum, .300 Win. Magnum and .338 Win. Magnum. Pre-1964 action. Bolt is jeweled and bolt handle knurled. Barrel lengths 24" and 26", depending on caliber. Weight about 8 lbs. In 2001, offered in .300 Win. Short Magnum (WSM).

NIB	Exc.	V.G.	Good	Fair	Poor
850	650	450	375	225	125

Model 70 Classic Camo Stainless

Features Sporter-style Mossy Oak Treestand camo stock, with 24" or 26" barrel. Chambered for .270 Win., .30-06, 7mm Rem. Magnum and .300 Win Magnum. Magazine capacity 5 rounds. Weight about 7.5 lbs. Introduced in 1998.

NIB	Exc.	V.G.	Good	Fair	Poor
850	650	450	375	225	125

Model 70 SM

Features synthetic stock, with black matte finish. Barrel length 24". Available in 10 calibers from .223 Rem. to .375 H&H Magnum. Weight between 7 and 8 lbs., depending on caliber.

NIB	Exc.	V.G.	Good	Fair	Poor
850	650	450	375	225	125

Model 70 DBM-S

Similar to Model 70 SM, but fitted with detachable box magazine. Metal parts are blued; stock synthetic. Offered in 8 calibers from .223 Rem. to .338 Win. Magnum. Furnished with scope bases; rings are open sights. Weight about 7.25 lbs., depending on caliber. Introduced in 1993.

NIB	Exc.	V.G.	Good	Fair	Poor
650	550	450	375	225	125

Model 70 Varmint

Similar to Model 70 Heavy Varmint, but furnished with traditional walnut stock and 26" medium-heavy barrel. Offered in .223 Rem., .22-250, .243 and .308. Weight 9 lbs.

NIB	Exc.	V.G.	Good	Fair	Poor
700	600	450	325	225	150

Model 70 DBM

DBM stands for (detachable box magazine). Fitted with straight-comb walnut stock. Jeweled bolt, with blued receiver. Shipped with scope bases and rings or open sights. Offered in 8 calibers from .223 Rem. to .300 Win. Magnum. Weight about 7.35 lbs., depending on caliber. Introduced in 1993.

NIB	Exc.	V.G.	Good	Fair	Poor
700	600	450	325	225	150

Model 70 Sporter

U.S.R.A.'s basic Model 70. Standard offerings: straight-comb walnut stock, with checkering; jeweled bolt; blued receiver and barrel. Available in 12 calibers from .223 Rem. to .338 Win. Magnum, including .270 Wby. Magnum and .300 Wby. Magnum. Barrel length 24". Available with scope bases and rings or open sights. Weight about 7.5 lbs.

NIB	Exc.	V.G.	Good	Fair	Poor
700	600	450	325	225	150

Model 70 WinTuff

Similar to Sporter, except fitted with laminated hardwood straight-comb stock, with cheekpiece. Barrel length 24". Choice of 6 calibers from .270 Win. to .338 Win. Magnum. Furnished with scope bases and rings. Weight about 7.65 lbs., depending on caliber.

NIB	Exc.	V.G.	Good	Fair	Poor
700	600	450	325	225	150

Model 70 Lightweight

Similar to Model 70 Winlight. Offered with straight-comb checkered walnut stock, with knurled bolt. Blued 22" barrel and receiver. No sights. Offered in 5 calibers: .223, .243, .270, .308 and .30-06. Weight about 7 lbs., depending on caliber.

NIB	Exc.	V.G.	Good	Fair	Poor
700	600	450	325	225	150

Model 70 Black Shadow

Chambered for .270, .30-06, 7mm Rem. Magnum and .300 Win. Magnum. Fitted with 22" or 24" barrel, depending on caliber. Finish matte black, with composite stock. Push-feed action. Weight 7.25 lbs. Introduced in 1998.

NIB	Exc.	V.G.	Good	Fair	Poor
550	450	375	325	225	150

Model 70 Ultimate Shadow

Introduced in 2003. Bolt-action model features new black synthetic stock design, with improved gripping surfaces and soft recoil pad. Has blued action and barrel. Chambered for .300 WSM, .270 WSM or 7mm WSM cartridges. Fitted with 24" barrel. Weight about 6.75 lbs. Offered with stainless action and barrel. **NOTE:** Add $45 for stainless steel.

NIB	Exc.	V.G.	Good	Fair	Poor
800	700	425	350	275	125

Model 70 Ultimate Shadow Camo

As above, with Mossy Oak New Break-Up camo. Introduced in 2004.

NIB	Exc.	V.G.	Good	Fair	Poor
900	800	525	450	375	150

Model 70 Super Shadow Super Short

Similar to above model, but chambered for .223 WSM or .243 WSM cartridge. Fitted with 22" barrel and blind magazine. Weight about 6 lbs. Introduced in 2003.

NIB	Exc.	V.G.	Good	Fair	Poor
700	600	450	325	225	150

Model 70 Super Shadow

Similar to Ultimate Shadow, but fitted with controlled round push-feed bolt. Chambered for .300 WSM, .270 WSM or 7mm WSM cartridge. Fitted with 22" barrel, composite stock and blind magazine. Weight about 6.75 lbs. Introduced in 2003. In 2006, new calibers .243, .308, .270, .30-06, .300WM. Model discontinued in 2007.

NIB	Exc.	V.G.	Good	Fair	Poor
700	600	450	325	225	150

Model 70 Stealth

Varmint model, with 26" heavy barrel. Chambered for .223 Rem., .22-250 or .308 Win. Has push-feed bolt-action. Black synthetic stock. Matte black finish. Weight about 10.85 lbs. In 2004, .223 WSSM, .243 WSSM and .25 WSSM calibers added.

NIB	Exc.	V.G.	Good	Fair	Poor
850	650	450	375	225	125

Model 70 Coyote

Introduced in 2000. Has push-feed bolt-action. Chambered for .223

Rem, .22-250 and .243 Win. Fitted with medium-heavy 24" stainless steel barrel, with laminated stock and large fore-end. Weight about 9 lbs. In 2002, offered in .270 WSM, 7mm WSM and .300 WSM. In 2005, .325 WSM was added. Discontinued 2006.

NIB	Exc.	V.G.	Good	Fair	Poor
750	650	450	375	225	125

Model 70 Coyote Lite

Introduced in 2005. Features lightweight composite stock, with skeletonized aluminum block bedding. Recoil pad. Fluted 24" medium-heavy barrel, with no sights. Offered in .223 Rem and all WSSM and WSM calibers. New calibers: .22-250, .243, .308. **NOTE:** Add $40 for stainless steel.

NIB	Exc.	V.G.	Good	Fair	Poor
850	650	450	375	225	125

Model 70 Ladies/Youth Ranger

Scaled-down version of Ranger. Length of pull 1" shorter than standard. Weight 6.5 lbs. Chambered in .243 and .308. In 1997, offered in .223 Rem. and 7mm-08 Rem.

NIB	Exc.	V.G.	Good	Fair	Poor
450	300	275	225	150	100

Model 70 Shadow Elite Stainless

Bolt-action rifle. Calibers: .22-250, .243, .308, .270, .30-06, .300 WM, .338 WM, .375 H&H, .270 WSM, 7mm WSM, .300 WSM, .325 WSM. Barrel stainless steel 24" or 26" (.300, .338 WM). Stock overmolded composite. Weight 6.5 to 7.75 lbs. Magazine capacity 3 or 5 rounds (.22-250, .243, .308, .270, .30-06). Introduced 2006.

NIB	Exc.	V.G.	Good	Fair	Poor
800	700	425	350	275	125

Model 70 Shadow Elite Camo Stainless

Similar to Shadow Elite Stainless, with Mossy Oak New Break Up camo synthetic stock.

NIB	Exc.	V.G.	Good	Fair	Poor
850	750	475	350	275	125

Model 70 Pro Shadow Blued

Bolt-action rifle. Calibers: .22-250, .243, .308, .270, .30-06, 7mm RM, .300 WM, .270 WSM, 7mm WSM, .300 WSM, .325 WSM. Barrel blued steel 22" (standard); 24" (Magnum). Stock overmolded composite. Weight 6.5 to 7 lbs. Magazine capacity 3 rounds (Magnum); 5 (standard). Introduced 2006.

NIB	Exc.	V.G.	Good	Fair	Poor
650	550	375	250	175	125

Model 70 Pro Shadow Stainless

Similar to Pro Shadow Blued, with stainless steel barrel. Chamberings .338 WM and .375 H&H.

NIB	Exc.	V.G.	Good	Fair	Poor
700	600	450	325	225	150

Model 70 Laminated Coyote Outback Stainless

Similar to Model 70 Coyote Lite, with skeletonized laminated stock and stainless steel only. Calibers: .22-250, .243, .308, .270, .30-06, 7mm RM, .300 WM, .270 WSM, 7mm WSM, .300 WSM, .325 WSM. Weight 7.75 lbs. Introduced 2006.

NIB	Exc.	V.G.	Good	Fair	Poor
750	650	450	375	225	125

Model 70 Laminated Coyote Gray or Brown Stainless

Similar to Model 70 Laminated Coyote Outback, with non-fluted barrel. Choice of brown or gray laminated stock.

NIB	Exc.	V.G.	Good	Fair	Poor
700	600	450	325	225	150

Model 670

Economy variation of Model 70 introduced in 1967; out of production in 1970. Features hardwood stock and blind magazine. Calibers: .225 Win., .243, .270, .308, .30-06; Magnum: .264 Win., 7mm Rem. Magnum, .300 Win. Magnum. **NOTE:** Add 10 percent for Magnum calibers or .225 Win.

NIB	Exc.	V.G.	Good	Fair	Poor
350	300	250	200	175	150

POST-2007 MODEL 70

In 2006, Winchester closed its factory in New Haven, CT. and discontinued production of Model 70 and Model 94 rifles. Late in 2007, it was announced that production of Model 70 would resume at FN plant in Columbia, SC. FN (Fabrique Nationale of Belgium) is parent company of Winchester. Following models are produced at South Carolina plant.

Model 70 Featherweight Deluxe

Pre-64 action; three-position safety; jeweled bolt; knurled bolt handle; walnut stock, with slight schnabel; cut checkering; Pachmayr Decelerator recoil pad; 22" or 24" barrel, depending on caliber. Chambered for a variety of cartridges from .243 to .325 WSM. Weight 6.5 to 7 lbs. Introduced in 2008. **NOTE:** Add $50 for Magnum calibers.

NIB	Exc.	V.G.	Good	Fair	Poor
800	650	525	450	375	325

Model 70 Sporter Deluxe

Similar to above, with non-schnabel fore-end and cheekpiece. **NOTE:** Add $50 for Magnum calibers.

NIB	Exc.	V.G.	Good	Fair	Poor
800	650	525	450	375	325

New Model 70 Super Grade Special Limited Edition

Very fancy version of Model 70. Featuring post-'64 action, ultra-premium walnut, gold-filled engraving, black fore-end cap, steel grip cap, shadow-line cheekpiece. Only 250 produced in 2008. Chambered in .300 Win. Magnum only.

NIB	Exc.	V.G.	Good	Fair	Poor
2400	2000	1650	1300	900	500

Model 70 Extreme Weather SS

Post-'64 style action, with 22", 24" or 26" barrel, depending on chambering. Three-position safety, fluted stainless barrel and Bell and Carlson composite stock. Chambered for a variety of cartridges from .243 to .325 WSM.

NIB	Exc.	V.G.	Good	Fair	Poor
1000	750	550	425	275	175

Model 70 FW Compact

Featherweight Compact made for smaller-framed shooters. Light mountain-type rifle, with 20" barrel. Weight 6.5 lbs. Pre-'64 controlled round feed and three-position safety. M.O.A. adjustable trigger system. Jeweled bolt body, with knurled bolt handle. Walnut stock, with fancy checkered pattern. Chambered for .22-250 Rem., .243 Win., 7mm-08 Rem. or .308 Win. Introduced in 2011.

NIB	Exc.	V.G.	Good	Fair	Poor
765	650	550	450	350	200

Model 70 Safari Express

Designed for dangerous game. Calibers .375 H&H, .416 Rem. Magnum, .458 Win. Magnum. Express sights, 24" barrel, satin finished, checkered walnut stock. Other features include reinforced crossbolts, dual recoil lugs and Pachmayr Decelerator recoil pad. Weight 9 lbs.

NIB	Exc.	V.G.	Good	Fair	Poor
1200	1000	800	650	500	350

Model 70 75th Anniversary Super Grade

Commemorates 75th Anniversary of rifle. Introduced in 2012, this special edition in .30-06 caliber. Grade IV/V Full Fancy walnut stock. One-piece bottom metal has engraving, with scroll pattern of 75th Model 70 emblem. Other features include pre-64 style controlled round feed, with claw extractor and Pachmayr Decelerator recoil pad.

NIB	Exc.	V.G.	Good	Fair	Poor
1800	1700	1600	—		

Model 70 Alaskan

Reintroduction of classic pre-64 Model in .30-06, .300 Win. Magnum, .338 Win. Magnum or .375 H&H. Checkered Monte Carlo walnut stock and fore-end. Barrel 25", with folding rear and gold bead front sights. Has pre-'64 controlled round feed and claw extractor. Available with gray laminate stock and stainless steel barrel. **NOTE:** Add $200 for laminate/stainless model.

NIB	Exc.	V.G.	Good	Fair	Poor
1100	900	750	600	500	400

Model 70 Jack O'Connor Tribute

Limited edition rifle honoring Jack O'Connor, dean of outdoor writers of the 20th century, who had a long association with Model 70. Chambered in his favorite caliber, .270 Win., with 22" hammer-forged barrel. Pre-64 style action, with controlled round feed; claw extractor; AA-grade French walnut stock, with shadowline cheekpiece; ebony fore-end tip. Other features include engraved pistol-grip cap and floorplate. O'Connor's signature in nickel on trigger guard. Offered in two grades, with higher-grade version having AAA-grade French walnut stock and checkered metal buttplate. Introduced in 2012, with limited production only in that year. **NOTE:** Add $500 for higher-grade model.

NIB	Exc.	V.G.	Good	Fair	Poor
2000	1900	1650	—	—	—

Model 70 150th Commemorative

To commemorate company's 150th Anniversary. Features Super Grade styling, with V/VI grade checkered walnut stock, shadow line cheekpiece, satin finish, black fore-end tip and special 150th grip cap. Deep relief scroll engraving, with gold embellishments highlight receiver, barrel, trigger guard and floorplate. Chambered for classic .270 Win., with 24" barrel. Introduced in 2016.

NIB	Exc.	V.G.	Good	Fair	Poor
1950	1800	—	—	—	—

WINCHESTER CUSTOM GUN SHOP

NOTE: There were a number of special order options offered by Custom shop, that greatly affect price. Such as: special-order engraving, stock carving, wood, sights, etc. Strongly suggest that an independent appraisal be secured prior to sale.

Model 94 Custom Limited Edition New Generation

Lever-action rifle stocked with fancy checkered walnut, with pistol-grip and long nose fore-end. Custom engraved, with gold inlaid moose on right side and gold inlaid buck and doe on left. Fitted with tang safety. Barrel 20". Chambered for .30-30 cartridge. Introduced in 2003. Weight about 6.25 lbs.

NIB	Exc.	V.G.	Good	Fair	Poor
3000	2500	2100	—	—	—

Model 70 Featherweight Ultra Grade

Limited to 1,000 rifles. Profusely engraved with game scene and gold line inlaid. Serial number inlaid in gold. Offered in .270-caliber. Very fine-figured walnut stock, with fine line checkering. Mahogany fitted case. Strongly suggest a qualified appraisal before sale.

NIB	Exc.	V.G.	Good	Fair	Poor
4000	3500	—	—	—	—

Model 70 Custom Featherweight

Introduced in 2003. Chambered for .270, 7mm Win. Magnum or .30-06. Fitted with 22" barrel. Semi-fancy walnut stock, with schnabel fore-end. Offered in blued or stainless steel finish in right-/left-hand models. Weight about 7.25 lbs.

NIB	Exc.	V.G.	Good	Fair	Poor
3500	—	—	—	—	—

Model 70 Custom Carbon

Features stainless steel action, with Shilen barrel wrapped in graphite epoxy. Fitted with black composite stock. Chambered for .270 WSM, 7mm WSM, .300 WSM, .25-06 Rem. or .338 Win. Magnum cartridge. Fitted with 24" barrel on all calibers, except .338 (26"). Weight about 6.5 lbs. on WSM calibers; 7 lbs. on others. Magazine capacity 3 rounds. Introduced in 2003.

NIB	Exc.	V.G.	Good	Fair	Poor
3200	—	—	—	—	—

Model 70 Custom Sharpshooter

A U.S.R.A. Custom Shop gun. Fitted with stainless steel Schneider barrel, with hand-honed action and hand-fitted. Custom McMillan A-2 glass bedded stock. Offered in .223 Rem., .22-250 Rem., .308 Win. and .300 Win. Magnum. Comes from factory with a hard case. Currently in production.

NIB	Exc.	V.G.	Good	Fair	Poor
2500	—	—	—	—	—

Model 70 Custom Classic Sharpshooter II

Same as above, with H-S heavy target stock, pre-1964 action and stainless steel H-S barrel. Weight about 11 lbs. Offered in .22-250, .308, .30-06 and .300 Win. Magnum. Introduced in 1996.

NIB	Exc.	V.G.	Good	Fair	Poor
2250	—	—	—	—	—

Model 70 Custom Sporting Sharpshooter

Essentially a take-off on Custom Sharpshooter, but configured for hunting. Fitted with McMillan sporter-style gray stock and Schneider stainless steel barrel. Offered in .270 Win., .300 Win. and 7mm STW. Introduced in 1993.

NIB	Exc.	V.G.	Good	Fair	Poor
2000	—	—	—	—	—

Model 70 Custom Classic Sporting Sharpshooter II

Introduced in 1996. Updated version of model above. Features pre-1964 action, with H-S special fiberglass stock and stainless steel barrel. Available in 7mm STW, .300 Win. Magnum. Weight about 8.5 lbs.

NIB	Exc.	V.G.	Good	Fair	Poor
2500	—	—	—	—	—

Model 70 Custom Grade

Custom built Model 70 is hand-finished, polished and fitted in Custom Shop. Internal parts are hand-honed, while barrel is lead lapped. Cus-

tomer can order individual items to his/her own taste, including engraving, special stock dimensions, carvings, etc. Each Custom Grade Model 70 should be priced on an individual basis.

Model 70 Custom Express

Also built in Custom Shop. Features figured walnut, hand-honed internal parts, bolt and follower are engine turned. Special 3-leaf rear sight also furnished. Offered in .375 H&H Magnum, .375 JRS, .416 Rem. Magnum, .458 Win. Magnum and .470 Capstick.

NIB	Exc.	V.G.	Good	Fair	Poor
3000	—	—	—	—	—

Model 70 Custom African Express

Introduced in 1999. Chambered for .340 Wby., .358 STA, .375 H&H, .416 Rem. Magnum and .458 Win. Magnum. Fitted with 24" barrel, select walnut stock and ebony pistol-grip cap. Magazine capacity 4 rounds. Express sights. Weight about 9.75 lbs.

NIB	Exc.	V.G.	Good	Fair	Poor
3850	—	—	—	—	—

Model 70 Custom Safari Express

Has a figured walnut stock, with bolt and follower engine turned. Express sights. Chambered in .340 Wby., .358 STA, .375 H&H, .416 Rem. Magnum and .458 Win. Magnum. Barrel length 24"; weight about 9.5 lbs. Introduced in 1999.

NIB	Exc.	V.G.	Good	Fair	Poor
2500	—	—	—	—	—

Model 70 Custom "Ultra Light" Mannlicher

Features full-length stock of figured walnut, with smooth tapered barrel and blued action. Chambered for .260 Rem., .308 Win. and 7mm-08. Fitted with 19" barrel and optional open sights. Weight about 6.75 lbs. Introduced in 1999.

NIB	Exc.	V.G.	Good	Fair	Poor
2500	—	—	—	—	—

Model 70 Ultimate Classic

Features a number of special options as standard. Included: pre-1964 action; choice of round, round fluted, half octagon half round, full tapered octagon, blued or stainless steel barrel actions; fancy American walnut stock; special Custom Shop serial numbers and proof stamp; inletted swivel bases; red recoil pad; fine cut checkering; hard case. Offered in a wide variety of calibers from .25-06 to .338 Win. Magnum. Weight about 7.5 to 7.75 lbs., depending on caliber. Available in stainless steel. In 1997, introduced in left-hand version.

NIB	Exc.	V.G.	Good	Fair	Poor
2450	—	—	—	—	—

Model 70 Custom Short Action

Custom Shop model fitted with 22" match-grade barrel controlled feed. Chambered for short-action calibers from .243 to .358. Semi-fancy walnut stock. Hand-cut checkering. Supplied with hard case. Weight about 7.5 lbs. Introduced in 2000. In 2003, offered in left-hand version.

NIB	Exc.	V.G.	Good	Fair	Poor
2700	—	—	—	—	—

Model 70 Custom Extreme Weather

Custom Shop model fitted with round or fluted 24" match-grade barrel. Both barrel and action are stainless steel. McMillan fiberglass stock, with cheekpiece. Chambered in calibers from .25-06 to .338 Win. Magnum. Weight about 7.5 lbs. Introduced in 2000. Lightweight Extreme Weather II model, introduced in 2006 (6.25 to 7 lbs.). MSRP: $2800.

NIB	Exc.	V.G.	Good	Fair	Poor
1950	—	—	—	—	—

Model 70 Custom Take Down

Introduced in 1998. This composite stock rifle has a special take-down feature. Chambered for .375 H&H, .416 Rem. Magnum, .300 Win Magnum, 7mm STW. Magazine capacity 3 rounds. Barrel length 26". Weight 8.5 to 9 lbs. Offered with fluted barrel in .300 Win. Magnum and 7mm STW.

NIB	Exc.	V.G.	Good	Fair	Poor
3300	—	—	—	—	—

Model 70 Custom 100th Anniversary .30-06

Semi-fancy walnut Featherweight stock, with single steel crossbolt, one-piece engraved floorplate, high-lustre blued and engraved 22" barrel. Commemorates centennial of .30-06 cartridge. Introduced 2006; only 100 manufactured.

NIB	Exc.	V.G.	Good	Fair	Poor
2700	—	—	—	—	—

Model 70 Custom Special "70 Years of the Model 70"

Calibers: .270, .30-06 Springfield, .300 WM. Barrel 24" or 26" (.300 WM), blued sightless. Engraved floorplate and barrel. Stock semi-fancy checkered walnut. Introduced 2006. Only 70 manufactured per caliber.

NIB	Exc.	V.G.	Good	Fair	Poor
2800	—	—	—	—	—

Model 70 Custom Maple

Calibers: .284, .270, .308, .30-06. Blued 24" barrel. Weight 7.75 lbs. Stocked in fiddleback maple, with pre-'64 pattern checkering. Quantities "very limited". Introduced 2006.

NIB	Exc.	V.G.	Good	Fair	Poor
4400	—	—	—	—	—

Model 70 Custom Continental Hunter

Calibers: .284, .270, .308, .30-06. Barrel 22" blued or stainless Krieger. Stock glossy claro walnut, round knob pistol-grip, schnabel fore-end.

NIB	Exc.	V.G.	Good	Fair	Poor
5300	—	—	—	—	—

Model 70 Custom Stainless Laminate

Calibers: .270 WSM, 7mm WSM, .300 WSM, .325 WSM. Barrel 24" stainless sporter. Stock black/gray or brown Featherweight laminated, with schnabel and Pachmayr pad.

NIB	Exc.	V.G.	Good	Fair	Poor
2300	—	—	—	—	—

Model 94 Custom Limited Edition

Essentially a special order Model 94, with choice of engraving and stock carving. Chambered for .44-40. Fitted with 24" octagonal barrel. Fancy walnut stock. Limited to 75 rifles. Weight about 7.75 lbs. Suggest an appraisal prior to sale.

NIB	Exc.	V.G.	Good	Fair	Poor
2300	—	—	—	—	—

Model 9410 Custom

Introduced in 2005. This .410 bore shotgun fitted with 24" round barrel and full length magazine. Case colored receiver, with semi-fancy checkered walnut stock. Weight about 7 lbs.

NIB	Exc.	V.G.	Good	Fair	Poor
2300	—	—	—	—	—

POST-1963 SHOTGUNS

MODEL 12 "Y" SERIES

Model 12 Field Grade

Later version of slide-action Model 12. Chambered for 12-gauge only. Offered with 26", 28" or 30" ventilated rib barrel and various chokes. Finish blued, with jeweled bolt and hand-checkered select walnut stock. This version easily recognizable as it has letter "Y" serial number prefix. Manufactured between 1972 and 1976.

NIB	Exc.	V.G.	Good	Fair	Poor
—	950	800	650	485	300

Model 12 Super Pigeon Grade

Deluxe version that features extensive engraving and fancy checkering. Offered with turned action and select fancy-grade walnut. Limited production item produced between 1964 and 1972. Briefly reintroduced in 1984; discontinued again in 1985.

NIB	Exc.	V.G.	Good	Fair	Poor
—	3000	2400	1850	1400	950

Model 12 Skeet

Similar to Field Grade, but offered with 26" ventilated rib and skeet-bored barrel. Finish blued, with skeet-type stock and recoil pad. Manufactured between 1972 and 1975.

NIB	Exc.	V.G.	Good	Fair	Poor
—	950	850	750	450	300

Model 12 Trap Grade

Features 30" ventilated rib barrel, with Full choke. Blued, with standard or Monte Carlo trap-style stock and recoil pad. Manufactured between 1972 and 1980.

NIB	Exc.	V.G.	Good	Fair	Poor
—	935	830	725	425	215

Model 12 (Limited Edition)

Available in 20-gauge only. Furnished with 26" ventilated rib barrel choked Improved Cylinder. Walnut stock checkered, with pistol-grip. Introduced in 1993. Available in three different grades.

Grade I

4,000 guns.

NIB	Exc.	V.G.	Good	Fair	Poor
1000	800	650	450	200	100

Grade IV

1,000 guns; gold highlights.

NIB	Exc.	V.G.	Good	Fair	Poor
1400	1100	850	500	200	100

Model 42 (Limited Edition)

Reproduction of famous Winchester Model 42, .410 bore slide-action shotgun. Furnished with 26" ventilated rib barrel choked Full. Receiver engraved with gold border. Introduced in 1993. Limited to 850 guns.

NIB	Exc.	V.G.	Good	Fair	Poor
1800	1400	1000	500	300	150

Model 1200

Slide-action shotgun chambered for 12-, 16- or 20-gauge. Offered with 26", 28" or 30" ventilated rib barrel, with various chokes. Has a blued alloy receiver. Checkered walnut stock and recoil pad. Manufactured between 1964 and 1981. Offered with plastic Hydrocoil stock. **NOTE:** Add 35 percent for plastic Hydrocoil stock.

NIB	Exc.	V.G.	Good	Fair	Poor
—	300	250	200	150	100

Ducks Unlimited Model

Available through Ducks Unlimited chapters. An independent appraisal is suggested.

MODEL 1300 SERIES

Discontinued in 2006.

Model 1300 XTR

Chambered for 12- and 20-gauge, with 3" chambers. Take-down gun offered with various length ventilated rib barrels, with screw-in choke tubes. Has blued alloy frame, with walnut stock. Introduced in 1978.

NIB	Exc.	V.G.	Good	Fair	Poor
475	350	275	200	150	100

Model 1300 Waterfowl

Chambered for 12-gauge 3" only. Has 30" ventilated rib barrel, with screw-in choke tubes. Matte-blued, with satin-finished walnut stock and recoil pad. Introduced in 1984. Laminated WinTuff stock made available in 1988. **NOTE:** Add $10 for laminated WinTuff stock.

NIB	Exc.	V.G.	Good	Fair	Poor
400	300	250	200	150	100

Model 1300 New Shadow Grass

Introduced in 2004. This 12-gauge 3" gun fitted with 26" or 28" ventilated rib barrel, with choke tubes. Composite stock has New Shadow Grass camo pattern. Weight about 7 lbs.

NIB	Exc.	V.G.	Good	Fair	Poor
470	370	250	200	150	100

Model 1300 WinCam Turkey Gun

Similar to Model 1300 Turkey Gun, with green laminated hardwood stock. Introduced in 1987. WinTuff version available. **NOTE:** Add $20 for WinTuff version.

NIB	Exc.	V.G.	Good	Fair	Poor
475	350	275	200	150	100

Model 1300 Stainless Security

Chambered for 12- or 20-gauge. Constructed of stainless steel. Has an 18" cylinder-bore barrel; 7- or 8-shot tubular magazine. Available with pistol-grip stock. **NOTE:** Add 50 percent for pistol-grip stock.

NIB	Exc.	V.G.	Good	Fair	Poor
475	350	275	200	150	100

Model 1300 Turkey

Slide-action model features 22" ventilated rib barrel. Chambered for 3" 12-gauge shells. Supplied with choke tubes. Weight 7.25 lbs.

NIB	Exc.	V.G.	Good	Fair	Poor
475	350	275	200	150	100

Model 1300 Realtree Turkey

Introduced in 1994. Features synthetic stock camouflaged with Realtree. Receiver and 22" barrel are matte finish.

NIB	Exc.	V.G.	Good	Fair	Poor
475	350	275	200	150	100

Model 1300 Mossy Oak Break-Up Turkey

Same as above, with Mossy Oak Break-Up camo stock and gun. Introduced in 2000.

NIB	Exc.	V.G.	Good	Fair	Poor
475	350	275	200	150	100

Model 1300 Black Shadow Turkey

Introduced in 1994. Features black composite stock, with non-glare finish on barrel, receiver, bolt and magazine. Barrel has 22" ventilated rib.

NIB	Exc.	V.G.	Good	Fair	Poor
475	350	275	200	150	100

Model 1300 National Wild Turkey Federation Series III

Engraved receiver, camo stock, open sights on a 22" plain barrel. All metal and wood parts are non-glare. Comes with quick detachable sling. Offered in 12-gauge only. Weight 7.25 lbs.

NIB	Exc.	V.G.	Good	Fair	Poor
575	420	350	250	150	100

Model 1300 National Wild Turkey Federation Series IV

Introduced in 1993. Similar to Series II, with addition of 22" ventilated rib barrel. Stock is black laminated. Comes with quick detachable sling. Weight 7 lbs.

NIB	Exc.	V.G.	Good	Fair	Poor
600	520	350	250	150	100

Model 1300 NWTF Short Turkey

This 12-gauge fitted with an 18" barrel and extended choke tubes. Fiber Optic sights. Mossy Oak camo stock. NWTF medallion on pistol-grip cap. Weight about 6.5 lbs. Introduced in 2005.

NIB	Exc.	V.G.	Good	Fair	Poor
475	350	275	200	150	100

Model 1300 Whitetails Unlimited Slug Hunter

Slide-action model features full-length rifle barrel. Chambered for 3" 12-gauge shells. Barrel choked Cylinder. Fitted with checkered walnut stock. Engraved receiver drilled and tapped for bases and rings, which are included. Comes equipped with camo sling. Weight 7.25 lbs.

NIB	Exc.	V.G.	Good	Fair	Poor
475	350	275	200	150	100

Model 1300 Slug Hunter

Similar to Whitetails Unlimited model, without engraved receiver.

NIB	Exc.	V.G.	Good	Fair	Poor
475	350	275	200	150	100

Model 1300 Buck and Tom

Introduced in 2002. Camo stock fitted with 22" barrel and choke tubes for deer and turkey. Receiver drilled and tapped for scope mount. Weight about 6.75 lbs.

NIB	Exc.	V.G.	Good	Fair	Poor
525	400	325	250	175	125

Model 1300 Universal Hunter

Introduced in 2002. Features camo stock, with 26" ventilated rib barrel. Choke tubes. Weight about 7 lbs.

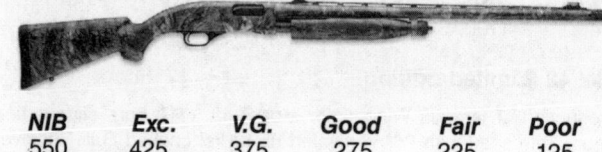

NIB	Exc.	V.G.	Good	Fair	Poor
550	425	375	275	225	125

Model 1300 Black Shadow Deer

Introduced in 1994. This 12-gauge features black composite stock, with non-glare finish on bolt, barrel, receiver and magazine. Barrel 22", with ramp front sight and adjustable rear. In 2000, offered with rifled barrel for shooting sabot slugs. **NOTE:** Add $25 for rifled barrel.

NIB	Exc.	V.G.	Good	Fair	Poor
475	350	275	200	150	100

Model 1300 Black Shadow Field

Same as above, but fitted with 26" or 28" ventilated rib barrel. Chambered for 3" Magnum shells. Weight about 7 lbs.

NIB	Exc.	V.G.	Good	Fair	Poor
475	350	275	200	150	100

Model 1300 Sporting/Field

This 12-gauge has 28" ventilated rib barrel, with five choke tubes. Checkered walnut stock. Black recoil pad. Weight about 7.5 lbs. Introduced in 2002.

NIB	Exc.	V.G.	Good	Fair	Poor
475	350	275	200	150	100

Model 1300 Sporting/Field Compact

As above, with 24" barrel and 1" shorter length of pull. Introduced in 2002.

NIB	Exc.	V.G.	Good	Fair	Poor
475	350	275	200	150	100

Model 1300 Walnut Field

This 12-gauge 3" gun fitted with 26" or 28" ventilated rib barrels, with choke tubes. Checkered walnut stock, with recoil pad. Weight about 7.25 lbs. Introduced in 2004.

NIB	Exc.	V.G.	Good	Fair	Poor
475	350	275	200	150	100

Model 1300 Slug Hunter Sabot (Smoothbore)

Similar to Slug Hunter, but furnished with smoothbore barrel. Special extended screw-in choke tube that is rifled.

NIB	Exc.	V.G.	Good	Fair	Poor
425	300	225	150	125	100

Model 1300 Upland Special

This 12-gauge slide-action shotgun fitted with 24" ventilated rib barrel. Straight-grip walnut stock. Weight about 7 lbs. Introduced in 1999. In 2000, offered in 20-gauge.

NIB	Exc.	V.G.	Good	Fair	Poor
600	500	400	300	200	100

Model 1300 Upland Special Field

Introduced in 2004. Features 12- or 20-gauge 3" guns, with 24" ventilated rib barrel and choke tube. Checkered walnut stock, with straight-grip. Weight about 6.75 lbs.

NIB	Exc.	V.G.	Good	Fair	Poor
600	500	400	300	200	100

Model 1300 Ranger

Slide-action shotgun is a lower-cost version of Model 1300. Furnished with hardwood stock. Available in 12- or 20-gauge, with 26" or 28" ventilated rib barrel. WinChokes are included.

NIB	Exc.	V.G.	Good	Fair	Poor
300	225	190	165	125	100

Model 1300 Ranger Ladies/Youth-Compact

Available in 20-gauge only. Has 1" shorter than standard length of pull and 22" ventilated rib barrel. Choke tubes are included. Weight 6.75 lbs.

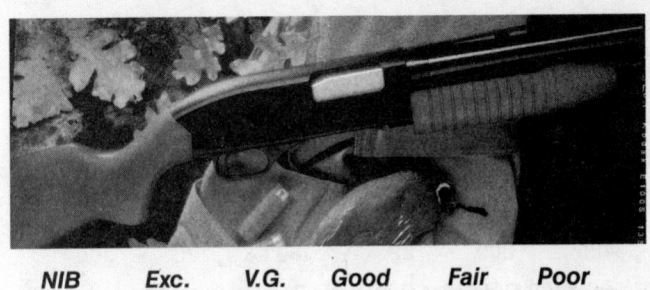

NIB	Exc.	V.G.	Good	Fair	Poor
300	225	190	165	125	100

Model 1300 Ranger Deer Slug

Comes in two principal configurations: 12-gauge 22" smooth barrel, with Cylinder choke; 12-gauge 22" rifled barrel. Both chambered for 3" shells. Weight 6.75 lbs.

NIB	Exc.	V.G.	Good	Fair	Poor
300	200	175	150	125	100

Model 1300 Ranger Deer Combo

Available in three different configurations. One: 12-gauge 22" smooth barrel. Two: 12-gauge 22" rifled barrel. Three: 20-gauge 22" smooth barrel. All configurations come with 28" ventilated rib barrel and WinChokes.

12 Gauge Combo

NIB	Exc.	V.G.	Good	Fair	Poor
375	275	225	190	165	100

20 Gauge Combo

NIB	Exc.	V.G.	Good	Fair	Poor
375	275	225	190	165	100

Model 1300 Defender Combo

Personal defense slide-action shotgun. Features 18" Cylinder choked barrel and 28" ventilated rib barrel, with modified WinChoke. Hardwood stock comes fitted to gun, with accessory pistol-grip.

NIB	Exc.	V.G.	Good	Fair	Poor
425	300	225	150	125	100

Model 1300 Defender 5-Shot

Same as above, but furnished with hardwood stock only and 18" barrel.

NIB	Exc.	V.G.	Good	Fair	Poor
425	300	225	150	125	100

Model 1300 Camp Defender

Introduced in 1999. This 12-gauge features a 22" barrel, with walnut stock. Magazine capacity 5 rounds. Barrel fitted with rifle sights. Weight about 7 lbs. Comes with Cylinder choke tube.

NIB	Exc.	V.G.	Good	Fair	Poor
425	300	225	150	125	100

Model 1300 Defender 8-Shot

Same as above, but furnished with an 18" barrel, with extended magazine tube.

NIB	Exc.	V.G.	Good	Fair	Poor
425	300	225	150	125	100

Model 1300 Defender Synthetic Stock

Same as above. Fitted with black synthetic full stock. Available in 12- or 20-gauge.

NIB	Exc.	V.G.	Good	Fair	Poor
425	300	225	150	125	100

Model 1300 Defender Pistol Grip

Same as above. Fitted with black synthetic pistol-grip and extended magazine tube.

NIB	Exc.	V.G.	Good	Fair	Poor
425	300	225	150	125	100

Model 1300 Lady Defender

Chambered for 20-gauge shell. Features an 18" barrel, with 8-round capacity. Pistol-grip stock. Introduced in 1997.

NIB	Exc.	V.G.	Good	Fair	Poor
425	300	225	150	125	100

Model 1300 Stainless Marine

This 12-gauge slide-action shotgun comes with a black synthetic full stock. All metal parts chrome plated. Barrel 18". Magazine tube holds 7 rounds. Weight 6.75 lbs.

NIB	Exc.	V.G.	Good	Fair	Poor
600	500	400	300	200	100

Model 1300 Stainless Marine with Pistol Grip

Same as above, with black synthetic pistol-grip in place of full buttstock. Weight 5.75 lbs.

NIB	Exc.	V.G.	Good	Fair	Poor
600	500	400	300	200	100

SPEED PUMP SERIES

This family of inertia-assisted slide-action shotguns was introduced in 2008. They took the place of discontinued Model 1300. The 3" 12-gauge available with 26" or 28" barrel. Three choke tubes included. Weight 7 to 7.25 lbs.

Speed Pump Walnut Field

High-gloss walnut, with traditional checkering.

NIB	Exc.	V.G.	Good	Fair	Poor
375	325	275	200	150	100

Speed Pump Black Shadow Field

Synthetic stock and fore-end, with matte black metal.

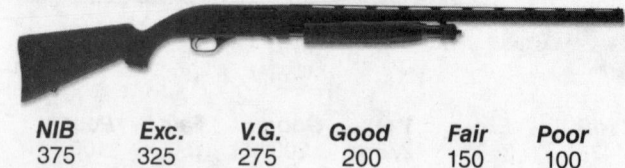

NIB	Exc.	V.G.	Good	Fair	Poor
375	325	275	200	150	100

Speed Pump Defender

This home-security 12-gauge, has an 18" Cylinder choke barrel and 5-round magazine tube. Weight about 6.5 lbs.

NIB	Exc.	V.G.	Good	Fair	Poor
375	325	275	200	150	100

Model SXP Series

Super X Pump is successor to Speed Pump series. Features same inertia-assisted action. Comes in 12-gauge only, with 3" chamber, 26" or 28" back-bored barrel with Invector choke tubes. Weight about 6.8 lbs. Field grade model has Black Shadow composite stock. Waterfowl variation (shown) has full coverage Mossy Oak Duck Blind camo. Also available with 18" straight cylinder barrel as Defender model. Prices are for Black Shadow field model. **NOTE:** Add 20 percent for Waterfowl. Deduct 20 percent for Defender.

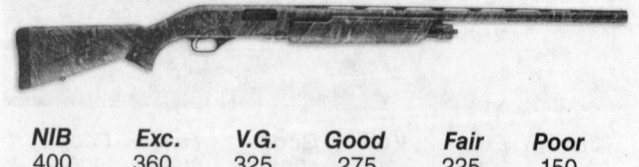

NIB	Exc.	V.G.	Good	Fair	Poor
400	360	325	275	225	150

Model 9410

Variation of Model 94 lever-action rifle. Chambered for .410 bore shotgun. Available in several versions. SEE: Model 9400 Series in lever-action rifle section.

Model 1500 XTR

Gas-operated semi-automatic shotgun. Chambered for 12- or 20-gauge, with 28" ventilated rib barrel with screw-in chokes. Finish blued, with walnut stock. Manufactured between 1978 and 1982.

NIB	Exc.	V.G.	Good	Fair	Poor
550	425	325	225	175	150

Super X Model 1

Self-compensating gas-operated semi-automatic shotgun. Chambered for 12-gauge. Offered with 26", 28" or 30" ventilated rib barrel, with various chokes. Features all-steel construction. Blued, with checkered walnut stock. Manufactured between 1974 and 1981.

NIB	Exc.	V.G.	Good	Fair	Poor
—	800	675	525	400	250

Super X Model 1 Custom Competition

Custom-order trap or skeet gun. Features self-compensating gas-operated action. Available in 12-gauge only from Custom Shop. Offered with a heavy degree of engraving on receiver. Fancy checkered walnut stock. Gold inlays are available. Would add approximately 50 percent to values given. Introduced in 1987.

NIB	Exc.	V.G.	Good	Fair	Poor
1450	1100	925	775	650	500

Super X2 3.5" Magnum

Introduced in 1999. Gas-operated design chambered for 3.5" 12-gauge shells. Fitted with black synthetic stock. Choice of 24", 26" or 28" ventilated rib barrels. Invector chokes. Magazine capacity 5 rounds. Weight about 7.5 lbs., depending on barrel length. Matte black finish.

NIB	Exc.	V.G.	Good	Fair	Poor
950	875	700	525	450	300

Super X2 Turkey

Similar to X2 Magnum, with 24" ventilated rib barrel with TruGlo sights. Extra-Full choke. Weight about 7.25 lbs. Black synthetic stock. Introduced in 1999.

NIB	Exc.	V.G.	Good	Fair	Poor
950	875	700	525	450	300

Super X2 Turkey Mossy Oak Break-Up

Same as above, with Mossy Oak Break-Up camo on stock and gun. Introduced in 2000.

NIB	Exc.	V.G.	Good	Fair	Poor
1025	900	700	525	450	350

Super X2 NWTF Turkey

Introduced in 2005. This 3.5" 12-gauge fitted with 24" ventilated rib barrel, with Extra Full extended choke tubes. Three dot TruGlo sights. Mossy Oak camo stock. Brass NWTF medallion on pistol-grip cap. Weight about 7.5 lbs.

NIB	Exc.	V.G.	Good	Fair	Poor
1235	950	1025	900	700	450

Super X2 Universal Hunter

Similar to Super X2 Turkey, with 26" barrel with Extra Full choke tube. Weight about 7.75 lbs. Introduced in 2002.

NIB	Exc.	V.G.	Good	Fair	Poor
1025	900	700	525	450	350

Super X2 Camo Waterfowl

Chambered for 12-gauge 3.5" shells. Fitted with 28" ventilated rib barrel. Features Mossy Oak camo finish. Weight about 8 lbs. Introduced in 1999. In 2004, New Shadow Grass camo pattern was added.

NIB	Exc.	V.G.	Good	Fair	Poor
1025	900	700	525	450	350

Super X2 Magnum Greenhead

Introduced in 2002. Chambered for 12-gauge 3.5" shell. Has composite stock that is green in color. Fitted with 28" barrel. Weight about 8 lbs.

NIB	Exc.	V.G.	Good	Fair	Poor
1025	900	700	525	450	350

Super X2 Magnum Field

Chambered for 12-gauge 3" shell. Offered with walnut or black synthetic stock. Choice of 26" or 28" ventilated rib barrel, with Invector chokes. Weight about 7.25 lbs. Introduced in 1999.

NIB	Exc.	V.G.	Good	Fair	Poor
950	875	700	525	450	300

Super X2 Light Field

Checkered walnut stock. Choice of 26" or 28" ventilated rib barrel, with choke tubes. Chambered for 12-gauge. Weight about 6.5 lbs. Introduced in 2005.

Super X2 Cantilever Deer

This 12-gauge has 22" fully rifled barrel, with fold-down rear sight and scope mount. Black composite stock. Weight about 7.25 lbs. Introduced in 2002.

NIB	Exc.	V.G.	Good	Fair	Poor
950	875	700	525	450	300

Super X2 Practical

Introduced in 2002. Designed for competition shooting. Fitted with a 22" barrel, with ghost ring sight and 8-round magazine. Black composite stock. Weight about 8 lbs.

NIB	Exc.	V.G.	Good	Fair	Poor
1025	900	700	525	450	350

Super X2 Sporting Clays

Introduced in 2001. Features 12-gauge. Choice of 28" or 30" barrels, with high post rib. Barrels are back-bored, with Invector chokes. Adjustable comb. Weight about 8 lbs.

NIB	Exc.	V.G.	Good	Fair	Poor
1200	950	750	575	500	350

Super X2 Sporting Clays Signature II

This 3" 12-gauge fitted with a 30" barrel, with choke tubes. Hardwood stock painted black metallic. Receiver a red anodized alloy. Weight about 8.25 lbs. Introduced in 2005.

NIB	Exc.	V.G.	Good	Fair	Poor
1025	900	700	525	450	350

Super X2 Signature Red Sporting

This 12-gauge 3" shell model features hardwood stock, with red Dura-Touch coating. Fitted with a 30" ventilated rib barrel, with five choke tubes. Weight about 8 lbs. Introduced in 2003.

NIB	Exc.	V.G.	Good	Fair	Poor
950	875	700	525	450	300

SUPER X3 (SX3) SERIES

Introduced in 2006. Super X3 12-gauge features weight and recoil reducing features and .742" back-bored barrel. Available in a variety of configurations. Weight under 7 lbs. in 3" Field model; about 7.5 lbs. in Composite, Camo and 3.5" models. All models, except Cantilever Deer, included three choke tubes.

Super X3 Field

Walnut stock and 26" or 28" barrel.

NIB	Exc.	V.G.	Good	Fair	Poor
1200	950	750	575	500	350

Super X3 Composite

Matte black stock and fore-end. Available in 26" or 28" barrel. Chambered 3" or 3.5". **NOTE:** Add $100 for 3.5" model.

NIB	Exc.	V.G.	Good	Fair	Poor
1200	950	750	575	500	350

Super X3 Camo

Composite camo stock, with 3.5" chamber. Available in various camo patterns, with 26" or 28" barrel.

NIB	Exc.	V.G.	Good	Fair	Poor
1200	950	750	575	500	350

Super X3 Cantilever Deer

Slug gun, with 22" barrel. Cantilever scope mount and 3" chamber.

NIB	Exc.	V.G.	Good	Fair	Poor
950	875	700	525	450	300

Super X3 "Flanigun" Exhibition/Sporting

With red receiver and fore-end cap, this is a duplicate of gun used by exhibition shooter Patrick Flanigan, with a shorter magazine tube. Has a 3" chamber and 28" barrel.

NIB	Exc.	V.G.	Good	Fair	Poor
1200	950	750	575	500	350

Super X3 Classic Field

Introduced in 2008. Similar to Super X3 Field, with traditional sharp checkering on pistol-grip and fore-end. Barrel length 26" or 28".

NIB	Exc.	V.G.	Good	Fair	Poor
950	875	700	525	450	300

Super X3 Turkey

New in 2008. Dedicated turkey model has a 3.5" chamber, 24" barrel, Extra Full choke tube. Complete coverage in Mossy Oak New Breakup camo. Price includes TruGlo red-dot scope. Weight 7.5 lbs.

NIB	Exc.	V.G.	Good	Fair	Poor
1200	950	750	575	500	350

Super X3 Universal Hunter

Designed for versatility, this model chambered for 12-gauge (3.5") or 20-gauge (3") ammunition. Synthetic stock covered with Mossy Oak Break-Up Country camo. Barrel 26" or 28", with Invector-Plus choke tubes and back-bored. Introduced in 2015.

NIB	Exc.	V.G.	Good	Fair	Poor
1075	900	—	—	—	—

Model 1400

Gas-operated semi-automatic shotgun. Chambered for 12-, 16- or 20-gauge. Offered with 26", 28" or 30" ventilated rib barrel, with various chokes. Finish blued, with checkered walnut stock. Manufactured between 1964 and 1981. Hydrocoil plastic stock available. Would add approximately 35 percent to values given.

NIB	Exc.	V.G.	Good	Fair	Poor
450	350	300	250	200	125

New Model 1400

Gas-operated semi-automatic shotgun. Chambered for 12- or 20-gauge. Offered with 22" or 28" ventilated rib barrel, with screw-in chokes. Finish blued, with checkered walnut stock. Introduced in 1989.

NIB	Exc.	V.G.	Good	Fair	Poor
450	350	300	250	200	125

Model 1400 Ranger

Utility-grade gas-operated semi-automatic shotgun. Chambered for 12- or 20-gauge. Offered with 28" ventilated rib barrel, with screw-in chokes or 24" slug barrel, with rifle sights. Finish blued, with checkered stock. Combination two-barrel set includes deer barrel. Would be worth approximately 20 percent additional. Introduced in 1983.

NIB	Exc.	V.G.	Good	Fair	Poor
400	300	250	200	150	100

Model 1400 Quail Unlimited

This 12-gauge semi-automatic shotgun introduced in 1993. Features compact engraved receiver, with 26" ventilated rib barrel supplied with WinChoke tubes. Stock checkered walnut. Weight 7.25 lbs.

NIB	Exc.	V.G.	Good	Fair	Poor
400	300	250	200	150	100

Model 1400 Ranger Deer Combo

Features 12-gauge 22" smooth barrel and 28" ventilated rib barrel, with three WinChokes.

NIB	Exc.	V.G.	Good	Fair	Poor
400	300	250	200	150	100

Model 37A

Introduced in 1973. Single-shot shotgun, with exposed hammer. Offered in 12-, 16-, 20-, 28-gauge and .410 bore. All guns choked Full, except youth model choked Modified. Walnut finish on hardwood stock. Pistol-grip cap, with white spacer. Weight about 6 lbs. About 395,000 produced until 1980.

NIB	Exc.	V.G.	Good	Fair	Poor
—	350	250	225	175	115

Model 22

Introduced in 1975. Side-by-side shotgun manufactured by Laurona in Spain, to Winchester's specifications for European market. Had an oil-finished stock, with checkered pistol-grip semi-beavertail forearm and hand engraved receiver. Finish black chrome. Fitted with double triggers and matted rib. Offered in 12-gauge only, with 28" barrels. Weight 6.75 lbs. RARE.

NIB	Exc.	V.G.	Good	Fair	Poor
1250	950	700	550	400	200

Model 91

Over/under shotgun built for Winchester by Laurona for its European markets. Offered in 12-gauge only, with 28" ventilated rib barrels and single/double triggers. Hand checkered oil-finished walnut stock, with hand engraved receiver. Finish was black chrome. Weight 7.5 lbs. RARE.

NIB	Exc.	V.G.	Good	Fair	Poor
1100	800	600	500	400	200

Supreme Field

Introduced in 2000. Over/under shotgun chambered for 12-gauge 3" shell. Fitted with 28" ventilated rib barrels, with Invector chokes. Walnut stock, with pistol-grip. Blued engraved receiver. Weight about 7.5 lbs.

NIB	Exc.	V.G.	Good	Fair	Poor
1025	900	700	525	450	350

Supreme Sporting

Similar to above model. Fitted with 28" or 30" blued ported barrels. Chambered for 12-gauge 2.75" shells. Polished silver receiver and adjustable trigger. Weight about 7.5 lbs. Introduced in 2000.

NIB	Exc.	V.G.	Good	Fair	Poor
1200	950	750	575	500	350

Supreme Elegance

Introduced in 2003. Over/under shotgun chambered for 12-gauge 3" shell. Choice of 26" or 28" ventilated rib barrels, with three choke tubes. Grayed receiver, with scroll and bird scenes. Weight about 7 lbs., depending on barrel length.

NIB	Exc.	V.G.	Good	Fair	Poor
1400	1100	850	500	200	100

MODEL 23 SERIES

Model 23 XTR

Side-by-side boxlock double-barrel shotgun. Chambered for 12- or 20-gauge. Offered with 25.5", 26", 28" or 30" ventilated rib barrels, with 3" chambers. Various choke combinations. Features single trigger and automatic ejectors. Scroll-engraved, with coin-finished receiver, blued barrels and checkered select walnut stock. Introduced in 1978. Available in a number of configurations. Differ in amount of ornamentation, quality of materials and workmanship utilized in their construction. Models and values listed. Discontinued.

NIB	Exc.	V.G.	Good	Fair	Poor
2000	1800	1400	1050	850	500

Pigeon Grade

With WinChokes.

NIB	Exc.	V.G.	Good	Fair	Poor
—	2300	1950	1600	1300	5000

Pigeon Grade Lightweight

Straight stock.

NIB	Exc.	V.G.	Good	Fair	Poor
—	2450	2100	1750	1400	500

Model 23 Golden Quail

This series available in 12-, 20-, 28-gauge and .410 bore. Features 25.5" barrels that are choked Improved Cylinder/Modified and straight-grip English-style stock, with recoil pad. Series discontinued in 1987. **NOTE:** Add 20 percent for 20-gauge; 50 percent for 28-gauge or .410 bore.

NIB	Exc.	V.G.	Good	Fair	Poor
3000	2700	2400	2000	1200	500

Model 23 Light Duck

Chambered for 20-gauge. Offered with 28" Full and Full-choked barrel. Manufactured 500 in 1985.

NIB	Exc.	V.G.	Good	Fair	Poor
3100	2900	2600	1800	800	500

Model 23 Heavy Duck

Chambered for 12-gauge, with 30" Full and Full-choked barrels. Manufactured 500 in 1984.

NIB	Exc.	V.G.	Good	Fair	Poor
3200	3000	2600	1800	800	500

MODEL 101 SERIES

Model 101 Field Grade

Over/under boxlock double-barrel shotgun. Chambered for 12-, 20-, 28-gauge and .410 bore. Offered with 26", 28" or 30" ventilated rib barrels, with various choke combinations. Since 1983, screw-in chokes have been standard and models so furnished would be worth approximately $50 additional. Single-selective trigger and automatic ejectors. Receiver engraved; finish blued, with checkered walnut stock. Manufactured between 1963 and 1987. **NOTE:** Add 40 percent for 28-gauge; 50 percent for .410 bore.

NIB	Exc.	V.G.	Good	Fair	Poor
1500	1350	1200	1050	850	500

Model 101 Waterfowl

Chambered for 12-gauge 3" shell. Has 30" or 32" ventilated rib barrels and matte finish.

NIB	Exc.	V.G.	Good	Fair	Poor
—	1900	1675	1400	800	400

Model 101 Magnum

Similar to Field Grade. Chambered for 12- or 20-gauge, with 3" Magnum chambers. Offered with 30" barrels and various chokes. Stock furnished with a recoil pad. Manufactured between 1966 and 1981.

Model 101 Skeet Grade

Offered with 26" skeet-bored barrels, with competition rib and skeet-type walnut stock. Manufactured between 1966 and 1984.

NIB	Exc.	V.G.	Good	Fair	Poor
—	1500	1250	1050	850	500

Model 101 Three-Gauge Skeet Set

Combination set offered with three barrels. Chambered for 20-, 28-gauge and .410 bore. Furnished with a fitted case. Manufactured between 1974 and 1984.

NIB	Exc.	V.G.	Good	Fair	Poor
—	3500	2600	1800	800	500

Model 101 Trap Grade

Chambered for 12-gauge only. Offered with 30" or 32" competition ribbed barrels choked for trap shooting. Furnished with competition-type stock. Manufactured between 1966 and 1984.

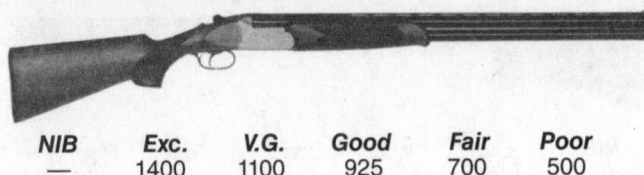

NIB	Exc.	V.G.	Good	Fair	Poor
—	1400	1100	925	700	500

Model 101 Pigeon Grade

More deluxe-engraved version of Model 101. Chambered for 12-, 20-, 28-gauge and .410 bore. Features coin-finished receiver, with fancy checkered walnut stock. Introduced in 1974.

NIB	Exc.	V.G.	Good	Fair	Poor
—	3000	2600	1800	1275	750

Model 101 Super Pigeon Grade

Deluxe version of Model 101. Chambered for 12-gauge. Heavily engraved, with several gold inlays. Receiver blued. Features high-grade walnut stock, with fleur-de-lis checkering. Imported between 1985 and 1987.

NIB	Exc.	V.G.	Good	Fair	Poor
—	5500	4200	3500	2800	1000

Model 101 Diamond Grade

Competition model chambered for all four gauges. Offered in trap or skeet configuration, with screw-in chokes. Engraved matte-finished receiver. Select checkered walnut stock. Skeet model features recoil-reducing muzzle vents.

NIB	Exc.	V.G.	Good	Fair	Poor
—	2000	1625	1250	900	680

Model 101 Pigeon Grade Trap

Deluxe dedicated trap gun introduced in 2008. Features Grade III/IV walnut stock, with high-gloss finish and raised comb. Barrels are 30" or 32". Three choke tubes included. Weight 7.5 to 7.75 lbs. **NOTE:** Add 5 percent for adjustable comb stock.

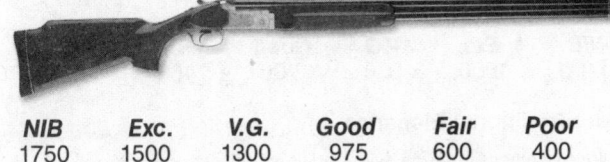

NIB	Exc.	V.G.	Good	Fair	Poor
1750	1500	1300	975	600	400

Model 101 150th Anniversary Commemorative

In 12-gauge, with deep relief scroll engraving, gold inlays, silver nitride receiver, trigger guard, safety and Winchester trademark. Barrels 28", with ventilated rib, ivory bead front sight and Winchester's Invector-Plus choke tubes. Grade IV/V walnut stock has 24 lpi checkering. Introduced in 2016.

NIB	Exc.	V.G.	Good	Fair	Poor
2800	2400	—	—	—	—

Model 501 Grand European

Over/under double-barrel shotgun. Chambered for 12- or 20-gauge. Available in trap or skeet configurations. Offered with 27", 30" or 32" ventilated rib barrels. Heavily engraved and matte finish, with select checkered walnut stock. Manufactured between 1981 and 1986.

NIB	Exc.	V.G.	Good	Fair	Poor
—	2700	2100	1700	1300	500

Model 501 Presentation Grade

Deluxe version chambered in 12-gauge only. Ornately engraved and gold-inlaid. Stock made out of presentation-grade walnut. Furnished with a fitted case. Manufactured between 1984 and 1987.

NIB	Exc.	V.G.	Good	Fair	Poor
—	3400	2750	2200	1600	500

Select Model 101 Field

Belgian-made version of Winchesters popular Model 101. Features Grade II/III walnut; 26" or 28" barrels; deep-relief engraving; blued receiver that mimics original 101. Classic white line spacer and vented recoil pad. Three choke tubes. Weight about 7.2 lbs. Introduced in 2007.

NIB	Exc.	V.G.	Good	Fair	Poor
1600	1400	1150	900	650	400

Select Model 101 Sporting

Similar to Field model plus competition features, such as, wider rib, adjustable trigger, white mid-bead and five extended Signature choke tubes. Ported barrels are 28", 30" or 32".

NIB	Exc.	V.G.	Good	Fair	Poor
1675	1475	1225	1050	775	450

Combination Gun

Over/under rifle/shotgun combination. Chambered for 12-gauge over .222, .223, .30-06 and 9.3x74R cartridges. Features 25" barrels and select checkered walnut stock. Shotgun tube has screw-in choke. Engraved in fashion of Model 501 Grand European. Manufactured between 1983 and 1985.

NIB	Exc.	V.G.	Good	Fair	Poor
—	3000	2500	1600	1200	700

Express Rifle

Over/under double-barreled rifle. Chambered for .257 Roberts, .270, 7.7x65R, .30-06 and 9.3x74R cartridges. Features 23.5" barrels, with solid rib and express sights. Engraved with game scenes. Has a satin-finished receiver. Stock checkered select walnut. Manufactured in 1984 and 1985.

NIB	Exc.	V.G.	Good	Fair	Poor
—	3500	3000	2100	1700	900

Model 96 Xpert

Utility-grade over/under double-barrel shotgun. Mechanically similar to Model 101. Chambered for 12- or 20-gauge. Offered with various barrel lengths and choke combinations. Boxlock action, with single-selective trigger and automatic ejectors. Plain receiver blued, with checkered walnut stock. Manufactured between 1976 and 1982. Competition-grade model for trap or skeet was also available. Would be worth approximately the same amount.

NIB	Exc.	V.G.	Good	Fair	Poor
—	1025	900	700	525	350

Model 1001 Field

New addition to U.S.R.A. product line for 1993. Over/under shotgun available in 12-gauge only, with 28" ventilated rib barrel. Furnished with WinPlus choke tubes. Walnut checkered pistol stock standard. Finish blued, with scroll engraving on receiver. Matte finish on receiver top. Weight 7 lbs. Subject to a 1995 recall.

NIB	Exc.	V.G.	Good	Fair	Poor
1000	850	700	500	350	200

Model 1001 Sporting Clays I & II

This model features: different stock dimensions; fuller pistol-grip; radiused recoil pad; wider ventilated rib. Fitted on 28" barrel (Sporting Clays I); 30" (Sporting Clays II). Comes complete with choke tubes. Frame has silver nitrate finish. Special engraving features a flying clay target. Introduced in 1993. Weight 7.75 lbs. Subject to a 1995 recall.

NIB	Exc.	V.G.	Good	Fair	Poor
1100	950	800	600	350	200

SELECT OVER/UNDER SERIES

This series of over/under shotguns was introduced into Winchester line in 2004. Series features a low-profile receiver, with unique engraving and lightweight barrels. Contoured walnut stocks, with distinctive checkering patterns.

Select Midnight

High-gloss bluing on receiver. Barrels with gold accent game bird pattern on both sides and bottom of receiver. Satin finished Grade II/III walnut. Oval checkering pattern. Choke tubes. Introduced 2006. Available in 26" and 28" barrels.

NIB	Exc.	V.G.	Good	Fair	Poor
1600	1400	1150	900	650	400

Select White Field

An engraved silver nitride receiver featured on both versions of White Field. Traditional Model: has traditional checkering; Extreme Model: features Select Series' unique oval checkering pattern. Both versions have choke tubes. Available in 26" and 28" barrels. Introduced 2006.

NIB	Exc.	V.G.	Good	Fair	Poor
1300	1200	1100	900	650	400

Select Energy Sporting

Chambered for 12-gauge 2.75" shell. Choice of 28", 30" or 32" ventilated rib barrels, with choke tubes and porting. TruGlo front sight. Adjustable trigger shoe. Walnut stock, with recoil pad. Weight about 7.62 lbs. Adjustable comb available. **NOTE:** Add $150 for adjustable comb.

NIB	Exc.	V.G.	Good	Fair	Poor
1600	1400	1150	900	650	400

Select Energy Trap

This 12-gauge model fitted with choice of 30" or 32" back-bored ported barrels. Wide ventilated rib. Choke tubes. Walnut stock, with Monte Carlo comb. Weight about 7.8 lbs. Adjustable comb available. **NOTE:** Add $150 for adjustable comb.

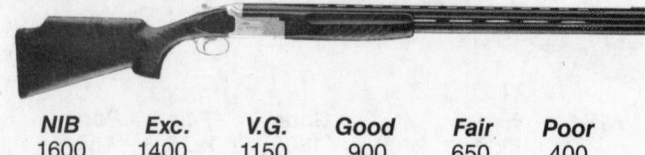

NIB	Exc.	V.G.	Good	Fair	Poor
1600	1400	1150	900	650	400

Select Elegance (Supreme)

This 12-gauge features full coverage engraving, with game scenes. Choice of 26" or 28" ventilated rib barrels, with choke tubes. Walnut stock, with unique checkering pattern. Weight about 7 lbs.

NIB	Exc.	V.G.	Good	Fair	Poor
1800	1400	1150	900	650	400

Select Field

This 12-gauge 3" gun fitted with choice of 26" or 28" ventilated rib barrels, with choke tubes. Engraved receiver, with oval checkering pattern. Weight about 7 lbs.

NIB	Exc.	V.G.	Good	Fair	Poor
1400	1200	950	700	450	300

Select Traditional Elegance

Similar to Select Elegance, with traditional checkering pattern.

NIB	Exc.	V.G.	Good	Fair	Poor
1400	1200	950	700	450	300

Select Deluxe Field

New in 2007. Belgian-made 3" 12-gauge features engraved steel receiver, with silver nitride finish and Grade II walnut. Barrels are 26", 28" or 30". Three chokes included. Weight about 7.25 lbs.

NIB	Exc.	V.G.	Good	Fair	Poor
1600	1400	1150	900	650	400

Select Platinum Field

This 3" 12-gauge introduced in 2007. Belgian-made and comes with 28" or 30" barrels, Grade II/III walnut and deep relief engraving. Includes three Signature extended choke tubes and hard case.

NIB	Exc.	V.G.	Good	Fair	Poor
2050	1800	1575	1200	900	500

Select Platinum Sporting

Similar to Platinum Field, with 28", 30" or 32" ported barrels, wide rib and adjustable trigger shoe. Five Signature extended choke tubes and hard case.

NIB	Exc.	V.G.	Good	Fair	Poor
2200	1950	1725	1375	1075	500

WINCHESTER COMMEMORATIVE RIFLES

Beginning in early 1960s, Winchester produced a number of special Model 1894 rifles and carbines that commemorated certain historic events, places or individuals. In some cases, they are slightly embellished and in others quite ornate. If a Winchester commemorative rifle has been cocked leaving a line on the hammer or lever, many collectors will show little or no interest in its acquisition. If they have been fired, they will realize little premium over standard Post-1964 Model 94. A number of commemorative's have been ordered by outside concerns and technically are not factory issues. Most have less collectibility than factory-issued models. There are a number of concerns that specialize in marketing the total range of Winchester commemorative rifles. Listed are factory-issue commemorative's with their current value, issue price and number manufactured.

CURRENT VALUE	ISSUE PRICE	NO. MANUFACTURED
1964 Wyoming Diamond Jubilee—Carbine		
1200	100	1,500
1966 Centennial—Rifle		
700	125	102,309
1966 Centennial—Carbine		
700	125	102,309
1966 Nebraska Centennial—Rifle		
1200	100	2,500
1967 Canadian Centennial—Rifle		
650	125	—
1967 Canadian Centennial—Carbine		
650	125	90,301
1967 Alaskan Purchase Centennial—Carbine		
1250	125	1,500
1968 Illinois Sesquicentennial—Carbine		
600	110	37,648
1968 Buffalo Bill—Carbine		
700	130	112,923
1968 Buffalo Bill—Rifle		
700	130	—
1968 Buffalo Bill "1 of 300" —Rifle		
3500	1000	300
1969 Theodore Roosevelt—Rifle		
700	135	—

CURRENT VALUE	ISSUE PRICE	NO. MANUFACTURED
1969 Theodore Roosevelt—Carbine		
700	135	52,386
1969 Golden Spike Carbine		
700	120	69,996
1970 Cowboy Commemorative Carbine		
750	125	27,549
1970 Cowboy Carbine "1 of 300"		
3500	1000	300
1970 Northwest Territories (Canadian)		
1000	150	2,500
1970 Northwest Territories Deluxe (Canadian)		
1300	250	500
1970 Lone Star—Rifle		
700	140	—
1970 Lone Star—Carbine		
700	140	38,385
1971 NRA Centennial—Rifle		
700	150	21,000
1971 NRA Centennial—Musket		
700	150	23,400
1971 Yellow Boy		
1300	250	4,900
1971 Royal Canadian Mounted Police (Canadian)		
900	190	9,500
1971 Mounted Police (Canadian)		
1000	190	5,100
1971 Mounted Police, Presentation		
10000	—	10
1974 Texas Ranger—Carbine		
800	135	4,850
1974 Texas Ranger Presentation Model		
3500	1000	150
1974 Apache (Canadian)		
900	150	8,600
1974 Commanche (Canadian)		
900	230	11,500
1974 Klondike Gold Rush (Canadian)		
900	240	10,200
1975 Klondike Gold Rush—Dawson City Issue (Canadian)		
8500	—	25
1976 Sioux (Canadian)		
900	280	10,000
1976 Little Bighorn (Canadian)		
1000	300	11,000
1976 U.S. Bicentennial Carbine		
800	325	19,999
1977 Wells Fargo		
800	350	19,999
1977 Legendary Lawman		
800	375	19,999
1977 Limited Edition I		
1600	1500	1,500

Current Value	Issue Price	No. Manufactured
1977 Cheyenne—.22 Cal. (Canadian)		
1100	320	5,000
1977 Cheyenne—.44-40 Cal. (Canadian)		
900	300	11,225
1977 Cherokee—.22 Cal. (Canadian)		
1100	385	3,950
1977 Cherokee—.30-30 Cal. (Canadian)		
900	385	9,000
1978 "One of One Thousand" (European)		
8250	5000	250
1978 Antler Game Carbine		
800	375	19,999
1979 Limited Edition II		
1600	1500	1,500
1979 Legendary Frontiersman Rifle		
800	425	19,999
1979 Matched Set of 1,000		
2800	3000	1,000
1979 Bat Masterson (Canadian)		
900	650	8,000
1980 Alberta Diamond Jubilee (Canadian)		
1000	650	2,700
1980 Alberta Diamond Jubilee Deluxe (Canadian)		
1800	1900	300
1980 Saskatchewan Diamond Jubilee (Canadian)		
1000	695	2,700
1980 Saskatchewan Diamond Jubilee Deluxe (Canadian)		
1800	1995	300
1980 Oliver Winchester		
900	375	19,999
1981 U.S. Border Patrol		
1000	1195	1,000
1981 U.S. Border Patrol—Member's Model		
1000	695	800
1981 Calgary Stampede (Canadian)		
1800	2200	1,000
1981 Canadian Pacific Centennial (Canadian)		
900	800	2,000
1981 Canadian Pacific Centennial Presentation (Canadian)		
1800	2200	300
1981 Canadian Pacific Employee's Model (Canadian)		
900	800	2,000
1981 John Wayne (Canadian)		
1600	600	1,000
1981 John Wayne		
1600	600	49,000
1981 Duke		
3750	2250	1,000
1981 John Wayne "1 of 300" Set		
7500	10000	300
1982 Great Western Artist I		
1550	2200	999

Current Value	Issue Price	No. Manufactured
1982 Great Western Artist II		
1500	2200	999
1982 Annie Oakley		
1300	699	6,000
1983 Chief Crazy Horse		
800	600	19,999
1983 American Bald Eagle		
800	895	2,800
1983 American Bald Eagle—Deluxe		
4000	2995	200
1983 Oklahoma Diamond Jubilee		
1750	2250	1,001
1984 Winchester—Colt Commemorative Set		
2750	3995	3,250
1985 Boy Scout 75th Anniversary .22 Cal.		
1100	615	15,000
1985 Boy Scout 75th Anniversary—Eagle Scout		
6000	2140	1,000
Texas Sesquicentennial Model—Rifle .38-55 Cal.		
2750	2995	1,500
Texas Sesquicentennial Model—Carbine .38-55 Cal.		
1000	695	15,000
Texas Sesquicentennial Model Set with Bowie Knife		
6500	7995	150
1986 Model 94 Ducks Unlimited		
900	—	2,800
1986 Statue of Liberty		
9000	6500	100
1986 120th Anniversary Model—Carbine .44-40 Cal.		
950	995	1,000
1986 European 1 of 1,000 Second Series (European)		
1000	6000	150
1987 U.S. Constitution 200th Anniversary .44-40		
15000	12000	17
1990 Wyoming Centennial—30-30		
1600	895	500
1991 Winchester 125th Anniversary		
6500	4995	61
1992 Arapaho—30-30		
1600	895	500
1992 Ontario Conservation—30-30		
1600	1195	400
1992 Kentucky Bicentennial—30-30		
1600	995	500
1993 Nez Perce—30-30		
1600	995	600
1995 Florida Sesquicentennial Carbine		
1600	1195	360
1996 Wild Bill Hickok Carbine		
1600	1195	350
2008 John Wayne 1892 .44-40		
2000	2000	N/A

WINDSOR
Windsor, Vermont
Robbins & Lawrence
Hartford, Connecticut

Windsor Rifle-Musket

A .577-caliber single-shot percussion rifle, with 39" round barrel secured by three barrel bands. Lock marked "Windsor". Rifles of this pattern were contracted for/by the British Government. Lock and barrel finished in white brass furniture and walnut stock. Approximately 16,000 made from 1855 to 1858.

NIB	Exc.	V.G.	Good	Fair	Poor
—	—	3750	3000	950	300

WINSLOW ARMS CO.
Camden, South Carolina

Bolt Action Rifle

High-grade semi-custom sporting rifle built upon a number of actions. Offered in all popular calibers from .17 Rem. to .458 Win. Magnum, with 24" barrel and 3-shot magazine. Larger Magnum models have 26" barrel and 2-shot magazine. Two basic stocks are offered—Conventional Bushmaster, which features a standard pistol-grip and beavertail forearm; Plainsmaster, which has a full curled hooked pistol-grip and wide flat beavertail forearm. Both have Monte Carlo-style stocks, with recoil pads and sling swivels. Offered in a choice of popular woods, with rosewood fore-end tips and pistol-grip caps. Eight different grades of this rifle are available. Following lists the values applicable for each.

Commander Grade

Figured walnut stock. Rosewood forearm tip and grip cap. White line recoil pad. FN Supreme action.

NIB	Exc.	V.G.	Good	Fair	Poor
—	1450	1050	925	700	550

Regal Grade

All features of Commander Grade plus ivory and ebony inlay on stock, French-style checkering, jeweled bolt.

NIB	Exc.	V.G.	Good	Fair	Poor
—	2200	1800	1225	900	600

Regent Grade

As above, with addition of hand-carved checkering.

NIB	Exc.	V.G.	Good	Fair	Poor
—	2375	1850	1250	900	600

Regimental Grade

As above, with addition of basket weave carving, two ivory stock inlays and large ivory and ebony inlay on both sides of buttstock with animal silhouette.

NIB	Exc.	V.G.	Good	Fair	Poor
—	3000	2200	1500	1200	650

Crown Grade

As above, with more elaborate ivory inlays on stock.

NIB	Exc.	V.G.	Good	Fair	Poor
—	3700	2550	1800	1500	650

Royal Grade

As above, with addition of even more elaborate stock carving and ivory and ebony inlay.

NIB	Exc.	V.G.	Good	Fair	Poor
—	4500	3250	2000	1600	650

Imperial Grade

As above, with addition of engraved barrel from receiver to 11" forward. Engraved receiver ring, bolt handle and trigger guard. Engraved scope mounts and rings.

NIB	Exc.	V.G.	Good	Fair	Poor
—	5000	3750	2500	2000	700

Emperor Grade

As above, with addition of gold raised relief animals, engraved receiver and forward part of barrel with muzzle tip engraved as well. Highest Winslow grade.

NIB	Exc.	V.G.	Good	Fair	Poor
—	6250	5000	4000	3000	700

WISEMAN, BILL & CO.
Bryan, Texas

Rifle

Custom order bolt-action rifle utilizing a Sako action. McMillan stainless steel barrel and laminated stock. Action components are Teflon coated. Made in four styles: Hunter, Hunter Deluxe, Maverick and Varminter.

NIB	Exc.	V.G.	Good	Fair	Poor
—	2500	2150	1750	1500	600

Silhouette Pistol

Custom made single-shot pistol produced in a variety of calibers, with 14" fluted stainless steel barrel and laminated pistol-grip stock. Furnished without sights. Introduced in 1989.

NIB	Exc.	V.G.	Good	Fair	Poor
—	1750	1450	1100	800	600

WITNESS
See—European American Armory

WOLF SPORTING PISTOLS
Importer—Handgunner Gunshop
Topton, Pennsylvania

Wolf SV Target

Chambered for 9x19, 9x21, 9x23, .38 Super, .40 S&W or .45 ACP. Barrel 4.5" long. Weight 44 oz. Many special features. Built in Austria. Price listed for basic pistol. A number of special order items are offered. Check with importer before a sale. First imported in 1998.

NIB	Exc.	V.G.	Good	Fair	Poor
2000	1600	1250	1000	750	600

Wolf SV Match

Chambered for 9x19, 9x21, 9x23, .38 Super, .40 S&W or .45 ACP. Barrel 5.5" long. Weight 44 oz. Many special features. Built in Austria. Price listed for basic pistol. A number of special order items are offered. Check with importer before a sale. First imported in 1998.

NIB	Exc.	V.G.	Good	Fair	Poor
2000	1600	1250	1000	750	600

WOODWARD, JAMES & SONS
London, England

Prior to WWII, this company produced a variety of boxlock and sidelock shotguns that are regarded as some of the best made. Prospective purchasers should secure a qualified appraisal prior to acquisition.

WURFFLEIN, ANDREW & WILLIAM
Philadelphia, Pennsylvania

Pocket Pistol

A .41-caliber percussion single-shot pocket pistol, with 2.5" or 3" barrel, German silver furniture and checkered walnut stock. Lock marked "A. Wurfflein / Phila.". Manufactured during 1850s and 1860s.

NIB	Exc.	V.G.	Good	Fair	Poor
—	—	2600	1750	700	200

Single-Shot Target Pistol

A .22-caliber single-shot pistol, with half-octagonal barrels measuring from 8" to 16" in length. Barrel pivots downward for loading and marked "W. Wurfflein Philad'a Pa. U.S.A. Patented June 24th, 1884". Blued, with walnut grips. Also available with detachable shoulder stock, which if present, would add approximately 35 percent to values listed. Manufactured from 1884 to 1890.

NIB	Exc.	V.G.	Good	Fair	Poor
—	—	2600	1750	700	200

Single-Shot Rifle

Single-shot rifle produced in a variety of calibers, with octagonal barrel lengths of 24" to 28". Available with a wide variety of optional features.

NIB	Exc.	V.G.	Good	Fair	Poor
—	—	2400	1250	350	150

Mid-range Model

As above, with 28" or 30" half-octagonal barrel.

NIB	Exc.	V.G.	Good	Fair	Poor
—	—	4250	3000	950	400

Model No. 25

Highest grade rifle manufactured by Wurfflein.

NIB	Exc.	V.G.	Good	Fair	Poor
—	—	4500	3500	1250	600

XL
HOPKINS & ALLEN
Norwich, Connecticut

Derringer

.41-caliber spur trigger single-shot pistol, with 2.75" octagonal barrel. Iron or brass frame. Blued nickel-plated, with rosewood grips. Barrel marked "XL Derringer". Manufactured during 1870s.

NIB	Exc.	V.G.	Good	Fair	Poor
—	1650	1295	950	500	150

Vest Pocket Derringer

As above in .22-caliber, with 2.25" round barrel normally full nickel-plated. Barrel marked "XL Vest Pocket". Manufactured from 1870s to 1890s.

NIB	Exc.	V.G.	Good	Fair	Poor
—	—	1350	750	325	125

XPERT
HOPKINS & ALLEN
Norwich, Connecticut

Xpert Derringer

.22- or .30-caliber spur trigger single-shot pistol, with round barrels 2.25" to 6" in length. Nickel-plated finish, with rosewood grips. Breechblock pivots to left side for loading. Barrel marked "Xpert-Pat. Sep. 23. 1878". Manufactured during 1870s.

NIB	Exc.	V.G.	Good	Fair	Poor
—	—	875	700	400	125

Xpert Pocket Rifle

Similar to derringer, with same size frame fitted with 7.5" barrel. Chambered for .22 cartridge, as well as .30-caliber rimfire. Supplied with wire stock. Values for gun with stock. Produced from about 1870 to 1890s.

NIB	Exc.	V.G.	Good	Fair	Poor
—	—	1475	1150	500	150

Z

Z-B RIFLE CO.
Brno, Czechoslovakia

Model ZKW-465 Varmint Rifle

Mauser bolt-action rifle chambered for .22 Hornet cartridge. Has 23" barrel, with three-leaf folding rear sight. Offered standard with double-set triggers. Finish blued, with select walnut checkered stock.

NIB	Exc.	V.G.	Good	Fair	Poor
—	1600	1150	975	800	500

ZANOTTI, FABIO
Brescia, Italy

Model 625

12-gauge to .410 bore boxlock double-barrel shotgun, with automatic ejectors and single-selective trigger. Blued, with checkered walnut stock.

NIB	Exc.	V.G.	Good	Fair	Poor
6500	5200	4700	3500	2500	500

Model 626

As above, engraved with scroll work or hunting scenes.

NIB	Exc.	V.G.	Good	Fair	Poor
7000	5700	5200	4000	2800	500

Giacinto

External hammer boxlock shotgun produced in a variety of gauges, with double triggers.

NIB	Exc.	V.G.	Good	Fair	Poor
6500	5200	4700	3500	2500	500

Maxim

Similar to Model 625 fitted with detachable sidelocks.

NIB	Exc.	V.G.	Good	Fair	Poor
7000	5700	5200	4000	2800	500

Edward

As above, but more intricately engraved.

NIB	Exc.	V.G.	Good	Fair	Poor
12000	9000	6500	4500	3000	1500

Cassiano I

As above, with exhibition grade engraving.

NIB	Exc.	V.G.	Good	Fair	Poor
13000	9000	7000	6000	4000	2000

Cassiano II

As above, with gold inlays.

NIB	Exc.	V.G.	Good	Fair	Poor
14500	12000	9500	7000	5000	2500

Cassiano Executive

Strictly custom-made shotgun produced to client's specifications.

NIB	Exc.	V.G.	Good	Fair	Poor
45000	—	—	—	—	—

ZEHNER, E. WAFFENFABRIK
Suhl, Germany

Zehna

6.35mm semi-automatic pistol, with 2.5" barrel and 5-shot magazine. Slide marked "Zehna DRPA", and caliber on later production models. Blued, with black plastic grips bearing monogram "EZ". Approximately 20,000 made from 1921 to 1927.

NIB	Exc.	V.G.	Good	Fair	Poor
—	395	300	250	175	100

ZEPHYR
Eibar, Spain
Importer—Stoegers

Woodlander II

12- or 20-gauge boxlock shotgun, with varying barrel lengths, double triggers and extractors. Blued, with walnut stock.

NIB	Exc.	V.G.	Good	Fair	Poor
600	450	400	300	200	100

Uplander

12-, 16-, 20-, 28-gauge or .410 bore sidelock double-barrel shotgun, with varying barrel lengths, double triggers and automatic ejectors. Blued, with walnut stock.

NIB	Exc.	V.G.	Good	Fair	Poor
850	700	500	400	300	150

Upland King

As above in 12- or 16-gauge, with ventilated rib barrels.

NIB	Exc.	V.G.	Good	Fair	Poor
1150	800	700	600	400	250

Vandalia

12-gauge single-barrel trap gun, with 32" full choked barrel. Blued, with walnut stock.

NIB	Exc.	V.G.	Good	Fair	Poor
750	600	550	450	300	150

Sterlingworth II

Identical to Woodlander, with sidelocks.

NIB	Exc.	V.G.	Good	Fair	Poor
850	700	550	450	300	150

Victor Special

12-gauge boxlock double-barrel shotgun, with 25", 28" or 30" barrels, double triggers and extractors. Blued, with walnut stock.

NIB	Exc.	V.G.	Good	Fair	Poor
525	400	300	250	175	100

Thunderbird

10-gauge Magnum boxlock double-barrel shotgun, with 32" full choked barrels, double triggers and automatic ejectors. Blued, with walnut stock.

NIB	Exc.	V.G.	Good	Fair	Poor
950	700	600	500	400	200

Honker

10-gauge Magnum single-barrel shotgun, with 36" full choked and ventilated rib barrel. Blued, with walnut stock.

NIB	Exc.	V.G.	Good	Fair	Poor
600	450	400	300	200	100

ZM WEAPONS
Bernardton, Massachusetts

LR-300 Sport Rifle

Highly modified AR-15 chambered for .223 cartridge. Fitted with 16.25" barrel and true folding stock. Ghost ring rear sight and adjustable post front, with tritium insert standard. Weight about 7.2 lbs. Introduced in 1997.

NIB	Exc.	V.G.	Good	Fair	Poor
—	1600	1200	950	775	500

ZOLI, ANTONIO
Brescia, Italy

Silver Hawk

12- or 20-gauge boxlock double-barrel shotgun. Produced in a variety of barrel lengths and chokes, with double trigger. Engraved blued, with walnut stock.

NIB	Exc.	V.G.	Good	Fair	Poor
—	1025	900	850	600	450

Ariete M2

12-gauge boxlock double-barrel shotgun, with 26" or 28" barrels, non-selective single trigger and automatic ejectors. Engraved blued, with walnut stock.

NIB	Exc.	V.G.	Good	Fair	Poor
—	1150	1000	850	700	350

Empire

As above in 12- or 20-gauge, with 27" or 28" barrels. Engraved French case-hardened blued, with walnut stock.

NIB	Exc.	V.G.	Good	Fair	Poor
—	2300	1950	1400	1250	400

Volcano Record

12-gauge sidelock double-barrel shotgun, with 28" barrels. Available in a variety of chokes, single-selective trigger and automatic ejectors. Engraved French case-hardened blued, with walnut stock.

NIB	Exc.	V.G.	Good	Fair	Poor
—	7000	6000	5000	4000	500

Volcano Record ELM

Strictly custom-ordered shotgun produced to purchaser's specifications. Value speculative.

NIB	Exc.	V.G.	Good	Fair	Poor
—	16000	13500	10500	8500	500

Silver Snipe

12- or 20-gauge over/under shotgun. Produced with varying lengths, ventilated rib barrels, single trigger and extractors. Engraved blued, with walnut stock.

NIB	Exc.	V.G.	Good	Fair	Poor
—	600	450	400	325	275

Golden Snipe

As above more finely finished. Fitted with automatic ejectors.

NIB	Exc.	V.G.	Good	Fair	Poor
—	650	500	450	350	300

Delfino

As above in 12- or 20-gauge Magnum, with 26" or 28" ventilated rib barrels, non-selective single trigger and automatic ejectors. Engraved blued, with walnut stock.

NIB	Exc.	V.G.	Good	Fair	Poor
—	575	425	325	275	250

Ritmo Hunting Gun

As above in 12-gauge Magnum, with 26" or 28" separated ventilated rib barrels, single-selective trigger and automatic ejectors. Engraved blued, with walnut stock.

NIB	Exc.	V.G.	Good	Fair	Poor
—	650	500	450	400	350

Condor Model

As above in 12-gauge, with 28" skeet bored barrels. Wide competition rib, single-selective trigger and automatic ejectors. Engraved French case-hardened blued, with walnut stock.

NIB	Exc.	V.G.	Good	Fair	Poor
—	1100	800	650	500	400

Angel Model

As above in field grade version.

NIB	Exc.	V.G.	Good	Fair	Poor
—	1100	800	600	500	400

Ritmo Pigeon Grade IV

As above, with 28" separated ventilated rib barrels, single-selective trigger, automatic ejectors and extensively engraved. French case-hardened blued, with finely figured walnut stock.

NIB	Exc.	V.G.	Good	Fair	Poor
—	2250	1600	1200	800	600

Model 208 Target

As above, with 28" or 30" trap or skeet bored barrels. Fitted with a wide ventilated rib.

NIB	Exc.	V.G.	Good	Fair	Poor
—	1200	850	700	600	500

Model 308 Target

As above, but more finely finished.

NIB	Exc.	V.G.	Good	Fair	Poor
—	1500	1100	850	700	500

Combinato

.222 or .243 and 12- or 20-gauge over/under combination rifle/shotgun, with engraved boxlock-action, double triggers and folding rear sight. French case-hardened blued, with walnut stock.

NIB	Exc.	V.G.	Good	Fair	Poor
—	2500	1700	1250	950	500

Safari Deluxe

As above, with false sidelocks engraved with scrolls or hunting scenes.

NIB	Exc.	V.G.	Good	Fair	Poor
—	5000	4000	2850	1500	650

ZOLI USA, ANGELO
Brescia, Italy

Slide-Action Shotgun

12-gauge Magnum slide-action shotgun. Produced with a variety of barrel lengths, with detachable choke tubes. Blued, with walnut stock.

NIB	Exc.	V.G.	Good	Fair	Poor
400	300	250	200	150	100

Diano I

12-, 20-gauge or .410 bore single-shot folding barrel shotgun. Produced in a variety of barrel lengths. Blued, with walnut stock.

NIB	Exc.	V.G.	Good	Fair	Poor
175	100	90	80	60	40

Diano II

As above, with bottom lever instead of top release lever.

NIB	Exc.	V.G.	Good	Fair	Poor
175	100	90	80	60	40

Apache

12-gauge Magnum lever-action shotgun, with 20" barrel. Fitted with detachable choke tubes. Blued, with walnut stock.

NIB	Exc.	V.G.	Good	Fair	Poor
500	400	350	300	250	150

Quail Special

.410 Magnum bore double-barrel shotgun, with 28" barrels and single trigger. Blued, with walnut stock.

NIB	Exc.	V.G.	Good	Fair	Poor
325	200	150	125	100	75

Falcon II

As above, with 26" or 28" barrels and double triggers.

NIB	Exc.	V.G.	Good	Fair	Poor
325	200	150	125	100	75

Pheasant

12-gauge Magnum double-barrel shotgun, with 28" barrels, single trigger and automatic ejectors. Blued, with walnut stock.

NIB	Exc.	V.G.	Good	Fair	Poor
450	350	300	250	200	150

Classic

As above, with 26" to 30" barrels fitted with detachable choke tubes, single-selective trigger and automatic ejectors. Blued, with walnut stock.

NIB	Exc.	V.G.	Good	Fair	Poor
850	700	600	500	300	200

Snipe

.410 bore over/under shotgun, with 26" or 28" barrels and single trigger.

NIB	Exc.	V.G.	Good	Fair	Poor
400	300	200	175	150	100

Dove

Similar to above.

NIB	Exc.	V.G.	Good	Fair	Poor
400	300	200	175	150	100

Texas

12-, 20-gauge or .410 bore over/under shotgun, with 26" or 28" barrels, double triggers and bottom barrel release lever.

NIB	Exc.	V.G.	Good	Fair	Poor
350	250	200	150	100	75

Field Special

12- or 20-gauge Magnum double-barrel shotgun. Produced in a variety of barrel lengths. Single trigger and extractors. Blued, with walnut stock.

NIB	Exc.	V.G.	Good	Fair	Poor
550	400	300	250	200	100

Pigeon Model

As above, but more finely finished.

NIB	Exc.	V.G.	Good	Fair	Poor
550	400	300	250	200	100

Standard Model

Similar to above in 12- and 20-gauge only.

NIB	Exc.	V.G.	Good	Fair	Poor
500	400	300	250	200	100

Special Model

As above, with detachable choke tubes and single-selective trigger.

NIB	Exc.	V.G.	Good	Fair	Poor
600	450	300	250	200	100

Deluxe Model
As above, but engraved with better quality walnut.

NIB	Exc.	V.G.	Good	Fair	Poor
800	600	500	400	300	150

Presentation Model
As above, with false sidelocks and finely figured walnut stock.

NIB	Exc.	V.G.	Good	Fair	Poor
950	700	600	450	350	200

St. George's Target
12-gauge over/under shotgun trap or skeet bore, with various barrel lengths, single-selective trigger and automatic ejectors. Blued, with walnut stock.

NIB	Exc.	V.G.	Good	Fair	Poor
1200	900	700	600	550	250

St. George Competition
12-gauge single-barrel gun, with extra set of over/under barrels.

NIB	Exc.	V.G.	Good	Fair	Poor
1950	1600	1200	950	500	300

Express Rifle
.30-06, 7x65Rmm or 9.3x74Rmm over/under double-barrel rifle, with single triggers and automatic ejectors. Blued, with walnut stock.

NIB	Exc.	V.G.	Good	Fair	Poor
4250	3500	2500	1750	1200	600

Express EM
As above, but more finely finished.

NIB	Exc.	V.G.	Good	Fair	Poor
5500	4000	3000	1500	1000	750

Savana E
As above, with double triggers.

NIB	Exc.	V.G.	Good	Fair	Poor
6500	5250	4500	3500	2750	1500

Savana Deluxe
As above, engraved with hunting scenes.

NIB	Exc.	V.G.	Good	Fair	Poor
8000	7000	6000	4750	3500	2000

AZ 1900C
.243, .270, 6.5x55mm, .308 or .30-06 bolt-action rifle, with 24" barrel and open sights. Blued, with walnut stock.

NIB	Exc.	V.G.	Good	Fair	Poor
850	700	500	400	300	150

AZ 1900M
Same as above, with Bell & Carlson composite stock.

NIB	Exc.	V.G.	Good	Fair	Poor
750	600	450	350	275	200

AZ 1900 Deluxe
As above, but more finely finished.

NIB	Exc.	V.G.	Good	Fair	Poor
1100	800	650	500	400	200

AZ 1900 Super Deluxe
As above, engraved with finely figured walnut stock.

NIB	Exc.	V.G.	Good	Fair	Poor
1500	1000	800	600	450	250

Patricia Model
As above in .410 Magnum bore, with 28" ventilated rib barrels, various chokes, single-selective trigger and automatic ejectors. Engraved blued, with finely figured walnut stock.

NIB	Exc.	V.G.	Good	Fair	Poor
1500	1100	950	750	650	400

Condor
.30-06 or .308 and 12-gauge over/under combination shotgun/rifle, with double triggers, extractors and sling swivels. Blued, with walnut stock.

NIB	Exc.	V.G.	Good	Fair	Poor
1500	1050	850	700	500	300

Airone
As above, with false sidelocks.

NIB	Exc.	V.G.	Good	Fair	Poor
1650	1250	1000	800	600	300

Leopard Express
.30-06, .308, 7x65Rmm or .375 H&H over/under double-barrel rifle, with 24" barrels. Express sights, double triggers and extractors. Blued, with walnut stock.

NIB	Exc.	V.G.	Good	Fair	Poor
1750	1400	1000	800	600	300

ZULAICA, M.
Eibar, Spain
Zulaica
Solid-frame .22-caliber revolver, with 6-shot cylinder that has zigzag grooves on its exterior surface. Fired by an external hammer. Frame is hollow, with a rod inside of it that connects to breechblock. Serrated cocking piece connected to this rod that is found at top rear of frame. When fired, cartridge case blows from cylinder and activates breechblock similar to a semi-automatic pistol.

NIB	Exc.	V.G.	Good	Fair	Poor
—	1000	800	600	350	250

ROYAL
Royal was applied to a number of pistols produced by this company as listed.

Royal
6.35mm or 7.65mm semi-automatic pistol. Normally marked on slide "Automatic Pistol 6.35 Royal" or "Automatic Pistol 7.65 Royal".

NIB	Exc.	V.G.	Good	Fair	Poor
—	300	175	100	75	50

7.65mm
As above in 7.65mm caliber, with 5.5" barrel and 12-shot magazine.

NIB	Exc.	V.G.	Good	Fair	Poor
—	325	200	125	100	75

6.35mm
Rather poor copy of Mauser Model C/96 semi-automatic pistol, with fixed lockwork.

NIB	Exc.	V.G.	Good	Fair	Poor
—	900	700	500	300	150

Vincitor
6.35mm or 7.65mm caliber semi-automatic pistol. Patterned after Model 1906 Browning. Slide marked "SA Royal Vincitor". Blued, with plastic grips.

NIB	Exc.	V.G.	Good	Fair	Poor
—	300	175	100	75	50

FIREARMS TRADE NAMES

A.A. Co.: Inexpensive pocket revolvers of unknown manufacture.

Acme:
a) Trade name used by the W.H. Davenport Firearms Co. on shotguns.
b) Trade name used by the Hopkins and Allen Co. on revolvers produced for the Merwin, Hulbert and Co. and the Herman Boker Co. of New York.
c) Trade name used by the Maltby, Henley and Co. of New York on inexpensive pocket revolvers.

Acme Arms Company: Trade name used by the J. Stevens Arms and Tool Co. on pistols and shotguns produced for the Cornwall Hardware Co. of New York.

Aetna: Trade name used by the firm of Harrington and Richardson on inexpensive pocket revolvers.

Alamo Ranger: The name found on inexpensive Spanish revolvers.

Alaska: Trade name used by the Hood Firearms Co. on inexpensive pocket revolvers.

Alert: Trade name used by the Hood Firearms Co. on inexpensive pocket revolvers.

Alexander Gun Company: Trade name believed to have been used by E.K. Tryon of Philadelphia on imported shotguns.

Alexis: Trade name used by the Hood Firearms Co. on inexpensive pocket revolvers.

Allen 22: Trade name used by the Hopkins and Allen Co. on inexpensive pocket revolvers.

America: Trade name used by the Crescent Firearms Co. on inexpensive pocket revolvers.

American: Trade name used by the Ely and Wray on inexpensive pocket revolvers.

American Barlock Wonder: Trade name used by the H. & D. Folsom Arms Co. on shotguns made for the Sears, Roebuck Co. of Chicago.

American Boy: Trade name used on firearms retailed by the Townley Metal and Hardware Co. of Kansas City, Missouri.

American Bulldog: Trade name used by the Iver Johnson Arms and Cycle Works on inexpensive pocket revolvers.

American Bulldog Revolver: Trade name used by Harrington and Richardson Arms Co. on an inexpensive pocket revolver.

American Eagle: Trade name used by the Hopkins and Allen Co. on inexpensive pocket revolvers.

American Gun Company: Trade name used by H. & D. Folsom Arms Co. on pistols and shotguns that firm retailed.

American Gun Barrel Company: Trade name used by R. Avis of West Haven, Connecticut, between 1916 and 1920.

American Nitro: Trade name used by H. & D. Folsom Arms Co. on shotguns.

Americus: Trade name used by the Hopkins and Allen Co. on inexpensive pocket revolvers.

Angel: Trade name found on inexpensive pocket revolvers of unknown manufacture.

Arab, The: Trade name used by the Harrington and Richardson Arms Co. on shotguns.

Aristocrat:
a) Trade name used by the Hopkins and Allen Co. on inexpensive pocket revolvers.
b) Trade name used by the Supplee-Biddle Hardware Co. of Philadelphia on firearms they retailed.

Armory Gun Company: Trade name used by H. & D. Folsom Arms Co. on shotguns.

Aubrey Shotgun: Trade name found on shotguns made for the Sears, Roebuck and Co. of Chicago by Albert Aubrey of Meriden, Connecticut.

Audax: Trade name used by the Manufacture d'Armes Pyrenees on semiautomatic pistols.

Aurora: Trade name found on inexpensive Spanish semiautomatic pistols.

Autogarde: Trade name used by the Societe Francaise des Munitions on semiautomatic pistols.

Automatic:
a) Trade name used by the Forehand and Wadsworth Co. on inexpensive pocket revolvers.
b) Trade name used by the Harrington and Richardson Arms Co. on inexpensive pocket revolvers.
c) Trade name used by the Iver Johnson Arms and Cycle Works on inexpensive pocket revolvers.

Auto Stand: Trade name used by the Manufacture Francaise d'Armes et Cycles, St. Etiene on semiautomatic pistols.

Avenger: Trade name found on inexpensive pocket revolvers of unknown manufacture.

Baby Hammerless: Trade mark used successively by Henry Kolb and R.F. Sedgley on pocket revolvers they manufactured.

Baby Russian: Trade name used by the American Arms Co. on revolvers they manufactured.

Baker Gun Company: Trade name used by the H. & D. Folsom Arms Co. on shotguns they retailed.

Baker Gun and Forging Company: Trade name used by the H. & D. Folsom Arms Co. on shotguns they retailed.

Bang: Trade name found on inexpensive pocket revolvers of unknown manufacture.

Bang Up: Trade name used on inexpensive pocket revolvers retailed by the Graham and Haines Co. of New York.

Bartlett Field: Trade name used on shotguns retailed by Hibbard, Spencer, Bartlett and Co. of Chicago.

Batavia: Trade name used on shotguns produced by the Baker Gun Co.

Batavia Leader: Trade name used on shotguns produced by the Baker Gun Co.

Bay State: Trade name used by the Harrington and Richardson Arms Co. on both inexpensive pocket revolvers and shotguns.

Belknap: Trade name used by the Belknap Hardware Co. of Louisville, Kentucky, on shotguns made by the Crescent Fire Arms Co., which they retailed.

Bellmore Gun Company: Trade name used by the H. & D. Folsom Arms Co. on shotguns made for them by the Crescent Fire Arms Co.

Berkshire: Trade name used by the H. & D. Folsom Arms Co. on shotguns made for the Shapleigh Hardware Co. of St. Louis, Missouri.

Bicycle: Trade name used on firearms made by the Harrington and Richardson Arms Co.

Big All Right: Trade name used on shotguns manufactured by the Wright Arms Co.

Big Bonanza: Trade name found on inexpensive pocket revolvers of unknown manufacture.

Bismarck: Trade name found on inexpensive pocket revolvers of unknown manufacture.

Black Beauty: Trade name used by the Sears, Roebuck and Co. on imported shotguns they retailed.

Black Diamond: Trade name found on Belgian made shotguns retailed by an unknown American wholesale house.

Black Diana: Trade name used by the Baker Gun Co. on shotguns.

Blackfield: Trade name used by the Hibbard, Spencer, Bartlett and Co. of Chicago on shotguns they retailed.

Blackhawk: Trade name found on inexpensive pocket revolvers of unknown manufacture.

Black Prince: Trade name used by the Hopkins and Allen Co. on inexpensive pocket revolvers.

Bliss: Trade name believed to have been used by the Norwich Arms Co.

Blood Hound: Trade name found on inexpensive pocket revolvers of unknown manufacture.

Bluefield: Trade name used by the W.H. Davenport Firearms Co. on shotguns.

Bluegrass: Trade name used by the Belknap Hardware Co. of Louisville, Kentucky, on shotguns they retailed.

Bluegrass Arms Company: Trade name of shotguns made by H. & D. Folsom Arms Co. for Belknap Hardware of Louisville, Kentucky.

Blue Jacket: Trade name used by the Hopkins and Allen Co. on inexpensive pocket revolvers they made for the Merwin, Hulbert and Co. of New York.

Blue Leader: Trade name found on inexpensive pocket revolvers of unknown manufacture.

Blue Whistler: Trade name used by the Hopkins and Allen Co. on inexpensive pocket revolvers they made for the Merwin, Hulbert and Co. of New York.

Bogardus Club Gun: Trade name found on Belgian made shotguns retailed by an unknown American wholesaler (possibly B. Kittredge and Co. of Cincinnati, Ohio).

Boltun: Trade name used by F. Arizmendi on semiautomatic pistols.

Bonanza: Trade name used by the Bacon Arms Co. on inexpensive pocket revolvers.

Boom: Trade name used by the Shattuck Arms Co. on inexpensive pocket revolvers.

Boone Gun Company: Trade name used by the Belknap Hardware Co. of Louisville, Kentucky, on firearms they retailed.

Boss:
a) Trade name used by E.H. and A.A. Buckland of Springfield, Massachusetts, on single-shot derringers designed by Holt & Marshall.
b) Trade name used on inexpensive pocket revolvers of unknown American manufacture.

Boys Choice: Trade name used by the Hood Firearms Co. on inexpensive pocket revolvers.

Bride Black Prince: Trade name used by H. & D. Folsom Arms Co. on shotguns.

Bridge Gun Company: Registered trade name of the Shapleigh Hardware Co., St. Louis, Missouri.

Bridgeport Arms Company: Trade name used by H. & D. Folsom Arms Co. on shotguns.

Bright Arms Company: Trade name used by H. & D. Folsom Arms Co.

British Bulldog: Trade name found on inexpensive pocket revolvers of unknown American and English manufacture.

Brownie:
a) Trade name used by the W.H. Davenport Firearms Co. on shotguns.
b) Trade name used by the O.F. Mossberg Firearms Co. on a four-shot pocket pistol.

Brutus: Trade name used by the Hood Firearms Co. on inexpensive pocket revolvers.

Buckeye: Trade name used by the Hopkins and Allen Co. on inexpensive pocket revolvers.

Buffalo: Trade name used by Gabilongo y Urresti on semiautomatic pistols.

Buffalo: Trade name found on bolt action rifles made in France.

Buffalo: Trade name used by the Western Arms Co. on an inexpensive pocket revolver.

Buffalo Bill: Trade name used by the Iver Johnson Arms and Cycle Works on an inexpensive pocket revolver.

Buffalo Stand: Trade name used by the Manufacture Francaise d'Armes et Cycles on target pistols.

Bull Dog: Trade name used by the Forehand and Wadsworth Co. on inexpensive pocket revolvers.

Bull Dozer:
a) Trade name used by the Norwich Pistol Co. on inexpensive pocket revolvers.
b) Trade name used by the Forehand and Wadsworth Co. on inexpensive pocket revolvers.
c) Trade name on Hammond Patent pistols made by the Connecticut Arms and Manufacturing Co.

Bull Frog: Trade name used by the Hopkins and Allen Co. on rifles.

Bulls Eye: Trade name used by the Norwich Falls Pistol Co. (O.A. Smith) on inexpensive pocket revolvers.

Burdick: Trade name used by the H. & D. Folsom Arms Co. on shotguns made for the Sears, Roebuck and Co. of Chicago.

Cadet: Trade name used by the Crescent Firearms Co. on rifles.

Canadian Belle: Trade name used by H. & D. Folsom Arms Co. on shotguns.

Cannon Breech: Trade name used by the Hopkins and Allen Co. on shotguns.

Captain: Trade name used by Manufacture d'Armes de Pyrenees on semiautomatic pistols.

Captain Jack: Trade name used by Hopkins & Allen on inexpensive pocket revolvers.

Carolina Arms Company: Trade name used by the H. & D. Folsom Arms Co. on shotguns produced for the Smith, Wadsworth Hardware Co. of Charlotte, North Carolina.

Caroline Arms: Trade name used by the H. & D. Folsom Arms Co.

Caruso: Trade name used by the Crescent Firearms Co. on shotguns made for the Hibbard, Spencer, Bartlett and Co. of Chicago.

Centennial 1876:
a) Trade name used by the Deringer Pistol Co. on inexpensive pocket revolvers.

b) Trade name used by the Hood Firearms Co. on inexpensive pocket revolvers.

Central Arms Company: Trade name used by the W. H. Davenport Firearms Co. on shotguns made for the Shapleigh Hardware Co. of St. Louis, Missouri.

Century Arms Company: Trade name used by the W. H. Davenport Firearms Co. on shotguns made for the Shapleigh Hardware Co. of St. Louis, Missouri.

Challenge:
a) Trade name found on inexpensive pocket revolvers of unknown manufacture.
b) Trade name used by the Sears, Roebuck and Co. of Chicago on shotguns made by Albert Aubrey of Meriden, Connecticut.

Challenge Ejector: Trade name used by the Sears, Roebuck and Co. of Chicago on shotguns made by Albert Aubrey of Meriden, Connecticut.

Champion:
a) Trade name used by H.C. Squires on shotguns.
b) Trade name used by J.P. Lovell on shotguns.
c) Trade name used by the Iver Johnson Arms and Cycle Works on shotguns and inexpensive pocket revolvers.
d) Trade name used by the Norwich Arms Co. on inexpensive pocket revolvers.

Chantecler: Trade name used by Manufacture d'Armes de Pyrenees on semiautomatic pistols.

Charles Richter Company: Trade name used by the H. & D. Folsom Arms Co. on firearms made for the New York Sporting Goods Co. of New York.

Chatham Arms Company: Trade name used by H. & D. Folsom Arms Co. used on shotguns.

Cherokee Arms Company: Trade name used by the H. & D. Folsom Arms Co. on shotguns made for C.M. McLung and Co. of Knoxville, Tennessee.

Chesapeake Gun Company: Trade name used by the H. & D. Folsom Arms Co. of New York.

Chicago: Trade name found on shotguns retailed by the Hibbard, Spencer, Bartlett and Co. of Chicago.

Chicago Ledger: Trade name used by the Chicago Firearms Co. on inexpensive pocket revolvers.

Chicago Long Range Wonder: Trade name used by the H. & D. Folsom Arms Co. on shotguns made for the Sears, Roebuck and Co. of Chicago.

Chichester: Trade name used by Hopkins & Allen on inexpensive pocket revolvers.

Chicopee Arms Company: Trade name used by the H. & D. Folsom Arms Co. of New York.

Chieftan: Trade name found on inexpensive pocket revolvers of unknown manufacture.

Christian Protector: Trade name found on inexpensive pocket revolvers of unknown manufacture.

Climax XL: Trade name used by Herman Boker and Co. of New York on revolvers, rifles and shotguns.

Club Gun: Trade name used by B. Kittredge and Co. of Cincinnati, Ohio, on shotguns they retailed.

Cock Robin: Trade name used by the Hood Firearms Co. on inexpensive pocket revolvers.

Colonial: Trade name used by Manufacture d'Armes de Pyrenees on semiautomatic pistols.

Colonial: Trade name used by H. & D. Folsom Co. on shotguns.

Columbian Automatic: Trade name used by Foehl & Weeks on inexpensive pocket revolvers.

Colton Arms Company: Trade name used by the Shapleigh Hardware Co. of St. Louis, Missouri, on imported shotguns they retailed.

Colton Firearms Company: Trade name used by the Sears, Roebuck and Co. of Chicago on shotguns they retailed.

Columbia:
a) Trade name found on inexpensive pocket revolvers of unknown manufacture.
b) Trade name used by H.C. Squires on shotguns.

Columbia Arms Company: Registered trade name of Henry Keidel, Baltimore, Maryland.

Columbian: Trade name found on inexpensive pocket revolvers of unknown manufacture.

Columbian Firearms Company:
a) Trade name used by the Maltby, Henly and Co. on inexpensive pocket revolvers.
b) Trade name used by the Crescent Firearms Co. on shotguns.

Combat: Trade name used by Randall Firearms Co. for its service model with a flat rib top and fixed sights.

Comet: Trade name used by the Prescott Pistol Co. on inexpensive pocket revolvers.

Commander: Trade name used by the Norwich Arms Co. on inexpensive pocket revolvers.

Commercial: Trade name used by the Norwich Falls Pistol Co. (O.A. Smith) on inexpensive pocket revolvers.

Compeer: Trade name used by the H. & D. Folsom Arms Co. on firearms made for the Van Camp Hardware and Iron Co. of Indianapolis, Indiana.

Competition: Trade name used by John Meunier of Milwaukee, Wisconsin, on rifles.

Conestoga Rifle Works: Trade name of Henry Leman, Philadelphia, Pennsylvania.

Connecticut Arms Company: Trade name used by H. & D. Folsom Arms Co. on shotguns.

Constable: Trade name used by Astra on semiautomatic pistols.

Constabulary: Trade name used by L. Ancion-Marx of Liege on revolvers.

Continental: Trade name used by the Great Western Gun Works of Pittsburgh, Pennsylvania, on firearms they retailed.

Continental Arms Company: Trade name used by the Marshall Wells Co. of Duluth, Minnesota, on firearms they retailed.

Cotton King: Trade name found on inexpensive pocket revolvers of unknown manufacture.

Cowboy: Trade name used by the Hibbard, Spencer, Bartlett and Co. of Chicago on imported, inexpensive pocket revolvers they retailed.

Cowboy Ranger: Trade name used by the Rohde Spencer Co. of Chicago on inexpensive pocket revolvers.

Crack Shot: Trade name used by the J. Stevens Arms and Tool Co. on rifles.

Cracker Jack: Trade name used by the J. Stevens Arms and Tool Co. on pistols.

Creedmoore:
a) Trade name used by the Hopkins and Allen

Co. on inexpensive pocket revolvers.
b) Trade name used by the Chicago Firearms Co. on inexpensive pocket revolvers.
c) Trade name used by William Wurflein on rifles.

Creedmoore Armory: Trade name used by A.D. McAusland of Omaha, Nebraska on rifles.

Creedmoore Arms Company: Trade name found on imported shotguns retailed by an unknown American wholesaler.

Crescent: Trade name used by the Crescent Arms Co. on inexpensive pocket revolvers.

Crescent International 1XL: Trade name used by Herman Boker and Co. of New York on shotguns.

Creve Coeur: Trade name used by the Isaac Walker Hardware Co. of Peoria, Illinois, on imported shotguns they retailed.

Crown: Trade name used by the Harrington and Richardson Arms Co. on inexpensive pocket revolvers.

Crown Jewel: Trade name used by the Norwich Arms Co. on inexpensive pocket revolvers.

Cruso: Trade name used by the H. & D. Folsom Arms Co. on shotguns made for Hibbard, Spencer, Bartlett and Co. of Chicago.

Cumberland Arms Company: Trade name used by the H. & D. Folsom Arms Co. on shotguns made for the Gray and Dudley Hardware Co. of Nashville, Tennessee.

Czar:
a) Trade name used by the Hopkins and Allen Co. on inexpensive pocket revolvers.
b) Trade name used by the Hood Firearms Co. on inexpensive pocket revolvers.

Daisy:
a) Trade name used by the Bacon Arms Co. on inexpensive pocket revolvers.
b) Registered proprietary trade name engraved on firearms made by the Winchester Repeating Arms Co. for the F. Lassetter and Co., Limited of Sydney, Australia.

Daniel Boone Gun Company: Trade name used by H. & D. Folsom Arms Co. on shotguns made for Belknap Hardware Co. of Louisville, Kentucky.

Daredevel: Trade name used by Lou J. Eppinger of Detroit, Michigan, on pistols.

Dash: Trade name found on inexpensive pocket revolvers of unknown manufacture.

Davis Guns: Trade names used successively by N.R. Davis, Davis Warner, and the Crescent-Davis Arms Co. on various firearms.

Dead Shot:
a) Trade name found on inexpensive pocket revolvers of unknown manufacture.
b) Trade name used by the Meriden Firearms Co. on rifles.

Deer Slayer: Trade name used by J. Henry and Son of Boulton, Pennsylvania on rifles.

Defender:
a) Trade name used by the Iver Johnson Arms and Cycle Works on inexpensive pocket revolvers.
b) Trade name used by the U.S. Small Arms Co. on knife pistols.

Defiance: Trade name used by the Norwich Arms Co. on inexpensive pocket revolvers.

Delphian Arms Company:
a) Trade name used by the Supplee-Biddle Hardware Co. of Philadelphia, Pennsylvania, on shotguns they retailed that were supplied by the H. & D. Folsom Co. of New York.
b) Trade name used by the H. & D. Folsom Arms Co. of New York on shotguns.

Delphian Manufacturing Company: Trade name used by the H. & D. Folsom Arms Co. of New York on shotguns.

Demon: Trade name used by Manufacture d'Armes de Pyrenees on semiautomatic pistols.

Demon Marine: As above.

Dexter: Trade name found on inexpensive pocket revolvers of unknown manufacture.

Diamond Arms Company: Trade name used by the Shapleigh Hardware Co. of St. Louis, Missouri, on imported shotguns they retailed.

Dictator: Trade name used by the Hopkins and Allen Co. on inexpensive pocket revolvers.

Dominion Pistol: Trade name found on inexpensive pocket revolvers of unknown manufacture.

Double Header: Trade name used by E.S. Renwick on Perry and Goddard Patent derringers.

Douglas Arms Company: Trade name used by the Hopkins and Allen Co. on shotguns.

Dreadnought: Trade name used by the Hopkins and Allen Co. on shotguns and inexpensive pocket revolvers.

Duchess: Trade name used by the Hopkins and Allen Co. on inexpensive pocket revolvers.

Duke: Trade name found on inexpensive pocket revolvers which may have been made by the Hopkins and Allen Co.

Dunlop Special: Trade name used by the Davis Warner Arms Co. on shotguns made for the Dunlop Hardware Co. of Macon, Georgia.

Duplex: Trade name used by the Osgood Gun Works of Norwich, Connecticut.

E.B.A.C.: Trade name used by Manufacture d'Armes de Pyrenees on semiautomatic pistols.

Eagle: Trade name used by the Iver Johnson Arms and Cycle Works on inexpensive pocket revolvers.

Eagle Arms Company: Trade name used by the Iver Johnson Arms and Cycle Works on inexpensive pocket revolvers.

Earlhood: Trade name used by E.L. Dickinson on inexpensive pocket revolvers.

Earnest Companion: Trade name found on inexpensive pocket revolvers of unknown manufacture.

Earthquake: Trade name used by E.L. Dickinson on inexpensive pocket revolvers.

Eastern Arms Company: Trade name used by the Sears, Roebuck and Co. of Chicago on both shotguns and inexpensive revolvers made by the Iver Johnson Arms and Cycle Works.

Eclipse:
a) Trade name found on single-shot derringers of unknown manufacture.
b) Trade name used by E.C. Meacham on imported shotguns.

Electric: Trade name found on inexpensive pocket revolvers of unknown manufacture.

Electric City Single Hammer: Trade name found on single-shot shotguns retailed by the Wyeth Hardware and Manufacturing Co. of St. Joseph, Missouri.

Elector: Trade name found on inexpensive pocket revolvers of unknown manufacture.

Elgin Arms Company: Trade name used by the H. & D. Folsom Arms Co. on shotguns made for the Strauss and Schram Co. of Chicago.

Elita: Trade name used by the W.H. Davenport Fire Arms Co. on shotguns.

Empire:
a) Trade name used by the Rupertus Patented Pistol Manufacturing Co. on inexpensive pocket revolvers.
b) Trade name used by the Crescent Firearms Co. on shotguns.

Empire Arms Company: Trade name used by the H. & D. Folsom Arms Co. on firearms made for the Sears, Roebuck and Co. of Chicago.

Enders Royal Shotgun: Trade name used by the Crescent Davis Firearms Co. on shotguns made for the Simmons Hardware Co. of St. Louis, Missouri.

Enders Special Service: Trade name used by the Crescent Davis Firearms Co. on shotguns made for the Simmons Hardware Co. of St. Louis, Missouri.

Enterprise: Trade name used by the Enterprise Gun Works on inexpensive pocket revolvers.

Essex Gun Works: Trade name used by the Crescent - Davis Firearms Co. on shotguns made for the Belknap Hardware Co. of Louisville, Kentucky.

Eureka: Trade name used by the Iver Johnson Arms and Cycle Works on inexpensive pocket revolvers.

Excel: Trade name used by both the H. & D. Folsom Arms Co. and the Iver Johnson Arms and Cycle Works on shotguns made for the Montgomery Ward and Co. of Chicago.

Excelsior:
a) Trade name found on inexpensive pocket revolvers of unknown manufacture.
b) Trade name used by the Iver Johnson Arms and Cycle Works on shotguns.

Expert:
a) Trade name found on single-shot derringers of unknown manufacture.
b) Trade name used by the W.J. Davenport Firearms Co. on shotguns made for the Witte Hardware Co. of St. Louis, Missouri.

Express: Trade name used by the Bacon Arms Co. on inexpensive pocket revolvers.

Express: Trade name used by Tomas de Urizar on a variety of semiautomatic pistols.

Farwell Arms Company: Trade name used by the Farwell, Ozmun, Kirk and Co. of St. Paul, Minnesota, on shotguns.

Fashion: Trade name found on inexpensive pocket revolvers of unknown manufacture.

Faultless: Trade name used by the H. & D. Folsom Arms Co. on shotguns made for the John M. Smythe Merchandise Co. of Chicago.

Faultless Goose Gun: Trade name used by the H. & D. Folsom Arms Co. on shotguns made for the John M. Smythe Merchandise Co. of Chicago.

Favorite:
a) Trade name used by the J. Stevens Arms and Tool Co. on rifles.
b) Trade name used by the Iver Johnson Arms and Cycle Works on inexpensive pocket revolvers.

Favorite Navy: Trade name used by the Iver Johnson Arms and Cycle Works on inexpensive pocket revolvers.

Featherlight: Trade name used by the Sears, Roebuck and Co. of Chicago on firearms they retailed.

Federal Arms Company: Trade name used by Meriden Firearms Co.

Folks Gun Works: Trade name of William and Samuel Folk of Bryan, Ohio on rifles and shotguns.

Frank Harrison Arms Company: Trade name used by the Sickles and Preston Co. of Davenport, Iowa, on firearms they retailed.

Freemont Arms Company: Trade name found on shotguns distributed by an unknown retailer.

Frontier: Trade name used by the Norwich Falls Pistol Co. (O.A. Smith) on inexpensive pocket revolvers made for the firm of Maltby, Curtis and Co. of New York.

Fulton: Trade name used by the Hunter Arms Co. on shotguns.

Fulton Arms Company: Trade name used by the W.H. Davenport Firearms Co. on shotguns.

Furor: Trade name used by Manufacture d'Armes de Pyrenees on semiautomatic pistols.

Gallia: Trade name used by Manufacture d'Armes de Pyrenees on semiautomatic pistols.

Game Getter: Registered trade mark of the Marble Arms and Manufacturing Co. on combination rifle-shotguns.

Gaulois: Trade name used by Manufacture d'Armes et Cycles on squeezer type pistols (see also Mitrailleuse).

Gem:
a) Trade name used by the J. Stevens Arms and Tool Co. on single-shot pocket pistols.
b) Trade name used by the Bacon Arms Co. on inexpensive pocket revolvers.

Gen Curtis E. LeMay: Trade name used for Randall Firearms Co. for its small compact pistol made from the General's own gun.

General: Trade name used by the Rupertus Patented Pistol Manufacturing Co. on inexpensive pocket revolvers.

General Butler: Trade name found on inexpensive pocket revolvers of unknown manufacture.

Gerrish: Trade name of G.W. Gerrish of Twin Falls, Idaho, used on shotguns.

Gibralter: Trade name of Albert Aubrey on shotguns made for the Sears, Roebuck and Co. of Chicago.

Gladiator: Trade name of Albert Aubrey on shotguns made for the Sears, Roebuck and Co. of Chicago.

Gold Field: Trade name found on inexpensive pocket revolvers of unknown manufacture.

Gold Hibbard: Trade name used by Hibbard, Spencer, Bartlett and Co. of Chicago on firearms they retailed.

Gold Medal Wonder: Trade name used by H. & D. Folsom Arms Co. on shotguns.

Governor: Trade name used by the Bacon Arms Co. on inexpensive pocket revolvers.

Guardian: Trade name used by the Bacon Arms Co. on inexpensive pocket revolvers.

Gut Buster: Trade name found on inexpensive pocket revolvers of unknown manufacture.

Gypsy: Trade name found on inexpensive pocket revolvers of unknown manufacture.

Half Breed: Trade name found on inexpensive pocket revolvers of unknown manufacture.

Hamilton Arms: Registered trade name of the Wiebusch and Hilger Co., New York.

Hammerless Auto Ejecting Revolver: Trade name of the Meriden Firearms Co. used on revolvers made for the Sears, Roebuck and Co. of New York.

Hanover Arms Co.: If no foreign proofmarks then trade name used by H. & D. Folsom Arms Co.

Hardpan: Trade name found on inexpensive American pocket revolver.

Hard Pan: Trade name used by Hood Arms Co. on inexpensive pocket revolvers.

Hart Arms Company: Trade name used by a Cleveland, Ohio, wholesaler (possibly the George Worthington Co.).

Hartford Arms Company: Trade name used by the H. & D. Folsom Arms on shotguns made for the Simmons Hardware Co. of St. Louis, Missouri.

Harvard: Trade name used by the H. & D. Folsom Arms Co. on shotguns made for the George Worthington Co. of Cleveland, Ohio.

Hercules: Trade name used by the Iver Johnson Arms and Cycle Works on shotguns made for the Montgomery Ward and Co. of Chicago.

Hermitage Arms Company: Trade name used by the H. & D. Folsom Arms Co. on shotguns made for the Gray and Dudley Hardware Co. of Nashville, Tennessee.

Hero:
a) Trade name used by the American Standard Tool Co. on percussion pistols.
b) Trade name used by the Manhattan Firearms Manufacturing Co. on percussion pistols.

Hexagon: Trade name used by the Sears, Roebuck and Co. of Chicago on shotguns they retailed.

Hinsdale: Trade name used by the Hopkins and Allen Co. on inexpensive pocket revolvers.

Hornet: Trade name used by the Prescott Pistol Co. on inexpensive pocket revolvers.

Howard Arms Company: Trade name used by the H. & D. Folsom Arms Co. on shotguns they distributed.

Hudson: Trade name used by the Hibbard, Spencer, Bartlett and Co. of Chicago on shotguns they retailed.

Hunter: Trade name used by the H. & D. Folsom Arms Co. on shotguns made for the Belknap Hardware Co. of Louisville, Kentucky.

Hunter, The: Trade name used by the Hunter Arms Co. on shotguns.

Hurricane: Trade name found on inexpensive pocket revolvers of unknown manufacture.

I.O.A.: Trade name used by the Brown, Camp Hardware Co. of Des Moines, Iowa on firearms they retailed.

I.X.L.:
a) Trade name used by B.J. Hart on percussion revolvers.
b) Trade name used by the W.H. Davenport Firearms Co. on shotguns made for the Witte Hardware Co. of St. Louis, Missouri.

Illinois Arms Company: Trade name used by the Rohde, Spencer Co. of Chicago on firearms they retailed.

Imperial: Trade name used by the Lee Arms Co. on inexpensive pocket revolvers.

Imperial Arms Company: Trade name used by the Hopkins and Allen Co. on inexpensive pocket revolvers.

Infallible: Trade name used by the Lancaster Arms Co. of Lancaster, Pennsylvania on shotguns they retailed.

Infallible Automatic Pistol: Trade name used by the Kirtland Brothers Co. of New York on inexpensive pistols they retailed.

International:
a) Trade name found on inexpensive pocket revolvers of unknown manufacture.

b) Trade name used by E.C. Meacham on shotguns.

Interstate Arms Company: Trade name used by the H. & D. Folsom Arms Co. on shotguns made for the Townley Metal and Hardware Co. of Kansas City, Missouri.

Invincible: Trade name used by the Iver Johnson Arms and Cycle Works on both shotguns and inexpensive pocket revolvers.

Ixor: Trade name used by Manufacture d'Armes de Pyrenees on semiautomatic pistols.

J.J. Weston: Trade name used by the H. & D. Folsom Arms Co. on shotguns.

J.S.T. & Company: Trade name used by the Iver Johnson Arms and Cycle Works on inexpensive pocket revolvers.

Jackson Arms Company: Trade name used by the H. & D. Folsom Arms Co. on shotguns made for C.M. McLung and Co. of Knoxville, Tennessee.

Jewel: Trade name used by the Hood Fire Arms Co. on inexpensive pocket revolvers.

John M. Smythe & Company: Trade name used by H. & D. Folsom Arms Co. for shotguns made for John M. Smythe Hardware Co. of Chicago.

John W. Price: Trade name used by the Belknap Hardware Co. of Louisville, Kentucky, on firearms they retailed.

Joker: Trade name used by the Marlin Firearms Co. on inexpensive pocket revolvers.

Joseph Arms Company (Norwich, Connecticut): Trade name used by H. & D. Folsom Arms Co.

Judge: Trade name found on inexpensive pocket revolvers of unknown manufacture.

Jupitor: Trade name used by Fabrique d'Armes de Grand Precision, Eibar, Spain, on semiautomatic pistols.

K.K.: Trade name used by the Hopkins and Allen Co. on shotguns made for the Shapleigh Hardware Co. of St. Louis, Missouri.

Keno: Trade name found on inexpensive pocket revolvers of unknown manufacture.

Kentucky: Trade name used by the Iver Johnson Arms and Cycle Works on inexpensive pocket revolvers.

Keystone Arms Company: Trade name used by the W.H. Davenport Firearms Co. on shotguns made for the E.K. Tryon Co. of Philadelphia, Pennsylvania.

Kill Buck: Trade name of the Enterprise Gun Works (James Bown), Pittsburgh, Pennsylvania.

Killdeer: Trade name used by the Sears, Roebuck and Co. of Chicago on firearms bearing their trade name Western Arms Co.

King Nitro: Trade name used by the W.H. Davenport Firearms Co. on shotguns made for the Shapleigh Hardware Co. of St. Louis, Missouri.

King Pin: Trade name found on inexpensive single-shot and revolving pocket pistols.

Kingsland Gun Company: Trade name used by the H. & D. Folsom Arms Co. on shotguns made for the Geller, Ward and Hasner Co. of St. Louis, Missouri.

Kirk Gun Company: Trade name used by Farwell, Ozmun, and Kirk Co. of St. Paul, Minnesota.

Knickerbocker: Trade name used by the Crescent-Davis Firearms Co. on shotguns.

Knickerbocker Club Gun: Trade name used by Charles Godfrey of New York on imported shotguns he retailed.

Knockabout: Trade name used by the Montgomery Ward and Co. of Chicago on shotguns they retailed.

Knox-All: Trade name used by the Iver Johnson Arms and Cycle Works on firearms they made for the H. & D. Folsom Arms Co. of New York.

L'Agent: Trade name used by Manufacture Francaises d'Armes et Cycles on revolvers.

Lakeside: Trade name used by the H. & D. Folsom Arms Co. on firearms they made for the Montgomery Ward and Co. of Chicago.

Le Colonial: Trade name used by Manufacture Francaises d'Armes et Cycles on revolvers.

Le Colonial: As above.

Le Francais: Trade name used by Manufacture Francaises d'Armes et Cycles on semiautomatic pistols.

Le Francais: As above on semiautomatic pistols.

Le Petit Forminable: Trade name used by Manufacture Francaises d'Armes et Cycles on revolvers.

Le Petit Forminable: As above on revolvers.

Le Protecteur: Trade name used by J.E. Turbiaux of Paris on squeezer pistols of the type later made by the Ames Sword Co.

Le Terrible: Trade name used by Manufacture Francaises d'Armes et Cycles on revolvers.

Leader:
a) Trade name used by the Shattuck Arms Co. on inexpensive pocket revolvers.
b) Trade name used by the Harrington and Richardson Arms Co. on inexpensive pocket revolvers.

Leader Gun Company: Trade name used by the H. & D. Folsom Arms Co. on shotguns they made for the Charles Williams Stores, Inc. of New York.

Lee's Hummer: Trade name used by the H. & D. Folsom Arms Co. on firearms they made for the Lee Hardware Co. of Salina, Kansas.

Lee's Special: Trade name used by the H. & D. Folsom Arms Co. on firearms they made for the Lee Hardware Co. of Salina, Kansas.

Liberty: Trade name used by the Norwich Falls Pistol Co. (O.A. Smith) on inexpensive pocket revolvers.

Liege Gun Company: Trade name used by the Hibbard, Spencer, Bartlett and Co. of Chicago on imported shotguns they retailed.

Lion: Trade name used by the Iver Johnson Arms and Cycle Works on inexpensive pocket revolvers.

Little Giant: Trade name used by the Bacon Arms Co. on inexpensive pocket revolvers.

Little John: Trade name used by the Hood Firearms Co. on inexpensive pocket revolvers.

Little Joker: Trade name found on inexpensive pocket revolvers of unknown manufacture.

Little Pal: Registered trade name for knife pistols made by L.E. Pulhemus.

Little Pet: Trade name used by the Sears, Roebuck and Co. of Chicago on inexpensive pocket revolvers they retailed.

London Revolver: Trade name found on inexpensive pocket revolvers of unknown manufacture.

Lone Star: Trade name found on inexpensive pocket revolvers of unknown manufacture.

Long Range Winner: Trade name used by the Sears, Roebuck and Co. of Chicago on shotguns they retailed.

Long Range Wonder: Trade name used by the Sears, Roebuck and Co. of Chicago on shotguns they retailed.

Long Tom: Trade name used by the Sears, Roebuck and Co. of Chicago on shotguns they retailed.

Looking Glass: Trade name used on semiautomatic pistols of unknown Spanish manufacture.

Marquis of Horne: Trade name used by Hood Arms Co. on inexpensive pocket revolvers.

Mars: Trade name used by Manufacture d'Armes de Pyrenees on semiautomatic pistols.

Marshwood: Trade name used by the H. & D. Folsom Arms Co. on shotguns they made for the Charles Williams Stores Inc. of New York.

Marvel: Trade name used by the J. Stevens Arms and Tool Co. on various firearms.

Massachusetts Arms Company: Trade name used by both the J. Stevens Arms and Tool Co. and the H. & D. Folsom Arms Co. on firearms made for the Blish, Mizet and Silliman Hardware Co. of Atchinson, Kansas.

Maximum: Trade name found on inexpensive pocket revolvers of unknown manufacture.

Metropolitan: Trade name used by the H. & D. Folsom Arms Co. on firearms they made for the Siegal-Cooper Co. of New York.

Metropolitan Police:
a) Trade name used by the Maltby, Curtiss and Co. on inexpensive pocket revolvers.
b) Trade name used by the Rohde-Spencer Co. of Chicago on inexpensive pocket revolvers.

Midget Hammerless: Trade name used by the Rohde-Spencer Co. of Chicago on inexpensive pocket revolvers.

Mikros: Trade name used by Manufacture d'Armes de Pyrenees on semiautomatic pistols.

Minnesota Arms Company: Trade name used by the H. & D. Folsom Arms Co. on shotguns they made for the Farwell, Ozmun, Kirk and Co. of St. Paul, Minnesota.

Missaubi Arms Company: Trade name used by the Hunter Arms Co., possibly for the Farwell, Ozmun, Kirk and Co. of St. Paul, Minnesota.

Mississippi Arms Company: Trade name used by the H. & D. Folsom Arms Co. on firearms made for the Shapleigh Hardware Co. of St. Louis, Missouri.

Mississippi Valley Arms Company: Trade name used by the H. & D. Folsom Arms Co. on firearms made for the Shapleigh Hardware Co. of St. Louis, Missouri.

Mitrailleuse: Alternate trade name of the Gauluis squeezer pistol.

Mohawk: Trade name used by the H. & D. Folsom Arms Co. on firearms made for the Blish, Mizet and Silliman Hardware Co. of Atchinson, Kansas.

Mohegan: Trade name used by the Hood Firearms Co. on inexpensive pocket revolvers.

Monarch:
a) Trade name used by the Hopkins and Allen Co. on inexpensive pocket revolvers.
b) Trade name used by the Osgood Gun Works on Duplex revolvers.

Monitor:
a) Trade name used by the Whitneyville Armory on inexpensive pocket revolvers.
b) Trade name used by the H. & D. Folsom Arms Co. on firearms made for the Paxton and Gallagher Co. of Omaha, Nebraska.

Montgomery Arms Company: Trade name used by the H. & D. Folsom Arms Co. on a variety of firearms.

Mountain Eagle: Trade name used by the Hopkins and Allen Co. on inexpensive pocket revolvers.

Mount Vernon Arms Company: Trade name used by the H. & D. Folsom Arms Co. on firearms made for the Carlin, Hullfish Co. of Alexandria, Virginia.

My Companion: Trade name found on inexpensive pocket revolvers of unknown manufacture.

My Friend: Trade name used by James Reid of New York.

N.R. Adams: Trade name used by the N.R. Davis and Co. on shotguns.

Napoleon: Trade name used by the Thomas J. Ryan Pistol Manufacturing Co. of Norwich, Connecticut, on inexpensive pocket revolvers.

National Arms Company: Trade name used by the H. & D. Folsom Arms Co. on firearms made both for the May Hardware Co. of Washington, D.C., and the Moskowitz and Herbach Co. of Philadelphia, Pennsylvania.

Nevermiss: Trade name used by the Marlin Firearms Co. on single-shot pocket pistols.

New Aubrey: Trade name used by Albert Aubrey of Meriden, Connecticut, on both revolvers and shotguns made for the Sears, Roebuck and Co. of Chicago.

New Britain Arms Company: Trade name used by H. & D. Folsom Arms Co.

New Defender: Trade name used by Harrington & Richardson on revolvers.

New Elgin Arms Company: Trade name used by H. & D. Folsom Arms Co.

New Empire: Trade name used by H. & D. Folsom Arms Co.

New England Arms Company: Trade name believed to have been used by Charles Godfrey on shotguns made for the Rohde-Spencer Co. of Chicago.

New Era Gun Works: Trade name used by the Baker Gun Co. on firearms made for an unknown retailer.

New Haven Arms Company: Trade name found on Belgian shotguns imported by either E.K. Tryon of Philadelphia or the Great Western Gun Works of Pittsburgh, Pennsylvania.

New Liberty: Trade name used by the Sears, Roebuck and Co. of Chicago on inexpensive pocket revolvers they retailed.

New Rival: Trade name used by the H. & D. Folsom Arms Co. on firearms made for the Van Camp Hardware and Iron Co. of Indianapolis, Indiana.

New Worcester: Trade name used by the Torkalson Manufacturing Co. of Worcester, Massachusetts.

New York Arms Company: Trade name used by the H. & D. Folsom Arms Co. on firearms made for the Garnet Carter Co. of Chattanooga, Tennessee.

New York Gun Company: Trade name used by the H. & D. Folsom Arms Co. on firearms made for the Garnet Carter Co. of Chattanooga, Tennessee.

New York Club: Trade name used by the H. & D. Folsom Arms Co. on rifles.

New York Machine Made: Trade name used by the H. & D. Folsom Arms Co.

New York Pistol Company: Trade name used by the Norwich Falls Pistol Co. (O.A. Smith) on inexpensive pocket revolvers.

Newport:
a) Trade name found on inexpensive pocket revolvers of unknown manufacture.
b) Trade name used by the H. & D. Folsom Arms Co. on shotguns made for Hibbard, Spencer, Bartlett and Co. of Chicago.

Nightingale: Trade name found on inexpensive pocket revolvers of unknown manufacture.

Nitro Bird: Trade name used by the Richards and Conover Hardware Co. of Kansas City, Missouri.

Nitro Hunter: Trade name used by the H. & D. Folsom Arms Co. on shotguns made for the Belknap Hardware Co. of Louisville, Kentucky.

Nitro King: Trade name used by the Sears, Roebuck and Co. of Chicago on shotguns of unknown manufacture.

Nitro Special: Trade name used by the J. Stevens Arms and Tool Co. on shotguns.

Northfield Knife Company: Trade name used by the Rome Revolver and Novelty Works of Rome, New York, on inexpensive pocket revolvers.

Norwich Arms Company:
a) Trade name used by the Hood Firearms Co. on inexpensive pocket revolvers.
b) Trade name found on shotguns retailed by the Marshall, Wells Co. of Duluth, Minnesota, and Winnipeg, Manitoba, Canada.

Norwich Falls Pistol Company: Trade name used by the O.A. Smith Co. on inexpensive pocket revolvers made for Maltby, Curtis and Co. of New York.

Norwich Lock Manufacturing Company: Trade name used by F.W. Hood Firearms Co. on inexpensive pocket revolvers.

Not-Nac Manufacturing Company: Trade name used by the H. & D. Folsom Arms Co. on firearms made for the Canton Hardware Co. of Canton, Ohio.

Novelty: Trade name used by D.F. Mossberg & Sons on Shattuck Unique pistols.

OK:
a) Trade name used by the Marlin Firearms Co. on single-shot pocket pistols.
b) Trade name used by Cowles and Son of Chicopee Falls, Massachusetts, on single-shot pocket pistols.
c) Trade name found on inexpensive pocket revolvers of unknown manufacture.

Old Hickory:
a) Trade name found on inexpensive pocket revolvers of unknown manufacture.
b) Trade name used by the Hibbard, Spencer, Bartlett and Co. of Chicago on shotguns they retailed.

Old Reliable: Trade name used by the Sharps Rifle Co.

Olympic:
a) Trade name used by the J. Stevens Arms and Tool Co. on rifles and pistols.
b) Trade name used by the Morley and Murphy Hardware Co. of Green Bay, Wisconsin, on firearms they retailed (possibly made by the J. Stevens Arms and Tool Co.).

Osprey: Trade name used by Lou J. Eppinger of Detroit, Michigan, on firearms he made.

Our Jake: Trade name used by E.L. and J. Dickinson of Springfield, Massachusetts, on inexpensive pocket revolvers.

Oxford Arms Company: Trade name used by the H. & D. Folsom Arms Co. on firearms made for the Belknap Hardware Co. of Louisville, Kentucky.

Pagoma: Trade name used by the H. & D. Folsom Arms Co. on firearms made for the Paxton and Gallagher Co. of Omaha, Nebraska.

Peoria Chief: Trade name found on inexpensive pocket revolvers.

Perfect: Trade name used by the Foehl and Weeks Firearms Manufacturing Co. of Philadelphia, Pennsylvania, on inexpensive pocket revolvers.

Perfect: Trade name used by Manufacture d'Armes de Pyrenees on semiautomatic pistols.

Perfection:
a) Trade name used by the H. & D. Folsom Arms Co. on firearms made for the H.G. Lipscomb and Co. of Nashville, Tennessee.
b) Trade name used by the John M. Smythe Merchandise Co. of Chicago on firearms they retailed.

Pet: Trade name found on inexpensive pocket revolvers of unknown manufacture.

Petrel: Trade name found on inexpensive pocket revolvers of unknown manufacture.

Phenix: Trade name used by J. Reid of New York on revolvers.

Phoenix:
a) Trade name used by J. Reid of New York on revolvers.
b) Trade name used by the Whitneyville Armory on percussion revolvers.

Piedmont: Trade name used by the H. & D. Folsom Arms Co. on firearms made for the Piedmont Hardware Co. of Danville, Pennsylvania.

Pinafore: Trade name used by the Norwich Falls Pistol Co. (O.A. Smith) on inexpensive pocket revolvers.

Pioneer: Trade name found on inexpensive pocket revolvers of unknown manufacture.

Pioneer Arms Company: Trade name used by the H. & D. Folsom Arms Co. on firearms made for the Kruse and Baklmann Hardware Co. of Cincinnati, Ohio.

Pittsfield: Trade name used by the Hibbard, Spencer, Bartlett and Co. of Chicago on firearms probably made by the H. & D. Folsom Arms Co.

Plug Ugly: Trade name found on inexpensive pocket revolvers of unknown manufacture.

Plymouth: Trade name used by Spear and Co. of Pittsburgh, Pennsylvania, on firearms they retailed.

Pocahontas: Trade name found on inexpensive pocket revolvers of unknown manufacture.

Pointer: Trade name found on single-shot pocket pistols of unknown manufacture.

Prairie Fire: Trade name found on inexpensive pocket revolvers of unknown manufacture.

Prairie King:
a) Trade name used by the Bacon Arms Co. on inexpensive pocket revolvers.
b) Trade name used by the H. & D. Folsom Arms Co. on inexpensive pocket revolvers.

Premier:
a) Trade name used by the Thomas E. Ryan Co. on inexpensive pocket revolvers.
b) Trade name used by the Harrington and Richardson Arms Co. on revolvers.
c) Trade name used by the Montgomery Ward and Co. of Chicago on firearms they retailed.
d) Registered trade name of Edward K. Tryon and Co. of Philadelphia, Pennsylvania.

Premium: Trade name used by the Iver Johnson Arms and Cycle Works on inexpensive pocket revolvers.

Princess: Trade name found on inexpensive pocket revolvers of unknown American manufacture.

Progress: Trade name used by Charles J. Godfrey of New York on shotguns.

Protection: Trade name used by the Whitneyville Armory on revolvers.

Protector:
a) Trade name found on inexpensive pocket revolvers of unknown manufacture.
b) Trade name used by the Chicago Firearms Co. on inexpensive pocket revolvers.

Protector Arms Company: Trade name used by the Rupertus Patented Pistol Manufacturing Co. on inexpensive pocket revolvers.

Providence: Trade name found on inexpensive pocket revolvers of unknown manufacture.

Puppy: Trade name found on inexpensive pocket revolvers made by several European makers.

Quail: Trade name used by the Crescent-Davis Arms Co. on shotguns.

Queen:
a) Trade name used by the Hood Firearms Co. on inexpensive pocket revolvers.
b) Trade name used by the Hyde and Shattuck Co. on inexpensive single-shot pocket pistols.

Queen City: Trade name used by the H. & D. Folsom Arms Co. on firearms made for the Elmira Arms Co. of Elmira, New York.

Raider: Randall Firearms Co. Commander size pistol named after Gen Randall's flight squadron; "Randall's Raiders".

Ranger:
a) Trade name found on inexpensive pocket revolvers of unknown manufacture.
b) Trade name used by the Eastern Arms Co. on various firearms made for the Sears, Roebuck and Co. of Chicago.
c) Trade name of the Sears, Roebuck and Co. of Chicago on a wide variety of firearms marketed by that firm.

Rapid-Maxim: Trade name used by Manufacture d'Armes de Pyrenees on semiautomatic pistols.

Reassurance: Trade name found on inexpensive pocket revolvers of unknown manufacture.

Red Chieftan: Trade name used by the Supplee Biddle Hardware Co. of Philadelphia, Pennsylvania, on inexpensive pocket pistols they retailed.

Red Cloud: Trade name used by the Ryan Pistol Manufacturing Co. on inexpensive pocket revolvers.

Red Hot: Trade name found on inexpensive pocket revolvers of unknown manufacture.

Red Jacket:
a) Trade name used by the Lee Arms Co. on inexpensive pocket revolvers.
b) Trade name used by the Hopkins and Allen Co. on inexpensive pocket revolvers.

Reliable: Trade name found on inexpensive pocket revolvers of unknown manufacture.

Reliance: Trade name used by John Meunier of Milwaukee, Wisconsin, on rifles.

Rev-O-Noc: Trade name used by the H. & D. Folsom Arms Co. on firearms made for the Hibbard, Spencer, Bartlett and Co. of Chicago.

Rich-Con: Trade name used by the H. & D. Folsom Arms Co. for shotguns made for Richardson & Conover Hardware Co.

Richmond Arms Company: Trade name used by the H. & D. Folsom Arms Co. on firearms made for an unknown retailer.

Rickard Arms Company: Trade name used by the H. & D. Folsom Arms Co. on firearms made for the J.A. Rickard Co. of Schenectady, New York.

Rip Rap: Trade name used by the Bacon Arms Co. on inexpensive pocket revolvers.

Rival: Trade name used by the H. & D. Folsom Arms Co. on firearms made for the Van Camp Hardware and Iron Co. of Indianapolis, Indiana.

Riverside Arms Company: Trade name used by the J. Stevens Arms and Tool Co. on various types of firearms.

Robin Hood: Trade name used by the Hood Firearms Co. on inexpensive pocket revolvers.

Rocky Hill: Trade name found on inexpensive cast iron percussion pocket pistols made in Rocky Hill, Connecticut.

Rodgers Arms Company: Trade name used by the Hood Firearms Co. on firearms made for an unknown retailer.

Royal Gun Company: Trade name used by the Three Barrel Gun Co.

Royal Service: Trade name used by the Shapleigh Hardware Co. of St. Louis, Missouri, on firearms they retailed.

Rummel Arms Company: Trade name used by the H. & D. Folsom Arms Co. on firearms made for the A.J. Rummel Arms Co. of Toledo, Ohio.

Russel Arms Company: Registered trade name of the Wiebusch and Hilger Co. of New York.

Russian Model: Trade name used by the Forehand and Wadsworth Co. on inexpensive pocket revolvers.

S. Holt Arms Company: Trade name used by the Sears, Roebuck and Co. of Chicago on shotguns they retailed.

S.A.: Trade mark of the Societe d'Armes Francaises.

S.H. Harrington: If no foreign proofmarks then trade name used by H. & D. Folsom Arms Co.

Safe Guard: Trade name found on inexpensive pocket revolvers of unknown manufacture.

Safety Police: Trade name used by the Hopkins and Allen Co. on inexpensive pocket revolvers.

Scott: Trade name used by the Hopkins and Allen Co. on inexpensive pocket revolvers.

Secret Service Special: Trade name used by the Rohde-Spencer Co. of Chicago on inexpensive pocket revolvers.

Selecta: Trade name used by Manufacture d'Armes de Pyrenees on semiautomatic pistols.

Senator: Trade name found on inexpensive pocket revolvers of unknown manufacture.

Sentinal: Trade name found on inexpensive pocket revolvers of unknown manufacture.

Service Model C: The predecessor to the "Raider" pistol.

Sheffield, The: Trade name used by the A. Baldwin and Co., Limited of New Orleans, Louisiana, on shotguns they retailed.

Sickels-Arms Company: Trade name used by the Sickels and Preston Co. of Davenport, Iowa, on firearms they retailed.

Simson: Trade name used by the Iver Johnson Arms and Cycle Works on firearms made for the Iver Johnson Sporting Goods Co. of Boston, Massachusetts.

Sitting Bull: Trade name found on inexpensive pocket revolvers of unknown manufacture.

Skue's Special: Trade name used by Ira M. Skue of Hanover, Pennsylvania, on shotguns.

Smoker: Trade name used by the Iver Johnson Arms and Cycle Works on inexpensive pocket revolvers.

Southern Arms Company: Trade name used by the H. & D. Folsom Arms Co. on firearms made for an unknown retailer.

Southerner:
a) Trade name used by the Brown Manufacturing Co. and the Merrimac Arms Manufacturing Co. on single-shot pocket pistols.
b) Registered trade name of Asa Farr of New York on pistols.

Southron: Trade name found on inexpensive pocket pistols of unknown manufacture.

Special Service: Trade name used by the Shapleigh Hardware Co. of St. Louis, Missouri, on inexpensive pocket revolvers.

Spencer Gun Company: Trade name used by the H. & D. Folsom Arms Co.

Splendor: Trade name found on inexpensive pocket revolvers of unknown manufacture.

Sportsman, The: Trade name used by the H. & D. Folsom Arms Co. on firearms made for the W. Bingham Co. of Cleveland, Ohio.

Springfield Arms Company: Trade name used by the J. Stevens Arms and Tool Co.

Spy: Trade name found on inexpensive pocket revolvers of unknown manufacture.

Square Deal: Trade name used by the H. & D. Folsom Arms Co. on firearms made for the Stratton, Warren Hardware Co. of Memphis, Tennessee.

St. Louis Arms Company: Trade name used by the H. & D. Folsom Arms Co. on firearms made for the Shapleigh Hardware Co. of St. Louis, Missouri.

Standard: Trade name used by the Marlin Firearms Co. on revolvers.

Stanley Arms: Registered trade name of the Wiebusch and Hilger Co. of New York on firearms they retailed.

Stanley Double Gun: Trade name used by the H. & D. Folsom Arms Co. on shotguns they retailed.

Star:
a) Trade name found on inexpensive single-shot pocket pistols of unknown manufacture.
b) Trade name used by the Prescott Pistol Co. on inexpensive pocket revolvers.
c) Trade name used by Johnson & Bye on single-shot cartridge derringers.

State Arms Company: Trade name used by the H. & D. Folsom Arms Co. on firearms made for the J.H. Lau and Co. of New York.

Sterling:
a) Trade name used by E.L. and J. Dickinson of Springfield, Massachusetts, on single-shot pistols.
b) Trade name used by the H. & D. Folsom Arms Co. on shotguns they retailed.

Stinger: Registered proprietary trade name engraved on firearms made by the Winchester Repeating Arms Co. for the Perry Brothers Limited of Brisbane, Australia.

Stonewall:
a) Trade name used by the Marlin Firearms Co. on single-shot derringers.
b) Trade name used by T.F. Guion of Lycoming, Pennsylvania, on single-shot percussion pistols he retailed.

Striker: Trade name found on inexpensive pocket revolvers of unknown manufacture.

Sullivan Arms Company: Trade name used by the H. & D. Folsom Arms Co. on firearms made for the Sullivan Hardware Co. of Anderson, South Carolina.

Superior: Trade name of the Paxton and Gallagher Co. of Omaha, Nebraska, on revolvers and shotguns.

Super Range: Trade name of the Sears, Roebuck and Co. of Chicago on shotguns.

Sure Fire: Trade name found on inexpensive pocket revolvers of unknown manufacture.

Swamp Angel: Trade name used by the Forehand and Wadsworth Co. on inexpensive pocket revolvers.

Swift: Trade name used by the Iver Johnson Arms and Cycle Works on firearms made for the John P. Lovell & Sons, Boston, Massachusetts.

Syco: Trade name used by the Wyeth Hardware Co. of St. Joseph, Missouri, on firearms they retailed.

Sympathique: Trade name used by Manufacture d'Armes de Pyrenees on semiautomatic pistols.

T. Barker: Trade name used by the H. & D. Folsom Arms Co. of New York on shotguns they retailed.

Ten Star: Trade name used by the H. & D. Folsom Arms Co. on firearms made for the Geller, Ward and Hasner Co. of St. Louis, Missouri.

Terrier: Trade name used by the Rupertus Patented Pistol Manufacturing Co. on inexpensive pocket revolvers.

Terror: Trade name used by the Forehand and Wadsworth Co. on inexpensive pocket revolvers.

Texas Ranger: Trade name used by the Montgomery Ward and Co. of Chicago on inexpensive pocket revolvers they retailed.

Thames Arms Company: Trade name used by the Harrington and Richardson Arms Co. on firearms they made for an unknown wholesaler.

Tiger:
a) Trade name used by the Iver Johnson Arms and Cycle Works on inexpensive pocket revolvers.
b) Trade name used by the J.H. Hall and Co. of Nashville, Tennessee, on shotguns they retailed.

Tobin Simplex: Trade name used on shotguns of unknown manufacture that were retailed by the G.B. Crandall Co., Limited of Woodstock, Ontario, Canada.

Toledo Firearms Company:
a) Trade name used by the Hopkins and Allen Co. on inexpensive pocket revolvers.
b) Trade name used by E.L. and J. Dickinson on inexpensive pocket revolvers.

Toronto Belle: Trade name found on inexpensive pocket revolvers of unknown manufacture.

Touriste: Trade name used by Manufacture d'Armes de Pyrenees on semiautomatic pistols.

Tower's Police Safety: Trade name used by Hopkins & Allen on inexpensive pocket revolvers.

Townley's Pal and Townley's American Boy: Trade name used by H. & D. Folsom Arms Co. for shotguns made for Townley Metal and Hardware Co. of Kansas City, Missouri.

Tramps Terror: Trade name used by the Forehand and Wadsworth Co. on inexpensive pocket revolvers.

Traps Best: Trade name believed to have been used by the H. & D. Folsom Arms Co. on firearms made for the Watkins, Cottrell Co. of Richmond, Virginia.

Triumph: Trade name used by the H. & D. Folsom Arms Co. on shotguns.

Trojan: Trade name found on inexpensive pocket revolvers of unknown manufacture.

True Blue: Trade name found on inexpensive pocket revolvers of unknown manufacture.

Tryon Special: Trade name used by the Edward K. Tryon Co. of Philadelphia, Pennsylvania, on shotguns they retailed.

Tycoon: Trade name used by the Iver Johnson Arms and Cycle Works on inexpensive pocket revolvers.

U.S. Arms Company: Trade name used successively by the Alexander Waller and Co. (1877), the Barton and Co. (1878) and the H. & D. Folsom Arms Co. (1879 forward) on a variety of firearms.

U.S. Revolver: Trade name used by the Iver Johnson Arms and Cycle Works on inexpensive pocket revolvers.

U.S. Single Gun: Trade name used by the Iver Johnson Arms and Cycle Works on single barrel shotguns.

Uncle Sam: Trade name used by Johnson & Bye on percussion pocket pistols.

Union:
a) Trade name found on inexpensive single-shot pocket pistols of unknown manufacture.
b) Trade name used by the Hood Firearms Co. on inexpensive pocket revolvers.
c) Trade name used by the Prescott Pistol Co. on inexpensive pocket revolvers.

Union Arms Company: Trade name used by the H. & D. Folsom Arms Co. on firearms made for the Bostwick, Braun Co. of Toledo, Ohio.

Union Jack: Trade name found on inexpensive pocket revolvers of unknown manufacture.

Union N.Y.: Trade name used by the Whitneyville Armory on inexpensive pocket revolvers.

Unique: Trade name used by the C.S. Shattuck Arms Co. on revolvers and four barrel pocket pistols.

United States Arms Company: Trade name used by Norwich Falls Pistol Co. (O.A. Smith) on inexpensive pocket revolvers.

Universal: Trade name used by the Hopkins and Allen Co. on inexpensive pocket revolvers.

Utica Firearms Company: Trade name used by the Simmons Hardware Co. of St. Louis, Missouri, on firearms they retailed.

Valient: Trade name used by the Spear and Co. of Pittsburgh, Pennsylvania, on firearms they retailed.

Veiled Prophet: Trade name used by the T.E. Ryan Pistol Manufacturing Co. on inexpensive pocket revolvers.

Venus: Trade name used by the American Novelty Co. of Chicago on inexpensive pocket revolvers.

Veteran: Trade name found on inexpensive pocket revolvers of unknown manufacture.

Veto: Trade name found on inexpensive pocket revolvers of unknown manufacture.

Victor:
a) Trade name used by the Marlin Firearms Co. on single-shot pocket pistols.
b) Trade name used by the Harrington and Richardson Arms Co. on inexpensive pocket revolvers.
c) Trade name used by the H. & D. Folsom Arms Co. on inexpensive pocket pistols and revolvers.

Victor Arms Company: Trade name used by the H. & D. Folsom Arms Co. on firearms made for the Hibbard, Spencer, Bartlett and Co. of Chicago.

Victor Special: Trade name used by the H. & D. Folsom Arms Co. on firearms made for the Hibbard, Spencer, Bartlett and Co. of Chicago.

Victoria: Trade name used by the Hood Firearms Co. on inexpensive pocket revolvers.

Vindix: Trade name used by Manufacture d'Armes de Pyrenees on semiautomatic pistols.

Viper: Trade name used on inexpensive pocket revolvers of unknown American manufacture.

Virginia Arms Company: Trade name used by the H. & D. Folsom Arms Co. and later the Davis-Warner Arms Co. on firearms made for the Virginia-Carolina Co. of Richmond, Virginia.

Volunteer: Trade name used by the H. & D. Folsom Arms Co. on inexpensive pocket revolvers made for the Belknap Hardware Co. of Louisville, Kentucky.

Vulcan: Trade name used by the H. & D. Folsom Arms Co. on firearms made for the Edward K. Tryon Co. of Philadelphia, Pennsylvania.

Walnut Hill: Trade name used by the J. Stevens Arms and Tool Co. on rifles.

Warner Arms Corporation: Trade name used by the H. & D. Folsom Arms Co. on firearms made for the Kirtland Brothers, Inc. of New York.

Wasp: Trade name found on inexpensive pocket revolvers of unknown manufacture.

Wautauga: Trade name used by the Whitaker, Holtsinger Hardware Co. of Morristown, Tennessee on firearms they retailed.

Western: Trade name used by the H. & D. Folsom Arms Co. on firearms made for the Paxton and Gallagher Co. of Omaha, Nebraska.

Western Arms Company:
a) Trade name used by the Bacon Arms on various types of firearms.
b) Trade name used by W.W. Marston on revolvers.
c) Trade name used by Henry Kolb and later R.F. Sedgly of Philadelphia, Pennsylvania, on Baby Hammerless revolvers.
d) Trade name used by the Ithaca Gun Co. on shotguns believed to have been made for the Montgomery Ward and Co. of Chicago.

Western Field: Trade name used by Montgomery Ward and Co. of Chicago on shotguns of various makes that they retailed.

Western Field: Trade name used by Manufacture d'Armes de Pyrenees on revolvers.

Whippet: Trade name used by the H. & D. Folsom Arms Co. on firearms made for the Hibbard, Spencer, Bartlett and Co. of Chicago.

Whistler: Trade name used by the Hood Firearms Co. on inexpensive pocket revolvers.

White Powder Wonder: Trade name used by Albert Aubrey of Meriden, Connecticut on shotguns made for the Sears, Roebuck and Co. of Chicago.

Wildwood: Trade name used by the H. & D. Folsom Arms Co. for shotguns made for Sears, Roebuck & Co.

Wilkinson Arms Company: Trade name used by the H. & D. Folsom Arms Co. on firearms made for the Richmond Hardware Co. of Richmond, Virginia.

Wiltshire Arms Company: Trade name used by the H. & D. Folsom Arms Co. on firearms made for the Stauffer, Eshleman and Co. of New Orleans, Louisiana.

Winfield Arms Company: Trade name used by the H. & D. Folsom Arms Co. on various types of firearms.

Winner: Trade name found on inexpensive pocket revolvers of unknown manufacture.

Winoca Arms Company: Trade name used by the H. & D. Folsom Arms Co. on firearms made for the N. Jacobi Hardware Co. of Wilmington, North Carolina.

Witte's Expert: Trade name used by the Witte Hardware Co. of St. Louis, Missouri, on shotguns they retailed.

Witte's IXL: Trade name used by the Witte Hardware Co. of St. Louis, Missouri, on shotguns they retailed.

Wolverine Arms Company: Trade name used by the H. & D. Folsom Arms Co. on firearms made for the Fletcher Hardware Co. of Wilmington, North Carolina.

Woodmaster: Trade name found on Belgian shotguns imported by an unknown wholesaler.

Worlds Fair: Trade name used by the Hopkins and Allen Co. on shotguns.

Worthington Arms Company: Trade name used by the H. & D. Folsom Arms Co. on various types of firearms.

Wyco: Trade name used by the Wyeth Hardware and Manufacturing Co. of St. Joseph, Missouri, on firearms they retailed.

XL:
a) Trade name used by the Hopkins and Allen Co. on inexpensive pocket revolvers.
b) Trade name used by the Marlin Firearms Co. on single-shot pocket pistols.

Xpert:
a) Trade name used by the Hopkins and Allen Co. on inexpensive pocket revolvers.
b) Trade name used by the Iver Johnson Arms and Cycle Works on inexpensive single-shot pocket pistols.

XXX Standard: Trade name used by the Marlin Firearms Co. on revolvers.

You Bet: Trade name used on inexpensive pocket revolvers of unknown American manufacture.

Young America: Trade name used by J.P. Lindsay of New York on superimposed - load percussion pistols.

Young American: Trade name used by the Harrington and Richardson Arms Co. on revolvers.

MODEL INDEX

A.A.
A.A. 17
Reims 17

A.A.A.
Modelo 1919 17

A-SQUARE
Hannibal Grade 17
Caesar Grade 17
Hamilcar Grade 17
Genghis Khan Model 17

A & R SALES SOUTH
45 Auto 18
Mark IV Sporter 18

ABADIE
Abadie Model 1878 18
Abadie Model 1886 18

ABBEY, F.J. & CO.
Rifle 18
Shotgun 18

ABBEY, GEORGE T.
Single-Barrel Shotgun 18
Side-by-Side Shotgun 18
Over/Under Shotgun 18

ABESSER & MERKEL
Crown Grade 18
Diamond Grade 18
Empire Grade 18
Excelsior Grade 19
Diana Grade 19
Vandalia Grade 19
Nimrod 19
Magazine Rifle 19

ACCU-MATCH
Accu-Match Custom Pistol 19

ACCU-TEK
AT-380SS 19
AT-380 II 20
CP-9SS 20
CP-45SS 20
CP-40SS 20
BL-9 20
BL-380 20
HC-380SS 20
AT-32SS 21
LT-380 21

ACCURACY INTERNATIONAL
Palmamaster 21
Cismmaster 21
AE 21
AT 21

AW 21
AX 21
AXMC 21
AX50 21

ACHA
Atlas 21
Looking Glass (Ruby-Style) 22
Looking Glass 22

ACME ARMS
.22 Revolver 22
.32 Revolver 22
Shotgun 22

ACME HAMMERLESS
Acme Hammerless 22

ACTION ARMS LTD.
AT-84, AT-88 22
AT-84P, AT-88P 22
AT-84H, AT-88H 22
Timber Wolf Carbine 22
Action Arms/IMI Uzi Carbine
 Models A and B 23

ADAMS / DEANE, ADAMS & DEANE
Adams Model 1851 Self-Cocking
 Revolver 23
Adams Pocket Revolver 23
Beaumont-Adams Revolver 23

ADAMY GEBRUDER
Over/Under Shotgun 23

ADCO ARMS
Diamond Double Over/Under 23
 Field Grade 23
 Imperial Grade 23
 Double Side-by-Side 23
 Imperial Semi-Automatic 23
 Imperial Pump 23

ADIRONDACK ARMS CO. / A.S. BABBITT CO.
Orvil M. Robinson Patent Rifle 23
 First Model 24
 Second Model 24

ADVANCED SMALL ARMS INDUSTRIES
one Pro .45 24

ADVANTAGE ARMS U.S.A., INC.
Model 422 24

AERO
Model 1914 (Aero) 24

AFC
Model 1895 25

Trainer 25
Semi-Auto 25

AGNER (SAXHOJ PRODUCTS, INC.)
Model M 80 25

AGUIRRE
Basculant 26
LeDragon 26

AGUIRRE Y ARANZABAL (AYA)
Matador 26
Matador II 26
Matador III 26
Bolero 26
Iberia 26
Iberia II 26
Model 106 26
Model 107-LI 26
Model 116 27
Model 117 27
Model 117 "Quail Unlimited" 27
Model 210 27
Model 711 Boxlock 27
Model 711 Sidelock 27
Senior 27
Model 79 "A" 27
Model 79 "B" 27
Model 79 "C" 27
Model 77 27
Coral "A" 27
Coral "B" 27
Model No. 1 28
Model No. 1 Round Body 28
Model No. 1 Deluxe 28
Model No. 2 28
Model No. 2 Round Body 28
Model No. 53 29
Model No. 56 29
Model XXV Sidelock 29
Adarra 29
Model XXV Boxlock 29
Model No. 4 29
Model No. 4 Deluxe 29
Model No. 37 Super 30
Model Augusta 30

AIR MATCH
Air Match 500 30

AJAX ARMY
Single-Action 30

AKDAL
Ghost 30
MKA 1919 30

ALASKA MAGNUM
Kodiak or Grizzly Model 30
Wolverine Model 30

ALDAZABAL
Model 1919 31
Military Model 31
Aldazabal 31

ALEXANDER ARMS
R-BEOPREC .50 Beowulf
 Precision Rifle 31
R-BEOENTRY .50 Beowulf Entry 31
R-50 .50 Beowulf Hunter 31
R-65 HUNT 6.5 Grendel 31
R-GSR 6.5 Grendel Sniper Rifle 31
R-338 Ulfbehrt .338 Lapua 31
R-556 5.56 NATO Incursion 31
R-300 16ST .300 AAC 31
R-17 .17 HMR 31

ALKARTASUNA FABRICA DE ARMAS
Alkar 32
Alkar (Ruby-Style) 32

ALL RIGHT FIREARMS CO.
Little All Right Palm Pistol 32

ALLEN, ETHAN
First Model Pocket Rifle 32
Second Model Pocket Rifle 32
Bar Hammer Pistol 32
Tube Hammer Pistol 32
Side Hammer Pistol 32
Center Hammer Pistol 33
Double-Barrel Pistol 33
Allen & Wheelock Center
 Hammer Pistol 33
Allen Thurber & Company
 Target Pistol 33
Ethan Allen Pepperboxes 33
Large Frame Pocket Revolver 33
Small Frame Pocket Revolver 33
Side Hammer Belt Revolver 33
Standard Model 33
Side Hammer Pocket Revolver 34
 Early Production 34
 Standard Production 34
Side Hammer Navy Revolver 34
 Early Production 34
 Standard Model 34
Center Hammer Army Revolver 34
Center Hammer Navy Revolver 34
Center Hammer Percussion Revolver ..34
Lipfire Army Revolver 34
 Early Model 34
 Late Model 34
Lipfire Navy Revolver 34
Lipfire Pocket Revolver 34
.32 Side Hammer Rimfire Revolver 35
 First Model 35
 Second Model 35
 Third Model 35
.22 Side Hammer Rimfire Revolver 35
 Early Model First Issue 35

Second Issue................................35
Third Issue.................................35
Fourth to Eighth Issue 35
Single-Shot Center Hammer............35
Early Issue...............................35
Standard Issue 35
.32 Single-Shot Center Hammer.......35
Vest Pocket Derringer 35
.32 Derringer 35
.41 Derringer 35
Center Hammer Muzzleloading Rifle ..35
Side Hammer Muzzleloading Rifle......36
Combination Gun 36
Side Hammer Breechloading Rifle......36
Drop Breech Rifle 36
Lipfire Revolving Rifle 36
Double-Barrel Shotgun 36

ALPHA ARMS CO.
Jaguar Grade I 36
Jaguar Grade II 36
Jaguar Grade III 36
Jaguar Grade IV 36
Alpha Big-Five................................36
Alpha Grand Slam 37
Alpha Custom 37
Alpha Alaskan 37

ALSOP, C.R.
First Model Navy Revolver 37
Standard Model Navy Revolver 37
Pocket Model Revolver 37

AMAC
U.S. Carbine .22.............................37
Wagonmaster Lever-Action Rifle........37
Wagonmaster .22 Magnum 37
Targetmaster Pump-Action Rifle........37
Li'L Champ Bolt-Action Rifle 37
M .30 Cal. Carbine 37
Paratrooper .30 Carbine 37
Enforcer .30 Carbine 37
Long Range Rifle System/
    AMAC Model 5100 37
TP-22 and TP-25............................38
AMAC 22 Compact or 25 Compact....38

AMERICAN ARMS, INC.
York/Gentry...................................38
10 Gauge Magnum Shotgun 38
12 Gauge Magnum Shotgun 38
Brittany...38
Turkey Special................................38
Waterfowl Special...........................38
Specialty Model..............................38
Derby 38
Grulla #2 38
F.S. 200...39
F.S. 300...39
F.S. 400...39
F.S. 500...39
Waterfowl Special...........................39
Waterfowl 10 Gauge........................39
Turkey Special................................39
Lince 39
Silver Model...................................39

Silver I 39
Silver II 39
Silver II Lite 39
Silver Competition/Sporting.............39
Silver Hunter 40
Bristol/Sterling...............................40
Sir..40
Royal 40
Excelsior 40
AASB...40
Campers Special.............................40
Youth Model...................................40
Slugger 40
10 Gauge Model 40
Combo Model 40
Phantom Field 40
Phantom Synthetic 40
Phantom HP...................................40
ZCY.308..41
AKY39...41
AKF39...41
AKC47...41
AKF47...41
EXP-64 Survival Rifle 41
SM-64 TD Sporter 41
1860 Henry 41
1866 Winchester.............................41
1873 Winchester.............................41
1885 Single-Shot High Wall 41
Sharps Cavalry Carbine 41
Sharps Frontier Carbine 41
Sharps Sporting Rifle 41
Sharps 1874 Deluxe Sporting Rifle 41
Model EP-.380................................41
Model PK-22 42
Model CX-22 42
Model TT Tokarev 42
Model ZC-.380 42
Aussie Model 42
Regulator 42
Regulator Deluxe 42

AMERICAN ARMS
Eagle .380......................................42

AMERICAN ARMS CO.
Fox Model "Swing Out"
    Hammer Double 42
Semi-Hammerless Double 42
Whitmore Model Hammerless
    Double 42
Semi-Hammerless Single-Barrel........43
Spur Trigger Single-Action
    Five-Shot Revolver 43
Standard Trigger Double-Action
    Model 1886 Revolver....................43
Hammerless Model 1890
    Double-Action 43
Combination .22 caliber R.F. and
    .32 caliber R.F. 43
.32 caliber R.F., Both Barrels............43
.32 caliber R.F., Both Barrels
    (2.625" barrel).............................43
.38 caliber R.F., Both Barrels............43
.41 caliber R.F., Both Barrels............43

AMERICAN CLASSIC
American Classic 1911-A1 43
American Classic
    Commander/Amigo......................44
American Classic Trophy Model.........44
American Classic .22 Model 44

AMERICAN DERRINGER CORP.
Model 1 Derringer 44
    Caliber: .22 Long Rifle through
        .357 Magnum and .45 ACP......44
    Calibers: .41 Mag., .44-40,
        .44 Special, .44 Mag.,
        .45 Long Colt, .410 Bore,
        .22 Hornet, .223 Rem.,
        30-30, and .45-70 Gov't.........44
Model 1 Lady Derringer 44
    Deluxe 44
    Deluxe Engraved........................44
Model 1 NRA 500 Series 44
Model 1 Texas Commemorative........44
    Caliber: .38 Special 45
    Calibers: .45 Colt and .44-40.......45
    Deluxe Engraved........................45
Model 1 125th Anniversary
    Commemorative 45
    Deluxe Engraved........................45
Model 2 Pen Pistol 45
Model 3...45
Model 4...45
    Engraved...................................45
Alaskan Survival Model....................45
Model 6...45
    Engraved...................................46
Double-Action Derringer 46
DA 38 Double-Action Derringer 46
Mini Cop 4-Shot.............................46
Cop 4-Shot....................................46
Model 7 Derringer—Lightweight........46
    .32 S&W Long / .32 Magnum 46
    .38 S&W and .380 ACP 46
    .22 LR and .38 Special 46
    .44 Special................................46
Model 8...46
    Engraved...................................46
Model 10 Derringer 46
Model 11 Derringer 46
Semmerling LM-4 47
LM-5...47
Millennium Series 2000...................47
Gambler Millennium 2000 47
Women of Texas Series....................47
Cowboy Series 2000 47

**AMERICAN FIRE ARMS
MFG. CO., INC.**
American .38 Special Derringer.........47
American .25 Automatic 47
American .380 Automatic 47

AMERICAN FRONTIER FIREARMS
1871, 72 Open Top Standard Model... 48
Richards & Mason Conversion 1851
    Navy Standard Model..................48
1860 Richards Army Model..............48

AMERICAN GUN CO., NEW YORK
Side-by-Side Shotgun......................48
Knickerbocker Pistol—See
    Knickerbocker 48

AMERICAN INDUSTRIES
Calico M-100..................................48
Calico M-100P/M-110 48
Calico M-100S Sporter/M-105..........48
Calico M-101 Solid Stock Carbine 48
Calico M-900..................................48
Calico M-950 Pistol.........................49
Calico M-951 49
Calico M-951S................................49

AMERICAN INTERNATIONAL
180 Carbine (SAM-180) 49

AMERICAN TACTICAL IMPORTS
AT CS/FS Series 49
AT MS380 49
GSG-522..49
GSG-AK 49
FX Series 49
ATI GSG 1911 49
SX Cavalry Shotgun 49
TAC-P, TAC-S Shotgun Series 49
    TAC-P 49
    TAC-S 49

**AMERICAN WESTERN ARMS INC.
(AWA)**
Lightning Rifle LE 50
Lightning Rifle 50
Lightning Carbine 50
Lightningbolt...................................50
Model 1892 Lever Action 50
Peacekeeper 50
Longhorn 50

AMES SWORD CO.
Turbiaux Le Protector......................50

AMT
Lightning 51
Bull's Eye Regulation Target 51
Baby Automag.................................51
Automag II 51
Automag III 51
Automag IV 51
Automag V......................................52
Javelina...52
Back Up Pistol................................52
    .45 ACP, .40 S&W, 9mm 52
    .38 Super, .357 SIG,
        .400 CorBon...........................53
    9mm, .38 Super, .40 S&W,
        .45 ACP 53
.380 Back Up II 53
Hardballer/Government Model...........53
    Hardballer 53
    Government Model 53
    Longslide 53
.400 Accelerator 53
Commando 53
On Duty 53

Skipper 54
Combat Skipper 54
Lightning 54
Small Game Hunter 54
Small Game Hunter II 54
Hunter 54
Magnum Hunter 54
Target Model............................54
Challenge Edition 54
Single-Shot Standard.................54
Single-Shot Deluxe....................54
Bolt-Action Repeating—Standard......54
Bolt-Action Repeating—Deluxe........54

ANDERSON
Under Hammer Pistol.........................55

ANDRUS & OSBORN
Under Hammer Pistol.........................55

ANSCHÜTZ, J.G. GMBH
Mark 10 Target 55
Model 1403D.............................55
Model 1407...............................55
Model 1408...............................55
Model 1411...............................55
Model 1413 Match......................55
Model 1416D HB Classic..............55
Model 1416D KL Classic...............55
Model 1416D Custom...................55
Model 1418D KL Mannlicher 55
Model 1418/19...........................56
Model 1433D.............................56
Model 1533...............................56
Model 1449D Youth.....................56
Model Woodchucker....................56
Model 1451E Target....................56
Model 1451R Sporter Target 56
Model 1451D Custom...................56
Model 1451D Classic...................56
Model 1516D KL Classic...............56
Model 1516D KL Custom...............56
Model 1517D Classic...................56
Model 1517D HB Classic...............56
Model 1517D Monte Carlo.............56
Model 1517MPR
  Multi-Purpose Rifle 57
Model 1518D Mannlicher 57
Model 184.................................57
Model 54 Sporter.......................57
Model 54M................................57
Model 141.................................57
Model 141M...............................57
Model 164.................................57
Model 164M...............................57
Model 153.................................57
Model 153-S..............................57
Model 64...................................57
Model 64MS...............................57
Model 64 MPR............................57
Model 64P.................................57
Model 64P Mag...........................57
Model 54.18MS...........................58
Model 54.MS REP 58
Model 2000 MK...........................58
Model 2007 Supermatch................58

Model 2013 Supermatch 58
Model 1903D..............................58
Model 1803D..............................58
Model 1808D RT Super 58
Model 1907ISU Standard Match......58
Model 1910 Super Match II 58
Model 1911 Prone Match 58
Model 1913 Super Match 58
Model 1827B Biathlon...................58
Model 1827BT Biathlon 59
Achiever 59
Achiever Super Target...................59
Bavarian 1700 59
Classic 1700 59
Custom 1700 59
Model 1700 Mannlicher 59
Model 1700 FWT 59
Model 1700 FWT Deluxe 59
Model 1710 D Classic 59
Model 1710 D HB Classic 59
Model 1710 D KL Monte Carlo..........59
Model 1710 D HB Classic
  150 Years Anniversary Version.......59
Model 1712 Silhouette Sporter........60
Model 1702 D HB Classic 60
Model 1502 D HB Classic 60
Model 1907 Club 60
Model 1717 D Classic 60
Model 1717 D HB Classic 60
Model 1727...............................60
Model 1730 D Classic 60
Model 1730 D HB Classic 60
Model 1730 D KL Monte Carlo..........60
Model 1733D KL Mannlicher 60
Model 1740 D Classic 60
Model 1743D..............................60
Model 1740 D HB Classic 61
Model 1740 D KL Monte Carlo..........61
Model 1770D..............................61
Model 1780D..............................61
Model 520/61 61
Model 525 Sporter 61
Model RX22................................61
Exemplar 61
Exemplar XIV 61
Exemplar Hornet.........................61

ANZIO IRON WORKS
Takedown Competition.....................62
  .338 Lapua 62
  .50 BMG 62
20/50 Rifle 62

APALOZO HERMANOS
Apaloza 62
Paramount.................................62
Triomphe 62

AR-7 INDUSTRIES
AR-7 Explorer 62
AR-7C Explorer 62
AR-7 Sporter 62
AR-7 Target 62
AR-7 Bolt-Action 62

ARCUS
Arcus-94 62

ARIZAGA, G.
Arizaga (Model 1915) 62
Mondial 63
Pinkerton 63
Warwick 63

ARIZMENDI, FRANCISCO
Singer 63
  6.35mm 63
  7.65mm 63
Teuf Teuf 63
  6.35mm 63
  7.65mm 63
Walman 63
  6.35mm 63
  7.65mm 63
  .380 64
Arizmendi 64
Boltun—1st Variation 64
  6.35mm 64
  7.65mm 64
Boltun—2nd Variation 64
Roland 64
  6.35mm 64
  7.65mm 64
Puppy 64
Pistolet Automatique.....................64
Kaba Spezial 64
Ydeal 64
  6.35mm 65
  7.65mm 65
  .380 65

ARIZMENDI, ZULAICA
Cebra Pistol 65
Cebra Revolver............................65

ARLINGTON ORDNANCE
M1 Garand 65
M1 Carbne 65

ARMALITE, INC.
AR-24 Pistol 65
AR-24 Tactical Custom 65
AR-17 Shotgun 66
AR-7 Explorer Rifle 66
AR-7 Custom 66
AR-180 66
  Howa 66
  Sterling 66
AR-180B 66
AR-10A4 Rifle 66
AR-10A4 Carbine 66
AR-10A2 Rifle 66
AR-10A2 Carbine 66
AR-10B 66
AR-10(T) Rifle 66
AR-10(T) Carbine 66
AR-10(T) Ultra 66
AR-10 SOF 66
AR-10 .338 Federal 67
M15 SOF 67
M15A2 HBAR 67

M15A2 National Match...................67
M15A2-M4A1C Carbine 67
M15A2-M4C Carbine 67
M15A4(T) Eagle Eye 67
M15A4 Special Purpose Rifle (SPR)...67
M15A4 Action Master 67
M15A4 Eagle Spirit 67
M15A4 Carbine 6.8 & 7.62x39........68
M15-22......................................68
AR-30M 68
AR-30A1 Standard........................68
AR-31 68
AR-50 68
Golden Eagle..............................68
HBAR 68
M4C Carbine...............................68

ARMERO ESPECIALISTAS
Alfa 68
Omega 69

ARMES DE CHASSE
Model EJ 69
Model EU 69
Highlander 69
Chesapeake 69
Balmoral 69
Model 70E 69
Model 74E 69
Model 76E 69

ARMINEX LTD.
Tri-Fire......................................69
Target Model...............................69

ARMITAGE INTERNATIONAL, LTD.
Scarab Skorpion..........................69

ARMSCO FIREARMS CORP.
Model 301A.................................70
Model 202B.................................70
Model 202A.................................70
Model 201A.................................70
Model 200A.................................70
Model 205A.................................70
Model 210AE...............................70
Model 210BE...............................70
Model 104A.................................70
Model 103D.................................70
Model 103DE...............................70
Model 103C.................................70
Model 103CE...............................70
Model 103F.................................70
Model 103FE...............................70
Model 101SE...............................70
Model 101BE...............................70
Model 401A.................................70
Model 401B.................................71
Model 501GA...............................71
Model 501GB...............................71
Model 601GB...............................71
Model 601GA...............................71
Model 701GA...............................71
Model 701GB...............................71
Model 801A.................................71
Model 801B.................................71

ARMSCOR PRECISION INTERNATIONAL

M14R 71
M14 National Match 71
FAL 71
M36 Israeli Sniper Rifle 71
Expert Model 71
Model M14P 71
Model M14D 71
Model 14Y 71
Model 12Y 71
Model 1400 71
Model M1500 72
Model M1600 72
Model M1600R 72
Model M1600C 72
Model M1600W 72
Model M1800 72
Model 20C 72
Model M20P 72
Model M2000 72
Model AK22S 72
Model AK22F 72
Hi-Power 72
Detective HP—Compact 72
P22 72
SD9 72
Armscor 1911A1-45 FS GI 73
Model M100 73
Model 200P 73
Model 200TC 73
Model 200DC 73
Model 201S 73
Model 202 73
Model 206 73
Model 210 73
MAP1 FS 73
MAPP1 FS 73
Model 1911-A1 73
Model 1911-A2 73
Model 30D 73
Model 30DG 73
Model 30R 73
Model 30RP 74
Model 30 SAS1 74

ARNOLD ARMS

Varminter I 74
Varminter II 74
Alaskan 74
Alaskan Trophy 74
Alaskan Guide 74
  Synthetic Stock 74
  Walnut Stock 74
Grand Alaskan 74
  "AAA" English Walnut 74
  "Exhibition" Grade Walnut 74
Safari 74
  "A" Fancy English Walnut 75
  "AA" Fancy English Walnut 75
African Trophy 75
Grand African 75
Serengeti Synthetic 75
African Synthetic 75
Neutralizer Mark I 75

Neutralizer Mark II 75
Benchrest Rifles 75
Prone Rifles 75
X-Course Rifles 75
1,000 Yard Match Rifles 75
Fully Accurized Production Rifles ...75

AROSTEGUI, EULOGIO

Azul Royal (Model 31) 75
Super Azul (M-34) 76
Azul 6.35mm 76
Azul 7.65mm 76
Velo-Dog 76

ARRIETA S.L.

490 Eder 76
500 Titan 76
501 Palomara 76
505 Alaska 76
510 Montana 76
550 Field 76
557 Standard 76
558 Patria 76
560 Cumbre 76
570 Lieja 76
575 Sport 77
578 Victoria 77
585 Liria 77
588 Cima 77
590 Regina 77
595 Principe 77
600 Imperial 77
601 Imperial Tiro 77
801 77
802 77
803 77
871 77
872 78
873 78
874 78
875 78
R-1 Double Rifle 78
R-2 Double Rifle 78

ARRIZABALAGA, HIJOS DE C.

Arrizabalaga 78
Campeon 78
Jo Lo Ar 78
Sharpshooter 79

ARSENAL, INC.

SA M-7 79
SA M-7 Classic 79
SA M-7S 79
SA RPK-5 79
SA RPK-7 79
SAS M-7 79
SAS M-7 Classic 79
SLR-104 79
SLR-106 79
SLR-107 79

ASCASO

Spanish Rebublican Government ...79

ASHEVILLE ARMORY

Enfield-Type Rifle 80

ASHTON, PETER & WILLIAM

Under Hammer Pistol 80

ASTRA-UNCETA SA

Victoria 80
Astra 1911 80
Astra 1924 80
Astra 100 (Old Model) 80
Astra 200 81
Astra 400 or Model 1921 81
Astra 300 81
Astra 600 81
Astra 700 81
Astra 800 81
Astra 900 82
Astra 1000 82
Astra 2000 82
Astra 3000 82
Astra 4000 Falcon 82
Astra 5000 Constable 82
Astra 7000 82
Astra A-80 82
Astra A-90 83
Constable A-60 83
Astra Cadix 83
.357 Double-Action Revolver 83
.44/.45 Double-Action Revolver ...83
Terminator 83
Convertible Revolver 83
Model A-70 83
Model A-75 84
Model A-100 84
Model A-100 Carry Comp 84

ATCSA

Colt Police Positive Copy 84
Target Pistol 84

AUBREY, A.J.

Double-Barrel Shotguns 84

AUER, B.

Pocket Pistol 84

AUGUSTA MACHINE WORKS

1851 Colt Navy Copy 84

AUSTIN & HALLECK, INC.

Model 320 LR BLU 84
Model 320 S/S 84
Model 420 LR Classic 84
Model 420 LR Monte Carlo 85
Mountain Rifle 85

AUSTRALIAN AUTOMATIC ARMS LTD.

SAR 85
SAP 85
SP 85

AUTAUGA ARMS INC.

MK II 85

AUTO MAG

.44 AMP 85
.44 AMP 85
.44 AMP 85
.357 AMP 85
.357 AMP 85
.44 AMP 85
.357 AMP 86
.44 AMP 86
.357 AMP 86
.44 AMP 86

AUTO ORDNANCE CORP.

Auto Ordnance 1911A1 86
Thompson Model 1911TC 86
Thompson Model 1911CAF 86
Thompson 1911 A1—Standard 86
Thompson 1911 A1—Parkerized ...87
Thompson 1911 A1—Deluxe 87
Thompson 1911 A1—
  Custom High Polish 87
Thompson 1911 A1—10mm 87
Thompson 1911 A1—Duo Tone 87
Thompson 1911 A1—Satin Nickel ...87
Thompson 1911 A1—Competition ...87
Thompson 1911 A1—Pit Bull 87
Thompson 1911 A1—General 87
ZG-51 "Pit Bull" 87
Auto-Ordnance Thompson Semi-
  Automatic Model 1927 Series 87
Second Generation Auto Ordnance
  Thompson Model 1927 87
1927 A1 Deluxe Model 87
1927 A1 Deluxe Model (First 932
  Carbines) 88
1927 A1 Standard Model 88
1927 A3 88
1927 A5 .45 ACP Caliber Auto
  Ordnance Semi-Automatic Pistol ...88
M-1 Semi-Automatic Carbine 88
Third Generation Auto Ordnance
  Thompson Model 1927 Semi-
  Automatic Carbine 88
TA5100D 88
T1B 88
T150D 88
T5 88
TA510D 88
T1SB 88
M1SB 88
M1 Carbine 89

AUTO POINTER

Auto Pointer Shotgun 89

AXTELL RIFLE CO.

#1 Long Range Creedmore 89
New Model Sharps 1877 89
#2 Long Range 89
Lower Sporting Rifle 89
Business Rifle 89
Overbaugh Schuetzen 89

AZPIRI

Avion 89
Colon 89

B.R.F.
B.R.F. 90

BABCOCK, MOSES
Babcock Under Hammer Cane Gun ...90

BAER CUSTOM, LES
Baer 1911 Ultimate Master Combat
Pistol-Compensated.......................90
Baer 1911 Ultimate Master Steel
Special 90
Baer 1911 Ultimate Master Combat
Pistol 90
6" Model 90
5" Model 91
Baer 1911 Ultimate Master Para 91
Unlimited Model 91
Limited Model 91
Baer 1911 Bullseye
Wadcutter Pistol 91
Baer 1911 National Match
Hardball Pistol 91
Baer 1911 Target Master 91
Baer 1911 IPSC Action Pistol 91
Baer 1911 P.P.C.
Distinguished Match 91
Baer 1911 P.P.C. Open Class 91
Baer 1911 Premier II 92
Baer 1911 Premier II—6" barrel 92
Baer 1911 Premier II—Light Weight
(LW1) 92
Baer 1911 Premier II—Light Weight
(LW2) 92
Baer 1911 Premier II—Super-Tac 92
Baer 1911 Prowler III 92
Baer 1911 Prowler IV 93
Baer 1911 Custom Carry—
Commanche Length......................93
Baer 1911 Custom Carry—5 93
Baer 1911 Thunder Ranch Special 93
Baer 1911 Thunder Ranch Special
Engraved Model 93
Baer S.R.P. (Swift Response Pistol) 93
Baer 1911 Monolith 93
Baer 1911 Monolith Heavyweight......94
Baer 1911 Monolith Tactical
Illuminator 94
Baer 1911 Monolith Commanche......94
Baer 1911 Monolith Commanche
Heavyweight 94
Baer 1911 Stinger............................94
Baer 1911 Stinger Stainless 94
Baer 1911 .38 Super Stinger 94
Black Baer 1911 94
Baer 1911 Concept I 94
Baer 1911 Concept II 95
Baer 1911 Concept III.......................95
Baer 1911 Concept IV 95
Baer 1911 Concept V 95
Baer 1911 Concept V 6" 95
Baer 1911 Concept VI 95
Baer 1911 Concept VI L.W. 95
Baer 1911 Conicept VII.....................96
Baer 1911 Concept VIII.....................96
Baer 1911 Concept IX 96
Baer 1911 Concept X........................96

Baer Lightweight .22-caliber 1911
Models...96
4.5" Model with fixed sights 96
5" Model with fixed sights 96
5" Model with Bo-Mar sights 96
Baer Limited Edition
Presentation Grade 1911 96
Model 1911
Twenty-Fifth Anniversary 96
Ultimate Recon...............................97
AR .223 Ultimate Super Varmint 97
AR .223 Ultimate Super Match 97
AR .223 M4-A2 Flattop 97
AR .223 IPSC Action Model...............97
AR .223 Ultimate NRA Match 97
Bullpup Muzzleloader......................97
Thunder Ranch Rifle 97
Monolith .308 S.W.A.T. 97

BAFORD ARMS, INC.
Thunder Derringer 98
Fire Power Model 35 98

BAIKAL
IJ-27E1C 98
TOZ - 34 98
Model MC-8-0 98
Model MC-5-105 98
Model MC-7 98
IZH18/MP18 98
IZK18MAX 98
IZH43 98
IZH43K 98
MP213 Coach Gun 98
IZH27 98
MP233 99
IZH94/MP94 99
IZH81 99
MP131K 99
MP133 99
MP153 99
IZH35 99
MP310 99
MP220 99

BAILONS GUNMAKERS, LTD.
Hunting Rifle 100

BAKER GUN & FORGING CO.
Baker Trap Gun 100
Elite Grade 100
Superba 100
Expert Grade Double Shotgun 100
Deluxe Grade Double Shotgun........100
Black Beauty Double Shotgun 101
Grade S Double Shotgun 101
Grade R Double Shotgun 101
Paragon Grade Shotgun..................101
Paragon Grade—Model NN 101
Batavia Special..............................101
Batavia Brush Gun 101
Batavia Leader 101
Batavia Damascus..........................101
Baker Hammer Gun 101
Batavia Automatic Rifle 102

BALL REPEATING CARBINE
Ball Repeating Carbine 102

BALLARD, C. H.
Single-Shot Derringer 102

BALLARD PATENT ARMS
Ballard (Ball & Williams)
Sporting Rifles, First Type
(Serial numbers 1-100)...............102
Ballard (Ball & Williams) Sporting
Rifles, Second Type
(Serial numbers 200-1600,
and 1600-14,000, interspersed
with martial production)...............102
Ballard (Ball & Williams) Sporting
Rifles, Third Type (Serial numbers
14,000-15,000) 102
Ballard (Ball & Williams) Military
Carbines (Serial numbers
1500-7500, and 8500-10500) ...103
Ballard (Ball & Williams) "Kentucky"
Half-Stock Rifles 103
Ballard (Ball & Williams) "Kentucky"
Full-Stock Rifles 103
Ballard (Dwight, Chapin & Co.)
Carbines 103
Ballard (Dwight, Chapin & Co.)
Full-Stock Rifles 103
Ballard (R. Ball & Co.)
Sporting Rifles 103
Ballard (R. Ball & Co.) Carbines 104
Ballard (Merrimack Arms &
Manufacturing Co.) Sporting
Rifles 104
Ballard (Merrimack Arms &
Manufacturing Co.) Carbines 104
Ballard (Brown Mfg. Co.)
Sporting Rifles 104
Ballard (Brown Mfg. Co.) Full-Stock
Military Rifles 104

BALLARD RIFLE AND CARTRIDGE CO.
No. 1-1/2 Hunter's Rifle 104
No. 1-3/4 Far West Rifle 104
No. 2 Sporting Model......................104
No. 3 Gallery Rifle..........................104
No. 3F Fine Gallery Rifle..................104
No. 4 Perfection Model 104
No. 4-1/2 Mid-Range Model 105
No. 5 Pacific Model 105
No. 5-1/2 Montana Model................105
No. 6 Off-Hand Rifle Model
(Schuetzen) 105
No. 7 Long Range Model 105
No. 8 Union Hill Model 105
Model 1885 High Wall 105

BAR-STO PRECISION MACHINE
Bar-Sto 25 ....,..105

BARRETT, F.A. MFG. CO.
Barrett MRAD.................................105
Model 82 Rifle 105
Model 82A1 105
Model 95M 106
Model 99 106
Model 107 106

Model 468 106
REC7 Gen II 106
Barrett Sovereign shotgun...............106
Albany O/U 106
Beltrami SxS 106

BARRETT, J. B. AND A.B. & CO.
Barrett Muskets and Rifled Muskets 106

BASCARAN, MARTIN A.
Martian 6.35mm 107
Martian 7.65mm 107
Thunder...107

BAUER, F. A. CORP.
The Rabbit 107
Bauer 25 Automatic.........................107

BAYONNE, MANUFACTURE D'ARMES
Model A 107
Model B 107
Model C 108
Model D 108
Model E 108
Model F 108
Model G 108
Model GZ 108
Model P-8 & P-15 108
Model P-15 M1 Target.....................109
Model R..109
.22 Long Rifle.............................109
7.65mm & 7.65mm
Long & .380 109
9mm Parabellum 109
Model R PARA Experimental...........109
Model "Le Chasseur".......................109

BEATTIE, J.
Beattie Gas Seal Revolver 110

BEAUMONT
1873 Dutch Service Revolver,
Old Model 110
1873 Dutch Service Revolver,
New Model 110
1873 KIM, Small Model 110

BECKER AND HOLLANDER
Beholla 110

BEEMAN PRECISION ARMS, INC.
MP-08...110
P-08 110
SP Standard....................................110
SP Deluxe.......................................110

BEERSTECHER, FREDERICK
Superposed Load Pocket Pistol 110

BENELLI
Model SL-121 V 111
Model SL-121 Slug 111
Model SL-123 V 111
Model SL-201 111
M3 Super 90 111
M3 Super 90 Folding Stock..............111
M4 111

M1014 Limited Edition 111
M1 Practical 111
M1 Super 90 Tactical....................112
M1 Super 90 Slug Gun 112
M1 Super 90 Entry Gun 112
M1 Super 90 Defense Gun 112
M1 Super 90 Field 112
M1 Super 90 Camo Field 112
M1 Field Steady Grip 112
M1 Super 90 Sporting Special 112
M2 Practical with ComforTech.........112
M2 Tactical 113
M2 Field with ComforTech 113
M2 Field without ComforTech 113
Montefeltro Super 90 113
Montefeltro 20 Gauge...................113
Montefeltro 20 Gauge Camo 113
Montefeltro 20 Gauge Limited.........113
Montefeltro Silver 113
Montefeltro (2005) 113
Montefeltro Compact 113
Montefeltro Synthetic...................113
Black Eagle Competition Gun 113
Black Eagle 114
Black Eagle Executive Series 114
    Grade I...............................114
    Grade II..............................114
    Grade III.............................114
Super Black Eagle 114
Super Black Eagle Left-Hand...........114
Super Black Eagle Custom
    Slug Gun 114
Super Black Eagle Camo Gun..........114
Super Black Eagle Steady Grip 114
Super Black Eagle Limited Edition.....114
Super Black Eagle II
    with ComforTech.....................115
Super Black Eagle II
    without ComforTech.................115
Super Black Eagle II Rifled Slug
    with ComforTech.....................115
Super Black Eagle II Turkey Gun 115
Super Black Eagle II Steady Grip......115
Legacy 115
Legacy Limited Edition..................115
Legacy (2005)............................115
Nova.......................................115
Nova Slug.................................116
Nova Rifled Slug 116
Nova Field Slug Combo..................116
Nova H2O Pump 116
Supernova 116
Supernova SteadyGrip...................116
Supernova Tactical 116
Sport Model..............................116
SuperSport with ComforTech...........116
Sport II Model............................116
Cordoba...................................117
Vinci 117
Super Vinci 117
Ultra Light................................117
Executive Series 117
    Type 1 117
    Type 2 117
    Type 3 117
Raffaello Series..........................117

Ethos......................................117
Ethos Small Gauge 117
828 U 117
828 U w/nickel-plated receiver........117
Model R1 Rifle 117
R1 Limited Edition Rifle.................118
Model R1 Carbine 118
Model R1 ComforTech Rifle.............118
Model MR1 Rifle 118
Model B-76 118
Model B-76S 118
Model B-77 118
Model B-80 118
Model B-80S 118
Model MP90S Match (World Cup)....118
Model MP95E Match (Atlanta).........118

BENTLEY, JOSEPH
Bentley Revolver..........................119

BERETTA, DR. FRANCO
Black Diamond Field Model.............119
    Grade One 119
    Grade Two 119
    Grade Three 119
    Grade Four 119
Gamma Standard 119
Gamma Deluxe 119
Gamma Target 119
America Standard 119
America Deluxe 119
Europa.....................................119
Europa Deluxe............................119
Francia Standard 119
Alpha Three 119
Beta Three 119

BERETTA, PIETRO
Model 1915 119
Model 1915/1917.........................120
Model 1919 120
Model 1923 120
Model 1931 120
Model 1934...............................121
    Air Force "RA" marked 121
    Navy "RM" marked 121
Model 1934 Romanian Contract.......121
Model 1935 121
Model 318.................................121
Model 418:................................121
Model 420.................................121
Model 421.................................121
Model 948.................................121
Model 949 Olympic Target 121
U22 Neos 4.5/6.0 122
U22 Neos 4.5 Inox/6.0 Inox 122
U22 Neos 6.0/7.5 DLX 122
U22 Neos 6.0/7.5 Inox DLX 122
Model 70 (Model 100) 122
Model 70S.................................122
Model 71/Jaguar (Model 101).........122
Model 72..................................122
Model 76 (102)...........................123
Model 950/Minx...........................123
Model 950B/Jetfire.......................123
Model 950 Jetfire Inox...................123

Model 3032 Tomcat 123
Model 3032 Tomcat Inox.................123
Model 3032 Tomcat Titanium..........124
Alley Cat...................................124
Model 951 124
Model 20...................................124
Model 21 Bobcat.........................124
    Standard Model......................124
Model 21EL 124
Model 21 Inox 125
Model 90...................................125
Model 92...................................125
Model 92SB-P 125
Model 92SB Compact.....................125
Model 92FS 125
Model 92FS Inox 125
Model 96...................................125
Model 96 Combat 125
Model 96 Stock...........................126
Model 96A1 126
Model 92/96FS Inox......................126
Model 92/96FS Centurion...............126
Model 92FS/96 Brigadier................126
Model 92FS/96 Brigadier Inox..........126
Model 92G-SD/96G-SD 126
Model 92F.................................127
Model 92F U.S. Marked Slide..........127
Model 92F Compact 127
Model 92/96 Compact "Type M" 127
Model 92/96M Compact Inox...........127
Model 92D Compact "Type M" 127
Model 92FS Deluxe 128
Model 92FS "470th Anniversary"
    Limited Edition.......................128
Model 92/96D 128
Model 92/96DS 128
Model 92G/96G 128
Model 92/96 Vertec......................128
Model 92 Competition
    Conversion Kit 128
Model 92/96 Combo 128
Model M9 Limited Edition 128
    Standard Model......................128
    Deluxe Model 128
Model 92 Billennium......................129
92 Steel-I 129
M9A1 129
Model 92/96 Custom Carry............129
Model 92/96 Border Marshall 129
Model 92G/96G Elite 130
Model 92G Elite II 130
Model 92FS Inox Tactical 130
Model 8000/8040/8045 Cougar 130
Model 8000/8040/8045
    Mini Cougar 130
Model 8000F—Cougar L................130
Model 9000F 131
Model 9000D 131
Model 9000S 131
Model 84/Cheetah 131
Model 84BB...............................132
Model 85/Cheetah 132
Model 86/Cheetah 132
Model 87/Cheetah 132
Model 87 Target 132
Model 89/Gold Standard................132

Model PX4 Storm Pistol 133
Model PX4 Storm Inox 133
Model PX4 Storm Subcompact........133
Model PX4 Storm SD
    (Special Duty) 133
90-Two.....................................133
BU9 Nano 133
Pico..133
Stampede 134
Stampede Buntline 134
Stampede Nickel 134
Stampede Deluxe 134
Stampede Patton Model.................134
Stampede Bisley 134
Laramie....................................134
1873 Renegade
    Short Lever-Action Rifle..............134
Gold Rush Slide-Action Rifle and
    Carbine 134
Cx4 Storm 134
AR-70 134
ARX 100...................................135
ARX 160...................................135
BM-59 Garand............................135
Model 500 Custom.......................135
    Model 500S 135
    Model 500DL 135
    Model 500DEELL....................135
    Model 500DEELLS..................135
Model 501 135
Model 502 135
Mato Standard 135
Mato Deluxe..............................135
Model S689 Sable........................135
    Silver Sable 136
    Gold Sable 136
    Diamond Sable 136
SSO Express 136
SSO5 Express 136
SSO6.......................................136
SSO6 EELL 136
Model 455 136
Model 455 EELL..........................136
BL-1..136
BL-2..136
BL-2/S (Speed Trigger) 136
BL-2 Stakeout 137
BL-3..137
BL-3 Competition 137
BL-4..137
BL-4 Competition 137
BL-5..137
BL-5 Competition 137
BL-6..137
BL-6 Competition 137
Model S55 B..............................137
Model S56 E..............................137
Model S58 Competition 137
Silver Snipe...............................137
Golden Snipe 137
Model 57 E................................137
ASEL Model 137
Model 409 PB.............................137
Model 410 137
Model 410 E..............................137
Model 411 E..............................137

Model 424 138
Model 426 E 138
Model 625 138
Model 626 Field Grade 138
Model 626 Onyx 138
Model 627 EL 138
Model 627 EELL 138
GR Series 138
  GR-1 138
  GR-2 138
  GR-3 138
Silver Hawk 138
Silver Hawk Featherweight ...138
Model 470 Silver Hawk 138
Model 470 Silver Hawk EL ...138
Model 471 Silver Hawk 139
Model 471 EL 139
Model 486 Parallelo 139
SO-1 139
SO-2 139
SO-3 139
SO-4 (Garcia SO3EL) 139
SO-5 (Garcia SO-3 EELL) 139
SO-6 (450 or 451 EL)
  Side-by-Side 139
SO-7 (451 EELL) Side-by-Side ...139
SO-5 Trap 139
SO-5 Trap 2 Barrel Set 139
SO-5 Sporting Clays 139
SO-5 Skeet 140
SO-6 EL 140
SO-6 Trap 140
SO-6 Skeet 140
SO-6 Sporting Clays 140
SO-6 EELL 140
SO-6 EESS 140
SO-7 140
SO-9 141
SO-10 141
Jubilee Field Grade (Giubileo) ...141
  Single Gun 141
  Matched Pair 141
Jubilee Sporting Grade 141
Jubilee II (Giublio) 141
  Single Gun 141
  Matched Pair 141
ASE Deluxe Sporting 141
Model 687 EELL Gallery Special ...141
  Single Gun 142
  Special Combo—20/28 Gauge ..142
  Matched Pair 142
Imperiale Montecarlo 142
Diana 142
Model 451 Series 142
Model 450 Series 142
Model 452 142
Model 452 EELL 142
Onyx 142
Onyx Waterfowler 3.5 142
White Onyx 142
Onyx Pro 142
Onyx Pro 3.5 142
682/682 Gold 142
682 Super Skeet 143
682 Gold Skeet 143

682 4 Barrel Set 143
682 Super Sporting/682
  Gold Sporting Ported 143
682 Gold Sporting 143
682 Sporting Combo 143
682 Super Trap 143
682 Top Single Super Trap ...143
682 Top Combo Super Trap ...143
682 Trap 143
682 Top Single Trap 143
682 Mono Combo Trap 143
682 Top Combo 143
682 Gold Trap
  with Adjustable Stock 144
682 Gold Skeet
  with Adjustable Stock 144
682 Gold "Live Bird" 144
S682 Gold E Trap 144
S682 Gold E Trap Combo 144
S682 Gold E Skeet 144
S682 Gold E Sporting 144
Model 685 144
686/686 Silver Perdiz Sporting ...144
686 Essential/Silver Essential ...144
686 Ultra Light Onyx 145
686 Onyx 145
686 Onyx 2 Barrel Set 145
686 Silver Receiver 145
686 L/686 Silver Perdiz 145
686 Silver Pigeon 145
  Sporting 145
  Trap (30") 145
  Trap Top Mono (32" or 34") ...145
686 Silver Pigeon S 145
686E Sporting 145
686 EL/Gold Perdiz 145
686 Hunter Sport 145
686 Onyx Hunter Sport 146
686 Whitewing 146
686 Blackwing 146
686 Sporting Combo 146
686 Collection Trap 146
686 Collection Sport 146
686 Quail Unlimited 2002 Covey
  Limited Edition 146
686 Ringneck Pheasants Forever ...146
Ultralight 146
Ultralight Deluxe 146
687/687 Silver Pigeon Sporting ...146
687 L/Silver Pigeon 146
687 Silver Pigeon II 147
687 Silver Pigeon Sporting ...147
687 Silver Pigeon II Sporting ...147
Silver Pigeon S 147
Silver Pigeon S Combo 147
687 Sporting Combo 147
687 Silver Pigeon IV 147
687 Silver Pigeon V 147
687 EL/687 Gold Pigeon 147
  12 and 20 gauge 147
  28 gauge and .410 bore 147
687 EL Gold Pigeon Sporting ...147
687 EELL/Diamond Pigeon 147
  12 and 20 gauge 148
  28 gauge and .410 bore 148
  Combo 148

687 EELL Diamond Pigeon Skeet 148
  12 gauge 148
  4 Barrel Set 148
  With Adjustable Stock 148
687 EELL Diamond Pigeon
  Sporting 148
687 EELL Trap 148
687 EELL Top Combo 148
687 EELL King Ranch 148
Model 692 148
  692 Sporting 148
  692 Trap 148
  692 Skeet 148
Model FS-1 148
TR-1 Trap 148
TR-2 Trap 149
Mark II Trap 149
ASE 90 Pigeon 149
ASE 90 Trap 149
ASE 90 Gold X Trap Combo ...149
ASE 90 Skeet 149
ASE 90 Sporting Clay 149
Model SL-2 149
Pigeon Series 149
  Silver Pigeon 149
  Gold Pigeon 149
  Ruby Pigeon 149
DT 10 Trident Trap 149
DT 10 Trident Trap Combo Top ...149
DT 10 Trident Trap Bottom Single ...149
DT 10 Trident Skeet 149
DT 10 Trident Sporting 150
DT 11 150
  Sporting 150
  Skeet 150
  Trap 150
  International Trap 150
SV10 Perennia 150
AL-1 150
AL-2 150
AL-2 Competition 150
AL-2 Magnum 150
AL-3 150
AL-3 Deluxe Trap 150
Model 301 150
Model 1200 Field Grade 150
Model 1200 Magnum 150
Model 1200 Riot 150
Model 1201 150
  Field Grade 151
  Riot Model 151
Model 1301 Comp 151
Model 302 151
Model 302 Super Lusso 151
Model Vittoria/Pintail 151
ES100 Pintail Synthetic 151
ES100 Pintail Rifled Slug 151
ES100 Rifled Slug 151
ES100 Rifled Slug Combo 151
ES100 NWTF Special Camo 151
Model A-303 151
Model A-303 Upland 152
Model A-303 Sporting Clay 152
Model A-303 Competition
  (Trap or Skeet) 152
Model A-303 Slug Gun 152

Model A-303 Youth Gun 152
Model A-303 Ducks Unlimited ...152
  12 Gauge 152
  20 Gauge 152
  Field Grade 152
  Slug Gun 152
  Synthetic Stock 152
  Camouflage 152
  Deluxe Grade/Gold Mallard ...152
AL390 Trap 152
AL390 Super Trap 152
AL390 Skeet 152
AL390 Super Skeet 152
AL390 Sporting 152
  20 gauge 152
  Ported 152
AL390 Sport Gold Sporting 153
AL390 Sport Sporting Youth ...153
AL390 NWTF Special Youth 153
AL390 Sport Sporting Youth
  Collection 153
AL390 Sport Diamond Sporting ...153
AL390 Camo 153
AL390 Waterfowl/Turkey Model ...153
AL390 NWTF Special Camo 153
AL390 NWTF Special Synthetic ...153
Super Trap 153
Super Skeet 153
Model 3901 153
Model 3901 RL 153
Model 3901 Camo 153
Model 3901 Citizen 154
Model 3901 Statesman 154
Model 3901 Ambassador 154
Model 3901 Target RL 154
Urika 154
Urika Synthetic 154
Urika Camo 154
Urika Gold 154
Urika Youth 154
Urika Sporting 154
Urika Gold Sporting 154
Urika Trap 154
Urika Gold Trap 154
Urika Parallel Target RL/SL 154
Urika Optima 155
Urika Synthetic Optima 155
Urika Optima Camo 155
Urika 2 X-Tra Grain 155
Urika 2 Gold 155
Urika 2 Kick-Off 155
Urika 2 Sporting X-Tra Grain ...155
Urika 2 Gold Sporting 155
Urika 2 Parallel Target X-Tra Grain ...155
Urika 2 Gold Parallel Target ...155
AL391 Covey 155
AL391 Ringneck 155
AL391 Teknys 155
AL391 Teknys Gold 156
AL391 Teknys Gold Target 156
AL391 Teknys King Ranch 156
AL391 Xtrema 3.5 156
AL391 Xtrema2 156
AL391 Xtrema2 Slug Gun 156
UGB25 XCEL 156

A400 Xplor Unico 156
A400 Xcel Sporting 156
A400 Extreme KO 156
TX4 Storm 156

BERGARA

B-14 Hunter...................................156
BCR-13 Sport Hunter......................157
BC-15 Long Range Hunter..............157
BX-11 Takedown Hunter 157
BCR-19 Tactical Rifle......................157
BCR-17 Medium Tactical 157
Mountain Hunter 157
Premier Series Classic 157

BERGER, JEAN MARIUS

Berger 157

BERGMANN, THEODOR

Model 1894 Bergmann Schmeisser . 157
Model 1896 Number 2 158
   Folding Trigger............................158
   Conventional 158
Model 1896 Number 3 158
   First Variation 158
   Second Variation 158
   Third Variation 158
   Holster and Stock Model 159
Model 1896 Number 4 159
Model 1897 Number 5 159
Model 1897 Number 5 Carbine.......159
Bergmann Simplex 159
Bergmann Mars 159
Bergmann Bayard Model 1908 159
Bergmann Post War Pistols.............160
   Model 2 and 3............................160
   Model 2a and 3a.........................160
Bergmann Erben Pistols...................160
Bergmann Erben Spezial..................160
Bergmann Erben Model II Pistol.......160

BERNARDELLI, VINCENZO

Vest Pocket Model...........................160
Pocket Model..................................161
Baby Model.....................................161
Sporter Model 161
Revolvers 161
Model 60 161
Model 68 161
Model 80 161
Model AMR 161
Model 69 161
Model PO10.....................................162
Model PO18.....................................162
Model PO18 Compact 162
Model P. One...................................162
Model P. One-Compact 162
Practical VB Target 162
Practical VB Custom 163
Model USA......................................163
Model 115.......................................163
Model 115S.....................................163
Model 115L......................................163
Model 115E......................................163
Model 115 Trap................................163
Model 115S Trap..............................163

Model 115E Trap..............................163
Model 190.......................................163
Model 190MC..................................163
Model 190 Special 163
Model 190 Combo Gun 163
Orione 163
Orione S 163
Orione L 163
Orione E 163
S. Uberto I Gamecock 163
Brescia 163
Italia 164
Italia Extra......................................164
S. Uberto 1......................................164
S. Uberto 1E....................................164
S. Uberto 2......................................164
S. Uberto 2E....................................164
S. Uberto F.S...................................164
S. Uberto F.S.E................................164
Roma 3...164
Roma 3E..164
Roma 4...164
Roma 4E..164
Roma 6...164
Roma 6E..164
Roma 7...164
Roma 8...164
Roma 9...165
Elio...165
Elio E..165
Hemingway.....................................165
Hemingway Deluxe..........................165
Las Palomas Pigeon Model 165
Holland V.B. Liscio 165
Holland V.B. Inciso 165
Holland V.B. Lusso 165
Holland V.B. Extra 165
Holland V.B. Gold 165
Luck..165
Giardino/Garden Gun
   (9mm Rimfire) 165
Carbina VB Target...........................165
Comb 2000 165
Express 2000 165
Express VB......................................165
Express VB Deluxe...........................166
Minerva 166

BERNARDON MARTIN

1907/8 Model..................................166
1908/9 Model..................................166

BERNEDO, VINCENZO

B C...166
Bernado..166

BERSA

Model 644.......................................166
Model 622.......................................167
Model 97...167
Model 23...167
Model 223.......................................167
Model 224.......................................167
Model 225.......................................167
Model 226.......................................167
Model 323.......................................167

Model 383.......................................167
Model 383A.....................................167
Model 83...167
Model 85...168
Model 86...168
Thunder 9..168
Series 95/Thunder 380 168
Thunder 380 Matte Plus 168
Thunder Pro Ultra Compact.............168
Thunder 9/40 High Capacity Series .. 168
Thunder Deluxe...............................169
Thunder 22......................................169

BERTRAND, JULES

Le Novo 169
Lincoln 169
Le Rapide 169

BERTUZZI

Zeus..169
Zeus Extra Lusso 169
Zeus Boss System............................169
Gull Wing 169
Ariete Extra Lusso 169
Orione 169
Venere 169
Ariete 169
Gull Wing 169

BIG HORN ARMORY

Big Horn Armory Model 89 Rifle
   and Carbine 169

BIGHORN ARMS CO.

Target Pistol...................................169
Shotgun..169

BIGHORN RIFLE CO.

Bighorn Rifle 169

BILHARZ, HALL & CO.

Breechloading ("Rising Breech")
   Carbine 170
Muzzleloading Carbine....................170

BILLINGHURST, WILLIAM

Under Hammer Pistol.......................170
Revolving Rifle................................170

BILLINGS

Pocket Pistol 170

BINGHAM LTD.

PPS 50 170
AK-22 170
Bantam..170

BISMARCK

Pocket Revolver..............................170

BITTNER, GUSTAV

Bittner 171

BLAKE, J. H.

Blake Bolt-Action Rifle 171

BLANCH, JOHN

Blanch Percussion Pistol.................171

BLASER JAGDWAFFEN

Model K77.......................................171
Model R-84 171
Model R-93 LX.................................171
Model R-93 Prestige 171
Model R-93 Classic 171
Model R-93 Luxus............................172
Model R-93 Synthetic 172
Model R-93 Attache 172
Model R-93 Safari Synthetic 172
Model R-93 Safari LX 172
Model R-93 Safari Classic 172
Model R-93 Safari Attache 172
Model R-93 Grand Luxe...................172
Model R-8 Professional 172
Model R-8 Professional Success 172
Model R-8 Professional Hunter........172
Model K-95 Standard 172
Model K-95 Luxus............................172
Model K-95 Stutzen.........................172
Ultimate Bolt-Action.......................172
Model R-93 Long Range Sporter 173
Model R-93 (LRS2)..........................173
Blaser S2 Double Rifle 173
   Standard...................................173
   Safari 173
F3 Series...173
   Game Standard 173
   Sporting Standard and Skeet......173
   Super Trap and Super Sport 173
Blaser HHS......................................173

BLISS, F. D.

Bliss Pocket Revolver......................173

BLISS & GOODYEAR

Pocket Model Revolver 173

BLUNT & SYMS

Under Hammer Pepperbox..............174
   Small Frame Round Handle
     .25-.28-Caliber 174
   Medium Frame Round Handle
     .31-Caliber............................174
   Round Handle Dragoon
     .36-Caliber............................174
   Medium Frame Saw Handle
     .31-Caliber............................174
   Saw Handle Dragoon
     .36-Caliber............................174
Dueling Pistol.................................174
Single-Shot Bar Hammer 174
Side Hammer Pocket Pistol 174
Side Hammer Belt Pistol 174
Ring Trigger Pistol 174
Double Barrel Pistol 174
Double Barrel Under
   Hammer Pistol...........................174
Derringer Style Pistol 174

BOBERG ARMS CORP.

XR9...174
XR45...174

BODEO
Italian Service Revolver 175
  System Bodeo Modello 1889
    (Enlisted Model) 175
  Modello 1889 (Officer's Model)...175

BOLUMBURO, G.
Bristol..175
Marina 6.35mm 175
Marina 7.65mm 175
Rex 175

BOND ARMS INC.
Texas Defender 175
Bond Patriot..................................176
Snake Slayer IV 176
Snake Slayer 176
Cowboy Defender..........................176
Century 2000 176

BORCHARDT
Borchardt......................................176
  Pistol Only..................................176
  Pistol with Case
    and Accessories.....................177

BOSIS, LUCIANO
Over/Under 177
Side-by-Side..................................177

BOSWELL, CHARLES
Double Rifle, Boxlock....................177
Double Rifle, Sidelock...................177

BOSWORTH, B. M.
Under Hammer Pistol.....................177

BRAND
Brand Breech Loading Carbine........177

BREDA, ERNESTO
Andromeda Special 177
Vega Special 177
Vega Special Trap.........................177
Sirio Standard 178
Standard Semi-Automatic...............178
  Grade I......................................178
  Grade II.....................................178
  Grade III....................................178
Magnum Model 178
Gold Series Antares Standard..........178
Gold Series Argus.........................178
Gold Series Aries 178
M1 Garand 178

BREN 10
Standard Bren 10...........................178
M & P Model.................................178
Special Forces Model 178
Dual-Master Presentation Model 178
Marksman Model 178
Jeff Cooper Commemorative...........179
Bren 10 (2010 Series) 179

BRETTON
Baby Standard 179

Deluxe Grade 179

BRIGGS, H. A.
Briggs Single-Shot Pistol...............179

BRILEY MANUFACTURING INC.
El Presidente Model—Unlimited......179
Versatility Plus Model—Limited.......179
Versatility Model—Limited..............179
Lightning Model—Action Pistol 179
Carry Comp Model—Defense 180

BRIXIA
Model 12.......................................180

BRNO ARMS
ZG-47 180
  Standard....................................180
  Deluxe 180
ZH-300 180
ZH-301 180
ZH-302 180
ZH-303 12 180
ZH-304 180
ZH-305 180
ZH-306 180
ZH-308 180
ZH-309 180
ZH-321 181
ZH-324 181
ZH-328 181
Model 300 Combo 181
Model 500 181
ZP-49...181
ZP-149...181
ZP-349...181
ZBK-100 181
ZKW-465 (Hornet Sporter) 181
Model 21H 181
Model 22F 181
Model I 181
Model II 181
ZKM 611 181
ZKM 451 181
ZKM 451 LUX 181
ZBK 680 181
Super Express Rifle 181
  Standard Model 181
  Grade I......................................181
  Grade II.....................................182
  Grade III....................................182
  Grade IV....................................182
  Grade V.....................................182
  Grade VI....................................182
ZH-344/348/349 182
Model 98 Standard.........................182
Model 98 Full Stock.......................182
ZK 99 182
ZBK 110 182
ZBK 110 LUX 182
ZBK 110 Super Lux 182
ZKR 551 182

BROLIN ARMS
L45—Standard Auto Pistol 182
L45C—Compact Auto Pistol 182

L45T 182
P45 Comp—
  Standard Carry Comp 182
P45C Comp—
  Compact Carry Comp..................183
P45T 183
TAC-11 183
MS45 183
M45 183
M40 183
M90 183
MC40 183
MC90 183
MB40 183
MB90 183
Pro-Stock—Competition Pistol........183
Pro-Comp—Competition Pistol 184
HL18SB..184
HL18SR..184
HL18SBN..184
HL18WB...184
HL18WR...184
HF24SB..184
HF28SB..184
HF24WB...184
HF28WB...184
Slug Special 184
Turkey Special 184
HC28SB..184
HC28SR..185
HC28WB...185
HC28WR...185
BL-12 Security...............................185
BL-12 Field 185
SAS-12 Security.............................185
Legacy 185
Mitchell PPS-50.............................185
Lightning Model 185
Lightning Hunter Model 185
Lightning Hunter All Weather Model.. 185
Lightning Varmint Model 185
Lightning Sniper 185
Lightning Professional 185
2000 Classic 185
2000 Varmint 185
2000 Sniper 186
2000 Professional 186
20/22 186
1898 Commemorative 186
98 186
Formula One RZ 186
Formula One RS 186
Formula Z 186
Single-Action Army Model..............186

BROOKLYN F. A. CO.
Slocum Pocket Revolver..................186
Slocum Unfluted Cylinder Pocket
  Revolver....................................186

BROWN, E.A. MANUFACTURING CO.
Brown Classic Single-Shot Pistol 186
Brown Model 97D Single-Shot Rifle.. 186

BROWN, ED PRODUCTS
Commander Bobtail.......................187
Classic Custom 187
Class A Limited 187
Kobra Custom .45 187
Kobra Carry .45 187
Executive Target 187
Executive Elite 187
Executive Carry 187
Special Forces 187
Jim Wilson Limited Edition 187
Jeff Cooper Commemorative
  Limited Edition..........................187
Massad Ayoob Limited Edition.........187
Savanna 188
Damara 188
Varmint..188
Bushveld..188
Express 188
Marine Sniper 188
Light Tactical.................................188
Tactical..188
Ozark 188
Denali..188
Peacekeeper..................................188

BROWN MANUFACTURING CO.
Southerner Derringer.....................189
  Brass Framed 189
  Iron Frame 189
  Brass Frame 4" Barrel...............189
Brown Mfg. Co./Merrill Patent
  Breechloading Rifles 189

BROWN PRECISION, INC.
Custom High Country.....................189
Pro Hunter 189
Pro Hunter Elite 189
Pro Varminter/Light Varminter 189
Tactical Elite..................................189
Open Country Varmint Rifle
  (disc. 1992)...............................189
Law Enforcement Model
  (disc. 1992)...............................189
Blaser Action Model (disc. 1989).....189

BROWNING ARMS CO.
Early Semi-Automatic Pistols...........189
Hi-Power Modern Production 189
  Spur Hammer Version 190
  Round Hammer Version...............190
Hi-Power—.30 Luger......................190
Tangent Sight Model......................190
Renaissance Hi-Power....................190
  Spur Hammer Model 190
  Ring Hammer Model 190
  Adjustable Sight Spur Hammer
    Model 190
  Renaissance .25-Caliber 190
  Renaissance .380-Caliber 190
  Renaissance .380-Caliber
    (Model 1971)..........................190
  Cased Renaissance Set...............190
Louis XVI Model 190
  Diamond Grip Model 190
  Medallion Grip Model..................190
Hi-Power Centennial Model............191

Hi-Power Capitan 191
Hi-Power Practical........................191
Hi-Power Silver Chrome Model........191
Hi-Power .40 S&W 191
Hi-Power Mark III.........................191
Hi-Power Gold Classic 191
Hi-Power Classic 191
Baby Browning..............................191
Browning Model 1955 191
Pro-9/Pro-40 192
BDA-380 192
BDA 192
BDM Pistol..................................192
BDM Silver Chrome 192
BDM Practical 192
BPM-D 192
BRM-DAO....................................192
Nomad 193
Challenger 193
Renaissance Challenger................193
Gold Line Challenger 193
Challenger II...............................193
Challenger III..............................193
Browning
    Collector's Association Edition......193
Medalist 193
International Medalist 194
Second Model International
    Medalist..................................194
Gold Line Medalist.......................194
Renaissance Medalist...................194
Buck Mark 194
Buck Mark Plus............................194
    Nickel 194
Buck Mark Varmint.......................194
Buck Mark Silhouette 195
Buck Mark 22 Micro......................195
    Plus 195
    Plus Nickel 195
Buck Mark 5.5 195
    Blued Target..............................195
    Blued Target (2005) 195
    Gold Target...............................195
    Field 195
    Field (2005) 195
Buck Field Plus 196
Buck Mark Bullseye.......................196
Buck Mark Unlimited Match 196
Buck Mark Challenge 196
Buck Mark Camper 196
Buck Mark Camper Cocobola UDX...196
Buck Mark Camper Stainless UFX....196
Buck Mark Practical URX
    Fiber Optic 196
Buck Mark Hunter 197
Buck Mark Limited Edition 25th
    Anniversary...............................197
Buck Mark Bullseye Target.............197
Buck Mark Bullseye Target URX.......197
Buck Mark Contour 5.5 URX 197
Buck Mark Contour Lite 5.5 URX 197
Buck Mark FLD Plus
    Rosewood UDX...........................197
Buck Mark Lite Splash 5.5 URX.......197
Buck Mark Micro Standard
    Stainless URX............................197

Buck Mark Micro Bull 197
Buck Mark Plus Stainless Black
    Laminated UDX...........................197
Buck Mark Plus UDX......................197
Full Line Dealer Buck Mark Plus
    Rosewood UDX...........................198
Buck Mark Plus Stainless UDX 198
Buck Mark Standard Stainless URX..198
Browning 1911-22..........................198
Browning 1911-22 A1
    Polymer Frame w/Rail 198
Browning 1911-22 Polymer
    Desert Tan................................198
Browning 1911-22 Black Label.......198
Browning 1911-380.......................198
Browning 1911-380 Black Label.....198
    Grade I.....................................199
    Pigeon 199
    Diana 199
    Midas.......................................199
    Grade I.....................................199
    Grade II....................................199
    Grade III...................................199
    Grade IV...................................199
    Grade V....................................199
    Grade VI...................................199
    Grade I Standard Weight 200
    Grade I Lightweight....................200
    Pigeon Grade 200
    Pointer Grade—(Rare)..................200
    Diana Grade 200
    Midas Grade..............................200
Superposed Superlight 200
    Grade I.....................................200
    Pigeon Grade 200
    Pointer Grade—(Rare) 200
    Diana Grade 200
    Midas Grade..............................200
    Presentation 1
        (without gold inlays) 201
    Presentation 1 Gold-inlaid 201
    Presentation 2
        (without gold inlays) 201
    Presentation 2 Gold-inlaid 201
    Presentation 3 Gold-inlaid 201
    Presentation 4 Gold-inlaid 201
    1981 Mallard Issue....................201
    1982 Pintail Issue.....................201
    1983 Black Duck Issue 201
Bicentennial Model 202
Classic 202
Gold Classic 202
Custom Shop B25 & B125
    Superposed..............................202
B-125 Hunting or
    Sporting Clays Model 202
    A-Style Engraving 202
    B-Style Engraving 202
    C-Style Engraving 202
B-125 Trap Model 202
    C-Style Engraving 202
B-25 202
    Grade 1 202
    Pigeon Grade 202
    Pointer Grade 202
    Diana Grade 202
    Midas Grade..............................202

Custom Shop BSL 202
    Case Colored Receiver
        (BSL Grade LC1) 202
    Engraved Gray Receiver
        (BSL Grade LC2) 202
Liege...202
B27 203
    Standard..................................203
    Deluxe 203
    Deluxe Trap 203
    Deluxe Skeet 203
    Grand Deluxe 203
    City of Liege Commemorative 203
ST-100 203
    Grade I.....................................203
    Upland Special—Grade I............203
    Grade II—1978 to 1983............203
    Grade II—Choke Tubes.............203
    Grade V—1978 to 1984............203
    Grade V with sideplates—
        1981 to 1984......................204
    Grade VI—Choke Tubes............204
Citori Hunter 204
Citori Sporting Hunter 204
Citori Satin Hunter 204
Citori Satin Hunter Micro Midas.......204
Citori Lightning 204
    Grade I.....................................204
    Grade III...................................204
    Grade IV...................................204
    Grade VI...................................205
    Grade VII..................................205
Citori Lightning Feather................205
Citori Lightning Feather Combo 205
Citori Feather XS 205
Citori Superlight Feather 205
Citori Super Lightning Grade I 205
Citori Classic Lightning Grade I.......205
Citori Classic Lightning Feather
    Grade I.....................................205
Citori 525 Sporting 205
Citori 525 Field 206
Citori 525 Golden Clays Sporting.....206
Citori 525 Feather 206
Citori 625 Sporting 206
Citori 625 Sporting Left-Hand 206
Citori 625 Field 206
Citori Model 725 Field 206
    Grade III...................................206
    Grade V....................................206
    Grade VII Small Gauge 206
    725 Feather 206
    725 Skeet 206
    725 Skeet w/adjustable comb 206
    725 Sporting 206
    725 Sporting
        w/adjustable comb...............206
    725 Trap 206
Citori Esprit 206
Citori Sporting Clays 207
Citori Lightning Sporting 207
    Pigeon Grade 207
    Golden Clays 207
Citori Privilege............................207
Citori XS Sporting Clays 207
Citori Ultra XS Skeet 207

Citori XS Special..........................208
Citori Plus 208
    Grade I.....................................208
    Pigeon Grade 208
    Signature Grade 208
    Golden Clays 208
Citori Trap Combination Set............208
GTI Model 208
    Grade I.....................................208
    Signature Grade 208
    Golden Clays 208
Ultra Sporter - (Sporting Clays) 208
    Golden Clays 208
Citori Superlight 208
Citori Superlight Feather 208
Micro Lightning 208
Gran Lightning 209
Gran Lightning 16 Gauge 209
Citori White Lightning 209
Citori White Upland Special 209
Citori Skeet 209
    Grade I.....................................209
    Grade II....................................209
    Grade III...................................209
    Grade V....................................209
    Grade VI...................................209
    Golden Clays 209
3 Gauge Sets 209
    Grade I.....................................209
    Grade III...................................209
    Grade VI...................................209
4 Gauge Sets 209
    Grade I.....................................209
    Grade III...................................209
    Grade VI...................................209
Citori Trap 209
    Grade I.....................................210
    Plus Trap 210
    Grade II....................................210
    Grade III...................................210
    Grade V....................................210
    Grade VI...................................210
Citori XT Trap 210
    Golden Clays 210
    Signature Grade 210
Citori XT Trap Gold........................210
Model 325 Sporting Clays...............210
Special Sporting 210
    Grade I.....................................210
    Signature Grade 210
    Pigeon Grade 210
    Golden Clays 210
Model 425 Sporting Clays...............210
Model 425 Golden Clays.................210
Light Sporting 802ES
    (Extended Swing)........................210
Citori Plus Combo.........................211
Citori Ultra XS Prestige..................211
BT-99...211
BT-99 Stainless.............................211
BT-99 Signature Grade I 211
BT-99 Pigeon Grade 211
BT-99 Golden Clays.......................211
BT-99 Plus...................................211
BT-99 Plus—Pigeon Grade.............211
BT-99 Plus—Signature Grade........211

BT-99 Plus Stainless—Grade I........211
BT-99 Plus—Golden Clays 211
BT-99 Plus Micro 211
BT-99 Grade III 211
BT-100 211
BT-100 Satin 212
BT-100 Thumbhole 212
Recoilless Trap 212
BSS 212
BSS Grade II 212
BSS Sporter 212
BSS Sidelock 212
Cynergy Field 212
Cynergy Classic Field....................213
Cynergy Field Small Gauge 213
Cynergy Sporting 213
Cynergy Classic Sporting 213
Cynergy Classic Field Grade III.......213
Cynergy Classic Field Grade VI 213
Cynergy Sporting Adjustable Comb..213
Cynergy Sporting Small Gauge 213
Cynergy Feather 213
Cynergy Feather Composite 213
Cynergy Euro Sporting 213
Cynergy Euro Field 214
Cynergy Euro Sporting Composite
  with Adjustable Comb 214
Cynergy Classic Trap
  Unsingle Combo 214
  Grade I—Plain Barrel..................214
  Grade I—Matte Rib 214
  Grade I—Vent Rib 214
  Grade II—Plain Barrel..................214
  Grade II—Matte Rib....................214
  Grade II—Vent Rib......................214
  Grade III—Plain Barrel.................214
  Grade III—Matte Rib....................214
  Grade III—Vent Rib.....................214
  Grade IV—Plain Barrel..................214
  Grade IV—Matte Rib....................214
  Grade IV—Vent Rib.....................214
American Browning Auto-5 214
  Plain Barrel 215
  Matte Rib 215
  Vent Rib 215
Auto-5 Lightweight.......................215
Auto-5 Magnum...........................215
Auto-5 Skeet..............................215
Auto-5 Trap Model.......................215
Sweet Sixteen 215
Buck Special 215
Two Millionth Commemorative........215
Auto-5 Light 12...........................215
Auto-5 Light 20...........................215
Auto-5 Magnum...........................215
Auto-5 Buck Special 215
Auto-5 Skeet..............................215
Sweet Sixteen 215
A-5 DU 50th Anniversary 215
A-5 DU Sweet Sixteen 216
Auto-5 Classic 216
  Classic 216
  Gold Classic 216
Auto-5 Light Buck Special..............216
Auto-5 Stalker 216
  Light Stalker..............................216

Magnum Stalker 216
Auto-5 Final Tribute
  Limited Edition..........................216
Browning A5 216
Browning A5 Ultimate 216
Browning A5 Sweet Sixteen 216
Double Automatic Shotgun..............216
Twelvette Double Auto 217
Twentyweight Double Auto 217
B-2000 217
B-2000 Magnum 217
B-2000 Buck Special 217
B-2000 Trap 217
B-2000 Skeet 217
B-80 217
B-80 Buck Special 217
B-80 DU Commemorative 217
Gold 10 217
Gold Evolve 218
Gold Light 10 Gauge Camo 218
Gold 10 Gauge Combo 218
Gold Stalker 218
Gold Classic Stalker 218
Gold 3-1/2" 12 Gauge 218
Gold 12 Gauge Hunter 218
Gold Classic Hunter 218
Gold Classic 20 Gauge 218
Gold Classic High Grade 219
Gold Deer Hunter 219
Gold Deer Hunter 20 Gauge 219
Gold Deer Stalker 219
Gold Deer Mossy Oak 219
Gold Waterfowl Mossy Oak
  Shadow Grass 219
Gold Waterfowl
  Mossy Oak Breakup....................219
Gold Turkey/Waterfowl Mossy Oak...219
Gold Turkey/Waterfowl Stalker.........219
Gold Turkey/Waterfowl Hunter 219
Gold NWTF Series 219
Gold Light 10 Gauge.....................219
Gold 12 Gauge............................219
  3.5" Chamber, Shadow Grass.....219
  3" Chamber 220
  3.5" Chamber
    Ultimate Turkey Gun 220
Gold Hunter 220
Gold Sporting Clays 220
Gold Ladies/Youth Sporting Clays 220
Gold "Golden Clays" Ladies
  Sporting Clays 220
Gold "Golden Clays"
  Sporting Clays 220
Gold Micro 220
Gold Upland 220
Gold Fusion 220
Gold Fusion High Grade 220
Golden Clays 221
Gold Superlite Hunter 221
Gold Superlite FLD Hunter.............221
Gold Superlite Micro 221
A-500G/A-500R 221
A-500G Sporting Clays 221
A-500R Hunting Model 221
A-500R Buck Special 221
Silver Hunter 221

Silver Stalker 221
Silver Micro 221
Silver Sporting Micro 221
Silver NWTF 222
Silver Rifled Deer 222
Silver—Mossy Oak.......................222
Maxus 222
Maxus Stalker 222
Maxus Mossy Oak Duck Blind 222
Maxus Hunter 222
Maxus Sporting Carbon 222
Maxus Sporting Golden Clays.........222
BPS Field Grade 222
  28 Gauge 222
BPS Magnum 222
BPS Waterfowl 12 Gauge Camo 222
BPS Waterfowl 12 Gauge
  Mossy Oak Break-Up 223
BPS Mossy Oak New Break-up........223
BPS Mossy Oak Duck Blind 223
BPS Rifled Deer Mossy Oak
  New Break-up 223
BPS NWTF Series 223
  10 Gauge 223
  12 Gauge 3.5" Chamber 223
  12 Gauge 3" Chamber 223
BPS Stalker.................................223
BPS Stalker—Combo 223
BPS Game Gun 223
  Game Gun Deer Special
    (shown above) 223
  Game Gun Turkey Special...........223
BPS 10 Gauge Mossy Oak Shadow
  Grass Camo 223
BPS 10 Gauge Turkey...................223
BPS Micro 20 Gauge 223
BPS Upland Special 223
BPS Small Gauge 224
BPS Pigeon Grade 224
BPS Buck Special 224
BPS Trap Model...........................224
BPS Micro Trap 224
BPS Youth Model 224
BPS Waterfowl Deluxe 224
BPS Ducks Unlimited Versions........224
  Grade I....................................224
  Grade V...................................224
  Grade I....................................224
  Grade V...................................224
  Hunter Version 225
  Stalker Version 225
High-Power Bolt-Action Rifle 225
  Safari Grade 225
  Medallion Grade 225
  Olympian Grade........................225
Model BBR..................................225
BOSS™ SYSTEM 225
X-Bolt Composite Stalker 225
X-Bolt Stainless Stalker 225
X-Bolt Hunter 226
X-Bolt Medallion 226
X-Bolt Micro Hunter 226
X-Bolt Eclipse Hunter 226
X-Bolt Varmint Stalker 226
X-Bolt RMEF White Gold 226
X-Bolt RMEF Special Hunter 226

X-Bolt Hell's Canyon 226
A-Bolt Hunter 226
A-Bolt II Hunter 226
A-Bolt II Hunter WSSM 226
A-Bolt II Micro Hunter 227
A-Bolt II Classic Hunter 227
A-Bolt Stainless Hunter 227
A-Bolt Classic Hunter WSSM 227
A-Bolt Mountain Ti 227
A-Bolt Composite Stalker 227
A-Bolt II Composite Stalker 227
A-Bolt Composite Stalker WSSM 227
A-Bolt Stainless Stalker 227
A-Bolt II Composite
  Stainless Stalker 227
A-Bolt Stainless Stalker WSSM........228
A-Bolt Carbon Fiber
  Stainless Stalker 228
A-Bolt II Heavy Barrel Varmint..........228
A-Bolt Varmint Stalker 228
A-Bolt Varmint Stalker WSSM..........228
A-Bolt Eclipse M-1000 228
A-Bolt Eclipse M-1000 WSM
  & Stainless 228
A-Bolt Eclipse Varmint 228
Euro-Bolt 228
A-Bolt II Euro Bolt 228
NRA A-Bolt Wildlife Conservation
  Collection 228
A-Bolt Medallion Model..................228
A-Bolt II Medallion 229
A-Bolt II Medallion WSSM 229
A-Bolt Gold Medallion 229
A-Bolt II Gold Medallion 229
A-Bolt II White Gold Medallion 229
A-Bolt White Gold Medallion RMEF ..229
A-Bolt Custom Trophy 229
A-Bolt Big Horn Sheep Issue 229
A-Bolt Micro-Medallion 229
A-Bolt II Micro-Medallion 229
A-Bolt Pronghorn Issue 229
A-Bolt Special Hunter RMEF...........230
A-Bolt White Gold RMEF 230
A-Bolt Target 230
A-Bolt Target Stainless..................230
A-Bolt .22 Grade I 230
A-Bolt .22 Gold Medallion 230
AB3 Composite Stalker 230
T-Bolt Model T-1 230
T-Bolt Model T-2 230
T-Bolt (2006) 231
T-Bolt Target/Varmint....................231
T-Bolt Target/Varmint Stainless........231
T-Bolt Composite Hunter 231
T-Bolt Composite Target/Varmint 231
T-Bolt Composite Target/Varmint
  Left-Hand.................................231
T-Bolt Sporter.............................231
T-Bolt Sporter Left-Hand 231
T-Bolt Composite Sporter
  Left-Hand.................................231
Acera Straight Pull Rifle 231
Model 52 Limited Edition 231
BPR-22 231
BPR-22 Grade II 232
Trombone Model 232

Semi-Automatic .22 (SA-22) 232
    Grade I 232
    Grade II 232
    Grade III 232
Semi-Auto .22
    (SA-22, Miroku Mfg.) 232
    Grade I 232
    Grade II 232
    Grade III 232
    Grade VI 232
Semi-Auto .22 High Grade
    100th Anniversary 233
BAR-22 233
BAR-22 Grade II 233
Buck Mark Rifle 233
    Target Model 233
    Sporter Model 233
Buck Mark Field Target
    Gray Laminate 233
Patent 1900 High Power 233
Bar High Power Rifle 233
    Grade I 233
    Grade I Magnum 233
    Grade II Deluxe 233
    Grade II Deluxe Magnum 234
    Grade III 234
    Grade III Magnum 234
    Grade IV 234
    Grade IV Magnum 234
    Grade V 234
    Grade V Magnum 234
North American Deer Rifle Issue 234
BAR Mark II Safari Rifle 234
BAR Mark II Lightweight 234
BAR Composite Stalker 234
BAR High Grade Models 234
BAR ShortTrac 235
BAR ShortTrac Stalker 235
BAR ShortTrac Left-Hand 235
BAR ShortTrac Mossy Oak
    New Break-up 235
BAR ShortTrac Digital Green 235
BAR LongTrac 235
BAR LongTrac Stalker 235
BAR LongTrac Left-Hand 235
BAR LongTrac Mossy Oak
    New Break-up 235
Model BPR 235
BL-22 Grade I 235
BL-22 Grade II 236
BL-22 Field Series Grade I 236
BL-17 Field Series Grade I 236
BL-22 Field Series Grade II 236
BL-17 Field Series Grade II 236
BL-22 Grade II Octagon 236
BL-17 Grade II Octagon 236
BL-22 Classic 236
BL-22 NRA Grade 1 236
BL-22 Gray Laminate Stainless 236
BL-22 Micro Midas 236
Model 81 BLR 236
BLR Lightning (Lightweight) 237
BLR Lightweight '81 237
BLR Lightweight Takedown 237
BLR Lightweight '81
    Stainless Takedown 237

Model B-78 237
Model 53 237
Model 65 Grade I 237
Model 65 High Grade 237
Model 71 Grade I 237
Model 71 High Grade 237
Jonathan Browning Centennial
    Mountain Rifle 238
Jonathan Browning Mountain Rifle ..238
Model 1878 (Original) 238
Model 1885 High Wall 238
Model 1885 Low Wall 238
Model 1885 Low Wall
    Traditional Hunter 238
Model 1885 BPCR (Black Powder
    Cartridge Rifle) 238
Model 1885 BPCR
    Creedmoor Type 238
Model 1885 High Wall
    Traditional Hunter 238
Model 1886 Grade I 238
    Carbine 238
Model 1886 High Grade 238
    Carbine 239
Model 1886 Montana Centennial ...239
B-92 Carbine 239
Model 1895 Grade I 239
Model 1895 High Grade 239
Express Rifle 239
Custom Shop Express Rifles 239
Continental Set 239

BRUCE & DAVIS
Double-Barreled Pistol 239

BRUCHET
Model A Shotgun 239
Model B 239

BRUFF, R.P.
Pocket Pistol 240

BSA GUNS LTD.
No. 12 Cadet Martini 240
Centurian Match Rifle 240
Model 13 Sporter 240
Martini International Match 240
Martini International Light 240
Martini International ISU 240
Royal 240
Majestic Deluxe 240
Majestic Deluxe Featherweight 240
Monarch Deluxe 240
Sporter/Classic 240
Varminter 240
Stutzen Rifle 240
Regal Custom 241
CFT Target Rifle 241
Royal 241
Classic 241
Falcon 241
Falcon Sporting 241
Silver Eagle 241
Silver Eagle II 241
200 Series 241
300 SM Series 241

BUCO
Buco Gas Pistol 241

BUDISCHOWSKY
TP-70 241
    .22 Rimfire Caliber 242
    .25 ACP Caliber 242

BUL TRANSMARK LTD.
Model M5 242

BULLARD REPEATING ARMS CO.
Small Frame 242
Large Frame 242
Carbine 242
Musket 242

BULLDOG SINGLE-SHOT PISTOL
Bulldog 242

BURGESS GUN CO.
12 Gauge Slide Action Shotgun 242
    Burgess engraving grades (1-4) ..242
Folding Shotgun 242
Slide Action Rifle 242

BURGSMULLER, K.
Burgo 243
Regent 243

BURNSIDE RIFLE CO.
Bristol, Rhode Island 243
Burnside Carbine 1st Model 243
2nd Model 243
3rd Model 243
4th Model 243

**BUSHMASTER FIREARMS
INTERNATIONAL**
ACR (Adaptive Combat Rifle) 243
ACR Enhanced 243
XM15-E2S Target Model 243
XM15-E2S V-Match
    Competition Rifle 243
XM15-E2S V-Match Carbine 244
XM15 3-Gun Enhanced Carbine 244
XM15-E2S Shorty Carbine 244
XM15-E2S Dissipator 244
XM15 Patrolman's Pistol 244
M4 Post-Ban Carbine 244
M4A3 Post-Ban Carbine 244
MOE Series 244
DCM Competition Rifle 244
11.5" Barrel Carbine 244
Heavy-Barreled Carbine 244
Modular Carbine 245
M17S Bullpup 245
Gas Piston Rifle 245
6.8 SPC Carbine 245
Carbon 15 9mm Carbine 245
Carbon 15 Top Loading Rifle 245
Carbon 15 Quad Rail Flattop 245
Predator 245
Carbon 15 .22 Rimfire Rifle 245
.308 Hunter 245
ORC Series 245

Quick Response Carbine 245
.450 Carbine 246
Bushmaster AK Carbine 246
Bushmaster .300 AAC Blackout 246
BA50 .50 BMG Rifle and Carbine 246
Carbon 15 .223 Pistol 246
Carbon 15 9mm Pistol 246
Type 97 Pistol 246

BUTLER, WM. S.
Butler Single-Shot Pistol 246

BUTTERFIELD, JESSE
Butterfield Army Revolver 246
Butterfield Pocket Pistol 246

CABANAS, INDUSTRIAS S.A.
Mini-82 Youth 247
R-83 Larger Youth 247
Safari A 247
Varmint 247
Espronceda IV 247
Leyre 247
Master 247

CAMPO GIRO
Esperanza y Unceta Model 1904 247
Model 1910 247
Model 1913 247
Model 1913/16 247

CARACAL
Caracal-F 248

CARD, S. W.
Under Hammer Pistol 248

CARLTON, M.
Under Hammer Pistol 248

CASARTELLI, CARLO
Sidelock Shotgun 248
Kenya Double Rifle 248
Africa Model 248
Safari Model 248

CASE WILLARD & CO.
Under Hammer Pistol 248

CASPIAN ARMS, LTD.
Vietnam Commemorative 248

CASULL ARMS, INC.
CA 2000 249
CA 3800 249

CENTURY GUN COMPANY
Model 100 249

**CENTURY
INTERNATIONAL ARMS CO.**
Centurion 39 AK Pistol 249
Centurion UC-9 Carbine 249
Centurion Over/Under Shotgun 249
Centurion 98 Sporter 249
Century Centurion 14 249
C93 Pistol 250

CZ 999 / CZ 40...........................250
Enfield Sporter No. I Mark III...........250
Enfield Sporter No. 4 Mark I............250
TOZ-17......................................250
TOZ-17-1...................................250
Mexican Mauser Model 1910
  Sporter 250
FAL Sporter................................250
M-14 Rifle..................................250
M85 Mini Mauser..........................250
Tiger Dragunov Rifle......................250
GP WASR 10 Rifle.........................250
Pietta SAA Millenium.....................250
Pietta Semi-Auto Shotgun...............251
PW 87.......................................251
Shooter's Arms 1911 Pistol.............251
Saiga Semi-auto Shotgun...............251
S.A.R. Series...............................251

CETME

Cetme Autoloading Rifle..................251

CHAMPLIN FIREARMS

Bolt-Action Rifle 251

CHAPMAN, G. & J.

Chapman Pocket Revolver 251

CHAPUIS ARMES

RGP Shotgun 251
RG Express Model 89 Rifle..............251
Utility Grade Express Model Rifle 251
St. Bonnet Model Shotgun 251
Super Orion Rifle Series.................251
African PH Model Grade I Rifle 252
  .470 Nitro & .416 Rigby.............252
  .375 H&H..............................252
  .300 Win. Magnum...................252
  .30-06, 9.3x74R.....................252
African PH Model Grade II...............252

CHARTER ARMS

Bulldog......................................252
Police Bulldog 252
Undercover 252
Off Duty.....................................252
Pathfinder..................................252
Mag Pug.....................................252
Dixie Derringer 252
Field King Rifle 252
Field King Carbine 252

CHARTER ARMS CORP.

Police Undercover 252
Undercover Stainless Steel..............252
Undercover Lite............................252
Undercoverette.............................253
Bulldog......................................253
Stainless Steel Bulldog 253
Heller Commemorative Bulldog 253
Target Bulldog 253
Pathfinder..................................253
Pathfinder Stainless Steel 253
Bulldog Pug 253
Stainless Steel Bulldog 253
Bulldog Tracker 253

Police Bulldog 253
Stainless Steel Police Bulldog..........254
Off Duty.....................................254
Pit Bull......................................254
Pitbull Rimless 254
Pitbull .45..................................254
The Mag Pug 254
Charter Arms Southpaw..................255
Pink Lady...................................255
Goldfinger 255
Patriot 255
Dixie Derringer,
  Current Production......................255
Explorer II Pistol...........................255
Model 40....................................255
Model 79K...................................256
Model 42T...................................256
AR-7 Explorer Rifle 256

CHEYTAC

M-200.......................................256
M-310.......................................256

CHIAPPA ARMS

1911-22.....................................256
M9...256
M9-22..256
Rhino..256
1873-22.....................................256
1873-22-10.................................256
Model 1886 Kodiak Rifle.................256
Model 1886 Rifle...........................257
Model 1892 Rifle...........................257
Model 39 Rifle..............................257
Model LA322 Rifle.........................257
Little Sharps Rifle 257
Sharps Down Under 257
Model 1887 Shotgun......................257

CHICAGO, F. A. CO.

Protector Palm Pistol—
  Standard Model 257
Nickel-Plated/Black Grips...............257

**CHIPMUNK RIFLES/
ROGUE RIFLE CO.**

Chipmunk Single-Shot
  Standard Rifle............................257
Deluxe Chipmunk 257
Chipmunk .17 HMR.........................257
Chipmunk TM 257
Silhouette Pistol 257

CHRISTENSEN ARMS

Carbon One 257
Carbon Lite.................................258
Carbon King.................................258
Carbon Cannon 258
Carbon Challenge I 258
Carbon Challenge II 258
Carbon Tactical 258
Carbon Conquest 258
Carbon One Hunter........................258
Carbon Ranger Repeater.................258
Carbon Ranger Single Shot 258
Summit Carbon.............................258

Summit Steel...............................258
CA-15.......................................259
CA-10 DMR.................................259
1911 Officer................................259
1911 Damascus............................259

CHURCHILL, E. J. LTD.

One of One Thousand Rifle..............259
Premier Over/Under.......................259
Premier Side-by-Side.....................259
Premier Double Rifle......................259
Baronet Magazine Rifle...................259

CHURCHILL

Windsor I....................................259
Windsor II...................................259
Windsor VI..................................260
Royal...260
Monarch.....................................260
Windsor III..................................260
Windsor IV..................................260
Regent..260
Regent II....................................260
Regent Shotgun/Rifle Combination ..260
Windsor Grade Semi-Automatic 260
Regent Grade Semi-Automatic 260
Windsor Grade Slide-Action 260
Highlander..................................260
Regent.......................................260

CIMARRON, F. A. CO.

Model No. 3 Schofield 261
  Civilian Model...........................261
  Military Model 261
  Wells Fargo..............................261
Model 1872 Open Top 261
General Custer 7th Cavalry Model ...261
Rough Rider U.S. Artillery Model......261
Frontier Six Shooter 261
Sheriff's Model no ejector 261
New Sheriff's Model w/ejector.........261
Wyatt Earp Buntline 262
New Thunderer 262
Thunderer Long Tom 262
Thunderstorm 262
Lightning 262
Lightning .32s.............................262
New Model P...............................262
Stainless Frontier Model P 263
A.P. Casey Model P U.S. Cavalry......263
Rinaldo A. Carr Model P U.S.
  Artillery 263
Evil Roy Model.............................263
Model P Jr. 263
Model P Jr. .32s...........................263
Cimarron 1880 Frontier Flat Top......263
Cimarron Bisley............................263
Cimarron Bisley Flat Top 263
El Pistolero.................................264
Doc Holliday Thunderer..................264
Rooster Shooter SAA 264
Man With No Name SAA 264
Model 1851................................264
Model 1861................................264
Model 1860................................264
Model 1911A1.............................264

Wild Bunch 1911 264
Titan Derringer 264
Diablo Derringer 264
Model 1865 Spencer......................264
Henry Civil War Model....................264
Henry Civilian Model......................264
Model 1866 Yellowboy Carbine 264
Model 1866 Yellowboy Rifle............264
Model 1866 Yellowboy Trapper........264
Model 1873 Winchester Rifle 265
Model 1873 Long Range Rifle 265
Model 1873 Carbine 265
Model 1873 Short Rifle 265
Model 1873 Trapper 265
Model 1873 Deluxe
  Sporting Rifle............................265
Model 1873 Evil Roy Rifle 265
Model 1873 Larry Crow
  Signature Series Rifle..................265
Model 1892 Solid Frame Rifle 265
Model 1892 Takedown Rifle............265
Model 1886................................265
Billy Dixon Model 1874 Sharps 265
Remington Rolling Block 265
Adobe Walls Rolling Block..............265
Model 1885 High Wall 265
Model 1885 Deluxe High Wall 265
Model 1885 Low Wall 265
Texas Ranger Carbine....................266
Sharps Silhouette 266
Quigley Sharps Sporting Rifle 266
Sharp's No. 1 Sporting Rifle 266
Pride of the Plains Model 266
Professional Hunter Model 266
Big Fifty Model 266
Springfield Trapdoor Carbine 266
Springfield Trapdoor
  Officer's Model 266
U.S. Shooting Team
  Creedmoor Sharps......................266
1878 Coach Gun 266
1881 Coach Gun 267
Model 1887 Shotgun......................267
Model 1897 Shotgun......................267

CLARK, F. H.

Pocket Pistol...............................267

CLASSIC DOUBLES

Model 201 Classic 267
Model 201 Small Bore Set 267
Model 101 Classic Field Grade I......267
Classic Field Grade II.....................267
Classic Sporter............................267
Waterfowl Model 267
Classic Trap Over/Under.................267
Classic Trap Single 267
Classic Trap Combo.......................267
Classic Skeet 267
Classic Skeet 4 Gauge Set.............267

CLEMENT, CHAS.

Model 1903................................268
Model 1907................................268
Model 1908................................268
Model 1909................................268

Model 1910 268
Model 1912 268
American Model 269

CLERKE PRODUCTS

Hi-Wall 269
Deluxe Hi-Wall 269

COBRA ENTERPRISES, INC.

Standard Series 269
Long Bore Series 269
Big Bore Series 269
C-32/C-380 269
C-9mm 270
Patriot .45 270

COBRAY INDUSTRIES

M-11 Pistol 270
M-12 270
TM-11 Carbine 270
TM-12 Carbine 270
Terminator Shotgun 270

COCHRAN TURRET

Under Hammer Turret Rifle 270
1st Type 270
2nd Type 270
3rd Type 270
Pistol 270

COFER, T. W.

Cofer Navy Revolver 271

COGSWELL

Cogswell Pepperbox Pistol 271

**COLT'S PATENT FIRE ARMS
MANUFACTURING COMPANY**

Pocket or Baby Paterson
Model No. 1 271
Belt Model Paterson No. 2 271
Belt Model Paterson No. 3 271
Ehlers Model Pocket Paterson 272
Ehlers Belt Model Paterson 272
Texas Paterson Model No. 5 272
Colt Model 1860 Army 272
Fluted Cylinder 272

COLT REVOLVING LONG GUNS
1837-1847

First Model Ring Lever Rifle 272
Second Model Ring Lever Rifle 272
Model 1839 Shotgun 272
Model 1839 Carbine 272
Model 1839/1848 Carbine 273
Model 1854 Russian Contract
Musket 273

COLT WALKER-DRAGOON MODELS

Walker Model Revolver 273
Civilian Walker Revolver 273
Whitneyville Hartford Dragoon 273
Walker Replacement Dragoon 273
First Model Dragoon 273
Military Model 273
Civilian Model 273
Second Model Dragoon 273

Civilian Model 274
Military Model 274
Militia Model 274
Third Model Dragoon 274
Civilian Model 274
Military Model 274
Shoulder Stock Cut Revolvers 274
Shoulder Stocks 274
C.L. Dragoon 274
8" Barrel Late Issue 274
Hartford English Dragoon 274
Model 1848 Baby Dragoon 274
Texas Ranger/Indian Scene 274
Stagecoach Holdup Scene 275
Model 1849 Pocket Revolver 275
London Model 1849
Pocket Revolver 275
Model 1851 Navy Revolver 275
Square Back Trigger Guard, 1st
Model, Serial #1-1000 275
Square Back Trigger Guard, 2nd
Model, Serial #1001-4200 275
Small Round Trigger Guard,
3rd Model,
Serial #4201-85000 275
Large Round Trigger Guard, 4th
Model,
Serial #85001-215000 276
Martial Model 276
Shoulder Stock Variations 276
Stock Only 276
3rd Model Cut For Stock 276
Stock 276
London Model 1851 Navy Revolver .. 276
1st Model 276
2nd Model 276
Hartford Manufactured Variation 276

COLT SIDE HAMMER MODELS

Model 1855 Side Hammer
"Root" Pocket Revolver 276
Model 1 and 1A
Serial #1-384 276
Model 2 Serial #476-25000 276
Model 3 Serial #25001-30000 ... 276
Model 3A and 4
Serial #1-2400 276
Model 5 Serial #2401-8000 276
Model 5A Serial #2401-8000 276
Models 6 and 6A
Serial #8001-11074 276
Models 7 and 7A
Serial #11075-14000 276

COLT SIDE HAMMER LONG GUNS

Model 1855 Sporting Rifle,
1st Model 276
Early Model 277
Production Model 277
Model 1855 1st Model Carbine 277
Model 1855 Half Stock
Sporting Rifle 277
Model 1855 Full Stock
Military Rifle 277
Martially Marked Models 277
Without Martial Markings 277
Model 1855 Full Stock
Sporting Rifle 277

Model 1855 Revolving Carbine 277
Model 1855 Artillery Carbine 277
Model 1855 British Carbine 277
Model 1855 Revolving Shotgun 277
.60 Caliber (20 gauge) 278
.75 Caliber (10 gauge) 278
Model 1861 Single-Shot
Rifled Musket 278
Production Model 278

COLT PERCUSSION REVOLVERS

Model 1860 Army Revolver 278
Martial Marked Model 278
Civilian Model 278
Full Fluted Cylinder Model 278
Model 1861 Navy Revolver 278
Fluted Cylinder Model 279
Military Model 279
Shoulder Stock Model 279
Revolver 279
Stock 279
Civilian Model 279
Model 1862 Pocket Navy Revolver .. 279
Standard Production Model 279
Model 1862 Police Revolver 279
Standard Production Model 279

COLT METALLIC CARTRIDGE
CONVERSIONS

Thuer Conversion Revolver 279
Model 1849 Pocket 279
Model 1851 Navy 279
Model 1860 Army 279
Model 1861 Navy 279
Model 1862 Police 279
Model 1862 Pocket Navy 280
Richards Conversion,
1860 Army Revolver 280
Civilian Model 280
Martially Marked 280
Transition Richards Model 280
Richards-Mason Conversion,
1860 Army Revolver 280
Richards-Mason Conversions
1851 Navy Revolver 280
Production Model
Serial #1-3800 280
U.S. Navy Model
Serial #41000-91000 280
Richards-Mason Conversion 1861
Navy Revolver 280
Standard Production Model
Serial #100-3300 280
U.S. Navy Model
Serial #1000-9999 281
Model 1862 Police and Pocket
Navy Conversions 281
Round Barrel Pocket Navy
with Ejector 281
3.5" Round Barrel
Without Ejector 281
4.5" Octagonal Barrel
Without Ejector 281
Model 1862 Pocket Navy
Octagon Barrel with Ejector ... 281
Model 1862 Police Round Barrel
with Ejector 281

Model 1871-1872
Open Top Revolver 281
1860 Army Grip Frame 281
1851 Navy Grip Frame 281
First Model Derringer 281
Second Model Derringer 281
Third Model Derringer 282
First Variation, Early Production .. 282
First Variation, Late Production ... 282
Production Model 282
House Model Revolver 282
Cloverleaf with 1.5"
Round Barrel 282
Cloverleaf with 3" Barrel 282
House Pistol with 5-Shot
Round Cylinder 282
Open Top Pocket Revolver 282
Early Model with Ejector Rod 282
Production Model without
Ejector Rod 282
New Line Revolver .22 282
1st Model 283
2nd Model 283
New Line Revolver .30 283
New Line Revolver .32 283
New Line Revolver .38 283
New Line Revolver .41 283
New House Model Revolver 284
New Police Revolver 284
Long Barrel Model with Ejector ... 284
1st Year Production
"Pinched Frame" 1873 Only 284
Early Military Model 1873-1877 285
Early Civilian Model 1873-1877 285
.44 Rimfire Model 1875-1880 285
Late Military Model 1878-1891 285
Artillery Model 1895-1903 285
London Model 285
Frontier Six-Shooter 1878-1882 285
Sheriff's or Storekeeper's
Model 1882-1898 285
Flattop Target Model 1888-1896 286
Bisley Model 1894-1915 286
Bisley Model Flattop Target
1894-1913 286
Standard Civilian Production
Models 1876-1898 286
Standard Production Pre-war
Models (1899-1940) 286
1896-1899, Serial numbers
165000-182000 286
1899-1908, Serial numbers
182000-300000 286
1908-1914, Serial numbers
300000-328000 286
1914-1920, Serial numbers
328000-339000 286
1920-1940, Serial numbers
339000-357000 286
Long Fluted Cylinder Model
(1913-1915) 287
Standard Post-war Model
(1956-1975) 287
.38 Special 287
.357 Magnum 287
.44 Special 287
.45 Colt 287
Sheriff's Model (1960-1975) 287

Buntline Special (1957-1975) 287
New Frontier (1961-1975) 287
New Frontier Buntline Special
 (1962-1967) 287
 .357 Magnum 288
 .44-40 288
 .44-40 Black Powder Frame
  (Screw Retaining Cylinder Pin) .288
 .44 Special 288
 .45 Colt 288
Sheriff's Model 3rd Generation 288
Buntline Special 3rd Generation 288
New Frontier 3rd Generation 288
Standard Single Action Army
 Optional Features 289
Colt Cowboy (CB1850) 289
Colt Single Action Army
 "Legend Rodeo" 289
Frontier Six Shooter (2008) 289
Sheriff's and Storekeeper's Model
 (2008) 289
175th Anniversary SAA
 Limited Edition 289
New Frontier Third Generation,
 Current Production 289
Frontier Scout (1957-1971) 289
Peacemaker & New Frontier .22 290
Scout Model SAA (1962-1971) 290

COLT ANTIQUE LONG ARMS

Berdan Single-Shot Rifle 290
 Russian Order 290
 Carbine Russian Order 290
 U.S. Sales 290
 Carbine U.S. Sales 290
Colt-Franklin Military Rifle 290
Colt-Burgess Lever-Action Rifle 290
 Rifle - Octagonal Barrel 291
 Rifle - Round Barrel 291
 Carbine 291
 Baby Carbine 291
Lightning Slide-Action,
 Medium-Frame 291
 Rifle 291
 Carbine 291
 Military Rifle or Carbine 291
 Baby Carbine 291
 San Francisco Police Rifle 291
Lightning Slide-Action Small-Frame .291
Lightning Slide-Action, Large-Frame
 (Express) 291
 Rifle - Octagonal Barrel 291
 Rifle - Round Barrel 291
 Carbine 291
 Baby Carbine 291
Model 1878 Double-Barrel Shotgun 291
Model 1883 Double-Barrel Shotgun 291
Double-Barrel Rifle 291

COLT DOUBLE-ACTION REVOLVERS

Model 1877 "Lightning" and
 "Thunderer" 292
 Without Ejector, 2.5" and
  3.5" Barrel 292
 With Ejector, 4.5" and 6" Barrel ..292
Model 1878 "Frontier" 292
 Standard 292

Omnipotent 292
 Sheriff's Model 292
Model 1902 (Philippine or Alaskan
 Model) 292
Model 1889 Navy—Civilian Model ..293
Model 1889 U.S. Navy—
 Martial Model 293
Model 1892 "New Army and Navy"
 —Civilian Model 293
 Model 1892 U.S. Navy—
  Martial Model 293
 Model 1892 U.S. Army—
  Martial Model 293
 Model 1894/1896 Army 293
Model 1905 Marine Corps 293
New Service Model 293
 Early Model, #1-21000 294
 Early Model Target,
  #6000-15000 294
 Improved Model,
  #21000-325000 294
 Improved Target Model,
  #21000-325000 294
 U.S. Army Model 1909,
  #30000-50000 294
 U.S. Navy Model 1909,
  #50000-52000 294
 U.S. Marine Corps Model 1909,
  #21000-23000 294
 U.S. Army Model 1917,
  #150000-301000 294
 Model 1917 Civilian,
  #335000-336000 294
 Late Model New Service,
  #325000-356000 294
 Shooting Master,
  #333000-350000 294
 Magnum Model New Service,
  Over #340000 295
New Pocket Model 295
Pocket Positive 295
Army Special Model 295
New Police Model 295
Police Positive 295
Police Positive Target 295
Police Positive Special 295
 .22 Caliber in Short Action—
  Single-Action-Only 296
Official Police 296
Commando Model 296
Marshal Model 297
Colt .38 SF-VI 297
Colt .38 SF-VI Special Lady 297
Detective Special
 1st Issue / 2nd Issue 297
Detective Special 3rd Issue 297
Detective Special II (DS-II) 297
Cobra 2nd Issue 298
Agent 1st Issue 298
Border Patrol 298
Agent L.W. 2nd Issue 298
Aircrewman Special 298
Courier 298
Trooper 298
Colt .357 Magnum 299
Diamondback 299
 .38 Special 299
 .22 Long Rifle 299

Viper 299
Python 299
 Blue or Royal Blue Finish 299
 Polished Nickel Finish 299
 Matte Stainless Steel 299
 Ultimate Bright Stainless 299
Python Elite 300
Python .38 Special 300
Python Hunter 300
Python Silhouette 300
Python Ten Pointer 300
Python Grizzly 300
Metropolitan MK III 300
Lawman MK III 300
Lawman MK V 300
Trooper MK III 300
Trooper MK V 300
Boa 300
Peacekeeper 301
King Cobra 301
 Blued 301
 Stainless Steel 301
 High Polish Stainless Steel 301
Anaconda 301
 .44 Magnum 301
 .45 Colt 301
 Realtree Camo Model—
  Adjustable Sights 301
 Realtree Camo Model—
  Scope Mounts 302
Model 1900 302
 Standard Civilian Production 302
 U.S. Navy Military Model 302
 U.S. Army Military Model—
  1st Contract 302
 U.S. Army Military Model—
  2nd Contract 302
Model 1902 Sporting Pistol 302
Model 1902 Military Pistol 302
 Early Model with Front
  of Slide Serrated 302
 Standard Model with Rear
  of Slide Serrated 302
 U.S. Army Marked,
  #15001-15200 with Front
  Serrations 302
Model 1903 Pocket Hammer
 Pistol 302
Model 1903 Hammerless,
 .32 Pocket Pistol (Model M) 303
 U.S. Military Model 303
Model 1908 Hammerless
 .380 Pocket Pistol 303
 Standard Civilian Model 303
 Military Model 303
Model 1908 Hammerless
 .25 Vest Pocket Model 303
 Civilian Model 303
 Military Model 303
Model 1905 .45 Automatic Pistol 303
 Civilian Model 304
 Military Model, Serial #1-201 304
Early Colt 1911 "Commercial
 Government Model" 304
Standard Colt "1911 Commercial
 Model" with Un-numbered Slide ..305

Standard Colt 1911 Commercial
 "Government Model" with
 Numbered Slide 305
Colt 1911 Commercial "Government
 Model" Argentine Contracts 305
Colt 1911 Commercial "Government
 Model" Russian Order 305
Colt 1911 Commercial "Government
 Model" Canadian Contract 305
Colt 1911 Commercial "Government
 Model" British Contract 305
Norwegian Kongsberg Vapenfabrikk
 Pistol Model 1912
 (Extremely Rare) 306
Norwegian Kongsberg Vapenfabrikk
 Pistol Model 1914 306
Norwegian Kongsberg Vapenfabrikk
 Model 1914 (Copy) 306
Colt 1912 306
Colt 1913-1915 306
Colt 1917-1918 306
Springfield Armory 1914-1916 306
Remington-UMC 1918-1919 306
North American Arms 1918 306
Standard Colt "1911A1 Commercial
 Government Model"
 Domestic Sales 307
Standard Colt "1911A1 Commercial
 Government Model"
 Export Sales 307
Argentine Colt-made 1911A1 model
 pistols without Swartz safeties 307
Brazilian, Mexican, and other South
 American (except Argentina) 307
Colt National Match Caliber .45,
 Pre-WWII, .45 (without Swartz
 safeties) 307
 With Adjustable Sights 307
 Fixed Sights 307
Swartz Safeties, Pre-WWII,
 Firing Pin and Hammer/Sear 307
Standard Colt 1911A1 Commercial
 "GOVERNMENT MODEL" Marked
 Pistol with Numbered Slide and
 Swartz Safeties 308
Colt National Match Caliber
 Pre-WWII, .45. Pre-WWII (with
 "Swartz Safeties") 308
 Stevens Adjustable Sights 308
 Fixed Sights 308
Standard 1911A1 Pre-WWII,
 "GOVERNMENT MODEL"
 Export Sales 308
Normal Brazilian and
 Mexican Pistols 308
Argentine Contract Pistols
 "Modelo Argentino 1927,
 Calibre .45" 308
Military to Commercial Conversions .308
Super .38 1929 Model, Pre-WWII ...308
Super Match .38 1935 Model,
 Pre-WWII 308
 Adjustable Sights 309
 Fixed Sights 309
Colt 309
Ithaca 309
Remington Rand 309
Union Switch & Signal 309
Singer Mfg. Co. 309
SN C220,000 to about C220,500 ...309

SN C220,500 to about C249,000 verified proof and "GOVERNMENT MODEL" marking 309
SN 255,000-C to about 258,000-C Slide Factory Roll Marked "PROPERTY OF THE STATE OF NEW YORK", verified proof, and "GOVERNMENT MODEL" marking (250 pistols total)......309
SN 249,500-C to about 335,000-C, verified proof and "GOVERNMENT MODEL" marking 309
SN 334,500-C to about 336,169-C, BB (Barrel Bushing) marked......309

ACE AND SERVICE MODEL ACE

Ace Model .22 Pistol 309
Pre-1945 Service Model Ace .22 R. F. Pistol 310
Blued pistols (before about SN SM 3840)...310
Parkerized pistols (after about SN SM 3840)......310
Service Model Ace-Post-War......310
Conversion Units .22-.45, .45-.22...310
Pre-war and Post-war "U" numbered Service Model Ace Conversion Unit, .22-.45 (to convert .45 cal. to .22 cal.)....310
Post-war Conversion Units 310
Pre-war Service Model Ace (Re-) Conversion Unit, .45-22 310
Post-war .22 Conversion Unit Unnumbered......310
Military National Match .45 Pistols ..310
Military National Match Pistols (Drake Slide)......311
Gold Cup National Match (pre-Series 70) 311
Gold Cup MKIII National Match 311
Colt 1911A1 AMU (Army Marksmanship Unit) 311

COLT LICENSED AND UNLICENSED FOREIGN-MADE 1911A1 AND VARIATIONS

Argentine D.G.F.M. 311
Argentine-Made Ballester Molina.....312
Brazilian Models 1911A1......312

COLT MODEL 1911A1 1970 - CURRENT

MKIV Series 70 Government Model ..312
Series 70 Gunsite Pistol Commander 312

COLT ENHANCED GOVERNMENT MODELS

Pre-70 Series (1949-1969)......313
Series 70 (1970-1983)......313
Series 80 (1983-1996)......313
Combat Commander 313
Blued......313
Nickel Plated 313
Stainless Steel......313
Polished Stainless Steel 313
Colt 1991A1 313
M1991A1 Commander......314
M1991A1 Compact......314

M1991A1 .38 Super 314
MK IV Series 80 Gold Cup National Match 314
Blued......314
Stainless Steel......314
Polished Stainless Steel 314
Officer's ACP......315
Blued......315
Matte Blued 315
Satin Nickel......315
Stainless Steel......315
Lightweight Officer's ACP......315
Concealed Carry Officer's Model 315
Delta Gold Cup......315
Delta Elite......315
Blued......315
Stainless Steel......315
Polished Stainless Steel 315
Combat Elite......315
Combat Target Model 316
Combat Target Commander......316
Combat Target Officer's ACP......316
Special Combat Government 316
Special Combat Government Carry Model 316
Close Quarters Battle (CQB) Pistol ...316
XSE Model O Government (01070XS) 316
XSE Model O Concealed Carry Officer's (09850XS) 316
XSE Model O Commander (04012XS) 317
XSE Model O Lightweight Commander (04860XS) 317
Colt Defender......317
Colt Defender Model O (07000D) 317
1911 – WWI Replica 317
1911 - WWI 1918 Replica 317
1911A1 - WWII Replica 317
Colt New Agent Double Action Only..317
Colt Model 1991 DAO 317
Colt Model 1911 100th Anniversary Series 318
1911ANVII 318
1911ANVIII......318
Gunsite Model 1911 318
Colt Government Model 1911 .22 LR Series 318
Colt Concealed Carry......318
New Agent 318
Colt Rail Gun 318
Competition Pistol 318
Double Eagle......318
Double Eagle Officer's Model 319
Double Eagle Combat Commander ...319
Double Eagle First Edition 319
Pocket Nine 319
Tac Nine 319
Mustang 319
Mustang PocketLite......320
Mustang Lite......320
Government Pocketlite LW 320
Mustang Pocketlite XSP......320
Mustang Plus II 320
Colt Pony 320
Colt Pony PocketLite......320
.380 Series 80 Government Model ...320

Colt CZ40 321
Colt Model 2000 321

COLT .22 RIMFIRE SEMI-AUTOMATIC PISTOLS

Pre-Woodsman 322
Woodsman Target 322
Woodsman Sport......322
Woodsman Match Target 323
Military Woodsman Match Target.....323
Woodsman Target 6" barrel......323
Woodsman Sport 4.5" barrel......323
Woodsman Match Target 6" barrel 323
Woodsman Match Target 4.5" barrel 324
Challenger 4.5" barrel 324
Challenger 6" barrel 324
Woodsman Target 6" barrel......324
Woodsman Sport 4.5" barrel......325
Woodsman Match Target 6" barrel ..325
Woodsman Match Target 4.5" barrel 325
Huntsman 6" or 4.5" barrel......325
Targetsman 6" barrel......325
Colt Junior Pocket Model 325
Cadet / Colt .22 325
Colt .22 Target 326

COLT MODERN LONG ARMS

Colteer I-22 326
Stagecoach 326
Courier 326
Colteer 326
Colt "57" Bolt-Action Rifle 326
Coltsman Bolt-Action Rifle 326
Coltsman Pump Shotgun 326
Semi-Automatic Shotgun 326
Double-Barrel Shotgun 326
Colt Light Rifle 327
Colt Sauer Bolt-Action Rifle 327
Colt Sauer Short Action 327
Colt Model 2012 SA308 327
SA308 327
MT308T......327
LT 327

COLT AR-15 & SPORTER RIFLES

AR-15 Sporter (Model #6000)......328
Sporter Lightweight Rifle......328
Sporter Target Model Rifle (Model #6551) 328
Sporter Match H-BAR (Model #6601) 328
AR-15 (XM16E1) 329
Sporter Match Delta H-BAR (Model #6601 DH)......329
Match Target H-BAR Compensated (Model #6601C)......329
Colt Match Target M4 329
Sporter Competition H-BAR (Model #6700) 329
Sporter Competition H-BAR Select w/scope (Model #6700CH)......329
Match Target Competition H-BAR Compensated (Model #6700C)....329

AR-15 Carbine Flat-top Heavyweight/ Match Target Competition (Model #6731) 329
AR-15 Tactical Carbine (Model #6721) 329
Sporter H-BAR Elite/Accurized Rifle (Model #6724) 329
Colt SP6920 329
Colt SP6940 330
Match Target Competition H-BAR (Model 6700) 330
Match Target Lightweight......330
Match Target M4 Carbine......330
Match Target H-BAR Rifle......330
Colt Carbine......330
M.A.R.C. 901 330
LE901 330
AR901 330
LE6920 330
LE6940 330
Expanse M4 330
COLT CUSTOM SHOP 330
U.S. Shooting Team Gold Cup......330

COLT REPRODUCTION PERCUSSION REVOLVERS

Walker......336

COLT BLACKPOWDER ARMS

1842 Paterson Colt No. 5 Holster Model 337
Walker......337
Steel Backstrap 337
Fluted Cylinder 337
Colt 1849 Model Pocket 337
Colt 1851 Model Navy 337
Dual Cylinder......337
Colt Model 1860 Army......337
Dual Cylinder......337
Colt Model 1860 Officer's Model 337
Colt Model 1860 Army Gold U.S. Cavalry 338
Stainless Steel......338
Colt 1860 Heirloom Edition 338
Colt Model 1861 Navy 338
General Custer 338
Colt Model 1862 Pocket Navy 338
Colt Model 1862 Trapper-Pocket Police......338
Artillery Model 338
Presentation 1 of 1000 338
Presentation 1 of 1000 Artillery Model 338
Colt Gamemaster .50 338

COLUMBUS F. A. MFG. CO.

Columbus Revolver......339

COMANCHE

Comanche I 339
Comanche II......339
Comanche III......339
Super Comanche 339

COMMANDO ARMS

Mark III Carbine......339
Mark 9 Carbine 339

Mark .45 339

COMPETITOR CORP.

Competitor Single-Shot..................339

CONNECTICUT ARMS CO.

Pocket Revolver.............................340

CONNECTICUT SHOTGUN MANUFACTURING COMPANY

RBL Side-By-Side Shotgun..............340
A-10 American...............................340
Model 21......................................340
Model 21 Grand American 340
Model 21 Over/Under 340
Model 21 Side-By-Side Rifle 340
A.H. Fox.......................................340

CONNECTICUT VALLEY ARMS CO.

Express Rifle.................................340
Over/Under Rifle............................340
Hawken Rifle.................................341
Presentation Grade Hawken 341
Pennsylvania Long Rifle 341
Kentucky Rifle...............................341
Mountain Rifle...............................341
Blazer Rifle...................................341
Apollo Shadow SS 341
Apollo Classic...............................341
Apollo Carbelite............................341
Apollo Starfire...............................341
Apollo Eclipse Rifle 341
Apollo Dominator...........................341
Apollo Brown Bear.........................341
Frontier Carbine 341
Plainsman Rifle.............................341
Panther Carbine 341
Bushwacker Rifle 342
Trophy Carbine 342
Varmint Rifle.................................342
Woodsman Rifle LS 342
Frontier Hunter Carbine 342
Grey Wolf Rifle..............................342
Lone Grey Wolf Rifle 342
Timber Wolf Rifle...........................342
Tracker Carbine LS 342
Stag Horn 342
Electra...343
Accura MR....................................343
Optima V2.....................................343
Brittany 11 Shotgun.......................343
1858 Remington Target 344

CONSTABLE, R.

Pocket Pistol 344

CONTENTO/VENTUR

Model 51.......................................344
Model 64.......................................344

CONTINENTAL

Continental Pocket Pistol
   (6.35mm)..................................345
Continental Pocket Pistol
   (7.65mm)..................................345

CONTINENTAL ARMS CO.

Pepperbox 345

CONTINENTAL ARMS CO.

Double Rifle 345

COOK & BROTHER RIFLES AND CARBINES

Cook & Brother Rifles (New Orleans
   & Selma production) 345
Cook & Brother Carbines
   (New Orleans production)............345
Cook & Brother Rifles (Athens
   production).................................345
Cook & Brother Carbines (Athens
   production).................................346

COONAN ARMS/COONAN INC.

Model A..346
Model B..346
Comp I...346
Comp I Deluxe..............................346
Classic (Current Production)...........346
Cadet 346
Cadet II..347
Coonan .45 ACP............................347

COOPER, J. M. & CO.

Pocket Revolver.............................347

COOPER ARMS

Model 36 Marksman 347
   Standard..................................347
   Classic.....................................347
   Custom Classic..........................347
   Western Classic.........................347
   BR-50 w/Jewell Trigger...............347
   IR-50-50 w/Jewell Trigger...........347
   Featherweight
     w/Jewell Trigger......................347
Model 38/40..................................347
   Classic.....................................347
   Custom Classic 347
   Western Classic
     (octagon barrel) 347
   Mannlicher Model 347
Model 21.......................................347
   Varmint Extreme........................348
   Classic.....................................348
   Custom Classic...........................348
   Western Classic..........................348
   Benchrest w/Jewell Trigger..........348
Model 22.......................................348
   Pro Varmint Extreme 348
   Benchrest w/Jewell Trigger..........348
Model 22 Repeater.........................348
   Classic.....................................348
   Custom Classic...........................348
   Western Classic..........................348
Model 52 Classic 348
Model 54.......................................348
Model 57.......................................348
Model 58 Classic 348

COOPERATIVA OBRERA

Longines.......................................348

COPELAND, FRANK

Copeland Pocket Revolver .22.........348
Copeland .32 Revolver....................348

COSMI, A. & F.

Semi-Automatic 348
   Standard Model..........................348
   Deluxe Model 349

COSMOPOLITAN ARMS CO.

Breech Loading Rifle 349

COWLES & SON

Single-Shot...................................349

CPA RIFLES

Schuetzen Rifle 349
Silhouette Rifle..............................349
Sporting Rifle 349
Varmint Rifle.................................349

CRAUSE, CARL PHILLIP MUSKETS AND RIFLES

Hanseatic League M1840
   Rifled Musket 349
Oldenberg M1849 Rifled Musket.....349

CRESCENT F. A. CO.

American Gun Co. No. 3—
   Damascus Barrels Hammer
   Sidelock...................................350
New Knickerbocker Damascus
   Barrels—Hammerless Sidelock....350
American Gun Co. Small Bore
   No. 28—Straight Stock Hammer
   Sidelock...................................351
Crescent Firearms Co. No. 0—
   Nickel—Hammer Sidelock..........351
Crescent Certified Empire No. 60—
   Hammerless Sidelock.................352
Crescent Certified Shotgun NFA,
   Curio or Relic 352
Brand Names Used by
   Crescent Arms..........................352

CRISPIN, SILAS

Crispin Revolver 353

CROSSFIRE

MK-1..354

CZ - STRAKONICE

Model TT 40/45/9 354

CZ

Fox...354
CZ 1921 Praga 354
Army Pistol 1922 (Nickl-Pistole) 355
CZ 1922..355
CZ 1924..355
CZ 1927..355
Model 52 (7.62 x 45) Carbine 356
Model 52/57 (7.62 x 39) 356
CZ Model 3....................................356
CZ 452-2E LUX..............................356
CZ ZKM-452D 356
CZ 452-2E ZKM Style.....................356
CZ 452 Training Rifle......................357

CZ 452 American Classic.................357
CZ 452 Varmint..............................357
CZ 452 Scout 357
CZ 452 Style.................................357
CZ 452 Silhouette..........................357
CZ 452 FS 357
CZ 455 American............................357
CZ 512..357
CZ 513 Basic.................................357
CZ 527 FS.....................................358
CZ 550 American Classic.................358
CZ 550..359
CZ 550 Battue Lux 359
CZ 550 FS Battue...........................359
CZ 550 Minnesota..........................359
CZ 550 Minnesota DM 359
CZ 550 Prestige.............................359
CZ 550 Lux....................................359
CZ 550 Varmint..............................359
CZ 550 Varmint Laminate 359
CZ 550 Safari Magnum 359
CZ 550 American Safari Magnum ...359
CZ 550 Ultimate Hunting Rifle 360
CZ 550 Premium............................360
CZ 550 Medium Magnum................360
CZ 550 Safari Classic Custom........360
CZ 557..360
CZ 584..360
CZ ZKK 600 360
CZ ZKK 601 360
CZ ZKK 602 360
CZ 700 Sniper M1..........................360
CZ 750 Sniper 360
CZ 550 Urban Sniper......................361
CZ 581..361
CZ 712..361
CZ 712 3-Gun 361
CZ 720..361
CZ 612/620...................................361
Redhead.......................................361
Canvasback...................................361
Woodcock.....................................361
Woodcock Custom Grade................361
Mallard...361
Durango..361
Amarillo..362
Ringneck.......................................362
Ringneck Custom Grade.................362
Bobwhite......................................362
Partridge.......................................362
Grouse 362
CZ Sporting...................................362
Hammer Coach 362
CZ 75...362
CZ 75 B..363
CZ 75 30th Anniversary..................363
CZ 75 Compact..............................363
CZ 75 Compact D 363
CZ 75 B Tactical 363
CZ 75 Tactical Sport 363
CZ 75 BD......................................364
CZ BD Compact.............................364
CZ BD Compact Carry 364
CZ 75 B SA...................................364
CZ 75 Semi-Compact.....................364

CZ 75 D PCR Compact 364
CZ 75 Champion 364
CZ 75 DAO 365
CZ P-01 365
CZ P-06 365
CZ P-09 Duty 365
CZ 75 Standard IPSC (ST) 365
CZ 75 M IPSC 365
CZ 75 Silver Anniversary 366
CZ 75 Stainless 366
CZ 75 SP-01 Shadow 366
CZ 75 SP-01 Shadow Custom 366
CZ 75 TS Czechmate 366
CZ 75 Tactical Sport 366
CZ 85 B 366
CZ 85 Combat 367
CZ 40B 367
CZ Kadet 367
CZ 75 Kadet Conversion 367
CZ 2075 RAMI 367
CZ 83 367
CZ 97 B 368
CZ 100 368
CZ 1911 A1 368
CZ Scorpion Evo 368

D. W. M.
Model 22 369

DAEWOO
DH-40 369
DP-51B 369
DP-51SB 369
DP-51CB 369
DP-52 369
DH380 369
DR200 370
K-2/AR-100 (Max I) 370
K1A1 (Max II) 370

DAISY
VL Rifle 370
VL Presentation Model 370
VL Cased Presentation Model 370
Model 2201/2211 370
Model 2202/2212 370
Model 2203/2213 370

DAKIN GUN CO.
Model 100 370
Model 147 370
Model 160 370
Model 215 370
Model 170 370

DAKOTA ARMS, INC.
Dakota 76 Classic 371
Dakota 76 Professional Hunter 371
Dakota 76 Varmint Grade 371
Model 97 Varmint Hunter 371
Model 76 Safari Grade 371
Model 76 Alpine Grade 371
Model 76 African Grade 371
Model 10 Single Shot 371
Model 10 Single Shot Magnum 371
Dakota .22 Long Rifle Sporter 371

Dakota .22 Long Rifle Sporter
   (New Model) 371
Model 97 Long Range Hunter 371
Model 97 Lightweight Hunter 372
Model T-76 Longbow Tactical Rifle ..372
Model 76 Traveler 372
   Classic 372
   Safari 372
   African 372
Classic Predator 372
   Serious Predator 372
   All-Weather Predator 372
Double Rifle 372
Little Sharps Rifle 372
Limited Edition .30-06 Model 76 372
Limited Edition .30-06 Model 10 373
Classic Grade 373
Premier Grade 373
Dakota American Legend 373
Dakota Shotgun 373
Model 7 373
Prince Model 373
Prince Model Side-Lever 373
Rex 373
Premier 373
Sideplate Model 373
Sideplate Model with Gold 373
Sideplate with Scroll 373
Hammer Gun 373
H.H. Model—no engraving 373
Esposizione 373
L'Inglesina 373
Model E "Fantasy 373
Boss—no engraving 374
Field 374
Grade II 374
Grade III 374

DALY, CHARLES
Commander Over/Under
   Model 100 374
Commander Over/Under
   Model 200 374
Superior Side-by-Side 374
Empire Side-by-Side 374
Diamond Grade Side-by-Side 374
Regent Diamond Grade
   Side-by-Side 374
Empire Over/Under 374
Diamond Grade Over/Under 374
Empire Grade 374
Regent Diamond Grade 375
Superior Grade 375
Diamond Grade 375
Regent Diamond Grade 375
Empire Grade Side-by-Side 375
Superior Grade Single Barrel Trap 375
Over/Unders 375
   Venture Grade 375
   Venture Grade Skeet or Trap 375
   Field Grade 375
   Superior Grade 375
   Superior Grade Trap 375
   Diamond Grade 375
   Diamond Grade Trap or Skeet 375
Novamatic Lightweight 375

Novamatic Trap 375
Charles Daly Automatic 375
Field Grade 375
Superior Grade Hunter 376
Superior Grade Sporting 376
Superior Grade Trap 376
Field Hunter VR-MC 376
Field Hunter VR-MC Youth 376
Superior II 376
   Hunter 376
   Sport 376
   Trap 376
Field Hunter Maxi-Mag VR-MC
   Semi-Auto 376
Model 105 376
Model 106/206 376
Model 306 376
Field Grade 377
Field Tactical 377
Field Hunter MM (Maxi-Mag) 377
Field Hunter Maxi-Mag VR-MC
   Pump 377
Country Squire Over/Under
   Folding 377
Field II Hunter 377
Field Ultra Light 377
Field III 377
Empire 377
Empire II EDL Hunter 377
Empire Sporting 377
Empire Grade Combination 378
Empire Trap 378
Empire Grade Trap Combo 378
Diamond GTX DL Hunter 378
Diamond GTX Sporting 378
Diamond GTX Trap or Skeet 378
Diamond GTX Trap Combo 378
Presentation Grade 378
Superior II 378
Superior II Sporting 378
Superior Grade Trap 378
Superior Grade Combination 378
Empire Trap Mono 378
Diamond GTX Mono 378
Field Hunter 379
Superior Hunter 379
Empire Hunter 379
Diamond DL 379
Diamond Regent DL 379
Country Squire Side-by-Side
   Folding 379
Model 306 379
Classic Coach 379
Field Grade Mauser 98 379
Field Grade Mini-Mauser 98 379
Superior Grade Mauser 98 379
Superior Grade Mini-Mauser 98 379
Field Grade Rimfires 379
Superior Grade Rimfires 380
Superior II Grade Rimfire 380
Empire Grade Rimfires 380
Superior Grade Express 380
Empire Express 380
DM-4 Series 380
Daly ZDA 380
Field 1911-A1 FS/MS/CS 380

Superior 1911-A1 EFS/EMS/ECS 380
Empire 1911-A1 EFS 380
Field 1911-A2P 381
.22 Caliber Conversion Kit 381
Field 1911-A1 PC 381
Superior 1911-A1 PC 381
Field 1911 Target EFST 381
Empire 1911 Target EFST 381
Empire Custom Match Target 381
Daly HP 381
Daly M-5 Government 381
Daly M-5 Commander 382
Daly M-5 Ultra-X 382
Daly M-5 IPSC 382
Daly Classic 1873 Single-Action
   Revolver 382
Model 600 382
Model 300 382
Model 206 382
   206 Field Grade 382
   206S Sporting Model 382
   206T Trap Model 382

DAN ARMS OF AMERICA
Field Grade 382
Deluxe Field Grade 382
Lux Grade I 383
Lux Grade II 383
Lux Grade III 383
Lux Grade IV 383
Silver Snipe 383

DANCE & BROTHERS
CONFEDERATE REVOLVERS
.36 Caliber 383
.44 Caliber 383

DANIEL DEFENSE
DDM4 383
MK 12 383

DANSK REKYLRIFFEL SYNDIKAT
Schouboe Model 1902 383
Schouboe Model 1904 383
Schouboe Model 1907 384
Schouboe Model 1907 9mm 384
Schouboe Model 1910/12 384
Schouboe Model 1916 384

DARDICK CORP.
Series 110 384
Series 1500 384

DARLING, B. & B. M.
Pepperbox Pistol 385

DARNE, S. A.
Model R11 385
Model R13 385
Model R15 385
Model V19 385
Model V22 385
Model V Hors Series No. I 385

DAVENPORT FIREARMS CO.
Double-Barrel Shotguns 385

1st Model.............................385
2nd Model 385
3rd Model 385
4th Model 385
Single-Barrel Shotgun....................385
8 Gauge Goose Gun 385
Falling Block Single-Shot Rifle........385

DAVIDSON, F.A.

Model 63B.............................385
Model 69 SL 386
Stagecoach Model 73.................386

DAVIS, A. JR.

Under Hammer Pistol.....................386

DAVIS, N.R. & CO./ DAVIS, N.R. & SONS

Grade A and B Hammerless Shotguns 386
Grade C Hammerless Shotgun 386
Grade D and DS Hammer Shotguns 386
Grade E and F Single- Barrel Shotguns.......................386
1st Button Opener— Hammer Boxlock 386
1st Sidelever—Hammer Boxlock.....386
2nd Sidelever—Hammer Boxlock....386
1st Toplever—Hammer Boxlock......386
2nd Toplever—Hammer Boxlock.....387
3rd Toplever—Hammer Boxlock.....387
1879 1st Model— Hammer Boxlock 387
1879 2nd Model—Damascus Barrel—Hammer Boxlock 387
1885—Hammerless Boxlock..........387
1886 Rival—Hammerless Boxlock ..387
1886 Rival Improved— Hammerless Boxlock.................387
1897 "G" —Hammer Sidelock........387
Hammerless 1900—Boxlock 387
Hammerless A—Damascus Barrel—Boxlock.......................387
Hammerless B—Boxlock............387
Hammerless C—Engraved Damascus Barrel—Boxlock....387
Hammerless D—Engraved— Boxlock 387
New Model— Hammerless Boxlock..................387
"D.S." Straight Stock—Engraved— Hammerless Boxlock.................387
Davis Special—Hammerless Boxlock................................387
Davis "B" Manga Steel— Hammerless Boxlock.................387
Model No. 600— Hammerless Boxlock..................387
Model No. 900— Hammerless Boxlock..................387

DAVIS-WARNER ARMS CORPORATION

Davis Grade B.S. Hammerless Shotgun.............................387
Davis-Warner Expert Hammerless ...387
"BS"—Hammerless Boxlock..........387
"Maximin"—Hammerless Boxlock...388
"DS"—Hammerless Boxlock..........388

Deluxe—Hammerless Boxlock........388
Premier—Hammerless Boxlock.......388
Peerless Ejector— Hammerless Boxlock..................388
Hypower—Hammerless Boxlock 388
Ajax (Model 800)......................388
Ajax—Hammerless Boxlock...........388
Certified (Savage)....................388
Deluxe Special (Model 805) 388
Premier Special (Model 802)........388
Premier (Model 801) 388
Warner Infallible Semi-Automatic Pistol.................388
Davis-Warner Swing-Out Revolver ...388
Davis-Warner Semi-Automatic Pistols 388

DAVIS & BOZEMAN

Pattern 1841 Rifle 388

DAVIS INDUSTRIES

D-Series Deringer.......................388
Big Bore D-Series......................389
Long Bore D-Series 389
P-32 389
P-380 389

DAW, G. H.

Daw Revolver 389

DEANE-HARDING

Revolver 389

DECKER, WILHELM

Revolver 390

DEMIRETT, J.

Under-Hammer Pistol 390

DEMRO

XF-7 Wasp Carbine 390
T.A.C. Model 1 390

DERINGER REVOLVER AND PISTOL CO.

Deringer Model I.......................390
Deringer Model II......................390
Centennial 1876 390

DERINGER RIFLES AND PISTOLS, HENRY

Deringer U.S. M1814 Military Rifle...........................390
Deringer U.S. M1817 Military Rifle (Types I & II) 390
In Flintlock 390
Altered to Percussion 390
Deringer Original Percussion Martial Rifles (Types I & II) 390
Deringer Original Percussion Rifle- Muskets............................391
Deringer U.S. Navy Contract "Boxlock" Pistols...................391
Deringer Percussion Pocket Pistols....................391
Principal Makers of Deringer- Style Pocket Pistols...............391

Agent Names Found On Deringer Pocket Pistols 392

DESENZANI, LABORATORIES ARMI

Over/Under 392
Side-By-Side 392

DESERT EAGLE

Desert Eagle .357 Magnum 392
Desert Eagle .41 Magnum/ .44 Magnum........................392
Desert Eagle .50 Action Express 392
Desert Eagle Mark XIX 392
.50A.E. w/6" Barrel.................393
.50A.E. w/10" Barrel................393
.44 Mag. w/6" Barrel...............393
.44 Mag. w/10" Barrel..............393
.357 Mag. w/6" Barrel..............393
.357 Mag. w/10" Barrel.............393
.440 CorBon w/6" Barrel (1999).............................393
.440 CorBon w/10" Barrel (1999).............................393
Bolt Assembly—.44/.50 or .357 .393
Mark XIX Component System 393
6" & 10" Component System......393
6" Component System 393
10" Component System 393
Baby Eagle............................393
.40 S&W (Standard)................393
9mm (Standard) 393
.41 Action Express..................393
Short Barrel (Semi-Compact)......393
Short Barrel/Short Grip (Compact)........................393
Semi-Compact Polymer 394
Compact Polymer 394
Mountain Eagle 394
Mountain Eagle Target Edition 394
Mountain Eagle Compact Edition 394
Desert Eagle L5........................394
Lone Eagle.............................394
Lone Eagle (New Model) 394
Micro Desert Eagle Pistol 395
Model 1911 Desert Eagle 395
MR9 / MR40...........................395
Mountain Eagle Rifle...................395
Mountain Eagle Varmint Edition 395
Magnum Lite Rimfire Rifles............395
Hogue and Fajen Scope- Hi Stock 395
Fajen Thumbhole Sporter 395
Fajen Thumbhole Silhouette 396
Turner Barracuda.................396
Magnum Lite Centerfire Rifles.........396
Heavy Barrel.....................396
Sport Taper Barrel................396
Tactical Rifle 396

DESTROYER CARBINE

Destroyer Carbine 396

DETONICS DEFENSE TECHNOLOGIES

Combat Master 396
Nemesis HT 396
DTX..................................396

DETONICS FIREARMS INDUSTRIES / NEW DETONICS / DECTONICS USA LLC

Mark I................................396
Mark II...............................396
Mark III..............................396
Mark IV...............................397
Combat Master 397
Combat Master Mark V 397
Combat Master Mark VI................397
Combat Master Mark VII 397
Military Combat MC2 397
Scoremaster 397
Janus Competition Scoremaster 397
Servicemaster 397
Pocket 9..............................397
Combat Master 397
Street Master 397
Model 9-11-01.........................397

DEUTSCHE WERKE

Ortgies 397
Ortgies 9mm 398

DIAMOND

Gold Series Semi-Automatic Shotgun............................398
Gold Series Pump-Action Shotgun ...398
Silver Series Mariner Semi-Automatic Shotgun 398
Silver Series Mariner Pump-Action Shotgun............................398
Diamond Elite Semi-Automatic Shotgun............................398
Diamond Panther Pump-Action Shotgun............................398
Diamond Panther Semi-Automatic Shotgun............................398
Diamond Elite Pump-Action Shotgun............................398

DIAMONDBACK FIREARMS

DB9 Semi-Automatic Pistol 398
DB380 Semi-Automatic Pistol 399
DB9 FS...............................399
DB15.................................399
DB15 NB.............................399
DB10.................................399

DICKINSON, E. L. & J.

Ranger 399
Single-Shot...........................399

DICKSON, NELSON & CO.

Rifle 399

DIMICK, H.E.

Percussion Pistol..........................399

DOMINO

Model OP 601 Match Pistol 399
Model SP 602 Match Pistol.............399

DORNHEIM, G.C.

Gecado Model 11.......................399
Gecado 7.65mm 400

DOUBLESTAR CORP.

Star EM-4 400
Star-15 400
Star Lightweight Tactical Rifle 400
Star Carbine 400
Star DS-4 Carbine 400
Star Super Match Rifle 400
Star Critterslayer 400
DSC Expedition Rifle 400
DSC Star-15 CMP Service Rifle 400
DSC Star CMP Improved
    Service Rifle 400
DSC Star 15 Lightweight Tactical 400
DSC Star Dissipator 400
DSC Star 15 9mm Carbine 400
1911 Combat Pistol 401
1911 C2 401
1911 C2G 401
DSC .300 Blackout AR Pistol 401

DOUBLETAP DEFENSE

Doubletap 401

DOUG TURNBULL MANUFACTURING CO.

Year Offered—1998 401
Year Offered—1999 401
Year Offered—2000 401
EHBM Colt 401
Smith & Wesson No. 3 Schofield 401
Colt/Winchester Cased Set 401
General Patton Colt 401
Theodore Roosevelt Colt 402
Theodore Roosevelt Winchester
    Model 1876 402
Cowboy Classic 402
Model 1911 Heritage 402

DOWNSIZER CORPORATION

Model WSP 402

DPMS

Panther Bull A-15 402
Panther Bull 24 402
Panther Deluxe Bull 24 Special 403
Panther Extreme Super Bull 24 403
Panther Bulldog 403
Panther Bull Sweet 16 403
Panther Bull SST 16 403
Panther Bull Classic 403
TAC 2/TAC 20 403
GII AP4 404
GII Hunter 404
Panther Arctic 404
Panther Classic 404
Panther DCM 404
Panther Classic 16 Post Ban 404
Panther Free Float 16 Post Ban 404
Panther Southpaw Post Ban 404
Panther Race Gun 404
Panther Tuber 404
Single Shot Rifle 405
Panther Pardus 405
Panther 20th Anniversary Rifle 405
Panther 6.8 Rifle 405
Panther Mark 12 405
Panther SDM-R 405

LRT-SASS 405
LR-260 405
LR-243 405
LR-204 405
Panther Arms 5.56 Oracle 405
Panther 3G1 405
Prairie Panther 405
Panther RAPTR 406
Panther REPR 406
Panther 308 Mk12 406
Panther A-15 Pump Rifle 406
Panther A-15 Pump Pistol 406
Panther DCM .22 LR 406
Panther Lite 308/338 406
Panther 6.5 406
6.8 SPCII Hunter 406
300 AAC Blackout 406
308 Recon 406

DRISCOLL, J.B.

Single-Shot Pocket Pistol 406

DRULOV

Model 70 Standard 406
Model 70 Special 406
Model 75 406
Pav 407

DSA, INC.

SA58 24" Bull 407
SA58 21" Bull 407
SA58 Medium Contour 407
SA58 Carbine 407
SA58 Standard 407
SA58 Tactical 407
SA58 Congo 407
SA58 Para Congo 407
SA58 Predator 407
SA58 Graywolf 407
SA58 T48 Replica 408
S1 Rifle 408
CVI Carbine 408
LE4 Carbine 408
DS-AR S Series Rifle 408
DS-AR Carbine 408
DS-AR Rifle 408
DS-AR DCM Rifle 408
DS-AR CQB MRP 408
DSA Z4 Gas Trap Carbine (GTC) 408
ZM-4 Series 409
RPD Traditional Rifle 409
RPD Carbine 409
DS-MP1 409
B&T TP9 Tactical Pistol 409
SA58TAC 409

DUMOULIN

Europa Model 409
Leige Model 409
Continental Model 409
Etendart Model 409
Superposed Express International 409
Boss Royal Model 410
Eagle Model Combination Gun 410
Europa I 410
Continental I Model 410

Pionnier Express Rifle 410
Aristocrat Model 410
Centurion Model 410
Centurion Classic 410
Diane 410
Amazone 410
Bavaria Deluxe 410
Safari Model 410
Safari Sportsman 410
African Pro 410

DUSEK, F.

Perla 410
Duo 410

84 GUN CO.

Classic Rifle 411
Lobo Rifle 411
Pennsylvania Rifle 411

E.M.F. CO., INC.

Hartford Bisley 411
Hartford Express 411
Hartford Pinkerton 411
Russian Model 1875 411
Remington Model 1875 Army
    Frontier 411
Schofield Model 411
Dakota Old Model 411
Dakota New Model 411
Dakota II 411
Citadel 1911 412
Lightning Standard 412
Rolling Block 412
1874 Sharps Sporting or
    Militay Rifle 412
Down Under Sharps Model 1874 412
Winchester Lever Actions 412
    Model 1860 412
    Model 1866 412
    Model 1873 412
    Model 1886/71 412
    Model 1892 412

EAGLE ARMS,
DIVISION OF ARMALITE

Golden Eagle 412
HBAR 412
SPR 412
M4C Carbine 412
M4A1C Carbine 412
Golden Eagle 412
AR-10 Match Rifle 412
Model M15 Series 412

ECHAVE & ARIZMENDI

Basque, Echasa, Dickson, or Dickson
    Special Agent 412
Bronco Model 1913 413
Bronco Model 1918 413
Echasa 413
Lightning 413
Lur Panzer 413
Pathfinder 413
Protector Model 1915 and 1918 413
Selecta Model 1918 413

ECHEVERRIA, STAR-BONIFACIO SA
(STAR)

Star Model 1908 414
Star Model 1914 414
Star Model 1919 414
Star Model 1919 New Variation 414
Modelo Militar 414
Star Model A 414
Star Model B 415
Star Model C 415
Star Model CO 415
Star Model D 415
Star Model DK Starfire 415
Star Model E 415
Star Model F 415
Star Model F Target 415
Star Model F Sport 416
Star Model F Olympic 416
Star Model F Olympic Rapid Fire 416
Star Model FR 416
Star Model FRS 416
Star Model FM 416
Star Model H 416
Star Model HK 416
Star Model HN 416
Star Model I 416
Star Model M 416
Star Model P 416
Star Model CU "Starlet" 416
Star Model 1941 S 416
Star Model BKS "Starlight" 417
Star Model PD 417
Star Model BM 417
Star Model BKM 417
Star Model 28 417
Star Model 30M 417
Star Model 30/PK 417
Megastar 418
Firestar M43, M40, and M45 418
Starfire Model 31P 418
Starfire Model 31PK 418
Ultrastar 418

ECLIPSE

Single-Shot Derringer 418

ELGIN CUTLASS

U.S. Navy Elgin Cutlass Pistol 418
Civilian Model 419
Small Model 419
Large Model 419

ELLS, JOSIAH

Model 1 419
Model 2 419
Model 3 419

ENDERS, CARL

Side-by-Side Shotgun 419

ENFIELD AMERICAN, INC.

MP-45 419

ENTERPRISE ARMS, INC.

Elite P500 420
Elite P425 420

Elite P325................................420
Tactical P500..........................420
Tactical P425..........................420
Tactical P325..........................420
Tactical P325 Plus...................420
Titleist P500...........................420
Boxer Model...........................420
TSM I.....................................420
TSM II....................................420
TSM III...................................421

ERA

ERA Side-by-Side Shotgun.............421
ERA Over/Under Shotgun................421

ERICHSON, G.

Pocket Pistol...........................421

ERMA WERKE WAFFENFABRIK

Erma .22 Luger Conversion Unit......421
.22 Target Pistol (Old Model)...........421
.22 Target Pistol (New Model)
    Master Model.......................421
KGP-68...................................421
KGP-69...................................422
KGP-22...................................422
KGP-32 & KGP-38....................422
ET-22 "Navy Luger" Long-Barreled
    Pistol.................................422
ESP 85A.................................422
EP-25.....................................422
RX-22 and PX-22.....................422
ER-772 Match.........................422
ER-773 Match.........................422
ER-777...................................423
EM1.22..................................423
EG-72, EG-722........................423
EG-712, EG-73........................423
SR-100...................................423

ERQUIAGA

Fiel...423
Fiel 6.35.................................423
Marte......................................423

ERRASTI, A.

Velo Dog.................................424
M1889....................................424
Errasti....................................424
Errasti Oscillante.....................424
Dreadnaught, Goliath and Smith
    Americano...........................424

ESCORT

Model AS................................424
Model PS................................424
Model PS AimGuard................424
Combo Model..........................424
Escort Semi-Auto Slug Gun......424
Escort Extreme Series.............425
    Extreme 3.5........................425
    Extreme 3...........................425
    Extreme Waterfowl Youth......425
Field Hunter............................425
AimGuard...............................425
Escort Pump Slug Gun.............425

ESPIRIN, HERMANOS

Euskaro..................................425

EUROARMS OF AMERICA

1851 Navy..............................425
1853 Enfield Rifled Musket.........426
Duck Gun................................426

EUROPEAN AMERICAN ARMORY CORP./ U.S. SPORTING GOODS, INC.

EAA Witness P-Series Full Size.......426
EAA Witness P-Series Carry-Comp...426
EAA Witness P-Series Compact......426
EAA Witness P-S Series.............426
EAA Witness Carry Comp...........427
    New Configuration................427
EAA Witness Standard..............427
    New Configuration................427
EAA Witness Subcompact..........427
    New Configuration................427
EAA Witness Sport L/S.............427
    New Configuration................427
EAA Witness Combo 9/40..........427
EAA Witness Silver Team Match....427
EAA Witness Sport...................428
    New Configuration................428
EAA Witness Hunter..................428
EAA Witness Gold Team Match....428
EAA Witness Limited Class Pistol.....428
EAA Witness Stock...................428
EAA Witness Multi Class Pistol
    ackage...............................428
EAA Witness Elite Match............429
EAA Witness 1911....................429
Zastava EZ Pistol.....................429
Thor.......................................429
BUL Government......................429
    Commander.........................429
    Stinger...............................429
EAA Big Bore Bounty Hunter.......429
EAA Small Bore Bounty Hunter....430
EAA Bounty Hunter Shotgun—
    External Hammers.................430
EAA Bounty Hunter Shotgun—
    Traditional...........................430
EAA F.A.B. 92 Pistol.................430
EAA European Standard Pistol......430
EAA European Target Pistol........430
EAA Windicator Standard Grade....430
EAA Windicator Basic Grade........430
EAA Windicator Tactical Grade.....430
    2" Barrel.............................430
    4" Barrel.............................430
EAA Windicator Target Grade.......430
EAA PM2 Shotgun....................431
EAA HW 60 Rifle......................431
    Target Grade........................431
    Match Grade........................431
EAA Sabatti Falcon...................431
    12/20 Gauge........................431
    28/.410..............................431
EAA SP 1822...........................431
EAA SP 1822H.........................431
EAA SP 1822TH........................431
EAA Sporting Clay Basic............431
EAA Sporting Clay Pro...............431

EAA Sporting Clay Pro Gold.........431
EAA Saba.................................431
EAA/Saiga Shotgun...................431
EAA/Saiga Rifle........................431
EAA Rover 870.........................431
EAA Benelli Silhouette Pistol........432
MP94 Combo Gun......................432
Model .410/22 LR......................432
Model 221 Double Rifle..............432

EVANS, J. E.

Pocket Pistol...........................432

EVANS REPEATING RIFLE CO.

Old Model...............................432
    Military Musket.....................432
    Sporting Rifle.......................432
    Carbine...............................432
Transitional Model....................433
    Military Musket.....................433
    Carbine...............................433
    Sporting Rifle.......................433
    Montreal Carbine..................433
New Model..............................433
    Military Musket.....................433
    Carbine...............................433
    Sporting Rifle.......................433

EXCAM

TA 76.....................................433
TA 38 Over/Under Derringer........433
TA 90.....................................433
BTA-90B.................................433
TA 90 SS................................433
TA 41, 41C, and 41 SS..............433
Warrior Model W 722.................433
Model W384.............................433
Model W357.............................434
Targa GT 26............................434
    Steel Frame Version..............434
    Alloy Frame Version..............434
GT 22.....................................434
GT 22T...................................434
GT 32.....................................434
GT 380...................................434
GT 380XE...............................434

EXCEL INDUSTRIES

Accelerator Pistol....................434
Accelerator Rifle......................434
X-22.......................................434
X-57 / X-30.............................434

F.A.S.

Model 601...............................435
Model 602...............................435
Model 603...............................435

F.I.E.

TZ 75.....................................435
TZ 75 Series 88.......................435
KG-99.....................................435
Spectre Assault Pistol...............435
Titan II .22.............................435
Titan E32................................435
Super Titan 11.........................435

Titan 25..................................435
Titan Tigress...........................436
D38 Derringer..........................436
D86 Derringer..........................436
Cowboy..................................436
Gold Rush...............................436
Texas Ranger..........................436
Buffalo Scout..........................436
Legend S.A.A..........................436
Hombre...................................436
Model 522TB...........................436
722..436
532TB.....................................437
732B.......................................437
Standard Revolver....................437
Models 384TB and 386TB..........437
Model 357TB...........................437
222, 232, and 382TB................437
Model 3572.............................437
Model 122...............................437
Single-Shot.............................437
S.O.B......................................437
Sturdy Over/Under....................437
Brute......................................437
SPAS-12.................................437
LAW-12..................................437
SAS-12...................................438

FABARM

Ellegi Standard........................438
    Ellegi Multichoke.................438
    Ellegi Innerchoke.................438
    Ellegi Magnum....................438
    Ellegi Super Goose..............438
    Ellegi Slug..........................438
    Ellegi Police........................438
XLR5 Velocity..........................438
    LR (Long Rib).......................438
    AR (Adjustable Rib)..............438
L4S Initial Hunter.....................438
Model S.D.A.S.S......................438
    Special Police......................438
    Martial Model......................438
Omega Standard......................438
Omega Goose Gun...................438
Beta Model..............................438
Beta Europe............................438
Field Model..............................439
Gamma Field...........................439
Gamma Paradox Gun.................439
Gamma Trap or Skeet................439
Gamma Sporting
    Competition Model...............439
Elos.......................................439
Axis Competition......................439
    Sporting.............................439
    Trap...................................439
Camo Lion...............................439
Red Lion..................................439
Red Lion Ducks Unlimited 2001....439
Gold Lion................................439
Gold Lion Mark III....................440
Sporting Clays Lion..................440
Rex Lion..................................440
Sporting Clays Extra.................440
Tactical Semi-Auto...................440

Home Security HD 440
H368 440
FP6 Field Pump 440
FP6 440
FP6 with Rail 440
Max Lion 441
Max Lion Light 441
Max Lion Paradox 441
Sporting Clays Competition Lion 441
Sporting Clays Max Lion 441
Sporting Clays Competition Extra 441
Black Lion Competition 441
Monotrap 441
Silver Lion 441
Silver Lion Youth 442
Super Light Lion Youth 442
Ultra Mag Lion 442
Super Light Lion 442
Camo Turkey Mag 442
Ultra Camo Mag Lion 442
Classic Lion Grade I 442
Classic Lion Grade II 442
Classic Lion Elite 442

FABBRI, ARMI
Side-by-Side Shotgun 442
Over/Under Shotgun 442

FABRIQUE NATIONALE
Model 1900 443
Model 1903 443
Model 1905 443
  1st Variation, Under Serial
   Number 100000 443
  2nd Variation, Over Serial
   Number 100000 443
Model 1910 444
Model 1922 444
"Baby" Model 444
Pre-War Commercial Model 444
  Tangent Sight Version 444
Pre-War Military Contract 444
  Belgium 444
  Canada and China 444
  Great Britain 444
  Estonia 444
  Holland 444
  Latvia 444
  Lithuania 444
  Romania 444
German Military Pistole
  Model 640(b) 444
  Fixed Sight Model 445
  Tangent Sight Model 445
Captured Pre-war
  Commercial Model 445
Post-War Military Contract 445
  Fixed Sight 445
  Tangent Sight 445
  Slotted and Tangent Sight 445
Post-War Commercial Model 445
  Fixed Sight 445
  Tangent Sight 445
  Slotted and Tangent Sight 445
Model 1889 445
Model 1949 or SAFN 49 445

Model 30-11 Sniper Rifle 445
FN-FAL 445
  50.00—21" Rifle Model 445
  50.63—18" Paratrooper Model 445
  50.64—21" Paratrooper Model 445
  50.41—Synthetic Butt H-Bar 445
  50.42—Wood Butt H-Bar 445
FN-FAL "G" Series
  (Type I Receiver) 445
  Standard 445
  Lightweight 445
  FN CAL 445
FNC 445
  Standard 445
  Paratrooper Model 445
Musketeer Sporting Rifles 445
Deluxe Sporter 446
FN Supreme 446
Supreme Magnum Model 446

FAIRBANKS, A. B.
Fairbanks All Metal Pistol 446

FALCON FIREARMS
Portsider 446
Portsider Set 446
Gold Falcon 446

FAMARS, A. & S.
Engraving Pattern Descriptions
  (Older Discontinued Patterns) 446
Zeus 446
  In the white 446
  D2 pattern 446
  S3 pattern 446
Tribute 446
  In the white 446
  D2 pattern 446
  S3 pattern 446
Venus 447
  In the white 447
  D2 pattern 447
  D3 pattern 447
  D4 pattern 447
  D5 pattern 447
  D4E pattern 447
  D5E pattern 447
  DXO pattern 447
Veneri 447
  D2 pattern 447
Jorema Royal 447
  In the white 447
  S2 pattern 447
  S3 pattern 447
  S4 pattern 447
  S5 pattern 447
  S4E pattern 447
  S5E pattern 447
  SXO pattern 447
Excaliber BL 447
Excalibur BL Extra 447
Excalibur BL Prestige 447
Excalibur BLX 447
Excalibur BLX Extra 447
Excalibur BLX Prestige 448
Excalibur SL 448

Excalibur SL Extra 448
Excalibur SL Prestige 448
Excalibur Express 448
Excalibur Express Extra 448
Excalibur Express Prestige 448
African Express 448
Venus Express Professional 448
Venus Express Extra 448

FARROW ARMS CO.
Farrow Falling Block Rifle 448
  No. 1 Model 448
  No. 2 Model 448

FAUSTI, STEFANO
Caledon 448
Caledon SL 448
Class 449
Class SL 449
Round Body 449
Magnificent Field 449
Magnificent Sporting 449
Model DEA 449
Classic Express Rifle 449

**FAYETTEVILLE ARMORY PISTOLS
AND RIFLES**
Fayetteville Armory Percussion
  Pistols 449
  (U.S. M1836 Pistols, Altered) 449
Fayetteville Armory Rifles
  (Types I through IV) 449

FEATHER INDUSTRIES, INC.
AT-22 450
AT-9 450
KG-9 450
KG-22 450
SAR-180 450
Mini-AT 450
Guardian Angel 450

FEDERAL ENGINEERING CORP.
XC-220 450
XC-450 450
XC-900 450

FEDERAL ORDNANCE, INC.
M-14 Semi-Automatic 450
Model 714 Broomhandle Mauser 451
Model 713 Mauser Carbine 451
Model 713 Deluxe 451
Standard Broomhandle 451
Ranger 1911A1 451

**FEG
(FEGYVER ES GAZKESZULEKGYAR)**
Model 1901 451
Model 1906 451
Model 1910 451
Frommer Stop Model 1912 451
Frommer Baby Model 452
Frommer Lilliput 452
Model 1929 452
  .22 Caliber 452
Model 1937 452
  Nazi Proofed 7.65mm Version 452

9mm Short Hungarian Military
  Version 452
Model R-9 452
Model AP-9 452
Model PPH 453
Model B9R 453
Model PA-63 453
Model FP-9 453
Model P9R 453
  Blue 453
  Chrome 453
Model P9RK 453
SA-2000-M 454
AMD-65 AK47 454

FEINWERKBAU
Model 2000 Universal 454
Mini 2000 454
Running Boar Rifle 454
Match Rifle 454
Model 2600 Ultra Match
  Free Rifle 454

FEMARU
Model 37 454
Hege 454
Tokagypt 454
Walam 454

FERLIB
Model F.VI 454
Model F.VII 455
Model F.VII/SC 455
Model F.VII Sideplate 455
Model F.VII/SC Sideplate 455
Hammer Gun 455

FERRY, ANDREWS & CO.
Under Hammer Pistol 455

FIALA ARMS COMPANY
Fiala Repeating Target Pistol 455
  Complete, Three Barrels, Stock,
   Tools, and Case 455
  Gun Only 455

FINNISH LION
ISU Target Rifle 456
Champion Free Rifle 456
Match Rifle 456

FIRESTORM
Firestorm .22 LR 456
Firestorm .32 456
Firestorm .380 456
Mini Firestorm 9mm 456
Mini Firestorm .40 S&W 456
Firestorm .45 Government 456
Compact Firestorm .45
  Government 457
Mini Firestorm .45 Government 457
1911 Mil-Spec Standard
  Government 457

FLETCHER BIDWELL, LLC
Spencer 1860 Military Carbine 457

FNH USA, INC.

Model Forty-Nine............457
Model FNP-9/FNP-40............457
FNP-45............458
FNP-45 Tactical............458
FNP-45 Competition............458
FNX-9, FNX-40............458
FNX-45............458
FNS-9............458
FNH Five-seveN............458
Model HP-SA............458
Model HP-SA-SFS............459
Model HP-DA/HP-DAO............459
Model HP-DA/HP-DAO Compact............459
Model BDA/BDAO Compact............459
FNAR............459
FN A1 SPR............459
FN A1a SPR............459
FN A2 SPR............459
FN A3 SPR............460
FN A4 SPR............460
FN A5 SPR............460
FN A5M............460
FN PS90............460
FNH-USA Ballista............460
FNH-USA SCAR 16S/17S............460
FN A5a SPR............460
FN PBR (Patrol Bolt Rifle)............460
Ultima Ratio Intervention............460
Ultima Ratio Commando I............461
Ultima Ratio Commando II............461
FN-Mini-Hecate............461
.338 Lapua............461
FS 2000............461
FNH-USA SC1............461
FN Police Shotgun............461
FN Tactical Police............461
FN Self-Loading Police............461

FOEHL, C.

Derringer............462

FOEHL & WEEKS

Columbian............462
Columbian Automatic............462
Perfect............462

FOGARTY

Fogarty Repeating Rifle
and Carbine............462
Rifle............462
Carbine............462

FOLSOM, H.

Derringer............462

FORBES RIFLES, LLC

Model 24B............462

FOREHAND & WADSWORTH

Single-Shot Derringer............462
Single-Shot .41 Derringer............462
Side-Hammer .22............462
Center Hammer............462
Old Model Army
Single-Action Revolver............463

New Model Army Single-Action
Revolver............463
Double-Action Revolver............463
British Bulldog............463
British Bulldog .44............463
Swamp Angel............463
Perfection Automatic............463
Double-Barrel Shotguns............463

FOWLER, B. JR.

Percussion Pistol............463

FOX, A. H.

Sterlingworth............463
Sterlingworth Deluxe............463
SP Grade............463
HE Grade............463
High Grade Guns A-FE............463
A Grade............463
AE Grade (Automatic Ejectors)............464
B Grade............464
BE Grade............464
C Grade............464
CE Grade............464
XE Grade............464
D Grade............464
DE Grade............464
F Grade............464
FE Grade............464
Single Barrel Trap Guns............464
J Grade............464
K Grade............464
L Grade............464
M Grade............464
CE Grade............465
XE Grade............465
DE Grade............465
FE Grade............465
Exhibition Grade............465

FRANCHI, L.

Astore............465
Astore II............465
Astore 5............465
Airone............465
Condor............465
Imperial............465
Imperiales............465
No. 5 Imperial Monte Carlo............465
No. 11 Imperial Monte Carlo............466
Imperial Monte Carlo Extra............466
Highlander............466
Priti Deluxe Model............466
Falconet............466
Falconet Skeet............466
Falconet International Skeet............466
Falconet Trap............466
Falconet International Trap............466
Peregrine Model 451............466
Peregrine Model 400............466
Aristocrat............466
Aristocrat Magnum............466
Aristocrat Silver King............466
Aristocrat Deluxe............466
Aristocrat Supreme............466
Aristocrat Imperial............467

Aristocrat Monte Carlo............467
Model 2003 Trap............467
Model 2004 Trap............467
Model 2005 Combination Trap............467
Model 3000 "Undergun"............467
Alcione Classic............467
Alcione T (Titanium)............467
Alcione T Two-Barrel Set............467
Alcione Field Model............467
Alcione Sporting............467
Alcione LF............467
Alcione SL Sport............467
Alcione SP............467
ALCIONE SIDEPLATES............468
Alcione Classic SX............468
Alcione Field SX............468
Veloce............468
Veloce English Stock............468
Veloce Grade II............468
Veloce Squire Set............468
Renaissance............469
Field............469
Classic............469
Elite............469
Sporting............469
Aspire............469
Instinct............469
AL48............469
AL 48 Short Stock (Modern)............469
AL 48 Deluxe English Stock
(Modern)............469
Hunter Model AL48 (1950-1970)............469
Eldorado AL48 (1954-1975)............469
Crown Grade............470
Diamond Grade............470
Imperial Grade............470
Model 500............470
Model 520 "Eldorado Gold"............470
Model 530 Trap............470
Prestige Model............470
Elite Model............470
SPAS12............470
Black Magic Game Model............470
Black Magic Hunter............470
Black Magic Lightweight Hunter............470
Variomax 912............470
Variomax 912 Camo............471
Variomax 912 SteadyGrip............471
Variopress 612 Sporting............471
Variopress 612 Field............471
Variopress 612 Defense............471
Variopress 620 Field............471
Variopress 620 Short Stock............471
Model 712............471
Weathercoat............471
Camo............471
Synthetic............471
Model 720............471
Camo............471
Walnut Short Stock............471
Weathercoat............472
I-12............472
I-12 White Gold............472
Fenice............472
Intensity............472

Affinity............472
Centennial Semi-Automatic............472

FRANCOTTE, A.

Jubilee............472
No. 14............472
No. 18............472
No. 20............472
No. 25............473
No. 30............473
Eagle Grade No. 45............473
Knockabout............473
Sidelock Side-by-Side............473
Deluxe Sidelock Side-by-Side............473
Custom Side-by-Side Shotguns............473
Custom Double Rifles............473
Custom Single-Shot
Mountain Rifles............473
Custom Bolt-Action Rifles............473

FRANKLIN, C. W.

Single-Barrel............474
Damascus Barrel Double............474
Steel Barrel Double............474

FRANKONIA JAGD

Favorit Standard............474
Favorit Deluxe............474
Safari Model............474
Heeren Rifle............474

FRASER F. A. CORP.

Fraser .25 cal............474

FREEDOM ARMS

Percussion Mini-Revolver............474
Bostonian (aka Boot Gun)............474
Patriot (aka Boot Gun)............474
Minuteman............474
Ironsides............474
Celebrity............474
Casull Field Grade Model 83............474
Casull Premier Grade Model 83............475
Model 97............475
Model 353............475
Field Grade............475
Premier Grade............475
Signature Edition............475
Model 252............475
Silhouette Class............475
Varmint Class............475
Model 757............475
Field Grade............475
Premier Grade............475
Model 654............475
Field Grade............475
Premier Grade............475
Model 83 .500 Wyoming Express............475

FREEMAN, AUSTIN T.

Freeman Army Model Revolver............476

FRIGON

FT I............476
FTC............476
FS-4............476

FRUHWIRTH

M1872 Fruhwirth System Rifle........476

FUNK, CHRISTOPH

Double Rifles................................476
Prewar Drilling in 16 or 12 gauge....476

FYRBERG, ANDREW

Double-Barrel Shotguns.................476
Revolvers..................................476

GABBET-FAIRFAX, H.

Mars 477

GABILONDO Y URRESTI

Velo-Dog Revolver 477
Radium....................................477
Ruby.......................................477
Bufalo 6.35mm............................477
Bufalo 7.65mm............................477
Bufalo 9mmK..............................478
Danton 6.35mm............................478
Danton War Model.........................478
　Nine-Round Magazine..................478
　Twenty-Round Magazine 478
Perfect 478
Plus Ultra.................................478

GALAND, C.F.

Galand, Galand & Sommerville, Galand
　Perrin
　(Galand M1872) 479
Velo-Dog 479
Le Novo 479
Tue-Tue 479

GALEF (ZABALA)

Zabala Double.............................479
Companion 479
Monte Carlo Trap..........................479
Silver Snipe, Golden Snipe,
　and Silver Hawk........................479

GALENA INDUSTRIES INC.

AMT Backup 479
Automag II 479
Automag III 480
Automag IV 480
Automag .440 CorBon......................480
Galena Accelerator 480
Galena Hardballer..........................480
Galena Longslide...........................480
Galena Commando...........................480

GALESI, INDUSTRIA ARMI

Model 1923 481
Model 1930 481
　9mm Parabellum........................481
Model 6 481
Model 9 481

GALIL

Model AR (.223) 481
Model ARM 481
Sniper Rifle...............................481
Hadar II...................................482

GALLAGER

Gallager Carbine 482
Percussion Model 482
Spencer Cartridge Model 482

GAMBA, RENATO

Hunter Super 482
Principessa................................482
Oxford 90..................................482
Oxford Extra...............................482
Gamba 624 Prince..........................482
Gamba 624 Extra...........................482
London 482
London Royal...............................482
Ambassador Gold and Black 482
Ambassador Executive......................482
Country Model 482
Grifone Model 482
Europa 2000................................482
Grinta Trap and Skeet 483
Victory Trap and Skeet 483
Edinburg Match.............................483
Boyern 88 Combination Gun 483
Daytona Trap...............................483
Daytona Sporting...........................483
Daytona Skeet..............................483
Daytona America Trap......................483
Daytona Game 483
Daytona Grade 6 Engraving.................483
　Daytona Trap and Skeet Models..483
　Daytona Sporting Model.............483
Daytona Grade 5 Engraving.................483
　Daytona Trap and Skeet Models..483
　Daytona Sporting Model.............483
Daytona Grade 4 Engraving.................483
　Daytona Trap and Skeet Models..483
　Daytona Sporting Model.............484
Daytona SL Grade 3 Engraving.............484
　Daytona Trap and Skeet Models..484
　Daytona Sporting Model.............484
　Daytona Game.........................484
Daytona SLHH Grade 2 Engraving....484
Daytona SLHH Grade 1
　Gold Engraving........................484
Daytona SLHH "One of Thousand" ...484
Concorde Trap..............................484
Concorde Skeet.............................484
Concorde Sporting..........................484
Concorde Game Grade 7
　Engraving...............................484
Concorde Game Grade 8
　Engraving...............................484
Concorde 2nd Generation 484
Le Mans 484
Hunter II..................................484
Safari Express.............................484
Mustang 485
RGZ 1000...................................485
RGX 1000 Express 485
SAB G90 485
SAB G91 Compact 485
Trident Fast Action........................485
Trident Super 485
Trident Match 900.........................485

GARAND

Rebuilt Rifle, any manufacture.........485
DCM Rifles.................................485
Navy Trophy Rifles U.S.N.
　Crane Depot Rebuild..................485
AMF Rebuild 486
H&R Rebuild 486
　Gas trap sn: ca 81-52,000.........486
　Gas trap/modified to gas port 486
　Pre-Dec. 7, 1941 gas port
　　production sn: ca 410,000 486
　WWII Production
　　sn: ca 410,000-3,880,000 ...486
　Post-WWII Production sn: ca
　　4,200,000-6,099,361 486
Winchester Educational Contract
　sn: 100,000-100,500................486
Winchester sn: 100,501-165,000...486
Winchester
　sn: 1,200,00-1,380,000............486
Winchester
　sn: 2,305,850-2,536,493..........486
Winchester
　sn: 1,601,150-1,640,000
　"win-13" 486
Harrington & Richardson
　Production 486
International Harvester Production ...486
International Harvester/
　with Springfield Receiver
　(postage stamp).......................486
International Harvester/
　with Springfield Receiver
　(arrow head).........................486
International Harvester/
　with Springfield Receiver
　(Gap letter)..........................486
International Harvester/
　with Harrington & Richardson
　Receiver...............................486
British Garands (Lend Lease)..........486
M1 Garand Cutaway.......................486
　M1C...................................486
　M1D (USMC Issue) MC 1952 486
National Match..............................486
　Type I.................................486
　Type II................................486

GARATE, ANITUA/G.A.C.

Charola....................................486
Cosmopolite................................486
El Lunar 487
G.A.C......................................487
Modelo Militar 487
Express or Danton 487
British Service Old Pattern No.2
　Mk. I Trocaola Aranzabal
　Military Revolver 487
L'Eclair 487
Sprinter 487
La Lira 487
Triumph 487

GARATE, HERMANOS

Cantabria..................................487
Velo-Stark.................................487

GARBI

Model 51-B 487

GARCIA

Garcia Bronco 488
Garcia Bronco .22/.410 488
Garcia Musketeer 488

GARRET, J. & F. CO.

Garrett Single-Shot Pistol...............489

GASSER, LEOPOLD

M1870......................................489
M1870/74..................................489
Gasser-Kropatschek M1876 489
Montenegrin Gasser 489
Rast & Gasser M1898 489

GATLING ARMS CO.

Kynoch-Dimancea 489

GAUCHER

GN 1 489

GAZANAGA, ISIDRO

Destroyer M1913...........................490
Destroyer M1916...........................490
Destroyer Revolver 490
Super Destroyer 490
Surete 490

GEM

Gem Pocket Revolver......................490

GENEZ, A. G.

Double-Barrel Shotgun 490
Pocket Pistol 490

GENSCHOW, G.

Geco 491
German Bulldog 491

GERING, H. M. & CO.

Leonhardt..................................491

GERSTENBERGER & EBERWEIN

Em-Ge, G.& E., Omega & Pic 491

GEVARM

Model A-6..................................491
E-1 Autoloading Rifle 491

GIB

10 Gauge Shotgun 491

Model 62-B 487
Model 71 487
Model 100 487
Model 101 488
Model 102 488
Model 103A 488
Model 103A Royal 488
Model 103B 488
Model 103B Royal 488
Model 120 488
Model 200 488
Model Special 488
Express Rifle 488

GIBBS
Gibbs Carbine 491
Gibbs Pistol 491

GIBBS GUNS, INC.
Mark 45 Carbine 492

GIBBS RIFLE COMPANY
Enfield No. 5 Jungle Carbine 492
Enfield No. 7 Jungle Carbine 492
Quest Extreme Carbine 492
Quest II Extreme Carbine 492
Quest III Extreme Carbine 492
Summit 45-70 Carbine 492
Mauser M71/84 492
Mauser M88 Commission Rifle 492
M98K Israeli Mauser 492
M1903-A4 Springfield
   Sniper Model 492

GIBBS TIFFANY & CO.
Under Hammer Pistol 492

GILLESPIE
Derringer Type Pocket Pistol 492

GLOCK
Glock 17 493
Glock 17C 493
Glock 17CC 493
Glock 17L Competition Model 493
Glock 19 493
Glock 19C 493
Glock 19CC 493
Glock 20 and Glock 21 493
Glock 20 SF Short Frame Pistol 494
Glock 21 SF 494
Glock 20C and 21C 494
Glock 20CC and 21CC 494
Glock 22 494
Glock 22C 494
Glock 22CC 494
Glock 23 494
Glock 23C 494
Glock 23CC 494
Glock 24 495
Glock 24C 495
Glock 24CC 495
Glock 26 and Glock 27 495
Glock 29 and Glock 30 495
Glock 29 SF Short Frame Pistol 495
Glock 31 495
Glock 31C 496
Glock 31CC 496
Glock 32 496
Glock 32C 496
Glock 32CC 496
Glock 33 496
Glock 34 496
Glock 35 496
Glock 36 496
Glock 37 497
Glock 38 497
Glock 39 497
Glock 41 Sport/Service
   Competition 497

Glock 42 497
Glock 43 497

GOLDEN EAGLE
Golden Eagle Model 5000 Grade I ...497
   Grade I Skeet 498
   Grade I Trap 498
Model 5000 Grade II 498
Grandee Grade III 498
Model 7000 Grade I 498
Model 7000 African 498
Model 7000 Grade II 498

GONCZ CO.
GC Carbine 498

GOVERNOR
Governor Pocket Revolver 499

GRAND POWER
K100 Mk12 499

GRAND PRECISION, FABRIQUE D'ARMES DE
Bulwark Model 1913 499
Bulwark Model 1914 499
Bulwark 6.35mm 499
Libia 6.35mm 500
Libia 7.65mm 500

GRANGER, G.
Side-by-Side Shotgun 500

GRAS
Model 1874 500

GREAT WESTERN ARMS COMPANY
Centerfire Single-Action 500
.22 Long Rifle Single-Action 500
Target Model (.22 LR) 500
Fast Draw Model 500
Deputy Model 501
Derringer Models 501
   Engraved Model 501
   Standard Model 501

GREAT WESTERN II
Custom 1873 SA 501
Stainless 1873 SA 501
Paladin Model 501
Liberty Model 501

GREEN, E.
Green 501

GREENE
Greene Breechloading Rifle 501

GREIFELT & CO.
Grade No. 1 502
Grade No. 3 502
Model 143E 502
Combination Gun 502
Model 22 502
Model 22E 502
Model 103 502
Model 103E 502

Drilling 502

GRENDEL, INC.
P-10 Pistol 502
P-12 502
P-30 503
P-30L 503
P-30M 503
P-31 503
SRT-20F Compact Rifle 503
SRT-24 503
R-31 Carbine 503

GRIFFON
Griffon 1911 A1 Combat 503

GRISWOLD & GUNNISON
1851 Navy Type 503

GROSS ARMS CO.
Pocket Revolver 504

GRUBB, J. C. & CO.
Pocket Pistol 504

GRULLA
Model 216RL 504
Royal 504
Consort 504

GUERINI, CAESAR
Flyway 504
Woodlander 504
Magnus Light 504
Magnus 504
Magnus Sporting 505
Maxum 505
Tempio 505
Forum/Forum Sporting 505
Summit Sporting/Summit Limited 505
Essex 505
Ellipse Evo 505
Apex 505
Invictus I Sporting 505

GUION, T. F.
Pocket Pistol 505

GUNCRAFTER INDUSTRIES
Model No. 1 505

GUNWORKS LTD.
Model 9 Derringer 506

GUSTAF, CARL
Bolt-Action Rifle 506
   Grade II 506
   Grade III 506
Deluxe Bolt-Action 506
Varmint Model 506
Grand Prix Target 506
Model 2000 506

GWYN & CAMPBELL
Union Carbine 506

H.J.S. INDUSTRIES, INC.
Frontier Four Derringer 507
Lone Star Derringer 507

H-S PRECISION, INC.
SPR Sporter Rifle 507
SPL Lightweight Sporter 507
PHR Professional Hunter Rifle 507
BHR Big Game Professional
   Hunter Rifle 507
PHL Professional Hunter
   Lightweight Rifle 507
VAR Varmint Rifle 507
Varmint Take-Down Rifle 507
Professional Hunter
   Take-Down Rifle 507
Varmint Pistol 507
Silhouette Pistol 508
HTR Heavy Tactical Rifle 508
Short Tactical 508
RDR Rapid Deployment Rifle 508
TTD Tactical Take-Down System 508

HAENEL, C. G.
Model 1 508
Model 2 508

HAFDASA
Ballester-Molina 508
Criolla 508
Hafdasa 509
Zonda 509
Rigaud 509
Campeon 509

HAHN, WILLIAM
Pocket Pistol 509

HALE, H. J.
Under Hammer Pistol 509

HALE & TULLER
Under Hammer Pistol 509

HALL, ALEXANDER
Revolving Rifle 509

HALL-NORTH
Type 1 Carbine 509
Type 2 Carbine 509

HAMBUSH, JOSEPH
Boxlock Side-by-Side Shotgun 509

HAMILTON RIFLE COMPANY

HAMMERLI, SA
Model 45 Smallbore Rifle 511
Model 54 Smallbore Rifle 511
Model 503 Smallbore Free Rifle 511
Model 104 512
Model 105 512
Model 106 512
Model 107 512
Model 107 Deluxe 512
Model 120-1 Free Pistol 512
Model 120-2 512

Model 120 Heavy Barrel 512
Model 150 512
Model 152 512
International Model 206 512
International Model 207 512
International Model 208 513
International Model 208 Deluxe 513
International Model 209 513
Model 230 513
Model 232 513
Model 280 513
Model SP 20 513

HAMMERLI-WALTHER

Olympia Model 200 Type 1952 514

HAMMOND BULLDOG

Hammond Bulldog 514

HAMMOND MFG. CO., GRANT

Military Automatic Pistol 514
Grant Hammond 7.65mm Pistol 514

HANKINS, WILLIAM

Pocket Revolver 514

HANUS, BILL

Bill Hanus Classic 515

HARRINGTON & RICHARDSON, INC.

Model No. 1 515
Model No. 1-1/2 515
Model No. 2-1/2 515
Model No. 3-1/2 515
Model No. 4-1/2 515
Model 1880 515
The American Double-Action 515
The Young America Double-Action ...515
Hunter 515
Trapper 515
New Defender 516
.22 U.S.R.A./Model 195
  Single-Shot Match Target Pistol ...517
  .22 U.S.R.A./Model 195 Pistol,
    Variations 1 to 3 517
  .22 U.S.R.A./Model 195 Pistol,
    Variation 4 517
Model 504 517
Model 532 517
Model 622 518
Model 905 519
Model 922 Second Issue 519
Model 923 519
Model 925 519
Model 935 519
Model 929 519
Model 929 Sidekick—New Model ...519
Model 929 Sidekick Trapper Edition .. 519
Model 930 519
Model 939 Ultra Sidekick 519
Model 939 Premier 519
Model 940 520
Model 949 520
Model 949 Western 520
Model 950 520
Model 976 520

Model 999 Sportsman 520
Model 999 Engraved 520
Amtec 2000 520
Hammerless Double 520
  D Grade 520
  C Grade 520
  B Grade 520
  A Grade 520
Harrich No. 1 520
Single-Barrel Shotguns 520
Turkey Mag 520
Youth Turkey Gun 521
Topper (New Production) 521
Topper Deluxe 521
Topper Jr. in 20 Gauge and
  .410 Bore Only 521
Topper Jr. Classic 521
Topper Deluxe Slug 521
Topper Deluxe Classic 521
Topper Trap Gun 521
Tamer 521
Ultra Slug Hunter 521
Ultra Slug Hunter Deluxe
  20 Gauge 521
Ultra Slug Hunter Deluxe
  12 Gauge 521
Ultra Slug Youth Model 521
Ultra Slug Hunter Bull Barrel 521
Ultra Slug Hunter
  Thumbhole Stock 521
Ultra Slug Youth Bull Barrel 522
Ultra Lite Slug Hunter 522
Camo Laminate Turkey
  NWTF Edition 522
Camo Laminate Turkey Youth
  NWTF Edition 522
  .32-20 W.C.F. serial range mostly
    from 43851 (?) to 43937 (?)..522
  .22 rimfire serial range from
    1 (?) to 223 (?) 522
H&R Handy-Gun (smooth bore)
  NFA, Curio or Relic 522
  .410 bore, Model 2,
    Types II and III 522
  28 gauge, Model 2, Type I 522
Topper (Old Production) 523
Model 401 523
Model 402 523
Model 440 523
Model 442 523
Model 403 523
Model 404 523
Pardner Pump Field Gun
  Full-Dip Camo 523
Excell 524
Excell Waterfowl 524
Excell Turkey 524
Excell Combo 524
Pinnacle 524
Model 1212 524
Long Tom Classic 524
H&R/NEF Handi-Rifle/Slug
  Gun Combo 524
Model 058 524
Model 258 524
Reising Model 60 524
Model 65 Military (Model 58C) 524

Model 155 (Shikari) 525
Model 301 Carbine 525
Model 317 Ultra Wildcat 525
H&R Handi-Rifle
  (current production) 525
H&R Survivor 525
Synthetic 525
Stainless 525
Synthetic Handi-Rifle/Slug
  Gun Combo 526
Superlite Compact 526
Ultra Varmint Rifle 526
Ultra Varmint Thumbhole 526
Stainless Steel Ultra Varmint
  Thumbhole 526
Ultra Varmint Fluted 526
Model 317P 526
Ultra Rifle—Hunting 526
Harrington & Richardson/
  New England Firearms
  Stainless Ultra Hunter with
  Thumbhole Stock 526
Ultra Rifle—Varmint 526
Ultra .22 Magnum Rifle 526
Ultra Rifle—Comp 526
Ultra Rifle Rocky Mountain Elk
  Foundation Commemorative 527
Sportster .17 HMR 527
Sportster 527
Sportster Compact 527
Buffalo Classic 527
Wesson & Harrington Brand
  125th Anniversary Rifle 527
Ultra Rifle Whitetails Unlimited
  1997 Commemorative Edition 527
CR Carbine 527
Model 333 527
Model 340 527
Model 360 Ultra Automatic 527
Model 451 Medalist 527
Model 700 527
100th Anniversary Officer's Model ...528
Custer Memorial Issue 528
  Officer's Model 528
  Enlisted Men's Model 528
Model 171 528
Model 171-DL 528
Model 174 528
Model 178 528

HARRIS GUNWORKS

National Match Rifle 528
Model 86 Sniper Rifle 529
Model 87 Series 529
Model 88 529
Model 89 Sniper Rifle 529
Model 93 529
Model 95 529
Model 96 529
Long Range Rifle 530
Target/Benchrest Rifle 530
Antietam Sharps Rifle 530
Signature Classic Sporter 530
Signature Classic Stainless Sporter .. 530
Signature Alaskan 530
Signature Titanium Mountain Rifle .. 530
Talon Safari Rifle 531

Talon Sporter Rifle 531
Double Rifle/Shotgun 531
  Boxlock 531
  Side Lock 531

HAWES

Trophy 532
Silver City 532

HDH, SA.

Cobold 533
Puppy 533
Lincoln 533
Lincoln-Bossu 533
Left Wheeler 533

HEAVY EXPRESS INC.

Heavy Express Premier—
  Ruger M77 Mk II 534
Heavy Express Monarch—
  Winchester M70 Classic 534
Heavy Express Monarch—
  Ruger 77 MK II 534
Heavy Express Single-Shot—
  Ruger #1 534

HECKLER & KOCH

Model 91 A2 534
Model 91 A3 534
Model 93 A2 534
Model 93 A3 534
Model 94 A2 535
Model 94 A3 535
Model 270 535
Model 300 535
Model 630 535
Model 770 535
Model 940 535
Model SL6 535
Model SL7 535
Model SR9 535
Model SR9 (T) Target 536
Model SR9 (TC)
  Target Competition 536
BASR Model 536
PSG-1 536
Model SL8-1 536
SLB 2000 536
Model USC 536
Model MR556A1 536
MR762A1 Carbine 536
HK4 536
  .22 Caliber or .380 Caliber 537
  .25 Caliber or .32 Caliber 537
  Conversion Units 537
P9 537
P9S 537
P9S Target Model 537
P9S Competition 537
VP 70Z 537
P7 PSP 537
P7 K3 537
  .22 Caliber Conversion Kit 538
  .32 ACP Caliber Conversion Kit ...538
P7 M8 538
P7 M10 538

P7 M13 538
SP89 538
USP 40 539
USP 9 539
USP 9SD 539
USP 40 Compact 539
USP 45 539
USP 9 Compact 540
USP Compact LEM
(Law Enforcement Modification) ...540
USP 45 Match 540
USP 45 Compact 540
USP 45 Compact Tactical 540
USP .357 Compact 541
USP 45 Expert 541
USP 45 Tactical 541
USP Elite 541
USP 45 50th Anniversary
Commemorative 541
P2000 GPM 541
P2000 SK 541
Mark 23 542
HK45 542
HK45 Compact 542
P30 542
VP9/VP40 542

HEINZELMANN, C.E.

Heim 543

HEIZER DEFENSE

PS1 Pocket Shotgun 543

HELFRICHT

Model 3 Pocket Pistol 543
Model 4 Pocket Pistol 543

HENRION & DASSY

Semi-Automatic 543

HENRY, ALEXANDER

Single-Shot Rifle 543
Double Rifle 543

HENRY REPEATING ARMS COMPANY

Lever-Action 543
Carbine 544
Youth Model 544
Lever-Action .22 Magnum 544
Lever-Action Frontier Model 544
Golden Boy 544
Golden Boy Deluxe 544
Deluxe Engraved Golden Boy
Magnum 544
Silver Boy 544
Varmint Express 544
Big Boy 544
Big Boy Deluxe Engraved
.44 Magnum 544
Big Boy .44 Magnum
"Wildlife Edition" 544
Big Boy .45 Colt "Cowboy Edition" ...544
.30-30 544
Mare's Leg 545
.45 Colt 545
.22 545

Original Henry Rifle 545
Long Ranger 545
Pump-Action Rifle 545
U.S. Survival Rifle 545
Pump-Action .22 Octagon Rifle 545
Mini Bolt 545
Acu-Bolt 545

HERITAGE MANUFACTURING, INC.

Stealth 545
Model H25S 546
Sentry 546
Rough Rider 546
With Combination Cylinder—
.22 Magnum 546
With Bird's-Head Grip & Combo
Cylinder 546
Rough Rider .17 HMR 546
Rough Rider Big-Bore Series 546

HEROLD

Bolt-Action Rifle 547

HERTER'S

Guide 547
Power-Mag Revolver 547
Western 547
J-9 or U-9 Hunter 547
J-9 or U-9 Presentation
or Supreme 547

HEYM, F. W.

Model HR-30 547
Model HR-38 547
Model 77B/55B Over/Under Rifle 547
Model 55BSS 547
Model 88 Safari 548
Model 33 Deluxe 548
Model 37 548
Model 37 Deluxe 548
Model SR-20 548
Model SR-20 Alpine 549
SR-20 Classic Safari 549
SR-20 Classic Sportsman 549
SR-20 Trophy 549
Heym Magnum Express 549

HI-POINT FIREARMS

Model C 549
Model C Polymer 549
Model C Comp 549
Model JH 549
Model 40SW 549
Model 9mm Polymer
(Model 916) 549
Model .45 Polymer 549
Model .40 Polymer 550
Model CF 550
.380 ACP Compensated 550
Model 4095 Carbine 550
Model 995 Carbine 550
Model 4595 Carbine 550

HIGH STANDARD

Model B 550
Model B-US 550

Model C 551
Model A 551
Model D 551
Model E 551
Model S 551
Model H-B, Type 1 Pre-War 551
Model H-B, Type 2 Post-War 551
Model H-A 552
Model H-D 552
Model H-E 552
Model USA—Model HD 552
Model USA—Model HD-MS 552
Model H-D Military 552
G-.380 552
G-B 553
G-D 553
G-E 553
Olympic (commonly called "G-O") 553
Supermatic 553
Olympic 553
Field King 554
Sport King 554
Supermatic S-100 554
Olympic O-100 554
Field King FK-100 554
Sport King SK-100 554
Sport King Lightweight SK-100 555
Flite King LW-100 555
Dura-Matic M-100 555
Olympic O-101 555
Supermatic S-101 555
Field King FK-101 555
Dura-Matic M-101 556
Conversion Kits 556
Supermatic Trophy 556
Supermatic Citation 556
Supermatic Tournament 556
Olympic 556
Olympic ISU 556
Olympic Trophy ISU 556
Sport King 557
Flite King 557
Sharpshooter 557
Conversion Kits 557
Supermatic Trophy 557
Supermatic Citation 557
Olympic 557
Olympic ISU 557
Victor (Slant Grip) 557
Supermatic Trophy 558
Supermatic Citation 558
Supermatic Tournament 558
Olympic 558
Olympic ISU 558
Olympic ISU 558
Olympic ISU
1980 Commemorative 558
Supermatic Trophy 558
Supermatic Trophy 1972
Commemorative 558
Supermatic Citation 558
Supermatic Tournament 558
Sport King 558
Sharpshooter 558
Survival Kit 558

Victor 558
10-X 559
Supermatic Trophy 559
Supermatic Citation 559
Citation II 559
Sport King-M 559
Type 1 Markings 560
Type 2 Markings 560
Type 3 Markings 560
Blued finish, white or black grips,
1962-1984 560
Nickel Finish black grips,
introduced 1970 560
Electroless Nickel Finish with
checkered walnut grips 560
Silver-Plated Derringer 560
Gold-Plated Derringer 560
Sentinel Aluminum Frames 560
Gold 560
Turquoise 560
Pink 560
Sentinel Imperial 560
Sentinel Deluxe 560
Sentinel Snub 560
Camp Gun 561
Sentinel Mark I 561
Sentinel Mark IV 561
Sentinel Mark II 561
Sentinel Mark III 561
Power Plus 561
Crusader 561
.45 Colt (s/n 000 to 050) 562
.45 Colt (s/n over 050) 562
Double Nine
with Aluminum Frame 562
Double Nine with Steel Frame 562
Longhorn 562
Marshal 562
Posse 562
Natchez 562
Hombre 562
Durango 562
The Gun/High Sierra 563
Griswold & Gunnison 563
Leech & Rigdon 563
Schneider & Glassick 563
Bicentennial 1776-1976 563
Special Presentation Bicentennial 563
Supermatic Field 563
Supermatic Special 563
Supermatic Deluxe 563
Supermatic Citation 563
Supermatic Trophy 563
Supermatic Duck 564
Supermatic Deer 564
Supermatic Skeet 564
Supermatic Trap 564
Model 200 564
Flite King Field 564
Flite King Brush 564
Flite King Special 564
Flite King Deluxe 564
Flite King Citation 564
Flite King Trophy 564
Flite King Skeet 565
Flite King Trap 565

Model 514 565
Semi-Automatic 565
Model 10-A 565
Model 10-B 565
Pump 565
Supermatic Shadow Automatic 565
Supermatic Shadow Indy
    Over/Under 565
Supermatic Shadow Seven
    Over/Under 565
Sport King/Flite King 565
Sport King Field 565
Sport King Special 565
Sport King Deluxe/Sport King Rifle ... 566
Sport King Carbine 566
Hi-Power Field Grade 566
Hi-Power Deluxe 566

HIGH STANDARD MANUFACTURING CO.

Supermatic Citation 566
Supermatic Citation MS 566
Supermatic Tournament 566
Supermatic Trophy 566
Olympic Model 566
Olympic ISU 566
Olympic Rapid Fire 566
Sport King 566
Victor 566
10-X 566
10-X—Shea Model 567
Olympic Trophy Space Gun 567
Model 1911A1 567
HAS-15 567
HAS-15 Enforcer 567
HAS-15 National Match 567

HILL, W.J.

Hill's Self-Extracting Revolver 567

HILLIARD, D. H.

Under Hammer Pistol 567

HOFFMAN, LOUIS

Pocket Pistol 567

HOLDEN, C. B.

Open Frame Rifle 567

HOLECK, EMANUEL

Holeck Rifle 567

HOLLAND & HOLLAND, LTD.

No. 2 Grade Double Rifle 568
Royal Side-by-Side Rifle 568
H&H .700 Bore Side-by-Side Rifle ... 568
Best Quality Rifle 568

HOLLOWAY ARMS CO.

HAC Model 7 568
HAC Model 7C 568
HAC Model 7S 568

HOLMES FIREARMS

MP-22 568
MP-83 568

HOPKINS & ALLEN

Dictator 569
Double-Barrel Shotguns 569

HOWA MACHINE COMPANY

Model 1500 Hunter 569
Model 1500 JRS Classic 569
Model 1500 Mountain 569
Model 1500 Trophy 570
Model 1500 Varmint 570
Model 1500 Varmint Supreme 570
Model 1500 Lightning Rifle 570
Model 1500 Youth 570
Model 1500 Thumbhole Sporter 570
Model 1500 Custom 570
Realtree Camo Rifle 570
Texas Safari Rifle 570
Model 1500 PCS
    (Police Counter Sniper) 570

HUGLU

Bobwhite 570
Ringneck 570
Woodcock 571
Woodcock Deluxe 571
Redhead 571
Redhead Deluxe 571
Mallard 571
Canvasback 571
Canvasback Deluxe 571
Cottontail 571
Durango 571
Amarillo 571
Sharptail 571
Canadian 572
Teal 572
Vandalia Trap 572
English Sporter 572
Custom Grade II 572
Custom Grade IV 572
Custom Grade IV with Upgrade 572
Custom Grade VI 572

HUNGARY

SA-85M 572

HUSQVARNA

Model 1907 572
Lahti 573
Hi-Power 573
Model 1100 Deluxe 573
Model 1000 Super Grade 573
Model 3100 Crown Grade 573
Model 4100 Lightweight 573
Model 456 573
Model 6000 573
Model 9000 Crown Grade 573
Model 8000 Imperial Grade 573

HY-HUNTER, INC.

Chicago Cub 573
Detective 573
Frontier Six Shooter (rimfire) 573
Frontier Six Shooter(centerfire) 573
Maxim 573
Military 573

Stingray 574
Panzer 574
Stuka 574
Automatic Derringer 574
Accurate Ace 574
Favorite 574
Gold Rush Derringer 574
Target Model 574

HYDE & SHATTUCK

Queen Derringer 574

HYPER

Single-Shot Rifle 574

I.G.I.

Domino SP602 575

IAB

S-300 575
C-300 Super Combo 575

IAI-AMERICAN LEGENDS

M-888 M1 Carbine 575
M-999 575
M-777 575
M-6000 575
M-5000 575

IGA

Single-Barrel Shotgun 575
Single-Barrel Shotgun
    Youth Model 575
Coach Gun 575
Standard Side-by-Side Uplander 576
Uplander Youth 576
Uplander Supreme 576
Standard Over/Under Condor I 576
Condor II 576
Condor Supreme Deluxe 576
Deluxe Over/Under ERA 2000 576

INDIAN ARMS CORP.

Indian Arms .380 576

INGRAM

MAC 11 576

INTERARMS

Mark X Viscount 577
Mark X Lightweight 577
Mini Mark X 577
Mark X American Field 577
Whitworth Express Rifle 577
Whitworth Mannlicher Carbine 577
Mannlicher Carbine 577
Continental Carbine 577
FEG R-9 577
FEG PPH 577
Mark II AP 577
Mark II APK 578
Virginian .22 Convertible 578
Virginian Stainless
    .22 Convertible 578

INTERARMS/HIGH STANDARD

AK-47 (7.62x39mm) 578
AKM Series (7.62x39mm) 578
AK-74 (5.45x39mm) 578

INTERDYNAMICS OF AMERICA

KG-9 578
KG-99 578
KG-99 Stainless 578
KG-99M 578

INTRATEC USA, INC.

TEC-9 578
TEC-9C 579
TEC-9M 579
TEC-22 "Scorpion" 579
TEC-38 579

IRVING, W.

Single-Shot Derringer 579
Pocket Revolver 1st Model 579
Pocket Revolver 2nd Model 579

ITHACA GUN CO.

Ithaca Baker Model 579
    Quality A 579
    Quality B 580
New Ithaca Gun 580
    Quality A 580
    Quality AA 580
    Quality B 580
    Quality X 580
The "New Double Bolted
    Hammer Gun" 580
    Quality A 580
    Quality AA 580
    Quality B 580
    Quality X 580
Crass Model 580
    Quality 1 580
    Quality 1-1/2 580
    Quality 1P 580
    Quality 2 580
    Quality 3 580
    Quality 4 580
Lewis Model 581
    Quality 1 581
    Quality 1 Special 581
    Quality 1-1/2 581
    Quality 2 581
    Quality 3 581
    Quality 4 581
    Quality 5 581
    Quality 6 581
    Quality 7 581
Minier Model 581
    Field Grade 581
    Quality 1 581
    Quality 1 Special 581
    Quality 1-1/2 581
    Quality 2 581
    Quality 3 581
    Quality 4 581
    Quality 5 581
    Quality 6 581
    Quality 7 581

Flues Model 581
  Field Grade 582
  Grade 1 582
  Grade 1 Special.........................582
  Grade 1-1/2............................582
  Grade 2 582
  Grade 3 582
  Grade 4 582
  Grade 5 582
  Grade 6 582
  Grade 7 582
  Sousa 582
The New Ithaca Double................582
  Field Grade 582
  Grade 1 582
  Grade 2 582
  Grade 3 582
  Grade 4 583
  Grade 5 583
  Grade 7 583
  Sousa Grade 583
Special Field Grade....................583
Grade 4E 583
Grade 7E 583
Sousa Grade 583
The Long Range Double................583
The Long Range Double Deluxe.......584
Flues Model Single-Barrel
  Trap Gun (1914 to 1922) 584
  Victory Grade 584
  Grade 4E 584
  Grade 5E 584
  Grade 6E 584
  Grade 7E 584
  Sousa Grade 584
Knick Model Single-Barrel Trap........584
  Victory Grade 584
  Grade 4E 584
  Grade 5E 584
  Grade 7E 585
  Sousa Grade 585
  $1,000 to $2,500 Grades 585
  $3,000 through the
    Dollar Grade 585
Century Grade Trap (SKB).............585
Century II (SKB).......................585
Model 66 Supersingle—
  1963-1978...........................585
Model 66 Youth Grade 585
Model 66 Buck Buster (RS Barrel) ..585
Model 66 Vent Rib 585
Model A..............................585
  Serial numbered from
    343336 to 398365............585
Model B..............................586
  Serial numbered from
    425000 to 464699.............586
Model 37/Standard
  Grade—1937-1983................586
Model 37S/Skeet Grade—
  1937-1953...........................586
Model 37T/Trap—1937-1953.......586
Model 37T/Target—1954-1961 586
Model 37R/Solid Rib—
  1940-1967...........................586
Model 37 Military Marked (WWII).....586

Model 37RD/Deluxe Solid Rib—
  1954-1962...........................586
Model 37 Deerslayer—
  1959-1987...........................586
Model 37 Deluxe
  Deerslayer—1959-1971 586
Model 37 Super Deluxe
  Deerslayer—1959-1987 586
Model 37 Supreme Grade—
  1967-1987...........................586
Model 37 Field Grade
  Standard—1983-1985 586
Model 37 Field Grade Vent Rib—
  1983-1986...........................586
Model 37 Basic
  Featherlight—1979-1983 587
Model 37V/Vent Rib—
  1961-1983...........................587
Model 37RV/Deluxe Vent Rib—
  1961-1966...........................587
Model 37D/Deluxe—1955-1977 ...587
Model 37DV/Deluxe Vent Rib—
  1961-1987...........................587
Model 37 Magnum 3"
  Chamber—1978-1987 587
Model 37 Field Grade
  Magnum—1984-1987..............587
Model 37 UltraLight—
  1978 to 1987 587
Model 37 English
  UltraLight—1982-1987.............587
Model 37 Camo 587
Model 37 Bicentennial.................587
Model 37 Ducks Unlimited
  Commemorative, Auction Grade...587
Model 37 Ducks Unlimited
  Commemorative, Trade Grade......587
Model 37 2500 Series Centennial ...587
Model 37 Presentation Series
  Centennial............................587
Hi-Grade Ithaca Model 37 Guns 587
  $1,000 Grade 588
  $2,000 Grade 588
  $3,000 Grade 588
Model 37
  Law Enforcement Weapons 588
  Military and Police (M&P)—
    1962-1986 588
  DS Police Special—
    1962-1986.........................588
Model 87 Basic—1989-1994 588
Model 87 Magnum 588
Model 87 Field Grade—
  1987-1990...........................588
Model 87 Camo—1987-1994.......588
Model 87 Turkey Gun—
  1987-1996...........................588
Model 87 Deluxe—1987-1996 588
Model 87 Ultralite—1987-1990 ...588
Model 87 English—1993-1996.....588
Model 87 Ultralite Deluxe.............588
Model 87 Supreme Grade—
  1987-1996...........................588
Model 87 Deerslayer
  Basic—1989-1996.................588
Model 87 Deerslayer—
  1989-1996...........................589
Model 87 Deluxe
  Deerslayer—1989-1996 589

Model 87 Deerslayer II—
  1988-1996...........................589
Model 87 Home Protection
  and Law Enforcement 589
  Military & Police—1987-1996...589
  DS Police Special—
    1987-1996.........................589
Model 37 Deerslayer II—
  Smooth Bore Deluxe 589
  Rifled Deluxe 589
Deerslayer III 589
Model 37 28 Gauge 589
Model 37 Deluxe Field 589
Model 37 Deluxe Field
  English Style..........................589
Model 37 Ultra Featherlight Grouse
  Special................................590
Model 37 Ultra Featherlight Youth....590
Model 37 Sporting Clays..............590
Model 37 Trap.......................590
Model 37 Women's Endowment
  Shotgun 590
Model 37 Waterfowler 590
Model 37 New Classic 590
Model 37 Turkeyslayer................590
Model 51A Standard 590
Model 51A Waterfowler 590
Model 51 Supreme Trap 591
Model 51 Supreme Skeet 591
Model 51 Ducks Unlimited
  Commemorative 591
Model 51 Presentation 591
  Standard Grade 591
  Standard Vent Rib Grade 591
  Deluxe Vent Rib Grade 591
  Supreme Grade 591
  Roadblocker—Military and
    Police Model........................591
  Presentation Grade 591
  National Wild Turkey Federation ..591
Model X5-C 591
Model X5T Lightning..................591
Model X-15 Lightning 591
Model 49 Saddlegun—
  1961-1979...........................591
  Deluxe Grade 591
  Presentation Grade 591
Model 49R—1968-1971.............591
Model 72 Saddlegun—
  1973-1979...........................591
LSA-55 or 65.........................591
  LSA-55 Standard....................591
  LSA-55 Deluxe 591
  LSA-55 Varmint Heavy Barrel 592
  LSA-55 Turkey Gun..................592
  LSA-65 Long Action 592
  LSA-65 Deluxe 592
Model 1911 592
X-Caliber 592

IVER JOHNSON ARMS, INC.
Frontier Four Derringer 592
Eagle Target Series 1911 .45.........592
Eagle Target Series 1911 .22 LR....592
Raven Series 1911 .45...............592
Raven Series 1911 .22 LR............592
1911A1..............................592

PAS Shotgun..........................592

**IVER JOHNSON ARMS &
CYCLE WORKS**
Trade Name Revolvers 592
Safety Automatic Double-Action 593
Model 1900 593
Supershot Sealed 8 593
Protector Sealed 8....................593
.22 Target Single-Action 593
Model 57A Target 594
Model 66 Trailsman 594
Model 67S Viking Snub..............594
Model X300 Pony...................595
Trailsman............................595
TP22/TP25 Pistol...................595
Model X.............................595
Model XA............................595
Model 2X............................595
Li'L Champ 595
Long Range Rifle.....................595
JJ 9mm Carbine 595
Delta-786 Carbine 595
Carbine .30 Caliber 595
U.S. Carbine .22 Caliber 595
Slide Action Targetmaster.............595
Wagonmaster Model EW .22 HBL
  Lever Action 595
Model IJ .22 HB Semi-Automatic
  (Trail Blazer) 595
Champion............................595
Matted Rib Grade 595
Trap Grade...........................596
Hercules Grade 596
Skeeter Model........................596
Super Trap 596
Silver Shadow 596

IXL
Pocket Revolver........................596
Navy Revolver 596

JACQUESMART, JULES
Le Monobloc 597

JACQUITH, ELIJAH
Revolving Under Hammer Rifle 597

JAGER WAFFENFABIK
Jager Semi-Automatic Pistol 597

JEFFERY, W. J. & CO. LTD.
Single-Shot............................597
Boxlock Double Rifle 597
Sidelock Double Rifle...................597

JENISON, J. & CO.
Under Hammer Pistol...................597

JENKS-HERKIMER
Jenks Carbine 597

JENKS CARBINE
Jenks "Mule Ear" Carbine 598
Jenks Navy Rifle........................598

JENNINGS F. A., INC.

J-22 598
Bryco Model 25 598
Bryco Model 38 598
Bryco Model 48 598

JERICHO

Jericho 599

JOHNSON, STAN, BYE & CO.

Defender, Eagle, Encore, Eureka,
  Favorite, Lion, Smoker,
  and Tycoon 599
Eclipse 599
American Bulldog 599

JOSLYN

Joslyn Breechloading Rifle 599
Model 1855 Carbine 599
.50-70 Alteration 599
Model 1855 Rifle 599

JOSLYN FIREARMS COMPANY

Model 1862 Carbine 599
Model 1864 Carbine 599
Army Model Revolver 600
  First Model 600
  Second Model 600

JURRAS, LEE

Howdah Pistol 600

JUSTICE, P. S.

Percussion Rifle 600

K.F.C.
(KAWAGUCHIYA FIREARMS CO.)

E-1 Trap or Skeet Over/Under 601
E-2 Trap or Skeet Over/Under 601
Field Grade Over/Under 601
Model 250 601

KAHR ARMS

K9 601
Lady K9 601
K9 Elite 601
MK9 Elite 601
P9 Compact Polymer 601
K9 Compact Polymer Covert 601
TP9 601
TP40 602
TP45 602
PM9 602
PM9 Micro 602
CM Series 602
CW380 602
K40 603
K40 Elite 603
K40 Covert 603
MK40 603
MK40 Elite 603
P40 603
P45 603
MK9 604
CW9 604
CW40 604

Wilson Combat Kahr Pistols 604
Model 1911PKZ 604
Model 1911 Standard 604
Model 1911C 604
Model 1911WGS Deluxe 604
P380 .380 ACP Pistol 604
CT45 605

KASSNAR IMPORTS, INC.

Standard Over/Under 605
Deluxe Over/Under 605
Standard Side-by-Side 605
Deluxe Side-by-Side 605

KBI, INC.

Kassnar PSP-25 605

KEBERST INTERNATIONAL

Model 1A 605

KEL-TEC CNC INDUSTRIES

Kel-Tec PMR-30 605
P-11 606
P-32 606
P-3AT 606
P-40 606
SUB-2000 Rifle 606
SU-16 606
PLR-16 606
RFB Rifle 606

KENDALL, NICANOR

Under Hammer Pistol 607

KENO

Derringer 607

KERR

Kerr Revolver 607

KESSLER ARMS
CORPORATION

Bolt-Action Shotgun 607
Levermatic Shotgun 607

KETTNER, EDWARD

Drilling 607

KIMBALL ARMS COMPANY

Semi-Automatic Pistol 607

KIMBER MFG., INC.

Model 82 Classic 608
Cascade 608
Custom Classic 608
Mini Classic 608
Deluxe Grade 608
Model 82A Government 608
Continental 608
Super Continental 608
Super America 608
Super Grade 608
Centennial 608
Brownell 608
Classic 608
Custom Classic 608

Deluxe Grade Sporter 608
Continental 608
Super Continental 608
Super America 608
Super Grade 608
Ultra Varmint 608
Super Varmint 608
Predator 609
  Hunter Grade 609
  Super Grade 609
Classic 609
Custom Classic 609
Deluxe Grade 609
Super America 609
Super Grade 609
African Grade 609
Classic 609
Super America 609
Custom Match 609
Custom Shop Super America
  (Basic) 609
Stainless Classic Limited Edition 609
SVT (Short Varmint/Target) 609
HS (Hunter Silhouette) 609
Single-Shot Varmint 610
Sporterized Model 98
  Swedish Mausers 610
Sporterized Model 96
  Swedish Mausers 610
Hunter 610
SVT (Short Varmint/Target)
  (Centerfire) 610
Pro Varmint 610
Classic Varmint 610
Classic 610
Custom Classic 610
Super America 610
SVT (Short Varmint/Target) 610
Classic Varmint 611
Pro Varmint 611
HS (Hunter Silhouette) 611
Youth 611
Hunter 611
Custom Match Limited Edition 611
Classic 611
Montana 611
Super America 611
Pro Varmint 611
Varmint 612
SVT 612
LongMaster VT 612
LongMaster Classic 612
LongMaster Pro 612
Light Police Tactical 612
Model 84L Classic Rifle 612
Model 84L Montana 612
Classic 612
Montana 612
Sonora 612
Caprivi 613
Talkeetna 613
Super America 613
Classic Select Grade 613
Tactical 613
Advanced Tactical 613
Advanced Tactical II 613

Patrol Rifle 613
Sporting 613
Field 613
Trap 613
Skeet 613
Grade I 614
Grade II 614
Grade I 614
Grade II 614
Custom 614
Custom II 614
Custom Heritage Edition 614
Custom Stainless II 614
Stainless Limited Edition 615
Custom Target 615
Custom TLE II (Tactical Law
  Enforcement) 615
Custom TLE/RL II 615
Stainless II 615
Stainless II (polished) 615
Stainless Ultra TLE II 615
Stainless Target II 615
Stainless Target II 9mm/10mm 615
Stainless Target II (polished) 616
Stainless Target Limited Edition 616
Custom Royal 616
Custom Royal II 616
Custom TLE/RL II Special Edition 616
Warrior 616
Desert Warrior 616
Anniversary Custom 616
Anniversary Gold Match 617
Anniversary Match Pair Custom 617
Gold Match 617
Gold Match II 617
Stainless Gold Match 617
Gold Team Match II 617
Team Match II .38 Super 617
Polymer 617
Polymer Stainless 618
Polymer Target 618
Polymer Stainless Target 618
Polymer Pro Carry Stainless 618
Polymer Stainless Gold Match 618
Pro Carry Ten II 618
Ultra Ten CDP II 619
Gold Match Ten II 619
BP Ten II 619
Pro BP Ten II 619
Compact 619
Compact Aluminum 619
Compact Stainless 619
Compact Stainless II 620
Compact Stainless Aluminum 620
Pro Carry II 620
Pro Carry II Night Sights 620
Pro Carry Stainless 620
Pro Carry Stainless Night Sights 620
Pro TLE/RL II 620
Stainless Pro TLE/RL II 620
Super Carry Pro 620
Pro TLE II TFS 620
Sapphire Pro II 620
Super Carry Custom HD 621
Super Carry Ultra Plus 621

Solo Carry STS.............................621
Ultra Carry.................................621
Ultra Carry II..............................621
Ultra Carry Stainless 621
Ultra Carry Stainless II 622
Micro Carry................................622
Micro Raptor..............................622
Warrior SOC...............................622
Master Carry Series.......................622
Centennial Edition 1911 622
Royal Carry................................622
Elite Carry................................622
Gold Guardian.............................623
Combat Carry..............................623
Gold Combat...............................623
Gold Combat II............................623
Gold Combat Stainless.....................623
Gold Combat Stainless II 623
Super Match...............................623
Super Match II............................624
LTP II....................................624
Raptor II.................................624
Pro Raptor II.............................624
Grand Raptor II...........................624
Ultra Raptor II...........................624
Ultra RCP II..............................624
Gold Combat RL II 625
Target Match..............................625
Super America 625
Ultra CDP.................................625
Ultra CDP II..............................625
Compact CDP 625
Compact CDP II............................625
Pro CDP...................................625
Pro CDP II................................626
Custom CDP 626
Custom CDP II.............................626
Eclipse Custom II.........................626
Eclipse Target II.........................626
Eclipse Ultra II..........................626
Eclipse Pro II............................626
Eclipse Pro Target II 626
Tactical Custom II........................627
Tactical Pro II...........................627
Tactical Ultra II.........................627
Custom Covert II..........................627
Pro Covert II.............................627
Ultra Covert II...........................627
Pro Aegis II 627
Custom Aegis II...........................628
Ultra Aegis II............................628
Ultra Onyx II Special Edition.............628
Model K6s.................................628
Rimfire Custom 628
Rimfire Target 628
Rimfire Super.............................629
.22 LR Conversion Kit.....................629

KING PIN

Derringer.................................629

KIRRIKALE, ENDUSTRISI

Kirrikale Pistol..........................629

KLEINGUENTHER/KDF, INC.

Condor 629
Brescia 629
K-14 Insta Fire Rifle.....................629
K-15 629
K-15 Pro-Hunter...........................629
K-15 Swat Rifle 629
K-15 Dangerous Game 630
K-16 630
Titan Menor 630
Titan II Standard 630
Titan II Magnum 630
Titan .411 KDF Mag. 630
K-22 630
  Deluxe 630
  Deluxe Custom 630
  Deluxe Special Select...................630
Model 2005 630
Model 2107 630
Model 2112 630

KLIPZIG & COMPANY

Pocket Pistol 630

KNICKERBOCKER

Knickerbocker Pistol NFA..................630
Double-Barrel Shotgun 630

KNIGHT RIFLES

Disc Magnum...............................630
Bighorn Magnum 631
T-Bolt Magnum 631
LK-93 Wolverine...........................631
LK-93 Wolverine Youth.....................631
American Knight...........................631
MK-85 Hunter 631
MK-85 Predator 631
MK-85 Stalker 631
MK-85 Knight Hawk 631
MK-86 Shotgun 631
HK-94 Hawkeye Pistol 631
Rolling Block Rifle 631
Long Range Hunter 631

KNIGHT'S ARMAMENT COMPANY

SR-15 Match 631
SR-15 M-5 Rifle 632
SR-15 E3 URX Carbine 632
SR-15 M-4 Carbine 632
SR-25 Match 632
SR-25 Lightweight Match 632
SR-25 Stoner Carbine 632
SR-25 APC 632
SR-25 Competition Match...................632
SR-25 Mk11 Mod 0 Match Rifle......632
SR-50 Rifle 632

KOHOUT & SPOLECNOST

Mars 632
Niva, PZK.................................633

KOLB, HENRY M.

Baby Hammerless 633
New Baby Hammerless.......................633

KOLIBRI/FREDERICH PFANNL

2.7mm 633
3mm 633

KOMMER, THEODOR WAFFENFABRIK

Model 1 633
Model 2 633
Model 3 634
Model 4 634

KONGSBERG

Thumbhole Sporter.........................634
Classic Rifle 634

KORRIPHILA

HSP 634
  HSP—Single-Action Only..........634
Odin's Eye................................634

KORTH

Semi-Automatic Pistol 634
Combat Revolver 635
Match Revolver 635

KRAG-JORGENSEN

Model of 1892 635
  1st Type,
    Serial number 1 — 1500......635
  2nd Type, Serial number
    1501 — 24562 635
Model 1892, altered to 1896 635
Model 1896 635
Model 1898 635
Model 1898 Practice Rifle
  (.22 rimfire)...........................635
Model 1899 Carbine.......................635

KRAUSER, ALFRED

Helfricht or Helkra 635

KRICO

Sporting Rifle 635
Sporting Carbine 635
Varmint Special Rifle 635
Model 300 635
Model 302 and 304 635
Model 311 Smallbore 635
Model 320 636
Model 340 636
Model 340 Mini-Sniper 636
Model 340 Kricotronic 636
Model 360S Biathlon Rifle.................636
Model 360S2 Biathlon Rifle........636
Model 400 Match 636
Model 400 Sporter 636
Model 420 636
Model 440 636
Model 500 Kricotronic Match Rifle...636
Model 600 Sporter 636
Model 600 Sniper Rifle 636
Model 600 Match Rifle 636
Model 620 637
Model 640 Varmint Rifle 637
Model 640 Sniper Rifle 637
Model 640 Deluxe Sniper Rifle 637
Model 700 Sporter 637

Model 720.................................637
Model 720 Limited Edition 637

KRIDER, J. H.

Pocket Pistol 637
Militia Rifle.............................637

KRIEGHOFF, HEINRICH, GUN CO.

Plus Model................................637
Trumpf Model 637
Trumpf Dural 637
Neptun 637
Neptun Dural..............................638
Neptun Primus 638
Neptun Primus Dural 638
Optima 638
Teck Over/Under 638
Ulm Model 638
Ulm Primus 638
Ultra 638
Classic 638
Classic Big Five 638
Model 32 Standard.........................638
  San Remo Grade 638
  Monte Carlo Grade 638
  Crown Grade 638
  Super Crown Grade 639
  Single Barrel Trap Gun 639
Teck Over/Under 639
Teck Dural 639
Ulm 639
Ulm Dural 639
Ulm Primus 639
Ulm Primus Dural 639
Ultra 639
KS-5 Single Barrel Trap...................639
KS-5 Special 639
K-80 Trap 639
  Over/Under Trap 639
  Unsingle Trap 639
  Top Single Trap 639
  Trap Combos 639
K-20 Sporting and Field..................639
K-80 Sporting Clays 639
K-80 Skeet 639
  Standard Weight Skeet...................640
  Lightweight Skeet 640
  International Skeet......................640
  4 Barrel Set 640
Essencia Boxlock..........................640
Essencia Sidelock.........................640

KRNKA, KAREL

Model 1892................................640

KSN INDUSTRIES

Golan 640
Kareen MK II 641
Kareen MK II—Compact 641
GAL.......................................641

KUFAHL, G. L.

Kufahl Needle-Fire Revolver 641

KYNOCH GUN FACTORY

Early Double Trigger Revolver 641

LINS, A. F.
Pocket Pistol 658
Rifled Musket 658

LITTLE SHARPS RIFLE MFG. CO.
Little Sharps Rifle 658

LJUTIC INDUSTRIES
Bi-Matic Semi-Automatic 658
Dynatrap Single-Barrel 658
Model X-73 Single-Barrel 658
Mono Gun Single-Barrel 658
LTX Model 658
Space Gun 658
Bi-Gun Over/Under 659
Bi-Gun Combo 659
LM-6 Super Deluxe 659

LLAMA
Model I-A 659
Model II 659
Model III 659
Model III-A 659
Model XII-B 660
Model Max-I 661
  Previous Production
    Prior to 2006 661
  New Production 661
Model Mini-Max 661
Mini-Max Sub Compact 661
Model Max-I with Compensator 661
Micro-Max 661
Model 82 661
Model 87 Competition 661
Compact Frame Semi-Automatic 661
Small Frame Semi-Automatic 662
Large Frame Semi-Automatic 662
Mugica 662
Tauler 662
Comanche I 663
Comanche II 663
Comanche III 663
Super Comanche 663

LOEWE, LUDWIG & CO.
Loewe Smith & Wesson Russian
  Revolver 663

LOHNER, C.
Pocket Pistol 663

LOMBARD, H. C. & CO.
Pocket Pistol 663

LONE STAR RIFLE COMPANY
Sporting Rifle 664
Target Rifle 664

LORCIN ENGINEERING CO., INC.
Model L-25 664
Model LT-25 664
Model L-22 664
Model L-380 664
Model L-380 10th Anniversary 664
Model L-32 664
Model LH-380 664

Model L-9mm 664
Derringer 664

LUGERS
1899/1900 Swiss Test Model 665
1900 Swiss Contract 665
1900 Commercial 665
1900 American Eagle 665
1900 Test Eagle 665
1900 Bulgarian Contract 665
1900 Carbine 666
1902 Prototype 666
1902 Commercial—"Fat Barrel" 666
1902 American Eagle 666
1902 American Eagle
  Cartridge Counter 666
1902 Carbine 666
1902 Presentation Carbine 666
1902/06 Carbine (Transitional) 666
1903 Commercial 666
1904 Navy 666
1906 Navy Commercial 666
1906 Commercial 667
1906 Commercial
  (Marked Safety) 667
1906 American Eagle 667
1906 American Eagle
  (Marked Safety) 667
1906 American Eagle 4.75" Barrel ..667
1906 U.S. Army Test Luger
  .45 Caliber 667
1906 Swiss Commercial 667
1906 Swiss Military 667
1906 Swiss Police Cross in Shield ..667
1906 Dutch Contract 668
1906 Royal Portuguese Navy 668
1906 Royal Portuguese Army (M2) ..668
1906 Republic of Portugal Navy 668
1906 Brazilian Contract 668
1906 Bulgarian Contract 668
1906 Russian Contract 668
1906 Navy 1st Issue 668
1906 Navy 2nd Issue 669
1908 Commercial 669
1908 Bulgarian 669
1908 Navy Commercial 669
1908 Navy 669
1914 Navy 669
1908 Military 1st Issue 669
1908 Military Dated Chamber
  (1910-1913) 669
1913 Commercial 669
1914 Military 670
1914 Artillery 670
DWM Double Dated 670
1920 Police Rework 670
1920 Commercial 670
1920 Commercial Navy 670
1920 Commercial Artillery 670
1920 Long Barrel Commercial 670
1920 Carbine 670
1920 Navy Carbine 670
1920 Swiss Commercial 670
1923 Stoeger Commercial 671
Abercrombie & Fitch
  Commercial 100 671

1923 Commercial 671
1923 Commercial Safe & Loaded 671
1923 Dutch
  Commercial & Military 671
Royal Dutch Air Force 671
1906 Vickers Dutch 671
1908 Erfurt 672
1914 Erfurt Military 672
1914 Erfurt Artillery 672
Double Date Erfurt 672
Simson & Co. Rework 672
Simson Grip Safety Rework 672
Simson Dated Military 672
Simson S Code 672
Deaths Head Rework 672
Kadetten Institute Rework 672
Mauser Unmarked Rework 672
Mauser Oberndorf 672
1934/06 Swiss
  Commercial Mauser 672
1935/06 Portuguese "GNR" 673
1934 Mauser Commercial 673
S/42 K Date 673
S/42 G Date 673
Dated Chamber S/42 673
S/42 Commercial Contract 673
Code 42 Dated Chamber 673
41/42 Code 673
byf Code 673
Persian Contract 4 673
Persian Contract Artillery 673
1934/06 Dated Commercial 673
1934 Mauser Dutch Contract 673
1934 Mauser Swedish Contract 674
1934 Mauser
  Swedish Commercial 674
1934 Mauser German Contract 674
Austrian Bundes Heer
  (Federal Army) 674
Mauser 2 Digit Date 674
Ku Luger (Prefix or suffix) 674
1923 DWM/Krieghoff Commercial ..674
DWM/Krieghoff Commercial 674
Krieghoff Commercial
  Inscribed Side Frame 674
S Code Krieghoff 674
Grip Safety Krieghoff 674
36 Date Krieghoff 674
4 Digit Dated Krieghoff 674
2nd Series Krieghoff Commercial 675
Post-War Krieghoff 675
Krieghoff Post-War Commercial 675
East German Luger Rework,
  aka VOPO 675
Detachable Carbine Stocks 675
P.08 Interarms 675
Cartridge Counter 675
Commemorative Bulgarian 676

LUNA
Model 200 Free Pistol 676
Model 300 Free Pistol 676
Target Rifle 676

LWRC INTERNATIONAL
M6-A2 676

PSD-Pistol 676
SIX8 677
REPR 677

LYMAN
Lyman In-Line 677
Deerstalker Rifle 677
Deerstalker Carbine 677
Great Plains Rifle 677
Trade Rifle 677
Plains Pistol 677
Model 1878 Sharps 677
Little Sharps 677

M. B. ASSOCIATES-GYROJET
Mark I Model A Carbine 678
Mark I Model B Carbine 678

MAGNUM RESEARCH, INC.
BFR Little Max (Short Cylinder) 679
IMI SP-21 679

MAKAROV PISTOL
Makarov 679
Bulgarian Makarov 679
East German Makarov 679

MALIN, F. E.
Boxlock Basic Model 680
Sidelock Basic Model 680

MALTBY, HENLEY AND CO.
Spencer Safety Hammerless
  Revolver 680

MANHATTAN FIREARMS COMPANY
Bar Hammer Pistol 680
Shotgun Hammer Pistol 680
Pepperbox 680
  Three-shot with 3" Barrel 680
  Five-shot with 3", 4", 5" Barrel 680
  Six-shot with 3" or 4" Barrel 680
  Six-shot with 5" Barrel 680
Pocket Revolver 680
  First Model—Five-Shot 680
  Second Model—Six-Shot 680
London Pistol Company 680
.36 Caliber Percussion Revolver 681
  Model I 681
  Model II 681
  Model III 681
  Model IV 681
  Model V 681
.22 Caliber Pocket Revolver 681
Manhattan-American Standard
  Hero 681
  Manhattan Manufactured 681
  American Standard
    Manufactured 681

MANN, FRITZ
6.35mm Pocket Pistol 681
7.65mm Pocket Pistol 681

MANNLICHER SCHOENAUER
Model 1903 Carbine 681
Model 1905 Carbine 681

Model 1908 Carbine......................681
Model 1910 Carbine.....................681
Model 1924 Carbine.....................682
High Velocity Rifle........................682
Model 1950.................................682
Model 1950 Carbine.....................682
Model 1950 6.5 Carbine...............682
Model 1952.................................682
Model 1952 Carbine.....................682
Model 1952 6.5mm Carbine.........682
Model 1956 Rifle.........................682
Model 1956 Carbine.....................682
Model 1961 MCA Rifle..................682
Model 1961 MCA Carbine 682
Alpine Model...............................682
Model M72 LM Rifle 682

MANUFRANCE

Auto Stand..................................682
Buffalo Stand 682
Le Agent 683
Le Colonial.................................683
LeFrancais 683

MANURHIN

Model PP.....................................683
Model PPK/S...............................683
Model PP Sports 683
Model 73 Defense Revolver 683
Model 73 Gendarmerie 683
Model 73 Sport 683
Model 73 Convertible 684
Model 73 Silhouette 684

MARATHON PRODUCTS, INC.

.22 First Shot..............................684
.22 Super Shot............................684
.22 Hot Shot Pistol 684
Centerfire Rifle............................684

MARBLE'S ARMS & MFG. CO.

Marble's Game Getter Gun—
    NFA, curio or relic 684
Model 1908.................................684
Model 1921.................................685
Marble's Game Getter Pistol
    and other special-order or
    experimental Game Getters—
    NFA, curio or relic 685

MARGOLIN

Model MT Sports.........................685
Model MTS-1...............................686
Model MTS-2...............................686

MARIETTE BREVETTE

4" Barrel Pepperbox 686
6" Barrel Pepperbox 686

MARLIN FIREARMS CO.

First Model..................................686
Military Rifle................................686
Civil War Military Carbine 686
Sporting Rifle 687
Sporting Carbine 687
Sporting Rifle 687
Ballard Hunters Rifle....................687

Ballard No. 1-1/2 Hunters Rifle 687
Ballard No. 1-3/4 "Far West"
    Hunters Rifle...........................687
Ballard No. 2 Sporting Rifle...........687
Ballard No. 3 Gallery Rifle.............688
Ballard No. 3F Gallery Rifle............688
Ballard No. 4 Perfection Rifle..........688
Ballard No. 3-1/2 Target Rifle.........688
Ballard No. 4-1/2 Mid Range Rifle ...688
Ballard No. 4-1/2 A-1
    Mid Range Target Rifle 688
Ballard No. 5 Pacific Rifle.............688
Ballard No. 5-1/2 Montana Rifle......688
Ballard No. 6 Schuetzen
    Off Hand Rifle..........................688
Ballard No. 6 Schuetzen Rifle........688
Ballard No. 6-1/2 Rigby
    Off Hand Mid Range Rifle 689
Ballard No. 7 "Creedmore A-1"
    Long Range Rifle 689
Ballard No. 7A-1 Long Range Rifle ..689
Ballard No. 7A-1 Extra Grade
    Long Range Rifle 689
Ballard No. 8 Union Hill Rifle.........689
Ballard No. 9 Union Hill Rifle.........689
Victor Model Derringer...................690
Nevermiss Model Derringer............690
    .22 Caliber Model.....................690
    .32 Caliber Model.....................690
    .41 Caliber Model.....................691
Stonewall Model Derringer.............691
O.K. Pocket Revolver 691
Marlin XXX Standard
    1872 Pocket Revolver 691
    Octagon Barrel—
        Early Variation.....................691
    Round Barrel—
        Non-Fluted Cylinder 691
    Round Barrel—
        Short Fluted Cylinder............692
    Round Barrel—
        Long Fluted Cylinder 692
    Early Octagon Barrel Model 692
    Round Barrel—Fluted Cylinder ...692
    Round Barrel—
        Non-Fluted Cylinder 692
Marlin No. 32 Standard
    1875 Pocket Revolver 692
Marlin 38 Standard 1878 Pocket
    Revolver..................................692
Marlin 1887 Double-Action
    Revolver..................................693
Model 1881 Lever-Action Rifle.......693
    Lightweight Model 693
Model 1888 Lever-Action Rifle.......693
Model 1889 Lever-Action Rifle.......693
    Production Model 693
    Short Carbine 693
    Carbine 20" Barrel
        and Saddle Ring on Left Side
        of Receiver...........................693
    Musket 694
    1st Variation 694
    2nd Variation 694
    .22 Rimfire..............................694
    .32 Rimfire and Centerfire..........694
    Antique Production (Pre-1898) ...694
    Modern Production 1899-1935..694

Antique Production (Pre-1898) ...694
Modern Production
    (1899-1935) 695
Antique Production (Pre-1898) ...695
Modern Production
    (1899-1917) 695
    Standard Production Rifle...........695
    Deluxe Rifle.............................695
Model 20.....................................695
Model 25.....................................695
Model 27.....................................695
Model 27S...................................695
Model 29.....................................696
Model 32.....................................696
Model 37.....................................696
Model 38.....................................696
Model 40.....................................696
Model 47.....................................696
Model 1936, Rifle or Carbine.........696
    1st Variation (early 1936) 696
    2nd Variation (late 1936-1947) ..696
Model 36 Rifle or Carbine
    (1937-1948) 696
    1st & 2nd Variations 697
    3rd Variation—Blued Receiver....697
Model 36 Sporting Carbine 697
Model 36A-DL Rifle 697
Model 336 Carbine
    (R.C. Regular Carbine)...............697
Model 336C.................................697
Model 336A.................................697
Model 336ADL.............................697
Model 336SD
    (Sporting Deluxe Carbine)...........697
Model 336 MicroGroove Zipper 697
Model 336T (Texan)......................697
Model 336DT................................697
Model 336 "Marauder"...................697
Model 336 .44 Magnum.................697
Model 336 "Centennial".................697
1970 100th Year Commemorative
    Matched Pair............................698
Model 336 "Zane Grey Century"......698
Model 336 Octagon........................698
Model 336ER (Extra Range) 698
Model 336C.................................698
Model 336SS................................698
Model 336LTS..............................698
Model 336 Cowboy 698
Model 336M.................................698
Model 336CC...............................698
Model 336W.................................698
Model 336Y "Spike Horn" 699
Model 336XLR..............................699
Model 336BL................................699
Model 30AS.................................699
Model 375...................................699
Model 444...................................699
Model 444S.................................699
Model 444SS................................699
Model 444P Outfitter.....................699
Model 444XLR..............................699
Model 1894.................................700
Model 1894 Octagon Barrel...........700
Model 1894 Sporter......................700
Model 1894P...............................700

Model 1894CS.............................700
Model 1894M...............................700
Model 1894S................................700
Model 1894CL (Classic).................700
Model 1894CL (Classic) New 700
Model 1894 Century Limited...........700
Model 1894 Century
    Limited Employee Edition 700
Model 1894 Cowboy 700
Model 1894 Cowboy 32 701
Model 1894 Cowboy II...................701
Model 1894CP..............................701
Model 1894SS..............................701
Model 1894PG..............................701
Model 1894FG..............................701
Model 1894 Cowboy 701
Marlin 1894 Deluxe.......................701
Marlin 1894CSS............................701
Marlin 1894 CSBL.........................701
Model 1895 and 1895SS...............702
Model 1895M...............................702
Model 1895 Century Limited...........702
Model 1895 Century
    Limited Employee Edition 702
Model 1895G Guide Gun.................702
Model 1895GS Guide Gun 702
Model 1895 Cowboy 702
Model 1895XLR.............................702
Model 1895MXLR..........................702
Model 1895 SBLR..........................702
Model 1895GBL.............................702
Model 308MXLR............................702
Model 308MX...............................703
Model 338MXLR............................703
Model 338MX...............................703
Model 1897 Century Limited...........703
Model 1897 Century
    Limited Employee Edition 703
Model 1897 Cowboy 703
Model 1897 Annie Oakley...............703
Glenfield Lever-Action Rifles...........703
Model 30AW.................................703
Model 39.....................................704
    Standard Rifle...........................704
    Deluxe Rifle.............................704
Model 39A....................................704
    Pre-war Variations
        (1939-1941) 704
    Post-war Variations
        (1945-1953) 704
    Post-war Variations
        (1954-1956) 704
    Golden 39A's" (1954-1963) 704
Model 39A Mountie........................704
    1st Variation 704
    Standard.................................704
Model 39A 1960 Presentation
    Model......................................704
Model 39M Mountie 1960
    Presentation Model.....................704
Model 39ADL................................704
Model Golden 39A.........................704
Model 39 Carbine..........................705
Model 39 Century Limited...............705
Model 39A Article II.......................705
Model 39M Article II 705
Model 39A Octagon 705

Model 39M Octagon......................705
Model 39AWL 705
Model 56 Levermatic....................705
Model 56 "Clipper King"
 Levermatic 705
Model 57 Levermatic....................706
Model 57M Levermatic..................706
Model 62 Levermatic....................706
Model 70P "Papoose"...................706
Model 70PSS..............................706
Model 70HC................................706
Model 9 Camp Carbine 706
Model 9N...................................706
Model 45 Camp Carbine 706
Model 922M................................707
Model 995...................................707
Model 995SS..............................707
Model 990L.................................707
Model 7000................................707
Model 60SS................................707
Model 60SN................................708
Model 60DLX..............................708
Model 2000................................708
Model 2000A..............................708
Model 2000L..............................708
Model 880..................................708
Model 880SS..............................709
Model 880SQ..............................709
Model 881..................................709
Model 882SS..............................709
Model 25N..................................709
Model 25NC 709
Model 25MN...............................709
Model 25MNC.............................709
Model 17V..................................709
Model 17VS................................709
Model 15YN "Little Buckaroo" 709
Model 15N..................................710
Model 15YS (Youth) 710
Model 81TS................................710
Model 882..................................710
Model 882L.................................710
Model 882SS..............................710
Model 882SSV............................710
Model 83TS................................710
Model 883..................................710
Model 883N................................710
Model 883SS..............................711
Model 717M2..............................711
Model 983T.................................711
Model 983S.................................711
Model 983...................................711
Model 917...................................711
Model 917V.................................711
Model 917VR..............................711
Model 917VS..............................711
Model 917VS-CF.........................711
Model 917VSF.............................711
Model 917VT...............................711
Model 917VST.............................711
Model 917M2..............................712
Model 917M2S............................712
Model 982S.................................712
Model 982L.................................712
Model 982...................................712

Model 982VS..............................712
Model 982VS-CF.........................712
Model 925M................................712
Model 925RM..............................712
Model 925R.................................713
Model XL7C................................713
Model XS7 Short-Action................714
Model XS7Y Youth Rifle................714
Model XS7C Camo 714
Model XS7S................................714
Model XL7..................................714
Model 1898................................714
 Grade A 714
 Grade A Brush or Riot 714
 Grade B 714
 Grade C 714
 Grade D 714
Model 16....................................714
 Grade A 714
 Grade B 714
 Grade C 714
 Grade D 714
Model 17....................................714
Model 19....................................714
 Grade A 715
 Grade B 715
 Grade C 715
 Grade D 715
Model 21 "Trap"..........................715
 Grade A 715
 Grade B 715
 Grade C 715
 Grade D 715
Model 24....................................715
 Grade A 715
 Grade B 715
 Grade C 715
 Grade D 715
Marlin "Trap Gun".......................715
Model 26....................................715
Model 26 Brush Gun 715
Model 26 Riot Gun 715
Model 28 Hammerless 715
 Grade A 715
 Grade B 715
 Grade C 715
 Grade D 715
Model 28TS Trap Gun 716
Model 28T Trap Gun 716
Model 30....................................716
 Grade A 716
 Grade B 716
 Grade C 716
 Grade D 716
Model 30 Field Grade 716
Model 31....................................716
 Grade A 716
 Grade B 716
 Grade C 716
 Grade D 716
Model 42/42A.............................716
Model 43A..................................716
Model 43T..................................716
Model 53....................................717
Model 63....................................717
Model 63T..................................717

Model 63TS 717
Premier Mark I............................717
Premier Mark II...........................717
Premier Mark IV..........................717
Model 120..................................717
Model 778 (Glenfield) 717
Model 60 Single-Barrel Shotgun......717
Model 90 Over/Under Shotgun 717
Model .410 Lever-Action Shotgun
 (Original)................................718
Model .410 Deluxe (Original)..........718
Model .410 (New)........................718
Model 410XLR 410 XLR................718
Model 50DL................................718
Model 55....................................718
Model 55 Swamp Gun..................718
Model 55 Goose Gun...................718
Model 55S Slug Gun 718
Model 5510 Goose Gun 719
Model 55GDL..............................719
Model 512 Slugmaster 719
Model 512DL Slugmaster 719
Model 512P.................................719
Model 25MG...............................719
Model LC410-DB.........................719
Model LC28-DB...........................719
Model LC12-DB...........................719
Model LC20-DB...........................719
Model LC12-OU...........................720
Model LC20-OU...........................720
Model MLS-50/54........................720

MAROCCHI ARMI

Model 2000................................720
Field Master I..............................720
Field Master II.............................720
Sporting Clays Model....................720
 Grade I....................................720
 Grade II...................................720
 Grade III..................................720
Sporting Light—Grade I.................720
Sporting Clays Left-Hand Model—
 Grade I....................................720
Lady Sport Model 720
 Grade I....................................720
 Spectrum Grade—
  Colored Frame 720
Lady Sport Left-Handed................720
 Grade I....................................720
 Spectrum Grade 720
Trap Model.................................720
 Grade I....................................720
 Grade II...................................720
 Grade III..................................720
Skeet Model...............................721
 Grade I....................................721
 Grade II...................................721
 Grade III..................................721

MARSTON, S.W.

Double-Action Pepperbox 721

MARSTON, W. W. & CO.

Double-Action Single-Shot Pistol 721
Pocket Revolver...........................721
Single-Action Pistol 721

Breech-Loading Pistol...................721
 Brass Frame..............................721
 Iron Frame 721
Double-Action Pepperbox 721
3-Barrel Derringer 722
 Knife Blade Model......................722
 Without Knife 722
3-Barrel Derringer .32 Caliber.........722

MASQUELIER, S. A.

Carpathe....................................722
Express 722
Ardennes 722
Boxlock Side-by-Side Shotgun.......722
Sidelock Side-by-Side Shotgun 722

MASSACHUSETTS ARMS CO.

Wesson & Leavitt Dragoon.............722
 Early Model with 6" Barrel 722
 Fully Marked 7" Barrel
  Standard Model 722
Wesson & Leavitt Belt Revolver 722
Maynard Primed Belt Revolver.........722
Maynard Primed Pocket Revolver 723
Single-Shot Pocket Pistol 723
1st Model 723
 U.S. Martially Marked..................723
 Commercial Model......................723
2nd Model 723
Maynard Patent Sporting Rifle 723

MATEBA ARMS

AutoRevolver...............................724
AutoRevolver Carbine 724

MAUNZ MFG., INC.

Model 77 Service Match Rifle 724
Model 87 Maunz Match Rifle 724
Model 57 M1A.............................724
Model 67 Match Grade
 for Practice 724

MAUSER WERKE

Early Model 98 Sporting Rifles 724
 Type A—Short Action 724
 Type A—Medium Action 724
 Type A—Long Action 724
 Type B.....................................724
 Type K.....................................724
 Type M.....................................724
 Type S.....................................724
Six-Shot Step-Barrel
 Cone Hammer 725
Twenty-Shot Step-Barrel
 Cone Hammer 725
System Mauser 10-Shot
 Cone Hammer 725
Six-Shot Standard Cone Hammer 725
Twenty-Shot Cone Hammer............725
Early Transitional
 Large Ring Hammer....................726
Model 1899 Flat Side—
 Italian Contract 726
Late Flat Side..............................726
Early Small Ring Hammer Model,
 Transitional...............................727

Early Small Ring
   Hammer Bolo Model 727
Six-Shot Small Ring
   Hammer Model 727
Standard Pre-war Commercial 727
9mm Export Model............................727
Mauser Banner Model 727
Persian Contract 727
Standard Wartime Commercial 727
9mm Parabellum Military Contract ..727
1920 Rework.....................................728
Luger Barreled 1920 Rework 728
Early Post-war Bolo Model 728
Late Post-war Bolo Model 728
French Gendarme Model 728
Early Model 1930..............................729
Late Model 1930................................729
Model 1930 Removable Magazine...729
Cone Hammer Flat Side Carbine......729
Large Ring Hammer Transitional
   Carbine.....................................729
Large Ring Hammer Flatside
   Carbine.....................................729
Small Ring Hammer Carbine 729
Chinese Marked,
   Handmade Copies 729
Taku-Naval Dockyard Model............729
   Sidelatch Model.........................729
   Later Production
     (Model 1910/14) 729
   Model 1914 "Humpback".............730
   Model 1914 (later)......................730
Model WTP I 730
Model 1934 730
   6.35mm 731
   7.65mm Commercial...................731
   7.65mm Eagle L proofed 731
   7.56mm Large Eagle over M
     (Navy)....................................731
Low Grip Screw Model.....................731
Early Commercial Model 731
Transition Model...............................731
Early Nazi Army Model 731
Late Nazi Army Model.......................731
Early Nazi Navy Model 732
Wartime Nazi Navy Model 732
Early Nazi Police Model...................732
Wartime Nazi Police Model..............732
Wartime Commercial Model 732
French Manufactured Model 732
Model HSc Post-war Production 732
   Mauser Production (.32)............732
   Gamba Production 732
Model 2000.......................................732
Model 3000.......................................732
Model 3000 Magnum.........................732
Model 4000.......................................732
Model 225..732
Model ES340 732
Model DSM34....................................732
Model MS420B..................................733
Model ES350.....................................733
Model M410 733
Model M420 733
Model EN310 733
Model EL320 733

Model KKW 733
Model MS350B..................................733
Model ES340B...................................733
Model MM410BN 733
Model MS420B..................................733
Model 107..733
Model 201 Standard..........................733
Model 66 Standard............................733
Model 66 Magnum 734
Model 66 Safari 734
Model 66 Stuzen 734
IDF Mauser Rifle Model 66SP.........734
Model 77 734
Model 77 Ultra 734
Model 77 Mannlicher 734
Model 77 Big Game 734
Model 86-SR 734
Model 93 SR 734
Model 96 734
Model 98 Standard............................734
Model 99 Standard............................734
Model 99 Magnum 735
Model M2
   (Imported by SIG ARMS) 735

MAVERICK ARMS, INC.
Model 88..735

MAYNARD/PERRY
Brass Framed Carbine 735

MCMILLAN & CO. INC., G.
Competition Model 736
Model 86 Sniper's Rifle.....................736
Model 86 System 736
Model 87
   Long Range Sniper's Rifle ...736
Model 87 System 736
Signature Model................................736
Signature Stainless...........................736
Signature Alaskan 736
Signature Titanium Mountain...........736
Signature Varminter 736
Talon Safari.......................................736
Talon Sporter 736
Model 300 Phoenix
   Long Range Rifle 737
Model 40 Sniper 737
Model 92 Bullpup 737
Model 93 SN 737
McMillan LRHR 737

MCMILLAN FIREARMS
Legacy 737
Heritage..737
TAC-Series...737

MENDENHALL, JONES & GARDNER
Muzzle Loading Rifle.........................737

MERIDEN FIREARMS CO.
Single-Barrel Shotguns and Rifles ...738

MERKEL, GEBRUDER
Model 8..738
Model 117/117E.................................738

Model 118/118E.................................738
Model 124/125...................................739
   Model 124 739
   Model 125 739
Model 130 739
Model 170 739
Model 127 739
Model 47E 739
Model 147 739
Model 147E 739
Model 147EL 739
Model 122 739
Model 47SL 740
Model 147SL 740
Model 147SSL 740
Models 247S/347S 740
   Model 247S 740
   Model 347S 740
Model 447SL 740
Model 280 740
Model 280EL 740
Model 280SL 740
Model 360 740
Model 360EL 741
Model 360SL 741
Model 280/360 Two Barrel Set........741
Model 280/360EL Two Barrel Set....741
Model 280/360SL Two Barrel Set....741
Model 1620 741
Model 1620E 741
Model 1620EL 741
Model 1620SL 741
Model 1622 741
Model 1622E 741
Model 1622EL 741
Model 102E 741
Model 103E 742
Model 204E 742
Model 301E 742
Model 302E 742
Model 303 Luxus 742
Model 304E 742
Model 401E 742
Model 200E 742
Model 200ES 742
Model 200SC (Sporting Clays)........743
Model 201E 743
Model 201ES 743
Model 201ET 743
Model 202E 743
Model 203E 743
Model 2000EL Sporter 744
Model 2000CL 744
Model 2000CL Sporter 744
Model 2001EL 744
Model 2001EL Sporter 744
Model 2002EL 744
Model 180 745
Model 300 745
Model 128E 745
Model 132E 745
Model 140-1 746
Model 140-1.1 746
Model 140-2 746

Model 140-2.1 746
Model 150-1 746
Model 150-1.1 746
Model 160S Luxus Double Rifle.......746
Model 160S-2.1 746
Model 211E Rifle/Shotgun
   Combination...............................746
Model 210E Rifle/Shotgun
   Combination...............................746
Model 211E Rifle/Shotgun
   Combination...............................746
Model 213E Rifle/Shotgun
   Combination...............................746
Model 313E Rifle/Shotgun
   Combination...............................746
Model 220E Over/Under
   Double Rifle...............................746
Model 221E Over/Under
   Double Rifle...............................746
Model 323E Over/Under
   Double Rifle...............................747
Model 95K Drilling.............................747
Model 96K 747
Model 96K—Engraved 747
K1 (K3) Jagd 747
K2 (K4) 747
KR-1 Premium 747
KR-1 Weimar 747

MERRILL, JAMES H.
Merrill Rifle 748
   1st Type 748
   2nd Type 748

MERRILL
Sportsman..749

MERWIN & BRAY
Merwin & Bray Pocket Pistol 749

MERWIN HULBERT & CO.
First Model Frontier Army,
   .44 Open Top 750
Second Model Frontier Army,
   .44 Open Top 750
Second Model Pocket Army,
   .44 Open Top 750
Third Model Frontier Army,
   Single-Action, .44 Topstrap 750
Third Model Frontier Army,
   Double-Action, .44 Topstrap 750
Third Model Pocket Army,
   Single-Action, .44 Topstrap 750
Third Model Pocket Army,
   Double-Action, .44 Topstrap 750
Fourth Model Frontier Army, Single-
   Action, .44 Topstrap....................750
Fourth Model Frontier Army,
   Double-Action, .44 Topstrap 750
First Pocket Model Single-Action 750
Second Pocket Model
   Single-Action..............................750
Third Pocket Model Single-Action
   Spur-Trigger 750
Third Pocket Model Single-Action
   w/Trigger Guard..........................750
Double-Action Pocket Model,
   Small Frame...............................750
Tip-Up .22 Spur-Trigger 751

METROPOLITAN ARMS CO.

1851 Navy Revolver 751
   Standard Navy Model.................751
   H.E. Dimick Navy Model 751

MIIDA

Model 612 751
Model 612 Skeet...........................751
Model 2100 Skeet.........................751
Model 2200 Trap or Skeet 751

MILLER ARMS

Standard Rifle 751

MINNEAPOLIS F. A. CO.

Palm Pistol...................................752

MITCHELL ARMS, INC.

Galil...752
MAS 752
AK-22 752
Sharpshooter II.............................753
Olympic I.S.U. 753
Victor II 753
Victor II with Weaver Rib 754
High Standard Collectors'
   Association Special Editions 754
Trophy II.......................................754
Victor II 754
Citation II 754
Three Gun Set 754
Six Gun Set 754
Skorpion 754
Spectre...754

MITCHELL'S MAUSERS

Black Arrow 754
Centurion......................................754
Valkyrie 754
Gold Series '03 754
Escalade 754
Sabre 754
Mauser M98 North American 754
Mauser M98 Varmint......................754
Mauser M98 African/Alaskan 754

MK ARMS, INC.

Model 760.....................................754

MOORE'S PATENT FIREARMS CO.

1st Variation Marked
   "Patent Applied For"....................755
2nd Variation Marked "D. Moore
   Patented Feb. 19 1861"........755
Standard Model Marked
   "Moore's Pat F.A. Co." 755
National Arms Co. Production. 755
Iron Model.................................755

MORGAN & CLAPP

Single-Shot Pocket Pistol 756

MORINI

C-80 Standard 756
CM-80 Super Competition 756
Model 84E Free Pistol.....................756

MORSE

Morse Carbine 756

MOSSBERG, O. F. & SONS, INC.

Brownie 756
Model 715P...................................756
Model K 757
Model M 757
Model L 757
Bolt-Action Rifles 757
Semi-Automatic Rifles 757
Targo Smoothbore Series 757
Model 400 Palomino 757
Model 702 Plinkster 757
Model 702 International Plinkster 758
Flex 22 Tactical 758
Model 817 Varmint.........................758
Tactical .22 758
Blaze 758
Blaze-47.......................................758
Model 715T Flat-Top 758
Model 100 ATR (All-Terrain Rifle).....758
Model 100 ATR Night Train..............759
Model 100 ATR Super Bantam 759
Model 800.....................................759
Model 800D...................................759
Model 800V...................................759
Model 800M...................................759
Model 800SM.................................759
Model 801 Half-Pint Plinkster 759
Model 802 Plinkster 759
Model 817 Plinkster 759
Model 810.....................................759
Model 472C...................................759
Model 479 PCA..............................759
Model 479 RR (Roy Rogers) 760
Model 464 Lever-Action Centerfire ..760
Model 464 Lever-Action Rimfire 760
SSi-One Sporter 760
SSi-One Varmint.............................760
SSi-One Slug 760
SSi-One Turkey 760
Model 1500 760
   Mountaineer Grade I 760
   Mountaineer Grade II 760
   Varmint.....................................760
Mossberg 4X4 Classic Stock
   Synthetic...................................760
Mossberg 4X4 Scoped Combo 761
Mossberg 4X4 Classic
   Walnut Stock.............................761
Patriot 761
Patriot Vortex Scoped Combo 761
Patriot Night Train I 761
Model MMR Hunter 761
Model MVP Flex 761
Miscellaneous Bolt-Action
   Shotguns 761
Model 695 761
Model 695 Camo 762
Model 200K 762
Model 500 Regal............................762
Model 500 Field Grade 762
Model 500 Steel Shot......................762
Model 500 Slugster 762
Model 500 Camper 762

Model 500 Mariner 762
Model 500 Muzzleloader Combo 762
Model 500 Bantam 762
Model 500 Super Bantam Field 762
Model 500 Super Bantam Turkey 763
Model 500 Super Bantam Slug 763
Model 500 Super Bantam Combo ...763
Model 500 Bullpup 763
Model 500 Slug Gun Viking Grade ...763
Model 500 Grand Slam Turkey 763
   Flex Hunting 763
   Flex Tactical 763
   Flex Deer/Security Combo 763
   Flex Turkey/Security; Waterfowl/
     Security.................................763
   Flex Duck Commander................763
Model 500 Combo 763
Model 500 USA..............................764
Model 500 HS (Home Security) 764
Model 500 Rolling Thunder 764
Model 500 Tactical Cruiser
   "Door Buster" 764
Model 500 Tactical 764
Model 500 ATI Scorpion..................764
Model 500 Magpul 764
Model 500 JIC (Just In Case) 764
Model 505 Youth............................764
Model 510 Mini Shotgun 764
Model 535 ATS
   (All Terrain Shotgun) Field............765
Model 535 ATS Turkey.....................765
Model 535 ATS Waterfowl................765
Model 535 ATS Slugster 765
Model 535 ATS Combos 765
Model 590 Special Purpose 765
Model 590 Mariner 765
Model 590DA..................................765
Model 590 Bullpup 765
Model 590A1 Blackwater..................765
Model 590 Tri Rail 765
Model 590 A1 765
Model 835 Ulti-Mag 766
Model 835 Ulti-Mag Viking Grade....766
Model 835 Ulti-Mag Crown Grade ...766
Model 835 Ulti-Mag Crown Grade
   Combo Model............................766
Model 835 Ulti-Mag
   Grand Slam Turkey....................766
Model 835 Ulti-Mag
   Thumbhole Turkey 766
Model 835 Ulti-Mag
   Tactical Turkey..........................766
Model 835 Wild Turkey Federation...766
Model 835 American Field 766
Model 835 Ulti-Mag
   Duck Commander......................766
Model 935 Magnum
   Waterfowl Camo 767
Model 935 Magnum Slugster...........767
Model 935 Magnum
   Turkey/Deer Comb.....................767
Model 935 Magnum
   Turkey Camo 767
Model 935 Magnum
   Turkey Pistol Grip.......................767
Model 935 Magnum Waterfowl
   Synthetic...................................767

Model 935 Magnum
   Turkey Synthetic 767
Model 935 Grand Slam Turkey 767
Model 930 Turkey 768
Model 930 Turkey Pistol Grip 768
Model 930 Waterfowl 768
Model 930 Pro Waterfowl 768
Model 930 Pro Sporting 768
Model 930 Slugster 768
Model 930 Tactical 768
Model 930 Road Blocker 768
Model 930 SPX...............................768
Model 930 Home Security/
   Field Combo..............................768
Model 3000 768
Model 3000 Waterfowl 768
Model 3000 Law Enforcement 768
Model 1000 769
Model 9200 Viking Grade 769
Model 9200 USST Crown Grade.......769
Model 9200 Combos 769
Model 9200 Special Hunter 769
Model 5500 MKI I...........................770
Silver Reserve Field Over/Under 770
Silver Reserve Sporting
   Over/Under................................770
Silver Reserve II Field......................770
Onyx Reserve Sporting
   Side-by-Side 770

MUSGRAVE

RSA NR I Single-Shot Target Rifle 771

NATIONAL ARMS CO.

Large Frame Teat-Fire Revolver 772
No. 2 Derringer 772

NAVY ARMS COMPANY

Model 83.......................................772
Model 93.......................................772
Model 95.......................................772
Model 96 Sportsman 772
Model 100 772
Model 100 Side-by-Side..................772
Model 150 772
Model 105 772
Model 105 Deluxe...........................772
Harpers Ferry Flint Rifle 773
Harpers Ferry
   "Journey of Discovery" Rifle 773
Brown Bess Musket.........................773
Brown Bess Carbine 773
1777 Charleville Musket 773
1777 Standard Charleville Musket...773
1816 M.T. Wickham Musket 773
1808 Springfield Musket 773
Pennsylvania Long Rifle 773
   Percussion 773
   Flintlock....................................773
Kentucky Rifle 773
   Percussion 773
   Flintlock....................................773
Mortimer Flintlock Rifle 773
Tryon Creedmoor Rifle 773
Standard Tryon Rifle 773
Deluxe Tryon Rifle..........................773

Parker-Hale Whitworth Rifle 774
Parker-Hale Volunteer Rifle.............774
Parker-Hale 3 Band Volunteer Rifle ..774
Rigby Target Rifle 774
1861 Springfield Rifle.....................774
Model 1873 Springfield Officer's
     Trapdoor 774
1862 C.S. Richmond Rifle...............774
Parker-Hale Three Band Musket 774
1873 Sharps Quigley......................775
1874 Sharps Infantry Rifle 775
1874 Sharps Sniper Rifle................775
Sharps Cavalry Carbine 775
Sharps Cavalry Carbine
     Cartridge Model........................775
1874 Sharps Plains Rifle 775
1874 Sharps Sporting Rifle 775
1874 Sharps Buffalo Rifle 775
1874 Sharps No. 3
     Long Range Rifle 775
1873 Winchester Rifle 776
Lightning Slide Action 776
1866 "Yellowboy" Rifle..................776
1866 "Yellowboy" Carbine.............776
1866 "Yellowboy" Short Rifle.........776
Iron Frame Henry 776
Blued Iron Frame Henry 776
Military Henry...............................776
Henry Carbine 777
Henry Trapper 777
1892 Rifle....................................777
1892 Short Rifle...........................777
1892 Carbine...............................777
1892 Brass Frame Carbine 777
1892 Brass Frame Rifle 777
No. 2 Creedmoor Target Rifle 777
Rolling Block Buffalo Rifle 777
     Half Octagon Barrel Model 777
"John Bodine" Rolling Block Rifle.....777
1885 High Wall 777
1873 Springfield Infantry Rifle.........777
1873 Springfield Cavalry Carbine 777
Ithaca/Navy Hawken Rifle..............778
Navy Arms Steel Shot Magnum 778
T&T Shotgun................................778
Japanese Tanegashima Matchlock ..778
Le Page Pistol..............................778
     Single Cased Set 778
     Double Cased Set.....................778
     Flintlock 778
     Smoothbore Flintlock Pistol 778
     Smoothbore Flintlock Pistol
          Single Cased Set.................778
     Smoothbore Flintlock Pistol
          Double Cased Set 778
Kentucky Pistol............................778
     Single Cased Set 779
     Double Cased Set.....................779
     Flintlock Pistol........................779
     Flintlock Pistol
          Single Cased Set.................779
     Flintlock Pistol
          Double Cased Set 779
     Pistol Single Cased Set 779
Beauregard Le Mat Pistol...............779
Starr Single-Action
     Model 1863 Army.....................779

1862 New Model Police.................779
1862 New Model Book-Style
     Cased Set 779
Paterson Revolver 779
     Single Cased Set 780
     Double Cased Set.....................780
1851 Navy Conversion 780
Augusta 1851 Navy Pistol..............780
Model 1851 Navy Frontiersman 780
Reb Model 1860 Pistol 780
1847 Walker Dragoon 780
     Single Cased Set 780
     Single Deluxe Cased Set 780
1860 Army Pistol 780
     Single Cased Set 780
     Double Cased Set,....................780
1860 Army Conversion 780
1858 New Model
     Remington-Style Pistol..............780
     Single Cased Set 781
     Double Cased Set.....................781
     Single Cased Set 781
     Double Cased Set.....................781
     Single Cased Set 781
     Double Cased Set.....................781
Spiller and Burr Pistol....................781
     Single Cased Set 781
     Double Cased Set.....................781
Rogers and Spencer 781
"London Gray" Rogers and
     Spencer Pistol 781
Rogers and Spencer Target Model ...781
1861 Navy Conversion 781
1872 Colt Open Top 781
1873 Colt-Style
     Single-Action Army 781
Model 1873 SAA Stainless
     Gunfighter...............................782
     Economy Model 1873 S.A.A.......782
     Nickel 1873 S.A.A. 782
1873 U.S. Cavalry Model 782
1873 Pinched Frame Model............782
1873 Flat Top Target.....................782
Deluxe 1873 Colt Revolver.............782
Bisley Model 782
Bisley Flat Top Target 783
1875 Remington-Style Revolver 783
1890 Remington-Style Revolver 783
Model 1875 Schofield—
     Wells Fargo 5" barrel 783
Model 1875 Schofield—Cavalry 7"
     barrel 783
Model 1875 Schofield—Deluxe 783
Model 1875 Schofield—
     B Engraved 783
Model 1875 Schofield—
     C Engraved 783
Model 1875 Schofield
     Founder's Model.......................783
Model 1875 Schofield—Hideout 783
New Model Russian 783
SKS Type 56 w/Scope Rail 783
Standard SKS Type 56 784
Standard SKS Type 56 With Scope
     and Bipod 784
SKS "Cowboy's Companion"
     Carbine 784

Military Version............................784
SKS "Hunter" Carbine 784
TT-Olympia Pistol 784
TU-90 Pistol 784
TU-111 Mauser.............................784
TU-KKW Training Rifle....................784
TU-KKW Sniper Trainer 784
TU-33/40 Carbine.........................784
JW-15 Rifle..................................784
Martini Target Rifle 784
Parker-Hale Sniper Rifle.................784
RPKS-74 784
No. 5 Enfield Jungle Carbine 784
No. 6 Enfield Jungle Carbine 801
Ishapore 2A No. 1 MK III Rifle.........801
2A Tanker Carbine........................801
MK III Tanker Carbine....................801
Lithgow No. 1 MK III Rifle 801
No. 1 MK III Enfield Rifle................801
No. 4 Tanker Carbine 801
No. 4 MK I Enfield Rifle 801
Savage No. 4 MK I Rifle 801
Luger 801
Grand Prix Silhouette Pistol 801

NEAL, W.
Under Hammer Pistol.....................801

NEPPERHAN FIREARMS CO.
Pocket Revolver.............................801

NESIKA BAY PRECISION, INC.
Hunting Rifles...............................801
Varmint Rifles...............................801
Urban Tactical Rifle 801

NEW ENGLAND FIREARMS CO.
Pardner 802
Pardner Youth 802
Special Purpose 802
Pardner Pump Turkey 802
Pardner Pump Walnut Shotgun........802
Pardner Pump Synthetic Shotgun 802
Pardner Pump Field Shotgun...........803
Pardner Pump Compact
     Field Shotgun 803
Pardner Pump Compact
     Walnut Shotgun 803
Pardner Pump Compact Synthetic
     Shotgun 803
Pardner Pump Combo 803
Pardner Pump Protector 803
Survivor.......................................803
Handi-Rifle (aka Handi-Gun)...........803
Tracker 803
Super Light Rifle...........................803
Huntsman 803
Tracker II.....................................804
Handi-Rifle Combo 804
Sportster......................................804
Sportster Youth.............................804
Sportster .17 HMR.........................804
Sportster .17 M2...........................804
Sportster SL 804
Sportster Versa-Pack.....................804
Sidekick Muzzleloader 804

NEW ULTRA LIGHT ARMS
Model 20 (Short Action) 804
Model 20 RF Rimfire.......................804
Model 20 Hunter's Pistol 805
Model 24 (Long Action)...................805
Model 28 Magnum..........................805
Model 40 Magnum..........................805
Model 90......................................805
Model 290.....................................805

NEWBURY ARMS CO.
Pocket Pistol 805
Pocket Revolver.............................805

NEWCOMB, H. G.
Pocket Pistol 805

NEWTON ARMS CO.
Newton-Mauser Rifle......................805
Standard Rifle First Type 805
Standard Rifle Second Model 805
Buffalo Newton Rifle 805

NICHOLS & CHILDS
Percussion Belt Revolver.................805
Revolving Percussion Rifle 805

NIGHTHAWK CUSTOM
Custom Talon/Talon II....................805
Custom Predator 806
GRP..806
Heinie Signature Series...................806
Lady Hawk....................................806
War Hawk Series...........................807
Kestrel...807
VIP 807

NOBLE
Model 275....................................808
Model 40......................................808
Model 50......................................808
Model 60......................................808
Model 65......................................808
Model 66CLP................................808
Model 66RCLP..............................808
Model 66RLP................................808
Model 66XL..................................808
Model 70RCLP..............................808
Model 70RLP................................808
Model 70XL..................................808
Model 602RCLP.............................808
Model 602CLP..............................808
Model 602RLP..............................808
Model 602XL................................808
Model 662....................................809
Model 80......................................809
Model 166L...................................809
Model 420....................................809
Model 450E..................................809

NORINCO
ATD .22.......................................809
EM-321..809
Model HL-12-203 Shotgun 809
Model HL-12-102 Shotgun 809
Model 97 Hammer Pump................809

Type 54-1 Tokarev......................809
1911 A1....................................809
Model 213 Pistol.....................810
Type 59 Makarov 810
SKS Rifle.................................810
Type 84S AK............................810
Type 84S-1..............................810
Type 84S-3..............................810

NORTH & COUCH

Animal Trap Gun......................810
   Disk Hammer Model 810
   Spur Hammer Model...............810

NORTH AMERICAN ARMS

Mini-Revolver..........................810
   Standard Rimfire Version.........810
   2 Cylinder Magnum Convertible
     Version................................810
   Viper Belt Buckle Version.........810
   Magnum Version 810
   Standard 3 Gun Set.................810
   Deluxe 3 Gun Set....................811
   Cased .22 Magnum..................811
Companion 811
Super Companion......................811
Black Widow 811
Mini-Master 811
"The Earl" Single-Action Revolver 811
   .22 Magnum only 811
   .22 convertible 811
Sidewinder..............................811
Single-Action Revolver 811
Guardian.................................811
Guardian .380..........................812

NORTH AMERICAN ARMS CORP.

Brigadier.................................812

NOSLER CUSTOM

Nosler Custom Model 48 Sporter.....812
Nosler Model 48 Professional.........812
Nosler Custom Rifle
   (Limited Edition)......................812
Nosler Varmageddon 812

NOWLIN MANUFACTURING COMPANY

Match Classic 812
Compact Carry.........................812
Match Master 812

O.D.I.

Viking.....................................813
Viking Combat..........................813

O'CONNELL, DAVID

Pocket Pistol 813

O'DELL, STEPHEN

Pocket Pistol 813

OHIO ORDNANCE INC.

Model 1918A3 Self-Loading Rifle....813
Colt Browning Water Cooled Gun.....813
1919A4...................................813

OJANGUREN Y VIDOSA

Apache (Model 1920)....................813
   7.65mm 814
Ojanguren................................814
Tanque 814

OLYMPIC ARMS, INC.

Black Widow 814
Enforcer..................................814
Match Master 814
Match Master 6".......................814
Cohort 814
Safari G.I.................................814
Schuetzen Pistol Works Big Deuce...814
Schuetzen Pistol Works Crest........814
Schuetzen Pistol Works Griffon.......815
Custom Journeyman 815
Model OA-93-PT.......................815
K4B-A4 817
Model OA-93-PT.......................817

OSBORN, S.

Under Hammer Pistol.....................818

OWA

OWA Pocket Pistol..........................818

P.38

H Prefix
   w/rectangular firing pin 819
Early w/High Gloss Blue 819
.30 caliber, extremely rare..........819
Early w/High Gloss Blue
   & Alloy Frame 819
Croatian Contract 819
Late w/Military Blue Finish 819
MOD P38—
   Late with Military Blue..............819
"ac45" Zero Series.....................819
   First Issue 819
   Second Issue..........................819
   Third Issue 819
"AC" (no date) 819
"AC40"....................................819
   Added....................................819
   Standard................................819
   1st Variation 819
   2nd Variation 819
   3rd Variation 819
   1st Variation 819
   2nd Variation 819
   1st Variation 819
   2nd Variation 819
   Single Line Slide......................819
"AC45"....................................820
   1st Variation 820
   2nd Variation 820
   3rd Variation 820
   German Proofed 820
   French Proofed 820
   Eagle /211 on frame 820
   1st Variation 820
   Standard Variation 820
   Zero Series 820

PALMER

Palmer Bolt-Action Carbine............821

PARA USA (PARA-ORDNANCE)

Para 1911 100th Anniversary 821
Model P14.45............................821
Model P14.45 Limited 821
Model P14.45 LDA/P14.45 LDA
   Stainless...............................821
Model P16.40............................822
Model P16.40 Limited 822
Model P16.40 LDA.....................822
Model P13.45............................822
Model P13.45/P12.45 Limited........822
Model P12.45 LDA/P12.45 LDA 822
Model P12.45/P12.40.................822
Model P10.45/P10.40/P10.9........823
Model P10.45 Limited 823
Model P18.9..............................823
Model P18.9 LDA.......................823
Model C7.45 LDA
   (Para Companion) 823
Model C6.45 LDA (Para Carry) 823
Model Stealth Carry....................823
Model Para CCW........................824
Model Para Companion
   Carry Option...........................824
Model Tac-Four.........................824
Model Tac-Four LE 824
Model LTC................................824
Model LTC Alloy.........................825
Model LTC Stainless 825
Hawg 9....................................825
Hawg 7....................................825
Model OPS...............................825
Model 1911..............................825
1911 SSP.................................825
GI Expert LTC............................825
1911 Wild Bunch 826
Warthog...................................826
Stainless Warthog 826
Stealth Warthog 826
Slim Hawg 826
Lite Hawg 9 826
P12.45....................................826
P13.45....................................827
Midnight Blue P14-45 827
Hi-Cap LTC...............................827
Stealth P14.45..........................827
P14.45....................................827
14.45 Tactical...........................827
P18.45....................................828
S12.45 Limited 828
S13.45 Limited 828
Stealth S14.45 Limited 828
S14.45 Limited 828
Long Slide Limited......................828
Stealth S16.40 Limited 828
S16.40 Limited 828
18.9 Limited 828
Todd Jarrett .40 USPSA P-16..........828
Todd Jarrett .45 USPSA 829
Companion II.............................829
Carry Model 829
Stealth Carry............................829

CCO (Companion Carry Option) 829
CCW.......................................829
Black Watch Companion 829
TAC-S.....................................829
Black Watch SSP.......................830
SSP..830
Stealth Limited 830
Limited 830
Carry 12 830
Tac-Four..................................830
Tac-Five...................................830
Stealth Hi-Cap .45......................830
Hi-Cap .45...............................831
Colonel....................................831
Hi-Cap .40...............................831
Stealth Hi-Cap 9........................831
Hi-Cap 9 831
Covert Black Nite-Tac..................831
Nite-Tac...................................831
Nite-Tac .40..............................831
Nite-Tac 9.................................831
Hi-Cap Limited .40......................831
Stealth Hi-Cap Limited 9...............832
Hi-Cap Limited 9........................832
Stealth Hi-Cap Ltd .45.................832
Hi-Cap Limited .45......................832

PARDINI

Standard Target Pistol.................832
Rapidfire Pistol..........................832
Centerfire Pistol 832
Free Pistol 832

PARKER-HALE LTD.

S&W Victory Conversion...............832
Model 1200..............................832
Model 1100 Lightweight...............832
Model 81 Classic 832
Model 81 African........................832
Model 84 Target 832
Model 85 Sniper 833
Model 640E Shotgun...................833
Model 640A..............................833
Model 645E..............................833
Model 670E..............................833
Model 680E—XXV......................833
1853 Enfield Rifle Musket..............833
1858 Enfield Naval Pattern Rifle......833
1861 Enfield Artillery Carbine
   Musketoon.............................833
Whitworth Military Target Rifle........833
Whitworth Sniping Rifle.................833
Volunteer Percussion Target Rifle.....833

PARKER

4-Shot Pistol............................833

PARKER BROS.

VH..834
PH..834
CH..835
BH..835
AH..835
AAH..835
A-1 Special...............................836
Single-Barrel Trap......................836

S.C. Grade 836
S.B. Grade 836
S.A. Grade 836
S.A.A. Grade 836
S.A-1 Special Grade 836
Under Lifter Hammer Gun 836
Trojan 836

PARKER FIELD & SONS
Gas Seal Revolver 836

PARKER REPRODUCTIONS
DHE Grade 836
  12 Gauge 837
  16/20 Combination 837
  28 Gauge 837
  28 Gauge/.410 Bore
    Combination 837
DHE Grade Steel-Shot Special 837
BHE Grade Limited Edition 837
  2-Barrel Set 837
A-1 Special 837
  12 or 20 Gauge 837
  28 Gauge 837
  28 Gauge & .410 Combination ...837
  16 Gauge and 20 Gauge
    Combination 837
  A-1 Special Custom Engraved 837

PEABODY
Peabody Rifle and Carbine 837
Sporting Rifle 837
Creedmoor 837
Creedmoor Mid-Range 838
What Cheer 838
What Cheer Mid-Range 838
Kill Deer 838

PEAVY, A. J.
Knife-Pistol 838

PECARE & SMITH
Pepperbox 838
  Ten-Shot Pepperbox (rare) 838

PEDERSEN, JOHN D.
Pedersen Rifle 838

PEDERSEN CUSTOM GUNS
Model 1500 838
Model 1000 839
  Grade I 839
  Grade II 839
Model 1000 Magnum 839
  Grade I 839
  Grade II 839
Model 1000 Skeet 839
  Grade I 839
  Grade II 839
Model 1000 Trap 839
  Grade I 839
  Grade II 839
Model 2000 839
  Grade I 839
  Grade II 839
Model 2500 839
  Grade III—Plain 839

Grade II 839
Grade I 839

PEDERSOLI, DAVIDE
Mang In Graz Pistol 839
Carleton Underhammer Pistol 840
Remington Pattern Target
  Revolver 840
Rogers & Spencer Target
  Percussion Target Revolver 840
Kentucky Pistol 840
Bounty Pistol 840
Navy Moll Pistol 841
Harper's Ferry Pistol 841
Queen Anne Pistol 841
An IX Pistol 841
An XIII Pistol 841
Remington Rider Derringer 841
Derringer Liegi 841
Zimmer Pistol 841
Saloon Pistol 841
Swivel-Breech Rifle 842
Bristlen A. Morges Target Rifle 842
Waadtlander Target Rifle 842
Swiss Rifle 842
Wurttemberg Mauser 842
Gibbs Rifle 842
Tryon Rifle 842
Mortimer Rifle 842
Indian Trade Musket 842
Frontier Rifle 842
Kentucky Rifle 842
Alamo Rifle 842
Cub 842
Country Hunter 843
Jager Rifle 843
Leger 1763 Charleville Musket 843
Revolutionnaire 1777 Musket 843
Corrige An IX 843
An IX Dragoon Musket 843
Austrian 1798 Flintlock Musket 843
Prussian 1809 Flintlock Musket 843
Brown Bess Flintlock Musket 843
Springfield 1795 Musket 843
Harper's Ferry 1816 Musket 843
Rocky Mountain Hawken 843
Springfield 1861 Rifle 843
Kodiak Combination Gun 844
Kodiak Double Rifle 844
Rolling Block Rifle 844
1859 Sharps Cavalry Carbine 844
1862 Robinson Confederate
  Sharps 844
Sharps 1863 Sporting Rifle 844
1874 Sharps 844
1873 Trapdoor Springfield 844
Kodiak Mark IV Express Rifle 844
Pedersoli Lightning Rifle 844
Double Percussion Shotgun 844
Coach Shotgun 844
Mortimer Shotgun 844
Denali 845
Brutus 94 845
Brutus Ovation 845
Rolling Block Percussion Rifle 845

PERAZZI
COMP 1-SB TRAP
  (Standard Grade) 845
COMP 1-TRAP (Standard Grade) 845
Light Game Model
  (Standard Grade) 845
MT-6 Model (Standard Grade) 845
MX3 845
  Standard Grade 845
  SC3 Grade 845
  SCO Grade 845
  Gold Grade 845
Grand American Special 846
  Standard Grade 846
  SC3 Grade 846
  SCO Grade 846
  Gold Grade 846
  SCO Grade w/Sideplates 846
  Gold Grade w/Sideplates 846
SHO Model 846
DHO Model 846
DHO Extra Gold 846
MX9 846
  Standard Grade 846
  SC3 Grade 846
  SCO Grade 846
  Standard Grade Trap Combo 846
MX10 846
  Standard Grade 846
  SC3 Grade 846
  SCO Grade 846
  Standard Grade Combo Model 846
TM1 Special Standard Grade 846
TMX Special 846
  Standard Grade 847
  SCO Grade 847
TM9 847
MX8 Special 847
  Standard Grade 847
  SC3 Grade 847
  SCO Grade 847
  Standard Grade Trap Combo 847
MX8/20 847
  Standard Grade 847
  SC3 Grade 847
  SCO Grade 847
MX8/20-8/20C 847
  Standard Grade 847
  SC3 Grade 847
  SCO Grade 847
MX7 Standard Grade 847
MX7C Standard Grade 847
DB81 Special 847
  Standard Grade 848
  SC3 Grade 848
  SCO Grade 848
Mirage Special Standard Grade 848
Mirage Special Sporting
  Standard Grade 848
Mirage Special Sporting Classic
  Standard Grade 848
Mirage MX8 Sporting
  Standard Grade 848
SCO Model 848
Mirage Special 4-Gauge Set 848
  Standard Grade 848

SC3 Grade 848
SCO Grade 848
MX12/12C 848
  Standard Grade 848
  SC3 Grade 848
  SCO Grade 848
MX20/20C 848
  Standard Grade 848
  SC3 Grade 848
  SCO Grade 849
MX28 and MX410 849
  Standard Grade 849
  SCO Grade 849
MX-2000 849
MX-2005 849

PERRY & GODDARD
Derringer 849

PERRY PATENT FIREARMS CO.
Perry Single-Shot Pistol 849
  1st Type 849
  2nd Type 849
Perry Carbine 849

PERUGINI & VISINI
Liberty Model 849
Classic Model 849
Bolt-Action Rifle 849
Deluxe Bolt-Action Rifle 849
Eagle Single-Shot 849
Boxlock Express Rifle 850
Magnum Over/Under 850
Super Express Rifle 850
Victoria Side-by-Side Rifle 850
Selous Side-by-Side Rifle 850

PETTINGILL C. S.
Pocket Revolver 850
  1st Model 850
  2nd Model 850
  3rd Model 850
Navy Revolver 850
Army Revolver 850

PFANNL, FRANCOIS
Erika 850

PGM PRECISION
Model PGM 850

PHILLIPS & RODGERS INC.
Medusa Model 47 851
Ruger 50 Conversion 851

PHOENIX ARMS
HP25 851
HP22/HP25 Target 851
Raven 851

PICKERT, FRIEDRICH
Arminius 7.65mm 852
Arminius Single-Shot Target Pistol ...852
Pickert Revolver 852

PIEPER, HENRI & NICOLAS
Pieper Model 1907......................852
Model 1908/Basculant 852
Pieper Bayard Revolver................853
Legia...853
Bayard...853

PILSEN, ZBROVKA
Pocket Pistol 853

PIOTTI
Model Piuma (BSEE)......................853
Westlake Model 853
Over/Under Gun 853
Model King No. I...........................853
Monte Carlo Model.......................853
Model King Extra 854
Model Lunik..................................854
Model Monaco..............................854
No. 1 or No. 2...............................854
No. 3 854
No. 4 854

PLAINFIELD MACHINE CO.
Super Enforcer 854
M1 Carbine...................................854
M1 Paratrooper Carbine 854

PLAINFIELD ORDNANCE CO.
Conversion Kit 854
.22 or .25 Caliber Pistol 854

PLANT'S MANUFACTURING CO.
Army Model Revolver.....................854
1st Model Brass Frame.............854
1st Model Iron Frame................855
2nd Model Rounded
  Brass Frame..........................855
2nd Model Iron Frame................855
3rd Model 855

POINTER
Single-Shot Derringer 855

POLY-TECHNOLOGIES, INC./POLY-TECH
SKS...855

POND, LUCIUS, W.
Brass Framed Revolver 856
Iron Framed Revolver 856
Separate Chamber Revolver............856
.22 Caliber Version 856
.32 Caliber Version 856

PORTER, P. W.
Turret Revolver 856
Turret Rifle 856
1st Model
  with Canister Magazine 856
2nd Model (New York)................856
3rd Model (New York)................856
4th Model (New York)................856

PRANDELLI & GASPARINI
Boxlock Side-by-Side Shotgun 856
Sidelock Side-by-Side Shotgun 856

Boxlock Over/Under Shotgun..........856
Sidelock Over/Under Shotgun.........857

PRATT, H.
Under Hammer Pistol.....................857

PRECISION SMALL ARMS
Diplomat Model 857
Montreaux Model 857
Renaissance Model 857
Imperiale 857

PREMIER
Regent Side-by-Side Shotgun 857
Regent Magnum 857
Brush King 857
Ambassador Model 858
Presentation Custom Grade 858

PRESCOTT, E. A.
Percussion Pocket Revolver 858
Pocket Revolver............................858
Navy Revolver 858
Army Revolver 858

PRINZ
Grade 1 Bolt-Action Rifle 858
Grade 2 Bolt-Action Rifle 858
Tip Up Rifle 858
Model 85 "Princess" 858

PROFESSIONAL ORDNANCE, INC.
Carbon-15 Pistol—Type 97 858
Carbon-15 Rifle—Type 97.............859
Carbon-15 Rifle—Type 97S.............859
Carbon-15 Pistol—Type 21.............859
Carbon-15 Rifle—Type 21.............859

PROTECTION
Protection Pocket Revolver.............859
1st Model..................................859
2nd Model 859

PUMA
Model 92 Rifle 859
Model 92 Carbine..........................859
Model 92 Trapper 859
PPS22..859

PURDEY, J. & SONS LTD.
Hammerless Ejector
  Side-by-Side Game Gun.............860
Hammerless Ejector
  Over/Under Gun.........................860
Double-Barreled Rifle 860
Best Quality Game Gun 860
Double Rifle 860
.300 H&H.................................860
.375 H&H.................................860
.470 N.E..................................860
.600 N.E..................................860

PYRENEES
Model 10 Unique..........................860
Model BCF66................................861
Model C.......................................861
Model DES 69..............................861

QUACKENBUSH
Quackenbush
  Safety Cartridge Rifle 862
Junior Safety Rifle 862
Bicycle Rifle 862

QUINABAUG MFG. CO.
Under Hammer Pistol......................862

R. G. INDUSTRIES
RG-25 863
RG-16 863
RG-17 863
RG-14 863
RG-30 863
RG-40 863
RG-57 863
RG-63 863
RG-66 863
RG-66T 863
RG-74 863
RG-88 863

RADOM
VIS-35 Reissue 864
FB P-64..864
FB P-83..864

RANDALL FIREARMS CO.
Model A111....................................864
Model A121....................................864
Model A131....................................864
Model B331....................................866
Model C311....................................866
Model C332....................................866
Model B321 SET 866
Model A111/111 Matched Set 867
Austrian Randall............................867
.45 LeMay—Right-Hand............867
.45 LeMay—Dogleg
  Right-Hand...........................867
.45 LeMay—Left-Hand............867
.45 LeMay—Dogleg
  Left-Hand..............................867
.45 Service—Right-Hand........867
.45 Service—Left-Hand........867
9mm Service—Right-Hand........867
9mm Service—Left-Hand........867

RANGER ARMS, INC.
.22 Rifle 867

RAPTOR ARMS CO.
Raptor Bolt-Action Rifle...................867
Peregrine Bolt-Action Rifle 867

RAST & GASSER

RAU ARMS CORP.
Model 500 868
Model 600 Deluxe 868

RECORD-MATCH ANSCHUTZ
Model 210 Free Pistol 868
Model 210A..................................868
Model 200 Free Pistol 868

REEDER, GARY CUSTOM GUNS
Arizona Ranger Classic 868
Badlands Classic..........................868
Black Widow 868
Night Rider..................................870
Coyote Classic 870
Classic Hunter.............................870
Alaskan Grizzly 870
Ultimate Back Up 2......................870
Ultimate 44 871

REFORM
Reform Pistol 872

REID, JAMES
Model 1 Revolver 872
Model 2 Revolver 872
Model 3 Revolver 872
Model 4 Revolver 873
"My Friend" Knuckle Duster 873
Brass Frame.............................873
Iron Frame 873
.32 Caliber Knuckle Duster 873
Brass Frame.............................873
Iron Frame 873
.41 Caliber Knuckle Duster 873
Model No. 1 Knuckle Duster 873
Model No. 2 Knuckle Duster 873
Model No. 3 Derringer 873
Model No. 4 Derringer 873
New Model Knuckle Duster 873

REISING ARMS CO.
Standard Model.............................873
New York Manufacture...............874
Hartford Manufacture................874

REMINGTON ARMS COMPANY, INC.
1st Model Remington-Beals
  Revolver..................................874
2nd Model Remington-Beals
  Revolver..................................874
3rd Model Remington-Beals
  Revolver..................................874
Remington-Rider Revolver..............874
Remington-Beals Army Revolver......874
Remington-Beals Navy Revolver 874
1861 Army Revolver 875
1861 Navy Revolver 875
New Model Army Revolver 875
Standard Model—
  Military Version 875
Civilian Model—No Government
  Inspector's Markings 875
.44 or .46 Cartridge Conversion .875
New Model Navy Revolver..............875
Military Version..........................875
Civilian Version.........................875
.38 Cartridge Conversion—
  1873 to 1888.....................875
New Model Single-Action
  Belt Revolver...........................875
Remington-Rider Double-Action
  Belt Revolver...........................876
New Model Police Revolver 876
New Model Pocket Revolver...........876
1st Version 876

2nd Version 876
3rd Version 876
.32 Cartridge Conversion 876
Remington-Rider Derringer 876
Zig-Zag Derringer......................876
Remington-Elliot Derringer 877
5-shot .22 caliber...................877
4-shot .32 caliber...................877
Vest Pocket Pistol.....................877
Large-Bore Vest Pocket Pistol 877
Remington-Elliot
Single-Shot Derringer 877
Early Type I 877
Model 1865 Navy Rolling Block
Pistol 878
Model 1867 Navy Rolling Block
Pistol 878
Model 1871 Army Rolling Block
Pistol 878
Remington-Smoot No. 1 Revolver 878
Remington-Smoot No. 2 Revolver 879
Remington-Smoot No. 3 Revolver 879
New No. 4 Revolver 879
Remington Iroquois Revolver 879
Model 1875 Single-Action
Revolver 879
Model 1890 Single-Action
Revolver 879
Model 1891 Target Rolling Block
Pistol 880
Model 1901 Target Rolling Block 880
Mark III Signal Pistol 880
Model 51 880
Model 53 880
Model 1911R1 881
Model 1911R1 Centennial 881
Model 1911R1 Centennial
Limited Edition.......................881
Model 1911R1 Enhanced 881
Model 1911R1 Carry....................881
Remington-UMC
Commemorative 1911 881
Model R51 881
Model RM380 882
Remington-Beals Rifle 883
U.S. Navy Rolling Block Carbine......883
Model 1867 Navy Cadet Rifle.........883
Rolling Block Military Rifles 883
Standard No. 1 Sporting Rifle 883
Long-Range Creedmoor Rifle 883
Mid-Range Target Rifle 883
Short-Range Rifle 883
Black Hills Rifle 883
Shotgun................................883
Baby Carbine 883
Model 1-1/2 Sporting Rifle.............883
No. 5 Sporting or Target Rifle 884
Model 1897 884
Carbine.................................884
No. 6 Falling Block Rifle 884
No. 7 Rolling Block Rifle 884
Remington-Hepburn No. 3 Rifle.....884
Remington-Hepburn No. 3
Match Rifle............................885
A Quality 885
B Quality 885

Remington-Hepburn No. 3
Long-Range Creedmoor Rifle.......885
Remington-Hepburn No. 3
Mid-Range Creedmoor Rifle 885
Remington-Hepburn No. 3
Long-Range Military Rifle 885
Plain Grade 885
Fancy Grade 885
Remington-Hepburn No. 3
Schuetzen Match Rifle 885
Breechloading Version................885
Muzzleloading Version 885
Remington-Hepburn No. 3
High-Power Rifle......................885
Sporting Rifle 886
Army Rifle 886
Navy Rifle 886
Carbine................................886
Frontier Model
(aka Indiana Scout Carbine).........886
Remington-Lee Magazine Rifle.......886
Remington-Lee Model 1879
Sharps Mfg. 886
Remington-Lee Model 1879
U.S. Navy Model 886
Remington-Lee Model 1879
Sporting Rifle 886
Remington-Lee Model 1879
Military Rifle 886
Remington-Lee Model 1882
Army Contract 886
Remington-Lee Model 1885
Navy Contract 886
Remington-Lee Model 1882 &
1885 Military Rifles 886
Remington-Lee Model 1882 &
1885 Sporting Rifle...................886
Remington-Lee Model 1882 &
1885 Carbine..........................886
Remington-Lee Model 1899 886
Military Rifle 886
Military Carbine 887
Remington Lebel Bolt-Action Rifle....887
Remington-Whitmore Model 1874 ...887
Shotgun................................887
Combination Gun (Rare) 887
Double Rifle...........................887
Model 1882 Shotgun....................887
Model 1883 through 1889
Shotgun................................887
Model 1893 (No. 9)....................887
Hammerless Shotgun Model 1894 ..887
Model 1900 Shotgun...................887
Model 8 Rifle 887
Standard Grade 887
Model 8A 888
Model 8C 888
8D Peerless 888
8E Expert 888
8F Premier 888
Standard Grade 888
Model 81A 888
81D Peerless 888
81F Premier 888
Model 12A 888
Model 12B 888
Model 12C 888
12C N.R.A. Target 888

Model 12CS 888
12D Peerless 888
12E Expert 888
12F Premier 888
Standard Grade 888
121D Peerless 888
121F Premier 889
Model 121S 889
121SB—Smoothbore 889
Model 14 or 14A 889
Model 14R 889
Model 141 889
Model 141 Special Grade 889
Model 25 889
Model 24 889
Model 241 Speedmaster 889
Model 241 889
241D Peerless 889
241E Expert 890
241F Premier 890
Model 550A 890
Model 41P 890
Model 41SB 890
Miscellaneous Remington Bolt Action
Rimfires, 1930-1970 890
Model 37 890
Model 37-1940 890
Model 504 891
Model 504 Custom.....................891
Model 504-T LS HB....................891
Model 541 S Custom 891
Model 541T 891
Model 541T Heavy Barrel 891
Model 547 891
Model 511 Scoremaster 891
Model 512 891
Model 513 TR Matchmaster...........891
Model 513 S 891
Model 514 891
Model 521 TL Jr. 892
Model 760 892
Standard Model 892
Carbine................................892
760D Peerless 892
760F Premier 892
760F Gold Inlaid 892
Bicentennial 892
ADL 892
BDL 892
Model 552A Speedmaster 892
Model 552 BDL.........................892
Model 552 BDL Deluxe Speedmaster
NRA Edition 892
Model 572 Fieldmaster.................892
Model 580 893
Model 591 893
Model 592 893
Model 740 893
ADL 893
BDL 893
Peerless Grade 893
Premier Grade 893
Model 742 893
BDL Standard Grade 894
742D Peerless 894
742F Premier (Game Scene) 894

742F Premier (Gold Inlaid)............894
Bicentennial 894
Standard Grade 894
7600D Peerless 894
7600F Premier 894
Premier 894
Synthetic 894
Special Purpose........................894
7600P Patrol 894
Buckmasters ADF
(American Deer Foundation).....894
Model Six...............................895
Model 7615 Tactical Pump
Carbine 895
Model 7615 Special Purpose
Synthetic 895
Model 7615 Camo Hunter 895
Model 7615 Ranch Carbine 895
Model 74 Sportsman 895
Model Four 895
Model 7400 895
Synthetic 895
Weathermaster........................895
Carbine................................895
Special Purpose.......................896
Buckmasters ADF
(American Deer Foundation) ..896
Model 7400 Custom Grade............896
F Grade................................896
F Grade with Gold Inlay 896
Model 750 Woodsmaster................896
Model 750 Synthetic 896
Model R-15 VTR Predator Rifle.......896
Model R-15 VTR Predator Carbine...896
Model R-15CS VTR Predator
Carbine 896
Model R-15 Hunter.....................896
Model R-15 VTR
Byron South Edition 896
Model R-15 VTR SS Varmint...........896
Model R-15 MOE 897
Model R-25 Modular
Repeating Rifle 897
Model R-25 GII.........................897
Model 10 Nylon 897
10 (model) 897
10 (SB) 897
Model 11 Nylon 897
Model 12 Nylon 897
Model 66 Nylon 897
66 (MB) "Mohawk" Brown 897
66 (SG) "Seneca" Green.............897
66 (AB) "Apache" Black 897
66 (BD) "Black Diamond" 897
66 (GS) "Gallery Special"............897
66 (AN)
"150th Anniversary Rifle" 898
66 (BI) "Bicentennial Rifle" 898
Model 76 Nylon 898
76 (MB) "Trailrider" 898
76 (AB) "Trailrider" 898
76 (not cataloged) 898
Model 77 Nylon........................898
HB 899
HB Magnum 899
Magnum 899
Magnum LS 899

Custom Target.................................899
Custom Target Magnum...................899
Yellow Jacket..................................899
Blaze Camo.....................................899
Pink Camo.......................................899
FLX..900
AAC..900
VTR - Quad Rail...............................900
VTR A-2 Fixed Stock.........................900
VTR Collapsible Stock.......................900
VTR A-TACS Camo............................900
Model Five.......................................900
Target Rifle......................................900
Centerfire Target..............................900
40XB Rangemaster Centerfire...........900
40XB BR..900
40XB Tactical Rifle...........................900
40XS Tactical...................................900
40XR KS Sporter...............................901
40XR Custom Sporter.......................901
Model XR-100 Rangemaster...............901
Model XC KS....................................901
Model 673 Guide Rifle.......................901
Model 720A......................................901
  Standard Version...........................901
  ADL...901
  BDL...901
Model 725 Kodiak.............................901
Model 600..902
Model 700 ADL..................................902
Model 700 ADL Synthetic Youth.........902
Model 700 BDL..................................902
Model 700 BDL LH (Left-Hand).........902
Model 700 BDL (DM)..........................902
Model 700 BDL LSS...........................902
Model 700 BDL SS DM—
  Magnum Rifle................................903
Model 700 BDL SS Short Action.........903
Model 700 BDL SS Camo Special
  Edition (RMEF)..............................903
Model 700 50th Anniversary Edition.903
Model 700 EtronX..............................903
Model 700 Mountain Rifle (DM).........904
Model 700 Safari Grade.....................904
Model 700 RS....................................904
Model 700 FS....................................904
Model 700 BDL European...................904
Model 700 BDL Stainless
  Synthetic......................................904
Model 700 BDL Stainless
  Synthetic (DM)..............................904
Model 700 CDL..................................904
Model 700 CDL
  Boone and Crockett.......................904
Model 700 CDL SF Ltd.......................904
Model 700 Mountain Rifle Stainless
  Synthetic......................................904
Model 700 LSS Mountain Rifle...........904
Model 700 Titanium..........................905
Model 700 Varmint Special
  Synthetic......................................905
Model 700 VS SF (Varmint Synthetic
  Stainless Fluted)...........................905
Model 700 Varmint Special Wood....905
Model 700 Varmint Laminated Stock
  (VLS)..905

Model 700 VS Composite
  (Varmint Synthetic Composite).....905
Model 700 LV SF (Light Varmint).....905
Model 700 VS SF II...........................905
Model 700 VSF.................................905
Model 700 LSS LH
  (Laminated Stock SS Left-Hand)...905
Model 700 SPS.................................905
Model 700 SPS Synthetic
  Left hand.....................................906
Model 700 SPS Varmint....................906
Model 700 SPS Dangerous Game.....906
Model 700 SPS Stainless...................906
Model 700 SPS DM............................906
Model 700 SPS Youth........................906
Model 700 SPS Tactical....................906
Model 700 SPS Tactical AAC............906
Model 700 XCR II RMEF
  Limited Edition.............................906
Model 700 SPS Tactical II................907
Remington 700 XCR II.......................907
Remington 700 XCR II -
  Bone Collector Edition...................907
Model 700 Classic............................907
Model 700 Custom............................907
Model 700 Custom "C" Grade..........907
AWR (Alaskan Wilderness Rifle).......907
APR (African Plains Rifle)................907
ABG (African Big Game)...................907
Model 700 Safari KS Stainless.........907
Model 700 Police..............................907
Model 700 Police DM.........................908
Model 700 Police Lightweight
  Tactical..908
Model 700 XCR Tactical
  Long Range Rifle...........................908
Model 700 XCR Compact Tactical....908
Model 700 Target Tactical Rifle........908
Model 700 Tactical Chassis..............908
Model 700 VTR Varmint-
  Tactical Rifle................................908
Model 700 VTR Desert Recon..........908
Model 700 XHR Extreme
  Hunting Rifle.................................908
Model 700 SPS Buckmasters
  Edition...908
Model 700 Alaskan Ti......................908
Model 700 LSS 50th Anniversary
  of .280 Remington.........................909
Model 700 VL SS Thumbhole............909
Model 710..909
Model Seven FS................................909
Model Seven MS...............................910
Model Seven AWR.............................910
Model Seven Youth...........................910
Model Seven CDL..............................910
Model Seven XCR Camo....................910
Model Seven
  25th Anniversary Version...............910
Model Seven Predator.......................910
Model 770 Youth..............................910
Model 715 Sportsman.......................910
Model 798..911
Model 798 Stainless Laminate.........911
Model 798 SPS.................................911
Model 798 Safari..............................911
Model 799..911

Model 1816 Commemorative
  Flint Lock Rifle.............................911
Remington No. 1 Rolling Block
  Mid-Range....................................911
Remington Mid-Range Sporter
  Rolling Block.................................911
Model SPR18 Single Shot Rifle.........911
Model SPR22 Double Rifle.................911
Model SPR94 Combo Gun..................911
Model 412..912
Model 700 ML...................................912
Model 700 ML Custom.......................912
Model 700 MLS.................................912
Model 700 MLS Custom.....................912
Model 700 ML Youth.........................912
Model 700 Ultimate
  Muzzle Loader..............................912
Genesis Muzzleloaders.....................912
Model 11..912
  11B Special...................................912
  11C Trap.......................................912
  11D Tournament............................913
  11E Expert....................................913
  11F Premier..................................913
  11R..913
Model 10A..913
Model 17..913
Model 29..913
Model 31..913
Model 870 Wingmaster......................913
Model 870 Field Wingmaster.............913
Model 870 Field Wingmaster
  16 Gauge......................................913
Model 870 Wingmaster
  NRA Edition...................................913
Model 870 Wingmaster Jr.................913
Model 870 Field Wingmaster
  Small Bores..................................914
Model 870 Express Super Magnum
  Fall Flight.....................................914
Model 870 Express Synthetic Super
  Mag Turkey-Waterfowl Camo.........914
Model 870 Super Mag
  Turkey-Predator Camo
  with Scope....................................914
Model 870TA Trap.............................914
Model 870TB Trap.............................914
Model 870TC Trap.............................914
Model 870 Express Deer Gun............915
Model 870 Express
  Deer/Turkey Combo.......................915
Model 870 Express Left-Hand...........915
Model 870 Express Synthetic
  Turkey Camo.................................915
Model 870 Express Super Magnum
  Turkey..915
Model 870 Express Synthetic Deer..915
Model 870 Express Compact Deer..915
Model 870 Express Compact
  Pink Camo....................................915
Model 870 Express Compact
  Synthetic......................................915
Model 870 Express
  Compact Camo..............................915
Model 870 Express Compact Jr.......915
Model 870 Express Combos.............915
Model 870 Express Youth Gun.........915
Model 870 Express Turkey...............916

Model 870 Express Camo Turkey....916
Model 870 20 Gauge Express
  Youth Camo Turkey.......................916
Model 870 Express Small Game......916
Model 870 Express HD
  (Home Defense)............................916
Model 870 Classic Trap...................916
Model 870 Special Field..................916
Model 870 Rifle Deer Gun...............916
Model 870 Brushmaster
  Deer Gun.....................................916
Model 870 Express Youth
  Turkey Camo.................................916
Model 870 Youth Deer Gun.............916
Model 870 Security..........................916
Model 870 SPS-Camo.......................916
Model 870 SPS Super Magnum
  Camo..917
Model 870 SPS-BG Camo..................917
Model 870 SPS
  Fully Rifled Deer Gun....................917
Model 870 SPS Super Slug
  Deer Gun.....................................917
Model 870 SPS-T...............................917
Model 870 SPS-T Camo.....................917
Model 870 SPS-T Youth
  Turkey Camo.................................917
Model 870 SPS-T Super Magnum
  Camo..917
Model 870 SPS-T Camo
  NWTF 25th Anniversary.................917
Model 870 SPS-T Super Mag............917
Model 870 SPS-T/20..........................917
Model 870 SPS-T Camo.....................918
Model 870 SP-T Super Magnum
  Thumbhole....................................918
Model 870 Tac-3 Speedfeed IV.......918
Model 870 Tac-3 Folder...................918
Model 870 Express Tactical A-TACS
  Camo..918
Model 870 Custom Grade.................918
  D Grade..918
  F Grade..918
  F Grade with Gold Inlay................918
Model 870 SP-T Thumbhole.............919
Model 870 Special Purpose
  Thumbhole....................................919
Model 870 XCS Marine Magnum.....919
Model 870 SPS MAX Gobbler.........919
Model 870 20 Gauge Lightweight
  Magnum..919
Model 870 Wingmaster 100th
  Anniversary..................................919
Model 870 American Classic...........919
Model 870 with Claro Walnut.........919
Model 870 Express Magnum
  ShurShot Cantilever.......................919
Model 870 SPS ShurShot Synthetic
  Super Slug....................................919
Model 870 Express Super Magnum
  Waterfowl.....................................920
Model 870 Express Magnum
  ShurShot Turkey............................920
Model 870 SPS ShurShot Turkey.....920
Model 870 Express Tactical.............920
Model 870 Express Tactical
  with Ghost Ring Sights..................920
Model 870 Tactical Desert Recon....920

Model 887 Nitro Mag
   Pump Shotgun 920
Model 887 Nitro Mag Waterfowl......920
Model 887 Bone Collector Edition....920
Model 887 Nitro Mag Camo
   Combo 920
Model 887 Nitro Mag Tactical.........920
Model 48 Sportsman 920
Model 11-48 921
Model 58 Sportsman 921
Model 878 Automaster 921
Model 1100 Classic Field 921
Model 1100 Small Game 921
Model 1100 Youth Gun 921
Model 1100 Youth Synthetic 921
Model 1100 Youth Synthetic Camo..921
Model 1100 Tournament Skeet 921
Model 1100 Tournament Skeet,
   12 Gauge 922
Model 1100 Classic Trap 922
Model 1100 Sporting 12................922
Model 1100 Sporting 20................922
Model 1100 Sporting 28................922
Model 1100 Competition Master 922
Model 1100 Competition 922
Model 1100 LT-20 922
Model 1100 LT-20 "Limited" 922
Model 1100 1 OF 3000 922
Model 1100 Special Field 922
Model 1100 TBMC Trap Gun 922
Model 1100 LT-20 Deer Gun 923
Model 1100 LT-20 Synthetic 923
Model 1100 LT-20 Magnum 923
Model 1100 LT-20 Synthetic Camo
   NWTF 25th Anniversary 923
Model 1100 Synthetic 923
Model 1100 Synthetic Deer Gun 923
Model 1100 Competition
   Synthetic...................................923
Model 1100 Custom Grade.............923
   D Grade 923
   F Grade....................................923
   F Grade with Gold Inlay 923
Model 1100 G3.............................923
Model 1100 Tactical
   Speedfeed IV 923
Model 1100 Tactical
   Standard Stock...........................923
Model 1100 Premier Sporting 923
Model 1100 50th Anniversary
   Limited Edition...........................924
Model 1100 American Classic.........924
Model 11-87 Premier 924
Model 11-87 Premier 20 Gauge 924
Model 11-87
   Dale Earnhardt Tribute...............924
Model 11-87 Upland Special...........924
Model 11-87 Premier Cantilever
   Scope Mount Deer Gun 924
Model 11-87 Premier Trap..............924
Model 11-87 Premier SC
   (Sporting Clays) 924
Model 11-87 SC NP
   (Sporting Clays Nickel-Plated)......925
Model 11-87 SPS-BG Camo 925
Model 11-87 SPS-T Camo...............925
Model 11-87 SPS 925

Model 11-87 SPS-Deer 925
Model 11-87 Waterfowl..................925
Model 11-87 SPS-T 925
Model 11-87 SPS-T Camo
   NWTF 25th Anniversary 925
Model 11-87 SP Super Magnum.....925
Model 11-87 SPS Super Magnum...925
Model 11-87 SPS-T Super Magnum
   (NWTF Edition) 925
Model 11-87 Police.......................926
Model 11-87 Custom Grade 926
   D Grade 926
   F Grade....................................926
   F Grade with Gold Inlay 926
Model 11-87 Sportsman Synthetic ... 926
Model 11-87 Sportsman Super
   Magnum 926
Model 11-87 Sportsman Rifled 926
Model 11-87 Sportsman Youth........926
Model 11-87 Sportsman Compact
   Synthetic...................................926
Model 11-87 Sportsman Youth
   Camo..926
Model 11-87 Sportsman
   NRA Edition 926
Model 11-87 SP Thumbhole 926
Model 11-87 SPS-T Super Magnum926
Model 11-87 SP-T Thumbhole 926
Model 11-87 Sportsman Camo 926
Model 11-87 Sportsman Camo
   Rifled.......................................927
Model 11-87 SPS Super Magnum
   Waterfowl..................................927
Model 11-87 Sportsman Super Mag
   ShurShot Turkey........................ 927
Model 11-87 Sportsman Super
   Magnum Waterfowl.....................927
Model 11-87 Sportsman ShurShot
   Cantilever..................................927
Model 11-96 Euro Lightweight........927
Model SP-10 927
Model SP-10 Magnum Camo..........927
Model SP-10 Magnum Camo NWTF
   25th Anniversary 927
Model SP-10 Synthetic 928
Model SP-10 RC/VT 928
Model SP-10 Custom Grade 928
Model SP-10 Magnum Waterfowl 928
Model SP-10 Magnum Thumbhole
   Camo..928
Model 105CTi 928
Versa Max....................................928
   Standard Grade 928
   Skeet..928
   TC 928
   TC 32D Grade 928
   TC 32F Grade............................928
   TC 32E Expert 928
   Field Grade 928
   Magnum 929
   Skeet..929
   4-Gauge Set...............................929
   Trap..929
   Special Trap 929
   Competition Trap 929
   Premier.....................................929
   "One of One Thousand" 929
Model 300 Ideal...........................929

Model 90-T Single-Barrel Trap 929
Model 90-T Single-Barrel Trap
   (High Rib) 929
Model 332 929
Remington Peerless......................929
Model 396 Sporting......................929
Model 396 Skeet...........................929
Model 396 Custom Grade..............930
STS Competition 930
Field Grade 930
Upland Grade 930
RGS...930
Remington Parker AAHE Double 930
Model XP-100...............................930
Model XP-100 Silhouette 930
Model XP-100 Custom 930
Model XP-100 Hunter 931
Model XP-100R Repeater 931
Model SPR 210.............................931
Model SPR 220.............................931
Model SPR 310.............................931
Model SPR 310S...........................931
Model SPR 100/Sporting...............931
Model SPR 18...............................931
Model SPR 22...............................931
Model SPR 94...............................931

RENETTE, GASTINNE
Model 105....................................932
Model 98......................................932
Model 202....................................932
Model 353....................................932
Type G Rifle 932

REPUBLIC ARMS, INC.
RAP 440.......................................932
Republic Patriot............................932

REUNIES
Dictator 933
Texas Ranger or Cowboy Ranger 933

REUTH, F.
Animal Trap Gun...........................933

REXIO DE ARMAS (COMANCHE)
RS 22 933
RS 22M..933
RJ 22 933
RJ 38 933
RS 357 933
Outfitter Single-Shot 934
Outfitter Single-Shot Compact........934

RHEINMETALL
Dreyse 6.35mm Model 1907 934
Dreyse 7.65mm Model 1907 934
Dreyse 9mm 934
Rheinmetall 32.............................934
Rheinmetall 9mm 934
Dreyse Light Rifle or Carbine...........934

RICHLAND ARMS CO.
Model 80 LS 935
Model 200 935
Model 202 935

Model 711 Magnum......................935
Model 707 Deluxe.........................935

RICHMOND ARMORY
Carbine..935

RIGBY, JOHN & CO., LTD.
Magazine Rifle 936
Big Game Rifle 936
London Best Rifle 936
African Express 936
Single-Shot Rifle 936
Second Quality Boxlock
   Double Rifle...............................936
Best Quality Boxlock
   Double Rifle...............................936
Best Quality Sidelock
   Double Rifle...............................936
Sidelock Double 936

RIGDON, ANSLEY & CO.
Early Production Model 937
Standard Production Model 937

RIPOMANTI, GUY
Side-by-Side Double Rifles.............937
Over/Under Double Rifle................937

RIZZINI, BATTISTA
Aurum Light.................................937
Artemis Classic 937
Artemis Deluxe.............................938
Artemis EL....................................938
Upland EL.....................................938
S780 Emel....................................938
S782 Emel Field Classic 938
S790 Emel Field............................938
S792 Emel Field............................938
Express 90 L.................................939
Express 92 EL...............................939

RIZZINI, FRATELLI
12 gauge 939
20 gauge 939
28 gauge and .410 bore 940
Extra Lusso Grade—
   Scalloped receiver 940
   12 gauge 940
   20 gauge 940
   28 gauge 940
   .410 bore 940
   12, 16, or 20 gauge 940
   28 gauge or .410 bore...............940

ROBAR AND DE KIRKHAVE
Melior Model 1907........................940
Melior Pocket Model......................941
Melior Model .22 Long Rifle 941
Melior Model .22 Target.................941
New Model Jieffeco (7.65mm) 941
New Model Jieffeco (6.35mm) 941

ROBAR COMPANIES
Robar SR60 Precision Rifle 942

ROBERTS DEFENSE
Super Grade Custom Series 942

ROBERTSON
Pocket Pistol 943

ROBINSON, S.C.
Robinson Sharps 943
Confederate Sharps 943

ROBINSON ARMAMENT CO.
Super VEPR 943
M-96 Expeditonary Rifle 943
M-96 Carbine 943
M-96 Top Fed 943

ROCK ISLAND ARMORY (TRADE NAME OF ARMSCOR)
M1911-A1 FSP 943
TCM 943
M2011-A1 943
MAPP 943
TCM Rifle 943

ROCK RIVER ARMS, INC.
Bullseye Wadcutter 944
Basic Limited Match 944
Limited Match 944
Hi-Cap Basic Limited 945
Ultimate Match Achiever 945
Match Master Steel 945
Basic Carry 945
Pro Carry 945
Tactical Pistol 945
Limited Police Competition 9mm 946
Unlimited Police
    Competition 9mm 946
CAR A2 946
CAR A2M 946
CAR A4 946
CAR A4M 946
Standard A2 946
National Match A2 946
Standard A4 Flattop 947
Varmint Rifle 947
Varmint EOP
    (Elevated Optical Platform) 947
Advanced Tactical Hunter 947
NM A2-DCM Legal 947
Government Model 947
Tactical CAR A4 947
Elite CAR A4 947
Tactical CAR UTE
    (Universal Tactical Entry) 2 947
Elite CAR UTE 2 947
Entry Tactical 947
TASC Rifle 947
LAR-15 Lightweight 948
LAR-15 X-1 Rifle 948
    X-1 .223 Wylde 948
    X-1 6.8 SPCII, .300 AAC or
        .458 Socom 948
    X-1 7.62 NATO 948
Texas Rifle 948
LAR 47 X-1 948

ROGERS & SPENCER
Army Revolver 948

ROGUE RIVER RIFLEWORKS
Boxlock Double Rifle 948
Sidelock Double Rifle 948

ROHRBAUGH
R9/R9S 949
380/380S 949

ROSS RIFLE CO.
Mark I 949
Mark I Carbine 949
Mark II 949
Mark III (Military) 949
Mark III/M-10 Sporter Rifle 949
    .280 Ross Caliber 950
    .303 British Caliber 950

ROSSI, AMADEO
Squire Shotgun 950
Field Grade Shotgun 950
Stainless Matched Pair
    Combo Guns 950
Trifecta 950
Turkey Gun 950
Rossi Circuit Judge 950
Model 62 950
Model 92 951
Model 92 Rifle 951
Rossi Rio Grande 951
Model 92 Large Loop 951
Model 65 951
Single-Shot Rifle 951
Single Shot Rifle—Heavy Barrel 951
Muzzleloading Rifle 951
Muzzleloader Matched Pair 951
Rossi Blued Synthetic
    Matched Pair 951
Rossi Stainless Synthetic
    Matched Pair 952
Rossi Wizard 952
Rossi Ranch Hand 952
Model 51 952
Model 511 Sportsman 952
Model 461 952
Model 462 952
Model 68S 952
Model 69 952
Model 70 952
Model 84 953
Model 851 953
Model 68 953
Model 31 953
Model 677 953
Model 88S 953
Model 351 953
Model 352 953
Model 951 953
Model 971 954
Model 971 Comp 954
Model 971 Comp Stainless 954
Model 972 954
Model 877 954
Model 89 954
Model 988 Cyclops 954
Model 720 955

ROTTWEIL
Model 650 955

RUPERTUS, JACOB
Single-Shot Pocket Pistol 956

RWS
Model 820 S 956
Model 820 SF 956
Model 820 K 956

S.A.E.
Model 210S 957
Model 340X 957
Model 209E 957
Model 70 957
Model 66C 957

S.E.A.M.
Praga 957
S.E.A.M. 957
Silesia 957

S.W.D., INC.
Cobray M-11 957
M-11 Carbine 957
Terminator 957

SACKET, D. D.
Under Hammer Pistol 957

SAFARI ARMS
Enforcer 957
Match Master 958
Black Widow 958
Model 81 958
Model 81L 958
Ultimate Unlimited 958

SAIGA
Model 100 958

SAKO
Standard Sporter 959
Deluxe Model 959
Finnbear 959
Forester 959
Vixen 959
FN Action 959
FN Magnum Action 959
Anniversary Model 959
Sako Quad Combo 960
Hunter 960
    Medium Action 960
    Short Action 960
    Long Action 960
    Carbine 960
Long Range Hunting Rifle 960
    Medium Action 960
    Long Action 960
FiberClass 960
FiberClass Carbine 960
Carbine 960
    Medium Action 960
    Long Action 961
Varmint-Heavy Barrel 961

Short Action 961
Medium Action 961
PPC Bench Rest/Varmint 961
Classic Grade 961
Deluxe Grade 961
    Medium Action 961
    Short Action 961
    Long Action 961
Super Grade/Super Deluxe 961
    Medium Action 961
    Short Action 961
    Long Action 961
Safari Grade 961
Model 75 Hunter 961
Model 75 Stainless Synthetic 962
Model 75 Deluxe 962
Model 75 Big Game Deluxe 962
Model 75 Varmint 962
Model 75 Varmint Set Trigger 962
Model 75 Varmint Stainless 962
Model 75 Varmint Stainless
    Set Trigger 962
Model 75 Finnlight 962
Model 75 Grey Wolf 962
Model 75 Custom Deluxe 962
Model 75 Custom Single Shot 962
Model 75 Super Deluxe 963
Model 78 963
Model 2700 Finnsport 963
Safari 80th Anniversary Model 963
Sako 85 Hunter 963
Sako 85 Stainless Synthetic 963
Sako 85 Synthetic 963
Sako 85 Finnlight 963
Sako 85 Varmint 963
Sako 85 Laminated SS Varmint 963
A-7 American Bolt-Action Rifle 963
A-7 Big Game Roughtech 963
A-7 Long Range Roughtech 964
A-7 Tecomate 964
Sako Classic Deluxe 964
Sako 85 Bavarian 964
Sako 85 Kodiak 964
Sako Black Bear Series 964
TRG-S 964
TRG-21 964
TRG-22 964
TRG-41 965
TRG-42 965

SAM, INC.
Model 88 Crossfire 965

SARASQUETA, FELIX
Merke 965

SARASQUETA, J. J.
Model 119E 965
Model 130E 965
Model 131E 965

SARSILMAZ
Professional 966
Kama Sport 966
Kama 966
Kilinc 2000 Mega 966

Kilinc 2000 Light.............................966
Hancer 2000/2000 Light 966
Bernardelli 966

SAUER & SON, J. P.

Bolt-Action Rifle 967
Model 200 967
Model 200 Lightweight 967
Model 200 Lux...............................967
Model 200 Carbon Fiber 967
Model 202 Supreme........................967
Model 202 Takedown......................967
Model S202 Wolverine 967
Model S202 Highland 967
Model S202 Forest..........................967
Model S202 Hardwood 967
Model S202 Match..........................967
Model S202 Outback.......................967
Model S202 Team Sauer 967
Model 90 967
Model 90 Stutzen 967
Model 90 Safari 968
Model 90 Supreme..........................968
SSG-3000 968
SG 550 Sniper 968
Luftwaffe M30 Survival Drilling........968
Model 3000 Drilling........................968
Model 54 Combo 968
Model 60 968
Royal Model 968
Grade I Artemis 968
Grade II Artemis 968
Model 66 968
    Grade I....................................968
    Grade II...................................968
    Grade III..................................968
Bär Pistol 968
Roth-Sauer Model 969
    A. European variation: 969
    B. English Export variation 969
Commercial variation......................969
    Caliber 7.65mm variation............969
    Caliber 7.65 variation with
        all words in English
        (i.e Son, Prussia, etc.)............969
Police Variations............................969
    Caliber 6.35mm police marked
        with Zusatzsicherung 969
    Caliber 7.65mm police marked
        without Zusatzsicherung........969
    Caliber 7.65mm police marked
        with Zusatzsicherung 969
R.F.V. (Reich Finanz Verwaltung) 969
    Caliber 6.35mm R.F.V. marked
        pistols 969
    Caliber 7.65mm R.F.V. marked
        pistols 969
Imperial Military Variations 970
    Caliber 7.65mm Imperial Military
        accepted pistols....................970
    Caliber 7.65mm Commercial
        with Zusatzsicherung 970
    Police with Zusatzsicherung and
        police grip-strap markings.....970
Paramilitary marked Sauer pistols
    of the 1925-35 period 970
Model 19 in 6.35mm.......................970

Caliber 6.35mm first
    sub-variation 970
Caliber 6.35mm second sub-
    variation 970
Caliber 6.35mm third
    sub-variation 970
Caliber 6.35mm English export
    variation 970
1926 Export Model 970
W.T.M.-Westentaschen Model—
    Vest Pocket Model 971
    Model 1920 971
    Model 1928 971
    Model 1933 971
Dutch Models.................................971
    Dutch Police 971
    Amsterdam Police 971
    Navy 971
    S.M.N. 971
    Department of Finance.............971
1930 Commercial Model 971
    Standard Commercial 971
    Standard Commercial
        with NIROSTA marked barrel,
        7.65mm...............................971
    Standard Commercial in .22 LR
        (.22 Long) 971
    Duralumin (Dural) Variation,
        7.65mm...............................971
Behorden Commercial 972
    Blue Anodized Variation 972
    Nonanodized Variation..............972
    Presentation Examples of
        Anodized and Nonanodized
        Variations 972
Police Models 972
    Sunburst K Police Acceptance 972
    Sunburst K Police Acceptance 972
    Diamond in Sunburst Police
        Acceptance 972
    Grip Strap Marked Variations 972
Model 38 972
    One Line Slide Legend Variation
        (pinned magazine release
        button - no screw).................972
    Two Line Slide Legend Variation
        (pinned magazine release
        button - no screw).................972
    Two Line Slide Legend Variation
        (magazine release button -
        with screw)...........................972
    SA der NSDAP Gruppe Thuringen
        Marked Variation 973
Model 38 pistols converted to
    H Models by Sauer factory 973
Model 38-H or H Model 973
    Standard Commercial Variation...973
    SA der NSDAP
        Gruppe Thuringia Variation.....973
    L.M. Model...............................973
    Flash Light Model 973
    Police Accepted Variation 973
H Model - Type Two 973
    Standard Commercial 973
    .22 Caliber Variation 973
    Jager Model 973
    Police Eagle C and Eagle F
        Acceptance Variations 973

German Military Variation
    Double Eagle 37 973
    Second Military Variation 974
    Police Eagle C Acceptance 974
H Model - Type Three 974
    Military Accepted 974
    Commercial..............................974
    Police Accepted with the
        Police Eagle C Acceptance 974
H Model - Type Four 974
    Military Accepted 974
    Commercial..............................974
    Police Accepted with the
        Police Eagle C Acceptance 974
    Eigentum NSDAP SA Gruppe
        Alpenland Slide Marked
        Pistols 974
    NSDAP SA Gruppe Alpenland
        Slide Marked Pistols..............975
    Himmler Presentation Pistols.....975
Model 38 975
    Military Accepted 975
    Commercial..............................975
    Police Accepted with
        Police Eagle C Acceptance 975
    Police Accepted with
        Police Eagle F Acceptance 975
First Variation 975
Second Variation 975

SAVAGE & NORTH

Figure 8 Revolver 975
    First Model...............................976
    Second Model 976
    Third Model..............................976
    Fourth Model............................976

SAVAGE ARMS CORPORATION

Model 1895.....................................976
Model 1899-A 22" Barrel
    Short Rifle 976
Model 1899-A 26"
    Round Barrel Rifle......................976
Model 1899-B 26"
    Octagon Barrel Rifle...................976
Model 1899-C 26" Half
    Octagon Barrel Rifle...................976
Model 1899-D Military Musket.........976
Model 1899-F Saddle Ring Carbine.. 976
Model 1899-CD Deluxe Rifle............976
Model 99-R Heavy Stocked Rifle 978
Model 99-RS Special Sights............978
Model 99-EG
    Standard Weight Rifle.................978
Model 99-C Clip Magazine Rifle 979
Model 99-PE
    Presentation Grade Rifle.............979
Model 1895 Anniversary Edition 979
Model 99-A Saddle Gun 979
Model 99-.358 and 99-.375
    Brush Guns 979
Model 99-CD Deluxe Clip Model......979
Model 99-CE (Centennial Edition) ...979
Model 1903 979
Model 1903 Gallery Model..............979
Model 1903
    Factory Engraved Models 979
    Grade EF.................................980

Expert Grade 980
Grade GH 980
Gold Medal Grade..........................980
Model 1909....................................980
Model 1911....................................980
Model 1912....................................980
Model 25..980
Model 29..980
Model 170......................................980
Model 1904....................................980
Model 1905....................................980
Model 4M......................................981
Model 5..981
Model 1920....................................981
Model 1922....................................981
Model 23A......................................981
Model 23AA....................................981
Model 23B......................................982
Model 23C......................................982
Model 23D......................................982
Model 40 (Old Model)......................982
Model 35..982
Model 46..982
Model 340......................................982
Model 110 Sporter 982
Model 110-M..................................982
Model 110-D..................................982
Model 110-P Premier Grade 982
Model 110-PE.................................982
Model 110-F...................................982
Model 110-FX.................................982
Model 110-FP.................................982
Model 110-G...................................983
Model 110-GX.................................983
Model 110-CY.................................983
Model 110-FP Tactical.....................983
Model 110-FP Duty 983
Model 110-FP-LE1...........................983
Model 110-FP-LE2...........................983
Model 110-Fiftieth Anniversary 983
Model 110 BA
    Law Enforcement Rifle 983
Model 111 Classic Hunter Series.....983
Model 111G....................................983
Model 111GCNS 983
Model 111GC..................................983
Model 111GL..................................984
Model 111F....................................984
Model 111FL..................................984
Model 111FC..................................984
Model 111FCNS..............................984
Model 111FXP3...............................984
Model 111FCXP3.............................984
Model 111FAK.................................984
Model 112BT / 112BT-S
    (Long Action) 984
Model 112 Series Varmint Rifles......984
Model 112BVSS (Long Action).........984
Model 112BVSS-S 984
Model 112FVSS...............................984
Model 112FVSS-S...........................985
Model 112FV..................................985
Model 112BT—
    Competition Grade....................985
Model 114C—Classic 985
Model 114CE—Classic European ...985

Model 114CU....985
Model 116FCSAK (Long Action)....985
Model 116FCS....986
Model 116FSK—Kodiak (Long Action)....986
Model 116SE—Safari Express....986
Model 116US....986
Model 12BVSS....986
Model 12BVSS-S....986
Model 12BVSS-SXP....986
Model 12FVSS-S....986
Model 12FV (Short Action)....986
Model 12FLV....986
Model 12VSS—Varminter (Short Action)....986
Model 12 Varminter Low Profile....987
Model 12 LRPV Long Range Precision Varminter....987
Model 12 Varminter Low Profile....987
Model 12 FCV Varmint Rifle....987
Model 12 F-Class Target Rifle....987
Model 12 Long Range Precision....987
Model 12 Palma....987
Model 40 Varmint Hunter....987
Model 10FP—Tactical (Short Action)....987
Model 10FCM—Scout Rifle....987
Model 10FP-LE1....988
Model 10FP-LE2....988
Model 10FCP-HS Precision....989
Model 10FCP Choate....989
Model 10FCP McMillan....989
Model 10FPXP-HS Precision....989
Model 10FP-HS....989
Model 10 Precision Carbine....989
Model 10FLCP....989
Model 10 BAS Law Enforcement Bolt-Action Rifle....989
Model 10 BAT-S....989
Model 10ML-II....989
Model 10MLSS-II....989
Model 10ML-II Camo....989
Model 10MLSS-II Camo....989
Model 10MLBSS-II....989
Model 10ML-IIXP....989
Model 10MLSS-IIXP....990
Model 11F....990
Model 11FCNS....990
Model 11 Lightweight Hunter....990
Model 11G....990
Model 11BTH....990
Model 11FYCAK....990
Model 14 Classic....990
Model 14 Left Hand....990
Model 114 Classic....990
Model 14 Euro Classic....991
Model 114 Euro Classic....991
Model 14 / 114 American Classic Stainless....991
Model 16FSS....991
Model 16FLSS....991
Model 16FCSAK....991
Model 16FCSS....991
Model 16BSS....991
Model 25 Lightweight Varminter Thumbhole....991

Model 25 Classic Sporter....991
Model 25 Walking Varminter....992
Model 60....992
Model 64GXP....992
Model 64BTV....992
Model 64F....992
Model 64FSS....992
Model 64FV....992
Model 64FVXP....992
Model 64FVSS....993
Model 64FXP....993
Model 88....993
Model 90 Carbine....993
Model A-17....993
Model 93G....993
Model 93 Classic Thumbhole....993
Model 93XP....993
Model 93FVSS....993
Model 93R17-Camo....994
Model 93R17-FVSS....994
Model 93R17-GV....994
Model 93R17-BV....994
Model Mark II BRJ....994
Model Mark II TRR-SR....995
Model CUB-G (Mini-Youth)....995
Model CUB-T....995
Model B Mag....995
Model 30G "Stevens Favorite"....995
Model 30G "Favorite" Takedown....995
Mark I-G....995
Mark I-FVT....995
Mark I-GY (Youth Model)....995
Mark I-GSB Smoothbore....995
Mark II-G....995
Mark II-GY (Youth Model)....995
Mark II-FSS....996
Mark II-LV....996
Mark II-F....996
Mark II-FXP....996
Mark II Camo....996
Mark II-FV....996
Mark II-FVXP....996
Mark II-FVT....996
Mark II-BV....996
Mark II BTV....996
Mark II BVTS....996
Mark II Classic....996
Model 900B—Biathlon....997
Model 900 TR—Target....997
Model 900S—Silhouette....997
Model 24....997
Model 24S....997
Model 24MS....997
Model 24DL....997
Model 24 Field—Lightweight Version....997
Model 24C....997
Model 24VS....997
Model 24F....997
Model 2400....997
Model 389....997
Model 42....997
Model 411 Upland Sporter....997
Model 420....997
Model 420 with Single Trigger....998

Model 430 with Single Trigger....998
Model 412F....998
Model 220....998
Model 210F....998
Model 210FT....998
Model 720....998
Model 726 Upland Sporter....998
Model 740C Skeet....998
Model 775....999
Model 750....999
Model FA-1....999
Model FP-1....999
Model 21....999
Model 28....999
Model 30....999
Model 242....999
Model 550....999
Model 440....999
Model 440A....999
Model 440B-T....1000
Model 333....1000
Model 333T....1000
Model 312 Field Over/Under....1000
Model 312 Trap....1000
Model 312 Sporting Clay....1000
Model 320 Field....1000
Fox Model B—Utica, NY....1000
Fox Model B—Chicopee Falls, Mass. (later Westfield, Mass.)....1000
Fox Model B—Single Trigger....1000
Fox Model BDL....1000
Fox Model BDE....1000
Fox Model BSE....1001
Fox Model BE....1001
Milano....1001
Model 1907....1001
Model 1907 Portugese Contract....1001
Model 1915 Hammerless....1001
  .32 Caliber....1001
  .380 Caliber....1001
Model 1917....1001
Model 6.35mm....1002
Model 1907 Test Pistol....1002
Model 1910 Test Pistol....1002
Model 1911 Test Pistol....1002
Model 101....1002
Model 501F—Sport Striker....1002
Model 501FXP....1002
Model 502F—Sport Striker....1003
Model 503F—Sport Striker....1003
Model 503FSS—Sport Striker....1003
Model 510F Striker....1003
Model 516FSS....1003
Model 516FSAK....1003
Model 516FSAK Camo....1003
Model 516BSS....1003
Model 516BSAK....1003

SAVAGE REVOLVING FIREARMS CO.
Navy Revolver....1004

SCATTERGUN TECHNOLOGIES
TR-870....1004
Standard Model....1004
Border Patrol Model....1004

Professional Model....1004
Entry Model....1004
K-9 Model....1004
SWAT Model....1005

SCCY INDUSTRIES
SCCY CPX....1005
SCCY CPX-3....1005

SCHALK, G. S.
Rifle Musket....1005

SCHALL & CO.
Repeating Pistol....1005

SCHMIDT, HERBERT
Model 11, Liberty 11, and Eig Model E-8....1005
Model 11 Target....1005
Frontier Model or Texas Scout....1005

SCHMIDT & COMPANY, E.
Pocket Pistol....1005

SCHNEIDER & CO.
Pocket Pistol....1006

SCHNEIDER & GLASSICK
Pocket Pistols....1006

SCHUERMAN ARMS, LTD.
Model SA40....1006

SCHULER, AUGUST
Reform....1006

SCHULTZ & LARSEN
Model 47 Match Rifle....1006
Model 61 Match Rifle....1006
Model 62 Match Rifle....1006
Model 54 Free Rifle....1006
Model 68 DL....1006

SCHWARZLOSE, ANDREAS
Military Model 1898 (Standard)....1006

SEARS, ROEBUCK & CO. BRAND
Double-Barrel Shotguns....1006

SEAVER, E.R.
Pocket Pistol....1007

SECURITY INDUSTRIES
Model PSS....1007
Model PM357....1007

SEDCO INDUSTRIES, INC.
Model SP22....1007

SEECAMP, L. W. CO., INC.
LWS .25 ACP Model....1007
LWS .32 ACP Model....1007
Matched Pair....1007

SERBU FIREARMS
BFG-50 Rifle....1007
BFG-50 Carbine....1007

BFG-50A 1008

SHARPS ARMS CO., C.
Model 1874 Sharps Hartford
   Sporting Rifle.............................1008
Model 1874 Bridgeport
   Sporting Rifle.............................1008
Model 1875 Carbine—
   Hunters Rifle 1008
Model 1874 Boss Gun.................1008
Model 1875 Target &
   Sporting Rifle............................1008
Model 1875 Classic Rifle 1008
Model 1885 High Wall
   Sporting Rifle............................1008
Model 1885 High Wall
   Classic Rifle 1008

SHARPS RIFLE COMPANY
SRC 25-45 Rifle...........................1008

SHARPS RIFLE MANUFACTURING COMPANY
Model 1849................................1008
Model 1850................................1008
Model 1851 Carbine.....................1008
   Military Carbine 1009
   Military Rifle 1009
   Sporting Rifle...........................1009
   Shotgun 1009
   Military Carbine 1009
   Military Rifle 1009
   Sporting Rifle...........................1009
   Shotgun 1009
Model 1855................................1009
Model 1855 U.S. Navy Rifle 1009
Model 1855 British Carbine 1009
Model 1859 Carbine.....................1009
   22" Barrel, Brass Mountings.....1009
   Iron Mountings 1010
   30" Barrel 1010
   36" Barrel 1010
Sporting Rifle..............................1010
Coffee-Mill Model........................1010
   Carbine....................................1010
   Military Rifle 1010
   Sporting Rifle...........................1010
   First Type 1010
   Second Type.............................1010
   Carbine....................................1010
   Military Carbine 1011
   Military Rifle 1011
   Hunter's Rifle 1011
   Business Rifle...........................1011
   Sporting Rifle...........................1011
   Creedmoor Rifle 1011
   Mid-Range Rifle........................1011
   Long-Range Rifle......................1011
   Schuetzen Rifle.........................1011
Carbine......................................1011
Military Rifle...............................1011
Sporting Rifle..............................1011
C. Sharps & Company and Sharps &
   Hankins Company Breechloading,
   Single-Shot Pistol 1012
Pistol-Grip Rifle 1012
Percussion Revolver 1012

4-Shot Pepperbox Pistols...........1012
   Model 1 1012
   Model 2 1013
   Model 3 1013
   Model 4 1013

SHATTUCK, C. S.
Double-Barrel Shotguns...............1013
Boom 1013
Pocket Revolver..........................1013

SHAW & LEDOYT
Under Hammer Pistol...................1013

SHAWK & MCLANAHAN
Navy Revolver 1013

SHERIDAN PRODUCTS, INC.
Knockabout/Model D 1014

SHILEN RIFLES, INC.
Model DGA Bench Rest Rifle 1014
Model DGA Sporter......................1014
Model DGA Silhouette Rifle 1014

SHILOH RIFLE MFG. CO., INC.
Model 1863 Military Rifle..............1014
Model 1863 Sporting Rifle 1014
Model 1863 Military Carbine.........1014
Model 1862 Confederate
   Robinson..................................1014
Model 1874 Creedmoor
   Target Rifle..............................1014
Model 1874 Buffalo Rifle
   (Quigley)..................................1014
Model 1874 Long Range
   Express Rifle............................1014
Model 1874 Montana
   Roughrider Rifle.......................1015
Saddle Rifle 1015
No. 1 Sporter Deluxe Rifle.............1015
No. 3 Standard Sporter 1015
Business Rifle.............................1015
Model 1874 Military Rifle..............1015
Hartford Model 1015

SIG-HAMMERLI
Model P240 Target Pistol..............1015

SIG
P210 Danish Army Model M49 1016

SIGARMS/SIG-SAUER
P210..1017
P210 Legend 1017
P220..1017
P220 Sport 1018
P220R Equinox 1018
P220R Carry Equinox 1018
P220 Langdon Edition 1018
P220 Combat 1018
P220 Match 1019
P220 Super Match 1019
P220 Compact 1019
P220 Elite 1019
P220 Elite Stainless.....................1019
P225..1020

P225 Limited 1020
P225-A 1020
P226..1020
P226BR .22.................................1020
P226 Navy Seal 1020
P226 ST 1020
P226 Sport Stock 1020
P226 Sport 1021
JP226 Jubilee Pistol.....................1021
P226R DAK 1021
P226 X-Five................................1021
P226 Tactical 1021
P226 Elite 1022
P226 SAO 1022
P226 Legion 1022
P226 MK25 Navy Model...............1022
P227..1023
P228..1023
P228 (New Model).......................1023
P229..1023
P229 Sport 1023
P229 Limited 1024
P229 Platinum Elite......................1024
1911 C3.....................................1024
Model GSR.................................1025
1911 STX 1025
1911 TACOPS TB 1025
Revolution..................................1025
Revolution Custom STX................1025
Revolution TTT 1025
Revolution Compact.....................1025
Revolution Compact SAS 1025
Revolution Compact C3 1025
P245 Custom Shop 1027
P320..1028
SP2340 1028
SP2009 1028
SP2022 1028
Model SA3 Hunter 1028
Model SA3 Sporting.....................1028
Model SA5 Sporting.....................1028
Aurora TR Field Shotguns.............1029
TR 20U.......................................1029
TR 20...1029
TR 30...1029
TR 40 Silver 1029
TR 40 Gold 1029
New Englander.............................1029
TT 25 Competition.......................1029
TT45 1029
SIG AMT 1029
SIG PE-57...................................1030
SIG 550......................................1030
SIG 551......................................1030
SSG 2000...................................1030
SSG 3000...................................1030
   Level I......................................1030
   Level II.....................................1030
   Level III....................................1030
   Conversion Kit—.22 LR 1030
Model 202 Supreme.....................1031
Model 202 Supreme Magnum.......1031
SIG 556......................................1031
SIG 556 SWAT............................1031
SIG 556 HOLO 1031

SIG 556 DMR..............................1031
SIG516 Gas Piston Rifle...............1031
SIG716 Tactical Patrol Rifle 1031
SIG M400 1031
SIG MCX 1031
Sauer SSG 3000 1032
SIG 50 1032

SILMA
Model 70 EJ 1032
   12 Gauge.................................1032
   20 Gauge.................................1032
Model 70 EJ 1032
   12 Gauge.................................1032
   20 Gauge.................................1032
   28 and .410 Gauge 1032
Superlight..................................1032
Clays Model 1032

SIMPLEX
Simplex 1032

SIMPSON, R. J.
Pocket Pistol 1032

SIMSON & COMPANY
Model 235..................................1033
Model 73....................................1033
Model 74....................................1033
Model 74E..................................1033
Model 1922................................1033
Model 1927................................1034

SIRKIS INDUSTRIES, LTD.
SD9..1034
Model 35 Match Rifle 1034
Model 36 Sniper's Rifle................1034

SKB ARMS COMPANY
Model 100..................................1034
Model 150..................................1034
Model 200..................................1034
Model 200E................................1034
Model 280..................................1034
Model 300..................................1034
Model 385..................................1034
Model 385 2 Barrel Set 1034
Model 385 Sporting Clays.............1034
Model 400E 1034
Model 480E................................1035
Model 85TSS Trap.......................1035
Model 85TSS Trap Unsingle 1035
Model 85TSS Trap Unsingle
   Combo.....................................1035
Model 85TSS Skeet......................1035
Model 500..................................1035
Model 505 Field...........................1035
Model 505 3-Gauge Skeet Set......1036
Model 585..................................1036
Model 585 Gold Package..............1036
Model 585 Skeet..........................1036
Model 585—3 Barrel Skeet Set....1036
Model 585—3 Barrel Skeet Set
   Gold Package 1036
Model 585 Youth/Ladies 1036
Model 585 Youth Gold Package.....1036

Model 585 Upland.........................1036
Model 585 Upland Gold Package ...1036
Model 600 1036
Model 600 Magnum......................1036
Model 600 Trap Gun.....................1036
Model 600 Skeet Gun....................1036
Model 600 Skeet Combo Set 1036
Model 605 1036
Model 605 3-Gauge Skeet Set......1037
Model 680E 1037
Model 685 1037
Model 700 Trap Gun.....................1037
Model 700 Skeet Gun....................1037
Model 785 1037
Model 785—2 Barrel Set 1037
Model 785 Sporting Clays............1037
Model 785 Skeet...........................1037
Model 785 3-Gauge Skeet Set......1037
Model 785 Trap.............................1037
Model 785 Trap Combo 1037
Model 800 Trap Gun.....................1037
Model 800 Skeet Gun....................1037
Model 880 Crown Grade...............1037
Model 885 1037
Model 5600 1037
Model 5700 1037
   Game Bird...............................1038
   Clays and Trap........................1038
Model 7300 1038
Model 1900 1038
Model 3000 1038
Model 200 Field 1038
Model 200 Sporting......................1038
Model 250 Field 1038
Model 590 1038
Model 90 TSS 1038
Model 7000 SL 1038
Century III 1038
Model IS300 1039

SLOTTER & CO.

Pocket Pistol 1039

SMITH, L. C.

Early Hammerless Shotguns..........1039
   00 Grade.................................1039
   0 Grade...................................1039
   No. 1 Grade.............................1039
   No. 2 Grade.............................1039
   No. 3 Grade.............................1039
   Pigeon Grade 1039
   No. 4 Grade.............................1039
   A-1 Grade................................1039
   No. 5 Grade.............................1039
   Monogram Grade 1039
   A-2 Grade................................1039
   A-3 Grade................................1039
Later Production Hammerless
   Shotguns 1039
   Field Grade 1040
   Specialty Grade 1040
   Skeet Special Grade.................1040
   Premier Skeet Grade.................1040
   Eagle Grade 1040
   Crown Grade 1040
   Ideal Grade 1040

Trap Grade 1040
Monogram Grade 1040
Fulton Model...............................1040
Fulton Special 1041
Hunter Special 1041
Single Barrel Trap Guns 1041
   Olympic Grade.........................1041
   Specialty Grade 1041
   Crown Grade 1041
   Monogram Grade 1041
1968 Model 1041
1968 Deluxe Model......................1041

SMITH, OTIS

Model 1883 Shell-Ejector 1041
Model 1892 1041

SMITH & WESSON

Model 1, 1st Issue Revolver 1041
   1st Type 1042
   2nd Type 1042
   3rd Type 1042
   4th Type 1042
   5th Type 1042
   6th Type 1042
Model 1, 2nd Issue......................1042
Model 1, 3rd Issue.......................1042
   Shorter Barreled Version 1042
   Longer Barreled Version 1042
Model 1-1/2 1st Issue
   (1-1/2 Old Model) 1042
Model 1-1/2 2nd Issue
   (1-1/2 New Model) 1043
   3.5" Barrel 1043
   2.5" Barrel 1043
Model 1-1/2 Transitional Model.....1043
Model 2 Army or Old Model 1043
   5" or 6" Barrel 1043
   4" Barrel 1043
   Early Model w/o Strain Screw—
      Under #6500 1043
   Later Model with Strain Screw ..1044
   8" or 10" Barrel 1044
.38 Single-Action 2nd Model.........1044
   8" and 10" Barrel 1044
   3.25", 4", 5", and 6"
      Barrel Lengths 1044
.38 Single-Action
   Mexican Model........................1044
.32 Double-Action 1st Model 1044
.32 Double-Action 2nd Model 1044
.32 Double-Action 3rd Model 1045
.32 Double-Action 4th Model 1045
.32 Double-Action 5th Model 1045
.32 Safety Hammerless
   (aka .32 New Departure or
   .32 Lemon Squeezer)
   1st Model................................1045
   8" and 10" Barrel 1046
   Standard Barrel 1046
.38 Double-Action 4th Model 1046
   Standard Production Model 1047
   Transition Model 1047
   U.S. Army Order.......................1047
   .44 Rimfire Henry Model 1047
Model 3 American 2nd Model 1047
   .44 Henry Rimfire 1047

Standard 8" Model,
   .44 American Centerfire 1047
Model 3 Russian 1st Model...........1047
   Russian Contract Model,
      Cyrillic Barrel Address 1047
   Commercial Model....................1047
   Rejected Russian Contract
      Model 1048
   Commercial Model....................1048
   .44 Rimfire Henry Model 1048
   Russian Contract Model 1048
   1st Model Turkish Contract........1048
   2nd Model Turkish Contract......1048
   Japanese Govt. Contract 1048
   Commercial Model....................1048
   .44 Henry Rimfire Model 1048
   Turkish Model..........................1048
   Japanese Contract Model.........1048
   Russian Contract Model 1048
Model 3 Russian 3rd Model
   (Loewe & Tula Copies)............1048
   Loewe......................................1048
   Tula...1048
Model 3 Schofield 1st Model.........1049
   "US" Contract 1049
   Civilian Model..........................1049
Model 3 Schofield 2nd Model.......1049
   "US" Contract 1049
   Civilian Model..........................1049
Model 3 Schofield—
   Surplus Models 1049
   Wells Fargo & Co. Model 1049
   Surplus Cut Barrel—
      Not Wells Fargo 1049
New Model No. 3 Single-Action 1049
   Standard Model 1049
   Japanese Naval Contract..........1049
   Japanese Artillery Contract.......1049
   Maryland Militia Model.............1049
   Argentine Model 1050
   Australian Contract 1050
   Revolver with Stock and
      Holsters...............................1050
   Turkish Model..........................1050
New Model No. 3 Target
   Single-Action...........................1050
New Model No. 3 Frontier
   Single-Action...........................1050
   .44-40—Commercial Model 1051
   Japanese Purchase
      Converted to .44 S&W
      Russian...............................1051
   Standard .44 S&W Russian 1051
   .22 L.R. 1051
   .32 S&W...................................1051
   .38 S&W...................................1051
3rd Model Single-Shot..................1052
Straight Line Single-Shot 1052
.32 Hand Ejector Model of
   1896 or .32 Hand Ejector
   1st Model................................1052
Hand Ejector Model of 1903 1052
.32 Hand Ejector Model of 1903
   2nd Change 1052
.32 Hand Ejector Model of 1903
   3rd Change 1052
.32 Hand Ejector Model of 1903
   4th Change 1052

.32 Hand Ejector Model of 1903
   5th Change 1052
.32 Hand Ejector Third Model........1052
K-32 Hand Ejector First Model 1053
.22 Ladysmith 1st Model 1053
.22 Ladysmith 2nd Model 1053
.22 Ladysmith 3rd Model..............1053
K-22 Outdoorsman/Masterpiece ...1053
.38 Hand Ejector Military & Police
   1st Model or Model of 1899......1053
   Commercial Model....................1053
   U.S. Navy Model 1053
   U.S. Army Model 1053
.38 Hand Ejector M&P 2nd Model
   or Model of 1902 1053
.38 Hand Ejector Model of 1905 ...1054
   1st Change 1054
   2nd Change 1054
   3rd Change 1054
   4th Change 1054
.22-32 Hand Ejector 1054
   Bekeart Model 1054
   Standard Model 1054
   .22-32 Kit Gun (Pre WWII) 1054
.44 Hand Ejector 1st Model 1054
   .44 S&W Special 1055
   Other Calibers (Rare) 1055
.44 Hand Ejector 2nd Model 1055
   .44 S&W Special 1055
   .38-40, .44-40 or .45 Colt.......1055
.44 Hand Ejector 3rd Model or
   Model of 1926 1055
   .44 S&W Special 1055
   .44-40 or .45 Colt....................1055
.45 Hand Ejector U.S. Service
   Model of 1917 1055
   Military Model 1055
   Brazilian Contract 1055
   Commercial Model....................1055
.455 Mark II Hand Ejector
   1st Model................................1056
Model 10 (.38 Military & Police) 1056
Victory Model 1057
Model 11 (.38/200 British)............1057
Model 12 (.38 Military & Police
   Airweight)...............................1057
USAF M-13 (Aircrewman) 1057
Model 13 (.357 Military & Police) ..1057
Model 14 (K-38 Masterpiece)........1057
Model 15
   (K-38 Combat Masterpiece).......1057
Model 16 (K-32 Masterpiece)........1058
Model 16 (.32 Magnum) 1058
K-32 Combat Masterpiece 1058
Model 17 (K-22) 1058
Model 647 1058
Model 648 1059
Model 648 (New Model) 1059
Model 18
   (K-22 Combat Masterpiece).......1059
Model 19
   (.357 Combat Magnum)............1059
   Combat Magnum
      (Pre-Model 19, 1954-1958)..1059
   Model 19, 19-1 1059
   Model 19-2, 19-3.....................1059

Oregon State Police Cased with Buckle..........................1059
Texas Ranger Cased with Knife..........................1059
Model 20 (.38/.44 Heavy Duty).....1059
Model 21 (1950 Military)..............1059
Model 21 Thunder Ranch..............1059
Model 696..................................1059
Model 25 (.45 Target Model of 1950)........1060
Model 25-3 125th Anniversary with Case..................................1060
Model 25-2..................................1060
Model 25 Mountain Gun................1060
Model 625-2..................................1061
Factory Registered .357 Magnum............................1061
Pre-war .357 Magnum..................1061
Model 27 (.357 Magnum)..............1061
Model 627....................................1062
Model 627 Pro Series....................1062
Model 28 (Highway Patrolman)......1062
Model 29 (.44 Magnum)................1062
Early 5-Inch Barrel Model 29.........1063
Model 629....................................1063
Model 629 Classic........................1063
Model 629 Classic DX...................1063
Model 629 Mountain Gun..............1063
Model 629 Backpacker..................1063
Model 629 Classic Powerport........1063
Fiftieth Anniversary Model 29........1064
Model 310 Night Guard.................1064
Model 327 Night Guard.................1064
Model 329 Night Guard.................1064
Model 386 Night Guard.................1064
Model 396 Night Guard.................1064
Model 315 Night Guard.................1064
Model 30 (The .32 Hand Ejector)...1064
Model 31 (.32 Regulation Police)...1065
Model 31 (.32 Regulation Police Target)....1065
Model 32 (.38/.32 Terrier)............1065
Model 33 (.38 Regulation Police)...1065
Model 34 (.22/.32 Kit Gun)............1065
1946-1952 Production.............1065
1953-1991 Production.............1065
Model 317 AirLite.........................1065
Model 317 AirLite Kit Gun..............1066
Model 317 AirLite Ladysmith..........1066
Model 331 AirLite.........................1066
Model 332 AirLite.........................1066
Model 337 AirLite.........................1066
Model 342 AirLite.........................1066
Model 325PD................................1067
Model 337 Kit Gun........................1067
Model 337 PD..............................1067
Model 340....................................1067
Model 342 PD..............................1067
Model 351PD................................1067
Model 360....................................1068
Model 360 Kit Gun........................1068
Model 386....................................1068
Model 386 PD..............................1068
Model 386 Sc/S............................1068
Model 386 XL Hunter....................1068
Model 396 Mountain Lite..............1068

Model 242..................................1069
Model 296..................................1069
Model 586..................................1069
Model 686..................................1069
Model 329PD..............................1069
Model 610 (2007 Reintroduction)..1069
Model 36 (.38 Chief's Special).......1069
Model 36LS (.38 Ladysmith).........1070
Model 36 (Chief's Special Target)..1070
Model 37....................................1070
Model 637....................................1070
Model 637 Carry Combo...............1070
Model 637 Power Port Pro Series..................................1070
Model 637CT..............................1070
Model 38 (Airweight Bodyguard)...............1071
Model 638..................................1071
Model 640 Centennial .357 Magnum............................1072
Model 642 Centennial Airweight....1072
Model 642CT (Crimson Trace).......1072
Model 642LS Ladysmith...............1072
Model 642 PowerPort Pro Series...1072
Model 631 Lady Smith..................1072
Model 632 PowerPort Pro Series...1073
Models 637 CT/638 CT/642 CT....1073
Model 042 Centennial Airweight....1073
Model 442 Centennial Lightweight...............................1073
Model 442/642/640/632 Pro Series..................................1073
Model 438..................................1073
Model 51 (.22/.32 Kit Gun Magnum)........1073
Model 53 (Magnum Jet)...............1074
Model 56 (KXT-38 USAF)..............1074
Model 500..................................1075
Model 60....................................1075
2" Barrel................................1075
3" Barrel................................1076
5" Barrel................................1076
Model 60LS (LadySmith)..............1076
Model 60 with Hi-Viz Sight...........1076
Model 60 Pro Series....................1076
Model 65 (.357 Military & Police Heavy Barrel Stainless)..............1076
Model 66 (.357 Combat Magnum Stainless)............................1077
Model 67 (.38 Combat Masterpiece Stainless)..............1077
Model 69....................................1077
Model 650..................................1077
Model 651..................................1077
Model 686 Powerport..................1077
Model 686 Plus Mountain Gun......1077
Model 686 Plus Pro Series...........1078
Model M986................................1078
Model 619..................................1078
Model 3 Schofield........................1079
Model 1917................................1079
Model 15....................................1079
Model 15 McGivern......................1079
Model 17....................................1079
Model 24....................................1079
Model 25....................................1079

Model 29....................................1079
Model 14 Classic.........................1079
Model 14 Classic (nickel)..............1079
Model 15 Classic.........................1079
Model 17 Masterpiece Classic......1079
Model 36 Classic.........................1079
Model 21 Classic.........................1080
Model 22 Classic.........................1080
Model 22 of 1917 Classic.............1080
Model 25 Classic.........................1080
Model 27 Classic.........................1080
Model 29 Classic.........................1080
Model 10 Classic.........................1081
M&P 340....................................1081
Model 39....................................1082
Model 39 Steel Frame..................1082
Model 59....................................1082
Model 439..................................1082
Model 669..................................1083
Model 645..................................1083
Model 745—IPSC.........................1083
Model 41....................................1083
Model 41 (New Model).................1083
Model 41-1................................1083
Model 41 Fiftieth Anniversary Edition.........1084
Model 46....................................1084
Model 61 Escort..........................1084
Model 52A..................................1084
Model 52 (.38 Master)..................1084
Model 52-1................................1084
Model 52-2................................1084
Model 2214 (The Sportsman)........1085
Model 2206................................1085
Model 2206 TGT (Target)..............1085
Model 422 Field..........................1085
Model 422 Target........................1085
Model 622 Field..........................1085
Model 622 Target........................1085
Model 622VR..............................1085
Model 22A Sport.........................1086
Model 22S Sport.........................1086
Model 22A Target........................1086
Model 22S Target........................1086
Model 22A Camo.........................1086
SW22 Victory..............................1086
Model 3904................................1086
Model 3906................................1087
Model 3914................................1087
Model 3913................................1087
Model 3914LS.............................1087
Model 3913LS.............................1087
Model 3954................................1088
Model 915..................................1088
Model 5904................................1088
Model 5903................................1088
Model 5946................................1089
Model 5967................................1089
Model 6904................................1089
Model 6906................................1089
Model 6946................................1089
Model 4003................................1089
Model 4004................................1089
Model 4006................................1089
Model 4026................................1090

Model 4046................................1090
Model 4013................................1090
Model 4014................................1090
Model 4053................................1090
Model 4054................................1090
Model 411..................................1091
Model 1006................................1091
Model 1076................................1091
Model 1086................................1091
Model 1026................................1091
Model 4506................................1091
Model 4505................................1092
Model 4516................................1092
Model 4536................................1092
Model 4546................................1092
Model 4040PD.............................1092
Model SW1911............................1092
Model SW1911 Adjustable............1093
Model SW1911Sc.........................1093
Model 1911 PD............................1093
Model SW1911 E Series...............1093
Model SW1911 DK (Doug Koenig)..........................1093
Model SW1911 Pro Series...........1093
Model SW1911 Pro Sub-Compact.........................1093
3913/3953 TSW.........................1094
4013/4053 TSW.........................1094
4513/4553 TSW.........................1094
4563/4566/4583/4586 TSW.......1095
CS9...1095
SW40F.......................................1095
Compact SW9C...........................1095
SW9M..1095
SW9P...1096
SW9G...1096
SW40V.......................................1096
SW40P.......................................1096
SW40G.......................................1096
SW380.......................................1096
SW9E...1097
SW40VE.....................................1097
SW40VE Allied Forces..................1097
SW99...1097
410 Two-Tone.............................1098
410S..1098
457..1098
457S..1099
908..1099
908S..1099
908S Carry Combo......................1099
909..1099
910..1099
910S..1100
M&P 9mm..................................1100
M&P 9-JG..................................1100
M&P 9 Pro Series........................1100
M&P 9L......................................1100
M&P 40......................................1100
M&P .357 SIG.............................1100
M&P 45......................................1100
M&P 45 with Thumb Safety..........1101
M&P 9c......................................1101
M&P 40c....................................1101
M&P Shield.................................1101

M&P BG380 1102
Model 14 Texas Ranger Comm......1102
Model 25-3 S&W
    125th Anniversary Comm.........1102
Model 26-4
    Georgia State Police Comm.......1102
Model 27 .357
    50th Anniversary Comm...........1102
Model 29-3 Elmer Keith Comm. 1102
Model 544 Texas Wagon Train
    150th Anniversary Comm.........1102
Model 586
    Mass. State Police Comm.........1102
Model 629-1 Alaska 1988 Iditarod
    Comm...................................1102
Model 745 IPSC Comm. 1102
Model 4516-1
    U.S. Marshall Comm. 1102
Model SW1911 PD Gunsite
    Commemorative 1102
Model SW1911 – Rolling Thunder
    Commemorative 1103
.40 S&W Tactical.........................1103
.40 S&W Compensated 1103
.40 S&W Performance
    Action Pistol 1103
Model 681 Quadport 1103
Model 686 Competitor..................1103
Model 686 Hunter........................1103
Model 686 Carry Comp 4 1103
Model 686 Carry Comp 3 1104
Model 686 Plus...........................1104
Model 686 - .38 Super..................1104
Model 629 Hunter........................1104
Model 629 Hunter II......................1104
Model 629 Comped Hunter...........1104
Model 629 12" Hunter/
    7.5" Hunter 1104
Model 629 Magnum Hunter
    Trail Boss 1104
Model 629 Compensated Hunter....1104
Model 629 Stealth Hunter.............1104
Model 629 Extreme......................1104
Model 629 Carry Comp 1104
Model 629 Carry Comp II..............1105
Model 629 Comped Hunter...........1105
Model 610 1105
Model 640 Carry Comp 1105
Model 640 .357 Quadport 1105
Model 460 Airweight 1105
Model 625 Light Hunter...............1105
Model 625 1105
Model 625 V-Comp 1105
Model 625—5.25 1105
Model 627—8 Shot 1105
Model 627 Defensive—8 Shot.......1105
Model 651 1106
"Shorty-Forty" .40 S&W................1106
Model 647 Varminter....................1106
Model 500 Magnum Hunter 1106
"Shorty Forty" Mark III..................1106
Shorty .45..................................1106
Shorty Nine................................1106
9 Recon.....................................1106
Performance Center .45 Limited....1107
45 Recon...................................1107
Shorty .356 TSW.........................1107

Model .356 TSW
    "Limited" Series.......................1107
Model 5906 Performance Center ...1107
Model 845 of 1998 1107
Model .45 CQB Combat................1107
Model 945 1108
Model 945 Micro.........................1108
Model SW945.............................1108
Model SW1911 1108
Model SW1911 DK.......................1108
Model SW1911 Tactical Rail..........1108
Model 66 .357 Magnum
    F-Comp 1108
Model 66 1109
Model 681 Quad Port 1109
Model 25 1109
Model 657 1109
Model 657 Classic 1109
Model 657 Defensive 1109
Model 657 Hunter 1109
Model 19 .357 Magnum
    K-Comp 1109
Model 60 Carry Comp 1109
Paxton Quigley Model 640 1110
Model 640 Centennial
    Powerport...............................1110
Model 327 Carry 1110
Model 13 .357 1110
Model .845 Single-Action 1110
Model 952 1110
Model 1911 1110
.320 Revolving Rifle Model 1110
Model A Rifle..............................1111
Model B.....................................1111
Model C.....................................1111
Model D.....................................1111
Model 1500 Series......................1111
M&P 15VTAC Viking Tactics 1111
M&P 15 300 Whisper...................1112

**SMITH AMERICAN ARMS
COMPANY**

Smith Carbine 1112

SNAKE CHARMER

Snake Charmer 1112

SNEIDER, CHARLES E.

Two-Cylinder Revolver 1112

**SOKOLOVSKY CORP.
SPORT ARMS**

.45 Automaster 1113

SPALDING & FISHER

Double Barreled Pistol 1113

SPANG & WALLACE

Pocket Pistol 1113

SPENCER

Spencer Carbine 1113
Military Rifle—Navy Model 1113
Springfield Armory
    Post-war Alteration 1113

SPENCER REVOLVER

Safety Hammerless Revolver 1114

SPHINX

AT-2000S/SDA...........................1114
AT-2000H/HDA 1115
AT-2000C...................................1115
AT-2000CS.................................1115
AT-2000GM................................1115
3000 1115

SPIES, A. W.

Pocket Pistol 1115

SPITFIRE

Super Sterling (G7) 1116
Competition Model (G3) 1116
Battle of Britain Commemorative ...1116

SPRINGFIELD ARMORY INC.

Iwo Jima M1 Garand 1116
M1A Basic Rifle..........................1116
D-Day M1 Garand
    Limited Edition........................1117
M1A Standard Rifle 1117
M1A-A1 Bush Rifle......................1117
M1A Scout Squad Rifle 1117
M1A National Match 1117
M1A Super Match 1117
M1A Model 25 Carlos Hathcock 1117
M21 Law Enforcement/
    Tactical Rifle...........................1117
M1A SOCOM 16 1117
M1A SOCOM II...........................1117
M1A SOCOM Urban Rifle 1118
IDF Mauser Rifle Model 66SP.......1118
SAR-48 1118
SAR-4800 1118
SAR-8 1118
SAR-8 Tactical 1118
M6 Scout...................................1118
M6 Scout—Stainless Steel 1118
M6 Scout Pistol..........................1118
Model 1911-A1 1118
Model 1911-A1 Service Model......1118
Model 1911-A1 Service
    Mil-Spec 1118
Model 1911-A1 Service Model
    Lightweight 1119
Model 1911-A1 Stainless 1119
Model 1911-A1 Factory Comp......1119
Model 1911-A1 Factory Comp
    High Capacity 1119
Model 1911-A2 S.A.S.S. 1119
Model 1911-A1 Defender 1119
Model 1911-A1 Loaded Defender
    Lightweight 1119
Model 1911-A1 Compact 1119
Model 1911-A1 Champion
    Mil-Spec 1120
Model 1911-A1 Loaded Champion
    Stainless 1120
Champion Compact......................1120
Model 1911 Loaded Champion
    Lightweight 1120
Ultra Compact 1911-A1 1120
Ultra Compact Lightweight MD-1...1121

Ultra Compact 1911-A1
    Mil-Spec 1121
V10 Ultra Compact 1911-A1.........1121
V10 Ultra Compact 1911-A1
    Mil-Spec 1121
Model 1911-A1 High Capacity 1121
Compact High Capacity................1121
Ultra Compact High Capacity........1121
Micro Compact—Parkerized 1121
Micro Compact—Stainless 1121
Micro Compact—O.D. Green 1121
Micro Compact—Black Stainless ..1121
Micro Compact Lightweight...........1122
Loaded Micro Compact
    Lightweight 1122
Model 1911-A1
    Mil-Spec Operator...................1122
Model 1911-A1
    Loaded Operator.....................1122
Combat Commander 1122
Trophy Match 1122
Loaded Leatham Trophy Match......1122
Full Size....................................1123
Full Size High-Capacity 1123
Champion 1123
Champion Lightweight..................1123
P9 Standard...............................1124
P9 Ultra (IPSC Approved).............1124
Super Tuned Champion 1124
Super Tuned V10.........................1124
Super Tuned Standard 1124
Range Officer 1124
Tactical Response Pistol (TRP).......1124
XD 4" 1125
XD 5" Bi-Tone Tactical 1126
XD Sub-Compact 1126
XD 45 ACP 1126
XD(M)..1126
XDM-3.8 1126
XD-S 1126
XD Mod. 2 1126
TGO 1 1126
TGO 2 1127
Custom Carry.............................1127
Basic Competition Model 1127
N.R.A. PPC 1127
Trophy Master Expert
    Limited Class 1127
Expert Pistol...............................1127
Bureau Model 1911-A1 1128
Springfield Formula "Squirtgun" ...1128
Bullseye Wadcutter......................1128
Trophy Master
    Distinguished Pistol 1128
CMC Formula "Squirtgun" 1128
National Match Model...................1128
A Model Master Grade
    Competition Pistol....................1129
Model B-1 Master Grade
    Competition Pistol....................1129
Omega 1129
XD Custom Pro 1129
XD Carry Pro 1129

SPRINGFIELD ARMS COMPANY

Belt Model 1129
Late Model Revolver 1130

SSK INDUSTRIES
SSK-XP100..................................1130

STAG ARMS
Stag-15 Model 3 Pre-Ban............1131
Stag-15 Model 4 Pre-Ban............1131
Stag 6.8 Model 5 Pre-Ban 1131
Stag-15 Model 6 Pre-Ban
  Super Varminter.....................1131
Stag-8T...................................1132

STANDARD ARMS CO.
Model G...................................1132
Model M...................................1132

STARR, EBAN T.
Single-Shot Derringer 1132
  First Model............................1132
  Second Model 1132
  Third Model............................1132
  Fourth Model..........................1132
  Fifth Model............................1132
  Sixth Model............................1132

STARR ARMS COMPANY
1858 Navy Revolver 1132
  Standard Model.......................1133
  Martially Marked (JT) 1133
Cartridge Carbine 1133

STEEL CITY ARMS, INC.
Double Deuce 1133

STENDA WAFFENFABRIK
Pocket Pistol..............................1133

STERLING ARMAMENT LTD.
Parapistol MK 7 C4 1134

STERLING ARMS CORPORATION
Model 283 Target 300 1134
Model 284 Target 300L 1134
Model 285 Husky......................1134
Model 286 Trapper....................1134
Model 287 PPL .380 1134
Model PPL .22 1134
Model 300................................1134
Model 300S..............................1134
Model 302................................1134
Model 302S..............................1135
Model 400................................1135
Model 400S..............................1135
Model 402................................1135
Model X-Caliber 1135

STEVENS ARMS CO., J.
Vest Pocket Pistol......................1135
Pocket Pistol.............................1135
  .22 Caliber............................1135
  .41 Caliber............................1135
No. 41 Pistol.............................1136
Single-Shot Pistol......................1136
Tip Up Rifles.............................1136
  Ladies Model—
    .22 or .25 Rimfire Only, 24"
    or 26" Barrel........................1136

Tip Up Rifle—
  Without Fore-end................1136
Tip Up Rifle—
  With Fore-end, Swiss-Type
  Buttplate 1136
Tip Up Shotgun—
  All Gauges, 30" or 32"
  Barrel................................1136
Ideal Single-Shot Rifle...............1136
No. 44 1136
No. 44-1/2 1136
No. 044-1/2 1136
No. 45 1136
No. 46 1137
No. 47 1137
No. 48 1137
No. 49 1137
Model 50................................1137
Model 51................................1137
No. 52 1137
No. 53 1137
No. 54 1137
No. 55 1137
No. 56 1137
No. 404 1138
No. 414 1138
No. 417 Walnut Hill Model 1138
No. 417 1/2 Walnut Hill Model 1138
No. 418 Walnut Hill Jr. 1138
No. 418 1/2 Walnut Hill Jr. 1138
1st Model Favorite.....................1138
No. 20 1138
No. 21 1138
No. 21 Ladies Model 1138
No. 16 1138
No. 16-1/2 1139
No. 23—Sure Shot 1139
Model 72................................1139
Model 70................................1140
High Power Rifle........................1140
  No. 425 1140
  No. 430 1140
  No. 435 1140
  No. 440 1140
Six-inch Pocket Rifle..................1140
No. 36 1140
First Issue Stevens-Conlin..........1140
Second Issue Stevens-Conlin
  No. 38 1140
No. 37 1140
No. 35 1141
No. 35 Target 1141
No. 35 Off-Hand/Auto-Shot
  Shotgun...............................1141
  No. 35 Off-Hand Shot Gun 1141
  No. 35 Auto-Shot....................1141
No. 43 1141
No. 10 Target Pistol 1141
Old Model Pocket Rifle...............1141
Reliable Pocket Rifle 1142
No. 42 Reliable Pocket Rifle 1142
First Issue New Model
  Pocket Rifle..........................1142
Second Issue New Model
  Pocket Rifle..........................1142
Vernier Model...........................1142
No. 40 1142

No. 40-1/2 1142
No. 34 (Hunter's Pet) 1142
No. 34-1/2 1142
Model 416................................1142
Model 322................................1143
Model 322-S.............................1143
Model 89.................................1143
Model 87M...............................1143
Model 987................................1143
Model 200XP Long or
  Short Action Package Rifle 1143
Model 200XP Camo 1143
Model 1877—Hammer Boxlock....1144
Model 250—Hammer Sidelock....1144
Model 335 (Late)—
  Hammerless Boxlock................1145
Model 330—Hammerless
  Boxlock...............................1145
Model 311H—Hammerless
  Boxlock...............................1146
Model 311H—Vent Rib
  Hammerless Boxlock................1146
Model 311J/R—Hammerless
  Boxlock...............................1146
Model 311J/R—Solid Rib
  Hammerless Boxlock................1146
Model 311H—Waterfowler
  Hammerless Boxlock................1146
Model 240—.410 Over/Under
  Hammer Tenite......................1146
Model 215—Hammer Boxlock......1146
Model 315 (Early)—Hammerless
  Boxlock...............................1147
Model 511—Hammerless
  Boxlock...............................1147
Model 215—Hammer Boxlock......1147
Model 315—Hammerless
  Boxlock...............................1147
Model 3151—Single Trigger
  Hammerless Boxlock................1147
Model 311—Single Trigger
  Hammerless Boxlock................1147
Model 5151—Hammerless
  Boxlock...............................1147
Model 5151—Single Trigger
  Hammerless Boxlock................1147
Model 311—New Style
  Hammerless Boxlock................1147
Model 311—New Style Tenite
  Hammerless Boxlock................1147
Model 511—Sunken Rib
  Hammerless Boxlock................1147
Model 511—Hammerless
  Boxlock...............................1147
Model 511A—Hammerless
  Boxlock...............................1147
Model 411 Upland Sporter 1147
Model 620 U.S. Marked
  Trench Gun 1148

STEYR
Schoenberger 1148
Mannlicher Model 1894 1148
  Argentine Contract..................1149
Steyr Model 1908 Pocket Pistol 1150
Steyr Hahn Model 1911
  Commercially Marked 1150
Steyr Model SP 1150
Steyr Model GB 1150

Rogak P-18..............................1150
Steyr GB 1150
Model M72 L/M.........................1150
Model SL.................................1150
Model L...................................1151
Luxus Series 1151
  Luxus Model L.......................1151
  Luxus Model M......................1151
  Luxus Model S.......................1151
Model M...................................1151
Professional Model M 1151
SBS ProHunter..........................1151
SBS ProHunter Stainless Steel......1151
SBS ProHunter Camo 1152
SBS ProHunter Camo
  Stainless Steel.......................1152
SBS ProHunter Mountain Rifle 1152
SBS ProHunter Mountain
  Stainless Steel.......................1152
SBS ProHunter Mountain Camo.....1152
SBS ProHunter Mountain Camo
  Stainless Steel.......................1152
SBS ProHunter (Youth/Ladies) 1152
SBS ProHunter Compact..............1152
SBS ProHunter 376 Steyr.............1152
SBS Forester............................1152
SBS Classic American.................1152
SBS Classic Mannlicher 1153
Steyr Scout Package 1153
Scout......................................1153
Steyr Scout Tactical 1153
Model SSG-PI...........................1153
SSG-PII Police Rifle....................1153
SSK-PIIK Police Kurz..................1153
SSG-PII & PIIK McMillan..............1154
SSG-PIV..................................1154
  Match..................................1154
SSG 08...................................1154
SSG Carbon Fiber......................1154
Match UIT................................1154
JAGD Match 1154
SBS Tactical.............................1154
SBS Tactical Heavy Barrel 1154
SBS Tactical Heavy Barrel
  Carbine................................1154
SBS Tactical McMillan.................1154
SBS CISM Rifle.........................1154
SBS Tactical Elite Heavy Barrel 1155
SBS Tactical Elite Heavy Barrel
  Carbine................................1155
Steyr AUG...............................1155
Steyr AUG—Police Model 1155
Steyr AUG Special Receiver..........1155
Steyr USR 1155
Steyr Zephyr 1155
Model SPP...............................1155
Model M...................................1155
Model M-A1.............................1155

STI INTERNATIONAL
LS9 & LS40 1156
BLS9 & BLS40 1156
Ranger 1156
Ranger II..................................1156
Trojan.....................................1157
Tactical 4.15.............................1157

Tactical 1157
Trubor 1157
Lawman 1157
Xcaliber Single Stack 1157
Xcaliber Double Stack 1157
Executive 1158
VIP 1158
Edge 1158
Eagle 1158
Duty One 1158
Duty CT 1158
Competitor 1159
Grandmaster 1159
Rangemaster 1159
Rangemaster II 1159
Targetmaster 1159
Stinger 1159
Hawk 4.3 1159
Night Hawk 4.3 1159
Falcon 3.9 1159
Sparrow 5.0 1160
Edge 5.1 1160
Eagle 5.1 1160
Eagle 5.5 1160
Eagle 6.0 1160
Hunter 6.0 1160
Special Edition 1160
I.P.S.C. 30th Anniversary 1160
TruSight 1160
Legacy 1160
GP6 1161
Sentinel Premier 1161
Limited Edition 20th Anniversary ...1161
Duty One 1161
Apeiro 1161
Eclipse 1161
DVC Open 1161
DVC Limited 1161
Texican Single Action Revolver 1161
FPI 2260 Rifle 1161
Sporting Competition Rifle 1162

STOCK, FRANZ
Stock 1162

STOCKING & CO.
Single-Shot Pistol 1162

STOEGER, A. F./STOEGER INDUSTRIES
.22 Luger 1162
American Eagle Luger 1162
American Eagle Navy Model 1162
Cougar 1162
Pro Series 95 1163
Model 2000 1163
Model 2000 Deluxe 1163
Model 2000 Camo 1163
Model 2000 Slug 1163
Model 2000 Synthetic 1163
Model 3000 1163
Uplander Youth 1164
Condor Combo 1164
    Field 1164
    Special 1164
    Supreme 1164

Single Barrel Classic Youth 1165
P-350 Defense 1165

STURM, RUGER & CO.
Standard Model
  "Red Eagle Grips" 1165
Standard Model 1165
Standard Model—
  Marked "Hecho en Mexico" 1166
Mark I Target Model 1166
  Red Eagle 6-7/8" barrel 1166
  Black or Silver Eagle
    6-7/8" barrel 1166
  5-1/4" Tapered Barrel Model 1166
  5-1/2" Bull Barrel Model 1166
  Rollmarked with U.S. on
    Top of Frame 1166
Stainless Steel 1 of 5,000 1166
Model KMK4 1167
Model KMK6 1167
Target Model 1167
Stainless Steel Target Model 1167
Government Model 1167
Stainless Steel
  Government Model 1167
Competition Model KMK678GC 1167
KP4 1168
P512 1169
22/45 Lite 1169
Standard Pistol 1169
Hunter 1169
Competition 1169
Mark III 22/45 Standard Pistol 1169
Mark III 22/45 Stainless 1169
Mark III 512 Pistol 1169
Mark III 22/45 Hunter 1170
Mark III 22/45RP Pistol 1170
Charger 1170
Charger — New Model 1170
Single Six Revolver 1170
Flat Gate Model 1170
Spanish Engraved
  (serial no. 7 and 8; and
  5100 to 5119) 1171
Silver Anodized Frame with Aluminum
  Cylinder Model
    with Martin Hardcoat Finish ...1171
Black Anodized Aluminum Frame
  and Cylinder Model 1171
Black Anodized Frame with
  Blue Steel Cylinder Model 1171
Silver Anodized Aluminum Frame
  with Blue Steel Cylinder
  and "S" Marking 1171
Super Single Six 1171
  4-5/8" Barrel 1171
  Nickel-Plated Model 1171
Bearcat (Old Model) 1171
Flattop—.357 Magnum 1172
  4-5/8" Barrel 1172
  6-1/2" Barrel 1172
  10" Barrel 1172
  6-1/2" Barrel 1172
  7-1/2" Barrel 1172
  10" Barrel 1172
Blackhawk 1172
  .357/9mm 1173
  .45 L.C./.45 ACP 1173

Early Model in
  Wood Presentation Case 1173
In Fitted White
  Cardboard Case 1173
Long Grip Frame in
  Wood Case 1173
Factory Verified 6-1/2" Barrel ...1173
Super Single Six Convertible
  (New Model) 1173
Stainless Steel Single Six
  Convertible 1174
New Model Single Six (.22 LR only)
  "Star" Model
  Blue Variation 5.5" or
    6.5" Barrel 1174
  9.5" Barrel—Rare 1174
  4.62" Barrel—Very Rare 1174
  Stainless Variation 5.5" or
    6.5" Barrel 1174
  9.5" Barrel 1174
  4.62" Barrel—Rare 1174
Fixed Sight New Model Single Six ..1174
  Blued Finish 1174
  Stainless Steel 1174
New Model Single Six
  50th Anniversary Model 1174
New Model Super Single Six 1175
New Model Super Single Six,
  .17 HMR 1175
New Model Single Six Hunter
  Convertible 1175
Single-Ten 1175
New Model Blackhawk Bisley 1175
50th Anniversary New Model
  Blackhawk NVB34-50 1176
Stainless Steel Blackhawk
  (New Model) 1176
Blackhawk Convertible
  (New Model) 1176
  .45 ACP & .45 Long Colt
    Convertible (1998) 1176
  Stainless Model .357/9mm 1176
Fiftieth Anniversary
  .44 Magnum Flattop New Model
  Blackhawk 1176
Model SRM Blackhawk
  .357 Maximum 1176
Super Blackhawk (New Model) 1176
Super Blackhawk Stainless Steel ...1176
Super Blackhawk Hunter 1176
50th Anniversary Matched Set
  .357 and .44 Magnum 1177
Bisley Model 1177
  .22 LR and .32 H&R Magnum ..1177
  .357 Magnum, .41 Magnum,
    .44 Magnum, .45 Colt 1177
Shootists Bisley 1177
Old Army Percussion Revolver 1177
Old Army Stainless Steel 1177
Ruger Vaquero 1177
Ruger Bisley Vaquero 1178
Ruger Vaquero Bird's-head 1178
Ruger New Vaquero 1178
SASS Vaquero Set 1178
Ruger New Model Bisley Vaquero ..1178
New Ruger Bearcat
  (Super Bearcat) 1179
  Blue 1179
  Stainless Steel 1179

Convertible (Recalled) 1179
Adjustable Sights
  (Lipsey's Exclusive) 1179
New Model Super Bearcat 1179
Fiftieth Anniversary New Bearcat ...1179
Security Six 1179
Speed Six 1179
Models 737, 738, 739 1179
GP-100 1179
GP-100 Stainless 1179
GP-100 Match Champion 1179
SP-101 1180
SP-101 Spurless-Hammer 1180
Redhawk 1180
Redhawk Stainless Steel 1180
Redhawk 4-Inch .45 Colt (2008) ..1180
Redhawk .45 ACP/.45 Colt 1181
Super Redhawk 1181
Super Redhawk Alaskan 1181
Police Service-Six 1181
Model 707 and 708 1181
LCR Lightweight
  Compact Revolver 1181
LCRX 1181
KP93DC 1183
KP944 1183
KP944DC 1183
KP944DAO 1183
P95 1183
KP95DC 1183
P95DAO 1183
KP95DAO 1184
KP97D 1184
KP97DAO 1184
KP345 1184
KP345PR 1184
SR9 / SR40 1184
SR45 1184
9E 1184
SR22 1184
LCP (Lightweight Compact Pistol) ...1185
LCP Crimson Trace 1185
LC9 1185
LC380 1185
American Pistol 1185
SR 1911 1185
SR 1911 LW Cmdr. 1186
10/22 Standard Carbine
  With Walnut Stock 1186
10/22 Standard Carbine
  Stainless Steel 1186
10/22 Magnum 1186
10/22 Sporter (Finger Groove Old
  Model) 1186
10/22 Deluxe Sporter 1186
10/22 International Carbine 1186
10/22T 1186
10/22 Canadian Centennial 1186
  Two Gun Set 1186
  10/22 Only 1186
10/22 Laminated Stock Carbine 1186
10/22 Laminated Stock
  International 1187
  Blue 1187
  Stainless Steel 1187
10/22 All Weather 1187

10/22 Carbine 40th Anniversary ...1187
10/22 50th Anniversary..................1187
10/22 Compact Rifle 10/22 CRR...1187
K10/22T Ruger 10/22 Target
    Stainless..................................1187
10/22-T 1187
10/22RPFCARH
    (Lipsey's Distributor's Special) ...1187
10/22VLEH Target Tactical 1187
10/22 Takedown 1187
Model 10/17 1188
SR-22 Rifle 1188
Model 44 Carbine.........................1188
Deerstalker Model 1188
Model 44 RS 1188
Model 44 Sporter
    (Finger Groove Old Model) 1188
Model 44 International Carbine 1188
Model 44
    25th Anniversary Model 1188
Model 99/44 Deerfield Carbine 1188
Mini-14 1188
Mini-14 Stainless Steel.................1188
Mini-14 Target 1188
Mini-14 Ranch 1188
Mini-14 Stainless
    All-Weather Ranch....................1188
Mini-14 NRA 1189
Mini-14 ATI Stock.........................1189
Mini-14 Tactical 1189
SR-556 1189
AR-556 1189
SR-762 1189
Mini-Thirty 1189
Mini-Thirty Stainless
    with Synthetic Stock 1189
GB Model....................................1189
PC4/PC9 Carbine 1190
No. 1 Light Sporter (1-A)...............1190
No, 1 Light Standard (1-AB)..........1190
No. 1 Standard (1-B) 1190
No. 1 Standard Stainless
    (1-B-BBZ) 1190
No. 1 Tropical (1-H) 1190
No. 1 International (1-RSI).............1190
No. 1 Medium Sporter (1-S) 1190
No. 1 Special Varminter (1-V) 1191
No. 1 Stainless Varminter
    (1-V-BBZ)................................1191
No. 3 Carbine..............................1191
Model 77-R/RS 1191
Model 77-RS 1191
Model 77 Flat Bolt........................1191
Model 77/17 Synthetic 1191
Model 77/17 Varmint....................1192
Model 77/17RM2..........................1192
Model 77/17RM2 Stainless Steel ..1192
Model 77/22................................1192
Model 77/22 Synthetic Stock........1192
Model 77/22 Stainless
    Steel/Synthetic Stock 1192
Model 77/22 Varmint....................1192
Model 77/22M Stainless Steel 1192
Model 77/22—.22 Hornet 1192
Model 77RL MKII..........................1193
Model 77LR MKII..........................1193
Model 77RLP MKII........................1193

Model 77VT MKII..........................1193
Model 77RBZ MKII........................1193
Model 77RSBZ MKII......................1193
Model 77CR MKII Compact Rifle....1193
Model 77 Express MKII..................1193
Model 77/44RS............................1194
Model 77/44RSP...........................1194
Model 77/357..............................1194
HM77R Hawkeye...........................1194
M77 Hawkeye Ultra-Light 1194
M77 Hawkeye All-Weather
    Ultra-Light..............................1194
M77 Hawkeye Compact.................1195
M77 Hawkeye Laminate
    Compact 1195
M77 Hawkeye All-Weather............1195
M77PRCM Hawkeye Compact
    Magnum 1195
M77RCM Hawkeye Compact
    Magnum 1195
M77 Hawkeye Magnum Hunter 1195
M77 Hawkeye Alaskan 1195
M77 Hawkeye African...................1195
M77 Hawkeye Tactical 1195
M77 Hawkeye Predator 1195
M77 Hawkeye International............1195
M77 Hawkeye Varmint Target........1195
American Rifle Compact 1196
Model 77/50RS............................1196
Model 77/50RSP...........................1196
Model 96/17................................1196
Red Label 2014 Model 1197
Red Label Sporting Clays 1197
Red Label All-Weather 1197
Red Label Series —
    Hand Engraved 1197
    Grade 1...................................1197
    Grade 2 (1/3 coverage)..............1197
    Grade 3 (2/3 coverage) 1197
Red Label Engraved......................1197
Red Label All-Weather Engraved ...1198
Woodside Over/Under....................1198
Trap Model..................................1198
Gold Label Side-by-Side 1198

SUNDANCE INDUSTRIES, INC.
Model D-22M 1198
Model BOA 1198
Model A-25..................................1198
Model Laser 25.............................1198
Sundance Point Blank...................1199

SUPER SIX LTD.
Bison Bull 1199

SUTHERLAND, S.
Pocket Pistol................................1199

SYMS, J. G.
Pocket Pistol................................1199

SYREN SHOTGUNS
Syren Tempio 1199
XLR5 Sporter 1199

TACONIC FIREARMS LTD.
M98 Ultimate Hunter 1200

TALLASSEE
Carbine.......................................1200

TANFOGLIO
Sata 1200
Titan 1200
Super Titan 1200

TANNER, ANDRE
Model 300S 1201
Model 50F 1201

**TARPLEY J. & F. AND
E. T. GARRETT & CO.**
Carbine.......................................1201

TAURUS INTERNATIONAL MFG. CO.
PT-92C..1201
PT-92..1201
PT-99..1201
PT-100..1202
PT-101..1202
Deluxe Shooter's Pak....................1202
PT-138..1202
    Blue.......................................1202
    Stainless Steel.........................1202
PT-908..1202
PT-911..1202
PT-111..1203
PT-140..1203
PT-140 Millennium.......................1203
    Blue.......................................1203
    Stainless Steel.........................1203
PT-145 Millennium.......................1203
    Blue.......................................1203
    Stainless Steel.........................1203
Millennium Pro.............................1203
Millennium G2..............................1203
Model 609TI-PRO 1203
PT-400/400SS.............................1203
    Blue.......................................1203
    Stainless Steel.........................1203
PT-132..1204
PT-58..1204
PT-145..1204
PT-45..1204
    Blue.......................................1204
    Stainless Steel.........................1204
PT-24/7-PRO Standard..................1204
PT-24/7-PRO Compact...................1205
PT-24/7-PRO Long Slide................1205
PT-24/7-9B..................................1205
PT-24/7-40B................................1205
PT-24/7PLS-9SSCTi-17 1205
PT-24/7PLS.................................1205
2045 Large Frame Pistol 1205
809-B 9mm.................................1205
800 Series Compact......................1205
PT191140B.................................1205
PT1911 1206
Model 1911B-9 1206
Model 1911B-38 1206
Model 1911HC.............................1206
PT-745GB....................................1206
PT745B/SS-LS.............................1206
PT917B20....................................1206

PT609Ti-13 1206
PT138BP12 Millennium Pro..........1206
PT-38B/SS...................................1206
PT-38SSSPRL..............................1207
738 TCP Compact Pistol...............1207
709 "Slim"..................................1207
638 Pro Compact.........................1207
DT Hybrid 1207
PT-945C......................................1207
    Blue.......................................1208
    Stainless Steel.........................1208
PT-945S......................................1208
    Blue.......................................1208
    Stainless Steel.........................1208
PT-940..1208
PT-938..1208
922 Sport....................................1208
PT-22..1208
PT-922..1208
PT-25..1209
22PLY/25PLY Small
    Polymer Frame Pistols 1209
Taurus Curve................................1209
Model 17MB2/MSS2.....................1209
Model 827SS4..............................1210
Model 83.....................................1210
Model 86.....................................1210
Model 85.....................................1211
Model 85 Stainless.......................1211
Model 85CH.................................1211
Model 85 Hy-Lite Magnesium 1211
Model 85 Ultra-Lite Gray...............1211
Model 85 Ultra-Lite Titanium.........1211
Model 85 View.............................1211
Model 850...................................1211
Model 850 Ultra-Lite Blue.............1212
Model 850 Ultra-Lite
    Stainless Steel.........................1212
Model 605...................................1212
Taurus Polymer Protector..............1212
Model 650...................................1212
Taurus 405 Revolver.....................1212
    Blue.......................................1212
    Stainless Steel.........................1212
Model 941...................................1213
    Blue.......................................1213
    Stainless Steel.........................1213
Model 941 UL...............................1213
Model 96.....................................1213
Model 741...................................1213
Model 761...................................1213
Model 65.....................................1213
Model 605...................................1213
    Blue.......................................1213
    Stainless Steel.........................1213
Model 605 Custom (B2C) 1213
    Blue.......................................1214
    Stainless Steel.........................1214
Model 605CHB2/SS2....................1214
    Blue.......................................1214
    Stainless Steel.........................1214
    Blue.......................................1214
    Stainless Steel.........................1214
Model 66.....................................1214
Model 66CP.................................1214
Model 66B4/SS4..........................1214

Blue 1214
Stainless Steel 1214
Model 607 1214
Blue 1214
Stainless Steel 1214
Model 606 1214
Model 608 1215
Blue 1215
Stainless Steel 1215
Model 689 1215
Model 617 1215
Blue 1215
Stainless Steel 1215
Ported Barrel 1215
Blue 1215
Stainless Steel 1215
Model 627 Tracker 1216
Model 669 1216
Model 669CP 1216
Model 415 1216
Model 431 1216
Model 817 (Ultra-Lite) 1216
Blue 1216
Stainless Steel 1216
Model 441 1216
Model 444 Multi 1216
Model 218 Raging Bee 1217
Blue 1217
Stainless Steel 1218
Black Stainless Steel 1218
Model 500 Magnum Raging Bull ... 1218
Model 500MSS2 Raging Bull 1218
Model 44/444 1218
Blue 1218
Stainless Steel 1218
Model 17 1218
Model 970 1218
Tracker .22/.22 Mag 1219
Model 425 Tracker 1219
Model 44 Tracker 1219
Tracker .45 1219
Model 445 1219
Model 460 1219
Model 45 1220
Blue 1220
Stainless Steel 1220
Model 627 1220
Tracker 10SS8 1220
Tracker 4510TKR 1220
Tracker 590 5mm 1220
Judge 1220
Model 4510TKR-SSR 1220
Judge Public Defender Polymer 1220
Judge Public Defender Ultra-Lite ... 1220
Model 17-12 1221
Model 85Ti 1221
Model 731Ti 1221
Model 617Ti 1221
Model 627Ti 1222
S/A-45, B/S/SM 1222
S/A-45-B12, S/SM12, S/S12,
    CHSA12 1223
Model 62 1223
Model 62 Carbine 1223
Model 62 Upstart 1223
Model 72 1223

Model 72 Carbine 1223
Model 63 1223
Model 62LAR-SS 1224
Thunderbolt 1224
CT9G2 1224

TAYLOR, L.B.
Pocket Pistol 1224

TAYLOR'S & CO., INC.
Napoleon Le Page Pistol
    (Model 551) 1224
Kentucky Pistol (Model 550) 1224
Colt Model 1847 Walker
    (Model 500A) 1224
Colt Model 1851 Navy 1224
    Brass Frame (Model 210) 1224
    Steel Frame (Model 245) 1224
Remington Model 1858 1224
    Brass Frame (Model 410) 1224
    Steel Frame (Model 430) 1224
Colt Model 1848 Baby Dragoon
    (Models 470, 471, 472) 1224
Starr Model 1858
    (Model 510, 511) 1224
Colt Model 1860 Army 1225
    Brass Frame (Model 300) 1225
    Steel Frame
        (Model 310, 312, 315) 1225
Colt Dragoon
    (Models 485A, 490A, 495A) 1225
Colt Model 1861 Navy
    (Model 210) 1225
Colt Model 1862 Police
    (Model 315B) 1225
Colt Model 1862 Pocket
    (Model 315C) 1225
Remington Model 1863 Pocket
    (Model 435) 1225
Colt Model 1873 Cattleman
    (Models 700, 701, 702) 1225
Colt Model 1873 Bird's-head
    (Models 703A, 703B, 703C) 1225
Colt Model 1873 "Outfitter" 1225
Remington Model 1875 1225
Remington Model 1890 1225
1911-A1 Model 1225
Kentucky Rifle 1225
    Flintlock (Model 183) 1225
    Percussion (Model 182) 1225
Model 1842 U.S.
    Percussion Musket
        (Model 125) 1225
    Smoothbore 1225
    Rifled with Rear Sight
        (Model 126) 1226
Model 1855 U.S.
    Percussion Musket
        (Model 116) 1226
Model 1853 3-Band
    Enfield Musket (Model 120) 1226
Model 1858 2-Band
    Enfield Musket (Model 121) 1226
Model 1861 Springfield Musket
    (Model 110) 1226
Model 1862 C.S. Richmond
    Musket (Model 115) 1226
Model 1863 Remington Zouave
    (Model 140) 1226

Henry Rifle 1226
    Brass Frame (Model 198) 1226
    Iron Frame (Model 199) 1226
Winchester Model 1866
    (Model 201) 1226
Winchester Model 1866 Yellowboy
    Carbine (Model 202) 1226
Winchester Model 1873
    (Model 200) 1226
Winchester Model 1873 Carbine
    (Model 200B) 1226
Winchester Model 1873
    Sporting Rifle (Model 200C) ... 1226
Winchester Model 1885 High Wall
    (Model 203) 1226
Winchester Model 1885 Low Wall
    Sporting Rifle (Model 204) 1227
Sharps Model 1859 Berdan
    Military (Model 152) 1227
Sharps Model 1863 Cavalry
    (Model 154) 1227
Sharps Model 1863 Sporting Rifle
    (Model 131) 1227
Sharps Model 1874 Sporting Rifle
    (Model 138) 1227
Sharps Model 1874 Deluxe
    Sporting Rifle (Model 155) 1227
Sharps Model 1874 Infantry Rifle
    (Model 157) 1227
Spencer Model 1865 Rifle 1227

TEXAS LONGHORN ARMS, INC.
Texas Border Special 1228
Mason Commemorative 1228
South Texas Army 1228
West Texas Target 1228
Grover's Improved Number Five ... 1228
Texas Sesquicentennial
    Commemorative 1229

THOMPSON/CENTER ARMS
10" Octagon Barrel Model 1229
10" Bull Barrel Model 1229
10" Vent Rib Model 1230
Super 14" Model 1230
Super 14" Vent Rib Model 1230
Super 16" Model 1230
Super 16" Vent Rib Model 1230
G2 Contender Rifle 1231
Standard 21" Carbine 1231
21" Carbine .410 Bore 1231
16" Youth Model Carbine 1231
Encore Pistol 1231
HotShot Youth Rifle 1231
Encore Rifle 1231
Encore Katahdin Carbine 1232
Encore Katahdin Turkey Gun 1232
Encore Shotgun 20 Gauge 1232
Encore Camo Shotgun 12 Gauge ... 1232
Encore Shotgun 12 Gauge 1232
Encore Rifled Shotgun 20 Gauge ... 1232
Encore Rifled Shotgun 12 Gauge ... 1232
Encore Turkey Gun 1232
Pro Hunter 1232
Pro Hunter Predator Rifle 1232
Pro Hunter Turkey Gun 1232
Pro Hunter Katahdin 1232
Icon 1232

Icon Classic Long Action Rifle 1233
Icon Weathershield
    Medium Action Rifle 1233
Venture Medium Action Rifle 1233
Venture Predator PDX Rifle 1233
Venture Weather Shield 1233
Dimension 1233
Thunder Hawk 1234
Thunder Hawk Shadow 1234
Grey Hawk 1234
Hawken Caplock Rifle 1234
Hawken Flintlock Rifle 1234
Hawken Custom/Elite 1234
Omega 45/Omega 50 1234
Omega Pivoting Breech Rifle 1234
Renegade Caplock Rifle 1234
Renegade Flintlock 1234
Big Boar Rifle 1235
High Plains Sporter 1235
    Rifle 1235
    Shotgun 1235
White Mountain Carbine 1235
Black Mountain Magnum 1235
Pennsylvania Hunter 1235
    Rifle 1235
    Carbine 1235
Pennsylvania Match Rifle 1235
New Englander Rifle 1235
New Englander Shotgun 1235
New Englander Composite 1235
    Rifle 1235
    Shotgun 1235
Scout Carbine 1235
    Walnut Stock 1235
    Composite Stock 1235
Scout Rifle 1235
    Walnut Stock 1236
    Composite Stock 1236
Scout Pistol 1236
Fire Hawk Deluxe 1236
Fire Hawk 1236
    Thumbhole Stock 1236
    Camo Stock 1236
    Bantam 1236
    .32 & .58 caliber models 1236
Fire Storm 1236
Black Diamond XR 1236
Triumph 1236
G2 Contender Muzzleloader 1236
Encore 209x50 Mag Carbine 1237
Encore 209x50 Pistol 1237

THUNDER FIVE
Thunder-Five 1237

TIKKA
Whitetail Hunter 1237
Whitetail Hunter Deluxe 1237
Whitetail/Battue Rifle 1237
Varmint/Continental Rifle 1237
Long Range Hunting 1237
Sporter 1237
412S Shotgun 1238
412S Shotgun/Rifle 1238
412S Sporting Clays 1238
512S Field Grade 1238

TISAS
(TRABZON GUN INDUSTRY CORP.)
Kanuni 16.....................................1239
Kanuni S.......................................1239
Zigana M16..................................1239
Zigana T.......................................1240
Zigana Sport................................1240
Zigana C45...................................1240
Zigana F.......................................1240

TODD, GEORGE H.
Rifled Musket...............................1240

TOKAREV
Russian Tokarev 1241
Chinese Licenses Tokarev.............1241
Polish Licensed Tokarev................1241
M48 Hungarian Tokarev................1241
Pakistani TT-33 Tokarev...............1241

TORKELSON ARMS CO.
Double-Barrel Shotguns...............1242

TRADEWINDS
Model 311-A 1242
Model 5000 "Husky" 1242

TRADITIONS
Hunter 1242
Field I...1242
Field II..1243
Waterfowl II..................................1243
Turkey II.......................................1243
Mag Hunter II...............................1243
Real 16 1243
Real 16 Gold................................1243
Gold Wing II Silver 1243
Elite I ST 1244
Elite Hunter 1244
Elite Field III ST............................1244
Uplander II Silver 1244
Uplander III Silver 1244
Uplander V Silver 1244
ALS Field 1244
ALS Hunter 1245
ALS Waterfowl..............................1245
ALS Turkey...................................1245

TRANTER, WILLIAM
Model 1872..................................1245
Model 1878..................................1245

TRIPLETT & SCOTT/MERIDEN MANUFACTURING COMPANY
Repeating Carbine........................1245

TRISTAR SPORTING ARMS
Silver Sporting..............................1245
Specialty Magnums.......................1245
Silver Hunter 1245
Silver II 1246
Silver Classic 1246
Brittany Sporting...........................1246
Brittany..1246
Brittany Classic 1246
York..1246

Hunter Lite...................................1246
Hunter 1246
Field Hunter 1246
Gentry/Gentry Coach 1246
Derby Classic 1246
TSA Field 1246
TSA Synthetic and Synthetic Mag ...1247
Model 333....................................1247
Model 333SC................................1247
Model 333SCL..............................1247
Model 333L...................................1247
Model 330....................................1247
Model 330D..................................1247
Model 300....................................1247
Model 311....................................1247
TR-L...1247
TR-SC..1247
TR-Mag..1248
TTR-Royal.....................................1248
TR-Class SL..................................1248
Model 411.....................................1248
Model 411R...................................1248
Model 411D..................................1248
Phantom Field...............................1248
Phantom Synthetic 1248
Phantom HP..................................1248
Ermes...1248
   Gold.....................................1249
   Silver 1249
   Nickel 1249
   Black 1249
Astra 20 1249
Mira Sporting 1249
Mira Camo 1249
CD Diana Field 1249
CD Diana Synthetic.......................1249
CD Diana Slug..............................1249
CD Diana Camo Mag 1249
Pee Wee 1249
Model C-100 1249
Model L-120..................................1250

TROCAOLA (TAC)
Break-Top Revolvers.....................1250

TRYON, EDWARD K. & COMPANY
Pocket Pistol 1250

TUCKER SHERARD & COMPANY
Dragoon 1250

TUFTS & COLLEY
Pocket Pistol 1250

TURNER, THOMAS
Pepperbox 1250

TYLER ORDNANCE WORKS
Tyler Texas Rifle............................1250
Hill Rifle.......................................1250

U.S. M1 CARBINE
Inland 1251
Underwood 1251
S.G. Saginaw 1251
IBM 1251

Quality Hardware..........................1251
National Postal Meter 1251
Standard Products........................1251
Rockola 1251
SG Grand Rapids..........................1251
Winchester 1251
Irwin Pedersen 1251
M1 Carbine Cutaway 1251
M1 Carbine Sniper
   with infra red conversion 1251
U.S. M1 A1 Paratrooper Model......1251

U.S. ORDNANCE
M-60...1251
M-60E3...1251
Browning Model 1919 1251
Vickers 1252

UBERTI, ALDO/UBERTI USA
Paterson Revolver 1252
Walker Colt Revolver.....................1252
Colt 2nd Model Dragoon
   Revolver....................................1252
Colt Model 1849 Wells Fargo 1253
   Pocket Revolver.........................1253
Colt Model 1848 Baby Dragoon 1253
Model 1851 Navy Colt 1253
Model 1861 Navy Colt 1253
   Military Model 1253
   Civilian Model 1253
Colt Model 1860 Army...................1253
   Military 1253
   Fluted Cylinder Military.............1253
   Civilian 1253
Colt Model 1862 Pocket
   Navy Revolver...........................1254
Colt Model 1868 Army Thuer
   Conversion 1254
Remington Model 1858 New Army
   .44 Caliber................................1254
Remington Model 1858
   New Army .36 Caliber 1254
Remington Model 1858
   New Army .44 Caliber Target 1254
Remington Model 1858
   New Army .44 Caliber
   Stainless Steel...........................1254
Remington Model 1858
   New Army .44 Cal. SS Target.....1254
Remington Model 1858
   Target Revolving Carbine...........1254
1875 Remington "Outlaw" 1254
Remington Model 1875 Frontier....1254
Remington Model 1890 Police 1255
Model 1871 Rolling Block Pistol 1255
Model 1871 Rolling Block
   Carbine.....................................1255
Henry Rifle 1255
Winchester Model 1866 1255
1866 Yellowboy Carbine 1255
Winchester Model 1873 Carbine ...1255
Winchester Model 1873 Rifle........1255
Winchester 1873 Short
   Sporting Rifle............................1256
Winchester 1873
   Half-Octagon Rifle 1256
Winchester 1873 Musket..............1256

Model 1885 High Wall
   Single-Shot Carbine..................1256
Model 1885 High Wall
   Single-Shot Rifle.......................1256
Model 1885 High Wall
   Single-Shot Rifle Pistol Grip.......1256
Winchester 1885 Low Wall
   Sporting Rifle............................1256
Winchester 1885 Low Wall
   Schuetzen 1256
Hawken Santa Fe 1256
Cattleman 1256
Cattleman .22 1256
   Flattop 1257
Buckhorn Target 1258
1873 Stallion 1258
Tornado 1258
No. 3 Schofield Revolver 1258
No. 3 New Model Russian 1258
Inspector Model 1259

UGARTECHEA, ARMAS
Upland Classic Model 110 1259
Custom Grade Models 1259
Upland Classic Grade III Model
   40 NEX 1259

UHLINGER, WILLIAM P.
Pocket Revolver.............................1259
   Long Cylinder (1-3/16") 1259
   Short Cylinder (1") 1259
   .32 Rimfire Model
   (5", 6", or 7" Barrel) 1259

UMAREX USA
Umarex Colt Tactical Rimfire
   M4 Ops Carbine 1259
Umarex H&K 416-22......................1259
Umarex H&K MP5 A5 1259

UNION
Pocket Pistol 1260

UNION FIRE ARMS COMPANY
Double Barrel Shotguns 1260
Model 24.......................................1260

UNITED SPORTING ARMS, INC.
Blued Guns (Seville, etc.) 1261

UNITED STATES ARMS
Single-Action Revolver...................1261

UNITED STATES FIRE ARMS MFG.
Single-Action Army Revolver 1261
Rodeo..1261
Rodeo II 1262
Buntline 1262
Buntline Special 1262
China Camp Cowboy Action Gun ...1262
Henry Nettleton Revolver...............1262
.22 Plinker 1262
Gunslinger 1262
Custer Battlefield Gun...................1262
Hunter 1262
Sheriff's Model 1262
Omni-Potent Bird's-Head Model 1263

Omni-Potent Snubnose 1263
Omni-Potent Target 1263
Bisley Model 1263
  Target 1263
Pony Express 1263
Model 1911 Army or Navy 1264
Ace .22 LR 1264
Super .38 1264
Cowboy Action Lightning 1264
Cowboy Action Carbine 1264
Lightning Magazine Rifle 1264
Lightning Magazine Carbine 1264
Lightning Baby Carbine 1264

UNITED STATES SMALL ARMS CO.

Huntsman Model Knife Pistol 1264

UNIVERSAL FIREARMS

Model 7112 1265
Double Wing 1265
Model 7212 1265
Model 1000 Military Carbine 1265
Model 2200 Leatherneck 1266

URIZAR, TOMAS

Celta, J. Cesar, Premier, Puma,
  and Union 1266
Dek-Du 1266
Express 1266
Imperial 1266
Le Secours or Phoenix 1266
Princeps 1266
Venus 1266

**USAS 12 DAEWOO
PRECISION IND., LTD.**

USAS 12 1266

USELTON ARMS INC.

Compact Classic 1266
Ultra Compact Classic 1266
Compact Classic Companion 1266
Carry Classic 1266
Ultra Carry 1266
Tactical 1911 1266
Classic National Match 1267

UZI ISRAELI MILITARY INDUSTRIES

Uzi Carbine Model A 1267
Uzi Carbine Model B 1267
Uzi Mini-Carbine 1267
Uzi Pistol 1267

VALKYRIE ARMS, LTD.

Browning 1919 A4 .30 Caliber 1268
U.S. M3-A1 1268
DeLisle Carbine 1268

VALMET, INC.

M-62S 1268
M-71S 1268
Model 76s 1268
  5.56mm 1268
  7.62x39mm 1268
Model 78 1268
Model 212 Lion 1268

Model 412 Combination Gun 1268

VALTRO

1998 A1 1268
Tactical 98 Shotgun 1268

VARNER SPORTING ARMS, INC.

Hunter Deluxe 1269
Presentation Grade 1269
  No. 1 Grade 1269
  No. 2 Grade 1269
  No. 3 Grade 1269

VECTOR ARMS, INC.

Pre-Ban 1269
Post-Ban 1269
Uzi 1269
  Pre-Ban 1269
  Post-Ban 1269

VEKTOR

Model Z88 1269
Model SP1 Service Pistol 1269
Model SP1 Sport 1269
Model SP1 Tuned Sport 1270
Model SP1 Target 1270
Model SP1 Compact
  (General's Model) 1270
Model SP2 1270
Model SP2 Ultra Sport 1271
Model SP2 Conversion Kit 1271
Model CP-1 Compact 1271
Vektor H5 Pump-Action Rifle 1271
Vektor 98 1271
Vektor Lyttelton 1271

VENUS WAFFENWERKE

Venus 1271

VERNEY-CARRON

Concours 1271
Skeet Model 1271
Snake Charmer II 1272

VERONA

Model SX401/S 1272
Model SX405/S/L 1272
Model SX405W/H/SW/SH 1272
LX501 1272
LX692G 1272
LX692G-20/28 1272
Model LX1001 Express Combo 1272
LX702G 1272
Model SS662GL 1272
Model SS772GL 1272
LX680 1273
LX692GS 1273
LX680C S&T 1273
LX692GC S&T 1273
LX702GC S&T 1273
Model SX801/L 1273
Model SX801G/GL 1273

VOERE

Model 1007 1274
Model 1013 1274

Model 2107 1274
Model 2107 Deluxe 1274
Model 2114S 1274
Model 2165 1274
Model 2185 1274
Model 2185 Match 1274
Model Titan 1274
Model Titan Menor 1274

VOLQUARTSEN CUSTOM

Standard 1275
VG-1 1275
Fusion Takedown Model 1275
  One barrel: .22 LR 1275
  One barrel: .17 WMR or
    .22 WMR 1275
  All three barrels included 1275
Evolution Model 1275
VX-2500 1275
VX-5000 1276
Black Cheetah Pistol 1276
Compact 1276
Olympic 1276
Stingray 1276
V-6 1276
V-2000 1277
V-Magic II 1277

VOUZELAUD

Model 315 E 1277
Model 315 EL 1277
Model 315 EGL 1277
Model 315 EGL-S 1277

WALCH, JOHN

Navy Revolver 1278
Pocket Revolver 1278

WALDMAN

Waldman 1278

WALLIS & BIRCH

Pocket Pistol 1278

WALTHER, CARL

Model 1 1278
  Fixed Sights 1278
  Pop Up Sights 1278
Model 3 1279
Model 6 1279
Model 7 1279
Model 8 1279
  Blue, Silver or Gold Finish 1280
  Engraved Slide 1280
  Engraved Slide and Frame 1280
  Engraved, Complete Coverage ..1280
Sport Model 1926/
  Walther Hammerless Target 22/
  Walther Standard Sport/ Walther
  1932 Olympia/ Sport Model
  Target/ Special Stoeger Model ...1280
Model MP 1280
Model AP 1280
Model PP 1280
  .22 Caliber 1281
  .25 Caliber 1281

.32 Caliber,
  High Polished Finish 1281
.32 Caliber, Milled Finish 1281
.380 Caliber 1281
.32 Caliber,
  with Duraluminum Frame 1281
.32 Caliber, with Bottom
  Magazine Release 1281
.32 Caliber,
  with Verchromt Finish 1281
.32 Caliber, Allemagne
  Marked 1281
.32 Caliber, A. F. Stoeger
  Contract 1281
.32 Caliber,
  with Waffenampt Proofs,
  High Polished Finish 1281
.32 Caliber,
  with Waffenampt Proofs,
  Milled Finish 1281
.32 Caliber, in Blue Finish and
  Full Coverage Engraving 1281
.32 Caliber, in Silver Finish and
  Full Coverage Engraving 1281
.32 Caliber, in Gold Finish and
  Full Coverage Engraving 1281
.32 Caliber,
  Police Eagle/C Proofed,
  High Polished Finish 1281
.32 Caliber, Police Eagle/C
  and Police Eagle/F Proofed,
  Milled Finish 1281
.32 Caliber, NSKK Marked
  on the Slide 1281
.32 Caliber, NSDAP Gruppe
  Markings 1281
.32 Caliber, PDM Marked with
  Bottom Magazine Release ...1281
.32 Caliber, RJ Marked 1281
.32 Caliber, RFV Marked, High
  Polished or Milled Finish 1281
.32 Caliber,
  RBD Munster Marked 1282
.32 Caliber, RpLt Marked 1282
.32 Caliber, Statens Vattenfallsverk
  Marked 1282
.32 Caliber, AC Marked 1282
.32 Caliber,
  Duraluminum Frame 1282
.380 Caliber, Bottom Magazine
  Release and Waffenampt
  Proofs 1282
.22 Caliber 1282
.25 Caliber 1282
.32 Caliber,
  High Polished Finish 1282
.32 Caliber, Milled Finish 1282
.380 Caliber 1282
.32 Caliber,
  with Duraluminum Frame 1282
.32 Caliber, Marked Mod. PP
  on Slide 1282
.32 Caliber,
  with Panagraphed Slide 1282
.32 Caliber,
  with Verchromt Finish 1282
.32 Caliber, in Blue Finish and
  Full Coverage Engraving 1282
.32 Caliber, in Silver Finish and
  Full Coverage Engraving 1282

.32 Caliber, in Gold Finish and
Full Coverage Engraving 1282
.32 Caliber, Czechoslovakian
Contract 1282
.32 Caliber,
Allemagne Marked..............1283
.32 Caliber,
with Waffenampt Proofs and
a High Polished Finish 1283
.32 Caliber, with Waffenampt
Proofs and a Milled Finish ...1283
.32 Caliber,
Police Eagle/C Proofed,
High Polished Finish............1283
.32 Caliber, Police Eagle/C
Proofed. Milled Finish 1283
.32 Caliber, Police Eagle/F
Proofed, Duraluminum
Frame, Milled Finish 1283
.22 Caliber, Late War,
Black Grips 1283
.32 Caliber, Party Leader Grips,
Brown 1283
.32 Caliber, Party Leader Grips,
Black 1283
.32 Caliber, RZM Marked 1283
.32 Caliber, PDM Marked with
Duraluminum Frame
and Bottom Magazine
Release 1283
.32 Caliber, RFV Marked 1283
.32 Caliber, DRP Marked.........1283
.32 Caliber,
Statens Vattenfallsverk 1283
Model PP—Some with Duraluminum
Frames 1283
.22 Caliber 1283
.32 Caliber 1283
.380 Caliber 1283
Model PP—All Three Calibers
Finished In Blue, Silver and Gold
with Full Coverage Engraving.....1283
Blue 1283
Silver 1283
Gold 1283
Model PP Manurhin..................1283
Model PP Sport, Manurhin 1283
Model PP Sport C, Manurhin 1283
Model PP Sport, Walther 1283
Model PP 50th Anniversary
Commemorative Model 1284
Model PPK—Some with
Duraluminum Frames 1284
.22 Caliber 1284
.32 Caliber 1284
.380 Caliber 1284
Model PPK—All Three Calibers
Finished In Blue, Silver
and Gold With Full Coverage
Engraving 1284
Blue 1284
Silver 1284
Gold 1284
Model PPK Mark II....................1284
Model PPK Manurhin................1284
Model PPK 50th Anniversary
Commemorative Model 1284
Model PPK American 1284
Model PPK/S..........................1284
Model PPK/S American 1284

Model TP 1284
Model TPH 1284
.22 Caliber 1285
Other Calibers 1285
Steel-Framed
(Introduced 1987) 1285
Model P.38K 1285
Model P.38 II 1285
Model P.38 IV 1285
Model P5, Compact..................1286
Model P5 One Hundred Year
Commemorative 1286
Model P88..............................1286
Model P88 Compact.................1286
Model P99..............................1287
Model P99 Compact AS/QA 1287
Model P990 QPQ.....................1287
Model P99 QA 1287
Model P99 Military 1287
Model P99 La Chasse DU 1287
Model P99 La Chasse 1288
CCP.......................................1288
Model P22 Standard.................1288
Model P22 Target....................1289
Free Pistol 1289
Model R99..............................1289
Model SP22-M1.......................1289
Model SP22-M2.......................1289
Model SP22-M3.......................1289
Package A1 with Walther
rifle scope 1291
Package A2 with laser 1291
Package A3 with Walther
rifle scope & laser 1291
Package A4 with Walther PS22
red-dot sight.......................1291
Model SF 1291
Model SFD.............................1291

WARNANT, L. AND J.
Revolver 1291

WARNER, CHAS.
Pocket Revolver.......................1291

WARNER, JAMES
Manually Revolved
Grooved Cylinder..................1292
Retractable Cylinder Model.......1292
Automatic Revolving Cylinder....1292
Second Model 1292
Third Model 1292
Single-Shot Derringer 1292
Pocket Revolver.......................1292

WARNER ARMS CORPORATION
Single Trigger Hammerless
Utica Special Double-Barrel 1292
Double Trigger Hammerless
Double-Barrel.......................1292
Grade X, SF, XT, SFT, XD
and XDF Hammer Guns...........1292
Field Grade Hammer Gun...........1292
Boxlock Hammerless 1292
Number 532 1293
Double-Action Hammerless.........1293

"Faultless": Warner-Schwarzlose
Model C, .32 ACP 1293

WEATHERBY
Mark V Deluxe..........................1293
Mark V Sporter 1293
Mark V .375
Weatherby Magnum................1293
Mark V .378
Weatherby Magnum................1293
Mark V .416
Weatherby Magnum................1293
Mark V .460
Weatherby Magnum................1293
Mark V Varmint 1294
Mark V Fibermark Composite 1294
Mark V Accumark.....................1295
50th Anniversary Commemorative
Mark V 1295
70th Anniversary Commemorative
Mark V 1295
1984 Olympic Commemorative
Mark V 1295
Safari Grade Mark V 1295
Crown Grade Mark V 1295
Mark V Super Varmint Master
(SVM)..................................1295
Mark V Special Varmint Rifle
(SVR) 1295
Mark V Synthetic Lightweight 1295
Mark V Stainless Lightweight 1295
Mark V Sporter Lightweight 1296
Mark V Accumark Lightweight 1296
Mark V Ultra Lightweight 1296
Mark V Deluxe Lightweight.........1296
Mark V SPM
(Super Predator Master)...........1296
Mark V SBGM
(Super Big Game Master) 1296
Mark V Arroyo 1296
Mark V Outfitter.......................1296
Mark V Tacmark 1296
TRR.......................................1296
TRR Magnum...........................1296
Vanguard VGX Deluxe 1297
Vanguard Weatherguard 1297
Vanguard Synthetic 1297
Vanguard Sub-MOA Matte
or Stainless 1298
Vanguard Sub-MOA Varmint 1298
Vanguard Compact...................1298
Vanguard Youth Compact............1298
Vanguard Deluxe 1298
Vanguard Series 2 Back Country ...1299
Vanguard Series 2 Sporter 1299
Vanguard Series 2 Synthetic 1299
Vanguard Series 2 Varmint
Special...............................1299
Weathermark 1299
Weathermark Alaskan.................1299
WBY-X...................................1299
Mark XXII 1299
Mark XXII Bolt Action 1299
Vanguard Sage Country Custom....1300
Vanguard Back Country Custom....1300
Classic Custom 1300
Safari Grade Custom 1300
Crown Custom 1300

Royal Custom...........................1300
Outfitter Custom.......................1300
Outfitter Krieger Custom 1300
Chris Kyle Limited Edition.............1300
PA-08 Upland 1301
PA-08 Knoxx Strutter X................1301
PA-08 Knoxx HD 1301
PA-08 Field/Slug Combo..............1301
PA-459 Turkey Camo..................1301
Centurion 1301
Centurion Deluxe 1301
Model 82................................1301
Model SAS Field.......................1301
Model SAS Camo......................1301
Shadow Grass.....................1301
Superflauge........................1301
Model SAS Sporting Clays..........1302
Model SAS Synthetic 1302
SA-08 Upland 1302
SA-08 Youth 1302
SA-08 Entré Rios......................1302
SA-459 TR..............................1302
Element Deluxe 1302
Model 92................................1302
Athena SBS 1303
Regency Field Grade...................1303
Orion Grade I —
New Production 1303
Orion Grade II Skeet 1303
Orion Grade II Classic Field 1304
Orion Grade II Classic
Sporting Clays 1304
Orion Super Sporting Clays (SSC) ..1304
Orion Grade III.........................1304
Orion Grade III Classic Field.........1304
Orion Grade III Classic
English Field.........................1304
Orion D'Italia 1305
Athena Grade III Classic Field........1305
Athena Grade IV 1305
Athena Grade V Classic Field.........1305
Competition Model Athena 1305

WEAVER ARMS
Nighthawk Assault Pistol..............1305

WEBLEY & SCOTT, LTD.
Model 1884 R.I.C. Naval..............1306
British Bulldog..........................1306
Pug 1306
Model 1878 Army Express
Revolver...............................1306
Webley Kaufmann Model 1880 1306
Webley-Fosbery
Automatic Revolver 1307
.455 Caliber 1307
.38 Caliber 1307
Model 1904 1307
Model 1905 1307
Model 1907 1308
Model 1908 1308
Model 1909 1308
Model 1910 .380 1308
Model 1910 .38 ACP 1308
Model 1911 1308
Model 1912 1309

Model 1913 1309
(RHA model) 1309
Model 1922 1309
Model 2000 O/U 1309

WEIHRAUCH, HANS HERMANN
Model HW 60M 1309
Model HW 66 1309
Model HW-3 1309
Model HW-5 1309
Model HW-7 1309
Model HW-9 1309

WEISBURGER, A.
Pocket Pistol 1310

WESSON, EDWIN
Dragoon 1310

WESSON, FRANK
Manual Extractor Model 1310
1870 Medium Frame Pocket Rifle
First Type 1310
1870 Medium Frame Pocket Rifle
Second Type............................1310
1870 Medium Frame Pocket Rifle
Third Type 1310
1870 Large Frame Pocket Rifle
First Type 1310
1870 Large Frame Pocket Rifle
Second Type............................1310
Medium Frame Superposed Pistol ...1310
First Type Marked
"Patent Applied For"...........1311
Second Type Marked "Patent
December 15, 1868" 1311
Third Type Full-Length
Fluted Barrels 1311
No. 2 Mid-Range or Hunting Rifle ..1311

WESSON & LEAVITT
Revolving Rifle.............................1311

WESSON FIREARMS, DAN
Model 41/741..............................1312
Model 414/7414...........................1313
Model 445/7445...........................1313
Model 15/715...............................1313
Model 41/741...............................1313
Model 44/744...............................1313
Model 45/745...............................1313
Model 360/7360...........................1313
Model 445/7445
(Alaskan Guide) 1313
Model 460/7460...........................1313
Model 722 VH10...........................1313
Model 744 V10S...........................1313
Model 740 V8S..............................1314
Model 722 VH10 SRS1 1314
Model 741 V10S SRS1 1314
Model 744 V8S SRS1 1314
Model 744 V10S SRS1 1314
Model 740 V8S SRS1 1314
Model 7414 V8S SRS1 1314
Model 7445 V8S SS1 1314
Model 22/722...............................1314
Model 32/732...............................1314

Model 3220/73220.......................1314
Model 15/715...............................1314
Model 41/741...............................1315
Model 22/722...............................1315
Model 44/744...............................1315
Model 45/745...............................1315
Model 460/7460...........................1315
Model 40/740...............................1315
Model 414/7414...........................1315
Model 445/7445...........................1315
Pointman Major............................1315
Pointman Seven...........................1315
Pointman Minor............................1315
Pointman Hi-Cap..........................1316
Pointman Dave Pruitt
Signature Series 1316
RZ-10 1316
RZ-45 Heritage 1316
ECO..1317
Patriot Marksman.........................1317
Coyote Classic 1318

WESSON FIREARMS CO., INC.
Model 11 1318
Model 12 1318
Model 14 1318
Model 15 1318
Model 8 1318
Model 9 1318
Model 22 1318
Model 22M 1318
Model 722M 1318
Standard Rib Shroud.................1318
Ventilated Rib Shroud................1318
Ventilated Heavy Rib Shroud.....1319
Standard Rib Shroud.................1319
Ventilated Rib Shroud................1319
Ventilated Heavy Rib Shroud.....1319
Model 732....................................1319
Model 322....................................1319
Model 7322..................................1319
Standard Rib Shroud.................1319
Ventilated Rib Shroud................1319
Ventilated Heavy Rib Shroud.....1319
Standard Rib Shroud.................1319
Ventilated Rib Shroud................1319
Ventilated Heavy Rib Shroud.....1319
Model 714....................................1320
Model 8.......................................1320
Model 708....................................1320
P14/8 Pistol Pac 1320
Model 15......................................1320
Model 715....................................1320
Model 9.......................................1320
Model 709....................................1320
Standard Rib Shroud.................1320
Ventilated Rib Shroud................1320
Ventilated Heavy Rib Shroud.....1320
330HP15 Hunter Pac 1320
331Model 40/Supermag...............1320
Ventilated Rib Shroud................1320
Ventilated Slotted Shroud—
8" barrel only.....................1320
Ventilated Heavy Rib Shroud.....1320
332HP40 Hunter Pac 1320
Model 375....................................1320

Ventilated Rib Shroud...............1321
Ventilated Heavy Rib Shroud.....1321
Ventilated Slotted Shroud—
8" barrel only.....................1321
P15/9 Pistol Pac 1321
Standard Rib Shroud.................1321
Ventilated Rib Shroud...............1321
Ventilated Heavy Rib Shroud.....1321
354HP375 Hunter Pac 1321
Model 744....................................1321
301 Model 41...............................1321
Model 45......................................1321
Model 745....................................1321
Ventilated Rib Shroud...............1321
Ventilated Heavy Rib Shroud.....1321
P44/P41/P45 Pistol Pac 1321
Ventilated Rib Shroud...............1322
Ventilated Heavy Rib Shroud.....1322
359 Model 445.............................1322
Model 7445..................................1322
Ventilated Rib Shroud...............1322
Ventilated Heavy Rib Shroud.....1322
Model 7445
Alaskan Guide Special...............1322
HP455 Hunter Pac 1322
Model 38P....................................1322
Ventilated Rib Shroud...............1322
Ventilated Heavy Rib Shroud.....1322
Model 738P..................................1323
Model 45/745 Pin Gun 1323
Ventilated Rib Shroud...............1323
Ventilated Heavy Rib Shroud.....1323
Model 15/715 Fixed Barrel
Target 1323

WESTLEY RICHARDS & CO., LTD.
B Model SxS Boxlock, Pre-WWII 1323
Best Quality Sidelock,
Current Model 1323
Magazine Rifle 1323
Boxlock Double Rifle 1323
Best Quality Over/Under Shotgun,
Current Model 1324

WHITE, ROLLIN
Pocket Pistol 1324

WHITNEY ARMS COMPANY
Eli Whitney, Sr. Armory
Muskets, 1798-1824. 1798
U.S. Contract Muskets,
Types I-IV..............................1324
Whitney Connecticut, New York,
and U.S. 1812
Contract Muskets 1324
Whitney (and P. & E.W. Blake)
U.S. M1816/1822 Contract
Muskets..................................1325
Whitney Armory U.S. M1816/M1822
Muskets, Flintlock or Altered to
Percussion and Adapted
with "Sea Fencible"
Heavy Buttplates.....................1325
Whitney Armory U.S. M1816/M1822
Muskets, Altered to
Percussion 1325
Whitney Armory Muskets,
1825-1842...............................1325

Eli Whitney, Jr. Armory Rifles and
Rifle-Muskets, 1842-1865........1325
Whitney U.S. M1841 Contract Rifle
(unaltered)...............................1326
Whitney U.S. M1841/1855 Contract
Rifle, Adapted to Saber Bayonet
and Long Range Sights 1326
Whitney U.S. M1841 Contract Rifles,
Adapted to Saber Bayonets and
Long Range Rear Sights
(Colt 1862 Adaptation) 1326
Whitney South Carolina Contract
M1841 Rifle.............................1326
Whitney "Good & Serviceable"
M1841 Derivatives 1326
Whitney P1853 "Long Enfield"
Rifle-Musket Derivative 1327
Whitney M1861 Connecticut
Contract Rifle-Musket
Derivative................................1328
Whitney "High Humpback"
Lockplate M1861 Rifle-Musket
Derivative................................1328
Whitney "Manton" M1861
Rifle-Musket Derivative 1329
Whitney "Direct Vent" M1861
Rifle-Musket Derivatives...........1329
Whitney U.S. M1861 Contract
Rifle-Musket.............................1329
Whitney U.S. Navy Contract Rifle ...1329
The Whitney Arms Company,
1865-1888..............................1329
Single Barreled Percussion
Shotgun 1329
Double-Barreled Percussion
Shotgun 1330
Whitney-Howard Lever Action
(Thunderbolt)...........................1330
Shotgun 1330
Rifle..1330
Carbine 1330
Whitney Phoenix..........................1330
Gallery Rifle.............................1330
Shotgun 1330
Military Rifle.............................1330
Schuetzen Rifle........................1330
Civilian Carbine 1330
Military Carbine 1331
Whitney-Laidley Model I
Rolling Block 1331
Military Carbine 1331
Civilian Carbine 1331
Military Rifle.............................1331
Gallery Rifle.............................1331
Sporting Rifle...........................1331
Creedmoor No. 1 Rifle...............1331
Creedmoor No. 2 Rifle...............1331
Whitney-Remington Model 2
Rolling Block 1331
Shotgun 1331
Military Carbine 1331
Civilian Carbine 1331
Military Rifle.............................1331
No. 1 Sporting Rifle...................1332
No. 2 Sporting Rifle...................1332
Sporting Rifle...........................1332
Military Rifle.............................1332
Carbine 1332
Small Frame Sporting Rifle.......1332

Large Frame Sporting Rifle.......1332
Military Rifle.............................1332
Military Carbine.......................1332
Whitney-Beals Patent Revolver......1333
First Model............................1333
.31 Caliber Model...................1333
.28 Caliber Model...................1333
First Model................................1333
First Variation.......................1333
Second Variation.....................1333
Third Variation.......................1333
Fourth Variation.....................1333
Second Model...........................1333
First Variation.......................1333
Second Variation.....................1333
Third Variation.......................1333
Fourth Variation.....................1333
Fifth Variation.......................1333
Sixth Variation.......................1333
First Model................................1334
First Variation.......................1334
Second Variation.....................1334
Third Variation.......................1334
Fourth Variation.....................1334
Fifth Variation.......................1334
Second Model...........................1334
First Variation.......................1334
Second Variation.....................1334
Third Variation.......................1334
Fourth Variation.....................1334

WHITNEY FIREARMS COMPANY
Blue Finish.............................1334
Nickel-Plated..........................1334

WICHITA ARMS, INC.
Classic Rifle.............................1334
Wichita International Pistol...........1335
Wichita Silhouette Pistol..............1335
Wichita MK40..........................1335

WICKLIFFE RIFLES
Model 76................................1335
Model 76 Deluxe.....................1335
Traditionalist.........................1335
Stinger Deluxe........................1335

WILDEY FIREARMS CO., INC.
Wildey Auto Pistol....................1336
Cheshire, Connecticut, Address.....1336
Serial No. 1 through 200..........1336
Survivor Model........................1336
Hunter Model..........................1336
Presentation Model..................1336

WILKINSON ARMS CO.
Terry Carbine..............................1337

WILLIAMSON
Derringer....................................1337

WILSON COMBAT
Model 1996A2............................1337
Protector....................................1338
Protector Compact.....................1338
Sentinel Ultra Compact...............1338

Tactical.....................................1338
Classic.....................................1338
Service Grade Target................1338
Beretta/Wilson 92G Brigadier
Tactical................................1339
Custom Carry Revolver.............1339
.22 Classic Rimfire Pistol..........1339
Combat Classic Super Grade
(Tactical Super Grade).............1339
Tactical Super Grade Compact......1339
Wilson X-TAC...........................1339
CQB Light-Rail Lightweight...........1340
Competition Pistols...................1340
UT-15 Urban Tactical.................1340
Tactical Hunter LW 6.8...............1340
M-4T Tactical Carbine................1341

WINCHESTER REPEATING ARMS
Jennings......................................1341
First Model............................1341
Second Model.........................1341
Third Model...........................1341
Smith & Wesson
Volcanic Firearms....................1341
4" Pistol................................1342
8" Pistol................................1342
6" Barrel................................1342
8" Barrel................................1342
16" Barrel..............................1342
Volcanic Firearms
(New Haven Arms Company)......1342
3-1/2" Barrel..........................1342
6" Barrel................................1342
Lever Action Carbine................1342
16" Barrel..............................1342
20" Barrel..............................1342
24" Barrel..............................1342
Iron Frame Rifle......................1343
Brass Frame Rifle....................1343
First Model Rifle.....................1343
First Model Carbine.................1343
Second Model Rifle..................1343
Second Model Carbine.............1344
Third Model Rifle....................1344
Third Model Carbine................1344
Third Model Musket.................1344
Fourth Model Rifle..................1344
Fourth Model Carbine..............1344
Fourth Model Musket...............1344
Model 1866 Iron Frame
Rifle Musket...........................1344
Model 1866 Iron Frame Swiss
Sharpshooters Rifle................1344
Model 1867 Iron Frame Carbine....1344
Model 1868 Iron Frame
Rifle Musket...........................1344
First Model Rifle.....................1344
First Model Carbine.................1345
First Model Musket.................1345
Second Model Rifle..................1345
Second Model Carbine.............1345
Second Model Musket.............1345
Third Model Rifle....................1345
Third Model Carbine................1345
Third Model Musket.................1345
Model 1873 .22 Rimfire Rifle........1345
First Model Rifle.....................1345

First Model Carbine.................1345
First Model Musket.................1345
Second Model Rifle..................1345
Second Model Carbine.............1345
Second Model Musket.............1345
Second Model Northwest
Mounted Police Carbine.......1345
Third Model Rifle....................1345
Third Model Carbine................1346
Third Model Musket.................1346
Winchester Hotchkiss
Bolt-Action Rifle......................1346
First Model Sporting Rifle.........1346
First Model Carbine.................1346
First Model Musket.................1346
Second Model Sporting Rifle.....1346
Second Model Carbine.............1346
Second Model Musket.............1346
Third Model Sporting Rifle........1346
Third Model Carbine................1346
Third Model Musket.................1346
Standard High Wall Rifle...........1347
Standard Low Wall Rifle............1347
High Wall Musket.....................1347
Low Wall Musket
(Winder Musket)...................1347
High Wall Schuetzen Rifle.........1347
Low Wall Carbine.....................1347
High Wall Shotgun....................1347
Model 1886..............................1347
Sporting Rifle..........................1348
Fancy Sporting Rifle................1348
Takedown Rifle—Standard.......1348
Extra Lightweight Takedown
Rifle—.33 caliber................1348
Extra Lightweight Takedown
Rifle—Other Calibers...........1348
Extra Lightweight Rifle—
.33 caliber..........................1348
Extra Lightweight Rifle—
Other Calibers....................1348
Carbine..................................1348
Musket...................................1348
Standard Rifle.........................1348
Standard Rifle (Carbine)...........1348
Deluxe Rifle............................1348
Deluxe Rifle (Carbine).............1348
Sporting Rifle..........................1349
Fancy Sporting Rifle................1349
Carbine..................................1349
Trapper's Carbine....................1349
Musket...................................1349
Model 1894..............................1349
First Model Sporting Rifle.........1349
Sporting Rifle..........................1349
Fancy Sporting Rifle................1349
Extra Lightweight Rifle............1350
Carbine..................................1350
Trapper's Carbine....................1350
Model 53..................................1350
Deluxe Model.........................1350
Model 55..................................1350
Model 64..................................1350
Carbine..................................1350
Model 65..................................1350
Model 1895..............................1350
Sporting Rifle..........................1351

Fancy Sporting Rifles...............1351
Carbine..................................1351
Standard Musket.....................1351
U.S. Army N.R.A. Musket..........1351
N.R.A. Musket,
Model 1903 and 1906.......1351
U.S. Army Musket....................1351
Russian Musket.......................1351
Class A, B, C, and D.................1351
Match Gun..............................1351
Standard Shotgun....................1351
Riot Shotgun...........................1351
Model 1901 Shotgun..................1351
Model 1893..............................1352
Standard Gun.........................1352
Trap Gun................................1352
Pigeon Gun/High Grade...........1352
Tournament Gun......................1352
Brush Gun..............................1352
Riot Gun.................................1352
Trench Gun.............................1352
Winchester-Lee
Straight Pull Rifle....................1352
U.S. Navy Musket....................1352
Commercial Musket.................1352
Sporting Rifle..........................1352
Model 1890..............................1353
First Model—Standard Grade...1353
Second Model—Case
Hardened Frame Standard...1353
Deluxe....................................1353
Second Model—
Blued Frame Standard..........1353
Deluxe....................................1353
Third Model Standard..............1353
Deluxe....................................1353
Model 1906..............................1353
.22 Short Only........................1353
Standard.................................1353
Expert....................................1353
Model 61..................................1354
Pre-war..................................1354
Post-war.................................1354
Magnum.................................1354
Model 62 and 62A.....................1354
Pre-war..................................1354
Post-war.................................1354
Model 62 Gallery.......................1354
Model 1903..............................1354
Standard.................................1354
Deluxe....................................1354
20" Barrel...............................1355
23" Barrel...............................1355
Model 1905..............................1355
Sporting.................................1355
Fancy Sporting........................1355
Sporting.................................1355
Fancy Sporting........................1355
Police....................................1355
Model 1910..............................1355
Sporting.................................1355
Fancy Sporting........................1355
Model 55 (Rimfire Rifle)............1355
Model 74..................................1355
Sporting.................................1355
Gallery Special—
.22 Short Only....................1356

Model 77 1356
Model 100 1356
  Rifle................................1356
  Carbine...........................1356
Model 88 1356
  Rifle................................1356
  1955-1963 Rifle Production.....1356
  1964-1973 Rifle Production.....1356
  Carbine...........................1356
Model 99 or Thumb Trigger...........1356
Model D Military Rifle 1357
Imperial Bolt-Action Magazine
  Rifle (Model 51)........................1357
Model 43 1357
  Standard.............................1357
  Special or Deluxe -...................1357
Model 47 1357
  Target Rifle..........................1357
Model 52 1357
  Standard.............................1357
  Target...............................1357
  Target—Speed Lock...............1357
  Model 52A Target Heavy Barrel—
    Rare............................1357
  Model 52B Target Heavy &
    Standard Barrel..................1358
  Model 52B Target Bull Barrel....1358
  Model 52C Target 1358
  Model 52D Target 1358
  Model 52B Bull Gun................1358
  Model 52C Bull Gun................1358
  International Match -
    Free Style.......................1358
  International Match - Prone......1358
  Model 52A Sporter 1358
  Model 52B Sporter 1358
  Model 52C Sporter 1358
Model 54 1358
  Standard.............................1358
  Carbine.............................1358
  Sniper's Rifle.......................1358
  N.R.A...............................1358
  Super Grade 1358
  Target...............................1358
  National Match 1359
  Sporting.............................1359
  Fancy Sporting 1359
Model 59 1359
Model 60 and 60A 1359
  Model 60 1359
  Model 60A 1359
Model 67 1359
  Sporting.............................1359
  Smoothbore 1359
  Junior...............................1359
  Miniature Target 1359
  With Scope 1360
  Without Scope.......................1360
Model 69 and 69A 1360
Model 697 1360
Model 70 1360
Standard Rifle .30-06 Springfield
  (1937-1963) 1360
  Pre-War 1360
  Post-War.............................1360
  Pre-War 1360
  Post-War.............................1361

Pre-War 1361
Post-War.............................1361
Pre-War 1361
Post-War.............................1361
Pre-War 1361
Post-War.............................1361
Pre-War 1361
Post-War.............................1361
Pre-War 1361
Post-War.............................1361
.338 Win. Magnum
  (1959-1963) 1361
Super Grade 1361
Target...............................1361
  Sporter 1362
  Target...............................1362
  Standard Grade—12 gauge.....1362
  Featherweight 1362
  Riot Gun 1362
  Trench Gun 1362
  Skeet Grade 1363
  Trap Grade 1363
  Heavy Duck Gun 1363
  Pigeon Grade 1363
Model 25 1363
Model 20 1363
Model 36 1363
Model 41 1363
Model 21—1931 to 1959 1363
  Standard Grade - 12 gauge......1364
  Standard Grade - 16 gauge......1364
  Standard Grade - 20 gauge......1364
  Tournament Grade -
    12 gauge 1364
  Tournament Grade -
    16 gauge 1364
  Tournament Grade -
    20 gauge 1364
  Trap Grade - 12 gauge.............1364
  Trap Grade - 16 gauge.............1364
  Trap Grade - 20 gauge.............1364
  Skeet Grade - 12 gauge............1364
  Skeet Grade - 16 gauge............1364
  Skeet Grade - 20 gauge............1364
  Duck/Magnum Gun..................1364
  12 gauge 1364
  16 gauge 1364
  20 gauge 1364
  .410 Bore 1364
Custom Shop Model 21s—
  1960 to 1981 1364
  Custom Grade—12 Gauge 1364
  Pigeon Grade—12 Gauge........1364
  Grand American—12 Gauge....1364
Custom Shop Model 21s—
  1982 to 1993 1365
  Standard Custom Built 1365
  Grand American 1365
  Grand American Small Gauge
    Set—28 or .410 bore 1365
Model 24 1365
  12 gauge 1365
  16 gauge 1365
  20 gauge 1365
  28 gauge 1365
  .410 bore 1365
  Youth Model 1365

Model 42 1365
  Standard Grade 1366
  Skeet Grade—Solid Rib 1366
  Skeet Grade—Ventilated Rib....1366
  Trap Grade - Plain or Solid Rib..1366
  Deluxe Grade—Solid Rib 1366
  Deluxe Grade—Ventilated Rib ..1366
  Plain...............................1366
  Fancy...............................1366
  Standard Grade 1366
  Skeet Grade 1366
  Standard Grade 1366
  Skeet Grade 1367
  Trap Grade 1367
  Pigeon Grade 1367
  Featherweight 1367
Model 59 1367
  Standard Grade 1367
  Pigeon Grade 1367
Model 121 1367
Model 131 1367
Model 310 1367
  Grade I..............................1368
  High Grade..........................1368
Wildcat..............................1368
Model 94 1368
Model 94 Traditional—CW...........1368
Model 94 Ranger 1368
Model 94 Ranger Compact 1368
Model 94 Black Shadow 1368
Model 94 Deluxe 1369
Model 94 Win-Tuff....................1369
Model 94 XTR 1369
Model 94 XTR Deluxe 1369
Model 94 Trapper 1369
Model 94 Legacy 20-inch 1369
Model 94 Legacy 24-inch 1369
Model 94 Legacy 26-inch 1369
Model 94 XTR Big Bore 1369
Model 94 Centennial
  Limited Editions......................1370
  Grade I..............................1370
  High Grade..........................1370
  Custom High Grade 1370
Model 94 Heritage—
  Limited 1 of 1000...................1370
Model 94 Heritage—
  Custom 1 of 100....................1370
Model 94 Trails End 1370
Model 94 Trails End Octagon.........1370
Model 94 Trails End Hunter 1370
Model 94 Timber Carbine 1370
Model 94 Timber Scout 1370
Model 94 Pack Rifle 1370
Model 1894 Custom Grade...........1371
Model 1894 High Grade 1371
Model 71 1371
Model 94 Short Rifle 1371
Model 94 Sporter 1371
Model 94 150th Commemorative....1371
Model 1886 Short Rifle...............1371
Model 1892 Carbine..................1371
Model 9410 1371
Model 9410 Semi-Fancy 1372
Model 9410 Packer 1372
Model 9410 Packer Compact........1372

Model 9410 Ranger 1372
Model 9422 High Grade 1373
Model 9422
  25th Anniversary Rifle..............1373
  Grade I..............................1373
  High Grade..........................1373
Model 9422 Legacy 1373
Model 9422 Large Loop
  & Walnut............................1373
Model 9422 High Grade Series II...1373
Model 9417 Traditional 1373
Model 9417 Legacy 1373
Traditional Tribute 1373
Legacy Tribute 1373
Custom Traditional Tribute 1374
Special Edition Traditional Tribute...1374
Special Edition Legacy Tribute 1374
Model 64 (Post-'64) 1374
Model 1885 Low Wall................1374
  Grade I..............................1374
  High Grade..........................1374
Model 1885 High Wall Hunter 1374
Model 1885 .30-06 Centennial
  High Wall Hunter 1374
Model 1885 Low Wall Classic 1374
Model 1885 Low Wall
  17 Mach 2 1374
Model 1892 1374
  Grade I..............................1375
  High Grade..........................1375
  Grade I..............................1375
  High Grade..........................1375
  Grade I (3,500).......................1375
  High Grade (1,000)...................1375
  Grade I..............................1375
  High Grade..........................1375
Model 1895—Limited Edition
  for the year 2000 1375
  Grade I..............................1375
  High Grade..........................1375
Model 1895 Saddle Ring Carbine... 1375
Model 1895 Theodore Roosevelt
  Safari Centennial High Grade.....1376
  Custom Grade 1376
Model 73.............................1376
  Short Rifle 1376
  Sporter 1376
Model 1866
  150th Commemorative 1376
Model 1873
  150th Commemorative 1376
Model 52B Sporting Rifle:
  1993-1997 Production 1376
Model XPR...........................1376
Model 70—Standard Grade.........1376
Model 70 Varmint.....................1376
Model 70 Westerner 1377
Model 70 African......................1377
Model 70 Magnum....................1377
Model 70 Deluxe 1377
Model 70 Mannlicher 1377
Model 70 Target Rifle 1377
Model 70 International Match
  Army...............................1377
Model 70A............................1377
Model 670 1377
Model 70 XTR Featherweight 1377

Model 70 Fiftieth Anniversary........1377
Model 70 XTR Super Express.......1377
Model 70 XTR Varmint.................1377
Model 70 Featherweight Classic
   All-Terrain 1378
Model 70 Featherweight
   Super Short............................1378
Model 70 Classic Laredo 1378
Model 70 Classic Compact 1378
Model 70 Classic Sporter LT 1378
Model 70 Classic Safari Express....1378
Model 70 Super Grade 1378
Model 70 RMEF Super Grade.......1379
Model 70 RMEF Super Grade III.....1379
Model 70 Classic Super Grade III....1379
Model 70 Super Express...............1379
Model 70 Heavy Varmint...............1379
Model 70 Classic Laminated
   Stainless 1379
Model 70 Classic Camo Stainless...1379
Model 70 SM 1379
Model 70 DBM-S 1379
Model 70 Varmint.........................1380
Model 70 DBM.............................1380
Model 70 Sporter 1380
Model 70 WinTuff........................1380
Model 70 Lightweight...................1380
Model 70 Black Shadow 1380
Model 70 Ultimate Shadow 1380
Model 70 Ultimate Shadow Camo..1380
Model 70 Super Shadow
   Super Short............................1380
Model 70 Super Shadow 1380
Model 70 Stealth.........................1380
Model 70 Coyote.........................1380
Model 70 Shadow Elite Stainless...1381
Model 70 Shadow Elite
   Camo Stainless 1381
Model 70 Pro Shadow Blued.........1381
Model 70 Pro Shadow Stainless 1381
Model 70 Laminated Coyote
   Outback Stainless.....................1381
Model 70 Laminated Coyote Gray
   or Brown Stainless....................1381
Model 670 1381
Model 70 Featherweight Deluxe 1381
Model 70 Sporter Deluxe 1381
New Model 70 Super Grade
   Special Limited Edition...............1381
Model 70 Extreme Weather SS.......1382
Model 70 FW Compact.................1382
Model 70 Safari Express...............1382
Model 70 75th Anniversary
   Super Grade............................1382
Model 70 Alaskan 1382
Model 70 Jack O'Connor Tribute ...1382
Model 70 150th Commemorative ..1382
Model 94 Custom Limited Edition
   New Generation........................1382
Model 70 Featherweight
   Ultra Grade..............................1382
Model 70 Custom Featherweight....1382
Model 70 Custom Carbon 1383
Model 70 Custom Sharpshooter 1383
Model 70 Custom Classic
   Sharpshooter II 1383

Model 70 Custom Sporting
   Sharpshooter...........................1383
Model 70 Custom Classic Sporting
   Sharpshooter II 1383
Model 70 Custom Grade...............1383
Model 70 Custom Express 1383
Model 70 Custom African
   Express..................................1383
Model 70 Custom Safari Express....1383
Model 70 Custom "Ultra Light"
   Mannlicher...............................1383
Model 70 Ultimate Classic 1383
Model 70 Custom
   Extreme Weather 1384
Model 70 Custom
   Stainless Laminate 1384
Model 12 Field Grade 1384
Model 12 Super Pigeon Grade 1384
Model 12 Skeet...........................1384
Model 12 Trap Grade...................1385
Model 12 (Limited Edition) 1385
   Grade I..................................1385
   Grade IV.................................1385
Model 42 (Limited Edition) 1385
Model 1200.................................1385
Ducks Unlimited Model 1385
Model 1300 XTR..........................1385
Model 1300 Waterfowl 1385
Model 1300 New Shadow Grass ...1385
Model 1300 WinCam Turkey Gun ...1385
Model 1300 Stainless Security......1385
Model 1300 Turkey 1386
Model 1300 Realtree Turkey 1386
Model 1300 Mossy Oak Break-Up
   Turkey....................................1386
Model 1300 Black Shadow Turkey..1386
Model 1300 National Wild Turkey
   Federation Series III 1386
Model 1300 National Wild Turkey
   Federation Series IV.................1386
Model 1300 NWTF Short Turkey....1386
Model 1300 Whitetails Unlimited
   Slug Hunter 1386
Model 1300 Slug Hunter...............1386
Model 1300 Buck and Tom...........1386
Model 1300 Universal Hunter........1386
Model 1300 Black Shadow Deer...1386
Model 1300 Black Shadow Field ...1386
Model 1300 Sporting/Field 1387
Model 1300 Sporting/Field
   Compact.................................1387
Model 1300 Walnut Field.............1387
Model 1300 Slug Hunter Sabot
   (Smoothbore)...........................1387
Model 1300 Upland Special 1387
Model 1300 Upland Special Field ..1387
Model 1300 Ranger 1387
Model 1300 Ranger Ladies/
   Youth-Compact........................1387
Model 1300 Ranger Deer Slug 1387
Model 1300 Ranger Deer Combo... 1387
   12 Gauge Combo 1387
   20 Gauge Combo 1387
Model 1300 Defender Combo 1387
Model 1300 Defender 5-Shot 1388
Speed Pump Walnut Field 1388
Model SXP Series........................

Model 9410....................................1388
Model 1500 XTR...........................1389
Super X Model 1 1389
Super X Model 1
   Custom Competition 1389
Super X2 3.5" Magnum 1389
Super X2 Turkey 1389
Super X2 Turkey Mossy Oak
   Break-Up.................................1389
Super X2 NWTF Turkey 1389
Super X2 Universal Hunter 1389
Super X2 Camo Waterfowl 1389
Super X2 Magnum Greenhead 1389
Super X2 Magnum Field 1389
Super X2 Light Field 1390
Super X2 Cantilever Deer 1390
Super X2 Practical........................1390
Super X2 Sporting Clays 1390
Super X2 Sporting Clays
   Signature II..............................1390
Super X2 Signature Red Sporting ... 1390
Super X3 Field 1390
Super X3 Composite......................1390
Super X3 Camo.............................1390
Super X3 Cantilever Deer 1390
Super X3 "Flanigun" Exhibition/
   Sporting..................................1390
Super X3 Classic Field 1390
Super X3 Turkey 1391
Model 1400 Quail Unlimited...........1391
Supreme Sporting 1392
Supreme Elegance 1392
Model 23 XTR..............................1392
   Pigeon Grade 1392
   Pigeon Grade Lightweight 1392
Model 23 Golden Quail 1392
Model 23 Light Duck 1392
Model 101 Field Grade 1392
Model 101 Three-Gauge
   Skeet Set................................1392
Model 101 Trap Grade..................1392
Model 101 Pigeon Grade Trap.......1393
Model 101 150th Anniversary
   Commemorative.......................1393
Model 501 Grand European 1393
Model 501 Presentation Grade......1393
Select Model 101 Field 1393
Select Model 101 Sporting 1393
Combination Gun 1393
Express Rifle 1393
Model 96 Xpert 1393
Model 1001 Field 1394
Model 1001 Sporting Clays I & II 1394
Select Midnight 1394
Select White Field 1394
Select Energy Sporting.................1394
Select Energy Trap.......................1394
Select Elegance (Supreme) 1394
Select Field 1394
Select Traditional Elegance...........1394
Select Platinum Field 1395
Select Platinum Sporting...............1395

WINDSOR

Rifle-Musket 1397

WINSLOW ARMS CO.
Bolt Action Rifle...........................1397
   Commander Grade 1397
   Regal Grade 1397
   Regent Grade 1397
   Regimental Grade 1397
   Crown Grade 1397
   Royal Grade 1397
   Imperial Grade.........................1397
   Emperor Grade 1397

WISEMAN, BILL & CO.
Rifle 1397
Silhouette Pistol 1397

WOLF SPORTING PISTOLS
Wolf SV Target.............................1397
Wolf SV Match 1397

XL
Derringer 1398
Vest Pocket Derringer 1398

XPERT
Xpert Derringer 1398
Xpert Pocket Rifle.........................1398

Z-B RIFLE CO.
Model ZKW-465 Varmint Rifle.......1399

ZANOTTI, FABIO
Model 625...................................1399

ZEPHYR
Woodlander II................................1399
Uplander.......................................1399
Upland King 1399
Vandalia 1399
Sterlingworth II 1399
Victor Special 1399
Thunderbird 1399
Honker 1399

ZM WEAPONS
LR-300 Sport Rifle 1399

ZOLI, ANTONIO
Ritmo Hunting Gun 1400
Condor Model 1400
Safari Deluxe 1401

ZOLI USA, ANGELO
Diano I..1401
AZ 1900C......................................1402

ZULAICA, M.
Royal 1402
   7.65mm 1402
   6.35mm 1402